All our love
& thanks always
God Bless Lisa

Much love,
Margot

Thanks for all of
your prayers. God
bless you
Judy

God bless you and yours
every day in every way —
Love Larry

Thank you
for keeping us
in His grip!
gratefully yours Pam

Much love to you!
Joy

May 8/85

Dear Alycemary,

Thank you for the "sinfully" rich, delicious lunch at the Steamers.

Only one with your Angelic charm could sell it right.

Was good fun!

:)

Barbara Tyndall
(sigh)

THE LIFE
AND TIMES OF
JESUS THE MESSIAH

Alfred Edersheim

AUTHOR OF

The Temple — Its Ministry and Services,
Sketches of Jewish Social Life in the Days of Christ,
Prophecy and History in Relation to the Messiah,
Bible History, Old Testament, etc.

PART ONE

Wm. B. Eerdmans Publishing Co., Grand Rapids, Michigan

First printing, One- volume Edition, November 1971

Reprinted, May 1984

ISBN 0-8028-8027-4

PHOTOLITHOPRINTED BY EERDMANS PRINTING COMPANY
GRAND RAPIDS, MICHIGAN, UNITED STATES OF AMERICA

TO THE CHANCELLOR, MASTERS AND SCHOLARS OF
THE UNIVERSITY OF OXFORD

These Volumes are Respectfully Dedicated

PREFACE

SECOND AND THIRD EDITIONS.

———

In issuing a new edition of this book I wish, in the first place, again to record, as the expression of permanent convictions and feelings, some remarks with which I had prefaced the Second Edition, although happily they are not at present so urgently called for.

With the feelings of sincere thankfulness for the kindness with which this book was received by all branches of the Church, only one element of pain mingled. Although I am well convinced that a careful or impartial reader could not arrive at any such conclusion, yet it was suggested that a perverse ingenuity might abuse certain statements and quotations for what in modern parlance are termed 'Anti-Semitic' purposes. That any such thoughts could possibly attach to a book concerning Him, Who was Himself a Jew; Who in the love of His compassion wept tears of bitter anguish over the Jerusalem that was about to crucify Him, and Whose first utterance and prayer when nailed to the Cross was: 'Father, forgive them, for they know not what they do —would seem terribly incongruous and painful. Nor can it surely be necessary to point out that the love of Christ, or the understanding of His Work and Mission, must call forth feelings far different from those to which reference has been made. To me, indeed, it is difficult to associate the so-called Anti-Semitic movement with any but the lowest causes: envy, jealousy, and cupidity on the one hand; or, on the other, ignorance, prejudice, bigotry, and hatred of race. But as these are times when it is necessary to speak unmistakably, I avail myself of the present opportunity to point out the reasons why any Talmudic quotations, even if fair, can have no application for 'Anti-Semitic' purposes.

First: It is a mistake to regard everything in Talmudic writings about 'the Gentiles' as presently applying to Christians. Those spoken of are characterised as 'the worshippers of idols,' 'of stars and planets,' and by similar designations. That 'the heathens' of those days and lands should have been .suspected of almost any abomination, deemed capable of any treachery or cruelty towards Israel—no student of history can deem strange, especially when the experience of so many terrible wrongs (would they had been confined to the heathen and to those times!) would naturally lead to morbidly excited suspicions and apprehensions.

Secondly: We must remember the times, the education, and the general standpoint of that period as compared with our own. No one would measure the belief of Christians by certain statements in the Fathers, nor judge the moral principles of Roman Catholics by prurient quotations from the Casuists; nor yet estimate the Lutherans by the utterances and deeds of the early successors of Luther, nor Calvinists by the burning of Servetus. In all such cases the general standpoint of the times has to be first taken into account. And no educated Jew would share the follies and superstitions, nor yet sympathise with the suspicions or feelings towards even the most hostile and depraved heathens, that may be quoted from the Talmud.

Thirdly: Absolutely the contrary of all this has been again and again set forth by modern Jewish writers. Even their attempts to explain away certain quotations from the Talmud—unsuccessful though, in my view, some of them are—afford evidence of their present repudiation of all such sentiments. I would here specially refer to such work as Dr. *Grünebaum's* 'Ethics of Judaism' ('Sittenlehre d. Judenthums')—a book deeply interesting also as setting forth the modern Jewish view of Christ and His Teaching, and accordant (though on different grounds) with some of the conclusions expressed in this book, as regards certain incidents in the History of Christ. The principles expressed by Dr. *Grünebaum*, and other writers, are such as for ever to give the lie to Anti-Semitic charges. And although he and others, with quite proper loyalty, labour to explain certain Talmudic citations, yet it ultimately comes to the admission that Talmudic sayings are not the criterion and rule of present duty, even as regards the heathen—still less Christians, to whom they do not apply.

What has just been stated, while it fully disposes of all 'Anti-Semitism,' only the more clearly sets forth the argument which forms the main proposition of this book. Here also we have the highest example.   None loved Israel so intensely, even unto death, as Jesus of Nazareth; none made such withering denunciations as He of Jewish Traditionalism, in all its branches, and of its Representatives.   It is with Traditionalism, not the Jews, that our controversy lies.   And here we cannot speak too plainly nor decidedly.   It might, indeed, be argued, apart from any proposed different applications, that on one or another point opinions of a different kind may also be adduced from other Rabbis.   Nor is it intended to convey unanimity of opinion on every subject.   For, indeed, such scarcely existed on any one point— not on matters of fact, nor even often on *Halakhic* questions.   And this also is characteristic of Rabbinism.   But it must be remembered that we are here dealing with the very text-book of that sacred and Divine Traditionalism, the basis and substance of Rabbinism, for which such unlimited authority and absolute submission are claimed; and hence, that any statement admitted into its pages, even though a different view were also to be adduced, possesses an authoritative and a representative character.   And this further appears from the fact that the same statements are often repeated in other documents, besides that in which they were originally made, and that they are also supported by other statements, kindred and parallel in spirit.

In truth, it has throughout been my aim to present, not one nor another isolated statement or aspect of Rabbinism, but its general teaching and tendency.   In so doing I have, however, purposely left aside certain passages which, while they might have most fully brought out the sad and strange extravagances to which Rabbinism could go, would have involved the unnecessary quotation of what is not only very painful in itself, but might have furnished an occasion to enemies of Israel.   Alike the one and the other it was my most earnest desire to avoid.   And by the side of these extravagances there is so much in Jewish writings and life—the outcome of Old Testament training—that is noblest and most touching, especially as regards the social virtues, such as purity, kindness, and charity, and the acknowledgment of God in sufferings, as well as their patient endurance.   On the other hand, it is difficult to believe that even the vehement assertions of partisans on the other side, supported by isolated sayings, sometimes torn from their context, or by such coincidences as are historically to be expected, will persuade those who keep in view either the words of Christ or His history and that of the Apostles, that the relation between Christianity in its origin, as the fulfilment of the Old Testament, and Traditionalism, as the externalised development of its letter, is other than that of which these volumes furnish both the explanation and the evidence.   In point of fact, the attentive student of history will observe that a similar protest against the bare letter underlies Alexandrianism and Philo—although there from the side of *reason* and apologetically, in the New Testament from the aspect of spiritual life and for its full presentation.

Thus much—somewhat reluctantly written, because approaching controversy—seemed necessary by way of explanation.   The brief interval between the First and Second Editions rendered only a superficial revision possible, as then indicated.   For the present edition the whole work has once more been revised, chiefly with the view of removing from the numerous marginal Talmudic references such misprints as were observed.   In the text and notes, also, a few *errata* have been corrected, or else the meaning rendered more clear. In one or two places fresh notes have been made; some references have been struck out, and others added.   These notes will furnish evidence that the literature of the subject, since the first appearance of these volumes, has not been neglected, although it seemed unnecessary to swell the 'List of Authorities' by the names of all the books since published or perused.   Life is too busy and too short to be always going back on one's traces.   Nor, indeed, would this be profitable. The further results of reading and study will best be embodied in further labours, please God, in continuation of those now completed. Opportunity may then also occur for the discussion of some questions which had certainly not been overlooked, although this seemed not the proper place for them: such as that of the composition of the Apostolic writings.

And so, with great thankfulness for what service this book has been already allowed to perform, I would now send it forth on its new journey, with this as my most earnest hope and desire: that, in however humble a manner, it may be helpful for the fuller and clearer setting forth of the Life of Him Who is the Life of all our life.

A. E.

OXFORD: *March* 1886.

PREFACE

TO

THE FIRST EDITION.

IN presenting these volumes to the reader, I must offer an explanation,—though I would fain hope that such may not be absolutely necessary. The title of this book must not be understood as implying any pretence on my part to write a 'Life of Christ' in the strict sense. To take the lowest view, the materials for it do not exist. Evidently the Evangelists did not intend to give a full record of even the outward events in that History; far less could they have thought of compassing the sphere or sounding the depths of the Life of Him, Whom they present to us as the God-Man and the Eternal Son of the Eternal Father. Rather must the Gospels be regarded as four different aspects in which the Evangelists viewed the historical Jesus of Nazareth as the fulfilment of the Divine promise of old, the Messiah of Israel and the Saviour of man, and presented Him to the Jewish and Gentile world for their acknowledgment as the Sent of God, Who revealed the Father, and was Himself the Way to Him, the Truth, and the Life. And this view of the Gospel-narratives underlies the figurative representation of the Evangelist in Christian Symbolism.[1]

In thus guarding my meaning in the choice of the title, I have already indicated my own standpoint in this book. But in another respect I wish to disclaim having taken any predetermined dogmatic standpoint at the outset of my investigations. I wished

-----

[1] Comp. the historical account of these symbols in *Zahn*, Forsch. z. Gesch. d. Neu-Test. Kanons, ii. pp. 257-275.

to write, not for a definite purpose, be it even that of the defence of the faith—but rather to let that purpose grow out of the book, as would be pointed out by the course of independent study, in which arguments on both sides should be impartially weighed and facts ascertained. In this manner I hoped best to attain what must be the first object in all research, but especially in such as the present: to ascertain, as far as we can, the truth, irrespective of consequences. And thus also I hoped to help others, by going, as it were, before them, in the path which their enquiries must take, and removing the difficulties and entanglements which beset it. So might I honestly, confidently, and, in such a matter, earnestly, ask them to follow me, pointing to the height to which such enquiries must lead up. I know, indeed, that there is something beyond and apart from this; even the restful sense on that height, and the happy outlook from it. But this is not within the province of one man to give to another, nor yet does it come in the way of study, however earnest and careful; it depends upon, and implies the existence of a subjective state which comes only by the direction given to our enquiries by the true ὁδηγός (St. John xvi. 13).

This statement of the general object in view will explain the course pursued in these enquiries. First and foremost, this book was to be a study of the Life of Jesus the Messiah, retaining the general designation, as best conveying to others the subject to be treated.

But, *secondly*, since Jesus of Nazareth was a Jew, spoke to, and moved among Jews, in Palestine, and at a definite period of its history, it was absolutely necessary to view that Life and Teaching in all its surroundings of place, society, popular life, and intellectual or religious development. This would form not only the frame in which to set the picture of the Christ, but the very background of the picture itself. It is, indeed, most true that Christ spoke not only to the Jews, to Palestine, and to that time, but—of which history has given the evidence—to all men and to all times. Still He spoke first and directly to the Jews, and His words must have been intelligible to them, His teaching have reached upwards from their intellectual and religious standpoint, even although it infinitely extended the horizon so as, in its full application, to make it wide as the bounds of earth and time. Nay, to explain the bearing of the religious leaders of Israel, from the first, towards Jesus, it seemed also necessary to trace the historical development of thought and religious belief, till it issued in that system of Traditionalism, which, by an internal necessity, was irreconcilably antagonistic to the Christ of the Gospels.

On other grounds also, such a full portraiture of Jewish life, society, and thinking seemed requisite. It furnishes alike a vindication and an illustration of the Gospel-narratives. A vindication —because in measure as we transport ourselves into that time, we feel that the Gospels present to us a real, historical scene; that the men and the circumstances to which we are introduced are real— not a fancy picture, but just such as we know and now recognize them, and would expect them to have spoken, or to have been. Again, we shall thus vividly realise another and most important aspect of the words of Christ. We shall perceive that their form is wholly of the times, their cast Jewish—while by the side of this similarity of form there is not only essential difference but absolute contrariety of substance and spirit. Jesus spoke as truly a Jew to the Jews, but He spoke not as they—no, not as their highest and best Teachers would have spoken. And this contrariety of spirit with manifest similarity of form is, to my mind, one of the strongest evidences of the claims of Christ, since it raises the all-important question, whence the Teacher of Nazareth—or, shall we say, the humble Child of the Carpenter-home in a far-off little place of Galilee —had drawn His inspiration? And clearly to set this forth has been the first object of the detailed Rabbinic quotations in this book.

But their further object, besides this vindication, has been the illustration of the Gospel-narratives. Even the general reader must be aware that some knowledge of Jewish life and society at the time is requisite for the understanding of the Gospel-history. Those who have consulted the works of *Lightfoot, Schöttgen, Meuschen, Wetstein* and *Wünsche,* or even the extracts from them presented in Commentaries, know that the help derived from their Jewish references is very great. And yet, despite the immense learning and industry of these writers, there are serious drawbacks to their use. Sometimes the references are critically not quite accurate; sometimes they are derived from works that should not have been adduced in evidence; occasionally, either the rendering, or the application of what is separated from its context, is not reliable. A still more serious objection is, that these quotations are not unfrequently one sided; but chiefly this—perhaps, as the necessary consequence of being merely illustrative notes to certain verses in the Gospels—that they do not present a full and connected picture. And yet it is this which so often gives the most varied and welcome illustration of the

Gospel-narratives. In truth, we know not only the leading personages in Church and State in Palestine at that time, their views, teaching, pursuits, and aims; the state of parties; the character of popular opinion; the proverbs, the customs, the daily life of the country—but we can, in imagination, enter their dwellings, associate with them in familiar intercourse, or follow them to the Temple, the Synagogue, the Academy, or to the market-place and the workshop. We know what clothes they wore, what dishes they ate, what wines they drank, what they produced and what they imported: nay, the cost of every article of their dress or food, the price of houses and of living; in short, every detail that can give vividness to a picture of life.

All this is so important for the understanding of the Gospel-history as, I hope, to justify the fulness of archæological detail in this book. And yet I have used only a portion of the materials which I had collected for the purpose. And here I must frankly own, as another reason for this fulness of detail, that many erroneous and misleading statements on this subject, and these even on elementary points, have of late been made. Supported by references to the labours of truly learned German writers, they have been sometimes set forth with such confidence as to impose the laborious and unwelcome duty of carefully examining and testing them. But to this only the briefest possible reference has been made, and chiefly in the beginning of these volumes.

Another explanation seems more necessary in this connection. In describing the Traditionalism of the time of Christ, I must have said what, I fear, may, most unwillingly on my part, wound the feelings of some who still cling, if not to the faith of, yet to what now represents the ancient Synagogue. But let me appeal to their fairness. I must needs state what I believe to be the facts; and I could neither keep them back nor soften them, since it was of the very essence of my argument to present Christ as both in contact and in contrast with Jewish Traditionalism. No educated Western Jew would, in these days, confess himself as occupying the exact standpoint of Rabbinic Traditionalism. Some will select parts of the system; others will allegorise, explain, or modify it; very many will, in heart—often also openly—repudiate the whole. And here it is surely not necessary for me to rebut or disown those vile falsehoods about the Jews which ignorance, cupidity, and bigoted hatred have of late again so strangely raised. But I would go further, and assert that, in reference to Jesus of Nazareth, no educated Israelite of to-day would identify himself with the religious leaders of the people eighteen centuries ago. Yet is not this disclaimer of that Traditionalism which not only explains the rejection of Jesus, but is the sole logical *raison d'être* of the Synagogue, also its condemnation?

I know, indeed, that from this negative there is a vast step in advance to the positive in the reception of the Gospel, and that many continue in the Synagogue, because they are not so convinced of the other as truthfully to profess it. And perhaps the means we have taken to present it have not always been the wisest. The mere appeal to the literal fulfilment of certain prophetic passages in the Old Testament not only leads chiefly to critical discussions, but rests the case on what is, after all, a secondary line of argumentation. In the New Testament prophecies are not made to point to facts, but facts to point back to prophecies. The New Testament presents the fulfilment of all prophecy rather than of prophecies, and individual predictions serve as fingerposts to great outstanding facts, which mark where the roads meet and part. And here, as it seems to me, we are at one with the ancient Synagogue. In proof, I would call special attention to Appendix IX., which gives a list of all the Old Testament passages Messianically applied in Jewish writings. We, as well as they, appeal to all Scripture, to all prophecy, as that of which the reality is in the Messiah. But we also appeal to the whole tendency and new direction which the Gospel presents in opposition to that of Traditionalism; to the new revelation of the Father, to the new brotherhood of man, and to the satisfaction of the deepest wants of the heart, which Christ has brought—in short, to the Scriptural, the moral, and the spiritual elements; and we would ask whether all this could have been only the outcome of a Carpenter's Son at Nazareth at the time, and amidst the surroundings which we so well know.

In seeking to reproduce in detail the life, opinions, and teaching of the contemporaries of Christ, we have also in great measure addressed ourselves to what was the *third special object* in view in this History. This was to clear the path of difficulties — in other words, to meet such objections as might be raised to the Gospel-narratives. And this, as regards principle—not details and minor questions, which will cause little uneasiness to the thoughtful and calm reader; quite irrespective also of any theory of inspiration which may be proposed, and hence of any harmonistic or kindred attempts which may be made. Broadly speaking, the attacks on the Gospel-narratives may be grouped under these three particulars:

they may be represented as intentional fraud by the writers, and imposition on the readers; or, secondly, a rationalistic explanation may be sought of them, showing how what originally had been quite simple and natural was misunderstood by ignorance, or perverted by superstition; or, thirdly, they may be represented as the outcome of ideas and expectations at the time, which gathered around the beloved Teacher of Nazareth, and, so to speak, found body in legends that clustered around the Person and Life of Him Who was regarded as the Messiah. . . . And this is supposed to account for the preaching of the Apostles, for their life-witness, for their martyr-death, for the Church, for the course which history has taken, as well as for the dearest hopes and experiences of Christian life!

Of the three modes of criticism just indicated, importance attaches only to the third, which has been broadly designated as the mythical theory. The fraud-theory seems—as even *Strauss* admits —psychologically so incompatible with admitted facts as regards the early Disciples and the Church, and it does such violence to the first requirements of historical enquiry, as to make it—at least to me— difficult to understand how any thoughtful student could be swayed by objections which too often are merely an appeal to the vulgar, intellectually and morally, in us. For—to take the historical view of the question—even if every concession were made to negative criticism, sufficient would still be left in the Christian documents to establish a *consensus* of the earliest belief as to all the great facts of the Gospel-History, on which both the preaching of the Apostles and the primitive Church have been historically based. And with this *consensus* at least, and its practical outcome, historical enquiry has to reckon. And here I may take leave to point out the infinite importance, as regards the very foundation of our faith, attaching to the historical Church—truly in this also the ἐκκλησία Θεοῦ ζῶντος, στύλος καὶ ἑδραίωμα [*columna et fulcrum*] τῆς ἀληθείας (the Church of the Living God, the pillar and stay [support] of the truth).

As regards the second class of interpretation—the rationalistic— it is altogether so superficial, shadowy and unreal that it can at most be only regarded as a passing phase of light-minded attempts to set aside felt difficulties.

But the third mode of explanation, commonly, though perhaps not always quite fairly, designated as the mythical, deserves and demands, at least in its sober presentation, the serious consideration of the historical student. Happily it is also that which, in the nature of it, is most capable of being subjected to the test of historical examination. For, as previously stated, we possess ample materials for ascertaining the state of thought, belief, and expectancy in the time of Christ, and of His Apostles. And to this aspect of objections to the Gospels the main line of argumentation in this book has been addressed. For, if the historical analysis here attempted has any logical force, it leads up to this conclusion, that Jesus Christ was, alike in the fundamental direction of His teaching and work, and in its details, antithetic to the Synagogue in its doctrine, practice, and expectancies.

But even so, one difficulty—we all feel it—remaineth. It is that connected with miracles, or rather with the miraculous, since the designation, and the difficulty to which it points, must not be limited to outward and tangible phenomena. But herein, I venture to say, lies also its solution, at least so far as such is possible—since the difficulty itself, the miraculous, is of the very essence of our thinking about the Divine, and, therefore one of the conditions of it: at least, in all religions of which the origin is not from within us, subjective, but from without us, objective, or, if I may so say, in all that claim to be universal religions (catholic thinking). But, to my mind, the evidential value of miracles (as frequently set forth in these volumes) lies not in what, without intending offence, I may call their barely super-naturalistic aspect, but in this, that they are the manifestations of the miraculous, in the widest sense, as the essential element in revealed religion. Miracles are of chief evidential value, not in themselves, but as instances and proof of the direct communication between Heaven and earth. And such direct communication is, at least, the postulate and first position in all religions. They all present to the worshipper some *medium* of personal communication from Heaven to earth—some prophet or other channel of the Divine—and some *medium* for our communication with Heaven. And this is the fundamental principle of the miraculous as the essential postulate in all religion that purposes again to bind man to God. It proceeds on the twofold principle that communication must first come to man *from Heaven*, and then that it does so come. Rather, perhaps, let us say, that all religion turns on these two great factors of our inner experience: man's felt need and (as implied in it, if we are God's creatures) his felt expectancy. And in the Christian Church this is not merely matter of the past—it has attained its fullest reality, and is a constant present in the indwelling of the Paraclete.

Yet another part of the task in writing this book remains to be mentioned. In the nature of it, such a book must necessarily have been more or less of a Commentary on the Gospels. But I have sought to follow the text of the Gospels throughout, and separately to consider every passage in them, so that, I hope, I may truthfully designate it also a Commentary on the Four Gospels—though an informal one. And here I may be allowed to state that throughout I have had the general reader in view, reserving for the foot-notes and *Appendices* what may be of special interest to students. While thankfully availing myself of all critical help within my reach—and here I may perhaps take the liberty of specially singling out Professor Westcott's Commentary on St. John—I have thought it right to make the sacred text the subject of fresh and independent study. The conclusions at which I arrived I would present with the more deference, that, from my isolated position, I had not, in writing these volumes, the inestimable advantage of personal contact, on these subjects, with other students of the sacred text.

It only remains to add a few sentences in regard to other matters —perhaps of more interest to myself than to the reader. For many years I had wished and planned writing such a book, and all my previous studies were really in preparation for this. But the task was actually undertaken at the request of the Publishers, of whose kindness and patience I must here make public acknowledgment. For, the original term fixed for writing it was two or three years. It has taken me seven years of continual and earnest labour—and, even so, I feel as if I would fain, and ought to, spend other seven years upon what could, at most, be touching the fringe of this great subject. What these seven years have been to me I could not attempt to tell. In a remote country parish, entirely isolated from all social intercourse, and amidst not a few trials, parochial duty has been diversified and relieved by many hours of daily work and of study—delightful in and for itself. If any point seemed not clear to my own mind, or required protracted investigation, I could give days of undisturbed work to what to others might perhaps seem secondary, but was all-important to me. And so these seven years passed—with no other companion in study than my daughter, to whom I am indebted, not only for the *Index Rerum*, but for much else, especially for a renewed revision, in the proof-sheets, of the references made throughout these volumes. What labour and patience this required every reader will perceive—although even so I cannot hope that no misprint or slip of the pen has escaped our detection.

And now I part from this book with thankfulness to Almighty

God for sparing me to complete it, with lingering regret that the task is ended, but also with unfeigned diffidence. I have, indeed, sought to give my best and most earnest labour to it, and to write what I believed to be true, irrespective of party or received opinions. This, in such a book, was only sacred duty. But where study necessarily extended to so many, and sometimes new, departments, I cannot hope always to carry the reader with me, or—which is far more serious—to have escaped all error. My deepest and most earnest prayer is that He, in Whose Service I have desired to write this book, would graciously accept the humble service—forgive what is mistaken and bless what is true. And if anything personal may intrude into these concluding lines, I would fain also designate what I have written as *Apologia pro vitâ meâ* (alike in its fundamental direction and even ecclesiastically)—if, indeed, that may be called an *Apologia* which is the confession of this inmost conviction of mind and heart: 'Lord, to Whom shall we go? The words of eternal life hast Thou! And we have believed and know that Thou art the Holy One of God.'

ALFRED EDERSHEIM.

8 BRADMORE ROAD, OXFORD:
September 1883

LIST OF AUTHORITIES

CHIEFLY USED IN WRITING THIS BOOK.

Alford: Greek Testament.
Von der Alm: Heidn. u. jüd. Urtheile über Jesu u. die alten Christen.
Altingius: Dissertationes et Orationes.
Apocrypha: S. P. C. K. Commentary on. The Apocryphal Gospels.
Auerbach: Berith Abraham.

Bacher: Die Agada der Babylon. Amoräer.
Bäck: Geschichte des Jüd. Volkes u. seiner Literatur.
Baedeker: Syrien u. Palästina.
Bähr: Gesetz über Falsche Zeugen nach Bible u. Talmud.
Barclay: City of the Great King.
Beer: Leben Abraham's.
Beer: Leben Mosis.
Beer, P.: Geschichte d. relig. Sekten d. Juden.
Bengel: Gnomon Novi Testamenti.
Bengel: Alter der jüdischen Proselytentaufe.
Bergel: Naturwissenschaftliche Kenntnisse d. Talmudisten.
Bergel: Der Himmel u. seine Wunder.
Bergel: Die Eheverhältnisse der alten Juden.
Berliner, Dr. A.: Targum Onkelos.
Bertholdt: Christologia Judæorum.
Beyschlag: Die Christologie des Neuen Testaments.
Beyschlag: Zur Johanneischen Frage.
Bickell: Die Entstehung der Liturgie aus der Einsetzungsfeier.
Bleek: Einleitung in das Neue Testament, ed. Mangold.
Bleek: Synoptische Erklärung d. drei Evangelien.
Bloch: Studien z. Gesch. der Sammlung d althebr. Literatur.
Bloch: Das Mosaisch-talmud. Polizeirecht.
Bloch: Civilprocess-Ordnung nach Mos. rabb. Rechte.
Bochartus: Hierozoicon.
Bodek: Marcus Aurelius u. R. Jehudah.
Bodenschatz: Kirchliche Verfassung der heutigen Juden.

Böhl: Forschungen nach einer Volks bibel zur Zeit Jesu.
Böhl: Alttestamentliche Citate im N. T.
Bonar: The Land of Promise.
Braun: Die Söhne des Herodes.
Braunius: De Vestitu Hebræorum.
Brecher: DasTranscendentaleimTalmud.
Bredow: Rabbinische Mythen, &c.
Brückner: Die Versuchungsgeschichte unseres Herrn Jesu Christi.
Brück: Rabbinische Ceremonialgebräuche.
Brüll: Fremdsprachliche Redensarten im Talmud.
Brüll: Trachten der Juden.
Buber: Pesikta.
Bucher: Des Apostels Johannes Lehre vom Logos.
Burgon: The Last Twelve Verses of St. Mark.
Buxtorf: Exercitationes.
Buxtorf: Synagoga Judaica.
Buxtorf; Lexicon Talmud.

Calvin: Comment. (*passim*).
Cahen: Repertorium Talmudicum.
Carpzov: Chuppa Hebræorium.
Caspari: Einleitung in das Leben Jesu Christi.
Cassel: Das Buch Kusari.
Cassel: Lehrbuch der Jüd. Gesch, u. Literatur.
Castelli: Commento di Sabbatai Donnolo sul libro della Creazione.
Castelli: Il Messia secondo gli Ebrei.
Cavedoni: Biblische Numismatik.
Charteris: Canonicity.
Chasronoth Hashas.
Cheyne: Prophecies of Isaiah.
Chijs: De Herode Magno.
Cohen: Les Déicides.
Commentaries, Speaker's, on the Gospels; Camb. Bible on the Gospels.
Conder: Tent Work in Palestine.
Conder: Handbook to the Bible.
Conforte: Liber Kore ha-Dorot.
Cook: The Rev.Version of the Gospels.
Creizenach: Shulcan Aruch.

Cremer: New Testament Dictionary.
Cureton: Syriac Gospels.

Dähne: Jüdisch-Alex. Religionsphilos.
Davidson: Introduction to the Study of the New Testament.
Davidson: The Last Things.
Dachs: Codex SuccaTalmudis Babylonici.
Danko: HistoriaRevelationis DivinæN.T.
Danko: De Sacra Scriptura ejusque interpretatione Commentarius.
Delaunay: Moines et Sibylles dans l'antiquité Judéo-Grecque.
Delitzsch: Handwerkerleben zur Zeit Jesu.
Delitzsch: Geschichte der jüd. Poesie.
Delitzsch: Durch Krankheit zur Genesung.
Delitzsch: Ein Tag in Capernaum.
Delitzsch: Untersuchungen üb. die Entsteh. u. Anlage d. Matth.-Evang.
Delitzsch; Talmudische Studien.
Delitzsch: Jesus und Hillel.
Derenbourg: Essai sur l'Histoire et la Géographie de la Palestine.
Deutsch: Literary Remains.
Deylingius: Observationes Sacræ.
Dillmann: Das Buch Henoch.
Döllinger: Heidenthum und Judenthum.
Drummond: The Jewish Messiah.
Dukes: Zur Rabbinischen Sprachkunde.
Dukes: Rabbinische Blumenlese.
Duschak: Zur Botanik des Talmud.
Duschak: Die Moral der Evangelien und des Talmud.
Duschak: Jüdischer Cultus.
Duschak: Schulgesetzgebung.

Ebrard: Wissenschaftliche Kritik der evangel. Geschichte.
Edersheim: History of the Jewish Nation.
Edersheim: The Temple, its Ministry and its Services.
Edersheim: Sketches of Jewish Social Life.
Ehrmann: Geschichte der Schulen u. der Cultur unter den Juden.
Eisenmenger: Entdecktes Judenthum.
Eisler: Beiträge zur Rabb. Sprach- u. Alterthums-kunde.
Ellicott: New Testament Commentary: Gospels.
Ellicott: Lectures on the Life of our Lord.
    Encyclopædia Britannica (*passim*).
Etheridge: The Targums on the Pentateuch.
Eusebius: Ecclesiastical History.
Ewald: Abodah Sarah.
Ewald: Geschichte des Volkes Israel.
Ewald: Bibl. Jahrb. (*passim*).

Fabricius: Codex Pseudepigraphus V.T.
Farrar: Life of Christ.
Farrar: Eternal Hope.
Fassel: Das Mos. rabb. Civilrecht.
Fassel: Gerichts-Verf.
Field: Otium Norvicense.
Filipowski: Liber Juchassin.
Fisher: Beginnings of Christianity.
Frankel: Targum der Proph.
Frankel: Ueb.d. Einfl.d. paläst. Exegese auf die Alexandr. Hermeneutik.
Frankel: Monatschrift für das Judenthum (*passim*).
Frankel: Vorstudien zu der Septuaginta.
Frankel: Einleitung in d. Jerusalem Talmud.
Franck: d. Kabbala.
Freudenthal: Hellenistische Studien.
Friedenthal: Jessode haddat weikere Haemuna.
Friedlaender: Sittengeschichte Roms.
Friedlaender: Ben Dosa u. seine Zeit.
Friedlaender: Patristische u. Talmudische Studien.
Friedlieb: Oracula Sibyllina.
Friedlieb: Archäologie der Leidensgeschichte.
Friedmann: Siphré debe Rab.
Fritzsche u. Grimm: Handbuch zu den Apokryphen.
Fritzsche u. Grimm: Libri V. T. Pseudepigraphi Selecti.
Fuller: Harmony of the Four Gospels.
Fürst: Der Kanon des A. T.
Fürst: Kultur u. Literaturgeschichte der Juden in Asien.
Fürst: Biblioth. Jüd. (*passim*).
Fürstenthal: Menorath Hammaor.
Fürstenthal: Jessode haddat.

Geier: De Ebræorum Luctu Lugentiumque Ritibus.
Geiger: Das Judenthum u. seine Geschichte.
Geiger: Beiträge z. Jüd. Literatur-Gesch.
Geiger: Zeitschrift für Jüd. Theol. (*passim*).
Geiger: Urschrift u. Uebersetzungen der Bibel.
Geikie: Life and Words of Christ.
Gelpke: Die Jugendgesch. des Herrn.
Gerlach: Die Röm. Statthälter in Syrien u Judäa.
Gfrörer: Philo.
Gfrörer: Jahrh. d. Heils.
Ginsburg: Ben Chajim's Introd.
Ginsburg: Massoreth Ha-Massoreth.
Ginsburg: The Essenes.
Ginsburg: The Kabbalah.
Godet: Commentar.

Godet: Bibl. Studies.
Goebel: Die Parabeln Jesu.
Goldberg: The Language of Christ.
Graetz: Geschichte der Juden.
Green: Handbk. to the Grammar of the Grk. Test.
Grimm: Die Samariter.
Grimm: Clavis N. T.
Gronemann: Die Jonathansche Pentateuch-Uebersetzung.
Grünebaum: Sittenlehre desJudenthums.
Guérin: Description de la Palestine et Samarie.
Guillemard: Hebraisms in the Greek Testament.
Günzburg: Beleuchtung des alten Judenthums.

Hamburger: Real Encyklopädie f. Bibel u. Talmud.
Hamelsveld: Dissertatio de ædibus vet. Hebr.
Haneberg: Die relig. Alterth. der Bibel.
Harnoch: De Philonis Judæi Log. Inquisitio.
Hartmann: Die Hebräerin am Putztische u. als Braut.
Hartmann: Die enge Verbindung des A. T. mit dem Neuen.
Hase: Leben Jesu.
Haupt: Die A. T. Citate in den 4 Evangelien.
Hausrath: Neutestamentliche Zeitgeschichte.
Herzfeld: Geschichte Israels.
Herzfeld: Handelsgeschichte der Juden des Alterthums.
Herzog: Real-Encyklopädie (*passim*).
Hildesheimer: Der Herod. Tempel n. d. Talmud u. Josephus.
Hilgenfeld: Jüdische Apokalyptik.
Hirschfeld: Halach. u. Hagad. Exegese.
Hirschfeld: Tractatus Macot.
Hitzig: Geschichte des Volkes Israel.
Hoffmann: Leben Jesu.
Hofmann: Schriftbeweis.
Hofmann: Weissagung u. Erfüllung.
Hoffmann: Abhandlungen üb. die Pentat. Gesetze.
Holdheim: d. Cerem. Ges.
Hottinger: Juris Hebr. Leges.
Huschke: Ueb. d. Census u. die Steuerverf. d. früh. Röm. Kaiserzeit.
Huschke: Ueb. d. z. Zeit d. Geb. Jesu Christi gehaltenen Census.
Havercamp: Flavius Josephus.

Ideler: Chronologie.
Ikenius: Antiquitates Hebraicæ.
Ikenius: Dissertationes Philologico-theologicæ.

Jellinek: Beth ha-Midrash.
Joel: Blick in d. Religionsgesch. d. 2ten Christlichen Jahrh.
Joel: Religionsphilos. des Sohar.
Jost: Gesch. d. Judenth. u. seiner Sekten.
Jowett: Epistles of St. Paul, Romans, Galatians, Thessalonians.
Josephus Gorionides: ed. Breithaupt.
Juynboll: Comment. in Hist. Gentis Samaritanæ.

Keil: Einl. in. d. Kanon. u. Apokryph. Schriften des A. T.
Keim: Geschichte Jesu von Nazara.
Kennedy: Resurrection of Jesus Christ.
Kirchheim: Septem Libri Talmudici parvi Hierosol.
Kirchner: Jüd. Passahf.
Kitto: Cyclopædia of Biblical Literature (*passim*).
Kobut: Jüdische Angelologie u. Daemonologie.
König: Die Menschwerdung Gottes.
Köster: Nachw. d. Spur. einer Trinitätslehre vor Christo.
Krafft: Jüdische Sagen u. Dichtungen.
Krauss: Die Grosse Synode.
Krebs: Decreta Athen in honor Hyrcani P. M. Judæorum.
Krebs: Decreta Roman. pro Judæis.
Krebs: Observationes in Nov. Test.
Kuhn: Städt. u. bürgerl. Verfass d. Röm. Reichs.

Landau: Arukh.
Lange: Bibelwerk (on Gospels).
Langen: Judenthum in Palästina z. Zeit Christi.
Lange: Leben Jesu.
Langfelder: Symbolik des Judenthums.
Lattes: Saggio di Giunte e Correzzioni al Lessico Talmudico.
Lavadeur: Krit. Beleucht. d. jüd Kalenderwesens.
Lenormant: Chaldean Magic.
Levi: Historia Religionis Judæorum.
Levy: Neuhebr. u. Chaldäisch. Wörterbuch.
Levy: Chaldäisch. Wörterb. über die Targumim.
Levy: Gesch. der Jüdisch. Münzen.
Levyssohn: Disputatio de Jud. sub. Cæs. Conditione.
Lewin: Fasti Sacri.
Lewin: Siege of Jerusalem.
Lewyssohn: Zoologie des Talmuds.
Lightfoot: Horæ Hebraicæ et Talmudicæ in 4 Evangel.
Lightfoot: Commentary on Galatians.
Lightfoot: Commentary on Colossians.
Lisco: Die Wunder Jesu Christi.

Low: Beiträge z. jüd Alterthumskunde.
Low: Lebensalter in d. jüd. Literatur.
Löwe: Schulchan Aruch.
Lowy: Biggoreth ha Talmud.
Lucius: Essenismus in sein Verhältn z. Judenth.
Lücke: Johannes (Gospel).
Lundius: Jüdische Heiligthümer.
Luthardt: Johann. Evangelium.
Luthardt: Die modern. Darstell. d. Lebens Jesu.
Lutterbeck: Neutestamentliche Lehrbegriffe.

McLellan: New Testament (Gospels).
Madden: Coins of the Jews.
Maimonides: Yad haChazzakah.
Marcus: Pädagogik des Talmud.
Marquardt: Röm, Staatsverwaltung.
Martinus: Fidei Pugio.
Maybaum: Die Anthropomorph. u. Anthropopath. bei Onkelos.
    Megillath Taanith.
Meier: Judaica.
Meuschen: Nov. Test ex Talmude et Joseph.
Meyer: Seder Olam Rabba et Suta.
Meyer: Buch Jezira.
Meyer: Kommentar. (on Gospels).
Meyer: Arbeit u. Handwerk. im Talmud.
    Midrash Rabboth.
    Midrashim. (See List in Rabb. Abbrev.)
Mill: On the Mythical Interpretation of the Gospels.
    Mishnah.
Molitor: Philosophie der Geschichte.
Moscovitor: Het N. T. en de Talmud.
Müller: Mess. Erwart. d. Jud. Philo.
Müller: Zur Johann Frage.
Müller, J.: Massech. Sopher.
Münter: Stern der Weisen

Nanz: Die Besessenen im N. T.
Neander: Life of Christ.
Nebe: Leidensgesch. unser. Herrn Jesu Christi.
Nebe: Auferstehungsgesch. unser. Herrn Jesu Christi.
Neubauer: La Géographie du Talmud.
Neubauer and Driver: Jewish Interpreters of Isaiah. liii.
Neumann: Messian. Erschein. bei d. Juden.
Neumann: Gesch. d. Mess. Weissag. im A. T.
    New Testament. Ed. Scrivener. Ed. Westcott and Hort. Ed. Gebhardt.
Nicolai: De Sepulchris Hebræorum.
    Nizzachon Vetus. et Toledoth Jeshu.

Nicholson: The Gospel accord. to the Hebrews.
Norris: New Testament (Gospels).
Nork: Rabbinische Quellen u. Parallelen.
Nutt: Samaritan History.

Otho: Lexicon Rabbin. Philolog.
Outram: De Sacrificiis Judæor et Christi.
    Othijoth de R. Akiba.
Oxlee: Doc. of Trinity on Princips. of Judaism.

Pagninus: Thesaurus Linguæ Sanctæ.
    Palestine Exploration Fund Quarterly Statements (*passim*).
Perles: Liechenfeierlichk. im Nachbibl, Judenth.
Philippson: Haben wirklich die Jud. Jesum gekreuzigt?
Philippson: Israelit. Religionslehre.
Philo Judæus: Opera.
    Pictorial Palestine (*passim*).
    Picturesque Palestine.
Pinner: Berachoth.
Pinner: Compend. des Hieros. u. Babyl. Thalm.
    Pirké de R. Elieser.
Plumptre: Comment. on the Gospels.
Plumptre: Bible Educator (*passim*).
Pocock: Porta Mosis.
Prayer-books, Jewish: i. Arnheim. ii. Mannheimer. iii. Polak (Frankfort ed.). iv. Friedländer. v. F. A. Euchel. vi. Jacobson. vii. Pesach Haggadah. viii. Rodelheim ed.
Pressensé: Jesus Christ: His Time, Life, and Works.
Prideaux: Connec. of O. and N.T.
Pusey: What is of Faith as to Everlasting Punishment?

Rabbinowicz: Einleit. in d. Gesetzgeb. u. Medicin d. Talm.
Ravuis: Dissertat. de. aedib. vet. Hebr.
Redslob: Die Kanonisch. Evangelien.
Reland: Antiquit. Sacr. veter. Hebr.
Reland: Palæstina.
Remond: Ausbreit. d. Judenthums.
Renan: L'Antéchrist.
Renan: Vie de Jésus.
Renan: Marc-Aurèle.
Rhenferd et Vitringa: De Decem Otiosis Synagogæ.
Riehm: Handwörterb. d. bibl. Alterth. (*passim*).
Riehm: Lehrbegriff d. Hebräerbriefs.
Riess: Geburtsjahr Christi.
Ritter: Philo u. die Halacha.
Roberts: Discussion on the Gospels.

Robinson: Biblical Researches in Palestine.
Roeth: Epistoia ad Hebræos.
Rohr: Palästina z. Zeit Christi.
Rönsch: Buch Jubiläen.
Roos: Lehre u. Lebensgesch. Jesu Christi.
Rösch: Jesus-Mythen d. Talmudist.
Rosenmüller: Biblisch. Geographie.
Rossi, *Azarjah de*: Meor Enajim.
Rossi, *Giambernardo de*: Della Lingua Propria di Christo.

Sachs: Beiträge z. Sprach u. Alterthumskunde.
Saalschütz: Musik bei d. Hebräern.
Saalschütz: Mos. Recht.
Salvador: Römerherrschaft in Judæa.
Salvador: Gesch. d. Jüd. Volkes.
Sammter: Baba Mezia.
Schenkel: Bibel-Lexicon (*passim*).
Schleusner: Lexicon Gr. Lat. in N.T.
Schmer: De Chuppa Hebræorum.
Schmilg: Der Siegeskalender Megill Taanith.
Schneckenburger: Neutestament. Zeitgeschichte.
Schoettgen: Horæ Hebraicæ et Talmudicæ.
Schreiber: Principien des Judenthums.
Schroederus: Comment. de Vestitu Mulier. Hebr.
Schürer: Neutestam. Zeitgesch.
Schürer: Gemeindeverfass. d. Juden in Rom in d. Kaiserzeit.
Schwab: Le Talmud de Jérusalem.
Schwarz: D. Heilige Land.
Schwarz: Tosifta Shabbath.
Scrivener: Introduction to the Criticism of the New Testament.
Seder Hadoroth.
Selden: De Synedriis Ebr.
Selden: De Jure Naturali et Gent. Hebr.
Selden: Uxor Ebraica.
Sepp: Leben Jesu.
Sevin: Chronologie des Lebens Jesu.
Sheringham: Joma.
Siegfried: Philo von Alexandria.
Singer: Onkelos u. seine Verhältn. z. Halacha.
Sion Ledorosh.
Smith: Dictionary of the Bible (*passim*).
Smith and Wace: Dictionary of Christian Biography (*passim*).
Sohar.
Tikkuné haSohar.
Saloweyczyk: Bibel, Talmud, u. Evangelium.
Sommer: Mispar haSohar.
Spencer: De Legib. Hebr. Ritual.
Spiess: Das Jerusalem des Josephus.
Spitzer: Das Mahl bei den Hebräern.

Stanley: Sinai and Palestine.
Steinmeyer: Geburt des Herrn u. seinerste Schritte im Leben.
Steinmeyer: Die Parabeln des Herrn
Stein: Schrift des Lebens.
Stern: Die Frau im Talmud.
Stern: Gesch. des Judenthums.
Stier: Reden des Herrn Jesu.
Strack: Pirké Aboth.
Strack: Proleg. Crit. in V.T. Hebr.
Strauss: Leben Jesu.
Supernatural Religion.
Surenhusius: Biblos Katallages.
Surenhusius: Mishnah.

Talmud, Babylon and Jerusalem.
Targum, the Targumim in the Mikraoth gedoloth.
Taylor: Sayings of the Jewish Fathers (Pirqé Ab., &c.), with critical and illustrative Notes.
Taylor: Great Exemplar.
Tauchuma: Midrash.
Thein: Der Talmud.
Theologische Studien u. Kritiken (*passim*).
Tholuck: Bergpredigt Christi.
Tholuck: Das Alt. Test. im Neu. Test.
Tischendorf: When were our Gospels written?
Toetterman: R. Eliezer ben Hyrcanus.
Traill: Josephus.
Trench: Notes on the Miracles
Trench: Notes on the Parables.
Tristram: Natural History of the Bible.
Tristram: Land of Israel.
Tristram: Land of Moab.
Trusen: Sitten, Gebräuche u. Krankheiten. d. alt. Hebr.

Ugolinus: Thesaurus Antiquitatum Sacrarum (*passim*).
Unruh: Das alte Jerusalem u. seine Bauwerke.

Vernes: Histoire des Idées Messianiques.
Vitringa: De Synagoga Vetere.
Volkmar: Einleitung in die Apokryphen.
Volkmar: Marcus.
Volkmar: Mose Prophetie u. Himmelfahrt.
Vorstius: De Hebraisms Nov. Test.

Wace: The Gospel and its Witnesses.
Wagenseil: Sota.
Wahl: Clavis Nov. Test. Philologica.
Warneck: Pontius Pilatus.
Watkins: Gospel of St. John.
Weber: Johannes der Täufer u. die Parteien seiner Zeit.

Weber: System der altsynagog. paläst. Theologie.
B. Weiss: Lehrb. d. bibl. Theol. des N.T.
Weiss: Mechilta.
Weiss: Siphra
B. Weiss: Matthäusevangelium.
B. Weiss: Leben Jesu.
Weiss: Geschichte. der jüd. Tradition.
Weizsäcker: Untersuch. üb. die evangel. Geschichte.
Wellhausen: Die Pharisäer u. die Sadducäer.
Westcott: Introduction to the Study of the Gospels.
Westcott: On the Canon of the New Testament.
Westcott: Gospel of St. John.
Wetstein: Novum Testamentum Græcum (Gospels).
Wichelhaus: Kommentar zur Leidensgeschichte.
Wieseler: Beiträge zu den Evang. u. der Evangel. Gesch.
Wieseler: Chronol. Synopse der 4 Evangelien.
Wiesner: d. Bann in s. Gesch. Entwickelung.
Winer: Biblisches Realwörterbuch (*passim*).

Winer: De Onkeloso.
Wilson: Recovery of Jerusalem.
Wittichen: Die Idee des Reiches Gottes.
Wittichen: Leben Jesu.
Wolfius: Bibliotheca Hebræa (*passim*).
Wordsworth: Commentary (Gospels).
Wunderbar: Bibl. talmud. Medecin.
Wünsche: Die Leiden des Messias.
Wünsche: Neue Beiträge z. Erläut. der Evangel.
Wünsche: Der Jerusalemische Talmud.
Wünsche: Bibliotheca Rabbinica.

Yalkut Shimeoni.
Yalkut Rubeni.
Young: Christology of the Targums.

Zahn: Forsch. zur Gesch. d. N.T. Kanons.
Zeller: Philosophie der Griechen.
Zemach David.
Zimmermann: Karten u. Pläne z. Topographie des alten Jerusalems.
Zöckler: Handb. d.Theol.Wissenschaften.
Zumpt: Geburtsjahr Christi.
Zunz: Zur Geschichte u. Literatur.
Zunz: Die Gottesdienstl. Vortr. d. Juden.
Zunz: Synagogale Poesie.
Zunz: Ritus d.Synagogalen-Gottesdienst.
Zuckermandel: Tosephta.

LIST OF ABBREVIATIONS USED IN REFERENCE TO RABBINIC WRITINGS QUOTED IN THIS WORK.

THE *Mishnah* is always quoted according to *Tractate, Chapter (Pereq)* and *Para-graph* (Mishnah), the Chapter being marked in *Roman*, the paragraph in ordinary Numerals. Thus Ber. ii. 4 means the Mishnic Tractate *Berakhoth*, second Chapter, fourth Paragraph.

The *Jerusalem Talmud* is distinguished by the abbreviation *Jer.* before the name of the Tractate. Thus, Jer. Ber. is the Jer. Gemara, or Talmud, of the Tractate *Berakhoth*. The edition, from which quotations are made, is that commonly used, Krotoschin, 1866, 1 vol. fol. The quotations are made either by Chapter and Para-graph (Jer. Ber. ii. 4), or, in these volumes mostly, by page and column. It ought to be noted that in Rabbinic writings each page is really a double one, distinguished respectively as *a* and *b*: *a* being the page to the left hand of the reader, and *b* the reverse one (on turning over the page) to the right hand of the reader. But in the *Jerusalem* Gemara (and in *Yalkut* [see below], as in all works where the page and column (*col.*) are mentioned) the quotation is often—in these volumes, mostly—made by page and column (two columns being on each side of a page). Thus, while Jer. Ber. ii. 4 would be Chapter II. Par. 4, the corresponding quotation by page and col-umn would in that instance be, Jer. Ber. 4 *d*; *d* marking that it is the fourth column in *b* (or the off-side) of page 4.

The *Babyl. Talmud* is, in all its editions, equally paged, so that a quotation made applies to all editions. It is double-paged, and quoted with the name of the Tractate, the number of the page, and *a* or *b* according as one or another side of the page is referred to. The quotations are distinguished from those of the Mishnah by this, that in the Mishnah Roman and ordinary numerals are employed (to mark Chapters and Paragraphs), while in the Babylon Talmud the name of the Tractate is followed by an ordinary numeral, indicating the page, together with *a* or *b*, to mark which side of the page is referred to. Thus Ber. 4 *a* means: Tractate *Berachoth*, p. 4, first or left-hand side of the page.

I have used the Vienna edition, but this, as already explained, is not a point of any importance. To facilitate the verification of passages quoted I have in very many instances quoted also the *lines*, either from top or bottom.

The abbreviation *Tos.* (*Tosephta*, additamentum) before the name of a Tractate refers to the additions made to the *Mishnah* after its redaction. This redaction dates from the third century of our era. The *Tos.* extends only over 52 of the Mishnic Tractates. They are inserted in the Talmud at the end of each Tractate, and are printed on the double pages in double columns (col. *a* and *b* on p. *a*, col. *e* and *d* on p. *b*). They are generally quoted by *Pereq* and *Mishnah*: thus, Tos. Gitt. i. 1, or (more rarely) by page and column, Tos. Gitt. p. 150 *a*. The ed. *Zuckermandel* is, when quoted, specially indicated.

Besides, the Tractate *Aboth de Rabbi Nathan* (Ab. de. R. Math.), and the smaller Tractates, *Sopherim* (*Sopher.*), *Semachoth* (*Semach.*), *Kallah* (*Kall. or Chall.*[1]),

---

[1] It is to be noted that in the marginal and note-references the old mode of indicating a reference (as in the first ed. of this book) and the, perhaps, more correct mode of translitera-tion have been promiscuously employed. But the reader can have no difficulty in under-standing the reference.

Derekh Erets (*Der Er.*), *Derekh Erets Zuta* (commonly *Der Er. S.*), and *Pereq Shalom* (*Per. Shal.*) are inserted at the close of vol. ix. of the Talmud. They are printed in four columns (on double pages), and quoted by Pereq and Mishnah.

The so-called Septem Libri Talmudici parvi Hierosolymitani are published separately (ed. *Raphael Kirchheim*, Frcf 1851). They are the *Massecheth Sepher Torah* (*Mass. Seph. Tor.*), *Mass. Mezuzah* (*Mass. Mesus.*), *Mass. Tephillin* (*Mass. Tephill.*), *Mass. Tsitsith* (*Mass. Ziz.*), *Mass. Abhadim* (*Mass. Abad.*), *Mass. Kuthim* (*Mass. Cuth.*), and *Mass. Gerim* (*Mass. Ger.*). They are printed and quoted according to double pages (*a* and *b*).

To these must be added the so-called *Chesronoth haShas*, a collection of passages expurgated in the ordinary editions from the various Tractates of the Talmud. Here we must close, what might else assume undue proportions, by an alphabetical list of the abbreviations, although only of the principal books referred to:—

Ab. Zar. [1] . . The Talmudic Tractate *Abhodah Zarah*, on Idolatry.
Ab. . . . " " " *Pirqey Abhoth*, Sayings of the Fathers.
Ab. de R Nath. The Tractate *Abhoth de Rabbi Nathan* at the close of vol. ix. in the Bab. Talm.
Arakh. . . The Talmudic Tractate *Arakhin*, on the redemption of persons or things consecrated to the Sanctuary.

Bab. K. . . " " " *Babha Qamma* ('First Gate'), the first,
Bab. Mets. [or *Mez.*] " " *Babha Metsia* ('Middle Gate'), the second,
Bab. B. . . " " " *Babha Bathra* ('Last Gate'), the third of the great Tractates on Common Law.
Bechor. . . " " " *Bekhoroth*, on the consecration to the Sanctuary of the First-born.
Bemid R. . . The Midrash (or Commentary (*Bemidbar Rabba*, on Numbers.
Ber. . . The Talmudic Tractate *Berakhoth*, on Prayers and Benedictions.
Ber. R. . . The Midrash (or Commentary) *Bereshith Rabba*, on Genesis.
Bets. [or *Bez.*] . . The Talmudic Tractate *Betsah*, laws about an egg laid on Sabbath and Fast-days, and on similar points connected with the sanctifying of such seasons.
Biccur. . . " " " *Bikkurim*, on First-fruits.

Chag. . . " " " *Chagigah*, on the festive offerings at the three Great Feasts.
Chall. . . " " " *Challah*, on the first of the dough (Numb. xv. 17).
Chull. . . " " " *Chullin*, the rubric as to the mode of killing meat and kindred subjects.

Debar R. . . The Midrash *Debharim Rabba*, on Deuteronomy.
Dem. . . The Talmudic Tractate *Demai*, regarding Produce, the tithing of which is not certain.

Ech. R. . . The Midrash *Ekhah Rabbathi*, on Lamentations (also quoted as Mid. on Lament).
Eduy. . . The Talmudic Tractate *Eduyoth* (Testimonies), the legal determinations enacted or confirmed on a certain occasion, decisive in Jewish History.
Erub. . . The Talmudic Tractate *Erubhin*, on the conjunction of Sabbath boundaries. (See Appendix XVII.)

Midr. Esth. . . The Midrash on Esther.

---

[1] Mark the note on previous page.

Gitt. . . . The Talmudic Tractate *Gittin,* on Divorce.

Horay. . . . The Taldmudic Tractate *Horayoth* 'Decisions' on certain uninten tional transgressions.

Jad. [or *Yad.*] " " " *Yadayim,* on the Washing of Hands.

Jebam. [or Yebam.] } " " " *Yebhamoth,* on the Levirate.

Jom. [mostly Yom.] } " " " *Yoma,* on the Day of Atonement.

Kel. . . . " " " *Kelim,* on the purification of furniture and vessels.

Kerith. . . " " " *Kerithuth,* on the punishment of 'cutting off.'

Kethub. . . " " " *Kethubhoth,* on marriage-contracts.

Kidd. . . " " " *Qiddushin,* on Betrothal.

Kil. . . . " " " *Kilayim,* on the unlawful commixtures (Lev. xix. 19; Deut. xxii. 9–11).

Kinn. . . " " " *Qinnim,* on the offering of doves (Lev. v. 1–10; xii. 8).

Midr. Kohel. . The Midrash on *Qoheleth* or Eccles.

Maas. . . . The Talmudic Tractate *Maaseroth,* on Levitical Tithes.

Maas Sh. . . " " " *Maaser Sheni,* on second Tithes (Deut. xiv. 22, &c.).

Machsh. . . " " " *Makhshirin,* on fluids that may render products 'defiled,' or that leave them undefiled (Lev. xi. 34, 38).

Makk. [or *Macc.*] " " " *Makkoth,* on the punishment of Stripes.

Mechil. . . " " " *Mekhilta,* a Commentary on part of Exo- dus, dating at the latest from the first half of the second century.

Megill. . . " " " *Megillah.* referring to the reading of the ('roll') Book of Esther and on the Feast of Esther.

Meil. . . " " " *Meilah,* on the defilement of things con- secrated.

Menach. . . " " " *Menachoth,* on Meat-offerings.

Midd. . . " " " *Middoth,* on the Temple-measurements and arrangements.

Mikv. . . " " " *Miqvaoth,* on ablutions and immersions.

Moed K. . . " " " *Moed Qatan,* on Half-holidays

Naz. . . . " " " *Nazir,* on the Nasirate.

Ned. . . . " " " *Nedarim,* on Vowing.

Neg. . . . " " " *Negaim,* on Leprosy.

Nidd. . . " " " *Niddah,* on female levitical impurity (*menstrua*).

Ohol. . . " " " *Oholoth,* on the defilement of tents and houses, specially by death.

Orl. . . . " " " *Orlah,* on the ordinances connected with Lev. xix. 23.

Par. . . . " " " *Parah,* on the Red Heifer and purification by its ashes.

Peah . . " " " *Peah,* on the corner to be left for the poor in harvesting.

Pes. . . " " " *Pesachim,* on the Paschal Feast.

Pesiqta . . The Book *Pesiqta*, an exceedingly interesting series of Meditations or brief discussions and Lectures on certain portions of the Lectionary for the principal Sabbaths and Feast Days.

Pirqé de R. Eliez. The Haggadic *Pirqé de Rabbi Eliezer*, in 54 chapters, a discursive Tractate on the History of Israel from the creation to the time of Moses, with the insertion of three chapters (xlix.-li.) on the history of Haman and the future Messianic deliverance.

Rosh haSh. . The Talmudic Tractate *Rosh haShanah*, on the Feast of New Year.

Sab. . . " " " *Zabhim*, on certain levitically defiling issues.
Sanh. . . " " " *Sanhedrin*, on the Sanhedrim and Criminal Jurisprudence.
Sebach. . . " " " *Zebhachim*, on Sacrifices.
Shabb. . . " " " *Shabbath*, on Sabbath-observance.
Shebh. . . " " " *Shebhiith*, on the Sabbatic Year.
Shebu. . . " " " *Shebhuoth*, on Oaths, &c.
Sheqal. . . " " " *Sheqalim*, on the Temple-Tribute, &c.
Shem R. . . The Midrash *Shemoth Rabba* on Exodus.
Shir haSh R. . " " *Shir haShirim Rabba*, on the Song of Solomon.
Siphra . . The ancient Commentary on Leviticus, dating from the second century.
Siphré . . The still somewhat older Commentary on Numb. and Deuter.
Sot. . . The Talmudic Tractate *Sotah*, on the Woman accused of Adultery.
Sukk. . . " " " *Sukkah*, on the Feast of Tabernacles.

Taan. . . " " " *Taanith*, on Fasting and Fast-Days.
Tam. . . " " " *Tamid*, on the daily Service and Sacrifice in the Temple.
Teb. Yom. . " " " *Tebhul Yom* (' bathed of the day '), on impurities, where there is immersion on the evening of the same day.
Tem. . . " " " *Temurah*, on substitution for things consecrated (Lev. xxvii. 10).
Ter. . . " " " *Terumoth*, on the priestly dues in produce.
Tohar. . . " " " *Toharoth*, on minor kinds of defilement.
Tanch. . . The Midrashic Commentary *Tanchuma* (or *Yelamdenu*), on the Pentateuch.

Ukz. . . The Talmudic Tractate *Uqtsin*, on the defilement of fruits through their envelopes, stalks, &c.

Vayyik. R. . The Midrash *Vayyikra Rabba*, on Leviticus.

Yalk. . . The great *collectaneum*: *Yalkut Shimeoni*, which is a *catena* on the whole Old Testament, containing also quotations from works lost to us.[1]

---

[1] It will, of course, be understood that we have only given the briefest, and, indeed, imperfect, indications of the contents of the various Talmudic Tractates. Besides giving the Laws connected with each of the subjects of which they treat, all kindred topics are taken up, nay, the discussion often passes to quite other than the subjects primarily treated of in a Tractate.

CONTENTS

OF

THE FIRST VOLUME

BOOK I.

INTRODUCTORY.

THE PREPARATION FOR THE GOSPEL:
THE JEWISH WORLD IN THE DAYS OF CHRIST.

BOOK II.

FROM THE MANGER IN BETHLEHEM TO THE

BAPTISM IN JORDAN.

BOOK III.

THE ASCENT:

FROM THE RIVER JORDAN TO THE MOUNT OF TRANSFIGURATION.

CONTENTS OF THE FIRST VOLUME.

Book I.

INTRODUCTORY.

THE PREPARATION FOR THE GOSPEL:
THE JEWISH WORLD IN THE DAYS OF CHRIST

כל הנביאים כולן לא נתנבאו אלא לימות המשיח

All the prophets prophesied not but of the days of the Messiah.'—SANH. **99** *a*.

לא אברי עלמא אלא . . . . למשיח

'The world was not created but only for the Messiah.'—SANH. **98** *b*.

CHAPTER I.

THE JEWISH WORLD IN THE DAYS OF CHRIST—THE JEWISH DISPERSION IN THE EAST.

AMONG the outward means by which the religion of Israel was preserved, one of the most important was the centralisation and localisation of its worship in Jerusalem. If to some the ordinances of the Old Testament may in this respect seem narrow and exclusive, it is at least doubtful, whether without such a provision Monotheism itself could have continued as a creed or a worship. In view of the state of the ancient world, and of the tendencies of Israel during the earlier stages of their history, the strictest isolation was necessary in order to preserve the religion of the Old Testament from that mixture with foreign elements which would speedily have proved fatal to its existence. And if one source of that danger had ceased after the seventy years' exile in Babylonia, the dispersion of the greater part of the nation among those whose manners and civilisation would necessarily influence them, rendered the continuance of this separation of as great importance as before. In this respect, even traditionalism had its mission and use, as a hedge around the Law to render its infringement or modification impossible.

Wherever a Roman, a Greek, or an Asiatic might wander, he could take his gods with him, or find rites kindred to his own. It was far otherwise with the Jew. He had only one Temple, that in Jerusalem; only one God, Him Who had once throned there between the Cherubim, and Who was still King over Zion. That Temple was the only place where a God-appointed, pure priesthood could offer acceptable sacrifices, whether for forgiveness of sin, or for fellowship with God. Here, in the impenetrable gloom of the innermost sanctuary, which the High-Priest alone might enter once a year for most solemn expiation, had stood the Ark, the leader of the people into the Land of Promise, and the footstool on which the Shechinah had rested. From that golden altar rose the sweet cloud of incense, symbol of Israel's accepted prayers; that seven-branched candlestick shed its perpetual light, indicative of the brightness of God's Covenant Presence; on that table, as it were before the face of Jehovah, was laid, week by week, 'the Bread of the Face,'[1] a constant sacrificial meal which Israel offered unto God, and wherewith God in turn fed His chosen priesthood.   On the great blood-sprinkled altar of sacrifice smoked the daily and festive burnt-offerings, brought by all Israel, and for all Israel, wherever scattered; while the vast courts of the Temple were thronged not only by native Palestinians, but literally by 'Jews out of every nation under heaven.'   Around this Temple gathered the sacred memories of the past; to it clung the yet brighter hopes of the future.   The history of Israel and all their prospects were intertwined with their religion; so that it may be said that without their religion they had no history, and without their history no religion.   Thus, history, patriotism, religion, and hope alike pointed to Jerusalem and the Temple as the centre of Israel's unity.

Nor could the depressed state of the nation alter their views or shake their confidence.   What mattered it, that the Idumæan, Herod, had usurped the throne of David, except so far as his own guilt and their present subjection were concerned?   Israel had passed through deeper waters, and stood triumphant on the other shore.   For centuries seemingly hopeless bondsmen in Egypt, they had not only been delivered, but had raised the God-inspired morning-song of jubilee, as they looked back upon the sea cleft for them, and which had buried their oppressors in their might and pride.   Again, for weary years had their captives hung Zion's harps by the rivers of that city and empire whose colossal grandeur, wherever they turned, must have carried to the scattered strangers the desolate feeling of utter hopelessness.   And yet that empire had crumbled into dust, while Israel had again taken root and sprung up.   And now little more than a century and a half had passed, since a danger greater even than any of these had threatened the faith and the very existence of Israel.   In his daring madness, the Syrian king, Antiochus IV. (Epiphanes) had forbidden their religion, sought to destroy their sacred books, with unsparing ferocity forced on them conformity to heathen rites, desecrated the Temple by dedicating it to Zeus Olympios, and even reared a heathen altar upon that of burnt-offering.[2]   Worst of all, his wicked schemes had been aided by two apostate High-Priests, who had outvied each other in buying and then prostituting

---

[1] Such is the literal meaning of what is translated by 'shewbread.'
[2] 1 Macc. i. 54, 59; *Jos.* Ant. xii. 5. 4.

the sacred office of God's anointed.[1] Yet far away in the mountains
of Ephraim[2] God had raised for them most unlooked-for and unlikely
help. Only three years later, and, after a series of brilliant victories
by undisciplined men over the flower of the Syrian army, Judas the
Maccabee—truly God's Hammer[3]—had purified the Temple, and
restored its altar on the very same day[4] on which the 'abomination
of desolation'[5] had been set up in its place. In all their history the
darkest hour of their night had ever preceded the dawn of a morning
brighter than any that had yet broken. It was thus that with one
voice all their prophets had bidden them wait and hope. Their
sayings had been more than fulfilled as regarded the past. Would
they not equally become true in reference to that far more glorious
future for Zion and for Israel, which was to be ushered in by the
coming of the Messiah?

Nor were such the feelings of the Palestinian Jews only. These
indeed were now a minority. The majority of the nation constituted
what was known as the dispersion; a term which, however, no longer
expressed its original meaning of banishment by the judgment of
God,[6] since absence from Palestine was now entirely voluntary. But
all the more that it referred not to outward suffering,[7] did its continued
use indicate a deep feeling of religious sorrow, of social isolation, and of
political strangership[8] in the midst of a heathen world. For although,
as Josephus reminded his countrymen,[a] there was 'no nation in the
world which had not among them part of the Jewish people,' since it
was 'widely dispersed over all the world among its inhabitants,'[b] yet
they had nowhere found a real home. A century and a half before

[a] Jew. W
ii. 16. 4

[b] vii. 3. 3

[1] After the deposition of Onias III.
through the bribery of his own brother
Jason, the latter and Menelaus outvied
each other in bribery for, and prostitu-
tion of, the holy office.

[2] Modin, the birthplace of the Maccabees, has been identified with the modern
El-Medyeh, about sixteen miles north-
west of Jerusalem, in the ancient territory of Ephraim. Comp. Conder's Handbook of the Bible, p. 291; and for a full
reference to the whole literature of the
subject, see Schürer (Neutest. Zeitgesch.
p. 78, note 1).

[3] On the meaning of the name Maccabee, comp. Grimm's Kurzgef. Exeget.
Handb. z. d. Apokr. Lief. iii., pp. ix. x.
We adopt the derivation from Maqqabha,
a hammer, like Charles Martel.

[4] 1 Macc. iv. 52–54: Megill. Taan. 23.

[5] 1 Macc. 1. 54.

[6] Alike the verb גָּלָה in Hebrew. and
διασπείρω in Greek, with their deriv-
atives, are used in the Old Testament,
and in the rendering of the LXX., with
reference to punitive banishment. See,
for example, Judg. xviii. 30; 1 Sam. iv.
21; and in the LXX. Deut. xxx. 4; Ps.
cxlvii. 2; Is. xlix. 6, and other passages.

[7] There is some truth, although greatly
exaggerated, in the bitter remarks of
Hausrath (Neutest. Zeitgesch. ii. p. 93),
as to the sensitiveness of the Jews in
the διασπορά, and the loud outcry of
all its members at any interference with
them, however trivial. But events
unfortunately too often proved how
real and near was their danger, and
how necessary the caution 'Obsta prin-
cipiis.'

[8] St. Peter seems to have used it in
that sense, 1 Pet. i. 1.

BOOK
I

our era comes to us from Egypt[1]—where the Jews possessed exceptional privileges—professedly from the heathen, but really from the Jewish[2] Sibyl, this lament of Israel:—

> Crowding with thy numbers every ocean and country—
> Yet an offense to all around thy presence and customs ![3]

Sixty years later the Greek geographer and historian Strabo bears the like witness to their presence in every land, but in language that shows how true had been the complaint of the Sibyl.[4] The reasons for this state of feeling will by-and-by appear. Suffice it for the present that, all unconsciously, Philo tells its deepest ground, and that of Israel's loneliness in the heathen world, when speaking, like the others, of his countrymen as in 'all the cities of Europe, in the provinces of Asia and in the islands,' he describes them as, wherever sojourning, having but one metropolis—not Alexandria, Antioch, or Rome—but 'the Holy City with its Temple, dedicated to the Most High God.'[5] A nation, the vast majority of which was dispersed over the whole inhabited earth, had ceased to be a special, and become a world-nation.[6] Yet its heart beat in Jerusalem, and thence the life-blood passed to its most distant members. And this, indeed, if we rightly understand it, was the grand object of the 'Jewish dispersion' throughout the world.

What has been said applies, perhaps, in a special manner, to the *Western*, rather than to the *Eastern* 'dispersion.' The connection of the latter with Palestine was so close as almost to seem one of continuity. In the account of the truly representative gathering in Jerusalem on that ever-memorable Feast of Weeks,[a] the division of the 'dispersion' into two grand sections—the Eastern or Trans-Euphratic, and the Western or Hellenist—seems clearly marked.[7] In this arrangement the former would include 'the Parthians, Medes, Elamites, and dwellers in Mesopotamia,' Judæa standing, so to speak, in the middle, while 'the Bretes and Arabians' would typically represent the farthest outrunners respectively of the Western and the Eastern Diaspora. The former, as we know from the New Testament,

[a] Acts ii. 9-11

---

[1] Comp. the remarks of *Schneckenburger* (Vorles ü. Neutest. Zeitg. p. 95).

[2] Comp. *Friedlieb*, D. Sibyll. Weissag. xxii. 39.

[3] Orac Sibyll. iii. 271, 272, apud Friedlieb, p. 62.

[4] *Strabo* apud *Jos.* Ant. xiv. 7. 2: 'It is not easy to find a place in the world that has not admitted this race, and is not mastered by it.'

[5] *Philo* in Flaccum (ed. Francf.), p. 971.

[6] Comp. *Jos.* Ant. xii. 3; xiii. 10. 4; 13. 1; xiv. 6. 2; 8. 1; 10. 8; *Sueton.* Cæs. 85.

[7] *Grimm* (Clavis N. T. p. 113) quotes two passages from Philo, in one of which he contradistinguishes 'us,' the Hellenist Jews, from 'the Hebrews,' and speaks of the Greek as 'our language.'

commonly bore in Palestine the name of the 'dispersion of the Greeks,'[a] and of 'Hellenists' or 'Grecians.'[b] On the other hand, the Trans-Euphratic Jews, who 'inhabited Babylon and many of the other satrapies,'[c] were included with the Palestinians and the Syrians under the term 'Hebrews,' from the common language which they spoke.

But the difference between the 'Grecians' and the 'Hebrews' was far deeper than merely of language, and extended to the whole direction of thought. There were mental influences at work in the Greek world from which, in the nature of things, it was impossible even for Jews to withdraw themselves, and which, indeed, were as necessary for the fulfilment of their mission as their isolation from heathenism, and their connection with Jerusalem. At the same time it was only natural that the Hellenists, placed as they were in the midst of such hostile elements, should intensely wish to be Jews, equal to their Eastern brethren. On the other hand, Pharisaism, in its pride of legal purity and of the possession of traditional lore, with all that it involved, made no secret of its contempt for the Hellenists, and openly declared the Grecian far inferior to the Babylonian 'dispersion.'[1] That such feelings, and the suspicions which they engendered, had struck deep into the popular mind, appears from the fact, that even in the Apostolic Church, and that in her earliest days, disputes could break out between the Hellenists and the Hebrews, arising from suspicion of unkind and unfair dealings grounded on these sectional prejudices.[d]

Far other was the estimate in which the Babylonians were held by the leaders of Judaism. Indeed, according to one view of it, Babylonia, as well as 'Syria' as far north as Antioch, was regarded as forming part of the land of Israel.[2] Every other country was considered outside 'the land,' as Palestine was called, with the exception of Babylonia, which was reckoned as part of it.[e] For Syria and Mesopotamia, eastwards to the banks of the Tigris, were supposed to have been in the territory which King David had conquered, and this made them ideally for ever like the land of Israel. But it was just between the Euphrates and the Tigris that the largest and wealthiest settlements of the Jews were, to such extent that a later writer actually designated them 'the land of Israel.' Here *Nehardaa,* on the *Nahar Malka,* or royal canal, which passed from the

CHAP.
I

[a] St. John vii. 35
[b] Acts vi. 1; ix. 29; xi. 20
[c] *Philo* ad Cajum, p. 1023; *Jos.* Ant. xv. 3. 1

[d] Acts vi. 1

[e] Erub. 21 a Gitt. 6 a

---

[1] Similarly we have (in Men. 110a) this curious explanation of Is. xliii. 6: 'My sons from afar'—these are the exiles in Babylon, whose minds were settled, like men, 'and my daughters from the ends of the earth'—these are the exiles in other lands, whose minds were not settled, like women.

[2] Ber. R. 17.

Euphrates to the Tigris, was the oldest Jewish settlement. It boasted of a Synagogue, said to have been built by King Jechoniah with stones that had been brought from the Temple.[1] In this fortified city the vast contributions intended for the Temple were deposited by the Eastern Jews, and thence conveyed to their destination under escort of thousands of armed men. Another of these Jewish treasure-cities was Nisibis, in northern Mesopotamia. Even the fact that wealth, which must have sorely tempted the cupidity of the heathen, could be safely stored in these cities and transported to Palestine, shows how large the Jewish population must have been, and how great their general influence.

In general, it is of the greatest importance to remember in regard to this Eastern dispersion, that only a minority of the Jews, consisting in all of about 50,000, originally returned from Babylon, first under Zerubbabel and afterwards under Ezra.[a] Nor was their inferiority confined to numbers. The wealthiest and most influential of the Jews remained behind. According to Josephus,[b] with whom Philo substantially agrees, vast numbers, estimated at millions, inhabited the Trans-Euphratic provinces. To judge even by the number of those slain in popular risings (50,000 in Seleucia alone[2]), these figures do not seem greatly exaggerated. A later tradition had it, that so dense was the Jewish population in the Persian Empire, that Cyrus forbade the further return of the exiles, lest the country should be depopulated.[3] So large and compact a body soon became a political power. Kindly treated under the Persian monarchy, they were, after the fall of that empire,[c] favoured by the successors of Alexander. When in turn the Macedono-Syrian rule gave place to the Parthian Empire,[d] the Jews formed, from their national opposition to Rome, an important element in the East. Such was their influence that, as late as the year 40 A.D., the Roman legate shrank from provoking their hostility.[4] At the same time it must not be thought that, even in these favoured regions, they were wholly without persecution. Here also history records more than one tale of bloody strife on the part of those among whom they dwelt.[5]

To the Palestinians, their brethren of the East and of Syria—to which they had wandered under the fostering rule of the Macedono-

[a] 537 B.C., and 459-'8 B.C.

[b] Ant. xi. 5. 2; xv. 2. 2; xviii. 9

[c] 330 B.C.

[d] 63 B.C.

---

[1] Comp. *Fürst*, Kult. u. Literaturgesch d. Jud. in Asien, vol. i. p. 8.

[2] *Jos.* Ant. xviii. 9. 9.

[3] Midrash on Cant. v. 5, ed. Warsh. p. 26 *a.*

[4] *Philo* ad Caj.

[5] The following are the chief passages in Josephus relating to that part of Jewish history: Ant. xi. 5. 2; xiv. 13. 5; xv. 2. 7; 3. 1; xvii. 2. 1–3; xviii. 9. 1, &c.; xx. 4. Jew. W. i. 13. 3.

Syrian monarchs (the Seleucidæ)—were indeed pre-eminently the Golah, or 'dispersion.' To them the Sanhedrin in Jerusalem intimated by fire-signals from mountain-top to mountain-top the commencement of each month for the regulation of the festive calendar,[1] even as they afterwards despatched messengers into Syria for the same purpose.[2] In some respects the Eastern dispersion was placed on the same footing; in others, on even a higher level than the mother-country. Tithes and *Terumoth*, or first-fruits in a prepared condition,[3] were due from them, while the *Bikkurim*, or first-fruits in a fresh state, were to be brought from Syria to Jerusalem. Unlike the heathen countries, whose very dust defiled, the soil of Syria was declared clean, like that of Palestine itself.[a] So far as purity of descent was concerned, the Babylonians, indeed, considered themselves superior to their Palestinian brethren. They had it, that when Ezra took with him those who went to Palestine, he had left the land behind him as pure as fine flour.[b] To express it in their own fashion: In regard to the genealogical purity of their Jewish inhabitants, all other countries were, compared to Palestine, like dough mixed with leaven; but Palestine itself was such by the side of Babylonia.[4] It was even maintained, that the exact boundaries could be traced in a district, within which the Jewish population had preserved itself unmixed. Great merit was in this respect also ascribed to Ezra. In the usual mode of exaggeration, it was asserted, that, if all the genealogical studies and researches[5] had been put together, they would have amounted to many hundred camel-loads. There was for it, however, at least this foundation in truth, that great care and labour were bestowed on preserving full and accurate records so as to establish purity of descent. What importance attached to it, we know from the action of Ezra[c] in that respect, and from the stress which Josephus lays on this point.[d] Official records of descent as regarded the priesthood were kept in the Temple. Besides, the Jewish authorities seem to have possessed a general official register, which Herod afterwards ordered to be burnt, from reasons which it is not difficult to infer. But from that day, laments a Rabbi, the glory of the Jews decreased![6]

Nor was it merely purity of descent of which the Eastern dispersion could boast. In truth, Palestine owed everything to Ezra,

[a] Ohol. xxiii. 7

[b] Kidd. 69 *b*

[c] Chs. ix. x.

[d] Lifei.; Ag Apion i. 7

---

[1] Rosh. haSh. ii. 4; comp. the Jer. Gemara on it, and in the Bab. Talmud 23 *b*.

[2] Rosh. haSh. i. 4.

[3] Shev. vi. *passim*; Gitt. 8 *a*.

[4] Cheth. 111 *a*.

[5] As comments upon the genealogies from 'Azel' in 1 Chr. viii. 37 to 'Azel' in ix. 44. Pes. 62 *b*.

[6] Pes. 62 *b*; *Sachs*, Beitr. vol. ii. p. 157.

BOOK
I

the Babylonian,[1] a man so distinguished that, according to tradition, the Law would have been given by him, if Moses had not previously obtained that honor. Putting aside the various traditional ordinances which the Talmud ascribes to him,[2] we know from the Scriptures what his activity for good had been. Altered circumstances had brought many changes to the new Jewish State. Even the language, spoken and written, was other than formerly. Instead of the characters anciently employed, the exiles brought with them, on their return, those now common, the so-called square Hebrew letters, which gradually came into general use."[3] The language spoken by the Jews was no longer Hebrew, but Aramæan, both in Palestine and in Babylonia;[4] in the former the Western, in the latter the Eastern dialect. In fact, the common people were ignorant of pure Hebrew, which henceforth became the language of students and of the Synagogue. Even there a *Methurgeman,* or interpreter, had to be employed to translate into the vernacular the portions of Scripture read in the public services,[5] and the addresses delivered by the Rabbis. This was the origin of the so-called *Targumim,* or paraphrases of Scripture. In earliest times, indeed, it was forbidden to the Methurgeman to read his translation or to write down a Targum, lest

ᵃ Sanh. 21 *b*

---

[1] According to tradition he returned to Babylon, and died there. Josephus says that he died in Jerusalem (Ant. xi. 5. 5).

[2] *Herzfeld* has given a very clear historical arrangement of the order in which, and the persons by whom, the various legal determinations were supposed to have been given. See Gesch. d. V. Isr. vol. iii. pp. 240 &c.

[3] Although thus introduced under Ezra, the ancient Hebrew characters, which resemble the Samaritan, only very gradually gave way. They are found on monuments and coins.

[4] *Herzfeld* (u. s. vol. iii. p. 46) happily designates the Palestinian as the Hebræo-Aramaic, from its Hebraistic tinge. The Hebrew, as well as the Aramæan, belongs to the Semitic group of languages, which has thus been arranged: 1. North Semitic: Punico-Phœnician, Hebrew, and Aramaic (Western and Eastern dialects). 2. South Semitic: Arabic, Himyaritic, and Ethiopian. 3. East Semitic: The Assyro-Babylonian cuneiform. When we speak of the dialect used in Palestine, we do not, of course, forget the great influence of Syria, exerted long before and after the Exile. Of these three branches the Aramaic is the most closely connected

with the Hebrew. Hebrew occupies an intermediate position between the Aramaic and the Arabic, and may be said to be the oldest, certainly from a literary point of view. Together with the introduction of the new dialect into Palestine, we mark that of the new, or square, characters of writing. The Mishnah and all the kindred literature up to the fourth century are in Hebrew, or rather in a modern development and adaptation of that language; the Talmud is in Aramæan. Comp. on this subject: *De Wette-Schrader,* Lehrb. d. hist. kr. Einl. (8 ed.) pp. 71–88; *Herzog's* Real-Encykl. vol. i. 466, 468; v. 614 &c., 710; *Zunz,* Gottesd. Vortr. d. Jud. pp. 7–9; *Herzfeld,* u. s. pp. 44 &c., 58 &c.

[5] Could St. Paul have had this in mind when, in referring to the miraculous gift of speaking in other languages, he directs that one shall always interpret (1 Cor. xiv. 27)? At any rate, the word *targum* in Ezra iv. 7 is rendered in the LXX. by ἑρμηνεύω. The following from the Talmud (Ber. 8 *a* and *b*) affords a curious illustration of 1 Cor. xiv. 27: 'Let a man always finish his Parashah (the daily lesson from the Law) with the congregation (at the same time)—twice the text, and once targum.'

the paraphrase should be regarded as of equal authority with the
original. It was said that, when Jonathan brought out his Targum
on the Prophets, a voice from heaven was heard to utter: 'Who is
this that has revealed My secrets to men?'ᵃ Still, such *Targu-*
mim seem to have existed from a very early period, and, amid
the varying and often incorrect renderings, their necessity must
have made itself increasingly felt. Accordingly, their use was
authoritatively sanctioned before the end of the second century after
Christ. This is the origin of our two oldest extant *Targumim*:
that of Onkelos (as it is called), on the Pentateuch; and that on
the Prophets, attributed to Jonathan the son of Uzziel. These names
do not, indeed, accurately represent the authorship of the oldest Targumim, which may more correctly be regarded as later and authoritative recensions of what, in some form, had existed before. But
although these works had their origin in Palestine, it is noteworthy
that, in the form in which at present we possess them, they are the
outcome of the schools of Babylon.

But Palestine owed, if possible, a still greater debt to Babylonia.
The new circumstances in which the Jews were placed on their
return seemed to render necessary an adaptation of the Mosaic Law,
if not new legislation. Besides, piety and zeal now attached themselves to the outward observance and study of the letter of the Law.
This is the origin of the *Mishnah*, or Second Law, which was intended
to explain and supplement the first. This constituted the only
Jewish dogmatics, in the real sense, in the study of which the sage,
Rabbi, scholar, scribe, and *Darshan*,[1] were engaged. The result of
it was the *Midrash*, or investigation, a term which afterwards was
popularly applied to commentaries on the Scriptures and preaching.
From the outset, Jewish theology divided into two branches: the
Halakhah and the *Haggadah*. The former (from *halakh*, to go) was,
so to speak, the Rule of the Spiritual Road, and, when fixed, had
even greater authority than the Scriptures of the Old Testament,
since it explained and applied them. On the other hand, the
Haggadah[2] (from *nagad*, to tell) was only the personal saying of
the teacher, more or less valuable according to his learning and
popularity, or the authorities which he could quote in his support.
Unlike the *Halakhah*, the *Haggadah* had no absolute authority,
either as to doctrine practice, or exegesis. But all the greater would

---

[1] From *darash*, to search out, literally,
to tread out. The preacher was afterwards called the *Darshan*.

[2] The *Halakhah* might be described as
the apocryphal Pentateuch, the *Haggadah* as the apocryphal Prophets.

be its popular influence,[1] and all the more dangerous the doctrinal license which it allowed. In fact, strange as it may sound, almost all the doctrinal teaching of the Synagogue is to be derived from the Haggadah—and this also is characteristic of Jewish traditionalism. But, alike in Halakhah and Haggadah, Palestine was under the deepest obligation to Babylonia. For the father of Halakhic study was Hillel, the Babylonian, and among the popular Haggadists there is not a name better known than that of Eleazar the Mede, who flourished in the first century of our era.

After this, it seems almost idle to inquire whether, during the first period after the return of the exiles from Babylon, there were regular theological academies in Babylon. Although it is, of course, impossible to furnish historical proof, we can scarcely doubt that a community so large and so intensely Hebrew would not have been indifferent to that study, which constituted the main thought and engagement of their brethren in Palestine. We can understand that, since the great Sanhedrin in Palestine exercised supreme spiritual authority, and in that capacity ultimately settled all religious questions—at least for a time—the study and discussion of these subjects should also have been chiefly carried on in the schools of Palestine; and that even the great Hillel himself, when still a poor and unknown student, should have wandered thither to acquire the learning and authority, which at that period he could not have found in his own country. But even this circumstance implies, that such studies were at least carried on and encouraged in Babylonia. How rapidly soon afterwards the authority of the Babylonian schools increased, till they not only overshadowed those of Palestine, but finally inherited their prerogatives, is well known. However, therefore, the Palestinians in their pride or jealousy might sneer,[2] that the Babylonians were stupid, proud, and poor ('they ate bread upon bread'),[3] even they had to acknowledge that, 'when the Law had fallen into oblivion, it was restored by Ezra of Babylon; when it was a second time forgotten, Hillel the Babylonian came and recovered it; and when yet a third time it fell into oblivion, Rabbi Chija came from Babylon and gave it back once more.'[4]

[1] We may here remind ourselves of 1 Tim. v. 17. St. Paul, as always, writes with the familiar Jewish phrases ever recurring to his mind. The expression διδασκαλία seems to be equivalent to Halakhic teaching. Comp. *Grimm*, Clavis N. T. pp. 98, 99.

[2] In Moed Q. 25 *a*. sojourn in Babylon

is mentioned as a reason why the Shekhinah could not rest upon a certain Rabbi.

[3] Pes. 34 *b*; Men. 52 *a*; Sanh. 24 *a*; Bets. 16 *a*—apud *Neubauer*, Géog. du Talmud, p. 323. In Keth. 75 *a*, they are styled the 'silly Babylonians.' See also Jer. Pes. 32 *a*.

[4] Sukk. 20 *a*. R. Chija, one of the

Such then was that Hebrew dispersion which, from the first, constituted really the chief part and the strength of the Jewish nation, and with which its religious future was also to lie. For it is one of those strangely significant, almost symbolical, facts in history, that after the destruction of Jerusalem the spiritual supremacy of Palestine passed to Babylonia, and that Rabbinical Judaism, under the stress of political adversity, voluntarily transferred itself to the seats of Israel's ancient dispersion, as if to ratify by its own act what the judgment of God had formerly executed. But long before that time the Babylonian 'dispersion' had already stretched out its hands in every direction. Northwards, it had spread through Armenia, the Caucasus, and to the shores of the Black Sea, and through Media to those of the Caspian. Southwards, it had extended to the Persian Gulf and through the vast extent of Arabia, although Arabia Felix and the land of the Homerites may have received their first Jewish colonies from the opposite shores of Ethiopia. Eastwards it had passed as far as India.[1] Everywhere we have distinct notices of these wanderers, and everywhere they appear as in closest connection with the Rabbinical hierarchy of Palestine. Thus the Mishnah, in an extremely curious section,[2] tells us how on Sabbaths the Jewesses of Arabia might wear their long veils, and those of India the kerchief round the head, customary in those countries, without incurring the guilt of desecrating the holy day by needlessly carrying what, in the eyes of the law, would be a burden;[a] while in the rubric for the Day of Atonement we have it noted that the dress which the High-Priest wore 'between the evenings' of the great fast—that is, as afternoon darkened into evening— was of most costly 'Indian' stuff.[b]

[a] Shabb. vi. 6

[b] Yoma iii. 7

That among such a vast community there should have been poverty, and that at one time, as the Palestinians sneered, learning may have been left to pine in want, we can readily believe. For, as one of the Rabbis had it in explanation of Deut. xxx. 13: 'Wisdom is not "beyond the sea"—that is, it will not be found among traders or merchants,'[c] whose mind must be engrossed by gain. And it was

[c] Er. 55 a

teachers of the second century, is among the most-celebrated Rabbinical authorities, around whose memory legend has thrown a special halo.

[1] In this, as in so many respects, Dr. Neubauer has collated very interesting information, to which we refer. See his Géogr. du Talm., pp. 369–399.

[2] The whole section gives a most curious glimpse of the dress and ornaments worn by the Jews at that time. The reader interested in the subject will find special information in the three little volumes of Hartmann (Die Hebräerin am Putztische), in N. G. Schröder's somewhat heavy work: De Vestitu Mulier. Hebr., and especially in that interesting tractate, Trachten d. Juden, by Dr. A. Brüll, of which, unfortunately, only one part has appeared.

BOOK I

ᵃ Kidd. iv. 14

trade and commerce which procured to the Babylonians their wealth and influence, although agriculture was not neglected. Their caravans—of whose camel drivers, by the way, no very flattering account is given ᵃ—carried the rich carpets and woven stuffs of the East, as well as its precious spices, to the West: generally through Palestine to the Phœnician harbours, where a fleet of merchantmen belonging to Jewish bankers and shippers lay ready to convey them to every quarter of the world. These merchant princes were keenly alive to all that passed, not only in the financial, but in the political world. We know that they were in possession of State secrets, and entrusted with the intricacies of diplomacy. Yet, whatever its condition, this Eastern Jewish community was intensely Hebrew. Only eight days' journey—though, according to Philo's western ideas of it, by a difficult road ¹—separated them from Palestine; and every pulsation there vibrated in Babylonia. It was in the most outlying part of that colony, in the wide plains of Arabia, that Saul of Tarsus spent those three years of silent thought and unknown labour, which preceded his re-appearance in Jerusalem, when from the burning longing to labour among his brethren, kindled by long residence among these Hebrews of the Hebrews, he was directed to that strange work which was his

ᵇ Gal. 1. 17; ᶜ 1 Pet. v. 13

life's mission.ᵇ And it was among the same community that Peter wrote and laboured,ᶜ amidst discouragements of which we can form some conception from the sad boast of Nehardaa, that up to the end of the third century it had not numbered among its members any convert to Christianity.²

In what has been said, no notice has been taken of those wanderers of the ten tribes, whose trackless footsteps seem as mysterious as their after-fate. The Talmudists name four countries as their seats. But, even if we were to attach historic credence to their vague statements, at least two of these localities cannot with any certainty be identified.³ Only thus far all agree as to point us northwards, through India, Armenia, the Kurdish mountains, and the Caucasus. And with this tallies a curious reference in what is known as IV. Esdras, which locates them in a land called Arzareth, a term which has, with some probability, been identified with the land of Ararat.⁴

---

¹ *Philo* ad Cajum, ed. Frcf. p. 1023.
² Pes. 56 *a*, apud *Neubauer*, u. s., p. 351.
³ Comp. *Neubauer*, pp. 315, 372; *Hamburger*, Real-Encykl. p. 135.
⁴ Comp. *Volkmar*, Handb. d. Einl. in d. Apokr. ii^te Abth., pp. 193, 194, notes.

For the reasons there stated, I prefer this to the ingenious interpretation proposed by Dr. Schiller-Szinessy (Journ. of Philol. for 1870, pp. 113, 114), who regards it as a contraction of *Erez achereth*, 'another land,' referred to in Deut. xxix. 27 (28).

Josephus [a] describes them as an innumerable multitude, and vaguely locates them beyond the Euphrates. The Mishnah is silent as to their seats, but discusses their future restoration; Rabbi Akiba denying and Rabbi Eliezer anticipating it.[b][1] Another Jewish tradition [c] locates them by the fabled river Sabbatyon, which was supposed to cease its flow on the weekly Sabbath. This, of course, is an implied admission of ignorance of their seats. Similarly, the Talmud [d] speaks of three localities whither they had been banished : the district around the river Sabbatyon; Daphne, near Antioch; while the third was overshadowed and hidden by a cloud.

Later Jewish notices connect the final discovery and the return of the 'lost tribes' with their conversion under that second Messiah who, in contradistinction to 'the Son of David' is styled 'the Son of Joseph,' to whom Jewish tradition ascribes what it cannot reconcile with the royal dignity of 'the Son of David,' and which, if applied to Him, would almost inevitably lead up to the most wide concessions in the Christian argument.[2] As regards the ten tribes there is this truth underlying the strange hypothesis, that, as their persistent apostacy from the God of Israel and His worship had cut them off from his people, so the fulfilment of the Divine promises to them in the latter days would imply, as it were, a second birth to make them once more Israel. Beyond this we are travelling chiefly into the region of conjecture. Modern investigations have pointed to the Nestorians,[3] and latterly with almost convincing evidence (so far as such is possible) to the Afghans, as descended from the lost tribes.[4] Such mixture with, and lapse into, Gentile nationalities seems to have been before the minds of those Rabbis who ordered that, if at present a non-Jew weds a Jewess, such a union was to be respected, since the stranger might be a descendant of the ten tribes.[e] Besides, there is reason to believe that part of them, at least, had coalesced with their brethren of the later exile;[5] while we know that individuals who had settled in Palestine and, presumably, elsewhere, were

CHAP.
I

[a] Ant. xi. 5. 2
[b] Sanh. x. 3
[c] Ber. R. 73

[d] Jer. Sanh. 29 c

[e] Yebam 16 b

---

[1] R. Eliezer seems to connect their return with the dawn of the new Messianic day.

[2] This is not the place to discuss the later Jewish fiction of a second or 'suffering' Messiah, 'the son of Joseph,' whose special mission it would be to bring back the ten tribes, and to subject them to Messiah, 'the son of David,' but who would perish in the war against Gog and Magog.

[3] Comp. the work of Dr. *Asahel Grant* on the Nestorians. His arguments have been well summarised and expanded in an interesting note in Mr. *Nutt's* Sketch of Samaritan History, pp. 2–4.

[4] I would here call special attention to a most interesting paper on the subject ('A New Afghan Question'), by Mr. *H. W. Bellew*, in the 'Journal of the United Service Institution of India,' for 1881, pp. 49–97.   [5] Kidd. 69 *b*.

able to trace descent from them.[1] Still the great mass of the ten tribes was in the days of Christ, as in our own, lost to the Hebrew nation.

[1] So Anna from the tribe of Aser, St. Luke ii. 36. *Lutterbeck* (Neutest. Lehrbegr. pp. 102, 103) argues that the ten tribes had become wholly undistinguishable from the other two. But his arguments are not convincing, and his opinion was certainly not that of those who lived in the time of Christ, or who reflected their ideas.

CHAPTER II.

THE JEWISH DISPERSION IN THE WEST—THE HELLENISTS—ORIGIN OF HELLENIST LITERATURE IN THE GREEK TRANSLATION OF THE BIBLE—CHARACTER OF THE SEPTUAGINT.

WHEN we turn from the Jewish 'dispersion' in the East to that in the West, we seem to breathe quite a different atmosphere. Despite their intense nationalism, all unconsciously to themselves, their mental characteristics and tendencies were in the opposite direction from those of their brethren. With those of the East rested the future of Judaism; with them of the West, in a sense, that of the world. The one represented old Israel groping back into the darkness of the past; the other young Israel, stretching forth its hands to where the dawn of a new day was about to break. These Jews of the West are known by the term *Hellenists*—from ἑλληνίζειν, to conform to the language and manners of the Greeks.[1]

Whatever their religious and social isolation, it was, in the nature of things, impossible that the Jewish communities in the West should remain unaffected by Grecian culture and modes of thought; just as, on the other hand, the Greek world, despite popular hatred and the contempt of the higher classes, could not wholly withdraw itself from Jewish influences. Witness here the many converts to Judaism among the Gentiles;[2] witness also the evident preparedness of the lands of this 'dispersion' for the new doctrine which was to come from Judæa. Many causes contributed to render the Jews of the West accessible to Greek influences. They had not a long local history to look back upon, nor did they form a compact body, like their brethren in the East. They were craftsmen, traders, merchants, settled for a

CHAP.
II

[1] Indeed, the word *Alnisti* (or *Alunistin*)—'Greek'—actually occurs, as in Jer. Sot. 21 *b*, line 14 from bottom. *Böhl* (Forsch. n. ein. Volksb. p. 7) quotes Philo (Leg. ad Caj. p. 1023) in proof that he regarded the Eastern dispersion as a branch separate from the Palestinians. But the passage does not convey to me the inference which he draws from it. Dr. Guillemard (Hebraisms in the Greek Test.) on Acts vi. 1, agreeing with Dr. Roberts, argues that the term 'Hellenist' indicated only principles, and not birthplace, and that there were Hebrews and Hellenists in and out of Palestine. But this view is untenable.

[2] An account of this propaganda of Judaism and of its results will be given in another connection.

time here or there—units which might combine into communities, but could not form one people. Then their position was not favourable to the sway of traditionalism. Their occupations, the very reasons for their being in a 'strange land,' were purely secular. That lofty absorption of thought and life in the study of the Law, written and oral, which characterised the East, was to them something in the dim distance, sacred, like the soil and the institutions of Palestine, but unattainable. In Palestine or Babylonia numberless influences from his earliest years, all that he saw and heard, the very force of circumstances, would tend to make an earnest Jew a disciple of the Rabbis; in the West it would lead him to 'hellenise.' It was, so to speak, 'in the air'; and he could no more shut his mind against Greek thought than he could withdraw his body from atmospheric influences. That restless, searching, subtle Greek intellect would penetrate everywhere, and flash its light into the innermost recesses of his home and Synagogue.

To be sure, they were intensely Jewish, these communities of strangers. Like our scattered colonists in distant lands, they would cling with double affection to the customs of their home, and invest with the halo of tender memories the sacred traditions of their faith. The Grecian Jew might well look with contempt, not unmingled with pity, on the idolatrous rites practised around, from which long ago the pitiless irony of Isaiah had torn the veil of beauty, to show the hideousness and unreality beneath. The dissoluteness of public and private life, the frivolity and aimlessness of their pursuits, political aspirations, popular assemblies, amusements—in short, the utter decay of society, in all its phases, would lie open to his gaze. It is in terms of lofty scorn, not unmingled with indignation, which only occasionally gives way to the softer mood of warning, or even invitation, that Jewish Hellenistic literature, whether in the Apocrypha or in its Apocalyptic utterances, addresses heathenism.

From that spectacle the Grecian Jew would turn with infinite satisfaction—not to say, pride—to his own community, to think of its spiritual enlightenment, and to pass in review its exclusive privileges.[1] It was with no uncertain steps that he would go past those splendid temples to his own humbler Synagogue, pleased to find himself there surrounded by those who shared his descent, his faith, his hopes; and gratified to see their number swelled by many who, heathens by birth, had learned the error of their ways, and now, so to speak, humbly stood as suppliant 'strangers of the gate,' to seek

[1] St. Paul fully describes these feelings in the Epistle to the Romans.

admission into his sanctuary.[1] How different were the rites which he practised, hallowed in their Divine origin, rational in themselves, and at the same time deeply significant, from the absurd superstitions around. Who could have compared with the voiceless, meaningless, blasphemous heathen worship, if it deserved the name, that of the Synagogue, with its pathetic hymns, its sublime liturgy, its Divine Scriptures, and those ' stated sermons ' which ' instructed in virtue and piety,' of which not only Philo,[a] Agrippa,[b] and Josephus,[c] speak as a regular institution, but whose antiquity and general prevalence is attested in Jewish writings,[2] and nowhere more strongly than in the book of the Acts of the Apostles?

And in these Synagogues, how would ' brotherly love ' be called out, since, if one member suffered, all might soon be affected, and the danger which threatened one community would, unless averted, ere long overwhelm the rest. There was little need for the admonition not to ' forget, the love of strangers.'[3] To entertain them was not merely a virtue; in the Hellenist dispersion it was a religious necessity. And by such means not a few whom they would regard as ' heavenly messengers ' might be welcomed. From the Acts of the Apostles we knew with what eagerness they would receive, and with what readiness they would invite, the passing Rabbi or teacher, who came from the home of their faith, to speak, if there were in them a word of comforting exhortation for the people.[d] We can scarcely doubt, considering the state of things, that this often bore on ' the consolation of Israel.' But, indeed, all that came from Jerusalem, all that helped them to realise their living connection with it, or bound it more closely, was precious. ' Letters out of Judæa,' the tidings which some one might bring on his return from festive pilgrimage or business journey, especially about anything connected with that grand expectation—the star which was to rise on the Eastern sky—would soon spread, till the Jewish pedlar in his wanderings had carried the news to the most distant and isolated Jewish home, where he might find a Sabbath-welcome and Sabbath-rest.

CHAP.
II

[a] De Vita
Mosis,
p. 685; Leg
ad Caj.
p. 1014
[b] Leg. ad
Caj. p. 1035
[c] Ag. Apion
ii. 17

[d] λόγος πα-
ρακλήσεως
πρὸς τὸν
λαόν,
Acts xiii. 18

[1] The ' *Gerey haShaar*,' proselytes of the gate, a designation which some have derived from the circumstance that Gentiles were not allowed to advance beyond the Temple Court, but more likely to be traced to such passages as Ex. xx. 10; Deut. xiv. 21; xxiv. 14.

[2] Comp. here Targ. Jon. on Judg. v. 2, 9. I feel more hesitation in appealing to such passages as Ber. 19 *a*, where we read of a Rabbi in Rome, Thodos (Theudos?), who flourished several generations before Hillel, for reasons which the passage itself will suggest to the student. At the time of Philo, however, such instructions in the Synagogues at Rome were a long-established institution (Ad Caj. p. 1014).

[3] φιλοξενία, Hebr. xiii. 2.

Such undoubtedly was the case. And yet, when the Jew stepped out of the narrow circle which he had drawn around him, he was confronted on every side by Grecianism. It was in the forum, in the market, in the counting-house, in the street; in all that he saw, and in all to whom he spoke. It was refined; it was elegant; it was profound; it was supremely attractive. He might resist, but he could not push it aside. Even in resisting, he had already yielded to it. For, once open the door to the questions which it brought, if it were only to expel, or repel them, he must give up that principle of simple authority on which traditionalism as a system rested. Hellenic criticism could not so be silenced, nor its searching light be extinguished by the breath of a Rabbi. If he attempted this, the truth would not only be worsted before its enemies, but suffer detriment in his own eyes. He must meet argument with argument, and that not only for those who were without, but in order to be himself quite sure of what he believed. He must be able to hold it, not only in controversy with others, where pride might bid him stand fast, but in that much more serious contest within, where a man meets the old adversary alone in the secret arena of his own mind, and has to sustain that terrible hand-to-hand fight, in which he is uncheered by outward help. But why *should* he shrink from the contest, when he was sure that his was Divine truth, and that therefore victory must be on his side? As in our modern conflicts against the onesided inferences from physical investigations we are wont to say that the truths of nature cannot contradict those of revelation—both being of God—and as we are apt to regard as truths of nature what sometimes are only deductions from partially ascertained facts, and as truths of revelation what, after all, may be only our own inferences, sometimes from imperfectly apprehended premises, so the Hellenist would seek to conciliate the truths of Divine revelation with those others which, he thought, he recognised in Hellenism. But what were the truths of Divine revelation? Was it only the substance of Scripture, or also its form—the truth itself which was conveyed, or the manner in which it was presented to the Jews; or, if both, then did the two stand on exactly the same footing? On the answer to these questions would depend how little or how much he would ' hellenise.'

One thing at any rate was quite certain. The Old Testament, leastwise, the Law of Moses, was directly and wholly from God; and if so, then its form also—its letter—must be authentic and authoritative. Thus much on the surface, and for all. But the student must search deeper into it, his senses, as it were, quickened by Greek criticism; he must 'meditate' and penetrate into the Divine mysteries. The Palestinian also searched into them, and the result was the *Midrash.* But, whichever of his methods he had applied—the *Peshat,* or simple criticism of the words, the *Derush,* or search into the possible applications of the text, what might be 'trodden out' of it; or the *Sod,* the hidden, mystical, supranatural bearing of the words—it was still only the *letter* of the text that had been studied. There was, indeed, yet another understanding of the Scriptures, to which St. Paul directed his disciples: the spiritual bearing of its spiritual truths. But that needed another qualification, and tended in another direction from those of which the Jewish student knew. On the other hand, there was the intellectual view of the Scriptures—their philosophical understanding, the application to them of the results of Grecian thought and criticism. It was this which was peculiarly Hellenistic. Apply that method, and the deeper the explorer proceeded in his search, the more would he feel himself alone, far from the outside crowd; but the brighter also would that light of criticism, which he carried, shine in the growing darkness, or, as he held it up, would the precious ore, which he laid bare, glitter and sparkle with a thousand varying hues of brilliancy. What was Jewish, Palestinian, individual, concrete in the Scriptures, was only the outside—true in itself, but not *the* truth. There were depths beneath. Strip these stories of their nationalism; idealise the individual of the persons introduced, and you came upon abstract ideas and realities, true to all time and to all nations. But this deep symbolism was Pythagorean; this pre-existence of ideas which were the types of all outward actuality, was Platonism! Broken rays in them, but the focus of truth in the Scriptures. Yet these were rays, and could only have come from the Sun. All truth was of God; hence theirs must have been of that origin. Then were the sages of the heathen also in a sense God-taught—and God-teaching, or inspiration, was rather a question of degree than of kind!

One step only remained; and that, as we imagine, if not the easiest, yet, as we reflect upon it, that which in practice would be most readily taken. It was simply to advance towards Grecianism; frankly to recognise truth in the results of Greek thought. There is that within us, name it mental consciousness, or as you will, which, all unbidden, rises to answer to the voice of intellectual truth, come whence it may, just as conscience answers to the cause of moral truth or duty. But in this case there was more. There was the mighty spell which Greek philosophy exercised on all kindred minds, and the special adaptation of the Jewish intellect to such subtle, if not deep, thinking. And, in general, and more powerful than the rest, because penetrating everywhere, was the charm of Greek literature, with its brilliancy; of Greek civilisation and culture, with their polish and attractiveness; and of what, in one word, we may call the 'time-spirit,' that *tyrannos*, who rules all in their thinking, speaking, doing, whether they list or not.

Why, his sway extended even to Palestine itself, and was felt in the innermost circle of the most exclusive Rabbinism. We are not here referring to the fact that the very language spoken in Palestine came to be very largely charged with Greek, and even Latin, words Hebraised, since this is easily accounted for by the new circumstances, and the necessities of intercourse with the dominant or resident foreigners. Nor is it requisite to point out how impossible it would have been, in presence of so many from the Greek and Roman world, and after the long and persistent struggle of their rulers to Grecianise Palestine, nay, even in view of so many magnificent heathen temples on the very soil of Palestine, to exclude all knowledge of, or contact with Grecianism. But not to be able to exclude was to have in sight the dazzle of that unknown, which as such, and in itself, must have had peculiar attractions to the Jewish mind. It needed stern principle to repress the curiosity thus awakened. When a young Rabbi, *Ben Dama*, asked his uncle whether he might not study Greek philosophy, since he had mastered the 'Law' in every aspect of it, the older Rabbi replied by a reference to Josh. i. 8: 'Go and search what is the hour which is neither of the day nor of the night, and in it thou mayest study Greek philosophy.'[a] Yet even the Jewish patriarch, Gamaliel II., who may have sat with Saul of Tarsus at the feet of his grandfather, was said to have busied himself with Greek, as he certainly held liberal views on many points connected with Grecianism. To be sure, tradition justified him on the ground that his position brought him into contact with the ruling powers, and, perhaps, to further vindicate him, ascribed similar pursuits to the elder Gamaliel, although groundlessly, to judge from the circumstance that he was so impressed even with the wrong of possessing a Targum on Job in Aramæan, that he had it buried deep in the ground.

But all these are indications of a tendency existing. How wide it must have spread, appears from the fact that the ban had to be pronounced on all who studied 'Greek wisdom.' One of the greatest Rabbis, Elisha ben Abujah, seems to have been actually led to apostacy by such studies. True, he appears as the '*Acher*'—the 'other'—in Talmudic writings, whom it was not proper even to

name. But he was not yet an apostate from the Synagogue when
those 'Greek songs' ever flowed from his lips; and it was in the very
Beth-ha-Midrash, or theological academy, that a multitude of *Siphrey
Minim* (heretical books) flew from his breast, where they had lain
concealed.[a] It may be so, that the expression '*Siphrey Homeros*'
(Homeric writings), which occur not only in the Talmud[b] but even
in the Mishnah[c] referred pre-eminently, if not exclusively, to the
religious or semi-religious Jewish Hellenistic literature, outside even
the Apocrypha.[1] But its occurrence proves, at any rate, that the
Hellenists were credited with the study of Greek literature, and that
through them, if not more directly, the Palestinians had become
acquainted with it.

This sketch will prepare us for a rapid survey of that Hellenistic
literature which Judæa so much dreaded. Its importance, not only to
the Hellenists but to the world at large, can scarcely be over-estimated.
First and foremost, we have here the Greek translation of the Old
Testament, venerable not only as the oldest, but as that which at the
time of Jesus held the place of our 'Authorized Version,' and as
such is so often, although freely, quoted, in the New Testament. Nor
need we wonder that it should have been the people's Bible, not
merely among the Hellenists, but in Galilee, and even in Judæa. It
was not only, as already explained, that Hebrew was no longer the
'vulgar tongue' in Palestine, and that written Targumim were prohibited. But most, if not all—at least in towns—would understand
the Greek version; it might be quoted in intercourse with Hellenist
brethren or with the Gentiles; and, what was perhaps equally, if not
more important, it was the most readily procurable. From the extreme
labour and care bestowed on them, Hebrew manuscripts of the Bible
were enormously dear, as we infer from a curious Talmudical notice,[d]
where a common woollen wrap, which of course was very cheap, a copy
of the Psalms, of Job, and torn pieces from Proverbs, are together
valued at five *maneh*—say, about 19*l.* Although this notice dates from
the third or fourth century, it is not likely that the cost of Hebrew
Biblical MSS. was much lower at the time of Jesus. This would, of
course, put their possession well nigh out of common reach. On the

CHAP.
II

a Jer. Chag.
ii. 1; comp.
Chag. 15
b Jer. Sanh.
x. 28 a
c Yad. iv. 6

d Gitt. 35
last line
and b

---

[1] Through this literature, which as
being Jewish might have passed unsuspected, a dangerous acquaintance might
have been introduced with Greek writings—the more readily, that for example
Aristobulus described Homer and Hesiod
as having 'drawn from our books' (ap.
Euseb. Præpar. Evang. xiii. 12). According to *Hamburger* (Real-Encykl. für
Bibel u. Talmud, vol. ii. pp. 68, 69), the
expression *Siphrey Homeros* applies
exclusively to the Judæo-Alexandrian
heretical writings; according to *Fürst*
(Kanon d. A. Test. p. 98), simply to
Homeric literature. But see the discussion in *Levy*, Neuhebr. u. Chald.Wörterb.,
vol. i. p. 476 *a* and *b*.

other hand, we are able to form an idea of the cheapness of Greek
manuscripts from what we know of the price of books in Rome at the
beginning of our era. Hundreds of slaves were there engaged copying
what one dictated. The result was not only the publication of as
large editions as in our days, but their production at only about double
the cost of what are now known as 'cheap' or 'people's editions.'
Probably it would be safe to compute, that as much matter as would
cover sixteen pages of small print might, in such cases, be sold at the
rate of about sixpence, and in that ratio.[1] Accordingly, manuscripts
in Greek or Latin, although often incorrect, must have been easily
attainable, and this would have considerable influence on making the
Greek version of the Old Testament the 'people's Bible.'[2]

The Greek version, like the Targum of the Palestinians, originated,
no doubt, in the first place, in a felt national want on the part of the
Hellenists, who as a body were ignorant of Hebrew. Hence we find
notices of very early Greek versions of at least parts of the Pentateuch.[3] But this, of course, could not suffice. On the other hand,
there existed, as we may suppose, a natural curiosity on the part of
students, especially in Alexandria, which had so large a Jewish population, to know the sacred books on which the religion and history of
Israel were founded. Even more than this, we must take into
account the literary tastes of the first three Ptolemies (successors in
Egypt of Alexander the Great), and the exceptional favour which
the Jews for a time enjoyed. Ptolemy I. (Lagi) was a great patron
of learning. He projected the Museum in Alexandria, which was a
home for literature and study, and founded the great library. In
these undertakings Demetrius Phalereus was his chief adviser. The
tastes of the first Ptolemy were inherited by his son, Ptolemy II.
(Philadelphus), who had for two years been co-regent.[a] In fact,
ultimately that monarch became literally book-mad, and the sums
spent on rare MSS., which too often proved spurious, almost pass
belief. The same may be said of the third of these monarchs,
Ptolemy III. (Euergetes). It would have been strange, indeed, if
these monarchs had not sought to enrich their library with an
authentic rendering of the Jewish sacred books, or not encouraged
such a translation.

---

[1] Comp. *Friedlander*, Sitteng. Roms,
vol. iii. p. 315.

[2] To these causes there should perhaps
be added the attempt to introduce Grecianism by force into Palestine, the consequences which it may have left, and the
existence of a Grecian party in the land.

[3] *Aristobulus* in Euseb. Præpar. Evang.
ix. 6; xiii. 12. The doubts raised by
Hody against this testimony have been
generally repudiated by critics since the
treatise by *Valkenaer* (Diatr. de Aristob.
Jud. appended to *Gaisford's* ed. of the
Præpar. Evang.).

These circumstances will account for the different elements which we can trace in the Greek version of the Old Testament, and explain the historical, or rather legendary, notices which we have of its composition. To begin with the latter. Josephus has preserved what, no doubt in its present form, is a spurious letter from one Aristeas to his brother Philocrates,[1] in which we are told how, by the advice of his librarian (?), Demetrius Phalereus, Ptolemy II. had sent by him (Aristeas) and another officer, a letter, with rich presents, to Eleazar, the High-Priest at Jerusalem; who in turn had selected seventy-two translators (six out of each tribe), and furnished them with a most valuable manuscript of the Old Testament. The letter then gives further details of their splendid reception at the Egyptian court, and of their sojourn in the island of Pharos, where they accomplished their work in seventy-two days, when they returned to Jerusalem laden with rich presents, their translation having received the formal approval of the Jewish Sanhedrin at Alexandria. From this account we may at least derive as historical these facts: that the Pentateuch—for to it only the testimony refers—was translated into Greek, at the suggestion of Demetrius Phalereus, in the reign and under the patronage—if not by direction—of Ptolemy II. (Philadelphus).[2] With this the Jewish accounts agree, which describe the translation of the Pentateuch under Ptolemy—the Jerusalem Talmud[a] in a simpler narrative, the Babylonian[b] with additions apparently derived from the Alexandrian legends; the former expressly noting thirteen, the latter marking fifteen, variations from the original text.[3]

The Pentateuch once translated, whether by one, or more likely by several persons,[4] the other books of the Old Testament would

---

[1] Comp. Josephi Opera, ed. Havercamp, vol. ii. App. pp. 103–132. The best and most critical edition of this letter by Prof. *M. Schmidt*, in Merx' Archiv. i. pp. 252–310. The story is found in *Jos.* Ant. xii. 2. 2; Ag. Ap. ii. 4; *Philo*, de Vita Mosis, lib. ii. § 5–7. The extracts are most fully given in *Euseb.* Præpar. Evang. Some of the Fathers give the story, with additional embellishments. It was first critically called in question by *Hody* (Contra Historiam Aristeæ de L. X. interpret. dissert. Oxon. 1685), and has since been generally regarded as legendary. But its foundation in fact has of late been recognized by well nigh all critics, though the letter itself is pseudonymic, and full of fabulous details.

[2] This is also otherwise attested. See

Keil, Lehrb. d. hist. kr. Einl. d. A. T., p. 551, note 5.

[3] It is scarcely worth while to refute the view of Tychsen, *Jost* (Gesch. d. Judenth.), and others, that the Jewish writers only wrote down for Ptolemy the Hebrew words in Greek letters. But the word לכתב cannot possibly bear that meaning in this connection. Comp. also *Frankel*, Vorstudien, p. 31.

[4] According to Sopher. i. 8, by five persons, but that seems a round number to correspond to the five books of Moses. *Frankel* (Ueber d. Einfl. d. paläst. Exeg.) labours, however, to show in detail the differences between the different translators. But his criticism is often strained, and the solution of the question is apparently impossible.

BOOK
I

naturally soon receive the same treatment. They were evidently rendered by a number of persons, who possessed very different qualifications for their work—the translation of the Book of Daniel having been so defective, that in its place another by Theodotion was afterwards substituted. The version, as a whole, bears the name of the LXX.—as some have supposed from the number of its translators according to Aristeas' account—only that in that case it should have been seventy-two; or from the approval of the Alexandrian Sannedrin[1]—although in that case it should have been seventy-one; or perhaps because, in the popular idea, the number of the Gentile nations, of which the Greek (Japheth) was regarded as typical, was seventy. We have, however, one fixed date by which to compute the completion of this translation. From the prologue to the Apocryphal 'Wisdom of Jesus the son of Sirach,' we learn that in his days the Canon of Scripture was closed; and that on his arrival, in his thirty-eighth year,[2] in Egypt, which was then under the rule of Euergetes, he found the so-called LXX. version completed, when he set himself to a similar translation of the Hebrew work of his grandfather. But in the 50th chapter of that work we have a description of the High-Priest Simon, which is evidently written by an eye-witness. We have therefore as one term the pontificate of Simon, during which the earlier Jesus lived; and as the other, the reign of Euergetes, in which the grandson was at Alexandria. Now, although there were two High-Priests who bore the name Simon, and two Egyptian kings with the surname Euergetes, yet on purely historical grounds, and apart from critical prejudices, we conclude that the Simon of Ecclus. L. was Simon I., the Just, one of the greatest names in Jewish traditional history; and similarly, that the Euergetes of the younger Jesus was the first of that name, Ptolemy III., who reigned from 247 to 221 B.C.[3] In his reign, therefore, we must regard the LXX. version as, at least substantially, completed.

[1] *Böhl* would have it, 'the Jerusalem Sanhedrin!'

[2] But the expression has also been referred to the thirty-eighth year of the reign of *Euergetes*.

[3] To my mind, at least, the historical evidence, apart from critical considerations, seems very strong. Modern writers on the other side have confessedly been influenced by the consideration that the earlier date of the Book of Sirach would also involve a much earlier date for the close of the O. T. Canon than they are disposed to admit. More especially would it bear on the question of the so-called 'Maccabean Psalms,' and the authorship and date of the Book of Daniel. But historical questions should be treated independently of critical prejudices. *Winer* (Bibl. Realwörterb. i. p. 555), and others after him admit that the Simon of Ecclus. ch. L. was indeed Simon the Just (i.), but maintain that the Euergetes of the Prologue was the second of that name, Ptolemy VII., popularly nicknamed Kakergetes. Comp. the remarks of *Fritzsche* on this view in the Kurzgef. Exeg. Handb. z. d. Apokr. 5te Lief. p. xvii

From this it would, of course, follow that the Canon of the Old
Testament was then practically fixed in Palestine.[1] That Canon was
accepted by the Alexandrian translators, although the more loose
views of the Hellenists on 'inspiration,' and the absence of that close
watchfulness exercised over the text in Palestine, led to additions and
alterations, and ultimately even to the admission of the Apocrypha
into the Greek Bible. Unlike the Hebrew arrangement of the tex
into the Law, the Prophets,[2] and the (sacred) Writings, or Hagiographa, the LXX. arrange them into historical, prophetical, and
poetic books, and count twenty-two, after the Hebrew alphabet,
instead of twenty-four, as the Hebrews. But perhaps both these
may have been later arrangements, since Philo evidently knew the
Jewish order of the books.[a] What text the translators may have
used we can only conjecture. It differs in almost innumerable
instances from our own, though the more important deviations are
comparatively few.[3] In the great majority of the lesser variations
our Hebrew must be regarded as the correct text.[4]

[a] De Vita
ContempL
§ 3

Putting aside clerical mistakes and misreadings, and making
allowance for errors of translation, ignorance, and haste, we note
certain outstanding facts as characteristic of the Greek version. It
bears evident marks of its origin in Egypt in its use of Egyptian
words and references, and equally evident traces of its Jewish composition. By the side of slavish and false literalism there is great
liberty, if not licence, in handling the original; gross mistakes occur
along with happy renderings of very difficult passages, suggesting
the aid of some able scholars. Distinct Jewish elements are un-
deniably there, which can only be explained by reference to Jewish
tradition, although they are much fewer than some critics have
supposed.[5] This we can easily understand, since only those tradi-

---

[1] Comp. here, besides the passages
quoted in the previous note, Baba B. 13 b
and 14 b; for the cessation of revelation in the Maccabean period, 1 Macc. iv.
46; ix. 27; xiv. 41; and, in general, for
the Jewish view on the subject at the
time of Christ, Jos. Ag. Ap. i. 8.

[2] Anterior: Josh., Judg., 1 and 2 Sam.
1 and 2 Kings. Posterior: Major: Is.,
Jer., and Ezek.; and the Minor Prophets.

[3] They occur chiefly in 1 Kings, the
books of Esther, Job, Proverbs, Jeremiah,
and Daniel. In the Pentateuch we find
them only in four passages in the Book of
Exodus.

[4] There is also a curious correspondence

between the Samaritan version of the
Pentateuch and that of the LXX., which
in no less than about 2,000 passages agree
as against our Hebrew, although in other
instances the Greek text either agrees
with the Hebrew against the Samaritan,
or else is independent of both. On the
connection between Samaritan literature
and Hellenism there are some very interesting notices in Freudenthal, Hell. Stud.
pp. 82–103, 130–136, 186, &c.

[5] The extravagant computations in
this respect of Frankel (both in his work,
Ueber d. Einfl. d. Paläst. Exeg., and
also in the Vorstud. z. Sept. pp. 189–191)
have been rectified by Herzfeld (Gesch.
d. Vol. Isr. vol. iii.), who, perhaps, goes to

BOOK
I

tions would find a place which at that early time were not only received, but in general circulation. The distinctively Grecian elements, however, are at present of chief interest to us. They consist of allusions to Greek mythological terms, and adaptations of Greek philosophical ideas. However few,[1] even one well-authenticated instance would lead us to suspect others, and in general give to the version the character of Jewish Hellenising. In the same class we reckon what constitutes the prominent characteristic of the LXX. version, which, for want of better terms, we would designate as rationalistic and apologetic. Difficulties—or what seemed such—are removed by the most bold methods, and by free handling of the text; it need scarcely be said, often very unsatisfactorily. More especially a strenuous effort is made to banish all anthropomorphisms, as inconsistent with their ideas of the Deity. The superficial observer might be tempted to regard this as not strictly Hellenistic, since the same may be noted, and indeed is much more consistently carried out, in the Targum of Onkelos. Perhaps such alterations had even been introduced into the Hebrew text itself.[2] But there is this vital difference between Palestinianism and Alexandrianism, that, broadly speaking, the Hebrew avoidance of anthropomorphisms depends on objective—theological and dogmatic—the Hellenistic on subjective —philosophical and apologetic—grounds. The Hebrew avoids them as he does what seems to him inconsistent with the dignity of Biblical heroes and of Israel. 'Great is the power of the prophets,' he writes,

ᵃ Mechilta
on Ex. xix.

'who liken the Creator to the creature;' or else[a] 'a thing is written only to break it to the ear'—to adapt it to our human modes of

ᵇBer. 31 b

speaking and understanding; and again,[b] the 'words of the Torah are like the speech of the children of men.' But for this very purpose the words of Scripture may be presented in another form, if need

---

the other extreme. Herzfeld (pp. 548–550) admits—and even this with hesitation—of only six distinct references to Halakhoth in the following passages in the LXX.: Gen. ix. 4; xxxii. 32; Lev. xix. 19; xxiv. 7; Deut. xxv. 5; xxvi. 12. As instances of Haggadah we may mention the renderings in Gen. v. 24 and Ex. x. 23.

[1] *Dähne* and *Gfrörer* have in this respect gone to the same extreme as *Frankel* on the Jewish side. But even *Siegfried* (Philo v.Alex. p. 8) is obliged to admit that the LXX. rendering, ἡ δὲ γῆ ἦν ἀόρατος ἀκαὶ κατασκεύαστος Gen. i. 2), bears undeniable mark of Grecian philosophic views. And certainly

this is not the sole instance of the kind.

[2] As in the so-called ' *Tiqquney Sopherim*,' or 'emendations of the scribes.' Comp. here generally the investigations of *Geiger* (Urschrift u. Ueberse z. d. Bibel). But these, however learned and ingenious, require, like so many of the dicta of modern Jewish criticism, to be taken with the utmost caution, and in each case subjected to fresh examination, since so large a proportion of their writings are what is best designated by the German *Tendenz-Schriften*, and their inferences *Tendenz-Schlüsse*. But the critic and the historian should have no *Tendenz*—except towards simple fact and historical truth.

be even modified, so as to obviate possible misunderstanding, or dogmatic error. The Alexandrians arrived at the same conclusion, but from an opposite direction. They had not theological but philosophical axioms in their minds—truths which the *highest* truth could not, and, as they held, did not contravene. Only dig deeper; get beyond the letter to that to which it pointed; divest abstract truth of its concrete, national, Judaistic envelope—penetrate through the dim porch into the temple, and you were surrounded by a blaze of light, of which, as its portals had been thrown open, single rays had fallen into the night of heathendom. And so the truth would appear glorious—more than vindicated in their own sight, triumphant in that of others!

In such manner the LXX. version became really the people's Bible to that large Jewish world through which Christianity was afterwards to address itself to mankind. It was part of the case, that this translation should be regarded by the Hellenists as inspired like the original. Otherwise it would have been impossible to make final appeal to the very words of the Greek; still less, to find in them a mystical and allegorical meaning. Only that we must not regard their views of inspiration—except as applying to Moses, and even there only partially—as identical with ours. To their minds inspiration differed quantitatively, not qualitatively, from what the rapt soul might at any time experience, so that even heathen philosophers might ultimately be regarded as at times inspired. So far as the version of the Bible was concerned (and probably on like grounds), similar views obtained at a later period even in Hebrew circles, where it was laid down that the Chaldee Targum on the Pentateuch had been originally spoken to Moses on Sinai,[a] though afterwards forgotten, till restored and re-introduced.[b]

Whether or not the LXX. was read in the Hellenist Synagogues, and the worship conducted, wholly or partly, in Greek, must be matter of conjecture. We find, however, a significant notice[c] to the effect that among those who spoke a barbarous language (not Hebrew —the term referring specially to Greek), it was the custom for one person to read the whole *Parashah* (or lesson for the day), while among the Hebrew-speaking Jews this was done by seven persons, successively called up. This seems to imply that either the Greek text alone was read, or that it followed a Hebrew reading, like the Targum of the Easterns. More probably, however, the former would be the case, since both Hebrew manuscripts, and persons qualified to read them, would be difficult to procure. At any rate, we know that

[a] Ned. 37 *b*; Kidd. 49 *a*

[b] Meg. 3 *a*

[c] Jer. Meg. iv. 3, ed. Krot. p. 75*a*

BOOK
I

the Greek Scriptures were authoritatively acknowledged in Palestine,[1] and that the ordinary daily prayers might be said in Greek.[2] The LXX. deserved this distinction from its general faithfulness—at least, in regard to the Pentateuch—and from its preservation of ancient doctrine. Thus, without further referring to its full acknowledgment of the doctrine of Angels (comp. Deut. xxxii. 8, xxxiii. 2), we specially mark that it preserved the Messianic interpretation of Gen. xlix. 10, and Numb. xxiv. 7, 17, 23, bringing us evidence of what had been the generally received view two and a half centuries before the birth of Jesus. It must have been on the ground of the use made of the LXX. in argument, that later voices in the Synagogue declared this version to have been as great a calamity to Israel as the making of the golden calf,[a] and that its completion had been followed by the terrible omen of an eclipse, that lasted three days.[b] For the Rabbis declared that upon investigation it had been found that the Torah could be adequately translated only into Greek, and they are most extravagant in their praise of the Greek version of *Akylas*, or Aquila, the proselyte, which was made to counteract the influence of the LXX.[c] But in Egypt the anniversary of the completion of the LXX. was celebrated by a feast in the island of Pharos, in which ultimately even heathens seem to have taken part.[d]

[a] Mass. Sopher i. Hal. 7—at the close of vol. ix. of the Bab. Talmud

[b] Hilch. Ged. Taan.

[c] Jer. Meg. i. 11, ed. Krot. p. 71 b and c

[d] *Philo*, Vita Mos. ii. ed. Francf. p. 660

[1] Meg. i. 8. It is, however, fair to confess strong doubt, on my part, whether this passage may not refer to the Greek translation of *Akylas*. At the same time it simply speaks of a translation into Greek. And before the version of Aquila the LXX. alone held that place. It is one of the most daring modern Jewish perversions of history to identify this Akylas, who flourished about 130 after Christ, with the Aquila of the Book of Acts. It wants even the excuse of a colourable perversion of the confused story about Akylas, which *Epiphanius* who is so generally inaccurate, gives in

De Pond. et Mensur. c. xiv.

[2] The 'Shema' (Jewish creed), with its collects, the eighteen 'benedictions,' and 'the grace at meat.' A later Rabbi vindicated the use of the 'Shema' in Greek by the argument that the word *Shema* meant not only 'Hear,' but also 'understand' (Jer. Sotah vii. 1.) Comp. Sotah vii. 1, 2. In Ber. 40 b, it is said that the Parashah connected with the woman suspected of adultery, the prayer and confession at the bringing of the tithes, and the various benedictions over food, may be said not only in Hebrew, but in any other languages.

CHAPTER III.

THE OLD FAITH PREPARING FOR THE NEW—DEVELOPMENT OF HELLENIST THEOLOGY: THE APOCRYPHA, ARISTEAS, ARISTOBULUS, AND THE PSEUD-EPIGRAPHIC WRITINGS.

THE translation of the Old Testament into Greek may be regarded as the starting-point of Hellenism. It rendered possible the hope that what in its original form had been confined to the few, might become accessible to the world at large.[a] But much yet remained to be done. If the religion of the Old Testament had been brought near to the Grecian world of thought, the latter had still to be brought near to Judaism. Some intermediate stage must be found; some common ground on which the two might meet; some original kindredness of spirit to which their later divergences might be carried back, and where they might finally be reconciled. As the first attempt in this direction—first in order, if not always in time—we mark the so-called Apocryphal literature, most of which was either written in Greek, or is the product of Hellenising Jews.[1] Its general object was twofold. First, of course, it was apologetic—intended to fill gaps in Jewish history or thought, but especially to strengthen the Jewish mind against attacks from without, and generally to extol the dignity of Israel. Thus, more withering sarcasm could scarcely be poured on heathenism than in the apocryphal story of ‘Bel and the Dragon,’ or in the so-called ‘Epistle of Jeremy,’ with which the Book of ‘Baruch’ closes. The same strain, only in more lofty tones, resounds through the Book of the ‘Wisdom of Solomon,’[b] along with the constantly implied contrast between the righteous, or Israel, and sinners, or the heathen. But the next object was to show that the deeper and purer thinking of heathenism in its highest philosophy supported—nay, in some respects, was identical with—the fundamental teaching of the Old Testament. This, of course, was apologetic of the Old Testament, but it also prepared the way for a

CHAP. III

[a] *Philo,* de Vita Mos. ed. Mangey, ii. p. 140

[b] Comp. x.-xx.

[1] All the Apocrypha were originally written in Greek, except 1 Macc., Judith, part of Baruch, probably Tobit, and, of course, the ‘Wisdom of Jesus the Son of Sirach.’

reconciliation with Greek philosophy. We notice this especially in the so-called Fourth Book of Maccabees, so long erroneously attributed to Josephus,[1] and in the 'Wisdom of Solomon.' The first postulate here would be the acknowledgment of truth among the Gentiles, which was the outcome of Wisdom—and Wisdom was the revelation of God. This seems already implied in so thoroughly Jewish a book as that of Jesus the Son of Sirach.[a] Of course there could be no alliance with Epicureanism, which was at the opposite pole of the Old Testament. But the brilliancy of Plato's speculations would charm, while the stern self-abnegation of Stoicism would prove almost equally attractive. The one would show why they believed, the other why they lived, as they did. Thus the theology of the Old Testament would find a rational basis in the ontology of Plato, and its ethics in the moral philosophy of the Stoics. Indeed, this is the very line of argument which Josephus follows in the conclusion of his treatise against Apion.[b] This, then, was an unassailable position to take: contempt poured on heathenism as such,[c] and a rational philosophical basis for Judaism. They were not deep, only acute thinkers, these Alexandrians, and the result of their speculations was a curious Eclecticism, in which Platonism and Stoicism are found, often heterogeneously, side by side. Thus, without further details, it may be said that the Fourth Book of Maccabees is a Jewish Stoical treatise on the Stoical theme of 'the supremacy of reason'—the proposition, stated at the outset, that 'pious reason bears absolute sway over the passions,' being illustrated by the story of the martyrdom of Eleazar, and of the mother and her seven sons.[d] On the other hand, that sublime work, the 'Wisdom of Solomon,' contains Platonic and Stoic elements [2]—chiefly perhaps the latter—the two occurring side by side. Thus [e] 'Wisdom,' which is so concretely presented as to be almost hypostatised,[3] is first described in the language of Stoicism,[f] and afterwards set forth, in that of Platonism,[g] as 'the breath of the power of God;' as 'a pure influence flowing from the glory of the Almighty;' 'the brightness of the everlasting light, the unspotted mirror of the power of God, and the image of His goodness.' Simi-

a Comp. for ex. Ecclus. xxiv. 6

b ii. 39, 40
c Comp. al- so *Jos.* Ag. Ap. ii. 34

d Comp. 2 Macc. vi.18- vii. 41

e Ch. vii. 22- 27
f Vv. 22-24
g Vv. 25-29

---

[1] It is printed in Havercamp's edition of Josephus, vol. ii. pp. 497–520. The best edition is in *Fritzsche*, Libri Apocryphi Vet. Test. (Lips. 1871).

[2] *Ewald* (Gesch. d. Volkes Isr., vol. iv. pp. 626–632) has given a glowing sketch of it. Ewald rightly says that its Grecian elements have been exaggerated; but *Bucher* (Lehre vom Logos, pp. 59–62) utterly fails in denying their presence altogether.

[3] Compare especially ix. 1; xviii. 14–16, where the idea of σοφία passes into that of the λόγος. Of course the above remarks are not intended to depreciate the great value of this book, alike in itself, and in its practical teaching, in its clear enunciation of a retribution as awaiting man, and in its important bearing on the New Testament revelation of the λόγος.

larly, we have[a] a Stoical enumeration of the four cardinal virtues, temperance, prudence, justice, and fortitude, and close by it the Platonic idea of the soul's pre-existence,[b] and of earth and matter pressing it down.[c] How such views would point in the direction of the need of a perfect revelation from on high, as in the Bible, and of its rational possibility, need scarcely be shown.

But how did Eastern Judaism bear itself towards this Apocryphal literature? We find it described by a term which seems to correspond to our 'Apocrypha,' as *Sepharim Genuzim,*' 'hidden books,' *i.e.,* either such whose origin was hidden, or, more likely, books withdrawn from common or congregational use. Although they were, of course, carefully distinguished from the canonical Scriptures, as not being sacred, their use was not only allowed, but many of them are quoted in Talmudical writings.[1] In this respect they are placed on a very different footing from the so-called *Sepharim Chitsonim,* or 'outside books,' which probably included both the products of a certain class of Jewish Hellenistic literature, and the *Siphrey Minim,* or writings of the heretics. Against these Rabbinism can scarcely find terms of sufficient violence, even debarring from share in the world to come those who read them.[d] This, not only because they were used in controversy, but because their secret influence on orthodox Judaism was dreaded. For similar reasons, later Judaism forbade the use of the Apocrypha in the same manner as that of the *Sepharim Chitsonim.* But their influence had already made itself felt. The Apocrypha, the more greedily perused, not only for their glorification of Judaism, but that they were, so to speak, doubtful reading, which yet afforded a glimpse into that forbidden Greek world, opened the way for other Hellenistic literature, of which unacknowledged but frequent traces occur in Talmudical writings.[2]

To those who thus sought to weld Grecian thought with Hebrew revelation, two objects would naturally present themselves. They must try to connect their Greek philosophers with the Bible, and they must find beneath the letter of Scripture a deeper meaning, which would accord with philosophic truth. So far as the text of Scripture was concerned, they had a method ready to hand. The Stoic philosophers had busied themselves in finding a deeper *allegorical* meaning, especially in the writings of Homer. By applying it to

CHAP.
III

[a] In ch. viii. 7

[b] In vv. 19, 20

[c] ix. 15

[d] Sanh 10♦

---

[1] Some Apocryphal books which have not been preserved to us are mentioned in Talmudical writings, among them one, 'The roll of the building of the Temple,' alas, lost to us! Comp. *Ham-*
burger, vol. ii. pp. 66–70.

[2] Comp. *Siegfried,* Philo von Alex. pp. 275–299, who, however, perhaps overstates the matter.

mythical stories, or to the popular beliefs, and by tracing the supposed symbolical meaning of names, numbers, &c., it became easy to prove almost anything, or to extract from these philosophical truths ethical principles, and even the later results of natural science.[1] Such a process was peculiarly pleasing to the imagination, and the results alike astounding and satisfactory, since as they could not be proved, so neither could they be disproved. This allegorical method[2] was the welcome key by which the Hellenists might unlock the hidden treasury of Scripture. In point of fact, we find it applied so early as in the 'Wisdom of Solomon.'[3]

But as yet Hellenism had scarcely left the domain of sober inter-pretation. It is otherwise in the letter of the Pseudo-Aristeas, to which reference has already been made.[4] Here the wildest symbolism is put into the mouth of the High-Priest Eleazar, to convince Aristeas and his fellow-ambassador that the Mosaic ordinances concerning food had not only a political reason—to keep Israel separate from impious nations—and a sanitary one, but chiefly a mystical meaning. The birds allowed for food were all tame and pure, and they fed on corn or vegetable products, the opposite being the case with those forbidden. The first lesson which this was intended to teach was, that Israel must be just, and not seek to obtain aught from others by violence; but, so to speak, imitate the habits of those birds which were allowed them. The next lesson would be, that each must learn to govern his passions and inclinations. Similarly, the direction about cloven hoofs pointed to the need of making separation—that is, between good and evil; and that about chewing the cud to the need of remembering, viz. God

---

[1] Comp. *Siegfried*, pp. 9–16; *Hart-mann*, Enge Verb. d. A. Test. mit d. N., pp. 568–572.

[2] This is to be carefully distinguished from the typical interpretation and from the mystical—the type being prophetic, the mystery spiritually understood.

[3] Not to speak of such sounder inter-pretations as that of the brazen serpent (Wisd. xvi. 6, 7), and of the Fall (ii. 24), or of the view presented of the early history of the chosen race in ch. x., we may mention as instances of allegorical interpretation that of the manna (xvi. 26–28), and of the high-priestly dress (xviii. 24), to which, no doubt, others might be added. But I cannot find sufficient evidence of this allegorical method in the Wisdom of Jesus the Son of Sirach. The reasoning of *Hartmann* (u. s., pp. 542–547) seems to me greatly strained.

Of the existence of allegorical inter-pretations in the Synoptic Gospels, or of any connection with Hellenism, such as Hartmann, Siegfried, and *Loesner* (Obs. ad. N.T. e Phil. Alex.) put into them, I cannot, on examination, discover any evidence. Similarity of expressions, or even of thought, afford no evidence of inward connection. Of the Gospel by St. John we shall speak in the sequel. In the Paul ne Epistles we find, as might be expected, some allegorical interpre-tations, chiefly in those to the Corin-thians, perhaps owing to the connection of that church with Apollos. Comp. here 1 Cor. ix. 9; x. 4 (Philo, Quod de-ter. potiori insid. 31); 2 Cor. iii. 16; Gal. iv. 21. Of the Epistle to the He-brews and the Apocalypse we cannot here speak.

[4] See p. 25.

and His will.[1] In such manner, according to Aristeas, did the High
Priest go through the catalogue of things forbidden, and of animals to
be sacrificed, showing from their 'hidden meaning' the majesty and
sanctity of the Law.[2]

CHAP.
III

This was an important line to take, and it differed in principle
from the allegorical method adopted by the Eastern Jews. Not only
the *Dorshey Reshumoth*,[3] or searchers out of the subtleties of Scripture,
of their indications, but even the ordinary Haggadist employed, indeed,
allegoric interpretations. Thereby Akiba vindicated for the 'Song of
Songs' its place in the Canon. Did not Scripture say: 'One thing
spake God, twofold is what I heard,'[a] and did not this imply a twofold
meaning; nay, could not the Torah be explained by many different
methods?[4] What, for example, was the water which Israel sought in
the wilderness, or the bread and raiment which Jacob asked in Bethel,
but the *Torah* and the dignity which it conferred? But in all these,
and innumerable similar instances, the allegorical interpretation was
only an application of Scripture for homiletical purposes, not a searching into a *rationale* beneath, such as that of the Hellenists. The
latter the Rabbis would have utterly repudiated, on their express principle that 'Scripture goes not beyond its plain meaning.'[5] They
sternly insisted, that we ought not to search into the ulterior object
and rationale of a law, but simply obey it. But it was this very
rationale of the Law which the Alexandrians sought to find under its
letter. It was in this sense that Aristobulus, a Hellenist Jew of
Alexandria,[b] sought to explain Scripture. Only a fragment of his

[a] Ps. lxii. 11;
Sanh. 34 *a*

[b] About 160
B.C.

[1] A similar principle applied to the prohibition of such species as the mouse or the weasel, not only because they destroyed everything, but because the latter, from its mode of conceiving and bearing, symbolized listening to evil tales, and exaggerated, lying, or mali-cious speech.

[2] Of course this method is constantly adopted by Josephus. Comp. for exam-ple, Ant. iii. 1. 6; 7. 7.

[3] Or *Dorshey Chamuroth*, searchers of difficult passages. *Zunz*. Gottesd. Vortr. p. 323, note *b*.

[4] The seventy languages in which the Law was supposed to have been written below Mount Ebal (Sotah vii. 5). I can-not help feeling this may in part also refer to the various modes of interpret-ing Holy Scripture, and that there is an allusion to this in Shabb. 88 *b*, where Ps. lxviii. 12. and Jer. xxiii. 29, are quoted, the latter to show that the word

of God is like a hammer that breaks the rock in a thousand pieces. Comp. Rashi on Gen. xxxiii. 20.

[5] Perhaps we ought here to point out one of the most important principles of Rabbinism, which has been almost en-tirely overlooked in modern criticism of the Talmud. It is this: that any ordi-nance, not only of the Divine law, but of the Rabbis, even though only given for a particular time or occasion, or for a special reason, remains in full force for all time unless it be expressly recalled (Betsah 5 *b*). Thus *Maimonides* (Sepher ha Mitsv.) declares the law to extirpate the Canaanites as continuing in its obli-gations. The inferences as to the *per-petual obligation*, not only of the cere-monial law, but of sacrifices, will be obvious, and their bearing on the Jewish controversy need not be explained. Comp. Chief Rabbi *Holdheim*, d. Cere-monial Gesetz in Messiasreich, 1845.

BOOK
I

ᵃ Præpar.
Evang. vii.
14. 1; viii.
10. 1–17;
xiii. 12

work, which seems to have been a Commentary on the Pentateuch, dedicated to King Ptolemy (Philometor), has been preserved to us (by Clement of Alexandria, and by Eusebius ᵃ). According to Clement of Alexandria, his aim was, ' to bring the Peripatetic philosophy out of the law of Moses, and out of the other prophets.' Thus, when we read that God stood, it meant the stable order of the world; that He created the world in six days, the orderly succession of time; the rest of the Sabbath, the preservation of what was created. And in such manner could the whole system of Aristotle be found in the Bible. But how was this to be accounted for? Of course, the Bible had not learned from Aristotle, but he and all the other philosophers had learned from the Bible. Thus, according to Aristobulus, Pythagoras, Plato, and all the other sages had really learned from Moses, and the broken rays found in their writings were united in all their glory in the Torah.

It was a tempting path on which to enter, and one on which there was no standing still. It only remained to give fixedness to the allegorical method by reducing it to certain principles, or canons of criticism, and to form the heterogeneous mass of Grecian philosophemes and Jewish theologumena into a compact, if not homogeneous system. This was the work of Philo of Alexandria, born about 20 B.C. It concerns us not here to inquire what were the intermediate links between Aristobulus and Philo. Another and more important point claims our attention. If ancient Greek philosophy knew the teaching of Moses, where was the historic evidence for it? If such did not exist, it must somehow be invented. Orpheus was a name which had

ᵇ As Val-
kenaer puts
it, Diatr. de
Aristob.
Jud. p. 73

always lent itself to literary fraud,ᵇ and so Aristobulus boldly produces (whether of his own or of others' making) a number of spurious citations from Hesiod, Homer, Linus, but especially from Orpheus, all Biblical and Jewish in their cast. Aristobulus was neither the first nor the last to commit such fraud. The Jewish Sibyl boldly, and, as we shall see, successfully personated the heathen oracles. And this opens, generally, quite a vista of Jewish-Grecian literature. In the second, and even in the third century before Christ, there were Hellenist historians, such as Eupolemus, Artapanus, Demetrius, and Aristeas; tragic and epic poets, such as Ezekiel, Pseudo-Philo, and Theodotus, who, after the manner of the ancient classical writers, but for their own purposes, described certain periods of Jewish history, or sang of such themes as the Exodus, Jerusalem, or the rape of Dinah.

The mention of these spurious quotations naturally leads us to another class of spurious literature, which, although not Hellenistic, has many elements in common with it, and, even when originating with Palestinian Jews is not Palestinian, nor yet has been preserved in its language.   We allude to what are known as the Pseudepigraphic, or Pseudonymic Writings, so called because, with one exception, they bear false names of authorship. It is difficult to arrange them otherwise than chronologically—and even here the greatest difference of opinions prevails. Their general character (with one exception) may be described as anti-heathen, perhaps missionary, but chiefly as Apocalyptic. They are attempts at taking up the key-note struck in the prophecies of Daniel; rather, we should say, to lift the veil only partially raised by him, and to point—alike as concerned Israel, and the kingdoms of the world—to the past, the present, and the future, in the light of the Kingship of the Messiah.   Here, if anywhere, we might expect to find traces of New Testament teaching; and yet, side by side with frequent similarity of form, the greatest difference—we had almost said contrast—in spirit, prevails.

Many of these works must have perished. In one of the latest of them [a] they are put down at seventy, probably a round number, having reference to the supposed number of the nations of the earth, or to every possible mode of interpreting Scripture. They are described as intended for 'the wise among the people,' probably those whom St. Paul, in the Christian sense, designates as 'knowing the time' [b][1] of the Advent of the Messiah. Viewed in this light, they embody the ardent aspirations and the inmost hopes[2] of those who longed for the 'consolation of Israel,' as they understood it. Nor should we judge their personations of authorship according to our Western ideas.[3] Pseudonymic writings were common in that age, and a Jew might perhaps plead that, even in the Old Testament, books had been headed by names which confessedly were not those of their authors (such as Samuel, Ruth, Esther). If those inspired poets who sang in the spirit, and echoed the strains, of Asaph, adopted that designation, and the sons of Korah preferred to be known by that title, might not they, who could no longer claim the authority of inspiration seek attention for their utterances by adopting the names of those in whose spirit they professed to write?

The most interesting as well as the oldest of these books are

[a] 4 Esdras xiv. 44, 46

[b] Rom. xiii. 11

---

[1] The καιρός of St. Paul seems here used in exactly the same sense as in later Hebrew זְמַן. The LXX. render it so in five passages (Ezr. v. 3; Dan. iv. 33; vi. 10; vii. 22, 25).

[2] Of course, it suits Jewish writers, like Dr. Jost, to deprecate the value of the Pseudepigrapha. Their ardour of expectancy ill agrees with the modern theories, which would eliminate, if possible, the Messianic hope from ancient Judaism.

[3] Comp. *Dillmann* in Herzog's Real-Encykl. vol. xii. p. 301.

those known as the *Book of Enoch*, the *Sibylline Oracles*, the *Psalter of Solomon*, and the *Book of Jubilees*, or *Little Genesis*. Only the briefest notice of them can here find a place.[1]

The *Book of Enoch*, the oldest parts of which date a century and a half before Christ, comes to us from Palestine. It professes to be a vision vouchsafed to that Patriarch, and tells of the fall of the Angels and its consequences, and of what he saw and heard in his rapt journeys through heaven and earth. Of deepest, though often sad, interest, is what it says of the Kingdom of Heaven, of the advent of Messiah and His Kingdom, and of the last things.

On the other hand, the *Sibylline Oracles*, of which the oldest portions date from about 160 B.C., come to us from Egypt. It is to the latter only that we here refer. Their most interesting parts are also the most characteristic. In them the ancient heathen myths of the first ages of man are welded together with Old Testament notices, while the heathen Theogony is recast in a Jewish mould. Thus Noah becomes Uranos, Shem Saturn, Ham Titan, and Japheth Japetus. Similarly, we have fragments of ancient heathen oracles, so to speak, recast in a Jewish edition. The strangest circumstance is, that the utterances of this Judaising and Jewish Sibyl seem to have passed as the oracles of the ancient Erythræan, which had predicted the fall of Troy, and as those of the Sibyl of Cumæ, which, in the infancy of Rome, Tarquinius Superbus had deposited in the Capitol.

The collection of eighteen hymns known as the *Psalter of Solomon* dates from more than half a century before our era. No doubt the original was Hebrew, though they breathe a somewhat Hellenistic spirit. They express ardent Messianic aspirations, and a firm faith in the Resurrection, and in eternal rewards and punishments.

Different in character from the preceding works is *The Book of Jubilees*—so called from its chronological arrangement into 'Jubilee-periods'—or '*Little Genesis*.' It is chiefly a kind of legendary supplement to the Book of Genesis, intended to explain some of its historic difficulties, and to fill up its historic *lacunæ*. It was probably written about the time of Christ—and this gives it a special interest—by a Palestinian, and in Hebrew, or rather Aramæan. But, like the rest of the Apocryphal and Pseudepigraphic literature which comes from Palestine, or was originally written in Hebrew, we possess it no longer in that language, but only in translation.

If from this brief review of Hellenist and Pseudepigraphic literature we turn to take a retrospect, we can scarcely fail to perceive,

---

[1] For a brief review of the 'Pseudepigraphic Writings,' see Appendix I.

on the one hand, the development of the old, and on the other the CHAP.
preparation for the new—in other words, the grand expectancy III
awakened, and the grand preparation made.   One step only remained
to complete what Hellenism had already begun.   That completion
came through one who, although himself untouched by the Gospel,
perhaps more than any other prepared alike his co-religionists the
Jews, and his countrymen the Greeks, for the new teaching, which,
indeed, was presented by many of its early advocates in the forms
which they had learned from him.   That man was Philo the Jew, of
Alexandria.

CHAPTER IV.

PHILO OF ALEXANDRIA, THE RABBIS, AND THE GOSPELS—THE FINAL DE-
VELOPMENT OF HELLENISM IN ITS RELATION TO RABBINISM AND THE
GOSPEL ACCORDING TO ST. JOHN.

BOOK
I

IT is strange how little we know of the personal history of the greatest of uninspired Jewish writers of old, though he occupied so prominent a position in his time.[1] Philo was born in Alexandria, about the year 20 before Christ. He was a descendant of Aaron, and belonged to one of the wealthiest and most influential families among the Jewish merchant-princes of Egypt. His brother was the political head of that community in Alexandria, and he himself on one occasion represented his co-religionists—though unsuccessfully—at Rome,[a] as the head of an embassy to entreat the Emperor Caligula for protection from the persecutions consequent on the Jewish resistance to placing statues of the Emperor in their Synagogues. But it is not with Philo, the wealthy aristocratic Jew of Alexandria, but with the great writer and thinker who, so to speak, completed Jewish Hellenism, that we have here to do. Let us see what was his relation alike to heathen philosophy and to the Jewish faith, of both of which he was the ardent advocate, and how in his system he combined the teaching of the two.

a 39 or 40
A.D.

To begin with, Philo united in rare measure Greek learning with Jewish enthusiasm. In his writings he very frequently uses classical modes of expression;[2] he names not fewer than sixty-four Greek writers;[3] and he either alludes to, or quotes frequently from, such sources as Homer, Hesiod, Pindar, Solon, the great Greek tragedians, Plato, and others. But to him these men were scarcely 'heathen.' He had sat at their feet, and learned to weave a system from Pythagoras, Plato, Aristotle, and the Stoics. The gatherings of these

---

[1] *Hausrath* (N.T. Zeitg. vol. ii. p. 222 &c.) has given a highly imaginative picture of Philo—as, indeed, of many other persons and things.

[2] *Siegfried* has, with immense labor, collected a vast number of parallel expressions, chiefly from Plato and Plutarch (pp. 39–47).

[3] Comp. *Grossmann*, Quæst. Phil. i. p. 5 &c.

philosophers were 'holy,' and Plato was 'the great.' But holier than
all was the gathering of the true Israel; and incomparably greater
than any, Moses. From him had all sages learned, and with him
alone was all truth to be found—not, indeed, *in* the letter, but *under*
the letter, of Holy Scripture. If in Numb. xxiii. 19 we read 'God
is not a man,' and in Deut. i. 31 that the Lord was 'as a man,' did
it not imply, on the one hand, the revelation of absolute truth by
God, and, on the other, accommodation to those who were weak?
Here, then, was the principle of a twofold interpretation of the Word
of God—the literal and the allegorical. The letter of the text must
be held fast; and Biblical personages and histories were real. But
only narrow-minded slaves of the letter would stop here; the more so,
as sometimes the literal meaning alone would be tame, even absurd;
while the allegorical interpretation gave the true sense, even though
it might occasionally run counter to the letter. Thus, the patriarchs
represented states of the soul; and, whatever the letter might bear,
Joseph represented one given to the fleshly, whom his brothers rightly
hated; Simeon the soul aiming after the higher; the killing of the
Egyptian by Moses, the subjugation of passion, and so on. But this
allegorical interpretation—by the side of the literal (the *Peshat* of the
Palestinians)—though only for the few, was not arbitrary. It had its
'laws,' and 'canons'—some of which excluded the literal interpretation, while others admitted it by the side of the higher meaning.[1]

To begin with the former: the literal sense must be wholly set
aside, when it implied anything unworthy of the Deity, anything unmeaning, impossible, or contrary to reason. Manifestly, this canon,
if strictly applied, would do away not only with all anthropomorphisms,
but cut the knot wherever difficulties seemed insuperable. Again, Philo
would find an allegorical, along with the literal, interpretation indicated
in the reduplication of a word, and in seemingly superfluous words,
particles, or expressions.[2] These could, of course, only bear such a
meaning on Philo's assumption of the actual inspiration of the LXX.
version. Similarly, in exact accordance with a Talmudical canon,[a]
any repetition of what had been already stated would point to something new. These were comparatively sober rules of exegesis. Not
so the licence which he claimed of freely altering the punctuation[3] of

CHAP.
IV

[a] Baba K
64 a

---

[1] In this sketch of the system of Philo
I have largely availed myself of the
careful analysis of *Siegfried*.

[2] It should be noted that these are
also Talmudical canons, not indeed for
allegorical interpretation, but as point-

ing to some special meaning, since there
was not a word or particle in Scripture without a definite meaning and
object.

[3] To illustrate what use might be
made of such alterations, the Midrash

BOOK
I

sentences, and his notion that, if one from among several synonymous words was chosen in a passage, this pointed to some special meaning attaching to it. Even more extravagant was the idea, that a word which occurred in the LXX. might be interpreted according to every shade of meaning which it bore in the Greek, and that even another meaning might be given it by slightly altering the letters. However, like other of Philo's allegorical canons, these were also adopted by the Rabbis, and Haggadic interpretations were frequently prefaced by: 'Read not thus—but thus.' If such violence might be done to the text, we need not wonder at interpretations based on a play upon words, or even upon parts of a word. Of course, all seemingly strange or peculiar modes of expression, or of designation, occurring in Scripture, must have their special meaning, and so also every particle, adverb, or preposition. Again, the position of a verse, its succession by another, the apparently unaccountable presence or absence of a word, might furnish hints for some deeper meaning, and so would an unexpected singular for a plural, or *vice versâ*, the use of a tense, even the gender of a word. Most serious of all, an allegorical inter-pretation might be again employed as the basis of another.[1]

We repeat, that these allegorical canons of Philo are essentially the same as those of Jewish traditionalism in the Haggadah,[2] only the latter were not rationalising, and far more brilliant in their application.[3] In another respect also the Palestinian had the advantage of the Alexandrian exegesis. Reverently and cautiously it indicated what might be omitted in public reading, and why; what expressions of the original might be modified by the Meturgeman, and how; so as to avoid alike one danger by giving a passage in its literality, and another by adding to the sacred text, or conveying a wrong impression of the Divine Being, or else giving occasion to the unlearned and

---

(Ber. R. 65) would have us punctuate Gen. xxvii. 19, as follows: 'And Jacob said unto his father, I (viz. am he who will receive the ten commandments)—(but) Esau (is) thy firstborn.' In Yalkut there is the still more curious explanation that in heaven the soul of Jacob was the firstborn!

[1] Each of these positions is capable of ample proof from Philo's writings, as shown by Siegfried. But only a bare statement of these canons was here possible.

[2] Comp. our above outline with the 'xxv. theses de modis et formulis quibus pr. Hebr. doctores SS. interpretari etc. soliti fuerunt,' in *Surenhusius, Βίβλος*

καταλλαγῆς, pp. 57–88.

[3] For a comparison between Philo and Rabbinic theology, see Appendix II.: 'Philo and Rabbinic Theology.' *Freudenthal* (Hellen. Studien, pp. 67 &c.) aptly designates this mixture of the two as 'Hellenistic Midrash,' it being difficult sometimes to distinguish whether it originated in Palestine or in Egypt, or else in both independently. Freudenthal gives a number of curious instances in which Hellenism and Rabbinism agree in their interpretations. For other interesting comparisons between Haggadic interpretations and those of Philo, see *Joel*, Blick in d. Religionsgesch. i. p. 3 &c.

unwary of becoming entangled in dangerous speculations. Jewish tradition here lays down some principles which would be of great practical use. Thus we are told,[a] that Scripture uses the modes of expression common among men. This would, of course, include all anthropomorphisms. Again, sometimes with considerable ingenuity, a suggestion is taken from a word, such as that Moses knew the serpent was to be made of brass from the similarity of the two words (*nachash*, a serpent, and *nechosheth*, brass.[b] Similarly, it is noted that Scripture uses euphemistic language, so as to preserve the greatest delicacy.[c] These instances might be multiplied, but the above will suffice.

CHAP.
IV

[a] Ber. 31 *b*

[b] Ber. R. 31

[c] Ber. R. 70

In his symbolical interpretations Philo only partially took the same road as the Rabbis. The symbolism of numbers and, so far as the Sanctuary was concerned, that of colours, and even materials, may, indeed, be said to have its foundation in the Old Testament itself. The same remark applies partially to that of names. The Rabbis certainly so interpreted them.[1] But the application which Philo made of this symbolism was very different. Everything became symbolical in his hands, if it suited his purpose: numbers (in a very arbitrary manner), beasts, birds, fowls, creeping things, plants, stones, elements, substances, conditions, even sex—and so a term or an expression might even have several and contradictory meanings, from which the interpreter was at liberty to choose.

From the consideration of the method by which Philo derived from Scriptures his theological views, we turn to a brief analysis of these views.[2]

1. *Theology.*—In reference to God, we find, side by side, the apparently contradictory views of the Platonic and the Stoic schools. Following the former, the sharpest distinction was drawn between God and the world. God existed neither in space, nor in time; He had neither human qualities nor affections; in fact, He was without

---

[1] Thus, to give only a few out of many examples, Ruth is derived from *ravah*, to satiate to give to drink, because David, her descendant, satiated God with his Psalms of praise (Ber. 7 *b*). Here the principle of the significance of Bible-names is deduced from Ps. xlvi. 8 (9 in the Hebrew): 'Come, behold the works of the Lord, who hath made names on earth,' the word 'desolations,' SHAMOTH, being altered to SHEMOTH, 'names.' In general, that section, from Ber. 3 *b*, to the end of 8 *a*, is full of Haggadic Scripture interpretations. On fol. 4 *a* there

is the curious symbolical derivation of *Mephibosheth*, who is supposed to have set David right on halakhic questions, as *Mippi bosheth*: 'from my mouth shaming,' 'because he put to shame the face of David in the Halakhah.' Similarly in Siphré (Par. Behaalothekha, ed. Friedmann, p. 20 *a*) we have very beautiful and ingenious interpretations of the names *Reuel, Hobab* and *Jethro*.

[2] It would be impossible here to give the references, which would occupy too much space.

any qualities (ἄποιος), and even without any name (ἄρρητος); hence, wholly uncognisable by man (ἀκατάληπτος). Thus, changing the punctuation and the accents, the LXX. of Gen. iii. 9 was made to read: 'Adam, thou art somewhere;' but God had no somewhere, as Adam seemed to think when he hid himself from Him. In the above sense, also, Ex. iii. 14, and vi. 3, were explained, and the two names *Elohim* and *Jehovah* belonged really to the two supreme Divine 'Potencies,' while the fact of God's being uncognisable appeared from Ex. xx. 21.

But side by side with this we have, to save the Jewish, or rather Old Testament, idea of creation and providence, the Stoic notion of God as immanent in the world—in fact, as that alone which is real in it, as always working: in short, to use his own Pantheistic expression, as 'Himself one and the all' (εἷς καὶ τὸ πᾶν). Chief in His Being is His goodness, the forthgoing of which was the ground of creation. Only the good comes from Him. With matter He can have nothing to do—hence the plural number in the account of creation. God only created the soul, and that only of the good. In the sense of being 'immanent,' God is everywhere—nay, all things are really only in Him, or rather He is the real in all. But chiefly is God the wellspring and the light of the soul—its 'Saviour' from the 'Egypt' of passion. Two things follow. With Philo's ideas of the separation between God and matter, it was impossible always to account for miracles or interpositions. Accordingly, these are sometimes allegorised, sometimes rationalistically explained. Further, the God of Philo, whatever he might say to the contrary, was *not* the God of that Israel which was His chosen people.

2. *Intermediary Beings.*—Potencies (δυνάμεις, λόγοι). If, in what has preceded, we have once and again noticed a remarkable similarity between Philo and the Rabbis, there is a still more curious analogy between his teaching and that of Jewish Mysticism, as ultimately fully developed in the 'Kabbalah.' The very term *Kabbalah* (from *qibbel,* to hand down) seems to point out not only its *de*scent by oral tradition, but also its *a*scent to ancient sources.[1] Its existence is presupposed, and its leading ideas are sketched in the Mishnah.[a] The Targums also bear at least one remarkable trace of it. May it not be, that as Philo frequently refers to ancient tradition, so both Eastern and Western Judaism may here have drawn from one and the same source—we will not venture to suggest, how high up—

[1] For want of handier material I must take leave to refer to my brief sketch of the Kabbalah in the 'History of the Jewish Nation,' pp. 434-446.

while each made such use of it as suited their distinctive tendencies?
At any rate the Kabbalah also, likening Scripture to a person, compares those who study merely the letter, to them who attend only to
the dress; those who consider the moral of a fact, to them who attend
to the body; while the initiated alone, who regard the hidden
meaning, are those who attend to the soul. Again, as Philo, so the
oldest part of the Mishnah[a] designates God as *Maqom*—'the place'— ^a Ab. v. 4
the τόπος, the all-comprehending, what the Kabbalists called the *En-
Soph*, 'the boundless,' that God, without any quality, Who becomes
cognisable only by His manifestations.[1]

The manifestations of God! But neither Eastern mystical
Judaism, nor the philosophy of Philo, could admit of any direct
contact between God and creation. The Kabbalah solved the difficulty by their *Sephiroth*,[2] or emanations from God, through which
this contact was ultimately brought about, and of which the *En-
Soph*, or crown, was the spring: 'the source from which the infinite
light issued.' If Philo found greater difficulties, he had also more
ready help from the philosophical systems to hand. His *Sephiroth*
were 'Potencies' (δυνάμεις), 'Words' (λόγοι), intermediate powers.
'Potencies,' as we imagine, when viewed Godwards; 'Words,' as
viewed creationwards. They were not emanations, but, according to
Plato, 'archetypal ideas,' on the model of which all that exists was
formed; and also, according to the Stoic idea, the cause of all, pervading all, forming all, and sustaining all. Thus these 'Potencies'
were wholly in God, and yet wholly out of God. If we divest all
this of its philosophical colouring, did not Eastern Judaism also
teach that there was a distinction between the Unapproachable God,
and God manifest?[3]

Another remark will show the parallelism between Philo and
Rabbinism.[4] As the latter speaks of the two qualities (*Middoth*) of
Mercy and Judgment in the Divine Being,[b] and distinguishes between ^b Jer. Ber.
ix. 7
Elohim as the God of Justice, and *Jehovah* as the God of Mercy
and Grace, so Philo places next to the Divine Word (θεῖος λόγος),
Goodness (ἀγαθότης), as the Creative Potency (ποιητικὴ δύναμις),

---

[1] In short, the λόγος σπερματικός of
the Stoics.

[2] Supposed to mean either *numera-
tiones*, or splendour. But why not derive
the word from σφαίρα? The ten are:
*Crown, Wisdom, Intelligence, Mercy,
Judgment, Beauty, Triumph, Praise,
Foundation, Kingdom*.

[3] For the teaching of Eastern Judaism
in this respect, see Appendix II.: 'Philo

and Rabbinic Theology.'

[4] A very interesting question arises:
how far Philo was acquainted with, and
influenced by, the Jewish traditional law
or the Halakhah. This has been treated
by Dr. *B. Ritter* in an able tractate (Philo
u. die Halach.), although he attributes
more to Philo than the evidence seems to
admit.

BOOK   and Power (ἐξουσια), as the Ruling Potency (βασιλικὴ δύναμις),
I   proving this by a curious etymological derivation of the words for
'God' and 'Lord' (Θεός and κύριος)—apparently unconscious that
the LXX., in direct contradiction, translated Jehovah by Lord
(κύριος), and Elohim by God (Θεός)! These two potencies of goodness and power, Philo sees in the two Cherubim, and in the two
'Angels' which accompanied God (the Divine Word), when on his
way to destroy the cities of the plain. But there were more than
these two Potencies. In one place Philo enumerates six, according to
the number of the cities of refuge. The Potencies issued from God
as the beams from the light, as the waters from the spring, as the
breath from a person; they were immanent in God, and yet also
without Him—motions on the part of God, and yet independent
beings. They were the ideal world, which in its impulse outwards,
meeting matter, produced this material world of ours. They were
also the angels of God—His messengers to man, the *media* through
whom He revealed Himself.[1]

3. *The Logos.*—Viewed in its bearing on New Testament teaching, this part of Philo's system raises the most interesting questions.
But it is just here that our difficulties are greatest. We can understand the Platonic conception of the Logos as the 'archetypal idea,'
and that of the Stoics as of the 'world-reason' pervading matter.
Similarly, we can perceive, how the Apocrypha—especially the Book
of Wisdom—following up the Old Testament typical truth concerning 'Wisdom' (as specially set forth in the Book of Proverbs) almost
arrived so far as to present 'Wisdom' as a special 'Subsistence' (hy-
postatising it). More than this, in Talmudical writings, we find mention not only of the *Shem*, or 'Name,'[2] but also of the Shekhinah,'
God as manifest and present, which is sometimes also presented as
the *Ruach ha Qodesh*, or Holy Spirit.[a] But in the Targumim we
meet yet another expression, which, strange to say, *never occurs in the*

ᵃ Or *Ruach
ham Maqom,*
Ab. iii. 10,
and fre-
quently in
the Tal-
mud.

[1] At the same time there is a remarkable difference here between Philo and
Rabbinism. Philo holds that the creation of the world was brought about by
the *Potencies*, but that the Law was given
directly through Moses, and *not* by the
mediation of angels. But this latter was
certainly the view generally entertained
in Palestine as expressed in the LXX.
rendering of Deut. xxxii. 2, in the Targumim on that passage, and more fully
still in *Jos. Ant.* xv. 5. 3, in the Midrashim and in the Talmud, where we are

told (Macc. 24 *a*) that only the opening
words, 'I am the Lord thy God, thou
shalt have no other gods but Me,' were
spoken by God Himself. Comp. also
Acts vii. 38, 53; Gal. iii. 19; Heb. ii. 2.
[2] *Hammejuchad,* 'appropriatum;' *ham-
mephorash,* 'expositum,' 'separatum,' the
'tetragrammaton,' or four-lettered name,
יהוה. There was also a *Shem* with
'twelve,' and one with 'forty-two' letters (Kidd. 71 *a*).

Talmud.[1] It is that of the *Memra*, Logos, or 'Word.' Not that the term   CHAP.
is exclusively applied to the Divine Logos.[2] But it stands out as perhaps   IV
the most remarkable fact in this literature, that God—not as in His permanent manifestation, or manifest Presence—but as revealing Himself,
is designated *Memra.* Altogether that term, as applied to God, occurs
in the Targum Onkelos 179 times, in the so-called Jerusalem Targum 99
times, and in the Targum Pseudo-Jonathan 321 times. A critical analysis shows that in 82 instances in Onkelos, in 71 instances in the Jerusalem Targum, and in 213 instances in the Targum Pseudo-Jonathan,
the designation *Memra* is not only distinguished from God, but evidently refers to God as revealing Himself.[3] But what does this imply? The distinction between God and the *Memra of Jehovah* is marked
in many passages.[4] Similarly, the *Memra of Jehovah* is distinguished
from the *Shekhinah.*[5] Nor is the term used instead of the sacred word
Jehovah;[6] nor for the well-known Old Testament expression 'the Angel
of the Lord;'[7] nor yet for the *Metatron* of the Targum Pseudo-Jonathan
and of the Talmud.[8] Does it then represent an older tradition underlying all these?[9] Beyond this Rabbinic theology has not preserved to
us the doctrine of Personal distinctions in the Godhead. And yet, if

[1] *Levy* (Neuhebr. Wörterb. i. p. 374 *a*)
seems to imply that in the Midrash the
term *dibbur* occupies the same place and
meaning. But with all deference I cannot agree with this opinion, nor do the
passages quoted bear it out.

[2] The 'word,' as spoken, is distinguished from the 'Word' as speaking, or
revealing Himself. The former is generally designated by the term *pithgama.*'
Thus in Gen. xv. 1, 'After these words
(things) came the "pithgama" of Jehovah
to Abram in prophecy, saying, Fear not,
Abram, My "Memra" shall be thy
strength, and thy very great reward.' Still,
the term *Memra*, as applied not only to
man, but also in reference to God, is not
always the equivalent of 'the Logos.'

[3] The various passages in the Targum
of Onkelos, the Jerusalem, and the
Pseudo-Jonathan Targum on the Pentateuch will be found enumerated and
classified, as those in which it is a *doubtful*, a *fair*, or an *unquestionable* inference, that the word *Memra* is intended
for God revealing Himself, in Appendix
II.: 'Philo and Rabbinic Theology.'

[4] As, for example, Gen. xxviii. 21, 'the
Memra of Jehovah shall be my God.'

[5] As, for example, Num. xxiii. 21, 'the
Memra of Jehovah their God is their
helper, and the Shekhinah of their King

is in the midst of them.'

[6] That term is often used by Onkelos.
Besides, the expression itself is 'the
Memra of Jehovah.'

[7] Onkelos only once (in Ex. iv. 24)
paraphrases Jehovah by 'Malakha.'

[8] Metatron, either = μετὰ θρόνον, or
μετὰ τύραννον. In the Talmud it is applied to the Angel of Jehovah (Ex. xxiii.
20), 'the Prince of the World,' 'the
Prince of the Face' or 'of the Presence,'
as they call him; he who sits in the innermost chamber before God, while the other
angels only hear His commands from behind the veil (Chag. 15 *a*; 16 *a*; Toseft. ad
Chull. 60 *a*; Jeb. 16 *b*). This *Metatron* of
the Talmud and the Kabbalah is also the
Adam Qadmon, or archetypal man.

[9] Of deep interest is Onkelos' rendering of Deut. xxxiii. 27, where, instead of
'underneath are the everlasting arms,'
Onkelos has, 'and by His Memra was
the world created,' exactly as in St. John
i. 10. Now this divergence of Onkelos
from the Hebrew text seems unaccountable. *Winer*, whose inaugural dissertation, 'De Onkeloso ejusque paraph.
Chald.' Lips. 1820, most modern writers
have followed (with amplifications, chiefly
from *Luzzato's* Philoxenus), makes no
reference to this passage, nor do his successors, so far as I know. It is curious

words have any meaning, the *Memra* is a hypostasis, though the dis tinction of permanent, personal Subsistence is not marked. Nor yet, to complete this subject, is the *Memra* identified with the Messiah. In the Targum Onkelos distinct mention is twice made of Him,[a] while in the other Targumim no fewer than seventy-one Biblical passages are rendered with explicit reference to Him.

If we now turn to the views expressed by Philo about the Logos we find that they are hesitating, and even contradictory. One thing, however, is plain: the Logos of Philo is *not* the Memra of the Targumim. For, the expression *Memra* ultimately rests on theological, that of *Logos* on philosophical grounds. Again, the Logos of Philo approximates more closely to the *Metatron* of the Talmud and Kabbalah. As they speak of him as the ' Prince of the Face,' who bore the name of his Lord, so Philo represents the Logos as ' the eldest Angel,' ' the many-named Archangel,' in accordance with the Jewish view that the name JeHoVaH unfolded its meaning in seventy names for the Godhead.[1] As they speak of the ' Adam Qadmon,' so Philo of the Logos as the human reflection of the eternal God. And in both these respects, it is worthy of notice that he appeals to ancient teaching.[2]

What, then, is the Logos of Philo ? Not a concrete personality, and yet, from another point of view, not strictly impersonal, nor merely a pro-

that, as our present Hebrew text of this verse consists of three words, so does the rendering of Onkelos, and that both end with the same word. Is the rendering of Onkelos then a paraphrase, or does it represent another reading? Another interesting passage is Deut. viii. 3. Its quotation by Christ in St. Matt. iv. 4 is deeply interesting, as read in the light of the rendering of Onkelos, ' Not by bread alone is man sustained, but by every forthcoming Memra from before Jehovah shall man live.' Yet another rendering of Onkelos is significantly illustrative of 1 Cor. x. 1-4. He renders Deut. xxxiii. 3 ' with power He brought them out of Egypt; they were led under thy cloud; they journeyed according to (by) thy Memra.' Does this represent a difference in the Hebrew from the admittedly difficult text in our present Bible? Winer refers to it as an instance in which Onkelos 'suopte ingenio et copiose admodum eloquitur vatum divinorum mentem,' adding, ' ita ut de his, quas singulis vocibus inesse crediderit, significationibus non possit recte judicari;' and Winer's successors say much the same. But this is to state, not to explain, the difficulty. In general, we may here be allowed to say that the question of the Targum

has scarcely received as yet sufficient treatment. Mr. *Deutsch's* Article in Smith's ' Dictionary of the Bible ' (since reprinted in his ' Remains ') is, though brilliantly written, unsatisfactory. Dr. *Davidson* (in Kitto's Cyclop., vol. iii. pp. 948–966) is, as always, careful, laborious, and learned. Dr. *Volck's* article (in Herzog's Real-Encykl., vol. xv. pp. 672–683) is without much intrinsic value, though painstaking. We mention these articles, besides the treatment of the subject in the Introduction to the Old Testament (Keil, De Wette-Schrader, Bleek-Kamphausen, Reuss), and the works of Zunz, Geiger, Nöldeke, and others, to whom partial reference has already been made. *Frankel's* interesting and learned book (Zu dem Targum der Propheten) deals almost exclusively with the Targum Jonathan, on which it was impossible to enter within our limits. As modern brochures of interest the following three may be mentioned: *Maybaum,* Anthropomorphien bei Onkelos; *Grönemann,* Die Jonath. Pentat. Uebers. im Verhältn. z. Halacha; and *Singer,* Onkelos im Verhältn. z. Halacha.
[1] See the enumeration of these 70 Names in the Baal-ha-Turim on Numb. xi. 16.
[2] Comp. *Siegfried,* u. s., pp. 221–223.

perty of the Deity, but the shadow, as it were, which the light of God casts—and if Himself light, only the manifested reflection of God, His spiritual, even as the world is His material, habitation. Moreover, the Logos is 'the image of God' (εἰκών), upon which man was made,[a] or, to use the platonic term, 'the archetypal idea.' As regards the relation between the Logos and the two fundamental Potencies (from which all others issue), the latter are variously represented—on the one hand, as proceeding from the Logos; and on the other, as themselves constituting the Logos. As regards the world, the Logos is its real being. He is also its archetype; moreover the instrument (ὄργανον) through Whom God created all things. If the Logos separates between God and the world, it is rather as intermediary; He separates, but He also unites. But chiefly does this hold true as regards the relation between God and man. The Logos announces and interprets to man the will and mind of God (ἑρμηνεὺς καὶ προφήτης); He acts as mediator; He is the real High-Priest, and as such by His purity takes away the sins of man, and by His intercession procures for us the mercy of God. Hence Philo designates Him not only as the High-Priest, but as the 'Paraclete.' He is also the sun whose rays enlighten man, the medium of Divine revelation to the soul; the Manna, or support of spiritual life; He Who dwells in the soul. And so the Logos is, in the fullest sense, Melchisedek, the priest of the most high God, the king of righteousness (βασιλεὺς δίκαιος), and the king of Salem (βασιλεὺς εἰρήνης), Who brings righteousness and peace to the soul.[b] But the Logos 'does not come into any soul that is dead in sin.' That there is close similarity of form between these Alexandrian views and much in the argumentation of the Epistle to the Hebrews, must be evident to all—no less than that there is the widest possible divergence in substance and spirit.[1] The Logos of Philo is shadowy, unreal, not a Person;[2] there is no need of an atonement; the High-Priest intercedes, but has no sacrifice to offer as the basis of His intercession, least of all that of Himself; the old Testament types are only typical ideas,

[a] Gen. i. 27

[b] De Leg.
Alleg. iii.
25, 26

---

[1] For a full discussion of this similarity of form and divergence of spirit, between Philo—or, rather, between Alexandrianism—and the Epistle to the Hebrews, the reader is referred to the masterly treatise by *Riehm* (Der Lehrbegriff d. Hebräerbr. ed. 1867, especially pp. 247–268, 411–424, 658–670, and 855–860). The author's general view on the subject is well and convincingly formulated on p. 249. We must, however, add, in opposition to Riehm, that, by his own showing, the writer of the Epistle to the Hebrews displays few traces of a *Palestinian* training.

[2] On the subject of Philo's Logos generally the brochure of *Harnoch* (Königsberg, 1879) deserves perusal, although it does not furnish much that is new. In general, the student of Philo ought especially to study the sketch by *Zeller* in his Philosophie der Gr., vol. iii. pt. ii. 3rd ed. pp. 338–418.

BOOK   not typical facts; they point to a Prototypal Idea in the eternal past,
I   not to an Antitypal Person and Fact in history; there is no cleansing
of the soul by blood, no sprinkling of the Mercy Seat, no access for all
through the rent veil into the immediate Presence of God; nor yet a
quickening of the soul from dead works to serve the living God. If
the argumentation of the Epistle to the Hebrews is Alexandrian, it is
an Alexandrianism which is overcome and past, which only furnishes
the form, not the substance, the vessel, not its contents. The closer
therefore the outward similarity, the greater is the contrast in
substance.

The vast difference between Alexandrianism and the New Testament will appear still more clearly in the views of Philo on *Cosmology*
and *Anthropology*. In regard to the former, his results in some respects
run parallel to those of the students of mysticism in the Talmud, and
of the Kabbalists. Together with the Stoic view, which represented
God as 'the active cause' of this world, and matter as 'the passive,'
Philo holds the Platonic idea, that matter was something existent, and
that it resisted God.[1] Such speculations must have been current
among the Jews long before, to judge by certain warnings given by the
Son of Sirach.[a][2] And Stoic views of the origin of the world seem
implied even in the Book of the Wisdom of Solomon (i. 7; vii. 24;
viii. 1; xii. 1).[3] The mystics in the Talmud arrived at similar
conclusions, not through Greek, but through Persian teaching. Their
speculations[4] boldly entered on the dangerous ground,[5] forbidden to
the many, scarcely allowed to the few,[6] where such deep questions as
the origin of our world and its connection with God were discussed.
It was, perhaps, only a beautiful poetic figure that God had taken of
the dust under the throne of His glory, and cast it upon the waters,
which thus became earth.[b] But so far did isolated teachers become

[a] As for example Ecclus. iii. 21-24

[b] Shem. R. 13

---

[1] With singular and characteristic inconsistency, Philo, however, ascribes
also to God the creation of matter (de
Somn. i. 13).

[2] So the Talmudists certainly understood it, Jer. Chag. ii. 1.

[3] Comp. *Grimm*, Exeg. Handb. zu d.
Apokr., Lief. vi. pp. 55, 56.

[4] They were arranged into those concerning the *Maasey Bereshith* (Creation),
and the *Maasey Merkabhah*, 'the chariot'
of Ezekiel's vision (Providence in the
widest sense, or God's manifestation in
the created world).

[5] Of the four celebrities who entered
the 'Pardes,' or enclosed Paradise of

theosophic speculation, one became an
apostate, another died, a third went
wrong (Ben Soma), and only Akiba escaped unscathed, according to the
Scripture saying, 'Draw me, and we will
run' (Chag. 14 *b*).

[6] 'It is not lawful to enter upon the
Maasey Bereshith in presence of two,
nor upon the *Merkabhah* in presence of
one, unless he be a "sage," and understands of his own knowledge. Any one
who ratiocinates on these four things, it
were better for him that he had not been
born: What is above and what is below;
what was afore, and what shall be hereafter.' (Chag. ii. 1.)

intoxicated[1] by the new wine of these strange speculations, that they whispered it to one another that water was the original element of the world,[2] which had successively been hardened into snow and then into earth.[a][3] Other and later teachers fixed upon the air or the fire as the original element, arguing the pre-existence of matter from the use of the word 'made' in Gen. i. 7. instead of 'created.' Some modified this view, and suggested that God had originally created the three elements of water, air or spirit, and fire, from which all else was developed.[4] Traces also occur of the doctrine of the pre-existence of things, in a sense similar to that of Plato.[b]

[a] Jer. Chag.
77 a

[b] Ber. R. 1.

Like Plato and the Stoics, Philo regarded matter as devoid of all quality, and even form. Matter in itself was dead—more than that, it was *evil*. This matter, which was already existing, God formed (not made), like an architect who uses his materials according to a pre-existing plan—which in this case was the archetypal world.

This was creation, or rather formation, brought about not by God Himself, but by the Potencies, especially by the Logos, Who was the connecting bond of all. As for God, His only direct work was the soul, and that only of the good, not of the evil. Man's immaterial part had a twofold aspect: earthwards, as Sensuousness ($a\check{\iota}\sigma\theta\eta\sigma\iota\varsigma$); and heavenwards, as Reason ($\nu o\hat{v}\varsigma$). The sensuous part of the soul was connected with the body. It had no heavenly past, and would have no future. But 'Reason' ($\nu o\hat{v}\varsigma$) was that breath of true life which God had breathed into man ($\pi\nu\epsilon\hat{v}\mu a$) whereby the earthy became the higher, living spirit, with its various faculties. Before time began the soul was without body, an archetype, the 'heavenly man,' pure spirit in Paradise (virtue), yet even so longing after its ultimate archetype, God. Some of these pure spirits descended into

---

[1] 'Ben Soma went astray (mentally): he shook the (Jewish) world.'

[2] That criticism, which one would designate as impertinent, which would find this view in 2 Peter iii. 5, is, alas! not confined to Jewish writers, but hazarded even by De Wette.

[3] Judah bar Pazi, in the second century. Ben Soma lived in the first century of our era.

[4] According to the Jerusalem Talmud (Ber. i. I) the firmament was at first soft, and only gradually became hard. According to Ber. R. 10, God created the world from a mixture of fire and snow, other Rabbis suggesting four original elements, according to the quarters of the globe, or else six, adding to them that which is above and that which is below.

A very curious idea is that of R. Joshua ben Levi, according to which all the works of creation were really finished on the first day, and only, as it were, extended on the other days. This also represents really a doubt of the Biblical account of creation. Strange though it may sound, the doctrine of development was derived from the words (Gen. ii. 4). 'These are the generations of heaven and earth when they were created, in the day when Jahveh Elohim made earth and heavens.' It was argued, that the expression implied, they were developed from the day in which they had been created. Others seem to have held, that the three principal things that were created—earth, heaven, and water—remained, each for three days, at the end

bodies and so lost their purity. Or else, the union was brought about by God and by powers lower than God (dæmons, δημιουργοί). To the latter is due our earthly part. God breathed on the formation, and the 'earthly Reason' became 'intelligent' 'spiritual' soul (ψυχη νοερά). Our earthly part alone is the seat of sin.[1]

This leads us to the great question of Original Sin. Here the views of Philo are those of the Eastern Rabbis. But both are entirely different from those on which the argument in the Epistle to the Romans turns. It was neither at the feet of Gamaliel, nor yet from Jewish Hellenism, that Saul of Tarsus learned the doctrine of original sin. The statement that as in Adam all spiritually died, so in Messiah all should be made alive,[2] finds absolutely no parallel in Jewish writings.[3] What may be called the starting point of Christian theology, the doctrine of hereditary guilt and sin, through the fall of Adam, and of the consequent entire and helpless corruption of our nature, is entirely unknown to Rabbinical Judaism. The reign of physical death was indeed traced to the sin of our first parents.[4] But the Talmud expressly teaches,[a] that God originally created man with two propensities,[5] one to good and one to evil (Yetser tobh, and Yetser hara[6]). The evil impulse began immediately after birth.[b][7] But it

[a] Ber. 61 a

[b] Sanh. 91 b

of which they respectively developed what is connected with them (Ber. R. 12).

[1] For further notices on the Cosmology and Anthropology of Philo, see Appendix II.: 'Philo and Rabbinic Theology.'

[2] We cannot help quoting the beautiful Haggadic explanation of the name Adam, according to its three letters, A, D, M—as including these three names, Adam, David, Messiah.

[3] Raymundus Martini, in his 'Pugio Fidei' (orig. ed. p. 675; ed. Voisin et Carpzov, pp. 866, 867), quotes from the book Siphré: 'Go and learn the merit of Messiah the King, and the reward of the righteous from the first Adam, on whom was laid only one commandment of a prohibitive character, and he transgressed it. See how many deaths were appointed on him, and on his generations, and on the generations of his generations to the end of all generations. (Wünsche, Leiden d. Mess. p. 65, makes here an unwarrantable addition, in his translation.) But which attribute (measuring?) is the greater—the attribute of goodness or the attribute of punishment (retribution)? He answered, the attribute of goodness is the greater, and the attribute of punishment the less. And Messiah the King, who was chastened and suffered for the transgressors, as it is said, "He was wounded for our

transgressions," and so on—how much more shall He justify (make righteous—by His merit) all generations; and this is what is meant when it is written, "And Jehovah made to meet upon Him the sin of us all."' We have rendered this passage as literally as possible, but we are bound to add that it is not found in any now existing copy of Siphré.

[4] Death is not considered an absolute evil. In short, all the various consequences which Rabbinical writings ascribe to the sin of Adam may be designated either as physical, or, if mental, as amounting only to detriment, loss, or imperfectness. These results had been partially counteracted by Abraham, and would be fully removed by the Messiah. Neither Enoch nor Elijah had sinned, and accordingly they did not die. Comp. generally, Hamburger, Geist d. Agada, pp. 81–84, and in regard to death as connected with Adam, p. 85.

[5] These are also hypostatised as Angels. Comp. Levy, Chald. Wörterb. p. 342 a; Neuhebr. Wörterb. p. 259, a, b.

[6] Or with 'two reins,' the one, advising to good, being at his right, the other, counselling evil, at his left, according to Eccles. x. 2 (Ber. 61 a, towards the end of the page).

[7] In a sense its existence was necessary for the continuance of this world.

was within the power of man to vanquish sin, and to attain perfect righteousness; in fact, this stage had actually been attained.[1]

Similarly, Philo regarded the soul of the child as 'naked' (Adam and Eve), a sort of *tabula rasa*, as wax which God would fain form and mould. But this state ceased when 'affection' presented itself to reason, and thus sensuous lust arose, which was the spring of all sin. The grand task, then, was to get rid of the sensuous, and to rise to the spiritual. In this, the ethical part of his system, Philo was most under the influence of Stoic philosophy. We might almost say, it is no longer the Hebrew who Hellenises, but the Hellene who Hebraises. And yet it is here also that the most ingenious and wide-reaching allegorisms of Scripture are introduced. It is scarcely possible to convey an idea of how brilliant this method becomes in the hands of Philo, how universal its application, or how captivating it must have proved. Philo describes man's state as, first one of sensuousness, but also of unrest, misery and unsatisfied longing. If persisted in, it would end in complete spiritual insensibility.[2] But from this state the soul must pass to one of devotion to reason.[3] This change might be accomplished in one of three ways: first, by study —of which physical was the lowest; next, that which embraced the ordinary circle of knowledge; and lastly, the highest, that of Divine philosophy. The second method was *Askesis*: discipline, or practice, when the soul turned from the lower to the higher. But the best of all was the third way: the free unfolding of that spiritual life which cometh neither from study nor discipline, but from a natural good disposition. And in that state the soul had true rest[4] and joy.[5]

Here we must for the present pause.[6] Brief as this sketch of Hellenism has been, it must have brought the question vividly before the mind, whether and how far certain parts of the New Testament, especially the fourth Gospel,[7] are connected with the direction of

The conflict between these two impulses constituted the moral life of man.

[1] The solitary exception here is 4 Esdras, where the Christian doctrine of original sin is most strongly expressed, being evidently derived from New Testament teaching. Comp. especially 4 Esdras (our Apocryphal 2 Esdras) vii. 46–53, and other passages. Wherein the hope of safety lay, appears in ch. ix.

[2] Symbolised by Lot's wife.

[3] Symbolised by *Ebher*, Hebrew.

[4] The Sabbath, Jerusalem.

[5] For further details on these points see Appendix II.: 'Philo and Rabbinic Theology.'

[6] The views of Philo on the Messiah will be presented in another connection.

[7] This is not the place to enter on the question of the composition, date, and authorship of the four Gospels. But as regards the point on which negative criticism has of late spoken strongest—and on which, indeed (as Weiss rightly remarks) the very existence of 'the Tübingen School' depends—that of the Johannine authorship of the fourth Gospel, I would refer to *Weiss*, Leben Jesu (1882: vol. i. pp. 84–139), and to *Dr. Salmon's* Introd. to the New Test. pp. 266–365.

thought described in the preceding pages. Without yielding to that school of critics, whose perverse ingenuity discerns everywhere a sinister motive or tendency in the Evangelic writers,[1] it is evident that each of them had a special object in view in constructing his narrative of the One Life; and primarily addressed himself to a special audience. If, without entering into elaborate discussion, we might, according to St. Luke i. 2, regard the narrative of St. Mark as the grand representative of that authentic 'narration' ($\delta\iota\acute{\eta}\gamma\eta\sigma\iota\varsigma$), though not by Apostles,[2] which was in circulation, and the Gospel by St. Matthew as representing the 'tradition' handed down (the $\pi\alpha\rho\acute{\alpha}\delta\sigma\sigma\iota\varsigma$), by the Apostolic eye-witnesses and ministers of the Word,[3] we should reach the following results. Our oldest Gospel-narrative is that by St. Mark, which, addressing itself to no class in particular, sketches in rapid outlines the picture of Jesus as the Messiah, alike for all men. Next in order of time comes our present Gospel by St. Matthew. It goes a step further back than that by St. Mark, and gives not only the genealogy, but the history of the miraculous birth of Jesus. Even if we had not the *consensus* of tradition, every one must feel that this Gospel is Hebrew in its cast, in its citations from the Old Testament, and in its whole bearing. Taking its key-note from the Book of Daniel, that grand Messianic text-book of Eastern Judaism at the time, and as re-echoed in the Book of Enoch—which expresses the popular apprehension of Daniel's Messianic idea—it presents the Messiah chiefly as ' the Son of Man,' ' the Son of David,' ' the Son of God.' We have here the fulfilment of Old Testament law and prophecy; the realisation of Old Testament life, faith, and hope. Third in point of time is the Gospel by St. Luke, which, passing back another step, gives us not only the history of the birth of Jesus, but also that of John, 'the preparer of the way.' It is Pauline, and addresses itself, or rather, we should say, presents the Person of the Messiah, it may be ' to the Jew first,' but certainly ' also to the Greek.' The term which St. Luke, alone of all Gospel writers,[4] applies to

---

[1] No one not acquainted with this literature can imagine the character of the arguments sometimes used by a certain class of critics. To say that they proceed on the most forced perversion of the natural and obvious meaning of passages, is but little. But one cannot restrain moral indignation on finding that to Evangelists and Apostles is imputed, on such grounds, not only systematic falsehood, but falsehood with the most sinister motives.

[2] I do not, of course, mean that the narration of St. Mark was not itself derived chiefly from Apostolic preaching, especially that of St. Peter. In general, the question of the authorship and source of the various Gospels must be reserved for separate treatment in another place.

[3] Comp. *Mangold's* ed. of *Bleek*, Einl. in d. N.T. (3te Aufl. 1875), p. 346.

[4] With the sole exception of St. Matt. xii. 18, where the expression is a quotation from the LXX. of Is. xlii. 1.

Jesus, is that of the παῖς or 'servant' of God, in the sense in which
Isaiah has spoken of the Messiah as the 'Ebhed Jehovah,' 'servant of
the Lord.' St. Luke's is, so to speak, the Isaiah-Gospel, presenting
the Christ in His bearing on the history of God's Kingdom and of the
world—as God's Elect Servant in Whom He delighted. In the Old
Testament, to adopt a beautiful figure,[1] the idea of the Servant of the
Lord is set before us like a pyramid: at its base it is all Israel, at its
central section Israel after the Spirit (the circumcised in heart), represented by David, the man after God's own heart; while at its apex
it is the 'Elect' Servant, the Messiah.[2] And these three ideas, with
their sequences, are presented in the third Gospel as centring in Jesus
the Messiah. By the side of this pyramid is the other: the Son of
Man, the Son of David, the Son of God. The Servant of the Lord of
Isaiah and of Luke is the Enlightener, the Consoler, the victorious
Deliverer; the Messiah or Anointed: the Prophet, the Priest, the
King.

Yet another tendency—shall we say, want?—remained, so to
speak, unmet and unsatisfied. That large world of latest and most
promising Jewish thought, whose task it seemed to bridge over the
chasm between heathenism and Judaism—the Western Jewish world,
must have the Christ presented to them. For in every direction is
He the Christ. And not only they, but that larger Greek world, so
far as Jewish Hellenism could bring it to the threshold of the Church.
This Hellenistic and Hellenic world now stood in waiting to enter it,
though as it were by its northern porch, and to be baptized at its
font. All this must have forced itself on the mind of St. John, re-
siding in the midst of them at Ephesus, even as St. Paul's Epistles
contain almost as many allusions to Hellenism as to Rabbinism.[3]
And so the fourth Gospel became, not the supplement, but the com-

---

[1] First expressed by *Delitzsch* (Bibl.
Comm. ii. d. Proph. Jes. p. 414), and then
adopted by *Oehler* (Theol. d. A. Test.
vol. ii. pp. 270–272).
[2] The two fundamental principles in
the history of the Kingdom of God are
selection and *development*. It is surely
remarkable, not strange, that these are
also the two fundamental truths in the
history of that other Kingdom of God,
Nature, if modern science has read them
correctly. These two *substantives* would
mark the *facts* as ascertained; the *adjectives*, which are added to them by a
certain class of students, mark only their
inferences from these facts. These facts
may be true, even if as yet incomplete,
although the inferences may be false.
Theology should not here rashly interfere. But whatever the ultimate result,
these two are certainly the fundamental
facts in the history of the Kingdom of
God, and, marking them as such, the
devout philosopher may rest contented.
[3] The Gnostics, to whom, in the opinion
of many, so frequent references are made
in the writings of St. John and St. Paul,
were only an offspring (rather, as the
Germans would term it, an *Abart*) of
Alexandrianism on the one hand, and
on the other of Eastern notions, which
are so largely embodied in the later
Kabbalah.

plement, of the other three.[1] There is no other Gospel more Palestinian than this in its modes of expression, allusions, and references.
Yet we must all feel how thoroughly Hellenistic it also is in its cast,[2]
in what it reports and what it omits—in short, in its whole aim;
how adapted to Hellenist wants its presentation of deep central
truths; how suitably, in the report of His Discourses—even so far
as their form is concerned—the promise was here fulfilled, of bringing
all things to remembrance whatsoever He had said.[a] It is the true
Light which shineth, of which the full meridian-blaze lies on the
Hellenist and Hellenic world. There is Alexandrian form of thought,
not only in the whole conception, but in the Logos,[3] and in His
presentation as the Light, the Life, the Wellspring of the world.[4]
But these forms are filled in the fourth Gospel with quite other substance. God is not afar off, uncognisable by man, without properties,
without name. He is the Father. Instead of a nebulous reflection
of the Deity we have the Person of the Logos; not a Logos with
the two potencies of goodness and power, but full of grace and
truth. The Gospel of St. John also begins with a 'Bereshith'—but
it is the theological, not the cosmic Bereshith, when the Logos was
with God and was God. Matter is not pre-existent; far less is it
evil. St. John strikes the pen through Alexandrianism when he lays
it down as the fundamental fact of New Testament history that 'the

---

[1] A complement, not a supplement, as
many critics put it (*Ewald, Weizsäcker,*
and even *Hengstenberg*)—least of all a
rectification (*Godet,* Evang. Joh. p. 633).

[2] *Keim* (Leben Jesu von Nazara, i. *a*,
pp. 112–114) fully recognises this; but I
entirely differ from the conclusions of
his analytical comparison of Philo with
the fourth Gospel.

[3] The student who has carefully considered the views expressed by Philo
about the Logos, and analysed, as in
the Appendix, the passages in the Targumim in which the word *Memra* occurs, cannot fail to perceive the immense difference in the presentation of
the Logos by St. John. Yet M. *Renan,*
in an article in the 'Contemporary Review' for September 1877, with utter
disregard of the historical evidence on
the question, maintains not only the
identity of these three sets of ideas, but
actually grounds on it his argument
against the authenticity of the fourth
Gospel. Considering the importance of
the subject, it is not easy to speak with
moderation of assertions so bold based
on statements so entirely inaccurate.

[4] Dr. *Bucher,* whose book, Des Apostels Johannes Lehre vom Logos, deserves
careful perusal, tries to trace the reason
of these peculiarities as indicated in the
Prologue of the fourth Gospel. Bucher
differentiates at great length between the
Logos of Philo and of the fourth Gospel.
He sums up his views by stating that in
the Prologue of St. John the Logos is
presented as the fulness of Divine Light
and Life. This is, so to speak, the theme,
while the Gospel history is intended to
present the Logos as the *giver* of this
Divine Light and Life. While the other
Evangelists ascend from the manifestation to the idea of the Son of God, St.
John descends from the idea of the Logos,
as expressed in the Prologue, to its concrete realisation in His history. The
latest tractate (at the present writing,
1882) on the Gospel of St. John, by Dr.
Müller, Die Johann. Frage, gives a
good summary of the argument on both
sides, and deserves the careful attention
of students of the question.

Logos was made flesh,' just as St. Paul does when he proclaims the great mystery of 'God manifest in the flesh.' Best of all, it is not by a long course of study, nor by wearing discipline, least of all by an inborn good disposition, that the soul attains the new life, but by a birth from above, by the Holy Ghost, and by simple faith which is brought within reach of the fallen and the lost.[1]

Philo had no successor. In him Hellenism had completed its cycle. Its message and its mission were ended. Henceforth it needed, like Apollos, its great representative in the Christian Church, two things: the baptism of John to the knowledge of sin and need, and to have the way of God more perfectly expounded.[a] On the other hand, Eastern Judaism had entered with Hillel on a new stage. This direction led farther and farther away from that which the New Testament had taken in following up and unfolding the spiritual elements of the Old. That development was incapable of transformation or renovation. It must go on to its final completion—and be either true, or else be swept away and destroyed.

---

[1] I cannot agree with *Weiss* (u. s., p. 122) that the great object of the fourth Gospel was to oppose the rising Gnostic movement. This may have been present to the Apostle's mind, as evidenced in his Epistle, but the object in view could not have been mainly, nor even primarily, negative and controversial.

CHAPTER V.

ALEXANDRIA AND ROME—THE JEWISH COMMUNITIES IN THE CAPITALS OF WESTERN CIVILISATION.

BOOK
I

WE have spoken of Alexandria as the capital of the Jewish world in the West. Antioch was, indeed, nearer to Palestine, and its Jewish population—including the floating part of it—as numerous as that of Alexandria. But the wealth, the thought, and the influence of Western Judaism centred in the modern capital of the land of the Pharaohs. In those days Greece was the land of the past, to which the student might resort as the home of beauty and of art, the time-hallowed temple of thought and of poetry. But it was also the land of desolateness and of ruins, where fields of corn waved over the remains of classic antiquity. The ancient Greeks had in great measure sunk to a nation of traders, in keen competition with the Jews. Indeed, Roman sway had levelled the ancient world, and buried its national characteristics. It was otherwise in the far East; it was otherwise also in Egypt. Egypt was not a land to be largely inhabited, or to be 'civilised' in the then sense of the term: soil, climate, history, nature forbade it. Still, as now, and even more than now, was it the dream-land of untold attractions to the traveller. The ancient, mysterious Nile still rolled its healing waters out into the blue sea, where (so it was supposed) they changed its taste within a radius farther than the eye could reach. To be gently borne in bark or ship on its waters, to watch the strange vegetation and fauna of its banks; to gaze beyond, where they merged into the trackless desert; to wander under the shade of its gigantic monuments, or within the wierd avenues of its colossal temples, to see the scroll of mysterious hieroglyphics; to note the sameness of manner and of people as of old, and to watch the unique rites of its ancient religion —this was indeed to be again in the old far-away world, and that amidst a dreaminess bewitching the senses, and a gorgeousness dazzling the imagination.[1]

---

[1] What charm Egypt had for the Romans may be gathered from so many of their mosaics and frescoes. Comp. *Friedländer*, u. s. vol. ii. pp. 134–136.

We are still far out at sea, making for the port of Alexandria— the only safe shelter all along the coast of Asia and Africa. Quite thirty miles out the silver sheen of the lighthouse on the island of Pharos[1]—connected by a mole with Alexandria—is burning like a star on the edge of the horizon. Now we catch sight of the palm-groves of Pharos; presently the anchor rattles and grates on the sand, and we are ashore. What a crowd of vessels of all sizes, shapes, and nationalities; what a multitude of busy people; what a very Babel of languages; what a commingling of old and new world civilisation; and what a variety of wares piled up, loading or unloading!

Alexandria itself was not an old Egyptian, but a comparatively modern, city; in Egypt and yet not of Egypt. Everything was in character—the city, its inhabitants, public life, art, literature, study, amusements, the very aspect of the place. Nothing original anywhere, but combination of all that had been in the ancient world, or that was at the time—most fitting place therefore to be the capital of Jewish Hellenism.

As its name indicates, the city was founded by Alexander the Great. It was built in the form of an open fan, or rather, of the outspread cloak of a Macedonian horseman. Altogether, it measured (16,360 paces) 3,160 paces more than Rome; but its houses were neither so crowded nor so many-storied. It had been a large city when Rome was still inconsiderable, and to the last held the second place in the Empire. One of the five quarters into which the city was divided, and which were named according to the first letters of the alphabet, was wholly covered by the royal palaces, with their gardens, and similar buildings, including the royal mausoleum, where the body of Alexander the Great, preserved in honey, was kept in a glass coffin. But these, and its three miles of colonnades along the principal highway, were only some of the magnificent architectural adornments of a city full of palaces. The population amounted, probably, to nearly a million, drawn from the East and West by trade, the attractions of wealth, the facilities for study, or the amusements of a singularly frivolous city. A strange mixture of elements among the people, combining the quickness and versatility of the Greek with the gravity, the conservatism, the dream-grandeur, and the luxury of the Eastern.

Three worlds met in Alexandria: Europe, Asia, and Africa; and

[1] This immense lighthouse was square up to the middle, then covered by an octagon, the top being round. The last recorded repairs to this magnificent structure of blocks of marble were made in the year 1303 of our era.

brought to it, or fetched from it, their treasures.   Above all, it was a commercial city, furnished with an excellent harbour—or rather with five harbours.   A special fleet carried, as tribute, from Alexandria to Italy, two-tenths of the corn produce of Egypt, which sufficed to feed the capital for four months of the year.   A magnificent fleet it was, from the light quick sailer to those immense corn-ships which hoisted a special flag, and whose early arrival was awaited at Puteoli[1] with more eagerness than that of any modern ocean-steamer.[2]   The commerce of India was in the hands of the Alexandrian shippers.[3]   Since the days of the Ptolemies the Indian trade alone had increased sixfold.[4]   Nor was the native industry inconsiderable.   Linen goods, to suit the tastes or costumes of all countries; woolen stuffs of every hue, some curiously wrought with figures, and even scenes; glass of every shade and in every shape; paper from the thinnest sheet to the coarsest packing paper; essences, perfumeries—such were the native products.   However idly or luxuriously inclined, still every one seemed busy, in a city where (as the Emperor Hadrian expressed it) 'money was the people's god;' and every one seemed well-to-do in his own way, from the waif in the streets, who with little trouble to himself could pick up sufficient to go to the restaurant and enjoy a comfortable dinner of fresh or smoked fish with garlic, and his pudding, washed down with the favourite Egyptian barley beer, up to the millionaire banker, who owned a palace in the city and a villa by the canal that connected Alexandria with Canobus.   What a jostling crowd of all nations in the streets, in the market (where, according to the joke of a contemporary, anything might be got except snow), or by the harbours; what cool shades, delicious retreats, vast halls, magnificent libraries, where the savants of Alexandria assembled and taught every conceivable branch of learning, and its far-famed physicians prescribed

[1] The average passage from Alexandria to Puteoli was twelve days, the ships touching at Malta and in Sicily.   It was in such a ship, the 'Castor and Pollux,' carrying wheat, that St. Paul sailed from Malta to Puteoli, where it would be among the first arrivals of the season.

[2] They bore, painted on the two sides of the prow, the emblems of the gods to whom they were dedicated, and were navigated by Egyptian pilots, the most renowned in the world.   One of these vessels is described as 180 by .45 feet, and of about 1,575 tons, and is computed to have returned to its owner nearly 3,000l. annually.   (Comp. *Friedländer*, u. s. vol. ii. p. 131, &c.)   And yet these

were small ships compared with those built for the conveyance of marble blocks and columns, and especially of obelisks.   One of these is said to have carried, besides an obelisk, 1,200 passengers, a freight of paper, nitre, pepper, linen, and a large cargo of wheat.

[3] The journey took about three months, either up the Nile, thence by caravan, and again by sea; or else perhaps by the Ptolemy Canal and the Red Sea.

[4] It included gold-dust, ivory, and mother-of-pearl from the interior of Africa, spices from Arabia, pearls from the Gulf of Persia, precious stones and byssus from India, and silk from China.

for the poor consumptive patients sent thither from all parts of
Italy! What bustle and noise among that ever excitable, chatty, con-
ceited, vain, pleasure-loving multitude, whose highest enjoyment was
the theatre and singers; what scenes on that long canal to Canobus,
lined with luxurious inns, where barks full of pleasure-seekers revelled
in the cool shade of the banks, or sped to Canobus, that scene of all
dissipation and luxury, proverbial even in those days! And yet, close
by, on the shores of Lake Mareotis, as if in grim contrast, were the
chosen retreats of that sternly ascetic Jewish party, the Therapeutæ,[a]
whose views and practices in so many points were kindred to those
of the Essenes in Palestine!

This sketch of Alexandria will help us to understand the surroundings of the large mass of Jews settled in the Egyptian capital.
Altogether more than an eighth of the population of the country
(one million in 7,800,000) was Jewish. Whether or not a Jewish
colony had gone into Egypt at the time of Nebuchadnezzar, or even
earlier, the great mass of its residents had been attracted by Alexander
the Great,[b] who had granted the Jews equally exceptional privileges
with the Macedonians. The later troubles of Palestine under the
Syrian kings greatly swelled their number, the more so that the
Ptolemies, with one exception, favoured them. Originally a special
quarter had been assigned to the Jews in the city—the ' Delta' by the
eastern harbour and the Canobus canal—probably alike to keep the
community separate, and from its convenience for commercial purposes.
The privileges which the Ptolemies had accorded to the Jews were
confirmed, and even enlarged, by Julius Cæsar. The export trade in
grain was now in their hands, and the harbour and river police committed to their charge. Two quarters in the city are named as specially Jewish—not, however, in the sense of their being confined to
them. Their Synagogues, surrounded by shady trees, stood in all
parts of the city. But the chief glory of the Jewish community in
Egypt, of which even the Palestinians boasted, was the great central
Synagogue, built in the shape of a basilica, with double colonnade,
and so large that it needed a signal for those most distant to know
the proper moment for the responses. The different trade guilds sat
there together, so that a stranger would at once know where to find
Jewish employers or fellow-workmen.[c] In the choir of this Jewish
cathedral stood seventy chairs of state, encrusted with precious stones,
for the seventy elders who constituted the eldership of Alexandria, on
the model of the great Sanhedrin in Jerusalem.

It is a strange, almost inexplicable fact, that the Egyptian Jews

CHAP.
V

[a] On the ex-
istence of
the Thera-
peutes
comp. Art.
Philo in
Smith &
Wace's
Dict. of
Chr. Biogr.
vol. iv.

[b] *Mommsen*
(Röm.
Gesch. v. p.
489)
ascribes
this rather
to Ptolemy
I.

[c] Sukk. 51 b

BOOK
I

had actually built a schismatic Temple. During the terrible Syrian persecutions in Palestine Onias, the son of the murdered High-Priest Onias III., had sought safety in Egypt. Ptolemy Philometor not only received him kindly, but gave a disused heathen temple in the town of Leontopolis for a Jewish sanctuary. Here a new Aaronic priesthood ministered, their support being derived from the revenues of the district around. The new Temple, however, resembled not that of Jerusalem either in outward appearance nor in all its internal fittings.[1] At first the Egyptian Jews were very proud of their new sanctuary, and professed to see in it the fulfilment of the prediction,[a] that five cities in the land of Egypt should speak the language of Canaan, of which one was to be called Ir-ha-Heres, which the LXX. (in their original form, or by some later emendation) altered into 'the city of righteousness.' This temple continued from about 160 B.C. to shortly after the destruction of Jerusalem. It could scarcely be called a rival to that on Mount Moriah, since the Egyptian Jews also owned that of Jerusalem as their central sanctuary, to which they made pilgrimages and brought their contributions,[b] while the priests at Leontopolis, before marrying, always consulted the official archives in Jerusalem to ascertain the purity of descent of their intended wives.[c] The Palestinians designated it contemptuously as 'the house of Chonyi' (Onias), and declared the priesthood of Leontopolis incapable of serving in Jerusalem, although on a par with those who were disqualified only by some bodily defect. Offerings brought in Leontopolis were considered null, unless in the case of vows to which the name of this Temple had been expressly attached.[d] This qualified condemnation seems, however, strangely mild, except on the supposition that the statements we have quoted only date from a time when both Temples had long passed away.

Nor were such feelings unreasonable. The Egyptian Jews had spread on all sides—southward to Abyssinia and Ethiopia, and westward to, and beyond, the province of Cyrene. In the city of that name they formed one of the four classes into which its inhabitants were divided.[e] A Jewish inscription at Berenice, apparently dating from the year 13 B.C., shows that the Cyrenian Jews formed a distinct community under nine 'rulers' of their own, who no doubt attended to the communal affairs—not always an easy matter, since the Cyrenian Jews were noted, if not for turbulence, yet for strong anti-

[a] Is. xix. 18

[b] Philo, ii. 646, ed. Mangey
[c] Jos. Ag. Ap. i. 7

[d] Men. xiii. 10, and the Gemara, 109 a and b

[e] Strabo in Jos. Ant. xiv. 7, 2

---

[1] Instead of the seven-branched golden candlestick there was a golden lamp, suspended from a chain of the same metal.

Roman feeling, which more than once was cruelly quenched in blood.[1] Other inscriptions prove,[2] that in other places of their dispersion also the Jews had their own *Archontes* or 'rulers,' while the special direction of public worship was always entrusted to the *Archisynagogos*, or 'chief ruler of the Synagogue,' both titles occurring side by side.[3] It is, to say the least, very doubtful, whether the High-Priest at Leontopolis was ever regarded as, in any real sense, the head of the Jewish community in Egypt.[4] In Alexandria, the Jews were under the rule of a Jewish *Ethnarch*,[5] whose authority was similar to that of 'the *Archon*' of independent cities.[a] But his authority[6] was transferred, by Augustus, to the whole 'eldership.'[b] Another, probably Roman, office, though for obvious reasons often filled by Jews, was that of the *Alabarch*, or rather *Arabarch*, who was set over the Arab population.[7] Among others, Alexander, the brother of Philo, held this post. If we may judge of the position of the wealthy Jewish families in Alexandria by that of this Alabarch, their influence must have been very great. The firm of Alexander was probably as rich as the great Jewish banking and shipping house of Saramalla in Antioch.[c] Its chief was entrusted with the management of the affairs of Antonia, the much respected sister-in-law of the Emperor Tiberius.[d] It was a small thing for such a man to lend King Agrippa, when his fortunes were very low, a sum of about 7,000*l.* with which to resort to Italy,[e] since he advanced it on the guarantee of Agrippa's wife, whom he highly esteemed, and at the same time made provision that the money should not be all spent before the Prince met the Emperor. Besides, he had his own plans in the matter. Two of his sons married daughters of King Agrippa; while a third, at the price of apostasy, rose successively to the posts of Procurator of Palestine, and finally of Governor of Egypt.[f] The Temple at Jerusalem bore evidence of the wealth and munificence of this Jewish millionaire. The gold and silver with which the nine massive gates

Marginal notes:

[a] *Strabo* in *Jos. Ant.* xiv. 7. 2

[b] *Philo*, in Flacc. ed. Mangey, ii. 527

[c] *Jos. Ant.* xiv. 13. 5; War. i. 13, 5

[d] Ant. xix 5. 1

[e] Ant. xviii. 6. 3

[f] Ant. xix. 5. 1; xx. 5. 3

---

[1] Could there have been any such meaning in laying the Roman cross which Jesus had to bear upon a Cyrenian (St. Luke xxiii. 26)? A symbolical meaning it certainly has, as we remember that the last Jewish rebellion (132–135 A.D.), which had Bar Cochba for its Messiah, first broke out in Cyrene. What terrible vengeance was taken on those who followed the false Christ, cannot here be told.

[2] Jewish inscriptions have also been found in Mauritania and Algiers.

[3] On a tombstone at Capua (*Mommsen,* Inscr. R. Neap. 3,657, apud *Schürer,* p.

629). The subject is of great importance as illustrating the rule of the Synagogue in the days of Christ. Another designation on the gravestones πατήρ συναγωγῆς seems to refer solely to age—one being described as 110 years old.

[4] *Jost,* Gesch. d. Judenth. i. p. 345.

[5] *Marquardt* (Röm. Staatsverwalt. vol. i. p. 297). Note 5 suggests that ἔθνος may here mean *classes, ordo.*

[6] The office itself would seem to have been continued. (*Jos.* Ant. xix. 5. 2.)

[7] Comp. *Wesseling,* de Jud. Archont. pp. 63, &c., apud *Schürer,* pp. 627, 628.

BOOK
I

were covered, which led into the Temple, were the gift of the great Alexandrian banker.

The possession of such wealth, coupled no doubt with pride and self-assertion, and openly spoken contempt of the superstitions around,[1] would naturally excite the hatred of the Alexandrian populace against the Jews. The greater number of those silly stories about the origin, early history, and religion of the Jews, which even the philosophers and historians of Rome record as genuine, originated in Egypt. A whole series of writers, beginning with Manetho,[a] made it their business to give a kind of historical travesty of the events recorded in the books of Moses. The boldest of these scribblers was Apion, to whom Josephus replied—a world-famed charlatan and liar, who wrote or lectured, with equal presumption and falseness, on every conceivable object. He was just the man to suit the Alexandrians, on whom his unblushing assurance imposed. In Rome he soon found his level, and the Emperor Tiberius well characterised the irrepressible boastful talker as the ' tinkling cymbal of the world.' He had studied, seen, and heard everything—even, on three occasions, the mysterious sound on the Colossus of Memnon, as the sun rose upon it! At least, so he graved upon the Colossus itself, for the information of all generations.[2] Such was the man on whom the Alexandrians conferred the freedom of their city, to whom they entrusted their most important affairs, and whom they extolled as the victorious, the laborious, the new Homer.[3] There can be little doubt, that the popular favour was partly due to Apion's virulent attacks upon the Jews. His grotesque accounts of their history and religion held them up to contempt. But his real object was to rouse the fanaticism of the populace against the Jews. Every year, so he told them, it was the practice of the Jews to get hold of some unfortunate Hellene, whom ill-chance might bring into their hands, to fatten him for the year, and then to sacrifice him, partaking of his entrails, and burying the body, while during these horrible rites they took a fearful oath of perpetual enmity to the Greeks. These were the people who battened on the wealth of Alexandria, who had usurped quarters of the city to which they had no right, and claimed exceptional privileges; a people who had proved traitors to, and the ruin of every one who had trusted them. ' If the Jews,' he exclaimed, ' are citizens of Alexandria, why do they not worship the same gods as the Alexandrians ? ' And, if they wished

[a] Probably about 200 B.C.

---

[1] Comp., for example, such a trenchant chapter as Baruch vi., or the 2nd Fragm. of the Erythr. Sibyl, vv. 21–33.

[2] Comp. *Friedländer*, u. s. ii. p. 155.

[3] A very good sketch of Apion is given by *Hausrath*, Neutest. Zeitg. vol. ii. pp. 187–195.

to enjoy the protection of the Cæsars, why did they not erect statues, and pay Divine honor to them?[1] There is nothing strange in these appeals to the fanaticism of mankind. In one form or another, they have only too often been repeated in all lands and ages, and, alas! by the representatives of all creeds. Well might the Jews, as Philo mourns,[a] wish no better for themselves than to be treated like other men!

We have already seen, that the ideas entertained in Rome about the Jews were chiefly derived from Alexandrian sources. But it is not easy to understand, how a Tacitus, Cicero, or Pliny could have credited such absurdities as that the Jews had come from Crete (Mount Ida—Idæi=Judæi), been expelled on account of leprosy from Egypt, and emigrated under an apostate priest, Moses; or that the Sabbath-rest originated in sores, which had obliged the wanderers to stop short on the seventh day; or that the Jews worshipped the head of an ass, or else Bacchus; that their abstinence from swine's flesh was due to remembrance and fear of leprosy, or else to the worship of that animal—and other puerilities of the like kind.[b] The educated Roman regarded the Jew with a mixture of contempt and anger, all the more keen that, according to his notions, the Jew had, since his subjection to Rome, no longer a right to his religion; and all the more bitter that, do what he might, that despised race confronted him everywhere, with a religion so uncompromising as to form a wall of separation, and with rites so exclusive as to make them not only strangers, but enemies. Such a phenomenon was nowhere else to be encountered. The Romans were intensely practical. In their view, political life and religion were not only intertwined, but the one formed part of the other. A religion apart from a political organisation, or which offered not, as a *quid pro quo*, some direct return from the Deity to his votaries, seemed utterly inconceivable. Every country has its own religion, argued Cicero, in his appeal for Flaccus. So long as Jerusalem was unvanquished, Judaism might claim toleration; but had not the immortal gods shown what they thought of it, when the Jewish race was conquered? This was a kind of logic that appealed to the humblest in the crowd, which thronged to hear the great orator defending his client, among others, against the charge of preventing the transport from Asia to Jerusalem of the annual Temple-tribute. This was not a popular accusation to bring against a man in such an assembly. And as the Jews—who, to create a disturbance, had (we are told) distributed themselves among the audience in such numbers,

CHAP.
V

[a] Leg. ad Caj. ed. Fref.

[b] Comp. Tacitus, Hist. v. 2-4; Plut. Sympos. iv. 5

[1] *Jos.* Ag. Ap. ii. 4, 5, 6.

that Cicero somewhat rhetorically declared, he would fain have spoken with bated breath, so as to be only audible to the judges—listened to the great orator, they must have felt a keen pang shoot to their hearts while he held them up to the scorn of the heathen, and touched, with rough finger, their open sore, as he urged the ruin of their nation as the one unanswerable argument, which Materialism could bring against the religion of the Unseen.

And that religion—was it not, in the words of Cicero, a ' barbarous superstition,' and were not its adherents, as Pliny had it,[a] ' a race distinguished for its contempt of the gods ' ?　To begin with their theology.　The Roman philosopher would sympathise with disbelief of all spiritual realities, as, on the other hand, he could understand the popular modes of worship and superstition.　But what was to be said for a worship of something quite unseen, an adoration, as it seemed to him, of the clouds and of the sky, without any visible symbol, conjoined with an utter rejection of every other form of religion—Asiatic, Egyptian, Greek, Roman—and the refusal even to pay the customary Divine honor to the Cæsars, as the incarnation of Roman power? Next, as to their rites.　Foremost among them was the initiatory rite of circumcision, a constant subject for coarse jests.　What could be the meaning of it; or of what seemed like some ancestral veneration for the pig, or dread of it, since they made it a religious duty not to partake of its flesh?　Their Sabbath-observance, however it had originated, was merely an indulgence in idleness.　The fast young Roman *literati* would find their amusement in wandering on the Sabbath-eve through the tangled, narrow streets of the Ghetto, watching how the dim lamp within shed its unsavory light, while the inmates mumbled prayers ' with blanched lips;'[b] or they would, like Ovid, seek in the Synagogue occasion for their dissolute amusements. The Thursday fast was another target for their wit.　In short, at the best, the Jew was a constant theme of popular merriment, and the theatre would resound with laughter as his religion was lampooned, no matter how absurd the stories, or how poor the punning.[1]

And then, as the proud Roman passed on the Sabbath through the streets, Judaism would obtrude itself upon his notice, by the shops that were shut, and by the strange figures that idly moved about in holiday attire.　They were strangers in a strange land, not only without sympathy with what passed around, but with marked contempt and abhorrence of it, while there was that about their whole bearing, which expressed the unspoken feeling, that the time

[1] Comp. the quotation of such scenes in the Introd. to the Midrash on Lamentations.

of Rome's fall, and of their own supremacy, was at hand. To put
the general feeling in the words of Tacitus, the Jews kept close together, and were ever most liberal to one another ; but they were filled
with bitter hatred of all others. They would neither eat nor sleep
with strangers ; and the first thing which they taught their proselytes
was to despise the gods, to renounce their own country, and to rend
the bonds which had bound them to parents, children or kindred.
To be sure, there was some ground of distorted truth in these charges.
For, the Jew, as such, was only intended for Palestine. By a necessity, not of his own making, he was now, so to speak, the negative
element in the heathen world; yet one which, do what he might,
would always obtrude itself upon public notice. But the Roman
satirists went further. They accused the Jews of such hatred of all
other religionists, that they would not even show the way to any who
worshipped otherwise, nor point out the cooling spring to the thirsty.[a]   [a] *Juv.* Sat.
xiv. 103, 104
According to Tacitus, there was a political and religious reason for
this. In order to keep the Jews separate from all other nations,
Moses had given them rites, contrary to those of any other race, that
they might regard as unholy what was sacred to others, and as lawful
what they held in abomination.[b]   Such a people deserved neither   [b] Hist. v. 13
consideration nor pity ; and when the historian tells how thousands
of their number had been banished by Tiberius to Sardinia, he
dismisses the probability of their perishing in that severe climate
with the cynical remark, that it entailed a 'poor loss'[c] (*vile*   [c] Ann. ii.85,
Comp. *Suet.*
Tib. 36
damnum).

Still, the Jew was there in the midst of them. It is impossible
to fix the date when the first Jewish wanderers found their way to the
capital of the world. We know, that in the wars under Pompey,
Cassius, and Antonius, many were brought captive to Rome, and sold
as slaves. In general, the Republican party was hostile, the Cæsars
were friendly, to the Jews. The Jewish slaves in Rome proved an
unprofitable and troublesome acquisition. They clung so tenaciously
to their ancestral customs, that it was impossible to make them con-
form to the ways of heathen households.[d]   How far they would carry   [d] *Philo,* Leg.
ad Caj. ed.
their passive resistance, appears from a story told by Josephus,[e] about   Frcf. p. 101
[e] Life 3
some Jewish priests of his acquaintance, who, during their captivity
in Rome, refused to eat anything but figs and nuts, so as to avoid the
defilement of Gentile food.[1]   Their Roman masters deemed it prudent

---

[1] *Lutterbeck* (Neutest. Lehrbegr. p.
119), following up the suggestions of
Wieseler (Chron. d. Apost. Zeitalt. pp.
384, 402, etc.), regards these priests as
the accusers of St. Paul, who brought
about his martyrdom.

to give their Jewish slaves their freedom, either at a small ransom, or even without it. These freedmen (*liberti*) formed the nucleus of the Jewish community in Rome, and in great measure determined its social character. Of course they were, as always, industrious, sober, pushing. In course of time many of them acquired wealth. By-and-by Jewish immigrants of greater distinction swelled their number. Still their social position was inferior to that of their co-religionists in other lands. A Jewish population so large as 40,000 in the time of Augustus, and 60,000 in that of Tiberius, would naturally include all ranks—merchants, bankers, *literati*, even actors.[1] In a city which offered such temptations, they would number among them those of every degree of religious profession ; nay, some who would not only imitate the habits of those around, but try to outdo their gross licentiousness.[2] Yet, even so, they would vainly endeavor to efface the hateful mark of being Jews.

Augustus had assigned to the Jews as their special quarter the 'fourteenth region' across the Tiber, which stretched from the slope of the Vatican onwards and across the Tiber-island, where the boats from Ostia were wont to unload. This seems to have been their poor quarter, chiefly inhabited by hawkers, sellers of matches,[a] glass, old clothes and second-hand wares. The Jewish burying-ground in that quarter[3] gives evidence of their condition. The whole appointments and the graves are mean. There is neither marble nor any trace of painting, unless it be a rough representation of the seven-branched candlestick in red coloring. Another Jewish quarter was by the *Porta Capena*, where the Appian Way entered the city. Close by, the ancient sanctuary of Egeria was utilized at the time of Juvenal[4] as a Jewish hawking place. But there must have been richer Jews also in that neighborhood, since the burying-place there discovered has paintings—some even of mythological figures, of which the meaning has not yet been ascertained. A third Jewish burying-ground was near the ancient Christian catacombs.

But indeed, the Jewish residents in Rome must have spread over every quarter of the city—even the best—to judge by the location of their Synagogues. From inscriptions, we have been made acquainted not only with the existence, but with the names, of not fewer than

ᵃMart. i.41;
xii. 57

---

[1] Comp., for example, *Mart.* xi. 94; *Jos.* Life 3.

[2] *Martialis*, u. s. The '*Anchialus*' by whom the poet would have the Jew swear, is a corruption of *Anochi Elohim* ('I am God') in Ex. xx. 2. Comp. *Ewald*,

Gesch. Isr. vol. vii. p. 27.

[3] Described by *Bosio*, but since unknown. Comp. *Friedländer*, u. s. vol. iii. pp. 510, 511.

[4] Sat. iii. 13; vi. 542.

seven of these Synagogues. Three of them respectively bear the
names of Augustus, Agrippa, and Volumnius, either as their patrons,
or because the worshippers were chiefly their attendants and clients;
while two of them derived their names from the *Campus Martius*, and
the quarter *Subura* in which they stood.[1] The *'Synagoge Elaias'*
may have been so called from bearing on its front the device of an
olive-tree, a favourite, and in Rome specially significant, emblem of
Israel, whose fruit, crushed beneath heavy weight, would yield the
precious oil by which the Divine light would shed its brightness
through the night of heathendom.[2] Of course, there must have
been other Synagogues besides those whose names have been discovered.

One other mode of tracking the footsteps of Israel's wanderings
seems strangely significant. It is by tracing their records among the
dead, reading them on broken tombstones, and in ruined monuments.
They are rude, and the inscriptions—most of them in bad Greek, or
still worse Latin, none in Hebrew—are like the stammering of
strangers. Yet what a contrast between the simple faith and earnest
hope which they express, and the grim proclamation of utter disbelief
in any future to the soul, not unmixed with language of coarsest
materialism, on the graves of so many of the polished Romans!
Truly the pen of God in history has, as so often, ratified the sentence
which a nation had pronounced upon itself. That civilisation was
doomed which could inscribe over its dead such words as: 'To eternal
sleep;' 'To perpetual rest;' or more coarsely express it thus, 'I was
not, and I became; I was, and am no more. Thus much is true; who
says other, lies; for I shall not be,' adding, as it were by way of
moral, 'And thou who livest, drink, play, come.' Not so did God
teach His people; and, as we pick our way among these broken
stones, we can understand how a religion, which proclaimed a hope
so different, must have spoken to the hearts of many even at Rome,
and much more, how that blessed assurance of life and immortality,
which Christianity afterwards brought, could win its thousands,
though it were at the cost of poverty, shame, torture, and the
arena.

Wandering from graveyard to graveyard, and deciphering the
records of the dead, we can almost read the history of Israel in the
days of the Cæsars, or when Paul the prisoner set foot on the soil of
Italy. When St. Paul, on the journey of the 'Castor and Pollux,'
touched at Syracuse, he would, during his stay of three days, find

---

[1] Comp. *Friedländer*, u. s. vol. iii. p. 510.   [2] Midr. R. on Ex. 36.

BOOK
I

ᵃ *Jos.* Ant.
xvii. 12. 1;
War ii. 7. 1

ᵇ Acts
xxviii. 17

himself in the midst of a Jewish community, as we learn from an
inscription. When he disembarked at Puteoli, he was in the oldest
Jewish settlement next to that of Rome,ᵃ where the loving hospitality
of Christian Israelites constrained him to tarry over a Sabbath. As
he 'went towards Rome,' and reached Capua, he would meet Jews
there, as we infer from the tombstone of one ' Alfius Juda,' who had
been 'Archon' of the Jews, and 'Archisynagogus' in Capua. As he
neared the city, he found in Anxur (Terracina) a Synagogue.[1] In Rome
itself the Jewish community was organized as in other places.ᵇ It
sounds strange, as after these many centuries we again read the
names of the Archons of their various Synagogues, all Roman, such as
Claudius, Asteris, Julian (who was Archon alike of the Campesian and
the Agrippesian Synagogue priest, the son of Julian the Archisynagogus, or chief of the eldership of the Augustesian Synagogue).
And so in other places. On these tombstones we find names of
Jewish Synagogue-dignitaries, in every centre of population—in
Pompeii, in Venusia, the birthplace of Horace; in Jewish catacombs;
and similarly Jewish inscriptions in Africa, in Asia, in the islands of
the Mediterranean, in Ægina, in Patræ, in Athens. Even where as
yet records of their early settlements have not been discovered, we
still infer their presence, as we remember the almost incredible extent
of Roman commerce, which led to such large settlements in Britain,
or as we discover among the tombstones those of ' Syrian' merchants,
as in Spain (where St. Paul hoped to preach, no doubt, also to his own
countrymen), throughout Gaul, and even in the remotest parts of
Germany.[2] Thus the statements of Josephus and of Philo, as to the
dispersion of Israel throughout all lands of the known world, are
fully borne out.

But the special importance of the Jewish community in Rome lay
in its contiguity to the seat of the government of the world, where
every movement could be watched and influenced, and where it could
lend support to the wants and wishes of that compact body which,
however widely scattered, was one in heart and feeling, in thought
and purpose, in faith and practice, in suffering and in prosperity.[3]
Thus, when upon the death of Herod a deputation from Palestine
appeared in the capital to seek the restoration of their Theocracy

[1] Comp. *Cassel*, in Ersch u. Gruber's
Encyclop. 2d sect. vol. xxvii. p. 147.
[2] Comp. *Friedländer*, u. s. vol. ii.
pp. 17–204 passim.
[3] It was probably this unity of Israelitish interests which *Cicero* had in view
(Pro Flacco, 28) when he took such
credit for his boldness in daring to stand
up against the Jews—unless, indeed, the
orator only meant to make a point in
favour of his client.

under a Roman protectorate,[a] no less than 8,000 of the Roman Jews joined it. And in case of need they could find powerful friends, not only among the Herodian princes, but among court favourites who were Jews, like the actor of whom Josephus speaks;[b] among those who were inclined towards Judaism, like Poppæa, the dissolute wife of Nero, whose coffin as that of a Jewess was laid among the urns of the emperors;[1] or among real proselytes, like those of all ranks who, from superstition or conviction, had identified themselves with the Synagogue.[2]

In truth, there was no law to prevent the spread of Judaism. Excepting the brief period when Tiberius[c] banished the Jews from Rome and sent 4,000 of their number to fight the banditti in Sardinia, the Jews enjoyed not only perfect liberty, but exceptional privileges. In the reign of Cæsar and of Augustus we have quite a series of edicts, which secured the full exercise of their religion and their communal rights.[3] In virtue of these they were not to be disturbed in their religious ceremonies, nor in the observance of their sabbaths and feasts. The annual Temple-tribute was allowed to be transported to Jerusalem, and the alienation of these funds by the civil magistrates treated as sacrilege. As the Jews objected to bear arms, or march, on the Sabbath, they were freed from military service. On similar grounds, they were not obliged to appear in courts of law on their holy days. Augustus even ordered that, when the public distribution of corn or of money among the citizens fell on a Sabbath, the Jews were to receive their share on the following day. In a similar spirit the Roman authorities confirmed a decree by which the founder of Antioch, Seleucus I. (Nicator),[d] had granted the Jews the right of citizenship in all the cities of Asia Minor and Syria which he had built, and the privilege of receiving, instead of the oil that was distributed, which their religion forbade them to use,[e] an equivalent in money.[f] These rights were maintained by Vespasian and Titus even after the last Jewish war, notwithstanding the earnest remonstrances of these cities. No wonder, that at the death of Cæsar[g] the Jews of Rome gathered for many nights, waking strange feelings of awe in the city, as they chanted in mournful melodies their Psalms around the pyre on which the body of their benefactor

CHAP.
V

[a] *Jos.* Ant. xvii. 11. 1; War. ii. 6. 1
[b] Life 3

[c] 19 A.D.

[d] Ob. 280 B.C.

[e] Ab. Sar ii. 6
[f] *Jos.* Ant. xii. 3. 1

[g] 44 B.C.

---

[1] *Schiller* (Gesch. d. Röm. Kaiserreichs, p. 583) denies that Poppæa was a proselyte. It is, indeed, true, as he argues, that the fact of her entombment affords no absolute evidence of this, if taken by itself; but comp. *Jos.* Ant. xx. 8. 11; Life 3.

[2] The question of Jewish proselytes will be treated in another place.

[3] Comp. *Jos.* Ant. xiv. 10, passim, and xvi. 6. These edicts are collated in *Krebs*. Decreta Romanor. pro Jud. facta, with long comments by the author, and by *Levyssohn*.

ᵃ *Suet.* Cæs.
84

had been burnt, and raised their pathetic dirges.ᵃ The measures of Tiberius against them were due to the influence of his favourite Sejanus, and ceased with his sway. Besides, they were the outcome of public feeling at the time against all foreign rites, which had been roused by the vile conduct of the priests of Isis towards a Roman matron, and was again provoked by a gross imposture upon Fulvia, a noble Roman proselyte, on the part of some vagabond Rabbis. But even so, there is no reason to believe that literally all Jews had left Rome. Many would find means to remain secretly behind. At any rate, twenty years afterwards Philo found a large community there, ready to support him in his mission on behalf of his Egyptian countrymen. Any temporary measures against the Jews can, therefore, scarcely be regarded as a serious interference with their privileges, or a cessation of the Imperial favour shown to them.

CHAPTER VI

POLITICAL AND RELIGIOUS LIFE OF THE JEWISH DISPERSION IN THE WEST
THEIR UNION IN THE GREAT HOPE OF THE COMING DELIVERER.

IT was not only in the capital of the Empire that the Jews enjoyed the rights of Roman citizenship. Many in Asia Minor could boast of the same privilege.[a] The Seleucidic rulers of Syria had previously bestowed kindred privileges on the Jews in many places. Thus, they possessed in some cities twofold rights: the status of Roman and the privileges of Asiatic, citizenship. Those who enjoyed the former were entitled to a civil government of their own, under archons of their choosing, quite independent of the rule and tribunals of the cities in which they lived. As instances, we may mention the Jews of Sardis, Ephesus, Delos, and apparently also of Antioch. But, whether legally entitled to it or not, they probably everywhere claimed the right of self-government, and exercised it, except in times of persecution. But, as already stated, they also possessed, besides this, at least in many places, the privileges of Asiatic citizenship, to the same extent as their heathen fellow-citizens. This twofold status and jurisdiction might have led to serious complications, if the archons had not confined their authority to strictly communal interests,[b] without interfering with the ordinary administration of justice, and the Jews willingly submitted to the sentences pronounced by their own tribunals.

But, in truth, they enjoyed even more than religious liberty and communal privileges. It was quite in the spirit of the times, that potentates friendly to Israel bestowed largesses alike on the Temple in Jerusalem, and on the Synagogues in the provinces. The magnificent porch of the Temple was 'adorned' with many such 'dedicated gifts.' Thus, we read of repeated costly offerings by the Ptolemies, of a golden wreath which Sosius offered after he had taken Jerusalem in conjunction with Herod, and of rich flagons which Augustus and his wife had given to the Sanctuary.[c] And, although this same Emperor praised his grandson for leaving Jerusalem unvisited on his journey from Egypt to Syria, yet he himself made provision for a

[a] *Jos.* Ant. xiv. 10, passim; Acts xxii. 25-29

[b] Co. ap. Acts xix. 14 ix. 2

[c] *Jos.* Ant. xii. 2. 5; xiii. 3. 4; Ag. Ap. ii. 5; Ant. xiv 16. 4; War v. 13

daily sacrifice on his behalf, which only ceased when the last war against Rome was proclaimed.[a] Even the circumstance that there was a 'Court of the Gentiles,' with marble screen beautifully ornamented, bearing tablets which, in Latin and Greek, warned Gentiles not to proceed further,[1] proves that the Sanctuary was largely attended by others than Jews, or, in the words of Josephus, that 'it was held in reverence by nations from the ends of the earth.'[b]

In Syria also, where, according to Josephus, the largest number of Jews lived,[2] they experienced special favour. In Antioch their rights and immunities were recorded on tables of brass.[3]

But, indeed, the capital of Syria was one of their favourite resorts. It will be remembered what importance attached to it in the early history of the Christian Church. Antioch was the third city of the Empire, and lay just outside what the Rabbinists designated as 'Syria' and still regarded as holy ground. Thus it formed, so to speak, an advanced post between the Palestinian and the Gentile world. Its chief Synagogue was a magnificent building, to which the successors of Antiochus Epiphanes had given the spoils which that monarch had brought from the Temple. The connection between Jerusalem and Antioch was very close. All that occurred in that city was eagerly watched in the Jewish capital. The spread of Christianity there must have excited deep concern. Careful as the Talmud is not to afford unwelcome information, which might have led to further mischief, we know that three of the principal Rabbis went thither on a mission—we can scarcely doubt for the purpose of arresting the progress of Christianity. Again, we find at a later period a record of religious controversy in Antioch between Rabbis and Christians.[4] Yet the Jews of Antioch were strictly Hellenistic, and on one occasion a great Rabbi was unable to find among them a copy of even the Book of Esther in Hebrew, which, accordingly, he had to write out from memory for his use in their Synagogue. A fit place this great border-city, crowded by Hellenists, in close connection with Jerusalem, to be the birthplace of the name 'Christian,' to send forth a Paul on his mission to the Gentile world, and to obtain for it a charter of citizenship far nobler than that of which the record was graven on tablets of brass.

But, whatever privileges Israel might enjoy, history records an

[a] *Jos.* War ii. 10. 4; ii. 17. 2

[b] War iv. 4. 3; comp. War ii. 17. 2-4

---

[1] One of these tablets has lately been excavated. Comp. 'The Temple: its Ministry and Services in the Time of Christ,' p. 24.

[2] War, vii. 3. 3.
[3] War, vii. 5. 2.
[4] Comp. generally *Neubauer*, Géogr. du Talmud, pp. 312, 313.

almost continuous series of attempts, on the part of the communities among whom they lived, to deprive them not only of their immunities, but even of their common rights. Foremost among the reasons of this antagonism we place the absolute contrariety between heathenism and the Synagogue, and the social isolation which Judaism rendered necessary. It was avowedly unlawful for the Jew even ' to keep company, or come unto one of another nation.' [a] To quarrel with this, was to find fault with the law and the religion which made him a Jew. But besides, there was that pride of descent, creed, enlightenment, and national privileges, which St. Paul so graphically sums up as ' making boast of God and of the law.' [b] However differently they might have expressed it, Philo and Hillel would have been at one as to the absolute superiority of the Jew as such. Pretensions of this kind must have been the more provocative, that the populace at any rate envied tne prosperity which Jewish industry, talent, and capital everywhere secured. Why should that close, foreign corporation possess every civic right, and yet be free from many of its burdens? Why should their meetings be excepted from the ' collegia illicita ' ? why should they alone be allowed to export part of the national wealth, to dedicate it to their superstition in Jerusalem ? The Jew could not well feign any real interest in what gave its greatness to Ephesus, its attractiveness to Corinth, its influence to Athens. He was ready to profit by it ; but his inmost thought must have been contempt, and all he wanted was quietness and protection in his own pursuits. What concern had he with those petty squabbles, ambitions, or designs, which agitated the turbulent populace in those Grecian cities ? what cared he for their popular meetings and noisy discussions ? The recognition of the fact that, as Jews, they were strangers in a strange land, made them so loyal to the ruling powers, and procured them the protection of kings and Cæsars. But it also roused the hatred of the populace.

That such should have been the case, and these widely scattered members have been united in one body, is a unique fact in history. Its only true explanation must be sought in a higher Divine impulse. The links which bound them together were: a common *creed*, a common *life*, a common *centre*, and a common *hope*.

Wherever the Jew sojourned, or however he might differ from his brethren, Monotheism, the Divine mission of Moses, and the authority of the Old Testament, were equally to all unquestioned articles of belief. It may well have been that the Hellenistic Jew, living in the midst of a hostile, curious, and scurrilous population, did

[a] Acts x. 28

[b] Comp.
Rom. ii. 17-24

BOOK   not care to exhibit over his house and doorposts, at the right of the
I   entrance, the *Mezuzah*,[1] which enclosed the folded parchment that, on
        twenty-two lines, bore the words from Deut. iv. 4–9 and xi.
13–21, or to call attention by their breadth to the *Tephillin*,[2] or phylacteries
on his left arm and forehead, or even to make observable the *Tsitsith*,[3]
or fringes on the borders of his garments.[4]   Perhaps, indeed, all these
observances may at that time not have been deemed incumbent on
every Jew.[5] At any rate, we do not find mention of them in
heathen writers. Similarly, they could easily keep out of view, or
they may not have had conveniences for, their prescribed purifications.
But in every place, as we have abundant evidence, where there were
at least ten *Batlanim*—male householders who had leisure to give
a Acts xv. 21 themselves to regular attendance—they had, from ancient times,[a]
one, and, if possible, more Synagogues.[6] Where there was no Syn-
b Acts xvi. agogue there was at least a *Proseuche*,[b 7] or meeting-place, under the
13   open sky, after the form of a theatre, generally outside the town, near
a river or the sea, for the sake of lustrations. These, as we know
from classical writers, were well known to the heathen, and even
frequented by them. Their Sabbath observance, their fasting on
Thursdays, their Day of Atonement, their laws relating to food, and
their pilgrimages to Jerusalem—all found sympathisers among Judaising Gentiles.[8] They even watched to see, how the Sabbath lamp
was kindled, and the solemn prayers spoken which marked the
beginning of the Sabbath.[9] But to the Jew the Synagogue was the

---

[1] Ber. iii. 3; Meg. i. 8; Moed K. iii. 4;
Men. iii. 7. Comp. *Jos.* Ant. iv. 8. 13; and
the tractate Mezuzah in *Kirchheim*, Septem libri Talmud. parvi Hierosol. pp.
12–17.

[2] St. Matt. xxiii. 5; Ber. i. 3; Shabb. vi.
2; vii. 3; xvi. 1; Er. x. 1, 2; Sheq. iii. 2;
Meg. i. 8; iv. 8; Moed. Q. iii. 4; Sanh.
xi. 3; Men. iii. 7; iv. 1; Kel. xviii. 8;
Miqv. x. 3; Yad. iii. 3. Comp. *Kirchheim*, Tract. Tephillin, u. s. pp. 18–21.

[3] Moed K. iii. 4; Eduy. iv. 10; Men.
lii. 7; iv. 1. Comp. *Kirchheim*, Tract.
Tsitsith, u. s. pp. 22–24.

[4] The *Tephillin* enclosed a transcript
of Exod. xiii. 1–10, 11–16; Deut. vi. 4–9;
xi. 13–21. The *Tsitsith* were worn in
obedience to the injunction in Num. xv.
37 etc.; Deut. xxii. 12 (comp. St. Matt.
ix. 20; xiv. 36; St. Mark v. 27; St. Luke
viii. 44).

[5] It is remarkable that Aristeas seems
to speak only of the phylacteries on the
arm, and Philo of those for the head,
while the LXX. takes the command entirely in a metaphorical sense. This has

already been pointed out in that book
of gigantic learning, *Spencer*, De Leg.
Hebr. p. 1213. *Frankel* (Ueber d. Einfl.
d. Pal. Exeg., pp. 89, 90) tries in vain to
controvert the statement. The insuffi-
ciency of his arguments has been fully
shown by *Herzfeld* (Gesch. d. Volk. Isr.
vol. iii. p. 224).

[6] συναγωγή, *Jos.* Ant. xix. 6. 3; War,
ii. 14. 4, 5; vii. 3. 3; *Philo*, Quod omnis
probus liber, ed. Mangey, ii. p. 458;
συναγώγιον, *Philo*, Ad Caj. ii. p. 591;
σαββατεῖον, *Jos.* Ant. xvi. 6. 2; προ-
σευκτήριον, *Philo*, Vita Mosis, lib. iii.,
ii. p. 168.

[7] προσευχή, *Jos.* Ant. xiv. 10. 23,
Life 54; *Philo*, In Flacc. ii. p. 523; Ad
Caj. ii. pp. 565, 596; *Epiphan.* Hær.
lxxx. 1. Comp. *Juven.* Sat. iii. 296: 'Ede
ubi consistas? in qua te quæro pros-
eucha?'

[8] Comp., among others, *Ovid*, Ars
Amat. i. 76; *Juv.* Sat. xiv. 96, 97; *Hor.*
Sat. i. 5. 100; 9. 70; *Suet.* Aug. 93.

[9] *Persius* v. 180.

bond of union throughout the world. There, on Sabbath and feast days they met to read, from the same Lectionary, the same Scripture-lessons which their brethren read throughout the world, and to say, in the words of the same liturgy, their common prayers, catching echoes of the gorgeous Temple-services in Jerusalem. The heathen must have been struck with awe as they listened, and watched in the gloom of the Synagogue the mysterious light at the far curtained end, where the sacred oracles were reverently kept, wrapped in costly coverings. Here the stranger Jew also would find himself at home: the same arrangements as in his own land, and the well-known services and prayers. A hospitable welcome at the Sabbath-meal, and in many a home, would be pressed on him, and ready aid be proffered in work or trial.

For, deepest of all convictions was that of their common *centre*; strongest of all feelings was the love which bound them to Palestine and to Jerusalem, the city of God, the joy of all the earth, the glory of His people Israel. 'If I forget thee, O Jerusalem, let my right hand forget her cunning; let my tongue cleave to the roof of my mouth.' Hellenist and Eastern equally realised this. As the soil of his native land, the deeds of his people, or the graves of his fathers draw the far-off wanderer to the home of his childhood, or fill the mountaineer in his exile with irrepressible longing, so the sounds which the Jew heard in his Synagogue, and the observances which he kept. Nor was it with him merely matter of patriotism, of history, or of association. It was a religious principle, a spiritual hope. No truth more firmly rooted in the consciousness of all, than that in Jerusalem alone men could truly worship.[a] As Daniel of old had in his hour of worship turned towards the Holy City, so in the Synagogue and in his prayers every Jew turned towards Jerusalem; and anything that might imply want of reverence, when looking in that direction, was considered a grievous sin. From every Synagogue in the Diaspora the annual Temple-tribute went up to Jerusalem,[1] no doubt often accompanied by rich votive offerings. Few, who could undertake or afford the journey, but had at some time or other gone up to the Holy City to attend one of the great feasts.[2] Philo, who was held by the same spell as the most bigoted Rabbinist, had himself been one of those deputed by his fellow-citizens to offer prayers and sacrifices in the great Sanctuary.[3] Views and feelings of this kind help us to un-

[a] St. John iv. 20

[1] Comp. *Jos.* Ant. xiv. 7. 2; xvi. 6, passium; *Philo*, De Monarchia, ed. Mangey, ii. p. 224; Ad Caj. ii. p. 568; Contra Flacc. ii. p. 524.

[2] *Philo*, De Monarchia, ii. p. 223.
[3] *Philo*, in a fragment preserved in *Euseb.*, Præpar. Ev. viii. 13. What the Temple was in the estimation of Israel,

BOOK
I

ª War vi. 9.
3; comp. ii.
14. 3

derstand, how, on some great feast, as Josephus states on sufficient
authority, the population of Jerusalem—within its *ecclesiastical*
boundaries—could have swelled to the enormous number of nearly
three millions.ª

And still, there was an even stronger bond in their common *hope.*
That hope pointed them all, wherever scattered, back to Palestine.
To them the coming of the Messiah undoubtedly implied the restoration of Israel's kingdom, and, as a first part in it, the return of 'the
dispersed.'¹ Indeed, every devout Jew prayed, day by day: ' Proclaim
by Thy loud trumpet our deliverance, and raise up a banner to
gather our dispersed, and gather us together from the four ends of
the earth. Blessed be Thou, O Lord! Who gatherest the outcasts
of Thy people Israel.'² That prayer included in its generality also

ᵇ Hos. xi. 11

the lost ten tribes. So, for example, the prophecy ᵇ was rendered:
'They hasten hither, like a bird out of Egypt,'—referring to Israel
of old; 'and like a dove out of the land of Assyria'—referring to

ᶜ Midr. on
Cant. i. 15,
ed. War-
shau, p. 11ᵇ

the ten tribes. ᶜ³ And thus even these wanderers, so long lost, were
to be reckoned in the field of the Good Shepherd. ⁴

It is worth while to trace, how universally and warmly both
Eastern and Western Judaism cherished this hope of all Israel's
return to their own land. The Targumim bear repeated reference to
it;⁵ and although there may be question as to the exact date of
these paraphrases, it cannot be doubted, that in this respect they
represented the views of the Synagogue at the time of Jesus. For
the same reason we may gather from the Talmud and earliest commentaries, what Israel's hope was in regard to the return of the
'dispersed.'⁶ It was a beautiful idea to liken Israel to the olive-tree,

ᵈ Men. 53 ᵇ

which is never stripped of its leaves.ᵈ The storm of trial that had swept
over it was, indeed, sent in judgment, but not to destroy, only to
purify. Even so, Israel's persecutions had served to keep them from

and what its loss boded, not only to
them, but to the whole world, will be
shown in a later part of this book.
¹ Even Maimonides, in spite of his
desire to minimise the Messianic expectancy, admits this.
² This is the tenth of the eighteen (or
rather nineteen) benedictions in the daily
prayers. Of these the first and the last
three are certainly the oldest. But this
tenth also dates from before the destruction of Jerusalem. Comp. *Zunz,*
Gottesd. Vortr. d. Juden, p. 368.
³ Comp. Jer. Sanh. x. 6; Sanh. 110 ᵇ:
Yalk. Shim.
⁴ The suggestion is made by *Castelli,*

Il Messia, p. 253.
⁵ Notably in connection with Ex. xii.
42 (both in the Pseudo-Jon. and Jer.
Targum); Numb. xxiv. 7 (Jer. Targ.);
Deut. xxx. 4 (Targ. Ps.-Jon.); Is. xiv. 29;
Jer. xxxiii. 13; Hos. xiv. 7; Zech. x. 6.
Dr. *Drummond,* in his ' Jewish Messiah,'
p. 335, quotes from the Targum on
Lamentations. But this dates from long
after the Talmudic period.
⁶ As each sentence which follows
would necessitate one or more references
to different works, the reader, who may
be desirous to verify the statements in
the text, is generally referred to *Castelli,*
u. s. pp. 251–255.

becoming mixed with the Gentiles. Heaven and earth might be CHAP.
destroyed, but not Israel; and their final deliverance would far out-VI
strip in marvellousness that from Egypt. The winds would blow to
bring together the dispersed; nay, if there were a single Israelite in a
land, however distant, he would be restored. With every honour would
the nations bring them back. The patriarchs and all the just would
rise to share in the joys of the new possession of their land; new
hymns as well as the old ones would rise to the praise of God. Nay,
the bounds of the land would be extended far beyond what they had
ever been, and made as wide as originally promised to Abraham.
Nor would that possession be ever taken from them, nor those joys
be ever succeeded by sorrows.[1] In view of such general expectations
we cannot fail to mark with what wonderful sobriety the Apostles put
the question to Jesus: 'Wilt Thou at this time restore the kingdom
to Israel?'[a] [a] Acts i. 6

Hopes and expectations such as these are expressed not only in
Talmudical writings. We find them throughout that very interesting Apocalyptic class of literature, the Pseudepigrapha, to which
reference has already been made. The two earliest of them, the
Book of Enoch and the Sibylline Oracles, are equally emphatic on
this subject. The seer in the Book of Enoch beholds Israel in the
Messianic time as coming in carriages, and as borne on the wings of
the wind from East, and West, and South.[b] Fuller details of that [b] Book of
En.ch.lvii.;
happy event are furnished by the Jewish Sibyl. In her utterances comp. xc.33
these three events are connected together: the coming of the Mes-
siah, the rebuilding of the Temple,[c] and the restoration of the dis- [c] B. iii. 286-
294; comp.
persed,[d] when all nations would bring their wealth to the House of B. v. 414-
433
God.[e][2] The latter trait specially reminds us of their Hellenistic origin. [d] iii. 732-735
A century later the same joyous confidence, only perhaps more clearly [e] iii. 766-783
worded, appears in the so-called 'Psalter of Solomon.' Thus the
seventeenth Psalm bursts into this strain: 'Blessed are they who shall
live in those days—in the reunion of the tribes, which God brings
about.'[f] And no wonder, since they are the days when 'the King, [f] Ps. of Sol.
vxii. 50;
comp. also
Ps. xi.

---

[1] The fiction of two Messiahs—one
the Son of David, the other the Son of
Joseph, the latter being connected with
the restoration of the ten tribes—has been
conclusively shown to be the post-Christian date (comp. *Schöttgen*, Horæ Hebr.
i. p. 359; and *Wünsche*, Leiden d. Mess.
p. 109). Possibly it was invented to
find an explanation for Zech. xii. 10
(comp. Succ. 52 *a*), just as the Socinian
doctrine of the assumption of Christ into

heaven at the beginning of His ministry
was invented to account for St. John iii.
13.

[2] M. *Maurice Vernes* (Hist. des Idées
Messian. pp. 43-119) maintains that the
writers of Enoch and Or. Sib. iii. expected this period under the rule of the
Maccabees, and regarded one of them as
the Messiah. It implies a peculiar reading of history, and a lively imagination,
to arrive at such a conclusion.

ᵃ Ps. Sal.
xviii. 23

ᵇ v. 25

ᶜ v. 27

ᵈ v. 28

ᵉ vv. 30, 31

the Son of David,'ᵃ having purged Jerusalemᵇ and destroyed the heathen by the word of His mouth,ᶜ would gather together a holy people which He would rule with justice, and judge the tribes of His people,ᵈ 'dividing them over the land according to tribes;' when 'no stranger would any longer dwell among them.'ᵉ

Another pause, and we reach the time when Jesus the Messiah appeared. Knowing the characteristics of that time, we scarcely wonder that the Book of Jubilees, which dates from that period, should have been Rabbinic in its cast rather than Apocalyptic. Yet even there the reference to the future glory is distinct. Thus we are told, that, though for its wickedness Israel had been scattered, God would 'gather them all from the midst of the heathen,' 'build among them His Sanctuary, and dwell with them.' That Sanctuary was to 'be for ever and ever, and God would appear to the eye of every one, and every one acknowledge that He was the God of Israel, and the Father of all the Children of Jacob, and King upon Mount Zion, from ever-

ᶠ Book of
Jub. ch. i.;
comp. also
ch. xxiii.

lasting to everlasting. And Zion and Jerusalem shall be holy.'ᶠ When listening to this language of, perhaps, a contemporary of Jesus, we can in some measure understand the popular indignation which such a charge would call forth, as that the Man of Nazareth had proposed to destroy

ᵍ St. John
ii. 19

the Temple,ᵍ or that he thought merely of the children of Jacob.

There is an ominous pause of a century before we come to the next work of this class, which bears the title of the Fourth Book of Esdras. That century had been decisive in the history of Israel. Jesus had lived and died; His Apostles had gone forth to bear the tidings of the new Kingdom of God; the Church had been founded and separated from the Synagogue; and the Temple had been destroyed, the Holy City laid waste, and Israel undergone sufferings, compared with which the former troubles might almost be forgotten. But already the new doctrine had struck its roots deep alike in Eastern and in Hellenistic soil. It were strange indeed if, in such circumstances, this book should not have been different from any that had preceded it; stranger still, if earnest Jewish minds and ardent Jewish hearts had re-mained wholly unaffected by the new teaching, even though the doctrine of the Cross still continued a stumbling-block, and the Gospel-announcement a rock of offence. But perhaps we could scarcely have been prepared to find, as in the Fourth Book of Esdras, doctrinal views which were wholly foreign to Judaism, and evidently derived from the New Testament, and which, in logical consistency, would seem to lead up to it.[1] The greater part of the book may be described

---

[1] The doctrinal part of IV. Esdras may be said to be saturated with the dogma of original sin, which is wholly foreign to the theology alike of Rabbinic and

as restless tossing, the seer being agitated by the problem and the consequences of sin, which here for the first and only time is presented as in the New Testament; by the question, why there are so few who are saved; and especially by what to a Jew must have seemed the inscrutable, terrible mystery of Israel's sufferings and banishment.[1] Yet, so far as we can see, no other way of salvation is indicated than that by works and personal righteousness. Throughout there is a tone of deep sadness and intense earnestness. It almost seems sometimes, as if one heard the wind of the new dispensation sweeping before it the withered leaves of Israel's autumn. Thus far for the principal portion of the book. The second, or Apocalyptic, part, endeavors to solve the mystery of Israel's state by foretelling their future. Here also there are echoes of New Testament utterances. What the end is to be, we are told in unmistakable language. His 'Son,' Whom the Highest has for a long time preserved, to deliver 'the creature' by Him, is suddenly to appear in the form of a Man. From His mouth shall proceed alike woe, fire, and storm, which are the tribulations of the last days. And as they shall gather for war against Him, He shall stand on Mount Zion, and the Holy City shall come down from heaven, prepared and ready, and He shall destroy all His enemies. But a peaceable multitude shall now be gathered to Him. These are the ten tribes, who, to separate themselves from the ways of the heathen, had wandered far away, miraculously helped, a journey of one and a half years, and who were now similarly restored by God to their own land. But as for the 'Son,' or those who accompanied him, no one on earth would be able to see or know them, till the day of His appearing.[a][2]

It seems scarcely necessary to complete the series of testimony by referring in detail to a book, called 'The Prophecy and Assumption of Moses,' and to what is known as the Apocalypse of Baruch, the servant of Jeremiah. Both date from probably a somewhat later period than the Fourth Book of Esdras, and both are fragmentary. The one distinctly anticipates the return of the ten tribes;[b] the other, in the letter to the nine and a half tribes, far beyond the Euphrates,[c] with which the book closes, preserves an ominous silence on that point, or rather alludes to it in language which so strongly reminds us of the

[a] Vis. vi. ch. xiii. 27-52

[b] Prophet. et Ass. Mos. iv. 7-14; vii. 20

[c] Ap. Bar. xxvii. 22

Hellenistic Judaism. Comp. *Vis.* i. ch. iii. 21, 22; iv. 30, 38; *Vis.* iii. ch. vi, 18, 19 (ed. Fritzsche, p. 607); 33-41; vii. 46-48; viii. 34-35.

[1] It almost seems as if there were a parallelism between this book and the Epistle to the Romans, which in its dog-matic part, seems successively to take up these three subjects, although from quite another point of view. How different the treatment is, need not be told.

[2] The better reading is 'in tempore diei ejus. (v. 52).'

adverse opinion expressed in the Talmud, that we cannot help sus-
pecting some internal connection between the two.[1]

The writings to which we have referred have all a decidedly
Hellenistic tinge of thought.[2] Still they are not the outcome of
pure Hellenism. It is therefore with peculiar interest that we turn
to Philo, the great representative of that direction, to see whether he
would admit an idea so purely national and, as it might seem, exclusive. Nor are we here left in doubt. So universal was this belief,
so deep-seated the conviction, not only in the mind, but in the heart
of Israel, that we could scarcely find it more distinctly expressed than
by the great Alexandrian. However low the condition of Israel
might be, he tells us,[a] or however scattered the people to the ends of
the earth, the banished would, on a given sign, be set free in one day.
In consistency with his system, he traces this wondrous event to
their sudden conversion to virtue, which would make their masters
ashamed to hold any longer in bondage those who were so much
better than themselves. Then, gathering as by one impulse, the dispersed would return from Hellas, from the lands of the barbarians,
from the isles, and from the continents, led by a Divine, superhuman
apparition invisible to others, and visible only to themselves. On
their arrival in Palestine the waste places and the wilderness would be
inhabited, and the barren land transformed into fruitfulness.

Whatever shades of difference, then, we may note in the expression of these views, all anticipate the deliverance of Israel, their restoration, and future pre-eminent glory, and they all connect these
events with the coming of the Messiah. This was 'the promise'
unto which, in their 'instant service night and day, the twelve tribes,'
however grievously oppressed, hoped to come.[b] To this 'sure word
of prophecy' 'the strangers scattered' throughout all lands would
'take heed, as unto a light that shineth in a dark place,' until the

ᵃ De Exe-
crat.
ed. Frcf.
pp. 936, 937

ᵇ Acts
xxvi. 7

---

[1] In Sanh. 110 b we read, 'Our Rabbis teach, that the Ten Tribes have no part in the era to come, because it is written "The Lord drave them out of their land in anger, and in wrath, and in great indignation, and cast them into another land." " The Lord drave them from their land "—in the present era—"and cast them into another land "—in the era to come.' In curious agreement with this, Pseudo-Baruch writes to the nine and a half tribes to 'prepare their hearts to that which they had formerly believed,' lest they should suffer ' in both eras (ab utroque sæculo),' being led captive in the one, and tormented in the other (Apoc. Bar. lxxxiii. 8).

[2] Thus, for example, the assertion that there had been individuals who fulfilled the commandments of God, Vis. i. ch. iii. 36; the domain of reason, iv. 22; v. 9; general Messianic blessings to the world at large, Vis. i. ch. iv. 27, 28; the idea of a law within their minds, like that of which St. Paul speaks in the case of the heathen, Vis. iii. ch. vi. 45–47 (ed. Fritzsche, p. 609). These are only in-stances, and we refer besides to the gen-eral cast of the reasoning.

day dawned. and the day-star rose in their hearts.[a] It was this
which gave meaning to their worship, filled them with patience in
suffering, kept them separate from the nations around, and ever fixed
their hearts and thoughts upon Jerusalem. For the 'Jerusalem'
which was above was 'the mother' of them all. Yet a little while,
and He that would come should come, and not tarry—and then all
the blessing and glory would be theirs. At any moment the gladsome tidings might burst upon them, that He had come, when their
glory would shine out from one end of the heavens to the other. All
the signs of His Advent had come to pass. Perhaps, indeed, the
Messiah might even now be there, ready to manifest Himself, so soon
as the voice of Israel's repentance called Him from His hiding. Any
hour might that banner be planted on the top of the mountains;
that glittering sword be unsheathed; that trumpet sound. Closer
then, and still closer, must be their connection with Jerusalem, as
their salvation drew nigh; more earnest their longing, and more
eager their gaze, till the dawn of that long expected day tinged the
Eastern sky with its brightness.

CHAPTER VII.

IN PALESTINE—JEWS AND GENTILES IN 'THE LAND'—THEIR MUTUAL
RELATIONS AND FEELINGS—'THE WALL OF SEPARATION.'

BOOK
I

THE pilgrim who, leaving other countries, entered Palestine, must
have felt as if he had crossed the threshold of another world.
Manners, customs, institutions, law, life, nay, the very intercourse
between man and man, were quite different. All was dominated by
the one all-absorbing idea of religion. It penetrated every relation
of life. Moreover, it was inseparably connected with the soil, as well
as the people of Palestine, at least so long as the Temple stood.
Nowhere else could the Shekhinah dwell or manifest itself; nor could,
unless under exceptional circumstances, and for 'the merit of the
fathers,' the spirit of prophecy be granted outside its bounds. To
the orthodox Jew the mental and spiritual horizon was bounded by
Palestine. It was 'the land'; all the rest of the world, except
Babylonia, was 'outside the land.' No need to designate it specially
as 'holy'; for all here bore the impress of sanctity, as he understood
it. Not that the soil itself, irrespective of the people, was holy; it
was Israel that made it such. For, had not God given so many commandments and ordinances, some of them apparently needless, simply
to call forth the righteousness of Israel; [a] did not Israel possess the
merits of 'the fathers,' [b] and specially that of Abraham, itself so
valuable that, even if his descendants had, morally speaking, been as
a dead body, his merit would have been imputed to them? [c] More
than that, God had created the world on account of Israel, [d] and for
their merit, making preparation for them long before their appearance on the scene, just as a king who foresees the birth of his son;
nay, Israel had been in God's thoughts not only before anything had
actually been created, but even before every other creative thought. [e]
If these distinctions seem excessive, they were, at least, not out of
proportion to the estimate formed of Israel's merits. In theory, the
latter might be supposed to flow from 'good works,' of course, including the strict practice of legal piety, and from 'study of the law.'

[a] Mac. 23 b
[b] Rosh
HaSh. 11 a
[c] Ber. R. 44
[d] Yalkut § 2

[e] Ber. R. 1

But in reality it was 'study' alone to which such supreme merit attached. Practice required knowledge for its direction; such as the *Am-ha-arets* (' country people,' plebeians, in the Jewish sense of being unlearned) could not possess,[a] who had bartered away the highest crown for a spade with which to dig. And ' the school of Arum '— the sages—the ' great ones of the world ' had long settled it, that study was before works.[b] And how could it well be otherwise, since the studies, which engaged His chosen children on earth, equally occupied their Almighty Father in heaven?[c] Could anything, then, be higher than the peculiar calling of Israel, or better qualify them for being the sons of God?

It is necessary to transport oneself into this atmosphere to understand the views entertained at the time of Jesus, or to form any conception of their infinite contrast in spirit to the new doctrine. The abhorrence, not unmingled with contempt, of all Gentile ways, thoughts and associations; the worship of the letter of the Law; the self-righteousness, and pride of descent, and still more of knowledge, become thus intelligible to us, and, equally so, the absolute antagonism to the claims of a Messiah, so unlike themselves and their own ideal. His first announcement might, indeed, excite hope, soon felt to have been vain; and His miracles might startle for a time. But the boundary lines of the Kingdom which He traced were essentially different from those which they had fixed, and within which they had arranged everything, alike for the present and the future. Had He been content to step within them, to complete and realise what they had indicated, it might have been different. Nay, once admit their fundamental ideas, and there was much that was beautiful, true, and even grand in the details. But it was exactly in the former that the divergence lay. Nor was there any possibility of reform or progress here. The past, the present, and the future, alike as regarded the Gentile world and Israel, were irrevocably fixed; or rather, it might almost be said, there were not such—all continuing as they had been from the creation of the world, nay, long before it. The Torah had really existed 2,000 years before Creation;[d] the patriarchs had had their Academies of study, and they had known and observed all the ordinances; and traditionalism had the same origin, both as to time and authority, as the Law itself. As for the heathen nations, the Law had been offered by God to them, but refused, and even their after repentance would prove hypocritical, as all their excuses would be shown to be futile. But as for Israel, even though their good deeds should be few, yet, by cumulating them from among all the people, they would appear

[a] Comp. Ab. ii. 5

[b] Jer. Chag. i. hal. 7, towards the end; Jer. Pes. iii. 7

[c] Ab. Z. 3 b

[d] Shir haShir. R. on Cant. v. 11, ed War shau, p. 26 b

BOOK
I

great in the end, and God would exact payment for their sins as a man does from his friends, taking little sums at a time. It was in this sense, that the Rabbis employed that sublime figure, representing the Church as one body, of which all the members suffered and joyed together, which St. Paul adopted and applied in a vastly different and spiritual sense.[a]

a Eph. iv. 16

If, on the one hand, the pre-eminence of Israel depended on the Land, and, on the other, that of the Land on the presence of Israel in it, the Rabbinical complaint was, indeed, well grounded, that its 'boundaries were becoming narrow.' We can scarcely expect any accurate demarcation of them, since the question, what belonged to it, was determined by ritual and theological, not by geographical considerations. Not only the immediate neighborhood (as in the case of Ascalon), but the very wall of a city (as of Acco and of Cæsarea) might be Palestinian, and yet the city itself be regarded as 'outside' the sacred limits. All depended on who had originally possessed, and now held a place, and hence what ritual obligations lay upon it. Ideally, as we may say, 'the land of promise' included all which God had covenanted to give to Israel, although never yet actually possessed by them. Then, in a more restricted sense, the 'land' comprised what 'they who came up from Egypt took possession of, from Chezib [about three hours north of Acre] and unto the river [Euphrates], and unto Amanah.' This included, of course, the conquests made by David in the most prosperous times of the Jewish commonwealth, supposed to have extended over Mesopotamia, Syria, Zobah, Achlah, &c. To all these districts the general name of *Soria*, or Syria, was afterwards given. This formed, at the time of which we write, a sort of inner band around 'the land,' in its narrowest and only real sense; just as the countries in which Israel was specially interested, such as Egypt, Babylon, Ammon, and Moab, formed an outer band. These lands were heathen, and yet not quite heathen, since the dedication of the so-called *Terumoth*, or first-fruits in a prepared state, was expected from them, while *Soria* shared almost all the obligations of Palestine, except those of the 'second tithes,' and the fourth year's product of plants.[b] But the wavesheaf at the Paschal Feast, and the two loaves at Pentecost, could only be brought from what had grown on the holy soil itself. This latter was roughly defined, as 'all which they who came up from Babylon took possession of, in the land of Israel, and unto Chezib.' Viewed in this light, there was a special significance in the fact that Antioch, where the name 'Christian' first marked the new 'Sect' which had sprung up in Palestine,[c] and where the first

b Lev. xix. 24

c Acts xi. 26

Gentile Church was formed,[a] lay just outside the northern boundary
of 'the land.' Similarly, we understand, why those Jewish zealots
who would fain have imposed on the new Church the yoke of the Law,[b]
concentrated their first efforts on that *Soria* which was regarded as a
kind of outer Palestine.

[a] Acts xi. 20, 21
[b] Acts xv. 1

But, even so, there was a gradation of sanctity in the Holy Land
itself, in accordance with ritual distinctions. Ten degrees are here
enumerated, beginning with the bare soil of Palestine, and culminat-
ing in the Most Holy Place in the Temple—each implying some ritual
distinction, which did not attach to a lower degree. And yet, although
the very dust of heathen soil was supposed to carry defilement, like
corruption or the grave, the spots most sacred were everywhere surrounded by heathenism ; nay, its traces were visible in Jerusalem
itself. The reasons of this are to be sought in the political circumstances of Palestine, and in the persistent endeavour of its rulers—
with the exception of a very brief period under the Maccabees—to
Grecianise the country, so as to eradicate that Jewish particularism
which must always be antagonistic to every foreign element. In
general, Palestine might be divided into the strictly Jewish territory,
and the so-called Hellenic cities. The latter had been built at different
periods, and were politically constituted after the model of the Greek
cities, having their own senates (generally consisting of several hundred
persons) and magistrates, each city with its adjoining territory forming
a sort of commonwealth of its own. But it must not be imagined,
that these districts were inhabited exclusively, or even chiefly, by
Greeks. One of these groups, that towards Peræa, was really Syrian,
and formed part of *Syria Decapolis*;[1] while the other, along the coast
of the Mediterranean, was Phœnician. Thus 'the land' was hemmed
in, east and west, within its own borders, while south and north
stretched heathen or semi-heathen districts. The strictly Jewish
territory consisted of Judæa proper, to which 'Galilee, Samaria and
Peræa were joined as Toparchies. These Toparchies consisted of a
group of townships, under a Metropolis. The villages and townships
themselves had neither magistrates of their own, nor civic constitution, nor lawful popular assemblies. Such civil adminstration as
they required devolved on 'Scribes' (the so-called κωμογραμματεῖς
or τοπογραμματεῖς). Thus Jerusalem was really, as well as nominally,

---

[1] The following cities probably formed
the *Decapolis*, though it is difficult to
feel quite sure in reference to one or the
other of them: Damascus, Philadelphia,
Raphana, Scythopolis, Gadara, Hippos

Dion, Pella, Gerasa, and Canatha. On
these cities, comp. *Caspari*, Chronol.
Geogr. Einl. in d. Leben J. Christi, pp.
83–90.

BOOK   the capital of the whole land. Judæa itself was arranged into eleven,
  I   or rather, more exactly, into nine Toparchies, of which Jerusalem was
        the chief. While, therefore, the Hellenic cities were each independent of
the other, the whole Jewish territory formed only one ' *Civitas*.' Rule,
government, tribute—in short, political life—centred in Jerusalem.

But this is not all. From motives similar to those which led to
the founding of other Hellenic cities, Herod the Great and his immediate successors built a number of towns, which were inhabited chiefly
by Gentiles, and had independent constitutions, like those of the Hellenic cities. Thus, Herod himself built Sebaste (Samaria), in the
centre of the country; Cæsarea in the west, commanding the sea-coast;
Gaba in Galilee, close to the great plain of Esdraelon; and Esbonitis
in Peræa.[1] Similarly, Philip the Tetrarch built Cæsarea Philippi
and Julias (Bethsaida-Julias, on the western shore of the lake); and
Herod Antipas another Julias, and Tiberias.[2] The object of these
cities was twofold. As Herod, well knowing his unpopularity, surrounded himself by foreign mercenaries, and reared fortresses around
his palace and the Temple which he built, so he erected these fortified posts, which he populated with strangers, as so many outworks,
to surround and command Jerusalem and the Jews on all sides. Again,
as, despite his profession of Judaism, he reared magnificent heathen
temples in honour of Augustus at Sebaste and Cæsarea, so those
cities were really intended to form centres of Grecian influence within
the sacred territory itself. At the same time, the Herodian cities enjoyed not the same amount of liberty as the ' Hellenic,' which, with
the exception of certain imposts, were entirely self-governed, while in
the former there were representatives of the Herodian rulers.[3]

Although each of these towns and districts had its special deities
and rites, some being determined by local traditions, their prevailing
character may be described as a mixture of Greek and Syrian worship,
the former preponderating, as might be expected.[4] On the other
hand, Herod and his successors encouraged the worship of the Emperor
and of Rome, which, characteristically, was chiefly practised in the
East.[5] Thus, in the temple which Herod built to Augustus in

---

[1] Herod rebuilt or built other cities, such as Antipatris, Cypros, Phasaelis, Anthedon, &c. Schürer describes the two first as *built*, but they were only *re*built or fortified (comp. Ant. xiii. 15. 1; War i. 21. 8.) by Herod.

[2] He also rebuilt Sepphoris.

[3] Comp. on the subject of the civic institutions of the Roman Empire, *Kuhn*,

Die Städt. u. bürgerl. Vert. d. Röm. Reichs, 2 vols.; and for this part, vol. ii. pp. 336–354, and pp. 370–372.

[4] A good sketch of the various rites prevailing in different places is given by *Schürer*, Neutest. Zeitg. pp. 378–385.

[5] Comp. *Weiseler*, Beitr. z richt. Würdig. d. Evang. pp. 90 91.

Cæsarea, there were statues of the Emperor as Olympian Zeus, and of Rome as Hera.[a] He was wont to excuse this conformity to heathenism before his own people on the ground of political necessity. Yet, even if his religious inclinations had not been in that direction, he would have earnestly striven to Grecianise the people. Not only in Cæsarea, but even in Jerusalem, he built a theatre and amphitheatre, where at great expense games were held every four years in honour of Augustus.[1] Nay, he placed over the great gate of the Temple at Jerusalem a massive golden eagle, the symbol of Roman dominion, as a sort of counterpart to that gigantic golden vine, the symbol of Israel, which hung above the entrance to the Holy Place. These measures, indeed, led to popular indignation, and even to conspiracies and tumults,[b] though not of the same general and intense character, as when, at a later period, Pilate sought to introduce into Jerusalem images of the Emperor, or when the statue of Caligula was to be placed in the Temple. In connection with this, it is curious to notice that the Talmud, while on the whole disapproving of attendance at theatres and amphitheatres—chiefly on the ground that it implies 'sitting in the seat of scorners,' and might involve contributions to the maintenance of idol-worship—does *not* expressly prohibit it, nor indeed speak very decidedly on the subject.[c]

The views of the Rabbis in regard to pictorial representations are still more interesting, as illustrating their abhorrence of all contact with idolatry. We mark here differences at two, if not at three periods, according to the outward circumstances of the people. The earliest and strictest opinions[d] absolutely forbade any representation of things in heaven, on earth, or in the waters. But the Mishnah[e] seems to relax these prohibitions by subtle distinctions, which are still further carried out in the Talmud.[2]

To those who held such stringent views, it must have been peculiarly galling to see their most sacred feelings openly outraged by their own rulers. Thus, the Asmonean princess, Alexandra, the mother-in-law of Herod, could so far forget the traditions of her house, as to send portraits of her son and daughter to Mark Antony for infamous purposes, in hope of thereby winning him for her ambitious plans.[f] One would be curious to know who painted these pictures, for, when the statue of Caligula was to be made for the Temple at Jerusalem, no

Marginal notes:

CHAP. VII

[a] *Jos.* Ant. xv. 9. 6; War i. 21. 5-8

[b] Ant. xv. 8. 1-4; xvii. 6. 2

[c] So at least in a Boraitha. Comp. the discussion and the very curious arguments in favour of attendance in Ab. Zar. 18 *b*, and following

[d] Mechilta on Ex. xx. 4 ed. Weiss, p. 75 *a*

[e] Ab. Zar. iii.

[f] *Jos.* Ant. xv. 2. 5 and 6

---

[1] The Actian games took place every fifth year, three years always intervening. The games in Jerusalem were held in the year 28 B.C. (*Jos.* Ant. xv. 8. 1); the first games in Cæsarea in the year 12 B.C.

[2] For a full statement of the Talmudical views as to images, representations on coins, and the most ancient Jewish coins, see Appendix III.

(Ant. xvi. 5. 1; comp. War i. 21. 8).

BOOK
I

ᵃ *Jos.* War v.
4. 4

ᵇ Acts xii.23

ᶜ An⸚. xix.
9. 7

ᵈ Dan. vii.
23

ᵉ Midr. R.
on Ex. Par.
23

ᶠ Ab. Z. 2 *b*

ᵍ Ab. Z. 10 *a;*
Gitt. 80 *a*

ʰ Ps. lxxvi.
3

Shabb. 88 *a*

native artist could be found, and the work was entrusted to Phœnicians. It must have been these foreigners also who made the 'figures,' with which Herod adorned his palace at Jerusalem, and 'the brazen statues' in the gardens 'through which the water ran out,'ᵃ as well as the colossal statues at Cæsarea, and those of the three daughters of Agrippa, which after his deathᵇ were so shamefully abused by the soldiery at Sebaste and Cæsarea.ᶜ

This abhorrence of all connected with idolatry, and the contempt entertained for all that was non-Jewish, will in great measure explain the code of legislation intended to keep the Jew and Gentile apart. If Judæa had to submit to the power of Rome, it could at least avenge itself in the Academies of its sages. Almost innumerable stories are told in which Jewish sages, always easily, confute Roman and Greek philosophers; and others, in which even a certain Emperor (Antoninus) is represented as constantly in the most menial relation of self-abasement before a Rabbi.[1] Rome, which was the fourth beast of Daniel,ᵈ would in the age to come,[2] when Jerusalem would be the metropolis of all lands,ᵉ be the first to excuse herself on false though vain pleas for her wrongs to Israel.ᶠ But on worldly grounds also, Rome was contemptible, having derived her language and writing from the Greeks, and not possessing even a hereditary succession in her empire.ᵍ If such was the estimate of dreaded Rome, it may be imagined in what contempt other nations were held. Well might 'the earth tremble,'ʰ for, if Israel had not accepted the Law at Sinai, the whole world would have been destroyed, while it once more 'was still' when that happy event took place, although God in a manner forced Israel to it.[1] And so Israel was purified at Mount Sinai from the impurity which clung to our race in consequence of the unclean union between Eve and the serpent, and which still adhered to all other nations![3]

To begin with, every Gentile child, so soon as born, was to be regarded as unclean. Those who actually worshipped mountains, hills, bushes, &c.—in short, gross idolaters—should be cut down with the sword. But as it was impossible to exterminate heathenism, Rabbinic legislation kept certain definite objects in view, which may be thus summarised : To prevent Jews from being inadvertently led into

---

[1] Comp. here the interesting tractate of Dr. *Bodek,* 'Marc. Aur. Anton. als Freund u. Zeitgenosse des R. Jehuda ha Nasi.'

[2] The *Athid labho,* 'sæculum futurum,' to be distinguished from the *Olam habba,* 'the world to come.'

[3] Ab. Z. 22 *b.* But as in what follows the quotations would be too numerous, they will be omitted. Each statement, however, advanced in the text or notes is derived from part of the Talmudic tractate Abodah Zarah.

idolatry; to avoid all participation in idolatry; not to do anything which might aid the heathen in their worship; and, beyond all this, not to give pleasure, nor even help, to heathens. The latter involved a most dangerous principle, capable of almost indefinite application by fanaticism. Even the Mishnah goes so far[a] as to forbid aid to a mother in the hour of her need, or nourishment to her babe, in order not to bring up a child for idolatry![1] But this is not all. Heathens were, indeed, not to be precipitated into danger, but yet not to be delivered from it. Indeed, an isolated teacher ventures even upon this statement: 'The best among the Gentiles, kill; the best among serpents, crush its head.'[b] Still more terrible was the fanaticism which directed, that heretics, traitors, and those who had left the Jewish faith should be thrown into actual danger, and, if they were in it, all means for their escape removed. No intercourse of any kind was to be had with such—not even to invoke their medical aid in case of danger to life,[2] since it was deemed, that he who had to do with heretics was in imminent peril of becoming one himself,[3] and that, if a heretic returned to the true faith, he should die at once— partly, probably, to expiate his guilt, and partly from fear of relapse. Terrible as all this sounds, it was probably not worse than the fanaticism displayed in what are called more enlightened times. Impartial history must chronicle it, however painful, to show the circumstances in which teaching so far different was propounded by Christ.[4]

In truth, the bitter hatred which the Jew bore to the Gentile can only be explained from the estimate entertained of his character. The

CHAP.
VII

[a] Ab. Z. ii. 1

[b] Mechilta, ed. Weiss, p. 33 b, line 8 from top

---

[1] The Talmud declares it only lawful if done to avoid exciting hatred against the Jews.

[2] There is a well-known story told of a Rabbi who was bitten by a serpent, and about to be cured by the invocation of the name of Jesus by a Jewish Christian, which was, however, interdicted.

[3] Yet, such is the moral obliquity, that even idolatry is allowed to save life, provided it be done in secret!

[4] Against this, although somewhat doubtfully, such concessions may be put as that, outside Palestine, Gentiles were not to be considered as idolators, but as observing the customs of their fathers (Chull. 13 b), and that the poor of the Gentiles were to be equally supported with those of Israel, their sick visited, and their dead buried; it being, however, significantly added, 'on account of the arrangements of the world' (Gitt. 61 a). The quotation so often made (Ab. Z. 3 a), that a Gentile who occupied himself with the Torah was to be regarded as equal to the High-Priest, proves nothing, since in the case supposed the Gentile acts like a Rabbinic Jew. But, and this is a more serious point, it is difficult to believe that those who make this quotation are not aware, how the Talmud (Ab. Z. 3 a) immediately labours to prove that their reward is *not* equal to that of Israelites. A somewhat similar charge of one-sidedness, if not of unfairness, must be brought against *Deutsch* (Lecture on the Talmud, Remains, pp. 146, 147), whose sketch of Judaism should be compared, for example, with the first Perek of the Talmudic tractate Abodah Zarah.

most vile, and even unnatural, crimes were imputed to them. It was not safe to leave cattle in their charge, to allow their women to nurse infants, or their physicians to attend the sick, nor to walk in their company, without taking precautions against sudden and unprovoked attacks. They should, so far as possible, be altogether avoided, except in cases of necessity or for the sake of business. They and theirs were defiled; their houses unclean, as containing idols or things dedicated to them; their feasts, their joyous occasions, their very contact, was polluted by idolatry; and there was no security, if a heathen were left alone in a room, that he might not, in wantonness or by carelessness, defile the wine or meat on the table, or the oil and wheat in the store. Under such circumstances, therefore, everything must be regarded as having been rendered unclean. Three days before a heathen festival (according to some, also three days after) every business transaction with them was prohibited, for fear of giving either help or pleasure. Jews were to avoid passing through a city where there was an idolatrous feast—nay, they were not even to sit down within the shadow of a tree dedicated to idol-worship. Its wood was polluted; if used in baking, the bread was unclean; if a shuttle had been made of it, not only was all cloth woven on it forbidden, but if such had been inadvertently mixed with other pieces of cloth, or a garment made from it placed with other garments, the whole became unclean. Jewish workmen were not to assist in building basilicas, nor stadia, nor places where judicial sentences were pronounced by the heathen. Of course, it was not lawful to let houses or fields, nor to sell cattle to them. Milk drawn by a heathen, if a Jew had not been present to watch it,[a] bread and oil prepared by them, were unlawful. Their wine was wholly interdicted [1]—the mere touch of a heathen polluted a whole cask; nay, even to put one's nose to heathen wine was strictly prohibited !

Painful as these details are, they might be multiplied. And yet the bigotry of these Rabbis was, perhaps, not worse than that of other sectaries. It was a painful logical necessity of their system, against which their heart, no doubt, often rebelled; and, it must be truthfully added, it was in measure accounted for by the terrible history of Israel.

---

[1] According to R. Asi, there was a threefold distinction. If wine had been dedicated to an idol, to carry, even on a stick, so much as the weight of an olive of it, defiled a man. Other wine, if prepared by a heathen, was prohibited, whether for personal use or for trading. Lastly, wine prepared by a Jew, but deposited in custody of a Gentile, was prohibited for personal use, but allowed for traffic.

CHAPTER VIII.

TRADITIONALISM, ITS ORIGIN, CHARACTER, AND LITERATURE—THE MISH-
NAH AND TALMUD—THE GOSPEL OF CHRIST—THE DAWN OF A NEW
DAY.

IN trying to picture to ourselves New Testament scenes, the figure most prominent, next to those of the chief actors, is that of the *Scribe* (סופר, γραμματεύς, *literatus*). He seems ubiquitous; we meet him in Jerusalem, in Judæa, and even in Galilee.[a] Indeed, he is indispensable, not only in Babylon, which may have been the birthplace of his order, but among the 'dispersion' also.[b] Everywhere he appears as the mouthpiece and representative of the people; he pushes to the front, the crowd respectfully giving way, and eagerly hanging on his utterances, as those of a recognised authority. He has been solemnly ordained by the laying on of hands; and is the *Rabbi*,[1] 'my great one,' Master, *amplitudo*. He puts questions; he urges objections; he expects full explanations and respectful demeanour. Indeed, his hyper-ingenuity in questioning has become a proverb. There is not measure of his dignity, nor yet limit to his importance. He is the 'lawyer,'[c] the 'well-plastered pit,' filled with the water of knowledge 'out of which not a drop can escape,'[d] in opposition to the weeds of untilled soil' (בורים) of ignorance.[e] He is the Divine aristocrat, among the vulgar herd of rude and profane 'country-people,' who 'know not the Law' and are 'cursed.' More than that, his order constitutes the ultimate authority on all questions of faith and practice; he is 'the Exegete of the Laws,'[f] the 'teacher of the Law,'[g] and along with 'the chief priests' and 'elders' a judge in the ecclesiastical tribunals, whether of the capital or in the provinces.[h] Although generally appearing in company with 'the Pharisees,' he is not necessarily one of them—for they represent a

CHAP.
VIII

[a] St. Luke
v. 17

[b] *Jos.* Ant.
xviii. 3. 5;
xx. 11. 2

[c] νομικός,
the legis
Divinæ
peritus, St.
Matt. xxii.
35; St.Luke
vii. 30; x.
25; xi. 45;
xiv. 3

[d] Ab. ii. 8

[e] Ber. 45 *b* 2;
Ab. ii. 5;
Bemid. R. 3

[f] *Jos.* Ant.
xvii. 6. 2

[g] νομοδιδάς
καλος, St.
Luke v. 17;
Acts v. 34;
comp. also
1 Tim. i. 7

[h] St. Matt.
ii. 4; xx.18;
xxi. 15;
xxvi. 57;
xxvii. 41;
St. Mark
xiv.1.43;xv.
1; St. Luke
xxii. 2, 66;
xxiii. 10;
Acts iv. 5

---

[1] The title *Rabbon* (*our* Master) occurs first in connection with Gamaliel i. (Acts v. 34). The N.T. expression *Rabboni* or *Rabbouni* (St. Mark x. 51; St. John xx. 16) takes the word *Rabbon* or *Rabban* (here in the absolute sense)=

Rabh, and adds to it the personal suffix 'my,' pronouncing the *Kamez* in the Syriac manner.

[2] Not 45 *a*, as apud *Derenbourg*. Similarly, his rendering 'littéralement, "citerne vide"' seems to me erroneous.

BOOK
I

^a *Siphré* or
Numb. פ
25 b

^b *Siphré* on
Deut. p.
105 a

^c Ezra vii.6,
10, 11, 12

^d לִדְרֹשׁ
וְלַעֲשֹׂות
וּלְלַמֵּד

^e Nedar. iv.
8

^f Neh. xiii.

religious party, while he has a status, and holds an office.[1] In short, he is the *Talmid* or learned student, the *Chakham* or sage, whose honour is to be great in the future world. Each Scribe outweighed all the common people, who must accordingly pay him every honour. Nay, they were honoured of God Himself, and their praises proclaimed by the angels; and in heaven also, each of them would hold the same rank and distinction as on earth.[a] Such was to be the respect paid to their sayings, that they were to be absolutely believed, even if they were to declare that to be at the right hand which was at the left, or *vice versâ*.[b]

An institution which had attained such proportions, and wielded such power, could not have been of recent growth. In point of fact, its rise was very gradual, and stretched back to the time of Nehemiah, if not beyond it. Although from the utter confusion of historical notices in Rabbinic writings and their constant practice of ante-dating events, it is impossible to furnish satisfactory details, the general development of the institution can be traced with sufficient precision. If Ezra is described in Holy Writ[c] as 'a ready (*expertus*) Scribe,' who had 'set his heart to seek (seek out the full meaning of) the law of the Lord, and to do it, and to teach in Israel,'[d] this might indicate to his successors, the *Sopherim* (Scribes), the threefold direction which their studies afterwards took: the *Midrash*, the *Halakhah*, and the *Haggadah*,[e][2] of which the one pointed to Scriptural investigation, the other to what was to be observed, and the third to oral teaching in the widest sense. But Ezra left his work uncompleted. On Nehemiah's second arrival in Palestine, he found matters again in a state of utmost confusion.[f] He must have felt the need of establishing some permanent authority to watch over religious affairs. This we take to have been 'the Great Assembly,' or, as it is commonly called, the 'Great Synagogue.' It is impossible with certainty to determine,[3] either who composed this assembly, or of how many members it consisted.[4] Probably it comprised the leading men in

[1] The distinction between 'Pharisees' and 'Scribes,' is marked in many passages in the N.T., for example, St. Matt. xxiii. passim; St. Luke vii. 30; xiv. 3; and especially in St. Luke xi. 43, comp. with v. 46. The words 'Scribes and Pharisees, hypocrites,' in ver. 44, are, according to all evidence, spurious.

[2] In Ned. iv. 3 this is the actual division. Of course, in another sense the Midrash might be considered as the source of both the Halakhah and the Haggadah.

[3] Very strange and ungrounded conjec-tures on this subject have been hazarded, which need not here find a place. Comp. for ex. the two articles of *Grätz* in *Frankel's* Monatsschrift for 1857, pp. 31 etc. 61 etc., the main positions of which have, however, been adopted by some learned English writers.

[4] The Talmudic notices are often inconsistent. The number as given in them amounts to about 120. But the modern doubts (of *Kuenen* and others) against the institution itself cannot be sustained.

Church and State, the chief priests, elders, and 'judges'— the latter two classes including 'the Scribes,' if, indeed, that order was already separately organised.[a] Probably also the term 'Great Assembly' refers rather to a succession of men than to one Synod; the ingenuity of later times filling such parts of the historical canvas as had been left blank with fictitious notices. In the nature of things such an assembly could not exercise permanent sway in a sparsely populated country, without a strong central authority. Nor could they have wielded real power during the political difficulties and troubles of foreign domination. The oldest tradition[b] sums up the result of their activity in this sentence ascribed to them: 'Be careful in judgment, set up many *Talmidim*, and make a hedge about the *Torah* (Law).'

In the course of time this rope of sand dissolved. The High-Priest, *Simon the Just*,[c] is already designated as 'of the remnants of the Great Assembly.' But even this expression does not necessarily imply that he actually belonged to it. In the troublous times which followed his Pontificate, the sacred study seems to have been left to solitary individuals. The Mishnic tractate Aboth, which records 'the sayings of the Fathers,' here gives us only the name of Antigonus of Socho. It is significant, that for the first time we now meet a Greek name among Rabbinic authorities, together with an indistinct allusion to his disciples.[d][1] The long interval between Simon the Just and Antigonus and his disciples, brings us to the terrible time of Antiochus Epiphanes and the great Syrian persecution. The very sayings attributed to these two sound like an echo of the political state of the country. On three things, Simon was wont to say, the permanency of the (Jewish?) world depends: on the Torah (faithfulness to the Law and its pursuit), on worship (the non-participation in Grecianism), and on works of righteousness.[e] They were dark times, when God's persecuted people were tempted to think, that it might be vain to serve Him, in which Antigonus had it: 'Be not like servants who serve their master for the sake of reward, but be like servants who serve their lord without a view to the getting of reward, and let the fear of heaven be upon you.'[f] After these two names come those of the so-called five *Zugoth*, or 'couples,' of whom Hillel and Shammai are the last. Later tradition has represented these successive couples as,

CHAP.
VIII

[a] Ezra x. 14;
Neh. v. 7

[b] Ab. 1. 1

[c] In the beginning of the third century B.C.

[d] Ab. 1. 3, 4

[e] Ab. 1. 2

Ab. 1. 3

[1] Zunz has well pointed out that, if in Ab. i. 4 the first 'couple' is said to have 'received from them'—while only Antigonus is mentioned in the preceding Mishnah, it must imply Antigonus and his unnamed disciples and followers. In general, I may take this opportunity of stating that, except for special reasons, I shall not refer to previous writers on this subject, partly because it would necessitate too many quotations, but chiefly because the line of argument I have taken differs from that of my predecessors.

BOOK
I

respectively, the *Nasi* (president), and *Ab-beth-din* (vice-president, of the *Sanhedrin*). Of the first three of these 'couples' it may be said that, except significant allusions to the circumstances and dangers of their times, their recorded utterances clearly point to the development of the purely *Sopheric* teaching, that is, to the Rabbinistic part of their functions. From the fourth 'couple,' which consists of Simon ben Shetach, who figured so largely in the political history of the later Maccabees[1] (as *Ab-beth-din*), and his superior in learning and judgment, Jehudah ben Tabbai (as *Nasi*), we have again utterances which show, in harmony with the political history of the time, that judicial functions had been once more restored to the Rabbis. The last of the five couples brings us to the time of Herod and of Christ.

We have seen that, during the period of severe domestic troubles, beginning with the persecutions under the Seleucidæ, which marked the mortal struggle between Judaism and Grecianism, the 'Great Assembly' had disappeared from the scene. The *Sopherim* had ceased to be a party in power. They had become the *Zeqenim*, 'Elders,' whose task was purely ecclesiastical — the preservation of their religion, such as the dogmatic labours of their predecessors had made it. Yet another period opened with the advent of the Maccabees. These had been raised into power by the enthusiasm of the *Chasidim*, or 'pious ones,' who formed the nationalist party in the land, and who had gathered around the liberators of their faith and country. But the later bearing of the Maccabees had alienated the nationalists. Henceforth they sink out of view, or, rather, the extreme section of them merged in the extreme section of the Pharisees, till fresh national calamities awakened a new nationalist party. Instead of the *Chasidim*, we see now two religious parties within the Synagogue — the Pharisees and the Sadducees. The latter originally represented a reaction from the Pharisees — the moderate men, who sympathised with the later tendencies of the Maccabees. Josephus places the origin of these two schools in the time of Jonathan, the successor of Judas

a 160–143 B.C.

Maccabee,[a] and with this other Jewish notices agree. Jonathan accepted from the foreigner (the Syrian) the High-Priestly dignity, and combined with it that of secular ruler. But this is not all. The earlier Maccabees surrounded themselves with a governing

b The Γε-
ρουσία,
1 Macc. xii.
6; xiii. 36;
xiv. 28; Jos.
Ant. xiii. 4.
9; 5. 8

eldership.[b][2] On the coins of their reigns this is designated as the *Chebher*, or eldership (association) of the Jews. Thus, theirs was what

---

[1] See Appendix IV.: 'Political History of the Jews from the Reign of Alexander to the Accession of Herod.'

[2] At the same time some kind of ruling λερουσία existed earlier than at this period, if we may judge from *Jos.*Ant. xii 3. 3.

Josephus designates as an aristocratic government,[a] and of which he somewhat vaguely says, that it lasted 'from the Captivity until the descendants of the Asmoneans set up kingly government.' In this aristocratic government the High-Priest would rather be the chief of a representative ecclesiastical body of rulers. This state of things continued until the great breach between Hyrcanus, the fourth from Judas Maccabee, and the Pharisaical party,[1] which is equally recorded by Josephus [b] and the Talmud,[c] with only variations of names and details. The dispute apparently arose from the desire of the Pharisees, that Hyrcanus should be content with the secular power, and resign the Pontificate. But it ended in the persecution, and removal from power, of the Pharisees. Very significantly, Jewish tradition introduces again at this time those purely ecclesiastical authorities which are designated as 'the couples.'[d] In accordance with this, altered state of things, the name 'Chebher' now disappears from the coins of the Maccabees, and the Rabbinical celebrities ('the couples' or *Zugoth*) are only teachers of traditionalism, and ecclesiastical authorities. The 'eldership,'[e] which under the earlier Maccabees was called 'the tribunal of the Asmoneans,'[f][2] now passed into the *Sanhedrin*.[3][g] Thus we place the origin of this institution about the time of Hyrcanus. With this Jewish tradition fully agrees.[4] The power of the Sanhedrin would, of course, vary with political circumstances, being at times almost absolute, as in the reign of the Pharisaic devotee-Queen, Alexandra, while at others it was shorn of all but ecclesiastical authority. But as the Sanhedrin was in full force at the time of Jesus, its organisation will claim our attention in the sequel.

After this brief outline of the origin and development of an institution which exerted such decisive influence on the future of Israel, it seems necessary similarly to trace the growth of the 'traditions of the Elders,' so as to understand what, alas! so effectually, opposed the new doctrine of the Kingdom. The first place must here be assigned to those legal determinations, which traditionalism declared absolutely binding on all—not only of equal, but even greater obligation than Scripture itself.[5] And this not illogically, since tradition was equally

CHAP.
VIII

[a] Ant. xi. 4. 8

[b] Ant. xiii. 10. 5. 6
[c] Kidd. 66 a

[d] Jer. Maas Sheni v. end, p. 56 d
Jer. Sot. ix. p. 24 a

[e] γερουσια

[f] בית
רינו של
חשמונאים
Sanh 82 a;
Ab. Z. 36 b

[g] συνέδριον
בית דין
in the N.T also once γερουσία, Acts v. 21, and twice πρεσβυτέριον St. Luke xxii. 66; Acts xxii 5

But he uses the term somewhat vaguely, applying it even to the time of Jaddua (Ant. xi. 8. 2).

[1] Even Ber. 48 a furnishes evidence of this 'enmity.' On the hostile relations between the Pharisaical party and the Maccabees see *Hamburger*, Real-Enc. ii. p. 367. Comp. Jer. Taan. iv. 5.

[2] *Derenbourg* takes a different view, and identifies the tribunal of the Asmoneans with the Sanhedrin. This seems

to me, historically, impossible. But his opinion to that effect (u. s. p. 87) is apparently contradicted at p. 93.

[3] *Schürer*, following *Wieseler*, supposes the Sanhedrin to have been of Roman institution. But the arguments of *Wieseler* on this point (Beitr. zur richt. Würd. d. Evang. p. 224) are inconclusive.

[4] Comp. *Derenbourg*, u. s. p. 95.

[5] Thus we read: 'The sayings of the

BOOK
I

of Divine origin with Holy Scripture, and authoritatively explained its meaning.; supplemented it; gave it application to cases not expressly provided for, perhaps not even foreseen in Biblical times ; and generally guarded its sanctity by extending and adding to its provisions, drawing ' a hedge,' around its ' garden enclosed.' Thus, in new and dangerous circumstances, would the full meaning of God's Law, to its every tittle and iota, be elicited and obeyed. Thus also would their feet be arrested, who might stray from within, or break in from without. Accordingly, so important was tradition, that the greatest merit a Rabbi could claim was the strictest adherence to the traditions, which he had received from his teacher. Nor might one Sanhedrin annul, or set aside, the decrees of its predecessors. To such length did they go in this worship of the letter, that the great Hillel was actually wont to mispronounce a word, because his teacher before him had done so.[a]

a Eduy. 1. 3.
See the
comment of
Maimon-
ides

These traditional ordinances, as already stated, bear the general name of the *Halakhah*, as indicating alike the way in which the fathers had walked, and that which their children were bound to follow.[1] These *Halakhoth* were either simply the laws laid down in Scripture; or else derived from, or traced to it by some ingenious and artificial method of exegesis ; or added to it, by way of amplification and for safety's sake; or, finally, legalised customs. They provided for every possible and impossible case, entered into every detail of private, family, and public life ; and with iron logic, unbending rigour, and most minute analysis pursued and dominated man, turn whither he might, laying on him a yoke which was truly unbearable. The return which it offered was the pleasure and distinction of knowledge, the acquisition of righteousness, and the final attainment of rewards ; one of its chief advantages over our modern traditionalism, that it was expressly forbidden to draw inferences from these traditions, which should have the force of fresh legal determinations.[2]

In describing the historical growth of the *Halakhah*,[3] we may

elders have more weight than those of the prophets ' (Jer. Ber. i. 7); ' an offence against the sayings of the Scribes is worse than one against those of Scripture ' (Sanh. xi. 3). Compare also Er. 21 *b* The comparison between such claims and those sometimes set up on behalf of ' creeds ' and ' articles ' (*Kitto's* Cyclop., 2nd ed., p. 786, col *a*) does not seem to me applicable. In the introduction to the Midr. on Lament. it is inferred from Jer. ix. 12, 13, that to forsake the law—in the Rabbinic sense—was worse than adolatry, uncleanness, or the shedding of blood. See generally that Introduction.

[1] It is so explained in the *Aruch* (ed *Landau*, vol. ii. p. 529, col *b*).

[2] Comp. *Hamburger*, u. s. p. 343.

[3] Comp. here especially the detailed description by *Herzfeld* (u. s. vol. iii. pp. 226, 263); also the Introduction of Maimonides, and the very able and learned works (not sufficiently appre-

dismiss in a few sentences the legends of Jewish tradition about patriarchal times. They assure us, that there was an Academy and a Rabbinic tribunal of Shem, and they speak of traditions delivered by that Patriarch to Jacob; of diligent attendance by the latter on the Rabbinic College; of a tractate (in 400 sections) on idolatry by Abraham, and of his observance of the whole traditional law; of the introduction of the three daily times of prayer, successively by Abraham, Isaac, and Jacob; of the three benedictions in the customary 'grace at meat,' as propounded by Moses, Joshua, and David and Solomon; of the Mosaic introduction of the practice of reading lessons from the law on Sabbaths, New Moons, and Feast Days, and even on the Mondays and Thursdays ; and of that, by the same authority, of preaching on the three great festivals about those feasts. Further, they ascribe to Moses the arrangement of the priesthood into eight courses (that into sixteen to Samuel, and that into twenty-four to David), as also, the duration of the time for marriage festivities, and for mourning. But evidently these are vague statements, with the object of tracing traditionalism and its observances to primæval times, even as legend had it, that Adam was born circumcised,[a] and later writers that he had kept all the ordinances.

But other principles apply to the traditions, from Moses downwards. According to the Jewish view, God had given Moses on Mount Sinai alike the oral and the written Law, that is, the Law with all its interpretations and applications. From Ex. xx. 1, it was inferred, that God had communicated to Moses the Bible, the Mishnah, and Talmud, and the Haggadah, even to that which scholars would in latest times propound.[1] In answer to the somewhat natural objection, why the Bible alone had been written, it was said that Moses had proposed to write down all the teaching entrusted to him, but the Almighty had refused, on account of the future subjection of Israel to the nations, who would take from them the written Law. Then the unwritten traditions would remain to separate between Israel and the Gentiles. Popular exegesis found this indicated even in the language of prophecy.[b]

CHAP. VIII

[a] Midr. Shochar Tobh on Ps. ix. 6. ed. Warshau, p. 14 *b*; Ab. de R. Nath. 2

[b] Hos. viii. 12; comp. Shem. R. 47

ciated) by Dr. *H. S. Hirschfeld*, Hala-chische Exegese (Berlin, 1840), and Hagadische Exegese (Berlin, 1847). Perhaps I may also take leave to refer to the corresponding chapters in my 'History of the Jewish Nation.'
[1] Similarly, the expressions in Ex. xxiv. 12 were thus explained: 'the tables of stone,' the ten commandments; the 'law,' the written Law; the 'commandments,' the Mishnah; 'which I have written,' the Prophets and Hagiographa; 'that thou mayest teach them,' the Talmud—'which shows that they were all given to Moses on Sinai' (Ber. 5 *a*, lines 11–16). A like application was made of the various clauses in Cant. vii. 12 (Erub. 21 *b*). Nay, by an alteration of the words in Hos. viii. 10, it was shown that the banished had been brought back for the merit of their study [of the sacrificial sections] of the Mishnah (Vayyik R. 7).

BOOK
I

ᵃ Ex. xxxiv.
27
ᵇ Jer. Chag.
p. 76 d

But traditionalism went further, and placed the oral actually above the written Law. The expression,ᵃ 'After the tenor of these words I have made a covenant with thee and with Israel,' was explained as meaning, that God's covenant was founded on the *spoken*, in opposition to the written words.ᵇ If the written was thus placed below the oral Law, we can scarcely wonder that the reading of the Hagiographa was actually prohibited to the people on the Sabbath, from fear that it might divert attention from the learned discourses of the Rabbis. The study of them on that day was only allowed for the purpose of learned investigation and discussions.ᶜ¹

ᶜ Tos.
Shabb. xiv.

But if traditionalism was not to be committed to writing by Moses, measures had been taken to prevent oblivion or inaccuracy. Moses had always repeated a traditional law successively to Aaron, to his sons, and to the elders of the people, and they again in turn to each other, in such wise, that Aaron heard the Mishnah four times, his sons three times, the Elders twice, and the people once. But even this was not all, for by successive repetitions (of Aaron, his sons, and the Elders) the people also heard it four times.ᵈ And, before his death, Moses had summoned any one to come forward, if he had forgotten aught of what he had heard and learned.ᵉ But these 'Halakhoth of Moses from Sinai' do not make up the whole of traditionalism. According to Maimonides, it consists of five, but more critically of three classes.² The *first* of these comprises both such ordinances as are found in the Bible itself, and the so-called *Halakhoth of Moses from Sinai*—that is, such laws and usages as prevailed from time immemorial, and which, according to the Jewish view, had been *orally* delivered to, but not written down by Moses. *For these*, therefore, *no proof was to be sought in Scripture*—at most support, or confirmatory allusion (*Asmakhtu*).³ Nor were these open to discussion. The *second* class formed the 'oral law,'ᶠ or the 'traditional teaching'ᵍ in the stricter sense. To this class belonged all that was supposed to be implied in, or that could be deduced from, the Law of Moses.⁴ The latter contained, indeed, in substance or

ⁱ Erub. 54b

Deut. 1. 5

ᶠ תורה
שבעל פה
ᵍ דברי
קבלה

---

¹ Another reason also is, however, mentioned for his prohibition.

² *Hirschfeld*, u. s. pp. 92–99.

³ From סמך, to lean against. At the same time the ordinances, for which an appeal could be made to *Asmakhta*, were better liked than those which rested on tradition alone (Jer. Chag. p. 76, col *d*).

⁴ In connection with this it is very significant that R. Jochanan ben Zaccai,

who taught not many years after the Crucifixion of Christ, was wont to say, that, in the future, Halakhahs in regard to purity, which had not the support of Scripture, would be repeated (Sot. 27 *b*, line 16 from top). In general, the teaching of R. Jochanan should be studied to understand the unacknowledged influence which Christianity exercised upon the Synagogue.

germ, everything; but it had not been brought out, till circumstances CHAP.
successfully evolved what from the first had been provided in princi- VIII
ple. *For this class of ordinances reference to, and proof from, Scripture*
was required. Not so for the *third* class of ordinances, which were
'the hedge' drawn by the Rabbis around the Law, to prevent any
breach of the Law or customs, to ensure their exact observance, or to
meet peculiar circumstances and dangers. These ordinances constituted 'the sayings of the Scribes'[a] or 'of the Rabbis'[b][1]—and were
either *positive* in their character (*Teqqanoth*), or else *negative* (*Gezeroth*
from *gazar* to cut off'). Perhaps the distinction of these two
cannot always be strictly carried out. But it was probably to this
third class especially, confessedly unsupported by Scripture, that
these words of Christ referred:[c] 'All therefore whatsoever they
tell you, that do and observe; but do not ye after their works: for
they say, and do not. For they bind heavy burdens and grievous to
be borne, and lay them on men's shoulders; but with their finger
they will not move them away (set in motion).'[2] This view has twofold confirmation. For, this third class of Halakhic ordinances was
the only one open to the discussion of the learned, the ultimate decision being according to the majority. Yet it possessed practically
(though not theoretically) the same authority as the other two classes.
In further confirmation of our view the following may be quoted: 'A
Gezerah (*i.e.* this third class of ordinances) is not to be laid on the
congregation, unless the majority of the congregation is able to bear
it'[d]—words which read like a commentary on those of Jesus, and
show that these burdens could be laid on, or moved away, according
to the varying judgment or severity of a Rabbinic College.[3]

This body of traditional ordinances forms the subject of the *Mish-*
nah, or second, repeated law. We have here to place on one side the

[a] דִּבְרֵי
סוֹפְרִים
[b] דְּרַבָּנָן

[c] St. Matt.
xxiii. 3, 4

[d] B. Kam.79
b

---

[1] But this is not always.
[2] To elucidate the meaning of Christ, it
seemed necessary to submit an avowedly
difficult text to fresh criticism. I have
taken the word κινεῖν, *moveo* in the
sense of *ire facio* (*Grimm*, Clavis N.T. ed.
2[da], p. 241 *a*), but I have not adopted
the inference of *Meyer* (Krit. Exeget.
Handb. p. 455). In classical Greek also
κινεῖν is used for 'to remove, to alter.'
My reasons against what may be called
the traditional interpretation of St. Matt.
xxiii. 3, 4, are: 1. It seems scarcely possible to suppose that, before such an audience, Christ would have contemplated
the possibility of not observing either of

the two first classes of *Halakhoth*, which
were regarded as beyond controversy.
2. It could scarcely be truthfully charged
against the Scribes and Pharisees, that
they did not attempt to keep themselves
the ordinances which they imposed upon
others. The expression in the parallel
passage (St. Luke xi. 46) must be explained in accordance with the commentation on St. Matt. xxiii. 4. Nor is
there any serious difficulty about it.
[3] For the classification, arrangement,
origin, and enumeration of these Halakhoth, see Appendix V.: 'Rabbinic
Theology and literature.'

Law of Moses as recorded in the Pentateuch, as standing by itself. All else—even the teaching of the Prophets and of the Hagiographa, as well as the oral traditions—bore the general name of *Qabbalah*—'that which has been received.' The sacred study—or *Midrash*, in the original application of the term—concerned either the *Halakhah*, traditional *ordinance*, which was always 'that which had been heard' (*Shematha*), or else the *Haggadah*, 'that which was said' upon the authority of individuals, not as legal ordinance. It was illustration, commentary, anecdote, clever or learned saying, &c. At first the *Halakhah* remained unwritten, probably owing to the disputes between Pharisees and Sadducees. But the necessity of fixedness and order led in course of time to more or less complete collections of the *Halakhoth*.[1] The oldest of these is ascribed to R. Akiba, in the time

of the Emperor Hadrian.[a2] But the authoritative collection in the so-called *Mishnah* is the work of Jehudah the Holy, who died about the end of the second century of our era.

Altogether, the Mishnah comprises six 'Orders' (*Sedarim*), each devoted to a special class of subjects.[3] These 'Orders' are divided into tractates (*Massikhtoth, Massekhtiyoth*, 'textures, webs'), of which there are sixty-three (or else sixty-two) in all. These tractates are again subdivided into chapters (*Peraqim*)—in all 525, which severally consist of a certain number of verses, or *Mishnahs* (*Mishnayoth*, in all 4,187). Considering the variety and complexity of the subjects treated, the Mishnah is arranged with remarkable logical perspicuity. The

---

[1] See the learned remarks of *Levy* about the reasons for the earlier prohibition of writing down the oral law, and the final collection of the Mishnah (Neuhebr. u. Chald. Wörterb. vol. ii. p. 435).

[2] These collections are enumerated in the Midrash on Eccles. xii. 3. They are also distinguished as 'the former' and 'the later' Mishnah (Nedar. 91 *a*).

[3] The first 'Order' (*Zeraim*, 'seeds') begins with the ordinances concerning 'benedictions,' or the time, mode, manner, and character of the prayers prescribed. It then goes on to detail what may be called the religio-agrarian laws (such as tithing, Sabbatical years, first fruits, &c.). The second 'Order' (*Moed*, 'festive time') discusses all connected with the Sabbath observance and the other festivals. The third 'Order' (*Nashim*, 'women') treats of all that concerns betrothal, marriage and divorce, but also includes a tractate on the Nasirate. The fourth 'Order' (*Neziqin*, 'damages') contains the civil and criminal law. Characteristically, it includes all the ordinances concerning idol-worship (in the tractate *Abhodah Zarah*) and 'the sayings of the Fathers' (*Abhoth*). The fifth 'Order' (*Qodashim*, 'holy things') treats of the various classes of sacrifices, offerings, and things belonging (as the first-born), or dedicated, to God, and of all questions which can be grouped under 'sacred things' (such as the redemption, exchange, or alienation of what had been dedicated to God). It also includes the laws concerning the daily morning and evening service (*Tamid*), and a description of the structure and arrangements of the Temple (*Middoth*, 'the measurements'). Finally, the sixth 'Order' (*Toharoth*, 'cleannesses') gives every ordinance connected with the questions of 'clean and unclean,' alike as regards human beings, animals, and inanimate things.-

language is Hebrew, though of course not that of the Old Testament.
The words rendered necessary by the new circumstances are chiefly
derived from the Greek, the Syriac, and the Latin, with Hebrew terminations.[1] But all connected with social intercourse, or ordinary life
(such as contracts), is written, not in Hebrew, but in Aramæan, as
the language of the people.

But the traditional law embodied other materials than the
Halakhoth collected in the Mishnah. Some that had not been
recorded there, found a place in the works of certain Rabbis, or were
derived from their schools. These are called *Boraithas*—that is, traditions *external* to the Mishnah. Finally, there were ' additions' (or
Tosephtoth), dating after the completion of the Mishnah, but probably
not later than the third century of our era. Such there are to not
fewer than fifty-two out of the sixty-three Mishnic tractates. When
speaking of the *Halakhah* as distinguished from the *Haggadah*, we
must not, however, suppose that the latter could be entirely separated
from it. In point of fact, one whole tractate in the *Mishnah* (Aboth:
The Sayings of the ' Fathers') is entirely *Haggadah*; a second (*Middoth*:
the ' Measurements of the Temple') has *Halakhah* in only fourteen
places; while in the rest of the tractates *Haggadah* occurs in not
fewer than 207 places. [2] Only thirteen out of the sixty-three tractates
of the *Mishnah* are entirely free from *Haggadah*.

Hitherto we have only spoken of the Mishnah. But this comprises only a very small part of traditionalism. In course of time the
discussions, illustrations, explanations, and additions to which the
Mishnah gave rise, whether in its application, or in the Academies of
the Rabbis, were authoritatively collected and edited in what are
known as the two *Talmuds* or *Gemaras*. [3] If we imagine something
combining law reports, a Rabbinical ' Hansard,' and notes of a theological debating club—all thoroughly Oriental, full of digressions,
anecdotes, quaint sayings, fancies, legends, and too often of what,
from its profanity, superstition, and even obscenity, could scarcely be
quoted, we may form some general idea of what the Talmud is. The
oldest of these two Talmuds dates from about the close of the fourth
century of our era. It is the product of the Palestinian Academies,
and hence called the *Jerusalem* Talmud. The second is about a century
younger, and the outcome of the Babylonian schools, hence called the

---

[1] Comp. the very interesting tractate
by Dr. *Brüll* (Fremdspr Redensart in d.
Talmud), as well as Dr. *Eisler's* Beiträge
z. Rabb. u. Alterthumsk., 3 fascic; *Sachs*,
Beitr. z. Rabb u. Alterthumsk.

[2] Comp. the enumeration in *Pinner*,
u. s.
[3] *Talmud*: that which is learned, doctrine. *Gemara*: either the same, or else
' perfection,' ' completion.'

Babylon (afterwards also 'our') Talmud. We do not possess either of these works complete.[1] The most defective is the Jerusalem Talmud, which is also much briefer, and contains far fewer discussions than that of Babylon. The Babylon Talmud, which in its present form extends over thirty-six out of the sixty-three tractates of the Mishnah, is about ten or eleven times the size of the latter, and more than four times that of the Jerusalem Talmud. It occupies (in our editions), with marginal commentations, 2,947 folio leaves (pages *a* and *b*). Both Talmuds are written in Aramæan; the one in its western, the other in its eastern dialect, and in both the Mishnah is discussed *seriatim*, and clause by clause. Of the character of these discussions it would be impossible to convey an adequate idea. When we bear in mind the many sparkling, beautiful, and occasionally almost sublime passages in the Talmud, but especially that its forms of thought and expression so often recall those of the New Testament, only prejudice and hatred could indulge in indiscriminate vituperation. On the other hand, it seems unaccountable how any one who has read a Talmudic tractate, or even part of one, could compare the Talmud with the New Testament, or find in the one the origin of the other.

To complete our brief survey, it should be added that our editions of the Babylon Talmud contain (at the close of vol. ix. and after the fourth 'Order') certain Boraithas. Of these there were originally *nine*, but two of the smaller tractates (on 'the memorial fringes,' and on 'non-Israelites') have not been preserved. The first of these Boraithas is entitled *Abhoth de Rabbi Nathan*, and partially corresponds with a tractate of a similar name in the Mishnah.[2] Next

---

[1] The following will explain our meaning: On the *first* 'order' we have the Jerusalem Talmud complete, that is, on every tractate (comprising in all 65 folio leaves), while the Babylon Talmud extends only over its first tractate (*Berakhoth*). On the *second* order, the four last chapters of one tractate (*Shabbath*) are wanting in the *Jerusalem*, and one whole tractate (*Sheqalim*) in the *Babylon* Talmud. The *third* order is complete in both Gemaras. On the *fourth* order a chapter is wanting in one tractate (*Makkoth*) in the *Jerusalem*, and two whole tractates (*Eduyoth* and *Abhoth*) in both Gemaras. The *fifth* order is wholly wanting in the *Jerusalem*, and two and a half tractates of it (*Middoth, Qinnim*, and half *Tamid*) in the Babylon Talmud. Of the sixth order only one tractate (*Niddah*) exists in both Gemaras. The principal Hala-

khoth were collected in a work (dating from about 800 A.D.) entitled *Halakhoth Gedoloth*. They are arranged to correspond with the weekly lectionary of the Pentateuch in a work entitled *Sheeltoth* ('Questions:' best ed. *Dghernfurth*, 1786). The Jerusalem Talmud extends over 39, the Babylonian over 36½ tractates—15½ tractates have no Gemara at all.

[2] The last ten chapters curiously group together events or things under numerals from 10 downwards. The most generally interesting of these is that of the 10 *Nequdoth*, or passages of Scripture in which letters are marked by dots, together with the explanation of their reasons (ch. xxxiv.). The whole Boraitha seems composed of parts of three different works, and consists of forty (or forty-one) chapters, and occupies ten folio leaves.

follow six minor tractates. These are respectively entitled *Sopherim* (Scribes),[1] detailing the ordinances about copying the Scriptures, the ritual of the Lectionary, and festive prayers; *Ebhel Rabbathi* or *Semakhoth*,[2] containing Halakhah and Haggadah about funeral and mourning observances; *Kallah*,[3] on the married relationship; *Derekh Erets*,[4] embodying moral directions and the rules and customs of social intercourse; *Derekh Erets Zuta*,[5] treating of similar subjects, but as regards learned students; and, lastly, the *Pereq ha Shalom*,[6] which is a eulogy on *peace*. All these tractates date, at least in their present form, later than the Talmudic period.[7]

But when the *Halakhah*, however varied in its application, was something fixed and stable, the utmost latitude was claimed and given in the *Haggadah*. It is sadly characteristic, that, practically, the main body of Jewish dogmatic and moral theology is really only *Haggadah*, and hence of no absolute authority. The *Halakhah* indicated with the most minute and painful punctiliousness every legal ordinance as to outward observances, and it explained every bearing of the Law of Moses. But beyond this it left the inner man, the spring of actions, untouched. What he was to believe and what to feel, was chiefly matter of the Haggadah. Of course the laws of morality, and religion, as laid down in the Pentateuch, were fixed principles, but there was the greatest divergence and latitude in the explanation and application of many of them. A man might hold or propound almost any views, so long as he contravened not the Law of Moses, as it was understood, and adhered in teaching and practice to the traditional ordinances. In principle it was the same liberty which the Romish Church accords to its professing members—only with much wider application, since the debatable ground embraced so many matters of faith, and the liberty given was not only that of private opinion but of public utterance. We emphasise this, because the absence of authoritative direction and the latitude in matters of faith

---

[1] In twenty-one chapters, each containing a number of Halakhahs, and occupying in all four folio leaves.
[2] In fourteen chapters, occupying rather more than three folio leaves.
[3] It fills little more than a folio page.
[4] In eleven chapters, covering about 1¾ folio leaves.
[5] In nine chapters, filling one folio leaf.
[6] Little more than a folio column.
[7] Besides these, *Raphael Kirchheim* has published (Frankfort, 1851) the so-called seven smaller tractates, covering

altogether, with abundant notes, only forty-four small pages, which treat of the copying of the Bible (*Sepher Torah*, in five chapters), of the *Mezuzah*, or memorial on the doorposts (in two chapters), of *Phylacteries* (*Tephillin*, in one chapter), of the *Tsitsith*, or memorial-fringes (in one chapter), of *Slaves* (*Abhadim*, in three chapters), of the *Cutheans*, or Samaritans (in two chapters), and, finally, a curious tractate on *Proselytes* (*Gerim*, in four chapters).

and inner feeling stand side by side, and in such sharp contrast, with the most minute punctiliousness in all matters of outward observance. And here we may mark the fundamental distinction between the teaching of Jesus and Rabbinism. He left the *Halakhah* untouched, putting it, as it were, on one side, as something quite secondary, while He insisted as primary on that which to them was chiefly matter of Haggadah. And this rightly so, for, in His own words, 'Not that which goeth into the mouth defileth a man; but that which cometh out of the mouth,' since 'those things which proceed out of the mouth come forth from the heart, and they defile the man.'[a] The difference was one of fundamental principle, and not merely of development, form, or detail. The one developed the Law in its outward direction as ordinances and commandments; the other in its inward application as life and liberty. Thus Rabbinism occupied one pole—and the outcome of its tendency to pure externalism was the Halakhah, all that was internal and higher being merely Haggadic. The teaching of Jesus occupied the opposite pole. Its starting-point was the inner sanctuary in which God was known and worshipped, and it might well leave the Rabbinic Halakhoth aside, as not worth controversy, to be in the meantime 'done and observed,' in the firm assurance that, in the course of its development, the spirit would create its own appropriate forms, or, to use a New Testament figure, the new wine burst the old bottles. And, lastly, as closely connected with all this, and marking the climax of contrariety: Rabbinism started with demand of outward obedience and righteousness, and pointed to sonship as its goal; the Gospel started with the free gift of forgiveness through faith and of sonship, and pointed to obedience and righteousness as its goal.

In truth, Rabbinism, as such, had no system of theology; only what ideas, conjectures, or fancies the Haggadah yielded concerning God, Angels, demons, man, his future destiny and present position, and Israel, with its past history and coming glory. Accordingly, by the side of what is noble and pure, what a terrible mass of utter incongruities, of conflicting statements and too often debasing superstitions, the outcome of ignorance and narrow nationalism; of legendary colouring of Biblical narratives and scenes, profane, coarse, and degrading to them; the Almighty Himself and His Angels taking part in the conversations of Rabbis, and the discussions of Academies; nay, forming a kind of heavenly Sanhedrin, which occasionally requires the aid of an earthly Rabbi.[1] The miraculous merges into the ridiculous, and

---

[1] Thus, in B. Mez. 86 *a*, we read of a   the subject of purity, when Rabbah was
discussion in the heavenly Academy on   summoned to heaven by death, although

even the revolting. Miraculous cures, miraculous supplies, miraculous help, all for the glory of great Rabbis,[1] who by a look or word can kill, and restore to life. At their bidding the eyes of a rival fall out, and are again inserted. Nay, such was the veneration due to Rabbis, that R. Joshua used to kiss the stone on which R. Eliezer had sat and lectured, saying: 'This stone is like Mount Sinai, and he who sat on it like the Ark.' Modern ingenuity has, indeed, striven to suggest deeper symbolical meaning for such stories. It should own the terrible contrast existing side by side: Hebrewism and Judaism, the Old Testament and traditionalism; and it should recognise its deeper cause in the absence of that element of spiritual and inner life which Christ has brought. Thus as between the two—the old and the new —it may be fearlessly asserted that, as regards their substance and spirit, there is not a difference, but a total divergence, of fundamental principle between Rabbinism and the New Testament, so that comparison between them is not possible. Here there is absolute contrariety.

The painful fact just referred to is only too clearly illustrated by the relation in which traditionalism places itself to the Scriptures of the Old Testament, even though it acknowledges their inspiration and authority. The Talmud has it,[a] that he who busies himself with Scripture only (*i.e.* without either the *Mishnah* or *Gemara*) has merit, and yet no merit.[2] Even the comparative paucity of references to the Bible in the Mishnah[3] is significant Israel had made void

[a] Baba
Mets. 33 *a*

---

this required a miracle, since he was constantly engaged in sacred study. Shocking to write, it needed the authority of Rabbah to attest the correctness of the Almighty's statement on the Halakhic question discussed.

[1] Some of these miracles are detailed in B. Mets. 85 *b*. 86 *a*. Thus, Resh Lakish, when searching for the tomb of R. Chija, found that it was miraculously removed from his sight, as being too sacred for ordinary eyes. The same Rabbi claimed such merit, that for his sake the Law should never be forgotten in Israel. Such was the power of the patriarchs that, if they had been raised up together, they would have brought Messiah before His time. When R. Chija prayed, successively a storm arose, the rain descended, and the earth trembled. Again, Rabbah, when about to be arrested, caused the face of the messenger to be turned to his back, and again restored it; next, by his prayer he made a wall burst, and so

escaped. In Abhod. Zar. 17 *b*, a miracle is recorded in favour of R. Eleazar, to set him free from his persecutors, or, rather, to attest a false statement which he made in order to escape martyrdom. For further extravagant praises of the Rabbis, comp. Sanh. 101 *a*.

[2] Similarly we read in Aboth d. R. Nathan 29: 'He who is master of the Midrash, but knows no Halakhahs, is like a hero, but there are no arms in his hand. He that is master of the Halakhoth, but knows nothing of the Midrashim, is a weak person who is provided with arms. But he that is master of both is both a hero and armed.'

[3] Most of these, of course, are from the Pentateuch. References to any other Old Testament books are generally loosely made, and serve chiefly as *points d'appui* for Rabbinical sayings. Scriptural quotations occur in 51 out of the 63 tractates of the Mishnah, the number of verses quoted being 430. A quotation in the

the Law by its traditions.   Under a load of outward ordinances and observances its spirit had been crushed.   The religion as well as the grand hope of the Old Testament had become externalized.   And so alike Heathenism and Judaism—for it was no longer the pure religion of the Old Testament—each following its own direction, had reached its goal.   All was prepared and waiting.   The very porch had been built, through which the new, and yet old, religion was to pass into the ancient world, and the ancient world into the new religion. Only one thing was needed: the Coming of the Christ.   As yet darkness covered the earth, and gross darkness lay upon the people. But far away the golden light of the new day was already tingeing the edge of the horizon.   Presently would the Lord arise upon Zion, and His glory be seen upon her.   Presently would the Voice from out the wilderness prepare the way of the Lord; presently would it herald the Coming of His Christ to Jew and Gentile, and that Kingdom of heaven, which, established upon earth, is righteousness, and peace, and joy in the Holy Ghost.[1]

Mishnah is generally introduced by the formula 'as it is said.' This in all but sixteen instances, where the quotation is prefaced by, 'Scripture means to say.' But, in general, the difference in the mode of quotation in Rabbinic writings seems to depend partly on the context, but chiefly on the place and time. Thus, 'as it is written' is a Chaldee mode of quotation. Half the quotations in the Talmud are prefaced by 'as it is said;' a fifth of them by 'as it is written;' a tenth by 'Scripture means to say;' and the remaining fifth by various other formulas. Comp. *Pinner's* Introduction to Berakhoth. In the Jerusalem Talmud no *al-tikré* ('read not so, but read so') occurs, for the purposes of textual criticism. In the Talmud a favourite mode of quoting from the Pentateuch, made in about 600 passages, is by introducing it as spoken or written by רֶחֱמָנָא. The various modes in which Biblical quotations are made in Jewish writings are enumerated in *Surenhusius Bίβλος καταλλαγῆς*, pp. 1–56.

[1] For details on the Jewish views on the Canon, and historical and mystical theology, see Appendix V.: 'Rabbinic Theology and Literature.'

Book II.

FROM THE MANGER IN BETHLEHEM TO THE BAPTISM IN JORDAN.

'Fortitudo infirmatur,
Parva fit immensitas;
Liberator alligatur,
Nascitur æternitas.
O quam mira perpetrasti
Jesu propter hominem!
Tam ardenter quem amasti
Paradiso exulem.'—*Ancient Latin Hymn*

CHAPTER I.

IN JERUSALEM WHEN HEROD REIGNED.

IF the dust of ten centuries could have been wiped from the eyelids of those sleepers, and one of them who thronged Jerusalem in the highday of its glory, during the reign of King Solomon, had returned to its streets, he would scarcely have recognised the once familiar city. Then, as now, a Jewish king reigned, who bore undivided rule over the whole land ; then, as now, the city was filled with riches and adorned with palaces and architectural monuments ; then, as now, Jerusalem was crowded with strangers from all lands. Solomon and Herod were each the last Jewish king over the Land of Promise;[1] Solomon and Herod, each, built the Temple. But with the son of David began, and with the Idumæan ended, ' the kingdom '; or rather, having fulfilled its mission, it gave place to the spiritual world-kingdom of ' David's greater Son.' The sceptre departed from Judah to where the nations were to gather under its sway. And the Temple which Solomon built was the first. In it the Shekhinah dwelt visibly. The Temple which Herod reared was the last. The ruins of its burning, which the torch of the Romans had kindled, were never to be restored. Herod was not the antitype, he was the Barabbas, of David's Royal Son.

In other respects, also, the difference was almost equally great. The four 'companion-like' hills on which the city was built,[a] the a **Ps.** cxxii deep clefts by which it was surrounded, the Mount of Olives rising in the the east, were the same as a thousand years ago. There, as of old were the Pool of Siloam and the royal gardens—nay, the very wall that had then surrounded the city. And yet all was so altered as to be scarcely recognisable. The ancient Jebusite fort, the City of David, Mount Zion,[2] was now the priests' quarter, Ophel, and the old royal palace and stables had been thrown into the Temple area—now com-

---

[1] I do not here reckon the brief reign of King Agrippa.

[2] It will be seen that, with the most recent explorers, I locate Mount Zion *not* on the traditional site, on the western hill of Jerusalem, but on the eastern, south of the Temple area.

pletely levelled—where they formed the magnificent treble colonnade, known as the Royal Porch. Passing through it, and out by the Western Gate of the Temple, we stand on the immense bridge which spans the 'Valley of the Cheesemongers,' or the Tyropœon, and connects the Eastern with the Western hills of the city. It is perhaps here that we can best mark the outstanding features, and note the changes. On the right, as we look northward, are (on the Eastern hill) Ophel, the Priest-quarter, and the Temple—oh, how wondrously beautiful and enlarged, and rising terrace upon terrace, surrounded by massive walls: a palace, a fortress, a Sanctuary of shining marble and glittering gold. And beyond it frowns the old fortress of Baris, rebuilt by Herod, and named after his patron, Antonia. This is the Hill of Zion. Right below us is the cleft of the Tyropœon—and here creeps up northwards the 'Lower City' or Acra, in the form of a crescent, widening into an almost square 'suburb.' Across the Tyropœon, westward, rises the 'Upper City.' If the Lower City and suburb form the business-quarter with its markets, bazaars, and streets of trades and guilds, the 'Upper City' is that of palaces. Here, at the other end of the great bridge which connects the Temple with the 'Upper City,' is the palace of the Maccabees; beyond it, the Xystos, or vast colonnaded enclosure, where popular assemblies are held ; then the Palace of Ananias the High-Priest, and nearest to the Temple, 'the Council Chamber' and public Archives. Behind it, westwards, rise, terrace upon terrace, the stately mansions of the Upper City, till, quite in the north-west corner of the old city, we reach the Palace which Herod had built for himself—almost a city and fortress, flanked by three high towers, and enclosing spacious gardens. Beyond it again, and outside the city walls, both of the first and the second, stretches all north of the city the new suburb of Bezetha. Here on every side are gardens and villas; here passes the great northern road; out there must they have laid hold on Simon the Cyrenian, and here must have led the way to the place of the Crucifixion.

Changes that marked the chequered course of Israel's history had come even over the city walls. The first and oldest—that of David and Solomon—ran round the west side of the Upper City, then crossed south to the Pool of Siloam, and ran up east, round Ophel, till it reached the eastern enclosure of the Temple, whence it passed in a straight line to the point from which it had started, forming the northern boundary of the ancient city. But although this wall still existed, there was now a marked addition to it. When the Maccabee Jonathan finally cleared Jerusalem of the Syrian garrison that lay in Fort Acra,[a] he built a wall right 'through the middle of the city,' so as to shut out the foe.[b] This wall probably ran from the western angle of the Temple southwards, to near the pool of Siloam, following the winding course of the Tyropœon, but on the other side of it, where the declivity of the Upper City merged in the valley. Another monument of the Syrian Wars, of the Maccabees, and of Herod, was the fortress Antonia. Part of it had, probably, been formerly occupied by what was known as Fort Acra, of such unhappy prominence in the wars that preceded and marked the early Maccabean period. It had passed from the Ptolemies to the Syrians, and always formed the central spot round which the fight for the city turned. Judas Maccabee had not been able to take it. Jonathan had laid siege to it, and built the wall, to which reference has just been made, so as to isolate its garrison. It was at last taken by Simon, the brother and successor of Jonathan, and levelled with the ground.[c] Fort Baris, which was constructed by his successor Hyrcanus I.,[d] covered a much wider space. It lay on the north-western angle of the Temple, slightly jutting beyond it in the west, but not covering the whole northern area of the Temple. The rock on which it stood was higher than the Temple,[1] although lower than the hill up which the new suburb Bezetha crept, which, accordingly, was cut off by a deep ditch, for the safety of the fortress. Herod greatly enlarged and strengthened it. Within encircling walls the fort rose to a height of sixty feet, and was flanked by four towers, of which three had a height of seventy, the fourth (S.E.), which jutted into the Temple area, of 105 feet, so as to command the sacred enclosure. A subterranean passage led into the Temple itself,[e] which was also connected with it by colonnades and stairs. Herod had adorned as well as strengthened and enlarged, this fort (now Antonia), and made it a palace, an armed camp, and almost a city.[f]

Hitherto we have only spoken of the first, or old wall, which was fortified by sixty towers. The second wall, which had only fourteen towers, began at some point in the northern wall at the Gate Gennath, whence it ran north, and then east, so as to enclose Acra and the Suburb. It terminated at Fort Antonia. Beyond, and all around this second wall stretched, as already noticed, the new, as yet unenclosed suburb Bezetha, rising towards the north-east. But

CHAP.
I

[a] 1 Macc. i. 33, and often; but the precise situation of this 'fort' is in dispute

[b] 1 Macc. xii. 36; *Jos.* Ant. xiii. 5. 11; comp. with it xiv. 16. 2; War vi. 7. 2; 8. 1

[c] 141 B.C.

[d] 135-106 B.C.

[e] Ant. xv. 11. 7

[f] *Jos.* War v. 5. 8

---

[1] It is, to say the least, doubtful, whether the numeral 50 cubits (75 feet), which *Josephus* assigns to this rock (War v. 5. 8), applies to its height (comp. *Speiss,* Das Jerus. d. Jos. p. 66).

these changes were as nothing compared with those within the city itself. First and foremost was the great transformation in the Temple itself,[1] which, from a small building, little larger than an ordinary church, in the time of Solomon,[2] had become that great and glorious House which excited the admiration of the foreigner, and kindled the enthusiasm of every son of Israel. At the time of Christ it had been already forty-six years in building, and workmen were still, and for a long time, engaged on it.[3] But what a heterogeneous crowd thronged its porches and courts! Hellenists; scattered wanderers from the most distant parts of the earth—east, west, north, and south; Galileans, quick of temper and uncouth of Jewish speech; Judæans and Jerusalemites; white-robed Priests and Levites; Temple officials; broad-phylacteried, wide-fringed Pharisees, and courtly, ironical Sadducees; and, in the outer court, curious Gentiles! Some had come to worship; others to pay vows, or bring offerings, or to seek purification; some to meet friends, and discourse on religious subjects in those colonnaded porches, which ran round the Sanctuary; or else to have their questions answered, or their causes heard and decided, by the smaller Sanhedrin of twenty-three, that sat in the entering of the gate or by the Great Sanhedrin. The latter no longer occupied the Hall of Hewn Stones, Gazith, but met in some chamber attached to those 'shops,' or booths, on the Temple Mount, which belonged to the High-Priestly family of Ananias, and where such profitable trade was driven by those who, in their cupidity and covetousness, were worthy successors of the sons of Eli. In the Court of the Gentiles (or in its porches) sat the official money-changers, who for a fixed discount changed all foreign coins into those of the Sanctuary. Here also was that great mart for sacrificial animals, and all that was requisite for offerings. How the simple, earnest country people, who came to pay vows, or bring offerings for purifying, must have wondered, and felt oppressed in that atmosphere of strangely blended religious rigorism and utter worldliness; and how they must have been taxed, imposed upon, and treated with utmost curtness, nay, rudeness, by those who laughed at their boorishness, and despised them as cursed, ignorant country people, little better than heathens, or, for that matter, than brute beasts. Here also there lay about a crowd of noisy beggars, unsightly from disease, and clamorous for help. And close by passed the luxurious scion of the High-

---

[1] I must take leave to refer to the description of Jerusalem, and especially of the Temple, in the 'Temple and its Services at the Time of Jesus Christ.'

[2] Dr. *Mühlau*, in Riehm's Handwörterb.

Part viii. p. 682 *b*, speaks of the dimensions of the old Sanctuary as little more than those of a village church.

[3] It was only finished in 64 A.D., that is, six years before its destruction.

Priestly families; the proud, intensely self-conscious Teacher of the
Law, respectfully followed by his disciples; and the quick-witted,
subtle Scribe.   These were men who, on Sabbaths and feast-days,
would come out on the Temple-terrace to teach the people, or condescend to answer their questions; who in the Synagogues would
hold their puzzled hearers spell-bound by their traditional lore and
subtle argumentation, or tickle the fancy of the entranced multitude,
that thronged every available space, by their ingenious frivolities,
their marvellous legends, or their clever sayings; but who would, if
occasion required, quell an opponent by well-poised questions, or crush
him beneath the sheer weight of authority.   Yet others were there
who, despite the utterly lowering influence which the frivolities of
the prevalent religion, and the elaborate trifling of its endless observances, must have exercised on the moral and religious feelings of
all—perhaps, because of them—turned aside, and looked back with
loving gaze to the spiritual promises of the past, and forward with
longing expectancy to the near 'consolation of Israel,' waiting for it
in prayerful fellowship, and with bright, heaven-granted gleams of its
dawning light amidst the encircling gloom.

Descending from the Temple into the city, there was more than
enlargement, due to the increased population.   Altogether, Jerusalem
covered, at its greatest, about 300 acres.[1]   As of old there were still
the same narrow streets in the business quarters; but in close contiguity to bazaars and shops rose stately mansions of wealthy merchants,
and palaces of princes.[2]   And what a change in the aspect of these
streets, in the character of those shops, and, above all, in the appearance of the restless Eastern crowd that surged to and fro! Outside their
shops in the streets, or at least in sight of the passers, and within reach
of their talk, was the shoemaker hammering his sandals, the tailor
plying his needle, the carpenter, or the worker in iron and brass. Those
who were less busy, or more enterprising, passed along, wearing some
emblem of their trade: the dyer, variously coloured threads; the carpenter, a rule: the writer, a reed behind his ear; the tailor, with a
needle prominently stuck in his dress. In the side streets the less
attractive occupations of the butcher, the wool-comber, or the flax-
spinner were carried on. In these large, shady halls, artistic trades
were pursued: the elegant workmanship of the goldsmith and jeweller;
the various *articles de luxe*, that adorned the houses of the rich; the
work of the designer, the moulder, or the artificer in iron or brass.

[1] See *Conder*, Heth and Moab, p. 94.
[2] Such as the Palace of Grapte, and that of Queen Helena of Adiabene.

BOOK
II

In these streets and lanes everything might be purchased: the production of Palestine, or imported from foreign lands—nay, the rarest articles from the remotest parts. Exquisitely shaped, curiously designed and jewelled cups, rings and other workmanship of precious metals; glass, silks, fine linen, woollen stuffs, purple, and costly hangings; essences, ointments, and perfumes, as precious as gold; articles of food and drink from foreign lands—in short, what India, Persia, Arabia, Media, Egypt, Italy, Greece, and even the far-off lands of the Gentiles yielded, might be had in these bazaars.

Ancient Jewish writings enable us to identify no fewer than 118 different articles of import from foreign lands, covering more than even modern luxury has devised. Articles of luxury, especially from abroad, fetched indeed enormous prices; and a lady might spend 36*l*. on a

ᵃ Baba B.
ix. 7

cloak; ᵃ silk would be paid by its weight in gold; purple wool at 3*l*. 5*s*. the pound, or, if double-dyed, at almost ten times that amount; while the price of the best balsam and nard was most exorbitant. On the other hand, the cost of common living was very low. In the bazaars you might get a complete suit for your slave for eighteen or nineteen

ᵇ Arakh. vi.
5
ᶜ Baba K.
x. 4
ᵈ Men. xiii.
8; Baba K.
iii. 9
ᵉ Tos. Sheq.
ii. ; Tos.
Ar. iv.
ᶠ Men. xiii.
8

shillings,ᵇ and a tolerable outfit for yourself from 3*l*. to 6*l*. For the same sum you might purchase an ass,ᶜ an ox,ᵈ or a cow,ᵉ and, for little more, a horse. A calf might be had for less than fifteen shillings, a goat for five or six.ᶠ Sheep were dearer, and fetched from four to fifteen or sixteen shillings, while a lamb might sometimes be had as low as two pence. No wonder living and labour were so cheap. Corn of all kinds, fruit, wine, and oil, cost very little. Meat was about a penny a pound; a man might get himself a small, of course unfurnished,

ᵍ Tos. Baba
Mets. iv

lodging for about sixpence a week.ᵍ A day labourer was paid about 7½*d*. a day, though skilled labour would fetch a good deal more. Indeed, the great Hillel was popularly supposed to have supported his

ʰ Yoma 35 b

family on less than twopence a day,ʰ while property to the amount of about 6*l*., or trade with 2*l*. or 3*l*. of goods, was supposed to exclude a person from charity, or a claim on what was left in the corners of

ⁱ Peah viii.
8, 9

fields and to the gleaners.ⁱ

To these many like details might be added.[1] Sufficient has been said to show the two ends of society: the exceeding dearness of luxuries, and the corresponding cheapness of necessaries. Such extremes would meet especially at Jerusalem. Its population, computed at from 200,000 to 250,000,[2] was enormously swelled by travellers, and by

---

[1] Comp. *Herzfeld's* Handelsgesch.
[2] Ancient Jerusalem is supposed to have covered about double the area of the

modern city. Comp. Dr. *Schick* in *A. M. Luncz*, 'Jerusalem,' for 1882.

pilgrims during the great festivals.[1] The great Palace was the residence of King and Court, with all their following and luxury; in Antonia lay afterwards the Roman garrison. The Temple called thousands of priests, many of them with their families, to Jerusalem; while the learned Academies were filled with hundreds, though it may have been mostly poor, scholars and students. In Jerusalem must have been many of the large warehouses for the near commercial harbour of Joppa; and thence, as from the industrial centres of busy Galilee, would the pedlar go forth to carry his wares over the land. More especially would the markets of Jerusalem, held, however, in bazaars and streets rather than in squares, be thronged with noisy sellers and bargaining buyers. Thither would Galilee send not only its manufactures, but its provisions: fish (fresh or salted), fruit[a] known for its lusciousness, oil, grape-syrup, and wine. There were special inspectors for these markets—the *Agardemis* or *Agronimos*—who tested weights and measures, and officially stamped them,[b] tried the soundness of food or drink,[c] and occasionally fixed or lowered the market-prices, enforcing their decision,[d] if need were, even with the stick.[e 2] Not only was there an upper and a lower market in Jerusalem,[f] but we read of at least seven special markets: those for cattle,[g] wool, iron-ware,[h] clothes, wood,[i] bread, and fruit and vegetables. The original market-days were Monday and Tuesday, afterwards Friday.[k] The large fairs (*Yeridin*) were naturally confined to the centres of import and export—the borders of Egypt (Gaza), the ancient Phœnician maritime towns (Tyre and Acco), and the Emporium across the Jordan (Botnah). Besides, every caravansary, or khan *(qatlis, atlis, κατάλυσις)*, was a sort of mart, where goods were unloaded, and *especially cattle set out*[l] for sale, and purchases made. But in Jerusalem one may suppose the sellers to have been every day in the market; and the magazines, in which greengrocery and all kinds of meat were sold (the *Beth haShevaqim)*,[m] must have been always open. Besides, there were the many shops *(Chanuyoth)* either fronting the streets, or in courtyards, or else movable wooden booths in the streets. Strangely enough, occasionally Jewish

---

CHAP.
I

[a] Maaser. ii.
3

[b] Baba B.
89 a
[c] Jer. Ab. Z
44 b; Ab. Z.
58 a
[d] Jer. Dem
22 c
[e] Yoma 9 a
[f] Sanh. 89 a
[g] Erub. x. 9
[h] Jos. War
v. 8. 1
[i] Ibid. ii.
19. 4
[k] Tos. Baba
Mets. iii.

[l] Kerith.
iii. 7;
Temur. iii.
5

[m] Makhsh.
vi. 2

---

[1] Although Jerusalem covered only about 300 acres, yet, from the narrowness of Oriental streets, it would hold a very much larger population than any Western city of the same extent. Besides, we must remember that its ecclesiastical boundaries extended beyond the city.

[2] On the question of officially fixing the market-price, diverging opinions are expressed, Baba B. 89 b. It was thought that the market-price should leave to the producer a profit of one-sixth on the cost (Baba B. 90 a). In general, the laws on these subjects form a most interesting study. *Bloch* (Mos. Talm. Polizeir.) holds, that there were two classes of market-officials. But this is not supported by sufficient evidence, nor, indeed, would such an arrangement seem likely.

[3] That of Botnah was the largest, Jer. Ab. Z. 39 d.

ᵃ Kethub.
ix. 4

women were employed in selling.ᵃ Business was also done in the restaurants and wineshops, of which there were many; where you might be served with some dish: fresh or salted fish, fried locusts, a mess of vegetables, a dish of soup, pastry, sweetmeats, or a piece of a fruit-cake, to be washed down with Judæan or Galilean wine, Idumæan vinegar, or foreign beer.

If from these busy scenes we turn to the more aristocratic quarters of the Upper City,[1] we still see the same narrow streets, but tenanted by another class. First, we pass the High-Priest's palace on the slope of the hill, with a lower story under the principal apartments, and a porch in front. Here, on the night of the Betrayal, Peter was

ᵃ St. Mark
xiv. 66

'beneath in the Palace.'ᵃ Next, we come to Xystos, and then pause for a moment at the Palace of the Maccabees. It lies higher up the hill, and westward from the Xystos. From its halls you can look into the city, and even into the Temple. We know not which of the Maccabees had built this palace. But it was occupied, not by the actually reigning prince, who always resided in the fortress (Baris, afterwards Antonia), but by some other member of the family. From them it passed into the possession of Herod. There Herod Antipas was when, on that terrible Passover, Pilate sent Jesus from the old

ᵇ St. Luke
xxiii. 6, 7

palace of Herod to be examined by the Ruler of Galilee.ᵇ If these buildings pointed to the difference between the past and present, two structures of Herod's were, perhaps, more eloquent than any words in their accusations of the Idumæan. One of these, at least, would come in sight in passing along the slopes of the Upper City. The Maccabean rule had been preceded by that of corrupt High-Priests, who had prostituted their office to the vilest purposes. One of them, who had changed his Jewish name of Joshua into Jason, had gone so far, in his attempts to Grecianise the people, as to build a Hippodrome and Gymnasium for heathen games. We infer, it stood where the Western hill sloped into the Tyropœon, to the south-west of the Temple.ᶜ

ᶜ Jos. War
ii. 3. 1

It was probably this which Herod afterwards enlarged and beautified, and turned into a theatre. No expense was spared on the great games held there. The theatre itself was magnificently adorned with gold, silver, precious stones, and trophies of arms and records of the victories of Augustus. But to the Jews this essentially heathen place, over against

ᵈ Ant. xv.
8. 1

their Temple, was cause of deep indignation and plots.ᵈ Besides this theatre, Herod also built an immense amphitheatre, which we must

ᵉ Ant. xvii.
10. 2; War
ii. 3. 1, 2

locate somewhere in the north-west, and outside the second city wall.ᵉ

All this was Jerusalem above ground. But there was an under.

[1] Compare here generally *Unruh*, D. alte Jerusalem.

ground Jerusalem also, which burrowed everywhere under the city— under the Upper City, under the Temple, beyond the city walls. Its extent may be gathered from the circumstance that, after the capture of the city, besides the living who had sought shelter there, no fewer than 2,000 dead bodies were found in those subterranean streets.

Close by the tracks of heathenism in Jerusalem, and in sharp contrast, was what gave to Jerusalem its intensely Jewish character. It was not only the Temple, nor the festive pilgrims to its feasts and services. But there were hundreds of Synagogues,[1] some for different nationalities—such as the Alexandrians, or the Cyrenians; some for, or perhaps founded by, certain trade-guilds. If possible, the Jewish schools were even more numerous than the Synagogues. Then there were the many Rabbinic Academies ; and, besides, you might also see in Jerusalem that mysterious sect, the Essenes, of which the members were easily recognized by their white dress. Essenes, Pharisees, stranger Jews of all hues, and of many dresses and languages! One could have imagined himself almost in another world, a sort of enchanted land, in this Jewish metropolis, and metropolis of Judaism. When the silver trumpets of the Priests woke the city to prayer, or the strain of Levite music swept over it, or the smoke of the sacrifices hung like another Shekhinah over the Temple, against the green background of Olivet; or when in every street, court, and housetop rose the booths at the Feast of Tabernacles, and at night the sheen of the Temple illumination threw long fantastic shadows over the city; or when, at the Passover, tens of thousands crowded up the Mount with their Paschal lambs, and hundreds of thousands sat down to the Paschal supper—it would be almost difficult to believe, that heathenism was so near, that the Roman was virtually, and would soon be really, master of the land, or that a Herod occupied the Jewish throne.

Yet there he was; in the pride of his power, and the reckless cruelty of his ever-watchful tyranny. Everywhere was his mark. Temples to the gods and to Cæsar, magnificent, and magnificently adorned, outside Palestine and in its non-Jewish cities; towns rebuilt or built: *Sebaste* for the ancient Samaria, the splendid city and harbour of *Cæsarea* in the west, *Antipatris* (after his father) in the north, *Kypros* and *Phasaelis* (after his mother and brother), and

---

[1] Tradition exaggerates their number as 460 (Jer. Kethub. 35 c.) or even 480 (Jer. Meg. 73 d). But even the large number (proportionally to the size of the city) mentioned in the text need not surprise us when we remember that *ten* men were sufficient to form a Synagogue, and how many—what may be called 'private'—Synagogues exist at present in every town where there is a large and orthodox Jewish population.

BOOK
II

Agrippeion; unconquerable fortresses, such as *Essebonitis* and *Machœ-rus* in Peræa, *Alexandreion, Herodeion, Hyrcania,* and *Masada* in Judæa—proclaimed his name and sway. But in Jerusalem it seemed as if he had gathered up all his strength. The theatre and amphitheatre spoke of his Grecianism; Antonia was the representative fortress; for his religion he had built that glorious Temple, and for his residence the noblest of palaces, at the north-western angle of the Upper City, close by where Milo had been in the days of David. It seems almost incredible, that a Herod should have reared the Temple, and yet we can understand his motives. Jewish tradition had it, that a Rabbi (Baba ben Buta) had advised him in this manner to conciliate the people,[a] or else thereby to expiate the slaughter of so many Rabbis.[b][1] Probably a desire to gain popularity, and superstition, may alike have contributed, as also the wish to gratify his love for splendour and building. At the same time, he may have wished to show himself a better Jew than that rabble of Pharisees and Rabbis, who perpetually would cast it in his teeth, that he was an Idumæan. Whatever his origin, he was a true king of the Jews—as great, nay greater, than Solomon himself. Certainly, neither labour nor money had been spared on the Temple. A thousand vehicles carried up the stone; 10,000 workmen, under the guidance of 1,000 priests, wrought all the costly material gathered into that house, of which Jewish tradition could say, 'He that has not seen the Temple of Herod, has never known what beauty is.'[c] And yet Israel despised and abhorred the builder! Nor could his apparent work for the God of Israel have deceived the most credulous. In youth he had browbeaten the venerable Sanhedrin, and threatened the city with slaughter and destruction; again and again had he murdered her venerable sages; he had shed like water the blood of her Asmonean princes, and of every one who dared to be free; had stifled every national aspiration in the groans of the torture, and quenched it in the gore of his victims. Not once, nor twice, but six times did he change the High-Priesthood, to bestow it at last on one who bears no good name in Jewish theology, a foreigner in Judæa, an Alexandrian. And yet the power of that Idumæan was but of yesterday, and of mushroom growth!

[a] Baba B.
3 *b*
[b] Bemid.
R. 14

[c] Baba B. 4*a*

---

[1] The occasion is said to have been, that the Rabbis, in answer to Herod's question, quoted Deut. xvii. 15. Baba ben Buta himself is said to have escaped the slaughter, indeed, but to have been deprived of his eyes.

CHAPTER II.

THE PERSONAL HISTORY OF HEROD—THE TWO WORLDS IN JERUSALEM.

It is an intensely painful history,[1] in the course of which Herod made his way to the throne. We look back nearly two and a half centuries to where, with the empire of Alexander, Palestine fell to his successors. For nearly a century and a half it continued the battle-field of the Egyptian and Syrian kings (the Ptolemies and the Seleucidæ). At last it was a corrupt High-Priesthood—with which virtually the government of the land had all along lain—that betrayed Israel's precious trust. The great-grandson of so noble a figure in Jewish history as Simon the Just (compare Ecclus. l.) bought from the Syrians the High-Priestly office of his brother, adopted the heathen name Jason, and sought to Grecianise the people. The sacred office fell, if possible, even lower when, through bribery, it was transferred to his brother Menelaus. Then followed the brief period of the terrible persecutions of Antiochus Epiphanes, when Judaism was all but exterminated in Palestine. The glorious uprising of the Maccabees called forth all the national elements left in Israel, and kindled afresh the smouldering religious feeling. It seemed like a revival of Old Testament times. And when Judas the Maccabee, with a band so inferior in numbers and discipline, defeated the best of the Syrian soldiery, led by its ablest generals, and, on the anniversary of its desecration by heathen rites, set up again the great altar of burnt-offering, it appeared as if a new Theocracy were to be inaugurated. The ceremonial of that feast of the new 'dedication of the Temple,' when each night the number of lights grew larger in the winter's darkness, seemed symbolic of what was before Israel. But the Maccabees were not the Messiah; nor yet the Kingdom, which their sword would have restored —that of Heaven, with its blessings and peace. If ever, Israel might then have learned what Saviour to look for.

The period even of promise was more brief than might have been expected. The fervour and purity of the movement ceased almost

---

[1] For a fuller sketch of this history see Appendix IV.

BOOK
II

with its success.   It was certainly never the golden age of Israel—not even among those who remained faithful to its God—which those seem to imagine who, forgetful of its history and contests, would trace to it so much that is most precious and spiritual in the Old Testament.   It may have been the pressure of circumstances, but it was anything but a pious, or even a 'happy' thought[1] of Judas the Maccabee, to seek the alliance of the Romans.   From their entrance on the scene dates the decline of Israel's national cause.   For a time, indeed—though after varying fortunes of war—all seemed prosperous.   The Maccabees became both High-Priests and Kings.   But party-strife and worldliness, ambition and corruption, and Grecianism on the throne, soon brought their sequel in the decline of *morale* and vigour, and led to the decay and decadence of the Maccabean house.   It is a story as old as the Old Testament, and as wide as the history of the world.   Contention for the throne among the Maccabees led to the interference of the foreigner.   When, after capturing Jerusalem, and violating the sanctity of the Temple, although not plundering its treasures, Pompey placed Hyrcanus II. in possession of the High-Priesthood, the last of the Maccabean rulers[2] was virtually shorn of power.   The country was now tributary to Rome, and subject to the Governor of Syria.   Even the shadow of political power passed from the feeble hands of Hyrcanus when, shortly afterwards, Gabinius (one of the Roman governors) divided the land into five districts, independent of each other.

But already a person had appeared on the stage of Jewish affairs, who was to give them their last decisive turn.   About fifty years before this, the district of Idumæa had been conquered by the Maccabean King Hyrcanus I., and its inhabitants forced to adopt Judaism.   By this Idumæa we are not, however, to understand the ancient or Eastern Edom, which was now in the hands of the Nabatæans, but parts of Southern Palestine which the Edomites had occupied since the Babylonian Exile, and especially a small district on the northern and eastern boundary of Judæa, and below Samaria.[a]   After it became Judæan, its administration was entrusted to a governor.   In the reign of the last of the Maccabees this office devolved on one Antipater, a man of equal cunning and determination.   He successfully interfered in the unhappy dispute for the crown, which was at last decided by the sword of Pompey.   Antipater took the part of the utterly weak Hyrcanus in that contest with his energetic brother Aristobulus.   He

[a] Comp.
1 Macc. vi.
31

[1] So *Schürer* in his Neutestam. Zeit-gesch.

[2] A table of the Maccabean and Herodian families is given in Appendix VI.

soon became the virtual ruler, and Hyrcanus II. only a puppet in his
hands. From the accession of Judas Maccabæus, in 166 B.C., to the
year 63 B.C., when Jerusalem was taken by Pompey, only about a
century had elapsed. Other twenty-four years, and the last of the
Maccabees had given place to the son of Antipater: Herod, surnamed
the Great.

The settlement of Pompey did not prove lasting. Aristobulus, the
brother and defeated rival of Hyrcanus, was still alive, and his sons
were even more energetic than he. The risings attempted by them,
the interference of the Parthians on behalf of those who were hostile
to Rome, and, lastly, the contentions for supremacy in Rome itself,
made this period one of confusion, turmoil, and constant warfare in
Palestine. When Pompey was finally defeated by Cæsar, the prospects of Antipater and Hyrcanus seemed dark. But they quickly
changed sides; and timely help given to Cæsar in Egypt brought to
Antipater the title of Procurator of Judæa, while Hyrcanus was left
in the High-Priesthood, and, at least, nominal head of the people. The
two sons of Antipater were now made governors: the elder, Phasaelus,
of Jerusalem; the younger, Herod, only twenty-five years old, of
Galilee. Here he displayed the energy and determination which
were his characteristics, in crushing a guerilla warfare, of which the
deeper springs were probably nationalist. The execution of its
leader brought Herod a summons to appear before the Great Sanhedrin of Jerusalem, for having arrogated to himself the power of
life and death. He came, but arrayed in purple, surrounded by a
body-guard, and supported by the express direction of the Roman
Governor to Hyrcanus, that he was to be acquitted. Even so he
would have fallen a victim to the apprehensions of the Sanhedrin—
only too well grounded—had he not been persuaded to withdraw from
the city. He returned at the head of an army, and was with difficulty
persuaded by his father to spare Jerusalem. Meantime Cæsar had
named him Governor of Cœlesyria.

On the murder of Cæsar, and the possession of Syria by Cassius,
Antipater and Herod again changed sides. But they rendered such
substantial service as to secure favour, and Herod was continued in
the position conferred on him by Cæsar. Antipater was, indeed,
poisoned by a rival, but his sons Herod and Phasaelus repressed and
extinguished all opposition. When the battle of Philippi placed the
Roman world in the hands of Antony and Octavius, the former
obtained Asia. Once more the Idumæans knew how to gain the new
ruler, and Phasaelus and Herod were named Tetrarchs of Judæa.

Afterwards, when Antony was held in the toils of Cleopatra, matters seemed, indeed, to assume a different aspect. The Parthians entered the land, in support of the rival Maccabean prince Antigonus, the son of Aristobulus. By treachery, Phasaelus and Hyrcanus were induced to go to the Parthian camp, and made captives. Phasaelus shortly afterwards destroyed himself in his prison,[1] while Hyrcanus was deprived of his ears, to unfit him for the High-Priestly office. And so Antigonus for a short time succeeded both to the High-Priesthood and royalty in Jerusalem. Meantime Herod, who had in vain warned his brother and Hyrcanus against the Parthian, had been able to make his escape from Jerusalem. His family he left to the defence of his brother Joseph, in the inaccessible fortress of Masada; himself fled into Arabia, and finally made his way to Rome. There he succeeded, not only with Antony, but obtained the consent of Octavius, and was proclaimed by the Senate King of Judæa. A sacrifice on the Capitol, and a banquet by Antony, celebrated the accession of the new successor of David.

But he had yet to conquer his kingdom. At first he made way by the help of the Romans. Such success, however, as he had gained, was more than lost during his brief absence on a visit to Antony. Joseph, the brother of Herod, was defeated and slain, and Galilee, which had been subdued, revolted again. But the aid which the Romans rendered, after Herod's return from Antony, was much more hearty, and his losses were more than retrieved. Soon all Palestine, with the exception of Jerusalem, was in his hands. While laying siege to it, he went to Samaria, there to wed the beautiful Maccabean princess Mariamme, who had been betrothed to him five years before.[2] That ill-fated Queen, and her elder brother Aristobulus, united in themselves the two rival branches of the Maccabean family. Their father was Alexander, the eldest son of Aristobulus, and brother of that Antigonus whom Herod now besieged in Jerusalem; and their mother, Alexandra, the daughter of Hyrcanus II. The uncle of Mariamme was not long able to hold out against the combined forces of Rome and Herod. The carnage was terrible. When Herod, by rich presents, at length induced the Romans to leave Jerusalem, they took Antigonus with them. By desire of Herod he was executed.

This was the first of the Maccabees who fell victim to his jealousy and cruelty. The history which now follows is one of sickening carnage. The next to experience his vengeance were the principal ad-

[1] By dashing out his brains against the prison walls.
[2] He had previously been married to one Doris, the issue of the marriage being a son, Antipater.

herents in Jerusalem of his rival Antigonus. Forty-five of the noblest and richest were executed. His next step was to appoint an obscure Babylonian to the High-Priesthood. This awakened the active hostility of Alexandra, the mother of Mariamme, Herod's wife. The Maccabean princess claimed the High-Priesthood for her son Aristobulus. Her intrigues with Cleopatra—and through her with Antony —and the entreaties of Mariamme, the only being whom Herod loved, though in his own mad way, prevailed. At the age of seventeen Aristobulus was made High-Priest. But Herod, who well knew the hatred and contempt of the Maccabean members of his family, had his mother-in-law watched, a precaution increased after the vain attempt of Alexandra to have herself and her son removed in coffins from Jerusalem, to flee to Cleopatra. Soon the jealousy and suspicions of Herod were raised to murderous madness, by the acclamations which greeted the young Aristobulus at the Feast of Tabernacles. So dangerous a Maccabean rival must be got rid of; and, by secret order of Herod, Aristobulus was drowned while bathing. His mother denounced the murderer, and her influence with Cleopatra, who also hated Herod, led to his being summoned before Antony. Once more bribery, indeed, prevailed; but other troubles awaited Herod.

When obeying the summons of Antony, Herod had committed the government to his uncle Joseph, who was also his brother-in-law, having wedded Salome, the sister of Herod. His mad jealousy had prompted him to direct that, in case of his condemnation, Mariamme was to be killed, that she might not become the wife of another. Unfortunately, Joseph told this to Mariamme, to show how much she was loved. But on the return of Herod, the infamous Salome accused her old husband of impropriety with Mariamme. When it appeared that Joseph had told the Queen of his commission, Herod, regarding it as confirming his sister's charge, ordered him to be executed, without even a hearing. External complications of the gravest kind now supervened. Herod had to cede to Cleopatra the districts of Phœnice and Philistia, and that of Jericho with its rich balsam plantations. Then the dissensions between Antony and Octavius involved him, in the cause of the former, in a war with Arabia, whose king had failed to pay tribute to Cleopatra. Herod was victorious; but he had now to reckon with another master. The battle of Actium[a] decided the fate of Antony, and Herod had to make his peace with Octavius. Happily, he was able to do good service to the new cause, ere presenting himself before Augustus. But, in order to be secure from all possible rivals, he had the aged Hyrcanus II. executed, on pretence of intrigues with the Arabs.

[a] 31 B.C.

Herod was successful with Augustus; and when, in the following summer, he furnished him supplies on his march to Egypt, he was rewarded by a substantial addition of territory.

When about to appear before Augustus, Herod had entrusted to one Soëmus the charge of Mariamme, with the same fatal directions as formerly to Joseph. Again Mariamme learnt the secret; again the old calumnies were raised—this time not only by Salome, but also by Kypros, Herod's mother; and again Herod imagined he had found corroborative evidence. Soëmus was slain without a hearing, and the beautiful Mariamme executed after a mock trial. The most fearful paroxysm of remorse, passion, and longing for his murdered wife now seized the tyrant, and brought him to the brink of the grave. Alexandra, the mother of Mariamme, deemed the moment favorable for her plots—but she was discovered, and executed. Of the Maccabean race there now remained only distant members, the sons of Babas, who had found an asylum with Costobarus, the Governor of Idumæa, who had wedded Salome after the death of her first husband. Tired of him, as she had been of Joseph, Salome denounced her second husband ; and Costobarus, as well as the sons of Babas, fell victims to Herod. Thus perished the family of the Maccabees.

The hand of the maddened tyrant was next turned against his own family. Of his ten wives, we mention only those whose children occupy a place in this history. The son of Doris was Antipater; those of the Maccabean Mariamme, Alexander and Aristobulus; another Mariamme, whose father Herod had made High-Priest, bore him a son named Herod (a name which other of the sons shared); Malthake, a Samaritan, was the mother of Archelaus and Herod Antipas; and, lastly, Cleopatra of Jerusalem bore Philip. The sons of the Maccabean princess, as heirs presumptive, were sent to Rome for their education. On this occasion Herod received, as reward for many services, the country east of the Jordan, and was allowed to appoint his still remaining brother, Pheroras, Tetrarch of Peræa. On their return from Rome the young princes were married : Alexander to a daughter of the King of Cappadocia, and Aristobulus to his cousin Berenice, the daughter of Salome. But neither kinship, nor the yet nearer relation in which Aristobulus now stood to her, could extinguish the hatred of Salome towards the dead Maccabean princess or her children. Nor did the young princes, in their pride of descent, disguise their feelings towards the house of their father. At first, Herod gave not heed to the denunciations of his sister. Presently he yielded to vague apprehensions. As a first step, Antipater, the son of Doris, was recalled from exile, and sent to Rome for education. So the breach became open; and Herod took his sons to Italy, to lay formal accusation against them before Augustus. The wise counsels of the Emperor restored peace for a time. But Antipater now returned to Palestine, and joined his calumnies to those of Salome. Once more the King of Cappadocia succeeded in reconciling Herod and his sons. But in the end the intrigues of Salome, Antipater, and of an infamous foreigner who had made his way at Court, prevailed. Alexander and Aristobulus were imprisoned, and an accusation of high treason laid against them before the Emperor. Augustus gave Herod full powers, but advised the convocation of a mixed tribunal of Jews and Romans to try the case. As might have been expected, the two princes were condemned to death, and when some old soldiers ventured to intercede for them, 300 of the supposed adherents of the cause were cut down, and the two princes strangled in prison. This happened in Samaria, where, thirty years before, Herod had wedded their ill-fated mother.

Antipater was now the heir presumptive. But, impatient of the throne, he plotted with Herod's brother, Pheroras, against his father. Again Salome denounced her nephew and her brother. Antipater withdrew to Rome; but when, after the death of Pheroras, Herod obtained indubitable evidence that his son had plotted against his life, he lured Antipater to Palestine, where on his arrival he was cast into prison. All that was needed was the permission of Augustus for his execution. It arrived, and was carried out only five days before the death of Herod himself. So ended a reign almost unparalleled for reckless cruelty and bloodshed, in which the murder of the Innocents in Bethlehem formed but so trifling an episode among the many deeds of blood, as to have seemed not deserving of record on the page of the Jewish historian.

But we can understand the feelings of the people towards such a King. They hated the Idumæan; they detested his semi-heathen reign; they abhorred his deeds of cruelty. The King had surrounded himself with foreign councillors, and was protected by foreign mercenaries from Thracia, Germany, and Gaul. [a] So long as he lived, no woman's honour was safe, no man's life secure. An army of all-powerful spies pervaded Jerusalem—nay, the King himself was said to stoop to that office. [b] If pique or private enmity led to denunciation, the torture would extract any confession from the most innocent. What his relation to Judaism had been, may easily be inferred. He would be a Jew—even build the Temple, advocate the cause of the Jews in other lands, and, in a certain sense, conform to the Law of

[a] *Jos. Ant.* vxii. 8. 3

[b] Ant. xv. 10. 4

BOOK
II

Judaism. In building the Temple, he was so anxious to conciliate national prejudice, that the Sanctuary itself was entrusted to the workmanship of priests only. Nor did he ever intrude into the Holy Place, nor interfere with any functions of the priesthood. None of his coins bear devices which could have shocked popular feeling, nor did any of the buildings he erected in Jerusalem exhibit any forbidden emblems. The Sanhedrin did exist during his reign, [1] though it must have been shorn of all real power, and its activity confined to ecclesiastical, or semi-ecclesiastical, causes. Strangest of all, he seems to have had at least the passive support of two of the greatest Rabbis—the Pollio and Sameas of Josephus[a]—supposed to represent those great figures in Jewish tradition, Abtalion and Shemajah. [b][2] We can but conjecture, that they preferred even his rule to what had preceded; and hoped it might lead to a Roman Protectorate, which would leave Judæa practically independent, or rather under Rabbinic rule.

It was also under the government of Herod, that Hillel and Shammai lived and taught in Jerusalem:[3] the two, whom tradition designates as 'the fathers of old.'[c] Both gave their names to 'schools,' whose direction was generally different—not unfrequently, it seems, chiefly for the sake of opposition. But it is not correct to describe the former as consistently the more liberal and mild. [4] The teaching of both was supposed to have been declared by the 'Voice from Heaven' (*the Bath-Qol*) as 'the words of the living God;' yet the Law was to be henceforth according to the teaching of Hillel. [d] But to us Hillel is so intensely interesting, not merely as the mild and gentle, nor only as the earnest student who came from Babylon to learn in the Academies of Jerusalem; who would support his family on a third of his scanty wages as a day labourer, that he might pay for entrance into the schools; and whose zeal and merits were only discovered when, after a severe night, in which, from poverty, he had been unable to gain admittance into the Academy, his benumbed form was taken down from the window-sill, to which he had crept up

[a] Ant. xiv.
9. 4; xv. 1
1 10. 4

[1] Ab. 1, 10,
11

[c] Eduj. 1. 4

[d] Jer. Ber.
3 *b*, lines 3
and 2 from
bottom

---

[1] Comp. the discussion of this question in *Wieseler*, Beitr. pp. 215 &c.

[2] Even their recorded fundamental principles bear this out. That of Shemajah was : ' Love labour, hate lordship, and do not push forward to the authorities.' That of Abtalion was: ' Ye sages, be careful in your words, lest perchance ye incur banishment, and are exiled to a place of bad waters, and the disciples who follow you drink of them and die,

and so in the end the name of God be profaned.'

[3] On Hillel and Shammai see the article in *Herzog's* Real-Encyklop.; that in *Hamburger's; Delitzsch*, Jesus u. Hillel, and books on Jewish history generally.

[4] A number of points on which the ordinances of Hillel were more severe than those of Shammai are enumerated in Eduj. iv. 1–12; v. 1–4; Ber. 36 *a*, end. Comp. also Ber. R. 1.

not to lose aught of the precious instruction. And for his sake did
they gladly break on that Sabbath the sacred rest. Nor do we think
of him, as tradition fables him—the descendant of David,[a] possessed
of every great quality of body, mind, and heart; nor yet as the second
Ezra, whose learning placed him at the head of the Sanhedrin, who
laid down the principles afterwards applied and developed by Rabbinism, and who was the real founder of traditionalism. Still less do
we think of him, as he is falsely represented by some: as he whose
principles closely resemble the teaching of Jesus, or, according to certain writers, were its source. By the side of Jesus we think of him
otherwise than this. We remember that, in his extreme old age and
near his end, he may have presided over that meeting of Sanhedrin
which, in answer to Herod's inquiry, pointed to Bethlehem as the
birthplace of the Messiah.[b][1] We think of him also as the grandfather of that Gamaliel, at whose feet Saul of Tarsus sat. And to us
he is the representative Jewish reformer, in the spirit of those times,
and in the sense of restoring rather than removing; while we think
of Jesus as the Messiah of Israel, in the sense of bringing the
Kingdom of God to all men, and opening it to all believers.

And so there were two worlds in Jerusalem, side by side. On
the one hand, was Grecianism with its theatre and amphitheatre;
foreigners filling the Court, and crowding the city; foreign tendencies
and ways, from the foreign King downwards. On the other hand,
was the old Jewish world, becoming now set and ossified in the Schools
of Hillel and Shammai, and overshadowed by Temple and Synagogue.
And each was pursuing its course, by the side of the other. If Herod
had everywhere his spies, the Jewish law provided its two police magistrates in Jerusalem, the only judges who received remuneration.[c][2]
If Herod judged cruelly and despotically, the Sanhedrin weighed
most deliberately, the balance always inclining to mercy. If Greek
was the language of the court and camp, and indeed must have been
understood and spoken by most in the land, the language of the
people, spoken also by Christ and His Apostles, was a dialect of the
ancient Hebrew, the Western or Palestinian Aramaic.[3] It seems
strange, that this could ever have been doubted.[4] A Jewish Messiah

CHAP.
II

[a] Ber. R. 98

[b] St. Matt.
ii. 4

[c] Jer,
Kethub.
35 c;
Kethub.
104 b

---

[1] On the chronology of the life of Hillel
&c., see also *Schmilg*, Ueb. d. Entsteh.
&c. der Megillath Taanith, especially p.
34. Hillel is said to have become Chief
of the Sanhedrin in 30 B.C., and to have
held the office for forty years. These
numbers, however, are no doubt somewhat exaggerated.

[2] The police laws of the Rabbis might
well serve as a model for all similar legislation.

[3] At the same time I can scarcely agree
with Delitzsch and others, that this was
the dialect called *Sursi*. The latter was
rather Syriac. Comp. *Levy*, ad voc.

[4] Professor *Roberts* has advocated, with

Who would urge His claim upon Israel in Greek, seems almost a contradiction in terms. We know, that the language of the Temple and the Synagogue was Hebrew, and that the addresses of the Rabbis had to be 'targumed' into the vernacular Aramæan—and can we believe that, in a Hebrew service, the Messiah could have risen to address the people in Greek, or that He would have argued with the Pharisees and Scribes in that tongue, especially remembering that its study was actually forbidden by the Rabbis?[1]

Indeed, it was a peculiar mixture of two worlds in Jerusalem: not only of the Grecian and the Jewish, but of piety and frivolity also. The devotion of the people and the liberality of the rich were unbounded. Fortunes were lavished on the support of Jewish learning, the promotion of piety, or the advance of the national cause. Thousands of votive offerings, and the costly gifts in the Temple, bore evidence of this. If priestly avarice had artificially raised the price of sacrificial animals, a rich man would bring into the Temple at his own cost the number requisite for the poor. Charity was not only open-handed, but most delicate, and one who had been in good circumstances would actually be enabled to live according to his former station.[2] Then these Jerusalemites—townspeople, as they called themselves—were so polished, so witty, so pleasant. There was a tact in their social intercourse, and a considerateness and delicacy in their public arrangements and provisions, nowhere else to be found.

*Bemid. R.
14; ed.
Warsh.p.
59a
b Baba K.

Their very language was different. There was a Jerusalem dialect,[a] quicker, shorter, 'lighter' (*Lishna Qalila*).[b] And their hospitality, especially at festive seasons, was unlimited. No one considered his house his own, and no stranger or pilgrim but found reception. And how much there was to be seen and heard in those luxuriously furnished houses, and at those sumptuous entertainments! In the women's apartments, friends from the country would see every novelty in dress, adornment, and jewellery, and have the benefit of examining themselves in looking-glasses. To be sure, as being womanish vanity, their use was interdicted to men, except it were to the members of

great ingenuity, the view that Christ and His Apostles used the Greek language. See especially his 'Discussions on the Gospels.' The Roman Catholic Church sometimes maintained, that Jesus and His disciples spoke Latin, and in 1822 a work appeared by *Black* to prove that the N.T. Greek showed a Latin origin.
[1] For a full statement of the arguments on this subject we refer the student to *Böhl*, Forsch. n. e. Volksbibel z. Zeit

Jesu, pp. 4–28; to the latter work by the same writer (Atttestam. Citate im N. Test.); to a very interesting article by Professor *Delitzsch* in the 'Daheim' for 1874 (No. 27); to *Buxtorf*, sub Gelil; to *J. D. Goldberg*, 'The Language of Christ'; but especially to *G. de Rossi*, Della lingua prop. di Cristo (Parma 1772).
[2] Thus Hillel was said to have hired a horse, and even an outrunner, for a decayed rich man '

the family of the President of the Sanhedrin, on account of their CHAP.
II intercourse with those in authority, just as for the same reason they were allowed to learn Greek.[a] Nor might even women look in the glass on the Sabbath.[b] But that could only apply to those carried in the hand, since one might be tempted, on the holy day, to do such servile work as to pull out a grey hair with the pincers attached to the end of the glass; but not to a glass fixed in the lid of a basket;[c] nor to such as hung on the wall.[d] And then the lady-visitor might get anything in Jerusalem; from a false tooth to an Arabian veil, a Persian shawl, or an Indian dress!

While the women so learned Jerusalem manners in the inner apartments, the men would converse on the news of the day, or on politics. For the Jerusalemites had friends and correspondents in the most distant parts of the world, and letters were carried by special messengers,[e] in a kind of post-bag. Nay, there seem to have been some sort of receiving-offices in towns,[f] and even something resembling our parcel-post.[g] And, strange as it may sound, even a species of newspapers, or broadsheets, appears to have been circulating (*Mikhtabhin*), not allowed, however, on the Sabbath, unless they treated of public affairs.[h]

Of course, it is difficult accurately to determine which of these things were in use in the earliest times, or else introduced at a later period. Perhaps, however, it was safer to bring them into a picture of Jewish society. Undoubted, and, alas, too painful evidence comes to us of the luxuriousness of Jerusalem at that time, and of the moral corruption to which it led. It seems only too clear, that such commentations as the Talmud[i] gives of Is. iii. 16-24, in regard to the manners and modes of attraction practised by a certain class of the female population in Jerusalem, applied to a far later period than that of the prophet. With this agrees only too well the recorded covert lascivious expressions used by the men, which gives a lamentable picture of the state of morals of many in the city,[k] and the notices of the indecent dress worn not only by women,[l] but even by corrupt High-Priestly youths. Nor do the exaggerated descriptions of what the Midrash on Lamentations[m] describes as the dignity of the Jerusalemites; of the wealth which they lavished on their marriages; of the ceremony which insisted on repeated invitations to the guests to a banquet, and that men inferior in rank should not be bidden to it; of the dress in which they appeared; the manner in which the dishes were served, the wine in white crystal vases; and the punishment of the cook who had failed in his duty, and which was to be commen-

[a] Jer.Shabb. 7 d
[b] Shabb. 149 a
[c] Kel. xiv. 6
[d] Tos. Shabb.xiii. ed. Zuckerm. p. 130
[e] Shabb.x.4
[f] Shabb.19a
[g] Rosh haSh. 9 b
[h] Tos. Shabb. xviii.
[i] Shabb. 62 b
[k] Comp. Shabb. 62 b, last line and first of 63 a
[l] Kel. xxiv. 16; xxviii. 9
[m] On ch. iv 2

surate to the dignity of the party—give a better impression of the great world in Jerusalem.

And yet it was the City of God, over whose destruction not only the Patriarch and Moses, but the Angelic hosts—nay, the Almighty Himself and His Shekhinah—had made bitterest lamentation.[1] The City of the Prophets, also—since each of them whose birthplace had not been mentioned, must be regarded as having sprung from it.[a] Equally, even more, marked, but now for joy and triumph, would be the hour of Jerusalem's uprising, when it would welcome its Messiah. Oh, when would He come? In the feverish excitement of expectancy they were only too ready to listen to the voice of any pretender, however coarse and clumsy the imposture. Yet He was at hand—even now coming: only quite other than the Messiah of their dreams. ' He came unto His own, and His own received Him not. But as many as received Him, to them gave He power to become children of God, even to them that believe on His Name.'

[a] Meg. 15 a

---

[1] See the Introduction to the Midrash on Lamentations. But some of the descriptions are so painful—even blasphemous—that we do not venture on quotation.

CHAPTER III.

THE ANNUNCIATION OF ST. JOHN THE BAPTIST.

(St. Luke i. 5-25.)

IT was the time of the Morning Sacrifice.[1] As the massive Temple-gates slowly swung on their hinges, a three-fold blast from the silver trumpets of the Priests seemed to waken the City, as with the Voice of God, to the life of another day. As its echoes came in the still air across the cleft of the Tyropœon, up the slopes of the Upper City, down the busy quarters below, or away to the new suburb beyond, they must, if but for a moment, have brought holier thoughts to all. For, did it not seem to link the present to the past and the future, as with the golden chain of promises that bound the Holy City to the Jerusalem that was above, which in type had already, and in reality would soon descend from heaven? Patriot, saint, or stranger, he could not have heard it unmoved, as thrice the summons from within the Temple-gates rose and fell.

It had not come too soon. The Levites on ministry, and those of the laity, whose 'course' it was to act as the representatives of Israel, whether in Palestine or far away, in a sacrifice provided by, and offered for, all Israel, hastened to their duties.[2] For already the blush of dawn, for which the Priest on the highest pinnacle of the Temple had watched, to give the signal for beginning the services of the day, had shot its brightness far away to Hebron and beyond. Within the Courts below all had long been busy. At some time previously, unknown to those who waited for the morning—whether at cock-crowing, or a little earlier or later,[a] the superintending Priest had summoned to their sacred functions those who had 'washed,' according

CHAP.
III

[a] Tamid i. 2

---

[1] We presume, that the ministration of Zacharias (St. Luke i. 9) took place in the morning, as the principal service. But *Meyer* (Komm. i. 2, p. 242) is mistaken in supposing, that this follows from the reference to the lot. It is, indeed, true that, of the four lots for the priestly functions, three took place only in the morn-ing. But that for incensing was repeated in the evening (Yoma 26 a). Even Bishop *Haneberg* (Die Relig. Alterth. p. 609) is not accurate in this respect.

[2] For a description of the details of that service, see 'The Temple and its Services,' &c.

BOOK
II

ᵃ Yoma 25 a

ᵇ Tamid v. 2

to the ordinance. There must have been each day about fifty priests on duty.¹ Such of them as were ready now divided into two parties, to make inspection of the Temple courts by torchlight. Presently they met, and trooped tó the well-known Hall of Hewn Polished Stones,ᵃ where formerly the Sanhedrin had been wont to sit. The ministry for the day was there apportioned. To prevent the disputes of carnal zeal, the 'lot' was to assign to each his function. Four times was it resorted to: twice before, and twice after the Temple-gates were opened. The first act of their ministry had to be done in the grey dawn, by the fitful red light that glowed on the altar of burnt offering, ere the priests had stirred it into fresh flame. It was scarcely daybreak, when a second time they met for the 'lot,' which designated those who were to take part in the sacrifice itself, and who were to trim the golden candlestick, and make ready the altar of incense within the Holy Place. And now morn had broken, and nothing remained before the admission of worshippers but to bring out the lamb, once again to make sure of its fitness for sacrifice, to water it from a golden bowl, and then to lay it in mystic fashion—as tradition described the binding of Isaac—on the north side of the altar, with its face to the west.

All, priests and laity, were present as the Priest, standing on the east side of the altar, from a golden bowl sprinkled with sacrificial blood two sides of the altar, below the red line which marked the difference between ordinary sacrifices and those that were to be wholly consumed. While the sacrifice was prepared for the altar, the priests, whose lot it was, had made ready all within the Holy Place, where the most solemn part of the day's service was to take place—that of offering the incense, which symbolised Israel's accepted prayers. Again was the lot (the third) cast to indicate him, who was to be honoured with this highest mediatorial act. Only once in a lifetime might any one enjoy that privilege.ᵇ Henceforth he was called 'rich,'² and must leave to his brethren the hope of the distinction which had been granted him. It was fitting that, as the

---

¹ If we reckon the total number in the twenty-four courses of, presumably, the officiating priesthood, at 20,000, according to *Josephus* (Ag. Ap. ii. 8), which is very much below the exaggerated Talmudic computation of 85,000 for the smallest course (Jer. Taan. 69 *a*), and suppose, that little more than one-third of each course had come up for duty, this would give fifty priests for each week-day, while on the Sabbath the whole course would be on duty. This is, of course, considerably more than the number requisite, since, except for the incensing priest, the lot for the morning also held good for the evening sacrifice.

² Yoma 26 *a*. The designation 'rich' is derived from the promise which, in Deut. xxxiii. 11, follows on the service referred to in verse 10. But probably a spiritual application was also intended.

custom was, such lot should be preceded by prayer and confession of their faith [1] on the part of the assembled priests.

It was the first week in October 748 A.U.C., [2] that is, in the sixth year before our present era, when 'the course of Abia' [3]—the eighth in the original arrangement of the weekly service—was on duty in the Temple. True this, as indeed most of the twenty-four 'courses' into which the Priesthood had been arranged, could not claim identity, only continuity, with those whose names they bore. For only three, or at most four, of the ancient 'courses' had returned from Babylon. But the original arrangement had been preserved, the names of the missing courses being retained, and their number filled up by lot from among those who had come back to Palestine. In our ignorance of the number of 'houses of their father,' or families,' which constituted the 'course of Abia,' it is impossible to determine, how the services of that week had been apportioned among them. But this is of comparatively small importance, since there is no doubt about the central figure in the scene.

In the group ranged that autumn morning around the superintending Priest was one, on whom the snows of at least sixty winters had fallen. [4] But never during these many years had he been honoured with the office of incensing—and it was perhaps well he should have learned, that this distinction came direct from God. Yet the venerable figure of Zacharias must have been well known in the Temple For, each course was twice a year on ministry, and, unlike the Levites, the priests were not disqualified by age, but only by infirmity. In many respects he seemed different from those around. His home was not in either of the great priest-centres— the Ophel-quarter in Jerusalem, nor in Jericho [5]—but in some small town in those uplands, south of Jerusalem: the historic 'hill-country of Judæa.' And yet he might have claimed distinction. To be a priest, and married to the daughter of a priest, was supposed to convey twofold honour. [6] That he was surrounded by relatives and friends, and that he was well known and respected throughout his

---

[1] The so-called *Shema*, consisting of Deut. vi. 4–9; xi. 13–21; Num. xv. 37–41.

[2] The question of this date is, of course, intimately connected with that of the Nativity of Christ, and could therefore not be treated in the text. It is discussed in Appendix VII.: 'On the Date of the Nativity of our Lord.'

[3] This was the eighth course in the original arrangement (1 Chr. xxiv. 10).

[4] According to St. Luke i. 7, they were

both 'well stricken in years.' But from Aboth v. 21 we learn, that sixty years was considered 'the commencement of agedness.'

[5] According to tradition, about one-fourth of the priesthood was resident in Jericho. But, even limiting this to those who were in the habit of officiating, the statement seems greatly exaggerated.

[6] Comp. Ber. 44 *a*; Pes. 49 *a*; Vayyikra R. 4.

BOOK
II

ª St. Luke 1.
58, 59, 61, 65,
66

district, appears incidentally from the narrative.[1]   It would, indeed, have been strange had it been otherwise.   There was much in the popular habits of thought, as well as in the office and privileges of the Priesthood, if worthily represented, to invest it with a venera- tion which the aggressive claims of Rabbinism could not wholly monopolise.   And in this instance Zacharias and Elisabeth, his wife, were truly 'righteous,'[1] in the sense of walking, so far as man could judge, 'blamelessly,' alike in those commandments which were specially binding on Israel, and in those statutes that were of universal bearing on mankind.[2]   No doubt their piety assumed in some measure the form of the time, being, if we must use the expression, Pharisaic, though in the good, not the evil sense of it.

There is much about those earlier Rabbis—Hillel, Gamaliel, and others—to attract us, and their spirit ofttimes sharply contrasts with the narrow bigotry, the self-glory, and the unspiritual externalism of their successors.   We may not unreasonably infer, that the *Tsaddiq* in the quiet home of the hill-country was quite other than the self- asserting Rabbi, whose dress and gait, voice and manner, words and even prayers, were those of the religious *parvenu*, pushing his claims to distinction before angels and men.   Such a household as that of Zacharias and Elisabeth would have all that was beautiful in the religion of the time: devotion towards God; a home of affection and purity; reverence towards all that was sacred in things Divine and human; ungrudging, self-denying, loving charity to the poor; the tenderest regard for the feelings of others, so as not to raise a blush, nor to wound their hearts;[3] above all, intense faith and hope in the higher and better future of Israel.   Of such, indeed, there must have been not a few in the land—the quiet, the prayerful, the pious, who, though certainly not Sadducees nor Essenes, but reckoned with the Pharisaic party, waited for the consolation of Israel, and received it with joy when manifested.   Nor could aught more certainly have marked the difference between the one and the other

---

[1] δίκαιος—of course not in the strict sense in which the word is sometimes used, especially by St. Paul, but as *pius et bonus.* See *Vorstius* (De Hebraism. N.T. pp. 55 &c.).   As the account of the Evangelist seems derived from an orig- inal Hebrew source, the word must have corresponded to that of *Tsaddiq* in the then popular signification.

[2] ἐντολαί and δικαιώματα evidently mark an essential division of the Law at the time.   But it is almost impossible to determine their exact Hebrew equiva- lents.   The LXX. render by these two terms not always the same Hebrew words.   Comp. Gen. xxvi. 5 with Deut. iv. 40.   They cannot refer to the division of the law into affirmative (248) and pro- hibitive (365) commandments.

[3] There is, perhaps, no point on which the Rabbinic Law is more explicit or stringent than on that of tenderest regard for the feelings of others, especially of the poor.

section than on a matter, which must almost daily, and most painfully,
have forced itself on Zacharias and Elisabeth.   There were among
the Rabbis those who, remembering the words of the prophet,[a] spoke
in most pathetic language of the wrong of parting from the wife of   [a] Mal. ii. 13
youth,[b] and there were those to whom the bare fact of childlessness   16
rendered separation a religious duty.[c]   Elisabeth was childless.   For   [b] Gitt. 90 b
many a year this must have been the burden of Zacharias' prayer;   [c] Yeb. 64 a
the burden also of reproach, which Elisabeth seemed always to carry
with her.   They had waited together these many years, till in the
evening of life the flower of hope had closed its fragrant cup; and
still the two sat together in the twilight, content to wait in loneliness,
till night would close around them.

But on that bright autumn morning in the Temple no such
thoughts would come to Zacharias.   For the first, and for the last
time in life the lot had marked him for incensing, and every thought
must have centred on what was before him.   Even outwardly, all
attention would be requisite for the proper performance of his office.
First, he had to choose two of his special friends or relatives, to
assist in his sacred service.   Their duties were comparatively simple.
One reverently removed what had been left on the altar from the
previous evening's service; then, worshipping, retired backwards.
The second assistant now advanced, and, having spread to the utmost
verge of the golden altar the live coals taken from that of burnt-
offering, worshipped and retired.   Meanwhile the sound of the
'organ' (the Magrephah), heard to the most distant parts of the
Temple, and, according to tradition, far beyond its precincts, had
summoned priests, Levites, and people to prepare for whatever service or duty was before them.   For, this was the innermost part
of the worship of the day.   But the celebrant Priest, bearing the
golden censer, stood alone within the Holy Place, lit by the sheen of
the seven-branched candlestick.   Before him—somewhat farther away,
towards the heavy Veil that hung before the Holy of Holies, was the
golden altar of incense, on which the red coals glowed.   To his right
(the left of the altar—that is, on the north side) was the table of
shewbread; to his left, on the right or south side of the altar, was the
golden candlestick.   And still he waited, as instructed to do, till a
special signal indicated, that the moment had come to spread the
incense on the altar, as near as possible to the Holy of Holies.
Priests and people had reverently withdrawn from the neighbourhood
of the altar, and were prostrate before the Lord, offering unspoken
worship, in which record of past deliverance, longing for mercies

BOOK
II

promised in the future, and entreaty for present blessing and peace,[1] seemed the ingredients of the incense, that rose in a fragrant cloud of praise and prayer.   Deep silence had fallen on the worshippers, as if they watched to heaven the prayers of Israel, ascending in the cloud of 'odours' that rose from the golden altar in the Holy Place.[a] Zacharias waited, until he saw the incense kindling.   Then he also would have 'bowed down in worship,' and reverently withdrawn,[b] had not a wondrous sight arrested his steps.

On the right (or south) side of the altar, between it and the golden candlestick, stood what he could not but recognise as an Angelic form.[2]   Never, indeed, had even tradition reported such a vision to an ordinary Priest in the act of incensing.   The two supernatural apparitions recorded—one of an Angel each year of the Pontificate of Simon the Just; the other in that blasphemous account of the vision of the Almighty by Ishmael, the son of Elisha, and of the conversation which then ensued[c][3]—had both been vouchsafed to High-Priests, and on the Day of Atonement.   Still, there was always uneasiness among the people as any mortal approached the immediate Presence of God, and every delay in his return seemed ominous.[d]   No wonder, then, that Zacharias 'was troubled, and fear fell on him,' as of a sudden—probably just after he had spread the incense on the altar, and was about to offer his parting prayer—he beheld what afterwards he knew to be the Angel Gabriel ('the might of God'). Apart from higher considerations, there could perhaps be no better evidence of the truth of this narrative than its accord with psychological facts.   An Apocryphal narrative would probably have painted the scene in agreement with what, in the view of such a writer, should have been the feelings of Zacharias, and the language of the Angel.[4]   The Angel would have commenced by referring to Zacharias' prayers for the coming of a Messiah, and Zacharias would have been represented in a highly enthusiastic state.   Instead of the strangely prosaic objection which he offered to the Angelic announcement, there would have been a burst of spiritual sentiment, or what passed for such.   But all this would have been psychologically untrue.   There

[a] Rev. v. 8; viii. 1, 3, 4

[b] Tamid vi. 3

[c] Ber. 7 a

[d] Jer. Yoma 42 c

---

[1] For the prayers offered by the people during the incensing, see 'The Temple,' pp. 139, 140.

[2] The following extract from Yalkut (vol. i. p. 113 d, close) affords a curious illustration of this Divine communication from beside the altar of incense: 'From what place did the Shekhinah speak to Moses? R. Nathan said: From the altar of incense, according to Ex. xxx. 6.

Simeon ben Asai said: From the side of the altar of incense.'

[3] According to the Talmud, Ishmael once went into the innermost Sanctuary, when he had a vision of God, Who called upon the priest to pronounce a benediction.   The token of God's acceptance had better not be quoted.

[4] Instances of an analogous kind frequently occur in the Apocryphal Gospels.

are moments of moral faintness, so to speak, when the vital powers
of the spiritual heart are depressed, and, as in the case of the Disciples on the Mount of Transfiguration and in the Garden of Gethsemane, the physical part of our being and all that is weakest in us
assert their power.

It was true to this state of semi-consciousness, that the Angel
first awakened within Zacharias the remembrance of life-long prayers
and hopes, which had now passed into the background of his being,
and then suddenly startled him by the promise of their realisation.
But that Child of so many prayers, who was to bear the significant
name of John (Jehochanan, or Jochanan), 'the Lord is gracious,' was
to be the source of joy and gladness to a far wider circle than that of
the family. This might be called the first rung of the ladder by
which the Angel would take the priest upwards. Nor was even this
followed by an immediate disclosure of what, in such a place, and
from such a messenger, must have carried to a believing heart the
thrill of almost unspeakable emotion. Rather was Zacharias led
upwards, step by step. The Child was to be great before the Lord;
not only an ordinary, but a life-Nazarite,[1] as Samson and Samuel of
old had been. Like them, he was not to consecrate himself, but from
the inception of life wholly to belong to God, for His work. And,
greater than either of these representatives of the symbolical import
of Nazarism, he would combine the twofold meaning of their mission
—outward and inward might in God, only in a higher and more
spiritual sense. For this life-work he would be filled with the
Holy Ghost, from the moment life woke within him. Then, as
another Samson, would he, in the strength of God, lift the axe to each
tree to be felled, and, like another Samuel, turn many of the children
of Israel to the Lord their God. Nay, combining these two missions,
as did Elijah on Mount Carmel, he should, in accordance with
prophecy,[a] precede the Messianic manifestation, and, not indeed in the
person or form, but in the spirit and power of Elijah, accomplish the
typical meaning of his mission, as on that day of decision it had risen
as the burden of his prayer[b]—that is, in the words of prophecy,[c]
'turn the heart of the fathers to the children,' which, in view of the
coming dispensation, would be 'the disobedient (to walk) in the
wisdom of the just.'[d] Thus would this new Elijah 'make ready for
the Lord a people prepared.'

If the apparition of the Angel, in that place, and at that time,
had overwhelmed the aged priest, the words which he heard must

a Mal. iii. 1

b 1 Kings
xviii. 37
c Mal. iv. 5,
6

d St. Luke
i. 17; comp.
St. Matt. xi.
19

---

[1] On the different classes of Nazarites, see 'The Temple, &c.,' pp. 322–331.

BOOK
II

have filled him with such bewilderment, that for the moment he scarcely realised their meaning. One idea alone, which had struck its roots so long in his consciousness, stood out: A son—while, as it were in the dim distance beyond, stretched, as covered with a mist of glory, all those marvellous things that were to be connected with him. So, when age or strong feeling renders us almost insensible to the present, it is ever that which connects itself with the past, rather than with the present, which emerges first and strongest in our consciousness. And so it was the obvious doubt, that would suggest itself, which fell from his lips—almost unconscious of what he said. Yet there was in his words an element of faith also, or at least of hope, as he asked for some pledge or confirmation of what he had heard.

It is this demand of some visible sign, by which to 'know' all that the Angel had promised, which distinguishes the doubt of Zacharias from that of Abraham,[a] or of Manoah and his wife,[b] under somewhat similar circumstances—although, otherwise also, even a cursory reading must convey the impression of most marked differences. Nor ought we perhaps to forget, that we are on the threshold of a dispensation, to which faith is the only entrance. This door Zacharias was now to hold ajar, a dumb messenger. He that would not speak the praises of God, but asked a sign, received it. His dumbness was a sign—though the sign, as it were the dumb child of the prayer of unbelief, was its punishment also. And yet, when rightly applied, a sign in another sense also—a sign to the waiting multitude in the Temple; a sign to Elisabeth; to all who knew Zacharias in the hill-country; and to the priest himself, during those nine months of retirement and inward solitude; a sign also that would kindle into fiery flame in the day when God would loosen his tongue.

A period of unusual length had passed, since the signal for incensing had been given. The prayers of the people had been offered, and their anxious gaze was directed towards the Holy Place. At last Zacharias emerged to take his stand on the top of the steps which led from the Porch to the Court of the Priests, waiting to lead in the priestly benediction,[c] that preceded the daily meat-offering and the chant of the Psalms of praise, accompanied with joyous sound of music, as the drink-offering was poured out. But already the sign of Zacharias was to be a sign to all the people. The pieces of the sacrifices had been ranged in due order on the altar of burnt-offering; the priests stood on the steps to the porch, and the people

a Gen. xvii. 17, 18
b Judg. xiii 2-21

c Numb. vi. 24-26

were in waiting. Zacharias essayed to speak the words of benediction, unconscious that the stroke had fallen. But the people knew
it by his silence, that he had seen a vision in the Temple. Yet as he
stood helpless, trying by signs to indicate it to the awestruck assembly, he remained dumb.

Wondering, they had dispersed—people and priests. The day's
service over, another family of ministrants took the place of those
among whom Zacharias had been; and again, at the close of the
week's service, another 'course' that of Abia. They returned to
their homes—some to Ophel, some to Jericho, some to their quiet
dwellings in the country. But God fulfilled the word which He had
spoken by His Angel.

Before leaving this subject, it may be well to inquire into the
relation between the events just described, and the customs and expectations of the time. The scene in the Temple, and all the surroundings, are in strictest accordance with what we know of the
services of the Sanctuary. In a narrative that lays hold on some
details of a very complex service, such entire accuracy conveys the
impression of general truthfulness. Similarly, the sketch of Zacharias
and Elisabeth is true to the history of the time—though Zacharias
could not have been one of the 'learned,' nor to the Rabbinists, a
model priest. They would have described him as an 'idiot,'[1] or common, and as an *Amha-arets*, a 'rustic' priest, and treated him
with benevolent contempt.[2] The Angelic apparition, which he saw, was
wholly unprecedented, and could therefore not have lain within range
of common expectation; though the possibility, or rather the fear, of
some contact with the Divine was always present to the popular mind.
But it is difficult to conceive how, if not true, the invention of such
a vision in such circumstances could have suggested itself. This
difficulty is enhanced by the obvious differences between the Evangelic
narrative, and the popular ideas of the time. Far too much importance has here been attached by a certain class of writers to a Rab-
binic saying,[a] that the names of the Angels were brought from Babylon.   [a] Jer.
haSh. 56 d,
line 10 from
bottom
For, not only was this saying (of Ben Lakish) only a clever Scriptural
deduction (as the context shows), and not even an actual tradition,
but no competent critic would venture to lay down the principle, that
isolated Rabbinic sayings in the Talmud are to be regarded as
sufficient foundation for historical facts. On the other hand, Rab-

---

[1] The word עם הארץ, or 'idiot,' when conjoined with 'priest' ordinarily means a
common priest, in distinction to the High
priest. But the word unquestionably
also signifies vulgar, ignorant, and illit-

erate. See Jer. Sot. 21 b, line 3 from
bottom; Sanh. 21 b. Comp. also Meg.
12 b; Ber. R. 96.

[2] According to Sanh. 90 b, such an one
was not even allowed to get the Terumah.

BOOK
II

ᵃ Judg. xiii.
18

ᵇ Dan. ix. 21
ᶜ x. 21

binic tradition does lay it down, that the names of the Angels were derived from their mission, and might be changed with it. Thus the reply of the Angel to the inquiry of Manoah ᵃ is explained as implying, that he knew not what other name might be given him in the future. In the Book of Daniel, to which the son of Lakish refers, the only two Angelic names mentioned are Gabriel ᵇ and Michael,ᶜ while the appeal to the Book of Daniel, as evidence of the Babylonish origin of Jewish Angelology, comes with strange inconsistency from writers who date it in Maccabean times.[1] But the question of Angelic nomenclature is quite secondary. The real point at issue is, whether or not the Angelology and Demonology of the New Testament was derived from contemporary Judaism. The opinion, that such was the case, has been so dogmatically asserted, as to have almost passed among a certain class as a settled fact. That nevertheless such was *not* the case, is capable of the most ample proof. Here also, with similarity of form, slighter than usually, there is absolute contrast of substance.[2]

Admitting that the names of Gabriel and Michael must have been familiar to the mind of Zacharias, some not unimportant differences must be kept in view. Thus, Gabriel was regarded in tradition as inferior to Michael; and, though both were connected with Israel, Gabriel was represented as chiefly the minister of justice, and Michael of mercy; while, thirdly, Gabriel was supposed to stand on the left, and not (as in the Evangelic narrative) on the right, side of the throne of glory. Small as these divergences may seem, they are all-important, when derivation of one set of opinions from another is in question. Finally, as regarded the coming of Elijah as forerunner of the Messiah, it is to be observed that, according to Jewish notions, he was to appear *personally*, and not merely ' in spirit and power.' In fact, tradition represents his ministry and appearances as almost continuous—not only immediately before the coming of Messiah, but at all times. Rabbinic writings introduce him on the scene, not only frequently, but on the most incongruous occasions, and for the most diverse

ᵈ Moed K.
26 a

ᵉ 1 Kings
xviii. 37 (in
Hebr. without ' that '
and
' again ');
see Ber.
31 b, last
two lines

ᶠ Bemidbar
R. 14. Another view
in Par. 13

purposes. In this sense it is said of him, that he always liveth.ᵈ Sometimes, indeed, he is blamed, as for the closing words in his prayer about the turning of the heart of the people,ᵉ and even his sacrifice on Carmel was only excused on the ground of express command.ᶠ But his great activity as precursor of the Messiah is to resolve doubts of all kinds; to reintroduce those who had been violently and improperly extruded

[1] Two other Angels are mentioned, but not named, in Dan. x. 13, 20.

[2] The Jewish ideas and teaching about angels are fully given in Appendix XIII. ' Jewish Angelology and Demonology.'

from the congregation of Israel, and vice-versâ; to make peace; while, finally, he was connected with the raising of the dead.[a][1] But nowhere is he prominently designated as intended 'to make ready for the Lord a people prepared.'[2]

CHAP.
III

[a] This in Shir haSh R. i. ed. Warshau, p. 3 a

Thus, from whatever source the narrative may be supposed to have been derived, its details certainly differ, in almost all particulars, from the theological notions current at the time. And the more Zacharias meditated on this in the long solitude of his enforced silence, the more fully must new spiritual thoughts have come to him. As for Elisabeth, those tender feelings of woman, which ever shrink from the disclosure of the dearest secret of motherhood, were intensely deepened and sanctified in the knowledge of all that had passed. Little as she might understand the full meaning of the future, it must have been to her, as if she also now stood in the Holy Place, gazing towards the Veil which concealed the innermost Presence. Meantime she was content with, nay, felt the need of, absolute retirement from other fellowship than that of God and her own heart. Like her husband, she too would be silent and alone—till another voice called her forth. Whatever the future might bring, sufficient for the present, that thus the Lord had done to her, in days in which He looked down to remove her reproach among men. The removal of that burden, its manner, its meaning, its end, were all from God, and with God; and it was fitting to be quite alone and silent, till God's voice would again wake the echoes within. And so five months passed in absolute retirement.

[1] All the Rabbinic traditions about 'Elijah as the Forerunner of the Messiah' are collated in Appendix VIII.

[2] I should, however, remark, that that very curious chapter on Repentance, in the Pirké de R. Elieser (c. 43), closes with these words: ' And Israel will not make great repentance till Elijah—his memory for blessing!—come, as it is said, Mal. iv. 6,' &c. From this isolated and enigmatic sentence, Professor *Delitzsch's* implied inference (Zeitschr. für Luther. Theol. 1875, p. 593) seems too sweeping.

CHAPTER IV.

THE ANNUNCIATION OF JESUS THE MESSIAH, AND THE BIRTH OF HIS FORERUNNER.

(St. Matt. i.; St. Luke i. 26–80.)

BOOK
II

FROM the Temple to Nazareth! It seems indeed most fitting that the Evangelic story should have taken its beginning within the Sanctuary, and at the time of sacrifice. Despite its outward veneration for them, the Temple, its services, and specially its sacrifices, were, by an inward logical necessity, fast becoming a superfluity for Rabbinism. But the new development, passing over the intruded elements, which were, after all, of rationalistic origin, connected its beginning directly with the Old Testament dispensation—its sacrifices, priesthood, and promises. In the Sanctuary, in connection with sacrifice, and through the priesthood — such was significantly the beginning of the era of fulfillment. And so the great religious reformation of Israel under Samuel had also begun in the Tabernacle, which had so long been in the background. But if, even in this Temple-beginning, and in the communication to, and selection of an idiot 'priest,' there was marked divergence from the Rabbinic ideal, that difference widens into the sharpest contrast, as we pass from the Forerunner to the Messiah, from the Temple to Galilee, from the 'idiot' priest to the humble, unlettered family of Nazareth. It is necessary here to recall our general impression of Rabbinism: its conception of God,[1] and of the highest good and ultimate object of all things, as concentrated in learned study, pursued in Academies; and then to think of the unmitigated contempt with which they were wont to speak of Galilee, and of the Galileans, whose very *patois* was an offence; of the utter abhorrence with which they regarded the unlettered country-people,

---

[1] Terrible as it may sound, it is certainly the teaching of Rabbinism, that God occupied so many hours every day in the study of the Law. Comp. Targ. Ps.-Jonathan on Deut. xxxii. 4, and Abhod. Z. 3 b. Nay, Rabbinism goes farther in its daring, and speaks of the Almighty as arrayed in a white dress, or as occupying himself by day with the study of the Bible, and by night with that of the six tractates of the Mishnah. Comp. also the Targum on Cant. v. 10

in order to realise, how such an household as that of Joseph and Mary would be regarded by the leaders of Israel.   A Messianic announce- ment, not the result of learned investigation, nor connected with the Academies, but in the Sanctuary, to a 'rustic' priest; an Elijah unable to untie the intellectual or ecclesiastical knots, of whose mission, indeed, this formed no part at all; and a Messiah, the off- spring of a Virgin in Galilee betrothed to a humble workman— assuredly, such a picture of the fulfillment of Israel's hope could never have been conceived by contemporary Judaism.   There was in such a Messiah absolutely nothing—past, present, or possible; intellectually, religiously, or even nationally—to attract, but all to repel.   And so we can, at the very outset of this history, understand the infinite contrast which it embodied—with all the difficulties to its reception, even to those who became disciples, as at almost every step of its pro- gress they were, with ever fresh surprise, recalled from all that they had formerly thought, to that which was so entirely new and strange.

And yet, just as Zacharias may be described as the representative of the good and the true in the Priesthood at that time, so the family of Nazareth as a typical Israelitish household.   We feel, that the scantiness of particulars here supplied by the Gospels, was intended to prevent the human interest from overshadowing the grand central Fact, to which alone attention was to be directed.   For, the design of the Gospels was manifestly not to furnish a biography of Jesus the Messiah, [1] but, in organic connection with the Old Testament, to tell the history of the long-promised establishment of the Kingdom of God upon earth.   Yet what scanty details we possess of the ' Holy Family ' and its surroundings may here find a place.

The highlands which form the central portion of Palestine are broken by the wide, rich plain of Jezreel, which severs Galilee from the rest of the land.   This was always the great battle-field of Israel. Appropriately, it is shut in as between mountain-walls.   That along the north of the plain is formed by the mountains of Lower Galilee, cleft about the middle by a valley that widens, till, after an hour's journey, we stand within an enclosure which seems almost one of Nature's own sanctuaries.   As in an amphitheatre, fifteen hill-tops rise around.   That to the west is the highest—about 500 feet.   On its lower slopes nestles a little town, its narrow streets ranged like terraces.   This is Nazareth, probably the ancient Sarid (or En-Sarid),

---

[1] The object which the Evangelists had in view was certainly not that of bio- graphy, even as the Old Testament con- tains no biography.   The twofold object of their narratives is indicated by St. Luke i. 4, and by St. John xx. 31.

which, in the time of Joshua, marked the northern boundary of
Zebulun. ᵃ¹

Climbing this steep hill, fragrant with aromatic plants, and bright
with rich-coloured flowers, a view almost unsurpassed opens before us.
For, the Galilee of the time of Jesus was not only of the richest
fertility, cultivated to the utmost, and thickly covered with populous
towns and villages, but the centre of every known industry, and the
busy road of the world's commerce. Northward the eye would sweep
over a rich plain; rest here and there on white towns, glittering in
the sunlight; then quickly travel over the romantic hills and glens
which form the scenes of Solomon's Song, till, passing beyond Safed
(the Tsephath of the Rabbis—the 'city set on an hill'), the view is
bounded by that giant of the far-off mountain-chain, snow-tipped
Hermon. Westward stretched a like scene of beauty and wealth—a
land not lonely, but wedded; not desolate, but teeming with life;
while, on the edge of the horizon, lay purple Carmel; beyond it a
fringe of silver sand, and then the dazzling sheen of the Great Sea.
In the farthest distance, white sails, like wings outspread towards the
ends of the world; nearer, busy ports; then, centres of industry;
and close by, travelled roads, all bright in the pure Eastern air and
rich glow of the sun. But if you turned eastwards, the eye would
soon be arrested by the wooded height of Tabor, yet not before attention had been riveted by the long, narrow string of fantastic caravans, and curiosity roused by the motley figures, of all nationalities
and in all costumes, busy binding the East to the West by that line
of commerce that passed along the route winding around Tabor. And
when, weary with the gaze, you looked once more down on little
Nazareth nestling on the breast of the mountain, the eye would rest
on a scene of tranquil, homely beauty. Just outside the town, in the
north-west, bubbled the spring or well, the trysting-spot of townspeople, and welcome resting-place of travellers. Beyond it stretched
lines of houses, each with its flat roof standing out distinctly against
the clear sky; watered, terraced gardens, gnarled wide-spreading fig-
trees, graceful feathery palms, scented oranges, silvery olive-trees,
thick hedges, rich pasture-land, then the bounding hills to the south;

¹ The name *Nazareth* may best be regarded as the equivalent of נְצֶרֶת,
'watch' or 'watcheress.' The name does
not occur in the Talmud, nor in those
Midrashim which have been preserved.
But the elegy of Eleazar ha Kallir—
written before the close of the Talmud—
in which Nazareth is mentioned as a Priest-
centre, is based upon an ancient Midrash,
now lost (comp. *Neubauer*, Géogr. du
Talmud, p. 117, note 5). It is, however,
possible, as Dr. *Neubauer* suggests (u. s.
p. 190, note 5), that the name נצחנה in
Midr. on Eccl. ii. 8 should read נצרנה,
and refers to Nazareth.

and beyond, the seemingly unbounded expanse of the wide plain of Esdraelon!

And yet, withdrawn from the world as, in its enclosure of mountains, Nazareth might seem, we must not think of it as a lonely village which only faint echoes reached of what roused the land beyond. With reverence be it said: such a place might have suited the training of the contemplative hermit, not the upbringing of Him Whose sympathies were to be with every clime and race. Nor would such an abode have furnished what (with all due acknowledgment of the supernatural) we mark as a constant, because a rationally necessary, element in Scripture history: that of inward preparedness in which the higher and the Divine afterwards find their ready points of contact.

Nor was it otherwise in Nazareth. The two great interests which stirred the land, the two great factors in the religious future of Israel, constantly met in the retirement of Nazareth. The great caravan-route which led from Acco on the sea to Damascus divided at its commencement into three roads: the most northern passing through Cæsarea Philippi; the Upper Galilean; and the Lower Galilean. The latter, the ancient *Via Maris* led through Nazareth, and thence either by Cana, or else along the northern shoulder of Mount Tabor, to the Lake of Gennesaret—each of these roads soon uniting with the Upper Galilean.[1] Hence, although the stream of commerce between Acco and the East was divided into three channels, yet, as one of these passed through Nazareth, the quiet little town was not a stagnant pool of rustic seclusion. Men of all nations, busy with another life than that of Israel, would appear in the streets of Nazareth; and through them thoughts, associations, and hopes connected with the great outside world be stirred. But, on the other hand, Nazareth was also one of the great centers of Jewish Temple-life. It has already been indicated that the Priesthood was divided into twenty-four 'courses,' which, in turn, ministered in the Temple. The Priests of the 'course' which was to be on duty always gathered in certain towns, whence they went up in company to Jerusalem, while those of their number who were unable to go spent the week in fasting and prayer. Now Nazareth was one of these Priest-centres,[2] and although it may well have been, that comparatively few in distant Galilee conformed to the Priestly regulations—some must have assembled there in preparation for the sacred functions, or appeared in its Synagogue.

---

[1] Comp. the detailed description of these roads, and the references in *Herzog's* Real-Encykl. vol. xv. pp. 160, 161.

[2] Comp. *Neubauer*, u. s. p. 190. See a detailed account in 'Sketches of Jewish Social Life,' &c. p. 36.

BOOK
II

Even the fact, so well known to all, of this living connection between Nazareth and the Temple, must have wakened peculiar feelings. Thus, to take the wider view, a double symbolic significance attached to Nazareth, since through it passed alike those who carried on the traffic of the world, and those who ministered in the Temple.[1]

We may take it, that the people of Nazareth were like those of other little towns similarly circumstanced:[2] with all the peculiarities of the impulsive, straight-spoken, hot-blooded, brave, intensely national Galileans;[3] with the deeper feelings and almost instinctive habits of thought and life, which were the outcome of long centuries of Old Testament training; but also with the petty interests and jealousies of such places, and with all the ceremonialism and punctilious self-assertion of Orientals. The cast of Judaism prevalent in Nazareth would, of course, be the same as in Galilee generally. We know, that there were marked divergences from the observances in that stronghold of Rabbinism,[4] Judæa—indicating greater simplicity and freedom from the constant intrusion of traditional ordinances. The home-life would be all the purer, that the veil of wedded life was not so coarsely lifted as in Judæa, nor its sacred secrecy interfered with by an Argus-eyed legislation.[5] The purity of betrothal in Galilee was less likely to be sullied,[a] and weddings were more simple than in Judæa—without the dubious institution of groomsmen,[b][6] or 'friends of the bridegroom,'[c] whose office must not unfrequently have degenerated into utter coarseness. The bride was chosen, not as in Judæa, where money was too often the motive, but as in Jerusalem, with chief regard to 'a fair degree;' and widows were (as in Jerusalem) more tenderly cared for, as we gather even from the fact, that they had a life-right of residence in their husband's house.[d]

Such a home was that to which Joseph was about to bring the maiden, to whom he had been betrothed. Whatever view may be taken of the genealogies in the Gospels according to St. Matthew and St. Luke—whether they be regarded as those of Joseph and of

a Keth. 12 a
b Keth. 12 a,
and often
c St. John
iii. 29

---

[1] It is strange, that these two circumstances have not been noticed. *Keim* (Jesu von Nazara i. 2, pp. 322, 323) only cursorily refers to the great road which passed through Nazareth.

[2] The inference, that the expression of Nathanael (St. John i. 46) implies a lower state of the people of Nazareth, is unfounded. Even *Keim* points out, that it only marks disbelief that the Messiah would come from such a place.

[3] Our description of them is derived

from notices by *Josephus* (such as War iii. 3, 2), and many passages in the Talmud,

[4] These differences are marked in Pes. iv. 5; Keth. iv. 12; Ned. ii. 4; Chull. 62 *a*; Baba K. 80 *a*; Keth. 12 *a*.

[5] The reader who wishes to understand what we have only ventured to hint, is referred to the Mishnic tractate Niddah.

[6] Comp. 'Sketches of Jewish Social Life,' &c., pp. 152 &c.

Mary,[1] or, which seems the more likely,[2] as those of Joseph only, marking his natural and his legal descent[3] from David, or vice versâ[4]—there can be no question, that both Joseph and Mary were of the royal lineage of David.[5] Most probably the two were nearly related,[6] while Mary could also claim kinship with the Priesthood, being, no doubt on her mother's side, a 'blood-relative' of Elisabeth, the Priest-wife of Zacharias.[a][7] Even this seems to imply, that Mary's family must shortly before have held higher rank, for only with such did custom sanction any alliance on the part of Priests.[8] But at the time of their betrothal, alike Joseph and Mary were extremely poor, as appears—not indeed from his being a carpenter, since a trade was regarded as almost a religious duty—but from the offering at the presentation of Jesus in the Temple.[b] Accordingly, their betrothal must have been of the simplest, and the dowry settled the smallest possible.[9] Whichever of the two modes of betrothal[10] may have been adopted: in the presence of witnesses—either by solemn word of mouth, in due prescribed formality, with the added pledge of a piece of money, however small, or of money's worth for use; or else by writing (the so-called *Shitre Erusin*)—there would be no sumptuous feast to follow; and the ceremony would conclude with some such benediction as that afterwards in use: 'Blessed art Thou, O Lord our God, King of the World, Who hath sanctified us by His Commandments, and enjoined us about incest, and forbidden the betrothed, but allowed us those wedded by *Chuppah* (the marriage-baldachino) and betrothal. Blessed art Thou, Who sanctifiest Israel

CHAP.
IV

[a] St. Luke i. 36

[b] St. Luke ii. 24

[1] The best defence of this view is that by *Wieseler*, Beitr. zur Würdig. d. Evang. pp. 133 &c. It is also virtually adopted by *Weiss* (Leben Jesu, vol. i. 1882).

[2] This view is adopted almost unanimously by modern writers.

[3] This view is defended with much skill by Mr. *McClellan* in his New Testament, vol. i. pp. 409–422.

[4] So Grotius, Bishop Lord Arthur Hervey, and after him most modern English writers.

[5] The Davidic descent of the Virgin-Mother—which is questioned by some even among orthodox interpreters—seems implied in the Gospel (St. Luke i. 27, 32, 69; ii. 4), and an almost *necessary* inference from such passages as Rom. i. 3; 2 Tim. ii. 8; Hebr. vii. 14. The Davidic descent of Jesus is not only admitted, but elaborately proved—on purely rationalistic grounds—by *Keim* (u. s. pp. 327–329).

[6] This is the general view of antiquity.

[7] Reference to this union of Levi and Judah in the Messiah is made in the Test. xii. Patriarch., Test. Simeonis vii. (apud *Fabr.* Cod. Pseudepigr. vol. ii. p. 542). Curiously, the great Hillel was also said by some to have descended, through his father and mother, from the tribes of Judah and Levi—all, however, asserting his Davidic origin (comp. Jer. Taan. iv. 2; Ber. R. 98 and 33).

[8] Comp. *Maimonides*, Yad haChaz Hil. Sanh. ii. The inference would, of course, be the same, whether we suppose Mary's mother to have been the sister-in-law, or the sister, of Elisabeth's father.

[9] Comp. 'Sketches of Jewish Social Life in the Days of Christ,' pp. 143–149. Also the article on 'Marriage' in *Cassell's* Bible-Educator, vol. iv. pp. 267–270.

[10] There was a third mode, by cohabitation; but this was highly disapproved of even by the Rabbis.

BOOK
II

by Chuppah and betrothal'—the whole being perhaps concluded by a benediction over the statutory cup of wine, which was tasted in turn by the betrothed. From that moment Mary was the betrothed wife of Joseph; their relationship as sacred, as if they had already been wedded. Any breach of it would be treated as adultery; nor could the band be dissolved except, as after marriage, by regular divorce. Yet months might intervene between the betrothal and marriage.[1]

Five months of Elisabeth's sacred retirement had passed, when a strange messenger brought its first tidings to her kinswoman in far-off Galilee. It was not in the solemn grandeur of the Temple, between the golden altar of incense and the seven-branched candlesticks that the Angel Gabriel now appeared, but in the privacy of a humble home at Nazareth. The greatest honor bestowed on man was to come amidst circumstances of deepest human lowliness, as if the more clearly to mark the exclusively Divine character of what was to happen. And, although the awe of the Supernatural must unconsciously have fallen upon her, it was not so much the sudden appearance of the mysterious stranger in her retirement that startled the maiden, as the words of his greeting, implying unthought blessing. The 'Peace to thee'[2] was, indeed, the well-known salutation, while the words, 'The Lord is with thee' might waken the remembrance of the Angelic call, to great deliverance in the past.[a] But this designation of 'highly favored'[3] came upon her with bewildering surprise, perhaps not so much from its contrast to the humbleness of her estate, as from the self-conscious humility of her heart. And it was intended so, for of all feelings this would now most become her. Accordingly, it is this story of special 'favour' or grace, which the Angel traces in rapid outline, from the conception of the Virgin-Mother to the distinctive, Divinely-given Name, symbolic of the meaning of His coming; His absolute greatness; His acknowledgment as the Son of God; and the fulfillment in Him of the great

a Judg. vi. 12

---

[1] The assertion of Professor *Wünsche* (Neue Beitr. zur Erläuter. d. Evang. p. 7) that the practice of betrothal was confined exclusively, or almost so, to Judæa, is quite ungrounded. The passages to which he refers (Kethub. i. 5—not 3—and especially Keth. 12 *a*) are irrelevant. Keth. 12 *a* marks the simpler and purer customs of Galilee, but does *not* refer to betrothals.

[2] I have rendered the Greek χαῖρε by the Hebrew שָׁלוֹם and for the correctness of it refer the reader to *Grimm's* remarks on 1 Macc. x. 18 (Exeget. Handb. zu d. Apokryph. 3ᵗᵉ Lief. p. 149).

[3] *Bengel* aptly remarks, 'Non ut mater gratiæ, sed ut filia gratiæ.' Even *Jeremy Taylor's* remarks (Life of Christ, ed. Pickering, vol. i. p. 56) would here require modification. Following the best critical authorities, I have omitted the words, 'Blessed art thou among women.'

Davidic hope, with its never-ceasing royalty,[1] and its never-ending, boundless Kingdom.[2]

In all this, however marvellous, there could be nothing strange to those who cherished in their hearts Israel's great hope, not merely as an article of abstract belief, but as matter of certain fact—least of all to the maiden of the lineage of David, betrothed to him of the house and lineage of David. So long as the hand of prophetic blessing rested on the house of David, and before its finger had pointed to the individual who 'found favor' in the highest sense, the consciousness of possibilities, which scarce dared shape themselves into definite thoughts, must at times have stirred nameless feelings—perhaps the more often in circumstances of outward depression and humility, such as those of the 'Holy Family.' Nor was there anything strange even in the naming of the yet unconceived Child. It sounds like a saying current among the people of old, this of the Rabbis,[a] concerning the six whose names were given before their birth: Isaac, Ishmael, Moses, Solomon, Josiah, and 'the Name of the Messiah, Whom may the Holy One, blessed be His Name, bring quickly in our days!'[3] But as for the deeper meaning of the name Jesus,[b] which, like an unopened bud, enclosed the flower of His Passion, that was mercifully yet the unthought-of secret of that word, which should pierce the soul of the Virgin-Mother, and which only His future history would lay open to her and to others.

Thus, on the supposition of the readiness of her believing heart, and her entire self-unconsciousness, it would have been only the glorious announcement of the impending event, which would absorb her thinking—with nothing strange about it, or that needed further light, than the *how* of her own connection with it.[4] And the words,

[a] Pirqé de R. El. 32, at the beginning

[b] St. Matt. i. 21

---

[1] We here refer, as an interesting corroboration, to the Targum on Ps. xlv. 7 6 in our A.V.). But this interest is intensely increased when we read it, not as in our editions of the Targum, but as found in a MS. copy of the year 1208 given by *Levy* in his Targum. Wörterb. vol. i. p. 390 *a*). Translating it from that reading, the Targum thus renders Ps. xlv. 7, 'Thy throne, O God, in the heaven' (Levy renders, 'Thy throne from God in heaven,' but in either case it refers to the throne of the Messiah) 'is for ever and ever' (for 'world without end,' עלמין עלמי 'a rule of righteousness is the rule of Thy kingdom, O Thou King Messiah!'

[2] In Pirqé de R. El. c. 11, the same boundless dominion is ascribed to Messiah the King. In that curious passage dominion is ascribed to 'ten kings,' the first being God, the ninth the Messiah, and the tenth again God, to Whom the kingdom would be delivered in the end, according to Is. xliv. 6; Zechar. xiv. 9; Ezek. xxxiv. 24, with the result described in Is. lii. 9.

[3] Professor *Wünsche's* quotation is here not exact (u. s. p. 414).

[4] *Weiss* (Leben Jesu, 1882, vol. i. p. 213) rightly calls attention to the humility of her self-surrender, when she willingly submitted to what her heart would feel hardest to bear—that of incurring suspicion of her purity in the sight of all.

BOOK
II

which she spake, were not of trembling doubt, that required to lean on the staff of a 'sign,' but rather those of enquiry, for the further guidance of a willing self-surrender. The Angel had pointed her opened eyes to the shining path: that was not strange; only, that *She* should walk in it, seemed so. And now the Angel still further unfolded it in words which, however little she may have understood their full meaning, had again nothing strange about them, save once more that *she* should be thus 'favoured'; words which, even to her understanding, must have carried yet further thoughts of Divine *favour*, and so deepened her humility. For, the idea of the activity of the Holy Ghost in all great events was quite familiar to Israel at the time,[1] even though the Individuation of the Holy Ghost may not have been fully apprehended. Only, that they expected such influences to rest exclusively upon those who were either mighty, or rich, or wise.[a] And of this twofold manifestation of miraculous 'favour'—that she, and as a Virgin, should be its subject—Gabriel, 'the might of God,' gave this unasked sign, in what had happened to her kinswoman Elisabeth.

Nedar. 38 a

The sign was at the same time a direction. The first, but also the ever-deepening desire in the heart of Mary, when the Angel left her, must have been to be away from Nazareth, and for the relief of opening her heart to a woman, in all things like-minded, who perhaps might speak blessed words to her. And to such an one the Angel himself seemed to have directed her. It is only what we would have expected, that 'with haste' she should have resorted to her kins-woman, without loss of time, and before she would speak to her betrothed of what even in wedded life is the first secret whispered.[2]

It could have been no ordinary welcome that would greet the Virgin-Mother, on entering the house of her kinswoman. Elisabeth must have learnt from her husband the destiny of their son, and hence the near Advent of the Messiah. But she could not have known either *when*, or *of whom* He would be born. When, by a sign not quite strange to Jewish expectancy,[3] she recognised in her

but especially in that of her betrothed. The whole account, as we gather from St. Luke ii. 19, 51, must have been derived from the personal recollections of the Virgin-Mother.

[1] So in almost innumerable Rabbinic passages.

[2] This in answer to the objection, so pertinaciously urged, of inconsistency with the narrative in St. Matt. i. 19 &c.

It is clear, that Mary went 'with haste' to her kinswoman, and that any communication to Joseph *could* only have taken place after that, and after the Angelic prediction was in all its parts confirmed by her visit to Elisabeth. *Jeremy Taylor* (u. s. p. 64) has already arranged the narrative as in the text.

[3] According to Jewish tradition, the yet unborn infants in their mother's

near kinswoman the Mother of her Lord, her salutation was that of a
mother to a mother—the mother of the 'preparer' to the mother of
Him for Whom he would prepare. To be more precise: the words
which, filled with the Holy Ghost, she spake, were the mother's
utterance, to the mother, of the homage which her unborn babe
offered to his Lord; while the answering hymn of Mary was the
offering of that homage unto God. It was the antiphonal morning-
psalmody of the Messianic day as it broke, of which the words were
still all of the old dispensation,[1] but their music of the new; the
keynote being that of 'favour,' 'grace,' struck by the Angel in his
first salutation: 'favour' to the Virgin;[a] 'favour,' eternal 'favour'
to all His humble and poor ones;[b] and 'favour' to Israel, stretching
in golden line from the calling of Abraham to the glorious future
that now opened.[c] Not one of these fundamental ideas but lay
strictly within the range of the Old Testament; and yet all of them
now lay beyond it, bathed in the golden light of the new day.
Miraculous it all is, and professes to be; not indeed in the connection
of these events, which succeed each other with psychological truthfulness; nor yet in their language, which is of the times and the
circumstances; but in the underlying facts.[2] And for these there
can be no other evidence than the Life, the Death, and the Resurrection of Jesus the Messiah. If He was such, and if He really rose
from the dead, then, with all soberness and solemnity, such inception
of His appearance seems almost a logical necessity. But of this
whole narrative it may be said, that such inception of the Messianic
appearance, such announcement of it, and such manner of His Coming,
could never have been invented by contemporary Judaism; indeed,
ran directly counter to all its preconceptions.[3]

CHAP.
IV

[a] 1st stanza
vv. 46-49
[b] 2nd stan-
za, vv. 50-53
[c] 3rd stan-
za, vv. 54-55

---

wombs responded by an Amen to the
hymn of praise at the Red Sea. This is
supposed to be indicated by the words
ממקור ישראל (Ps. lxviii. 27; see also
the Targum on that verse). Comp. Keth.
7 b and Sotah 30 b (last line) and 31 a,
though the coarse legendary explanation
of R. Tanchuma mars the poetic beauty
of the whole.
[1] The poetic grandeur and the Old
Testament cast of the Virgin's hymn
(comp. the Song of Hannah, 1 Sam. ii.
1-10), need scarcely be pointed out.
Perhaps it would read fullest and best
by trying to recall what must have been
its Hebrew original.
[2] Weiss, while denying the historical
accuracy of much in the Gospel-narrative

of it, unhesitatingly accepts the fact of
the supernatural birth of Jesus.
[3] Keim elaborately discusses the origin
of what he calls the legend of Christ's
supernatural conception. He arrives at
the conclusion that it was a *Jewish*-
Christian legend—as if a *Jewish* invention of such a 'legend' were not the most
unlikely of all possible hypotheses! But
negative criticism is at least bound to
furnish some historical basis for the
origination of such an unlikely legend.
Whence was the idea of it first derived?
How did it find such ready acceptance
in the Church? Weiss has, at considerable length, and very fully, shown the
impossibility of its origin either in Jewish or heathen legend.

Three months had passed since the Virgin-Mother entered the home of her kinswoman. And now she must return to Nazareth. Soon Elisabeth's neighbours and kinsfolk would gather with sympathetic joy around a home which, as they thought, had experienced unexpected mercy—little thinking, how wide-reaching its consequences would be. But the Virgin-Mother must not be exposed to the publicity of such meetings. However conscious of what had led to her condition, it must have been as the first sharp pang of the sword which was to pierce her soul, when she told it all to her betrothed. For, however deep his trust in her whom he had chosen for wife, only a direct Divine communication could have chased all questioning from his heart, and given him that assurance, which was needful in the future history of the Messiah. Brief as, with exquisite delicacy, the narrative is, we can read in the 'thoughts' of Joseph the anxious contending of feelings, the scarcely established, and yet delayed, resolve to 'put her away,' which could only be done by regular divorce; this one determination only standing out clearly, that, if it must be, her letter of divorce shall be handed to her privately, only in the presence of two witnesses. The humble *Tsaddiq* of Nazareth would not willingly have brought the blush to any face, least of all would he make of her 'a public exhibition of shame.'[1] It was a relief that he could legally divorce her either publicly or privately, whether from change of feeling, or because he had found just cause for it, but hesitated to make it known, either from regard for his own character, or because he had not sufficient *legal* evidence[2] of the charge. He would follow, all unconscious of it, the truer manly feeling of R. Eliezar,[a] R. Jochanan, and R. Zera,[b] according to which a man would not like to put his wife to shame before a Court of Justice, rather than the opposite sentence of R. Meir.

The assurance, which Joseph could scarcely dare to hope for, was miraculously conveyed to him in a dream-vision. All would now be clear; even the terms in which he was addressed ('thou son of David'), so utterly unusual in ordinary circumstances, would prepare him for the Angel's message. The naming of the unborn Messiah would accord with popular notions;[3] the symbolism of such a name

a Keth. 74 b
75 a
b Keth. 97 b

---

[1] I have thus paraphrased the verb παραδειγματίζω, rendered in Heb. vi. 6 (A.V.) 'put to an open shame.' Comp. also LXX. Num. xxv. 4; Jer. xiii. 22; Ezek. xxviii. 17 (see *Grimm*, Clavis N.T. p. 333 b) Archdeacon *Farrar* adopts the reading δειγματίσαι.

[2] For example, if he had not sufficient witnesses, or if their testimony could be invalidated by any of those provisions in favour of the accused, of which traditionalism had not a few. Thus, as indicated in the text, Joseph might have privately divorced Mary, leaving it open to doubt on what ground he had so acted.

[3] See a former note.

was deeply rooted in Jewish belief;[1] while the explanation of *Jehoshua* or *Jeshua (Jesus)*, as He who would save His people (primarily, as he would understand it, Israel) from their sins, described at least one generally expected aspect of His Mission,[2] although Joseph may not have known that it was the basis of all the rest. And perhaps it was not without deeper meaning and insight into His character, that the Angel laid stress on this very element in His communication to Joseph, and not to Mary.

The fact that such an announcement came to Him in a *dream*, would dispose Joseph all the more readily to receive it. 'A good dream' was one of the three things[3] popularly regarded as marks of God's favour; and so general was the belief in their significance, as to have passed into this popular saying: 'If any one sleeps seven days without dreaming (or rather, remembering his dream for interpretation), call him wicked' (as being unremembered of God[a][4]). Thus Divinely set at rest, Joseph could no longer hesitate. The highest duty towards the Virgin-Mother and the unborn Jesus demanded an immediate marriage, which would afford not only outward, but moral protection to both.[5]

a Ber. 55 b

---

[1] Thus we read in (*Shocher Tobh*) the Midrash on Prov. xix. 21 (closing part; ed. Lemberg. p. 16 *b*) of eight names given to the Messiah, viz. *Yinnon* (Ps. xxii. 17, 'His name shall sprout [bear sprouts] before the Sun;' comp. also Pirqé de R. El. c. 2); *Jehovah; Our Righteousness; Tsemach* (the Branch, Zech. iii. 8); *Menachem* (the Comforter, Is. li. 3); *David* (Ps. xviii. 50); *Shiloh* (Gen. xlix. 10); *Elijah* (Mal. iv. 5). The Messiah is also called *Anani* (He that cometh in the clouds, Dan. vii. 13; see Tanch. Par. Toledoth 14); *Chaninah*, with reference to Jer. xvi. 13; *the Leprous*, with reference to Is. liii. 4 (Sanh. 96 *b*). It is a curious instance of the Jewish mode of explaining a meaning by *gi-matreya*, or numerical calculation, that they prove *Tsemach* (Branch) and *Mena-chem* (Comforter) to be the same, because the numerical equivalents of the one word are equal to those of the other: מ=40, צ=50, ח=8, מ=40, = 138 ; צ= 90, מ= 40, ח=8,=138.

[2] Professor *Wünsche*(Erläuter.d.Evang. p. 10) proposes to strike out the words 'from their sins' as an un-Jewish interpolation. In answer, it would suffice to point him to the passages on this very subject which he has collated in a previous work: Die Leiden des Messias, pp.

63–108. To these I will only add a comment in the Midrash on Cant. i. 14 (ed. Warshau, p. 11 *a* and *b*), where the reference is undoubtedly to the Messiah (in the words of R. Berakhyah, line 8 from bottom; and again in the words of R. Levi, 11 *b*, line 5 from top, &c.). The expression כפר is there explained as meaning 'He Who makes expiation for the sins of Israel,' and it is distinctly added that this expiation bears reference to the transgressions and evil deeds of the children of Abraham, for which God provides this Man as the Atonement.

[3] 'A good king, a fruitful year, and a good dream.'

[4] Rabbi Zera proves this by a reference to Prov. xix. 23, the reading *Sabhea* (satisfied) being altered into *Shebha*—both written שבע—while ילין is understood as of spending the night. Ber. 55 *a* to 57 *b* contains a long, and sometimes very coarse, discussion of dreams, giving their various interpretations, rules for avoiding the consequences of evil dreams, &c. The fundamental principle is, that 'a dream is according to its interpretation' (Ber. 55 *b*). Such views about dreams would, no doubt, have long been matter of popular belief, before being formally expressed in the Talmud.

[5] The objection, that the account of

BOOK
II

Viewing events, not as isolated, but as links welded in the golden chain of the history of the Kingdom of God, 'all this'—not only the birth of Jesus from a Virgin, nor even His symbolic Name with its import, but also the unrestful questioning of Joseph,—'happened'[1] in fulfilment[2] of what had been prefigured.ᵃ The promise of a Virgin-born son as a sign of the firmness of God's covenant of old with David and his house; the now unfolded meaning of the former symbolic name *Immanuel*; even the unbelief of Ahaz, with its counterpart in the questioning of Joseph- -'all this' could now be clearly read in the light of the breaking day. Never had the house of David sunk morally lower than when, in the words of Ahaz, it seemed to renounce the very foundation of its claim to continuance; never had the fortunes of the house of David fallen lower, than when a Herod sat on its throne, and its lineal representative was a humble village carpenter, from whose heart doubts of the Virgin-Mother had to be Divinely chased. And never, not even when God gave to the doubts of Moses this as the sign of Israel's future deliverance, that in that mountain they should worship ᵇ—had unbelief been answered by more strange evidence. But as, nevertheless, the stability of the Davidic house was ensured by the future advent of *Immanuel*—and with such certainty, that before even such a child could discern between choice of good and evil, the land would be freed of its dangers; so now all that was then prefigured was to become literally true, and Israel to be saved from its real danger by the Advent of Jesus, Immanuel.[3] And so it had all been intended. The golden

Joseph and Mary's immediate marriage is inconsistent with the designation of Mary in St. Luke ii. 5, is sufficiently refuted by the consideration that, in any other case, Jewish custom would not have allowed Mary to travel to Bethlehem in company with Joseph. The expression used in St. Luke ii. 5, must be read in connection with St. Matt. i. 25.

[1] *Haupt* (Alttestam. Citate in d. vier Evang. pp. 207–215) rightly lays stress on the words, '*all this was done.*' He even extends its reference to the three-fold arrangement of the genealogy by St. Matthew, as implying the ascending splendour of the line of David, its midday glory, and its decline.

[2] The correct Hebrew equivalent of the expression 'that it might be fulfilled' ἵνα πληρωθῇ is not, as *Surenhusius* (Biblos Katallages, p. 151) and other writers have it, לקיים מה ויאמר, still

loss (Wünsche) הרא הוא דכתיב, but, as Professor Delitzsch renders it, in his new translation of St. Matthew, למלאות את אשר דבר יי. The difference is important, and Delitzsch's translation completely established by the similar rendering of the LXX. of 1 Kings ii. 27 and 2 Chron. xxxvi. 22.

[3] A critical discussion of Is. vii. 14 would here be out of place; though I have attempted to express my views in the text. (The nearest approach to them is that by *Engelhardt* in the Zeitschr. für Luth. Theol. für 1872, Heft iv.). The quotation of St. Matthew follows, with scarcely any variation, the rendering of the LXX. That *they* should have translated the Hebrew עלמה by παρθένος, 'a Virgin,' is surely sufficient evidence of the admissibility of such a rendering. The idea that the promised Son was to be

cup of prophecy which Isaiah had placed empty on the Holy Table, waiting for the time of the end, was now full filled, up to its brim, with the new wine of the Kingdom.

Meanwhile the long-looked-for event had taken place in the home of Zacharias. No domestic solemnity so important or so joyous as that in which, by circumcision, the child had, as it were, laid upon it the yoke of the Law, with all of duty and privilege which this implied. Even the circumstance, that it took place at early morning [a] might indicate this. It was, so tradition has it, as if the father had acted sacrificially as High-Priest, [b] offering his child to God in gratitude and love; [c] and it symbolised this deeper moral truth, that man must by his own act complete what God had first instituted. [d] To Zacharias and Elisabeth the rite would have even more than this significance, as administered to the child of their old age, so miraculously given, and who was connected with such a future. Besides, the legend which associates circumcision with Elijah, as the restorer of this rite in the apostate period of the Kings of Israel, [e] was probably in circulation at the time. [1] We can scarcely be mistaken in supposing, that then, as now, a benediction was spoken before circumcision, and that the ceremony closed with the usual grace over the cup of wine, [2] when the child received his name in a prayer that probably did not much differ from this at present in use: 'Our God, and the God of our fathers, raise up this child to his father and mother, and let his name be called in Israel Zacharias, the son of Zacharias.[3] Let his father re-

CHAP.
IV

[a] Pes. 4 a

Yalkut
Sh. i. par.
81

[c] Tanch. P
Tetsavveh.
at the be-
ginning,
ed. War-
shau. p. 111
[a]

[d] Tanch.
u. s.

[e] Pirq de
R. Elies. c.
29

either that of Ahaz, or else of the prophet, cannot stand the test of critical investigation (see *Haupt*, u. s., and *Böhl*, Alttest. Citate im N.T. pp. 3–6). Our difficulties of interpretation are, in great part, due to the abruptness of Isaiah's prophetic language, and to our ignorance of surrounding circumstances. *Steinmeyer* ingeniously argues against the mythical theory that, since Is. vii. 14 was *not* interpreted by the ancient Synagogue in a Messianic sense, that passage could not have led to the origination of 'the legend' about the 'Virgin's Son ' (Gesch. d. Geb. d. Herrn, p. 95). We add this further question, *Whence* did it originate?

[1] Probably the designation of 'chair' or 'throne of Elijah,' for the chair on which the godparent holding the child sits, and certainly the invocation of Elijah, are of later date. Indeed, the institution of godparents is itself of later origin. Curiously enough, the Council of Terracina, in 1330 had to interdict

Christians acting as godparents at circumcision ! Even the great Buxtorf acted as godparent in 1619 to a Jewish child, and was condemned to a fine of 100 florins for his offence. See *Löw*, Lebensalter, p. 86.

[2] According to *Josephus* (Ag. Ap. ii. 26) circumcision was not followed by a feast. But, if this be true, the practice was soon altered, and the feast took place on the eve of circumcision (Jer. Keth. i. 5; B. Kama 80 *a*; B. Bath. 60 *b*, &c.). Later Midrashim traced it up to the history of Abraham and the feast at the weaning of Isaac, which they represented as one at circumcision (Pirqé d. R. Eliez. 29).

[3] Wünsche reiterates the groundless objection of Rabbi Löw (u. s. p. 96), that a family-name was only given in remembrance of the grandfather, *deceased* father, or other member of the family ! Strange, that such a statement should ever have been hazarded ; stranger still, that it should be repeated after having been fully refuted by Delitzsch. It certainly

BOOK
II

joice in the issue of his loins, and his mother in the fruit of her womb, as it is written in Prov. xxiii. 25, and as it is said in Ezek. xvi. 6, and again in Ps. cv. 8, and Gen. xxi. 4;' the passages being, of course, quoted in full. The prayer closed with the hope that the child might grow up, and successfully, 'attain to the Torah, the marriage-baldachino, and good works.'[1]

Of all this Zacharias was, though a deeply interested, yet a deaf and dumb[2] witness. This only had he noticed, that, in the benediction in which the child's name was inserted, the mother had interrupted the prayer. Without explaining her reason, she insisted that his name should not be that of his aged father, as in the peculiar circumstances might have been expected, but John (*Jochanan*). A reference to the father only deepened the general astonishment, when he also gave the same name. But this was not the sole cause for marvel. For, forthwith the tongue of the dumb was loosed, and he, who could not utter the name of the child, now burst into praise of the name of the Lord. His last words had been those of unbelief, his first were those of praise; his last words had been a question of doubt, his first were a hymn of assurance. Strictly Hebrew in its cast, and closely following Old Testament prophecy, it is remarkable —and yet almost natural—that this hymn of the Priest closely follows, and, if the expression be allowable, spiritualises a great part of the most ancient Jewish prayer: the so-called Eighteen Benedictions; rather perhaps, that it transforms the expectancy of that prayer into praise of its realisation. And if we bear in mind, that a great portion of these prayers was said by the Priests before the lot was cast for incensing, or by the people in the time of incensing, it almost seems as if, during the long period of his enforced solitude, the aged Priest had meditated on, and learned to understand, what so often he had repeated. Opening with the common form of benediction, his hymn struck, one by one, the deepest chords of that prayer, specially this the most significant of all (the fifteenth Eulogy), ' Speedily make to shoot forth the Branch[3] of David, Thy servant, and

---

is contrary to *Josephus* (War iv. 3, 9), and to the circumstance that both the father and brother of Josephus bore the name of Matthias. See also *Zunz* (Z. Gesch. u. Liter. p. 318).

[1] The reader will find *B. H. Auerbach's* Berith Abraham (with a Hebrew introduction) an interesting tractate on the subject. For another and younger version of these prayers, see *Löw*, u. s. p. 102.

[2] From St. Luke i. 62 we gather, that Zacharias was what the Rabbis understood by חרש—one deaf as well as dumb. Accordingly they communicated with him by רמזים ' signs '—as *Delitzsch* correctly renders it: וַיִּרְמְזוּ אֶל־אָבִיו

[3] Although almost all modern authorities are against me, I cannot persuade myself that the expression (St. Luke i. 78) rendered ' dayspring ' in our A.V. is here not the equivalent of the Hebrew צמח

exalt Thou his horn by Thy salvation, for in Thy salvation we trust CHAP.
all the day long. Blessed art Thou, Jehovah! Who causeth to spring IV
forth the Horn of Salvation' (literally, to branch forth). This analogy
between the hymn of Zacharias and the prayers of Israel will best
appear from the benedictions with which these eulogies closed. For,
when thus examined, their leading thoughts will be found to be as
follows: God as the *Shield of Abraham*; He that raises the dead, and
causes salvation to shoot forth; the Holy One; Who graciously *giveth
knowledge*; Who taketh pleasure in *repentance*; Who multiplieth
forgiveness; Who *redeemeth Israel*; Who *healeth their* (spiritual)
diseases; Who *blesseth the years*; Who *gathereth the outcasts of His
people*; Who loveth *righteousness and judgment*; Who is the *abode
and stay of the righteous*; Who *buildeth Jerusalem*; Who causeth the
Horn of Salvation to shoot forth; Who *heareth prayer*; Who *bringeth
back His Shekhinah to Zion*; God the *Gracious One*, to Whom praise
is due; Who *blesseth* His people *Israel with peace*.

It was all most fitting. The question of unbelief had struck the
Priest dumb, for most truly unbelief cannot speak; and the answer
of faith restored to him speech, for most truly does faith loosen the
tongue. The first evidence of his dumbness had been, that his
tongue refused to speak the benediction to the people; and the first
evidence of his restored power was, that he spoke the benediction of
God in a rapturous burst of praise and thanksgiving. The sign of
the unbelieving Priest standing before the awe-struck people, vainly
essaying to make himself understood by signs, was most fitting; most
fitting also that, when 'they made signs' to him, the believing father
should burst in their hearing into a prophetic hymn.

But far and wide, as these marvellous tidings spread throughout
the hill-country of Judæa, fear fell on all—the fear also of a nameless
hope. The silence of a long-clouded day had been broken, and the
light which had suddenly riven its gloom, laid itself on their hearts
in expectancy: 'What then shall this Child be? For the Hand of
the Lord also was with Him!' [2]

'Branch.' The LXX. at any rate rendered צֶמַח in Jer. xxiii. 5; Ezek. xvi. 7;
xvii. 10; Zech. iii. 8; vi. 12, by ἀνατολή.
[1] The italics mark the points of correspondence with the hymn of Zacharias.
Comp. the best edition of the Jewish
Prayer Book (Frankfort, 5601), pp. 21–28.

The Eighteen Eulogies are given in full
in the 'History of the Jewish Nation,'
pp. 363–367.
[2] The insertion of γάρ seems critically
established, and gives the fuller meaning.

CHAPTER V.

WHAT MESSIAH DID THE JEWS EXPECT?

BOOK
II

It were an extremely narrow, and, indeed, false view, to regard the difference between Judaism and Christianity as confined to the question of the fulfillment of certain prophecies in Jesus of Nazareth. These predictions could only outline individual features in the Person and history of the Messiah. It is not thus that a likeness is recognised, but rather by the combination of the various features into a unity, and by the expression which gives it meaning. So far as we can gather from the Gospel narratives, no objection was ever taken to the fulfillment of individual prophecies in Jesus. But the general conception which the Rabbis had formed of the Messiah, differed totally from what was presented by the Prophet of Nazareth. Thus, what is the fundamental divergence between the two may be said to have existed long before the events which finally divided them. It is the combination of letters which constitute words, and the same letters may be combined into different words. Similarly, both Rabbinism and—what, by anticipation, we designate—Christianity might regard the same predictions as Messianic, and look for their fulfillment; while at the same time the Messianic ideal of the Synagogue might be quite other than that, to which the faith and hope of the Church have clung.

1. The most important point here is to keep in mind the organic *unity* of the Old Testament. Its predictions are not isolated, but features of one grand prophetic picture; its ritual and institutions parts of one great system; its history, not loosely connected events, but an organic development tending towards a definite end. Viewed in its innermost substance, the history of the Old Testament is not different from its typical institutions, nor yet these two from its predictions. The idea, underlying all, is God's gracious manifestation in the world—the Kingdom of God; the meaning of all—the establishment of this Kingdom upon earth. That gracious purpose was, so to speak, individualized, and the Kingdom actually established in the

Messiah.   Both the fundamental and the final relationship in view was
that of God towards man, and of man towards God: the former as expressed by the word Father; the latter by that of Servant—or rather
the combination of the two ideas: 'Son-Servant.' This was already implied in the so-called Protevangel;[a] and in this sense also the words   [a] Gen. iii.13
of Jesus hold true: 'Before Abraham came into being, I am.'

.But, narrowing our survey to where the history of the Kingdom
of God begins with that of Abraham, it was indeed as Jesus said:
'Your father Abraham rejoiced that he should see My day, and he
saw it, and was glad.'[b]   For, all that followed from Abraham to the   [b] St. John
Messiah was one, and bore this twofold impress: heavenwards, that of   viii. 56
Son; earthwards, that of Servant.   Israel was God's Son—His 'first-
born'; their history that of the children of God; their institutions those
of the family of God; their predictions those of the household of God.
And Israel was also the Servant of God—'Jacob My Servant'; and its
history, institutions, and predictions those of the Servant of the Lord.
Yet not merely Servant, but Son-Servant—'anointed' to such service.
This idea was, so to speak, crystallised in the three great representative institutions of Israel.   The 'Servant of the Lord' in relation
to Israel's history was Kingship in Israel; the 'Servant of the Lord'
in relation to Israel's ritual ordinances was the Priesthood in Israel;
the 'Servant of the Lord' in relation to prediction was the Prophetic
order.   But all sprang from the same fundamental idea: that of the
'Servant of Jehovah.'

One step still remains.   The Messiah and His history are not
presented in the Old Testament as something separate from, or
superadded to, Israel.   The history, the institutions, and the predictions of Israel run up into Him.[1]   He is the typical Israelite, nay,
typical Israel itself—alike the crown, the completion, and the representative of Israel.   He is the Son of God and the Servant of the
Lord; but in that highest and only true sense, which had given its
meaning to all the preparatory development.   As He was 'anointed'
to be the 'Servant of the Lord,' not with the typical oil, but by 'the
Spirit of Jehovah' 'upon' Him, so was He also the 'Son' in a
unique sense.   His organic connection with Israel is marked by the
designations 'Seed of Abraham' and 'Son of David,' while at the
same time He was essentially, what Israel was subordinately and

---

[1] In this respect there is deep significance in the Jewish legend (frequently
introduced; see, for example, Tanch. ii.
99 *a*; Deb. R. 1), that all the miracles

which God had shown to Israel in the
wilderness would be done again to redeemed Zion in the 'latter days.'

BOOK
II

ᵃ St. Matt.
ii. 15

typically: 'Thou art My Son—this day have I begotten Thee.' Hence also, in strictest truthfulness, the Evangelist could apply to the Messiah what referred to Israel, and see it fulfilled in His history: 'Out of Egypt have I called my Son.'ᵃ And this other correlate idea, of Israel as 'the Servant of the Lord,' is also fully concentrated in the Messiah as the Representative Israelite, so that the Book of Isaiah, as the series of predictions in which His picture is most fully outlined, might be summarised as that concerning 'the Servant of Jehovah.' Moreover, the Messiah, as Representative Israelite, combined in Himself as 'the Servant of the Lord' the threefold office of Prophet, Priest, and King, and joined together the two

ᵇ Phil. ii.
6-11

ideas of 'Son' and 'Servant.'ᵇ And the final combination and full exhibition of these two ideas was the fulfillment of the typical mission of Israel, and the establishment of the Kingdom of God among men.

ᶜ Gen. iii.15

Thus, in its final, as in its initial,ᶜ stage it was the establishment of the Kingdom of God upon earth—brought about by the 'Servant' of the Lord, Who was to stricken humanity the God-sent 'Anointed Comforter' (*Mashiach ha-Menachem*): in this twofold sense of 'Comforter' of individuals ('the friend of sinners'), and 'Comforter' of Israel and of the world, reconciling the two, and bringing to both eternal salvation. And here the mission of Israel ended. It had passed through three stages. The first, or *historical,* was the preparation of the Kingdom of God; the second, or *ritual*, the typical presentation of that Kingdom; while the third, or *prophetic*, brought that Kingdom into actual contact with the kingdoms of the world. Accordingly, it is during the latter that the designation 'Son of David' (typical Israel) enlarged in the visions of Daniel into that of 'Son of Man' (the Head of redeemed humanity). It were a onesided view to regard the Babylonish exile as only a punishment for Israel's sin. There is, in truth, nothing in all God's dealings in history exclusively *punitive*. That were a merely negative element. But there is always a positive element also of actual progress; a step forward, even though in the taking of it something should have to be crushed. And this step forward was the development of the idea of the Kingdom of God in its relation to the world.

2. This organic unity of Israel and the Messiah explains how events, institutions, and predictions, which initially were purely Israelitish, could with truth be regarded as finding their full accomplishment in the Messiah. From this point of view the whole Old Testament becomes the perspective in which the figure of the Messiah stands out. And perhaps the most valuable element in Rabbinic

commentation on Messianic times is that in which, as so frequently,   CHAP.
it is explained, that all the miracles and deliverances of Israel's past   V
would be re-enacted, only in a much wider manner, in the days of
the Messiah. Thus the whole past was symbolic, and typical of the
future—the Old Testament the glass, through which the universal
blessings of the latter days were seen. It is in this sense that we
would understand the two sayings of the Talmud: ' All the prophets
prophesied only of the days of the Messiah,'ª and ' The world was   ª Sanh. 99 a
created only for the Messiah.' ᵇ   ᵇ Sanh. 98 b

In accordance with all this, the ancient Synagogue found references to the Messiah in many more passages of the Old Testament
than those verbal predictions, to which we generally appeal; and the
latter formed (as in the New Testament) a proportionately small, and
secondary, element in the conception of the Messianic era. This
is fully borne out by a detailed analysis of those passages in the
Old Testament to which the ancient Synagogue referred as Messianic.[1]
Their number amounts to upwards of 456 (75 from the Pentateuch,
243 from the Prophets, and 138 from the Hagiographa), and their
Messianic application is supported by more than 558 references to
the most ancient Rabbinic writings.[2] But comparatively few of these
are what would be termed verbal predictions. Rather would it seem as
if every event were regarded as prophetic, and every prophecy, whether
by fact, or by word (prediction), as a light to cast its sheen on the
future, until the picture of the Messianic age in the far back-ground
stood out in the hundredfold variegated brightness of prophetic events,
and prophetic utterances; or, as regarded the then state of Israel,
till the darkness of their present night was lit up by a hundred constellations kindling in the sky overhead, and its lonely silence broken
by echoes of heavenly voices, and strains of prophetic hymns borne on
the breeze.

Of course, there was the danger that, amidst these dazzling lights,
or in the crowd of figures, each so attractive, or else in the absorbing
interest of the general picture, the grand central Personality should
not engage the attention it claimed, and so the meaning of the whole

[1] See Appendix IX., where a detailed
list is given of all the Old Testament
passages which the ancient Synagogue
applied Messianically, together with the
references to the Rabbinic works where
they are quoted.
[2] Large as this number is, I do not
present the list as complete. Thus, out
of the thirty-seven Parashahs constituting the Midrash on Leviticus, no fewer
than twenty-five close with an outlook on
Messianic times. The same may be said
of the close of many of the Parashahs in
the Midrashim known as Pesiqta and
Tanchuma (*Zunz,* u. s. pp. 181, 234). Besides, the oldest portions of the Jewish
liturgy are full of Messianic aspirations.

be lost in the contemplation of its details. This danger was the greater from the absence of any deeper spiritual elements. All that Israel needed: 'study of the Law and good works,' lay within the reach of every one; and all that Israel hoped for, was national restoration and glory. Everything else was but means to these ends; the Messiah Himself only the grand instrument in attaining them. Thus viewed, the picture presented would be of Israel's exaltation, rather than of the salvation of the world. To this, and to the idea of Israel's exclusive spiritual position in the world, must be traced much, that otherwise would seem utterly irrational in the Rabbinic pictures of the latter days. But in such a picture there would be neither room nor occasion for a Messiah-Saviour, in the only sense in which such a heavenly mission could be rational, or the heart of humanity respond to it. The Rabbinic ideal of the Messiah was not that of 'a light to lighten the Gentiles, and the glory of His people Israel'—the satisfaction of the wants of humanity, and the completion of Israel's mission —but quite different, even to contrariety. Accordingly, there was a fundamental antagonism between the Rabbis ·and Christ, quite irrespective of the manner in which He carried out His Messianic work. On the other hand, it is equally noteworthy, that the purely national elements, which well nigh formed the sum total of Rabbinic expectation, scarcely entered into the teaching of Jesus about the Kingdom of God. And the more we realise, that Jesus so fundamentally separated Himself from all the ideas of His time, the more evidential is it of the fact, that He was not the Messiah of Jewish conception, but derived His mission from a source unknown to, or at least ignored by, the leaders of His people.

3. But still, as the Rabbinic ideas were at least based on the Old Testament, we need not wonder that they also embodied the chief features of the Messianic history. Accordingly, a careful perusal of their Scripture quotations[1] shows, that the main postulates of the New Testament concerning the Messiah are fully supported by Rabbinic statements. Thus, such doctrines as the *pre-mundane existence* of the Messiah; His *elevation* above Moses, and even above the Angels; His *representative* character; His cruel *sufferings* and *derision*; His *violent death*, and that *for His people*; His *work* on behalf of the living and of the dead; His *redemption*, and restoration of Israel; the *opposition* of the Gentiles; their partial *judgment* and *conversion*; the *prevalence* of His *Law*; the *universal blessings* of the latter days; and His *Kingdom*—can be clearly deduced from un-

[1] For these, see Appendix IX.

questioned passages in ancient Rabbinic writings. Only, as we might expect, all is there indistinct, incoherent, unexplained, and from a much lower standpoint. At best, it is the lower stage of yet unfulfilled prophecy—the haze when the sun is about to rise, not the blaze when it has risen. Most painfully is this felt in connection with the one element on which the New Testament most insists. There is, indeed, in Rabbinic writings frequent reference to the sufferings, and even the death of the Messiah, and these are brought into connection with our sins—as how could it be otherwise in view of Isaiah liii. and other passages—and in one most remarkable comment[a] the Messiah is represented as willingly taking upon Himself all these sufferings, on condition that all Israel—the living, the dead, and those yet unborn—should be saved, and that, in consequence of His work, God and Israel should be reconciled, and Satan cast into hell. But there is only the most indistinct reference to the removal of sin by the Messiah, in the sense of vicarious sufferings.

In connection with what has been stated, one most important point must be kept in view. So far as their opinions can be gathered from their writings, the great doctrines of Original Sin, and of the sinfulness of our whole nature, were not held by the ancient Rabbis.[1] Of course, it is not meant that they denied the consequences of sin, either as concerned Adam himself, or his descendants; but the final result is far from that seriousness which attaches to the Fall in the New Testament, where it is presented as the basis of the need of a Redeemer, Who, as the Second Adam, restored what the first had lost. The difference is so fundamental as to render further explanation necessary.[2]

The fall of Adam is ascribed to the envy of the Angels[3]—not the fallen ones, for none were fallen, till God cast them down in consequence of their seduction of man. The Angels, having in vain tried to prevent the creation of man, at last conspired to lead him into sin as the only means of his ruin—the task being undertaken by *Sammael* (and his Angels), who in many respects was superior to the other Angelic princes.[b] The instrument employed was the serpent, of whose original condition the strangest legends are told, probably to make the Biblical narrative appear more rational.[c] The details of the story of the Fall, as told by the Rabbis, need not be here repeated, save to indicate its consequences. The first of these was the with-

CHAP.
V

[a] Yalkut on Is. ix. 1

[b] Pirqe de R. El. c. 13, Yalkut i. p. 8 c

Comp. Pirqé de R. El. and Yalkut, u.s.; also Ber. R. 19

[1] This is the view expressed by *all* Jewish dogmatic writers. See also *Weber*. Altsynag. Theol. p. 217.
[2] Comp. on the subject. Ber. R. 12–16.
[3] In Ber. R., however, it has seemed to me, as if sometimes a mystical and symbolical view of the history of the Fall were insinuated—evil concupiscence being the occasion of it.

BOOK
II

a Ber. R. 19,
ed. War-
shau, p. 37a

b Bemidb.
R. 13

c Vayyikra
R. 27

d Ber. R. 16
21, and
often

e Ber. R. 5,
12, 10;
comp. also
Midr. on
Eccl. vii. 13;
and viii. 1,
and Baba
B. 17 a

f Ber. R. 9

g Bemidb.
R. 19

h According
to Deut.
xxxiii. 2;
Hab. iii. 3

i Ab. Zar.
2 b

k Ab. Z. 5 a

drawal of the Shekhinah from earth to the first heaven, while sub-sequent sins successively led to its further removal to the seventh heaven. This, however, can scarcely be considered a permanent sequel of sin, since the good deeds of seven righteous men, beginning with Abraham, brought it again, in the time of Moses, to earth.[a] Six things Adam is said to have lost by his sin; but even these are to be restored to man by the Messiah.[b][1] That the physical death of Adam was the consequence of his sin, is certainly taught. Other-wise he would have lived forever, like Enoch and Elijah.[c] But although the fate which overtook Adam was to rest on all the world,[d] and death came not only on our first father but on his descendants, and all creation lost its perfectness,[e] yet even these temporal sequences are not universally admitted. It rather seems taught, that death was intended to be the fate of all, or sent to show the folly of men claiming Divine worship, or to test whether piety was real,[f] the more so that with death the weary struggle with our evil inclination ceased. It was needful to die when our work was done, that others might enter upon it. In each case death was the consequence of our own, not of Adam's sin.[g] In fact, over these six—Abraham, Isaac, Jacob, Moses, Aaron, and Miriam—the Angel of Death had had no absolute power. Nay, there was a time when all Israel were not only free from death, but like the Angels, and even higher than they. For, originally God had offered the Law to all Gentile nations,[h] but they had refused to submit to it.[i] But when Israel took on themselves the Law at Mount Sinai, the description in Psalm lxxxii. 6 applied literally to them. They would not have died, and were 'the sons of God.'[k] But all this was lost by the sin of making the golden calf—although the Talmud marks that, if Israel had continued in that Angelic state, the nation would have ceased with that generation.[2] Thus there were two divergent opinions—the one ascribing death to personal, the other tracing it to Adam's guilt.[3]

---

[1] They are: the shining splendour of his person, even his heels being like suns; his gigantic size, from east to west, from earth to heaven; the spontaneous splendid products of the ground, and of all fruit-trees; an infinitely greater measure of light on the part of the heavenly bodies; and, finally, endless duration of life (Ber. R. 12, ed. Warsh. p. 24 b; Ber. R. 21; Sanh. 38 b; Chag. 12 a; and for their restoration by the Messiah, Bem. R. 13).
[2] By a most ingenious theological arti-fice the sin of the golden calf, and that of David are made matter for thanksgiving;

the one as showing that, even if the whole people sinned, God was willing to for-give; the other as proving, that God gra-ciously condescended to each individual sinner, and that to each the door of repentance was open.
[3] In the Talmud (Shabb. 55 a and b) each view is supported in discussion, the one by a reference to Ezek. xviii. 20, the other to Eccles. ix. 2 (comp. also Siphré on Deut. xxxii. 49). The final conclu-sion, however, greatly inclines towards the connection between death and the fall (see especially the clear statement in

When, however, we pass from the physical to the moral sequences of the fall, our Jewish authorities wholly fail us. They teach, that man is created with two inclinations—that to evil (the *Yetser ha-ra*), and that to good;[a] the first working in him from the beginning, the latter coming gradually in the course of time.[b] Yet, so far from guilt attaching to the *Yetser ha-ra*, its existence is absolutely necessary, if the world is to continue.[c] In fact, as the Talmud expressly teaches,[d] the evil desire or impulse was created by God Himself; while it is also asserted[e] that, on seeing the consequences, God actually repented having done so. This gives quite another character to sin, as due to causes for which no blame attaches to man.[f] On the other hand, as it is in the power of each wholly to overcome sin, and to gain life by study and works;[g] as Israel at Mount Sinai had actually got rid of the *Yetser ha-ra*; and as there had been those, who were entirely righteous,[h]—there scarcely remains any moral sequence of Adam's fall to be considered. Similarly, the Apocrypha are silent on the subject, the only exception being the very strong language used in II. Esdras, which dates after the Christian era.[i1]

4. In the absence of felt need of deliverance from sin, we can understand, how Rabbinic tradition found no place for the Priestly office of the Messiah, and how even His claims to be the Prophet of His people are almost entirely overshadowed by His appearance as their King and Deliverer. This, indeed, was the ever-present want, pressing the more heavily as Israel's national sufferings seemed almost inexplicable, while they contrasted so sharply with the glory expected by the Rabbis. *Whence these sufferings?* From sin[k]—national sin; the idolatry of former times;[l] the prevalence of crimes and vices; the dereliction of God's ordinances;[m] the neglect of instruction, of study, and of proper practice of His Law; and, in later days, the love of money and party strife.[n] *But the seventy years' captivity had ceased, why not the present dispersion?* Because hypocrisy had been added to all other sins;[o] because there had not been proper repentance;[p]

CHAP.
V

[a] Targum Ps.-Jon. on Gen. ii. 7
[b] Nedar. 32 b; Midr. on Eccl. iv. 13, 14,ed. W. p. 89 a; ix. 15; ib. p. 101 a
[c] Ber. R. 9
[d] Ber. 61 a
[e] Sukk. 52 a, and Yalkut ii. p. 149 b
[f] Comp. also Jer. Targum on Ex. xxxii. 22
[g] Ab. Z. 5 b; Kidd. 30 b
[h] For example, Yoma 28 b; Chag. 4 b
[i] Comp. IV. Esd. iii. 21, 22, 26; iv. 30; especially vii. 46–53

[k] Men. 53 b
[l] Gitt. 7 a
[m] Gitt. 88 a
[n] Jer. Yoma i. 1; Yoma 9 a, and many other passages
[o] Yoma 9 b
[p] Jer. Yoma i. 1

Debar. R. 9, ed. Warsh., p. 20 a). This view is also supported by such passages in the Apocrypha as Wisdom ii. 23, 24; iii. 1, &c.; while, on the other hand, Ecclus. xv. 11–17 seems rather to point in a different direction.

[i1] There can be no question that, despite its strong polemical tendency against Christianity, the Fourth Book of Esdras (II. Esdras in our Apocrypha), written at the close of the first century of our era, is deeply tinged with Christian doctrine.

Of course, the first two and the last two chapters in our Apocryphal II. Esdras are later spurious additions of Christian authorship. But in proof of the influence of the Christian teaching on the writer of the Fourth Book of Esdras we may call attention, besides the adoption of the doctrine of original sin, to the remarkable application to Israel of such N.T. expressions as the 'firstborn,' the 'only-begotten,' and the 'Well-beloved' (IV. Esdras vi. 58—in our Apocr. II. Esdras iv. 58).

BOOK
II

ª Nidd. 13 b
b Yoma 19 b

c For all
these
points
comp. Ber.
58 b; 59 a;
Sot. 48 a;
Shabb.
138 b; Baba
B. 12 a, b

d Vayyikra
R. 19

e Sukk. 55 b

f Pesiqta, 1
ed. Buber,
p. 145 a,
last lines

g Midr, on
Ps.cxxxvii.

h Pesiqta
148 b

i Chag. 13 b

k Shemoth
R. 2. ed.
Warsh. p.
7 b, lines 12
&c.

m Ber. 3 a;
59 a

n Pesiqta
119 b; 120 a

because of the half-heartedness of the Jewish proselytes; because of improper marriages, and other evil customs;ª and because of the gross dissoluteness of certain cities.b The consequences appeared not only in the political condition of Israel, but in the land itself, in the absence of rain and dew, of fruitfulness and of plenty; in the general disorder of society; the cessation of piety and of religious study; and the silence of prophecy.c As significantly summed up, Israel was without Priesthood, without law, without God.d Nay, the world itself suffered in consequence of the destruction of the Temple. In a very remarkable passage,e where it is explained, that the seventy bullocks offered during the Feast of Tabernacles were for the nations of the world, R. Jochanan deplores their fate, since while the Temple had stood the altar had atoned for the Gentiles, but who was now to do so? The light, which had shone from out the Temple windows into the world, had been extinguished.f Indeed, but for the intercession of the Angels the world would now be destroyed.g In the poetic language of the time, the heavens, sun, moon and stars, trees and mountains, even the Angels, mourned over the desolation of the Temple,h and the very Angelic hosts had since been diminished.i But, though the Divine Presence had been withdrawn, it still lingered near His own; it had followed them in all their banishments; it had suffered with them in all their sorrows.2 It is a touching legend, which represents the Shekhinah as still lingering over the western wall of the Templek— the only one supposed to be still standing.3 Nay, in language still bolder, and which cannot be fully reproduced, God Himself is represented as mourning over Jerusalem and the Temple. He has not entered His Palace since then, and His hair is wet with the dew.4 He weeps over His children and their desolateness,m and displays in the heavens tokens of mourning, corresponding to those which an earthly monarch would show.n

All this is to be gloriously set right, when the Lord turneth the captivity of Zion, and the Messiah cometh. *But when may He be expected, and what are the signs of His coming?* Or perhaps the question should thus be put: *Why are the redemption of Israel and the coming of the Messiah so unaccountably delayed?* It is here

---

1 This is *the* Pesiqta. not that which is generally quoted either as *Rabbathi* or *Sutarta.*

2 This in very many Rabbinical passages. Comp. *Castelli*, Il Messia, p. 176, note 4.

2 In proof they appeal to such passages as 2 Chr. vii. 16; Ps. iii. 4; Cant. ii. 9, proving it even from the decree of Cyrus (Ezra i. 3, 4), in which God is spoken of as still in desolate Jerusalem.

4 The passage from Yalkut on Is. lx. 1 is quoted in full in Appendix IX.

that the Synagogue finds itself in presence of an insoluble mystery. The explanations attempted are, confessedly, guesses, or rather attempts to evade the issue. The only course left is, authoritatively to impose silence on all such inquiries—the silence, as they would put it, of implicit, mournful submission to the inexplicable, in faith that somehow, when least expected, deliverance would come; or, as we would put it, the silence of ever-recurring disappointment and despair. Thus the grand hope of the Synagogue is, as it were, written in an epitaph on a broken tombstone, to be repeated by the thousands who, for these long centuries, have washed the ruins of the Sanctuary with unavailing tears.

CHAP.
V

5. *Why delayeth the Messiah His coming?* Since the brief and broken sunshine of the days of Ezra and Nehemiah, the sky overhead has ever grown darker, nor have even the terrible storms, which have burst over Israel, reft the canopy of cloud. The first captivity passed, why not the second? This is the painful question ever and again discussed by the Rabbis.[a] Can they mean it seriously, that the sins of the second, are more grievous than those which caused the first dispersion; or that they of the first captivity repented, but not they of the second? What constitutes this repentance which yet remains to be made? But the reasoning becomes absolutely self-contradictory when, together with the assertion that, if Israel repented but one day, the Messiah would come,[b] we are told, that Israel will not repent till Elijah comes.[c] Besides, bold as the language is, there is truth in the expostulation, which the Midrash[d] puts into the mouth of the congregation of Israel: 'Lord of the world, it depends on Thee that we repent.' Such truth, that, although at first the Divine reply is a repetition of Zechar. i. 3, yet, when Israel reiterates the words, 'Turn Thou us unto Thee, O Lord, and we shall be turned,' supporting them by Ps. lxxxv. 4, the argument proves unanswerable.

[a] Jer. Yoma i. 1, ed. Krot. p 38 c, last part. Sanh. 97 b, 98 a

[b] Midr. on Cant. v. 2, ed. Warsh. p. 25 a; Sanh. 98 a

[c] Pirqe de R. Eliez. 43 end

[d] On Lam. v. 21, ed. Warsh. vol iii. p. 77 a

Other conditions of Israel's deliverance are, indeed, mentioned. But we can scarcely regard the Synagogue as seriously making the coming of Messiah dependent on their realisation. Among the most touching of these is a beautiful passage (almost reminding us of Heb. xi.), in which Israel's future deliverance is described as the reward of faith.[e] Similarly beautiful is the thought,[f] that, when God redeems Israel, it will be amidst their weeping.[g] But neither can this be regarded as the condition of Messiah's coming; nor yet such generalities as the observance of the Law, or of some special commandments. The very variety of suggestions[h][1] shows, how utterly unable the

[e] Tanch. on Ex. xv. 1, ed. Warsh. p. 86 b

[f] On Jer.' xxxi. 9

[g] Tanch. on Gen. xlv. 2, ed. Warsh.

[h] Sanh. 97 b 98 a

[1] The reader will find these discussions summarised at the close of Appendix IX.

BOOK
II

ᵃ Sanh. 98 a
and b

Synagogue felt to indicate any condition to be fulfilled by Israel. Such vague statements, as that the salvation of Israel depended on the merits of the patriarchs, or on that of one of them, cannot help us to a solution; and the long discussion in the Talmud ᵃ leaves no doubt, that the final and most sober opinion was, that the time of Messiah's coming depended not on repentance, nor any other condition, but on the mercy of God, when the time fixed had arrived. But even so, we are again thrown into doubt by the statement, that it might be either hastened or retarded by Israel's bearing![1]

In these circumstances, any attempt at determining the date of Messiah's coming would be even more hypothetical than such calculations generally are.[2] Guesses on the subject could only be grounded on imaginary symbolisms. Of such we have examples in the Talmud.[3] Thus, some fixed the date at 4000 years after the Creation—curiously enough, about the era of Christ—though Israel's sin had blotted out the whole past from the reckoning; others at 4291 from the Creation; ᵇ others again expected it at the beginning, or end, of the eighty-fifth Jubilee—with this proviso, that it it would not take place earlier; and so on, through equally groundless conjectures. A comparatively late work speaks of five monarchies—Babylon, Medo-Persia, Greece, Rome and Ishmael. During the last of these God would hear the cry of Israel, ᶜ and the Messiah come, after a terrible war between Rome and Ishmael (the West and the East).ᵈ But as the rule of these monarchies was to last altogether one day (=1000 years), less two-thirds of an hour (1 hour=83⅓ years), ᵉ it would follow, that their domination would last 944⅘ years.[4] Again, according to Jewish tradition, the rule of Babylon had lasted 70, that of Medo-Persia 34, and that of Greece 180 years, leaving 660⅘ years for Rome and Ishmael. Thus the date for the expected Advent of the Messiah would have been about 661 after the destruction of Jerusalem, or about the year 729 of the Christian era.[5]

In the category of guesses we must also place such vague statements, as that the Messiah would come, when all were righteous, or all wicked; or else nine months after the empire of Rome had ex-

ᵇ Sanh. 97 b

ᶜ Pirqé de
R. Elies. 32
ᵈ u. s. 30

ᵉ Comp.
Pirqé de R.
El. 48

---

[1] See, on the whole subject, also Debar. R. 2.

[2] We put aside, as universally repudiated, the opinion expressed by one Rabbi, that Israel's Messianic era was past, the promises having been fulfilled in King Hezekiah (Sanh. 98 b; 99 a).

[3] See, in Appendix IX. the extracts from Sanh.

[4] Pirqé de R. El. 28. The reasoning by which this duration of the monarchies is derived from Lament. i. 13 and Zech. xiv. 7, is a very curious specimen of Rabbinic argumentation.

[5] Comp. Zunz, Gottesd. Vortr. p. 277.

tended over the whole world;[a] or when all the souls, predestined to inhabit bodies, had been on earth.[b] But as, after years of unrelieved sufferings, the Synagogue had to acknowledge that, one by one, all the terms had passed, and as despair settled on the heart of Israel, it came to be generally thought, that the time of Messiah's Advent could not be known beforehand,[c] and that speculation on the subject was dangerous, sinful, even damnable. The time of the end had, indeed, been revealed to two sons of Adam, Jacob and David; but neither of them had been allowed to make it known.[d] In view of this, it can scarcely be regarded as more than a symbolical, though significant guess, when the future redemption of Israel is expected on the Paschal Day, the 15th of Nisan.[e][2]

6. We now approach this most difficult and delicate question: What was the expectation of the ancient Synagogue, as regarded the Nature, Person, and qualifications of the Messiah? In answering it—not at present from the Old Testament, but from the views expressed in Rabbinic literature, and, so far as we can gather from the Gospel-narratives, from those cherished by the contemporaries of Christ—two inferences seem evident. First, the idea of a Divine Personality, and of the union of the two Natures in the Messiah, seems to have been foreign to the Jewish auditory of Jesus of Nazareth, and even at first to His disciples. Secondly, they appear to have regarded the Messiah as far above the ordinary human, royal, prophetic, and even Angelic type, to such extent, that the boundary-line separating it from Divine Personality is of the narrowest, so that, when the conviction of the reality of the Messianic manifestation in Jesus burst on their minds, this boundary-line was easily, almost naturally, overstepped, and those who would have shrunk from framing their belief in such dogmatic form, readily owned and worshipped Him as the Son of God. Nor need we wonder at this, even taking the highest view of Old Testament prophecy. For here also the principle applies, which underlies one of St. Paul's most wide-reaching utterances: 'We prophesy in part'[3] (ἐκ μέρους προφητεύομεν).[f] In the nature of it, all prophecy presents but disjecta membra, and it almost seems, as if we had to take our stand in the prophet's valley of vision (Ezek. xxxvii.), waiting till, at the bidding of the Lord,

CHAP.
V

[a] Sanh. 98 b 1
[b] Ab. Z. 5 a, Ber. R. 24
[c] Targum Pseudo-Jon. on Gen. xlix. 1
[d] Midrash on Ps. xxxi. ed. Warsh. p. 41 a, lines 18 to 15 from bottom
[e] Pesikta, ed. Buber, 47 b, 48 a, Sopher. xxi. Hal. 2. Shir. haShir. R. ii. 8, ed. Warsh. vol. iii. p. 15 a

[f] 1 Cor. xiii. 9

---

[1] See Appendix IX.
[2] Solitary opinions, however, place the future redemption in the month Tishri (Tanch. on Ex. xii. 37, ed. Warsh. p. 81 b, line 2 from bottom).
[3] See the telling remarks of Oehler in Herzog's Real-Encykl., vol. ix. p. 417.

We would add, that there is always a 'hereafter' of further development in the history of the individual believer, as in that of the Church—growing brighter and brighter, with increased spiritual communication and knowledge, till at last the perfect light is reached.

CHAP
II

the scattered bones should be joined into a body, to which the breath of the Spirit would give life.

These two inferences, derived from the Gospel-narratives, are in exact accordance with the whole line of ancient Jewish teaching. Beginning with the LXX. rendering of Genesis xlix. 10, and especially of Numbers xxiv. 7, 17, we gather, that the Kingdom of the Messiah[1] was higher than any that is earthly, and destined to subdue them all. But the rendering of Psalm lxxii. 5, 7; Psalm cx. 3; and especially of Isaiah ix., carries us much farther. They convey the idea, that the existence of this Messiah was regarded as premundane (before the moon,[a] before the morning-star[b]), and eternal,[c] and His Person and dignity as superior to that of men and Angels: 'the Angel of the Great Council,'[d] probably 'the Angel of the Face'—a view fully confirmed by the rendering of the Targum.[3]　The silence of the Apocrypha about the Person of the Messiah is so strange, as to be scarcely explained by the consideration, that those books were composed when the need of a Messiah for the deliverance of Israel was not painfully felt.[4]　All the more striking are the allusions in the Pseudepigraphic Writings, although these also do not carry us beyond our two inferences. Thus, the third book of the Sibylline Oracles —which, with few exceptions,[5] dates from more than a century and a half before Christ—presents a picture of Messianic times,[e] generally admitted to have formed the basis of Virgil's description of the Golden Age, and of similar heathen expectations. In these Oracles, 170 years before Christ, the Messiah is '*the King sent from heaven*' who would 'judge every man in blood and splendour of fire.'[f]　Similarly, the vision of Messianic times opens with a reference to 'the King Whom *God will send from the sun.*[g][6]　That a superhuman King-

ᵃ Ps. lxxii.
ᵇ Ps. cx.
ᶜ Ps. lxxii.
ᵈ Is. ix. 6 2

ᵉ vv. 652-807

ᶠ vv. 285, 286

ᵍ v. 652

---

[1] No reasonable doubt can be left on the mind, that the LXX. translators have here the Messiah in view.

[2] The criticism of Mr. Drummond on these three passages (Jewish Messiah, pp. 290, 291) cannot be supported on critical grounds.

[3] Three, if not four, different renderings of the Targum on Is. ix. 6 are possible. But the *minimum* conveyed to my mind implies the premundane existence, the eternal continuance, and the superhuman dignity of the Messiah. (See also the Targum on Micah v. 2.)

[4] This is the view of *Grimm*, and more fully carried out by *Oehler*. The argument of Hengstenberg, that the mention of such a Messiah was restrained from

fear of the heathen, does not deserve serious refutation.

[5] These exceptions are, according to *Friedlieb* (Die Sibyllin. Weissag.) vv. 1–45, vv. 47–96 (dating from 40–31 before Christ), and vv. 818–828. On the subject generally, see our previous remarks in Book I.

[6] Mr. Drummond defends (at pp. 274, 275) Holtzmann's view, that the expression applies to Simon the Maccabee, although on p. 291 he argues on the opposite supposition that the text refers to the Messiah. It is difficult to understand, how on reading the whole passage the hypothesis of Holtzmann could be entertained. While referring to the 3rd Book of the Sib. Or., another point of

dom of eternal duration, such as this vision paints,[a] should have a superhuman King, seems almost a necessary corollary.[1]

Even more distinct are the statements in the so-called ' Book of Enoch.' Critics are substantially agreed, that the oldest part of it[b] dates from between 150 and 130 B.C.[2] The part next in date is full of Messianic allusions; but, as a certain class of modern writers has ascribed to it a post-Christian date, and, however ungrounded,[3] to Christian authorship, it may be better not to refer to it in the present argument, the more so as we have other testimony from the time of Herod. Not to speak, therefore, of such peculiar designations of the Messiah as ' the Woman's Son,'[c] ' the Son of Man,'[d] ' the Elect,' and ' the Just One,' we mark that the Messiah is expressly designated in the oldest portion as ' the Son of God ' (' I and My Son ').[e] That this implies, not, indeed, essential Sonship, but infinite superiority over all other servants of God, and rule over them, appears from the mystic description of the Messiah as ' the first of the [now changed] white bulls,' ' the great Animal among them, having great and black

CHAP.
V

[a] vv. 652-807

[b] ch. i.–xxxvi. and lxxii.-cv.

[c] lxii. 5

[d] For ex. xlviii. 2; lxii. 7; lxix 29

[e] cv. 2

---

considerable interest deserves notice. According to the theory which places the authorship of Daniel in the time of Antiochus Epiphanes—or say about 165 B.C.—the ' fourth kingdom ' of Daniel must be the Grecian. But, on the other hand, such certainly was *not* the view entertained by Apocalypts of the year 165, since the 3d Book of the Sib. Or., *which dates from precisely that period*, not only takes notice of the rising power of Rome, but anticipates the destruction of the Grecian Empire by Rome, which in turn is to be vanquished by Israel (vv. 175-195; 520-544; 638-807). This most important fact would require to be accounted for by the opponents of the authenticity of Daniel.

[1] I have purposely omitted all references to controverted passages. But see *Langen*, D. Judenth. in Palest. pp.401 &c.

[2] The next oldest portion, consisting of the so-called Similitudes (ch. xxxvii.-lxxi.), excepting what are termed ' the Noachic[4] parts, dates from about the time of Herod the Great.

[3] *Schürer* (Lehrb. d. Neutest. Zeitg. pp. 534, 535) has, I think, conclusively shown that this portion of the Book of Enoch is of *Jewish* authorship, and *pre-Christian* date. If so, it were deeply interesting to follow its account of the Messiah. He appears by the side of the Ancient of Days, His face like the ap-

pearance of a man, and yet so lovely, like that of one of the holy Angels. This ' Son of Man ' has, and with Him dwells, all righteousness: He reveals the treasures of all that is hidden, being chosen by the Lord, is superior to all, and destined to subdue and destroy all the powers and kingdoms of wickedness (ch. xlvi.). Although only revealed at the last, His Name had been named before God, before sun or stars were created. He is the staff on which the righteous lean, the light of nations. and the hope of all who mourn in spirit. All are to bow down before Him, and adore Him, and for this He was chosen and hidden with God before the world was created, and will continue before Him for ever (ch. xlviii.). This ' Elect One ' is to sit on the throne of glory, and dwell among His saints. Heaven and earth would be removed, and only the saints would abide on the renewed earth (ch. xlv.). He is mighty in all the secrets of righteousness, and unrighteousness would flee as a shadow, because His glory lasted from eternity to eternity, and His power from generation to generation (ch. xlix.). Then would the earth, Hades, and hell give up their dead, and Messiah, sitting on His throne, would select and own the just, and open up all secrets of wisdom, amidst the universal joy of ransomed earth (ch. li., lxi., lxii.).

horns on His head ' ᵃ—Whom ' all the beasts of the field and all the fowls of heaven dread, and to Whom they cry at all times.'

Still more explicit is that beautiful collection of eighteen Psalms, dating from about half a century before Christ, which bears the name of 'the Psalter of Solomon.' A chaste anticipation of the Messianic Kingdom ᵇ is followed by a full description of its need and its blessings,ᶜ to which the concluding Psalm ᵈ forms an apt epilogue. The King Who reigns is of the house of David.ᵉ He is the Son of David, Who comes at the time known to God only, to reign over Israel.ᶠ He is a righteous King, taught of God.ᵍ He is Christ the Lord ($X\rho\iota\sigma\tau\grave{o}\varsigma K\acute{v}\rho\iota o\varsigma$,ʰ exactly as in the LXX. translation of Lamentations iv. 20). ' He is pure from sin,' which qualifies Him for ruling His people, and banishing sinners ᵇy His word.ⁱ ' Never in His days will He be infirm towards His God, since God renders Him strong in the Holy Ghost,' wise in counsel, with might and righteousness (' mighty in deed and word '). The blessing of the Lord being upon Him, He does not fail.ᵏ ' This is the beauty of the King of Israel, Whom God hath chosen, to set Him over the house of Israel to rule it.' ᵐ Thus invincible, not by outward might, but in His God, He will bring His people the blessings of restoration to their tribal possessions, and of righteousness, but break in pieces His enemies, not by outward weapons, but by the word of His mouth; purify Jerusalem, and judge the nations, who will be subject to His rule, and behold and own His glory.ⁿ Manifestly, this is not an earthly Kingdom, nor yet an earthly King.

If we now turn to works dating after the Christian era, we would naturally expect them, either simply to reproduce earlier opinions, or, from opposition to Christ, to present the Messiah in a less exalted manner.[1] But since, strange to say, they even more strongly assert the high dignity of the Messiah, we are warranted in regarding this as the rooted belief of the Synagogue.[2] This estimate of the Messiah may be gathered from IV Esdras,ᵒ[3] with which the kindred picture of

---

[1] In illustration of this tendency we may quote the following, evidently polemical saying, of R. Abbahu. ' If any man saith to thee, "I am God," he is a liar; "I am the Son of Man," he will at last repent of it; "I go up to heaven," hath he said, and shall he not do it?' [or, he hath said, and shall not make it good] (Jer. Taan. p. 65 b. line 7 from bottom). This R. Abbahu (279–320 of our era) seems to have largely engaged in controversy with Jewish Christians. Thus he sought to argue against the

Sonship of Christ, by commenting, as follows, on Is. xliv. 6: ' " I am the first " —because He has no father; "I am the last "—because He has no Son; " and beside me there is no God "—because He has no brother (equal)' (Shem. R. 29, ed. Warsh. vol. ii. p. 41 a, line 8 from bottom).

[2] It is, to say the least, a pity that Mr. Drummond should have imagined that the question could be so easily settled on the premises which he presents.

[3] The 4th Book of Esdras (in our Apocr.

the Messiah and His reign in the Apocalypse of Baruch[a] may be compared. But even in strictly Rabbinic documents, the *premundane*, if not the eternal *existence of the Messiah* appears as matter of common belief. Such is the view expressed in the Targum on Is. ix. 6, and in that on Micah v. 2. But the Midrash on Prov. viii. 9[b] expressly mentions the Messiah among the seven things created before the world.[1] The passage is the more important, as it throws light on quite a series of others, in which the *Name of the Messiah* is said to have been created before the world.[c][2] Even if this were an ideal conception, it would prove the Messiah to be elevated above the ordinary conditions of humanity. But it means much more than this, since not only the existence of the Messiah long before His actual appearance, but His *premundane* state are clearly taught in other places. In the Talmud[d] it is not only implied, that the Messiah may already be among the living, but a strange story is related, according to which He had actually been born in the royal palace at Bethlehem, bore the name *Menachem* (Comforter), was discovered by one R. Judan through a peculiar device, but had been carried away by a storm. Similarly, the Babylon Talmud represents Him as sitting at the gate of Imperial Rome.[e] In general, the idea of the Messiah's appearance and concealment is familiar to Jewish tradition.[f] But the Rabbis go much farther back, and declare that from the time of Judah's marriage,[g] 'God busied Himself with creating the light of the Messiah,' it being significantly added that, 'before the first oppressor [Pharaoh] was born, the final deliverer [Messiah, the son of David] was already born.'[h] In another passage the Messiah is expressly identified with *Anani*,[1] and therefore represented as pre-existent long before his actual manifestation.[k] The same inference may be drawn from His emphatic designation as the First.[m] Lastly, in Yalkut on Is. lx., the words 'In Thy light shall we see light' (Ps. xxxvi. 9) are

CHAP.
V

[a] lxx. 9-lxxiv.

[b] Ed. Lemb. p. 7 a

[c] Pirqé de R. E. 3; Midr.on Ps. xciii. 1; Ps. 54 a; Nedar. 39 b; Ber. R. 1; Tanch. on Numb. vii. 14, ed. Warsh. vol. ii. p. 56 b, at the bottom

[d] Jer. Ber. ii. 4, p. 5 a

[e] Sanh. 98 a; comp. also Jerus. Targ. on Ex. xii. 42, Pirqé de R. El. 30, and other passages

[f] See for example Pesiqta, ed Buber, p. 49 b b

[g] Gen.. xxxviii. 1, 2

[h] Ber. R. 85, ed. Warsh. p. 151 b

[i] Mentioned in 1 Chr.iii. 24 b

[k] Tanch. Par. Toledoth, 14. ed. Warsh. p. 37 b

[m] Ber. R. 65. ed.Warsh. p. 114 b; Vayyikra R. 30, ed. W. vol. ii⁴, p. 47 a; Pes. 5 a

---

II. Esdras) dates from the end of the first century of our era—and so does the Apocalypse of Baruch.
[1] These are: the Throne of Glory, Messiah the King, the Torah, (ideal) Israel, the Temple, repentance, and Gehenna.
[2] In Pirqé de R. El. and the other authorities these seven things are: the Torah, Gehenna, Paradise, the Throne of Glory, the Temple, repentance, and the Name of the Messiah.
[3] In Ber. R. six things are mentioned: two actually created (the Torah and the Throne of Glory), and four which

came into His Mind to create them (the Fathers, Israel, the Temple, and the Name of the Messiah).
[4] In Tanch. seven things are enumerated (the six as in Ber. R., with the addition of repentance), 'and some say: also Paradise and Gehenna.'
[5] In that passage the time of Messiah's concealment is calculated at forty-five days, from a comparison of Dan. xii. 11 with v. 12.
[6] The comment on this passage is curiously mystical, but clearly implies not only the pre-existence, but the superhuman character of the Messiah.

BOOK
II

explained as meaning, that this is the light of the Messiah,—the same which God had at the first pronounced to be very good, and which, before the world was created, He had hid beneath the throne of His glory for the Messiah and His age. When Satan asked for whom it was reserved, he was told that it was destined for Him Who would put him to shame, and destroy him. And when, at his request, he was shown the Messiah, he fell on his face and owned, that the Messiah would in the future cast him and the Gentiles into Gehenna.[a] Whatever else may be inferred from it, this passage clearly implies not only the pre-existence, but the premundane existence of the Messiah.[1]

But, indeed, it carries us much farther. For, a Messiah, pre-existent, in the Presence of God, and destined to subdue Satan and cast him into hell, could not have been regarded as *an ordinary man.* It is indeed true that, as the history of Elijah, so that of the Messiah is throughout compared with that of Moses, the 'first' with 'the last Redeemer.' As Moses was educated at the court of Pharaoh, so the Messiah dwells in Rome (or Edom) among His enemies.[b] Like Moses He comes, withdraws, and comes again.[c] Like Moses He works deliverance. But here the analogy ceases, for, whereas the redemption by Moses was temporary and comparatively small, that of the Messiah would be eternal and absolute. All the marvels connected with Moses were to be intensified in the Messiah. The ass on which the Messiah would ride—and this humble estate was only caused by Israel's sin[d]—would be not only that on which Moses had come back to Egypt, but also that which Abraham had used when he went to offer up Isaac, and which had been specially created on the eve of the world's first Sabbath.[e] Similarly, the horns of the ram caught in the thicket, which was offered instead of Isaac, were destined for blowing —the left one by the Almighty on Mount Sinai, the right and larger one by the Messiah, when He would gather the outcasts of Israel (Is. xxvii. 13).[f] Again, the 'rod' of the Messiah was that of Aaron, which had budded, blossomed, and burst into fruit; as also that on which Jacob had leaned, and which, through Judah, had passed to all the kings of Israel, till the destruction of the Temple.[g] And so the principle that 'the later Deliverer would be like the first' was carried into every detail. *As the first Deliverer brought down the Manna, so the Messiah;* [h] *as the first Deliverer had made a spring of water to rise, so would the second.*[i]

[a] Yalkut ii. p. 56 c

[b] Shem.R.1, ed.W. vol. ii. p. 5 b; Tanch.Par. Tazrya, 8, ed.W.vol. ii. p. 20 a Pesiqta, ed. Buber, p. 49 b; Midr. Ruth,Par.5, ed.W. p. 43 b
[d] Sanh. 98 a

[e] Pirqé de R. El. 31, ed. Lemb. p. 38 a

[f] Pirqé de R. El. u. s., p. 39 a, close
[g] Bemid. R. 18, close of the Par.
[h] Ps. lxxii. 16
[i] According to the last clause of (English version) Joel iii. 18 (Midr. on Eccles. i. 9. ed. Warsh, vol. iv. p. 80 b)

[1] The whole of this very remarkable passage is given in Appendix IX., in the notes on Is. xxv. 8; lx 1; lxiv. 4; Jer. xxxi. 8.

But even this is not all. That the Messiah had, without any instruction, attained to knowledge of God;[a] and that He had received, directly from Him, all wisdom, knowledge, counsel, and grace,[b] is comparatively little, since the same was claimed for Abraham, Job, and Hezekiah. But we are told that, when God showed Moses all his successors, the spirit of wisdom and knowledge in the Messiah equalled that of all the others together.[c] The Messiah would be 'greater than the Patriarchs,' higher than Moses,[1] and even *loftier than the ministering Angels.*[d] In view of this we can understand, how the Midrash on Psalm xxi. 3 should apply to the Messiah, in all its literality, that 'God would set His own crown on His head,' and clothe Him with His 'honour and majesty.' It is only consistent that the same Midrash should assign to the Messiah the Divine designations: 'Jehovah is a Man of War,' and 'Jehovah our Righteousness.'[e] One other quotation, from perhaps the most spiritual Jewish commentary, must be added, reminding us of that outburst of adoring wonder which once greeted Jesus of Nazareth. The passage first refers to the seven garments with which God successively robed Himself—the first of 'honour and glory,' at creation;[f] the second of 'majesty,' at the Red Sea;[g] the third of 'strength,' at the giving of the Law;[h] the fourth 'white,' when He blotteth out the sins of Israel;[i] the fifth of 'zeal,' when He avengeth them of their enemies;[k] the sixth of 'righteousness,' at the time when the Messiah should be revealed;[m] and the seventh 'red,' when He would take vengeance on Edom (Rome).[n] 'But,' continues the commentary, 'the garment with which in the future He will clothe the Messiah, its splendour will extend from one end of the world to the other, as it is written:[o] "As a bridegroom priestly in headgear." And Israel are astounded at His light, and say: Blessed the hour in which the Messiah was created; blessed the womb whence He issued; blessed the generation that sees Him; blessed the eye that is worthy to behold Him; because the opening of His lips is blessing and peace, and His speech quieting of the spirit. Glory and majesty are in His appearance (vesture), and confidence and tranquillity in His words; and on His tongue compassion and forgiveness; His prayer is a sweet-smelling odour, and His supplication holiness and purity. Happy Israel, what is reserved for you! Thus it is written:[p] "How manifold is Thy goodness, which Thou hast reserved to them that fear Thee."'[q] Such a King Messiah might well be represented as sitting at the Right

CHAP.
V

[a] Bemid. R. 14, ed. Warsh. p. 55 *a*

[b] Bemid. R. 13

[c] Yalkut on Numb. xxvii. 16. vol. i. p. 247 *d*

[d] Tanch., Par. Toledoth 14

[e] Midr. Tehill. ed. Warsh. p. 30 *b*

[f] Ps. civ. 1
[g] Ps. xciii. 1
[h] Ps. xciii. 1
[i] Dan. vii. 9
[k] Is. lix. 17
[m] Is. lix. 17
[n] Is. lxiii.

[o] Is. lxi. 10

[p] Ps. xxxi. 19
[q] Pesiqta. ed. Buber. pp. 149, *a, b*

---

[1] This is the more noteworthy as, according to Sotah 9 *b*, none in Israel was so great as Moses, who was only inferior to the Almighty.

BOOK
II

Hand of God, while Abraham was only at His left; ᵃ nay, as throwing forth His Right Hand, while God stood up to war for Him. ᵇ

It is not without hesitation, that we make reference to Jewish
allusions to the miraculous birth of the Saviour.   Yet there are two
expressions, which convey the idea, if not of superhuman origin, yet
of some great mystery attaching to His birth.   The first occurs in
connection with the birth of Seth.   'Rabbi Tanchuma said, in the
name of Rabbi Samuel: Eve had respect [had regard, looked for-
ward] to that Seed which is to come from another place.   And who
is this?   This is Messiah the King.' ᶜ   The second appears in the
narrative of the crime of Lot's daughters: ᵈ 'It is not written, "that
we may preserve a son from our father," but "seed from our father."
This is that seed which is coming from another place.   And who is
this?   This is the King Messiah.' ᵉ¹

That a superhuman character attached, if not to the Personality,
yet to the Mission of the Messiah, appears from three passages, in
which the expression, 'The Spirit of the Lord moved upon the face
of the deep,' is thus paraphrased: 'This is the Spirit of the King
Messiah.' ᶠ²   Whether this implies some activity of the Messiah in
connection with creation,³ or only that, from the first, His Mission
was to have a bearing on all creation, it elevates His character and
work above every other agency, human or Angelic.   And, without
pressing the argument, it is at least very remarkable that even the
Ineffable Name *Jehovah* is expressly attributed to the Messiah. ᵍ   The

---

¹ I am, of course, aware that certain
Rabbinists explain the expression 'Seed
from another place,' as referring to the
descent of the Messiah from Ruth—a
non-Israelite.   But if this explanation
could be offered in reference to the
daughters of Lot, it is difficult to see its
meaning in reference to Eve and the
birth of Seth.   The connection there with
the words (Gen. iv. 25), 'God hath appointed me another Seed,' would be the
very loosest.

² I am surprised, that *Castelli* (u. s.
p. 207) should have contended, that the
reading in Ber. R. 8 and Vay. R. 14
should be 'the Spirit of Adam.'   For (1)
the attempted correction gives neither
sense, nor proper meaning.   (2) The
passage Ber. R. 1 is not impugned; yet
that passage is the basis of the other
two.   (3) Ber. R. 8 must read, 'The
Spirit of God moved on the deep—that
is, the Spirit of Messiah the King,' because
the proof-passage is immediately added,

'and the spirit of the Lord shall rest
upon Him,' which is a Messianic passage;
and because, only two lines before the
impugned passage, we are told, that Gen.
i. 26, 1st clause, refers to the 'spirit of the
first man.'   The latter remark applies
also to Vayyikra R. 14, where the context
equally forbids the proposed correction.

³ It would be very interesting to compare with this the statements of Philo as
to the agency of the *Logos* in Creation.
The subject is very well treated by *Riehm*
(Lehrbegr. d. Hebr. Br. pp. 414–420),
although I cannot agree with all his conclusions.

⁴ The whole of this passage, beginning
at p. 147 b, is very curious and deeply interesting.   It would lead too far to quote
it, or other parallel passages which might
be adduced.   The passage in the Midrash
on Lament. i. 16 is also extremely interesting.   After the statement quoted in
the text, there follows a discussion on
the names of the Messiah, and then the

fact becomes the more significant, when we recall that one of the most familiar names of the Messiah was *Anani*—He Who cometh in the clouds of heaven.[a]

In what has been stated, no reference has been made to the final conquests of Messiah, to His reign with all its wonders, or to the subdual of all nations—in short, to what are commonly called 'the last things.' This will be treated in another connection. Nor is it contended that, whatever individuals may have expected, the Synagogue taught the doctrine of the Divine Personality of the Messiah, as held by the Christian Church. On the other hand, the cumulative evidence just presented must leave on the mind at least this conviction, that the Messiah expected was far above the conditions of the most exalted of God's servants, even His Angels; in short, so closely bordering on the Divine, that it was almost impossible to distinguish Him therefrom. In such circumstances, it only needed the personal conviction, that He, Who taught and wrought as none other, was really the Messiah, to kindle at His word into the adoring confession, that He was indeed 'the Son of the Living God.' And once that point reached, the mind, looking back through the teaching of the Synagogue, would, with increasing clearness, perceive that, however ill-understood in the past, this had been all along the sum of the whole Old Testament. Thus, we can understand alike the preparedness for, and yet the gradualness of conviction on this point; then, the increasing clearness with which it emerged in the consciousness of the disciples; and, finally, the unhesitating distinctness with which it was put forward in Apostolic teaching as the fundamental article of belief to the Church Catholic.[1]

---

curious story about the Messiah having already been born in Bethlehem.

[1] It will be noticed, that the cumulative argument presented in the foregoing pages follows closely that in the first chapter of the Epistle to the Hebrews; only, that the latter carries it up to its final conclusion, that the Messiah was truly the Son of God, while it has been our purpose simply to state, *what was the expectation of the ancient Synagogue*, not what it *should have been* according to the Old Testament.

CHAPTER VI.

THE NATIVITY OF JESUS THE MESSIAH.

(St. Matthew i. 25; St. Luke ii. 1-20.)

BOOK
II

SUCH then was 'the hope of the promise made of God unto the fathers,' for which the twelve tribes, 'instantly serving (God) night and day,' longed—with such vividness, that they read it in almost every event and promise; with such earnestness, that it ever was the burden of their prayers; with such intensity, that many and long centuries of disappointment have not quenched it. Its light, comparatively dim in days of sunshine and calm, seemed to burn brightest in the dark and lonely nights of suffering, as if each gust that swept over Israel only kindled it into fresh flame.

To the question, whether this hope has ever been realised—or rather, whether One has appeared Whose claims to the Messiahship have stood the test of investigation and of time—impartial history can make only one answer. It points to Bethlehem and to Nazareth. If the claims of Jesus have been rejected by the Jewish Nation, He has at least, undoubtedly, fulfilled one part of the Mission prophetically assigned to the Messiah. Whether or not He be the Lion of the tribe of Judah, to Him, assuredly, has been the gathering of the nations, and the isles have waited for His law. Passing the narrow bounds of obscure Judæa, and breaking down the walls of national prejudice and isolation, He has made the sublimer teaching of the Old Testament the common possession of the world, and founded a great Brotherhood, of which the God of Israel is the Father. He alone also has exhibited a life, in which absolutely no fault could be found; and promulgated a teaching, to which absolutely no exception can be taken. Admittedly, He was *the One perfect Man*—the ideal of humanity, His doctrine the one absolute teaching. The world has known none other, none equal. And the world has owned it, if not by the testimony of words, yet by the evidence of facts. Springing from such a people; born, living, and dying in circumstances, and using means, the most unlikely of such results—the Man of Nazareth

has, by universal consent, been the mightiest Factor in our world's
history: alike politically, socially, intellectually, and morally. If
He be not the Messiah, He has at least thus far done the Messiah's
work. If He be not the Messiah, there has at least been none other,
before or after Him. If He be not the Messiah, the world has not,
and never can have, a Messiah.

To Bethlehem as the birthplace of Messiah, not only Old Testa-
ment prediction,[a] but the testimony of Rabbinic teaching, unhesi-   [a] Micah v. 2
tatingly pointed. Yet nothing could be imagined more directly contrary
to Jewish thoughts and feelings—and hence nothing less likely to
suggest itself to Jewish invention[1]—than the circumstances which,
according to the Gospel-narrative, brought about the birth of the
Messiah in Bethlehem. A counting of the people, or Census; and
that Census taken at the bidding of a heathen Emperor, and
executed by one so universally hated as Herod, would represent the *ne
plus ultra* of all that was most repugnant to Jewish feeling.[2] If the
account of the circumstances, which brought Joseph and Mary to
Bethlehem, has no basis in fact, but is a legend invented to locate
the birth of the Nazarene in the royal City of David, it must be
pronounced most clumsily devised. There is absolutely nothing to
account for its origination—either from parallel events in the past, or
from contemporary expectancy. Why then connect the birth of
their Messiah with what was most repugnant to Israel, especially if,
as the advocates of the legendary hypothesis contend, it did not
occur at a time when any Jewish Census was taken, but ten years
previously?

But if it be impossible rationally to account for any legendary
origin of the narrative of Joseph and Mary's journey to Bethlehem,
the historical grounds, on which its accuracy has been impugned, are
equally insufficient. They resolve themselves into this: that (beyond
the Gospel-narrative) we have no solid evidence that Cyrenius was at
that time occupying the needful official position in the East, to order
such a registration for Herod to carry out. But even this feeble contention is by no means historically unassailable.[3] At any rate, there

---

[1] The advocates of the mythical theory
have not answered, not even faced or
understood, what to us seems, on their
hypothesis, an insuperable difficulty.
Granting, that Jewish expectancy would
suggest the birth of Jesus at Bethlehem,
why invent such circumstances to bring
Mary to Bethlehem ? *Keim* may be right
in saying: 'The belief in the birth at
Bethlehem originated very simply (Le-

ben Jesu i. 2, p. 393); but all the more
complicated and inexplicable is the origination of the legend, which accounts for
the journey thither of Mary and Joseph.
[2] In evidence of these feelings, we
have the account of *Josephus* of the consequences of the taxation of Cyrenius
(Ant. xviii. 1. 1. Comp. Acts v. 37).
[3] The arguments on what may be called
the orthodox side have, from different

BOOK
II

ᵃ Comp.
Acts v. 37

are two facts, which render any historical mistake by St. Luke on this point extremely difficult to believe. First, he was evidently aware of a Census under Cyrenius, ten years later;ᵃ secondly, whatever rendering of St. Luke ii. 2 may be adopted, it will at least be admitted, that the intercalated sentence about Cyrenius was not necessary for the narrative, and that the writer must have intended thereby emphatically to mark a certain event. But an author would not be likely to call special attention to a fact, of which he had only indistinct knowledge; rather, if it *must* be mentioned, would he do so in the most indefinite terms. This presumption in favour of St. Luke's statement is strengthened by the consideration, that such an event as the taxing of Judæa must have been so easily ascertainable by him.

We are, however, not left to the presumptive reasoning just set forth. That the Emperor Augustus made registers of the Roman Empire, and of subject and tributary states, is now generally admitted. This registration—for the purpose of future taxation— would also embrace Palestine. Even if no actual order to that effect had been issued during the lifetime of Herod, we can understand that he would deem it most expedient, both on account of his relations to the Emperor, and in view of the probable excitement which a heathen Census would cause in Palestine, to take steps for making a registration, and that rather according to the Jewish than the Roman manner. This Census, then, arranged by Augustus, and taken by Herod in his own manner, was, according to St. Luke, 'first [really] carried out when Cyrenius was Governor of Syria,' some years after Herod's death and when Judæa had become a Roman province. [1]

We are now prepared to follow the course of the Gospel-narrative. In consequence of 'the decree of Cæsar Augustus,' Herod directed a general registration to be made after the Jewish, rather than the Roman, manner. Practically the two would, indeed, in this instance, be very similar. According to the Roman law, all country-people were to be registered in their 'own city'—meaning thereby the town to which the village or place, where they were born, was attached. In

points of view, been so often and well stated—latterly by Wieseler, Huschke, Zumpt, and Steinmeyer—and on the other side almost *ad nauseam* by negative critics of every school, that it seems unnecessary to go again over them. The reader will find the whole subject stated by Canon *Cook*, whose views we substantially adopt, in the 'Speaker's Commentary' (N.T. i. pp. 326–329). The reasoning of *Mommsen* (Res gestæ D. Aug. pp. 175, 176) does not seem to me to affect the view taken in the text.

[1] For the textual explanation we again refer to Canon *Cook*, only we would mark, with Steinmeyer, that the meaning of the expression ἐγένετο, in St. Luke ii. 2, is determined by the similar use of

so doing, the 'house and lineage' (the *nomen* and *cognomen*) of each
were marked.[1] According to the Jewish mode of registration, the
people would have been enrolled according to *tribes* (מטות), *families* or
clans (משפחות), and the *house* of their fathers (בית אבות). But as
the ten tribes had not returned to Palestine, this could only take
place to a very limited extent,[2] while it would be easy for each to be
registered in 'his own city.' In the case of Joseph and Mary, whose
descent from David was not only known, but where, for the sake of
the unborn Messiah, it was most important that this should be distinctly
noted, it was natural that, in accordance with Jewish law, they
should have gone to Bethlehem. Perhaps also, for many reasons
which will readily suggest themselves, Joseph and Mary might be
glad to leave Nazareth, and seek, if possible, a home in Bethlehem.
Indeed, so strong was this feeling, that it afterwards required special
Divine direction to induce Joseph to relinquish this chosen place of
residence, and to return into Galilee.[a] In these circumstances, Mary,
now the 'wife' of Joseph, though standing to him only in the actual
relationship of 'betrothed,'[b] would, of course, accompany her husband
to Bethlehem. Irrespective of this, every feeling and hope in her
must have prompted such a course, and there is no need to discuss
whether Roman or Jewish Census-usage required her presence—a
question which, if put, would have to be answered in the negative.

The short winter's day was probably closing in,[3] as the two travellers from Nazareth, bringing with them the few necessaries of a
poor Eastern household, neared their journey's end. If we think of
Jesus as the Messiah from heaven, the surroundings of outward
poverty, so far from detracting, seem most congruous to His Divine
character. Earthly splendor would here seem like tawdry tinsel,
and the utmost simplicity like that clothing of the lilies, which far
surpassed all the glory of Solomon's court. But only in the East
would the most absolute simplicity be possible, and yet neither it,
nor the poverty from which it sprang, necessarily imply even the
slightest taint of social inferiority. The way had been long and

[a] St. Matt
ii. 22

[b] St. Luke
ii. 5

it in Acts xi. 28, where what was predicted is said to have actually taken place
(ἐγένετο) at the time of Claudius Cæsar.
[1] Comp. *Huschke*, Ueber d. z. Zeit d.
Geb. J. C. gehalt. Census pp. 119, 120.
Most critics have written very confusedly
on this point.
[2] The reader will now be able to appreciate the value of *Keim's* objections
against such a Census, as involving a
'wahre Volkswanderung' (!), and being

'eine Sache der Unmöglichkeit.'
[3] This, of course, is only a conjecture;
but I call it 'probable,' partly because
one would naturally so arrange a journey
of several days, to make its stages as
slow and easy as possible, and partly
from the circumstance, that, on their arrival, they found the khan full, which
would scarcely have been the case had
they reached Bethlehem early in the
day.

BOOK
II

weary—at the very least, three days' journey, whatever route had been taken from Galilee. Most probably it would be that so commonly followed, from a desire to avoid Samaria, along the eastern banks of the Jordan, and by the fords of Jericho.[1] Although passing through one of the warmest parts of the country, the season of the year must, even in most favorable circumstances, have greatly increased the difficulties of such a journey. A sense of rest and peace must, almost unconsciously, have crept over the travellers when at last they reached the rich fields that surrounded the ancient 'House of Bread,' and, passing through the valley which, like an amphitheatre, sweeps up to the twin heights along which Bethlehem stretches (2,704 feet above the sea), ascended through the terraced vineyards and gardens. Winter though it was, the green and silvery foliage of the olive might, even at that season, mingle with the pale pink of the almond—nature's 'early waker'[2]—and with the darker coloring of the opening peach-buds. The chaste beauty and sweet quiet of the place would recall memories of Boaz, of Jesse, and of David. All the more would such thoughts suggest themselves, from the contrast between the past and the present. For, as the travellers reached the heights of Bethlehem, and, indeed, long before, the most prominent object in view must have been the great castle which Herod had built, and called after his own name. Perched on the highest hill south-east of Bethlehem, it was, at the same time

a *Jos*. Ant. xiv. 13. 9; xv. 9. 4; War. i. 13. 8: 21, 10

magnificent palace, strongest fortress, and almost courtier-city.[a] With a sense of relief the travellers would turn from this, to mark the undulating outlines of the highland wilderness of Judæa, till the horizon was bounded by the mountain-ridges of Tekoa. Through the break of the hills eastward the heavy molten surface of the Sea of Judgment would appear in view; westward wound the road to Hebron; behind them lay the valleys and hills which separated Bethlehem from Jerusalem, and concealed the Holy City.

But for the present such thoughts would give way to the pressing necessity of finding shelter and rest. The little town of Bethlehem was crowded with those who had come from all the outlying district to register their names. Even if the strangers from far-off Galilee had been personally acquainted with any one in Bethlehem, who could have shown them hospitality, they would have found every

---

[1] Comp. the account of the roads, inns, &c. in the 'History of the Jewish Nation,' p. 275; and the chapter on Travelling in Palestine,' in 'Sketches of Jewish Social Life in the Days of Christ.'

[2] The almond is called, in Hebrew, שָׁקֵד, 'the waker.' from the word 'to be awake.' It is quite possible, that many of the earliest spring flowers already made the landscape bright.

house fully occupied. The very inn was filled, and the only available CHAP.
space was, where ordinarily the cattle were stabled.[1] Bearing in mind VI
the simple habits of the East, this scarcely implies, what it would
in the West; and perhaps the seclusion and privacy from the noisy,
chattering crowd, which thronged the khan, would be all the more
welcome. Scanty as these particulars are, even thus much is
gathered rather by inference than from the narrative itself. Thus
early in this history does the absence of details, which painfully
increases as we proceed, remind us, that the Gospels were not
intended to furnish a biography of Jesus, nor even the materials for
it; but had only this twofold object: that those who read them
'might believe that Jesus is the Christ, the Son of God,' and that
believing they 'might have life through His Name.'[a] The Christian
heart and imagination, indeed, long to be able to localise the scene of
such surpassing importance, and linger with fond reverence over that
Cave, which is now covered by 'the Church of the Nativity.' It may
be—nay, it seems likely—that this, to which the most venerable
tradition points, was the sacred spot of the world's greatest event.[2]
But certainty we have not. It is better, that it should be so. As to
all that passed in the seclusion of that 'stable'—the circumstances
of the 'Nativity,' even its exact time after the arrival of Mary (brief
as it must have been)—the Gospel-narrative is silent. This only is
told, that then and there the Virgin-Mother 'brought forth her first-
born Son, and wrapped Him in swaddling clothes, and laid Him in a
manger.' Beyond this announcement of the bare fact, Holy Scripture,
with indescribable appropriateness and delicacy, draws a veil over
that most sacred mystery. Two impressions only are left on the
mind: that of utmost earthly humility, in the surrounding circum-

* St. John
xx. 31;
comp.
St. Luke i. 4

---

[1] Dr. *Geikie* indeed '*feels sure*' that the καταλύμα was *not* an inn, but a guest-chamber, because the word is used in that sense in St. Mark xiv.14, Luke xxii. 11. But this inference is critically untenable. The Greek word is of very wide application, and means (as Schleusner puts it) 'omnis locus quieti aptus.' In the LXX. καταλύμα is the equivalent of not less than *five* Hebrew words, which have widely different meanings. In the LXX. rendering of Ex. iv. 24 it is used for the Hebrew מָלוֹן, which certainly cannot mean a guest-chamber, but an inn. No one could imagine that. if private hospitality had been extended to the Virgin-Mother, she would have been left in such circumstances in a stable. The same

term occurs in Aramaic form, in Rabbinic writings, as אַכְסַנְיָא or צָלֵילִי=צָלֵילִי. καταλύμα, an inn. *Delitzsch*, in his Hebrew N.T., uses the more common מָלוֹן. Bazaars and markets were also held in those hostelries; animals killed, and meat sold there; also wine and cider; so that they were a much more public place of resort than might at first be imagined. Comp. *Herzfeld*, Handelsgesch. p. 325.

[2] Perhaps the best authenticated of all local traditions is that which fixes on this cave as the place of the Nativity. The evidence in its favour is well given by Dr. *Farrar* in his 'Life of Christ.' Dean Stanley, however, and others, have questioned it.

stances; and that of inward fitness, in the contrast suggested by them. Instinctively, reverently, we feel that it is well it should have been so. It best befits the birth of the Christ—if He be what the New Testament declares Him.

On the other hand, the circumstances just noted afford the strongest indirect evidence of the truth of this narrative. For, if it were the outcome of Jewish imagination, where is the basis for it in contemporary expectation? Would Jewish legend have ever presented its Messiah as born in a stable, to which chance circumstances had consigned His Mother? The whole current of Jewish opinion would run in the contrary direction. The opponents of the authenticity of this narrative are bound to face this. Further, it may safely be asserted, that no Apocryphal or legendary narrative of such a (legendary) event would have been characterised by such scantiness, or rather absence, of details. For, the two essential features, alike of legend and of tradition, are, that they ever seek to surround their heroes with a halo of glory, and that they attempt to supply details, which are otherwise wanting. And in both these respects a more sharply-marked contrast could scarcely be presented, than in the Gospel-narrative.

But as we pass from the sacred gloom of the cave out into the night, its sky all aglow with starry brightness, its loneliness is peopled, and its silence made vocal from heaven. There is nothing now to conceal, but much to reveal, though the manner of it would seem strangely incongruous to Jewish thinking. And yet Jewish tradition may here prove both illustrative and helpful. That the Messiah was to be born in Bethlehem,[1] was a settled conviction. Equally so was the belief, that He was to be revealed from *Migdal Eder*, 'the tower of the flock.'[a] This *Migdal Eder* was *not* the watch-tower for the ordinary flocks which pastured on the barren sheep-ground beyond Bethlehem, but lay close to the town, on the road to Jerusalem. A passage in the Mishnah [b] leads to the conclusion, that the flocks, which pastured there, were destined for Temple-sacrifices,[2] and, accordingly, that the shepherds, who watched over them, were

a Targum Pseudo-Jon.onGen. xxxv 21

b Shek. vii. 4

[1] In the curious story of His birth, related in the Jer. Talmud (Ber. ii. 3), He is said to have been born in 'the royal castle of Bethlehem;' while in the parallel narrative in the Midr. on Lament. i. 16, ed. W. p. 64 *b*) the somewhat mysterious expression is used כְּבִירַת עַרְבָא. But we must keep in view the Rabbinic statement that, even if a castle falls down, it is still called a castle (Yalkut, vol. ii. p. 60 *b*).

[2] In fact the Mishnah (Baba K. vii. 7) expressly forbids the keeping of flocks throughout the land of Israel, except in the wildernesses—and the only flocks otherwise kept, would be those for the Temple-services (Baba K. 80 *a*).

not ordinary shepherds. The latter were under the ban of Rabbinism,[1] on account of their necessary isolation from religious ordinances, and their manner of life, which rendered strict legal observance unlikely, if not absolutely impossible. The same Mishnic passage also leads us to infer, that these flocks lay out *all the year round*, since they are spoken of as in the fields thirty days before the Passover—that is, in the month of February, when in Palestine the average rainfall is nearly greatest.[2] Thus, Jewish tradition in some dim manner apprehended the first revelation of the Messiah from that *Migdal Eder*, where shepherds watched the Temple-flocks all the year round. Of the deep symbolic significance of such a coincidence, it is needless to speak.

It was, then, on that 'wintry night' of the 25th of December,[3] that shepherds watched the flocks destined for sacrificial services, in the very place consecrated by tradition as that where the Messiah was to be first revealed. Of a sudden came the long-delayed, unthought-of announcement. Heaven and earth seemed to mingle, as suddenly an Angel stood before their dazzled eyes, while the outstreaming glory of the Lord seemed to enwrap them, as in a mantle of light.[4]

[1] This disposes of an inapt quotation (from Delitzsch) by Dr. Geikie. No one could imagine, that the Talmudic passages in question could apply to such shepherds as these.

[2] The mean of 22 seasons in Jerusalem amounted to 4·718 inches in December, 5·479 in January, and 5·207 in February (see a very interesting paper by Dr. *Chaplin* in Quart. Stat. of Pal. Explor. Fund, January, 1883). For 1876–77 we have these startling figures: mean for December, ·490; for January, 1·595; for February, 8·750—and, similarly, in other years. And so we read: 'Good the year in which *Tebheth* (December) is without rain' (Taan. 6 *b*). Those who have copied Lightfoot's quotations about the flocks not lying out during the winter months ought, at least, to have known that the reference in the Talmudic passages is *expressly* to the flocks which pastured in 'the wilderness' (אלו הן מדבריות). But even so, the statement, as so many others of the kind, is not accurate. For, in the Talmud two opinions are expressed. According to one, the 'Midbariyoth,' or 'animals of the wilderness,' are those which go to the open at the Passover-time, and return at the first rains (about November); while, on the other hand, Rabbi maintains, and, as it seems, more authoritatively, that *the wilderness-flocks*

remain in the open alike in the hottest days and in the rainy season—*i.e.* all the year round (Bezah 40 *a*). Comp. also Tosephta Bezah iv. 6. A somewhat different explanation is given in Jer. Bezah 63 *b*.

[3] There is no adequate reason for questioning the historical accuracy of this date. The objections generally made rest on grounds, which seem to me historically untenable. The subject has been fully discussed in an article by *Cassel* in Herzog's Real. Ency. xvii. pp. 588–594. But a curious piece of evidence comes to us from a Jewish source. In the addition to the Megillath Taanith (ed. Warsh. p. 20 *a*), the 9th Tebheth is marked as a fast day, and it is added, that the reason for this is not stated. Now, Jewish chronologists have fixed on that day as that of Christ's birth, and it is remarkable that, between the years 500 and 816 A.D. the 25th of December fell no less than twelve times on the 9th Tebheth. If the 9th Tebheth, or 25th December, was regarded as the birthday of Christ, we can understand the concealment about it. Comp. *Zunz*, Ritus d. Synag. Gottesd. p. 126.

[4] In illustration we may here quote Shem. R. 2 (ed. W. vol. ii. p. 8 *a*), where it is said that, wherever Michael appears, there also is the glory of the Shekhinah. In the same section we read, in reference

Surprise, awe, fear would be hushed into calm and expectancy, as from the Angel they heard, that what they saw boded not judgment, but ushered in to waiting Israel the great joy of those good tidings which he brought: that the long-promised Saviour, Messiah, Lord, was born in the City of David, and that they themselves might go and see, and recognize Him by the humbleness of the circumstances surrounding His Nativity.

It was, as if attendant angels had only waited the signal. As, when the sacrifice was laid on the altar, the Temple-music burst forth in three sections, each marked by the blast of the priests' silver trumpets, as if each Psalm were to be a *Tris-Hagion*;[1] so, when the Herald-Angel had spoken, a multitude of heaven's host[2] stood forth to hymn the good tidings he had brought. What they sang was but the reflex of what had been announced. It told in the language of praise the character, the meaning, the result, of what had taken place. Heaven took up the strain of 'glory'; earth echoed it as 'peace'; it fell on the ears and hearts of men as 'good pleasure':

> Glory to God in the highest—
> And upon earth peace—
> Among men good pleasure![3]

Only once before had the words of the Angels' hymn fallen upon mortal's ears, when, to Isaiah's rapt vision, Heaven's high Temple had opened, and the glory of Jehovah swept its courts, almost breaking down the trembling posts that bore its boundary gates. Now the same glory enwrapt the shepherds on Bethlehem's plains. Then the Angels' hymn

---

to the appearance in the bush, that, 'at first only one Angel came,' who stood in the burning bush, and after that the Shekhinah came, and spoke to Moses from out the bush. (It is a curious illustration of Acts ix. 7, that Moses alone is said in Jewish tradition to have seen the vision, but not the men who were with him.) Wetstein gives an erroneous reference to a Talmudic statement, to the effect that, at the birth of Moses, the room was filled with heavenly light. The statement really occurs in Sotah 12 *a*; Shem. R. 1; Yalkut i. 51 *c*. This must be the foundation of the Christian legend, that the cave, in which Christ was born, was filled with heavenly light. Similarly, the Romish legend about the Virgin Mother not feeling the pangs of maternity is derived from the Jewish legend, which asserts the same of the mother of Moses. The same authority

maintains, that the birth of Moses remained unknown for three months, because he was a child of seven months. There are other legends about the sinlessness of Moses' father, and the maidenhood of his mother (at 103 years), which remind us of Christian traditions.

[1] According to tradition, the three blasts symbolically proclaimed the kingdom of God, the providence of God, and the final judgment.

[2] Curiously enough, the word στρα τιά is Hebraised in the same connection אסטרטיא של מעלה. See Yalkut on Ps. xlv. (vol. ii. p. 105 *a*, about the middle).

[3] I have unhesitatingly retained the reading of the *textus receptus*. The arguments in its favor are sufficiently set forth by Canon Cook in his 'Revised Version of the First Three Gospels,' pp. 27–32.

had heralded the announcement of the Kingdom coming; now that of the King come. Then it had been the *Tris-Hagion* of prophetic anticipation; now that of Evangelic fulfilment.

The hymn had ceased; the light faded out of the sky; and the shepherds were alone. But the Angelic message remained with them; and the sign, which was to guide them to the Infant Christ, lighted their rapid way up the terraced height to where, at the entering of Bethlehem, the lamp swinging over the hostelry directed them to the strangers of the house of David, who had come from Nazareth. Though it seems as if, in the hour of her utmost need, the Virgin-Mother had not been ministered to by loving hands,[1] yet what had happened in the stable must soon have become known in the Khan. Perhaps friendly women were still passing to and fro on errands of mercy, when the shepherds reached the 'stable.'[2] There they found, perhaps not what they had expected, but as they had been told. The holy group only consisted of the humble Virgin-Mother, the lowly carpenter of Nazareth, and the Babe laid in the manger. What further passed we know not, save that, having seen it for themselves, the shepherds told what had been spoken to them about this Child, to all around[3]—in the 'stable,' in the fields, probably also in the Temple, to which they would bring their flocks, thereby preparing the minds of a Simeon, of an Anna, and of all them that looked for salvation in Israel.[4]

And now the hush of wondering expectancy fell once more on all, who heard what was told by the shepherds—this time not only in the hill-country of Judæa, but within the wider circle that embraced Bethlehem and the Holy City. And yet it seemed all so sudden, so strange. That on such slender thread, as the feeble throb of an Infant-life, the salvation of the world should hang—and no special care watch over its safety, no better shelter be provided it than a 'stable,' no other cradle than a manger! And still it is ever so. On what slender thread has the continued life of the Church often seemed to hang; on what feeble throbbing that of every child of God—with

---

[1] This appears to me implied in the emphatic statement, that Mary—as I gather, herself—'wrapped Him in swaddling clothes' (St. Luke ii. 7, 12). Otherwise the remark would seem needless and meaningless.

[2] It seems difficult to understand how, on Dr. Geikie's theory, the shepherds could have found the Infant-Saviour, since, manifestly, they could not during that night have roused every household

in Bethlehem, to inquire whether any child had been born among their guests.

[3] The term διαγνωρίζω implies more than to 'make known abroad.' Wahl renders it *'ultro citroque narro'*; Schleusner: *'divulgo aliquid ut aliis innotescat, spargo rumorem.'*

[4] This may have prepared not only those who welcomed Jesus on His presentation in the Temple, but filled many others with expectancy.

BOOK
II

no visible outward means to ward off danger, no home of comfort, no rest of ease. But, 'Lo, children are Jehovah's heritage!'—and: 'So giveth He to His beloved in *his* sleep!'[1]

[1] The following remarkable extract from the Jerusalem Targum on Ex. xii. 42 may interest the reader:—

'It is a night to be observed and exalted. . . . Four nights are there written in the Book of Memorial. Night first: when the Memra of Jehovah was revealed upon the world for its creation; when the world was without form and void, and darkness was spread upon the face of the deep, and the Memra of Jehovah illuminated and made it light; and He called it the first night. Night second: when the Memra of Jehovah was revealed unto Abraham between the divided pieces; when Abraham was a hundred years, and Sarah was ninety years, and to confirm thereby that which the Scripture saith,—Abraham a hundred years old, can he beget? and Sarah, ninety years old, can she bear? Was not our father Isaac thirty-seven years old at the time he was offered upon the altar? Then the heavens were bowed down and brought low, and Isaac saw their foundations, and his eyes were blinded owing to that sight; and He called it the second night. The third night: when the Memra of Jehovah was revealed upon the Egyptians, at the dividing of the night; His right hand slew the first-born of the Egyptians, and His right hand spared the first-born of Israel; to fulfil what the Scripture hath said, Israel is My first-born well-beloved son. And He called it the third night. Night the fourth: when the end of the world will be accomplished, that it might be dissolved, the bands of wickedness destroyed, and the iron yoke broken. Moses came forth from the midst of the desert, and the King Messiah from the midst of Rome. This one shall lead at the head of a Cloud, and that one shall lead at the head of a Cloud; and the Memra of Jehovah will lead between both, and they two shall come as one (*Cachada*).' (For explan. see vol. ii. p. 100, note.)

CHAPTER VII.

THE PURIFICATION OF THE VIRGIN AND THE PRESENTATION IN THE TEMPLE.

(St. Luke ii. 21–38.)

FOREMOST amongst those who. wondering, had heard what the shep- CHAP.
herds told, was she whom most it concerned, who laid it up deepest VII
in her heart, and brought to it treasured stores of memory. It was
the Mother of Jesus. These many months, all connected with this
Child could never have been far away from her thoughts. And now
that He was hers, yet not hers—belonged, yet did not seem to belong,
to her—He would be the more dear to her Mother-heart for what
made Him so near, and yet parted Him so far from her. And upon
all His history seemed to lie such wondrous light, that she could
only see the path behind, so far as she had trodden it; while upon
that on which she was to move, was such dazzling brightness, that
she could scarce look upon the present, and dared not gaze towards
the future.

At the very outset of this history, and increasingly in its course,
the question meets us, how, if the Angelic message to the Virgin
was a reality, and her motherhood so supernatural, she could have
been apparently so ignorant of what was to come—nay, so often have
even misunderstood it? Strange, that she should have 'pondered
in her heart' the shepherd's account; stranger, that afterwards she
should have wondered at His lingering in the Temple among Israel's
teachers; strangest, that, at the very first of His miracles, a mother's
fond pride should have so harshly broken in upon the Divine melody
of His work, by striking a keynote so different from that, to which
His life had been set; or that afterwards, in the height of his activity,
loving fears, if not doubts, should have prompted her to interrupt,
what evidently she had not as yet comprehended in the fulness of its
meaning. Might we not rather have expected, that the Virgin-
Mother from the inception of this Child's life would have understood, that He was truly the Son of God? The question, like so
many others, requires only to be clearly stated, to find its emphatic
answer. For. had it been so. His history. His human life, of which

every step is of such infinite importance to mankind, would not have been possible. Apart from all thoughts of the deeper necessity, both as regarded His Mission and the salvation of the world, of a true human development of gradual consciousness and personal life, Christ could not, in any true sense, have been subject to His Parents, if they had fully understood that He was Divine; nor could He, in that case, have been watched, as He 'grew in wisdom and in favour with God and men.' Such knowledge would have broken the bond of His Humanity to ours, by severing that which bound Him as a child to His mother. We could not have become His brethren, had He not been truly the Virgin's Son. The mystery of the Incarnation would have been needless and fruitless, had His humanity not been subject to all its right and ordinary conditions. And, applying the same principle more widely, we can thus, in some measure, understand why the mystery of His Divinity had to be kept while He was on earth. Had it been otherwise, the thought of His Divinity would have proved so all-absorbing, as to render impossible that of His Humanity, with all its lessons. The Son of God Most High, Whom they worshipped, could never have been the loving Man, with Whom they could hold such close converse. The bond which bound the Master to His disciples—the Son of Man to humanity—would have been dissolved; His teaching as a Man, the Incarnation, and the Tabernacling among men, in place of the former Old Testament Revelation from heaven, would have become wholly impossible. In short, one, and that the distinctive New Testament, element in our salvation would have been taken away. At the beginning of His life He would have anticipated the lessons of its end—nay, not those of His Death only, but of His Resurrection and Ascension, and of the coming of the Holy Ghost.

In all this we have only been taking the subjective, not the objective, view of the question; considered the earthward, not the heavenward, aspect of His life. The latter, though very real, lies beyond our present horizon. Not so the question as to the development of the Virgin-Mother's spiritual knowledge. Assuming her to have occupied, in the fullest sense, the standpoint of Jewish Messianic expectancy, and remembering, also, that she was so 'highly favoured' of God, still, there was not as yet anything, nor could there be for many years, to lead her beyond what might be called the utmost height of Jewish belief. On the contrary, there was much connected with His true Humanity to keep her back. For narrow as, to our retrospective thinking, the boundary-line seems between Jewish belief and that in the hypostatic union of the two Natures, the passage from the one to the other represented such tremendous mental revolution, as to imply direct Divine teaching.[a] An illustrative instance will prove this better than argument. We read, in a commentary on the opening words of Gen. xv. 18,[b] that when God made the covenant with Abram, He 'revealed to him both this *Olam* (dispensation) and the *Olam* to come,' which latter expression is correctly explained as referring to the days of the Messiah. Jewish tradition, therefore, here asserts exactly what Jesus stated in these words: 'Your father Abraham rejoiced to see My day; and he saw it, and was glad.'[c] Yet we know what storm of indignation the enunciation of it called forth among the Jews!

Thus it was, that every event connected with the Messianic manifestation of Jesus would come to the Virgin-Mother as a fresh discovery and a new surprise. Each event, as it took place, stood isolated in her mind; not as part of a whole which she would anticipate, nor as only one link in a chain; but as something quite by itself. She knew the beginning, and she knew the end; but she knew not the path which led from the one to the other; and each step in it was a new revelation. Hence it was, that she so carefully treasured in her heart every new fact,[d] piecing each to the other, till she could read from it the great mystery that He, Whom Incarnate she had borne, was, indeed, the Son of the living God. And as it was natural, so it was well that it should be so. For, thus only could she truly, because self-unconsciously, as a Jewish woman and mother, fulfil all the requirements of the Law, alike as regarded herself and her Child

The first of these was Circumcision, representing voluntary subjection to the conditions of the Law, and acceptance of the obligations, but also of the privileges, of the Covenant between God and Abraham and his seed. Any attempt to show the deep significance of such a rite in the case of Jesus, could only weaken the impression which the fact itself conveys. The ceremony took place, as in all ordinary circumstances, on the eighth day, when the Child received the Angel-given name *Jeshua* (Jesus). Two other legal ordinances still remained to be observed. The firstborn son of every household was, according to the Law, to be 'redeemed' of the priest at the price of five shekels of the Sanctuary.[e] Rabbinic casuistry here added many needless, and even repulsive, details. The following, however, are of practical interest. The earliest period of presentation was thirty-one days after birth. so as to make the legal month quite

CHAP.
VII

[a] 1 Cor. xii. 3

[b] Ber. R. 44, ed. Warsh. p. 81 b

[c] St. John viii. 56

[d] St. Luke ii. 19, 51

[e] Numb. xviii. 16

complete. The child must have been the firstborn of his mother (according to some writers, of his father also);[1] neither father nor mother[2] must be of Levitic descent; and the child must be free from all such bodily blemishes as would have disqualified him for the priesthood — or, as it was expressed: 'the firstborn for the priesthood.' It was a thing much dreaded, that the child should die before his redemption; but if his father died in the interval, the child had to redeem himself when of age. As the Rabbinic law expressly states, that the shekels were to be of 'Tyrian weight,'[a] the value of the 'redemption money' would amount to about ten or twelve shillings. The redemption could be made from any priest, and attendance in the Temple was not requisite. It was otherwise with the 'purification' of the mother.[b] The Rabbinic law fixed this at forty-one days after the birth of a son, and eighty-one after that of a daughter,[3] so as to make the Biblical terms quite complete.[c] But it might take place any time later—notably, when attendance on any of the great feasts brought a family to Jerusalem. Thus, we read of cases when a mother would offer several sacrifices of purification at the same time.[4] But, indeed, the woman was not required to be personally present at all, when her offering was presented, or, rather (as we shall see), provided for—say, by the representatives of the laity, who daily took part in the services for the various districts from which they came. This also is specially provided for in the Talmud.[5] But mothers who were within convenient distance of the Temple, and especially the more earnest among them, would naturally attend personally in the Temple;[6] and in such cases, when practicable, the redemption of the firstborn, and the purification of his mother, would be combined. Such was undoubtedly the case with the Virgin-Mother and her Son.

a Bechor.
viii. 7

b Lev. xii.

c Comp.
Sifra, ed.
Weiss, p. 59
a and b;
Maimon-
ides, Yad
haChaz.
Hal.
Mechusré
Capp., ed.
Amst., vol.
iii. p. 255
a and b

---

[1] So *Lundius*, Jüd. Alterth. p. 621, and *Buxtorf*, Lex. Talmud. p. 1699. But I am bound to say, that this seems contrary to the sayings of the Rabbis.

[2] This disposes of the idea, that the Virgin-Mother was of direct Aaronic or Levitic descent.

[3] Archdeacon Farrar is mistaken in supposing, that the 'thirty-three days' were counted 'after the circumcision.' The idea must have arisen from a misunderstanding of the English version of Lev. xii. 4. There was no connection between the time of the circumcision of the child, and that of the purification of his mother. In certain circumstances circumcision might have to be delayed

for days—in case of sickness, till recovery. It is equally a mistake to suppose, that a Jewish mother could not leave the house till *after* the forty days of her purification.

[4] Comp. Kerith. i. 7.

[5] Jer. Sheq. 50 *b*.

[6] There is no ground whatever for the objection which Rabbi *Löw* (Lebensalter, p. 112) raises against the account of St. Luke. Jewish documents only prove, that a mother *need* not personally attend in the Temple; not that they *did* not do so, when attendance was possible. The contrary impression is conveyed to us by Jewish notices.

For this twofold purpose the Holy Family went up to the Temple, when the prescribed days were completed.[1] The ceremony at the redemption of a firstborn son was, no doubt, more simple than that at present in use. It consisted of the formal presentation of the child to the priest, accompanied by two short 'benedictions'—the one for the law of redemption, the other for the gift of a firstborn son, after which the redemption money was paid.[2] Most solemn, as in such a place, and remembering its symbolic significance as the expression of God's claim over each family in Israel, must this rite have been.

As regards the rite at the purification of the mother, the scantiness of information has led to serious misstatements. Any comparison with our modern 'churching' of women[3] is inapplicable, since the latter consists of thanksgiving, and the former primarily of a sin-offering for the Levitical defilement symbolically attaching to the beginning of life, and a burnt-offering, that marked the restoration of communion with God. Besides, as already stated, the sacrifice for purification might be brought in the absence of the mother. Similar mistakes prevail as to the rubric. It is not the case, as generally stated, that the woman was sprinkled with blood, and then pronounced clean by the priest, or that prayers were offered on the occasion.[4] The service simply consisted of the statutory sacrifice. This was what, in ecclesiastical language, was termed an offering *oleh veyored*, that is, 'ascending and descending,' according to the means of the offerer. The sin-offering was, in all cases, a turtle-dove or a young pigeon. But, while the more wealthy brought a lamb for a burnt-offering, the poor might substitute for it a turtle-dove, or a young pigeon.[5] The rubric directed that the neck of the sin-offering was to

---

[1] The expression τοῦ καθαρισμοῦ αὐτῶν cannot refer to the Purification of the Virgin and *her Babe* (Farrar), nor to that of the Virgin and Joseph (Meyer), because neither the Babe nor Joseph needed, nor were they included in, the purification. It can only refer to 'their' (*i.e.* the Jews') purification. But this does not imply any Romish inferences (*Sepp,* Leben Jesu, ii. 1, p. 131) as to the superhuman condition or origin of the Blessed Virgin; on the contrary, the offering of the sin-offering points in the other direction.

[2] Comp. the rubric and the prayers in *Maimonides,* Yad haChaz. Hilch. Biccur. xi. 5.

[3] So Dr. Geikie.

[4] So Dr. Geikie, taking his account from *Herzog's* Real-Encykl. The mistake about the mother being sprinkled with sacrificial blood originated with Lightfoot (Horæ Hebr. on St. Luke ii. 22). Later writers have followed the lead. Tamid v. 6, quoted by Lightfoot, refers only to the cleansing of the leper. The 'prayers' supposed to be spoken, and the pronouncing clean by the priests, are the embellishments of later writers, for which Lightfoot is not responsible.

[5] According to Sifra (Par. Tazria, Per. iv. 3): 'Whenever the sin-offering is changed, it precedes [as on ordinary occasions] the burnt-offering; but when the burnt-offering is changed [as on this occasion], it precedes the sin-offering.'

BOOK
II

be broken, but the head not wholly severed; that some of the blood should be sprinkled at the south-western angle of the altar,[1] below the red line,[2] which ran round the middle of the altar, and that the rest should be poured out at the base of the altar. The whole of the flesh belonged to the priests, and had to be eaten within the enclosure of the Sanctuary. The rubric for the burnt-offering of a turtle-dove

a Sebach.
vi. 5

or a young pigeon was somewhat more intricate.[a] The substitution of the latter for a young lamb was expressly designated 'the poor's offering.' And rightly so, since, while a lamb would probably cost about three shillings, the average value of a pair of turtle-doves, for

b Comp.
Kerith. i. 7

both the sin- and burnt-offering, would be about eightpence,[b] and on one occasion fell so low as twopence. The Temple-price of the meat- and drink-offerings was fixed once a month; and special officials instructed the intending offerers, and provided them with what was

c Sheq. iv. 9

needed.[c] There was also a special 'superintendent of turtle-doves and pigeons,' required for certain purifications, and the holder of that office

d Sheq. v. 1

is mentioned with praise in the Mishnah.[d] Much, indeed, depended upon his uprightness. For, at any rate as regarded those who brought the poor's offering, the purchasers of pigeons or turtle-doves would, as a rule, have to deal with him. In the Court of the Women there were thirteen trumpet-shaped chests for pecuniary contributions, called 'trumpets.'[3] Into the third of these they who brought the poor's offering, like the Virgin-Mother, were to drop the price of the sacri-

e Tosepht.
Sheq. iii. 2

fices which were needed for their purification.[4] As we infer,[e] the superintending priest must have been stationed here, alike to inform the offerer of the price of the turtle-doves, and to see that all was in order. For, the offerer of the poor's offering would not require to deal directly with the sacrificing priest. At a certain time in the day this third chest was opened, and half of its contents applied to burnt-, the other half to sin-offerings. Thus sacrifices were provided for a corresponding number of those who were to be purified, without either shaming the poor, needlessly disclosing the character of impurity, or causing unnecessary bustle and work. Though this mode of procedure could, of course, not be obligatory, it would, no doubt, be that generally followed.

We can now, in imagination, follow the Virgin-Mother in the

---

[1] But this precise spot was not matter of absolute necessity (Seb. vi. 2). Directions are given as to the manner in which the priest was to perform the sacrificial act.

[2] Kinnim i. 1. If the sin-offering was

a four-footed animal, the blood was sprinkled *above* the red line.

[3] Comp. St. Matt. vi. 2. See 'The Temple and its Services,' &c. pp. 26, 27.

[4] Comp. Shekal. vi. 5, the Commentaries, and Jer. Shek. 50 b.

Temple.[1] Her child had been given up to the Lord, and received back from Him. She had entered the Court of the Women, probably by the 'Gate of the Women,'[2] on the north side, and deposited the price of her sacrifices in Trumpet No. 3, which was close to the raised dais or gallery where the women worshipped, apart from the men. And now the sound of the organ, which announced throughout the vast Temple-buildings that the incense was about to be kindled on the Golden Altar, summoned those who were to be purified. The chief of the ministrant lay-representatives of Israel on duty (the so-called 'station-men') ranged those, who presented themselves before the Lord as offerers of special sacrifices, within the wickets on either side the great Nicanor Gate, at the top of the fifteen steps which led up from the Court of the Women to that of Israel. It was, as if they were to be brought nearest to the Sanctuary; as if theirs were to be specially the 'prayers' that rose in the cloud of incense from the Golden Altar; as if for them specially the sacrifices were laid on the Altar of Burnt-offering; as if theirs was a larger share of the benediction which, spoken by the lips of the priests, seemed like Jehovah's answer to the prayers of the people; theirs especially the expression of joy symbolised in the drink-offering, and the hymn of praise whose *Tris-Hagion* filled the Temple. From where they stood they could see it all,[3] share in it, rejoice in it. And now the general service was over, and only those remained who brought special sacrifices, or who lingered near them that had such, or whose loved abode was ever in the Temple. The purification-service, with such unspoken prayer and praise as would be the outcome of a grateful heart,[4] was soon ended, and they who had shared in it were Levitically clean. Now all stain was removed, and, as the Law put it, they might again partake of sacred offerings.

And in such sacred offering, better than any of which priest's

---

[1] According to Dr. Geikie, 'the Golden Gate at the head of the long flight of steps that led to the valley of the Kedron opened into the Court of the Women.' But there was no Golden Gate, neither was there any flight of steps into the valley of the Kedron, while between the Court of the Women and any outer gate (such as *could* have led into Kedron), the Court of the Gentiles and a colonnade must have intervened.

[2] Or else, 'the gate of the firstlings.' Comp. generally, 'The Temple, its Ministry and Services.'

[3] This they could not have done from the elevated platform on which they commonly worshipped.

[4] This is stated by the Rabbis to have been the object of the burnt-offering. That suggested for the sin-offering is too ridiculous to mention. The language used about the burnt-offering reminds us of that in the exhortation in the office for the 'Churching of Women': 'that she might be stirred up to give thanks to Almighty God, Who has delivered her from the pains and perils of childbirth (שֶׁהַצִּילָהּ מֵחֶבְלֵי יוֹלֵדָה), which is matter of miracle.' (Comp. *Hottingerus*, Juris Hebr. Leges, ed. Tiguri, p. 233.)

family had ever partaken, was the Virgin-Mother immediately to share. It has been observed, that by the side of every humiliation connected with the Humanity of the Messiah, the glory of His Divinity was also made to shine forth. The coincidences are manifestly undesigned on the part of the Evangelic writers, and hence all the more striking. Thus, if he was born of the humble Maiden of Nazareth, an Angel announced His birth; if the Infant-Saviour was cradled in a manger, the shining host of heaven hymned His Advent. And so afterwards—if He hungered and was tempted in the wilderness, Angels ministered to Him, even as an Angel strengthened Him in the agony of the garden. If He submitted to baptism, the Voice and vision from heaven attested His Sonship; if enemies threatened. He could miraculously pass through them; if the Jews assailed, there was the Voice of God to glorify Him; if He was nailed to the cross, the sun craped his brightness, and earth quaked; if He was laid in the tomb, Angels kept its watches, and heralded His rising. And so, when now the Mother of Jesus, in her humbleness, could only bring the 'poor's offering,' the witness to the greatness of Him Whom she had borne was not wanting. A 'eucharistic offering'—so to speak—was brought, the record of which is the more precious that Rabbinic writings make no allusion to the existence of the party, whose representatives we here meet. Yet they were the true outcome of the spirit of the Old Testament, and, as such, at this time, the special recipients of the 'Spirit' of the Old Testament.

The 'parents' of Jesus had brought Him into the Temple for presentation and redemption, when they were met by one, whose venerable figure must have been well known in the city and the Sanctuary. Simeon combined the three characteristics of Old Testament piety: '*Justice*,' as regarded his relation and bearing to God and man;[1] '*fear of God*,'[2] in opposition to the boastful self-righteousness of Pharisaism; and, above all, *longing expectancy* of the near fulfilment of the great promises, and that in their *spiritual* import as 'the Consolation of Israel.'[3] The Holy Spirit was upon

---

[1] Comp. *Josephus*, Ant. xii. 2. 5.

[2] The expression, εὐλαβής, unquestionably refers to 'fear of God.' Comp. *Delitzsch*, Hebr. Br. pp. 191, 192; and *Grimm*, Clavis N.T. p. 180 *b*.

[3] The expression נֶחָמָה 'consolation,' for the great Messianic hope—whence the Messianic title of *Menachem*—is of very frequent occurrence (so in the Targum on Isaiah and Jeremiah, and in many Rabbinical passages). Curiously enough,

it is several times put into the mouth of a *Simeon* (Chag. 16 *b*; Macc. 5 *b*; Shev. 34 *a*)—although, of course, not the one mentioned by St. Luke. The suggestion, that the latter was the son of the great Hillel and the father of Gamaliel, St. Paul's teacher, though not impossible as regards time, is unsupported, though it does seem strange that the Mishnah has nothing to say about him: '*lo niscar bamishnah.*'

him; and by that same Spirit[1] the gracious Divine answer to his
heart's longing had been communicated him.   And now it was as
had been promised him.   Coming 'in the Spirit' into the Temple,
just as His parents were bringing the Infant Jesus, he took Him
into his arms, and burst into rapt thanksgiving.   Now, indeed, had
God fulfilled His word.   He was not to see death, till he had seen
the Lord's Christ.   Now did his Lord 'dismiss' him 'in peace'[2]—
release him[3] in blessed comfort from work and watch—since he had
actually seen that salvation,[4] so long preparing for a waiting weary
world: a glorious light, Whose rising would light up heathen darkness, and be the outshining glory around Israel's mission.   With this
Infant in his arms, it was as if he stood on the mountain-height of
prophetic vision, and watched the golden beams of sunrise far away
over the isles of the Gentiles, and then gathering their full glow
over his own beloved land and people.   There was nothing Judaic—
quite the contrary: only what was of the Old Testament—in what
he first said.[a]

But his unexpected appearance, the more unexpected deed and
words, and that most unexpected form in which what was said of the
Infant Christ was presented to their minds, filled the hearts of His
parents with wonderment.   And it was, as if their silent wonderment
had been an unspoken question, to which the answer now came in
words of blessing from the aged watcher.   Mystic they seemed, yet
prophetic.   But now it was the personal, or rather the Judaic, aspect
which, in broken utterances, was set before the Virgin-Mother—as
if the whole history of the Christ upon earth were passing in rapid
vision before Simeon.   That Infant, now again in the Virgin-Mother's
arms: It was to be a stone of decision; a foundation and corner-
stone,[b] for fall or for uprising; a sign spoken against; the sword of
deep personal sorrow would pierce the Mother's heart; and so to the

CHAP.
VII

[a] St. Luke
ii. 29–32

[b] Is. viii. 14

---

[1] The mention of the 'Holy Spirit,' as
speaking to individuals, is frequent in
Rabbinic writings.   This, of course, does
not imply their belief in the Personality
of the Holy Spirit (comp. Bemidb. R. 15;
20; Midr. on Ruth ii. 9; Yalkut, vol. i.
pp. 221 *b* and 265 *d*).

[2] The Talmud (Ber. last page) has a
curious conceit, to the effect that, in taking leave of a person, one ought to say:
'Go *to* peace,' not '*in* peace ' (לְשָׁלוֹם,
not בְּשָׁלוֹם), the former having been
said by Jethro to Moses (Ex. iv. 18), on
which he prospered; the latter by David
to Absalom (2 Sam. xv. 9), on which he

perished.   On the other hand, on taking
leave of a dead friend, we are to say
'Go *in* peace,' according to Gen. xv. 15,
and *not* 'Go *to* peace.'

[3] The expression, ἀπολύειν, *absolvere,
liberare, demittere,* is most graphic.   It
corresponds to the Hebrew פָּטַר, which
is also used of death; as in regard to
Simeon the Just, Menach. 109 *b*; comp.
Ber. 17 *a*; Targum on Cant. i. 7.

[4] *Godet* seems to strain the meaning
of σωτήριον, when he renders it by the
neuter of the adjective.   It is frequently
used in the LXX. for יְשׁוּעָה.

terrible end, when the veil of externalism which had so long covered the hearts of Israel's leaders would be rent, and the deep evil of their thoughts[1] laid bare. Such, as regarded Israel, was the history of Jesus, from His Baptism to the Cross; and such is still the history of Jesus, as ever present to the heart of the believing, loving Church.

Nor was Simeon's the only hymn of praise on that day. A special interest attaches to her who, coming that very moment, responded in praise to God[2] for the pledge she saw of the near redemption. A kind of mystery seems to invest this Anna (*Channah*). A widow, whose early desolateness had been followed by a long life of solitary mourning; one of those in whose home the tribal genealogy had been preserved.[3] We infer from this, and from the fact that it was that of a tribe which had *not* returned to Palestine, that hers was a family of some distinction. Curiously enough, the tribe of Asher alone is celebrated in tradition for the beauty of its women, and their fitness to be wedded to High-Priest or King.[a]

But Anna had better claim to distinction than family-descent, or long, faithful memory of brief home-joys. These many years she had spent in the Sanctuary,[4] and spent in fasting and prayer—yet not of that self-righteous, self-satisfied kind which was of the essence of popular religion. Nor, as to the Pharisees around, was it the Synagogue which was her constant and loved resort; but the Temple, with its symbolic and unspoken worship, which Rabbinic self-assertion and rationalism were rapidly superseding, and for whose services, indeed, Rabbinism could find no real basis. Nor yet were 'fasting and prayer' to her the all-in-all of religion, sufficient in themselves; sufficient also before God. Deepest in her soul was longing waiting for the 'redemption' promised, and now surely nigh. To her widowed heart the great hope of Israel appeared not so much, as to Simeon, in the light of 'consolation,' as rather in that of 'redemption.' The seemingly hopeless exile of her own tribe, the political state of Judæa, the condition—social, moral, and religious—of her own Jerusalem: all kindled in her, as in those who were like-minded, deep, earnest longing for the time of promised 'redemption.' No

ᵃ Bər. R. 71,
ed. Warsh.
p. 131 b
end; 99.
p. 179 a,
lines 13 and
12 from
bottom

---

[1] διαλογισμός, generally used in an evil sense.

[2] The verb ἀνθομολογεῖσθαι may mean responsive praise, or simply praise (הוֹדָה), which in this case, however, would equally be 'in response' to that of Simeon, whether responsive in form or not.

[3] The whole subject of 'genealogies' is briefly, but well treated by *Hamburger*, Real Encykl., section ii. pp. 291 &c.

It is a pity, that *Hamburger* so often treats his subjects from a Judæo-apologetic standpoint.

[4] It is scarcely necessary to discuss the curious suggestion, that Anna actually *lived* in the Temple. No one, least of all a woman, permanently resided in the Temple, though the High Priest had chambers there.

place so suited to such an one as the Temple, with its services—the
only thing free, pure, undefiled, and pointing forward and upward;
no occupation so befitting as 'fasting and prayer.' And, blessed be
God, there were others, perhaps many such, in Jerusalem. Though
Rabbinic tradition ignored them, they were the salt which preserved
the mass from festering corruption. To her as the representative,
the example, friend, and adviser of such, was it granted as prophetess
to recognise Him, Whose Advent had been the burden of Simeon's
praise. And, day by day, to those who looked for redemption in
Jerusalem, would she speak of Him Whom her eyes had seen, though
it must be in whispers and with bated breath. For they were in the
city of Herod, and the stronghold of Pharisaism.

CHAPTER VIII.

THE VISIT AND HOMAGE OF THE MAGI, AND THE FLIGHT INTO EGYPT.

(St. Matt. ii. 1-18.)

BOOK
II

WITH the Presentation of the Infant Saviour in the Temple, and His acknowledgment—not indeed by the leaders of Israel, but, characteristically, by the representatives of those earnest men and women who looked for His Advent—the Prologue, if such it may be called, to the third Gospel closes. From whatever source its information was derived—perhaps, as has been suggested, its earlier portion from the Virgin-Mother, the later from Anna; or else both alike from her, who with loving reverence and wonderment treasured it all in her heart—its marvellous details could not have been told with greater simplicity, nor yet with more exquisitely delicate grace. [1] On the other hand, the Prologue to the first Gospel, while omitting these, records other incidents of the infancy of the Saviour. The plan of these narratives, or the sources whence they may originally have been derived, may account for the omissions in either case. At first sight it may seem strange, that the cosmopolitan Gospel by St. Luke should have described what took place in the Temple, and the homage of the Jews, while the Gospel by St. Matthew, which was primarily intended for Hebrews, records only the homage of the Gentiles, and the circumstances which led to the flight into Egypt. But of such seeming contrasts there are not a few in the Gospel-history—discords, which soon resolve themselves into glorious harmony.

The story of the homage to the Infant Saviour by the *Magi* is told by St. Matthew, in language of which the brevity constitutes the

---

[1] It is scarcely necessary to point out, how evidential this is of the truthfulness of the Gospel-narrative. In this respect also the so-called Apocryphal Gospels, with their gross and often repulsive legendary adornments, form a striking contrast. I have purposely abstained from reproducing any of these narratives, partly because previous writers have done so, and partly because the only object served by repeating, what must so deeply shock the Christian mind, would be to point the contrast between the canonical and the Apocryphal Gospels. But this can, I think, be as well done by a single sentence, as by pages of quotations.

chief difficulty. Even their designation is not free from ambiguity. The term *Magi* is used in the LXX., by Philo, Josephus, and by profane writers, alike in an evil and, so to speak, in a good sense[1]— in the former case as implying the practice of magical arts;[a] in the latter, as referring to those Eastern (especially Chaldee) priest-sages, whose researches, in great measure as yet mysterious and unknown to us, seem to have embraced much deep knowledge, though not untinged with superstition. It is to these latter, that the Magi spoken of by St. Matthew must have belonged. Their number—to which, however, no importance attaches—cannot be ascertained.[2] Various suggestions have been made as to the country of 'the East,' whence they came. At the period in question the sacerdotal caste of the Medes and Persians was dispersed over various parts of the East,[3] and the presence in those lands of a large Jewish *diaspora*, through which they might, and probably would, gain knowledge of the great hope of Israel,[4] is sufficiently attested by Jewish history. The oldest opinion traces the Magi—though partially on insufficient grounds[5]—to *Arabia*. And there is this in favor of it, that not only the closest intercourse existed between Palestine and Arabia, but that from about 120 B.C. to the sixth century of our era, the kings of *Yemen* professed the Jewish faith.[6] For if, on the one hand, it seems unlikely, that Eastern Magi would spontaneously connect a celestial phenomenon with the birth of a Jewish king,

CHAP.
VIII

[a] So also in
Acts viii. 9;
xiii. 6, 8

---

[1] The evidence on this point is furnished by *J. G. Müller* in Herzog's Real-Enc., vol. viii. p. 682. The whole subject of the visit of the Magi is treated with the greatest ability and learning (as against *Strauss*) by Dr. *Mill* ('On the Mythical Interpretation of the Gospels,' part ii. pp. 275 &c.).

[2] They are variously stated as twelve (Aug. Chrysost.) and three, the latter on account of the number of the gifts. Other legends on the subject need not be repeated.

[3] *Mill*, u. s., p. 303.

[4] There is no historical evidence that at the time of Christ there was among the nations any widespread expectancy of the Advent of a Messiah in Palestine. Where the knowledge of such a hope existed, it must have been entirely derived from Jewish sources. The allusions to it by *Tacitus* (Hist. v. 13) and *Suetonius* (Vesp. 4) are evidently derived from Josephus, and admittedly refer to the Flavian dynasty, and to a period seventy years or more after the Advent

of Christ. 'The splendid vaticination in the Fourth Eclogue of Virgil,' which Archdeacon Farrar regards as among the 'unconscious prophecies of heathendom,' is confessedly derived from the Cumæan Sibyl, and based on the Sibylline Oracles, book iii. lines 784–794 (ed. *Friedlieb*, p. 86; see Einl. p. xxxix.). Almost the whole of book iii., inclusive of these verses, is of *Jewish* authorship, and dates probably from about 160 B.C. Archdeacon Farrar holds that, *besides the above references*, 'there is ample proof, both in Jewish and Pagan writings, that a guilty and weary world was dimly expecting the advent of its Deliverer.' But he offers no evidence of it, either from Jewish or Pagan writings.

[5] Comp. *Mill*, u. s., p. 308, note 66. The *grounds* adduced by some are such references as to Is. viii. 4; Ps. lxxii. 10, &c.; and the character of the gifts.

[6] Comp. the account of this Jewish monarchy in the 'History of the Jewish Nation,' pp. 67–71; also *Remond's* Vers. e. Gesch. d. Ausbreit. d. Judenth. pp. 81 &c.; and *Jost*, Gesch. d. Isr. vol. v. pp. 236 &c.

evidence will, on the other hand, be presented to connect the mean-ing attached to the appearance of 'the star' at that particular time with Jewish expectancy of the Messiah. But we are anticipating.

Shortly after the Presentation of the Infant Saviour in the Temple, certain Magi from the East arrived in Jerusalem with strange tidings. They had seen at its 'rising'[1] a sidereal appear-ance,[2] which they regarded as betokening the birth of the Messiah King of the Jews, in the sense which at the time attached to that designation. Accordingly, they had come to Jerusalem to pay homage[3] to Him, probably not because they imagined He must be born in the Jewish capital[4] but because they would naturally expect there to obtain authentic information, 'where' He might be found. In their simplicity of heart, the Magi addressed themselves in the first place to the official head of the nation. The rumor of such an inquiry, and by such persons, would rapidly spread throughout the city. But it produced on King Herod, and in the capital, a far dif-ferent impression from the feeling of the Magi. Unscrupulously cruel as Herod had always proved, even the slightest suspicion of danger to his rule—the bare possibility of the Advent of One, Who had such claims upon the allegiance of Israel, and Who, if acknow-ledged, would evoke the most intense movement on their part—must have struck terror to his heart. Not that he could believe the tidings, though a dread of their possibility might creep over a nature such as Herod's; but the bare thought of a Pretender, with such claims, would fill him with suspicion, apprehension, and impotent rage. Nor is it difficult to understand, that the whole city should, although on different grounds, have shared the 'trouble' of the king. It was certainly not, as some have suggested, from appre-hension of 'the woes' which, according to popular notions, were to accompany the Advent of Messiah. Throughout the history of Christ the absence of such 'woes' was never made a ground of objection to

---

[1] This is the correct rendering, and not, as in A.V., 'in the East,' the latter be-ing expressed by the plural of ἀνατολή, in v. 1, while in vv. 2 and 9 the word is used in the singular.

[2] *Schleusner* has abundantly proved that the word ἀστήρ, though primarily meaning a *star*, is also used of constella-tions, meteors, and comets—in short, has the widest application: 'omne designare, quod aliquem splendorem habet et emit-tit' (Lex. in N.T., t. i. pp. 390, 391).

[3] Not, as in the A.V., 'to worship,' which at this stage of the history would

seem most incongruous, but as an equiva-lent of the Hebrew הִשְׁתַּחֲוֹת, as in Gen. xix. 1. So often in the LXX. and by profane writers (comp. *Schleusner*, u. s., t. ii. pp. 749, 750, and *Vorstius*, De Hebraismis N.T. pp. 637–641).

[4] This is the view generally, but as I think erroneously, entertained. Any Jew would have told them, that the Messiah was not to be born in Jerusalem. Be-sides, the question of the Magi implies their ignorance of the 'where' of the Messiah.

His Messianic claims; and this, because these 'woes' were not asso- **CHAP.**
ciated with the first Advent of the Messiah, but with His final mani- **VIII**
festation in power. And between these two periods a more or less
long interval was supposed to intervene, during which the Messiah
would be 'hidden,' either in the literal sense, or perhaps as to His
power, or else in both respects.[1] This enables us to understand the
question of the disciples, as to the sign of His coming and the end of
the world, and the answer of the Master.[a] But the people of Jeru- ^a As re-
salem had far other reason to fear. They knew only too well the ported in St. Matt.
character of Herod, and what the consequences would be to them, or xxiv. 3–29
to any one who might be suspected, however unjustly, of sympathy
with any claimant to the royal throne of David.[2]

Herod took immediate measures, characterised by his usual cunning. He called together all the High-Priests—past and present—
and all the learned Rabbis,[3] and, without committing himself as to
whether the Messiah was already born, or only expected,[4] simply propounded to them the question of His birthplace. This would show
him where Jewish expectancy looked for the appearance of his rival,
and thus enable him to watch alike that place and the people generally, while it might possibly bring to light the feelings of the leaders
of Israel. At the same time he took care diligently to inquire the
precise time, when the sidereal appearance had first attracted the
attention of the Magi.[b] This would enable him to judge, how far ^b St. Matt.
back he would have to make his own inquiries, since the birth of the ii. 7
Pretender might be made to synchronise with the earliest appearance of the sidereal phenomenon. So long as any one lived, who was
born in Bethlehem between the *earliest* appearance of this 'star'
and the time of the arrival of the Magi, he was not safe. The subsequent conduct of Herod[c] shows, that the Magi must have told him, ^c v. 16
that their earliest observation of the sidereal phenomenon had taken
place two years before their arrival in Jerusalem.

The assembled authorities of Israel could only return one answer

---

[1] Christian writers on these subjects have generally conjoined the so-called 'woes of the Messiah' with His first appearance. It seems not to have occurred to them, that, if such had been the Jewish expectation, a preliminary objection would have lain against the claims of Jesus from their absence.

[2] Their feelings on this matter would be represented, *mutatis mutandis*, by the expressions in the Sanhedrin, recorded in St. John xi. 47–50.

[3] Both Meyer and Weiss have shown, that this was not a meeting of the Sanhedrin, if, indeed, that body had anything more than a shadowy existence during the reign of Herod.

[4] The question propounded by Herod (v. 4), 'where Christ should be born,' is put neither in the past nor in the future, but in the *present* tense. In other words, he laid before them a *case*—a theological problem—but not a *fact*, either past or future.

BOOK
II

ª Jer. Ber.
ii. 4, p. 5 a

ᵇ St. Matt.
ii. 6

to the question submitted by Herod. As shown by the rendering of the *Targum Jonathan*, the prediction in Micah v. 2 was at the time universally understood as pointing to Bethlehem, as the birthplace of the Messiah. That such was the general expectation, appears from the Talmud,ª where, in an imaginary conversation between an Arab and a Jew, Bethlehem is authoritatively named as Messiah's birthplace. St. Matthew reproduces the prophetic utterance of Micah, exactly as such quotations were popularly made at that time. It will be remembered that, Hebrew being a dead language so far as the people were concerned, the Holy Scriptures were always translated into the popular dialect, the person so doing being designated *Methurgeman* (*dragoman*) or interpreter. These renderings, which at the time of St. Matthew were not yet allowed to be written down, formed the precedent for, if not the basis of, our later *Targum*. In short, at that time each one *Targumed* for himself, and these *Targumim* (as our existing one on the Prophets shows) were neither literal versions,[1] nor yet paraphrases, but something between them, a sort of interpreting translation. That, when Targuming, the New Testament writers should in preference make use of such a well-known and widely-spread version as the Translation of the LXX. needs no explanation. That they did not confine themselves to it, but, when it seemed necessary, literally or Targumically rendered a verse, appears from the actual quotations in the New Testament. Such *Targuming* of the Old Testament was entirely in accordance with the then universal method of setting Holy Scripture before a popular audience. It is needless to remark, that the New Testament writers would *Targum* as Christians. These remarks apply not only to the case under immediate consideration,ᵇ but generally to the quotations from the Old Testament in the New.[2]

[1] In point of fact, the Talmud expressly lays it down, that 'whosoever targums a verse in its closely literal form [without due regard to its meaning], is a liar.' (Kidd. 49 a; comp. on the subject *Deutsch's* 'Literary Remains,' p. 327).

[2] The general principle, that St. Matthew rendered Mic. v. 2 *targumically*, would, it seems, cover all the differences between his quotation and the Hebrew text. But it may be worth while, in this instance at least, to examine the differences in detail. *Two* of them are trivial, viz., 'Bethlehem, land of Juda,' instead of 'Ephratah;' 'princes' instead of 'thousands,' though St. Matthew may, *possibly*, have pointed בְּאַלְפֵי ('princes'),

instead of בְּאַלְפֵי,' as in *our* Hebrew text. Perhaps he rendered the word more correctly than we do, since אֶלֶף means not only a 'thousand' but also a part of a tribe (Is. lx. 22), a clan, or *Beth Abh* (Judg. vi. 15); comp. also Numb. i. 16; x. 4, 36; Deut. xxxiii. 17; Josh. xxii. 21, 30; 1 Sam. x. 19; xxiii. 23; in which case the personification of these 'thousands' (=our 'hundreds') by their chieftains or 'princes' would be a very apt Targumic rendering. Two other of the divergences are more important, viz., (1) 'Art not the least,' instead of 'though thou be little.' But the Hebrew words have also been otherwise rendered: in

The further conduct of Herod was in keeping with his plans. He sent for the Magi—for various reasons, *secretly*. After ascertaining the precise time, when they had first observed the 'star,' he directed them to Bethlehem, with the request to inform him when they had found the Child ; on pretence, that he was equally desirous with them to pay Him homage. As they left Jerusalem[1] for the goal of their pilgrimage, to their surprise and joy, the 'star,' which had attracted their attention at its 'rising,'[2] and which, as seems implied in the narrative, they had not seen of late, once more appeared on the horizon, and seemed to move before them, till 'it stood over where the young child was'—that is, of course, over Bethlehem, not over any special house in it. Whether at a turn of the road, close to Bethlehem, they lost sight of it, or they no longer heeded its position, since it had seemed to go before them to the goal that had been pointed out—for, surely, they needed not the star to *guide* them to Bethlehem—or whether the celestial phenomenon now disappeared, is neither stated in the Gospel-narrative, nor is indeed of any importance. Sufficient for them, and for us: they had been authoritatively directed to Bethlehem; as they had set out for it, the sidereal phenomenon had once more appeared; and it had seemed to go before them, till it actually stood over Bethlehem. And, since in ancient times such extraordinary 'guidance' by a 'star' was matter of belief and expectancy,[3] the Magi would, from their standpoint, regard it as the fullest confirmation that they had been rightly directed to Bethlehem—and 'they rejoiced with exceeding great joy.' It could not be difficult to learn in Bethlehem, where the Infant, around Whose Birth marvels had gathered, might be found. It appears that the temporary shelter of the 'stable' had been exchanged by the Holy Family for the more permanent abode of a 'house;'[a] and there the Magi found the Infant-Saviour with His Mother. With exquisite tact and reverence the narrative attempts

ᵃ v. 11

---

the Syriac *interrogatively* ('art thou little?'), which suggests the rendering of St. Matthew; and in the Arabic just as by St. Matthew (vide *Pocock*, Porta Mosis, Notæ, c. ii. ; but Pocock does not give the Targum accurately). *Credner* ingeniously suggested, that the rendering of St. Matthew may have been caused by a Targumic rendering of the Hebrew צָעִיר by בְּעִיר ; but he does not seem to have noticed, that this is the *actual* rendering in the Targum Jon. on the passage. As for the second and more serious

divergence in the latter part of the verse, it may be best here simply to give for comparison the rendering of the passage in the Targum Jonathan: 'Out of thee shall come forth before Me Messiah to exercise rule over Israel.'

[1] Not *necessarily* by *night*, as most writers suppose.

[2] So correctly, and not 'in the East,' as in A.V.

[3] Proof of this is abundantly furnished by *Wetstein*, Nov. Test. t. i. pp. 247 and 248.

BOOK
II

ᵃ 2 Cor. v
16

not the faintest description of the scene.   It is as if the sacred writer
had fully entered into the spirit of St. Paul, ' Yea, though we have
known Christ after the flesh, yet now henceforth know we Him no
more.'ᵃ And thus it should ever be. It is the great fact of the
manifestation of Christ—not its outward surroundings, however precious or touching they might be in connection with any ordinary
earthly being—to which our gaze must be directed. The externals
may, indeed, attract our sensuous nature; but they detract from the
unmatched glory of the great supersensuous Reality.[1] Around the
Person of the God-Man, in the hour when the homage of the heathen
world was first offered Him, we need not, and want not, the drapery
of outward circumstances. That scene is best realized, not by description, but by silently joining in the silent homage and the silent
offerings of 'the wise men from the East.'

Before proceeding further, we must ask ourselves two questions:
What relationship does this narrative bear to Jewish expectancy?
and, Is there any astronomical confirmation of this account? Besides
their intrinsic interest, the answer to the first question will determine, whether any legendary basis could be assigned to the narrative;
while on the second will depend, whether the account can be truthfully charged with an accommodation on the part of God to the
superstitions and errors of astrology. For, if the whole was extra-
natural, and the sidereal appearance specially produced in order to
meet the astrological views of the Magi, it would not be a sufficient
answer to the difficulty, 'that great catastrophes and unusual phenomena in nature have synchronised in a remarkable manner with
great events in human history.'[2] On the other hand, if the sidereal
appearance was not of supernatural origin, and would equally have
taken place whether or not there had been Magi to direct to Bethlehem, the difficulty is not only entirely removed, but the narrative
affords another instance, alike of the condescension of God to the
lower standpoint of the Magi, and of His wisdom and goodness in
the combination of circumstances.

As regards the question of Jewish expectancy, sufficient has been
said in the preceding pages, to show that Rabbinism looked for a
very different kind and manner of the world's homage to the Messiah

---

[1] In this seems to lie the strongest
condemnation of Romish and Romanis-
ing tendencies, that they ever seek to
present—or, perhaps, rather obtrude—
the external circumstances. It is not
thus that the Gospel most fully presents

to us the spiritual, nor yet thus that the
deepest and holiest impressions are made.
True religion is ever *objectivistic*, sensuous *subjectivistic*.

[2] Archdeacon Farrar.

than that of a few Magi, guided by a star to His Infant-Home. Indeed, so far from serving as historical basis for the origin of such a 'legend,' a more gross caricature of Jewish Messianic anticipation could scarcely be imagined. Similarly futile would it be to seek a background for this narrative in Balaam's prediction,[a] since it is incredible that any one could have understood it as referring to a brief sidereal apparition to a few Magi, in order to bring them to look for the Messiah.[1] Nor can it be represented as intended to fulfil the prophecy of Isaiah,[b][2] that 'they shall bring gold and incense, and they shall show forth the praises of the Lord.' For, supposing this figurative language to have been grossly literalised,[3] what would become of the other part of that prophecy,[4] which must, of course, have been treated in the same manner; not to speak of the fact, that the whole evidently refers not to the Messiah (least of all in His Infancy), but to Jerusalem in her latter-day glory. Thus, we fail to perceive any historical basis for a legendary origin of St. Matthew's narrative, either in the Old Testament or, still less, in Jewish tradition. And we are warranted in asking: If the account be not true, what rational explanation can be given of its origin, since its invention would never have occurred to any contemporary Jew?

But this is not all. There seems, indeed, no logical connection between this astrological interpretation of the Magi, and any supposed practice of astrology among the Jews. Yet, strange to say, writers have largely insisted on this.[5] The charge is, to say the least, grossly exaggerated. That Jewish—as other Eastern—impostors pretended to astrological knowledge, and that such investigations may have been secretly carried on by certain Jewish students, is readily admitted.

CHAP. VIII

[a] Numb. xxiv. 17

[b] Ix. 6 last clauses

---

[1] *Strauss* (Leben Jesu, i. pp. 224–249) finds a legendary basis for the Evangelic account in Numb. xxiv. 17, and also appeals to the legendary stories of profane writers about stars appearing at the birth of great men.

[2] *Keim* (Jesu von Nazara, i. 2, p. 377) drops the appeal to legends of profane writers, ascribes only a secondary influence to Numb. xxiv. 17, and lays the main stress of 'the legend' on Is. lx.— with what success the reader may judge.

[3] Can it be imagined that any person would invent such a 'legend' on the strength of Is. lx. 6 ? On the other hand, if the event really took place, it is easy to understand how Christian symbolism would—though uncritically—have seen an adumbration of it in that prophecy.

[4] The 'multitude of camels and drome-daries,' the 'flocks of Kedar and the rams of Nebaioth' (v. 7), and 'the isles,' and 'the ships of Tarshish' (v. 9).

[5] The subject of Jewish astrology is well treated by Dr. *Hamburger*, both in the first and second volumes of his Real-Encykl. The ablest summary, though brief, is that in Dr. *Gideon Brecher's* book, 'Das Transcendentale im Talmud.' *Gfrörer* is, as usually, one-sided, and not always trustworthy in his translations. A curious brochure by Rabbi *Thein* (Der Talmud, od. das Prinzip d. planet. Einfl.) is one of the boldest attempts at special pleading, to the ignoration of palpable facts on the other side. *Hausrath's* dicta on this subject are, as on many others, assertions unsupported by historical evidence.

BOOK
II

ᵃ Deb. R. 8
ᵇ Comp.
Shabb. 75 a
ᶜ See for ex.
Jos. War
vi. 5. 3
ᵈ Shabb.
156 a

ᵉ Shabb,
u. s.
ᶠ Moed K.
16 a

ᵍ Shabb. 145
b; 146 a
comp. Yeb.
103 b
ʰ Moed K.
28 a
ⁱ Comp.
Baba K.
2 b; Shabb.
121 b

ᵏ Ned. 39 b

But the language of disapproval in which these pursuits are referred to —such as that knowledge of the Law is not found with astrologers [a]— and the emphatic statement, that he who learned even one thing from a *Mage* deserved death, show what views were authoritatively held.[b][1] Of course, the Jews (or many of them), like most ancients, believed in the influence of the planets upon the destiny of man.[c] But it was a principle strongly expressed, and frequently illustrated in the Talmud, that such planetary influence did *not* extend to Israel.[d] It must be admitted, that this was not always consistently carried out; and there were Rabbis who computed a man's future from the constellation (the *Mazzal*), either of the day, or the hour, under which he was born.[e] It was supposed, that some persons had a star of their own,[f] and the (representative) stars of all proselytes were said to have been present at Mount Sinai. Accordingly, they also, like Israel, had lost the defilement of the serpent (sin).[g] One Rabbi even had it, that success, wisdom, the duration of life, and a posterity, depended upon the constellation.[h] Such views were carried out till they merged in a kind of fatalism,[i] or else in the idea of a 'natal affinity,' by which persons born under the same constellation were thought to stand in sympathetic *rapport*.[k] The further statement, that conjunctions of the planets [2]

[1] I cannot, however, see that Buxtorf charges so many Rabbis with giving themselves to astrology as Dr. Geikie imputes to him—nor how *Humboldt* can be quoted as corroborating the Chinese record of the appearance of a new star in 750 (see the passage in the Cosmos, Engl. transl. vol. i. pp. 92, 93).

[2] Jewish astronomy distinguishes the seven planets (called 'wandering stars'); the twelve signs of the Zodiac, *Mazzaloth* (Aries, Taurus, Gemini, Cancer, Leo, Virgo, Libra, Scorpio, Sagittarius, Capricornus, Aquarius, Pisces)—arranged by astrologers into four trigons: that of fire (1, 5, 9); of earth (2, 6, 10); of air (3, 7, 11); and of water (4, 8, 12); and the stars. The Kabbalistic book Raziel (dating from the eleventh century) arranges them into three quadrons. The comets, which are called arrows or star-rods, proved a great difficulty to students. The planets (in their order) were: *Shabbathai* (the Sabbatic, Saturn); *Tsedeq* (righteousness, Jupiter); *Maadim* (the red, blood-coloured, Mars); *Chammah* (the Sun); *Nogah* (splendour, Venus); *Cokhabh* (the star, Mercury); *Lebhanah* (the Moon). Kabbalistic works depict our system as a circle, the lower arc consisting of *Oceanos*, and the upper filled by the sphere of the earth; next comes that of the surrounding atmosphere; then successively the seven semicircles of the planets, each fitting on the other—to use the Kabbalistic illustration—like the successive layers in an onion (see Sepher Raziel, ed. Lemb. 1873, pp. 9 b, 10 a). Day and night were divided each into twelve hours (from 6 A.M. to 6 P.M., and from 6 P.M. to 6 A.M.). Each hour was under the influence of successive planets: thus, *Sunday*, 7 A.M., the Sun; 8 A.M., Venus; 9 A.M., Mercury; 10 A.M., Moon; 11 A.M., Saturn; 12 A.M., Jupiter, and so on. Similarly, we have for *Monday*, 7 A.M., the Moon, &c.; for *Tuesday*, 7 A.M., Mars; for *Wednesday*, 7 A.M., Mercury; for *Thursday*, 7 A.M., Jupiter; for *Friday*, 7 A.M., Venus; and for *Saturday*, 7 A.M., Saturn. Most important were the *Tequphoth*, in which the Sun entered respectively Aries (Tek. *Nisan*, spring-equinox, 'harvest'), Cancer (Tek. *Tammuz*, summer solstice, 'warmth'), Libra (Tek. *Tishri*, autumn-equinox, seed-time), Capricornus (Tek. *Tebheth*, winter-solstice, 'cold'). Comp. Targ. Pseudo-Jon. on Gen. viii. 22. From one Tequphah to the other were 91 days 7½ hours. By a

affected the products of the earth [a] is scarcely astrological; nor perhaps this, that an eclipse of the sun betokened evil to the nations, an eclipse of the moon to Israel, because the former calculated time by the sun, the latter by the moon.

But there is one illustrative Jewish statement which, though not astrological, is of the greatest importance, although it seems to have been hitherto overlooked. Since the appearance of *Münter's* well known tractate on the Star of the Magi,[1] writers have endeavoured to show, that Jewish expectancy of a Messiah was connected with a peculiar sidereal conjunction, such as that which occurred two years before the birth of our Lord,[b] and this on the ground of a quotation from the well-known Jewish commentator Abarbanel (or rather *Abrabanel*).[c] In his Commentary on Daniel that Rabbi laid it down, that the conjunction of Jupiter and Saturn in the constellation Pisces betokened not only the most important events, but referred especially to Israel (for which he gives five mystic reasons). He further argues that, as that conjunction had taken place three years before the birth of Moses, which heralded the first deliverance of Israel, so it would also precede the birth of the Messiah, and the final deliverance of Israel. But the argument fails, not only because Abarbanel's calculations are inconclusive and even erroneous,[2] but because it is manifestly unfair to infer the state of Jewish belief at the time of Christ from a haphazard astrological conceit of a Rabbi of the fifteenth century. There is, however, testimony which seems to us not only reliable, but embodies most ancient Jewish tradition. It is contained in one of the smaller *Midrashim*, of which a collection has lately been published.[3] On account of its importance, one quotation at least from it should be made in full. The so-called Messiah-Haggadah (*Aggadoth Mashiach*) opens as follows: '*A star shall come out of Jacob.* There is a Boraita in the name of the Rabbis: The heptad in which the Son of David cometh—in the *first* year, there will not be sufficient nourish-

CHAP.
VIII

[a] Erub.56 a;
Ber. R. 10

[b] In 747
A.U.C., or
7 B.C.

[c] Born 143,
died 1508

---

beautiful figure the sundust is called ' filings of the day ' (as the word ξύσμα— that which falls off from the sunwheel as it turns (Yoma 20 *b*).

[1] 'Der Stern der Weisen,' Copenhagen, 1827. The tractate, though so frequently quoted, seems scarcely to have been sufficiently studied, most writers having apparently rather read the references to it in *Ideler's* Handb. d. Math. u. techn. Chronol. *Münter's* work contains much that is interesting and important.

[2] To form an adequate conception of the untrustworthiness of such a testimony, it is necessary to study the history of the astronomical and astrological pursuits of the Jews during that period, of which a masterly summary is given in *Steinschneider's* History of Jewish Literature (*Ersch* u. *Gruber*, Encykl. vol. xxvii.). Comp. also *Sachs*, Relig. Poes. d. Juden in Spanien, pp. 230 &c.

[3] By Dr. *Jellinek*, in a work in six parts, entitled ' Beth ha-Midrash,' Leipz, and Vienna, 1853–1878.

ment; in the *second* year the arrows of famine are launched; in the *third*, a great famine; in the *fourth*, neither famine nor plenty; in the *fifth*, great abundance, and *the Star shall shine forth from the East, and this is the Star of the Messiah.* And it will shine from the East for fifteen days, and if it be prolonged, it will be for the good of Israel; in the *sixth*, sayings (voices), and announcements (hearings); in the *seventh*, wars, and at the close of the seventh the Messiah is to be expected.' A similar statement occurs at the close of a collection of three Midrashim—respectively entitled, 'The Book of Elijah,' 'Chapters about the Messiah,' and 'The Mysteries of R. Simon, the son of Jochai' [a]—where we read that a Star in the East was to appear two years before the birth of the Messiah. The statement is almost equally remarkable, whether it represents a tradition previous to the birth of Jesus, or originated after that event. But *two years* before the birth of Christ, which, as we have calculated, took place in December 749 A.U.C., or 5 before the Christian era, brings us to the year 747 A.U.C., or 7 before Christ, in which such a Star should appear in the East.[1]

[a] Jellinek,
Beth ha-
Midrash,
fasc. iii. p.
8

Did such a Star, then, really appear in the East seven years before the Christian era? Astronomically speaking, and without any reference to controversy, there can be no doubt that the most remarkable conjunction of planets—that of Jupiter and Saturn in the constellation of Pisces, which occurs only once in 800 years—*did* take place no less than three times in the year 747 A.U.C., or two years before the birth of Christ (in May, October and December). This conjunction is admitted by all astronomers. It was not only extraordinary, but presented the most brilliant spectacle in the night-sky, such as could not but attract the attention of all who watched the sidereal heavens, but especially of those who busied themselves with astrology. In the year following, that is, in 748 A.U.C., another planet, Mars, joined this conjunction. The merit of first discovering these facts—of which it is unnecessary here to present the literary history [2]—belongs to the

---

[1] It would, of course, be possible to argue, that the Evangelic account arose from this Jewish tradition about the appearance of a star two years before the birth of the Messiah. But it has been already shown, that the hypothesis of a Jewish legendary origin is utterly untenable. Besides, if St. Matthew ii. had been derived from this tradition, the narrative would have been quite differently shaped, and more especially the two years' interval between the rising of the star and the Advent of the Messiah

would have been emphasized, instead of being, as now, rather matter of inference.

[2] The chief writers on the subject have been: *Münter* (u.s.), *Ideler* (u.s.) and *Wieseler* (Chronol. Synopse d. 4 Evang. (1843), and again in *Herzog's* Real-Enc. vol. xxi p. 544, and finally in his Beitr. z. Würd. d Ev. 1869). In our own country, writers have, since the appearance of Professor *Pritchard's* art. (' Star of the Wise Men') in Dr. *Smith's* Bible Dict. vol. iii., generally given up the astronomical argument, without, however, clearly indicating

great *Kepler*,[a] who, accordingly, placed the Nativity of Christ in the year 748 A.U.C.   This date, however, is not only well nigh impossible; but it has also been shown that such a conjunction would, for various reasons, not answer the requirements of the Evangelical narrative, so far as the guidance to Bethlehem is concerned. But it does fully account for the attention of the Magi being aroused, and—even if they had not possessed knowledge of the Jewish expectancy above described —for their making inquiry of all around, and certainly, among others, of the Jews.   Here we leave the domain of the *certain*, and enter upon that of the *probable*.   Kepler, who was led to the discovery by observing a similar conjunction in 1603–4, also noticed, that when the three planets came into conjunction, a new, extraordinary, brilliant, and peculiarly colored evanescent star was visible between Jupiter and Saturn, and he suggested that a similar star had appeared under the same circumstances in the conjunction preceding the Nativity.   Of this, of course, there is not, and cannot be, absolute certainty.   But, if so, this would be ' the star ' of the Magi, ' in its rising.'   There is yet another remarkable statement, which, however, must also be assigned only to the domain of the *probable*.   In the astronomical tables of the Chinese—to whose general trustworthiness so high an authority as *Humboldt* bears testimony [b]—the appearance of an evanescent star was noted.   Pingré and others have designated it as a comet, and calculated its first appearance in February 750 A.U.C., which is just the time when the Magi would, in all probability, leave Jerusalem for Bethlehem, since this must have preceded the death of Herod, which took place in March 750.   Moreover, it has been astronomically ascertained, that such a sidereal apparition would be visible to those who left Jerusalem, and that it would point—almost seem to go before —in the direction of, and stand over, Bethlehem.[1]   Such, impartially stated, are the facts of the case—and here the subject must, in the present state of our information, be left.[2]

Only two things are recorded of this visit of the Magi to Bethlehem: their humblest Eastern homage, and their offerings.[3]   Viewed

[a] De Stella Nova &c., Pragæ, 160

[b] Cosmos, vol. 1. p. 92

whether they regard the star as a *miraculous* guidance. I do not, of course, presume to enter on an astronomical discussion with Professor Pritchard; but as his reasoning proceeds on the idea that the planetary conjunction of 747 A.U.C., is regarded as 'the Star of the Magi,' his arguments do not apply either to the view presented in the text nor even to that of Wieseler. Besides, I must guard myself against accepting his interpretation of the narrative in St. Matthew.

[1] By the astronomer, Dr. Goldschmidt. (See *Wieseler*, Chron. Syn. p. 72.)

[2] A somewhat different view is presented in the laborious and learned edition of the New Testament by Mr. *Brown McClellan* (vol. i. pp. 400–402).

[3] Our A.V. curiously translates in v. 11, 'treasures,' instead of 'treasury-cases.' The expression is exactly the same as in Deut. xxviii. 12, for which the

BOOK
II

as gifts, the incense and the myrrh would, indeed, have been strangely inappropriate. But their offerings were evidently intended as specimens of the products of their country, and their presentation was, even as in our own days, expressive of the homage of their country to the new-found King. In this sense, then, the Magi may truly be regarded as the representatives of the Gentile world; their homage as the first and typical acknowledgment of Christ by those who hitherto had been 'far off;' and their offerings as symbolic of the world's tribute. This deeper significance the ancient Church has rightly apprehended, though, perhaps, mistaking its grounds. Its symbolism, twining, like the convolvulus, around the Divine Plant, has traced in the gold the emblem of His Royalty; in the myrrh, of His Humanity, and that in the fullest evidence of it, in His burying; and in the incense, that of His Divinity.[1]

As always in the history of Christ, so here also, glory and suffering appear in juxtaposition. It could not be, that these Magi should become the innocent instruments of Herod's murderous designs; nor yet that the Infant-Saviour should fall a victim to the tyrant. Warned of God in a dream, the 'wise men' returned 'into their own country another way;' and, warned by the angel of the Lord in a dream, the Holy Family sought temporary shelter in Egypt. Baffled in the hope of attaining his object through the Magi, the reckless tyrant sought to secure it by an indiscriminate slaughter of all the children in Bethlehem and its immediate neighborhood, from two years and under. True, considering the population of Bethlehem, their number could only have been small, probably twenty at most.[2] But the deed was none the less atrocious; and these infants may justly be regarded as the 'protomartyrs,' the first witnesses, of Christ, 'the blossom of martyrdom' ('flores martyrum,' as *Prudentius* calls them). The slaughter was entirely in accordance with the character and former measures of Herod.[3] Nor do we wonder, that it remained unrecorded by Josephus, since on other occasions also he has omitted

---

LXX. use the same words as the Evangelist. The expression is also used in this sense in the Apocr. and by profane writers. Cömp. *Wetstein* and *Meyer* ad locum. Jewish tradition also expresses the expectancy that the nations of the world would offer gifts unto the Messiah. (Comp. Pes. 118 *b*; Ber. R. 78.)

[1] So not only in ancient hymns (by *Sedulius, Juvencus,* and *Claudian*), but by the Fathers and later writers. (Comp. *Sepp*, Leben Jesu, ii. 1, pp. 102, 103.)

[2] So Archdeacon Farrar rightly computes it.

[3] An illustrative instance of the ruthless destruction of whole families on suspicion that his crown was in danger, occurs in Ant. xv. 8. 4. But the suggestion that Bagoas had suffered at the hands of Herod for Messianic predictions is entirely an invention of *Keim*. (*Schenkel*, Bibel Lex., vol. iii. p. 37. Comp. Ant. xvii. 2. 4.)

events which to us seem important.[1] The murder of a few infants in an insignificant village might appear scarcely worth notice in a reign stained by so much bloodshed. Besides, he had, perhaps, a special motive for this silence. Josephus always carefully suppresses, so far as possible, all that refers to the Christ[2]—probably not only in accordance with his own religious views, but because mention of a Christ might have been dangerous, certainly would have been inconvenient, in a work written by an intense self-seeker, mainly for readers in Rome.

Of two passages in his own Old Testament Scriptures the Evangelist sees a fulfilment in these events. The flight into Egypt is to him the fulfilment of this expression by Hosea, ' Out of Egypt have I called My Son.'[a] In the murder of 'the Innocents,' he sees the fulfilment of Rachel's lament[b] (who died and was buried in Ramah)[3] over her children, the men of Benjamin, when the exiles to Babylon met in Ramah,[c] and there was bitter wailing at the prospect of parting for hopeless captivity, and yet bitterer lament, as they who might have encumbered the onward march were pitilessly slaughtered. Those who have attentively followed the course of Jewish thinking, and marked how the ancient Synagogue, and that rightly, read the Old Testament in its unity, as ever pointing to the Messiah as the fulfilment of Israel's history, will not wonder at, but fully accord with, St. Matthew's retrospective view. The words of Hosea were in the highest sense 'fulfilled' in the flight to, and return of, the Saviour from Egypt.[4] To an inspired writer, nay, to a true Jewish reader of the Old Testament, the question in regard to any prophecy could not be: What did *the prophet*—but, What did the *prophecy* —mean? And this could only be unfolded in the course of Israel's history. Similarly, those who ever saw in the past the prototype of the future, and recognised in events, not only the principle, but the very features, of that which was to come, could not fail to perceive, in the bitter wail of the mothers of Bethlehem over their slaughtered children, the full realisation of the prophetic description of the scene

[a] Hos. xi. 1

[b] Jer. xxxi. 15

[c] Jer. xl. 1

---

[1] There are, in Josephus' history of Herod, besides omissions, inconsistencies of narrative, such as about the execution of Mariamme (Ant. xv. 3, 5–9 &c. ; comp. War i. 22. 3, 4), and of chronology (as War i. 18. 2, comp. v. 9. 4; Ant. xiv. 16. 2, comp. xv. 1. 2, and others.)

[2] Comp. on article on Josephus in *Smith* and *Wace's* Dict. of Christian Biogr.

[3] See the evidence for it summarized in 'Sketches of Jewish Social Life in the Days of Christ,' p. 60.

[4] In point of fact the ancient Synagogue *did* actually apply to the Messiah Ex. iv. 22, on which the words of Hosea are based. See the Midrash on Ps. ii. 7. The quotation is given in full in our remarks on Ps. ii. 7 in Appendix IX.

BOOK
II

enacted in Jeremiah's days.   Had not the prophet himself heard, in the lament of the captives to Babylon, the echoes of Rachel's voice in the past?   In neither one nor the other case had the utterances of the prophets (Hosea and Jeremiah) been *predictions*: they were *prophetic*. In neither one nor the other case was the 'fulfilment' literal: it was Scriptural, and that in the truest Old Testament sense.

CHAPTER IX.

THE CHILD-LIFE IN NAZARETH.

(St. Matt. ii. 19-23; St. Luke ii. 39, 40.)

THE stay of the Holy Family in Egypt must have been of brief duration. The cup of Herod's misdeeds, but also of his misery, was full. During the whole latter part of his life, the dread of a rival to the throne had haunted him, and he had sacrificed thousands, among them those nearest and dearest to him, to lay that ghost.[1] And still the tyrant was not at rest. A more terrible scene is not pre. sented in history than that of the closing days of Herod. Tormented by nameless fears; ever and again a prey to vain remorse, when he would frantically call for his passionately-loved, murdered wife Mariamme, and her sons; even making attempts on his own life; the *delirium* of tyranny, the passion for blood, drove him to the verge of madness. The most loathsome disease, such as can scarcely be described, had fastened on his body,[2] and his sufferings were at times agonizing. By the advice of his physicians, he had himself carried to the baths of Callirhoe (east of the Jordan), trying all remedies with the determination of one who will do hard battle for life. It was in vain. The namelessly horrible distemper, which had seized the old man of seventy, held him fast in its grasp, and, so to speak, played death on the living. He knew it, that his hour was come, and had himself conveyed back to his palace under the palm-trees of Jericho. They had known it also in Jerusalem, and, even before the last stage of his disease, two of the most honored and loved Rabbis—Judas and Matthias—had headed the wild band, which would sweep away all traces of Herod's idolatrous rule. They began by pulling down the immense golden eagle, which hung over the great gate of the Temple. The two ringleaders, and forty of their followers,

---

[1] And yet *Keim* speaks of his *Hoch-herzigkeit* and *natürlicher Edelsinn!* (Leben Jesu, i. 1. p. 184.) A much truer estimate is that of *Schürer*, Neu-test. Zeitgesch. pp. 197, 198.

[2] See the horrible description of his living death in *Jos.* Ant. xvii. 6. 5.

allowed themselves to be taken by Herod's guards. A mock public trial in the theatre at Jericho followed. Herod, carried out on a couch, was both accuser and judge. The zealots, who had made noble answer to the tyrant, were burnt alive; and the High-Priest, who was suspected of connivance, deposed.

After that the end came rapidly. On his return from Callirhoe, feeling his death approaching, the King had summoned the noblest of Israel throughout the land of Jericho, and shut them up in the Hippodrome, with orders to his sister to have them slain immediately upon his death, in the grim hope that the joy of the people at his decease would thus be changed into mourning. Five days before his death one ray of passing joy lighted his couch. Terrible to say, it was caused by a letter from Augustus allowing Herod to execute his son Antipater—the false accuser and real murderer of his half-brothers Alexander and Aristobulus. The death of the wretched prince was hastened by his attempt to bribe the jailer, as the noise in the palace, caused by an attempted suicide of Herod, led him to suppose his father was actually dead. And now the terrible drama was hastening to a close. The fresh access of rage shortened the life which was already running out. Five days more, and the terror of Judæa lay dead. He had reigned thirty-seven years—thirty-four since his conquest of Jerusalem. Soon the rule for which he had so long plotted, striven, and stained himself with untold crimes, passed from his descendants. A century more, and the whole race of Herod had been swept away.

We pass by the empty pageant and barbaric splendor of his burying in the Castle of Herodium, close to Bethlehem. The events of the last few weeks formed a lurid back-ground to the murder of 'the Innocents.' As we have reckoned it, the visit of the Magi took place in February 750 A.U.C. On the 12th of March the Rabbis and their adherents suffered. On the following night (or rather early morning) there was a lunar eclipse; the execution of Antipater preceded the death of his father by five days, and the latter occurred from seven to fourteen days before the Passover, which in 750 took place on the 12th of April.[1]

---

[1] See the calculation in *Wieseler's* Synopse, pp. 56 and 444. The 'Dissertatio de Herode Magno, by *J. A. van der Chijs* (Leyden, 1855), is very clear and accurate. Dr. Geikie adopts the manifest mistake of Caspari, that Herod died in January, 753, and holds that the Holy Family spent three years in Egypt. The repeated statement of Josephus that Herod died close upon the Passover should have sufficed to show the impossibility of that hypothesis. Indeed, there is scarcely any historical date on which competent writers are more agreed than that of Herod's death. See *Schürer*, Neutest. Zeitg., pp. 222, 223.

It need scarcely be said, that Salome (Herod's sister) and her husband were too wise to execute Herod's direction in regard to the noble Jews shut up in the Hippodrome. Their liberation, and the death of Herod, were marked by the leaders of the people as joyous events in the so-called *Megillath Taanith*, or Roll of Fasts, although the date is not exactly marked.[a] Henceforth this was to be a *Yom Tobh* (feast-day), on which mourning was interdicted.[1]

Herod had three times before changed his testament. By the first will Antipater, the successful calumniator of Alexander and Aristobulus, had been appointed his successor, while the latter two were named kings, though we know not of what districts.[b] After the execution of the two sons of Mariamme, Antipater was named king, and, in case of his death, Herod, the son of Mariamme II. When the treachery of Antipater was proved, Herod made a third will, in which Antipas (the Herod Antipas of the New Testament) was named his successor.[c] But a few days before his death he made yet another disposition, by which Archelaus, the elder brother of Antipas (both sons of Malthake, a Samaritan), was appointed king; Antipas tetrarch of Galilee and Peræa; and Philip (the son of Cleopatra, of Jerusalem [2]), tetrarch of the territory east of the Jordan.[3] These testaments reflected the varying phases of suspicion and family-hatred through which Herod had passed. Although the Emperor seems to have authorised him to appoint his successor,[d] Herod wisely made his disposition dependent on the approval of Augustus.[e] But the latter was not by any means to be taken for granted. Archelaus had, indeed, been immediately proclaimed King by the army; but he prudently declined the title, till it had been confirmed by the Emperor. The night of his father's death, and those that followed, were characteristically spent by Archelaus in rioting with his friends.[f] But the people of Jerusalem were not easily satisfied. At first liberal promises of amnesty and reforms had assuaged the populace.[g] But the indignation excited by the late murder of the Rabbis soon burst

CHAP.
IX

[a] Meg.Taan
xi. 1, ed
Warsh,
p. 16 *a*

[b] *Jos.*War
i. 23. 5

[c] *Jos.* Ant.
xvii. 6. 1;
War i. 32. 7

[d] *Jos.*War
i. 23. 5
[e] Ant. xvii
8. 2

[f] Ant. xvii
8. 4; 9. 5

[g] Ant. xvii.
8. 4

---

[1] The Megillath Taanith itself, or 'Roll of Fasts,' does not mention the death of Herod. But the commentator adds to the dates 7th *Kislev* (Nov.) and 2nd *Shebhat* (Jan.), both manifestly incorrect, the notice that Herod had died—on the 2nd Shebhat. Jannai also—at the same time telling a story about the incarceration and liberation of 'seventy of the Elders of Israel,' evidently a modification of Josephus' account of what passed in the Hiprodrome of Jericho. Accordingly,

Grätz (Gesch. vol. iii. p. 427) and *Derenbourg* (pp. 101, 164) have regarded the 1st of Shebhat as really that of Herod's death. But this is impossible; and we know enough of the historical inaccuracy of the Rabbis not to attach any serious importance to their precise dates.

[2] Herod had married no less than ten times. See his genealogical table.

[3] Batanæa, Trachonitis, Auranitis, and Panias.

BOOK
II

into a storm of lamentation, and then of rebellion, which Archelaus silenced by the slaughter of not less than three thousand, and that within the sacred precincts of the Temple itself.[a]

Ant. xvii. 9 1–3

Other and more serious difficulties awaited him in Rome, whither he went in company with his mother, his aunt Salome, and other relatives. These, however, presently deserted him to espouse the claims of Antipas, who likewise appeared before Augustus to plead for the royal succession, assigned to him in a former testament. The Herodian family, while intriguing and clamouring each on his own account, were, for reasons easily understood, agreed that they would rather not have a king at all, but be under the suzerainty of Rome; though, if king there must be, they preferred Antipas to Archelaus. Meanwhile, fresh troubles broke out in Palestine, which were suppressed by fire, sword, and crucifixions. And now two other deputations arrived in the Imperial City. Philip, the step-brother of Archelaus, to whom the latter had left the administration of his kingdom, came to look after his own interests, as well as to support Archelaus.[b][1] At the same time, a Jewish deputation of fifty, from Palestine, accompanied by eight thousand Roman Jews, clamoured for the deposition of the entire Herodian race, on account of their crimes,[2] and the incorporation of Palestine with Syria—no doubt in hope of the same semi-independence under their own authorities, enjoyed by their fellow-religionists in the Grecian cities. Augustus decided to confirm the last testament of Herod, with certain slight modifications, of which the most important was that Archelaus should bear the title of *Ethnarch*, which, if he deserved it, would by-and-by be exchanged for that of King. His dominions were to be Judæa, Idumæa, and Samaria, with a revenue of 600 talents[3] (about 230,000*l*. to 240,000*l*). It is needless to follow the fortunes of the new Ethnarch. He began his rule by crushing all resistance by the wholesale slaughter of his opponents. Of the High-Priestly office he disposed after the manner of his father. But he far surpassed him in cruelty, oppression, luxury, the grossest egotism, and the lowest sensuality, and that, without possessing the talent or the energy of Herod.[4] His brief reign ceased in the year 6 of our era, when the Emperor banished him, on account of his crimes, to Gaul.

[b] Ant. xvii. 11. 1; War ii. 6. 1

---

[1] I cannot conceive on what ground *Keim* (both in *Schenkel's* Bibel Lex, and in his 'Jesu von Nazara') speaks of him as a pretender to the throne.

[2] This may have been the historical basis of the parable of our Lord in St. Luke xix. 12–27.

[3] The revenues of Antipas were 200 talents, and those of Philip 100 talents.

[4] This is admitted even by *Braun* (Söhne d. Herodes, p. 8). Despite its pretentiousness this tractate is untrustworthy, being written in a party spirit (Jewish).

It must have been soon after the accession of Archelaus,[1] but before tidings of it had actually reached Joseph in Egypt, that the Holy Family returned to Palestine. The first intention of Joseph seems to have been to settle in Bethlehem, where he had lived since the birth of Jesus. Obvious reasons would incline him to choose this, and, if possible, to avoid Nazareth as the place of his residence. His trade, even had he been unknown in Bethlehem, would have easily supplied the modest wants of his household. But when, on reaching Palestine, he learned who the successor of Herod was, and also, no doubt, in what manner he had inaugurated his reign, common prudence would have dictated the withdrawal of the Infant-Saviour from the dominions of Archelaus. But it needed Divine direction to determine his return to Nazareth.[2]

Of the many years spent in Nazareth, during which Jesus passed from infancy to childhood, from childhood to youth, and from youth to manhood, the Evangelic narrative has left us but briefest notice. Of His *childhood*: that 'He grew and waxed strong in spirit, filled with wisdom, and the grace of God was upon Him;'[a] of His *youth*: besides the account of His questioning the Rabbis in the Temple, the year before he attained Jewish majority—that 'He was subject to His parents,' and that 'He increased in wisdom and in stature, and in favour with God and man.' Considering what loving care watched over Jewish child-life, tenderly marking by not fewer than eight designations the various stages of its development,[3] and the deep interest naturally attaching to the early life of the Messiah, that silence, in contrast to the almost blasphemous absurdities of the Apocryphal Gospels, teaches us once more, and most impressively, that the Gospels furnish a history of the Saviour, not a biography of Jesus of Nazareth.

a St. Luke ii. 40

St. Matthew, indeed, summarises the whole outward history of

---

[1] We gather this from the expression, 'When he heard that Archelaus did reign.' Evidently Joseph had *not* heard who was Herod's successor, when he left Egypt. Archdeacon Farrar suggests, that the expression 'reigned' ('as a king, βασιλεύει—St. Matt. ii. 22) refers to the period before Augustus had changed his title from 'King' to Ethnarch. But this can scarcely be pressed, the word being used of other rule than that of a *king*, not only in the New Testament and in the Apocrypha, but by Josephus, and even by classical writers.

[2] The language of St. Matthew (ii. 22, 23) seems to imply express Divine direc-tion not to enter the territory of Judæa. In that case he would travel along the coast-line till he passed into Galilee. The impression left is, that the settle-ment at Nazareth whs not of his own choice.

[2] *Yeled*, the newborn babe, as in Is. ix. 6; *Yoneq*, the suckling, Is. xi. 8; *Olel*, the suckling beginning to ask for food, Lam. iv. 4; *Gamul*, the weaned child, Is. xxviii. 9; *Taph*, the child clinging to its mother, Jer. xl. 7; *Elem*, a child becoming firm; *Naar*, the lad, literally, 'one who shakes himself free;' and *Bachur*, the ripened one. (See 'Sketches of Jewish Social Life,' pp. 103, 104.)

BOOK
II

the life in Nazareth in one sentence. Henceforth Jesus would stand out before the Jews of His time — and, as we know, of all times [1] — by the distinctive designation: 'of Nazareth,' נצרי (*Notsri*), Ναζω-ραῖος, 'the Nazarene.' In the mind of a Palestinian a peculiar significance would attach to the by-Name of the Messiah, especially in its connection with the general teaching of prophetic Scripture. And here we must remember, that St. Matthew primarily addressed his Gospel to Palestinian readers, and that it is the Jewish presentation of the Messiah as meeting Jewish expectancy. In this there is nothing derogatory to the character of the Gospel, no accommodation in the sense of adaptation, since Jesus was not only the Saviour of the world, but especially also the King of the Jews, and we are now considering how He would stand out before the Jewish mind. On one point all were agreed: His Name was *Notsri* (of Nazareth). St. Matthew proceeds to point out, how entirely this accorded with prophetic Scripture—not, indeed, with any single prediction, but with the whole language of the prophets. From this [2] the Jews derived not fewer than eight designations or Names by which the Messiah was to be called. The most prominent among them was that of *Tsemach*,

[a] In accordance with Jer. xxiii. 5; xxxiii. 15; and especially Zech iii. 18

or 'Branch.' [a] We call it the most prominent, not only because it is based upon the clearest Scripture-testimony, but because it evidently occupied the foremost rank in Jewish thinking, being embodied in this earliest portion of their daily liturgy: 'The *Branch* of David, Thy Servant, speedily make to shoot forth, and His Horn exalt Thou by Thy Salvation. . . . Blessed art Thou Jehovah, Who causeth to spring forth (literally: to branch forth) the Horn of Salvation' (15th Eulogy). Now, what is expressed by the word *Tsemach* is also conveyed by the term *Netser*, 'Branch,' in such passages as Isaiah xi. 1, which was likewise applied to the Messiah. [3] Thus, starting from Isaiah xi. 1, *Netser*

[b] So in Bei. R. 76

being equivalent to *Tsemach*, Jesus would, as *Notsri* or *Ben Netser*, [b][4] bear in popular parlance, and that on the ground of prophetic Scriptures, the exact equivalent of the best-known designation of the Messiah. [5] The more significant this, that it was not a self-chosen nor man-given name, but arose, in the providence of God, from what otherwise might have been called the accident of His residence. We

---

[1] This is still the common, almost universal, designation of Christ among the Jews.

[2] Comp. ch. iv. of this book.

[3] See Appendix IX.

[4] Comp. *Buxtorf*, Lexicon Talm. p. 1383.

[5] All this becomes more evident by *Delitzsch's* ingenious suggestion (Zeitschr. für luther. Theol. 1876, part iii. p. 402), that the real meaning, though not the literal rendering, of the words of St. Matthew, would be כי נצר שמו—'for Nezer ['branch'] is His Name.'

admit that this is a Jewish view; but then this Gospel *is* the Jewish view of the Jewish Messiah.

But, taking this Jewish title in its Jewish significance, it has also a deeper meaning, and that not only to Jews, but to all men. The idea of Christ as the Divinely placed 'Branch' (symbolised by His Divinely-appointed early residence), small and despised in its forth-shooting, or then visible appearance (like Nazareth and the Nazarenes), but destined to grow as the Branch sprung out of Jesse's roots, is most marvellously true to the whole history of the Christ, alike as sketched 'by the prophets,' and as exhibited in reality. And thus to us all, Jews or Gentiles, the Divine guidance to Nazareth and the name Nazarene present the truest fulfilment of the prophecies of His history.

Greater contrast could scarcely be imagined than between the intricate scholastic studies of the Judæans, and the active pursuits that engaged men in Galilee. It was a common saying: 'If a person wishes to be rich, let him go north; if he wants to be wise, let him come south'—and to Judæa, accordingly, flocked, from ploughshare and workshop, whoever wished to become 'learned in the Law.' The very neighbourhood of the Gentile world, the contact with the great commercial centres close by, and the constant intercourse with foreigners, who passed through Galilee along one of the world's great highways, would render the narrow exclusiveness of the Southerners impossible. Galilee was to Judaism 'the Court of the Gentiles'—the Rabbinic Schools of Judæa its innermost Sanctuary. The natural disposition of the people, even the soil and climate of Galilee, were not favourable to the all-engrossing passion for Rabbinic study. In Judæa all seemed to invite to retrospection and introspection; to favour habits of solitary thought and study, till it kindled into fanaticism. Mile by mile as you travelled southwards, memories of the past would crowd around, and thoughts of the future would rise within. Avoiding the great towns as the centres of hated heathenism, the traveller would meet few foreigners, but everywhere encounter those gaunt representatives of what was regarded as the superlative excellency of his religion. These were the embodiment of Jewish piety and asceticism, the possessors and expounders of the mysteries of his faith, the fountain-head of wisdom, who were not only sure of heaven themselves, but knew its secrets, and were its very aristocracy; men who could tell him all about his own religion, practised its most minute injunctions, and could interpret every stroke and letter of the Law—nay, whose it actually was to 'loose and to bind,' to pronounce an action lawful or unlawful, and to 'remit or retain sins,' by declaring a man liable to, or free from, expiatory sacrifices, or else punishment in this or the next world. No Hindoo fanatic would more humbly bend before Brahmin saints, nor devout Romanist more venerate the members of a holy fraternity, than the Jew his great Rabbis.[1] Reason, duty, and precept, alike bound him to reverence them, as he reverenced the God Whose interpreters, representatives, deputies, intimate companions, almost colleagues in the heavenly Sanhedrin, they were. And all around, even nature itself, might seem to foster such tendencies. Even at that time Judæa was comparatively desolate, barren, grey. The decaying cities of ancient renown; the lone highland scenery; the bare, rugged hills; the rocky terraces from which only artificial culture could woo a return; the wide solitary plains, deep glens, limestone heights—with distant glorious Jerusalem ever in the far background, would all favour solitary thought and religious abstraction.

It was quite otherwise in Galilee. The smiling landscape of Lower Galilee invited the easy labour of the agriculturist. Even the highlands of Upper Galilee[2] were not, like those of Judæa, sombre, lonely, enthusiasm-killing, but gloriously grand, free, fresh, and bracing. A more beautiful country—hill, dale, and lake—could scarcely be imagined than Galilee Proper. It was here that Asher had 'dipped his foot in oil.' According to the Rabbis, it was easier to rear a forest of olive-trees in Galilee than one child in Judæa. Corn grew in abundance; the wine, though not so plentiful as the oil, was rich and generous. Proverbially, all fruit grew in perfection, and altogether the cost of living was about one-fifth that in Judæa. And then, what a teeming, busy population! Making every allowance for exaggeration, we cannot wholly ignore the account of Josephus about the 240 towns and villages of Galilee, each with not less than 15,000 inhabitants. In the centres of industry all then known trades were busily carried on; the husbandman pursued his happy toil on

---

[1] One of the most absurdly curious illustrations of this is the following: 'He who blows his nose in the presence of his Rabbi is worthy of death' (Erub. 99 a, line 11 from bottom). The *dictum* is supported by an alteration in the reading of Prov. viii. 36.

[2] Galilee covered the ancient possessions of Issachar, Zebulun, Naphtali, and Asher. 'In the time of Christ it stretched northwards to the possessions of Tyre on the one side, and to Syria on the other.

On the south it was bounded by Samaria —Mount Carmel on the Western, and the district of Scythopolis on the eastern side, being here landmarks; while the Jordan and the Lake of Gennesaret formed the general eastern boundary line.' (Sketches of Jewish Soc. Life. p. 33.) It was divided into Upper and Lower Galilee—the former beginning 'where sycomores (*not* our sycamores) cease to grow.' Fishing in the Lake of Galilee was free to all (Baba K. 81 b).

genial soil, while by the Lake of Gennesaret, with its unrivalled beauty, its rich villages, and lovely retreats, the fisherman plied his healthy avocation. By those waters, overarched by a deep blue sky, spangled with the brilliancy of innumerable stars, a man might feel constrained by nature itself to meditate and pray; he would not be likely to indulge in a morbid fanaticism.

Assuredly, in its then condition, Galilee was not the home of Rabbinism, though that of generous spirits, of warm, impulsive hearts, of intense nationalism, of simple manners, and of earnest piety. Of course, there would be a reverse side to the picture. Such a race would be excitable, passionate, violent. The Talmud accuses them of being quarrelsome,[a] but admits that they cared more for honour than for money. The great ideal teacher of Palestinian schools was Akiba, and one of his most outspoken opponents a Galilean, Rabbi José.[b] In religious observances their practice was simpler; as regarded canon-law they often took independent views, and generally followed the interpretations of those who, in opposition to Akiba, inclined to the more mild and rational—we had almost said, the more human—application of traditionalism.[1] The Talmud mentions several points in which the practice of the Galileans differed from that of Judæa—all either in the direction of more practical earnestness,[2] or of alleviation of Rabbinic rigorism.[3] On the other hand, they were looked down upon as neglecting traditionalism, unable to rise to its speculative heights, and preferring the attractions of the Haggadah to the logical subtleties of the Halakhah.[4] There was a general contempt in Rabbinic circles for all that was Galilean. Although the Judæan or Jerusalem dialect was far from pure,[5] the people of Galilee were especially blamed for neglecting the study of their language, charged with errors in grammar, and especially with absurd malpronunciation, sometimes leading to ridiculous mistakes.[6]

קנטרנין
[a] 'cantan-
kerous' (?),
Ned. 48 a

[b] Siphré on
Numb. x.
19, ed.
Fried-
mann, 4 a;
Chag. 14 a

---

[1] Of which Jochanan, the son of Nuri, may here be regarded as the exponent.

[2] As in the relation between bridegroom and bride, the cessation of work the day before the Passover, &c.

[3] As in regard to animals lawful to be eaten, vows, &c.

[4] The doctrinal, or rather Halakhic, differences between Galilee and Judæa are partially noted by *Lightfoot* (Chronogr. Matth. præm. lxxxvi.), and by *Hamburger* (Real-Enc. i. p. 395).

[5] See *Deutsch's* Remains, p. 358.

[5] The differences of pronunciation and language are indicated by *Lightfoot* (u. s.

lxxxvii.), and by *Deutsch* (u. s. pp. 357, 358). Several instances of ridiculous mistakes arising from it are recorded. Thus, a woman cooked for her husband two lentils (טלפחי) instead of two feet (of an animal, טלפי), as desired (*Nedar.* 66 *b*). On another occasion a woman malpronounced 'Come, I will give thee milk,' into 'Companion, butter devour thee!' (Erub. 53 *b*). In the same connection other similar stories are told. Comp. also *Neubauer,* Géogr. du Talmud, p. 184, *G. de Rossi,* della lingua prop. di Cristo, Dissert. I. *passim.*

'Galilean—Fool!' was so common an expression, that a learned lady turned with it upon so great a man as R. José, the Galilean, because he had used two needless words in asking her the road to Lydda.[a][1] Indeed, this R. José had considerable prejudices to overcome, before his remarkable talents and learning were fully acknowledged.[2]

Among such a people, and in that country, Jesus spent by far the longest part of His life upon earth. Generally, this period may be described as that of His true and full Human Development—physical, intellectual, spiritual—of outward submission to man, and inward submission to God, with the attendant results of 'wisdom,' 'favour,' and 'grace.' Necessary, therefore, as this period was, if the Christ was to be TRUE MAN, it cannot be said that it was lost, even so far as His Work as Saviour was concerned. .It was more than the preparation for that work; it was the commencement of it: *subjectively* (and passively), the self-abnegation of humiliation in His willing submission; and *objectively* (and actively), the fulfilment of all righteousness through it. But into this 'mystery of piety' we may only look afar off—simply remarking, that it almost needed for us also these thirty years of *Human Life*, that the overpowering thought of His Divinity might not overshadow that of His Humanity. But if He was subject to such conditions, they must, in the nature of things, have affected His development. It is therefore not presumption when, without breaking the silence of Holy Scripture, we follow the various stages of the Nazareth life, as each is, so to speak, initialled by the brief but emphatic summaries of the third Gospel.

In regard to the *Child-Life*,[3] we read: 'And the Child grew, and waxed strong in spirit,[4] being filled with wisdom, and the grace of God was upon Him.'[b] This marks, so to speak, the lowest rung in the ladder. Having entered upon life as the Divine Infant, He began it as the Human Child, subject to all its conditions, yet perfect in them.

These conditions were, indeed, for that time, the happiest conceivable, and such as only centuries of Old Testament life-training could have made them. The Gentile world here presented terrible contrast,

---

[1] The Rabbi asked: *What road leads to Lydda?*—using *four* words. The woman pointed out that, since it was not lawful to multiply speech with a woman, he should have asked: *Whither to Lydda?*—in *two* words.

[2] In fact, only four great Galilean Rabbis are mentioned. The Galileans are said to have inclined towards mystical (Kabbalistic?) pursuits.

[3] *Gelpke*, Jugendgesch, des Herrn, has, at least in our days, little value beyond its title.

[4] The words 'in spirit' are of doubtful authority. But their omission can be of no consequence, since the 'waxing strong' evidently refers to the mental development, as the subsequent clause shows.

alike in regard to the relation of parents and children, and the
character and moral object of their upbringing.   Education begins
in the *home*, and there were not homes like those in Israel; it is
imparted by influence and example, before it comes by teaching; it
is acquired by what is seen and heard, before it is laboriously learned
from books; its real object becomes instinctively felt, before its
goal is consciously sought.   What Jewish fathers and mothers were;
what they felt towards their children; and with what reverence,
affection, and care the latter returned what they had received, is
known to every reader of the Old Testament.   The relationship of
father has its highest sanction and embodiment in that of God
towards Israel; the tenderness and care of a mother in that of the
watchfulness and pity of the Lord over His people.   The semi-Divine
relationship between children and parents appears in the location, the
far more than outward duties which it implies in the wording, of the
Fifth Commandment.   No punishment more prompt than that of its
breach;[a] no description more terribly realistic than that of the vengeance which overtakes such sin.[b]

[a] Deut. xxi.
18–21
[b] Prov. xxx.
17

From the first days of its existence, a religious atmosphere surrounded the child of Jewish parents.   Admitted in the number of
God's chosen people by the deeply significant rite of circumcision,
when its name was first spoken in the accents of prayer,[1] it was
henceforth separated unto God.   Whether or not it accepted the
privileges and obligations implied in this dedication, they came to
him directly from God, as much as the circumstances of his birth.
The God of Abraham, Isaac, and Jacob, the God of Israel, the God
of the promises, claimed him, with all of blessing which this conveyed,
and of responsibility which resulted from it.   And the first wish
expressed for him was that, 'as he had been joined to the covenant,'
so it might also be to him in regard to the 'Torah' (Law), to 'the
Chuppah' (the marriage-baldachino), and 'to good works;' in other
words, that he might live 'godly, soberly, and righteously in this
present world'—a holy, happy, and God-devoted life.   And what
this was, could not for a moment be in doubt.   Putting aside the
overlying Rabbinic interpretations, the ideal of life was presented to
the mind of the Jew in a hundred different forms—in none perhaps
more popularly than in the words, 'These are the things of which
a man enjoys the fruit in this world, but their possession continueth
for the next: to honour father and mother, pious works, peacemaking

---

[1] See the notice of these rites at the circumcision of John the Baptist, in ch. iv. of
his Book.

BOOK
II

ª Peah i. 1

Ber. 63 b

ᶜ On which
Deut. vi. 4–9
and xi. 13–
21 were
inscribed
ᵈ Jos. Ant.
iv. 8. 13;
Ber. iii. 3;
Megill. i. 8;
Moed K. iii.

ᵉ Ps. cxxi. 8

between man and man, and the study of the Law, which is equivalent
to them all.' ª This devotion to the Law was, indeed, to the Jew the all
in all—the sum of intellectual pursuits, the aim of life.   What better
thing could a father seek for his child than this inestimable boon?
The first education was necessarily the mother's.[1]   Even the
Talmud owns this, when, among the memorable sayings of the sages,
it records one of the School of Rabbi Jannai, to the effect that knowledge of the Law may be looked for in those, who have sucked it in
at their mother's breast.ᵇ   And what the true mothers in Israel were,
is known not only from instances in the Old Testament, from the
praise of woman in the Book of Proverbs, and from the sayings of
the son of Sirach (Ecclus. iii.[2]), but from the Jewish women of the
New Testament.[3]   If, according to a somewhat curious traditional
principle, women were dispensed from all such positive obligations as
were incumbent at fixed periods of time (such as putting on phylacteries), other religious duties devolved exclusively upon them.   The
Sabbath meal, the kindling of the Sabbath lamp, and the setting
apart a portion of the dough from the bread for the household,—
these are but instances, with which every 'Taph,' as he clung to
his mother's skirts, must have been familiar.   Even before he could
follow her in such religious household duties, his eyes must have
been attracted by the *Mezuzah* attached to the door-post, as the name
of the Most High on the outside of the little folded parchment ᶜ was
reverently touched by each who came or went, and then the fingers
kissed that had come in contact with the Holy Name.ᵈ   Indeed, the
duty of the *Mezuzah* was incumbent on women also, and one can
imagine it to have been in the heathen-home of Lois and Eunice
in the far-off 'dispersion,' where Timothy would first learn to
wonder at, then to understand, its meaning.   And what lessons for
the past and for the present might not be connected with it !   In
popular opinion it was the symbol of the Divine guard over Israel's
homes, the visible emblem of this joyous hymn: 'The Lord shall
preserve thy going out and coming in, from this time forth, and even
for evermore.' ᵉ

There could not be national history, nor even romance, to compare
with that by which a Jewish mother might hold her child entranced.

---

[1] Comp. 'Sketches of Jewish Social
Life,' pp. 86–160, the literature there
quoted: *Duschak*, Schulgesetzgebung d.
alten Isr. ; and Dr. *Marcus*, Pædagog. d.
Isr. Volkes.

[2] The counterpart is in Ecclus. xxx.

[3] Besides the holy women who are
named in the Gospels, we would refer to
the mothers of Zebedee's children and
of Mark, to Dorcas, Lydia, Lois, Eunice,
Priscilla, St. John's 'elect lady,' and
others.

And it was his own history—that of his tribe, clan, perhaps family; of the past, indeed, but yet of the present, and still more of the glorious future. Long before he could go to school, or even Synagogue, the private and united prayers and the domestic rites, whether of the weekly Sabbath or of festive seasons, would indelibly impress themselves upon his mind. In mid-winter there was the festive illumination in each home. In most houses, the first night only one candle was lit, the next two, and so on to the eighth day; and the child would learn that this was symbolic, and commemorative of the *Dedication of the Temple*, its purgation, and the restoration of its services by the lion-hearted Judas the Maccabee. Next came, in earliest spring, the merry time of *Purim*, the Feast of Esther and of Israel's deliverance through her, with its good cheer and boisterous enjoyments.[1] Although the Passover might call the rest of the family to Jerusalem, the rigid exclusion of all leaven during the whole week could not pass without its impressions. Then, after the Feast of Weeks, came bright summer. But its golden harvest and its rich fruits would remind of the early dedication of the first and best to the Lord, and of those solemn processions in which it was carried up to Jerusalem. As autumn seared the leaves, the Feast of the New Year spoke of the casting up of man's accounts in the great Book of Judgment, and the fixing of destiny for good or for evil. Then followed the Fast of the Day of Atonement, with its tremendous solemnities, the memory of which could never fade from mind or imagination; and, last of all, in the week of the Feast of Tabernacles, there were the strange leafy booths in which they lived and joyed, keeping their harvest-thanksgiving; and praying and longing for the better harvest of a renewed world.

But it was not only through sight and hearing that, from its very inception, life in Israel became religious. There was also from the first positive teaching, of which the commencement would necessarily devolve on the mother. It needed not the extravagant laudations, nor the promises held out by the Rabbis, to incite Jewish women to this duty. If they were true to their descent, it would come almost naturally to them. Scripture set before them a continuous succession of noble Hebrew mothers. How well they followed their example, we learn from the instance of her, whose son, the child of a Gentile father, and reared far away, where there was not even a Synagogue to sustain religious life, had 'from an infant[2] known the Holy Scriptures,' and

---

[1] Some of its customs almost remind us of our 5th of November.

[2] The word βρέφος has no other meaning than that of 'infant' or 'babe.'

BOOK
II

that in their life-moulding influence.[a] It was, indeed, no idle boast that the Jews 'were from their swaddling-clothes . . . trained to recognise God as their Father, and as the Maker of the world;' that, 'having been taught the knowledge (of the laws) from earliest youth, they bore in their souls the image of the commandments;'[b] that 'from their earliest consciousness they learned the laws, so as to have them, as it were, engraven upon the soul;'[c] and that they were 'brought up in learning,' 'exercised in the laws,' 'and made acquainted with the acts of their predecessors in order to their imitation of them.'[d]

But while the earliest religious teaching would, of necessity, come from the lips of the mother, it was the father who was 'bound to teach his son.'[e] To impart to the child knowledge of the Torah conferred as great spiritual distinction, as if a man had received the Law itself on Mount Horeb.[f] Every other engagement, even the necessary meal, should give place to this paramount duty;[g] nor should it be forgotten that, while here real labour was necessary, it would never prove fruitless.[h] That man was of the profane vulgar (an *Am ha-arets*), who had sons, but failed to bring them up in knowledge of the Law.[i] Directly the child learned to speak, his religious instruction was to begin[k]—no doubt, with such verses of Holy Scripture as composed that part of the Jewish liturgy, which answers to our Creed.[1] Then would follow other passages from the Bible, short prayers, and select sayings of the sages. Special attention was given to the culture of the *memory*, since forgetfulness might prove as fatal in its consequences as ignorance or neglect of the Law.[m] Very early the child must have been taught what might be called his birthday-text—some verse of Scripture beginning, or ending with, or at least containing, the same letters as his Hebrew name. This guardian-promise the child would insert in its daily prayers.[2] The earliest hymns taught would be the Psalms for the days of the week, or festive Psalms, such as the *Hallel*,[n] or those connected with the festive pilgrimages to Zion.

The regular instruction commenced with the fifth or sixth year (according to strength), when every child was sent to school.[o] There can be no reasonable doubt that at that time such schools existed throughout the land. We find references to them at almost every period; indeed, the existence of higher schools and Academies would not have been possible without such primary instruction. Two Rabbis

Marginal notes:

[a] 2 Tim. iii. 15; 1. 5
[b] *Philo,* Legat. ad Cajum, sec. 16. 31
[c] *Jos.* Ag. Apion ii. 19
[d] *Jos.* Ag. Apion ii.26; comp. 1. 8. 12; ii. 27
[e] Kidd, 29 a
[f] Sanh. 99 b
[g] Kidd, 30 a
[h] Meg. 6 b
[i] Sot. 22 a
Succ. 42 a
[p] Ab. iii. 9
[n] Ps. cxiii.–cxviii.
[o] Baba B. 21 a; Keth. 50 a

---

[1] The *Shema.*

[2] Comp. 'Sketches of Jewish Social Life,' pp. 159 &c. The enigmatic mode of wording and writing was very common. Thus, the year is marked by a verse, generally from Scripture, which contains the letters that give the numerical value of the year. These letters are indicated by marks above them.

of Jerusalem, specially distinguished and beloved on account of their
educational labours, were among the last victims of Herod's cruelty.[a]
Later on, tradition ascribes to Joshua the son of Gamla the introduction of schools in every town, and the compulsory education in them
of all children above the age of six.[b] Such was the transcendent
merit attaching to this act, that it seemed to blot out the guilt of the
purchase for him of the High-Priestly office by his wife Martha, shortly
before the commencement of the great Jewish war.[c][1] To pass over
the fabulous number of schools supposed to have existed in Jerusalem,
tradition had it that, despite of this, the City only fell because of the
neglect of the education of children.[d] It was even deemed unlawful
to live in a place where there was no school.[e] Such a city deserved
to be either destroyed or excommunicated.[f]

It would lead too far to give details about the appointment of,
and provision for, teachers, the arrangements of the schools, the method
of teaching, or the subjects of study, the more so as many of these
regulations date from a period later than that under review. Suffice
it that, from the teaching of the alphabet or of writing, onwards to
the farthest limit of instruction in the most advanced Academies of
the Rabbis, all is marked by extreme care, wisdom, accuracy, and a
moral and religious purpose as the ultimate object. For a long time it
was not uncommon to teach in the open air;[g] but this must have been
chiefly in connection with theological discussions, and the instruction of youths. But the children were gathered in the Synagogues,
or in School-houses,[2] where at first they either stood, teacher and
pupils alike, or else sat on the ground in a semicircle, facing the
teacher, as it were, literally to carry into practice the prophetic saying: 'Thine eyes shall see thy teachers.'[h] The introduction of benches
or chairs was of later date; but the principle was always the same,
that in respect of accommodation there was no distinction between
teacher and taught.[3] Thus, encircled by his pupils, as by a crown of
glory (to use the language of Maimonides), the teacher—generally the
Chazzan, or Officer of the Synagogue[i]—should impart to them the
precious knowledge of the Law, with constant adaptation to their capacity, with unwearied patience, intense earnestness, strictness tempered
by kindness, but, above all, with the highest object of their training
ever in view. To keep children from all contact with vice; to train them

CHAP.
IX

[a] *Jos.* Ant.
xvii. 6. 2
[b] Baba B.
21 *a*

[c] Yebam.
61 *a*; Yoma
18 *a*

[d] Shabb.
119 *b*
[e] Sanh. 17 *b*
[f]Shabb.u.s.

[g] Shabb.
127 *a*;
Moed K.16 *a*

[h] Is. xxx. 20

[i] For ex-
ample,
Shabb. 11 *a*

---

[1] He was succeeded by Matthias, the
son of Theophilos, under whose Pontificate the war against Rome began.
[2] Among the names by which the
schools are designated there is also that
of *Ischoli*, with its various derivations,
evidently from the Greek σχολή, *schola*.
[3] The proof-passages from the Talmud
are collated by Dr. *Marcus* (Pædagog.
d. Isr. Volkes, ii. pp. 16, 17).

BOOK
II

to gentleness, even when bitterest wrong had been received; to show sin in its repulsiveness, rather than to terrify by its consequences; to train to strict truthfulness; to avoid all that might lead to disagreeable or indelicate thoughts; and to do all this without showing partiality, without either undue severity, or laxity of discipline, with judicious increase of study and work, with careful attention to thoroughness in acquiring knowledge—all this and more constituted the ideal set before the teacher, and made his office of such high esteem in Israel.

Roughly classifying the subjects of study, it was held, that, up to ten years of age, the Bible exclusively should be the text-book; from ten to fifteen, the Mishnah, or traditional law; after that age, the student should enter on those theological discussions which occupied

ª Ab. v. 21

time and attention in the higher Academies of the Rabbis.ª Not that this progression would always be made. For, if after three, or, at most, five years of tuition—that is, after having fairly entered on Mishnic studies—the child had not shown decided aptitude, little hope was to be entertained of his future. The study of the Bible commenced with that of the Book of Leviticus.[1] Thence it passed to the other parts of the Pentateuch; then to the Prophets; and, finally, to the Hagiographa. What now constitutes the Gemara or Talmud was taught in the Academies, to which access could not be gained till after the age of fifteen. Care was taken not to send a child too early to school, nor to overwork him when there. For this purpose the school-hours were fixed, and attendance shortened during the summer-months.

The teaching in school would, of course, be greatly aided by the services of the Synagogue, and the deeper influences of home-life. We know that, even in the troublous times which preceded the rising of the Maccabees, the possession of parts or the whole of the Old Testament (whether in the original or the LXX. rendering) was so common, that during the great persecutions a regular search was made throughout the land for every copy of the Holy Scriptures, and

ᵇ 1 Macc. 1.
57; comp.
Jos.Ant.xii.
5. 4

those punished who possessed them.ᵇ After the triumph of the Maccabees, these copies of the Bible would, of course, be greatly multiplied. And, although perhaps only the wealthy could have purchased

---

[1] *Altingius* (Academic. Dissert. p. 335) curiously suggests, that this was done to teach a child its guilt and the need of justification. The Rabbinical interpretation (Vayyikra R. 7) is at least equally far-fetched: that, as children are pure and sacrifices pure, it is fitting that the pure should busy themselves with the pure. The obvious reason seems, that Leviticus treated of the ordinances with which every Jew ought to have been acquainted.

a MS. of the whole Old Testament in Hebrew, yet some portion or portions of the Word of God, in the original, would form the most cherished treasure of every pious household.   Besides, a school for Bible-study was attached to every academy,[a] in which copies of the Holy Scripture would be kept.   From anxious care to preserve the integrity of the text, it was deemed unlawful to make copies of small portions of a book of Scripture.[1]   But exception was made of certain sections which were copied for the instruction of children.   Among them, the history of the Creation to that of the Flood; Lev. i.–ix.; and Numb. i.–x. 35, are specially mentioned.[b]

It was in such circumstances, and under such influences, that the early years of Jesus passed.   To go beyond this, and to attempt lifting the veil which lies over His Child-History, would not only be presumptuous,[2] but involve us in anachronisms.   Fain would we know it, whether the Child Jesus frequented the Synagogue School; who was His teacher, and who those who sat beside Him on the ground, earnestly gazing on the face of Him Who repeated the sacrificial ordinances in the Book of Leviticus, that were all to be fulfilled in Him. But it is all ' a mystery of Godliness.'   We do not even know quite certainly whether the school-system had, at that time, extended to far-off Nazareth; nor whether the order and method which have been described were universally observed at that time.   In all probability, however, there was such a school in Nazareth, and, if so, the Child-Saviour would conform to the general practice of attendance.   We may thus, still with deepest reverence, think of Him as learning His earliest earthly lesson from the Book of Leviticus.   Learned Rabbis there were not in Nazareth—either then or afterwards.[3]   He would attend the services of the Synagogue, where Moses and the prophets

[a] Jer. Meg. iii. 1, p. 73 d

[b] Sopher. v. 9, p. 25 b; Gitt. 60 a; Jer. Meg. 74 a; Tos. Yad. 2

---

[1] *Herzfeld* (Gesch. d. V. Isr. iii. p.267, note) strangely misquotes and misinterprets this matter.   Comp. Dr. *Müller*, Massech. Sofer. p. 75.

[2] The most painful instances of these are the legendary accounts of the early history of Christ in the Apocryphal Gospels (well collated by *Keim*, i. 2, pp. 413–468, *passim*).   But later writers are unfortunately not wholly free from the charge.

[3] I must here protest against the introduction of imaginary ' Evening Scenes in Nazareth,' when, according to Dr. Geikie, ' friends or neighbours of Joseph's circle would meet for an hour's quiet gossip.'   Dr. Geikie here introduces as specimens of this ' quiet gossip ' a number of Rabbinic quotations from the German translation in *Dukes*' ' Rabbinische Blumenlese.'   To this it is sufficient answer: 1. There were no such learned Rabbis in Nazareth.   2. If there had been, they would not have been visitors in the house of Joseph.   3. If they had been visitors there, they would not have spoken what Dr. Geikie quotes from Dukes, since some of the extracts are from mediæval books, and only one a proverbial expression. 4.   Even if they had so spoken, it would at least have been in the words which Dukes has translated, without the changes and additions which Dr. Geikie has introduced in some instances.

were read, and, as afterwards by Himself,ᵃ occasional addresses delivered.[1] That His was pre-eminently a pious home in the highest sense, it seems almost irreverent to say. From His intimate familiarity with Holy Scripture, in its every detail, we may be allowed to infer that the home of Nazareth, however humble, possessed a precious copy of the Sacred Volume in its entirety. At any rate, we know that from earliest childhood it must have formed the meat and drink of the God-Man. The words of the Lord, as recorded by St. Matthew ᵇ and St. Luke,ᶜ also imply that the Holy Scriptures which He read were in the original Hebrew, and that they were written in the square, or Assyrian, characters.[2] Indeed, as the Pharisees and Sadducees always appealed to the Scriptures in the original, Jesus could not have met them on any other ground, and it was this which gave such point to His frequent expostulations with them: ‘Have ye not read?’

But far other thoughts than theirs gathered around His study of the Old Testament Scriptures. When comparing their long discussions on the letter and law of Scripture with His references to the Word of God, it seems as if it were quite another book which was handled. As we gaze into the vast glory of meaning which He opens to us; follow the shining track of heavenward living to which He points; behold the lines of symbol, type, and prediction converging in the grand unity of that Kingdom which became reality in Him; or listen as, alternately, some question of His seems to rive the darkness, as with flash of sudden light, or some sweet promise of old to lull the storm, some earnest lesson to quiet the tossing waves—we catch faint, it may be far-off, glimpses of how, in that early Child-life, when the Holy Scriptures were His special study, He must have read them, and what thoughts must have been kindled by their light. And thus better than before can we understand it: ‘And the Child grew, and waxed strong in spirit, filled with wisdom, and the grace of God was upon Him.’

[1] See Book III., the chapter on ‘The Synagogue of Nazareth.’

[2] This may be gathered even from such an expression as ‘One iota, or one little hook,’—not ‘tittle’ as in the A. V.

CHAPTER X.

IN THE HOUSE OF HIS HEAVENLY, AND IN THE HOME OF HIS EARTHLY
FATHER—THE TEMPLE OF JERUSALEM—THE RETIREMENT AT NAZA-
RETH.

(St. Luke ii. 41–52.)

ONCE only is the great silence, which lies on the history of Christ's
early life, broken.   It is to record what took place on His first visit to
the Temple.   What this meant, even to an ordinary devout Jew, may
easily be imagined.   Where life and religion were so intertwined,
and both in such organic connection with the Temple and the people
of Israel, every thoughtful Israelite must have felt as if his real life
were not in what was around, but ran up into the grand unity of the
people of God, and were compassed by the halo of its sanctity.   To him
it would be true in the deepest sense, that, so to speak, each Israelite
was born in Zion, as, assuredly, all the well-springs of his life were
there.[a]   It was, therefore, not merely the natural eagerness to see the
City of their God and of their fathers, glorious Jerusalem; nor yet the
lawful enthusiasm, national or religious, which would kindle at the
thought of ' our feet ' standing within those gates, through which
priests, prophets, and kings had passed; but far deeper feelings which
would make glad, when it was said: ' Let us go into the house of
Jehovah.'   They were not ruins to which precious memories clung,
nor did the great hope seem to lie afar off, behind the evening-mist.
But 'glorious things were spoken of Zion, the City of God'—in the
past, and in the near future 'the thrones of David' were to be set
within her walls, and amidst her palaces.[b]

In strict law, personal observance of the ordinances, and hence attendance on the feasts at Jerusalem, devolved on a youth only when
he was of age, that is, at thirteen years.   Then he became what was
called ' a son of the Commandment,' or ' of the Torah.'[c]   But, as a
matter of fact, the legal age was in this respect anticipated by two
years, or at least by one.[d]   It was in accordance with this custom, that,[1]

CHAP.
X

[a] Ps.lxxxvii.
5-7

[b] Ps. cxxii.
1-5

[c] Ab. v. 21

[d] Yoma 82a

---

[1] Comp. also *Maimonides*, Hilkh.Chag.
ii.   The common statement, that Jesus
went to the Temple because He was ' a
Son of the Commandment,' is obviously

BOOK
II

ᵃ Jer Kidd.
61 c

ᵇ From 4
B.C. to 6 A.D.

ᶜ 6-11 (?)
A.D.

ᵈ Acts v. 37;
Jos. Ant.
xviii. 1. 1

on the first Pascha after Jesus had passed His twelfth year, His Parents took Him with them in the 'company' of the Nazarenes to Jerusalem. The text seems to indicate, that it was their wont [1] to go up to the Temple; and we mark that, although women were not bound to make such personal appearance,ᵃ Mary gladly availed herself of what seems to have been the direction of Hillel (followed also by other religious women, mentioned in Rabbinic writings), to go up to the solemn services of the Sanctuary. Politically, times had changed. The weak and wicked rule of Archelaus had lasted only nine years,ᵇ when, in consequence of the charges against him, he was banished to Gaul. Judæa, Samaria and Idumæa were now incorporated into the Roman province of Syria, under its Governor, or *Legate*. The special administration of that part of Palestine was, however, entrusted to a *Procurator*, whose ordinary residence was at Cæsarea. It will be remembered, that the Jews themselves had desired some such arrangement, in the vain hope that, freed from the tyranny of the Herodians, they might enjoy the semi-independence of their brethren in the Grecian cities. But they found it otherwise. Their privileges were not secured to them; their religious feelings and prejudices were constantly, though perhaps not intentionally, outraged; [2] and their Sanhedrin shorn of its real power, though the Romans would probably not interfere in what might be regarded as purely religious questions. Indeed, the very presence of the Roman power in Jerusalem was a constant offence, and must necessarily have issued in a life and death struggle. One of the first measures of the new Legate of Syria, P. Sulpicius Quirinius,ᶜ after confiscating the ill-gotten wealth of Archelaus, was to order a census in Palestine, with the view of fixing the taxation of the country.ᵈ The popular excitement which this called forth was due, probably, not so much to opposition on principle, [3] as to this, that the census was regarded as the badge of servitude, and

erroneous. All the more remarkable, on the other hand, is St. Luke's accurate knowledge of Jewish customs, and all the more antithetic to the mythical theory the circumstance, that he places this remarkable event in the twelfth year of Jesus' life, and not when He became 'a Son of the Law.'

[1] We take as the more correct reading that which puts the participle in the present tense (ἀναβαινόντων), and not in the aorist.

[2] The Romans were tolerant of the religion of all subject nations—excepting only Gaul and Carthage. This for reasons which cannot here be discussed.

But what rendered Rome so obnoxious to Palestine was the *cultus* of the Emperor, as the symbol and impersonation of Imperial Rome. On this *cultus* Rome insisted in all countries, not perhaps so much on religious grounds as on political, as being the expression of loyalty to the empire. But in Judæa this *cultus* necessarily met resistance to the death. (Comp. *Schneckenburger*, Neutest. Zeitgesch. pp. 40–61.)

[3] This view, for which there is no historic foundation. is urged by those whose interest it is to deny the possibility of a census during the reign of Herod.

incompatible with the Theocratic character of Israel.[1] Had a census been considered absolutely contrary to the Law, the leading Rabbis would never have submitted to it;[2] nor would the popular resistance to the measure of Quirinius have been quelled by the representations of the High-Priest Joazar. But, although through his influence the census was allowed to be taken, the popular agitation was not suppressed. Indeed, that movement formed part of the history of the time, and not only affected political and religious parties in the land, but must have been presented to the mind of Jesus Himself, since, as will be shown, it had a representative within His own family circle.

This accession of Herod, misnamed the Great, marked a period in Jewish history, which closed with the war of despair against Rome and the flames of Jerusalem and the Temple. It gave rise to the appearance of what Josephus, despite his misrepresentation of them, rightly calls a *fourth* party—besides the Pharisees, Sadducees, and Essenes—that of the *Nationalists.*[a] A deeper and more independent view of the history of the times would, perhaps, lead us to regard the whole country as ranged either with or against that party. As afterwards expressed in its purest and simplest form, their watchword was, *negatively,* to call no human being their absolute lord;[b] *positively,* that God alone was to lead as absolute Lord.[c] It was, in fact, a revival of the Maccabean movement, perhaps more fully in its national than in its religious aspect, although the two could scarcely be separated in Israel, and their motto almost reads like that which according to some, furnished the letters whence the name *Maccabee*[d] was composed: *Mi Camochah Baelim Jehovah,* 'Who like Thee among the gods, Jehovah?'[e] It is characteristic of the times and religious tendencies, that their followers were no more called, as before, *Assideans* or *Chasidim,* 'the pious,' but *Zealots* (Ζηλωταί), or by the Hebrew equivalent *Qannaim* (*Cananœans,* not '*Canaanites,*' as in A.V.) The real home of that party was not Judæa nor Jerusalem, but Galilee.

Quite other, and indeed antagonistic, tendencies prevailed in the stronghold of the Herodians, Sadducees, and Pharisees. Of the latter only a small portion had any real sympathy with the national movement. Each party followed its own direction. The Essenes, absorbed in theosophic speculations, not untinged with Eastern mysticism, withdrew from all contact with the world, and practiced an ascetic life. With them, whatever individuals may have felt, no such movement could have originated; nor yet with the Herodians or Boethusians, who

CHAP.
X

[a] Ant. xviii.
1. 6

[b] Ant. xviii.
1. 6
[c] u. s. and
Jew. War
vii. 10. 1

[d] מכבי

[e] Ex. xv. 11

---

[1] That these were the sole grounds of resistance to the census, appears from   *Jos.* Ant. xviii. 1. 1, 6.
[2] As unquestionably they did.

BOOK
II

ᵃ Judg. xi.
3–6

ᵇ Ant. xiv.
9. 2–5

ᵉ Sanh. 19 a

ᵈ Yoma 39 b

combined strictly Pharisaic views with Herodian political partisanship; nor yet with the Sadducees; nor, finally, with what constituted
the great bulk of the Rabbinist party, the School of Hillel. But the
brave, free Highlanders of Galilee, and of the region across their
glorious lake, seemed to have inherited the spirit of Jephthah,ᵃ and
to have treasured as their ideal—alas! often wrongly apprehended—
their own Elijah, as, descending in wild, shaggy garb from the mountains of Gilead, he did battle against all the might of Ahab and
Jezebel. Their enthusiasm could not be kindled by the logical
subtleties of the Schools, but their hearts burned within them for their
God, their land, their people, their religion, and their freedom.

It was in Galilee, accordingly, that such wild, irregular resistance
to Herod at the outset of his career, as could be offered, was organised
by guerilla bands, which traversed the country, and owned one Ezekias
as their leader. Although Josephus calls them 'robbers,' a far different
estimate of them obtained in Jerusalem, where, as we remember, the
Sanhedrin summoned Herod to answer for the execution of Esekias.
What followed is told in substantially the same manner, though with
difference of form[1] and, sometimes, nomenclature, by Josephus,ᵇ and
in the Talmud.ᵉ The story has already been related in another
connection. Suffice it that, after the accession of Herod, the Sanhedrin became a shadow of itself. It was packed with Sadducees and
Priests of the King's nomination, and with Doctors of the canon-law,
whose only aim was to pursue in peace their subtleties; who had not,
and, from their contempt of the people, could not have, any real
sympathy with national aspirations; and whose ideal heavenly Kingdom was a miraculous, heaven-instituted, absolute rule of Rabbis.
Accordingly, the national movement, as it afterwards developed,
received neither the sympathy nor the support of leading Rabbis.
Perhaps the most gross manifestation of this was exhibited, shortly
before the taking of Jerusalem, by R. Jochanan ben Saccai, the most
renowned among its teachers. Almost unmoved he had witnessed the
portent of the opening of the Temple-doors by an unseen Hand,
which, by an interpretation of Zech. xi. 1, was popularly regarded as
betokening its speedy destruction.ᵈ [2] There is cynicism, as well as
want of sympathy, in the story recorded by tradition, that when, in
the straits of famine during the siege, Jochanan saw people eagerly

---

[1] The Talmud is never to be trusted
as to historical details. Often it seems
purposely to alter, when it intends the
experienced student to read between
the lines, while at other times it presents

a story in what may be called an alle
gorical form.
[2] The designation 'Lebanon' is often
applied in Talmudic writings to the
Temple.

feasting on soup made from straw, he scouted the idea of such a garrison resisting Vespasian and immediately resolved to leave the city.[a] In fact, we have distinct evidence that R. Jochanan had, as leader of the School of Hillel, used all his influence, although in vain, to persuade the people to submission to Rome.[b]

We can understand it, how this school had taken so little interest in anything purely national. Generally only one side of the character of Hillel has been presented by writers, and even this in greatly exaggerated language. His much lauded gentleness, peacefulness, and charity were rather negative than positive qualities. He was a philosophic Rabbi, whose real interest lay in a far other direction than that of sympathy with the people—and whose motto seemed, indeed, to imply, ' We, the sages, are the people of God; but this people, who know not the Law, are cursed.'[c] A far deeper feeling, and intense, though misguided earnestness pervaded the School of Shammai. It was in the minority, but it sympathised with the aspirations of the people. It was not philosophic nor eclectic, but intensely national. It opposed all approach to, and by, strangers; it dealt harshly with proselytes,[d] even the most distinguished (such as Akylas or Onkelos);[e] it passed, by first murdering a number of Hillelites who had come to the deliberative assembly, eighteen decrees, of which the object was to prevent all intercourse with Gentiles;[1] and it furnished leaders or supporters of the national movement.

We have marked the rise of the Nationalist party in Galilee at the time of Herod's first appearance on the scene, and learned how

CHAP.
X

[a] Midr. R.
on Lament.
i. 5; ed.
Warsh. vol.
iii. p. 60 a
[b] Ab. de R.
Nathan 4

[c] Comp. Ab
ii. 5

[d] Shabb. 31 a
[e] Ber. R. 70

---

[1] This celebrated meeting, of which, however, but scant and incoherent notices are left us (Shabb. i. 7 and specially in the Jer. Talmud on the passage p. 3 c, d; and Shabb. 17 a; Tos. Shabb. i. 2), took place in the house of Chananyah, ben Chizqiyah, ben Garon, a noted Shammaite. On arriving, many of the Hillelites were killed in the lower room, and then a majority of Shammaites carried the so-called *eighteen decrees*. The first twelve forbade the purchase of the most necessary articles of diet from Gentiles; the next five forbade the learning of their language, declared their testimony invalid, and their offerings unlawful, and interdicted all intercourse with them; while the last referred to first fruits. It was on the ground of these decrees that the hitherto customary burnt-offering for the Emperor was intermitted, which was really a declaration of war against Rome. The date of these decrees was probably about four years before the destruction of the Temple (See *Grätz*, Gesch. d. Juden, vol. iii. pp. 494–502). These decrees were carried by the influence of R. Eleazar, son of Chananyah the High-Priest, a very wealthy man, whose father and brother belonged to the opposite or peace party. It was on the proposal of this strict Shammaite that the offering for the Emperor was intermitted (*Jos*. Jew. War ii. 17. 2, 3). Indeed, it is impossible to over-estimate the influence of these Shammaite decrees on the great war with Rome. Eleazar, though opposed to the extreme party, one of whose chiefs he took and killed, was one of the leaders of the national party in the war (War ii. 17. 9, 10). There is, however, some confusion about various persons who bore the same name. It is impossible in this place to mention the various Shammaites who took part in the last Jewish war. Suffice it to indicate the tendency of that School.

mercilessly he tried to suppress it: first, by the execution of Ezekias and his adherents, and afterwards, when he became King of Judæa, by the slaughter of the Sanhedrists. The consequence of this unsparing severity was to give Rabbinism a different direction. The School of Hillel which henceforth commanded the majority, were men of no political colour, theological theorists, self-seeking Jurists, vain rather than ambitious. The minority, represented by the School of Shammai, were Nationalists. Defective and even false as both tendencies were, there was certainly more hope, as regarded the Kingdom of God, of the Nationalists than of the Sophists and Jurists. It was, of course, the policy of Herod to suppress all national aspirations. No one understood the meaning of Jewish Nationalism so well as he; no one ever opposed it so systematically. There was internal fitness, so to speak, in his attempt to kill the King of the Jews among the infants of Bethlehem. The murder of the Sanhedrists, with the consequent new anti-Messianic tendency of Rabbinism, was one measure in that direction; the various appointments which Herod made to the High-Priesthood another. And yet it was not easy, even in those times, to deprive the Pontificate of its power and influence. The High-Priest was still the representative of the religious life of the people, and he acted on all occasions, when the question under discussion was not one exclusively of subtle canon-law, as the President of the Sanhedrin, in which, indeed, the members of his family had evidently seat and vote.[a] The four families[1] from which, with few exceptions, the High-Priest—however often changed—were chosen, absorbed the wealth, and commanded the influence, of a state-endowed establishment, in its worst times. It was, therefore, of the utmost importance to make wise choice of the High-Priest. With the exception of the brief tenure by Aristobulus, the last of the Maccabees—whose appointment, too soon followed by his murder, was at the time a necessity—all the Herodian High-Priests were non-Palestinians. A keener blow than this could not have been dealt at Nationalism.

The same contempt for the High-Priesthood characterised the brief reign of Archelaus. On his death-bed, Herod had appointed to the Pontificate Joazar, a son of Boethos, the wealthy Alexandrian priest, whose daughter, Mariamme II., he had married. The Boethusian family, allied to Herod, formed a party—the Herodians—who combined strict Pharisaic views with devotion to the reigning family.[2] Joazar took the popular part against Archelaus, on his accession.

[a] Acts iv. 6

---

[1] See the list of High-Priests in Appendix VI.
[2] The Boethusians furnished no fewer than four High-Priests during the period between the reign of Herod and that of Agrippa I. (41 A.D.).

For this he was deprived of his dignity in favour of another son of
Boethos, Eleazar by name. But the mood of Archelaus was fickle
—perhaps he was distrustful of the family of Boethos. At any rate,
Eleazar had to give place to Jesus, the son of Sië, an otherwise unknown individual. At the time of the taxing of Quirinius we find
Joazar again in office,[a] apparently restored to it by the multitude,
which, having taken matters into its own hands at the change of
government, recalled one who had formerly favoured national aspirations.[b] It is thus that we explain his influence with the people, in
persuading them to submit to the Roman taxation.

But if Joazar had succeeded with the unthinking populace, he
failed to conciliate the more advanced of his own party, and, as the
event proved, the Roman authorities also, whose favour he had
hoped to gain. It will be remembered, that the Nationalist party
—or ' Zealots, ' as they were afterwards called—first appeared in
those guerilla-bands which traversed Galilee under the leadership
of Ezekias, whom Herod executed. But the National party was
not destroyed, only held in check, during his iron reign. It was
once more the family of Ezekias that headed the movement.
During the civil war which followed the accession of Archelaus, or
rather was carried on while he was pleading his cause in Rome, the
standard of the Nationalists was again raised in Galilee. Judas,
the son of Ezekias, took possession of the city of Sepphoris, and
armed his followers from the royal arsenal there. At that time, as
we know, the High-Priest Joazar sympathised, at least indirectly,
with the Nationalists. The rising, which indeed was general throughout Palestine, was suppressed by fire and sword, and the sons of
Herod were enabled to enter on their possessions. But when, after the
deposition of Archelaus, Joazar persuaded the people to submit to
the taxing of Quirinius, Judas was not disposed to follow what he
regarded as the treacherous lead of the Pontiff. In conjunction
with a Shammaite Rabbi, Sadduk, he raised again the standard of
revolt, although once more unsuccessfully.[c] How the Hillelites looked
upon this movement, we gather even from the slighting allusion of
Gamaliel.[d] The family of Ezekias furnished other martyrs to the
National cause. The two sons of Judas died for it on the cross in
46 A.D.[e] Yet a third son, Manahem, who, from the commencement
of the war against Rome, was one of the leaders of the most fanatical
Nationalists, the Sicarii—the Jacobins of the party, as they have
been aptly designated—died under unspeakable sufferings,[f] while a
fourth member of the family, Eleazar, was the leader of Israel's

CHAP.
X

[a] Ant. xviii.
1. 1

[b] Ant. xviii.
2. 1

[c] Ant. xviii
1. 1
[d] Acts v. 37

[e] Ant. xx.
5. 2

[f] Jewish
War ii. 17
8 and 9

forlorn hope, and nobly died at Masada, in the closing drama of the
Jewish war of independence.ᵃ Of such stuff were the Galilean
Zealots made. But we have to take this intense Nationalist tendency
also into account in the history of Jesus, the more so that at least
one of His disciples, and he a member of His family, had at one time
belonged to the party. Only the Kingdom of which Jesus was the
King was, as He Himself said, not of this world, and of far different
conception from that for which the Nationalists longed.

At the time when Jesus went up to the feast, Quirinius was, as
already stated, Governor of Syria. The taxing and the rising of
Judas were alike past; and the Roman Governor, dissatisfied with the
trimming of Joazar, and distrustful of him, had appointed in his
stead Ananos, the son of Seth, the Annas of infamous memory in the
New Testament. With brief interruption, he or his son held the
Pontifical office till, under the Procuratorship of Pilate, Caiaphas, the
son-in-law of Annas, succeeded to that dignity. It has already been
stated that, subject to the Roman Governors of Syria, the rule of
Palestine devolved on Procurators, of whom Coponius was the first.

Of him and his immediate successors—Marcus Ambivius,ᵇ Annius
Rufus,ᶜ and Valerius Gratus,ᵈ we know little. They were, indeed,
guilty of the most grievous fiscal oppressions, but they seem to have
respected, so far as was in them, the religious feelings of the Jews.
We know, that they even removed the image of the Emperor from
the standards of the Roman soldiers before marching them into
Jerusalem, so as to avoid the appearance of a *cultus* of the Cæsars.
It was reserved for Pontius Pilate to force this hated emblem on the
Jews, and otherwise to set their most sacred feelings at defiance. But
we may notice, even at this stage, with what critical periods in Jewish
history the public appearance of Christ synchronised. His first visit
to the Temple followed upon the Roman possession of Judæa, the
taxing, and the national rising, as also the institution of Annas to
the High-Priesthood. And the commencement of His public Ministry was contemporaneous with the accession of Pilate, and the
institution of Caiaphas. Whether viewed subjectively or objectively,
these things also have a deep bearing upon the history of the Christ.

It was, as we reckon it, in spring A.D. 9, that Jesus for the first
time went up to the Paschal Feast in Jerusalem. Coponius would
be there as the Procurator; and Annas ruled in the Temple as High-
Priest, when He appeared among its doctors. But far other than
political thoughts must have occupied the mind of Christ. Indeed,
for a time a brief calm had fallen upon the land. There was nothing

to provoke active resistance, and the party of the Zealots, although
existing, and striking deeper root in the hearts of the people, was, for
the time, rather what Josephus called it, 'the philosophical party'—
their minds busy with an ideal, which their hands were not yet preparing to make a reality.   And so, when, according to ancient wont,[a]   [a] Ps. xlii.
the festive company from Nazareth, soon swelled by other festive bands,   Is. xxx. 29
went up to Jerusalem, chanting by the way those ' Psalms of Ascent '[b]   [b] A.V.
to the accompaniment of the flute, they might implicitly yield them-   'Degrees';
selves to the spiritual thoughts kindled by such words.   Ps. cxx.-
cxxxiv.

When the pilgrims' feet stood within the gates of Jerusalem, there
could have been no difficulty in finding hospitality, however crowded
the City may have been on such occasions [1]—the more so when we
remember the extreme simplicity of Eastern manners and wants, and
the abundance of provisions which the many sacrifices of the season
would supply.   But on this subject, also, the Evangelic narrative keeps
silence.   Glorious as a view of Jerusalem must have seemed to a child
coming to it for the first time from the retirement of a Galilean village,
we must bear in mind, that He Who now looked upon it was not an
ordinary Child.   Nor are we, perhaps, mistaken in the idea that the
sight of its grandeur would, as on another occasion,[c] awaken in Him   [c] St. Luke
not so much feelings of admiration, which might have been akin to   xix. 41
those of pride, as of sadness, though He may as yet have been scarcely
conscious of its deeper reason.   But the one all-engrossing thought
would be of the *Temple*.   This, his first visit to its halls, seems also
to have called out the first outspoken—and may we not infer, the first
conscious—thought of that Temple as the House of His Father, and
with it the first conscious impulse of his Mission and Being.   Here also
it would be the higher meaning, rather than the structure and appearance, of the Temple, that would absorb the mind.   And yet there
was sufficient, even in the latter, to kindle enthusiasm.   As the pilgrim ascended the Mount, crested by that symmetrically proportioned
building, which could hold within its gigantic girdle not fewer than
210,000 persons, his wonder might well increase at every step.   The
Mount itself seemed like an island, abruptly rising from out deep
valleys, surrounded by a sea of walls, palaces, streets, and houses, and
crowned by a mass of snowy marble and glittering gold, rising terrace
upon terrace.   Altogether it measured a square of about 1,000 feet,
or, to give a more exact equivalent of the measurements furnished by

---

[1] It seems, however, that the Feast of
Pentecost would see even more pilgrims
—at least from a distance—in Jerusalem,
than that of the Passover (comp. Acts ii.
9-11).

the Rabbis, 927 feet. At its north-western angle, and connected with it, frowned the Castle of Antonia, held by the Roman garrison. The lofty walls were pierced by massive gates—the unused gate *(Tedi)* on the north; the Susa Gate on the east, which opened on the arched roadway to the Mount of Olives;[1] the two so-called ' Huldah ' (probably, ' weasel ') gates, which led by tunnels[2] from the priest-suburb Ophel into the outer Court; and, finally, four gates on the west.

Within the gates ran all around covered double colonnades, with here and there benches for those who resorted thither for prayer or for conference. The most magnificent of those was the southern, or twofold double colonnade, with a wide space between; the most venerable, the ancient ' Solomon's Porch,' or eastern colonnade. Entering from the Xystus bridge, and under the tower of John,[a] one would pass along the southern colonnade (over the tunnel of the Huldah-gates) to its eastern extremity, over which another tower rose, probably ' the pinnacle' of the history of the Temptation. From this height yawned the Kedron valley 450 feet beneath. From that lofty pinnacle the priest each morning watched and announced the earliest streak of day. Passing along the eastern colonnade, or Solomon's Porch, we would, if the description of the Rabbis is trustworthy, have reached the Susa Gate, the carved representation of that city over the gateway reminding us of the *Eastern* Dispersion. Here the standard measures of the Temple are said to have been kept; and here, also, we have to locate the first or lowest of the three Sanhedrins, which, according to the Mishnah,[b] held their meetings in the Temple; the second, or intermediate Court of Appeal, being in the ' Court of the Priests ' (probably close to the Nicanor Gate); and the highest, that of the Great Sanhedrin, at one time in the ' Hall of Hewn Square Stones ' *(Lishkath ha-Gazith.)*

Passing out of these ' colonnades,' or ' porches,' you entered the ' Court of the Gentiles,' or what the Rabbis called ' the Mount of the House,' which was widest on the west side. and more and more narrow respectively on the east, the south, and the north. This was called the *Chol*, or ' profane ' place to which Gentiles had access. Here must have been the market for the sale of sacrificial animals, the tables of the money-changers, and places for the sale of other needful articles.[c][3]

[a] *Jos.* War
vi. 3. 2

[b] Sanh. xi.2

[c] St. John
ii. 14; St.
Matt. xxi.
12; Jerus.
Chag. p. 78
a; comp.
Neh. xiii. 4
&c.

[1] So according to the Rabbis; Josephus does not mention it. In general, the account here given is according to the Rabbis.

[2] These tunnels were divided by colonnades respectively into three and into two, the double colonnade being probably used by the priests, since its place of exit was close to the entrance into the Court of the Priests.

[3] The question what was sold in this ' market ') and its relation to ' the bazaar' of the family of Annas (the *Chanuyoth beney Chanan*) will be discussed in a later part.

Advancing within this Court, you reached a low breast-wall (the *Soreg*), which marked the space beyond which no Gentile, nor Levitically unclean person, might proceed—tablets, bearing inscriptions to that effect, warning them off. Thirteen openings admitted into the inner part of the Court. Thence fourteen steps led up to the *Chel* or Terrace, which was bounded by the wall of the Temple-buildings in the stricter sense. A flight of steps led up to the massive, splendid gates. The two on the west side seem to have been of no importance, so far as the worshippers were concerned, and probably intended for the use of workmen. North and south were four gates.[1] But the most splendid gate was that to the east, termed 'the Beautiful.'[a]

Entering by the latter, you came into the Court of the Women, so called because the women occupied in it two elevated and separated galleries, which, however, filled only part of the Court. Fifteen steps led up to the Upper Court, which was bounded by a wall, and where was the celebrated Nicanor Gate, covered with Corinthian brass. Here the Levites, who conducted the musical part of the service, were placed. In the Court of the Women were the Treasury and the thirteen 'Trumpets,' while at each corner were chambers or halls, destined for various purposes. Similarly, beyond the fifteen steps, there were repositories for the musical instruments. The Upper Court was divided into two parts by a boundary—the narrow part forming the Court of Israel, and the wider that of the Priests, in which were the great Altar and the Laver.

The Sanctuary itself was on a higher terrace than the Court of the Priests. Twelve steps led up to its Porch, which extended beyond it on either side (north and south). Here, in separate chambers, all that was necessary for the sacrificial service was kept. On two marble tables near the entrance the old shewbread which was taken out, and the new that was brought in, were respectively placed. The Porch was adorned by votive presents, conspicuous among them a massive golden vine. A two-leaved gate opened into the Sanctuary itself, which was divided into two parts. The *Holy Place* had the Golden Candlestick (south), the Table of Shewbread (north), and the Golden Altar of Incense between them. A heavy double veil concealed the entrance to the *Most Holy Place*, which in the second

---

[1] The question as to their names and arrangement is not without difficulty. The subject is fully treated in 'The Temple and its Services.' Although I have followed in the text the arrangements of the Rabbis, I must express my grave doubts as to their historical trustworthiness. It seems to me that the Rabbis always give rather the *ideal* than the *real*—what, according to their theory, should have been, rather than what actually was.

Temple was empty, nothing being there but the piece of rock, called the *Ebhen Shethiyah*, or Foundation Stone, which, according to tradition, covered the mouth of the pit, and on which, it was thought, the world was founded. Nor does all this convey an adequate idea of the vastness of the Temple-buildings. For all around the Sanctuary and each of the Courts were various chambers and out-buildings, which served different purposes connected with the Services of the Temple.[1]

In some part of this Temple, 'sitting in the midst of the Doctors,[2] both hearing them and asking them questions,' we must look for the Child Jesus on the third and the two following days of the Feast on which He first visited the Sanctuary. Only on the two first days of the Feast of Passover was personal attendance in the Temple necessary. With the third day commenced the so-called half-holydays, when it was lawful to return to one's home[a]—a provision of which, no doubt, many availed themselves. Indeed, there was really nothing of special interest to detain the pilgrims. For, the Passover had been eaten, the festive sacrifice (or *Chagigah*) offered, and the first ripe barley reaped and brought to the Temple, and waved as the Omer of first flour before the Lord. Hence, in view of the well-known Rabbinic provision, the expression in the Gospel-narrative concerning the 'Parents' of Jesus, 'when they had fulfilled the days,'[b] cannot necessarily imply that Joseph and the Mother of Jesus had remained in Jerusalem during the whole Paschal week.[3] On the other hand, the circumstances connected with the presence of Jesus in the Temple render this supposition impossible. For, Jesus could not have been found among the Doctors after the close of the Feast. The first question here is as to the locality in the Temple, where the scene has to be laid. It has, indeed, been commonly supposed that there was a Synagogue in the Temple; but of this there is, to say the least, no historical evidence. But even if such had existed, the worship and addresses of the Synagogue would not have offered any opportunity for the questioning on the part of Jesus which the narrative implies. Still more groundless is the idea that there was in the Temple something like a *Beth ha-*

a So according to the Rabbis generally. Comp. *Hoffmann, Abh.* ii. d. pent. Ges. pp. 65, 66

b St. Luke ii. 43

---

[1] For a full description, I must refer to 'The Temple, its Ministry and Services at the time of Jesus Christ.' Some repetition of what had been alluded to in previous chapters has been unavoidable in the present description of the Temple.

[2] Although comparatively few really great authorities in Jewish Canon Law lived at that time, more than a dozen names could be given of Rabbis celebrated in Jewish literature, who must have been His contemporaries at one or another period of His life.

[3] In fact, an attentive consideration of what in the tractate Moed K. (comp. also Chag. 17 *b*), is declared to be lawful occupation during the half-holydays, leads us to infer that a very large proportion must have returned to their homes.

[4] For a full discussion of this important question, see Appendix X.: 'The Supposed Temple-Synagogue.'

Midrash, or theological Academy, not to speak of the circumstance that a child of twelve would not, at any time, have been allowed to take part in its discussions. But there were occasions on which the Temple became virtually, though not formally, a *Beth ha-Midrash.* For we read in the Talmud,[a] that the members of the Temple-Sanhedrin, who on ordinary days sat as a Court of Appeal, from the close of the Morning- to the time of the Evening-Sacrifice, were wont on Sabbaths and *feast-days* to come out upon 'the Terrace' of the Temple, and there to teach. In such popular instruction the utmost latitude of questioning would be given. It is in this audience, which sat on the ground, surrounding and mingling with the Doctors—and hence *during,* not *after* the Feast—that we must seek the Child Jesus.

But we have yet to show that the presence and questioning of a Child of that age did not necessarily imply anything so extraordinary, as to convey the idea of supernaturalness to those Doctors or others in the audience. Jewish tradition gives other instances of precocious and strangely advanced students. Besides, scientific theological learning would not be necessary to take part in such popular discussions. If we may judge from later arrangements, not only in Babylon, but in Palestine, there were two kinds of public lectures, and two kinds of students. The first, or more scientific class, was designated *Kallah* (literally, bride), and its attendants *Beney-Kallah* (children of the bride). These lectures were delivered in the last month of summer (Elul), before the Feast of the New Year, and in the last winter month (Adar), immediately before the Feast of Passover. They implied considerable preparation on the part of the lecturing Rabbis, and at least some Talmudic knowledge on the part of the attendants. On the other hand, there were Students of the Court (*Chatsatsta,* and in Babylon *Tarbitsa*), who during ordinary lectures sat separated from the regular students by a kind of hedge, outside, as it were in the Court, some of whom seem to have been ignorant even of the Bible. The lectures addressed to such a general audience would, of course, be of a very different character.[b]

But if there was nothing so unprecedented as to render His Presence and questioning marvellous, yet all who heard Him 'were amazed' at His 'combinative insight'[1] and 'discerning answers.'[2]

CHAP.
X

[a] Sanh. 88 *b*

[b] Comp.Jer.
Ber. iv. p. 7
d, and other
passages

---

[1] The expression σύνεσις means originally *concursus,* and (as *Schleusner* rightly puts it) *intelligentia* in the sense of perspicacia qua res probe cognitæ subtiliter ac diligenter a se invicem discernuntur. The LXX. render by it no less than eight different Hebrew terms.

[2] The primary meaning of the verb, from which the word is derived, is *secerno, discerno.*

BOOK
II

ᵃ Jer. Pes.
vi. 1; Pes.
66 a

ᵇ St. Matt.
xxii. 42-45

ᶜ Jos. Ant.
xv. 8. 5
ᵈ Maas. Sh.
v. 2

We scarcely venture to inquire towards what His questioning had been directed. Judging by what we know of such discussions, we infer that they may have been connected with the Paschal solemnities. Grave Paschal questions *did* arise. Indeed, the great Hillel obtained his rank as chief when he proved to the assembled Doctors that the Passover might be offered even on the Sabbath.ᵃ Many other questions might arise on the subject of the Passover. Or did the Child Jesus—as afterwards, in connection with the Messianic teaching ᵇ—lead up by His questions to the deeper meaning of the Paschal solemnities, as it was to be unfolded, when Himself was offered up, 'the Lamb of God, Which taketh away the sin of the world'?

Other questions also almost force themselves on the mind—most notably this: whether on the occasion of this His first visit to the Temple, the Virgin-Mother had told her Son the history of His Infancy, and of what had happened when, for the first time, He had been brought to the Temple. It would almost seem so, if we might judge from the contrast between the Virgin-Mother's complaint about the search of His father and of her, and His own emphatic appeal to the business of His Father. But most surprising—truly wonderful it must have seemed to Joseph, and even to the Mother of Jesus, that the meek, quiet Child should have been found in such company, and so engaged. It must have been quite other than what, from His past, they would have expected; or they would not have taken it for granted, when they left Jerusalem, that He was among their kinsfolk and acquaintance, perhaps mingling with the children. Nor yet would they, in such case, after they missed Him at the first night's halt—at Sichem,ᶜ if the direct road north, through Samaria,¹ was taken (or, according to the Mishnah, at Akrabah ᵈ)—have so anxiously sought Him by the way,² and in Jerusalem; nor yet would they have been 'amazed' when they found Him in the assembly of the Doctors. The reply of Jesus to the half-reproachful, half-relieved expostulation of them who had sought Him 'sorrowing' these three days,³ sets clearly these three things before us. He had been so entirely absorbed by the awakening thought of His Being and Mission, however kindled, as to be not only neglectful, but forgetful of all around. Nay, it even seemed to Him impossible to understand how they could have sought Him, and not known where He

---

¹ According to Jer. Ab. Z. 44 *d*, the soil, the fountains, the houses, and the roads of Samaria were 'clean.'

² This is implied in the use of the present participle.

³ The first day would be that of missing Him, the second that of the return, and the third that of the search in Jerusalem.

had lingered. *Secondly*: we may venture to say, that He now realised that this was emphatically *His* Father's House. And, *thirdly*: so far as we can judge, it was then and there that, for the first time, He felt the strong and irresistible impulse—that Divine necessity of His Being—to be 'about His Father's business.'[1] We all, when first awakening to spiritual consciousness—or, perhaps, when for the first time taking part in the feast of the Lord's House —may, and, learning from His example, should, make this the hour of decision, in which heart and life shall be wholly consecrated to the 'business' of our Father. But there was far more than this in the bearing of Christ on this occasion. That forgetfulness of His Child-life was a sacrifice—a sacrifice of self; that entire absorption in His Father's business, without a thought of self, either in the gratification of curiosity, the acquisition of knowledge, or personal ambition—a consecration of Himself unto God. It was the first manifestation of His passive and active obedience to the Will of God. Even at this stage, it was the forth-bursting of the inmost meaning of His Life: 'My meat is to do the Will of Him that sent Me, and to finish His work.' And yet this awakening of the Christ-consciousness on His first visit to the Temple, partial, and perhaps even temporary, as it may have been, seems itself like the morning-dawn, which from the pinnacle of the Temple the Priest watched, ere he summoned his waiting brethren beneath to offer the early sacrifice.

From what we have already learned of this History, we do not wonder that the answer of Jesus came to His parents as a fresh surprise. For, we can only understand what we perceive in its totality. But here each fresh manifestation came as something separate and new—not as part of a whole; and therefore as a surprise, of which the purport and meaning could not be understood, except in its organic connection and as a whole. And for the true human development of the God-Man, what was the natural was also the needful process, even as it was best for the learning of Mary herself, and for the future reception of His teaching. These three

---

[1] The expression ἐν τοῖς τοῦ πατρός μου may be equally rendered, or rather supplemented, by 'in My Father's house,' and 'about My Father's business.' The former is adopted by most modern commentators. But (1) it does not accord with the word that must be supplemented in the two analogous passages in the LXX. Neither in Esth. vii. 9, nor in Ecclus. xlii. 10, is it strictly 'the *house*.'

(2) It seems unaccountable how the word 'house' could have been left out in the Greek rendering of the Aramæan words of Christ—but quite natural, if the word to be supplemented was 'things' or 'business.' (3) A reference to the Temple as His Father's *house* could not have seemed so strange on the lips of Jesus—nor, indeed, of any Jewish child—as to fill Joseph and Mary with astonishment.

subsidiary reasons may once more be indicated here in explanation of the Virgin-Mother's seeming ignorance of her Son's true character: the necessary gradualness of such a revelation; the necessary development of His own consciousness; and the fact, that Jesus could not have been subject to His Parents, nor had true and proper human training, if they had clearly known that He was the essential Son of God.

A further, though to us it seems a downward step, was His quiet, immediate, unquestioning return to Nazareth with His Parents, and His willing submission[1] to them while there. It was self-denial, self-sacrifice, self-consecration to His Mission, with all that it implied. It was not self-exinanition but self-submission, all the more glorious in proportion to the greatness of that *Self*. This constant contrast before her eyes only deepened in the heart of Mary the ever-present impression of ' all those matters,'[2] of which she was the most cognisant. She was learning to spell out the word Messiah, as each of ' those matters ' taught her one fresh letter in it, and she looked at them all in the light of the Nazareth-Sun.

With His return to Nazareth began Jesus' Life of youth and early manhood, with all of inward and outward development, of heavenly and earthly approbation which it carried.[a] Whether or not He went to Jerusalem on recurring Feasts, we know not, and need not inquire. For only once during that period—on His first visit to the Temple, and in the awakening of His Youth-Life— could there have been such outward forth-bursting of His real Being and Mission. Other influences were at their silent work to weld His inward and outward development, and to determine the manner of His later Manifesting of Himself. We assume that the School-education of Jesus must have ceased soon after His return to Nazareth. Henceforth the Nazareth-influences on the Life and Thinking of Jesus may be grouped—and progressively as He advanced from youth to manhood—under these particulars: *Home*, *Nature*, and *Prevailing Ideas*.

1. *Home*. Jewish Home-Life, especially in the country, was of the simplest. Even in luxurious Alexandria it seems often to have been such, alike as regarded the furnishing of the house, and the provisions of the table.[3] The morning and midday meal must have been of the plainest, and even the larger evening meal of the

---

[1] The voluntariness of His submission is implied by the present part. mid. of the verb.

[2] The Authorised Version renders 'sayings.' But I think the expression is clearly equivalent to the Hebrew כָּל־הַדְּבָרִים= all these things. St. Luke uses the word דבר in that sense in i. 65; ii. 15, 19, 51; Acts v. 32; x. 37; xiii. 42.

[3] Comp. Philo in Flacc.ed. Fcf. p.977 &c.

simplest, in the home at Nazareth. Only the Sabbath and festivals, whether ·domestic or public, brought what of the best lay within reach. But Nazareth was not the city of the wealthy or influential, and such festive evening-entertainments, with elaborate ceremoniousness of reception, arranging of guests according to rank, and rich spread of board, would but rarely, if ever, be witnessed in those quiet homes. The same simplicity would prevail in dress and manners.[1] But close and loving were the bonds which drew together the members of a family, and deep the influence which they exercised on each other. We cannot here discuss the vexed question whether 'the brothers and sisters' of Jesus were such in the real sense, or step-brothers and sisters, or else cousins, though it seems to us as if the primary meaning of the terms would scarcely have been called in question, but for a theory of false asceticism, and an undervaluing of the sanctity of the married estate.[a] But, whatever the precise relationship between Jesus and these 'brothers and sisters,' it must, on any theory, have been of the closest, and exercised its influence upon Him.[2]

Passing over Joses or Joseph, of whose history we know next to nothing, we have sufficient materials to enable us to form some judgment of what must have been the tendencies and thoughts of two of His brothers *James* and *Jude*, before they were heart and soul followers of the Messiah, and of His cousin *Simon*.[3] If we might venture on a general characterisation, we would infer from the Epistle of St. James, that his religious views had originally been cast in the mould of *Shammai*. Certainly, there is nothing of the Hillelite direction about it, but all to remind us of the earnestness, directness, vigour, and rigour of Shammai. Of *Simon* we know that he had belonged to the Nationalist party, since he is expressly so designated (*Zelotes*,[b] *Canancean*).[c] Lastly, there are in the Epistle of St. Jude, one undoubted, and another probable reference to two of those (Pseudepigraphic) Apocalyptic books, which at that time marked one deeply interesting phase of the Messianic outlook of Israel.[d] We have thus within the narrow circle of Christ's Family-Life—not to speak of any intercourse with the sons of Zebedee, who probably were also His cousins[4]—the three most

[a] Comp. St. Matt. i. 24; St. Luke ii. 7; St. Matt. xii. 46; xiii. 55, 56; St. Mark iii. 31; vi. 3; Acts i. 14; 1 Cor. ix. 5; Gal. i 19

[b] St. Luke vi. 15; Acts i. 13

[c] St. Mark iii. 18

[d] St. Jude xv. 14, 15 to the book of Enoch, and v. 9 probably to the Assum. of Moses

---

[1] For details as to dress, food, and manners in Palestine, I must refer to other parts of this book.

[2] The question of the real relationship of Christ to His 'brothers' has been so often discussed in the various Cyclopædias that it seems unnecessary here to enter upon the matter in detail. See also *Dr. Lightfoot's* Dissertation in his Comment. on Galat. pp. 282–291.

[3] I regard this Simon (Zelotes) as the son of Clopas (brother of Joseph, the Virgin's husband) and of Mary. For the reasons of this view, see Book III. ch. xvii. and Book V. ch. xv.

[4] On the maternal side. We read St. John xix. 25 as indicating four women— His Mother's sister being Salome, according to St. Mark xv. 40.

BOOK
II

hopeful and pure Jewish tendencies, brought into constant contact with Jesus: in Pharisaism, the teaching of Shammai; then, the Nationalist ideal; and, finally, the hope of a glorious Messianic future. To these there should probably be added, at least knowledge of the lonely preparation of His kinsman John, who, though certainly *not* an Essene, had, from the necessity of his calling, much in his outward bearing that was akin to them.

But we are anticipating. From what are, necessarily, only suggestions, we turn again to what is certain in connection with His Family-Life and its influences. From St. Mark vi. 3, we may infer with great probability, though not with absolute certainty,[a] that He had adopted the trade of Joseph. Among the Jews the contempt for manual labour, which was one of the painful characteristics of heathenism, did not exist. On the contrary, it was deemed a religious duty, frequently and most earnestly insisted upon, to learn some trade, provided it did not minister to luxury, nor tend to lead away from personal observance of the Law.[b] There was not such separation between rich and poor as with us, and while wealth might confer social distinction, the absence of it in no way implied social inferiority. Nor could it be otherwise where wants were so few, life was so simple, and its highest aim so ever present to the mind.

We have already spoken of the religious influences in the family, so blessedly different from that neglect, exposure, and even murder of children among the heathen, or their education by slaves, who corrupted the mind from its earliest opening.[2] The love of parents to children, appearing even in the curse which was felt to attach to childlessness; the reverence towards parents, as a duty higher than any of outward observance; and the love of brethren, which Jesus had learned in His home, form, so to speak, the natural basis of many of the teachings of Jesus. They give us also an insight into the family-life of Nazareth. And yet there is nothing sombre nor morose about it; and even the joyous games of children, as well as festive gatherings of families, find their record in the words and the life of Christ. This also is characteristic of His past. And so are His deep sympathy with all sorrow and suffering, and His love for the family circle, as evidenced in the home of Lazarus. That He spoke Hebrew, and used

[a] Comp.
St. Matt.
xiii. 55;
St. John vi.
42

[b] Comp.
Ab. i. 10;
Kidd. 29 b1

---

[1] See the chapter on 'Trades and Tradesmen,' in the 'Sketches of Jewish Social Life.'

[2] Comp. this subject in *Döllinger*, 'Heidenthum u. Judenthum,' in regard to the Greeks, p. 692; in regard to the Romans, pp. 716-722: in regard to education and its abominations, pp. 723-726. Nothing can cast a more lurid light on the need for Christianity, if the world was not to perish of utter rottenness, than a study of ancient Hellas and Rome, as presented by Döllinger in his admirable work.

and quoted the Scriptures in the original, has already been shown,
although, no doubt, He understood Greek, possibly also Latin.

Secondly: Nature and Every-day Life. The most superficial
perusal of the teaching of Christ must convince how deeply sympathetic
He was with nature, and how keenly observant of man. Here there
is no contrast between love of the country and the habits of city life;
the two are found side by side. On His lonely walks He must have
had an eye for the beauty of the lilies of the field, and thought of it,
how the birds of the air received their food from an Unseen Hand,
and with what maternal affection the hen gathered her chickens
under her wing. He had watched the sower or the vinedresser as he
went forth to his labour, and read the teaching of the tares which
sprang up among the wheat. To Him the vocation of the shepherd
must have been full of meaning, as he led, and fed, and watched his
flock, spoke to his sheep with well-known voice, brought them to the
fold, or followed, and tenderly carried back, those that had strayed,
ever ready to defend them, even at the cost of his own life. Nay, He
even seems to have watched the habits of the fox in its secret lair.
But he also equally knew the joys, the sorrows, the wants and
sufferings of the busy multitude. The play in the market, the
marriage processions, the funeral rites, the wrongs of injustice and
oppression, the urgent harshness of the creditor, the bonds and
prison of the debtor, the palaces and luxury of princes and courtiers,
the self-indulgence of the rich, the avarice of the covetous, the
exactions of the tax-gatherer, and the oppression of the widow by
unjust judges, had all made an indelible impression on His mind.
And yet this evil world was not one which He hated, and from which
He would withdraw Himself with His disciples, though ever and
again He felt the need of periods of meditation and prayer. On the
contrary, while He confronted all the evil in it, He would fain pervade
the mass with the new leaven; not cast it away, but renew it. He
recognised the good and the hopeful, even in those who seemed most
lost. He quenched not the dimly burning flax, nor brake the
bruised reed. It was not contempt of the world, but sadness over
it; not condemnation of man, but drawing him to His Heavenly
Father; not despising of the little and the poor, whether ontwardly or
inwardly such, but encouragement and adoption of them—together
with keen insight into the real under the mask of the apparent, and
withering denunciation and unsparing exposure of all that was evil,
mean, and unreal, wherever it might appear. Such were some of the
results gathered from His past life, as presented in His teaching.

Thirdly: Of the *prevailing ideas* around, with which He was brought in contact, some have already been mentioned. Surely, the earnestness of His Shammaite brother, if such we may venture to designate him; the idea of the Kingdom suggested by the Nationalists, only in its purest and most spiritual form, as not of this world, and as truly realising the sovereignty of God in the individual, who-ever he might be; even the dreamy thoughts of the prophetic litera-ture of those times, which sought to read the mysteries of the coming Kingdom; as well as the prophet-like asceticism of His forerunner and kinsman, formed at least so many points of contact for His teaching. Thus, Christ was in sympathy with all the highest ten-dencies of His people and time. Above all, there was His intimate converse with the Scriptures of the Old Testament. If, in the Syna-gogue, He saw much to show the hollowness, self-seeking, pride, and literalism which a mere external observance of the Law fostered, He would ever turn from what man or devils said to what He read, to what was 'written.' Not one dot or hook of it could fall to the ground—all must be established and fulfilled. The Law of Moses in all its bearings, the utterances of the prophets—Isaiah, Jeremiah, Ezekiel, Daniel, Hosea, Micah, Zechariah, Malachi—and the hopes and consolations of the Psalms, were all to Him literally true, and cast their light upon the building which Moses had reared. It was all one, a grand unity; not an aggregation of different parts, but the unfolding of a living organism. Chiefest of all, it was the thought of the Messianic bearing of all Scripture to its unity, the idea of the King-dom of God and the King of Zion, which was the life and light of all. Beyond this, into the mystery of His inner converse with God, the unfolding of His spiritual receptiveness, and the increasing communication from above, we dare not enter. Even what His bodily appearance may have been, we scarcely venture to imagine.[1] It could not but be that His outer man in some measure bodied forth His 'Inner Being.' Yet we dread gathering around our thoughts of Him the artificial flowers of legend.[2] What His manner and mode of re-ceiving and dealing with men were, we can portray to ourselves from His life. And so it is best to remain content with the simple account of the Evangelic narrative: 'Jesus increased in favour with God and Man.'

---

[1] Even the poetic conception of the painter can only furnish his own ideal, and that of one special mood. Speaking as one who has no claim to knowledge of art, only one picture of Christ ever really impressed me. It was that of an 'Ecce Homo,' by Carlo Dolci, in the Pitti Gal-lery at Florence. For an account of the early pictorial representations, comp.

Gieseler. Kirchengesch. i. pp. 85, 86.
[2] Of these there are, alas! only too many. The reader interested in the matter will find a good summary in *Keim*, i. 2, pp. 460–463. One of the few note-worthy remarks recorded is this descrip-tion of Christ, in the spurious Epistle of *Lentulus*. 'Who was never seen to laugh, but often to weep.'

CHAPTER XI.

IN THE FIFTEENTH YEAR OF TIBERIUS CÆSAR AND UNDER THE PONTIFI-CATE OF ANNAS AND CAIAPHAS—A VOICE IN THE WILDERNESS.

(St. Matthew iii. 1–12; St. Mark i. 2–8; St. Luke iii. 1–18.)

THERE is something grand, even awful, in the almost absolute silence which lies upon the thirty years between the Birth and the first Messianic Manifestation of Jesus. In a narrative like that of the Gospels, this must have been designed; and, if so, affords presumptive evidence of the authenticity of what follows, and is intended to teach, that what had preceded concerned only the inner History of Jesus, and the preparation of the Christ. At last that solemn silence was broken by an appearance, a proclamation, a rite, and a ministry as startling as that of Elijah had been. In many respects, indeed, the two messengers and their times bore singular likeness. It was to a society secure, prosperous, and luxurious, yet in imminent danger of perishing from hidden, festering disease; and to a religious community which presented the appearance of hopeless perversion, and yet contained the germs of a possible regeneration, that both Elijah and John the Baptist came. Both suddenly appeared to threaten terrible judgment, but also to open unthought-of possibilities of good. And, as if to deepen still more the impression of this contrast, both appeared in a manner unexpected, and even antithetic to the habits of their contemporaries. John came suddenly out of the wilderness of Judæa, as Elijah from the wilds of Gilead; John bore the same strange ascetic appearance as his predecessor; the message of John was the counterpart of that of Elijah; his baptism that of Elijah's novel rite on Mount Carmel. And, as if to make complete the parallelism, with all of memory and hope which it awakened, even the more minute details surrounding the life of Elijah found their counterpart in that of John. Yet history never repeats itself. It fulfils in its development that of which it gave indication at its commencement. Thus, the history of John the Baptist was the fulfilment of that of Elijah in 'the fulness of time.'

For, alike in the Roman world and in Palestine, the time had fully come; not, indeed, in the sense of any special expectancy, but of absolute need. The reign of Augustus marked, not only the climax, but the crisis, of Roman history. Whatever of good or of evil the ancient world contained, had become fully ripe. As regarded politics, philosophy, religion, and society, the utmost limits had been reached.[1] Beyond them lay, as only alternatives, ruin or regeneration. It was felt that the boundaries of the Empire could be no further extended, and that henceforth the highest aim must be to preserve what had been conquered. The destinies of Rome were in the hands of one man, who was at the same time general-in-chief of a standing army of about three hundred and forty thousand men, head of a Senate (now sunk into a mere court for registering the commands of Cæsar), and High-Priest of a religion, of which the highest expression was the apotheosis of the State in the person of the Emperor. Thus, all power within, without, and above lay in his hands. Within the city, which in one short reign was transformed from brick into marble, were, side by side, the most abject misery and almost boundless luxury. Of a population of about two millions, well-nigh one half were slaves; and, of the rest, the greater part either freedmen and their descendants, or foreigners. Each class contributed its share to the common decay. Slavery was not even what we know it, but a seething mass of cruelty and oppression on the one side, and of cunning and corruption on the other. More than any other cause, it contributed to the ruin of Roman society. The freedmen, who had very often acquired their liberty by the most disreputable courses, and had prospered in them, combined in shameless manner the vices of the free with the vileness of the slave. The foreigners—especially Greeks and Syrians—who crowded the city, poisoned the springs of its life by the corruption which they brought. The free citizens were idle, dissipated, sunken; their chief thoughts of the theatre and the arena; and they were mostly supported at the public cost. While, even in the time of Augustus, more than two hundred thousand persons were thus maintained by the State, what of the old Roman stock remained was rapidly decaying, partly from corruption, but chiefly from the increasing cessation of marriage, and the nameless abominations of what remained of family-life.

[1] Instead of detailed quotations I would here generally refer to works on Roman history, especially to *Friedländer's* Sittengeschichte Roms, and to *Döllinger's* exhaustive work, Heidenthum and Judenthum.

The state of the provinces was in every respect more favourable.
But it was the settled policy of the Empire, which only too surely
succeeded, to destroy all separate nationalities, or rather to absorb
and to Grecianise all.   The only real resistance came from the Jews.
Their tenacity was religious, and, even in its extreme of intolerant
exclusiveness, served a most important Providential purpose.   And
so Rome became to all the centre of attraction, but also of fast-spread-
ing destructive corruption.   Yet this unity also, and the common
bond of the Greek language, served another important Providential
purpose.   So did, in another direction, the conscious despair of any
possible internal reformation.   This, indeed, seemed the last word
of all the institutions in the Roman world: It is not in me!   Religion, philosophy, and society had passed through every stage, to that
of despair.   Without tracing the various phases of ancient thought,
it may be generally said that, in Rome at least, the issue lay between
Stoicism and Epicureanism.   The one flattered its pride, the other
gratified its sensuality; the one was in accordance with the
original national character, the other with its later decay and corruption.   Both ultimately led to atheism and despair—the one, by
turning all higher aspirations self-ward, the other, by quenching
them in the enjoyment of the moment; the one, by making the extinction of all feeling and self-deification, the other, the indulgence
of every passion and the worship of matter, its ideal.

That, under such conditions, all real belief in a personal con
tinuance after death must have ceased among the educated classes,
needs not demonstration.   If the older Stoics held that, after death,
the soul would continue for some time a separate existence—in the
case of sages till the general destruction of the world by fire, it was
the doctrine of most of their successors that, immediately after death,
the soul returned into 'the world-soul' of which it was part.   But
even this hope was beset by so many doubts and misgivings, as to
make it practically without influence or comfort.   Cicero was the
only one who, following Plato, defended the immortality of the soul,
while the Peripatetics denied the existence of a soul, and leading
Stoics at least its continuance after death.   But even Cicero writes
as one overwhelmed by doubts.   With his contemporaries this doubt
deepened into absolute despair, the only comfort lying in present
indulgence of the passions.   Even among the Greeks, who were most
tenacious of belief in the non-extinction of the individual, the practical upshot was the same.   The only healthier tendency, however
mixed with error, came from the Neo-Platonic School, which accord-

ingly offered a point of contact between ancient philosophy and the new faith.

In such circumstances, anything like real religion was manifestly impossible. Rome tolerated, and, indeed, incorporated,. all national rites. But among the populace religion had degenerated into abject superstition. In the East, much of it consisted of the vilest rites; while, among the philosophers, all religions were considered equally false or equally true—the outcome of ignorance, or else the unconscious modifications of some one fundamental thought. The only religion on which the State insisted was the deification and worship of the Emperor.[1] These apotheoses attained almost incredible development. Soon not only the Emperors, but their wives, paramours, children, and the creatures of their vilest lusts, were deified; nay, any private person might attain that distinction, if the survivors possessed sufficient means.[2] Mingled with all this was an increasing amount of superstition—by which term some understood the worship of foreign gods, the most part the existence of fear in religion. The ancient Roman religion had long given place to foreign rites, the more mysterious and unintelligible the more enticing. It was thus that Judaism made its converts in Rome; its chief recommendation with many being its contrast to the old, and the unknown possibilities which its seemingly incredible doctrines opened. Among the most repulsive symptoms of the general religious decay may be reckoned prayers for the death of a rich relative, or even for the satisfaction of unnatural lusts, along with horrible blasphemies when such prayers remained unanswered. We may here contrast the spirit of the Old and New Testaments with such sentiments as this, on the tomb of a child: 'To the unjust gods who robbed me of life;' or on that of a girl of twenty: 'I lift my hands against the god who took me away, innocent as I am. '

It would be unsavoury to describe how far the worship of in decency was carried; how public morals were corrupted by the mimic representations of everything that was vile, and even by the pandering of a corrupt art. The personation of gods, oracles, divination, dreams, astrology, magic, necromancy, and theurgy,[3] all

---

[1] The only thorough resistance to this worship came from hated Judæa, and, we may add, from Britain (*Döllinger*, p. 611).

[2] From the time of Cæsar to that of Diocletian, fifty-three such apotheoses took place, including those of fifteen women belonging to the Imperial families.

[3] One of the most painful, and to the Christian almost incredible, manifestations of religious decay was the unblushing manner in which the priests practised imposture upon the people. Numerous and terrible instances of this could be given. The evidence of this is not only

contributed to the general decay. It has been rightly said, that the idea of conscience, as we understand it, was unknown to heathenism. Absolute right did not exist. Might was right. The social relations exhibited, if possible, even deeper corruption. The sanctity of marriage had ceased. Female dissipation and the general dissoluteness led at last to an almost entire cessation of marriage. Abortion, and the exposure and murder of newly-born children, were common and tolerated; unnatural vices, which even the greatest philosophers practised, if not advocated, attained proportions which defy description.

But among these sad signs of the times three must be specially mentioned: the treatment of slaves; the bearing towards the poor; and public amusements. The slave was entirely unprotected; males and females were exposed to nameless cruelties, compared to which death by being thrown to the wild beasts, or fighting in the arena, might seem absolute relief. Sick or old slaves were cast out to perish from want. But what the influence of the slaves must have been on the free population, and especially upon the young—whose tutors they generally were—may readily be imagined. The heartlessness towards the poor who crowded the city is another well-known feature of ancient Roman society. Of course, there was neither hospitals, nor provision for the poor; charity and brotherly love in their every manifestation are purely Old and New Testament ideas. But even the bestowal of the smallest alms on the needy was regarded as very questionable; best, not to afford them the means of protracting a useless existence. Lastly, the account which Seneca has to give of what occupied and amused the idle multitude—for all manual labour, except agriculture, was looked upon with utmost contempt —horrified even himself. And so the only escape which remained for the philosopher, the satiated, or the miserable, seemed the power of self-destruction! What is worse, the noblest spirits of the time felt, that the state of things was utterly hopeless. Society could not reform itself; philosophy and religion had nothing to offer: they had been tried and found wanting. Seneca longed for some hand from without to lift up from the mire of despair; Cicero pictured the enthusiasm which would greet the embodiment of true virtue, should it ever appear on earth; Tacitus declared human life one

derived from the Fathers, but a work has been preserved in which formal instructions are given, how temples and altars are to be constructed in order to produce false miracles, and by what means impostures of this kind may be successfully practised. (Comp. 'The Pneumatics of Hero,' translated by *B. Woodcroft.*) The worst was, that this kind of imposture on the ignorant populace was openly approved by the educated. (*Döllinger*, p. 647.)

great farce, and expressed his conviction that the Roman world lay under some terrible curse. All around, despair, conscious need, and unconscious longing. Can greater contrast be imagined, than the proclamation of a coming Kingdom of God amid such a world; or clearer evidence be afforded of the reality of this Divine message, than that it came to seek and to save that which was thus lost? One synchronism, as remarkable as that of the Star in the East and the Birth of the Messiah, here claims the reverent attention of the student of history. On the 19th of December A.D. 69, the Roman Capitol, with its ancient sanctuaries, was set on fire. Eight months later, on the 9th of Ab A.D. 70, the Temple of Jerusalem was given to the flames. It is not a coincidence but a conjunction, for upon the ruins of heathenism and of apostate Judaism was the Church of Christ to be reared.

A silence, even more complete than that concerning the early life of Jesus, rests on the thirty years and more, which intervened between the birth and the open forthshowing[1] of John in his character as Forerunner of the Messiah. Only his outward and inward develop-
ment, and his being 'in the deserts,'[2] are briefly indicated.[a] The latter, assuredly, not in order to learn from the *Essenes*,[3] but to attain really, in lonely fellowship with God, what they sought extern-ally. It is characteristic that, while Jesus could go straight from the home and workshop of Nazareth to the Baptism of Jordan, His Forerunner required so long and peculiar preparation: characteristic of the difference of their Persons and Mission, characteristic also of the greatness of the work to be inaugurated. St. Luke furnishes precise notices of the time of the Baptist's public appearance—not merely to fix the exact chronology, which would not have required so many details, but for a higher purpose. For, they indicate, more clearly than the most elaborate discussion, the fitness of the moment for the Advent of 'the Kingdom of Heaven.' For the first time since the Babylonish Captivity, the foreigner, the Chief of the hated Roman Empire—according to the Rabbis, the fourth beast of Daniel's vision[b]—was absolute and undisputed master of Judæa; and the

[a] St. Luke i. 80

[b] Ab.Zar.2b

---

[1] This seems the full meaning of the word, St. Luke i. 80. Comp. Acts i. 24 (in the A.V. 'shew ').

[2] The plural indicates that St. John was not always in the same 'wilder-ness.' The plural form in regard to the 'wildernesses which are in the land of Israel,' is common in Rabbinic writings (comp. Baba K. vii. 7 and the Gemaras

on the passage). On the fulfilment by the Baptist of Is. xl. 3, see the discussion of that passage in Appendix XI.

[3] *Godet* has, in a few forcible sentences, traced what may be called not merely the difference, but the contrast between the teaching and aims of the Essenes and those of John.

chief religious office divided between two, equally unworthy of its
functions. And it deserves, at least, notice, that of the Rulers
mentioned by St. Luke, Pilate entered on his office[a] only shortly
before the public appearance of John, and that they all continued
till after the Crucifixion of Christ. There was thus, so to speak, a
continuity of these powers during the whole Messianic period.

As regards Palestine, the ancient kingdom of Herod was now
divided into four parts, Judæa being under the direct administration
of Rome, two other tetrarchies under the rule of Herod's sons (Herod
Antipas and Philip), while the small principality of Abilene was
governed by Lysanias.[1] Of the latter no details can be furnished,
nor are they necessary in this history. It is otherwise as regards the
sons of Herod, and especially the character of the Roman government
at that time.

Herod Antipas, whose rule extended over forty-three years,
reigned over Galilee and Peræa—the districts which were respectively the principal sphere of the Ministry of Jesus and of John the
Baptist. Like his brother Archelaus, Herod Antipas possessed in an
even aggravated form most of the vices, without any of the greater
qualities, of his father. Of deeper religious feelings or convictions
he was entirely destitute, though his conscience occasionally misgave,
if it did not restrain, him. The inherent weakness of his character
left him in the absolute control of his wife, to the final ruin of his fortunes. He was covetous, avaricious, luxurious, and utterly dissipated;
suspicious, and with a good deal of that fox-cunning which, especially
in the East, often forms the sum total of state-craft. Like his father,
he indulged a taste for building—always taking care to propitiate
Rome by dedicating all to the Emperor. The most extensive of his
undertakings was the building, in 22 A.D., of the city of Tiberias, at
the upper end of the Lake of Galilee. The site was under the
disadvantage of having formerly been a burying-place, which, as
implying Levitical uncleanness, for some time deterred pious Jews
from settling there. Nevertheless, it rose in great magnificence from
among the reeds which had but lately covered the neighbourhood
(the ensigns armorial of the city were 'reeds'). Herod Antipas made
it his residence, and built there a strong castle and a palace of

---

[1] Till quite lately, those who impugn
the veracity of the Gospels—*Strauss*, and
even *Keim*—have pointed to this notice
of Lysanias as an instance of the unhistorical character of St. Luke's Gospel.
But it is now admitted on all hands that
the notice of St. Luke is strictly correct;
and that, besides the other Lysanias, one
of the same name had reigned over
Abilene at the time of Christ. Comp.
Wieseler, Beitr. pp.196–204, and *Schürer*
in *Riehm's* Handwörterb, p. 931.

unrivalled splendour. The city, which was peopled chiefly by adventurers, was mainly Grecian, and adorned with an amphitheatre, of which the ruins can still be traced.

A happier account can be given of Philip, the son of Herod the Great and Cleopatra of Jerusalem. He was undoubtedly the best of Herod's sons. He showed, indeed, the same abject submission as the rest of his family to the Roman Emperor, after whom he named the city of Cæsarea Philippi, which he built at the sources of the Jordan; just as he changed the name of Bethsaida, a village of which he made an opulent city, into Julias, after the daughter of Augustus. But he was a moderate and just ruler, and his reign of thirty-seven years contrasted favourably with that of his kinsmen. The land was quiet and prosperous, and the people contented and happy.

As regards the Roman rule, matters had greatly changed for the worse since the mild sway of Augustus, under which, in the language of Philo, no one throughout the Empire dared to molest the Jews.[a] The only innovations to which Israel had then to submit were, the daily sacrifices for the Emperor and the Roman people, offerings on festive days, prayers for them in the Synagogues, and such participation in national joy or sorrow as their religion allowed.[b]

It was far other when Tiberius succeeded to the Empire, and Judæa was a province. Merciless harshness characterised the administration of Palestine; while the Emperor himself was bitterly hostile to Judaism and the Jews, and that although, personally, openly careless of all religion.[c] Under his reign the persecution of the Roman Jews occurred, and Palestine suffered almost to the verge of endurance. The first Procurator whom Tiberius appointed over Judæa, changed the occupancy of the High-Priesthood four times, till he found in Caiaphas a sufficiently submissive instrument of Roman tyranny. The exactions, and the reckless disregard of all Jewish feelings and interests, might have been characterised as reaching the extreme limit, if worse had not followed when Pontius Pilate succeeded to the procuratorship. Venality, violence, robbery, persecutions, wanton malicious insults, judicial murders without even the formality of a legal process, and cruelty—such are the charges brought against his administration.[d] If former governors had, to some extent, respected the religious scruples of the Jews, Pilate set them purposely at defiance; and this not only once, but again and again, in Jerusalem,[e] in Galilee,[f] and even in Samaria,[g] until the Emperor himself interposed.[h]

Such, then, was the political condition of the land, when John

a *Philo*,
ed. Frcf.,
Leg. 1015

b u. s. 1031,
1041

c *Suet.* Tiber.
69

d *Philo*, u.s.
1034

e *Jos.* Ant.
xviii. 3. 1, 2

f St. Luke
xiii. 1

g Ant. xviii.
4. 1, 2.

h *Philo*,Leg.
1033

appeared to preach the near Advent of a Kingdom with which
Israel associated all that was happy and glorious, even beyond the
dreams of the religious enthusiast. And equally loud was the call
for help in reference to those who held chief spiritual rule over the
people. St. Luke significantly joins together, as the highest religious
authority in the land, the names of Annas and Caiaphas.[1] The
former had been appointed by Quirinius. After holding the Pontificate for nine years, he was deposed, and succeeded by others, of
whom the fourth was his son-in-law Caiaphas. The character of the
High-Priests during the whole of that period is described in the
Talmud[a] in terrible language. And although there is no evidence
that 'the house of Annas'[2] was guilty of the same gross self-
indulgence, violence,[b] luxury, and even public indecency,[c] as some of
their successors, they are included in the woes pronounced on the
corrupt leaders of the priesthood, whom the Sanctuary is represented
as bidding depart from the sacred precincts, which their presence
defiled.[d] It deserves notice, that the special sin with which the
house of Annas is charged is that of 'whispering'—or hissing like
vipers—which seems to refer[3] to private influence on the judges
in their administration of justice, whereby 'morals were corrupted,
judgment perverted, and the Shekhinah withdrawn from Israel.'[e]
In illustration of this, we recall the terrorism which prevented Sanhedrists from taking the part of Jesus,[f] and especially the violence
which seems to have determined the final action of the Sanhedrin,[g]
against which not only such men as Nicodemus and Joseph of Arimathæa, but even a Gamaliel, would feel themselves powerless. But
although the expression 'High-Priest' appears sometimes to have
been used in a general sense, as designating the sons of the High-
Priests, and even the principal members of their families,[h] there could,

CHAP.
XI

[a] Pes. 57 a

[b] Jos. Ant.
xx. 8. 8
[c] Yoma 35 b

[d] Pes. u.s.

[e] Tos. Set.
xiv.

[f] St. John
vii. 50–52
[g] St. John
xi. 47–50

[h] Jos. Jewish
War vi. 2.2

---

[1] The Procurators were Imperial financial officers, with absolute power of
government in smaller territories. The
office was generally in the hands of the
Roman knights, which chiefly consisted
of financial men, bankers, chief publicans, &c. The order of knighthood had
sunk to a low state, and the exactions of
such a rule, especially in Judæa, can better be imagined than described. Comp.
on the whole subject, *Friedländer*, Sit-
tengesch. Rom, vol. i. p. 268 &c.

[2] Annas, either *Chanan* (חנן), or else
Chana or *Channa*, a common name. Professor *Delitzsch* has rightly shown that
the Hebrew equivalent for Caiaphas is
not *Keypha* (כיפא) =Peter, but *Kayapha*

(קיפא), or perhaps rather—according to
the reading Καϊφᾶς—קיפה, Kaipha, or
Kaiphah. The name occurs in the Mishnah
as *Kayaph* [so, and not *Kuph*, correctly]
(Parah iii. 5). Professor *Delitzsch* does
not venture to explain its meaning.
Would it be too bold to suggest a derivation from קף, and the meaning to be:
He who is 'at the top'?
[3] If we may take a statement in the
Talmud, where the same word occurs, as
a commentary.
[4] I do not, however, feel sure that the
word 'high-priests' in this passage should
be closely pressed. It is just one of those
instances in which it would suit Josephus

BOOK
II

ᵃ St. John
xi. 49
ᵇ St. John
xviii. 13

779 A.U.C.

ᵈ St. Luke
iii. 3
ᵉ St. John i.
28

ᶠ 2 Kings i.
8

of course, be only one actual High-Priest. The conjunction of the two names of Annas and Caiaphas[1] probably indicates that, although Annas was deprived of the Pontificate, he still continued to preside over the Sanhedrin—a conclusion not only borne out by Acts iv. 6, where Annas appears as the actual President, and by the terms in which Caiaphas is spoken of, as merely ' one of them,'ᵃ but by the part which Annas took in the final condemnation of Jesus.ᵇ

Such a combination of political and religious distress, surely, constituted the time of Israel's utmost need. As yet, no attempt had been made by the people to right themselves by armed force. In these circumstances, the cry that the Kingdom of Heaven was near at hand, and the call to preparation for it, must have awakened echoes throughout the land, and startled the most careless and unbelieving. It was, according to St. Luke's exact statement, in the fifteenth year of the reign of Tiberius Cæsar—reckoning, as provincials would do,[2] from his co-regency with Augustus (which commenced two years before his sole reign), in the year 26 A.D.ᶜ According to our former computation, Jesus would then be in His thirtieth year.[3] The scene of John's first public appearance was in 'the wilderness of Judæa,' that is, the wild, desolate district around the mouth of the Jordan. We know not whether John baptized in this place,[4] nor yet how long he continued there; but we are expressly told, that his stay was not confined to that locality.ᵈ Soon afterwards we find him at Bethabara,ᵉ which is farther up the stream. The outward appearance and the habits of the Messenger corresponded to the character and object of his Mission. Neither his dress nor his food was that of the Essenes;[5] and the former, at least, like that of Elijah,ᶠ whose mission he was now to ' fulfil.'

to give such a grandiose title to those who joined the Romans.

[1] This only in St. Luke.

[2] *Wieseler* has, I think, satisfactorily established this. Comp. Beitr. pp. 191–194.

[3] St. Luke speaks of Christ being ' about thirty years old ' at the time of His baptism. If John began His public ministry in the autumn, and some months elapsed before Jesus was baptized, our Lord would have just passed His thirtieth year when He appeared at Bethabara. We have positive evidence that the expression ' about' before a numeral meant either a little more or a little less than that exact number. See Midr. on Ruth i. 4 ed. Warsh. p. 39 *b*.

[4] Here tradition, though evidently falsely, locates the Baptism of Jesus.

[5] In reference not only to this point, but in general, I would refer to Bishop *Lightfoot's* masterly essay on the Essenes in his Appendix to his Commentary on Colossians (especially here, pp. 388, 400). It is a remarkable confirmation of the fact that, if John had been an Essene, his food could not have been ' locusts' that the Gospel of the Ebionites, who, like the Essenes, abstained from animal food, omits the mention of the ' locusts,' of St. Matt. iii. 4. (see Mr. *Nicholson's* ' The Gospel of the Hebrews,' pp. 34, 35). But proof positive is derived from Jer. Nedar. 40 *b*, where, in case of a vow of abstinence from flesh, fish and locusts are interdicted.

[6] Our A.V. wrongly translates ' a hairy man,' instead of a man with a hairy

This was evinced alike by what he preached, and by the new
symbolic rite, from which he derived the name of 'Baptist.' The
grand burden of his message was: the announcement of the
approach of 'the Kingdom of Heaven,' and the needed preparation
of his hearers for that Kingdom. The latter he sought, positively,
by admonition, and negatively, by warnings, while he directed all
to the Coming One, in Whom that Kingdom would become, so
to speak, individualised. Thus, from the first, it was 'the good
news of the Kingdom,' to which all else in John's preaching was
but subsidiary.

Concerning this 'Kingdom of Heaven,' which was the great message of John, and the great work of Christ Himself,[1] we may here
say, that it is the whole Old Testament *sublimated*, and the whole
New Testament *realised*. The idea of it did not lie hidden in
the Old, to be opened up in the New Testament—as did the mystery
of its realisation.[a] But this rule of heaven and Kingship of
Jehovah was the very substance of the Old Testament; the object
of the calling and mission of Israel; the meaning of all its
ordinances, whether civil or religious;[2] the underlying idea of all
its institutions.[3] It explained alike the history of the people, the
dealings of God with them, and the prospects opened up by the
prophets. Without it the Old Testament could not be understood;
it gave perpetuity to its teaching, and dignity to its representations.
This constituted alike the real contrast between Israel and the
nations of antiquity, and Israel's real title to distinction. Thus the
whole Old Testament was the preparatory presentation of the rule
of heaven and of the Kingship of its Lord.

But preparatory not only in the sense of typical, but also in that
of inchoative. Even the twofold hindrance—internal and external—
which 'the Kingdom' encountered, indicated this. The former arose
from the resistance of Israel to their King; the latter from the opposition of the surrounding kingdoms of this world. All the more
intense became the longing through thousands of years, that these

CHAP.
XI

[a] Rom. xvi
25, 26;
Eph. i. 9;
Col. i. 26, 27

(camel's hair) raiment.' This seems afterwards to have become the distinctive
dress of the prophets (comp. Zech. xiii. 4).

[1] *Keim* beautifully designates it: *Das
Lieblingswort Jesu*.

[2] If, indeed, in the preliminary dispensation these two can be well separated.

[3] I confess myself utterly unable to
understand, how anyone writing a History of the Jewish Church can apparently eliminate from it what even *Keim*

designates as the 'treibenden Gedanken
des Alten Testamentes'—those of the
Kingdom and the King. A Kingdom of
God without a King; a Theocracy without the rule of God; a perpetual Davidic
Kingdom without a 'Son of David'—
these are *antinomies* (to borrow the
term of *Kant*) of which neither the Old
Testament, the Apocrypha, the Pseudepigraphic writings, nor Rabbinism were
guilty.

BOOK
II

hindrances might be swept away by the Advent of the promised Messiah, Who would permanently establish (by His spirit) the right relationship between the King and His Kingdom, by bringing in an everlasting righteousness, and also cast down existing barriers, by calling the kingdoms of this world to be the Kingdom of our God. This would, indeed, be the Advent of the Kingdom of God, such as had been the glowing hope held out by Zechariah,[a] the glorious vision beheld by Daniel.[b] Three ideas especially did this Kingdom of God imply: *universality, heavenliness,* and *permanency.* Wide as God's domain would be His Dominion; holy, as heaven in contrast to earth, and God to man, would be his character; and triumphantly lasting its continuance. Such was the teaching of the Old Testament, and the great hope of Israel. It scarcely needs mental compass, only moral and spiritual capacity, to see its matchless grandeur, in contrast with even the highest aspirations of heathenism, and the blanched ideas of modern culture.

a xiv. 9 [1]
b vii. 13, 14 [2]

How imperfectly Israel understood this Kingdom, our previous investigations have shown. In truth, the men of that period possessed only the term—as it were, the form. What explained its meaning, filled, and fulfilled it, came once more from heaven. Rabbinism and Alexandrianism kept alive the thought of it; and in their own way filled the soul with its longing—just as the distress in Church and State carried the need of it to every heart with the keenness of anguish. As throughout this history, the *form* was of that time; the substance and the spirit were of Him Whose coming was the Advent of that Kingdom. Perhaps the nearest approach to it lay in the higher aspirations of the Nationalist party, only that it sought their realisation, not spiritually, but outwardly. Taking the sword, it perished by the sword. It was probably to this that both Pilate and Jesus referred in that memorable question: 'Art Thou then a King?' to which our Lord, unfolding the deepest meaning of His mission, replied: 'My Kingdom is not of this world: if My Kingdom were of this world, then would My servants fight.'[c]

c St. John
xviii. 33-37

According to the Rabbinic views of the time, the terms 'Kingdom,' 'Kingdom of heaven,'[3] and 'Kingdom of God' (in the Targum

---

[1] 'And the Lord shall be King over all the earth: in that day shall there be one Lord, and His Name one.'

[2] 'I saw in the night visions, and, behold, One like the Son of Man came with the clouds of heaven, and came to the Ancient of Days, and they brought Him near before Him. And there was given Him dominion, and glory, and a kingdom, that all people, nations, and languages, should serve Him: His dominion is an everlasting dominion, which shall not pass away, and His kingdom that which shall not be destroyed.'

[3] Occasionally we find, instead of *Malkhuth Shamayim* ('Kingdom of

on Micah iv. 7 ‘Kingdom of Jehovah’), were equivalent. In fact, the word ‘heaven’ was very often used instead of ‘God,’ so as to avoid unduly familiarising the ear with the Sacred Name.[1] This, probably, accounts for the exclusive use of the expression ‘Kingdom of Heaven’ in the Gospel by St. Matthew.[2] And the term did imply a contrast to earth, as the expression ‘the Kingdom of God’ did to this world. The consciousness of its contrast to earth or the world was distinctly expressed in Rabbinic writings.[a]

This ‘Kingdom of Heaven,’ or ‘of God,’ must, however, be distinguished from such terms as ‘the Kingdom of the Messiah’ (*Malkhutha dimeshicha*[b]), ‘the future age (world) of the Messiah’ (*Alma deathey dimeshicha*[c]), ‘the days of the Messiah,’ ‘the age to come’ (*sœculum futurum*, the *Athid labho*[3]—both this and the previous expression[d]), ‘the end of days,’[e] and ‘the end of the extremity of days’ *Soph Eqebh Yomaya*[f]). This is the more important, since the ‘Kingdom of Heaven’ has so often been confounded with the period of its triumphant manifestation in ‘the days,’ or in ‘the Kingdom, of the Messiah.’ Between the Advent and the final manifestation of ‘the Kingdom,’ Jewish expectancy placed a temporary obscuration of the Messiah.[4] Not His first appearance, but His triumphant manifestation, was to be preceded by the so-called ‘sorrows of the Messiah’ (the *Chebhley shel Mashiach*), ‘the tribulations of the latter days.’[5]

A review of many passages on the subject shows that, in the Jewish mind the expression ‘Kingdom of Heaven’ referred, not so much to any particular period, as in general to *the Rule of God*—as acknowledged, manifested, and eventually perfected. Very often it is the equivalent for personal acknowledgment of God: the taking upon oneself of the ‘yoke’ of ‘the Kingdom,’ or of the commandments—the former preceding and conditioning the latter.[g] Accord-

a As in Shebhu 35 b; Ber. R. 9, ed. Warsh, pp. 19 b, 20 a

b As in the Targum on Ps. xiv. 7, and on Is. liii. 10

c As in Targum on 1 Kings iv. 33 (v. 13)

d For ex ample, in Ber. R. 88, ed. Warsh. p. 157 a

e Targ. Pseudo-Jon. on Ex. xl. 9, 11

f Jer. Targ. on Gen. iii. 15; Jer. and Pseudo-Jon. Targ on Numb. xxiv. 14

g So expressly in Mechilta, p. 75 a; Yalkut, vol. ii. p. 14 a, last line

---

Heaven’), *Malkhutha direqiya* (‘Kingdom of the firmament’), as in Ber. 58 a, Shebhu. 35 b. But in the former passage, at least, it seems to apply rather to God’s Providential government than to His moral reign.

[1] The Talmud (Shebhu. 35 b) analyses the various passages of Scripture in which it is used in a sacred and in the common sense.

[2] In St. Matthew the expression occurs thirty-two times; six times that of ‘the Kingdom;’ five times that of ‘Kingdom of God.’

[3] The distinction between the *Olam* habba (the world to come), and the *Athid labho* (the age to come), is important. It will be more fully referred to by-and-by. In the meantime, suffice it, that the *Athid labho* is the more specific designation of Messianic times. The two terms are expressly distinguished, for example, in Mechilta (ed. *Weiss*), p. 74 a, lines 2, 3.

[4] This will be more fully explained and shown in the sequel. For the present we refer only to Yalkut, vol. ii. p. 75 d, and the Midr. on Ruth ii. 14.

[5] The whole subject is fully treated in Book V. ch. vi.

ingly, the Mishnah[a] gives this as the reason why, in the collection of Scripture passages which forms the prayer called 'Shema,'[1] the confession, Deut. vi. 4 &c., precedes the admonition, Deut. xi. 13 &c., because a man takes upon himself first the yoke of the Kingdom of Heaven, and afterwards that of the commandments. And in this sense, the repetition of this Shema, as the personal acknowledgment of the Rule of Jehovah, is itself often designated as 'taking upon oneself the Kingdom of Heaven.'[b] Similarly, the putting on of phylacteries, and the washing of hands, are also described as taking upon oneself the yoke of the Kingdom of God.[2] To give other instances: Israel is said to have taken up the yoke of the Kingdom of God at Mount Sinai;[c] the children of Jacob at their last interview with their father;[d] and Isaiah on his call to the prophetic office,[e] where it is also noted that this must be done willingly and gladly. On the other hand, the sons of Eli and the sons of Ahab are said to have cast off the Kingdom of Heaven.[f] While thus the acknowledgment of the Rule of God, both in profession and practice, was considered to constitute the Kingdom of God, its full manifestation was expected only in the time of the Advent of Messiah. Thus in the Targum on Isaiah xl. 9, the words 'Behold your God!' are paraphrased: 'The Kingdom of your God is revealed.' Similarly,[g] we read: 'When the time approaches that the Kingdom of Heaven shall be manifested, then shall be fulfilled that "the Lord shall be King over all the earth."'[h][3] On the other hand, the unbelief of Israel would appear in that they would reject these three things: the Kingdom of Heaven, the Kingdom of the House of David, and the building of the Temple, according to the prediction in Hos. iii. 5.[i] It follows that, after the period of unbelief, the Messianic deliverances and blessings of the 'Athid Labho,' or future age, were expected. But the final completion of all still remained for the 'Olam Habba,' or world to come. And that there is a distinction between the time of the Messiah and this 'world to come' is frequently indicated in Rabbinic writings.[4]

[a] Ber. ii. 2

[b] For example, Ber. 13 b, 14 b; Ber. ii. 5; and the touching story of Rabbi Akiba thus taking upon himself the yoke of the Law in the hour of his martyrdom, Ber. 61 b

[c] So often. Comp. Siphré p. 142 b, 143 b

[d] Ber. R. 98

[e] Yalkut, vol. ii. p. 43 a

[f] Midr. on 1 Sam. ii. 12; Midr. on Eccl. i. 18

[g] In Yalkut ii. p. 178 a

[h] Zech. xiv. 9

[i] Midr. on 1 Sam. viii. 7. Comp. also generally Midr. on Ps. cxlvii. 1

[1] The Shema, which was repeated twice every day, was regarded as distinctive of Jewish profession (Ber. iii. 3).

[2] In Ber. 14 b, last line, and 15 a, first line, there is a shocking definition of what constitutes the Kingdom of Heaven in its completeness. For the sake of those who would derive Christianity from Rabbinism, I would have quoted it, but am restrained by its profanity.

[3] The same passage is similarly referred to in the Midr. on Song. ii. 12, where the words 'the time of the singing has come,' are paraphrased; 'the time of the Kingdom of Heaven that it shall be manifested, hath come' (in R. Martini Pugio Fidei, p. 782).

[4] As in Shabb. 63 a, where at least three differences between them are mentioned. For, while all prophecy pointed to the days of the Messiah, concerning

As we pass from the Jewish ideas of the time to the teaching of the New Testament, we feel that while there is *complete change of spirit*, the form in which the idea of the Kingdom of Heaven is presented is substantially similar. Accordingly, we must dismiss the notion that the expression refers to the Church, whether visible (according to the Roman Catholic view) or invisible (according to certain Protestant writers).[1] 'The Kingdom of God,' or Kingly Rule of God, is an *objective fact*. The visible Church can only be the *subjective* attempt at its outward realisation, of which the invisible Church is the true counterpart. When Christ says,[a] that 'except a man be born from above, he cannot see the Kingdom of God,' He teaches, in opposition to the Rabbinic representation of how 'the Kingdom' was taken up, that a man cannot even comprehend that glorious idea of the Reign of God, and of becoming, by conscious self-surrender, one of His subjects, except he be first born from above. Similarly, the meaning of Christ's further teaching on this subject[b] seems to be that, except a man be born of water (profession, with baptism[2] as its

a St. John iii. 3

b in ver. 5

---

the world to come we are told (Is. lxiv. 4) that 'eye hath not seen, &c.'; in the days of the Messiah weapons would be borne, but not in the world to come; and while Is. xxiv. 21 applied to the days of the Messiah, the seemingly contradictory passage, Is. xxx. 26, referred to the world to come. In Targum Pseudo-Jonathan on Exod. xvii. 16, we read of three generations: that of this world, that of the Messiah, and that of the world to come (Aram: Alma deathey=*olam habba*). Comp. Ar. 13 *b*, and Midr. on Ps. lxxxi. 2 (3 in A.V.), ed. *Warsh.* p. 63 *a*, where the harp of the Sanctuary is described as of seven strings (according to Ps. cxix. 164); in the days of the Messiah as of eight strings (according to the inscription of Ps. xii.); and in the world to come (here *Athid labho*) as of ten strings (according to Ps. xcii. 3). The references of *Gfrörer* (Jahrh. d. Heils, vol. ii. p. 213) contain, as not unfrequently, mistakes. I may here say that *Rhenferdius* carries the argument about the *Olam habba*, as distinguished from the days of the Messiah, beyond what I believe to be established. See his Dissertation in *Meuschen*, Nov. Test. pp. 1116 &c.

[1] It is difficult to conceive, how the idea of the identity of the Kingdom of God with the Church could have originated. Such parables as those about the Sower, and about the Net (St. Matt. xiii. 3-9; 47, 48), and such admonitions as those of Christ to His disciples in St. Matt. xix. 12; vi. 33; and vi. 10, are utterly inconsistent with it.

[2] The passage which seems to me most fully to explain the import of baptism, in its *subjective* bearing, is 1 Peter, iii. 21, which I would thus render: 'which (water) also, as the antitype, now saves you, *even* baptism; not the putting away of the filth of the flesh, but the inquiry (the searching, *perhaps* the entreaty), for a good conscience towards God, through the resurrection of Christ.' It is in this sense that baptism is designated in Tit. iii. 5, as the 'washing,' or 'bath of regeneration,' the baptized person stepping out of the waters of baptism with this openly spoken new search after a good conscience towards God; and in this sense also that baptism—not the act of baptizing, nor yet that of being baptized—saves us, but this through the Resurrection of Christ. And this leads us up to the *objective* aspect of baptism. This consists in the *promise* and the *gift* on the part of the Risen Saviour, Who, by and with His Holy Spirit, is ever present with his Church. These remarks leave, of course, aside the question of Infant-Baptism, which rests on another and, in my view most solid basis.

symbol) and the Spirit, he cannot really enter into the fellowship of that Kingdom.

In fact, an analysis of 119 passages in the New Testament where the expression 'Kingdom' occurs, shows that it means *the rule of God*;[1] which was *manifested in and through Christ*;[2] is *apparent in 'the Church*';[3] *gradually develops amidst hindrances*;[4] is *triumphant at the second coming of Christ*[5] ('the end'); and, finally, *perfected in the world to come.*[6] Thus viewed, the announcement of John of the near Advent of this Kingdom had deepest meaning, although, as so often in the case of prophetism, the stages intervening between the Advent of the Christ and the triumph of that Kingdom seem to have been hidden from the preacher. He came to call Israel to submit to the Reign of God, about to be manifested in Christ. Hence, on the one hand, he called them to repentance—a 'change of mind'—with all that this implied; and, on the other, pointed them to the Christ, in the exaltation of His Person and Office. Or rather, the two combined might be summed up in the call: 'Change your mind'—repent, which implies, not only a turning from the past, but a turning to the Christ in newness of mind.[7] And thus the symbolic action by which this preaching was accompanied might be designated 'the baptism of repentance.'

The account given by St. Luke bears, on the face of it, that it was a summary, not only of the first, but of all John's preaching.[a] The very presence of his hearers at this call to, and baptism of, repentance, gave point to his words. Did they who, notwithstanding their

a iii. 18

[1] In this view the expression occurs thirty-four times, viz.: St. Matt. vi. 33; xii. 28; xiii. 38; xix. 24; xxi. 31; St. Mark i. 14; x. 15, 23, 24, 25; xii. 34; St. Luke i. 33; iv. 43; ix. 11; x. 9, 11; xi. 20; xii. 31; xvii. 20, 21; xviii. 17, 24, 25, 29; St. John iii. 3; Acts i. 3; viii. 12; xx. 25; xxviii. 31; Rom. xiv. 17; 1 Cor. iv. 20; Col. iv. 11; 1 Thess. ii. 12; Rev. i. 9.

[2] As in the following seventeen passages, viz.: St. Matt. iii. 2; iv. 17, 23; v. 3, 10; ix. 35; x. 7; St. Mark i. 15; xi. 10; St. Luke viii. 1; ix. 2; xvi. 16; xix. 12, 15; Acts i. 3; xxviii. 23; Rev. i. 9.

[3] As in the following eleven passages: St. Matt. xi. 11; xiii. 41; xvi. 19; xviii. 1; xxi. 43; xxiii. 13; St. Luke vii. 28; St. John iii. 5; Acts i. 3; Col. i. 13; Rev. i. 9.

[4] As in the following twenty-four pas-

sages: St. Matt. xi. 12; xiii. 11, 19, 24, 31, 33, 44, 45, 47, 52; xviii. 23; xx. 1; xxii. 2; xxv. 1, 14; St. Mark iv. 11, 26, 30; St. Luke viii. 10; ix. 62; xiii. 18, 20; Acts i. 3; Rev. i. 9.

[5] As in the following twelve passages: St. Mark xvi. 28; St. Mark ix. 1; xv. 43; St. Luke xvii. 27; xix. 11; xxi. 31; xxii. 16, 18; Acts i. 3; 2 Tim. iv. 1; Heb. xii. 28; Rev. i. 9.

[6] As in the following thirty-one passages: St. Matt. v. 19, 20; vii. 21; viii. 11; xiii. 43; xviii. 3; xxv. 34; xxvi. 29; St. Mark ix. 47; x. 14; xiv. 25; St. Luke vi. 20; xii. 32; xiii. 28, 29; xiv. 15; xviii. 16; xxii. 29; Acts i. 3; xiv. 22; 1 Cor. vi. 9, 10; xv. 24, 50; Gal. v. 21; Eph. v. 5; 2 Thess. i. 5; St. James ii. 5; 2 Peter i. 11; Rev. i. 9; xii. 10.

[7] The term 'repentance' includes faith in Christ, as in St. Luke xxiv. 47; Acts v. 31.

sins,[1] lived in such security of carelessness and self-righteousness, really understand and fear the final consequences of resistance to the coming 'Kingdom'? If so, theirs must be a repentance not only in profession, but of heart and mind, such as would yield fruit, both good and visible. Or else did they imagine that, according to the common notion of the time, the vials of wrath were to be poured out only on the Gentiles,[2] while they, as Abraham's children, were sure of escape—in the words of the Talmud, that 'the night' (Is. xxi. 12) was 'only to the nations of the world, but the morning to Israel'?[a]

For, no principle was more fully established in the popular conviction, than that all Israel had part in the world to come (Sanh. x. 1), and this, specifically, because of their connection with Abraham. This appears not only from the New Testament,[b] from Philo, and Josephus, but from many Rabbinic passages. 'The merits of the Fathers,' is one of the commonest phrases in the mouth of the Rabbis.[3] Abraham was represented as sitting at the gate of Gehenna, to deliver any Israelite[4] who otherwise might have been consigned to its terrors.[c] In fact, by their descent from Abraham, all the children of Israel were nobles,[d] infinitely higher than any proselytes. 'What,' exclaims the Talmud, 'shall the born Israelite stand upon the earth, and the proselyte be in heaven?'[e] In fact, the ships on the sea were preserved through the merit of Abraham; the rain descended on account of it.[f] For his sake alone had Moses been allowed to ascend into heaven, and to receive the Law; for his sake the sin of the golden calf had been forgiven;[g] his righteousness had on many occasions been the support of Israel's cause;[h] Daniel had been heard for the sake of Abraham;[i] nay, his merit availed even for the wicked.[k][5] In its extravagance the Midrash thus apostrophises Abraham: 'If thy

CHAP.
XI

[a] Jer. Taan. 64 a

[b] St. John viii. 33, 39, 53

[c] Ber. R. 48; comp. Midr. on Ps. vi. 1; Pirké d. R. Elies. c. 29; Shem. R. 19 Yalkut i. p. 23 b

[d] Baba Mez. vii. 1; Baba K. 91 a

[e] Jer. Chag. 76 a

[f] Ber. R. 39

[g] Shem R. 44

[h] Vayyikra R. 36

[i] Ber. 7 b

[k] Shabb. 55 a; comp Beer, Leben Abr. p. 88

---

[1] I cannot, with *Schöttgen* and others, regard the expression 'generation of vipers' as an allusion to the filthy legend about the children of Eve and the serpent, but believe that it refers to such passages as Ps. lviii. 4.

[2] In proof that such was the common view, I shall here refer to only a few passages, and these exclusively from the Targumim: Jer. Targ. on Gen. xlix. 11; Targ. on Is. xi. 4; Targ. on Amos ix. 11; Targ. on Nah. i. 6; on Zech. x. 3, 4. See also Ab. Z. 2 b, Yalkut i. p. 64 a; also 56 b (where it is shown how plagues exactly corresponding to those of Egypt

were to come upon Rome).

[3] 'Everything comes to Israel on account of the merits of the fathers' (Siphré on Deut. p. 108 b). In the same category we place the extraordinary attempts to show that the sins of Biblical personages were not sins at all, as in Shabb. 55 b, and the idea of Israel's merits as works of supererogation (as in Baba B. 10 a).

[4] I will not mention the profane device by which apostate and wicked Jews are at that time to be converted into non-Jews.

[5] Professor *Wünsche* quotes an inapt passage from Shabb. 89 b, but ignores, or is ignorant of the evidence above given.

BOOK
II

ᵃ Ber. R. ed.
Warsh.
p. 80 b, par.
44
ᵇ Perhaps
with refer-
ence to Is.
ii. 1, 2

ᶜ For ex.
Jer. Taan.
64 a

children were even (morally) dead bodies, without bloodvessels or bones, thy merit would avail for them!'ᵃ

But if such had been the inner thoughts of his hearers, John warned them, that God was able of those stones that strewed the river-bank to raise up children unto Abraham;ᵇ¹ or, reverting to his former illustration of 'fruits meet for repentance,' that the proclamation of the Kingdom was, at the same time, the laying of the axe to the root of every tree that bore not fruit. Then making application of it, in answer to the specific inquiry of various classes, the preacher gave them such practical advice as applied to the well-known sins of their past;² yet in this also not going beyond the merely negative, or preparatory element of 'repentance.' The positive, and all-important aspect of it, was to be presented by the Christ. It was only natural that the hearers wondered whether John himself was the Christ, since he thus urged repentance. For this was so closely connected in their thoughts with the Advent of the Messiah, that it was said, 'If Israel repented but one day, the Son of David would immediately come.'ᶜ But here John pointed them to the difference between himself and his work, and the Person and Mission of the Christ. In deepest reverence he declared himself not worthy to do Him the service of a slave or of a disciple.³ His Baptism would not be of preparatory repentance and with water, but the Divine Baptism in⁴ the Holy Spirit and fire⁵—in the Spirit Who sanctified, and the Divine Light which purified,⁶ and so effectively qualified for the

¹ *Lightfoot* aptly points out a play on the words 'children'— *banim* — and 'stones'—*abhanim*. Both words are derived from *bana*, to build, which is also used by the Rabbis in a moral sense like our own 'upbuilding,' and in that of the gift or adoption of children. It is not necessary, indeed almost detracts from the general impression, to see in the stones an allusion to the Gentiles.

² Thus the view that charity delivered from Gehenna was very commonly entertained (see, for example, Baba B. 10 a). Similarly, it was the main charge against the publicans that they exacted more than their due (see, for example, Baba K. 113 a). The Greek ὀψώνιον, or wage of the soldiers, has its Rabbinic equivalent of *Afsanya* (a similar word also in the Syriac).

³ *Volkmar* is mistaken in regarding this as the duty of the house-porter towards arriving guests. It is expressly mentioned as one of the characteristic duties of slaves in Pes. 4 a; Jer Kidd. i. 3; Kidd. 22 b. In Kethub. 96 a it is described as also the duty of a disciple towards his teacher. In Mechilta on Ex. xxi. 2 (ed. *Weiss*, p. 82 a) it is qualified as only lawful for a teacher so to employ his disciple, while, lastly, in Pesiqta x. it is described as the common practice.

⁴ *Godet* aptly calls attention to the use of the preposition *in* here, while as regards the baptism of water no preposition is used, as denoting merely an instrumentality.

⁵ The same writer points out that the want of the preposition before 'fire' shows that it cannot refer to the fire of judgment, but must be a further enlargement of the word 'Spirit.' Probably it denotes the negative or purgative effect of this baptism, as the word 'holy' indicates its positive and sanctifying effect.

⁶ The expression 'baptism of fire' was certainly not unknown to the Jews.

'Kingdom.' And there was still another contrast. John's was but preparing work, the Christ's that of final decision; after it came the
harvest. His was the harvest, and His the garner; His also the fan, with
which He would sift the wheat from the straw and chaff—the one to
be garnered, the other burned with fire unextinguished and inextin-
guishable.[1] Thus early in the history of the Kingdom of God was it
indicated, that alike that which would prove useless straw and the
good corn were inseparably connected in God's harvest-field till the
reaping time; that both belonged to Him; and that the final separation would only come at the last, and by His own Hand.

What John preached, that he also symbolised by a rite which,
though not in itself, yet in its application, was wholly new. Hitherto
the Law had it, that those who had contracted Levitical defilement
were to immerse before offering sacrifice. Again, it was prescribed
that such Gentiles as became 'proselytes of righteousness,' or 'proselytes of the Covenant' (*Gerey hatstsedeq* or *Gerey habberith*), were to
be admitted to full participation in the privileges of Israel by the
threefold rites of circumcision, baptism,[2] and sacrifice—the immersion
being, as it were, the acknowledgment and symbolic removal of
moral defilement, corresponding to that of Levitical uncleanness. But
never before had it been proposed that Israel should undergo a
'baptism of repentance,' although there are indications of a deeper
insight into the meaning of Levitical baptisms.[3] Was it intended,

In Sanh. 39 *a* (last lines) we read of an immersion of God in fire, based on Is. lxvi. 15. An immersion or baptism of fire is proved from Numb. xxxi. 23. More apt, perhaps, as illustration is the statement, Jer. Sot. 22 *d*, that the Torah (the Law) its parchment was white fire, the writing black fire, itself fire mixed with fire, hewn out of fire, and given by fire, according to Deut. xxxiii. 2.

[1] This is the meaning of ἄσβεστος. The word occurs only in St. Matt. iii. 12; St. Luke iii. 17; St. Mark ix. 43, 45 (?), but frequently in the classics. The question of 'eternal punishment' will be dis-cussed in another place. The simile of the fan and the garner is derived from the Eastern practice of threshing out the corn in the open by means of oxen, after which, what of the straw had been tram-pled under foot (not merely the *chaff*, as in the A.V.) was burned. This use of the straw for fire is referred to in the Mishnah, as in Shabb. iii. 1; Par. iv. 3. But in that case the Hebrew equivalent for it is שׁק (*Qash*)—as in the above

passages, and not *Tebhen* (*Meyer*), nor even as Professor *Delitzsch* renders it in his Hebrew N.T.: *Mots*. The three terms are, however, combined in a curiously illustrative parable (Ber. R. 83), referring to the destruction of Rome and the pres-ervation of Israel, when the grain refers the straw, stubble, and chaff, in their dispute for whose sake the field existed, to the time when the owner would gather the corn into his barn, but burn the straw, stubble, and chaff.

[2] For a full discussion of the question of the baptism of proselytes, see Appen-dix XII.

[3] The following very significant pas-sage may here be quoted: 'A man who is guilty of sin, and makes confession, and does not turn from it, to whom is he like? To a man who has in his hand a defiling reptile, who, even if he immerses in all the waters of the world, his bap-tism avails him nothing ; but let him cast it from his hand, and if he immerses in only forty seah of water, immediately his baptism avails him.' On the same

that the hearers of John should give this as evidence of their repentance, that, like persons defiled, they sought purification, and, like strangers, they sought admission among the people who took on themselves the Rule of God? These two ideas would, indeed, have made it truly a 'baptism of repentance.' But it seems difficult to suppose, that the people would have been prepared for such admissions; or, at least, that there should have been no record of the mode in which a change so deeply spiritual was brought about. May it not rather have been that as, when the first Covenant was made, Moses was directed to prepare Israel by symbolic baptism of their persons [a] and their garments,[b] so the initiation of the new Covenant, by which the people were to enter into the Kingdom of God, was preceded by another general symbolic baptism of those who would be the true Israel, and receive, or take on themselves, the Law from God?[1] In that case the rite would have acquired not only a new significance, but be deeply and truly the answer to John's call. In such case also, no special explanation would have been needed on the part of the Baptist, nor yet such spiritual insight on that of the people as we can scarcely suppose them to have possessed at that stage. Lastly, in that case nothing could have been more suitable, nor more solemn, than Israel in waiting for the Messiah and the Rule of God, preparing as their fathers had done at the foot of Mount Sinai.[2]

[a] Comp. Gen. xxxv. 2

[b] Ex. xix. 10, 14

page of the Talmud there are some very apt and beautiful remarks on the subject of repentance (Taan. 16 *a*, towards the end).

[1] It is remarkable, that *Maimonides* traces even the practice of baptizing proselytes to Ex. xix. 10, 14 (Hilc Issurey Biah xiii. 3; Yad haCh. vol. ii. p. 142 *b*). He also gives reasons for the 'baptism' of Israel before entering into covenant with God. In Kerith, 9 *a* 'the baptism' of Israel is proved from Ex. xxiv. 5, since every sprinkling of blood was supposed to be preceded by immersion. In Siphré on Numb. (ed.

Weiss, p. 30 *b*) we are also distinctly told of 'baptism' as one of the three things by which Israel was admitted into the Covenant.

[2] This may help us, even at this stage, to understand why our Lord, in the fulfilment of all righteousness, submitted to baptism. It seems also to explain why, after the coming of Christ, the baptism of John was alike unavailing and even meaningless (Acts xix. 3–5). Lastly, it also shows how he that is least in the Kingdom of God is really greater than John himself (St. Luke vii. 28).

CHAPTER XII.

THE BAPTISM OF JESUS: ITS HIGHER MEANING.

(St. Matt. iii. 13–17; St. Mark i. 7–11; St. Luke iii. 21–23; St. John i. 32–34.)

THE more we think of it, the better do we seem to understand how that 'Voice crying in the wilderness: Repent! for the Kingdom of Heaven is at hand,' awakened echoes throughout the land, and brought from city, village, and hamlet strangest hearers.   For once, every distinction was levelled.   Pharisee and Sadducee, outcast publican and semi-heathen soldier, met here as on common ground.   Their bond of union was the common 'hope of Israel'—the only hope that remained: that of 'the Kingdom.'   The long winter of disappointment had not destroyed, nor the storms of suffering swept away, nor yet could any plant of spurious growth overshadow, what had struck its roots so deep in the soil of Israel's heart.

That Kingdom had been the last word of the Old Testament.   As the thoughtful Israelite, whether Eastern or Western,[1] viewed even the central part of his worship in sacrifices, and remembered that his own Scriptures had spoken of them in terms which pointed to something beyond their offering,[2] he must have felt that 'the blood of bulls and of goats, and the ashes of an heifer sprinkling the unclean,' could

---

[1] It may be said that the fundamental tendency of Rabbinism was anti-sacrificial, as regarded the value of sacrifices in commending the offerer to God. After the destruction of the Temple it was, of course, the task of Rabbinism to show that sacrifices had no intrinsic importance, and that their place was taken by prayer, penitence, and good works.   So against objectors on the ground of Jer. xxxiii. 18—but see the answer in Yalkut on the passage (vol. ii. p. 67 *a*, towards the end) dogmatically (Bab. B. 10 *b*; Vayyikra R. 7, ed. *Warsh.* vol. iii. p. 12 *a*): 'he that doeth repentance, it is imputed to him as if he went up to Jerusalem, built the Temple and altar, and wrought all the sacrifices in the Law';

and in view of the cessation of sacrifices in the 'Athid·labho' (Vay, u. s.; Tanch. on Par. Shemini).   Soon, prayer or study were put even above sacrifices (Ber. 32 *b*; Men. 110 *a*), and an isolated teacher went so far as to regard the introduction of sacrificial worship as merely intended to preserve Israel from conforming to heathen worship (Vayyikra R. 22, u. s. p. 34 *b*, close).   On the other hand, individuals seemed to have offered sacrifices even after the destruction of the Temple (Eduy. viii. 6; Mechilta on Ex. xviii. 27, ed. *Weiss*, p. 68 *b*).

[2] Comp. 1 Sam. xv. 22; Ps. xl. 6–8; li. 7, 17; Is. i. 11–13; Jer. vii. 22, 23; Amos v. 21, 22; Ecclus. vii. 9; xxxiv. 18, 19; xxxv. 1, 7.

only ' sanctify to the purifying of the flesh;' that, indeed, the whole body of ceremonial and ritual ordinances 'could not make him that did the service perfect as pertaining to the conscience.' They were only 'the shadow of good things to come;' of 'a new' and 'better covenant, established upon better promises.'[1] It was otherwise with the thought of the Kingdom. Each successive link in the chain of prophecy bound Israel anew to this hope, and each seemed only more firmly welded than the other. And when the voice of prophecy had ceased, the sweetness of its melody still held the people spell-bound, even when broken in the wild fantasies of Apocalyptic literature. Yet that ' root of Jesse,' whence this Kingdom was to spring, was buried deep under ground, as the remains of ancient Jerusalem are now under the desolations of many generations. Egyptian, Syrian, Greek, and Roman had trodden it under foot; the Maccabees had come and gone, and it was not in them; the Herodian kingdom had risen and fallen; Pharisaism, with its learning, had overshadowed thoughts of the priesthood and of prophetism; but the hope of that Davidic Kingdom, of which there was not a single trace or representative left, was even stronger than before. So closely has it been intertwined with the very life of the nation, that, to all believing Israelites, this hope has through the long night of ages, been like that eternal lamp which burns in the darkness of the Synagogue, in front of the heavy veil that shrines the Sanctuary, which holds and conceals the precious rolls of the Law and the Prophets.

This great expectancy would be strung to utmost tension during the pressure of outward circumstances more hopeless than any hitherto experienced. Witness here the ready credence which impostors found, whose promises and schemes were of the wildest character; witness the repeated attempts at risings, which only despair could have prompted; witness, also, the last terrible war against Rome, and, despite the horrors of its end, the rebellion of Bar-Kokhabh, the false Messiah. And now the cry had been suddenly raised: 'The Kingdom of Heaven is at hand!' It was heard in the wilderness of Judæa, within a few hours' distance from Jerusalem. No wonder Pharisee and Sadducee flocked to the spot. How many of them came to inquire, how many remained to be baptized, or how many went away disappointed in their hopes of 'the Kingdom,' we know not.[2] But they would not see anything in the messenger that

[1] Hebr. ix. 13, 9; x. 1; viii. 6, 13. On this subject we refer to the classical work of *Riehm* (Lehrbegriff des Hebräer-

briefes, 1867).
[2] Ancient commentators supposed that they came from hostile motives; later

could have given their expectations a rude shock. His was not a call
to armed resistance, but to repentance, such as all knew and felt must
precede the Kingdom. The hope which he held out was not of
earthly possessions, but of purity. There was nothing negative or
controversial in what he spoke; nothing to excite prejudice or passion.
His appearance would command respect, and his character was in
accordance with his appearance. Not rich nor yet Pharisaic garb
with wide *Tsitsith*,[1] bound with many-coloured or even priestly girdle,
but the old prophet's poor raiment held in by a leathern girdle. Not
luxurious life, but one of meanest fare.[2] And then, all in the man was
true and real. ' Not a reed shaken by the wind,' but unbendingly firm
in deep and settled conviction; not ambitious nor self-seeking, but
most humble in his self-estimate, discarding all claim but that of
lowliest service, and pointing away from himself to Him Who was to
come, and Whom as yet he did not even know. Above all, there was
the deepest earnestness, the most utter disregard of man, the most
firm belief in what he announced. For himself he sought nothing;
for them he had only one absorbing thought: The Kingdom was at
hand, the King was coming—let them prepare!

Such entire absorption in his mission, which leaves us in ignorance
of even the details of his later activity, must have given force to his
message.[3] And still the voice, everywhere proclaiming the same mes-

writers that curiosity prompted them.
Neither of these views is admissible, nor
does St. Luke vii. 30 imply, that all the
Pharisees who come to him rejected his
baptism.

[1] Comp. St. Matt. xxiii. 5. The *Tsitsith*
(*plural, Tsitsiyoth*), or borders (corners,
' wings ') of the garments, or rather the
fringes fastened to them. The observance was based on Numb. xv. 38–41,
and the Jewish practice of it is indicated
not only in the N.T. (u. s., comp. also
St. Matt. ix. 20; xiv. 36) but in the Targumim on Numb. xv. 38, 39 (comp. also
Targ. Pseudo-Jon. on Numb. xvi. 1, 2,
where the peculiar colour of the Tsitsith
is represented as the cause of the controversy between Moses and Korah. But
see the version of this story in Jer. Sanh.
x. p. 27 *d*, end). The *Tsitsith* were originally directed to be of white threads,
with one thread of deep blue in each
fringe. According to tradition, each of
these white fringes is to consist of
eight threads, one of them wound round
the others; first, *seven times* with a
double knot; then *eight times* with a
double knot (7 + 8 numerically = הי‎);

then *eleven times* with a double knot
(11 numerically = הו‎;) and lastly, *thirteen times* (13 numerically = אחד‎; or, altogether יהוה אחד‎, *Jehovah One*). Again,
it is pointed out that as Tsitsith is
numerically equal to 600 (ציצית‎), this,
with the eight threads and five knots,
gives the number 613, which is that of
the Commandments. At present the
Tsitsith are worn as a special under-
garment (the ארבע כנפות‎) or on the
Tallith or prayer-mantle, but anciently
they seem to have been worn on the
outer garment itself. In Bemidbar R.
17, end (ed. *Warsh*, vol. iv. p. 69 *a*), the
blue is represented as emblematic of the
sky, and the latter as of the throne of
God (Ex. xxiv. 10). Hence to look upon
the Tsitsith was like looking at the throne
of glory (*Schürer* is mistaken in supposing that the tractate *Tsitsith* in the
Septem Libri Talmud. par. pp. 22, 23, contains much information on the subject).

[2] Such certainly was John the Baptist's. Some locusts were lawful to be
eaten, Lev. xi. 22. Comp. Terum. 59 *a*;
and, on the various species, Chull. 65.

[3] Deeply as we appreciate the beauty

BOOK
II

sage, travelled upward, along the winding Jordan which cleft the land of promise. It was probably the autumn of the year 779 (A.U.C.), which, it may be noted, was a Sabbatic year.[1] Released from business and agriculture, the multitudes flocked around him as he passed on his Mission. Rapidly the tidings spread from town and village to distant homestead, still swelling the numbers that hastened to the banks of the sacred river. He had now reached what seems to have been the most northern point of his Mission-journey,[2] *Beth-Abara* ('the house of passage,' or 'of shipping')—according to the ancient reading, Bethany ('the house of shipping')—one of the best known fords across the Jordan into Peræa.[3] Here he baptized.[a] The ford was little more than twenty miles from Nazareth. But long before John had reached that spot, tidings of his word and work must have come even into the retirement of Jesus' Home-Life.

* St. John i.
28.

It was now, as we take it, the early winter of the year 780.[4] Jesus had waited those months. Although there seems not to have been any personal acquaintance between Jesus and John—and how could there be, when their spheres lay so widely apart?—each must have heard and known of the other. Thirty years of silence weaken most human impressions—or, if they deepen, the enthusiasm that had accompanied them passes away. Yet, when the two met, and perhaps had brief conversation, each bore himself in accordance with his previous history. With John it was deepest, reverent humility— even to the verge of misunderstanding his special Mission, and work of initiation and preparation for the Kingdom. He had heard of Him before by the hearing of the ear, and when now he saw Him,

of *Keim's* remarks about the character and views of John, we feel only the more that such a man *could* not have taken the public position nor made such public proclamation of the Kingdom as at hand, without a direct and objective call to it from God. The treatment of John's earlier history by *Keim* is, of course, without historical basis.

[1] The year from *Tishri* (autumn) 779 to *Tishri* 780 was a Sabbatic year. Comp. the evidence in *Wieseler*, Synopse d. Evang. pp. 204, 205.

[2] We read of three places where John baptized: 'the wilderness of Judæa'— probably the traditional site near Jericho; Ænon, near Salim, on the boundary between Samaria and Judæa (*Conder's* Handbook of the Bible, p. 320); and Beth-Abara, the modern Abârah, 'one of the main Jordan fords, a little north of Beisân' (u. s.).

[3] It is one of the merits of Lieut. *Conder* to have identified the site of Beth-Abara. The word probably means 'the house of passage' (fords), but may also mean 'the house of shipping,' the word *Abarah* in Hebrew meaning 'ferry-boat,' 2 Sam. xix. 18. The reading *Bethania* instead of *Bethabara* seems undoubtedly the original one, only the word must not be derived (as by Mr. *Conder*, whose explanations and comments are often untenable), from the province *Batanea*, but explained as *Beth-Oniyah*, the 'house of shipping.' (See *Lücke*, Comment. ü. d. Evang. Joh. i. pp. 392. 393.)

[4] Considerable probability attaches to the tradition of the Basilideans, that our Lord's Baptism took place on the 6th or 10th of January. (See Bp. *Ellicott's* Histor. Lect. on the Life of our Lord Jesus Christ, p. 105, note 2.

that look of quiet dignity, of the majesty of unsullied purity in the
only Unfallen, Unsinning Man, made him forget even the express
command of God, which had sent him from his solitude to preach and
baptize, and that very sign which had been given him by which to
recognise the Messiah.[a][1]   In that Presence it only became to him a
question of the more 'worthy' to the misunderstanding of the
nature of his special calling.

But Jesus, as He had not made haste, so was He not capable of
misunderstanding.   To Him it was 'the fulfilling of all righteousness.'
From earliest ages it has been a question why Jesus went to be
baptized.   The heretical Gospels put into the mouth of the Virgin-
Mother an invitation to go to that baptism, to which Jesus is
supposed to have replied by pointing to His own sinlessness, except
it might be on the score of ignorance, in regard to a limitation of
knowledge.[2]   Objections lie to most of the explanations offered by
modern writers.   They include a bold denial of the fact of Jesus'
Baptism; the profane suggestion of collusion between John and
Jesus; or such suppositions, as that of His personal sinfulness, of
His coming as the Representative of a guilty race, or as the bearer of
the sins of others, or of acting in solidarity with His people—or else
to separate Himself from the sins of Israel; of His surrendering
Himself thereby unto death for man; of His purpose to do honour to
the baptism of John; or thus to elicit a token of His Messiahship;
or to bind Himself to the observance of the Law; or in this manner
to commence His Messianic Work; or to consecrate Himself solemnly
to it; or, lastly, to receive the spiritual qualification for it.[3]   To these
and similar views must be added the latest conceit of *Renan*,[4] who
arranges a scene between Jesus, who comes with some disciples, and
John, when Jesus is content for a time to grow in the shadow of
John, and to submit to a rite which was evidently so generally
acknowledged.   But the most reverent of these explanations involve
a twofold mistake.   They represent the Baptism of John as one of
repentance, and they imply an ulterior motive in the coming of
Christ to the banks of Jordan.   But, as already shown, the Baptism
of John was in itself only a consecration to, and preparatory

[1] The superficial objection on the supposed discrepancy between St. Matthew
iii. 14 and St. John i. 33 has been well
put aside by Bp. *Ellicott* (u. s. p. 107,
note).

[2] Comp. *Nicholson*, Gospel according
to the Hebrews, pp. 38, 92, 93.

[3] It would occupy too much space to
give the names of the authors of these

theories.   The views of *Godet* come
nearest to what we regard as the true
explanation.

[4] I must here, once for all, express my
astonishment that a book so frivolous
and fantastic in its treatment of the Life
of Jesus, and so superficial and often
inaccurate, should have excited so much
public attention.

initiation for, the new Covenant of the Kingdom. *As applied to* *sinful men* it *was* indeed necessarily a 'baptism of repentance;' but not as applied to the sinless Jesus. Had it primarily and always been a 'baptism of repentance,' He could not have submitted to it.

Again, and most important of all, we must not seek for any ulterior motive in the coming of Jesus to this Baptism. *He had no* *ulterior motive of any kind*: it was an act of simple submissive obedience on the part of the Perfect One—and submissive obedience has no motive beyond itself. It asks no reasons; it cherishes no ulterior purpose. And thus it was 'the *ful*filment of all righteousness.' And it was in perfect harmony with all His previous life. Our difficulty here lies—if we are unbelievers, in thinking simply of the Humanity of the Man of Nazareth; if we are believers, in making abstraction of his Divinity. But thus much, at least, all must concede, that the Gospels always present Him as the God-Man, in an inseparable mystical union of the two natures, and that they present to us the even more mysterious idea of His Self-exinanition, of the voluntary obscuration of His Divinity, as part of His Humiliation. Placing ourselves on this standpoint—which is, at any rate, that of the Evangelic narrative—we may arrive at a more correct view of this great event. It seems as if, in the Divine Self-exinanition, apparently necessarily connected with the perfect human development of Jesus, some corresponding outward event were ever the occasion of a fresh advance in the Messianic consciousness and work. The first event of that kind had been his appearance in the Temple. These two things then stood out vividly before Him—not in the ordinary human, but in the Messianic sense: that the Temple was the House of His Father, and that to be busy about it was His Life-work. With this He returned to Nazareth, and in willing subjection to His Parents fulfilled all righteousness. And still, as He grew in years, in wisdom, and in favour with God and Man, this thought—rather this burning consciousness, was the inmost spring of His Life. *What* this business specially was, He knew not yet, and waited to learn; the *how* and the *when* of His life-consecration, He left unasked and unanswered in the still waiting for Him. And in this also we see the Sinless, the Perfect One.

When tidings of John's Baptism reached His home, there could be no haste on His part. Even with knowledge of all that concerned John's relation to Him, there was in the 'fulfilment of all righteousness' quiet waiting. The one question with Him was, as He afterwards put it: 'The Baptism of John, whence was it? from heaven, or of men?' (St. Matt. xxi. 25). That question once answered, there could be no longer doubt nor hesitation. He went—not for any ulterior purpose, nor from any other motive than that it *was of God.* He went voluntarily, because it was such—and because 'it became Him' in so doing 'to fulfil all righteousness.' There is this great difference between His going to that Baptism, and afterwards into the wilderness: in the former case, His act was of preconceived purpose; in the latter it was not so, but 'He was driven'—without previous purpose to that effect—under the constraining power 'of the Spirit,' without premeditation and resolve of it; without even knowledge of its object. In the one case He was active, in the other passive; in the one case He fulfilled righteousness, in the other His righteousness was tried. But as, on His first visit to the Temple, this consciousness about His Life-business came to Him in His Father's House, ripening slowly and fully those long years of quiet submission and growing wisdom and grace at Nazareth, so at His Baptism, with the accompanying descent of the Holy Ghost, His abiding in Him, and the heard testimony from His Father, the knowledge came to Him, and, in and with[1] that knowledge, the qualification for the business of His Father's House. In that hour He learned the *when*, and in part the *how*, of His Life-business; the latter to be still farther, and from another aspect, seen in the wilderness, then in His life, in His suffering, and, finally, in His death. In man the subjective and the objective, alike intellectually and morally, are ever separate; in God they are one. What He is, that He wills. And in the God-Man also we must not separate the subjective and the objective. The consciousness of the *when* and the *how* of His Life-business was necessarily accompanied, while He prayed, by the descent, and the abiding in Him, of the Holy Ghost, and by the testifying Voice from heaven. His inner knowledge was real qualification—the forth-bursting of His Power; and it was inseparably accompanied by outward qualification, in what took place at His Baptism. But the first step to all was His voluntary *descent* to Jordan, and in it the fulfilling of all righteousness. His previous life had been that of the Perfect Ideal Israelite—believing, unquestioning, submissive—in preparation for that which, in His thirteenth year, He had learned as its business. The Baptism of Christ was the last act of His private life; and, emerging from its waters in prayer, He learned: *when* His business was to commence, and *how* it would be done.

---

[1] But the latter must be firmly upheld.

That one outstanding thought, then, 'I must be about My Father's business,' which had been the principle of His Nazareth life, had come to full ripeness when He knew that the cry, 'The Kingdom of Heaven is at hand,' was from God. The first great question was now answered. His Father's business was the Kingdom of Heaven. It only remained for Him 'to be about it,' and in this determination He went to submit to its initiatory rite of Baptism. We have, as we understand it, distinct evidence—even if it were not otherwise necessary to suppose this—that 'all the people had been baptized,'[a] when Jesus came to John. Alone the two met —probably for the first time in their lives. Over that which passed between them Holy Scripture has laid the veil of reverent silence, save as regards the beginning and the outcome of their meeting, which it was necessary for us to know. When Jesus came, John knew Him not. And even when He knew Him, that was not enough. Not remembrance of what he had heard and of past transactions, nor the overwhelming power of that spotless Purity and Majesty of willing submission, were sufficient. For so great a witness as that which John was to bear, a present and visible demonstration from heaven was to be given. Not that God sent the Spirit-Dove, or heaven uttered its voice, for the purpose of giving this as a sign to John. These manifestations were necessary in themselves, and, we might say, would have taken place quite irrespective of the Baptist. But, while necessary in themselves, they were also to be a sign to John. And this may perhaps explain why one Gospel (that of St. John) seems to describe the scene as enacted before the Baptist, whilst others (St. Matthew and St. Mark) tell it as if only visible to Jesus.[1] The one bears reference to 'the record,' the other to the deeper and absolutely necessary fact which underlay 'the record.' And, beyond this, it may help us to perceive at least one aspect of what to man is the miraculous: as in itself the higher Necessary, with casual and secondary manifestation to man.

We can understand how what he knew of Jesus, and what he now saw and heard, must have overwhelmed John with the sense of Christ's transcendentally higher dignity, and led him to hesitate about, if not to refuse, administering to Him the rite of Baptism.[2] Not because it was 'the baptism of repentance,' but because he stood

---

[1] The account by St. Luke seems to me to include both. The common objection on the score of the supposed divergence between St. John and the Synoptists is thus met.

[2] The expression διεκώλυεν (St. Matt iii. 14: 'John forbade Him') implies earnest resistance (comp. *Meyer* ad locum).

in the presence of Him 'the latchet of Whose shoes' he was 'not worthy to loose.' Had he not so felt, the narrative would not have been psychologically true; and, had it not been recorded, there would have been serious difficulty to our reception of it. And yet, withal, in so 'forbidding' Him, and even suggesting his own baptism by Jesus, John forgot and misunderstood his mission. John himself was never to be baptized; he only held open the door of the new Kingdom; himself entered it not, and he that was least in that Kingdom was greater than he. Such lowliest place on earth seems ever conjoined with greatest work for God. Yet this misunderstanding and suggestion on the part of John might almost be regarded as a temptation to Christ. Not, perhaps, His first, nor yet this His first victory, since the 'sorrow' of His Parents about His absence from them when in the Temple must to the absolute submissiveness of Jesus have been a temptation to turn aside from His path, all the more felt in the tenderness of His years, and the inexperience of a first public appearance. He then overcame by the clear consciousness of His Life-business, which could not be contravened by any apparent call of duty, however specious. And He now overcame by falling back upon the simple and clear principle which had brought him to Jordan: 'It becometh us to fulfil all righteousness.' Thus, simply putting aside, without argument, the objection of the Baptist, He followed the Hand that pointed Him to the open door of 'the Kingdom.'

Jesus stepped out of the baptismal waters 'praying.'[a] One prayer, the only one which He taught His disciples, recurs to our minds.[1] We must here individualise and emphasise in their special application its opening sentences: 'Our Father Which art in heaven, hallowed be Thy Name! Thy Kingdom come! Thy will be done in earth, as it is in heaven!' The first thought and the first petition had been the conscious outcome of the Temple-visit, ripened during the long years at Nazareth. The others were now the full expression of His submission to Baptism. He knew His Mission; He had consecrated Himself to it in His Baptism; 'Father Which art in heaven, hallowed be Thy Name.' The unlimited petition for the doing of God's Will on earth with the same absoluteness as in heaven, *was* His self-consecration: the prayer of His Baptism, as the other was its

[a] 1 St. Luke iii. 21

---

[1] It seems to me that the prayer which the Lord taught His disciples must have had its root in, and taken its start from, His own inner Life. At the same time it is adapted to our wants. Much in that prayer has, of course, no application to Him, but is His application of the doctrine of the Kingdom to our state and wants.

confession. And the 'hallowed be Thy Name' was the eulogy, because the ripened and experimental principle of His Life. *How* this Will, connected with 'the Kingdom,' was to be done by Him, and *when*, He was to learn *after* His Baptism. But strange, that the petition which followed those which must have been on the lips of Jesus in that hour should have been the subject of the *first temptation* or assault by the Enemy; strange also, that the other two temptations should have rolled back the force of the assault upon the two great experiences He had gained, and which formed the burden of the petitions, 'Thy Kingdom come; Hallowed be Thy Name.' Was it then so, that all the assaults which Jesus bore only concerned and tested the reality of a past and already attained experience, save those last in the Garden and on the Cross, which were 'sufferings' by which He 'was made perfect'?

But, as we have already seen, such inward forth-bursting of Messianic consciousness could not be separated from objective qualification for, and testimony to it. As the prayer of Jesus winged heavenwards, His solemn response to the call of the Kingdom—'Here am I;' 'Lo, I come to do Thy Will'—the answer came, which at the same time was also the predicted sign to the Baptist. Heaven seemed cleft, and in bodily shape like a dove, the Holy Ghost descended on [1] Jesus, remaining on him. It was as if, symbolically, in the words of St. Peter,[a] that Baptism had been a new flood, and He Who now emerged from it, the Noah—or rest, and comfort-bringer—Who took into His Ark the dove bearing the olive-branch, indicative of a new life. Here, at these waters, was the Kingdom, into which Jesus had entered in the fulfilment of all righteousness; and from them he emerged as its Heaven-designated, Heaven-qualified, and Heaven-proclaimed King. As such he had received the fulness of the Spirit for His Messianic Work—a fulness abiding in Him—that out of it we might receive, and grace for grace. As such also the voice from Heaven proclaimed it, to Him and to John: 'Thou art ('this is') My Beloved Son, in Whom I am well pleased.' The ratification of the great Davidic promise, the announcement of the fulfilment of its predictive import in Psalm ii.[2] was God's solemn declaration of Jesus

[a] 1 St. Pet.
iii. 21

---

[1] Whether or not we adopt the reading εἰς αὐτόν in St. Mark i. 10, the *remaining* of the Holy Spirit upon Jesus is clearly expressed in St. John i. 32.

[2] Here the Targum on Ps. ii. 7, which is evidently intended to weaken the Messianic interpretation, gives us wel-
come help. It paraphrases: 'Beloved as a son to his father art Thou to Me.' Keim regards the words, 'Thou art my beloved Son,' &c., as a mixture of Is. xlii. 1 and Ps. ii. 7. I cannot agree with this view, though this history is the fulfilment of the prediction in Isaiah.

as the Messiah, His public proclamation of it, and the beginning of Jesus' Messianic work. And so the Baptist understood it, when he 'bare record' that He was 'the Son of God.'[a]

Quite intelligible as all this is, it is certainly miraculous; not, indeed, in the sense of contravention of the Laws of Nature (illogical as that phrase is), but in that of having nothing analogous in our present knowledge and experience. But would we not have expected the supra-empirical, the directly heavenly, to attend such an event— that is, if the narrative itself be true, and Jesus what the Gospels represent Him? To reject, therefore, the narrative because of its supra-empirical accompaniment seems, after all, a sad inversion of reasoning, and begging the question. But, to go a step further: if there be no reality in the narrative, whence the invention of the legend? It certainly had no basis in contemporary Jewish teaching; and, equally certainly, it would not have spontaneously occurred to Jewish minds. Nowhere in Rabbinic writings do we find any hint of a Baptism of the Messiah, nor of a descent upon Him of the Spirit in the form of a dove. Rather would such views seem, à priori, repugnant to Jewish thinking. An attempt has, however, been made in the direction of identifying two traits in this narrative with Rabbinic notices. The 'Voice from heaven' has been represented as the '*Bath-Qol*,' or 'Daughter-Voice,' of which we read in Rabbinic writings, as bringing heaven's testimony or decision to perplexed or hardly bestead Rabbis. And it has been further asserted, that among the Jews 'the dove' was regarded as the emblem of the Spirit. In taking notice of these assertions some warmth of language may be forgiven.

We make bold to maintain that no one, who has impartially examined the matter,[1] could find any real analogy between the so-called *Bath-Qol*, and the 'Voice from heaven' of which record is made in the New Testament. However opinions might differ, on one thing all were agreed: the *Bath-Qol* had come *after* the voice of prophecy and the Holy Ghost had ceased in Israel,[b] and, so to speak, had taken, their place.[2] *But at the Baptism of Jesus the descent of the Holy*

CHAP.
XII

[a] St. John i. 34

[b] Jer. Sot. ix. 14; Yoma 9 b; Sotah 33 a; 48 b; Sanh. 11 a

---

[1] Dr. *Wünsche's* Rabbinic notes on the Bath-Qol (Neue Beitr. pp. 22, 23) are taken from *Hamburger's* Real-Encykl. (Abth. ii. pp. 92 &c.).

[2] *Hamburger*, indeed maintains, on the ground of Macc. 23 b, that occasionally it was identified with the Holy Spirit. But carefully read, neither this passage, nor the other, in which the same mis-translation and profane misinterpretation of the words 'She has been more righteous' (Gen. xxxviii. 26) occur (Jer. Sot. ix. 7), at all bears out this suggestion. It is quite untenable in view of the distinct statements (Jer. Sot. ix. 14; Sot. 48 b; and Sanh. 11 a), that after the cessation of the Holy Spirit the Bath-Qol took His place.

BOOK
II

Ghost was accompanied by the Voice from Heaven. Even on this ground, therefore, it could not have been the Rabbinic Bath-Qol. But, further, this ' Daughter-Voice' was regarded rather as the echo of, than as the Voice of God itself[1] (Toseph. Sanh. xi. 1). The occasions on which this ' Daughter-Voice' was supposed to have been heard are so various and sometimes so shocking, both to common and to moral sense, that a comparison with the Gospels is wholly out of the question. And here it also deserves notice, that references to this *Bath-Qol* increase the farther we remove from the age of Christ.[2]

We have reserved to the last the consideration of the statement, that among the Jews the Holy Spirit was presented under the symbol of a dove. It is admitted, that there is no support for this idea either in the Old Testament or in the writings of Philo (*Lücke,* Evang. Joh. i. pp. 425, 426); that, indeed, such animal symbolism of the Divine is foreign to the Old Testament. But all the more confident appeal is made to Rabbinic writings. The suggestion was, apparently, first made by *Wetstein.*[a] It is dwelt upon with much confidence by *Gfrörer*[3] and others, as evidence of the mythical origin of the Gospels;[b] it is repeated by *Wünsche,* and even reproduced by writers who, had they known the real state of matters, would not

[a] Nov. Test. i. p. 268.

[b] Jahrh. des Heils, vol. ii. p. 433

[1] Comp. on the subject *Pinner* in his Introduction to the tractate Berakhoth.

[2] In the Targum Onkelos it is not at all mentioned. In the Targum Pseudo-Jon. it occurs four times (Gen. xxxviii. 26; Numb. xxi. 6; Deut. xxviii. 15; xxxiv. 5), and four times in the Targum on the Hagiographa (twice in Ecclesiastes, once in Lamentations, and once in Esther). In Mechilta and Siphra it does not occur at all, and in Siphré only once, in the absurd legend that the Bath-Qol was heard a distance of twelve times twelve miles proclaiming the death of Moses (ed. *Friedmann,* p. 149 *b*). In the Mishnah it is only twice mentioned (Yeb. xvi. 6, where the sound of a Bath-Qol is supposed to be sufficient attestation of a man's death to enable his wife to marry again; and in Abhoth vi. 2, where it is impossible to understand the language otherwise than figuratively). In the Jerusalem Talmud the Bath-Qol is referred to twenty times, and in the Babylon Talmud sixty-nine times. Sometimes the Bath-Qol gives sentence in favour of a popular Rabbi, sometimes it attempts to decide controversies, or bears witness; or eise it is said every day to proclaim: Such an one's daughter is destined for

such an one (Moed Kat. 18 *b*; Sot. 2 *a*; Sanh. 22 *a*). Occasionally it utters curious or profane interpretations of Scripture (as in Yoma 22 *b*; Sot. 10 *b*), or silly legends, as in regard to the insect *Yattush* which was to torture Titus (Gitt. 56 *b*), or as warning against a place where a hatchet had fallen into the water, descending for seven years without reaching the bottom. Indeed, so strong became the feeling against this superstition, that the more rational Rabbis protested against any appeal to the Bath-Qol (Baba Metsia 59 *b*).

[3] The force of *Gfrörer's* attacks upon the Gospels lies in his cumulative attempts to prove that the individual miraculous facts recorded in the Gospels are based upon Jewish notions. It is, therefore, necessary to examine each of them separately, and such examination, if careful and conscientious, shows that his quotations are often untrustworthy, and his conclusions fallacies. None the less taking are they to those who are imperfectly acquainted with Rabbinic literature. *Wünsche's* Talmudic and Midrashic Notes on the N.T. (Göttingen, 1878) are also too often misleading.

have lent their authority to it. Of the *two* passages by which this strange hypothesis is supported, that in the Targum on Cant. ii. 12 may at once be dismissed, as dating considerably after the close of the Talmud. There remains, therefore, only the one passage in the Talmud,[a] which is generally thus quoted: 'The Spirit of God moved on the face of the waters, like a dove.'[b] That this quotation is incomplete, omitting the most important part, is only a light charge against it. For, if fully made, it would only the more clearly be seen to be *inapplicable*. The passage (Chag. 15 *a*) treats of the supposed distance between 'the upper and the lower waters,' which is stated to amount to only three fingerbreadths. This is proved by a reference to Gen. i. 2, where the Spirit of God is said to brood over the face of the waters, 'just as a dove broodeth over her young without touching them.' It will be noticed, that the comparison is not between the Spirit and the dove, but between the *closeness* with which a dove broods over her young without touching them, and the supposed proximity of the Spirit to the lower waters without touching them.[1] But, if any doubt could still exist, it would be removed by the fact that in a parallel passage,[c] the expression used is not 'dove' but 'that bird.' Thus much for this oft-misquoted passage. But we go farther, and assert, that the dove was *not* the symbol of the Holy Spirit, but that of Israel. As such it is so universally adopted as to have become almost historical.[d] If, therefore, Rabbinic illustration of the descent of the Holy Spirit with the visible appearance of a dove must be sought for, it would lie in the acknowledgment of Jesus as the ideal typical Israelite, the Representative of His People.

The lengthened details, which have been necessary for the exposure of the mythical theory, will not have been without use, if they carry to the mind the conviction that this history had no basis in existing Jewish belief. Its origin cannot, therefore, be rationally accounted for—except by the answer which Jesus, when He came to Jordan, gave to that grand fundamental question: 'The Baptism of John, whence was it? From Heaven, or of men?'[e]

CHAP.
XII

[a] Chag. 15 *a*

[b] *Farrar,* Life of Christ, i p. 117

[c] Ber. R. 2

[d] Comp. the long illustrations in the Midr. 15: Sanh. 95 *a*: Ber. R. 39; Yalkut on Ps. lv. 7, and other passages

[e] St. Matt xxi. 25

---

[1] The saying in Chag. 15 *a* is of *Ben Soma,* who is described in Rabbinic literature as tainted with Christian views, and whose belief in the possibility of the supernatural birth of the Messiah is so coarsely satirised in the Talmud. Rabbi *Löw* (Lebensalter. p. 58) suggests that in Ben Soma's figure of the dove there may have been a Christian reminiscence

Book III.

THE ASCENT:

FROM THE RIVER JORDAN TO THE MOUNT OF TRANSFIGURATION.

כל מקום שאתה מוצא גבורתו של הקב״ה אתה מוצא ענוותנותו דבר זה כתוב בתורה ושנוי בנביאים ומשולש בכתובים

'In every passage of Scripture where thou findest the Majesty of God, thou also findest close by His Condescension (Humility). So it is written down in the Law [Deut. x. 17, followed by verse 18], repeated in the Prophets [Is. lvii. 15], and reiterated in the Hagiographa [Ps. lxviii. 4, followed by verse 5].'—MEGILL. 31 a.

CHAPTER I.

THE TEMPTATION OF JESUS.

(St. Matt. iv. 1–11; St. Mark i. 12, 13; St. Luke iv. 1–13.)

THE proclamation and inauguration of the 'Kingdom of Heaven' at such a time, and under such circumstances, was one of the great *antitheses* of history. With reverence be it said, it is only God Who would thus begin His Kingdom. A similar, even greater antithesis, was the commencement of the Ministry of Christ. From the Jordan to the wilderness with its wild beasts; from the devout acknowledgment of the Baptist, the consecration and filial prayer of Jesus, the descent of the Holy Spirit, and the heard testimony of Heaven, to the utter forsakenness, the felt want and weakness of Jesus, and the assaults of the Devil—no contrast more startling could be conceived. And yet, as we think of it, what followed upon the Baptism, and that it so followed, was necessary, as regarded the Person of Jesus, His Work, and that which was to result from it.

Psychologically, and as regarded the Work of Jesus, even reverent negative Critics [1] have perceived its higher need. That at His consecration to the Kingship of the Kingdom, Jesus should have become clearly conscious of all that it implied in a world of sin; that the Divine method by which that Kingdom should be established, should have been clearly brought out, and its reality tested; and that the King, as Representative and Founder of the Kingdom, should have encountered and defeated the representative, founder, and holder of the opposite power, 'the prince of this world'—these are thoughts which must arise in everyone who believes in any Mission of the Christ. Yet this only as, after the events, we have learned to know the character of that Mission, not as we might have preconceived it. We can understand, how a Life and Work such as

[1] No other terms would correctly describe the book of Keim to which I specially refer. How widely it differs, not only from the superficial trivialities of a Renan, but from the stale arguments of Strauss, or the picturesque inaccuracies of a Hausrath, no serious student need be told. Perhaps on that ground it is only the more dangerous.

BOOK
III

that of Jesus, would commence with 'the Temptation,' but none other than His. Judaism never conceived such an idea; because it never conceived a Messiah like Jesus. It is quite true that long previous Biblical teaching, and even the psychological necessity of the case, must have pointed to temptation and victory as the condition of spiritual greatness. It could not have been otherwise in a world hostile to God, nor yet in man, whose conscious choice determines his position. No crown of victory without previous contest, and that proportionately to its brightness; no moral ideal without personal attainment and probation. The patriarchs had been tried and proved; so had Moses, and all the heroes of faith in Israel. And Rabbinic legend, enlarging upon the Biblical narratives, has much to tell of the original envy of the Angels; of the assaults of Satan upon Abraham, when about to offer up Isaac; of attempted resistance by the Angels to Israel's reception of the Law; and of the final vain endeavour of Satan to take away the soul of Moses.[1] Foolish, repulsive, and even blasphemous as some of these legends are, thus much at least clearly stood out, that spiritual trials must precede spiritual elevation. In their own language: 'The Holy One, blessed be His Name, does not elevate a man to dignity till He has first tried and searched him; and if he stands in temptation, then He raises him to dignity.'[a]

Thus far as regards man. But in reference to the Messiah there is not a hint of any temptation or assault by Satan. It is of such importance to mark this clearly at the outset of this wonderful history, that proof must be offered even at this stage. In whatever manner negative critics may seek to account for the introduction of Christ's Temptation at the commencement of His Ministry, it cannot have been derived from Jewish legend. The 'mythical' interpretation of the Gospel-narratives breaks down in this almost more manifestly than in any other instance.[2] So far from any idea obtaining that Satan was to assault the Messiah, in a well-known passage, which has been previously quoted,[b] the Arch-enemy is represented as overwhelmed and falling on his face at sight of Him, and owning

[a] Bemidb. R. 15, ed. Warsh. vol. iv. p. 63 a, lines 5 and 4 from bottom

[b] Yalkut on Is. lx. 1, vol. ii. p. 56

---

[1] On the temptations of Abraham see Book of Jubilees, ch. xvii.; Sanh. 89 b (and differently but not less blasphemously in Pirké de R. Elies. 31); Pirké de R. Elies. 26, 31, 32 (where also about Satan's temptation of Sarah, who dies in consequence of his tidings); Ab. de R. N. 33; Ber. R. 32, 56; Yalkut, i. c. 98, p. 28 b; and Tanchuma, where the story is related with most repulsive details. As to Moses, see for example Shabb. 89 a; and especially the truly horrible story of the death of Moses in Debar R. 11 (ed. Warsh. iii. p. 22 a and b). But I am not aware of any temptation of Moses by Satan.

[2] Thus Gfrörer can only hope that some Jewish parallelism may yet be discovered (!); while Keim suggests, of course without a tittle of evidence, additions by the early Jewish Christians. But whence and why these imaginary additions?

his complete defeat.[1] On another point in this history we find the same inversion of thought current in Jewish legend. In the Commentary just referred to,[a] the placing of Messiah on the pinnacle of the Temple, so far from being of Satanic temptation, is said to mark the hour of deliverance, of Messianic proclamation, and of Gentile voluntary submission. 'Our Rabbis give this tradition: In the hour when King Messiah cometh, He standeth upon the roof of the Sanctuary, and proclaims to Israel, saying, Ye poor (suffering), the time of your redemption draweth nigh. And if ye believe, rejoice in My Light, which is risen upon you. . . . . Is. lx. 1. . . . . upon you only . . . . Is. lx. 2. . . . . In that hour will the Holy One, blessed be His Name, make the Light of the Messiah and of Israel to shine forth; and all shall come to the Light of the King Messiah and of Israel, as it is written . . . . . Is. lx. 3. . . . . And they shall come and lick the dust from under the feet of the King Messiah, as it is written, Is. xlix. 23. . . . . . And all shall come and fall on their faces before Messiah and before Israel, and say, We will be servants to Him and to Israel. And every one in Israel shall have 2,800 servants,[2] as it is written, Zech. viii. 23.' One more quotation from the same Commentary:[b] 'In that hour, the Holy One, blessed be His Name, exalts the Messiah to the heaven of heavens, and spreads over Him of the splendour of His glory because of the nations of the world, because of the wicked Persians. They say to Him, Ephraim, Messiah, our Righteousness, execute judgment upon them, and do to them what Thy soul desireth.'

In another respect these quotations are important. They show that such ideas were, indeed, present to the Jewish mind, but in a sense opposite to the Gospel-narratives. In other words, they were regarded as the rightful manifestation of Messiah's dignity; whereas in the Evangelic record they are presented as the suggestions of Satan, and the Temptation of Christ. Thus the Messiah of Judaism is the Anti-Christ of the Gospels. But if the narrative cannot be traced to Rabbinic legend, may it not be an adaptation of an Old Testament narrative, such as the account of the forty days' fast of Moses on the mount, or of Elijah in the wilderness? Viewing the Old Testament in its unity, and the Messiah as the apex in the column of its history, we admit—or rather, we must expect—

---

[1] *Keim* (Jesu von Naz. i. *b*, p. 564) seems not to have perused the whole passage, and, quoting it at second-hand, has misapplied it. The passage (Yalkut on Is. lx. 1) has been given before.

[2] The number is thus reached: as there are *seventy* nations, and *ten* of each are to take hold on each of the *four* corners of a Jew's garment, we have 70 × 10 × 4 =2,800.

throughout points of correspondence between Moses, Elijah, and the Messiah. In fact, these may be described as marking the three stages in the history of the Covenant. Moses was its giver, Elijah its restorer, the Messiah its renewer and perfecter. And as such they all had, in a sense, a similar outward consecration for their work. But that neither Moses nor Elijah was assailed by the Devil, constitutes not the only, though a vital, difference between the fast of Moses and Elijah, and that of Jesus. Moses fasted in the middle, Elijah at the end, Jesus at the beginning of His ministry. Moses fasted in the Presence of God;[1] Elijah alone; Jesus assaulted by the Devil. Moses had been called up by God; Elijah had gone forth in the bitterness of his own spirit; Jesus was driven by the Spirit. Moses failed after his forty days' fast, when in indignation he cast the Tables of the Law from him; Elijah failed before his forty days' fast; Jesus was assailed for forty days and endured the trial. Moses was angry against Israel; Elijah despaired of Israel; Jesus overcame for Israel.

Nor must we forget that to each the trial came not only in his human, but in his representative capacity—as giver, restorer, or perfecter of the Covenant. When Moses and Elijah failed, it was not only as individuals, but as giving or restoring the Covenant. And when Jesus conquered, it was not only as the Unfallen and Perfect Man, but as the Messiah. His Temptation and Victory have therefore a twofold aspect: the general human and the Messianic, and these two are closely connected. Hence we draw also this happy inference: in whatever Jesus overcame, we can overcome. Each victory which He has gained secures its fruits for us who are His disciples (and this alike objectively and subjectively). We walk in His foot-prints; we can ascend by the rock-hewn steps which His Agony has cut. He is the perfect man; and as each temptation marks a human assault (assault on humanity), so it also marks a human victory (of humanity). But He is also the Messiah; and alike the assault and the victory were of the Messiah. Thus, each victory of humanity becomes a victory *for* humanity; and so is fulfilled, in this respect also, that ancient hymn of royal victory, 'Thou hast ascended on high; Thou hast led captivity captive; Thou hast received gifts for men; yea, for the rebellious also, that Jehovah God, might dwell among them.'[a][2]

---

[1] The Rabbis have it, that a man must accommodate himself to the ways of the place where he is. When Moses was on the Mount he lived of 'the bread of the Torah' (Shem. R. 47).

[2] The quotation in Eph. iv. 8 resem-

But even so, there are other considerations necessarily preliminary to the study of one of the most important parts in the life of Christ. They concern these two questions, so closely connected that they can scarcely be kept quite apart: Is the Evangelic narrative to be regarded as the account of a *real* and *outward* event ? And if so, how was it possible—or, in what sense can it be asserted—that Jesus Christ, set before us as the Son of God, was ' tempted of the Devil ' ? All subsidiary questions run up into these two.

As regards the *reality* and *outwardness* of the temptation of Jesus, several suggestions may be set aside as unnatural, and *ex post facto* attempts to remove a felt difficulty. *Renan's* frivolous conceit scarcely deserves serious notice, that Jesus went into the wilderness in order to imitate the Baptist and others, since such solitude was at the time regarded as a necessary preparation for great things. We equally dismiss as more reverent, but not better grounded, such suggestions as that an interview there with the deputies of the Sanhedrin, or with a Priest, or with a Pharisee, formed the historical basis of the Satanic Temptation; or that it was a vision, a dream, the reflection of the ideas of the time; or that it was a parabolic form in which Jesus afterwards presented to His disciples His conception of the Kingdom, and how they were to preach it.[1] Of all such explanations it may be said, that the narrative does not warrant them, and that they would probably never have been suggested, if their authors had been able simply to accept the Evangelic history. But if so it would have been both better and wiser wholly to reject (as some have done) the authenticity of this, as of the whole early history of the Life of Christ, rather than transform what, if true, is so unspeakably grand into a series of modern platitudes. And yet (as *Keim* has felt) it seems impossible to deny, that such a transaction at the beginning of Christ's Messianic Ministry is not only credible, but almost a necessity; and that such a transaction must have assumed the form of a contest with Satan. Besides, throughout the Gospels there is not only allusion to this first great conflict (so that it does *not* belong only to the early history of Christ's Life), but constant reference to the power of Satan in the world, as a kingdom opposed to that of God, and of which the Devil is the King.[2] And the reality of such a kingdom of evil no earnest mind would call in question, nor would it pronounce à

bles the rendering of the Targum (see *Delitzsch* Comm. ü. d. Psalter, vol. i. p. 503).

[1] We refrain from naming the indi-

vidual writers who have broached these and other equally untenable hypotheses.

[2] The former notably in St. Matt. xii. 25–28; St. Luke xi. 17 &c. The import

priori against the personality of its king. Reasoning *à priori*, its credibility rests on the same kind of, only, perhaps, on more generally patent, evidence as that of the beneficent Author of all Good, so that —with reverence be it said—we have, apart from Holy Scripture, and, as regards one branch of the argument, as much evidence for believing in a personal Satan, as in a Personal God. Holding, therefore, by the reality of this transaction, and finding it equally impossible to trace it to Jewish legend, or to explain it by the coarse hypothesis of misunder-standing, exaggeration, and the like, this one question arises: Might it not have been a purely inward transaction,—or does the narrative present an account of what was objectively real ?

At the outset, it is only truthful to state, that the distinction does not seem of quite so vital importance as it has appeared to some, who have used in regard to it the strongest language.[1] On the other hand it must be admitted that the narrative, if naturally interpreted, suggests an outward and real event, not an inward trans-action;[2] that there is no other instance of ecstatic state or of vision recorded in the life of Jesus, and that (as Bishop *Ellicott* has shown),[3] the special expressions used are all in accordance with the natural view. To this we add, that some of the objections raised—notably that of the impossibility of showing from one spot all the kingdoms of the world—cannot bear close investigation. For no rational interpretation would insist on the absolute literality of this statement, any more than on that of the survey of the *whole* extent of the land of Israel by Moses from Pisgah.[a][4] All the requirements of the narrative would be met by supposing Jesus to have been placed on a very high mountain, whence south, the land of Judæa and far-off Edom; east, the swelling plains towards Euphrates; north, snow-capped Lebanon; and west, the cities of Herod, the coast of the Gentiles, and beyond, the wide sea dotted with sails, gave far-off prospect of the kingdoms of this world. To His piercing gaze all their grandeur would seem to unroll, and pass before Him like a moving scene, in which the sparkle of beauty and wealth dazzled the eye, the sheen of arms glittered in the far

a Deut.
xxxiv. 1-3

of this, as looking back upon the history of the Temptation, has not always been sufficiently recognised. In regard to Satan and his power many passages will occur to the reader, such as St. Matt. vi. 13; xii. 22; xiii. 19, 25, 39; xxvi. 41; St. Luke x. 18; xxii. 3, 28, 31; St. John viii. 44; xii. 31; xiii. 27; xiv. 30; xvi. 11.

[1] So Bishop *Ellicott*, Histor. Lectures, p. 111.

[2] Professor *Godet's* views on this sub-ject are very far from satisfactory,

whether exegetically or dogmatically. Happily, they fall far short of the notion of any internal solicitation to sin in the case of Jesus, which Bishop Ellicott so justly denounces in strongest language

[3] U. s. p. 110, note 2.

[4] According to Siphré (ed. *Friedmann* p. 149 *a* and *b*), God showed to Moses Israel in its happiness, wars, and misfor-tunes; the whole world from the Day of Creation to that of the Resurrection; Paradise, and Gehenna.

distance, the tramp of armed men, the hum of busy cities, and the
sound of many voices fell on the ear like the far-off rush of the sea,
while the restful harmony of thought, or the music of art, held and
bewitched the senses—and all seemed to pour forth its fullness in
tribute of homage at His feet in Whom all is perfect, and to Whom
all belongs.

But in saying this we have already indicated that, in such circumstances, the boundary-line between the outward and the inward must
have been both narrow and faint. Indeed, with Christ it can scarcely
be conceived to have existed at such a moment. The past, the present,
and the future must have been open before Him like a map unrolling.
Shall we venture to say that such a vision was only inward, and not
outwardly and objectively real? In truth we are using terms which
have no application to Christ. If we may venture once more to speak
in this wise of the Divine Being: With Him what we view as the
opposite poles of subjective and objective are absolutely one. To go
a step further: many even of *our* temptations are only (contrastedly)
inward, for these two reasons, that they have their basis or else their
point of contact within us, and that from the limitations of our bodily
condition we do not see the enemy, nor can take active part in the
scene around. But in both respects it was not so with the Christ.
If this be so, the whole question seems almost irrelevant, and the distinction of *outward* and *inward* inapplicable to the present case. Or
rather, we must keep by these two landmarks: First, it was not inward in the sense of being merely subjective; but it was all *real*—a
real assault by a real Satan, really under these three forms, and it constituted a real Temptation to Christ. Secondly, it was not merely
outward in the sense of being only a present assault by Satan; but it
must have reached beyond the outward into the inward, and have had
for its further object that of influencing the future Work of Christ, as
it stood out before His Mind.

A still more difficult and solemn question is this: In what respect
could Jesus Christ, the Perfect Sinless Man, the Son of God, have
been tempted of the Devil? That He was so tempted is of the very
essence of this narrative, confirmed throughout His after-life, and
laid down as a fundamental principle in the teaching and faith of the
Church.[a] On the other hand, temptation without the inward corre- [a] Heb. iv. 15
spondence of existent sin is not only unthinkable, so far as man is
concerned,[b] but temptation without the possibility of sin seems unreal [b] St. James i. 14
—a kind of Docetism.[1] Yet the very passage of Holy Scripture in

[1] The heresy which represents the Body of Christ as only apparent, not real.

BOOK
III

which Christ's equality with us as regards all temptation is expressed, also emphatically excepts from it this one particular *sin*,[a] not only in the sense that Christ actually did not sin, nor merely in this, that 'our concupiscence'[b] had no part in His temptations, but emphatically in this also, that the notion of sin has to be wholly excluded from our thoughts of Christ's temptations.'

To obtain, if we can, a clearer understanding of this subject, two points must be kept in view. Christ's was real, though unfallen Human Nature; and Christ's Human was in inseparable union with His Divine Nature. We are not attempting to explain these mysteries, nor at present to vindicate them; we are only arguing from the standpoint of the Gospels and of Apostolic teaching, which proceeds on these premisses—and proceeding on them, we are trying to understand the Temptation of Christ. Now it is clear, that human nature, that of Adam before his fall, was created both sinless and peccable. If Christ's Human Nature was not like ours, but, morally, like that of Adam before his fall, then must it likewise have been both sinless and in itself peccable. We say, in itself—for there is a great difference between the statement that human nature, as Adam and Christ had it, was capable of sinning, and this other, that Christ was peccable. From the latter the Christian mind instinctively recoils, even as it is metaphysically impossible to imagine the Son of God peccable. Jesus voluntarily took upon Himself human nature with all its infirmities and weaknesses—but without the moral taint of the Fall: without sin. It was human nature, in itself capable of sinning, but not having sinned. If He was absolutely sinless, He must have been unfallen. The position of the first Adam was that of being capable of not sinning, not that of being incapable of sinning. The Second Adam also had a nature capable of not sinning, but not incapable of sinning. This explains the possibility of 'temptation' or assault upon Him, just as Adam could be tempted before there was in him any inward *consensus* to it.[2] The first Adam would have been 'perfected'—or passed from the capability of not sinning to the incapability of sinning—by obedience. That 'obedience'—or absolute submission to the Will of God—was the grand outstanding characteristic of Christ's work;

---

[1] Comp. *Riehm*, Lehrbegr. d. Hebr. Br. p. 364. But I cannot agree with the views which this learned theologian expresses. Indeed, it seems to me that he does not meet the real difficulties of the question; on the contrary, rather aggravates them. They lie in this: How could One Who (according to *Riehm*) stood on the same level with us in regard to all temptations have been exempt from sin?

[2] The latter was already sin. Yet 'temptation' means more than mere 'assault.' There may be conditional mental *assensus* without moral *consensus*—and so temptation without sin. See p. 301, *note*.

but it was so, because He was not only the Unsinning, Unfallen Man, CHAP.
but also the Son of God. Because God was His Father, therefore He I
must be about His Business, which was to do the Will of His Father.
With a peccable Human Nature He was impeccable; not because He
obeyed, but being impeccable He so obeyed, because His Human was
inseparably connected with His Divine Nature. To keep this Union
of the two Natures out of view would be Nestorianism.[1] To sum up:
The Second Adam, morally unfallen, though voluntarily subject to all
the conditions of our Nature, was, with a peccable Human Nature,
absolutely impeccable as being also the Son of God—a peccable
Nature, yet an impeccable Person: the God-Man, 'tempted in regard to all (things) in like manner (as we), without (excepting) sin.'

All this sounds, after all, like the stammering of Divine words
by a babe, and yet it may in some measure help us to understand the
character of Christ's first great Temptation.

Before proceeding, a few sentences are required in explanation of
seeming differences in the Evangelic narration of the event. The
historical part of St. John's Gospel begins after the Temptation—that
is, with the actual Ministry of Christ; since it was not within the
purport of that work to detail the earlier history. That had been
sufficiently done in the Synoptic Gospels. Impartial and serious
critics will admit that these are in accord. For, if St. Mark only
summarises, in his own brief manner, he supplies the two-fold notice
that Jesus was 'driven' into the wilderness, 'and was with the wild
beasts,' which is in fullest internal agreement with the detailed narratives of St. Matthew and St. Luke. The only noteworthy difference
between these two is, that St. Matthew places the Temple-temptation
before that of the world-kingdom, while St. Luke inverts this order,
probably because his narrative was primarily intended for Gentile
readers, to whose mind this might present itself as to them the true
gradation of temptation. To St. Matthew we owe the notice, that
after the Temptation 'Angels came and ministered' unto Jesus; to
St. Luke, that the Tempter only 'departed from Him for a season.'

To restate in order our former conclusions, Jesus had deliberately,
of His own accord and of set firm purpose, gone to be baptized. That
one grand outstanding fact of His early life, that He must be about
His Father's Business, had found its explanation when He knew that
the Baptist's cry, 'the Kingdom of Heaven is at hand,' was from God.
His Father's Business, then, was 'the Kingdom of Heaven,' and to it

[1] The heresy which unduly separated the two Natures.

He consecrated Himself, so fulfilling all righteousness. But **His** 'being about it' was quite other than that of any Israelite, however devout, who came to Jordan. It was His consecration, not only to the Kingdom, but to the Kingship, in the anointing and permanent possession of the Holy Ghost, and in His proclamation from heaven. That Kingdom was His Father's Business; its Kingship, the manner in which He was to be 'about it.' The next step was not, like the first, voluntary, and of preconceived purpose. Jesus went to Jordan; He was driven of the Spirit into the wilderness. Not, indeed, in the sense of His being unwilling to go,[1] or having had other purpose, such as that of immediate return into Galilee, but in that of not being willing, of having no will or purpose in the matter, but being 'led up,' unconscious of its purpose, with irresistible force, by the Spirit. In that wilderness He had to test what He had learned, and to learn what He had tested. So would He have full proof for His Work of the *What*—His Call and Kingship; so would He see its *How*—the manner of it; so, also, would, from the outset, the final issue of His Work appear.

Again—banishing from our minds all thought of sin in connection with Christ's Temptation,[a] He is presented to us as the Second Adam, both as regarded Himself, and His relation to man. In these two respects, which, indeed, are one, He is now to be tried. Like the first, the Second Adam, sinless, is to be tempted, but under the existing conditions of the Fall: in the wilderness, not in Eden; not in the enjoyment of all good, but in the pressing want of all that is necessary for the sustenance of life, and in the felt weakness consequent upon it. For (unlike the first) the Second Adam was, in His Temptation, to be placed on an absolute equality with us, except as regarded sin. Yet even so, there must have been some point of inward connection to make the outward assault a temptation. It is here that opponents (such as *Strauss* and *Keim*) have strangely missed the mark, when objecting, either that the forty days' fast was intrinsically unnecessary, or that the assaults of Satan were clumsy suggestions, incapable of being temptations to Jesus. He is 'driven' into the wilderness by the Spirit to be tempted.[2] The history of humanity

a Hebr. iv.
15

---

[1] This is evident even from the terms used by St. Matthew (ἀνήχθη) and St. Luke (ἤγετο). I cannot agree with *Godet*, that Jesus would have been inclined to return to Galilee and begin teaching. Jesus had no inclination save this—to do the Will of His Father. And yet the expression 'driven' used by St.

Mark seems to imply some human shrinking on His part—at least at the outset.

[2] The place of the Temptation could not, of course, have been the traditional 'Quarantania,' but must have been near Bethabara. See also *Stanley's* Sinai and Palestine, p. 308.

is taken up anew at the point where first the kingdom of Satan was
founded, only under new conditions. It is not now a choice, but a
contest, for Satan *is* the prince of this world. During the whole
forty days of Christ's stay in the wilderness His Temptation continued,
though it only attained its high point at the last, when, after the long
fast, He felt the weariness and weakness of hunger. As fasting occupies but a very subordinate, we might almost say a tolerated, place
in the teaching of Jesus; and as, so far as we know, He exercised on
no other occasion such ascetic practices, we are left to infer internal,
as well as external, necessity for it in the present instance. The former is easily understood in His pre-occupation; the latter must have
had for its object to reduce Him to utmost outward weakness, by the
depression of all the vital powers. We regard it as a psychological
fact that, under such circumstances, of all mental faculties the memory
alone is active, indeed, almost preternaturally active. During the
preceding thirty-nine days the plan, or rather the future, of the Work
to which He had been consecrated, must have been always before Him.
In this respect, then, He must have been tempted. It is wholly impossible that He hesitated for a moment as to the means by which He
was to establish the Kingdom of God. He could not have felt tempted
to adopt carnal means, opposed to the nature of that Kingdom, and
to the Will of God. The unchangeable convictions which He had
already attained must have stood out before Him: that His Father's
business was the Kingdom of God; that He was furnished to it, not
by outward weapons, but by the abiding Presence of the Spirit;
above all, that absolute submission to the Will of God was the way to
it, nay, itself the Kingdom of God. It will be observed, that it was
on these very points that the final attack of the Enemy was directed
in the utmost weakness of Jesus. But, on the other hand, the Tempter
could not have failed to assault Him with considerations which He
must have felt to be true. How could He hope, alone, and with such
principles, to stand against Israel? He knew their views and feelings; and as, day by day, the sense of utter loneliness and forsakenness increasingly gathered around Him, in His increasing faintness
and weakness, the seeming hopelessness of such a task as He had
undertaken must have grown upon Him with almost overwhelming
power.[1] Alternately, the temptation to despair, presumption, or the
cutting short of the contest in some decisive manner, must have

---

[1] It was this which would make the
'assault' a 'temptation' by vividly setting before the mind the reality and rationality of these considerations—a mental *assensus*—without implying any inward *consensus* to the manner in which
the Enemy proposed to have them set
aside.

presented itself to His mind, or rather have been presented to it by the Tempter.

And this was, indeed, the essence of His last three great temptations; which, as the whole contest, resolved themselves into the one question of absolute submission to the Will of God,[1] which is the sum and substance of all obedience. If He submitted to it, it must be suffering, and only suffering—helpless, hopeless suffering to the bitter end; to the extinction of life, in the agonies of the Cross, as a malefactor; denounced, betrayed, rejected by His people; alone, in very God-forsakenness. And when thus beaten about by temptation, His powers reduced to the lowest ebb of faintness, all the more vividly would memory hold out the facts so well known, so keenly realised at that moment, in the almost utter cessation of every other mental faculty:[2] the scene lately enacted by the banks of Jordan, and the two great expectations of His own people, that the Messiah was to head Israel from the Sanctuary of the Temple, and that all kingdoms of the world were to become subject to Him. Here, then, is the inward basis of the Temptation of Christ, in which the fast was not unnecessary, nor yet the special assaults of the Enemy either 'clumsy suggestions,' or unworthy of Jesus.

He is weary with the contest, faint with hunger, alone in that wilderness. His voice falls on no sympathising ear; no voice reaches Him but that of the Tempter. There is nothing bracing, strengthening in this featureless, barren, stony wilderness—only the picture of desolateness, hopelessness, despair. He must, He will absolutely submit to the Will of God. But can this be the Will of God? One word of power, and the scene would be changed. Let Him despair of all men, of everything—*He* can do it. By His Will the Son of God, as the Tempter suggests—not, however, calling thereby in question His Sonship, but rather proceeding on its admitted reality[3]—can change the stones into bread. He can do miracles—put an end to present want and question, and, as visibly the possessor of absolute miraculous power, the goal is reached! But this would really have been to change the idea of Old Testament miracle into the heathen conception of magic, which was absolute power inherent in an indi-

---

[1] All the assaults of Satan were really directed against Christ's absolute submission to the Will of God, which was His Perfectness. Hence, by every one of these temptations, as *Weiss* says in regard to the first, '*rüttelt er an Seiner Vollkommenheit.*'

[2] I regard the memory as affording the basis for the Temptation. What was so vividly in Christ's memory at that moment, that was flashed before Him as in a mirror under the dazzling light of temptation.

[3] Satan's 'if' was rather a taunt than a doubt. Nor could it have been intended to call in question His ability to do miracles. Doubt on that point would already have been a fall.

vidual, without moral purpose.   The moral purpose—the grand moral
purpose in all that was of God—was absolute submission to the Will
of God.   His Spirit had driven Him into that wilderness.   His circumstances were God-appointed; and where He so appoints them,
He will support us in them, even as, in the failure of bread, He supported Israel by the manna.[a][1]   And Jesus absolutely submitted to
that Will of God by continuing in His present circumstances.   To
have set himself free from what they implied, would have been *despair*
of God, and rebellion.   He does more than not succumb: He conquers.
The Scriptural reference to a better life upon the Word of God marks
more than the end of the contest; it marks the *conquest* of Satan.
He emerges on the other side triumphant, with this expression of His
assured conviction of the sufficiency of God.

It cannot be despair—and He cannot take up His Kingdom alone,
in the exercise of mere power!   Absolutely submitting to the Will
of God, He must, and He can, absolutely trust Him.   But if so, then
let Him really trust Himself upon God, and make experiment—nay
more, public demonstration—of it.   If it be not despair of God, let
it be *presumption!*   He will not do the work alone!   Then God-up-
borne, according to His promise, let the Son of God suddenly, from
that height, descend and head His people, and that not in any profane
manner, but in the midst of the Sanctuary, where God was specially
near, in sight of incensing priests and worshipping people.   So also
will the goal at once be reached.

The Spirit of God had driven Jesus into the wilderness; the spirit
of the Devil now carried Him to Jerusalem.   Jesus stands on the lofty
pinnacle of the Tower, or of the Temple-porch,[2] presumably that on
which every day a Priest was stationed to watch, as the pale morning
light passed over the hills of Judæa far off to Hebron, to announce it as
the signal for offering the morning sacrifice.[3]   If we might indulge our
imagination, the moment chosen would be just as the Priest had quitted

---

[1] The supply of the manna was only
an exemplification and application of the
general principle, that man really lives
by the Word of God.

[2] It cannot be regarded as certain, that
the πτερύγιον τοῦ ἱεροῦ was, as commentators generally suppose, the Tower
at the southeastern angle of the Temple
Cloisters, where the Royal (southern) and
Solomon's (the eastern) Porch met, and
whence the view into the Kedron Valley
beneath was to the stupendous depth of
450 feet.   Would this angle be called 'a
wing' (πτερύγιον)?   Nor can I agree
with Delitzsch, that it was the 'roof' of

the Sanctuary, where indeed there would
scarcely have been standing-room.   It
certainly formed the watch-post of the
Priest.   Possibly it may have been the
extreme corner of the 'wing-like' porch,
or *ulam*, which led into the Sanctuary.
Thence a Priest could easily have communicated with his brethren in the court
beneath.   To this there is, however, the
objection that in that case it should have
been τοῦ ναοῦ.   At p. 244, the ordinary
view of this locality has been taken.

[3] Comp. 'The Temple, its Ministry and
Services,' p. 132.

that station. The first desert-temptation had been in the grey of break-ing light, when to the faint and weary looker the stones of the wilder-ness seemed to take fantastic shapes, like the bread for which the faint body hungered. In the next temptation Jesus stands on the watch-post which the white-robed priest had just quitted. Fast the rosy morning-light, deepening into crimson, and edged with gold, is spreading over the land. In the Priests' Court below Him the morning-sacrifice has been offered. The massive Temple-gates are slowly opening, and the blasts of the priests' silver trumpets is summoning Israel to begin a new day by appearing before their Lord. Now then let Him descend, Heaven-borne, into the midst of priests and people. What shouts of acclamation would greet His appearance! What homage of worship would be His! The goal can at once be reached, and that at the head of believing Israel. Jesus is surveying the scene. By His side is the Tempter, watching the features that mark the work-ing of the spirit within. And now he has whispered it. Jesus had overcome in the first temptation by simple, absolute trust. This was the time, and this the place to act upon this trust, even as the very Scriptures to which Jesus had appealed warranted. But so to have done would have been not trust—far less the heroism of faith—but *presumption*. The goal might indeed have been reached; but not the Divine goal, nor in God's way—and, as so often, Scripture itself explained and guarded the Divine promise by a preceding Divine command.[1] And thus once more Jesus not only is not overcome, but He overcomes by absolute submission to the Will of God.

To submit to the Will of God! But is not this to acknowledge His authority, and the order and disposition which He has made of all things? Once more the scene changes. They have turned their back upon Jerusalem and the Temple. Behind are also all popular prejudices, narrow nationalism, and limitations. They no longer

---

[1] *Bengel*: 'Scriptura per Scripturam interpretanda et concilianda.' This is also a Rabbinic canon. The Rabbis fre-quently insist on the duty of not expos-ing oneself to danger, in presumptuous expectation of miraculous deliverance. It is a curious saying: Do not stand over against an ox when he comes from the fodder; Satan jumps out from between his horns. (Pes. 112 *b*.) David had been presumptuous in Ps. xxvi. 2—and failed. (Sanh. 107 *a*.) But the most apt illus-tration is this: On one occasion the child of a Rabbi was asked by R. Jochanan to quote a verse. The child quoted Deut. xiv. 22, at the same time pro-pounding the question, why the second clause virtually repeated the first. The Rabbi replied, 'To teach us that the giv-ing of tithes maketh rich.' 'How do you know it?' asked the child. 'By experi-ence,' answered the Rabbi. 'But,' said the child, 'such experiment is not lawful, since we are not to tempt the Lord our God.' (See the very curious book of Rabbi *So oweyczgk*, Die Bibel, d. Talm. u. d. Evang. p. 132.)

breathe the stifled air, thick with the perfume of incense. They have taken their flight into God's wide world. There they stand on the top of some very high mountain. It is in the full blaze of sunlight that He now gazes upon a wondrous scene. Before Him rise, from out the cloud-land at the edge of the horizon, forms, figures, scenes—come words, sounds, harmonies. The world in all its glory, beauty, strength, majesty, is unveiled. Its work, its might, its greatness, its art, its thought, emerge into clear view. And still the horizon seems to widen as He gazes; and more and more, and beyond it still more and still brighter appears. It is a world quite other than that which the retiring Son of the retired Nazareth-home had ever seen, could ever have imagined, that opens its enlarging wonders. To us in the circumstances the temptation, which at first sight seems, so to speak, the clumsiest, would have been well nigh irresistible. In measure as our intellect was enlarged, our heart attuned to this world-melody, we would have gazed with bewitched wonderment on that sight, surrendered ourselves to the harmony of those sounds, and quenched the thirst of our soul with maddening draught. But passively sublime as it must have appeared to the Perfect Man, the God-Man—and to Him far more than to us from His infinitely deeper appreciation of, and wider sympathy with the good, the true, and the beautiful—He had already overcome. It was, indeed, not 'worship,' but homage which the Evil One claimed from Jesus, and that on the truly stated and apparently rational ground, that, in its present state, all this world 'was delivered' unto him, and he exercised the power of giving it to whom he would. But in this very fact lay the answer to the suggestion. High above this moving scene of glory and beauty arched the deep blue of God's heaven, and brighter than the sun, which poured its light over the sheen and dazzle beneath, stood out the fact: 'I must be about My Father's business;' above the din of far-off sounds rose the voice: 'Thy Kingdom come!' Was not all this the Devil's to have and to give, because it was not the Father's Kingdom, to which Jesus had consecrated Himself? What Satan sought was, 'My kingdom come' —a Satanic Messianic time, a Satanic Messiah; the final realisation of an empire of which his present possession was only temporary, caused by the alienation of man from God. To destroy all this: to destroy the works of the Devil, to abolish his kingdom, to set man free from his dominion, was the very object of Christ's Mission. On the ruins of the past shall the new arise, in proportions of grandeur and beauty hitherto unseen, only gazed at afar by prophets' rapt sight.

It is to become the Kingdom of God; and Christ's consecration to it is to be the corner-stone of its new Temple. Those scenes are to be transformed into one of higher worship; those sounds to mingle and melt into a melody of praise. An endless train, unnumbered multitudes from afar, are to bring their gifts, to pour their wealth, to consecrate their wisdom, to dedicate their beauty—to lay it all in lowly worship as humble offering at His feet: a world God-restored, God-dedicated, in which dwells God's peace, over which rests God's glory. It is to be the bringing of worship, not the crowning of rebellion, which is the *Kingdom.* And so Satan's greatest becomes to Christ his coarsest temptation,[1] which He casts from Him; and the words: ' Thou shalt worship the Lord thy God, and Him only shalt thou serve,' which now receive their highest fulfilment, mark not only Satan's defeat and Christ's triumph, but the principle of His Kingdom—of all victory and all triumph.

Foiled, defeated, the Enemy has spread his dark pinions towards that far-off world of his, and covered it with their shadow. The sun no longer glows with melting heat; the mists have gathered or the edge of the horizon, and enwrapped the scene which has faded from view. And in the cool and shade that followed have the Angels[2] come and ministered to His wants, both bodily and mental. He has refused to assert power; He has not yielded to despair; He would not fight and conquer alone in His own strength; and He has received power and refreshment, and Heaven's company unnumbered in their ministry of worship. He would not yield to Jewish dream; He did not pass from despair to presumption; and lo, after the contest, with no reward as its object, all is His. He would not have Satan's vassals as His legions, and all Heaven's hosts are at His command. It had been victory; it is now shout of triumphant praise. He Whom God had anointed by His Spirit had conquered by the Spirit; He Whom Heaven's Voice had proclaimed God's beloved Son, in Whom He was well pleased, had proved such, and done His good pleasure.

They had been all overcome, these three temptations against submission to the Will of God, present, personal, and specifically Messianic. Yet all His life long there were echoes of them: of the first, in the suggestion of His brethren to show Himself;[a] of the second, in the popular attempt to make Him a king, and perhaps also in what constituted the final idea of Judas Iscariot; of the

---

[1] Sin always intensifies in the coarseness of its assaults.

[2] For the Jewish views on Angelology and Demonology, see Appendix XIII.: 'Jewish Angelology and Demonology.'

third, as being most plainly Satanic, in the question of Pilate: 'Art Thou then a king?'

The enemy 'departed from Him'—yet only 'for a season.' But this first contest and victory of Jesus decided all others to the last. These were, perhaps not as to the shaping of His Messianic plan, nor through memory of Jewish expectancy, yet still in substance the same contest about absolute obedience, absolute submission to the Will of God, which constitutes the Kingdom of God. And so also from first to last was this the victory: 'Not My will, but Thine, be done.' But as, in the first three petitions which He has taught us, Christ has enfolded us in the mantle of His royalty, so has He Who shared our nature and our temptations gone up with us, want-pressed, sin-laden, and temptation-stricken as we are, to the Mount of Temptation in the four human petitions which follow the first. And over us is spread, as the sheltering folds of His mantle, this as the outcome of His royal contest and glorious victory, 'For Thine is the Kingdom, and the power, and the glory, for ever and ever!'[1]

[1] This quotation of the Doxology leaves, of course, the critical question undetermined, whether the words were part of the 'Lord's Prayer' in its original form.

CHAPTER II.

THE DEPUTATION FROM JERUSALEM—THE THREE SECTS OF THE PHARI-
SEES, SADDUCEES, AND ESSENES—EXAMINATION OF THEIR DISTINC-
TIVE DOCTRINES.[1]

(St. John i. 19–24.)

BOOK
III

APART from the repulsively carnal form which it had taken, there is something absolutely sublime in the continuance and intensity of the Jewish expectation of the Messiah. It outlived not only the delay of long centuries, but the persecutions and scattering of the people; it continued under the disappointment of the Maccabees, the rule of a Herod, the administration of a corrupt and contemptible Priesthood, and, finally, the government of Rome as represented by a Pilate; nay, it grew in intensity almost in proportion as it seemed unlikely of realisation. These are facts which show that the doctrine of the Kingdom, as the sum and substance of Old Testament teaching, was the very heart of Jewish religious life; while, at the same time, they evidence a moral elevation which placed abstract religious conviction far beyond the reach of passing events, and clung to it with a tenacity which nothing could loosen.

Tidings of what these many months had occurred by the banks of the Jordan must have early reached Jerusalem, and ultimately stirred to the depths its religious society, whatever its preoccupation with ritual questions or political matters. For it was not an ordinary movement, nor in connection with any of the existing parties, religious or political. An extraordinary preacher, of extraordinary appearance and habits, not aiming, like others, after renewed zeal in legal observances, or increased Levitical purity, but preaching repentance and moral renovation in preparation for the coming Kingdom, and sealing this novel doctrine with an equally novel rite, had drawn

---

[1] This chapter contains, among other matter, a detailed and critical examination of the great Jewish Sects, such as was necessary in a work on 'The Times,' as well as 'The Life,' of Christ.

from town and country multitudes of all classes—inquirers, penitents
and novices. The great and burning question seemed, what the real
character and meaning of it was? or rather, whence did it issue,
and whither did it tend? The religious leaders of the people proposed to answer this by instituting an inquiry through a trustworthy deputation. In the account of this by St. John certain
points seem clearly implied;[a] on others only suggestions can be
ventured.

That the interview referred to occurred *after* the Baptism of
Jesus, appears from the whole context.[1] Similarly, the statement that
the deputation which came to John was 'sent from Jerusalem' by
'the Jews,' implies that it proceeded from authority, even if it did
not bear more than a semi-official character. For, although the expression '*Jews*' in the fourth Gospel generally conveys the idea of
contrast to the disciples of Christ (for ex. St. John vii. 15), yet it
refers to the people in their corporate capacity, that is, as represented by their constituted religious authorities.[b] On the other
hand, although the term 'scribes and elders' does not occur in the
Gospel of St. John,[2] it by no means follows that 'the Priests and
Levites' sent from the capital either represented the two great
divisions of the Sanhedrin, or, indeed, that the deputation issued
from the Great Sanhedrin itself. The former suggestion is entirely
ungrounded; the latter at least problematic. It seems a legitimate
inference that, considering their own tendencies, and the political
dangers connected with such a step, the Sanhedrin of Jerusalem
would not have come to the formal resolution of sending a regular
deputation on such an inquiry. Moreover, a measure like this
would have been entirely outside their recognised mode of procedure.
The Sanhedrin did not, and could not, originate charges. It only
investigated those brought before it. It is quite true that judgment
upon false prophets and religious seducers lay with it;[c] but the
Baptist had not as yet said or done anything to lay him open to such
an accusation. He had in no way infringed the Law by word or deed,
nor had he even claimed to be a prophet.[3] If, nevertheless, it seems
most probable that 'the Priests and Levites' came from the Sanhedrin,
we are led to the conclusion that theirs was an informal mission,
rather privately arranged than publicly determined upon.

CHAP.
II

[a] 1. 19–28

[b] Comp. St
John v. 15,
16; ix. 18,
22; xviii.
12, 31

[d] Sanh. 1. 5

---

[1] This point is fully discussed by
Lücke, Evang. Joh., vol. i. pp. 396–398.
[2] So Professor *Westcott*, in his Commentary on the passage (Speaker's Comment., N.T., vol. ii. p. 18), where he
notes that the expression in St. John
viii. 3 is unauthentic.
[4] Of this the Sanhedrin must have
been perfectly aware. Comp. St. Matt.
iii. 7; St. Luke iii. 15 &c.

And with this the character of the deputies agrees. 'Priests and Levites'—the colleagues of John the Priest—would be selected for such an errand, rather than leading Rabbinic authorities. The presence of the latter would, indeed, have given to the movement an importance, if not a sanction, which the Sanhedrin could not have wished. The only other authority in Jerusalem from which such a deputation could have issued was the so-called 'Council of the Temple,' 'Judicature of the Priests,' or 'Elders of the Priesthood,'[a] which consisted of the fourteen chief officers of the Temple. But although they may afterwards have taken their full part in the condemnation of Jesus, ordinarily their duty was only connected with the services of the Sanctuary, and not with criminal questions or doctrinal investigations.[1] It would be too much to suppose, that they would take the initiative in such a matter on the ground that the Baptist was a member of the Priesthood. Finally, it seems quite natural that such an informal inquiry, set on foot most probably by the Sanhedrists, should have been entrusted exclusively to the Pharisaic party. It would in no way have interested the Sadducees; and what members of that party had seen of John[b] must have convinced them that his views and aims lay entirely beyond their horizon.

The origin of the two great parties of Pharisees and Sadducees has already been traced.[2] They mark, not sects, but mental directions, such as in their principles are natural and universal, and, indeed, appear in connection with all metaphysical[3] questions. They are the different modes in which the human mind views supersensuous problems, and which afterwards, when one-sidedly followed out, harden into diverging schools of thought. If Pharisees and Sadducees were not 'sects' in the sense of separation from the unity of the Jewish ecclesiastical community, neither were theirs 'heresies' in the conventional, but only in the original sense of tendency, direction, or, at most, views, differing from those commonly entertained.[4] Our sources of information here are: the New Testament,

a For cx.
Yoma 1. 5

b St. Matt.
iii. 7, &c.

---

[1] Comp. 'The Temple, its Ministry and Services,' p. 75. Dr. *Geiger* (Urschr. u. Uebersetz. d. Bibel, pp. 113, 114) ascribes to them, however, a much wider jurisdiction. Some of his inferences (such as at pp. 115, 116) seem to me historically unsupported.

[2] Comp. Book I. ch. viii.

[3] I use the term metaphysical here in the sense of all that is above the natural, not merely the speculative, but the supersensuous generally.

[4] The word $\alpha\H{i}\rho\varepsilon\sigma\iota\varsigma$ has received its present meaning chiefly from the adjective attaching to it in 2 Pet. ii. 1. In Acts xxiv. 5, 14, xxviii. 22, it is vituperatively applied to Christians; in 1 Cor. xi. 19, Gal. v. 20, it seems to apply to diverging practices of a sinful kind; in Titus iii. 10, the 'heretic' seems one who held or taught diverging opinions or practices. Besides, it occurs in the N.T. once to mark the Sadducees, and twice the Pharisees (Acts v. 17; xv. 5, and xxvi. 5).

Josephus, and Rabbinic writings. The New Testament only marks,
in broad outlines and popularly, the peculiarities of each party; but
from the absence of bias it may safely be regarded[1] as the most
trustworthy authority on the matter. The inferences which we
derive from the statements of Josephus,[2] though always to be
qualified by our general estimate of his *animus*,[3] accord with those
from the New Testament. In regard to Rabbinic writings, we have
to bear in mind the admittedly unhistorical character of most of
their notices, the strong party-bias which coloured almost all their
statements regarding opponents, and their constant tendency to trace
later views and practices to earlier times.

Without entering on the principles and supposed practices of
the fraternity' or 'association' (*Chebher, Chabhurah, Chabhurta*) of
Pharisees, which was comparatively small, numbering only about
5,000 members,[a] the following particulars may be of interest. The
object of the association was twofold: to observe in the strictest
manner, and according to traditional law, all the ordinances concerning Levitical purity, and to be extremely punctilious in all connected
with religious dues (tithes and all other dues). A person might undertake only the second, without the first of these obligations. In that
case he was simply a *Neeman*, an 'accredited one' with whom one
might enter freely into commerce, as he was supposed to have paid
all dues. But a person could not undertake the vow of Levitical
purity without also taking the obligation of all religious dues. If
he undertook both vows he was a *Chabher*, or associate. Here there
were four degrees, marking an ascending scale of Levitical purity, or
separation from all that was profane.[b] In opposition to these was the
Am ha-arets, or 'country people' (the people which knew not, or
cared not for the Law, and were regarded as 'cursed'). But it must
not be thought that every *Chabher* was either a learned Scribe, or that
every Scribe was a *Chabher*. On the contrary, as a man might be a
Chabher without being either a Scribe or an elder,[c] so there must have
been sages, and even teachers, who did not belong to the association,
since special rules are laid down for the reception of such.[d] Candidates
had to be formally admitted into the ' fraternity ' in the presence of
three members. But every accredited public ' teacher ' was, unless
anything was known to the contrary, supposed to have taken upon

[a] *Jos.* Ant.
xvii. 2. 4

[b] Chag. ii.
5. 7; comp.
Tohor. vii.
5

[c] For ex.
Kidd. 33 *b*

[d] Bekh. 30

---

[1] I mean on historical, not on theological grounds.
[2] I here refer to the following passages:
Jewish War ii. 8. 14; Ant. xiii. 5. 9;
0. 5, 6; xvii. 2. 4; xviii. 1, 2, 3, 4.

[3] For a full discussion of the character
and writings of Josephus, I would refer
to the article in Dr. *Smith's* Dict. of Chr.
Biogr. vol. iii.

BOOK
III

> Bekhor. 30

b Dem. ii. 2

c Demai ii.3

d In St.
Luke xi.42;
xviii. 12;
St. Matt.
xxiii. 23

e In St.
Luke xi. 39,
41; St.Matt.
xxiii. 25, 26

f Sot. 22 b;
Jer. Ber.
ix. 7

g Sot. iii. 4

h Pes. 70 b

i Abhoth de
R.Nathan 5

k Jer. Chag.
79 d; Tos.
Chag. iii.

him the obligations referred to.[1] The family of a *Chabher* belonged, as a matter of course, to the community;[a] but this ordinance was afterwards altered.[2] The *Neeman* undertook these four obligations: to tithe what he ate, what he sold, and what he bought, and not to be a guest with an *Am ha-arets*.[b] The full *Chabher* undertook not to sell to an 'Am ha-arets' any fluid or dry substance (nutriment or fruit), not to buy from him any such fluid, not to be a guest with him, not to entertain him as a guest in his own clothes (on account of their possible impurity)—to which one authority adds other particulars, which, however, were not recognised by the Rabbis generally as of primary importance.[c]

These two great obligations of the 'official' Pharisee, or 'Associate' are pointedly referred to by Christ—both that in regard to *tithing* (the vow of the *Neeman*);[d] and that in regard to Levitical purity (the special vow of the *Chabher*).[e] In both cases they are associated with a want of corresponding inward reality, and with hypocrisy. These charges cannot have come upon the people by surprise, and they may account for the circumstance that so many of the learned kept aloof from the 'Association' as such. Indeed, the sayings of some of the Rabbis in regard to Pharisaism and the professional Pharisee are more withering than any in the New Testament. It is not necessary here to repeat the well-known description, both in the Jerusalem and the Babylon Talmud, of the seven kinds of 'Pharisees,' of whom six (the 'Shechemite,' the 'stumbling,' the 'bleeding,' the 'mortar,' the 'I want to know what is incumbent on me,' and 'the Pharisee from fear') mark various kinds of unreality, and only one is 'the Pharisee from love.'[f] Such an expression as 'the plague of Pharisaism' is not uncommon; and a silly pietist, a clever sinner, and a female Pharisee are ranked among 'the troubles of life.'[g] 'Shall we then explain a verse according to the opinions of the Pharisees?' asks a Rabbi, in supreme contempt for the arrogance of the fraternity.[h] 'It is as a tradition among the Pharisees[i] to torment themselves in this world and yet they will gain nothing by it in the next.' The Sadducees had some reason for the taunt, that 'the Pharisees would by-and-by subject the globe of the sun itself to their purifications,'[k] the more so that their assertions of purity were sometimes conjoined with Epicurean maxims, betokening a very different state of mind, such as, 'Make haste to eat and drink, for the world which we qui

---

[1] Abba Saul would also have freed all students from that formality.

[2] Comp. the suggestion as to the sig-nificant time when this alteration was introduced, in 'Sketches of Jewish Social Life,' pp. 228, 229.

resembles a wedding feast;' or this: 'My son, if thou possess any- CHAP.
thing, enjoy thyself, for there is no pleasure in Hades,[1] and death II
grants no respite. But if thou sayest, What then would I leave to
my sons and daughters? Who will thank thee for this appointment
in Hades?' Maxims these to which, alas! too many of their recorded
stories and deeds form a painful commentary.[2]

But it would be grossly unjust to identify Pharisaism, as a
religious direction, with such embodiments of it or even with the
official 'fraternity.' While it may be granted that the tendency and
logical sequence of their views and practices were such, their system,
as opposed to Sadduceeism, had very serious bearings: dogmatic,
ritual, and legal. It is, however, erroneous to suppose, either that
their system represented traditionalism itself, or that Scribes and
Pharisees are convertible terms,[3] while the Sadducees represented the
civil and political element. The Pharisees represented only the prevailing system of, not traditionalism itself; while the Sadducees also
numbered among them many learned men. They were able to enter
into controversy, often protracted and fierce, with their opponents,
and they acted as members of the Sanhedrin, although they had
diverging traditions of their own, and even, as it would appear, at
one time a complete code of canon-law.[a][4] Moreover, the admitted [a] Megill.
fact, that when in office the Sadducees conformed to the principles Taan. Per.
and practices of the Pharisees, proves at least that they must have iv. ed.
been acquainted with the ordinances of traditionalism.[5] Lastly, Warsh. p. 8
there were certain traditional ordinances on which both parties were a
at one.[b] Thus it seems Sadduceeism was in a sense rather a specula- [b] Sanh.33 t
tive than a practical system, starting from simple and well-defined Horay 4 a
principles, but wide-reaching in its possible consequences. Perhaps
it may best be described as a general reaction against the extremes of
Pharisaism, springing from moderate and rationalistic tendencies;
intended to secure a footing within the recognised bounds of
Judaism; and seeking to defend its principles by a strict literalism of

[1] Erub. 54 a. I give the latter clause,
not as in our edition of the Talmud, but
according to a more correct reading
(Levy, Neuhebr. Wörterb. vol. ii. p. 102).
[2] It could serve no good purpose to
give instances. They are readily accessible to those who have taste or curiosity
in that direction.
[3] So, erroneously, Wellhausen, in his
treatise 'Pharisäer u. Sadduc.'; and partially, as it seems to me, even Schürer
(Neutest. Zeitgesch.). In other respects
also these two learned men seem too

much under the influence of Geiger and
Kuenen.
[4] Wellhausen has carried his criticisms
and doubts of the Hebrew Scholion on
the Megill. Taan. (or 'Roll of Fasts')
too far.
[5] Even such a book as the Meg. Taan.
does not accuse them of absolute ignorance, but only of being unable to prove
their dicta from Scripture (comp. Pereq
x. p. 15 b, which may well mark the extreme of Anti-Sadduceeism).

interpretation and application.   If so, these interpretations would be intended rather for defensive than offensive purposes, and the great aim of the party would be after rational freedom—or, it might be, free rationality.   Practically, the party would, of course, tend in broad, and often grossly unorthodox, directions.

The fundamental *dogmatic* differences between the Pharisees and Sadducees concerned: the rule of faith and practice; the 'after death;' the existence of angels and spirits; and free will and pre-destination.   In regard to the first of these points, it has already been stated that the Sadducees did not lay down the principle of absolute rejection of all traditions as such, but that they were opposed to traditionalism as represented and carried out by the Pharisees.   When put down by sheer weight of authority, they would probably carry the controversy further, and retort on their opponents by an appeal to Scripture as against their traditions, per-haps ultimately even by an attack on traditionalism; but always as represented by the Pharisees.[1]   A careful examination of the state-ments of Josephus on this subject will show that they convey no more than this.[2]   The Pharisaic view of this aspect of the contro-versy appears, perhaps, most satisfactorily, because indirectly, in cer-tain sayings of the Mishnah, which attribute all national calamities to those persons, whom they adjudge to eternal perdition, who interpret

a Ab. iii. 11; v 8 Scripture 'not as does the *Halakhah*,' or established Pharisaic rule.[a] In this respect, then, the commonly received idea concerning the Pharisees and Sadducees will require to be seriously modified.   As regards the *practice* of the Pharisees, as distinguished from that of the Sadducees, we may safely treat the statements of Josephus as the exaggerated representations of a partisan, who wishes to place his party in the best light.   It is, indeed, true that the Pharisees,

b Jos. War i. 5. 2
c Ant. xviii. 1. 3
'interpreting the legal ordinances with rigour,'[b3] imposed on them-selves the necessity of much self-denial, especially in regard to food,[c] but that their practice was under the guidance of *reason*, as Josephus

---

[1] Some traditional explanation of the Law of Moses was absolutely necessary, if it was to be applied to existing cir-cumstances.   It would be a great his-torical inaccuracy to imagine that the Sadducees rejected the whole παράδοσις τῶν πρεσβυτέρων (St. Matt. xv. 2) from Ezra downwards.

[2] This is the meaning of Ant. xiii. 10. 6, and clearly implied in xviii. 1, 3, 4, and War ii. 8. 14.

[3] M. *Derenbourg* (Hist. de la Palest., p. 122, note) rightly remarks, that the Rab-binic equivalent for Josephus' ἀκρίβεια is חֻומְרָא, heaviness, and that the Phar-isees were the מַחְמִירִין, or 'makers heavy.'   What a commentary this on the charge of Jesus about 'the heavy bur-dens' of the Pharisees!   St. Paul uses the same term as Josephus to describe the Pharisaic system, where our A.V. renders 'the perfect manner' (Acts xxii. 3).   Comp. also Acts xxvi. 5: κατὰ τὴν ἀκριβεστάτην αἵρεσιν.

asserts, is one of those bold mis-statements with which he has too often to be credited. His vindication of their special reverence for age and authority[a] must refer to the honours paid by the party to 'the Elders,' not to the old. And that there was sufficient ground for Sadducean opposition to Pharisaic traditionalism, alike in principle and in practice, will appear from the following quotation, to which we add, by way of explanation, that the wearing of phylacteries was deemed by that party of Scriptural obligation, and that the phylactery for the head was to consist (according to tradition) of four compartments. 'Against the words of the Scribes is more punishable than against the words of Scripture. He who says, No phylacteries, so as to transgress the words of Scripture, is not guilty (free); five compartments—to add to the words of the Scribes—he is guilty.'[b][1]

The second doctrinal difference between Pharisees and Sadducees concerned the 'after death.' According to the New Testament,[c] the Sadducees denied the resurrection of the dead, while Josephus, going further, imputes to them denial of reward or punishment after death,[d] and even the doctrine that the soul perishes with the body.[e] The latter statement may be dismissed as among those inferences which theological controversialists are too fond of imputing to their opponents. This is fully borne out by the account of a later work,[f] to the effect, that by successive misunderstandings of the saying of Antigonus of Socho, that men were to serve God without regard to reward, his *later* pupils had arrived at the inference that there was no other world—which, however, *might* only refer to the Pharisaic ideal of 'the world to come,' not to the denial of the immortality of the soul—and no resurrection of the dead. We may therefore credit Josephus with merely reporting the common inference of his party. But it is otherwise in regard to their denial of the resurrection of the dead. Not only Josephus, but the New Testament and Rabbinic writings attest this. The Mishnah expressly states[g] that the formula 'from age to age,' or rather 'from world to world,' had been introduced as a protest against the opposite theory; while the Talmud, which records disputations between Gamaliel and the Sadducees[2] on the subject of the resurrection, expressly imputes the

a Ant. xviii.
1. 3

b Sanh. xi. 3

c St. Matt
xxii. 23,
and paral-
lel pas-
sages; Acts
iv. 1, 2;
xxiii. 8

d War ii. 8.
14

e Ant. xviii.
1. 4
f Ab. d. R.
Nath. 5

g Ber ix. 5

---

[1] The subject is discussed at length in Jer. Ber. i. 7 (p. 3 *b*), where the superiority of the Scribe over the Prophet is shown (1) from Mic. ii. 6 (without the words in *italics*), the one class being the Prophets ('prophesy not'), the other the Scribes ('prophesy'); (2) from the fact that the Prophets needed the attestation of miracles. (Deut. xiii. 2), but not the Scribes (Deut. xvii. 11).

[2] This is admitted even by *Geiger* (Urschr. u. Uebers. p. 130, note), though

denial of this doctrine to the 'Scribes of the Sadducees.' In fairness it is perhaps only right to add that, in the discussion, the Sadducees seem only to have actually denied that there was proof for this doctrine in the Pentateuch, and that they ultimately professed themselves convinced by the reasoning of Gamaliel.[1] Still the concurrent testimony of the New Testament and of Josephus leaves no doubt, that in this instance their views had not been misrepresented. Whether or not their opposition to the doctrine of the Resurrection arose in the first instance from, or was prompted by, Rationalistic views, which they endeavoured to support by an appeal to the letter of the Pentateuch, as the source of traditionalism, it deserves notice that in His controversy with the Sadducees Christ appealed to the Pentateuch in proof of His teaching.[2]

Connected with this was the equally Rationalistic opposition to belief in Angels and Spirits. It is only mentioned in the New Testament,[a] but seems almost to follow as a corollary. Remembering what the Jewish Angelology was, one can scarcely wonder that in controversy the Sadducees should have been led to the opposite extreme.

The last dogmatic difference between the two 'sects' concerned that problem which has at all times engaged religious thinkers: man's free will and God's pre-ordination, or rather their compatibility. Josephus—or the reviser whom he employed—indeed, uses the purely heathen expression 'fate' ($\varepsilon i\mu\alpha\rho\mu\acute{\varepsilon}\nu\eta$)[3] to designate the Jewish idea of the pre-ordination of God. But, properly understood, the real difference between the Pharisees and Sadducees seems to have amounted to this: that the former accentuated God's pre-

[a] Acts xxiii.

---

in the passage above referred to he would emendate: 'Scribes of the Samaritans.' The passage, however, implies that these were *Sadducean Scribes*, and that they were both willing and able to enter into theological controversy with their opponents.

[1] Rabbi Gamaliel's proof was taken from Deut. i. 8: 'Which Jehovah sware unto your fathers to give unto them.' It is not said ' unto you,' but unto ' *them*,' which implies the resurrection of the dead. The argument is kindred in character, but far inferior in solemnity and weight, to that employed by our Lord, St. Matt. xxii. 32, from which it is evidently taken. (See book v. ch. iv., the remarks on that passage.)

[2] It is a curious circumstance in con-

nection with the question of the Sadducees, that it raised another point in controversy between the Pharisees and the 'Samaritans,' or, as I would read it, the Sadducees, since ' the Samaritans ' (Sadducees ?) only allowed marriage with the *betrothed*, not the actually *wedded* wife of a deceased childless brother (Jer Yebam. i. 6, p. 3 *a*). The Sadducees in the Gospel argue on the Pharisaic theory, apparently for the twofold object of casting ridicule on the doctrine of the Resurrection, and on the Pharisaic practice of marriage with the *espoused* wife of a deceased brother.

[3] The expression is used in the heathen (philosophical) sense of *fate* by *Philo*, De Incorrupt. Mundi. § 10. ed. Mangey, vol. ii. p. 496 (ed. Fref. p. 947).

ordination, the latter man's free will; and that, while the Pharisees admitted only a partial influence of the human element on what happened, or the co-operation of the human with the Divine, the Sadducees denied all absolute pre-ordination, and made man's choice of evil or good, with its consequences of misery or happiness, to depend entirely on the exercise of free will and self-determination. And in this, like many opponents of 'Predestinarianism,' they seem to have started from the principle, that it was impossible for God 'either to commit or to foresee [in the sense of fore-ordaining] anything evil.' The mutual misunderstanding here was that common in all such controversies. Although [a] Josephus writes as if, according to the Pharisees, the chief part in every good action depended upon fate [pre-ordination] rather than on man's doing, yet in another place [b] he disclaims for them the notion that the will of man was destitute of spontaneous activity, and speaks somewhat confusedly— for he is by no means a good reasoner—of 'a mixture' of the Divine and human elements, in which the human will, with its sequence of virtue or wickedness, is subject to the will of fate. A yet further modification of this statement occurs in another place,[c] where we are told that, according to the Pharisees, some things depended upon fate, and more on man himself. Manifestly, there is not a very wide difference between this and the fundamental principle of the Sadducees in what we may suppose its primitive form.

But something more will have to be said as illustrative of Pharisaic teaching on this subject. No one who has entered into the spirit of the Old Testament can doubt that its outcome was *faith*, in its twofold aspect of acknowledgment of the absolute Rule, and simple submission to the Will, of God. What distinguished this so widely from fatalism was what may be termed *Jehovahism*—that is, the *moral* element in its thoughts of God, and that He was ever presented as in *paternal relationship* to men. But the Pharisees carried their accentuation of the Divine to the verge of fatalism. Even the idea that God had created man with two impulses, the one to good, the other to evil; and that the latter was absolutely necessary for the continuance of this world, would in some measure trace the causation of moral evil to the Divine Being. The absolute and unalterable pre-ordination of every event, to its minutest details, is frequently insisted upon. Adam had been shown all the generations that were to spring from him. Every incident in the history of Israel had been foreordained, and the actors in it—for good or for evil—were only instruments for carrying out the Divine Will. What were ever

[a] In Jewish War ii. 8. 14

[b] Ant. xviii. 1. 3

[c] Ant. xiii. 5. 9

Moses and Aaron? God would have delivered Israel out of Egypt, and given them the Law, had there been no such persons. Similarly was it in regard to Solomon, to Esther, to Nebuchadnezzar, and others. Nay, it was because man was predestined to die that the serpent came to seduce our first parents. And as regarded the history of each individual: all that concerned his mental and physical capacity, or that would betide him, was prearranged. His name, place, position, circumstances, the very name of her whom he was to wed, were proclaimed in heaven, just as the hour of his death was foreordered. There might be seven years of pestilence in the land, and yet no one died before his time.[a] Even if a man inflicted a cut on his finger, he might be sure that this also had been preordered.[b] Nay, 'wheresoever a man was destined to die, thither would his feet carry him.'[1] We can well understand how the Sadducees would oppose notions like these, and all such coarse expressions of fatalism. And it is significant of the exaggeration of Josephus,[2] that neither the New Testament, nor Rabbinic writings, bring the charge of the denial of God's prevision against the Sadducees.

But 'there is another aspect of this question also. While the Pharisees thus held the doctrine of absolute preordination, side by side with it they were anxious to insist on man's freedom of choice, his personal responsibility, and moral obligation.[3] Although every event depended upon God, whether a man served God or not was entirely in his own choice. As a logical sequence of this, fate had no influence as regarded Israel, since all depended on prayer, repentance, and good works. Indeed, otherwise that repentance, on which Rabbinism so largely insists, would have had no meaning. Moreover, it seems as if it had been intended to convey that, while our evil actions were entirely our own choice, if a man sought to amend his ways, he would be helped of God.[c] It was, indeed, true that God had created

---

[1] The following curious instance of this is given. On one occasion King Solomon, ·when attended by his two Scribes, Elihoreph and Ahiah (both supposed to have been Ethiopians), suddenly perceived the Angel of Death. As he looked so sad, Solomon ascertained as its reason, that the two Scribes had been demanded at his hands. On this Solomon transported them by magic into the land of *Luz*, where, according to legend, no man ever died. Next morning Solomon again perceived the Angel of Death, but this time laughing, because, as he said. Solomon had sent these men to the very place whence he had been ordered to fetch them (Sukk, 53 a).

[2] Those who understand the character of Josephus' writings will be at no loss for his reasons in this. It would suit his purpose to speak often of the fatalism of the Pharisees, and to represent them as a philosophical sect like the Stoics. The latter, indeed, he does in so many words.

[3] For details comp. *Hamburger*, Real-Encykl. ii. pp. 103–106—though there is some tendency to 'colouring' in this as in other articles of the work.

the evil impulse in us; but He had also given the remedy in the Law.[a] This is parabolically represented under the figure of a man seated at the parting of two ways, who warned all passers that if they chose one road it would lead them among the thorns, while on the other brief difficulties would end in a plain path (joy).[b] Or, to put it in the language of the great Akiba[c]: 'Everything is foreseen; free determination is accorded to man; and the world is judged in goodness.' With this simple juxtaposition of two propositions equally true, but incapable of metaphysical combination, as are most things in which the empirically cognisable and uncognisable are joined together, we are content to leave the matter.

The other differences between the Pharisees and Sadducees can be easily and briefly summed up. They concern ceremonial, ritual, and juridical questions. In regard to the first, the opposition of the Sadducees to the excessive scruples of the Pharisees on the subject of Levitical defilements led to frequent controversy. Four points in dispute are mentioned, of which, however, three read more like ironical comments than serious divergences. Thus, the Sadducees taunted their opponents with their many lustrations, including that of the Golden Candlestick in the Temple.[d] Two other similar instances are mentioned.[e] By way of guarding against the possibility of profanation, the Pharisees enacted, that the touch of any thing sacred 'defiled' the hands. The Sadducees, on the other hand, ridiculed the idea that the Holy Scriptures 'defiled' the hands, but not such a book as Homer.[1] In the same spirit, the Sadducees would ask the Pharisees how it came, that water pouring from a clean into an unclean vessel did not lose its purity and purifying power.[2] If these represent no serious controversies, on another ceremonial question there was real difference, though its existence shows how far party-spirit could lead the Pharisees. No ceremony was surrounded with greater care to prevent defilement than that of preparing the ashes of the Red Heifer.[3]

[a] Baba B. 16 a
[b] Siphré on Deut. xi. 26, § 53, ed. Friedmann. p. 86 a
[c] Ab. iii. 15

[d] Jer. Chag iii. 8; Tos. Chag. iii., where the reader will find sufficient proof that the Sadducees were not in the wrong
[e] In Yad. iv. 6, 7

---

[1] The Pharisees replied by asking on what ground the bones of a High-Priest 'defiled,' but not those of a donkey. And when the Sadducees ascribed it to the great value of the former, lest a man should profane the bones of his parents by making spoons of them, the Pharisees pointed out that the same argument applied to defilement by the Holy Scriptures. In general, it seems that the Pharisees were afraid of the satirical comments of the Sadducees on their doings (comp. Parah iii. 3).

[2] *Wellhausen* rightly denounces the strained interpretation of *Geiger*, who would find here—as in other points—hidden political allusions.

[3] Comp. 'The Temple, its Ministry and Services,' pp. 309, 312. The rubrics are in the Mishnic tractate Parah, and in Tos. Par.

BOOK
III

ᵃ Parah iii,;
Tos. Par. 3

What seem the original ordinances,ᵃ directed that, for seven days previous to the burning of the Red Heifer, the priest was to be kept in separation in the Temple, sprinkled with the ashes of all sin-offerings, and kept from the touch of his brother-priests, with even greater rigour than the High-Priest in his preparation for the Day of Atonement. The Sadducees insisted that, as 'till sundown' was the rule in all purification, the priest must be in cleanliness till then, before burning the Red Heifer. But, apparently for the sake of opposition, and in contravention to their own principles, the Pharisees would ac-tually 'defile' the priest on his way to the place of burning, and then immediately make him take a bath of purification which had been

ᵇ Parah iii.
7

prepared, so as to show that the Sadducees were in error.ᵇ ¹ In the same spirit, the Sadducees seem to have prohibited the use of any-thing made from animals which were either interdicted as food, or by reason of their not having been properly slaughtered; while the Pharisees allowed it, and, in the case of Levitically clean animals which had died or been torn, even made their skin into parchment,

ᶜ Shabb.
108 a

which might be used for sacred purposes.ᶜ

These may seem trifling distinctions, but they sufficed to kindle the passions. Even greater importance attached to differences on *ritual* questions, although the controversy here was purely theoreti-cal. For, the Sadducees, when in office, always conformed to the pre-vailing Pharisaic practices. Thus the Sadducees would have interpreted Lev. xxiii. 11, 15, 16, as meaning that the wave-sheaf (or, rather, the *Omer*) was to be offered on 'the morrow after the weekly Sabbath'— that is, on the Sunday in Easter week—which would have brought

ᵈ Vv. 15, 16

ᵉ Men. x. 3;
65 a; Chag.
ii. 4

the Feast of Pentacost always on a Sunday;ᵈ while the Pharisees un-derstood the term 'Sabbath' of the festive Paschal day.ᵉ ² Connected with this were disputes about the examination of the witnesses who testified to the appearance of the new moon, and whom the Phari-

ᶠ Rosh
haSh. i. 7;
ii. 1;
Tos. Rosh
haSh. ed. Z.
i. 15.

sees accused of having been suborned by their opponents.ᶠ

The Sadducean objection to pouring the water of libation upon the altar on the Feast of Tabernacles, led to riot and bloody repris-als on the only occasion on which it seems to have been carried into

ᵍ Sukk.48 b;
comp. *Jos.*
Ant. xiii
13. 5

practice.ᵍ ³ Similarly, the Sadducees objected to the beating

---

¹ The Mishnic passage is difficult, but I believe I have given the sense cor-rectly.

² This difference, which is more intri-cate than appears at first sight, requires

a longer discussion than can be given in this place.

³ For details about the observances on this festival I must refer to 'The Temple, its Ministry and Services.'

off the willow-branches after the procession round the altar on the last day of the Feast of Tabernacles, if it were a Sabbath.[a] Again, the Sadducees would have had the High-Priest, on the Day of Atonement, kindle the incense *before* entering the Most Holy Place; the Pharisees *after* he had entered the Sanctuary.[b] Lastly, the Pharisees contended that the cost of the daily Sacrifices should be discharged from the general Temple treasury, while the Sadducees would have paid it from free-will offerings. Other differences, which seem not so well established, need not here be discussed.

Among the divergences on *juridical* questions, reference has already been made to that in regard to marriage with the 'betrothed,' or else actually espoused widow of a deceased, childless brother. Josephus, indeed, charges the Sadducees with extreme severity in criminal matters;[c] but this must refer to the fact that the ingenuity or punctiliousness of the Pharisees would afford to most offenders a loophole of escape. On the other hand, such of the diverging juridical principles of the Sadducees, as are attested on trustworthy authority,[1] seem more in accordance with justice than those of the Pharisees. They concerned (besides the Levirate marriage) chiefly three points. According to the Sadducees, the punishment[d] against false witnesses was only to be executed if the innocent person, condemned on their testimony, had actually suffered punishment, while the Pharisees held that this was to be done if the sentence had been actually pronounced, although not carried out.[e] Again, according to Jewish law, only a son, but not a daughter, inherited the father's property. From this the Pharisees argued, that if, at the time of his father's decease, that son were dead, leaving only a daughter, this granddaughter would (as representative of the son) be the heir, while the daughter would be excluded. On the other hand, the Sadducees held that, in such a case, daughter and granddaughter should share alike.[f] Lastly, the Sadducees argued that if, according to Exodus xxi. 28,29, a man was responsible for damage done by his cattle, he was equally, if not more, responsible for damage done by his slave. while the Pharisees refused to recognise any responsibility on the latter score.[g][2]

For the sake of completeness it has been necessary to enter into

CHAP.
II

a Sukk.43 b
and in the
Jerus.
Talm. and
Tos. Sukk.
iii. 1
b Jer. Yoma
i. 5; Yoma
19 b; 53 a

c Specially
Ant. xx. 9

d Decreed
in Deut.
xix. 21

e Makk. 1. 6

f Baba B.
115 b;
Tos.Yad.
ii. 20

g Yad. iv. 7
and Tos.
Yad.

---

[1] Other differences, which rest merely on the authority of the Hebrew Commentary on 'The Roll of Fasts,' I have discarded as unsupported by historical evidence. I am sorry to have in this respect, and on some other aspects of the question, to differ from the learned Article on 'The Sadducees,' in *Kitto's* Bibl. Encycl.

[2] *Geiger*, and even *Derenbourg*, see in these things deep political allusions—which, as it seems to me, have no other existence than in the ingenuity of these writers.

BOOK
III

ª Ant. xiii. 10. 6
Ant. xvii. 2. 4

ᶜ Acts v. 17; Ant. xx. 9.]

ᵈ Sheqal. iv. 4; vi. 1; Eduy. viii. 2: Ab. ii. 8 &c.

St. John i. 24

In the Ab. de R. Nath. c. 5

details, which may not possess a general interest. This, however, will be marked, that, with the exception of dogmatic differences, the controversy turned on questions of 'canon-law.' Josephus tells us that the Pharisees commanded the masses,ª and especially the female world,ᵇ while the Sadducees attached to their ranks only a minority, and that belonging to the highest class. The leading priests in Jerusalem formed, of course, part of that highest class of society; and from the New Testament and Josephus we learn that the High-Priestly families belonged to the Sadducean party.ᶜ But to conclude from this,[1] either that the Sadducees represented the civil and political aspect of society, and the Pharisees the religious; or, that the Sadducees were the priest-party,[2] in opposition to the popular and democratic Pharisees, are inferences not only unsupported, but opposed to historical facts. For, not a few of the Pharisaic leaders were actually priests,ᵈ while the Pharisaic ordinances make more than ample recognition of the privileges and rights of the Priesthood. This would certainly not have been the case if, as some have maintained, Sadducean and priest-party had been convertible terms. Even as regards the deputation to the Baptist of ' Priests and Levites ' from Jerusalem, we are expressely told that they ' were of the Pharisees.'ᵉ

This bold hypothesis seems, indeed, to have been invented chiefly for the sake of another, still more unhistorical. The derivation of the name ' Sadducee ' has always been in dispute. According to a Jewish legend of about the seventh century of our era,ᶠ the name was derived from one Tsadoq (Zadok),[3] a disciple of Antigonus of Socho, whose principle of not serving God for reward had gradually misinterpreted into Sadduceeism. But, apart from the objection that in such case the party should rather have taken the name of Antigonites, the story itself receives no support either from Josephus or from early Jewish writings. Accordingly modern critics have adopted another hypothesis, which seems at least equally untenable. On the supposition that the Sadducees were the 'priest-party,' the name of the sect is derived from Zadok (Tsadoq), the High-Priest in the time of Solomon.[4] But the objections to this are insuperable. Not to speak of the linguistic difficulty of deriving Tsadduqim (Zaddukim, Sadducees) from Tsadoq (Zadok),[5]

---

[1] So Wellhausen, u. s.
[2] So Geiger, u. s.
[3] Tseduqim and Tsadduqim mark different transliterations of the name Sadducees.
[4] This theory, defended with ingenuity by Geiger, had been of late adopted by most writers, and even by Schürer. But

not a few of the statements hazarded by Dr. Geiger seem to me to have no historical foundation, and the passages quoted in support either do not convey such meaning, or else are of no authority.
[5] So Dr. Löw, as quoted in Dr. Ginsburg's article.

neither Josephus nor the Rabbis know anything of such a connection between Tsadoq and the Sadducees, of which, indeed, the *rationale* would be difficult to perceive.   Besides, is it likely that a party would have gone back so many centuries for a name, which had no connection with their distinctive principles?   The name of a party is, if self-chosen (which is rarely the case), derived from its founder or place of origin, or else from what it claims as distinctive principles or practices.   Opponents might either pervert such a name, or else give a designation, generally opprobrious, which would express their own relation to the party, or to some of its supposed peculiarities.   But on none of these principles can the origin of the name of Sadducees from Tsadoq be accounted for.   Lastly, on the supposition mentioned, the Sadducees must have given the name to their party, since it cannot be imagined that the Pharisees would have connected their opponents with the honoured name of the High-Priest Tsadoq.

If it is highly improbable that the Sadducees, who, of course, professed to be the right interpreters of Scripture, would choose any party-name, thereby stamping themselves as sectaries, this derivation of their name is also contrary to historical analogy.   For even the name Pharisees, '*Perushim*,' 'separated ones,' was not taken by the party itself, but given to it by their opponents.[a][1]   From 1 Macc. ii. 42; vii. 13; 2 Macc. xiv. 6, it appears that originally they had taken the sacred name of *Chasidim*, or 'the pious.'[b]   This, no doubt, on the ground that they were truly those who, according to the directions of Ezra,[c] had separated themselves (become *nibhdalim*) 'from the filthiness of the heathen' (all heathen defilement) by carrying out the traditional ordinances.[2]   In fact, Ezra marked the beginning of the 'later,' in contradistinction to the 'earlier,' or Scripture-*Chasidim*.[d]   If we are correct in supposing that their opponents had called them *Perushim*, instead of the Scriptural designation of *Nibhdalim*, the inference is at hand, that, while the 'Pharisees' would arrogate to themselves the Scriptural name of *Chasidim*, or 'the pious,' their opponents would retort that they were satisfied to be *Tsaddiqim*,[3] or 'righteous.'   Thus the name of *Tsaddiqim* would become that of the party opposing the Pharisees, that is, of the *Sadducees*.

[a] Yad. iv. 6 &c.

[b] Ps. xxx. 4; xxxi. 23; xxxvii. 28

[c] vi. 21; ix. 1; x. 11; Neh. ix. 2

[d] Ber. v. 1; comp. with Vayyikra R. 2, ed. Warsh. t. iii. p. 5 a

---

[1] The argument as against the derivation of the term *Sadducee* would, of course, hold equally good, even if each party had assumed, not received from the other, its characteristic name.

[2] Comp. generally, 'Sketches of Jewish Social Life,' pp. 230, 231.

[3] Here it deserves special notice that the Old Testament term *Chasid*, which the Pharisees arrogated to themselves, is rendered in the Peshito by *Zaddîq*.   Thus, as it were, the opponents of Pharisaism would play off the equivalent *Tsaddiq* against the Pharisaic arrogation of *Chasid*.

BOOK
III

There is, indeed, an admitted linguistic difficulty in the change of the sound *i* into *u* (*Tsaddiqim* into *Tsadduqim*), but may it not have been that this was accomplished, not grammatically, but by popular witticism? Such mode of giving a ' by-name ' to a party or government is, at least, not irrational, nor is it uncommon.[1] Some wit might have suggested: Read not *Tsaddiqim*, the 'righteous,' but *Tsadduqim* (from *Tsadu*, צָדוּ), 'desolation,' 'destruction.' Whether or not this suggestion approve itself to critics, the derivation of Sadducees from *Tsaddiqim* is certainly that which offers most probability.[2]

This uncertainty as to the origin of the name of a party leads almost naturally to the mention of another, which, indeed, could not be omitted in any description of those times. But while the Pharisees and Sadducees were parties *within* the Synagogue, the Essenes (Εσσηνοί, or 'Εσσαῖοι—the latter always in Philo) were, although strict Jews, yet separatists, and, alike in doctrine, worship, and practice, *outside* the Jewish body ecclesiastic. Their numbers amounted to only about 4,000.[a] They are not mentioned in the New Testament, and only very indirectly referred to in Rabbinic writings, perhaps without clear knowledge on the part of the Rabbis. If the conclusion concerning them, which we shall by-and-by indicate, be correct, we can scarcely wonder at this. Indeed, their entire separation from all who did not belong to their sect, the terrible oaths by which they bound themselves to secrecy about their doctrines, and which would prevent any free religious discussion, as well as the character of what is known of their views, would account for the scanty notices about them. Josephus and Philo,[3] who speak of them in the most sympathetic manner, had, no doubt, taken special pains to ascertain all that could be learned. For this Josephus seems to have enjoyed special opportunities.[4] Still, the secrecy of their doctrines renders us dependent on writers, of whom at least one (Josephus) lies open to the suspicion of colouring and

a Philo, Quod omnis probus liber, § 12, ed, Mang. ii. p. 457 ; *Jos.* Ant. xviii. 1. 5

---

[1] Such by-names, by a play on a word, are not unfrequent. Thus, in Shem. R. 5 (ed. *Warsh.* p. 14 *a*, lines 7 and 8 from top), Pharaoh's charge that the Israelites were נִרְפִּים, 'idle,' is, by a transposition of letters made to mean that they were πόρνοι.

[2] It seems strange, that so accurate a scholar as *Schürer* should have regarded the 'national party' as merely an offshoot from the Pharisees (Neutest. Zeitgesch. p. 431), and appealed in proof to a

passage in *Josephus* (Ant. xviii. 1. 6), which expressly calls the Nationalists a *fourth* party, by the side of the Pharisees, Sadducees, and Essenes. That in practice they would carry out the strict Judaism of the Pharisees, does not make them Pharisees.

[3] They are also mentioned by *Pliny* (Hist. Natur. v. 16).

[4] This may be inferred from *Josephus'* Life, c. 2.

exaggeration. But of one thing we may feel certain: neither John CHAP.
the Baptist, and his Baptism, nor the teaching of Christianity, had II
any connection with Essenism. It were utterly unhistorical to infer
such from a few points of contact—and these only of similarity, not
identity—when the differences between them are so fundamental.
That an Essene would have preached repentance and the Kingdom
of God to multitudes, baptized the uninitiated, and given supreme
testimony to One like Jesus, are assertions only less extravagant than
this, that One Who mingled with society as Jesus did, and Whose
teaching, alike in that respect, and in all its tendencies, was so
utterly Non-, and even Anti-Essenic, had derived any part of His
doctrine from Essenism. Besides, when we remember the views of
the Essenes on purification, and on Sabbath observance, and their
denial of the Resurrection, we feel that, whatever points of resemblance
critical ingenuity may emphasise, the teaching of Christianity was in
a direction opposite from that of Essenism.[1]

We possess no *data* for the history of the origin and development
(if such there was) of Essenism. We may admit a certain connection between Pharisaism and Essenism, though it has been
greatly exaggerated by modern Jewish writers. Both directions
originated from a desire after 'purity,' though there seems a fundamental difference between them, alike in the idea of what constituted purity, and in the means for attaining it. To the Pharisee it
was Levitical and legal purity, secured by the 'hedge' of ordinances
which they drew around themselves. To the Essene it was absolute
purity in separation from the 'material,' which in itself was defiling.
The Pharisee attained in this manner the distinctive merit of a saint;
the Essene obtained a higher fellowship with the Divine, 'inward'
purity, and not only freedom from the detracting, degrading influence of matter, but command over matter and nature. As the result
of this higher fellowship with the Divine, the adept possessed the
power of prediction; as the result of his freedom from, and command

---

[1] This point is conclusively disposed
of by Bishop *Lightfoot* in the third Dissertation appended to his Commentary
on the Colossians (pp. 397–419). In
general, the masterly discussion of the
whole subject by Bishop *Lightfoot*, alike
in the body of the Commentary and in
the three Dissertations appended, may be
said to form a new era in the treatment
of the whole question, the points on
which we would venture to express
dissent being few and unimportant. The
reader who wishes to see a statement of
the supposed analogy between Essenism
and the teaching of Christ will find it in
Dr. *Ginsburg's* Article 'Essenes,' in
Smith and *Wace's* Dictionary of Christian
Biography. The same line of argument
has been followed by *Frankel* and *Gärtz*.
The reasons for the opposite view are
set forth in the text.

BOOK
III

over matter, the power of miraculous cures. That their purifications, strictest Sabbath observance, and other practices, would form points of contact with Pharisaism, follows as a matter of course; and a little reflection will show, that such observances would naturally be adopted by the Essenes, since they were within the lines of Judaism, although separatists from its body ecclesiastic. On the other hand, their fundamental tendency was quite other than that of Pharisaism, and strongly tinged with Eastern (Parsee) elements. After this the inquiry as to the precise date of its origin, and whether Essenism was an offshoot from the original (ancient) Assideans or *Chasidim*, seems needless. Certain it is that we find its first mention about 150 B.C.,[a] and that we meet the first Essene in the reign of Aristobulus I.[b]

a *Jos.* Ant. xiii. 5. 9
b 105–104
B.C.; Ant. xiii. 11. 2; War i. 3. 5

Before stating our conclusions as to its relation to Judaism and the meaning of the name, we shall put together what information may be derived of the sect from the writings of Josephus, Philo, and Pliny.[1] Even its outward organisation and the mode of life must have made as deep, and, considering the habits and circumstances of the time, even deeper impression than does the strictest asceticism on the part of any modern monastic order, without the unnatural and repulsive characteristics of the latter. There were no vows of absolute silence, broken only by weird chaunt of prayer or 'memento mori;' no penances, nor self-chastisement. But the person who had entered the 'order' was as effectually separated from all outside as if he had lived in another world. Avoiding the large cities as the centres of immorality,[c] they chose for their settlements chiefly villages, one of their largest colonies being by the shore of the Dead Sea.[d] At the same time they had also 'houses' in most, if not all the cities of Palestine,[e] notably in Jerusalem,[f] where, indeed, one of the gates was named after them.[g] In these 'houses' they lived in common,[h] under officials of their own. The affairs of 'the order' were administered by a tribunal of at least a hundred members.[i] They wore a common dress, engaged in common labor, united in common prayers, partook of common meals, and devoted themselves to works of charity, for which each had liberty to draw from the com-

c *Philo,* ii. p. 457
d *Pliny,* Hist. Nat. v. 16, 17
e *Philo,* u.s. p. 632; *Jos.* Jewish War ii. 8. 4
f Ant. xiii. 11. 2; xv. 10. 5; xvii. 13. 3
g War v. 4. 2
h *Philo,* u.s. p. 632
i War ii. 8. 9

---

[1] Compare *Josephus*, Ant. xiii. 5, 9; xv. 10. 4, 5; xviii. 1. 5; Jewish War, ii. 8, 2–13; *Philo,* Quod omnis probus liber, § 12, 13 (ed. *Mangey,* ii. 457–459; ed. Par. and Fref. pp. 876–879; ed. *Richter,* vol. v. pp. 285–288); *Pliny,* N.H. v. 16, 17. For references in the Fathers see Bp. *Lightfoot* on Colossians, pp. 83, 84 (note). Comp. the literature there and in *Schürer* (Neutest. Zeitgesch. p. 599), to which I would add Dr. *Ginburg's* Art. 'Essenes' in *Smith's* and *Wace's* Dict. of Chr. Biogr., vol. ii.

mon treasury at his own discretion, except in the case of relatives.[a] It scarcely needs mention that they extended fullest hospitality to strangers belonging to the order; in fact, a special official was appointed for this purpose in every city.[b] Everything was of the simplest character, and intended to purify the soul by the greatest possible avoidance, not only of what was sinful, but of what was material. Rising at dawn, no profane word was spoken till they had offered their prayers. These were addressed towards, if not to, the rising son—probably, as they would have explained it, as the emblem of the Divine Light, but implying invocation, if not adoration, of the sun.[1] After that they were dismissed by their officers to common work. The morning meal was preceded by a lustration, or bath. Then they put on their 'festive' linen garments, and entered, purified, the common hall as their Sanctuary. For each meal was sacrificial, in fact, the only sacrifices which they acknowleged. The 'baker,' who was really their priest—and naturally so, since he prepared the sacrifice—set before each bread, and the cook a mess of vegetables. The meal began with prayer by the presiding priest, for those who presided at these 'sacrifices' were also 'priests,' although in neither case probably of Aaronic descent, but consecrated by themselves.[c] The sacrificial meal was again concluded by prayer, when they put off their sacred dress, and returned to their labour. The evening meal was of exactly the same description, and partaken of with the same rites as that of the morning.

Although the Essenes, who, with the exception of a small party among them, repudiated marriage, adopted children to train them in the principles of their sect,[2] yet admission to the order was only granted to adults, and after a novitiate which lasted three years. On entering, the novice received the three symbols of purity: an axe, or rather a *spade*, with which to dig a pit, a foot deep, to cover up the excrements; an *apron*, to bind round the loins in bathing; and a *white dress*, which was always worn, the festive garment at meals being of linen. At the end of the first year the novice was

CHAP. II

[a] War ii. 8.6
[b] u. s. § 4

[c] *Jos.* War ii 8. 5; Ant. xviii. 1. 5

---

[1] The distinction is *Schürer's*, although he is disposed to minimise this point. More on this in the sequel.

[2] *Schürer* regards these children as forming the first of the four 'classes' or 'grades' into which the Essenes were arranged. But this is contrary to the express statement of *Philo*, that only adults were admitted into the order, and hence only such could have formed a 'grade' or 'class' of the community.

(Comp. ed. *Mangey*, ii. p. 632, from *Eusebius'* Præpar. Evang. lib. viii. cap. 8.) I have adopted the view of Bishop *Lightfoot* on the subject. Even the marrying order of the Essenes, however, only admitted of wedlock under great restrictions, and as a necessary evil (War, u. s. § 13). Bishop *Lightfoot* suggests, that these were not Essenes in the strict sense, but only 'like the third order of a Benedictine or Franciscan brotherhood.

admitted to the lustrations. He had now entered on the *second* grade, in which he remained for another year. After its lapse, he was advanced to the *third* grade, but still continued a novice, until, at the close of the third year of his probation, he was admitted to the *fourth* grade—that of full member, when, for the first time, he was admitted to the sacrifice of the common meals. The mere touch of one of a lower grade in the order defiled the Essene, and necessitated the lustration of a bath. Before admission to full membership, a terrible oath was taken. As, among other things, it bound to the most absolute secrecy, we can scarcely suppose that its form, as given by Josephus,[a] contains much beyond what was generally allowed to transpire. Thus the long list given by the Jewish historian of moral obligations which the Essenes undertook, is probably only a rhetorical enlargement of some simple formula. More credit attaches to the alleged undertaking of avoidance of all vanity, falsehood, dishonesty, and unlawful gains. The last parts of the oath alone indicate the peculiar vows of the sect, that is, so far as they could be learned by the outside world, probably chiefly through the practice of the Essenes. They bound each member not to conceal anything from his own sect, nor, even on peril of death, to disclose their doctrines to others; to hand down their doctrines exactly as they had received them; to abstain from robbery;[1] and *to guard the books belonging to their sect, and the names of the Angels.*

[a] War ii. 8.7

It is evident that, while all else was intended as safeguards of a rigorous sect of purists, and with the view of strictly keeping it a secret order, the last-mentioned particulars furnish significant indications of their peculiar doctrines. Some of these may be regarded as only exaggerations of Judaism, though not of the Pharisaic kind.[2] Among them we reckon the extravagant reverence for the name of their legislator (presumably Moses), whom to blaspheme was a capital offence; their rigid abstinence from all prohibited food; and their exaggerated Sabbath-observance, when, not only no food was prepared, but not a vessel moved, nay, not even nature eased.[3] But this latter was connected with their fundamental idea of inherent im-

---

[1] Can this possibly have any connection in the mind of Josephus with the later Nationalist movement? This would agree with his insistance on their respect for those in authority. Otherwise the emphasis laid on abstinence from robbery seems strange in such a sect.

[2] I venture to think that even Bishop *Lightfoot* lays too much stress on the affinity to Pharisaism. I can discover few, if any, traces of Pharisaism in the distinctive sense of the term. Even their frequent washings had a different object from those of the Pharisees.

[3] For a similar reason, and in order 'not to affront the Divine rays of light'—the light as symbol, if not outcome, of the Deity—they covered themselves, in such circumstances, with the mantle which was their ordinary dress in winter.

purity in the body, and, indeed, in all that is material. Hence, also,
their asceticism, their repudiation of marriage, and their frequent
lustrations in clean water, not only before their sacrificial meals, but
upon contact even with an Essene of a lower grade, and after attending to the calls of nature. Their undoubted *denial of the resurrection
of the body* seems only the logical sequence from it. If the soul
was a substance of the subtlest ether, drawn by certain natural
enticement into the body, which was its prison, a state of perfectness
could not have consisted in the restoration of that which, being
material, was in itself impure. And, indeed, what we have called
the exaggerated Judaism of the sect—its rigid abstinence from all
forbidden food, and peculiar Sabbath-observance—may all have had
the same object, that of tending towards an external purism, which
the Divine legislator would have introduced, but the 'carnally-
minded' could not receive. Hence, also, the strict separation of the
order, its grades, its rigorous discipline, as well as its abstinence from
wine, meat, and all ointments—from every luxury, even from trades
which would encourage this, or any vice. This aim after external
purity explains many of their outward arrangements, such as that
their labour was of the simplest kind, and the commonality of
all property in the order; perhaps, also, what may seem more
ethical ordinances, such as the repudiation of slavery, their refusal
to take an oath, and even their scrupulous care of truth. The white
garments, which they always wore, seem to have been but a symbol
of that purity which they sought. For this purpose they submitted,
not only to strict asceticism, but to a discipline which gave the
officials authority to expel all offenders, even though in so doing
they virtually condemned them to death by starvation, since the
most terrible oaths had bound all entrants into the order not to
partake of any food other than that prepared by their 'priests.'

In such a system there would, of course, be *no place for either
an Aaronic priesthood, or bloody sacrifices.* In fact, they repudiated
both. Without formally rejecting the Temple and its services, there
was no room in their system for such ordinances. They sent, indeed,
thank-offerings to the Temple, but what part had they in bloody
sacrifices and an Aaronic ministry, which constituted the main business of the Temple? Their 'priests' were their bakers and presidents;
their sacrifices those of fellowship, their sacred meals of purity. It
is quite in accordance with this tendency when we learn from Philo
that, in their diligent study of the Scriptures, they chiefly adopted
the allegorical mode of interpretation.[a]

[a] Ed. *Mang*
ii. p. 458

BOOK
III

We can scarcely wonder that such Jews as Josephus and Philo, and such heathens as Pliny, were attracted by such an unworldly and lofty sect. Here were about 4,000 men, who deliberately separated themselves, not only from all that made life pleasant, but from all around; who, after passing a long and strict novitiate, were content to live under the most rigid rule, obedient to their superiors; who gave up all their possessions, as well as the earnings of their daily toil in the fields, or of their simple trades; who held all things for the common benefit, entertained strangers, nursed their sick, and tended their aged as if their own parents, and were charitable to all men; who renounced all animal passions, eschewed anger, ate and drank in strictest moderation, accumulated neither wealth nor possessions, wore the simplest white dress till it was no longer fit for use; repudiated slavery, oaths, marriage; abstained from meat and wine, even from the common Eastern anointing with oil; used mystic lustrations, had mystic rites and mystic prayers, an esoteric literature and doctrines; whose every meal was a sacrifice, and every act one of self-denial; who, besides, were strictly truthful, honest, upright, virtuous, chaste, and charitable—in short, whose life meant, positively and negatively, a continual purification of the soul by mortification of the body. To the astonished onlookers this mode of life was rendered even more sacred by doctrines, a literature, and magic power known only to the initiated. Their mysterious conditions made them cognisant of the names of Angels, by which we are, no doubt, to understand a theosophic knowledge, fellowship with the Angelic world, and the power of employing its ministry. Their constant purifications, and the study of their prophetic writings, gave them the power of prediction;[a] the same mystic writings revealed the secret remedies of plants and stones for the healing of the body,[1] as well as what was needed for the cure of souls.

Jos. War ii. 8, 12; comp. Ant. xiii. 11. 2; xv. 10. 5; xvii. 13. 3

It deserves special notice that this intercourse with Angels, this secret traditional literature, and its teaching concerning mysterious remedies in plants and stones, are not unfrequently referred to in that Apocalyptic literature known as the 'Pseudepigraphic Writings.' Confining ourselves to undoubtedly Jewish and pre-Christian documents,[2] we know what development the doctrine of Angels received both in the Book of Enoch (alike in its earlier and in its later portion[b]) and in the Book of Jubilees,[3] and how the 'seers' received Angelic

[b] Ch. xxxi.- lxxi.

---

[1] There can be no question that these Essene cures were magical, and their knowledge of remedies esoteric.

[2] Bishop *Lightfoot* refers to a part of the Sibylline books which seems of Christian authorship.

[3] Comp. *Lucius,* Essenismus, p. 109. This brochure, the latest on the subject,

instruction and revelations. The distinctively Rabbinic teaching on these subjects is fully set forth in another part of this work.[1] Here we would only specially notice that in the Book of Jubilees [a] Angels are represented as teaching Noah all 'herbal remedies' for diseases,[b] while in the later Pirqé de R. Eliezer [c] this instruction is said to have been given to Moses. These two points (relation to the Angels, and knowledge of the remedial power of plants—not to speak of visions and prophecies) seem to connect the secret writings of the Essenes with that 'outside' literature which in Rabbinic writings is known as *Sepharim haChitsonim*, 'outside writings.'[2] The point is of greatest importance, as will presently appear.

It needs no demonstration, that a system which proceeded from a contempt of the body and of all that is material; in some manner identified the Divine manifestation with the Sun; denied the Resurrection, the Temple-priesthood, and sacrifices; preached abstinence from meats and from marriage; decreed such entire separation from all around that their very contact defiled, and that its adherents would have perished of hunger rather than join in the meals of the outside world; which, moreover, contained not a trace of Messianic elements —indeed, had no room for them—could have had no internal connection with the origin of Christianity. Equally certain is it that, in respect of doctrine, life, and worship, it really stood *outside* Judaism, as represented by either Pharisees or Sadducees. The question whence the foreign elements were derived, which were its distinctive characteristics, has of late been so learnedly discussed, that only the conclusions arrived at require to be stated. Of the two theories, of which the one traces Essenism to Neo-Pythagorean,[3] the other to Persian sources,[4] the latter seems fully established—without, however, wholly denying at least the possibility of Neo-Pythagorean influences. To the grounds which have been so conclusively urged in support of the Eastern origin of Essenism,[5] in its distinctive features, may be added this, that Jewish Angelology, which played so great a part in the system, was derived from Chaldee and Persian sources, and perhaps also the curious notion, that the knowledge of medicaments, originally

though interesting, adds little to our knowledge.

[1] See Appendix XIII. on the Angelology, Satanology, and Demonology of the Jews.

[2] Only after writing the above I have noticed, that *Jellinek* arrives at the same conclusion as to the Essene character of the Book of Jubilees (Beth ha-Midr. iii. p. xxxiv., xxxv.), and of the Book of Enoch (u. s. ii. p. xxx.).

[3] So *Zeller*, Philosophie d. Griechen, ed. 1881, iii. pp. 277–337.

[4] So Bishop *Lightfoot*, in his masterly treatment of the whole subject in his Commentary on the Ep. to the Colossians.

[5] By Bishop *Lightfoot*, u. s. pp. 382–396. In general, I prefer on many points —such as the connection between Essenism and Gnosticism &c., simply to refer readers to the classic work of Bishop *Lightfoot.*

a Sepher
Noach ap.
Jellinek iij
p. 156

derived by Noah from the angels, came to the Egyptians chiefly through the magic books of the Chaldees.[a][1]

It is only at the conclusion of these investigations that we are prepared to enter on the question of the origin and meaning of the name *Essenes*, important as this inquiry is, not only in itself, but in regard to the relation of the sect to orthodox Judaism. The eighteen or nineteen proposed explanations of a term, which must undoubtedly be of Hebrew etymology, all proceed on the idea of its derivation from something which implied praise of the sect, the two least objectionable explaining the name as equivalent either to 'the pious,' or else to 'the silent ones.' But against all such derivations there is the obvious objection, that the Pharisees, who had the moulding of the theological language, and who were in the habit of giving the hardest names to those who differed from them, would certainly not have bestowed a title implying encomium on a sect which, in principle and practices, stood so entirely *outside*, not only of their own views, but even of the Synagogue itself. Again, if they had given a name of encomium to the sect, it is only reasonable to suppose that they would not have kept, in regard to their doctrines and practices, a silence which is only broken by dim and indirect allusions. Yet, as we examine it, the origin and meaning of the name seem implied in their very position towards the Synagogue. They were the only real *sect,* strictly *outsiders,* and their name *Essenes* ('Εσσηνοί, 'Εσσαῖοι) seems the Greek equivalent for *Chitsonim* (חיצונים), 'the outsiders.' Even the circumstance that the axe, or rather spade (ἀξινάριον), which every novice received, has for its Rabbinic equivalent the word *Chatsina*, is here not without significance. Linguistically, the words *Essenoi* and *Chitsonim* are equivalents, as admittedly are the similar designations *Chasidim* (חסידים) and Asidaioi ('Ασιδαῖοι). For, in rendering Hebrew into Greek, the *ch* (ח) is 'often entirely omitted, or represented by a *spiritus lenis* in the beginning,' while 'in regard to the vowels no distinct rule is to be laid down.'[b] Instances of a change of the Hebrew *i* into the Greek *e* are frequent, and of the Hebrew *o* into the Greek *e* not rare. As one instance will suffice, we select a case in which exactly the same transmutation of the two vowel-sounds occurs—that of the Rabbinic Abhg*i*nos (אבגינוס) for the Greek(εὐγενής)Eugenēs ('well-born').[2]

b Deutsch,
Remains,
pp. 359, 360

---

[1] As regards any connection between the Essenes and the *Therapeutai, Lucius* has denied the existence of such a sect and the Philonic authorship of *de V.cont.* The latter we have sought to defend in the Art. *Philo* (*Smith* and *Wace's* Dict. of Chr. Biogr. iv.), and to show that the Therapeutes were not a 'sect' but an esoteric circle of Alexandrian Jews.

[2] As other instances may be quoted such as Istagioth (אסטגיות) = στέγη, roof; Istuli (אסטולי)=στήλη, a pillar; Dikhsumini (דכסומיני)=δεξαμενή, cistern.

This derivation of the name *Essenes,* which strictly expresses the character and standing of the sect relatively to orthodox Judaism, and, indeed, is the Greek form of the Hebrew term for ' outsiders,' is also otherwise confirmed.   It has already been said, that no direct statement concerning the Essenes occurs in Rabbinic writings. Nor need this surprise us, when we remember the general reluctance of the Rabbis to refer to their opponents, except in actual controversy; and, that, when traditionalism was reduced to writing, Essenism, as a Jewish sect, had ceased to exist. Some of its elements had passed into the Synagogue, influencing its general teaching (as in regard to Angelology, magic, &c.), and greatly contributing to that mystic direction which afterwards found expression in what is now known as the *Kabbalah.* But the general movement had passed beyond the bounds of Judaism, and appeared in some forms of the Gnostic heresy. But still there are Rabbinic references to the 'Chitsonim,' which seem to identify them with the sect of the Essenes. Thus, in one passage[a] certain practices of the Sadducees and of the Chitsonim are mentioned together, and it is difficult to see who could be meant by the latter if not the Essenes. Besides, the practices there referred to seem to contain covert allusions to those of the Essenes. Thus, the Mishnah begins by prohibiting the public reading of the Law by those who would not appear in a coloured, but only in a *white* dress. Again, the curious statement is made that the manner of the *Chitsonim* was to cover the phylacteries with gold—a statement unexplained in the Gemara, and inexplicable, unless we see in it an allusion to the Essene practice of facing the rising Sun in their morning prayers.[1] Again, we know with what bitterness Rabbinism denounced the use of the *externe writings* (the *Sepharim haChitsonim*) to the extent of excluding from eternal life those who studied them.[b] But one of the best ascertained facts concerning the Essenes is that they possessed secret, ' outside,' holy writings of their own, which they guarded with special care. And, although it is not maintained that the *Sepharim haChitsonim* were exclusively Essene writings,[2] the latter must have been included among them. We have already seen reason for believ-

[a] Megill. 24 *b*, lines 4 and 5 from bottom

[b] Sanh. x. 1

---

[1] The practice of beginning prayers before, and ending them as the sun had just risen, seems to have passed from the Essenes to a party in the Synagogue itself, and is pointedly alluded to as a characteristic of the so-called *Vethikin,* Ber. 9 *b*; 25 *b*; 26 *a.* But another peculiarity about them, noticed in Rosh haSh. 32 *b* (the repetition of all the verses in the Pentateuch containing the record of God in the so-called *Malkhiyoth, Zikhronoth,* and *Shophroth*), shows that they were not Essenes, since such Rabbinic practices must have been alien to their system.

[2] In Sanh. 100 *b* they are explained as ' the writings of the Sadducees,' and by another Rabbi as ' the Book of Sirach ' (Ecclus. in the Apocrypha). *Hamburger,* as sometimes, makes assertions on this

BOOK
III

ᵃ In Sanh.
x. 1
ᵇ Meg. 24 b

ᶜ Sanh. 101
a; Jer. Sanh.
p. 28 b

ing, that even the so-called Pseudepigraphic literature, notably such
works as the Book of Jubilees, was strongly tainted with Essene views;
if, indeed, in perhaps another than its present form, part of it was
not actually Essene. Lastly, we find what seems to us yet another
covert allusion[a] to Essene practices, similar to that which has already
been noticed.[b] For, immediately after consigning to destruction all
who denied that there was proof in the Pentateuch for the Resurrection (evidently the Sadducees), those who denied that the Law was
from heaven (the *Minim*, or heretics—probably the Jewish Christians),
and all 'Epicureans'[1] (materialists), the same punishment is assigned
to those 'who read externe writings' (*Sepharim haChitsonim*) and
'who whispered' (a magical formula) 'over a wound.'[2] Both the
Babylonian and the Jerusalem Talmud[c] offer a strange explanation
of this practice; perhaps, because they either did not, or else would
not, understand the allusion. But to us it seems at least significant
that as, in the first quoted instance, the mention of the *Chitsonim* is
conjoined with a condemnation of the exclusive use of white garments
in worship, which we know to have been an Essene peculiarity, so the
condemnation of the use of *Chitsonim* writings with that of magical
cures.[3] At the same time, we are less bound to insist on these
allusions as essential to our argument, since those, who have given
another derivation than ours to the name *Essenes*, express themselves
unable to find in ancient Jewish writings any trustworthy reference
to the sect.

On one point, at least, our inquiry into the three 'parties' can
leave no doubt. The Essenes could never have been drawn either to
the person, or the preaching of John the Baptist. Similarly, the
Sadducees would, after they knew its real character and goal, turn

---

point which cannot be supported (Real-
Wörterb. ii. p. 70). Jer. Sanh. 28 *a* ex-
plains, 'Such as the books of Ben Sirach
and of Ben La'nah'—the latter apparently
also an Apocryphal book, for which the
Midr. Kohel. (ed. *Warsh.* iii. p. 106 *b*) has
'the book of Ben Tagla' 'La'nah' and
'Tagla' could scarcely be symbolic names.
On the other hand, I cannot agree with
Fürst (Kanon d. A.T. p. 99), who identi-
fies them with Apollonius of Tyana and
Empedocles. Dr. *Neubauer* suggests that
Ben La'nah may be a corruption of *Sibyl-
line* Oracles.

[1] The 'Epicureans,' or 'freethinkers,'
are explained to be such as speak contemptuously of the Scriptures, or of the
Rabbis (Jer. Sanh. 27 *d*). In Sanh. 38 *b*

a distinction is made between 'stranger'
(heathen) Epicureans, and Israelitish Epicureans. With the latter it is unwise to
enter into argument.

[2] Both in the Jer. and Bab. Talm. it is
conjoined with 'spitting,' which was a
mode of healing, usual at the time. The
Talmud forbids the magical formula, only
in connection with this 'spitting'—and
then for the curious reason that the Divine Name is not to be recorded while
'spitting.' But, while in the Bab. Talm.
the prohibition bears against such 'spitting' *before* pronouncing the formula, in
the Jer. Talm. it is *after* uttering it.

[3] Bishop *Lightfoot* has shown that the
Essene cures were magical (u. s. pp. 91
&c. and p. 377).

contemptuously from a movement which would awaken no sympathy in them, and could only become of interest when it threatened to endanger their class by awakening popular enthusiasm, and so rousing the suspicions of the Romans. To the Pharisees there were questions of dogmatic, ritual, and even national importance involved, which made the barest possibility of what John announced a question of supreme moment. And, although we judge that the report which the earliest Pharisaic hearers of John ᵃ brought to Jerusalem—no doubt, detailed and accurate—and which led to the despatch of the deputation, would entirely predispose them against the Baptist, yet it behooved them, as leaders of public opinion, to take such cognisance of it, as would not only finally determine their own relation to the movement, but enable them effectually to direct that of others also.

ᵃ St. Matt.
iii. 7

CHAPTER III.

THE TWOFOLD TESTIMONY OF JOHN—THE FIRST SABBATH OF JESUS'S MINISTRY—THE FIRST SUNDAY—THE FIRST DISCIPLES.

(St. John i. 15-51.)

BOOK III

THE forty days, which had passed since Jesus had first come to him, must have been to the Baptist a time of soul-quickening, of unfolding understanding, and of ripened decision. We see it in his more emphasised testimony to the Christ; in his fuller comprehension of those prophecies which had formed the warrant and substance of his Mission; but specially in the yet more entire self-abnegation, which led him to take up a still lowlier position, and acquiescingly to realise that his task of heralding was ending, and that what remained was to point those nearest to him, and who had most deeply drunk of his spirit, to Him Who had come. And how could it be otherwise? On first meeting Jesus by the banks of Jordan, he had felt the seeming incongruity of baptizing One of Whom he had rather need to be baptized. Yet this, perhaps, because he had beheld himself by the Brightness of Christ, rather than looked at the Christ Himself. What he needed was not to be baptized, but to learn that it became the Christ to fulfil all righteousness. This was the first lesson. The next, and completing one, came when, after the Baptism, the heavens opened, the Spirit descended, and the Divine Voice of Testimony pointed to, and explained the promised sign.[1] It told him, that the work, which he had begun in the obedience of faith, had reached the reality of fulfilment. The first was a lesson about the Kingdom; the second about the King. And then Jesus was parted from him, and led of the Spirit into the wilderness.

Forty days since then—with these events, this vision, those words ever present to his mind! It had been the mightiest impulse; nay, it must have been a direct call from above, which first brought John from his life-preparation of lonely communing with God to the task of preparing Israel for that which he knew was preparing for them.

[1] St. John 1. 33.

He had entered upon it, not only without illusions, but with such entire self-forgetfulness, as only deepest conviction of the reality of what he announced could have wrought. He knew those to whom he was to speak—the preoccupation, the spiritual dulness, the sins of the great mass; the hypocrisy, the unreality, the inward impenitence of their spiritual leaders; the perverseness of their direction; the hollowness and delusiveness of their confidence as being descended from Abraham. He saw only too clearly their real character, and knew the near end of it all: how the axe was laid to the barren tree, and how terribly the fan would sift the chaff from the wheat. And yet he preached and baptized; for, deepest in his heart was the conviction, that there was a Kingdom at hand, and a King coming. As we gather the elements of that conviction, we find them chiefly in the Book of Isaiah. His speech and its imagery, and, especially, the burden of his message, were taken from those prophecies.[1] Indeed, his mind seems saturated with them; they must have formed his own religious training; and they were the preparation for his work. This gathering up of the Old Testament rays of light and glory into the burning-glass of Evangelic prophecy had set his soul on fire. No wonder that, recoiling equally from the externalism of the Pharisees, and the merely material purism of the Essenes, he preached quite another doctrine, of inward repentance and renewal of life.

One picture was most brightly reflected on those pages of Isaiah. It was that of the Anointed, Messiah, Christ, the Representative Israelite, the Priest, King, and Prophet,[a] in Whom the institution and sacramental meaning of the Priesthood, and of Sacrifices, found their fulfilment.[b] In his announcement of the Kingdom, in his call to inward repentance, even in his symbolic Baptism, that Great Personality always stood out before the mind of John, as the One all-overtopping and overshadowing Figure in the background. It was the Isaiah-picture of 'the King in His beauty,' the vision of 'the

[a] Is. ix. 6 &c.; xi.; xlii.; lii. 13 &c. [iii.]; lxi.

[b] Is. liii.

---

[1] This is insisted upon by *Keim*, in his beautiful sketch of the Baptist. Would that he had known the Master in the glory of His Divinity, as he understood the Forerunner in the beauty of his humanity! To show how the whole teaching of the Baptist was, so to speak, saturated with Isaiah-language and thoughts, comp. not only Is. xl. 3, as the burden of his mission, but as to his imagery (after *Keim*): *Generation of vipers*, Is. lix. 5; *planting of the Lord*, Is. v. 7; *trees*, vi. 13; x. 15, 18, 33; xl. 24; *fire*, i. 31; ix. 18; x. 17; v. 24; xlvii. 14; *floor and fan*, xxi. 10; xxviii. 27 &c.; xxx. 24; xl. 24; xli. 15 &c.; *bread and coat to the poor*, lviii. 7; *the garner*, xxi. 10. Besides these, the Isaiah reference in his Baptism (Is. lii. 15; i. 16), and that to the Lamb of God—indeed many others of a more indirect character, will readily occur to the reader. Similarly, when our Lord would afterwards instruct him in his hour of darkness (St. Matt. xi. 2), He points for the solution of his doubts to the well-remembered prophecies of Isaiah (Is. xxxv. 5, 6; lxi. 1; viii. 14, 15).

land of far distances'ᵃ¹—to him a reality, of which Sadducee and Essene had no conception, and the Pharisee only the grossest misconception. This also explains how the greatest of those born of women was also the most humble, the most retiring, and self-forgetful. In a picture such as that which filled his whole vision, there was no room for self. By the side of such a Figure all else appeared in its real littleness, and, indeed, seemed at best but as shadows cast by its light. All the more would the bare suggestion on the part of the Jerusalem deputation, that he might be the Christ, seem like a blasphemy, from which, in utter self-abasement, he would seek shelter in the scarce-ventured claim to the meanest office which a slave could discharge. He was not Elijah. Even the fact that Jesus afterwards, in significant language, pointed to the possibility of his becoming such to Israel (St. Matt. xi. 14), proves that he claimed it not;² not 'that prophet'; not even a prophet. He professed not visions, revelations, special messages. All else was absorbed in the great fact: he was only the voice of one that cried, 'Prepare ye the way!' Viewed especially in the light of those self-glorious times, this reads not like a fictitious account of a fictitious mission; nor was such the profession of an impostor, an associate in a plot, or an enthusiast. There was deep reality of all-engrossing conviction which underlay such self-denial of mission.

And all this must have ripened during the forty days of probably comparative solitude,³ only relieved by the presence of such 'disciples' as, learning the same hope, would gather around him. What he had seen and what he had heard threw him back upon what he had expected and believed. It not only fulfilled, it transfigured it. Not that, probably, he always maintained the same height which he then attained. It was not in the nature of things that it should be so. We often attain, at the outset of our climbing, a glimpse, afterwards hid from us in our laborious upward toil till the supreme height is reached. Mentally and spiritually we may attain almost at a bound results, too often lost to us till again secured by long

¹ I cannot agree with Mr. *Cheyne* (Prophecies of Is. vol. i. p. 183), that there is no Messianic reference here. It may not be in the most literal sense '*personally* Messianic;' but surely this ideal presentation of Israel in the perfectness of its kingdom, and the glory of its happiness, is one of the fullest Messianic pictures (comp. vv. 17 to end).
² This is well pointed out by *Keim*.

³ We have in a previous chapter suggested that the baptism of Jesus had taken place at Bethabara, that is, the furthest northern point of his activity, and probably at the close of his *baptismal* ministry. It is not possible in this place to detail the reasons for this view. But the learned reader will find remarks on it in *Keim*, i. 2, p. 524.

reflection, or in the course of painful development. This in some
measure explains the fulness of John's testimony to the Christ as 'the Lamb of God, Which taketh away the sin of the world,' when at the beginning we find ourselves almost at the goal of New Testament teaching. It also explains that last strife of doubt and fear, when the weary wrestler laid himself down to find refreshment and strength in the shadow of those prophecies, which had first called him to the contest. But during those forty days, and in the first meetings with Jesus which followed, all lay bathed in the morning-light of that heavenly vision, and that Divine truth wakened in him the echoes of all those prophecies, which these thirty years had been the music of his soul.

And now, on the last of those forty days, simultaneously with the final great Temptation of Jesus [1] which must have summed up all that had preceded it in the previous days, came the hour of John's temptation by the deputation from Jerusalem.[2] Very gently it came to him, like the tempered wind that fans the fire into flame, not like that keen, desolating storm-blast which swept over the Master. To John, as now to us, it was only the fellowship of His sufferings, which he bore in the shelter of that great Rock over which its intense-ness had spent itself. Yet a very real temptation it was, this pro-voking to the assumption of successively lower grades of self-asser-tion, where only entire self-abnegation was the rightful feeling. Each suggestion of lower office (like the temptations of Christ) marked an increased measure of temptation, as the human in his mission was more and more closely neared. And greatest temptation it was when, after the first victory, came the not unnatural challenge of his authority for what he said and did. This was, of all others, the question which must at all times, from the beginning of his mission to the hour of his death, have pressed most closely upon him, since it touched not only his conscience, but the very ground of his mission, nay, of his life. That it was such temptation is evidenced by the fact that, in the hour of his greatest loneliness and depression, it formed his final contest, in which he temporarily paused, like Jacob in his Israel-struggle, though, like him, he failed not in it. For what was the meaning of that question which the disciples of John brought to

---

[1] This, of course, on the supposition that the Baptism of Jesus took place at Bethabara, and hence that the 'wilder-ness' into which He was driven, was close by. It is difficult to see why, on any other supposition, Jesus returned to Bethabara, since evidently it was not for the sake of any personal intercourse with John.

[2] This is most beautifully suggested by Canon *Westcott* in his Commentary on the passage.

BOOK
III

Jesus: 'Art Thou He that should come, or do we look for another?' other than doubt of his own warrant and authority for what he had said and done? But in that first time of his trial at Bethabara he overcame—the first temptation by the humility of his intense sincerity, the second by the absolute simplicity of his own experimental conviction; the first by what he had seen, the second by what he had heard concerning the Christ at the banks of Jordan. And so, also, although perhaps 'afar off,' it must ever be to us in like temptation.

Yet, as we view it, and without needlessly imputing malice prepense to the Pharisaic deputation, their questions seemed but natural. After his previous emphatic disclaimer at the beginning of his preaching (St. Luke iii. 15), of which they in Jerusalem could scarcely have been ignorant, the suggestion of his Messiahship—not indeed expressly made, but sufficiently implied to elicit what the language of St. John [1] shows to have been the most energetic denial—could scarcely have been more than tentative. It was otherwise with their question whether he was 'Elijah'? Yet, bearing in mind what we know of the Jewish expectations of Elijah, and how his appearance was always readily recognised,[2] this also could scarcely have been meant in its full literality—but rather as ground for the further question after the goal and warrant of his mission. Hence also John's disavowing of such claims is not satisfactorily accounted for by the common explanation, that he denied being Elijah in the sense of not being what the Jews expected of the Forerunner of the Messiah: the real, identical Elijah of the days of Ahab; or else, that he denied being such in the sense of the peculiar Jewish hopes attaching to his reappearance in the 'last days.' There is much deeper truth in the disclaimer of the Baptist. It was, indeed, true that, as foretold in the

[a] St. Luke i. 17

Angelic announcement,[a] he was sent 'in the spirit and power of Elias,' that is, with the same object and the same qualifications. Similarly, it is true what, in His mournful retrospect of the result of John's mission, and in the prospect of His own end, the Saviour said of him, 'Elias is indeed come,' but 'they knew him not, but have done

[b] St. Mark ix. 13; St. Matt. xvii. 12

unto him whatsoever they listed.'[b] But on this very recognition and reception of him by the Jews depended his being to them Elijah —who should 'turn the hearts of the fathers to the children, and the

---

[1] 'He confessed, and denied not' (St. John i. 20). Canon *Westcott* points out, that 'the combination of a positive and negative' is intended to 'express the fulness of truth,' and that 'the first term

marks the readiness of his testimony, the second its completeness.'

[2] See Appendix VIII.: 'Rabbinic Traditions about Elijah, the Forerunner of the Messiah.'

disobedient to the wisdom of the just,' and so 'restore all things.' Between the Elijah of Ahab's reign, and him of Messianic times, lay the wide cleft of quite another dispensation. The 'spirit and power of Elijah' could 'restore all things,' because it was the dispensation of the Old Testament, in which the result was outward, and by outward means. But 'the spirit and power' of the Elijah of the New Testament, which was to accomplish the inward restoration through penitent reception of the Kingdom of God in its reality, could only accomplish that object if 'they received it'—if 'they knew him.' And as in his own view, and looking around and forward, so also in very fact the Baptist, though Divinely such, was *not* really Elijah *to Israel*—and this is the meaning of the words of Jesus: 'And if ye will receive it, this is Elias, which was for to come.'[a]

[a] St. Matt. xi. 14

More natural still—indeed, almost quite truthful, seems the third question of the Pharisees, whether the Baptist was 'that prophet.' The reference here is undoubtedly to Deut. xviii. 15, 18. Not that the reappearance of Moses as lawgiver was expected. But as the prediction of the eighteenth chapter of Deuteronomy, especially when taken in connection with the promise[b] of a 'new covenant' with a 'new law' written in the hearts of the people, implied a change in this respect, it was but natural that it should have been expected in Messianic days by the instrumentality of 'that prophet.'[1] Even the various opinions broached in the Mishnah,[c] as to what were to be the reformatory and legislative functions of Elijah, prove that such expectations were connected with the Forerunner of the Messiah.

[b] Jer. xxxi. 31 &c.

[c] Eduy. viii, 7

But whatever views the Jewish embassy might have entertained concerning the abrogation, renewal, or renovation of the Law[2] in Messianic times, the Baptist repelled the suggestion of his being 'that prophet' with the same energy as those of his being either the Christ or Elijah. And just as we notice, as the result of those forty days' communing, yet deeper humility and self-abnegation on the part of the Baptist, so we also mark increased intensity and directness in the testimony which he now bears to the Christ before the Jerusalem deputies.[d] 'His eye is fixed on the Coming One.' 'He is as a voice not to be inquired about, but heard;' and its clear and

[d] St. John i. 22–28

---

[1] Can the reference in St. Stephen's speech (Acts vii. 37) apply to this expected alteration of the Law? At any rate St. Stephen is on his defence for teaching the abolition by Jesus of the Old Testament economy. It is remarkable that he does not deny the charge, and that his contention is, that the Jews wickedly resisted the authority of Jesus (vv. 51–53).

[2] For the Jewish views on the Law in Messianic times, see Appendix XIV.; 'The Law in Messianic Days.'

BOOK
III

unmistakable, but deeply reverent utterance is: 'The Coming One has come.'[1]

The reward of his overcoming temptation—yet with it also the fitting for still fiercer conflict (which two, indeed, are always conjoined), was at hand. After His victorious contest with the Devil, Angels had come to minister to Jesus in body and soul. But better than Angels' vision came to refresh and strengthen His faithful witness John. On the very day of the Baptist's temptation Jesus had left the wilderness. On the morrow after it, 'John seeth Jesus coming unto him, and saith, Behold, the Lamb of God, Which taketh away the sin of the world!' We cannot doubt, that the thought here present to the mind of John was the description of 'The Servant of Jehovah,'[a] as set forth in Is. liii. If all along the Baptist had been filled with Isaiah-thoughts of the Kingdom, surely in the forty days after he had seen the King, a new 'morning' must have risen upon them,[b] and the halo of His glory shone around the well-remembered prophecy. It must always have been Messianically understood;[c] it formed the groundwork of Messianic thought to the New Testament writers[d]—nor did the Synagogue read it otherwise, till the necessities of controversy diverted its application, not indeed from the *times*, but from the *Person* of the Messiah.[2] But we can understand how, during those forty days, this greatest height of Isaiah's conception of the Messiah was the one outstanding fact before his view. And what he believed, that he spake, when again, and unexpectedly, he saw Jesus.

Yet, while regarding his words as an appeal to the prophecy of Isaiah, two other references must not be excluded from them: those to the Paschal Lamb, and to the Daily Sacrifice. These are, if not directly pointed to, yet implied. For the Paschal Lamb was, in a sense, the basis of all the sacrifices of the Old Testament, not only from its saving import to Israel, but as that which really made them 'the Church,'[3] and people of God. Hence the institution of the Paschal Lamb was, so to speak, only enlarged and applied in the daily sacrifice of a Lamb, in which this twofold idea of redemption and fellowship was exhibited. Lastly, the prophecy of Isaiah liii. was

a Is. liii. 13

b Is. viii. 20

c Is. liii. 13-liii.

d Comp. St. Matt. viii. 17; St. Luke xxii. 37; Acts viii. 32; 1 Pet. ii. 22

---

[1] The words within quotations are those of Archdeacon *Watkins*, in his Commentary on St. John.

[2] Manifestly, whatever interpretation is made of Is. iii. 13-liii., it applies to Messianic *times*, even if the sufferer were, as the Synagogue now contends, Israel. On the whole subject comp. the most learned and exhaustive discussions by Dr. *Pusey* in his introduction to the catena of Jewish Interpretations of Is. liii.

[3] To those persons who deny to the people of God under the Old Testament the designation *Church*, we commend the use of that term by St. Stephen in Acts vii. 38.

but the complete realisation of these two ideas in the Messiah. Neither could the Paschal Lamb, with its completion in the Daily Sacrifice, be properly viewed without this prophecy of Isaiah, nor yet that prophecy properly understood without its reference to its two great types. And here one Jewish comment in regard to the Daily Sacrifice (not previously pointed out) is the more significant, that it dates from the very time of Jesus. The passage reads almost like a Christian interpretation of sacrifice. It explains how the morning and evening sacrifices were intended to atone, the one for the sins of the night, the other for those of the day, so as ever to leave Israel guiltless before God; and it expressly ascribes to them the efficacy of a *Paraclete*—that being the word used.[a] Without further following this remarkable Rabbinic commentation,[b] which stretches back its view of sacrifices to the Paschal Lamb, and, beyond it, to that offering of Isaac by Abraham which, in the Rabbinic view, was the *substratum* of all sacrifices, we turn again to its teaching about the Lamb of the Daily Sacrifice. Here we have the express statement, that both the school of Shammai and that of Hillel—the latter more fully—insisted on the symbolic import of this sacrifice in regard to the forgiveness of sin. ' Kebhasim' (the Hebrew word for 'lambs'), explained the school of Shammai, 'because, according to Micah vii. 19, they suppress [in the A.V. ' subdue '] our iniquities (the Hebrew word *Kabhash* meaning he who suppresseth).'[1] Still more strong is the statement of the school of Hillel, to the effect that the sacrificial lambs were termed *Kebhasim* (from *kabhas*, ' to wash '), ' because they wash away the sins of Israel.'[c] The quotation just made gains additional interest from the circumstance, that it occurs in a ' meditation' (if such it may be called) for the new moon of the Passover-month (Nisan). In view of such clear testimony from the time of Christ, less positiveness of assertion might, not unreasonably, be expected from those who declare that the sacrifices bore no reference to the forgiveness of sins, just as, in the face of the application made by the Baptist and other New Testament writers, more exegetical modesty seems called for on the part of those who deny the Messianic references in Isaiah.

If further proof were required that, when John pointed the by-standers to the Figure of Jesus walking towards them, with these words : ' Behold, the Lamb of God,' he meant more than His gentleness, meekness, and humility, it would be supplied by the qualifying

CHAP.
III

[a] Pesiqta, ed. *Buber*, p. 61
[b] comp. more fully in Yalkut p. 248 *d*
[b] In i. p. 249 *a*

[c] And this with special reference to Is. i. 18

[1] This appears more clearly in the Hebrew, where both words (' lambs' and ' suppressors ') are written exactly the same, כבשים. In Hillel's derivation it is identified with the root כבס = כבש.

BOOK
III

explanation, 'Which taketh away the sin of the world.' We prefer rendering the expression 'taketh away' instead of 'beareth,' because it is in that sense that the LXX. uniformly use the Greek term. Of course, as *we* view it, the taking away presupposes the taking upon Himself of the sin of the world. But it is not necessary to suppose that the Baptist clearly understood that manner of His Saviourship, which only long afterwards, and reluctantly, came to the followers of the Lamb.[1] That he understood the application of His ministry to the whole world, is only what might have been expected of one taught by Isaiah; and what, indeed, in one or another form, the Synagogue has always believed of the Messiah. What was distinctive in the words of the Baptist, seems his view of *sin* as a totality, rather than sins: implying the removal of that great barrier between God and man, and the triumph in that great contest indicated in Gen. iii. 15, which Israel after the flesh failed to perceive. Nor should we omit here to notice an undesigned evidence of the Hebraic origin of the fourth Gospel; for an Ephesian Gospel, dating from the close of the second century, would not have placed in its forefront, as the first public testimony of the Baptist (if, indeed, it would have introduced him at all), a quotation from Isaiah—still less a sacrificial reference.

The motives which brought Jesus back to Bethabara must remain in the indefiniteness in which Scripture has left them. So far as we know, there was no personal interview between Jesus and the Baptist. Jesus had then and there nothing further to say to the Baptist; and yet on the day following that on which John had, in such manner, pointed Him out to the bystanders, He was still there, only returning to Galilee the next day. Here, at least, a definite object becomes apparent. This was not merely the calling of His first disciples, but the necessary Sabbath rest; for, in this instance, the narrative supplies the means of ascertaining the days of the week on which each event took place. We have only to assume, that the marriage in Cana of Galilee was that of a maiden, not a widow. The great festivities which accompanied it were unlikely, according to Jewish ideas, in the case of a widow; in fact, the whole *mise en scène* of the marriage renders this most improbable. Besides, if it had been the marriage of a widow, this (as will immediately appear) would imply that Jesus had returned

---

[1] This meets the objection of *Keim* (i. 2, p. 552), which proceeds on the assumption that the words of the Baptist imply that he knew not merely *that*, but *how*, Jesus would take away the sin of the world. But his words certainly do not oblige us to think, that he had the Cross in view. But, surely, it is a most strange idea of *Godet*, that at His Baptism Jesus, like all others, made confession of sins; that, as He had none of His own, He set before the Baptist the picture of the sin of Israel and of the world; and that this had led to the designation: 'The Lamb of God.'

from the wilderness on a Saturday, which, as being the Jewish Sabbath, could not have been the case. For uniform custom fixed the marriage of a maiden on Wednesdays, that of a widow on Thursday.[1] Counting backwards from the day of the marriage in Cana, we arrive at the following results. The interview between John and the Sanhedrin-deputation took place on a *Thursday*. 'The next day,' *Friday,* Jesus returned from the wilderness of the Temptation, and John bore his first testimony to 'the Lamb of God.' The following day, when Jesus appeared a second time in view, and when the first two disciples joined Him, was the *Saturday*, or Jewish Sabbath. It was, therefore, only the following day, or *Sunday*,[a] that Jesus returned to Galilee,[2] calling others by the way. 'And the third day' after it[b]—that is, on the *Wednesday*—was the marriage in Cana.[3]

a St. John 1
43
b St. John
ii. 1

If we group around these days the recorded events of each, they almost seem to intensify in significance. The *Friday* of John's first pointing to Jesus as the Lamb of God, which taketh away the sin of the world, recalls that other Friday, when the full import of that testimony appeared. The *Sabbath* of John's last personal view and testimony to Christ is symbolic in its retrospect upon the old economy. It seems to close the ministry of John, and to open that of Jesus; it is the leave-taking of the nearest disciples of John from the old, their search after the new. And then on the first *Sunday*—the beginning of Christ's active ministry, the call of the first disciples, the first preaching of Jesus.

As we picture it to ourselves: in the early morning of that *Sabbath* John stood, with the two of his disciples who most shared his thoughts and feelings. One of them we know to have been *Andrew* (v. 40); the other, unnamed one, could have been no other than John himself, the beloved disciple.[4] They had heard what their teacher had, on the previous day, said of Jesus. But then He seemed to them but as a passing Figure. To hear more of Him, as well as in deepest sympathy, these two had gathered to their Teacher on that Sabbath morning, while the other disciples of John were probably engaged with that, and with those, which formed the surroundings of an ordinary Jewish Sabbath.[5] And now that Figure once more appeared in view. None

Which taketh away the sin of the world.'
[1] For the reasons of this, comp. 'Sketches of Jewish Social Life,' p. 151.
[2] This may be regarded as another of the undesigned evidences of the Hebraic origin of the fourth Gospel. Indeed, it might also be almost called an evidence of the truth of the whole narrative.

[3] Yet *Renan* speaks of the first chapters of St. John's Gospel as scattered notices, without chronological order!
[4] This reticence seems another undesigned evidence of Johannine authorship.
[5] The Greek has it: 'John was standing, and from among his disciples two.'

with the Baptist but these two. He is not teaching now, but learning, as the intensity and penetration of his gaze[1] calls from him the now worshipful repetition of what, on the previous day, he had explained and enforced. There was no leave-taking on the part of these two— perhaps they meant not to leave John. Only an irresistible impulse, a heavenly instinct, bade them follow His steps. It needed no direction of John, no call from Jesus. But as they went in modest silence, in the dawn of their rising faith, scarce conscious of the *what* and the *why*, He turned Him. It was not because He discerned it not, but just because He knew the real goal of their yet unconscious search, and would bring them to know *what* they sought, that He put to them the question, ' What seek ye? ' which elicited a reply so simple, so real, as to carry its own evidence. He is still to them the Rabbi—the most honoured title they can find—yet marking still the strictly Jewish view, as well as their own standpoint of ' *What* seek ye?' They wish, yet scarcely dare, to say what was their object, and only put it in a form most modest, suggestive rather than expressive. There is strict correspondence to their view in the words of Jesus. Their very Hebraism of ' Rabbi ' is met by the equally Hebraic ' Come and see; '[2] their unspoken, but half-conscious longing by what the invitation implied (according to the most probable reading, ' Come and ye shall see '[3]).

It was but early morning—ten o'clock.[4] What passed on that long Sabbath-day we know not save from what happened in its

---

[1] The word implies earnest, penetrating gaze.

[2] The precise date of the origin of this designation is not quite clear. We find it in threefold development: *Rab, Rabbi,* and *Rabban*—' amplitudo,' ' amplitudo mea,' ' amplitudo nostra,' which mark successive stages. As the *last* of these titles was borne by the grandson of Hillel (A.D. 30–50), it is only reasonable to suppose that the two preceding ones were current a generation and more before that. Again, we have to distinguish the original and earlier use of the title when it only applied to *teachers,* and the later usage when, like the word *'Doctor,'* it was given indiscriminately to men of supposed learning. When Jesus is so addressed it is in the sense of ' my Teacher.' Nor can there be any reasonable doubt, that thus it was generally current in and before the time noted in the Gospels. A still higher title than any of these three seems to have been *Beribbi,* or *Berabbi,*

by which Rabban Gamaliel is designated in Shabb. 115 *a.* It literally means ' belonging to the house of a Rabbi,'—as we would say, a Rabbi of Rabbis. On the other hand, the expression ' Come and see ' is among the most common Rabbinic formulas, although generally connected with the acquisition of special and important information.

[3] Comp. Canon *Westcott's* note.

[4] The common supposition is, that the time must be computed according to the Jewish method, in which case the tenth hour would represent 4 P.M. But remembering that the Jewish day ended with sunset, it could, in that case, have been scarcely marked, that ' they abode with Him that day.' The correct interpretation would therefore point in this, as in the other passages of St. John, to the Asiatic numeration of hours, corresponding to our own. Comp. J. B. Mc-Lellan's New Testament, pp. 740-742.

course. From it issued the two, not learners now but teachers, bearing what they had found to those nearest and dearest. The form of
the narrative and its very words convey, that the two had gone, each
to search for his brother—Andrew for Simon Peter, and John for
James, though here already, at the outset of this history, the haste
of energy characteristic of the sons of Jona outdistanced the more
quiet intenseness of John:[a] 'He (Andrew) first findeth his own   [a] v. 41
brother.'[1] But Andrew and John equally brought the same announcement, still markedly Hebraic in its form, yet filled with the new
wine, not only of conviction, but of joyous apprehension: 'We have
found the Messias.'[2] This, then, was the outcome to them of that
day—He was the Messiah; and this the goal which their longing
had reached, 'We have found Him.' Quite beyond what they had
heard from the Baptist; nay, what only personal contact with Jesus
can carry to any heart.

And still this day of first marvellous discovery had not closed. It
almost seems, as if this 'Come and see' call of Jesus were emblematic,
not merely of all that followed in His own ministry, but of the
manner in which to all time the 'What seek ye?' of the soul is
answered. It could scarcely have been but that Andrew had told
Jesus of his brother, and even asked leave to bring him. The searching, penetrating glance[3] of the Saviour now read in Peter's inmost
character his future call and work: 'Thou art Simon, the son of
John[4]—thou shalt be called[5] Cephas, which is interpreted (Grecianised) Peter.'[6]

It must not, of course, be supposed that this represents all that
had passed between Jesus and Peter, any more than that the
recorded expression was all that Andrew and John had said of Jesus
to their brothers. Of the interview between John and James his
brother, the writer, with his usual self-reticence, forbears to speak.
But we know its result; and, knowing it, can form some conception
of what passed on that holy evening between the new-found Messiah
and His first four disciples: of teaching manifestation on His part,
and of satisfied heart-peace on theirs. As yet they were only

---

[1] This appears from the word 'first,'
used as an adjective here, v. 41 (although
the reading is doubtful), and from the implied reference to some one else later on.
[2] On the reading of the Aramaic
Meshicha by Messias, see *Delitzsch* in
the Luther. Zeitschr. for 1876, p. 603.
Of course, both Messias and Christ mean
'the Anointed.'

[3] The same word as that used in regard
to the Baptist looking upon Jesus.
[4] So according to the best text, and
not *Jona*.
[5] 'Hereafter thou shalt win the name.'
—*Westcott.*
[6] So in the Greek, of which the English
interpretation is 'a stone'—*Keyph*, or
Keypha, 'a rock.'

followers, learners, not yet called to be Apostles, with all of entire renunciation of home, family, and other calling which this implied. This, in the course of proper development, remained for quite another period. Alike their knowledge and their faith for the present needed, and could only bear, the call to personal attachment.[1]

It was Sunday morning, the first of Christ's Mission-work, the first of His Preaching. He was purposing to return to Galilee. It was fitting He should do so: for the sake of His new disciples; for what He was to do in Galilee; for His own sake. The first Jerusalem-visit must be prepared for by them all; and He would not go there till the right time—for the Paschal Feast. It was probably a distance of about twenty miles from Bethabara to Cana. By the way, two other disciples were to be gained—this time not brought, but called, where, and in what precise circumstances, we know not. But the notice that Philip was a fellow-townsman of Andrew and Peter, seems to imply some instrumentality on their part. Similarly, we gather that, afterwards, Philip was somewhat in advance of the rest, when he found his acquaintance Nathanael, and engaged in conversation with him just as Jesus and the others came up. But here also we mark, as another characteristic trait of John, that he, and his brother with him, seem to have clung close to the Person of Christ, just as did Mary afterwards in the house of her brother. It was this intense exclusiveness of fellowship with Jesus which traced on his mind that fullest picture of the God-Man, which his narrative reflects.

The call to Philip from the lips of the Saviour met, we know not under what circumstances, immediate responsive obedience. Yet, though no special obstacles had to be overcome, and hence no special narrative was called for, it must have implied much of learning, to judge from what he did, and from what he said to Nathanael. There is something special about Nathanael's conquest by Christ—rather implied, perhaps, than expressed—and of which the Lord's words give significant hints. They seem to point to what had passed in his mind just before Philip found him. Alike the expression 'an Israelite in truth, in whom is no guile'[a]—looking back on what changed the name of Jacob into Israel—and the evident reference to

---

[1] The evidence for the great historic difference between this call to personal attachment, and that to the Apostolate, is shown—I should think beyond the power of cavil—by *Godet*, and especially by Canon *Westcott*. To these and other commentators the reader must be referred on this and many points, which it would be out of place to discuss at length in this book.

the full realisation of Jacob's vision in Bethel,[a] may be an indication that this very vision had engaged his thoughts. As the Synagogue understood the narrative, its application to the then state of Israel and the Messianic hope would most readily suggest itself. Putting aside all extravagances, the Synagogue thought, in connection with it, of the rising power of the Gentiles, but concluded with the precious comfort of the assurance, in Jer. xxx. 11, of Israel's final restoration.[b] Nathanael (Theodore, 'the gift of God,') had, as we often read of Rabbis,[1] rested for prayer, meditation, or study, in the shadow of that wide-spreading tree so common in Palestine, the fig-tree.[2] The approaching Passover-season, perhaps mingling with thoughts of John's announcement by the banks of Jordan, would naturally suggest the great deliverance of Israel in 'the age to come;'[c] all the more, perhaps, from the painful contrast in the present. Such a verse as that with which, in a well-known Rabbinic work,[d] the meditation for the New Moon of Nisan, the Passover month, closes: 'Happy is he that hath the God of Jacob for his help,'[e] would recur, and so lead back the mind to the suggestive symbol of Jacob's vision, and its realisation in 'the age to come.'[f]

These are, of course, only suppositions; but it might well be that Philip had found him while still busy with such thoughts. Possibly their outcome, and that quite in accordance with Jewish belief at the time, may have been, that all that was needed to bring that happy 'age to come' was, that Jacob should become Israel in truth. In such case he would himself have been ripening for 'the Kingdom' that was at hand. It must have seemed a startling answer to his thoughts, this announcement, made with the freshness of new and joyous conviction: 'We have found Him of Whom Moses in the Law, and the Prophets, did write.' But this addition about the Man of Nazareth, the Son of Joseph,[3] would appear a terrible anti-climax. It was so different from anything that he had associated either with the great hope of Israel, or with the Nazareth of his own neighbourhood, that his exclamation, without implying any special imputation on the little town which he knew so well, seems not only natural, but, psychologically, deeply true. There was but one

CHAP.
III

[a] v. 51

[b] Tanchuma on the passage, ed. Warsh. p. 38 a, b

[c] So in Tanchuma

[d] Pesiqta

[e] Ps. cxlvi 5; Pesiqta, ed. Buber, p. 62 a

[f] Tanchuma, u. s.

---

[1] Corroborative and illustrative passages are here too numerous, perhaps also not sufficiently important, to be quoted in detail.

[2] Ewald imagines that this 'fig-tree' had been in the garden of Nathanael's house at Cana, and Archdeacon Watkins seems to adopt this view, but, as it seems to me, without historical ground.

[3] This, as it would seem, needless addition (if the narrative were fictitious) is of the highest evidential value. In an Ephesian Gospel of the end of the second century it would have been well-nigh impossible.

answer to this—that which Philip made, which Jesus had made to Andrew and John, and which has ever since been the best answer to all Christian inquiry: 'Come and see.' And, despite the disappointment, there must have been such moving power in the answer which Philip's sudden announcement had given to his unspoken thoughts, that he went with him. And now, as ever, when in such spirit we come, evidences irrefragable multiplied at every step. As he neared Jesus, he heard Him speak to the disciples words concerning him, which recalled, truly and actually, what had passed in his soul. But could it really be so, that Jesus knew it all? The question, intended to elicit it, brought such proof that he could not but burst into the immediate and full ackowledgment: 'Thou art the Son of God,' Who hast read my inmost being; 'Thou art the King of Israel,' Who dost meet its longing and hope. And is it not ever so, that the faith of the heart springs to the lips, as did the water from the riven rock at the touch of the God-gifted rod? It needs not long course of argumentation, nor intricate chain of evidences, welded link to link, when the secret thoughts of the heart are laid bare, and its inmost longings met. Then, as in a moment, it is day, and joyous voice of song greets its birth.

And yet that painful path of slower learning to enduring conviction must still be trodden, whether in the sufferings of the heart, or the struggle of the mind. This it is which seems implied in the half-sad question of the Master,[a] yet with full view of the final triumph ('thou shalt see greater things than these'), and of the true realisation in it of that glorious symbol of Jacob's vision.[b]

And so Nathanael, 'the God-given'—or, as we know him in after-history, Bartholomew, 'the son of Telamyon'[1]—was added to the disciples. Such was on that first Sunday the small beginning of the great Church Catholic; these the tiny springs that swelled into the mighty river which, in its course, has enriched and fertilised the barrenness of the far-off lands of the Gentiles.

[a] v. 50, comp. the words to Peter in St. John xiii. 36–38; and to the disciples, St. John xvi. 31, 32

[b] v. 51

---

[1] So, at least, most probably. Comp. St. John xxi. 2, and the various commentaries.

CHAPTER IV.

THE MARRIAGE FEAST IN CANA OF GALILEE—THE MIRACLE THAT IS 'A SIGN.'

(St. John ii. 1–12.)

AT the close of His Discourse to Nathanael—His first sermon—
Jesus had made use of an expression which received its symbolic fulfilment in His first deed. His first testimony about Himself had
been to call Himself the 'Son of Man.'[a][1] We cannot but feel that
this bore reference to the confession of Nathanael: 'Thou art the Son
of God; Thou art the King of Israel.' It is, as if He would have
turned the disciples from thoughts of His being the Son of God and
King of Israel to the voluntary humiliation of His Humanity, as
being the necessary basis of His work, without knowledge of which
that of His Divinity would have been a barren, speculative abstraction, and that of His Kingship a Jewish fleshly dream. But it was not
only knowledge of His humiliation in His Humanity. For, as in the
history of the Christ humiliation and glory are always connected, the
one enwrapped in the other as the flower in the bud, so here also His
humiliation as the Son of Man is the exaltation of humanity, the
realisation of its ideal destiny as created in the likeness of God. It
should never be forgotten, that such teaching of His exaltation and
Kingship through humiliation and representation of humanity was
needful. It was the teaching which was the outcome of the Temptation and of its victory, the very teaching of the whole Evangelic
history. Any other real learning of Christ would, as we see it, have
been impossible to the disciples—alike mentally, as regards foundation and progression, and spiritually. A Christ: God, King, and not
primarily 'the Son of Man,' would not have been the Christ of
Prophecy, nor the Christ of Humanity, nor the Christ of salvation,

CHAP.
IV

[a] St. John i.
51

---

[1] For a full discussion of that most
important and significant appellation
'Son of Man,' comp. *Lücke*, u. s. pp.
459–466; *Godet* (German transl.), pp.
104–108; and especially *Westcott*, pp.
33–35. The main point is here first to
ascertain the Old Testament import of
the title, and then to view it as present
to later Jewish thinking in the Pseudepigraphic writings (Book of Enoch).
Finally, its full realisation must be
studied in the Gospel-history.

BOOK
III

nor yet the Christ of sympathy, help, and example. A Christ, God and King, Who had suddenly risen like the fierce Eastern sun in midday brightness, would have blinded by his dazzling rays (as it did Saul on the way to Damascus), not risen 'with kindly light' to chase away darkness and mists, and with genial growing warmth to woo life and beauty into our barren world. And so, as 'it became Him,' for the carrying out of the work, 'to make the Captain of Salvation perfect through sufferings,' [a] so it was needful for *them* that He should veil, even from their view who followed Him, the glory of His Divinity and the power of His Kingship, till they had learned all that the designation 'Son of Man' implied, as placed below 'Son of God' and 'King of Israel.

a Hebr. ii. 10

This idea of the 'Son of Man,' although in its full and prophetic meaning, seems to furnish the explanation of the miracle at the marriage of Cana. We are now entering on the Ministry of 'The Son of Man,' first and chiefly in its contrast to the preparatory call of the Baptist, with the asceticism symbolic of it. We behold Him now as freely mingling with humanity, sharing its joys and engagements, entering into its family life, sanctioning and hallowing all by His Presents and blessing; then as transforming the 'water of legal purification' into the wine of the new dispensation, and, more than this, the water of our felt want into the wine of His giving; and, lastly, as having absolute power as the 'Son of Man,' being also 'the Son of God' and 'the King of Israel.' Not that it is intended to convey, that it was the primary purpose of the miracle of Cana to exhibit the contrast between His own Ministry and the asceticism of the Baptist, although greater could scarcely be imagined than between the wilderness and the supply of wine at the marriage-feast. Rather, since this essential difference really existed, it naturally appeared at the very commencement of Christ's Ministry.[1] And so in regard to the other meaning, also, which this history carries to our minds.

At the same time it must be borne in mind, that marriage conveyed to the Jews much higher thoughts than merely those of festivity and merriment. The pious fasted before it, confessing their sins. It was regarded almost as a Sacrament. Entrance into the married state

---

[1] We may, however, here again notice that, if this narrative had been fictitious, it would seem most clumsily put together. To introduce the Forerunner with fasting, and as an ascetic, and Him to Whom he pointed with a marriage-feast, is an incongruity which no writer of a legend would have perpetrated. But the writer of the fourth Gospel does not seem conscious of any incongruity, and this because he has no ideal story nor characters to introduce. In this sense it may be said, that the introduction of the story of the marriage-feast of Cana is in itself the best proof of its truthfulness, and of the miracle which it records.

was thought to carry the forgiveness of sins.[a][1] It almost seems as if the relationship of Husband and Bride between Jehovah and His people, so frequently insisted upon, not only in the Bible, but in Rabbinic writings, had always been standing out in the background. Thus the bridal pair on the marriage-day symbolised the union of God with Israel.[2] Hence, though it may in part have been national pride, which considered the birth of every Israelite as almost outweighing the rest of the world, it scarcely wholly accounts for the ardent insistance on marriage, from the first prayer at the circumcision of a child, onwards through the many and varied admonitions to the same effect. Similarly, it may have been the deep feeling of brotherhood in Israel, leading to sympathy with all that most touched the heart, which invested with such sacredness participation in the gladness of marriage,[3] or the sadness of burial. To use the bold allegory of the times, God Himself had spoken the words of blessing over the cup at the union of our first parents, when Michael and Gabriel acted as groomsmen,[b] and the Angelic choir sang the wedding hymn.[c] So also He had shown the example of visiting the sick (in the case of Abraham), comforting the mourners (in that of Isaac), and burying the dead (in that of Moses).[d] Every man who met it, was bound to rise and join the marriage procession, or the funeral march. It was specially related of King Agrippa that he had done this, and a curious Haggadah sets forth that, when Jezebel was eaten of dogs, her hands and feet were spared,[e] because, amidst all her wickedness, she had been wont to greet every marriage-procession by clapping of hands, and to accompany the mourners a certain distance on their way to the burying.[f] And so we also read it, that, in the burying of the widow's son of Nain, 'much people of the city was with her.'[g]

In such circumstances, we would naturally expect that all connected with marriage was planned with care, so as to bear the impress of sanctity, and also to wear the aspect of gladness.[4] A special formality,

CHAP.
IV

[a] Yalkut on 1 Sam. xiii. 1 vol ii. p. 16 d

[b] Ber. R. 8
[c] Ab. de R. Nath. iv.

[d] Sot. 14 a

[e] 2 Kings. ix. 35

[f] Yalkut on 2 Kings ix 35,vol. ii. p. 36 a and b
[g] St. Luke vii. 12

---

[1] The Biblical proofs adduced for attaching this benefit to a sage, a bridegroom, and a prince on entering on their new state, are certainly peculiar. In the case of a bridegroom it is based on the name of Esau's bride, Machalath (Gen. xxviii. 9), a name which is derived from the Rabbinic 'Machal,' to forgive. In Jer. Biccur. iii. p. 65 d, where this is also related, it is pointed out that the original name of Esau's wife had been Basemath (Gen. xxxvi. 3), the name Machalath, therefore, having been given when Esau married.

[2] In Yalcut on Is. lxi. 10 (vol. ii. p. 57 d) Israel is said to have been ten times called in Scripture 'bride' (six times in Canticles, three times in Isaiah, and once in Jeremiah). Attention is also called to the 'ten garments' with which successively the Holy One arrayed Himself; to the symbolic priestly dignity of the bridegroom, &c.

[3] Everything, even a funeral, had to give way to a marriage-procession.

[4] For details I must refer to the Ency-

that of 'betrothal' (*Erusin Qiddushin*), preceded the actual marriage by a period varying in length, but not exceeding a twelvemonth in the case of a maiden.[1] At the betrothal, the bridegroom, personally or by deputy, handed to the bride a piece of money or a letter, it being expressly stated in each case that the man thereby espoused the woman. From the moment of betrothal both parties were regarded, and treated in law (as to inheritance, adultery, need of formal divorce), as if they had been actually married, except as regarded their living together. A legal document (the *Shitré Erusin*) fixed the dowry which each brought, the mutual obligations, and all other legal points.[2] Generally a festive meal closed the ceremony of betrothal—*but not in Galilee*, where, habits being more simple and pure, that which some-times ended in sin was avoided.

On the evening of the actual marriage (*Nissuin, Chathnuth*), the bride was led from her paternal home to that of her husband. First came the merry sounds of music; then they who distributed among the people wine and oil, and nuts among the children; next the bride, covered with the bridal veil, her long hair flowing, surrounded by her companions, and led by 'the friends of the bridegroom,' and 'the children of the bride-chamber.' All around were in festive array; some carried torches, or lamps on poles; those nearest had myrtle-branches and chaplets of flowers. Every one rose to salute the procession, or join it; and it was deemed almost a religious duty to break into praise of the beauty, the modesty, or the virtues of the bride. Arrived at her new home, she was led to her husband. Some such formula as 'Take her according to the Law of Moses and of Israel,'[a] would be spoken, and the bride and bridegroom crowned with garlands.[3] Then a formal legal instrument, called the *Kethubah*, was signed,[b] which set forth that the bridegroom undertook to work for her, to honour, keep, and care for her,[4] as is the manner of the men of Israel; that he promised to give his maiden-wife at least two hundred *Zuz*[5] (or more it might be),[6] and to increase her own dowry

ᵃ Jer. Yeb.
Md.

ᵇ Comp.
Tob. vii. 14

clopædias, to the article in *Cassell's* 'Bible Educator,' and to the corresponding chapters in 'Sketches of Jewish Social Life.'

[1] Pesiq. R. 15 applies the first clause of Prov. xiii. 12 to a long engagement, the second to a short one.

[2] The reader who is curious to see these and other legal documents *in extenso*, is referred to Dr. *Sammter's* ed. ·of the tractate Baba Metsia (notes at the end, fol. pp. 144-148).

[3] Some of these joyous demonstrations, such as the wearing of crowns, and even the bridal music, were for a time pro-hibited after the destruction of Jeru-salem, in token of national mourning (Sot. ix. 14). On these crowns comp. *Wagenseil*, Sota, pp. 965-967.

[4] I quote the very words of the formula, which, it will be noticed, closely agree with those in our own Marriage Service.

[5] If the *Zuz* be reckoned at 7*d*., about 5*l*. 16*s*. 8*d*.

[6] This, of course, represents only the *minimum*. In the case of a priest's daughter the ordinary legal minimum was doubled.

(which, in the case of a poor orphan, the authorities supplied) by at
least one half, and that he also undertook to lay it out for her to the
best advantage, all his own possessions being guarantee for it.[1] Then,
after the prescribed washing of hands and benediction, the marriage-
supper began—the cup being filled, and the solemn prayer of bridal
benediction spoken over it. And so the feast lasted—it might be
more than one day—while each sought to contribute, sometimes
coarsely,[2] sometimes wisely, to the general enjoyment,[a] till at last 'the   [a] Comp.
Ber. 6 b
friends of the bridegroom' led the bridal pair to the *Cheder* and the
Chuppah, or the bridal chamber and bed. Here it ought to be
specially noticed, as a striking evidence that the writer of the fourth
Gospel was not only a Hebrew, but intimately acquainted with the
varying customs prevailing in Galilee and in Judæa, that at the
marriage of Cana no 'friend of the bridegroom,' or 'groomsman'
(*Shoshebheyna*), is mentioned, while he *is* referred to in St. John iii. 29,
where the words are spoken outside the boundaries of Galilee. For
among the simpler and purer Galileans the practice of having 'friends
of the bridegroom,' which must so often have led to gross impropriety,[b]   [b] Comp.
Kethub.
did not obtain,[3] though all the invited guests bore the general name   12 a; Jer.
Kethub, 1.
of 'children of the bridechamber' (*bené Chuppah*).[c]   p. 25 a

It was the marriage in Cana of Galilee. All connected with the   [c] Comp. St.
Matt. ix. 15
account of it is strictly Jewish—the feast, the guests, the invitation
of the stranger Rabbi, and its acceptance by Jesus. Any Jewish
Rabbi would have gone, but how differently from Him would he have
spoken and acted ! Let us first think of the scenic details of the
narrative. Strangely, we are not able to fix with certainty the site of
the little town of Cana.[4] But if we adopt the most probable indentifi-
cation of it with the modern pleasant village of *Kefr Kenna*,[5] a few
miles north-east of Nazareth, on the road to the Lake of Galilee, we
picture it to ourselves as on the slope of a hill, its houses rising terrace

---

[1] The Talmud (Tos. Kethub.) here puts
the not inapt question, 'How if the
bridegroom has no goods and chattels ?'
but ultimately comforts itself with the
thought that every man has some property, if it were only the six feet of ground
in which he is to be buried.

[2] Not a few such instances of riotous
merriment, and even dubious jokes, on
the part of the greatest Rabbis are mentioned, to check which some were wont
to adopt the curious device of breaking
valuable vases, &c.

[3] This, and the other great differences
in favour of morality and decency which

distinguished the customs of Galilee from
those of the rest of Palestine, are enumerated in Jer. Kethub. i. 1, p. 25 a, about
the middle.

[4] Two such sites have been proposed—
that by Dr. Robinson being very unlikely
to represent the ancient ' Cana of Galilee.'

[5] Comp. the memoir on the subject
by *Zeller* in the Quarterly Report of the
Palestine Explor. Fund (for 1869, No. iii.,
and for April 1878, by Mr. *Hepworth
Dixon*); and Lieut. *Conder*, Tent-Work.
in Palestine, vol. i. pp. 150–155. *Zeller*
makes it five miles from Nazareth,
Conder only three and three-quarters.

upon terrace, looking north and west over a large plain (that of Battauf),
and south upon a valley, beyond which the hills rise that separate it
from Mount Tabor and the plain of Jezreel. As we approach the
little town through that smiling valley, we come upon a fountain of
excellent water, around which the village gardens and orchards
clustered, that produced in great abundance the best pomegranates in
Palestine. Here was the home of Nathanael-Bartholomew, and it seems
not unlikely, that with him Jesus had passed the time intervening
between His arrival and 'the marriage,' to which His Mother had
come—the omission of all mention of Joseph leading to the supposition, that he had died before that time. The inquiry, what had brought
Jesus to Cana, seems almost worse than idle, remembering what had
passed between Him and Nathanael, and what was to happen in the
first 'sign,' which was to manifest His glory. It is needless to specu-
late, whether He had known beforehand of 'the marriage.' But we
can understand the longing of the 'Israelite indeed' to have Him
under his roof, though we can only imagine what the Heavenly Guest
would now teach him, and those others who accompanied Him. Nor
is there any difficulty in understanding, that on His arrival He would
hear of this 'marriage,' of the presence of His Mother in what seems
to have been the house of a friend, if not a relative; that Jesus
and His disciples would be bidden to the feast; and that He resolved
not only to comply with the request) but to use it as a leave-taking
from home and friends—similar, though also far other, than that of
Elisha, when he entered on his mission. Yet it seems deeply significant, that the 'true Israelite' should have been honoured to be the
first host of 'Israel's King.'

And truly a leave-taking it was for Christ from former friends and
home—a leave-taking also from His past life. If one part of the
narrative—that of His dealing with His Mother—has any special
meaning, it is that of leave-taking, or rather of leaving home and
family, just as with this first 'sign' He took leave of all the past.
When he had returned from His first Temple-visit, it had been in the
self-exinanition of voluntary humility: to 'be subject to His Parents.'
That period was now ended, and a new one had begun—that of
active consecration of the whole life to His 'Father's business.' And
what passed at the marriage-feast marks the beginning of this
period. We stand on the threshold, over which we pass from the old
to the new—to use a New Testament figure: to the marriage-supper
of the Lamb.

Viewed in this light, what passed at the marriage in Cana seems

like taking up the thread, where it had been dropped at the first
manifestation of His Messianic consciousness. In the Temple at
Jerusalem He had said in answer to the misapprehensive *question* of
His Mother: 'Wist ye not that I must be about My Father's business?' and now when about to take in hand that 'business,' He tells
her so again, and decisively, in reply to her misapprehensive *suggestion*. It is a truth which we must ever learn, and yet are ever slow
to learn in our questionings and suggestings, alike as concerns His
dealings with ourselves and His rule of His Church, that the highest
and only true point of view is ' the Father's business,' not our personal
relationship to Christ. This thread, then, is taken up again at Cana
in the circle of friends, as immediately afterwards in His public
manifestation, in the purifying of the Temple. What He had first
uttered as a Child, on His first visit to the Temple, that He manifested
forth when a Man, entering on His active work—negatively, in His
reply to His Mother; positively, in the 'sign' He wrought. It all
meant: 'Wist ye not that I must be about My Father's business?'
And, positively and negatively, His first appearance in Jerusalem [a]
meant just the same. For, there is ever deepest unity and harmony
in that truest Life, the Life of Life.

[a] St. John ii
13-17, and
vv. 18-23

As we pass through the court of that house in Cana, and reach
the covered gallery which opens on the various rooms—in this instance,
particularly, on the great reception room—all is festively adorned. In
the gallery the servants move about, and there the 'water-pots' are
ranged, 'after the manner of the Jews,' for purification—for the washing not only of hands before and after eating, but also of the vessels
used.[b] How detailed Rabbinic ordinances were in these respects, will
be shown in another connection. 'Purification' was one of the
main points in Rabbinic sanctity. By far the largest and most
elaborate[1] of the six books into which the Mishnah is divided, is exclusively devoted to this subject (the *'Seder Tohoroth,'* purifications).
Not to speak of references in other parts of the Talmud, we have
two special tractates to instruct us about the purification of 'Hands'
(*Yadayim*) and of 'Vessels' (*Kelim*). The latter is the most elaborate
in all the Mishnah, and consists of not less than thirty chapters.
Their perusal proves, alike the strict accuracy of the Evangelic nar-

[b] Comp. St.
Mark vii
1-4

---

[1] The whole Mishnah is divided into
six *Sedarim* (Orders), of which the last
is the *Seder Tohoroth*, treating of 'purifications.' It consists of twelve tractates
(*Massikhtoth*), 126 chapters (*Peraqim*),
and contains no fewer than 1001 separate
Mishnayoth (the next largest *Seder*—
Neziqin—contains 689 Mishnayoth). The
first tractate in this 'Order of Purifications' treats of the purification of
vessels (*Kelim*), and contains no fewer
than thirty chapters; '*Yadayim*' ('hands')
is the eleventh tractate, and contains
four chapters.

BOOK
III

ratives, and the justice of Christ's denunciations of the unreality and gross hypocrisy of this elaborateness of ordinances.[1] This the more so, when we recall that it was actually vaunted as a special qualification for a seat in the Sanhedrin, to be so acute and learned as to know how to prove clean creeping things (which were declared unclean by the Law).[a] And the mass of the people would have regarded neglect of the ordinances of purification as betokening either gross ignorance, or daring impiety.

ᵃ Sanh. 17 a

At any rate, such would not be exhibited on an occasion like the present; and outside the reception-room, as St. John with graphic minuteness of details relates, six of those stone pots, which we know from Rabbinic writings,[2] were ranged. Here it may be well to add, as against objectors, that it is impossible to state with certainty the exact measure represented by the 'two or three firkins apiece.' For, although we know that the term *metretes* (A.V. 'firkin') was intended as an equivalent for the Hebrew '*bath*,'[b] yet three different kinds of '*bath*' were at the time used in Palestine: the common Palestinian or 'wilderness' bath, that of Jersusalem, and that of Sepphoris.[3] The common Palestinian 'bath' was equal to the Roman *amphora*, containing about 5¼ gallons, while the Sepphoris 'bath' corresponded to the Attic *metretes*, and would contain about 8½ gallons. In the former case, therefore, each of these pots might have held from 10½ to 15¾ gallons; in the latter, from 17 to 25½. Reasoning on the general ground that the so-called Sepphoris measurement was common in Galilee, the larger quantity seems the more likely, though by no means certain. It is almost like trifling on the threshold of such a history, and yet so many cavils have been raised, that we must here remind ourselves, that neither the size, nor the number of these vessels has anything extraordinary about it. For such an occasion the family would produce or borrow the largest and handsomest stone-vessels that could be procured; nor is it necessary to suppose that they were filled to the brim; nor should we forget that, from a Talmudic notice,[c] it seems to have been the practice to set apart some of these vessels exclusively for the use of the bride and of the more distinguished guests, while the rest were used by the general company.

ᵇ Jos. Ant. viii. 2. 9

ᶜ Shabb. 77 b. So Lightfoot *in loc.*

Entering the spacious, lofty dining-room,[4] which would be bril-

---

[1] Comp. St. Mark vii. 2–5; St. Matt. xxiii. 25, 26; St. Luke xi. 38, 39.

[2] These 'stone-vessels' (*Keley Abhanim*) are often spoken of (for example, Chel. x. 1). In Yaday. i. 2 they are expressly mentioned for the purification of the

hands.

[3] For further details we refer to the *excursus* on Palestinian money, weights, and measures, in *Herzfeld's* Handelsgesch. d. Juden, pp. 171–185.

[4] The *Teraqlin*, from which the other

liantly lighted with lamps and candlesticks, the guests are disposed round tables on couches, soft with cushions or covered with tapestry, or seated on chairs. The bridal blessing has been spoken, and the bridal cup emptied. The feast is proceeding—not the common meal, which was generally taken about even, according to the Rabbinic saying,[a] that he who postponed it beyond that hour was as if he swallowed a stone—but a festive evening meal. If there had been disposition to those exhibitions of, or incitement to, indecorous and light merriment,[1] such as even the more earnest Rabbis deprecated, surely the presence of Jesus would have restrained it. And now there must have been a painful pause, or something like it, when the Mother of Jesus whispered to Him that 'the wine failed.'[2] There could, perhaps, be the less cause for reticence on this point towards her Son, not merely because this failure may have arisen from the accession of guests in the persons of Jesus and his disciples, for whom no provision had been originally made, but because the gift of wine or oil on such occasions was regarded a meritorious work of charity.[b]

But all this still leaves the main incidents in the narrative untouched. How are we to understand the implied request of the Mother of Jesus? how His reply? and what was the meaning of the miracle? It seems scarcely possible to imagine that, remembering the miraculous circumstances connected with His Birth, and informed of what had passed at Jordan, she now anticipated, and by her suggestion wished to prompt, this as His Royal Messianic manifestation.[3] With reverence be it said, such a beginning of Royalty and triumph would have been paltry: rather that of the Jewish miracle-monger than that of the Christ of the Gospels. Not so, if it was only 'a sign,' pointing to something beyond itself. Again, such anticipations on the part of Mary seem psychologically untrue—that is, untrue to her history. She could not, indeed, have ever forgotten the circum-

CHAP.
IV

[a] Pes. 18 b

[b] Baba B
ix.

---

side-rooms opened (Jer. Rosh haSh. 59 b; Yoma 15 b). From Baba B. vi. 4 we learn, that such an apartment was at least 15 feet square and 15 feet high. Height of ceiling was characteristic of Palestinian houses. It was always half the breadth and length put together. Thus, in a small house consisting of one room: length, 12 feet, breadth, 9 feet, the height would be 10½ feet. In a large house: length, 15 feet, breadth, 12 feet, the height would be 13½ feet. From Jer. Kethub. p. 28 d we learn, that the bride was considered as actually married the

moment she had entered the *Teraqlin*, before she had actually gone to the *Chuppah*.

[1] Thus it was customary, and deemed meritorious, to sing and perform a kind of play with myrtle branches (Jer. Peah 15 d); although one Rabbi was visited with sudden death for excess in this respect.

[2] St. John ii. 3, A.V.: 'when they wanted wine.'

[3] This is the view of many commentators, ancient and modern.

stances which had surrounded His Birth; but the deeper she 'kept all these things in her heart,' the more mysterious would they seem, as time passed in the dull round of the most simple and uneventful country-life, and in the discharge of every-day duties, without even the faintest appearance of anything beyond it. Only twelve years had passed since His Birth, and yet they had not understood His saying in the Temple! How much more difficult would it be after thirty years, when the Child had grown into Youth and Manhood, with still the same silence of Divine Voices around? It is difficult to believe in fierce sunshine on the afternoon of a long, grey day. Although we have no absolute certainty of it, we have the strongest internal reasons for believing, that Jesus had done no miracles these thirty years in the home at Nazareth,[1] but lived the life of quiet submission and obedient waiting. That was the then part of His Work. It may, indeed, have been that Mary knew of what had passed at Jordan; and that, when she saw Him returning with His first disciples, who, assuredly, would make no secret of their convictions —whatever these may have conveyed to outsiders—she felt that a new period in His Life had opened. But what was there in all this to suggest such a miracle? and if it had been suggested, why not ask for it in express terms, if it was to be the commencement, certainly in strangely incongruous circumstances, of a Royal manifestation?

On the other hand, there was one thing which she had learned, and one thing which she was to unlearn, after those thirty years of the Nazareth-Life. What she had learned—what she must have learned —was absolute confidence in Jesus. What she had to unlearn, was the natural, yet entirely mistaken, impression which His meekness, stillness, and long home-submission had wrought on her as to His relationship to the family. It was, as we find from her after-history, a very hard, very slow, and very painful thing to learn it;[2] yet very needful, not only for her own sake, but because it was a lesson of absolute truth. And so when she told Him of the want that had arisen, it was simply in absolute confidence in her Son, probably without any conscious expectancy of a miracle on His part.[3] Yet

---

[1] *Tholuck* and *Lücke*, however, hold the opposite view.

[2] *Luthardt* rightly calls it the commencement of a very painful education, of which the next stage is marked in St. Luke viii. 19, and the last in St. John xix. 26.

[3] This meets the objection of *Strauss* and others, that Mary could not have expected a miracle. It is scarcely conceivable, how *Calvin* could have imagined that Mary had intended Jesus to deliver an address with the view of turning away thought from the want of wine; or

not without a touch of maternal self-consciousness, almost pride, that He, Whom she could trust to do anything that was needed, was her Son, Whom she could solicit in the friendly family whose guests they were—and if not for her sake, yet at her request. It was a true earth-view to take of their relationship; only, an earth-view which must now for ever cease: the outcome of His misunderstood meekness and weakness, and which yet, strangely enough, the Romish Church puts in the forefront as the most powerful plea for Jesus' acting. But the fundamental mistake in what she attempted is just this, that she spake as His Mother, and placed that maternal relationship in connection with His Work. And therefore it was that as, on the first misunderstanding in the Temple, He had said: 'Wist ye not that I must be about my Father's business?' so now: 'Woman, what have I to do with thee?' With that 'business' earthly relationship, however tender, had no connection. With everything else it had, down to the utter self-forgetfulness of that tenderest commendation of her to John, in the bitterest agonies of the Cross; but not with this. No, not now, nor ever henceforth, with this. As in His first manifestation in the Temple, so in this the first manifestation of His glory, the finger that pointed to 'His hour' was not, and could not be, that of an earthly parent, but of His Father in Heaven.[1] There was, in truth, a twofold relationship in that Life, of which none other but the Christ could have preserved the harmony.

This is one main point—we had almost called it the negative one; the other, and positive one, was the miracle itself. All else is but accidental and circumstantial. No one who either knows the use of the language,[2] or remembers that, when commending her to John on the Cross, He used the same mode of expression,[a] will imagine, that there was anything derogatory to her, or harsh on His part, in addressing her as 'woman' rather than 'mother.' But the language is to us significant of the teaching intended to be conveyed, and as the beginning of this further teaching: 'Who is My mother? and My brethren? And He stretched forth His hand toward His disciples, and said, Behold My mother and My brethren!'[b]

And Mary did not, and yet she did, understand Him, when she turned to the servants with the direction, implicitly to follow His behests. What happened is well known: how, in the excess of their zeal, they filled the water-pots to the brim—an accidental circum-

[a] St. John xix. 26

[b] St. Matt xii. 46–50

Bengel, that she intended to give a hint that the company should break up.
[1] *Godet* aptly says, 'His motto hence-

forth is: My Father and I.'
[2] Comp. the passages from the classics quoted by *Wetstein* in his Commentary.

stance, yet useful, as much that seems accidental, to show that there could be neither delusion nor collusion; how, probably in the drawing of it, the water became best wine—'the conscious water saw its God, and blushed;' then the coarse proverbial joke of what was probably the master of ceremonies and purveyor of the feast,ᵃ intended, of course, not literally to apply to the present company, and yet in its accidentalness an evidence of the reality of the miracle; after which the narrative abruptly closes with a retrospective remark on the part of him who relates it. What the bridegroom said; whether what had been done became known to the guests, and, if so, what impression it wrought; how long Jesus remained; what His Mother felt—of this and much more that might be asked, Scripture, with that reverent reticence which we so often mark, in contrast to our shallow talkativeness, takes no further notice. And best that it should be so. St. John meant to tell us, what the Synoptists, who begin their account with the later Galilean ministry, have not recorded,[1] of the first of His miracles as a 'sign,'[2] pointing to the deeper and higher that was to be revealed, and of the first forth-manifesting of 'His glory.'[3] That is all; and that object was attained. Witness the calm, grateful retrospect upon that first day of miracles, summed up in these simple but intensely conscious words: 'And His disciples believed on Him.'

A sign it was, from whatever point we view its meaning, as previously indicated. For, like the diamond that shines with many colours, it has many meanings; none of them designed, in the coarse sense of the term, but all real, because the outcome of a real Divine Life and history. And a real miracle also, not only historically, but as viewed in its many meanings; the beginning of all others, which in a sense are but the unfolding of this first. A miracle it is, which cannot be explained, but is only enhanced by the almost incredible platitudes to which negative criticism has sunk in its commentation,[4]

---

[1] On the omission of certain parts of St. John's narrative by the Synoptists, and *vice versâ*, and on the supposed differences, I can do no better than refer the reader to the admirable remarks of Canon *Westcott*, Introduction to the Study of the Gospels, pp. 280 &c.

[2] According to the best reading, and literally, 'This did—beginning of signs —Jesus in Cana.' Upon a careful review the Rabbinic expression *Simana* (taken from the Greek word here used) would seem to me more fully to render the idea than the Hebrew *Oth*. But the significant use of the word *sign* should be well marked. See Canon *Westcott* on the

passage.

[3] In this, the first of his miracles, it was all the more necessary that He should manifest his glory.

[4] Thus *Schenkel* regards Christ's answer to Mary as a proof that He was not on good terms with His family; *Paulus* suggests, that Jesus had brought the wine, and that it was afterwards mixed with the water in the stone-vessels; *Gfrörer*, that Mary had brought it as a present, and at the feast given Jesus the appropriate hint when to have it set on. The gloss of *Renan* seems to me even more untenable and repulsive.

for which there assuredly exists no legendary basis, either in Old CHAP.
Testament history, or in contemporary Jewish expectation;[1] which IV
cannot be sublimated into nineteenth-century idealism;[2] least of all
can be conceived as an after-thought of His disciples, invented by an
Ephesian writer of the second century.[3] But even the allegorical
illustration of St. Augustine, who reminds us that in the grape the
water of rain is ever changed into wine, is scarcely true, save as a
bare illustration, and only lowers our view of the miracle. For *miracle*
it is,[4] and will ever remain; not, indeed, magic,[5] nor arbitrary power,
but power with a moral purpose, and that the highest.[6] And we
believe it, because this 'sign' is the first of all those miracles in which
the Miracle of Miracles gave 'a sign,' and manifested forth His
glory—the glory of His Person, the glory of His Purpose, and the
glory of His Work.

[1] Against this view of *Strauss*, see *Lücke*, u. s. p. 477.

[2] So *Lange*, in his 'Life of Christ,' imagining that converse with Jesus had put all in that higher ecstasy in which He gave them to drink from the fulness of Himself. Similar spiritualisation—though by each in his own manner—has been attempted by *Baur*, *Keim*, *Ewald*, *Hilgenfeld*, and others. But it seems more rational, with *Schweizer* and *Weisse*, to deny the historical accuracy of the whole, than to resort to such expedients.

[3] *Hilgenfeld*, however, sees in this miracle an evidence that the Christ of the fourth Gospel proclaimed another and a higher than the God of the Old Testament—in short, evidence of the Gnostic taint of the fourth Gospel.

[4] *Meyer* well reminds us that 'physical incomprehensibility is not identical with absolute impossibility.'

[5] *Godet* has scarcely rightly marked the difference.

[6] If I rightly understand the meaning of Dr. *Abbott's* remarks on the miracles in the fourth Gospel (Encycl. Britan. vol. x. p. 825 *b*), they imply that the change of the water into wine was an emblematic reference to the Eucharistic wine, this view being supported by a reference to 1 John v. 8. But could this be considered sufficient ground for the inference, that no historic reality attaches to the whole history? In that case it would have to be seriously maintained, that an Ephesian writer at the end of the second century had invented the fiction of the miraculous change of water into wine, for the purpose of certain Eucharistic teaching!

CHAPTER V.

THE CLEANSING OF THE TEMPLE—'THE SIGN,' WHICH IS NOT A SIGN.

(St. John ii. 13–25.)

BOOK
III

a St. Matt. iv.
13; ix. 1;
St. Mark ii. 1

b St. Mark
vi. 3

IT has been said that Mary understood, and yet did not understand Jesus. And of this there seems fresh evidence in the circumstance that, immediately after the marriage of Cana, she and the 'brethren of Jesus' went with Him, or followed Him, to Capernaum, which henceforth became 'His own city,'a during His stay by the Lake of Galilee. The question, whether He had first returned to Nazareth, seems almost trifling. It may have been so, and it may be that His brothers had joined Him there, while His 'sisters,' being married, remained at Nazareth.b For the departure of the family from Nazareth many reasons will, in the peculiar circumstances, suggest themselves. And yet one feels, that their following Jesus and His disciples to their new home had something to do with their understanding, and yet not understanding, of Him, which had been characteristic of Mary's silent withdrawal after the reply she had received at the feast of Cana, and her significant direction to the servants, implicitly to do what He bade them. Equally in character is the willingness of Jesus to allow His family to join Him—not ashamed of their humbleness, as a Jewish Messiah might have been, nor impatient of their ignorance: tenderly near to them, in all that concerned the humanness of His feelings; sublimely far from them, in all connected with His Work and Mission.

It is almost a relief to turn from the long discussion (to which reference has already been made): whether those who bore that designation were His 'brothers' and 'sisters' in the real sense, or the children of Joseph by an earlier marriage, or else His cousins—and to leave it in the indefiniteness which rests upon it.[1] But the observant

---

[1] In support of the natural interpretation of these terms (which I frankly own to be my view) not only St. Matt. i. 25 and St. Luke ii. 7 may be urged, but these two questions may be put, suggested by Archdeacon *Norris* (who himself holds them to have been the children of Joseph by a former marriage): How could our Lord have been, through Joseph, the heir of David's throne (according to the genealogies), if Joseph had elder sons? And again, What became of the six young motherless children when Joseph and the Virgin went first to Bethlehem, and then into Egypt, and why are the elder sons not mentioned on the occasion of the

reader will probably mark, in connection with this controversy, that
it is, to say the least, strange that 'brothers' of Jesus should, without further explanation, have been introduced in the fourth Gospel,
if it was an Ephesian production, if not a fiction of spiritualistic
tendency; strange also, that the fourth Gospel alone should have
recorded the removal to Capernaum of the 'mother and brothers' of
Jesus, in company with Him. But this by the way, and in reference
to recent controversies about the authorship of the fourth Gospel.

If we could only feel quite sure—and not merely deem it most
probable—that the *Tell Hûm* of modern exploration marks the site of
the ancient *Capernaum, Kephar Nachum,* or *Tanchumin* (the latter,
perhaps, 'village of consolation'), with what solemn interest would
we wander over its ruins.[1] We know it from New Testament history,
and from the writings of Josephus.[a] A rancorous notice and certain
vile insinuations[2] of the Rabbis,[b] connecting it with 'heresy,' presumably that of Christianity, seem also to point to *Kephar Nachum*
as the home of Jesus, where so many of His miracles were done.
At the time it could have been of only recent origin, since its Synagogue had but lately been reared, through the friendly liberality of
that true and faithful Centurion.[c] But already its importance was
such, that it had become the station of a garrison, and of one of the
principal custom-houses. Its soft, sweet air, by the glorious Lake of
Galilee, with snow-capped Hermon full in view in the North—from a
distance, like Mount Blanc over the Lake of Geneva;[3] the fertility of
the country—notably of the plain of Gennesaret close by; and the
merry babble, and fertilising proximity of a spring which, from its
teeming with fish like that of the Nile, was popularly regarded as
springing from the river of Egypt—this and more must have made
Capernaum one of the most delightful places in these 'Gardens of
Princes,' as the Rabbis interpreted the word 'Gennesaret,' by the
'cither-shaped lake' of that name.[4] The town lay quite up on its
north-western shore, only two miles from where the Jordan falls into
the lake. As we wander over that field of ruins, about half a mile in

a Jewish
War iii. 10.
8; Life 72

b Midr. on
Eccl. i. 8.
and vii 26.
ed. Warsh.
vol. iii. p.80
a and 97 a

c St. Matt.
viii. 5, &c.

---

visit to the Temple? (Commentary on the
New Testament, vol. i. p. 117.)

[1] *Robinson, Sepp,* and, if I understand
him aright, Lieut. *Conder,* regard *Khan
Minyeh* (Tent-Work in Palest. vol. ii.
pp. 182 &c.) as the site of Capernaum;
but most modern writers are agreed in
fixing it at *Tell Hûm.*

[2] The stories are too foolish, and the
insinuations too vile, to be here repeated.

The second of the two notices evidently
refers to the first. The 'heretic' Jacob
spoken of, is the *bête noire* of the Rabbis.
The implied charges against the Christians remind one of the description, Rev.
ii. 20–24.

[3] The comparison is Canon *Tristram's*
(Land of Israel, p. 427).

[4] This is another Rabbinic interpretation of the term Gennesaret.

BOOK
III

length by a quarter in breadth, which in all probability mark the site of ancient Capernaum, we can scarcely realise it, that the desolateness all around has taken the place of the life and beauty of eighteen centuries ago. Yet the scene is the same, though the breath of judgment has long swept the freshness from its face. Here lies in unruffled stillness, or wildly surges, lashed by sudden storms, the deep blue lake, 600 or 700 feet below the level of the Mediterranean. We can look up and down its extent, about twelve miles, or across it, about six miles. Right over on the other side from where we stand —somewhere there, is the place where Jesus miraculously fed the five thousand. Over here came the little ship, its timbers still trembling, and its sides and deck wet with the spray of that awful night of storm, when He came to the weary rowers, and brought with Him calm. Up that beach they drew the boat. Here, close by the shore, stood the Synagogue, built of white limestone on dark basalt foundation. North of it, up the gentle slopes, stretched the town. East and south is the lake, in almost continuous succession of lovely small bays, of which more than seventeen may be counted within six miles, and in one of which nestled Capernaum. All its houses are gone, scarce one stone left on the other: the good Centurion's house, that of Matthew the publican,[a] that of Simon Peter,[b] the temporary home which first sheltered the Master and His loved ones. All are unrecognisable—a confused mass of ruins—save only that white Synagogue in which He taught. From its ruins we can still measure its dimensions, and trace its fallen pillars; nay, we discover over the lintel of its entrance the device of a pot of manna, which may have lent its form to His teaching there[c]—a device different from that of the seven-branched candlestick, or that other most significant one of the Paschal Lamb, which seem to have been so frequent over the Synagogues in Galilee.[1]

[a] St. Mark
ii. 15;
comp.
iii. 20, 31
[b] St. Matt.
viii. 14

[c] St. John
vi. 49, 59

And this, then, is Capernaum—the first and the chief home of Jesus, when He had entered on His active work. But, on this occasion, He 'continued there not many days.' For, already, 'the Jews' Passover was at hand,' and He must needs keep that feast in Jerusalem. If our former computations are right—and, in the nature of things, it is impossible to be absolutely certain about exact dates—and John began his preaching in the autumn of the year 779 from the building of Rome, or in 26 of our present reckoning, while Jesus was baptized in the early winter following,[d][2] then

[d] A.D. 27

---

[1] Comp. especially *Warren's* Recovery of Jerusalem, pp. 337–351.

[2] *Wieseler* and most modern writers place the Baptism of Jesus in the *summer*

this Passover must have taken place in the spring (about April) of CHAP.
the same year.[a] The preparations for it had, indeed, commenced a V
month before. Not to speak of the needful domestic arrangements
for the journey of pilgrims to Jerusalem, the whole land seemed in [a] 780 A.U.C.
a state of preparation. A month before the feast (on the 15th Adar) or 27 A.D.
bridges and roads were put in repair, and sepulchres whitened, to
prevent accidental pollution to the pilgrims. Then, some would
select this out of the three great annual feasts for the tithing of
their flocks and herds, which, in such case, had to be done two
weeks before the Passover; while others would fix on it as the time
for going up to Jerusalem before the feast ' to purify themselves ' [b]— [b] St. John
that is, to undergo the prescribed purification in any case of Levitical xi. 55
defilement. But what must have appealed to every one in the land
was the appearance of the ' money-changers' (Shulchanim), who
opened their stalls in every country-town on the 15th of Adar (just a
month before the feast). They were, no doubt, regularly accredited
and duly authorised. For, all Jews and proselytes—women, slaves,
and minors excepted—had to pay the annual Temple-tribute of half
a shekel, according to the 'sacred' standard, equal to a common
Galilean shekel (two denars), or about 1s. 2d. of our money. From
this tax many of the priests—to the chagrin of the Rabbis—claimed
exemption, on the ingenious plea that in Lev. vi. 23 (A.V.) every
offering of a priest was ordered to be burnt, and not eaten; while
from the Temple-tribute such offerings were paid for as the two wave
loaves and the shewbread, which were afterwards eaten by priests.
Hence, it was argued, their payment of Temple-tribute would have
been incompatible with Lev. vi. 23!

But to return. This Temple-tribute had to be paid in exact
half-shekels of the Sanctuary, or ordinary Galilean shekels. When
it is remembered that, besides strictly Palestinian silver and especially
copper coin,[1] Persian, Tyrian, Syrian, Egyptian, Grecian, and Roman

of 27 A.D., and, accordingly, the first
Passover in spring, 28 A.D. But it seems
to me highly improbable, that so long an
interval as nine or ten months should
have elapsed between John's first preaching and the Baptism of Jesus. Besides,
in that case, how are we to account for
the eight or nine months between the
Baptism and the Passover ? So far as I
know, the only reason for this strange
hypothesis is St. John ii. 20, which will
be explained in its proper place.
[1] Simon Maccabee had copper money
coined; the so-called copper shekel, a

little more than a penny, and also half
and quarter shekels (about a half-penny,
and a farthing). His successors coined
even smaller copper money. During the
whole period from the death of Simon
to the last Jewish war no Jewish silver
coins issued from the Palestinian mint,
but only copper coins. Herzfeld (Handelsgesch. pp. 178, 179) suggests that
there was sufficient foreign silver coinage circulating in the country, while
naturally only a very small amount of
foreign copper coin would be brought to
Palestine.

money circulated in the country, it will be understood what work these 'money-changers' must have had.   From the 15th to the 25th Adar they had stalls in every country-town.   On the latter date, which must therefore be considered as marking the first arrivals of festive pilgrims in the city, the stalls in the country were closed, and the money-changers henceforth sat within the precincts of the Temple.   All who refused to pay the Temple-tribute (except priests) were liable to distraint of their goods.   The 'money-changers' made a statutory fixed charge of a *Maah*, or from $1\frac{1}{2}d$. to $2d$. [1] (or, according to others, of half a maah) on every half-shekel.   This was called *qolbon*.   But if a person tendered a *Sela* (a four-denar piece, in value two half-shekels of the Sanctuary, or two Galilean shekels), he had to pay double *qolbon*; one for his half-shekel of tribute-money, the other for his change.   Although not only priests, but all other non-obligatory officers, and those who paid for their poorer brethren, were exempted from the charge of *qolbon*, it must have brought in an immense revenue, since not only many native Palestinians might come without the statutory coin, but a vast number of foreign Jews presented themselves on such occasions in the Temple. Indeed, if we compute the annual Temple-tribute at about 75,000*l*., the bankers' profits may have amounted to from 8,000*l*. to 9,000*l*., an immense sum in the circumstances of the country. [2]

But even this does not represent all the facts of the case.   We have already seen, that the 'money-changers' in the Temple gave change, when larger amounts than were equivalent to the Temple-tribute were proffered.   It is a reasonable, nay, an almost necessary inference, that many of the foreign Jews arriving in Jerusalem would take the opportunity of changing at these tables their foreign money, and for this, of course, fresh charges would be made.   For, there was a great deal to be bought within the Temple-area, needful for the feast (in the way of sacrifices and their adjuncts), or for purification, and it would be better to get the right money from the authorised changers, than have disputes with the dealers.   We can picture to ourselves the scene around the table of an Eastern money-changer— the weighing of the coins, deductions for loss of weight, arguing, disputing, bargaining—and we can realise the terrible truthfulness of

---

[1] It is extremely difficult to fix the *exact* equivalent.   *Cassel* computes it at one-fifth, *Herzfeld* at one-sixth, *Zunz* at one-third, and *Winer* at one-fourth of a denar.

[2] Comp. *Winer's* Real-Worterb.   I have taken a low estimate, so as to be well within bounds.   All the regulations about the *Tribute* and *Qolbon* are enumerated in Sheqal. i.   I have not given references for each of the statements advanced, not because they are not to hand in regard to almost every detail, but to avoid needless quotations.

our Lord's charge that they had made the Father's House a mart and place of traffic. But even so, the business of the Temple money-changers would not be exhausted. Through their hands would pass the immense votive offerings of foreign Jews, or of proselytes, to the Temple; indeed, they probably transacted all business matters connected with the Sanctuary. It is difficult to realise the vast accumulation of wealth in the Temple-treasury. But some idea of it may be formed from the circumstance that, despite many previous spoliations, the value of the gold and silver which Crassus[a] carried from the Temple-treasury amounted to the enormous sum of about two and a half millions sterling. Whether or not these Temple money-changers may have transacted other banking business, given drafts, or cashed those from correspondents, received and lent money at interest—all which was common at the time—must remain undetermined.

CHAP.
V

[a] 54–53 B.C.

Readers of the New Testament know, that the noisy and incongruous business of an Eastern money-lender was not the only one carried on within the sacred Temple-enclosure. It was a great accommodation, that a person bringing a sacrifice might not only learn, but actually obtain, in the Temple from its officials what was required for the meat- and 'drink-offering. The prices were fixed by tariff every month, and on payment of the stated amount the offerer received one of four counterfoils, which respectively indicated, and, on handing it to the proper official, procured the prescribed complement of his sacrifice.[1] The Priests and Levites in charge of this made up their accounts every evening, and these (though necessary) transactions must have left a considerable margin of profit to the treasury. This would soon lead to another kind of traffic. Offerers might, of course, bring their sacrificial animals with them, and we know that on the Mount of Olives there were four shops, specially for the sale of pigeons and other things requisite for sacrificial purposes.[b][2] But then, when an animal was brought, it had to be examined as to its Levitical fitness by persons regularly qualified and appointed. Disputes might here arise, due to the ignorance of the purchaser, or the greed of the examiner. A regularly qualified examiner was called *mumcheh* (one approved), and how much labour was given to the acquisition of

[b] Jer. Taan iv. 8

---

[1] Comp. 'The Temple and its Services, &c.,' pp. 118, 119.

[2] M. *Derenbourg* (Histoire de Palest., p. 467) holds that these shops were kept by priests, or at any rate that the profits went to them. But I cannot agree with

him that these were the *Chanuyoth*, or shops, of the family of Annas, to which the Sanhedrin migrated forty years before the destruction of Jerusalem. See farther on.

BOOK
III

ᵃ Sanh. 5 b

ᵇ Bekhor.
iv. 5

ᶜ Ker. i. 7

ᵈ Jerus.
Chag. 78 a

the requisite knowledge appears from the circumstance, that a certain
teacher is said to have spent eighteen months with a farmer, to learn
what faults in an animal were temporary, and which permanent.ᵃ
Now, as we are informed that a certain *mumcheh* of firstlings had
been authorised to charge for his inspection from four to six *Isar*
(1¼d. to about 2d.), according to the animal inspected,ᵇ it is but
reasonable to suppose that a similar fee may have been exacted
for examining the ordinary sacrificial animals.   But all trouble and
difficulty would be avoided by a regular market within the Temple-
enclosure, where sacrificial animals could be purchased, having
presumably been duly inspected, and all fees paid before being
offered for sale.[1]   It needs no comment to show how utterly the
Temple would be profaned by such traffic, and to what scenes it
might lead.   From Jewish writings we know, that most improper
transactions were carried on, to the taking undue advantage of the
poor people who came to offer their sacrifices.   Thus we read,ᶜ that
on one occasion the price of a couple of pigeons was run up to the
enormous figure of a gold denar (a Roman gold denar, about 15s. 3d.),
when, through the intervention of Simeon, the grandson of the great
Hillel, it was brought down before night to a quarter of a silver
denar, or about 2d. each.   Since Simeon is represented as introducing his resolve to this effect with the adjuration, ' by the Temple,'
it is not unfair to infer that these prices had ruled within the sacred
enclosure.   It was probably not merely controversial zeal for the
peculiar teaching of his master Shammai, but a motive similar to
that of Simeon, which on another occasion induced Baba ben Buta
(well known as giving Herod the advice of rebuilding the Temple),
when he found the Temple-court empty of sacrificial animals, through
the greed of those who had ' thus desolated the House of God,' to
bring in no less than three thousand sheep, so that the people might
offer sacrifices.ᵈ [2]

This leads up to another question, most important in this connection.   The whole of this traffic—money-changing, selling of doves,
and market for sheep and oxen—was in itself, and from its attendant
circumstances, a terrible desecration; it was also liable to gross

---

[1] It is certain that this Temple-market
could not have been ' on both sides of
the Eastern Gate— the gate Shushan—as
far as Solomon's Porch ' (Dr. *Farrar*).
If it had been on both sides of this gate,
it must have been in Solomon's Porch.
But this supposition is out of the question.   There would have been no room

there for a market, and it formed the
principal access into the Sanctuary. The
Temple-market was undoubtedly somewhere in the ' Court of the Gentiles.'

[2] It is, however, quite certain that Baba
ben Buta had not ' been the first to introduce ' (Dr. *Farrar*) this traffic.   A perusal
of Jer. Chag. 78 a shows this sufficiently.

abuses. But was there about the time of Christ anything to make it specially obnoxious and unpopular? The priesthood must always have derived considerable profit from it—of course, not the ordinary priests, who came up in their 'orders' to minister in the Temple, but the permanent priestly officials, the resident leaders of the priesthood, and especially the High-Priestly family. This opens up a most interesting inquiry, closely connected, as we shall show, with Christ's visit to the Temple at this Passover. But the materials here at our command are so disjointed, that, in attempting to put them together, we can only suggest what seems most probable, not state what is absolutely certain. What became of the profits of the money-changers, and who were the real owners of the Temple-market?

To the first of these questions the Jerusalem Talmud [a] gives no less than five different answers, showing that there was no fixed rule as to the employment of these profits, or, at least, that it was no longer known at that time. Although four of these answers point to their use for the public service, yet that which seems most likely assigns the whole profits to the money-changers themselves. But in that case it can scarcely be doubted, that they had to pay a considerable rental or percentage to the leading Temple-officials. The profits from the sale of meat- and drink-offerings went to the Temple-treasury. But it can hardly be believed, that such was the case in regard to the Temple-market. On the other hand, there can be little doubt, that this market was what in Rabbinic writings is styled 'the Bazaars of the sons of Annas' (*Chanuyoth beney Chanan*), the sons of that High-Priest Annas, who is so infamous in New Testament history. When we read that the Sanhedrin, forty years before the destruction of Jerusalem, transferred its meeting-place from 'the Hall of Hewn Stones' (on the south side of the Court of the Priests, and therefore partly within the Sanctuary itself) to 'the Bazaars,' and then afterwards to the City, [b] the inference is plain, that these Bazaars were those of the sons of Annas the High-Priest, and that they occupied part of the Temple-court; in short, that the Temple-market and the Bazaars of the sons of Annas are identical.

If this inference, which is in accordance with received Jewish opinion, be admitted, we gain much light as regards the purification of the Temple by Jesus, and the words which He spake on that occasion. For, our next position is that, from the unrighteousness of the traffic carried on in these Bazaars, and the greed of their owners, the 'Temple-market' was at the time most unpopular. This appears, not only from the conduct and words of the patriarch Simeon and of

[a] Jer. Sheq.
i. 7, last 4
lines, p. 46
b

[b] Rosh
haSh.31 a,b

BOOK
III

a Siphre on
Deut. § 105,
end. ed.
Friedmann,
p. 95 b; Jer.
Peah i. 6

b St. Matt.
xxi. 12

c Ant. xx. 9.
2–4

d Pes. 57 a

e Pes. u. s.

Baba ben Buta (as above quoted), but from the fact that popular indignation, three years before the destruction of Jerusalem, swept away
the Bazaars of the family of Annas,[a] and this, as expressly stated, on
account of the sinful greed which characterised their dealings.   And
if any doubt should still linger in the mind, it would surely be removed
by our Lord's open denunciation of the Temple-market as ' a den of
robbers.'[b] Of the avarice and corruption of this infamous High-
Priestly family, alike Josephus and the Rabbis give a most terrible
picture.   Josephus describes Annas (or Ananus), the son of the
Annas of the New Testament, as ' a great hoarder up of money,'
very rich, and as despoiling by open violence the common priests of
their official revenues.[c]   The Talmud also records the curse which
a distinguished Rabbi of Jerusalem (Abba Shaul) pronounced upon
the High-Priestly families (including that of Annas), who were
' themselves High-Priests, their sons treasurers (Gizbarin), their
sons-in-law assistant-treasurers (Ammarkalin), while their servants
beat the people with sticks.'[d]   What a comment this passage offers
on the bearing of Jesus, as He made a scourge to drive out the very
servants who ' beat the people with sticks,' and upset their unholy
traffic!   It were easy to add from Rabbinic sources repulsive details of
their luxuriousness, wastefulness, gluttony, and general dissoluteness.
No wonder that, in the figurative language of the Talmud, the Temple
is represented as crying out against them: ' Go hence, ye sons of
Eli, ye defile the Temple of Jehovah!'[e]   These painful notices of
the state of matters at that time help us better to understand what
Christ did, and who they were that opposed His doing.

These Temple-Bazaars, the property, and one of the principal
sources of income, of the family of Annas, were the scene of the
purification of the Temple by Jesus; and in the private *locale*
attached to these very Bazaars, where the Sanhedrin held its meetings
at the time, the final condemnation of Jesus may have been planned,
if not actually pronounced.   All this has its deep significance.   But
we can now also understand why the Temple officials, to whom these
Bazaars belonged, only challenged the authority of Christ in thus
purging the Temple.   The unpopularity of the whole traffic, if not
their consciences, prevented their proceeding to actual violence.
Lastly, we can also better perceive the significance, alike of Christ's
action, and of His reply to their challenge, spoken as it was close
to the spot where He was so soon to be condemned by them.
Nor do we any longer wonder that no resistance was offered by
the people to the action of Jesus. and that even the remonstrances

of the priests were not direct, but in the form of a perplexing question.

For it is in the direction just indicated, and in no other, that objections have been raised to the narrative of Christ's first public act in Jerusalem: the purgation of the Temple. Commentators have sufficiently pointed out the differences between this and the purgation of the Temple at the close of His Ministry.[a][1] Indeed, on comparison, these are so obvious, that every reader can mark them. Nor does it seem difficult to understand, rather does it seem not only fitting, but almost logically necessary, that, if any such event had occurred, it should have taken place both at the beginning and at the close of His public ministry in the Temple. Nor yet is there anything either 'abrupt' or 'tactless' in such a commencement of his Ministry. It is not only profane, but unhistorical, to look for calculation and policy in the Life of Jesus. Had there been such, He would not have died on the Cross. And 'abrupt' it certainly was not. Jesus took up the thread where he had dropped it on His first recorded appearance in the Temple, when he had spoken His wonder, that those who knew Him should have been ignorant, that He must be about His Father's business. He was now about His Father's business, and, as we may so say, in the most elementary manner. To put an end to this desecration of His Father's House, which, by a nefarious traffic, had been made a place of mart, nay, 'a den of robbers,' was, what all who knew Mis Mission must have felt, a most suitable and almost necessary beginning of His Messianic Work.

And many of those present must have known Jesus. The zeal of His early disciples, who, on their first recognition of Him, proclaimed the new-found Messiah, could not have given place to absolute silence. The many Galilean pilgrims in the Temple could not but have spread the tidings, and the report must soon have passed from one to the other in the Temple-courts, as He first entered their sacred enclosure. They would follow Him, and watch what He did. Nor were they disappointed. He inaugurated His Mission by fulfilling the prediction concerning Him Who was to be Israel's refiner and purifier (Mal. iii. 1-3). Scarce had He entered the Temple-porch, and trod the Court of the Gentiles, than He drove thence what profanely defiled it.[2] There was not a hand lifted, not a word spoken

CHAP.
V

[a] St. Matt. xxi. 12, &c.; St. Mark xi 11, &c.; St. Luke xix. 45 &c.

[1] It must, however, be admitted, that even *Luther* had grave doubts whether the narrative of the Synoptists and that of the fourth Gospel did not refer to one and the same event. Comp. *Meyer,* Komment. (on St. John), p. 142, notes.

[2] And so He ever does, beginning His Ministry by purifying, whether as regards the individual or the Church.

to arrest Him, as He made the scourge of small cords (even this not without significance) and with it drove out of the Temple both the sheep and the oxen; not a word said, nor a hand raised, as He poured into their receptacles the changers' money, and overthrew their tables.[1] His Presence awed them, His words awakened even their consciences; they knew, only too well, how true His denunciations were. And behind Him was gathered the wondering multitude, that could not but sympathise with such bold, right royal, and Messianic vindication of Temple sanctity from the nefarious traffic of a hated, corrupt, and avaricious Priesthood. It was a scene worth witnessing by any true Israelite, a protest and an act which, even among a less emotional people, would have gained Him respect, approbation, and admiration, and which, at any rate, secured his safety.[2]

For when 'the Jews,' by which here, as in so many other places, we are to understand the rulers of the people—in this instance, the Temple officials—did gather courage to come forward, they ventured not to lay hands on Him. It was not yet the time for it. In presence of that multitude they would not then have dared it, even if policy had not dictated quietness within the Temple-enclosure, when the Roman garrison so close by, in Fort Antonia, kept jealous watch for the first appearance of a tumult.[a] Still more strangely, they did not even reprove Him for what He had done, as if it had been wrong or improper. With infinite cunning, as appealing to the multitude, they only asked for 'a sign' which would warrant such assumption of authority. But this question of challenge marked two things: the essential opposition between the Jewish authorities and Jesus, and the manner in which they would carry on the contest, which was henceforth to be waged between Him and the rulers of the people. That first action of Jesus determined their mutual positions; and with and in that first conflict its end was already involved. The action of Jesus as against the rulers must develop into a life-opposition; their first step against Him must lead on to the last in His condemnation to the Cross.

And Jesus then and there knew it all, foresaw, or rather saw it all. His answer told it. It was—as all His teaching to those who seeing do not see, and hearing do not hear, whose understanding is

[a] Acts xxi.
31, 32

---

[1] Canon *Westcott* calls attention to the use of two different terms for money-changers in vv. 14, 15. In the latter only it is κολλυβιστής, of which the Aramaic form is *qolbon*. It is this *qolbon*-taking against which the Hand of Christ is specially directed.

[2] Yet *Renan* ventures to characterise this as a sudden, ill-advised outburst of ill-humour.

darkened and heart hardened—in parabolic language, which only the
after-event would make clear.[a] As for 'the sign,' then and ever again
sought by an 'evil and adulterous generation'—evil in their thoughts
and ways and adulterous to the God of Israel—He had then, as
afterwards,[b] only one 'sign' to give: 'Destroy this Temple, and in
three days I will raise it up.' Thus He met their challenge for a
sign by the challenge of a sign: Crucify Him, and He would rise
again; let them suppress the Christ, He would triumph.[1] A sign
this which they understood not, but misunderstood, and by making
it the ground of their false charge in His final trial, themselves
unwittingly fulfilled.

CHAP.
V

[a] St. Matt.
xiii. 11–15;
St. Mark iv,
11, 12
[b] St. Matt.
xii. 38–40

And yet to all time this is the sign, and the only sign, which the
Christ has given, which He still gives to every 'evil and adulterous
generation,' to all sin-lovers and God-forsakers. They will destroy,
so far as their power reaches, the Christ, crucify Him, give His words
the lie, suppress, sweep away Christianity—and they shall not succeed: He shall triumph. As on that first Easter-day, so now and
ever in history, He raises up the Temple, which they break down.
This is the 'sign,' the evidence, the only 'sign,' which the Christ
gives to His enemies; a sign which, as an historical fact, has been
patent to all men, and seen by them; which might have been evidence,
but being of the nature of miracle, not explicable by natural agencies,
they have misunderstood, viewing 'the Temple' merely as a building,
of which they fully know the architecture, manner, and time of
construction,[2] but of whose spiritual character and upbuilding they
have no knowledge nor thought. And thus, as to that generation, so

---

[1] 'I cannot see in the words of Jesus
any direct reference to the abrogation of
the material Temple and its services, and
the substitution of the Church for it. Of
course, such was the case, and implied in
His Crucifixion and Resurrection, though
not alluded to here.

[2] From the expression (St. John ii. 20)
'Forty and six years was this Temple in
building,' it has been inferred by most
writers that this Passover was of the
year 791 A.U.C., or 28 A.D., and not, as
we have argued, of the year 780 A.U.C.,
or 27 A.D. But their calculation rests on
an oversight. Admittedly the rebuilding of the Temple began in the autumn
of the eighteenth year of Herod's reign
(Jos. Ant. xv. 11. 1–6). As Herod's reign
dates from 717 A.U.C., the Temple-
building must have commenced in the

autumn of the year 734–35. But it has
already been explained that, in Jewish
reckoning, the beginning of a new year
was reckoned as a year. Thus if, according to universal opinion (comp. Wieseler,
Chronolog. Synopse, pp. 165, 166), the
Temple-building began in Kislev 734,
forty-nine years after it would bring us
to the autumn 779, and the Passover of
780, or 27 A.D., would be regarded and
spoken of as 'forty and six years.' If a
Jew had calculated the time at the Passover 781, he would not have said 'forty-
six' but 'forty-seven years' 'was this
Temple in building.' The mistake of
writers lies in forgetting that a fresh
year had begun after the autumn—or at
any rate at the Passover. It may here
be added, that the Temple was not finally
completed till 63 A.D.

BOOK
III

ᵃ Acts xiii.
41

to all which have followed, this is still the 'sign,' if they understand it—the only sign, the Great Miracle, which, as they only calculate from the visible and to them ascertained, these 'despisers behold, and wonder, and perish,' for He worketh 'a work in their days, a work which they shall in no wise believe.'ᵃ

CHAPTER VI.

THE TEACHER COME FROM GOD AND THE TEACHER FROM JERUSALEM—
JESUS AND NICODEMUS.

(St. John iii. 1–21.)

BUT there were those who beheld, and heard His words, and did in some measure understand them.   Even before Jesus had spoken to the Temple-officials, His disciples, as silently they watched Him, saw an old Scripture-saying kindled into light by the halo of His glory.   It was that of the suffering, self-forgetful, God-dedicated Servant of Jehovah, as His figure stood out against the Old Testament sky, realising in a hostile world only this, as the deepest element of His being and calling: entire inward and outward consecration to God, a burnt-offering, such as Isaac would have been.   Within their minds sprang up unbidden, as when the light of the Urim and Thummim fell on the letters graven on the precious stones of the High-Priest's breastplate, those words of old: 'The zeal of Thine house eateth me up. ᵃ   Thus, even in those days of their early learning, Jesus purging the Temple in view of a hostile rulership was the full realisation of that picture, which must be prophetic, since no mere man ever bore those lineaments: that of the ideal Nazarite, whom the zeal of God's house was consuming.   And then long afterwards, after His Passion and Death, after those dark days of loneliness and doubt, after the misty dawn of the first recognition—this word, which He had spoken to the rulers at the first, came to them, with all the convincing power of prediction fulfilled by fact, as an assured conviction, which in its strong grasp held not only the past, but the present, because the present is ever the *fulfilment* of the past: 'When therefore He was risen from the dead, His disciples remembered that He had said this unto them; and they believed the Scripture, and the word which Jesus had said.'

Again, as we think of the meaning of His refusing 'a sign' to the rulers of Israel—or rather think of the only 'sign' which He did give them—we see nothing incompatible with it in the fact that, at the

CHAP.
VI

ᵃ Ps. lxix. 9

same feast, He did many 'signs'[1] in sight of the people. For it was only the rulers who had entered on that conflict, of which, from the character and aims of the two parties engaged, the beginning involved the terrible end as its logical sequence. In presence of such a foe only one 'sign' could be given: that of reading their inmost hearts, and in them their real motives and final action, and again of setting forth His own final triumph—a predictive description, a 'no sign' that was, and is, a sign to all time. But neither challenge nor hostile demand for a sign had been addressed to Him by the people. Indeed even at the last, when incited by their rulers, and blindly following them, 'they knew not what they did.' And it was to them that Jesus now, on the morning of His Work, spoke by 'signs.'

The Feast of the Passover commenced on the 15th Nisan, dating it, of course, from the preceding evening. But before that—before the slaying of the Paschal Lamb, on the afternoon of the 14th Nisan —the visitor to the Temple would mark something peculiar.[2] On the evening of the 13th Nisan, with which the 14th, or 'preparation-day,' commenced, the head of each household would, with lighted candle and in solemn silence, search out all leaven in his house, prefacing his search with solemn thanksgiving and appeal to God, and closing it by an equally solemn declaration that he had accomplished it, so far as within his knowledge, and disavowing responsibility for what lay beyond it. And as the worshippers went to the Temple, they would see prominently exposed, on a bench in one of the porches, two desecrated cakes of some thankoffering, indicating that it was still lawful to eat of that which was leavened. At ten, or at latest eleven o'clock, one of those cakes was removed, and then they knew that it was no longer lawful to eat of it. At twelve o'clock the second cake was removed, and this was the signal for solemnly burning all the leaven that had been gathered. Was it on the eve of the 14th, when each head of a house sought for and put aside the leaven, or else as the people watched these two cakes, and then the removal of the last of them, which marked that all leaven was to be 'purged out,' that Jesus, in real fulfilment of its national meaning, 'cleansed' the Temple of its leaven?

We can only suggest the question. But the 'cleansing of the Temple' undoubtedly preceded the actual festive Paschal week.[a] To

ª St. John ii.

---

[1] Although our A.V. translates in ver. 18 'sign' and in ver. 23 'miracles,' the Greek word is the same in both cases, and means a 'sign.'

[2] We reserve a detailed account of the Paschal celebration for our account of the last Passover of Jesus.

those who were in Jerusalem it was a week such as had never been
before, a week when 'they saw the signs which He did,' and when, stirred by a strange impulse, 'they believed in His Name' as the Messiah. 'A milk-faith,' as Luther pithily calls it, which fed on, and required for its sustenance, 'signs.' And like a vision it passed with the thing seen. Not a faith to which the sign was only the fingerpost, but a faith of which the sign, not the thing signified, was the substance; a faith which dazzled the mental sight, but reached not down to the heart. And Jesus, Who with heart-searching glance saw what was in man, Who needed not any to tell Him, but with immediateness knew all, did not commit Himself to them. They were not like His first Galilean disciples, true of heart and in heart. The Messiah Whom these found, and He Whom those saw, met different conceptions. The faith of the Jerusalem sign-seers would not have compassed what the Galileans experienced; it would not have understood nor endured, had He committed Himself to them. And yet He did, in wondrous love, condescend and speak to them in the only language they could understand, in that of 'signs.' Nor was it all in vain.

Unrecorded as these miracles are—because the words they spoke were not recorded on many hearts—it was not only here and there, by this or that miracle, that their power was felt. Their grand general effect was, to make the more spiritually minded and thoughtful feel that Jesus was indeed 'a teacher come from God.' In thinking of the miracles of Jesus, and generally of the miraculous in the New Testament, we are too apt to overlook the principal consideration in the matter. We regard it from our present circumstances, not from those of the Jews and people of that time; we judge it from our standpoint, not from theirs. And yet the main gist of the matter lies here. We would not expect to be convinced of the truth of religion, nor converted to it, by outward miracles; we would not expect them at all. Not but that, if a notable miracle really did occur, its impression and effect would be overwhelming; although, unless a miracle submitted itself to the strictest scientific tests, when in the nature of things it would cease to be a miracle, it would scarcely find general credence. Hence, truth to say, the miraculous in the New Testament constitutes to modern thought not its strong, but its weak point; not its convincing evidence, but its point of attack and difficulty. Accordingly, treating of, or contemplating the miracles of the New Testament, it is always their moral, not their natural (or supra-

natural), aspect which has its chief influence upon us. But what is
this but to say that ours is *modern*, not ancient thought, and that the
evidential power of Christ's miracles has given place to the age and
dispensation of the Holy Ghost?   With us the process is the reverse
of what it was with them of old.   They approached the moral and
spiritual through the miraculous; we the miraculous through the
moral and spiritual. His Presence, that one grand Presence is, indeed,
ever the same.   But God always adapts His teaching to our learning;
else it were not teaching at all, least of all Divine teaching.   Only
what carries it now to us is not the same as what carried it to them
of old: it is no more the fingerpost of 'signs,' but the finger of the
Spirit.   To them the miraculous was the *expected*—that miraculous
which to us also is so truly and Divinely miraculous, just because it
applies to all time, since it carries to us the *moral*, as to them the
physical, aspect of the miracle; in each case, Divine reality Divinely
conveyed.   It may therefore safely be asserted, that to the men of
that time no teaching of the new faith would have been real without
the evidence of miracles.

In those days, when the idea of the miraculous was, so to speak,
fluid—passing from the natural into the supernatural—and men regarded all that was above their view-point of nature as supernatural,
the idea of the miraculous would, by its constant recurrence, always
and prominently suggest itself.   Other teachers also, among the Jews
at least, claimed the power of doing miracles, and were popularly
credited with them.   But what an obvious contrast between theirs
and the 'signs' which Jesus did!   In thinking of this, it is necessary
to remember, that the Talmud and the New Testament alike embody
teaching Jewish in its form, and addressed to Jews, and—at least so far
as regards the subject of miracles—at periods not far apart, and brought
still nearer by the singular theological conservatism of the people.
If, with this in our minds, we recall some of the absurd Rabbinic pretensions to miracles—such as the creation of a calf by two Rabbis
every Sabbath eve for their Sabbath meal,[a] or the repulsive, and in
part blasphemous, account of a series of prodigies in testimony of the
subtleties of some great Rabbi[b]—we are almost overwhelmed by the
evidential force of the contrast between them and the 'signs' which
Jesus did.   We seem to be in an entirely new world, and we can
understand the conclusion at which every earnest and thoughtful mind
must have arrived in witnessing them, that He was, indeed, ' a Teacher
from God.'

[a] Sanh. 65 b

[b] Baba
Mez. 59 b

Such an observer was Nicodemus (*Naqdimon*),[1] one of the Pharisees and a member of the Jerusalem Sanhedrin. And, as we gather
from his mode of expression,[2] not he only, but others with him.
From the Gospel-history we know him to have been cautious by nature and education, and timid of character; yet, as in other cases,
it was the greatest offence to his Jewish thinking, the Cross, which
at last brought him to the light of decision, and the vigour of bold
confession.[a] And this in itself would show the real character of his
inquiry, and the effect of what Jesus had first taught him. It is, at
any rate, altogether rash to speak of the manner of his first approach
to Christ as most commentators have done. We can scarcely
realise the difficulties which he had to overcome. It must have been
a mighty power of conviction, to break down prejudice so far as to
lead this old Sanhedrist to acknowledge a Galilean, untrained in the
Schools, as a Teacher come from God, and to repair to Him for
direction on, perhaps, the most delicate and important point in Jewish
theology. But, even so, we cannot wonder that he should have
wished to shroud his first visit in the utmost possible secrecy. It was
a most compromising step for a Sanhedrist to take. With that first
bold purgation of the Temple a deadly feud between Jesus and the
Jewish authorities had begun, of which the sequel could not be
doubtful. It was involved in that first encounter in the Temple, and
it needed not the experience and wisdom of an aged Sanhedrist to
forecast the end.

Nevertheless, Nicodemus came. If this is evidence of his intense
earnestness, so is the bearing of Jesus of His Divine Character, and
of the truth of the narrative. As he was not depressed by the resistance of the authorities, nor by the 'milk-faith' of the multitude,
so He was not elated by the possibility of making such a convert as a
member of the great Sanhedrin. There is no excitement, no undue
deference, nor eager politeness; no compromise, nor attempted per-
suasiveness; not even accommodation. Nor, on the other hand, is
there assumed superiority, irony, or dogmatism. There is not even
a reference to the miracles, the evidential power of which had wrought

[1] A Nicodemus is spoken of in the
Talmud as one of the richest and most
distinguished citisens of Jerusalem (Taan.
20 *a*: Kethub. 66 *b*: Gitt. 56 *a*; Ab. de
R. Nath. 6 comp. Ber. R. 42. Midr. on
Eccles. vii. 12, and on Lament. i. 5). But
this name was only given him on account
of a miracle which happened at his request, his real name being *Bunai*, the
son of Gorion. A *Bunai* is mentioned in
the Talmud among the disciples of Jesus,
and a story is related how his daughter,
after immense wealth, came to most abject poverty. But there can scarcely be
a doubt that this somewhat legendary
Naqdimon was *not* the Nicodemus of the
Gospel.

[2] '*We* know that Thou art a Teacher
come from God.'

BOOK
III

in His visitor the initial conviction, that He was a Teacher come from God. All is calm, earnest, dignified—if we may reverently say it—as became the God-Man in the humiliation of His personal teaching. To say that it is all un-Jewish were a mere truism: it is Divine. No fabricated narrative would have invented such a scene, nor so represented the actors in it.[1]

Dangerous as it may be to indulge the imagination, we can almost picture the scene. The report of what passed reads, more than almost any other in the Gospels, like notes taken at the time by one who was present. We can almost put it again into the form of brief notes, by heading what each said in this manner, *Nicodemus:*—or, *Jesus:*. They are only the outlines of the conversation, given, in each case, the really important gist, and leaving abrupt gaps between, as would be the manner in such notes. Yet quite sufficient to tell us all that is important for us to know. We can scarcely doubt that it was the narrator, John, who was the witness that took the notes. His own reflections upon it, or rather his after-look upon it, in the light of later facts, and under the teaching of the Holy Ghost, is described in the verses with which the writer follows his account of what had passed between Jesus and Nicodemus (St. John iii. 16–21). In the same manner he winds up with similar reflections (ib. vv. 31–36) the reported conversation between the Baptist and his disciples. In neither case are the verses to which

---

[1] This, of course, is not the view of the Tübingen School, which regards the whole of this narrative as representing a later development. Dr. *Abbott* (Encycl. Brit., Art. 'Gospels,' p. 821) regards the expression, 'born of water and of the Spirit,' as a reference to Christian Baptism, and this again as evidence for the late authorship of the fourth Gospel. His reasoning is, that the *earliest* reference to regeneration is contained in St. Matt. xviii. 3. Then he supposes a reference in *Justin's* Apologia (i. 61) to be a *further* development of this doctrine, and he denies what is generally regarded as Justin's quotation from St. John iii. 5 to be such, because it omits the word 'water.' A *third* stage he supposes to be implied in 1 Pet. i. 3, 23; with which he connects 1 Pet. iii. 21. The *fourth* stage of development he regards as embodied in the words of St. John iii. 5. All these hypotheses—for they are no more than such—are built on Justin's omission of the word 'water,' which, as Dr. Abbott argues, proves that Justin must have been unacquainted with the fourth Gospel, since otherwise it were impossible that, when expressly treating of Baptism, he should have omitted it. To us, on the other hand, the opposite seems the legitimate inference. Treating confessedly of Baptism, it was only necessary for his argument, which identified regeneration with Baptism, to introduce the reference to the Spirit. Otherwise the quotation is so exactly that from the fourth Gospel, including even the objection of Nicodemus, that it is almost impossible to imagine that so literal a transcription could have originated otherwise than from the fourth Gospel itself, and that it is the result of a supposed series of developments in which Justin would represent the second, and the fourth Gospel the fourth stage. But besides, the attentive reader of the chapter in *Justin's* Apology cannot fail to remark that Justin represents a *later*, and not an *earlier*, stage than the fourth Gospel. For, with Justin, Baptism and regeneration are manifestly identified, not with renovation of our nature, but with the forgiveness of sins.

we refer, part of what either Jesus or John said at the time, but what,
in view of it, John says in name of, and to the Church of the New
Testament.[1]

If from St. John xix. 27 we might infer that St. John had 'a
home' in Jerusalem itself—which, considering the simplicity of living
at the time, and the cost of houses, would not necessarily imply that
he was rich—the scene about to be described would have taken place
under the roof of him who has given us its record. In any case, the
circumstances of life at the time are so well known, that we have no
difficulty in realising the surroundings. It was night—one of the
nights in that Easter week so full of marvels. Perhaps we may be
allowed to suppose that, as so often in analogous circumstances, the
spring-wind, sweeping up the narrow streets of the City, had suggested
the comparison,[2] which was so full of deepest teaching to Nicodemus.   [2] St. John
Up in the simply furnished *Aliyah*—the guest-chamber on the roof   iii. 8
—the lamp was still burning, and the Heavenly Guest still busy with
thought and words.   There was no need for Nicodemus to pass through
the house, for an outside stair led to the upper room.   It was night,
when Jewish superstition would keep men at home; a wild, gusty
spring night, when loiterers would not be in the streets; and no one
would see him as at that hour he ascended the outside steps that led
up to the *Aliyah*.   His errand was soon told: one sentence, that which
admitted the Divine Teachership of Jesus, implied all the questions
he could wish to ask.   Nay, his very presence there spoke them.
Or, if otherwise, the answer of Jesus spoke them.   Throughout,
Jesus never descended to the standpoint of Nicodemus, but rather
sought to lift him to His own.   It was all about 'the Kingdom of
God,'[3] so connected with that Teacher come from God, that Nicodemus
would inquire.

And yet, though Christ never descended to the standpoint of
Nicodemus, we must bear in mind what his views as a Jew would be,
if we would understand the interview.   Jesus took him straight to
whence alone that 'Kingdom' could be seen.   'Except a man be
born from above,[4] he cannot see the Kingdom of God.'   It has been

---

[1] For detailed examination and proof
I must here refer the reader to Canon
Westcott's Commentary.

[2] I cannot agree with Archdeacon
Watkins, who would render it, 'The
Spirit breathes'—an opinion, so far as I
know, unsupported, and which seems to
me ill-accordant with the whole context.

[3] The expression, 'Kingdom of God,'
occurs only in iii. 3 and iii. 5 of the fourth

Gospel.   Otherwise the expression 'My
Kingdom' is used in xviii. 36.   This exceptional use of the Synoptic term, 'Kingdom of God,' is noteworthy in this connection, and not without its important
bearing on the question of the authorship
of the fourth Gospel.

[4] Notwithstanding the high authority
of Professor *Westcott*, I must still hold
that this, and now 'anew,' is the right

BOOK
III

a Yebam.
62 a

b Yalkut on
1 Sam. xiii.

c As in
Yalkut

thought by commentators, that there is here an allusion to a Jewish mode of expression in regard to proselytes, who were viewed as ' new-born.' But in that case Nicodemus would have understood it, and answered differently—or, rather, not expressed his utter inability to understand it. It is, indeed, true that a Gentile on becoming a proselyte—though not, as has been suggested, an ordinary penitent[1] —was likened to a child just born.[a] It is also true, that persons in certain circumstances—the bridegroom on his marriage, the Chief of the Academy on his promotion, the king on his enthronement— were likened to those newly born.[b] The expression, therefore, was not only common, but, so to speak, fluid; only, both it and what it implied must be rightly understood. In the first place, it was only a simile, and never meant to convey a real regeneration ('as a child'). So far as proselytes were concerned, it meant that, having entered into a new relation to God, they also entered into new relationship to man, just as if they had at that moment been newly born. All the old relations had ceased—a man's father, brother, mother, sister were no longer his nearest of kin: he was a new and another man. Then, secondly,[c] it implied a new state, when all a man's past was past, and his sins forgiven him as belonging to that past. It will now be perceived, how impossible it was for Nicodemus to understand the teaching of Jesus, and yet how all-important to him was that teaching. For, even if he could have imagined that Jesus pointed to repentance, as that which would give him the figurative standing of 'born from above,' or even 'born anew,' it would not have helped him. For, first, this second birth was only a simile. Secondly, according to the Jewish view, this second birth was the consequence of having taken upon oneself 'the Kingdom;' not, as Jesus put it, the cause and condition of it. The proselyte had taken upon himself 'the Kingdom,' and therefore he was 'born' anew, while Jesus put it

rendering. The word ἄνωθεν has always the meaning 'above' in the fourth Gospel (ch. iii. 3, 7, 31; xix. 11, 23); and otherwise also St. John always speaks of 'a birth' from God (St. John i. 13; 1 John ii. 29; iii. 9; iv. 7; v. 1, 4, 18).
[1] This is at least implied by *Wünsche*, and taken for granted by others. But ancient Jewish tradition and the Talmud do not speak of it. Comp. Yebam. 22 a, 62 a; 97 a and b; Bekhor. 47 a. Proselytes are always spoken of as 'new creatures,' Ber. R. 39, ed. Warsh. p. 72 a; Bemidb. R. 11. In Vayyikra R. 30, Ps. cii. 18, 'the people that shall be created' is explained:

'For the Holy One, blessed be His Name, will create them a new creature.' In Yalkut on Judg. vi. 1 (vol. ii. p. 10 c, about the middle) this new creation is connected with the forgiveness of sins, it being maintained that whoever has a miracle done, and praises God for it, his sins are forgiven, and he is made a new creature. This is illustrated by the history of Israel at the Red Sea, by that of Deborah and Barak, and by that of David. In Shem. R. 3 (ed. Warsh. ii. p. 11 a) the words Ex. iv. 12, 'teach thee what thou shalt say,' are explained as equivalent to 'I will create thee a new creation.'

that he must be born again in order to see the Kingdom of God. CHAP.
Lastly, it was 'a birth from above' to which reference was made. VI
Judaism could understand a new relationship towards God and man,
and even the forgiveness of sins. But it had no conception of a
moral renovation, a spiritual birth, as the initial condition for reformation, far less as that for seeing the Kingdom of God. And it was
because it had no idea of such 'birth from above,' of its reality or
even possibility, that Judaism could not be the Kingdom of God.

Or, to take another view of it, for Divine truth is many-sided—
perhaps some would say, to make 'Western' application of what
was first spoken to the Jew—in one respect Nicodemus and Jesus
had started from the same premiss: *The Kingdom of God.* But
how different were their conceptions of what constituted that Kingdom, and of what was its door of entrance! What Nicodemus had
seen of Jesus had not only shaken the confidence which his former
views on these subjects had engendered in him, but opened dim
possibilities, the very suggestion of which filled him with uneasiness
as to the past, and vague hopes as to the future. And so it ever is
with us also, when, like Nicodemus, we first arrive at the conviction
that Jesus is the Teacher come from God. What He teaches is so
entirely different from what Nicodemus, or any of us could, from any
other standpoint than that of Jesus, have learned or known concerning
the Kingdom and entrance into it. The admission, however reached,
of the Divine Mission of this Teacher, implies, unspoken, the grand
question about the Kingdom. It is the opening of the door through
which the Grand Presence will enter in. To such a man, as to us in
like unspoken questioning, Jesus ever has but one thing to say:
'Except a man be born from above, he cannot see the Kingdom of
God.' The Kingdom is other, the entrance to it is other, than you know
or think. That which is of the flesh is flesh. Man may rise to high
possibilities—mental, even moral: self-development, self-improvement,
self-restraint, submission to a grand idea or a higher law, refined
moral egotism, æsthetic even moral altruism. But to see the *Kingdom
of God*: to understand what means the absolute rule of God, the one
high calling of our humanity, by which a man becomes a child of
God—to perceive this, not as an improvement upon our present
state, but as the submission of heart, mind, and life to Him as our
Divine King, an existence which is, and which means, proclaiming
unto the world the Kingship of God: this can only be learned from
Christ, and needs even for its perception a kinship of spirit—for that
which is born of the Spirit is spirit. To *see* it, needs the birth from

BOOK
III

a ver. 4

above; to *enter* it, the double baptismal birth of what John's Baptism had meant, and of what Christ's Baptism was.

Accordingly, all this sounded quite strange and unintelligible to Nicodemus. He could understand how a man might *become* other, and so ultimately *be* other; but how a man could first *be* other in order to *become* other—more than that, needed to be 'born from above,' in order to 'see the Kingdom of God'—passed alike his experience and his Jewish learning. Only one possibility of *being* occurred to him: that given him in his natural disposition, or as a Jew would have put it, in his original innocency when he first entered the world. And this—so to express ourselves—he thought aloud.ᵃ But there was another world of being than that of which Nicodemus thought. That world was the 'Kingdom of God' in its essential contrariety to the kingdom of this world, whether in the general sense of that expression, or even in the special Judaistic sense attaching to the 'Kingdom' of the Messiah. There was only one gate by which a man could pass into that Kingdom of God—for that which was of the flesh could ever be only fleshly. Here a man might strive, as did the Jews, by outward conformity to *become*, but he would never attain to *being*. But that 'Kingdom' was *spiritual*, and here a man must *be* in order to *become*. How was he to attain that new being? The Baptist had pointed it out in its negative aspect of repentance and putting away the old by his Baptism of water; and as regarded its positive aspect he had pointed to Him Who was to baptize with the Holy Ghost and with fire. This was the gate of *being* through which a man must enter into the Kingdom, which was of the Messiah, because it was of God and the Messiah was of God, and in *that* sense 'the Teacher come from God'—that is, being sent of God, He taught of God by bringing to God. This but a few who had gone to the Baptist had perceived, or indeed could perceive, because the Baptist could in his Baptism only convey the negative, not the positive, aspect of it. And it needed that positive aspect—the being born from above—in order to see the Kingdom of God. But as to the mystery of this *being* in order to *become*—hark! did he hear the sound of that wind as it swept past the *Aliyah*? He heard its voice; but he neither knew whence it came, nor whither it went. So was every one that was born of the Spirit. You heard the voice of the Spirit Who originated the new being, but the origination of that new being, or its further development into all that it might and would become, lay beyond man's observation.

Nicodemus now understood in some measure *what* entrance into

the Kingdom meant; but its *how* seemed only involved in greater
mystery. That it was such a mystery, unthought and unimagined
in Jewish theology, was a terribly sad manifestation of what the
teaching in Israel was. Yet it had all been told them, as of personal
knowledge, by the Baptist and by Jesus; nay, if they could only have
received it, by the whole Old Testament. He wanted to know the
how of these things before he believed them. He believed them
not, though they passed on earth, because he knew not their *how*.
How then could he believe that *how*, of which the agency was
unseen and in heaven? To that spring of being no one could ascend
but He that had come down from heaven,[1] and Who, to bring to us
that spring of being, had appeared as 'the Son of Man,' the Ideal
Man, the embodiment of the Kingdom of Heaven, and thus the only
true Teacher come from God. Or did Nicodemus think of another
Teacher—hitherto their only Teacher, Moses—whom Jewish tradition generally believed to have ascended into the very heavens, in order
to bring the teaching unto them?[2] Let the history of Moses, then,
teach them! They thought they understood his teaching, but there
was one symbol in his history before which tradition literally stood
dumb. They had heard what Moses had taught them; they had
seen 'the earthly things' of God in the Manna which had rained
from heaven—and, in view and hearing of it all, they had not believed,
but murmured and rebelled. Then came the judgment of the fiery
serpents, and, in answer to repentant prayer, the symbol of new
being, a life restored from death, as they looked on their no longer
living but dead death lifted up before them. A symbol this, showing
forth two elements: negatively, the putting away of the past in their
dead death (the serpent no longer living, but a brazen serpent); and
positively, in their look of faith and hope. Before this symbol, as has
been said, tradition has stood dumb. It could only suggest one
meaning, and draw from it one lesson. Both these were true, and
yet both insufficient. The meaning which tradition attached to it
was, that Israel lifted up their eyes, not merely to the serpent, but
rather to their Father in heaven, and had regard to His mercy.
This,[3] as St. John afterwards shows (ver. 16), was a true interpreta-

---

[1] The clause 'Who is in heaven' is regarded, on critical grounds, as a *gloss.*
But, even so, it seems almost a necessary
gloss, in view of the Jewish notions about
the ascent of Moses into heaven. Strange
to say, the passage referred to forced *So-
cinus* to the curious dogma that before the
commencement of His ministry Jesus had

been rapt in spirit to heaven. (Comp. 'The
History and Development of Socinian-
ism,' in the North. Brit. Rev. May 1859.)
[2] This in many places. Comp., for ex.,
Jer. Targ. on Deut. xxx. 12, and the
shocking notice in Bemid. R. 19.
Another view, however, Sukk. 5 *a.*
[3] So already in Wisdom of Solomon

tion; but it left wholly out of sight the Antitype, in gazing on Whom our hearts are uplifted to the love of God, Who gave His only-begotten Son, and we learn to know and love the Father in His Son. And the lesson which tradition drew from it was, that this symbol taught, the dead would live again; for, as it is argued,[a] 'behold, if God made it that, through the similitude of the serpent which brought death, the dying should be restored to life, how much more shall He, Who is Life, restore the dead to life.' And here lies the true interpretation of what Jesus taught. If the uplifted serpent, as symbol, brought life to the believing look which was fixed upon the giving, pardoning love of God, then, in the truest sense, shall the uplifted Son of Man give true life to everyone that believeth, looking up in Him to the giving and forgiving love of God, which His Son came to bring, to declare, and to manifest. 'For as Moses lifted up the serpent in the wilderness, so must the Son of Man be lifted up, that whosoever believeth should in Him have eternal life.'[1]

With this final and highest teaching, which contains all that Nicodemus, or, indeed, the whole Church, could require or be able to know, He explained to him and to us the *how* of the new birth—alike the source and the flow of its spring. Ours it is now only to 'believe,' where we cannot further know, and, looking up to the Son of Man in His perfected work, to perceive, and to receive the gift of God's love for our healing. In this teaching it is not the serpent and the Son of Man that are held side by side, though we cannot fail to see the symbolic reference of the one to the other, but the uplifting of the one and the other—the one by the sin, the other through the sin of the people: both on account of it—the forthgoing of God's pardoning mercy, the look of faith, and the higher recognition of God's love in it all.

And so the record of this interview abruptly closes. It tells all, but no more than the Church requires to know. Of Nicodemus we shall hear again in the sequel, not needlessly, nor yet to complete

xvi. 7; still more clearly in the Targum Pseudo-Jonathan on Numb. xxi. 8, 9: 'He who lifted up his heart to the name of the Memra of Jehovah, lived;' and in the Jerusalem Targum on the passage: 'And Moses made a serpent of brass, and set it on a place aloft [of uplifting] (*talé* —the same term, curiously, which is applied by the Jews to Christ as the 'Uplifted' or 'Crucified' One). And it was that every one that was bitten with the serpent, and lifted his face in prayer (the word implies humbled prayer) unto His Father Who is in heaven, and looked unto the brazen serpent, he was healed.' Similarly Rosh haSh iii. 8. *Buxtorf's* learned tractate on the Brazen Serpent (Exercitationes, pp. 458–492) adds little to our knowledge.
[1] This seems the correct reading. Comp. Canon *Westcott's* note on the passage, and in general his most full and thorough criticism of the various readings in this chapter.

a biography, were it even that of Jesus; but as is necessary for the understanding of this History. What follows[a] are not the words of Christ, but of St. John. In them, looking back many years afterwards in the light of completed events, the Apostle takes his stand, as becomes the circumstances, where Jesus had ended His teaching of Nicodemus—under the Cross. In the Gift, unutterable in its preciousness, he now sees the Giver and the Source of all.[b] Then, following that teaching of Jesus backward, he sees how true it has proved concerning the world, that 'that which is of the flesh is flesh;' how true, also, concerning the Spirit-born, and what need there is to us of 'this birth from above.'

But to all time, through the gusty night of our world's early spring, flashes, as the lamp in that *Aliyah* through the darkened streets of silent Jerusalem, that light; sounds through its stillness, like the Voice of the Teacher come from God, this eternal Gospel-message to us and to all men: 'God so loved the world, that He gave His only-begotten Son, that whosoever believeth in Him should not perish, but have everlasting life.'

CHAP.
VI

[a] St. John iii. 16-21

[b] ver. 16

CHAPTER VII.

IN JUDÆA AND THROUGH SAMARIA—A SKETCH OF SAMARITAN HISTORY AND THEOLOGY—JEWS AND SAMARITANS.

(St. John iv. 1-4.)

BOOK
III

^a St. John iii. 22

^b St. John vi. 2

^c St. John iv. 1

^d Rom. vi. 3

WE have no means of determining how long Jesus may have tarried in Jerusalem after the events recorded in the previous two chapters. The Evangelic narrative[a] only marks an indefinite period of time, which, as we judge from internal probability, cannot have been protracted. From the city He retired with His disciples to 'the country,' which formed the province of Judæa. There He taught and His disciples baptized.[b][1] From what had been so lately witnessed in Jerusalem, as well as from what must have been known as to the previous testimony of the Baptist concerning Him, the number of those who professed adhesion to the expected new Kingdom, and were consequently baptized, was as large, in that locality, as had submitted to the preaching and Baptism of John—perhaps even larger. An exaggerated report was carried to the Pharisaic authorities:[2] 'Jesus maketh and baptizeth more disciples than John.'[c] From which, at least, we infer, that the opposition of the leaders of the party to the Baptist was now settled, and that it extended to Jesus; and also, what careful watch they kept over the new movement.

But what seems at first sight strange is the twofold circumstance, that Jesus should for a time have established Himself in such apparently close proximity to the Baptist, and that on this occasion, and on this only, He should have allowed His disciples to administer the rite of Baptism. That the latter must not be confounded with Christian Baptism, which was only introduced after the Death of Christ,[d] or, to speak more accurately, after the outpouring of the Holy Ghost, needs no special explanation. But our difficulties only

---

[1] The Baptism of preparation for the Kingdom could not have been administered by Him Who *opened* the Kingdom of Heaven.

[2] The Evangelist reports the message which was brought to the Pharisees in the very words in which it was delivered.

increase, as we remember the essential difference between them, grounded on that between the Mission of John and the Teaching of Jesus. In the former, the Baptism of repentant preparation for the coming Kingdom had its deepest meaning; not so in presence of that Kingdom itself, and in the teaching of its King. But, even were it otherwise, the administration of the same rite by John and by the disciples of Jesus in apparently close proximity, seems not only unnecessary, but it might give rise to misconception on the part of enemies, and misunderstanding or jealousy on the part of weak disciples.

Such was actually the case when, on one occasion, a discussion arose 'on the part of John's disciples with a Jew,'[1] on the subject of purification.[a] We know not the special point in dispute, nor does it seem of much importance, since such 'questions' would naturally suggest themselves to a caviller or opponent[2] who encountered those who were administering Baptism. What really interests us is, that somehow this Jewish objector must have connected what he said with a reference to the Baptism of Jesus' disciples. For, immediately afterwards, the disciples of John, in their sore zeal for the honour of their master, brought him tidings, in the language of doubt, if not of complaint, of what to them seemed interference with the work of the Baptist, and almost presumption on the part of Jesus. While fully alive to their grievous error, perhaps in proportion as we are so, we cannot but honour and sympathise with this loving care for their master. The toilsome mission of the great Ascetic was drawing to its close, and that without any tangible success so far as he was concerned. Yet, to souls susceptible of the higher, to see him would be to be arrested; to hear him, to be convinced; to know, would be to love and venerate him. Never before had such deep earnestness and reality been witnessed, such devotedness, such humility and self-abnegation, and all in that great cause which set every Jewish heart on fire. And then, in the high-day of his power, when all men had gathered around him and hung on his lips; when all wondered whether he would announce himself as the Christ, or, at least, as His Forerunner, or as one of the great Prophets; when a word from him would have kindled that multitude into a

---

[1] This, and not 'the Jews,' is the better reading.

[2] Probably the discussion originated with John's disciples—the objector being a Jew or a professing disciple of Christ, who deprecated their views. In the one case they would in his opinion be too low; in the other too high. In either case the subject in dispute would not be *baptisms*, but the general subject of *purifications*—a subject of such wide range in Jewish theology, that one of the six sections into which the Mishnah or traditional Law is divided, is specially devoted to it.

frenzy of enthusiasm—he had disclaimed everything for himself, and pointed to Another! But this 'Coming One,' to whom he had borne witness, had hitherto been quite other than their Master. And, as if this had not been enough, the multitudes, which had formerly come to John, now flocked around Jesus; nay, He had even usurped the one distinctive function still left to their master, humble as it was. It was evident that, hated and watched by the Pharisees; watched, also, by the ruthless jealousy of a Herod; overlooked, if not supplanted, by Jesus, the mission of their master was nearing its close. It had been a life and work of suffering and self-denial; it was about to end in loneliness and sorrow. They said nothing expressly to complain of Him to Whom John had borne witness, but they told of what He did, and how all men came to Him.

The answer which the Baptist made, may be said to mark the high point of his life and witness. Never before was he so tender, almost sad; never before more humble and self-denying, more earnest and faithful. The setting of his own life-sun was to be the rising of One infinitely more bright; the end of his Mission the beginning of another far higher. In the silence, which was now gathering around him, he heard but one Voice, that of the Bridegroom, and he rejoiced in it, though he must listen to it in stillness and loneliness. For it he had waited and worked. Not his own, but this had he sought. And now that it had come, he was content; more than content: his 'joy was now fulfilled.' 'He must increase, but I must decrease.' It was the right and good order. With these as his last words publicly spoken,[1] this Aaron of the New Testament unrobed himself ere he lay down to die. Surely among those born of women there was not one greater than John.

That these were his last words, publicly spoken and recorded, may, however, explain to us why on this exceptional occasion Jesus sanctioned the administration by His disciples of the Baptism of John. It was not a retrogression from the position He had taken in Jerusalem, nor caused by the refusal of His Messianic claims in the Temple.[2] There is no retrogression, only progression, in the Life of Jesus. And yet it was only on this occasion that the rite was administered under His sanction. But the circumstances were exceptional. It was John's last testimony to Jesus, and it was preceded by this testimony of Jesus to John. Far divergent, almost opposite, as from the first their paths had been, this practical sanction on the

---

[1] The next event was John's imprisonment by Herod.

[2] This strange suggestion is made by *Godet*.

part of Jesus of John's Baptism, when the Baptist was about to CHAP. VII
be forsaken, betrayed, and murdered, was Christ's highest testimony
to him. Jesus adopted his Baptism, ere its waters for ever ceased to
flow, and thus He blessed and consecrated them. He took up the
work of His Forerunner, and continued it. The baptismal rite of
John administered with the sanction of Jesus, was the highest witness
that could be borne to it.

There is no necessity for supposing that John and the disciples of
Jesus baptized at, or quite close to, the same place. On the contrary,
such immediate juxtaposition seems, for obvious reasons, unlikely.
Jesus was within the boundaries of the province of Judæa, while
John baptized at Ænon (the springs), near to Salim. The latter site
has not been identified. But the oldest tradition, which places it a
few miles to the south of Bethshean (Scythopolis), on the border of
Samaria and Galilee, has this in its favour, that it locates the scene of
John's last public work close to the seat of Herod Antipas, into whose
power the Baptist was so soon to be delivered.[1] But already there
were causes at work to remove both Jesus and His Forerunner from
their present spheres of activity. As regards Christ, we have the
express statement,[a] that the machinations of the Pharisaic party in
Jerusalem led Him to withdraw into Galilee. And, as we gather from
the notice of St. John, the Baptist was now involved in this hostility,
as being so closely connected with Jesus. Indeed, we venture the
suggestion that the imprisonment of the Baptist, although occasioned
by his outspoken rebuke of Herod, was in great part due to the
intrigues of the Pharisees. Of such a connection between them and
Herod Antipas, we have direct evidence in a similar attempt to bring
about the removal of Jesus from his territory.[b] It would not have
been difficult to rouse the suspicions of a nature so mean and jealous
as that of Antipas, and this may explain the account of Josephus,[c]
who attributes the imprisonment and death of the Baptist simply to

[a] St. John iv. 1

[b] St. Luke xiii. 31, 32

[c] Ant. xviii. 5. 2

[1] No fewer than four localities have been identified with Ænon and Salim. *Ewald, Hengstenberg, Wieseler,* and *Godet,* seek it on the *southern* border of Judæa (*En-rimmon,* Neh. xi. 29, comp. Josh. xv. 1, 32). This seems so improbable as scarcely to require discussion. Dr. *Barclay* (City of the Great King, pp. 558-571) finds it a few miles from Jerusalem in the *Wady Fâr'ah,* but admits (p. 565) that there are doubts about the Arab pronunciation of this *Salim.* Lieut. *Conder* (Tent-Work in Palest., vol. i. pp. 91-93) finds it in the Wady *Fâr'ah,* which leads from Samaria to the Jordan. Here he describes most pictorially 'the springs' 'in the open valley surrounded by desolate and shapeless hills,' with the village of *Salim* three miles south of the valley, and the village of 'Ainân four miles north of the stream. Against this there are, however, two objections. First, both Ænon and Salim would have been in Samaria. Secondly, so far from being close to each other, Ænon would have been seven miles from Salim.

BOOK
III

Herod's suspicious fear of John's unbounded influence with the people.[1]

Leaving for the present the Baptist, we follow the footsteps of the Master. They are only traced by the disciple who best understood their direction, and who alone has left us a record of the beginning of Christ's ministry. For St. Matthew and St. Mark expressly indicate the imprisonment of the Baptist as their starting-point,[a] and, though St. Luke does not say this in so many words, he characteristically commences with Christ's public Evangelic teaching in the Synagogues of Galilee. Yet the narrative of St. Matthew[b] reads rather like a brief summary;[2] that of St. Mark seems like a succession of rapid sketches; and even that of St. Luke, though with deeper historic purpose than the others, outlines, rather than tells, the history. St. John alone does not profess to give a narrative at all in the ordinary sense; but he selects incidents which are characteristic as unfolding the meaning of that Life, and records discourses which open its inmost teaching;[c] and he alone tells of that early Judæan ministry and the journey through Samaria, which preceded the Galilean work.

The shorter road from Judæa to Galilee led through Samaria;[d] and this, if we may credit Josephus,[e] was generally taken by the Galileans on their way to the capital. On the other hand, the Judæans seem chiefly to have made a *détour* through Peræa, in order to avoid hostile and impure Samaria. It lay not within the scope of our Lord to extend His personal Ministry, especially at its commencement, beyond the boundaries of Israel,[f] and the expression, 'He must needs go through Samaria,'[g] can only refer to the advisability

a St. Mark i. 14; St. Mark iv. 12

b See specially St. Matt. iv. 13 to end

c St. John xx. 30, 31; xxi. 25

d Jos. Life, 52

e Ant. xx. 6. 1

f St. Matt. x. 5

g St. John iv. 4

---

[1] Ant. xviii. 5. 2: 'But to some of the Jews it appeared, that the destruction of Herod's army came from God, and, indeed, as a righteous punishment on account of what had been done to John, who was surnamed the Baptist. For Herod ordered him to be killed, a good man, and who commanded the Jews to exercise virtue, both as to righteousness towards one another, and piety towards God, and so to come to baptism. For that the baptizing would be acceptable to Him, if they made use of it, not for the putting away (remission) of some sins, but for the purification of the body, after that the soul had been previously cleansed by righteousness. And when others had come in crowds, for they were exceedingly moved by hearing these words, Herod, fearing lest such influence of his over the people might lead to some re-bellion, for they seemed ready to do anything by his counsel, deemed it best, before anything new should happen through him, to put him to death, rather than that, when a change should arise in affairs, he might have to repent.' Comp. also *Krebs*. Observationes in Nov. Test. e Fl. Jos. pp. 35, 36.

[2] I am so strongly impressed with this, that I do not feel sure about *Godet's* theory, that the calling of the four Apostles recorded by the Synoptists (St. Matt. iv. 18–22; St. Mark i. 16–20; St. Luke v. 1–11), had really taken place during our Lord's first stay in Capernaum (St. John ii. 12). On the whole, however, the circumstances recorded by the Synoptists seem to indicate a period in the Lord's Ministry beyond that early stay in Capernaum.

in the circumstances of taking the most direct road,[1] or else to the
wish of avoiding Peræa as the seat of Herod's government.[2] Such
prejudices in regard to Samaria, as those which affected the ordinary
Judæan devotee, would, of course, not influence the conduct of Jesus.
But great as these undoubtedly were, they have been unduly exaggerated by modern writers. misled by one-sided quotations from Rabbinic
works.[3]

The Biblical history of that part of Palestine which bore the name
of Samaria need not here be repeated.[a] Before the final deportation
of Israel by Shalmaneser, or rather Sargon,[4] the 'Samaria' to which
his operations extended must have considerably shrunk in dimensions,
not only owing to previous conquests, but from the circumstance that
the authority of the kings of Judah seems to have extended over a
considerable portion of what once constituted the kingdom of Israel.[b]
Probably the Samaria of that time included little more than the city
of that name, together with some adjoining towns and villages. It is
of considerable interest to remember that the places, to which the
inhabitants of Samaria were transported,[c] have been identified with
such clearness as to leave no reasonable doubt, that at least some of
the descendants of the ten tribes, whether mixed or unmixed with
Gentiles, must be sought among what are now known as the Nestorian
Christians.[5] On the other hand, it is of no practical importance for
our present purpose to ascertain the exact localities, whence the new
'Samaritans' were brought to take the place of the Israelitish exiles.[d]
Suffice it, that one of them, perhaps that which contributed the
principal settlers, *Cuthah*, furnished the name *Cuthim*, by which the
Jews afterwards persistently designated the Samaritans. It was intended as a term of reproach,[e] to mark that they were of foreign
race,[f][6] and to repudiate all connection between them and the Jews.
Yet it is impossible to believe that, at least in later times, they did
not contain a considerable admixture of Israelitish elements. It is
difficult to suppose, that the original deportation was so complete as
to leave behind no traces of the original Israelitish inhabitants.[g]

[a] Comp. 1
Kings xiii.
32; xvi. 24
&c.; Tig-
lath-
pileser, 2
Kings xv.
29; Shal-
maneser,
xvii. 3-5;
xviii. 9-11;
Sargon,
xvii. 6, &c.

[b] 2 Chron.
xxx. 1-26;
xxxiv. 6

[c] 2 Kings
xvii. 6

[d] 2 Kings
xvii. 24-26;
comp. Ezr.
iv. 2, 10

[e] St. John
viii. 48

[f] St. Luke
xvii. 16.

[g] Comp. 2
Chron.
xxxiv. 6, 9
Jer. xli. 5;
Amos v. 3

[1] I cannot agree with Archdeacon
Watkins, that the 'needs go' was in
order ' to teach in Samaria, as in Judæa,
the principles of true religion and worship.'
[2] So *Bengel* and *Luthardt*.
[3] Much as has been written about
Samaria, the subject has not been quite
satisfactorily treated. Some of the
passages referred to by *Deutsch* (*Smith's*
Dict. of the Bible, vol. iii., Art. Samaritan

Pentat. p. 1118) cannot be verified—probably owing to printer's mistakes.
[4] Comp. *Smith's* Bible Dict., Art. Sargon; and *Schrader*, Keil-Inschr. u. d.
Alte Test. p. 158 &c.
[5] Of course, not *all* the ten tribes.
Comp. previous remarks on their migra-
tions.
[6] The expression cannot, however, be
pressed as implying that the Samaritans
were of entirely Gentile blood.

BOOK
III

ᵃ Jos. Ant.
xi. 8, 2, 6, 7

ᵇ 2 Kings
xvii. 30, 31

ᶜ vv. 28-41

Their number would probably be swelled by fugitives from Assyria, and by Jewish settlers in the troublous times that followed. Afterwards, as we know, they were largely increased by apostates and rebels against the order of things established by Ezra and Nehemiah.[a] Similarly, during the period of internal political and religious troubles, which marked the period to the accession of the Maccabees, the separation between Jews and Samaritans could scarcely have been generally observed, the more so that Alexander the Great placed them in close juxtaposition.[1]

The first foreign colonists of Samaria brought their peculiar forms of idolatry with them.[b] But the Providential judgments, by which they were visited, led to the introduction of a spurious Judaism, consisting of a mixture of their former superstitions with Jewish doctrines and rites.[c] Although this state of matters resembled that which had obtained in the original kingdom of Israel, perhaps just because of this, Ezra and Nehemiah, when reconstructing the Jewish commonwealth, insisted on a strict separation between those who had returned from Babylon and the Samaritans, resisting equally their offers of co-operation and their attempts at hindrance. This embittered the national feeling of jealousy already existing, and led to that constant hostility between Jews and Samaritans which has continued to this day. The religious separation became final when (at a date which cannot be precisely fixed[2]) the Samaritans built a rival temple on Mount Gerizim, and Manasseh,[3] the brother of Jaddua, the Jewish High-Priest, having refused to annul his marriage with the daughter of Sanballat, was forced to flee, and became the High-Priest of the new Sanctuary. Henceforth, by impudent assertion and falsification of the text of the Pentateuch,[4] Gerizim was declared the rightful centre of worship, and the doctrines and rites of the Samaritans exhibited a curious imitation and adaptation of those prevalent in Judæa.

We cannot here follow in detail the history of the Samaritans, nor explain the dogmas and practices peculiar to them. The latter would be the more difficult, because so many of their views were simply corruptions of those of the Jews, and because, from the want of an authenticated ancient literature,[5] the origin and meaning of many of

---

[1] Comp. *Herzfeld*, Gesch. d. Volkes Isr. ii. p. 120.

[2] *Jost* thinks it existed even before the time of Alexander. Comp. *Nutt*, Samar. Hist. p. 16, note 2.

[3] The difficult question, whether this is the Sanballat of the Book of Nehemiah, is fully discussed by *Petermann* (*Herzog's* Real-Enc. vol. xiii. p. 366).

[4] For a very full criticism of that Pentateuch, see Mr. *Deutsch's* Art. in *Smith's* Bible-Dict.

[5] Comp. the sketch of it in *Nutt's* Samar. Hist., and *Petermann's* Art.

them have been forgotten.[1] Sufficient, however, must be said to explain the mutual relations at the time when the Lord, sitting on Jacob's well, first spake to the Samaritans of the better worship 'in spirit and truth,' and opened that well of living water which has never since ceased to flow.

CHAP.
VII

The political history of the people can be told in a few sentences. Their Temple,[2] to which reference has been made, was built, not in Samaria but at Shechem—probably on account of the position held by that city in the former history of Israel—and on Mount Gerizim, which in the Samaritan Pentateuch was substituted for Mount Ebal in Deut. xxvii. 4. It was Shechem also, with its sacred associations of Abraham, Jacob, and Joseph, which became the real capital of the Samaritans. The fate of the city of Samaria under the reign of Alexander is uncertain—one account speaking of the rebellion of the city, the murder of the Macedonian governor, the consequent destruction of Samaria, and the slaughter of part, and transportation of the rest, of its inhabitants to Shechem,[3] while Josephus is silent on these events. When, after the death of Alexander, Palestine became the field of battle between the rulers of Egypt and Syria, Samaria suffered even more than other parts of the country. In 320 B.C. it passed from the rule of Syria to that of Egypt (Ptolemy Lagi). Six years later[a] it again became Syrian (Antigonus). Only three years afterwards,[b] Ptolemy reconquered and held it for a very short time. On his retreat, he destroyed the walls of Samaria and of other towns. In 301 it passed again by treaty into the hands of Ptolemy, out in 298 it was once more ravaged by the son of Antigonus. After that it enjoyed a season of quiet under Egyptian rule, till the reign of Antiochus (III.) the Great, when it again passed temporarily, and under his successor, Seleucus IV. (Philopator),[c] permanently under Syrian dominion. In the troublous times of Antiochus IV. Epiphanes,[d] the Samaritans escaped the fate of the Jews by repudiating all con-

[a] In 314
[b] In 311
[c] 187-175
[d] 175-164

---

[1] As instances we may mention the names of the Angels and devils. One of the latter is called *Yatsara* (יצרא), which *Petermann* derives from Deut. xxxi. 21, and *Nutt* from Ex. xxiii. 28. I have little doubt, it is only a corruption of *Yetser haRa*. Indeed, the latter and Satan are expressly identified in Baba B. 16 *a*. Many of the Samaritan views seem only corruptions and adaptations of those current in Palestine, which, indeed, in the circumstances, might have been expected.

[2] The Jews termed it פלטנוס (Ber. R. 81). *Frankel* ridicules the derivation of

Reland (de Monte Garis iii., apud *Ugolini*, Thes. vol. vii. pp. 717, 718), who explains the name as πελεθοῦ ναός, *stercoreum delubrum*, corresponding to the Samaritan designation of the Temple at Jerusalem as בית קלקלתא *œdes stercorea*. *Frankel* himself (Paläst. Ex. p. 248) derives the expression from πλάτανος with reference to Gen. xxxv. 4. But this seems quite untenable. May not the term be a compound of פלט, *to spit out*, and ναός?

[3] Comp. *Herzfeld*, u. s. ii. p. 120.

BOOK
III

ᵃ According to *Jos.* Ant. xii. 5. 5, ἐλλύνιος; according to 2 Macc. vi. 2 2, ξένιος

ᵇ Between 113 and 105

ᶜ Ant xiv. 5. 3

ᵈ Ant. xx. 8. 5; Jewish War i. 21. 2

ᵉ Ant. xviii. 4. 2

ᶠ See specially War iii. 3. 4, 5

ᵍ For ex. Baba B. iii. 2

ʰ For ex. Jer. Chag. iii. 4

ⁱ Gitt. vii. 7

ᵏ War iii. 3. 4, 5

nection with Israel, and dedicating their temple to Jupiter.ᵃ In the contest between Syria and the Maccabees which followed, the Samaritans, as might be expected, took the part of the former. In 130 B.C. John Hyrcanus destroyed the Temple on Mount Gerizim,[1] which was never rebuilt. The city of Samaria was taken several years afterwardsᵇ[2] by the sons of Hyrcanus (Antigonus and Aristobulus), after a year's siege, and the successive defeat of Syrian and Egyptian armies of relief. Although the city was now not only destroyed, but actually laid under water to complete its ruin, it was rebuilt by Gabinius shortly before our era,ᶜ and greatly enlarged and beautified by Herod, who called it *Sebaste* in honour of Augustus, to whom he reared a magnificent temple.ᵈ Under Roman rule the city enjoyed great privileges—had even a Senate of its own.ᵉ By one of those striking coincidences which mark the Rule of God in history, it was the accusation brought against him by that Samaritan Senate which led to the deposition of Pilate. By the side of Samaria, or Sebaste, we have already marked as perhaps more important, and as the religious capital, the ancient Shechem, which, in honour of the Imperial family of Rome, ultimately obtained the name of Flavia Neapolis, which has survived in the modern Nablus. It is interesting to notice that the Samaritans also had colonies, although not to the same extent as the Jews. Among them we may name those of Alexandria, Damascus, in Babylonia, and even some by the shores of the Red Sea.[3]

Although not only in the New Testament, but in 1 Macc. x. 30, and in the writings of Josephus,ᶠ Western Palestine is divided into the provinces of Judæa, Samaria, and Galilee, the Rabbis, whose ideas were shaped by the observances of Judaism, ignore this division. For them Palestine consisted only of Judæa, Peræa, and Galilee.ᵍ Samaria appears merely as a strip intervening between Judæa and Galilee, being 'the land of the Cuthæans.'ʰ Nevertheless, it was not regarded like heathen lands, but pronounced clean. Both the Mishnahⁱ and Josephusᵏ mark *Anuath* (כפר עותנאי) as the southern boundary of Samaria (towards Judæa). Northward it extended to

---

[1] It is very probable that the date 25 Marcheshvan (Nov.) in the Megill. Taan. refers to the capture of Samaria. Both the Talmud (Jer. Sot. ix. 14; Sot. 33 *a*) and *Josephus* (Ant. xiii. 10. 7) refers to a *Bath Qol* announcing this victory to Hyrcanus while he ministered in the Sanctuary at Jerusalem.

[2] Not a few of the events of Herod's

life were connected with Samaria. There he married the beautiful and ill-fated Mariamme (Ant. xiv. 12. 1); and there, thirty years later, her two sons were strangled by order of the jealous tyrant (Ant. xvi. 11. 2–7).

[3] Comp. *Nutt*, Samar. Hist. p. 26, note, and the authorities there quoted.

Ginæa (the ancient En-Gannim) on the south side of the plain of Jezreel; on the east it was bounded by the Jordan; and on the west by the plain of Sharon, which was reckoned as belonging to Judæa. Thus it occupied the ancient territories of Manasseh and Ephraim, and extended about forty-eight miles (north and south) by forty (east and west). In aspect and climate it resembled Judæa, only that the scenery was more beautiful and the soil more fertile. The political enmity and religious separation between the Jews and Samaritans account for their mutual jealousy. On all public occasions the Samaritans took the part hostile to the Jews, while they seized every opportunity of injuring and insulting them. Thus, in the time of Antiochus III. they sold many Jews into slavery.[a] Afterwards they sought to mislead the Jews at a distance, to whom the beginning of every month (so important in the Jewish festive arrangements) was intimated by beacon fires, by kindling spurious signals.[b] We also read that they tried to desecrate the Temple on the eve of the Passover;[c] and that they waylaid and killed pilgrims on their road to Jerusalem.[d] The Jews retaliated by treating the Samaritans with every mark of contempt; by accusing them of falsehood, folly, and irreligion; and, what they felt most keenly, by disowning them as of the same race or religion, and this in the most offensive terms of assumed superiority and self-righteous fanaticism.

In view of these relations, we almost wonder at the candour and moderation occasionally displayed towards the Samaritans in Jewish writings. These statements are of practical importance in this history, since elaborate attempts have been made to show what articles of food the disciples of Jesus might have bought in Samaria, in ignorance that almost all would have been lawful. Our inquiry here is, however, somewhat complicated by the circumstance that in Rabbinic writings, as at present existing, the term Samaritans (Cuthim[1]) has, to avoid the censorship of the press, been often purposely substituted for 'Sadducees,' or 'heretics,' i.e. Christians. Thus, when[e] the Samaritans are charged with denying in their books that the Resurrection can be proved from the Pentateuch, the real reference is supposed to have been to Sadducean or Christian heretical writings. Indeed, the terms Samaritans, Sadducees, and heretics are used so interchangeably, that a careful inquiry is necessary, to show in each case which of them is really meant. Still more frequent is the use

CHAP. VII

[a] Ant. xii. 4. 1

[b] Rosh haSh. ii. 2

[c] Ant. xviii. 2. 2

[d] Ant. xx. 6. 1

[e] In Sanh. 90 b

---

[1] The more exact translation would, of course, be Kuthim, but I have written Cuthim on account of the reference to 2 Kings xxvii. 24. Indeed, for various reasons, it is impossible always to adopt a uniform or exact system of transliteration.

[2] Thus in Ber. 57 b Cuthæan is evi-

BOOK
III

of the term 'Samaritan' (כותי) for 'stranger' (נכרי), the latter, and not strictly Samaritan descent being meant.[1] The popular interchange of these terms casts light on the designation of the Samaritan as 'a stranger' by our Lord in St. Luke xvii. 18.

In general it may be said that, while on certain points Jewish opinion remained always the same, the judgment passed on the Samaritans, and especially as to intercourse with them, varied, according as they showed more or less active hostility towards the Jews. Thus the Son of Sirach would correctly express the feeling of contempt and dislike, when he characterised the Samaritans as 'the foolish people' which his 'heart abhorred.'[a]   The same sentiment appears in early Christian Pseudepigraphic and in Rabbinic writings. In the so-called 'Testament of the Twelve Patriarchs' (which probably dates from the beginning of the second century), 'Sichem' is the City of Fools, derided by all men.[b]   It was only natural, that Jews should be forbidden to respond by an *Amen* to the benediction of Samaritans, at any rate till they were sure it had been correctly spoken,[c] since they were neither in practice nor in theory regarded as co-religionists.[d][2]   Yet they were not treated as heathens, and their land, their springs, baths, houses, and roads were declared clean.[e]

The question was discussed, whether or not they were to be considered 'lion-proselytes' (from fear of the lions), or as genuine converts;[f] and, again, whether or not they were to be regarded as heathens.[g]   This, and the circumstance that different teachers at different times gave directly opposite replies to these questions, proves that there was no settled principle on the subject, but that opinions varied according to the national bearing of the Samaritans.   Thus, we are expressly told,[h] that at one time both their testimony and their religious orthodoxy were more credited than at others, and they are not treated as Gentiles, but placed on the same level as an ignorant Jew.   A marked difference of opinion here prevails.   The older tradition, as represented by Simon the son of Gamaliel, regards them as in every respect like Israelites;[i] whilst later authority (Rabbi

[a] Ecclus. 1. 25, 26

[b] Test. Levi. vii.

[c] Ber. viii. 8

[d] Sheq. i. 5

[e] Jer. Abhod. Z. v. 4, p. 44 d

[f] Sanh. 85 b; Chull. 3 b; Kidd, 75 b

[g] Jer. Sheq. 46 b

[h] Jer. Demai iii. 4

[i] Comp. also Jer. Dem. vi. 11; Jer. Ber. vii. 1; and Jer. Keth. 27 a

dently used for 'idolator.' An instance of the Jewish use of the term Cuthæan for Christian occurs in Ber. R. 64, where the Imperial permission to rebuild the Temple of Jerusalem is said to have been frustrated by Cuthæan intrigue, the text here evidently referring by that expression not to Samaritans, but to Christians, however silly the charge against them. See *Joël*, Blicke in d. Relig. Gesch. p. 17.   Comp. also *Frankel* u. s. p. 244;

Jost, Gesch. d. Judenth. i. p. 49, note 2.
    [1] *Frankel* quotes as a notable instance of it, Ber. viii. 8, and refers in proof to the Jerus. Talmud on this Mishnah. But, for reasons soon to be explained, I am not prepared in this instance to adopt his view.
    [2] As in the case of heathens, neither Temple-tribute, nor any other than free-will and votive offerings were received from them.

Jehuda the Holy) would have them considered and treated as heathens. Again, it is expressly stated in the Babylon Talmud,[a] that the Samaritans observed the letter of the Pentateuch, while one authority adds, that in that which they observed they were more strict than the Jews themselves.[b] Of this, indeed, there is evidence as regards several ordinances. On the other hand, later authorities again reproach them with falsification of the Pentateuch, charge them with worshipping a dove,[c] and even when, on further inquiry, they absolve them from this accusation, ascribe their excessive veneration for Mount Gerizim to the circumstance that they worshipped the idols which Jacob had buried under the oak at Shechem. To the same hatred, caused by national persecution, we must impute such expressions as[d] that he, whose hospitality receives a foreigner, has himself to blame if his children have to go into captivity.

The expression, 'the Jews have no dealings with the Samaritans,'[e] finds its exact counterpart[f] in this: 'May I never set eyes on a Samaritan;' or else, 'May I never be thrown into company with him!' A Rabbi in Cæsarea explains, as the cause of these changes of opinion, that formerly the Samaritans had been observant of the Law, which they no longer were; a statement repeated in another form to the effect, that their observance of it lasted as long as they were in their own cities.[g] Matters proceeded so far, that they were entirely excluded from fellowship.[h] The extreme limit of this direction,[1] if, indeed, the statement applies to the Samaritans,[i] is marked by the declaration, that to partake of their bread was like eating swine's flesh. This is further improved upon in a later Rabbinic work,[k] which gives a detailed story of how the Samaritans had conspired against Ezra and Nehemiah, and the ban been laid upon them, so that now not only was all intercourse with them forbidden, but their bread declared like swine's flesh; proselytes were not to be received from them; nor would they have part in the Resurrection of the dead.[2] But there is a great difference between all this extravagance and the opinions prevailing at the time of Jesus. Even in the Rabbinic tractate on the Samaritans[m] it is admitted, that in most of their usages they resembled Israelites, and many rights and privileges are conceded to them, from which a heathen would have been excluded. They are to be 'cred-

CHAP.
VII

[a] Ber. 47 b

[b] Comp. Chull. 4 a

[c] Chull. 6 a

[d] Sanh. 104 a

[e] St. John iv. 9
[f] Megill. 2

[g] Jer. Abhod. Zar. v. 4
[h] Chull. 6 a
[i] Shebhyith viii. 10

[k] Yalkut ii. p. 36 d

[m] Masse-cheth Kuthim, in Kirchheim, Septem Libri parvi Talmudici, pp. 31-36

[1] The expression literally applies to idolaters.

[2] In Jer. Kil. ix. 4, p. 32 c (middle) the question of the Resurrection is discussed, when it is said that the Samaritan inhabitants of Palestine, far from enjoying the blessings of that period, would be made into sections (or, made like cloth [?]), and then burnt up.

BOOK
III

d Chull. 3 *b*

b Jer.
Abhod.
Zar. v. 4

c Gitt. 10 *b*;
Nidd. 33 *b*

d Siphrè on
Numb. xv.
31; Sanh.
90 *b*

ited' on many points; their meat is declared clean, if an Israelite had witnessed its killing, or a Samaritan ate of it;[a] their bread[1] and, under certain conditions, even their wine, are allowed; and the final prospect is held out of their reception into the Synagogue, when they shall have given up their faith in Mount Gerizim, and acknowledged Jerusalem and the Resurrection of the dead. But Jewish toleration went even further. At the time of Christ all their food was declared lawful.[b] There could, therefore, be no difficulty as regarded the purchase of victuals on the part of the disciples of Jesus.

It has already been stated, that most of the peculiar doctrines of the Samaritans were derived from Jewish sources. As might be expected, their tendency was Sadducean rather than Pharisaic.[2] Nevertheless, Samaritan 'sages' are referred to.[c] But it is difficult to form any decided opinion about the doctrinal views of the sect, partly from the comparative lateness of their literature, and partly because the Rabbinist charges against them cannot be absolutely trusted. It seems at least doubtful, whether they really denied the Resurrection, as asserted by the Rabbis,[d] from whom the Fathers have copied the charge.[3] Certainly, they hold that doctrine at present. They strongly believed in the Unity of God; they held the doctrine of Angels and devils;[4] they received the Pentateuch as of sole Divine authority;[5] they regarded Mount Gerizim as the place chosen of God, maintaining that it alone had not been covered by the flood, as the Jews asserted of Mount Moriah; they were most strict and zealous in what of Biblical or traditional Law they

[1] In Jer. Orlah ii. 7 the question is discussed, how long after the Passover it is not lawful to use bread baked by Samaritans, showing that ordinarily it was lawful.

[2] The doctrinal views, the festive observances, and the literature of the Samaritans of a later period, cannot be discussed in this place. For further information we refer to the following:—The Articles in *Smith's* Dictionary of the Bible, in *Winer's* Bibl. Real-Wörterb., and especially in *Herzog's* Real-Encykl. (by *Petermann*); to *Juynboll*, Comment. in Hist. Gentis Samarit.; *Jost*, Gesch. des Judenth.; *Herzfeld*, Gesch. des jüdisch. Volkes, *passim*; *Frankel*, Einfluss der Paläst. Exeg. pp. 237–254; *Nutt*, Sketch of Samaritan History, &c.

[3] *Epiphanius*, Hæres. ix., xiv.; *Leontius*, De Sectis viii.; *Gregory the Great*, Moral. i. xv. *Grimm* (Die Samariter &c., pp. 91 &c.), not only strongly defends

the position of the Fathers, but holds that the Samaritans did not even believe in the immortality of the soul, and maintained that the world was eternal. The 'Samaritan Chronicle' dates from the thirteenth century, but *Grimm* maintains that it embodies the earlier views of that people (u. s. p. 107).

[4] This seems inconsistent with their disbelief of the Resurrection, and also casts doubt on the patristic testimony about them, since *Leontius* falsely accuses them of rejecting the doctrine of Angels. *Epiphanius*, on the other hand, attributes to them belief in Angels. *Reland* maintains, that they regarded the Angels as merely 'powers'—a sort of impersonal abstractions; *Grimm* thinks there were two sects of Samaritans—one believing, the other disbelieving, in Angels.

[5] For their horrible distortion of later Jewish Biblical history, see *Grimm* (u. s.), p. 107.

received; and lastly, and most important of all, they looked for the coming of a Messiah, in Whom the promise would be fulfilled, that the Lord God would raise up a Prophet from the midst of them, like unto Moses, in Whom his words were to be, and unto Whom they should hearken.[a][1] Thus, while, in some respects, access to them would be more difficult than to His own countrymen, yet in others Jesus would find there a soil better prepared for the Divine Seed, or, at least, less encumbered by the thistles and tares of traditionalism and Pharisaic bigotry.

CHAP.
VII

a Deut.
xviii. 15, 18

[1] They expected that this Messiah would finally convert all nations to Samaritanism (*Grimm*, p. 99). But there is no historic ground for the view of Mr. *Nutt* (Sketch of Samar. Hist. pp. 40, 69) that the idea of a Messiah the Son of Joseph, which holds so large a place in later Rabbinic theology, was of Samaritan origin.

CHAPTER VIII.

JESUS AT THE WELL OF SYCHAR.

(St. John iv. 1–42.)

BOOK III

THERE is not a district in 'the Land of Promise' which presents a scene more fair or rich than the plain of Samaria (the modern *El Mukhna*). As we stand on the summit of the ridge, on the way from Shiloh, the eye travels over the wide sweep, extending more than seven miles northward, till it rests on the twin heights of Gerizim and Ebal, which enclose the valley of Shechem. Following the straight olive-shaded road from the south, to where a spur of Gerizim, jutting south-east, forms the Vale of Shechem, we stand by that 'Well of Jacob' to which so many sacred memories attach. Here, in 'the parcel of ground' afterwards given to Joseph,[1] which Jacob had bought from the people of the land, the patriarch had, at great labour and cost, sunk a well through the limestone rock. At present it is partially filled with rubbish and stones, but originally it must have gone down about 150 feet.[2] As the whole district abounds in springs, the object of the patriarch must have been to avoid occasion of strife with the Amorite herdsmen around. That well marks the boundary of the Great Plain, or rather its extensions bear other names. To the left (westwards), between Gerizim (on the south) and Ebal (on the north), winds the valley of olive-clad Shechem, the modern Nablus, though that town is not in view from the Well of Sychar. Still higher up the same valley, the mud hovels of

---

[1] The reference here is to Gen. xlviii. 22. *Wünsche*, indeed, objects that this application of the passage is inaccurate, and contrary to universal Rabbinic tradition. But in this, as in other instances, it is not the Gospel, but rather Dr. *Wünsche*, who is inaccurate. If the reader will refer to *Geiger's* Urschr. p. 80, he will find *proof* that the Evangelist's rendering of Gen. xlviii. 22 *was* in accordance with ancient Rabbinic tradition, which was only afterwards altered for anti-Samaritan purposes. On the other

[2] The present depth of the well is about seventy-five feet. Most travellers have given more or less pictorial accounts of Jacob's Well. We refer here especially to Mr. *King's* Report (Quarterly Stat. of the Pal. Explor. Fund, Ap. 1879), although it contains the strange mistake that Jesus had that day come from Jerusalem, and reached Jacob's Well by midday.

hand, this may be regarded as another undesigned proof of the Johannine authorship of the Fourth Gospel.

Sebastiyeh mark the site of ancient Samaria, the magnificent Sebaste of Herod. North of the entrance to the Vale of Shechem rises Mount Ebal, which also forms. so to speak, the western wall of the northern extension of the Plain of Samaria. Here it bears the name of *El 'Askar*, from Askar, the ancient Sychar, which nestles at the foot of Ebal, at a distance of about two miles from Shechem. Similarly, the eastern extension of the plain bears the name of the Valley of Shalem, from the hamlet of that name, which probably occupies the site of the ancient city before which Jacob pitched his tent on his return to Canaan.[a]

At 'the Well of Jacob' which, for our present purpose, may be regarded as the centre of the scene, several ancient Roman roads meet and part. That southward, to which reference has already been made, leads close by Shiloh to Jerusalem; that westward traverses the vale of Shechem; that northward brings us to the ancient Sychar, only about half a mile from 'the Well.' Eastward there are two ancient Roman roads: one winds south-east, till it merges in the main road; the other strikes first due east, and then descends in a south-easterly direction through *Wady Farâh*, which debouches into the Jordan. We can trace it as it crosses the waters of that Wâdy, and we infer, that its immediate neighbourhood must have been the scene where Jesus had taught, and His disciples baptized. It is still in Judæa, and yet sufficiently removed from Jerusalem; and the Wâdy is so full of springs that one spot near it actually bears the name of *'Ainûn*, 'springs,' like the ancient *Ænon*. But, from the spot which we have indicated, it is about twenty miles, across a somewhat difficult country to Jacob's Well. It would be a long and toilsome day's journey thither on a summer day, and we can understand how, at its end, Jesus would rest weary on the low parapet which enclosed the Well, while His disciples went to buy the necessary provisions in the neighbouring Sychar.

And it was, as we judge, the evening of a day in early summer,[1] when Jesus, accompanied by the small band which formed His disciples,[2] emerged into the rich Plain of Samaria. Far as the eye could sweep, 'the fields' were 'already white unto the harvest.'

[a] Gen. xxxiii. 18 19

---

[1] For 'the location of Sychar,' and the vindication of the view that the event took place at the beginning of the wheat harvest, or about the middle of May, see Appendix XV. The question is of considerable importance.

[2] From the silence of the Synoptists, and the general designation of the disciples without naming them, *Caspari* concludes that only John, and perhaps Nathanael, but none of the other apostles, had accompanied Jesus on this journey (Chronol. Geogr. Einl. p. 104).

They had reached 'the Well of Jacob.' There Jesus waited, while the others went to Sychar on their work of ministry. Probably John remained with the Master. They would scarcely have left Him alone, especially in that place; and the whole narrative reads like that of one who had been present at what passed.[1] More than any other, perhaps, in the Fourth Gospel, it bears the mark, not only of Judæan, but of contemporary authorship. It seems utterly incompatible with the modern theory of its Ephesian origin at the end of the second century. The location of the scene, not in Sebaste or Shechem, but at Sychar,[2] which in the fourth century at least had so entirely ceased to be Samaritan, that it had become the home of some celebrated Rabbis;[3] the intimate knowledge of Samaritan and Jewish relations, which at the time of Christ allowed the purchase of food, but would certainly not have conceded it two centuries later; even the introduction of such a statement as 'Salvation is of the Jews,' wholly inconsistent with the supposed scope of an Ephesian Gospel—these are only some of the facts which will occur to the student of that period, as bearing unsolicited testimony to the date and nationality of the writer.

Indeed, there is such minuteness of detail about the narrative, and with it such charm of simplicity, affectionateness, reverence, and depth of spiritual insight, as to carry not only the conviction of its truthfulness, but almost instinctively to suggest to us 'the beloved disciple' as its witness. Already he had taken the place nearest to Jesus and saw and spake as none other of the disciples. Jesus weary, and resting while the disciples go to buy food, is not an Ephesian, but a truly Evangelic presentation of the Christ in His human weakness and want.

All around would awaken in the Divinely-attuned soul of the Divine Redeemer the thoughts which so soon afterwards found appropriate words and deeds. He is sitting by Jacob's Well—the very well which the ancestor of Israel had digged, and left as a memorial of his first and symbolic possession of the land. Yet this was also the scene of Israel's first rebellion against God's order, against the Davidic line and the Temple. And now Christ is here, among those who are not of Israel, and who persecute it. Surely this, of all others, would be

---

[1] *Caspari* (u. s. p. 103) thinks that John only related that of which he himself was an eyewitness, except, perhaps, in ch. xviii. 33, &c.

[2] It is very characteristic when *Schenkel*, in ignorance of the fact that Sychar is mentioned by the Rabbis, argues that the use of the name Sychar for Shechem affords evidence that the Fourth Gospel is of Gentile-Christian origin.

[3] See Appendix XV.

the place where the Son of David, cast out of Jerusalem and the CHAP.
Temple, would think of the breach, and of what alone could heal it. VIII
He is hungry, and those fields are white to the harvest; yet far more
hungering for that spiritual harvest which is the food of His soul.
Over against Him, sheer up 800 feet, rises Mount Gerizim, with the
ruins of the Samaritan rival Temple on it; just as far behind Him,
already overhung by the dark cloud of judgment, are that Temple and
City which knew not the day of their visitation. The one inquiring
woman, and she a Samaritan, and the few only partially comprehending and much misunderstanding disciples; their inward thinking that
for the spiritual harvest it was but seed-time, and the reaping yet
'four months distant,' while in reality, as even their eyes might see if
they but lifted them, the fields were white unto the harvest: all this,
and much more, forms a unique background to the picture of this
narrative.

To take another view of the varying lights on that picture: Jesus
weary and thirsty by Jacob's Well, and the water of life which was to
spring from, and by that Well, with its unfailing supply and its unending refreshment! The spiritual in all this bears deepest symbolic
analogy to the outward—yet with such contrasts also, as the woman
giving to Christ the one, He to her the other; she unconsciously beginning to learn, He unintendingly (for He had not even entered
Sychar) beginning to teach, and that, what He could not yet teach in
Judæa, scarcely even to His own disciples; then the complete change
in the woman, and the misapprehension[a] and non-reception[b] of the [a] St. John
disciples—and over it all the weary form of the Man Jesus, opening iv. 33
as the Divine Christ the well of everlasting life, the God-Man *satisfied*
with the meat of doing the Will, and finishing the Work, of Him
that sent Him: such are some of the thoughts suggested by the
scene.

And still others rise, as we think of the connection in the narrative of St. John of this with what preceded and with what follows.
It almost seems as if that Gospel were constructed in cycles, each
beginning, or at least connected, with Jerusalem, and leading up to a
grand climax. Thus, the first cycle[b] might be called that of *purifi-* [b] ii. 13–iv.
cation : first, that of the Temple; then, inward purification by the 54
Baptism from above; next, the symbolic Baptism of water; lastly, the
real water of life given by Jesus; and the climax—Jesus the Restorer
of life to them that believe. Similarly, the second cycle,[c] beginning [c] v.–vi. 3
with the idea of water in its symbolic application to real worship and
life from Jesus, would carry us a stage further; and so onward through-

BOOK
III

out the Gospel. Along with this we may note, as another peculiarity of the Fourth Gospel, that it seems arranged according to this definite plan of grouping together in each instance the *work* of Christ, as followed by the illustrative *word* of Christ. Thus the fourth would, both externally and internally, be the pre-eminently *Judæan* Gospel, characterised by cyclical *order*, illustrative *conjunction of work and word*, and progressively leading up to the grand climax of Christ's last discourses, and finally of His Death and Resurrection, with the teaching that flows from the one and the other.

It was about six o'clock in the evening,[1] when the travel-stained pilgrims reached that ' parcel of ground ' which, according to ancient Jewish tradition, Jacob had given to his son Joseph.[2] Here (as already stated) by the ' Well of Jacob ' where the three roads—south, to Shechem, and to Sychar (Askar)—meet and part, Jesus sat down, while the disciples (probably with the exception of John) went on to the closely adjoining little town of Sychar to buy food. Even this latter circumstance marks that it was evening, since noon was not the time either for the sale of provisions, nor for their purchase by travellers. Once more it is when the true Humanity of Jesus is set before us, in the weakness of His hunger and weariness,[3] that the glory of His Divine Personality suddenly shines through it. This time it was a poor, ignorant Samaritan woman,[4] who came, not for any religious purpose—indeed, to whom religious thought, except within her own very narrow circle, was almost unintelligible—who became the occasion of it. She had come—like so many of us, who find the pearl in the field which we occupy in the business of everyday-life—on humble, ordinary duty and work. Men call it *common* ; but there is nothing common and unclean that God has sanctified by making use of it, or which His Presence and teaching may transform into a vision from heaven.

[1] We have already expressed our belief, that in the Fourth Gospel time is reckoned not according to the Jewish mode, but according to the Roman civil day, from midnight to midnight. For a full discussion and proof of this, with notice of objections, see *McLellan's* New Test. vol. i. pp. 737–743. It must surely be a *lapsus* when at p. 288 (note *o*), the same author seems to assume the contrary. *Meyer* objects, that, if it had been 6 P.M., there would not have been time for the after-events recorded. But they could easily find a place in the delicious cool of a summer's evening, and both the coming up of the Samaritans (most unlikely at noon-time), and their invitation to Jesus ' to tarry ' with them (v. 40), are in favour of our view. Indeed, St. John xix. 14 renders it impossible to adopt the Jewish mode of reckoning.

[2] See a previous note on p. 404.

[3] *Godet* rightly asks what, in view of this, becomes of the supposed Docetism which, according to the Tübingen school, is one of the characteristics of the Fourth Gospel ?

[4] By which we are to understand a woman from the *country*, not the town of Samaria, a Samaritaness. The suggestion, that she resorted to Jacob's Well on account of its sanctity, scarcely requires refutation.

There was another well (the '*Ain 'Askar*), on the east side of the little town, and much nearer to Sychar than ' Jacob's Well; ' and to it probably the women of Sychar generally resorted. It should also be borne in mind, that in those days such work no longer de-volved, as in early times, on the matrons and maidens of fair degree, but on women in much humbler station. This Samaritaness may have chosen ' Jacob's Well,' perhaps, because she had been at work in the fields close by; or else, because her abode was nearer in that direction— for the *ancient* Sychar may have extended southward; perhaps, because, if her character was what seems implied in verse 18, the concourse of the more common women at the village-well of an evening might scarcely be a pleasant place of resort to one with her history. In any case, we may here mark those Providential leadings in our everyday life, to which we are so often almost as much spiritually indebted, as to grace itself; which, indeed, form part of the dispensation of grace. Perhaps we should note how, all unconsciously to her (as so often to us), poverty and sin sometimes bring to the well by which Jesus sits weary, when on His return from self-righteous Judæa.

But these are only symbols; the barest facts of the narrative are themselves sufficiently full of spiritual interest. Both to Jesus and to the woman, the meeting was unsought, Providential in the truest sense—God-brought. Reverently, so far as the Christ is concerned, we add, that both acted truly—according to what was in them. The request: ' Give Me to drink,' was natural on the part of the thirsty traveller, when the woman had come to draw water, and they who usually ministered to Him were away.ᵃ Even if He had not spoken, the Samaritaness would have recognised the Jew by His appearance[1] and dress, if, as seems likely, He wore the fringes on the border of His garment.[2] His speech would, by its pronunciation, place His nationality beyond doubt.[3] Any kindly address, conveying a request not absolutely necessary, would naturally surprise the woman; for, as

ᵃ ver. 8

---

[1] According to the testimony of travel-lers the Samaritans, with the exception of the High-Priestly family, have *not* the common, well-known type of Jewish face and feature.

[2] The ' fringes ' on the *Tallith* of the Samaritans are blue, while those worn by the Jews, whether on the *Arba Kanphoth* or the *Tallith*, are white. The Samaritans do not seem to have worn *phylacteries* (Menach. 42 *b*). But neither did many of the Jews of old—nor, I feel persuaded, our Lord (comp. *Jost*, Gesch. d. Judenth. vol. i. p. 60).

[3] There were, undoubtedly, marked differences of pronunciation between the Jews and the Samaritans. Without entering into details, it may be said, that they chiefly concern the vowel-sounds; and among consonants the *gutturals* (which are generally not pronounced), the *aspirates*, and the letter ע, which is not, as in Hebrew, either ש (pro-nounced *s*), or שׁ (pronounced *sh*), but is always pronounced as '*sh*.' In connection with this we may notice one of those instances, how a strange mistake comes ' by tradition' to be commonly received. It

the Evangelist explanatively adds: 'Jews have no dealings with Samaritans,'[1] or rather, as the expression implies, no needless, friendly, nor familiar intercourse with them—a statement true at all times. Besides, we must remember that this was an ignorant Samaritaness of the lower order. In the mind of such an one, two points would mainly stand out: that the Jews in their wicked pride would have no intercourse with them; and that Gerizim, not Jerusalem, as the Jews falsely asserted, was the place of rightful worship. It was, therefore, genuine surprise which expressed itself in the question: 'How is it, Thou, being a Jew, of me askest to drink?' It was the first lesson she learned, even before He taught her. Here was a Jew, not like ordinary Jews, not like what she had hitherto thought them: what was the cause of this difference?

Before we mark how the answer of Jesus met this very question, and so as to direct it to spiritual profit, another and more general reflection presses on our minds. Although Jesus may not have come to Sychar with the conscious purpose of that which ensued, yet, given the meeting with the Samaritan woman, what followed seems almost matter of necessity. For it is certain that the Christ, such as the Gospels describe Him, could not have been brought into contact with spiritual ignorance and want, any more than with physical distress, without offering it relief. It was, so to speak, a necessity, alike of His Mission and of His Nature (as the God-Man). In the language of another Gospel, 'power went out from Him;' and this, whether consciously sought, or unconsciously felt after in the stretching forth of the hands of the sightless or in the upward look of the speechless. The Incarnate Son of God could not but bring health and life amidst disease and death; the Saviour had come to seek and to save that which was lost.

And so it was, that the 'How is it?' of the Samaritan woman so soon, and so fully, found its answer. 'How is it?' In this, that He, Who had spoken to her, was not like what she thought and knew

---

has been asserted that, if Jesus had said to the woman: *Teni li lishtoth* ('Give me to drink'), a Samaritan would have pronounced it *listoth*, since the Samaritans pronounced the *sh* as *s*. But the reverse of this is the fact. The Samaritans pronounced the *s* ('*sin*') as *sh* ('*shin*')— and not the *sh* as *s*. The mistake arose from confounding the old Ephraimite (Judg. xii. 5, 6) with the Samaritan mode of pronouncing. The suggestion seems

first to have been made—though *very doubtfully*—by *Stier* (Reden Jesu, iv. p 134). Stier, however, at least rendered the words of Jesus: *Teni li lishtoth*. *Gode* (ad loc.) accepts Stier's suggestions, but renders the words: Teni li lish*ch*oth. Later writers have repeated this, only altering *lishchoth* into lish*k*oth.

[1] The article is wanting in the original.

of the Jews. He was what Israel was intended to have become to mankind; what it was the final object of Israel to have been. In Him was God's gift to mankind. Had she but known it, the present relation between them would have been reversed; the Well of Jacob would have been a symbol, yet but a symbol, of the living water, which she would have asked and He given. As always, the seen is to Christ the emblem of the unseen and spiritual; Nature, that in and through which, in manifold and divers colouring, He ever sees the supernatural, even as the light lies in varying hues on the mountain, or glows in changeful colouring on the edge of the horizon. A view this of all things existent, which Hellenism, even in its sublimest poetic conception of creation as the impress of heavenly archetypes, has only materialised and reserved. But to Jesus it all pointed upward, because the God of Nature was the God of Grace, the One Living and True God in Whom all matter and spirit lives, Whose world is one in design, workmanship, and purpose. And so nature was but the echo of God's heard Voice, which ever, to all and in all, speaks the same, if there be but listening ears. And so He would have it speak to men in parables, that, to them who see, it might be the Jacob's ladder leading from earth to heaven, while they, whose sight and hearing are bound in the sleep of heart-hardening, would see but not perceive, and hear but not understand.

It was with the ignorant woman of Sychar, as it had been with the learned 'Master in Israel.' As Nicodemus had seen, and yet not seen, so this Samaritaness. In the birth of which Jesus spoke, *he* had failed to apprehend the 'from above' and ' of the Spirit; ' *she* now the thought suggested by the contrast between the cistern in the limerock and the well of living water. The 'How can these things be ? ' of Nicodemus finds its parallel in the bewilderment of the woman. Jesus had nothing wherewith to draw from the deep well. Whence, then, the 'living water' ? To outward appearance there was a physical impossibility. This was one aspect of it. And yet, as Nicodemus' question not only similarly pointed to a physical impossibility, but also indicated dim searching after higher meaning and spiritual reality, so that of the woman: 'No ! art Thou greater than our father Jacob ? ' who, at such labour, had dug this well, finding no other means than this of supplying his own wants and those of his descendants. Nor did the answer of Jesus now differ in spirit from that which He had given to the Rabbi of Jerusalem, though it lacked the rebuke, designed to show how thoroughly the religious system, of

BOOK
III

which Nicodemus was a teacher, failed in its highest object. But to this woman His answer must be much simpler and plainer than to the Rabbi. And yet, if it be Divine teaching, it cannot be quite plain, but must contain that which will point upward, and lead to further inquiry. And so the Divine Teacher explained, not only the difference between ordinary water and that of which He had spoken, but in a manner to bring her to the threshold of still higher truth. It was not water like that of Jacob's Well which He would give, but 'living water.' In the Old Testament a perennial *spring* had, in figurative language, been thus designated,[a] in significant contrast to water accumulated in a cistern.[b] But there was more than this: it was water which for ever quenched the thirst, by meeting all the inward wants of the soul; water also, which, in him who had drunk of it, became a well, not merely quenching the thirst on this side time, but 'springing up into everlasting life.' It was not only the meeting of wants felt, but a new life, and that not essentially different, but the same as that of the future, and merging in it.

[a] Gen. xxvi.
19; Lev.
xiv. 5
[b] Jer. ii. 13

The question has sometimes been asked, to what Jesus referred by that well of living water springing up into everlasting life. Of the various strange answers given, that, surely, is almost the worst, which would apply it to the doctrine of Jesus, supporting such explanation by a reference to Rabbinic sayings in which doctrine is compared to 'water.' This is one of those not unfrequent instances in which Rabbinic references mislead rather than lead, being insufficiently known, imperfectly understood, or misapplied. It is quite true, that in many passages the teaching of the Rabbis is compared to *water*,[1] but never to a 'well of water springing up.' The difference is very great. For it is the boast of Rabbinism, that its disciples drink of the waters of their teachers; chief merit lies in receptiveness, not spontaneity, and higher praise cannot be given than that of being 'a well-plastered cistern, which lets not out a drop of water,'[c] and in that sense to 'a spring whose waters ever grow stronger.' But this is quite the opposite of what our Lord teaches. For, it is only true of what man can give when we read this (in Ecclus. xxiv. 21): 'They that drink me shall yet be thirsty.'[2] More closely related to the words of Christ

[c] Ab. ii. 9

---

[1] Those who wish to see the well-worn Rabbinic references will find them in *Lightfoot* and *Schöttgen* ad loc.

[2] There is much spurious religious sentiment which, in contravention to our Lord's saving, delights in such expressions as that of *St. Bernard of Clairvaux* (followed by so many modern hymnologists):

'Qui Te gustant esuriunt,
Qui bibunt adhuc sitiunt.'
(Ap. *Daniel*, Thes. i. p. 223.)

is it, when we read[a] of a ' fountain of wisdom;' while, in the Targum on Cant. iv. 14, ' the words of the Law' are likened ' unto a well of living waters.' The same idea was carried perhaps even further, when, at the Feast of Tabernacles, amidst universal rejoicing, water from Siloam was poured from a golden pitcher on the altar, as emblem of the outpouring of the Holy Ghost.[1] But the saying of our Lord to the Samaritaness referred neither to His teaching, nor to the Holy Ghost, nor yet to faith, but to the gift of that new spiritual life in Him, of which faith is but the outcome.

If the humble, ignorant Samaritaness had formerly not seen, though she had imperfectly guessed, that there was a higher meaning in the words of Him Who spake to her, a like mixture of ill-apprehension and rising faith seems to underlie her request for this water, that she might thirst no more, neither again come thither to draw.[2] She now believes in the incredible; believes it, because of Him and in Him; believes, also, in a satisfaction through Him of outward wants, reaching up beyond this to the everlasting life. But all these elements are yet in strange confusion. Those who know how difficult it is to lodge any new idea in the mind of uneducated rustics in our own land, after all our advantages of civilising contact and education, will understand, how utterly at a loss this Samaritan countrywoman must have been to grasp the meaning of Jesus. But He taught, not as we teach. And thus He reached her heart in that dimly conscious longing which she expressed, though her intellect was incapable of distinguishing the new truth.

Surely, it is a strange mistake to find in her words[b] ' a touch of irony,' while, on the other hand, it seems an exaggeration to regard them simply as the cry of realised spiritual need. Though reluctantly, a somewhat similar conclusion is forced upon us with reference to the question of Jesus about the woman's husband, her reply, and the Saviour's rejoinder. It is difficult to suppose, that Christ asked the woman to call her husband with the primary object of awakening in her a sense of sin. This might follow, but the text gives no hint of it. Nor does anything in the bearing of the woman

The theology of this is not only sickly, but untrue and misleading.

[1] See ' The Temple and its Ministry,' pp. 241–243.

[2] I cannot bring myself to see, as some commentators, any extraordinary mark of rising reverence in the use by her of the word 'Sir' in vv. 11 and 15. It seems only natural in the circumstances.

a ver. 19
b ver. 29

c St. John i.
48, 49

d Comp
St. John
vi. 6

indicate any such effect; indeed, her reply [a] and her after-reference to it [b] rather imply the contrary. We do not even know for certain, whether the five previous husbands had died or divorced her, and, if the latter, with whom the blame lay, although not only the peculiar mode in which our Lord refers to it, but the present condition of the woman, seem to point to a sinful life in the past. In Judæa a course like hers would have been almost impossible; but we know too little of the social and moral condition of Samaria to judge of what might there be tolerated. On the other hand, we have abundant evidence that, when the Saviour so unexpectedly laid open to her a past, which He could only supernaturally have known, the conviction at once arose in her that He was a Prophet, just as in similar circumstances it had been forced upon Nathanael.[c] But to be a Prophet meant to a Samaritan that He was the Messiah, since they acknowledged none other after Moses. Whether or not the Messiah was known by the present Samaritan designation of Him as ' the Converter ' and ' the Returner ' (Restorer?), is of comparatively small importance, though, if we felt certain of this, the influence of the new conviction on the mind of the woman would appear even more clearly. In any case it was an immense, almost immeasurable, advance, when this Samaritan recognised in the stranger Jew, Who had first awakened within her higher thoughts, and pointed her to spiritual and eternal realities, the Messiah, and this on the strength of evidence the most powerfully convincing to a mind like hers: that of telling her, suddenly and startlingly, what He could not have known, except through higher than human means of information.

It is another, and much more difficult question, why Jesus should have asked for the presence of her husband. The objection, that to do so, knowing the while that she had had no husband, seems un-worthy of our Lord, may, indeed, be answered by the consideration, that such ' proving ' of those who were in His training was in accord-ance with His mode of teaching, leading upwards by a series of moral questions.[d] But perhaps a more simple explanation may offer even a better reply. It seems, as if the answer of verse 15 marked the utmost limit of the woman's comprehension. We can scarcely form an ade-quate notion of the narrowness of such a mental horizon as hers. This also explains, at least from one aspect, the reason of His speaking to her about His own Messiahship, and the worship of the future, in words far more plain than He used to His own disciples. None but the plainest statements could she grasp; and it is not unnatural to suppose that, having reached the utmost limits of which she was

capable, the Saviour now asked for her husband, in order that, through CHAP.
the introduction of another so near to her, the horizon might be VIII
enlarged. This is also substantially the view of some of the Fathers.[1]
But, if Christ was in earnest in asking for the presence of her husband,
it surely cannot be irreverent to add, that at that moment the peculiar
relationship between the man and the woman did not stand out before
His mind. Nor is there anything strange in this. The man was,
and was not, her husband. Nor can we be sure that, although unmarried, the relationship involved anything absolutely contrary to the
law; and to all intents the man might be known as her husband.
The woman's answer at once drew the attention of the Christ to this
aspect of her history, which immediately stood out fully before His
Divine knowledge. At the same time her words seemed like a
confession—perhaps we should say, a concession to the demands of
her own conscience, rather than a confession. Here, then, was the
required opportunity, both for carrying further truth to her mind, by
proving to her that He Who spake to her was a Prophet, and at the
same time for reaching her heart.

But whether or not this view of the history be taken, it is difficult
to understand, how any sober interpreter could see in the five
husbands of the woman either a symbolical, or a mythical, reference
to the five deities whom the ancestors of the Samaritans worshipped,[a] [a] 2 Kings
the spurious service of Jehovah representing the husband, yet no xvii. 24 &c.
husband, of the woman. It is not worth while discussing this
strange suggestion from any other than the mythical standpoint.
Those who regard the incidents of the Gospel-narratives as myths,
having their origin in Jewish ideas, are put to even greater straits
by the whole of this narrative than they who regard this Gospel as of
Ephesian authorship. We may put aside the general objections
raised by *Strauss*, since none of his successors has ventured seriously
to urge them. It is more important to notice, how signally the
author of the mythical theory has failed in suggesting any historical
basis for this 'myth.' To speak of meetings at the well, such as those
with Rebekah or Zipporah, is as much beside the question as an appeal
to Jewish expectancy of an omniscient Messiah. Out of these two
elements almost any story might be constructed. Again, to say that
this story of Jesus' success among the Samaritans was invented, in
order to vindicate the later activity of the Apostles among that
people, is simply to beg the whole question. In these straits so

[1] Comp. *Lücke*, Evang. Joh. vol. l. p. 588.

BOOK
III

distinguished a writer as *Keim*[1] has hazarded the statement: 'The meeting with the Samaritaness has, for every one who has eyes, only a symbolical meaning, by the side of which no historical fact exists.' An assertion this, which is perhaps best refuted by being simply quoted.[2] On the other hand, of all the myths likely to enter into Jewish imagination, the most unlikely would be one representing the Christ in familiar converse with a woman, and she a Samaritan, offering to her a well of water springing into everlasting life, and setting before her a spiritual worship of which Jerusalem was not the centre. Where both the Ephesian and the mythical theory so signally fail, shall we not fall back upon the natural explanation, borne out by the simplicity and naturalness of the narrative—that the story here related is real and true? And, if so, shall we not all the more thankfully gather its lessons?

The conviction, sudden but firm, that He Who had laid open the past to her was really a Prophet, *was already faith in Him*; and so the goal had been attained—not, perhaps, faith in His Messiahship, about which she might have only very vague notions, but *in Him*. And faith in the Christ, not in anything about Him, but in Himself, *has* eternal life. Such faith also leads to further inquiry and knowledge. As it has been the traditional practice to detect irony in this or that saying of the woman, or else to impute to her spiritual feelings far in advance of her possible experience, so, on the other hand, has her inquiry about the place of proper worship, Jerusalem or Gerizim, been unduly depreciated. It is indeed too true that those, whose consciences are touched by a presentation of their sin, often seek to turn the conversation into another and quasi-religious channel. But of neither the one nor the other is there evidence in the present case. Similarly, it is also only too true, that their one point of difference is, to narrow-minded sectarians, their all-in-all of religion. But in this instance we feel that the woman has no after-thought, no covert purpose in what she asks. All her life long she had heard that Gerizim was the mount of worship, the holy hill which the waters of the Flood had never covered,[3] and that the Jews were in deadly error.

---

[1] The references here are to *Strauss*, vol. i. pp. 510-519, and to *Keim* i. 1, p. 116.

[2] Meyer, *Komment.* vol. ii. p. 208, rightly remarks on the theory of *Baur*, *Hilgenfeld*, &c. According to them, the whole of this history is only a type of heathenism as receptive to faith, in contrast to Nicodemus, the type of Judaism

shutting itself up against faith. But. in that case why make the principal person a Samaritan, and not a heathen, and why attribute to her belief in a Messiah, which was entirely foreign to heathen ism?

[3] Curiously enough, several instances are related in Rabbinic writings in which Samaritans enter into dispute with

But here was an undoubted Prophet, and He a Jew. Were they then in error about the right place of worship, and what was she to think, and to do? To apply with such a question to Jesus was already to find the right solution, even although the question itself might indicate a lower mental and religious standpoint. It reminds us of the inquiry which the healed Naaman put to Elisha about the Temple of Rimmon, and of his request for a mule's burden of earth from the land of the True God, and for true worship.

Once more the Lord answers her question by leading her far beyond it—beyond all controversy: even on to the goal of all His teaching. So marvellously does He speak to the simple in heart. It is best here to sit at the feet of Jesus, and, realising the scene, to follow as His Finger points onwards and upwards. ' There cometh an hour, when neither in this mountain, nor yet in Jerusalem, ye shall worship the Father.' Words of sad warning, these; words of prophecy also, that already pointed to the higher solution in the worship of a common Father, which would be the worship neither of Jews nor of Samaritans, but of children. And yet there was truth in their present differences. ' Ye worship ye know not what: we worship what we know, since salvation is from out the Jews.'[1] The Samaritan was aimless worship, because it wanted the goal of all the Old Testament institutions, that Messiah ' Who was to be of the seed of David '[a]—for, of the Jews, ' as concerning the flesh,' was Christ to come.[b] But only of present interest could such distinctions be; for an hour would come, nay, already was, when the true worshippers would ' worship the Father in spirit and in truth, for the Father also seeketh such for His worshippers. Spirit is God '[2]—and only worship in spirit and in truth could be acceptable to such a God.

a Rom. i. 3
b Rom. ix. 5

Higher or more Christlike teaching than this could not be uttered. And she who heard, thus far understood it, that in the glorious pict-

---

Rabbis who pass by Mount Gerizim on their way to Jerusalem, to convince them that Gerizim was the proper place of worship. One instance may here be mentioned,.when a Samaritan maintained that Gerizim was the mount of blessing, because it was not covered by the Flood, quoting in proof Ezek. xxii. 24. The Rabbi replied, that if such had been the case, God would have told Noah to flee there, instead of making an ark. The Samaritan retorted, that this was done to try him. The Rabbi was silenced, but his muleteer appealed to Gen. vii. 19, according to which all the high hills under the heavens were covered, and so silenced the Samaritan. (Deb. R. 3; comp. Ber. R. 32.) On the other hand, it ought to be added, that in Ber. R. 33 the Mount of Olives is said not to have been covered by the Flood, and that Ezek. xxii. 24 is applied to this.

[1] He had formerly taught her the ' where,' and now teaches her the ' what,' of true worship.

[2] It is remarkable, that most of the alterations in the Samaritan Pentateuch are with the view of removing anthropomorphisms.

BOOK
III

ure, which was set before her, she saw the coming of the Kingdom of the Messiah. 'I know that Messiah cometh.[1] When He cometh, He will tell us all things.' It was then that, according to the need of that untutored woman, He told her plainly what in Judæa, and even by His disciples, would have been carnally misinterpreted and misapplied: that He was the Messiah. So true is it, that 'babes' can receive what often must remain long hidden 'from the wise and prudent.'

It was the crowning lesson of that day. Nothing more could be said; nothing more need be said. The disciples had returned from Sychar. That Jesus should converse with a woman, was so contrary to all Judæan notions of a Rabbi,[2] that they wondered. Yet, in their reverence for Him, they dared not ask any questions. Meanwhile the woman, forgetful of her errand, and only conscious of that new well-spring of life which had risen within her, had left the unfilled water-pot by the Well, and hurried into 'the City.' They were strange tidings which she brought; the very mode of her announcement affording evidence of their truth: 'Come, see a man who told me all that I have done. No—is this the Christ?' We are led to infer, that these strange tidings soon gathered many around her; that they questioned, and, as they ascertained from her the indisputable fact of His superhuman knowledge, believed on Him, so far as the

vv. 39, 40

woman could set Him before them as object of faith.[a] Under this impression 'they went out of the City, and came on their way to-

b ver. 30

wards Him.[b 3]

Meantime the disciples had urged the Master to eat of the food which they had brought. But His Soul was otherwise engaged. Thoughts were present of the glorious future, of a universal worship of the Father by those whom He had taught, and of which He had just seen such unexpected earnest. These mingled with feelings of pain at the spiritual dulness of those by whom He was surrounded, who could see in that conversation with a Samaritan woman nothing but a strange innovation on Rabbinic custom and dignity, and now

---

[1] The words 'which is called Christ' should be within brackets, and are the explanation of the writer.

[2] In the original, ver. 31 has it: 'Rabbi (not Master), eat.' Surely such an address to Christ is sufficiently anti-Ephesian. Readers know how thoroughly opposed to Jewish notions was any needless converse with a woman (comp. Ab. i. 5; Ber. 43 *b*; Kidd. 70 *a*; also Erub. 53 *b*). To instruct a woman in the Law was for-

bidden; comp. the story in Bemid. R. 9.

[3] Following the suggestion of Professor *Westcott*, I would thus give the real meaning of the original. It may save needless notes if I add, that where the rendering differs from the A.V. the change has been intentional, to bring out the meaning of the Greek; and that where words in the A.V. are omitted, it is because they are either spurious, or doubtful.

thought of nothing beyond the immediate errand on which they had gone to Sychar. Even His words of rebuke only made them wonder whether, unknown to them, some one had brought Him food. It was not the only, nor the last, instance of their dulness to spiritual realities.[a]

[a] St. Matt. xvi. 6, 7

Yet with Divine patience He bore with them: 'My meat is, that I may do the Will of Him that sent Me, and that I may accomplish (bring to a perfect end) His work.' To the disciples that work appeared still in the far future. To them it seemed as yet little more than seed-time; the green blade was only sprouting; the harvest of such a Messianic Kingdom as they expected was still months distant. To correct their mistake, the Divine Teacher, as so often, and as best adapted to His hearers, chose His illustration from what was visible around. To show their meaning more clearly, we venture to reverse the order of the sentences which Jesus spoke: 'Behold, I say unto you, lift up your eyes and look [observantly] at the fields, that they are white to the harvest. [But] do ye not say (viz. in your hearts[1]) that there are yet four months, and the harvest cometh?' The words will appear the more striking, if (with Professor Westcott) we bear in mind that, perhaps at that very moment, the Samaritans, coming to Him from Sychar, were appearing in sight.

But we also regard it as marking the time, when this conversation took place. Generally the words, 'yet four months, and then cometh the harvest,' are regarded either as a proverbial expression, or as indicating, that the Lord spake at the Well of Jacob four months before the harvest-time—that is, about the month of January, if the barley-harvest, or in February, if the wheat-harvest, was meant. The suggestion that it was a proverb may be dismissed, first, because there is not a trace of such a proverb, and then because, to give it even the scantiest meaning, it is necessary to supply: 'Between seed-time and harvest there are four months,' which is not true, since in Palestine about six months intervene between them. On the other hand, for reasons explained in another place,[2] we conclude, that it could not have been January or February, when Jesus was in Sychar. But why not reverse the common theory, and see in the second clause, introduced by the words, 'Behold! lift up your eyes and observe,' a mark of the time and circumstances; while the expression, 'Do ye not say, There are yet four months, and the

---

[1] This is a Hebraism.   [2] See them in Appendix XV.

BOOK
III

cometh harvest,' would be understood as parabolically spoken? Admittedly, one of the two clauses is a literal mark of time, and the other is spoken parabolically.   But there is no reason why the second clause may not mark the time, while on independent grounds we must conclude,[1] that Christ returned from Judæa to Galilee in the early summer.

Passing from this point, we notice how the Lord further unfolded His own lesson of present harvesting, and their inversion of what was sowing, and what reaping time.   'Already'[2] he that reaped received wages, and gathered fruit unto eternal life (which is the real reward of the Great Reaper, the seeing of the travail of His soul), so that in this instance the sower rejoiced equally[3] as the reaper.   And, in this respect, the otherwise cynical proverb, that one was the sower, another the reaper of his sowing, found a true application.   It was indeed so, that the servants of Christ were sent to reap what others had sown, and to enter into their labour.   One had sowed, another would reap.   And yet, as in this instance of the Samaritans, the sower would rejoice as well as the reaper; nay, both would rejoice together, in the gathered fruit unto eternal life.   And so the sowing in tears is on the spiritual field often mingled with the harvest of gladness, and to the spiritual view both are really one. 'Four months' do not intervene between them; so that, although one may sow and another reap, yet the sower seeth that harvest for which the harvester gets wages, and rejoices with him in the fruit which is gathered into the eternal storehouse.

It was as Christ had said.   The Samaritans, who believed 'because of the word' (speech) 'of the woman [what she said] as she testified' of the Christ, 'when they came' to that well, 'asked Him to abide with them.   And He abode there two days.   And many more believed because of His own word (speech, discourse), and said unto the woman: No longer because of thy speaking[4] do we believe.

---

[1] Comp. Appendix XV.

[2] We follow Canon *Westcott*, who, for reasons explained by him, joins the word 'already' to ver. 36, omitting the particle 'and.'

[3] It will be noticed that, in ver. 36, ἵνα has been translated 'so that,' the καί omitted, and ὁμοῦ rendered 'equally as.' Linguistically, no apology is required for these renderings. I, however, hesitate between this and the rendering: 'in order that the sower may rejoice along with the reaper.' But the translation in the text seems to agree better with what follows.   The whole passage is perhaps one of the most difficult, from the curtness and rapid transition of the sentences. The only apology which I can offer for proposing a new rendering and a new interpretation is, that those with which I am acquainted have not conveyed any distinct or connected meaning to my own mind.

[4] λαλιά, speech, talking.

For we ourselves have heard, and know, that this is truly the Saviour
of the world.'[1]

We know not what passed these two days.   Apparently no miracles
were wrought, but those of His Word only.   It was the deepest and
purest truth they learned, these simple men of simple faith, who had
not learned of man, but listened to His Word only.   The sower as
well as the reaper rejoiced, and rejoiced together.   Seed-time and
harvest mingled, when for themselves they knew and confessed, that
this was truly the Saviour of the world.

---

[1] We have omitted the words 'the   as faithfully as possible, so as to bring
Christ,' in ver. 42, as apparently spurious.   out the real meaning.
In general, the text has been rendered

CHAPTER IX.

THE SECOND VISIT TO CANA—CURE OF THE 'NOBLEMAN'S' SON AT CAPERNAUM.

(St. Matt. iv. 12; St. Mark i. 14; St. Luke iv. 14, 15; St. John iv. 43–54.)

BOOK
III

a St. John
iv. 45

b St. Matt.
iv. 12
c St. Mark
i. 14

d St. Luke
iv. 1t

e St. Matt.
iv. 17

f St. Mark i.
15

THE brief harvest in Samaria was, as Jesus had indicated to His disciples, in another sense also the beginning of sowing-time, or at least that when the green blade first appeared above ground. It formed the introduction to that Galilean ministry, when 'the Galileans received Him, having seen all the things that He did at Jerusalem at the Feast.'[a] Nay, in some respects, it was the real beginning of His Work also, which, viewed as separate and distinct, commenced when the Baptist was cast into prison.[1] Accordingly, this circumstance is specially marked by St. Matthew,[b] and by St. Mark,[c] while St. Luke, as if to give greater emphasis to it, abruptly connects this beginning of Christ's sole and separate Work with the history of the Temptation.[d] All that intervened seems to him but introductory, that 'beginning' which might be summed up by the words, 'in the power of the Spirit,' with which he describes His return to Galilee. In accordance with this view, Christ is presented as taking up the message of His Forerunner,[e] only with wider sweep, since, instead of adding to His announcement of the Kingdom of Heaven and call to repentance that to a Baptism of preparation, He called those who heard Him to 'believe the Gospel' which He brought them.[f]

But here also,—as Eusebius had already noted[2]—the Fourth Gospel, in its more comprehensive presentation of the Christ, as adding, not merely in the external succession of events, but in their internal connection, feature to feature in the portraiture of the Divine Redeemer, supplies the gap in the Synoptic narratives, which so often read only like brief historical summaries, with here and there special

---

[1] The history of the Baptist's imprisonment will be given in the sequel.

[2] The origin, authorship, and occasion of the Synoptic Gospels and of that by St. John, as well as their interrelation, is discussed in *Euseb.* Hist. Eccles. iii. 24, the discussion being the more important that Eusebius throughout appeals for his statements to 'the testimony of the ancients.'

episodes or reports of teaching inserted. For St. John not only tells us of that early Ministry, which the Synoptists designedly pass over, but while, like them, referring to the captivity of John as the occasion of Christ's withdrawal from the machinations of the Pharisaic party in Judæa, he joins this departure from Judæa with the return to Galilee by supplying, as connecting link, the brief stay in Samaria with its eventful results. St. John, also, alone supplies the first-recorded event of this Galilean ministry.[a] We therefore follow his guidance, simply noting that the various stages of this Galilean residence should be grouped as follows: Cana,[b] Nazareth,[c] and Capernaum, with general itineration from that centre.[d] The period occupied, by what is thus briefly indicated in the Gospels, was from early summer, say, the beginning of June, to the unnamed 'feast of the Jews.'[e] If it is objected, that the events seem too few for a period of about three months, the obvious answer is, that, during most of this time, Jesus was in great measure unattended, since the call of the Apostles[f] only took place *after* the 'unnamed feast;' that, indeed, they had probably returned to their homes and ordinary occupations when Jesus went to Nazareth,[g] and that therefore, not having themselves been eye-witnesses of what had passed, they confined themselves to a general summary. At the same time, St. Luke expressly marks that Jesus taught in the various Synagogues of Galilee,[h] and also that He made a longer stay in Capernaum.[i]

When Jesus returned to Galilee, it was in circumstances entirely different from those under which He had left it. As He Himself said,[k] there had, perhaps naturally, been prejudices connected with the humbleness of His upbringing, and the familarity engendered by knowledge[1] of His home-surroundings. These were overcome, when the Galileans had witnessed at the feast in Jerusalem, what He had done. Accordingly, they were now prepared to receive Him with the reverent attention which His Word claimed. We may conjecture, that it was partially for reasons such as these that He first bent His steps to Cana. The miracle, which had there been wrought,[m] would still further prepare the people for His preaching. Besides, this was the home of Nathanael, who had probably followed Him to Jerusalem, and in whose house a gladsome homage of welcome would now await Him. It was here that the second recorded miracle of His Galilean ministry was wrought, with what effect upon the whole district, may

[a] St. John iv. 43–54

[b] St. John iv. 45–54

[c] St. Luke iv. 16–30

[d] St. Matt. iv. 13–17; St. Mark 1. 14, 15; St. Luke iv. 31, 32

[e] St. John v. 1

[f] St. Matt. iv. 18–22 &c.

[g] St. Luke iv. 16

[h] St. Luke iv. 15

[i] St. Luke iv. 31; comp. St. Matt. iv. 13–16

[k] St. John iv. 44

[m] St. John ii. 1–11

---

[1] I cannot believe that the expression 'His own country,' refers to Judæa. Such an explanation is not only unnatural, but contrary to the usage of the expression ἴδιος ('his own'). Comp. St. Matt. ix. 1; also St. John vii. 40–42. *Strauss's* arguments (Leben Jesu, i. p. 659) seem here conclusive.

be judged from the expectancies which the fame of it excited even in Nazareth, the city of His early upbringing.ᵃ

It appears that the son of one of Herod Antipas' officers, either civil or military,[1] was sick, and at the point of death. When tidings reached the father that the Prophet, or more than Prophet, Whose fame had preceded Him to Galilee, had come to Cana, he resolved, in his despair of other means, to apply to Him for the cure of His child. Nothing can be gained for the spiritual interest of this or any other Biblical narrative, by exaggeration; but much is lost, when the historical demands of the case are overlooked. It is not from any disbelief in the supernatural agency at work, that we insist on the natural and rational sequence of events. And having done so, we can all the more clearly mark, by the side of the natural, the distinctively higher elements at work. Accordingly, we do not assume that this 'court-officer' was actuated by spiritual belief in the Son of God, when applying to Him for help. Rather would we go to almost the opposite extreme, and regard him as simply actuated by what, in the circumstances, might be the views of a devout Jew. Instances are recorded in the Talmud, which may here serve as our guide. Various cases are related in which those seriously ill, and even at the point of death, were restored by the prayers of celebrated Rabbis. One instance is specially illustrative.ᵇ We read that, when the son of Rabban Gamaliel was dangerously ill, he sent two of his disciples to one Chanina ben Dosa to entreat his prayers for the restoration of his son. On this, Chanina is said to have gone up to the *Aliyah* (upper chamber) to pray. On his return, he assured the messengers that the young man was restored, grounding his confidence, not on the possession of any prophetic gift, but on the circumstance that he knew his request was answered from the freedom he had in prayer. The messengers noted down the hour, and on their arrival at the house of Gamaliel found, that at that very hour 'the fever left him, and he asked for water.' Thus far the Rabbinic story. Even supposing that it was either invented or coloured in imitation of the New Testament, it shows, at least, what a devout Jew might deem lawful to expect from a celebrated Rabbi, who was regarded as having power in prayer.

Having indicated the illustrated part of this story, we may now mark the contrast between it and the event in the Gospels. There restoration is not merely asked, but expected, and that, not in answer

---

[1] βασιλικός, used by Josephus in the general sense of officers in the service of Herod Antipas. Comp. *Krebs*, Obs. in N. Test. e Fl. Josepho, pp. 144, 145, who notes that the expression occurs 600 times in the writings of Josephus.

to prayer, but by Christ's Personal presence. But the great and CHAP.
vital contrast lies, alike in what was thought of Him Who was instru- IX
mental in the cure—performed it—and in the moral effects which it
wrought. The history just quoted from the Talmud is immediately
followed by another of similar import, when a celebrated Rabbi
accounts on this wise for his inability to do that in which Chanina
had succeeded, that Chanina was like ' a servant of the King,' who went
in and out familiarly, and so might beg favours; while he (the failing
Rabbi) was ' like a lord before the King,' who would not be accorded
mere favours, but discussed matters on a footing of equality. This
profane representation of the relation between God and His servants,
the utterly unspiritual view of prayer which it displays, and the daring
self-exaltation of the Rabbi, surely mark sufficiently an absolute
contrast in spirit between the Jewish view and that which underlies
the Evangelic narrative.

Enough has been said to show, that the application to Jesus on
the part of the ' royal officer' did not, in the peculiar circumstances,
lie absolutely beyond the range of Jewish ideas. What the ' court-
officer' exactly expected to be done, is a question secondary to that
of his state of receptiveness, as it may be called, which was the moral
condition alike of the outward help, and of the inward blessing which
he received. One thing, however, it is of importance to notice. We
must not suppose, that when, to the request that Jesus would come
down to Capernaum to perform the cure, the Master replied, that
unless they saw [1] signs and wonders they would not believe, He
meant thereby to convey that his Jewish hearers, in opposition to
the Samaritans, required 'signs and wonders' in order to believe.
For the application of ' the officer' was itself an expression of faith,
although imperfect. Besides, the cure, which was the object of the
application, could not have been performed without a miracle. What
the Saviour reproved was not the request for a miracle, which was
necessary, but the urgent plea that He should come down to Capernaum for that purpose, which the father afterwards so earnestly
repeated.[a] That request argued ignorance of the real character of [a] ver. 49
the Christ, as if He were either merely a Rabbi endowed with special
power, or else a miracle-monger. What He intended to teach this
man was, that He, Who had life in Himself, could restore life at a
distance as easily as by His Presence; by the word of his Power as
readily as by personal application. A lesson this of the deepest im-

---

[1] The emphasis must lie on the word 'see,' yet not exclusively. *Lücke's* objec-tions to this (Ev. Joh. i. p. 622) are not well founded.

BOOK
III

ᵃ ver. 50
ᵇ ver. 53

ᶜ St. John i.
vi. 50, 51

ᵈ St. Matt.
viii. 5 &c.;
St. Luke
vii. 1 &c.

portance, as regarded the Person of Christ; a lesson, also, of the widest application to us and for all circumstances, temporal and spiritual. When the 'court-officer' had learned this lesson, he became 'obedient unto the faith,' and 'went his way,' ᵃ presently to find his faith both crowned and perfected.ᵇ And when both ' he and his house' had learned that lesson, they would never afterwards think of the Christ either as the Jews did, who simply witnessed His miracles, or unspiritually. It was the completion of that teaching which had first come to Nathanael, the first believer of Cana.ᶜ So, also, is it when we have learned that lesson, that we come to know alike the meaning and the blessedness of believing in Jesus.

Indeed, so far as its moral import is concerned, the whole history turns upon this point. It also marks the fundamental difference between this and the somewhat similar history of the healing of the Centurion's servant in Capernaum.ᵈ Critics have noticed marked divergences in almost every detail of the two narratives,[1] which some—both orthodox and negative interpreters—have so strangely represented as only different presentations of one and the same event.[2] But, besides these marked differences of detail, there is also fundamental difference in the substance of the narratives, and in the spirit of the two applicants, which made the Saviour in the one instance reprove as the requirement of sight, which by itself could only produce a transitory faith, that which in the other He marvelled at as greatness of faith, for which He had in vain looked in Israel. The great point in the history of the 'court-officer' is Israel's mistaken view of the Person and Work of the Christ. That in the narrative of the Centurion is the preparedness of a simple faith, unencumbered by Jewish realism, although the outcome of Jewish teaching. The carnal realism of the one, which looks for signs and wonders, is contrasted with the simplicity and straightforwardness of the other. Lastly, the point in the history of the Syro-Phœnician woman, which is sometimes confounded with it,[3] is the intensity of

---

[1] These will readily occur on comparison of the two narratives. Archdeacon *Watkins* (*ad loc.*) has grouped these under eight distinct particulars. Comp. *Lücke* (Ev. Joh.) i. p. 626.

[2] So partially and hesitatingly *Origen*, *Chrysostom*, and more decidedly *Theophilus*, *Euthymius*, *Irenæus*, and *Eusebius*. All modern negative critics hold this view; but *Gfrörer* regards the narrative of St. John, *Strauss* and *Weiss* that of St. Matthew, as the original ac-

count. And yet *Keim* ventures to assert: ' Ohne allen Zweifel (!) ist das die selbe Geschichte.'

[3] Alike *Strauss* and *Keim* discuss this at some length from the point of view of seeming contradiction between the reception of the heathen Centurion and the first refusal of the Syro-Phœnician woman. *Keim's* treatment of the whole subject seems to me inconsistent with itself.

the same faith which, despite discouragements, nay, seeming improbabilities, holds fast by the conviction which her spiritual instinct had grasped—that such an One as Jesus must be not only the Messiah of the Jews, but the Saviour of the world.

We may as well here complete our critical notices, at least as concerns those views which have of late been propounded. The extreme school of negative critics seems here involved in hopeless self-contradiction. For, if this narrative of a Jewish courtier is really only another recension of that of the heathen centurion, how comes it that the 'Jewish' Gospel of St. Matthew makes a *Gentile*, while the so-called 'anti-Jewish,' 'Ephesian' Gospel of St. John makes a *Jew*, the hero of the story? As signally does the 'mythical' theory break down. For, admittedly, there is no Rabbinic basis for the invention of such a story; and by far the ablest representative of the negative school[1] has conclusively shown, that it could not have originated in an imitation of the Old Testament account of Naaman's cure by Elisha the prophet.[2] But, if Christ had really spoken those words to the courtier, as this critic seems to admit, there remains only, as he puts it, this '*trilemma:*' either He could really work the miracle in question; or, He spoke as a mere fanatic; or else, He was simply a deceiver. It is a relief to find that the two last hypotheses are discarded. But, as negative criticism—may we not say, from the same spirit which Jesus reproved in the courtier—is unwilling to admit that Jesus really wrought this miracle, it is suggested in explanation of the cure, that the sick child, to whom the father had communicated his intended application to Jesus, had been in a state of expectancy which, when the courtier returned with the joyous assurance that the request was granted, issued in actual recovery.[3] To this there is the obvious answer, that the explanation wants the first requirement—that of an historical basis. There is not a tittle of evidence that the child expected a cure; while, on the other hand, the narrative expressly states that he was cured *before* his father's return. And, if the narrative may be altered at will to suit the necessities of a groundless hypothesis, it is difficult to see which, or whether any, part of it should be retained. It is not so that the origin of a faith, which has transformed the world, can be

---

[1] *Keim*, Jesu v. Nazara, II. i. pp. 179–185. I regret to say, that the language of Keim at p. 181 is among the most painful in his book.

[2] So *Strauss*, Leben Jesu, vol. ii. pp. 121, 122 (1st ed.).

[3] At least I so understand *Keim*, unless he means that the faith of the child alone brought about the cure, in which case there was no need for the father's journey. *Keim* naïvely asks, what objections there can be to this view, unless for the 'wording of St. John'? But the whole narrative is derived from that 'wording.'

explained. But we have here another evidence of the fact, that objections which, when regarded as part of a connected system, seem so formidable to some, utterly break down, when each narrative is carefully examined in detail.

There are other circumstances in this history, which require at least passing consideration. Of these the principal are the time when the servants of the court-officer met him, on his return journey, with the joyful tidings that his son lived; and, connected with it, the time when 'he began to do nicely;'[a][1] and, lastly, that when the 'court-official' applied to Jesus. The two latter events were evidently contemporaneous.[b] The exact time indicated by the servants as the commencement of the improvement is, 'Yesterday, at the seventh hour.' Now, however the Jewish servants may originally have expressed themselves, it seems impossible to assume, that St. John intended any other than the Roman notation of the civil day, or that he meant any other hour than 7 P.M. The opposite view, that it marks Jewish notation of time, or 1 P.M., is beset by almost unsurmountable difficulties.[2] For it must be borne in mind, that, as the distance between Capernaum and Cana is about twenty-five miles, it would have been extremely difficult, if not impossible, for the courtier, leaving his home that morning, not only to have reached Cana, but to have had the interview with Jesus by 1 P.M. The difficulty is only increased, when we are asked to believe, that after such a journey the courtier had immediately set out on his return. But this is absolutely necessary for the theory, since a Jew would not have set out on such a journey after dusk. But farther, on the above supposition, the servants of the court official must have taken the road immediately, or very soon after, the improvement *commenced*. This is itself unlikely, and, indeed, counter-indicated by the terms of the conversation between the courtier and the servants, which imply that they had waited till they were sure that it was recovery, and not merely a temporary improvement.[c] Again, on the theory combated, the servants, meeting the 'courtier,' as we must suppose, midway, if not near to Capernaum, would have said, 'Yesterday at the seventh hour the fever left him,' meaning thereby, that, as they spoke in the evening, when another Jewish day had begun, the fever had left him on the afternoon of the same day, although, according to Jewish

a ver. 52

b ver. 53

ver. 52

---

[1] So literally; the A.V. has: 'began to amend.'

[2] The Jewish servants may have expressed the time according to Jewish notation, though in such a house in Galilee such might not have been the usual practice. However this be, we contend that St. John's notation of time was according to the Roman civil day, or rather according to that of Asia Minor

reckoning, 'yesterday,' since 1 P.M. would be reckoned as the previous day. But it may be safely affirmed, that no Jew would have so expressed himself. If, on the evening of a day, they had referred to what had taken place five or six hours previously, at 1 P.M., they would have said: 'At the seventh hour the fever left him;' and *not* '*Yesterday* at the seventh hour.'

CHAP. IX

It is needless to follow the matter further. We can understand how, leaving Capernaum in the morning, the interview with Jesus and the simultaneous cure of the child would have taken place about seven o'clock of the evening. Its result was, not only the restoration of the child, but that, no longer requiring to *see* signs and wonders, 'the man believed the word which Jesus had spoken unto him.' In this joyous assurance, which needed no more ocular demonstration, he 'went his way,' either to the hospitable home of a friend, or to some near lodging-place on the way, to be next day met by the gladsome tidings, that it had been to him according to his faith. As already noted, the whole *morale* of the history lies in this very matter, and it marks the spiritual receptiveness of the courtier, which, in turn, was the moral condition of his desire being granted. Again, we learn how, by the very granting of his desire, the spiritual object of Christ in the teaching of the courtier was accomplished, how, under certain spiritual conditions in him and upon him, the temporal benefit accomplished its spiritual object. And in this also, as in other points which will occur to the devout reader, there are lessons of deepest teaching to us, and for all times and circumstances.

Whether this 'royal officer' was *Chuza*, Herod's steward, whose wife, under the abiding impression of this miracle to her child, afterwards humbly, gratefully ministered to Jesus,[a] must remain undetermined on this side time. Suffice it, to mark the progress in the 'royal officer' from belief in the power of Jesus to faith in His word,[b] and thence to absolute faith in Him,[c] with its blessed expansive effect on that whole household. And so are we ever led faithfully and effectually, yet gently, by His benefits, upwards from the lower stage of belief by what we see Him *do*, to that higher faith which is absolute and unseeing trust, springing from experimental knowledge of what He *is*.

[a] St. Luke viii. 3
[b] ver. 50
[c] ver. 53

CHAPTER X

THE SYNAGOGUE AT NAZARETH—SYNAGOGUE–WORSHIP AND ARRANGE
MENTS.

(St. Luke iv. 16.)

BOOK
III

THE stay in Cana, though we have no means of determining its
length, was probably of only short duration. Perhaps the Sabbath
of the same week already found Jesus in the Synagogue of Nazareth.
We will not seek irreverently to lift the veil of sacred silence, which
here, as elsewhere, the Gospel-narratives have laid over the Sanctuary
of His inner Life. That silence is itself *theopneustic,* of Divine
breathing and inspiration; it is more eloquent than any eloquence,
a guarantee of the truthfulness of what is said. And against this
silence, as the dark background, stands out as the Figure of Light
the Person of the Christ. Yet, as we follow Jesus to the city of His
Childhood and home of His humility, we can scarcely repress thoughts
of what must have stirred His soul, as He once more entered the
well-known valley, and beheld the scenes to each of which some early
memory must have attached.

Only a few months since He had left Nazareth, but how much
that was all-decisive to Him, to Israel, and to the world had passed !
As the lengthening shadows of Friday's sun closed around the quiet
valley, He would hear the well-remembered double blast of the
trumpet from the roof of the Synagogue-minister's house, proclaiming the advent of the holy day.[a] Once more it sounded through the
still summer-air, to tell all, that work must be laid aside.[b] Yet a
third time it was heard, ere the ' minister ' put it aside close by
where he stood, not to profane the Sabbath by carrying it; for now
the Sabbath had really commenced, and the festive Sabbath-lamp
was lit.

Sabbath morn dawned, and early He repaired to that Synagogue
where, as a Child, a Youth, a Man, He had so often worshipped in
the humble retirement of His rank, sitting, not up there among the
elders and the honoured, but far back. The old well-known faces
were around Him, the old well-remembered words and services fell

[a] Shabb.35 b
[b] Jer.Shabb
xvii. p. 16 a

on His ear. How different they had always been to Him than to CHAP.
them, with whom He had thus mingled in common worship! And X
now He was again among them, truly a stranger among His own
countrymen; this time, to be looked at, listened to, tested, tried,
used or cast aside, as the case might be. It was the first time,[1] so
far as we know, that He taught in a Synagogue, and this Synagogue
that of His own Nazareth.

It was, surely, a wondrously linked chain of circumstances, which
bound the Synagogue to the Church. Such a result could never have
been foreseen, as that, what really was the consequence of Israel's
dispersion, and, therefore, indirectly the punishment of their sin,
should become the means of fulfilling Israel's world-mission. Another
instance this, of how Divine judgment always bears in its bosom
larger mercy; another illustration how the dying of Israel is ever
life to the world; another manifestation of that supernatural Rule
of God, in which all is rule, that is, law and order, and all the supernatural, bringing to pass, in the orderly succession of events, what at
the outset would have seemed, and really is, miraculous. For the
Synagogue became the cradle of the Church. Without it, as indeed
without Israel's dispersion, the Church Universal would, humanly
speaking, have been impossible, and the conversation of the Gentiles
have required a succession of millennial miracles.

That Synagogues originated during, or in consequence of the
Babylonish captivity, is admitted by all. The Old Testament contains no allusion to their existence,[2] and the Rabbinic attempts to
trace them even to Patriarchal times[3] deserve, of course, no serious

[1] The remark in the 'Speaker's Commentary' (St. Luke iv. 16), that Jesus
had been in the habit of expounding the
Scriptures in Nazareth, is not only
groundless, but inconsistent with the
narrative. See ver. 22. Still more
strange is the supposition, that 'Jesus
offered to read and to expound, and signified this intention by standing up.
This might be done by any member of
the congregation.' Most assuredly such
would not be the case.

[2] This seems at first sight inconsistent
with Ps. lxxiv. 8. But the term rendered
'Synagogues' in the A.V. has never been
used in that sense. The solution of the
difficulty here comes to us through the
LXX. Their rendering, καταπαύσωμεν
(let us make to cease), shows that in their
Hebrew MSS. they read שׁבתו. If so,
then the ו probably belonged to the
next word, and the text would read:

שַׁבַּת וְכָל־מוֹעֲדֵי־אֵל. 'Let us suppress
altogether—the Sabbath and all the festive seasons in the land.' Comp. *Ehrt,*
Abfass. Zeit. u. Abschl. d. Psalt. pp.
17–19.

[3] The introduction of morning, midday, and afternoon prayers is respectively ascribed to Abraham, Isaac, and
Jacob. The Targum of Onkelos and
the Targum Ps.-Jon. on Gen. xxv. 27
imply their existence in the time of
Jacob. In B. Kama 82 *a,* and Jer. Megill. 75 *a,* its services are traced to the
time of Moses. According to Sanh. 94 *b,*
Synagogues existed in the time of Hezekiah. It is needless to follow the subject further. We take the present opportunity of adding, that, as the Rabbinic
quotations in this chapter would be so
numerous, only those will be given which
refer to points hitherto unnoticed, or of
special importance.

consideration. We can readily understand how during the long years of exile in Babylon, places and opportunities for common worship on Sabbaths and feast-days must have been felt almost a necessity. This would furnish, at least, the basis for the institution of the Synagogue. After the return to Palestine, and still more by 'the dispersed abroad,' such 'meeting-houses' (*Battey Khenesiyoth, do- mus congregationum, Synagogues*) would become absolutely requisite. Here those who were ignorant even of the language of the Old Testament would have the Scriptures read and 'targumed' to them.[1] It was but natural that prayers, and, lastly, addresses, should in course of time be added. Thus the regular Synagogue- service would gradually arise; first on Sabbaths and on feast- or fast-days, then on ordinary days, at the same hours as, and with a sort of internal correspondence to, the worship of the Temple. The services on Mondays and Thursdays were special, these being the ordinary market-days, when the country-people came into the towns, and would avail themselves of the opportunity for bringing any case that might require legal decision before the local Sanhedrin, which met in the Synagogue, and consisted of its authorities.   Naturally, these two days would be utilised to afford the country-people, who lived far from the Synagogues, opportunities for worship;[a] and the services on those days were of a somewhat more elaborate character. Accordingly, Monday and Thursday were called 'the days of congre- gation' or 'Synagogue' (*Yom ha-Kenisah*).

In another place[2] it has been shown, how rapidly and generally the institution of Synagogues spread among the Jews of the Disper- sion in all lands, and what important purposes they served.   In Palestine they were scattered over the whole country, though it is only reasonable to suppose, that their number greatly increased after the destruction of the Temple, and this without crediting the Jewish legend as to their extraordinary number in certain cities, such as 480, or 460, in Jerusalem.[3]   In the capital, and probably in some other large cities, there were not only several Synagogues, but these arranged according to nationalities, and even crafts.[4] At the same time it deserves notice, that even in so important a place as Capernaum

a Baba K.
82 a

---

[1] The expressions 'Targum' and 'tar- guming' have been previously explained. The first indication of such paraphras- ing in the vernacular is found in Neh. viii. 7, 8.

[2] See Book I. pp. 19, 77.

[3] These numbers, however, seem to have been symbolical. The number 480 is, by *Gimatreya*, deduced from the word 'She that was full of' (meleathi) in Is. i. 21. Comp. Yalkut, vol. ii. p. 40 *d*, towards the end, or else 480 = 4 × 10 × 12.

[4] Comp. Megill. 26.

there seems either not to have been a Synagogue, or that it was utterly insignificant, till the want was supplied by the pious Gentile centurion.[a] This would seem to dispose of the question whether, as is generally assumed, a Jewish community in a place, if numbering ten heads of families, was obliged to build a Synagogue, and could enforce local taxation for the purpose. Such was undoubtedly the later Rabbinic ordinance,[b] but there is no evidence that it obtained in Palestine, or in early times.

Generally, of course, a community would build its own Synagogue, or else depend on the charitable assistance of neighbours, or on private munificence. If this failed, they might meet for worship in a private dwelling, a sort of 'Synagogue in the house.'[c] For, in early times the institution would be much more simple than at a later period. In this, as in other respects, we must remember that later Jewish arrangements afford no evidence of those which prevailed while the Temple stood, nor yet the ordinances of the chiefs of Babylonian Academies of the customs existing in Palestine, and, lastly, that the Rabbinic directions mark rather an ideal than the actual state of things. Thus—to mention an instance of some importance, because the error has been so often repeated as to be generally believed, and to have misled recent explorers in Palestine—there is no evidence that in Palestine Synagogues always required to be built in the highest situation in a town, or, at least, so as to overtop the other houses. To judge from a doubtful[1] passage in the Talmud,[d] this seems to have been the case in Persia, while a later notice[e] appeals in support of it to Prov. viii. 2. But even where the Jews were most powerful and influential, the rule could not have been universally enforced, although later Rabbis lay it down as a principle.[f] Hence, the inference, that the Galilean Synagogues lately excavated cannot date from an early period, because they are not in prominent positions, is erroneous.[2]

But there were two rules observed, which seem to have been enforced from early times. One of these enjoined, that a Synagogue should not be erected in a place, unless it contained ten *Batlanim*,[3] or men of leisure, who could devote their time to the Synagogue

CHAP.
X

[a] St. Luke vii. 5

[b] *Maimonides,* Hilc. Tephill, xi 1

[c] Comp. Philem. 2

[d] Shabb. 11 a
[e] Tos. Még. ed. Z iv. 23

[f] *Maimonides,* Hilc. Tephill. xi. 2

---

[1] See the notes in *Maimonides,* Hilc. Tephill. xi. 2; p. 75 b.
[2] Comp. Lieut. *Kitchener's* article on the Synagogues of Galilee (P.E.F. Report, July 1878, pp. 126 &c.). The inference, that they date from the beginning of the third century, when the Jews were in high favour with the Emperor Alexander Severus, is all the more ungrounded, that at that time, if ever, the Jewish authorities would strictly adhere to Talmudic directions as to the structure of Synagogues.

[3] From '*battel,*' which here seems to have the same meaning as the Latin *vacare rei,* to have leisure for a thing.

BOOK
III

worship and administration.[1] This was proved by the consideration, that common worship implied a congregation, which, according to Jewish Law, must consist of at least ten men.[2] Another, and perhaps more important rule was as to the direction in which Synagogues were to be built, and which worshippers should occupy during prayer. Here two points must be kept in view: 1st. Prayer towards the east was condemned, on the ground of the false worship towards the east mentioned in Ezek. viii. 16.[a] 2ndly. The prevailing direction in Palestine was towards the west, as in the Temple. Thus, we read[b] that the entrance into the Synagogue was by the east, as the entrance through the Beautiful Gate into the Sanctuary. This, however, may refer, not to the door, but to the passage (aisle) into the interior of the building. In other places,[c] the advice is simply given to turn towards Jerusalem, in whatever direction it be. In general, however, it was considered that since the Shekhinah was everywhere in Palestine, direction was not of paramount importance.

If we combine these notices, and keep in view the general desire to conform to the Temple arrangements, the ruined Synagogues lately excavated in the north of Galilee seem, in a remarkable manner, to meet the Talmudic requirements. With the exception of one (at 'Irbid, which has its door to the east), they all have their entrances on the south. We conjecture that the worshippers, imitating in this the practice in the Temple, made a circuit, either completely to the north, or else entered at the middle of the eastern aisle, where, in the ground-plan of the Synagogue at Capernaum, which seems the most fully preserved ruin, two pillars in the colonnade are wanting.[3] The so-called ' Ark ' would be at the south end; the seats for the elders and honourable in front of it, facing the people, and with their back to the Ark.[d] Here two pillars are wanting in the Synagogue at Capernaum. The lectern of the reader would be in the centre, close to where the entrance was into the double colonnade which formed the Synagogue, where, at present, a single pillar is marked in the plan of the Capernaum Synagogue; while the women's gallery was at the north end, where two columns and pillars of peculiar shape,

[a] Comp.Jer.
Ber. iv. 5;
Baba B. 25 a
[b] Tos.
Megill.iii. 3

[c] Baba B.
25 a and b;
Jer. Ber. iv.
5

[d] Tos.
Meg. iii. 3

---

[1] This is expressly stated in Jer. Megill. i. 6, p. 70 b, towards the end.

[2] Comp. Megill. iv. 3; Sanh. i. 6. That ten constituted a congregation was derived from Numb. xiv. 27. Similarly, it was thought to be implied in the fact, that if ten righteous men had been in Sodom, the city would not have been destroyed. But in case of necessity the number ten might be made up by a male child under age (Ber. R. 91, pp. 160 a and b).

[3] On the next page we give a plan of the Synagogue excavated at Tell Hûm (Capernaum). It is adapted from Capt. Wilson's plan in the P.E.F. Quarterly Statement, No. 2.

which may have supported the gallery, are traceable. For it is a
mistake to suppose that the men and women sat in opposite aisles,
separated by a low wall. *Philo* notices, indeed, this arrangement in
connection with the Therapeutæ;[a] but there is no indication that the
practice prevailed in the Synagogues, or in Palestine.

We can now, with the help given by recent excavations, form a
conception of these ancient Synagogues. The Synagogue is built of
the stone of the country. On the lintels over the doors there are

CHAP.
X

a De Vit.
Contempl.3
and 9, ed.
Mang. ii.
pp. 476, 482

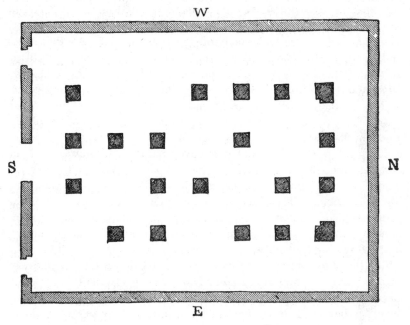

W

S   N

E

PLAN OF SYNAGOGUE AT 'TELL HÛM.'

various ornamentations—a seven-branched candlestick, an open flower
between two Paschal lambs, or vine-leaves with bunches of grapes,
or, as at Capernaum, a pot of manna between representations of
Aaron's rod. Only glancing at the internal decorations of mould-
ings or cornice, we notice that the inside plan is generally that of
two double colonnades, which seem to have formed the body of the
Synagogue, the aisles east and west being probably used as passages.
The intercolumnar distance is very small, never greater than 9½ feet.[1]

---

[1] Comp. Palestine Exploration Fund Report, Quarterly Statement, ii. p. 42 &c.

The 'two corner columns at the northern end invariably have their two exterior faces square like pillars, and the two interior ones formed by half-engaged pillars.' Here we suppose the women's gallery to have risen. The flooring is formed of slabs of white limestone;[1] the walls are solid (from 2 even to 7 feet in thickness), and well built of stones, rough in the exterior, but plastered in the interior. The Synagogue is furnished with sufficient windows to admit light. The roof is flat, the columns being. sometimes connected by blocks of stone, on which massive rafters rest.

Entering by the door at the southern end, and making the circuit to the north, we take our position in front of the women's gallery. These colonnades form the body of the Synagogue.[2] At the south end, facing north, is a movable ' Ark,' containing the sacred rolls of the Law and the Prophets. It is called the Holy Chest or Ark, *Aron*

[a] Shabb. 32 a

haqqodesh (to call it simply ' *aron* ' was sinful),[a] but chiefly the *Tebhah*, Ark.[3] It was made movable, so that it might be carried out, as on

[b] Megill. 26 b; Taan. 15 a

public fasts.[b] Steps generally led up to it (the *Darga* or *Saphsel*). In front hangs (this probably from an early period) the *Vilon* or curtain. But the Holy Lamp is never wanting, in imitation of the

[c] Exod. xxvii. 20

undying light in the Temple.[c] Right before the Ark, and facing the people, are the seats of honour, for the rulers of the Synagogue and

[d] St. Matt. xxiii. 6; Tos. Megill. ed. Z. iv. 21

the honourable.[d] The place for him who leads the devotion of the people is also in front of the Ark, either elevated, or else, to mark humility, lowered.[4] In the middle of the Synagogue (so generally)

[e] Megill. 32 a

is the *Bima*,[5] or elevation, on which there is the *Luach*, or desk,[e] from which the Law is read. This is also called the *Kurseya*, chair, or

[f] Megill. 26 b

throne,[f] or *Kissé*, and *Pergulah*. Those who are to read the Law will stand, while he who is to preach or deliver an address will sit. Beside them will be the *Methurgeman*, either to interpret, or to repeat aloud, what is said.

As yet the Synagogue is empty, and we may therefore call to mind what we ought to think, and how to bear ourselves. To neglect attendance on its services would not only involve personal

---

[1] Comp. *Warren's* ' Recovery of Jerusalem,' p. 343 &c.

[2] There is a curious passage in Ber. 8 *a*, which states that although there were thirteen Synagogues in Tiberias, it was the practice of the Rabbis only to pray ' between the columns where they studied.' This seems to imply that the Academy consisted also of colonnades. For it would be difficult to believe that all the supposed Synagogues exca-

vated in Galilee were Academies.

[3] It was also called Argas and Qomtar (Megill. 26 *b*), but more generally Chest.

[4] Hence the expression ' yored liphney hattebhah,' and ' obhed liphney hattebhah.'

[5] Seems also to have been called ' Kathedrah,' just as by our Lord (St. Matt. xxiii. 2). Comp. *Buxtorf's* Lexicon, p. 2164.

guilt, but bring punishment upon the whole district. Indeed, to be effectual, prayer must be offered in the Synagogue.[a] At the same time, the more strict ordinances in regard to the Temple, such as, that we must not enter it carrying a staff, nor with shoes, nor even dust on the feet, nor with scrip or purse, do not apply to the Synagogue, as of comparatively inferior sanctity.[b] However, the Synagogue must not be made a thoroughfare. We must not behave lightly in it.[c] We may not joke, laugh, eat, talk, dress, nor resort there for shelter from sun or rain. Only Rabbis and their disciples, to whom so many things are lawful, and who, indeed, must look upon the Synagogue as if it were their own dwelling, may eat, drink, perhaps even sleep there. Under certain circumstances, also, the poor and strangers may be fed there.[d] But, in general, the Synagogue must be regarded as consecrated to God. Even if a new one be built, care must be taken not to leave the old edifice till the other is finished. Money collected for the building may, in cases of necessity, be used for other purposes, but things dedicated for it are inalienable by sale. A Synagogue may be converted into an Academy, because the latter is regarded as more sacred, but not *vice versâ*. Village Synagogues may be disposed of, under the direction of the local Sanhedrin, provided the *locale* be not afterwards used for incongruous purposes, such as public baths, a wash-house, a tannery, &c. But town Synagogues are inalienable, because strangers may have contributed to them; and, even if otherwise, they have a right to look for some place of worship. At the same time, we must bear in mind that this rule had its exceptions; notably that, at one time, the guild of coppersmiths in Jerusalem sold their Synagogue.[e]

All this, irrespective of any Rabbinic legends, shows with what reverence these 'houses of congregation' were regarded. And now the weekly Sabbath, the pledge between Israel and God, had once more come. To meet it as a bride or queen, each house was adorned on the Friday evening. The Sabbath lamp was lighted; the festive garments put on; the table provided with the best which the family could afford; and the *Qiddush*, or benediction, spoken over the cup of wine, which, as always, was mixed with water.[1] And as Sabbath morning broke, they hastened with quick steps to the Synagogue; for such was the Rabbinic rule in going, while it was prescribed to return with slow and lingering steps. Jewish punctiliousness defined every

[a] Comp. Ber. 6 *a* and *b*; 8 *a*

[b] Ber. 63 *a*

[c] Tos. Megill. ed. Z. iii. 7

[d] Pes. 101 *a*

[e] Megill. 26*a*

---

[1] This, not for symbolical reasons, but probably on account of the strength of the wine. It is needless here to give the rules how the cup is to be held, or even the liturgical formula of the Qiddush. Comp. Jer. Ber. p. 3 *c*, *d*; vii. 6, p. 11 *c*, *d*.

movement and attitude in prayer. If those rules were ever observed in their entirety, devotion must have been crushed under their weight. But we have evidence that, in the time of our Lord, and even later, there was much personal freedom left;[1] for, not only was much in the services determined by the usage of each place, but the leader of the devotions might preface the regular service by free prayer, or insert such between certain parts of the liturgy.

We are now in the Nazareth Synagogue. The officials are all assembled. The lowest of these is the *Chazzan*, or minister,[a] who often acts also as schoolmaster. For this reason, and because the conduct of the services may frequently devolve upon him, great care is taken in his selection. He must be not only irreproachable, but, if possible, his family also. Humility, modesty, knowledge of the Scriptures, distinctness and correctness in pronunciation, simplicity and neatness in dress, and an absence of self-assertion, are qualities sought for, and which, in some measure, remind us of the higher qualifications insisted on by St. Paul in the choice of ecclesiastical officers. Then there are the elders (*Zeqenim*), or rulers (ἄρχοντες), whose chief is the *Archisynagogos*, or *Rosh ha-Keneseth*. These are the rulers (*Parnasim*) or shepherds (ποιμένες). There can be no question (from the inscriptions on the Jewish tombstones in Rome),[b] that the *Archisynagogos*[b] was *chief* among the rulers, and that, whether or not there was, as in the community at Rome, and probably also among the dispersed in the West, besides him, a sort of political chief of the elders, or *Gerousiarch*.[c] All the rulers of the Synagogue were duly examined as to their knowledge, and ordained to the office. They formed the local Sanhedrin or tribunal. But their election depended on the choice of the congregation; and absence of pride, as also gentleness and humility, are mentioned as special qualifications.[d] Sometimes the office was held by regular teachers.[e]

If, as in Rome, there was an apparently unordained eldership (*Gerousia*), it had probably only the charge of outward affairs, and acted rather as a committee of management. Indeed, in foreign Synagogues, the rulers seem to have been chosen, sometimes for a specified period, at others for life. But, although it may be admitted

a St. Luke
iv. 20

b Comp.
Schürer,
Gemeind.
Verfass. in
Rom, pp. 27
&c.

c *Schürer,*
u.s., pp. 18-
20

d Sanh. 92 a;
Chag. 5 b
e Gitt. 60 a

---

[1] As to all this, and the great liberty in prayer, comp. *Zunz*, Gottesd. Vortr. d. Jud. pp. 368, 369, and notes *a*, *b*, and *d*; and Ritus des Synag. Gottesd. pp. 2 and 3.

[2] In St. Mark v. 22, several *Archisynagogoi* seem to be spoken of. But the expression may only mean, as *Weiss* suggests, one of the order of the *Archi-*synagogoi. The passage in Acts xiii. 15 is more difficult. Possibly it may depend upon local circumstances—the term *Archisynagogoi* including others beside the *Archisynagogoi* in the strictest sense, such as the *Gerousiarchs* of the Roman inscriptions.

that the *Archisynagogos,* or chief ruler of the Synagogue, was only the CHAP.
X first among his equals, there can be no doubt that the virtual rule of the Synagogue devolved upon him. He would have the superintendence of Divine service, and, as this was not conducted by regular officials, he would in each case determine who were to be called up to read from the Law and the Prophets, who was to conduct the prayers, and act as *Sheliach Tsibbur,* or messenger of the congregation, and who, if any, was to deliver an address. He would also see to it that nothing improper took place in the Synagogue,[a] and that the prayers were properly conducted. In short, the supreme care, both of the services and of the building, would devolve upon him. To these regular officials we have to add those who officiated during the service, the *Sheliach Tsibbur,* or delegate of the congregation—who, as its mouthpiece, conducted the devotions—the Interpreter or *Methurgeman,* and those who were called on to read in the Law and the Prophets, or else to preach.

a St. Luke xiii. 14

We are now in some measure prepared to follow the worship on that Sabbath in Nazareth. On His entrance into the Synagogue, or perhaps before that, the chief ruler would request Jesus to act for that Sabbath as the *Sheliach Tsibbur.* For according to the Mishnah,[b] the person who read in the Synagogue the portion from the Prophets, was also expected to conduct the devotions, at least in greater part.[1] If this rule was enforced at that time, then Jesus would ascend the *Bima,* and standing at the lectern, begin the service by two prayers, which in their most ancient form, as they probably obtained in the time of our Lord, were as follows:—

b Megill. v. 5

I. 'Blessed be Thou, O Lord, King of the world, Who formest the light and createst the darkness, Who makest peace, and createst everything; Who, in mercy, givest light to the earth, and to those who dwell upon it, and in Thy goodness, day by day, and every day, renewest the works of creation. Blessed be the Lord our God for the glory of His handiworks, and for the light-giving lights which He has made for His praise. Selah. Blessed be the Lord our God, Who has formed the lights.'

II. 'With great love hast Thou loved us, O Lord our God, and with much overflowing pity hast Thou pitied us, our Father and our King. For the sake of our fathers who trusted in Thee, and Thou taughtest them the statutes of life, have mercy upon us, and teach us. Enlighten our eyes in Thy Law; cause our hearts to cleave to Thy commandments; unite our hearts to love and fear Thy Name,

---

[1] Part of the *Shema,* and the whole of the Eulogies.

and we shall not be put to shame, world without end. For Thou art a God Who preparest salvation, and us hast Thou chosen from among all nations and tongues, and hast in truth brought us near to Thy great Name—Selah—that we may lovingly praise Thee and Thy Unity. Blessed be the Lord, Who in love chose His people Israel.'

After this followed what may be designated as the Jewish Creed, called the *Shema,* from the word '*shema,*' or 'hear,' with which it begins. It consisted of three passages from the Pentateuch,[a] so arranged, as the Mishnah notes,[b] that the worshipper took upon himself first the yoke of the Kingdom of Heaven, and only after it the yoke of the commandments; and in the latter, again, first those that applied to night and day, and then those that applied to the day only. They were probably but later determinations, conceived in a spirit of hostility to what was regarded as the heresy of Christianity, which insisted that, as the first sentence in the *Shema,* asserting the Unity of God, was the most important, special emphasis should be laid on certain words in it. The recitation of the *Shema* was followed by this prayer:—

'True it is that Thou art Jehovah, our God, and the God of our fathers, our King, and the King of our fathers, our Saviour, and the Saviour of our fathers, our Creator, the Rock of our Salvation, our Help and our Deliverer. Thy Name is from everlasting, and there is no God beside Thee. A new song did they that were delivered sing to Thy Name by the sea-shore; together did all praise and own Thee King, and say, Jehovah shall reign, world without end! Blessed be the God Who saveth Israel.'

This prayer finished, he who officiated took his place before the Ark, and there repeated what formed the prayer in the strictest sense, or certain 'Eulogies' or Benedictions. These are eighteen, or rather nineteen, in number, and date from different periods. But as on Sabbaths only the three first and the three last of them, which are also those undoubtedly of greatest age, were repeated, and between them certain other prayers inserted, only these six, with which the series respectively began and ended, need here find a place. The first Benediction was said with bent body. It was as follows:—

I. 'Blessed be the Lord our God, and the God of our fathers, the God of Abraham, and the God of Isaac, and the God of Jacob; the Great, the Mighty, and the Terrible God, the Most High God, Who showeth mercy and kindness. Who createth all things, Who remembereth the gracious promises to the fathers, and bringeth a Saviour to their children's children, for His own Name's sake, in

a Deut. vi.
4-9; xi. 13-
21; Numb.
xv. 37-41
b Ber. ii. 2

love. O King, Helper, Saviour, and Shield! Blessed art Thou,
O Jehovah, the Shield of Abraham.'

II. 'Thou O Lord, art mighty for ever; Thou. Who quickenest
the dead, art mighty to save. In Thy mercy Thou preservest the
living, Thou quickenest the dead; in Thine abundant pity Thou
bearest up those who fall, and healest those who are diseased, and
loosest those who are bound, and fulfillest Thy faithful word to those
who sleep in the dust. Who is like unto Thee, Lord of strength, and
who can be compared to Thee, Who killest and makest alive, and
causest salvation to spring forth? And faithful art Thou to give
life to the dead. Blessed art Thou, Jehovah, Who quickenest the
dead!'

III. 'Thou art Holy, and Thy name is Holy. Selah. Blessed
art Thou Jehovah God, the Holy One.'

After this, such prayers were inserted as were suited to the day.
And here it may be noticed that considerable latitude was allowed.
For, although[a] it was not lawful to insert any petition in the three _[a] According to Ber. 34 a_
first or the three last Eulogies, but only in the intermediate Benedic-
tions, in practice this was certainly not observed. Thus, although,
by the rubric, prayer for rain and dew was to be inserted up to the
season of the Passover in the ninth Benediction, yet occasionally
reference to this seems also to have been made in the second Benediction, as connected with the quickening of that which is dead.[b] Nay, _[b] Ber. 33 a_
some Rabbis went so far as to recommend a brief summary of the
eighteen Eulogies, while yet another (R. Eliezer) repudiated all
fixed forms of prayer.[1] But gradually, and especially after the insertion of the well-known prayer against the heretics or rather Christian
converts (Eulogy XI.[2]), the present order of the eighteen Eulogies
(_Amidah_) seems to have been established. Both the Jerusalem[c] and _[c] Jer. Ber. iv. 3 to end_
the Babylon Talmud[d] contain much on this subject which is of very _[d] Ber. 33 a &c._
great interest.[3]

Following the order of the service, we now come to the concluding Eulogies, which were as follows :—

XVII. (XVI.) 'Take gracious pleasure, O Jehovah our God, in

---

[1] There is even doubt, whether the exact words of at least some of the Benedictions were fixed at an early period.
See _Zunz_, u. s.

[2] Originally the eulogies were eighteen
in number. The addition of that against
the heretics would have made them nineteen. Accordingly, Eulogy xv., which
prayed for the coming of the Branch of

David, was joined to the previous one in
order to preserve the number eighteen.
Comp. Jer. Ber. iv. 3. It is sadly characteristic that, together with a curse
upon Christian converts, the Messianic
hope of Israel should thus have been
pushed into the background.

[3] For the sake of brevity, I can only
here refer the reader to the passages.

BOOK
III

Thy people Israel and in their prayers, and in love accept the burnt-offerings of Israel, and their prayers with Thy good pleasure, and may the services of Thy people be ever acceptable unto Thee. And O that our eyes may see it, as Thou turnest in mercy to Zion. Blessed be Thou, O Jehovah, Who restoreth His Shekhinah to Zion.'

XVIII. (XVII.) In saying this Eulogy, which was simply one of thanks, it was ordered that all should bend down. It was as follows : —' We give praise to Thee, because Thou art He, Jehovah, our God, and the God of our fathers, for ever and ever. The Rock of our life, the Shield of our salvation, Thou art He, from generation to generation. We laud Thee, and declare Thy praise. For our lives which are bound up in Thine Hand, for our souls which are committed to Thee, and for Thy wonders which are with us every day and for Thy marvellous deeds and Thy goodnesses which are at all seasons, evening, and morning, and midday—Thou Gracious One, for Thy compassions never end, Thou Pitying One, for Thy mercies never cease, for ever do we put our trust in Thee. And for all this, blessed and exalted be Thy Name, our King, always, world without end. And all the living bless Thee—Selah—and praise Thy Name in truth, O God, our Salvation and our Help. Selah. Blessed art Thou, Jehovah. The Gracious One is Thy Name, and to Thee it is pleasant to give praise.'

After this the priests, if any were in the Synagogue, spoke the blessing, elevating their hands up to the shoulders [a] (in the Temple above the head). This was called the lifting up of hands.[b] In the Synagogue the priestly blessing was spoken in three sections, the people each time responding by an Amen.[c] Lastly, in the Synagogue, the word 'Adonai' was substituted for Jehovah.[d][1] If no descendants of Aaron were present, the leader of the devotions repeated the usual priestly benediction.[e] After the benediction followed the last Eulogy, which, in its abbreviated form (as presently used in the Evening Service), is as follows :—

XIX. (XVIII.) 'O bestow on Thy people Israel great peace for ever. For Thou art King, and Lord of all peace. And it is good in Thine eyes to bless Thy people Israel at all times and at every hour with Thy peace. Blessed art Thou, Jehovah, Who blesseth His people Israel with peace!'

It was the practice of leading Rabbis, probably dating from very early times, to add at the close of this Eulogy certain prayers of their

[a] Sot. vii. 6
[b] Comp. 1 Tim. ii. 8
[c] Sot. 37 b 38 a
[d] Siphré on Numb. par. 39, p. 12 a
[e] Numb. vi. 23-26

---

[1] Minor differences need not here be detailed, especially as they are by no means certain.

own, either fixed or free, of which the Talmud gives specimens. From very early times also, the custom seems to have obtained that the descendants of Aaron, before pronouncing the blessing, put off their shoes. In the benediction the priests turned towards the people, while he who led the ordinary prayers stood with his back to the people, looking towards the Sanctuary. The superstition, that it was unlawful to look at the priests while they spoke the blessing,[a] must be regarded as of later date. According to the Mishnah, they who pronounce the benediction must have no blemish on their hands, face, or feet, so as not to attract attention; but this presumably refers to those officiating in the Temple.[1] It is a curious statement, that priests from certain cities in Galilee were not allowed to speak the words of blessing, because their pronounciation of the gutturals was misleading.[b] According to the Jerusalem Talmud,[c] moral blemishes, or even sin, did not disqualify a priest from pronouncing the benediction, since it was really God, and not man, Who gave the blessing.[2] On the other hand, strict sobriety was insisted on on such occasions. Later Judaism used the priestly benediction as a means for counteracting the effects of evil dreams. The public prayers closed with an Amen, spoken by the congregation.

The liturgical part being thus completed, one of the most important, indeed, what had been the primary object of the Synagogue service, began. The *Chazzan*, or minister, approached the Ark, and brought out a roll of the Law. It was taken from its case (*têq, teqah*), and unwound from those cloths *(mitpachoth)* which held it. The time had now come for the reading of portions from the Law and the Prophets. On the Sabbath, at least seven persons were called upon successively to read portions from the Law, none of them consisting of less than three verses. On the 'days of congregation' (Monday and Thursday), three persons were called up; on New Moon's Day, and on the intermediate days of a festive week, four; on feast days, five; and on the Day of Atonement, six.[3] No doubt, there was even

CHAP.
X

[a] Chag. 16 *a*

[b] Megill. 24 *b*
[c] Jer. Gitt.
v. 9. p 47 *b*;
comp.
Duschak,
Jüd. Kultus, p. 270

---

[1] It seems also to have been the rule, that they must wash their hands before pronouncing the benediction (Sot. 39 *a*).

[2] The question is discussed: first, who blessed the priests ? and, secondly, what part God had in that benediction ? The answer will readily be guessed (Chull. 49 *a*). In Siphré on Numbers, par. 43, the words are quoted (Numb. vi. 27) to show that the blessing came from God, and not from, although through, the priests. In Bemidb. R. 11 ed. Warsh. iv. p. 40 *a*

there is a beautiful prayer, in which Israel declares that it only needs the blessing of God, according to Deut. xxvi. 15, on which the answer comes, that although the priests bring the benediction, it is God Who stands and blesses His people. Accordingly, the benediction of the priests is only the symbol of God's blessing.

[3] For these different numbers very curious symbolical reasons are assigned (Megill. 23 *a*).

BOOK
III

a Meg. 29 b
b Jer.
Shabb.
xvi. 1;
Sopher.xvi.
10

in ancient times a lectionary, though certainly not that presently in use, which occupies exactly a year.[1] On the contrary, the Palestinian lectionary occupied three[a] or, according to some, three and a half years,[b] half a Sabbatic period. Accordingly, we find that the *Massorah* divides the Pentateuch into 154 sections. In regard to the lectionary of three and a half years we read of 175 sections. It requires, however, to be borne in mind, that preparatory to, and on certain festive days, the ordinary reading was interrupted, and portions substituted which bore on the subject of the feast. Possibly, at different periods different cycles may have obtained—those for three

c Comp.
Megill. 31 b
d Gitt. 59 b

and a half years, three years, and even for one year.[c][2] According to the Talmud,[d] a descendant of Aaron was always called up first to the reading;[3] then followed a Levite, and afterwards five ordinary Israelites. As this practice, as well as that of priestly benediction,[4] has been continued in the Synagogue from father to son, it is possible still to know who are descendants of Aaron, and who Levites. The reading of the Law was both preceded and followed by brief Benedictions.

Upon the Law followed a section from the Prophets,[5] the so-called *Haphtarah*.[6] The origin of this practice is not known, although it is one that must evidently have met a requirement on the part of the worshippers. Certain it is, that the present lectionary from the Prophets did not exist in early times; nor does it seem unlikely that the choice of the passage was left to the reader himself. At any rate,

e Megill iv.
4

as regarded the ordinary Sabbath days,[e] we are told that a reader might omit one or more verses, provided there was no break. As the Hebrew was not generally understood, the *Methurgeman*, or Interpreter, stood

f Comp.
1 Cor. xiv.
27, 28

by the side of the reader,[f] and translated into the Aramæan verse by verse, and in the section from the Prophets, or *Haphtarah*,

---

[1] This division seems to have originated in Babylon. Comp. *Zunz*, Gottesd. Vortr. pp. 3, 4.

[2] Comp. *Duschak*, Gesch. des jüd. Cultus, pp. 251–258.

[3] Some of the leading Rabbis resisted this practice, and declared that a Rabbi who yielded to it deserved death (Megill. 28 a; comp. Megill. 22 a. See generally *Duschak*, u. s. p. 255).

[4] Every descendant of Aaron in the Synagogue is bound to join in the act of benediction, on pain of forfeiture of the blessing on himself, according to Gen. xii. 3. Otherwise he transgresses three commands, contained in Numb. vi. 27 (Sot. 38 b). The present mode of dividing the fingers when pronouncing the blessing is justified by an appeal to Cant. ii. 9 (Bemidb. R. 11), although no doubt the origin of the practice is mystical.

[5] The reasons commonly assigned for it are unhistorical. Comp. 'Sketches of Jewish Life,' p. 278. The term Haphtarah, or rather *Aphtarah* and *Aphtarta* is derived from *patar*, to dismiss—either, like the Latin *Missa*, because it ended the general service, or else because the valedictory discourse, called *Aphtarah*, was connected with it.

[6] In a few places in Babylon (Shabb. 116 b), lessons from the Hagiographa were read at afternoon services. Besides, on Purim the whole Book of Esther was read.

after every three verses.[a] But the *Methurgeman* was not allowed to read his translation, lest it might popularly be regarded as authoritative. This may help us in some measure to understand the popular mode of Old Testament quotations in the New Testament. So long as the substance of the text was given correctly, the *Methurgeman* might paraphrase for better popular understanding. Again, it is but natural to suppose, that the *Methurgeman* would prepare himself for his work by such materials as he would find to hand, among which, of course, the translation of the LXX. would hold a prominent place. This may in part account alike for the employment of the LXX., and for its Targumic modifications, in the New Testament quotations.

The reading of the section from the Prophets (the *Haphtarah*) was in olden times immediately followed by an address, discourse, or sermon (*Derashah*), that is, where a Rabbi capable of giving such instruction, or a distinguished stranger, was present. Neither the leader of the devotions ('the delegate of the congregation' in this matter, or *Sheliach Tsibbur*), nor the *Methurgeman*, nor yet the preacher, required ordination.[1] That was reserved for the *rule* of the congregation, whether in legislation or administration, doctrine or discipline.

The only points required in the preacher were the necessary qualifications, both mental and moral.[2] When a great Rabbi employed a *Methurgeman* to explain to the people his sermon, he would, of course, select him for the purpose. Such an interpreter was also called *Amora*, or speaker. Perhaps the Rabbi would whisper to him his remarks, while he would repeat them aloud; or else he would only condescend to give hints, which the *Amora* would amplify; or he would speak in Hebrew, and the *Amora* translate it into Aramæan, Greek, Latin, or whatever the language of the people might be, for the sermon must reach the people in the vulgar tongue. The *Amora* would also, at the close of the sermon, answer questions or meet objections. If the preacher was a *very* great man, he would, perhaps, not condescend to communicate with the *Amora* directly, but employ one of his students as a middleman. This was also the practice when the preacher was in mourning for a very near relative—for so important was his office that it must not be interrupted, even by the sorrows or the religious obligations of 'mourning.'[b]

---

[1] At a later period, however, ordination seems to have been required for preaching. By a curious Rabbinic exegesis, the first clause of Prov. vii. 26 was applied to those who preached without ordination, and the second clause to those who were ordained and did not preach (Sot. 22 a).

[2] Thus, we have a saying of the first century 'You preach beautifully, but you do not practice beautifully' (Chag. 14 b; Yebam. 63 b).

BOOK
III

Indeed, Jewish tradition uses the most extravagant terms to extol the institution of preaching. To say that it glorified God, and brought men back, or at least nearer to Him, or that it quenched the soul's thirst, was as nothing. The little city, weak and besieged, but

* Eccl. ix. 15

delivered by the wise man in it,[a] served as symbol of the benefit which the preacher conferred on his hearers. The Divine Spirit rested on him, and his office conferred as much merit on him as if he had

b Ab. de R. Nath. 4

offered both the blood and the fat upon the altar of burnt offering.[b] No wonder that tradition traced the institution back to Moses, who had directed that, previous to, and on the various festivals, addresses, explanatory of their rites, and enforcing them, should be delivered to

c Meg. 4 a

the people.[c] The Targum Jonathan assumes the practice in the

d Targum on Judg. v. 2, 9

time of the Judges;[d] the men of the Great Synagogue are, of course, credited with it, and Shemayah and Abhtalyon are expressly desig-

e Darsha-nin, Pes. 70 b

nated as 'preachers.'[e] How general the practice was in the time of Jesus and His Apostles, the reader of the New Testament need not

f Ag. Ap. ii. 18

be told, and its witness is fully borne out by *Josephus*[f] and *Philo*.[g]

g In Flacc., ed. Frcf., p. 972; de Vita Mos. p. 688; Leg. ad Caj. pp. 1014, 1035

Both the Jerusalem and the Babylon Talmud assume it as so common, that in several passages 'Sabbath-observance' and the 'Sabbath-sermon' are identified. Long before Hillel we read of Rabbis preaching—in Greek or Latin—in the Jewish Synagogues of Rome,[h]

h For ex. Pes. 53 b

just as the Apostles preached in Greek in the Synagogues of the dispersed. That this practice, and the absolute liberty of teaching, subject to the authority of the 'chief ruler of the Synagogue,' formed important links in the Christianisation of the world, is another evidence of that wonder-working Rule of God, which brings about marvellous results through the orderly and natural succession of events —nay, orders these means with the view to their ultimate issue.

But this is not all. We have materials for drawing an accurate picture of the preacher, the congregation, and the sermon, as in those days. We are, of course, only speaking of the public addresses in the Synagogues on Sabbaths—not of those delivered at other times or in other places. Some great Rabbi, or famed preacher, or else a distinguished stranger, is known to be in the town. He would, of course, be asked by the ruler of the Synagogue to deliver a discourse. But who is a great preacher? We know that such a reputation was much coveted, and conferred on its possessor great distinction. The popular preacher was a power, and quite as much an object of popular homage and flattery as in our days. Many a learned Rabbi bitterly complained on finding his ponderous expositions neglected, while the multitude pushed and crowded into the neighoouring Synagogue to hear the declamations of some shallow popular Haggadist.[1] And so it came, that many cultivated this branch of theology. When a popular preacher was expected, men crowded the area of the Synagogue, while women filled the gallery.[a] On such occasions, there was the additional satisfaction of feeling that they had done something specially meritorious in running with quick steps, and crowding into the Synagogue.[b] For, was it not to carry out the spirit of Hos. vi. 3; xi. 10—at least, as Rabbinically understood? Even grave Rabbis joined in this 'pursuit to know the Lord,' and one of them comes to the somewhat caustic conclusion, that 'the reward of a discourse is the haste.'[c] However, more unworthy motives sometimes influenced some of the audience, and a Talmudic passage[d] traces the cause of many fasts to the meetings of the two sexes on such occasions.

The type of a popular preacher was not very different from what in our days would form his chief requisites. He ought to have a good figure,[e] a pleasant expression, and melodious voice (his words ought to be 'like those of the bride to the bridegroom'), fluency, speech 'sweet as honey,' 'pleasant as milk and honey'—'finely sifted like fine flour,' a diction richly adorned, 'like a bride on her wedding-day;' and sufficient confidence in his own knowledge and self-assurance never to be disconcerted. Above all he must be conciliatory, and avoid being too personal. Moses had addressed Israel as rebellious and hard-hearted, and he was not allowed to bring them into the land of promise. Elijah had upbraided them with having broken the covenant, and Elisha was immediately appointed his successor. Even Isaiah had his lips touched with burning coals, because he spoke of dwelling among a people of sinful lips.[f 2] As for the mental qualifications of the preacher, he must know his Bible well. As a bride knows

CHAP.
X

[a] Succ. 51 b

[b] Ber. 6 b

[c] Ber. 6 b

[d] Kidd. 81 a

[e] Taan. 16 a.
See *Dus-chak*, u. s. p. 285.

[f] Yalkut ii.
p. 43 a, be-
ginning

---

[1] In Sot. 40 a we have an account of how a popular preacher comforted his deserted brother theologian by the following parable: 'Two men met in a city, the one to sell jewels and precious things, the other toys, tinsel, and trifles. Then all the people ran to the latter shop, because they did not understand the wares of the former. A curious instance of popular wit is the following: It was expected that a person lately ordained should deliver a discourse before the people. The time came, but the *Methurge-man* in vain bent his ear closer and closer. It was evident that the new preacher had nothing to say. On which the *Methurgeman* quoted Habak. ii. 19:

'Woe unto him that saith to the wood, Awake; to the dumb stone, Arise, it shall teach!' (Sanh. 7 b). It was probably on account of such scenes, that the Nasi was not allowed afterwards to ordain without the consent of the Sanhedrin.

[2] In connection with this the proverb quoted in the New Testament is thus used by Rabbi Tarphon: 'I wonder whether anyone at present would accept reproof. If you said, Remove the mote from thine eye, he would immediately reply, First remove the beam out of thine own eye' (Arach. 16 b). May this not indicate how very widely the sayings of Christ had spread among the people?

properly to make use of her twenty-four ornaments, so must the preacher of the twenty-four books of the Bible. He must carefully prepare his subject—he is ' to hear himself' before the people hear him. But whatever else he may be or do, *he must be attractive*.[1] In earlier times the sermon might have consisted of a simple exposition of some passages from Scripture, or the Book of Sirach, which latter was treated and quoted by some of the Rabbis almost as if it had been canonical.[a] But this, or the full discussion of a single text[2] (קרה, to bore), would probably not be so attractive as the adaptation of a text to present circumstances, or even its modification and alteration for such purposes. There were scarcely bounds to the liberties taken by the preacher. He would divide a sentence, cut off one or two syllables from a word and join them to the next, so producing a different meaning, or giving a new interpretation to a text. Perhaps the strangest method was that of introducing Greek words and expressions into the Hebrew, and this not only to give a witty repartee,[b] but in illustration of Scripture.[c] Nay, many instances occur, in which a Hebrew word is, from the similarity of its sound with the Greek, rendered as if it were actually Greek, and thus a new meaning is given to a passage.[3]

If such licence was taken, it seems a comparatively small thing that a doctrine was derived from a word, a particle, or even a letter. But, as already stated, the great point was to attract the hearers. Parables, stories, allegories, witticisms, strange and foreign words, absurd legends, in short, anything that might startle an audience, was introduced.[4] Sometimes a discourse was entirely Haggadic; at

[1] Even the celebrated R. Eliezer had the misfortune that, at a festival, his hearers one by one stole out during the sermon (Bez. 15 *b*). On the other hand, it is said of R. Akiba, although his success as a preacher was very varied, that his application to Israel of the sufferings of Job and of his final deliverance moved his hearers to tears (Ber. R. 33).

[2] See *Zunz*, Gottesd. Vortr. p. 352, Note *b*.

[3] Thus, in Tanch. on Ex. xxii. 24 (ed. Warsh. p. 105 *a* and *b*, sect. 15, towards the end), the expression in Deut. xv. 7, ' Meachikha,' from thy brother, is rendered '*μὴ* achikha,' not thy brother. Similarly, in the Pesiqta, the statement in Gen. xxii. 7, 8, ' God will provide Himself a lamb for a burnt-offering,' is paraphrased. ' And if not a *Seh* (lamb) for a burnt-offering, my son, *σε* (thee) for a burnt offering. It is added, ' se leolah is

Greek, meaning, thou art the burnt-offering.' But the Greek in the former passage is also explained by rendering the ' achikha ' as an Aramaic form of *ἔοικα*, in which case it would targumically mean ' Withhold not thy hand from the poor, who is like to thee.' Comp. the interesting tractate of *Brüll* (Fremdspr. Redens. p. 21). A play upon Greek words is also supposed to occur in the Midrash on Cant. ii. 9, where the word ' dodi,' by omitting the second *d*, and transposing the *yod* and the *vav*, is made into the Greek *διος*, divine. But I confess I do not feel quite sure about this, although it has the countenance of *Levy*. In the Midrash on Cant. ii. 15, a whole Greek sentence is inserted, only Aramaically written. See also *Sachs*, Beitr. pp. 19 &c.

[4] Thus, when on one occasion the hearers of Akiba were going to sleep during his sermon, he called out: ' Why was Esther

others, the Haggadah served to introduce the Halakhah. Sometimes CHAP.
the object of the preacher was purely homiletical; at others, he dealt X
chiefly with the explanation of Scripture, or of the rites and meaning
of festivals. A favourite method was that which derived its name
from the stringing together of pearls (*Charaz*), when a preacher,
having quoted a passage or section from the Pentateuch, strung on
to it another and like-sounding, or really similar, from the Prophets
and the Hagiographa. Or else he would divide a sentence, generally
under three heads, and connect with each of the clauses a separate
doctrine, and then try to support it by Scripture. It is easy to
imagine to what lengths such preachers might go in their misinterpretation and misrepresentations of the plain text of Holy Scripture.
And yet a collection of short expositions (the *Pesiqta*), which, though
not dating from that period, may yet fairly be taken as giving a good
idea of this method of exposition, contains not a little that is fresh,
earnest, useful, and devotional. It is interesting to know that, at
the close of his address, the preacher very generally referred to the
great Messianic hope of Israel. The service closed with a short
prayer, or what we would term an 'ascription.'

We can now picture to ourselves the Synagogue, its worship, and
teaching. We can see the leader of the people's devotions as (according to Talmudic direction) he first refuses, with mock-modesty, the
honour conferred on him by the chief ruler; then, when urged, prepares to go; and when pressed a third time, goes up with slow and
measured steps to the lectern, and then before the Ark. We can
imagine how one after another, standing and facing the people, un-
rolls and holds in his hand a copy of the Law or of the Prophets, and
reads from the Sacred Word, the *Methurgeman* interpreting. Finally,
we can picture it, how the preacher would sit down and begin his discourse, none interrupting him with questions till he had finished,
when a succession of objections, answers, or inquiries might await the
Amora, if the preacher had employed such help. And help it certainly was not in many cases, to judge by the depreciatory and caustic
remarks, which not unfrequently occur, as to the manners, tone,
vanity, self-conceit, and silliness of the *Amora*[a] who, as he stood

[a] Midr. on
Eccl. vii. 5;
ix. 17 b

Queen in Persia over 127 provinces?
Answer: She was a descendant of Sarah,
who lived 127 years' (Ber. R. 58). On
a similar occasion R. Jehudah startled
the sleepers by the question: 'One woman
in Egypt bore 600,000 men in one birth.'
One of his hearers immediately replied
to the question, who she was: 'It was
Jochebed, who bore Moses, who is reckoned equal to all the 600,000 of Israel'
(Midr. Shir haSh. R., ed. Warsh., p. 11
b, towards the end, on Cant. i. 15).

[1] In both these passages 'the fools' are
explained to refer to the *Methurgeman*.

beside the Rabbi, thought far more of attracting attention and applause to himself, then of benefiting his hearers.   Hence some Rabbis would only employ special and trusted interpreters of their own, who were above fifty years of age.ᵃ   In short, so far as the sermon was concerned, the impression it produced must have been very similar to what we know the addresses of the monks in the Middle Ages to have wrought.   All the better can we understand, even from the human aspect, how the teaching of Jesus, alike in its substance and form, in its manner and matter, differed from that of the scribes; how multitudes would hang entranced on His word; and how, everywhere and by all, its impression was felt to be over-powering.

But it is certainly not the human aspect alone which here claims our attention.   The perplexed inquiry: 'Whence hath this man this wisdom and this knowledge?' must find another answer than the men of Nazareth could suggest, although to those in our days also who deny His Divine character, this must ever seem an unanswered and unanswerable question.

CHAPTER XI.

THE FIRST GALILEAN MINISTRY.

(St. Matt. iv. 13–17; St. Mark i. 14, 15; St. Luke iv. 15–32.)

THE visit to Nazareth was in many respects decisive. It presented by anticipation an epitome of the history of the Christ. He came to His own, and His own received Him not. The first time He taught in the Synagogue, as the first time He taught in the Temple, they cast Him out. On the one and the other occasion, they questioned His authority, and they asked for a 'sign.' In both instances, the power which they challenged was, indeed, claimed by Christ, but its display, in the manner which they expected, refused. The analogy seems to extend even farther—and if a misrepresentation of what Jesus had said when purifying the Temple formed the ground of the final false charge against Him,[a] the taunt of the Nazarenes: 'Physician, heal thyself!' found an echo in the mocking cry, as He hung on the Cross: 'He saved others, Himself He cannot save.'[b]

It is difficult to understand how, either on historical grounds, or after study of the character of Christ, the idea could have arisen[1] that Jesus had offered, or that He had claimed, to teach on that Sabbath in the Synagogue of Nazareth. Had He attempted what, alike in spirit and form, was so contrary to all Jewish notions, the whole character of the act would have been changed. As it was, the contrast with those by whom He was surrounded is almost as striking, as the part which He bore in the scene. We take it for granted, that what had so lately taken place in Cana, at only four miles' distance, or, to speak more accurately, in Capernaum, had become known in Nazareth. It raised to the highest pitch of expectancy the interest and curiosity previously awakened by the reports, which the Galileans had brought from Jerusalem, and by the general fame which had spread about Jesus. They were now to test, whether their

CHAP.
XI

[a] St. Matt. xxvi. 60, 61

[b] St. Matt. xxvii. 40-42

---

[1] And yet most commentators—following, I suppose, the lead of *Meyer*—hold that Christ had 'stood up' in the sense of offering or claiming to read.

countryman would be equal to the occasion, and do in His own city what they had heard had been done for Capernaum. To any ordinary man the return to Nazareth in such circumstances must have been an ordeal. Not so to the Christ, Who, in utter self-forgetfulness, had only this one aim of life—to do the Will of Him that sent Him. And so His bearing that day in the Synagogue is itself evidence, that while *in*, He was not *of*, that time.

Realising the scene on such occasions, we mark the contrast. As there could be no un-Jewish forwardness on the part of Jesus, so, assuredly, would there be none of that mock-humility of reluctance to officiate, in which Rabbinism delighted. If, as in the circumstances seems likely, Jesus commenced the first part of the service, and then pronounced before the 'Ark' those Eulogies which were regarded as, in the strictest sense, the prayer (*Tephillah*), we can imagine—though we can scarcely realise—the reverent solemnity, which would seem to give a new meaning to each well-remembered sentence. And in His mouth it all *had* a new meaning. We cannot know what, if any, petitions He inserted, though we can imagine what their spirit would have been. And now, one by one, Priest, Levite, and, in succession, five Israelites, had read from the Law. There is no reason to disturb the almost traditional idea, that Jesus Himself read the concluding portion from the Prophets, or the so-called *Haphtarah*. The whole narrative seems to imply this. Similarly, it is most likely that the *Haphtarah* for that day was taken from the prophecies of Isaiah,[1] and

ᵃ Is. lxi. 1, 2
ᵇ St. Luke
iv. 18, 19
ᶜ Baba B.
18 b

that it included the passage ᵃ quoted by the Evangelist as read by the Lord Jesus.ᵇ We know that the 'rolls' on which the Law was written were distinct from those of the Prophets; ᶜ and every probability points to it, that those of the Prophets, at least the Greater, were also written on separate scrolls. In this instance we are expressly told, that the minister 'delivered unto Him the book of the prophet Esaias,' we doubt not, for the *Haphtarah*,[2] and that, 'when He had unrolled the book,' He 'found' the place from which the Evangelist makes quotation.

---

[1] Although we cannot feel quite sure of this.

[2] I infer this from the fact, that the Book of the Prophet Isaiah was *given* to Him by the Minister of the Synagogue. Since the time of *Bengel* it has been a kind of traditional idea that, if this was the *Haphtarah* for the day, the sermon of Christ in Nazareth must have taken place on the Day of Atonement, for which in the modern Jewish lectionary Is. lviii. 6 forms part of the *Haphtarah*. There are, however, two objections to this view: 1. Our modern lectionary of *Haphtarahs* is certainly *not* the same as that in the time of Christ. 2. Even in our modern lectionary, Is. lxi. 1, 2 forms *no* part of the *Haphtarah*, either for the Day of Atonement, nor for any other Sabbath or festive day. In the modern lectionary Is. lvii. 14 to Is. lviii. 14 is the *Haphtarah* for the Day of Atonement.

When unrolling, and holding the scroll, much more than the sixty-first chapter of Isaiah must have been within range of His eyes. On the other hand, it is quite certain that the verses quoted by the Evangelist could not have formed the whole *Haphtarah*. According to traditional rule,[a] the *Haphtarah* ordinarily consisted of not less than twenty-one verses,[1] though, if the passage was to be 'targumed,' or a sermon to follow, that number might be shortened to seven, five, or even three verses. Now the passage quoted by St. Luke consists really of only one verse (Is. lxi. 1), together with a clause from Is. lviii. 6,[2] and the first clause of Is. lxi. 2. This could scarcely have formed the whole *Haphtarah*. There are other reasons also against this supposition. No doubt Jesus read alike the *Haphtarah* and the text of His discourse in Hebrew, and then 'targumed' or translated it: while St. Luke, as might be expected, quotes (with but two trifling alterations[3]) from the rendering of the LXX. But, on investigation, it appears that one clause is omitted from Is. lxi. 1,[4] and that between the close of Is. lxi. 1 and the clause of verse 2, which is added, a clause is inserted from the LXX. of Is. lviii. 6.[5] This could scarcely have been done in reading the *Haphtarah*. But if, as we suppose, the passages quoted formed the introductory text of Christ's discourse, such quotation and combination were not only in accordance with Jewish custom, but formed part of the favourite mode of teaching—the *Charaz*—or stringing, like pearls, passage to passage, illustrative of each other.[6] In the present instance, the portion of the scroll which Jesus unrolled may have exhibited in close proximity the two passages which formed the introductory text (the so-called *Pethichah*). But this is of comparatively small interest, since both the omission of a clause from Is. lxi. 1, and the insertion of another adapted from Is. lviii. 6, were evidently intentional. It might be presumptuous to attempt stating the reasons which may have influenced the Saviour in this, and yet some of them will instinctively occur to every thoughtful reader.

[a] Massech. Soph. xii. 7

---

[1] This symbolically: 7 × 3, since each of the seven readers in the Law had to read at least three verses.

[2] 'To set at liberty those that are bruised.' The words are taken, with but a slight necessary alteration in the verb, from the LXX. rendering of Is. lviii. 6. The clause from Is. lxi. 2 is: ' To preach the acceptable year of the Lord.'

[3] *Preaching* instead of *proclaiming*, in Is. lxi. 2, and in the form of the verb in the clause from Is. lviii. 6. Besides, the insertion of the clause: ' to heal the

broken-hearted,' is spurious.

[4] All the best MSS. omit the words, ' To heal the broken-hearted.'

[5] See above, Note 2.

[6] See the remarks on this point in the previous chapter. If I rightly understand the somewhat obscure language of *Surenhusius* (Biblos Katallages, pp. 339–345), such is also the view of that learned writer. This peculiarly Jewish method of Scriptural quotation by 'stringing together' is employed by St. Paul in Rom. iii. 10–18.

BOOK
III

^a The other
two being
Is. xxxii.
14, 15, and
Lament.
iii. 50

It was, indeed, Divine 'wisdom'—'the Spirit of the Lord' upon Him, which directed Jesus in the choice of such a text for His first Messianic Sermon. It struck the key-note to the whole of His Galilean ministry. The ancient Synagogue regarded Is. lxi. 1, 2, as one of the three passages,^a in which mention of the Holy Ghost was connected with the promised redemption.[1] In this view, the application which the passage received in the discourse of our Lord was peculiarly suitable. For the words in which St. Luke reports what followed the *Pethichah*, or introductory text, seem rather a summary, than either the introduction or part of the discourse of Christ. 'This day is this Scripture fulfilled in your ears.' A summary this, which may well serve to guide in all preaching. As regards its form, it would be: so to present the teaching of Holy Scripture, as that it can be drawn together in the focus of one sentence; as regards its substance, that this be the one focus: all Scripture fulfilled by a present Christ. And this—in the Gospel which He bears to the poor, the release which He announces to the captives, the healing which He offers to those whom sin had blinded, and the freedom He brings to them who were bruised; and all as the trumpet-blast of God's Jubilee into His world of misery, sin, and want! A year thus begun would be glorious indeed in the blessings it gave.

There was not a word in all this of what common Jewish expectancy would have connected with, nay, chiefly accentuated in an announcement of the Messianic redemption; not a word to raise carnal hopes, or flatter Jewish pride. Truly, it was the most un-Jewish discourse for a Jewish Messiah of those days, with which to open His Ministry. And yet such was the power of these 'words of grace.' that the hearers hung spell-bound upon them. Every eye was fastened on Him with hungry eagerness. For the time they forgot all else— Who it was that addressed them, even the strangeness of the message, so unspeakably in contrast to any preaching of Rabbi or Teacher that had been heard in that Synagogue. Indeed, one can scarcely conceive the impression which the Words of Christ must have produced, when promise and fulfilment, hope and reality, mingled, and wants of the heart, hitherto unrealised, were wakened, only to be more than satisfied. It was another sphere, another life. Truly, the anointing of the Holy Ghost was on the Preacher, from Whose lips dropped these 'words of grace.' And if such was the announcement of the Year of God's Jubilee, what blessings must it bear in its bosom!

---

[1] See the Appendix on the Messianic passages.

The discourse had been spoken, and the breathless silence with which, even according to Jewish custom, it had been listened to,[1] gave place to the usual after-sermon hum of an Eastern Synagogue. On one point all were agreed: that they were marvellous words of grace, which had proceeded out of His mouth. And still the Preacher waited, with deep longing of soul, for some question, which would have marked the spiritual application of what He had spoken. Such deep longing of soul is kindred to, and passes into almost sternness, just because he who so longs is so intensely in earnest, in the conviction of the reality of his message. It was so with Jesus in Nazareth. They were indeed making application of the Sermon to the Preacher, but in quite different manner from that to which His discourse had pointed. It was not the fulfilment of the Scripture in Him, but the circumstance, that such an one as the Son of Joseph, their village carpenter, should have spoken such words, that attracted their attention. Not, as we take it, in a malevolent spirit, but altogether unspiritually, as regarded the effect of Christ's words, did one and another, here and there, express wonderment to his neighbour.

They had *heard*, and now they would fain have *seen*. But already the holy indignation of Him, Whom they only knew as Joseph's son, was kindled. The turn of matters; their very admiration and expectation; their vulgar, unspiritual comments: it was all so entirely contrary to the Character, the Mission, and the Words of Jesus. No doubt they would next expect, that here in His own city, and all the more because it was such, He would do what they had heard had taken place in Capernaum. It was the world-old saying, as false, except to the ear, and as speciously popular as most such sayings: 'Charity begins at home'—or, according to the Jewish proverb, and in application to the special circumstances: 'Physician, heal thyself.'[2] Whereas, if there is any meaning in truth and principle; if there was any meaning and reality in Christ's Mission, and in the discourse He had just spoken, Charity does *not* begin at home; and 'Physician, heal thyself' is not of the Gospel for the poor, nor yet the preaching of God's Jubilee, but that of the Devil, whose works Jesus had come to destroy. How could He, in His holy abhorrence and indignation, say this better than by again repeating, though now with different application, that sad experience, 'No prophet is accepted in his own country,' which He could have hoped was for ever behind Him;[a] and

CHAP.
XI

[a] St. John
iv. 44

---

[1] See the previous chapter. It was the universal rule to listen to the sermon in perfect silence (Pes. 110 *a*; Moed K. *a*). The questions and objections commenced afterwards.

[2] The proverb really is: 'Physician, heal thine own lameness' (Ber. R. 23, ed. Warsh. p. 45 *b*).

by pointing to those two Old Testament instances of it, whose names and authority were most frequently on Jewish lips? Not they who were 'their own,' but they who were most receptive in faith—not Israel, but Gentiles, were those most markedly favoured in the ministry of Elijah and of Elisha.[1]

As we read the report of Jesus' words, we perceive only dimly that aspect of them which stirred the wrath of His hearers to the utmost, and yet we do understand it. That He should have turned so fully the light upon the Gentiles, and flung its large shadows upon them; that ' Joseph's Son ' should have taken up this position towards them; that He would make to them spiritual application unto death of His sermon, since they would not make it unto life: it stung them to the quick. Away He must out of His city; it could not bear His Presence any longer, not even on that holy Sabbath. Out they thrust Him from the Synagogue; forth they pressed Him out of the city; on they followed, and around they beset Him along the road by the brow of the hill on which the city is built—perhaps to that western angle, at present pointed out as the site.[2] This, with the unspoken intention of crowding Him over the cliff,[3] which there rises abruptly about forty feet out of the valley beneath.[4] If we are correct in indicating the locality, the road here bifurcates,[5] and we can conceive how Jesus, Who had hitherto, in the silence of sadness, allowed Himself almost mechanically to be pressed onwards by the surrounding crowd, now turned, and by that look of commanding majesty, the forthbreaking of His Divine Being, which ever and again wrought on those around miracles of subjection, constrained them to halt and give way before Him, while unharmed He passed through their midst.[6] So did Israel of old pass through the cleft waves of the sea, which the wonder-working rod of Moses had converted into

---

[1] The statement that the famine in the time of Elijah lasted three and a half years is in accordance with universal Jewish tradition. Comp. Yalkut on 1 Kings xvi., vol. ii. p. 32 *b*.

[2] See *Stanley*, Sinai and Palestine, p. 363. But surely it could not have been the *south*-western corner (*Conder*, Tent-Work, i. p. 140, and all later writers).

[3] The provision, which awarded instant death without formal trial in case of open blasphemy or profanation (Sanh. 81 *b*), would not apply in this instance. Probably the purpose was, that the crowd around should, as it were accidentally, push Him over the cliff.

[4] The spot is just above the Maronite

Church.

[5] See the plan of Nazareth in *Bädeker's* (*Socin's*) Palæstina, p. 255. The road to the left goes westward, that through the northern part of the town, towards Capernaum. Our localisation gains in probability, if the ancient Synagogue stood where tradition places it. At present it is in the hands of the Maronites.

[6] The circumstance that the Nazarenes did not avow the purpose of casting Him over the cliff, but intended accidentally to crowd Him over, explains how, when He turned sharply round to the right, and passed through the crowd, they did not follow Him.

a wall of safety.   Yet, although He parted from it in judgment,
not thus could the Christ have finally and for ever left His own
Nazareth.[1]

Cast out of His own city, Jesus pursued His solitary way towards
Capernaum.[2]   There, at least, devoted friends and believing disciples
would welcome Him.   There, also, a large draught of souls would fill
the Gospel-net.   Capernaum would be His Galilean home.[a]   Here He   [a] St. Matt.
                                                                        ix. 1
would, on the Sabbath-days, preach in that Synagogue, of which the
good centurion was the builder,[b] and Jairus the chief ruler.[c]   These   [b] St. Luke
                                                                             vii. 5
names, and the memories connected with them, are a sufficient com-   [c] St. Mark
ment on the effect of His preaching: that 'His word was with power.'   v. 22
In Capernaum, also, was the now believing and devoted household
of the court-officer, whose only son the Word of Christ, spoken at a
distance, had restored to life.   Here also, or in the immediate neighbourhood, was the home of His earliest and closest disciples, the
brothers Simon and Andrew, and of James and John, the sons of
Zebedee.

From the character of the narrative, and still more from the later
call of these four,[d] it would seem that, after the return of Jesus from   [d] St. Matt.
                                                                            iv. 18, 22,
Judæa into Galilee, His disciples had left Him, probably in Cana, and   and paral-
                                                                          lels
returned to their homes and ordinary avocations.   They were not yet
called to forsake all and follow Him—not merely to discipleship, but
to fellowship and Apostolate.   When He went from Cana to Nazareth,
they returned to Capernaum.   They knew He was near them.
Presently He came; and now His Ministry was in their own Capernaum, or in its immediate neighbourhood.

[1] Many, even orthodox commentators, hold that this history is the same as that related in St. Matt. xiii. 54–58, and St. Mark vi. 1–6. But, for the reasons about to be stated, I have come, although somewhat hesitatingly, to the conclusion, that the narrative of St. Luke and those of St. Matthew and St. Mark refer to different events. 1. The narrative in St. Luke (which we shall call A) refers to the commencement of Christ's Ministry, while those of St. Matthew and St. Mark (which we shall call B) are placed at a later period. Nor does it seem likely, that our Lord would have entirely abandoned Nazareth after one rejection. 2. In narrative A, Christ is without disciples; in narrative B He is accompanied by them. 3. In narrative A no miracles are recorded—in fact, His words about Elijah and Elisha preclude any idea of them; while in narrative B there are a few, though

not many. 4. In narrative A He is thrust out of the city immediately after His sermon, while narrative B implies, that He continued for some time in Nazareth, only wondering at their unbelief.
If it be objected, that Jesus could scarcely have returned to Nazareth after the attempt on His life, we must bear in mind that this purpose had not been avowed, and that His growing fame during the intervening period may have rendered such a return not only possible, but even advisable.
The coincidences as regards our Lord's statement about the Prophet, and their objection as to His being the carpenter's son, are only natural in the circumstances.

[2] Probably resting in the immediate neighbourhood of Nazareth, and pursuing His journey next day, when the Sabbath was past.

For Capernaum was not the only place where He taught. Rather
was it the centre for itinerancy through all that district, to preach in
its Synagogues.ᵃ Amidst such ministry of quiet 'power,' chiefly
alone and unattended by His disciples, the summer passed. Truly,
it was summer in the ancient land of Zebulun and Naphtali, in the
Galilee of the Gentiles, when the glorious Light that had risen chased
away the long winter's darkness, and those who had been the first
exiles in Assyrian bondage were the first brought back to Israel's true
liberty, and by Israel's Messiah-King. To the writer of the first
Gospel, as, long years afterwards, he looked back on this, the happy
time when he had first seen the Light, till it had sprung up even to
him 'in the region and shadow of death,' it must have been a time of
peculiarly bright memories. How often, as he sat at the receipt of
custom, must he have seen Jesus passing by; how often must he
have heard His Words, some, perhaps, spoken to himself, but all
falling like good seed into the field of his heart, and preparing him
at once and joyously to obey the summons when it came: *Follow Me.*
And not to him only, but to many more, would it be a glowing, growing time of heaven's own summer.

There was a dim tradition in the Synagogue, that this prediction,ᵇ
'The people that walk in the darkness see a great light,' referred to the
new light, with which God would enlighten the eyes of those who had
penetrated into the mysteries of Rabbinic lore, enabling them to
perceive concerning 'loosing and binding, concerning what was clean

and what was unclean.'ᶜ Others[1] regarded it as a promise to the
early exiles, fulfilled when the great liberty came to them. To Levi-
Matthew it seemed as if both interpretations had come true in those
days of Christ's first Galilean ministry. Nay, he saw them combined
in a higher unity when to their eyes, enlightened by the great Light,
came the new knowledge of what was bound and what loosed, what
unclean and clean, though quite differently from what Judaism had
declared it to them; and when, in that orient Sun, the promise of
liberty to long-banished Israel was at last· seen fulfilled. It was,
indeed, the highest and only true fulfilment of that prediction of
Isaiah,[2] in a history where all was prophetic, every partial fulfilment
only an unfolding and opening of the bud, and each symbolic of
further unfolding till, in the fulness of time, the great Reality came,

---

[1] See *Mikraoth Gedoloth* on the passage.
[2] The words, 'That it might be fulfilled which was spoken by Esaias,' do
not bear the meaning, that this was their
primary and literal purpose. They represent a frequent mode of citation
among Jewish writers, indicating a *real*
fulfilment of the spirit, though not always
of the letter, of a prophecy. On this sub-

to which all that was prophetic in Israel's history and predictions   CHAP.
pointed.   And so as, in the evening of his days, Levi-Matthew looked   XI
back to distant Galilee, the glow of the setting sun seemed once more
to rest on that lake, as it lay bathed in its sheen of gold.   It lit up
that city, those shores, that custom-house; it spread far off, over
those hills, and across the Jordan.   Truly, and in the only true sense,
had then the promise been fulfilled:[a] 'To them which sat in the re-   [a] St. Matt.
gion and shadow of death, light is sprung up.'   ix. 16

ject see also *Surenhusius*, u. s., p. 218,   might be fulfilled which was spoken '), u.
and his admirable exposition of the Jew-   s., pp. 2–4.
ish formula לקיים מה שנאמר ('that it

CHAPTER XII.

AT THE 'UNKNOWN' FEAST IN JERUSALEM, AND BY THE POOL OF BETHESDA.

(St. John v.)

BOOK
III

THE shorter days of early autumn had come,[1] and the country stood in all its luxurious wealth of beauty and fruitfulness, as Jesus passed from Galilee to what, in the absence of any certain evidence, we must still be content to call 'the Unknown Feast' in Jerusalem. Thus much, however, seems clear that it was either the 'Feast of Wood-offering' on the 15th of Abh (in August), when, amidst demonstrations of joy, willing givers brought from all parts of the country the wood required for the service of the Altar; or else the 'Feast of Trumpets' on the 1st of Tishri (about the middle of September), which marked the beginning of the New (civil) Year.[2] The journey of Christ to that Feast and its results are not mentioned in the Synoptic Gospels, because that Judæan ministry which, if the illustration be lawful, was the historical thread on which St. John strung his record of what the Word spake, lay, in great measure, beyond their historical standpoint. Besides, this and similar events belonged, indeed, to that grand Self-Manifestation of Christ, with the corresponding growth of opposition consequent upon it, which it was the object of the Fourth Gospel to set forth; but it led to no permanent results, and so was outside the scope of the more popular, pragmatic record, which the other Gospels had in view.

There may in this instance, however, have been other reasons also for their silence. It has already been indicated that, during the summer of Christ's first Galilean ministry, when Capernaum was His centre of action, the disciples had returned to their homes and usual avocations, while Jesus moved about chiefly alone and unattended. This explains the circumstance of a second call, even to His most intimate and closest followers. It also accords best with that gradual

---

[1] Both *Godet* and Prof. *Westcott* (the latter more fully) have pointed out the distinction between μετὰ ταῦτα (literally: 'after those things—as in St. John v. 1'),and μετὰ τοῦτο. The former does not indicate immediate succession of time.

[2] For a full discussion of the question see vol. ii. App. XV. pp. 765, 766; for the 'Feast of Wood-offering,' 'The Temple and its Services,&c.,' pp.295, 296.

development in Christ's activity, which commencing with the more private teaching of the new Preacher of Righteousness in the villages by the lake, or in the Synagogues, expanded into that publicity in which He at last appears, surrounded by His Apostles, attended by the loving ministry of those to whom He had brought healing of body or soul, and followed by a multitude which everywhere pressed around Him for teaching and help.

This more public activity commenced with the return of Jesus from 'the Unknown Feast' in Jerusalem. There He had, in answer to the challenge of the Jewish authorities, for the first time set forth His Messianic claims in all their fulness. And there, also, He had for the first time encountered that active persecution unto death, of which Golgotha was the logical outcome. This Feast, then, was the time of critical decision. Accordingly, as involving the separation from the old state and the commencement of a new condition of things, it was immediately followed by the call of His disciples to a new Apostle-ship. In this view, we can also better understand the briefness of the notices of His first Galilean ministry, and how, after Christ's return from that Feast, His teaching became more full, and the display of His miraculous power more constant and public.

It seems only congruous, accordant with all the great decisive steps of Him in Whose footprints the disciples trod, only after He had marked them, as it were, with His Blood—that He should have gone up to that Feast alone and unattended. That such had been the case, has been inferred by some from this, that the narrative of the healing of the impotent man reads so Jewish, that the account of it appears to have been derived by St. John from a Jew at Jerusalem.[a][1] Others[2] *Wetstein* have come to the same conclusion from the meagreness of details about the event. But it seems implied in the narrative itself, and the marked and exceptional absence of any reference to disciples leads to the obvious conclusion, that they had not been with their Master.

But, if Jesus was alone and unattended at the Feast, the question arises, whence the report was derived of what He said in reply to the challenge of the Jews? Here the answer naturally suggests itself, that the Master Himself may, at some later period of His life—perhaps during His last stay in Jerusalem—have communicated to His disciples, or else to him who stood nearest to Him, the details of what

---

[1] The reader will have no difficulty in finding not a few points in St. John v. utterly irreconcilable with the theory of a second century Ephesian Gospel. It would take too much space to particularise them.

[2] So *Gess, Godet,* and others.

had passed on the first occasion when the Jewish authorities had sought to extinguish His Messianic claims in His blood. If that communication was made when Jesus was about to be offered up, it would also account for what otherwise might seem a difficulty: the very developed form of expression in which His relation to the Father, and His own Office and Power, are presented. We can understand how, from the very first, all this should have been laid before the teachers of Israel. But in view of the organic development of Christ's teaching, we could scarcely expect it to have been expressed in such very full terms, till near the close of His Ministry.[1]

But we are anticipating. The narrative transports us at once to what, at the time, seems to have been a well-known locality in Jerusalem, though all attempts to identify it, or even to explain the name *Bethesda*, have hitherto failed. All we know is, that it was a pool enclosed within five porches, by the sheep-market, presumably close to the 'Sheep-Gate.'[a] This, as seems most likely, opened from the busy northern suburb of markets, bazaars, and workshops, eastwards upon the road which led over the Mount of Olives and Bethany to Jericho.[2] In that case, most probability would attach to the identification of the Pool Bethesda with a pool somewhat north of the so-called *Birket Israîl*. At present it is wholly filled with rubbish, but in the time of the Crusaders it seems to have borne the name of the Sheep-pond, and, it was thought, traces of the five porches could still be detected. Be this as it may, it certainly bore in the 'Hebrew' —or rather Aramæan—'tongue,' the name *Bethesda*. No doubt this name was designative, though the common explanations—*Beth Chisda* (so most modern writers, and *Watkins*) 'House of Mercy' (?), *Beth Istebha* (אִסְטְבָא, *Delitzsch*), 'House of Porches,' and *Beth Zeytha* (*Westcott*) 'House of the Olive '—seem all unsatisfactory. More probability attaches to the rendering *Beth Asutha* (*Wünsche*), or *Beth Asyatha*, 'House of Healing.' But as this derivation offers linguistic difficulties, we would suggest that the second part of the name (Beth-*Esda*) was really a Greek word Aramaised. Here two different derivations suggest themselves. The root-word of *Esda* might either express to '*become well*'—Beth ἰᾶσθαι—or something akin to the Rabbinic *Zit*[3] (זִיט=ζῆθι). In that case, the designation would agree with an

---

[1] Even *Strauss* admits, that the discourse contains nothing which *might* not have been spoken by Christ. His objection to its authenticity, on the ground of the analogies to it in certain portions of the Fourth Gospel and of the Epistles of St. John, is a curious instance of critical argumentation (Leben Jesu, i. p. 646).

[2] Comp. specially *Riehm's* Handwörterb. *ad voc.*

[3] Said when people sneezed, like '*Prosit!* '

ancient reading of the name, *Bethzatha.* Or else, the name Bethesda CHAP.
might combine, according to a not uncommon Rabbinic practice, the XII
Hebrew *Beth* with some Aramaised form derived from the Greek word
ζέω, ' to boil ' or ' bubble up ' (subst. ζέσις); in which case it would
mean ' the House of Bubbling-up,' viz. water. Any of the three
derivations just suggested would not only give an apt designation for
the pool, but explain why St. John, contrary to his usual practice,
does not give a Greek equivalent for a Hebrew term.

All this is, however, of very subordinate importance, compared with
the marvellous facts of the narrative itself. In the five porches surrounding this pool lay ' a great multitude of the impotent,' in anxious
hope of a miraculous cure. We can picture to ourselves the scene.
The popular superstitions,[1] which gave rise to what we would regard as
a peculiarly painful exhibition of human misery of body and soul, is
strictly true to the times and the people. Even now travellers describe a similar concourse of poor crippled sufferers, on their miserable
pallets or on rugs, around the mineral springs near Tiberias, filling, in
true Oriental fashion, the air with their lamentations. In the present
instance there would be even more occasion for this than around any
ordinary thermal spring. For the popular idea was, that an Angel
descended into the water, causing it to bubble up, and that only he
who *first* stepped into the pool would be cured. As thus only one
person could obtain benefit, we may imagine the lamentations of the
' many ' who would, perhaps, day by day, be disappointed in their
hopes. This bubbling up of the water was, of course, due not to
supernatural but to physical causes. Such intermittent springs are
not uncommon, and to this day the so-called ' Fountain of the Virgin '
in Jerusalem exhibits the phenomenon. It is scarcely necessary
to say, that the Gospel-narrative does not ascribe this ' troubling of
the waters ' to Angelic agency, nor endorses the belief, that only the
first who afterwards entered them, could be healed. This was evidently
the belief of the impotent man, as of all the waiting multitude.[a] But _{*St. John v 7*}
the words in verse 4 of our Authorised Version, and perhaps, also,
the last clause of verse 3, are admittedly an interpolation.[2]

In another part of this book it is explained at length,[3] how Jewish
belief at the time attached such agency to Angels, and how it localised

---

[1] Indeed, belief in ' holy wells ' seems
to have been very common in ancient
times. From the cuneiform inscriptions
it appears to have been even entertained
by the ancient Babylonians.

[2] I must here refer to the critical dis-

cussion in Canon *Westcott's* Commentary
on St. John. I only wish I could without
unfairness transport to these pages the
results of his masterly criticism of this
chapter.

[3] See the Appendix on ' Angels.'

(so to speak) special Angels in springs and rivers; and we shall have presently to show, what were the popular notions about miraculous cures. If, however, the belief about Bethesda arose merely from the mistaken ideas about the cause of this bubbling of the water, the question would naturally suggest itself, whether any such cases as those described had ever really occurred, and, if not, how such a superstition could have continued. But that such healing might actually occur in the circumstances, no one would be prepared to deny, who has read the accounts of pilgrimages to places of miraculous cure, or who considers the influence of a firm expectancy on the imagination, especially in diseases which have their origin in the nervous system. This view of the matter is confirmed, and Scripture still further vindicated from even the faintest appearance of endorsing the popular superstition, by the use of the article in the expression ' a multitude of the impotent ' ($\pi\lambda\tilde{\eta}\theta o\varsigma$ $\tau\tilde{\omega}\nu$ $\dot{\alpha}\sigma\theta\epsilon\nu o\acute{\nu}\nu\tau\omega\nu$), which marks this impotence as used in the generic sense, while the special diseases, afterwards enumerated without the article, are ranged under it as instances of those who were thus impotent. Such use of the Greek term, as not applying to any one specific malady, is vindicated by a reference to St. Matt. viii. 17 and St. Mark vi. 56, and by its employment by the physician Luke. It is, of course, not intended to imply, that the distempers to which this designation is given had *all* their origin in the nervous system; but we argue that, if the term ' impotent ' was the general, of which the diseases mentioned in verse 3 were the specific —in other words, that, if it was an ' impotence,' of which these were the various manifestations—it may indicate, that they all, so far as relieved, had one common source, and this, as we would suggest, in the nervous system.[1]

With all reverence, we can in some measure understand, what feelings must have stirred the heart of Jesus, in view of this suffering, waiting ' great multitude.' Why, indeed, did He go into those five porches, since He had neither disease to cure, nor cry for help had come to Him from those who looked for relief to far other means? Not, surely, from curiosity. But as one longs to escape from the stifling atmosphere of a scene of worldly pomp, with its glitter and unreality, into the clearness of the evening-air, so our Lord may have longed to pass from the glitter and unreality of those who held rule

---

[1] Another term for 'sick' in the N. T. is $\overset{}{\alpha}\rho\rho\omega\sigma\tau o\varsigma$ (St. Matt. xiv. 14; St. Mark vi. 5, 13; xvi. 18; (comp. Ecclus. vii. 35). This corresponds to the Hebrew חָלָה. Mal. i. 8. In 1 Cor. xi. 30 the two words are used together, $\overset{}{\alpha}\rho\rho\omega\sigma\tau o\varsigma$ and $\dot{\alpha}\sigma\theta\epsilon\nu\acute{\eta}\varsigma$.

in the Temple, or who occupied the seat of Moses in their Academies, CHAP.
to what was the atmosphere of His Life on earth, His real Work, XII
among that suffering, ignorant multitude, which, in its sorrow, raised
a piteous, longing cry for help where it had been misdirected to seek it.

And thus we can here also perceive the deep internal connection
between Christ's miracle of healing 'the impotent man' and the
address of mingled sadness and severity,[a] in which He afterwards set [a] St. John
before the Masters in Israel the one truth fundamental in all things. v. 17–47
We have only, so to speak, to reverse the formal order and succession
of that discourse, to gain an insight into what prompted Jesus to go
to Bethesda, and by His power to perform this healing.[1] He had
been in the Temple at the Feast; He had necessarily been in contact
—it could not be otherwise, when in the Temple—with the great ones
of Israel. What a stifling atmosphere there of glitter and unreality!
What had He in common with those who 'received glory one of
another, and the glory which cometh from the One only God' they
sought not?[b] How could such men believe? The first meaning, and [b] ver. 44
the object of His Life and Work, was as entirely different from their
aims and perceptions, as were the respective springs of their inner
being. They clung and appealed to Moses; to Moses, whose successors
they claimed to be, let them go![c] Their elaborate searching and [c] vv. 45–47
sifting of the Law in hope that, by a subtle analysis of its every
particle and letter, by inferences from, and a careful drawing of a prohibitive hedge around, its letter, they would possess themselves of
eternal life,[d] what did it all come to? Utterly self-deceived, and far [d] ver. 39
from the truth in their elaborate attempts to outdo each other in
local ingenuity, they would, while rejecting the Messiah sent from
God, at last become the victims of a coarse Messianic impostor.[e] And [e] vv. 40–43
even in the present, what was it all? Only the letter—the outward!
All the lessons of their past miraculous history had been utterly lost
on them. What had there been of the merely outward in its miracles
and revelations?[f] It had been the witness of the Father; but this [f] ver. 37
was the very element which, amidst their handling of the external
form, they perceived not. Nay, not only the unheard Voice of the
Father, but also the heard voice of the Prophets—a voice which they
might have heard even in John the Baptist. They heard, but did not
perceive it—just as, in increasing measure, Christ's sayings and doings,
and the Father and His testimony, were not perceived. And so all
hastened on to the judgment of final unbelief, irretrievable loss, and

---

[1] Such a logical inversion seems necessary in passing from the objective to the
subjective.

BOOK
III

ᵃ vv. 30-38

self-caused condemnation.ᵃ It was all utterly mistaken; utter, and, alas! guilty perversion, their elaborate trifling with the most sacred things, while around them were suffering, perishing men, stretching 'lame hands' into emptiness, and wailing out their mistaken hopes into the eternal silence.

While they were discussing the niceties of what constituted labour on a Sabbath, such as what infringed its sacred rest or what constituted a burden, multitudes of them who laboured and were heavy laden were left to perish in their ignorance. That was the Sabbath, and the God of the Sabbath of Pharisaism; this the rest, the enlightenment, the hope for them who laboured and were heavy laden, and who longed and knew not where to find the true *Sabbatismos*! Nay, if the Christ had not been the very opposite of all that Pharisaism sought, He would not have been the Orient Sun of the Eternal Sabbath. But the God Who ever worked in love, Whose rest was to give rest, Whose Sabbath to remove burdens, was His Father. He knew Him; He saw His working; He was in fellowship of love, of work, of power with Him. He had come to loose every yoke, to give life, to bring life, to be life—because He had life: life in its fullest sense. For, contact with Him, whatever it may be, gives life: to the diseased, health; to the spiritually dead, the life of the soul; to the dead in their graves, the life of resurrection. And all this was the meaning of Holy Scripture, when it pointed forward to the Lord's Anointed; and all this was not merely His own, but the Father's Will—the Mission which He had given Him, the Work which He had sent Him to do.ᵇ

ᵇ vv. 19-32

Translate this into deed, as all His teachings have been, are, and will be, and we have the miraculous cure of the impotent man, with its attendant circumstances. Or, conversely, translate that deed, with its attendant circumstances, into words, and we have the discourse of our Lord. Moreover, all this is fundamental to the highest understanding of our Lord's history. And, therefore, we understand how, many years afterwards, the beloved disciple gave a place to this miracle, when, in the full ripeness of spiritual discernment, he chose for record in his Gospel from among those 'many signs,' which Jesus truly did,ᶜ only *five* as typical, like the five porches of the great Bethesda of His help to the impotent, or like the five divisions into which the Psalter of praise was arranged. As he looked back, from the height where he stood at his journey's end, to where the sun was setting in purple and golden glory far across the intervening landscape, amidst its varying scenes this must have stood out before his sight, as what

ᶜ St. John
xx. 30

might show to us that 'Jesus was the Christ, the Son of God, and that believing we might have life through His Name.[a]

And so, understanding from what He afterwards said to 'the Jews' what He thought and felt in going thither, we are better prepared to follow the Christ to Bethesda. Two pictures must have been here simultaneously present to His mind. On the one side, a multitude whose sufferings and false expectancies rose, like the wail of the starving for bread ; and, on the other side, the neighbouring Temple, with its priesthood and teachers, who, in their self-seeking and the trifling of their religious externalism, neither understood, heard, nor would have cared for such a cry. If there was an Israel, Prince with God, and if there was a God of the Covenant, this must not, cannot be ; and Christ goes to Bethesda as Israel's Messiah, the Truth, and the Life. There was twofold suffering there, and it were difficult to know which would have stirred Him most : that of the body, or the mistaken earnestness which so trustfully looked for Heaven's relief— yet within such narrow limits as the accident or good fortune of being first pushed into the Angel-troubled waters. But this was also a true picture of His people in their misery, and in their narrow notions of God and of the conditions of His blessing. And now Israel's Messiah had at last come. What would we expect Him to have done? Surely not to preach controversial or reformatory doctrines; but to *do*, if it were in Him, and in doing to speak. And so in this also the Gospel-narrative proves itself true, by telling that He did, what alone would be true in a Messiah, the Son of God. It is, indeed, impossible to think of Incarnate Deity—and this, be it remembered, is the fundamental postulate of the Gospels—as brought into contact with misery, disease, and death without their being removed. That power went forth from Him always, everywhere, and to all, is absolutely necessary, if He was the Son of God, the Saviour of the world. And so the miracles, as we mistakingly term the result of the contact of God with man, of the *Immanuel* (God with us), are not only the golden ladder which leads up to *the Miracle*, God manifest in the flesh, but the steps by which He descends from His height to our lowliness.

The waters had not yet been 'troubled,' when He stood among that multitude of sufferers and their attendant friends. It was in those breathless moments of the intense suspense of expectancy, when every eye was fixed on the *pool*, that the eye of the Saviour searched for the most wretched object among them all. In him, as a typical case, could He best do and teach that for which He had come. This 'impotent' man, for thirty-eight years a hopeless sufferer, with-

out attendant or friend ᵃ among those whom misery—in this also the
true outcome of sin—made so intensely selfish; and whose sickness
was really the consequence of his sin,ᵇ and not merely in the sense
which the Jews attached to it ᶜ—this now seemed the fittest object for
power and grace.   For, most marked in this history is the entire
spontaneity of our Lord's help.¹   It is idle to speak either of faith or
of receptiveness on the man's part.   The essence of the whole lies in the
utter absence of both; in Christ's raising, as it were, the dead, and
calling the things that are not as though they were.   This, the fundamental thought concerning His Mission and power as the Christ
shines forth as the historical background in Christ's subsequent,
explanatory discourse.   The ' Wilt thou be made whole ? ' with which
Jesus drew the man's attention to Himself, was only to probe and lay
bare his misery.   And then came the word of power, or rather the
power spoken forth, which made him whole every whit.   Away from
this pool, in which there was no healing; away—for the Son of God
had come to him with the outflowing of His power and pitying help,
and he *was* made whole.   Away with his bed, not, although it was the
holy Sabbath, but just because it was the Sabbath of holy rest and
holy delight !

In the general absorbedness of all around, no ear, but that to
which it had been spoken, had heard what the Saviour had said.
The waters had not been troubled, and the healing had been all unseen.   Before the healed man, scarcely conscious of what had passed,
had, with new-born vigour, gathered himself up and rolled together
his coverlet to hasten after Him, Jesus had already withdrawn.ᵈ ²
In that multitude, all thinking only of their own sorrows and wants,
He had come and gone unobserved.   But they all now knew and
observed this miracle of healing, as they saw this unbefriended and
most wretched of them all healed, without the troubling of waters or
first immersion in them.   Then there was really help in Israel, and
help not limited to such external means! How could Christ have
taught that multitude, nay, all Jerusalem and Jewry, all this, as well
as all about Himself, but by what He did ?   And so we learn here also
another aspect of miracles, as necessary for those who, weary of
Rabbinic wrangling, could, in their felt impotence, only learn by what
He did that which He would say.

We know it not, but we cannot believe that on that day, nor,
perhaps, thenceforth on any other day, any man stepped for healing

¹ This characteristic is specially marked   ² The meaning of the expression is
by Canon *Westcott.*   ' retired ' or ' withdrawn ' Himself.

into the bubbling waters of Bethesda. Rather would they ask the healed man, Whose was the word that had brought him healing? But he knew Him not. Forth he stepped into God's free air, a new man. It was truly the holy Sabbath within, as around him; but he thought not of the day, only of the rest and relief it had brought. It was the holy Sabbath, and he carried on it his bed. If he remembered that it was the Sabbath, on which it was unlawful to carry forth anything—a burden, he would not be conscious that it was a burden, or that he had any burden; but very conscious that He, Who had made him whole, had bidden him take up his bed and walk. These directions had been bound up with the very word ('Rise') in which his healing had come. That was enough for him. And in this lay the beginning and root of his inward healing. Here was simple trust, unquestioning obedience to the unseen, unknown, but real Saviour. For he believed Him,[1] and therefore trusted in Him, that He must be right; and so, trusting without questioning, he obeyed.

The Jews saw him, as from Bethesda he carried home his 'burden.' Such as that he carried were their only burdens. Although the law of Sabbath-observance must have been made stricter in later Rabbinic development, when even the labour of moving the sick into the waters of Bethesda would have been unlawful, unless there had been present danger to life,[2] yet, admittedly, this carrying of the bed was an infringement of the Sabbatic law, as interpreted by traditionalism. Most characteristically, it was this external infringement which they saw, and nothing else; it was the Person Who had commanded it Whom they would know, not Him Who had made whole the impotent man. Yet this is quite natural, and perhaps not so different from what we may still witness among ourselves.

It could not have been long after this—most likely, as soon as possible—that the healed man and his Healer met in the Temple. What He then said to him, completed the inward healing. On the ground of his having been healed, let him be whole. As he trusted and obeyed Jesus in the outward cure, so let him now inwardly and morally trust and obey. Here also this looking through the external to the internal, through the temporal to the spiritual and eternal, which is so characteristic of the after-discourse of Jesus, nay, of all

[1] In connection with this see ver. 24, where the expression is 'believeth Him,' not 'on Him' as in the A.V., which occasionally obliterates the difference between the two, which is so important, the one implying credit, the other its outcoming trust (comp. St. John vi. 29, 30; viii. 30, 31; 1 John v. 10).

[2] The whole subject of the Sabbath-Law will be specially discussed in a later chapter. See also Appendix XVII. on 'The Law of the Sabbath' according to the Mishnah and Talmud.

His discourses and of His deeds, is most marked. The healed man now knew to Whom he owed faith, gratitude, and trust of obedience; and the consequences of this knowledge must have been incalculable. It would make him a disciple in the truest sense. And this was the only additional lesson which he, as each of us, must learn individually and personally: that the man healed by Christ stands in quite another position, as regards the morally right, from what he did before—not only before his healing, but even before his felt sickness, so that, if he were to go back to sin, or rather, as the original implies, 'continue to sin,'[1] a thing infinitely worse would come to him.

It seems an idle question, why the healed man told the Jews that it was Jesus. It was only natural that he should do so. Rather do we ask, How did he know that He Who had spoken to him was *Jesus*? Was it by the surrounding of keen-eyed, watchful Rabbis, or by the contradiction of sinners? Certain we are, that it was far better Jesus should have silently withdrawn from the porches of Bethesda to make it known in the Temple, Who it was that had done this miracle. Far more effectually could He so preach its lesson to those who had been in Bethesda, and to all Jewry.

And yet something further was required. He must speak it out in clear, open words, what was the hidden inward meaning of this miracle. As so often, it was the bitter hatred of His persecutors which gave Him the opportunity. The first forthbursting of His Messianic Mission and Character had come in that Temple, when He realised it as His Father's House, and His Life as about His Father's business. Again had these thoughts about His Father kindled within Him in that Temple, when, on the first occasion of His Messianic appearance there, He had sought to purge it, that it might be a House of Prayer. And now, once more in that House, it was the same consciousness about God as His Father, and His Life as the business of His Father, which furnished the answer to the angry invectives about His breach of the Sabbath-Law. The Father's Sabbath was His; the Father worked hitherto and He worked; the Father's work and His were the same; He was the Son of the Father.[a] And in this He also taught, what the Jews had never understood, the true meaning of the Sabbath-Law, by emphasising that which was the fundamental thought of the Sabbath—'Wherefore the Lord blessed the Sabbath day, and *hallowed it*:' not the rest of inactivity, but of blessing and hallowing.

Once more it was not His whole meaning, but only this one

a ver. 17

---

[1] See *Westcott* ad loc.

point, that He claimed to be equal with God, of which they took hold. As we understand it, the discourse beginning with verse 19 is not a continuation of that which had been begun in verse 17, but was delivered on another, though probably proximate occasion. By what He had said about the Father working hitherto and His working, He had silenced the multitude, who must have felt that God's rest was truly that of beneficence, not of inactivity. But He had raised another question, that of His equality with God, and for this He was taken to task by the Masters in Israel. To them it was that He addressed that discourse which, so to speak, preached His miracle at the Pool of Bethesda. Into its details we cannot enter further than has already been done. Some of its reasonings can be clearly traced, as starting from certain fundamental positions, held in common alike by the Sanhedrists and by Christ. Others, such as probably in answer to unreported objections, we may guess at. This may also account for what may seem occasional abruptness of transitions.

But what most impresses us, is the majestic grandeur of Christ's self-consciousness in presence of His enemies, and yet withal the tone of pitying sadness which pervades His discourse. The time of the judgment of silence had not yet come. And for the present the majesty of His bearing overawed them, even as it did His enemies to the end, and Christ could pass unharmed from among them. And so ended that day in Jerusalem. And this is all that is needful for us to know of His stay at the Unknown Feast. With this inward separation, and the gathering of hostile parties closes the first and begins the second, stage of Christ's Ministry.

CHAPTER XIII.

BY THE SEA OF GALILEE—THE FINAL CALL OF THE FIRST DISCIPLES, AND THE MIRACULOUS DRAUGHT OF FISHES.

(St. Matt. iv. 18-22; St. Mark i. 16-20; St. Luke v. 1-11.)

BOOK
III

WE are once again out of the stifling spiritual atmosphere of the great City, and by the glorious Lake of Galilee. They were other men, these honest, simple, earnest, impulsive Galileans, than that self-seeking, sophistical, heartless assemblage of Rabbis, whose first active persecution Jesus had just encountered, and for the time overawed by the majesty of His bearing. His return to Capernaum could not have remained unknown. Close by, on either side of the city, the country was studded with villages and towns, a busy, thriving, happy multitude. During that bright summer He had walked along that Lake, and by its shore and in the various Synagogues preached His Gospel. And they had been 'astonished at His doctrine, for His word was with power.' For the first time they had heard what they felt to be 'the Word of God,' and they had learned to love its sound. What wonder that, immediately on His return, 'the people pressed upon Him to hear' it.

If we surrender ourselves to the impression which the Evangelic narratives give us when pieced together,[1] it would almost seem, as if what we are about to relate had occurred while Jesus was returning from Jerusalem. For, the better reading of St. Mark i. 16 gives this as the mark of time: ' As He was passing on by the Sea of Galilee. But perhaps, viewed in connection with what follows, the impression may be so far modified, that we may think of it as on the first morning after His return. It had probably been a night of storm on the

---

[1] The accounts in the three Synoptic Gospels must be carefully pieced together. It will be seen that only thus can they be understood. The narratives of St. Matthew and St. Mark are almost literally the same, only adding in St. Mark i. 20 a notice about 'the hired servants,' which is evidential of the Petrine origin of the information. St. Luke seems to have made special inquiry, and, while adopting the narrative of the others, supplements it with what without them would be almost unintelligible.

Lake. For, the toil of the fishermen had brought them no draught of fishes,[a] and they stood by the shore, or in the boats drawn up on the beach, casting in their nets to 'wash' them[1] of the sand and pebbles, with which such a night's work would clog them, or to mend what had been torn by the violence of the waves. It was a busy scene; for, among the many industries by the Lake of Galilee, that of fishing was not only the most generally pursued, but perhaps the most lucrative.

Tradition had it, that since the days of Joshua, and by one of his ten ordinances, fishing in the Lake, though under certain necessary restrictions, was free to all.[2] And as fish was among the favourite articles of diet, in health and sickness, on week-days and especially at the Sabbath-meal, many must have been employed in connection with this trade. Frequent, and sometimes strange, are the Rabbinic advices, what kinds of fish to eat at different times, and in what state of preparation. They were eaten fresh, dried, or pickled;[b] a kind of 'relish' or sauce was made of them, and the roe also prepared.[c] We are told, how the large fish was carried to market slung on a ring or twine,[d] and the smaller fish in baskets or casks. In truth, these Rabbis are veritable connoisseurs in this delicacy; they discuss their size with exaggerations, advise when they are in season, discern a peculiar flavour in the same kinds if caught in different waters, and tell us how to prepare them most tastfully, cautioning us to wash them down, if it cannot be with water, with beer rather than wine.[e][3] It is one of their usual exaggerations, when we read of 300 different kinds of fish at a dinner given to a great Rabbi,[f] although the common proverb had it, to denote what was abundant, that it was like 'bringing fish to Acco.'[g] Besides, fish was also largely imported from abroad.[4] It indicates the importance of this traffic, that one of the gates of Jerusalem was called 'the fish-gate.'[h] Indeed, there is a legend[i] to the effect, that not less than 600,000 casks of sardines were every week supplied for the fig-dressers of King Jannæus. But, apart from such exaggerations, so considerable was this trade that, at a later period, one of the Patriarchs of the Sanhedrin engaged in it, and actually freighted ships for the transport of fish.[k]

CHAP.
XIII

[a] St. Luke v. 5

[b] St. Matt. vii. 10; xiii. 47; xv. 36
[c] Ab. Z. 39 a
[d] Bab. Mez. ii. 1

[e] Moed K. 11 a, last line
[f] Jer. Sheq. vi. 2, p. 50 a

[g] Shem. R. 9

[h] Neh. iii. 3
[i] Ber. 44 a

[k] Jer. Ab. Z. ii. 10, p. 42 a

---

[1] St. Matt. iv. 18 &c.; St. Mark i. 16 &c. as compared with St. Luke v. 2.

[2] In order not to impede navigation, it was forbidden to fix nets. For these two ordinances, see Baba K. 80 b, last line &c. The reference to the fishing in the lake is in 81 b. But see Tos. Baba K. viii. 17, 18.

[3] Three lines before that we read this saying of a fisherman: 'Roast fish with his brother (salt), lay it beside his father (water), eat it with his son (fish-juice), and drink upon it his father ' (water).

[4] Specially from Egypt and Spain, Machsh. vi. 3.

BOOK
III

These notices, which might be largely multiplied, are of more than antiquarian interest. They give a more vivid idea of life by the Lake of Galilee, and show that those engaged in that trade, like Zebedee and his sons (זְבַדְיָה, 'the God-given,' like Theodore and Dorothea), were not unfrequently men of means and standing. This irrespective of the fact, that the Rabbis enjoined some trade or industrial occupation on every man, whatever his station. We can picture to ourselves, on that bright autumn morning, after a stormy night of bootless toil, the busy scene by the Lake, with the fishermen cleaning and mending their nets. Amidst their work they would scarcely notice the gathering crowd. As we have suggested from the better reading of St. Mark i. 16, it was Christ's first walk by the Lake on the morning after His return from Judæa. Engaged in their fishing on the afternoon, evening, and night of His arrival in Capernaum, they would probably not have known of His presence till He spake to them. But He had come that morning specially to seek four of these fishers, that He might, now that the time for it had come, call them to permanent discipleship—and, what is more, fit them for the work to which he would call them.

Jewish customs and modes of thinking at that time do not help us further to understand the Lord's call of them, except so far as they enable us more clearly to apprehend what the words of Jesus would convey to them. The expression 'Follow Me' would be readily understood, as implying a call to become the *permanent* disciple of a teacher.[a] Similarly, it was not only the practice of the Rabbis, but regarded as one of the most sacred duties, for a Master to gather around him a circle of disciples.[b] Thus, neither Peter and Andrew, nor the sons of Zebedee, could have misunderstood the call of Christ, or even regarded it as strange. On that memorable return from His Temptation in the wilderness they had learned to know Him as the Messiah,[c] and they followed Him. And, now that the time had come for gathering around Him a separate discipleship, when, with the visit to the Unknown Feast, the Messianic activity of Jesus had passed into another stage, that call would not come as a surprise to their minds or hearts.

So far as the Master was concerned, we mark three points. First, the call came *after* the open breach with, and initial persecution of, the Jewish authorities. It was, therefore, a call to fellowship in His peculiar relationship to the Synagogue. Secondly, it necessitated the abandonment of all their former occupations, and, indeed, of all earthly ties.[d] Thirdly, it was from the first, and clearly, marked as

[a] So in Erub. 30 a

[b] Ab. i. 1; Sanh. 91 b

[c] St. John i. 37 &c.

[d] St. Matt. iv. 20, 22

totally different from a call to such discipleship, as that of any other Master in Israel. It was not to learn more of doctrine, nor more fully to follow out a life-direction already taken, but to begin, and to become, something quite new, of which their former occupation offered an emblem. The disciples of the Rabbis, even those of John the Baptist, 'followed,' in order to learn; they, in order to do, and to enter into fellowship with His Work. 'Follow Me, and I will make you fishers of men.' It was then quite a new call this, which at the same time indicated its real aim and its untold difficulties. Such a call could not have been addressed to them, if they had not already been disciples of Jesus, understood His Mission, and the character of the Kingdom of God. But, the more we think of it, the more do we perceive the magnitude of the call and of the decision which it implied —for, without doubt, they understood what it implied, as clearly, in some respects perhaps more clearly, than we do. All the deeper, then, must have been their loving belief in Him, and their earnest attachment, when, with such unquestioning trust, and such absolute simplicity and entireness of self-surrender, that it needed not even a spoken *Yea* on their part, they forsook ship and home to follow Him. And so, successively, Simon[1] and Andrew, and John and James— those who had been the first to hear, were also the first to follow Jesus. And ever afterwards did they remain closest to Him, who had been the first fruits of His Ministry.

It is not well to speak too much of the faith of men. With all the singleness of spiritual resolve—perhaps, as yet, rather impulse— which it implied, they probably had not themselves full or adequate conception of what it really meant. That would evolve in the course of Christ's further teaching, and of their learning in mind and heart. But, even thus, we perceive, that in their own call they had already, in measure, lived the miracle of the draught of fishes which they were about to witness. What had passed between Jesus and, first, the sons of Jona, and then those of Zebedee, can scarcely have occupied many minutes. But already the people were pressing around the Master in eager hunger for the Word; for, all the livelong night their own teachers had toiled, and taken nothing which they could give them as food. To such call the Fisher of Men could not be deaf.

---

[1] The name *Peter* occurs also among the Jews, but not that of *Paul*. Thus, in Pesiqta (ed. *Buber*, p. 158 *a*, line 8 from bottom, see also the Note there) we read of a R. José the son of Peytros, and similarly in the fragments from Tan- chuma in *Jellinek's* Beth ha-Midr. vol. vi. p. 95, where, however, he is called *Ben Petio*. In Menor. Hamm. the name is changed into *Phinehas*. Comp. *Jelli- nek*, Beth ha-Midr. vol. vi. Pref. xi.

The boat of Peter shall be His pulpit; He had consecrated it by consecrating its owner. The boat has been thrust out a little from the land, and over the soft ripple of the waters comes the strange melody of that Word. We need scarcely ask what He spake. It would be of the Father, of the Kingdom, and of those who entered it —like what He spake from the Mount, or to those who laboured and were heavy laden. But it would carry to the hearers the wondrous beauty and glory of that opening Kingdom, and, by contrast, the deep poverty and need of their souls. And Peter had heard it all in the boat, as he sat close by, in the shadow of His Majesty. Then, this was the teaching of which he had become a disciple; this, the net and the fishing to which he was just called. How utterly miserable, in one respect, must it have made him. Could such an one as he ever hope, with whatever toil, to be a successful fisher?

Jesus had read his thoughts, and much more than read them. It was all needed for the qualifying of Peter especially, but also of the others who had been called to be fishers of men. Presently it shall be all brought to light; not only that it may be made clear, but that, alike, the lesson and the help may be seen. And this is another object in Christ's miracles to His disciples: to make clear their inmost thoughts and longings, and to point them to the right goal. 'Launch out into the deep, and let down your nets for a draught.' That they toil in vain all life's night, only teaches the need of another beginning. The 'neverthless, at Thy word,' marks the new trust, and the new work as springing from that trust. When Christ is in the boat and bids us let down the net, there *must* be 'a great multitude of fishes.' And all this in this symbolic miracle. Already 'the net was breaking,' when they beckoned to their partners in the other ship, that they should come and help them. And now both ships are burdened to the water's edge.

But what did it all mean to Simon Peter? He had been called to full discipleship, and he had obeyed the call. He had been in his boat beside the Saviour, and heard what He had spoken, and it had gone to his heart. And now this miracle which he had witnessed! Such shoal of fish in one spot on the Lake of Galilee was not strange. The miraculous was, that the Lord had seen through those waters down where the multitude of fishes was, and bidden him let down for a draught. He could see through the intervening waters, right down to the bottom of that sea; He could see through him, to the very bottom of Peter's heart. He did see it—and all that Jesus had just spoken meant it, and showed him what was there. And could *he*

then be a fisher of men, out of whose heart, after a life's night of toil,
the net would come up empty, or rather only clogged with sand and
torn with pebbles? This is what he meant when ' he fell down at
Jesus' knees, saying: Depart from me, for I am a sinful man, O Lord.'
And this is why Jesus comforted him: ' Fear not; from henceforth
thou shalt catch men.' And so also. and so only, do we, each of us,
learn the lesson of our calling, and receive the true comfort in it.
Nor yet can anyone become a true fisher of men in any other than
such manner.

The teaching and the comfort required not to be repeated in the
life of Peter, nor in that of the others who witnessed and shared in
what had passed. Many are the truths which shine out from the
symbolism of this scene, when the first disciples were first called.
That call itself; the boat; the command of Christ, despite the night
of vain toil; the unlikely success; the net and its cast at the bidding
of Christ, with the absolute certitude of result, where He is and when
He bids; the miraculous direction to the spot; the multitude of fishes
enclosed; the net about to break, yet not breaking; the surprise, as
strange perhaps as the miracle itself; and then, last of all, the lesson
of self-knowledge and humiliation: all these and much more has the
Church most truly read in this history. And as we turn from it,
this stands out to us as its final outcome and lesson: ' And when
they had brought their ships to land, they forsook all and followed
Him.' [1]

[1] We would call special attention to
the arrangement of this narrative. The
explanation given in the text will, it is
hoped, be sufficient answer to the difficulties raised by some commentators.
Strauss' attempt to indicate the mythic
origin of this narrative forms one of the
weakest parts of his book. *Keim* holds
the genuineness of the account of the two
first Evangelists, but rejects that of the
third, on grounds which neither admit nor
require detailed examination. The latest
and most curious idea of the Tübingen
school has been, to see in the account of
St. Luke a reflection on Peter as Judaistically cramped, and to understand the
beckoning to his partners as implying
the calling in of Pauline teachers.

CHAPTER XIV.

A SABBATH IN CAPERNAUM.

(St. Matt. viii 14–17; St. Mark i. 21–34; St. Luke iv. 33–41.)

BOOK
III

IT was the Holy Sabbath—the first after He had called around Him His first permanent disciples; the first, also, after His return from the Feast at Jerusalem. Of both we can trace indications in the account of that morning, noon, and evening which the Evangelists furnish. The greater detail with which St. Mark, who wrote under the influence of St. Peter, tells these events, shows the freshness and vividness of impression on the mind of Peter of those early days of his new life. As indicating that what is here recorded took place immediately after the return of Jesus from Jerusalem, we mark, that as yet there were no watchful enemies in waiting to entrap Him in such breach of the Law, as might furnish ground for judicial pro-

ᵃ St. Luke
v. 21; vi. 2;
vi. 7

cedure. But, from their presence and activity so soon afterwards,ᵃ we infer, that the authorities of Jerusalem had sent some of their familiars to track His steps in Galilee.

But as yet all seemed calm and undisturbed. Those simple, warm-hearted Galileans yielded themselves to the power of His words and works, not discerning hidden blasphemy in what He said, nor yet Sabbath-desecration in His healing on God's holy day. It is morning, and Jesus goes to the Synagogue at Capernaum.[1] To teach there, was now His wont. But frequency could not lessen the impression. In describing the Influence of His Person or words the Evangelists use a term, which really means *amazement*.[2] And when we find the

ᵇ St. Matt.
vii. 28

same word to describe the impression of the 'Sermon on the Mount,'ᵇ the inference is naturally suggested, that it presents the type, if it does not sum up the contents, of some of His Synagogue-discourses.

---

[1] The accounts of this given by St. Mark and St. Luke chronologically precede what is related in St. Matt. viii. 14–17. The reader is requested in each case to peruse the Biblical narratives before, or along with their commentation in the chapters of the present work.

[2] The following are the passages in which the same term is used: St. Matt. vii. 28; xiii. 54; xix. 25; xxii. 33; St. Mark i. 22; vi. 2; vii. 37; x. 26; xi. 18; St. Luke ii. 48; iv. 32; ix. 43; Acts xiii. 12.

It is not necessary to suppose that, what held His hearers spell-bound, had necessarily also its effect on their hearts and lives. Men may be enraptured by the ideal without trying to make it the real. Too often it is even in inverse proportion; so that those who lead not the most moral lives even dare to denounce the New Testament stand-point, as below their own conceptions of right and duty. But there is that in man, evidence of his origin and destiny, which always and involuntarily responds to the presentation of the higher. And in this instance it was not only what He taught, but the contrast with that to which they had been accustomed on the part of 'the Scribes,' which filled them with amazement. There was no appeal to human authority, other than that of the conscience; no subtle logical dis-tinctions, legal niceties, nor clever sayings. Clear, limpid, and crys-talline, flowed His words from out the spring of the Divine Life that was in Him.

Among the hearers in the Synagogue that Sabbath morning was one of a class, concerning whose condition, whatever difficulties may attach to our proper understanding of it, the reader of the New Testament must form some definite idea. The term 'demoniacal possession' occurs not in the New Testament. We owe it to Josephus,[a] from whom it has passed into ecclesiastical language. We dismiss it the more readily, that, in our view, it conveys a wrong impression. The New Testament speaks of those who had a spirit, or a demon, or demons, or an unclean spirit, or the spirit of an unclean demon, but chiefly of persons who were 'demonised.'[1] Similarly, it seems a strange inaccuracy on the part of commentators to exclude from the Gospel of St. John all notice of the 'demonised.' That the Fourth Gospel, although not reporting any healing of the demonised, shares the fundamental view of the Synoptists, appears not only from St. John vii. 20, viii. 48, 52, but especially from viii. 49 and x. 20, 21.[2] We cannot believe that the writer of the Fourth Gospel would have put into the mouth of Jesus the answer 'I am not a demon,' or have allowed Him to be described by His

[a] Comp. *Delitzsch* in *Riehm's* Hand-wörter-buch

---

[1] The word 'spirit' or 'spirits' occurs *twice* in St. Matthew, *thrice* in St. Mark and *twice* in St. Luke; with the addition 'evil,' *twice* in St. Luke; with that of 'un-clean,' *once* in St. Matthew, *eleven* times in St. Mark, and *four* times in St. Luke. The word δαίμων in singular or plural occurs once in each of the Synoptists; while δαιμόνιον, in singular or plural, occurs nine times in St. Matthew, three times in St. Mark, fourteen times in St.

Luke, and six times in St. John. The expression 'the spirit of an unclean de-mon' occurs once in St. Luke, while the verb 'to be demonised' occurs, in one form or another, seven times in St. Mat-thew, four times in St. Mark, once in St. Luke, and once in St. John. Comp. also the careful *brochure* of Pastor *Nanz*, Die Besessenen im N.T., although we differ from his conclusions.

[2] Comp. also *Weiss*, Leben Jesu i. p. 457.

friends as not one 'demonised,' without a single word to show dissent from the popular view, if he had not shared the ideas of the Synoptists. In discussing a question of such very serious import in the study and criticism of the Gospels, the precise facts of the case should in the first place be clearly ascertained.

The first question here is, whether Christ Himself shared the views, not indeed of His contemporaries (for these, as we shall see, were very different), but of the Evangelists in regard to what they call the 'demonised'? This has been extensively denied, and Christ represented as only unwilling needlessly to disturb a popular prejudice, which He could not at the time effectually combat. But the theory requires more than this; and, since Christ not only tolerated, but in addressing the demonised actually adopted, or seemed to adopt, the prevailing view, it has been argued, that, for the sake of these poor afflicted persons, He acted like a physician who appears to enter into the fancy of his patient, in order the more effectually to heal him of it. This view seems, however, scarcely worth refuting, since it imputes to Jesus, on a point so important, a conduct not only unworthy of Him, or indeed of any truly great man, but implies a canon of ' accommodation' which might equally be applied to His Miracles, or to anything else that contravened the notions of an interpreter, and so might transform the whole Gospel-narratives into a series of historically untrustworthy legends. But we will not rest the case on what might be represented as an appeal to prejudice. For, we find that Jesus not only tolerated the popular 'prejudice,' or that He ' adopted it for the sake of more readily healing those thus afflicted'—but that He even made it part of His disciples' commission to ' cast out demons,'[a] and that, when the disciples afterwards reported their success in this, Christ actually made it a matter of thanksgiving to God.[b] The same view underlies His reproof to the disciples, when failing in this part of their work;[c] while in St. Luke xi. 19, 24, He adopts, and argues on this view as against the Pharisees. Regarded therefore in the light of history, impartial criticism can arrive at no other conclusion, than that Jesus of Nazareth shared the views of the Evangelists as regards the ' demonised.'[1]

Our next inquiry must be as to the character of the phenomenon thus designated. In view of the fact that in St. Mark ix. 21, the demonised had been such ' of a child,' it is scarcely possible to ascribe it simply to *moral* causes. Similarly, personal faith does not

[a] St. Matt.
x. 8

[b] St. Luke
x. 17, 18

[c] St. Matt.
xvii. 21;
comp. also
xii. 43 &c.,
also
spoken to
the dis-
ciples

---

[1] This is also the conclusion arrived at by *Weiss*, u. s.

seem to have been a requisite condition of healing. Again, as other
diseases are mentioned without being attributed to demoniacal
influence, and as *all* who were dumb, deaf, or paralysed would not
have been described as ' demonised,' it is evident that all physical,
or even mental distempers of the same class were not ascribed to the
same cause: some might be natural, while others were demoniacal.
On the other hand, there were more or less violent symptoms of
disease in every demonised person, and these were greatly aggravated
in the last paroxysm, when the demon quitted his habitation. We
have, therefore, to regard the phenomena described as caused by the
influence of such ' spirits,' primarily, upon that which forms the *nexus*
between body and mind, the nervous system, and as producing different physical effects, according to the part of the nervous system affected. To this must be added a certain impersonality of consciousness,
so that for the time the consciousness was not that of the demonised,
but the demoniser, just as in certain mesmeric states the consciousness of the mesmerised is really that of the mesmeriser. We might
carry the analogy farther, and say, that the two states are exactly
parallel—the demon or demons taking the place of the mesmeriser,
only that the effects were more powerful and extensive, perhaps more
enduring. But one point seems to have been assumed, for which
there is, to say the least, no evidence, viz., that because, at least in
many cases, the disease caused by the demon was permanent, therefore those who were so affected were *permanently* or constantly
under the power of the demon. Neither the New Testament, nor
even Rabbinic literature, conveys the idea of permanent demoniac
indwelling, to which the later term ' possession ' owes its origin.[1] On
the contrary, such accounts, as that of the scene in the Synagogue
of Capernaum, convey the impression of a sudden influence, which
in most cases seems occasioned by the spiritual effect of the Person
or of the Words of the Christ. To this historical sketch we have only
to add, that the phenomenon is not referred to either in the Old
Testament,[2] or in the Apocrypha,[3] nor, for that matter, in the
Mishnah,[4] where, indeed, from the character of its contents, one

---

[1] The nearest approach to it, so far as
I am aware, occurs in Pirqé de R. El. c.
13 (ed. Lemberg, p. 16 *b*, 17 *a*), where
the influence of Satan over the serpent
(in the history of the Fall) is likened to
that of an evil spirit over a man, all
whose deeds and words are done under
the influence of the demon, so that he
only acts at his bidding.

[2] Surely *Strauss* (Leben Jesu, ii. 10)

could not have remembered the expressions in 1 Sam. xvi. 14, 15, &c., when he
sees a parallel to demoniacal possessions
in the case of Saul.

[3] Tob. viii. 2, 3, is *not* a case in point.

[4] *Gfrörer* (Jahrh. d. Heils, i. pp. 410,
412) quotes Erub. iv. 1 and Gitt. vii. 1;
but neither of these passages implies
anything like demoniac possession.

would scarcely expect to find it. But we find it mentioned not only in the New Testament, but in the writings of *Josephus*.[1] The references in heathen or in Christian writings posterior to those of the New Testament lie beyond our present inquiry.[2]

In view of these facts, we may arrive at some more definite conclusions. Those who contend that the representations of the Evangelists are identical with the popular Jewish notions of the time, must be ill acquainted with the latter. What these were, is explained in another place.[3] Suffice it here to state that, whatever want of clearness there may be about the Jewish ideas of demoniac influences, there is none as to the means proposed for their removal. These may be broadly classified as: *magical means* for the prevention of such influences (such as the avoidance of certain places, times, numbers, or circumstances; amulets, &c.); *magical means* for the cure of diseases; and direct *exorcism* (either by certain outward means, or else by formulas of incantation). Again, while the New Testament furnishes no data by which to learn the views of Jesus or of the Evangelists regarding the exact character of the phenomenon, it furnishes the fullest details as to the manner in which the demonised were set free. This was always the same. It consisted neither in magical means nor formulas of exorcism, but always in the Word of Power which Jesus spake, or entrusted to His disciples, and which the demons always obeyed. There is here not only difference, but contrariety in comparison with the current Jewish notions, and it leads to the conclusion that there was the same contrast in His views, as in His treatment of the ' demonised.'

Jewish superstition in regard to the demoniacal state can, therefore, no more affect the question of the credibility of the Gospel-accounts of it, than can quotations from heathen or from post-Apostolic Christian writers. In truth, it must be decided purely on New Testament grounds; and resolves itself into that of the general trustworthiness of the Evangelic narratives, and of our estimate of the Person of Christ. Thus viewed, he who regards Jesus as the Messiah and the Son of God can be in no doubt. If we are asked to explain the *rationale* of the phenomenon, or of its cessation—if, indeed, it has wholly and everywhere ceased—we might simply decline to attempt that for which we have not sufficient data, and

---

[1] See, for example, Ant. vi. 8. 2; 11. 3; viii. 2. 5; War vii. 6. 3.

[2] The reader will find full references in the Encyclopædias, in *Wetstein* (Nov. Test. i. pp. 279–284), and in *Nanz's* brochure.

[3] See Appendix XVI.: ' Jewish Views about Demons and the demonised.'

this, without implying that such did not exist, or that, if known, they would not wholly vindicate the facts of the case. At any rate, it does not follow that there are no such data because we do not possess them; nor is there any ground for the contention that, if they existed, we ought to possess them. For, admittedly, the phenomenon was only a temporary one.

And yet certain considerations will occur to the thoughtful reader, which, if they do not explain, will at least make him hesitate to designate as inexplicable, the facts in question. In our view, at least, he would be a bold interpreter who would ascribe all the phenomena even of heathen magic to jugglery, or else to purely physical causes. Admittedly they have ceased, or perhaps, as much else, assumed other forms, just as, so far as evidence goes, demoniac influence has—at least in the form presented in the New Testament. But, that it has so ceased, does not prove that it never existed. If we believe that the Son of God came to destroy the works of the Devil, we can understand the developed enmity of the kingdom of darkness; and if we regard Christ as Very God, taking, in manner to us mysterious, Humanity, we can also perceive how the Prince of Darkness might, in counterfeit, seek through the demonised a temporary dwelling in Humanity for purposes of injury and destruction, as Christ for healing and salvation. In any case, holding as we do that this demoniac influence was not *permanent* in the demonised, the analogy of certain mesmeric influences seems exactly to apply. No reference is here made to other supernatural spirit-influences of which many in our days speak, and which, despite the lying and imposture probably connected with them, have a background of truth and reality, which, at least in the present writer's experience, cannot be absolutely denied. In the mysterious connection between the sensuous and supersensuous, spirit and matter, there are many things which the vulgar ' bread-and-butter philosophy ' fails rightly to apportion, or satisfactorily to explain. That, without the intervention of sensuous media, mind can, may, and does affect mind; that even animals, in proportion to their sensitiveness, or in special circumstances, are affected by that which is not, or else not yet, seen, and this quite independently of man ; that, in short, there are not a few phenomena ' in heaven and earth ' of which our philosophy dreams not—these are considerations which, however the superficial sciolist may smile at them, no earnest inquirer would care to dismiss with peremptory denial. And superstition only begins when we look for them, or else when we attempt to account for and explain them, not in the admission of their possibility.

But, in our view, it is of the deepest importance always to keep in mind, that the 'demonised' was not a *permanent* state, or possession by the powers of darkness. For, it establishes a *moral* element, since, during the period of their temporary liberty, the demonised might have shaken themselves free from the overshadowing power, or sought release from it. Thus the demonised state involved personal responsibility, although that of a diseased and disturbed consciousness.

In one respect those who were 'demonised' exhibited the same phenomenon. They all owned the Power of Jesus. It was not otherwise in the Synagogue at Capernaum on that Sabbath-morning. What Jesus had spoken produced an immediate effect on the demonised, though one which could scarcely have been anticipated. For, there is authority for inserting the word 'straightway'[a] immediately after the account of Jesus' preaching. Yet, as we think of it, we cannot imagine that the demon would have continued silent nor yet that he could have spoken other than the truth in the Presence of the God-Man. There must be, and yet there cannot be, resistance. The very Presence of the Christ meant the destruction of this work of the Devil. Involuntarily, in his confessed inability of disguise or resistance, he owns defeat, even before the contest. 'What have we to do with Thee, Jesus of Nazareth?[1] Thou art come to destroy us![2] I know Thee Who Thou art, the Holy One of God.' And yet there seems in these words already an emergence of the consciousness of the demonised, at least in so far that there is no longer confusion between him and his tormenter, and the latter speaks in his own name. One stronger than the demon had affected the higher part in the demonised. It was the Holy One of God, in Whose Presence the powers of moral destruction cannot be silent, but must speak, and own their subjection and doom. The Christ needs not to contend : that He is the Christ, is itself victory.

But this was not all. He had come not only to destroy the works of the Devil. His Incarnation meant this—and more: to set the prisoners free. By a word of command He gagged[3] the confessions of the demon, unwillingly made, and even so with hostile

[a] In St.
Mark i. 23

---

[1] I have omitted, on critical grounds, the clause, 'Let us alone.' The expression, 'What between us and Thee, Jesu Nazarene,' contains a well-known Hebraism.

[2] This seems the more córrect rendering.

[3] This is the real meaning of the expression rendered, 'Hold thy peace.' It stills the raging of the powers of evil, just as, characteristically, it is again employed in the stilling of the storm, St. Mark iv. 39.

intent. It was not by such voices that He would have His Messiah-ship ever proclaimed. Such testimony was wholly unfitting and incongruous; it would have been a strange discord on the witness of the Baptist and the Voice Which had proclaimed Him from heaven. And, truly, had it been admitted, it would have strangely jarred in a Life which needed not, and asked not even the witness of men, but appealed straightway to God Himself. Nor can we fail to perceive how, had it been allowed, it would have given a true ground to what the Pharisees sought to assign as the interpretation of His Power, that by the Prince of Demons He cast out demons. And thus there is here also deep accord with the fundamental idea which was the outcome of His Temptation: that not the seemingly shortest, but the Divine way must lead Him to the goal, and that goal not Royal pro-clamation, but the Resurrection.

The same power which gagged the confession also bade the demon relinquish his prey. One wild paroxysm—and the sufferer was for ever free. But on them all who saw and heard it fell the utter stupor and confusion of astonishment.[1] Each turned to his neighbour with the inquiry: 'What is this? A new doctrine with authority! And He commandeth the unclean spirits, and they obey Him.'[2] Well might they inquire. It had been a threefold miracle: 'a new doctrine;' 'with authority;' and obedience of the unclean spirits to His command. There is throughout, and especially in the account of the casting out of the demon, such un-Jewish simplicity, with entire absence of what would have been characteristic in a Jewish exorcist; such want of all that one would have expected, if the event had been invented, or coloured for a purpose, or tinged by contemporary notions; and, withal, such sublimity and majesty, that it is difficult to under-stand how any one can resist the impression of its reality, or that He Who so spake and did was in truth the Son of God.

From the Synagogue we follow the Saviour, in company with His called disciples, to Peter's wedded home. But no festive meal, as was Jewish wont, awaited them there. A sudden access of violent 'burn-ing fever,'[3] such as is even now common in that district, had laid Peter's mother-in-law prostrate. If we had still any lingering

---

[1] The Greek term implies this. Be-sides its use in this narrative (St. Mark i. 27; St. Luke iv. 36, in the latter in the substantive form), it occurs in St. Mark x. 24, 32; Acts ix. 6; and as a substan-tive in Acts iii. 10.

[2] This seems the better rendering.
[3] Such is the meaning of the Greek word. I cannot understand, why the corresponding term in St. Luke should have been interpreted in 'The Speaker's Commentary as 'typhoid fever.'

thought of Jewish magical cures as connected with those of Jesus, what is now related must dispel it. The Talmud gives this disease precisely the same name (אשתא צמירתא, *Eshatha Tsemirta*), 'burning fever,' and prescribes for it a magical remedy, of which the principal part is to tie a knife wholly of iron by a braid of hair to a thornbush, and to repeat on successive days Exod. iii. 2, 3, then ver. 4, and finally ver. 5, after which the bush is to be cut down, while a certain magical formula is pronounced.[a] How different from this, alike in its sublime simplicity and in the majestic bearing of Him Who healed, is the Evangelic narrative of the cure of Peter's mother-in-law. To ignore, in our estimate of the trustworthiness of the Gospels, this essential contrast, would be a grave historical mistake. Jesus is 'told' of the sickness; He is besought for her who is stricken down. In His Presence disease and misery cannot continue. Bending over the sufferer, He 'rebuked the fever,' just as He had rebuked[1] 'the demon' in the Synagogue, and for the same reason, since all disease, in the view of the Divine Healer, is the outcome of sin. Then lifting her by the hand, she rose up, healed, to 'minister' unto them. It was the first *Diaconate*[2] of woman in the Church—might we not almost say, in the world?—a Diaconate to Christ, and to those that were His; the Diaconate of one healed by Christ; a Diaconate immediately following such healing. The first, this, of a long course of woman's Diaconate to Christ, in which, for the first time, woman attained her true position. And what a Sabbath-meal it must have been, after that scene in the Synagogue and after that healing in the house, when Jesus was the Guest, they who had witnessed it all sat at meat with Him, and she who had been healed was the *Deaconess.* Would that such were ever our Christian festive meals!

It was evening. The sun was setting, and the Sabbath past. All that day it had been told from home to home what had been done in the Synagogue; it had been whispered what had taken place in the house of their neighbour Simon. This one conviction had been borne in upon them all, that '*with authority*' He spake, with authority and power He commanded even the unclean spirits, and they obeyed. No scene more characteristic of the Christ than that on this autumn evening at Capernaum. One by one the stars had shone out over the tranquil Lake and the festive city, lighting up earth's

---

[1] The word is the same in both cases.   marks of *Volkmar* (Marcus, pp. 99, 100).
[2] The term is the same. See the re-

darkness with heaven's soft brilliancy, as if they stood there witnesses, that God had fulfilled His good promise to Abraham.[a] On that evening no one in Capernaum thought of business, pleasure, or rest. There must have been many homes of sorrow, care, and sickness there, and in the populous neighbourhood around. To them, to all, had the door of hope now been opened. Truly, a new Sun had risen on them, with healing in His wings. No disease too desperate, when even the demons owned the authority of His mere rebuke. From all parts they bring them: mothers, widows, wives, fathers, children, husbands—their loved ones, the treasures they had almost lost; and the whole city throngs—a hushed, solemnised, overawed multitude—expectant, waiting at the door of Simon's dwelling. There they laid them, along the street up to the market-place, on their beds; or brought them, with beseeching look and word. What a symbol of this world's misery, need, and hope; what a symbol, also, of what the Christ really is as the Consoler in the world's manifold woe! Never, surely, was He more truly the Christ; nor is He in symbol more truly such to us and to all time, than when, in the stillness of that evening, under the starlit sky, He went through that suffering throng, laying His hands in the blessing of healing on every one of them, and casting out many devils. No picture of the Christ more dear to us, than this of the unlimited healing of whatever disease of body or soul. In its blessed indefiniteness it conveys the infinite potentiality of relief, whatever misery have fallen on us, or whatever care or sorrow oppress us. He must be blind, indeed, who sees not in this Physician the Divine Healer; in this Christ the Light of the World; the Restorer of what sin had blighted; the Joy in our world's deep sorrow. Never was prophecy more truly fulfilled than, on that evening, this of Isaiah: 'Himself took our infirmities, and bare our sicknesses.'[b] By His Incarnation and Coming, by His taking our infirmities, and bearing our sicknesses—for this in the truest and widest sense is the meaning of the Incarnation of the Christ—did He become the Healer, the Consoler of humanity, its Saviour in all ills of time, and from all ills of eternity. The most real fulfilment this, that can be conceived, of Isaiah's rapt vision of Who and what the Messiah was to be, and to do; not, indeed, what is sometimes called fulfilment, or expected as such, in a literal and verbal correspondence with the prediction. An utterly mechanical, external, and unspiritual view this of prophecy, in which, in quite Jewish literalism, the spirit is crushed by the letter. But, viewed in its real bearing on mankind with its wants, Christ, on that evening, was the

CHAP. XIV

[a] Gen. xxii. 17, 18

[b] Is. liii.

real, though as yet only initial, fulfilment of the world's great hope, to which, centuries before, the God-directed hand of the prophet had pointed.[1]

So ended that Sabbath in Capernaum: a Sabbath of healing, joy, and true rest. But far and wide, into every place of the country around, throughout all the region of Galilee, spread the tidings, and with them the fame of Him Whom demons must obey, though they dare not pronounce Him the Son of God. And on men's ears fell His Name with sweet softness of infinite promise, 'like rain upon the mown grass, as showers that water the earth.'

[1] I can scarcely find words strong enough to express my dissent from those who would limit Is. liii. 4, either on the one hand to spiritual, or on the other to physical 'sicknesses.' The promise is one of future deliverance from both, of a Restorer from all the woe which sin had brought. In the same way the expression 'taking upon Himself,' and 'bearing' refers to the Christ as our Deliverer, because our Substitute. Because He took upon Himself our infirmities, therefore He bore our sicknesses. That the view here given is that of the N.T., appears from a comparison of the application of the passage in St. Matt. viii. 17 with that in St. John i. 29 and 1 Pet. ii. 24. The words, as given by St. Matthew, are most truly a N.T. 'Targum' of the original. The LXX. renders, 'This man carries our sins and is pained for us;' Symmachus, 'Surely He took up our sins, and endured our labors;' the Targum Jon., 'Thus for our sins He will pray, and our iniquities will for His sake be forgiven.' (Comp. Driver and Neubauer, The Jewish Interpreters on Isaiah liii., vol. ii.) Lastly, it is with reference to this passage that the Messiah bears in the Talmud the designation, 'The Leprous One,' and 'the Sick One' (Sanh. 98 b).

CHAPTER XV.

SECOND JOURNEY THROUGH GALILEE—THE HEALING OF THE LEPER.

(St. Matt. iv. 23; viii. 2–4; St. Mark i. 35–45; St. Luke iv. 42–44; v. 12–16.)

A DAY and an evening such as of that Sabbath of healing in Capernaum must, with reverence be it written, have been followed by what
opens the next section.[1] To the thoughtful observer there is such
unbroken harmony in the Life of Jesus, such accord of the inward
and outward, as to carry instinctive conviction of the truth of its record. It was, so to speak, an inward necessity that the God-Man,
when brought into contact with disease and misery, whether from
physical or supernatural causes, should remove it by His Presence,
by His touch, by His Word. An outward necessity also, because no
other mode of teaching equally convincing would have reached those
accustomed to Rabbinic disputations, and who must have looked for
such a manifestation from One Who claimed such authority. And
yet, so far from being a mere worker of miracles, as we should have
expected if the history of His miracles had been of legendary origin,
there is nothing more marked than the pain, we had almost said the
humiliation, which their necessity seems to have carried to His heart.
'Except ye see signs and wonders, ye will not believe;' 'an evil and
adulterous generation seeketh a sign;' 'blessed are they that have
not seen, and yet have believed'—such are the utterances of Him
Who sighed when He opened the ears of the deaf,[a] and bade His
Apostles look for higher and better things than power over all diseases or even over evil spirits.[b][2] So would not the Messiah of Jewish legend have spoken or done; nor would they who invented such
miracles have so referred to them.

In truth, when, through the rift in His outward history, we catch
a glimpse of Christ's inner Being, these miracles, so far as not the
outcome of the mystic union of the Divine and the Human in His
Person, but as part of His Mission, form part of His Humiliation.

CHAP.
XV

[a] St. Mark
vii. 34

[b] St. Luke
x. 17-20

---

[1] So both in St. Mark (i. 35–39) and in
St. Luke (iv. 42–44), and in substantial

accord even in St. Matthew (iv. 23).
[2] So also St. Paul, 1 Cor. xii. 31: xiii. 1.

They also belong to that way which He had chosen in his initial conquest of the Tempter in the Wilderness, when He chose, not the sudden display of absolute power for the subdual of His people, but the
painful, slow method of meeting the wants, and addressing Himself
to the understanding and capacity of those over Whom He would
reign.   In this view, it seems as if we could gain a fresh understanding, not only of the expediency of His final departure, so far as
concerned the future teaching of the disciples by the Holy Spirit, but
of His own longing for the Advent of the Comforter.   In truth, the
two teachers and the two modes of teaching could not be together,
and the Ascension of the Christ, as the end of His Humiliation,
marked the Advent of the Holy Ghost, as bestowing another mode of
teaching than that of the days of His Humiliation.

And so, thinking of the scene on the evening before, we can un-
ᵃ St. Mark
i. 35
derstand how, 'very early, while it was still very dark,'ᵃ Jesus rose
up, and went into a solitary place to pray.   The use of the same expression[1] in St. Mark xiii. 35 enables us to fix the time as that of
the fourth night-watch, or between three and six o'clock of the morning.   It was not till some time afterwards, that even those, who had
so lately been called to His closest fellowship, rose, and, missing
Him, followed.   Jesus had prayed in that solitude, and consecrated
it.   After such a day, and in prospect of entering on His second
journey through Galilee[2]—this time in so far different circumstances
—He must prevent the dawn of the morning in prayer.   And by this
also would they learn, that He was not merely a worker of miracles,
but that He, Whose Word demons obeyed, lived a Life, not of outward but of inward power, in fellowship with His Father, and baptized his work with prayer.   But as yet, and, indeed, in measure all
through His Life on earth, it seemed difficult for them in any measure
to realise this.   'All men seek for Thee,' and therefore they would
have had Him return to Capernaum.   But this was the very reason
why He had withdrawn ere dawn of day.   He had come forth, and
that,[3] not to attract the crowds, and be proclaimed a King, but to
preach the Kingdom of God.   Once more we say it: so speaks not,
nor acts the hero of Jewish legend!

As the three Synoptists accordantly state, Jesus now entered on
His second Galilean journey.   There can be little doubt, that the
chronological succession of events is here accurately indicated by the

---

[1] πρωΐ.
[2] The circumstances will be referred to
in the sequel.
[3] The expression in St. Luke iv. 43

shows, that the 'coming forth' (St. Mark
i. 38) cannot be limited to His leaving
Capernaum.

more circumstantial narrative in St. Mark's Gospel.[1] The arrange-   CHAP.
ment of St. Luke appears that of historical grouping, while that of   XV
St. Matthew is determined by the Hebraic plan of his Gospel, which
seems constructed on the model of the Pentateuch,[2] as if the establishment of the Kingdom by the Messiah were presented as the fulfilment of its preparatory planting in Israel.   But this second journey
through Galilee, which the three Gospels connect with the stay at
Capernaum, marks a turning-point in the working of the Christ. As
already stated, the occurrences at the ' Unknown Feast,'[3] in Jerusalem, formed a new point of departure.   Christ had fully presented
His claims to the Sanhedrists, and they had been fully rejected by
the Scribes and the people.   Henceforth He separated Himself from
that 'untoward generation;' henceforth, also, began His systematic
persecution by the authorities, when His movements were tracked
and watched.   Jesus went alone to Jerusalem.   This, also, was
fitting.   Equally so, that on His return He called His disciples to be
His followers; and that from Capernaum He entered, in their company, on a new phase in His Work.

Significantly, His Work began where that of the Rabbis, we had
almost said of the Old Testament saints, ended.   Whatever remedies,
medical, magical, or sympathetic, Rabbinic writings may indicate for
various kinds of disease, leprosy is not included in the catalogue.
They left aside what even the Old Testament marked as moral death,
by enjoining those so stricken to avoid all contact with the living,
and even to bear the appearance of mourners.   As the leper passed
by, his clothes rent, his hair dishevelled,[4] and the lower part of his   a Lev. xiii.
face and his upper lip covered,[a] it was as one going to death who   45
reads his own burial-service, while the mournful words, ' Unclean!
Unclean!' which he uttered, proclaimed that his was both living and
moral death.   Again, the Old Testament, and even Rabbinism, took,

---

[1] The following are, briefly, some of
the considerations which determine the
chronological order here adopted: (1.)
This event could not have taken place
after the Sermon on the Mount, since
then the twelve Apostles were already
called, nor yet after the call of St.
Matthew.   (2.) From the similes employed (about the lilies of the field, &c.),
the Sermon on the Mount seems to have
taken place in spring; this event in early
autumn.   On the other hand, the order
in St. Mark exactly fits in, and also in
the main agrees, with that in St. Luke,
while, lastly, it exhibits the growing per-

secutions from Jerusalem, of which we
have here the first traces.
[2] This is ingeniously indicated in Professor *Delitzsch's* Entsteh. d. Kanon.
Evang., although, in my view, the theory
cannot be carried out in the full details
attempted by the Professor.   But such a
general conception of the Gospel by St.
Matthew is not only reasonable in itself,
but explains his peculiar arrangement of
events.
[3] On the date of this feast comp. Appendix XV.
[4] From this women were excepted,
Sot. iii. 8.

BOOK
III

in the measures prescribed in leprosy, primarily a moral, or rather a ritual, and only secondarily a sanitary, view of the case. The isolation already indicated, which banished lepers from all intercourse except with those similarly stricken,[1] and forebade their entering not only the Temple or Jerusalem, but any walled city,[2] could not have been merely prompted by the wish to prevent infection. For all the laws in regard to leprosy are expressly stated not to have application in the case of heathens, proselytes before their conversion, and even of Israelites on their birth.[3] The same inference must also be drawn from the circumstance, that the priestly examination and subsequent isolation of the leper were not to commence during the marriage-

^a Neg. iii. 2

week, or on festive days,[a] since, evidently, infection would have been most likely to spread in such circumstances.[4]

It has already been stated, that Rabbinism confessed itself powerless in presence of this living death. Although, as *Michaelis* rightly

^b Das Mos.
Recht, vol.
iv. p. 195

suggests,[b] the sacrificial ritual for the cleansed leper implies, at least, the possibility of a cure, it is in every instance traced to the direct agency of God.[5] Hence the mythical theory, which, to be rational, must show some precedent to account for the origination of the narrative in the Gospel, here once more breaks down.[6] *Keim* cannot deny the evident authenticity of the Evangelic narrative, and has no better explanation to offer than that of the old Rationalists—which *Strauss* had already so fully refuted[7]—that the poor sufferer only asked of Jesus to *declare*, not to *make*, him clean.[8] In truth, the possibility of any cure through human agency was never contemplated by the

^c Ant. iii.
11. 3

Jews. *Josephus* speaks of it as possibly granted to prayer,[c] but in a manner betokening a pious phraseology without serious meaning. We may go further, and say that not only did Rabbinism never suggest the cure of a leper, but that its treatment of those sufferers presents the most marked contrast to that of the Saviour. And yet, as if

---

[1] They were not allowed to hold intercourse with persons under other defilement than leprosy, Pes. 67 *a*.

[2] These were considered as walled since the time of Joshua, Kel. i. 7, and their sanctity equal to that of the camp of Israel, and greater than that of unwalled towns.

[3] Neg. iii. 1; vii. 1; xi. 1; xii. 1.

[4] The following parts are declared in the Mishnah as untainted by leprosy: within the eye, ear, nose, and mouth; the folds of the skin, especially those of the neck; under the female breast; the armpit; the sole of the foot, the nails, the head,ᐧand the beard (Neg. vi. 8).

[5] *Michaelis* views the whole question chiefly from the standpoint of sanitary police.

[6] It is, though I think hesitatingly, propounded by *Strauss* (vol. ii. pp. 56, 57). He has been satisfactorily answered by *Volkmar* (Marcus, p. 110).

[7] u. s. pp. 53, 54.

[8] Jesu von Naz. ii. p. 174. This is among the weakest portions of the book. *Keim* must have strongly felt ' the telling marks of the authenticity of this narrative,' when he was driven to an explanation which makes Jesus ' present Himself as a Scribe.'

writing its own condemnation, one of the titles which it gives to the   CHAP.
Messiah is 'the Leprous,' the King Messiah being represented as seated   XV
in the entrance to Rome, surrounded by, and relieving all misery and   ‿‿‿
disease, in fulfilment of Is. liii. 4.[a] [1]   [a] Sanh. 98 *b*

We need not here enumerate the various symptoms, by which the
Rabbinic law teaches us to recognise true leprosy.[2] Any one capable
of it might make the medical inspection, although only a descendant
of Aaron could formally pronounce clean or unclean.[b] Once declared   [b] Neg. iii. 1
leprous, the sufferer was soon made to feel the utter heartlessness of
Rabbinism. To banish him outside walled towns[c] may have been a   [c] Kel. i. 7
necessity, which, perhaps, required to be enforced by the threatened
penalty of forty stripes save one.[d] Similarly, it might be a right,   [d] Pes. 67
even merciful, provision, that in the Synagogues lepers were to be the
first to enter and the last to leave, and that they should occupy a
separate compartment (*Mechitsah*), ten palms high, and six feet wide.[e] [e] Neg. xiii
For, from the symbolism and connection between the physical and the   12
psychical,[3] the Old Testament, in its rites and institutions, laid the
greatest stress on 'clean and unclean.' To sum it up in briefest
compass, and leaving out of view leprosy of clothes or houses,[4]
according to the Old Testament, defilement was conveyed only by the
animal body, and attached to no other living body than that of man,
nor could any other living body than that of man communicate defilement. The Old Testament mentioned eleven principal kinds of defilement. These, as being capable of communicating further defilement,
were designated *Abhoth hattumeoth*—'fathers of defilements'—the
defilement which they produced being either itself an *Abh hattumeah*,
or else a 'Child,' or a 'Child's Child of defilement' (וְלֹר וְלֹר הַטּוּמָאה).
We find in Scripture thirty-two *Abhoth hattumeoth*, as they are called.
To this Rabbinic tradition added other twenty-nine. Again, according to Scripture, these 'fathers of defilements' affected only in two
degrees; the direct effect produced by them being designated 'the
beginning,' or 'the first,' and that further propagated, 'the second'
degree. But Rabbinic ordinances added a third, fourth, and even
fifth degree of defilement.[5] From this, as well as the equally intricate

---

[1] See the passage in full in the Appendix on Messianic Prophecies.
[2] These are detailed in Neg. i. 1–4; ii.
1; iii. 3–6; vii. 1; ix. 2, 3.
[3] Undoubtedly the deepest and most
philosophical treatment of this subject is
that in the now somewhat rare, and unfortunately uncompleted, work of *Molitor*,
Philosophie d. Gesch. (see vol. iii. pp. 126

&c., and 253 &c.). The author is, however, perhaps too much imbued with the
views of the Kabbalah.
[4] According to Tos. Neg. vi. no case of
leprosy of houses had ever occurred, but
was only mentioned in Scripture, in order
to give occasion to legal studies, so as to
procure a Divine reward.
[5] I have here followed, or rather sum-

arrangements about purification, the Mishnic section about 'clean and unclean' is at the same time the largest and most intricate in the Rabbinic code, while its provisions touched and interfered, more than any others, with every department of life.

In the elaborate code of defilements leprosy was not only one of 'the fathers of uncleanness,' but, next to defilement from the dead, stood foremost amongst them. Not merely actual contact with the leper, but even his entrance defiled a habitation,[a] and everything in it, to the beams of the roof.[b] But beyond this, Rabbinic harshness or fear carried its provisions to the utmost sequences of an unbending logic. It is, indeed, true that, as in general so especially in this instance, Rabbinism loved to trace disease to moral causes. 'No death without sin, and no pain without transgression;'[c] 'the sick is not healed, till all his sins are forgiven him.'[d] These are oft-repeated sayings; but, when closely examined, they are not quite so spiritual as they sound. For, first, they represent a reaction against the doctrine of original sin, in the sense that it is not the Fall of man, but one's actual transgression, to which disease and death are to be traced according to the saying: 'Not the serpent kills, but sin.'[e][1] But their real unspirituality appears most clearly, when we remember how special diseases were traced to particular sins. Thus,[f] child-lessness and leprosy are described as chastisements, which indeed procure for the sufferer forgiveness of sins, but cannot, like other chastisements, be regarded as the outcome of love, nor be received in love.[2] And even such sentiments in regard to sufferings[g] are immediately followed by such cynical declarations on the part of Rabbis so afflicted, as that they loved neither the chastisement, nor its reward.[h] And in regard to leprosy, tradition had it that, as leprosy attached to the house, the dress, or the person, these were to be regarded as always heavier strokes, following as each successive warning had been neglected, and a reference to this was seen in Prov. xix. 29.[1][3] Eleven sins are mentioned[k] which bring leprosy, among them pre-eminently those of which the tongue is the organ.[m]

[a] Kel. 1. 1-4

[b] Neg. xiii. 11

[c] Shabb. 55 a
[d] Nedar. 41 a

[e] Ber. 33 a

[f] Ber. 5 b

[g] Ber. 5 a

[h] Ber. 5 b
[i] Bemidb. R. 13
[k] Tanch. on Hammet-sora 4; ed. Lemberg ii. p. 24 a

[m] u. s., 2, p. 23 a;
Arach. 15 b;
and in many passages

marised, *Maimonides*. It was, of course, impossible to give even the briefest de-tails.

[1] The story, of which this saying is the moral, is that of the crushing of a ser-pent by the great miracle-monger Cha-nina ben Dosa, without his being hurt. But I cannot help feeling that a *double entendre* is here intended—on the one hand, that even a serpent could not hurt one like Chanina, and, on the other, the wider bearing on the real cause of death: not our original state, but our actual sin.

[2] The Midrash enumerates four as in that category: the poor, the blind, the childless, and the leprous.

[3] From Zech. xiv. 12 it was inferred, that this leprosy would smite the Gen-tiles even in the Messianic age (Tan-chuma, Tazria, end).

Still, if such had been the real views of Rabbinism one might have expected that Divine compassion would have been extended to those, who bore such heavy burden of their sins. Instead of this, their burdens were needlessly increased. True, as wrapped in mourner's garb the leper passed by, his cry ' Unclean!' was to incite others to pray for him—but also to avoid him.[a] No one was even to salute him; his bed was to be low, inclining towards the ground.[b] If he even put his head into a place, it became unclean. No less a distance than four cubits (six feet) must be kept from a leper; or, if the wind came from that direction, a hundred were scarcely sufficient. Rabbi Meir would not eat an egg purchased in a street where there was a leper. Another Rabbi boasted, that he always threw stones at them to keep them far off, while others hid themselves or ran away.[c][1] To such extent did Rabbinism carry its inhuman logic in considering the leper as a mourner, that it even forbade him to wash his face.[d]

We can now in some measure appreciate the contrast between Jesus and His contemporaries in His bearing towards the leper. Or, conversely, we can judge by the healing of this leper of the impression which the Saviour had made upon the people. He would have fled from a Rabbi; he came in lowliest attitude of entreaty to Jesus. Criticism need not so anxiously seek for an explanation of his approach. There was no Old Testament precedent for it: not in the case of Moses, nor even in that of Elisha, and there was no Jewish expectancy of it. But to have heard Him teach, to have seen or known Him as healing all manner of disease, must have carried to the heart the conviction of His absolute power. And so one can understand this lowly reverence of approach, this cry which has so often since been wrung from those who have despaired of all other help: ' If Thou wilt, Thou canst make me clean.' It is not a prayer, but the ground-tone of all prayer—faith in His Power, and absolute committal to Him of our helpless, hopeless need. And Jesus, touched with compassion, willed it. It almost seems, as if it were in the very exuberance of power that Jesus, acting in so direct contravention of Jewish usage, touched the leper. It was fitting that Elisha should disappoint Naaman's expectancy, that the prophet would heal his leprosy by the touch of his hand. It was even more fitting that Jesus should surprise the Jewish leper by touching, ere by His

CHAP. XV

[a] Moed K. 5 a
[b] u. s. 15 a

[c] Vayyik. R. 16. [Leprosy is there brought into connection with calumny]
[d] Moed. K. 15 a

---

[1] And yet Jewish symbolism saw in the sufferings of Israel and the destruction of the Temple the real fulfilment of the punishment of leprosy with its attendant ordinances, while it also traced in the healing of that disease and the provisions for declaring the leper clean, a close analogy to what would happen in Israel's restoration (Vayyikra R. 15, 17; Yalkut i. par. 551, 563).

Word He cleansed him.   And so, experience ever finds that in Christ the real is far beyond the ideal.   We can understand, how, from his standpoint, *Strauss* should have found it impossible to understand the healing of leprosy by the touch and Word of Jesus.   Its explanation lies in the fact, that He was the God-Man.   And yet, as our inner tending after God and the voice of conscience indicate that man is capable of adoption into God's family, so the marked power which in disease mind has over body points to a higher capability in Man Perfect, the Ideal Man, the God-Man, of vanquishing disease by His Will.

It is not quite so easy at first sight to understand, why Christ should with such intense earnestness, almost vehemence,[1] have sent the healed man away—as the term bears, 'cast him out.'[2]   Certainly not (as *Volkmar*—fantastically in error on this, as on so many other points—imagines) because He disapproved of his worship.   Rather do we once more gather, how the God-Man shrank from the fame connected with miracles—specially with such an one—which as we have seen, were rather of inward and outward necessity than of choice in His Mission.   Not so—followed by a curious crowd, or thronged by eager multitudes of sight-seers, or aspirants for temporal benefits— was the Kingdom of Heaven to be preached and advanced.   It would have been the way of a Jewish Messiah, and have led up to His royal proclamation by the populace.   But as we study the character of the Christ, no contrast seems more glaring—let us add, more painful—than that of such a scene.   And so we read that, when, notwithstanding the Saviour's charge to the healed leper to keep silence, it was nevertheless—nay, as might perhaps have been expected —all the more made known by him—as, indeed, in some measure it could scarcely have remained entirely unknown, He could no more, as before, enter the cities, but remained without in desert places, whither they came to Him from every quarter.   And in that withdrawal He spoke, and healed, 'and prayed.'

Yet another motive of Christ's conduct may be suggested.   His injunction of silence was combined with that of presenting himself to the priest and conforming to the ritual requirements of the

---

[1] On this term see the first note in this chapter.

[2] This, however, as *Godet* has shown (Comm. on St. Luke, German transl., p. 137), does not imply that the event took place either in a house or in a town, as most commentators suppose.   It is strange that the 'Speaker's Commentary,' following *Weiss*, should have located the incident in a Synagogue.   It could not possibly have occurred there, unless all Jewish ordinances and customs had been reversed.

Mosaic Law in such cases.[1] It is scarcely necessary to refute the notion, that in this Christ was prompted either by the desire to see the healed man restored to the society of his fellows, or by the wish to have some officially recognised miracle, to which He might afterwards appeal. Not to speak of the un-Christlikeness of such a wish or purpose, as a matter of fact, He did *not* appeal to it, and the healed leper wholly disappears from the Gospel-narrative. And yet his conforming to the Mosaic Ritual was to be 'a testimony unto them.' The Lord, certainly, did not wish to have the Law of Moses broken—and broken, not superseded, it would have been, if its provisions had been infringed before His Death, Ascension, and the Coming of the Holy Ghost had brought their fulfilment.

But there is something else here. The course of this history shows, that the open rupture between Jesus and the Jewish authorities, which had commenced at the Unknown Feast at Jerusalem, was to lead to practical sequences. On the part of the Jewish authorities, it led to measures of active hostility. The Synagogues of Galilee are no longer the quiet scenes of His teaching and miracles; His Word and deeds no longer pass unchallenged. It had never occurred to these Galileans, as they implicitly surrendered themselves to the power of His words, to question their orthodoxy. But now, immediately after this occurrence, we find Him accused of blasphemy.[a] They had not thought it breach of God's Law when, on that Sabbath, He had healed in the Synagogue of Capernaum and in the home of Peter; but after this it became sinful to extend like mercy on the Sabbath to him whose hand was withered.[b] They had never thought of questioning the condescension of his intercourse with the poor and needy; but now they sought to sap the commencing allegiance of His disciples by charging Him with undue intercourse with publicans and sinners,[c] and by inciting against Him even the prejudices and doubts of the half-enlightened followers of His own Forerunner.[d] All these new incidents are due to one and the same cause; the presence and hostile watchfulness of the Scribes and Pharisees, who now for the first time appear on the scene of His ministry. Is it too much then to infer, that, immediately after that Feast at Jerusalem, the

CHAP. XV

[a] St. Luke v. 21

[b] St. Luke vi. 7

[c] St. Luke v. 30

[d] St. Luke v. 33

---

[1] The Rabbinic ordinances as to the ritual in such cases are in Neg. xiv. See 'The Temple and its Services' pp. 315–317. Special attention was to be given, that the water with which the purified leper was sprinkled was from a pure, flowing spring (six different collections of water, suited to different kinds of impurity, being .described in Miqv. i. 1–8). From Parah viii. 10 we gather, that among other rivers even the Jordan was not deemed sufficiently pure, because in its course other streams, which were not lawful for such purification, had mingled with it.

Jewish authorities sent their familiars into Galilee after Jesus, and that it was to the presence and influence of this informal deputation that the opposition to Christ, which now increasingly appeared, was due? If so, then we see not only an additional motive for Christ's injunction of silence on those whom He had healed, and for His own withdrawal from the cities and their throng, but we can understand how, as He afterwards answered those, whom John had sent to lay before Christ his doubts, by pointing to His works, so He replied to the sending forth of the Scribes of Jerusalem to watch, oppose, and arrest Him, by sending to Jerusalem as His embassy the healed leper, to submit to all the requirements of the Law. It was *His* testimony unto them—His, Who was meek and lowly in heart; and it was in deepest accord with what He had done, and was doing. Assuredly, He, Who brake not the bruised reed, did not cry nor lift up His Voice in the streets, but brought forth judgment unto truth. And in Him shall the nations trust!

CHAPTER XVI.

THE RETURN TO CAPERNAUM—CONCERNING THE FORGIVENESS OF SINS—
THE HEALING OF THE PARALYSED.

(St. Matt. ix. 1–8; St. Mark ii. 1–12; St. Luke v. 17–26.)

IT is a remarkable instance of the reserve of the Gospel-narratives, that of the second journey of Jesus in Galilee no other special event is recorded than the healing of the leper.   And it seems also to indicate, that this one miracle had been so selected for a special purpose. But if, as we have suggèsted, after the ' Unknown Feast,' the activity of Jesus assumed a new and what, for want of a better name, may be called an anti-Judaic character, we can perceive the reason of it. The healing of leprosy was recorded as typical.   With this agrees also what immediately follows.   For, as Rabbinism stood confessedly powerless in face of the living death of leprosy, so it had no word of forgiveness to speak to the conscience burdened with sin, nor yet word of welcome to the sinner.   But this was the inmost meaning of the two events which the Gospel-history places next to the healing of the leper: the forgiveness of sins in the case of the paralytic, and the welcome to the chief of sinners in the call of Levi-Matthew.

CHAP.
XVI

We are still mainly following the lead of St. Mark,[1] alike as regards the succession of events and their details.   And here it is noteworthy, how the account in St. Mark confirms that by St. John [a] of what had occurred at the Unknown Feast.   Not that either Evangelist could have derived it from the other.   But if we establish the trustworthiness of the narrative in St. John v., which is unconfirmed by any of the Synoptists, we strengthen not only the evidence in favour of the Fourth Gospel generally, but that in one of its points of chief difficulty, since such advanced teaching on the part of Jesus, and such developed hostility from the Jewish authorities, might scarcely have been looked for at so early a stage.   But when we com-

[a] St. John v

---

[1] The same order is followed by St. Luke.   From the connection between St. Mark and St. Peter, we should naturally look for the fullest account of that early Capernaum-Ministry in the Second Gospel.

BOOK
III

* St. Mark
ii. 6, 7

b St. John
v. 27

c St. Mark
ii. 9
d In St.
John v. 8

e St. John v.
36; comp.
St. Mark
ii. 10

pare the language of St. Mark with the narrative in the fifth chapter of St. John's Gospel, at least four points of contact prominently appear. For, first, the unspoken charge of the Scribes,[a] that in forgiving sins Jesus blasphemed by making Himself equal with God, has its exact counterpart in the similar charge against Him in St. John v. 18, which kindled in them the wish to kill Jesus. Secondly, as in that case the final reply of Jesus pointed to 'the authority' ($\dot{\epsilon}\xi o v \sigma \iota a$) which the Father had given Him for Divine administration on earth,[b] so the healing of the paralytic was to show the Scribes that He had 'authority' ($\dot{\epsilon}\xi o v \sigma \iota a$)[1] for the dispensation upon earth of the forgiveness of sins, which the Jews rightly regarded as the Divine prerogative. Thirdly, the words which Jesus spake to the paralytic: 'Rise, take up thy bed, and walk,'[c] are to the very letter the same[2] which are recorded[d] as used by Him when He healed the impotent man at the Pool of Bethesda. Lastly, alike in the words which Jesus addressed to the Scribes at the healing of the paralytic, and in those at the Unknown Feast, He made final appeal to His works as evidential of His being sent by, and having received of, the Father 'the authority' to which He laid claim.[e] It would be utterly irrational to regard these as coincidences, and not references. And their evidential force becomes the stronger, as we remember the entire absence of design on the part of St. Mark.[3] But this correspondence not only supports the trustworthiness of the two independent narratives in St. Mark and in St. John, but also confirms alike that historical order in which we have arranged the events, and the suggestion that, after the encounter at the Unknown Feast, the authorities of Jerusalem had sent representatives to watch, oppose, and, if possible, entrap Jesus.

In another manner, also, the succession of events, as we have traced it, seems confirmed by the account of the healing of the

---

[1] The A.V. mars the meaning by rendering it: 'power.'

[2] So according to the best readings.

[3] It is, of course, not pretended by negative critics that the Fourth Gospel borrowed from St. Mark. On the contrary, the supposed differences in form and spirit between the Synoptists and the Fourth Gospel form one of the main arguments against the authenticity of the latter. In regard to the 5th chap. of St. John, Dr. *Abbott* writes (Art. 'Gospels,' Encycl. Brit. p. 833 *b*): 'That part of the discourse in which Christ describes Himself in the presence of the multitude as having received all power

to judge and to quicken the dead, does not resemble anything in the Synoptic narrative'—except St. Matt. xi. 27; St. Luke x. 22, and 'that was uttered privately to the disciples.' To complete the irony of criticism, Dr. *Abbott* contrasts the 'faith of the Synoptists,' such as 'that half-physical thrill of trust in the presence of Jesus, which enables the limbs of a paralysed man to make the due physical response to the emotional shock consequent on the word "Arise," so that in the strength of that shock the paralytic is enabled to shake off the disease of many years,' with faith such as the Fourth Gospel presents it.

paralytic. The second journey of Jesus through Galilee had commenced in autumn; the return to Capernaum was 'after days,' which, in common Jewish phraseology,[1] meant a considerable interval. As we reckon, it was winter, which would equally account for Christ's return to Capernaum, and for His teaching in the house. For, no sooner 'was it heard that He was in the house,' or, as some have rendered it, 'that He was at home,' than so many flocked to the dwelling of Peter, which at that period may have been 'the house' or temporary 'home' of the Saviour, as to fill its limited space to over flowing, and even to crowd out to the door and beyond it. The general impression on our minds is, that this audience was rather in a state of indecision than of sympathy with Jesus. It included 'Pharisees and doctors of the Law,' who had come on purpose from the towns of Galilee, from Judæa, and from Jerusalem. These occupied the 'uppermost rooms,' sitting, no doubt, near to Jesus. Their influence must have been felt by the people. Although irresistibly attracted by Jesus, an element of curiosity, if not of doubt, would mingle with their feelings, as they looked at their leaders, to whom long habit attached the most superstitious veneration. If one might so say, it was like the gathering of Israel on Mount Carmel, to witness the issue as between Elijah and the priests of Baal.

Although in no wise necessary to the understanding of the event, it is helpful to try and realise the scene. We can picture to ourselves the Saviour 'speaking the Word' to that eager, interested crowd, which would soon become forgetful even of the presence of the watchful 'Scribes.' Though we know a good deal of the structure of Jewish houses,[2] we feel it difficult to be sure of the exact place which the Saviour occupied on this occasion. Meetings for religious study and discussion were certainly held in the *Aliyah* or upper chamber.[a] But, on many grounds, such a *locale* seems utterly unsuited to the requirements of the narrative.[3] Similar objections attach to the idea, that it was the front room of one of those low houses occupied by the poor.[4] Nor is there any reason for supposing that the house occupied by Peter was one of those low buildings,

[a] Shabb. 1.
4; Jer.
Sanh. 21 b;
Jer. Pes. 30
b, and often

---

[1] לימים. See *Wetstein* in loc.
[2] 'Sketches of Jewish life,' pp. 93–96.
[3] Such a crowd could scarcely have assembled there—and where were those about and beyond the door?
[4] This is the suggestion of Dr. *Thomson* ('The Land and the Book,' pp. 358, 359). But even he sees difficulties in it. Besides, was Christ inside the small room

of such a house, and if so, how did the multitude see and hear Him? Nor can I see any reason for representing Peter as so poor. Professor *Delitzsch's* conception of the scene (in his 'Ein Tag in Capern,') seems to me, so far as I follow it, though exceedingly beautiful, too imaginative.

which formed the dwellings of the very poor. It must, at any rate, have contained, besides a large family room, accommodation for Peter and his wife, for Peter's mother-in-law, and for Jesus as the honoured guest. The Mishnah calls a small house one that is 9 feet long by 12 broad, and a large house one that is 12 feet long by 15 broad, and adds that a dining-hall is 15 feet square, the height being always computed at half the length and breadth.[a] But these notices seem rather to apply to a single room. They are part of a legal discussion, in which reference is made to a building which might be erected by a man for his son on his marriage, or as a dwelling for his widowed daughter. Another source of information is derived from what we know of the price and rental of houses. We read[b] of a house as costing ten (of course, gold) dinars, which would make the price 250 silver dinars, or between 7l. and 8l. of our money. This must, however, have been 'a small house,' since the rental of such is stated to have been from 7s. to 28s. a year,[c] while that of a large house is computed at about 9l. a year,[d] and that of a courtyard at about 14s. a year.[e]

All this is so far of present interest as it will help to show, that the house of Peter could not have been a 'small one.' We regard it as one of the better dwellings of the middle classes. In that case all the circumstances fully accord with the narrative in the Gospels. Jesus is speaking the Word, standing in the covered gallery that ran round the courtyard of such houses, and opened into the various apartments. Perhaps He was standing within the entrance of the guest-chamber, while the Scribes were sitting within that apartment, or beside Him in the gallery. The court before Him is thronged, out into the street. All are absorbedly listening to the Master, when of a sudden those appear who are bearing a paralytic on his pallet. It had of late become too common a scene to see the sick thus carried to Jesus to attract special attention. And yet one can scarcely conceive that, if the crowd had merely filled an apartment and gathered around its door, it would not have made way for the sick, or that somehow the bearers could not have come within sight, or been able to attract the attention of Christ. But with a courtyard crowded out into the street, all this would be, of course, out of the question. In such circumstances, what was to be done? Access to Jesus was simply impossible. Shall they wait till the multitude disperses, or for another and more convenient season? Only those would have acted thus who have never felt the preciousness of an opportunity, because they have never known what real need is. Inmost in

a Baba B. vi. 4

b In Jer. Keth. iv. 14, p. 29 b

c Tos. B. Mets. c. iv. 2

d u. s., c. viii. 31, ed. Z.

e Baba Mets. v. 2

the hearts of those who bore the paralysed was the belief, that Jesus could, and that he would, heal. They must have heard it from others; they must have witnessed it themselves in other instances. And in-most in the heart of the paralytic was, as we infer from the first words of Jesus to him, not only the same conviction, but with it weighed a terrible fear, born of Jewish belief, lest his sins might hinder his healing. And this would make him doubly anxious not to lose the present opportunity.

And so their resolve was quickly taken. If they cannot approach Jesus with their burden, they can let it down from above at His feet. Outside the house, as well as inside, a stair led up to the roof. They may have ascended it in this wise, or else reached it by what the Rabbis called 'the road of the roofs,'[a] passing from roof to roof, if the house adjoined others in the same street. The roof itself, which had hard beaten earth or rubble underneath it, was paved with brick, stone, or any other hard substance, and surrounded by a balustrade which, according to Jewish Law, was at least three feet high. It is scarcely possible to imagine, that the bearers of the paralytic would have attempted to dig through this into a room below, not to speak of the interruption and inconvenience caused to those below by such an operation. But no such objection attaches if we regard it, not as the main roof of the house, but as that of the covered gallery under which we are supposing the Lord to have stood. This could, of course, have been readily reached from above. In such case it would have been comparatively easy to 'unroof' the covering of 'tiles,' and then, 'having dug out' an opening through the lighter framework which supported the tiles, to let down their burden 'into the midst before Jesus.' All this, as done by four strong men, would be but the work of a few minutes. But we can imagine the arresting of the discourse of Jesus, and the breathless surprise of the crowd as this opening through the tiles appeared, and slowly a pallet was let down before them. Busy hands would help to steady it, and bring it safe to the ground. And on that pallet lay one paralysed—his fevered face and glistening eyes upturned to Jesus.

It must have been a marvellous sight, even at a time and in circumstances when the marvellous might be said to have become of every-day occurrence. This energy and determination of faith ex-ceeded aught that had been witnessed before. Jesus saw it, and He spake. For, as yet, the blanched lips of the sufferer had not parted to utter his petition. He believed, indeed, in the power of Jesus to heal, with all the certitude that issued, not only in the determina-

[a] *Jos, Ant.* xiii. 5. 3; Bab. Mez 88 *a*

tion to be laid at His feet, but at whatever trouble and in any circumstances, however novel or strange. It needed, indeed, faith to overcome all the hindrances in the present instance; and still more faith to be so absorbed and forgetful of all around, as to be let down from the roof through the broken tiling into the midst of such an assembly. And this open outburst of faith shone out the more brightly, from its contrast with the covered darkness and clouds of unbelief within the breast of those Scribes, who had come to watch and ensnare Jesus.

As yet no one had spoken, for the silence of expectancy had fallen on them all. *Could* He, and, if He could, *would* He help—and *what* would He do? But He, Who perceived man's unspoken thoughts, knew that there was not only faith, but also fear, in the heart of that man. Hence the first words which the Saviour spake to him were:

ª St. Matt.
ix. 2

'Be of good cheer.'ª He had, indeed, got beyond the coarse Judaic standpoint, from which suffering seemed an expiation of sin. It was argued by the Rabbis, that, if the loss of an eye or a tooth liberated a slave from bondage, much more would the sufferings of the whole body free the soul from guilt; and, again, that Scripture itself indicated this by the use of the word 'covenant,' alike in connection

ᵇ Lev. ii. 13
ᶜ Deut.
xxviii. 69 b
ᵈ Ber. 5 a
ᵉ Ber. 5 b

with the salt which rendered the sacrifices meet for the altar,ᵇ and sufferings,ᶜ which did the like for the soul by cleansing away sin.ᵈ We can readily believe. as the recorded experience of the Rabbis shows,ᵉ that such sayings brought neither relief to the body, nor comfort to the soul of real sufferers. But this other Jewish idea was even more deeply rooted, had more of underlying truth, and would, especially in presence of the felt holiness of Jesus, have a deep influence on the soul, that recovery would not be granted to the sick

Nedar. 41 a

unless his sins had first been forgiven him.ᶠ It was this deepest, though, perhaps, as yet only partially conscious, want of the sufferer before Him, which Jesus met when, in words of tenderest kindness, He spoke forgiveness to his soul, and that not as something to come, but as an act already past: 'Child, thy sins have been forgiven.'² We should almost say, that He needed first to speak these words, before He gave healing: needed, in the psychological order of things; needed, also, if the inward sickness was to be healed, and because the inward stroke, or paralysis, in the consciousness of guilt, must be removed, before the outward could be taken away.

---

¹ In our A.V. it is erroneously Deut. xxix. 1.
² So according to the greater number of MSS., which have the verb in the *perfect* tense.

In another sense, also, there was a higher 'need be' for the word CHAP. which brought forgiveness, before that which gave healing.　Although XVI it is not for a moment to be supposed, that, in what Jesus did, He had primary intention in regard to the Scribes, yet here also, as in all Divine acts, the undesigned adaptation and the undesigned sequences are as fitting as what we call the designed.　For, with God there is neither past nor future; neither immediate nor mediate; but all is one, the eternally and God-pervaded Present.　Let us recall, that Jesus was in the presence of those in whom the Scribes would feign have wrought disbelief, not of His power to cure disease—which was patent to all—but in His Person and authority; that, perhaps, such doubts had already been excited.　And here it deserves special notice, that, by first speaking forgiveness, Christ not only presented the deeper moral aspect of His miracles, as against their ascription to magic or Satanic agency, but also established that very claim, as regarded His Person and authority, which it was sought to invalidate. In this forgiveness of sins He presented His Person and authority as Divine, and He proved it such by the miracle of healing which immediately followed.　Had the two been inverted, there would have been evidence, indeed, of His power, but not of His Divine Personality, nor of His having authority to forgive sins; and this, not the doing of miracles, was the object of His Teaching and Mission, of which the miracles were only secondary evidence.

Thus the inward reasoning of the Scribes,[1] which was open and known to Him Who readeth all thoughts,[2] issued in quite the opposite of what they could have expected.　Most unwarranted, indeed, was the feeling of contempt which we trace in their unspoken words, whether we read them: 'Why doth this one thus speak blasphemies?' or, according to a more correct transcript of them: 'Why doth this one speak thus?　He blasphemeth!'　Yet from their point of view they were right, for God alone can forgive sins; nor has that power ever been given or delegated to man.　But was He a mere man, like even the most honoured of God's servants?　Man, indeed; but 'the Son of Man'[3] in the emphatic and well-understood sense of being

---

[1] The expression, 'reasoning in their hearts,' corresponds *exactly* to the Rabbinic מהרהר בלבו. Ber. 22 *a*. The word הרהר is frequently used in contradistinction to speaking.

[2] In Sanh. 93 *b* this reading of the thoughts is regarded as the fulfilment of Is. xi. 3, and as one of the marks of the Messiah, which Bar Kokhabh not possessing was killed.

[3] That the expression 'Son of Man' (בן אדם) was well understood as referring to the Messiah, appears from the following remarkable anti-Christian passage (Jer. Taan 65 *b*, at the bottom): 'If a man shall say to thee, I am God, he lies; if he says, I am the Son of Man, his end will be to repent it; if he says,

the Representative Man, who was to bring a new life to humanity; the Second Adam, the Lord from Heaven. It seemed easy to *say*: 'Thy sins have been forgiven.' But to Him, Who had 'authority' to do so on earth, it was neither more easy nor more difficult than to say: 'Rise, take up thy bed, and walk.' Yet this latter, assuredly, proved the former, and gave it in the sight of all men unquestioned reality. And so it was the thoughts of these Scribes, which, as applied to Christ, were 'evil'—since they imputed to Him blasphemy —that gave occasion for offering real evidence of what they would have impugned and denied. In no other manner could the object alike of miracles and of this special miracle have been so attained as by the 'evil thoughts' of these Scribes, when, miraculously brought to light, they spoke out the inmost possible doubt, and pointed to the highest of all questions concerning the Christ. And so it was once more the wrath of man which praised Him!

'And the remainder of wrath did he restrain.' As the healed man slowly rose, and, still silent, rolled up his pallet, a way was made for him between this multitude which followed him with wondering eyes. Then, as first mingled wonderment and fear fell on Israel on Mount Carmel, when the fire had leaped from heaven, devoured the sacrifice, licked up the water in the trench, and even consumed the stones of the altar, and then all fell prostrate, and the shout rose to heaven: 'Jehovah, He is the Elohim!' so now, in view of this manifestation of the Divine Presence among them. The amazement of fear fell on them in this Presence, and they glorified God, and they said: 'We have never seen it on this wise!'

I go up into heaven (to this applies Numb. xxiii. 19), hath he said and shall he not do it? [or, hath he spoken, and shall he make it good?] Indeed, the whole passage, as will be seen, is an attempt to adapt. Numb. xxiii. 19 to the Christian controversy.

CHAPTER XVII.

THE CALL OF MATTHEW—THE SAVIOUR'S WELCOME TO SINNERS—RAB-
BINIC THEOLOGY AS REGARDS THE DOCTRINE OF FORGIVENESS IN
CONTRAST TO THE GOSPEL OF CHRIST—THE CALL OF THE TWELVE
APOSTLES.

(St. Matt. ix. 9–13; St. Mark ii. 13–17; St. Luke v. 27–32; St. Matt. x. 2–4;
St. Mark iii. 13–19; St. Luke vi. 12–19.)

IN two things chiefly does the fundamental difference appear between CHAP.
XVII Christianity and all other religious systems, notably Rabbinism. And in these two things, therefore, lies the main characteristic of Christ's work; or, taking a wider view, the fundamental idea of all religions. Subjectively, they concern *sin* and the *sinner*; or, to put it objectively, the forgiveness of sin and the welcome to the sinner. But Rabbinism, and every other system down to modern humanitarianism —if it rises so high in its idea of God as to reach that of sin, which is its shadow—can only generally point to God for the forgiveness of sin. What here is merely an abstraction, has become a concrete reality in Christ. He speaks forgiveness on earth, because He is its embodiment. As regards the second idea, that of the sinner, all other systems know of no welcome to him till, by some means (inward or outward), he have ceased to be a sinner and become a penitent. They would first make him a penitent, and then bid him welcome to God; Christ first welcomes him to God, and so makes him a penitent. The one demands, the other imparts life. And so Christ is the Physician, Whom they that are in health need not, but they that are sick. And so Christ came not to call the righteous but sinners—not to repentance, as our common text erroneously puts it in St. Matthew ix. 13, and St. Mark ii. 17,[1] but to Himself, to the Kingdom; and this is the beginning of repentance.

Thus it is that Jesus, when His teaching becomes distinctive from that of Judaism, puts these two points in the foreground: the one at

---

[1] The words 'to repentance' are certainly spurious in St. Matt. and St. Mark. I regard theirs as the original and authentic report of the words of Christ. In St. Luke v. 32, the words 'unto repentance' do certainly occur. But, with *Godet*, I regard them as referring to 'the righteous,' and as used, in a sense, ironically.

the cure of the paralytic, the other in the call of Levi-Matthew. And this, also, further explains His miracles of healing as for the higher presentation of Himself as the Great Physician, while it gives some insight into the *nexus* of these two events, and explains their chronological succession.[1] It was fitting that at the very outset, when Rabbinism followed and challenged Jesus with hostile intent, these two spiritual facts should be brought out, and that, not in a controversial, but in a positive and practical manner. For, as these two questions of sin and of the possible relation of the sinner to God are the great burden of the soul in its upward striving after God, so the answer to them forms the substance of all religions. Indeed, all the cumbrous observances of Rabbinism—its whole law—were only an attempted answer to the question: How can a man be just with God?

But, as Rabbinism stood self-confessedly silent and powerless as regarded the forgiveness of sins, so it had emphatically no word of welcome or help for the sinner. The very term 'Pharisee,' or 'separated one,' implied the exclusion of sinners. With this the whole character of Pharisaism accorded; perhaps, we should have said, that of Rabbinism, since the Sadducean would here agree with the Pharisaic Rabbi. The contempt and avoidance of the unlearned, which was so characteristic of the system, arose not from mere pride of knowledge, but from the thought that, as 'the Law' was the glory and privilege of Israel—indeed, the object for which the world was created and preserved—ignorance of it was culpable. Thus, the unlearned blasphemed his Creator, and missed or perverted his own destiny. It was a principle, that 'the ignorant cannot be pious.' On the principles of Rabbinism, there was logic in all this, and reason also, though sadly perverted. The yoke of 'the Kingdom of God' was the high destiny of every true Israelite. Only, to them it lay in external, not internal conformity to the Law of God: 'in meat and drink,' not 'in righteousness, peace, and joy in the Holy Ghost.' True, they also perceived, that 'sins of thought' and purpose, though uncommitted, were 'more grievous than even sins of outward deed;'[a] but only in this sense, that each outward sin was traceable to inward dereliction or denial of the Law—'no man sinneth, unless the spirit of error has first entered into him.'[b] On this ground the punishment of infidelity or apostasy in the next world was endless, while that of actual transgressions was limited in duration.[c][2]

As 'righteousness came by the Law,' so also return to it on the

a Yoma 29 a

b Sot. 3 a

c Rosh haSh. 17 a

---

[1] So in all the three Gospels.   [2] Comp. Sepher Iqqarim iv. 28.

part of the sinner.   Hence, although Rabbinism had no welcome to the sinner, it was unceasing in its call to repentance and in extolling its merits.   All the prophets had prophesied only of repentance.[a] The last pages of the Tractate on the Day of Atonement are full of praises of repentance.   It not only averted punishment and prolonged life, but brought good, even the final redemption to Israel and the world at large.   It surpassed the observance of all the commandments, and was as meritorious as if one had restored the Temple and Altar, and offered all sacrifices.[b] One hour of penitence and good works outweighed the whole world to come.   These are only a few of the extravagant statements by which Rabbinism extolled repentance.   But, when more closely examined, we find that this repentance, as preceding the free welcome of invitation to the sinner, was only another form of work-righteousness.   This is, at any rate, one meaning[1] of the saying which conjoined the Law and repentance, and represented them as preceding the Creation.[c]   Another would seem derived from a kind of Manichæan view of sin.   According to it, God Himself was really the author of the *Yetser haRa*, or evil impulse[2] ('the law in our members'), for which, indeed, there was an absolute necessity, if the world was to continue.[d][3]   Hence, 'the penitent' was really 'the great one,' since his strong nature had more in it of the 'evil impulse,' and the conquest of it by the penitent was really of greater merit than abstinence from sin.[e]   Thus it came, that the true penitent really occupied a higher place—'stood where the perfectly righteous could not stand.'[f]   There is then both work and merit in penitence; and we can understand, how 'the gate of penitence is open, even when that of prayer is shut,'[g] and that these two sentences are not only consistent, but almost cover each other—that the Messianic deliverance would come, if all Israel did righteousness,[h] and, again, if all Israel repented for only one day;[i] or, to put it otherwise—if Israel were all saints, or all sinners.[k]

We have already touched the point where, as regards repentance, as formerly in regard to forgiveness, the teaching of Christ is in absolute and fundamental contrariety to that of the Rabbis.   According to Jesus Christ, when we have done all, we are to feel that we are but unprofitable servants.[m]   According to the Rabbis, as

CHAP.
XVII

[a] Ber. 34 *h*

[b] Vayyik. R. 7

[c] Pes. 54 *a*; Ber. R. 1

[d] Yoma 69 *b*; Ber. R. 9, and in many places

[e] Sanh. 99 *a*; *Maimon.* Hil. Tesh. Per. 7

[f] Sanh. 99 *a*; Ber. 34 *b*

[g] Yalkut on Ps. xxxii.- p. 101 *b*

[h] Sanh. 98 *a*

[i] Sanh. 98 *a*; Jer. Taan. 64 a

[k] Sanh. 98 *a*

[m] St. Luke xvii. 10

---

[1] It would be quite one-sided to represent this as the *only* meaning, as, it seems to me, *Weber* has done in his 'System d. altsynagog, palæst. Theol.' This, and a certain defectiveness in the treatment, are among the blemishes in this otherwise interesting and very able

posthumous work.
[2] So in too many passages for enumeration.
[3] Some of these points have already been stated.   But it was necessary to repeat them so as to give a connected view.

St. Paul puts it, 'righteousness cometh by the Law;' and, when it is lost, the Law alone can restore life;[1] while, according to Christian teaching, it only bringeth death. Thus there was, at the very foundation of religious life, absolute contrariety between Jesus and His contemporaries. Whence, if not from heaven, came a doctrine so novel as that which Jesus made the basis of His Kingdom?

In one respect, indeed, the Rabbinic view was in some measure derived from the Old Testament, though by an external and, therefore, false interpretation of its teaching. In the Old Testament, also, 'repentance' was Teshubhah (תשובה), 'return;' while, in the New Testament, it is 'change of mind' (μετανοια). It would not be fair here to argue, that the common expression for repenting was 'to do penitence' (עשה תשובה), since by its side we frequently meet that other: 'to return in penitence' (שוב בתשובה). Indeed, other terms for repentance also occur. Thus Tohu (תהו) means repentance in the sense of regret; Charatah, perhaps, more in that of a change of mind; while Teyubha or Teshubhah is the return of repentance. Yet, according to the very common Rabbinic expression, there is a 'gate of repentance' (שער תשובה, תייבא) through which a man must enter, and, even if Charatah be the sorrowing change of mind, it is at most only that gate. Thus, after all, there is more in the 'doing of penitence' than appears at first sight. In point of fact, the full meaning of repentance as Teshubhah, or 'return,' is only realised, when a man has returned from dereliction to observance of the Law. Then, sins of purpose are looked upon as if they had been unintentional—nay, they become even virtuous actions.[a]

We are not now speaking of the forgiveness of sins. In truth, Rabbinism knew nothing of a forgiveness of sin, free and unconditional, unless in the case of those who had not the power of doing anything for their atonement. Even in the passage which extols most the freeness and the benefits of repentance (the last pages of the Tractate on the Day of Atonement), there is the most painful discussion about sins great and small, about repentance from fear or from love, about sins against commands or against prohibitions; and, in what cases repentance averted, or else only deferred, judgment, leaving final expiation to be wrought by other means. These were: personal sufferings,[b] death,[c] or the Day of Atonement.[d] Besides these, there were always the 'merits of the fathers;'[e] or, perhaps, some one good work done;[f] or, at any rate, the brief period of purgatorial

a Yoma 86

b Ber. 5 a, b; Kidd. 81 b

c Yoma u. s.

d Yoma u. s., and many passages

e In almost innumerable passages

f Ab. Zar. 5 a

[1] So, according to Rabbinism, both in the Sepher Iqqar. and in Menor. Hammaor.

pain, which might open the gate of mercy.   These are the so-called
'advocates' (Peraqlitin, פרקליטין) of the penitent sinner.   In a classical passage on the subject,[a] repentance is viewed in its bearing on
four different spiritual[1] conditions, which are supposed to be respectively referred to in Jer. iii. 22; Lev. xvi. 30; Is. xxii. 14; and
Ps. lxxxix. 32.   The first of these refers to a breach of a *command*,
with immediate and persistent cry for forgiveness, which is at
once granted.   The second is that of a breach of a *prohibition*,
when, besides repentance, the Day of Atonement is required.   The
third is that of *purposed sin*, on which death or cutting off had been
threatened, when, besides repentance and the Day of Atonement,
sufferings are required; while in *open profanation* of the Name of
God, only death can make final atonement.[b]

But the nature of repentance has yet to be more fully explained.
Its gate is sorrow and shame.[c]   In that sense repentance may be the
work of a moment, ' as in the twinkling of an eye,'[d] and a life's sins may
obtain mercy by the tears and prayers of a few minutes' repentance.'[2]
To this also refers the beautiful saying, that all which rendered a
sacrifice unfit for the altar, such as that it was broken, fitted the
penitent for acceptance, since 'the sacrifices of God were a broken
and contrite heart.'[f]   By the side of what may be called contrition,
Jewish theology places *confession* (*Viddui*, וידוי).   This was deemed so
integral a part of repentance, that those about to be executed,[g]
or to die,[h] were admonished to it.   Achan of old had thus obtained
pardon.[i]   But in the case of the living all this could only be regarded
as repentance in the sense of being its preparation or beginning.
Even if it were *Charatah*, or regret at the past, it would not yet be
Teshubhah, or return to God; and even if it changed purposed into
unintentional sin, arrested judgment, and stayed or banished its Angel,
it would still leave a man without those works which are not only his
real destiny and merit heaven, but constitute true repentance.   For,
as sin is ultimately dereliction of the Law, beginning within, so

CHAP.
XVII

[a] Mechilta, 76 a

[b] See also Yoma 86 and following

[c] Ber. 12 b; Chag. 5 a
[d] Pesiqta ed. Bub. p. 163 b
[e] Ab. Zar. 17 a

[f] Vayyik. R. 7

[g] Sanh. vi. 2
[h] Shabb. 32 a
[i] Sanh. u. s.

---

[1] In *Menorath Hammaor* (Ner v. 1. 1,
2) seven kinds of repentance in regard to
seven different conditions are mentioned.
They are repentance immediately after
the commission of sin; after a course of
sin, but while there is still the power of
sinning; where there is no longer the
occasion for sinning ; where it is caused
by admonition, or fear of danger; where
it is caused by actual affliction; where a
man is old, and unable to sin; and,
lastly, repentance in prospect of death.

[2] This is illustrated, among other
things, by the history of a Rabbi who, at
the close of a dissolute life, became a
convert by repentance. The story of the
occasion of his repentance is not at all
nice in its realistic details, and the tears
with which a self-righteous colleague saw
the beatification of the penitent are painfully illustrative of the elder brother in
the Parable of the Prodigal Son (Ab. Z.
17 a).

BOOK
III

ª Ps. xcii.
ᵇ Ber. R. 22
ᶜ 2 Chron.
xxxiii. 12,
13

ᵈ Debar. R.
2; ed.
Warsh. p. 7
a; comp.
Sanh. 102 b,
last lines,
and 103 a
ᵉ Ex. xv. 11

ᶠ Taan. 16 a

ᵍ Rosh
haSh. 17 b

ʰ BabaMez.
85 a
ⁱ Ber. 17 a
ᵏ u. s.

ᵐ Baba
Mez. 85 a

ⁿ Tanch.
Noach 4
ᵒ See the
discussion
in B. Mez.
37 a

repentance is ultimately return to the Law. In this sense there is a higher and meritorious confession, which not only owns sin but God, and is therefore an inward return to Him. So Adam, when he saw the penitence of Cain, burst into this Psalm,[a] 'It is a good thing to confess[1] unto the Lord.'[b][2] Manasseh, when in trouble, called upon God and was heard,[c] although it is added, that this was only done in order to prove that the door of repentance was open to all. Indeed, the Angels had closed the windows of Heaven against his prayers, but God opened a place for their entrance beneath His throne of glory.[d] Similarly, even Pharaoh, who, according to Jewish tradition, made in the Red Sea confession of God,[e] was preserved, became king of Nineveh, and so brought the Ninevites to true repentance, which verily consisted not merely in sackcloth and fasting, but in restitution, so that every one who had stolen a beam pulled down his whole palace to restore it.[f]

But, after all, inward repentance only arrested the decrees of justice.[g] That which really put the penitent into right relationship with God was *good deeds*. The term must here be taken in its widest sense. *Fasting* is meritorious in a threefold sense: as the expression of humiliation,[h] as an offering to God, similar to, but better than the fat of sacrifices on the altar,[i] and as preventing further sins by chastening and keeping under the body.[k] A similar view must be taken of self-inflicted penances.[m][3] On the other hand, there was restitution to those who had been wronged—as a woman once put it to her husband, to the surrender of one's 'girdle.'[n][4] Nay, it must be of even more than was due in strict law.[o] To this must be added public acknowledgment of public sins. If a person had sinned in one direction, he must not only avoid it for the future,[5] but aim at doing all the more in the opposite direction, or of overcoming sin in the same circumstances of temptation.[6] Beyond all this were the really *good*

---

[1] So it would need to be rendered in this context.

[2] Another beautiful allegory is that, in the fear of Adam, as the night closed in upon his guilt, God gave him two stones to rub against each other, which produced the spark of light—the rubbing of these two stones being emblematic of repentance (Pes. 54 a; Ber. R. 11, 12).

[3] Baba Mez. 84 b (quoted by *Weber*) is scarcely an instance. The whole of that part of the Talmud is specially repugnant, from its unsavory character and grossly absurd stories. In one of the stories in Baba Mez. 85, a Rabbi tries by sitting over the fire in an oven, whether

he has become impervious to the fire of Gehinnom. For thirty days he was successful, but after that it was noticed his thighs were singed, whence he was called 'the little one with the singed thighs.'

[4] But such restitution was sometimes not insisted on, for the sake of encouraging penitents.

[5] Rabbinism has an apt illustration of this in the saying, that all the baths of lustration would not cleanse a man, so long as he continued holding in his hand that which had polluted him (Taan. 16 a).

[6] These statements are all so thoroughly Rabbinic that it is needless to make special references.

works, whether occupation with the Law [a] or outward deeds, which constituted perfect repentance. Thus we read,[b] that every time Israel gave alms or did any kindness, they made in this world great peace, and procured great Paracletes between Israel and their Father in Heaven. Still farther, we are told [c] what a sinner must do who would be pardoned. If he had been accustomed daily to read one column in the Bible, let him read two; if to learn one chapter in the Mishnah, let him learn two. But if he be not learned enough to do either, let him become an administrator for the congregation, or a public distributor of alms. Nay, so far was the doctrine of external merit carried, that to be buried in the land of Israel was supposed to ensure forgiveness of sins.[d] This may, finally, be illustrated by an instance, which also throws some light on the parable of Dives in Hades. Rabbi Simeon ben Lakish had in early life been the associate of two robbers. But he repented, 'returned to his God with all his heart, with fasting and prayer, was early and late before God, and busied himself with the *Torah* (Law) and the commandments.' Then both he and his former companions died, when they saw him in glory, while themselves were in the lowest hell. And when they reminded God, that with Him there was no regard of persons, He pointed to the Rabbi's penitence and their own impenitence. On this they asked for respite, that they might 'do great penitence,' when they were told that there was no space for repentance after death. This is farther enforced by a parable to the effect, that a man, who is going into the wilderness, must provide himself with bread and water while in the inhabited country, if he would not perish in the desert.

Thus, in one and another respect, Rabbinic teaching about the need of repentance runs close to that of the Bible. But the vital difference between Rabbinism and the Gospel lies in this: that whereas Jesus Christ freely invited *all* sinners, whatever their past, assuring them of welcome and grace, the last word of Rabbinism is only despair, and a kind of Pessimism. For, it is expressly and repeatedly declared in the case of certain sins, and, characteristically, of heresy, that, even if a man genuinely and truly repented, he must expect immediately to die—indeed, his death would be the evidence that his repentance was genuine, since, though such a sinner might turn from his evil, it would be impossible for him, if he lived, to lay hold on the good, and to do it.[e]

It is in the light of what we have just learned concerning the Rabbinic views of forgiveness and repentance that the call of Levi-Matthew must be read, if we would perceive its full meaning. There

CHAP.
XVII

[a] Vayyik.
R. 3,
towards
the end
[b] In B. Bab.
10 a
[c] Vayyik.
R. 25, beg.
ed. Warsh.
p. 38 a

[d] Tanch. on
Gen. xlviii.

[e] Ab. Zar.
17 a

BOOK
III

ᵃ St. Mark
ii. 13

ᵇ Gitt. 84 b

ᶜ Sheq. v. 1
ᵈ Eduy. ii.
5; Yoma
84 a
ᵉ Sanh. 43 a,
in the older
editions;
comp.
Chesron.
haShas,
p. 22 b

is no need to suppose that it took place immediately on the cure of the paralytic. On the contrary, the more circumstantial account of St. Mark implies, that some time had intervened.ᵃ If our suggestion be correct, that it was winter when the paralytic was healed at Capernaum, we may suppose it to have been the early spring-time of that favoured district, when Jesus 'went forth again by the seaside.' And with this, as we shall see, best agrees the succession of after-events.

Few, if any, could have enjoyed better opportunities for hearing, and quietly thinking over the teaching of the Prophet of Nazareth, than Levi-Matthew. There is no occasion for speculating which was his original, or whether the second name was added after his conversion, since in Galilee it was common to have two names—one the strictly Jewish, the other the Galilean.ᵇ Nor do we wonder, that in the sequel the first or purely Jewish name of *Levi* was dropped, and only that of Matthew (*Matti, Mattai, Matteya, Mattithyah*), retained. The latter which is the equivalent of Nathanael, or of the Greek Theodore (gift of God), seems to have been frequent. We read that it was that of a former Temple-official,ᶜ and of several Rabbis.ᵈ It is perhaps of more interest, that the Talmudᵉ names five as the disciples of Jesus, and among them these two whom we can clearly identify: Matthew [1] and Thaddæus. [2]

Sitting before [3] his custom-house, as on that day when Jesus called him, Matthew must have frequently heard Him as He taught

---

[1] A ridiculous story is told that Matthew endeavored to avert sentence of death by a play on his name, quoting Ps. xlii. 2: '*Mathai* (in our version, 'When') I shall come and appear before God;' to which the judges replied by similarly adapting Ps. xli. 5: '*Mathai* (in our version, 'When') he shall die, and his name perish.'

The other three disciples are named: *Neqai, Netser,* and *Boni,* or *Buni.* In Taan. 20 a a miracle is related which gave to Boni the name of Nicodemus (Naqdimon). But I regard this as some confusion, of which there is much in connection with the name of Nicodemus in the Talmud. According to the Talmud, like Matthew, the other three tried to save their lives by punning appeals to Scripture, similar to that of St. Matthew. Thus, Neqai quotes Exod. xxiii. 7, 'Naqi ('the innocent' in our version) and the righteous shalt thou not slay,' to which the judges replied by Ps. x. 8, 'in the

secret places he shall slay Naqi ('the innocent' in our version'). Again, Netser pleads Is. xi. 1: 'Netser (a branch) shall grow out of his roots,' to which the judges reply, Is. xiv. 19: 'Thou art cast out of thy grave like an abominable Netser' (branch), while Boni tries to save his life by a pun on Exod. iv. 22: 'My first-born *Beni* (in our version, 'my son') is Israel,' to which the judges reply by quoting the next verse, 'I will slay *Binkha* (in our version, 'thy son'), thy first-born!' If the Hebrew *Beni* was sometimes pronounced *Boni,* this may account for the Grecianised form *Boanerges* ('sons of thunder') for *Beney-Regosh,* or *Regasha.* In Hebrew the root scarcely means even 'noise' (see *Gesenius* sub רגש), but it has that meaning in the Aramæan. *Kautzsch* (Gram. d. Bibl.-Aram.) suggests the word *regaz,* 'anger,' 'angry impetuosity.' But the suggestion does not commend itself.

[3] ἐπὶ τὸ τελώνιον.

by the sea-shore. For this would be the best, and therefore often CHAP.
chosen, place for the purpose. Thither not only the multitude from XVII
Capernaum could easily follow; but here was the landing-place for
the many ships which traversed the Lake, or coasted from town to
town. And this not only for them who had business in Capernaum
or that neighbourhood, but also for those who would then strike
the great road of Eastern commerce, which led from Damascus to the
harbours of the West. Touching the Lake in that very neighbourhood, it turned thence, northwards and westwards, to join what was
termed the Upper Galilean road.

We know much, and yet, as regards details, perhaps too little
about those 'tolls, dues, and customs,' which made the Roman administration such sore and vexatious exaction to all 'Provincials,' and
which in Judæa loaded the very name of publican with contempt and
hatred. They who cherished the gravest religious doubts as to the
lawfulness of paying any tribute to Cæsar, as involving in principle
recognition of a bondage to which they would fain have closed their
eyes, and the substitution of heathen kingship for that of Jehovah,
must have looked on the publican as the very embodiment of anti-
nationalism. But perhaps men do not always act under the constant
consciousness of such abstract principles. Yet the endless vexatious
interferences, the unjust and cruel exactions, the petty tyranny, and
the extortionate avarice, from which there was neither defence nor
appeal, would make it always well-nigh unbearable. It is to this
that the Rabbis so often refer. If 'publicans' were disqualified from
being judges or witnesses, it was, at least so far as regarded witness-
bearing, because 'they exacted more than was due.'[a] Hence also it [a] Sanh. 25 b
was said, that repentance was specially difficult for tax-gatherers and
custom-house officers.[b][1] [b] Baba K. 94 b

It is of importance to notice, that the Talmud distinguishes two
classes of 'publicans': the tax-gatherer in general (*Gabbai*), and the
Mokhes, or *Mokhsa*, who was specially the *douanier* or custom-house
official.[2] Although both classes fall under the Rabbinic ban, the
douanier—such as Matthew was—is the object of chief execration.
And this, because his exactions were more vexatious, and gave more
scope to rapacity. The *Gabbai*, or tax-gatherer, collected the regular
dues, which consisted of ground-, income-, and poll-tax. The ground-

---

[1] With them herdsmen were conjoined, on account of their frequent temptations to dishonesty, and their wild lives far from ordinances.

[2] *Wünsche* is mistaken in making the *Gabbai* the superior, and the *Mokhes* the subordinate, tax-collector. See *Levy*, Neuhebr. Wörterb. iii. p. 116 *a*.

tax amounted to one-tenth of all grain and one-fifth of the wine and fruit grown; partly paid in kind, and partly commuted into money. The income-tax amounted to 1 per cent.; while the head-money, or poll-tax, was levied on all persons, bond and free, in the case of men from the age of fourteen, in that of women from the age of twelve, up to that of sixty-five.

If this offered many opportunities for vexatious exactions and rapacious injustice, the *Mokhes* might inflict much greater hardship upon the poor people. There was tax and duty upon all imports and exports; on all that was bought and sold; bridge-money, road-money, harbour-dues, town-dues, &c. The classical reader knows the ingenuity which could invent a tax, and find a name for every kind of exaction, such as on axles, wheels, pack-animals, pedestrians, roads, highways; on admission to markets; on carriers, bridges, ships, and quays; on crossing rivers, on dams, on licences, in short, on such a variety of objects, that even the research of modern scholars has not been able to identify all the names. On goods the *ad valorem* duty amounted to from $2\frac{1}{2}$ to 5, and on articles of luxury to even $12\frac{1}{2}$ per cent. But even this was as nothing, compared to the vexation of being constantly stopped on the journey, having to unload all one's pack-animals, when every bale and package was opened, and the contents tumbled about, private letters opened, and the *Mokhes* ruled supreme in his insolence and rapacity.

The very word *Mokhes* seems, in its root-meaning, associated with the idea of oppression and injustice. He was literally, as really, an oppressor. The Talmud charges them with gross partiality, remitting in the case of those to whom they wished to show favour, and exacting from those who were not their favourites. They were a criminal race, to which Lev. xx. 5 applied. It was said, that there never was a family which numbered a *Mokhes*, in which all did not become such. Still, cases are recorded when a religious publican would extend favour to Rabbis, or give them timely notice to go into hiding. If one belonging to the sacred association (a *Chabher*) became either a *Gabbai* or a *Mokhes*, he was at once expelled, although he might be restored on repentance.[a] That there was ground for such rigour, appears from such an occurrence,[b] as when a *Mokhes* took from a defenceless person his ass, giving him another, and very inferior, animal for it. Against such unscrupulous oppressors every kind of deception was allowed; goods might be declared to be votive offerings,[c] or a person pass his slave as his son.[d]

The *Mokhes* was called 'great'[e] if he employed substitutes, and

[a] Jer. Dem. 23 a; comp. Bekhor. 31 a

[b] In B. Kamma x. 2

[c] Nedar. iii. 4

[d] Jer. Kidd. 66 b

[e] Shabb. 78 b

'small' if he stood himself at the receipt of custom. Till the time of Cæsar the taxes were farmed in Rome, at the highest bidding, mostly by a joint-stock company of the knightly order, which employed publicans under them. But by a decree of Cæsar, the taxes of Judæa were no longer farmed, but levied by publicans in Judæa, and paid directly to the Government, the officials being appointed by the provincials themselves.[a][1] This was, indeed, a great alleviation, although it perhaps made the tax-gatherers only more unpopular, as being the direct officials of the heathen power. This also explains how, if the Mishnah forbids[b] even the changing of money from the guilt-laden chest of a *Mokhes*, or *douanier*, the Gemara[c] adds, that such applied to custom-house officers who either did not keep to the tax appointed by the Government, or indeed to any fixed tax, and to those who appointed themselves to such office—that is, as we take it, who would volunteer for the service, in the hope of making profit on their own account. An instance is, however, related of a *Gabbai*, or tax-gatherer, becoming a celebrated Rabbi, though the taint of his former calling deterred the more rigid of his colleagues from intercourse with him.[d] On heathen feast days toll was remitted to those who came to the festival.[e] Sometimes this was also done from kindness.[f] The following story may serve as a final illustration of the popular notions, alike about publicans and about the merit of good works. The son of a *Mokhes* and that of a very pious man had died. The former received from his townsmen all honour at his burial, while the latter was carried unmourned to the grave. This anomaly was Divinely explained by the circumstance, that the pious man had committed one transgression, and the publican had done one good deed. But a few days afterwards a further vision and dream was vouchsafed to the survivors, when the pious was seen walking in gardens beside water-brooks, while the publican was descried stretching out his tongue towards the river to quench his thirst, but unable to reach the refreshing stream.[g]

What has been described in such detail, will cast a peculiar light on the call of Matthew by the Saviour of sinners. For, we remember that Levi-Matthew was not only a 'publican,' but of the worst kind: a '*Mokhes*' or *douanier*; a 'little Mokhes,' who himself stood at his custom-house; one of the class to whom, as we are told, repentance offered special difficulties. And, of all such officials, those who had to take toll from ships were perhaps the worst, if we are to

[a] *Jos.* Ant. xiv. 10. 5

[b] B. Kamma x. 1
[c] Baba K. 113 a

[d] Bekhor. 31 a
[e] Ab. Zar. 13 a
[f] Tos. B. Mets. viii. 25, ed. Zuck.

[g] Jer. Chag. 77 d; comp Jer. Sanh. 23 c, and Sanh. 44 b

---

[1] Comp. *Wieseler's* Beitr. pp. 75–78. Hence the 'publicans' were not subordinates, but direct officials of the Government.

judge by the proverb: 'Woe to the ship which sails without having paid the dues.'ᵃ And yet, after all, Matthew may have been only one of that numerous class to whom religion is merely a matter quite outside of, and in another region from life, and who, having first gone astray through ignorance, feel themselves ever farther repelled, or rather shut out, by the narrow, harsh uncharitableness of those whom they look upon as the religious and pious.

But now quite another day had dawned on him. The Prophet of Nazareth was not like those other great Rabbis, or their pietist, self-righteous imitators. There was that about Him which not only aroused the conscience, but drew the heart—compelling, not repelling. What He said opened a new world. His very appearance bespoke Him not harsh, self-righteous, far away, but the Helper, if not even the Friend, of sinners. There was not between Him and one like Matthew, the great, almost impassable gap of repentance. He had seen and heard Him in the Synagogue—and who that had heard His Words, or witnessed His power, could ever forget, or lose the impression? The people, the rulers, even the evil spirits, had owned His authority. But in the Synagogue Jesus was still the Great One, far-away from him; and he, Levi-Matthew, the 'little Mokhes' of Capernaum, to whom, as the Rabbis told him, repentance was next to impossible. But out there, in the open, by the seashore, it was otherwise. All unobserved by others, he observed all, and could yield himself, without reserve, to the impression. Now, it was an eager multitude that came from Capernaum; then, a long train bearing sufferers, to whom gracious, full, immediate relief was granted—whether they were Rabbinic saints, or sinners. And still more gracious than His deeds were His Words.

And so Matthew sat before his custom-house, and hearkened and hoped. Those white-sailed ships would bring crowds of listeners; the busy caravan on that highway would stop, and its wayfarers turn aside to join the eager multitude—to hear the Word or see the Word. Surely, it was not 'a time for buying and selling,' and Levi would have little work, and less heart for it at his custom-house. Perhaps he may have witnessed the call of the first Apostles; he certainly must have known the fishermen and shipowners of Capernaum. And now it appeared, as if Jesus had been brought still nearer to Matthew. For, the great ones of Israel, 'the Scribes of the Pharisees,'[1] and their pietest followers, had combined against Him, and would exclude

---

[1] This is perhaps the better reading of St. Mark ii. 16.

Him, not on account of sin, but on account of the sinners. And so, CHAP.
we take it, long before that eventful day which for ever decided his XVII
life, Matthew had, in heart, become the disciple of Jesus. Only he
dared not, could not, have hoped for personal recognition—far less
for call to discipleship. But when it came, and Jesus fixed on him
that look of love which searched the inmost deep of the soul, and
made Him the true Fisher of men, it needed not a moment's thought
or consideration. When he spake it, ' Follow Me,' the past seemed all
swallowed up in the present heaven of bliss. He said not a word,
for his soul was in the speechless surprise of unexpected love and
grace; but he rose up, left the custom-house, and followed Him. That
was a gain that day, not of Matthew alone, but of all the poor and
needy in Israel—nay, of all sinners from among men, to whom the
door of heaven was opened. And, verily, by the side of Peter, as the
stone, we place Levi-Matthew, as typical of those rafters laid on the
great foundation, and on which is placed the flooring of that habitation of the Lord, which is His Church.

It could not have been long after this—probably almost immediately—that the memorable gathering took place in the house of
Matthew, which gave occasion to that cavil of the Pharisaic Scribes,
which served further to bring out the meaning of Levi's call. For,
opposition ever brings into clearer light positive truth, just as
judgment comes never alone, but always conjoined with display of
higher mercy. It was natural that all the publicans around should,
after the call of Matthew, have come to his house to meet Jesus.
Even from the lowest point of view, the event would give them
a new standing in the Jewish world, in relation to the Prophet of
Nazareth. And it was characteristic that Jesus should improve
such opportunity. When we read of ' sinners ' as in company with
these publicans, it is not necessary to think of gross or open offenders,
though such may have been included. For, we know what such
a term may have included in the Pharisaic vocabulary. Equally
characteristic was it, that the Rabbinists should have addressed their
objection as to fellowship with such, not to the Master, but to the
disciples. Perhaps, it was not only, nor chiefly, from moral cowardice,
though they must have known what the reply of Jesus would have
been. On the other hand, there was wisdom, or rather cunning,
in putting it to the disciples. They were but initial learners—and
the question was one not so much of principle, as of acknowledged
Jewish propriety. Had they been able to lodge this cavil in their
minds, it would have fatally shaken the confidence of the disciples

BOOK
III

*St. Matt.
ix. 14-17

in the Master; and, if they could have been turned aside, the cause of the new Christ would have been grievously injured, if not destroyed. It was with the same object, that they shortly afterwards enlisted the aid of the well-meaning, but only partially-instructed disciples of John on the question of fasting,[a] which presented a still stronger *consensus* of Jewish opinion as against Christ, all the more telling, that here the practice of John seemed to clash with that of Jesus.

But then John was at the time in prison, and passing through the temporary darkness of a thick cloud towards the fuller light. But Jesus could not leave His disciples to answer for themselves. What, indeed, could or would they have had to say? And He ever speaks for us, when we cannot answer for ourselves. From their own standpoint and contention—nay, also in their own form of speech— He answered the Pharisees. And He not only silenced their gainsaying, but further opened up the meaning of His acting—nay, His very purpose and Mission. 'No need have they who are strong and in health[b] of a physician, but they who are ill.' It was the very principle of Pharisaism which He thus set forth, alike as regarded their self-exclusion from Him and His consorting with the diseased. And, as the more Hebraic St. Matthew adds, applying the very Rabbinic formula, so often used when superficial speciousness of knowledge is directed to further thought and information: 'Go and learn!'[1] Learn what? What their own Scriptures meant; what was implied in the further prophetic teaching, as correction of a one-sided literalism and externalism that misinterpreted the doctrine of sacrifices—learn that fundamental principle of the spiritual meaning of the Law as explanatory of its mere letter, 'I will have mercy, and not sacrifice.' They knew no mercy that was not sacrifice[2]—with merit attaching; He no sacrifice, real and acceptable to God, that was not mercy. And this also is a fundamental principle of the Old Testament, as spiritually understood; and, being such a fundamental principle, He afterwards again applied this saying of the prophet[c] to His own mode of viewing and treating the Sabbath-question.[d]

This was one aspect of it, as Jesus opened up anew the Old Testament, of which their key of knowledge had only locked the

*b The latter
in St. Luke
v. 31*

c Hos. vi. 6

*d St. Matt.
xii. 7*

---

[1] צֵא וּלְמַד, a very common formula, where further thought and instruction are required. So common, indeed, is it, that it is applied in the sense of 'let,' such, or such thing 'come and teach' (יצֵא וּלְמַד). Sometimes the formula is varied, as בּוֹא וּרְאֵה, 'come and see' (Baba Bath. 10 *a*), or צֵאוּ וּרְאוּ, 'go and

see' (u. s., *b*).
[2] Even in that beautiful page in the Talmud (Succ. 49 *b*) righteousness and sacrifices are compared, the former being declared the greater; and then righteousness is compared with works of kindness, with alms, &c.

door. There was yet another and higher, quite explaining and applying alike this saying and the whole Old Testament, and thus His Own Mission. And this was the fullest unfolding and highest vindication of it: 'For, I am not come to call righteous men, but sinners.'[1] The introduction of the words 'to repentance' in some manuscripts of St. Matthew and St. Mark shows, how early the full meaning of Christ's words was misinterpreted by prosaic apologetic attempts, that failed to fathom their depth. For, Christ called sinners to better and higher than repentance, even to Himself and His Kingdom; and to 'emendate' the original record by introducing these words from another Gospel[2] marks a purpose, indicative of retrogression. And this saying of Christ concerning the purpose of His Incarnation and Work: 'to call not righteous men, but sinners,' also marks the standpoint of the Christ, and the relation which each of us, according to his view of self, of righteousness, and of sin—personally, voluntarily, and deliberately—occupies towards the Kingdom and the Christ.

The history of the call of St. Matthew has also another, to some extent subordinate, historical interest, for it was no doubt speedily followed by the calling of the other Apostles.[a] This is the chronological succession in the Synoptic narratives. It also affords some insight into the history of those, whom the Lord chose as bearers of His Gospel. The difficulties connected with tracing the family descent or possible relationship between the Apostles are so great, that we must forego all hope of arriving at any certain conclusion. Without, therefore, entering on details about the genealogy of the Apostles, and the varied arrangement of their names in the Gospels, which, with whatever uncertainty remaining in the end, may be learned from any work on the subject, some points at least seem clear. First, it appears that only the calling of those to the Apostolate is related, which in some sense is typical, viz. that of Peter and Andrew, of James and John, of Philip and Bartholomew (or Bar Telamyon, or Temalyon,[b] generally supposed the same as Nathanael), and of Matthew the publican. Yet, secondly, there is something which attaches to each of the others. Thomas, who is called Didymus (which means 'twin'), is closely connected with Matthew, both in St. Luke's Gospel and in that of St. Matthew himself. James is expressly named as the son of Alphæus or Clopas.[c][3] This

CHAP.
XVII

[a] St. Matt. x. 2–4; St. Mark iii. 13–19; St. Luke vi. 12–19

[b] Vayyik. R. 6; Pesiq. R. 22, ed. Friedm. p. 113 a

[c] St. John xix. 25

---

[1] Mark the absence of the Article.
[2] See the note on p. 507.
[3] Thus he would be the same as 'James the Less,' or rather 'the Little,' a son of Mary, the sister-in-law of the Virgin-Mother.

BOOK
III

we know to have been also the name of Matthew-Levi's father. But, as the name was a common one, no inference can be drawn from it, and it does not seem likely that the father of Matthew was also that of James, Judas, and Simon, for these three seem to have been brothers. Judas is designated by St. Matthew as Lebbæus, from the Hebrew *lebh*, a heart, and is also named, both by him and by St. Mark, Thaddæus—a term which, however, we would not derive, as is commonly done, from *thad*, the 'female breast,' but following the analogy of the Jewish name *Thodah*, from '*praise.*' [1] In that case both Lebbæus and Thaddæus would point to the heartiness and the Thanksgiving of the Apostle, and hence to his character. St. Luke simply designates him Judas of James, which means that he was the brother (less probably, the son) of James. [a] Thus his real name would have been Judas Lebbæus, and his surname Thaddæus. Closely connected with these two we have in all-the Gospels, Simon, surnamed Zelotes or Cananæan (not Canaanite), both terms indicating his original connection with the Galilean Zealot party, the ' Zealots for the Law.' [b] His position in the Apostolic Catalogue, and the testimony of Hegesippus, [c] seem to point him out as the son of Clopas, and brother of James, and of Judas Lebbæus. These three were, in a sense, cousins of Christ, since, according to Hegesippus, Clopas was the brother of Joseph, while the sons of Zebedee were real cousins, their mother Salome being a sister of the Virgin. [2] Lastly, we have Judas Iscariot, or *Ish Kerioth*, 'a man of Kerioth,' a town in Judah. [d] Thus the betrayer alone would be of Judæan origin, the others all of Galilean; and this may throw light on not a little in his after-history.

No further reference than this briefest sketch seems necessary, although on comparison it is clear that the Apostolic Catalogues in the Gospels are ranged in three groups, each of them beginning with respectively the same name (Simon, Philip, and James the son of Alphæus). This, however, we may remark—how narrow, after all, was the Apostolic circle, and how closely connected most of its members. And yet, as we remember the history of their calling, or those notices attached to their names which afford a glimpse into their history, it was a circle, thoroughly representative of those who would

[a] St. Luke vi. 15; comp. St. John xiv. 22

[b] War. iv. 3, 9

[c] Euseb. H. E. iii. 11; iv. 22

[d] Josh. xv. 25

---

[1] As is done in the Rabbinic story where Thaddæus appeals to Ps. c. 1 (superscription) to save his life, while the Rabbis reply by appealing to Ps. 1. 23: 'Whoso offereth praise (*thodah*) glorifieth Me' (Sanh. 43 *a*, *Chesr. haSh.*).

[2] As to the identity of the names Alphæus and Clopas, comp. *Wetzel* in the Theol. Stud. u. Krit. for 1883, Heft iii. See also further remarks on the sons of Clopas, in the comment on St. John xix. 25 in Book V. ch. xv.

gather around the Christ. Most marked and most solemn of all, it was
after a night of solitary prayer on the mountain-side, that Jesus at
early dawn 'called His disciples, and of them He chose twelve, whom
also He named Apostles,' 'that they should be with Him, and that
He might send them forth to preach, and to have power to heal
sickness and to cast out devils.' [1]

[1] As to the designation Boanerges (sons of thunder), see note 2, p. 514.

CHAPTER XVIII.

THE SERMON ON THE MOUNT—THE KINGDOM OF CHRIST AND RABBINIC TEACHING.[1]

(St. Matt. v.-vii.)

BOOK
III

a St. Luke
vi. 13

IT was probably on one of those mountain-ranges, which stretch to the north of Capernaum, that Jesus had spent the night of lonely prayer, which preceded the designation of the twelve to the Apostolate. As the soft spring morning broke, He called up those who had learned to follow Him, and from among them chose the twelve, who were to be His Ambassadors and Representatives.[a][2] But already the early light had guided the eager multitude which, from all parts, had come to the broad level plateau beneath to bring to Him their need of soul or body. To them He now descended with words of comfort and power of healing. But better yet had He to say, and to do for them, and for us all. As they pressed around Him for that touch which brought virtue of healing to all, He retired again to the mountain-height, and through the clear air of the bright spring day spake, what has ever since been known as the 'Sermon on the Mount,' from the place where He sat, or as that 'in the plain' (St. Luke vi. 17), from the place where He had first met the multitude, and which so many must have continued to occupy while He taught.

The first and most obvious, perhaps, also, most superficial thought, is that which brings this teaching of Christ into comparison, we shall not say with that of His contemporaries—since scarcely any who lived in the time of Jesus said aught that can be compared with it—but with the best of the wisdom and piety of the Jewish sages, as

---

[1] As it was impossible to quote separately the different verses in the Sermon on the Mount, the reader is requested to have the Bible before him, so as to compare the verses referred to with their commentation in this chapter.

[2] It is so that we group together St. Luke vi. 12, 13, 17–19, compared with St. Mark iii. 13–15 and St. Matthew v. 1, 2.

[3] According to traditional view this mountain was the so-called 'Karn Hattin' (Horns of Hattin) on the road from Tiberias to Nazareth, about 1½ hours to the north-west of Tiberias. But the tradition dates only from late Crusading times, and the locality is, for many reasons, unsuitable.

preserved in Rabbinic writings. Its essential difference, or rather
contrariety, in spirit and substance, not only when viewed as a whole,
but in almost each of its individual parts, will be briefly shown in the
sequel. For the present we only express this as deepest conviction,
that it were difficult to say which brings greater astonishment(though
of opposite kind): a first reading of the 'Sermon on the Mount,' or
that of any section of the Talmud. The general reader is here at a
double disadvantage. From his upbringing in an atmosphere which
Christ's Words have filled with heaven's music, he knows not, and
cannot know, the nameless feeling which steals over a receptive soul
when, in the silence of our moral wilderness, those voices first break
on the ear, that had never before been wakened to them. How they
hold the soul entranced, calling up echoes of inmost yet unrealised
aspiration, itself the outcome of the God-born and God-tending within
us, and which renders us capable of new birth into the Kingdom;
call up, also, visions and longings of that world of heavenly song, so
far away and yet so near us; and fill the soul with subduedness,
expectancy, and ecstasy! So the travel-stained wanderer flings him
down on the nearest height, to feast his eyes with the first sight of
home in the still valley beneath; so the far-of exile sees in his dreams
visions of his child-life, all transfigured; so the weary prodigal leans
his head in silent musing of mingled longing and rest on a mother's
knee. So, and much more; for, it is the Voice of God Which speaks
to us in the cool of the evening, amidst the trees of the lost Garden;
to us who, in very shame and sorrow, hide, and yet even so hear, not
words of judgment but of mercy, not concerning an irrevocable, and
impossible past, but concerning a real and to us possible future, which
is that past, only better, nearer, dearer,—for, that it is not the human
which has now to rise to the Divine, but the Divine which has come
down to the human.

Or else, turn from this to a first reading of the wisdom of the
Jewish Fathers in their Talmud. It little matters, what part be
chosen for the purpose. Here, also, the reader is at disadvantage,
since his instructors present to him too frequently broken sentences,
extracts torn from their connection, words often mistranslated as regards their real meaning, or misapplied as regards their bearing and
spirit; at best, only isolated sentences. Take these in their connection and real meaning, and what a terrible awakening! Who, that
has read half-a-dozen pages successively of any part of the Talmud,
can feel otherwise than by turns shocked, pained, amused, or astounded?
There is here wit and logic, quickness and readiness, earnestness and

zeal, but by the side of it terrible profanity, uncleanness, superstition.
and folly.   Taken as a whole, it is not only utterly unspiritual, but
anti-spiritual.   Not that the Talmud is worse than might be expected
of such writings in such times and circumstances, perhaps in many
respects much better—always bearing in mind the particular standpoint of narrow nationalism, without which Talmudism itself could not
have existed, and which therefore is not an accretion, but an essential
part of it.   But, taken not in abrupt sentences and quotations, but
as a whole, it is so utterly and immeasurably unlike the New Testament, that it is not easy to determine which, as the case may be, is
greater, the ignorance or the presumption of those who put them
side by side.   Even where spiritual life pulsates, it seems propelled
through valves that are diseased, and to send the life-blood gurgling
back upon the heart, or along ossified arteries that quiver not with
life at its touch.   And to the reader of such disjointed Rabbinic
quotations there is this further source of misunderstanding, that the
form and *sound of words* is so often the same as that of the sayings of
Jesus, however different their spirit.   For, necessarily, the wine—be
it new or old—made in Judæa, comes to us in Palestinian vessels.
The new teaching, to be historically true, must have employed the old
forms and spoken the old language.   But the ideas underlying terms
equally employed by Jesus and the teachers of Israel are, in everything
that concerns the relation of souls to God, so absolutely different as
not to bear comparison.   Whence otherwise the enmity and opposition to Jesus from the first, and not only after His Divine claim had
been pronounced?   These two, starting from principles alien and
hostile, follow opposite directions, and lead to other goals.   He who
has thirsted and quenched his thirst at the living fount of Christ's
Teaching, can never again stoop to seek drink at the broken cisterns
of Rabbinism.

　　We take here our standpoint on St. Matthew's account of the
'Sermon on the Mount,' to which we can scarcely doubt that by St.
Luke [a] is parallel.   Not that it is easy, or perhaps even possible, to
determine, whether all that is now grouped in the 'Sermon on the
Mount' was really spoken by Jesus on this one occasion.   From the
plan and structure of St. Matthew's Gospel, the presumption seems
rather to the contrary.   For, isolated parts of it are introduced by
St. Luke in other connections, yet quite fitly.[1]   On the other hand,

a St. Luke
vi.

---

[1] The reader will find these parallelisms in Dean *Plumptre's* Notes on St. Mat-thew v. 1 (in Bishop *Ellicott's* Commen- tary for English Readers, vol. i. of the N.T. p. 20).

even in accordance with the traditional characterisation of St. Matthew's narrative, we expect in it the fullest account of our Lord's Discourses,[1] while we also notice that His Galilean Ministry forms the main subject of the First Gospel.[2] And there is one characteristic of the 'Sermon on the Mount' which, indeed, throws light on the plan of St. Matthew's work in its apparent chronological inversion of events, such as in its placing the 'Sermon on the Mount' before the calling of the Apostles. We will not designate the 'Sermon on the Mount' as the promulgation of the New Law, since that would be a far too narrow, if not erroneous, view of it. But it certainly seems to correspond to the Divine Revelation in the 'Ten Words' from Mount Sinai. Accordingly, it seems appropriate that the Genesis-part of St. Matthew's Gospel should be immediately followed by the Exodus-part, in which the new Revelation is placed in the forefront, to the seeming breach of historical order, leaving it afterwards to be followed by an appropriate grouping of miracles and events, which we know to have really preceded the 'Sermon on the Mount.'

Very many-sided is that 'Sermon on the Mount,' so that different writers, each viewing it from his standpoint, have differently sketched its general outline, and yet carried to our minds the feeling that thus far they had correctly understood it. We also might attempt humble contribution towards the same end. Viewing it in the light of the time, we might mark in it alike advancement on the Old Testament (or rather, unfolding of its inmost, yet hidden meaning), and contrast to contemporary Jewish teaching. And here we would regard it as presenting the full delineation of the ideal man of God, of prayer, and of righteousness—in short, of the inward and outward manifestation of discipleship. Or else, keeping before us the different standpoint of His hearers, we might in this 'Sermon' follow up this contrast to its underlying ideas as regards: First, the right relationship between man and God, or true righteousness—what inward graces characterise and what prospects attach to it, in opposition to Jewish views of merit and of reward. Secondly, we would mark the same contrast as regards sin (*hamartology*), temptation, &c. Thirdly, we would note it, as regards salvation (*soteriology*); and, lastly, as regards what may be termed moral theology: personal feelings, married and other relations, discipleship, and the like. And in this great contrast

---

[1] Comp. *Euseb.* H. Eccl. iii. 39.

[2] Thus St. Matthew passes over those earlier events in the Gospel-history of which Judæa was the scene, and even over the visits of Jesus to Jerusalem previous to the last Passover, while he devotes not less than fourteen chapters and a half to the half-year's activity in Galilee. If St. John's is the Judæan, St. Matthew's is the Galilean Gospel.

two points would prominently stand out : New Testament humility, as opposed to Jewish (the latter being really pride, as only the con- sciousness of failure, or rather, of inadequate perfectness, while New Testament humility is really despair of self); and again, Jewish as opposed to New Testament perfectness (the former being an attempt by means external or internal to strive up to God: the latter a new life, springing from God, and in God). Or, lastly, we might view it as *upward* teaching in regard to God: the *King*; *inward* teaching in regard to man: the *subjects of the King*; and *outward* teaching in regard to the Church and the world: *the boundaries of the Kingdom.*

This brings us to what alone we can here attempt: a general outline of the ' Sermon on the Mount.' Its great subject is neither righteousness, nor yet the New Law (if such designation be proper in regard to what in no real sense is a Law), but that which was innermost and uppermost in the Mind of Christ—the Kingdom of God. Notably, the Sermon on the Mount contains not any detailed or systematic doctrinal,[1] nor any ritual teaching, nor yet does it prescribe the form of any outward observances. This marks, at least negatively, a difference in principle from all other teaching. Christ came to found a Kingdom, not a School; to institute a fellowship, not to propound a system. To the first disciples all doctrinal teaching sprang out of fellowship with Him. They saw Him, and therefore believed; they believed, and therefore learned the truths connected with Him, and springing out of Him. So to speak, the seed of truth which fell on their hearts was carried thither from the flower of His Person and Life.

Again, as from this point of view the Sermon on the Mount differs from all contemporary Jewish teaching, so also is it impossible to compare it with any other system of morality. The difference here is one not of degree, nor even of kind, but of standpoint. It is indeed true, that the Words of Jesus, properly understood, marks the utmost limit of all possible moral conception. But this point does not come in question. Every moral system is a road by which, through self-denial, discipline, and effort, men seek to reach the goal. Christ begins with this goal, and places His disciples at once in the position to which all other teachers point as the end. They work up to the

---

[1] On this point there seems to me some confusion of language on the part of controversialists. Those who main- tain that the Sermon on the Mount con- tains no doctrinal elements at all must mean systematic teaching—what are commonly called dogmas—since, besides St. Matt. vii. 22, 23, as Professor *Wace* has so well urged, love to God and to our neighbour mark both the starting-point and the final outcome of all theology.

goal of becoming the 'children of the Kingdom;' He makes men CHAP.
such, freely, and of His grace: and this *is* the Kingdom. What the XVIII
others labour for, He gives. They begin by demanding, He by bestowing: because he brings good tidings of forgiveness and mercy.
Accordingly, in the real sense, there is neither new law nor moral
system here, but entrance into a new life: 'Be ye therefore perfect,
as your Father Which is in heaven is perfect.'

But if the Sermon on the Mount contains not a new, nor, indeed,
any system of morality, and addresses itself to a new condition of
things, it follows that the promises attaching, for example, to the so-
called ' Beatitudes ' must not be regarded as the *reward* of the spiritual
state with which they are respectively connected, nor yet as their
result. It is not *because* a man is poor in spirit that his is the Kingdom of Heaven, in the sense that the one state will grow into the other,
or be its result; still less is the one the reward of the other.[1] The
connecting link—so to speak, the theological copula between the ' state'
and the promise—is in each case Christ Himself: because He stands
between our present and our future, and 'has opened the Kingdom of
Heaven to all believers.' Thus the promise represents the gift of
grace by Christ in the new Kingdom, as adapted to each case.

It is Christ, then, as the King, Who is here flinging open the gates
of His Kingdom. To study it more closely: in the three chapters,
under which the Sermon on the Mount is grouped in the first Gospel,[a] a chs.v.-vii
the Kingdom of God is presented *successively, progressively,* and *extensively.* Let us trace this with the help of the text itself.

In the first part of the Sermon on the Mount[b] the Kingdom of b St. Matt.v
God is delineated generally, first *positively,* and then *negatively,* marking especially how its righteousness goes deeper than the mere letter
of even the Old Testament Law. It opens with ten Beatitudes, which
are the New Testament counterpart to the Ten Commandments. These
present to us, not the observance of the Law written on stone, but
the realisation of that Law which, by the Spirit, is written on the
fleshly tables of the heart.[c] c St. Matt.
v. 3–12

These Ten Commandments in the Old Covenant were preceded by a
Prologue.[d] The ten Beatitudes have, characteristically, not a Prologue d Ex. xix.
3–6
but an Epilogue,[e] which corresponds to the Old Testament Prologue. e St. Matt.
v. 13–16
This closes the first section, of which the object was to present

---

[1] To adopt the language of St. Thomas Aquinas—it is neither *meritum ex con-gruo,* nor yet is it *ex condigno.* The Re-formers fully showed not only the error of Romanism in this respect, but the untenableness of the theological dis-tinction.

BOOK
III

the Kingdom of God in its characteristic features. But here it was necessary, in order to mark the real continuity of the New Testament with the Old, to show the relation of the one to the other. And this is the object of verses 17 to 20, the last-mentioned verse forming at the same time a grand climax and transition to the criticism of the Old Testament-Law in its merely literal application, such as the Scribes and Pharisees made.[a] For, taking even the letter of the Law, there is not only progression, but almost contrast, between the righteousness of the Kingdom and that set forth by the teachers of Israel. Accordingly, a detailed criticism of the Law now follows—and that not as interpreted and applied by 'tradition,' but in its barely literal meaning. In this part of the 'Sermon on the Mount' the careful reader will mark an analogy to Exod. xxi. and xxii.

a vv. 21 to end of ch. v.

This closes the first part of the 'Sermon on the Mount.' The second part is contained in St. Matt. vi. In this the criticism of the Law is carried deeper. The question now is not as concerns the Law in its literality, but as to what constituted more than a mere observance of the outward commandments: *piety, spirituality, sanctity.* Three points here stood out specially—nay, stand out still, and in all ages. Hence this criticism was not only of special application to the Jews, but is universal, we might almost say, prophetic. These three high points are *alms, prayer*, and *fasting*—or, to put the latter more generally, the relation of the physical to the spiritual. These three are successively presented, negatively and positively.[b] But even so, this would have been but the external aspect of them. The Kingdom of God carries all back to the grand underlying ideas. What were this or that mode of giving alms, unless the right idea be apprehended, of what constitutes riches, and where they should be sought? This is indicated in verses 19 to 21. Again, as to *prayer*: what matters it if we avoid the externalism of the Pharisees, or even catch the right form as set forth in the 'Lord's Prayer,' unless we realise what underlies prayer? It is to lay our inner man wholly open to the light of God in genuine, earnest simplicity, to be quite shone through by Him.[c] It is, moreover, absolute and undivided self-dedication to God.[d] And in this lies its connection, alike with the spirit that prompts *almsgiving*, and with that which prompts real *fasting*. That which underlies all such fasting is a right view of the relation in which the body with its wants stands to God—the temporal to the spiritual.[e] It is the spirit of prayer which must rule alike alms and fasting, and pervade them: the upward look and self-dedication to God, the seeking first after the Kingdom of God and His Righteousness, that man, and self, and life

b *Alms*, vi. 1-4; *Prayer*, vv. 5-15; *Fasting*, 16-18

c vv. 22, 23

d vv. 22-24

e vv. 25 to end of ch. vi.

may be baptized in it. Such are the real alms, the real prayers, the real fasts of the Kingdom of God.

If we have rightly apprehended the meaning of the two first parts of the 'Sermon on the Mount,' we cannot be at a loss to understand its *third* part, as set forth in the seventh chapter of St. Matthew's Gospel. Briefly, it is this, as addressed to His contemporaries, nay, with wider application to the men of all times: *First,* the Kingdom of God cannot be *circumscribed,* as you would do it.[a] *Secondly,* it cannot be *extended,* as you would do it, by external means,[b] but cometh to us from God,[c] and is entered by personal determination and sepa-ration.[d] *Thirdly,* it is not *preached,* as too often is attempted, when thoughts of it are merely of the external.[e] *Lastly,* it is not *mani-fested* in life in the manner too common among religionists, but is very real, and true, and good in its effects.[f] And this Kingdom, as received by each of us, is like a solid house on a solid foundation, which nothing from without can shake or destroy.[g]

The infinite contrast, just set forth, between the Kingdom as pre-sented by the Christ and Jewish contemporary teaching is the more striking, that it was expressed in a form, and clothed in words with which all His hearers were familiar; indeed, in modes of expression current at the time. It is this which has misled so many in their quotations of Rabbinic parallels to the 'Sermon on the Mount.' They perceive outward similarity, and they straightway set it down to identity of spirit, not understanding that often those things are most unlike in the spirit of them, which are most like in their form. No part of the New Testament has had a larger array of Rabbinic parallels adduced than the 'Sermon on the Mount;' and this, as we might expect, because, in teaching addressed to His contemporaries, Jesus would naturally use the forms with which they were familiar. Many of these Rabbinic quotations are, however, entirely inapt, the similarity lying in an expression or turn of words.[1] Occasionally, the misleading error goes even further, and that is quoted in illustration of Jesus' sayings which, either by itself or in the context, implies quite the opposite. A detailed analysis would lead too far, but a few speci-mens will sufficiently illustrate our meaning.

To begin with the first Beatitude, to the poor in spirit, since theirs is the Kingdom of Heaven, this early Jewish saying[h] is its very counterpart, marking not the optimism, but the pessimism of life: 'Ever be more and more lowly in spirit, since the expectancy of man

[a] vii. 1–5
[b] ver. 6
[c] vv. 7–12
[d] vv. 13, 14
[e] vv. 15, 16
[f] vv. 17–20
[g] vv. 24–27
[h] Ab. iv. 4

---

[1] So in the quotations of many writers on the subject, notably those of *Wünsche.*

BOOK
III

R. 1, ed.
Warsh. p.
2 b

ᶜ Abhodah
Zarah

is to become the food of worms.' Another contrast to Christ's promise of grace to the 'poor in spirit' is presented in this utterance of self-righteousness ᵃ on the part of Rabbi Joshua, who compares the reward (שכר) formerly given to him who brought one or another offering to the Temple with that of him who is of a lowly mind (השירעתו שפל), to whom it is reckoned as if he had brought all the sacrifices. To this the saying of the great Hillel ᵇ seems exactly parallel: ' My humility is my greatness, and my greatness my humility,' which, be it observed, is elicited by a Rabbinic accommodation of Ps. cxiii., 5, 6: 'Who is exalted to sit, who humbleth himself to behold.' It is the omission on the part of modern writers of this explanatory addition, which has given the saying of Hillel even the faintest likeness to the first Beatitude.

But even so, what of the promise of 'the Kingdom of Heaven?' What is the meaning which Rabbinism attaches to that phrase, and would it have entered the mind of a Rabbi to promise what he understood as the Kingdom to all men, Gentiles as well as Jews, who were poor in spirit? We recall here the fate of the Gentiles in Messianic days, and, to prevent misstatements, summarise the opening pages of the Talmudic tractate on Idolatry.ᶜ At the beginning of the coming era of the Kingdom, God is represented as opening the Torah, and inviting all who had busied themselves with it to come for their reward. On this, nation by nation appears—first, the Romans, insisting that all the great things they had done were only done for the sake of Israel, in order that they might the better busy themselves with the Torah. Being harshly repulsed, the Persians next come forward with similar claims, encouraged by the fact that, unlike the Romans, they had not destroyed the Temple. But they also are in turn repelled. Then all the Gentile nations urge that the Law had not been offered to them, which is proved to be a vain contention, since God had actually offered it to them, but only Israel had accepted it. On this the nations reply by a peculiar Rabbinic explanation of Exod. xix. 17, according to which God is actually represented as having lifted Mount Sinai like a cask, and threatened to put it over Israel unless they accepted the Law. Israel's obedience, therefore, was not willing, but enforced. On this the Almighty proposes to judge the Gentiles by the Noachic commandments, although it is added, that, even had they observed them, these would have carried no reward. And, although it is a principle that even a heathen, if he studied the Law, was to be esteemed like the High-Priest, yet it is argued, with the most perverse logic, that the reward of heathens who observed the Law must be less than

that of those who did so because the Law was given them, since the
former acted from impulse, and not from obedience!

Even thus far the contrast to the teaching of Jesus is tremendous. A few further extracts will finally point the difference between the largeness of Christ's World-Kingdom, and the narrowness of Judaism. Most painful as the exhibition of profanity and national conceit is, it is needful in order to refute what we must call the daring assertion, that the teaching of Jesus, or the Sermon on the Mount, had been derived from Jewish sources. At the same time it must carry to the mind, with almost irresistible force, the question whence, if not from God, Jesus had derived His teaching, or how else it came so to differ, not in detail, but in principle and direction, from that of all His contemporaries.

In the Talmudic passages from which quotation has already been made, we further read that the Gentiles would enter into controversy with the Almighty about Israel. They would urge, that Israel had not observed the Law. On this the Almighty would propose Himself to bear witness for them. But the Gentiles would object, that a father could not give testimony for his son. Similarly, they would object to the proposed testimony of heaven and earth, since self-interest might compel them to be partial. For, according to Ps. lxxvi. 8, 'the earth was afraid,' because, if Israel had not accepted the Law, it would have been destroyed, but it 'became still' when at Sinai they consented to it. On this the heathen would be silenced out of the mouth of their own witnesses, such as Nimrod, Laban, Potiphar, Nebuchadnezzar, &c. They would then ask, that the Law might be given them, and promise to observe it. Although this was now impossible, yet God would, in His mercy, try them by giving them the Feast of Tabernacles, as perhaps the easiest of all observances. But as they were in their tabernacles, God would cause the sun to shine forth in his strength, when they would forsake their tabernacles in great indignation, according to Ps. ii. 3. And it is in this manner that Rabbinism looked for the fulfilment of those words in Ps. ii. 4: 'He that sitteth in the heavens shall laugh, the Lord shall have them in derision,' this being the only occasion on which God laughed! And if it were urged, that at the time of the Messiah all nations would become Jews, this was indeed true; but although they would adopt Jewish practices, they would apostatise in the war of Gog and Magog, when again Ps. ii. 4 would be realised: 'The Lord shall laugh at them.' And this is the teaching which some writers would compare with that of Christ! In view of such statements, we can

BOOK
III

only ask with astonishment: What fellowship of spirit can there be between Jewish teaching and the first Beatitude?

It is the same sad self-righteousness and utter carnalness of view which underlies the other Rabbinic parallels to the Beatitudes, pointing to contrast rather than likeness. Thus the Rabbinic blessedness of mourning consists in this, that much misery here *Erub. 41 b* makes up for punishment hereafter.[a] We scarcely wonder that no Rabbinic parallel can be found to the third Beatitude, unless we recall the contrast which assigns in Messianic days the possession of earth to Israel as a nation. Nor could we expect any parallel to the fourth Beatitude, to those who hunger and thirst after righteousness. Rabbinism would have quite a different idea of 'righteousness,' considered as 'good works,' and chiefly as almsgiving (designated as *Tsedaqah*, or righteousness). To such the most special reward is *b Baba B.* promised, and that *ex opere operato*.[b] Similarly, Rabbinism speaks *10 a* of the perfectly righteous (צדיק גמור) and the perfectly unrighteous, or else of the righteous and unrighteous (according as the good or the evil might weigh heaviest in the scale); and, besides these, of a kind of middle state. But such a conception as that of 'hunger' and 'thirst' after righteousness would have no place in the system. And, that no doubt may obtain, this sentence may be quoted: 'He that says, I give this "Sela" as alms, in order that (בשביל) my sons may live, and that I may merit the world to come, behold, this is the *c Baba B.* perfectly righteous.'[c] Along with such assertions of work-righteous-*10 b; comp.* ness we have this principle often repeated, that all such merit at-*Pes. 8 a;* taches only to Israel, while the good works and mercy of the Gentiles *Rosh haSh.* are actually reckoned to them as sin,[d] though it is only fair to add *4 a* that one voice (that of Jochanan ben Zakkai) is raised in contradic-*d B. Bath.* tion of such horrible teaching. *u. s.*

It seems almost needless to prosecute this subject; yet it may be well to remark, that the same self-righteousness attaches to the quality of mercy, so highly prized among the Jews, and which is *e B. Bath.* supposed not only to bring reward,[e] but to atone for sins.[f1] With *9 b* regard to purity of heart, there is, indeed, a discussion between the *f Chag. 27 a* school of Shammai and that of Hillel—the former teaching that

[1] In Jer. B. Kamma 6 c, we have this saying in the name of R. Gamaliel, and therefore near Christian times: 'Whensoever thou hast mercy, God will have mercy upon thee; if thou hast not mercy, neither will God have mercy upon thee;' to which, however, this saying of Rab must be put as a pendent, that if a man has in vain sought forgiveness from his neighbour, he is to get a whole row of men to try to assuage his wrath, to which Job xxxiii. 28 applies; the exception, however, being, according to R. José, that if one had brought an evil name upon his neighbour, he would never obtain forgiveness. See also Shabb. 151 b.

guilty thoughts constitute sin, while the latter expressly confines it to guilty deeds.[a] The Beatitude attaching to peace-making has many analogies in Rabbinism; but the latter would never have connected the designation of 'children of God' with any but Israel.[b] A similar remark applies to the use of the expression 'Kingdom of Heaven' in the next Beatitude.

A more full comparison than has been made would almost require a separate treatise. One by one, as we place the sayings of the Rabbis by the side of those of Jesus in this Sermon on the Mount, we mark the same essential contrariety of spirit, whether as regards righteousness, sin, repentance, faith, the Kingdom, alms, prayer, or fasting. Only two points may be specially selected, because they are so frequently brought forward by writers as proof, that the sayings of Jesus did not rise above those of the chief Talmudic authorities. The first of these refers to the well-known words of our Lord:[c] 'Therefore all things whatsoever ye would that men should do to you, do ye even so to them: for this is the law and the prophets.' This is compared with the following Rabbinic parallel,[d] in which the gentleness of Hillel is contrasted with the opposite disposition of Shammai. The latter is said to have harshly repelled an intending proselyte, who wished to be taught the whole Law while standing on one foot, while Hillel received him with this saying: 'What is hateful to thee, do not to another. This is the whole Law, all else is only its explanation.' But it will be noticed that the words in which the Law is thus summed up are really only a quotation from Tob. iv. 15, although their presentation as the substance of the Law is, of course, original. But apart from this, the merest beginner in logic must perceive, that there is a vast difference between this negative injunction, or the prohibition to do to others what is hateful to ourselves, and the positive direction to do unto others as we would have them do unto us.[1] The one does not rise above the standpoint of the Law, being as yet far from that love which would lavish on others the good we ourselves desire, while the Christian saying embodies the nearest approach to absolute love of which human nature is capable, making that the test of our conduct to others which we ourselves desire to possess. And, be it observed, the Lord does not put self-love as the principle of our conduct, but only as its ready test. Besides, the further explanation in St. Luke vi. 38 should here be kept in view,

CHAP. XVIII

[a] B. Mez. 43 b and 44 a; comp also Kidd. 42 b

[b] Ab. iii 14

[c] St. Matt. vii. 12

[d] Shabb. 31 a

[1] As already stated, it occurs in this negative and unspiritual form in Tob. iv. 15, and is also so quoted in the lately published Διδαχὴ τῶν δώδεκα ἀποσ-τόλων (ed. Bryennios) ch. i. It occurs in the same form in Clem. Strom. ii. c. 23.

BOOK
III .

ᵃ St. Matt.
vi. 9-13

ᵇ Berak-
hoth

ᶜ Ber. 34 a,
b; 32 a; 58 b
ᵈ Jer. Ber.
8 b
ᵉ Is.
xxxviii. 2.
Beautiful
prayers in
Ber. 16 b, 17
a; but most
painful
instances
very fre-
quently
occur in
the
Midrashim,
such as in
Shem. R. 43
ᶠ Jer. Ber.
8 c

Ber. 29 b

as also what may be regarded as the explanatory additions in St.
Matt. v. 42–48.

The second instance, to which it seems desirable to advert, is the
supposed similarity between petitions in the Lord's Prayer ᵃ and
Rabbinic prayers.   Here, we may remark, at the outset, that both
the spirit and the manner of prayer are presented by the Rabbis
so externally, and with such details, as to make it quite different
from prayer as our Lord taught His disciples.   This appears from
the Talmudic tractate specially devoted to that subject,ᵇ where the
exact position, the degree of inclination, and other trivialities, never
referred to by Christ, are dwelt upon at length as of primary
importance.ᶜ   Most painful, for example, is it ᵈ to find this interpretation of Hezekiah's prayer,ᵉ when the King is represented as
appealing to the merit of his fathers, detailing their greatness in
contrast to Rahab or the Shunammite, who yet had received a reward,
and closing with this: ' Lord of the world, I have searched the 248
members which Thou hast given me, and not found that I have
provoked Thee to anger with any one of them, how much more
then shouldest Thou on account of these prolong my life?'   After
this, it is scarcely necessary to point to the self-righteousness which,
in this as in other respects, is the most painful characteristic of
Rabbinism.   That the warning against prayers at the corner of streets
was taken from life, appears from the well-known anecdote ᶠ concerning one, Rabbi Jannai, who was observed saying his prayers in
the public streets of Sepphoris, and then advancing four cubits to
make the so-called supplementary prayer.   Again, a perusal of some
of the recorded prayers of the Rabbis ᵍ will show, how vastly different
many of them were from the petitions which our Lord taught.
Without insisting on this, nor on the circumstance that all recorded
Talmudic prayers are of much later date than the time of Jesus, it
may, at the same time, be freely admitted that here also the form,
and sometimes even the spirit, approached closely to the words of
our Lord.   On the other hand, it would be folly to deny that the
Lord's Prayer, in its sublime spirit, tendency, combination, and succession of petitions, is unique; and that such expressions in it as
' Our Father,' ' the Kingdom,'' forgiveness,' ' temptation,' and others,
represent in Rabbinism something entirely different from that which
our Lord had in view.   But, even so, such petitions as ' forgive us
our debts,' could, as has been shown in a previous chapter, have no
true parallel in Jewish theology.¹

¹ For some interesting Rabbinic parallels to the Lord's Prayer, see Dr.

Further details would lead beyond our present scope. It must suffice to indicate that such sayings as St. Matt. v. 6, 15, 17, 25, 29, 31, 46, 47; vi. 8, 12, 18, 22, 24, 32; vii. 8, 9, 10, 15, 17–19, 22, 23, have no parallel, in any real sense, in Jewish writings, whose teaching, indeed, often embodies opposite ideas. Here it may be interesting, by one instance, to show what kind of Messianic teaching would have interested a Rabbi. In a passage [a] which describes the great danger of intercourse with Jewish Christians, as leading to heresy, a Rabbi is introduced, who, at Sepphoris, had met one of Jesus' disciples, named Jacob, a 'man of Kefr Sekanya,' reputed as working miraculous cures in the name of his Master.[1] It is said, that at a later period the Rabbi suffered grievous persecution, in punishment for the delight he had taken in a comment on a certain passage of Scripture, which Jacob attributed to his Master. It need scarcely be said, that the whole story is a fabrication; indeed, the supposed Christian interpretation is not even fit to be reproduced; and we only mention the circumstance as indicating the contrast between what Talmudism would have delighted in hearing from its Messiah, and what Jesus spoke.

But there are points of view which may be gained from Rabbinic writings, helpful to the understanding of the 'Sermon on the Mount,' although not of its spirit. Some of these may here be mentioned. Thus, when [b] we read that not one jot or tittle shall pass from the Law, it is painfully interesting to find in the Talmud the following quotation and mistranslation of St. Matt. v. 17: ' I have come not to diminish from the Law of Moses, nor yet have I come to add to the Law of Moses.'[c][2] But the Talmud here significantly omits the addition made by Christ, on which all depends: ' till all be fulfilled.' Jewish tradition mentions this very letter *Yod* as irremovable,[d] adding, that if all men in the world were gathered together to abolish the least letter in the Law, they would not succeed.[e] Not a letter could be removed from the Law [f]—a saying illustrated by this curious conceit,

CHAP.
XVIII

[a] Abhod.
Zar. 17 a
and 27 b

[b] In St.
Matt. v. 18

[c] Shabb.
116 b

[d] Jer. Sanh.
p. 20 c

[e] Shir.
haSh. R. on
ch. v. 11, ed.
Warsh.
p. 27 a

[f] Shem. R. 6

Taylor's learned edition of the 'Sayings of the Jewish Fathers,' *Excursus V.* (pp. 138–145). The reader will also find much to interest him in *Excursus IV.*

[1] Comp. the more full account of this Jacob's proposal to heal Eleazar ben Dama when bitten by a serpent in Jer. Shabb. xiv. end. Kefr Sekanya seems to have been the same as Kefr Simai, between Sepphoris and Acco (comp. *Neubauer*, Geogr. p. 234).

[2] *Delitzsch* accepts a different reading, which furnishes this meaning, ' but I am come to add.' The passage occurs in a very curious connection, and for the purpose of showing the utter dishonesty of Christians—a Christian philosopher first arguing from interested motives, that since the dispersion of the Jews the Law of Moses was abrogated, and a new Law given; and the next day, having received a larger bribe, reversing his decision, and appealing to this rendering of St. Matt. v. 17.

BOOK
III

a Sanh.
107 a, and
other pas-
sages
b InVayyik.
R. 19

that the *Yod* which was taken by God out of the name of Sarah (Sarai), was added to that of Hoshea, making him Joshua (Jehoshua).[a] Similarly,[b] the guilt of changing those little hooks ('tittles') which make the distinction between such Hebrew letters as ר and ד, ה and ח, ב and כ, is declared so great, that, if such were done, the world would be destroyed.[1] Again the thought about the danger of those who broke the least commandment is so frequently expressed in Jewish writings, as scarcely to need special quotation. Only, there it is put on the ground, that we know not what reward may attach to one or another commandment. The expression 'they of old,'[c] quite corresponds to the Rabbinic appeal to those that had preceded, the *Zeqenim* or *Rishonim*. In regard to St. Matt. v. 22, we remember that the term 'brother' applied only to Jews, while the Rabbis used to designate the ignorant[d]—or those who did not believe such exaggerations, as that in the future God would build up the gates of Jerusalem with gems thirty cubits high and broad—as *Reyqa*,[e] with this additional remark, that on one such occasion the look of a Rabbi had immediately turned the unbeliever into a heap of bones!

c St. Matt.
v. 21

d B. Kam-
ma 50 b

e Sanh. 100 a

Again, the opprobrious term 'fool' was by no means of uncommon occurrence among the sages;[f] and yet they themselves state, that to give an opprobrious by-name, or to put another openly to shame, was one of the three things which deserved Gehenna.[g] To verse 26 the following is an instructive parallel: 'To one who had defrauded the custom-house, it was said: "Pay the duty." He said to them: "Take all that I have with me." But the tax-gatherer answered him, "Thinkest thou, we ask only this one payment of duty? Nay, rather, that duty be paid for all the times in which according to thy wont, thou hast defrauded the custom-house."'[h] The mode of swearing mentioned in verse 35 was very frequently adopted, in order to avoid pronouncing the Divine Name. Accordingly, they swore by the Covenant, by the Service of the Temple, or by the Temple. But perhaps the usual mode of swearing, which is attributed even to the Almighty, is 'By thy life' (חייך). Lastly, as regards our Lord's admonition, it is mentioned[i] as characteristic of the pious, that their 'yea is yea,' and their 'nay nay.'

f Sotah iii.
4; Shabb.
13 b

g Bab. Mez.
58 b, at
bottom

h Pesiqt. ed.
Bub. 164 a

i In the
Midrash on
Ruth iii. 18

---

[1] The following are mentioned as instances: The change of ד into ר in Deut. vi. 4; of ר into ד in Exod. xxxiv. 14; of ח into ה Lev. xxii. 32; of ה into ח first verse of Ps. cl.; of ב into כ in Jer. v. 12; כ into ב 1 Sam. ii. 2. It ought to be marked, that *Wünsche's* quotations of these passages (Bibl. Rabb. on Shir haSh. R. v. 11) are not always correct.

Passing to St. Matt. vi., we remember, in regard to verse 2, that the boxes for charitable contributions in the Temple were trumpet-shaped, and we can understand the figurative allusion of Christ to demonstrative piety.[1] The parallelisms in the language of the Lord's Prayer—at least so far as the wording, not the spirit, is concerned, —have been frequently shown. If the closing doxology, ' Thine is the Kingdom, and the power, and the glory,'[a] were genuine, it would correspond to the common Jewish ascription, from which, in all probability, it has been derived. In regard to verses 14 and 15, although there are many Jewish parallels concerning the need of forgiving those that have offended us, or else asking forgiveness, we know what meaning Rabbinism attached to the forgiveness of sins. Similarly, it is scarcely necessary to discuss the Jewish views concerning fasting. In regard to verses 25 and 34, we may remark this exact parallel:[b] ' Every one who has a loaf in his basket, and says, What shall I eat to-morrow? is one of little faith.' But Christianity goes further than this. While the Rabbinic saying only forbids care when there is bread in the basket, our Lord would banish anxious care even if there were no bread in the basket. The expression in verse 34 seems to be a Rabbinic proverb. Thus,[c] we read: ' Care not for the morrow, for ye know not what a day may bring forth. Perhaps he may not be on the morrow, and so have cared for a world that does not exist for him.' Only here, also, we mark that Christ significantly says not as the Rabbis, but, ' the morrow shall take thought for the things of itself.'

In chapter vii., verse 2, the saying about having it measured to us with the same measure that we mete, occurs in precisely the same manner in the Talmud,[d] and, indeed, seems to have been a proverbial expression. The illustration in verses 3 and 4, about the mote and the beam, appears thus in Rabbinic literature:[e] ' I wonder if there is any one in this generation who would take reproof. If one said, Take the mote out of thine eye, he would answer, Take the beam from out thine own eye.' On which the additional question is raised, whether any one in that generation were capable of reproving. As it also occurs with only trifling variations in other passages,[f] we conclude that this also was a proverbial expression. The same may be said of gathering ' grapes of thorns.'[g] Similarly, the designation of ' pearls '(verse 6) for the valuable sayings of sages is common. To verse 11 there is a realistic parallel,[h] when it is related, that at a certain fast, on account of drought, a Rabbi admonished the people to good deeds, on which a man gave money to the woman from whom he had been di-

[a] ver. 13

[b] In Sot. 48 b

[c] Sanh. 100 b

[d] Sot. i. 7

[e] Arach. 16 b

[f] B. Bath. 15 b; Bekhor. 38 b; Yalk. on Ruth

[g] Pes. 49 a

[h] In Ber. R 33

CHAP. XVIII

[1] See 'The Temple. its Ministry and Services,' &c., pp. 26, 27.

vorced, because she was in want. This deed was made a plea in prayer by the Rabbi, that if such a man cared for his wife who no more belonged to him, how much more should the Almighty care for the descendants of Abraham, Isaac, and Jacob. Upon this, it is added, the rain descended plentifully. If difference, and even contrast of spirit, together with similarity of form, were to be further pointed out, we should find it in connection with verse 14, which speaks of the fewness of those saved, and also verse 26, which refers to the absolute need of doing, as evidence of sonship. We compare

ᵃ Jer. Ber. 13 d, towards the end

with this what the Talmud ᵃ says of Rabbi Simeon ben Jochai, whose worthiness was so great, that during his whole lifetime no rainbow was needed to ensure immunity from a flood, and whose power was such that he could say to a valley: Be filled with gold dinars. The same Rabbi was wont to say: ' I have seen the children of the world to come, and they are few. If there are three, I and my son are of their number; if they are two, I and my son are they.' After such expression of boastful self-righteousness, so opposed to the passage in the Sermon on the Mount, of which it is supposed to be the parallel, we scarcely wonder to read that, if Abraham had redeemed all generations to that of Rabbi Simon, the latter claimed to redeem by his own merits all that followed to the end of the world—nay, that if Abraham were reluctant, he (Simon) would take Ahijah the Shilo-

ᵇ In Sukk. 45 b he proposes to conjoin with himself his son, instead of Abraham.

nite with him, and reconcile the whole world!ᵇ Yet we are asked by some to see in such Rabbinic passages parallels to the sublime teaching of Christ!

ᶜ In Ab. iii. 17

The ' Sermon on the Mount ' closes with a parabolic illustration, which in similar form occurs in Rabbinic writings. Thus,ᶜ the man whose wisdom exceeds his works is compared to a tree whose branches are many, but its roots few, and which is thus easily upturned by the wind; while he whose works exceed his wisdom is likened to a tree, whose branches are few, and its roots many, against which all the winds in the world would strive in vain. A still more close parallel

ᵈ Ab. de R. Nath. 24

is that ᵈ in which the man who has good works, and learns much in the Law, is likened to one, who in building his house lays stones first, and on them bricks, so that when the flood cometh the house is not destroyed; while he who has not good work, yet busies himself much with the Law, is like one who puts bricks below, and stones above which are swept away by the waters. Or else the former is like one who puts mortar between the bricks, fastening them one to the other; and the other to one who merely puts mortar outside, which the rain dissolves and washes away.

The above comparisons of Rabbinic sayings with those of our Lord lay no claim to completeness. They will, however, suffice to explain and amply to vindicate the account of the impression left on the hearers of Jesus. But what, even more than all else, must have filled them with wonderment and awe was, that He Who so taught also claimed to be the God-appointed final Judge of all, whose fate would be decided not merely by professed discipleship, but by their real relation to Him (St. Matt. vii. 21–23). And so we can understand it, that, alike in regard to what He taught and what He claimed, 'The people were astonished at His doctrine: for He taught them as One having authority—*and not as the Scribes.*' [1]

[1] I had collected a large number of supposed or real Rabbinic parallels to the 'Sermon on the Mount.' But as they would have occupied by far too large a space, I have been obliged to omit all but such as would illustrate the fundamental position taken in this chapter, and, indeed, in this book: the contrariety of spirit, by the side of similarity of form and expressions, between the teaching of Jesus and that of Rabbinism.

CHAPTER XIX.

THE RETURN TO CAPERNAUM—HEALING OF THE CENTURION'S SERVANT.

(St. Matt. viii. 1, 5–15; St. Mark iii. 20, 21; St. Luke vii. 1–10.)

BOOK
III

WE are once again in Capernaum. It is remarkable how much, connected not only with the Ministry of Jesus, but with His innermost Life, gathers around that little fishing town. In all probability its prosperity was chiefly due to the neighbouring Tiberias, which Herod Antipas[1] had built, about ten years previously. Noteworthy is it also, how many of the most attractive characters and incidents in the Gospel-history are connected with that Capernaum, which, as a city, rejected its own real glory, and, like Israel, and for the same reason, at last incurred a prophetic doom commensurate to its former privileges.[a]

a St. Luke
x 15

But as yet Capernaum was still 'exalted up to heaven.' Here was the home of that believing Court-official, whose child Jesus had healed.[b] Here also was the household of Peter; and here the paralytic had found, together with forgiveness of his sins, health of body. Its streets, with their outlook on the deep blue Lake, had been thronged by eager multitudes in search of life to body and soul. Here Matthew-Levi had heard and followed the call of Jesus; and here the good Centurion had in stillness learned to love Israel, and serve Israel's King, and built with no niggard hand that Synagogue, most splendid of those yet exhumed in Galilee, which had been consecrated by the Presence and Teaching of Jesus, and by prayers, of which the conversion of Jairus, its chief ruler, seems the blessed answer. And now, from the Mount of Beatitudes, it was again to His temporary home at Capernaum that Jesus retired.[c] Yet not either to solitude or to rest. For, of that multitude which had hung entranced on His Words many followed Him, and there was now such constant pressure around Him, that, in the zeal of their attendance upon the wants and demands of those who hungered

b St. John
iv.

c St. Mark
iii. 19–21

---

[1] For a discussion of the precise date of the building of Tiberias, see *Schürer*, Neutest. Zeitgesch. p. 234, note 2. For details, comp. *Jos*. Ant. xviii. 2. 3; 6. 2; xix. 8. 1; War ii. 9. 1; 21. 3, 6, 9; Life 9, 12, 17, 66, and many other places.

after the Bread of Life, alike Master and disciples found not leisure so much as for the necessary sustenance of the body.

The circumstances, the incessant work, and the all-consuming zeal which even 'His friends' could but ill understand, led to the apprehension—the like of which is so often entertained by well-meaning persons in all ages, in their practical ignorance of the all-engrossing but also sustaining character of engagements about the Kingdom— that the balance of judgment might be overweighted, and high reason brought into bondage to the poverty of our earthly frame. In its briefness, the account of what these 'friends,' or rather 'those from Him'— His home—said and did, is most pictorial. On tidings reaching them,[1] with reiterated, growing, and perhaps Orientally exaggerating details, they hastened out of their house in a neighbouring street[2] to take possession of Him, as if He had needed their charge. It is not necessary to include the Mother of Jesus in the number of those who actually went. Indeed, the later express mention of His 'Mother and brethren'[a] seems rather opposed to the supposition. Still less does the objection deserve serious refutation,[3] that any such procedure, assumedly, on the part of the Virgin-Mother, would be incompatible with the history of Jesus' Nativity. For, all must have felt, that 'the zeal' of God's House was, literally, 'consuming' Him, and the other view of it, that it was setting on fire, not the physical, but the psychical framework of His humiliation, seems in no way inconsistent with what loftiest, though as yet dim, thought had come to the Virgin about her Divine Son. On the other hand, this idea, that He was 'beside Himself,' afforded the only explanation of what otherwise would have been to them well-nigh inexplicable. To the Eastern mind especially this want of self-possession, the being 'beside' oneself, would point to possession by another—God or Devil. It was on the ground of such supposition that the charge was so constantly raised by the Scribes, and unthinkingly taken up by the people, that Jesus was mad, and had a devil: not a demoniacal possession, be it marked, but possession by the Devil, in the absence of self-possessedness. And hence our Lord characterised this charge as really blasphemy against the Holy Ghost. And this also explains how, while unable to deny the reality of His Works, they could still resist their evidential force.

a St. Mark
iii. 31

[1] I take this as the general meaning, although the interpretation which paraphrases the ἔλεγον γάρ ('they said,' ver. 21) as referring to the report which reached the οἱ παρ αὐτοῦ, seems to me strained. Those who are curious will find all kinds of proposed interpretations collected in *Meyer*, ad loc.

[2] The idea that they were in Nazareth seems wholly unfounded.

[3] Urged even by *Meyer*

However that incident may for the present have ended, it could have caused but brief interruption to His Work. Presently there came the summons of the heathen Centurion and the healing of His servant, which both St. Matthew and St. Luke record, as specially bearing on the progressive unfolding of Christ's Mission. Notably— these two Evangelists; and notably—with variations due to the peculiar standpoint of their narratives. No really serious difficulties will be encountered in trying to harmonise the details of these two narratives; that is, if any one should attach importance to such precise harmony. At any rate, we cannot fail to perceive the reason of these variations. *Meyer* regards the account of St. Luke as the original, *Keim* that of St. Matthew—both on subjective rather than historical grounds.[1] But we may as well note, that the circumstance, that the event is passed over by St. Mark, militates against the favourite modern theory of the Gospels being derived from an original tradition (what is called the 'original Mark,' *Ur-Marcus*').[2]

If we keep in view the historical object of St. Matthew, as primarily addressing himself to Jewish, while St. Luke wrote more especially for Gentile readers, we arrive, at least, at one remarkable outcome of the variations in their narratives. Strange to say, the Judæan Gospel gives the pro-Gentile, the Gentile narrative the pro-Jewish, presentation of the event. Thus, in St. Matthew the history is throughout sketched as personal and direct dealing with the heathen Centurion on the part of Christ, while in the Gentile narrative of St. Luke the dealing with the heathen is throughout indirect, by the intervention of Jews, and on the ground of the Centurion's spiritual sympathy with Israel. Again, St. Matthew quotes the saying of the Lord which holds out to the faith of Gentiles a blessed equality with Israel in the great hope of the future, while it puts aside the mere claim of Israel after the flesh, and dooms Israel to certain judgment. On the other hand, St. Luke omits all this. A strange inversion it might seem, that the Judæan Gospel should contain what the Gentile account omits, except for this, that St. Matthew argues with his countrymen the real standing of the Gentiles, while St. Luke pleads with the Gentiles for sympathy and love with Jewish modes of thinking. The one is not only an exposition, but a justification, of the event as against Israel; the other an *Eirenicon*, as well

---

[1] The difficulties which *Keim* raises seem to me little deserving of serious treatment. Sometimes they rest on assumptions which, to say the least, are not grounded on evidence.

[2] *Godet* has some excellent remarks on this point.

as a touching representation of the plea of the younger with his elder brother at the door of the Father's House.

But the fundamental truth in both accounts is the same; nor is it just to say that in the narrative the Gentiles are preferred before Israel. So far from this, their faith is only put on an equality with that of believing Israel. It is not Israel, but Israel's fleshly claims and unbelief, that are rejected; and Gentile faith occupies, not a new position outside Israel, but shares with Abraham, Isaac and Jacob the fulfilment of the promise made to their faith. Thus we have here the widest Jewish universalism, the true interpretation of Israel's hope; and this, even by the admission of our opponents,[1] not as a later addition, but as forming part of Christ's original teaching. But if so, it revives, only in accentuated manner, the question: Whence this essential difference between the teaching of Christ on this subject, and that of contemporary Rabbinism.

Yet another point may be gained from the admissions of negative criticism, at least on the part of its more thoughtful representatives. *Keim* is obliged to acknowledge the authenticity of the narrative. It is immaterial here which 'recension' of it may be regarded as the original. The Christ *did* say what the Gospels represent! But *Strauss* has shown, that in such case any natural or semi-natural explanation of the healing is impossible. Accordingly, the '*Trilemma*' left is: either Christ was really what the Gospels represent Him, or He was a daring enthusiast, or (saddest of all) He must be regarded as a conscious impostor. If either of the two last alternatives were adopted, it would, in the first instance, be necessary to point out some ground for the claim of such power on the part of Jesus. What could have prompted Him to do so? Old Testament precedent there was none; certainly not in the cure of Naaman by Elisha.[2] And Rabbinic parallelism there was none. For, although a sudden cure, and at a distance, is related in connection with a Rabbi,[a] all the circumstances are absolutely different. In the Jewish story recourse was, indeed, had to a Rabbi; but for prayer that the sick might be healed of God, not for actual healing by the Rabbi. Having prayed, the Rabbi informed the messengers who had come to implore his help, that the fever had left the sick. But when asked by them whether he claimed to be a prophet, he expressly repudiated any prophetic knowledge, far more any supernatural power of healing, and explained that liberty in prayer always indicated to him that his prayer had been answered. All analogy thus failing,

ᵃ Ber. 34 b

---

[1] So notably *Keim*.   [2] The differences have been well marked by *Keim*.

the only explanation left to negative criticism, in view of the admitted authenticity of the narrative, is, that the cure was the result of the psychical influence of the Centurion's faith and of that of his servant. But what, in that case, of the words which Jesus admittedly spoke? Can we, as some would have it, rationally account for their use by the circumstance that Jesus had had experience of such psychical influences on disease? or that Christ's words were, so to speak, only an affirmation of the Centurion's faith—something between a 'benedictory wish' and an act? Surely, suggestions like these carry their own refutation.

Apart, then, from explanations which have been shown untenable, what is the impression left on our minds of an event, the record of which is admitted to be authentic? The heathen Centurion is a real historical personage. He was captain of the troop quartered in Capernaum, and in the service of Herod Antipas. We know that such troops were chiefly recruited from Samaritans and Gentiles of Cæsarea.[a] Nor is there the slightest evidence that this Centurion was a 'proselyte of righteousness.' The accounts both in St. Matthew and in St. Luke are incompatible with this idea. A 'proselyte of righteousness' could have had no reason for not approaching Christ directly, nor would he have spoken of himself as 'unfit' that Christ should come under his roof. But such language quite accorded with Jewish notions of a *Gentile,* since the houses of Gentiles were considered as defiled, and as defiling those who entered them.[b] On the other hand, the 'proselytes of righteousness' were in all respects equal to Jews, so that the words of Christ concerning Jews and Gentiles, as reported by St. Matthew, would not have been applicable to them. The Centurion was simply one who had learned to love Israel and to reverence Israel's God; one who, not only in his official position, but from love and reverence, had built that Synagogue, of which, strangely enough, now after eighteen centuries, the remains,[1] in their rich and elaborate carvings of cornices and entablatures, of capitals and niches, show with what liberal hand he had dealt his votive offerings.

We know too little of the history of the man, to judge what earlier impulses had led him to such reverence for Israel's God. There might have been something to incline him towards it in his early upbringing, perhaps in Cæsarea; or in his family relationships; perhaps in that very servant (possibly a Jew) whose implicit obedience to his master seems in part to have led him up to faith in analogous

[a] *Jos. Ant.* xix. 9. 1, 2

[b] Ohal xxviii. 7

---

[1] Comp. *Warren,* Recovery of Jerusalem, p. 385 &c.

submission of all things to the behests of Christ.[a] The circumstances, the times, the place, the very position of the man, make such suppositions rational, even suggest them. In that case, his whole bearing would be consistent with itself, and with what we know of the views and feelings of the time. In the place where the son of his fellow-official at the Court of Herod had been healed by the Word of Jesus, spoken at a distance,[b] in the Capernaum which was the home of Jesus and the scene of so many miracles, it was only what we might expect, that in such a case he should turn to Jesus and ask His help. Quite consistent with his character is the straightforwardness of his expectancy, characteristically illustrated by his military experience—what *Bengel* designates as the wisdom of his faith beautifully shining out in the bluffness of the soldier. When he had learned to own Israel's God, and to believe in the absolute unlimited power of Jesus, no such difficulties would come to him, nor, assuredly, such cavils rise, as in the minds of the Scribes, or even of the Jewish laity. Nor is it even necessary to suppose that, in his unlimited faith in Jesus, the Centurion had distinct apprehension of His essential Divinity. In general, it holds true, that, throughout the Evangelic history, belief in the Divinity of our Lord was the outcome of experience of His Person and Work, not the condition and postulate of it, as is the case since the Pentecostal descent of the Holy Ghost and His indwelling in the Church.

In view of these facts, the question with the Centurion would be: not, *Could* Jesus heal his servant, but, *Would* He do so? And again, this other specifically: Since, so far as he knew, no application from any in Israel, be it even publican or sinner, had been doomed to disappointment, would he, as a Gentile, be barred from share in this blessing? was he 'unworthy,' or, rather, 'unfit' for it? Thus this history presents a crucial question, not only as regarded the character of Christ's work, but the relation to it of the Gentile world. Quite consistent with this—nay, its necessary outcome—were the scruples of the Centurion to make direct, personal application to Jesus. In measure as he reverenced Jesus, would these scruples, from his own standpoint, increase. As the houses of Gentiles were 'unclean,'[c] entrance into them, and still more familiar fellowship, would 'defile.' The Centurion must have known this; and the higher he placed Jesus on the pinnacle of Judaism, the more natural was it for him to communicate with Christ through the elders of the Jews, and not to expect the Personal Presence of the Master, even if the application to him were attended with success. And here it is important

CHAP.
XIX

[a] St. Luke vii. 8, last clause

[b] St. John iv. 46-53

[c] Ohal xviii. 7

(for the criticism of this history) to mark that, alike in the view of the Centurion, and even in that of the Jewish elders who undertook his commission, Jesus as yet occupied the purely Jewish standpoint.

Closely considered, whatever verbal differences, there is not any *real* discrepancy in this respect between the Judæan presentation of the event in St. Matthew and the fuller Gentile account of it by St. Luke. From both narratives we are led to infer that the house of the Centurion was not in Capernaum itself, but in its immediate neighbourhood, probably on the road to Tiberias. And so in St. Matt. viii. 7, we read the words of our Saviour when consenting: ' I, having come, will heal him; ' just as in St. Luke's narrative a space of time intervenes, in which intimation is conveyed to the Centurion, when he sends ' friends ' to arrest Christ's actual coming into his house.[a] Nor does St. Matthew speak of any actual request on the part of the Centurion, even though at first sight his narrative seems to imply a personal appearance.[b] The general statement ' beseeching Him '—although it is not added in what manner, with what words, nor for what special thing—must be explained by the more detailed narrative of the embassy of Jewish Elders.[1] There is another marked agreement in the seeming difference of the two accounts. In St. Luke's narrative, the second message of the Centurion embodies two different expressions, which our Authorised Version unfortunately renders by the same word. It should read: ' Trouble not Thyself, for I am not fit (Levitically speaking) that Thou shouldest enter under my roof;' Levitically, or Judaistically speaking, my house is not a fit place for Thy entrance; ' wherefore neither did I judge myself worthy (spiritually, morally, religiously) [ἠξίωσα, pondus habens, ejusdem ponderis cum aliquo, pretio æquans] to come unto Thee.' Now, markedly, in St. Matthew's presentation of the same event to the Jews, this latter ' worthiness ' is omitted, and we only have St. Luke's first term, ' fit ' (ἱκανός): ' I am not fit that thou shouldest come under my roof,' my house is unfitting Thine entrance. This seems to bear out the reasons previously indicated for the characteristic peculiarities of the two narratives.

[a] St. Luke
vii. 6

[b] St. Matt.
viii. 5

But in their grand leading features the two narratives entirely agree. There is earnest supplication for his sick, seemingly dying servant.[2] Again, the Centurion in the fullest sense believes in the power

---

[1] Without the article; perhaps only some of them went on this errand of mercy.

[2] St. Matt. viii. 6, literally, ' my servant has been thrown down (by disease) in the house, paralytic.' The βέβληται

of Jesus to heal, in the same manner as he knows his own commands as
an officer would be implicitly obeyed; for, surely, no thoughtful reader
would seriously entertain the suggestion, that the military language
of the Centurion only meant, that he regarded disease as caused by
evil demons or noxious powers who obeyed Jesus, as soldiers or
servants do their officer or master. Such might have been the underlying Jewish view of the times; but the fact, that in this very thing
Jesus contrasted the faith of the Gentile with that of Israel, indicates
that the language in question must be taken in its obvious sense.
But in his self-acknowledged ' unfitness' lay the real ' fitness ' of this
good soldier for membership with the true Israel; and in his deep-felt
' unworthiness' the real 'worthiness' (the *ejusdem ponderis*) for 'the
Kingdom ' and its blessings. It was this utter disclaimer of all claim,
outward or inward, which prompted that absoluteness of trust which
deemed all things possible with Jesus, and marked the real faith of
the true Israel. Here was one, who was in the state described in the
first clauses of the ' Beatitudes,' and to whom came the promise of the
second clauses; because Christ *is* the connecting link between the
two, and because He consciously was such to the Centurion, and,
indeed, the only possible connecting link between them.

And so we mark it, in what must be regarded as the high-point in
this history, so far as its teaching to us all, and therefore the reason
of its record in the New Testament, is concerned: that participation
in the blessedness of the Kingdom is not connected with any outward
relationship towards it, nor belongs to our inward consciousness in
regard to it; but is granted by the King to that faith which in
deepest simplicity realises, and holds fast by Him. And yet, although
discarding every Jewish claim to them—or, it may be, in our days,
everything that is merely *outwardly* Christian—these blessings are
not outside, still less beyond, what was the hope of the Old Testament, nor in our days the expectancy of the Church, but are literally
its fulfilment: the sitting down ' *with Abraham, and Isaac, and Jacob
in the Kingdom of Heaven.*' Higher than, and beyond this not even
Christ's provision can take us.

But for the fuller understanding of the words of Christ, the
Jewish modes of thought, which He used in illustration, require to be
briefly explained. It was a common belief, that in the day of the
Messiah redeemed Israel would be gathered to a great feast, together
with the patriarchs and heroes of the Jewish faith. This notion,
which was but a coarsely literal application of such prophetic figures

corresponds to the Hebrew טוּט. The Peter's mother-in-law is described as
same word is used in ver. 14, when ' thrown down and fever-burning.'

BOOK
III

as in Is. xxv. 6, had perhaps yet another and deeper meaning. As each weekly Sabbath was to be honoured by a feast, in which the best which the family could procure was to be placed on the board, so would the world's great Sabbath be marked by a feast in which the Great Householder, Israel's King, would entertain His household and guests. Into the painfully, and, from the notions of the times, grossly realistic description of this feast,[1] it is needless here to enter. One thing, however, was clear: Gentiles could have no part in that feast. In fact, the shame and anger of ' these ' foes on seeing the ' table spread ' for this Jewish feast was among the points specially noticed as fulfilling the predictions of Ps. xxiii. 5.[a] On this point, then, the words of Jesus in reference to the believing Centurion formed the most marked contrast to Jewish teaching.

a Bemid.
R. 21, ed.
Warsh. iv.
p. 85 a, 57 a

In another respect also we mark similar contrariety. When our Lord consigned the unbelieving to ' outer darkness, where there is weeping and gnashing of teeth,' he once more used Jewish language, only with opposite application of it. Gehinnom—of which the entrance, marked by ever-ascending smoke,[b] was in the valley of Hinnom, between two palm trees—lay beyond ' the mountains of darkness.'[c] It was a place of darkness,[d] to which, in the day of the Lord,[e] the Gentiles would be consigned.[f] On the other hand, the merit of circumcision would in the day of the Messiah deliver Jewish sinners from Gehinnom.[g] It seems a moot question, whether the expression ' outer darkness '[h][2] may not have been intended to designate—besides the darkness outside the lighted house of the Father, and even beyond the darkness of Gehinnom—a place of hopeless, endless night. Associated with it is ' the weeping [3] and the gnashing of teeth.' In Rabbinic thought the former was connected with sorrow,[4] the latter almost always with anger [5]—not, as generally supposed, with anguish.

b Erub. 19 a

c Tamid.
32 b
d Targ. on
1 Sam. ii.
9; Ps.
lxxxviii. 12
e Amos.v. 20
f Yalkut ii.
p. 42 c
g u. s. nine
lines
higher up
h St. Matt.
viii. 12

---

[1] One might say that all the species of animals are put in requisition for this great feast: Leviathan (B. Bath. 75 a); Behemoth (Pirké d. R. Eliez. 11); the gigantic bird Bar Jochani (B. Bath. 73 b; Bekhor. 57 b, and other passages). Similarly, fabulous fatted geese are mentioned —probably for that feast (B. Bath. 73 b). The wine there dispensed had been kept in the grapes from the creation of the world (Sanh. 99 a; Targum on Cant. viii. 2); while there is difficulty as to who is worthy to return' thanks, when at last the duty is undertaken by David, according to Ps. cxvi. 13 (Pes. 119 b).
[2] All commentators regard this as a contrast to the light in the palace, but so far as I know the Messianic feast is not described as taking place in a palace.
[3] The use of the article makes it emphatic—as Bengel has it: In hac vita dolor nondum est dolor.
[4] In Succ. 52 a it is said that in the age to come (Athid labho) God would bring out the Yetser haRa (evil impulse), and slaughter it before the just and before the wicked. To the one he would appear like a great mountain, to the other like a small thread. Both would weep—the righteous for joy, that they had been able to subdue so great a mountain; the wicked for sorrow, that they had not been able even to break so small a thread.
[5] This is also the meaning of the expression in Ps. cxii. 10. The verb is used

To complete our apprehension of the contrast between the views of the Jews and the teaching of Jesus, we must bear in mind that, as the Gentiles could not possibly share in the feast of the Messiah, so Israel had claim and title to it. To use Rabbinic terms, the former were 'children of Gehinnom,' but Israel 'children of the Kingdom,'[a] or, in strictly Rabbinic language, 'royal children,'[b] 'children of God,' 'of heaven,'[c] 'children of the upper chamber' (the *Aliyah*)[d] and 'of the world to come.'[e] In fact, in their view, God had first sat down on His throne as King, when the hymn of deliverance (Ex. xv. 1) was raised by Israel—the people which took upon itself that yoke of the Law which all other nations of the world had rejected.[f]

Never, surely, could the Judaism of His hearers have received more rude shock than by this inversion of all their cherished beliefs. There was a feast of Messianic fellowship, a recognition on the part of the King of all His faithful subjects, a joyous festive gathering with the fathers of the faith. But this fellowship was not of outward, but of spiritual kinship. There were 'children of the Kingdom,' and there was an 'outer darkness' with its anguish and despair. But this childship was of the Kingdom, such as He had opened it to all believers; and that outer darkness theirs, who had only outward claims to present. And so this history of the believing Centurion is at the same time an application of the 'Sermon on the Mount'—in this also aptly following the order of its record—and a further carrying out of its teaching. Negatively, it differentiated the Kingdom from Israel; while, positively, it placed the hope of Israel, and fellowship with its promises, within reach of all faith, whether of Jew or Gentile. He Who taught such new and strange truth could never be called a mere reformer of Judaism. There cannot be 'reform,' where all the fundamental principles are different. Surely He was the Son of God, the Messiah of men, Who, in such surrounding, could so speak to Jew and Gentile of God and His Kingdom. And surely also, He, Who could so bring spiritual life to the dead, could have no difficulty by the same word, 'in the self-same hour,' to restore life and health to the servant of him, whose faith had inherited the Kingdom. The first grafted tree of heathendom that had so blossomed could not shake off unripe fruit. If the teaching of Christ was new and was true, so must His work have been. And in this lies the highest vindication of this miracle,—that He is the Miracle.

CHAP.
XIX

[a] St. Matt. viii. 12
[b] Shabb. xiv. 4
[c] בנים למקום Ab. iii. 14 comp. Jer. Kidd. 61 c middle
[d] Sanh. 97 b; Succ. 45 b
[e] Jer. Ber. 13 d, end
[f] Pesiqta 16 b; Shem. R. 23

with this idea in Acts vii. 54, and in the LXX., Job. xvi. 9; Ps. xxxv. 16; xxxvii. 12; and in Rabbinical writings, for example, Jer. Keth. 35 b; Shem. R. 5, &c.

CHAPTER XX.

THE RAISING OF THE YOUNG MAN OF NAIN—THE MEETING OF LIFE AND DEATH.

(St. Luke vii. 11–17.)

BOOK
III

* Cant. ii.
11-13

THAT early spring-tide in Galilee was surely the truest realisation of the picture in the Song of Solomon, when earth clad herself in garments of beauty, and the air was melodious with songs of new life.[a] It seemed as if each day marked a widening circle of deepest sympathy and largest power on the part of Jesus; as if each day also brought fresh surprise, new gladness; opened hitherto un-thought-of possibilities, and pointed Israel far beyond the horizon of their narrow expectancy. Yesterday it was the sorrow of the heathen Centurion which woke an echo in the heart of the Supreme Commander of life and death; faith called out, owned, and placed on the high platform of Israel's worthies. To-day it is the same sorrow of a Jewish mother, which touches the heart of the Son of Mary, and appeals to where denial is unthinkable. In that Presence grief and death cannot continue. As the defilement of a heathen house could not attach to Him, Whose contact changed the Gentile stranger into a true Israelite, so could the touch of death not render unclean Him, Whose Presence vanquished and changed it into life. Jesus could not enter Nain, and its people pass Him to carry one dead to the burying.

For our present purpose it matters little, whether it was the very 'day after' the healing of the Centurion's servant, or 'shortly afterwards,'[1] that Jesus left Capernaum for Nain. Probably it was the morrow of that miracle, and the fact that 'much people,' or rather 'a great multitude,' followed Him, seems confirmatory of it. The way was long—as we reckon, more than twenty-five miles; but, even if it was all taken on foot, there could be no difficulty in reach-ing Nain ere the evening, when so often funerals took place. Various

---

[1] This depends on whether we adopt the reading ἐν τῇ or ἐν τῷ ἑξῆς.

roads lead to, and from Nain;[1] that which stretches to the Lake of
Galilee and up to Capernaum is quite distinctly marked.   It is difficult to understand, how most of those who have visited the spot could
imagine the place, where Christ met the funeral procession, to have
been the rock-hewn tombs to the *west* of Nain and towards Nazareth.[2]   For, from Capernaum the Lord would not have come that
way, but approach it from the north-east by Endor.   Hence there
can be little doubt, that Canon *Tristram* correctly identifies the now
unfenced burying-ground, about ten minutes' walk to the east of
Nain, as that whither, on that spring afternoon, they were carrying
the widow's son.[3]   On the path leading to it the Lord of Life for the
first time burst open the gates of death.

It is all desolate now.   A few houses of mud and stone with low
doorways, scattered among heaps of stones and traces of walls, is all
that remains of what even these ruins show to have been once a
city, with walls and gates.[4]   The rich gardens are no more, the
fruit trees cut down, 'and there is a painful sense of desolation'
about the place, as if the breath of judgment had swept over it.
And yet even so we can understand its ancient name of Nain, 'the
pleasant,'[5] which the Rabbis regarded as fulfilling that part of the
promise to Issachar: 'he saw the land that it was pleasant.'[6]   From
the elevation on which the city stood we look northwards, across the
wide plain, to wooded Tabor, and in the far distance to snow-capped
Hermon.   On the left (in the west) rise the hills beyond which
Nazareth lies embosomed; to the right is Endor; southwards
Shunem, and beyond it the Plain of Jezreel.   By this path, from
Endor, comes Jesus with His disciples and the great following multitude.   Here, near by the city gate, on the road that leads eastwards
to the old burying-ground, has this procession of the 'great multitude,' which accompanied the Prince of Life, met that other 'great
multitude' that followed the dead to his burying.   Which of the
two shall give way to the other?   We know what ancient Jewish
usage would have demanded.   For, of all the duties enjoined, none

---

[1] I cannot understand what Dean
Stanley means, when he says (Sinai and
Palest. p. 352): 'One entrance alone it
could have had.'   I have counted not
fewer than six roads leading to Nain.
[2] So Dean *Stanley*, and even Captain
Conder.   Canon *Farrar* regards this as
one of 'the certain sites.'   But, even according to his own description of the
route taken from Capernaum, it is difficult to understand how Jesus could have

issued upon the rock-hewn tombs.
[3] 'Land of Israel,' pp. 129, 130.
[4] Captain *Conder* (Tent-Work in Pal. i.
pp. 121, 122) has failed to discover traces
of a wall.   But see the description of
Canon *Tristram* (Land of Isr. p. 129)
which I have followed in my account.
[5] I cannot accept the rendering of
Nain by '*pascuum*.'
[6] Ber. R. 98, ed. Warsh. p. 175 *b*:
‏יאת הארץ כי נעמה.‏ ‏זו נעים‏.

BOOK
III

* Ber. 18 a

b Ber. 28 b

c Nedar. 40
a, lines 6
and 7 from
bottom

d Ber. v. 5

e Moed K.
27 b
f Jer. Moed.
K. 83 d
g Moed K.
8 b

h Rosh
haSh 17 a
and other-
wise

more strictly enforced by every consideration of humanity and piety, even by the example of God Himself, than that of comforting the mourners and showing respect to the dead by accompanying him to the burying.[a][1] The popular idea, that the spirit of the dead hovered about the unburied remains, must have given intensity to such feelings.

Putting aside later superstitions, so little has changed in the Jewish rites and observances about the dead,[2] that from Talmudic and even earlier sources,[3] we can form a vivid conception of what had taken place in Nain. The watchful anxiety; the vain use of such means as were known, or within reach of the widow; the deepening care, the passionate longing of the mother to retain her one treasure, her sole earthly hope and stay; then the gradual fading out of the light, the farewell, the terrible burst of sorrow: all these would be common features in any such picture. But here we have, besides, the Jewish thoughts of death and after death; knowledge just sufficient to make afraid, but not to give firm consolation, which would make even the most pious Rabbi uncertain of his future;[b] and then the desolate thoughts connected in the Jewish mind with childlessness. We can realise it all: how Jewish ingenuity and wisdom would resort to remedies real or magical; how the neighbours would come in with reverent step, feeling as if the very *Shekhinah* were unseen at the head of the pallet in that humble home;[c] how they would whisper sayings about submission, which, when realisation of God's love is wanting, seem only to stir the heart to rebellion against absolute power; and how they would resort to the prayers of those who were deemed pious in Nain.[d]

But all was in vain. And now the well-known blast of the horn has carried tidings, that once more the Angel of Death has done his dire behest.[e] In passionate grief the mother has rent her upper garment.[f] The last sad offices have been rendered to the dead. The body has been laid on the ground; hair and nails have been cut,[g] and the body washed, anointed, and wrapped in the best the widow could procure; for, the ordinance which directed that the dead should be buried in 'wrappings' (*Takhrikhin*), or, as they significantly called it, the 'provision for the journey' (*Zevadatha*),[h] of the most inex-

---

[1] For the sake of brevity I must here refer to 'Sketches of Jewish Social Life,' ch. x., and to the article in 'The Bible Educator,' vol. iv. pp. 330–333.

[2] *Haneberg* (Relig. Alterth. pp. 502, 503) gives the apt reasons for this.

[3] The Tractate *Ebhel Rabbathi* ('Great

Mourning') euphemistically called *Masse-kheth Semachoth*, 'Tractate of Joys.' It is already quoted in the Talmud: comp. *Zunz*, Gottesd. Vortr. p. 90, note d. It is inserted in vol. ix. of the Bab. Talmud, pp. 28 a to 31 b.

pensive linen, is of later date than our period. It is impossible to say, whether the later practice already prevailed, of covering the body with metal, glass, or salt, and laying it either upon earth or salt.[a]

And now the mother was left *Oneneth* (moaning, lamenting)—a term which distinguished the mourning before from that after burial.[1] She would sit on the floor, neither eat meat, nor drink wine. What scanty meal she would take, must be without prayer, in the house of a neighbour, or in another room, or at least with her back to the dead.[b] Pious friends would render neighbourly offices, or busy themselves about the near funeral. If it was deemed duty for the poorest Jew, on the death of his wife, to provide at least two flutes and one mourning woman,[c] we may feel sure that the widowed mother had not neglected what, however incongruous or difficult to procure, might be regarded as the last tokens of affection. In all likelihood the custom obtained even then, though in modified form, to have funeral orations at the grave. For, even if charity provided for an unknown wayfarer the simplest funeral, mourning-women would be hired to chaunt in weird strains the lament: 'Alas, the lion! alas. the hero!' or similar words,[d] while great Rabbis were wont to bespeak for themselves a warm funeral oration' (*Hesped*, or *Hespeda*).[2] For, from the funeral oration a man's fate in the other world might be inferred;[e] and, indeed, 'the honour of a sage was in his funeral oration.'[f] And in this sense the Talmud answers the question, whether a funeral oration is intended to honour the survivors or the dead.[g]

But in all this painful pageantry there was nothing for the heart of the widow, bereft of her only child. We can follow in spirit the mournful procession, as it started from the desolate home. As it issued, chairs and couches were reversed, and laid low. Outside, the funeral orator, if such was employed, preceded the bier, proclaiming the good deeds of the dead.[h] Immediately before the dead came the women, this being peculiar to Galilee,[i] the Midrash giving this reason of it, that woman had introduced death into the world.[k] The body was not, as afterwards in preference,[m] carried in an ordinary coffin of wood (*Aron*), if possible, cedarwood—on one occasion, at least, made with holes beneath;[n] but laid on a bier, or in an open coffin (*Mittah*). In former times a distinction had been made in these biers between

CHAP
XX

[a] Shabb. 151 b; Semach. I

[b] Jer. Ber. 5 d

[c] Kethub. iv. 4

[d] Mass. Semach. i. 9

[e] Shabb. 153 a

[f] Moed K. 25 a

[g] Sanh. 46 b

[h] Shabb. 153 a

[i] Shabb. 153 a

[k] Ber. R. 17 end

[m] Ber. 19 c

[n] Jer. Kil. 32 b; Ber. R. 100

---

[1] The mourning up to the time of burial or during the first day was termed *Aninah* (widowed-mourning, moaning) Jer. Horay. 48 *a*. The following three, seven, or thirty days (as the case might be) were those of *Ebhel*, 'mourning.'

Other forms of the same word need not be mentioned.

[2] Of these a number of instances are given in the Talmud—though probably only of the prologue, or epilogue, or of the most striking thoughts.

BOOK
III

ᵃ Par. xii. 9

ᵇ Moed K.
27 a and b
ᶜ Semach.
c. 8

ᵈ Bez. 6 a
Nidd. 37 a
ᵉ Moed K.
27 b; Ber.
53 a
ᶠ Jer. Sheq.
ii. 7

ᵍ Ber. iii. 1

ʰ Ber. 18 a

i Jer. Sot.
17 b, end

rich and poor. The former were carried on the so-called *Dargash*—as it were, in state—while the poor were conveyed in a receptacle made of wickerwork (*Kelibha* or *Kelikhah*), having sometimes at the foot what was termed 'a horn,' to which the body was made fast.ᵃ But this distinction between rich and poor was abolished by Rabbinic ordinance, and both alike, if carried on a bier, were laid in that made of wickerwork.ᵇ Commonly, though not in later practice, the face of the dead body was uncovered.ᶜ The body lay with its face turned up, and his hands folded on the breast. We may add, that when a person had died unmarried or childless, it was customary to put into the coffin something distinctive of them, such as pen and ink, or a key. Over the coffins of bride or bridegroom a baldachino was carried. Sometimes the coffin was garlanded with myrtle.ᵈ In exceptional cases we read of the use of incense,ᵉ and even of a kind of libation.ᶠ

We cannot, then, be mistaken in supposing that the body of the widow's son was laid on the ' bed ' (*Mittah*), or in the ' willow basket,' already described (*Kelibha*, from *Kelubh*).¹ Nor can we doubt that the ends or handles were borne by friends and neighbours, different parties of bearers, all of them unshod, at frequent intervals relieving each other, so that as many as possible might share in the good work.ᵍ During these pauses there was loud lamentation; but this custom was not observed in the burial of women. Behind the bier walked the relatives, friends, and then the sympathising 'multitude.' For it was deemed like mocking one's Creator not to follow the dead to his last resting-place, and to all such want of reverence Prov. xvii. 5 was applied.ʰ If one were absolutely prevented from joining the procession, although for its sake all work, even study, should be interrupted, reverence should at least be shown by rising up before the dead.ⁱ And so they would go on to what the Hebrews beautifully designated as the ' house of assembly ' or ' meeting,' the ' hostelry,' the ' place of rest,' or ' of freedom,' the ' field of weepers,' the ' house of eternity,' or ' of life.'

We can now transport ourselves into that scene. Up from the city close by came this 'great multitude' that followed the dead, with lamentations, wild chaunts of mourning women,² accompanied

---

¹ It is evident the young man could not have been 'coffined,' or it would have been impossible for him to sit up at Christ's bidding. I must differ from the learned *Delitzsch*, who uses the word אָרוֹן in translating σορός. Very remarkable also it seems to me, that those who advocate wicker-basket interments are without knowing it, resorting to the old Jewish practice.

² Sometimes the lament was chaunted simply in chorus, at others one woman began and then the rest joined in chorus. The latter was distinctively termed the *Qinah*, see Moed K. iii. 9.

by flutes and the melancholy tinkle of cymbals, perhaps by trumpets,[a] amidst expressions of general sympathy. Along the road from Endor streamed the great multitude which followed the 'Prince of Life.' Here they met: Life and Death. The connecting link between them was the deep sorrow of the widowed mother. He recognised her as she went before the bier, leading him to the grave whom she had brought into life. He recognised her, but she recognised Him not, had not even seen Him. She was still weeping; even after He had hastened a step or two in advance of His followers, quite close to her, she did not heed Him, and was still weeping. But, 'beholding her,' the Lord[2] 'had compassion on her.' Those bitter, silent tears which blinded her eyes were strongest language of despair and utmost need, which never in vain appeals to His heart, Who has borne our sorrows. We remember, by way of contrast, the common formula used at funerals in Palestine, 'Weep with them, all ye who are bitter of heart!'[b] It was not so that Jesus spoke to those around, nor to her, but characteristically: 'Be not weeping.'[3] And what He said, that He wrought. He touched the bier—perhaps the very wicker basket in which the dead youth lay. He dreaded not the greatest of all defilements,—that of contact with the dead,[c] which Rabbinism, in its elaboration of the letter of the Law, had surrounded with endless terrors. His was other separation than of the Pharisees: not that of submission to ordinances, but of conquest of what made them necessary.

And as He touched the bier, they who bore it stood still. They could not have anticipated what would follow. But the awe of the coming wonder—as it were, the shadow of the opening gates of life, had fallen on them. One word of sovereign command, 'and he that was dead sat up, and began to speak.' Not of that world of which he had had brief glimpse. For, as one who suddenly passes from dream-vision to waking, in the abruptness of the transition, loses what he had seen, so he, who from that dazzling brightness was hurried back to the dim light to which his vision had been accustomed. It must have seemed to him, as if he woke from long sleep. Where was he now? who those around him? what this strange assemblage? and Who He, Whose Light and Life seemed to fall upon him?

And still was Jesus the link between the mother and the son, who

CHAP. XX
[a] Keth. 17 a; Moed K. 27 b
[b] Moed K. 8 a, lines 7 and 8 from bottom
[c] Kel. 1

[1] Apparently sometimes torches were used at funerals (Ber. 53 a).
[2] The term κύριος for 'the Lord' is peculiar to St. Luke and St. John—a significant conjunction. It occurs only once in St. Mark (xvi. 19).
[3] So literally. We here recall the unfeeling threats by R. Huna of further bereavements to a mother who wept very much, and their fulfilment (Moed. K. 27 b).

BOOK
III

had again found each other. And so, in the truest sense, 'He gave him[1] to his mother.' Can any one doubt that mother and son henceforth owned, loved, and trusted Him as the true Messiah? If there was no moral motive for this miracle, outside Christ's sympathy with intense suffering and the bereavement of death, was there no moral result as the outcome of it? If mother and son had not called upon Him before the miracle, would they not henceforth and for ever call upon Him? And if there was, so to speak, inward necessity, that Life Incarnate should conquer death—symbolic and typic necessity of it also—was not everything here congruous to the central fact in this history? The simplicity and absence of all extravagant details; the Divine calmness and majesty on the part of the Christ, so different from the manner in which legend would have coloured the scene, even from the intense agitation which characterised the conduct of an Elijah, an Elisha, or a Peter, in somewhat similar circumstances; and, lastly, the beauteous harmony where all is in accord, from the first touch of compassion till when, forgetful of the bystanders, heedless of 'effect,' He gives the son back to his mother—are not all these worthy of the event, and evidential of the truth of the narrative?

But, after all, may we regard this history as real—and, if so, what are its lessons?[2] On one point, at least, all serious critics are now agreed. It is impossible to ascribe it to exaggeration, or to explain it on natural grounds. The only alternative is to regard it either as true, or as *designedly* false. Be it, moreover, remembered, that not only one Gospel, but *all*, relate some story of raising the dead—whether that of this youth, of Jairus' daughter, or of Lazarus. They also all relate the Resurrection of the Christ, which really underlies those other miracles. But if this history of the raising of the young man is false, what motive can be suggested for its invention, for motive there must have been for it? Assuredly, it was no part of Jewish expectancy concerning the Messiah, that He would perform such a miracle. And negative criticism has admitted,[3] that the differences between this history and the raising of the dead by Elijah or Elisha are so numerous and great, that these narratives

---

[1] So literally—and very significantly.

[2] Minor difficulties may be readily dismissed. Such is the question, why this miracle has not been recorded by St. Matthew. Possibly St. Matthew may have remained a day behind in Capernaum. In any case, the omission cannot be of real importance as regards the question of the credibility of such a miracle, since similar miracles are related in all the four Gospels.

[3] So *Keim*, who finally arrives at the conclusion that the event is fictitious. His account seems to me painfully unfair, as well as unsatisfactory in the extreme.

cannot be regarded as suggesting that of the raising of the young
man of Nain. We ask again: Whence, then, this history, if it was
not true? It is an ingenious historical suggestion—rather an admission by negative criticism [1]—that so insignificant, and otherwise
unknown, a place as Nain would not have been fixed upon as the site
of this miracle, if some great event had not occurred there which
made lasting impression on the mind of the Church. What was
that event, and does not the reading of this record carry conviction
of its truth? Legends have not been so written. Once more, the
miracle is described as having taken place, not in the seclusion of a
chamber, nor before a few interested witnesses, but in sight of the
great multitude which had followed Jesus, and of that other great
multitude which came from Cana. In this twofold great multitude was
there none, from whom the enemies of Christianity could have wrung
contradiction, if the narrative was false? Still further, the history
is told with such circumstantiality of details, as to be inconsistent
with the theory of a later invention. Lastly, no one will question,
that belief in the reality of such 'raising from the dead' was a
primal article in the faith of the primitive Church, for which—as a
fact, not a possibility—all were ready to offer up their lives. Nor
should we forget that, in one of the earliest apologies addressed to
the Roman Emperor, *Quadratus* appealed to the fact, that, of those
who had been healed or raised from the dead by Christ, some were
still alive, and all were well known.[a] On the other hand, the only
real ground for rejecting this narrative is disbelief in the Miraculous,
including, of course, rejection of the Christ as the Miracle of
Miracles. But is it not vicious reasoning in a circle, as well as
begging the question, to reject the Miraculous because we discredit
the Miraculous? and does not such rejection involve much more of
the incredible than faith itself?

And so, with all Christendom, we gladly take it, in simplicity of
faith, as a true record by true men—all the more, that they who told
it knew it to be so incredible, as not only to provoke scorn,[b] but to
expose them to the charge of cunningly devising fables.[c] But they
who believe, see in this history, how the Divine Conqueror, in His
accidental meeting with Death, with mighty arm rolled back the
tide, and how through the portals of heaven which He opened stole
in upon our world the first beam of the new day. Yet another—in
some sense lower, in another, practically higher—lesson do we learn.
For, this meeting of the two processions outside the gate of Nain

[a] *Euseb.*
Hist. Eccl.
iv. 3

[b] Acts xvii.
32; xxvi. 8;
1 Cor. xv.
12-19
[c] 2 Pet 1. 16

---

[1] This is the admission of *Keim*.

was accidental, yet not in the conventional sense. Neither the arrival of Jesus at that place and time, nor that of the funeral procession from Nain, nor their meeting, was either designed or else miraculous. Both happened in the natural course of natural events, but their concurrence (συγκυρία[1]) was *designed*, and directly God-caused. In this God-caused, designed concurrence of events, in themselves ordinary and natural, lies the mystery of special Providences, which, to whomsoever they happen, he may and should regard them as miracles and answer to prayer. And this principle extends much farther: to the prayer for, and provision of, daily bread, nay, to mostly all things, so that, to those who have ears to hear, all things around speak in parables of the Kingdom of Heaven.

But on those who saw this miracle at Nain fell the fear[2] of the felt Divine Presence, and over their souls swept the hymn of Divine praise: fear, because[3] a great Prophet was risen up among them; praise, because God had visited[4] His people. And further and wider spread the wave—over Judæa, and beyond it, until it washed, and broke in faint murmur against the prison-walls, within which the Baptist awaited his martyrdom. Was He then the ' Coming One?' and, if so, why did, or how could, those walls keep His messenger within grasp of the tyrant?[5]

---

[1] The term συγκυρία rendered in the A.V. ' chance' (St. Luke x. 31), means literally, the coming together, the meeting, or concurrence of events.
[2] Lit. ' fear took all.'
[3] ὅτι.

[4] Significantly, the same expression as in St. Luke i. 68.
[5] The embassy of the Baptist will be described in connection with the account of his martyrdom.

CHAPTER XXI.

THE WOMAN WHICH WAS A SINNER.

(St. Luke vii. 36–50.)

THE precise date and place of the next recorded event in this Galilean journey of the Christ are left undetermined. It can scarcely have occurred in the quiet little town of Nain, indeed, is scarcely congruous with the scene which had been there enacted. And yet it must have followed almost immediately upon it. We infer this, not only from the silence of St. Matthew, which in this instance might have been due, not to the temporary detention of that Evangelist in Capernaum, while the others had followed Christ to Nain, but to what may be called the sparingness of detail in the Gospel-narratives, each Evangelist relating mostly only one in a group of kindred events.[1] But other indications determine our inference. The embassy of the Baptist's disciples (which will be described in another connection[2]) undoubtedly followed on the raising of the young man of Nain. This embassy would scarcely have come to Jesus in Nain. It probably reached Him on His farther Missionary journey, to which there seems some reference in the passage in the First Gospel [a] which succeeds the account of that embassy. The actual words there recorded can, indeed, scarcely have been spoken at that time. They belong to a later period on that Mission-journey, and mark more fully developed opposition and rejection of the Christ than in those early days. Chronologically, they are in their proper place in St. Luke's Gospel,[b] where they follow in connection with that Mission of the Seventy, which, in part at least, was prompted by the growing enmity to the Person of Jesus. On the other hand, this Mission of the Seventy, is *not* recorded by St. Matthew. Accordingly, he inserts those prophetic denunciations which, according to the plan of his Gospel, could not have been omitted, at the beginning of this Missionary journey,

CHAP.
XXI

[a] St. Matt. xi. 20–30

[b] St. Luke x. 13–22

---

[1] This is specially characteristic of the Gospel by St. Luke.
[2] See note in previous chapter.

because it marks the beginning of that systematic opposition,ᵃ the full development of which, as already stated, prompted the Mission of the Seventy.

Yet, even so, the impression left upon us by St. Matt. xi. 20–30 (which follows on the account of the Baptist's embassy) is, that Jesus was on a journey, and it may well be that those precious words of encouragement and invitation, spoken to the burdened and wearily labouring,ᵇ formed part, perhaps the substance, of His preaching on that journey. Truly these were 'good tidings,' and not only to those borne down by weight of conscious sinfulness or deep sorrow, who wearily toiled towards the light of far-off peace, or those dreamt-of heights where some comprehensive view might be gained of life with its labours and pangs. 'Good news,' also, to them who would fain have 'learned' according to their capacity, but whose teachers had weighted 'the yoke of the Kingdom'[1] to a heavy burden, and made the Will of God to them labour, weary and unaccomplishable. But, whether or not spoken at that special time, we cannot fail to recognise their special suitableness to the 'forgiven sinner' in the Pharisee's house,ᶜ and their inward, even if not outward, connection with her history.

Another point requires notice. It is how, in the unfolding of His Mission to Man, the Christ progressively placed Himself in antagonism to the Jewish religious thought of His time, from out of which He had historically sprung. In this part of His earthly course the antagonism appeared, indeed, so to speak, in a positive rather than negative form, that is, rather in what He affirmed than in what He combated, because the opposition to Him was not yet fully developed; whereas in the second part of His course it was, for a similar reason, rather negative than positive. From the first this antagonism was there in what He taught and did; and it appeared with increasing distinctness in proportion as He taught. We find it in the whole spirit and bearing of what he did and said—in the house at Capernaum, in the Synagogues, with the Gentile Centurion, at the gate of Nain, and especially here, in the history of the much forgiven woman who had much sinned. A Jewish Rabbi could not have so acted and spoken; he would not even have understood Jesus; nay, a Rabbi, however gentle and pitiful, would in word and deed have taken precisely the opposite direction from that of the Christ.

---

[1] Made 'the yoke of the Kingdom of Héaven' (עול מלכות שמים) equal to 'the yoke of ihe Law' (עול תורה) or to that 'of the commandments' (עול מצות).

As St. Gregory expresses it, this is perhaps a history more fit to be wept over than commented upon. For comments seem so often to interpose between the simple force of a narrative and our hearts, and few events in the Gospel-history have been so blunted and turned aside as this history, through verbal controversies and dogmatic wrangling.

The first impression on our minds is, that the history itself is but a fragment. We must try to learn from its structure, where and how it was broken off. We understand the infinite delicacy that left her unnamed, the record of whose 'much forgiveness' and great love had to be joined to that of her much sin. And we mark, in contrast, the coarse clumsiness which, without any reason for the assertion, to meet the cravings of morbid curiosity, or for saint-worship, has associated her history with the name of Mary Magdalene.[1] Another, and perhaps even more painful, mistake is the attempt of certain critics to identify this history with the much later anointing of Christ at Bethany,[a] and to determine which of the two is the simpler, and which the more ornate—which the truer of the accounts, and whence, or why, each of the Evangelists has framed his distinctive narrative. Yet the two narratives have really nothing in common, save that in each case there was a 'Simon'—perhaps the commonest of Jewish names; a woman who anointed; and that Christ, and those who were present, spoke and acted in accordance with other passages in the Gospel-history:[2] that is, true to their respective histories. But, such twofold anointing—the first, at the beginning of His works of mercy, of the Feet by a forgiven, loving sinner on whom the Sun had just risen; the second, of His Head, by a loving disciple, when the full-orbed Sun was setting in blood, at the close of His Ministry—is, as in the twofold purgation of the Temple at the beginning and close of His Work, only like the completing of the circle of His Life.

The invitation of Simon the Pharisee to his table does not necessarily indicate, that he had been impressed by the teaching of Jesus, any more than the supposed application to his case of what is called the 'parable' of the much and the little forgiven debtor implies, that he had received from the Saviour spiritual benefit, great or small. If Jesus had taught in the 'city,' and, as always,

[a] St. Matt. xxvi. 6 &c. and parallels.

---

[1] The untenableness of this strange hypothesis has been shown in almost all commentaries. There is not a tittle of evidence for it.

[2] The objections of *Keim*, though bulking largely when heaped together by him, seem not only unfair, but, when examined one by one, are seen to be groundless.

BOOK
III

ᵃ St. Luke
vii. 40

ᵇ Ab. iv. 16

irresistibly drawn to Him the multitude, it would be only in accordance with the manners of the time if the leading Pharisee invited the distinguished 'Teacher' to his table. As such he undoubtedly treated Him.ᵃ The question in Simon's mind was, whether He was more than 'Teacher'—even 'Prophet;' and that such question rose within·him indicates, not only that Christ openly claimed a position different from that of Rabbi, and that His followers regarded Him at least as a prophet, but also, within the breast of Simon, a struggle in which strong Jewish prejudice was bearing down the mighty impression of Christ's Presence.

They were all sitting, or rather 'lying' [1]—the Mishnah sometimes also calls it 'sitting down and leaning'—around the table, the body resting on the couch, the feet turned away from the table in the direction of the wall, while the left elbow rested on the table. And now, from the open courtyard, up the verandah-step, perhaps through an antechamber,ᵇ and by the open door, passed the figure of a woman into the festive reception-room and dining-hall—the *Teraqlin* (*triclinium*) of the Rabbis. [2] How did she obtain access? Had she mingled with the servants, or was access free to all—or had she, perhaps, known the house and its owner? [3] It little matters—as little as whether she 'had been,' or 'was' up to that day, 'a sinner,' [4] in the terrible acceptation of the term. But we must bear in mind the greatness of Jewish prejudice against any conversation with woman, however lofty her character, fully to realise the absolute incongruity on the part of such a woman in seeking access to the Rabbi, Whom so many regarded as the God-sent Prophet.

But this, also, is evidential, that here we are far beyond the Jewish standpoint. To this woman it was not incongruous, because to her Jesus had, indeed, been the Prophet sent from God. We have said before that this story is a fragment; and here, also, as in the invitation of Simon to Jesus, we have evidence of it. She had, no doubt, heard His words that day. What He had said would be,

---

[1] Ber. vi. 6 makes the following curious distinction: if they sit at the table, each says 'the grace' for himself; if they 'lie down' to table, one says it in the name of all. If wine is handed them during dinner, each says 'the grace' over it for himself; if after dinner, one says it for all.

[2] The *Teraqlin* was sometimes entered by an *antechamber* (*Prosedor*), Ab. iv. 16, and opened into one (Jer. Rosh haSh. 59 *b*), or more (Yom. 15 *b*), side- or bed-rooms. The common meas-

urement for such a hall was fifteen feet (ten cubits) breadth, length, and height (Baba B. vi. 4).

[3] The strangeness of the circumstance suggests this, which is, alas! by no means inconsistent with what we know of the morality of some of these Rabbis, although this page must not be stained by detailed references.

[4] The other and harsher reading, 'a woman which was in the city a sinner,' need scarcely be discussed.

in substance, if not in words: ' Come unto Me, all ye that labour and
are heavy laden, and I will give you rest. . . .   Learn of Me, for I am
meek and lowly in heart. . . .   Ye shall find rest unto your souls.
. . . .' This *was* to her the Prophet sent from God with the good
news that opened even to her the Kingdom of Heaven, and laid its
yoke upon her, not bearing her down to very hell, but easy of wear
and light of burden. She knew that it was all as He said, in regard
to the heavy load of her past; and, as she listened to those Words,
and looked on that Presence, she learned to believe that it was all as
He had promised to the heavy burdened. And she had watched, and
followed Him afar off to the Pharisee's house. Or, perhaps, if it be
thought that she had not that day heard for herself, still, the sound
of that message must have reached her, and wakened the echoes of
her heart. And still it was: Come to *Me*; learn of *Me*; *I* will give
rest. What mattered all else to her in the hunger of her soul, which
had just tasted of that Heavenly Bread?

The shadow of her form must have fallen on all who sat at meat.
But none spake; nor did she heed any but One. Like heaven's own
music, as Angels' songs that guide the wanderer home, it still sounded
in her ears. There are times when we forget all else in one absorbing
thought; when men's opinions—nay, our own feelings of shame—are
effaced by that one Presence; when the ' Come to *Me*; learn of *Me*; *I*
will give you rest,' are the all in all to us. Then it is, that the
fountains of the Great Deep within are broken open by the wonder-
working rod, with which God's Messenger to us—the better Moses—
has struck our hearts. She had come that day to ' learn' and to ' find
rest.' What mattered it to her who was there, or what they thought?
There was only One Whose Presence she dared not encounter—not
from fear of Him, but from knowledge of herself. It was He to Whom
she had come. And so she ' stood behind at His Feet.' She had
brought with her an *alabastron* (phial, or flask, commonly of alabaster)
of perfume.[1] It is a coarse suggestion, that this had originally been
bought for a far different purpose. We know that perfumes were
much sought after, and very largely in use. Some, such as true
balsam, were worth double their weight in silver; others, like the

[1] I have so translated the word μύρον, which the A.V. renders ' ointment.' The word is evidently the Hebrew and Rabbinic מוֹר, which, however, is not always the equivalent for myrrh, but seems also to mean *musk* and *mastic.* In short, I regard it as designating any fluid unguent —or, generally speaking, ' perfume.' So common was the use of perfumes, that Ber. vi. 6 mentions a *mugmar*, or a kind of incense, which was commonly burnt after a feast. As regards the word ' *alu-bastron*,' the name was given to perfume-phials in general, even if not made of alabaster, because the latter was so frequently used for such flasks.

BOOK
III

a Shebh. vii. 6

b Jer. Demai 22 b

c Ab. S. 35 b

d Shabb. vi. 3

e ver. 39

spikenard (whether as juice or unguent, along with other ingredients), though not equally costly, were also 'precious.' We have evidence that perfumed oils—notably oil of roses,[a] and of the iris plant, but chiefly the mixture known in antiquity as *foliatum,* were largely manufactured and used in Palestine.[b] A flask with this perfume was worn by women round the neck, and hung down below the breast (the *Tselochith shel Palyeton*).[c] So common was its use as to be allowed even on the Sabbath.[d] This 'flask '(possibly the *Chumarta de Philon* of Gitt. 69 *b*)—not always of glass, but of silver or gold, probably often also of alabaster—containing '*palyeton* '(evidently, the *foliatum* of Pliny) was used both to sweeten the breath and perfume the person. Hence it seems at least not unlikely, that the *alabastron* which she brought, who loved so much, was none other than the 'flask of foliatum,' so common among Jewish woman.[1]

As she stood behind Him at His Feet, reverently bending, a shower of tears, like sudden, quick summer-rain, that refreshes air and earth, 'bedewed '[2] His Feet. As if surprised, or else afraid to awaken His attention, or defile Him by her tears, she quickly[3] wiped them away with the long tresses of her hair that had fallen down and touched Him,[4] as she bent over His Feet. Nay, not to wash them in such impure waters had she come, but to show such loving gratefulness and reverence as in her poverty she could, and in her humility she might offer. And, now that her faith had grown bold in His Presence, she is continuing[5] to kiss those Feet which had brought to her the 'good tidings of peace,' and to anoint them out of the *alabastron* round her neck. And still she spake not, nor yet He. For, as on her part silence seemed most fitting utterance, so on His, that He suffered it in silence was best and most fitting answer to her.

Another there was whose thoughts, far other than hers or the Christ's, were also unuttered. A more painful contrast than that of 'the Pharisee ' in this scene, can scarcely be imagined. We do not insist that the designation 'this Man, '[e] given to Christ in his un-

---

[1] The derivation of the Rabbinic term in *Buxtorf's* Lexicon (p. 1724) is certainly incorrect. I have no doubt the פלייטון was the *foliatum* of *Pliny* (Hist. Nat. xiii. 1, 2). In Jew. War iv. 9, 10, *Josephus* seems to imply that women occasionally poured over themselves unguents. According to Kethub. vi. 4, a woman might apparently spend a tenth of her dowry on such things as unguents and perfumes. For, in Kethub. 66 *b* we have an exaggerated account of a woman spending upwards of 300*l.* on perfumes! This will at any rate prove their common and abundant use.
[2] This is the real meaning of the verb
[3] This is implied in the tense.
[4] It is certainly not implied, that she had her hair dishevelled as in mourning or as by women before drinking the waters of jealousy.
[5] The tense implies this.

spoken thoughts, or the manner in which afterwards he replied to
the Saviour's question by a supercilious 'I suppose,' or 'presume,'[a]
necessarily imply contempt. But they certainly indicate the mood
of his spirit. One thing, at least, seems now clear to this Pharisee:
If 'this Man,' this strange, wandering, popular idol, with His
strange, novel ways and words, Whom in politeness he must call
'Teacher,'[1] Rabbi, *were* a Prophet, He would have known who the
woman was, and, if He had known who she was, then would He
never have allowed such approach. So do we, also, often argue as
to what He would do, if He knew. But He *does* know; and it is just
because He knoweth that He doeth what, from our lower standpoint,
we cannot understand. Had He been a *Rabbi*, He would certainly,
and had he been merely a Prophet, He would probably, have repelled
such approach. The former, if not from self-righteousness, yet from
ignorance of sin and forgiveness; the latter, because such homage
was more than man's due.[2] But, He was more than a prophet—the
Saviour of sinners; and so she might quietly weep over His Feet, and
then quickly wipe away the 'dew' of the 'better morning,' and
then continue to kiss His Feet and to anoint them.

And yet Prophet He also was, and in far fuller sense than Simon
could have imagined. For, He had read Simon's unspoken thoughts.
Presently He would show it to him; yet not, as we might, by open
reproof, that would have put him to shame before his guests, but
with infinite delicacy towards His host, and still in manner that he
could not mistake. What follows is not, as generally supposed, a
parable but an illustration. Accordingly, it must in no way be
pressed. With this explanation vanish all the supposed difficulties
about the Pharisees being 'little forgiven,' and hence 'loving little.'
To convince Simon of the error of his conclusion, that, if the life of
that woman had been known, the prophet must have forbidden her
touch of love, Jesus entered into the Pharisee's own modes of reasoning. Of two debtors, one of whom owed ten times as much as the
other,[3] who would best love the creditor[4] who had freely[5] forgiven

---

[1] In the A.V.
[2] The Talmud, with its usual exaggeration, has this story when commenting
on the reverence due by children to their
parents, that R. Ishmael's mother had
complained her son would not allow her,
when he came from the Academy, to *wash
his feet* and then drink the water—on
which the sages made the Rabbi yield !
(Jer. Peah 15 c). Again, some one came
to *kiss R. Jonathan's feet*, because he

had induced filial reverence in his son
(u. s., col. d).
[3] The one sum=upwards of 15*l.* ; the
other=upwards of 1*l.* 10*s.*
[4] Money-lender—though perhaps not
in the evil sense which we attach to the
term. At the same time, the frequent
allusion to such and to their harsh ways
offers painful illustration of the social
state at the time.
[5] So rather than 'frankly' in the A.V.

them?[1] Though to both the debt might have been equally impos-sible of discharge, and both might love equally, yet a *Rabbi* would, according to his Jewish notions, say, that he would love most to whom most had been forgiven. If this was the undoubted outcome of Jewish theology—the so much for so much—let it be applied to the present case. If there were much benefit, there would be much love; if little benefit, little love. And conversely: in such case much love would argue much benefit; little love, small benefit. Let him then apply the reasoning by marking this woman, and contrast-ing her conduct with his own. To wash the feet of a guest, to give him the kiss of welcome, and especially to anoint him,[2] were not, indeed, necessary attentions at a feast. All the more did they indicate special care, affection, and respect.[3] None of these tokens of deep regard had marked the merely polite reception of Him by the Pharisee. But, in a twofold climax of which the intensity can only be indicated,[4] the Saviour now proceeds to show, how different it had been with her, to whom, for the first time, He now turned! On Simon's own reasoning, then, he must have received but little, she much benefit. Or, to apply the former illustration, and now to reality: 'Forgiven have been her sins, the many'[5]—not in ignorance, but with knowledge of their being 'many.' This, by Simon's former admission, would explain and account for her much love, as the effect of much forgiveness. On the other hand—though in delicacy the Lord does not actually express it—this other inference would also hold true, that Simon's little love showed that 'little is being forgiven.'[6]

What has been explained will dispose of another controversy which, with little judgment and less taste, has been connected with this marvellous history. It must not be made a question as between Romanist and Protestant, nor as between rival dogmatists, whether love had any meritorious part in her forgiveness, or whether, as after-wards stated, her 'faith' had 'saved' her. Undoubtedly, her faith *had* saved her. What she had heard from His lips, what she knew of Him, she had believed. She had believed in 'the good tidings of peace' which He had brought, in the love of God, and His Father-

---

[1] The points of resemblance and of difference with St. Matt. xviii. 23 will readily appear on comparison.

[2] Comp. for ex. St. John xiii. 4.

[3] Washing: Gen. xviii. 4; xix. 2; xxiv. 32; Judg. xix. 21; 1 Sam. xxv. 41; kissing: Ex. xviii. 7; 2 Sam. xv. 5; xix. 39; anointing: Eccl. ix. 8; Amos vi. 6, as well as Ps. xxiii. 5.

[4] Thou gavest me no water, she washed not with water but tears; no kiss, she kissed my feet; no oil, she unguent; not to the head, but to the feet. And yet: *emphatically*—into *thy* house I came, &c.

[5] So literally.

[6] Mark the tense.

hood of pity to the most sunken and needy; in Christ, as the Messenger of Reconciliation and Peace with God; in the Kingdom of Heaven which He had so suddenly and unexpectedly opened to her, from out of whose unfolded golden gates Heaven's light had fallen upon her, Heaven's voices had come to her. She had believed it all: the Father, the Son—Revealer, the Holy Ghost—Revealing. And it *had* saved her. When she came to that feast, and stood behind with humbled, loving gratefulness and reverence of heart-service, she *was* already saved. She needed not to be forgiven: she had been forgiven. And it was because she was forgiven that she bedewed His Feet with the summer-shower of her heart, and, quickly wiping away the flood with her tresses, continued kissing and anointing them. All this was the impulse of her heart, who, having come in heart, still came to Him, and learned of Him, and found rest to her soul. In that early springtide of her new-born life, it seemed that, as on Aaron's rod, leaf, bud, and flower were all together in tangled confusion of rich forthbursting. She had not yet reached order and clearness; perhaps, in the fulness of her feelings, knew not how great were her blessings, and felt not yet that conscious rest which grows out of faith in the forgiveness which it obtains.

And this was now the final gift of Jesus to her. As formerly for the first time He had turned so now for the first time He spoke to her—and once more with tenderest delicacy. ' Thy sins have been forgiven '[1]—not, *are* forgiven, and not now—' the many.' Nor does He now heed the murmuring thoughts of those around, who cannot understand Who this is that forgiveth sins also. But to her, and truly, though not literally, to them also, and to us, He said in explanation and application of it all: ' Thy faith has saved thee: go into peace.'[2] Our logical dogmatics would have had it: ' go *in* peace;' more truly He, ' *into* peace.'[3] And so she, the first who had come to Him for spiritual healing, the first of an unnumbered host, went out into the better light, into peace of heart, peace of faith, peace of rest, and into the eternal peace of the Kingdom of Heaven, and of the Heaven of the kingdom hereafter and for ever.

[1] So, properly rendered. Romanism, in this also arrogating to man more than Christ Himself ever spoke, has it: *Absolvo te*, not ' thy sins have been forgiven,' but I absolve thee!

[2] So literally.

[3] This distinction between the two modes of expression is marked in Moed. K. 29 *a:* '*into* peace,' as said to the living; '*in* peace,' as referring to the dead.

CHAPTER XXII.

THE MINISTRY OF LOVE, THE BLASPHEMY OF HATRED, AND THE MISTAKES
OF EARTHLY AFFECTION—THE RETURN TO CAPERNAUM—HEALING
OF THE DEMONISED DUMB—PHARISAIC CHARGE AGAINST CHRIST—
THE VISIT OF CHRIST'S MOTHER AND BRETHREN.

(St. Luke viii. 1–3; St. Matt. ix. 32–35; St. Mark iii. 22, &c.; St. Matt. xii. 46–50
and parallels.)

BOOK
III

HOWEVER interesting and important to follow the steps of our Lord
on His journey through Galilee, and to group in their order the
notices of it in the Gospels, the task seems almost hopeless. In
truth, since none of the Evangelists attempted—should we not say,
ventured—to write a 'Life' of the Christ, any strictly historical
arrangement lay outside their purpose. Their point of view was that
of the internal, rather than the external development of this history.
And so events, kindred in purpose, discourses bearing on the same
subject, or parables pointing to the same stretch of truth, were
grouped together; or, as in the present instance, the unfolding
teaching of Christ and the growing opposition of His enemies
exhibited by joining together notices which, perhaps, belong to
different periods. And the lesson to us is, that, just as the Old
Testament gives neither the national history of Israel, nor the
biography of its heroes, but a history of the Kingdom of God in its
progressive development, so the Gospels present not a 'Life of
Christ,' but the history of the Kingdom of God in its progressive
manifestation.

Yet, although there are difficulties connected with details, we
can trace in outline the general succession of events. We conclude,
that Christ was now returning to Capernaum from that Missionary
journey[a] of which Nain had been the southernmost point. On this
journey He was attended, not only by the Twelve, but by loving
grateful women, who ministered to Him of their substance. Among
them three are specially named. 'Mary, called Magdalene,' had

[a] St. Luke
viii. 1–3; St.
Matt. ix. 35

received from Him special benefit of healing to body and soul.[1] Her designation as Magdalene was probably derived from her native city, Magdala,[2] just as several Rabbis are spoken of in the Talmud as 'Magdalene' (*Magdelaah*, or *Magdelaya*[3]). Magdala, which was a Sabbath-day's journey from Tiberias,[a] was celebrated for its dye-works,[b] and its manufactories of fine woolen textures, of which eighty are mentioned.[c] Indeed, all that district seems to have been engaged in this industry.[4] It was also reputed for its traffic in turtle-doves and pigeons for purifications—tradition, with its usual exaggeration of numbers, mentioning three hundred such shops.[d] Accordingly, its wealth was very great, and it is named among the three cities whose contributions were so large as to be sent in a wagon to Jerusalem.[e] But its moral corruption was also great, and to this the Rabbis attributed its final destruction.[f] Magdala had a Synagogue.[g][5] Its name was probably derived from a strong tower which defended its approaches, or served for outlook. This suggestion is supported by the circumstance, that what seems to have formed part, or a suburb of Magdala,[6] bore the names of 'Fish-tower' and 'Tower of the Dyers.' One at least, if not both these towers, would be near the landing-place, by the Lake of Galilee, and overlook its waters. The necessity for such places of outlook and defence, making the town a *Magdala*, would be increased by the proximity of the magnificent plain of Gennesaret, of which Josephus speaks in such rapturous terms.[h] Moreover, only twenty minutes to the north of Magdala descended the so-called 'Valley of Doves' (the Wady Hamâm), through which passed the ancient caravan-road that led over Nazareth to Damascus. The name 'valley of doves' illustrates the substantial accuracy of the Rabbinic descriptions of ancient Magdala. Modern travelers (such as Dean *Stanley*, Professor *Robinson*,

a Jer. Erub. 22 d, end
b Ber. R. 79
c Jer. Taan. 69 a, line 15 from bottom
d Midr. on Lament. ii. 2
e Jer. Taan. 69 a
f Jer. Taan. u. s.; Midr. on Lament. ii. 2, ed. Warsh. p. 67 b middle
g Midr. on Eccl. x. 8, ed. Warsh p. 102 b
h Jewish War iii. 10

---

[1] 'Out of whom went seven devils.' Those who are curious to see one attempt at finding a 'rational' basis for some of the Talmudical legends about Mary Magdalene and others connected with the history of Christ, may consult the essay of *Rösch* in the Studien and Kritiken for 1873, pp. 77–115 (Die Jesus-Mythen d. Judenth.).

[2] The suggestion that the word meant 'curler of hair,' which is made by *Lightfoot*, and repeated by his modern followers, depends on entire misapprehension.

[3] In Baba Mets. 25 a, middle, R. Isaac the Magdalene is introduced in a highly characteristic discussion about coins that

are found. His remark about three coins laid on each other like a tower might, if it had not been connected with such a grave discussion, have almost seemed a pun on *Magdala*.

[4] Thus in regard to another village (not mentioned either by *Relandus* or *Neubauer*) in the Midr. ii. 2, ed. Warsh. p. 67 b, line 13 from bottom.

[5] This Synagogue is introduced in the almost blasphemous account of the miracles of Simon ben Jochai, when he declared Tiberias free from the defilement of dead bodies, buried there.

[6] This has been well shown by *Neubauer*, Géogr. de la Palestine, pp. 217, 218.

BOOK
III

Farrar, and others) have noticed the strange designation 'Valley of Doves' without being able to suggest the explanation of it, which the knowledge of its traffic in doves for purposes of purification at once supplies. Of the many towns and villages that dotted the shores of the Lake of Galilee, all have passed away except Magdala, which is still represented by the collection of mud hovels that bears the name of Mejdel. The ancient watch-tower which gave the place its name is still there, probably standing on the same site as that which looked down on Jesus and the Magdalene. To this day Magdala is celebrated for its springs and rivulets, which render it specially suitable for dyeworks; while the shell-fish with which these waters and the Lake are said to abound,[a] might supply some of the dye.[1]

ᵃ *Baedeker's Palästina*, pp. 268, 269

Such details may help us more clearly to realise the home, and with it, perhaps, also the upbringing and circumstances of her who not only ministered to Jesus in His Life, but, with eager avarice of love, watched 'afar off' His dying moments,[b] and then sat over against the new tomb of Joseph in which His Body was laid.[c] And the terrible time which followed she spent with her like-minded friends, who in Galilee had ministered to Christ,[d] in preparing those 'spices and ointments'[e] which the Risen Saviour would never require. For, on that Easter-morning the empty tomb of Jesus was only guarded by Angel-messengers, who announced to the Magdalene and Joanna, as well as the other women,[f] the gladsome tidings that His foretold Resurrection had become a reality. But however difficult the circumstances may have been, in which the Magdalene came to profess her faith in Jesus, those of *Joanna* (the Hebrew *Yochani*[g]) must have been even more trying. She was the wife of *Chuza*, Herod's Steward [2]— possibly, though not likely, the Court-official whose son Jesus had healed by the word spoken in Cana.[h] The absence of any reference to the event seems rather opposed to this supposition. Indeed, it seems doubtful, whether *Chuza* was a Jewish name. In Jewish writings[3] the designation (כּוּזָא)[i] seems rather used as a by-name

ᵇ St. Matt. xxvii. 56
ᶜ ver. 61

ᵈ St. Luke xxiii. 55
ᵉ ver. 56

ᶠ St. Luke xxiv. 10

ᵍ Seb. 62 *b*

ʰ St. John iv. 46–54

ⁱ Yebam. 10 *a*

---

[1] It is at any rate remarkable that the Talmud (Megill. 6 *a*) finds in the ancient territory of Zebulun the *Chilzon* (חִלָּזוֹן) so largely used in dyeing purple and scarlet, and so very precious. Spurious dyes of the same colour were also produced (comp. *Lewysohn*, Zool. d. Talm. pp. 281–283).

[2] Curiously enough, the Greek term ἐπίτροπος (steward) has passed into the Rabbinic *Aphiterophos*.

[3] *Delitzsch* (Zeitsch. für Luther Theol.

for 1876, p. 598), seems to regard *Kuzith* (כּוּזִית) as the Jewish equivalent of Chuza. The word is mentioned in the *Aruch* (ed. *Landau*, p. 801 *b*, where the references, however, are misquoted) as occurring in Ber. R. 23 and 51. No existing copy of the Midrash has these references, which seem to have been purposely omitted. It is curious that both occur in connection with Messianic passages. In any case, however, *Kuzith* was not a proper name, but some mystic designation.

('little pitcher') for a small, insignificant person, than as a proper name.[1] Only one other of those who ministered to Jesus is mentioned by name. It is *Susanna,* the 'lily.' The names of the other loving women are not written on the page of earth's history, but only on that of the 'Lamb's Book of Life.' And they 'ministered to Him of their substance.' So early did eternal riches appear in the garb of poverty; so soon did love to Christ find its treasure in consecrating it to His Ministry. And ever since has this been the law of His Kingdom, to our great humiliation and yet greater exaltation in fellowship with Him.

CHAP.
XXII

It was on this return-journey to Capernaum, probably not far from the latter place, that the two blind men had their sight restored.[a] It was then, also, that the healing of the demonised dumb took place, which is recorded in St. Matt. ix. 32–35, and alluded to in St. Mark iii. 22–30. This narrative must, of course, not be confounded with the somewhat similar event told in St. Matt. xii. 22–32, and in St. Luke xi. 14–26. The latter occurred at a much later period in our Lord's life, when, as the whole context shows, the opposition of the Pharisaic party had assumed much larger proportions, and the language of Jesus was more fully denunciatory of the character and guilt of His enemies. That charge of the Pharisees, therefore, that Jesus cast out the demons through the Prince of the demons,[b] as well as His reply to it, will best be considered when it shall appear in its fullest development. This all the more, that we believe at least the greater part of our Lord's answer to their blasphemous accusation, as given in St. Mark's Gospel,[c] to have been spoken at that later period.[2]

[a] St. Matt. ix. 27–31

[b] St. Matt. ix. 34

[c] St. Mark iii. 23–30

It was on this return-journey to Capernaum from the uttermost borders of Galilee, when for the first time He was not only followed by His twelve Apostles, but attended by the loving service of those who owed their all to His Ministry, that the demonized dumb was restored by the casting out of the demon. Even these circumstances show that a new stage in the Messianic course had begun. It is characterised by fuller unfolding of Christ's teaching and working,

---

Lightfoot (Horæ Hebr. on Luke viii. 3) reads in the genealogy of Haman (in Sopher. xiii. 6) *Bar Kuza.* But it is really *Bar Biza,* 'son of contempt'—all the names being intended as defamatory of Haman. Similarly, *Lightfoot* asserts that the designation does not occur in the genealogy of Haman in the Targum Esther. But in the Second Targum Esther (Miqraoth Gedol. Part vi. p. 5 *a*) the name does occur in the genealogy as

'*Bar Buzah.*'

[1] *Dr. Neubauer* (Studia Bibl. p. 225) regards *Chuza* as an Idumæan name, connected with the Edomite god *Kos.*

[2] I regard St. Mark iii. 23–30 as combining the event in St. Matt. ix. (see St. Mark iii. 23) with what is recorded in St. Matt. xii. and St. Luke xi., and I account for this combination by the circumstance that the latter is not related by St. Mark.

and, *pari passu,* by more fully developed opposition of the Pharisaic party. For the two went together, nor can they be distinguished as cause or effect. That new stage, as repeatedly noted, had opened on His return from the 'Unknown Feast' in Jerusalem, whence He seems to have been followed by the Pharisaic party. We have marked it so early as the call of the four disciples by the Lake of Galilee. But it first actively appeared at the healing of the paralytic in Capernaum, when, for the first time, we noticed the presence and murmuring of the Scribes, and, for the first time also, the distinct declaration about the forgiveness of sins on the part of Jesus. The same twofold element appeared in the call of the publican Matthew, and the cavil of the Pharisees at Christ's subsequent eating and drinking with 'sinners.' It was in further development of this separation from the old and now hostile element, that the twelve Apostles were next appointed, and that distinctive teaching of Jesus addressed to the people in the 'Sermon on the Mount,' which was alike a vindication and an appeal. On the journey through Galilee, which now followed. the hostile party does not seem to have actually attended Jesus; but their growing, and now outspoken opposition is heard in the discourse of Christ about John the Baptist after the dismissal of his disciples,[a] while its influence appears in the unspoken thoughts of Simon the Pharisee.

ᵃ St. Matt.
xi. 16–19

But even before these two events, that had happened which would induce the Pharisaic party to increased measures against Jesus. It has already been suggested, that the party, as such, did not attend Jesus on His Galilean journey. But we are emphatically told, that tidings of the raising of the dead at Nain had gone forth into Judæa.[b] No doubt they reached the leaders at Jerusalem. There seems just sufficient time between this and the healing of the demonised dumb on the return-journey to Capernaum, to account for the presence there of those Pharisees,[c] who are expressly described by St. Mark[d] as 'the Scribes which came down from Jerusalem.'

ᵇ St. Luke
vii. 17

ᶜ St. Matt.
ix. 34
ᵈ St. Mark
iii. 32

Other circumstances, also, are thus explained. Whatever view the leaders at Jerusalem may have taken of the raising at Nain, it could no longer be denied that miracles were wrought by Jesus. At least, what to *us* seem miracles, yet not to them, since, as we have seen, 'miraculous' cures and the expelling of demons lay within the sphere of their 'extraordinary ordinary'—were not miracles in our sense, since they were, or professed to be, done by their 'own children.' The mere fact, therefore, of such cures, would present no difficulty to them. To *us* a single well-ascertained miracle would form irrefragable evidence of the claims of Christ; to *them* it would not. They could believe in the 'miracles,' and yet not in the Christ. To them the question would not be, as to us, whether they were miracles—but, By what power, or in what Name, He did these deeds? From our standpoint, their opposition to the Christ would—in view of His Miracles—seem not only wicked. but rationally inexplicable. But ours was not their point of view. And here, again, we perceive that it was enmity to the *Person* and *Teaching* of Jesus which led to the denial of His claims. The inquiry: By what Power Jesus did these works? they met by the assertion, that it was through that of Satan, or the Chief of the Demons. They regarded Jesus, as not only temporarily, but permanently, possessed by a demon, that is, as the constant vehicle of Satanic influence. And this demon was, according to them, none other than Beelzebub, the prince of the devils.[a] Thus, in their view, it was really Satan who acted in and through Him; and Jesus, instead of being recognised as the Son of God, was regarded as an incarnation of Satan; instead of being owned as the Messiah, was denounced and treated as the representative of the Kingdom of Darkness. All this, because the Kingdom which He came to open, and which He preached, was precisely the opposite of what they regarded as the Kingdom of God. Thus it was the essential contrariety of Rabbinism to the Gospel of the Christ that lay at the foundation of their conduct towards the Person of Christ. We venture to assert, that this accounts for the whole after-history up to the Cross.

Thus viewed, the history of Pharisaic opposition appears not only consistent, but is, so to speak, morally accounted for. Their guilt lay in treating that as Satanic agency which was of the Holy Ghost; and this, because they were of their father the Devil, and knew not, nor understood, nor yet loved the Light, their deeds being evil. They were not children of the light, but of that darkness which comprehended Him not Who was the Light. And now we can also understand the growth of active opposition to Christ. Once arrived at the conclusion, that the miracles which Christ did were due to the power of Satan, and that He was the representative of the Evil One, their course was rationally and morally chosen. To regard every fresh manifestation of Christ's Power as only a fuller development of the power of Satan, and to oppose it with increasing determination and hostility, even to the Cross: such was henceforth the natural progress of this history. On the other hand, such a course once fully settled upon, there would, and could, be no further reasoning

a St. Mark
iii. 22

BOOK
III

with, or against it on the part of Jesus.   Henceforth His Discourses and attitude to such Judaism must be chiefly denunciatory, while still seeking—as, from the inward necessity of His Nature and the outward necessity of His Mission, He must—to save the elect remnant from this 'untoward generation,' and to lay broad and wide the foundations of the future Church.   But the old hostile Judaism must henceforth be left to the judgment of condemnation, except in those tears of Divine pity which the Jew-King and Jewish Messiah wept over the Jerusalem that knew not the day of its visitation.

But all this, when the now beginning movement shall have reached its full proportions.[a]   For the present, we mark only its first appearance.   The charge of Satanic agency was, indeed, not quite new.   It had been suggested, that John the Baptist had been under demoniacal influence, and this cunning pretext for resistance to his message had been eminently successful with the people.[b]   The same charge, only in much fuller form, was now raised against Jesus.   As 'the multitude marvelled, saying, it was never so seen in Israel,' the Pharisees, without denying the facts, had this explanation of them, to be presently developed to all its terrible consequences: that, both as regarded the casting out of the demon from the dumb man and all similar works, Jesus wrought it 'through the Ruler of the Demons.'[c] [1]

And so the edge of this manifestation of the Christ was blunted and broken.   But their besetment of the Christ did not cease.   It is to this that we attribute the visit of 'the mother and brethren' of Jesus, which is recorded in the three Synoptic Gospels.[d]   Even this circumstance shows its decisive importance.   It forms a parallel to the former attempts of the Pharisees to influence the disciples of Jesus,[e] and then to stir up the hostility of the disciples of John.[f] *both of which are recorded by the three Evangelists.*   It also brought to light another distinctive characteristic of the Mission of Jesus.   We place this visit of the 'mother and brethren' of Jesus immediately after His return to Capernaum, and we attribute it to Pharisaic opposition, which either filled those relatives of Jesus with fear for His safety, or made them sincerely concerned about His proceedings.   Only if it meant some kind of interference with His Mission, whether prompted by fear or affection, would Jesus have so disowned their relationship.

[a] St. Matt. xii. 22 &c.; St. Luke xi. 14 &c.

[b] St. Matt. xi. 17, 18; St. Luke vii. 31–32

[c] St. Matt. ix. 33, 34

[d] St. Matt. xii. 46 &c.; St. Mark iii. 31 &c. St. Luke viii. 19 &c.
[e] St. Matt. ix. 11
[f] u. s. ver. 14

---

[1] At the same time I have, with not a few authorities, strong doubts whether St. Matt. ix. 34 is not to be regarded as an interpolation (see *Westcott* and *Hort,* New Testament).   *Substantially,* the charge was there; but it seems doubtful whether, *in so many words,* it was made till a later period.

But it meant more than this. As always, the positive went side by side with the negative. Without going so far, as with some of the Fathers, to see pride or ostentation in this, that the Virgin-Mother summoned Jesus to her outside the house, since the opposite might as well have been her motive, we cannot but regard the words of Christ as the sternest prophetic rebuke of all Mariolatry, prayer for the Virgin's intercession, and, still more, of the strange doctrines about her freedom from actual and original sin, up to their prurient sequence in the dogma of the 'Immaculate Conception.'

On the other hand, we also remember the deep reverence among the Jews for parents, which found even exaggerated expression in the Talmud.[a][1] And we feel that, of all in Israel, He, Who was their King, could not have spoken nor done what might even seem disrespectful to a mother. There must have been higher meaning in His words. That meaning would be better understood after His Resurrection. But even before that it was needful, in presence of interference or hindrance by earthly relationships, even the nearest and tenderest, and perhaps all the more in their case, to point to the higher and stronger spiritual relationship. And beyond this, to still higher truth. For, had He not entered into earthly kinship solely for the sake of the higher spiritual relationship which He was about to found; and was it not, then, in the most literal sense, that not those in nearest earthly relationship, but they who sat 'about Him, nay, whoever shall do the will of God,' were really in closest kinship with Him? Thus, it was not that Christ set lightly by His Mother, but that He confounded not the means with the end, nor yet surrendered the spirit for the letter of the Law of Love, when, refusing to be arrested or turned aside from His Mission, even for a moment,[2] He elected to do the Will of His Father rather than neglect it by attending to the wishes of the Virgin-Mother. As *Bengel* aptly puts it: He contemns not the Mother, but He places the Father first.[3] And this is ever the right relationship in the Kingdom of Heaven!

[a] Jer. Peah
i. 1

---

[1] An instance of this has been given in the previous chapter, p. 567, note. Other examples of filial reverence are mentioned, some painfully ludicrous, others touching, and accompanied by sayings which sometimes rise to the sublime.

[2] *Bengel* remarks on St. Matt. xii. 46: 'Non plane hic congruebat sensus Mariæ cum sensu Filii.'

[3] 'Non spernit Matrem, sed anteponit Patrem.'

CHAPTER XXIII.

.EW TEACHING ' IN PARABLES '—THE PARABLES TO THE PEOPLE BY THE
LAKE OF GALILEE, AND THOSE TO THE DISCIPLES IN CAPERNAUM.

(St. Matt. xiii. 1–52; St. Mark iv. 1–34; St. Luke viii. 4–18.)

BOOK
III

* St. Matt.
vii. 26

b u. s. vi.
28–30
c vii. 16–20

WE are once more with Jesus and His disciples by the Lake of Galilee. We love to think that it was in the early morning, when the light laid its golden shadows on the still waters, and the fresh air, untainted by man, was fragrant of earth's morning sacrifice, when no voice of human discord marred the restfulness of holy silence, nor broke the Psalm of Nature's praise. It was a spring morning too, and of such spring-time as only the East, and chiefly the Galilean Lake, knows—not of mingled sunshine and showers, of warmth and storm, clouds and brightness, when life seems to return slowly and feebly to the palsied limbs of our northern climes, but when at the warm touch it bounds and throbs with the vigour of youth. The imagery of the 'Sermon on the Mount' indicates that winter's rain and storms were just past.* Under that sky Nature seems to meet the coming of spring by arraying herself in a garb more glorious than Solomon's royal pomp. Almost suddenly the blood-red anemones, the gay tulips, the spotless narcissus, and the golden ranunculus[1] deck with wondrous richness the grass of the fields—alas! so soon to wither[b]— while all trees put forth their fragrant promise of fruit.[c] As the imagery employed in the Sermon on the Mount confirmed the inference, otherwise derived, that it was spoken during the brief period after the winter rains, when the 'lilies' decked the fresh grass, so the scene depicted in the Parables spoken by the Lake of Galilee indicates a more advanced season, when the fields gave first promise

[1] It adds interest to these Solomon-like lilies that the Mishnah designates one class of them, growing in fields and vineyards, by the name 'royal lily' (Kil. v. 8, Bab. Talmud, p. 29 a). At the same time, the term used by our Lord need not be confined to 'lilies' in the strictest sense. It may represent the whole wild flora of spring, chiefly the anemones (comp. *Tristram*, Nat. Hist. of the Bible, pp. 462–465). A word with the same letters as κρίνος (though of different meaning) is the Rabbinic *Narkes*, the narcissus — of course that דרברא (of fields), not רגנויתא (of gardens).

of a harvest to be gathered in due time.   And as we know that the barley-harvest commenced with the Passover, we cannot be mistaken in supposing that the scene is laid a few weeks before that Feast.

Other evidence of this is not wanting.   From the opening verses[a] we infer, that Jesus had gone forth from 'the house' with His disciples only, and that, as He sat by the seaside, the gathering multitude had obliged Him to enter a ship, whence He spake unto them many things in Parables.   That this parabolic teaching did not follow, far less, was caused by, the fully developed enmity of the Pharisees,[b][1] will appear more clearly in the sequel.   Meantime it should be noticed, that the first series of Parables (those spoken by the Lake of Galilee) bear no distinct reference to it.   In this respect we mark an ascending scale in the three series of Parables, spoken respectively at three different periods in the History of Christ, and with reference to three different stages of Pharisaic opposition and popular feeling.   The first series is that,[c] when Pharisaic opposition had just devised the explanation that His works were of demoniac agency, and when misled affection would have converted the ties of earthly relationship into bonds to hold the Christ.   To this there was only one reply, when the Christ stretched out His Hand over those who had learned, by following Him, to do the Will of His Heavenly Father, and so become His nearest of kin.   *This* was the real answer to the attempt of His mother and brethren; *that* to the Pharisaic charge of Satanic agency.   And it was in this connection that, first to the multitude, then to His disciples, the first series of Parables was spoken, which exhibits the elementary truths concerning the planting of the Kingdom of God, its development, reality, value, and final vindication.

In the second series of Parables we mark a different stage.   The fifteen Parables of which it consists[d] were spoken after the Trans- figuration, on the descent into the Valley of Humiliation.   They also concern the Kingdom of God, but, although the prevailing character- istic is still *parenetic*,[2] or, rather, Evangelic, they have a controversial aspect also, as against some vital, active opposition to the Kingdom, chiefly on the part of the Pharisees.   Accordingly, they appear among 'the Discourses' of Christ,[e] and are connected with the climax of Pharisaic opposition as presented in the charge, in its

margin notes:
[a] St. Matt. xiii. 1, 2
[b] St. Matt. xii. 24 &c.
[c] St. Matt. xiii.
[d] St. Luke x.-xvi., xviii., passim
[e] St. Luke xi.-xiv.

---

[1] This seems to be the view of *Goebel* in his 'Parabeln Jesu,' a book to which I would here, in general, acknowledge my obligations.   The latest work on the subject (*F. L. Steinmeyer*, d. Par. d. Herrn, Berlin 1884) is very disappointing.

[2] Admonitory, hortatory—a term used in theology, of which it is not easy to give the exact equivalent.

BOOK
III

ᵃ St. Luke
xi. 14–36;
St. Matt.
xii. 22–45;
St. Mark
iii. 22–30

ᵇ St. Matt.
xviii., xx.,
xxi., xxii.
xxiv., xxv.;
St. Luke
xix.

ᶜ St. Mark
ɪv. 11

most fully developed form, that Jesus was, so to speak, the Incarnation of Satan, the constant medium and vehicle of his activity.ᵃ This *was* the blasphemy against the Holy Ghost. All the Parables spoken at that period bear more or less direct reference to it, though, as already stated, as yet in positive rather than negative form, the Evangelic element in them being primary, and the judicial only secondary.

This order is reversed in the third series, consisting of eight Parables.ᵇ Here the controversial has not only the ascendency over the Evangelic element, but the tone has become judicial, and the Evangelic element appears chiefly in the form of certain predictions connected with the coming end. The Kingdom of God is presented in its final stage of ingathering, separation, reward and loss, as, indeed, we might expect in the teaching of the Lord immediately before His final rejection by Israel and betrayal into the hands of the Gentiles.

This internal connection between the Parables and the History of Christ best explains their meaning. Their artificial grouping (as by mostly all modern critics [1]) is too ingenious to be true. One thing, however, is common to all the Parables, and forms a point of connection between them. They are all occasioned by some unreceptiveness on the part of the hearers, and that, even when the hearers are professing disciples. This seems indicated in the reason assigned by Christ to the disciples for His use of parabolic teaching: that unto them it was ' given to know the mystery of the Kingdom of God, but unto them that are without, all these things are done in parables.'ᶜ And this may lead up to such general remarks on the Parables as are necessary for their understanding.

Little information is to be gained from discussing the etymology of the word *Parable*.[2] The verb from which it is derived means *to project*; and the term itself, the placing of one thing by the side of another. Perhaps no other mode of teaching was so common among the Jews[3] as that by Parables. Only in their case, they were almost entirely illustrations of what had been said or taught;[4]

---

[1] Even *Goebel*, though rightly following the purely historical method, has, in the interest of so-called higher criticism, attempted such artificial grouping.

[2] From παραβάλλω, *projicio, admoveo rem rei comparationis causa* (*Grimm*). Little can be learned from the classical definitions of the παραβολή. See Archbishop *Trench* on the Parables.

[3] *F. L. Steinmeyer* has most strangely attempted to deny this. Yet every ancient Rabbinic work is literally *full* of parables. In Sanh. 38 *b* we read that R. Meir's discourses consisted in third of legal determinations, in third of Haggadah, and in third of parables.

[4] I am here referring only to the form, not the substance, of these Jewish parables.

while, in the case of Christ, they served as the foundation for His
teaching. In the one case, the light of earth was cast heavenwards, in the other, that of heaven earthwards; in the one case, it was intended to make spiritual teaching appear Jewish and national, in the other to convey spiritual teaching in a form adapted to the standpoint of the hearers. This distinction will be found to hold true, even in instances where there seems the closest parallelism between a Rabbinic and an Evangelic Parable. On further examination, the difference between them will appear not merely one of degree, but of kind, or rather of standpoint. This may be illustrated by the Parable of the woman who made anxious search for her lost coin,[a] to which there is an almost literal Jewish parallel.[b] But, whereas in the Jewish Parable the moral is, that a man ought to take much greater pains in the study of the Torah than in the search for coin, since the former procures an eternal reward, while the coin would, if found, at most only procure temporary enjoyment, the Parable of Christ is intended to set forth, not the merit of study or of works, but the compassion of the Saviour in seeking the lost, and the joy of Heaven in his recovery. It need scarcely be said, that comparison between such Parables, as regards their spirit, is scarcely possible, except by way of contrast.[1]

[a] St. Luke xv. 8-10
[b] In the Midrash on Cant. i. 1

But, to return. In Jewish writings a Parable (*Mimshal, Mashal, Mathla*) is introduced by some such formula as this: ' I will tell thee a parable ' (אמשול לך משל). ' To what is the thing like? To one,' &c. Often it begins more briefly, thus: ' A Parable. To what is the thing like?' or else, simply: ' To what is the thing like?' Sometimes even this is omitted, and the Parable is indicated by the preposition ' to ' at the beginning of the illustrative story. Jewish writers extol Parables, as placing the meaning of the Law within range of the comprehension of all men. The 'wise King ' had introduced this method, the usefulness of which is illustrated by the Parable of a great palace which had many doors, so that people lost their way in it, till one came who fastened a ball of thread at the chief entrance, when all could readily find their way in and out.[c] Even this will illustrate what has been said of the difference between Rabbinic Parables and those employed by our Lord.

[c] Midr. on Cant. i. 1

The general distinction between a Parable and a Proverb, Fable and Allegory, cannot here be discussed at length.[2] It will sufficiently

---

[1] It is, indeed, possible that the framework of some of Christ's Parables may have been adopted and adapted by later Rabbis. No one who knows the early intercourse between Jews and Jewish Christians would deny this *à priori*.

[2] I must here refer to the various Biblical Dictionaries, to Professor *West-*

ᵃ St. Matt.
xxiv. 32;
St. Mark
iii. 23;
St. Luke
v. 36
ᵇ St. Luke
iv. 23
ᶜ St. Matt.
xv. 15

appear from the character and the characteristics of the Parables of our Lord. That designation is, indeed, sometimes applied to what are not Parables, in the strictest sense; while it is wanting where we might have expected it. Thus, in the Synoptic Gospels illustrations,[a] and even proverbial sayings, such as 'Physician, heal thyself,'[b] or that about the blind leading the blind,[c] are designated Parables. Again, the term 'Parable,' although used in our Authorised Version, does not occur in the original of St. John's Gospel; and this, although not a few illustrations used in that Gospel might, on superficial examination, appear to be Parables. The term must, therefore, be here restricted to special conditions. The first of these is, that all Parables bear reference to well-known scenes, such as those of daily life; or to events, either real, or such as every one would expect in given circumstances, or as would be in accordance with prevailing notions.[1]

Such pictures, familiar to the popular mind, are in the Parable connected with corresponding spiritual realities. Yet, here also, there is that which distinguishes the Parable from the mere illustration. The latter conveys no more than—perhaps not so much as—that which was to be illustrated; while the Parable conveys this and a great deal beyond it to those, who can follow up its shadows to the light by which they have been cast. In truth, Parables are the outlined shadows—large, perhaps, and dim—as the light of heavenly things falls on well-known scenes, which correspond to, and have their higher counterpart in spiritual realities. For, earth and heaven are twin-parts of His works. And, as the same law, so the same order, prevails in them; and they form a grand unity in their relation to the Living God Who reigneth. And, just as there is ultimately but one Law, one Force, one Life, which, variously working, effects and affects all the Phenomenal in the material universe, however diverse it may seem, so is there but one Law and Life as regards the intellectual, moral—nay, and the spiritual. One Law, Force, and Life, binding the earthly and the heavenly into a Grand Unity—the outcome of the Divine Unity, of which it is the manifestation. Thus things in earth and heaven are kindred, and the one may become to us Parables of the other. And so, if the place of our resting be Bethel, they become Jacob's ladder, by which those from heaven come down to earth, and those from earth ascend to heaven.

Another characteristic of the Parables, in the stricter sense, is

---

cott's Introduction to the Study of the Gospels (pp. 28, 286), and to the works of Archbishop *Trench* and Dr. *Goebel*.

[1] Every reader of the Gospels will be able to distinguish these various classes.

that in them the whole picture or narrative is used in illustration of
some heavenly teaching, and not merely one feature or phase of it,[1]
as in some of the parabolic illustrations and proverbs of the Synoptists, or the parabolic narratives of the Fourth Gospel. Thus, in the
parabolic illustrations about the new piece of cloth on the old garment,[a] about the blind leading the blind,[b] about the forth-putting of
leaves on the fig-tree;[c] or in the parabolic proverb, ' Physician, heal
thyself;'[d] or in such parabolic narratives of St. John, as about the
Good Shepherd,[e] or the Vine '—in each case, only one part is selected
as parabolic. On the other hand, even in the shortest Parables, such
as those of the seed growing secretly,[g] the leaven in the meal,[h] and
the pearl of great price,[i] the picture is *complete*, and has not only in
one feature, but in its whole bearing, a counterpart in spiritual
realities. But, as shown in the Parable of the seed growing secretly,[k]
it is not necessary that the Parable should always contain some narrative, provided that not only one feature, but the whole thing related,
have its spiritual application.

In view of what has been explained, the arrangement of the
Parables into *symbolical* and *typical*[2] can only apply to their form,
not their substance. In the first of these classes a scene from nature
or from life serves as basis for exhibiting the corresponding spiritual
reality. In the latter, what is related serves as type ($\tau\acute{\upsilon}\pi o\varsigma$), not in
the ordinary sense of that term, but in that not unfrequent in
Scripture: as example—whether for imitation,[m] or in warning.[n] In
the typical Parables the illustration lies, so to speak, on the outside;
in the symbolical, within the narrative or scene. The former are to
be applied; the latter must be explained.

It is here that the characteristic difference between the various
classes of hearers lay. All the Parables, indeed, implied some background of opposition, or else of unreceptiveness. In the record of
this first series of them,[o] the fact that Jesus spake to the people in
Parables,[p] and *only* in Parables,[q] is strongly marked. It appears,
therefore, to have been the first time that this mode of popular
teaching was adopted by him.[3] Accordingly, the disciples not only
expressed their astonishment, but inquired the reason of this novel
method.[r] The answer of the Lord makes a distinction between those

CHAP.
XXIII

[a] St. Luke
v. 36
[b] St. Luke
vi. 39
[c] St. Matt.
xxiv. 32
[d] St. Luke
iv. 23
[e] St. John x.
[f] St. John
xv.
[g] St. Mark
iv. 26-29
[h] St. Matt.
xiii. 33
[i] vv. 45, 46
[k] St. Mark
iv. 26-29

[m] Phil. iii.
17; 1 Tim.
iv. 12
[n] 1 Cor. x. 6,
11

[o] St. Matt.
xiii.
[p] St. Matt.
xiii. 3, and
parallels
[q] St. Matt.
xiii. 34;
St. Mark
iv. 33, 34
[r] St. Matt.
xiii. 10, and
parallels

---

[1] *Cremer* (Lex. of N. T. Greek, p. 124)
lays stress on the idea of a *comparison*,
which is manifestly incorrect; *Goebel*,
with not much better reason, on that of
a narrative form.
[2] So by *Goebel*.

[3] In the Old Testament there are parabolic descriptions and utterances—especially in Ezekiel (xv.; xvi.; xvii.; xix.),
and a fable (Judg. ix. 7-15), but only
two Parables: the one *typical* (2 Sam.
xii. 1-6), the other *symbolical* (Is. v. 1-6).

BOOK to whom it is given to know the mysteries of the Kingdom, and
III those to whom all things were done in Parables. But, evidently,
this method of teaching could not have been adopted for the people,
in contradistinction to the disciples, and as a judicial measure, since
even in the first series of Parables three were addressed to the dis-
ᵃ St. Matt. ciples, after the people had been dismissed.ᵃ On the other hand, in
xiii. 36, 44–
52 answer to the disciples, the Lord specially marks this as the difference between the teaching vouchsafed to them and the Parables
spoken to the people, that the designed effect of the latter was
judicial: to complete that hardening which, in its commencement,
ᵇ St. Matt. had been caused by their voluntary rejection of what they had heard.ᵇ
xi. 13–17
But, as not only the people, but the disciples also, were taught by
Parables, the hardening effect must not be ascribed to the parabolic
mode of teaching, now for the first time adopted by Christ. Nor is
it a sufficient answer to the question, by what this darkening effect,
and hence hardening influence, of the Parable on the people was
ᶜ St. Matt. caused, that the first series, addressed to the multitude,ᶜ consisted
xiii. 1–9, 24–
33 of a cumulation of Parables, without any hint as to their meaning
or interpretation.[1] For, irrespective of other considerations, these
Parables were at least as easily understood as those spoken immediately afterwards to the disciples, on which, similarly, no comment
was given by Jesus. On the other hand, to us at least, it seems
clear, that the ground of the different effect of the Parables on the
unbelieving multitude and on the believing disciples was not objective, or caused by the substance or form of these Parables, but subjective, being caused by the different standpoint of the two classes of
hearers toward the Kingdom of God.

This explanation removes what otherwise would be a serious
difficulty. For, it seems impossible to believe, that Jesus had adopted
a special mode of teaching for the purpose of concealing the truth,
which might have saved those who heard Him. His words, indeed,
indicate that such *was* the effect of the Parables. But they also
indicate, with at least equal clearness, that the cause of this hardening lay, not in the parabolic method of teaching, but in the state of
spiritual insensibility at which, by their own guilt, they had previously arrived. Through this, what might, and, in other circumstances, would, have conveyed spiritual instruction, necessarily became that which still further and fatally darkened and dulled their
minds and hearts. Thus, their own hardening merged into the
St. Matt. judgment of hardening.ᵈ
xiii. 13–15

---

[1] So even *Goebel* (i. pp. 33–42, and especially p. 38.)

We are now in some measure able to understand, why Christ now for the first time adopted parabolic teaching. Its reason lay in the altered circumstances of the case. All his former teaching had been plain, although initial. In it He had set forth by Word, and exhibited by fact (in miracles), that Kingdom of God which He had come to open to all believers. The hearers had now ranged themselves into two parties. Those who, whether temporarily or permanently (as the result would show), had admitted these premisses, so far as they understood them, were His professing disciples. On the other hand, the Pharisaic party had now devised a consistent theory, according to which the acts, and hence also the teaching, of Jesus, were of Satanic origin. Christ must still preach the Kingdom; for that purpose had he come into the world. Only, the presentation of that Kingdom must now be for *decision*. It must separate the two classes, leading the one to clearer understanding of the mysteries of the Kingdom—of what not only seems, but to our limited thinking really *is*, mysterious; while the other class of hearers would now regard these mysteries as wholly unintelligible, incredible, and to be rejected. And the ground of this lay in the respective positions of these two classes towards the Kingdom. 'Whosoever hath, to him shall be given, and he shall have more abundance; but whosoever hath not, from him shall be taken away even that he hath.' And the mysterious manner in which they were presented in Parables was alike suited to, and corresponded with, the character of these 'mysteries of the Kingdom,' now set forth, not for initial instruction, but for final decision. As the light from heaven falls on earthly objects, the shadows are cast. But our perception of them, and its mode, depend on the position which we occupy relatively to that Light.

And so it was not only best, but most merciful, that these mysteries of substance should now, also, be presented as mysteries of form in Parables. Here each would see according to his standpoint towards the Kingdom. And this was in turn determined by previous acceptance or rejection of that truth, which had formerly been set forth in a plain form in the teaching and acting of the Christ. Thus, while to the opened eyes and hearing ears of the one class would be disclosed that, which prophets and righteous men of old had desired but not attained, to them who had voluntarily cast aside what they had, would only come, in their seeing and hearing, the final judgment of hardening. So would it be to each according to his standpoint. To the one would come the grace of final revelation, to the other the

BOOK
III

ᵃ Is. vi. 9, 10

ᵇ St. Matt.
xiii.

ᶜ St. Mark
iv. 26-29

ᵈ Arach.
25 a, line 18
from bottom

final judgment which, in the first place, had been of their own choice, but which, as they voluntarily occupied their position relatively to Christ, had grown into the fulfilment of the terrible prediction of Esaias concerning the final hardening of Israel.ᵃ

Thus much in general explanation. The record of the first series of Parablesᵇ contains three separate accounts: that of the Parables spoken to the people; that of the reason for the use of parabolic teaching, and the explanation of the first Parables (both addressed to the disciples); and, finally, another series of Parables spoken to the disciples. To each of these we must briefly address ourselves.

On that bright spring morning, when Jesus spoke from 'the ship' to the multitude that crowded the shore, He addressed to them these *four Parables*: concerning Him Who sowed,[1] concerning the Wheat and the Tares, concerning the Mustard-Seed, and concerning the Leaven. The first, or perhaps the two first of these, must be supplemented by what may be designated as a *fifth Parable*, that of the Seed growing unobservedly. This is the only Parable of which St. Mark alone has preserved the record.ᶜ All these Parables refer, as is expressly stated, to the Kingdom of God; that is, not to any special phase or characteristic of it, but to the Kingdom itself, or, in other words, to its history. They are all such as befit an open-air address at that season of the year, in that locality, and to those hearers. And yet there is such gradation and development in them as might well point upwards and onwards.

The first Parable is that of Him Who sowed. We can almost picture to ourselves the Saviour seated in the prow of the boat, as He points His hearers to the rich plain over against Him, where the young corn, still in the first green of its growing, is giving promise of harvest. Like this is the Kingdom of Heaven which He has come to proclaim. Like what? Not yet like that harvest, which is still in the future, but like that field over there. The Sower[2] has gone forth to sow the Good Seed. If we bear in mind a mode of sowing peculiar (if we are not mistaken) to those times, the Parable gains in vividness. According to Jewish authorities there was twofold sowing, as the seed was either cast by the hand (מפולת יד) or by means of cattle (מפולת שוורים ᵈ). In the latter case, a sack with holes was filled with corn and laid on the back of the animal, so that, as it moved onwards, the seed was thickly scattered. Thus it might well be, that it would fall indiscriminately on beaten roadway,[3] on

---

[1] The correct reading in St. Matt. xiii. 18 is τοῦ σπείραντος, not σπείροντος as in the T. R.

[2] With the definite article—not 'a Sower,' as in our A.V., but the Sower.

[3] παρὰ τὴν ὁδόν, not παρὰ τὸν

stony places but thinly covered with soil, or where the thorns had CHAP.
not been cleared away, or undergrowth from the thorn-hedge crept XXIII
into the field,[1] as well as on good ground. The result in each case
need not here be repeated. But what meaning would all this convey to the Jewish hearers of Jesus? How could this sowing and
growing be like the Kingdom of God? Certainly not in the sense
in which they expected it. To them it was only a rich harvest, when
all Israel would bear plenteous fruit. Again, what was the Seed,
and who the Sower? or what could be meant by the various kinds
of soil and their unproductiveness?

To us, as explained by the Lord, all this seems plain. But to
them there could be no possibility of understanding, but much occasion for misunderstanding it, unless, indeed, they stood in right
relationship to the 'Kingdom of God.' The initial condition requisite
was to believe that Jesus was the Divine Sower, and His Word the
Seed of the Kingdom: no other Sower than He, no other Seed of the
Kingdom than His Word. If this were admitted, they had at least
the right premisses for understanding 'this mystery of the Kingdom.'
According to Jewish view the Messiah was to appear in outward
pomp, and by display of power to establish the Kingdom. But this
was the very idea of the Kingdom, with which Satan had tempted
Jesus at the outset of His Ministry.[2] In opposition to it was this
'mystery of the Kingdom,' according to which it consisted in reception of the Seed of the Word. That reception would depend on the
nature of the soil, that is, on the mind and heart of the hearers.
The Kingdom of God was *within*: it came neither by a display of
power, nor even by this, that Israel, or else the Gospel-hearers, were
the field on which the Seed of the Kingdom was sown. *He* had
brought the Kingdom: the Sower had gone forth to sow. This was
of free grace—the Gospel. But the seed might fall on the roadside,
and so perish without even springing up. Or it might fall on rocky
soil, and so spring up rapidly, but wither before it showed promise of
fruit. Or it might fall where thorns grew along with, and more
rapidly than, it. And so it would, indeed, show promise of fruit;
the corn might appear in the ear; but that fruit would not come to
ripeness ('bring no fruit to perfection'[a]), because the thorns grow-   [a] St. Luke
ing more rapidly would choke the corn. Lastly, to this threefold   viii. 14

ἀγρὸν. I cannot understand how this   on the highway.
road could be within the ploughed and   [1] Comp. the slight variations in the
sowed field. Our view is further con-   three Gospels.
firmed by St. Luke viii. 5, where the seed is   [2] Comp. the chapter on the Tempta-
described as 'trodden down'—evidently   tion.

faultiness of soil, through which the seed did not spring up at all, or merely sprung up, or just reached the promise, but not the perfection of fruit, corresponded a threefold degree of fruit-bearing in the soil, according to which it brought forth thirtyfold, sixtyfold, or an hundredfold, in the varying measure of its capacity.

If even the disciples failed to comprehend the whole bearing of this 'Mystery of the Kingdom,' we can believe how utterly strange and un-Jewish such a Parable of the Messianic Kingdom must have sounded to them, who had been influenced by the Pharisaic representations of the Person and Teaching of Christ. And yet the while these very hearers were, unconsciously to themselves, fulfilling what Jesus was speaking to them in the Parable!

Whether or not the Parable recorded by St. Mark alone,[a] concerning the Seed growing unobservedly, was spoken afterwards in private to the disciples, or, as seems more likely, at the first, and to the people by the sea-shore, this appears the fittest place for inserting it. If the first Parable, concerning the Sower and the Field of Sowing, would prove to all who were outside the pale of discipleship a 'mystery,' while to those within it would unfold knowledge of the very mysteries of the Kingdom, this would even more fully be the case in regard to this second or supplementary Parable. In it we are only viewing that portion of the field, which the former Parable had described as good soil. ' So is the Kingdom of God, as if a man had cast the seed on the earth, and slept and rose, night and day, and the seed sprang up and grew: how, he knows not himself. Automatous [1] [self-acting] the earth beareth fruit: first blade, then ear, then full wheat in the ear! But when the fruit presents itself, immediately he sendeth forth [2] the sickle, because the harvest is come.' The meaning of all this seems plain. As the Sower, after the seed has been cast into the ground, can do no more; he goes to sleep at night, and rises by day, the seed the meanwhile growing, the Sower knows not how, and as his activity ceases till the time that the fruit is ripe, when immediately he thrusts in the sickle—so is the Kingdom of God. The seed is sown; but its growth goes on, dependent on the law inherent in seed and soil, dependent also on Heaven's blessing of sunshine and showers, till the moment of ripeness, when the harvest-time is come. We can only go about our

---

[1] I would here remark in general, that I have always adopted what seemed to me the best attested readings, and endeavoured to translate literally, preserving, where it seemed desirable, even the succession of the words.

[2] This is a Hebraism—explaining the Hebrew use of the verb שלח in analogous circumstances.

daily work, or lie down to rest, as day and night alternate; we see, but know not the *how* of the growth of the seed. Yet, assuredly it will ripen, and when that moment has arrived, immediately the sickle is thrust in, for the harvest is come. And so also with *the* Sower. His outward activity on earth was in the sowing, and it will be in the harvesting. What lies between them is of that other Dispensation of the Spirit, till He again send forth His reapers into His field. But all this must have been to those 'without' a great mystery, in no wise compatible with Jewish notions; while to them 'within' it proved a yet greater, and very needful unfolding of the mysteries of the Kingdom, with very wide application of them.

The 'mystery' is made still further mysterious, or else it is still further unfolded, in the next Parable concerning the Tares sown among the Wheat. According to the common view, these Tares represent what is botanically known as the 'bearded Darnel' (*Lolium temulentum*), a poisonous rye-grass, very common in the East, 'entirely like wheat until the ear appears,' or else (according to some), the 'creeping wheat' or 'couch-grass' (*Triticum repens*), of which the roots creep underground and become intertwined with those of the wheat. But the Parable gains in meaning if we bear in mind that, according to ancient Jewish (and, indeed, modern Eastern) ideas, the Tares were *not* of different seed,[a] but only a degenerate kind of wheat.[b] Whether in legend or symbol, Rabbinism has it that even the ground had been guilty of fornication before the judgment of the Flood, so that when wheat was sown tares sprang up.[c] The Jewish hearers of Jesus would, therefore, think of these tares as degenerate kind of wheat, originally sprung at the time of the Flood, through the corruptness of the earth, but now, alas! so common in their fields; wholly undistinguishable from the wheat, till the fruit appeared: noxious, poisonous, and requiring to be separated from the wheat, if the latter was not to become useless.

With these thoughts in mind, let us now try to realise the scene pictured. Once more we see the field on which the corn is growing —we know not how. The sowing time is past. 'The Kingdom of Heaven is become [1] like to a man who sowed good seed in his field. But in the *time* that men sleep came his enemy and over-sowed tares [2] in (upon) the midst [3] of the wheat, and went away.' Thus far the picture is true to nature, since such deeds of enmity were, and still

a Kil. i. 1

b Jer. Kil.
26 d

c Ber. R. 28
ed. Warsh.
p. 53 a,
about the
middle

---

[1] The tense should here be marked.
[2] The Greek ζιζάνιον is represented by the Hebrew זוּן or זוּנִין.

[3] The expression is of great importance. The right reading is ἐπίσπειρεν (*insuper sero*—to sow above), not ἔσπειρε (sowed).

BOOK
III

are, common in the East. And so matters would go on unobserved, since, whatever kind of 'tares' may be meant, it would, from their likeness, be for some time impossible to distinguish them from the wheat. 'But when the herbage grew and made fruit, then appeared (became manifest) also the tares.' What follows is equally true to fact, since, according to the testimony of travellers, most strenuous efforts are always made in the East to weed out the tares. Similarly, in the parable, the servants of the householder are introduced as inquiring whence these tares had come; and on the reply: 'A hostile person has done this,' they further ask: 'Wilt thou then that we go (straightway) and gather them together?' The absence of any reference to the rooting up or burning the tares, is intended to indicate, that the only object which the servants had in view was to keep the wheat pure and unmixed for the harvest. But this their final object would have been frustrated by the procedure, which their inconsiderate zeal suggested. It would, indeed, have been quite possible to distinguish the tares from the wheat—and the Parable proceeds on this very assumption—for, by their fruit they would be known. But in the present instance separation would have been impossible, without, at the same time, uprooting some of the wheat. For, the tares had been sown right into the midst, and not merely by the side, of the wheat; and their roots and blades must have become intertwined. And so they must grow together to the harvest. Then such danger would no longer exist, for the period of growing was past, and the wheat had to be gathered into the barn. Then would be the right time to bid the reapers first gather the tares into bundles for burning, that afterwards the wheat, pure and unmixed, might be stored in the garner.

True to life as the picture is, yet the Parable was, of all others, perhaps the most un-Jewish, and therefore mysterious and unintelligible. Hence the disciples specially asked explanation of this only, which from its main subject they rightly designated as the Parable 'of the Tares.'[a] Yet this was also perhaps the most important for them to understand. For already 'the Kingdom of Heaven is become like' this, although the appearance of fruit has not yet made it manifest, that tares have been sown right into the midst of the wheat. But they would soon have to learn it in bitter experience and as a grievous temptation,[b] and not only as regarded the impressionable, fickle multitude, nor even the narrower circle of professing followers of Jesus, but that, alas! in their very midst there was a traitor   And they would have to learn it more and more in the

[a] St. Matt.
xiii. 36

[b] St. John
vi. 66-70

time to come, as we have to learn it to all ages, till the 'Age-' or
'Æon-completion.' [1] Most needful, yet most mysterious also, is this
other lesson, as the experience of the Church has shown, since almost
every period of her history has witnessed, not only the recurrence of
the proposal to make the wheat unmixed, while growing, by gathering
out the tares, but actual attempts towards it. All such have proved
failures, because the field is the wide 'world,' not a narrow sect;
because the tares have been sown into the midst of the wheat, and
by the enemy; and because, if such gathering were to take place,
the roots and blades of tares and wheat would be found so intertwined, that harm would come to the wheat. But why try to gather the
tares together, unless from undiscerning zeal? Or what have we, who
are only the owner's servants, to do with it, since we are not bidden
of Him? The 'Æon-completion' will witness the harvest, when the
separation of tares and wheat may not only be accomplished with
safety, but shall become necessary. For the wheat must be garnered
in the heavenly storehouse, and the tares bound in bundles to be
burned. Then the harvesters shall be the Angels of Christ, the
gathered tares 'all the stumbling-blocks and those who do the
lawlessness,' and their burning the casting of them ·into the oven of
the fire.' [2]

More mysterious still, and, if possible, even more needful, was
the instruction that the Enemy who sowed the tares was the Devil.
To the Jews, nay, to us all, it may seem a mystery, that in 'the
Messianic Kingdom of Heaven' there should be a mixture of tares
with the wheat, the more mysterious, that the Baptist had predicted
that the coming Messiah would thoroughly purge His floor. But to
those who were capable of receiving it, it would be explained by the
fact that the Devil was 'the Enemy' of Christ, and of His Kingdom,
and that he had sowed those tares. This would, at the same time, be
the most effective answer to the Pharisaic charge, that Jesus was the
Incarnation of Satan, and the vehicle of his influence. And once instructed in this, they would have further to learn the lessons of faith
and patience, connected with the fact that the good seed of the
Kingdom grew in the field of the world, and hence that, by the very
conditions of its existence, separation by the hand of man was impossible so long as the wheat was still growing. Yet that separation would surely be made in the great harvest, to certain, terrible

---

[1] Æon, or 'age,' *without* the article
in ver. 40, and so it should also be in
ver. 39.

[2] With the two articles: the well-
known oven of the well-known fire—
Gehenna.

loss of the children of the wicked one,[1] and to the 'sun-like forthshin-
ing' in glory of the righteous in the Kingdom prepared by their Father.

The first Parables were intended to present the mysteries of the
Kingdom as illustrated by the sowing, growing, and intermixture of
the Seed. The concluding two Parables set forth another equally
mysterious characteristic of the Kingdom: that of its development
and power, as contrasted with its small and weak beginnings. In the
Parable of the Mustard-seed this is shown as regards the relation of
the Kingdom to the outer world; in that of the Leaven, in reference to the world within us. The one exhibits the *extensiveness*, the
other the *intensiveness*, of its power; in both cases at first hidden,
almost imperceptible, and seemingly wholly inadequate to the final
result. Once more we say it, that such Parables must have been
utterly unintelligible to all who did not see in the humble, despised,
Nazarene, and in His teaching, the Kingdom. But to those whose
eyes, ears and hearts had been opened, they would carry most
needed instruction and most precious comfort and assurance. Accordingly, we do not find that the disciples either asked or received
an interpretation of these Parables.

A few remarks will set the special meaning of these Parables
more clearly before us. Here also the illustrations used may have
been at hand. Close by the fields, covered with the fresh green or
growing corn, to which Jesus had pointed, may have been the garden
with its growing herbs, bushes and plants, and the home of the
householder, whose wife may at that moment have been in sight,
busy preparing the weekly provision of bread. At any rate, it is
necessary to keep in mind the *homeliness* of these illustrations.
The very idea of Parables implies, not strict scientific accuracy, but
popular pictorialness. It is characteristic of them to present vivid
sketches that appeal to the popular mind, and exhibit such analogies
of higher truths as can be readily perceived by all. Those addressed
were not to weigh every detail, either logically or scientifically, but
at once to recognise the aptness of the illustration as presented to
the popular mind. Thus, as regards the first of these two Parables,
the seed of the mustard-plant passed in popular parlance as the
smallest of seeds.[2] In fact, the expression, 'small as a mustard-seed,'

---

[1] Without here anticipating what may
have to be said as to Christ's teaching of
the final fate of the wicked, it cannot be
questioned that at that period the doctrine of endless punishment was the
common belief of the Jews. I am aware,
that dogmas should not be based upon
parabolic teaching, but in the present
instance the Parable would have been
differently worded, if such dogmatic
teaching had not been in the mind of
Speaker and hearers.

[2] Certainly the *Sinapis nigra*, and not
the *Salvadora persica*.

had become proverbial, and was used, not only by our Lord,[a] but fre-   CHAP.
quently by the Rabbis, to indicate the smallest amount, such as the   XXIII
least drop of blood,[b] the least defilement,[c] or the smallest remnant of
sun-glow in the sky.[d]   'But when it is grown, it is greater than the   [a] St. Matt.
garden-herbs.'   Indeed, it looks no longer like a large garden-herb   xvii. 20
or shrub, but 'becomes,' or rather, appears like, 'a tree '—as St. Luke   [b] Ber. 31 a
puts it, 'a great tree,' [e] of course, not in comparison with other trees,   [c] Nidd. v. 2
but with garden-shrubs.   Such growth of the mustard seed was also a   [d] Vayyik.
                                                                            R. 31, ed.
fact well known at the time, and, indeed, still observed in the East.[1]   Warsh.,
This is the first and main point in the Parable.   The other, con-   vol. iii. p.
cerning the birds which are attracted to its branches and 'lodge '—   48 a
                                                                            [e] St. Luke
literally, 'make tents' [2]—there, or else under the shadow of it,[f] is   xiii. 18, 19
subsidiary.   Pictorial, of course, this trait would be, and we can the   [f] St. Mark
more readily understand that birds would be attracted to the branches   iv. 32
or the shadow of the mustard-plant, when we know that mustard was
in Palestine mixed with, or used as food for pigeons,[g] and presumably   [g] Jer.
would be sought by other birds.   And the general meaning would the   Shabb. 16 c
more easily be apprehended, that a tree, whose wide-spreading branches
afforded lodgment to the birds of heaven, was a familiar Old Testament figure for a mighty kingdom that gave shelter to the nations.[h]   [h] Ezek.
Indeed, it is specifically used as an illustration of the Messianic   xxxi. 6, 12;
                                                                            Dan. iv. 12,
Kingdom.[i]   Thus the Parable would point to this, so full of mystery   14, 21, 22
to the Jews, so explanatory of the mystery to the disciples: that the   [i] Ezek. xvii.
Kingdom of Heaven, planted in the field of the world as the smallest   23
seed, in the most humble and unpromising manner, would grow till it
far outstripped all other similar plants, and gave shelter to all nations
under heaven.

To this *extensive* power of the Kingdom corresponded its *intensive*
character, whether in the world at large or in the individual.   This
formed the subject of the last of the Parables addressed at this time
to the people—that of the Leaven.   We need not here resort to
ingenious methods of explaining 'the three measures,' or *Seahs*, of
meal in which the leaven was hid.   Three Seahs were an Ephah,[k] of   [k] Men. vii.
which the exact capacity differed in various districts.   According to
the so-called 'wilderness,' or original Biblical, measurement, it was

---

[1] Comp. *Tristram*, Nat. Hist. of the
Bible, p. 472.   The quotations in *Buxtorf's* Lex. Rabb. pp. 822, 823, on which
the supposed Rabbinic illustrations of
the growth of the plant are based (*Lightfoot, Schöttgen, Wetstein*, even *Vorstius*
and *Winer*), are wholly inapt, being taken
from legendary descriptions of the future

glory of Palestine—the exaggerations
being of the grossest character.
[2] Canon *Tristram's* rendering of the
verb (u. s. p. 473) as merely perching or
resting does not give the real meaning of
it.   He has very aptly noticed how fond
birds are of the mustard-seed.

BOOK
III

ᵃ Erub. viii.
2; 83 a
ᵇ Comp.
Gen. xviii.
6; Judg. vi.
19; 1 Sam. i.
24; Jos. Ant.
ix. 4, 5;
Babha B.
9 a, &c.

supposed to be a space holding 432 eggs,ᵃ while the Jerusalem ephah was one-fifth, and the Sepphoris (or Galilean) ephah two-fifths, or, according to another authority, one-half larger.[1] To mix 'three measures' of meal was common in Biblical, as well as in later times.ᵇ Nothing further was therefore conveyed than the common process of ordinary, everyday life. And in this, indeed, lies the very point of the Parable, that the Kingdom of God, when received within, would seem like leaven hid, but would gradually pervade, assimilate, and transform the whole of our common life.

With this most un-Jewish, and, to the unbelieving multitude, most mysterious characterisation of the Kingdom of Heaven, the Saviour dismissed the people. Enough had been said to them and for them, if they had but ears to hear. And now He was again alone with the disciples 'in the house' at Capernaum, to which they had

ᶜ St. Matt.
xiii. 36;
comp. ver.
10, and St.
Mark iv. 10

returnedᶜ. Many new and deeper thoughts of the Kingdom had come to them. But why had He so spoken to the multitude, in a manner so different, as regarded not only the form, but even the substance of His teaching? And did they quite understand its solemn meaning themselves? More especially, who was the enemy whose activity would threaten the safety of the harvest? Of that

ᵈ St. John
iv. 35

harvest they had already heard on the way through Samaria.ᵈ And what were those 'tares,' which were to continue in their very midst till the judicial separation of the end? To these questions Jesus now made answer. His statement of the reason for adopting in the present instance the parabolic mode of teaching would, at the same time, give them farther insight into those very mysteries of the Kingdom which it had been the object of these Parables to set forth.[2] His unsolicited explanation of the details of the first Parable would call attention to points that might readily have escaped their

---

[1] Comp. *Herzfeld*, Handelsgesch. d. Juden, pp. 183–185.

[2] On Is. lxi. 10, we read the following beautiful illustration, alike of the words of our Lord in St. Matt. xiii. 16, and of the exclamation of the woman in St. Luke xi. 27: 'Seven garments there are with which the Holy One, blessed be His Name, clothed Himself, from the time the world was created to the hour when He will execute punishment on Edom the wicked (Rome). When He created the world, He clothed himself with glory and splendour (Ps. civ. 1); when He manifested Himself by the Red Sea, He clothed Himself with majesty (Ps. xciii. 1); when He gave the Law, He clothed Himself with strength (*ib.*); when He forgives the iniquity of Israel, He clothes Himself in white (Dan. vii. 9); when He executeth punishment on the nations of the world, He clothes himself with vengeance (Is. lix. 17). The sixth garment He will put on in the hour when the Messiah shall be revealed. Then shall He clothe Himself with righteousness (*ib.*). The seventh garment is when He taketh vengeance on Edom, then shall He be clothed in red (Is. lxiii. 2), and the garment with which in the future He will clothe Messiah shall shine forth from one end of the world to the other, according to Is. lxi. 10. And Israel shall enjoy His light, and say, Blessed the hour in

notice, but which, for warning and instruction, it most behoved them to keep in view.

The understanding of the first Parable seems to have shown them, how much hidden meaning this teaching conveyed, and to have stimulated their desire for comprehending what the presence and machinations of the hostile Pharisees might, in some measure, lead them to perceive in dim outline. Yet it was not to the Pharisees that the Lord referred. The Enemy was the Devil; the field, the world; the good seed, the children of the Kingdom; the tares, the children of the Wicked One. And most markedly did the Lord, in this instance, not explain the Parable, as the first one, in its details, but only indicate, so to speak, the stepping-stones for its understanding. This, not only to train the disciples, but because—unlike the first Parable—that of the Tares would only in the future and increasingly unfold its meaning.

But even this was not all. The disciples had now knowledge concerning the mysteries of the Kingdom. But that Kingdom was not matter of the understanding only, but of personal apprehension. This implied discovery of its value, personal acquisition of it, and surrender of all to its possession. And this mystery of the Kingdom was next conveyed to the disciples in those Parables specially addressed to, and suited only for, them.

Kindred, or rather closely connected, as are the two Parables of the Treasure hid in the Field and of the Pearl of Great Price—now spoken to the disciples—their differences are sufficiently marked. In the first, one who must probably be regarded as intending to buy a, if not this, field, discovers a treasure hidden there, and in his joy parts with all else to become owner [1] of the field and of the hidden treasure which he had so unexpectedly found. Some difficulty has been expressed in regard to the morality of such a transaction. In reply it may be observed, that it was, at least, in entire accordance with Jewish law.[a][2] If a man had found a treasure in loose coins

[a] B. Mets.
25 a, b.

which Messiah was born; blessed the womb which bare Him; blessed the generation which seeth, blessed the eye which is deemed worthy to behold Him, because that the opening of His lips is blessing and peace, His speech rest to the soul, and security and rest are in His Word. And on His tongue pardon and forgiveness; His prayer the incense of accepted sacrifice; His entreaty holiness and purity. Blessed are ye Israel—what is reserved for you! Even as it is written (Ps. xxxi. 20; 19 in our A.V.). (Pesiqta, ed. *Bub.*

p. 149 *a* and *b*.)

[1] The $\check{\epsilon}\mu\pi o\rho o\varsigma$—in opposition to the $\kappa\acute{\alpha}\pi\eta\lambda o\varsigma$, or huckster, small trader—is the *en gros* merchant who travels from place to place and across waters (from $\pi\acute{o}\rho o\varsigma$) to purchase.

[2] But the instance quoted by *Wetstein* (N. Test. i. p. 407) from Babha Mez. 28 *b* is inapt, and depends on entire misunderstanding of the passage. The Rabbi who found the treasure, so far from claiming, urged its owner to take it back.

among the corn, it would certainly be his, if he bought the corn. If he had found it on the ground, or in the soil, it would equally certainly belong to him, if he could claim ownership of the soil, and even if the field were not his own, unless others could *prove* their right to it. The law went so far as to adjudge to the purchaser of fruits anything found among these fruits. This will suffice to vindicate a question of detail, which, in any case, should not be too closely pressed in a parabolic history.

But to resume our analysis. In the second Parable we have a wise merchantman who travels in search of pearls, and when he finds one which in value exceeds all else, he returns and sells all that he has, in order to buy this unique gem. The supreme value of the Kingdom, the consequent desire to appropriate it, and the necessity of parting with all else for this purpose, are the points common to this and the previous Parable. But in the one case, it is marked that this treasure is hid from common view in the field, and the finder makes unexpected discovery of it, which fills him with joy. In the other case, the merchantman is, indeed, in search of pearls, but he has the wisdom to discover the transcendent value of this one gem, and the yet greater wisdom to give up all further search and to acquire it at the surrender of everything else. Thus, two different aspects of the Kingdom, and two different conditions, on the part of those who, for its sake, equally part with all, are here set before the disciples.

Nor was the closing Parable of the Draw-net less needful. Assuredly it became, and would more and more become, them to know, that mere discipleship—mere inclusion in the Gospel-net— was not sufficient. That net let down into the sea of this world would include much which, when the net was at last drawn to shore, would prove worthless or even hurtful. To be a disciple, then, was not enough. Even here there would be separation. Not only the tares, which the Enemy had designedly sown into the midst of the wheat, but even much that the Gospel-net, cast into the sea, had inclosed, would, when brought to land, prove fit only to be cast away, into ' the oven of the fire where there is the wailing and the gnashing of teeth. '

So ended that spring-day of first teaching in Parables, to the people by the Lake, and in the house at Capernaum to the disciples. Dim, shadowy outlines, growing larger and more faint in their tracings to the people; shadowy outlines, growing brighter and clearer to all who were disciples. Most wondrous instruction to all, and in all aspects of it; which even negative critics admit to have really formed part of Christ's own original teaching. But if this be the case, we have two questions of decisive character to ask. Undoubtedly, these Parables were un-Jewish. This appears, not only from a comparison with the Jewish views of the Kingdom, but from the fact that their meaning was unintelligible to the hearers of Jesus, and from this, that, rich as Jewish teaching is in Parables, none in the least parallel to them can be adduced.[1] Our first question, therefore, is: Whence this un-Jewish and anti-Jewish teaching concerning the Kingdom on the part of Jesus of Nazareth?

Our second question goes still farther. For, if Jesus was not a Prophet—and, if a Prophet, then also the Son of God—yet no more strangely unexpected prophecy, minutely true in all its details, could be conceived, than that concerning His Kingdom which His parabolic description of it conveyed. Has not History, in the

---

[1] The so-called Rabbinic illustrations are inapt, except as *per contra*. Thus, on St. Matt. xiii. 17 it is to be remarked, that in Rabbinic opinion revelation of God's mysteries would only be granted to those who were righteous or learned. The Midr. on Eccl. i. 7 contains the following Parable in illustration (comp. Dan. ii. 21): A matron is asked, to which of two that would borrow she would lend money—to a rich or a poor man. And when she answers: To a rich man, since even if he lost it, he would be able to repay, she is told that similarly God gives not wisdom to fools, who would employ it for theatres and baths, &c., but to the sages, who make use of it in the Academies. A similar and even more strange explanation of Exod. xv. 26 occurs Ber. 40 *a*, where it is shown that God supports the full, and not, as man, an empty vessel. Hence, if we begin to learn, or repeat what we have learned, we shall learn more, and conversely also. Further, on ver. 12 we note, that 'to have taken away what one hath' is a Jewish proverbial expression: 'that which is in their hand shall be taken from them' (Ber. R. 20, ed. Warsh. p. 38 *b*, last two lines). Expressions similar to ver. 16 are used by the Rabbis, for ex. Chag. 14 *b*. In regard to ver. 11, R. Eliezer inferred from Exod. xv. 2 that servant-maids saw at the Red Sea what neither Ezekiel nor the prophets had seen, which

he corroborates from Ezek. i. 1 and Hos. xii. 10 (Mechilta, ed. *Weiss* p. 44 *a*). Another and much more beautiful parallelism has been given before. On ver. 19 it ought to be remarked that the Wicked One was not so much represented by the Rabbis as the Enemy of the Kingdom of God, but as that of individuals—indeed, was often described as identical with the evil impulse (Yetser haRa, comp. Chag. 16 *a*; B. Bathr. 16 *a*; Succ. 52 *a*). On ver. 22 we remark, that not riches, but poverty, was regarded by the Rabbis as that which choked the good seed. On ver. 39, we may remark a somewhat similar expression in B. Mez. 83 *b*: 'Let the Lord of the Vineyard come and remove the thorns.' On ver. 42, the expression 'oven of fire,' for Gehenna, is the popular Jewish one (חמצן). Similarly, the expression, 'gnashing of teeth,' chiefly characteristic of the anger and jealousy of those in Gehinnom, occurs in the Midrash on Eccl. i. 15. On ver. 44 we refer to the remarks and note on that Parable (p. 595). In connection with ver. 46, we remember that, in Shabb. 119 *a*, a story is told concerning a pearl for which a man had given his whole fortune, hoping thereby to prevent the latter being alienated from him (comp. Ber. R. 11). Lastly, in connection with ver. 47 we notice, that the comparison of men with fishes is a common Jewish one (Abod. Zar. 3 *b*; 4 *a*).

BOOK
III

strange, unexpected fulfilling of that which no human ingenuity at the time could have forecast, and no pen have described with more minute accuracy of detail, proved Him to be more than a mere man —One sent from God, the Divine King of the Divine Kingdom, in all the vicissitudes which such a Divine Kingdom must experience when set up upon earth?

CHAPTER XXIV.

CHRIST STILLS THE STORM ON THE LAKE OF GALILEE.

(St. Matt. viii. 18, 23–27; St. Mark iv. 35–41; St. Luke viii. 22–25.)

It was the evening of that day of new teaching, and once more great multitudes were gathering to Him. What more, or, indeed, what else, could He have said to those to whom He had all that morning spoken in Parables, which hearing they had not heard nor understood? It was this, rather than weariness after a long day's working, which led to the resolve to pass to the other side. To merely physical weariness Jesus never subordinated his work. If, therefore, such had been the motive, the proposal to withdraw for rest would have come from the disciples, while here the Lord Himself gave command to pass to the other side. In truth, after that day's teaching it was better, alike for these multitudes and for His disciples, that He should withdraw. And so 'they took Him even as He was' —that is, probably without refreshment of food, or even preparation of it for the journey. This indicates how readily, nay, eagerly, the disciples obeyed the behest.

Whether in their haste they heeded not the signs of the coming storm; whether they had the secret feeling, that ship and sea which bore such burden were safe from tempest; or, whether it was one of those storms which so often rise suddenly, and sweep with such fury over the Lake of Galilee, must remain undetermined. He was in 'the ship'[1]—whether that of the sons of Jonas, or of Zebedee—the well-known boat, which was always ready for His service, whether as pulpit, resting-place, or means of journeying. But the departure had not been so rapid as to pass unobserved; and the ship was attended by other boats, which bore those that would fain follow Him. In the stern of the ship, on the low bench where the steersman sometimes takes rest, was pillowed the Head of Jesus. Weariness, faintness, hunger, exhaustion, asserted their mastery over His true humanity.

---

[1] The definite article (St. Mark iv. 36) marks it as 'the' ship—a well-known boat which always bore Him.

BOOK
III

a Phil. ii. 6

He, Whom earliest Apostolic testimony [a] proclaimed to have been in 'the form of God,' slept. Even this evidences the truth of the whole narrative. If Apostolic tradition had devised this narrative to exhibit His Divine Power, why represent Him as faint and asleep in the ship; and, if it would portray Him as deeply sleeping for very weariness, how could it ascribe to Him the power of stilling the storm by His rebuke? Each of these by themselves, but not the two in their combination, would be as legends are written. Their coincidence is due to the incidence of truth. Indeed, it is characteristic of the History of the Christ, and all the more evidential that it is so evidently undesigned in the structure of the narrative, that every deepest manifestation of His Humanity is immediately attended by highest display of His Divinity, and each special display of His Divine Power followed by some marks of His true Humanity. Assuredly, no narrative could be more consistent with the fundamental assumption that He is the God-Man.

Thus viewed, the picture is unspeakably sublime. Jesus is asleep, for very weariness and hunger, in the stern of the ship, His head on that low wooden bench, while the heavens darken, the wild wind swoops down those mountain-gorges, howling with hungry rage over the trembling sea; the waves rise and toss, and lash and break over the ship, and beat into it, and the white foam washes at His feet His Humanity here appears as true as when He lay cradled in the manger; His Divinity, as when the sages from the East laid their offerings at His Feet. But the danger is increasing—'so that the ship was now filling.' [b] They who watched it, might be tempted to regard the peaceful rest of Jesus, not as indicative of Divine Majesty —as it were, sublime consciousness of absolute safety—because they did not fully realize Who He was. In that case it would, therefore, rather mean absolute weakness in not being able, even at such a time, to overcome the demands of our lower nature; real indifference, also, to their fate—not from want of sympathy, but of power. In short, it might lead up to the inference that the Christ was a no-Christ, and the Kingdom of which he had spoken in Parables, not His, in the sense of being identified with His Person.

b St. Mark
iv. 37

In all this we perceive already, in part, the internal connection between the teaching of that day and the miracle of that evening. Both were quite novel: the teaching by Parables, and then the help in a Parable. Both were founded on the Old Testament: the teaching on its predictions, [c] the miracle on its proclamations of the special Divine Manifestations in the sea; [d] and both show that everything

c Is. vi. 9, 10
d Ps. cvi. 9;
cvii. 25;
Is. li. 10;
Nah. i. 4–7;
Hab. iii. 8

depended on the view taken of the Person of the Christ. Further
teaching comes to us from the details of the narrative which follows.
It has been asked, with which of the words recorded by the Synoptists the disciples had wakened the Lord: with those of entreaty to
save them,[a] or with those of impatience, perhaps uttered by Peter
himself?[b] But why may not both accounts represent what had
passed? Similarly, it has been asked, which came first—the Lord's
rebuke of the disciples, and after it that of the wind and sea,[c] or the
converse?[d] But, may it not be that each recorded that first which
had most impressed itself on his mind?—St. Matthew, who had been
in the ship that night, the needful rebuke to the disciples; St. Mark
and St. Luke, who had heard it from others,[e] the help first, and then
the rebuke?

Yet it is not easy to understand what the disciples had really expected, when they wakened the Christ with their 'Lord, save us—we
perish!' Certainly, not that which actually happened, since not only
wonder, but fear, came over them[1] as they witnessed it. Probably
theirs would be a vague, undefined belief in the unlimited possibility
of all in connection with the Christ. A belief this, which seems to
us quite natural as we think of the gradually emerging, but still partially cloud-capped height of His Divinity, of which, as yet, only the
dim outlines were visible to them. A belief this, which also accounts
for the co-existing, not of disbelief, nor even of unbelief, but of inability of apprehension, which, as we have seen, characterised the
bearing of the Virgin-Mother. And it equally characterised that of
the disciples up to the Resurrection-morning, bringing them to the
empty tomb, and filling them with unbelieving wonder that the tomb
was empty. Thus, we have come to that stage in the History of the
Christ when, in opposition to the now formulated charge of His
enemies as to His Person, neither His Teaching nor His Working
could be fully understood, except so far as his Personality was understood—that He was of God and Very God. And so we are gradually
reaching on towards the expediency and the need of the coming of
the Holy Ghost to reveal that mystery of His Person. Similarly, the
two great stages in the history of the Church's learning were: the
first—to come to knowledge of what He was, by experience of what
He did; the second—to come to experience of what He did and does,
by knowledge of what He is. The former, which corresponds, in the

CHAP.
XXIV

[a] St. Matt.
and
St. Luke
[b] St. Mark

[c] St. Matt.
[d] St. Mark
and
St. Luke

[e] St. Mark
probably
from
St. Peter

---

[1] From the size of these boats it seems
unlikely, that any but His closest followers would have found room in the
ship. Besides, the language of those
who called for help and the answer of
Christ imply the same thing.

Old Testament, to the patriarchal age, is that of the period when Jesus was on earth; the second, which answers to the history of Israel, is that of the period after His Ascension into Heaven and the Descent of the Holy Ghost.

ᵃ St. Mark
iv. 38
ᵇ Ps. cvi. 9;
Nah. i. 4
ᶜ St. Luke
iv. 39
ᵈ St. Mark
ix. 25

When 'He was awakened'ᵃ by the voice of His disciples, 'He rebuked the wind and the sea,' as Jehovah had of oldᵇ—just as He had 'rebuked' the fever,ᶜ and the paroxysm of the demonised.ᵈ For, all are His creatures, even when lashed to frenzy of the 'hostile power.' And the sea He commanded as if it were a sentient being: 'Be silent! Be silenced!' And immediately the wind was bound, the panting waves throbbed into stillness, and a great calm of rest fell upon the Lake. For, when Christ sleepeth, there is storm; when He waketh, great peace. But over these men who had erst wakened Him with their cry, now crept wonderment, awe, and fear. No longer,

as at His first wonder-working in Capernaum, was it: '*What* is this?'ᵉ but '*Who*, then, is this?'[1] And so the grand question, which the enmity of the Pharisees had raised, and which, in part, had been answered in the Parables of teaching, was still more fully and practically met in what, not only to the disciples, but to all time, was a Parable of help. And Jesus also did wonder, but at that which alone could call forth His wonder—the unreachingness of their faith: where was it? and how was it, they had no faith?

Thus far the history, related, often almost in the same words, by the three Evangelists. On all sides the narrative is admitted to form part of the primitive Evangelic tradition. But if so, then, even on the showing of our opponents, it must have had some foundation in an event surpassing the ordinary facts in the history of Jesus. Accordingly, of all negative critics, at most only two venture to dismiss it as unfounded on fact. But such a bold assumption would rather increase than diminish the difficulty. For, if legend it be, its invention and insertion into the primitive record must have had some historical reason. Such, however, it is absolutely impossible here to trace. The Old Testament contains no analogous history which it might have been wished to imitate; Jewish Messianic expectancy afforded no basis for it; and there is absolutely no Rabbinic parallel[2] which could be placed by its side. Similar objections apply to the suggestion of exaggeration of some real event (*Keim*). For, the essence of the narrative lies in its details, of which the origin and the universal acceptance in the primitive belief of the Church have to be accounted

---

[1] So literally.

[2] The supposed Rabbinic parallels in (Chull. 7 *a*) works are quite inapplicable.

Wetstein (Babha Mez. 59 *b*) and *Wünsche's*

for. Nor is the task of those negative critics more easy, who, admitting the foundation in fact for this narrative, have suggested various theories to account for its miraculous details. Most of these explanations are so unnatural,[1] as only to point the contrast between the ingenuity of the nineteenth century and the simple, vivid language of the original narrative. For it seems equally impossible to regard it as based either on a misunderstanding of the words of Jesus during a storm (*Paulus*), or on the calm faith of Jesus when even the helmsman despaired of safety (*Schenkel*), or to represent it as only in some way a symbol of analogous mental phenomena (*Ammon, Schleiermacher, Hase, Weiszäcker*, and others). The very variety of explanations proposed, of which not one agrees with the others, shows, that none of them has proved satisfactory to any but their own inventors. And of all it may be said, that they have no foundation whatever in the narrative itself. Thus the only alternative left is either wholly to reject, or wholly to accept, the narrative.

If our judgment is to be determined by the ordinary rules of historical criticism, we cannot long be in doubt which of these propositions is true. Here is a narrative, which has the *consensus* of the three Evangelists; which admittedly formed part of the original Evangelic tradition; for the invention of which no specific motive can possibly be assigned; and which is told with a simplicity of language and a pictorial vividness of detail that carry their own evidence. Other corroborative points, such as the unlikeliness of the invention of such a situation for the Christ, or of such bearing of the disciples, have been previously indicated. Absolute historical demonstration of the event is, of course, in the nature of things impossible. But, besides the congruousness to the Parabolic teaching which had preceded this Parabolic miracle, and the accord of the Saviour's rebuke with His mode of silencing the hostile elements on other occasions, some further considerations in evidence may be offered to the thoughtful reader.

For, first, in this 'dominion over the sea,' we recognise, not only the fullest refutation of the Pharisaic misrepresentation of the Person of Christ, but the realisation in the Ideal Man of the ideal of man as heaven-destined,[a] and the initial fulfilment of the promise which this destination implied. 'Creation' has, indeed, been 'made subject to vanity;'[b] but this 'evil,' which implies not merely decay but

[a] Ps. viii. 4–8

[b] Rom. viii 20

---

[1] The strangest commentation, perhaps, is that of *Volkmar* (Marcus, pp. 307–312). For I cannot here perceive any kind of parallelism with the history of Jonah, nor yet see any references to the history of St. Paul's shipwreck.

BOOK
III

* Ber. R. 12

rebellion, was directly due to the Fall of man, and will be removed at the final 'manifestation of the sons of God.' And here St. Paul so far stands on the same ground as Jewish theology, which also teaches that 'although all things were created in their perfectness, yet when the first Adam sinned, they were corrupted.'ª Christ's dominion over the sea was, therefore, only the Second and Unfallen Adam's real dominion over creation, and the pledge of its restoration, and of our dominion in the future. And this seems also to throw fresh light on Christ's *rebuke*, whether of storm, disease, or demoniac possession. Thus there is a grand consistency in this narrative, as regards the Scriptural presentation of the Christ.

Again, the narrative expresses very markedly, that the interposition of Christ, alike in itself, and in the manner of it, was wholly unexpected by, indeed, contrary to the expectation of, the disciples. This also holds true in regard to other of the great manifestations of Christ, up to His Resurrection from the dead. This, of course, proves that the narrative was not founded on existing Jewish ideas. But there is more than this. The gratuitous introduction of traits which, so far from glorifying, would rather detract from a legendary Christ, while at the same time they seriously reflect on the disciples, presumably the inventors of the legend, appears to us wholly inconsistent with the assumption that the narrative is spurious.

Nor ought we to overlook another circumstance. While we regard the narrative as that of an historical occurrence—indeed, because we do so—we cannot fail to perceive its permanent symbolic and typical bearing. It were, indeed, impossible to describe either the history of the Church of Christ, or the experience of individual disciples, more accurately, or with wider and deeper capability of application, than in the Parable of this Miracle. And thus it is morally true to all ages; just because it was historically true at the first.[1] And as we enter on this field of contemplation, many views open to us. The true Humanity of the Saviour, by the side of His Divine Power; the sleeping Jesus and the Almighty Word of rebuke and command to the elements, which lay them down obedient at His feet: this sharp-edged contrast resolved into a higher unity—how true is it to the fundamental thought of the Gospel-History! Then this other contrast of the failure of faith, and then the excitement of the disciples; and of

---

[1] A fact may be the basis of a symbol; but a symbol can never be the basis of a fact. The former is the principle of Divine history, the latter of human legend. But, even so, legend could never have arisen but for a belief in Divine history: it is the counterfeit coin of Revelation.

the calm of the sleeping, and then the Majesty of the wakening
Christ. And, lastly, yet this third contrast of the helplessness and
despondency of the disciples and the Divine certitude of conscious
Omnipotence.

We perceive only difficulties and the seemingly impossible, as
we compare what may be before us with that which we consciously
possess. He also makes this outlook: but only to know and show,
that with Him there can be no difficulty, since all is His—and all may
be ours, since He has come for our help and is in the ship. One thing
only He wonders at—the shortcomings of our faith; and one thing
only makes it impossible for Him to help—our unbelief.

CHAPTER XXV.

AT GERASA—THE HEALING OF THE DEMONISED.

(St. Matt. viii. 28–34; St. Mark v. 1–20; St. Luke viii. 26–39.)

BOOK
III

THAT day of wonders was not yet ended. Most writers have, indeed, suggested, that the healing of the demonised on the other side took place at early dawn of the day following the storm on the Lake. But the distance is so short that, even making allowance for the delay by the tempest, the passage could scarcely have occupied the whole night.[1] This supposition would be further confirmed, if 'the evening' when Jesus embarked was what the Jews were wont to call 'the first evening,' that is, the time when the sun was declining in the heaven, but before it had actually set, the latter time being 'the second evening.'[2] For, it seems most unlikely that multitudes would have resorted to Jesus at Capernaum after 'the second evening,' or that either the disciples or other boats would have put to sea after nightfall. On the other hand, the scene gains in grandeur—has, so to speak, a fitting background—if we suppose the Saviour and His disciples to have landed on the other side late in the evening, when perhaps the silvery moon was shedding her pale light on the weird scene, and laying her halo around the shadows cast upon the sea by the steep cliff down which the herd of swine hurried and fell. This would also give time afterwards for the dispersion, not only into 'the city,' but into 'the country' of them who had fed the swine. In that case, of course, it would be in the early morning that the Gerasenes afterwards resorted to Jesus and that He again returned to Capernaum.

---

[1] In the history related in St. Matt. xiv. 22, &c. the embarkation was much later (see next note), and it is expressly stated that 'the wind was contrary.' But even there, when it ceased they were 'immediately' on shore (St. John vi. 21), although the distance formerly traversed had been rather less than three-fourths of the way (twenty-five or thirty furlongs, St. John vi. 19). At that place the whole distance across would be five or six miles. But the passage from Capernaum to Gerasa would not be so long as that.

[2] The distinction between the two evenings seems marked in St. Matt. xiv. 15, as compared with verse 23. In both verses precisely the same expression is used. But between the first and the second evening a considerable interval of time must be placed.

And, lastly, this would allow sufficient time for those miracles which
took place on that same day in Capernaum after His return thither.
Thus, all the circumstances lead us to regard the healing of the
demonised at Gerasa as a night-scene, immediately on Christ's arrival
from Capernaum, and after the calming of the storm at sea.

It gives not only life to the narrative, but greatly illustrates it,
that we can with confidence describe the exact place where our Lord
and His disciples touched the other shore. The ruins right over
against the plain of Gennesaret, which still bear the name of *Kersa* or
Gersa, must represent the ancient Gerasa.[1] This is the correct reading
in St. Mark's, and probably in St. Luke's, perhaps also in St. Matthew's Gospel.[2] The locality entirely meets the requirements of the
narrative. About a quarter of an hour to the south of Gersa is a
steep bluff, which descends abruptly on a narrow ledge of shore. A
terrified herd running down this cliff could not have recovered its
foothold, and must inevitably have been hurled into the Lake beneath.
Again, the whole country around is burrowed with limestone caverns
and rock-chambers for the dead, such as those which were the dwelling of the demonised. Altogether the scene forms a fitting background to the narrative.

From these tombs the demonised, who is specially singled out by
St. Mark and St. Luke, as well as his less prominent companion,[a] [a] St. Matt
came forth to meet Jesus. Much that is both erroneous and mis- viii. 28
leading has been written on Jewish Demonology. According to
common Jewish superstition, the evil spirits dwelt especially in lonely
desolate places, and also among tombs.[3] We must here remember
what has previously been explained as to the confusion in the
consciousness of the demonised between their own notions and the
ideas imposed on them by the demons. It is quite in accordance
with the Jewish notions of the demonised, that, according to the

---

[1] Comp. *Tristram's* 'Land of Israel,'
p. 465; *Bädeker's* (*Socin*) Pälestina, p.
267. The objection in *Riehm's* Handwörterb. p. 454, that Gerasa did not form
part of the Decapolis manifestly derives
no real support from St. Mark v. 20. The
two facts are in no way inconsistent. All
other localisations are impossible, since
the text requires close proximity to the
lake. Professor *Socin* describes this cliff
as steep 'as nowhere else by the lake.'

[2] In this, as in all other instances, I
can only indicate the critical results at
which I have arrived. For the grounds
on which these conclusions are based, I
must refer to the works which bear on

the respective subjects.

[2] See Appendix XIII., 'Angelology
and Demonology:' and Appendix XVI.,
'Jewish Views about Demons and the Demonised.' Archdeacon *Farrar* has misunderstood the reference of *Otho* (Lex.
Rabb. 146). The affections mentioned
in Jer. Terum. 40 *b* are not treated as
'all demoniacs;' on the contrary, most
of them, indeed all, with one exception,
are expressly stated to be indications of
mental disease (comp. also Chag. 3 *b*).
The quotations of *Gfrörer* are, as too
often, for a purpose, and untrustworthy,
except after examination of the context.

more circumstantial account of St. Luke, he should feel as it were driven into the deserts, and that he was in the tombs, while, according to St. Mark, he was 'night and day in the tombs and in the mountains,' the very order of the words indicating the notion (as in Jewish belief), that it was chiefly at night that evil spirits were wont to haunt burying-places.

In calling attention to this and similar particulars, we repeat, that this must be kept in view as characteristic of the demonised, that they were incapable of separating their own consciousness and ideas from the influence of the demon, their own identity being merged, and to that extent lost, in that of their tormentors. In this respect the demonised state was also kindred to madness. Self-consciousness, or rather what may be termed *Individuism, i.e.* the consciousness of distinct and independent individuality, and with it the power of self-origination in matters mental and moral (which some might term an aspect of free volition), distinguish the human soul from the mere animal spirit. But in maniacal disease this power is in abeyance, or temporarily lost through physical causes, such as disease of the brain as the medium of communication between the mind and the world of sense; disease of the nervous system, through which ordinarily impressions are conveyed to and from the *sensorium*; or disease of both brain and nervous system, when previously existing impressions on the brain (in memory, and hence possibly imagination) may be excited without corresponding outward causes. If in such cases the absolute power of self-origination and self-action is lost to the mind, habits of sin and vice (or moral disease) may have an analogous effect as regards moral freedom—the power of moral self-origination and action. In the demonised state the two appear combined, the cause being neither disease nor vice, but the presence of a superior power of evil. This loss of individuism, and the subjection of one's identity to that of the demon might, while it lasted, be called *temporary* ' possession,' in so far as the mental and moral condition of the person was for the time not one of freedom and origination, but in the control of the possessing demon.

One practical inference may even now be drawn from this somewhat abstruse discussion. The language and conduct of the demonised, whether seemingly his own, or that of the demons who influenced him, must always be regarded as a mixture of the Jewish-human and the demoniacal. The demonised speaks and acts as a Jew under the control of a demon. Thus, if he chooses solitary places by day, and tombs by night, it is not that demons really preferred such habitations, but that the Jews imagined it, and that the demons, acting on the existing consciousness, would lead him, in accordance with his pre-conceived notions, to select such places. Here also mental disease offers points of analogy. For, the demonised would speak and act in accordance with his previous (Jewish) demonological ideas. He would not become a new man, but be the old man, only under the influence of the demon, just as in mania a person truly and con-sistently speaks and acts, although under the false impressions which a diseased brain conveys to him. The fact that in the demonised state a man's identity was not superseded, but controlled, enables us to account for many phenomena without either confounding demonism with mania, or else imputing to our Lord such accommodation to the notions of the times, as is not only untenable in itself, but forbidden even by the language of the present narrative.

The description of the demonised, coming out of the tombs to meet Jesus as He touched the shore at Gerasa, is vivid in the extreme. His violence, the impossibility of control by others,[1] the absence of self-control,[2] his homicidal,[3] and almost suicidal,[4] frenzy, are all depicted. Evidently, it was the object to set forth the extreme degree of the demonised state. Christ, Who had been charged by the Pharisees with being the embodiment and messenger of Satan, is here face to face with the extreme manifestation of demoniac power and influence. It is once more, then, a Miracle in Parable which is about to take place. The question, which had been raised by the enemies, is about to be brought to the issue of a practical demonstra-tion. We do not deny that the contest and the victory, this miracle, nay, the whole series of miracles of which it forms part, are extra-ordinary, even in the series of Christ's miracles. Our explanation proceeds on the very ground that such was, and must have been, the case. The teaching by Parables, and the parabolic miracles which follow, form, so to speak, an ascending climax, in contrast to the terrible charge which by-and-by would assume the proportions of blasphemy against the Holy Ghost, and issue in the betrayal and judicial murder of Jesus. There are critical epochs in the history of the Kingdom of God, when the power of evil, standing out in sharpest contrast, challenges that overwhelming manifestation of the Divine, as such, to bear down and crush that which opposes it.

---

[1] St. Mark v. 3, 4.
[2] 'Ware no clothes' (St. Luke viii. 27) may, however, refer only to the upper, not the under-garments.
[3] St. Matt. viii. 28.
[4] St. Mark v. 5.

Periods of that kind are characterised by miraculous interposition of power, unique even in Bible-history. Such a period was, under the Old Testament, that of Elijah and Elisha, with its altogether exceptional series of miracles; and,· under the New Testament, that after the first formulated charge of the Pharisees against the Christ.

With irresistible power the demonised was drawn to Jesus, as He touched the shore at Gerasa. As always, the first effect of the contact was a fresh paroxysm,[1] but in this peculiar case not physical, but moral. As always also, the demons knew Jesus, and His Presence seemed to constrain their confession of themselves—and therefore of Him. As in nature the introduction of a dominant element sometimes reveals the hidden presence of others, which are either attracted or repelled by it, so the Presence of Christ obliged the manifestation, and, in the case of these evil spirits, the self-confession, of the powers of evil. In some measure it is the same still. The introduction of grace brings to light and experience sin hitherto unknown, and the new life brings consciousness of, and provokes contest with, evil within, of which the very existence had previously been unsuspected. In the present instance the immediate effect was homage,[a] which presently manifested itself in language such as might have been expected.

ᵃ St. Mark
v. 6;
St. Luke
viii. 28

Here also it must be remembered, that both the act of homage, or ' worship,' and the words spoken, were not the outcome either of the demonised only, nor yet of the demons only, but a combination of the two: the control of the demons being absolute over the man such as he was. *Their* language led to *his* worship; *their* feelings and fears appeared in *his* language. It was the self-confession of the *demons*, when obliged to come into His Presence and do homage, which made the *man* fall down and, in the well-known Jewish formula, recorded by the three Evangelists, say: ' What have I to do with Thee,' or rather, ' What between me and Thee'—what have we in common (*Mah li valakh*)? Similarly, although it was consciousness of subjection and fear in His Presence, on the part of the demons, which underlay the adjuration not to inflict torment on them, yet the language itself, as the text shows, was that of the

---

[1] In his endeavour to represent the demonised state as a species of mania, which was affected by the Presence of Christ, Archdeacon *Farrar* makes the following statement: ' The presence, the look, the voice of Christ, even before He addressed these sufferers, seems always to have calmed and overawed them.' But surely the very opposite of this is the fact, and the first effect of contact with Christ was not calm, but a paroxysm.

demonised, and the form in which their fear expressed itself was
that of *his* thinking. The demons, in their hold on their victim,
could not but own their inferiority, and apprehend their defeat and
subjection, especially on such an occasion; and the Jew, whose consciousness was under their control—not unified, but identified with it
—exclaimed: ' I adjure Thee by God, that Thou torment me not.'

This strange mixture of the demoniac with the human, or rather,
this expression of underlying demoniac thought in the forms and
modes of thinking of the Jewish victim, explains the expressed fear
of present actual torment, or, as St. Matthew, who, from the briefness
of his account, does not seem to have been an eye-witness, expresses
it: ' Thou art come to torment us before the time;' and possibly also
for the 'adjuration by God.'[1] For, as immediately on the homage
and protestation of the demonised: 'What between me and Thee,
Jesus, Thou Son of the Most High God?' Christ had commanded
the unclean spirit to come out of the man, it may have been, that in
so doing He had used the Name of the Most High God; or else the
'adjuration' itself may have been the form in which the Jewish
speaker clothed the consciousness of the demons, with which his own
was identified.

It may be conjectured, that it was partly in order to break this
identification, or rather to show the demonised that it was not real,
and only the consequence of the control which the demons had over
him, that the Lord asked his name. To this the man made answer,
still in the dual consciousness, ' My name is Legion: for we are
many.'[2] Such might be the subjective motive for Christ's question.
Its objective reason may have been to show the power of the demoniac
possession in the present instance, thus marking it as an altogether
extreme case. The remembrance, that the answer is once more in
the forms of Jewish thinking, enables us to avoid the strange notion
(whether it express the opinion of some, or the difficulties of others),
that the word 'Legion' conveys the idea of six thousand armed and
strong warriors of evil. [3] For, it was a common Jewish idea, that,

---

[1] Both St. Mark and St. Luke have it:
' Jesus, Son of the Most High God.'

[2] So substantially in St. Luke, as in
St. Mark.

[3] This is one of the difficulties mentioned by Dean *Plumptre*. Archdeacon
Farrar seems to think that the man
imagined ' 6000 devils were in possession of his soul.' His statement, that it

' was a thoroughly Jewish belief' that
unclean spirits should pass into the
swine, I must take leave to deny. One
or another disease, such as *rabies*, were,
indeed, attributed by some Rabbis to
the agency of evil spirits—but there is
no ground for either the general or the
specific statement of Dr. Farrar as regards this ' Jewish belief.'

Ber. 51 a

under certain circumstances, 'a legion of hurtful spirits'[1] (of course not in the sense of a Roman legion) 'were on the watch for men, saying: When shall he fall into the hands of one of these things, and be taken?'[a]

This identification of the demons with the demonised, in consequence of which he thought with their consciousness, and they spoke not only through him but in his forms of thinking, may also account for the last and most difficult part of this narrative. Their main object and wish was not to be banished from the country and people, or, as St. Luke puts it—again to 'depart into the abyss.' Let us now try to realise the scene. On the very narrow strip of shore, between the steep cliff that rises in the background and the Lake, stand Jesus with His disciples and the demonised. The wish of the demons is not to be sent out of the country—not back into the abyss. The one is the cliff overhead, the other the Lake beneath: so, symbolically, and, to the demonised, really. Up on that cliff a great herd of swine is feeding; up that cliff, therefore, is 'into the swine;' and this also agrees with Jewish thoughts concerning uncleanness. The rendering of our Authorised Version,[b] that, in reply to the demoniac entreaty, 'forthwith Jesus gave them leave,' has led to misunderstanding. The distinction here to be made is, though narrow, yet real and important. The verb, which is the same in all the three Gospels, would be better rendered by 'suffered' than by 'gave them leave.' With the latter we associate positive permission. None such was either asked or given. The Lord suffered it—that is, He did not actually hinder it.[2] He only 'said unto them, Go!'

What followed belongs to the phenomena of supersensuous influences upon animals, of which many instances are recorded, but the *rationale* of which it is impossible to explain. How the unclean spirits could enter into the swine, is a question which cannot be entertained till we shall know more of the animal soul than is at present within our range. This, however, we can understand, that under such circumstances a panic would seize the herd, that it would madly rush down the steep on which it could not arrest itself, and so perish in the sea. And this also we can perceive, how the real object of the demons was thus attained; how they did *not* leave the country, when Christ was entreated to leave it.

[b] St. Mark
v. 13

---

[1] The common Rabbinic word for Legion is, indeed, *Ligyon* or *Ligyona*, but the expression (Ber. 51 *a*) אִסְטַלְגִּינִית (Istalginith) שַׂר מַלְאֲכֵי חַבָּלָה cannot mean anything else than a legion of hurtful spirits.

[2] The verb ἐπιτρέπω is used both in the active sense of permitting, and in that of not hindering. As to the latter use of the word, comp. specially St. Matt. xix. 8; St. Mark x. 4.

The weird scene over which the moon had shed her ghostlike light, was past.   The unearthly utterances of the demonised, the wild panic among the herd on the cliff, the mad rush down the steep, the splashing waters as the helpless animals were precipitated into the Lake—all this makes up a picture, unsurpassed for vivid, terrible realism.   And now sudden silence has fallen on them.   From above, the keepers of the herd had seen it all—alike what had passed with the demonised, and then the issue in the destruction of the herd.   From the first, as they saw the demonised, for fear of whom 'no man might pass that way,' running to Jesus, they must have watched with eager interest.   In the clear Eastern air not a word that was spoken could have been lost.   And now in wild terror they fled, into Gerasa—into the country round about, to tell what had happened.

It is morning, and a new morning-sacrifice and morning-Psalm are about to be offered.   He that had erst been the possession of foul and evil spirits—a very legion of them—and deprived of his human individuality, is now 'sitting at the feet of Jesus,' learning of Him, 'clothed and in his right mind.'   He has been brought to God, restored to self, to reason, and to human society—and all this by Jesus, at Whose Feet he is gratefully, humbly sitting, 'a disciple.' Is He not then the Very Son of God?   Viewing this miracle, as an historical fact, viewing it as a Parabolic Miracle, viewing it also as symbolic of what has happened in all ages—is He not the Son of the Most High God?   And is there not now, on His part, in the morning-light the same calmness and majesty of conscious Almighty Power as on the evening before, when He rebuked the storm and calmed the sea?

One other point as regards the healing of this domonism deserves special consideration.   Contrary to what was commonly the case, when the evil spirits came out of the demonised, there was no paroxysm of *physical* distress.   Was it then so, that the more complete and lasting the demoniac possession, the less of purely physical symptoms attended it?

But now from town and country have they come, who had been startled by the tidings which those who fed the swine had brought. We may contrast the scene with that of the shepherds when on Bethlehem's plains the great revelation had come to them, and they had seen the Divine Babe laid in the manger, and had worshipped. Far other were the tidings which these herdsmen brought, and their effect.   It is not necessary to suppose, that their request that Jesus would depart out of their coasts was prompted only by the loss of the herd of swine.[1]   There could be no doubt in their minds, that One possessing supreme and unlimited power was in their midst.   Among men superstitious, and unwilling to submit absolutely to the Kingdom which Christ brought, there could only be one effect of what they had heard, and now witnessed in the person of the healed demonised —awe and fear!   The 'Depart from me, for I am a sinful man,' is the natural expression of a mind conscious of sin when brought into contact with the Divine, Whose supreme and absolute Power is realised as hostile.   And this feeling would be greatly increased, in measure as the mind was under the influence of superstitious fears.

In such place and circumstances Jesus could not have continued. And, as He entered the ship, the healed demonised humbly, earnestly entreated, that he might go with his Saviour.   It would have seemed to him, as if he could not bear to lose his new found happiness; as if there were calm, safety, and happiness only in His Presence; not far from Him—not among those wild mountains and yet wilder men. Why should he be driven from His fellowship, who had so long been an outcast from that of his fellow-men, and why again left to himself? So, perhaps, should we have reasoned and spoken; so too often do we reason and speak, as regards ourselves or those we love.   Not so He Who appoints alike our discipline and our work.   To go back, now healed, to his own, and to publish there, in the city—nay, through the whole of the large district of the ten confederate cities, the Decapolis—how great things Jesus had done for him, such was henceforth to be his life-work.   In this there would be both safety and happiness.

'And all men did marvel.'   And presently Jesus Himself came back into that Decapolis, where the healed demonised had prepared the way for Him.[2]

---

[1] This is the view of Archdeacon *Farrar*. The Gadara of which the poets *Meleager* and *Philodemus* were natives was, of course, not the scene of this miracle.

[2] As this healing of the demonised may be regarded as the 'test-case' on the general question, I have entered more fully on the discussion. The arguments in favour of the general view taken of the demonised are so clearly and forcibly stated by Archbishop *Trench* (on 'The Miracles') and in 'The Speaker's Commentary' (N. Test. vol. i.

p. 44), that it seems needless to reiterate them. To me at least it seems difficult to understand, how any reader of the narrative, who comes to it without preconceived opinions, can arrive at any other conclusion than that either the whole must be rejected as mythical, or else be received as implying that there was a demonised state, different from madness; that Jesus treated the present as such; bade the unclean spirits go out, and by His word banished them. The objection as to the morality of the destruction of the herd seems scarcely more weighty than the sneer of *Strauss*, that the devils must have been stupid in immediately destroying their new habitations. The question of morality cannot even be raised, since Jesus did not command—only not hinder—the devils entering into the swine, and as for the destruction of their new dwellings, so far from being stupid, it certainly did secure their undisturbed continuance in the country and the withdrawal of Jesus. All attempts to adapt this miracle to our modern experience, and the ideas based upon it, by leaving out or rationalising one or another trait in the narrative, are emphatically failures. We repeat: the history must be received as it stands—or wholly rejected.

CHAPTER XXVI.

THE HEALING OF THE WOMAN—CHRIST'S PERSONAL APPEARANCE—
THE RAISING OF JAIRUS' DAUGHTER.

(St. Matt. ix. 18–26; St. Mark v. 21–43; St. Luke viii. 40–56.)

BOOK
III

THERE seems remarkable correspondence between the two miracles which Jesus had wrought on leaving Capernaum and those which He did on His return. In one sense they are complementary to each other. The stilling of the storm and the healing of the demonised were manifestations of the absolute power inherent in Christ; the recovery of the woman and the raising of Jairus' daughter, evidence of the absolute efficacy of faith. The unlikeliness of dominion over the storm, and of command over a legion of demons, answers to that of recovery obtained in such a manner, and of restoration when disease had passed into actual death. Even the circumstances seem to correspond, though at opposite poles; in the one case, the Word spoken to the unconscious element, in the other the touch of the unconscious Christ; in the one case the absolute command of Christ over a world of resisting demons, in the other absolute certainty of faith as against the hostile element, of actual fact. Thus the Divine character of the Saviour appears in the absoluteness of His Omnipotence, and the Divine character of His Mission in the all-powerfulness of faith which it called forth.

On the shore at Capernaum many were gathered on the morning after the storm. It may have been, that the boats which had accompanied His had returned to friendly shelter, ere the storm had risen to full fury, and had brought anxious tidings of the storm out on the Lake. There they were gathered now in the calm morning, friends eagerly looking out for the well-known boat that bore the Master and His disciples. And as it came in sight, making again for Capernaum, the multitude also would gather in waiting for the return of Him, Whose words and deeds were indeed mysteries, but mysteries of the Kingdom. And quickly, as He again stepped on the well-known shore, was He welcomed, surrounded, soon 'thronged,' inconveniently pressed upon,[1] by the crowd, eager, curious, expectant. It seemed as if they had been all 'waiting for Him,' and He had been away all too long for their impatience. The tidings rapidly spread, and reached two homes where His help was needed; where, indeed, it alone could now be of possible avail. The two most nearly concerned must have gone to seek that help about the same time, and prompted by the same feelings of expectancy. Both Jairus, the Ruler of the Synagogue, and the woman suffering these many years from disease, had faith. But the weakness of the one arose from excess, and threatened to merge into superstition, while the weakness of the other was due to defect, and threatened to end in despair. In both cases faith had to be called out, tried, purified, and so perfected; in both the thing sought for was, humanely speaking, unattainable, and the means employed seemingly powerless; yet, in both, the outward and inward results required were obtained through the power of Christ, and by the peculiar discipline to which, in His all-wise arranging, faith was subjected.

It sounds almost like a confession of absolute defeat, when negative critics (such as *Keim*) have to ground their mythical explanation of this history on the supposed symbolical meaning of what they designate as the fictitious name of the Ruler of the Synagogue— *Jair*, 'he will give light'[a]—and when they[b] further appeal to the correspondence between the age of the maiden and the years (twelve) during which the woman had suffered from the bloody flux. This coincidence is, indeed, so trivial as not to deserve serious notice; since there can be no conceivable connection between the age of the child and the duration of the woman's disease, nor, indeed, between the two cases, except in this, that both appealed to Jesus. As regards the name *Jairus*, the supposed symbolism is inapt; while internal reasons are opposed to the hypothesis of its fictitiousness. For, it seems most unlikely that St. Mark and St. Luke would have rendered the discovery of ' a myth ' easy by needlessly breaking the silence of St. Matthew, and giving the name of so well-known a person as a Synagogue-ruler of Capernaum. And this the more readily, that the name, though occurring in the Old Testament, and in the ranks of the Nationalist party in the last Jewish War,[c] was apparently not a common one.[2] But these are comparatively small difficulties in the way of the mythical interpretation.

CHAP.
XXVI

[a] Jesu v. Nazar. ii. 2, p. 472

[b] *Strauss,* Leben Jesu ii. p. 135

[c] *Jos.* Jewish War vi. 1. 8, close

---

[1] Comp. St. Luke viii. 45; St. Mark v. 31.

[2] The name, a well-known O.T. one

(Numb. xxxii. 41; Judg., x. 3), does not occur in Rabbinic literature till after the Middle Ages.

Jairus, one of the Synagogue-rulers [1] of Capernaum, had an only daughter, [2] who at the time of this narrative had just passed childhood, and reached the period when Jewish Law declared a woman of age. [3] Although St. Matthew, contracting the whole narrative into briefest summary, speaks of her as dead at the time of Jairus' application to Jesus, the other two Evangelists, giving fuller details, describe her as on the point of death, literally, ' at the last breath ' (*in extremis*). [4] Unless her disease had been both sudden and exceedingly rapid, which is barely possible, it is difficult to understand why her father had not on the previous day applied to Jesus, if his faith had been such as is generally supposed. But if, as the whole tenour of the history shows, his faith had been only general and scarcely formed, we can account the more easily for the delay. Only in the hour of supreme need, when his only child lay dying, did he resort to Jesus. There was need to perfect such faith, on the one side into perseverance of assurance, and on the other into energy of trustfulness. The one was accomplished through the delay caused by the application of the woman, the other by the supervention of death during this interval.

There was nothing unnatural or un-Jewish in the application of this Ruler to Jesus. He must have known of the healing of the son of the Court-official, and of the servant of the Centurion, there or in the immediate neighbourhood—as it was said, by the mere word of Christ. For there had been no imposition of silence in regard to them, even had such been possible. Yet in both cases the recovery might be ascribed by some to coincidence, by others to answer of prayer. And perhaps this may help us to understand one of the reasons for the prohibition of telling what had been done by Jesus, while in other instances silence was not enjoined. Of course, there were occasions—such as the raising of the young man at Nain and of Lazarus—when the miracle was done so publicly, that a command of this kind would have been impossible. But in other cases may this not be the line of demarcation, that silence was *not* enjoined when a result was achieved which, according to the notions of the time, *might* have been attributed to other than direct Divine Power,

---

[1] *Keim* starts the theory that, according to St. Matthew, Jairus was an ἄρχων in the sense of a civil magistrate. This, in order to make St. Matthew contradict St. Mark and St. Luke, as if ἄρχων were not one of the most common designations of Synagogue-rulers.

[2] The particulars of her history must be gathered from a comparison of the three Gospels.

[3] A woman came of age at twelve years and one day, boys at thirteen years and one day.

[4] *Godet* points out a like summarisation in St. Matthew's account of the Centurion's servant.

while in the latter cases [1] publicity was (whenever possible) forbidden? And this for the twofold reason, that Christ's Miracles were intended to aid, not to supersede, faith; to direct to the Person and Teaching of Christ, as that which proved the benefit to be real and Divine; not to excite the carnal Jewish expectancies of the people, but to lead in humble discipleship to the Feet of Jesus. In short, if only those were made known which would not necessarily imply *Divine Power* (according to Jewish notions), then would not only the distraction and tumult of popular excitement be avoided, but in each case faith in the Person of Christ be still required, ere the miracles were received as evidence of His Divine claims.[2] And this need of faith was the main point.

That, in view of his child's imminent death, and with the knowledge he had of the 'mighty deeds' commonly reported of Jesus, Jairus should have applied to Him, can the less surprise us, when we remember how often Jesus must, with consent and by invitation of this Ruler, have spoken in the Synagogue; and what irresistible impression His words had made. It is not necessary to suppose, that Jairus was among those elders of the Jews who interceded for the Centurion; the form of his present application seems rather opposed to it. But after all, there was nothing in what he said which a Jew in those days might not have spoken to a Rabbi, who was regarded as Jesus must have been by all in Capernaum who believed not the horrible charge, which the Judæan Pharisees had just raised. Though we cannot point to any instance where the laying on of a great Rabbi's hands was sought for healing, such, combined with prayer, would certainly be in entire accordance with Jewish views at the time. The confidence in the result, expressed by the father in the accounts of St. Mark and St. Matthew, is not mentioned by St. Luke. And perhaps, as being the language of an Eastern, it should not be taken in its strict literality as indicating actual conviction on the part of Jairus, that the laying on of Christ's Hands would certainly restore the maiden.

Be this as it may, when Jesus followed the Ruler to his house, the multitude 'thronging Him' in eager curiosity, another approached Him from out that crowd, whose inner history was far

---

[1] The following are the instances in which silence was enjoined:—St. Matt. viii. 4 (St. Mark i. 44; St. Luke v. 14); St. Matt. ix. 30; xii. 16; St. Mark iii. 12; v. 43 (St. Luke viii. 56); St. Mark vii. 36; viii. 26.

[2] In general, we would once more thus formulate our views: *In the Days of Christ men learned first to believe in His Person, and then in His Word; in the Dispensation of the Holy Spirit we learn first to believe in His Word, and then in His Person.*

BOOK
III

ᵃ Shabb.
110 a and b

different from that of Jairus. The disease from which this woman had suffered for twelve years would render her Levitically ' unclean.' It must have been not unfrequent in Palestine, and proved as intractable as modern science has found it, to judge by the number and variety of remedies prescribed, and by their character. On one leaf of the Talmud ᵃ not less than eleven different remedies are proposed, of which at most only six can possibly be regarded as astringents or tonics, while the rest are merely the outcome of superstition, to which resort is had in the absence of knowledge.¹ But what possesses real interest is, that, in all cases where astringents or tonics are prescribed, it is ordered, that, while the woman takes the remedy, she is to be addressed in the words: ' Arise (*Qum*) from thy flux.' It is not only that psychical means are apparently to accompany the therapeutical in this disease, but the coincidence in the command, Arise (*Qum*), with the words used by Christ in raising Jairus' daughter is striking. But here also we mark only contrast to the magical cures of the Rabbis. For Jesus neither used remedies, nor spoke the word *Qum* to her who had come ' in the press behind' to touch for her healing ' the fringe of His outer garment.'

As this is almost the only occasion on which we can obtain a glimpse of Christ's outward appearance and garb, it may be well to form such accurate conception of it, as is afforded by a knowledge of the dress of the ancient Hebrews. The Rabbis laid it down as a rule, that the learned ought to be most careful in their dress. It was a disgrace if a scholar walked abroad with clouted shoes;² to wear dirty clothes deserved death;ᵇ for ' the glory of God was man, and the glory of man was his dress.' ᶜ This held specially true of the Rabbi, whose appearance might otherwise reflect on the theological profession. It was the general rule to eat and drink below (or else according to) a man's means, but to dress and lodge above them.ᵈ ³ For, in these four things a man's character might be learned: at his cups, in money matters, when he was angry, and by his ragged dress.ᵉ Nay, ' The clothing of the wife of a *Chabher* (learned associate) is of greater importance than the life of the ignorant (rustic), for the sake of the dignity of the learned.' ᶠ Accordingly, the Rabbis were wont to wear such dress by which they might be distinguished. At a

ᵇ Shabb.
114 a
ᶜ Derekh
Erets S. x
towards
the end

ᵈ Babha
Mez. 52 a;
Chull. 84 b

ᵉ Erub. 65 b

ᶠ Jer.
Horay. 48 a,
4 lines from
bottom

---

¹ Such as the ashes of an Ostrich-Egg, carried in summer in a linen, in winter in a cotton rag; or a barley-corn found in the dung of a white she-ass, &c.

² In Ber. 43 b, it is explained to refer to such shoes as had ' clouts on the top of clouts.'

³ Accordingly, when a person applied for relief in food, inquiry was to be made as to his means, but not if he applied for raiment (Babha B 9 a).

later period they seem at their ordination to have been occasionally arrayed in a mantle of gold-stuff.[a] Perhaps a distinctive garment, most likely a head-gear, was worn, even by 'rulers' ('the elder,' זָקֵן), at their ordination.[1] The Palestinian *Nasi*, or President of the Sanhedrin, also had a distinctive dress,[b] and the head of the Jewish community in Babylon a distinctive girdle.[c][2]

In referring to the dress which may on a Sabbath be saved from a burning house—not, indeed, by carrying it, but by successively putting it on, no fewer than eighteen articles are mentioned.[d] If the meaning of all the terms could be accurately ascertained, we should know precisely what the Jews in the second century, and presumably earlier, wore, from the shoes and stockings on their feet to the gloves[3] on their hands. Unfortunately, many of these designations are in dispute. Nor must it be thought that, because there are eighteen names, the dress of an Israelite consisted of so many separate pieces. Several of them apply to different shapes or kinds of the same under or upper garments, while the list indicates their extreme number and variety rather than the ordinary dress worn. The latter consisted, to judge by the directions given for undressing and dressing in the bathroom, of six, or perhaps more generally, of five articles: the shoes, the head-covering, the *Tallith* or upper cloak, the girdle, the *Chaluq* or under-dress, and the *Aphqarsin* or innermost covering.[e] As regarded shoes, a man should sell his very roof-tree for them,[4] although he might have to part with them for food, if he were in a weak condition through blood-letting.[f] But it was *not* the practice to provide more than one pair of shoes,[g] and to this may have referred the injunction[h] of Christ to the Apostles not to provide shoes for their journey, or else to the well-known distinction between shoes (*Manalim*) and sandals (*Sandalim*). The former, which were sometimes made of very coarse material, covered the whole foot, and were specially intended for winter or rainy weather; while the sandals, which only protected the soles and sides of the feet, were specially for summer use.[1]

CHAP.
XXVI

[a] Babha Mez. 85 a
[b] Ber. 28 a
[c] Horay. 13 b

[d] Shabb. 120 a; Jer. Shabb. 15 d

[e] Derekh Erets R. x p. 33 d
[f] Shabb. 129 a; comp. Pes. 112 a
[g] Jer. Shabb. vi. 2
[h] St. Matt. x. 10

[1] B. Bathra 58 a, lines 2 and 3 from top

---

[1] But I admit that the passage (Vayyik. R. 2) is not quite clear. The *Maaphoreth* there mentioned may not have been an official dress, but one which the man otherwise used, and which was only specially endeared to him by the recollection that he had worn it at his ordination.

[2] In general, I would here acknowledge my indebtedness on the very difficult subject of dress to *Sachs*, Beiträge z. Sprach- u. Alterth.-Forsch.; to the Articles in *Levy's* Dictionaries; and espe-cially to *Brüll*, Trachten d. Juden. The Article in *Hamburger's* Real-Encykl. is little more than a repetition of *Brüll's*. From other writers I have not been able to derive any help.

[3] So *Landau* renders one of the words in Shabb. 120 a. I need scarcely say that the rendering is very doubtful.

[4] *Brüll* regards this as controversial to the practices of the early Christians. But he confounds sects with the Church.

BOOK
III

ª Exod.
xiv. 8

b Kel.
xxix. 1

c Pes. 111 b.
See also the
somewhat
profane
etymology
of סוּדְרָא in
Shabb. 77 b,
סוּד ה׳ •
לִירֵאָיו
d Jer. Sanh.
20 c, bottom
e Babha B.
67 b

f Moed K.
14 a
g St. Matt.
x. 10, and
parallels

h St. John
xix. 23

i Comp.
Rev. i. 13

In regard to the covering of the head, it was deemed a mark of disrespect to walk abroad, or to pass a person, with bared head.[1] Slaves covered their heads in presence of their masters, and the Targum Onkelos indicates Israel's freedom by paraphrasing the expression they 'went out with a high hand'ª by 'with uncovered head.'[2] The ordinary covering of the head was the so-called *Sudar* (or Sudarium), a kerchief twisted into a turban, and which might also be worn round the neck. A kind of hat was also in use, either of light material or of felt (*Aphilyon shel rosh*, or *Philyon*).b The *Sudar* was twisted by Rabbis in a peculiar manner to distinguish them from others.c We read besides of a sort of cap or hood attached to some kinds of outer or of inner garments.

Three, or else four articles commonly constituted the dress of the body. First came the under-garment, commonly the *Chaluq* or the *Kittuna*[3] (the Biblical *Kethoneth*), from which latter some have derived the word 'cotton.' The *Chaluq* might be of linen or of wool.d The sages wore it down to the feet. It was covered by the upper garment or *Tallith* to within about a handbreadth.e The *Chaluq* lay close to the body, and had no other opening than that round the neck and for the arms. At the bottom it had a kind of hem. To possess only one such 'coat' or inner garment was a mark of poverty.f Hence, when the Apostles were sent on their temporary mission, they were directed not to take 'two coats.'g Closely similar to, if not identical with, the *Chaluq*, was the ancient garment mentioned in the Old Testament as *Kethoneth*, to which the Greek 'Chiton' ($\chi\iota\tau\acute{\omega}\nu$) corresponds. As the garment which our Lord wore,h[4] and those of which He spoke to His Apostles are designated by that name, we conclude that it represents the well-known *Kethoneth* or Rabbinic *Kittuna*. This might be of almost any material, even leather, though it was generally of wool or flax. It was sleeved, close-fitting, reached to the ankles, and was fastened round the loins, or just under the breast,[1] by a girdle. One kind of the latter, the *Pundah* or *Aphundah*,[5] was provided with pockets or other receptacles,[6] and

---

[1] On the other hand, to walk about with shoes loosed was regarded as a mark of pride.
[2] The like expression occurs in the Targum on Judg. v. 9.
[3] Also, *Kittanitha*. and *Kittunitha*.
[4] As to the mode of weaving such garments, see the pictorial illustration in *Braunius*, Vest. Sacerd. Hebræor., which is reproduced, with full details from various other works, in *Hartmann's*

Hebr. am Putzt. vol. i., explanatory notes being added at the beginning of vol. iii. *Sammter's* note in his edition of B. Mezia, p. 151 *a*, is only a reproduction of *Hartmann's* remarks.
[5] It was worn outside (Jer. Ber. 14 *c*, top). This is the girdle which was not to be worn in the Temple, probably as being that of a person engaged in business.
[6] This is the explanation of the Aruch (ed. *Landau*, i. p. 157 *b*).

hence might not be worn outside by those who went into the Temple,[a] probably to indicate that he who went to worship should not be engaged in, nor bear mark of, any other occupation.

Of the two other garments mentioned as parts of a man's *toilette*, the *Aphqarsin* or *Aphikarsus* seems to have been an article of luxury rather than of necessity. Its precise purpose is difficult to determine. A comparison of the passages in which the term occurs conveys the impression, that it was a large kerchief used partly as a head-gear, and which hung down and was fastened under the right arm.[b][1] Probably it was also used for the upper part of the body. But the circumstance that, unlike the other articles of dress, it need not be rent in mourning,[c] and that, when worn by females, it was regarded as a mark of wealth,[d] shows that it was not a necessary article of dress, and hence that, in all likelihood, it was not worn by Christ. It was otherwise with the *upper garment*. Various shapes and kinds of such were in use, from the coarser *Boresin* and *Bardesin*—the modern *Burnoose*—upwards. The *Gelima* was a cloak of which 'the border,' or 'hem,' is specially mentioned (שיפולי גלימא).[e] The *Gunda* was a peculiarly Pharisaic garb.[f] But the upper garment which Jesus wore would be either the so-called *Goltha*, or, most likely, the *Tallith*. Both the *Goltha*[g] and the *Tallith*[h] were provided, on the four borders, with the so-called *Tsitsith*, or 'fringes.' These were attached to the four corners of the outer dress, in supposed fulfilment of the command, Numb. xv. 38–41; Deut. xxii. 12. At first, this observance seems to have been comparatively simple. The question as to the number of filaments on these 'fringes' was settled in accordance with the teaching of the School of Shammai. Four filaments (not three, as the Hillelites proposed), each of four finger-lengths (these, as later tradition put it, doubled), and attached to the four corners of what must be a strictly square garment—such were the earliest rules on the subject.[i] The Mishnah leaves it still a comparatively open question, whether these filaments were to be blue or white.[k] But the Targum makes a strong point of it as between Moses and Korah, that there was to be a filament of hyacinth colour among four of white.[m] It seems even to imply the peculiar symbolical mode of knotting them at present in use.[n] Further symbolic details were, of course, added in the course of time.[2] As these fringes were attached to the corners of any square garment, the

CHAP. XXVI

[a] Jer. Ber. 14 c, top

[b] Kel. xxix. 1; Ber. 23 b; 24 b, in the sense of kerchief worn in an accessible position; Pesiqt. 15 b, as lying close to the body and yet contracting dust; Jer. Ber. 4 c, line 14 from top, used for wrapping the upper part of the body

[c] Jer. Moed, K. 83 d

[d] Nidd. 48 b

[e] Sanh. 102 b, and often

[f] Sot. 22 b

[g] Jer. Sanh. 28 c

[h] Menach. 37 b

[i] Siphré, ed. Friedmann, p. 117 a

[k] Menach. iv. 1

[m] Targ. Ps.-Jon. on Numb. xvi. 2

[n] u. s. on Numb. xv. 38

---

[1] This passage is both curious and difficult. It seems to imply that the *Aphqarsin* was a garment worn in summer, close to the body, and having sleeves.

[2] The number of knots and threads at present counted are, of course, later additions. The little tractate *Tsitsith Kirchheim*, Septem Libri Talm. P. pp. 22–24)

question, whether the upper garment which Jesus wore was the *Goltha* or the *Tallith*, is of secondary importance. But as all that concerns His Sacred Person is of deepest interest, we may be allowed to state our belief in favour of the *Tallith*. Both are mentioned as distinctive dresses of teachers, but the *Goltha* (so far as it differed from the *Tallith*) seems the more peculiarly Rabbinic.

We can now form an approximate idea of the outward appearance of Jesus on that spring-morning amidst the throng at Capernaum. He would, we may safely assume, go about in the ordinary, although not in the more ostentatious, dress, worn by the Jewish teachers of Galilee. His head-gear would probably be the *Sudar* (Sudarium) wound into a kind of turban, or perhaps the *Maaphoreth*,[1] which seems to have served as a covering for the head, and to have descended over the back of the neck and shoulders, somewhat like the Indian pugaree. His feet were probably shod with *sandals*. The *Chaluq*, or more probably the *Kittuna*, which formed his inner garment, must have been close-fitting, and descended to His feet, since it was not only so worn by teachers, but was regarded as absolutely necessary for any one who would publicly read or 'Targum' the Scriptures, or exercise any function in the Synagogue.[a] As we know, it 'was without seam, woven from the top throughout;'[b] and this closely accords with the texture of these garments. Round the middle it would be fastened with a *girdle*.[2] Over this inner, He would most probably wear the square outer garment, or *Tallith*, with the customary fringes of four long white threads with one of hyacinth knotted together on each of the four corners. There is reason to believe, that three square garments were made with these 'fringes,' although, by way of ostentation, the Pharisees made them particularly wide so as to attract attention, just as they made their phylacteries broad.[c] Although Christ only denounced the latter practice, not the phylacteries themselves, it is impossible to believe that Himself ever wore them, either on the forehead or the arm.[3] There was certainly no warrant for them in Holy Scripture, and only Pharisee externalism could represent their use as fulfilling the import of

[a] Tos. Megill. iv. p.45 *b*, lines 17 and 16 from bottom
[b] St. John xix. 23
[c] St. Matt. xviii. 5

is merely a summary. The various authorities on the subject—and not a few have been consulted—are more or less wanting in clearness and defective. Comp. p. 277, note 2, of this volume.

[1] The difference between it and the *Aphqarsin* seems to be, that the latter was worn and fastened *inside* the dress. The *Maaphoreth* would in some measure combine the uses of the *Sudar* and the *Aphqarsin*.

[2] Canon *Westcott* (Speaker's Comment. on St. John xix. 23) seems to imply that the girdle was worn outside the loose outer garment. This was not the case.

[3] On this subject I must take leave to refer to the Bibl. Cyclopædias and to 'Sketches of Jewish Social Life,' pp. 220–224.

Exod. xiii. 9, 16; Deut. vi. 8; xi. 18.   The admission that neither the officiating priests, nor the representatives of the people, wore them in the Temple,[a] seems to imply that this practice was not quite universal.   For our part, we refuse to believe that Jesus, like the Pharisees, appeared wearing phylacteries every day and all day long, or at least a great part of the day.   For such was the ancient custom, and not merely, as the modern practice, to wear them only at prayer.[1]

One further remark may be allowed before dismissing this subject. Our inquiries enable us in this matter also to confirm the accuracy of the Fourth Gospel.   We read[b] that the quaternion of soldiers who crucified Christ made division of the riches of His poverty, taking each one part of His dress, while for the fifth, which, if divided, would have had to be rent in pieces, they cast lots.   This incidental remark carries evidence of the Judæan authorship of the Gospel in the accurate knowledge which it displays.   The four pieces of dress to be divided would be the head-gear, the more expensive sandals or shoes, the long girdle, and the coarse *Tallith*—all about equal in value.[2]   And the fifth undivided and, comparatively, most expensive garment, 'without seam, woven from the top throughout,' probably of wool, as befitted the season of the year, was the *Kittuna*, or inner garment.   How strange, that, what would have been of such priceless value to Christendom, should have been divided as the poor

---

[1] As the question is of considerable practical importance, the following, as bearing upon it, may be noticed. From Jer. Ber. 4 c, we gather: 1. That at one time it was the practice to wear the phylacteries all day long, in order to pass as pious. This is denounced as a mark of hypocrisy. 2. That it was settled, that phylacteries should be worn during a considerable part of the day, but not the whole day. [In Ber. 23 a to 24 a we have rules and discussions about depositing them under certain circumstances, and where to place them at night.] 3. That it was deemed objectionable to wear them only during prayer. 4. That celebrated Rabbis did not deem it necessary always to wear the phylacteries both on the head and on the arm. This seems to prove that their obligation could not have been regarded as absolutely binding. Thus, R. Jochanan wore those for the head only in winter, but not in summer, because then he did not wear a headgear. As another illustration, that the wearing of phylacteries was not deemed absolutely requisite, the following passage may be quoted (Sanh. xi. 3): 'It is more culpable to transgress the words of the Scribes than those of the Torah. He that says, There are no phylacteries, transgresses the word of the Torah, and is not to be regarded as a rebel (literally, is free); but he who says, There are five compartments (instead of four), to add to the words of the Scribes, he is guilty.

[2] I find that the lowest price mentioned for an upper garment was 7½ *dinars*, or about 4s. 7d. (Jer. Kilay. ix. 1). The more common price, however, seems to have been 12 dinars, or about 7s. 6d. The cost of making seems to have been 8 dinars, or about 5s. (Jer. Babha Mets. vi. 1), leaving 4 dinars, or 2s. 6d., for the material. Of course, the latter might be much more expensive, and the cost of the garment increased accordingly.

booty of a rough, unappreciative soldiery! Yet how well for us, since not even the sternest warning could have kept within the bounds of mere reverence the veneration with which we should have viewed and handled that which He wore, Who died for us on the Cross. Can we, then, wonder that this Jewish woman, 'having heard the things concerning Jesus,' with her imperfect knowledge, in the weakness of her strong faith, thought that, if she might but touch His garment, she would be made whole? It is but what we ourselves might think, if He were still walking on earth among men: it is but what, in some form or other, we still feel when in the weakness—the rebound or diastole—of our faith it seems to us, as if the want of this touch in not outwardly-perceived help or Presence left us miserable and sick, while even one real touch, if it were only of His garment, one real act of contact, however mediate, would bring us perfect healing. And in some sense it really is so. For, assuredly, the Lord cannot be touched by disease and misery, without healing coming from Him, for He is the God-Man. And He is also the loving, pitying Saviour. Who disdains not, nor turns from our weakness in the manifestation of our faith, even as He turned not from hers who touched His garment for her healing.

We can picture her to our minds as, mingling with those who thronged and pressed upon the Lord, she put forth her hand and 'touched the border of His garment,' most probably [1] the long *Tsitsith* of one of the corners of the *Tallith*. We can understand how, with a disease which not only rendered her Levitically defiling, but where womanly shamefacedness would make public speech so difficult, she, thinking of Him Whose Word, spoken at a distance, had brought healing, might thus seek to have her heart's desire. What strong faith to expect help where all human help, so long and earnestly sought, had so signally failed! And what strong faith to expect, that even contact with Him, the bare touch of His garment, would carry such Divine Power as to make her 'whole.' Yet in this very strength lay also its weakness. She believed so much in Him, that she felt as if it needed not personal appeal to Him; she felt so deeply the hindrances to her making request of Himself, that, believing so strongly in Him, she deemed it sufficient to touch, not even Himself, but that which in itself had no power nor value, except as it was in contact with His Divine Person. But it is here that her faith was

---

[1] This, however, does not necessarily follow, although in New Testament language $\kappa\rho\dot{\alpha}\sigma\pi\epsilon\delta o\nu$ seems to bear that meaning. Comp. the excellent work of *Braunius* (Vest. Sac. Heb. pp. 72, 73—not p. 55, as *Schleusner* notes).

beset by two-fold danger. In its excess it might degenerate into superstition, as trees in their vigour put forth shoots, which, unless they be cut off, will prevent the fruit-bearing, and even exhaust the life of the tree. Not the garments in which He appeared among men, and which touched His Sacred Body, nor even that Body, but Himself brings healing. Again, there was the danger of losing sight of that which, as the moral element, is necessary in faith: personal application to, and personal contact with, Christ.

And so it is to us also. As we realise the Mystery of the Incarnation, His love towards, and His Presence with, His own, and the Divine Power of the Christ, we cannot think too highly of all that is, or brings, in contact with Him. The Church, the Sacraments, the Apostolic Ministry of His Institution—in a word, the grand historic Church, which is alike His Dwelling-place, His Witness, and His Representative on earth, ever since He instituted it, endowed it with the gift of the Holy Spirit, and hallowed it by the fulfilled promise of His Eternal Presence, is to us what the garment He wore was to her who touched Him. We shall think highly of all this in measure as we consciously think highly of Him. His Bride the Church; the Sacraments which are the fellowship of His Body and Blood, of His Crucifixion and Resurrection; the Ministry and Embassy of Him, committed to the Apostles, and ever since continued with such direction and promise, cannot be of secondary importance— must be very real and full of power, since they are so connected, and bring us into such connection with Him: the spirituo-physical points of contact between Him, Who is the God-man, and those who, being men, are also the children of God. Yet in this strength of our faith may also lie its danger if not its weakness. Through excess it may pass into superstition, which is the attachment of power to anything other than the Living God; or else, in the consciousness of our great disease, want of courage might deprive faith of its moral element in personal dealing and personal contact with Christ.

Very significantly to us who, in our foolish judging and merciless condemning of one another, ever re-enacted the Parable of the Two Debtors, the Lord did not, as Pseudo-orthodoxy would prescribe it, disappoint her faith for the weakness of its manifestation. To have disappointed her faith, which was born of such high thoughts of Him, would have been to deny Himself—and he cannot deny Himself. But very significantly, also, while He disappointed not her faith, He corrected the error of its direction and manifestation.

And to this His subsequent bearing toward her was directed. No sooner had she so touched the border of His garment than 'she knew in the body that she was healed of the scourge.'[1] No sooner, also, had she so touched the border of His garment than *He* knew, 'perceived in Himself,' what had taken place: the forthgoing of the Power that is from out of Him.[2]

Taking this narrative in its true literality, there is no reason to overweight and mar it by adding what is not conveyed in the text. There is nothing in the language of St. Mark[3] (as correctly rendered), nor of St. Luke, to oblige us to conclude that this forthgoing of Power, which He perceived in Himself, had been through an act, of the full meaning of which Christ was unconscious—in other words, that He was ignorant of the person who, and the reason why, she Had touched Him. In short, 'the forthgoing of the Power that is out of Him' was neither unconscious nor unwilled on His part. It was caused by her faith, not by her touch. 'Thy faith hath made thee whole.' And the question of Jesus could not have been misleading, when 'straightway'[4] He 'turned Him about in the crowd and said, Who touched My garments?' That He knew who had done it, and only wished, through self-confession, to bring her to clearness in the exercise of her faith, appears from what is immediately added: 'And He looked round about,' not to see *who* had done it, but 'to see her that had done this thing.' And as His look of unspoken appeal was at last fixed on her alone in all that crowd, which, as Peter rightly said, was thronging and pressing Him, 'the
woman saw that she was not hid,'ᵃ and came forward to make full confession. Thus, while in His mercy He had borne with her weakness, and in His faithfulness not disappointed her faith, its twofold errror was also corrected. She learned that it was not from the garment, but from the Saviour, that the Power proceeded; she learned also, that it was not the touch of it, but the faith in Him, that made whole—and such faith must ever be of personal dealing with Him. And so He spoke to her the Word of twofold help and

---

[1] So literally in St. Mark's Gospel.

[2] This gives the full meaning—but it is difficult to give a literal translation which would give the entire meaning of the original.

[3] The Revised Version renders it: 'And straightway Jesus, perceiving in Himself that the power *proceeding* from Him had gone forth, turned Him about.' Mark the position of the first comma. In the Speaker's Commentary it is rendered:

'And immediately Jesus, having perceived in Himself that the virtue had gone forth from Him.' Dean *Plumptre* translates: 'Knowing fully in Himself the virtue that had gone out from Him.'

[4] The arrangement of the words in the A.V. is entirely misleading. The word 'immediately' refers to His turning round, *not* to His perceiving in Himself.

assurance: ' Thy faith hath made thee whole—go forth into peace,[1] **CHAP.** and be healed of thy scourge.' **XXVI**

Brief as is the record of this occurrence, it must have caused considerable delay in the progress of our Lord to the house of Jairus. For in the interval the maiden, who had been at the last gasp when her father went to entreat the help of Jesus, had not only died, but the house of mourning was already filled with relatives, hired mourners, wailing women, and musicians, in preparation for the funeral. The intentional delay of Jesus when summoned to Lazarus [a] leads us to ask, whether similar purpose may not have influenced His conduct in the present instance. But even were it otherwise, no outcome of God's Providence is of chance, but each is designed. The circumstances, which in their concurrence make up an event, may all be of natural occurrence, but their conjunction is of Divine ordering and to a higher purpose, and this constitutes Divine Providence. It was in the interval of this delay that the messengers came, who informed Jairus of the actual death of his child. Jesus overheard [2] it, as they whispered to the Ruler not to trouble the Rabbi any further,[3] but He heeded it not, save so far as it affected the father. The emphatic admonition, not to fear, only to believe, gives us an insight into the threatening failure of the Ruler's faith; perhaps, also, into the motive which prompted the delay of Christ. The utmost need, which would henceforth require the utmost faith on the part of Jairus had now come. But into that, which was to pass within the house, no stranger must intrude. Even of the Apostles only those, who now for the first time became, and henceforth continued, the innermost circle,[4] might witness, without present danger to themselves or others, what was about to take place. How Jesus dismissed the multitude, or else kept them at bay, or where He parted from all his disciples except Peter, James, and John, does not clearly appear, and, indeed, is of no importance. He may have left the nine Apostles with the people, or outside the house, or parted from them in the courtyard of Jairus' house before he entered the inner apartments.[5]

St. John xi. 6

---

[1] So literally.

[2] I adopt the reading παρακούσας, which seems to me better rendered by ' overhearing ' than by ' not heeding,' as in the Revised Version.

[3] The word unquestionably means, literally, Teacher—but in the sense of Rabbi, or Master.

[4] Those who believe in an ' anti-Petrine' tendency in the Gospel by St. Luke must find it difficult to account for the prominence given to him in the Third Gospel.

[5] I confess myself unable to see any real discrepancy between the accounts of St. Mark and St. Luke, such as *Strauss*, *Keim*, and others have tried to establish. In St. Mark it is: 'He suffered no man

Within, ' the tumult ' and weeping, the wail of the mourners, real or hired, and the melancholy sound of the mourning flutes [1]—sad preparation for, and pageantry of, an Eastern funeral—broke with dismal discord on the majestic calm of assured victory over death, with which Jesus had entered the house of mourning. But even so He would tell it them, as so often in like circumstances He tells it to us, that the damsel was not dead, but only sleeping. The Rabbis also frequently have the expression ' to sleep' (demakh רמך, or רמוך, when the sleep is overpowering and oppressive), instead of ' to die.' It may well have been that Jesus made use of this word of double meaning in some such manner as this: Talyetha dimkhath, 'the maiden sleepeth.' And they understood Him well in their own way, yet understood Him not at all.

As so many of those who now hear this word, they to whom it was then spoken, in their coarse realism, laughed Him to scorn. For did they not verily know that she had actually died, even before the messengers had been despatched to prevent the needless trouble of His coming? Yet even this their scorn served a higher purpose. For it showed these two things: that to the certain belief of those in the house the maiden was really dead, and that the Gospel-writers regarded the raising of the dead as not only beyond the ordinary range of Messianic activity, but as something miraculous even among the miracles of Christ. And this also is evidential, at least so far as to prove that the writers recorded the event not lightly, but with full knowledge of the demand which it makes on our faith.

The first thing to be done by Christ was to ' put out' the mourners, whose proper place this house no longer was, and who by their conduct had proved themselves unfit to be witnesses of Christ's great manifestation. The impression which the narrative leaves on the mind is, that all this while the father of the maiden was stupefied, passive, rather than active in the matter. The great fear, which had come upon him when the messengers apprised him of his only child's death, seemed still to numb his faith. He followed Christ without taking any part in what happened; he witnessed the pageantry or the approaching obsequies in his house without interfering; he heard the scorn which Christ's majestic declaration of the victory over death provoked, without checking it. The fire of his faith was that
[a] Is. xlii. 3 of ' dimly burning flax.'[a] But ' He will not quench ' it.

man to accompany Him ' (whither ?); in St. Luke: ' He suffered not any man to enter in with Him.'

[1] They are specially called ' flutes for the dead ' (B. Mez. vi. 1): חלילים למת.

He now led the father and the mother into the chamber where
the dead maiden lay, followed by the three Apostles, witnesses of
His chiefest working and of His utmost earthly glory, but also of
His inmost sufferings. Without doubt or hesitation He took her
by the hand and spoke only these two words: *Talyetha Qum* [*Kum*]
(טְלִיתָא קוּם [1]), Maiden, arise! 'And straightway the damsel arose.'
But the great astonishment which came upon them, as well as the
'strait charge' that no man should know it, are further evidence, if
such were required, how little their faith had been prepared for that
which in its weakness was granted to it. And thus Jesus, as He
had formerly corrected in the woman that weakness of faith which
came through very excess, so now in the Ruler of the Synagogue the
weakness which was by failure. And so 'He hath done all things
well: He maketh even the deaf to hear, and the dumb to speak.'[a]

[a] St. Mark
vii. 37.

How Jesus conveyed Himself away, whether through another
entrance into the house, or by 'the road of the roofs,' we are not told.
But assuredly, He must have avoided the multitude. Presently we
find Him far from Capernaum. Probably He had left it immediately
on quitting the house of Jairus. But what of that multitude? The
tidings must have speedily reached them, that the daughter of
the Synagogue-Ruler was not dead. Yet it had been straitly charged
that none of them should be informed, how it had come to pass that
she lived. They were then with this intended mystery before them.
She was not dead: thus much was certain. The Christ had, ere
leaving that chamber, given command that meat should be brought
her; and, as that direction must have been carried out by one of the
attendants, this would become immediately known to all that household. Had she then not really died, but only been sleeping? Did
Christ's words of double meaning refer to literal sleep? Here then
was another Parable of twofold different bearing: to them that had
hearts to understand, and to them who understood not. In any case,
their former scorn had been misplaced; in any case, the Teacher of

---

[1] The reading which accordingly seems
best is that adopted by *Westcott* and
Hort, Ταλειθά κούμ. The Aramaic or
Rabbinic for maiden is either *Talyetha*
or *Talyutha* (טְלִיתָא). In the second
Targum on Esther ii. 7, 8, the reading is
טְלוּתָא (*Talutha*), where *Levy* conjectures the reading טְלִיתָא (*Talitha*) or
else *Talyetha*. The latter seems also
the proper equivalent of ταλειθά. while

the reading 'Talitha' is very uncertain.
As regards the second word, *qum* [pro-
nounced *kum*], most writers have, without difficulty, shown that it should be
qumi, not *qum*. Nevertheless, the same
command is spelt קוּם in the Talmud (as
it is pronounced in the Syriac) when a
woman is addressed. In Shabb. 110 *b*,
the command *qum*, as addressed to a
woman suffering from a bloody flux,
occurs not less than seven times in that
one page (וקום מוזבך).

Nazareth was far other than all the Rabbis. In what Name, and by what Power, did He come and act ? Who was He really ? Had they but known of the ' *Talyetha Qum*,' and how these two words had burst open the two-leaved doors of death and Hades! Nay, but it would have only ended in utter excitement and complete misunderstanding, to the final impossibility of the carrying out of Christ's Mission. For, the full as well as the true knowledge, that He was the Son of God, could only come after His contest and suffering. And our faith also in Him is first of the suffering Saviour, and then of the Son of God. Thus was it also from the first. It was through what He did for them that they learned Who He was. Had it been otherwise, the full blaze of the Sun's glory would have so dazzled them, that they could not have seen the Cross.

Yet to all time has this question engaged the minds of men: Was the maiden really dead, or did she only sleep ? With it this other and kindred one is connected: Was the healing of the woman miraculous, or only caused by the influence of mind over body, such as is not unfrequently witnessed, and such as explains modern so-called miraculous cures, where only superstition perceives supernatural agency? But these very words ' Influence of mind over body,' with which we are so familiar, are they not, so to speak, symbolic and typical? Do they not point to the possibility, and, beyond it, to the fact of such influence of the God-Man, of the command which he wielded over the body ? May not command of soul over body be part of unfallen Man's original inheritance; all most fully realised in the Perfect Man, the God-Man, to Whom has been given the absolute rule of all things, and Who has it in virtue of His Nature ? These are only dim feelings after possible higher truths.

No one who carefully reads this history can doubt, that the Evangelists, at least, viewed this healing as a real miracle, and intended to tell it as such. Even the statement of Christ, that by the forthgoing of Power He knew the moment when the woman touched the hem of His garment, would render impossible the view of certain critics (*Keim* and others), that the cure was the effect of natural causes: expectation acting through the imagination on the nervous system, and so producing the physical results. But even so, and while these writers reiterate certain old cavils [1] propounded by *Strauss*, and by him often derived from the ancient armoury of our own Deists (such as *Woolston*), they admit being so impressed with the ' simple,' ' natural,' and ' life-like ' cast of the narrative, that they

---

[1] We cannot call the trivial objections urged other than 'cavils.'

contend for its historic truth. But the great leader of negativism, *Strauss*, has shown that any natural explanation of the event is opposed to the whole tenour of the narrative, indeed of the Gospel-history; so that the alternative is its simple acceptance or its rejection. *Strauss* boldly decides for the latter, but in so doing is met by the obvious objection, that his denial does not rest on any historical foundation. We can understand, how a legend could gather around historical facts and embellish them, but not how a narrative so entirely without precedent in the Old Testament, and so opposed, not only to the common Messianic expectation, but to Jewish thought, could have been invented to glorify a Jewish Messiah.[1]

As regards the restoration to life of Jairus' daughter, there is a like difference in the negative school (between *Keim* and *Strauss*). One party insists that the maiden only seemed, but was not really dead, a view open also to this objection, that it is manifestly impossible by such devices to account for the raising of the young man at Nain, or that of Lazarus. On the other hand, *Strauss* treats the whole as a myth. It is well, that in this case, he should have condescended to argument in support of his view, appealing to the expectancy created by like miracles of Elijah and Elisha, and to the general belief at that time, that the Messiah would raise the dead. For, the admitted differences between the recorded circumstances of the miracles of Elijah and Elisha and those of Christ are so great, that another negative critic (*Keim*) finds proof of imitation in their contrasts![a] But the appeal to Jewish belief at that time tells, if possible, even more strongly against the hypothesis in question (of *Keim* and *Strauss*). It is, to say the least, doubtful whether Jewish theology generally ascribed to the Messiah the raising of the dead.[2] There are isolated statements to that effect, but the majority of opinions is, that God would Himself raise the dead. But even those passages in which this is attributed to the Messiah tell against the assertions of *Strauss*. For, the resurrection to which they refer is that *of all the dead* (whether at the end of the present age, or of the world), and not of single individuals. To the latter there is not the

[a] Jesu v.
Nazar. ii. 2
p. 475

---

[1] According to *Eusebius* (Hist. Eccl. vii. 18) there was a statue in Paneas in commemoration of this event, which was said to have been erected by this woman to Christ.

[2] The passage which *Strauss* quotes from *Bertholdt* (Christol. Jud. p. 179), is from a later Midrash, that on Proverbs. No one would think of deriving purely Jewish doctrine either from the Sohar or from IV. Esdras, which is of post-Christian date, and strongly tinged with Christian elements. Other passages, however, might be quoted in favour of this view (comp. *Weber*, Altsynagog. Theol. pp. 351, 352), and on the other side, *Hamburger*, Real-Encykl. (II. Abth. 'Belebung der Todten'). The matter will be discussed in the sequel.

faintest allusion in Jewish writings, and it may be safely asserted that such a dogma would have been foreign, even incongruous, to Jewish theology.

The unpleasant task of stating and refuting these objections seemed necessary, if only to show that, as of old so now, this history cannot be either explained or accounted for. It must be accepted or rejected, accordingly as we think of Christ. Admittedly, it formed part of the original tradition and belief of the Church. And it is recorded with such details of names, circumstances, time and place, as almost to court inquiry, and to render fraud well-nigh impossible. And it is so recorded by all the three Evangelists, with such variations, or rather, additions, of details as only to confirm the credibility of the narrators, by showing their independence of each other. Lastly, it fits into the whole history of the Christ, and into this special period of it; and it sets before us the Christ and His bearing in a manner, which we instinctively feel to be accordant with what we know and expect. Assuredly, it implies determined rejection of the claims of the Christ, and that on grounds, not of history, but of preconceived opinions hostile to the Gospel, not to see and adore in it the full manifestation of the Divine Saviour of the world, ' Who hath abolished death, and hath brought life and immortality to light through the Gospel.' [a] And with this belief our highest thoughts of the potential for humanity, and our dearest hopes for ourselves and those we love, are inseparably connected.

[a] 2 Tim. 1. 10

CHAPTER XXVII.

SECOND VISIT TO NAZARETH—THE MISSION OF THE TWELVE.

(St. Matt. xiii. 54–58; x. 1, 5–42; xi. 1; St. Mark vi. 1–13; St. Luke ix. 1–6.)

IT almost seems, as if the departure of Jesus from Capernaum marked a crisis in the history of that town.   From henceforth it ceases to be the centre of His activity, and is only occasionally, and in passing, visited.   Indeed, the concentration and growing power of Pharisaic opposition, and the proximity of Herod's residence at Tiberias [1] would have rendered a permanent stay there impossible at this stage in our Lord's history.   Henceforth, His Life is, indeed, not purely missionary, but He has no certain dwelling-place: in the sublime pathos of His own language, ' He hath not where to lay His Head.'

CHAP XXVII

The notice in St. Mark's Gospel,[a] that His disciples followed Him, seems to connect the arrival of Jesus in ' His own country ' (at Nazareth) with the departure from the house of Jairus, into which He had allowed only three of His Apostles to accompany Him. The circumstances of the present visit, as well as the tone of His countrymen at this time, are entirely different from what is recorded of His former sojourn at Nazareth.[b][2]   The tenacious narrowness, and the prejudices, so characteristic of such a town, with its cliques and petty family-pride, all the more self-asserting that the gradation would be almost imperceptible to an outsider, are, of course, the same as on the former visit of Jesus.   Nazareth would have ceased to be Nazareth, had its people felt or spoken otherwise than nine or ten months before.   That His fame had so grown in the interval, would only stimulate the conceit of the village-town to try, as it were, to construct the great Prophet out of its own building materials, with this additional gratification that He was thoroughly their own, and that they possessed even better materials in their Nazareth.   All this is so quite according to life, that the substantial repetition of the former

[a] St. Mark vi. 1

[b] St. Luke iv. 16–31

[1] Although in Ber. R. 23 the origin of that name is rightly traced to the Emperor Tiberius, it is characteristic that the Talmud tries otherwise to derive the name of what afterwards was the sacred capital of Palestinian Rabbinism, some explaining that it lay in the navel (*tibura*) of the land, others paraphrasing the name ' because the view was good ' (Meg. 6 *a*).   Rabbinic ingenuity declared it one of the cities fortified since the time of Joshua, so as to give it the privileges attaching to such.

[3] Compare Chapters X. and XI.

scene in the Synagogue, so far from surprising us, seems only natural. What surprises us is, what He marvelled at: the unbelief of Nazareth, which lay at the foundation of its estimate and treatment of Jesus.

Upon their own showing their unbelief was most unwarrantable. If ever men had the means of testing the claims of Jesus, the Nazarenes possessed them. True, they were ignorant of the miraculous event of His Incarnation; and we can now perceive at least one of the reasons for the mystery, which was allowed to enwrap it, as well as the higher purpose in Divine Providence of His being born, not in Nazareth, but in Bethlehem of Judæa, and of the interval of time between that Birth and the return of His parents from Egypt to Nazareth. Apart from prophecy, it was needful for Nazareth that Christ should have been born in Bethlehem, otherwise the 'mystery of His Incarnation' must have become known. And yet it could not have been made known, alike for the sake of those most nearly concerned, and for that of those who, at that period of His History, could not have understood it; to whom, indeed, it would have been an absolute hindrance to belief in Him. And He could not have returned to Bethlehem, where He was born, to be brought up there, without calling attention to the miracle of His Birth. If, therefore, for reasons easily comprehended, the mystery of His Incarnation was not to be divulged, it was needful that the Incarnate of Nazareth should be born at Bethlehem, and the Infant of Bethlehem be brought up at Nazareth.

By thus withdrawing Him successively from one and the other place, there was really none on earth who knew of His miraculous Birth, except the Virgin-Mother, Joseph, Elizabeth, and probably Zacharias. The vision and guidance vouchsafed to the shepherds on that December night did not really disclose the mystery of His Incarnation. Remembering their religious notions, it would not leave on them quite the same impression as on us. It might mean much, or it might mean little, in the present: time would tell. In those lands the sand buries quickly and buries deep—preserving, indeed, but also hiding what it covers. And the sands of thirty years had buried the tale which the shepherds had brought; the wise men from the East had returned another way; the excitement which their arrival in Jerusalem and its object had caused, was long forgotten. Messianic expectations and movements were of constant recurrence: the religious atmosphere seemed charged with such elements; and the political changes and events of the day were too engrossing to allow of much attention to an isolated report, which, after all, might mean little, and which certainly was of the long past. To keep up attention, there must be communication; and that was precisely what was wanting in this instance. The reign of Herod was tarnished by many suspicions and murders such as those of Bethlehem. Then intervened the death of Herod,—while the carrying of Jesus into Egypt and His non-return to Bethlehem formed a complete break in the continuity of His History. Between obscure Bethlehem in the far south, and obscure Nazareth in the far north, there was no communication such as between towns in our own land, and they who had sought the Child's life, as well as they who might have worshipped Him, must have been dead. The aged parents of the Baptist cannot have survived the thirty years which lay between the Birth of Christ and the commencement of His Ministry. We have already seen reason for supposing that Joseph had died before. None, therefore, knew all except the Virgin-Mother; and she would hide it the deeper in her heart, the more years passed, and she increasingly felt, as they passed, that, both in His early obscurity and in His later manifestation, she could not penetrate into the real meaning of that mystery, with which she was so closely connected. She could not understand it; how dared she speak of it? She could not understand; nay, we can almost perceive, how she might even misunderstand—not the fact, but the meaning and the purport of what had passed.

But in Nazareth they knew nothing of all this; and of Him only as that Infant Whom His parents, Joseph the carpenter and Mary, had brought with them months after they had first left Nazareth. Jewish law and custom made it possible, that they might have been married long before. And now they only knew of this humble family, that they lived in retirement, and that sons and daughters had grown around their humble board. Of Jesus, indeed, they must have heard that He was not like others around—so quite different in all ways, as He grew in wisdom and stature, and in favour with God and man. Then came that strange tarrying behind on His first visit to Jerusalem, when His parents had to return to seek, and at last found Him in the Temple. This, also, was only strange, though perhaps not strange in a child such as Jesus; and of His own explanation of it, so full of deepest meaning, they might not have heard. If we may draw probable, though not certain, inferences, after that only these three outward circumstances in the history of the family might have been generally noticed: that Jesus followed the occupation of His adoptive father;[a] that Joseph had

[a] St. Mark
vi. 3

died; and that the mother and 'brethren' of Jesus had left Nazareth,[1] while His 'sisters' apparently continued there, being probably
married to Nazarenes. ª

When Jesus had first left Nazareth to seek Baptism at the hands
of John) it could scarcely have attracted much attention. Not only
did 'the whole world' go after the Baptist, but, considering what
was known of Jesus, His absence from, not His presence at the banks
of Jordan, would have surprised the Nazarenes. Then came vague
reports of His early doings, and, what probably His countrymen
would much more appreciate, the accounts which the Galileans
brought back from the Feast of what Jesus had done at Jerusalem.
His fame had preceded Him on that memorable Sabbath, when all
Nazareth had thronged the Synagogue, curious to hear what the
Child of Nazareth would have to say, and still more eager to see
what He could do. Of the charm of His words there could be no
question. Both what He said and how He said it, was quite other
than what they had ever listened to. The difference was not in
degree, but in kind: He spoke to them of the Kingdom; yet not as
for Israel's glory, but for unspeakable comfort in the soul's deepest
need. It was truly wonderful, and that not abstractly, but as on
the part of 'Joseph's Son.' That was all they perceived. Of that
which they had most come to see there was, and could be, no manifestation, so long as they measured the Prophet by His outward
antecedents, forgetful that it was inward kinship of faith, which connected Him that brought the blessing with those who received it.

But this seeming assumption of superiority on the part of
Joseph's Son was quite too much for the better classes of Nazareth.
It was intolerable, that He should not only claim equality with an
Elijah or an Elisha, but place them, the burghers of Nazareth, as it
were, outside the pale of Israel, below a heathen man or woman. And
so, if He had not, without the show of it, proved the authority and power
He possessed, they would have cast Him headlong over the ledge of
the hill of their insulted town. And now He had come back to
them, after nine or ten months, in totally different circumstances.
No one could any longer question His claims, whether for good or
for evil. As on the Sabbath He stood up once more in that Synagogue to teach, they were astonished. The rumour must have spread
that, notwithstanding all, His own kin—probably His 'sisters,' whom

[1] They seem to have settled in Capernaum, having followed Jesus to that
place on His first removal to it. We can
readily understand, that their continuance
in Nazareth would have been difficult.
The death of Joseph is implied in his
not being mentioned in the later history
of Jesus.

He might have been supposed by many to have come to visit—did CHAP.
not own and honour Him as a Prophet.   Or else, had they of His XXVII
own house purposely spread it, so as not to be involved in His Fate?
But the astonishment with which they heard Him on that Sabbath
was that of unbelief.   The cause was so apparently inadequate to the
effect!   They knew His supposed parentage and His brothers; His
sisters were still with them; and for these many years had they known
Him as the carpenter, the son of the carpenter.   Whence, then, had
'this One, ' 'these things, ' 'and what the wisdom which' was 'given
to this One'—and these mighty works done by His Hands?'ª   ª St. Mark
                                                                  vi. 2
    It was, indeed, more than a difficulty—an impossibility—to
account for it on their principles.   There could be no delusion, no
collusion, no deception.   In our modern cant-phraseology, theirs
might have been designated Agnosticism and philosophic doubt.
But philosophic it certainly was not, any more than much that now
passes, because it bears that name; at least, if, according to modern
negative criticism, the inexplicable is also the unthinkable.   Nor was
it really doubt or Agnosticism, any more than much that now covers
itself with that garb.   It was, what Christ designated it—unbelief,
since the questions would have been easily answered—indeed, never
have arisen—had they believed that He was the Christ.   And the
same alternative still holds true.   If 'this One' is what negative
criticism declares Him, which is all that it can know of Him by the
outside: the Son of Mary, the Carpenter and Son of the carpenter
of Nazareth, Whose family occupied the humblest position among
Galileans—then whence this wisdom which, say of it what you will,
underlies all modern thinking, and these mighty works, which have
moulded all modern history?   Whence—if He be only what you can
see by the outside, and yet His be such wisdom, and such mighty deeds
have been wrought by His Hands?   Is He only what you say and see,
seeing that such results are noways explicable on such principles; or
is He not much more than this—even the Christ of God?
    'And He marvelled because of their unbelief. '   In view of their
own reasoning it was most unreasonable.   And equally unreasonable
is modern unbelief.   For, the more strongly negative criticism asserts
its position as to the Person of Jesus, the more unaccountable are His
Teaching and the results of His Work.
    In such circumstances as at Nazareth, nothing could be done by
a Christ, in contradistinction to a miracle-monger.   It would have
been impossible to have finally given up His own town of Nazareth
without one further appeal and one further opportunity of repentance.

BOOK
III

~~~~~~~

As He had begun, so He closed this part of His Galilean Ministry, by preaching in His own Synagogue of Nazareth.   Save in the case of a few who were receptive, on whom He laid His Hands for healing, His visit passed away without such 'mighty works' as the Nazarenes had heard of. He will not return again to Nazareth.   Henceforth He will make commencement of sending forth His disciples, partly to disarm prejudices of a personal character, partly to spread the Gospel-tidings farther and wider than he alone could have carried them. For His Heart compassionated the many who were ignorant and out of the way.   And the harvest was near, and the harvesting was great, and it was His Harvest, into which He would send forth labourers.

For, although, in all likelihood, the words, from which quotation has just been made, [a] were spoken at a later time, [b] they are so entirely in the spirit of the present Mission of the Twelve, that they, or words to a similar effect, may also have been uttered on the present occasion. Of such seeming repetitions, when the circumstances were analogous, although sometimes with different application of the same many-sided words, there are not a few instances, of which one will presently come under notice. [c]   Truly those to whom the Twelve were sent forth were 'troubled' [1] as well as 'scattered,' like sheep that have not a Shepherd, and it was to deliver them from the 'distress' caused by 'grievous wolves,' and to gather into His fold those that had been scattered abroad, that Jesus sent forth the Twelve with the special commission to which attention will now be directed.   Viewing it in its fullest form, [d] it is to be noted:—

First: That this Discourse of Christ consists of *five* parts: vv. 5 to 15; vv. 16 to 23; vv. 24 to 33; vv. 34 to 39; vv. 40 to the end.

Secondly: That many passages in it occur in different connections in the other two Synoptic Gospels, specially in St. Mark xiii. and in St. Luke xii. and xxi.   From this it may be inferred, either that Jesus spake the same or similar words on more than one occasion (when the circumstances were analogous), or else that St. Matthew grouped together into one Discourse, as being internally connected, sayings that may have been spoken on different occasions.   Or else—and this seems to us the most likely—both these inferences may in part be correct. For,

Thirdly: It is evident, that the Discourse reported by St. Matthew goes far beyond that Mission of the Twelve, beyond even that of the Early Church, indeed, sketches the history of the Church's Mission in a hostile world, up 'to the end.'   At the same time it is equally

[a] St. Matt. ix. 36-38
[b] St. Luke x. 2

[c] Comp. St. Matt. x. 26 with St. Luke xii. 1, 2

[d] St. Matt. x. 5 to the end

----

[1] So in St. Matt. ix. 36.

evident, that the predictions, warnings, and promises applicable to a later period in the Church's history, hold equally true in principle in reference to the first Mission of the Twelve; and, conversely, that what specially applied to it, also holds true in principle of the whole subsequent history of the Church in its relation to a hostile world. Thus, what was specially spoken at this time to the Twelve, has ever since, and rightly, been applied to the Church; while that in it, which specially refers to the Church of the future, would in principle apply also to the Twelve.

Fourthly: This distinction of primary and secondary application in the different parts of the Discourse, and their union in the general principles underlying them, has to be kept in view, if we are to understand this Discourse of Christ. Hence, also, the present and the future seem in it so often to run into each other. The horizon is gradually enlarging throughout the Discourse, but there is no change in the standpoint originally occupied; and so the present merges into the future, and the future mingles with the present. And this, indeed, is also the characteristic of much of Old Testament prophecy, and which made the prophet ever a preacher of the present, even while he was a foreteller of the future.

Lastly: It is evidential of its authenticity, and deserves special notice, that this Discourse, while so un-Jewish in spirit, is more than any other, even more than that on the Mount, Jewish in its forms of thought and modes of expression.

With the help of these principles, it will be more easy to mark the general outline of this Discourse. Its first part[a] applies entirely to this first Mission of the Twelve, although the closing words point forward to ' the judgment.'[b] Accordingly it has its parallels, although in briefer form, in the other two Gospels.[c]

1. The Twelve were to go forth two and two,[d] furnished with authority[1]—or, as St. Luke more fully expresses it, with ' power and authority '—alike over all demons and to heal all manner of diseases. It is of secondary importance, whether this was conveyed to them by word only, or with some sacramental sign, such as breathing on them or the laying on of hands. The special commission, for which they received such power, was to proclaim the near advent of the Kingdom, and, in manifestation as well as in evidence of it, to heal the sick, cleanse the lepers, and cast out demons.[2] They were to speak good

[a] St. Matt. x. 5–15

[b] ver. 15

[c] St. Mark vi. 7–11; St. Luke ix. 1–5

[d] St. Mark vi. 7

---

[1] So also in St. Matthew and in St. Mark. But this ' authority ' sprang from the power which he gave them.

[2] Dean *Plumptre* remarks : ' The words (" raise the dead ") are omitted by the best MSS.'

BOOK
III

and to do good in the highest sense, and that in a manner which all would feel good: freely, even as they had received it. Again, they were not to make any special provision [1] for their journey, beyond the absolute immediate present.[2] They were but labourers, yet as such they had claim to support. Their Employer would provide, and the field in which they worked might well be expected to supply it.[a 3]

a Comp. for this latter aspect 1 Tim. v. 18

In accordance with this, singleness of purpose and an entire self-denial, which should lead them not to make provision 'for the flesh,' but as labourers to be content with daily food, were the further injunctions laid on them. Before entering into a city, they were to make inquiry, literally to 'search out,' who in it was 'worthy,' and of them to ask hospitality; not seeking during their stay a change for the gratification of vanity or for self-indulgence. If the report on which they had made choice of a host proved true, then the 'Peace with thee!' with which they had entered their temporary home, would become a reality. Christ would make it such. As He had given them 'power and authority,' so He would 'honour' the draft on Him, in acknowledgment of hospitable reception, which the Apostles' 'Peace with thee!' implied.

But even if the house should prove unworthy, the Lord would none the less own the words of His messengers and make them real; only, in such case the peace would return to them who had spoken it. Yet another case was possible. The house to which their inquiries had led them, or the city into which they had entered, might refuse to receive them, because they came as Christ's ambassadors. Greater, indeed, would be their guilt than that of the cities of the plain, since these had not known the character of the heavenly guests to whom they refused reception; and more terrible would be their future punishment. So Christ would vindicate their authority as well as His own, and show the reality of their commission: on the one hand, by making their Word of Peace a reality to those who had proved 'worthy;' and, on the other, by punishment if their message

---

[1] *Weiss* (Matth. Evang. p. 262) has the curious idea that the prohibitions about money, &c., refer to their not making gain on their journey.

[2] Sandals, but not shoes. As regards the marked difference about 'the staff,' *Ebrard* (Evang. Gesch. p. 459) points out the agreement of *thought* in all the Gospels. Nothing was to be taken—they were to go as they stood, without preparation or provision. Sometimes there was a secret receptacle at the top

of the staff to hold valuables, or, in the case of the poor, water (Kel. xvii. 16).

[3] According to Jewish Law, 'the labourers' (the פּוֹעֲלִים, at least), would be secured their food. Not so always, however, slaves (Gitt. 12 *a*). In general, the Rabbinic Law of slavery is exceeding harsh—far more so than that of the Pentateuch (comp. an abstract of the Laws of Slavery in *Fassel*, Mos.-Rabb. Civil-Recht, vol. ii. pp. 393-406).

was refused. Lastly, in their present Mission they were not to touch either Gentile or Samaritan territory. The direction—so different in spirit from what Jesus Himself had previously said and done, and from their own later commission—was, of course, only 'for the present necessity.'[1] For the present they were neither prepared nor fitted to go beyond the circuit indicated. It would have been a fatal anticipation of their inner and outer history to have attempted this, and it would have defeated the object of our Lord of disarming prejudices when making a final appeal to the Jews of Galilee.

Even these considerations lead us to expect a strictly Jewish cast in this Discourse to the Disciples. The command to abstain from any religious fellowship with Gentiles and Samaritans was in temporary accommodation to the prejudices of His disciples and of the Jews. And the distinction between 'the way of the Gentiles' and 'any city of the Samaritans' is the more significant, when we bear in mind that even the dust of a heathen road was regarded as defiling,[a] while the houses, springs, roads, and certain food of the Samaritans were declared clean.[b] At the same time, religiously and as regarded fellowship, the Samaritans were placed on the same footing with Gentiles.[c] Nor would the injunction, to impart their message freely, sound strange in Jewish ears. It was, in fact, what the Rabbis themselves most earnestly enjoined in regard to the teaching of the Law and traditions, however different their practice may have been.[d] Indeed, the very argument, that they were to impart freely, because they had received freely, is employed by the Rabbis, and derived from the language and example of Moses in Deut. iv. 5.[e][2] Again, the directions about not taking staff, shoes, nor money-purse, exactly correspond to the Rabbinic injunction not to enter the Temple-precincts with staff, shoes[3] (mark, not sandals), and a money-girdle.[f][4] The symbolic reasons underlying this command would, in both cases, be probably the same: to avoid even the appearance of being engaged on other business, when the whole being should be absorbed in the service of the Lord. At any rate, it would convey to the disciples the idea, that they were to consider themselves as if entering the Temple-

CHAP.
XXVII

[a] Sanh. 15 b; Ned. 53 b

[b] Jer. Abhod. Z 44 d

[c] Jer. Sheq. i. 5, p. 46 b

[d] Ab. i. 13

[e] Ab. iv. 5; Bekhor. 29 a

[f] Ber. ix. 5

---

[1] The direction is recorded by St. Matthew only. But St. Matt. xxviii. 19 would, if it were necessary, sufficiently prove that this is not a Judaistic limitation.

[2] At the same time the statement in Bekhor. 29 a, that 'if needful money was to be paid for the acquisition of learning,' according to Prov. xxiii. 23

('by the truth'), implies that the rule cannot always have been strictly observed.

[3] The *Manal* (מִנְעָל) or shoe, in contradistinction to the *Sandal* (סַנְדָּל), as in Jer. Shabb. 8 a.

[4] The *Pundah* (פּוּנְדָּה), or *Aphundah* (אֲפוּנְדָה). Comp. for ex. Jer. Shabb. 12 c.

BOOK
III

a St. Luke
ii. 49

b Sanh. x. 3

c Deut. xiii.
17

d Jer. Peah
16 a
e Sanh. 64 a

f According
to Gen.
xiii. 3
g Arach.
16 b, lines
12 and 11
from
bottom
h St. Matt.
x. 1–15
i St. Matt.
x. 16–23

k vv. 16–18

m ver. 23

precincts, thus carrying out the principle of Christ's first thought in the Temple: ' Wist ye not that I must be about My Father's business?' [a] Nor could they be in doubt what severity of final punishment a doom heavier than that of Sodom and Gomorrah would imply, since, according to early tradition, their inhabitants were to have no part in the world to come.[b] And most impressive to a Jewish mind would be the symbolic injunction, to shake off the dust of their feet for a testimony against such a house or city. The expression, no doubt, indicated that the ban of the Lord was resting on it, and the symbolic act would, as it were, be the solemn pronouncing that ' nought of the cursed thing ' clave to them.[c] [1] In this sense, anything that clave to a person was metaphorically called ' the dust,' as for example, ' the dust of an evil tongue,' [d] ' the dust of usury,' as, on the other hand, to ' dust to idolatry ' meant to cleave to it.[e] Even the injunction not to change the dwelling, where one had been received, was in accordance with Jewish views, the example of 'Abraham being quoted, who [f] ' returned to the place where his tent had been at the beginning.' [g] [2]

These remarks show how closely the Lord followed, in this first part of His charge to the disciples,[h] Jewish forms of thinking and modes of expression. It is not otherwise in the second, [i] although the difference is here very marked. We have no longer merely the original commission, as it is given in almost the same terms by St. Mark and St. Luke. But the horizon is now enlarged, and St. Matthew reports that which the other Evangelists record at a later stage of the Lord's Ministry. Whether or not when the Lord charged His disciples on their first mission, He was led gradually to enlarge the scope of His teaching so as to adapt it to all times, need not be discussed. For St. Matthew himself could not have intended to confine the words of Christ to this first journey of the Apostles, since they contain references to division in families, persecutions, and conflict with the civil power,[k] such as belong to a much later period in the history of the Church; and, besides, contain also that prediction which could not have applied to this first Mission of the Apostles, ' Ye shall not have gone over the cities of Israel, till the Son of Man be come.' [m]

---

[1] The explanations of this expression generally offered need not here be repeated.

[2] So common, indeed, was this view as to have become proverbial. Thus, it was said concerning learned descendants of a learned man, that 'the Torah returned into its *Akhsanya* (($\xi\varepsilon\nu\acute{\iota}\alpha$),' or hospice (Baba Mez. 85 a, bis, in the curious story about the successful attempts made to convert to study the dissolute son of a great Rabbi).

Witnout here anticipating the full inquiry into the promise of His immediate Coming, it is important to avoid, even at this stage, any possible misunderstanding on the point. The expectation of the Coming of 'the Son of Man' was grounded on a prophecy of Daniel,[a] in which that Advent, or rather manifestation, was associated with judgment. The same is the case in this Charge of our Lord. The disciples in their work are described 'as sheep in the midst of wolves,' a phrase which the Midrash[b] applies to the position of Israel amidst a hostile world, adding: How great is that Shepherd, Who delivers them, and vanquishes the wolves! Similarly, the admonition to 'be wise as serpents and harmless as doves' is reproduced in the Midrash,[c] where Israel is described as harmless as the dove towards God, and wise as serpents towards the hostile Gentile nations. Such and even greater would be the enmity which the disciples, as the true Israel, would have to encounter from Israel after the flesh. They would be handed over to the various Sanhedrin,[1] and visited with such punishments as these tribunals had power to inflict.[d] More than this, they would be brought before governors and kings—primarily, the Roman governors and the Herodian princes.[e] And so determined would be this persecution, as to break the ties of the closest kinship, and to bring on them the hatred of all men.[f] The only, but the all-sufficient, support in those terrible circumstances was the assurance of such help from above, that, although unlearned and humble, they need have no care, nor make preparation in their defence, which would be given them from above. And with this they had the promise, that he who endured to the end would be saved, and the prudential direction, so far as possible, to avoid persecution by timely withdrawal, which could be the more readily achieved, since they would not have completed their circuit of the cities of Israel before the 'Son of Man be come.'

It is of the greatest importance to keep in view that, at whatever period of Christ's Ministry this prediction and promise were spoken, and whether only once or oftener, they refer exclusively to a *Jewish* state of things. The persecutions are exclusively Jewish. This appears from verse 18, where the answer of the disciples is promised to be 'for a testimony against them,' who had delivered them up, that is, here evidently the Jews, as also against 'the Gentiles.' And the Evangelistic circuit of the disciples in their preaching was to be *primarily Jewish*; and not only so, but in the time when there were

Margin notes:

[a] Dan. vii. 13

[b] On Esther viii. 2, ed. Warsh. p. 120 b

[c] On Cant. ii. 14

[d] St. Matt. x. 17

[e] ver. 18

[f] vv. 21, 22

---

[1] The question of the constitution and jurisdiction of the various Sanhedrin will be discussed in another place.

BOOK
III

still 'cities of Israel,' that is, previous to the final destruction of the Jewish commonwealth. The reference, then, is to that period of Jewish persecution and of Apostolic preaching in the cities of Israel, which is bounded by the destruction of Jerusalem. Accordingly, the 'coming of the Son of Man,' and the 'end' here spoken of, must also have the same application. It was, as we have seen, according to Dan. vii. 13, a coming in judgment. To the Jewish persecuting authorities, who had rejected the Christ, in order, as they imagined, to save their City and Temple from the Romans,[a] and to whom Christ had testified that He would come again, this judgment on their city and state, this destruction of their polity, *was* 'the Coming of the Son of Man' in judgment, and the only coming which the Jews, as a state, could expect, the only one meet for them, even as, to them who look for Him, He will appear a second time, without sin unto salvation.

That this is the only natural meaning attaching to this prediction, especially when compared with the parallel utterances recorded in St. Mark xiii. 9–13, appears to us indubitable. It is another question how, or how far, those to whom these words were in the first place addressed would understand their full bearing, at least at that time. Even supposing, that the disciples who first heard did not distinguish between the Coming to Israel in judgment, and that to the world in mingled judgment and mercy, as it was afterwards conveyed to them in the Parable of the Forthshooting of the Fig-tree,[b] yet the early Christians must soon have become aware of it. For, the distinction is sharply marked. As regards its manner, the 'second' Coming of Christ may be said to correspond to the state of those to whom He cometh. To the Jews His first Coming was *visible*, and as claiming to be their King. They had asked for a sign; and no sign was given them at the time. They rejected Him, and placed the Jewish polity and nation in rebellion against 'the King.' To the Jews, who so rejected the first visible appearance of Christ as their King, the second appearance would be invisible but real; the sign which they had asked would be given them, but as a sign of judgment, and His Coming would be in judgment. Thus would His authority be vindicated, and He appear, not, indeed, visibly but really, as what He had claimed to be. That this was to be the manner and object of His Coming to Israel, was clearly set forth to the disciples in the Parable of the Unthankful Husbandmen.[c] The coming of the Lord of the vineyard would be the destruction of the wicked husbandmen. And to render misunderstanding impossible, the explanation is

ᵃ St. John
xi. 48

ᵇ St. Luke
xxi. 29-31

ᶜ St. Matt.
xxi. 33-46,
and the
parallels

immediately added, that the Kingdom of God was to be taken from them, and given to those who would bring forth the fruits thereof. Assuredly, this could not, even in the view of the disciples, which may have been formed on the Jewish model, have applied to the Coming of Christ at the end of the present Æon dispensation.

We bear in mind that this second, outwardly invisible but very real, Coming of the Son of Man to the Jews, as a state, could only be in judgment on their polity, in that 'Sign' which was once refused, but which, when it appeared, would only too clearly vindicate His claims and authority. Thus viewed, the passages, in which that second Coming is referred to, will yield their natural meaning. Neither the mission of the disciples, nor their journeying through the cities of Israel, was finished, before the Son of Man came. Nay, there were those standing there who would not taste death, till they had seen in the destruction of the city and state the vindication of the Kingship of Jesus, which Israel had disowned.[a] And even in those last Discourses in which the horizon gradually enlarges, and this Coming in judgment to Israel merges in the greater judgment on an unbelieving world,[b] this earlier Coming to the Jewish nation is clearly marked. The three Evangelists equally record it, that 'this generation' should not pass away, till all things were fulfilled.[c] To take the lowest view, it is scarcely conceivable that these sayings would have been allowed to stand in all the three Gospels, if the disciples and the early Church had understood the Coming of the Son of Man in any other sense than as to the Jews in the destruction of their polity. And it is most significant, that the final utterances of the Lord as to His Coming were elicited by questions arising from the predicted destruction of the Temple. This the early disciples associated with the final Coming of Christ. To explain more fully the distinction between them would have been impossible, in consistency with the Lord's general purpose about the doctrine of His Coming. Yet the Parables which in the Gospels (especially in that by St. Matthew) follow on these predictions,[d] and the teaching about the final Advent of 'the Son of Man,' point clearly to a difference and an interval between the one and the other.

The disciples must have the more readily applied this prediction of His Coming to Palestine, since 'the woes' connected with it so closely corresponded to those expected by the Jews before the Advent of Messiah.[e] Even the direction to flee from persecution is repeated by the Rabbis in similar circumstances and established by the example of Jacob,[f] of Moses,[g] and of David.[h]

a St. Matt.
xvi. 28, and
parallels

b St. Matt.
xxiv. and
parallels

c St. Matt.
xxiv. 34; St.
Mark xiii.
30; St. Luke
xxi. 32

d St. Matt.
xxv. 1-30

e Sot. ix. 15;
comp.
Sanh. 97 a
to 99 a,
passim

f Hos. xii.
12

g Ex. ii. 15

h 1 Sam.
xix. 12;
comp.
Bemidb. R.
23, ed.
Warsh. p.
86 b, and
Tanch.

BOOK
III

ᵃ St. Matt.
x. 24–34

In the next section of this Discourse of our Lord, as reported by St. Matthew,ᵃ the horizon is enlarged. The statements are still primarily applicable to the early disciples, and their preaching among the Jews and in Palestine. But their ultimate bearing is already wider, and includes predictions and principles true to all time. In view of the treatment which their Master received, the disciples must expect misrepresentation and evil-speaking. Nor could it seem strange to them, since even the common Rabbinic proverb had it:[1] ' It is enough for a servant to be as his lord ' (דיו לעבד שיהא כרבו). As we hear it from the lips of Christ, we remember that this saying afterwards comforted those, who mourned the downfall of wealthy and liberal homes in Israel, by thoughts of the greater calamity which had overthrown Jerusalem and the Temple. And very significant is its application by Christ: ' If they have called the Master of the house Beelzebul,[2] how much more them of His household.' This charge, brought of course by the Pharisaic party of Jerusalem, had a double significance. We believe, that the expression ' Master of the house ' looked back to the claims which Jesus had made on His first purification of the Temple. We almost seem to hear the coarse Rabbinic witticism in its play on the word Beelzebul. For, Zebhul, (זְבוּל) means in Rabbinic language, not any ordinary dwelling, but specifically the Temple,[3] ᵇ and Beel-Zebul would be the Master of the Temple.' On the other hand, Zibbul (זִבּוּל) means[4] sacrificing to idols;ᶜ and hence Beel-zebul would, in that sense, be equivalent to ' lord ' or ' chief of idolatrous sacrificing '[5]—the worst and chiefest of demons, who presided over, and incited to, idolatry. ' The Lord of the Temple ' (which truly was His Church) was to them ' the chief of idolatrous worship,' the Representative of God that of the worst of demons: Beelzebul was Beelzibbul![6] What then might ' His Household ' expect at their hands?

But they were not to fear such misrepresentations. In due time

ᵇ Jer. Ber.
13 b

ᶜ Abod. Z.
18 b, and
often

---

[1] So Ber. 58 b; Siphra on Lev. xxv. 23; Ber. R. 49; Shem. R. 42; Midr. on Ps. xxvii. 4.

[2] This is undoubtedly the correct reading, and not Beelzebub. Any reference to the Baalzebub, or ' fly-god ' of 2 Kings i. 2, seems, rationally, out of the question.

[3] Zebhul (זְבוּל) is also the name of the fourth of the seven heavens in which Jewish mysticism located the heavenly Jerusalem with its Temple, at whose altar Michael ministered (Chag. 12 b).

[4] The primary meaning is: manuring (land) with dung.

[5] It could not possibly mean, as has been supposed, ' lord of dung,' because dung is זֶבֶל and not זִבּוּל.

[6] This alone explains the meaning of Beelzebul. Neither Beelzebub nor Baalzebul were names given by the Jews to any demon, but Beelzebul, the ' lord of sacrificing to idols,' would certainly be the designation of what they regarded as the chief of the demons.

the Lord would make manifest both His and their true character.[a][1]
Nor were they to be deterred from announcing in the clearest and
most public manner, in broad daylight, and from the flat roofs of
houses, that which had been first told them in the darkness, as
Jewish teachers communicated the deepest and highest doctrines in
secret to their disciples, or as the preacher would whisper his discourse into the ear of the interpreter.   The deepest truths concerning
His Person, and the announcement of His Kingdom and Work, were
to be fully revealed, and loudly proclaimed.   But, from a much higher
point of view, how different was the teaching of Christ from that of
the Rabbis!   The latter laid it down as a principle, which they tried
to prove from Scripture,[b] that, in order to save one's life, it was
not only lawful, but even duty—if necessary, to commit any kind
of sin, except idolatry, incest, or murder.[c]   Nay, even idolatry was
allowed, if only it were done in secret, so as not to profane the Name
of the Lord—than which death was infinitely preferable.[2]   Christ, on
the other hand, not only ignored this vicious Jewish distinction of
public and private as regarded morality, but bade His followers set
aside all regard for personal safety, even in reference to the duty of
preaching the Gospel.   There was a higher fear than of men: that of
God—and it should drive out the fear of those who could only kill the
body.   Besides, why fear?   God's Providence extended even over
the meanest of His creatures.   Two sparrows cost only an *assàrion*
(אִסָּר), about the third of a penny.[3]   Yet even one of them would
not perish without the knowledge of God.   No illustration was more
familiar to the Jewish mind than that of His watchful care even
over the sparrows.   The beautiful allusion in Amos iii. 5 was
somewhat realistically carried out in a legend which occurs in more
than one Rabbinic passage.   We are told that, after that great
miracle-worker of Jewish legend, R. Simeon ben Jochai, had been
for thirteen years in hiding from his persecutors in a cave, where he
was miraculously fed, he observed that, when the bird-catcher laid
his snare, the bird escaped, or was caught, according as a voice from
heaven proclaimed, 'Mercy,' or else, 'Destruction.'   Arguing, that if
even a sparrow could not be caught without heaven's bidding, how

CHAP.
XXVII

[a] St. Matt.
x. 26

[b] Lev. xviii.
5

[c] Sanh. 74 *a*
comp.
Yoma 82 *a*

---

[1] Mark the same meaning of the expression in St. Luke viii. 17; xii. 2.
[2] I confess myself unable to understand the bearing of the special pleading
of *Wünsche* against this inference from
Sanh. 74 *a*.   His reasoning is certainly
incorrect.

[3] The *Isar* (אִיסָר), or assarion, is expressly and repeatedly stated in Rabbinic
writings to be the twenty-fourth part of
a dinar, and hence not a halfpenny farthing, but about the third of a penny.
Comp. *Herzfeld*, Handelsgeschichte, pp.
180–182.

much more safe was the life of a 'son of man' (נֶפֶשׁ דְבַר נַשׁ), he came forth.[a]

Nor could even the additional promise of Christ: 'But of you even the hairs of the head are all numbered,'[1] surprise His disciples. But it would convey to them the gladsome assurance that, in doing His Work, they were performing the Will of God, and were specially in His keeping. And it would carry home to them—with the comfort of a very different application, while engaged in doing the Work and Will of God—what Rabbinism expressed in a realistic manner by the common sayings, that whither a man was to go, thither his feet would carry him; and, that a man could not injure his finger

on earth, unless it had been so decreed of him in heaven.[b] And in later Rabbinic writings[c] we read, in almost the words of Christ: 'Do I not number all the hairs of every creature?' And yet an

even higher outlook was opened to the disciples. All preaching was confessing, and all confessing a preaching of Christ; and our confession or denial would, almost by a law of nature, meet with similar confession or denial on the part of Christ before His Father in heaven.[2] This, also, was an application of that fundamental principle, that 'nothing is covered that shall not be revealed,' which, indeed, extendeth to the inmost secrets of heart and life.

What follows in our Lord's Discourse[d] still further widens the horizon. It describes the condition and laws of His Kingdom, until the final revelation of that which is now covered and hidden. So long as His claims were set before a hostile world they could only provoke war.[3] On the other hand, so long as such decision was necessary, in the choice of either those nearest and dearest, of ease, nay, of life itself, or else of Christ, there could be no compromise. Not that, as is sometimes erroneously supposed, a very great *degree* of love to the dearest on earth amounts to loving them more than Christ. No degree of proper affection can ever make affection wrongful, even as no diminution of it could make wrongful affection right. The love which Christ condemneth differs not in degree, but in kind, from rightful affection. It is one which takes the place of love to Christ—not which is placed by the side of that of Christ. For, rightly viewed, the two occupy different provinces. Wherever and whenever the two affections come into comparison, they also

---

[1] This is the literal rendering.
[2] This appears more clearly when we translate literally (ver. 32): 'Who shall confess in Me'—and again: 'in him will I also confess.'

[3] The original is very peculiar: 'Think not that I came to cast peace on the earth,' as a sower casts the seed into the ground.

come into collision. And so the questions of not being worthy of
Him (and who can be positively worthy?), and of the true finding or
losing of our life, have their bearing on our daily life and profession.[1]
But even in this respect the disciples must, to some extent, have
been prepared to receive the teaching of Christ. It was generally
expected, that a time of great tribulation would precede the Advent
of the Messiah. Again, it was a Rabbinic axiom, that the cause of
the Teacher, to whom a man owed eternal life, was to be taken in
hand before that of his father, to whom he owed only the life of this
world.[a][2] Even the statement about taking up the cross in following   [a] B. Mets.
Christ, although prophetic, could not sound quite strange. Cruci-   33 a
fixion was, indeed, not a Jewish punishment, but the Jews must have
become sadly familiar with it. The Targum[b] speaks of it as one of   [b] On Ruth
the four modes of execution which Naomi described to Ruth as those   i. 17
in custom in Palestine, the other three being—stoning, burning, and
beheading. Indeed, the expression 'bearing the cross,' as indicative
of sorrow and suffering, is so common, that we read, Abraham
carried the wood for the sacrifice of Isaac, 'like one who bears his
cross on his shoulder.'[c]   [c] Ber. R. 56,
Nor could the disciples be in doubt as to the meaning of the last   on Gen.
                                                                         xxii. 6
part of Christ's address.[d] They were old Jewish forms of thought,   [d] St. Matt.
only filled with the new wine of the Gospel. The Rabbis taught,   x. 40-42
only in extravagant terms, the merit attaching to the reception and
entertainment of sages.[e] The very expression 'in the name of' a   [e] Comp. for
prophet, or a righteous man, is strictly Jewish (לשם), and means for   example
                                                                         the long
the sake of, or with intention, in regard to. It appears to us, that   discussion
Christ introduced His own distinctive teaching by the admitted   in Ber. 63 b
Jewish principle, that hospitable reception for the sake of, or with
the intention of doing it to, a prophet or a righteous man, would
procure a share in the prophet's or righteous man's reward. Thus,
tradition had it, that the Obadiah of King Ahab's court[f] had become   [f] 1 Kings
the prophet of that name, because he had provided for the hundred   xviii. 4
prophets.[g] And we are repeatedly assured, that to receive a sage, or [g] Sanh. 39 b
even an elder, was like receiving the Shekhinah itself. But the
concluding promise of Christ, concerning the reward of even 'a cup
of cold water' to 'one of these little ones' 'in the name of a disciple,'

---

[1] The meaning of the expression,   for My sake shall find it.'
losing and finding one's life, appears   [2] Especially if he taught him the
more markedly by attending to the   highest of all lore, the Talmud, or ex-
tenses in the text: 'He that found his   plained the reason or the meaning of
life shall lose it, and he that lost his life   what it contained.

goes far beyond the farthest conceptions of His contemporaries. Yet, even so, the expression would, so far as its form is concerned, perhaps bear a fuller meaning to them than to us. These 'little ones' (קְמִנִים) were 'the children,' who were still learning the elements of knowledge, and who would by-and-by grow into 'disciples.' For, as the Midrash has it: 'Where there are no little ones, there are no disciples; and where no disciples, no sages: where no sages, there no elders; where no elders, there no prophets; and where no prophets, there [a] does God not cause His Shekhinah to rest.' [b]

[a] According to Is. viii. 16
[b] Ber. R. 42, on Gen. xiv. 1

We have been so particular in marking the Jewish parallelisms in this Discourse, first, because it seemed important to show, that the words of the Lord were not beyond the comprehension of the disciples. Starting from forms of thought and expressions with which they were familiar, He carried them far beyond Jewish ideas and hopes. But, secondly, it is just in this similarity of form, which proves that it was of the time and to the time, as well as to us and to all times, that we best see, how far the teaching of Christ transcended all contemporary conception.

But the reality, the genuineness, the depth and fervour of self-surrender, which Christ expects, is met by equal fulness of acknowledgment on His part, alike in heaven and on earth. In fact, there is absolute identification with His ambassadors on the part of Christ. As He is the Ambassador of the Father, so are they His, and as such also the ambassadors of the Father. To receive them was, therefore, not only to receive Christ, but the Father, Who would own the humblest, even the meanest service of love to one of the learners, 'the little ones.' All the more painful is the contrast of Jewish pride and self-righteousness, which attributes supreme merit to ministering, not as to God, but as to man; not for God's sake, but for that of the man; a pride which could give utterance to such a saying, 'All the prophets have announced salvation only to the like of those who give their daughters in marriage to sages, or cause them to make gain, or give of their goods to them. But what the bliss of the sages themselves is, no mortal eye has seen.' [c]

[c] Sanh. 99 a

It was not with such sayings that Christ sent forth His disciples; nor in such spirit, that the world has been subdued to Him. The relinquishing of all that is nearest and dearest, cross-bearing, loss of life itself—such were the terms of His discipleship. Yet acknowledgment there would surely be, first, in the felt and assured sense of His Presence; then, in the reward of a prophet, a righteous man, or, it might be, a disciple. But all was to be in Him, and for Him, even the gift of ' a cup of cold water ' to ' a little one.' Nay, neither the ' little ones,' the learners, nor the cup of cold water given them, would be overlooked or forgotton.

But over all did the ' Meek and Lowly One ' cast the loftiness of His Humility.

CHAPTER XXVIII.

THE STORY OF JOHN THE BAPTIST, FROM HIS LAST TESTIMONY TO JESUS
TO HIS BEHEADING IN PRISON.

(1. St. John iii. 25–30. 2. St. Matt. ix. 14–17; St. Mark ii. 18–22; St. Luke v. 33–39.
3. St. Matt. xi. 2–14; St. Luke vii. 18–35. 4. St. Matt. xiv. 1–12; St. Mark vi.
14–29; St. Luke ix. 7–9.)

BOOK
III

ᵃ St. Matt.
xi. 1

ᵇ St. Mark
vi. 12, 13;
St. Luke ix.
6

WHILE the Apostles went forth by two and two on their first Mission,[1] Jesus Himself taught and preached in the towns around Capernaum.[a] This period of undisturbed activity seems, however, to have been of brief duration.[2] That it was eminently successful, we infer not only from direct notices,[b] but also from the circumstance that, for the first time, the attention of Herod Antipas was now called to the Person of Jesus. We suppose that, during the nine or ten months of Christ's Galilean Ministry, the Tetrarch had resided in his Peræan dominions (east of the Jordan), either at Julias or at Machærus, in which latter fortress the Baptist was beheaded. We infer, that the labours of the Apostles had also extended thus far, since they attracted the notice of Herod. In the popular excitement caused by the execution of the Baptist, the miraculous activity of the messengers of the Christ, Whom John had announced, would naturally attract wider interest, while Antipas would, under the influence of fear and superstition, give greater heed to them. We can scarcely be mistaken in supposing, that this accounts for the abrupt termination of the labours of the Apostles, and their return to Jesus. At any rate, the arrival of the disciples of John, with tidings of their master's death, and the return

ᶜ St. Matt.
xiv. 12, 13;
St. Mark
vi. 30

of the Apostles, seem to have been contemporaneous.[c] Finally, we conjecture, that it was among the motives which influenced the removal of Christ and His Apostles from Capernaum. Temporarily to withdraw Himself and His disciples from Herod, to give them a

---

[1] This is the only occasion on which they are designated as Apostles in the Gospel by St. Mark.

[2] Their mission seems to have been short, probably not more than two weeks

or so. But it seems impossible, in consistency with the facts, to confine it to two days, as Bishop *Ellicott* proposes (Hist. Lect. p. 193).

season of rest and further preparation after the excitement of the last
few weeks, and to avoid being involved in the popular movements
consequent on the murder of the Baptist—such we may venture to
indicate as among the reasons of the departure of Jesus and His
disciples, first into the dominions of the Tetrarch Philip, on the
eastern side of the Lake,[a] and after that 'into the borders of Tyre
and Sidon.'[b] Thus the fate of the Baptist was, as might have been
expected, decisive in its influence on the History of the Christ and of
His Kingdom. But we have yet to trace the incidents in the life of
John, so far as recorded in the Gospels, from the time of His last contact with Jesus to his execution.

1. It was[c] in the late spring, or rather early summer of the year
27 of our era, that John was baptizing in Ænon, near to Salim.
In the neighbourhood, Jesus and His disciples were similarly engaged.[1]
The Presence and activity of Jesus in Jerusalem at the Passover[d] had
determined the Pharisaic party to take active measures against Him
and His Forerunner. John.   As to the first outcome of this plan we
notice the discussions on the question of 'purification,' and the
attempt to separate between Christ and the Baptist by exciting the
jealousy of the latter.[e] But the result was far different. His disciples might have been influenced, but John himself was too true a
man, and too deeply convinced of the reality of Christ's Mission, to
yield even for a moment to such temptation. Nothing more noble
can be conceived than the self-abnegation of the Baptist in circumstances which would not only have turned aside an impostor or an
enthusiast, but must have severely tried the constancy of the truest
man.   At the end of a most trying career of constant self-denial its
scanty fruits seemed, as it were, snatched from Him, and the multitude, which he had hitherto swayed, turned after Another, to Whom
himself had first given testimony, but Who ever since had apparently
neglected him.   And now he had seemingly appropriated the one
distinctive badge of his preaching! Not to rebel, nor to murmur, but
even to rejoice in this as the right and proper thing, for which he had
longed as the end of his own work—this implies a purity, simplicity,
and grandeur of purpose, and a strength of conviction unsurpassed
among men.   The moral height of this testimony of John, and the
evidential force of the introduction of this narrative—utterly unaccountable, nay, unintelligible on the hypothesis that it is not true—
seem to us among the strongest evidences in favour of the Gospel-
history.

CHAP.
XXVIII

[a] St. John
vi. 1
[b] St. Mark
vii. 24

[c] St. John
iii. 22 to
iv. 3

[d] St. John
ii. 13 to iii.
21

[e] St. John
iii. 25 &c.

[1] Comp. chapter vii. of this Book. For   some points formerly referred to have
the sake of clearness and connection,   had to be here repeated.

BOOK
III

It was not the greatness of the Christ, to his own seeming loss, which could cloud the noonday of the Baptist's convictions. In simple Judæan illustration, he was only 'the friend of the Bridegroom' (the *'Shoshebheyna'*), with all that popular association or higher Jewish allegory connected with that relationship.[1] He claimed not the bride. His was another joy—that of hearing the Voice of her rightful Bridegroom, Whose 'groomsman' he was. In the sound of that Voice lay the fulfilment of his office. And St. John, looking back upon the relation between the Baptist and Jesus—on the reception of the testimony of the former and the unique position of 'the Bridegroom'—points out the lessons of the answer of the Baptist to his disciples (St. John iii. 31 to 36[2]) as formerly those of the conversa-

* St. John
iii. 16 to 21

tion with Nicodemus.*

This hour of the seeming abasement of the Baptist was, in truth, that of the highest exaltation, as marking the fulfilment of his office, and, therefore, of his joy. Hours of cloud and darkness were to follow.

2. The scene has changed, and the Baptist has become the prisoner of Herod Antipas. The dominions of the latter embraced, in the north: Galilee, *west* of the Jordan and of the Lake of Galilee; and in the south: Peræa, *east* of the Jordan. To realise events we must bear in mind that, crossing the Lake eastwards, we should pass from the possessions of Herod to those of the Tetrarch Philip, or else come upon the territory of the 'Ten Cities,' or Decapolis, a kind of confederation of townships, with constitution and liberties, such as those of the Grecian cities.[3] By a narrow strip northwards, Peræa just slipped in between the Decapolis and Samaria. It is impossible with certainty to localise the Ænon, near Salim, where John baptized. Ancient tradition placed the latter a few miles south of Scythopolis or Bethshean, on the borders of Galilee, or rather, the Decapolis, and Samaria. But as the eastern part of Samaria towards the Jordan was very narrow, one may well believe that the place was close to, perhaps actually in, the north-eastern angle of the province of Judæa, where it borders on Samaria. We are now on the western bank of Jordan. The other, or eastern, bank of the river would be that narrow northern strip of Peræa which formed part of the territory of Antipas. Thus a few miles, or the mere crossing of the river, would have brought

---

[1] Comp. 'Sketches of Jewish Social Life,' pp. 152, 153.

[2] These verses contain the reflections of the Evangelist, not the words of the Baptist, just as previously vv. 16 to 21

are no longer the words of Christ but those of St. John.

[3] Comp. *Caspari*, Chronolog. Geogr. Einl. pp. 83–91.

the Baptist into Peræa.   There can be no doubt but that the Baptist
must either have crossed into, or else that Ænon, near Salim, was
actually within the dominions of Herod.[1]   It was on that occasion
that Herod seized on his person, [a] and that Jesus, Who was still
within Judæan territory, withdrew from the intrigues of the Pharisees
and the proximity of Herod, through Samaria, into Galilee.[b]

For, although Galilee belonged to Herod Antipas, it was sufficiently far from the present residence of the Tetrarch in Peræa.
Tiberias, his Galilean residence, with its splendid royal palace, had
only been built a year or two before;[2] and it is impossible to suppose, that Herod would not have sooner heard of the fame of Jesus,[c]
if his court had been in Tiberias, in the immediate neighbourhood
of Capernaum.   We are, therefore, shut up to the conclusion, that,
during the nine or ten months of Christ's Ministry in Galilee, the
Tetrarch resided in Peræa.   Here he had two palaces, one at Julias,
or Livias, the other at Machærus.   The latter will be immediately
described as the place of the Baptist's imprisonment and martyrdom.
The Julias, or Livias, of Peræa must be distinguished from another
city of that name (also called Bethsaida) in the North (east of the
Jordan), and within the dominions of the Tetrarch Philip.   The
Julias of Peræa represented the ancient *Beth Haram* in the tribe of
Gad,[d] a name for which Josephus gives[e] *Betharamphtha*, and the
Rabbis *Beth Ramthah*.[f][3]   It still survives in the modern *Beit-harân*.
But of the fortress and palace which Herod had built, and named
after the Empress, 'all that remains' are ' a few traces of walls and
foundations.'[4]

Supposing Antipas to have been at the Peræan Julias, he would
have been in the closest proximity to the scene of the Baptist's last
recorded labours at Ænon.   We can now understand, not only how
John was imprisoned by Antipas, but also the threefold motives
which influenced it.   According to Josephus,[g] the Tetrarch was
afraid that his absolute influence over the people, who seemed disposed to carry out whatever he advised, might lead to a rebellion.
This circumstance is also indicated in the remark of St. Matthew,[h]
that Herod was afraid to put the Baptist to death on account of the
people's opinion of him.   On the other hand, the Evangelic statement,[i] that Herod had imprisoned John on account of his declaring

CHAP.
XXVIII

[a] St. John
iii. 24

[b] St. John
vi. 1

[c] St. Matt.
xiv. 1

[d] Numb.
xxxii. 36;
Josh.xiii.27
[e] Ant. xviii.
2. 1
[f] Jerus.
Shev. 38 d

[g] Ant. xviii
5, 2

[h] St. Matt.
xiv. 5

[i] St. Matt.
xiv. 3, 4;
St. Mark vi
17, 18

---

[1] Ænon may even have been in Peræa
itself—in that case, on the eastern bank
of the Jordan.
[2] Comp. *Schürer*, Neutest. Zeitgesch.
p. 233.   As to the name Tiberias, comp.

p. 635, note 1.
[3] Comp. the references in *Böttger*,
Lex. zu Jos. p. 58.
[4] See the description of the site in
Tristram, Land of Moab, p. 348.

BOOK
III

his marriage with Herodias unlawful, is in no way inconsistent with the reason assigned by Josephus. Not only might both motives have influenced Herod, but there is an obvious connection between them. For, John's open declaration of the unlawfulness of Herod's marriage, as unlike incestuous and adulterous, might, in view of the influence which the Baptist exercised, have easily led to a rebellion. In our view, the sacred text gives indication of yet a third cause which led to John's imprisonment, and which indeed, may have given final weight to the other two grounds of enmity against him. It has been suggested, that Herod must have been attached to the Sadducees, if to any religious party, because such a man would not have connected himself with the Pharisees. The reasoning is singularly inconclu, sive. On political grounds, a Herod would scarcely have lent his weight to the Sadducean or aristocratic priest-party in Jerusalem; while, religiously, only too many instances are on record of what the Talmud itself calls 'painted ones, who are like the Pharisees, and

ᵃ Sot. 22 b

who act like Zimri, but expect the reward of Phinehas.'ᵃ Besides, the Pharisees may have used Antipas as their tool, and worked upon his wretched superstition to effect their own purposes. And this is what we suppose to have been the case. The reference to the Pharisaic spying and to their comparisons between the influence of

ᵇ St. John iv. 1, 2

Jesus and John,ᵇ which led to the withdrawal of Christ into Galilee, seems to imply that the Pharisees had something to do with the imprisonment of John. Their connection with Herod appears even more clearly in the attempt to induce Christ's departure from Galilee, on pretext of Herod's machinations. It will be remembered that the Lord unmasked their hypocrisy by bidding them go back to Herod, showing that He fully knew that real danger threatened Him,

ᶜ St. Luke xiii. 31–33

not from the Tetrarch, but from the leaders of the party in Jerusalem.ᶜ Our inference therefore is, that Pharisaic intrigue had a very large share in giving effect to Herod's fear of the Baptist and of his reproofs.

3. We suppose, then, that Herod Antipas was at Julias, in the immediate neighbourhood of Ænon, at the time of John's imprisonment. But, according to Josephus, whose testimony there is no reason to question, the Baptist was committed to the strong

ᵈ Ant. xviii. 5, 2

fortress of Machærus.ᵈ¹ If Julias lay where the Wady of the Heshban debouches into the Jordan, east of that river, and a little north of the Dead Sea, Machærus is straight south of it, about

---

¹ A little before that it seems to have belonged to Aretas. We know not, how it again passed into the hands of Antipas, if, indeed, it ever was fully ceded by him to the Arabs. Comp. *Schürer*, u. s. p. 239, and *Wieseler*, Chron. Syn. p. 244, Beitr. pp. 5, &c., whose positions are, however, not always quite reliable.

two and a half hours north-west of the ancient *Kiriathaim* (the
modern *Kurêiyât*), the site of Chedorlaomer's victory.[a] Machærus
(the modern *M'khaur*) marked the extreme point south, as Pella that
north, in Peræa. As the boundary fortress in the south-east (towards [a]Gen. xiv. 5
Arabia), its safety was of the greatest importance, and everything
was done to make a place, exceedingly strong by nature, impregnable.
It had been built by Alexander Jannæus, but destroyed by Gabinius
in the wars of Pompey.[b] It was not only restored, but greatly [b] Jewish War i. 8. 5
enlarged, by Herod the Great, who surrounded it with the best defences known at that time. In fact, Herod the Great built a town
along the shoulder of the hill, and surrounded it by walls, fortified
by towers. From this town a farther height had to be climbed, on
which the castle stood, surrounded by walls, and flanked by towers
one hundred and sixty cubits high. Within the inclosure of the
castle Herod had built a magnificent palace. A large number of
cisterns, storehouses, and arsenals, containing every weapon of attack
or defence, had been provided to enable the garrison to stand a prolonged
siege. *Josephus* describes even its natural position as unassailable.
The highest point of the fort was on the west, where it looked sheer
down into a valley. North and south the fort was equally cut off by
valleys, which could not be filled up for siege purposes. On the east
there was, indeed, a valley one hundred cubits deep, but it terminated
in a mountain opposite to Machærus. This was evidently the weak
point of the situation.[1]

A late and very trustworthy traveller[2] has pronounced the descrip-
tion of Josephus[c] as sufficiently accurate, although exaggerated, and [c] War vii. 6 1, 2
as probably not derived from personal observation. He has also fur-
nished such pictorial details, that we can transport ourselves to that
rocky keep of the Baptist, perhaps the more vividly that, as we
wander over the vast field of stones, upturned foundations, and
broken walls around, we seem to view the scene in the lurid sunset
of judgment. 'A rugged line of upturned squared stones' shows
the old Roman paved road to Machærus. Ruins covering quite a
square mile, on a group of undulating hills, mark the site of the
ancient town of Machærus. Although surrounded by a wall and
towers, its position is supposed not to have been strategically de-
fensible. Only a mass of ruins here, with traces of a temple to

---

[1] Here Bassus made his attack in the last Jewish war (*Jos.* War vii. 6. 1–4).
[2] Canon *Tristram*, Land of Moab, pp. 255–265; comp. *Baedeker* (*Socin*) Palästina, p. 195 and, for the various pas-
sages in Josephus referring to Machærus, *Böttger*, u. s. pp. 165–167.

the Syrian Sun-God, broken cisterns, and desolateness all around. Crossing a narrow deep valley, about a mile wide, we climb up to the ancient fortress on a conical hill. Altogether it covered a ridge of more than a mile. The key of the position was a citadel to the extreme east of the fortress. It occupied the summit of the cone, was isolated, and almost impregnable, but very small. We shall return to examine it. Meanwhile, descending a steep slope about 150 yards towards the west, we reach the oblong flat plateau that formed the fortress, containing Herod's magnificent palace. Here, carefully collected, are piled up the stones of which the citadel was built. These immense heaps look like a terrible monument of judgment.

We pass on among the ruins. No traces of the royal palace are left, save foundations and enormous stones upturned. Quite at the end of this long fortress in the west, and looking southwards, is a square fort. We return, through what we regard as the ruins of the magnificent castle-palace of Herod, to the highest and strongest part of the defences—the eastern keep or the citadel, on the steep slope 150 yards up. The foundations of the walls all around, to the height of a yard or two above the ground, are still standing. As we clamber over them to examine the interior, we notice how small this keep is: exactly 100 yards in diameter. There are scarcely any remains of it left. A well of great depth, and a deep cemented cistern with the vaulting of the roof still complete, and—of most terrible interest to us—two dungeons, one of them deep down, its sides scarcely broken in, ' with small holes still visible in the masonry where staples of wood and iron had once been fixed'! As we look down into its hot darkness, we shudder in realising that this terrible keep had for nigh ten months been the prison of that son of the free ' wilderness,' the bold herald of the coming Kingdom, the humble, earnest, self-denying John the Baptist. Is this the man whose testimony about the Christ may be treated as a falsehood?

We withdraw our gaze from trying to pierce this gloom and to call up in it the figure of the camel-hair-clad and leather-girt preacher, and look over the ruins at the scene around. We are standing on a height not less than 3,800 feet above the Dead Sea. In a straight line it seems not more than four or five miles; and the road down to it leads, as it were, by a series of ledges and steps. We can see the whole extent of this Sea of Judgment, and its western shores from north to south. We can almost imagine the Baptist, as he stands surveying this noble prospect. Far to the south stretches the rugged

wilderness of Judæa, bounded by the hills of Hebron. Here nestles
Bethlehem, there is Jerusalem. Or, turning another way, and looking into the deep cleft of the Jordan valley: this oasis of beauty is
Jericho; beyond it, like a silver thread, Jordan winds through a
burnt, desolate-looking country, till it is lost to view in the haze
which lies upon the edge of the horizon. As the eye of the Baptist
travelled over it, he could follow all the scenes of His life and labours,
from the home of his childhood in the hill-country of Judæa, to those
many years of solitude and communing with God in the wilderness,
and then to the first place of his preaching and Baptism, and onwards
to that where he had last spoken of the Christ, just before his own
captivity. And now the deep dungeon in the citadel on the one
side, and, on the other, down that slope, the luxurious palace of
Herod and his adulterous, murderous wife, while the shouts of wild
revelry and drunken merriment rise around! Was this the Kingdom he had come to announce as near at hand; for which he had
longed, prayed, toiled, suffered, utterly denied himself and all that
made life pleasant, and the rosy morning of which he had hailed with
hymns of praise? Where was the Christ? Was He the Christ?
What was He doing? Was he eating and drinking all this while
with publicans and sinners, when he, the Baptist, was suffering for
Him? Was He in His Person and Work so quite different from
himself? and why was He so? And did the hot haze and mist
gather also over this silver thread in the deep cleft of Israel's barren
burnt-up desolateness?

4. In these circumstances we scarcely wonder at the feelings of
John's disciples, as months of this weary captivity passed. Uncertain
what to expect, they seem to have oscillated between Machærus and
Capernaum. Any hope in their Master's vindication and deliverance lay in the possibilities involved in the announcement he had
made of Jesus as the Christ. And it was to Him that their Master's
finger had pointed them. Indeed, some of Jesus' earliest and most
intimate disciples had come from their ranks; and, as themselves
had remarked, the multitude had turned to Jesus even before the
Baptist's imprisonment.[a] And yet, could He be the Christ? How [a] St. John
many things about Him that were strange and seemed inexplicable! iii. 26
In their view, there must have been a terrible contrast between him
who lay in the dungeon of Machærus, and Him Who sat down to eat
and drink at a feast of the publicans.

His reception of publicans and sinners they could understand;
their own Master had not rejected them. But why eat and drink

with them? Why feasting, and this in a time when fasting and prayer would have seemed specially appropriate? And, indeed, was not fasting always appropriate? And yet this new Messiah had not taught his disciples either to fast or what to pray! The Pharisees, in their anxiety to separate between Jesus and His Forerunner, must have told them all this again and again, and pointed to the contrast.

At any rate, it was at the instigation of the Pharisees, and in company with them,[1] that the disciples of John propounded to Jesus this question about fasting and prayer, immediately after the feast in the house of the converted Levi-Matthew.[a] We must bear in mind that fasting and prayer, or else fasting and alms, or all the three, were always combined. Fasting represented the negative, prayer and alms the positive element, in the forgiveness of sins. Fasting, as self-punishment and mortification, would avert the anger of God and calamities. Most extraordinary instances of the purposes in view in fasting, and of the results obtained are told in Jewish legend, which (as will be remembered) went so far as to relate how a Jewish saint was thereby rendered proof against the fire of Gehenna, of which a realistic demonstration was given when his body was rendered proof against ordinary fire.[b]

Even apart from such extravagances, Rabbinism gave an altogether external aspect to fasting. In this it only developed to its utmost consequences a theology against which the Prophets of old had already protested. Perhaps, however, the Jews are not solitary in their misconception and perversion of fasting. In their view, it was the readiest means of turning aside any threatening calamity, such as drought, pestilence, or national danger. This, *ex opere operato*: because fasting was self-punishment and mortification, not because a fast meant mourning (for sin, not for its punishment), and hence indicated humiliation, acknowledgment of sin, and repentance. The second and fifth days of the week (Monday and Thursday)[3] were those appointed for public fasts, because Moses was supposed to have gone up the Mount for the second Tables of the Law on a Thursday, and to have returned on a Monday. The self-introspection of Pharisaism led many to fast on these two days all the year round,[c] just as in Temple-times not a few would offer daily trespass-offering for sins of which they were ignorant. Then there were

a St. Matt.
ix. 14–17
and
parallels

b B. Mez. 85
a, 2 towards
the end

c Taan. 12 a;
St. Luke
xviii. 12

---

[1] Thus viewed there is no contradiction, not even real variation, between St. Matt. ix. 14, St. Mark ii. 18, and St. Luke v. 33.

[2] Altogether, Baba Mez, 84 *a* to 85 *a* contains a mixture of the strangest, grossest, and profanest absurdities.

[3] Thus a three days' fast would be on the second, fifth, and again on the second day of the week.

such painful minutiæ of externalism, as those which ruled how, on a less strict fast, a person might wash and anoint; while, on the strictest fast, it was prohibited even to salute one another.[a][1]

It may well have been, that it was on one of these weekly fasts that the feast of Levi-Matthew had taken place, and that this explains the expression: 'And John's disciples and the Pharisees were fasting.'[b][2] This would give point to their complaint, 'Thy disciples fast not.' Looking back upon the standpoint from which they viewed fasting, it is easy to perceive why Jesus could not have sanctioned, not even tolerated, the practice among His disciples, as little as St. Paul could tolerate among Judaising Christians the, in itself indifferent, practice of circumcision. But it was not so easy to explain this at the time to the disciples of John. For, to understand it, implied already entire transformation from the old to the new spirit. Still more difficult must it have been to do it in such manner, as at the same time to lay down principles that would rule all similar questions to all ages. But our Lord did both, and even thus proved His Divine Mission.

The last recorded testimony of the Baptist had pointed to Christ as the 'Bridegroom.'[c] As explained in a previous chapter, John applied this in a manner which appealed to popular custom. As he had pointed out, the Presence of Jesus marked the marriage-week. By universal consent and according to Rabbinic law, this was to be a time of unmixed festivity.[d] Even on the Day of Atonement a bride was allowed to relax one of the ordinances of that strictest fast.[e] During the marriage-week all mourning was to be suspended —even the obligation of the prescribed daily prayers ceased. It was regarded as a religious duty to gladden the bride and bridegroom. Was it not, then, inconsistent on the part of John's disciples to expect 'the sons of the bride-chamber' to fast, so long as the Bridegroom was with them?

This appeal of Christ is still further illustrated by the Talmudic ordinance[f] which absolved 'the friends of the bridegroom,' and all 'the sons of the bride-chamber,' even from the duty of dwelling in booths (at the Feast of Tabernacles). The expression, 'sons of the bride-chamber' (בְּנֵי חוּפָּה), which means all invited guests, has the more significance, when we remember that the Covenant-union between God and Israel was not only compared to a marriage, but the

CHAP.
XXVIII

[a] Taan i.
4-7

[b] St. Mark
ii. 18

[c] St. John
iii. 29

[d] Ber. 6 b

[e] Yoma viii.
1

[f] Jer. Sukk.
53 a, near
the middle

---

[1] Comp. 'The Temple, its Ministry and Services,' pp. 296-298.
[2] This is the real import of the original.

Tabernacle and Temple designated as 'the bridal chambers.'[a][1] And, as the institution of 'friends of the bridegroom' prevailed in Judæa, but *not* in Galilee, this marked distinction of the 'friends of the bridegroom,'[2] in the mouth of the Judæan John, and 'sons of the bride-chamber' in that of the Galilean Jesus, is itself evidential of historic accuracy, as well as of the Judæan authorship of the Fourth Gospel.

But let it not be thought that it was to be a time of unbroken joy to the disciples of Jesus. Nay, the ideas of the disciples of John concerning the Messianic Kingdom, as one of resistless outward victory and assertion of power, were altogether wrong. The Bridegroom would be violently taken from them, and then would be the time for mourning and fasting. Not that this necessarily implies literal fasting, any more than it excludes it, provided the great principles, more fully indicated immediately afterwards, are kept in view. Painfully minute, Judaistic self-introspection is contrary to the spirit of the joyous liberty of the children of God. It is only a sense of sin, and the felt absence of the Christ, which should lead to mourning and fasting, though not in order thereby to avert either the anger of God or outward calamity. Besides the evidential force of this highly spiritual, and thoroughly un-Jewish view of fasting, we notice some other points in confirmation of this, and of the Gospel-history generally. On the hypothesis of a Jewish invention of the Gospel-history, or of its Jewish embellishment, the introduction of this narrative would be incomprehensible. Again, on the theory of a fundamental difference in the Apostolic teaching, St. Matthew and St. Mark representing the original Judaic, St. Luke the freer Pauline development, the existence of this narrative in the first two Gospels would seem unaccountable. Or, to take another view—on the hypothesis of the much later and non-Judæan (Ephesian) authorship of the Fourth Gospel, the minute archæological touches, and the general fitting of the words of the Baptist[b] into the present narrative would be inexplicable. Lastly, as against all deniers and detractors of the Divine Mission of Jesus, this early anticipation of His violent removal by death, and of the consequent mourning of the Church, proves that it came not to Him from without, as by the accident of events, but that from the beginning He anticipated the end, and pursued it of set, steadfast purpose.

[1] 'All the bride-chambers were only within the portions of Benjamin' (the Tabernacle and the Temple). Hence Benjamin was called 'the host of the Lord.'

[2] Strangely, the two designations are treated as identical in most Commentaries.

Yet another point in evidence comes to us from the eternal and un-Jewish principles implied in the two illustrations, of which Christ here made use.[a] In truth, the Lord's teaching is now carried down to its ultimate principles. The slight variations which here occur in the Gospel of St. Luke, as, indeed, such exist in so many of the narratives of the same events by different Evangelists, should not be 'explained away.' For, the sound critic should never devise an explanation for the sake of a supposed difficulty, but truthfully study the text—as an interpreter, not an apologist. Such variations of detail present no difficulty. As against a merely mechanical, unspiritual accord, they afford evidence of truthful, independent witness, and irrefragable proof that, contrary to modern negative criticism, the three narratives are not merely different recensions of one and the same original document.

In general, the two illustrations employed—that of the piece of undressed cloth (or, according to St. Luke, a piece torn from a new garment) sewed upon the rent of an old garment, and that of the new wine put into the old wine-skins—must not be too closely pressed in regard to their language.[1] They seem chiefly to imply this: You ask, why do we fast often, but Thy disciples fast not? You are mistaken in supposing that the old garment can be retained, and merely its rents made good by patching it with a piece of new cloth. Not to speak of the incongruity, the effect would only be to make the rent ultimately worse. The old garment will not bear mending with the 'undressed cloth.' Christ's was not merely a reformation: all things must become new. Or, again, take the other view of it—as the old garment cannot be patched from the new, so, on the other hand, can the new wine of the Kingdom not be confined in the old forms. It would burst those wine-skins. The spirit must, indeed, have its corresponding form of expression; but that form must be adapted, and correspond to it. Not the old with a little of the new to hold it together where it is rent; but the new, and that not in the old wine-skins, but in a form corresponding to the substance. Such are the two final principles [2]—the one primarily addressed to the Pharisees, the other to the disciples of John, by which the illustrative teaching concerning the marriage-feast, with its bridal garment and wine of banquet, is carried far beyond the original question of the disciples of John, and receives an application to all time.

[1] *Godet* has shown objections against all previous interpretations. But his own view seems to me equally untenable.
[2] St. Luke v. 39 seems either a gloss of the writer, or may be (though very doubtfully) an interpolation. There is a curious parallel to the verse in Ab. iv. 20.

5. We are in spirit by the mount of God, and about to witness the breaking of a terrible storm.ᵃ It is one that uproots the great trees and rends the rocks; and we shall watch it solemnly, earnestly, as with bared head—or, like Elijah, with face wrapt in mantle. Weeks had passed, and the disciples of John had come back and showed their Master of all these things. He still lay in the dungeon of Machærus; his circumstances unchanged—perhaps, more hopeless than before. For, Herod was in that spiritually most desperate state: he had heard the Baptist, and was much perplexed. And still he heard—but only heard—him gladly.ᵇ ¹ It was a case by no means singular, and of which Felix, often sending for St. Paul, at whose preaching of righteousness, temperance, and the judgment to come, he had trembled, offers only one of many parallels. That, when hearing him, Herod was 'much perplexed,' we can understand, since he 'feared him, knowing that he was a righteous man and holy,' and thus fearing 'heard him.' But that being 'much perplexed,' he still 'heard him gladly,' constituted the hopelessness of his case. But was the Baptist right? Did it constitute part of his Divine calling to have not only denounced, but apparently directly confronted Herod on his adulterous marriage? Had he not attempted to lift himself the axe which seemed to have slipt from the grasp of Him, of Whom the Baptist had hoped and. said that He would lay it to the root of the tree?

Such thoughts may have been with him, as he passed from his dungeon to the audience of Herod, and from such bootless interviews back to his deep keep. Strange as it may seem, it was, perhaps, better for the Baptist when he was alone. Much as his disciples honoured and loved him, and truly zealous and jealous for him as they were, it was best when they were absent. There are times when affection only pains, by forcing on our notice inability to understand, and adding to our sorrow that of feeling our inmost being a stranger to those nearest, and who love us must. Then, indeed, is a man alone. It was so with the Baptist. The state of mind and experience of his disciples has already appeared, even in the slight notices concerning them. Indeed,. had they fully understood him, and not ended where he began—which, truly, is the characteristic of all sects, in their crystallisation, or, rather, ossification of truth—they would not have remained his disciples; and this consciousness must also have brought exquisite pain. Their very affection for him, and

---

¹ This is both the correct reading and rendering.

their zeal for his credit (as shown in the almost coarse language of their inquiry: 'John the Baptist hath sent us unto Thee, saying, Art Thou He that cometh, or look we for another?'), as well as their tenacity of unprogressiveness—were all, so to speak, marks of his failure. And, if he had failed with them, had he succeeded in anything?

And yet further and more terrible questions rose in that dark dungeon. Like serpents that crept out of its walls, they would uncoil and raise their heads with horrible hissing. What if, after all, there had been some terrible mistake on his part? At any rate the logic of events was against him. He was now the fast prisoner of that Herod, to whom he had spoken with authority; in the power of that bold adulteress, Herodias. If he were Elijah, the great Tishbite had never been in the hands of Ahab and Jezebel. And the Messiah, Whose Elijah he was, moved not; could not, or would not, move, but feasted with publicans and sinners! Was it all a reality? or—oh, thought too horrible for utterance—could it have been a dream, bright but fleeting, uncaused by any reality, only the reflection of his own imagination? It must have been a terrible hour, and the power of darkness. At the end of one's life, and that of such self-denial and suffering, and with a conscience so alive to God, which had—when a youth—driven him burning with holy zeal into the wilderness, to have such a question meeting him as: Art Thou He, or do we wait for another? Am I right, or in error and leading others into error? must have been truly awful. Not Paul, when forsaken of all he lay in the dungeon, the aged prisoner of Christ; not Huss, when alone at Constance he encountered the whole Catholic Council and the flames; only He, the God-Man, over Whose soul crept the death-coldness of great agony when, one by one, all light of God and man seemed to fade out, and only that one remained burning—His own faith in the Father, could have experienced bitterness like this. Let no one dare to say that the faith of John failed, at least till the dark waters have rolled up to his own soul. For mostly all and each of us must pass through some like experience; and only our own hearts and God know, how death-bitter are the doubts, whether of head or of heart, when question after question raises, as with devilish hissing, its head, and earth and heaven seem alike silent to us.

But here we must for a moment pause to ask ourselves this, which touches the question of all questions: Surely, such a man as this Baptist, so thoroughly disillusioned in that hour, could not have been an impostor, and his testimony to Christ a falsehood? Nor yet could the record, which gives us this insight into the weakness of the strong man and the doubts of the great Testimony-bearer, be a cunningly-invented fable. We cannot imagine the record of such a failure, if the narrative were an invention. And if this record be true, it is not only of present failure, but also of the previous testimony of John. To us, at least, the evidential force of this narrative seems irresistible. The testimony of the Baptist to Jesus offers the same kind of evidence as does that of the human soul to God: in both cases the one points to the other, and cannot be understood without it.

In that terrible conflict John overcame, as we all must overcome. His very despair opened the door of hope. The helpless doubt, which none could solve but One, he brought to Him around Whom it had gathered. Even in this there is evidence for Christ, as the unalterably True One. When John asked the question: Do we wait for another? light was already struggling through darkness. It was incipient victory even in defeat. When he sent his disciples with this question straight to Christ, he had already conquered; for such a question addressed to a possibly false Messiah has no meaning. And so must it ever be with us. Doubt is the offspring of our disease, diseased as is its paternity. And yet it cannot be cast aside. It may be the outcome of the worst, or the problems of the best souls. The twilight may fade into outer night, or it may usher in the day. The answer lies in this: whether doubt will lead us *to* Christ, or *from* Christ.

Thus viewed, the question: ' Art Thou the Coming One, or do we wait for another? ' indicated faith both in the great promise and in Him to Whom it was addressed. The designation ' The Coming One ' (*habba*), though a most truthful expression of Jewish expectancy, was not one ordinarily used of the Messiah. But it was invariably used in reference to the Messianic age, as the *Athid labho*, or coming future (literally, the prepared for to come), and the *Olam habba*, the coming world or Æon.[1] But then it implied the setting right of all things by the Messiah, the assumption and vindication of His Power. In the mouth of John it might therefore mean chiefly this : Art Thou He that is to establish the Messianic Kingdom in its outward power, or have we to wait for another? In that case, the manner in which the Lord answered it would be all the more sig-

---

[1] The distinction between the two expressions will be further explained in the sequel.

nificant.   The messengers came just as He was engaged in healing body and soul.[a1]   Without interrupting His work, or otherwise noticing their inquiry, He bade them tell John for answer what they had seen and heard, and that 'the poor,'[b] are evangelised.'   To this, as the inmost characteristic of the Messianic Kingdom, He only added, not by way of reproof nor even of warning, but as a fresh 'Beatitude:'   'Blessed is he, whosoever shall not be scandalised in Me.'   To faith, but only to faith, this was the most satisfactory and complete answer to John's inquiry.   And such a sight of Christ's distinctive Work and Word, with believing submission to the humble-ness of the Gospel, is the only true answer to our questions, whether of head or heart.

But a harder saying than this did the Lord speak amidst the forthpouring of His testimony to John, when his messengers had left. It pointed the hearers beyond their present horizon.   Several facts here stand out prominently.   First, He to Whom John had formerly borne testimony, now bore testimony to him; and that, not in the hour when John had testified for Him, but when his testimony had wavered and almost failed.   This is the opposite of what one would have expected, if the narrative had been a fiction, while it is exactly what we might expect if the narrative be true.   Next, we mark that the testimony of Christ is as from a higher standpoint.   And it is a full vindication as well as unstinted praise, spoken, not as in his hearing, but after his messengers—who had met a seemingly cold reception—had left.   The people were not coarsely to misunderstand the deep soul-agony, which had issued in John's inquiry.   It was not the outcome of a fickleness which, like the reed shaken by every wind, was moved by popular opinion.   Nor was it the result of fear of bodily consequences, such as one that pampered the flesh might entertain.   Let them look back to the time when, in thousands, they had gone into the wilderness to hear his preaching.   What had attracted them thither?   Surely it was, that he was the opposite of one swayed by popular opinion, 'a reed shaken by the wind.'   And when they had come to him, what had they witnessed?[2]   Surely, his dress and food betokened the opposite of pampering or care of the body, such as they saw in the courtiers of a Herod.   But what they did expect, that they really did see: a prophet, and much more than a

[a] St. Luke
vii. 21
[b] St. Matt.
xi. 5

---

[1] Negative criticism charges St. Luke with having inserted this trait, forgetting that it is referred to by St. Matthew.
[2] The two terms are different.   The query was: would they go out 'to gaze at' a reed, and 'to see' one in soft clothing.

BOOK
III

mere prophet, the very Herald of God and Preparer of Messiah's Way. [1] And yet—and this truly was a hard saying and utterly un-Judaic— it was neither self-denial nor position, no, not even that of the New Testament Elijah, which constituted real greatness, as Jesus viewed it, just as nearest relationship constituted not true kinship to Him. To those who sought the honour which is not of man's bestowing, but of God, to be a little one in the Kingdom of God was greater greatness than even the Baptist's.

But, even so, let there be no mistake. As afterwards St. Paul argued with the Jews, that their boast in the Law only increased their guilt as breakers of the Law, so here our Lord. The popular concourse to, and esteem of, the Baptist,[a][2] did not imply that spiritual reception which was due to his Mission.[b] It only brought out, in more marked contrast, the wide inward difference between the expectancy of the people as a whole, and the spiritual reality presented to them in the Forerunner of the Messiah and in the Messiah Himself.[c] Let them not be deceived by the crowds that had submitted to the Baptism of John. From the time that John began to preach the Kingdom, hindrances of every kind had been raised. To overcome them and enter the Kingdom, it required, as it were, violence like that to enter a city which was surrounded by a hostile army.[3] Even by Jewish admission,[4] the Law ' and all the prophets prophesied only of the days of Messiah.'[d] John, then, was the last link; and, if they would but have received it, he would have been to them the Elijah, the Restorer of all things. Selah—' he that hath ears, let him hear.'

Nay, but it was not so. The children of that generation expected quite another Elijah and quite another Christ, and disbelieved and complained, because the real Elijah and Christ did not meet their foolish thoughts. They were like children in a market-place, who expected their fellows to adapt themselves to the tunes they played. It was as if they said: We have expected great Messianic glory and national exaltation, and ye have not responded (' we have piped [5] unto you, and ye have not danced '); we have looked for deliverance from our national sufferings, and they stirred not your sympathies

[a] St. Luke vii. 29, 30
[b] St. Matt. xi. 12–14

[c] St. Matt. xi. 14–19

[d] Sanh. 99 a; Ber. 34 b; Shabb. 63 a

---

[1] The reader will mark the difference between the quotation as made by all the three Evangelists, and our present Hebrew text and the LXX., and possibly draw his own inferences.

[2] This is a sort of parenthetic note by St. Luke.

[3] The common interpretations of this verse have seemed to me singularly unsatisfactory.

[4] Comp. the Appendix on the Jewish Interpretation of Prophecy.

[5] The pipe was used both in feasts and at mourning. So the Messianic hope had both its joyous and its sorrowful aspect.

nor brought your help ('we have mourned to you, and ye have not lamented'). But you thought of the Messianic time as children, and of us, as if we were your fellows, and shared your thoughts and purposes! And so when John came with his stern asceticism, you felt he was not one of you. He was in one direction outside your boundary-line, and I, as the Friend of sinners, in the other direction. The axe which he wielded you would have laid to the tree of the Gentile world, not to that of Israel and of sin; the welcome and fellowship which I extended, you would have had to 'the wise' and 'the righteous,' not to sinners. Such was Israel as a whole. And yet there was an election according to grace: the violent, who had to fight their way through all this, and who took the Kingdom by violence—and so Heaven's Wisdom (in opposition to the children's folly) is vindicated [1] by all her children.[2] If anything were needed to show the internal harmony between the Synoptists and the Fourth Gospel, it would be this final appeal, which recalls those other words: 'He came unto His own (things or property), and his own (people, they who were His own) received Him not. But as many as received Him, to them gave He power (right, authority) to become children of God, which were born (begotten,) not . . . of the will of man, but of God.' [a]

[a] St. John i. 11-13

6. The scene once more changes, and we are again at Machærus.[3] Weeks have passed since the return of John's messengers. We cannot doubt that the sunlight of faith has again fallen into the dark dungeon, nor yet that the peace of restful conviction has filled the martyr of Christ. He must have known that his end was at hand, and been ready to be offered up. Those not unfrequent conversations, in which the weak, superstitious, wicked tyrant was 'perplexed' and yet 'heard him gladly,' could no longer have inspired even passing hopes of freedom. Nor would he any longer expect from the Messiah assertions of power on his behalf. He now understood that for which He had come;' he knew the better liberty, triumph, and victory which He brought. And what mattered it? His life-work had been done, and there was nothing further that fell to him or that he could do, and the weary servant of the Lord must have longed for his rest.

It was early spring, shortly before the Passover, the anniversary of the death of Herod the Great and of the accession of (his son)

---

[1] Literally, justified. The expression is a Hebraism.

[2] I cannot accept the reading 'works' in St. Mark.

[3] As, according to *Josephus*, John was executed at Machærus, the scene must have been there, and not either at Tiberias or at Julias.

Herod Antipas to the Tetrarchy.[1] A fit time this for a Belshazzar-feast, when such an one as Herod would gather to a grand banquet ' his lords,' and the military authorities, and the chief men of Galilee. It is evening, and the castle-palace is brilliantly lit up. The noise of music and the shouts of revelry come across the slope into the citadel, and fall into the deep dungeon where waits the prisoner of Christ. And now the merriment in the great banqueting-hall has reached its utmost height. The king has nothing further to offer his satiated guests, no fresh excitement. So let it be the sensuous stimulus of dubious dances, and, to complete it, let the dancer be the fair young daughter of the king's wife, the very descendant of the Asmonæan priest-princes! To viler depth of coarse familiarity even a Herod could not have descended.

She has come, and she has danced, this princely maiden, out of whom all maidenhood and all princeliness have been brazed by a degenerate mother, wretched offspring of the once noble Maccabees. And she has done her best in that wretched exhibition, and pleased Herod and them that sat at meat with him. And now, amidst the general plaudits, she shall have her reward—and the king swears it to her with loud voice, that all around hear it—even to the half of his kingdom. The maiden steals out of the banquet-hall to ask her mother what it shall be. Can there be doubt or hesitation in the mind of Herodias? If there was one object she had at heart, which these ten months she had in vain sought to attain: it was the death of John the Baptist. She remembered it all only too well—her stormy, reckless past. The daughter of Aristobulus, the ill-fated son of the ill-fated Asmonæan princess Mariamme (I.), she had been married to her half-uncle, Herod Philip,[2] the son of Herod the Great and of Mariamme

---

[1] The expression γενέσια leaves it doubtful, whether it was the birthday of Herod or the anniversary of his accession. *Wieseler* maintains that the Rabbinic equivalent (*Ginuseya*, or *Giniseya*) means the day of accession, *Meyer* the birthday. In truth it is used for both. But in Abod. Z. 10 *a* (about the middle) the *Yom Ginuseya* is expressly and elaborately shown to be the day of accession. Otherwise also the balance of evidence is in favour of this view. The event described in the text certainly took place *before* the Passover, and this was the time of Herod's death and of the accession of Antipas. It is not likely, that the Herodians would have celebrated their birthdays.

[2] From the circumstance that *Josephus* calls him Herod and not Philip, a certain class of critics have imputed error to the Evangelists (*Schürer*, u. s., p. 237). But it requires to be kept in view, that in that case the Evangelists would be guilty not of one but of two gross historical errors. They would (1) have confounded this Herod with his half-brother Philip, the Tetrarch, and (2) made him the husband of Herodias, instead of being her son-in-law, Philip the Tetrarch having married Salome. Two such errors are altogether inconceivable in so well-known a history, with which the Evangelists otherwise show such familiarity. On the other hand, there are internal reasons for believing that this Herod had a second name. Among the eight sons of Herod the Great there are three who

(II.), the daughter of the High-Priest (Boëthos). At one time it seemed as if Herod Philip would have been sole heir of his father's dominions. But the old tyrant had changed his testament, and Philip was left with great wealth, but as a private person living in Jerusalem. This little suited the woman's ambition. It was when his half-brother, Herod Antipas, came on a visit to him at Jerusalem, that an intrigue began between the Tetrarch and his brother's wife. It was agreed that, after the return of Antipas from his impending journey to Rome, he would repudiate his wife, the daughter of Aretas, king of Arabia, and wed Herodias. But Aretas' daughter heard of the plot, and having obtained her husband's consent to go to Machærus, she fled thence to her father. This, of course, led to enmity between Antipas and Aretas. Nevertheless, the adulterous marriage with Herodias followed. In a few sentences the story may be carried to its termination. The woman proved the curse and ruin of Antipas. First came the murder of the Baptist, which sent a thrill of horror through the people, and to which all the later misfortunes of Herod were attributed. Then followed a war with Aretas, in which the Tetrarch was worsted. And, last of all, his wife's ambition led him to Rome to solicit the title of King, lately given to Agrippa, the brother of Herodias. Antipas not only failed, but was deprived of his dominions, and banished to Lyons in Gaul. The pride of the woman in refusing favours from the Emperor, and her faithfulness to her husband in his fallen fortunes, are the only redeeming points in her history.[a] As for Salome, she was first married to her uncle, Philip the Tetrarch. Legend has it, that her death was retributive, being in consequence of a fall on the ice.

[a] *Jos.* Ant. xviii. 7. 1, 2; War ii. 9. 6

Such was the woman who had these many months sought with the vengefulness and determination of a Jezebel, to rid herself of the hated person, who alone had dared publicly denounce her sin, and whose words held her weak husband in awe. The opportunity had now

---

bear his name (Herod). Of only one, Herod Antipas, we know the second name (Antipas). But, as for example in the case of the Bonaparte family, it is most unlikely that the other two should have borne the name of Herod without any distinctive second name. Hence we conclude, that the name Philip, which occurs in the Gospels (in St. Luke iii. 19 it is spurious), was the second name of him whom *Josephus* simply names as Herod. If it be objected, that in such case Herod would have had two sons

named Philip, we answer (1) that he had two sons of the name Antipas, or Antipater, (2) that they were the sons of different mothers, and (3) that the full name of the one was Herod Philip (first husband of Herodias), and of the other simply Philip the Tetrarch (husband of Salome, and son-in-law of Herodias and of Herod Philip her first husband). Thus for distinction's sake the one might have been generally called simply Herod, the other Philip.

come for obtaining from the vacillating monarch what her entreaties could never have secured. As the Gospel puts it,ª 'instigated' by her mother, the damsel hesitated not. We can readily fill in the outlined picture of what followed. It only needed the mother's whispered suggestion, and still flushed from her dance, Salome re-entered the banqueting-hall. 'With haste,' as if no time were to be lost, she went up to the king: 'I would that thou forthwith give me in a charger, the head of John the Baptist!' Silence must have fallen on the assembly. Even into their hearts such a demand from the lips of little more than a child must have struck horror. They all knew John to be a righteous and holy man. Wicked as they were, in their superstition, if not religiousness, few, if any of them, would have willingly lent himself to such work. And they all knew, also, why Salome, or rather Herodias, had made this demand. What would Herod do? 'The king was exceeding sorry.' For months he had striven against this. His conscience, fear of the people, inward horror at the deed, all would have kept him from it. But he had sworn to the maiden, who now stood before him, claiming that the pledge be redeemed, and every eye in the assembly was now fixed upon him. Unfaithful to his God, to his conscience, to truth and righteousness; not ashamed of any crime or sin, he would yet be faithful to his half-drunken oath, and appear honorable and true before such companions!

It has been but the contest of a moment. 'Straightway' the king gives the order to one of the body-guard.[1] The maiden hath withdrawn to await the result with her mother. The guardsman has left the banqueting-hall. Out into the cold spring night, up that slope, and into the deep dungeon. As its door opens, the noise of the revelry comes with the light of the torch which the man bears. No time for preparation is given, nor needed. A few minutes more, and the gory head of the Baptist is brought to the maiden in a charger, and she gives the ghastly dish to her mother.

It is all over! As the pale morning light streams into the keep, the faithful disciples, who had been told of it, come reverently to bear the headless body to the burying. They go forth for ever from that accursed place, which is so soon to become a mass of shapeless ruins. They go to tell it to Jesus, and henceforth to remain with Him. We can imagine what welcome awaited them. But the people

---

[1] A σπεκουλάτωρ, speculator, one of a body-guard which had come into use, who attended the Cæsars, executed their behests and often their sudden sentences of death (from speculor). The same word occurs in RabbinicHebrew as Sephaqlator (סְפָקְלָטוֹר), or Isphaqlator (אִסְפְּקְלָטוֹר), and is applied to one who carries out the sentence of execution (Shabb. 108 a).

ever afterwards cursed the tyrant, and looked for those judgments of God to follow, which were so soon to descend on him. And he himself was ever afterwards restless, wretched, and full of apprehensions. He could scarcely believe that the Baptist was really dead, and when the fame of Jesus reached him, and those around suggested that this was Elijah, a prophet, or as one of them, Herod's mind, amidst its strange perplexities, still reverted to the man whom he had murdered. It was a new anxiety, perhaps, even so, a new hope; and as formerly he had often and gladly heard the Baptist, so now he would fain have seen Jesus.[a] He would see Him; but not now. In that dark night of betrayal, he, who at the bidding of the child of an adulteress, had murdered the Forerunner, might, with the approbation of a Pilate, have rescued Him whose faithful witness John had been. But night was to merge into yet darker night. For it was the time and the power of the Evil One. And yet: Jehovah reigneth.'

CHAP.
XXVIII

[a] St. Luke
ix. 9

CHAPTER XXIX.

THE MIRACULOUS FEEDING OF THE FIVE THOUSAND.

(St. Matt. xiv. 13–21; St. Mark vi. 30–44; St. Luke ix. 10–17; St. John vi. 1–14.)

BOOK
III

IN the circumstances described in the previous chapter, Jesus resolved at once to leave Capernaum; and this probably alike for the sake of His disciples, who needed rest; for that of the people, who might have attempted a rising after the murder of the Baptist; and temporarily to withdraw Himself and His followers from the power of Herod. For this purpose He chose the place outside the dominions of Antipas, nearest to Capernaum. This was Beth-Saida ('the house of fishing,' 'Fisher-town,'[1] as we might call it), on the eastern border of Galilee,[a] just within the territory of the Tetrarch Philip. Originally a small village, Philip had converted it into a town, and named it Julias, after Cæsar's daughter. It lay on the eastern bank of Jordan, just before that stream enters the Lake of Galilee.[b] It must, however, not be confounded with the other 'Fisher-town,' or Bethsaida, on the western shore of the Lake,[2] which the Fourth Gospel, evidencing by this local knowledge its Judæan, or rather Galilean, authorship, distinguishes from the eastern as Bethsaida of Galilee.'[c][3]

Other minute points of deep interest in the same direction will present themselves in the course of this narrative. Meantime we note, that this is the only history, previous to Christ's last visit to Jerusalem, which is recorded by all the four Evangelists; the only

a *Jos.* War iii. 3. 5

b *Jos.* Ant. xviii. 2. 1

c St. John xii. 21; comp. i. 44; St. Mark vi. 45

---

[1] The common reading, 'House of fishes,' is certainly inaccurate. Its Aramaic equivalent would be probably בֵּית צֵידָא. *Tseida* means literally hunting as well as fishing, having special reference to catching in a *snare* or net. Possibly, but not so likely, it may have been בֵּית צַיָּדָא (*Tsayyada*), house of a snarer-huntsman, here fisher. It will be

noticed, that we retain the *textus recep tus* of St. Luke ix. 10.

[2] I do not quite understand the reasoning of Captain *Conder* on this point (Handb. of the Bible, pp. 321, &c.), but I cannot agree with his conclusions.

[3] On the whole question comp. the Encyclopædias, *Caspari* u. s. pp. 81, 83; Baedeker (*Socin*), p. 267; *Tristram,* Land of Israel, p. 443 &c.

series of events also in the whole course of that Galilean Ministry, which commenced after His return from the ' Unknown Feast,' [a] which is referred to in the Fourth Gospel; [1] and that it contains two distinct notices as to time, which enable us to fit it exactly into the framework of this history. For, the statement of the Fourth Gospel,[b] that the ' Passover was nigh,' [2] is confirmed by the independent notice of St. Mark,[c] that those whom the Lord miraculously led were ranged ' on the green grass.' In that climate there would have been no ' green grass ' soon after the Passover. We must look upon the coincidence of these two notices as one of the undesigned confirmations of this narrative.

CHAP. XXIX

[a] St. John v.
[b] St. John vi. 4
[c] St. Mark vi. 39

For, miraculous it certainly is, and the attempts rationalistically to explain it, to sublimate it into a parable, to give it the spiritualistic meaning of spiritual feeding, or to account for its mythical origin by the precedent of the descent of the manna, or of the miracle of Elisha,[3] are even more palpable failures than those made to account for the miracle at Cana. The only alternative is to accept— or entirely to reject it. In view of the exceptional record of this history in all the four Gospels, no unbiassed historical student would treat it as a simple invention, for which there was no ground in reality. Nor can its origin be accounted for by previous Jewish expectancy, or Old Testament precedent. The only rational mode of explaining it is on the supposition of its truth. This miracle, and what follows, mark the climax in our Lord's doing, as the healing of the Syro-Phœnician maiden the utmost sweep of His activity, and the Transfiguration the highest point in regard to the miraculous about His Person. The only reason which can be assigned for the miracle of His feeding the five thousand was that of all His working: Man's need, and, in view of it, the stirring of the Pity and Power that were in Him. But even so, we cannot fail to mark the contrast between King Herod, and the banquet that ended with the murder of the Baptist, and King Jesus, and the banquet that ended with His lonely prayer on the mountain-side, the calming of the storm on the Lake, and the deliverance from death of His disciples.

[1] Professor *Westcott* notes, that the account of St. John could neither have been derived from those of the Synoptists, nor from any common original, from which their narratives are by some supposed to have been derived.

[2] There is no valid reason for doubting the genuineness of these words, or giving them another meaning than in the text. Comp. *Westcott*, ad. loc.

[3] Even those who hold such views assert them in this instance hesitatingly. It seems almost impossible to conceive, that a narrative recorded in all the four Gospels should not have an historical basis, and the appeal to the precedent of Elisha is the more inapt, that in common Jewish thinking he was *not* regarded as specially the type of the Messiah.

Only a few hours' sail from Capernaum, and even a shorter distance bv land (round the head of the Lake) lay the district of Bethsaida-Julias. It was natural that Christ, wishing to avoid public
attention, should have gone ' by ship,' and equally so that the many
' seeing them departing, and knowing '—viz., what direction the boat
was taking, should have followed on foot, and been joined by others
from the neighbouring villages,[1] as those from Capernaum passed
through them, perhaps, also, as they recognised on the Lake the now
well-known sail,[2] speeding towards the other shore.   It is an incidental
but interesting confirmation of the narrative, that the same notice
about this journey occurs, evidently undesignedly, in St. John vi. 22.
Yet another we find in the fact, that some of those who 'ran there

ᵃ St. Mark
vi. 33

on foot ' had reached the place before Jesus and His Apostles.[a]   Only
some, as we judge.   The largest proportion arrived later, and soon
swelled to the immense number of ' about 5,000 men,' 'besides
women and children.'   The circumstance that the Passover was nigh
at hand, so that many must have been starting on their journey to
Jerusalem, round the Lake and through Peræa, partly accounts for
the concourse of such multitudes.   And this, perhaps in conjunction
with the effect on the people of John's murder, may also explain
their ready and eager gathering to Christ, thus affording yet another
confirmation of the narrative.

It was a well-known spot where Jesus and His Apostles touched
the shore.   Not many miles south of it was the Gerasa or Gergesa,

ᵇ St. Mark
v. 1-16

where the great miracle of healing the demonised had been wrought.[b]
Just beyond Gerasa the mountains and hills recede, and the plain
along the shore enlarges, till it attains wide proportions on the
northern bank of the Lake.   The few ruins which mark the site of
Bethsaida-Julias—most of the basalt-stones having been removed
for building purposes—lie on the edge of a hill, three or four miles
north of the Lake.   The ford, by which those who came from Capernaum crossed the Jordan, was, no doubt, that still used, about two
miles from where the river enters the Lake.   About a mile further,
on that wide expanse of grass, would be the scene of the great
miracle.   In short, the locality thoroughly accords with the requirements of the Gospel-narrative.

As we picture it to ourselves, our Lord with His disciples, and

---

[1] This seems the fair meaning of St.
Mark vi. 31–33, comp. with St. Matt. xiv.
13.
[2] St. Mark vi. 32 has it 'by (or rather
ın) the ship,' with the definite article.

Probably it was the same boat that was
always at His disposal, perhaps belonging to the sons of Jonas or to the sons of
Zebedee.

perhaps followed by those who had outrun the rest, first retired to
the top of a height, and there rested in teaching converse with
them.[a] Presently, as He saw the great multitudes gathering, He
was 'moved with compassion towards them.'[b1] There could be no
question of retirement or rest in view of this. Surely, it was the
opportunity which God had given—a call which came to Him from
His Father. Every such opportunity was unspeakably precious to
Him, Who longed to gather the lost under His wings. It might be,
that even now they would learn what belonged to their peace. Oh,
that they would learn it! At least, He must work while it was called
to-day, ere the night of judgment came; work with that unending
patience and intense compassion which made Him weep, when He
could no longer work. It was this depth of longing and intenseness
of pity which now ended the Saviour's rest, and brought Him down
from the hill to meet the gathering multitude in the 'desert' plain
beneath.

And what a sight to meet His gaze—these thousands of strong
men, besides women and children; and what thoughts of the past,
the present, and the future, would be called up by the scene! 'The
Passover was nigh,'[c] with its remembrances of the Paschal night,
the Paschal Lamb, the Paschal Supper, the Paschal deliverance—
and most of them were Passover-pilgrims on their way to Jerusalem.
These Passover-pilgrims and God's guests, now streaming out into
this desert after Him; with a murdered John just buried, and
no earthly teacher, guide, or help left! Truly they were 'as sheep
having no shepherd.'[d] The very surroundings seemed to give to the
thought the vividness of a picture: this wandering, straying multitude, the desert sweep of country, the very want of provisions. A
Passover, indeed, but of which He would be the Paschal Lamb, the
Bread which He gave, the Supper, and around which He would gather
those scattered, shepherdless sheep into one flock of many 'companies,' to which His Apostles would bring the bread He had blessed
and broken, to their sufficient and more than sufficient nourishment;
from which, indeed, they would carry the remnant-baskets full, after
the flock had been fed, to the poor in the outlying places of far-off
heathendom. And so thoughts of the past, the present, and the
future must have mingled—thoughts of the Passover in the past, of
the Last, the Holy Supper in the future, and of the deeper inward

CHAP.
XXIX

[a] St. John
vi. 3
[b] St. Matt.
xiv. 14

[c] St. John
vi. 4

[d] St. Mark
vi. 34

---

[1] Canon *Westcott* supposes that 'a day
of teaching and healing must be intercalated before the miracle of feeding,' but
I cannot see any reason for this. All the
events fit well into one day.

BOOK
III

meaning and bearing of both the one and the other; thoughts also of this flock, and of that other flock which was yet to gather, and of the far-off places, and of the Apostles and their service, and of the provision which they were to carry from His Hands—a provision never exhausted by present need, and which always leaves enough to carry thence and far away.

There is, at least in our view, no doubt that thoughts of the Passover and of the Holy Supper, of their commingling and mystic meaning, were present to the Saviour, and that it is in this light the miraculous feeding of the multitude must be considered, if we are in any measure to understand it. Meantime the Saviour was moving among them—'beginning to teach them many things,'[a] and 'healing them that had need of healing.'[b] Yet, as He so moved and thought of it all, from the first, 'He Himself knew what He was about to do.[c] And now the sun had passed its meridian, and the shadows fell longer on the surging crowd. Full of the thoughts of the great Supper, which was symbolically to link the Passover of the past with that of the future, and its Sacramental continuation to all time, He turned to Philip with this question: 'Whence are we to buy bread, that these may eat?' It was to 'try him,' and show how he would view and meet what, alike spiritually and temporally, has so often been the great problem. Perhaps there was something in Philip which made it specially desirable, that the question should be put to him.[d] At any rate, the answer of Philip showed that there had been a 'need be' for it. This—'two hundred denarii (between six and seven pounds) worth of bread is not sufficient for them, that every one may take a little,' is the course realism, not of unbelief, but of an absence of faith which, entirely ignoring any higher possibility, has not even its hope left in a 'Thou knowest, Lord.'

But there is evidence, also, that the question of Christ worked deeper thinking and higher good. As we understand it, Philip told it to Andrew, and they to the others. While Jesus taught and healed, they must have spoken together of this strange question of the Master. They knew Him sufficiently to judge, that it implied some purpose on His part. Did He intend to provide for all that multitude? They counted them roughly—going along the edge and through the crowd—and reckoned them by thousands, besides women and children. They thought of all the means for feeding such a multitude. How much had they of their own? As we judge by combining the various statements, there was a lad there who carried the scant, humble provisions of the party—perhaps a fisher-lad

a St. Mark
vi. 34
b St. Luke
ix. 11
c St. John
vi. 6

d Comp.
St. John
xiv. 8, 9

brought for the purpose from the boat.[a] It would take quite what Philip had reckoned—about two hundred denarii—if the Master meant them to go and buy victuals for all that multitude. Probably the common stock—at any rate as computed by Judas, who carried the bag—did not contain that amount. In any case, the right and the wise thing was to dismiss the multitude, that they might go into the towns and villages and buy for themselves victuals, and find lodgment. For already the bright spring-day was declining, and what was called 'the first evening' had set in.[1] For the Jews reckoned two evenings, although it is not easy to determine the exact hour when each began and ended. But, in general, the first evening may be said to have begun when the sun declined, and it was probably reckoned as lasting to about the ninth hour, or three o'clock of the afternoon.[b] Then began the period known as 'between the evenings,' which would be longer or shorter according to the season of the year, and which terminated with 'the second evening'—the time from when the first star appeared to that when the third star was visible.[c] With the night began the reckoning of the following day.

It was the 'first evening' when the disciples, whose anxiety must have been growing with the progress of time, asked the Lord to dismiss the people. But it was as they had thought. He would have them give the people to eat! Were they, then, to go and buy two hundred denarii worth of loaves? No—they were not to buy, but to give of their own store! How many loaves had they! Let them go and see.[d] And when Andrew went to see what store the fisher-lad carried for them, he brought back the tidings, 'He hath five barley loaves and two small fishes,' to which he added, half in disbelief, half in faith's rising expectancy of impossible possibility: 'But what are they among so many?'[e] It is to the fourth Evangelist alone that we owe the record of this remark, which we instinctively feel gives to the whole the touch of truth and life. It is to him also that we owe other two minute traits of deepest interest, and of far greater importance than at first sight appears.

When we read that these five were *barley*-loaves, we learn that, no doubt from voluntary choice, the fare of the Lord and of His followers was the poorest. Indeed, barley-bread was, almost proverbially, the meanest. Hence, as the Mishnah puts it, while all other meat-offerings were of wheat, that brought by the woman accused of adultery was to be of barley, because (so R. Gamaliel puts it), 'as her deed is that of animals, so her offering is also of the

[a] Comp. St. John vi. 9 with St. Matt. xiv. 17; St. Mark vi. 38; St. Luke ix. 13

[b] Comp. *Jos.* Ant. xvi. 6. 2

[c] Orach-Chajim 261

[d] St. Mark vi. 38

[e] St. John vi. 9

---

[1] The expression in St. Mark vi. 35 is literally, 'a late hour,' ὥρα πολλή.

BOOK
III

● Sotah. ii. 1

b Babha. B.
740 b
c רגים
קטנים
Beza 16 a
d Ber. 40 a,
near the
middle

food of animals.' [a] The other minute trait in St. John's Gospel consists in the use of a peculiar word for 'fish' (ὀψάριον), 'opsarion, which properly means what was eaten along with the bread, and specially refers to the small, and generally dried or pickled fish eaten with bread, like our 'sardines,' or the 'caviar' of Russia, the pickled herrings of Holland and Germany, or a peculiar kind of small dried fish, eaten with the bones, in the North of Scotland. Now just as any one who would name that fish as eaten with bread, would display such minute knowledge of the habits of the North-east of Scotland as only personal residence could give, so in regard to the use of this term, which, be it marked, is *peculiar to the Fourth Gospel*, Dr. *Westcott* suggests, that ' it may have been a familiar Galilean word,' and his conjecture is correct, for *Ophsonin* (אָפְסוֹנִין), derived from the same Greek word (ὄψον), of which that used by St. John is the diminutive, means a ' savoury dish,' while *Aphyan* (אַפְיָאן) or *Aphits* (עְפִיץ), is the term for a kind of small fish, such as sardines. The importance of tracing accurate local knowledge in the Fourth Gospel warrants our pursuing the subject further. The Talmud, declares that of all kinds of meat, fish only becomes more savoury by salting,[b] and names certain kinds, specially designated as ' small fishes,' [c] which might be eaten without being cooked. Small fishes were recommended for health; [d] and a kind of pickle or savoury was also made of them. Now the Lake of Galilee was particularly rich in these fishes, and we know that both the salting and pickling of them was a special industry among its fishermen. For this purpose a small kind of them were specially selected, which bear the name *Terith* (טְרִית).[1] Now the diminutive used by St. John (ὀψάριον), of which our Authorized Version no doubt gives the meaning fairly by rendering it 'small fishes,' refers, no doubt, to those small fishes (probably a kind of sardine) of which millions were caught in the Lake, and which, dried and salted, would form the most common ' savoury ' with bread for the fisher-population along the shores.

If the Fourth Gospel in the use of this diminutive displays such special Lake-knowledge as evidences its Galilean origin, another touching trait connected with its use may here be mentioned. It has already been said that the term is used only by St. John, as if to mark the Lake of Galilee origin of the Fourth Gospel. But only once again does the expression occur in the Fourth Gospel. On that

---

[1] Comp. *Herzfeld*, Handelsgesch. pp. 305, 306. In my view he has established the meaning of this name as against   *Lewysohn*, Zool. d. Talm. pp. 255, 256, and *Levy*, Neuhebr. Wörterb. ii. 192 a.

morning, when the Risen One manifested Himself by the Lake of
Galilee to them who had all the night toiled in vain, He had provided for them miraculously the meal, when on the 'fire of charcoal'
they saw the well-remembered 'little fish' (the *opsarion*), and, as
He bade them bring of the 'little fish' (the *opsaria*) which they
had miraculously caught, Peter drew to shore the net full, not of
opsaria, but 'of great fishes' (ἰχθύων μεγάλων). And yet it was
not of those 'great fishes' that He gave them, but 'He took
the bread and gave them, and the *opsarion* likewise.'ᵃ Thus, in
infinite humility, the meal at which the Risen Saviour sat down
with His disciples was still of 'bread and small fishes'—even though
He gave them the draught of large fishes; and so at that last
meal He recalled that first miraculous feeding by the Lake of
Galilee. And this also is one of those undesigned, too often unobserved traits in the narrative, which yet carry almost irresistible
evidence.

There is one proof at least of the implicit faith or rather trust of
the disciples in their Master. They had given Him account of their
own scanty provision, and yet, as He bade them make the people sit
down to the meal, they hesitated not to obey. We can picture it to
ourselves, what is so exquisitely sketched: the expanse of 'grass,'ᵇ
'green,' and fresh,ᶜ 'much grass;'ᵈ then the people in their 'companies'ᵉ of fifties and hundreds, reclining,ᶠ and looking in their
regular divisions, and with their bright many-coloured dresses, like
'garden-beds'ᵍ¹ on the turf. But on One Figure must every eye
have been bent. Around Him stood His Apostles. They had laid
before Him the scant provision made for their own wants, and which
was now to feed this great multitude. As was wont at meals, on the
part of the head of the household, Jesus took the bread, 'blessed'ʰ
or, as St. John puts it, 'gave thanks,'² and 'brake' it. The expression
recalls that connected with the Holy Eucharist, and leaves little
doubt on the mind that, in the Discourse delivered in the Synagogue
of Capernaum,ⁱ there is also reference to the Lord's Supper. As of
comparatively secondary importance, yet helping us better to realise
the scene, we recall the Jewish ordinance, that the Head of the
House was only to speak the blessing if he himself shared in the
meal, yet if they who sat down to it were not merely guests, but his

CHAP.
XXIX

ᵃ St. John
xxi. 9, 10, 13

ᵇ St. Matt.
xiv. 19
ᶜ St. Mark
vi. 39
ᵈ St. John
vi. 10
ᵉ συμπόσια
St. Mark
vi. 39
ᶠ κλισίας, St.
Luke ix. 14
ᵍ St. Mark
vi. 40
ʰ Ber. 46 a

ⁱ St. John
vi. 48-58

---

¹ The literal rendering of πρασιά, is
'garden-bed.' In St. Mark vi. 40, πρασιαὶ
πρασιαί, 'garden-beds, garden-beds.'
In the A. V. 'in ranks.'
² The expression is different from that

used by the Synoptists; but in St. Matt.
xv. 36, and in St. Mark viii. 6, the term
is also that of *thanksgiving*, not *blessing*
(εὐχαριστέω, not εὐλογέω).

BOOK
III

ᵃ Rosh
haSh. 29 b
ᵇ Sot. vii. 1

ᶜ Jer. Sot.
p. 21 b

ᵈ Ber. 44 a

ᵉ Comp.
Sotah. ii. 1

children, or his household, then might he speak it, even if he himself did not partake of the bread which he had broken.ᵃ

We can scarcely be mistaken as to the words which Jesus spake when 'He gave thanks.' The Jewish Law ᵇ allows the grace at meat to be said, not only in Hebrew, but in any language, the Jerusalem Talmud aptly remarking, that it was proper a person should understand to Whom he was giving thanks (לְמִי מְבָרֵךְ).ᶜ Similarly, we have very distinct information as regards a case like the present. We gather, that the use of ' savoury ' with bread was specially common around the Lake of Galilee, and the Mishnah lays down the principle, that if bread and ' savoury ' were eaten, it would depend which of the two was the main article of diet, to determine whether ' thanksgiving' should be said for one or the other. In any case only one benediction was to be used.ᵈ In this case, of course, it would be spoken over the bread, the ' savoury ' being merely an addition. There can be little doubt, therefore, that the words which Jesus spake, whether in Aramæan, Greek, or Hebrew, were those so well known: ' Blessed art Thou, Jehovah our God, King of the world, Who causes to come forth (הַמּוֹצִיא) bread from the earth.' Assuredly it was this threefold thought: the upward thought (*sursum corda*), the recognition of the creative act as regards every piece of bread we eat, and the thanksgiving, which was realised anew in all its fulness, when, as He distributed to the disciples, the provision miraculously multiplied in His Hands. And still they bore it from His Hands from company to company, laying before each a store. When they were all filled, He that had provided the meal bade them gather up the fragments before each company. So doing, each of the twelve had his basket filled. Here also we have another life-touch. Those ' baskets' (κόφινοι), known in Jewish writings by a similar name (*Kephiphah*), made of wicker or willows ¹ (כְּפִיפָה מִצְרִית), were in common use, but considered of the poorest kind.ᵉ There is a sublimeness of contrast that passes description between this feast to the five thousand, besides women and children, and the poor's provision of barley bread and the two small fishes; and, again, between the quantity left and the coarse wicker baskets in which it was stored. Nor do we forget to draw mentally the parallel between this Messianic feast and that banquet of ' the latter days ' which Rabbinism pictured so realistically. But as the wondering multitude watched, as the disciples gathered from

¹ Not an Egyptian basket, as even *Jost* translates in his edition of the Mishnah. The word is derived from מֵצֶר (Metser), wicker or willow).

company to company the fragments into their baskets, the murmur ran through the ranks: 'This is truly the Prophet, "the Coming One" (*habba*, הבא) into the world.' And so the Baptist's last inquiry, 'Art Thou the Coming One?'[1] was fully and publicly answered, and that by the Jews themselves.

[1] See the meaning of that expression in the previous chapter.

CHAPTER XXX.

THE NIGHT OF MIRACLES ON THE LAKE OF GENNESARET.

(St. Matt. xiv. 22–36; St. Mark vi. 45–56; St. John vi. 15–21.)

BOOK
III

THE last question of the Baptist, spoken in public, had been: 'Art Thou the Coming One, or look we for another?' It had, in part, been answered, as the murmur had passed through the ranks: 'This One is truly the Prophet, the Coming One!' So, then, they had no longer to wait, nor to look for another! And this 'Prophet' was Israel's long expected Messiah. What this would imply to the people, in the intensity and longing of the great hope which, for centuries, nay, far beyond the time of Ezra, had swayed their hearts, it is impossible fully to conceive. Here, then, was the Great Reality at last before them. He, on Whose teaching they had hung entranced, was 'the Prophet,' nay, more, 'the Coming One:' He Who was coming all those many centuries, and yet had not come till now. Then, also, was He more than a Prophet—a King: Israel's King, the King of the world. An irresistible impulse seized the people. They would proclaim Him King, then and there; and as they knew, probably from previous utterances, perhaps when similar movements had to be checked, that He would resist, they would constrain Him to declare Himself, or at least to be proclaimed by them. Can we wonder at this; or that thoughts of a Messianic worldly kingdom should have filled, moved, and influenced to discipleship a Judas; or that, with such a representative of their own thoughts among the disciples, the rising waves of popular excitement should have swollen into the mighty billows?

'Jesus therefore, perceiving that they were about to come, and to take Him by force, that they might make Him King,[1] withdrew again into the mountain, Himself alone,' or, as it might be rendered,

---

[1] Note here the want of the article: ἵνα ποιήσωσιν αὐτὸν βασιλέα. We owe this notice to the Fourth Gospel, and it is in marked inconsistency with the theory of its late Ephesian authorship.

though not quite in the modern usage of the expression, 'became an anchorite again . . . Himself alone.'[a] This is another of those sublime contrasts, which render it well-nigh inconceivable to regard this history otherwise than as true and Divine. Yet another is the manner in which He stilled the multitude, and the purpose for which He became the lonely Anchorite on the mountain-top. He withdrew to pray; and He stilled the people, and sent them, no doubt solemnised, to their homes, by telling them that He withdrew to pray. And He did pray till far on, ' when the (second) evening had come,'[b] and the first stars shone out in the deep blue sky over the Lake of Galilee, with the far lights twinkling and trembling on the other side. And yet another sublime contrast—as He constrained the disciples to enter the ship, and that ship, which bore those who had been sharers in the miracle, could not make way against storm and waves, and was at last driven out of its course. And yet another contrast—as He walked on the storm-tossed waves and subdued them. And yet another, and another—for is not all this history one sublime contrast to the seen and the thought of by men, but withal most true and Divine in the sublimeness of these contrasts?

For whom and for what He prayed, alone on that mountain, we dare not, even in deepest reverence, inquire. Yet we think, in connection with it, of the Passover, the Manna, the Wilderness, the Lost Sheep, the Holy Supper, the Bread which is His Flesh, and the remnant in the Baskets to be carried to those afar off, and then also of the attempt to make Him a King, in all its spiritual unreality, ending in His View with the betrayal, the denial, and the cry: 'We have no King but Cæsar.' And as He prayed, the faithful stars in the heavens shone out. But there on the Lake, where the bark which bore His disciples made for the other shore, ' a great wind' ' contrary to them ' was rising. And still He was ' alone on the land,' but looking out into the evening after them, as the ship was ' in the midst of the sea,' and they toiling and ' distressed in rowing.'

Thus far, to the utmost verge of their need, but not farther. The Lake is altogether about forty furlongs or stadia (about six miles) wide, and they had as yet reached little more than half the distance (twenty-five or thirty furlongs). Already it was ' the fourth watch of the night.' There was some difference of opinion among the Jews, whether the night should be divided into three, or (as among the Romans) into four watches. The latter (which would count the night at twelve instead of nine hours) was adopted by many.[c] In any case it would be what might be termed the morning-

[a] St. John vi. 15

[b] St. Matt. xiv. 23

[c] Ber. 3 b

watch,[1] when the well-known Form seemed to be passing them, 'walking upon the sea.' There can, at least, be no question that such was the impression, not only of one or another, but that all saw Him. Nor yet can there be here question of any natural explanation. Once more the truth of the event must be either absolutely admitted, or absolutely rejected.[2] The difficulties of the latter hypothesis, which truly cuts the knot, would be very formidable. Not only would the origination of this narrative, as given by two of the Synoptists and by St. John, be utterly unaccountable—neither meeting Jewish expectancy, nor yet supposed Old Testament precedent—but, if legend it be, it seems purposeless and irrational. Moreover, there is this noticeable about it, as about so many of the records of the miraculous in the New Testament, that the writers by no means disguise from themselves or their readers the obvious difficulties involved. In the present instance they tell us, that they regarded His Form moving on the water as 'a spirit,' and cried out for fear; and again, that the impression produced by the whole scene, even on them that had witnessed the miracle of the previous evening, was one of overwhelming astonishment. This walking on the water, then, was even to them within the domain of the truly miraculous, and it affected their minds equally, perhaps even more than ours, from the fact that in their view so much, which to us seems miraculous, lay within the sphere of what might be expected in the course of such a history.

On the other hand, this miracle stands not isolated, but forms one of a series of similar manifestations. It is closely connected both with what had passed on the previous evening, and what was to follow; it is told with a minuteness of detail, and with such marked absence of any attempt at gloss, adornment, apology, or self-glorification, as to give the narrative (considered simply as such) the stamp of truth; while, lastly, it contains much that lifts the story from the merely miraculous into the domain of the sublime and deeply spiritual. As regards what may be termed its credibility, this at least

---

[1] Probably from 3 to about 6 A. M.

[2] Even the beautiful allegory into which *Keim* would resolve it—that the Church in her need knows not, whether her Saviour may not come in the last watch of the night—entirely surrenders the whole narrative. And why should three Evangelists have invented such a story, in order to teach or rather disguise a doctrine, which is otherwise so clearly expressed throughout the whole New Testament, as to form one of its primary principles? *Volkmar* (Marcus, p. 372) regards this whole history as an allegory of St. Paul's activity among the Gentiles! Strange in that case, that it was omitted in the Gospel by St. Luke. But the whole of that section of *Volkmar's* book (beginning at p. 327) contains an extraordinary congeries, of baseless hypotheses, of which it were difficult to say, whether the language is more painfully irreverent or the outcome more extravagant.

may again be stated, that this and similar instances of ' dominion
over the creature,' are not beyond the range of what God had
originally assigned to man, when He made him a little lower than
the angels, and crowned him with glory and honour, made him to
have dominion over the works of His Hands, and all things were
put under his feet.[a]   Indeed, this ' dominion over the sea ' seems ^a Ps. viii. 5,
6; comp.
to exhibit the Divinely human rather than the humanly Divine Hebr. ii. 6-9
aspect of His Person,[1] if such distinction may be lawfully made.
Of the physical possibility of such a miracle—not to speak of the
contradiction in terms which this implies—no explanation can be attempted, if it were only on the ground that we are utterly ignorant
of the conditions under which it took place.

This much, however, deserves special notice, that there is one
marked point of difference between the account of this miracle and
what will be found a general characteristic in legendary narratives.
In the latter, the miraculous, however extraordinary, is the expected;
it creates no surprise, and it is never mistaken for something that
might have occurred in the ordinary course of events.   For, it is characteristic of the mythical that the miraculous is not only introduced
in the most realistic manner, but forms the essential element in
the conception of things.   This is the very *raison d'être* of the myth
or legend, when it attaches itself to the real and historically true.
Now the opposite is the case in the present narrative.   Had it been
mythical or legendary, we should have expected that the disciples
would have been described as immediately recognising the Master
as He walked on the sea, and worshipping Him.   Instead of this,
they ' are troubled ' and ' afraid.'   ' They supposed it was an apparition,'[2] (this in accordance with popular Jewish notions), and ' cried
out for fear.'   Even afterwards, when they had received Him into
the ship, 'they were sore amazed in themselves,' and ' understood
not,' while those in the ship (in contradistinction to the disciples),
burst forth into an act of worship.   This much then is evident, that
the disciples expected not the miraculous; that they were unprepared for it; that they had explained it on what to them seemed natural
grounds; and that, even when convinced of its reality, the impression of wonder, which it made, was of the deepest.   And this also
follows is a corollary, that, when they recorded it, it was not in

[1] On the other hand, the miraculous
feeding of the multitude seems to exhibit
rather the humanly-Divine aspect of His
Person.

[2] Literally, a phantasma.   This word
is only used in this narrative (St. Matt.
xiv. 26 and St. Mark vi. 49).

BOOK
III

ignorance that they were writing that which sounded strangest, and which would affect those who should read it with even much greater wonderment—we had almost written, unbelief—than those who themselves had witnessed it.

Nor let it be forgotten, that what has just been remarked about this narrative holds equally true in regard to other miracles recorded in the New Testament. Thus, even so fundamental an article of the faith as the resurrection of Christ is described as having come upon the disciples themselves as a surprise—not only wholly unexpected, but so incredible, that it required repeated and indisputable evidence to command their acknowledgment. And nothing can be more plain, than that St. Paul himself was not only aware of the general resist-

a Acts xxvi. 8

b 1 Cor. xv. 12-19

c Acts xvii. 31, 32

d 1 Cor. xv. 1-8

ance which the announcement of such an event would raise,[a] but that he felt to the full the difficulties of what he so firmly believed,[b] and made the foundation of all his preaching.[c] Indeed, the elaborate exposition of the historical grounds, on which he had arrived at the conviction of reality,[d] affords an insight into the mental difficulties which it must at first have presented to him. And a similar inference may be drawn from the reference of St. Peter to the difficulties con-

e 2 Pet. iii. 4

nected with the Biblical predictions about the end of the world.[e][1]

It is not necessary to pursue this subject further. Its bearing on the miracle of Christ's walking on the Sea of Galilee will be sufficiently manifest. Yet other confirmatory evidence may be gathered from a closer study of the details of the narrative. When Jesus

f St. Matt. xiv. 22

' constrained the disciples to enter into the boat, and to go before Him unto the other side,[f] they must have thought, that His purpose was to join them by land, since there was no other boat there,

g St. John vi. 22

save that in which they crossed the Lake.[g] And possibly such had been his intention, till He saw their difficulty, if not danger, from the contrary wind.[2] This must have determined Him to come to their help. And so this miracle also was not a mere display of power, but, being caused by their need, had a moral object. And when it is asked, how from the mountain-height by the Lake He could have seen at night where the ship was labouring so far on the Lake,[3]

---

[1] The authenticity of the Second Epistle of St. Peter is here taken for granted, but the drift of the argument would be the same, to whatever authorship it be ascribed.

[2] Weiss (Matthäus-Evang. p. 372) sees a gross contradiction between what seems implied as to His original purpose and His walking on the sea, and hence

rejects the narrative. Such are the assumptions of negative criticism. But it seems forgotten that, according to St. Matt. xiv. 24, the journey seems at first to have been fairly prosperous.

[3] Weiss (u. s.) certainly argues on the impossibility of His having seen the boat so far out on the Lake.

it must surely have been forgotten that the scene is laid quite shortly before the Passover (the 15th of Nisan), when, of course, the moon would shine on an unclouded sky, all the more brightly on a windy spring-night, and light up the waters far across.

We can almost picture to ourselves the weird scene. The Christ is on that hill-top in solitary converse with His Father—praying after that miraculous breaking of bread: fully realising all that it implied to Him of self-surrender, of suffering, and of giving Himself as the Food of the World, and all that it implied to us of blessing and nourishment; praying also—with that scene fresh on His mind, of their seeking to make Him, even by force, their King—that the carnal might become spiritual reality (as in symbol it would be with the Breaking of Bread). Then, as He rises from His knees, knowing that, alas, it could not and would not be so to the many, He looks out over the Lake after that little company, which embodied and represented all there yet was of His Church, all that would really feed on the Bread from Heaven, and own Him their true King. Without presumption, we may venture to say, that there must have been indescribable sorrow and longing in His Heart, as His gaze was bent across the track which the little boat would follow. As we view it, it seems all symbolical: the night, the moonlight, the little boat, the contrary wind, and then also the lonely Saviour after prayer looking across to where the boatmen vainly labour to gain the other shore. As in the clear moonlight just that piece of water stands out, almost like burnished silver, with all else in shadows around, the sail-less mast is now rocking to and fro, without moving forward. They are in difficulty, in danger: and the Saviour cannot pursue His journey on foot by land; He must come to their help, though it be across the water. It is needful, and therefore it shall be *upon* the water; and so the storm and unsuccessful toil shall not prevent their reaching the shore, but shall also be to them for teaching concerning Him and His great power, and concerning His great deliverance; such teaching as, in another aspect of it, had been given them in symbol in the miraculous supply of food, with all that it implied (and not to them only, but to us also) of precious comfort and assurance, and as will for ever keep the Church from being overwhelmed by fear in the stormy night on the Lake of Galilee, when the labour of our oars cannot make way for us.

And they also who were in the boat must have been agitated by peculiar feelings. Against their will they had been 'constrained' by the Lord to embark and quit the scene; just as the multitude, under the influence of the great miracle, were surrounding their Master, with violent insistence to proclaim him the Messianic King of Israel. Not only a Judas Iscariot, but all of them, must have been under the strongest excitement: first of the great miracle, and then of the popular movement. It was the crisis in the history of the Messiah and of His Kingdom. Can we wonder, that, when the Lord in very mercy bade them quit a scene which could only have misled them, they were reluctant, nay, that it almost needed violence on His part? And yet—the more we consider it—was it not most truly needful for them, that they should leave? But, on the other hand, in this respect also, does there seem a 'need be' for His walking upon the sea, that they might learn not only His Almighty Power, and (symbolically) that He ruled the rising waves; but that, in their disappointment at His not being a King, they might learn that He *was* a King—only in a far higher, truer sense than the excited multitude would have proclaimed Him.

Thus we can imagine the feelings with which they had pushed the boat from the shore, and then eagerly looked back to descry what passed there. But soon the shadows of night were enwrapping all objects at a distance, and only the bright moon overhead shone on the track behind and before. And now the breeze from the other side of the Lake, of which they may have been unaware when they embarked on the eastern shore, had freshened into violent, contrary wind. All energies must have been engaged to keep the boat's head towards the shore.[1] Even so it seemed as if they could make no progress, when all at once, in the track that lay behind them, a Figure appeared. As it passed onwards over the water, seemingly upborne by the waves as they rose, not disappearing as they fell, but carried on as they rolled, the silvery moon laid upon the trembling waters the shadows of that Form as it moved, long and dark, on their track. St. John uses an expression,[2] which shows us in the pale light, those

---

[1] According to St. Matt. xiv. 24, they seem only to have encountered the full force of the wind when they were about the middle of the Lake. We imagine that soon after they embarked there may have been a fresh breeze from the other side of the Lake, which by and by rose into a violent contrary wind.

[2] St. John, in distinction to the Synoptists, here uses the expression θεωρεῖν (St. John vi.' 19), which in the Gospels has the *distinctive meaning of fixed, earnest, and intent gaze,* mostly outward, but sometimes also inward, in the

sense of earnest and attentive consideration. The use of this word as distinguished from merely *seeing,* is so important for the better understanding of the New Testament, that every reader should mark it. We accordingly append a list of the passages in the Gospels where this word is used: St. Matt. xxvii. 55; xxviii. 1; St. Mark iii. 11; v. 15, 38; xii. 41; xv. 40, 47; xvi. 4; St. Luke x. 18; xiv. 29; xxi. 6; xxiii. 35, 48; xxiv. 37, 39; St. John ii. 23; iv. 19; vi. 2 (*Lachm.* and ‛*reg.*), 19, 40, 62; vii. 3; viii. 51; ix. 8; x. 12; xii. 19, 45; xiv. 17,

in the boat, intently, fixedly, fearfully, gazing at the Apparition as It neared still closer and closer. We must remember their previous excitement, as also the presence, and, no doubt, the superstitious suggestions of the boatman, when we think how they cried out for fear, and deemed It an Apparition. And 'He would have passed by them,'ᵃ as He so often does in our case—bringing them, indeed, deliverance, pointing and smoothing their way, but not giving them His known Presence, if they had not cried out. But their fear, which made them almost hesitate to receive Him into the boat, ¹ even though the outcome of error and superstition, brought His ready sympathy and comfort, in language which has so often, and in all ages, converted foolish fears of misapprehension into gladsome, thankful assurance: ' It is I, be not afraid!'

And they were no longer afraid, though truly His walking upon the waters might seem more awesome than any 'apparition. ' The storm in their hearts, like that on the Lake, was commanded by His Presence. We must still bear in mind their former excitement, now greatly intensified by what they had just witnessed, in order to understand the request of Peter: 'Lord, if it be Thou, bid me come to Thee on the water.' They are the words of a man, whom the excitement of the moment has carried beyond all reflection. And yet this combination of doubt ('if it be Thou '), with presumption ('bid me come on the water'), is peculiarly characteristic of Peter. He is the Apostle of Hope—and hope is a combination of doubt and presumption, but also their transformation. With reverence be it said, Christ could not have left the request ungranted, even though it was the outcome of yet unreconciled and untransformed doubt and presumption. He would not have done so—or doubt would have remained doubt untransformed; and He could not have done so, without also correcting it, or presumption would have remained presumption untransformed, which is only upward growth, without deeper rooting in inward spiritual experience. And so He bade him come upon the water, ² to transform his doubt, but left him, unassured from without, to his own feelings as he saw the wind,³ to

ᵃ St. Mark.
vi. 48

19; xvi. 10, 16, 17, 19; xvii. 24; xx. 6, 12, 14. It will thus be seen, that the expression is more frequently used by St. John than in the other Gospels, and it is there also that its distinctive meaning is of greatest importance.

¹ This seems to me implied in the expression, St. John vi. 21: 'Then they were willing to take Him into the ship.'

Some negative critics have gone so far as to see in this graphic hint a contradiction to the statements of the Synoptists. (See Lücke, Comment. ii. d. Evang. Joh. ii. pp. 120-122.)

² As to the physical possibility of it, we have to refer to our former remarks.

³ The word 'boisterous' must be struck out as an interpolated gloss.

transform his presumption; while by stretching out His Hand to save him from sinking, and by the words of correction which He spake, He did actually so point to their transformation in that hope, of which St. Peter is the special representative, and the preacher in the Church.

And presently, as they two came into the boat, [1] the wind ceased, and immediately the ship was at the land. But ' they that were in the boat '—apparently in contradistinction to the disciples,[2] though the latter must have stood around in sympathetic reverence— ' worshipped Him, saying, Of a truth Thou art the Son of God.' The first full public confession this of the fact, and made not by the disciples, but by others. With the disciples it would have meant something far deeper. But as from the lips of these men, it seems like the echo of what had passed between them on that memorable passage across the Lake. They also must have mingled in the conversation, as the boat had pushed off from the shore on the previous evening, when they spake of the miracle of the feeding, and then of the popular attempt to proclaim Him Messianic King, of which they knew not yet the final issue, since they had been ' constrained to get into the boat,' while the Master remained behind. They would speak of all that He was and had done, and how the very devils had proclaimed Him to be the ' Son of God, 'on that other shore, close by where the miracle of feeding had taken place. Perhaps, having been somewhat driven out of their course, they may have passed close to the very spot, and, as they pointed to it recalled the incident. And this designation of ' Son of God, ' with the worship which followed, would come much more readily, because with much more superficial meaning, to the boatmen than to the disciples. But in them, also, the thought was striking deep root; and presently, by the Mount of Transfiguration, would it be spoken in the name of all by Peter, not as demon- nor as man-taught, but as taught of Christ's Father Who is in Heaven.

Yet another question suggests itself. The events of the night are not recorded by St. Luke—perhaps because they did not come within his general view-plan of that Life; perhaps from reverence, because neither he, nor his teacher St. Paul, were within that inner

---

[1] I cannot see (with *Meyer*) any variation in the narrative in St. John vi. 21. The expression, ' they were willing to take him into the ship,' certainly does *not* imply that, after the incident of Peter's failure, He did not actually enter the boat.

[2] *Weiss* (p. 373) assures us that this view is ' impossible; ' but on no better ground than that no others than ten disciples are mentioned in St. Matt. xiv. 22, as if it had been necessary to mention the embarkation of the boatmen.

circle, with which the events of that night were connected rather in
the way of reproof than otherwise.   At any rate, even negative
criticism cannot legitimately draw any adverse inference from it, in
view of its record not only by two of the Synoptists, but in the
Fourth Gospel.   St. Mark also does not mention the incident concerning St. Peter; and this we can readily understand from his
connection with that Apostle.   Of the two eyewitnesses, St. John
and St. Matthew, the former also is silent on that incident.   On any
view of the authorship of the Fourth Gospel, it could not have been
from ignorance, either of its occurrence, or else of its record by
St. Matthew.   Was it among those 'many other things which Jesus
did,' which were not written by him, since their complete chronicle
would have rendered a Gospel-sketch impossible?   Or did it lie
outside that special conception of his Gospel, which, as regards its
details, determined the insertion or else the omission of certain incidents?   Or was there some reason for this omission connected with
the special relation of John to Peter?   And, lastly, why was St.
Matthew in this instance more detailed than the others, and alone told
it with such circumstantiality?   Was it that it had made such deep
impression on his own mind; had he somehow any personal connection
with it; or did he feel, as if this bidding of Peter to come to Christ
out of the ship and on the water had some close inner analogy with
his own call to leave the custom-house, and follow Christ?   Such,
and other suggestions which may arise can only be put in the form
of questions.   Their answer awaits the morning and the other shore.

THE END OF THE FIRST VOLUME.

THE LIFE AND TIMES
OF JESUS THE MESSIAH

THE LIFE
AND TIMES OF
JESUS THE MESSIAH

Alfred Edersheim

AUTHOR OF

The Temple — Its Ministry and Services,
Sketches of Jewish Social Life in the Days of Christ,
Prophecy and History in Relation to the Messiah,
Bible History, Old Testament, etc.

PART TWO

Wm. B. Eerdmans Publishing Co., Grand Rapids, Michigan

CONTENTS

OF

THE SECOND VOLUME.

BOOK III.—*continued.*

THE ASCENT:

FROM THE RIVER JORDAN TO THE MOUNT OF TRANSFIGURATION.

BOOK IV.

THE DESCENT:

FROM THE MOUNT OF TRANSFIGURATION INTO THE
VALLEY OF HUMILIATION AND DEATH.

BOOK V.

THE CROSS AND THE CROWN.

APPENDICES.

Book III.

THE ASCENT:

FROM THE RIVER JORDAN TO THE MOUNT OF TRANSFIGURATION—*continued*

CHAPTER XXXI.

THE CAVILS OF THE PHARISEES CONCERNING PURIFICATION, AND THE
TEACHING OF THE LORD CONCERNING PURITY—THE TRADITIONS CON-
CERNING 'HAND-WASHING' AND 'VOWS.'

(St. Matt. xv. 1–20; St. Mark vii. 1–23.)

As we follow the narrative, confirmatory evidence of what had preceded springs up at almost every step. It is quite in accordance
with the abrupt departure of Jesus from Capernaum, and its motives,
that when, so far from finding rest and privacy at Bethsaida (east of
the Jordan), a greater multitude than ever had there gathered around
Him, which would fain have proclaimed Him King, He resolved
on immediate return to the western shore, with the view of seeking a quieter retreat, even though it were in 'the coasts of Tyre
and Sidon.'[a] According to St. Mark,[b] the Master had directed the
disciples to make for the other Bethsaida, or 'Fisherton,' on the
western shore of the Lake.[c] Remembering how common the corresponding name is in our own country,[1] and that fishing was the main
industry along the shores of the Lake, we need not wonder at the
existence of more than one Beth-Saida, or 'Fisherton.'[2] Nor yet
does it seem strange, that the site should be lost of what, probably,
except for the fishing, was quite an unimportant place. By the testimony both of Josephus and the Rabbis, the shores of Gennesaret
were thickly studded with little towns, villages, and hamlets, which
have all perished without leaving a trace, while even of the largest
the ruins are few and inconsiderable. We would, however, hazard a
geographical conjecture. From the fact that St. Mark[d] names
Bethsaida, and St. John[e] Capernaum, as the original destination
of the boat, we would infer that Bethsaida was the fishing quarter

[a] St. Matt.
xv. 21
[b] St. Mark
vi. 45
[c] St. John
xii. 21

[d] St. Mark
vi. 45
[e] St. John
vi. 17

[1] I have myself counted twelve different places in England bearing names
which might be freely rendered by 'Bethsaida,' not to speak of the many suburbs
and quarters which bear a like designation, and, of course, my list is anything
but complete.

[2] In Jer. Megill. (p. 70 *a*, line 15 from
bottom) we read of a צייירתה, but the
locality scarcely agrees with our Beth-
Saida.

of, or rather close to, Capernaum, even as we so often find in our own country a 'Fisherton' adjacent to larger towns.   With this would agree the circumstance, that no traces of an ancient harbour have been discovered at Tell Hûm, the site of Capernaum.[1] Further, it would explain, how Peter and Andrew, who, according to St. John,[a] were of Bethsaida, are described by St. Mark[b] as having their home in Capernaum.   It also deserves notice, that, as regards the house of St. Peter, St. Mark, who was so intimately connected with him, names Capernaum, while St. John, who was his fellow-townsman, names Bethsaida, and that the reverse difference obtains between the two Evangelists in regard to the direction of the ship.   This also suggests, that in a sense—as regarded the fishermen—the names were interchangeable, or rather, that Bethsaida was the 'Fisherton' of Capernaum.[2]

A superficial reader might object that, in the circumstances, we would scarcely have expected Christ and His disciples to have returned at once to the immediate neighbourhood of Capernaum, if not to that city itself.   But a fuller knowledge of the circumstances will not only, as so often, convert the supposed difficulty into most important confirmatory evidence, but supply some deeply interesting details.   The apparently trivial notice, that (at least) the concluding part of the Discourses, immediately on the return to Capernaum, was spoken by Christ 'in Synagogue,'[c][3] enables us not only to localise this address, but to fix the exact succession of events.   If this Discourse was spoken 'in Synagogue,' it must have been (as will be shown) on the Jewish Sabbath.   Reckoning backwards, we arrive at the conclusion, that Jesus with His disciples left Capernaum for Beth-saida-Julias on a Thursday; that the miraculous feeding of the multitude took place on Thursday evening; the passage of the disciples to the other side, and the walking of Christ on the sea, as well as the failure of Peter's faith, in the night of Thursday to Friday; the passage of the people to Capernaum in search of Jesus,[d] with all that followed, on the Friday; and, lastly, the final Discourses of Christ on the Saturday in Capernaum and in the Synagogue.

Two inferences will appear from this chronological arrangement. First, when our Lord had retraced His steps from the eastern shore in search of rest and retirement, it was so close on the Jewish Sabbath (Friday), that He was almost obliged to return to Capernaum to

a St. John i.
44; xii. 21
b St. Mark
i. 29

c St. John
vi. 59

d St. John
vi. 22–24

---

[1] Comp. *Baedeker* (*Socin*) Paläst. page 270.

[2] May this connection of Capernaum and Beth-Saida account for the mention of the latter as one of the places which had been the scene of so many of His mighty works (St. Matt. xi. 21; St. Luke x. 13)?

[3] There is no article in the original.

spend the holy day there, before undertaking the further journey to CHAP.
'the coasts of Tyre and Sidon.' And on the Sabbath no actual XXXI
danger, either from Herod Antipas or the Pharisees, need have been
apprehended. Thus (as before indicated), the sudden return to
Capernaum, so far from constituting a difficulty, serves as confirmation of the previous narrative. Again, we cannot but perceive a
peculiar correspondence of dates. Mark here: The miraculous
breaking of bread at Bethsaida on a Thursday evening, and the
breaking of Bread at the Last Supper on a Thursday evening; the
attempt to proclaim Him King, and the betrayal; Peter's bold assertion, and the failure of his faith, each in the night from Thursday
to Friday; and, lastly, Christ's walking on the angry, storm-tossed
waves, and commanding them, and bringing the boat that bore His
disciples safe to land, and His victory and triumph over Death and
him that had the power of Death.

These, surely, are more than coincidences; and in this respect
also may this history be regarded as symbolic. As we read it, Christ
directed the disciples to steer for Bethsaida, the 'Fisherton' of Capernaum, But, apart from the latter suggestion, we gather from the
expressions used,[a] that the boat which bore the disciples had drifted   [a] St. Mark
out of its course—probably owing to the wind—and touched land,   vi. 53
not where they had intended, but at Gennesaret, where they moored
it. There can be no question, that by this term is meant 'the plain
of Gennesaret,' the richness and beauty of which *Josephus*[b] and   [b] Jewish
the Rabbis[c] describe in such glowing language. To this day it bears   War iii. 10.
marks of having been the most favoured spot in this favoured region.   7, 8
Travelling northwards from Tiberias along the Lake, we follow, for   [c] Pes. 8 b;
about five or six miles, a narrow ledge of land shut in by mountains,   Meg. 6 a;
when we reach the home of the Magdalene, the ancient Magdala   Ber. R. 98
(the modern *Mejdel*). Right over against us, on the other side, is
Kersa (Gerasa), the scene of the great miracle. On leaving Magdala
the mountains recede, and form an amphitheatric plain, more than a
mile wide, and four or five miles long. This is 'the land of Gennesaret'
(*el Ghuweir*). We pass across the 'Valley of Doves,' which intersects
it about one mile to the north of Magdala, and pursue our journey
over the well-watered plain, till, after somewhat more than an hour,
we reach its northern boundary, a little beyond *Khân Minyeh*. The
latter has, in accordance with tradition, been regarded by some as
representing Bethsaida,[1] but seems both too far from the Lake, and
too much south of Capernaum, to answer the requirements.

[1] *Baedeker (Socin)* has grouped together the reasons against identifying *Khân Minyeh* with Capernaum itself.

BOOK
III

No sooner had the well-known boat, which bore Jesus and His disciples, been run up the gravel-beach in the early morning of that Friday, than His Presence must have become known throughout the district, all the more that the boatmen would soon spread the story of the miraculous occurrences of the preceding evening and night. With Eastern rapidity the tidings would pass along, and from all the country around the sick were brought on their pallets, if they might but touch the border of His garment. Nor could such touch, even though the outcome of an imperfect faith, be in vain—for He, Whose garment they sought leave to touch, was the God-Man, the Conqueror of Death, the Source and Spring of all Life. And so it was where He landed, and all the way up to Bethsaida and Capernaum.[a][1]

a St. Matt. xiv. 34–36; St. Mark vi 53–56

In what followed, we can still trace the succession of events, though there are considerable difficulties as to their precise order. Thus we are expressly told,[b] that those from 'the other side' came to Capernaum' on 'the day following' the miraculous feeding, and that one of the subsequent Discourses, of which the outline is preserved, was delivered 'in Synagogue.'[c] As this could only have been done either on a Sabbath or Feast-Day (in this instance, the Passover[d]), it follows, that in any case a day must have intervened between their arrival at Capernaum and the Discourse in Synagogue. Again, it is almost impossible to believe that it could have been on the Passover-day (15th Nisan).[2] For we cannot imagine, that any large number would have left their homes and festive preparations on the Eve of the Pascha (14th Nisan), not to speak of the circumstance that in Galilee, differently from Judæa, all labour, including, of course, that of a journey across the Lake, was intermitted on the Eve of the Passover.[e] Similarly, it is almost impossible to believe, that so many festive pilgrims would have been assembled till late in the evening preceding the 14th Nisan so far from Jerusalem as Bethsaida-Julias, since it would have been impossible after that to reach the city and Temple in time for the feast. It, therefore, only remains to regard the Synagogue-service at which Christ preached as that of an ordinary Sabbath, and the arrival of the multitude as having taken place on the Friday in the forenoon.

b St. John vi. 22–25

c ver. 59

d St. John vi. 4

e Pes. 55 a

Again, from the place which the narrative occupies in the Gospels of St. Matthew and St. Mark, as well as from certain internal

---

[1] Mr. *Brown McClellan* (N.T. vol. i. p. 570) holds, that both the Passover and Pentecost had intervened—I know not on what grounds. At the same time the language in St. Mark vi. 56, might imply more than one occasion on which the same thing happened.

[2] This is propounded in *Wieseler*, Chronolog. Synopse, pp. 276, 290, as a possible view.

evidence, it seems difficult to doubt, that the reproof of the Pharisees and Scribes on the subject of 'the unwashed hands,'[a] was not administered immediately after the miraculous feeding and the night of miracles. We cannot, however, feel equally sure, which of the two preceded the other: the Discourse in Capernaum,[b] or the Reproof of the Pharisees.[c] Several reasons have determined us to regard the Reproof as having preceded the Discourse. Without entering on a detailed discussion, the simple reading of the two sections will lead to the instinctive conclusion, that such a Discourse could not have been followed by such cavil and such Reproof, while it seems in the right order of things, that the Reproof which led to the 'offence' of the Pharisees, and apparently the withdrawal of some in the outer circle of discipleship,[d] should have been followed by the positive teaching of the Discourse, which in turn resulted in the going back of many who had been in the inner circle of disciples.

In these circumstances, we venture to suggest the following as the succession of events. Early on the Friday morning the boat which bore Jesus and His disciples grated on the sandy beach of the plain of Gennesaret. As the tidings spread of His arrival and of the miracles which had so lately been witnessed, the people from the neighbouring villages and towns flocked around Him, and brought their sick for the healing touch. So the greater part of the forenoon passed. Meantime, while they moved, as the concourse of the people by the way would allow, the first tidings of all this must have reached the neighbouring Capernaum. This brought immediately on the scene those Pharisees and Scribes 'who had come from Jerusalem' on purpose to watch, and, if possible, to compass the destruction of Jesus. As we conceive it, they met the Lord and His disciples on their way to Capernaum. Possibly they overtook them, as they rested by the way, and the disciples, or some of them, were partaking of some food—perhaps, some of the consecrated Bread of the previous evening. The Reproof of Christ would be administered there; then the Lord would, not only for their teaching, but for the purposes immediately to be indicated, turn to the multitude;[f] next would follow the remark of the disciples and the reply of the Lord, spoken, probably, when they were again on the way;[g] and, lastly, the final explanation of Christ, after they had entered the house at Capernaum.[h] In all probability a part of what is recorded in St. John vi. 24, &c. occurred also about the same time; the rest on the Sabbath which followed.

[a] St. Matt. xv. 1; St. Mark vii. 1
[b] St. John vi. 59
[c] St. Matt. xv. 1 &c.

[d] St. Matt. xv. 12–14

[e] St. John vi. 60–66

[f] St. Matt. xv. 10; St. Mark vii. 14, 15
[g] St. Matt. xv. 12–14
[h] St. Matt xv. 15–20; St. Mark vii. 17–23

Although the cavil of the Jerusalem Scribes may have been occasioned by seeing some of the disciples eating without first having washed their hands, we cannot banish the impression that it reflected on the miraculously provided meal of the previous evening, when thousands had sat down to food without the previous observance of the Rabbinic ordinance. Neither in that case, nor in the present, had the Master interposed. He was, therefore, guilty of participation in their offence. So this was all which these Pharisees and Scribes could see in the miracle of Christ's feeding the Multitude—that it had not been done according to Law! Most strange as it may seem, yet in the past history of the Church, and, perhaps, sometimes also in the present, this has been the only thing which some men have seen in the miraculous working of the Christ! Perhaps we should not wonder that the miracle itself made no deeper impression, since even the disciples 'understood not' (by reasoning) 'about the loaves' —however they may have accounted for it in a manner which might seem to them reasonable. But, in another aspect, the objection of the Scribes was not a mere cavil. In truth, it represented one of the great charges which the Pharisees brought against Jesus, and which determined them to seek His destruction.

It has already been shown, that they accounted for the miracles of Christ as wrought by the power of Satan, whose special representative—almost incarnation—they declared Jesus to be. This would not only turn the evidential force of these signs into an argument against Christ, but vindicate the resistance of the Pharisees to His claims. The second charge against Jesus was, that He was 'not of God;' that He was 'a sinner.'[a] If this could be established, it would, of course, prove that He was not the Messiah, but a deceiver who misled the people, and whom it was the duty of the Sanhedrin to unmask and arrest. The way in which they attempted to establish this, perhaps persuaded themselves that it was so, was by proving that He sanctioned in others, and Himself committed, breaches of the traditional law; which, according to their fundamental principles, involved heavier guilt than sins against the revealed Law of Moses. The third and last charge against Jesus, which finally decided the action of the Council, could only be fully made at the close of His career. It might be formulated so as to meet the views of either the Pharisees or Sadducees. To the former it might be presented as a blasphemous claim to equality with God—the Very Son of the Living God. To the Sadducees it would appear as a movement on the part of a most dangerous enthusiast—if honest and

a St. John
ix. 16, 24

self-deceived, all the more dangerous; one of those pseudo-Messiahs who led away the ignorant, superstitious, and excitable people; and which, if unchecked, would result in persecutions and terrible vengeance by the Romans, and in loss of the last remnants of their national independence. To each of these three charges, of which we are now watching the opening or development, there was (from the then standpoint) only one answer: Faith in His Person. And in our time, also, this is the final answer to all difficulties and objections. To this faith Jesus was now leading His disciples, till, fully realised in the great confession of Peter, it became, and has ever since proved, the Rock on which that Church is built, against which the very gates of Hades cannot prevail.

It was in support of the second of these charges, that the Scribes now blamed the Master for allowing His disciples to eat without having previously washed, or, as St. Mark—indicating, as we shall see, in the word the origin of the custom—expresses it with graphic accuracy: 'with common hands.'[1] Once more we have to mark, how minutely conversant the Gospel narratives are with Jewish Law and practice. This will best appear from a brief account of this 'tradition of the elders,'[2] the more needful that important differences prevail even among learned Jewish authorities, due probably to the circumstance that the brief Mishnic Tractate devoted to the subject[3] has no Gemara attached to it, and also largely treats of other matters. At the outset we have this confirmation of the Gospel language, that this practice is expressly admitted to have been, not a Law of Moses, but 'a tradition of the elders.'[4] Still, and perhaps on this very account, it was so strictly enjoined, that to neglect it was like being guilty of gross carnal defilement. Its omission would lead to temporal destruction,[a] or, at least, to poverty.[b] Bread

ᵃ Sot. 4 b
ᵇ Shabb.
62 b

---

[1] The word quite corresponds to the Jewish term. Notwithstanding the objection of the learned Bishop *Haneberg* (Relig. Alterth. p. 475, note 288) I believe it corresponds to the Rabbinic חֹל or חוּלָּא (Hebr. חֹל) *profanus*, in the sense of 'common,' 'not hallowed.'

[2] The fullest account of it within reach of ordinary readers is in the Notes to *Pocock's* Porta Mosis (pp. 350–402) though it is confused, not quite accurate, and based chiefly on later Jewish authorities. *Spencer* (de Leg. Hebr. pp. 1175–1179) only adds references to similar Gentile rites. *Goodwin*, even under the revision of *Hottinger* (pp. 182–188), is in

this instance inferior to *Pocock*. *Buxtorf* (Synag. pp. 179–184) gives chiefly illustrative Jewish legends; *Otho* (Lex. Rabb. pp. 335, 336) extracts from his predecessors, to little advantage. The Rabbinic notes of *Lightfoot*, *Wünsche*, *Schöttgen*, and *Wetstein* give no clear account; and the Biblical Dictionaries are either silent, or (as *Herzog's*) very meagre. Other accounts are, unfortunately, very inaccurate.

[3] *Yadayim*, in four chapters, which, however, touches on other subjects also, notably on the canonicity of certain parts of the O.T.

[4] We refer here generally to *Chull.* 105 a, b, 106 b.

BOOK
III

ᵃ Sot. 4 b
ᵇ Eduy. v. 6;
Ber. 19 a

ᶜ Chull. 106
a; Bemidb.
R. 20, ed.
Warsh. p.
81 b

ᵈ Chull.
106 a

ᵉ Chull.
106 a
ᶠ Lev xi. 44

ᵍ Ber. 53 b,
end

ʰ Erub. 17 b;
Chull. 105 b

ⁱ Chull.
105 a, b

מֵישָׁא ᵏ
(Chull. 107
a and b)

eaten with unwashen hands was as if it had been filth.ᵃ   Indeed, a Rabbi who had held this command in contempt was actually buried in excommunication.ᵇ   Thus, from their point of view, the charge of the Scribes against the disciples, so far from being exaggerated, is most moderately worded by the Evangelists.   In fact, although at one time it had only been one of the marks of a Pharisee, yet at a later period to wash before eating was regarded as affording the ready means of recognising a Jew.ᶜ [1]

It is somewhat more difficult to account for the origin of the ordinance.   So far as indicated, it seems to have been first enjoined in order to ensure that sacred offerings should not be eaten in defilement.   When once it became an ordinance of the elders, this was, of course, regarded as sufficient ground for obedience.ᵈ   Presently, Scriptural support was sought for it.   Some based it on the original ordinance of purification in Lev. xv. 11;ᵉ while others saw in the words ᶠ 'Sanctify yourselves,' the command to wash before meat; in the command, 'Be ye holy,' that of washing after meat; while the final clause, 'for I am the Lord your God,' was regarded as enjoining 'the grace at meat.'ᵍ   For, soon it was not merely a washing before, but also after meals.   The former alone was, however, regarded as 'a commandment' (Mitsvah), the other only as 'a duty' (Chobhah), which some, indeed, explained on sanitary grounds, as there might be left about the hands what might prove injurious to the eyes.ʰ [2]   Accordingly, soldiers might, in the urgency of campaigning, neglect the washing before, but they ought to be careful about that after meat.   By-and-by, the more rigorous actually washed between the courses, although this was declared to be purely voluntary.ⁱ   This washing before meals is regarded by some as referred to in Talmudic writings by the expression 'the first waters' (Mayim rishonim), while what is called 'the second' (sheniyim), or 'the other,' 'later,' or 'after-waters' (Mayim acharonim), is supposed to represent the washing after meals.

But there is another and more important aspect of the expression, which leads us to describe the rite itself.   The distinctive designation for it is Netilath Yadayim,[3] literally, the lifting of the hands; while for the washing before meat the term Meshi or Meshaᵏ is also used, which literally means 'to rub.'   Both these terms

---

[1] Many illustrative stories are given of its importance, on the one hand, and of the danger of neglecting it on the other. With these legends it is not necessary to cumber our pages.

[2] The danger from 'Salt of Sodom is

specially mentioned.

[3] נְטִילָה, sometimes though rarely, טהרת ידים, but not רחיצת, which refers to ordinary washing. Occasionally it is simply designated by the term Netilah.

point to the manner of the rite. The first question here was, whether
'second tithe,' prepared first-fruits (*Terumah*), or even common food
(*Chullin*), or else, 'holy,' i.e. sacrificial food, was to be partaken of. In
the latter case a complete immersion of the hands ('baptism,' *Tebh-
ilath Yadayim*), and not merely a *Netilath*, or 'uplifting,' was
prescribed.ᵃ The latter was really an affusion. As the purifications
were so frequent, and care had to be taken that the water had not
been used for other purposes, or something fallen into it that might
discolour or defile it, large vessels or jars were generally kept for the
purpose. These might be of any material, although stone is specially
mentioned.¹ It was the practice to draw water out of these with
what was called a *natla*, *antila*, or *antelaya*,ᵇ very often of glass, which
must hold (at least) a quarter of a log ᶜ—a measure equal to one
and a half 'egg-shells.' For, no less quantity than this might be
used for affusion. The water was poured on both hands, which must
be free of anything covering them, such as gravel, mortar, &c. The
hands were lifted up, so as to make the water run to the wrist, in
order to ensure that the whole hand was washed, and that the water
polluted by the hand did not again run down the fingers. Similarly,
each hand was rubbed with the other (the fist), provided the hand
that rubbed had been affused: otherwise, the rubbing might be done
against the head, or even against a wall. But there was one point on
which special stress was laid. In the 'first affusion,' which was all
that originally was required when the hands were Levitically
'defiled,' the water had to run down to the wrist ² (עַד הַפֶּרֶק, or עַד הַפֶּרֶק)
lappereq, or *ad happereq*). If the water remained short of the wrist
(*chuts lappereq*), the hands were not clean.ᵈ Accordingly, the words
of St. Markᵉ can only mean that the Pharisees eat not 'except they
wash their hands to the wrist.' ³

Allusion has already been made to what are called 'the first' and
'the second,' or 'other' 'waters.' But, in their original meaning,
these terms referred to something else than washing before and after
meals. The hands were deemed capable of contracting Levitical
defilement, which, in certain cases, might even render the whole

CHAP.
XXXI

ᵃ Chag. ii.
5, 6

ᵇ ἀντγίον

ᶜ Chull.
107 a; Baba
B. 58 b, and
often

ᵈ Comp.
Yad. ii. 3;
Chull. 106
a and b

ᵉ St. Mark
vii. 3

---

¹ This and what follows illustrates
St. John ii. 6.
  ² The language of the Mishnah shows
that the word פֶּרֶק, which bears as vague
and wide meaning as πυγμή, which seems
a literal translation of it, can only apply
to the wrist.
  ² The rendering 'wash diligently,'
gives no meaning; that 'with the fist'

is not in accordance with Jewish Law;
while that 'up to the elbow' is not only
contrary to Jewish Law, but apparently
based on a wrong rendering of the word
פֶּרֶק. This is fully shown by *Wetstein*
(N.T. i. p. 585), but his own explanation,
that πυγμή refers to the measure or
weight of the water for washing, is
inadmissible.

body 'unclean.' If the hands were 'defiled,' two affusions were required: the first, or 'first waters' (*mayim rishonim*) to remove the defilement, and the 'second,' or 'after waters' (*mayim sheniyim* or *acharonim*) to wash away the waters that had contracted the defilement of the hands. Accordingly, on the affusion of the first waters the hands were elevated, and the water made to run down at the wrist, while at the second waters the hands were depressed, so that the water might run off by the finger points and tips. By-and-by, it became the practice to have two affusions, whenever *Terumah* (prepared first-fruits) was to be eaten, and at last even when ordinary food (*Chullin*) was partaken of. The modern Jews have three affusions, and accompany the rite with a special benediction.

This idea of the 'defilement of the hands' received a very curious application. According to one of the eighteen decrees, which, as we shall presently show, date before the time of Christ, the Roll of the Pentateuch in the Temple defiled all kinds of meat that touched it. The alleged reason for this decree was, that the priests were wont to keep the *Terumah* (preserved first-fruits) close to the Roll of the Law, on which account the latter was injured by mice. The Rabbinic ordinance was intended to avert this danger.[a][1] To increase this precaution, it was next laid down as a principle, that all that renders the *Terumah* unfit, also defiles the hands.[b] Hence, the Holy Scriptures defiled not only the food but the hands that touched them, and this not merely in the Temple, but anywhere, while it was also explained that the Holy Scriptures included the whole of the inspired writings—the Law, Prophets, and Hagiographa. This gave rise to interesting discussions, whether the Song of Solomon, Ecclesiastes, or Esther were to be regarded as 'defiling the hands,' that is, as part of the Canon. The ultimate decision was in favour of these books: 'all the holy writings defile the hands; the Song of Songs and Ecclesiastes defile the hands.'[c] Nay, so far were sequences carried, that even a small portion of the Scriptures was declared to defile the hands if it contained eighty-five letters, because the smallest 'section' (*Parashah*) in the Law[d] consisted of exactly that number. Even the Phylacteries, because they contained portions of the sacred text, the very leather straps by which they were bound to the head and arm—nay, the blank margins around the text of the Scriptures,

[a] Shabb.
14 a

[b] Yad. iii. 2

[c] Yad. iii. 5

[d] Numb. x. 35, 36

---

[1] In Yad. iv. 6, the Pharisees in dispute with the Sadducees indicate what seems to me a far more likely reason, in the desire to protect the Scriptures from profane use.

or at the beginning and end of sections, were declared to defile the hands.[a1]

From this exposition it will be understood what importance the Scribes attached to the rite which the disciples had neglected. Yet at a later period Pharisaism, with characteristic ingenuity, found a way of evading even this obligation, by laying down what we would call the Popish (or semi-Popish) principle of 'intention.' It was ruled, that if anyone had performed the rite of handwashing in the morning, 'with intention' that it should apply to the meals of the whole day, this was (with certain precautions) valid.[b] But at the time of which we write the original ordinance was quite new. This touches one of the most important, but also most intricate questions in the history of Jewish dogmas. Jewish tradition traced, indeed, the command of washing the hands before eating—at least of sacrificial offerings—to Solomon,[c] in acknowledgment of which 'the voice from heaven' (Bath-Qol) had been heard to utter Prov. xxiii. 15, and xxvii. 11. But the earliest trace of this custom occurs in a portion of the Sibylline Books, which dates from about 160 B.C.,[d] where we find an allusion to the practice of continually washing the hands, in connection with prayer and thanksgiving.[2] It was reserved for Hillel and Shammai, the two great rival teachers and heroes of Jewish traditionalism, immediately before Christ, to fix the Rabbinic ordinance about the washing of hands (Netilath Yadayim), as previously described. This was one of the few points on which they were agreed,[e] and hence emphatically 'a tradition of the Elders,' since these two teachers bear, in Rabbinic writings, each the designation of 'the Elder.'[f] Then followed a period of developing traditionalism, and hatred of all that was Gentile. The tradition of the Elders was not yet so established as to command absolute and universal obedience, while the disputes of Hillel and Shammai, who seemed almost on principle to have taken divergent views on every question, must have disturbed the minds of many. We have an account of a stormy meeting between the two Schools, attended even with bloodshed. The story is so confusedly, and so differently told in

CHAP.
XXXI

[a] Yad. iii. 3–5

[b] Chull. 106 b

[c] Shabb. 14 b, end

[d] Or. Sib. iii. 591–593

[e] Shabb. 14 b, about the middle

[f] הזקן

---

[1] By a curious inversion the law ultimately came to be, that the Scriptures everywhere defiled the hands, except those of the Priests in the Temple (Kel. xv. 6). This on the ground that, taught by former enactments, they had learned to keep the Terumah far away from the sacred rolls, but really, as I believe, because the law, that the Priests' hands became defiled if they touched a copy of the sacred rules, must have involved constant difficulties.

[2] We must bear in mind, that it was the work of an Egyptian Jew, and I cannot help feeling that the language bears some likeness to what afterwards was one of the distinctive practices of the Essenes.

BOOK
III

ᵃ Jer.
Shabb. p. 3
z, d
ᵇ Shabb.
13 b to 14 b

ᶜ Jer.
Shabb. 3 c

ᵈ Jer.
Shabb. 3 d
ᵉ Shabb.
13 b; 14 b
ᶠ Shabb. 14
b, towards
end

ᵍ Ab. Z. 35 a

the Jerusalem ᵃ and in the Babylon Talmud,ᵇ that it is difficult to form a clear view of what really occurred. Thus much, however, appears —that the Shammaites had a majority of votes, and that 'eighteen decrees' (ר"ח דברים) were passed in which the two Schools agreed, while on other eighteen questions (perhaps a round number) the Shammaites carried their views by a majority, and yet other eighteen remained undecided. Each of the Schools spoke of that day according to its party-results. The Shammaites (such as Rabbi Eliezer) extolled it as that on which the measure of the Law had been filled up to the full,ᶜ while the Hillelites (like Rabbi Joshua) deplored, that on that day water had been poured into a vessel full of oil, by which some of the more precious fluid had been spilt. In general, the tendency of these eighteen decrees was of the most violently anti-Gentile, intolerant, and exclusive character. Yet such value was attached to them, that, while any other decree of the sages might be altered by a more grave, learned, and authoritative assembly, these eighteen decrees might not under any circumstances, be modified.ᵈ But, besides these eighteen decrees, the two Schools on that day ᵉ agreed in solemnly re-enacting 'the decrees about the Book (the copy of the Law), and the hands'(גזירות הספר והידים). The Babylon Talmud ᶠ notes that the latter decree, though first made by Hillel and Shammai, 'the Elders,' was not universally carried out until re-enacted by their colleges. It is important to notice, that this 'Decree' dates from the time just before, and was finally carried into force in the very days of Christ. This fully accounts for the zeal which the Scribes displayed—and explains 'the extreme minuteness of details' with which St. Mark 'calls attention' to this Pharisaic practice.[1] For, it was an express Rabbinic principle ᵍ that, if an ordinance had been only recently re-enacted (גזירה הרשה), it might not be called in question or 'invalidated' (אין מפקפקין בה).[2] Thus it will be seen, that the language employed by the Evangelist affords most valuable indirect confirmation of the trustworthiness of his Gospel, as not only showing intimate familiarity with the *minutiæ* of Jewish 'tradition,'

---

[1] In the 'Speaker's Commentary' (ad loc.) this 'extreme minuteness of details' is, it seems to me not correctly, accounted for on the ground of 'special reference to the Judaisers who at a very early period formed an influential party at Rome.'

[2] This is the more striking as the same expression is used in reference to the opposition or rather the 'invalidating' by R. Eliezer ben Chanokh of the ordinance of hand-washing, for which he was

excommunicated (שפקפק בטהרת ידים, Eduy. v. 6). The term פקק, which originally means to stop up by pouring or putting in something, is used for contemning or bringing into contempt, invalidating, or shaking a decree, with the same signification as זלזל. This is proved from the use of the latter in Ab. Z. 35 a, line 9 from bottom, and 36 a, line 12 from top.

but giving prominence to what was then a present controversy—and all this the more, that it needs intimate knowledge of that Law even fully to understand the language of the Evangelist.

After this full exposition, it can only be necessary to refer in briefest manner to those other observances which orthodox Judaism had 'received to hold.' They connect themselves with those eighteen decrees, intended to separate the Jew from all contact with Gentiles. Any contact with a heathen, even the touch of his dress, might involve such defilement, that on coming from the market the orthodox Jew would have to immerse. Only those who know the complicated arrangements about the defilements of vessels that were in any part, however small, hollow, as these are described in the Mishnah (Tractate *Kelim*), can form an adequate idea of the painful minuteness with which every little detail is treated. Earthen vessels that had contracted impurity were to be broken; those of wood, horn, glass, or brass immersed; while, if vessels were bought of Gentiles, they were (as the case might be) to be immersed, put into boiling water, purged with fire, or at least polished.[a]

Let us now try to realise the attitude of Christ in regard to these ordinances about purification, and seek to understand the reason of His bearing. That, in replying to the charge of the Scribes against His disciples, He neither vindicated their conduct, nor apologised for their breach of the Rabbinic ordinances, implied at least an attitude of indifference towards traditionalism. This is the more noticeable, since, as we know, the ordinances of the Scribes were declared more precious,[b][1] and of more binding importance than those of Holy Scripture itself.[c] But, even so, the question might arise, why Christ should have provoked such hostility by placing Himself in marked antagonism to what, after all, was indifferent in itself. The answer to this inquiry will require a disclosure of that aspect of Rabbinism which, from its painfulness, has hitherto been avoided. Yet it is necessary not only in itself, but as showing the infinite distance between Christ and the teaching of the Synagogue. It has already been told, how Rabbinism, in the madness of its self-exaltation, represented God as busying Himself by day with the study of the Scriptures, and by night with that of the Mishnah;[d] and how, in the heavenly Sanhedrin, over which the Almighty presided, the Rabbis sat in the order of their greatness, and the Halakhah was discussed, and decisions taken in accordance

[a] Ab. Zar. v *passim*

[b] Jer. Chag. 76 *d*

[c] Jer. Ber. 3 *b*; Sanh. xi. 3; Erub. 21 *b*

[d] Targum (ed. Ven.) on Cant. v. 10; comp. Ab. Z. 3 *b*

---

[1] In this passage there is a regular discussion, whether that which is written (the Pentateuch), or that which is oral (tradition is more precious and to be loved (אֵיזֶה מֵהֶן חֲבִיבִין). The opinion is in favour of the oral (אוֹתָן שֶׁבְּעַל פֶּה).

BOOK
III

ᵃ Baba
Mez. 86 a
ᵇ Ab. Z. u. s.
ᶜ Comp.
Chag. 5 b

ᵈ Ber. 3 a

ᵉ Ber. 59 a

ᶠ Ber. 7 a;
Ab. Z. 4 b

ᵍ Ber. 7 a

ʰ Shem. R.
42, comp.
Rosh
haSh. 17 b

ⁱ Ber. 6 a

ᵏ Shem. R.
15, ed.
Warsh.
p. 22 a, line
13 from top
ᵐ Is. lxvi.
15; comp.
Numb.
xxxi. 23

with it.ᵃ Terrible as this sounds, it is not nearly all. Anthropo-morphism of the coarsest kind is carried beyond the verge of pro-fanity, when God is represented as spending the last three hours of every day in playing with Leviathan,ᵇ and it is discussed, how, since the destruction of Jerusalem, God no longer laughs, but weeps, and that, in a secret place of His own, according to Jer. xiii. 17.ᶜ Nay, Jer. xxv. 30 is profanely misinterpreted as implying that, in His grief over the destruction of the Temple, the Almighty roars like a lion in each of the three watches of the night.ᵈ The two tears which He drops into the sea are the cause of earthquakes; although other, though not less coarsely realistic, explanations are offered of this phenomenon.ᵉ

Sentiments like these, which occur in different Rabbinic writings, cannot be explained away by any ingenuity of allegorical interpre-tation. There are others, equally painful, as regards the anger of the Almighty, which, as kindling specially in the morning, when the sun-worshippers offer their prayers, renders it even dangerous for an individual Israelite to say certain prayers on the morning of New Year's Day, on which the throne is set for judgment.ᶠ Such realistic anthropomorphism, combined with the extravagant ideas of the eternal and heavenly reality of Rabbinism and Rabbinic ordinances, help us to understand, how the Almighty was actually represented as saying prayers. This is proved from Is. lvi. 7. Sublime though the language of these prayers is, we cannot but notice that the all-covering mercy, for which He is represented as pleading, is extended only to Israel.ᵍ It is even more terrible to read of God wearing the *Tallith*,ʰ or that He puts on the Phylacteries, which is deduced from Is. lxii. 8. That this also is connected with the vain-glorious boast ing of Israel, appears from the passages supposed to be enclosed in these Phylacteries. We know that in the ordinary Phylacteries these are: Exod. xiii. 1–10; 10–16; Deut. vi. 4–10; xi. 13–22. In the Divine Phylacteries they were: 1 Chron. xvii. 21; Deut. iv. 7–8; xxxiii. 29; iv. 34; xxvi. 19.ⁱ Only one other point must be mentioned as connected with Purifications. To these also the Almighty is supposed to submit. Thus He was purified by Aaron, when He had contracted defilement by descending into Egypt.ᵏ This is deduced from Lev. xvi. 16. Similarly, He immersed in a bath of fire,ᵐ after the defilement of the burial of Moses.

These painful details, most reluctantly given, are certainly not intended to raise or strengthen ignorant prejudices against Israel, to whom ' blindness in part ' has truly happened; far less to encourage the wicked spirit of contempt and persecution which is characteristic, not of believing, but of negative theology.　But they will explain, how Jesus could not have assumed merely an attitude of indifference towards traditionalism.　For, even if such sentiments were ·repre-sented as a later development, they are the outcome of a direction, of which that of Jesus was the very opposite, and to which it was antagonistic.　But, if Jesus was not sent of God—not the Messiah—whence this wonderful contrast of highest spirituality in what He taught of God as our Father, and of His Kingdom as that over the hearts of all men?　The attitude of antagonism to traditionalism was never more pronounced than in what He said in reply to the charge of neglect of the ordinance about 'the washing of hands.'　Here it must be remembered, that it was an admitted Rabbinic principle that, while the ordinances of Scripture required no confirmation, those of the Scribes needed such,[a] and that no Halakhah (traditional law) might contradict Scripture.[1]　When Christ, therefore, next pro-ceeded to show, that in a very important point—nay, in 'many such like things'—the Halakhah was utterly incompatible with Scripture, that, indeed, they made 'void the Word of God' by their traditions which they had received,[b] He dealt the heaviest blow to tradition-alism.　Rabbinism stood self-condemned; on its own showing, it was to be rejected as incompatible with the Word of God.

It is not so easy to understand, why the Lord should, out of 'many such things,' have selected in illustration the Rabbinic ordinance concerning vows, as in certain circumstances, contravening the fifth commandment.　Of course, the 'Ten Words' were the Holy of Holies of the Law; nor was there any obligation more rigidly observed—indeed, carried in practice almost to the verge of absurdity[2]—than that of honour to parents.　In both respects, then, this was a specially vulnerable point, and it might well be argued that, if in this Law Rabbinic ordinances came into conflict with the demands of God's Word, the essential contrariety between them must, indeed, be great.　Still, we feel as if this were not all.　Was there any special instance in view, in which the Rabbinic law about votive offerings had led to such abuse?　Or was it only, that at this festive season the Galilean pilgrims would carry with them to Jerusalem their votive offerings?　Or, could the Rabbinic ordinances about 'the sanctification of the hands' (*Yadayim*) have recalled to the Lord another Rabbinic appli-

[a] Jer. Taan. 66 *a*, about the middle

[b] St. Matt. xv. 3, 6; St. Mark vii. 9. 13

---

[1] It was, however, admitted that the Halakhah sometimes went beyond the Pentateuch (Sot. 16 *a*).

[2] See the remarks on this point in vol. i. pp. 567, 576, 577.

BOOK
III

cation of the word 'hand' (*yad*) in connection with votive offerings? It is at least sufficiently curious to find mention here, and it will afford the opportunity of briefly explaining, what to a candid reader may seem almost inexplicable in the Jewish legal practice to which Christ refers.

At the outset it must be admitted, that Rabbinism did *not* encourage the practice of promiscuous vowing. As we view it, it belongs, at best, to a lower and legal standpoint. In this respect Rabbi Akiba put it concisely, in one of his truest sayings: 'Vows are a hedge to abstinence.'[a] On the other hand, if regarded as a kind of return for benefits received, or as a promise attaching to our prayers, a vow—unless it form part of our absolute and entire self-surrender —partakes either of work-righteousness, or appears almost a kind of religious gambling. And so the Jewish proverb has it: 'In the hour of need a vow; in time of ease excess.'[b] Towards such work-righteousness and religious gambling the Eastern, and especially the Rabbinic Jew, would be particularly inclined. But even the Rabbis saw that its encouragement would lead to the profanation of what was holy; to rash, idle, and wrong vows; and to the worst and most demoralising kind of perjury, as inconvenient consequences made themselves felt. Of many sayings, condemnatory of the practice, one will suffice to mark the general feeling: 'He who makes a vow, even if he keep it, deserves the name of wicked.'[c] Nevertheless, the practice must have attained terrible proportions, whether as regards the number of vows, the lightness with which they were made, or the kind of things which became their object. The larger part of the Mishnic Tractate on 'Vows' (*Nedarim*, in eleven chapters) describes what expressions were to be regarded as equivalent to vows, and what would either legally invalidate and annul a vow, or leave it binding. And here we learn, that those who were of full age, and not in a position of dependence (such as wives) would make almost any kind of vows, such as that they would not lie down to sleep, not speak to their wives or children, not have intercourse with their brethren, and even things more wrong or foolish—all of which were solemnly treated as binding on the conscience. Similarly, it was not necessary to use the express words of vowing. Not only the word 'Qorban' [*Korban*]— 'given to God'—but any similar expression, such as *Qonakh*, or *Qonam*[1] (the latter also a Phœnician expression, and probably an equivalent for *Qeyam*, 'let it be established') would suffice; the mention of anything

[a] Ab. iii. 18

[b] Ber. R. 81

[c] Nedar. 9 a; 22 a

---

[1] According to Nedar. 10 *a*, the Rabbis invented this word instead of 'Qorban to the Lord' (Lev. i. 2), in order that the Name of God might not be idly taken.

laid upon the altar (though not of the altar itself), such as the wood, or the fire, would constitute a vow,[a] nay, the repetition of the form which generally followed on the votive *Qonam or Qorban* had binding force, even though not preceded by these terms. Thus, if a man said: 'That I eat or taste of such a thing,' it constituted a vow, which bound him not to eat or taste it, because the common formula was: 'Qorban (or Qonam) that I eat or drink, or do such a thing,' and the omission of the votive word did not invalidate a vow, if it were otherwise regularly expressed.[b]

It is in explaining this strange provision, intended both to uphold the solemnity of vows, and to discourage the rash use of words, that the Talmud[c] makes use of the word '*hand*' in a connection which we have supposed might, by association of ideas, have suggested to Christ the contrast between what the Bible and what the Rabbis regarded as 'sanctified hands,' and hence between the commands of God and the traditions of the Elders. For the Talmud explains that, when a man simply says: 'That (or if) I eat or taste such a thing,' it is imputed as a vow, and he may not eat or taste of it, 'because the hand is on the Qorban'[d]—the mere touch of Qorban had sanctified it, and put it beyond his reach, just as if it had been laid on the altar itself. Here, then, was a contrast. According to the Rabbis, the touch of 'a common' hand defiled God's good gift of meat, while the touch of 'a sanctified' hand in rash or wicked words might render it impossible to give anything to a parent, and so involve the grossest breach of the Fifth Commandment! Such, according to Rabbinic Law, was the 'common' and such the 'sanctifying' touch of the hands—and did such traditionalism not truly 'make void the Word of God'?

A few further particulars may serve to set this in clearer light. It must not be thought that the pronunciation of the votive word '*Qorban*,' although meaning 'a gift,' or 'given to God,' necessarily dedicated a thing to the Temple. The meaning might simply be, and generally was, that it was to be regarded like *Qorban*—that is, that in regard to the person or persons named, the thing termed was to be considered as if it were *Qorban*, laid on the altar, and put entirely out of their reach. For, although included under the one name, there were really two kinds of vows: those of consecration to God, and those of personal obligation[1]—and the latter were the most frequent.

To continue. The legal distinction between a vow, an oath, and

---

[1] See *Maimonides*, Yad haChas., Hilkh. Nedar. i. 1, 2.

[a] Nedar. 1.
1-3

[b] Jer.
Nedar. 36 *d*,
line 20 from
top

[c] u. s.

[d] משם יד
לקרב
(Jer.
Nedar. 36 *d*,
line 22)

BOOK
III

שׁאני a
אוכל
לא אוכל b
a Jer. Ned.
u. s.

d Tos.
Arach. iv.

a they open
a door.'
f Nedar. ix.
passim

g Chag. i. 8

'the ban,' are clearly marked both in reason and in Jewish Law. The oath was an absolute, the vow a conditional undertaking—their difference being marked even by this, that the language of a vow ran thus: 'That' or 'if' 'I or another do such a thing,' 'if I eat;' a while that of the oath was a simple affirmation or negation, b 'I shall not eat.' c On the other hand, the 'ban' might refer to one of three things: those dedicated for the use of the priesthood, those dedicated to God, or else to a sentence pronounced by the Sanhedrin. d In any case it was not lawful to 'ban' the whole of one's property, nor even one class of one's property (such as all one's sheep), nor yet what could not, in the fullest sense, be called one's *property*, such as a child, a Hebrew slave, or a purchased field, which had to be restored in the Year of Jubilee; while an inherited field, if banned, would go in perpetuity for the use of the priesthood. Similarly, the Law limited vows. Those intended to incite to an act (as on the part of one who sold a thing), or by way of exaggeration, or in cases of mistake, and, lastly, vows which circumstances rendered impossible, were declared null. To these four classes the Mishnah added those made to escape murder, robbery, and the exactions of the publican. If a vow was regarded as rash or wrong, attempts were made e to open a door for repentance. f Absolutions from a vow might be obtained before a 'sage,' or, in his absence, before three laymen,[1] when all obligations became null and void. At the same time the Mishnah g admits, that this power of absolving from vows was a tradition hanging, as it were, in the air,[2] since it received little (or, as *Maimonides* puts it, no) support from Scripture.[3]

There can be no doubt, that the words of Christ referred to such vows of personal obligation. By these a person might bind himself in regard to men or things, or else put that which was another's out of his own reach, or that which was his own out of the reach of another, and this as completely as if the thing or things had been *Qorban*, a gift given to God. Thus, by simply saying, 'Qonam,' or 'Qorban, that by which I might be profited by thee,' a person bound himself never to touch, taste, or have anything that belonged to the person so addressed. Similarly, by saying 'Qorban, that by which

---

[1] *Maimonides* u. s. Hilk. Shebh. v. 1.
[2] This is altogether a very curious Mishnah. It adds to the remark quoted in the text this other significant admission, that the laws about the Sabbath, festive offerings, and the malversation of things devoted to God 'are like moun- tains hanging by one hair,' since Scripture is scant on these subjects, while the traditional Laws are many.
[3] On the subject of Vows see also 'The Temple and its Services,' pp. 322–326. The student should consult *Siphré*, Par. Mattoth, pp. 55 *b* to 58 *b*.

thou mightest be profited by me,' he would prevent the person so
addressed from ever deriving any benefit from that which belonged
to him. And so stringent was the ordinance that (almost in the
words of Christ) it is expressly stated that such a vow was binding,
even if what was vowed involved a breach of the Law.[a] It cannot be
denied that such vows, in regard to parents, would be binding, and
that they were actually made.[1] Indeed, the question is discussed
in the Mishnah in so many words, whether 'honour of father and
mother'[b] constituted a ground for invalidating a vow, and decided
in the negative against a solitary dissenting voice.[c] And if doubt
should still exist, a case is related in the Mishnah,[d] in which a father
was thus shut out by the vow of his son from anything by which
he might be profited by him (שֶׁהָיָה אָבִיו מֻדָּר הֵימֶנוּ הֲנָאָה)[2]. Thus the
charge brought by Christ is in fullest accordance with the facts of
the case. More than this, the manner in which it is put by St. Mark
shows the most intimate knowledge of Jewish customs and law.
For, the seemingly inappropriate addition to our Lord's mention of
the Fifth Commandment of the words: 'He that revileth father or
mother, he shall (let him) surely die,'[e] is not only explained but
vindicated by the common usage of the Rabbis,[3] to mention along
with a command the penalty attaching to its breach, so as to indicate
the importance which Scripture attached to it. On the other hand,
the words of St. Mark: 'Qorban (that is to say, gift [viz., to God])
that by which thou mightest be profited by me,' are a most exact
transcription into Greek of the common formula of vowing, as given
in the Mishnah and Talmud (קָרְבָּן שֶׁאַתָּה נֶהֱנֶה לִי).[4]

But Christ did not merely show the hypocrisy of the system of
traditionalism in conjoining in the name of religion the greatest
outward punctiliousness with the grossest breach of real duty.
Never, alas! was that aspect of prophecy, which in the present saw
the future, more clearly vindicated than as the words of Isaiah to
Israel now appeared in their final fulfilment: 'This people honoureth

CHAP.
XXXI

[a] Nedar.
ii. 2

כַּבֵּד
אָבִיו וְאִמּוֹ

[c] Ned. ix. 1
[d] Nedar. v.

[e] Ex. xxi. 17

---

[1] I can only express surprise, that
Wünsche should throw doubt upon it.
It is fully admitted by *Levy*, Targ.
Wörterb. sub קרבן.

[3] In this case the son, desirous that
his father should share in the festivities
at his marriage, proposed to give to a
friend the court in which the banquet
was to be held and the banquet itself,
but only for the purpose that his father
might eat and drink with him. The
proposal was refused as involving sin,
and the point afterwards discussed and

confirmed—implying, that in no circumstances could a parent partake of anything belonging to his son, if he had pronounced such a vow, the only relaxation
being that in case of actual starvation
('if he have not what to eat')the son might
make a present to a third person, when
the father might in turn receive of it.

[3] Comp. *Wünsche*, ad loc.

[4] Other translations have been proposed, but the above is taken from Nedar.
viii. 7, with the change only of *Qonam*
into *Qorban*.

Me with their lips, but their heart is far from Me. Howbeit, in vain do they worship Me, teaching for doctrines the commandments of men.'[1] But in thus setting forth for the first time the real character of traditionalism, and setting Himself in open opposition to its fundamental principles, the Christ enunciated also for the first time the fundamental principle of His own interpretation of the Law. That Law was not a system of externalism, in which outward things affected the inner man. It was moral and addressed itself to man as a moral being—to his heart and conscience. As the spring of all moral action was within, so the mode of affecting it would be inward. Not from without inwards, but from within outwards: such was the principle of the new Kingdom, as setting forth the Law in its fulness and fulfilling it. 'There is nothing from without the[2] man, that, entering into him, can defile him; but the things which proceed out of the man, those are they that defile the[2] man.'[3] Not only negatively, but positively, was this the fundamental principle of Christian practice in direct contrast to that of Pharisaic Judaism. It is in this essential contrariety of principle, rather than in any details, that the unspeakable difference between Christ and all contemporary teachers appears. Nor is even this all. For, the principle laid down by Christ concerning that which entereth from without and that which cometh from within, covers, in its full application, not only the principle of Christian liberty in regard to the Mosaic Law, but touches far deeper and permanent questions, affecting not only the Jew, but all men and to all times.

As we read it, the discussion, to which such full reference has been made, had taken place between the Scribes and the Lord, while the multitude perhaps stood aside. But when enunciating the grand principle of what constituted real defilement, 'He called to Him the multitude.'[a] It was probably while pursuing their way to Capernaum, when this conversation had taken place, that His disciples afterwards reported, that the Pharisees had been offended by that saying of His to the multitude. Even this implies the weakness of the disciples: that they were not only influenced by the good or evil opinion of these religious leaders of the people, but in some measure sympathised with their views. All this is quite natural, and as bringing before us real, not imaginary persons, so far evidential of the narrative. The answer which the Lord gave the disciples bore a

[a] St. Matt.
xv. 10;
St. Mark
vii. 14

---

[1] The quotation is a 'Targum,' which in the last clause follows almost entirely the LXX.

[2] Mark the definite article.
[3] The words in St. Mark vii. 16 are of very doubtful authenticity.

twofold aspect: that of solemn warning concerning the inevitable
fate of every plant which God had not planted, and that of warning
concerning the character and issue of Pharisaic teaching, as being
the leadership of the blind by the blind,[1] which must end in ruin to
both.

But even so the words of Christ are represented in the Gospel as
sounding strange and difficult to the disciples—so truthful and natural
is the narrative. But they were earnest, genuine men; and when
they reached the home in Capernaum, Peter, as the most courageous
of them, broke the reserve—half of fear and half of reverence—which,
despite their necessary familiarity, seems to have subsisted between
the Master and His disciples. And the existence of such reverential
reserve in such circumstances appears, the more it is considered, yet
another evidence of Christ's Divine Character, just as the implied
allusion to it in the narrative is another undesigned proof of its
truthfulness. And so Peter would seek for himself and his fellow-
disciples an explanation of what still seemed to him only parabolic
in the Master's teachings. He received it in the fullest manner.
There was, indeed, one part even in the teaching of the Lord, which
accorded with the higher views of the Rabbis. Those sins which
Christ set before them as sins of the outward and inward man,[2] and
of what connects the two: our relation to others, were the outcome
of evil thoughts.' And this, at least, the Rabbis also taught; explaining, with much detail, how the heart was alike the source of
strength and of weakness, of good and of evil thoughts, loved and
hated, envied, lusted and deceived, proving each statement from
Scripture.[a] But never before could they have realised, that anything
entering from without could not defile a man. Least of all could
they perceive the final inference which St. Mark long afterwards
derived from this teaching of the Lord: ' *This He said*, making all
meats clean.'[b] [3]

[a] Midr. on
Eccles. 1. 16

[b] St. Mark
vii. 19, last
clause

---

[1] Both these sayings seem to have
been proverbial at the time, although I
am not able to quote any passage in
Jewish writings in which they occur in
exactly the same form.

[2] In St. Mark vii. 21 these outcomings
of ' evil thoughts' are arranged in three
groups of four, characterised as in the
text; while in St. Matt. xv. 19 the order
of the ten commandments seems followed. The account of St. Mark is the
fuller. In both accounts the expression
'blasphemy' ($\beta\lambda\alpha\sigma\phi\eta\mu\dot{\iota}\alpha$)—rendered in
the Revised Version by ' railing '—seems

to refer to calumnious and evil speaking about our fellow-men.

[3] I have accepted this rendering of the
words, first propounded by St. Chrysostom, and now adopted in the Revised Version, although not without much misgiving. For there is strong objection to
it from the Jewish *usus* and views. The
statement in Ber. 61 *a*, last line, 'The
œsophagus which causeth to enter and
which casteth out all manner of meat.
(ושט מכניס ומוציא כל מיני מאכל)
seems to imply that *the words of Christ
were a proverbial expression.* The Tal-

Yet another time had Peter to learn that lesson, when his resistance to the teaching of the vision of the sheet let down from heaven was silenced by this: ' What God hath cleansed, make not thou common.' [a] Not only the spirit of legalism, but the very terms ' common ' (in reference to the unwashen hands) and ' making clean ' are the same. Nor can we wonder at this, if the vision of Peter was real, and not, as negative criticism would have it, invented so as to make an imaginary Peter—Apostle of the Jews—speak and act like Paul. On that hypothesis, the correspondence of thought and expression would seem, indeed, inexplicable; on the former, the Peter, who has had that vision, is telling through St. Mark the teaching that underlay it all, and, as he looked back upon it, drawing from it the inference which he understood not at the time: ' This He said, making all meats clean.'

A most difficult lesson this for a Jew, and for one like Peter, nay, for us all, to learn. And still a third time had Peter to learn it, when, in his fear of the Judaisers from Jerusalem, he made that common which God had made clean, had care of the unwashen hands, but forgot that the Lord had made clean all meats. Terrible, indeed, must have been that contention which followed between Paul and Peter. Eighteen centuries have passed, and that fatal strife is still the ground of theological contention against the truth.[1] Eighteen centuries, and within the Church also the strife still continues. Brethren sharply contend and are separated, because they will insist on that as of necessity which should be treated as of indifference: because of the not eating with unwashen hands, forgetful that He has made all meats clean to him who is inwardly and spiritually cleansed.

mudic idea is based on the curious physiological notion (Midr. on Eccles. vii. 19), that the food passed from tne œsophagus first into the larger intestine (*Hemses*, המסס, perhaps=*omasum*), where the food was supposed to be crushed as in a mill (Vayyik R. 4, 18; Midr. on Eccl. xii. 3), and thence only, through various organs, into the stomach proper. (As regards the process in animals, see *Lewysohn*, Zool. d. Talm. pp. 37–40). (The passage from Ber. 61 *a* has been so rendered by *Wünsche*, in his note on St. Matt. xv. 17, as to be in parts well nigh unintelligible.) It may interest students

that the strange word ἀφεδρῶν, rendered both in the A.V. and the R.V. by ' draught,' seems to correspond to the Rabbinic *Aphidra* (אפידרא), which *Levy* renders by ' the floor of a stable formed by the excrements of the animals which are soaked and stamped into a hard mass.'

[1] It is, of course, well known that the reasoning of the Tübingen school and of kindred negative theology is based on a supposed contrariety between the Petrine and Pauline direction, and that this again is chiefly based on the occurrence in Antioch recorded in Gal. ii. 11 &c.

CHAPTER XXXII.

THE GREAT CRISIS IN POPULAR FEELING—THE LAST DISCOURSES IN THE
SYNAGOGUE OF CAPERNAUM—CHRIST THE BREAD OF LIFE—'WILL
YE ALSO GO AWAY?'

(St. John vi. 22–71.)[1]

THE narrative now returns to those who, on the previous evening, had, after the miraculous meal, been 'sent away' to their homes. We remember, that this had been after an abortive attempt on their part to take Jesus by force and make Him their Messiah-King. We can understand that the effectual resistance of Jesus to their purpose not only weakened, but in great measure neutralised, the effect of the miracle which they had witnessed. In fact, we look upon this check as the first turning of the tide of popular enthusiasm. Let us bear in mind what ideas and expectations of an altogether external character those men connected with the Messiah of their dreams. At last, by some miracle more notable even than the giving of the Manna in the wilderness, enthusiasm has been raised to the highest pitch, and thousands were determined to give up their pilgrimage to the Passover, and then and there proclaim the Galilean Teacher Israel's King. If He were the Messiah, such was His rightful title. Why then did He so strenuously and effectually resist it? In ignorance of His real views concerning the Kingship, they would naturally conclude that it must have been from fear, from misgiving, from want of belief in Himself. At any rate, He could not be the Messiah, Who would not be Israel's King. Enthusiasm of this kind, once repressed, could never be kindled again. Henceforth there was continuous misunderstanding, doubt, and defection among former adherents, growing into opposition and hatred unto death. Even to those who took not this position, Jesus, His Words and Works, were henceforth a constant mystery.[2] And so it came, that the morn-

---

[1] It is specially requested, that this chapter be read along with the text of Scripture.

[2] We are here involuntarily reminded of the fate of Elijah on the morning after the miracle on Mount Carmel. But how different the bearing of Christ from that of the great prophet!

ing after the miraculous meal found the vast majority of those who had been fed, either in their homes or on their pilgrim-way to the Passover at Jerusalem. Only comparatively few came back to seek Him, where they had eaten bread at His Hand. And even to them, as the after-conversation shows, Jesus was a mystery. They could not disbelieve, and yet they could not believe; and they sought both 'a sign' to guide, and an explanation to give them its understanding. Yet out of them was there such selection of grace, that all that the Father had given would reach Him, and that they who, by a personal act of believing choice and by determination of conviction, would come, should in no wise be rejected of Him.

It is this view of the mental and moral state of those who, on the morning after the meal, came to seek Jesus, which alone explains the question and answers of the interview at Capernaum. As we read it: 'the day following the multitude which stood on the other [the eastern] side of the sea' 'saw that Jesus was not there, neither His disciples.'[a] But of two facts they were cognizant. They knew that, on the evening before, only one boat had come over, bringing Jesus and His disciples; and that Jesus had not returned in it with His disciples, for they had seen them depart, while Jesus remained to dismiss the people. In these circumstances they probably imagined, that Christ had returned on foot by land, being, of course, ignorant of the miracle of that night. But the wind which had been contrary to the disciples, had also driven over to the eastern shore a number of fishing-boats from Tiberias (and this is one of the undesigned confirmations of the narrative). These they now hired, and came to Capernaum, making inquiry for Jesus. Whether on that Friday afternoon they went to meet Him on His way from Gennesaret (which the wording of St. John vi. 25 makes likely), or awaited His arrival at Capernaum, is of little importance. Similarly, it is difficult to determine whether the conversation and outlined address of Christ took place on one or partly on several occasions: on the Friday afternoon or Sabbath morning, or only on the Sabbath. All that we know for certain is, that the *last* part (at any rate[b]) was spoken 'in Synagogue, as He taught in Capernaum.'[c] It has been well observed, that 'there are evident breaks after verse 40 and verse 51.'[1] Probably the succession of events may have been, that part of what is here recorded by St. John[d] had taken place when those from across the Lake had first met Jesus;[e] part on the way to, and entering, the Synagogue;[f] and part as what He spoke in His

vv. 22, 24

[b] St. John
vi. 53–58
[c] ver. 59

[d] vi. 25–65
[e] vv. 25–36
[f] vv. 41–52

[1] *Westcott,* ad. loc.

Discourse,[a] and then after the defection of some of His former dis- CHAP.
ciples.[b]   But we can only suggest such an arrangement, since it   XXXII
would have been quite consistent with Jewish practice, that the
greater part should have taken place in the Synagogue itself, the   [a] vv. 52-58
Jewish questions and objections representing either an irregular   [b] vv. 61-65
running commentary on His Words, or expressions during breaks in,
or at the conclusion of, His teaching.

   This, however, is a primary requirement, that, what Christ is
reported to have spoken, should appear suited to His hearers: such as
would appeal to what they knew, such also as they could understand.
This must be kept in view, even while admitting that the Evangelist
wrote his Gospel in the light of much later and fuller knowledge,
and for the instruction of the Christian Church, and that there may
be breaks and omissions in the reported, as compared with the original
Discourse, which, if supplied, would make its understanding much
easier to a Jew.   On the other hand, we have to bear in mind all the
circumstances of the case.   The Discourse in question was delivered
in the city, which had been the scene of so many of Christ's great
miracles, and the centre of His teaching, and in the Synagogue, built
by the good Centurion, and of which Jairus was the chief ruler.
Here we have the outward and inward conditions for even the most
advanced teaching of Christ.   Again, it was delivered under twofold
moral conditions, to which we may expect the Discourse of Christ to
be adapted.   For, first, it was after that miraculous feeding which
had raised the popular enthusiasm to the highest pitch, and also
after that chilling disappointment of their Judaistic hopes in Christ's
utmost resistance to His Messianic proclamation.   They now came
'seeking for Jesus,' in every sense of the word.   They knew not
what to make of those, to them, contradictory and irreconcilable
facts; they came, because they did eat of the loaves, without
seeing in them ' signs.'[c]   And therefore they came for such a 'sign'   [c] ver. 26
as they could perceive, and for such teaching in interpretation of it
as they could understand.   They were outwardly—by what had
happened—prepared for the very highest teaching, to which the
preceding events had led up, and therefore they must receive such,
if any.   But they were not inwardly prepared for it, and therefore
they could not understand it.   Secondly, and in connection with
it, we must remember that two high points had been reached—by
the people, that Jesus was the Messiah-King; by the ship's company,
that He was the Son of God.   However imperfectly these truths may
have been apprehended, yet the teaching of Christ, if it was to be pro-

BOOK
III

ª St. John
vi. 25-29

gressive, must start from them and then point onwards and upwards. In this expectation we shall not be disappointed. And if, by the side of all this, we shall find allusions to peculiarly Jewish thoughts and views, these will not only confirm the Evangelic narrative, but furnish additional evidence of the Jewish authorship of the Fourth Gospel.

1. The question ª : ' Rabbi, when camest Thou hither? ' with which they from the eastern shore greeted Jesus, seems to imply that they were perplexed about, and that some perhaps had heard a vague rumour of the miracle of His return to the western shore. It was the beginning of that unhealthy craving for the miraculous which the Lord had so sharply to reprove. In His own words: they sought Him not because they ' saw signs,' but because they ' ate of the loaves,' and, in their coarse love for the miraculous, ' were filled.' ¹ What brought them, was not that they had discerned either the higher meaning of that miracle, or the Son of God, but those carnal Judaistic expectancies which had led them to proclaim Him King. What they waited for, was a Kingdom of God—not in righteousness, joy, and peace in the Holy Ghost, but in meat and drink—a kingdom with miraculous wilderness-banquets to Israel, and coarse miraculous triumphs over the Gentiles. Not to speak of the fabulous Messianic banquet which a sensuous realism expected, or of the achievements for which it looked, every figure in which prophets had clothed the brightness of those days was first literalised, and then exaggerated, till the most glorious poetic descriptions became the most repulsively incongruous caricatures of spiritual Messianic expectancy. The fruit-trees were every day, or at least every week or two, to yield their riches, the fields their harvests; ᵇ the grain was to stand like palm trees, and to be reaped and winnowed without labour.ᶜ Similar blessings were to visit the vine; ordinary trees would bear like fruit trees, and every produce, of every clime, would be found in Palestine in such abundance and luxuriance as only the wildest imagination could conceive.

ᵇ Shabb.
30 b; Jer.
Sheqal.vi. 2
ᶜ Kethub.
111 b

Such were the carnal thoughts about the Messiah and His Kingdom of those who sought Jesus because they ' ate of the loaves, and were filled.' What a contrast between them and the Christ, as He pointed them from the search for *such* meat to ' work for the meat which He would give them,' not as a merely Jewish Messiah, but as ' the Son of Man.' And yet, in uttering this strange truth, Jesus could appeal to something they knew when He added, ' for Him the Father hath sealed, even God.' The words, which seem almost inexplicable in

---

¹ Canon *Westcott* notes the intended realism in the choice of words: ' Liter- ally, " were satisfied with food as animals with fodder." '—ἐχορτάσθητε.

this connection, become clear when we remember that this was a well-known Jewish expression. According to the Rabbis, 'the seal of God was *Truth* (*AeMeTH*),' the three letters of which this word is composed in Hebrew (אמת) being, as was significantly pointed out, respectively the first, the middle, and the last letters of the alphabet.[a] Thus the words of Christ would convey to His hearers that for the real meat, which would endure to eternal life—for the better Messianic banquet—they must come to Him, because God had impressed upon Him His own seal of truth, and so authenticated His Teaching and Mission.

In passing, we mark this as a Jewish allusion, which only a Jewish writer (not an Ephesian Gospel) would have recorded. But it is by no means the only one. It almost seems like a sudden gleam of light—as if they were putting their hand to this Divine Seal, when they now ask Him what they must do, in order to work the Works of God? Yet strangely refracted seems this ray of light, when they connect the Works of God with their own doing. And Christ directed them, as before, only more clearly, to Himself. To work the Works of God they must not do, but believe in Him Whom God had sent. Their twofold error consisted in imagining, that they could work the Works of God, and this by some doing of their own. On the other hand, Christ would have taught them that these Works of God were independent of man, and that they would be achieved through man's faith in the Mission of the Christ.

2. As it impresses itself on our minds, what now follows[b] took place at a somewhat different time—perhaps on the way to the Synagogue. It is a remarkable circumstance, that among the ruins of the Synagogue of Capernaum the lintel has been discovered, and that it bears the device of a pot of manna, ornamented with a flowing pattern of vine leaves and clusters of grapes.[1] Here then were the outward emblems, which would connect themselves with the Lord's teaching on that day. The miraculous feeding of the multitude in the 'desert place' the evening before, and the Messianic thoughts which clustered around it, would naturally suggest to their minds remembrance of the manna. That manna, which was Angels' food, distilled (as they imagined) from the upper light, 'the dew from above'[c]—miraculous food, of all manner of taste, and suited to every age, according to the wish or condition of him who ate it,[d] but bitterness to Gentile palates—they expected the Messiah to bring again from heaven. For, all that the first deliverer Moses had done, the

---

[1] Comp. 'Sketches of Jewish Social Life,' pp. 256, 257.

[a] Jer. Sanh. 18 *a*; Ber. R. 81

[b] St John vi. 30-36

[c] Yoma 75 *b*

[d] Shem. R. 25

BOOK
III

ᵃ Midr. on
Eccles. i. 9

ᵇ Targ.
Pseudo-
Jon. on
Deut.
xxxiv. 8;
Taan. 9 a

ᶜ Prov. ix. 5

ᵈ Shem. R.
25

ᵉ Comp.
Chag. 14 a

second—Messiah—would also do.ᵃ   And here, over their Synagogue, was the pot of manna—symbol of what God had done, earnest of what the Messiah would do: that pot of manna, which was now among the things hidden, but which Elijah, when he came, would restore again!

Here, then, was a real sign.   In their view the events of yesterday must lead up to some such sign, if they had any real meaning. They had been told to believe on Him, as the One authenticated by God with the seal of Truth, and Who would give them meat to eternal life.   By what sign would Christ corroborate His assertion, that they might see and believe?   What work would He do to vindicate His claim?   Their fathers had eaten manna in the wilderness.   To understand the reasoning of the Jews, implied but not fully expressed, as also the answer of Jesus, it is necessary to bear in mind (what forms another evidence of the Jewish authorship of the Fourth Gospel), that it was the oft and most anciently expressed opinion that, although God had given them this bread out of heaven, yet it was given through the merits of Moses, and ceased with his death.ᵇ This the Jews had probably in view, when they asked: 'What workest Thou?'; and this was the meaning of Christ's emphatic assertion, that it was *not* Moses who gave Israel that bread.   And then by what, with all reverence, may still be designated a peculiarly Jewish turn of reasoning—such as only those familiar with Jewish literature can fully appreciate (and which none but a Jewish reporter would have inserted in his Gospel)—the Saviour makes quite different, yet to them familiar, application of the manna.   Moses had not given it—his merits had not procured it—but His Father gave them the true bread out of heaven.   ' For,' as He explained, ' the bread of God is that ¹ which cometh down from heaven, and giveth life unto the world.'   Again, this very Rabbinic tradition, which described in such glowing language the wonders of that manna, also further explained its other and real meaning to be, that if Wisdom said, ' Eat of my bread and drink of my wine,'ᶜ it indicated that the manna and the miraculous water-supply were the sequence of Israel's receiving the Law and the Commandmentsᵈ—for the real bread from heaven was the Law. ᵉ ²

---

¹ Not as in the A.V. of ver. 33: 'He Which cometh down from heaven.' The alteration is most important in the argument as addressed to the Jews: the one they could understand and would admit, not so the other.

² In the Midrash on Eccl. ii. 24; iii. 12; viii. 15, we are told, that when in Ecclesiastes we read of eating and drinking, it always refers to the Law and good works.

It was an appeal which the Jews understood, and to which they could not but respond. Yet the mood was brief. As Jesus, in answer to the appeal that He would evermore give them this bread, once more directed them to Himself—from works of men to the Works of God and to faith—the passing gleam of spiritual hope had already died out, for they had seen Him and 'yet did not believe.'

CHAP. XXXII

With these words of mingled sadness and judgment, Jesus turned away from His questioners. The solemn sayings which now followed [a] could not have been spoken to, and they would not have been understood by, the multitude. And accordingly we find that, when the conversation of the Jews is once more introduced,[b] it takes up the thread where it had been broken off, when Jesus spake of Himself as the Bread Which had come down from heaven. Had they heard what, in our view, Jesus spake only to His disciples, their objections would have been to more than merely the incongruity of Christ's claim to have come down from heaven.[1]

[a] St. John vi. 37-40

[b] ver. 41

3. Regarding these words of Christ, then, as addressed to the disciples, there is really nothing in them beyond their standpoint, though they open views of the far horizon. They had the experience of the raising of the young man at Nain, and there, at Capernaum, of Jairus' daughter. Besides, believing that Jesus *was* the Messiah, it might perhaps not be quite strange nor new to them as Jews—although not commonly received—that He would at the end of the world raise the pious dead.[2] Indeed, one of the names given to the Messiah— that of *Yinnon*, according to Ps. lxxii. 17 [c]—has by some been derived from this very expectancy.[d] Again, He had said, that it was not any Law, but His Person, that was the bread which came down from heaven, and gave life, not to Jews only, but unto the world— and they had seen Him and believed not. But none the less would the loving purpose of God be accomplished in the totality of His true people, and its joyous reality be experienced by every individual among them: 'All that [the total number, $\pi \tilde{a} \nu$ $\overset{\text{\'o}}{o}$] which the Father giveth Me shall come unto Me [shall reach Me [3]], and him that cometh unto Me [the coming one to Me] I will not cast out outside.' What follows is merely the carrying out in all directions, and to its fullest consequences, of this twofold fundamental principle. The totality of the God-given would really reach Him, despite all

[c] Sanh. 98 b

[d] Midrash on Ps. xciii. 1; Pirké de R. Eliez. 32, ed. Lemb. p. 39 b

---

[1] After having arrived at this conclusion, I find that Canon *Westcott* has expressed the same views, and I rejoice in being fortified by so great an authority.

[2] But not here and there one dead.

In general, see vol. i. p. 633, where the question of Jewish belief on that subject is discussed.

[3] So Canon *Westcott*; and also *Godet* ad loc.

hindrances, for the object of His Coming was to do the Will of His Father; and those who came would not be cast outside, for the Will of Him that had sent Him, and which He had come to do, was that of '*the* all which He has given' Him, He 'should not lose *anything* out of this, but raise it up in the last day.' Again, the totality—the all—would reach Him, since it was the Will of Him that sent Him 'that everyone ($\pi\tilde{\alpha}\varsigma$) who intently looketh[1] at the Son, and believeth on Him, should have eternal life;' and the coming ones would not be cast outside, since this was His undertaking and promise as the Christ in regard to each: 'And raise him up will I at the last day.'[a]

ᵃ St. John
vi. 40

Although these wonderful statements reached in their full meaning far beyond the present horizon of His disciples, and even to the utmost bounds of later revelation and Christian knowledge, there is nothing in them which could have seemed absolutely strange or unintelligible to those who heard them. Given belief in the Messiahship of Jesus and His Mission by the Father; given experience of what He had done, and perhaps, to a certain extent, Jewish expectancy of what the Messiah would do in the last day; and all this directed or corrected by the knowledge concerning His work which His teaching had imparted, and the words were intelligible and most suitable, even though they would not convey to them all that they mean to us. If so seemingly incongruous an illustration might be used, they looked through a telescope that was not yet drawn out, and saw the same objects, through quite diminutively and far otherwise than we, as gradually the hand of Time has drawn out fully that through which both they and we, who believe, intently gaze on the Son.

ᵇ St. John
vi. 41–51

4. What now follows[b] is again spoken to 'the Jews,' and may have occurred just as they were entering the Synagogue. To those spiritually unenlightened, the point of difficulty seemed, how Christ could claim to be the Bread come down from heaven. Making the largest allowance, His known parentage and early history[2] forbade anything like a literal interpretation of His Words. But this inability to understand, ever brings out the highest teaching of Christ. We note the analogous fact, and even the analogous teaching, in the

---

[1] Mark the special meaning of $\theta\varepsilon\omega\rho\tilde{\omega}\nu$ as previously explained.

[2] This is not narrated in the Fourth Gospel. But allusions like this cover the whole early history of Jesus, and prove that omissions of the most important facts in the history of Jesus are neither due to ignorance of them on the part of the writer of the Fourth Gospel, nor to the desire to express by silence his dissent from the accounts of the Synoptists.

case of Nicodemus.[a][1] Only, his was the misunderstanding of ignorance, theirs of wilful resistance to His Manifestation; and so the
tone towards them was other than to the Rabbi.

Yet we also mark, that what Jesus now spake to 'the Jews' was
the same in substance, though different in application, from what
He had just uttered to the disciples. This, not merely in regard to
the Messianic prediction of the Resurrection, but even in what He
pronounced as the judgment on their murmuring. The words: ' No
man can come to Me, except the Father Which hath sent Me draw
him,' present only the converse aspect of those to the disciples: ' All
that which the Father giveth Me shall come unto Me, and him that
cometh unto Me I will in no wise cast out.' For, far from being
a judgment on, it would have been an excuse of, Jewish unbelief,
and, indeed, entirely discordant with all Christ's teaching, if the inability to come were regarded as other than personal and moral,
springing from man's ignorance and opposition to spiritual things.
No man can come to the Christ—such is the condition of the human
mind and heart, that coming to Christ as a disciple is, not an outward, but an inward, not a physical, but a moral impossibility—
except the Father ' draw him.' And this, again, not in the sense of
any constraint, but in that of the personal, moral, loving influence and
revelation, to which Christ afterwards refers when He saith: ' And I,
if I be lifted up from the earth, will draw all men unto Myself.'[b]

Nor did Jesus, even while uttering these high, entirely un-Jewish
truths, forget that He was speaking them to Jews. The appeal to
their own Prophets was the more telling, that Jewish tradition also
applied these two prophecies (Is. liv. 13; Jer. xxxi. 34) to the teaching by God in the Messianic Age.[c][2] But the explanation of the
manner and issue of God's teaching was new: ' Everyone that hath
heard from the Father, and learned, cometh unto Me.' And this, not
by some external or realistic contact with God, such as they regarded
that of Moses in the past, or expected for themselves in the latter
days; only ' He Which is from God, He hath seen the Father.' But
even this might sound general and without exclusive reference to
Christ. So, also, might this statement seem: ' He that believeth[3]
hath eternal life.' Not so the final application, in which the subject was
carried to its ultimate bearing, and all that might have seemed general
or mysterious plainly set forth. The Personality of Christ *was* the

---

[1] Canon *Westcott* has called attention
to this.

[2] For other Rabbinic applications of
these verses to the Messiah and His

times, see the Appendix on Messianic
passages.

[3] The words ' on Me ' are spurious.

Bread of Life: 'I am the Bread of Life.'ª The Manna had not been bread of life, for those who ate it had died, their carcasses had fallen in the wilderness.   Not so in regard to this, the true Bread from heaven. To share in that Food was to have everlasting life, a life which the sin and death of unbelief and judgment would not cut short, as it had that of them who had eaten the Manna and died in the wilderness.   It was another and a better Bread which came from heaven in Christ, and another, better, and deathless life which was connected with it: 'the Bread that I will give is My Flesh,[1] for the life of the world.'

5. These words, so deeply significant to us, as pointing out the true meaning of all His teaching, must, indeed, have sounded most mysterious.   Yet the fact that they strove about their meaning shows, that they must have had some glimmer of apprehension that they bore on His self-surrender, or, as they might view it, His martyrdom. This last point is set forth in the concluding Discourse,ᵇ which we know to have been delivered in the Synagogue, whether before, during, or after, His regular Sabbath address.   It was not a mere martyrdom for the life of the world, in which all who benefited by it would share— but personal fellowship with Him.   Eating the Flesh and drinking the Blood of the Son of Man, such was the necessary condition of securing eternal life.   It is impossible to mistake the primary reference of these words to our personal application of His Death and Passion to the deepest need and hunger of our souls; most difficult, also, to resist the feeling that, secondarily,[2] they referred to that Holy Feast which shows forth that Death and Passion, and is to all time its remembrance, symbol, seal, and fellowship.   In this, also, has the hand of History drawn out the telescope; and as we gaze through it, every sentence and word sheds light upon the Cross and light from the Cross, carrying to us this twofold meaning: His Death, and its Celebration in the great Christian Sacrament.

6. But to them that heard it, nay even to many of His disciples, this was an hard saying.   Who could bear it? For it was a thorough disenchantment of all their Judaic illusions, an entire upturning of all their Messianic thoughts, and that, not merely to those whose views were grossly carnal, but even to many who had hitherto been drawn closer to Him.   The 'meat' and 'drink' from heaven which had the Divine seal of 'truth' were, according to Christ's teaching, not 'the Law,' nor yet Israel's privileges, but fellowship with the

---

[1] The words in the A.V., which I will give,' are spurious.

[2] Canon *Westcott* (ad loc.) clearly shows, that the reference to the Holy Supper can only be secondary. Mark here specially, that in the latter we have 'the Body,' not 'the Flesh' of the Lord.

Person of Jesus in that state of humbleness ('the Son of Joseph,'[a]), nay, of martydom, which His words seemed to indicate, 'My Flesh is the true[1] meat, and My Blood is the true drink;'[b] and what even this fellowship secured, consisted only in abiding in Him and He in them;[c] or, as they would understand it, in inner communion with Him, and in sharing His condition and views. Truly, this was a totally different Messiah and Messianic Kingdom from what they either conceived or wished.

Though they spake it not, this was the rock of offence over which they stumbled and fell. And Jesus read their thoughts. How unfit were they to receive all that was yet to happen in connection with the Christ—how unprepared for it! If they stumbled at this, what when they came to contemplate[2] the far more mysterious and un-Jewish facts of the Messiah's Crucifixion and Ascension![d] Truly, not outward following, but only inward and spiritual life-quickening could be of profit—even in the case of those who heard the very Words of Christ, which were spirit and life. Thus it again appeared, and most fully, that, morally speaking, it was absolutely impossible to come to Him, even if His Words were heard, except under the gracious influence from above.[e]

And so this was the great crisis in the History of the Christ. We have traced the gradual growth and development of the popular movement, till the murder of the Baptist stirred popular feeling to its inmost depth. With his death it seemed as if the Messianic hope, awakened by his preaching and testimony to Christ, were fading from view. It was a terrible disappointment, not easily borne. Now must it be decided, whether Jesus was really the Messiah. His Works, notwithstanding what the Pharisees said, seemed to prove it. Then let it appear; let it come, stroke upon stroke—each louder and more effective than the other—till the land rang with the shout of victory and the world itself re-echoed it. And so it seemed. That miraculous feeding—that wilderness-cry of Hosanna to the Galilean King-Messiah from thousands of Galilean voices—what were they but its beginning? All the greater was the disappointment: first, in the repression of the movement—so to speak, the retreat of the Messiah, His voluntary abdication, rather, His defeat; then, next day, the incongruousness of a King, Whose few unlearned followers, in their ignorance and un-Jewish neglect of most sacred ordinances, outraged

CHAP. XXXII

[a] ver. 42
[b] ver. 55
[c] ver. 56

[d] ver. 62

[e] ver. 65; comp. vv. 37, 44

---

[1] Comp. here the remarks on ver. 27, about Truth as the seal with which God sealed the Christ.

[2] Mark here also the special meaning of θεωρῆτε.

BOOK
III

every Jewish feeling, and whose conduct was even vindicated by their Master in a general attack on all traditionalism, that basis of Judaism—as it might be represented, to the contempt of religion and even of common truthfulness in the denunciation of solemn vows! This was not the Messiah Whom the many—nay, Whom almost any —would own.[a]

[a] St. Matt. xv. 12

Here, then, we are at the parting of the two ways; and, just because it was the hour of decision, did Christ so clearly set forth the highest truths concerning Himself, in opposition to the views which the multitude entertained about the Messiah. The result was yet another and a sorer defection. ' Upon this many of His disciples went back, and walked no more with Him.'[b] Nay, the searching trial reached even unto the hearts of the Twelve. Would they also go away? It was an anticipation of Gethsemane—its first experience. But one thing kept them true. It was the experience of the past. This was the basis of their present faith and allegiance. They *could* not go back to their old past; they must cleave to Him. So Peter spake it in name of them all: ' Lord, to whom shall we go? Words of Eternal Life hast Thou!' Nay, and more than this, as the result of what they had learned: 'And we have believed and know that Thou art the Holy One of God.'[c][1] It is thus, also, that many of us, whose thoughts may have been sorely tossed, and whose foundations terribly assailed, may have found our first resting-place in the assured, unassailable spiritual experience of the past. Whither can we go for Words of Eternal Life, if not to Christ? If He fails us, then all hope of the Eternal is gone. But He *has* the Words of Eternal life—and we believed when they first came to us; nay, we know that He is the Holy One of God. And this conveys all that faith needs for further learning. The rest will He show, when He is transfigured in our sight.

[b] St. John vi. 66

[c] vv. 68, 69

But of these Twelve Christ knew one to be ' a devil '—like that Angel, fallen from highest height to lowest depth.[2] The apostasy of Judas had already commenced in his heart. And, the greater the popular expectancy and disappointment had been, the greater the reaction and the enmity that followed. The hour of decision was past, and the hand on the dial pointed to the hour of His Death.

---

[1] This is the reading of all the best MSS., and not as in the A.V. 'that Christ, the Son of the Living God.' For the history of the variations by which this change was brought about, see *Westcott*, ad loc.

[2] The right reading of ver. 71 is: ' Judas the son of Simon Iscariot,' that is, ' a man of Kerioth.' *Kerioth* was in Judæa (Josh. xv. 25), and Judas, it will be remembered, the only Judæan disciple of Jesus.

CHAPTER XXXIII.

JESUS AND THE SYRO-PHŒNICIAN WOMAN.

(St. Matt. xv. 21–28; St. Mark vii. 24–30.)

THE purpose of Christ to withdraw His disciples from the excitement of Galilee, and from what might follow the execution of the Baptist, had been interrupted by the events at Bethsaida-Julias, but it was not changed.   On the contrary, it must have been intensified.   That wild, popular outburst, which had almost forced upon Him a Jewish Messiah-Kingship; the discussion with the Jerusalem Scribes about the washing of hands on the following day; the Discourses of the Sabbath, and the spreading disaffection, defection, and opposition which were its consequences—all pointed more than ever to the necessity of a break in the publicity of His Work, and to withdrawal from that part of Galilee.   The nearness of the Sabbath, and the circumstance that the Capernaum-boat lay moored on the shore of Bethsaida, had obliged Him, when withdrawing from that neighbourhood, to return to Capernaum.   And there the Sabbath had to be spent— in what manner we know.   But as soon as its sacred rest was past, the journey was resumed.   For the reasons already explained, it extended much further than any other, and into regions which, we may venture to suggest, would not have been traversed but for the peculiar circumstances of the moment.

A comparatively short journey would bring Jesus and His companions from Capernaum 'into the parts,' or, as St. Mark more specifically calls them, 'the borders of Tyre and Sidon.'   At that time this district extended, north of Galilee,[a] from the Mediterranean to the Jordan.   But the event about to be related occurred, as all circumstances show, not within the territory of Tyre and Sidon, but on its borders, and within the limits of the Land of Israel.   If any doubt could attach to the objects which determined Christ's journey to those parts, it would be removed by the circumstance that St. Matthew[b] tells us, He 'withdrew'[1] thither, while St. Mark notes

CHAP.
XXXIII

[a] *Jos.* War
iii. 3. 1

[b] St. Matt
xv. 21

[1] So correctly rendered.

that He 'entered into an house, and would have no man know it.'
That house in which Jesus sought shelter and privacy would, of
course, be a Jewish home; and, that it was within the borders of
Israel, is further evidenced by the notice of St. Matthew, that 'the
Canaanitish woman' who sought His help 'came out from those borders'—that is, from out the Tyro-Sidonian district—into that Galilean
border where Jesus was.

The whole circumstances seem to point to more than a night's
rest in that distant home. Possibly, the two first Passover-days may
have been spent here. If the Saviour had left Capernaum on the
Sabbath evening, or the Sunday morning, He may have reached that
home on the borders before the Paschal Eve, and the Monday and
Tuesday [1] may have been the festive Paschal days, on which sacred
rest was enjoined. This would also give an adequate motive for such
a sojourn in that house, as seems required by the narrative of St.
Mark. According to that Evangelist, 'Jesus would have no man
know' His Presence in that place, 'but He could not be hid.' Manifestly, this could not apply to the rest of one night in a house. According to the same Evangelist, the fame of His Presence spread into
the neighbouring district of Tyre and Sidon, and reached the mother
of the demonised child, upon which she went from her home into
Galilee to apply for help to Jesus. All this implies a stay of two or
three days. And with this also agrees the after-complaint of the
disciples: 'Send her away, for she crieth after us.' [a] As the Saviour
apparently received the woman in the house, [b] it seems that she must
have followed some of the disciples, entreating their help or intercession in a manner that attracted the attention which, according to
the will of Jesus, they would fain have avoided, before, in her despair,
she ventured into the Presence of Christ within the house.

All this resolves into a higher harmony those small seeming discrepancies, which negative criticism had tried to magnify into contradictions. It also adds graphic details to the story. She who now
sought His help was, as St. Matthew calls her, from the Jewish
standpoint, 'a Canaanitish [c] woman,' by which term a Jew would designate a native of Phœnicia, or, as St. Mark calls her, a Syro-Phœnician
(to distinguish her country from Lybo-Phœnicia), and 'a Greek'—
that is, a heathen. But, we can understand how she who, as *Bengel*
says, made the misery of her little child her own, would, on hearing
of the Christ and His mighty deed, seek His help with the most

a St. Matt.
xv. 23
b St. Mark
vii. 24, 25

c Ezra ix. 1

---

[1] Or, the Passover-eve may have been Monday evening.

intense earnestness, and that, in so doing, she would approach Him
with lowliest reverence, falling at His Feet.ª But what in the circumstances seems so peculiar, and, in our view, furnishes the explanation of the Lord's bearing towards this woman, is her mode of
addressing Him: 'O Lord, Thou Son of David!' This was the most
distinctively Jewish appellation of the Messiah; and yet it is
emphatically stated of her, that she was a heathen. Tradition has
preserved a few reported sayings of Christ, of which that about to
be quoted seems, at least, quite Christ-like. It is reported that,
'having seen a man working on the Sabbath, He said: "O man, if
indeed thou knowest what thou doest, thou art blessed; but if thou
knowest not, thou art cursed, and art a transgressor of the Law."' [1]
The same principle applied to the address of this woman—only that,
in what followed, Christ imparted to her the knowledge needful to
make her blessed.

Spoken by a heathen, these words were an appeal, not to the
Messiah of Israel, but to an Israelitish Messiah—for David had
never reigned over her or her people. The title might be most
rightfully used, if the promises to David were fully and spiritually
apprehended—not otherwise. If used without that knowledge, it
was an address by a stranger to a Jewish Messiah, Whose works were
only miracles, and not also and primarily signs. Now this was
exactly the error of the Jews which Jesus had encountered and
combated, alike when He resisted the attempt to make Him King,
in His reply to the Jerusalem Scribes, and in His Discourses at
Capernaum. To have granted her the help she so entreated, would
have been, as it were, to reverse the whole of His Teaching, and to
make His works of healing merely works of power. For, it will not
be contended that this heathen woman had full spiritual knowledge
of the world-wide bearing of the Davidic promises, or of the world-
embracing designation of the Messiah as the Son of David. In her
mouth, then, it meant something to which Christ could not have
yielded. And yet He could not refuse her petition. And so He
first taught her, in such manner as she could understand—that which
she needed to know, before she could approach Him in such manner-—
the relation of the heathen to the Jewish world, and of both to the
Messiah, and then He gave her what she asked.

It is this, we feel convinced, which explains all. It could not have
been, that from His human standpoint He first kept silence, His
deep tenderness and sympathy forbidding Him to speak, while the

ª St. Mark
vii. 25

[1] Comp. Canon *Westcott*, Introduction to the Study of the Gospels, Appendix C.

CHAP.
XXXIII

normal limitation of His Mission forbade Him to act as she sought.[1] Such limitation could not have existed in His mind; nor can we suppose such an utter separation of His Human from His Divine consciousness in His Messianic acting. And we recoil from the opposite explanation, which supposes Christ to have either tried the faith of the woman, or else spoken with a view to drawing it out. We shrink from the idea of anything like an after-thought, even for a good purpose, on the part of the Divine Saviour. All such after-thoughts are, to our thinking, incompatible with His Divine Purity and absolute rectitude. God does not make us good by a device—and that is a very wrong view of trials, or of delayed answers to prayer, which men sometimes take. Nor can we imagine, that the Lord would have made such cruel trial of the poor agonised woman, or played on her feelings, when the issue would have been so unspeakably terrible, if in her weakness she had failed. There is nothing analogous in the case of this poor heathen coming to petition, and being tried by being told that she could not be heard, because she belonged to the dogs, not the children, and the trial of Abraham, who was a hero of faith, and had long walked with God. In any case, on any of the views just combated, the Words of Jesus would bear a needless and inconceivable harshness, which grates on all our feelings concerning Him. The Lord does not afflict willingly, nor try needlessly, nor disguise His loving thoughts and purposes, in order to bring about some effect in us. He needs not such means; and, with reverence be it said, we cannot believe that He ever uses them.

But, viewed as the teaching of Christ to this heathen concerning Israel's Messiah, all becomes clear, even in the very brief reports of the Evangelists, of which that by St. Matthew reads like that of one present, that of St. Mark rather like that of one who relates what he has heard from another (St. Peter). She had spoken, but Jesus had answered her not a word. When the disciples —in some measure, probably, still sharing the views of this heathen, that he was the Jewish Messiah—without, indeed, interceding for her, asked that she might be sent away, because she was troublesome to them, He replied, that His Mission was only to the lost sheep of the house of Israel. This was absolutely true, as regarded His Work

---

[1] This view is advocated by Dean *Plumptre* with remarkable beauty, tenderness, and reverence. It is also that of *Meyer* and of *Ewald*. The latter remarks, that our Lord showed twofold greatness: First, in his calm limitation to His special mission, and then in His equally calm overstepping of it, when a higher ground for so doing appeared.

while upon earth; and true, in every sense, as we keep in view the world-wide bearing of the Davidic reign and promises, and the real relation between Israel and the world. Thus baffled, as it might seem, she cried no longer 'Son of David,' but, 'Lord, help me.' It was then that the special teaching came in the manner she could understand. If it were as 'the Son of David' that He was entreated —if the heathen woman as such applied to the Jewish Messiah as such, what, in the Jewish view, were the heathens but 'dogs,' and what would be fellowship with them, but to cast to the dogs—house-dogs,[1] it may be—what should have been the children's bread? And, certainly, no expression more common in the mouth of the Jews, than that which designated the heathens as dogs.[a][2] Most harsh as it was, as the outcome of national pride and Jewish self-assertion, yet in a sense it was true, that those *within* were the children, and those '*without*' 'dogs.'[b] Only, who were they within and who they without? What made 'a child,' whose was the bread—and what characterised 'the dog,' that was 'without'?

CHAP.
XXXIII

[a] Midr. on
Ps. iv. 8;
Meg. 7 *b*

[b] Rev. xxii
15

Two lessons did she learn with that instinct-like rapidity which Christ's personal Presence—and it alone—seemed ever and again to call forth, just as the fire which fell from heaven consumed the sacrifice of Elijah. 'Yea, Lord,' it is as Thou sayest: heathenism stands related to Judaism as the house-dogs to the children, and it were not meet to rob the children of their bread in order to give it to dogs. But Thine own words show, that such would not now be the case. If they are house-dogs, then they are the Master's, and under His table, and when He breaks the bread to the children, in the breaking of it the crumbs must fall all around. As St. Matthew puts it: 'The dogs eat of the crumbs which fall from their Master's table;' as St. Mark puts it: 'The dogs under the table eat of the children's crumbs.' Both versions present different aspects of the same truth. Heathenism may be like the dogs, when compared with the children's place and privileges; but He is their Master still, and they under His table; and when He breaks the bread there is enough and to spare for them—even under the table they eat of the children's crumbs.

But in so saying she was no longer 'under the table,' but had sat down at the table with Abraham, Isaac, and Jacob, and was partaker of the children's bread. He was no longer to her the Jewish Messiah, but truly 'the Son of David.' She now understood what

---

[1] The term means 'little dogs,' or 'house-dogs.'

[2] Many passages might be quoted either similar, or based on this view of Gentiles.

she prayed, and she *was* a daughter of Abraham. And what had taught her all this was faith in His Person and Work, as not only just enough for the Jews, but enough and to spare for all—children at the table and dogs under it; that in and with Abraham, Isaac, Jacob, and David, all nations were blessed in Israel's King and Messiah. And so it was, that the Lord said it: 'O woman, great is thy faith: be it done unto thee even as thou wilt.' Or, as St. Mark puts it, not quoting the very sound of the Lord's words, but their impression upon Peter: 'For this saying go thy way; the devil is gone out of thy daughter.'[1] 'And her daughter was healed from that hour.'[a] 'And she went away unto her house, and found her daughter prostrate [indeed] upon the bed, and [but] the demon gone out.'

a St. Matt.
xv. 28

To us there is in this history even more than the solemn interest of Christ's compassion and mighty Messianic working, or the lessons of His teaching. We view it in connection with the scenes of the previous few days, and see how thoroughly it accords with them in spirit, thus recognising the deep internal unity of Christ's Words and Works, where least, perhaps, we might have looked for such harmony. And again we view it in its deeper bearing upon, and lessons to, all times. To how many, not only of all nations and conditions, but in all states of heart and mind, nay, in the very lowest depths of conscious guilt and alienation from God, must this have brought unspeakable comfort, the comfort of truth, and the comfort of His Teaching. Be it so, an outcast, 'dog;' not at the table, but under the table. Still we are at His Feet; it is our Master's Table; He is our Master; and, as He breaks the children's bread, it is of necessity that 'the children's crumbs' fall to us— enough, quite enough, and to spare. Never can we be outside His reach, nor of that of His gracious care, and of sufficient provision to eternal life.

Yet this lesson also must we learn, that as 'heathens' we may not call on Him as 'David's Son,' till we know why we so call Him. If there can be no despair, no being cast out by Him, no absolute distance that hopelessly separates from His Person and Provision, there must be no presumption, no forgetfulness of the right relation, no expectancy of magic-miracles, no viewing of Christ as a Jewish Messiah.

---

[1] Canon *Cook* (Speaker's Comm. on St. Mark vii. 26) regards this 'as one of the very few instances in which our Lord's words really differ in the two accounts.' With all deference, I venture to think it is not so, but that St. Mark gives what St. Peter had received as the impression of Christ's words on his mind.

We must learn it, and painfully, first by His silence, then by this,   CHAP.
that He is only sent to the lost sheep of the house of Israel, what we   XXXIII
are and where we are—that we may be prepared for the grace of God
and the gift of grace.   All men—Jews and Gentiles, 'children' and
'dogs'—are as before Christ and God equally undeserving and equally
sinners, but those who have fallen deep can only learn that they are
sinners by learning that they are great sinners, and will only taste of
the children's bread when they have felt, 'Yea, Lord,' 'for even the
dogs' 'under the table eat of the children's crumbs,' 'which fall from
their Master's table.'

CHAPTER XXXIV.

A GROUP OF MIRACLES AMONG A SEMI-HEATHEN POPULATION.

(St. Matt. xv. 29–31; St. Mark vii. 31–37; St. Mark viii. 22–26; St. Matt. xi. 27–31.)

BOOK
III

IF even the brief stay of Jesus in that friendly Jewish home by the borders of Tyre could not remain unknown, the fame of the healing of the Syro-Phœnician maiden would soon have rendered impossible that privacy and retirement, which had been the chief object of His leaving Capernaum. Accordingly, when the two Paschal days were ended, He resumed His journey, extending it far beyond any previously undertaken, perhaps beyond what had been originally intended. The borders of Palestine proper, though not of what the Rabbis reckoned as belonging to it,[1] were passed. Making a long circuit through the territory of Sidon,[2] He descended—probably through one of the passes of the Hermon range—into the country of the Tetrarch Philip. Thence He continued 'through the midst of the borders of Decapolis,' till He once more reached the eastern, or south-eastern, shore of the Lake of Galilee. It will be remembered that the Decapolis, or confederacy of ' the Ten Cities,'[3] was wedged in between the Tetrarchies of Philip and Antipas. It embraced ten cities, although that was not always their number, and their names are variously enumerated. Of these cities Hippos, on the south-eastern shore of the Lake, was the most northern, and Philadelphia, the ancient Rabbath-Ammon, the most southern. Scythopolis, the ancient Beth-Shean, with its district, was the only one of them on the western bank of the Jordan. This extensive ' Ten Cities ' district was essentially heathen territory. Their ancient monuments show, in which of them Zeus, Astarte, and Athene, or else Artemis,

---

[1] For the Rabbinic views of the boundaries of Palestine see 'Sketches of Jewish Social Life,' ch. ii.

[2] The correct reading of St. Mark vii. 31, is 'through Sidon.' By the latter I do not understand the town of that name, which would have been quite outside the

Saviour's route, but (with *Ewald* and *Lange*) the territory of Sidon.

[3] The fullest notice of the 'Ten Cities' is that of *Caspari*, Chronolog. Geogr. Einl. pp. 83–91, with which compare *Menke's* Bibel-Atlas, Map V.

Hercules, Dionysos, Demeter, or other Grecian divinities, were worshipped.[1] Their political constitution was that of the free Greek
cities. They were subject only to the Governor of Syria, and formed
part of Cœle-Syria, in contradistinction to Syro-Phœnicia. Their privileges dated from the time of Pompey, from which also they afterwards reckoned their era.

It is important to keep in view that, although Jesus was now
within the territory of ancient Israel, the district and all the
surroundings were essentially heathen, although in closest proximity
to, and intermingling with, that which was purely Jewish. St. Mat-
thew[a] gives only a general description of Christ's activity there, ^a St. Matt
concluding with a notice of the impression produced on those who xv. 29-31
witnessed His mighty deeds, as leading them to glorify 'the God of
Israel.' This, of course, confirms the impression that the scene is
laid among a population chiefly heathen, and agrees with the more
minute notice of the locality in the Gospel of St. Mark. One special
instance of miraculous healing is recorded in the latter, not only from
its intrinsic interest, but perhaps, also, as in some respects typical.

1. Among those brought to Him was one deaf, whose speech had,
probably in consequence of this, been so affected as practically to
deprive him of its power.[2] This circumstance, and that he is not
spoken of as so afflicted from his birth, leads us to infer that the
affection was—as not unfrequently—the result of disease, and not
congenital. Remembering, that alike the subject of the miracle
and they who brought him were heathens, but in constant and close
contact with Jews, what follows is vividly true to life. The entreaty
to 'lay His Hand upon him' was heathen, and yet semi-Jewish also.
Quite peculiar it is, when the Lord took him aside from the multitude;
and again that, in healing him, 'He spat,' applying it directly to the
diseased organ. We read of the direct application of saliva only here
and in the healing of the blind man at Bethsaida.[b][3] We are disposed ^b St. Mark
to regard this as peculiar to the healing of Gentiles. Peculiar, also, v. iii. 23
is the term expressive of burden on the mind, when, 'looking up to
heaven, He sighed.'[4] Peculiar, also, is the 'thrusting'[5] of His
Fingers into the man's ears, and the touch of his tongue. Only

---

[1] Comp. *Schürer*, pp. 382, 383.

[2] μογιλάλος or μογγιλάλος does
not mean one absolutely dumb. It is literally: *difficulter loquens*. The Rabbinic
designation of such a person would have
been *Cheresh* (Ter. i. 2) although different opinions obtain as to whether the
term includes impediment of speech
(comp. Meg. ii. 4; Gitt. 71 *a*).

[3] In St. John ix. 6 it is really application of clay.

[4] στενάζω occurs only here in the
Gospels. Otherwise it occurs in Rom.
viii. 23; 2 Cor. v. 2, 4; Hebr. xiii. 17;
James v. 9; the substantive in Acts vii.
34; Rom, viii. 26.

[5] So literally.

the upward look to Heaven and the command 'Ephphatha'—'be opened'—seem the same as in His every day wonders of healing. But we mark that all here seems much more elaborate than in Israel. The reason of this must, of course, be sought in the moral condition of the person healed. Certain characteristics about the action of the Lord may, perhaps, help us to understand it better. There is an accumulation of means, yet each and all inadequate to effect the purpose, but all connected with His Person. This elaborate use of such means would banish the idea of magic; it would arouse the attention, and fix it upon Christ, as using these means, which were all connected with His own person ; while, lastly, the sighing, and the word of absolute command, would all have here their special significance.

Let us try to realize the scene. They have heard of Him as the wonder-worker, these heathens in the land so near to, and yet so far from, Israel; and they have brought to Him 'the lame, blind, dumb, maimed,[1] and many others,' and laid them at His Feet. Oh, what wonder! All disease vanishes in presence of Heaven's Own Life Incarnate. Tongues long weighted are loosed, limbs maimed or bent by disease[1] are restored to health, the lame are stretched straight; the film of disease and the paralysis of nerve-impotence pass from eyes long insensible to the light. It is a new era—Israel conquers the heathen world, not by force, but by love; not by outward means, but by the manifestation of life-power from above. Truly, this is the Messianic conquest and reign: 'and they glorified the God of Israel. '

From amongst this mass of misery we single out and follow one,[a] whom the Saviour takes aside, that it may not merely be the breath of heaven's spring passing over them all, that wooeth him to new life, but that He may touch and handle him, and so give health to soul and body. The man is to be alone with Christ and the disciples. It is not magic; means are used, and such as might not seem wholly strange to the man. And quite a number of means! He thrust His Fingers into his deaf ears, as if to make a way for the sound: He spat on his tongue, using a means of healing accepted in popular opinion of Jew and Gentile;[b][2] He touched his tongue. Each act seemed a fresh incitement to his faith—and all connected itself with

[1] Κυλλός means here *incurvatus*, and not as in ix. 43 *mutilatus*.

[2] *Wünsche* (ad. loc.) is guilty of serious misapprehension when he says that the Talmud condemns to eternal punishment those who employ this mode of healing. This statement is incorrect.

What it condemns is the whispering of magical formulas over a wound (Sanh. 90 *a*), when it was the custom of some magicians to spit *before* (Sanh. 101 *a*), others *after* pronouncing the formula (Jer. Sanh. 28 *b*). There is no analogy whatever between this and what our

he Person of Christ. As yet there was not breath of life in it all. **CHAP.**
But when the man's eyes followed those of the Saviour to heaven, he **XXXIV**
would understand whence He expected, whence came to Him the power
—Who had sent Him, and Whose He was. And as he followed the movement of Christ's lips, as he groaned under the felt burden He had come
o remove, the sufferer would look up expectant. Once more the
Saviour's lips parted to speak the word of command: ' Be opened ' [a]—— *[a] ἐφφαθά =*
and straightway the gladsome sound would pass into ' his hearing,' [1] אתפתח
and the bond that seemed to have held his tongue was loosed. He
was in a new world, into which He had put him that had spoken
hat one Word; He, Who had been burdened under the load which He
had lifted up to His Father; to Whom all the means that had been
used had pointed, and with Whose Person they had been connected.

It was in vain to enjoin silence. Wider and wider spread the
unbidden fame, till it was caught up in this one hymn of praise,
which has remained to all time the jubilee of our experience of Christ
as the Divine Healer: ' He hath done all things well—He maketh
even the deaf to hear, and the dumb to speak.' This Jewish word,
Ephphatha, spoken to the Gentile Church by Him, Who, looking up
o heaven, sighed under the burden, even while He uplifted it, has
opened the hearing and loosed the bond of speech. Most significantly
was it spoken in the language of the Jews; and this also does it
each, that Jesus must always have spoken the Jews' language. For,
if ever, to a Grecian in Grecian territory would He have spoken in
Greek, not in the Jews' language, if the former and not the latter
had been that of which He made use in His Words and Working.

2. Another miracle is recorded by St. Mark,[b] as wrought by [b] St. Mark
Jesus in these parts, and, as we infer, on a heathen.[2] All the circum- viii. 22-26
stances are kindred to those just related. It was in Bethsaida-Julias,

---

Lord did, and the use of saliva for cures is universally recognised by the Rabbis.

[1] So literally, or rather 'hearings'—in the plural.

[2] Most commentators regard this as the *eastern* Bethsaida, or Bethsaida-Julias. The objection (in the Speaker's Commentary) that the text speaks of ' a village ' (vv. 23, 26) is obviated by the circumstance that similarly we read immediately afterwards (ver. 27) about the villages of Cæsarea Philippi.' Indeed, a knowledge of Jewish law enables us to see here a fresh proof of the genuineness of the Evangelic narrative. For, according to Meg. 3 *b* the villages about a town were reckoned as belonging to it, while, on the other hand, a town which had

not among its inhabitants ten *Batlanin* (persons who devoted themselves to the worship and affairs of the Synagogue) was to be regarded as a village. The Bethsaida of ver. 22 must refer to the district, in one of the hamlets of which the blind man met Jesus. It does not appear, that Jesus ever again wrought miracles, either in Capernaum or the western Bethsaida, if, indeed, He ever returned to that district. Lastly, the scene of that miracle must have been the eastern Bethsaida (Julias), since immediately afterwards the continuance of His journey to Cæsarea Philippi is related without any notice of crossing the Lake.

that one blind was brought unto Him, with the entreaty that He would touch him,—just as in the case of the deaf and dumb. Here, also, the Saviour took him aside—'led him out of the village '—and 'spat on his eyes, and put His Hands upon him. We mark not only the similarity of the means employed, but the same, and even greater elaborateness in the use of them, since a twofold touch is recorded before the man saw clearly.[1] On any theory—even that which would regard the Gospel-narratives as spurious—this trait must have been intended to mark a special purpose, since this is the only instance in which a miraculous cure was performed gradually, and not at once and completely. So far as we can judge, the object was, by a gradual process of healing, to disabuse the man of any idea of magical cure, while at the same time the process of healing again markedly centered in the Person of Jesus. With this also agrees (as in the case of the deaf and dumb) the use of spittle in the healing. We may here recall, that the use of saliva was a well-known Jewish remedy for affections of the eyes.[a] It was thus that the celebrated Rabbi Meir relieved one of his fair hearers, when her husband, in his anger at her long detention by the Rabbi's sermons, had ordered her to spit in the preacher's face. Pretending to suffer from his eyes, the Rabbi contrived that the woman publicly spat in his eyes, thus enabling her to obey her husband's command.[b] The anecdote at least proves, that the application of saliva was popularly regarded as a remedy for affections of the eyes.

a Jer.
Shabb. xiv.
4; Baba B.
126 b

b Jer. Sot.
16 d, about
the middle

Thus in this instance also, as in that of the deaf and dumb, there was the use of means, Jewish means, means manifestly insufficient (since their first application was only partially successful), and a multiplication of means—yet all centering in, and proceeding from, His Person. As further analogies between the two, we mark that the blindness does not seem to have been congenital, [c] but the consequence of disease, and that silence was enjoined after the healing.[d] Lastly, the confusedness of his sight, when first restored to him, surely conveyed, not only to him but to us all, both a spiritual lesson and a spiritual warning.

c Comp.
St. Mark
viii. 24

d ver. 26

3. Yet a third miracle of healing requires to be here considered, although related by St. Matthew in quite another connection.[e] But we have learned enough of the structure of the First Gospel to know, that its arrangement is determined by the plan of the writer rather than by the chronological succession of events.[2] The manner

e St. Matt.
ix. 27-31

---

[1] The better reading of the words is given in the Revised Version.
[2] Thus, the healing recorded imme- diately after this history, in St. Matt. ix. 32–35, belongs evidently to a later period. Comp. St. Luke xi. 14.

in which the Lord healed the two blind men, the injunction of
silence, and the notice that none the less they spread His fame in
all that land,[1] seem to imply that He was not on the ordinary scene
of His labours in Galilee.　Nor can we fail to mark an internal
analogy between this and the other two miracles enacted amidst a
chiefly Grecian population.　And, strange though it may sound, the
cry with which the two blind men who sought His help followed Him,
' Son of David, have mercy on us,' comes, as might be expected, more
frequently from Gentile than from Jewish lips.　It was, of course,
pre-eminently the Jewish designation of the Messiah, the basis of all
Jewish thought of Him.　But, perhaps on that very ground, it would
express in Israel rather the homage of popular conviction, than, as in
this case, the cry for help in bodily disease.　Besides, Jesus had not
as yet been hailed as the Messiah, except by His most intimate disciples; and, even by them, chiefly in the joy of their highest spiritual
attainments.　He was the Rabbi, Teacher, Wonder-worker, Son of
Man, even Son of God; but the idea of the Davidic Kingdom as
implying spiritual and Divine, not outwardly royal rule, lay as yet
on the utmost edge of the horizon, covered by the golden mist of
the Sun of Righteousness in His rising.　On the other hand, we can
understand, how to Gentiles, who resided in Palestine, the Messiah of
Israel would chiefly stand out as 'the Son of David.'　It was the
most ready, and, at the same time, the most universal, form in which
the great Jewish hope could be viewed by them.　It presented to
their minds the most marked contrast to Israel's present fallen state,
and it recalled the Golden Age of Israel's past, and that, as only the
symbol of a far wider and more glorious reign, the fulfilment of what
to David had only been promises.[2]

Peculiar to this history is the testing question of Christ, whether
they really believed what their petition implied, that He was able to
restore their sight; and, again, His stern, almost passionate, insistence[3] on their silence as to the mode of their cure.　Only on one
other occasion do we read of the same insistence.　It is, when the
leper had expressed the same absolute faith in Christ's ability to

---

[1] I admit that especially the latter
argument is inconclusive, but I appeal
to the general context and the setting of
this history.　It is impossible to regard
St. Matt. ix. as a chronological record of
events.

[2] He is *addressed* as 'Son of David,'
in this passage, by the Syro-Phœnician
woman (St. Matt. xv. 22), and by the

blind men near Jericho (St. Matt. xx.
30, 31; St. Mark x. 47, 48; St. Luke
xviii, 38, 39), and *proclaimed* as such
by the people in St. Matt. xii. 23; xxi.
9, 15.

[3] ἐμβριμάομαι—the word occurs in
that sense only here and in St. Mark i. 43;
otherwise also in St. Mark xiv. 5, and
in St. John xi. 33, 38.

ª St. Mark
1. 40, 41

heal if He willed it, and Jesus had, as in the case of those two blind men, conferred the benefit by the touch of His Hand.ª In both these cases, it is remarkable that, along with strongest faith of those who came to Him, there was rather an implied than an expressed petition on their part. The leper who knelt before Him only said: ' Lord, if Thou wilt, Thou canst make me clean; ' and the two blind men: ' Have mercy on us, Thou Son of David.' Thus it is the highest and most realising faith, which is most absolute in its trust and most reticent as regards the details of its request.

But as regards the two blind men (and the healed leper also), it is almost impossible not to connect Christ's peculiar insistence on their silence with their advanced faith. They had owned Jesus as ' the Son of David,' and that, not in the Judaic sense (as by the Syro-Phœnician woman[1]), but as able to do all things, even to open by His touch the eyes of the blind. And it had been done to them, as it always is—according to their faith. But a profession of faith so wide-reaching as theirs, and sealed by the attainment of what it sought, yet scarcely dared to ask, must not be publicly proclaimed. It would, and in point of fact did, bring to Him crowds which, unable spiritually to understand the meaning of such a confession, would only embarrass and hinder, and whose presence and homage would have to be avoided as much, if not more, than that of open enemies.ᵇ For confession of the mouth must ever be the outcome of heart-belief, and the acclamations of an excited Jewish crowd were as incongruous to the real Character of the Christ, and as obstructive to the progress of His Kingdom, as is the outward homage of a world which has not heart-belief in His Power, nor heart-experience of His ability and willingness to cleanse the leper and to open the eyes of the blind. Yet the leprosy of Israel and the blindness of the Gentile world are equally removed by the touch of His Hand at the cry of faith.

ᵇ St. Mark i.
45

The question has been needlessly discussed,[2] whether they were to praise or blame, who, despite the Saviour's words, spread His fame. We scarcely know what, or how much, they disobeyed. They could not but speak of His Person; and theirs was, perhaps, not yet that higher silence which is content simply to sit at His Feet.

---

[1] It should be borne in mind, that the country, surroundings, &c., place these men in a totally different category from the Syro-Phœnician woman.

[2] Roman Catholic writers mostly praise, while Protestants blame, their conduct.

CHAPTER XXXV.

THE TWO SABBATH-CONTROVERSIES—THE PLUCKING OF THE EARS OF CORN BY THE DISCIPLES, AND THE HEALING OF THE MAN WITH THE WITH-ERED HAND.

(St. Matt. xii. 1–21; St. Mark ii. 23—iii. 6; St. Luke vi. 1–11.)

IN grouping together the three miracles of healing described in the last chapter, we do not wish to convey that it is certain they had taken place in precisely that order. Nor do we feel sure, that they preceded what is about to be related. In the absence of exact data, the succession of events and their location must be matter of combination. From their position in the Evangelic narratives, and the manner in which all concerned speak and act, we inferred, that they took place at that particular period and east of the Jordan, in the Decapolis or else in the territory of Philip. They differ from the events about to be related by the absence of the Jerusalem Scribes, who hung on the footsteps of Jesus. While the Saviour tarried on the borders of Tyre, and thence passed through the territory of Sidon into the Decapolis and to the southern and eastern shores of the Lake of Galilee, they were in Jerusalem at the Passover. But after the two festive days, which would require their attendance in the Temple, they seem to have returned to their hateful task. It would not be difficult for them to discover the scene of such mighty works as His. Accordingly, we now find them once more confronting Christ. And the events about to be related are chronologically distinguished from those that had preceded, by this presence and opposition of the Pharisaic party. The contest now becomes more decided and sharp, and we are rapidly nearing the period when He, Who had hitherto been chiefly preaching the Kingdom, and healing body and soul, will, through the hostility of the leaders of Israel, enter on the second, or prevailingly negative stage of His Work, in which, according to the prophetic description, 'they compassed' Him 'about like bees,' but 'are quenched as the fire of thorns.'

Where fundamental principles were so directly contrary, the oc-

CHAP.
XXXV

BOOK
III

casion for conflict could not be long wanting. Indeed, all that Jesus taught must have seemed to these Pharisees strangely un-Jewish in cast and direction, even if not in form and words. But chiefly would this be the case in regard to that on which, of all else, the Pharisees laid most stress, the observance of the Sabbath. On no other subject is Rabbinic teaching more painfully minute and more manifestly incongruous to its professed object. For, if we rightly apprehend what underlay the complicated and intolerably burdensome laws and rules of Pharisaic Sabbath-observance, it was to secure, negatively, absolute rest from all labour, and, positively, to make the Sabbath a delight. The Mishnah includes Sabbath-desecration among those most heinous crimes for which a man was to be stoned.[a] This, then, was their first care: by a series of complicated ordinances to make a breach of the Sabbath-rest impossible. How far this was carried, we shall presently see. The next object was, in a similarly external manner, to make the Sabbath a delight. A special Sabbath dress, the best that could be procured; the choicest food, even though a man had to work for it all the week, or public charity were to supply it[b]—such were some of the means by which the day was to be honoured and men to find pleasure therein. The strangest stories are told, how, by the purchase of the most expensive dishes, the pious poor had gained unspeakable merit, and obtained, even on earth, Heaven's manifest reward. And yet, by the side of these and similar strange and sad misdirections of piety, we come also upon that which is touching, beautiful, and even spiritual. On the Sabbath there must be no mourning, for to the Sabbath applies this saying:[c] 'The blessing of the Lord, it maketh rich, and He addeth no sorrow with it.' Quite alone was the Sabbath among the measures of time. Every other day had been paired with its fellow: not so the Sabbath. And so any festival, even the Day of Atonement, might be transferred to another day: not so the observance of the Sabbath. Nay, when the Sabbath complained before God, that of all days it alone stood solitary, God had wedded it to Israel; and this holy union God had bidden His people 'remember,'[d] when it stood before the Mount. Even the tortures of Gehenna were intermitted on that holy, happy day.[e]

The terribly exaggerated views on the Sabbath entertained by the Rabbis, and the endless burdensome rules with which they encumbered everything connected with its sanctity, are fully set forth in another place.[1] The Jewish Law, as there summarised, sufficiently explains the controversies in which the Pharisaic party

a Sanh.
vii. 4

b Peah
viii. 7

c In Prov. x.
22

d Ex. xx. 8

e Comp.
Ber. R. 11
on Gen. ii. 3

[1] See Appendix XVII: The Ordinances and Law of the Sabbath.

now engaged with Jesus. Of these the first was when, going through the cornfields on the Sabbath, His disciples began to pluck and eat the ears of corn. Not, indeed, that this was the first Sabbath-controversy forced upon Christ.[a] But it was the first time that Jesus allowed, and afterwards Himself did, in presence of the Pharisees, what was contrary to Jewish notions, and that, in express and unmistakable terms, He vindicated His position in regard to the Sabbath. This also indicates that we have now reached a further stage in the history of our Lord's teaching.

CHAP.
XXXV

[a] Comp.
St. John v.
9, 16

This, however, is not the only reason for placing this event so late in the personal history of Christ. St. Matthew inserts it at a different period from the other two Synoptists; and although St. Mark and St. Luke introduce it amidst the same surroundings, the connection, in which it is told in all the three Gospels, shows that it is placed out of the historical order, with the view of grouping together what would exhibit Christ's relation to the Pharisees and their teaching. Accordingly, this first Sabbath-controversy is immediately followed by that connected with the healing of the man with the withered hand. From St. Matthew and St. Mark it might, indeed, appear as if this had occurred on the same day as the plucking of the ears of corn, but St. Luke corrects any possible misunderstanding, by telling us that it happened ' on another Sabbath '— perhaps that following the walk through the cornfields.

Dismissing the idea of inferring the precise time of these two events from their place in the Evangelic record, we have not much difficulty in finding the needful historical data for our present inquiry. The first and most obvious is, that the harvest was still standing— whether that of barley or of wheat. The former began immediately after the Passover, the latter after the Feast of Pentecost; the presentation of the wave-omer of barley making the beginning of the one, that of the two wave-loaves that of the other.[1] Here another historical notice comes to our aid. St. Luke describes the Sabbath of this occurrence as 'the second-first '—an expression so peculiar that it cannot be regarded as an interpolation,[2] but as designedly chosen by the Evangelist to indicate something well understood in Palestine at the time. Bearing in mind the limited number of Sabbaths between the commencement of the barley and the end of the wheat-harvest, our inquiry is here much narrowed. In Rabbinic writings the term 'second-first ' is not applied to any Sabbath.

---

[1] Comp. ' The Temple and its Services,' pp. 222, 226, 230, 231.

[2] The great majority of critics are agreed as to its authenticity.

BOOK
III

But we know that the fifty days between the Feast of Passover and that of Pentecost were counted from the presentation of the wave-omer on the Second Paschal Day, at the first, second, third day, &c., after the ' Omer.' Thus the ' second-first ' Sabbath might be either ' the first Sabbath after the second day, ' which was that of the presentation of the Omer, or else the second Sabbath after this first day of reckoning, or ' Sephirah,' as it was called (ספירת העמר). To us the first of these dates seems most in accord with the manner in which St. Luke would describe to Gentile readers the Sabbath which was the first after the second,' or, Sephirah-day.[1]

Assuming, then, that it was probably the first—possibly, the second—Sabbath after the 'reckoning,' or second Paschal Day, on which the disciples plucked the ears of corn, we have still to ascertain whether it was in the first or second Passover of Christ's Ministry.[2] The reasons against placing it between the first Passover and Pentecost are of the strongest character. Not to speak of the circumstance that such advanced teaching on the part of Christ, and such advanced knowledge on the part of His disciples, indicate a later period, our Lord did not call His twelve Apostles till long after the Feast of Pentecost, viz. after His return from the so-called ' Unknown Feast,'[a] which, as shown in another place,[3] must have been either that of ' Wood-Gathering,' in the end of the summer, or else New Year's Day, in the beginning of autumn. Thus, as by ' the disciples ' we must in this connection understand, in the first place, ' the Apostles,' the event could not have occurred between the first Passover and Pentecost of the Lord's Ministry.

The same result is reached by another process of reasoning. After the first Passover[b] our Lord, with such of His disciples as had then gathered to Him, tarried for some time—no doubt for several weeks—in Judæa.[c] The wheat was ripe for harvesting, when He

[a] St. John v.

[b] St. John ii. 13

[c] St. John iii. 22; v. 1–3

---

[1] The view which I have adopted is that of *Scaliger* and *Lightfoot*; the alternative one mentioned, that of *Delitzsch*. In regard to the many other explanations proposed, I would lay down this canon: No explanation can be satisfactory which rests not on some ascertained fact in Jewish life, but where the fact is merely ' supposed ' for the sake of the explanation which it would afford. Thus, there is not the slightest support in fact for the idea, that the first Sabbath of the second month was so called (*Wetstein*, Speaker's Commentary), or the first Sabbath in the second year of a septennial cycle, or the Sabbath of the Nisan (the sacred) year, in contradistinction to the Tishri or secular year, which began in autumn. Of these and similar interpretations it is enough to say, that the underlying fact is ' supposed ' for the sake of a 'supposed' explanation; in other words, they embody an hypothesis based on an hypothesis.

[2] There were only three Paschal feasts during the public ministry of Christ. Any other computation rests on the idea that the Unknown Feast was the Passover, or even the Feast of Esther.

[3] Comp. Appendix XV.

passed through Samaria.[a] And, on His return to Galilee, His dis-   CHAP.
ciples seem to have gone back to their homes and occupations, since   XXXV
it was some time afterwards when even His most intimate disciples—
Peter, Andrew, James, and John—were called a second time.[b] Chro-   [a] St. John iv. 35
nologically, therefore, there is no room for this event between the   [b] St. Matt. iv. 18-22
first Passover and Pentecost.[1] Lastly, we have here to bear in mind,
that, on His first appearance in Galilee, the Pharisees had not yet
taken up this position of determined hostility to Him. On the other
hand, all agrees with the circumstance, that the active hostility of
the Pharisees and Christ's separation from the ordinances of the
Synagogue commenced with His visit to Jerusalem in the early
autumn of that year.[c] If, therefore, we have to place the plucking of   [c] St. John v.
the ears of corn after the Feast recorded in St. John v., as can scarcely
be doubted, it must have taken place, not between the first, but between
the Second Passover and Pentecost of Christ's Public Ministry.

Another point deserves notice. The different 'setting' (chronologically speaking) in which the three Gospels present the event
about to be related, illustrates that the object of the Evangelists
was to present the events in the History of the Christ in their
succession, not of time, but of bearing upon final results. This,
because they do not attempt a Biography of Jesus, which, from their
point of view, would have been almost blasphemy, but a History of
the Kingdom which He brought; and because they write it, so to
speak, not by adjectives (expressive of qualities), nor adverbially,[2] but
by substantives. Lastly, it will be noted that the three Evangelists
relate the event about to be considered (as so many others), not,
indeed, with variations,[3] but with differences of detail, showing the
independence of their narratives, which, as we shall see, really supplement each other.

We are now in a position to examine the narrative itself. It was
on the Sabbath after the Second Paschal Day that Christ and His
disciples passed[4]—probably by a field-path—through cornfields, when

---

[1] Few would be disposed to place St.
Matt. xii. before St. Matt. iv.

[2] Adverbs answer to the questions,
How, When, Why, Where.

[3] *Meyer* insists that the ὁδὸν, ποιεῖν or
more correctly, ὁδ ὁποιεῖν (St. Mark ii. 23)
should be translated literally, that the
disciples began to make a way by plucking the ears of corn. Accordingly, he
maintains, that there is an essential difference between the account of St. Mark
and those of the two other Evangelists,

who attribute the plucking of the ears to
hunger. Canon *Cook* (Speaker's Commentary, New Testament i. p. 216) has to
my mind, conclusively shown the untenableness of *Meyer's* contention. He compares the expression of St. Mark to the
Latin '*iter facere.*' I would suggest the
French '*chemin faisant.*' *Godet* points
out the absurdity of plucking up ears in
order to make a way through the corn.

[4] In St. Mark also the better reading
is διαπορεύεσθαι.

His disciples, being hungry,ᵃ as they went,ᵇ plucked ears of corn and ate them, having rubbed off the husks in their hands.ᶜ On any ordinary day this would have been lawful,ᵈ but on the Sabbath it involved, according to Rabbinic statutes, at least two sins. For, according to the Talmud, what was really one labour, would, if made up of several acts, each of them forbidden, amount to several acts of labour, each involving sin, punishment, and a sin-offering.ᵉ[1] This so-called 'division' of labour applied only to infringement of the Sabbath-rest—not of that of feast-days.ᶠ Now in this case there were at least two such acts involved: that of plucking the ears of corn, ranged under the sin of reaping, and that of rubbing them, which might be ranged under sifting in a sieve, threshing, sifting out fruit, grinding, or fanning. The following Talmudic passage bears on this: 'In case a woman rolls wheat to remove the husks, it is considered as sifting; if she rubs the heads of wheat, it is regarded as threshing; if she cleans off the side-adherences, it is sifting out fruit; if she bruises the ears, it is grinding; if she throws them up in her hand, it is winnowing.'ᵍ One instance will suffice to show the externalism of all these ordinances. If a man wished to move a sheaf on his field, which of course implied labour, he had only to lay upon it a spoon that was in his common use, when, in order to remove the spoon, he might also remove the sheaf on which it lay!ʰ And yet it was forbidden to stop with a little wax the hole in a cask by which the fluid was running out,ⁱ or to wipe a wound!

Holding views like these, the Pharisees, who witnessed the conduct of the disciples, would naturally harshly condemn, what they must have regarded as gross desecration of the Sabbath. Yet it was clearly not a breach of the Biblical, but of the Rabbinic Law. Not only to show them their error, but to lay down principles which would for ever apply to this difficult question, was the object of Christ's reply. Unlike the others of the Ten Commandments, the Sabbath Law has in it two elements; the moral and the ceremonial: the eternal, and that which is subject to time and place; the inward and spiritual, and the outward (the one as the mode of realizing the other). In their distinction and separation lies the difficulty of the subject. In its spiritual and eternal element, the Sabbath Law embodied the two thoughts of rest for worship, and worship which

---

[1] Thus (Shabb. 74 b, lines 12, 11 from bottom), if a person were to pull out a feather from the wing of a bird, cut off the top, and then pluck off the fluff below it would involve three labours and three sin-offerings.

pointed to rest. The keeping of the seventh day, and the Jewish mode of its observance, were the temporal and outward form in which these eternal principles were presented. Even Rabbinism, in some measure, perceived this. It was a principle, that danger to life superseded the Sabbath Law,[1] and indeed all other obligations.[2] Among the curious Scriptural and other arguments by which this principle was supported, that which probably would most appeal to common sense was derived from Lev. xviii. 5. It was argued, that a man was to keep the commandments that he might live—certainly not, that by so doing he might die.[a] In other words, the outward mode of observation was subordinate to the object of the observance. Yet this other and kindred principle did Rabbinism lay down, that every positive commandment superseded the Sabbath-rest. This was the ultimate vindication of work in the Temple, although certainly not its explanation. Lastly, we should in this connection, include this important canon, laid down by the Rabbis: ' a single Rabbinic prohibition is not to be heeded, where a graver matter is in question.' [b]

All these points must be kept in view for the proper understanding of the words of Christ to the Scribes. For, while going far beyond the times and notions of His questioners, His reasoning must have been within their comprehension. Hence the first argument of our Lord, as recorded by all the Synoptists, was taken from Biblical History. When, on his flight from Saul, David had, ' when an hungered,' eaten of the shewbread, and given it to his followers,[3] although, by the letter of the Levitical Law,[c] it was only to be eaten by the priests, Jewish tradition vindicated his conduct on the plea that ' danger to life superseded the Sabbath-Law, and hence, all laws connected with it,[4] while, to show David's zeal for the Sabbath-Law, the legend was added, that he had reproved the priests of Nob, who had been baking the shewbread on the Sabbath.[d] To the first argument of Christ, St. Matthew adds this as His second, that the priests, in their services in the Temple, necessarily broke the Sabbath-

CHAP.
XXXV

[a] Jer.
Shabb. xiv.
4, pp. 14 d,
15 a

[b] Jer.
Shabb.
xvi. 1

[c] Lev. xxiv
5-9

[d] Yalkut ii.
par. 130,
p. 18 d

---

[1] But only where the life of an Israelite, not of a heathen or Samaritan, was in danger (Yoma 84 b).

[2] *Maimonides*, Hilkh. Shabb. ii. 1 (Yad haCh. vol. i. part iii. p. 141 a): ' The Sabbath is set aside on account of danger to life, as all other ordinances (המצות כשאר כל).'

[3] According to 1 Sam. xxii. 9 Ahimelech (or Ahijah, 1 Sam. xiv. 3) was the high Priest. We infer, that Abiathar was con-

joined with his father in the priesthood. Comp. the 'Bible-History,' vol. iv. p. 111.

[4] The question discussed in the Talmud is, whether, supposing an ordinary Israelite discharged priestly functions on the Sabbath in the temple, it would involve two sins: unlawful service and Sabbath-desecration; or only one sin, unlawful service.

Law without thereby incurring guilt. It is curious, that the Talmud discusses this very point, and that, by way of illustration, it introduces an argument from Lev. xxii. 10: 'There shall no stranger eat of things consecrated.' This, of course, embodies the principle underlying the prohibition of the shewbread to all who were not priests.[a] Without entering further on it, the discussion at least shows, that the Rabbis were by no means clear on the *rationale* of Sabbath-work in the Temple.

In truth, the reason why David was blameless in eating the shewbread was the same as that which made the Sabbath-labour of the priests lawful. The Sabbath-Law was not one merely of rest, but of rest for worship. The Service of the Lord was the object in view. The priests worked on the Sabbath, because this service was the object of the Sabbath; and David was allowed to eat of the shewbread, not because there was danger to life from starvation, but because he pleaded that he was on the service of the Lord and needed this provision. The disciples, when following the Lord, were similarly on the service of the Lord; ministering to Him was more than ministering in the Temple, for He was greater than the Temple. If the Pharisees had believed this, they would not have questioned their conduct, nor in so doing have themselves infringed that higher Law which enjoined mercy, not sacrifice.

To this St. Mark adds as corollary: 'The Sabbath was made for man, and not man for the Sabbath.' It is remarkable, that a similar argument is used by the Rabbis. When insisting that the Sabbath Law should be set aside to avoid danger to life, it is urged: 'the Sabbath is handed over to you; not, ye are handed over to the Sabbath.'[b] Lastly, the three Evangelists record this as the final outcome of His teaching on this subject, that 'the Son of Man is Lord of the Sabbath also.' The Service of God, and the Service of the Temple, by universal consent superseded the Sabbath-Law. But Christ was greater than the Temple, and His Service more truly that of God, and higher than that of the outward Temple—and the Sabbath was intended for man, to serve God: therefore Christ and His Service were superior to the Sabbath-Law. Thus much would be intelligible to these Pharisees, although they would not receive it, because they believed not on Him as the Sent of God.[1]

But to us the words mean more than this. They preach not only

a Jer.
Shabb. ii. 5,
p. 5 a

b Mechilt.
on Ex.
xxxi. 13,
ed. *Weiss*,
p. 109 b

[1] We may here again state, that Cod. D has this after St. Luke vi. 4: 'The same day, having beholden a man working on the Sabbath, He said to Him: "Man, if thou knowest what thou dost, blessed art thou: but if thou knowest not, thou

that the Service of Christ is that of God, but that, even more than in the Temple, all of work or of liberty is lawful which this service requires. We are free while we are doing anything for Christ; God loves mercy, and demands not sacrifice; His sacrifice is the service of Christ, in heart, and life, and work. We are not free to do anything we please; but we are free to do anything needful or helpful, while we are doing any service to Christ. He is the Lord of the Sabbath, Whom we serve in and through the Sabbath. And even this is significant, that, when designating Himself Lord of the Sabbath, it is as 'the Son of Man.' It shows, that the narrow Judaistic form regarding the day and the manner of observance is enlarged into the wider Law, which applies to all humanity. Under the New Testament the Sabbath has, as the Church, become *Catholic*, and its Lord is Christ as the Son of Man, to Whom the body Catholic offers the acceptable service of heart and life.

The question as between Christ and the Pharisees was not, however, to end here. 'On another Sabbath'—probably that following —He was in their Synagogue. Whether or not the Pharisees had brought 'the man with the withered hand' on purpose, or placed him in a conspicuous position, or otherwise raised the question, certain it is that their secret object was to commit Christ to some word or deed, which would lay Him open to the capital charge of breaking the Sabbath-law. It does not appear, whether the man with the withered hand was consciously or unconsciously their tool. But in this they judged rightly: that Christ would not witness disease without removing it—or, as we might express it, that disease *could* not continue in the Presence of Him, Who was the Life. He read their inward thoughts of evil, and yet he proceeded to do the good which He purposed. So God, in His majestic greatness, carries out the purpose which He has fixed—which we call the law of nature—whoever and whatever stand in the way; and so God, in His sovereign goodness, adapts it to the good of His creatures, notwithstanding their evil thoughts.

So much unclearness prevails as to the Jewish views about healing on the Sabbath, that some connected information on the subject seems needful. We have already seen, that in their view only actual danger to life warranted a breach of the Sabbath-Law. But this

art accursed and a transgressor of the Law"' (*Nicholson*, Gospel according to the Hebrews, p. 151). It need scarcely be said, that the words, as placed in St. Luke, are a spurious addition, although as Canon *Westcott* rightly infers, 'the saying [probably] rests on some real incident' (Introd. to the Study of the Gospels, p. 454, note.

BOOK
III

ᵃ Debar. R.
10
ᵇ Yoma
viii. 6
ᶜ Yoma 84 a
ᵈ Shabb.
xiv. 3

ᵉ u. s. 4

ᶠ Comp.
Jer.
Shabb. 14 d

ᵍ St. Mark
iii. 4
ʰ St. Matt.
xii. 12

opened a large field for discussion. Thus, according to some, disease of the ear,[a] according to some throat-disease,[b] while, according to others, such a disease as angina,[c] involved danger, and superseded the Sabbath-Law. All applications to the outside of the body were forbidden on the Sabbath. As regarded internal remedies, such substances as were used in health, but had also a remedial effect, might be taken,[d] although here also there was a way of evading the Law.[1] A person suffering from toothache might not gargle his mouth with vinegar, but he might use an ordinary toothbrush and dip it in vinegar.[e] The Gemara here adds, that gargling was lawful, if the substance was afterwards swallowed. It further explains, that affections extending from the lips, or else from the throat, inwards, may be attended to, being regarded as dangerous. Quite a number of these are enumerated, showing, that either the Rabbis were very lax in applying their canon about mortal diseases, or else that they reckoned in their number not a few which we would not regard as such.[2] External lesions also might be attended to, if they involved danger to life.[3] Similarly, medical aid might be called in, if a person had swallowed a piece of glass; a splinter might be removed from the eye, and even a thorn from the body.[f]

But although the man with the withered hand could not be classed with those dangerously ill, it could not have been difficult to silence the Rabbis on their own admissions. Clearly, their principle implied, that it was lawful on the Sabbath to do that which would save life or prevent death. To have taught otherwise, would virtually have involved murder. But if so, did it not also, in strictly logical sequence, imply this far wider principle, that it must be lawful to do good on the Sabbath? For, evidently, the omission of such good would have involved the doing of evil. Could this be the proper observance of God's holy day? There was no answer to such an argument; St. Mark expressly records that they dared not attempt a reply.[g] On the other hand, St. Matthew, while alluding to this terribly telling challenge,[h] records yet another and a personal argument. It seems that Christ publicly appealed to them: If any

[1] Thus, when a Rabbi was consulted, whether a man might on the Sabbath take a certain drink which had a purgative effect, he answered: 'If for pleasure it is lawful; if for healing forbidden' (Jer. Shabb. 14 c).

[2] Thus one of the Rabbis regarded fœtor of the breath as possibly dangerous

(u. s. 14 d).

[3] Displacement of the frontal bone, disease of the nerves leading from the ear to the upper jaw, an eye starting from its socket, severe inflammations, and swelling wounds, are specially mentioned.

poor man among them, who had one sheep, were in danger of losing CHAP
it through having fallen into a pit, would he not lift it out?   To be XXXV
sure, the Rabbinic Law ordered that food and drink should be lowered
to it, or else that some means should be furnished by which it might
either be kept up in the pit, or enabled to come out of it.ª   But even ª Shabb.
the Talmud discusses cases in which it was lawful to lift an animal 128 *b*
out of a pit on a Sabbath.ᵇ   There could be no doubt, at any rate, ᵇ Shabb.
that even if the Law was, at the time of Christ, as stringent as in the 117 *b*, about
Talmud, a man would have found some device, by which to recover the middle
the solitary sheep which constituted his possession.   And was not
the life of a human being to be more accounted of?   Surely, then,
on the Sabbath-day it was lawful to do good?   Yes—to do good, and
to neglect it, would have been to do evil.   Nay, according to their
own admission, should not a man, on the Sabbath, save life? or
should he, by omitting it, kill?

We can now imagine the scene in that Synagogue.   The place is
crowded.   Christ probably occupies a prominent position as leading
the prayers or teaching: a position whence He can see, and be seen
by all.   Here, eagerly bending forward, are the dark faces of the
Pharisees, expressive of curiosity, malice, cunning.   They are looking
round at a man whose right hand is withered,ᶜ perhaps putting him ᶜ St. Luke
forward, drawing attention to him, loudly whispering, ' Is it lawful vi. 6
to heal on the Sabbath-day?'   The Lord takes up the challenge.
He bids the man stand forth—right in the midst of them, where they
might all see and hear.   By one of those telling appeals, which go
straight to the conscience, He puts the analogous case of a poor man
who was in danger of losing his only sheep on the Sabbath: would
he not rescue it; and was not a man better than a sheep?   Nay, did
they not themselves enjoin a breach of the Sabbath-Law to save
human life?   Then, must He not do so; might He not do good
rather than evil?

They were speechless.   But a strange mixture of feeling was in
the Saviour's heart—strange to us, though it is but what Holy
Scripture always tells us of the manner in which God views sin and
the sinner, using terms, which, in their combination, seem grandly
incompatible: ' And when He had looked round about on them with
anger, being grieved at the hardening of their heart.   It was but
for a moment, and then, with life-giving power, He bade the man
stretch forth his hand.   Withered it was no longer, when the Word
had been spoken, and a new sap, a fresh life had streamed into it, as,
following the Saviour's Eye and Word, he slowly stretched it forth.

And as He stretched it forth, his hand was restored.[1] The Saviour had broken their Sabbath-Law, and yet He had not broken it, for neither by remedy, nor touch, nor outward application had He healed him. He had broken the Sabbath-rest, as God breaks it, when He sends, or sustains, or restores life, or does good: all unseen and unheard, without touch or outward application, by the Word of His Power, by the Presence of His Life.

But who after this will say, that it was Paul who first introduced into the Church either the idea that the Sabbath-Law in its Jewish form was no longer binding, or this, that the narrow forms of Judaism were burst by the new wine of that Kingdom, which is that of the Son of Man?

They had all seen it, this miracle of almost new creation. As He did it, He had been filled with sadness: as they saw it, 'they were filled with madness.'[a] So their hearts were hardened. They could not gainsay, but they went forth and took counsel with the Herodians against Him, how they might destroy Him. Presumably, then, He was within, or quite close by, the dominions of Herod, east of the Jordan. And the Lord withdrew once more, as it seems to us, into Gentile territory, probably that of the Decapolis. For, as He went about healing all, that needed it, in that great multitude that followed His steps, yet enjoining silence on them, this prophecy of Isaiah blazed into fulfilment: ' Behold My Servant, Whom I have chosen, My Beloved, in Whom My soul is well-pleased: I will put My Spirit upon Him, and He shall declare judgment to the Gentiles. He shall not strive nor cry aloud, neither shall any hear His Voice in the streets. A bruised reed shall He not break, and smoking flax shall He not quench, till He send forth judgment unto victory. And in His Name shall the Gentiles trust.'

And in His Name shall the Gentiles trust. Far out into the silence of those solitary upland hills of the Gentile world did the call, unheard and unheeded in Israel, travel. He had other sheep which were not of that fold. And down those hills, from the far-off lands, does the sound of the bells, as it comes nearer and nearer, tell that those other sheep, which are not of this fold, are gathering at His call to the Good Shepherd; and through these centuries, still louder and more manifold becomes this sound of nearing bells, till they shall all be gathered into one: one flock, one fold, one Shepherd.

---

[1] The tense indicates, that it was restored as he stretched it out. And this is spiritually significant. According to St. *Jerome* (Comm. in Matt. xii. 13), in the Gospel of the Nazarenes and Ebionites this man was described as a mason, and that he had besought Jesus to restore him, so that he might not have to beg for his bread.

CHAPTER XXXVI.

THE FEEDING OF THE FOUR THOUSAND—TO DALMANUTHA—'THE SIGN FROM HEAVEN'—JOURNEY TO CÆSAREA PHILIPPI—WHAT IS THE LEAVEN OF THE PHARISEES AND SADDUCEES?

(St. Matt. xv. 32—xvi. 12; St. Mark viii. 1-21.)

THEY might well gather to Jesus in their thousands, with their wants CHAP. of body and soul, these sheep wandering without a shepherd; for His XXXVI Ministry in that district, as formerly in Galilee, was about to draw to a close.   And here it is remarkable, that each time His prolonged stay and Ministry in a district were brought to a close with some supper, so to speak, some festive entertainment on his part.   The Galilean Ministry had closed with the feeding of the five thousand, the guests being mostly from Capernaum and the towns around, as far as Bethsaida (Julias), many in the number probably on their way to the Paschal feast at Jerusalem.[1]   But now at the second provision for the four thousand, with which His Decapolis Ministry closed, the guests were not strictly Jews, but semi-Gentile inhabitants of that district and its neighbourhood.   Lastly, his Judæan Ministry closed with the Last Supper.   At the first 'Supper,' the Jewish guests would fain have proclaimed Him Messiah-King; at the second, as 'the Son of Man,' He gave food to those Gentile multitudes which having been with Him those days, and consumed all their victuals during their stay with him, He could not send away fasting, lest they should faint by the way.   And on the last occasion, as the true Priest and Sacrifice, He fed His own with the true Paschal Feast, ere He sent them forth alone into the wilderness.   Thus these three 'Suppers' seem connected, each leading up, as it were, to the other.

There can, at any rate, be little doubt that this second feeding of the multitude took place in the Gentile Decapolis, and that those who sat down to the meal were chiefly the inhabitants of that district.[2]   If it be lawful, departing from strict history, to study the

---

[1] Comp. ch. xxix. of this Book.
[2] This appears from the whole context.

Comp. Bp. *Ellicott's* Histor. Lect. pp. 220, 221, and notes.

BOOK
III

symbolism of this event, as compared with the previous feeding of the five thousand who were Jews, somewhat singular differences will present themselves to the mind. On the former occasion there were five thousand fed with five loaves, when twelve baskets of fragments were left. On the second occasion, four thousand were fed from seven loaves, and seven baskets of fragments collected. It is at least curious, that the number *five* in the provision for the Jews is that of the Pentateuch, just as the number *twelve* corresponds to that of the tribes and of the Apostles. On the other hand, in the feeding of the Gentiles we mark the number *four*, which is the signature of the world, and *seven*, which is that of the Sanctuary. We would not by any means press it, as if these were, in the telling of the narrative, designed coincidences; but, just because they are undesigned, we value them, feeling that there is more of undesigned symbolism in all God's manifestations—in nature, in history, and in grace—than meets the eye of those who observe the merely phenomenal. Nay, does it not almost seem, as if all things were cast in the mould of heavenly realities, and all earth's 'shewbread' Bread of His Presence '?

On all general points the narratives of the two-fold miraculous feeding run so parallel, that it is not necessary again to consider this event in detail. But the attendant circumstances are so different, that only the most reckless negative criticism could insist, that one and the same event had been presented by the Evangelists as two separate occasions.[1] The broad lines of difference as to the number of persons, the provision, and the quantity of fragments left, cannot be overlooked. Besides, on the former occasion the repast was provided in the evening for those who had gone after Christ, and listened to Him all day, but who, in their eager haste, had come without victuals, when He would not dismiss them faint and hungry, because they had been so busy for the Bread of Life that they had forgotten that of earth. But on this second occasion, of the feeding of the Gentiles, the multitude had been three days with Him, and what sustenance they had brought must have failed, when, in His compassion, the Saviour would not send them to their homes fasting, lest they should faint by the way. This could not have befallen those Gentiles, who had come to the Christ for food to their souls. And, it must be kept in view, that Christ dismissed them, not, as before, because they would have made Him their King, but because Him-

---

[1] For a summary of the great differences between the two miracles, comp. Bp. *Ellicott*, u. s. pp. 221, 222. The statements of *Meyer* ad loc. are unsatisfactory.

self was about to depart from the place; and that, sending them CHAP.
to their homes, He could not send them to faint by the way. Yet XXXVI
another marked difference lies even in the designation of 'the
baskets' in which the fragments left were gathered. At the first
feeding, there were, as the Greek word shows, the small wicker-
baskets which each of the Twelve would carry in his hand. At the
second feeding they were the large baskets, in which provisions,
chiefly bread, were stored or carried for longer voyages.[1] For, on the
first occasion, when they passed into Israelitish territory—and, as
they might think, left their home for a very brief time—there was
not the same need to make provision for storing necessaries as on
the second, when they were on a lengthened journey, and passing
through, or tarrying in Gentile territory.

But the most noteworthy difference seems to us this—that on
the first occasion, they who were fed were Jews—on the second,
Gentiles. There is an exquisite little trait in the narrative which
affords striking, though utterly undesigned, evidence of it. In referring to the blessing which Jesus spake over the *first* meal, it was
noted,[2] that, in strict accordance with Jewish custom, He only
rendered thanks once, over the bread. But no such custom would
rule His conduct when dispensing the food to the Gentiles; and,
indeed, His speaking the blessing only over the bread, while He was
silent when distributing the fishes, would probably have given rise
to misunderstanding. Accordingly, we find it expressly stated that
He not only gave thanks over the bread, but also spake the blessing
over the fishes.[a] Nor should we, when marking such undesigned [a] St. Mark
evidences, omit to notice, that on the first occasion, which was imme- viii. 6, 7
diately before the Passover, the guests were, as three of the Evangelists expressly state, ranged on 'the grass,'[b] while, on the present [b] St. Matt.
occasion, which must have been several weeks later, when in the xiv. 19;
East the grass would be burnt up, we are told by the two Evangelists St. Mark
that they sat on 'the ground.'[3] Even the difficulty, raised by some, vi. 39; St.
as to the strange repetition of the disciples' reply, the outcome, in John vi. 10
part, of non-expectancy, and, hence, non-belief, and yet in part
also of such doubt as tends towards faith: 'Whence should we have,

---

[1] The κόφινος (St. Matt. xiv. 20) was the small handbasket (see ch. xxix), while the σπυρίς (the term used at the feeding of the four thousand) is the large provision-basket or hamper, such as that in which St. Paul was let down over the wall at Damascus (Acts ix. 25). What makes it more marked is, that the distinction of the two words is kept up in the reference to the two miracles (St. Matt. xvi. 9, 10).

[2] See ch. xxix.

[3] Literally, ' upon the earth.'

in a solitary place,[1] so many loaves as to fill so great a multitude?'
seems to us only confirmatory of the narrative, so psychologically
true is it.   There is no need for the ingenious apology,[2] that, in the
remembrance and tradition of the first and second feeding, the similarity of the two events had led to greater similarity in their narration than the actual circumstances would perhaps have warranted.
Interesting thoughts are here suggested by the remark,[3] that it is
not easy to transport ourselves into the position and feelings of those
who had witnessed such a miracle as that of the first feeding of the
multitude.   'We think of the Power as inherent, and, therefore,
permanent.   To them it might seem intermittent—a gift that came
and went.'   And this might seem borne out by the fact that, ever
since, their wants had been supplied in the ordinary way, and that,
even on the first occasion, they had been directed to gather up the
fragments of the heaven-supplied meal.

But more than this requires to be said.   First, we must here
once more remind ourselves, that the former provision was for Jews,
and the disciples might, from their standpoint, well doubt, or at least
not assume, that the same miracle would supply the need of the
Gentiles, and the same board be surrounded by Jew and Gentile.
But, further, the repetition of the same question by the disciples
really indicated only a sense of their own inability, and not a doubt
of the Saviour's power of supply, since on this occasion it was not,
as on the former, accompanied by a request on their part, to send
the multitude away.   Thus the very repetition of the question might
be a humble reference to the past, of which they dared not, in the
circumstances, ask the repetition.

Yet, even if it were otherwise, the strange forgetfulness of Christ's
late miracle on the part of the disciples, and their strange repetition
of the self-same question which had once—and, as it might seem to
us, for ever—been answered by wondrous deed, need not surprise
us.   To them the miraculous on the part of Christ must ever have
been the new, or else it would have ceased to be the miraculous.
Nor did they ever fully realise it, till after His Resurrection they
understood, and worshipped Him as God Incarnate.   And it is only
realising faith of this, which it was intended gradually to evolve
during Christ's Ministry on earth, that enables us to apprehend the
Divine Help as, so to speak, incarnate and ever actually present in
Christ.   And yet even thus, how often we do, who have so believed

---

[1] The word ἐρημια means a specially lonely place.   [2] Of *Bleek.*
[3] By Dean *Plumptre,* ad loc.

in Him, forget the Divine provision which has come to us so lately, and repeat, though perhaps not with the same doubt, yet with the same want of certainty, the questions with which we had at first met the Saviour's challenge of our faith. And even at the last it is met, as by the prophet, in sight of the apparently impossible, by: 'Lord, Thou knowest.'[a] More frequently, alas! is it met by non-belief, misbelief, disbelief, or doubt, engendered by misunderstanding or forgetfulness of that which past experience, as well as the knowledge of Him, should long ago have indelibly written on our minds.

On the occasion referred to in the preceding narrative, those who had lately taken counsel together against Jesus—the Pharisees and the Herodians, or, to put it otherwise, the Pharisees and Sadducees—were not present. For, those who, politically speaking, were 'Herodians,' might also, though perhaps not religiously speaking, yet from the Jewish standpoint of St. Matthew, be designated as, or else include, Sadducees.[1] But they were soon to reappear on the scene, as Jesus came close to the Jewish territory of Herod. We suppose the feeding of the multitude to have taken place in the Decapolis, and probably on, or close to, the Eastern shore of the Lake of Galilee. As Jesus sent away the multitude whom He had fed, He took ship with His disciples, and ' came into the borders of Magadan,'[b][2] or, as St. Mark puts it, ' the parts of Dalmanutha.' 'The borders of Magadan' must evidently refer to the same district as ' the parts of Dalmanutha.' The one may mark the extreme point of the district southwards, the other northwards—or else, the points west[3] and east—in the locality where He and His disciples landed. This is, of course, only a suggestion, since neither ' Magadan,' nor ' Dalmanutha,' has been identified. This only we infer, that the place was close to, yet not within the boundary of, strictly Jewish territory; since on His arrival there the Pharisees are said to ' come forth '[c]—a word ' which implies, that they resided elsewhere,'[4] though, of course, in the neighbourhood. Accordingly, we would seek Magadan south of the Lake of Tiberias, and near to the borders of Galilee, but within the Decapolis. Several sites bear at present somewhat similar names. In regard to the strange and un-Jewish name of *Dalmanutha*, such utterly unlikely conjectures have been made, that one based on ety-

a Ezek. xxxvii. 3

b St. Matt. xv. 39

c St. Mark viii. 11

---

[1] Compare, however, vol. i. pp. 238, 240, and Book V. ch. iii. Where the political element was dominant, the religious distinction might not be so clearly marked.

[2] It need scarcely be said that the best reading is Magadan, not Magdala.

[3] It has been ingeniously suggested, that Magadan might represent a Megiddo, being a form intermediate between the Hebrew Megiddon and the Asyrian Magadû.

[4] Canon *Cook* in the 'Speaker's Commentary,' ad loc.

mology may be hazarded.   If we take from *Dalmanutha* the Aramaic termination -*utha*, and regard the initial *de* as a prefix, we have the word *Laman, Limin,* or *Liminah* (לְמָן, לְמִין, לְמִינָה =λιμήν), which, in Rabbinic Hebrew, means *a bay,* or *port,* and Dalmanutha might have been the place of a small bay.   Possibly, it was the name given to the bay close to the ancient *Tarichœa,* the modern *Kerak,* so terribly famous for a sea-fight, or rather a horrible butchery of poor fugitives, when Tarichæa was taken by the Romans in the great Jewish war. Close by, the Lake forms a bay (*Laman*), and if, as a modern writer asserts,[1] the fortress of Tarichæa was surrounded by a ditch fed by the Jordan and the Lake, so that the fortress could be converted into an island, we see additional reason for the designation of *Lamanutha*.[2]

It was from the Jewish territory of Galilee, close by, that the Pharisees now came 'with the Sadducees' tempting Him with questions, and desiring that His claims should be put to the ultimate arbitrament of 'a sign from heaven.'   We can quite understand such a challenge on the part of Sadducees, who would disbelieve the heavenly Mission of Christ, or, indeed, to use a modern term, any supra-naturalistic connection between heaven and earth.   But, in the mouth of the Pharisees also, it had a special meaning. Certain supposed miracles had been either witnessed by, or testified to them, as done by Christ.   As they now represented it—since Christ laid claims which, in their view, were inconsistent with the doctrine received in Israel, preached a Kingdom quite other than that of Jewish expectancy—was at issue with all Jewish customs—more than this, was a breaker of the Law, in its most important commandments, as they understood them—it followed that, according to Deut. xiii., He was a false prophet, who was not to be listened to.   Then, also, must the miracles which He did have been wrought by the power of Beelzebul, 'the lord of idolatrous worship,' the very prince of devils. But had there been real signs, and might it not all have been an illusion?   Let Him show them 'a sign,'[3] and let that sign come direct from heaven!

Two striking instances from Rabbinic literature will show, that this demand of the Pharisees was in accordance with their notions and practice.   We read that, when a certain Rabbi was asked by his disciples about the time of Messiah's Coming, he replied: 'I am

---

[1] *Sepp,* ap. *Böttger,* Topogr. Lex. zu Fl. Josephus, p. 240.

[2] Bearing in mind that Tarichæa was the chief depôt for salting the fish for export, the disciples may have had some connections with the place. The word here used would, to judge

by analogous instances, be אוֹת (*Oth*), and not סִימָן (*Siman*), as *Wünsche* suggests, even though the word is formed from the Greek σημεῖον. But the Rabbinic *Siman* seems to me to have a different shade of meaning.

afraid that you will also ask me for a sign.' When they promised they would not do so, he told them that the gate of Rome would fall and be rebuilt, and fall again, when there would not be time to restore it, ere the Son of David came. On this they pressed him, despite his remonstrance, for 'a sign,' when this was given them— that the waters which issued from the cave of Pamias were turned into blood.[a][1] Again, as regards 'a sign from heaven,' it is said that Rabbi Eliezer, when his teaching was challenged, successively appealed to certain 'signs.' First, a locust-tree moved at his bidding one hundred, or, according to some, four hundred cubits. Next, the channels of water were made to flow backwards; then the walls of the Academy leaned forward, and were only arrested at the bidding of another Rabbi. Lastly, Eliezer exclaimed: 'If the Law is as I teach, let it be proved from heaven!' when a voice fell from the sky (the *Bath Qol*): 'What have ye to do with Rabbi Eliezer, for the Halakhah is as he teaches?'[b]

It was, therefore, no strange thing, when the Pharisees asked of Jesus 'a sign from heaven,' to attest His claims and teaching. The answer which He gave was among the most solemn which the leaders of Israel could have heard, and He spake it in deep sorrow of spirit.[c] They had asked Him virtually for some sign of His Messiahship; some striking vindication from heaven of His claims. It would be given them only too soon. We have already seen,[2] that there was a Coming of Christ in His Kingdom—a vindication of His kingly claim before His apostate rebellious subjects, when they who would not have Him to reign over them, but betrayed and crucified Him, would have their commonwealth and city, their polity and Temple, destroyed. By the lurid light of the flames of Jerusalem and the Sanctuary were the words on the cross to be read again. God would vindicate His claims by laying low the pride of their rebellion. The burning of Jerusalem was God's answer to the Jews' cry, 'Away with Him—we have no king but Cæsar;' the thousands of crosses on which the Romans hanged their captives, the terrible counterpart of the Cross on Golgotha.

It was to this, that Jesus referred in His reply to the Pharisees and 'Sadducean' Herodians. How strange! Men could discern by the appearance of the sky whether the day would be fair or stormy.[3]

Marginal notes:
[a] Sanh. 98 a last 4 lines
[b] Baba Mez. 59 b, line 4 from top, &c.
[c] St. Mark viii. 12

---

[1] However, this (and, for that matter, the next Haggadah also) may have been intended to be taken in an allegoric or parabolic sense, though there is no hint given to that effect,

[2] See ch. xxvii. vol. i. p. 647.

[3] Although some of the best MSS. omit St. Matt. xvi. 2, beginning 'When it is evening,' to the end of ver. 3, most critics are agreed that it should be retained. But the words in italics in vv. 2 and 3 should be left out, so as to mark exclamations.

BOOK
III

And yet, when all the signs of the gathering storm, that would destroy their city and people, were clearly visible, they, the leaders of
the people, failed to perceive them! Israel asked for 'a sign'! No
sign should be given the doomed land and city other than that which
had been given to Nineveh: 'the sign of Jonah.'[1]   The only sign to
Nineveh was Jonah's solemn warning of near judgment, and his call
to repentance—and the only sign now, or rather 'unto this generation no sign,'[a] was the warning cry of judgment and the loving call
to repentance.[b]

ᵃ St. Mark
viii. 12
ᵇ St. Luke
xix. 41–44

It was but a natural, almost necessary, sequence, that 'He left
them and departed.' Once more the ship, which bore Him and His
disciples, spread its sails towards the coast of Bethsaida-Julias. He
was on His way to the utmost limit of the land, to Cæsarea Philippi,
in pursuit of His purpose to delay the final conflict. For the great
crisis must begin, as it would end, in Jerusalem, and at the Feast;
it would begin at the Feast of Tabernacles,[c] and it would end at the
following Passover. But by the way, the disciples themselves showed
how little even they, who had so long and closely followed Christ, understood His teaching, and how prone to misapprehension their spiritual
dulness rendered them. Yet it was not so gross and altogether incomprehensible, as the common reading of what happened would imply.

ᶜ St. John
vii.

When the Lord touched the other shore, His mind and heart
were still full of the scene from which He had lately passed. For
truly, on this demand for a sign did the future of Israel seem to
hang. Perhaps it is not presumptuous to suppose, that the journey
across the Lake had been made in silence on His part, so deeply
were mind and heart engrossed with the fate of His own royal city.
And now, when they landed, they carried ashore the empty provision-
baskets; for, as, with his usual attention to details, St. Mark notes,
they had only brought one loaf of bread with them. In fact, in
the excitement and hurry 'they forgot to take bread' with them.
Whether or not something connected with this arrested the attention
of Christ, He at last broke the silence, speaking that which was so
much on His mind. He warned them, as greatly they needed it, of the
leaven with which Pharisees and Sadducees had, each in their own
manner, leavened, and so corrupted,[2] the holy bread of Scripture-
truth. The disciples, aware that in their hurry and excitement they

---

[1] So according to the best reading.
[2] The figurative meaning of leaven, as
that which morally corrupts, was familiar
to the Jews. Thus the word שְׂאוֹר
(Seor) is used in the sense of 'moral

leaven' hindering the good in Ber. 17 a
while the verb חָמֵץ (chamets) 'to be
come leavened,' is used to indicate moral
deterioration in Rosh haSh. 3 b, 4 a.

had forgotten bread, misunderstood these words of Christ—although not in the utterly unaccountable manner which commentators generally suppose: as implying 'a caution against procuring bread from His enemies.' It is well-nigh impossible, that the disciples could have understood the warning of Christ as meaning any such thing—even irrespective of the consideration, that a prohibition to buy bread from either the Pharisees or Sadducees would have involved an impossibility. The misunderstanding of the disciples was, if unwarrantable, at least rational. They thought the words of Christ implied, that in His view they had not *forgotten* to bring bread, but purposely omitted to do so, in order, like the Pharisees and Sadducees, to 'seek of Him a sign' of His Divine Messiahship— nay, to oblige Him to show such—that of miraculous provision in their want. The mere suspicion showed what was in their minds, and pointed to their danger. This explains how, in His reply, Jesus reproved them, not for utter want of discernment, but only for 'little faith.' It was their lack of faith—the very leaven of the Pharisees and Sadducees—which had suggested such a thought. Again, if the experience of the past—their own twice-repeated question, and the practical answer which it had received in the miraculous provision of not only enough, but to spare—had taught them anything, it should have been to believe, that the needful provision of their wants by Christ was not 'a sign,' such as the Pharisees had asked, but what faith might ever expect from Christ, when following after, or waiting upon, Him. Then understood they truly, that it was not of the leaven of bread that He had bidden them beware—that His mysterious words bore no reference to bread, nor to their supposed omission to bring it for the purpose of eliciting a sign from Him, but pointed to the far more real danger of 'the teaching of the Pharisees and Sadducees,' which had underlain the demand for a sign from heaven.

Here, as always, Christ rather suggests than gives the interpretation of His meaning. And this is the law of His teaching. Our modern Pharisees and Sadducees, also, too often ask of him a sign from heaven in evidence of His claims. And we also too often misunderstand His warning to us concerning their leaven. Seeing the scanty store in our basket, our little faith is busy with thoughts about possible signs in multiplying the one loaf which we have, forgetful that, where Christ is, faith may ever expect all that is needful, and that our care should only be in regard to the teaching which might leaven and corrupt that on which our souls are fed.

CHAPTER XXXVII.

THE GREAT CONFESSION—THE GREAT COMMISSION—THE GREAT INSTRUC-
TION—THE GREAT TEMPTATION—THE GREAT DECISION.

(St. Matt. xvi. 13-28; St. Mark viii. 27—ix. 1; St. Luke ix. 18-27.)

BOOK
III

IF we are right in identifying the little bay—Dalmanutha—with the
neighbourhood of Tarichæa, yet another link of strange coincidence
connects the prophetic warning spoken there with its fulfilment.
From Dalmanutha our Lord passed across the Lake to Cæsarea
Philippi. From Cæsarea Philippi did Vespasian pass through Tiberias to Tarichæa, when the town and people were destroyed, and the
blood of the fugitives reddened the Lake, and their bodies choked
its waters. Even amidst the horrors of the last Jewish war, few
spectacles could have been so sickening as that of the wild stand at
Tarichæa, ending with the butchery of 6,500 on land and sea, and
lastly, the vile treachery by which they, to whom mercy had been
promised, were lured into the circus at Tiberias, when the weak and
old, to the number of about 1,200, were slaughtered, and the rest

^a Jos. Jew.
War iii. 10

—upwards of 30,400—sold into slavery.ᵃ¹ Well might He, Who
foresaw and foretold that terrible end, standing on that spot, deeply
sigh in spirit as He spake to them who asked 'a sign,' and yet saw
not what even ordinary discernment might have perceived of the red
and lowering sky overhead.

From Dalmanutha, across the Lake, then by the plain where so
lately the five thousand had been fed, and near to Bethsaida, would
the road of Christ and His disciples lead to the capital of the Tetrarch Philip, the ancient Paneas, or, as it was then called, Cæsarea
Philippi, the modern Banias. Two days' journey would accomplish
the whole distance. There would be no need of taking the route
now usually followed, by Safed. Straight northwards from the Lake
of Galilee, a distance of about ten miles, leads the road to the

---

¹ If it were for no other reason than
the mode in which the ex-general of the
Galileans, *Josephus*, tells this story, he
would deserve our execration.

uppermost Jordan-Lake, that now called *Huleh*, the ancient Merom.[1]   CHAP.
As we ascend from the shores of Gennesaret, we have a receding   XXXVII
view of the whole Lake and the Jordan-valley beyond.   Before us
rise hills; over them, to the west, are the heights of Safed; beyond
them swells the undulating plain between the two ranges of Anti-
Libanus; far off is Hermon, with its twin snow-clad heads ('the
Hermons'), [a] and, in the dim far background, majestic Lebanon.   It   [a] Ps. xlii. 6
is scarcely likely, that Jesus and His disciples skirted the almost
impenetrable marsh and jungle by Lake Merom.   It was there, that
Joshua had fought the last and decisive battle against Jabin and his
confederates, by which Northern Palestine was gained to Israel.[b]   We   [b] Josh. xi. 1-5
turn north of the Lake, and west to Kedes, the Kedesh Naphtali of
the Bible, the home of Barak.   We have now passed from the limestone of Central Palestine into the dark basalt formation.   How
splendidly that ancient Priest-City of Refuge lay!   In the rich
heritage of Naphtali,[c] Kedesh was one of the fairest spots.   As we   [c] Deut. xxxiii. 23
climb the steep hill above the marshes of Merom, we have before us
one of the richest plains of about two thousand acres.   We next
pass through olive-groves and up a gentle slope.   On a knoll before
us, at the foot of which gushes a copious spring, lies the ancient
Kedesh.

The scenery is very similar, as we travel on towards Cæsarea
Philippi.   About an hour and a half farther, we strike the ancient
Roman road.   We are now amidst vines and mulberry-trees.   Passing
through a narrow rich valley, we ascend through a rocky wilderness
of hills, where the woodbine luxuriantly trails around the plane-
trees.   On the height there is a glorious view back to Lake Merom
and the Jordan-valley; forward, to the snowy peaks of Hermon; east,
to height on height, and west, to peaks now only crowned with
ruins.   We still continued along the height, then descended a steep
slope, leaving, on our left, the ancient Abel Beth Maachah,[d] the   [d] 2 Sam.xx. 14
modern *Abil*.   Another hour, and we are in a plain where all the
springs of the Jordan unite.   The view from here is splendid, and
the soil most rich, the wheat crops being quite ripe in the beginning
of May.   Half an hour more, and we cross a bridge over the bright
blue waters of the Jordan, or rather of the Hasbany, which, under a
very wilderness of oleanders, honeysuckle, clematis, and wild rose, rush
among huge boulders, between walls of basalt.   We leave aside, at

---

[1] For the geographical details I must
refer to the words of *Stanley* and *Tris-*
tram, and to *Bädeker*'s Palästina.   I
have not deemed it necessary to make
special quotation of my authority in each
case.

a distance of about half an hour to the east, the ancient Dan (the modern Tell-Kady), even more glorious in its beauty and richness than what we have passed. Dan lies on a hill above the plain. On the western side of it, under overhanging thickets of oleander and other trees, and amidst masses of basalt boulders, rise what are called ' the lower springs ' of Jordan, issuing as a stream from a basin sixty paces wide, and from a smaller source close by. The ' lower springs ' supply the largest proportion of what forms the Jordan. And from Dan olive-groves and oak-glades slope up to Banias, or Cæsarea Philippi.

The situation of the ancient Cæsarea Philippi (1,147 feet above the sea) is, indeed, magnificent. Nestling amid three valleys on a terrace in the angle of Hermon, it is almost shut out from view by cliffs and woods. 'Everywhere there is a wild medley of cascades, mulberry trees, fig-trees, dashing torrents, festoons of vines, bubbling fountains, reeds, and ruins, and the mingled music of birds and waters.' [1] The vegetation and fertility all around are extraordinary. The modern village of Banias is within the walls of the old fortifications, and the ruins show that it must anciently have extended far southwards. But the most remarkable points remain to be described. The western side of a steep mountain, crowned by the ruins of an ancient castle, forms an abrupt rock-wall. Here, from out an immense cavern, bursts a river. These are 'the upper sources' of the Jordan. This cave, an ancient heathen sanctuary of Pan, gave its earliest name of Paneas to the town. Here Herod, when receiving the tetrarchy from Augustus, built a temple in his honour. On the rocky wall close by, votive niches may still be traced, one of them bearing the Greek inscription, ' Priest of Pan.' When Herod's son, Philip, received the tetrarchy, he enlarged and greatly beautified the ancient Paneas, and called it in honour of the Emperor, Cæsarea Philippi. The castle-mount (about 1,000 feet above Paneas), takes nearly an hour to ascend, and is separated by a deep valley from the flank of Mount Hermon. The castle itself (about two miles from Banias) is one of the best preserved ruins, its immense bevelled structure resembling the ancient forts of Jerusalem, and showing its age. It followed the irregularities of the mountain, and was about 1,000 feet long by 200 wide. The eastern and higher part formed, as in Machærus, a citadel within the castle. In some parts the rock rises higher than the walls. The views, sheer down the precipitous sides of the mountain, into the valleys and far away, are magnificent.

[1] *Tristram*, Land of Israel, p. 586.

It seems worth while, even at such length, to describe the scenery along this journey, and the look and situation of Cæsarea, when we recall the importance of the events enacted there, or in the immediate neighbourhood.   It was into this chiefly Gentile district, that the Lord now withdrew with His disciples after that last and decisive question of the Pharisees.   It was here that, as His question, like Moses' rod, struck their hearts, there leaped from the lips of Peter the living, life-spreading waters of his confession.   It may have been, that this rock-wall below the castle, from under which sprang Jordan, or the rock on which the castle stood, supplied the material suggestion for Christ's words: ' Thou art Peter, and on this rock will I build My Church.' [1]   In Cæsarea, or its immediate neighbourhood,[2] did the Lord spend, with His disciples, six days after this confession; and here, close by, on one of the heights of snowy Hermon, was the scene of the Transfiguration, the light of which shone for ever into the hearts of the disciples on their dark and tangled path;[a] nay, far beyond that—beyond life and death—beyond the grave and the judgment, to the perfect brightness of the Resurrection-day.

As we think of it, there seems nothing strange in it, but all most wise and most gracious, that such events should have taken place far away from Galilee and Israel, in the lonely grandeur of the shadows of Hermon, and even amongst a chiefly Gentile population. Not in Judæa, nor even in Galilee—but far away from the Temple, the Synagogue, the Priests, Pharisees and Scribes, was the first confession of the Church made, and on this confession its first foundations laid.   Even this spoke of near judgment and doom to what had once been God's chosen congregation.   And all that happened, though Divinely shaped as regards the end, followed in a natural and orderly succession of events.   Let us briefly recall the circumstances, which in the previous chapters have been described in detail.

It had been needful to leave Capernaum.   The Galilean Ministry of the Christ was ended, and, alike the active persecutions of the Pharisees from Jerusalem, the inquiries of Herod, whose hands, stained with the blood of the Baptist, were tremblingly searching for his greater Successor, and the growing indecision and unfitness of the people—as well as the state of the disciples—pointed to the need for leaving Galilee.   Then followed ' the Last Supper ' to Israel on the eastern shore of Lake Gennesaret, when they would have

[a] 2 Pet. i. 19

---

[1] So Dean *Stanley*, with his usual charm of language, though topographically not quite correctly (Sinai and Palestine, p. 395).
[2] Nothing in the above obliges us to infer, that the words of Peter's confession were spoken in Cæsarea itself. The place might have been in view or in the memory.

made Him a King.   He must now withdraw quite away, out of the boundaries of Israel.   Then came that miraculous night-journey, the brief Sabbath-stay at Capernaum by the way, the journey through Tyrian and Sidonian territory, and round to the Decapolis, the teaching and healing there, the gathering of the multitude to Him, together with that 'Supper, ' which closed His Ministry there—and, finally, the withdrawal to Tarichæa, where His Apostles, as fishermen of the Lake, may have had business-connections, since the place was the great central depôt for selling and preparing the fish for export.

In that distant and obscure corner, on the boundary-line between Jew and Gentile, had that greatest crisis in the history of the world occurred, which sealed the doom of Israel, and in their place substituted the Gentiles as citizens of the Kingdom.   And, in this respect also, it is most significant, that the confession of the Church likewise took place in territory chiefly inhabited by Gentiles, and the Transfiguration on Mount Hermon.   That crisis had been the public challenge of the Pharisees and Sadducees, that Jesus should legitimate His claims to the Messiahship by a sign from heaven.   It is not too much to assert, that neither His questioners, nor even His disciples, understood the answer of Jesus, nor yet perceived the meaning of His 'sign.'   To the Pharisees Jesus would seem to have been defeated, and to stand self-convicted of having made Divine claims which, when challenged, He could not substantiate.   He had hitherto elected(as they, who understood not His teaching, would judge) to prove Himself the Messiah by the miracles which He had wrought—and now, when met on His own ground, He had publicly declined, or at least evaded, the challenge.   He had conspicuously—almost self-confessedly— failed!   At least, so it would appear to those who could not understand His reply and ' sigh. '   We note that a similar final challenge was addressed to Jesus by the High-Priest, when he adjured Him to say, whether He was what He claimed.   His answer then was an assertion—not a proof; and, unsupported as it seemed, His questioners would only regard it as blasphemy.

But what of the disciples, who (as we have seen) would probably understand 'the sign' of Christ little better than the Pharisees? That what might seem Christ's failure, in not daring to meet the challenge of His questioners, must have left some impression on them, is not only natural, but appears even from Christ's warning of the leaven—that is, of the teaching of the Pharisees and Sadducees. Indeed, that this unmet challenge and virtual defeat of Jesus *did* make lasting and deepest impression in His disfavour, is evident

from the later challenge of His own relatives to go and meet the
Pharisees at headquarters in Judæa, and to show openly, if He
could, by His works, that He was the Messiah.[a] All the more
remarkable appears Christ's dealing with His disciples, His demand
on, and training of their faith. It must be remembered, that His
last 'hard' sayings at Capernaum had led to the defection of many,
who till then had been His disciples.[b] Undoubtedly this had already
tried their faith, as appears from the question of Christ: 'Will ye
also go away?[c] It was this wise and gracious dealing with them—
this putting the one disappointment of doubt, engendered by what
they could not understand, against their whole past experience in
following Him, which enabled them to overcome. And it is this
which also enables us to answer the doubt, perhaps engendered by
inability to understand seemingly unintelligible, hard sayings of
Christ, such as that to the disciples about giving them His Flesh to
eat, or about His being the Living Bread from heaven. And, this
alternative being put to them: would they, could they, after their
experience of Him, go away from Him, they overcame, as we overcome, through what almost sounds like a cry of despair, yet is a shout
of victory: 'Lord, to whom shall we go? Thou hast the words of
eternal life.'

And all that followed only renewed and deepened the trial of
faith, which had commenced at Capernaum. We shall, perhaps, best
understand it when following the progress of this trial in him who,
at last, made shipwreck of his faith: Judas Iscariot. Without
attempting to gaze into the mysterious abyss of the Satanic element
in his apostasy, we may trace his course in its psychological development. We must not regard Judas as a monster, but as one with
passions like ourselves. True, there was one terrible master-passion
in his soul—covetousness; but that was only the downward, lower
aspect of what seems, and to many really is, that which leads to the
higher and better—ambition. It had been thoughts of Israel's King
which had first set his imagination on fire, and brought him to follow
the Messiah. Gradually, increasingly, came the disenchantment.
It was quite another Kingdom, that of Christ; quite another Kingship than what had set Judas aglow. This feeling was deepened as
events proceeded. His confidence must have been terribly shaken
when the Baptist was beheaded. What a contrast to the time when
his voice had bent the thousands of Israel, as trees in the wind! So
this had been nothing—and the Baptist must be written off, not as
for, but as really against, Christ. Then came the next disappoint-

[a] St. John
vii. 1–5

[b] St. John
vi. 60–66;
comp.
St. Matt.
xv. 12

[c] St. John
vi. 67

ment, when Jesus would not be made King. Why not—if He were King? And so on, step by step, till the final depth was reached, when Jesus would not, or could not—which was it?—meet the public challenge of the Pharisees. We take it, that it was then that the leaven pervaded and leavened Judas in heart and soul.

We repeat it, that what so, and permanently, penetrated Judas, could not (as Christ's warning shows) have left the others wholly unaffected. The very presence of Judas with them must have had its influence. And how did Christ deal with it? There was, first, the silent sail across the Lake, and then the warning which put them on their guard, lest the little leaven should corrupt the bread of the Sanctuary, on which they had learned to live. The littleness of their faith must be corrected; it must grow and become strong. And so we can understand what follows. It was after solitary prayer—no ᵃ St. Luke
ix. 18 doubt for them ᵃ—that, with reference to the challenge of the Pharisees, ' the leaven ' that threatened them, He now gathered up all their experience of the past by putting to them the question, what men, the people who had watched His Works and heard His Words, regarded Him as being. Even on them some conviction had been wrought by their observance of Him. It marked Him out (as the disciples said) as different from all around, nay, from all ordinary men: like the Baptist, or Elijah, or as if He were one of the old prophets alive again. But, if even the multitude had gathered such knowledge of Him, what was their experience, who had always been with Him? Answered he, who most truly represented the Church, because he combined with the most advanced experience of the three most intimate disciples the utmost boldness of confession: ' Thou art the Christ! '

And so in part was this 'leaven' of the Pharisees purged! Yet not wholly. For then it was, that Christ spake to them of His sufferings and death, and that the resistance of Peter showed how deeply that leaven had penetrated. And then followed the grand contrast presented by Christ, between minding the things of men and those of God, with the warning which it implied. and the monition as to the necessity of bearing the cross of contempt, and the absolute call to do so, as addressed to those who would be His disciples. Here, then, the contest about ' the sign,' or rather the challenge about the Messiahship, was carried from the mental into the moral sphere, and so decided. Six days more of quiet waiting and growth of faith, and it was met, rewarded, crowned, and perfected by the sight on the Mount of Transfiguration; yet, even so, perceived only as through the heaviness of sleep.

Thus far for the general arrangement of these events. We shall now be prepared better to understand the details. It was certainly not for personal reasons, but to call attention to the impression made even on the popular mind, to correct its defects, and to raise the minds of the Apostles to far higher thoughts, that He asked them about the opinions of men concerning Himself. Their difference proved not only their incompetence to form a right view, but also how many-sided Christ's teaching must have been. We are probably correct in supposing, that popular opinion did not point to Christ as literally the Baptist, Elijah, Jeremiah, or one of the other prophets who had long been dead. For, although the literal reappearance of Elijah, and probably also of Jeremiah,[1] was expected, the Pharisees did not teach, nor the Jews believe in, a transmigration of souls. Besides, no one looked for the return of any of the other old prophets, nor could any one have seriously imagined, that Jesus was, literally, John the Baptist, since all knew them to have been contemporaries.[2] Rather would it mean, that some saw in Him the continuation of the work of John, as heralding and preparing the way of the Messiah, or, if they did not believe in John, of that of Elijah; while to others He seemed a second Jeremiah, denouncing woe on Israel,[3] and calling to tardy repentance; or else one of those old prophets, who had spoken either of the near judgment or of the coming glory. But, however men differed on these points, in this all agreed, that they regarded Him not as an ordinary man or teacher, but His Mission as straight from heaven; and, alas, in this also, that they did *not* view Him as the Messiah. Thus far, then, there was already retrogression in popular opinion, and thus far had the Pharisees already succeeded.

There is a significant emphasis in the words, with which Jesus

---

[1] I confess, however, to strong doubts on this point. Legends of the hiding of the tabernacle, ark, and altar of incense on Mount Nebo by Jeremiah, were, indeed, combined with an expectation that these precious possessions would be restored in Messianic times (2 Macc. ii. 1–7), but it is expressly added in ver. 8, that 'the Lord' Himself, and not the prophet, would show their place of concealment. Dean *Plumptre's* statement, that the Pharisees taught, and the Jews believed in, the doctrine of the transmigration of souls must have arisen from the misapprehension of what Josephus said, to which reference has already been made in the chapter on 'The Pharisees, Sadducees, and Essenes.' The first distinct

mention of the reappearance of Jeremiah, along with Elijah, to restore the ark, &c., is in *Josippon ben Gorion* (lib. i. c. 21), but here also only in the Cod. *Munster.*, not in that used by *Breithaupt.* The age of the work of *Josippon* is in dispute; probably we may date it from the tenth century of our era. The only other testimony about the reappearance of Jeremiah is in 4 Esd. (2 Esd.) ii. 18. But the book is post-Christian, and, in that section especially, evidently borrows from the Christian Scriptures.

[2] On the vague fears of Herod, see vol. i. p. 675.

[3] A vision of Jeremiah in a dream was supposed to betoken chastisements (Ber. 57 *e*, line 7 from top).

BOOK
III

* St. Mark
viii. 27, 29

b St. Matt.
xvi. 16

c Rom. x. 10

turned from the opinion of ' the multitudes ' to elicit the faith of the disciples: ' But you, whom do *you* say that I am? ' It is the more marked, as the former question was equally emphasised by the use of the article (in the original): ' Who do the men say that I am? ' a In that moment it leaped, by the power of God, to the lips of Peter: ' Thou art the Christ (the Messiah), the Son of the Living God.' b St. Chrysostom has beautifully designated Peter as ' the mouth of the Apostles '—and we recall, in this connection, the words of St. Paul as casting light on the representative character of Peter's confession as that of the Church, and hence on the meaning of Christ's reply, and its equally representative application: ' With the mouth confession is made unto salvation.' c The words of the confession are given somewhat differently by the three Evangelists. From our standpoint, the briefest form (that of St. Mark): ' Thou art the Christ,' means quite as much as the fullest (that of St. Matthew): ' Thou art the Christ, the Son of the Living God.' We can thus understand, how the latter might be truthfully adopted, and, indeed, would be the most truthful, accurate, and suitable in a Gospel primarily written for the Jews. And here we notice, that the most exact form of the words seems that in the Gospel of St. Luke: ' The Christ of God.'

In saying this, so far from weakening, we strengthen the import of this glorious confession. For first, we must keep in view, that the confession: ' Thou art the Messiah ' is also that: ' Thou art the Son of the Living God.' If, according to the Gospels, we believe that Jesus was the true Messiah, promised to the fathers—' the Messiah of God '—we cannot but believe that He is ' the Son of the Living God.' Scripture and reason equally point to this conclusion from the premisses. But, further, we must view such a confession, even though made in the power of God, in its historical connection. The words must have been such as Peter could have uttered, and the disciples acquiesced in, at the time. Moreover, they should mark a distinct connection with, and yet progress upon, the past. All these conditions are fulfilled by the view here taken. The *full* knowledge, in the sense of really understanding, that He was the Son of the Living

d Comp.
Rom. i. 4

e St. Matt.
xiv. 33

God, came to the disciples only after the Resurrection. d Previously to the confession of Peter, the ship's company, that had witnessed His walking on the water, had owned: ' Of a truth Thou art the Son of God,' e but not in the sense in which a well-informed, believing Jew would hail Him as the Messiah, and ' the Son of the Living God,' designating both His Office and His Nature—and these two in their combination. Again, Peter himself had made a confession of Christ, when, after his discourse at Capernaum, so many of His disciples had forsaken Him. It had been: 'We have believed, and know that Thou art the Holy One of God.' [a][1] The mere mention of these words shows both their internal connection with those of his last and crowning confession: 'Thou art the Christ of God,' and the immense progress made.

[a] St. John vi. 69

The more closely we view it, the loftier appears the height of this confession. We think of it as an advance on Peter's past ; we think of it in its remembered contrast to the late challenge of the Pharisees, and as so soon following on the felt danger of their leaven. And we think of it, also, in its almost immeasurable distance from the appreciative opinion of the better disposed among the people. In the words of this confession Peter has consciously reached the firm ground of Messianic acknowledgment. All else is implied in this, and would follow from it. It is the first real confession of the Church. We can understand, how it followed after solitary prayer by Christ [b]—we can scarcely doubt, for that very revelation by the Father, which He afterwards joyously recognised in the words of Peter.

[b] St. Luke ix. 18

The reply of the Saviour is only recorded by St. Matthew. Its omission by St. Mark might be explained on the ground that St. Peter himself had furnished the information. But its absence there and in the Gospel of St. Luke [2] proves (as *Beza* remarks), that it could never have been intended as the foundation of so important a doctrine as that of the permanent supremacy of St. Peter. But even if it were such, it would not follow that this supremacy devolved on the successors of St. Peter, nor yet that the Pope of Rome is the successor of St. Peter; nor is there even solid evidence that St. Peter ever was Bishop of Rome. The dogmatic inferences from a certain interpretation of the words of Christ to Peter being therefore utterly untenable, we can, with less fear of bias, examine their meaning. The whole form here is Hebraistic. The 'blessed art thou' is Jewish in spirit and form; the address, 'Simon bar Jona,' proves that the Lord spake in Aramaic. Indeed, a Jewish Messiah responding, in the hour of his Messianic acknowledgment, in Greek to His Jewish confessor, seems utterly incongruous. Lastly, the expression 'flesh and blood,' as contrasted with God, occurs not only in that Apocryphon of strictly Jewish authorship, the Wisdom of the

[1] This is the correct reading.
[2] There could have been no anti-Petrine tendency in this, since it is equally omitted in the Petrine Gospel of St. Mark.

BOOK
III

a Ecclus.
xiv. 18;
xvii. 31
b 1 Cor. xv.
60; Gal. i.
16; Eph. vi.
12

c St. John
i. 42

d Pesiqta,
ed. Buber,
p.158 a, line
8 from
bottom

Son of Sirach,[a] and in the letters of St. Paul,[b] but in almost innumerable passages in Jewish writings, as denoting man in opposition to God; while the revelation of such a truth by ' the Father Which is in Heaven,' represents not only both Old and New Testament teaching, but is clothed in language familiar to Jewish ears (אָבִינוּ שֶׁבַּשָּׁמַיִם).

Not less Jewish in form are the succeeding words of Christ, ' Thou art Peter (*Petros*), and upon this rock (*Petra*) will I build my Church.' We notice in the original the change from the masculine gender, ' Peter' (Petros), to the feminine, ' Petra' (' Rock '), which seems the more significant, that *Petros* is used in Greek for ' stone,' and also sometimes for ' rock,' while *Petra* always means a ' rock.' The change of gender must therefore have a definite object which will presently be more fully explained. Meantime we recall that, when Peter first came to Christ, the Lord had said unto him: ' Thou shalt be called Cephas, which is, by interpretation, Peter [*Petros*, a Stone, or else a Rock] '[c]—the Aramaic word *Kepha* (כֵּיפָא, or כֵּיפָה) meaning, like Peter, both ' stone ' and ' rock." But both the Greek Petros and Petra have (as already stated) passed into Rabbinic language. Thus, the name *Peter*, or rather *Petros*, is Jewish, and occurs, for example, as that of the father of a certain Rabbi (José bar Petros).[d] When the Lord, therefore, prophetically gave the name Cephas, it may have been that by that term He gave only a prophetic interpretation to what had been his previous name Peter (פֵּיטְרוֹס). This seems the more likely, since, as we have previously seen, it was the practice in Galilee to have two names,[1] especially when the strictly Jewish name, such as Simon, had no equivalent among the Gentiles.[2] Again, the Greek word *Petra*—Rock—(' on this *Petra* [Rock] will I build my Church ') was used in the same sense in Rabbinic language. It occurs twice in a passage, which so fully illustrates the Jewish use, not only of the word, but of the whole figure, that it deserves a place here. According to Jewish ideas, the world would not have been created, unless it had rested, as it were, on some solid foundation of piety and acceptance of God's Law—in other words, it required a moral, before it could receive a physical foundation. Rabbinism here contrasts the Gentile world with Israel. It is, so runs the comment, as if a king were going to build a city. One and another site is tried for a foundation, but in digging they always come upon water. At last they come upon a *Rock*

---

[1] See the remarks on Matthew-Levi in vol. i. ch. xvii. p. 514 of this Book.

[2] Thus, for example, Andrew was both 'Ανδρέας and אַנְדְּרַאי (Anderai) = ' manly,' ' brave.' A family *Anderai* is mentioned Jer. Kethub. 33 *a*.

(*Petra*, פטרא). So, when God was about to build his world, He could not rear it on the generation of Enos nor on that of the flood, who brought destruction on the world; but 'when He beheld that Abraham would arise in the future, He said: Behold I have found a Rock (Petra, פטרא) to build on it, and to found the world,' whence also Abraham is called a Rock (*Tsur*, צור) as it is said:[a] 'Look unto the Rock whence ye are hewn.'[b][1] The parallel between Abraham and Peter might be carried even further. If, from a misunderstanding of the Lord's promise to Peter, later Christian legend represented the Apostle as sitting at the gate of heaven, Jewish legend represents Abraham as sitting at the gate of Gehenna, so as to prevent all who had the seal of circumcision from falling into its abyss.[c][2] To complete this sketch—in the curious Jewish legend about the Apostle Peter, which is outlined in an Appendix to this volume,[3] Peter is always designated as *Simon Kepha* (spelt קיפא), there being, however, some reminiscence of the meaning attached to his name in the statement made, that, after his death, they built a church and tower, and called it *Peter* (פטר) 'which is the name for stone, because he sat there upon a stone till his death'[1] (שישב שם על האבן).[4]

But to return. Believing, that Jesus spoke to Peter in the Aramic, we can now understand how the words *Petros* and *Petra* would be purposely used by Christ to mark the difference, which their choice would suggest. Perhaps it might be expressed in this somewhat clumsy paraphrase: 'Thou art Peter (Petros)—a Stone or Rock—and upon this Petra—the Rock, the Petrine—will I found My Church.' If, therefore, we would not entirely limit the reference to the words of Peter's confession, we would certainly apply them to that which was the Petrine in Peter: the heaven-given faith which manifested itself in his confession.[5] And we can further understand how, just as Christ's contemporaries may have regarded the world as reared on the rock of faithful Abraham, so Christ promised, that He would build His Church on the Petrine in Peter—on his faith and

CHAP. XXXVII

[a] Is. li. 1
[b] Yalkut on Numb. xxiii. 9, vol. i. p.243, b, last 6 lines, and c, first 3 lines
[c] Erub.19 a Ber. R. 48

---

[1] The same occurs in Shem. R. 15, only that there it is not only Abraham but 'the fathers' who are 'the Rocks' (the word used there is not *Petra* but *Tsur*) on whom the world is founded.
[2] There was a strange idea about Jewish children who had died uncircumcised and the sinners in Israel exchanging their position in regard to circumcision. Could this, only spiritually understood and applied, have been present to the mind of St. Paul when he wrote Romans ii. 25, 26, last clauses?
[3] See Appendix XVIII.
[4] The reader will have no difficulty in recognizing a reference to the See of Rome, perhaps 'the Chair of St. Peter,' mixed up with the meaning of the name of Peter.
[5] The other views of the words are (*a*) that Christ pointed to Himself as the Rock, (*b*) or to Peter as a person, (*c*) or to Peter's confession.

ᵃ Ecclus.
xxiv. 2
ᵇ Comp.
Acts vii. 38,
and even
St. Matt.
xviii. 17

confession.   Nor would the term 'Church' sound strange in Jewish ears.   The same Greek word (ἐκκλησία), as the equivalent of the Hebrew *Qahal*, 'convocation,' 'the called,'[1] occurs in the LXX. rendering of the Old Testament, and in 'the Wisdom of the Son of Sirach'[a] and was apparently in familiar use at the time.[b]   In Hebrew use it referred to Israel, not in their national but in their religious unity. As here employed, it would convey the prophecy, that His disciples would in the future be joined together in a religious unity; that this religious unity or 'Church' would be a building of which Christ was the Builder; that it would be founded on 'the Petrine' of heaven-taught faith and confession; and that this religious unity, this Church, was not only intended for a time, like a school of thought, but would last beyond death and the disembodied state: that, alike as regarded Christ and His Church—'the gates of Hades [2] shall not prevail against it.[c]

Viewing 'the Church' as a building founded upon 'the Petrine,'[3] it was not to vary, but to carry on the same metaphor, when Christ promised to give to him who had spoken as representative of the Apostles—'the stewards of the mysteries of God'—'the keys of the Kingdom of Heaven.'   For, as the religious unity of His disciples, or the Church, represented 'the royal rule of heaven,' so, figuratively, entrance into the gates of this building, submission to the rule of God —to that Kingdom of which Christ was the King.   And we remember how, in a special sense, this promise was fulfilled to Peter.   Even as he had been the first to utter the confession of the Church, so was he also privileged to be the first to open its hitherto closed gates to the Gentiles, when God made choice of him, that, through his mouth, the Gentiles should first hear the words of the Gospel,[c] and at his bidding first be baptized.[d]

ᶜ Acts xv. 7
ᵈ Acts x. 48

If hitherto it has appeared that what Christ said to Peter, though infinitely transcending Jewish ideas, was yet, in its expression and even cast of thought, such as to be quite intelligible to Jewish minds, nay, so familiar to them, that, as by well-marked steps, they might ascend to the higher Sanctuary, the difficult words with which our Lord closed must be read in the same light.   For, assuredly,

---

[1] The other word is *Edah*. Comp. Bible Hist. vol. ii. p. 177, note.

[2] It is important to notice that the word is *Hades*, and not *Gehenna*. Dean *Plumptre* calls attention to the wonderful character of such a prophecy at a time when all around seemed to fore-shadow only failure.

[3] Those who apply the words 'upon this Rock, &c.,' to Peter or to Christ must feel, that they introduce an abrupt and inelegant transition from one figure to another.

in interpreting such a saying of Christ to Peter, our first inquiry must be, what it would convey to the person to whom the promise was addressed. And here we recall, that no other terms were in more constant use in Rabbinic Canon-Law than those of 'binding' and 'loosing.' The words are the literal translation of the Hebrew equivalents *Asar* (אָסַר), which means 'to bind,' in the sense of prohibiting, and *Hittir* (הִתִּיר, from נְתַר) which means 'to loose,' in the sense of permitting. For the latter the term *Shera* or *Sheri* (שְׁרָא, or שְׁרֵי) is also used. But this expression is, both in Targumic and Talmudic diction, not merely the equivalent of permitting, but passes into that of remitting or pardoning. On the other hand, 'binding and loosing' referred simply to things or acts prohibiting or else permitting them, declaring them lawful or unlawful. This was one of the powers claimed by the Rabbis. As regards their *laws* (not decisions as to things or acts), it was a principle, that while in Scripture there were some that bound and some that loosed, all the laws of the Rabbis were in reference to 'binding.'[a] If this then represented the *legislative*, another pretension of the Rabbis, that of declaring 'free' or else 'liable,' i.e., guilty (*Patur* or *Chayyabh*), expressed their claim to the *judicial* power. By the first of these they 'bound' or 'loosed' acts or things; by the second they 'remitted' or 'retained,' declared a person free from, or liable to punishment. to compensation, or to sacrifice. These two powers—the legislative and judicial—which belonged to the Rabbinic office, Christ now transferred, and that not in their pretension, but in their reality, to His Apostles: the first here to Peter as their Representative, the second after His Resurrection to the Church.[b]

[a] Jer. Ber. 3 b; Jer. Meg. 71 a; Jer. Sanh. 30 a

[b] St. John xx. 23

On the second of these powers we need not at present dwell. That of 'binding' and 'loosing' included all the legislative functions for the new Church. And it was a reality. In the view of the Rabbis heaven was like earth, and questions were discussed and settled by a heavenly Sanhedrin. Now, in regard to some of their earthly decrees, they were wont to say that 'the Sanhedrin above' confirmed what 'the Sanhedrin beneath' had done. But the words of Christ, as they avoided the foolish conceit of His contemporaries, left it not doubtful, but conveyed the assurance that, under the guidance of the Holy Ghost, whatsoever they bound or loosed on earth would be bound or loosed in heaven.

But all this that had passed between them could not be matter of common talk—least of all, at that crisis in His History, and in that locality. Accordingly, all the three Evangelists record—eac

BOOK
III

with distinctive emphasis[1]—that the open confession of his Messiahship, which was virtually its proclamation, was not to be made public. Among the people it could only have led to results the opposite of those to be desired. How unprepared even that Apostle was, who had made proclamation of the Messiah, for what his confession implied, and how ignorant of the real meaning of Israel's Messiah, appeared only too soon. For, His proclamation as the Christ imposed on the Lord, so to speak, the necessity of setting forth the mode of His contest and victory—the Cross and the Crown. Such teaching was the needed sequence of Peter's confession—needed, not only for the correction of misunderstanding, but for direction. And yet significantly it is only said, that ' He began ' to teach them these things—no doubt, as regarded the *manner*, as well as the time of this teaching. The Evangelists, indeed, write it down in plain language, as fully taught them by later experience, that He was to be rejected by the rulers of Israel, slain, and to rise again the third day. And there can be as little doubt, that Christ's language (as afterwards they looked back upon it) must have clearly implied all this, as that at the time they did not fully understand it.[2] He was so constantly in the habit of using symbolic language, and had only lately reproved them for taking that about ' the leaven ' in a literal, which He had meant in a figurative sense, that it was but natural, they should have regarded in the same light announcements which, in their strict literality, would seem to them well nigh incredible. They could well understand His rejection by the Scribes—a sort of figurative death, or violent suppression of His claims and doctrines, and then, after briefest period, their resurrection, as it were—but not these terrible details in their full literality.

But, even so, there was enough of terrible realism in the words of Jesus to alarm Peter. His very affection, intensely human, to the Human Personality of his Master would lead him astray. That He, Whom he verily believed to be the Messiah, Whom he loved with all the intenseness of such an intense nature—that He should pass through such an ordeal—No! Never! He put it in the very strongest language, although the Evangelist gives only a literal translation of the Rabbinic expression[3]—God forbid it, ' *God* be

---

[1] The word used by St. Matthew (διε-στείλατο) means 'charged;' that by St. Mark (ἐπετίμησεν) implies rebuke; while the expression employed by St. Luke (ἐπιτιμήσας αὐτοῖς παρήγγειλε) conveys both rebuke and command.

[2] Otherwise they could not afterwards have been in such doubt about His Death and Resurrection.

[3] It is very remarkable that the expression ἵλεώς σοι. literally ' have mercy on thee,' is the exact transcript of the Rabbinic *Chas lecha* (חס לך). See *Levy*, Neuhebr. Wörterb. vol. ii, p. 85.

merciful to Thee:'[1] no, such never could, nor should be to the
Christ ! It was an appeal to the Human in Christ, just as Satan had, in
the great Temptation after the forty days' fast, appealed to the purely
Human in Jesus. Temptations these, with which we cannot reason,
but which we must put behind us as *behind*, or else they will be a
stumbling-block before us; temptations, which come to us often
through the love and care of others, Satan transforming himself
into an Angel of light; temptations, all the more dangerous, that
they appeal to the purely human, not the sinful, element in us, but
which arise from the circumstance, that they who so become our
stumbling-block, so long as they are *before* us, are prompted by an
affection which has regard to the purely human, and, in its one-
sided human intenseness, minds the things of man, and not those of
God.

Yet Peter's words were to be made useful, by affording to the
Master the opportunity of correcting what was amiss in the hearts of
all His- disciples, and teaching them such general principles about
His Kingdom, and about that implied in true discipleship, as
would, if received in the heart, enable them in due time victoriously
to bear those trials connected with that rejection and Death of the
Christ, which at the time they could not understand. Not a Messianic Kingdom, with glory to its heralds and chieftains—but self-
denial, and the voluntary bearing of that cross on which the powers
of this world would nail the followers of Christ. They knew the
torture which their masters—the power of the world—the Romans,
were wont to inflict: such must they, and similar must we all, be
prepared to bear,[2] and, in so doing, begin by denying self. In such
a contest, to lose life would be to gain it, to gain would be to lose
life. And, if the issue lay between these two, who could hesitate
what to choose, even if it were ours to gain or lose a whole world ?
For behind it all there was a reality—a Messianic triumph and
Kingdom—not, indeed, such as they imagined, but far higher, holier:
the Coming of the Son of Man in the glory of His Father, and with
His Angels, and then eternal gain or loss, according to our deeds.[a]   [a] St. Matt.
xvi. 24–27

But why speak of the future and distant? 'A sign'—a terrible
sign of it 'from heaven,' a vindication of Christ's 'rejected' claims,

---

The commoner expression is *Chas ve
Shalom*, 'mercy and peace,' viz. be to
thee, and the meaning is, God forbid, or
God avert, a thing or its continuance.
[1] So the Greek literally.
[2] In those days the extreme suffering
which a man might expect from the hostile power (the Romans) was the literal
cross; in ours, it is suffering not less
acute, the greatest which the present
hostile power can inflict: really, though
perhaps not literally, a cross.

a vindication of the Christ, Whom they had slain, invoking His Blood on their City and Nation, a vindication, such as alone these men could understand, of the reality of His Resurrection and Ascension, was in the near future.   The flames of the City and Temple would be the light in that nation's darkness, by which to read the inscription on the Cross.   All this not afar off.   Some of those whe stood there would not 'taste death,' [1] till in those judgments they would see that the Son of Man had come in His Kingdom. [a]

* St. Matt.
xvi. 28

Then—only then—at the burning of the City! Why not now, visibly, and immediately on their terrible sin?   Because God shows not 'signs from heaven' such as man seeks; because His long-suffering waiteth long; because, all unnoticed, the finger moves on the dial-plate of time till the hour strikes; because there is Divine grandeur and majesty in the slow, unheard, certain night-march of events under His direction.   God is content to wait, because He reigneth; man must be content to wait, because he believeth.

---

[1] This is an exact translation of the phrase טעם מיתה, which is of such very frequent occurrence in Rabbinic writings.   See our remarks on St. John viii. 52 in Book IV. ch. viii.

Book IV.

THE DESCENT:

FROM THE MOUNT OF TRANSFIGURATION INTO THE VALLEY OF HUMILIATION AND DEATH.

'But God forbede but men shulde leve
Wel mor thing then men han seen with eye
Men shall not wenen euery thing a lye
But yf him-selfe yt seeth or elles dooth
For god wot thing is neuer the lasse sooth
Thogh euery wight ne may it nat y-see.'

CHAUCER: *Prologue to the Legend of Good Women.*

CHAPTER I.

THE TRANSFIGURATION.

(St Matt. xvii. 1–8; St. Mark ix. 2–8; St. Luke ix. 28–36.)

THE great confession of Peter, as the representative Apostle, had laid the foundations of the Church as such. In contradistinction to the varying opinions of even those best disposed towards Christ, it openly declared that Jesus was the Very Christ of God, the fulfilment of all Old Testament prophecy, the heir of Old Testament promise, the realisation of the Old Testament hope for Israel, and, in Israel, for all mankind. Without this confession, Christians might have been a Jewish sect, a religious party, or a school of thought, and Jesus a Teacher, Rabbi, Reformer, or Leader of men. But the confession which marked Jesus as the Christ, also constituted His followers the Church. It separated them, as it separated Him, from all around; it gathered them into one, even Christ; and it marked out the foundation on which the building made without hands was to rise. Never was illustrative answer so exact as this: 'On this Rock' —bold, outstanding, well-defined, immovable—'will I build **My** Church.'

Without doubt this confession also marked the high-point of the Apostles' faith. Never afterwards, till His Resurrection, did it reach so high. Nay, what followed seems rather a retrogression from it: beginning with their unwillingness to receive the announcement of His decease, and ending with their unreadiness to share His sufferings or to believe in His Resurrection. And if we realise the circumstances, we shall understand at least, their initial difficulties. Their highest faith had been followed by the most crushing disappointment; the confession that He was the Christ, by the announcement of His approaching Sufferings and Death at Jerusalem. The proclamation that He was the Divine Messiah had not been met by promises of the near glory of the Messianic Kingdom, but by announcements of certain, public rejection and seeming terrible defeat. Such possibilities had never seriously entered into their thoughts of the Messiah; and the declaration of the very worst, and that in the near future, made at such a moment, must have been a staggering blow to all their hopes. It was as if they had reached the topmost height, only to be cast thence into the lowest depth.

On the other hand, it was necessary that at this stage in the History of the Christ, and immediately after His proclamation, the sufferings and the rejection of the Messiah should be prominently brought forward. It was needful for the Apostles, as the remonstrance of Peter showed; and, with reverence be it added, it was needful for the Lord Himself, as even His words to Peter seem to imply: 'Get thee behind Me; thou art a stumbling-block unto me.' For—as we have said—was not the remonstrance of the disciple in measure a re-enactment of the great initial Temptation by Satan after the forty days' fast in the wilderness? And, in view of all this, and of what immediately afterwards followed, we venture to say, it was fitting that an interval of 'six' days should intervene, or, as St. Luke puts it, including the day of Peter's confession and the night of Christ's Transfiguration, 'about eight days.' The Chronicle of these days is significantly left blank in the Gospels, but we cannot doubt, that it was filled up with thoughts and teaching concerning that Decease, leading up to the revelation on the Mount of Transfiguration.

There are other blanks in the narrative besides that just referred to. We shall try to fill them up, as best we can. Perhaps it was the Sabbath when Peter's great confession was made; and the 'six days' of St. Matthew and St. Mark become the 'about eight days' of St. Luke, when we reckon from that Sabbath to the close of another, and suppose that at even the Saviour ascended the Mount of Transfiguration with the three Apostles: Peter, James, and John. There can scarcely be a reasonable doubt that Christ and His disciples had not left the neighborhood of Cæsarea,[1] and hence, that 'the mountain' must have been one of the slopes of gigantic, snowy Hermon. In that quiet semi-Gentile retreat of Cæsarea Philippi could He best teach them, and they best learn, without interruption or temptation from Pharisees and Scribes, that terrible mystery of His Suffering. And on that gigantic mountain barrier which divided Jewish and

---

[1] According to an old tradition, Christ had left Cæsarea Philippi, and the scene of the Transfiguration was Mount Tabor. But (1) there is no notice of His departure, such as is generally made by St. Mark; (2) on the contrary, it is mentioned by St. Mark as after the Transfiguration (ix. 30); (3) Mount Tabor was at that time crowned by a fortified city, which would render it unsuitable for the scene of the Transfiguration.

Gentile lands, and while surveying, as Moses of old, the land to be occupied in all its extent, amidst the solemn solitude and majestic grandeur of Hermon, did it seem most fitting that, both by anticipatory fact and declamatory word, the Divine attestation should be given to the proclamation that He was the Messiah, and to this also, that, in a world that is in the power of sin and Satan, God's Elect must suffer, in order that, by ransoming, He may conquer it to God. But what a background, here, for the Transfiguration; what surroundings for the Vision, what echoes for the Voice from heaven!

It was evening,[1] and, as we have suggested, the evening after the Sabbath, when the Master and those three of His disciples, who were most closely linked to Him in heart and thought, climbed the path that led up to one of the heights of Hermon. In all the most solemn transactions of earth's history, there has been this selection and separation of the few to witness God's great doings. Alone with his son, as the destined sacrifice, did Abraham climb Moriah; alone did Moses behold, amid the awful loneliness of the wilderness, the burning bush, and alone on Sinai's height did he commune with God; alone was Elijah at Horeb, and with no other companion to view it than Elisha did he ascend into heaven. But Jesus, the Saviour of His people, could not be quite alone, save in those innermost transactions of His soul: in the great contest of His first Temptation, and in the solitary communings of His heart with God. These are mysteries which the outspread wings of Angels, as reverently they hide their faces, conceal from earth's, and even heaven's, vision. But otherwise, in the most solemn turning-points of this history, Jesus could not be alone, and yet was alone with those three chosen ones, most receptive of Him, and most representative of the Church. It was so in the house of Jairus, on the Mount of Transfiguration, and in the Garden of Gethsemane.

As St. Luke alone informs us, it was 'to pray' that Jesus took them apart up into that mountain. 'To pray,' no doubt in connection with 'those sayings;' since their reception required quite as much the direct teaching of the Heavenly Father, as had the previous confession of Peter, of which it was, indeed, the complement, the other aspect, the twin height. And the Transfiguration, with its attendant glorified Ministry and Voice from heaven, was God's answer to that prayer.

What has already been stated, has convinced us that it could not have been to one of the highest peaks of Hermon, as most modern

---

[1] This is implied not only in the disciples being heavy with sleep, but in the morning scene (St. Luke ix. 37) which followed.

writers suppose, that Jesus led His companions. There are three such peaks: those north and south, of about equal height (9,400 feet above the sea, and nearly 11,000 above the Jordan valley), are only 500 paces distant from each other, while the third, to the west (about 100 feet lower), is separated from the others by a narrow valley. Now, to climb the top of Hermon is, even from the nearest point, an Alpine ascent, trying and fatiguing, which would occupy a whole day (six hours in the ascent and four in the descent), and require provisions of food and water; while, from the keenness of the air, it would be impossible to spend the night on the top.[1] To all this there is no allusion in the text, nor slightest hint of either difficulties or preparations, such as otherwise would have been required. Indeed, a contrary impression is left on the mind.

'Up into an high mountain apart,' 'to pray.' The Sabbath-sun had set, and a delicious cool hung in the summer air, as Jesus and the three commenced their ascent. From all parts of the land, far as Jerusalem or Tyre, the one great object in view must always have been snow-clad Hermon. And now it stood out before them—as, to the memory of the traveller in the West, Monte Rosa or Mont Blanc[2]— in all the wondrous glory of a sunset: first rose-coloured, then deepening red, next 'the death-like pallor, and the darkness relieved by the snow, in quick succession.'[3] From high up there, as one describes it,[4] 'a deep ruby flush came over all the scene, and warm purple shadows crept slowly on. The sea of Galilee was lit up with a delicate greenish-yellow hue, between its dim walls of hill. The flush died out in a few minutes, and a pale, steel-coloured shade succeeded. . . . A long pyramidal shadow slid down to the eastern foot of Hermon, and crept across the great plain; Damascus was swallowed up by it; and finally the pointed end of the shadow stood out distinctly against the sky—a dusky cone of dull colour against the flush of the afterglow. It was the shadow of the mountain itself, stretching away for seventy miles across the plain—the most marvellous shadow perhaps to be seen anywhere. The sun underwent strange changes of shape in the thick vapours—now almost square, now like a domed Temple—until at length it slid into the sea, and went out like a blue spark.' And overhead shone out in the blue

---

[1] Canon *Tristram* writes: 'We were before long painfully affected by the rarity of the atmosphere.' In general, our description is derived from Canon *Tristram* ('Land of Israel'), Captain *Conder* ('Tent-Work in Palestine), and *Bädeker-Socin's* Palästina, p. 354.

[2] One of its names, *Shenir* (Deut. iii. 9; Cant. iv. 8; Ezek. xxvii. 5) means Mont Blanc. In Rabbinic writings it is designated as the 'snow-mountain.'

[3] *Tristram*, u. s., p. 607.

[4] *Conder*, u. s., vol. i. p. 264.

summer-sky, one by one, the stars in Eastern brilliancy. We know
not the exact direction which the climbers took, nor how far their
journey went. But there is only one road that leads from Cæsarea
Philippi to Hermon, and we cannot be mistaken in following it. First,
among vine-clad hills stocked with mulberry, apricot and fig-trees;
then, through corn-fields where the pear tree supplants the fig; next,
through oak coppice, and up rocky ravines to where the soil is dotted
with dwarf shrubs. And if we pursue the ascent, it still becomes
steeper, till the first ridge of snow is crossed, after which turfy banks,
gravelly slopes, and broad snow-patches alternate. The top of
Hermon in summer—and it can only be ascended in summer or autumn
—is free from snow, but broad patches run down the sides expanding
as they descend. To the very summit it is well earthed; to 500
feet below it, studded with countless plants, higher up with dwarf
clumps.[1]

As they ascend in the cool of that Sabbath evening, the keen
mountain air must have breathed strength into the climbers, and
the scent of snow—for which the parched tongue would long in
summer's heat[a]—have refreshed them. We know not what part [a] Prov. xxv.
13
may have been open to them of the glorious panorama from Hermon,
embracing as it does a great part of Syria from the sea to Damascus,
from the Lebanon and the gorge of the Litany to the mountains of
Moab; or down the Jordan valley to the Dead Sea; or over Galilee,
Samaria, and on to Jerusalem and beyond it. But such darkness as
that of a summer's night would creep on. And now the moon shone
out in dazzling splendour, cast long shadows over the mountain, and
lit up the broad patches of snow, reflecting their brilliancy on the
objects around.

On that mountain-top 'He prayed.' Although the text does not
expressly state it, we can scarcely doubt, that He prayed with them,
and still less, that He prayed for them, as did the Prophet for his
servant, when the city was surrounded by Syrian horsemen: that
his eyes might be opened to behold heaven's host—the far 'more
that are with us than they that are with them.'[b] And, with deep [b] 2 Kings
vi. 16, 17
reverence be it said, for Himself also did Jesus pray. For, as the pale
moonlight shone on the fields of snow in the deep passes of Hermon,
so did the light of the coming night shine on the cold glitter of Death
in the near future. He needed prayer, that in it His Soul might
lie calm and still—perfect, in the unruffled quiet of His Self-

---

[1] Our description is based on the graphic account of the ascent by Canon *Tristram* (u. s. pp. 609–613).

surrender, the absolute rest of His Faith, and the victory of His Sacrificial Obedience. And He needed prayer also, as the introduction to, and preparation for, His Transfiguration. Truly, He stood on Hermon.· It was the highest ascent, the widest prospect into the past, present, and future, in His Earthly Life. Yet was it but Hermon at night. And this is the human, or rather the Theanthropic view of this prayer, and of its consequence.

As we understand it, the prayer with them had ceased, or it had merged into silent prayer of each, or Jesus now prayed alone and apart, when what gives this scene such a truly human and truthful aspect ensued. It was but natural for these men of simple habits, at night, and after the long ascent, and in the·strong mountain-air, to be heavy with sleep. And we also know it as a psychological fact, that, in quick reaction after the overpowering influence of the strongest emotions, drowsiness would creep over their limbs and senses. 'They were heavy—weighted—with sleep,' as afterwards at Gethsemane their eyes were weighted.[a][1] Yet they struggled with it, and it is quite consistent with experience, that they should continue in that state of semi-stupor, during what passed between Moses and Elijah and Christ, and also be 'fully awake,'[2] 'to see His Glory, and the two men who stood with Him.' In any case this descriptive trait, so far from being (as negative critics would have it), a 'later embellishment,' could only have formed part of a primitive account, since it is impossible to conceive any rational motive for its later addition.[3]

What they saw was their Master, while praying, 'transformed.'[4] The 'form of God' shone through the 'form of a servant;' 'the appearance of His Face became other,'[b][5] it 'did shine as the sun.'[c][6] Nay, the whole Figure seemed bathed in light, the very garments whiter far than the snow on which the moon shone[7]—'so as no fuller on earth can white them,'[d] 'glittering,'[e] 'white as the light.' And

[a] St. Matt. xxvi. 43; St. Mark xiv. 40

[b] St. Luke

[c] St. Matthew

[d] St. Mark

[e] St. Luke

[1] The word is the same. It also occurs in a figurative sense in 2 Cor. i. 8; v. 4; 1 Tim. v. 16.

[2] *Meyer* strongly advocates the rendering: 'but having kept awake.' See, however, *Godet's* remarks ad loc.

[3] *Meyer* is in error in supposing that the tradition, on which St. Luke's account is founded, amplifies the narratives of St. Matthew and St. Mark. With Canon *Cook* I incline to the view of *Resch*, that, judging from the style, &c., St. Luke derived this notice from the same source as the materials for the large portion from ch. ix. 51 to xviii. 17.

[4] On the peculiar meaning of the word

μορφή comp. Bishop *Lightfoot* on Philip. pp. 127–133.

[5] This expression of St. Luke, so far from indicating embellishment of the other accounts, marks, if anything, rather retrogression.

[6] It is scarcely a Rabbinic parallel—hardly an illustration—that in Rabbinic writings also Moses' face before his death is said to have shone as the sun, for the comparison is a Biblical one. Such language would, of course, be familiar to St. Matthew.

[7] The words 'as snow,' in St. Mark ix. 3, are, however, spurious—an early gloss.

more than this they saw and heard. They saw 'with Him two men,'[a] whom, in their heightened sensitiveness to spiritual phenomena, they could have no difficulty in recognising, by such of their conversation as they heard, as Moses and Elijah.[1] The column was now complete: the base in the Law; the shaft in that Prophetism of which Elijah was the great Representative—in his first Mission, as fulfilling the primary object of the Prophets: to call Israel back to God; and, in his second Mission, this other aspect of the Prophets' work, to prepare the way for the Kingdom of God; and the apex in Christ Himself—a unity completely fitting together in all its parts. And they heard also, that they spake of ' His Exodus—outgoing— which He was about to fulfil at Jerusalem.'[b] Although the term ' Exodus,' ' outgoing,' occurs otherwise for ' death,'[2] we must bear in mind its meaning as contrasted with that in which the same Evangelic writer designates the Birth of Christ, as His ' incoming.'[c] In truth, it implies not only His Decease, but its manner, and even His Resurrection and Ascension. In that sense we can understand the better, as on the lips of Moses and Elijah, this about His *fulfilling* that Exodus: accomplishing it in all its fulness, and so completing Law and Prophecy, type and prediction.

And still that night of glory had not ended. A strange peculiarity has been noticed about Hermon in 'the extreme rapidity of the formation of cloud on the summit. In a few minutes a thick cap forms over the top of the mountain, and as quickly disperses and entirely disappears.'[3] It almost seems as if this, like the natural position of Hermon itself, was, if not to be connected with, yet, so to speak, to form the background to what was to be enacted. Suddenly a cloud passed over the clear brow of the mountain—not an ordinary, but ' a luminous cloud,' a cloud uplit, filled with light. As it laid itself between Jesus and the two Old Testament Representatives, it parted, and presently enwrapped them. Most significant is it, suggestive of the Presence of God, revealing, yet concealing—a cloud, yet luminous. And this cloud overshadowed the disciples: the shadow of its light fell upon them. A nameless terror seized them. Fain would they have held what seemed for ever to escape their grasp. Such vision had never before been vouchsafed to mortal man as had fallen on their sight; they had already heard Heaven's converse; they had tasted Angels' Food, the Bread of His Presence. Could the vision not be perpetuated—at

CHAP.
I

[a] St. Luke

[b] St. Luke

[c] εἴσοδος, Acts xiii. 24

---

[1] *Godet* points out the emphatic meaning of οἵτινες in St. Luke ix. 30=*quippe qui*: they were none other than.

[2] In some of the Apocrypha **and** *Josephus*, as well as in 2 Pet. i. 15.

[3] *Conder*, u. s. vol. i. p 265.

least prolonged? In the confusion of their terror they knew not how otherwise to word it, than by an expression of ecstatic longing for the continuance of what they had, of their earnest readiness to do their little best, if they could but secure it—make booths for the heavenly Visitants [1]—and themselves wait in humble service and reverent attention on what their dull heaviness had prevented their enjoying and profiting by, to the full. They knew and felt it: 'Lord'—'Rabbi'—'Master'—'it is good for us to be here'—and they longed to have it; yet how to secure it, their terror could not suggest, save in the language of ignorance and semi-conscious confusion. 'They wist not what they said.' In presence of the luminous cloud that enwrapt those glorified Saints, they spake from out that darkness which compassed them about.

And now the light-cloud was spreading; presently its fringe fell upon them.[2] Heaven's awe was upon them: for the touch of the heavenly strains, almost to breaking, the bond betwixt body and soul. 'And a Voice came out of the cloud, saying, This is My Beloved [3] Son: hear Him.' It had needed only One other Testimony to seal it all; One other Voice, to give both meaning and music to what had been the subject of Moses' and Elijah's speaking. That Voice had now come—not in testimony to any fact, but to a Person—that of Jesus as His 'Beloved Son,'[4] and in gracious direction to them. They heard it, falling on their faces in awestruck worship.

How long the silence had lasted, and the last rays of the cloud had passed, we know not. Presently, it was a gentle touch that roused them. It was the Hand of Jesus, as with words of comfort He reassured them: 'Arise, and be not afraid.' And as, startled,[5] they looked round about them, they saw no man save Jesus only. The Heavenly Visitants had gone, the last glow of the light-cloud had faded away, the echoes of Heaven's Voice had died out. It was night, and they were on the Mount with Jesus, and with Jesus only.

Is it truth or falsehood; was it reality or vision—or part of both, this Transfiguration-scene on Hermon? One thing, at least, must be

[1] *Wünsche* (ad loc.) quotes as it seems to me, very inaptly, the Rabbinic realistic idea of the fulfilment of Is. iv. 5, 6, that God would make for each of the righteous seven booths, varying according to their merits (Baba B. 75 a), or else one booth for each (Bemid. R. 21, ed. Warsh. p. 85a). Surely, there can be no similarity between this and the words of Peter.

[2] A comparison of the narratives leaves on us the impression that the disciples also were touched by the cloud. I cannot agree with *Godet*, that the question depends on whether we adopt in St. Luke ix. 34 the reading of the T.R. ἐκείνους, or that of the Alex. αὐτούς.

[3] The more correct reading in St. Luke seems to be 'Elect Son.'

[4] St. Matthew adds, 'in Whom I am well pleased.' The reason of this fuller account is not difficult to understand.

[5] St. Mark indicates this by the words: 'And suddenly, when they looked round about.'

evident: if it be a true narrative, it cannot possibly describe a merely CHAP.
I
subjective vision without objective reality. But, in that case, it
would be not only difficult, but impossible, to separate one part of the
narrative—the appearance of Moses and Elijah—from the other, the
Transfiguration of the Lord, and to assign to the latter objective
reality,[1] while regarding the former as merely a vision. But is the
account true? It certainly represents primitive tradition, since it is
not only told by all the three Evangelists, but referred to in 2 Peter i.
16–18,[2] and evidently implied in the words of St. John, both in his
Gospel,[a] and in the opening of his First Epistle. Few, if any, would a St. John i.
14
be so bold as to assert that the whole of this history had been
invented by the three Apostles, who professed to have been its
witnesses. Nor can any adequate motive be imagined for its invention. It could not have been intended to prepare the Jews for the
Crucifixion of the Messiah, since it was to be kept a secret till after
His Resurrection; and, after the event, it could not have been
necessary for the assurance of those who believed in the Resurrection,
while to others it would carry no weight. Again, the special traits
of this history are inconsistent with the theory of its invention. In
a legend, the witnesses of such an event would not have been represented as scarcely awake, and not knowing what they said. Manifestly, the object would have been to convey the opposite impression.
Lastly, it cannot be too often repeated, that, in view of the manifold
witness of the Evangelists, amply confirmed in all essentials by the
Epistles—preached, lived, and bloodsealed by the primitive Church,
and handed down as primitive tradition—the most untenable theory
seems that which imputes intentional fraud to their narratives, or, to
put it otherwise, non-belief on the part of the narrators of what they
related.

But can we suppose, if not fraud, yet mistake on the part of
these witnesses, so that an event, otherwise naturally explicable, may,
through their ignorance or imaginativeness, have assumed the proportions of this narrative? The investigation will be the more easy,
that, as regards all the main features of the narrative, the three
Evangelists are entirely agreed. Instead of examining in detail the
various rationalistic attempts made to explain this history on natural
grounds, it seems sufficient for refutation to ask the intelligent reader

---

[1] This part of the argument is well
worked out by *Meyer*, but his arguments
for regarding the appearance of Moses
and Elijah as merely a vision, because
the former at least had no resurrection-
body, are very weak. Are we sure, that
disembodied spirits have no kind of corporeity, or that they *cannot* assume a
visible appearance ?

[2] Even if that Epistle were not St.
Peter's, it would still represent the most
ancient tradition.

BOOK
IV

to attempt imagining any natural event, which by any possibility could have been mistaken for what the eyewitnesses related, and the Evangelists recorded.

There still remains the mythical theory of explanation, which, if it could be supported, would be the most attractive among those of a negative character.   But we cannot imagine a legend without some historical motive or basis for its origination.   The legend must be in character—that is, congruous to the ideas and expectancies entertained.   Such a history as that of the Transfiguration could not have been a pure invention; but if such or similar expectancies had existed about the Messiah, then such a legend might, without intentional fraud, have, by gradual accretion, gathered around the Person of Him Who was regarded as the Christ.   And this is the *rationale* of the so-called *mythical theory*.   But all such ideas vanish at the touch of history.   There was absolutely no Jewish expectancy that could have bodied itself forth in a narrative like that of the Transfiguration.   To begin with the accessories—the idea, that the coming of Moses was to be connected with that of the Messiah, rests not only on an exaggeration, but on a dubious and difficult passage in the Jerusalem Targum.[a1]   It is quite true, that the face of Moses shone when he came down from the Mount; but, if this is to be regarded as the basis of the Transfiguration of Jesus, the presence of Elijah would not be in point.   On the other hand—to pass over other inconsistencies—anything more un-Jewish could scarcely be imagined than a Messiah crucified, or that Moses and Elijah should appear to converse with Him on such a Death!   If it be suggested, that the

[a] On Ex.
xii.

---

[1] Moses and the Messiah are placed side by side, the one as coming from the desert, the other from Rome. 'This one shall lead at the head of a cloud, and that one shall lead at the head of a cloud, the Memra of Jehovah leading between them twain, and they going'—as I would render it—'as one' (*Ve-innun mehalkhin kachada*), or, as some render it, 'they shall walk together.'   The question here arises, whether this is to be understood as merely figurative language, or to be taken literally.   If literally, does the Targum refer to a kind of heavenly vision, or to something that was actually to take place, a kind of realism of what Philo had anticipated (see vol. i. p. 82)?   It may have been in this sense that Fr. Tayler renders the words by '*in culmine nubis equitabit*.'   But on careful consideration the many and obvious incongruities involved in it seem to render a literal interpretation well nigh impossible.

But all seems not only plain but accordant with other Rabbinic teaching (see vol. i. p. 176), if we regard the passage as only indicating a parallelism between the first and the second Deliverer and the deliverances wrought by them.   Again, although the parallel is often drawn in Rabbinic writings between Moses and Elijah, I know only one passage, and that a dubious one, in which they are conjoined in the days of the Messiah.   It occurs in Deb. R. 3 (seven lines before the close of it), and is to this effect, that, because Moses had in this world given his life for Israel, therefore in the Æon to come, when God would send Elijah the prophet, they two should come, *keachath*, either 'together' or 'as one,' the proof passage being Nah. i. 3, 'the whirlwind' there referring to Moses, and 'the storm' to Elijah.   Surely, no one would found on such a basis a Jewish mythical origin of the Transfiguration.

purpose was to represent the Law and the Prophets as bearing testimony to the Dying of the Messiah, we fully admit it. Certainly, this is the New Testament and the true idea concerning the Christ; but equally certainly, it was not and is not, that of the Jews concerning the Messiah.[1]

If it is impossible to regard this narrative as a fraud; hopeless, to attempt explaining it as a natural event; and utterly unaccountable, when viewed in connection with contemporary thought or expectancy —in short, if all negative theories fail, let us see whether, and how, on the supposition of its reality, it will fit into the general narrative. To begin with: if our previous investigations have rightly led us up to this result, that Jesus was the Very Christ of God, then this event can scarcely be described as miraculous—at least in such a history. If we would not expect it, it is certainly that which might have been expected. For, first, it was (and at that particular period) a necessary stage in the Lord's History, viewed in the light in which the Gospels present Him. Secondly, it was needful for His own strengthening, even as the Ministry of the Angels after the Temptation. Thirdly, it was 'good' for these three disciples to be there: not only for future witness, but for present help, and also with special reference to Peter's remonstrance against Christ's death-message. Lastly, the Voice from heaven, in hearing of His disciples, was of the deepest importance. Coming after the announcement of His Death and Passion, it sealed that testimony, and, in view of it, proclaimed Him as the Prophet to Whom Moses had bidden Israel hearken,[a] while it repeated the heavenly utterance concerning Him made at His Baptism.[b]

But, for us all, the interest of this history lies not only in the past; it is in the present also, and in the future. To all ages it is like the vision of the bush burning, in which was the Presence of God. And it points us forward to that transformation, of which that of Christ was the pledge, when 'this corruptible shall put on incorruption.' As of old the beacon-fires, lighted from hill to hill, announced to them far away from Jerusalem the advent of solemn feast, so does the glory kindled on the Mount of Transfiguration shine through the darkness of the world, and tell of the Resurrection-Day.

On Hermon the Lord and His disciples had reached the highest point in this history. Henceforth it is a descent into the Valley of Humiliation and Death!

CHAP.
I

[a] Deut. xviii. 15

[b] St. Matt. iii. 17

---

[1] *Godet* has also aptly pointed out, that the injunction of silence on the disciples as to this event is incompatible with the mythical theory. It could only point to a real event, not to a myth.

CHAPTER II.

ON THE MORROW OF THE TRANSFIGURATION.

(St. Matt. xvii. 9–21; St. Mark ix. 9–29: St. Luke ix. 37–43.)

BOOK
IV

IT was the early dawn of another summer's day when the Master and His disciples turned their steps once more towards the plain. They had seen His Glory; they had had the most solemn witness which, as Jews, they could have; and they had gained a new knowledge of the Old Testament. It all bore reference to the Christ, and it spake of His Decease. Perhaps on that morning better than in the previous night did they realise the vision, and feel its calm happiness. It was to their souls like the morning-air which they breathed on that mountain.

It would be only natural, that their thoughts should also wander to the companions and fellow-disciples whom, on the previous evening, they had left in the valley beneath. How much they had to tell them, and how glad they would be of the tidings they would hear! That one night had for ever answered so many questions about that most hard of all His sayings: concerning His Rejection and violent Death at Jerusalem; it had shed heavenly light into that terrible gloom! They—at least these three—had formerly simply submitted to the saying of Christ because it was His, without understanding it; but now they had learned to see it in quite another light. How they must have longed to impart it to those whose difficulties were at least as great, perhaps greater, who perhaps had not yet recovered from the rude shock which their Messianic thoughts and hopes had so lately received. We think here especially of those, whom, so far as individuality of thinking is concerned, we may designate as the representative three, and the counterpart of the three chosen Apostles: Philip, who ever sought firm standing-ground for faith; Thomas, who wanted evidence for believing; and Judas, whose burning Jewish zeal for a Jewish Messiah had already begun to consume his own soul, as the wind had driven back upon himself the flame that had been kindled. Every question of a Philip, every doubt of a Thomas, every despairing wild outburst of a Judas, would be met by what they had now to tell.

But it was not to be so. Evidently, it was not an event to be made generally known, either to the people or even to the great body of the disciples. They could not have understood its real meaning; they would have misunderstood, and in their ignorance misapplied to carnal Jewish purposes, its heavenly lessons. But even the rest of the Apostles must not know of it: that they were not qualified to witness it, proved that they were not prepared to hear of it. We cannot for a moment imagine, that there was favouritism in the selection of certain Apostles to share in what the others might not witness. It was not because these were better loved, but because they were better prepared [1]—more fully receptive, more readily acquiescing, more entirely self-surrendering. Too often we commit in our estimate the error of thinking of them exclusively as Apostles, not as disciples; as our teachers, not as His learners, with all the failings of men, the prejudices of Jews, and the unbelief natural to us all, but assuming in each individual special forms, and appearing as characteristic weaknesses.

And so it was that, when the silence of that morning-descent was broken, the Master laid on them the command to tell no man of this vision, till after the Son of Man were risen from the dead. This mysterious injunction of silence affords another presumptive evidence against the invention, or the rationalistic explanations, or the mythical origin of this narrative. It also teaches two further lessons. The silence thus enjoined was the first step into the Valley of Humiliation. It was also a test, whether they had understood the spiritual teaching of the vision. And their strict obedience, not questioning even the grounds of the injunction, proved that they had learned it. So entire, indeed, was their submission, that they dared not even ask the Master about a new and seemingly greater mystery than they had yet heard: the meaning of the Son of Man rising from the Dead.[a] Did it refer to the general Resurrection; was the Messiah to be the first to rise from the dead, and to waken the other sleepers—or was it only a figurative expression for His triumph and vindication? Evidently, they knew as yet nothing of Christ's Personal Resurrection, as separate from that of others, and on the third day after His Death. And yet it was no near! So ignorant were they, and so unprepared! And they dared not ask the Master of it. This much

---

[1] While writing this, we fully remember about the title of St. John as he 'whom Jesus loved' specially, even in that inner and closer circle.

they had already learned: not to question the mysteries of the future, but simply to receive them.　But in their inmost hearts they kept that saying—as the Virgin-Mother had kept many a like saying—carrying it about 'with them' as a precious living germ that would presently spring up and bear fruit, or as that which would kindle into light and chase all darkness.　But among themselves, then and many times afterwards, in secret converse, they questioned what the rising again from the dead should mean.[a]

ᵃ St. Mark
ix. 10

There was another question, and it they might ask of Jesus, since it concerned not the mysteries of the future, but the lessons of the past.　Thinking of that vision, of the appearance of Elijah and of his speaking of the Death of the Messiah, why did the Scribes say that Elijah should first come—and, as was the universal teaching, for the purpose of restoring all things?　If, as they had seen, Elijah had come—but only for a brief season, not to abide, along with Moses, as they had fondly wished when they proposed to rear them booths; if he had come not to the people but to Christ, in view of only them three—and they were not even to tell of it; and, if it had been, not to prepare for a spiritual restoration, but to speak of what implied the opposite: the Rejection and violent Death of the Messiah—then, were the Scribes right in their teaching, and what was its real meaning?　The question afforded the opportunity of presenting to the disciples not only a solution of their difficulties, but another insight into the necessity of His Rejection and Death. They had failed to distinguish between the coming of Elijah and its alternative sequence.　Truly 'Elias cometh first'—and Elijah had 'come already' in the person of John the Baptist.　The Divinely intended object of Elijah's coming *was* to 'restore all things.'　This, of course, implied a moral element in the submission of the people to God, and their willingness to receive his message.　Otherwise there was this Divine alternative in the prophecy of Malachi: 'Lest I come to smite the land with the ban' (*Cherem*).　Elijah *had* come; if the people had received his message, there would have been the promised restoration of all things.　As the Lord had said on a previous occa-

ᵇ St. Matt.
xi. 14

sion[b]: 'If ye are willing to receive *him*,[1] this is Elijah, which is to come.'　Similarly, if Israel had received the Christ, He would have gathered them as a hen her chickens for protection; He would not only have been, but have visibly appeared as, their King.　But Israel did not know their Elijah, and did unto him whatsoever they listed; and so, in logical sequence, would the Son of Man also suffer of

---

[1] The meaning remains substantially the same whether we insert 'him' or 'it.'

them. And thus has the other part of Malachi's prophecy been ful- CHAP.
filled: and the land of Israel been smitten with the ban.[1]   II

Amidst such conversation the descent from the mountain was
accomplished. Presently they found themselves in view of a scene,
which only too clearly showed that unfitness of the disciples for the
heavenly vision of the preceding night, to which reference has been
made. For, amidst the divergence of details between the narratives
of St. Matthew and St. Mark, and, so far as it goes, that of St. Luke,
the one point in which they almost literally and emphatically accord
is, when the Lord speaks of them, in language of bitter disappointment and sorrow, as a generation with whose want of faith, notwithstanding all that they had seen and learned, He had still to bear,
expressly attributing[a] their failure in restoring the lunatick, to their   [a] In St. Mat
'unbelief.'[2]   thew and
                                                                              St. Mark

It was, indeed, a terrible contrast between the scene below and
that vision of Moses and Elijah, when they had spoken of the Exodus
of the Christ, and the Divine Voice had attested the Christ from out
the luminous cloud. A concourse of excited people—among them
once more 'Scribes,' who had tracked the Lord and come upon His
weakest disciples in the hour of their greatest weakness—is gathered
about a man who had in vain brought his lunatick son for healing.
He is eagerly questioned by the multitude, and moodily answers; or,
as it might almost seem from St. Matthew,[b] he is leaving the crowd   [b] ver. 14
and those from whom he had vainly sought help. This was the hour
of triumph for these Scribes. The Master had refused the challenge
in Dalmanutha, and the disciples, accepting it, had signally failed.
There they were, 'questioning with them' noisily, discussing this
and all similar phenomena, but chiefly the power, authority, and
reality of the Master. It reminds us of Israel's temptation in the
wilderness, and we should scarcely wonder, if they had even questioned the return of Jesus, as they of old did that of Moses.

At that very moment, Jesus appeared with the three. We cannot wonder that, 'when they saw Him, they were greatly amazed,[3]
and running to Him saluted Him.'[c] He came—as always, and to us   [c] St. Mark
also—unexpectedly, most opportunely, and for the real decision of the

---

[1] The question, whether there is to be
a literal reappearance of Elijah before
the Second Advent of Christ does not
seem to be answered in the present passage. Perhaps it is purposely left unanswered.

[2] The reading 'little faith' instead of
'unbelief,' though highly attested, seems

only an early correction. On internal
grounds it is more likely, that the expression ' little faith ' is a correction by a later
apologete, than 'unbelief.' The latter also
corresponds to ' faithless generation.'

[3] There is no hint in the text, that their
amazement was due to the shining of
His Face.

question in hand.   There was immediate calm, preceding victory. Before the Master's inquiry about the cause of this violent discussion could be answered, the man who had been its occasion came forward.   With lowliest gesture ('kneeling to Him'ª) he addressed Jesus.   At last he had found Him, Whom he had come to seek; and, if possibility of help there were, oh! let it be granted.   Describing the symptoms of his son's distemper, which were those of epilepsy and mania—although both the father and Jesus rightly attributed the disease to demoniac influence—he told, how he had come in search of the Master, but only found the nine disciples, and how they had presumptuously attempted, and signally failed in the attempted cure.

Why had they failed?   For the same reason, that they had not been taken into the Mount of Transfiguration—because they were 'faithless,' because of their 'unbelief.'   They had that outward faith of the ' *probatum est* ' ('it is proved'); they believed because, and what, they had seen ; and they were drawn closer to Christ— at least almost all of them, though in varying measure—as to Him Who, and Who alone, spake 'the words of eternal life,' which, with wondrous power, had swayed their souls, or laid them to heaven's rest.   But that deeper, truer faith, which consisted in the spiritual view of that which was the unseen in Christ, and that higher power, which flows from such apprehension, they had not.   In such faith as they had, they spake, repeated forms of exorcism, tried to imitate their Master.   But they signally failed, as did those seven Jewish Priest-sons at Ephesus.   And it was intended that they should fail, that so to them and to us the higher meaning of faith as contrasted with power, the inward as contrasted with the merely outward qualification, might appear.   In that hour of crisis, in the presence of questioning Scribes and a wondering populace, and in the absence of the Christ, only one power could prevail, that of spiritual faith; and 'that kind ' could ' not come out but by prayer.' [2]

It is this lesson, viewed also in organic connection with all that had happened since the great temptation at Dalmanutha, which furnishes the explanation of the whole history.   For one moment we have a glimpse into the Saviour's soul: the poignant sorrow of His disappointment at the unbelief of the ' faithless and perverse genera-

---

[1] In St. Mark ix. 16 the better reading is, 'He asked them,' and not, as in the T.R., 'the Scribes.'

[2] The addition of the word 'fasting ' in St. Mark is probably spurious.   It reads like a later gloss.   It is not unlikely that St. Matt. xvii. 21 is merely a spurious insertion from St. Mark.   However, see *Meyer* on this point.

tion,'[1] with which He had so long borne; the infinite patience and condescension, the Divine 'need be' of His having thus to bear even with His own, together with the deep humiliation and keen pang which it involved; and the almost home-longing, as one has called it,[2] of His soul. These are mysteries to adore. The next moment Jesus turns Him to the father. At His command the lunatick is brought to Him. In the Presence of Jesus, and in view of the coming contest between Light and Darkness, one of those paroxysms of demoniac operation ensues, such as we have witnessed on all similar occasions. This was allowed to pass in view of all. But both this, and the question as to the length of time the lunatick had been afflicted, together with the answer, and the description of the dangers involved, which it elicited, were evidently intended to point the lesson of the need of a higher faith. To the father, however, who knew not the mode of treatment by the Heavenly Physician, they seemed like the questions of an earthly healer who must consider the symptoms before he could attempt to cure. 'If Thou canst do anything, have compassion on us, and help us.'

It was but natural—and yet it was the turning-point in this whole history, alike as regarded the healing of the lunatick, the better leading of his father, the teaching of the disciples, and that of the multitude and the Scribes. There is all the calm majesty of Divine self-consciousness, yet without trace of self-assertion, when Jesus, utterly ignoring the 'if Thou canst,' turns to the man and tells him that, while with the Divine Helper there is the possibility of all help, it is conditioned by a possibility in ourselves, by man's receptiveness, by his faith. Not, if the Christ can do anything or even everything, but, 'If thou canst believe,'[3] all things are possible to him that believeth.'[4] The question is not, it can never be, as the man had put it; it must not even be answered, but ignored. It must ever be,

---

[1] The expression 'generation' although embracing in its reproof all the people, is specially addressed to the disciples.

[2] *Godet.*

[3] The weight of the evidence from the MSS. accepted by most modern critics (though not by that very judicious commentator, Canon *Cook*) is in favour of the reading and rendering: 'If Thou canst! all things are possible,' &c. But it seems to me, that this mode of reply on the part of Christ is not only without any other parallel in the Gospels, but too artificial, too Western, if I may use the expression. While the age of a MS. or MSS. is,

of course, one of the outward grounds on which the criticism of the text must proceed, I confess to the feeling that, as age and purity are not identical, the interpreter must weigh all such evidence in the light of the internal grounds for or against its reception. Besides, in this instance, it seems to me that there is some difficulty about the τό if πιστεῦσαι is struck out, and which is not so easily cleared up as *Meyer* suggests.

[4] 'Omnipotentiæ Divinæ se fides hominis, quasi organon, accommodat ad recipiendum, vel etiam ad agendum.'—*Bengel.*

not what *He* can, but what *we* can. When the infinite fulness is poured forth, as it ever is in Christ, it is not the oil that is stayed, but the vessels which fail. He giveth richly, inexhaustibly, but not mechanically; there is only one condition, the moral one of the presence of absolute faith—our receptiveness. And so these words have to all time remained the teaching to every individual striver in the battle of the higher life, and to the Church as a whole—the ' *in hoc signo vinces*' [1] over the Cross, the victory that overcometh the world, even our faith.

It was a lesson, of which the reality was attested by the hold which it took on the man's whole nature. While by one great outgoing of his soul he overleapt all, to lay hold on the one fact set before him, he felt all the more the dark chasm of unbelief behind him, but he also clung to that Christ, Whose teaching of faith had shown him, together with the possibility, the source of faith. Thus through the felt unbelief of faith he attained true faith by laying hold on the Divine Saviour, when he cried out and said: [2] ' Lord, I believe; help Thou mine unbelief.' [3] These words have remained historic, marking all true faith, which, even as faith, is conscious of, nay implies, unbelief, but brings it to Christ for help. The most bold leap of faith and the timid resting at His Feet, the first beginning and the last ending of faith, have alike this as their watchword.

Such cry could not be, and never is, unheard. It was real demoniac influence which, continuing with this man from childhood onwards, had well-nigh crushed all moral individuality in him. In his many lucid intervals these many years, since he had grown from a child into a youth, he had never sought to shake off the yoke and regain his moral individuality, nor would he even now have come, if his father had not brought him. If any, this narrative shows the view which the Gospels and Jesus took of what are described as the ' demonised.' It was a reality, and not accommodation to Jewish views, when, as He saw ' the multitude running together, He rebuked the unclean spirit, saying to him: Dumb and deaf spirit, I command thee, come out of him, and no more come into him.'

Another and a more violent paroxysm, so that the bystanders almost thought him dead. But the unclean spirit had come out of

---

[1] ' In this sign shalt thou conquer '—the inscription on the supposed vision of the Cross by the Emperor Constantine before his great victory and conversion to Christianity.

[2] The words with ' tears,' in the T.R.

are apparently a spurious addition.

[3] The interpretation of *Meyer*: ' Do not withhold thy help, notwithstanding my unbelief ' seems as jejune as that of others: ' Help me in my unbelief.'

him.   And with strong gentle Hand the Saviour lifted him, and with
loving gesture delivered him to his father.

All things had been possible to faith; not to that external belief
of the disciples, which failed to reach 'that kind,'[1] and ever fails to
reach such kind, but to true spiritual faith in Him.   And so it is to
each of us individually, and to the Church, to all time.   'That kind,'
—whether it be of sin, of lust, of the world, or of science falsely so
called, of temptation, or of materialism—cometh not out by any of
our ready-made formulas or dead dogmas.   Not so are the flesh and
the Devil vanquished; not so is the world overcome.   It cometh out
by nothing but by prayer: 'Lord, I believe; help Thou mine unbelief.'   Then, although our faith were only what in popular language was described as the smallest—'like a grain of mustard-seed'
—and the result to be achieved the greatest, most difficult, seemingly transcending human ability to compass it—what in popular
language was designated as 'removing mountains'[2]—'nothing shall
be impossible' unto us.   And these eighteen centuries of suffering
in Christ, and deliverance through Christ, and work for Christ, have
proved it.   For all things are ours, if Christ is ours.

[1] But it is rather too wide an application, when *Euthymius Zygabenus* (one
of the great Byzantine theologians of the
twelfth century), and others after him,
note 'the kind of all demons.'

[2] The Rabbinic use of the expression,
'grain of mustard seed,' has already been
noted.   The expression 'tearing up' or
'removing' 'mountains' was also proverbial among the Rabbis.   Thus, a great
Rabbi might be designated as one who
'uprooted mountains' (Ber., last page,
line 5 from top; and Horay, 14 *a*), or as
one who pulverised them (Sanh. 24 *a*).
The expression is also used to indicate
apparently impossible things, such as
those which a heathen government may
order a man to do (Baba B. 3 *b*).

CHAPTER III.

THE LAST EVENTS IN GALILEE—THE TRIBUTE-MONEY, THE DISPUTE BY THE WAY, THE FORBIDDING OF HIM WHO COULD NOT FOLLOW WITH THE DISCIPLES, AND THE CONSEQUENT TEACHING OF CHRIST.

(St. Matt. xvii. 22—xviii. 22; St. Mark ix. 30-50; St. Luke ix. 43-50.)

BOOK
IV

Now that the Lord's retreat in the utmost borders of the land, at Cæsarea Philippi, was known to the Scribes, and that He was again surrounded and followed by the multitude, there could be no further object in His retirement. Indeed, the time was coming that He should meet that for which He had been, and was still, preparing the minds of His disciples—His Decease at Jerusalem. Accordingly, we find Him once more with His disciples in Galilee—not to abide there,[1] nor to traverse it as formerly for Missionary purposes, but preparatory to His journey to the Feast of Tabernacles. The few events of this brief stay, and the teaching connected with it, may be summed up as follows.

1. Prominently, perhaps, as the summary of all, we have now the clear and emphatic repetition of the prediction of His Death and Resurrection. While He would keep His present stay in Galilee as

ª St. Mark

private as possible,ª He would fain so emphasize this teaching to His disciples, that it should sink down into their ears and memories. For it was, indeed, the most needful for them in view of the immediate future. Yet the announcement only filled their loving hearts with exceeding sorrow; they comprehended it not; nay, they were—perhaps not unnaturally—afraid to ask Him about it. We remember, that even the three who had been with Jesus on the Mount, understood not what the rising from the dead should mean, and that, by direction of the Master, they kept the whole Vision from their fellow-disciples; and, thinking of it all, we scarcely wonder that, from their standpoint, it was hid from them, so that they might not perceive it.

---

[1] The expression in St. Matthew (xvii. 22) does not imply permanent abode, but a temporary stay—a going to and fro.

2. It is to the depression caused by His insistence on this terrible future, to the constant apprehension of near danger, and the consequent desire not to 'offend,' and so provoke those at whose hands, Christ had told them, He was to suffer, that we trace the incident about the tribute-money. We can scarcely believe, that Peter would have answered as he did, without previous permission of his Master, had it not been for such thoughts and fears. It was another mode of saying, 'That be far from Thee'—or, rather, trying to keep it as far as he could from Christ. Indeed, we can scarcely repress the feeling, that there was a certain amount of secretiveness on the part of Peter, as if he had apprehended that Jesus would not have wished him to act as he did, and would fain have kept the whole transaction from the knowledge of his Master.

It is well known that, on the ground of the injunction in Exod. xxx. 13 &c., every male in Israel, from twenty years upwards, was expected annually to contribute to the Temple-Treasury the sum of one half-shekel[1] of the Sanctuary,[a] that is, one common shekel, or two Attic drachms,[2] equivalent to about 1s. 2d. or 1s. 3d. of our money. Whether or not the original Biblical ordinance had been intended to institute a regular annual contribution, the Jews of the Dispersion would probably regard it in the light of a patriotic as well as religious act.

To the particulars previously given on this subject a few others may be added. The family of the Chief of the Sanhedrin (Gamaliel) seems to have enjoyed the curious distinction of bringing their contributions to the Temple-Treasury, not like others, but to have thrown them down before him who opened the Temple-Chest,[3] when they were immediately placed in the box from which, without delay, sacrifices were provided.[b] Again, the commentators explain a certain passage in the Mishnah[c] and the Talmud[d] as implying that, although the Jews in Palestine had to pay the tribute-money before the Passover, those from neighbouring lands might bring it before the Feast of Weeks, and those from such remote countries as Babylonia and Media as late as the Feast of Tabernacles.[4] Lastly, although

Marginal notes:
[a] Comp. 2 Kings xii. 4; 2 Chron. xxiv. 6; Neh. x. 32

[b] Sheq. iii. 3
[c] Sheq. iii. 4
[d] Yoma 64 a

---

[1] According to Neh. x. 32, immediately after the return from Babylon the contribution was a *third* of a shekel—probably on account of the poverty of the people.

[2] But only one Alexandrian (comp. LXX. Gen. xxiii. 15; Josh. vii. 21).

[3] Could there have been an intended, or—what would be still more striking—an unintended, but very real irony in this, when Judas afterwards cast down the pieces of silver in the Temple (St. Matt. xxvii. 5)?

[4] Dean *Plumptre* is mistaken in comparing, as regarded the Sadducees, the Temple-rate with the Church-rate question. There is no analogy between them, nor did the Sadducees ever question its propriety. The Dean is also in error in supposing, that the Palestinians were wont to bring it at one of the other feasts.

BOOK
IV

ᵃ Sheqal.
vi. 5
ᵇ Yoma 55 b

ᶜ Ps. ii. 4

ᵈ Jos. War
vii. 6. 6

the Mishnah lays it down, that the goods of those might be distrained, who had not paid the Temple-tribute by the 25th Adar, it is scarcely credible that this obtained at the time of Christ,[1] at any rate in Galilee. Indeed, this seems implied in the statement of the Mishnah and the Talmud,[b] that one of the 'thirteen trumpets' in the Temple, into which contributions were cast, was destined for the shekels of the current, and another for those of the preceding, year. Finally, these Temple-contributions were in the first place devoted to the purchase of all public sacrifices, that is, those which were offered in the name of the whole congregation of Israel, such as the morning and evening sacrifices. It will be remembered, that this was one of the points in fierce dispute between the Pharisees and Sadducees, and that the former perpetuated their triumph by marking its anniversary as a festive day in their calendar. It seems a terrible irony of judgment[c] when Vespasian ordered, after the destruction of the Temple, that this tribute should henceforth be paid for the rebuilding of the Temple of Jupiter Capitolinus.[d]

It will be remembered that, shortly before the previous Passover, Jesus with His disciples had left Capernaum,[2] that they returned to the latter city only for the Sabbath, and that, as we have suggested, they passed the first Paschal days on the borders of Tyre. We have, indeed, no means of knowing where the Master had tarried during the ten days between the 15th and the 25th Adar, supposing the Mishnic arrangements to have been in force in Capernaum. He was certainly not at Capernaum, and it must also have been known, that He had not gone up to Jerusalem for the Passover. Accordingly, when it was told in Capernaum, that the Rabbi of Nazareth had once more come to what seems to have been His Galilean home, it was only natural, that they who collected the Temple-tribute[3] should have applied for its payment. It is quite possible, that their application may have been, if not prompted, yet quickened, by the wish to involve Him in a breach of so well-known an obligation, or else by a hostile curiosity. Would He, Who took so strangely different views of Jewish observances, and Who made such extraordinary claims, own the duty of paying the Temple-tribute? Had it been

---

[1] The penalty of distraint had only been enacted less than a century before (about 78), during the reign of Queen Salome-Alexandra, who was entirely in the hands of the Pharisees.

[2] See Book III. ch. xxxi.

[3] If it were not for the authority of *Wieseler*, who supports it, the suggestion would scarcely deserve serious notice,

that the reference here is not to the Temple-tribute, but to the Roman poll-tax o census. Irrespective of the question whether a census was then levied in Galilee, the latter is designated both in St. Matt. xvii. 25, and in xxii. 17, as well as in St. Mark xii. 14, as κῆνσος, while here the well-known expression *did-rachma* is used.

owing to His absence, or from principle, that He had not paid it last CHAP.
Passover-season? The question which they put to Peter implies, at III
least, their doubt.

We have already seen what motives prompted the hasty reply of
Peter. He might, indeed, also otherwise, in his rashness, have given
an affirmative answer to the inquiry, without first consulting the
Master. For there seems little doubt, that Jesus had on former
occasions complied with the Jewish custom. But matters were now
wholly changed. Since the first Passover, which had marked His
first public appearance in the Temple at Jerusalem, He had stated—
and quite lately in most explicit terms—that He was the Christ, the
Son of God. To have now paid the Temple-tribute, without explanation, might have involved a very serious misapprehension. In view of
all this, the history before us seems alike simple and natural. There
is no pretext for the artificial construction put upon it by commentators,
any more than for the suggestion, that such was the poverty of the
Master and His disciples, that the small sum requisite for the Temple-
tribute had to be miraculously supplied.

We picture it to ourselves on this wise. Those who received the
Tribute-money had come to Peter, and perhaps met him in the
court or corridor, and asked him: 'Your Teacher (Rabbi), does He
not pay the didrachma?' While Peter hastily responded in the
affirmative, and then entered into the house to procure the coin, or
else to report what had passed, Jesus, Who had been in another part
of the house, but was cognisant of all, 'anticipated him.'[1] Addressing him in kindly language as 'Simon,' He pointed out the real state
of matters by an illustration which must, of course, not be too literally
pressed, and of which the meaning was: Whom does a King intend to tax for the maintenance of his palace and officers? Surely
not his own family, but others. The inference from this, as regarded
the Temple-tribute, was obvious. As in all similar Jewish parabolic
teaching, it was only indicated in general principle: 'Then are the
children free.' But even so, be it as Peter had wished, although not
from the same motive. Let no needless offence be given; for,
assuredly, they would not have understood the principle on which
Christ would have refused the Tribute money,[2] and all misunder-

[1] The Revised Version renders it by:
'spake first.' But the word (προφθάνω)
does not bear this meaning in any of
the fifteen passages in the LXX., where
it corresponds to the Hebrew Qiddem,
and means 'to anticipate' or 'to prevent' in the archaic sense of that word.

[2] In Succ. 30 a, we read a parable of a
king who paid toll, and being asked the
reason, replied that travellers were to
learn by his example not to seek to
withdraw themselves from paying all
dues.

standing on the part of Peter was now impossible.   Yet Christ would still further vindicate His royal title.   He will pay for Peter also, and pay, as heaven's King, with a *Stater*, or four-drachm piece, miraculously provided.

Thus viewed, there *is*, we submit, a moral purpose and spiritual instruction in the provision of the Stater out of the fish's mouth. The rationalistic explanation of it need not be seriously considered; for any mythical interpretation there is not the shadow of support in Biblical precedent or Jewish expectancy.   But the narrative in its literality has a true and high meaning.   And if we wished to mark the difference between its sober simplicity and the extravagances of legend, we would remind ourselves, not only of the well-known story of the Ring of Polycrates, but of two somewhat kindred Jewish Haggadahs.   They are both intended to glorify the Jewish mode of Sabbath observance.   One of them bears that one Joseph, known as 'the honourer' of the Sabbath, had a wealthy heathen neighbour, to whom the Chaldæans had prophesied that all his riches would come to Joseph.   To render this impossible, the wealthy man converted all his property into one magnificent gem, which he carefully concealed within his head-gear.   Then he took ship, so as for ever to avoid the dangerous vicinity of the Jew.   But the wind blew his head-gear into the sea, and the gem was swallowed by a fish.   And lo! it was the holy season, and they brought to the market a splendid fish.   Who would purchase it but Joseph, for none as he would prepare to honour the day by the best which he could provide.   But when they opened the fish, the gem was found in it—the moral being: ' He that borroweth for the Sabbath, the Sabbath will repay him.'[a]

ᵃ Shabb.
119 a, lines
20 &c. from
top

The other legend is similar.   It was in Rome (in the Christian world) that a poor tailor went to market to buy a fish for a festive meal.[1]   Only one was on sale, and for it there was keen competition between the servant of a Prince and the Jew, the latter at last buying it for not less than twelve dinars.   At the banquet, the Prince inquired of his servants why no fish had been provided. When he ascertained the cause, he sent for the Jew with the threatening inquiry, how a poor tailor could afford to pay twelve dinars for a fish?   'My Lord,' replied the Jew, 'there is a day on which all our sins are remitted us, and should we not honour it?'   The answer satisfied the Prince.   But God rewarded the Jew, for, when the fish

---

[1] In the Midrash: 'On the eve of the great fast' (the Day of Atonement). But from the connection it is evidently in-   tended to apply to the distinction to be put on the Sabbath-meal.

was opened, a precious gem was found in it, which he sold, and ever afterwards lived of the proceeds.[a]

The reader can scarcely fail to mark the absolute difference between even the most beautiful Jewish legends and any trait in the Evangelic history.

3. The event next recorded in the Gospels took place partly on the way from the Mount of Transfiguration to Capernaum, and partly in Capernaum itself, immediately after the scene connected with the Tribute-money. It is recorded by the three Evangelists, and it led to explanations and admonitions, which are told by St. Mark and St. Luke, but chiefly by St. Matthew. This circumstance seems to indicate, that the latter was the chief actor in that which occasioned this special teaching and warning of Christ, and that it must have sunk very deeply into his heart.

As we look at it, in the light of the then mental and spiritual state of the Apostles, not in that in which, perhaps naturally, we regard them, what happened seems not difficult to understand. As St. Mark puts it,[b] by the way they had disputed among themselves which of them would be the greatest—as St. Matthew explains,[c] in the Messianic Kingdom of Heaven. They might now the more confidently expect its near Advent from the mysterious announcement of the Resurrection on the third day,[d] which they would probably connect with the commencement of the last Judgment, following upon the violent Death of the Messiah. Of a dispute, serious and even violent, among the disciples, we have evidence in the exhortation of the Master, as reported by St. Mark,[e] in the direction of the Lord how to deal with an offending brother, and in the answering inquiry of Peter.[f] Nor can we be at a loss to perceive its occasion.» The distinction just bestowed on the three, in being taken up the Mount, may have roused feelings of jealousy in the others, perhaps of self-exaltation in the three. Alike the spirit which John displayed in his harsh prohibition of the man that did not follow with the disciples,[g] and the self-righteous bargaining of Peter about forgiving the supposed or real offences of a brother,[h] give evidence of anything but the frame of mind which we would have expected after the Vision on the Mount.

In truth, most incongruous as it may appear to us, looking back on it in the light of the Resurrection-day, nay, almost incredible— evidently, the Apostles were still greatly under the influence of the old spirit. It was the common Jewish view, that there would be distinctions of rank in the Kingdom of Heaven. It can scarcely be neccessary to prove this by Rabbinic quotations, since the whole

CHAP.
III

[a] Ber. R. 11 on Gen. ii. 3

[b] St. Mark ix. 34
[c] St. Matt. xviii. 1

[d] St. Matt. xvii. 23; St. Mark ix. 31

[e] St. Mark ix. 42-50

[f] St. Matt. xviii. 15, 21

[g] St. Mark ix. 38

[h] St. Matt. xviii. 21

BOOK
IV

ᵃ Taan.
iii. 8;
comp.
especially
Jer. Taan.
67 a
ᵇ Baba B.
75 a

ᶜ Ber. 34 b

ᵈ St. Matt.
xx. 20

system of Rabbinism and Pharisaism, with its separation from the vulgar and ignorant, rests upon it. But even within the charmed circle of Rabbinism, there would be distinctions, due to learning, merit, and even to favouritism. In this world there were His special favourites, who could command anything at His hand, to use the Rabbinic illustration, like a spoilt child from its father.ᵃ¹ And in the Messianic age God would assign booths to each according to his rank.ᵇ On the other hand, many passages could be quoted bearing on the duty of humility and self-abasement. But the stress laid on the merit attaching to this shows too clearly, that it was the pride that apes humility. One instance,ᶜ previously referred to, will suffice by way of illustration. When the child of the great Rabbi Jochanan ben Zakkai was dangerously ill, he was restored through the prayer of one Chanina ben Dosa. On this the father of the child remarked to his wife: ' If the son of Zakkai had all day long put his head between his knees, no heed would have been given to him.' ' How is that?' asked his wife; ' is Chanina greater than thou?' ' No, was the reply, ' he is like a servant before the King, while I am like a prince before the King' (he is always there, and has thus opportunities which I, as a lord, do not enjoy).

How deep-rooted were such thoughts and feelings, appears not only from the dispute of the disciples by the way, but from the request proffered by the mother of Zebedee's children and her sons at a later period, in terrible contrast to the near Passion of our Lord.ᵈ It does, indeed come upon us as a most painful surprise, and as sadly incongruous, this constant self-obtrusion, self-assertion, and low, carnal self-seeking; this Judaistic trifling in face of the utter self-abnegation and self-sacrifice of the Son of Man. Surely, the contrast between Christ and His disciples seems at times almost as great as between Him and the other Jews. If we would measure His Stature, or comprehend the infinite distance between His aims and teaching and those of His contemporaries, let it be by comparison with even the best of His disciples. It must have been part of His humiliation and self-exinanition to bear with them. And is it not, in a sense, still so as regards us all?

We have already seen, that there was quite sufficient occasion and material for such a dispute on the way from the Mount of Transfiguration to Capernaum. We suppose Peter to have been only at

---

¹ The almost blasphemous story of how Choni or Onias, ' the circle-drawer,' drew a circle around him, and refused to leave it till God had sent rain—and succes-sively objected to too little and too much, stands by no means alone. Jer. Taan. 67 a gives some very painful details about this power of even altering the decrees of God.

the first with the others. To judge by the later question, how often he was to forgive the brother who had sinned against him, he may have been so deeply hurt, that he left the other disciples, and hastened on with the Master, Who would, at any rate, sojourn in his house. For, neither he nor Christ seem to have been present when John and the others forbade the man, who would not follow with them, to cast out demons in Christ's name. Again, the other disciples only came into Capernaum, and entered the house, just as Peter had gone for the Stater, with which to pay the Temple-tribute for the Master and himself. And, if speculation be permissible, we would suggest that the brother, whose offences Peter found it so difficult to forgive, may have been none other than Judas. In such a dispute by the way, he, with his Judaistic views, would be specially interested; perhaps he may have been its chief instigator; certainly, he, whose natural character, amidst its sharp contrasts to that of Peter, presented so many points of resemblance to it, would, on many grounds, be specially jealous of, and antagonistic to him.

Quite natural in view of this dispute by the way is another incident of the journey, which is afterwards related.[a] As we judge, John seems to have been the principal actor in it; perhaps, in the absence of Peter, he claimed the leadership. They had met one who was casting out demons in the Name of Christ—whether successfully or not, we need scarcely inquire. So widely had faith in the power of Jesus extended; so real was the belief in the subjection of the demons to Him; so reverent was the acknowledgment of Him. A man, who, thus forsaking the methods of Jewish exorcists, owned Jesus in the face of the Jewish world, could not be far from the Kingdom of Heaven; at any rate, he could not quickly speak evil of Him. John had, in name of the disciples, forbidden him, because he had not cast in his lot wholly with them. It was quite in the spirit of their ideas about the Messianic Kingdom, and of their dispute, which of His close followers would be greatest there. And yet, they might deceive themselves as to the motives of their conduct. If it were not almost impertinence to use such terms, we would have said that there was infinite wisdom and kindness in the answer which the Saviour gave, when referred to on the subject. To forbid a man, in such circumstances, would be either prompted by the spirit of the dispute by the way—or else must be grounded on evidence that the motive was, or the effect would untimately be (as in the case of the sons of Sceva) to lead men 'to speak evil' of Christ, or to hinder the work of His disciples. Assuredly, such could not have been the case with

a St. Mark ix. 38; St. Luke ix. 49

BOOK
IV

a man, who invoked His Name, and perhaps experienced its efficacy. More than this—and here is an eternal principle: ' He that is not against us is for us; ' he that opposeth not the disciples, really is for them—a saying still more clear, when we adopt the better reading in St. Luke,[a] ' He that is not against you is for you. '[1]

a St. Luke
ix. 50

There was reproof in this, as well as instruction, deeply consistent with that other, though seemingly different, saying:[b] ' He that is not with Me is against Me.' The distinction between them is twofold. In the one case it is ' not against,' in the other it is ' not with;' but chiefly it lies in this: in the one case it is not against the disciples in their work, while in the other it is—not with Christ. A man who did what he could with such knowledge of Christ as he possessed, even although he did not absolutely follow with them, was ' not against ' them. Such an one should be regarded as thus far with them; at least be let alone, left to Him Who knew all things. Such a man would not lightly speak evil of Christ—and that was all the disciples should care for, unless, indeed, they sought their own. Quite other was it as regarded the relation of a person to the Christ Himself. There neutrality was impossible—and that which was not with Christ, by this very fact was against Him. The lesson is of the most deep-reaching character, and the distinction, alas! still overlooked—perhaps, because ours is too often the spirit of those who journeyed to Capernaum. Not, that it is unimportant to follow with the disciples, but that it is not ours to forbid any work done, however imperfectly, in His Name, and that only one question is really vital —whether or not a man is decidedly with Christ.

b St. Matt.
xii. 30

Such were the incidents by the way. And now, while withholding from Christ their dispute, and, indeed, anything that might seem personal in the question, the disciples, on entering the house where He was in Capernaum, addressed to Him this inquiry (which should be inserted from the opening words of St. Matthew's narrative): ' Who, then, is greatest in the Kingdom of Heaven? ' It was a general question—but Jesus perceived the thought of their hearts;[c] He knew about what they had disputed by the way,[d] and now asked them concerning it. The account of St. Mark is most graphic. We almost see the scene. Conscience-stricken ' they held their peace.' As we read the further words:[e] 'And He sat down,' it seems as if the

c St. Luke
d St. Mark
ix. 33

e ver. 35

---

[1] Readers of ordinary sobriety of judgment will form their opinions of the value of modern negative criticism, when we tell them that it has discovered in this man who did not follow with the disciples an allusion to ' Pauline Christianity,' of which St. Mark took a more charitable view than St. Matthew! By such treatment it would not be difficult to make anything of the facts of history.

Master had at first gone to welcome the disciples on their arrival, and they, ' full of their dispute,' had, without delay, addressed their inquiry to him in the court or antechamber, where they met Him, when, reading their thoughts, He had first put the searching counter-question, what had been the subject of their dispute. Then, leading the way into the house, ' He sat down,' not only to answer their inquiry, which was not a real inquiry, but to teach them what so much they needed to learn. He called a little child—perhaps Peter's little son—and put him in the midst of them. Not to strive who was to be greatest, but to be utterly without self-consciousness, like a child—thus, to become turned and entirely changed in mind: ' converted,' was the condition for entering into the Kingdom of Heaven. Then, as to the question of greatness there, it was really one of greatness of service—and that was greatest service which implied most self-denial. Suiting the action to the teaching, the Blessed Saviour took the happy child in His Arms. Not, to teach, to preach, to work miracles, nor to do great things, but to do the humblest service for Christ's sake—lovingly, earnestly, wholly, self-forgetfully, simply for Christ, was to receive Christ—nay, to receive the Father. And the smallest service, as it might seem—even the giving a cup of cold water in such spirit, would not lose its reward. Blessed teaching this to the disciples and to us; blessed lesson, which, these many centuries of scorching heat, has been of unspeakable refreshing, alike to the giver and the receiver of the cup of water in the Name of Christ, in the love of Christ, and for the sake of Christ.[1]

These words about receiving Christ, and ' receiving in the Name of Christ,' had stirred the memory and conscience of John, and made him half wonder, half fear, whether what they had done by the way, in forbidding the man to do what he could in the name of Christ, had been right. And so he told it, and received the further and higher teaching on the subject. And, more than this, St. Mark and, more fully, St. Matthew, record some further instruction in connection with it, to which St. Luke refers, in a slightly different form, at a somewhat later period.[a] But it seems so congruous to the present occasion, that we conclude it was then spoken, although, like other sayings,[b] it may have been afterwards repeated under similar circumstances.[2] Certainly, no more effective continuation,

CHAP.
III

[a] St. Luke xvii. 1-7

[b] Comp. for example St. Mark ix. 50 with St. Matt. v. 13

---

[1] *Verbal* parallels could easily be quoted, and naturally so, since Jesus spoke as a Jew to Jews—but no *real* parallel. Indeed, the point of the story lies in its being so utterly un-Jewish.

[2] Or else St. Luke may have gathered into connected discourses what may have been spoken at different times.

BOOK
IV

ᵃ St. Matt.
xviii. 2-6,
and
parallels

and application to Jewish minds, of the teaching of our Lord could be conceived than that which follows. For, the love of Christ goes deeper than the condescension of receiving a child, utterly un-Pharisaic and un-Rabbinic as this is.ᵃ To have regard to the weaknesses of such a child—to its mental and moral ignorance and folly, to adapt ourselves to it, to restrain our fuller knowledge and forego our felt liberty, so as not ' to offend '—not to give occasion for stumbling to ' one of these little ones,' that so through our knowledge the weak brother for whom Christ died should not perish: this is a lesson which reaches even deeper than the question, what is the condition of entrance into the Kingdom, or what service constitutes real greatness in it. A man may enter into the Kingdom and do service—yet, if in so doing he disregard the law of love to the little ones, far better his work should be abruptly cut short; better, one of those large millstones, turned by an ass, were hung about his neck and he cast into the sea! We pause to note, once more, the Judaic, and, therefore, evidential, setting of the Evangelic narrative. The Talmud also speaks of two kinds of millstones—the one turned by hand

ᵇ Kethub.
59 b, line 18
from
bottom
ᶜ Moed K.
10 b, first
line
ᵈ Kidd. 29 b,
lines 10 and
9 from
bottom
ᵉ Vayyikra
R. 26.

(רחיים דידא),ᵇ referred to in St. Luke xvii. 35; the other turned by an ass (μύλος ὀνικός), just as the Talmud also speaks of ' the ass of the millstone ' (חמר׳ דריחיא).ᶜ Similarly, the figure about a millstone hung round the neck occurs also in the Talmud—although there as figurative of almost insuperable difficulties.ᵈ Again, the expression, ' it were better for him,' is a well-known Rabbinic expression (*Mutabh hayah lo*).ᵉ Lastly, according to St. Jerome, the punishment which seems alluded to in the words of Christ, and which we know to have been inflicted by Augustus, was actually practised by the Romans in Galilee on some of the leaders of the insurrection under Judas of Galilee.

ᶠ St. Matt.
xviii. 8-9;
St. Mark,
ix. 43-48

And yet greater guilt would only too surely be incurred! Woe unto the world!ᶠ Occasions of stumbling and offence will surely come, but woe to the man through whom such havoc was wrought. What then is the alternative? If it be a question as between offence and some part of ourselves, a limb or member, however useful—the hand, the foot, the eye—then let it rather be severed from the body, however painful, or however seemingly great the loss. It cannot be so great as that of the whole being in the eternal fire of Gehenna, where their worm dieth not, and the fire is not quenched.¹ Be

---

¹ St. Mark ix. 44, the last clause of ver. 45, and ver. 46, seem to be spurious. But ver. 48 (except the words τοῦ πυρός, for which read simply: ' into Gehenna ') as well as the expression ' fire that never shall be quenched,' and in St. Matthew,

it hand, foot, or eye—practice, pursuit, or research—which consciously leads us to occasions of stumbling, it must be resolutely put aside in view of the incomparably greater loss of eternal remorse and anguish.

Here St. Mark abruptly breaks off with a saying in which the Saviour makes general application, although the narrative is further continued by St. Matthew. The words reported by St. Mark are so remarkable, so brief, we had almost said truncated, as to require special consideration.[a] It seems to us that, turning from this thought that even members which are intended for useful service may, in certain circumstances, have to be cut off to avoid the greatest loss, the Lord gave to His disciples this as the final summary and explanation of all: 'For every one shall be salted for the fire'[1]—or, as a very early gloss, which has strangely crept into the text,[2] paraphrased and explained it, 'Every sacrifice shall be salted with salt.'[b] No one is fit for the sacrificial fire, no one can himself be, nor offer anything as a sacrifice, unless it have been first, according to the Levitical Law, covered with salt, symbolic of the incorruptible. 'Salt is good; but if the salt,' with which the spiritual sacrifice is to be salted for the fire, 'have lost its savour, wherewith will ye season it?' Hence, 'have salt in yourselves,' but do not let that salt be corrupted by making it an occasion of offence to others, or among yourselves, as in the dispute by the way, or in the disposition of mind that led to it, or in forbidding others to work who follow not with you, but 'be at peace among yourselves.'

To this explanation of the words of Christ it may, perhaps, be added that, from their form, they must have conveyed a special meaning to the disciples. It is a well-known law, that every sacrifice burned on the Altar must be salted with salt.[c] Indeed, according to the Talmud, not only every such offering, but even the wood with which the sacrificial fire was kindled, was sprinkled with salt.[d] Salt symbolised to the Jews of that time the incorruptible and the higher. Thus, the soul was compared to the salt, and it was said concerning the dead: 'Shake off the salt, and throw the flesh to the dogs.'[e] The Bible was compared to salt; so was acuteness of intellect.[f] Lastly, the question: 'If the salt have lost its savour, wherewith will ye season it?' seems to have been proverbial, and occurs in

CHAP.
III

[a] St. Mark ix. 49, 50

[b] These words are spurious

[c] Lev. ii. 13

[d] Menach. 20 b

[e] Nidd. 31 a

[f] Kidd. 29 b

'everlasting fire,' are on all hands admitted to be genuine. The question of 'eternal punishment,' from the standpoint of Jewish theology, will be treated in a later part.

[1] The rendering 'Salted for the fire,' viz., as a sacrifice, has been adopted by

other critics.

[2] We can readily understand how that clause, which was one of the most ancient explanations, perhaps a marginal gloss on the text 'Everyone shall be salted for the fire,' crept into the text when its meaning was no longer understood.

exactly the same words in the Talmud, apparently to denote a thing that is impossible.[a][1]

Most thoroughly anti-Pharisaic and anti-Rabbinic as all this was, what St. Matthew further reports leads still farther in the same direction. We seem to see Jesus still holding this child, and, with evident reference to the Jewish contempt for that which is small, point to him and apply, in quite other manner than they had ever heard, the Rabbinic teaching about the Angels. In the Jewish view,[2] only the chiefest of the Angels were before the Face of God within the curtained Veil, or *Pargod*, while the others, ranged in different

classes, stood outside and awaited his behest.[b] The distinction which the former enjoyed was always to behold His Face, and to hear and know directly the Divine counsels and commands. This distinction was, therefore, one of knowledge; Christ taught that it was one of love. Not the more exalted in knowledge, and merit, or worth, but the simpler, the more unconscious of self, the more receptive and clinging—the nearer to God. Look up from earth to heaven; those representative, it may be, guardian, Angels nearest to God, are not those of deepest knowledge of God's counsel and commands, but those of simple, humble grace and faith—and so learn, not only not to despise one of these little ones, but who is truly greatest in the Kingdom of Heaven!

Viewed in this light, there is nothing incongruous in the transition: ' For the Son of Man is come to save that which was lost.'[c] This, His greatest condescension when He became the Babe of Bethlehem, is also His greatest exaltation. He Who is nearest the Father, and, in the most special and unique sense, always beholds His Face, is He that became a Child, and, as the Son of Man, stoops lowest, to save that which was lost. The words are, indeed, regarded as spurious by most critics, because certain leading manuscripts omit them, and they are supposed to have been imported from St. Luke xix. 10. But such a transference from a context wholly unconnected with this section[3] seems unaccountable, while, on the other hand, the verse in question forms, not only an apt, but almost necessary, transition to the Parable of the Lost Sheep. It seems, therefore, difficult to eliminate it without also striking out

---

[1] מילחא כי סרי׳ במאי מלחי לה—' the salt, when it becomes ill-savouring, with what shall it be seasoned ? ' The passage occurs in a very curious Haggadah, and the objection that salt would not become ill-savouring, would not apply to the proverb in the form given it by Christ.

[2] See the Appendix on 'Angelology and Demonology.'

[3] Except that the history of Zacchæus, in which the words occur, is really an application to real life of the Parable of the Lost Sheep.

that Parable; and yet it fits most beautifully into the whole context. Suffice it for the present to note this. The Parable itself is more fully repeated in another connection,[a] in which it will be more convenient to consider it.

Yet a further depth of Christian love remained to be shown, which, all self-forgetful, sought not its own, but the things of others. This also bore on the circumstances of the time, and the dispute between the disciples, but went far beyond it, and set forth eternal principles. Hitherto it had been a question of not seeking self, nor minding great things, but Christ-like and God-like, to condescend to the little ones. What if actual wrong had been done, and just offence given by a 'brother'?[b] In such case, also, the principle of the Kingdom—which, negatively, is that of self-forgetfulness, positively, that of service of love—would first seek the good of the offending brother. We mark, here, the contrast to Rabbinism, which directs that the first overtures must be made by the offender, not the offended;[c] and even prescribes this to be done in the presence of numerous witnesses, and, if needful, repeated three times.[d] As regards the duty of showing to a brother his fault, and the delicate tenderness of doing this in private, so as not to put him to shame, Rabbinism speaks the same as the Master of Nazareth.[e] In fact, according to Jewish criminal law, punishment could not be inflicted unless the offender (even the woman suspected of adultery) had previously been warned before witnesses. Yet, in practice, matters were very different: and neither could those be found who would take reproof, nor yet such as were worthy to administer it.[f]

b St. Matt.
xviii. 15

c Yoma
viii. 9
d Yoma
87 a

e Shabb.
119 b;
Tamid 28 a;
Arakh. 16 b

f Arakh.
u. s.

Quite other was it in the Kingdom of Christ, where the theory was left undefined, but the practice clearly marked. Here, by loving dealing, to convince of his wrong, him who had done it, was not humiliation nor loss of dignity or of right, but real gain: the gain of our brother to us, and eventually to Christ Himself. But even if this should fail, the offended must not desist from his service of love, but conjoin in it others with himself so as to give weight and authority to his remonstrances, as not being the outcome of personal feeling or prejudice—perhaps, also, to be witnesses before the Divine tribunal. If this failed, a final appeal should be made on the part of the Church as a whole, which, of course, could only be done through her representatives and rulers, to whom Divine authority had been committed. And if that were rejected, the offer of love would, as always in the Gospel, pass into danger of judgment. Not, indeed, that such was to be executed by man, but that such an offender, after the first and

BOOK
IV

a Titus
iii. 10

b St. Matt.
xviii. 19

c St. Matt.
xviii. 19, 20

d St. Matt.
xviii. 21

second admonition, was to be rejected.[a] He was to be treated as was the custom in regard to a heathen or a publican—not persecuted, despised, or avoided, but not received in Church-fellowship (a heathen), nor admitted to close familiar intercourse (a publican). And this, as we understand it, marks out the mode of what is called Church discipline in general, and specifically as regards wrongs done to a brother. Discipline so exercised (which may God restore to us) has the highest Divine sanction, and the most earnest reality attaches to it. For, in virtue of the authority which Christ has committed to the Church in the persons of her rulers and representatives,[1] what they bound or loosed—declared obligatory or non-obligatory—was ratified in heaven. Nor was this to be wondered at. The incarnation of Christ was the link which bound earth to heaven: through it whatever was agreed upon in the fellowship of Christ, as that which was to be asked, would be done for them of his Father Which was in heaven.[b] Thus, the power of the Church reached up to heaven through the power of prayer in His Name Who made God our Father. And so, beyond the exercise of discipline and authority, there was the omnipotence of prayer—' if two of you shall agree . . . as touching anything . . . it shall be done for them '—and, with it, also the infinite possibility of a higher service of love. For, in the smallest gathering in the Name of Christ, His Presence would be,[2] and with it the certainty of nearness to, and acceptance with, God.[c]

It is bitterly disappointing that, after such teaching, even a Peter could—either immediately afterwards, or perhaps after he had had time to think it over, and apply it—come to the Master with the question, how often he was to forgive an offending brother, imagining that he had more than satisfied the new requirements, if he extended it to seven times.[d] Such traits show better than elaborate discussions the need of the mission and the renewing of the Holy Ghost. And yet there is something touching in the simplicity and honesty with which Peter goes to the Master with such a misapprehension of His

---

[1] It is both curious and interesting to find that the question, whether the Priests exercised their functions as ' the sent of God ' or ' the sent of the congregation '—that is, held their commission directly from God, or only as being the representatives of the people, is discussed already in the Talmud (Yoma 18 b &c.; Nedar. 35 b). The Talmud replies that, as it is impossible to delegate what one does not possess, and since the laity might neither offer sacrifices nor do any like service, the Priests could not possibly have been the delegates of the Church, but must be those of God. (See the essay by Delitzsch in the Zeitschr. für Luther. Theol. for 1854, pp. 446–449.)

[2] The Mishnah (Ab. iii. 2), and the Talmud (Ber. 6 a), infer from Mal. iii. 16, that, when two are together and occupy themselves with the Law, the Shekhinah is between them. Similarly, it is argued from Lament. iii. 28, and Exod. xx. 21, that if even one alone is engaged in such pursuits, God is with him and will bless him.

teaching, as if he had fully entered into its spirit. Surely, the new
wine was bursting the old bottles. It was a principle of Rabbinism
that, even if the wrongdoer had made full restoration, he would not
obtain forgiveness till he had asked it of him whom he had wronged,
but that it was cruelty in such circumstances to refuse pardon.[a] The
Jerusalem Talmud[b] adds the beautiful remark: 'Let this be a token
in thine hand—each time that thou showest mercy, God will show
mercy on thee; and if thou showest not mercy, neither will God show
mercy on thee.'   And yet it was a settled rule, that forgiveness should
not be extended more than three times.[c] Even so, the practice was
terribly different. The Talmud relates, without blame, the conduct of
a Rabbi, who would not forgive a very small slight of his dignity,
though asked by the offender for thirteen successive years, and that
on the Day of Atonement—the reason being, that the offended Rabbi
had learned by a dream that his offending brother would attain the
highest dignity, whereupon he feigned himself irreconcilable, to force
the other to migrate from Palestine to Babylon, where, unenvied by
him, he might occupy the chief place![d]

And so it must have seemed to Peter, in his ignorance, quite a
stretch of charity to extend forgiveness to seven, instead of three
offences. It did not occur to him, that the very act of numbering
offences marked an externalism which had never entered into, nor
comprehended the spirit of Christ. Until seven times? Nay, until
seventy times seven![1] The evident purport of these words was to
efface all such landmarks. Peter had yet to learn, what we, alas! too
often forget: that as Christ's forgiveness, so that of the Christian,
must not be computed by numbers. It is *qualitative*, not *quantitative*:
Christ forgives sin, not sins—and he who has experienced it, follows
in His footsteps.[2]

CHAP.
III

[a] Babha K.
viii. 7
[b] Jer.
Babha K.
6 c

[c] Yoma 86 b

[d] Yoma 87

---

[1] It makes no difference in the argument, whether we translate seventy times seven, or else seventy times and seven.

[2] The Parable, with which the account in St. Matthew closes, will be explained by and by in the Second Series of Parables.

CHAPTER IV.

THE JOURNEY TO JERUSALEM—CHRONOLOGICAL ARRANGEMENT OF THE
LAST PART OF THE GOSPEL-NARRATIVES—FIRST INCIDENTS BY THE
WAY.

(St. John vii. 1–16; St. Luke ix. 1–56; 57–62; St. Matthew viii. 19–22.)

BOOK
IV

THE part in the Evangelic History which we have now reached has this peculiarity and difficulty, that the events are now recorded by only one of the Evangelists. The section in St. Luke's Gospel from chapter ix. 51 to chapter xviii. 14 stands absolutely alone. From the circumstance that St. Luke omits throughout his narrative all notation of time or place, the difficulty of arranging here the chronological succession of events is so great, that we can only suggest what seems most probable, without feeling certain of the details. Happily, the period embraced is a short one, while at the same time the narrative of St. Luke remarkably fits into that of St. John. St. John mentions three appearances of Christ in Jerusalem at that period: at the Feast of Tabernacles,[a] at that of the Dedication,[b] and His final entry, which is referred to by all the other Evangelists.[c] But, while the narrative of St. John confines itself exclusively to what happened in Jerusalem or its immediate neighborhood. it also either mentions or gives sufficient indication that on two out of these three occasions Jesus left Jerusalem for the country east of the Jordan (St. John x. 19–21; St. John x. 39–43, where the words in ver. 39, 'they sought again to take Him,' point to a previous similar attempt and flight). Besides these, St. John also records a journey to Bethany—though not to Jerusalem—for the raising of Lazarus,[d] and after that a council against Christ in Jerusalem, in consequence of which He withdrew out of Judæan territory into a district near 'the wilderness'[e]—as we infer, that in the north, where John had been baptizing and Christ been tempted, and whither He had afterwards withdrawn.[f] We regard this 'wilderness' as on the western bank of the Jordan, and extending northward towards the eastern shore of the Lake of Galilee.[g]

If St. John relates three appearances of Jesus at this time in

[a] St. John vii. to x.

[b] x. 22–42

[c] St. Matt. xx. 17 &c.; St. Mark x. 32 &c.; St. Luke xvii. 11 &c.

[d] St. John xi.

[e] xi. 54

[f] St. Luke iv. 1; v. 16; vii. 24

[g] St. Luke viii. 29

Jerusalem, St. Luke records three journeys to Jerusalem,[a] the last of which agrees, in regard to its starting point, with the notices of the other Evangelists,[b] always supposing that we have correctly indicated the locality of 'the wilderness' whither, according to St. John xi. 54, Christ retired previous to His last journey to Jerusalem. In this respect, although it is impossible with our present information to localise ' the City of Ephraim,'[c] the statement that it was ' near the wilderness,' affords us sufficient general notice of its situation. For, the New Testament speaks of only two ' wildernesses,' that of Judæa in the far South, and that in the far North of Peræa, or perhaps in the Decapolis, to which St. Luke refers as the scene of the Baptist's labours, where Jesus was tempted, and whither He afterwards withdrew. We can, therefore, have little doubt that St. John refers[d] to this district. And this entirely accords with the notices by the other Evangelists of Christ's last journey to Jerusalem, as through the borders of Galilee and Samaria, and then across the Jordan, and by Bethany to Jerusalem.

It follows (as previously stated) that St. Luke's account of the three journeys to Jerusalem fits into the narrative of Christ's three appearances in Jerusalem as described by St. John. *And the unique section in St. Luke[e] supplies the record of what took place before, during, and after those journeys, of which the upshot is told by St. John.* This much seems certain; the exact chronological succession must be, in part, matter of suggestion. But we have now some insight into the plan of St. Luke's Gospel, as compared with that of the others. We see that St. Luke forms a kind of transition, is a sort of connecting link between the other two Synoptists[f] and St. John. This is admitted even by negative critics.[g] The Gospel by St. Matthew has for its main object the Discourses or teaching of the Lord, around which the History groups itself. It is intended as a demonstration, primarily addressed to the Jews, and in a form peculiarly suited to them, that Jesus was the Messiah, the Son of the Living God. The Gospel by St. Mark is a rapid survey of the History of the Christ as such. *It deals mainly with the Galilean Ministry.* The Gospel by St. John, which gives the highest, the reflective, view of the Eternal Son as the Word, *deals almost exclusively with the Jerusalem Ministry.*[1] And the Gospel by St. Luke complements the narratives in the other two Gospels (St. Matthew and St. Mark), and it supplements them *by tracing, what is not done otherwise:*

[a] St. Luke ix. 51; xiii. 22; xviii. 31

[b] St. Matt. xix. 1; St. Mark x. 1

[c] Comp. the suggestions in *Neubauer*, Geog. de Talm. p. 155

[d] in St. John xi. 54

[e] St. Luke ix. 51–xviii. 14

[f] St. Matthew and St. Mark

[g] See *Renan*, Les Evangiles, p. 266

---

[1] This seems unaccountable on the modern negative theory of its being an Ephesian Gospel.

the Ministry in Peræa. Thus, it also forms a transition to the Fourth Gospel of the Judæan Ministry. If we may venture a step further: The Gospel by St. Mark gives the general view of the Christ; that by St. Matthew the Jewish, that by St. Luke the Gentile, and that by St. John the Church's view. Imagination might, indeed, go still further, and see the impress of the number *five*—that of the Pentateuch and the Book of Psalms—in the First Gospel; the numeral *four* (that of the world) in the Second Gospel (4×4=16 chapters); that of *three* in the Third (8×3=24 chapters); and that of *seven*, the sacred Church number, in the Fourth Gospel (7×3=21 chapters). And perhaps we might even succeed in arranging the Gospels into corresponding sections. But this would lead, not only beyond our present task, but from solid history and exegesis into the regions of speculation.

The subject, then, primarily before us, is the journeying of Jesus to Jerusalem. In that wider view which St. Luke takes of this whole history, he presents what really were three separate journeys as *one*—that towards the great end. In its conscious aim and object, all—from the moment of His finally quitting Galilee to His final Entry into Jerusalem—formed, in the highest sense, only one journey And this St. Luke designates in a peculiar manner. Just as [a] he had spoken, not of Christ's Death but of His ' Exodus,' or outgoing, which included His Resurrection and Ascension, so he now tells us that, ' when the days of His uptaking '—including and pointing to His Ascension [2]—' were being fulfilled, He also [3] steadfastly set [4] His Face to go to Jerusalem.'

[a] St. Luke
ix. 31

St. John, indeed, goes farther back, and speaks of the circumstances which preceded His journey to Jerusalem. There is an interval, or, as we might term it, a blank, of more than half a year between the last narrative in the Fourth Gospel and this. For, the events chronicled in the sixth chapter of St. John's Gospel took place immediately before the Passover,[b] which was on the fifteenth day of the first ecclesiastical month (*Nisan*), while the Feast of Taber-

[b] St. John
vi. 4

[1] Of course, putting aside the question of the arrangement into chapters, the reader might profitably make the experiment of arranging the Gospels into parts and sections, nor could he have a better guide to help his own investigations than Canon *Westcott's* Introduction to the Study of the Gospels.

[2] The substantive $\dot{\alpha}\nu\dot{\alpha}\lambda\eta\psi\iota\varsigma$ occurs only in this place, but the cognate verb repeatedly, as referring to the Ascension. The curious interpretation of *Wieseler* would not even call for notice, it it had not the authority of his name.

[3] The word $\kappa\alpha\acute{\iota}$, omitted in translations, seems to denote Christ's full determination by the side of the fulfilment of the time. It could scarcely be argued that it stands merely for the Hebrew copulative ;.

[4] The term is used in the LXX as denoting *firmly setting*. In connection with $\pi\rho\acute{o}\sigma\omega\pi o\nu$ it occurs twelve times.

nacles [a] began on the same day of the seventh ecclesiastical month (*Tishri*). But, except in regard to the commencement of Christ's Ministry, that sixth chapter is the only one in the Gospel of St. John which refers to the Galilean Ministry of Christ. We would suggest, that what it records is partly intended [1] to exhibit, by the side of Christ's fully developed teaching, the fully developed enmity of the Jerusalem Scribes, which led even to the defection of many former disciples. Thus, chapter vi. would be a connecting-link (both as regards the teaching of Christ and the opposition to Him) between chapter v., which tells of His visit at the 'Unknown Feast,' and chapter vii., which records that at the Feast of Tabernacles. The six or seven months between the Feast of Passover [b] and that of Tabernacles, [c] and all that passed within them, are covered by this brief remark: 'After these things Jesus walked in Galilee: for He would not walk in Judæa, because the Jews [the leaders of the people [2]] sought to kill Him.'

But now the Feast of Tabernacles was at hand. The pilgrims would probably arrive in Jerusalem before the opening day of the Festival. For, besides the needful preparations—which would require time, especially on this Feast, when booths had to be constructed in which to live during the festive week—it was (as we remember) the common practice to offer such sacrifices as might have previously become due at any of the great Feasts to which the people might go up. [3] Remembering that five months had elapsed since the last great Feast (that of Weeks), many such sacrifices must have been due. Accordingly, the ordinary festive companies of pilgrims, which would travel slowly, must have started from Galilee some time before the beginning of the Feast. These circumstances fully explain the details of the narrative. They also afford another most painful illustration of the loneliness of Christ in His Work. His disciples had failed to understand, they misapprehended His teaching. In the near prospect of His Death they either displayed gross ignorance, or else disputed about their future rank. And His own 'brethren' did not believe in Him. The whole course of late events, especially the unmet challenge of the Scribes for 'a sign from heaven,' had deeply

CHAP.
IV

[a] St. John vii. 2

[b] St. John vi.

[c] St. John vii.

---

[1] Other and deeper reasons will also suggest themselves, and have been hinted at when treating of this event.

[2] The term 'Jews' is generally used by St. John in that sense.

[3] According to Babha K. 113 *a*, regular festive lectures commenced in the Academies thirty days before each of the great Feasts. Those who attended them were called *Beney Rigla*, in distinction to the *Beney Khallah*, who attended the regular Sabbath lectures.

shaken them. What was the purpose of 'works,' if done in the privacy of the circle of Christ's Apostles, in a house, a remote district, or even before an ignorant multitude? If, claiming to be the Messiah, He wished to be openly[1] known as such, He must use other means. If He really did these things, let Him manifest Himself before the world—in Jerusalem, the capital of their world, and before those who could test the reality of His Works. Let Him come forward, at one of Israel's great Feasts, in the Temple, and especially at this Feast which pointed to the Messianic ingathering of all nations. Let Him now go up with them in the festive company into Judæa, that so His disciples—not the Galileans only, but all—might have the opportunity of 'gazing'[2] on His Works.[3]

As the challenge was not new,[4] so, from the worldly point of view, it can scarcely be called unreasonable. It is, in fact, the same in principle as that to which the world would now submit the claims of Christianity to men's acceptance. It has only this one fault, that it ignores the world's enmity to the Christ. Discipleship is not the result of any outward manifestation by 'evidences' or demonstration. It requires the conversion of a child-like spirit. To manifest Himself! This truly would He do, though not in their way. For this 'the season'[5] had not yet come, though it would soon arrive. Their 'season'—that for such Messianic manifestations as they contemplated—was 'always ready.' And this naturally, for 'the world' could not 'hate' them; they and their demonstrations were quite in accordance with the world and its views. But towards Him the world cherished personal hatred, because of their contrariety of principle, because Christ was manifested, not to restore an earthly kingdom to Israel, but to bring the Heavenly Kingdom upon earth—'to destroy the works of the Devil.' Hence, He must provoke the enmity of that world which lay in the Wicked One. Another manifestation than that which they sought would He make, when His 'season was fulfilled;' soon, beginning at this very Feast, continued at the next, and completed at the last Passover; such manifestation of Himself as the Christ, as could alone be made in view of the essential enmity of the world.

And so He let them go up in the festive company, while Himself tarried. When the noise and publicity (which He wished to avoid)

---

[1] The same term פרהסיא (*Parhesya*) occurs in Rabbinic language.

[2] The verb is the significant one, θεωρέω.

[3] *Godet* remarks, that the style of ver. 4

is peculiarly Hebraistic.

[4] See especially the cognate occurrence and expressions at the marriage feast in Cana.

[5] καιρός.

were no longer to be apprehended, He also went up, but privately,[1] CHAP.
not publicly, as they had suggested.   Here St. Luke's account begins.   IV
It almost reads like a commentary on what the Lord had just said
to His brethren, about the enmity of the world, and His mode of
manifestation—who would not, and who would receive Him, and why.
'He came unto His own, and His own received Him not.   But as
many as received Him, to them gave He power to become children of
God . . . which were born . . . of God.'

The first purpose of Christ seems to have been to take the more
direct road to Jerusalem, through Samaria, and not to follow that
of the festive pilgrim-bands, which travelled to Jerusalem through
Peræa, in order to avoid the band of their hated rivals.   But His
intention was soon frustrated.   In the very first Samaritan village to
which the Christ had sent beforehand to prepare for Himself and His
company,[2] His messengers were told that the Rabbi could not be
received; that neither hospitality nor friendly treatment could be
extended to One Who was going up to the Feast at Jerusalem.   The
messengers who brought back this strangely un-Oriental answer met
the Master and His followers on the road.   It was not only an outrage on common manners, but an act of open hostility to Israel,
as well as to Christ, and the 'Sons of Thunder,' whose feelings for
their Master were, perhaps, the more deeply stirred as opposition to
Him grew more fierce, proposed to vindicate the cause, alike of Israel
and its Messiah-King, by the open and Divine judgment of fire called
down from heaven to destroy that village.   Did they in this connection think of the vision of Elijah, ministering to Christ on the
Mount of Transfiguration—and was this their application of it?
Truly, they knew not of what Spirit they were to be the children and
messengers.   He Who had come, not to destroy, but to save, turned
and rebuked them, and passed from Samaritan into Jewish territory
to pursue His journey.[3]   Perhaps, indeed, He had only passed into
Samaria to teach His disciples this needful lesson.   The view of
this event just presented seems confirmed by the circumstance, that

---

[1] *Godet* infers from the word 'secretly,'
that the journey of St. Luke ix. 51 could
not have been that referred to by St.
John.   But the *qualified* expression, 'as
it were in secret,' conveys to my mind
only a contrast to the public pilgrim-
bands, in which it was the custom to travel
to the Feasts—a publicity, which His
'brethren' specially desired at this time.
Besides, the 'in secret' of St. John
might refer not so much to the journey
as to the appearance of Christ at the

Feast: comp. St. John vii. 11, 14.
[2] It does not necessarily follow, that
the company at starting was a large one.
But they would have no host nor quarters
ready to receive them in Samaria. Hence
the despatch of messengers.
[3] At the same time, according to the
best MSS. the words (in St. Luke ix. 54):
'Even as Elias did,' and those (in verses
55 and 56) from 'and said. . .' to 'save
them,' are interpolated. They are 'a
gloss,' though a correct one.

BOOK
IV

ª St. Matt.
viii. 18

ᵇ St. Matt.
viii. 19-22

ᶜ St. Luke
xi. 27

St. Matthew lays the scene immediately following ' on the other side '—that is, in the Decapolis.ª

It was a journey of deepest interest and importance. For, it was decisive not only as regarded the Master, but those who followed Him. Henceforth it must not be, as in former times, but wholly and exclusively, as into suffering and death. It is thus that we view the next three incidents of the way. Two of them find, also, a place in the Gospel by St. Matthew,ᵇ although in a different connection, in accordance with the plan of that Gospel, which groups together the Teaching of Christ, with but secondary attention to chronological succession.

It seems that, as, after the rebuff of these Samaritans, they ' were going ' towards another, and a Jewish village, ' one '[1] of the company, and, as we learn from St. Matthew, ' a Scribe,' in the generous enthusiasm of the moment—perhaps, stimulated by the wrong of the Samaritans, perhaps, touched by the love which would rebuke the zeal of the disciples, but had no word of blame for the unkindness of others—broke into a spontaneous declaration of readiness to follow Him absolutely and everywhere. Like the benediction of the woman who heard Him,ᶜ it was one of these outbursts of an enthusiasm which His Presence awakened in every susceptible heart. But there was one eventuality which that Scribe, and all of like enthusiasm, reckoned not with—the utter homelessness of the Christ in this world —and this, not from accidental circumstances, but because He was ' the Son of Man.'[2] And there is here also material for still deeper thought in the fact that this man was ' a Scribe,' and yet had not gone up to the Feast, but tarried near Christ—was ' one ' of those that followed Him now, and was capable of such feelings![3] How many whom *we* regard as Scribes, may be in analogous relation to the Christ, and yet how much of fair promise has failed to ripen into reality in view of the homelessness of Christ and Christianity in this world—the strangership of suffering which it involves to

[1] The word τις, here designates a certain one—one, viz., of the company. The arrangement of the words undoubtedly is, ' one *of the company* said unto Him by the way,' and not as either in the A.V. or R.V. Comp. Canon *Cook*, ad loc. in the ' Speaker's Commentary.'

[2] We mark, that the designation 'Son of Man ' is here for the first time applied to Christ by St. Matthew. May this history have been inserted in the First Gospel in that particular connection for the purpose of pointing out this contrast in the treat-

ment of the Son of Man by the sons of men—as if to say: Learn the meaning of the representative title: Son of Man, in a world of men who would not receive Him? It is the more marked, that it immediately precedes the first application on the part of men of the title ' Son of God' to Christ in this Gospel (St. Matt. vii. 29).

[3] It is scarcely necessary to discuss the suggestion, that the first two referred to in the narrative were either Bartholomew and Philip, or else Judas Iscariot and Thomas.

those who would follow, not somewhere, but absolutely, and everywhere?

The intenseness of the self-denial involved in following Christ, and its contrariety to all that was commonly received among men, was, purposely, immediately further brought out. This Scribe had proffered to follow Jesus. Another of his disciples He *asked* to follow Him, and that in circumstances of peculiar trial and diffi- culty.[a] The expression 'to follow' a Teacher would, in those days, be universally understood as implying discipleship. Again, no other duty would be regarded as more sacred than that they, on whom the obligation naturally devolved, should bury the dead. To this every- thing must give way—even prayer, and the study of the Law.[b] Lastly, we feel morally certain, that, when Christ called this disciple to follow Him, He was fully aware that at that very moment his father lay dead. Thus, He called him not only to homelessness—for this he might have been prepared—but to set aside what alike natural feeling and the Jewish Law seemed to impose on him as the most sacred duty. In the seemingly strange reply, which Christ made to the request to be allowed first to bury his father, we pass over the consideration that, according to Jewish law, the burial and mourning for a dead father, and the subsequent purifications, would have occupied many days, so that it might have been difficult, perhaps impossible, to overtake Christ. We would rather abide by the simple words of Christ. They teach us this very solemn and searching lesson, that there are higher duties than either those of the Jewish Law, or even of natural reverence, and a higher call than that of man. No doubt Christ had here in view the near call to the Seventy—of whom this disciple was to be one—to 'go and preach the Kingdom of God.' When the direct call of Christ to any work comes—that is, if we are *sure* of it from His own words, and not (as, alas! too often we do) only infer it by our own reasoning on His words—then every other call must give way. For, duties can never be in conflict—and this duty about the living and life must take precedence of that about death and the dead. Nor must we hesi- tate, because we know not in what form this work for Christ may come. There are critical moments in our inner history, when to post- pone the immediate call, is really to reject it; when to go and bury the dead—even though it were a dead father—were to die ourselves!

Yet another hindrance to following Christ was to be faced. Another in the company that followed Christ would go with Him, but he asked permission first to go and bid farewell to those whom

[a] St. Luke ix. 59

[b] Ber. iii. 1; 17 b, and other passages, but es- pecially Megill. 3

he had left in his home.   It almost seems as if this request had been one of those ' tempting ' questions, addressed to Christ.   But, even if otherwise, the farewell proposed was not like that of Elisha, nor like the supper of Levi-Matthew.   It was rather like the year which Jephtha's daughter would have with her companions, ere fulfilling the vow.   It shows, that to follow Christ was regarded as a *duty*, and to leave those in the earthly home as a *trial*; and it betokens, not merely a divided heart, but one not fit for the Kingdom of God.   For, how can he draw a straight furrow in which to cast the seed, who, as he puts his hand to the plough, looks around or behind him?

Thus, these are the three vital conditions of following Christ: absolute self-denial and homelessness in the world; immediate and entire self-surrender to Christ and His Work, and a heart and affections simple, undivided, and set on Christ and His Work, to which there is no other trial of parting like that which would involve parting from Him, no other or higher joy than that of following Him.   In such spirit let them now go after Christ in His last journey—and to such work as He will appoint them!

CHAPTER V.

FURTHER INCIDENTS OF THE JOURNEY TO JERUSALEM—THE MISSION
AND RETURN OF THE SEVENTY—THE HOME AT BETHANY—MARTHA
AND MARY.

(St. Luke x. 1–16; Matt. ix. 36–38; xi. 20–24; St. Luke x. 17–24; St. Matt. xi.
25–30 ; xiii. 16 ; St. Luke x. 25 ; 38–42.

ALTHOUGH, for the reasons explained in the previous chapter, the
exact succession of events cannot be absolutely determined, it seems
most likely, that it was on His progress southwards at this time that
Jesus 'designated'[1] those 'seventy'[2] 'others,' who were to herald
His arrival in every town and village. Even the circumstance, that
the instructions to them are so similar to, and yet distinct from, those
formerly given to the Twelve, seems to point to them as those from
whom the Seventy are to be distinguished as 'other.' We judge,
that they were sent forth at this time, first, from the Gospel of St.
Luke, where this whole section appears as a distinct and separate
record, presumably, chronologically arranged ; secondly, from the
fitness of such a mission at that particular period, when Jesus made
His last Missionary progress towards Jerusalem; and, thirdly, from
the unlikelihood, if not impossibility, of taking such a public step
after the persecution which broke out after His appearance at Jerusalem on the Feast of Tabernacles. At any rate, it could not have
taken place later than in the period between the Feast of Tabernacles and that of the Dedication of the Temple, since, after that, Jesus
'walked no more openly among the Jews.'[a]

With all their similarity, there are notable differences between
the Mission of the Twelve and this of 'the other Seventy.' Let it be
noted, that the former is recorded by the three Evangelists, so that
there could have been no confusion on the part of St. Luke.[b] But
the mission of the Twelve was on their appointment to the Apostolate; it was evangelistic and missionary; and it was in confirmation
and manifestation of the 'power and authority' given to them. We

CHAP.
V

[a] St. John
xi. 54

[b] St. Matt.
x. 5 &c.;
St. Mark vi.
7 &c.;
St. Luke ix.
1 &c.

[1] Perhaps this may be a fuller English
equivalent than 'appoint.'

[2] The reading: 'Seventy-two' seems a
correction, made for obvious reasons.

BOOK
IV

regard it, therefore, as symbolical of the Apostolate just instituted, with its work and authority. On the other hand, no power or authority was formally conferred on the Seventy, their mission being only temporary, and, indeed, for one definite purpose; its primary object was to prepare for the coming of the Master in the places to which they were sent; and their selection was from the wider circle of disciples, the number being now Seventy instead of Twelve. Even these two numbers, as well as the difference in the functions of the two classes of messengers, seem to indicate that the Twelve symbolised the princes of the tribes of Israel, while the Seventy were the symbolical representatives of these tribes, like the seventy elders appointed to assist Moses.ᵃ¹ This symbolical meaning of the number Seventy continued among the Jews. We can trace it in the LXX. (supposed) translators of the Bible into Greek, and in the seventy members of the Sanhedrin, or supreme court.²

There was something very significant in this appearance of Christ's messengers, by two and two, in every place He was about to visit. As John the Baptist had, at the first, heralded the Coming of Christ, so now two heralds appeared to solemnly announce His Advent at the close of His Ministry; as John had sought, as the representative of the Old Testament Church, to prepare His Way, so they, as the representatives of the New Testament Church. In both cases the preparation sought was a moral one. It was the national summons to open the gates to the rightful King, and accept His rule. Only, the need was now the greater for the failure of John's mission, through the misunderstanding and disbelief of the nation.ᵇ This conjunction with John the Baptist and the failure of his mission, as regarded *national* results, accounts for the insertion in St. Matthew's Gospel of part of the address delivered on the Mission of the Seventy, immediately after the record of Christ's rebuke of the national rejection of the Baptist.ᶜ For St. Matthew, who (as well as St. Mark) records not the Mission of the Seventy—simply because (as before explained) the whole section, of which it forms part, is peculiar to St. Luke's Gospel—reports ' the Discourses ' connected with it in other, and to them congruous, connections.

We mark, that, what may be termed ' the Preface ' to the Mission of the Seventy, is given by St. Matthew (in a somewhat fuller form)

¹ In Bemidb. R. 15, ed. Warsh. p. 64 *b*, the mode of electing these Seventy is thus described. Moses chose six from every tribe, and then put into an urn seventy-two lots, of which seventy had the word *Zaqen* (Elder) inscribed on them, while two were blanks. The latter are supposed to have been drawn by Eldad and Medad.

² Comp. Sanh. 1. 6.

as that to the appointment and mission of the Twelve Apostles;[a] and it may have been, that kindred words had preceded both. Partially, indeed, the expressions reported in St. Luke x. 2 had been employed long before.[b] Those 'multitudes' throughout Israel—nay, those also which 'are not of that flock'— appeared to His view like sheep without a true shepherd's care, 'distressed and prostrate,'[1] and their mute misery and only partly conscious longing appealed, and not in vain, to His Divine compassion. This constituted the ultimate ground of the Mission of the Apostles, and now of that of the Seventy, into a harvest that was truly great. Compared with the extent of the field, and the urgency of the work, how few were the labourers! Yet, as the field was God's, so also could He alone 'thrust forth labourers' willing and able to do His work, while it must be ours to pray that He would be pleased to do so.

On these introductory words,[c] which ever since have formed 'the bidding prayer' of the Church in her work for Christ, followed the commission and special directions to the thirty-five pairs of disciples who went on this embassy. In almost every particular they are the same as those formerly given to the Twelve.[2] We mark, however, that both the introductory and the concluding words addressed to the Apostles are wanting in what was said to the Seventy. It was not necessary to warn them against going to the Samaritans, since the direction of the Seventy was to those cities of Peræa and Judæa, on the road to Jerusalem, through which Christ was about to pass. Nor were they armed with precisely the same supernatural powers as the Twelve.[d] Naturally, the personal directions as to their conduct were in both cases substantially the same. We mark only three peculiarities in those addressed to the Seventy. The direction to 'salute no man by the way' was suitable to a temporary and rapid mission, which might have been sadly interrupted by making or renewing acquaintances. Both the Mishnah[e] and the Talmud[f] lay it down, that prayer was not to be interrupted to salute even a king, nay, to uncoil a serpent that had wound round the foot.[3] On the other hand, the Rabbis discussed the question, whether the reading of the *Shema* and of the portion of the Psalms called the *Hallel* might be interrupted at the close of a paragraph, from respect for a person, or interrupted in the middle, from motives of fear.[g] All agreed, that immediately before prayer no one should be saluted, to prevent

CHAP.
V

[a] St. Matt. ix. 36-38
[b] St. John iv. 35

[c] St. Luke x. 2

[d] St. Matt. x. 7, 8; comp. St. Luke x. 9

[e] Ber. 30 b
[f] u. s. 32 b

[g] Ber. 14 a

---

[1] The first word means literally 'torn.' The second occurs sixty-two times in the LXX. as equivalent for the Hebrew (Hiphil) *Hishlikh*, projicio, abjicio.

[2] See Book III. ch. xxvii.

[3] But it might be interrupted for a scorpion, Ber. 33 a. Comp. page 141, note 1.

BOOK
IV

distraction, and it was advised rather to summarise or to cut short than to break into prayer, though the latter might be admissible in case of absolute necessity.ᵃ None of these provisions, however, seems to have been in the mind of Christ. If any parallel is to be sought, it would be found in the similar direction of Elisha to Gehazi, when sent to lay the prophet's staff on the dead child of the Shunammite.

The other two peculiarities in the address to the Seventy seem verbal rather than real. The expression,ᵇ 'if the Son of Peace be there,' is a Hebraism, equivalent to 'if the house be worthy,'ᶜ and refers to the character of the head of the house and the tone of the household.[1] Lastly, the direction to eat and drink such things as were set before them ᵈ is only a further explanation of the command to abide in the house which had received them, without seeking for better entertainment.[2] On the other hand, the whole most important close of the address to the Twelve—which, indeed, forms by far the largest part of it ᵉ— is wanting in the commission to the Seventy, thus clearly marking its merely temporary character.

In St. Luke's Gospel, the address to the Seventy is followed by a denunciation of Chorazin and Bethsaida.ᶠ This is evidently in its right place there, after the Ministry of Christ in Galilee had been completed and finally rejected. In St. Matthew's Gospel, it stands (for a reason already indicated) immediately after the Lord's rebuke of the popular rejection of the Baptist's message.ᵍ The 'woe' pronounced on those cities, in which 'most of His mighty works were done,' is in proportion to the greatness of their privileges. The denunciation of Chorazin and Bethsaida is the more remarkable, that Chorazin is not otherwise mentioned in the Gospels, nor yet any miracles recorded as having taken place in (the western) Bethsaida. From this two inferences seem inevitable. First, this history must be real. If the whole were legendary, Jesus would not be represented as selecting the names of places, which the writer had not connected with the legend. Again, apparently no record has been preserved in the Gospels of most of Christ's miracles—only those being narrated which were necessary in order to present Jesus

---

[1] Comp. Job xxi. 9, both in the original and the Targum.

[2] Canon *Cook* (ad loc.) regards this as evidence that the Seventy were also sent to the Samaritans ; and as implying permission to eat of their food, which the Jews held to be forbidden. To me it conveys the opposite, since so fundamen-

tal an alteration would not have been introduced in such an indirect manner. Besides, the direction is not to eat their food, but any kind of food. Lastly, if Christ had introduced so vital a change, the later difficulty of St. Peter, and the vision on the subject, would not be intelligible.

as the Christ, in accordance with the respective plans on which each
of the Gospels was constructed.[a]

As already stated, the denunciations were in proportion to the
privileges, and hence to the guilt, of the unbelieving cities. Chorazin
and Bethsaida are compared with Tyre and Sidon, which under similar admonitions would have repented,[1] while Capernaum, which, as
for so long the home of Jesus, had truly 'been exalted to heaven,'[2]
is compared with Sodom. And such guilt involved greater punishment. The very site of Bethsaida and Chorazin cannot be fixed
with certainty. The former probably represents the 'Fisherton' of
Capernaum,[3] the latter seems to have almost disappeared from the
shore of the Lake. St. Jerome places it two miles from Capernaum.
If so, it may be represented by the modern Kerâzeh, somewhat to
the north-west of Capernaum. The site would correspond with the
name. For Kerâzeh is at present 'a spring with an insignificant
ruin above it,'[4] and the name Chorazin may well be derived from
Keroz (כְּרוֹז) a water-jar—Cherozin, or 'Chorazin,' the water-jars.
If so, we can readily understand that the 'Fisherton' on the south
side of Capernaum, and the well-known springs, 'Chorazin,' on the
other side of it, may have been the frequent scene of Christ's miracles. This explains also, in part, why the miracles there wrought
had not been told as well as those done in Capernaum itself. In the
Talmud a Chorazin, or rather Chorzim, is mentioned as celebrated for
its wheat.[b] But as for Capernaum itself—standing on that vast field
of ruins and upturned stones which marks the site of the modern
Tell Hûm, we feel that no description of it could be more pictorially
true than that in which Christ prophetically likened the city in its
downfall to the desolateness of death and 'Hades.'

Whether or not the Seventy actually returned to Jesus before the
Feast of Tabernacles,[5] it is convenient to consider in this connection
the result of their Mission. It had filled them with the 'joy' of assurance; nay, the result had exceeded their expectations, just as their
faith had gone beyond the mere letter unto the spirit of His Words.
As they reported it to Him, even the demons had been subject to
them through His Name. In this they had exceeded the letter of

CHAP.
V

[a] St. John
xxi. 25

[b] Menach.
85 a; comp.
Neubauer, p.
220

---

[1] Fasting 'in sackcloth and ashes'
was the practice in public humiliations
(Taan. ii. 1).

[2] The R.V., following what are regarded as some of the best MSS., renders
it interrogatively: 'Shalt thou be exalted,' &c.? But such a question is not
only without precedent, but really yields

no meaning. We have, therefore, adopted
the reading of Alford, Meyer, &c., which
only differs in tense from the A.V.

[3] See Book III. ch. xxxi.

[4] Canon Tristram.

[5] Godet infers this from the use of the
word 'returned,' St. Luke x. 17.

BOOK
IV
Christ's commission; but as they made experiment of it, their faith had grown, and they had applied His command to 'heal the sick' to the worst of all sufferers, those grievously vexed by demons. And, as always, their faith was not disappointed. Nor could it be other-wise. The great contest had been long decided; it only remained for the faith of the Church to gather the fruits of that victory. The Prince of Light and Life had vanquished the Prince of Darkness and Death. The Prince of this world must be cast out.[a] In spirit, Christ gazed on 'Satan fallen as lightning from heaven.' As one has aptly paraphrased it:[1] 'While you cast out his subjects, I saw the prince himself fall.' It has been asked, whether the words of Christ referred to any particular event, such as His Victory in the Temptation.[2] But any such limitation would imply grievous misunderstanding of the whole. So to speak, the fall of Satan is to the *bottomless* pit; ever going on to the final triumph of Christ. As the Lord beholds him, he *is* fallen from heaven—from the seat of power and of worship; for, his mastery is broken by the Stronger than he. And he is fallen like lightning, in its rapidity, dazzling splendour, and destructiveness.[b] Yet as we perceive it, it is only demons cast out in His Name. For still is this fight and sight continued, and to all ages of the present dispensation. Each time the faith of the Church casts out demons—whether as formerly, or as they presently vex men, whether in the lighter combat about possession of the body, or in the sorer fight about possession of the soul—as Christ beholds it, it is ever Satan fallen. For, he sees of the travail of His soul, and is satisfied. And so also is there joy in heaven over every sinner that repenteth.

The authority and power over 'the demons,' attained by faith, was not to pass away with the occasion that had called it forth. The Seventy were the representatives of the Church in her work of pre-paring for the Advent of Christ. As already indicated, the sight of Satan fallen from heaven is the continuous history of the Church. What the faith of the Seventy had attained was now to be made permanent to the Church, whose representatives they were. For, the words in which Christ now gave authority and power to tread on[3] serpents and scorpions, and over all the power of the Enemy, and the promise that nothing should hurt them, could not have been addressed to the Seventy for a Mission which had now come to an

[a] St. John xii. 31

[b] Rev. xii. 7–12

---

[1] *Godet*, ad loc.

[2] So far from seeing here, with *Wünsche* (ad loc.), Jewish notions about Satan, I hold that in the Satanology of the New Testament, perhaps more than anywhere else, do we mark not only difference, but *contrast*, to Jewish views.

[3] The word *over* (' on,' A.V.) must be connected with 'power.'

end, except in so far as they represented the Church Universal. It is almost needless to add, that those 'serpents and scorpions' are not to be literally but symbolically understood.[a][1] Yet it is not this power or authority which is to be the main joy either of the Church or the individual, but[2] the fact that our names are written in heaven.[3] And so Christ brings us back to His great teaching about the need of becoming children, and wherein lies the secret of true greatness in the Kingdom.

It is beautifully in the spirit of all this, when we read that the joy of the disciples was met by that of the Master, and that His teaching presently merged into a prayer of thanksgiving. Throughout the occurrences since the Transfiguration, we have noticed an increasing antithesis to the teaching of the Rabbis. But it almost reached its climax in the thanksgiving, that the Father in heaven had hid these things from the wise and the understanding, and revealed them unto babes. As we view it in the light of those times, we know that 'the wise and understanding'—the Rabbi and the Scribe—could not, from their standpoint, have perceived them; nay, that it is matter of never-ending thanks that, not what they, but what 'the babes,' understood, was—as alone it could be—the subject of the Heavenly Father's revelation. We even tremble to think how it would have fared with 'the babes,' if 'the wise and understanding' had had part with them in the knowledge revealed. And so it must ever be, not only the Law of the Kingdom and the fundamental principle of Divine Revelation, but matter for thanksgiving, that, not as 'wise and understanding,' but only as 'babes'—as 'converted,' 'like children'—we can share in that knowledge which maketh wise unto salvation. And this truly is the Gospel, and the Father's good pleasure.[4]

The words,[b] with which Christ turned from this Address to the Seventy and thanksgiving to God, seem almost like the Father's answer to the prayer of the Son. They refer to, and explain, the authority which Jesus had bestowed on His Church: 'All things were delivered[5] to Me of My Father;' and they afford the highest

CHAP.
V

[a] Comp. Ps. xci. 13; St. Mark xvi. 18

[b] St. Luke x. 22

---

[1] I presume, that in the same symbolical sense must be understood the Haggadah about a great Rabbinic Saint, whom a serpent bit without harming him, and then immediately died. The Rabbi brought it to his disciples with the words: It is not the serpent that killeth, but sin (Ber. 33 a).

[2] The word 'rather' in the A.V. is spurious.

[3] The figure is one current in Scripture (comp. Exod. xxxii. 32: Is. iv. 3; Dan. xii. 1). But the Rabbis took it in a grossly literal manner, and spoke of three books opened every New Year's Day—those of the pious, the wicked, and the intermediate (Rosh haSh. 16 b).

[4] This is a common Jewish formula: רצון לפניך.

[5] The tense should here be marked.

BOOK
IV

St. Matt.
xi. 28-30
b St. Luke
x. 23, 24
c Comp.
St. Matt.
xiii. 16

d Acts xv. 10

rationale for the fact, that these things had been hid from the wise and revealed unto babes. For, as no man, only the Father, could have full knowledge of the Son, and, conversely, no man, only the Son, had true knowledge of the Father, it followed, that this knowledge came to us, not of Wisdom or learning, but only through the Revelation of Christ: ' No one knoweth Who the Son is, save the Father; and Who the Father is, save the Son, and he to whomsoever the Son willeth to reveal Him.'

St. Matthew, who also records this—although in a different connection, immediately ofter the denunciation of the unbelief of Chorazin, Bethsaida, and Capernaum—concludes this section by words which have ever since been the grand text of those who, following in the wake of the Seventy, have been ambassadors for Christ.[a] On the other hand, St. Luke concludes this part of his narrative by adducing words equally congruous to the occasion,[b] which, indeed, are not new in the mouth of the Lord.[c] From their suitableness to what had preceded, we can have little doubt that both that which St. Matthew, and that which St. Luke, reports was spoken on this occasion. Because knowledge of the Father came only through the Son, and because these things were hidden from the wise and revealed to ' babes,' did the gracious Lord open His Arms so wide, and bid all [1] that laboured and were heavy laden come to Him. These were the sheep, distressed and prostrate, whom to gather, that He might give them rest, He had sent forth the Seventy on a work, for which He had prayed the Father to thrust forth labourers, and which He has since entrusted to the faith and service of love of the Church. And the true wisdom, which qualified for the Kingdom, was to take up His yoke, which would be found easy, and a lightsome burden, not like that unbearable yoke of Rabbinic conditions; [d] and the true understanding to be sought, was by learning of Him. In that wisdom of entering the Kingdom by taking up its yoke, and in that knowledge which came by learning of Him, Christ was Himself alike the true lesson and the best Teacher for those ' babes.' For He is meek and lowly in heart. He had done what He taught, and He taught what He had done; and so, by coming unto Him, would true rest be found for the soul.

These words, as recorded by St. Matthew—the Evangelist of the Jews—must have sunk the deeper into the hearts of Christ's Jewish

---

[1] *Melanchthon* writes: ' In this "*All*" thou art to include thyself, and not to think that thou dost not belong thereto;   thou art not to search for another register of God.'

hearers, that they came in their own old familiar form of speech, yet with such contrast of spirit. One of the most common figurative expressions of the time was that of 'the yoke' (עֹל), to indicate submission to an occupation or obligation. Thus, we read not only of the 'yoke of the Law,' but of that of 'earthly governments,' and ordinary 'civil obligations.'[a] Very instructive for the understanding of the figure is this paraphrase of Cant. i. 10: 'How beautiful is their neck for bearing the yoke of Thy statutes; and it shall be upon them like the yoke on the neck of the ox that plougheth in the field, and provideth food for himself and his master.'[b][1] This yoke might be 'cast off,' as the ten tribes had cast off that 'of God,' and thus brought on themselves their exile.[c] On the other hand, to 'take upon oneself the yoke' (קִבֵּל עֹל) meant to submit to it of free choice and deliberate resolution. Thus, in the allegorism of the Midrash, in the inscription, Prov. xxx. 1, concerning 'Agur, the son of Jakeh'—which is viewed as a symbolical designation of Solomon—the word 'Massa,' rendered in the Authorized Version 'prophecy,' is thus explained in reference to Solomon: 'Massa, because he lifted on himself (Nasa) the yoke of the Holy One, blessed be He.'[d] And of Isaiah it was said, that he had been privileged to prophesy of so many blessings, 'because he had taken upon himself the yoke of the Kingdom of Heaven with joy.'[e][2] And, as previously stated, it was set forth that in the 'Shema,' or Creed—which was repeated every day—the words, Deut. vi. 4–9, were recited before those in xi. 13–21, so as first generally to 'take upon ourselves the yoke of the Kingdom of Heaven, and only afterwards that of the commandments.'[f][3] And this yoke all Israel had taken upon itself, thereby gaining the merit ever afterwards imputed to them.

Yet, practically, 'the yoke of the Kingdom' was none other than that 'of the Law' and 'of the commandments;' one of laborious performances and of impossible self-righteousness. It was 'unbearable,' not 'the easy' and lightsome yoke of Christ, in which the Kingdom of God was of faith, not of works. And, as if themselves to bear witness to this, we have this saying of theirs, terribly significant in this connection: 'Not like those formerly (the first), who made for themselves the yoke of the Law easy and light; but like those after them (those afterwards), who made the yoke of the Law

CHAP.
V ,

[a] Abhoth. iii. 5

[b] Targum, ad loc.

[c] Shemoth R. 30

[d] Midr. Shoch. Tobh. ed. Lemb. p. 20 a

[e] Yalkut ii. p. 43 a, § 275, lines 10 &c. from bottom

[f] Ber. ii. 2

---

[1] Similarly we read of 'the yoke of repentance (Moed K. 16 b), of that 'of man,' or rather 'of flesh and blood' (Ab. de R. Nath. 20), &c.
[2] This is mentioned as an answer given in the great Academy of Jerusalem by Elijah the prophet to a question propounded to him by a student.
[3] Comp. 'Sketches of Jewish Social Life,' p. 270.

BOOK
IV

ᵃ Sanh.94 b,
middle
ᵇ St. Luke
x. 23, 24

ᶜ St. Luke
x. 25 &c.

upon them heavy!'ᵃ And, indeed, this voluntary making of the yoke as heavy as possible, the taking on themselves as many obligations as possible, was the ideal of Rabbinic piety. There was, therefore, peculiar teaching and comfort in the words of Christ; and well might He add, as St. Luke reports,ᵇ that blessed were they who saw and heard these things.[1] For, that Messianic Kingdom, which had been the object of rapt vision and earnest longing to prophets and kings of old had now become reality.[2]

Abounding as this history is in contrasts, it seems not unlikely, that the scene next recorded by St. Lukeᶜ stands in its right place. Such an inquiry on the part of a 'certain lawyer,' as to what he should do to inherit eternal life, together with Christ's Parabolic teaching about the Good Samaritan, is evidently congruous to the previous teaching of Christ about entering into the Kingdom of Heaven. Possibly, this Scribe may have understood the words of the Master about these things being hid from the wise, and the need of taking up the yoke of the Kingdom, as enforcing the views of those Rabbinic teachers, who laid more stress upon good works than upon study. Perhaps himself belonged to that minority, although his question was intended to tempt—to try whether the Master would stand the Rabbinic test, alike morally and dialectically. And, without at present entering on the Parable which gives Christ's final answer (and which will best be considered together with the others belonging to that period), it will be seen how peculiarly suited it was to the state of mind just supposed.

From this interruption, which, but for the teaching of Christ connected with it, would have formed a terrible discord in the heavenly harmony of this journey, we turn to a far other scene. It follows in the course of St. Luke's narrative, and we have no reason to consider it out of its proper place. If so, it must mark the close of Christ's journey to the Feast of Tabernacles, since the home of Martha and Mary, to which it introduces us, was in Bethany, close to Jerusalem, almost one of its suburbs. Other indications, confirmatory of this note of time, are not wanting. Thus, the history

---

[1] In a rapt description of the Messianic glory (Pesiqta, ed. *Buber.* 149 *a*, end) we read that Israel shall exult in His light, saying: 'Blessed the hour in which the Messsiah has been created; blessed the womb that bare Him; blessed the eye that sees Him; blessed the eye that is deemed worthy to behold Him, for the opening of his lips is blessing and peace,

&c.' It is a strange coincidence, to say the least, that this passage occurs in a 'Lecture' on the portion of the prophets (Is. lxi. 10), which at present is read in the Synagogues on a Sabbath close to the Feast of Tabernacles.

[2] The same words were spoken on a previous occasion (St. Matt. xiii. 16), after the Parable of the Sower.

which follows that of the home of Bethany, when one of His disciples asks Him to teach them to pray, as the Baptist had similarly taught his followers, seems to indicate, that they were then on the scene of John's former labours—north-east of Bethany; and, hence, that it occurred on Christ's return from Jerusalem. Again, from the narrative of Christ's reception in the house of Martha, we gather that Jesus had arrived in Bethany with His disciples, but that He alone was the guest of the two sisters.[a] We infer that Christ had dismissed His disciples to go into the neighbouring City for the Feast, while Himself tarried in Bethany. Lastly, with all this agrees the notice in St. John vii. 14, that it was not at the beginning, but ' about the midst of the feast,' that ' Jesus went up into the Temple.' Although travelling on the two first festive days was not actually unlawful, yet we can scarcely conceive that Jesus would have done so—especially on the Feast of Tabernacles; and the inference is obvious, that Jesus had tarried in the immediate neighbourhood, as we know He did at Bethany in the house of Martha and Mary.[1]

[a] St. Luke
x. 38

Other things, also, do so explain themselves—notably, the absence of the brother of Martha and Mary, who probably spent the festive days in the City itself. It was the beginning of the Feast of Tabernacles, and the scene recorded by St. Luke[b] would take place in the open leafy booth which served as the sitting apartment during the festive week. For, according to law, it was duty during the festive week to eat, sleep, pray, study—in short, to live—in these booths, which were to be constructed of the boughs of living trees.[2] And, although this was not absolutely obligatory on women,[c] yet, the rule which bade all make ' the booth the principal, and the house only the secondary dwelling,'[d] would induce them to make this leafy tent at least the sitting apartment alike for men and women. And, indeed, those autumn days were just the season when it would be joy to sit in these delightful cool retreats—the memorials of Israel's pilgrim-days! They were high enough, and yet not too high; chiefly open in front; close enough to be shady, and yet not so close as to exclude sunlight and air. Such would be the apartment in which what is recorded passed; and, if we add that this booth stood probably in the court, we can picture to ourselves Martha moving forwards and backwards on her busy errands, and seeing, as she passed again and again, Mary still sitting a rapt listener, not heeding what passed around; and,

[b] x. 38-42

[c] Sukk. ii. 8

[d] u. s. 9

---

[1] No one who impartially reads St. John xi. can doubt, that the persons there introduced are the Martha and Mary of this history, nor hence that their home was in Bethany.

[2] Comp. ' The Temple and its Services,' p. 237, &c.

lastly, how the elder sister could, as the language of verse 40 implies, enter so suddenly the Master's Presence, bringing her complaint.

To understand this history, we must dismiss from our minds preconceived, though, perhaps, attractive thoughts. There is no evidence that the household of Bethany had previously belonged to the circle of Christ's professed disciples. It was, as the whole history shows, a wealthy home. It consisted of two sisters—the elder, *Martha* (a not uncommon Jewish name,[1] being the feminine of *Mar*,[2] and equivalent to our word ' mistress '); the younger, *Mary*; and their brother *Lazarus*, or, *Laazar*.[3] Although we know not how it came, yet, evidently, the house was Martha's, and into it she received Jesus on His arrival in Bethany. It would have been no uncommon occurrence in Israel for a pious, wealthy lady to receive a great Rabbi into her house. But the present was not an ordinary case. Martha must have heard of Him, even if she had not seen Him. But, indeed, the whole narrative implies,[a] that Jesus had come to Bethany with the view of accepting the hospitality of Martha, which probably had been proffered when some of those ' Seventy,' sojourning in the worthiest house at Bethany, had announced the near arrival of the Master. Still, her bearing affords only indication of being drawn towards Christ—at most, of a sincere desire to learn the good news, not of actual discipleship.

ᵃ Comp. St.
Luke x. 38

And so Jesus came—and, with Him and in Him, Heaven's own Light and Peace. He was to lodge in one of the booths, the sisters in the house, and the great booth in the middle of the courtyard would be the common living apartment of all. It could not have been long after His arrival—it must have been almost immediately, that the sisters felt they had received more than an Angel unawares. How best to do Him honour, was equally the thought of both. To Martha it seemed, as if she could not do enough in showing Him all hospitality. And, indeed, this festive season was a busy time for the mistress of a wealthy household, especially in the near neighbourhood of Jerusalem, whence her brother might, after the first two festive days, bring with him, any time that week, honoured guests from the City. To these cares was now added that of doing sufficient honour to such a Guest—for she, also, deeply felt His greatness. And so she hurried to and fro through the courtyard, literally, ' distracted [4] about much serving.'

---

[1] See *Levy*, Neuhebr. Wörterb. ad voc.

[2] Martha occurs, however, also as a male name (in the Aramaic)

[3] The name Laazar (לְעָזָר), or Lazar,

occurs frequently in Talmudic writings as an abbreviated form of *Elazar* or *Eleazar* (אֶלְעָזָר).

[4] περιεσπᾶτο.

Her younger sister, also, would do Him all highest honour; but, not as Martha. Her homage consisted in forgetting all else but Him, Who spake as none had ever done. As truest courtesy or affection consists, nor in its demonstrations, but in being so absorbed in the object of it as to forget its demonstration, so with Mary in the Presence of Christ. And then a new Light, another Day had risen upon her; a fresh life had sprung up within her soul: 'She sat at the Lord's Feet,[1] and heard his Word.' We dare not inquire, and yet we well know, of what it would be. And so, time after time— perhaps, hour after hour—as Martha passed on her busy way, she still sat, listening and living. At last, the sister who, in her impatience, could not think that a woman could, in such manner, fulfil her duty, or show forth her religious profiting, broke in with what sounds like a querulous complaint: 'Lord, dost Thou not care that my sister did leave me to serve alone?' Mary *had* served with her, but she had now left her to do the work alone. Would the Master bid her resume her neglected work? But, with tone of gentle reproof and admonition, the affectionateness of which appeared even in the repetition of her name, Martha, Martha—as, similarly, on a later occasion, Simon, Simon—did He teach her in words which, however simple in their primary meaning, are so full, that they have ever since borne the most many-sided application: 'Thou art careful and anxious about many things; but one thing is needful;[2] and Mary hath chosen that good part, which shall not be taken away from her.'

It was, as we imagine, perhaps the first day of, or else the preparation for, the Feast. More than that one day did Jesus tarry in the home of Bethany. Whether Lazarus came then to see Him—and, still more, what both Martha and Mary learned, either then, or afterwards, we reverently forbear to search into. Suffice it, that though the natural disposition of the sisters remained what it had been, yet henceforth, 'Jesus loved Martha and her sister.'

---

[1] This, instead of 'Jesus,' is the reading more generally received as correct.

[2] Few would be disposed to adopt the proposed alternative reading (R.V., margin): 'but few things are needful, or one' —meaning, not much preparation, indeed, only one dish is necessary.

CHAPTER VI.

AT THE FEAST OF TABERNACLES—FIRST DISCOURSE IN THE TEMPLE.

(St. John vii. 11–36.)

BOOK
IV

It was *Chol ha Moed*—as the non-sacred part of the festive week, the half-holy days were called.[1] Jerusalem, the City of Solemnities, the City of Palaces, the City of beauty and glory, wore quite another than its usual aspect; other, even, than when its streets were thronged by festive pilgrims during the Passover-week, or at Pentecost. For this was pre-eminently the Feast for foreign pilgrims, coming from the farthest distance, whose Temple-contributions were then received and counted.[2] Despite the strange costumes of Media, Arabia, Persia, or India, and even further; or the Western speech and bearing of the pilgrims from Italy, Spain, the modern Crimea, and the banks of the Danube, if not from yet more strange and barbarous lands, it would not be difficult to recognise the lineaments of the Jew, nor to perceive that to change one's clime was not to change one's mind. As the Jerusalemite would look with proud self-consciousness, not unmingled with kindly patronage, on the swarthy strangers, yet fellow-country-men, or the eager-eyed Galilean curiously stare after them, the pilgrims would, in turn, gaze with mingled awe and wonderment on the novel scene. Here was the realisation of their fondest dreams ever since childhood, the home and spring of their holiest thoughts and best hopes—that which gave inward victory to the vanquished, and converted persecution into anticipated triumph.

They could come at this season of the year—not during the winter for the Passover, nor yet quite so readily in summer's heat for Pentecost. But now, in the delicious cool of early autumn, when all harvest-operations, the gathering in of luscious fruit and the vintage were past, and the first streaks of gold were tinting the foliage, strangers from afar off, and countrymen from Judæa, Peræa, and Galilee, would mingle in the streets of Jerusalem, under the

---

[1] Also *Cholo shel Moed* and *Moed Qaton*.   [2] See ch. iii. of this Book.

ever-present shadow of that glorious Sanctuary of marble, cedarwood, and gold, up there on high Moriah, symbol of the infinitely more glorious overshadowing Presence of Him, Who was the Holy One in the midst of Israel. How all day long, even till the stars lit up the deep blue canopy over head, the smoke of the burning, smouldering sacrifices rose in slowly-widening column, and hung between the Mount of Olives and Zion; how the chant of Levites, and the solemn responses of the *Hallel* were borne on the breeze, or the clear blast of the Priests' silver trumpets seemed to waken the echoes far away! And then, at night, how all these vast Temple-buildings stood out, illuminated by the great Candelabras that burned in the Court of the Women, and by the glare of torches, when strange sound of mystic hymns and dances came floating over the intervening darkness! Truly, well might Israel designate the Feast of Tabernacles as '*the* Feast' (*haChag*), and the Jewish historian describe it as 'the holiest and greatest.' [a1]

Early on the 14th Tishri (corresponding to our September or early October), all the festive pilgrims had arrived. Then it was, indeed, a scene of bustle and activity. Hospitality had to be sought and found; guests to be welcomed and entertained; all things required for the feast to be got ready. Above all, booths must be erected everywhere—in court and on housetop, in street and square, for the lodgment and entertainment of that vast multitude; leafy dwellings everywhere, to remind of the wilderness-journey, and now of the goodly land. Only that fierce castle, Antonia, which frowned above the Temple, was undecked by the festive spring into which the land had burst. To the Jew it must have been a hateful sight, that castle, which guarded and dominated his own City and Temple —hateful sight and sounds, that Roman garrison, with its foreign, heathen, ribald speech and manners. Yet, for all this, Israel could not read on the lowering sky the signs of the times, nor yet knew the day of their merciful visitation. And this, although of all festivals, that of Tabernacles should have most clearly pointed them to the future.

Indeed, the whole symbolism of the Feast, beginning with the completed harvest, for which it was a thanksgiving, pointed to the future. The Rabbis themselves admitted this. The strange number of sacrificial bullocks—seventy in all—they regarded as referring to 'the seventy nations' of heathendom. [b] The ceremony of the out-

CHAP.
VI

[a] *Jos. Ant.* viii. 4. 1

[b] *Sukk.* 55 *b*; Pesiqta, ed. *Buber*, p. 17 *a*; 194 *a*; Shabb. 88 *b*

---

[1] For a full description of the Feast of Tabernacles in the days of Christ, I must refer to 'The Temple and its Services.'

BOOK
IV

ᵃ Sukk. v. 1
ᵇ Jer. Sukk.
v. 1, p. 55 a

pouring of water, which was considered of such vital importance as to give to the whole festival the name of 'House of Outpouring,'ᵃ was symbolical of the outpouring of the Holy Spirit.ᵇ As the brief night of the great Temple-illumination closed, there was solemn testimony made before Jehovah against heathenism. It must have been a stirring scene, when from out of the mass of Levites, with their musical instruments, who crowded the fifteen steps that led from the Court of Israel to that of the Women, stepped two priests with their silver trumpets. As the first cockcrowing intimated the dawn of morn, they blew a threefold blast; another on the tenth step, and yet another threefold blast as they entered the Court of the Women. And still sounding their trumpets, they marched through the Court of the Women to the Beautiful Gate. Here, turning round and facing westwards to the Holy Place, they repeated: ' Our fathers, who were in this place, they turned their backs on the Sanctuary of Jehovah, and their faces eastward, for they worshipped eastward, the sun; but we, our eyes are towards Jehovah.' ' We

Sukk. v. 4

are Jehovah's—our eyes are towards Jehovah.'ᶜ¹ Nay, the whole of this night- and morning-scene was symbolical: the Temple-illumination, of the light which was to shine from out the Temple into the dark night of heathendom; then, at the first dawn of morn the blast of the priests' silver trumpets, of the army of God, as it advanced, with festive trumpet-sound and call, to awaken the sleepers, marching on to quite the utmost bounds of the Sanctuary, to the Beautiful Gate, which opened upon the Court of the Gentiles—and, then again, facing round to utter solemn protest against heathenism, and make solemn confession of Jehovah!

But Jesus did not appear in the Temple during the first two festive days. The pilgrims from all parts of the country—perhaps, they from abroad also—had expected Him there, for everyone would now speak of Him—'not openly,' in Jerusalem, for they were afraid of their rulers. It was hardly safe to speak of Him without reserve. But they sought Him, and inquired after Him—and they did speak of Him, though there was only a murmuring—a low, confused discussion of the *pro* and *con*, in this great controversy among the ' multitudes,'² or festive bands from various parts. Some said: He is a good man, while others declared that He only led astray the common, ignorant populace. And now, all at once, in *Chol ha*

---

¹ This second form is according to R. Jenudah's tradition.
² In the plural it occurs only in this place in St. John, and once in St. Mark (vi. 33), but sixteen times in St. Luke, and still more frequently in St. Matthew.

Moed,[1] Jesus Himself appeared in the Temple, and taught. We know that, on a later occasion,[a] He walked and taught in 'Solomon's Porch,' and, from the circumstance that the early disciples made this their common meeting-place,[b] we may draw the inference that it was here the people now found Him. Although neither Josephus nor the Mishnah mention this 'Porch' by name,[2] we have every reason for believing that it was the eastern colonnade, which abutted against the Mount of Olives and faced 'the Beautiful Gate,' that formed the principal entrance into the 'Court of the Women,' and so into the Sanctuary. For, all along the inside of the great wall which formed the Temple-enclosure ran a double colonnade—each column a monolith of white marble, 25 cubits high, covered with cedar-beams. That on the south side (leading from the western entrance to Solomon's Porch), known as the 'Royal Porch,' was a threefold colonnade, consisting of four rows of columns, each 27 cubits high, and surmounted by Corinthian capitals. We infer that the eastern was 'Solomon's Porch,' from the circumstance that it was the only relic left of Solomon's Temple.[c] These colonnades, which, from their ample space, formed alike places for quiet walk and for larger gatherings, had benches in them—and, from the liberty of speaking and teaching in Israel, Jesus might here address the people in the very face of His enemies.

We know not what was the subject of Christ's teaching on this occasion. But the effect on the people was one of general astonishment. They knew what common unlettered Galilean tradesmen were—but *this*, whence came it?[d] 'How does this one know literature (letters, learning),[e] never having learned?' To the Jews there was only one kind of learning—that of Theology; and only one road to it—the Schools of the Rabbis. Their *major* was true, but their *minor* false—and Jesus hastened to correct it. He had, indeed, 'learned,' but in a School quite other than those which alone they recognised. Yet, on their own showing, it claimed the most absolute submission. Among the Jews a Rabbi's teaching derived authority from the fact of its accordance with tradition—that it accurately represented what had been received from a previous great teacher, and so on upwards to Moses, and to God Himself. On this ground Christ claimed the highest authority. His doctrine was not His own invention—it was the teaching of Him that sent Him. The doctrine

CHAP. VI

[a] St. John x. 23
[b] Acts v. 12

[c] *Jos.* Ant. xv. 11. 5; xx. 9. 7

[d] St. John vii. 15
[e] Comp. Acts xxvi. 24

---

[1] See above, p. 148.
[2] This, as showing such local knowledge on the part of the Fourth Gospel, must be taken as additional evidence of its Johannine authorship, just as the mention of that Porch in the Book of Acts points to a Jerusalem source of information.

was God-received, and Christ was sent direct from God to bring it. He was God's messenger of it to them.[a] Of this twofold claim there was also twofold evidence. Did He assert that what He taught was God-received? Let trial be made of it. Everyone who in his soul felt drawn towards God; each one who really ' willeth to do His Will,' would know ' concerning this teaching, whether it is of God,' or whether it was of man.[1] It was this felt, though unrealised influence which had drawn all men after Him, so that they hung on His lips. It was this which, in the hour of greatest temptation and mental difficulty, had led Peter, in name of the others, to end the sore inner contest by laying hold on this fact: ' To whom shall we go? Thou hast the words of eternal life—and we have believed and know, that Thou art the Holy One of God.'[b] Marking, as we pass, that this inward connection between that teaching and learning and the present occasion, may be the deeper reason why, in the Gospel by St. John, the one narrative is immediately followed by the other, we pause to say, how real it hath proved in all ages and to all stages of Christian learning—that the *heart* makes the truly God-taught ('*pectus facit Theologum*'), and that inward, true aspiration after the Divine prepares the eye to behold the Divine Reality in the Christ. But, if it be so is there not evidence here, that He is the God-sent— that He is a real, true Ambassador of God? If Jesus' teaching meets and satisfies our moral nature, if it leads up to God, is He not the Christ?

And this brings us to the second claim which Christ made, that of being sent by God. There is yet another logical link in His reasoning. He had said: ' He shall know of the teaching, whether it be of God, or whether I speak from Myself.' From Myself? Why, there is this other test of it: ' Who speaketh from himself, seeketh his own glory—there can be no doubt or question of this, but do I seek My own glory?—' But He Who seeketh the glory of Him Who sent Him, He is true [a faithful messenger], and unrighteousness is not in Him.'[c] Thus did Christ appeal and prove it: My doctrine is of God, and I am sent of God!

Sent of God, no unrighteousness in Him! And yet at that very moment there hung over Him the charge of defiance of the Law of Moses, nay, of that of God, in an open breach of the Sabbath-commandment—there, in that very City, the last time He had been in Jerusalem; for which, as well as for His Divine claims, the Jews were

a St. John
vii. 16-17

b St. John
vi. 68, 69

c St. John
vii. 18

---

[1] The passage quoted by Canon *Westcott* from Ab. ii. 4 does not seem to be parallel.

even then seeking 'to kill Him.'[a]   And this forms the transition to what may be called the second part of Christ's address.   If, in the first part, the Jewish form of ratiocination was already apparent, it seems almost impossible for any one acquainted with those forms to understand how it can be overlooked in what follows.[1]   It is exactly the mode in which a Jew would argue with Jews, only the substance of the reasoning is to all times and people.   Christ is defending Himself against a charge which naturally came up, when He claimed that His Teaching was of God and Himself God's real and faithful Messenger.   In His reply the two threads of the former argument are taken up.   Doing is the condition of knowledge—and a messenger had been sent from God!   Admittedly, Moses was such, and yet every one of them was breaking the Law which he had given them; for, were they not seeking to kill Him without right or justice? This, put in the form of a double question,[b] represents a peculiarly Jewish mode of argumentation, behind which lay the terrible truth, that those, whose hearts were so little longing to do the Will of God, not only must remain ignorant of His Teaching as that of God, but had also rejected that of Moses.

A general disclaimer, a cry ' Thou hast a demon ' (art possessed), ' who seeks to kill Thee?' here broke in upon the Speaker.   But He would not be interrupted, and continued: ' One work I did, and all you wonder on account of it '[2]—referring to His healing on the Sabbath, and their utter inability to understand His conduct.   Well, then, Moses was a messenger of God, and I am sent of God.   Moses gave the law of circumcision—not, indeed, that it was of his authority, but had long before been God-given—and, to observe this law, no one hesitated to break the Sabbath,[3] since, according to Rabbinic principle, a positive ordinance superseded a negative.   And yet, when Christ, as sent from God, made a man every whit whole on the Sabbath (' made a whole man sound ') they were angry with Him![c]   Every argument which might have been urged in favour of the postponement of Christ's healing to a week-day, would equally apply to that of circumcision; while every reason that could be

CHAP.
VI

[a] St. John
v. 18

[b] St. John
vii. 19, 20

[c] vv. 21-24

---

[1] I regard this as almost overwhelming evidence against the theory of an Ephesian authority of the Fourth Gospel. Even the double question in ver. 19 is here significant.

[2] The words 'on account of it,' rendered in the A.V. 'therefore,' and placed in ver. 22 (St. John vii.), really form the close of ver. 21. At any rate, they cannot be taken in the sense of ' therefore.'

[3] This was a well-recognized Rabbinic principle. Comp. for example Shabb. 132 a, where the argument runs that, if circumcision, which applies to one of the 248 members, of which, according to the Rabbis, the human body consists, superseded the Sabbath, how much more the preservation of the whole body.

BOOK
IV
urged in favour of Sabbath-circumcision, would tell an hundredfold in favour of the act of Christ. Oh, then, let them not judge after the mere outward appearance, but 'judge the right judgment.' And, indeed, had it not been to convince them of the externalism of their views, that Jesus had on that Sabbath opened the great controversy between the letter that killeth and the spirit that maketh alive, when He directed the impotent man to carry home the bed on which he had lain?

If any doubt could obtain, how truly Jesus had gauged the existing state of things, when He contrasted heart-willingness to do the Will of God, as the necessary preparation for the reception of His God-sent Teaching, with their murderous designs, springing from blind literalism and ignorance of the spirit of their Law, the reported remarks of some Jerusalemites in the crowd would suffice to convince us.[a]   The fact that He, Whom they sought to kill, was suffered to speak openly, seemed to them incomprehensible. Could it be that the authorities were shaken in their former idea about Him, and now regarded Him as the Messiah? But it could not be.[1] It was a settled popular belief, and, in a sense, not quite unfounded, that the appearance of the Messiah would be sudden and unexpected. He might be there, and not be known; or He might come, and be again hidden for a time.[b][2] As they put it, when Messiah came, no one would know whence He was; but they all knew 'whence this One' was. And with this rough and ready argument of a coarse realism, they, like so many among us, settled off-hand and once for all the great question. But Jesus could not, even for the sake of His poor weak disciples, let it rest there. 'Therefore' He lifted up His voice,[3] that it reached the dispersing, receding multitude. Yes, they thought they knew both Him and whence He came. It would have been so had He come from Himself. But He had been sent, and He that sent Him 'was real;'[4] it was a real Mission, and Him, who had thus sent the Christ, they knew not. And so, with a reaffirmation of

a St. John
vii. 25-27

b Comp.
also Sanh.
97 a; Midr.
on Cant.
ll. 10

---

[1] In the original: 'Can it be?'

[2] See Book II. ch. v., and Appendix IX.

[3] 'Cried.'

[4] The word ἀληθινός has not an exact English equivalent, scarcely a German one (wahrhaftig?). It is a favourite word of St. John's, who uses it eight times in his Gospel, or, if the Revised reading viii. 16 be adopted, nine times (i. 9; iv. 23, 37; vi. 32; vii. 28; viii. 16?; xv. 1; xvii. 3; xix. 35); and four times in his First Epistle (ii. 8, and three times in ch. v. 20). Its Johannine meaning is perhaps best seen when in juxtaposition with ἀληθής (for example, 1 John ii. 8). But in the Book of Revelation, where it occurs ten times (iii. 7, 14; vi. 10; xv. 3; xvi. 7; xix. 2, 9, 11; xxi. 5; xxii. 6), it has another meaning, and can scarcely be distinguished from our English 'true.' It is used, in the same sense as in St. John's Gospel and Epistle, in St. Luke xvi. 11, in 1 Thess. i. 9; and three times in the Epistle to the Hebrews (viii. 2; ix. 24; x. 22). We may, therefore, regard it as a word to which a Grecian, not a Judæan meaning attaches. In our view it refers

His twofold claim, His Discourse closed.[a] But they had understood His allusions, and in their anger would fain have laid hands on Him, but His hour had not come. Yet others were deeply stirred to faith. As they parted they spoke of it among themselves, and the sum of it all was: 'The Christ, when He cometh, will He do more miracles (signs) than this One did?'

So ended the first teaching of that day in the Temple. And as the people dispersed, the leaders of the Pharisees—who, no doubt aware of the presence of Christ in the Temple, yet unwilling to be in the number of His hearers, had watched the effect of His Teaching —overheard the low, furtive, half-outspoken remarks ('the murmuring') of the people about Him. Presently they conferred with the heads of the priesthood and the chief Temple-officials.[1] Although there was neither meeting, nor decree of the Sanhedrin about it, nor, indeed, could be,[2] orders were given to the Temple-guard on the first possible occasion to seize Him. Jesus was aware of it, and as, either on this or another day, He was moving in the Temple, watched by the spies of the rulers and followed by a mingled crowd of disciples and enemies, deep sadness in view of the end filled His heart. 'Jesus therefore said'—no doubt to His disciples, though in the hearing of all—'yet a little while am I with you, then I go away[3] to Him that sent Me. Ye shall seek Me, and not find Me; and where I am, thither ye cannot come.'[b] Mournful words, these, which were only too soon to become true. But those who heard them naturally failed to comprehend their meaning. Was He about to leave Palestine, and go to the Diaspora of the Greeks, among the dispersed who lived in heathen lands, to teach the Greeks? Or what could be His meaning? But we, who hear it across these centuries, feel as if their question, like the suggestion of the High-Priest at a later period, nay, like so many suggestions of men, had been, all unconsciously, prophetic of the future.

to the true as the real, and the real as that which has become outwardly true. I do not quite understand—and, so far as I understand it, I do not agree with, the view of *Cremer* (Bibl. Theol. Lex., Engl. ed. p. 85), that 'ἀληθινός is related to ἀληθής as form to contents or substance.' The distinction between the Judæan and the Grecian meaning is not only borne out by the Book of Revelation (which uses it in the Judæan sense), but by Ecclus. xlii. 2. 11. In the LXX. it stands for not fewer than twelve Hebrew words.

[1] On the heads and chief officials of the Priesthood, see 'The Temple and its Services,' ch. iv., especially pp. 75–77.

[2] Only those unacquainted with the judicial procedure of the Sanhedrin could imagine that there had been a regular meeting and decree of that tribunal. That would have required a formal accusation, witnesses, examination, &c.

[3] Canon *Westcott* marks, that the word here used (ὑπάγω) indicates a personal act, while another word (πορεύομαι) marks a purpose or mission, and yet a third word (ἀπέρχομαι) expresses simple separation.

CHAPTER VII.

'IN THE LAST, THE GREAT DAY OF THE FEAST.

(St. John vii. 37—viii. 11.)

BOOK
IV

It was 'the last, the great day of the Feast,' and Jesus was once more in the Temple. We can scarcely doubt that it was the concluding day of the Feast, and not, as most modern writers suppose, its Octave, which, in Rabbinic language, was regarded as 'a festival by itself.'[a][1] But such solemn interest attaches to the Feast, and this occurrence on its last day, that we must try to realise the scene. We have here the only Old Testament type yet unfulfilled; the only Jewish festival which has no counterpart in the cycle of the Christian year,[2] just because it points forward to that great, yet unfulfilled hope of the Church: the ingathering of Earth's nations to the Christ.

[a] Comp. Yoma 3 a, and often

The celebration of the Feast corresponded to its great meaning. Not only did all the priestly families minister during that week, but it has been calculated that not fewer than 446 Priests, with, of course, a corresponding number of Levites, were required for its sacrificial worship. In general, the services were the same every day, except that the number of bullocks offered decreased daily from thirteen on the first, to seven on the seventh day. Only during the first two, and on the last festive day (as also on the Octave of the Feast), was strict Sabbatic rest enjoined. On the intervening half-holidays (*Chol haMoed*), although no new labour was to be undertaken, unless in the public service, the ordinary and necessary avocations of the home and of life were carried on, and especially all done that was required

---

[1] Hence the benediction said at the *beginning* of every Feast is not only said on the first of that of Tabernacles, but also on the *octave* of it (Sukk. 48 *a*). The sacrifices for that occasion were quite different from those for 'Tabernacles;' the 'booths' were removed; and the peculiar rites of the Feast of Tabernacles no longer observed. This is distinctly stated in Sukk. iv. 1, and the diverging opinion of R. Jehudah on this and another point is formally rejected in Tos. Sukk. iii. 16. For the six points of difference between the Feast of Tabernacles and its Octave, see note at the end of ch. viii.

[2] Bishop *Haneberg* speaks of the anniversaries of the Martyrs as part-fulfilment of the typical meaning of that Feast.

for the festive season. But 'the last, the Great Day of the Feast,' was marked by special observances.

Let us suppose ourselves in the number of worshippers, who on 'the last, the Great Day of the Feast,' are leaving their 'booths' at daybreak to take part in the service. The pilgrims are all in festive array. In his right hand each carries what is called the *Lulabh*,[1] which, although properly meaning 'a branch,' or 'palm-branch,' consisted of a myrtle and willow-branch tied together with a palm-branch between them. This was supposed to be in fulfilment of the command, Lev. xxiii. 40. 'The fruit (A.V. 'boughs') of the goodly trees,' mentioned in the same verse of Scripture, was supposed to be the *Ethrog*, the so-called Paradise-apple (according to Ber. R. 15, the fruit of the forbidden tree), a species of citron.[a] This *Ethrog* each worshipper carries in his left hand. It is scarcely necessary to add, that this interpretation of Lev. xxiii. 40 was given by the Rabbis;[b] perhaps more interesting to know, that this was one of the points in controversy between the Pharisees and Sadducees.

Thus armed with *Lulabh* in their right, and *Ethrog* in their left hands, the festive multitude would divide into three bands. Some would remain in the Temple to attend the preparation of the Morning Sacrifice. Another band would go in procession 'below Jerusalem'[c] to a place called Moza, the 'Kolonia' of the Jerusalem Talmud,[d] which some have sought to identify with the Emmaus of the Resurrection-Evening.[2] At Moza they cut down willow-branches, with which, amidst the blasts of the Priests' trumpets, they adorned the altar, forming a leafy canopy about it. Yet a third company were taking part in a still more interesting service. To the sound of music a procession started from the Temple. It followed a Priest who bore a golden pitcher, capable of holding three *log*.[3] Onwards it passed, probably, through Ophel, which recent investigations have shown to have been covered with buildings to the very verge of Siloam, down the edge of the Tyropœon Valley, where it merges into that of the Kedron. To this day terraces mark where the gardens, watered by the living spring, extended from the King's Gardens by the spring Rogel down to the entrance into the Tyropœon. Here was the so-called 'Fountain-Gate,' and still within the City-wall 'the Pool of Siloam,' the overflow of which fed a lower pool. As already stated it was at the merging of the Tyropœon into the Kedron Valley, in

[a] Targ. Onkelos, and Pseudo-Jon. and Jerus. on Lev. xxiii. 40; *Jos.* Ant. xiii. 13. 5

[b] Vayy. R. 30, towards end, ed. Warsh., p. 47 *a*

[c] Sukk. iv. 5

[d] Jer. Sukk. iv. 3, p. 54 *b*

---

[1] Also *Lulabha* and *Luleybha*.
[2] For a full discussion of this point, see p. 636, note 3.
[3] Rather more than two pints.

BOOK
IV

the south-eastern angle of Jerusalem. The Pool of Siloam was fed by the living spring farther up in the narrowest part of the Kedron Valley, which presently bears the name of 'the Virgin's Fountain,' but represents the ancient En-Rogel and Gihon. Indeed, the very canal which led from the one to the other, with the inscription of the workmen upon it, has lately been excavated.[1] Though chiefly of historical interest, a sentence may be added. The Pool of Siloam is the same as 'the King's Pool' of Neh. ii. 14.[a] It was made by King Hezekiah, in order both to divert from a besieging army the spring of Gihon, which could not be brought within the City-wall, and yet to bring its waters within the City.[b] This explains the origin of the name *Siloam*, 'sent'—a conduit[c]—or 'Siloah,' as Josephus calls it. Lastly, we remember that it was down in the valley at Gihon (or En-Rogel), that Solomon was proclaimed,[d] while the opposite faction held revel, and would have made Adonijah king, on the cliff *Zoheleth* (the modern *Zahweileh*) right over against it, not a hundred yards distant,[e] where they must, of course, have distinctly heard the sound of the trumpets and the shouts of the people as Solomon was proclaimed king.[f]

[a] Comp. Neh. iii. 15

[b] 2 Chron. xxxii. 30; [1] 2 Kings xx. 20

[c] St. John ix. 7

[d] 1 Kings i. 33, 38

[e] 1 Kings i. 9

[f] ver. 41

But to return. When the Temple-procession had reached the Pool of Siloam, the Priest filled his golden pitcher from its waters.[2] Then they went back to the Temple, so timing it, that they should arrive just as they were laying the pieces of the sacrifice on the great Altar of Burnt-offering,[g] towards the close of the ordinary Morning-Sacrifice service. A threefold blast of the Priests' trumpets welcomed the arrival of the Priest, as he entered through the 'Water-gate,'[3] which obtained its name from this ceremony, and passed straight into the Court of the Priests. Here he was joined by another Priest, who carried the wine for the drink-offering. The two Priests ascended 'the rise' of the altar, and turned to the left. There were two silver funnels here, with narrow openings, leading down to the base of the altar. Into that at the east, which was somewhat wider, the wine was poured, and, at the same time, the water into the western and narrower opening, the people shouting to the Priest to raise his hand, so as to make sure that he poured the water into the funnel. For, although it was held, that the water-pouring was an ordi-

[g] Tos. Sukk iii. 8

---

[1] Curiously, in that passage the spring of the river is designated by the word *Moza*.

[2] Except on a Sabbath, and on the first day of the Feast. On these occasions it had been provided the day before.

[3] One of the gates that opened from 'the terrace' on the south side of the Temple.

nance instituted by Moses, 'a Halakhah of Moses from Sinai,' [a] this was another of the points disputed by the Sadducees.[1]   And, indeed, to give practical effect to their views, the High-Priest Alexander Jannæus had on one occasion poured the water on the ground, when he was nearly murdered, and in the riot, that ensued, six thousand persons were killed in the Temple.[b]

Immediately after 'the pouring of water,' the great 'Hallel,' consisting of Psalms cxiii. to cxviii. (inclusive), was chanted antiphonally, or rather, with responses, to the accompaniment of the flute. As the Levites intoned the first line of each Psalm, the people repeated it; while to each of the other lines they responded by *Hallelu Yah* ('Praise ye the Lord'). But in Psalm cxviii. the people not only repeated the first line, 'O give thanks to the Lord,' but also these, 'O then, work now salvation, Jehovah,' [c] 'O Lord, send now prosperity;' [d] and again, at the close of the Psalm, 'O give thanks to the Lord.'   As they repeated these lines, they shook towards the altar the *Lulabh* which they held in their hands—as if with this token of the past to express the reality and cause of their praise, and to remind God of His promises.   It is this moment which should be chiefly kept in view.

The festive morning-service was followed by the offering of the special sacrifices for the day, with their drink-offerings, and by the Psalm for the day, which, on 'the last, the Great Day of the Feast,' was Psalm lxxxii. from verse 5. [e] [2]   The Psalm was, of course, chanted, as always, to instrumental accompaniment, and at the end of each of its three sections the Priests blew a threefold blast, while the people bowed down in worship.   In further symbolism of this Feast, as pointing to the ingathering of the heathen nations, the public services closed with a procession round the Altar by the Priests, who chanted 'O then, work now salvation, Jehovah!   O Jehovah, send now prosperity.' [f]   But on 'the last, the Great Day of the Feast,' this procession of Priests made the circuit of the altar, not only once, but seven times, as if they were again compassing, but now with prayer, the Gentile Jericho which barred their possession of the promised land. Hence the seventh or last day of the Feast was also called that of 'the Great Hosannah.'   As the people left the Temple, they saluted the altar with words of thanks,[g] and on the last day of the Feast

CHAP. VII

[a] Jer. Sukk. iv. 6; Sukk. 44 a

[b] Sukk. iv. 9; Jos. Ant. xiii. 13. 5

[c] Ps. cxviii. 25

[d] ver. 25

[e] Sukk. 55 a; *Maimonides*, Yad haChas. Hilkh. Temid. uMos. x. 11 (vol. iii. p. 204 a)

[f] Ps. cxviii. 25

[g] Sukk. iv. 5

---

[1] On the other hand, R. Akiba maintained, that the 'water-pouring' was prescribed in the *written* Law.

[2] For the Psalms chanted on the other days of the Feast, and a detailed description of the Feast itself, see 'The Temple and its Services,' ch. xiv.

BOOK
IV

ᵃ u. s. 1
and 6
ᵇ u. s. 8

they shook off the leaves on the willow-branches round the altar, and beat their palm-branches to pieces.ᵃ On the same afternoon the 'booths' were dismantled, and the Feast ended.ᵇ

We can have little difficulty in determining at what part of the services of 'the last, the Great Day of the Feast,' Jesus stood and cried, 'If any one thirst, let Him come unto Me and drink!' It must have been with special reference to the ceremony of the out-pouring of the water, which, as we have seen, was considered the central part of the service.[1] Moreover, all would understand that His words must refer to the Holy Spirit, since the rite was univer-sally regarded as symbolical of His outpouring. The forthpouring of the water was immediately followed by the chanting of the *Hallel*. But after that there must have been a short pause to prepare for the festive sacrifices (the *Musaph*). It was then, immediately after the symbolic rite of water-pouring, immediately after the people had responded by repeating those lines from Psalm cxviii.—given thanks, and prayed that Jehovah would send salvation and prosperity, and had shaken their *Lulabh* towards the altar, thus praising 'with heart, and mouth, and hands,' and then silence had fallen upon them—that there rose, so loud as to be heard throughout the Temple, the Voice of Jesus. He interrupted not the services, for they had for the moment ceased: He interpreted, and He fulfilled them.

Whether we realise it in connection with the deeply-stirring rites just concluded, and the song of praise that had scarcely died out of the air; or think of it as a vast step in advance in the history of Christ's Manifestation, the scene is equally wondrous. But yester-day they had been divided about Him, and the authorities had given directions to take Him; to-day He is not only in the Temple, but, at the close of the most solemn rites of the Feast, asserting, within the hearing of all, His claim to be regarded as the fulfilment of all, and the true Messiah! And yet there is neither harshness of com-mand nor violence of threat in His proclamation. It is the King, meek, gentle, and loving; the Messiah, Who will not break the bruised reed, Who will not lift up His Voice in tone of anger, but speak in accents of loving, condescending compassion, Who now bids, whosoever thirsteth, come unto Him and drink. And so the words have to all time remained the call of Christ to all that thirst,

---

[1] I must respectfully differ from Canon *Westcott* (ad loc.) when he regards it as a doubtful question whether or not the 'water-pouring' had taken place on the day when our Lord so pointed to the ful-filment of its symbolical meaning.

whence- or what-soever their need and longing of soul may be. But, as we listen to these words as originally spoken, we feel how they mark that Christ's hour was indeed coming: the preparation past; the manifestation in the present, unmistakable, urgent, and loving; and the final conflict at hand.

Of those who had heard Him, none but must have understood that, if the invitation were indeed real, and Christ the fulfilment of all, then the promise also had its deepest meaning, that he who believed on Him would not only receive the promised fulness of the Spirit, but give it forth to the fertilising of the barren waste around. It was, truly, the fulfilment of the Scripture-promise, not of one but of all: that in Messianic times the *Nabhi*, ' prophet,' literally the weller forth, viz., of the Divine, should not be one or another select individual, but that He would pour out on all His handmaidens and servants of His Holy Spirit, and thus the moral wilderness of this world be changed into a fruitful garden. Indeed, this is expressly stated in the Targum which thus paraphrases Is. xliv. 3: ' Behold, as the waters are poured on arid ground and spread over the dry soil, so will I give the Spirit of My Holiness on thy sons, and My blessing on thy children's children.' What was new to them was, that all this was treasured up in the Christ, that out of His fulness men might receive, and grace for grace. And yet even this was not quite new. For, was it not the fulfilment of that old prophetic cry: ' The Spirit of the Lord Jehovah is upon Me: therefore has He Messiahed (anointed) Me to preach good tidings unto the poor ' ? So then, it was nothing new, only the happy fulfilment of the old, when He thus ' spake of the Holy Spirit, which they who believed on Him should receive,' not then, but upon His Messianic exaltation.

And so we scarcely wonder that many, on hearing Him, said, though not with that heart-conviction which would have led to self-surrender, that He was the Prophet promised of old, even the Christ, while others, by their side, regarding Him as a Galilean, the Son of Joseph, raised the ignorant objection that He could not be the Messiah, since the latter must be of the seed of David and come from Bethlehem. Nay, such was the anger of some against what they regarded a dangerous seducer of the poor people, that they would fain have laid violent hands on Him. But amidst all this, the strongest testimony to His Person and Mission remains to be told. It came, as so often, from a quarter whence it could least have been expected. Those Temple-officers, whom the authorities had commissioned to watch an opportunity for seizing Jesus, came back

BOOK
IV

without having done their behest, and that, when, manifestly, the scene in the Temple might have offered the desired ground for His imprisonment. To the question of the Pharisees, they could only give this reply, which has ever since remained unquestionable fact of history, admitted alike by friend and foe: 'Never man so spake as this man.'[1] For, as all spiritual longing and all upward tending, not only of men but even of systems, consciously or unconsciously tends towards Christ,[a] so can we measure and judge all systems by this, which no sober student of history will gainsay, that no man or system ever so spake.

[a] St. John
vii. 17

It was not this which the Pharisees now gainsaid, but rather the obvious, and, we may add, logical, inference from it. The scene which followed is so thoroughly Jewish, that it alone would suffice to prove the Jewish, and hence Johannine, authorship of the Fourth Gospel. The harsh sneer: 'Are ye also led astray?' is succeeded by pointing to the authority of the learned and great, who with one accord were rejecting Jesus. 'But this people'—the country-people (*Am ha-arez*), the ignorant, unlettered rabble—'are cursed.' Sufficient has been shown in previous parts of this book to explain alike the Pharisaic claim of authority and their almost unutterable contempt of the unlettered. So far did the latter go, that it would refuse, not only all family connection and friendly intercourse,[b] but even the bread of charity, to the unlettered;[c] nay, that, in theory at least, it would have regarded their murder as no sin,[d] and even cut them off from the hope of the Resurrection.[e] [2] But is it not true, that, even in our days, this double sneer, rather than argument, of the Pharisees is the main reason of the disbelief of so many: Which of the learned believe on Him? but the ignorant multitude are led by superstition to ruin.

[b] Ps. 49 b

[c] Baba B.
8 b
[d] Pes. 49 d
[e] Kethub.
111 b

There was one standing among the Temple-authorities, whom an uneasy conscience would not allow to remain quite silent. It was the Sanhedrist Nicodemus, still a night-disciple, even in brightest noon-tide. He could not hold his peace, and yet he dared not speak for Christ. So he made compromise of both by taking the part of, and speaking as, a righteous, rigid Sanhedrist. 'Does our Law judge (pronounce sentence upon) a man, except it first hear from himself and know what he doeth?' From the Rabbinic point of view, no sounder judicial saying could have been uttered. Yet such common-

---

[1] Whether or not the last three words are spurious is, so far as the sense of the words is concerned, matter of comparative indifference

[2] For further details the reader is referred to *Wagenseil's* Sota, pp. 516–519.

places impose not on any one, nor even serve any good purpose. It helped not the cause of Jesus, and it disguised not the advocacy of Nicodemus. We know what was thought of Galilee in the Rabbinic world. 'Art thou also of Galilee? Search and see, for out of Galilee ariseth no prophet.'

And so ended this incident, which, to all concerned, might have been so fruitful of good. Once more Nicodemus was left alone, as every one who has dared and yet not dared for Christ is after all such bootless compromises; alone—with sore heart, stricken conscience, and a great longing.[1]

---

[1] The reader will observe, that the narrative of the woman taken in adultery, as also the previous verse (St. John vii. 53–viii. 11) have been left out in this History—although with great reluctance. By this it is not intended to characterise that section as Apocryphal, nor indeed to pronounce any opinion as to the reality of some such occurrence. For, it contains much which we instinctively feel to be like the Master, both in what Christ is represented as saying and as doing. All that we reluctantly feel bound to maintain is, that the narrative in its present form did *not* exist in the Gospel of St. John, and, indeed, *could* not have existed. For a summary of the external evidence against the Johannine authorship of the passage, I would refer to Canon *Westcott's* Note, ad loc., in the 'Speaker's Commentary.' But there is also *internal* evidence, and, to my mind at least, most cogent, against its authenticity—at any rate, in its present form. From first to last it is utterly un-Jewish. Accordingly, unbiassed critics who are conversant either with Jewish legal procedure, or with the habits and views of the people at the time, would feel obliged to reject it, even if the external evidence had been as strong in its favour as it is for its rejection. Archdeacon *Farrar* has, indeed, devoted to the illustration of this narrative some of his most pictorial pages. But, with all his ability and eloquence, his references to Jewish law and observances are not such as to satisfy the requirements of criticism. To this general objection to their correctness I must add a protest against the views which he presents of the moral state of Jewish society at the time. On the other hand, from whatever point we view this narrative—the accusers, the witnesses, the public examination, the bringing of the woman to Jesus, or the punishment claimed—it presents insuperable difficulties. That a woman taken in the act of adultery should have been brought before Jesus (and apparently without the witnesses to her crime); that such an utterly un-Jewish, as well as illegal, procedure should have been that of the 'Scribes and Pharisees'; that such a breach of law, and of what Judaism would regard as decency, should have been perpetrated to 'tempt' Him; or that the Scribes should have been so ignorant as to substitute stoning for strangulation, as the punishment of adultery; lastly, that this scene should have been enacted in the Temple, presents a veritable climax of impossibilities. I can only express surprise that Archdeacon *Farrar* should have suggested that the 'Feast of Tabernacles' had grown into a kind of vintage-festival, which would often degenerate into acts of licence and immorality,' or that the lives of the religious leaders of Israel 'were often stained' with such sins. The first statement is quite ungrounded; and as for the second, I do not recall a single instance in which a charge of adultery is brought against a Rabbi of that period. The quotations in *Sepp's* Leben Jesu (vol. v. p. 183), which Archdeacon *Farrar* adduces, are not to cases in point, however much, from the Christian point of view, we may reprobate the conduct of the Rabbis there mentioned.

CHAPTER VIII.

TEACHING IN THE TEMPLE ON THE OCTAVE OF THE FEAST OF TABERNACLES.

(St. John viii. 12–59.)

BOOK
IV

THE startling teaching on ‘the last, the Great Day of the Feast’ was not the only one delivered at that season. The impression left on the mind is, that after silencing, as they thought, Nicodemus, the leaders of the Pharisees had dispersed.[1] The addresses of Jesus which followed must, therefore, have been delivered, either later on that day, or, what on every account seems more likely, chiefly, or all, on the next day,[2] which was the Octave of the Feast, when the Temple would be once more thronged by worshippers.

a St. John
viii. 20
b ver. 21

On this occasion we find Christ, first in ‘The Treasury,’[a] and then[b] in some unnamed part of the sacred building, in all probability one of the ‘Porches.’ Greater freedom could be here enjoyed, since these ‘Porches,’ which enclosed the Court of the Gentiles, did not form part of the Sanctuary in the stricter sense. Discussions might take place, in which not, as in ‘the Treasury,’ only ‘the Phari-

c ver. 13

sees,’[c] but the people generally, might propound questions, answer, or assent. Again, as regards the requirements of the present narrative, since the Porches opened upon the Court, the Jews might there pick up stones to cast at Him (which would have been impossible in any part of the Sanctuary itself), while lastly, Jesus might easily pass out of the Temple in the crowd that moved through the Porches to the outer gates.[3]

---

[1] This, although St. John vii. 53 must be rejected as spurious. But the whole context seems to imply, that for the present the auditory of Jesus had dispersed. [2] It is, however, not unlikely that the first address (vv. 12–19) may have been delivered on the afternoon of the ‘Last Day of the Feast,’ when the cessation of preparations for the Temple-illumination may have given the outward occasion for the words: ‘I am the light of the World.’ The παλιν of vv. 12 and 21 seems in each case to indicate a fresh period of time. Besides, we can scarcely suppose that all from vii. 37 to viii. 59 had taken place the same day. For this and other arguments on the point, see *Lücke*, vol. ii. pp. 279–281. [3] The last clauses of ver. 59, ‘going through the midst of them went His way, and so passed by,’ must be omitted as spurious.

But the narrative first transports us into 'the Treasury,' where 'the Pharisees'—or leaders—would alone venture to speak. It ought to be specially marked, that if they laid not hands on Jesus when He dared to teach in this sacred locality, and that such unwelcome doctrine, His immunity must be ascribed to the higher appointment of God: 'because His hour had not yet come.'[a] An archæological question may here be raised as to the exact localisation of 'the Treasury,' whether it was the colonnade around 'the Court of the Women,' in which the receptacles for charitable contributions—the so-called *Shopharoth*, or 'trumpets'—were placed,[b] or one of the two 'chambers' in which, respectively, secret gifts[1] and votive offerings[2] were deposited.[c][3] The former seems the most likely. In any case, it would be within 'the Court of the Women,' the common meeting-place of the worshippers, and, as we may say, the most generally attended part of the Sanctuary.[4] Here, in the hearing of the leaders of the people, took place the first Dialogue between Christ and the Pharisees.

It opened with what probably was an allusion alike to one of the great ceremonies of the Feast of Tabernacles, to its symbolic meaning, and to an express Messianic expectation of the Rabbis. As the Mishnah states: On the first,[d] or, as the Talmud would have it,[e] on every night[5] of the festive week, 'the Court of the Women,' was brilliantly illuminated, and the night spent in the demonstrations already described. This was called 'the joy of the feast.' This 'festive joy,' of which the origin is obscure, was no doubt connected with the hope of earth's great harvest-joy in the conversion of the heathen world, and so pointed to 'the days of the Messiah.' In connection with this we mark, that the term 'light' was specially

CHAP.
VIII

[a] ver. 20

[b] Sheqal.
vi. 5

[c] Sheqal.
v. 6

[d] Sukk. v. 2
[e] Jer. Sukk.
55 b; Sukk.
53 a

---

[1] The so-called 'chamber of the silent' (*Chashaim*), Sheqal. v. 6.
[2] The 'chamber of the vessels' (*Kelim*). It was probably over, or in this chamber that Agrippi hung up the golden memorial-chain of his captivity (*Jos.* Antiq. xix. 6. 1).
[3] Comp. generally 'The Temple and its Services,' pp. 26, 27.
[4] The 'Court of the Women' (γυναικωνῖς, *Jos.* Jew.War v. 5. 3; comp. also v. 5. 2), so called, because women could not penetrate further. It was the real Court of the Sanctuary. Here Jeremiah also taught (xix. 14; xxvi. 2). But it is not correct to state (*Westcott*), that the Council Chamber of the Sanhedrin (*Gazith*) was 'between the Court of the Women and the inner court.' It was in the south-eastern angle of the Court of the Priests—and hence at a considerable distance from the Court of the Women. But, not to speak of the circumstance that the Sanhedrin no longer met in that Chamber—even if it had been nearer, Christ's teaching in the Treasury could not (at any period) 'have been within earshot of the Sanhedrin,' since it would not sit on that day.
[5] Although Rabbi Joshua tells (in the Talmud) that during all the nights of the festive week they 'did not taste sleep,' this seems scarcely credible, and the statement of the Mishnah is the more rational. *Maimonides*, however, adopts the view of the Talmud (Hilch. Lul. viii. 12).

ᵃ Bemidb.
R. 15, ed.
Warsh.
p. 62 a, b

ᵇ St. Luke
ii. 32

ᵉ Ber. R. 3

ᵈ Bemidb.
R. 15
ᵉ Yalk. on
Is. lx.
ᶠ On Lam. i.
16, ed.
Warsh. p.
64 a, b

ᵍ In Dan. ii.
22

ʰ St. Luke ii
32

applied to the Messiah. In a very interesting passage of the Midrash ᵃ we are told, that, while commonly windows were made wide within and narrow without, it was the opposite in the Temple of Solomon, because the light issuing from the Sanctuary was to lighten that which was without. This reminds us of the language of devout old Simeon in regard to the Messiah,ᵇ as 'a light to lighten the Gentiles, and the glory of His people Israel.' The Midrash further explains, that, if the light in the Sanctuary was to be always burning before Jehovah, the reason was, not that He needed such light, but that He honoured Israel with this as a symbolic command. In Messianic times God would, in fulfilment of the prophetic meaning of this rite, 'kindle for them the Great Light,' and the nations of the world would point to them, who had lit the light for Him Who lightened the whole world. But even this is not all. The Rabbis speak of the original light in which God had wrapped Himself as in a garment,ᶜ and which could not shine by day, because it would have dimmed the light of the sun. From this light that of the sun, moon, and stars had been kindled.ᵈ It was now reserved under the throne of God for the Messiah,ᵉ in Whose days it would shine forth once more. Lastly, we ought to refer to a passage in another Midrash,ᶠ where, after a remarkable discussion on such names of the Messiah as 'the Lord our Righteousness,' 'the Branch,' 'the Comforter,' 'Shiloh,' 'Compassion,' His Birth is connected with the destruction, and His return with the restoration of the Temple.[1] But in that very passage the Messiah is also specially designated as the 'Enlightener,' the words:ᵍ 'the light dwelleth with Him,' being applied to Him.

What has just been stated shows, that the Messianic hope of the aged Simeon ʰ most truly expressed the Messianic thoughts of the time. It also proves, that the Pharisees could not have mistaken the Messianic meaning in the words of Jesus, in their reference to the past festivity: 'I am the Light of the world.' This circumstance is itself evidential as regards this Discourse of Christ, the truth of this narrative, and even the Jewish authorship of the Fourth Gospel. But, indeed, the whole Address, the argumentation with the Pharisees which follows, as well as the subsequent Discourse to, and argumentation with, the Jews, are peculiarly Jewish in their form of reasoning. Substantially, these Discourses are a continuation of those previously delivered at this Feast. But they carry the argu-

---

[1] The passage is one of the most remarkable, as regards the Messianic views of the Rabbis. See Appendix IX.

ment one important step both backwards and forwards. The situation had now become quite clear, and neither party cared to conceal
it. What Jesus had gradually communicated to the disciples, who
were so unwilling to receive it, had now become an acknowledged
fact. It was no longer a secret that the leaders of Israel and Jerusalem were compassing the Death of Jesus. This underlies all His
Words. And He sought to turn them from their purpose, not by appealing to their pity nor to any lower motive, but by claiming as His
right that, for which they would condemn Him. He *was* the Sent of
God, the Messiah; although, to know Him and His Mission, it needed
moral kinship with Him that had sent Him. But this led to the very
root of the matter. It needed moral kinship with God: did Israel,
as such, possess it? *They did not*; nay, no man possessed it, till
given him of God. This was not exactly new in these Discourses of
Christ, but it was now far more clearly stated and developed, and in
that sense new.

We also are too apt to overlook this teaching of Christ—perhaps
have overlooked it. It is concerning the corruption of our whole
nature by sin, and hence the need of God-teaching, if we are to
receive the Christ, or understand His doctrine. That which is born
of the flesh is flesh; that which is born of the Spirit is Spirit; wherefore, 'marvel not that I said, Ye must be born again.' That had been
Christ's initial teaching to Nicodemus, and it became, with growing
emphasis, His final teaching to the teachers of Israel. It is not St.
Paul who first sets forth the doctrine of our entire moral ruin: he had
learned it from the Christ. It forms the very basis of Christianity;
it is the ultimate reason of the need of a Redeemer, and the *rationale*
of the work which Christ came to do. The Priesthood and the
Sacrificial Work of Christ, as well as the higher aspect of His
Prophetic Office, and the true meaning of His Kingship, as not of
this world, are based upon it. Very markedly, it constitutes the
starting-point in the fundamental divergence between the leaders of
the Synagogue and Christ—we might say, to all time between Christians and non-Christians. The teachers of Israel knew not, nor
believed in the total corruption of man—Jew as well as Gentile—
and, therefore, felt not the need of a Saviour. They could not
understand it, how 'Except a man'—at least a Jew—were 'born
again,' and, 'from above,' he could not enter, nor even see, the
Kingdom of God. They understood not their own Bible: the story
of the Fall—not Moses and the Prophets; and how could they understand Christ? they believed not them, and how could they believe

BOOK
IV

Him? And yet, from this point of view, but only from this, does all seem clear: the Incarnation, the History of the Temptation and Victory in the Wilderness, and even the Cross. Only he who has, in some measure, himself felt the agony of the first garden, can understand that *of the second garden*. Had they understood, by that personal experience which we must all have of it, the Proto-Evangel of the great contest, and of the great conquest by suffering, they would have followed its lines to their final goal in the Christ as the fulfilment of all. And so, here also, were the words of Christ true, that it needed heavenly teaching, and kinship to the Divine, to understand His doctrine.

This underlies, and is the main object of these Discourses of Christ. As a corollary He would teach, that Satan was not a merely malicious, impish being, working outward destruction, but that there was a moral power of evil which held us all—not the Gentile world only, but even the most favoured, learned, and exalted among the Jews. Of this power Satan was the concentration and impersonation; the prince of the power of 'darkness.' This opens up the reasoning of Christ, alike as expressed and implied. He presented Himself to them as the Messiah, and hence as the Light of the World. It resulted, that only in following Him would a man 'not walk in the darkness,'[1] but have the light—and that, be it marked, not the light of knowledge, but of life.[a] On the other hand, it also followed, that all, who were not within this light, were in darkness and in death.

ª St. John
viii. 12

It was an appeal to the moral in His hearers. The Pharisees sought to turn it aside by an appeal to the external and visible. They asked for some witness, or palpable evidence, of what they called His testimony about Himself,[b] well knowing that such could only be through some external, visible, miraculous manifestation, just as they had formerly asked for a sign from heaven. The Bible, and especially the Evangelic history, is full of what men ordinarily, and often thoughtlessly, call the miraculous. But, in this case, the miraculous would have become the magical, which it never is. If Christ had yielded to their appeal, and transferred the question from the moral to the coarsely external sphere, He would have ceased to be the Messiah of the Incarnation, Temptation, and Cross, the Messiah-Saviour. It would have been to un-Messiah the Messiah of the Gospel, for it was only, in another form, a repetition of the Temptation. A miracle or sign would at that moment have been a moral

ᵇ ver. 13

---

[1] Mark here the definite article.

anachronism—as much as any miracle would be in our days,[1] when the Christ makes His appeal to the moral, and is met by a demand for the external and material evidence of His Witness.

The interruption of the Pharisees [a] was thoroughly Jewish, and so was their objection. It had to be met, and that in the Jewish form[2] in which it had been raised, while the Christ must at the same time continue His former teaching to them concerning God and their own distance from Him. Their objection had proceeded on this fundamental judicial principle —'A person is not accredited about himself.' [b] Harsh and unjust as this principle sometimes was,[3] it evidently applied only in *judicial* cases, and hence implied that these Pharisees sat in judgment on Him as one suspected, and charged with guilt. The reply of Jesus was plain. Even if His testimony about Himself were unsupported, it would still be true, and He was competent to bear it, for He knew, as a matter of fact, whence He came and whither He went—His own part in this Mission, and its goal, as well as God's—whereas they knew[4] not either.[c] But, more than this: their demand for a witness had proceeded on the assumption of their being the judges, and He the panel—a relation which only arose from their judging after the flesh. Spiritual judgment upon that which was within belonged only to Him, that searcheth all secrets. Christ, while on earth, judged no man; and, even if He did so, it must be remembered that He did it not alone, but with, and as the Representative of, the Father. Hence, such judgment would be true.[d] But, as for their main charge, was it either true, or good in law? In accordance with the Law of God, there were two witnesses to the fact of His Mission: His own, and the frequently-shown attestation of His Father. And, if it were objected that a man could not bear witness in his own cause, the same Rabbinic canon laid it down, that this only applied if his testimony stood alone. But if it were corroborated (even in a matter of greatest delicacy),[5] although by only one male or female slave—who ordinarily were unfit for testimony—it would be credited.

[a] St. John viii. 13

[b] Kethub. ii. 9

[c] St. John viii. 14

[d] vv. 15, 16

---

[1] It is substantially the same evidence which is demanded by the negative physicists of our days. Nor can I imagine a more thorough misunderstanding of the character and teaching of Christianity than, for example, the proposal to test the efficacy of prayer, by asking for the recovery of those in a hospital ward! This would represent heathenism, not Christianity.

[2] We mark here again the evidence of the Jewish authorship of the Fourth Gospel.

[3] Thus the testimony of a man, that during the heathen occupancy of Jerusalem his wife had never left him, was not allowed, and the husband forbidden his wife (Kethub. ii. 9).

[4] Not, as in the A.V., 'tell.'

[5] Kethub. ii 9. Such solitary testimony only when favourable, not when adverse. On the law of testimony generally, comp. *Saalschütz*, Mos. Recht, pp. 604, 605.

The reasoning of Christ, without for a moment quitting the higher ground of His teaching, was quite unanswerable from the Jewish standpoint. The Pharisees felt it, and, though well knowing to Whom He referred, tried to evade it by the sneer—where (not Who) His Father was? This gave occasion for Christ to return to the main subject of His Address, that the reason of their ignorance of Him was, that they knew not the Father, and, in turn, that only acknowledgment of Him would bring true knowledge of the Father.[a]

ª St. John
viii. 19

Such words would only ripen in the hearts of such men the murderous resolve against Jesus. Yet, not till *His*, not their, hour had come! Presently, we find Him again, now in one of the Porches—probably that of Solomon—teaching, this time, 'the Jews.' We imagine they were chiefly, if not all, Judæans—perhaps Jerusalemites, aware of the murderous intent of their leaders—not His own Galileans, whom He addressed. It was in continuation of what had gone before—alike of what He had said to them and of what they felt towards Him. The words are intensely sad—Christ's farewell to His rebellious people, His tear-words over lost Israel; abrupt also, as if they were torn sentences, or, else, headings for special discourses: 'I go My way'—'Ye shall seek Me, and in your sin[1] shall ye die'—'Whither I go, ye cannot come!' And is it not all most true? These many centuries has Israel sought its Christ, and perished in its great sin of rejecting Him; and whither Christ and His kingdom tended, the Synagogue and Judaism never came. They thought that He spoke of His dying, and not, as He did, of that which came after it. But, how could His dying establish such separation between them? This was the next question which rose in their minds.[b] Would there be anything so peculiar about His dying, or, did His expression about *going* indicate a purpose of taking away His Own life?[2]

ᵇ St. John
viii. 22

It was this misunderstanding which Jesus briefly but emphatically corrected by telling them, that the ground of their separation was the difference of their nature: they were from beneath, He from above; they of this world, He not of this world. Hence they could

---

[1] Not 'sins,' as in the A.V.

[2] Generally this is understood as referring to the supposed Jewish belief, that suicides occupied the lowest place in Gehenna. But a glance at the context must convince that the Jews could not have understood Christ as meaning, that He would be separated from them by being sent to the lowest Gehenna. Besides, this supposed punishment of suicides is only derived from a rhetorical passage in *Josephus* (Jew. War iii. 8. 5), but unsupported by any Rabbinic statements. The Rabbinic definition—or rather limitation—of what constitutes suicide is remarkable. Thus, neither Saul, nor Ahitophel, nor Zimri, are regarded as suicides, because they did it to avoid falling into the hands of their enemies. For premeditated, real suicide the punishment is left with God. Some difference is to be made in the burial of such, yet not such as to put the survivors to shame.

not come where He would be, since they must die in their sin, as
He had told them—'if ye believe not that I am.'[a]

The words were intentionally mysteriously spoken, as to a Jewish
audience. Believe not that Thou art! But 'Who art Thou?'
Whether or not the words were spoken in scorn, their question condemned themselves. In His broken sentence, Jesus had tried them
—to see how they would complete it. Then it was so! All this time
they had not yet learned Who He was; had not even a conviction
on that point, either for or against Him, but were ready to be
swayed by their leaders! 'Who I am?'—am I not telling you it
even from the beginning; has My testimony by word or deed ever
swerved on this point? I am what all along, from the beginning, I
tell you.[1] Then, putting aside this interruption, He resumed His
argument.[b] Many other things had He to say and to judge concerning them, besides the bitter truth of their perishing if they believed
not that it was He—but He that had sent Him was true, and He
must ever speak into the world the message which He had received.
When Christ referred to it as that which 'He heard from Him,'[c] He
evidently wished thereby to emphasise the fact of His Mission from
God, as constituting His claim on their obedience of faith. But it
was this very point which, even at that moment, they were not
understanding.[d] And they would only learn it, not by His Words,
but by the event, when they had 'lifted Him up,' as they thought, to
the Cross, but really on the way to His Glory.[2][e] Then would they

[a] vv. 23, 24

[b] vv. 25, 26

[c] ver. 26

[d] ver. 27

[e] ver. 28

---

[1] It would be impossible here to enter
into a critical analysis or vindication of
the rendering of this much controverted
passage, adopted in the text. The
method followed has been to retranslate
literally into Hebrew:

מתחילה הוא שגם דברתי אליכם

This might be rendered either, 'To begin
with—He that I also tell you;' or, 'from
the beginning He that I also tell you.'
I prefer the latter, and its meaning seems
substantially that of our A.V.

[2] As Canon *Westcott* rightly points
out (St. John xii. 32), the term 'lifting
up' includes both the death and the
glory. If we ask ourselves what corresponding Hebrew word, including the
sensus malus as well as the *sensus bonus*
would have been used, the verb *Nasa*
(נשא) naturally occurs (comp. Gen xl.
19 with ver. 13). For we suppose, that
the word used by Christ at this early
part of His Ministry could not have
necessarily involved a prediction of His

Crucifixion, and that they who heard it
rather imagined it to refer to His Exaltation. There is a curiously illustrative
passage here (in Pesiqta R. 10), when a
king, having given orders that the head
of his son should be 'lifted up'(שאו את)
ראשו), that it should be hanged up (תלו
את ראשו), is exhorted by the tutor to spare
what was his 'moneginos'(only begotten).
On the king's replying that he was bound
by the orders he had given, the tutor
answers by pointing out that the verb
Nasa means lifting up in the sense of
exalting, as well as of executing. But,
besides the verb *Nasa*, there is also the
verb *Zeqaph* (זקף), which in the Aramaic
and in the Syriac is used both for lifting
up and for hanging—specifically for crucifying; and, lastly, the verb *Tela* (תְּלָא or
תְּלָה), which means in the first place to
lift up, and secondarily to hang or crucify
(see *Levy*, Targum, Wörterb. ii. p. 539 *a*
and *b*). If this latter verb was used,

BOOK
IV

ᵃ ver. 28
(comp. ver.
24)

perceive the meaning of the designation He had given of Himself, and the claim founded on it ᵃ : ‘ Then shall ye perceive that I am.’ Meantime : ‘ And of Myself do I nothing, but as the [1] Father taught Me, these things do I speak. And He that sent Me is with Me. He [2] hath not left Me alone, because what pleases Him I do always.’

If the Jews failed to understand the expression ‘lifting up,’ which might mean His Exaltation, though it did mean, in the first place, His Cross, there was that in His Appeal to His Words and Deeds as bearing witness to His Mission and to the Divine Help and Presence in it, which by its sincerity, earnestness, and reality, found its way to the hearts of many. Instinctively they felt and believed that His Mission must be Divine. Whether or not this found articulate expression, Jesus now addressed Himself to those who thus far—at least for the moment—believed on Him. They were at the crisis of their spiritual history, and He must press home on them what He had sought to teach at the first. By nature far from Him, they were bondsmen. Only if they *abode* in His Word would they know the truth, and the truth would make them free. The result of this knowledge would be moral, and hence that knowledge consisted not in merely believing on Him, but in making His Word and teaching

ᵇ vv. 30–32

their dwelling—abiding in it.ᵇ But it was this very moral application which they resisted. In this also Jesus had used their own forms of thinking and teaching, only in a much higher sense. For their own tradition had it, that he only was free who laboured in the

ᶜ Ab.
Baraitha
vi. 2, p.
23 b; Erub.
54 a, line 13
from
bottom

study of the Law.ᶜ Yet the liberty of which He spoke came not through study of the Law,[3] but from abiding in the Word of Jesus. But it was this very thing which they resisted. And so they ignored the spiritual, and fell back upon the national, application of the words of Christ. As this is once more evidential of the Jewish authorship of this Gospel, so also the characteristically Jewish boast, that as the children of Abraham they had never been, and never could be, in real servitude. It would take too long to enumerate all the benefits supposed to be derived from descent from Abraham. Suffice here the almost fun-

ᵈ Shabb. 67
a; 128 a

damental principle: ‘ All Israel are the children of Kings,’ᵈ and its application even to common life, that as ‘the children of Abraham,

ᵉ Baba
Mets. vii. 1

Isaac, and Jacob, not even Solomon’s feast could be too good for them.’ᵉ

---

then the Jewish expression *Taluy*, which is still opprobriously given to Jesus, would after all represent the original designation by which He described His own death as the ‘lifted-up One.’

[1] Not ‘ my,’ as in A.V.

[2] A new sentence; and He,’ not ‘ the

Father,’ as in the A.V.

[3] With reference to Exod. xxxii. 16, a play being made on the word *Charuth* (‘graven’) which is interpreted *Cheyruth* (‘liberty’). The passage quoted by *Wünsche* (Baba Mets. 85 b) is not applicable.

Not so, however, would the Lord allow them to pass it by. He
pointed them to another servitude which they knew not, that of sin, [a]
and, entering at the same time also on their own ideas, He told them
that continuance in this servitude would also lead to national bondage and rejection: 'For the servant abideth not in the house for
ever.'[1] On the other hand, the Son abode there for ever; whom
He made free by adoption into His family, they would be free in
reality and essentially.[b][2] Then for their very dulness, He would
turn to their favourite conceit of being Abraham's seed. There
was, indeed, an obvious sense in which, by their natural descent,
they were such. But there was a moral descent—and that alone
was of real value. Another, and to them wholly new, and heavenly
teaching this, which our Lord presently applied in a manner they
could neither misunderstand nor gainsay, while He at the same time
connected it with the general drift of His teaching. Abraham's seed?
But they entertained purposes of murder, and that, because the
Word of Christ had not free course, made not way in them.[3] His
Word was what He had *seen* with (before) the Father,[4] 'not heard—for
His presence was there Eternal. Their deeds were what they had
heard from their father[5]—the word 'seen' in our common text depend-
ing on a wrong reading. And thus He showed them—in answer to
their interpellation—that their father could not have been Abraham,
so far as spiritual descent was concerned.[c] They had now a glimpse
of His meaning, but only to misapply it, according to their Jewish prejudice. Their spiritual descent, they urged, must be of God, since
their descent from Abraham was legitimate.[d] But the Lord dispelled
even this conceit by showing, that if theirs were spiritual descent
from God, then would they not reject His Message, nor seek to kill
Him, but recognise and love him.[e]

But whence this misunderstanding of His speech?[6][1] Because
they are morally incapable of hearing it—and this because of the
sinfulness of their nature: an element which Judaism had never
taken into account. And so, with infinite Wisdom, Christ once more
brought back His Discourse to what He would teach them concerning man's need, whether he be Jew or Gentile, of a Saviour and of
renewing by the Holy Ghost. If the Jews were morally unable to

CHAP.
VIII

[a] St. John
viii. 34

[b] ver. 35

[c] vv. 37–40

[d] ver. 41

[e] ver. 42

[f] vv. 43 47

---

[1] Here there should be a full stop, and
not as in the A.V.
[2] ὄντως. Comp. *Westcott* ad loc.
[3] So Canon *Westcott* aptly renders it.
[4] Not 'My Father,' as in the A.V.
These little changes are most important,
as we remember that the hearers would
so far understand and could have sympathised, had the truth been in them.
[5] According to the proper reading, the
rendering must be 'from your father,
not 'with your father,' as in the A.V.
[6] The word here is λαλιά.

BOOK
IV

hear His Word and cherished murderous designs, it was because, morally speaking, their descent was of the Devil. Very differently from Jewish ideas [1] did He speak concerning the moral evil of Satan, as both a murderer and a liar—a murderer from the beginning of the history of our race, and one who ' stood not in the truth, because truth is not in him.' Hence ' whenever he speaketh a lie '—whether to our first parents, or now concerning the Christ—' he speaketh from out his own (things), for he (Satan) is a liar, and the father of such an one (who telleth or believeth lies).' [2] Which of them could convict Him of sin? If therefore He spake truth,[3] and they believed Him not, it was because they were not of God, but, as He had shown them, of their father, the Devil.

The argument was unanswerable, and there seemed only one way to turn it aside—a Jewish *Tu quoque*, an adaptation of the ' Physician, heal thyself': ' Do we not say rightly, that Thou art a Samaritan, and hast a demon?' It is strange that the first clause of this reproach should have been so misunderstood and yet its direct explanation lies on the surface. We have only to translate it into the language which the Jews had used. By no strain of ingenuity is it possible to account for the designation 'Samaritan,' as given by the Jews to Jesus, if it is regarded as referring to nationality. Even at the very Feast they had made it an objection to His Messianic claims, that He was (as they supposed) a Galilean.[a] Nor had He come to Jerusalem from Samaria;[b] nor could He be so called (as Commentators suggest) because He was ' a foe ' to Israel, or a ' breaker of the Law,' or ' unfit to bear witness ' [4]—for neither of these circumstances would have led the Jews to designate Him by the term ' Samaritan.' ' But, in the language which they spoke, what is rendered into Greek by 'Samaritan,' would have been either *Kuthi* (כותי), which, while literally meaning a Samaritan,[c] is almost as often used in the sense of ' heretic,' or else *Shomroni* (שמרוני). The latter word deserves special attention.[5] Literally, it also means, 'Samaritan;' but, the name *Shomron* (perhaps from its connection with Samaria), is also sometimes used as the equivalent of *Ashmedai*, the Prince of the demons.[d][6] According to the Kabbalists, *Shomron* was the father of Ashmedai, and hence the same as *Sammael*, or Satan. That this was a wide-spread

[a] vii. 52

[b] St. Luke ix. 53.

[c] from *Kuth* or *Kutha*; comp. 2 Kings xvii. 24, 30

[d] Ber. R. 36, ed. Warsh. p. 65 *b*, line 5 from bottom; Yalkut on Job xxi. vol. ii. p. 150 *b* line 16 from bottom

[1] See Book II. ch. v.
[2] I cannot here regard Canon *Westcott's* rendering, which is placed in the margin of the Revised Version, as satisfactory.
[3] In the text without the article.
[4] The passage quoted by *Schöttgen* (Yebam. 47 *a*) is inapplicable, as it

really refers to a non-Israelite. More apt, but also unsuitable, is Sot. 22 *a*, quoted by *Wetstein*.
[5] Comp. *Kohut,* Jüd. Angelol. p. 95.
[6] See the Appendix on Jewish-Angelology and Demonology.

Jewish belief, appears from the circumstance that in the Korân
(which, in such matters, would reproduce popular Jewish tradition),
Israel is said to have been seduced into idolatry by *Shomron*,[a] while,
in Jewish tradition, this is attributed to Sammael.[b] If, therefore,
the term applied by the Jews to Jesus was *Shomroni*—and not
Kuthi, 'heretic'—it would literally mean, 'Child of the Devil.'[1]

This would also explain why Christ only replied to the charge of
having a demon, since the two charges meant substantially the same:
'Thou art a child of the devil and hast a demon.' In wondrous
patience and mercy He almost passed it by, dwelling rather, for their
teaching, on the fact that, while they dishonoured Him, He honoured
His Father. He heeded not their charges. His concern was the
glory of His Father; the vindication of His own honour would be
brought about by the Father—though, alas! in judgment on those
who were casting such dishonour on the Sent of God.[c] Then, as if
lingering in deep compassion on the terrible issue, He once more
pressed home the great subject of His Discourse, that only 'if a man
keep'—both have regard to, and observe—His 'Word,' 'he shall
not gaze at death [intently behold it][2] unto eternity'—for ever shall
he not come within close and terrible gaze of what is really death, of
what became such to Adam in the hour of his Fall.

It was, as repeatedly observed, this death as the consequence of
the Fall, of which the Jews knew nothing. And so they once more
misunderstood it as of physical death,[3] and, since Abraham and the
prophets had died, regarded Christ as setting up a claim higher than
theirs.[d] The Discourse had contained all that He had wished to
bring before them, and their objections were degenerating into
wrangling. It was time to break it off by a general application.
The question, He added, was not of what *He* said, but of what God
said of Him—that God, Whom they claimed as theirs, and yet knew
not, but Whom He knew, and Whose Word He 'kept.'[4] But, as for

CHAP.
VIII

[a] L'Alcoran
trad. par le
*Sieur du
Ryer*, p. 247
[b] Pirqé de
R. Eliez. 45
ed. Lemb.
p. 59 *b*, line
10 from top

[c] St. John
viii. 50

[d] vv. 52, 53

---

[1] I need scarcely point out how strongly
evidential this is of the Jewish authorship of the Fourth Gospel.

[2] The word is that peculiar and remarkable one, θεώρεω, to gaze earnestly and
intently, to which I have already called
attention (see vol. i. p. 692).

[3] He spoke of 'seeing,' they of 'tasting'
death (vv. 51, 52). The word טעם 'taste,'
is used in precisely the same manner by
the Rabbis. Thus, in the Jer. Targum on
Deut. xxxii. 1. In Ber. R. 9, we are told,
that it was originally destined that the
first man should not taste death. Again,

'Elijah did not taste the taste of death'
(Ber. R. 21). And, tropically, in such a
passage as this: 'If any one would taste a
taste (here: have a foretaste) of death, let
him keep his shoes on while he goes to
sleep' (Yom. 78 *l*). It is also used of sleep,
as: 'All the days of the joy of the house
of drawing [Feast of Tabernacles] we did
not taste the taste of sleep' (Succ. 53 *a*).
It is needless to add other quotations.

[4] On the expression 'keep' (τηρεῖν)
His work,' *Bengel* beautifully observes:
*doctrinam Jesu, credendo; promissa,
sperando; facienda obediendo.*

BOOK
IV

* Gen. xv.
17

ᵇ Ber. R.
44, ed.
Warsh. p.
81 b, lines
8, 7, 6 from
bottom

Abraham—he had 'exulted' in the thought of the coming day of the Christ, and, seeing its glory, he was glad. Even Jewish tradition could scarcely gainsay this, since there were two parties in the Synagogue, of which one believed that, when that horror of great darkness fell on him, ª Abraham had, in vision, been shown not only this, but the coming world—and not only all events in the present 'age,' but also those in Messianic times.ᵇ ¹   And now, theirs was not misunderstanding, but wilful misinterpretation. He had spoken of Abraham seeing His day; they took it of His seeing Abraham's day, and challenged its possibility. Whether or not they intended thus to elicit an avowal of His claim to eternal duration, and hence to Divinity, it was not time any longer to forbear the full statement, and, with Divine emphasis, He spake the words which could not be mistaken: 'Verily, verily, I say unto you, before Abraham was, I AM.'

It was as if they had only waited for this. Furiously they rushed from the Porch into the Court of the Gentiles—with symbolic significance, even in this—to pick up stones, and to cast them at Him. But, once more, His hour had not yet come, and their fury proved impotent. Hiding Himself for the moment, as might so easily be done, in one of the many chambers, passages, or gateways of the Temple, He presently passed out.

It had been the first plain disclosure and avowal of His Divinity, and it was 'in the midst of His enemies,' and when most contempt was cast upon Him. Presently would that avowal be renewed both in Word and by Deed; for 'the end' of mercy and judgment had not yet come, but was drawing terribly nigh.

¹ In the Targum Jerusalem on Gen. xv. also it seems implied that Abraham saw in vision all that would befall his children in the future, and also Gehenna and its torments. So far as I can gather, only the latter, not the former, seems implied in the Targ. Pseudo-Jonathan.

Note on the differences between the Feast of Tabernacles and that of its Octave (see p. 156, note 1). The six points of difference which mark the Octave as a separate feast are indicated by the memorial words and letters קָשַׁבְ סֹל רֹדֹ. and are as follows: (1) During the seven days of Tabernacles the Priests of all the 'courses' officiated, while on the Octave the sacrificial services were appointed, as usually, by *lot* (פַּיִים). (2) The benediction at the *beginning* of a *feast* was spoken again at the Octave (זְמָן). (3) The Octave was designated in prayer, and by special ordinances, as a separate *feast* (רֶגֶל). (4) Difference in the *sacrifices* (קָרְבָּן). (5) Difference in the *Psalms*—on the Octave (Soph. xix. 2) probably Ps. xii. (שִׁיר). (6) According to 1 Kings viii. 66, difference as to the *blessing* (בְּרָכָה).

CHAPTER IX.

THE HEALING OF THE MAN BORN BLIND.

(St. John ix.)

AFTER the scene in the Temple described in the last chapter, and Christ's consequent withdrawal from His enemies, we can scarcely suppose any other great event to have taken place on that day within or near the precincts of the Sanctuary. And yet, from the close connection of the narratives, we are led to infer that no long interval of time can have elapsed before the healing of the man born blind.[1] Probably it happened the day after the events just recorded. We know that it was a Sabbath,[a] and this fresh mark of time, as well as the multiplicity of things done, and the whole style of the narrative, confirm our belief that it was not on the evening of the day when He had spoken to them first in 'the Treasury,' and then in the Porch.

On two other points there is strong presumption, though we cannot offer actual proof. Remembering, that the entrance to the Temple or its Courts was then—as that of churches is on the Continent—the chosen spot for those who, as objects of pity, solicited charity;[b] remembering, also, how rapidly the healing of the blind man became known, and how soon both his parents and the healed man himself appeared before the Pharisees—presumably, in the Temple; lastly, how readily the Saviour knew where again to find him,[c]—we can scarcely doubt that the miracle took place at the entering to the Temple, or on the Temple-Mount. Secondly, both the Work, and especially the Words of Christ, seem in such close connection with what had preceded, that we can scarcely be mistaken in regarding them as intended to form a continuation of it.

It is not difficult to realise the scene, nor to understand the remarks of all who had part in it. It was the Sabbath—the day

CHAP. IX

[a] St. John ix. 14

[b] Acts iii. 2

[c] St. John ix. 35

---

[1] *Godet* supposes that it had taken place on the evening of the Octave of the Feast. On the other hand, Canon *Westcott* would relegate both ch. ix. and x. to the 'Feast of the Dedication.' But his argument on the subject, from another rendering of St. John x. 22, has failed to convince me.

BOOK
IV

after the Octave of the Feast, and Christ with His disciples was passing—presumably when going into the Temple, where this blind beggar was wont to sit, probably soliciting alms, perhaps in some such terms as these, which were common at the time: 'Gain merit by me;' or, 'O tenderhearted, by me gain merit, to thine own benefit.' But on the Sabbath he would, of course, neither ask nor receive alms, though his presence in the wonted place would secure wider notice and perhaps lead to many private gifts. Indeed, the blind were regarded as specially entitled to charity;[a] and the Jerusalem Talmud[b] relates some touching instances of the delicacy displayed towards them. As the Master and His disciples passed the blind beggar, Jesus 'saw' him, with that look which they who followed Him knew to be full of meaning. Yet, so thoroughly Judaised were they by their late contact with the Pharisees, that no thought of possible mercy came to them, only a truly and characteristically Jewish question, addressed to Him expressly, and as 'Rabbi:'[1] through whose guilt this blindness had befallen him—through his own, or that of his parents.

For, thoroughly Jewish the question was. Many instances could be adduced, in which one or another sin is said to have been punished by some immediate stroke, disease, or even by death; and we constantly find Rabbis, when meeting such unfortunate persons, asking them, how or by what sin this had come to them. But, as this man was 'blind from his birth,' the possibility of some actual sin before birth would suggest itself, at least as a speculative question, since the 'evil impulse' (Yetser haRa), might even then be called into activity.[c] At the same time, both the Talmud and the later charge of the Pharisees, 'In sins wast thou born altogether,' imply that in such cases the alternative explanation would be considered, that the blindness might be caused by the sin of his parents.[2] It was a common Jewish view, that the merits or demerits of the parents would appear in the children. In fact, up to thirteen years of age a child was considered, as it were, part of his father, and as suffering for his guilt.[d] More than that, the thoughts of a mother might affect the moral state of her unborn offspring, and the terrible apostasy of one of the greatest Rabbis had, in popular belief, been caused by the sinful delight his mother had taken when passing through an idol-grove.[e] Lastly, certain special sins in the parents would result in

[a] Peah viii. 9

[b] Jer. Peah viii. 9, p. 21 b

[c] Sanh.91 b; Ber. R. 34

[d] Shabb. 32 b; 105 b; Yalkut on Ruth, vol. ii. par. 600, p. 163 c

[e] Midr. on Ruth. iii. 13.

---

[1] So in the original.

[2] This opinion has, however, nothing to do with 'the migration of souls'—a doctrine which has been generally, but quite erroneously, supposed that *Josephus* imputed to the Pharisees. The misunderstanding of Jew. War. ii. 8. 14, should be corrected by Antiq. xviii. 1. 3.

specific diseases in their offspring, and one is mentioned [a] as causing blindness in the children.[1] But the impression left on our minds is, that the disciples felt not sure as to either of these solutions of the difficulty. It seemed a mystery, inexplicable on the supposition of God's infinite goodness, and to which they sought to apply the common Jewish solution. Many similar mysteries meet us in the administration of God's Providence—questions, which seem unanswerable, but to which we try to give answers, perhaps, not much wiser than the explanations suggested by disciples.

But why seek to answer them at all, since we possess not all, perhaps very few of, the *data* requisite for it? There is one aspect, however, of adversity, and of a strange dispensation of evil, on which the light of Christ's Words here shines with the brightness of a new morning. There is a physical, natural reason for them. God has not specially sent them, in the sense of His interference or primary causation, although He *has* sent them in the sense of His knowledge, will, and reign. They have come in the ordinary course of things, and are traceable to causes which, if we only knew them, would appear to us the sequence of the laws which God has imposed on His creation, and which are necessary for its orderly continuance. And, further, all such evil consequences, from the operation of God's laws, are in the last instance to be traced back to the curse which sin has brought upon man and on earth. With these His Laws, and with their evil sequences to us through the curse of sin, God does *not* interfere in the ordinary course of His Providence; although he would be daring, who would negative the possibility of what may seem, though it is not, interference, since the natural causes which lead to these evil consequences may so easily, naturally, and rationally be affected. But there is another and a higher aspect of it, since Christ has come, and is really the Healer of all disease and evil by being the Remover of its ultimate moral cause. This is indicated in His words, when, putting aside the clumsy alternative suggested by the disciples, He told them that it was so in order ' that the works of God might be made manifest in him.' They wanted to know the ' why,' He told them the ' in order to,' of the man's calamity; they wished to understand its reason as regarded its origin, He told them its reasonableness in regard to the purpose which it, and all similar suffering, should serve, since Christ has come, the Healer of evil—

---

[1] At the same time those opinions, which are based on higher moral views of marriage, are only those of an individual teacher. The latter are cynically and coarsely set aside by ' the sages ' in Nedar. 20 *b*.

because the Saviour from sin. Thus He transferred the question from intellectual ground to that of the moral purpose which suffering might serve. And this not in itself, nor by any destiny or appointment, but because the Coming and Work of the Christ has made it possible to us all. Sin and its sequences are still the same, for ' the world is established that it cannot move.' But over it all has risen the Sun of Righteousness with healing in His wings; and, if we but open ourselves to His influence, these evils may serve this purpose, and so have this for their reason, not as, regards their genesis, but their continuance, ' that the works of God may be made manifest.'

To make this the reality to us, was ' the work of Him ' Who sent, and for which He sent, the Christ. And rapidly now must He work it, for perpetual example, during the few hours still left of His brief working-day.[a] This figure was not unfamiliar to the Jews,[b] though it may well be that, by thus emphasising the briefness of the time, He may also have anticipated any objection to His healing on the Sabbath. But it is of even more importance to notice, how the two leading thoughts of the previous day's Discourse were now again taken up and set forth in the miracle that followed. These were, that He did the Work which God had sent Him to do,[c] and that He was the Light of the world.[d] As its Light He could not but shine so long as He was in it. And this He presently symbolised (and is not every miracle a symbol?) in the healing of the blind.

Once more we notice, how in His Deeds, as in His Words, the Lord adopted the forms known and used by His contemporaries, while He filled them with quite other substance. It has already been stated,[1] that saliva was commonly regarded as a remedy for diseases of the eye, although, of course, not for the removal of blindness. With this He made clay, which He now used, adding to it the direction to go and wash in the Pool of Siloam, a term which literally meant ' sent.' [2] A symbolism, this, of Him Who was the Sent of the Father. For, all is here symbolical: the cure and its means. If we ask ourselves why means were used in this instance, we can only suggest, that it was partly for the sake of him who was to be healed, partly for theirs who afterwards heard of it. For, the blind man seems to have been ignorant of the character of his Healer,[e] and it needed the use of some means to make him, so to speak, receptive. On the other hand, not only the use of means, but their inadequacy to the object, must have impressed all. Symbolical, also, were these means.

---

[1] See Book III. ch. xxxiv. p. 48.

[2] The etymological correctness of the rendering *Siloam* by Sent ' is no longer called in question. As to the spring *Siloam*, see ch. vii. of this Book.

Sight was restored by clay, made out of the ground with the spittle
of Him, Whose breath had at the first breathed life into clay; and
this was then washed away in the Pool of Siloam, from whose waters
had been drawn on the Feast of Tabernacles that which symbolised
the forthpouring of the new life by the Spirit. Lastly, if it be
asked why such miracle should have been wrought on one who had
not previous faith, who does not even seem to have known about the
Christ, we can only repeat, that the man himself was intended to
be a symbol, 'that the works of God should be made manifest in
him.'

And so, what the Pharisees had sought in vain, was freely vouchsafed when there was need for it. With inimitable simplicity, itself
evidence that no legend is told, the man's obedience and healing are
recorded. We judge, that his first impulse when healed must have
been to seek for Jesus, naturally, where he had first met Him. On
his way, probably past his own house to tell his parents, and again
on the spot where he had so long sat begging, all who had known him
must have noticed the great change that had passed over him. So
marvellous, indeed, did it appear, that, while part of the crowd that
gathered would, of course, acknowledge his identity, others would
say: 'No, but he is like him;' in their suspiciousness looking for
some imposture. For there can be little doubt, that on his way he
must have learned more about Jesus than merely His Name,[a] and in   [a] ver. 11
turn have communicated to his informants the story of his healing.
Similarly, the formal question now put to him by the Jews was as
much, if not more, a preparatory inquisition than the outcome of a
wish to learn the circumstances of his healing. And so we notice in
his answer the cautious desire not to say anything that could incriminate his Benefactor. He tells the facts truthfully, plainly; he
accentuates by what means he had 'recovered,'[1] not *received*, sight;
but otherwise gives no clue by which either to discover or to incriminate Jesus.[b]   [b] ver. 12

Presently they bring him to the Pharisees, not to take notice of
his healing, but to found on it a charge against Christ. Such must
have been their motive, since it was universally known that the leaders of the people had, of course informally, agreed to take the strictest
measures, not only against the Christ, but against any one who professed to be His disciple.[c] The ground on which the present charge [c] ver. 22
against Jesus would rest was plain: the healing involved a manifold
breach of the Sabbath-Law. The first of these was that He had

---

[1] This is the proper rendering. The organs of sight existed, but could not be used.

BOOK
IV

ᵃ Shabb.
xxiv. 3
ᵇ Jerus.
Shabb. 14 d

ᶜ Jer.
Shabb.
u. s.

ᵈ St. John
ix. 15

ᵉ vv. 17 and
following

made clay.ᵃ Next, it would be a question whether any remedy might be applied on the holy day. Such could only be done in diseases of the internal organs (from the throat downwards), except when danger to life or the loss of an organ was involved.ᵇ It was, indeed, declared lawful to apply, for example, wine to the outside of the eyelid, on the ground that this might be treated as washing; but it was sinful to apply it to the inside of the eye. And as regards saliva, its application to the eye is expressly forbidden, on the ground that it was evidently intended as a remedy.ᶜ

There was, therefore, abundant legal ground for a criminal charge. And, although on the Sabbath the Sanhedrin would not hold any formal meeting, and, even had there been such, the testimony of one man would not have sufficed, yet 'the Pharisees' set the inquiry regularly on foot. First, as if not satisfied with the report of those who had brought the man, they made him repeat it.ᵈ The simplicity of the man's language left no room for evasion or subterfuge. Rabbinism was on its great trial. The wondrous fact could neither be denied nor explained, and the only ground for resisting the legitimate inference as to the character of Him Who had done it, was its inconsistence with their traditional law. The alternative was: whether their traditional law of Sabbath-observance, or else He Who had done such miracles, was Divine? Was Christ not of God, because He did not keep the Sabbath in their way? But, then; could an open transgressor of God's Law do such miracles? In this dilemma they turned to the simple man before them. 'Seeing that He opened' his eyes, what did he say of Him? what was the impression left on his mind, who had the best opportunity for judging?ᵉ

There is something very peculiar, and, in one sense, most instructive, as to the general opinion entertained even by the best-disposed, who had not yet been taught the higher truth, in his reply, so simple and solemn, so comprehensive in its sequences, and yet so utterly inadequate by itself: 'He is a Prophet.' One possibility still remained. After all, the man might not have been really blind; and they might, by cross-examining the parents, elicit that about his original condition which would explain the pretended cure. But on this most important point, the parents, with all their fear of the anger of the Pharisees, remained unshaken. He *had* been born blind; but as to the manner of his cure, they declined to offer any opinion. Thus, as so often, the machinations of the enemies of Christ led to results the opposite of those wished for. For, the evidential value of their attestation of their son's blindness was manifestly proportional to their fear of committing themselves to any testimony for Christ, well knowing what it would entail.

For to persons so wretchedly poor as to allow their son to live by begging,[1] the consequence of being ' un-Synagogued,' or put outside the congregation [2]—which was to be the punishment of any who confessed Jesus as the Messiah—would have been dreadful. Talmudic writings speak of two, or rather, we should say, of three, kinds of 'excommunication,' of which the two first were chiefly disciplinary, while the third was the real 'casting out,' ' un-Synagoguing,' 'cutting off from the congregation.'[3] The general designation[4] for ' excommunication' was *Shammatta*, although, according to its literal meaning, the term would only apply to the severest form of it.[5] The first and lightest degree was the so-called *Neziphah* or *Neziphutha*; properly, ' a rebuke,' an inveighing. Ordinarily, its duration extended over seven days; but, if pronounced by the Nasi, or Head of the Sanhedrin, it lasted for thirty days. In later times, however, it only rested for one day on the guilty person.[a] Perhaps St. Paul referred to this ' rebuke ' in the expression which he used about an offending Elder.[b] He certainly adopted the practice in Palestine,[6] when he would not have an Elder ' rebuked' although he went far beyond it when he would have such ' entreated.' In Palestine it was ordered, that an offending Rabbi should be scourged instead of being excommunicated.[c] Yet another direction of St. Paul's is evidently derived from these arrangements of the Synagogue, although applied in a far different spirit. When the Apostle wrote: ' An heretic after the first and second admonition reject;' there must have been in his mind the *second degree* of Jewish excommunication, the so-called *Niddui* (from the verb to thrust, thrust out, cast out). This lasted for thirty days at the least, although among the Babylonians only for seven days.[d] At the end of that term there was ' a second admonition,' which lasted other thirty days. If still unrepentant, the third, or real excommunication, was pronounced, which was called the *Cherem*, or ban, and of which the duration was indefinite. Any

[a] Moed K.
16 *a* and *b*

[b] 1 Tim. v.

[c] Moed K.
17 *a*; Nedar.
7 *b*; Pes.
52 *a*

[d] Moed K.
16 *a*

---

[1] It would lead too far to set these forth in detail. But the shrinking from receiving alms was in proportion to the duty of giving them. Only extreme necessity would warrant begging, and to solicit charity needlessly, or to simulate any disease for the purpose, would, deservedly, bring the reality in punishment on the guilty.

[2] ἀποσυνάγωγος γίνεσθαι. So also St. John xii. 42; xvi. 2.

[3] In Jer. Moed K. 81 *d*, line 20 from top: הוא יברל מקהל

[4] Both *Buxtorf* and *Levy* have made this abundantly clear, but Jewish authorities are not wanting which regard this as the worst kind of ban.

[5] *Levy* derives it from שמר, to destroy, to root out. The Rabbinic derivations in Moed K. 17 *a*, are only a play upon the word.

[6] But there certainly were notable exceptions to this rule, even in Palestine. Among the Babylonian Jews it did not obtain at all.

* Moed K.
16a; Shebh.
36a; Baba
Mez. 59 b

ᵇ Shebh. 36.
a; Sanh. 107
printed
in the Ches-
ronoth
ha-Shas,
p. 25 b

three persons, or even one duly authorised, could pronounce the lowest sentence. The greater excommunication (*Niddui*)—which, happily, could only be pronounced in an assembly of ten—must have been terrible, being accompanied by curses,ᵃ¹ and, at a later period, sometimes proclaimed with the blast of the horn.ᵇ If the person so visited occupied an honourable position, it was the custom to intimate his sentence in a euphemistic manner, such as: ' It seems to me that thy companions are separating themselves from thee.' He who was so, or similarly addressed, would only too well understand its meaning. Henceforth he would sit on the ground, and bear himself like one in deep mourning. He would allow his beard and hair to grow wild and shaggy; he would not bathe, nor anoint himself; he would not be admitted into an assembly of ten men, neither to public prayer, nor to the Academy; though he might either teach, or be taught by, single individuals. Nay, as if he were a leper, people would keep at a distance of four cubits from him. If he died, stones were cast on his coffin, nor was he allowed the honour of the ordinary funeral, nor were they to mourn for him. Still more terrible was the final excommunication, or *Cherem*, when a ban of indefinite duration was laid on a man. Henceforth he was like one dead. He was not allowed to study with others, no intercourse was to be held with him, he was not even to be shown the road. He might, indeed, buy the necessaries of life, but it was forbidden to eat or drink with such an one.ᶜ

ᶜ Comp.
1 Cor. v. 11

We can understand, how everyone would dread such an anathema. But when we remember, what it would involve to persons in the rank of life, and so miserably poor as the parents of that blind man, we no longer wonder at their evasion of the question put by the Sanhedrin. And if we ask ourselves, on what ground so terrible a punishment could be inflicted to all time and in every place—for the ban once pronounced applied everywhere—simply for the confession of Jesus as the Christ, the answer is not difficult. The Rabbinists enumerate twenty-four grounds for excommunication, of which more than one might serve the purpose of the Pharisees. But in general, to resist the authority of the Scribes, or any of their decrees, or to lead others either away from ' the commandments,' or to what was regarded as profanation of the Divine Name, was sufficient to incur the ban, while it must be borne in mind that excommunication by the President of the Sanhedrin extended to all places and persons.ᵈ

ᵈ Jer. Moed
K. 81 d,
about the
middle

---

¹ *Buxtorf* here reminds us of 1 Cor. v. 5.

² There our Lord is said to have been anathematised to the sound of 400 trumpets. The passage does not appear in the expurgated editions of the Talmud.

As nothing could be elicited from his parents, the man who had been blind was once more summoned before the Pharisees. It was no longer to inquire into the reality of his alleged blindness, nor to ask about the cure, but simply to demand of him recantation, though this was put in the most specious manner. Thou hast been healed: own that it was only by God's Hand miraculously stretched forth,[1] and that 'this man' had nothing to do with it, save that the coincidence may have been allowed to try the faith of Israel. It could not have been Jesus Who had done it, for they knew Him to be 'a sinner.' Of the two alternatives they had chosen that of the absolute rightness of their own Sabbath-traditions as against the evidence of His Miracles. Virtually, then, this was the condemnation of Christ and the apotheosis of traditionalism. And yet, false as their conclusion was, there was this truth in their premises, that they judged of miracles by the moral evidence in regard to Him, Who was represented as working them.

But he who had been healed of his blindness was not to be so betrayed into a denunciation of his great Physician. The simplicity and earnestness of his convictions enabled him to gain even a logical victory. It was his turn now to bring back the question to the issue which they had originally raised; and we admire it all the more, as we remember the consequences to this poor man of thus daring the Pharisees. As against their opinion about Jesus, as to the correctness of which neither he nor others could have direct knowledge,[2] there was the unquestionable fact of his healing of which he *had* personal knowledge. The renewed inquiry now by the Pharisees, as to the manner in which Jesus had healed him,[a] might have had for its object to betray the man into a positive confession, or to elicit something demoniacal in the mode of the cure. The blind man had now fully the advantage. He had already told them; why the renewed inquiry? As he put it half ironically: Was it because they felt the wrongness of their own position, and that they should become His disciples? It stung them to the quick; they lost all self-possession, and with this their moral defeat became complete. 'Thou art the disciple of that man, but we (according to the favourite phrase) are the disciples of Moses.' Of the Divine Mission of Moses they knew, but of the Mission of Jesus they knew nothing.[b] The unlettered

CHAP.
IX

[a] St. John
ix. 26

[b] ver. 29

---

[1] The common view (*Meyer, Watkins, Westcott*) is, that the expression, 'Give glory to God' was merely a formula of solemn adjuration, like Josh. vii. 19. But even so, as Canon *Westcott* remarks, it implies · that the cure was due directly to God.'

[2] In the original: 'If He is a sinner, I know not. One *thing* I know, that, being blind, now I see.'

BOOK
IV

man had now the full advantage in the controversy. 'In this, indeed,' there was 'the marvellous,' that the leaders of Israel should confess themselves ignorant of the authority of One, Who had power to open the eyes of the blind—a marvel which had never before been witnessed. If He had that power, *whence* had He obtained it, and *why*? It could only have been from God. They said, He was 'a sinner'—and yet there was no principle more frequently repeated by the Rabbis,ᵃ than that answers to prayer depended on a man being 'devout' and doing the Will of God. There could therefore by only one inference: If Jesus had not Divine Authority, He could not have had Divine Power.

ᵃ Ber. 6 b;
Taan. iii. 8;
Sukk. 14 a;
Yoma 29 a

The argument was unanswerable, and in its unanswerableness shows us, not indeed the purpose, but the evidential force of Christ's Miracles. In one sense they had no purpose, or rather were purpose to themselves, being the forthbursting of His Power and the manifestation of His Being and Mission, of which latter, as applied to things physical, they were part. But the truthful reasoning of that untutored man, which confounded the acuteness of the sages, shows the effect of these manifestations on all whose hearts were open to the truth. The Pharisees had nothing to answer, and, as not unfrequently in analogous cases, could only, in their fury, cast him out with bitter reproaches. Would he teach them—he, whose very disease showed him to have been a child conceived and born in sin, and who, ever since his birth, had been among ignorant, Law-neglecting 'sinners'?

But there was Another, Who watched and knew him: He Whom, so far as he knew, he had dared to confess, and for Whom he was content to suffer. Let him now have the reward of his faith, even its completion; and so shall it become manifest to all time, how, as we follow and cherish the better light, it riseth upon us in all its brightness, and that faithfulness in little bringeth the greater stewardship. Tenderly did Jesus seek him out, wherever it may have been: ᵇ and, as He found him, this one question did He ask, whether the conviction of his experience was not growing into the higher faith of the yet unseen: 'Dost thou believe on the Son of God?'¹ He had had personal experience of Him—was not that such as to lead up to the higher faith? And is it not always so, that the higher faith is

ᵇ St. John
ix. 35

---

¹ With all respect for such authority as that of Professors *Westcott* and *Hort* ('The N.T.' p. 212), I cannot accept the proposed reading 'Son of Man, instead of 'Son of God.' Admittedly, the evidence for the two readings is evenly balanced, and the *internal* evidence seems to be strongly in favour of the reading 'Son of God.'

based on the conviction of personal experience—that we believe on
Him as the Son of God, because we have experience of Him as the
God-sent, Who has Divine Power, and has opened the eyes of the
blind-born—and Who has done to us what had never been done by
any other in the world?   Thus is faith always the child of experience, and yet its father also; faith not without experience, and yet
beyond experience; faith not superseded by experience, but made
reasonable by it.

To such a soul it needed only the directing Word of Christ.   'And
Who is He, Lord, that I may believe on Him?'[a]   It seems as if
the question of Jesus had kindled in him the conviction of what
was the right answer.   We almost see how, like a well of living
water, the words sprang gladsome from his inmost heart, and how he
looked up expectant on Jesus.   To such readiness of faith there could
be only one answer.   In language more plain than He had ever
before used, Jesus answered, and with immediate confession of implicit faith the man lowly worshipped.[1]   And so it was, that the first
time he saw hisDeliverer, it was to worship Him.   It was the highest
stage yet attained.   What contrast this faith and worship of the
poor unlettered man, once blind, now in every sense seeing, to the
blindness of judgment which had fallen on those who were the
leaders of Israel![b]   The cause alike of the one and the other was
the Person of the Christ.   For our relationship to Him determines
sight or blindness, as we either receive the evidence of what He is
from what He indubitably does, or reject it, because we hold by our
own false conceptions of God, and of what His Will to us is.   And so
is Christ also for 'judgment.'

There were those who still followed Him—not convinced by, nor
as yet decided against Him—Pharisees, who well understood the
application of His Words.   Formally, it had been a contest between
traditionalism and the Work of Christ.   They also were traditionalists
—were they also blind?   But, nay, they had misunderstood Him by
leaving out the *moral* element, thus showing themselves blind
indeed.   It was not the calamity of blindness; but it was a blindness
in which they were guilty, and for which they were responsible,[c]
which indeed was the result of their deliberate choice: therefore
their sin—not their blindness only—remained!

*CHAP.
IX.*

[a] St. John
ix. 36

[b] ver. 39

[c] ver. 41

[1] προσεκύνησεν. The word is never
used by St. John of mere respect for
man, but always implies Divine worship.
In the Gospel it occurs ch. iv. 20-24; ix.
38; xii. 20; and twenty-three times in
the Book of Revelation, but always in
the sense of worship.

CHAPTER X.

THE 'GOOD SHEPHERD' AND HIS 'ONE FLOCK'—LAST DISCOURSE AT THE
FEAST OF TABERNACLES.

(St. John x. 1–21.)

BOOK
IV

THE closing words which Jesus had spoken to those Pharisees who followed Him breathe the sadness of expected near judgment, rather than the hopefulness of expostulation. And the Discourse which followed, ere He once more left Jerusalem, is of the same character. It seems, as if Jesus could not part from the City in holy anger, but ever, and only, with tears. All the topics of the former Discourses are now resumed and applied. They are not in any way softened or modified, but uttered in accents of loving sadness rather than of reproving monition. This connection with the past proves, that the Discourse was spoken immediately after, and in connection with, the events recorded in the previous chapters. At the same time, the tone adopted by Christ prepares us for His Peræan Ministry, which may be described as that of the last and fullest outgoing of His most intense pity. This, in contrast to what was exhibited by the rulers of Israel, and which would so soon bring terrible judgment on them. For, if such things were done in ' the green tree ' of Israel's Messiah-King, what would the end be in the dry wood of Israel's commonwealth and institutions?

It was in accordance with the character of the Discourse presently under consideration, that Jesus spake it, not, indeed, in Parables in the strict sense (for none such are recorded in the Fourth Gospel), but in an allegory[1] in the Parabolic form,[a] hiding the higher truths from those who, having eyes, had not seen, but revealing them to such whose eyes had been opened. If the scenes of the last few days had made anything plain, it was the utter unfitness of the teachers of Israel for their professed work of feeding the flock of God. The Rabbinists also called their spiritual leaders 'feeders,' *Parnasin*

* St. John
x. 6

---

[1] The word is not parable, but παροιμία, proverb or allegory. On the essential characteristics of the Parables, see Book III. ch. xxiii.

פרנסין)—a term by which the Targum renders some of the references to 'the Shepherds' in Ezek. xxxiv. and Zech xi.[1] The term comprised the two ideas of 'leading' and 'feeding,' which are separately insisted on in the Lord's allegory. As we think of it, no better illustration, nor more apt, could be found for those to whom 'the flock of God' was entrusted. It needed not therefore that a sheepfold should have been in view,[2] to explain the form of Christ's address.[a] It only required to recall the Old Testament language about the shepherding of God, and that of evil shepherds, to make the application to what had so lately happened. They were, surely, not shepherds, who had cast out the healed blind man, or who so judged of the Christ, and would cast out all His disciples. They had entered into God's Sheepfold, but not by the door by which the owner, God, had brought His flock into the fold. To it the entrance had been His free love, His gracious provision, His thoughts of pardoning, His purpose of saving mercy. That was God's Old Testament-door into His Sheepfold. Not by that door, as had so lately fully appeared, had Israel's rulers come in. They had climbed up to their place in the fold some other way—with the same right, or by the same wrong, as a thief or a robber. They had wrongfully taken what did not belong to them—cunningly and undetected, like a thief; they had allotted it to themselves, and usurped it by violence, like a robber. What more accurate description could be given of the means by which the Pharisees and Sadducees had attained the rule over God's flock, and claimed it for themselves? And what was true of them holds equally so of all, who, like them, enter by ' some other way.'

How different He, Who comes in and leads us through God's door of covenant-mercy and Gospel-promise—the door by which God had brought, and ever brings, His flock into His fold! This was the true Shepherd. The allegory must, of course, not be too closely pressed; but, as we remember how in the East the flocks are at night driven into a large fold, and charge of them is given to an under shepherd, we can understand how, when the shepherd comes in the morning, ' the doorkeeper'[3] or 'guardian' opens to him. In interpreting the allegory, stress must be laid not so much on any single phrase, be it the ' porter,' the ' door,' or the ' opening,' as on their combination. If the shepherd comes to the door, the porter hastens to open it to him from within, that he may obtain access to the flock; and when a

a St. John x. 1-5

CHAP.
X

---

[1] The figure of a shepherd is familiar in Rabbinic as in Biblical literature. Comp. Bemidb. R. 23; Yalkut i. p. 68 a.
[2] This is the view advocated by Archdeacon *Watkins*, ad loc.
[3] This is the proper reading: he who locked the door from within and guarded it.

true spiritual Shepherd comes to the true spiritual door, it is opened to him by the guardian from within, that is, he finds ready and immediate access. Equally pictorial is the progress of the allegory Having thus gained access to His flock, it has not been to steal or rob, but the Shepherd knows and calls them, each by his name, and leads them out. We mark that in the expression: 'when He has *put forth* all His own,'[1]—the word is a strong one. For they have to go each singly, and perhaps they are not willing to go out each by himself, or even to leave that fold, and so he 'puts' or thrusts them forth, and He does so to 'all His own.' Then the Eastern shepherd places himself at the head of his flock, and goes before them, guiding them, making sure of their following simply by his voice, which they know. So would His flock follow Christ, for they know His Voice, and in vain would strangers seek to lead them away, as the Pharisees had tried. It was not the known Voice of their own Shepherd, and they would only flee from it. [a]

^a St. John
x. 4, 5

We can scarcely wonder, that they who heard it did not understand the allegory, for they were not of His flock and knew not His Voice. But His own knew it then, and would know it for ever. 'Therefore,'[b] both for the sake of the one and the other, He continued, now dividing for greater clearness the two leading ideas of His allegory, and applying each separately for better comfort. These two ideas were: *entrance* by the *door*, and the characteristics of the *good Shepherd*—thus affording a twofold test by which to recognise the true, and distinguish it from the false.

^b ver. 7

^c vv. 7–9

    I. *The door*—Christ was the Door.[c] The entrance into God's fold and to God's flock was only through that, of which Christ was the reality. And it had ever been so. All the Old Testament institutions, prophecies, and promises, so far as they referred to access into God's fold, meant Christ. And all those who went before Him,[2] pretending to be the door—whether Pharisees, Sadducees, or Nationalists—were only thieves and robbers: that was not the door into the Kingdom of God. And the sheep, God's flock, did not hear them; for, although they might pretend to lead the flock, the voice was that of strangers. The transition now to another application of the allegorical idea of the 'door' was natural and almost necessary, though it appears somewhat abrupt. Even in this it is peculiarly Jewish. We must understand this transition as follows: I am the Door; those who professed otherwise to gain access to the fold have climbed in some other way. But if I am the only, I am also truly

---

[1] This is the literal rendering.
[2] The words 'who went before Me' are questioned by many.

the Door. And, dropping the figure, if any man enters by Me, he
shall be·saved, securely go out and in (where the language is not to
be closely pressed), in the sense of having liberty and finding pasture.
   II. This forms also the transition to the second leading idea of the
allegory: *the True and Good Shepherd.* Here we mark a fourfold
progression of thought, which reminds us of the poetry of the Book
of Psalms. There the thought expressed in one line or one couplet
is carried forward and developed in the next, forming what are called
the Psalms of Ascent ('of Degrees'). And in the Discourse of Christ
also the final thought of each couplet of verses is carried forward,
or rather leads upward in the next. Thus we have here a Psalm of
Degrees concerning the Good Shepherd and His Flock, and, at the
same time, a New Testament version of Psalm xxiii. Accordingly its
analysis might be formulated as follows:—
   1. *Christ, the Good Shepherd, in contrast to others who falsely
claimed to be the shepherds.*[a] Their object had been self, and they
had pursued it even at the cost of the sheep, of their life and safety.
He 'came'[1] for them, to give, not to take, 'that they may have life
and have abundance.'[2]
   '*Life*,'—nay, that they may have it, *I* ' *lay down*'[3] Mine: so
does it appear that ' I am the Good[4] Shepherd.'[5]
   2. *The Good Shepherd Who layeth down His life for His Sheep!*
What a contrast to a mere hireling, whose are not the sheep, and
who fleeth at sight of the wolf (danger), ' and the wolf seizeth them,
and scattereth (viz., the flock): (he fleeth) because he is a hireling,
and careth not for the sheep.' The simile of the wolf must not be
too closely pressed, but taken in a general sense, to point the contrast
to Him ' Who layeth down His Life for His sheep.'[6]
   Truly He is—is seen to be—'the fair Shepherder,'[7] Whose are
the sheep, and as such, ' *I know Mine*, and Mine know Me, even as
the Father knoweth Me, and I know the Father. And *I lay down
My Life for the sheep.*'

[a] ver. 10.

---

[1] Not as in the A.V., 'am come.'
[2] As Canon *Westcott* remarks, 'this points to something more than life.'
[3] This is the proper rendering.
[4] Literally ' fair.' As Canon *Westcott*, with his usual happiness, expresses it: ' not only good inwardly (ἀγαθός) but good as perceived (καλός).
[5] This would be all the more striking that, according to Rabbinic law, a shepherd was *not* called upon to expose his own life for the safety of his flock, nor responsible in such a case. The opposite view depends on a misunderstanding of a sentence quoted from Bab. Mez. 93 *b*. As the context there shows, if a shepherd leaves his flock, and in his absence the wolf comes, the shepherd is responsible, but only because he ought not to have left the flock, and his presence might have prevented the accident. In case of attack by *force supérieure* he is *not* responsible for his flock.
[6] See an important note at the end of this chapter.
[7] See Note 4.

3. *For the sheep that are Mine,* whom *I know, and for whom I lay down My Life!* But those sheep, they are not only ' of this fold,' not all of the Jewish ' fold,' but also scattered sheep of the Gentiles. They have all the characteristics of the flock: they are His; and they hear His Voice; but as yet they are outside the fold. Them also the Good Shepherd ' must lead,' and, in evidence that they are His, as He calls them and goes before them, they shall hear His Voice, and so, O most glorious consummation, ' they shall become one flock [1] and one Shepherd.'

And thus is the great goal of the Old Testament reached, and ' the good tidings of great joy ' which issue from Israel ' are unto all people.' The Kingdom of David, which is the Kingdom of God, is set up upon earth, and opened to all believers. We cannot help noticing—though it almost seems to detract from it—how different from the Jewish ideas of it is this Kingdom with its Shepherd-King, Who knows and Who lays down His Life for the sheep, and Who leads the Gentiles not to subjection nor to inferiority, but to equality of faith and privileges, taking the Jews out of their special fold and leading up the Gentiles, and so making of both ' one flock.' Whence did Jesus of Nazareth obtain these thoughts and views, towering so far aloft of all around?

But, on the other hand, they are utterly un-Gentile also—if by the term ' Gentile ' we mean the ' Gentile Churches,' in antagonism to the Jewish Christians, as a certain school of critics would represent them, which traces the origin of this Gospel to this separation. A Gospel written in that spirit would never have spoken on this wise of the mutual relation of Jews and Gentiles towards Christ and in the Church. The sublime words of Jesus are only compatible with one supposition: that He was indeed the Christ of God. Nay, although men have studied or cavilled at these words for eighteen and a half centuries, they have not yet reached unto this: ' They shall become one flock, one Shepherd.'

[a] St. John x. 17, 18

4. In the final Step of ' Ascent ' [a] the leading thoughts of the whole Discourse are taken up and carried to the last and highest thought. *The Good Shepherd that brings together the One Flock!* Yes—by laying down His Life, but also by taking it up again. Both are necessary for the work of the Good Shepherd—nay, the life is laid down in the surrender of sacrifice, in order that it may be taken up again, and much more fully, in the Resurrection-Power. And, therefore, His Father loveth Him as the Messiah-Shepherd,

[1] Not ' fold,' as in the A.V.

Who so fully does the work committed to Him, and so entirely surrenders Himself to it.

His Death, His Resurrection—let no one imagine that it comes
from without! It is His own act. He has 'power' in regard to both,
and both are His own, voluntary, Sovereign, and Divine acts.

And this, all this, in order to be the Shepherd-Saviour—to die,
and rise for His Sheep, and thus to gather them all, Jews and
Gentiles, into one flock, and to be their Shepherd. This, neither
more nor less, was the Mission which God had given Him; this,
'the *commandment*' which He had received of His Father—*that
which God had given Him to do.*[a]

It was a noble close of the series of those Discourses in the
Temple, which had it for their object to show, that He was truly
sent of God.

And, in a measure, they attained that object. To some, indeed, it
all seemed unintelligible, incoherent, madness; and they fell back
on the favourite explanation of all this strange drama—He hath a
demon! But others there were—let us hope, many, not yet His
disciples—to whose hearts these words went straight. And how could
they resist the impression? 'These utterances are not of a demonised'—and, then, it came back to them: 'Can a demon open the
eyes of the blind?'

And so, once again, the Light of His Words and His Person
fell upon His Works, and, as ever, revealed their character, and made
them clear.

NOTE.—It seems right here, in a kind of 'Postscript-Note,' to call attention to
what could not have been inserted in the text without breaking up its unity, and yet
seems too important to be relegated to an ordinary foot-note. In Yoma 66 *b*, lines
18 to 24 from top, we have a series of questions addressed to Rabbi Eliezer ben
Hyrcanos, designed—as it seems to me—to test his views about Jesus and his relation to the new doctrine. Rabbi Eliezer, one of the greatest Rabbis, was the
brother-in-law of Gamaliel II., the son of that Gamaliel at whose feet Paul sat.
He may, therefore, have been acquainted with the Apostle. And we have indubitable evidence that he had intercourse with Jewish Christians, and took pleasure in
their teaching; and, further, that he was accused of favouring Christianity. Under
these circumstances, the series of covered, enigmatic questions, reported as addressed to him, gains a new interest. I can only repeat, that I regard them as
referring to the Person and the Words of Christ. One of these questions is to this
effect: 'Is it [right, proper, duty] for the Shepherd to save a lamb from the lion?'
To this the Rabbi gives (as always in this series of questions) an evasive answer, as
follows: 'You have only asked me about the lamb.' On this the following question
is next put, I presume by way of forcing an express reply: 'Is it [right, proper,
duty] to save the Shepherd from the lion?' and to this the Rabbi once more

evasively replies: 'You have only asked me about the Shepherd.' Thus, as the words of Christ to which covert reference is made have only meaning when the two ideas of the Sheep and the Shepherd are combined, the Rabbi, by dividing them, cleverly evaded giving an answer to his questioners. But these inferences come to us, all of deepest importance: 1. I regard the questions above quoted as containing a distinct reference to the words of Christ in St. John x. 11. Indeed, the whole string of questions, of which the above form part, refers to Christ and His Words. 2. It casts a peculiar light, not only upon the personal history of this great Rabbi, the brother-in-law of the Patriarch Gamaliel II., but a side-light also, on the history of Nicodemus. Of course, such evasive answers are utterly unworthy of a disciple of Christ, and quite incompatible with the boldness of confession which must characterise them. But the question arises—now often seriously discussed by Jewish writers: how far many Rabbis and laymen may have gone in their belief of Christ, and yet—at least in too many instances—fallen short of discipleship; and, lastly, as to the relation between the early Church and the Jews, on which not a few things of deep interest have to be said, though it may not be on the present occasion. 3. Critically also, the quotation is of the deepest importance. For, does it not *furnish a reference*—and that on the lips of Jews—*to the Fourth Gospel, and that from the close of the first century?* There is here something which the opponents of its genuineness and authenticity will have to meet and answer.

Another series of similar allegorical questions in connection with R. Joshua b. Chananyah is recorded in Bekhor. 8 *a* and *b*, but answered by the Rabbi in an *anti-*Christian sense. See *Mandelstamm*, Talmud. Stud. i. But *Mandelstamm* goes too far in his view of the purely allegorical meaning, especially of the introductory part.

CHAPTER XI.

THE FIRST PERÆAN DISCOURSES—TO THE PHARISEES CONCERNING THE
TWO KINGDOMS—THEIR CONTEST—WHAT QUALIFIES A DISCIPLE FOR
THE KINGDOM OF GOD, AND HOW ISRAEL WAS BECOMING SUBJECT TO
THAT OF EVIL.

(St. Matt. xii. 22–45; St. Luke xi. 14–36.)

IT was well that Jesus should, for the present, have parted from
Jerusalem with words like these. They would cling about His
hearers like the odour of incense that had ascended. Even 'the
schism' that had come among them [a] concerning His Person made it
possible not only to continue His Teaching, but to return to the City
once more ere His final entrance. For, His Peræan Ministry, which
extended from after the Feast of Tabernacles to the week preceding
the last Passover, was, so to speak, cut in half by the brief visit of
Jesus to Jerusalem at the Feast of the Dedication. [b] Thus, each part
of the Peræan Ministry would last about three months; the first, from
about the end of September to the month of December; [c] the second,
from that period to the beginning of April. [d] Of these six months we
have (with the solitary exception of St. Matthew xii. 22–45), [1] no
other account than that furnished by St. Luke, [e] [2] although, as usually,
the Jerusalem and Judæan incidents of it are described by St. John. [f]
After that we have the account of His journey to the last Passover,
recorded, with more or less detail, in the three Synoptic Gospels.

It will be noticed that this section is peculiarly lacking in *incident*. It consists almost exclusively of Discourses and Parables, with
but few narrative portions interspersed. And this, not only because
the season of the year must have made itinerancy difficult, and thus
have hindered the introduction to new scenes and of new persons, but
chiefly from the character of His Ministry in Peræa. We remember
that, similarly, the beginning of Christ's Galilean Ministry had been

CHAP.
XI

[a] St. John x.
19

[b] St. John x.
22–39

[c] 28 A.D.

[d] 29 A.D.

[e] St. Luke
xi. 14 to
xvii. 11

[f] St. John
x. 22–42;
xi. 1–45;
xi. 46–54

---

[1] The reasons for his insertion of this
part must be sought in the character of
this Discourse and in the context in St.
Matthew's Gospel.

[2] On the characteristics of this Section,
Canon *Cook* has some very interesting
remarks in the Speaker's Commentary,
N.T. vol. i. p. 379.

BOOK
IV

chiefly marked by Discourses and Parables. Besides, after what had passed, and must now have been so well known, illustrative Deeds could scarcely have been so requisite in Peræa. In fact, His Peræan was, substantially, a resumption of His early Galilean Ministry, only modified and influenced by the much fuller knowledge of the people concerning Christ, and the greatly developed enmity of their leaders. This accounts for the recurrence, although in fuller, or else in modified, form, of many things recorded in the earlier part of this History. Thus, to begin with, we can understand how He would, at this initial stage of His Peræan, as in that of His Galilean Ministry, repeat, when asked for instruction concerning prayer, those sacred words ever since known as the Lord's Prayer. The variations are so slight as to be easily accounted for by the individuality of the reporter.[1] They afford, however, the occasion for remarking on the two principal differences. In St. Luke the prayer is for the forgiveness of ' sins,' while St. Matthew uses the Hebraic term ' debts,' which has passed even into the Jewish Liturgy, denoting our guilt as indebtedness (מחוק כל שטרי חובותינו). Again, the ' day by day ' of St. Luke, which further explains the petition for ' daily bread,' common both to St. Matthew and St. Luke, may be illustrated by the beautiful Rabbinic teaching, that the Manna fell only for each day, in order that thought of their daily dependence might call forth constant faith in our ' Father Which is in heaven.'[a][2] Another Rabbinic saying places [b] our nourishment on the same level with our redemption, as regards the thanks due to God and the fact that both are day by day.[c] Yet a third Rabbinic saying [d] notes the peculiar manner in which both nourishment and redemption are always mentioned in Scripture (by reduplicated expressions), and how, while redemption took place by an Angel,[e] nourishment is attributed directly to God.[f]

But to return. From the introductory expression: ' When (or whenever) ye pray, say '—we venture to infer, that this prayer was intended, not only as the model, but as furnishing the words for the future use of the Church. Yet another suggestion may be made. The request, ' Lord, teach us to pray, as John also taught his disciples,'[g] seems to indicate what was ' the certain place,' which, now consecrated by our Lord's prayer, became the school for ours. It

[a] Yoma 76 a, lines 14–16 from top

[b] According to Ps. cxxxvi. 24, 25

[c] Ber. R. 20, ed. Warsh. p. 39 b, last line

[d] Ber. R. 97

[e] Gen. xlviii. 16

[f] Ps. cxlv. 16

[g] St. Luke xi. 1

---

[1] The concluding Doxology should be omitted from St. Matthew's report of the prayer. As regards the different readings which have been adopted into the Revised Version, the reader is advised, before accepting the proposed altera-tions, to consult Canon *Cook's* judicious notes (in the Speaker's Commentary ad loc.).

[2] The same page of the Talmud contains, however, some absurdly profane legends about the manna.

seems at least likely, that the allusion of the disciples to the
Baptist may have been prompted by the circumstance, that the
locality was that which had been the scene of John's labours—of
course, in Peræa.   Such a note of place is the more interesting, that
St. Luke so rarely indicates localities.   In fact, he leaves us in ignorance of what was the central place in Christ's Peræan Ministry,
although there must have been such.   In the main, the events are,
indeed, most likely narrated in their chronological order.   But, as
Discourses, Parables, and incidents are so closely mixed up, it will
be better, in a work like the present, for clearness' and briefness'
sake, to separate and group them, so far as possible.   Accordingly,
this chapter will be devoted to the briefest summary of the Lord's Discourses in Peræa, previous to His return to Jerusalem for the Feast
of the Dedication of the Temple.

The first of these was on the occasion of His casting out a demon,[a]
and restoring speech to the demonised; or if, as seems likely, the
cure is the same as that recorded in St. Matt. xii. 22, both sight and
speech, which had probably been paralysed.   This is one of the
cases in which it is difficult to determine whether narratives in different Gospels, with slightly varying details, represent different events
or only differing modes of narration.   It needs no argument to prove,
that substantially the same event, such as the healing of a blind or
dumb demonised person, may, and probably would, have taken place
on more than one occasion, and that, when it occurred, it would elicit
substantially the same remarks by the people, and the same charge
against Christ of superior demoniac agency which the Pharisees had
now distinctly formulated.[b]   Again, when recording similar events,
the Evangelists would naturally come to tell them in much the same
manner.   Hence, it does not follow that two similar narratives in
different Gospels always represent the same event.   But in this instance, it seems likely.   The earlier place which it occupies in the
Gospel by St. Matthew may be explained by its position in a group
denunciatory of the Pharisees; and the notice there of their blasphemous charge of His being the instrument of Satan probably indicates
the outcome of their 'council,' how they might destroy Him.[c] [1]

It is this charge of the Pharisees which forms the main subject
of Christ's address, His language being now much more explicit than
formerly,[d] even as the opposition of the Pharisees had more fully
ripened.   In regard to the slight difference in the narratives of

Marginal notes:

CHAP.
XI

[a] St. Luke
xi. 14

[b] See Book
III. ch.
xxii

[c] St. Matt.
xii. 14

[d] St. Mark
iii. 22 ; see
Book III.
ch. xxii.

---

[1] It marks the chronological place of
this miracle that it seems suitably to
follow the popular charge against Jesus,
as expressed in St. John viii. 48 and x. 20.

a See for example St.
Luke xi.
22, 22

b St. Matt.
xii. 25

c vv. 27–30

St. Matthew and St. Luke, we mark that, as always, the Words of the Lord are more fully reported by the former, while the latter supplies some vivid pictorial touches.[a] The following are the leading features of Christ's reply to the Pharisaic charge: First, It was utterly unreasonable,[b] and inconsistent with their own premisses,[c] showing that their ascription of Satanic agency to what Christ did was only prompted by hostility to His Person. This mode of turning the argument against the arguer was peculiarly Hebraic, and it does not imply any assertion on the part of Christ, as to whether or not the disciples of the Pharisees really cast out demons. Mentally, we must supply—according to your own professions, your disciples cast out demons. If so, by whom are they doing it?

But, secondly, beneath this logical argumentation lies deep and spiritual instruction, closely connected with the late teaching during the festive days in Jerusalem. It is directed against the flimsy, superstitious, and unspiritual views entertained by Israel, alike of the Kingdom of evil and of that of God. For, if we ignore the moral aspect of Satan and his kingdom, all degenerates into the absurdities and superstitions of the Jewish view concerning demons and Satan, which are fully described in another place.[1] On the other hand, introduce the ideas of moral evil, of the concentration of its power in a kingdom of which Satan is the representative and ruler, and of our own inherent sinfulness, which makes us his subjects—and all becomes clear. Then, truly, can Satan not cast out Satan—else how could his kingdom stand; then, also, is the casting out of Satan only by 'God's Spirit,' or 'Finger:' and this *is* the Kingdom

d St. Matt.
xii. 25–28

e Yalkut on
Is. lx.

of God.[d] Nay, by their own admission, the casting out of Satan was part of the work of Messiah.[e] [2] Then had the Kingdom of God, indeed, come to them—for in this was the Kingdom of God; and He was the God-sent Messiah, come not for the glory of Israel, nor for anything outward or intellectual, but to engage in mortal conflict with moral evil, and with Satan as its representative. In that contest Christ, as the Stronger, bindeth 'the strong one,' spoils his house (divideth his spoil), and takes from him the armour in which

f v. 29

his strength lay ('he trusted') by taking away the power of sin.[f] This is the work of the Messiah—and, therefore also, no one can be indifferent towards Him, because all, being by nature in a certain relation towards Satan, must, since the Messiah had commenced His

---

[1] See the Appendix on Angelology and Demonology.

[2] See Book II. ch. v., and the Appendix to it, where the passage is given in full.

Work, occupy a definite relationship towards the Christ Who combats Satan.[1][a]

It follows, that the work of the Christ is a moral contest waged through the Spirit of God, in which, from their position, all must take a part. But it is conceivable that a man may not only try to be passively, but even be actively on the enemy's side, and this not by merely speaking against the Christ, which might be the outcome of ignorance or unbelief, but by representing that as Satanic which was the object of His Coming.[b] Such perversion of all that is highest and holiest, such opposition to, and denunciation of, the Holy Spirit as if He were the manifestation of Satan, represents sin in its absolute completeness, and for which there can be no pardon, since the state of mind of which it is the outcome admits not the possibility of repentance, because its essence lies in this, to call that Satanic which is the very object of repentance. It were unduly to press the Words of Christ, to draw from them such inferences as, whether sins unforgiven in this world might or might not be forgiven in the next, since, manifestly, it was not the intention of Christ to teach on this subject. On the other hand, His Words seem to imply that, at least as regards this sin, there is no room for forgiveness in the other world. For, the expression is not ' the age to come ' (עתיד לבוא), but, ' the world to come ' (עולם הבא, or, עלמא דאתי), which, as we know, does not strictly refer to Messianic times. but to the future and eternal, as distinguished both from this world (עולם הזה), and from 'the days of the Messiah ' (ימות המשיח).[c]

3. But this recognition of the spiritual, which was the opposite of the sin against the Holy Ghost, was, as Christ had so lately explained in Jerusalem, only to be attained by spiritual kinship with it.[d] The tree must be made good, if the fruit were to be good; tree and fruit would correspond to each other. How, then, could these Pharisees ' speak good things,' since the state of the heart determined speech and action? Hence, a man would have to give an account even of every idle word, since, however trifling it might appear to others or to oneself, it was really the outcome of ' the heart,' and showed the inner state. And thus, in reality. would a man's future in judgment be determined by his words; a conclusion the more solemn, when we remember its bearing on what His disciples on the

CHAP.
XI

[a] v. 30

[b] vv. 31, 32

[c] See Book II. ch. xi. vol. 1. p. 267

[d] St. Matt. xii. 33-37

---

[1] The reason of the difference between this and the somewhat similar passage, St. Luke ix 50, is, that there the relationship is to the *disciples*, here to the Person of the Christ.

BOOK
IV

one side, and the Pharisees on the other, said concerning Christ and the Spirit of God.

4. Both logically and morally the Words of Christ were unanswerable; and the Pharisees fell back on the old device of challenging proof of His Divine Mission by some visible sign.[a] But this was to avoid the appeal to the moral element which the Lord had made; it was an attempt to shift the argument from the moral to the physical. It was the moral that was at fault, or rather, wanting in them; and no amount of physical evidence or demonstration could have supplied that. All the signs from heaven would not have supplied the deep sense of sin and of the need for a mighty spiritual deliverance,[b] which alone would lead to the reception of the *Saviour* Christ. Hence, as under previous similar circumstances,[c] He would offer them only one sign, that of Jonas the prophet. But whereas on the former occasion Christ chiefly referred to Jonas' *preaching* (of repentance), on this He rather pointed to the allegorical *history* of Jonas as the Divine attestation of his Mission. As he appeared in Nineveh, he was himself ' a sign unto the Ninevites; '[d] the fact that he had been three days and nights in the whale's belly, and that thence he had, so to speak, been sent forth alive to preach in Nineveh, was evidence to them that he had been sent of God. And so would it be again. After three days and three nights ' in the heart of the earth '—which is a Hebraism for ' in the earth '[1]—would His Resurrection Divinely attest to this generation His Mission. The Ninevites did not question, but received this attestation of Jonas; nay, an authentic report of the wisdom of Solomon had been sufficient to bring the Queen of Sheba from so far; in the one case it was, because they felt their sin; in the other, because she felt need and longing for better wisdom than she possessed. But these were the very elements wanting in the men of this generation; and so both Nineveh and the Queen of Sheba would stand up, not only as mute witnesses against, but to condemn, them. For, the great Reality of which the preaching of Jonas had been only the type, and for which the wisdom of Solomon had been only the preparation, had been presented to them in Christ.[e]

5. And so, having put aside this cavil, Jesus returned to His

[a] St. Matt. xii. 38

[b] ver. 39
[c] St. Matt. xvi. 1–4

[d] St. Luke xi. 30

[e] St. Matt. xii. 39–42

---

[1] This is simply a Hebraism of which, as similar instances, may be quoted, Exod. xv. 8 ('the heart of the sea'); Deut. iv. 11 ('the heart of heaven'); 2 Sam. xviii. 14 ('the heart of the terebinth '). Hence, I cannot agree with Dean *Plumptre*, that the expression 'heart of the earth' bears any reference to Hades.

former teaching [a] concerning the Kingdom of Satan and the power
of evil; only now with application, not, as before, to the individual,
but, as prompted by a view of the unbelieving resistance of Israel, to
the Jewish commonwealth as a whole.   Here, also, it must be remembered, that, as the words used by our Lord were allegorical and
illustrative, they must not be too closely pressed.   As compared with
the other nations of the world, Israel was like a house from which
the demon of idolatry had gone out with all his attendants—really
the 'Beel-Zibbul' whom they dreaded.   And then the house had
been swept of all the foulness and uncleanness of idolatry, and garnished with all manner of Pharisaic adornments.   Yet all this while
the house was left really empty; God was not there; the Stronger
One, Who alone could have resisted the Strong One, held not rule
in it.   And so the demon returned to it again, to find the house
whence he had come out, swept and garnished indeed—but also
empty and defenceless.   The folly of Israel lay in this, that they
thought of only one demon—him of idolatry—Beel-Zibbul, with all
his foulness.   That was all very repulsive, and they had carefully
removed it.   But they knew that demons were only manifestations
of demoniac power, and that there was a Kingdom of *evil*.   So this
house, swept of the foulness of heathenism and adorned with all the
self-righteousness of Pharisaism, but empty of. God, would only become a more suitable and more secure habitation of Satan; because,
from its cleanness and beauty, his presence and rule there as an evil
spirit would not be suspected.   So, to continue the illustrative
language of Christ, he came back 'with seven other spirits more
wicked than himself'—pride, self-righteousness, unbelief, and the
like, the number seven being general—and thus the last state—
Israel without the foulness of gross idolatry and garnished with all
the adornments of Pharisaic devotion to the study and practice of
the Law—was really worse than had been the first with all its open
repulsiveness.

6. Once more was the Discourse interrupted, this time by a truly
Jewish incident.   A woman in the crowd burst into exclamations
about the blessedness of the Mother who had borne and nurtured
such a Son. [b]   The phraseology seems to have been not uncommon,
since it is equally applied by the Rabbis to Moses, [c] and even to a
great Rabbi. [d]   More striking, perhaps, is another Rabbinic passage
(previously quoted), in which Israel is described as breaking forth into
these words on beholding the Messiah: 'Blessed the hour in which
Messiah was created; blessed the womb whence He issued; blessed

BOOK
IV

ᵃ Persiqta, ed. *Buber*, p. 149 *a*, last lines

ᵇ St. Matt. xii. 46, 47

ᶜ St. Luke xi. 33–36

ᵈ St. Matt. v. 15; vi. 22, 23

the generation that sees Him; blessed the eye that is worthy to behold Him.'ᵃ[1]

And yet such praise must have been peculiarly unwelcome to Christ, as being the exaltation of only His Human Personal excellence, intellectual or moral. It quite looked away from that which He would present: His Work and Mission as the Saviour. Hence it was, although from the opposite direction, as great a misunderstanding as the Personal depreciation of the Pharisees. Or, to use another illustration, this praise of the Christ through His Virgin-Mother was as unacceptable and unsuitable as the depreciation of the Christ, which really, though unconsciously, underlay the loving care of the Virgin-Mother when she would have arrested Him in His Work,[2] and which (perhaps for this very reason) St. Matthew relates in the same connection.ᵇ Accordingly, the answer in both cases is substantially the same: to point away from His merely Human Personality to His Work and Mission—in the one case: ' Whosoever shall do the Will of My Father Which is in heaven, the same is My brother, and sister, and mother;' in the other: ' Yea rather, blessed are they that hear the Word of God and keep it.'[3]

7. And now the Discourse draws to a closeᶜ by a fresh application of what, in some other form or connection, Christ had taught at the outset of His public Ministry in the ' Sermon on the Mount.'ᵈ Rightly to understand its present connection, we must pass over the various interruptions of Christ's Discourse, and join this as the conclusion to the previous part, which contained the main subject. This was, that spiritual knowledge presupposed spiritual kinship.[4] Here, as becomes the close of a Discourse, the same truth is practically applied in a more popular and plain, one might almost say realistic, manner. As here put, it is, that spiritual receptiveness is ever the condition of spiritual reception. What was the object of lighting a lamp? Surely, that it may give light. But if so, no one would put it into a vault, nor under the bushel, but on the stand. Should we then expect that God would light the spiritual lamp, if it be put in a dark vault? Or, to take an illustration of it from the eye, which, as regards the body, serves the same purpose as the lamp in a house. Does it not depend on the state of the eye whether or not we have the sensation, enjoyment, and benefit of the light?

---

[1] For the full quotation, see Book II. ch. v., and the reference to it in Appendix IX.
[2] See Book III. ch. xxii.
[3] In view of such teaching, it is indeed difficult to understand the *cultus* of the Virgin—and even much of that tribute to the exclusively human in Christ which is so characteristic of Romanism.
[4] See above, page 199 &c.

Let us, therefore, take care, lest, by placing, as it were, the lamp in a vault, the light in us be really only darkness. [1] On the other hand, if by means of a good eye the light is transmitted through the whole system—if it is not turned into darkness, like a lamp that is put into a vault or under a bushel, instead of being set up to spread light through the house—then shall we be wholly full of light. And this, finally, explains the reception or rejection of Christ: how, in the words of an Apostle, the same Gospel would be both a savour of life unto life, and of death unto death.

It was a blessed lesson with which to close His Discourse, and one full of light, if only they had not put it into the vault of their darkened hearts. Yet presently would it shine forth again, and give light to those whose eyes were opened to receive it; for, according to the Divine rule and spiritual order, to him that hath shall be given, and from him that hath not shall be taken away even that he hath.

CHAP. XI

[1] In some measure like the demon who returned to find his house empty, swept and garnished.

CHAPTER XII.

THE MORNING-MEAL IN THE PHARISEE'S HOUSE—MEALS AND FEASTS
AMONG THE JEWS—CHRIST'S LAST PERÆAN WARNING TO PHARISAISM.

(St. Luke xi. 37–54.)

BOOK
IV

BITTER as was the enmity of the Pharisaic party against Jesus, it had not yet so far spread, nor become so avowed, as in every place to supersede the ordinary rules of courtesy. It is thus that we explain that invitation of a Pharisee to the morning-meal, which furnished the occasion for the second recorded Peræan Discourse of Christ. Alike in substance and tone, it is a continuation of His former address to the Pharisees. And it is probably here inserted in order to mark the further development of Christ's anti-Pharisaic teaching. It is the last address to the Pharisees, recorded in the Gospel of St. Luke.[1] A similar last appeal is recorded in a much later portion of St. Matthew's Gospel,[a] only that St. Luke reports that spoken in Peræa, St. Matthew that made in Jerusalem. This may also partly account for the similarity of language in the two Discourses. Not only were the circumstances parallel, but the language held at the end [b] may naturally have recurred to the writer, when reporting the last controversial Discourse in Peræa. Thus it may well have been, that Christ said substantially the same things on both occasions, and yet that, in the report of them, some of the later modes of expression may have been transferred to the earlier occasion. And because the later both represents and presents the fullest anti-Pharisaic Discourse of the Saviour, it will be better to postpone our analysis till we reach that period of His Life.[2]

Some distinctive points, however, must here be noted. The remarks already made will explain, how some time may have elapsed between this and the former Discourse, and that the expression, 'And as He spake'[c] must not be pressed as a mark of time (referring

a St. Matt.
xxiii.

b St. Matt.
xxiii.

c St. Luke
xi. 37

---

[1] Even St. Luke xx. 45–47 is not an exception. Christ, indeed, often afterwards answered their questions, but this is His last formal address to the Phari- sees.

[2] See the remarks on St. Luke xi. 39–52 in our analysis of St. Matt. xxiii. in chap. iv. of Book V.

to the immediately preceding Discourse), but rather be regarded as indicating the circumstances under which a Pharisee had bidden Him to the meal.[1] Indeed, we can scarcely imagine that, immediately after such a charge by the Pharisees as that Jesus acted as the representative of Beelzebul, and such a reply on the part of Jesus, a Pharisee would have invited Him to a friendly meal, or that 'Lawyers,' or, to use a modern term, 'Canonists,' would have been present at it. How different their feelings were after they had heard His denunciations, appears from the bitterness with which they afterwards sought to provoke Him into saying what might serve as ground for a criminal charge.[a] And there is absolutely no evidence that, as commentators suggest, the invitation of the Pharisee had been hypocritically given, for the purpose of getting up an accusation against Christ. More than this, it seems entirely inconsistent with the unexpressed astonishment of the Pharisee, when he saw Jesus sitting down to food without having first washed hands. Up to that moment, then, it would seem that he had only regarded Him as a celebrated Rabbi, though perhaps one who taught strange things.

But what makes it almost certain, that some time must have elapsed between this and the previous Discourse (or rather that, as we believe, the two events happened in different places), is, that the invitation of the Pharisee was to the 'morning-meal.'[2] We know that this took place early, immediately after the return from morning-prayers in the Synagogue.[3] It is, therefore, scarcely conceivable, that all that is recorded in connection with the first Discourse should have occurred before this first meal. On the other hand, it may well have been, that what passed at the Pharisee's table may have some connection with something that had occurred just before in the Synagogue, for we conjecture that it was the Sabbath-day. We infer this from the circumstance that the invitation was *not* to the principal meal, which on a Sabbath 'the Lawyers' (and, indeed, all householders) would, at least ordinarily, have in their own homes.[4] We can picture to ourselves the scene. The week-day family-meal was simple enough, whether breakfast or dinner—the latter towards evening, although sometimes also in the middle of the day, but always before actual darkness, in order, as it was expressed, that the sight of the dishes

CHAP.
XII

[a] St. Luke
xi. 53, 54

---

[1] The expression 'one of the Lawyers' (ver. 45) seems to imply that there were several at table.

[2] Not 'to dine' as in the A.V. Although in *later* Greek the word ἄριστον was used for *prandium*, yet its original meaning as 'breakfast' seems fixed by St. Luke xiv. 12, ἄριστον ἢ δεῖπνον.

[3] פַּת שַׁחֲרִית, of which the German *Morgenbrot* is a literal rendering. To take the first meal later in the day was deemed very unwholesome: 'like throwing a stone into a skin.'

[4] On the sacredness of the duty of hospitality, see 'Sketches of Jewish Social Life,' pp. 47–49.

BOOK
IV

Yoma 74 b
Bezeh 16 a

Ber. 41 b

Ber. 35 a
Ps. xxiv. 1

Ber. 36 a

Ber. vi. 6

by daylight might excite the appetite.ᵃ The Babylonian Jews were content to make a meal without meat; not so the Palestinians.ᵇ With the latter the favorite food was young meat: goats, lambs, calves. Beef was not so often used, and still more rarely fowls. Bread was regarded as the mainstay of life,[1] without which no entertainment was considered as a meal. Indeed, in a sense it constituted the meal. For the blessing was spoken over the bread, and this was supposed to cover all the rest of the food that followed, such as the meat, fish or vegetables—in short, all that made up the dinner, but not the dessert. Similarly, the blessing spoken over the wine included all other kinds of drink.ᶜ Otherwise it would have been necessary to pronounce a separate benediction over each different article eaten or drunk. He who neglected the prescribed benedictions was regarded as if he had eaten of things dedicated to God,ᵈ since it was written: 'The earth is the Lord's, and the fulness thereof.'ᵉ [2] Beautiful as this principle is, it degenerated into tedious questions of casuistry. Thus, if one kind of food was eaten as an addition to another, it was settled that the blessing should be spoken only over the principal kind. Again, there are elaborate disputations as to what should be regarded as fruit, and have the corresponding blessing, and how, for example, one blessing should be spoken over the leaves and blossom, and another over the berries of the caper.ᶠ Indeed, that bush gave rise to a serious controversy between the Schools of Hillel and Shammai. Another series of elaborate discussions arose, as to what blessing should be used when a dish consisted of various ingredients, some the product of the earth, others, like honey, derived from the animal world. Such and similar disquisitions, giving rise to endless argument and controversy, busied the minds of the Pharisees and Scribes.

Let us suppose the guests assembled. To such a morning-meal they would not be summoned by slaves, nor be received in such solemn state as at feasts. First, each would observe, as a religious rite, 'the washing of hands.' Next, the head of the house would cut a piece from the whole loaf—on the Sabbath there were two loaves—and speak the blessing.[3] But this, only if the company reclined at table, as at dinner. If they *sat*, as probably always at the early meal, each would speak the benediction for himself.ᵍ The same

---

[1] As always in the East, there were many kinds of bakemeat, from the coarse barley-bread or rice-cake to the finest pastry. We read even of a kind of biscuit, imported from India (the *Teritha*, Ber. 37 b).

[2] So rigid was this, that it was deemed duty to speak a blessing over a drink of water, if one was thirsty, Ber. vi. 8.

[3] This, also, was matter of controversy, but the Rabbis decided that the blessing must first be spoken, and then the loaf cut (Ber. 39 b).

rule applied in regard to the wine. Jewish casuistry had it, that one blessing sufficed for the wine intended as part of the meal. If other wine were brought in during the meal, then each one would have to say the blessing anew over it; if after the meal (as was done on Sabbaths and feast-days, to prolong the feast by drinking), one of the company spoke the benediction for all.

At the entertainment of this Pharisee, as indeed generally, our Lord omitted the prescribed 'washing of hands' before the meal. But as this rite was in itself indifferent, He must have had some definite object, which will be explained in the sequel. The externalism of all these practices will best appear from the following account which the Talmud gives of 'a feast.'[a] As the guests enter, they sit down on chairs, and water is brought to them, with which they wash one hand. After this the cup is taken, when each speaks the blessing over the wine partaken of before dinner. Presently they all lie down at table. Water is again brought them, with which they now wash both hands, preparatory to the meal, when the blessing is spoken over the bread, and then over the cup, by the chief person at the feast, or else by one selected by way of distinction. The company responded by *Amen*, always supposing the benediction to have been spoken by an Israelite, not a heathen, slave, nor law-breaker. Nor was it lawful to say it with an unlettered man, although it might be said with a Cuthæan[b] (heretic, or else Samaritan), who was learned. After dinner the crumbs, if any, are carefully gathered—hands are again washed, and he who first had done so leads in the prayer of thanksgiving. The formula in which he is to call on the rest to join him, by repeating the prayers after him, is prescribed, and differs according to the number of those present. The blessing and the thanksgiving are allowed to be said not only in Hebrew, but in any other language.[c]

In regard to the position of the guests, we know that the uppermost seats were occupied by the Rabbis. The Talmud formulates it[d] in this manner: That the worthiest lies down first, on his left side, with his feet stretching back. If there are two 'cushions' (divans), the next worthiest reclines above him, at his left hand; if there are three cushions, the third worthiest lies below him who had lain down first (at his right), so that the chief person is in the middle (between the worthiest guest at his left and the less worthy one at his right hand). The water before eating is first handed to the worthiest, and so in regard to the washing after meat. But if a very large number are present, you begin after dinner with the least worthy, till you come to the last five. when the worthiest in the company washes his hands,

a Ber. 43 a

b Ber. 47 b

c Ber. 40 b

d Ber. 46 b

and the other four after him.[1] The guests being thus arranged, the head of the house, or the chief person at table, speaks the blessing,[2] and then cuts the bread. By some it was not deemed etiquette to begin eating till after he who had said the prayer had done so, but this does not seem to have been the rule among the Palestinian Jews. Then, generally, the bread was dipped into salt, or something salted, etiquette demanding that where there were two they should wait one for the other, but not where there were three or more.

This is not the place to furnish what may be termed a list of *menus* at Jewish tables. In earlier times the meal was, no doubt, very simple. It became otherwise when intercourse with Rome, Greece, and the East made the people familiar with foreign luxury, while commerce supplied its requirements. Indeed, it would scarcely be possible to enumerate the various articles which seem to have been imported from different, and even distant, countries.

To begin with: the wine was mixed with water, and, indeed, some thought that the benediction should not be pronounced till the water had been added to the wine.[a] According to one statement, two parts,[b] according to another, three parts, of water were to be added to the wine.[c] Various vintages are mentioned: among them a red wine of Saron, and a black wine. Spiced wine was made with honey and pepper. Another mixture, chiefly used for invalids, consisted of old wine, water, and balsam; yet another was 'wine of myrrh;'[d] we also read of a wine in which capers had been soaked. To these we should add wine spiced, either with pepper, or with absinthe; and what is described as vinegar, a cooling drink made either of grapes that had not ripened, or of the lees. Besides these, palm-wine was also in use. Of foreign drinks, we read of wine from Ammon, and from the province Asia, the latter a kind of 'must' boiled down. Wine in ice came from the Lebanon; a certain kind of vinegar from Idumæa; beer from Media and Babylon; a barley-wine (*zythos*) from Egypt. Finally, we ought to mention Palestinian apple-cider,[e] and the juice of other fruits. If we adopt the rendering of some, even liqueurs were known and used.

Long as this catalogue is, that of the various articles of food, whether native or imported, would occupy a much larger space. Suffice it that, as regarded the various kinds of grain, meat, fish, and fruits.

---

[1] According to Ber. 46 *b*, the order in Persia was somewhat different. The arrangement indicated in the text is of importance as regards the places taken at the Last Supper, when there was a dispute among the disciples about the order in which they were to sit (comp. pp. 493—495).

[2] Tradition ascribes this benediction to Moses on the occasion when manna first fell.

either in their natural state or preserved, it embraced almost everything known to the ancient world. At feasts there was an introductory course, consisting of appetising salted meat, or of some light
dish. This was followed by the dinner itself, which finished with
dessert (*Aphiqomon* or *terugima*) consisting of pickled olives, radishes
and lettuce, and fruits, among which even preserved ginger from
India is mentioned.[a] The most diverse and even strange state- a Comp.
Ber. 40–44
ments are made as to the healthiness, or the reverse, of certain articles passim
of diet, especially vegetables. Fish was a favorite dish, and never
wanting at a Sabbath-meal. It was a saying, that both salt and
water should be used at every meal, if health was to be preserved.
Condiments, such as mustard or pepper, were to be sparingly used.
Very different were the meals of the poor. Locusts—fried in flour or
honey, or preserved—required, according to the Talmud, no blessing,
since the animal was really among the curses of the land. Eggs
were a common article of food, and sold in the shops. Then there
was a milk-dish into which people dipped their bread. Others, who
were better off, had a soup made of vegetables, especially onions,
and meat, while the very poor would satisfy the cravings of hunger
with bread and cheese, or bread and fruit, or some vegetables, such as
cucumbers, lentils, beans, peas, or onions.

At meals the rules of etiquette were strictly observed, especially as
regarded the sages. Indeed, two tractates are added to the Talmud,
of which the one describes the general etiquette, the other that of
'sages,' and the title of which may be translated by 'The Way of
the World' (*Derekh Erets*), being a sort of code of good manners.
According to some, it was not good breeding to speak while eating.
The learned and most honored occupied not only the chief places,
but were sometimes distinguished by a double portion. According
to Jewish etiquette, a guest should conform in everything to his
host, even though it were unpleasant. Although hospitality was the
greatest and most prized social virtue, which, to use a Rabbinic expression, might make every home a sanctuary and every table an
altar, an unbidden guest, or a guest who brought another guest, was
proverbially an unwelcome apparition. Sometimes, by way of self-
righteousness, the poor were brought in, and the best part of the
meal ostentatiously given to them. At ordinary entertainments,
people were to help themselves. It was not considered good manners to drink as soon as you were asked, but you ought to hold the
cup for a little in your hand. But it would be the height of rudeness,
either to wipe the plates, to scrape together the bread, as though you

BOOK
IV

had not had enough to eat, or to drop it, to the inconvenience of your neighbour. If a piece were taken out of a dish, it must of course not be put back; still less must you offer from your cup or plate to your neighbour. From the almost religious value attaching to bread, we scarcely wonder that these rules were laid down: not to steady a cup or plate upon bread, nor to throw away bread, and that after dinner the bread was to be carefully swept together. Otherwise, it was thought, demons would sit upon it. The 'Way of the World' for Sages,[a] lays down these as the marks of a Rabbi: that he does not eat standing; that he does not lick his fingers; that he sits down only beside his equals—in fact, many regarded it as wrong to eat with the unlearned; that he begins cutting the bread where it is best baked, nor ever breaks off a bit with his hand; and that, when drinking, he turns away his face from the company. Another saying was that the sage was known by four things: at his cups, in money matters, when angry, and in his jokes.[b] After dinner, the formalities concerning handwashing and prayer, already described, were gone through, and then frequently aromatic spices burnt, over which a special benediction was pronounced. We have only to add, that on Sabbaths it was deemed a religious duty to have three meals, and to procure the best that money could obtain, even though one were to save and fast for it all the week. Lastly, it was regarded as a special obligation and honor to entertain sages.

[a] Derekh
Erets Suta
v. and vii

[b] Erub. 65 b

We have no difficulty now in understanding what passed at the table of the Pharisee. When the water for purification was presented to Him, Jesus would either refuse it; or if, as seems more likely at a morning-meal, each guest repaired by himself for the prescribed purification, He would omit to do so, and sit down to meat without this formality. No one, who knows the stress which Pharisaism laid on this rite would argue that Jesus might have conformed to the practice.[1] Indeed, the controversy was long and bitter between the Schools of Shammai and Hillel, on such a point as whether the hands were to be washed *before* the cup was filled with wine, or *after* that, and where the towel was to be deposited. With such things the most serious ritual inferences were connected on both sides.[c] A religion which spent its energy on such trivialities must have lowered the moral tone. All the more that Jesus insisted so earnestly, as the substance of His Teaching, on that corruption of our nature which Judaism ignored, and on that spiritual purification

[c] Ber. 51 b
to 52 b

---

[1] For a full account of the laws concerning the washing of hands and the views entertained of the rite, see Book III. ch. xxxi.

which was needful for the reception of His doctrine, would He publicly and openly set aside ordinances of man which diverted thoughts of purity into questions of the most childish character. On the other hand, we can also understand what bitter thoughts must have filled the mind of the Pharisee, whose guest Jesus was, when he observed His neglect of the cherished rite. It was an insult to himself, a defiance of Jewish Law, a revolt against the most cherished tradltions of the Synagogue. Remembering that a Pharisee ought not to sit down to a meal with such, he might feel that he should not have asked Jesus to his table. All this, as well as the terrible contrast between the punctiliousness of Pharisaism in outward purifications, and the inward defilement which it never sought to remove, must have lain open before Him Who read the inmost secrets of the heart, and kindled His holy wrath. Probably taking occasion (as previously suggested) from something that had passed before, He spoke with the point and emphasis which a last appeal to Pharisaism demanded.

What our Lord said on this occasion will be considered in detail in another place.[1] Suffice it hear to mark, that He first exposed the mere externalism of the Pharisaic law of purification, to the utter ignoring of the higher need of inward purity, which lay at the foundation of all.[a] If the primary origin of the ordinance was to prevent the eating of sacred offerings in defilement,[2] were these outward offerings not a symbol of the inward sacrifice, and was there not an inward defilement as well as the outward?[b] To consecrate what we had to God in His poor, instead of selfishly enjoying it, would not, indeed, be a purification of them (for such was not needed), but it would, in the truest sense, be to eat God's offerings in cleanness.[c] We mark here a progress and a development, as compared with the former occasion when Jesus had publicly spoken on the same subject.[d] Formerly, He had treated the ordinance of the Elders as a matter not binding; now, He showed how this externalism militated against thoughts of the internal and spiritual. Formerly, He had shown how traditionalism came into conflict with the written Law of God: now, how it superseded the first principles which underlay that Law. Formerly, He had laid down the principle that defilement came not from without inwards, but from within outwards;[e] now, He unfolded this highest principle that higher consecration imparted purity.

CHAP.
XII

[a] St. Luke xi. 39

[b] ver. 40

[c] ver. 41

[d] St. Matt. xv. 1-9

[e] St. Matt. xv. 10, 11

---

[1] In connection with St. Matt. xxiii.
[2] On the origin and meaning of the ordinance, see Book III. ch. xxxi.

BOOK
IV

a St. Luke
xi. 42

b ver. 43

c St. Luke
xii. 1

The same principle, indeed, would apply to other things, such as to the Rabbinic law of tithing. At the same time it may have been, as already suggested, that something which had previously taken place, or was the subject of conversation at table, had given occasion for the further remarks of Christ.[a] Thus, the Pharisee may have wished to convey his rebuke of Christ by referring to the subject of tithing. And such covert mode of rebuking was very common among the Jews. It was regarded as utterly defiling to eat of that which had not been tithed. Indeed, the three distinctions of a Pharisee were:[1] not to make use nor to partake of anything that had not been tithed; to observe the laws of purification; and, as a consequence of these two, to abstain from familiar intercourse with all non-Pharisees. This separation formed the ground of their claim to distinction.[b] It will be noticed that it is exactly to these three things our Lord adverts: so that these sayings of His are not, as might seem, unconnected, but in the strictest internal relationship. Our Lord shows how Pharisaism, as regarded the outer, was connected with the opposite tendency as regarded the inner man: outward purification with ignorance of the need of that inward purity, which consisted in God-consecration, and with the neglect of it; strictness of outward tithing with ignorance and neglect of the principle which underlay it, viz., the acknowledgment of God's right over mind and heart (judgment and the love of God); while, lastly, the Pharisaic pretence of separation, and consequent claim to distinction, issued only in pride and self-assertion. Thus, tried by its own tests, Pharisaism[2] terribly failed. It was hypocrisy, although that word was not mentioned till afterwards;[c][3] and that both negatively and positively: the concealment of what it was, and the pretension to what it was not. And the Pharisaism which pretended to the highest purity, was, really, the greatest impurity—the defilement of graves, only covered up, not to be seen of men!

It was at this point that one of 'the Scribes' at table broke in. Remembering in what contempt some of the learned held the ignorant bigotry of the Pharisees,[4] we can understand that he might have listened with secret enjoyment to denunciations of their 'folly.' As the common saying had it, 'the silly pietist,' 'a woman Pharisee,' and the (self-inflicted) 'blows of Pharisaism,' were among the plagues

---

[1] On 'the Pharisees, Sadducees, and Essenes,' see Book III. ch. ii. In fact, the fraternity of the Pharisees were bound by these two vows, that of tithing, and that in regard to purifications.

[2] St. Luke xi. 44. The word 'Scribes

and Pharisees, hypocrites,' are an interpolation.

[3] See previous Note.

[4] As to the estimate of the Pharisees, comp. also 'Sketches of Jewish Social Life,' p. 237.

of life.[a] And we cannot help feeling, that there is sometimes a touch of quiet humour in the accounts which the Rabbis give of the encounters between the Pharisees and their opponents.[1] But, as the Scribe rightly remarked, by attacking, not merely their practice, but their principles, the whole system of traditionalism, which they represented, was condemned.[b] And so the Lord assuredly meant it. The 'Scribes' were the exponents of the traditional law; those who bound and loosed in Israel. They did bind on heavy burdens, but they never loosed one; all those grievous burdens of traditionalism they laid on the poor people, but not the slightest effort did they make to remove any of them.[c] Tradition, yes! the very profession of it bore witness against them. Tradition, the ordinances that had come down—they would not reform nor put aside anything, but claim and proclaim all that had come down from the fathers as a sacred inheritance to which they clung. So be it! let them be judged by their own words. The fathers had murdered the prophets, and they built their sepulchres; that, also, was a tradition—that of guilt which would be avenged. Tradition, learning, exclusiveness—alas! it was only taking away from the poor the key of knowledge; and while they themselves entered not by 'the door' into the Kingdom, they hindered those who would have gone in. And truly so did they prove that theirs was the inheritance, the 'tradition,' of guilt in hindering and banishing the Divine teaching of old, and murdering its Divine messengers.[d]

There was a terrible truth and solemnity in what Jesus spake, and in the Woe which He denounced on them. The history of the next few months would bear witness how truly they had taken upon them this tradition of guilt; and all the after-history of Israel shows how fully this 'Woe' has come upon them. But, after such denunciations, the entertainment in the Pharisee's house must have been broken up. The Christ was too terribly in earnest—too mournfully so over those whom they hindered from entering the Kingdom, to bear with the awful guilt of their trivialities. With what feelings they parted from Him, appears from the sequel.

'And when He was come out from thence, the Scribes and the Pharisees began to press upon Him vehemently, and to provoke Him to speak of many things; laying wait for Him, to catch something out of His Mouth.'[2]

CHAP.
XII

[a] Sot. iii. 4

[b] St. Luke xi. 45

[c] ver. 46

[d] vv. 47-52

---

[1] See previous Note.
[2] This is both the correct reading and rendering of St. Luke xi. 53, 54, as given in the Revised Version.

CHAPTER XIII.

TO THE DISCIPLES—TWO EVENTS AND THEIR MORAL.

(St. Luke xii. 1—xiii. 17.)

BOOK
IV

THE record of Christ's last warning to the Pharisees, and of the feelings of murderous hate which it called forth, is followed by a summary of Christ's teaching to His disciples. The tone is still that of warning, but entirely different from that to the Pharisees. It is a warning of *sin* that threatened, not of *judgment* that awaited; it was for prevention, not in denunciation. That such warnings were most seasonable, requires scarcely proof. They were prompted by circumstances around. The same teaching, because prompted by the same causes, had been mostly delivered, also, on other occasions. Yet there are notable, though seemingly slight, divergences, accounted for by the difference of the writers or of the circumstances, and which mark the independence of the narratives.

ᵃ St. Luke
xii. 1-12

1. The first of these Discourses ᵃ naturally connects itself with what had passed at the Pharisee's table, an account of which must soon have spread. Although the Lord is reported as having addressed the same language chiefly to the Twelve when sending them

ᵇ St. Matt.
x.

on their first Mission,ᵇ ¹ we shall presently mark several characteristic variations. The address—or so much of it as is reported, probably only its summary—is introduced by the following notice of the circumstances: ' In the mean time, when the many thousands of the people were gathered together, so that they trode upon each other, He began to say to His disciples: "First [above all, בתהלה],² beware of the leaven of the Pharisees, which is hypocrisy." ' There is no need to point out the connection between this warning and the denunciation of Pharisaism and traditionalism at the Pharisee's table. Although the word ' hypocrisy ' had not been spoken there, it was the

¹ With St. Luke xii. 2–9, comp. St. Matt. x. 26–33; with St. Luke xii. 10, comp. St. Matt. xii. 31, 32; and with St. Luke xii. 11, 12, comp. St. Matt. x. 18–20.

² I prefer this rendering to that which connects the word 'first' as a mark of time with the previous words.

sum and substance of His contention, that Pharisaism, while pretending to what it was not, concealed what it was. And it was this which, like 'leaven,' pervaded the whole system of Pharisaism. Not that as individuals they were all hypocrites, but that the system was hypocrisy. And here it is characteristic of Pharisaism, that Rabbinic Hebrew has not even a word equivalent to the term 'hypocrisy.' The only expression used refers either to flattery of, or pretence before men,[1] not to that unconscious hypocrisy towards God which our Lord so truly describes as 'the leaven' that pervaded all the Pharisees said and did. It is against this that He warned His disciples—and in this, rather than conscious deception, pretence, or flattery, lies the danger of the Church. Our common term, 'unreality,' but partially describes it. Its full meaning can only be gathered from Christ's teaching. But what precise term He may have used, it is impossible to suggest.[2]

After all, hypocrisy was only self-deception.[a] 'But,[3] there is nothing covered that shall not be revealed.' Hence, what they had said in the darkness would be revealed, and what they had spoken about in the store-rooms[4] would be proclaimed on the housetops. Nor should fear influence them.[b] Fear of whom? Man could only kill the body, but God held body and soul. And, as fear was foolish, so was it needless in view of that wondrous Providence which watched over even the meanest of God's creatures.[c] Rather let them, in the impending struggle with the powers of this world, rise to consciousness of its full import—how earth's voices would find their echo in heaven. And then this contest, what was it! Not only opposition to Christ, but, in it inmost essence, blasphemy against the Holy Ghost. Therefore, to succumb in that contest, implied the deepest spiritual danger.[d] Nay, but let them not be apprehensive; their acknowledgment would be not only in the future; even now, in the hour of their danger, would the Holy Ghost help them, and give them an answer before their accusers and judges, whoever they might be—Jews or Gentiles. Thus, if they fell victims, it would be with the knowledge—not by neglect—of their Father; here, there, everywhere—in their own hearts, before the Angels, before men, would He give testimony for those who were His witnesses.[e]

[a] St. Luke xii. 2

[b] ver. 4

[c] vv. 6, 7

[d] vv. 8-10

[e] vv. 11, 12

---

[1] *Wünsche* goes too far in saying that חנף and חנופה are only used in the sense of flattering. See *Levy*, sub verb.

[2] The Peshito paraphrases it

[3] Thus, and not 'for,' as in the A.V.

[4] St. Luke seems to use ταμεῖον in that sense (here and in ver. 24), St. Matthew in the sense of 'inner chamber' (St. Matt. vi. 6; xxiv. 26). In the LXX. it is used chiefly in the latter sense; in the Apocr. once in the sense of 'inner chamber' (Tob. vii. 16), and once in that of 'storeroom' (Ecclus. xxix. 12).

Before proceeding, we briefly mark the differences between this and the previous kindred address of Christ, when sending the Apostles on their Mission.^a There (after certain personal directions), the Discourse *began*^b with what it here *closes*. There it was in the form of warning prediction, here in that of comforting reassurance; there it was near the beginning, here near the close, of His Ministry. Again, as addressed to the Twelve on their Mission, it was followed by personal directions and consolations,^c and then, transition was made to the admonition to dismiss fear, and to speak out publicly what had been told them privately. On the other hand, when addressing His Peræan disciples, while the same admonition is given, and partly on the same grounds, yet, as spoken to disciples rather than to preachers, the reference to the similarity of their fate with that of Christ is omitted, while, to show the real character of the struggle, an admonition is added, which in His Galilean Ministry was given in another connection.^d Lastly, whereas the Twelve were admonished not to fear, and, therefore, to speak openly what they had learned privately, the Peræan disciples are forewarned that, although what they had spoken together in secret would be dragged into the light of greatest publicity, yet they were not to be afraid of the possible consequences to themselves.

2. The second Discourse recorded in this connection was occasioned by a request for judicial interposition on the part of Christ. This He answered by a Parable,[1] ^e which will be explained in conjunction with the other Parables of that period. The outcome of this Parable, as to the utter uncertainty of this life, and the consequent folly of being so careful for this world while neglectful of God, led Him to make warning application to His Peræan disciples.^f Only here the negative injunction that preceded the Parable, 'beware of covetousness,' is, when addressed to 'the disciples,' carried back to its positive underlying principle: to dismiss all anxiety, even for the necessaries of life, learning from the birds and the flowers to have absolute faith and trust in God, and to labour for only one thing—the Kingdom of God. But, even in this, they were not to be careful, but to have absolute faith and trust in their Father, 'Who was well pleased to give' them 'the Kingdom.'^g

With but slight variations the Lord had used the same language, even as the same admonition had been needed, at the beginning of His Galilean Ministry, in the Sermon on the Mount.^h Perhaps we may here, also, regard the allusion to the springing flowers as a mark of time. Only, whereas in Galilee this would mark the

a St. Matt. x.
b St. Matt. x. 18–20
c St. Matt. x. 21–25
d St. Luke xii. 10, comp. with St. Matt. xii. 31, 32
e St. Luke xii. 16–21
f St. Luke xii. 22–34
g St. Luke xii. 32
h St. Matt. vi. 25–33

---

[1] Concerning the foolish rich man.

beginning of spring, it would, in the more favoured climate of certain parts of Peræa, indicate the beginning of December, about the time of the Feast of the Dedication of the Temple.   More important, perhaps, is it to note, that the expression[a] rendered in the Authorised and Revised Versions, ' neither be ye of doubtful mind,' really means, ' neither be ye uplifted,' in the sense of not aiming, or seeking after great things.[b]   This rendering of the Greek word ($\mu\varepsilon\tau\varepsilon\omega\rho\iota\zeta\varepsilon\iota\nu$) is in accordance with its uniform use in the LXX.,[1] and in the Apocrypha; while, on the other hand, it occurs in *Josephus* and *Philo*, in the sense of ' being of a doubtful mind.'   But the context here shows, that the term must refer to the disciples coveting great things, since only to this the remark could apply, that the Gentile world sought such things, but that our Father knew what was really needful for us.

Of deepest importance is the final consolation, to dismiss all care and anxiety, since the Father was pleased to give to this ' little flock ' the Kingdom.   The expression ' flood ' carries us back to the language which Jesus had held ere parting from Jerusalem.[c]   Henceforth this designation would mark His people.   Even its occurrence fixes this Discourse as not a repetition of that which St. Matthew had formerly reported, but as spoken after the Jerusalem visit.   It designates Christ's people in distinction to their ecclesiastical (or outward) organisation in a ' fold,' and marks alike their individuality and their conjunction, their need and dependence, and their relation to Him as the ' Good Shepherd.'   Small and despised though it be in the eyes of men, ' the little flock' is unspeakably noble, and rich in the gift of the Father.

These admonitions, alike as against covetousness, and as to absolute trust and a self-surrender to God, which would count all loss for the Kingdom, are finally set forth, alike in their present application and their ultimate and permanent principle, in what we regard as the concluding part of this Discourse.[d]   Its first sentence: ' Sell that ye have, and give alms,' which is only recorded by St. Luke, indicates not a general principle, but its application to that particular period, when the faithful disciple required to follow the Lord, unencumbered by worldly cares or possessions.[e]   The general principle underlying it is that expressed by St. Paul,[f] and finally resolves itself into this: that the Christian should have as not holding, and use what he has not for self nor sin, but for necessity.   This conclusion of Christ's

CHAP.
XIII

[a] St. Luke
xii. 29

[b] Comp.
Jer. xiv. 5

[c] St. John x.

[d] St. Luke
xii. 33, 34

[e] comp.
St. Matt.
xix. 21

[f] 1 Cor. vii.
30, 31

---

[1] The word occurs in that sense twenty-five times in the LXX. of the old Testament (four times as a noun, thirteen times as an adjective, eight times as a verb), and seven times in the Apocrypha (twice as a verb and as an adjective, and three times as a noun).   This must fix the N.T. *usus.*

BOOK
IV

* St. Matt.
vi. 19-21

ᵇ St. Luke
xii.
ᶜ vv. 35-38

ᵈ St. Matt.
xxiv. 43, 44

Discourse, also, confirms the inference that it was delivered near the terrible time of the end. Most seasonable would be here the repetition—though in slightly different language—of an admonition, given in the beginning of Christ's Galilean Ministry,* to provide treasure in heaven, which could neither fail nor be taken away, for, assuredly, where the treasure was, there also would the heart be.

3. Closely connected with, and yet quite distinct from, the previous Discourse is that about the waiting attitude of the disciples in regard to their Master. Wholly detached from the things of the world, their hearts set on the Kingdom, only one thing should seem worthy their whole attention, and engage all their thoughts and energies: their Master! He was away at some joyous feast, and the uncertainty of the hour of His return must not lead the servants to indulge in surfeiting, nor to lie down in idleness, but to be faithful to their trust, and eagerly expectant of their Master. The Discourse itself consists of three parts and a practical application.

1. *The Disciples as Servants in the absence of their Master:* ᵇ *their duty and their reward.*ᶜ This part, containing what would be so needful to these Peræan disciples, is peculiar to St. Luke. The Master is supposed to be absent, at a wedding—a figure which must not be closely pressed, not being one of the essentials in the Parable. At most, it points to a joyous occasion, and its mention may chiefly indicate that such a feast might be protracted, so that the exact time of the Master's return could not be known to the servants who waited at home. In these circumstances, they should hold themselves in readiness, that, whatever hour it might be, they should be able to open the door at the first knocking. Such eagerness and devotion of service would naturally meet its reward, and the Master would, in turn, consult the comfort of those who had not allowed themselves their evening-meal, nor lain down, but watched for His return. Hungry and weary as they were from their zeal for Him, He would now, in turn, minister to their personal comfort. And this applied to servants who so watched—it mattered not how long, whether into the second or the third of the watches into which the night was divided.[1]

The 'Parable' now passes into another aspect of the case, which is again referred to in the last Discourses of Christ.ᵈ Conversely—suppose the other case, of people sleeping: the house might be

---

[1] The first is not mentioned, because it was so early, nor yet the fourth, because the feast would scarcely be protracted so long. Anciently, the Hebrews counted *three* night-watches; but after-wards, and probably at the time of Christ, they divided the night into *four* watches (see the discussion in Ber. 3 a). The latter arrangement was probably introduced from the Romans.

broken into. Of course, if one had known the hour when the thief
would come, sleep would not have been indulged in; but it is just this
uncertainty and suddenness—and the Coming of the Christ into His
Kingdom would be equally sudden—which should keep the people in
the house ever on their watch till Christ came.[a]

It was at this particular point that a question of Peter interrupted
the Discourse of Christ. To whom did this 'Parable' apply about
'the good man' and 'the servants' who were to watch: to the Apostles, or also to all? From the implied—for it is not an express—
answer of the Lord, we infer, that Peter expected some difference
between the Apostles and the rest of the disciples, whether as regarded the attitude of the servants that waited, or the reward. From
the words of Christ the former seems the more likely. We can understand how Peter might entertain the Jewish notion, that the
Apostles would come with the Master from the marriage-supper, rather
than wait for His return, and work while waiting. It is to this that the
reply of Christ refers. If the Apostles or others are rulers, it is as
stewards, and their reward of faithful and wise stewardship will be
advance to higher administration. But as stewards they are servants
—servants of Christ, and ministering servants in regard to the other
and general servants. What becomes them in this twofold capacity
is faithfulness to the absent, yet ever near, Lord, and to their work,
avoiding, on the one hand, the masterfulness of pride and of harshness,
and, on the other, the self-degradation of conformity to evil manners,
either of which would entail sudden and condign punishment in the
sudden and righteous reckoning at His appearing. The 'Parable,' therefore, alike as to the waiting and the reckoning, applied to
work for Christ, as well as to *personal relationship* towards Him.

Thus far this solemn warning would naturally be afterwards repeated in Christ's Last Discourses in Judæa, as equally needful, in
view of His near departure.[b] But in this Peræan Discourse, as reported by St. Luke, there now follows what must be regarded, not,
indeed, as a further answer to Peter's inquiry, but as specifically referring to the general question of the relation between special work
and general discipleship which had been raised. For, in one sense,
all disciples are servants, not only to wait, but to work. As regarded
those who, like the professed stewards or labourers, knew their work,
but neither 'made ready,'[1] nor did according to His Will, their punishment and loss (where the illustrative figure of 'many' and 'few
stripes' must not be too closely pressed) would naturally be greater

[1] So literally.

BOOK
IV

ᵃ St. Luke
xii. 47, 48

ᵇ St. Luke
xii. 49-53

vv. 49-50

ᵈ St. Matt.
x 34-36

ᵉ St. Luke
xii. 51-53

ᶠ ver. 54

ᵍ St. Matt.
xvi. 2, 3

ʰ St. Luke
xii. 56

ⁱ ver. 57

than that of them who knew not—though this also involves guilt—that their Lord had any will towards them, that is, any work for them. This, according to a well-understood principle, universally, almost instinctively, acted upon among men.ᵃ

2. In the absence of their master! *A period this of work*, as well as of waiting; *a period of trial also.*ᵇ Here, also, the two opening verses, in their evident connection with the subject-matter under the first head of this Discourse,[1] but especially with the closing sentences about work for the Master, are peculiar to St. Luke's narrative, and fit only into it. The Church had a work to do in His absence—the work for which He had come. He 'came to cast fire on earth,'—that fire which was kindled when the Risen Saviour sent the Holy Ghost, and of which the tongues of fire were the symbol.[2] Oh, how He longed,[3] that it were already kindled! But between Him and it lay the cold flood of His Passion, the terrible Passion in which He was to be baptized. Oh, how He felt the burden of that coming Agony!ᶜ That fire must they spread: this was the work in which, as disciples, each one must take part. Again, in that Baptismal Agony of His they also must be prepared to share. It was *fire*: burning up, as well as purifying and giving light. And here it was in place to repeat to His Peræan disciples the prediction already addressed to the Twelve when going on their Mission,ᵈ as to the certain and necessary trials connected with carrying 'the fire' which Christ had cast on earth, even to the burning up of the closest bonds of association and kinship.ᵉ

3. Thus far to the disciples. And now for its application to 'the multitudes'ᶠ—although here also He could only repeat what on a former occasion He had said to the Pharisees.ᵍ Let them not think that all this only concerned the disciples. No; it was a question between Israel and their Messiah, and the struggle would involve the widest consequences, alike to the people and the Sanctuary. Were they so blinded as not 'to know how to interpret the time'?ʰ Could they not read its signs—they who had no difficulty in interpreting it when a cloud rose from the sea, or the sirocco blew from the south?[4] Why then—and here St. Luke is again alone in his reportⁱ—did they not, in the circumstances, of themselves judge what was right and fitting and necessary, in view of the gathering tempest?

---

[1] Comp. before, under 1, p. 218.

[2] This clause is most important for the interpretation of that which precedes it, showing that it cannot be taken *in sensu malo*. It cannot therefore be 'the fire of judgment' (*Plumptre*.)

[3] Probably, as *Wünsche* suggests, the הלוֹאי. or else the וּלוֹאי of the Rabbis.

[4] The observant reader will notice how characteristic the small differences are. Thus. the sirocco would *not* be expected in Galilee, but in Peræa, and in the latter also the first flowers would appear much earlier.

What was it? Even what he had told them before in Galilee,[a] for the circumstances were the same. What common sense and common prudence would dictate to every one whom his accuser or creditor haled before the magistrate: to come to an agreement with him before it was too late, before sentence had been pronounced and executed.[b] Although the illustration must not be pressed as to details, its general meaning would be the more readily understood that there was a similar Rabbinic proverb,[c] although with very different practical application.

4. Besides these Discourses, two events are recorded before Christ's departure to the 'Feast of the Dedication.' Each of these led to a brief Discourse, ending in a Parable.

The first records two circumstances not mentioned by the Jewish historian *Josephus*,[1] nor in any other historical notice of the time, either by Rabbinic or other writers. This shows, on the one hand, how terribly common such events must have been, when they could be so generally omitted from the long catalogue of Pilate's misdeeds towards the Jews. On the other hand it also evidences that the narrative of St. Luke was derived from independent, authentic sources —in other words, the historical character of his narrative—when he could refer as well known to facts, which are not mentioned in any other record of the times; and, lastly, that we are not warranted in rejecting a notice, simply because we find no other mention of it than on the pages of the Third Gospel.

It appears that, just then, or quite soon afterwards, some persons told Christ about a number of His own Galileans, whom Pilate had ordered to be cut down, as we infer, in the Temple, while engaged in offering their sacrifices,[d] so that, in the pictorial language of the East, their blood had mingled with that of their sacrifices. Clearly, their narration of this event must be connected with the preceding Discourse of Jesus. He had asked them, whether they could not discern the signs of the terrible national storm that was nearing. And it was in reference to this, as we judge, that they repeated this story. To understand their object, we must attend to the answer of Christ. It is intended to refute the idea, that these Galileans had in this been visited by a special punishment of some special sin against God. Two questions here arise. Since between Christ's visit to Jerusalem at the Feast of Tabernacles and that at the Dedication of the Temple no Festival took place, it is most probable that this event had happened

CHAP.
XIII

[a] St. Matt. v. 25, 26

[b] St. Luke xii. 58, 59

[c] Sanh. 95 b. Its import is thus explained: *Prépare ta vengeance, sans que ton ennemi puisse s'en douter* (*Schuhl*, Sent. et. Prov. d. Talm. p. 3)

[d] St. Luke xiii. 1-5

---

[1] This omission goes far to prove the groundlessness of the charge brought by *Renan*, and lately by *Joël* (Bl. in d. Relig. Gesch. ii. pp. 52 &c.), that the writings of *Josephus* have been largely falsified by Christian copyists.

before Christ's visit to Jerusalem. But in that case it seems most likely—almost certain—that Christ had heard of it before. If so, or, at any rate, if it was not quite a recent event, why did these men tell Him of it then and there? Again, it seems strange that, although the Jews connected special sins with special punishments, they should have regarded it as the Divine punishment of a special sin to have been martyred by a Pilate in the Temple, while engaged in offering sacrifices.

All this becomes quite plain, if we regard these men as trying to turn the edge of Jesus' warning by a kind of ' *Tu quoque* ' argument. Very probably these Galileans were thus ruthlessly murdered, because of their real or suspected connection with the Nationalist movement, of which Galilee was the focus. It is as if these Jews had said to Jesus: Yes, signs of the times and of the coming storm! These Galileans of yours, your own countrymen, involved in a kind of Pseudo-Messianic movement, a kind of 'signs of the times' rising, something like that towards which you want us to look—was not their death a condign punishment? This latter inference they did not express in words, but implied in their narration of the fact. But the Lord read their thoughts and refuted their reasoning. For this purpose He adduced another instance,[a] when a tower at the Siloam-Pool had fallen on eighteen persons and killed them, perhaps in connection with that construction of an aqueduct into Jerusalem by Pilate, which called forth, on the part of the Jews, the violent opposition, which the Roman so terribly avenged. As good Jews, they would probably think that the fall of the tower, which had buried in its ruins these eighteen persons, who were perhaps engaged in the building of that cursed structure, was a just judgment of God! For Pilate had used for it the sacred money which had been devoted to Temple-purposes (the *Qorban*),[b] and many there were who perished in the tumult caused by the Jewish resistance to this act of profanation. But Christ argued, that it was as wrong to infer that Divine-judgment had overtaken His Galilean countrymen, as it would be to judge that the Tower of Siloam had fallen to punish these Jerusalemites. Not one party only, nor another; not the supposed Messianic tendency (in the shape of a national rising), nor, on the other hand, the opposite direction of absolute submission to Roman domination, was in fault. The whole nation was guilty; and the coming storm, to the signs of which He had pointed, would destroy all unless there were spiritual repentance on the part of the nation. And yet wider than this, and applying to all time, is the underlying principle, that, when a calamity befalls a district or an aggregation of individuals, we ought not to take to ourselves judgment as to its special causation, but to think spiritually of its general application— not so much seek to trace what is the character of its connection with a district or individuals, as to learn its lessons and to regard them as a call addressed to all. And conversely, also, this holds true in regard to deliverances.

Having thus answered the implied objection, the Lord next showed, in the Parable of the Fig-tree,[a] the need and urgency of national repentance.[1]

The second event recorded by St. Luke in this connection[b] recalls the incidents of the early Judæan[c] and of the Galilean Ministry.[d] We observe the same narrow views and externalism as before in regard to the Sabbath on the part of the Jewish authorities, and, on the part of Christ, the same wide principles and spiritual application. If we were in search of evidence of the Divine Mission of Jesus, we would find it in this contrariety on so fundamental a point, since no teacher in Israel nor Reformer of that time —not the most advanced Sadducee—would have defended, far less originated, the views as to the Sabbath which Christ now propounded.[2] Again, if we were in quest of evidence of the historical truthfulness of the Gospel-narratives, we would find it in a comparison of the narratives of the three Sabbath-controversies: in Jerusalem, in Galilee, and in Peræa. In all the spirit was the same. And, although the differences between them may seem slight, they are characteristic, and mark, as if they pointed to it with the finger, the locality and circumstances in which each took place. In Jerusalem there is neither reasoning nor rebuke on the part of the Jews, but absolute persecution. There also the Lord enters on the higher exposition of His action, motives, and Mission.[e] In Galilee there is questioning, and cunning intrigue against Him on the part of the Judæans who dogged His steps. But while no violence can be attempted against Him, the people do not venture openly to take His part.[f] But in Peræa we are confronted by the clumsy zeal of a country-Archisynagogos (Chief Ruler of a Synagogue), who is very angry, but not very wise; who admits Christ's healing power, and does not dare to attack Him directly, but, instead, rebukes, not Christ, not even the woman who had been healed, but the people who witnessed it, at the same time telling them to come fer healing on other days, not

CHAP.
XIII

[a] St. Luke xiii. 6-9

[b] St. Luke xiii. 10-17
[c] St. John v 16
[d] St. Matt. xii. 9-13

[e] St. John v 16, 17 &c.

[f] St. Matt. xii. 1-21

---

[1] For the exposition of this Parable, I refer to that of all the Parables of that period.

[2] On the Sabbath-Law, see Appendix XVII.

perceiving, in his narrow-minded bigotry, what this admission implied. This rustic Ruler had not the cunning, nor even the courage, of the Judæan Pharisees in Galilee, whom the Lord had formerly convicted and silenced. Enough, to show this obscure Peræan partisan of Pharisaism and the like of him their utter folly, and that by their own admissions.[a] And presently, not only were His adversaries ashamed, while in Galilee they went out and held a council against Him,[b] but the people were not afraid, as the Galileans had been in presence of their rulers, and openly rejoiced in the glorious working of the Christ.

ᵃ St. Luke
xiii. 15, 16

ᵇ St. Matt.
xii. 14

Little more requires to be added about this incident in 'one of the Synagogues' of Peræa. Let us only briefly recall the scene. Among those present in this Synagogue had been a poor woman, who for eighteen years had been a sufferer, as we learn, through demoniac agency. It is quite true that most, if not all, such diseases were connected with moral distemper, since demoniac possession was not permanent, and resistance might have been made in the lucid intervals, if there had been moral soundness. But it is ungrounded to distinguish between the 'spirit of infirmity' as the moral and psychical, and her being 'bent,' as indicating the physical disease, [1] or even to describe the latter as a 'permanent curvature of the spine.' [2] The Greek word here rendered 'infirmity' has passed into Rabbinic language (*Isteniseyah*, איסתניסיה), and there means, not any particular disease, but sickliness, sometimes weakliness. In fact, she was, both physically and morally, not sick, but sickly, and most truly was hers 'a spirit of infirmity,' so that 'she was bowed together, and could in no wise lift herself up.' For, we mark that hers was not demoniac possession at all—and yet, though she had not yielded, she had not effectually resisted, and so she was 'bound' by 'a spirit of infirmity,' both in body and soul.

We recognise the same 'spirit of infirmity' in the circumstances of her healing. When Christ, seeing her—probably a fit symbol of the Peræans in that Synagogue—called her, she came; when He said unto her, 'Woman, thou hast been loosed [3] from thy sickliness,' she *was* unbound, and yet in her weakliness she answered not, nor straightened herself, till Jesus 'laid His Hands on her,' and so strengthened her in body and soul, and then she was immediately 'made straight, and glorified God.'

---

[1] This is the view of *Godet*, who regards the 'Thou hast been loosed' as referring to the psychical ailment.

[2] So Dean *Plumptre*.
[3] So, and not as in the A.V.

As for the Archisynagogos, we have, as already hinted, such char- CHAP.
acteristic portraiture of him that we can almost see him: confused, XIII
irresolute, perplexed, and very angry, bustling forward and scolding
the people who had done nothing, yet not venturing to silence the
woman, now no longer infirm—far less, to reprove the great Rabbi,
Who had just done such a 'glorious thing,' but speaking at Him
through those who had been the astounded eye-witnesses. He was
easily and effectually silenced, and all who sympathised with him
put to shame.   'Hypocrites!' spake the Lord—on your own admissions your practice and your Law condemn your speech. Every one
on the Sabbath looseth his ox or ass, and leads him to the watering.
The Rabbinic law expressly allowed this,[1] and even to draw the
water, provided the vessel were not carried to the animal.[a] If, as [a] Erub. 17 b;
you admit, I have the power of 'loosing' from the bonds of Satan, 20 b
and she has been so bound these eighteen years, should she—a
daughter of Abraham—not have that done for her which you do for
your beasts of burden?

The retort was unanswerable and irresistible; it did what was
intended: it covered the adversaries with shame. And the Peræans
in that Synagogue felt also, at least for the time, the blessed freedom which had come to that woman. They took up the echoes of
her hymn of praise, and 'rejoiced for all the glorious things that
were done by Him.' And He answered their joy by rightly directing
it—by setting before them 'the Kingdom,' which He had come both
to preach and to bring, in all its freeness, reality, power, and all-
pervading energy, as exhibited in the two Parables of the 'Mustard-seed' and 'the Leaven,' spoken before in Galilee. These were
now repeated, as specially suited to the circumstances: first, to the
Miracle they had witnessed; then, to the contention that had
passed; and, lastly, to their own state of feeling. And the practical
application of these Parables must have been obvious to all.

---

[1] It was *not* contrary to the Rab-   poses. The rule is quite different from
binic law, as Canon *Cook* (ad loc.) sup-   that which applied in St. Matt. xii. 11.

CHAPTER XIV.

AT THE FEAST OF THE DEDICATION OF THE TEMPLE.

(St. Luke xiii. 22; St. John x. 22–42.)

BOOK
IV

28 A.D.

ABOUT two months had passed since Jesus had left Jerusalem after the Feast of Tabernacles. Although we must not commit ourselves to such calculations, we may here mention the computation which identifies the first day of the Feast of Tabernacles of that year[a] with Thursday the 23rd September; the last, 'the Great Day of the Feast,' with Wednesday the 29th; the Octave of the Feast with the 30th September; and the Sabbath when the man born blind was healed with the 2nd of October.[1] In that case, 'the Feast of the Dedication of the Temple,' which commenced on the 25th day of Chislev, and lasted eight days, would have begun on Wednesday the 1st, and closed on Wednesday the 8th December. But, possibly, it may have been a week or two later. At that Feast, or about two months after He had quitted the City, we find Christ once more in Jerusalem and in the Temple. His journey thither seems indicated in the Third Gospel (St. Luke xiii. 22), and is at least implied in the opening words with which St. John prefaces his narrative of what happened on that occasion.[b][2]

[b] St. John x. 22

As we think of it, there seems special fitness—presently to be pointed out—in Christ's spending what we regard as the last anniversary season of His Birth[3] in the Temple at that Feast. It was not of Biblical origin, but had been instituted by Judas Maccabæus in 164 B.C., when the Temple, which had been desecrated by Antiochus Epiphanes, was once more purified, and re-dedicated to the Service of Jehovah.[c] Accordingly, it was designated as 'the Dedication of the Altar.'[d] Josephus[e] calls it 'The Lights,' from one of the principal observances at the Feast, though he speaks in hesitating language of

[c] 1 Macc. vi. 52–59
[d] u. s. vv. 56–59
[e] Ant. xii. 7. 7

---

[1] Wieseler, Chronolog. Synopse, pp. 482, 483.

[2] It must, however, be admitted that some commentators draw an opposite inference from these words.

[3] The subject has been more fully treated in an article in the 'Leisure Hour' for Dec. 1873: 'Christmas, a Festival of Jewish Origin.'

the origin of the festival as connected with this observance—probably because, while he knew, he was ashamed to avow, and yet afraid to deny his belief in the Jewish legend connected with it. The Jews called it *Chanukkah*, ' dedication ' or ' consecration,' and, in much the same sense, *Enkainia* in the Greek of the LXX.,[a][1] and in the New Testament. During the eight days of the Feast the series of Psalms known as the *Hallel*[b] was chanted in the Temple, the people responding as at the Feast of Tabernacles. [2] Other rites resembled those of the latter Feast. Thus, originally, the people appeared with palm-branches. [c] This, however, does not seem to have been afterwards observed, while another rite, not mentioned in the Book of Maccabees—that of illuminating the Temple and private houses—became characteristic of the Feast. Thus, the two festivals, which indeed are put in juxtaposition in 2 Macc. x. 6, seem to have been both externally and internally connected. The Feast of the ' Dedication,' or of ' Lights,' derived from that of Tabernacles its duration of eight days, the chanting of the *Hallel*, and the practice of carrying palm-branches. On the other hand, the rite of the Temple-illumination may have passed from the Feast of the ' Dedication ' into the observances of that of ' Tabernacles.' Tradition had it, that, when the Temple-Services were restored by Judas Maccabæus, the oil was found to have been desecrated. Only one flagon was discovered of that which was pure, sealed with the very signet of the High-Priest. The supply proved just sufficient to feed for one day the Sacred Candlestick, but by a miracle the flagon was continually replenished during eight days, till a fresh supply could be brought from Thekoah. In memory of this, it was ordered the following year, that the Temple be illuminated for eight days on the anniversary of its ' Dedication.' [d] The Schools of Hillel and Shammai differed in regard to this, as on most other observances. The former would have begun the first night with the smallest number of lights, and increased it every night till on the eighth it was eight times as large as on the first. The School of Shammai, on the other hand, would have begun with the largest number, and diminished, till on the last night it amounted to an eighth of the first. Each party had its own—not very satisfactory— reasons for its distinctive practice, and its own adherents. [e] But the ' Lights ' in honour of the Feast were lit not only in the Temple, but

a Ezra vi. 16, 17; Neh. xii. 27; Dan. iii. 2
b Ps. cxiii. cxviii.

c 2 Macc. x. 7

d Shabb. 21 b, lines 11 to 8 from bottom

e Shabb. 21 b, about the middle

---

[1] Similarly, the cognate words ἐγκαίνισις and ἐγκαινισμός as well as the verb (ἐγκαινίζω), are frequently used both in the LXX. and the Apocrypha. The verb also occurs Heb. ix. 18; x. 20.

[2] See ch. vii. This was always the case when the *Hallel* was chanted.

BOOK
IV

in every home.   One would have sufficed for the whole household on the first evening, but pious householders lit a light for every inmate of the home, so that, if ten burned on the first, there would be eighty on the last night of the Festival.   According to the Talmud, the light might be placed at the entrance to the house or room, or, according to circumstances, in the window, or even on the table. According to modern practice the light is placed at the left on entering a room (the Mezuzah is on the right).   Certain benedictions are spoken on lighting these lights, all work is stayed, and the festive time spent in merriment.   The first night is specially kept in memory of Judith, who is supposed then to have slain Holofernes, and cheese is freely partaken of as the food of which, according to legend,[1] she gave him so largely, to incite him to thirst and drunkenness.[2] Lastly, during this Festival, all fasting and public mourning were prohibited, though some minor acts of private mourning were allowed.[a]

[a] Moed K. iii. 9; Shabb. 21 b

More interesting, perhaps, than this description of the outward observances is the meaning of this Festival and its connection with the Feast of Tabernacles, to both of which reference has already been made.   Like the Feast of Tabernacles, it commemorated a Divine Victory, which again gave to Israel their good land, after they had once more undergone sorrows like those of the wilderness; it was another harvest-feast, and pointed forward to yet another ingathering. As the once extinguished light was relit in the Temple—and, according to Scriptural imagery, might that not mean the Light of Israel, the Lamp of David?—it grew day by day in brightness, till it shone quite out into the heathen darkness, that once had threatened to quench it.   That He Who purified the Temple, was its True Light, and brought the Great Deliverance, should (as hinted) have spent the last anniversary season of His Birth at that Feast in the Sanctuary, shining into their darkness, seems most fitting, especially as we remember the Jewish legend, according to which the making of the Tabernacle had been completed on the 25th Chislev, although it was not set up till the 1st of Nisan (the Paschal month).[b]

[b] Bemidb. R. 13, ed. Warsh., p. 49 a, line 15 from top

Thoughts of the meaning of this Feast, and of what was associated with it, will be helpful as we listen to the words which Jesus spake to the people in ' Solomon's Porch.'   There is a pictorialness in the

---

[1] In regard to the latter Jewish legend, the learned reader will find full quotations (as, in general, much interesting information on the ' Feast of the Dedications') in *Selden*, de Synedriis (ed. Frcf. 1696) p. 1213, and in general from p. 1207 to 1214.

[2] The reader will find much that is curious in these four Midrashim (apud *Jellinek*, Beth haMidr. i. pp. 130-146): the Maaseh Jehudith, 2 Midr. for Chanukkah, and he Megillath Antiochos. See also the Megillath Taanith (ed. Warsh. 1874), pp. 14 a to 15 b.

description of the circumstances, which marks the eyewitness. It is winter, and Christ is walking in the covered Porch,[1] in front of the ' Beautiful Gate,' which formed the principal entrance into the ' Court of the Women.' As he walks up and down, the people are literally barring His Way—' came round about ' Him. From the whole circumstances we cannot doubt, that the question which they put: ' How long holdest Thou us in suspense? ' had not in it an element of truthfulness or genuine inquiry. Their desire, that He should tell them ' plainly ' if He were the Christ, had no other motive than that of grounding on it an accusation.[2] The more clearly we perceive this, the more wonderful appears the forbearance of Christ and the wisdom of His answer. Briefly he puts aside their hypocrisy. What need is there of fresh speech? He told them before, and they ' believe [3] not.' From words He appeals to the mute but indisputable witness of deeds: the works which He wrought in His Father's Name. Their non-belief in presence of these facts was due to their not being of His Sheep. As he had said unto them before,[4] it was characteristic of His Sheep (as generally of every flock in regard to its own shepherd) to hear—recognise, listen to—His Voice and follow Him. We mark in the words of Christ, a triplet of double parallelisms concerning the Sheep and the Shepherd, in ascending climax,[a] as follows:—[5]

* St. John
x. 27, 28

My sheep hear My Voice,	And I know them,
And they follow me:	And I give unto them eternal life:
And they shall never perish.	And no one shall snatch them out of My Hand.

A similar fourfold parallelism with descending and ascending climax, but of an antithetic character, has been noticed[6] in Christ's former Discourse in the Temple (St. John x. 13–15)—

The hireling	I
Is an hireling,	Am the good Shepherd,
Careth not for the sheep.	Know the sheep,
Fleeth	Lay down My Life.

---

[1] The location of this ' Porch ' in the passage under the present mosque *El Aksa* (proposed by *Caspari*, Chronol. Geogr. Einleit. p. 256, and adopted by Archdeacon *Watkins*) is contrary to all the well-known facts.

[2] Commentators mostly take quite a different view, and regard theirs as more or less honest inquiry.

[3] According to the better reading, in the *present* tense.

[4] This clause in ver. 26 of the A.V. must, *if retained*, be joined to ver. 27.

[5] So, after the precedent of *Bengel*, especially *Luthardt* and *Godet*, and after them others.

[6] By *Bengel*.

Richer or more comforting assurance than that recorded above could not have been given. But something special has here to be marked. The two first parallelisms always link the promise of Christ to the attitude of the sheep; not, perhaps, conditionally, for the relation is such as not to admit conditionalness, either in the form of 'because—therefore,' or even of 'if—then,' but as a matter of sequence and of fact. But in the third parallelism there is no reference to anything on the part of the sheep; it is all promise, and the second clause only explains and intensifies what is expressed in the first. If it indicates attack of the fiercest kind and by the strongest and most cunning of enemies, be they men or devils, it also marks the watchfulness and absolute superiority of Him Who hath them, as it were, in His Hand—perhaps a Hebraism for 'power'—and hence their absolute safety. And, as if to carry twofold assurance of it, He reminds His hearers that *His* Work being 'the Father's Commandment,' it is really the Father's Work, given to Christ to do, and no one could snatch them out of the Father's Hand. It is a poor cavil, to try to limit these assurances by seeking to grasp and to comprehend them in the hollow of our human logic. Do they convey what is commonly called 'the doctrine of perseverance'? Nay! but they teach us, not about *our* faith but about *His* faithfulness, and convey to us assurance concerning Him rather than ourselves; and this is the only aspect in which 'the doctrine of perseverance' is either safe, true, or Scriptural.

But one logical sequence is unavoidable. Rightly understood, it is not only the last and highest announcement, but it contains and implies everything else. If the Work of Christ is really that of the Father, and His Working also that of the Father, then it follows that He 'and the Father are One' ('one' is in the neuter). This identity of work (and purpose) implies the identity of Nature (Essence); that of working, the identity of power.[1] And so, evidently, the Jews understood it, when they again took up stones with the intention of stoning Him—no doubt, because He expressed, in yet more plain terms, what they regarded as His blasphemy. Once more the Lord appealed from His Words, which were doubted, to His Works, which were indubitable. And so He does to all time. His Divine Mission is evidence of His Divinity. And if His Divine Mission be doubted, He appeals to the 'many excellent works' (καλὰ

[1] St. *Augustine* marks, that the word 'one' tells against Arianism, and the plural 'are' against Sabellianism. And do they not equally tell against all heresy?

$\overset{"}{\epsilon}\rho\gamma\alpha$) which He hath 'showed from the Father,' any one of which
might, and, in the case of not a few, had, served as evidence of His
Mission. And when the Jews ignored, as so many in our days, this
line of evidence, and insisted that He had been guilty of blasphemy,
since, being a man, He had made Himself God, the Lord replied in a
manner that calls for our special attention. From the peculiarly
Hebraistic mode of designating a quotation from the Psalms[a] as
'written in the Law,'[1] we gather that we have here a literal transcript of the very words of our Lord.[2] But what we specially wish,
is, emphatically, to disclaim any interpretation of them, which would
seem to imply that Christ had wished to evade their inference: that
He claimed to be One with the Father—and to convey to them, that
nothing more had been meant than what might lawfully be applied
to an ordinary man. Such certainly is not the case. He had claimed
to be One with the Father in work and working: from which, of
course, the necessary inference was, that He was also One with Him
in Nature and Power. Let us see whether the claim was strange.
In Ps. lxxxii. 6 the titles 'God' (*Elohim*) and 'Sons of the Highest'
(*Beney Elyon*) had been given to Judges as the Representatives and
Vicegerents of God, wielding His delegated authority, since to them
had come His Word of authorisation. But here was authority not
transmitted by 'the word,' but personal and direct consecration, and
personal and direct Mission on the part of God. The comparison
made was not with prophets, because they only told the word and
message from God, but with Judges, who, as such, did the very *act* of
God. If those who, in so acting, had received an indirect commission,
were 'gods,' the very representatives of God,[3] could it be blasphemy
when He claimed to be the Son of God, Who had received, not
authority through a word transmitted through long centuries, but
direct personal command to do the Father's Work; had been directly
and personally consecrated to it by the Father, and directly and personally sent by Him, not to say, but to do, the work of the Father?
Was it not rather the true and necessary inference from these premisses?

[a] Ps.
lxxxii. 6

---

[1] In Rabbinic writings the word for
Law (*Torah*, or *Oreya*, or *Oreyan*) is
very frequently used to denote not only
the Law, but the whole Bible. Let one
example suffice: 'Blessed be the Merciful Who has given the threefold *Law*
(אוריין, Pentateuch, Prophets, and Hagiographa) to a threefold people (priests,
Levites, laity) by the hands of a third
(Moses, being the third born of his parents)
on the third day (after the preparation)
in the third month (Sivan),' Shabb. 88 *a*.

[2] We need scarcely call attention to the
evidence which it affords of the Judæan
authorship of the Fourth Gospel.

[3] We would call attention to the words
'The Scripture cannot be broken' (ver.
35) as evidential of the views which Jesus
took of the authority of the Old Testament, as well as of its inspiration.

BOOK
IV

ᵃ St. John
x. 37

All would, of course, depend on this, whether Christ really did the works of the Father.ᵃ That was the test; and, as we instinctively perceive, both rationally and truly. But if He did the works of His Father, then let them believe, if not the words yet the works, and thus would they arrive at the knowledge, ' and understand ' [1]—distinguishing here the act from the state [2]—that ' in Me is the Father, and I in the Father.' In other words, recognizing the Work as that of the Father, they would come to understand that the father worked in Him, and that the root of His Work was in the Father.

The stones, that had been taken up, were not thrown, for the words of Christ rendered impossible the charge of explicit blasphemy which alone would, according to Rabbinic law, have warranted such summary vengeance. But ' they sought again to sieze Him,' so as to drag Him before their tribunal. His time, however, had not yet come, ' and He went forth out of their hand '—how, we know not.

Once more the Jordan rolled between Him and His bitter persecutors. Far north, over against Galilee, in the place of John's early labours, probably close to where Jesus Himself had been baptized, was the scene of His last labours. And those, who so well remembered both the Baptist and the testimony which he had there borne to the Christ, recalled it all as they listened to His Words and saw His Works. As they crowded around Him, both the difference and the accord between John and Jesus carried conviction to their minds. The Baptist had done ' no sign,' [3] such as those which Jesus wrought: but all things which John had spoken of Him, they felt it, were true. And, undisturbed by the cavils of Pharisees and Scribes, many of these simple-minded, true-hearted men, far away from Jerusalem, believed on Him. To adapt a saying of *Bengel*: they were the posthumous children of the Baptist. Thus did he, being dead, yet speak. And so will all that is sown for Christ, though it lie buried and forgotten of men, spring up and ripen, as in one day, to the deep, grateful, and external joy of them who had laboured in faith and gone to rest in hope.

[1] Thus, according to the better reading.
[2] So *Meyer*.
[3] The circumstance, that, according to the Gospels, no miracle was wrought by John, is not only evidential of the trustworthiness of their report of our Lord's miracles, but otherwise also deeply significant. It shows that there is no craving for the miraculous, as in the Apocryphal and legendary narratives, and it proves that the Gospel-narratives were not cast in the mould of Jewish contemporary expectation, which would certainly have assigned another *rôle* to Elijah as the Forerunner of the Messiah than, first, that of solitary testimony, then of forsakenness, and, lastly, of cruel and unavenged murder at the hands of a Herodian. Truly, the history of Jesus is not that of the Messiah of Judaic conception !

CHAPTER XV.

THE SECOND SERIES OF PARABLES—THE TWO PARABLES OF HIM WHO
IS NEIGHBOUR TO US: THE FIRST, CONCERNING THE LOVE THAT,
UNASKed, GIVES IN OUR NEED; THE SECOND, CONCERNING THE
LOVE WHICH IS ELICITED BY OUR ASKING IN OUR NEED.

(St. Luke x. 25–37; xi. 5–13.)

THE period between Christ's return from the 'Feast of the Dedication' and His last entry into Jerusalem, may be arranged into two
parts, divided by the brief visit to Bethany for the purpose of raising
Lazarus from the dead. Even if it were possible, with any certainty,
chronologically to arrange the events of each of these periods, the
variety and briefness of what is recorded would prevent our closely
following them in this narrative. Accordingly, we prefer grouping
them together as the Parables of that period, its Discourses, and its
Events. And the record of the raising of Lazarus may serve as a
landmark between our Summary of the Parables and that of the
Discourses and Events which preceded the Lord's final appearance in
Jerusalem.

These last words help us to understand the necessary difference
between the Parables of this and of the preceding and the following
periods. The Parables of this period look back upon the past, and
forward into the future. Those spoken by the Lake of Galilee were
purely symbolical. They presented unseen heavenly realities under
emblems which required to be translated into earthly language. It
was quite easy to do so, if you possessed the key to the heavenly
mysteries; otherwise, they were dark and mysterious. So to speak,
they were easily read from above downwards. Viewed from below
upwards, only most dim and strangely intertwining outlines could be
perceived. It is quite otherwise with the second series of Parables.
They could, as they were intended, be understood by all. They required no translation. They were not symbolical but typical, using the
word 'type,' not in the sense of involving a predictive element,[a] but
as indicating an example, or, perhaps, more correctly, an exempli-

CHAP.
XV

[a] As in
Rom. v. 14

BOOK
IV

ᵃ As in
1 Cor. x. 6,
11; Phil. iii.
17; 1 Thess.
i. 7; 2
Thess.iii 9;
1 Tim. iv.
12; Tit. ii.
7; 1 Pet.v. 3

fication.ᵃ Accordingly, the Parables of this series are also intensely practical. Lastly, their prevailing character is not descriptive, but hortatory; and they bring the Gospel, in the sense of glad tidings to the lost, most closely and touchingly to the hearts of all who hear them. They are signs in words, as the miracles are signs in works, of what Christ has come to do and to teach. Most of them bear this character openly; and even those which do not, but seem more like warning, have still an undertone of love, as if Divine compassion lingered in tender pity over that which threatened, but might yet be averted.

Of the Parables of the third series it will for the present suffice to say, that they are neither symbolical nor typical, but their prevailing characteristic is prophetic. As befits their historical place in the teaching of Christ, they point to the near future. They are the fast falling, lengthening shadows cast by the events which are near at hand,

The Parables of the second (or Peræan) series, which are typical and hortatory, and ' Evangelical ' in character, are thirteen in number, and, with the exception of the last, are either peculiar to, or else most fully recorded in, the Gospel by St. Luke.

ᵇ St. Luke
x. 25-37

1. *The Parable of the Good Samaritan.*ᵇ—This Parable is connected with a question, addressed to Jesus by a ' lawyer '—not one of the Jerusalem Scribes or Teachers, but probably an expert in Jewish Canon Law,[1] who possibly made it more or less a profession in that district, though perhaps not for gain. Accordingly, there is a marked absence of that rancour and malice which charaterised his colleagues of Judæa. In a previous chapter it has been shown, that this narrative probably stands in its proper place in the Gospel of St. Luke.[2] We have also suggested, that the words of this lawyer referred, or else that himself belonged, to that small party among the Rabbinists who, at least in theory, attached greater value to good works than to study. At any rate, there is no occasion to impute directly evil motives to him. Knowing the habits of his class, we do not wonder that he put his question to ' tempt '—test, try—the great Rabbi of Nazareth. There are many similar instances in Rabbinic writings of meetings between great Teachers, when each tried to involve the other in dialectic difficulties and subtle disputations. Indeed, this was part of Rabbinism, and led to that painful and fatal trifling with

---

[1] A distinction between different classes of Scribes, of whom some gave themselves to the study of the Law, while others included with it that of the Prophets, such as Dean *Plumptre* suggests (on St. Matt. xxii. 35), did not exist.

[2] See generally ch. v. of this Book.

truth, when everything became matter of dialectic subtlety, and CHAP.
nothing was really sacred. What we require to keep in view is, that XV
to this lawyer the question which he propounded was only one of
theoretic, not of practical interest, nor matter of deep personal concern, as it was to the rich young ruler, who, not long afterwards,
addressed a similar inquiry to the Lord.[a]

We seem to witness the opening of a regular Rabbinic contest,
as we listen to this speculative problem: 'Teacher, what having done
shall I inherit eternal life ?' At the foundation lay the notion, that
eternal life was the reward of merit, of works: the only question was,
what these works were to be. The idea of guilt had not entered
his mind; he had no conception of sin within. It was the old Judaism
of self-righteousness speaking without disguise: that which was the
ultimate ground of the rejecting and crucifying of the Christ. There
certainly was a way in which a man might inherit eternal life, not
indeed as having absolute claim to it, but (as the Schoolmen might
have said: *de congruo*) in consequence of God's Covenant on Sinai.
And so our Lord, using the common Rabbinic expression 'what
readest thou?' (מאי קראת), pointed him to the Scriptures of the Old
Testament.

The reply of the 'lawyer' is remarkable, not only on its own
account, but as substantially, and even literally, that given on two
other occasions by the Lord Himself.[b] The question therefore
naturally arises, whence did this lawyer, who certainly had not
spiritual insight, derive his reply? As regarded the duty of absolute love to God, indicated by the quotation of Deut. vi. 5, there
could, of course, be no hesitation in the mind of a Jew. The
primary obligation of this is frequently referred to, and, indeed,
taken for granted, in Rabbinic teaching. The repetition of this
command, which in the Talmud receives the most elaborate and
strange interpretation,[1] formed part of the daily prayers. When
Jesus referred the lawyer to the Scriptures, he could scarcely fail to
quote this first paramount obligation. Similarly, he spoke as a
Rabbinic lawyer, when he referred in the next place to love to our
neighbour, as enjoined in Lev. xix. 18. Rabbinism is never weary
of quoting as one of the characteristic sayings of its greatest

[a] St. Luke xviii. 18-23

[b] St. Matt. xix. 16-22; xxii. 34-40

---

[1] Thus: ' "With all thy heart"—with both thy impulses, that to good and that to evil; "with all thy soul"—even if it takes away thy soul; "with all thy might" —"with all thy money." Another interpretation: "With all thy might"—in regard to every measure with which He measures to thee art thou bound to praise Him ' (there is here a play on the words which cannot be rendered), Ber. 54 *a*, about the middle.

BOOK
IV

ᵃ Shabb.
31 a, about
the middle

ᵇ Yalkut i.
174 a, end;
Siphra on
the pas-
sage, ed.
Weiss, p.
89 b;
also Ber. R.
24, end

ᶜ St. Matt.
vii. 12

teacher, Hillel (who, of course, lived before this time), that he had summed up the Law, in briefest compass, in these words: ' What is hateful to thee, that do not to another. This is the whole Law; the rest is only its explanation.' ᵃ Similarly, Rabbi Akiba taught, that Lev. xix. 18 was the principal rule, we might almost say, the chief summary of the Law (כלל גדו: בתורה).ᵇ Still, the two principles just mentioned are not enunciated in conjunction by Rabbinism, nor seriously propounded as either containing the whole Law or as securing heaven. They are also, as we shall presently see, sub jected to grave modifications. One of these, as regards the negative form in which Hillel put it, while Christ put it positively,ᶜ ¹ has been previously noticed. The existence of such Rabbinic modifications, and the circumstance, already mentioned, that on two other occasions the answer of Christ Himself to a similar inquiry was precisely that of this lawyer, suggests the inference, that this question may have been occasioned by some teaching of Christ, to which they had just listened, and that the reply of the lawyer may have been prompted by what Jesus had preached concerning the Law.

If it be asked, why Christ seemed to give His assent to the lawyer's answer, as if it really pointed to the right solution of the great question, we reply: No other answer could have been given him. On the ground of works—if that had been tenable—this was the way to heaven. To understand any other answer, would have required a sense of sin; and this could not be imparted by reasoning: it must be experienced. It is the preaching of the Law which

ᵈ Rom. vii.
awakens in the mind a sense of sin.ᵈ Besides, if not morally, yet mentally, the difficulty of this ' way ' would soon suggest itself to a Jew. Such, at least, is one aspect of the counter-question with which ' the lawyer ' now sought to retort on Jesus.

Whatever complexity of motives there may have been—for we know nothing of the circumstances, and there may have been that in the conduct or heart of the lawyer which was specially touched by what had just passed—there can be no doubt as to the maiu object of his question: ' But who is my neighbour? ' He wished ' to justify himself,' in the sense of vindicating his original question, and showing that it was not quite so easily settled as the answer of Jesus

---

¹ *Hamburger* (Real Encykl., Abth. ii. p. 411) makes the remarkable admission that the negative form was chosen to make the command ' possible ' and ' practical.' It is not so that Christ has accommodated the Divine Law to our sinfulness. See previous remarks on this Law in Book III. ch. xviii.

seemed to imply. And here it was that Christ could in a 'Parable'
show how far orthodox Judaism was from even a true understanding,
much more from such perfect observance of this Law as would gain
heaven. Thus might He bring even this man to feel his shortcomings and sins, and awaken in him a sense of his great need.
This, of course, would be the negative aspect of this Parable; the
positive is to all time and to all men.

That question: 'Who is my neighbour?' has ever been at the
same time the outcome of Judaism (as distinguished from the religion
of the Old Testament), and also its curse. On this point it is duty
to speak plainly, even in face of the wicked persecutions to which
the Jews have been exposed on account of it. Whatever modern
Judaism may say to the contrary, there is a foundation of truth
in the ancient heathen charge against the Jews of *odium generis
humani* (hatred of mankind). God had separated Israel unto Himself by purification and renovation—and this is the original meaning
of the word 'holy' and 'sanctify' in the Hebrew (קָדַשׁ). They
separated themselves in self-righteousness and pride—and that is
the original meaning of the word 'Pharisee' and 'Pharisaism' (פְּרוּשׁ).
In so saying no blame is cast on individuals; it is the system which
is at fault. This question: 'Who is my neighbour?' frequently
engages Rabbinism. The answer to it is only too clear. If a hypercriticism were to interpret away the passage[a] which directs that
idolators are not to be delivered when in imminent danger, while
heretics and apostates are even to be led into it, the painful discussion on the meaning of Exod. xxiii. 5 [b] would place it beyond question.
The sum of it is, that, except to avert hostility, a burden is only to
be unloaded, if the beast that lieth under it belongeth to an Israelite,
not if it belong to a Gentile; and so the expression,[c] 'the ass of
him that hateth thee,' must be understood of a Jewish, and not of a
Gentile enemy (שׂוֹנֵא יִשְׂרָאֵל וְלֹא שׂוֹנֵא א״ה).[d]

It is needless to follow the subject further. But more complete
rebuke of Judaistic narrowness, as well as more full, generous, and
spiritual world-teaching than that of Christ's Parable could not be
imagined. The scenery and colouring are purely local. And here
we should remember, that, while admitting the lawfulness of the
widest application of details for homiletical purposes, we must take
care not to press them in a strictly exegetical interpretation.[1]

[a] Ab Zar.
26 a

[b] Babha
Mets 32 b

[c] Ex. xxiii.5

[d] Babha
Mets. 32 b
line 3 from
bottom

---

[1] As to many of these allegorisations, *Calvin* rightly observes: 'Scripturæ major habenda est reverentia, quam ut germanum ejus sensum hac licentia transfigurare liceat.' In general, see *Goebel*, u. s.

BOOK
IV

Some one coming from the Holy City, the Metropolis of Judaism, is pursuing the solitary desert-road, those twenty-one miles to Jericho, a district notoriously insecure, when he 'fell among robbers, who, having both stripped and inflicted on him strokes, went away leaving him just as he was,[1] half dead.' This is the first scene. The second opens with an expression which, theologically, as well as exegetically, is of the greatest interest. The word rendered 'by chance' (συγκυρία) occurs only in this place,[2] for Scripture commonly views matters in relation to agents rather than to results. As already noted,[3] the real meaning of the word is 'concurrence,' much like the corresponding Hebrew term (מִקְרֶה). And better definition could not be given, not, indeed, of 'Providence,' which is a heathen abstraction for which the Bible has no equivalent, but for the concrete reality of God's providing. He provides through a concurrence of circumstances, all in themselves natural and in the succession of ordinary causation (and this distinguishes it from the miracle), but the concurring of which is directed and overruled by Him. And this helps us to put aside those coarse tests of the reality of prayer and of the direct rule of God, which men sometimes propose. Such stately ships ride not in such shallow waters.

It was by such a 'concurrence,' that, first a priest, then a Levite, came down that road, when each, successively, 'when he saw him, passed by over against (him).' It was the principle of questioning, 'Who is my neighbour?' which led both priest and Levite to such heartless conduct. Who knew what this wounded man was, and how he came to lie there: and were they called upon, in ignorance of this, to take all the trouble, perhaps incur the risk of life, which care of him would involve? Thus Judaism (in the persons of its chief representatives) had, by its exclusive attention to the letter, come to destroy the spirit of the Law. Happily, there came yet another that way, not only a stranger, but one despised, a semi-heathen Samaritan.[4] He asked not who the man was, but what was his need. Whatever the wounded Jew might have felt towards him, the Samaritan proved a true 'neighbour.' 'He came towards him, and beholding him, he was moved with compassion.' His resolution was soon taken. He first bound up his wounds, and then, taking from his travelling provision wine and oil, made of them, what was regarded as the common dressing for wounds.[a] Next, having

[1] 'ἡμιθανῆ τυγχάνοντα, Germ., wie er eben war,' Grimm, Clavis N.T.p. 438 b.
[2] I cannot (as some writers do) see any irony in the expression.

[3] Vol. i. p. 560.
[4] In the Greek, ver. 33 begins with 'A Samaritan, however,' to emphasise the contrast to the priest and Levite.

'set' (lifted) him on his own beast, he walked by his side, and
brought him to one of those houses of rest and entertainment, whose
designation (πανδοχεῖον) has passed into Rabbinic language (פונדקא).
These khans, or hostelries, by the side of unfrequented roads, afforded
free lodgment to the traveller. But generally they also offered
entertainment, in which case, of course, the host, commonly a non-
Israelite, charged for the victuals supplied to man or beast, or for the
care taken. In the present instance the Samaritan seems himself to
have tended the wounded man all that evening. But even thus his
care did not end. The next morning, before continuing his journey,
he gave to the host two dinars—about one shilling and threepence of
our money, the amount of a labourer's wages for two days,[a]—as it
were, two days' wages for his care of him, with this provision, that if
any further expense were incurred, either because the wounded man
was not sufficiently recovered to travel, or else because something
more had been supplied to him, the Good Samaritan would pay it
when he next came that way.

[a] St. Matt. xx. 2

So far the Parable: its lesson 'the lawyer' is made himself to
enunciate. 'Which of these three seems to thee to have become
neighbour of him that fell among the robbers?' Though unwilling
to take the hated name of Samaritan on his lips, especially as the
meaning of the Parable and its anti-Rabbinic bearing were so evident,
the 'lawyer' was obliged to reply, 'He that showed mercy on him,'
when the Saviour finally answered, 'Go, and do thou likewise.'

Some further lessons may be drawn. The Parable implies not a
mere enlargement of the Jewish ideas, but a complete change of them.
It is truly a Gospel-Parable, for the whole old relationship of mere
duty is changed into one of love. Thus, matters are placed on an
entirely different basis from that of Judaism. The question now is
not 'Who is my neighbour?' but 'Whose neighbour am I?' The
Gospel answers the question of duty by pointing us to love. Wouldst
thou know who is thy neighbour? Become a neighbour to all by the
utmost service thou canst do them in their need. And so the Gospel
would not only abolish man's enmity, but bridge over man's separation. Thus is the Parable truly Christian, and, more than this, points
up to Him Who, in our great need, became Neighbour to us, even at
the cost of all He had. And from Him, as well as by His Word, are
we to learn our lesson of love.

2. The Parable which follows in St. Luke's narrative[b] seems
closely connected with that just commented upon. It is also a story
of a good neighbour who gives in our need, but presents another

[b] St. Luke xi. 5-13

BOOK
IV

ver. 1

ver. 8

aspect of the truth to which the Parable of the Good Samaritan ha
pointed. Love bends to our need: this is the objective manifestatio
of the Gospel. Need looks up to love, and by its cry elicits th
boon which it seeks. And this is the subjective experience of th
Gospel. The one underlies the story of the first Parable, the othe
that of the second.

Some such internal connection between the two Parables seems
indeed, indicated even by the loose manner in which this secon
Parable is strung to the request of some disciples to be taught wha
to pray.ᵃ Like the Parable of the ' Good Samaritan,' it is typical, an
its application would be the more felt, that it not only points to a
exemplification, but appeals to every man's conciousness of what hin
self would do in certain given circumstances. The latter are as follows
A man has a friend wno, long after nightfall, unexpectedly comes t
him from a journey. He has nothing in the house, yet he must pr
vide for his need, for hospitality demands it. Accordingly, though i
be so late, he goes to his friend and neighbour to ask him for thre
loaves, stating the case. On the other hand, the friend so asked re
fuses, since, at that late hour, he has retired to bed with his children
and to grant his request would imply not only inconvenience t
himself, but the disturbing of the whole household. The main cir
cumstances therefore are: Sudden, unthought-of sense of imperativ
need, obliging to make what seems an unseasonable and unreasonabl
request, which, on the face of it, offers difficulties and has no clain
upon compliance. It is, therefore, not ordinary but, so to speak
extraordinary prayer, which is here alluded to.

To return to the Parable: the question (abruptly broken off fron
the beginning of the Parable in ver. 5), is what each of us would d
in the circumstances just detailed. The answer is implied in wha
follows.ᵇ It points to continued importunity, which would at las
obtain what it needs. ' I tell you, even if he will not give him
rising up, because he is his friend, yet at least ¹ on account of hi
importunity, he will rise up and give him as many as he needeth.
This literal rendering will, it is hoped, remove some of the seemin
difficulties of the Parable. It is a gross misunderstanding to describ
it as presenting a *mechanical* view of prayer: as if it implied, eithe
that God was unwilling to answer; or else, that prayer, otherwis
unheard, would be answered merely for its importunity. It must b
remembered, that he who is within is a friend, and that, under ordi

---

¹ διά γε, *Goebel,* ad loc.

nary circumstances, he would at once have complied with the request.
But, in this case, there were special difficulties, which are represented
as very great; it is midnight; he has retired to bed, and with his
children; the door is locked. And the lesson is, that where, for
some reasons, there are, or seem, special difficulties to an answer to
our prayers (it is very late, the door is no longer open, the children
have already been gathered in), the .importunity arising from the
sense of our absolute need, and the knowledge that He is our Friend,
and that He has bread, will ultimately prevail. The difficulty is not
as to the giving, but as to the giving *then*—'rising up,' and this is
overcome by perseverance, so that (to return to the Parable), if he
will not rise up because he is his friend, yet at least he will rise
because of his importunity, and not only give him 'three' loaves,
but, in general, ' as many as he needeth.'

So important is the teaching of this Parable, that Christ makes
detailed application of it. In the circumstances described a man
would persevere with his friend, and in the end succeed. And,
similarly, the Lord bids us 'ask,' and that earnestly and believingly;
'seek,' and that energetically and instantly; 'knock,' and that
intently and loudly. Ask—He is a Friend, and we shall 'receive;'
'seek,' it is there, and we shall 'find; '' knock,'—our need is absolute,
and it shall be opened to us. But the emphasis of the Parable and its
lesson are in the word 'every one' ($\pi \tilde{\alpha} s$). Not only this or that, but
'*every one*,' shall so experience it. The word points to the special
difficulties that may be in the way of answer to prayer—the difficulties of the 'rising up,' which have been previously indicated in the
Parable. These are met by perseverance which indicates the reality
of our need ('ask'), the reality of our belief that the supply is there
('seek '), and the intensity and energy of our spiritual longing
('knock '). Such importunity applies to '*every one*,' whoever he be,
and whatever the circumstances which would seem to render his prayer
specially difficult of answer. Though he feel that he has not and
needs, he 'asks; ' though he have lost—time, opportunities, mercies—
he 'seeks; ' though the door seem shut, he 'knocks.' Thus the Lord
is helper to 'every one; ' but, as for us, let us learn the lesson from
what we ourselves would do in analogous circumstances.

Nay, more than this, God will not deceive by the appearance of
what is not reality. He will even give the greatest gift. The Parabolic relation is now not that of friends, but of father and son. If
the son asks for bread, will the father give what seems such, but
is only a stone? If he asks for a fish, will he tender him what

looks such, but is a serpent? If he seek an egg, will he hand to him what breeds a scorpion? The need, the hunger, of the child will not, in answer to its prayer, receive at the Father's Hands, that which seems, but gives not the reality of satisfaction—rather is poison. Let us draw the inference. Such is our conduct—how much more shall our heavenly Father give His Holy Spirit to them that ask Him. That gift will not disappoint by the appearance of what is not reality; it will not deceive either by the promise of what it does not give, or by giving what would prove fatal. As we follow Christ's teaching, we ask for the Holy Spirit; and the Holy Spirit, in leading us to Him, leads us into all truth, to all life, and to what satisfies all need.

CHAPTER XVI.

THE THREE PARABLES OF WARNING: TO THE INDIVIDUAL, TO THE NATION,
AND TO THE THEOCRACY—THE FOOLISH RICH MAN—THE BARREN FIG-
TREE—THE GREAT SUPPER.

(St. Luke xii. 13-21; xiii. 6-9; xiv. 16-24.)

THE three Parables, which successively follow in St. Luke's Gospel, may generally be designated as those 'of warning.' This holds specially true of the last two of them, which refer to the civil and the ecclesiastical polity of Israel. Each of the three Parables is set in an historical frame, having been spoken under circumstances which gave occasion for such illustration.

1. *The Parable of the foolish rich man.*[a] It appears, that some one among them that listened to Jesus conceived the idea, that the authority of the Great Rabbi of Nazareth might be used for his own selfish purposes. This was all he had profited, that it seemed to open possibilities of gain—stirred thoughts of covetousness. But other inferences also come to us. Evidently, Christ must have attracted and deeply moved multitudes, or His interposition would not have been sought; and, equally evidently, what He preached had made upon this man the impression, that he might possibly enlist Him as his champion. The presumptive evidence which it affords as regards the effect and the subject-matter of Christ's preaching is exceedingly interesting. On the other hand, Christ had not only no legal authority for interfering, but the Jewish law of inheritance was so clearly defined, and, we may add, so just, that if this person had any just or good cause, there could have been no need for appealing to Jesus. Hence it must have been 'covetousness,' in the strictest sense, which prompted it—perhaps, a wish to have, besides his own share as a younger brother, half of that additional portion which, by law, came to the eldest son of the family.[b][1] Such an attempt for covetous purposes to make use of the pure unselfish preaching of love, and to

Marginal notes:

CHAP.
XVI

[a] St. Luke xii. 13-21

[b] Bekhor viii. 2; Baba B. viii.

---

[7] Cases might, however, arise when the claim was doubtful, and then the inheritance would be divided (Baba B. ix. 2). The double part of an eldest son was computed in the following manner. If five sons were left, the property was divided into six parts, and the eldest son had two parts, or one-third of the property. If nine sons were left, the property was divided into ten parts, and the eldest son

derive profit from His spiritual influence, accounts for the severity with which Christ rejected the demand, although, as we judge, He would, under any circumstances, have refused to interfere in purely civil disputes, with which the established tribunals were sufficient to deal.

All this accounts for the immediate reference of our Lord to *covetousness*, the folly of which He showed by this almost self-evident principle, too often forgotten—that 'not in the super-abounding to any one [not in that wherein he has more than enough] consisteth his life, from the things which he possesseth.'[1] In other words, that part of the things which a man possesseth by which his life is sustained, consists not in what is superabundant ; his life is sustained by that which he needs and uses; the rest, the super-abundance, forms no part of his life, and may, perhaps, never be of use to him.   Why, then, be covetous, or long for more than we need ? And this folly also involves danger.   For, the love of these things will engross mind and heart, and care about them will drive out higher thoughts and aims.   The moral as regarded the Kingdom of God, and the warning not to lose it for thought of what 'perisheth with the using,' are obvious.

The Parable itself bears on all these points.   It consists of two parts, of which the first shows the folly, the second the sin and danger, of that care for what is beyond our present need, which is the characteristic of covetousness.   The rich man is surveying his land, which is bearing plentifully—evidently beyond its former yield, since the old provision for storing the corn appears no longer sufficient. It seems implied—or, we may at least conjecture—that this was not only due to the labour and care of the master, but that he had devoted to it his whole thought and energy.   More than this, it seems as if, in the calculations which he now made, he looked into the future, and saw there progressive increase and riches.   As yet, the harvest was not reaped ; but he was already considering what to do, reckoning upon the riches that would come to him.   And so he resolved to pull down the old, and build larger barns, where he would store his future possessions.   From one aspect there would have been nothing wrong in an act of almost necessary foresight—only great folly in thinking, and speaking, and making plans, as if that were already absolutely his which might never come to him at all, which,

had two parts, or a fifth of the property. But there were important limitations to this.   Thus, the law did not apply to a posthumous son, nor yet in regard to the mother's property, nor to any increase or gain that might have accrued since the father's death.   For a brief sum-mary, see *Saalschütz*, Mos. Recht, pp. 820 &c.

[7] So literally.

was still unreaped, and might be garnered long after he was dead. His life was not sustained by that part of his possessions which were the 'superabounding.' But to this folly was also added sin. For, God was not in all his thoughts. In all his plans for the future— and it was his folly to make such absolutely—he thought not of God. His whole heart was set on the acquisition of earthly riches—not on the service of God. He remembered not his responsibility; all that he had, was for himself, and absolutely his own to batten upon; 'Soul, thou hast much goods laid up for many years; take thine ease, eat, drink, be merry.' He did not even remember, that there was a God Who might cut short his years.

So had he spoken in his heart—proud, selfish, self-indulgent, God-forgetting—as he looked forth upon what was not yet, even in an inferior sense, his own, but which he already treated as such, and that in the most absolute sense. And now comes the quick, sharp, contrast, which is purposely introduced quite abruptly. 'But God said unto Him'—not by revelation nor through inward presentiment, but, with awful suddenness, in those unspoken words of fact which cannot be gainsaid or answered: 'Thou fool! this very night'— which follows on thy plans and purposings—'thy soul is required of thee. But, the things which thou hast prepared, whose shall they be?' Here, with the obvious evidence of the *folly* of such state of mind, the Parable breaks off. Its *sinfulness*—nay, and beyond this negative aspect of it, the wisdom of righteousness in laying up the good treasure which cannot be taken from us, appears in this con- cluding remark of Christ—'So is he who layeth up treasure (trea- sureth) for himself, and is not rich towards God.'

It was a barbed arrow, we might say, out of the Jewish quiver, but directed by the Hand of the Lord. For, we read in the Talmud [a] that a Rabbi told his disciples, 'Repent the day before thy death;' and when his disciples asked him: 'Does a man know the day of his death?' he replied, that on that very ground he should repent to-day, lest he should die to-morrow. And so would all his days be days of repentance. Again, the Son of Sirach wrote: [b] 'There is that waxeth rich by his wariness and pinching, and this is the portion of his reward; whereas he saith, I have found rest, and now will eat continually of my goods; and yet he knoweth not what time shall come upon him, and that he must leave those things to others, and die.' But we sadly miss in all this the spiritual application which Christ made. Similarly, the Talmud,[c] by a play on the last word (חלד), in the first verse of Psalm xlix., compares man to the weasel,

[a] Shabb. 153 a, line 16 &c. from top

[b] Ecclus. xi. 18, 19

[c] Jer. Shabb. 14 c, top

BOOK
IV
⌣⌣⌣

a Debar. R.
9, ed.
Warsh. p.
19 b, line
6 from top
and
onwards

which laboriously gathers and deposits, not knowing for whom, while the Midrash[a] tells a story, how, when a Rabbi returned from a feast where the Host had made plans of storing his wine for a future occasion, the Angel of Death appeared to him, grieved for man, 'since you say, thus and thus shall we do in the future, while no one knoweth how soon he shall be called to die,' as would be the case with the host of that evening, who would die after the lapse of thirty days. But once more we ask, where is the spiritual application, such as was made by Christ? So far from it, the Midrash adds, that when the Rabbi challenged the Angel to show him the time of his own death, he received this reply, that he had not dominion over the like of him, since God took pleasure in their good works, and added to their days!

2. The special warning intended to be conveyed by the Parable of *the Barren Fig-tree*[b] sufficiently appears from the context. As explained in a previous chapter,[1] the Lord had not only corrected the erroneous interpretation which the Jews were giving to certain recent national occurrences, but pointed them to this higher moral of all such events, that, unless speedy national repentance followed, the whole people would perish. This Parable offers not merely an exemplification of this general prediction of Christ, but sets before us what underlies it: Israel in its relation to God; the need of repentance; Israel's danger; the nature of repentance, and its urgency; the relation of Christ to Israel; the Gospel; and the final judgment on impenitence.

b St. Luke
xiii. 6–9

As regards the details of this Parable, we mark that the fig-tree had been specially planted by the owner in his vineyard, which was the choicest situation. This, we know, was not unusual. Fig-trees, as well as palm and olive-trees, were regarded as so valuable, that to cut them down if they yielded even a small measure of fruit, was popularly deemed to deserve death at the Hand of God.[c] Ancient Jewish writings supply interesting particulars of this tree and its culture. According to *Josephus*, in favoured localities the ripe fruit hung on the tree for ten months of the year,[d] the two barren months being probably April and May, before the first of the three crops which it bore had ripened. The first figs[e] ripened towards the end of June, sometimes earlier. The second, which are those now dried and exported, ripened in August; the third, which were small and of comparatively little value, in September, and often hung all winter on the trees. A species (the *Benoth Shuach*) is mentioned, of which the fruit required three years for ripening.[f] The fig-tree was

c Baba K.
91 b

d War. iii.
10, 8

e Phaggim,
Shebh. iv. 7

f Shebh. v 1

---

[1] See ch. xiii. of this Book.

regarded as the most fruitful of all trees.[a] On account of its repeated crops, it was declared not subject to the ordinance which
enjoined that fruit should be left in the corners for the poor.[b] Its
artificial inoculation was known.[c] The practice mentioned in the
Parable, of digging about the tree (מעדרין), and dunging it (מזבלין),
is frequently mentioned in Rabbinic writings, and by the same
designations. Curiously, *Maimonides* mentions three years as the
utmost limit within which a tree should bear fruit in the land
of Israel.[d] Lastly, as trees were regarded as by their roots under-
mining and deteriorating the land,[e] a barren tree would be of threefold
disadvantage: it would yield no fruit; it would fill valuable space,
which a fruit-bearer might occupy; and it would needlessly deteriorate the land. Accordingly, while it was forbidden to destroy fruit-
bearing trees,[f] it would, on the grounds above stated, be duty to cut
down a 'barren' or 'empty' tree (*Ilan seraq*[g]).

These particulars will enable us more fully to understand the
details of the Parable. Allegorically, the fig-tree served in the Old
Testament as emblem of the Jewish nation[h]—in the Talmud, rather
as that of Israel's lore, and hence of the leaders and the pious
of the people.[i] The vineyard is in the New Testament the symbol
of the Kingdom of God, as distinct from the nation of Israel.[k]
Thus far, then, the Parable may be thus translated: God called Israel
as a nation, and planted it in the most favoured spot: as a fig-tree
in the vineyard of His own Kingdom. 'And He came seeking,' as
He had every right to do, 'fruit thereon, and found none.' It was
the third year[1] that He had vainly looked for fruit, when He turned
to His Vinedresser—the Messiah, to Whom the vineyard is committed
as its King—with this direction: 'Cut it down—why doth it also
deteriorate the soil?' It is barren, though in the best position; as
a fig-tree it ought to bear figs, and here the best; it fills the place
which a good tree might occupy; and besides, it deteriorates[2] the
soil (literally: מחליד את הקרקע). And its three years' barrenness has
established (as before explained) its utterly hopeless character. Then
it is that the Divine Vinedresser, in His infinite compassion, pleads,
and with far deeper reality than either Abraham or Moses could
have entreated, for the fig-tree which Himself had planted and
tended, that it should be spared 'this year also,' 'until then that I
shall dig about it, and dung it,'—till He labour otherwise than before,

CHAP.
XVI

[a] Shebh. i, 3
[b] Peah i. 4
[c] Shebh. ii.
5

[d] Moreh
Nebhukh.
iii. 37, apud
Wetstein,
ad loc.
[e] Baba B.
19 b

[f] Deut. xx,
19; Baba
K. 91 b; 92 a
[g] Kil. vi. 5

[h] Joel. i. 7

[i] Ber. 57 a;
Mikr. on
Cant. i. 1
[k] St. Matt.
xx. 1 &c.;
xxi. 33 &c.
In Jewish
thought
the two
were
scarcely
separated.

---

[1] Not after three years, but evidently
in the third year, when the third year's
crop should have appeared.

[2] καταργεῖ. *Grimm* renders the
word, *enervo, sterilem reddo.*

BOOK
IV

even by His Own Presence and Words, nay, by laying to its roots His most precious Blood. ' And if then it bear fruit '—here the text abruptly breaks off, as implying that in such case it would, of course, be allowed to remain; ' but if not, *then* against [1] the future (coming) *year* shalt thou cut it down.' The Parable needs no further commentation.[2] In the words of a recent writer: [3] ' Between the tree and the axe nothing intervenes but the intercession of the Gardener, Who would make a last effort, and even His petition applies only to a short and definite period, and, in case it pass without result, this petition itself merges in the proposal, " But if not, then cut it down." ' How speedily and terribly the warning came true, not only students of history, but all men and in all ages have been made to know. Of the lawfulness of a further application of this Parable to all kindred circumstances of nation, community, family, nay, even of individuals, it is not necessary to speak.

ᵃ St. Luke
xiv. 16–24.

3. The third Parable of warning—that of *the Great Supper* ᵃ— refers not to the political state of Israel, but to their ecclesiastical *status*, and their continuance as the possessors and representatives of the Kingdom of God. It was spoken after the return of Jesus from the Feast of the Dedication, and therefore carries us beyond the point in this history which we have reached. Accordingly, the attendant circumstances will be explained in the sequel. In regard to these we only note, how appropriately such a warning of Israel's spiritual danger, in consequence of their hardness of heart, misrepresentation, and perversion of God's truth, would come at a Sabbath-meal of the Pharisees, when they lay in wait against Him, and He first challenged their externalising of God's Day and Law to the subversion of its real meaning, and then rebuked the self-assertion, pride, and utter want of all real love on the part of these leaders of Israel.

What led up to the Parable of ' the Great Supper' happened after these things: after His healing of the man with the dropsy in sight of them all on the Sabbath, after His twofold rebuke of their perversion of the Sabbath-Law, and of those marked characteristics of Pharisaism, which showed how far they were from bringing forth fruit worthy of the Kingdom, and how, instead of representing, they mis-

---

[1] εἰς τὸ μέλλον. *Goebel* points to a similiar use of εἰς in St. Luke i. 20; Acts xiii. 42.

[2] Dean *Plumptre* regards the fig-tree as the symbol of a soul making fruitless profession; the vineyard as that of Israel. For homiletical purposes, or for practical application, this is, of course, perfectly fair; but not in strict exegesis. To waive other and obvious objections, it were to introduce modern, Christian ideas, which would have been wholly unintelligible to Christ's hearers.

[3] *Goebel.*

represented the Kingdom, and were utterly unfit ever to do otherwise.[a] The Lord had spoken of making a feast, not for one's kindred, nor for the rich—whether such outwardly, or mentally and spritually from the standpoint of the Pharisees—but for the poor and afflicted. This would imply true spirituality, because that fellowship of giving, which descends to others in order to raise them as brethren, not condescends, in order to be raised by them as their Master and Superior.[b] And He had concluded with these words: 'And thou shalt be blessed—because they have not to render back again to thee, for it shall be rendered back to thee again in the Resurrection of the Just.'[c]

It was this last clause—but separated, in true Pharisaic spirit, from that which had preceded, and indicated the motive—on which one of those present now commented, probably with a covert, perhaps a provocative, reference to what formed the subject of Christ's constant teaching: 'Blessed whoso shall eat bread in the Kingdom of Heaven.' An expression this, which to the Pharisee meant the common Jewish expectancy of a great feast [1] at the beginning of the Messianic Kingdom. So far he had rightly understood, and yet he had entirely misunderstood, the words of Christ. Jesus had, indeed, referred to the future retribution of (not, *for*) deeds of love, among which He had named as an instance, suggested by the circumstances, a feast for, or rather brotherly love and fellowship towards, the poor and suffering. But although the Pharisee referred to the Messianic Day, his words show that he did not own Jesus as the Messiah. Whether or not it was the object of his exclamation, as sometimes religious commonplaces or platitudes are in our days, to interrupt the course of Christ's rebukes, or, as before hinted, to provoke Him to unguarded speech, must be left undetermined. What is chiefly apparent is, that this Pharisee separated what Christ said about the blessings of the first Resurrection from that with which He had connected them—we do not say as their condition, but as logically their moral antecedent: viz., love, in opposition to self-assertion and self-seeking. The Pharisee's words imply that, like his class, he, at any rate, fully expected to share in these blessings, as a matter of course, and because he was a Pharisee. Thus to leave out Christ's anteceding words was not only to set them aside, but to pervert His saying, and to place the blessedness of the future on the very opposite basis from that on which Christ had rested it.

CHAP.
XVI

[a] St. Luke
xiv. 1-11

[b] vv. 12, 13

[b] St. Luke
xiv. 14

---

[1] The expression 'eating bread' is a well-known Hebraism, used both in the Old Testament and in Rabbinic writings for taking part in a meal.

BOOK
IV

ᵃ ver. 16

ᵇ Is. xxv. 6, 7

Accordingly, it was to this man personally ᵃ that the Parable was addressed.

There can be no difficulty in understanding the main ideas underlying the Parable. The man who made the 'Great Supper'[1] was He Who had, in the Old Testament, prepared ' a feast of fat things.' ᵇ The 'bidding many' preceded the actual announcement of the day and hour of the feast. We understand by it a preliminary intimation of the feast then preparing, and a general invitation of the guests, who were the chief people in the city; for, as we shall presently see, the scene is laid in a city. This general announcement was made in the Old Testament institutions and prophecies, and the guests bidden were those in the city, the chief men—not the ignorant and those out of the way, but the men who knew, and read, and expounded these prophecies. At last the preparations were ended, and the Master sent out His Servant, not necessarily to be understood of any one individual in particular—such as John the Baptist —but referring to whomsoever He would employ in His Service for that purpose. It was to intimate to the persons formerly bidden, that everything was now ready. Then it was that, however differing in their special grounds for it, or expressing it with more or less courtesy, they were all at one in declining to come. The feast, to which they had been bidden some time before, and to which they had apparently agreed to come (at least, this was implied), was, when actually announced as ready, not what they had expected, at any rate not what they regarded as more desirable than what they had, and must give up in order to come to it. For—and this seems one of the principal points in the Parable—to come to that feast, to enter into the Kingdom, implies the giving up of something that seems if not necessary yet most desirable, and the enjoyment of which appears only reasonable. Be it possession, business, and pleasure (*Stier*), or the priesthood, the magistracy, and the people generally (St. *Augustine*), or the priesthood, the Pharisees, and the Scribes, or the Pharisees, the Scribes, and the self-righteously virtuous, with reference to whom we are specially to think of the threefold excuse, the main point lies in this, that, when the time came, they all refused to enter in, each having some valid and reasonable excuse. But the ultimate ground of their refusal was, that they felt no real desire, and saw nothing attractive in such a feast; had no real reverence for the host; in short, that to them it was not a feast at all, but something much less to be desired than what they had, and

---

[1] Rather the *principal meal*, which was towards evening.

would have been obliged to give up, if they had complied with the invitation.

CHAP.
XVI

Then let the feast—for it was prepared by the goodness and liberality of the Host—be for those who were in need of it, and to whom it would be a feast: the poor and those afflicted—the maimed, and blind, and lame, on whom those great citizens who had been first bidden would look down. This, with reference to, and in higher spiritual explanation of, what Christ had previously said about bidding such to our feasts of fellowship and love.[a] Accordingly, the Servant is now directed to 'go out quickly into the (larger) streets and the (narrow) lanes of the City,—a trait which shows that the scene is laid in 'the City,' the professed habitation of God. The importance of this circumstance is evident. It not only explains who the first bidden chief citizens were, but also that these poor were the despised ignorant, and the maimed, lame, and blind—such as the publicans and sinners. These are they in 'the streets' and 'lanes;' and the Servant is directed, not only to invite, but to 'bring them in,' as otherwise they might naturally shrink from coming to such a feast. But even so, 'there is yet room;' for the great Lord of the house has, in His great liberality, prepared a very great feast for very many. And so the Servant is once more sent, so that the Master's 'house may be filled.' But now he is bidden to 'go out,' outside the City, outside the Theocracy, 'into the highways and hedges,' to those who travel along the world's great highway, or who have fallen down weary, and rest by its hedges; into the busy, or else weary, heathen world. This reference to the heathen world is the more apparent that, according to the Talmud,[b] there were commonly no hedges round the fields of the Jews. And this time the direction to the Servant is not, as in regard to those naturally bashful outcasts of the City—who would scarcely venture to the great house—to 'bring them in,' but 'constrain' [without a pronoun] 'to come in,' Not certainly as indicating their resistance and implying force,[1] but as the moral constraint of earnest, pressing invitation, coupled with assurance both of the reality of the feast and of their welcome to it. For, these wanderers on the world's highway had, before the Servant came to them, not known anything of the Master of the house, and all was quite new and unexpected. Their being invited by a Lord Whom they had not known, perhaps never heard of before, to a City in which they were strangers, and to a feast for

a St. Luke
xiv. 13

b B. Bathr
4 a, lines 8
10 from
bottom

---

[1] It is most sad, and seems almost incredible, that this 'constrain to come in' has from of old been quoted in justification of religious persecution.

which—as wayfarers, or as resting by the hedges, or else as working within their enclosure—they were wholly unprepared, required special urgency, ‘a constraining,’ to make them either believe in it, or come to it from where the messengers found them, and that with-out preparing for it by dress or otherwise. And so the house would be filled!

Here the Parable abruptly breaks off. What follows are the words of our Lord in explanation and application of it to the company then present: ‘For I say unto you, that none of those men which were bidden shall taste of My supper.’ And this was the final answer to this Pharisee and to those with him at that table, and to all such perversion of Christ’s Words and misapplication of God’s Promises as he and they were guilty of.

CHAPTER XVII.

THE THREE PARABLES OF THE GOSPEL: OF THE RECOVERY OF THE
LOST—OF THE LOST SHEEP, THE LOST DRACHM, THE LOST SON.

(St. Luke xv.)

A SIMPLE perusal of the three Parables, grouped together in the fifteenth chapter of St. Luke's Gospel, will convince us of their connection. Although they treat of 'repentance,' we can scarcely call them 'The Parables of Repentance;' for, except in the last of them, the aspect of repentance is subordinate to that of restoration, which is the moral effect of repentance. They are rather peculiarly Gospel-Parables 'of the recovery of the lost:' in the first instance, through the unwearied labour; in the second, through the anxious care, of the owner; and in the third Parable, through the never-ceasing love of the Father.

CHAP.
XVII

Properly to understand these Parables, the circumstance which elicited them must be kept in view. As Jesus preached the Gospel of God's call, not to those who had, as they imagined, prepared themselves for the Kingdom by study and good works, but as that to a door open, and a welcome free to all, 'all the publicans and sinners were [constantly] drawing near to Him.' It has formerly been shown,[1] that the Jewish teaching concerning repentance was quite other than, nay, contrary to, that of Christ. Theirs was not a Gospel to the lost: they had nothing to say to sinners. They called upon them to 'do penitence,' and then Divine Mercy, or rather Justice, would have its reward for the penitent. Christ's Gospel was to the lost as such. It told them of forgiveness, of what the Saviour was doing, and the Father purposed and felt for them; and that, not in the future and as reward of their penitence, but now in the immediate present. From what we know of the Pharisees, we can scarcely wonder that 'they were murmuring at Him, saying, This man receiveth "sinners," and eateth with them. Whether or not Christ

---

[1] See Book III. ch. xvii.

BOOK
IV

ᵃ St. Matt.
ix. 10, 11

had on this, as on other occasions,ᵃ joined at a meal with such persons—which, of course, in the eyes of the Pharisees would have been a great aggravation to His offence—their charge was so far true, that ' this One,' in contrariety to the principles and practice of Rabbinism, ' received sinners ' as such, and consorted with them. Nay, there was even more than they charged Him with: He not only received them when they sought Him, but He sought them, so as to bring them to Him; not, indeed, that they might remain ' sinners,' but that, by seeking and finding them, they might be restored to the Kingdom, and there might be joy in heaven over them. And so these are truly Gospel-Parables, although presenting only some aspects of it.

Besides their subject-matter, these three Parables have some other points in common. Two things are here of chief interest. They all proceed on the view that the work of the Father and of Christ, as regards ' the Kingdom,' is the same; that Christ was doing the work of the Father, and that they who know Christ know the Father also. That work was the restoration of the lost; Christ had come to do it, and it was the longing of the Father to welcome the lost home again. Further, and this is only second in importance, the lost was still God's property; and he who had wandered farthest was a child of the Father, and considered as such. And, although this may, in a wider sense, imply the general propriety of Christ in all men, and the universal Fatherhood of God, yet, remembering that this Parable was spoken to Jews, we, to whom these Parables now come, can scarcely be wrong in thinking, as we read them, with special thankfulness of our Christian privileges, as by Baptism numbered among the sheep of His Flock, the treasure of His Possession, and the children of His Home.[1]

In other particulars there are, however, differences, all the more marked that they are so finely shaded. These concern the *lost*, their *restoration*, and its *results*.

1. *The Parable of the Lost Sheep.*—At the outset we remark that this Parable and the next, that of the *Lost Drachm*. are intended as an answer to the Pharisees. Hence they are addressed to them: ' What man of you?'ᵇ ' or what woman?'ᶜ just as His late rebuke to them on the subject of their Sabbath-cavils had been couched:

ᵇ St. Luke
xv. 4
ᶜ ver. 8

---

[1] The only other alternative would seem, if one were to narrow the underlying ideas in a strictly Predestinarian sense. But this seems not only incompatible with the third Parable, where all turns on personal resolve, but runs contrary to the whole spirit of these Parables, which is not of the exclusion of any, but of the widest inclusion.

Which of you shall have a son or an ox fallen into a well?'[a] Not CHAP. XVII so the last Parable, of the *Lost Son*, in which He passed from defence, or rather explanation, of His conduct, to its higher reason, showing that He was doing the work of the Father.   Hence, while the element of comparison (with that which had not been lost) appears in most detailed form in the first Parable, it is generalised in the second, and wholly omitted in the third.

[a] St. Luke xiv. 5

Other differences have to be marked in the Parables themselves. In the first Parable (that of the *Lost Sheep*) the main interest centres in the *lost*; in the second (that of the *Lost Drachm*), in the *search*; in the third, in the *restoration*.   And although in the third Parable the Pharisees are not addressed, there is the highest personal application to them in the words which the Father speaks to the elder son—an application, not so much of warning, as of loving correction and entreaty, and which seems to imply, what otherwise these Parables convey, that at least these Pharisees had 'murmured,' not so much from bitter hostility to Christ, as from spiritual ignorance and misunderstanding.

Again, these Parables, and especially that of the Lost Sheep, are evidently connected with the preceding series, that 'of warnings.' The last of these showed how the poor, the blind, lame, and maimed, nay, even the wanderers on the world's highway, were to be the guests at the heavenly Feast.   And this, not only in the future, and after long and laborious preparation, but now, through the agency of the Saviour.   As previously stated, Rabbinism placed acceptance at the end of repentance, and made it its wages.   And this, because it knew not, nor felt the power of sin, nor yet the free grace of God. The Gospel places acceptance at the beginning of repentance, and as the free gift of God's love.   And this, because it not only knows the power of sin, but points to a Saviour, provided of God.

The Lost Sheep is only one among a hundred: not a very great loss.   Yet which among us would not, even from the common motives of ownership, leave the ninety-and-nine, and go after it, all the more that it has strayed into the wilderness?   And, to take these Pharisees on their own ground,[1] should not the Christ have done likewise to the straying and almost lost sheep of His own flock? Nay, quite generally and to all time, is this not the very work of the 'Good Shepherd,' and may we not, each of us, thus draw from it

---

[1] There is to some extent a Rabbinic parallel Parable (Ber. R. 86, ed. Warsh. p. 154 *b*, about the middle), where one who is driving twelve animals laden with wine, leaves the eleven and follows the twelfth into the shop of a Gentile, for fear that the wine which it bears might be mixed there.

BOOK
IV

precious comfort? As we think of it, we remember that it is natural for the foolish sheep so to wander and stray. And we think not only of those sheep which Jewish pride and superciliousness had left to go astray, but of our own natural tendency to wander. And we recall the saying of St. Peter, which, no doubt, looked back upon this Parable: 'Ye were as sheep going astray; but are now returned unto the Shepherd and Bishop of your souls.'[a] It is not difficult in imagination to follow the Parabolic picture: how in its folly and ignorance the sheep strayed further and further, and at last was lost in solitude and among stony places; how the shepherd followed and found it, weary and footsore; and then with tender care lifted it on his shoulder, and carried it home, gladsome that he had found the lost. And not only this, but when, after long absence, he returned home with his found sheep, that now nestled close to its Saviour, he called together his friends, and bade them rejoice with him over the erst lost and now found treasure.

*1 Pet. ii.25

It needs not, and would only diminish the pathos of this exquisite Parable, were we to attempt interpreting its details. They apply wherever and to whatever they can be applied. Of these three things we think: of the *lost sheep*; of the *Good Shepherd*, seeking, finding, bearing, rejoicing; and of the *sympathy* of all who are truly friends—like-minded with Him. These, then, are the emblems of heavenly things. In heaven—oh, how different the feeling from that of Pharisaism! View 'the flock' as do the Pharisees, and divide them into those who need and who need not repentance, the 'sinners' and the 'righteous,' as regards man's application of the Law—does not this Parable teach us that in heaven there shall be joy over the 'sinner that repenteth' more than over the 'ninety-and-nine' 'righteous,' which 'have not need of repentance'? And to mark the terrible contrast between the teaching of Christ and that of the Pharisees; to mark also, how directly from heaven must have been the message of Jesus, and how poor sinners must have felt it such, we put down in all its nakedness the message which Pharisaism brought to the lost. Christ said to them: 'There is joy in heaven over one sinner that repenteth.' Pharisaism said—and we quote here literally—'There is joy before God when those who provoke Him perish from the world.'[b]

b Siphre,
ed. Fried-
mann, p. 37
a, line 13
from top

2. In proceeding to the second Parable, that of *the Lost Drachm*, we must keep in mind that in the first the danger of being lost arose from the *natural tendency* of the sheep to wander.[1] In the second

---

[1] In St. Matt. xviii. 12–14, the same Parable is used, but with different appli-cation—not as here to the loss, but to what men might deem the smallness of the

Parable it is no longer our natural tendency to which our loss is attributable. The drachm (about $7\frac{1}{2}d$. of our money) has been lost, as the woman, its owner, was using or counting her money. The loss is the more sensible, as it is one out of only ten, which constitute the owner's property. But *it is still in the house*—not like the sheep that had gone astray—only covered by the dust that is continually accumulating from the work and accidents around. And so it is more and more likely to be buried under it, or swept into chinks and corners, and less and less likely to be found as time passes. But the woman lights a lamp, sweeps the house, and seeks diligently, *till* she has found it. And then she calleth together those around, and bids them rejoice with her over the finding of the lost part of her possessions. And so there is joy in the presence of the Angels over one sinner that repenteth. The comparison with others that need not such is now dropped, because, whereas formerly the sheep had strayed—though from the frowardness of its nature—here the money had simply been lost, fallen among the dust that accumulates—practically, was no longer money, or of use; became covered, hidden, and was in danger of being for ever out of sight, not serviceable, as it was intended to be and might have been.

We repeat, the interest of this Parable centres in the *search*, and the loss is caused, not by natural tendency, but by surrounding circumstances, which cover up the bright silver, hide it, and render it useless as regards its purpose, and lost to its owner.

3. If it has already appeared that the two first Parables are not merely a repetition, in different form, of the same thought, but represent two different aspects and causes of the 'being lost'— the essential difference between them appears even more clearly in the third Parable, that of *the Lost Son*. Before indicating it in detail, we may mark the similarity in form, and the contrast in spirit, of analogous Rabbinic Parables. The thoughtful reader will have noted this even in the Jewish parallel to the first Parable,[1] where the reason of the man following the straying animal is Pharisaic fear and distrust, lest the Jewish wine which it carried should become mingled with that of the Gentiles. Perhaps, however, this is a more apt parallel, when the Midrash[a] relates how, [a] on Ex. iii. 1 when Moses fed the sheep of Jethro in the wilderness, and a kid had gone astray, he went after it, and found it drinking at a spring. As he thought it might be weary, he laid it on his shoulder and

loss, with special reference to the command in ver. 10 (ver. 11 in the text of

our A.V. is spurious).
[1] See Note on p. 255 of this chapter.

BOOK
IV

ᵃ Shem. R.
2. ed.
Warsh. p.
7 b, about
the middle
ᵇ on Prov.
ii. 4

ᶜ Midr. on
Cant. i. 1,
ed. Warsh
p. 3 a,
about the
middle

ᵈ Ber. 34 b
about the
middle

ᵉ Is.lxiv. 4

ᶠ Jer. iii. 12
ᵍ Debar. R.
2, on Deut.
iii. 25,
which, in
general,
contains
several re-
ferences to
repent-
ance,
ed. Warsh.
p.7 b, about
the middle

brought it back, when God said that, because he had shown pity on the sheep of a man, He would give him His own sheep, Israel, to feed.ᵃ As a parallel to the second Parable, this may be quoted as similar in form, though very different in spirit, when a Rabbi notes,ᵇ that, if a man had lost a *Sela* (drachm) or anything else of value in his house, he would light ever so many lights (מדליק כמה נרות כמה פתילות) till he had found what provides for only one hour in this world. How much more, then, should he search, as for hidden treasures, for the words of the Law, on which depends the life of this and of the world to come!ᶜ And in regard to the high place which Christ assigned to the repenting sinner, we may note that, according to the leading Rabbis, the penitents would stand nearer to God than the 'perfectly righteous' (צדיקים גמורים), since, in Is. lvii. 19, peace was first bidden to those who had been afar off, and then only to those near. This opinion was, however, not shared by all, and one Rabbi maintained,ᵈ that, while all the prophets had only prophesied with reference to penitents (this had been the sole object of their mission), yet, as regarded the 'perfectly righteous,' ' eye hath not seen' O God, beside Thee, what He hath prepared' for them.ᵉ Lastly, it may, perhaps, be noted, that the expression 'there is joy before Him' (היתה שמחה לפניו) is not uncommon in Jewish writings with reference to events which take place on earth.

To complete these notes, it may be added that, besides illustrations, to which reference will be made in the sequel, Rabbinic tradition supplies a parallel to at least part of the third Parable, that of the Lost Son. It tells us that, while prayer may sometimes find the gate of access closed, it is never shut against repentance, and it introduces a Parable in which a king sends a tutor after his son, who, in his wickedness, had left the palace, with this message: ' Return, my son!' to which the latter replied: 'With what face can I return? I am ashamed!' On which the father sends this message: ' My son, is there a son who is ashamed to return to his father—and shalt thou not return to thy father? Thou shalt return.' So, continues the Midrash, had God sent Jeremiah after Israel in the hour of their sin with the call to return,ᶠ and the comforting reminder that it was to their Father.ᵍ

In the Parable of ' *the Lost Son*,' the main interest centres in his *restoration*. It is not now to the innate tendency of his nature, nor yet to the work and dust in the house that the loss is attributable, but to the personal, free choice of the individual. He does not stray; he does not fall aside—he wilfully departs, and under aggravated circumstances. It is the younger of two sons of a father, who is equally loving to both, and kind even to his hired servants, whose home, moreover, is one not only of sufficiency, but of super-abundance and wealth. The demand which he makes for the 'portion of property falling' to him is founded on the Jewish Law of Inheritance.[1] Presumably, the father had only these two sons. The eldest would receive two portions, the younger the third of all movable property. The father could not have disinherited the younger son, although, if there had been several younger sons, he might have divided the property falling to them as he wished, pro-vided he expressed only his disposition, and did not add that such or such of the children were to have a less share or none at all. On the other hand, a man might, during his lifetime, dispose of all his property by gift, as he chose, to the disadvantage, or even the total loss, of the first-born, or of any other children; nay, he might give all to strangers.[2] In such cases, as, indeed, in regard to all such dis-positions, greater latitude was allowed if the donor was regarded as dangerously ill, than if he was in good health. In the latter case a legal formality of actual seizure required to be gone through. With reference to the two eventualities just mentioned—that of diminishing or taking away the portion of younger children, and the right of gift —the Talmud speaks of Testaments,[3] which bear the name *Diyatiqi*, as in the New Testament.[a] These dispositions might be made either in writing or orally. But if the share of younger children was to be diminished or taken away, the disposition must be made by a person presumably near death (*Shekhibh mera*). But no one in good health (*Bari*) could diminish (except by gift) the legal portion of a younger son.[4]

It thus appears that the younger son was, by law, fully entitled to his share of the possessions, although, of course, he had no right to claim it during the lifetime of his father. That he did so, might have been due to the feeling that, after all, he must make his own way in the world; to dislike of the order and discipline of his home; to estrangement from his elder brother; or, most likely, to a desire for liberty and enjoyment, with the latent belief that he would

[a] Baba B. viii. 6; Moed K. iii. 3

---

[1] See ch. xvi. Note 1.

[2] But in regard to such disinheriting of children, even if they were bad, it was said, that the Spirit of Wisdom did not rest on them who made such disposition (Baba B. viii. 5).

[3] It may be interesting here to quote, in connection with the interpretation of

Heb. vii. 18, viii. 7–13, this Rabbinic principle: 'A testament makes void a [previous] testament,' Jer. Baba B. 16 *b*, below.

[4] The present Jewish Law of Inherit-ance is fully given in *Fassel*, Mos. Rabb. Civil-Recht, vol. i. pp. 274–412.

succeed well enough if left to himself. At any rate, his conduct, whatever his motives, was most heartless as regarded his father, and sinful as before God. Such a disposition could not prosper. The father had yielded to his demand, and, to be as free as possible from control and restraint, the younger son had gone into a far country. There the natural sequences soon appeared, and his property was wasted in riotous living. Regarding the demand for his inheritance as only a secondary trait in the Parable, designed, on the one hand, more forcibly to bring out the guilt of the son, and, on the other, the goodness, and afterwards the forgiveness, of the Father, we can scarcely doubt that by the younger son we are to understand those 'publicans and sinners' against whose reception by, and fellowship with, Christ the Pharisees had murmured.

The next scene in the history is misunderstood when the objection is raised, that the young man's misery is there represented as the result of Providential circumstances rather than of his own misdoing. To begin with, he would not have been driven to such straits in the famine, if he had not wasted his substance with riotous living. Again, the main object is to show, that absolute liberty and indulgence of sinful desires and passions ended in anything but happiness. The Providence of God had an important part in this. Far more frequently are folly and sin punished in the ordinary course of Providence than by special judgments. Indeed, it is contrary to the teaching of Christ,[a] and it would lead to an unmoral view of life, to regard such direct interpositions as necessary, or to substitute them for the ordinary government of God. Similarly, for our awakening also we are frequently indebted to what is called the Providence, but what is really the manifold working together of the grace, of God. And so we find special meaning in the occurrence of this famine. That, in his want, 'he clave [1] (ἐκολλήθη) to one of the citizens of that country,' seems to indicate that the man had been unwilling to engage the dissipated young stranger, and only yielded to his desperate importunity. This also explains how he employed him in the lowest menial service, that of feeding swine. To a Jew, there was more than degradation in this, since the keeping of swine (although perhaps the ownership rather than the feeding) was prohibited to Israelites under a curse.[b] [2] And even in this demeaning service he was so evil entreated, that for very hunger he would fain have 'filled his belly with the carob-pods that the swine did eat.' But here the same harshness, which had

b Baba K.
82 b, and
the reference to it
in the Midrash on
Eccles.
viii. 1

[1] More literally, 'was glued.' The LXX. translate thus the Hebrew דבק, 'to cleave.'

[2] This prohibition is connected by tradition with Maccabean times.

sent him to such employment, met him on the part of all the people of that country: ' and no man gave unto him,' even sufficient of such food. What perhaps gives additional meaning to this description is the Jewish saying: ' When Israel is reduced to the carob-tree, they become repentant.'[a][1]

It was this pressure of extreme want which first showed to the younger son the contrast between the country and the circumstances to which his sin had brought him, and the plentiful provision of the home he had left, and the kindness which provided bread enough and to spare for even the hired servants. There was only a step between what he said, ' having come into himself,' and his resolve to return, though its felt difficulty seems implied in the expression: ' I will arise.' Nor would he go back with the hope of being reinstated in his position as son, seeing he had already received, and wasted in sin, his portion of the patrimony. All he sought was to be made as one of the hired servants. And, alike from true feeling, and to show that this was all his pretence, he would preface his request by the confession, that he had sinned ' against heaven '—a frequent Hebraism for ' against God '[2]—and in the sight of his father, and hence could no longer lay claim to the name of son. The provision of the son he had, as stated, already spent, the name he no longer deserved. This favour only would he seek, to be as a hired servant in his father's house, instead of in that terrible, strange land of famine and harshness.

But the result was far other than he could have expected. When we read that, ' while he was yet afar off, his father saw him,' we must evidently understand it in the sense, that his father had been always on the outlook for him, an impression which is strengthened by the later command to the servants to ' bring the calf, the fatted one,'[b] as if it had been specially fattened against his return. As he now saw him, ' he was moved with compassion, and he ran, and he fell on his neck, and covered him with kisses.'[3] Such a reception rendered the purposed request, to be made as one of the hired

---

[1] The fruit of the carob-tree is regarded in Jewish and heathen literature as the poorest, and, indeed, only fit for animals. See *Wetstein* ad loc. According to Jewish ideas, it took seventy years before the carob-tree bore fruit (Bekhor. 8 *a*). It is at least doubtful whether the tree is mentioned in the Old Testament (the בוצ of 2 Sam. v. 23, 24). In the Mishnah it is frequently referred to (Peah i. 5; Shabb. xxiv. 2; Baba B. ii. 7). Its fruit seems to have been the food of ascetics, such as Chanina b. Dosa, &c. (Ber. 17 *b*), and Simeon b. Jochai (Shabb. 33 *b*), even as it had been that of John the Baptist. Its leaves seem on occasions to have been used as writing-material (Tos. Gitt. 2).

[2] Other terms were also substituted (such as ' Might,' ' Mercy,' &c.)—with the view of avoiding needless mention of the Deity.

[3] Or 'kissed him much,' κατεφίλησεν αὐτόν.

BOOK
IV

ᵃ ver. 21.
See marg.
of R. V.

ᵇ Siphré,
ed. *Friedm.*
p. 35 *a*

servants, impossible—and its spurious insertion in the text of some important manuscripts ᵃ affords sad evidence of the want of spiritual tact and insight of early copyists. The father's love had anticipated his confession, and rendered its self-spoken sentence of condemnation impossible. 'Perfect love casteth out fear,' and the hard thoughts concerning himself and his deserts on the part of the returning sinner were banished by the love of the father. And so he only made confession of his sin and wrong—not now as preface to the request to be taken in as a servant, but as the outgoing of a humbled, grateful, truly penitent heart. Him whom want had humbled, thought had brought to himself, and mingled need and hope led a suppliant servant—the love of a father, which anticipated his confession, and did not even speak the words of pardon, conquered, and so morally begat him a second time as his son. Here it deserves special notice, as marking the absolute contrast between the teaching of Christ and Rabbinism, that we have in one of the oldest Rabbinic works ᵇ a Parable exactly the reverse of this, when the son of a friend is redeemed from bondage, not as a son, but to be a slave, that so obedience might be demanded of him. The inference drawn is, that the obedience of the redeemed is not that of filial love of the pardoned, but the enforcement of the claim of a master. How otherwise in the Parable and teaching of Christ!

But even so the story of love has not come to an end. They have reached the house. And now the father would not only restore the son, but convey to him the evidence of it, and he would do so before, and by the servants. The three tokens of wealth and position are to be furnished him. 'Quickly' the servants are to bring forth the 'stola,' the upper garment of the higher classes, and that 'the first '—the best, and this instead of the tattered, coarse raiment of the foreign swineherd. Similarly, the finger-ring for his hand, and the sandals for his unshod feet, would indicate the son of the house. And to mark this still further, the servants were not only to bring these articles, but themselves to 'put them on ' the son, so as thereby to own his mastership. And yet further, the calf, 'the fatted one ' for this very occasion, was to be killed, and there was to be a joyous feast, for 'this ' his son 'was dead, and is come to life again; was lost, and is found.' [1]

Thus far for the reception of 'publicans and sinners,' and all in every time whom it may concern. Now for the other aspect of the

---

[1] Thus the text correctly. As it seems to me, the words do not, in the first place, point to a moral change. Dogmatically, the inference is no doubt cor- rect, but, as *Goebel* remarks, they would scarcely have, in that sense, been addressed to the servants.

history. While this was going on, so continues the Parable, the elder **CHAP.** brother was still in the field. On his return home, he inquired of **XVII** a servant the reason of the festivities which he heard within the house. Informed that his younger brother had come, and the calf long prepared against a feast had been killed, because his father had recovered him 'safe and sound,' he was angry, would not go in, and even refused the request to that effect of the father, who had come out for the purpose. The harsh words of reproach with which he set forth his own apparent wrongs could have only one meaning: his father had never rewarded him for his services. On the other hand, as soon as 'this' his 'son'—whom he will not even call his brother—had come back, notwithstanding all his disservice, he had made a feast of joy!

But in this very thing lay the error of the elder son, and—to apply it—the fatal mistake of Pharisaism. The elder son regarded all as of merit and reward, as work and return. But it is not so. We mark, first, that the same tenderness which had welcomed the returning son, now met the elder brother. He spoke to the angry man, not in the language of merited reproof, but addressed him lovingly as 'son,' and reasoned with him. And then, when he had shown him his wrong, he would fain recall him to better feeling by telling him of the other as his 'brother.'[a] But the main point is **ª St. Luke** this. There can be here no question of desert. So long as the son **xv. 32** is in His Father's house He gives in His great goodness to His child all that is the Father's. But this poor lost one—still a son and a brother—he has not got any reward, only been taken back again by a Father's love, when he had come back to Him in the deep misery of his felt need. This son, or rather, as the other should view him, this 'brother,' had been dead, and was come to life again; lost, and was found. And over this 'it was meet to make merry and be glad,' not to murmur. Such murmuring came from thoughts of work and pay—wrong in themselves, and foreign to the proper idea of Father and son; such joy, from a Father's heart. The elder brother's were the thoughts of a servant:[1] of service and return; the younger brother's was the welcome of a son in the mercy and everlasting love of a Father. And this to us, and to all time!

[1] It may be worth mentioning a somewhat similar parable in Bemidb. R. 15 (ed. Warsh. p. 62 b, near beginning). Reference is made to the fact, that, according to Numb. vii., all the twelve tribes brought gifts, except Levi. Upon that follows in Numb. viii. the consecration of the Levites to the service of the Lord. The Midrash likens it to a feast which a king had made for all the people, but to which he does not bid his special friend. And while the latter seems to fear that this exclusion may imply disfavour, the king has a special feast for his friend only, and shows him that while the common meal was for all, the special feast is for those he specially loves.

CHAPTER XVIII.

THE UNJUST STEWARD—DIVES AND LAZARUS—JEWISH AGRICULTURAL
NOTES—PRICES OF PRODUCE—WRITING AND LEGAL DOCUMENTS—
PURPLE AND FINE LINEN—JEWISH NOTIONS OF HADES.

(St. Luke xvi.)

BOOK
IV

ALTHOUGH widely differing in their object and teaching, the last group of Parables spoken during this part of Christ's Ministry are, at least outwardly, connected by a leading thought. The word by which we would string them together is *Righteousness.* There are three Parables of the *Un*righteous: the Unrighteous Steward, the Unrighteous Owner, and the Unrighteous Dispenser, or Judge. And these are followed by two other Parables of the *Self*-righteous: Self-righteousness in its Ignorance, and its dangers as regards oneself; and Self-righteousness in its Harshness, and its dangers as regards others. But when this outward connection has been marked, we have gone the utmost length. Much more close is the internal connection between some of them.

We note it, first and chiefly, between the two first Parables. Recorded in the same chapter,[a] and in the same connection, they were addressed to the same audience. True, the Parable of the *Unjust Steward* was primarily spoken 'to His disciples,'[b] that of *Dives and Lazarus* to the Pharisees.[c] But then the audience of Christ at that time consisted of disciples and Pharisees. And these two classes in the audience stood in peculiar relation to each other, which is exactly met in these two Parables, so that the one may be said to have sprung out of the other. For, the 'disciples,' to whom the first Parable was addressed, were not primarily the Apostles, but those 'publicans and sinners' whom Jesus had received, to the great displeasure of the Pharisees.[d] Them He would teach concerning the Mamon of unrighteousness. And, when the Pharisees sneered at this teaching, He would turn it against them, and show that, beneath the self-justification,[g] which made them forget that now the Kingdom of God was opened to all,[f] and imagine that they were the sole vindicators of a Law[g] which in their everyday practice they notoriously broke,[h] there lay as deep sin and as great alienation from God as that of the sinners

[a] St. Luke xvi.

[b] ver 1

[c] ver. 15

[d] St. Luke xv. 1, 2

[e] St. Luke xvi 15
[f] ver. 16
[g] ver. 17
[h] ver. 18

whom they despised. Theirs might not be the Mamon *of*, yet it might be that *for* unrighteousness; and, while they sneered at the idea of such men making of their Mamon friends that would receive them into everlasting tabernacles, themselves would experience that in the end a terrible readjustment before God would follow on their neglect of using for God, and their employment only for self of such Mamon as was theirs, coupled as it was with harsh and proud neglect of what they regarded as wretched, sore-covered Lazarus, who lay forsaken and starving at their very doors.

It will have been observed, that we lay once more special stress on the historical connection and the primary meaning of the Parables. We would read them in the light of the circumstances in which they were spoken—as addressed to a certain class of hearers, and as referring to what had just passed. The historical application once ascertained, the general lessons may afterwards be applied to the widest range. This historical view will help us to understand the introduction, connection, and meaning, of the two Parables which have been described as the most difficult: those of *the Unjust Steward*,[1] and of *Dives and Lazarus*.

At the outset we must recall, that they were addressed to two different classes in the same audience. In both the subject is *Unrighteousness*. In the first, which is addressed to the recently converted publicans and sinners, it is the Unrighteous Steward, making unrighteous use of what had been committed to his administration by his Master; in the second Parable, which is addressed to the self-justifying, sneering Pharisees, it is the Unrighteous Possessor, who uses only for himself and for time what he has, while he leaves Lazarus, who, in his view, is wretched and sore-covered, to starve or perish, unheeded, at his very door. In agreement with its object, and as suited to the part of the audience addressed, the first Parable points a lesson, while the second furnishes a warning. In the first Parable we are told, what the sinner when converted should learn from his previous life of sin; in the second, what the self-deceiving, proud Pharisee should learn as regarded the life which to him seemed so fair, but was in reality so empty of God and of love. It follows— and this is of greatest importance, especially in the interpretation of the first Parable—that we must not expect to find spiritual equivalents for each of the persons or incidents introduced. In each case, the Parable itself forms only an illustration of the lessons, spoken or

---

[1] The reader who wishes to see the different views and interpretations of this Parable is referred to the modern commentaries, and especially to Archbishop *Trench's* Notes on the Parables (13th ed.), pp. 427-452.

implied, which Christ would convey to the one and the other class in His audience.

I. *The Parable of the Unjust Steward.*—In accordance with the canon of interpretation just laid down, we distinguish—1. The illustrative Parable.[a] 2. Its moral.[b] 3. Its application in the combination of the moral with some of the features of the Parable.[c]

1. The illustrative Parable.[d] This may be said to converge to the point brought out in the concluding verse:[e] the prudence which characterises the dealings of the children of this world in regard to their own generation—or, to translate the Jewish forms of expression into our own phraseology, the wisdom with which those who care not for the world to come choose the means most effectual for attaining their worldly objects. It is this prudence by which their aims are so effectually secured, *and it alone,* which is set before 'the children of light,' as that by which to learn. And the lesson is the more practical, that those primarily addressed had hitherto been among these men of the world. Let them learn from the serpent its wisdom, and from the dove its harmlessness; from the children of this world, their prudence as regarded their generation, while, as children of the new light, they must remember the higher aim for which that prudence was to be employed. Thus would that Mamon which is 'of unrighteousness,' and which certainly 'faileth,' become to us treasure in the world to come—welcome us there, and, so far from 'failing,' prove permanent—welcome us in *everlasting* tabernacles. Thus, also, shall we have made friends of the 'Mamon of unrightousness,' and that, which from its nature must fail, become eternal gain—or, to translate it into Talmudic phraseology, it will be of the things of which a man enjoys the interest in this world, while the capital remains for the world to come.

It cannot now be difficult to understand the Parable. Its object is simply to show, in the most striking manner, the prudence of a worldly man, who is unrestrained by any other consideration than that of attaining his end. At the same time, with singular wisdom, the illustration is so chosen as that its matter (*materia*), 'the Mamon of unrighteousness,' may serve to point a life-lesson to those newly converted publicans and sinners, who had formerly sacrificed all for the sake, or in the enjoyment of, that Mamon. All else, such as the question, who is the master and who the steward, and such like, we dismiss, since the Parable is only intended as an illustration of the lesson to be afterwards taught.

The connection between this Parable and what the Lord had

previously said concerning returning sinners, to which our remarks CHAP.
have already pointed, is further evidenced by the use of the term XVIII
'wasting' (διασκορπίζων), in the charge against the steward, just
as the prodigal son had 'wasted' (διεσκόρπισε) his substance.[a] [a] St. Luke xv. 13
Only, in the present instance, the property had been entrusted to his
administration. As regards the owner, his designation as 'rich'
seems intended to mark how large was the property committed to
the steward. The 'steward' was not, as in St. Luke xii. 42–46, a
slave, but one employed for the administration of the rich man's
affairs, subject to notice of dismissal.[b] He was accused—the term [b] St. Luke xvi. 2, 3
implying malevolence, but not necessarily a false charge—not of
fraud, but of wasting, probably by riotous living and carelessness, his
master's goods. And his master seems to have convinced himself
that the charge was true, since he at once gives him notice of dismissal. The latter is absolute, and not made dependent on the
'account of his stewardship,' which is only asked as, of course,
necessary, when he gives up his office. Nor does the steward either
deny the charge or plead any extenuation. His great concern rather
is, during the time still left of his stewardship, before he gives up
his accounts, to provide for his future support. The only alternative
before him in the future is that of manual labour or mendicancy.
But for the former he has not strength; from the latter he is restrained by shame.

Then it is that his 'prudence' suggests a device by which, after
his dismissal, he may, without begging, be received into the houses
of those whom he has made friends.[1] It must be borne in mind,
that he is still steward, and, as such, has full power of disposing of
his master's affairs. When, therefore, he sends for one after another
of his master's debtors, and tells each to alter the sum in the bond,
he does not suggest to them forgery or fraud, but, in remitting part
of the debt—whether it had been incurred as rent in kind, or as the
price of produce purchased—he acts, although unrighteously, yet
strictly within his rights. Thus, neither the steward nor the debtors
could be charged with criminality, and the master must have been
struck with the cleverness of a man who had thus secured a future
provision by making friends, so long as he had the means of so doing
(ere his Mamon of unrighteousness failed).

---

[1] A somewhat similar parable occurs
in Vayyik. R. 5 (towards the close) about
a 'prudent' farmer. When matters go
badly with his farm, he dresses himself
in his best, puts on a cheerful mien, and
so appears before his landlord. By well
turned, flattering replies to the inquiries
about the cattle and the crops, he so
conciliates favour, that when the landlord finally inquires what he wished, and
he requests a loan, he receives double
the sum he had asked.

A few archæological notices may help the interpretation of details. From the context it seems more likely, that the 'bonds,' or rather 'writings,' of these debtors were written acknowledgments of debt, than, as some have supposed that they were, leases of farms. The debts over which the steward variously disposed, according as he wished to gain more or less favour, were considerable. In the first case they are stated at 'a hundred *Bath* of oil,' in the second as 'a hundred *Cor* of wheat.' In regard to these quantities we have the preliminary difficulty, that three kinds of measurement were in use in Palestine—that of the 'Wilderness,' or, the original Mosaic; that of 'Jerusalem,' which was more than a fifth larger; and that of Sepphoris, probably the common Galilean measurement, which, in turn, was more than a fifth larger than the Jerusalem measure.[1] To be more precise, one Galilean was equal to $\frac{3}{2}$ 'Wilderness' measures. Assuming the measurement to have been the Galilean, one *Bath*[2] would have been equal to an Attic *Metrêtês*, or about 39 *litres*. On the other hand, the so-called 'Wilderness measurement' would correspond with the Roman measures, and, in that case, the '*Bath*' would be the same as the *Amphora*, or amount to a little less than 26

ª Ant. viii.
2, 9; comp.
ix. 4, 5

litres.[3] The latter is the measurement adopted by Josephus.'[a] In the Parable, the first debtor was owing 100 of these 'Bath,' or, according to the Galilean measurement, about 3,900 *litres* of oil. As regards the value of a Bath of oil, little information can be derived from the statements of *Josephus*, since he only mentions prices under

ᵇ Jewish
War. ii. 21.
2

exceptional circumstances, either in particularly plentiful years,[b] or else at a time of war and siege.[c] In the former, an Amphora, or 26

ᶜ Life, 13

litres, of oil seems to have fetched about 9*d*.; but it must be added, that, even in such a year, this represents a rare stroke of business, since the oil was immediately afterwards re-sold for eight times the amount, and this—3*s*. for half an Amphora of about

---

[1] See *Herzfeld*, Handelsgesch, pp. 183–185. I have proceeded on his computation. I am bound to add, that there are few subjects on which the statements of writers are more inconsistent or confused. The statements made in the text are derived from *Jewish* sources.

[2] The writer in *Smith's* Bibl. Dict., vol. iii. p. 1740 *b*, is mistaken in saying that 'the *Bath* is the largest of liquid measures.' According to Ezek. xlv. 11, the *Chomer* or *Cor* = ten bath or ephah, was equally applied to liquid and dry measures. The Bath (one-tenth of the Chomer or Cor) = three seah: the seah = two hin; the hin = twelve log; the log = space of six eggs. Further,

one thirty-secondth of a log is reckoned equal to a large (table), one sixty-fourth to a small (dessert) spoon.

[3] This difference between the 'Wilderness,' or 'Mosaic,' and the 'Galilean measure removes the difficulty (raised by *Thenius*) about the capacity of the 'brazen sea' in Solomon's Temple (1 Kings vii. 23, 26). The *Bath* should be calculated, not according to the Galilean (= Metrêtês = about thirty-nine litres), but according to the 'Wilderness' measure (= amphora = about twenty-six litres).

[4] The reading in Ant. xv. 9. 2: 'The Attic Medimni,' is evidently a copyist's error for 'Metrêtai.'

13 litres—would probably represent an exceptionally high war-price. The fair price for it would probably have been 9*d.* For the Mishnah informs us, that the ordinary 'earthenware casks' (the *Gerabh*) held each 2 Seah, or 48 Log, or about 26 litres.[a] Again, according to a notice in the Talmud,[b] 100 such 'casks,' or, 200 Seah, were sold for 10 (presumably gold) dinars, or 250 silver dinars, equal to about 7*l.* 10*s.* of our money. And as the *Bath* (= 3 Seah) held a third more than one of those 'casks,' or *Gerabhin*, the value of the 100 Bath of oil would probably amount to about 10*l.* of our money, and the remission of the steward, of course, to 5*l.*

The second debtor owed 'a hundred Cor of wheat.'—that is, in dry measure, ten times the amount of the oil of the first debtor, since the *Cor* was ten *Ephah* or *Bath*, the *Ephah* three *Seah*, the *Seah* six *Qabh*, and the *Qabh* four *Log.* This must be borne in mind, since the dry and the fluid measures were precisely the same; and here, also, their threefold computation (the 'Wilderness,' the 'Jerusalem,' and the 'Galilean') obtained. As regards the value of wheat, we learn[c] that, on an average, four Seah of seed were expected to produce one Cor—that is, seven and a half times their amount; and that a field 1,500 cubits long and 50 wide was expected to grow a Cor. The average price of a Cor of wheat, bought *uncut*, amounted to about 25 dinars, or 15*s.* Striking an average between the lowest prices mentioned [d] and the highest,[e] we infer that the price of 3 Seah or an Ephah would be from two shillings to half-a-crown, and accordingly of a *Cor* (or 10 Ephah) from 20 to 25 shillings (probably this is rather more than it would cost). On this computation the hundred Cor would represent a debt of from 100*l.* to 125*l.*, and the remission of the steward (of 20 Cor), a sum of from 20*l.* to 25*l.* Comparatively small as these sums may seem, they are in reality large, remembering the value of money in Palestine, which, on a low computation, would be five times as great as in our own country.[1] These two debtors are only mentioned as instances, and so the unjust steward would easily secure for himself friends by the 'Mamon of unrighteousness,' the term *Mamon*,[2] we may note, being derived from the Syriac and Rabbinic word of the same kind (מָמוֹן, from מִנְיָ=מִין , מנה, 'to apportion).[3]

Another point on which acquaintance with the history and habits

CHAP.
XVIII

[a] Terum. x.
8
[b] Jer. Baba
M. iv. 2, p.
9 *d*

[c] from
Baba M.
105 *b*, about
the middle

[d] Peah viii.
7: Erub.
viii. 2:
Baba B. 92
b

[e] Baba B
91 a

---

[1] This will appear from the cost of living, labour, &c.
[2] The word should be written with one *m.* See *Grimm* s. v.
[3] *Grimm* (after *Drusius*) derives it from אמן, but this is most unlikely. The derivation of *Lagarde* (ap. *Kautzsch*, p. 173) seems very difficult. *Buxtorf* (s. v.) largely, but not very satisfactorily, discusses its etymology. The view in the text has the sanction of *Levy.*

BOOK
IV

of those times throws light is, how the debtors could so easily alter the sum mentioned in their respective bonds. For, the text implies that this, and not the writing of a new bond, is intended; since in that case the old one would have been destroyed, and not given back for alteration. It would be impossible, within the present limits, to enter fully on the interesting subject of writing, writing-materials, and written documents among the ancient Jews.[1] Suffice it to give here the briefest notices.

The materials on which the Jews wrote were of the most divers kind: leaves, as of olives, palms, the carob, &c.; the rind of the pomegranate, the shell of walnuts, &c.; the prepared skins of animals (leather and parchment); and the product of the papyrus, used long before the time of Alexander the Great for the manufacture of paper, and known in Talmudic writings by the same name, as *Papir*[a] or *Apipeir*,[b] but more frequently by that of *Nayyar*—probably from the stripes (*Nirin*) of the plant of which it was made.[2] But what interests us more, as we remember the 'tablet' ($\pi\iota\nu\alpha\kappa\iota\delta\iota\sigma\nu$) on which Zacharias wrote the name of the future Baptist,[c] is the circumstance that it bears not only the same name, *Pinaqes* or *Pinqesa*, but that it seems to have been of such common use in Palestine.[3] It consisted of thin pieces of wood (the *Luach*) fastened or strung together. The Mishnah[d] enumerates three kinds of them: those where the wood was covered with papyrus,[4] those where it was covered with wax, and those where the wood was left plain to be written on with ink. The latter was of different kinds. Black ink was prepared of soot (the *Deyo*), or of vegetable or mineral substances.[5] Gum Arabic and Egyptian (*Qumos* and *Quma*) and vitriol (*Qanqanthos*) seem also to have been used[e] in writing. It is curious to read of writing in colours and with red ink or *Siqra*,[f] and even of a kind of sympathetic ink, made from the bark of the ash, and brought out by a mixture of vitriol and gum.[g] We also read of a gold-ink, as that in which the copy of the Law was written which, according to the legend, the High-Priest had sent to Ptolemy Philadelphus for

a Sot. 49 b
b Kel. xxiv. 7
c St. Luke i. 63
d Kel. xxiv. 7
e Shabb. xii. 4
f u. s.
g Jer. Shabb 13 d. about the middle

---

[1] I must here refer generally to the monograph of *Löw* (Graphische Requis. u. Erzeugn., 2 vols.). Its statements require, however, occasionally to be rectified. See also *Herzfeld*, Handelsgesch. pp. 113 &c., and Note 17.

[2] *Löw*, u. s. vol. i. pp. 97, 98. It is curious to learn that in those days also waste paper went to the grocer. (Baba M. 56 *b*.)

[3] From earlier times comes to us notice of the *Gillayon* (Is. viii. 1)—a

smooth tablet of wood, metal, or stone —and of the *Cheret*, or stylus (Is. viii. 1), and the *Et*, which means probably not only a *stylus* but also a *calamus* (Ps. xlv. 2; Jer. viii. 8).

[4] So *Sachs*, Beitr. z. Sprach u. Alterth. Forsch. vol. i. p. 165; but *Löw* (u. s.) seems of different opinion.

[5] The *Deyo* seems to have been a dry substance which was made into black ink. Ink from gall-nuts appears to be of later invention.

the purpose of being translated into Greek by the LXX.[a] But the
Talmud prohibits copies of the Law in gold letters,[1] or more probably
such in which the Divine Name was written in gold letters.[b 2] In
writing, a pen, *Qolemos*, made of reed (*Qaneh*[c]) was used, and the
reference in an Apostolic Epistle[d] to writing ' with ink and pen ' (διὰ
μέλανος καὶ καλάμου) finds even its verbal counterpart in the Midrash, which speaks of *Milanin* and *Qolemin* (ink and pens). Indeed,
the public ' writer '—a trade very common in the East[3]—went about
with a *Qolemos*, or reed-pen, behind his ear, as a badge of his employment.[e 4] With the reed-pen we ought to mention its necessary accompaniments: the penknife,[f] the inkstand (which, when
double, for black and red ink, was sometimes made of earthenware,
Qalamarim[g]), and the ruler[h]—it being regarded by the stricter
set as unlawful to write any words of Holy Writ on any unlined
material, no doubt to ensure correct writing and reading.[i 5]

In all this we have not referred to the practice of writing on
leather specially prepared with salt and flour,[k] nor to the *Qelaph*, or
parchment in the stricter sense.[m] For we are here chiefly interested
in the common mode of writing, that on the *Pinaqes*, or ' tablet,'
and especially on that covered with wax. Indeed, a little vessel
holding wax was generally attached to it (*Pinaqes sheyesh bo beth
Qibbul shaavah*[n]). On such a tablet they wrote, of course, not with
a reed-pen, but with a *stylus*, generally of iron. This instrument

CHAP.
XVIII

[a] *Jos.* Ant.
xii. 2. 10
[b] Shabb.
103 *b*;
Sopher. i. 9
[c] Shabb.
viii. 5
[d] 3 John 13

[e] Shabb. i. 3
[f] Already
mentioned
in Jer.
xxxvi. 23,
and in the
Mishnah
called Olar.
אוֹלָר,
Kel. xii. 8
[g] Kel. ii. 7
[h] Kel. xii. 8
[i] Meg. 16 *b*
[k] Meg. 17 *a*;
19 *a*
[m] Shabb.
viii. 3

[n] Kel. xvii.
17

---

[1] But the learned *Relandus* asserts
that there were in his country such texts
written in gold letters, and that hence
the Talmudic prohibition could have
only applied to the copies used in the
Synagogues (*Havercamp's* ed. of *Josephus*, vol. i. p. 593, Note *e*).

[2] Not to make a distinction between
any portions of Scripture, and also from
the curious Kabbalistic idea that somehow every word in the Bible contained
the Divine Name.

[3] We read of one, Ben Qamtsar, who
wrote four letters (the Tetragram) at
once, holding four reeds (*Qolemosin*) at
the same time between his four fingers
(Yoma 38 *b*). The great R. Meir was
celebrated as a copyist, specially of the
Bible, at which work he is said to have
made about 8*s*. weekly, of which, it is
stated, he spent a third on his living, a
third on his dress, and a third on charity
to Rabbis (Midr. on Eccles. ii. 18, ed.
Warsh. p. 83 *b*, last two lines). The codices of R. Meir seem to have embodied
some variations of the common text.

Thus, in the Psalms he wrote *Halleluyah*
in one word, as if it had been an interjec-
tion, and not in the orthodox way, as two
words: *Hallelu Yah* (Jer. Meg. 72 *a*). His
codices seem also to have had marginal
notes. Thus, on the words ' very good '
(טוֹב מְאֹד), Gen. i. 31, he noted ' death is
good ' (טוֹב מוֹת), a sort of word-play, to
support his view, that death was originally of God and created by Him—a natural
necessity rather than a punishment (Ber.
R. 9). Similarly, on Gen. iii. 21, he altered in the margin the עוֹר, ' skin,' of the
text into אוֹר, ' light,' thus rendering
' garments of light ' (u. s. 20). Again, in
Gen. xlvi. 23, he left out the ו from וּבְנֵי,
rendering it ' And the *son* of Dan was
Chushim ' (u. s. 94). Similarly, he altered
the words, Is. xxi. 11, מַשָּׂא דוּמָה, ' the
burden of *Dumah* ' into *Roma*, רוֹמִי (Jer.
Taan. p. 64 *a*, line 10 from top).

[4] Similarly, the carpenter carried a
small wooden rule behind his ear.

[5] Letters, other documents, or bales of
merchandise, were sealed with a kind of
red clay.

BOOK
IV

ᵉ Kel. xiii. 2

ᵇ Ab. iii. 16

ᵉ Baba B.
161 b

ᵈ u. s. 163 a,
b; 164 a

ᵉ St. Luke
xvi. 7

ᶠ Shem. R.
15

ᵍ Baba M.
i. 8

ʰ Baba B.
163 a, b

consisted of two parts, which might be detached from each other:
the hard pointed 'writer' (*Kothebh*), and the 'blotter' (*Mocheq*)
which was flat and thick for smoothing out letters and words which
had been written or rather graven in the wax.ᵃ There can be no
question that acknowledgments of debt, and other transactions, were
ordinarily written down on such wax-covered tablets; for not only is
direct reference made to it,ᵇ but there are special provisions in regard to documents where there are such erasures, or rather efface-
ments: such as, that they require to be noted in the document,ᶜ
under what conditions and how the witnesses are in such cases to
affix their signatures,ᵈ just as there are particular injunctions how
witnesses who could not write are to affix their mark.

But although we have thus ascertained that 'the bonds' in the
Parable must have been written on wax—or else, possibly, on parchment—where the *Mocheq*, or blotter, could easily efface the numbers,
we have also evidence that they were not, as so often, written on
'tablets' (the *Pinaques*). For, the Greek term, by which these
'bonds' or 'writings' are designated in the Parable (γράμματαᵉ), is
the same as is sometimes used in Rabbinic writings (*Gerammation*)
for an acknowledgment of debt;ᶠ¹ the Hebraised Greek word corresponding to the more commonly used (Syriac) term *Shitre* (*Shetar*),
which also primarily denotes 'writings,' and is used specifically for
such acknowledgments.ᵍ² Of these there were two kinds. The most
formal *Shetar* was not signed by the debtor at all, but only by the
witnesses, who were to write their names (or marks) immediately
(not more than two lines) below the text of the document, to prevent
fraud. Otherwise, the document would not possess legal validity.
Generally, it was further attested by the Sanhedrin³ of three, who
signed in such manner as not to leave even one line vacant.ʰ Such
a document contained the names of creditor and debtor, the amount
owing, and the date, together with a clause attaching the property
of the debtor. In fact, it was a kind of mortgage; all sale of prop-

---

¹ The designations for the general
formulary (*Tophos*, or *Tiphos* (Gitt. iii.
2), = typos), and for the special clauses
(*Toreph* = Tropos) were of Greek derivation. For the full draft of the various
legal documents we refer the reader to
Note ix. at the end of *Sammter's* edition
of Baba Mets. pp. 144–148. How many
documents of this kind Jewish legalism
must have invented, may be gathered from
the circumstance that *Herzfeld* (u. s. p.
314) enumerates not fewer than thirty-
eight different kinds of them! It appears

that there were certain forms of these and
similar documents, prepared with spaces
left blank to be filled in (Gitt. iii. 2).
² The more full designation was *Shetar
Chobh*, a writing of debt (Baba M. i. 6),
or *Shetar Milvah* (Gitt. iii. 2), a writing
of loan.
³ The attestation of the court was
called *Qiyum Beth Din*, 'the establishment of the court,' *Ashra*, or *Asharta*,
strengthening, or *Henpheq* (Baba Mez.
7 b), literally, the production, viz. before
the court.

erty being, as with us, subject to such a mortgage,[a] which bore the name *Acharayuth* (probably, 'guarantee'[1]). When the debt was paid, the legal obligation was simply returned to the debtor; if paid in part, either a new bond was written, or a receipt given, which was called *Shobher* [b] or *Tebhara*, because it 'broke' the debt.

But in many respects different were those bonds which were acknowledgments of debt for purchases made, such as we suppose those to have been which are mentioned in the Parable. In such cases it was not uncommon to dispense altogether with witnesses, and the document was signed by the debtor himself. In bonds of this kind, the creditor had not the benefit of a mortgage in case of sale. We have expressed our belief that the Parable refers to such documents, and we are confirmed in this by the circumstance that they not only bear a different name from the more formal bonds (the *Shitre*), but one which is perhaps the most exact rendering of the Greek term (כתב ידו,[c] a 'writing of hand,' 'note of hand'[2]). For completeness' sake we add, in regard to the farming of land, that two kinds of leases were in use. Under the first, called *Shetar Arisuth*, the lessee (*Aris*=ούρος[3]) received a certain portion of the produce. He might be a lessee for life, for a specified number of years, or even a hereditary tiller of the ground; or he might sub-let it to another person.[d] Under the second kind of lease, the farmer—or *Meqabbel* —entered into a contract for payment either in kind, when he undertook to pay a stipulated and unvarying amount of produce, in which case he was called a *Chokher* (*Chakhur* or *Chakhira*[4]), or else a certain annual rental in money, when he was called a *Sokher*.[5]

2. From this somewhat lengthened digression, we return to notice the *moral* of the Parable.[e] It is put in these words: 'Make to yourselves friends out of [by means of] the Mamon of unrighteousness, that, when it shall fail,[6] they may receive you into everlasting tabernacles.' From what has been previously stated, the meaning of these words offers little serious difficulty. We must again recall the circum-

CHAP.
XVIII

[a] Babha B.
x. 8
[b] Babha M.
7

[c] Babha B.
x. 8

[d] Babha B
46 b

[e] St. Luke
xvi. 9

---

[1] For the derivation and legal bearing of the term, see *Löw*, vol. ii. p. 82.

[2] Although it is certain that letters of credit were used by the Jews of old, there is sufficient reason for believing that 'bills' were first introduced into commerce by the Italians, and not by Jews.

[3] But *Guisius* (in *Surenhusius*' Mishna, vol. i. pp. 56, 57) gives a different derivation and interpretation, which the learned reader may consult for himself.

[4] The difference between the *Aris* and the *Chokher* is stated in Jer. Bikkur. 64 b.

[5] The difference between the *Chokher* and the *Sokher* is expressed in Tos. Demai vi. 2. *Ugolini* (Thes. vol. xx. pp. cxix., cxx.) not only renders but copies this passage wrongly. A more composite bargain of letting land and lending money for its better cultivation is mentioned in B. Mez. 69 b.

[6] This, and not 'they shall fail,' is the correct reading.

BOOK
IV

stance, that they were primarily addressed to converted publicans and sinners, to whom the expression 'Mamon of unrighteousness'— of which there are close analogies, and even an exact transcript [1] in the Targum—would have an obvious meaning. Among us, also, there are not a few who may feel its aptness as they look back on the past, while to all it carries a much needed warning. Again, the addition of the definite article leaves no doubt, that 'the everlasting tabernacles' mean the well-known heavenly home; in which sense the term 'tabernacle' is, indeed, already used in the Old Testament.[a][2] But as a whole we regard it (as previously hinted) as an adaptation to the Parable of the well-known Rabbinic saying, that there were certain graces of which a man enjoyed the benefit here, while the capital, so to speak, remained for the next world. And if a more literal interpretation were demanded, we cannot but feel the duty incumbent on those converted publicans, nay, in a sense, on us all, to seek to make for ourselves of the Mamon—be it of money, of knowledge, of strength, or opportunities, which to many has, and to all may so easily, become that 'of unrighteousness'—such lasting and spiritual application: gain such friends by means of it, that, 'when it fails,' as fail it must when we die, all may not be lost, but rather meet us in heaven. Thus would each deed done for God with this Mamon become a friend to greet us as we enter the eternal world.

3. The suitableness both of the Parable and of its application to the audience of Christ appears from its similarity to what occurs in Jewish writings. Thus, the reasoning that the Law could not have been given to the nations of the world, since they have not observed the seven Noachic commandments (which Rabbinism supposes to have been given to the Gentiles), is illustrated by a Parable in which a king is represented as having employed two administrators (*Apiterophin*); one over the gold and silver, and the other over the straw. The latter rendered himself suspected, and—continues the Parable —when he complained that he had not been set over the gold and silver, they said unto him: Thou fool, if thou hast rendered thyself suspected in regard to the straw, shall they commit to thee the treasure of gold and silver?[b] And we almost seem to hear the very words of Christ: 'He that is faithful [2] in that which is least, is faithful also in much,' in this of the Midrash: 'The Holy One, blessed be His Name, does not give great things to a man until he has been

[a] Ps. xv. 1.; xxvii. 5, the latter being realistically understood in Siphra

[b] Yalkut, vol. i. p. 81 a, lines 19 &c. from top

---

[1] So in the Targ. on Hab. ii. 9, מָמוֹן דְּרִשְׁע.

[2] Comp. *Schöttgen* ad loc.

[3] No doubt the equivalent for the Rabbinic נָאמָן *accreditus*, and used in the same sense.

tried in a small matter;' which is illustrated by the history of Moses and of David, who were both called to rule from the faithful guiding of sheep.[a]

Considering that the Jewish mind would be familiar with such modes of illustration, there could have been no misunderstanding of the words of Christ. These converted publicans might think—and so may some of us—that theirs was a very narrow sphere of service, one of little importance; or else, like the Pharisees, and like so many others among us, that faithful administration of the things of this world ('the Mamon of unrighteousness') had no bearing on the possession of the true riches in the next world. In answer to the first difficulty, Christ points out that the principle of service is the same, whether applied to much or to little; that the one was, indeed, meet preparation for, and, in truth, the test of the other.[b] 'He that is faithful'—or, to paraphrase the word ($\pi\iota\sigma\tau\acute{o}s$), he that has proved himself, is accredited (answering to נאמן)—'in the least, is also faithful [accredited] in much; and who in the least is unjust is also in much unjust.' Therefore, if a man failed in faithful service of God in his worldly matters—in the language of the Parable, if he were not faithful in the Mamon of unrighteousness—could he look for the true Mamon, or riches of the world to come? Would not his unfaithfulness in the lower stewardship imply unfitness for the higher? And—still in the language of the Parable—if they had not proved faithful in mere stewardship, 'in that which was another's,' could it be expected that they would be exalted from stewardship to proprietorship? And the ultimate application of all was this, that dividedness was impossible in the service of God.[c] It is impossible for the disciple to make separation between spiritual matters and worldly, and to attempt serving God in the one and Mamon in the other. There is absolutely no such distinction to the disciple, and our common usage of the words *secular* and *spiritual* is derived from a terrible misunderstanding and mistake. To the secular, nothing is spiritual; and to the spiritual, nothing is secular: No servant *can* serve two Masters; ye cannot serve God and Mamon.

II. The Parable of *Dives and Lazarus.*[d]—Although primarily spoken to the Pharisees, and not *to* the disciples, yet, as will presently appear, it was spoken *for* the disciples. The words of Christ had touched more than one sore spot in the hearts of the Pharisees. This consecration of all to God as the necessary condition of high spiritual service, and then of higher spiritual standing—as it

[a] Shem. R., ed. Warsh., p. 7 b, about the middle

[b] St. Luke xvi. 10

[c] ver. 13

[d] St. Luke xvi. 14-31

were 'ownership'—such as they claimed, was a very hard saying. It touched their covetousness. They would have been quite ready to hear, nay, they believed that the 'true' treasure had been committed to their trust. But that its condition was, that they should prove themselves God-devoted in 'the unrighteous Mamon,' faithful in the employment of it in that for which it was entrusted to their stewardship, this was not to be borne. Nor yet, that such prospects should be held out to publicans and sinners, while they were withheld from those who were the custodians of the Law and of the Prophets. But were they faithful to the Law? And as to their claim of being the 'owners,' the Parable of the Rich Owner and of his bearing would exhibit how unfaithful they were in 'much' as well as in 'little,' in what they claimed as owners as well as in their stewardship—and this, on their own showing of their relations to publicans and sinners: the Lazarus who lay at their doors.

Thus viewed, the verses which introduce the second Parable (that of *Dives and Lazarus*) will appear, not 'detached sayings,' as some commentators would have us believe, but most closely connected with the Parable to which they form the Preface. Only, here especially, must we remember, that we have only Notes of Christ's Discourse, made years before by one who had heard it, and containing the barest outline—as it were, the stepping-stones—of the argument as it proceeded. Let us try to follow it. As the Pharisees heard what Christ said, their covetousness was touched. It is said, moreover, that they derided Him—literally, 'turned up their noses at Him.'[a] The mocking gestures, with which they pointed to His publican-disciples, would be accompanied by mocking words in which they would extol and favourably compare their own claims and standing with that of those new disciples of Christ. Not only to refute but to confute, to convict, and, if possible, to convince them, was the object of Christ's Discourse and Parable. One by one their pleas were taken up and shown to be utterly untenable. They were persons who by outward righteousness and pretences sought to appear just before men, but God knew their hearts; and that which was exalted among men, their Pharisaic standing and standing aloof, was abomination before Him.[b] These two points form the main subject of the Parable. Its *first* object was to show the great difference between the 'before men' and the 'before God;' between Dives as he appears to men in this world, and as he is before God and will be in the next world. Again, the *second* main object of the Parable was to illustrate that their Pharisaic standing and standing aloof—the

a St. Luke xvi. 14

b ver. 15

bearing of Dives in reference to a Lazarus—which was the glory of Pharisaism before men, was an abomination before God. Yet a third object of the Parable was in reference to their covetousness, the selfish use which they made of their possessions—their Mamon. But a selfish was an unrighteous use; and, as such, would meet with sorer retribution than in the case of an unfaithful steward.

But we leave for the present the comparative analysis of the Parable to return to the introductory words of Christ. Having shown that the claims of the Pharisees and their standing aloof from poor sinners were an abomination before God, Christ combats these grounds of their bearing, that they were the custodians and observers of the Law and of the Prophets, while those poor sinners had no claims upon the Kingdom of God. Yes—but the Law and the Prophets had their terminus ad quem in John the Baptist, who 'brought the good tidings of the Kingdom of God.' Since then 'every one' had to enter it by personal resolution and 'force.'[a] Yes—it was true that the Law could not fail in one tittle of it.[b] But, notoriously and in everyday life, the Pharisees, who thus spoke of the Law and appealed to it, were the constant and open breakers of it. Witness here their teaching and practice concerning divorce, which really involved a breach of the seventh commandment.[c]

[a] Comp. St. Matt. xi. 12, and our remarks on the passage
[b] St. Luke xvi. 16, 17
[c] ver. 18

Thus, when bearing in mind that, as previously stated, we have here only the 'heads,' or rather the 'stepping stones,' of Christ's argument—from notes by a hearer at the time, which were afterwards given to St. Luke—we clearly perceive, how closely connected are the seemingly disjointed sentences which preface the Parable, and how aptly they introduce it. The Parable itself is strictly of the Pharisees and their relation to the 'publicans and sinners' whom they despised, and to whose stewardship they opposed thoughts of their own proprietorship. With infinite wisdom and depth the Parable tells in two directions: in regard to their selfish use of the literal riches—their covetousness—and in regard to their selfish use of the figurative riches: their Pharisaic righteousness, which left poor Lazarus at their door to the dogs and to famine, not bestowing on him aught from their supposed rich festive banquets.

On the other hand, it will be necessary in the interpretation of this Parable to keep in mind, that its Parabolic details must not be exploited, nor doctrines of any kind derived from them, either as to the character of the other world, the question of the duration of future punishments, or the possible moral improvement of those in Gehinnom. All such things are foreign to the Parable, which is

BOOK
IV

only intended as a type, or exemplification and illustration, of what is intended to be taught. And, if proof were required, it would surely be enough to remind ourselves, that this Parable is addressed to the Pharisees, to whom Christ would scarcely have communicated details about the other world, on which He was so reticent in His teaching to the disciples. The Parable naturally falls into three parts.

ᵃ vv. 16-22

1. *Dives and Lazarus before and after death,*ᵃ or the contrast between 'before men' and 'before God;' the unrighteous use of riches—literal and figurative; and the relations of the Pharisaic Dives to the publican Lazarus, as before men and as before God: the 'exalted among men' an 'abomination before God.' And the application of the Parable is here the more telling, that *alms* were so highly esteemed among the Pharisees, and that the typical Pharisee is thus set before them as, on their own showing, the typical sinner.

The Parable opens by presenting to us 'a rich man' 'clothed in purple and byssus, joyously faring every day in splendour.' All here is in character. His dress is described as the finest and most costly, for byssus and purple were the most expensive materials, only inferior to silk, which, if genuine and unmixed—for at least three kinds of silk are mentioned in ancient Jewish writings—was worth its weight in gold. Both byssus—of which it is not yet quite certain, whether it was of hemp or cotton—and purple were indeed manufactured in Palestine, but the best byssus (at least at that time [1]) came from Egypt and India. The white garments of the High-

ᵇ Yoma iii. 6, 7

Priest on the Day of Atonement were made of it.ᵇ To pass over

ᶜ Jer. Yoma iii. 6, p. 40 d

exaggerated accounts of its costliness,ᶜ the High-Priest's dress of Pelusian linen for the morning service of the Day of Atonement was said to have cost about 36*l.*; that of Indian linen for the evening of the same day about 24*l.* Of course, this stuff would, if of

ᵈ Jer. Kidd. 62 c

home-manufacture, whether made in Galilee or in Judæa,ᵈ be much cheaper. As regarded purple, which was obtained from the coasts of

ᵉ Shabb.26 a

Tyre,ᵉ wool of violet-purple was sold about that period by weight [f]

ᶠ Kel. xxix.

at the rate of about 3*l.* the Roman pound, though it would, of course, considerably vary in price.

Quite in accordance with this luxuriousness—unfortunately not uncommon among the very high-placed Jews, since the Talmud (though, no doubt, exaggeratedly) speaks of the dress of a corrupt

---

[1] In later times Palestinian byssus seems to have been in great repute. See *Herzfeld,* Handelsgesch. p. 107.

High-Priest as having cost upwards of 300*l.*[a]—was the feasting every day, the description of which conveys the impression of *company, merriment,* and *splendour.* All this is, of course, intended to set forth the selfish use which this man made of his wealth, and to point the contrast of his bearing towards Lazarus. Here also every detail is meant to mark the pitiableness of the case, as it stood out before Dives. The very name—not often mentioned in any other real, and never in any other Parabolic story—tells it: *Lazarus, Laazar,* a common abbreviation of *Elazar,* as it were, 'God help *him*!' Then we read that he 'was cast'[1] (ἐβέβλητο) at his gateway, as if to mark that the bearers were glad to throw down their unwelcome burden.[2] Laid there, he was in full view of the Pharisee as he went out or came in, or sat in his courtyard. And as he looked at him, he was covered with a loathsome disease; as he heard him, he uttered a piteous request to be filled with what fell from the rich man's table. Yet nothing was done to help his bodily misery, and, as the word 'desiring' (ἐπιθυμῶν) implies, his longing for the 'crumbs' remained unsatisfied. So selfish in the use of his wealth was Dives, so wretched Lazarus in his view; so self-satisfied and unpitying was the Pharisee, so miserable in his sight and so needy the publican and sinner. 'Yea, even the dogs came and licked his sores'—for it is not to be understood as an alleviation, but as an aggravation of his ills, that he was left to the dogs, which in Scripture are always represented as unclean animals.

So it was before men. But how was it before God? There the relation was reversed. The beggar died—no more of him here. But the Angels 'carried him away into Abraham's bosom.' Leaving aside for the present[3] the Jewish teaching concerning the 'after death,' we are struck with the sublime simplicity of the figurative language used by Christ, as compared with the wild and sensuous fancies of later Rabbinic teaching on the subject. It is, indeed, true, that we must not look in this Parabolic language for Christ's teaching about the 'after death.' On the other hand, while He would say nothing that was essentially divergent from, at least, the

---

[1] The better reading of ver. 20 is that adopted in the Revised Version: 'And a certain beggar named Lazarus'—only that we should render 'was cast.'

[2] I cannot agree with Dean *Plumptre* that the name Lazarus had been chosen with special reference, and as a warning, to the brother of Martha and Mary. If Lazarus of Bethany was thus to be warned in regard to the proper use of his riches,

his name would have been given to Dives, and not to the beggar. But besides, can we for one moment believe that Christ would in such manner have introduced the name of Lazarus of Bethany into such a Parable, he being alive at the time? Nothing, surely, could be further from His general mode of teaching than the introduction of such personalities.

[3] For this see Book V. ch. vi.

BOOK
IV

purest views entertained on the subject at that time—since otherwise the object of the Parabolic illustration would have been lost—yet, whatever He did say must, when stripped of its Parabolic details, be consonant with fact. Thus, the carrying up of the soul of the righteous by Angels is certainly in accordance with Jewish teaching, though stripped of all legendary details, such as about the number and the greetings of the Angels.[a] But it is also fully in accordance with Christian thought of the ministry of Angels. Again, as regards the expression 'Abraham's bosom,' it occurs, although not frequently, in Jewish writings.[b][1] On the other hand, the appeal to Abraham as our father is so frequent, his presence and merits are so constantly invoked; notably, he is so expressly designated as he who receives (מקבל) the penitent into Paradise,[c] that we can see how congruous especially to the higher Jewish teaching, which dealt not in coarsely sensuous descriptions of *Gan Eden*, or Paradise, the phrase 'Abraham's bosom' must have been. Nor surely can it be necessary to vindicate the accord with Christian thinking of a figurative expression, that likens us to children lying lovingly in the bosom of Abraham as our spiritual father.

2. *Dives and Lazarus after death*[d]: The 'great contrast' fully realised, and how to enter into the Kingdom.—Here also the main interest centres in Dives. He also has died and been buried. Thus ends all his exaltedness before men. The next scene is in *Hades* or *Sheol*, the place of the disembodied spirits before the final Judgment. It consists of two divisions: the one of consolation, with all the faithful gathered unto Abraham as their father; the other of fiery torment. Thus far in accordance with the general teaching of the New Testament. As regards the details, they evidently represent the views current at the time among the Jews. According to them, the Garden of Eden and the Tree of Life were the abode of the blessed.[e] Nay, in common belief, the words of Gen. ii. 10: 'a river went out of Eden to water the garden,' indicated that this Eden was distinct from, and superior to, the garden in which Adam had been originally placed.[f] With reference to it, we read that the righteous in *Gan Eden* see the wicked in *Gehinnom*, and rejoice;[g] and, similarly, that the wicked in *Gehinnom* see the righteous sitting beatified in *Gan Eden*, and their souls are troubled.[h] Still more marked is the parallelism in a legend told[i] about two wicked companions, of whom one had died impenitent, while the other on seeing

[margin notes:]
[a] Kethub. 104 a; Bemidb. R. 11, ed. Warsh. p. 42 b; Targ. on Cant. iv. 12
[b] 4 Macc. xiii. 16; Kidd. 72 b, 1st line
[c] Erub. 19 a
[d] St. Luke xvi. 23-26
[e] Jer. Targ. on Gen. iii. 24
[f] Ber. 34 b
[g] Vayyik.R. 32, beginning
[h] u.s. p.48 b, lines 8 and 9 from top
[i] Midr. on Eccles. i.15, ed. Warsh. p. 81 b. about the middle

---

[1] But I cannot think with *Grimm* (Kurzgef. Exeg. Handb. z. d. Apokr. Lief. iv. p. 347) that the expression refers to a feast of fellowship.

it had repented. After death, the impenitent in Gehinnom saw the happiness of his former companion, and murmured. When told that the difference of their fate was due to the other's penitence, he wished to have space assigned for it, but was informed that this life (the eve of the Sabbath) was the time for making provision for the next (the Sabbath). Again, it is consonant with what were the views of the Jews, that conversations could be held between dead persons, of which several legendary instances are given in the Talmud.[a][1] The torment, especially of thirst, of the wicked, is repeatedly mentioned in Jewish writings. Thus, in one place,[b] the fable of *Tantalus* is apparently repeated. The righteous is seen beside delicious springs, and the wicked with his tongue parched at the brink of a river, the waves of which are constantly receding from him.[c] But there is this very marked and characteristic contrast, that in the Jewish legend the beatified is a Pharisee, while the sinner tormented with thirst is a Publican! Above all, and as marking the vast difference between Jewish ideas and Christ's teaching, we notice that there is no analogy in Rabbinic writings to the statement in the Parable, that there is a wide and impassable gulf between Paradise and Gehenna.

To return to the Parable. When we read that Dives in torments 'lifted up his eyes,' it was, no doubt, for help, or, at least, alleviation. Then he first perceived and recognised the reversed relationship. The text emphatically repeats here: 'And he,—literally, this one (καὶ αὐτός), as if now, for the first time, he realised, but only to misunderstand and misapply it, how easily superabundance might minister relief to extreme need—'calling (viz., upon = invoking) said: "Father Abraham, have mercy upon me, and send Lazarus."' The invocation of Abraham, as having the power, and of Abraham as 'Father,' was natural on the part of a Jew. And our Lord does not here express what really was, but only introduces Jews as speaking in accordance with the popular notions. Accordingly, it does not necessarily imply on the part of Dives either glorification of carnal descent (*gloriatio carnis*, as *Bengel* has it), nor a latent idea that he might still dispose of Lazarus. A Jew would have appealed to 'Father Abraham' under such or like circumstances, and many analogous statements might be quoted in proof. But all the more telling is it, that the rich Pharisee should behold in the bosom of Abraham, whose child he specially claimed to be, what, in his sight, had been poor Lazarus, covered with moral sores, and, religiously speaking, thrown down outside his gate—not only not admitted to

[a] Ber. 18 b

[b] Jer. Chag. 77 d

[c] Comp. also Jer. Sanh. 23 c about the middle

[1] According to some of the commentators these were, however, dreams.

the fellowship of his religious banquet, but not even to be fed by the crumbs that fell from his table, and to be left to the dogs. And it was the climax of the contrast that he should now have to invoke, and that in vain, his ministry, seeking it at the hands of Abraham. And here we also recall the previous Parable about making, ere it fail, friends by means of the Mamon of unrighteousness, that they may welcome us in the everlasting tabernacles.

It should be remembered that Dives now limits his request to the humblest dimensions, asking only that Lazarus might be sent to dip the tip of his finger in the cooling liquid, and thus give him even the smallest relief. To this Abraham replies, though in a tone of pity: 'Child,' yet decidedly—showing him, first, the rightness of the present position of things; and, secondly, the impossibility of any alteration, such as he had asked. Dives had, in his lifetime, received his good things; that had been *his* things, he had chosen them as his part, and used them for self, without communicating of them. And Lazarus had received evil things. Now Lazarus was comforted, and Dives in torment. It was the right order—not that Lazarus was comforted because in this world he had suffered, nor yet that Dives was in torment because in this world he had had riches. But Lazarus received there the comfort which had been refused to him on earth, and the man who had made this world his good, and obtained there his portion, of which he had refused even the crumbs to the most needy, now received the meet reward of his unpitying, unloving, selfish life. But, besides all this, which in itself was right and proper, Dives had asked what was impossible: no intercourse could be held between Paradise and Gehenna, and on this account[1] a great and impassable chasm existed between the two, so that, even if they would, they could not, pass from heaven to hell, nor yet from hell to those in bliss. And, although doctrinal statements should not be drawn from Parabolic illustrations, we would suggest that, at least so far as this Parable goes, it seems to preclude the hope of a gradual change or transition after a life lost in the service of sin and self.

3. *Application of the Parable*,ᵃ showing how the Law and the Prophets cannot fail, and how we must now press into the Kingdom. It seems a strange misconception on the part of some commentators, that the next request of Dives indicates a commencing change of mind on his part. To begin with, this part of the Parable is only

---

[1] The exact rendering in ver. 26 is; 'in order that (ὅπως, so also in ver. 28) they who would pass from hence to you,' &c.

intended to illustrate the need, and the sole means of conversion to CHAP.
God—the appeal to the Law and the Prophets being the more apt XVIII
that the Pharisees made their boast of them, and the refusal of any
special miraculous interposition the more emphatic, that the Pharisees
had been asking for ' a sign from heaven.' Besides, it would require
more than ordinary charity to discover a moral change in the desire
that his brothers might—not be converted, but not come to that
place of torment!

Dismissing, therefore, this idea, we now find Dives pleading that
Lazarus might be sent to his five brothers, who, as we infer, were of
the same disposition and life as himself had been, to 'testify unto
them'—the word implying more than ordinary, even earnest, testimony. Presumably, what he so earnestly asked to be attested was, that
he, Dives, was in torment; and the expected effect, not of the testimony but of the mission of Lazarus,[a] whom they are supposed to have [a] ver. 30
known, was, that these, his brothers, might not come to the same
place. At the same time, the request seems to imply an attempt at
self-justification, as if, during his life, he had not had sufficient
warning. Accordingly, the reply of Abraham is no longer couched
in a tone of pity, but implies stern rebuke of Dives. They need no
witness-bearer: they have Moses and the Prophets, let them hear
them. If testimony be needed, theirs has been given, and it is
sufficient—a reply this, which would specially appeal to the Pharisees.
And when Dives, now, perhaps, as much bent on self-justification as
on the message to his brothers, remonstrates that, although they had
not received such testimony, yet 'if one come to them from the
dead,' they would repent, the final, and, as, alas! history has shown
since the Resurrection of Christ, the true answer is, that 'if they hear
not [give not hearing to] Moses and the Prophets, neither will they
be influenced[1] [moved: their intellects to believe, their wills to
repent], if one rose from the dead.'

And here the Parable, and the warning to the Pharisees, abruptly
break off. When next we hear the Master's voice,[b] it is in loving [b] ch. xvii.
application to the disciples of some of the lessons which were implied
in what He had spoken to the Pharisees.

---

[1] This is the real meaning of the verb
πείθω in the passive voice. The rendering 'persuade' is already Targumic—
giving it the sense of moving or influencing the intellect. To us the other
sense, that of influencing the will to repentance, seems more likely to have
been intended.

CHAPTER XIX.

THE THREE LAST PARABLES OF THE PERÆAN SERIES: THE UNRIGHTEOUS JUDGE—THE SELF-RIGHTEOUS PHARISEE AND THE PUBLICAN—THE UNMERCIFUL SERVANT.

(St. Luke xviii. 1–14; St. Matt. xviii. 23–35.)

BOOK
IV

IF we were to seek confirmation of the suggestion, that these last and the two preceding Parables are grouped together under a common viewpoint, such as that of *Righteousness*, the character and position of the Parables now to be examined would supply it. For, while the Parable of the Unjust Judge evidently bears close affinity to those that had preceded—especially to that of him who persisted in his request for bread [a]—it evidently refers not, as the other, to man's present need, but to the Second Coming of Christ. The prayer, the perseverance, the delay, and the ultimate answer of which it speaks, are all connected with it.[b] Indeed, it follows on what had passed on this subject immediately before—first, between the Pharisees and Christ,[c] and then between Christ and the disciples.[d]

Again, we must bear in mind that between the Parable of *Dives and Lazarus* and that of the *Unjust Judge*, not, indeed, a great interval of time, but most momentous events, had intervened. These were: the visit of Jesus to Bethany, the raising of Lazarus, the Jerusalem council against Christ, the flight to Ephraim,[e] a brief stay and preaching there, and the commencement of His last journey to Jerusalem.[f] During this last slow journey from the borders of Galilee to Jerusalem, we suppose the Discourses[g] and the Parable about the Coming of the Son of Man to have been spoken. And although such utterances will be best considered in connection with Christ's later and full Discourses about ' The Last Things,' we readily perceive, even at this stage, how, when He set His Face towards Jerusalem, there to be offered up, thoughts and words concerning the ' End ' may have entered into all His teaching, and so have given occasion for the questions of the Pharisees and disciples, and for the answers of Christ, alike by Discourse and in Parable.

The most common and specious, but also the most serious mis-

^a St. Luke xi. 5 &c.

^b Comp. St. Luke xviii. 7, 8
^c xvii. 20, 21
^d vv. 22–37

^e St. John xi.

^f St. Luke xvii. 11
^g St. Luke xvii.

take in reference to the Parable of 'the Unjust Judge,' is to regard
it as implying that, just as the poor widow insisted in her petition and
was righted because of her insistence, so the disciples should persist
in prayer and would be heard because of their insistence.   But this
is an entirely false interpretation.   When treating of the Parable of
the *Unrighteous Steward*, we disclaimed all merely mechanical ideas
of prayer, as if God heard us for our many repetitions.   This error
must here also be carefully avoided.   The inference from the Parable
is not, that the Church will be ultimately vindicated because she perseveres in prayer, but that she so perseveres, because God will surely
right her cause: it is not, that insistence in prayer is the cause of its
answer, but that the certainty of that which is asked for should lead
to continuance in prayer, even when all around seems to forbid the
hope of answer.   This is the lesson to be learned from a comparison
of the Unjust Judge with the Just and Holy God in His dealings
with His own.   If the widow persevered, knowing that, although no
other consideration, human or Divine, would influence the Unjust
Judge, yet her insistence would secure its object, how much more
should we 'not faint,' but continue in prayer, who are appealing to
God, Who has His people and His cause at heart, even though He
delay, remembering also that even this is for their sakes who pray.
And this is fully expressed in the introductory words.   'He spake
also a Parable to them with reference [1] to the need be ($\pi\rho\grave{o}s$ $\tau\grave{o}$ $\delta\epsilon\widetilde{\iota}\nu$)
of their [2] always praying and not fainting.' [3]

The remarks just made will remove what otherwise might seem
another serious difficulty.   If it be asked, how the conduct of the
Unjust Judge could serve as illustration of what might be expected
from God, we answer, that the lesson in the Parable is not from the
similarity but from the contrast between the Unrighteous human and
the Righteous Divine Judge.   'Hear what the Unrighteous Judge
saith.   But God [mark the emphatic position of the word], shall He
not indeed [$o\grave{v}$ $\mu\acute{\eta}$] vindicate [the injuries of, do judgment for] His
elect . . .?'   In truth, this mode of argument is perhaps the most
common in Jewish Parables, and occurs on almost every page of
ancient Rabbinic commentaries.   It is called the *Qal vaChomer*, 'light
and heavy,' and answers to our reasoning *a fortiori* or *de minore ad
majus* (from the less to the greater). [4]   According to the Rabbis, *ten*

---

[1] Even this shows that it is intended
to mark an essential difference between
this and the preceding Parables.

[2] The word $a\grave{v}\tau o\acute{v}s$ should be inserted
in the text.

[3] The verbs are, of course, in the in-
finitive.

[4] Sometimes it is applied in the opposite direction, from the greater to the less.

BOOK
IV

a Ber. R. 92,
ed. Warsh.
p. 164 b
from about
the middle

instances of such reasoning occur in the Old Testament[1] itself.[a] Generally, such reasoning is introduced by the words *Qal vaChomer*; often it is prefaced by, *Al achath Kammah veKammah*, 'against one how much and how much,' that is, 'how much more.' Thus, it is argued that, 'if a King of flesh and blood' did so and so, shall not the King of Kings, &c.; or, if the sinner received such and such, shall not the righteous, &c.? In the present Parable the reasoning would be: 'If the Judge of Unrighteousness' said that he would vindicate, shall not the Judge of all Righteousness do judgment on behalf of His Elect? In fact, we have an exact Rabbinic parallel to the thought underlying, and the lesson derived from, this Parable. When describing, how at the preaching of Jonah Nineveh repented and cried to God, His answer to the loud persistent cry of the people is thus explained: 'The bold (he who is unabashed) conquers even a wicked person [to grant him his request], how much more the All-Good of the world!'[b]

b Pesquita,
ed. *Buber.*
p. 161 a,
lines 3 and
2 from
bóttom

The Parable opens by laying down as a general principle the necessity and duty of the Disciples always to pray—the precise meaning being defined by the opposite, or limited clause: 'not to faint,' that is, not 'to become weary.'[2] The word 'always' must not be understood in respect of time, as if it meant continuously, but at all times, in the sense of under all circumstances, however apparently adverse, when it might seem as if an answer could not come, and we would therefore be in danger of 'fainting' or becoming weary. This rule applies here primarily to that 'weariness' which might lead to the cessation of prayer for the Coming of the Lord, or of expectancy of it, during the long period when it seems as if He delayed His return, nay, as if increasingly there were no likelihood of it. But it may also be applied to all similar circumstances, when prayer seems so long unanswered that weariness in praying threatens to overtake us. Thus, it is argued, even in Jewish writings, that a man should never be deterred from, nor cease praying, the illustration by *Qal vaChomer* being from the case of Moses, who knew that it was decreed he should not enter the land, and yet continued praying about it.[c]

c Siphré. ed
Friedm. p.
50 b, line 7
from top

The Parable introduces to us a Judge in a city, and a widow. Except where a case was voluntarily submitted for arbitration rather than judgment, or judicial advice was sought of a sage, *one man*

---

[1] These *ten* passages are: Gen. xliv. 8; Exod. vi. 9, 12; Numb. xii. 14; Deut. xxxi. 27; two instances in Jerem. xii. 5; 1 Sam. xxiii. 3; Prov. xi. 31; Esth. ix. 12; and Ezek. xv. 5.

[2] The verb is used in the same sense wherever it occurs in the N.T.: viz., St. Luke xviii. 1; 2 Cor. iv. 1, 16; Gal. vi. 9; Eph. iii. 13; and 2 Thess. iii. 13. It is thus peculiar to St. Luke and to St. Paul.

could not have formed a Jewish tribunal. Besides, his mode of speaking and acting is inconsistent with such a hypothesis. He must therefore have been one of the Judges, or municipal authorities, appointed by Herod or the Romans—perhaps a Jew, but not a *Jewish* Judge. Possibly, he may have been a police-magistrate, or one who had some function of that kind delegated to him. We know that, at least in Jerusalem, there were two stipendiary magistrates (*Dayyaney Gezeroth* [a]), whose duty it was to see to the observance of all police-regulations and the prevention of crime. Unlike the regular Judges, who attended only on certain days and hours,[b] and were unpaid, these magistrates were, so to speak, always on duty, and hence unable to engage in any other occupation. It was probably for this reason that they were paid out of the Temple-Treasury,[c] and received so large a salary as 225*l.*, or, if needful, even more.[d] On account of this, perhaps also for their unjust exactions, Jewish wit designated them, by a play on the words, as *Dayyaney Gezeloth*— Robber-Judges, instead of their real title of *Dayyaney Gezeroth* (Judges of Prohibitions, or else of Punishments).[1] It may have been that there were such Jewish magistrates in other places also. *Josephus* speaks of local magistracies.[e][2] At any rate there were in every locality police-officials, who watched over order and law.[3] The Talmud speaks in very depreciatory terms of these 'village-Judges' (*Dayyaney deMegista*), in opposition to the town tribunals (*Bey Davar*), and accuses them of ignorance, arbitrariness, and covetousness, so that for a dish of meat they would pervert justice.[f] Frequent instances are also mentioned of gross injustice and bribery in regard to the non-Jewish Judges in Palestine.

It is to such a Judge that the Parable refers—one who was consciously, openly, and avowedly [g] inaccessible to the highest motive, the fear of God, and not even restrained by the lower consideration of regard for public opinion. It is an extreme case, intended to illustrate the exceeding unlikelihood of justice being done. For the same purpose, the party seeking justice at his hands is described as a poor, unprotected widow. But we must also bear in mind, in the interpretation of this Parable, that the Church, whom she represents, is also widowed in the absence of her Lord. To return—this widow 'came' to the Unjust Judge (the imperfect tense in the original in-

CHAP.
XIX

[a] Kethub. 104 b

[b] Shabb.10 a

[c] Jer. Sheq. 48 a
[d] Keth. 105 a ;Jer.Keth xiii. 1

[e] Ant. iv. 8, 14

[f] Babha K. 114 a

[g] St. Luke xviii. 4

---

[1] Comp. *Geiger*, Urschr. u. Uebers. pp. 119, 120, Note, with which, however, comp. the two Essays mentioned in Note 3.

[2] See *Geiger*, u. s. p. 115.

[3] Comp.*Bloch*, Mos.Talm. Polizeirecht, which is, however, only an enlargement of *Frankel's* essay in the Monatschr. für Gesch. d. Judenth. for 1852, pp. 243-261.

BOOK
IV

dicating repeated, even continuous coming), with the urgent demand to be vindicated of her adversary, that is, that the Judge should make legal inquiry, and by a decision set her right as against him at whose hands she was suffering wrong. For reasons of his own he would not; and this continued for a while. At last, not from any higher principle, nor even from regard for public opinion—both of which, indeed, as he avowed to himself, had no weight with him—he complied with her request, as the text (literally translated) has it:

^a Comp. St.
Luke xi. 8

' Yet at any rate ^a because this widow troubleth me, I will do justice for her, lest, in the end, coming she bruise me ' [1]—do personal violence to me, attack me bodily. Then follows the grand inference from it: If the ' Judge of Unrighteousness ' speak thus, shall not the Judge of all Righteousness—God—do judgment, vindicate [by His Coming to judgment and so setting right the wrong done to His Church] ' His Elect, which cry to Him day and night, although He suffer long on account of them '—delay His final interposition of judgment and mercy, and that, not as the Unjust Judge, but for their own sakes, in order that the number of the Elect may all be gathered in, and they fully prepared?

^b St. Luke
xviii. 8

^c ver. 7

Difficult as the rendering of this last clause admittedly is, our interpretation of it seems confirmed by the final application of this Parable.^b Taking the previous verse along with it, we would have this double Parallelism: ' But God, shall He not vindicate [do judgment on behalf of] His Elect? ' ^c ' I tell you, that He will do judgment on behalf of them shortly '—this word being chosen rather than ' speedily ' (as in the A. and R.V.), because the latter might convey the idea of a sudden interposition, such as is not implied in the expression. This would be the first Parallelism; the second this: ' Although He suffer long [delay His final interposition] on account of them ' (verse 7), to which the second clause of verse 8 would correspond, as offering the explanation and vindication: ' But the Son of Man, when He have come, shall He find the faith upon the earth? ' It is a terribly sad question, as put by Him Who is the Christ: After all this long-suffering delay, shall He find the faith upon the earth— intellectual belief on the part of one class, and on the part of the Church the faith of the heart which trusts in, longs, and prays, because it expects and looks for His Coming, all undisturbed by the prevailing unbelief around, only quickened by it to more intensity

---

[1] This, as the only possible rendering of the verb in this instance, is also vindicated by *Meyer* ad loc. The Judge seems afraid of bodily violence from the exasperated woman. For a significant pugilistic use of the verb, comp. 1 Cor. ix. 27.

of prayer! Shall He find it? Let the history of the Church, nay, each man's heart, make answer!

2. *The Parable of the Pharisee and the Publican*, which follows,[a] is only internally connected with that of 'the Unjust Judge.' It is not *un*righteousness, but of *self*-righteousness—and this, both in its positive and negative aspects: as trust in one's own state, and as contempt of others. Again, it has also this connection with the previous Parable, that, whereas that of the Unrighteous Judge pointed to continuance, this to humility in prayer.

The introductory clause shows that it has no connection in point of time with what had preceded, although the interval between the two may, of course, have been very short. Probably, something had taken place, which is not recorded, to occasion this Parable, which, if not directly addressed to the Pharisees,[1] is to such as are of Pharisaic spirit. It brings before us two men going up to the Temple— whether 'at the hour of prayer,' or otherwise, is not stated. Remembering that, with the exception of the Psalms for the day and the interval for a certain prescribed prayer, the service in the Temple was entirely sacrificial, we are thankful for such glimpses, which show that, both in the time of public service, and still more at other times, the Temple was made the place of private prayer.[b] On the present occasion the two men, who went together to the entrance of the Temple, represented the two religious extremes in Jewish society. To the entrance of the Temple, but no farther, did the Pharisee and the Publican go together. Within the sacred enclosure—before God, where man should least have made it, began their separation. 'The Pharisee put himself by himself,[2] and prayed thus: O God, I thank Thee that I am not as the rest of men—extortioners, unjust, adulterers—nor also as this Publican [there].' Never, perhaps, were words of thanksgiving spoken in less thankfulness than these. For, thankfulness implies the acknowledgment of a gift; hence, a sense of not having had ourselves what we have received; in other words,

CHAP.
XIX

a St. Luke
xviii. 9-14

b Comp. St.
Luke ii. 27,
37; Acts ii.
46; v. 12, 42

---

[1] The objection of *Schleiermacher* (followed by later commentators), that, in a Parable addressed to Pharisees, a Pharisee would not have been introduced as the chief figure, seems of little force.

[2] For the philological vindication of this rendering, see *Goebel*, Parabeln (i. p. 327). The arguments in its favour are as follows: 1. It corresponds to the description of the position of the Publican, who also stood by himself 'afar off.' 2. Otherwise, the mention that the Pharisee

'stood' would seem utterly idle. He *could* not have sat. 3. The rendering 'prayed with himself,' is not correct. The words mean: '*to* himself'—and this would give no meaning. But even were we to render it 'with himself' in the sense of silent prayer, the introduction of such a remark as that he prayed silently, would be both needless and aimless. But what decides us is the parallelism with the account of the posture of the Publican.

BOOK
IV

then, a sense of our personal need, or humility. But the very first act of this Pharisee had been to separate himself from all the other worshippers, and notably from the Publican, whom, as his words show, he had noticed, and looked down upon. His thanksgiving referred not to what he had received, but to the sins of others by which they were separated from him, and to his own meritorious deeds by which he was separated from them. Thus, his words expressed what his attitude indicated; and both were the expression, not of thankfulness, but of boastfulness. It was the same as their bearing at the feast and in public places; the same as their contempt and condemnation of ' the rest of men,' and especially ' the publicans; ' the same that even their designation—' Pharisees,' ' Separated ones,' implied. The ' rest of men ' might be either the Gentiles, or, more probably, the common unlearned people, the *Am haArets*, whom they accused or suspected of every possible sin, according to their fundamental principle: ' The unlearned cannot be pious.' And, in their sense of that term, they were right—and in this lies the condemnation of their righteousness. And, most painful though it be, remembering the downright earnestness and zeal of these men, it must be added that, as we read the Liturgy of the Synagogue, we come ever and again upon such and similar thanksgiving—that they are ' not as the rest of men.' [1]

But this was not all. From looking down upon others the Pharisee proceeded to look up to himself. Here Talmudic writings offer painful parallelisms. They are full of references to the merits of the just, to ' the merits and righteousness of the fathers,' or else of Israel in taking upon itself the Law. And for the sake of these merits and of that righteousness, Israel, as a nation, expects general acceptance, pardon, and temporal benefits [2]—for, all *spiritual* benefits Israel as a nation, and the pious in Israel individually, possess already, nor do they need to get them from heaven, since they can and do work them out for themselves. And here the Pharisee in the Parable significantly dropped even the form of thanksgiving. The

[1] Of this spirit are even such Eulogies as these in the ordinary morning-prayer: ' Blessed art Thou, Lord, our God, King of the world, that Thou hast not made me a stranger (a Gentile) . . . a servant . . . a woman.'

[2] The merit or *Zekhuth*. On this subject we must refer, as far too large for quotation. to the detailed account in such works as *Weber*, System d. altsynag. Theol. pp. 280 &c. Indeed, there is no limit to such extravagances. The world itself had been created on account of the merits of Israel, and is sustained by them, even as all nations only continue by reason of this (Shemoth R. 15, 28; Bemidb. R. 2). A most extraordinary account is given in Bemidb. R. 20 of the four merits for the sake of which Israel was delivered out of Egypt: they did not change their names; nor their language; nor reveal their secrets; nor were dissolute.

religious performances which he enumerated are those which mark the Pharisee among the Pharisees: 'I fast twice a week, and I give tithes of all that I acquire.'[1] The first of these was in pursuance of the custom of some 'more righteous than the rest,' who, as previously explained, fasted on the second and fifth days of the week (Mondays and Thursdays).[a] But, perhaps, we should not forget that these were also the regular market days, when the country-people came to the towns, and there were special Services in the Synagogues, and the local Sanhedrin met—so that these saints in Israel would, at the same time, attract and receive special notice for their fasts. As for the boast about giving tithes of all that he acquired—and not merely of his land, fruits, &c.—it has already been explained,[2] that this was one of the distinctive characteristics of 'the sect of the Pharisees.' Their practice in this respect may be summed up in these words of the Mishnah:[b] 'He tithes all that he eats, all that he sells, and all that he buys, and he is not a guest with an unlearned person [*Am haArets*, so as not possibly to partake of what may have been left untithed].'

Although it may not be necessary, yet one or two quotations will help to show how truly this picture of the Pharisee was taken from life. Thus, the following prayer of a Rabbi is recorded: 'I thank Thee, O Lord my God, that Thou hast put my part with those who sit in the Academy, and not with those who sit at the corners [money-changers and traders]. For, I rise early and they rise early: I rise early to the words of the Law, and they to vain things. I labour and they labour: I labour and receive a reward, they labour and receive no reward. I run and they run: I run to the life of the world to come, and they to the pit of destruction.'[c] Even more closely parallel is this thanksgiving, which a Rabbi puts into the mouth of Israel: 'Lord of the world, judge me not as those who dwell in the big towns [such as Rome]: among whom there is robbery, and uncleanness, and vain and false swearing.'[d] Lastly, as regards the boastful spirit of Rabbinism, we recall such painful sayings as those of Rabbi Simeon ben Jochai, to which reference has already been made[3]—notably this, that if there were only two righteous men in the world, he and his son were these; and if only one, it was he![e]

The second picture, or scene, in the Parable sets before us the reverse state of feeling from that of the Pharisee. Only, we must bear in mind, that, as the Pharisee is not blamed for his giving of

---

[1] Not 'possess,' as in the A.V. [2] See Book III. ch. ii.
[3] Comp. vol. i. p. 540.

Marginal notes:

[a] Taan. 12 a

[b] Demai ii 2

[c] Ber. 28 b

[d] Erub. 21 b, lines 12 and 11 from bottom

[e] Ber. R. 35 ed. Warsh. p. 64 b, end

Chapter marker: CHAP. XIX

thanks,, nor yet for his good-doing, real or imaginary, so the prayer of the Publican is not answered, because he was a sinner. In both cases what decides the rejection or acceptance of the prayer is, whether or not it was *prayer*. The Pharisee retains the righteousness which he had claimed for himself, whatever its value; and the Publican receives the righteousness which he asks: both have what they desire before God. If the Pharisee 'stood by himself,' apart from others, so did the Publican: 'standing afar off,' viz. from the Pharisee—quite far back, as became one who felt himself unworthy to mingle with God's people. In accordance with this: ' He would not so much as lift [1] his eyes to heaven,' as men generally do in prayer, 'but smote his [2] breast' —as the Jews still do in the most solemn part of their confession on the Day of Atonement—' saying, God be merciful to me the sinner.' The definite article is used to indicate that he felt, as if he alone were a sinner—nay, *the* sinner. Not only, as has been well remarked, [3] ' does he not think of any one else ' (*de nemine alio homine cogitat*), while the Pharisee had thought of every one else; but, as he had taken a position not in front of, but behind, every one else, so, in contrast to the Pharisee, who had regarded every one but himself as a sinner, the Publican regarded every one else as righteous compared with him ' the sinner.' And, while the Pharisee felt no need, and uttered no petition, the Publican felt only need, and uttered only petition. The one appealed to himself for justice, the other appealed to God for mercy.

More complete contrast, therefore, could not be imagined. And once more, as between the Pharisee and the Publican, the seeming and the real, that before men and before God, there is sharp contrast, and the lesson which Christ had so often pointed is again set forth, not only in regard to the feelings which the Pharisees entertained, but also to the gladsome tidings of pardon to the lost: ' I say unto you, This man went down to his house justified above the other ' [so according to the better reading, παρ᾽ ἐκεῖνον]. In other words, the sentence of righteousness as from God with which the Publican went home was above, far better than, the sentence of righteousness as pronounced by himself, with which the Pharisee returned. This saying casts also light on such comparisons as between ' the righteous' elder brother and the pardoned prodigal, or the ninety-nine that ' need no repentance ' and the lost that was found, or, on such an utterance as this: ' Except your righteousness shall

---

[1] This, and not 'lift so much as his eyes,' is the proper position of the words.

[2] The word ' upon ' should be left out.

[3] So *Bengel*.

exceed the righteousness of the Scribes and Pharisees, ye shall in no case enter into the Kingdom of Heaven.[a] And so the Parable ends with the general principle, so often enunciated: 'For every one that exalteth himself shall be abased; and he that humbleth himself shall be exalted. And with this general teaching of the Parable fully accords the instruction of Christ to His disciples concerning the reception of little children, which immediately follows.[b]

3. The Parable with which this series closes—that of the *Unmerciful Servant*,[c] can be treated more briefly, since the circumstances leading up to it have already been explained in chapter iii. of this Book. We are now reaching the point where the solitary narrative of St. Luke again merges with those of the other Evangelists. That the Parable was spoken before Christ's *final* journey to Jerusalem, appears from St. Matthew's Gospel.[d] On the other hand, as we compare what in the Gospel by St. Luke follows on the Parable of the Pharisee and Publican[e] with the circumstances in which the Parable of the Unmerciful Servant is introduced, we cannot fail to perceive inward connection between the narratives of the two Evangelists, confirming the conclusion, arrived at on other grounds, that the Parable of the Unmerciful Servant belongs to the Peræan series, and closes it.

Its connection with the Parable of the Pharisee and the Publican lies in this, that Pharisaic self-righteousness and contempt of others may easily lead to unforgiveness and unmercifulness, which are utterly incompatible with a sense of our own need of Divine mercy and forgiveness. And so in the Gospel of St. Matthew this Parable follows on the exhibition of a self-righteous, unmerciful spirit, which would reckon up how often we should forgive, forgetful of our own need of absolute and unlimited pardon at the hands of God[f]—a spirit, moreover, of harshness, that could look down upon Christ's 'little ones,' in forgetfulness of our own need perhaps of cutting off even a right hand or foot to enter the Kingdom of Heaven.[g]

In studying this Parable, we must once more remind ourselves of the general canon of the need of distinguishing between what is *essential* in a Parable, as directly bearing on its lessons, and what is merely introduced for the sake of the Parable itself, to give point to its main teaching. In the present instance, no sober interpreter would regard of the essence of the Parable the King's command to sell into slavery the first debtor, together with his wife and children. It is simply a historical trait, introducing what in analogous circum-

CHAP.
XIX

[a] St. Matt.
v. 20

[b] St. Luke
xviii. 15-17

[c] St. Matt.
xviii. 23-35

[d] St. Matt.
xix. 1

[e] St. Luke
xviii. 15-17

[f] St. Matt.
xviii. 15-22

[g] St. Matt.
xviii. 1-14,
passim

stances might happen in real life, in order to point the lesson, that a man's strict desert before God is utter, hopeless, and eternal ruin and loss. Similarly, when the promise of the debtor is thus introduced: 'Have patience with me, and I will pay thee all,' it can only be to complete in a natural manner the first part of the Parabolic history and to prepare for the second, in which forbearance is asked by a fellow-servant for the small debt which he owes. Lastly, in the same manner, the recall of the King's original forgiveness of the great debtor can only be intended to bring out the utter incompatibility of such harshness towards a brother on the part of one who has been consciously forgiven by God his great debt.

Thus keeping apart the essentials of the Parable from the accidents of its narration, we have three distinct scenes, or parts, in this story. In the *first*, our new feelings towards our brethren are traced to our new relation towards God, as the proper spring of all our thinking, speaking, and acting. Notably, as regards forgiveness, we are to remember the Kingdom of God: 'Therefore has the Kingdom of God become like'—'therefore': in order that thereby we may learn the duty of absolute, not limited, forgiveness—not that of 'seven,' but of 'seventy times seven.' And now this likeness of the Kingdom of Heaven is set forth in the Parable of 'a man, a King' (as the Rabbis would have expressed it, 'a king of flesh and blood'), who would 'make his reckoning' ($\sigma\upsilon\nu\alpha\iota\rho\epsilon\iota\nu$) 'with his servants'—certainly not his bondservants, but probably the governors of his provinces, or those who had charge of the revenue and finances. 'But after he had begun to reckon'—not necessarily at the very beginning of it—'one was brought to him, a debtor of ten thousand talents.' Reckoning them only as Attic talents (1 talent = 60 minas = 6,000 dinars) this would amount to the enormous sum of about two and a quarter millions sterling. No wonder, that one who during his administration had been guilty of such peculation, or else culpable negligence, should, as the words 'brought to him' imply, have been reluctant to face the king. The Parable further implies, that the debt was admitted; and hence, in the course of ordinary judicial procedure—according to the Law of Moses,[a] and the universal code of antiquity—that 'servant,' with his family and all his property, was ordered to be sold,[1] and the returns paid into the treasury.

Of course, it is not suggested that the 'payment' thus made

---

[1] Accordingly, these servants could not have been 'bondservants,' as in the margin of the R.V.

had met his debt. Even this would, if need were, confirm the view, previously expressed, that this trait belongs not to the essentials of the Parable, but to the details of the narrative. So does the promise, with which the now terrified 'servant,' as he cast himself at the feet of the King, supported his plea for patience: 'I will pay thee all.' In truth, the narrative takes no notice of this, but, on the other hand, states: 'But, being moved with compassion, the lord of that servant released him [from the bondage decreed, and which had virtually begun with his sentence], and the debt forgave he him.'[1] A more accurate representation of our relation to God could not be made. We are the debtors of our heavenly King, Who has entrusted to us the administration of what is His, and which we have purloined or misused, incurring an unspeakable debt, which we can never discharge, and of which, in the course of justice, unending bondage, misery, and utter ruin would be the proper sequence. But, if in humble repentance we cast ourselves at His Feet, He is ready, in infinite compassion, not only to release us from meet punishment, but—O blessed revelation of the Gospel!—to forgive us the debt.

It is this new relationship to God which must be the foundation and the rule for our new relationship towards our fellow-servants. And this brings us to the *second* part, or scene in this Parable. Here the lately pardoned servant finds one of his fellow-servants, who owes him the small sum of 100 dinars, about 4*l.* 10*s.* Mark now the sharp contrast, which is so drawn as to give point to the Parable. In the first case, it was the servant brought to *account*, and that before the *King*; here it is a *servant finding* and that his *fellow-servant*; in the first case, he owed talents, in the second dinars (a six-thousandth part of them); in the first, ten thousand talents; in the second, one hundred dinars. Again, in the first case payment is only demanded, while in the second the man takes his fellow-servant by the throat—a not uncommon mode of harshness on the part of Roman creditors—and says: 'Pay what,' or according to the better reading, 'if thou owest anything.' And, lastly, although the words of the second debtor are almost the same[2] as those in which the first debtor besought the King's patience, yet no mercy is shown, but he is 'cast' [with violence] into prison, till he have paid what was due.[3]

[1] Mark the emphatic position of the words in the original.

[2] According to the better reading, the word 'all' in ver. 29 should be left out —and the omission is significant. The servant who promised to pay 'all' (ver. 26) promised more than he could possibly perform; while he who undertook what he might reasonably perform, did *not* say 'all.'

[3] The Rabbinic Law was much more merciful than this apparently harsh (Roman or Herodian) administration of it. It laid it down that, just as when a

It can scarcely be necessary to show the incongruousness or the guilt of such conduct. But this is the object of the *third* part, or scene, in the Parable. Here—again for the sake of pictorialness—the other servants are introduced as exceedingly sorry, no doubt about the fate of their fellow-servant, especially in the circumstances of the case. Then they come to their lord, and 'clearly set forth,' or 'explain' (διασαφεῖν) what had happened, upon which the Unmerciful Servant is summoned, and addressed as 'wicked servant,' not only because he had not followed the example of his lord, but because, after having received such immense favour as the entire remission of his debt on entreating his master, to have refused to the entreaty of his fellow-servant even a brief delay in the payment of a small sum, argued want of all mercy and positive wickedness. And the words are followed by the manifestations of righteous anger. As he has done, so is it done to him—and this is the final application of the Parable.[a] He is delivered to the 'tormentors,' not in the sense of being tormented by them, which would scarcely have been just, but in that of being handed over to such keepers of the prison, to whom criminals who were to be tortured were delivered, and who executed such punishment on them: in other words he is sent to the hardest and severest prison, there to remain till he should pay all that was due by him—that is, in the circumstances, for ever. And here we may again remark, without drawing any dogmatic inferences from the language of the Parable, that it seems to proceed on these two assumptions: that suffering neither expiates guilt, nor in itself amends the guilty, and that as sin has incurred a debt that can never be discharged, so the banishment, or rather the loss and misery of it, will be endless.

We pause to notice, how near Rabbinism has come to this Parable, and yet how far it is from its sublime teaching. At the outset we recall that unlimited forgiveness—or, indeed, for more than the farthest limit of three times—was *not* the doctrine of Rabbinism. It did, indeed, teach how freely God would forgive Israel, and it introduces a similar Parable of a debtor appealing to

person had owed to the Sanctuary a certain sum or his property, his goods might be distrained, but so much was to be deducted and left to the person, or given to him, as was needful for his sustenance, so was it to be between creditor and debtor. If a creditor distrained the goods of his debtor, he was bound to leave to the latter, if he had been a rich man, a sofa [to recline at table] and a couch and pillow; if the debtor had been a poor man, a sofa and a couch with a reed-mat [for coverlet] (Bab. Mets. 113 *a* and *b*). Nay, certain tools had to be returned for his use, nor was either the Sheriff-officer nor the creditor allowed to enter the house to make distraint. (As regards distraints for Vows, see Arach. 23 *b*, 24 *a*).

his creditor, and receiving the fullest and freest release of mercy,[a] and it also draws from it the moral, that man should similarly show mercy: but it is not the mercy of forgiveness from the heart, but of forgiveness of money debts to the poor,[b] or of various injuries,[c] and the mercy of benevolence and beneficence to the wretched.[d] But, however beautifully Rabbinism at times speaks on the subject, the Gospel conception of forgiveness, even as that of mercy, could only come by blessed experience of the infinitely higher forgiveness, and the incomparably greater mercy, which the pardoned sinner has received in Christ from our Father in Heaven.

But to us all there is the deepest seriousness in the warning against unmercifulness; and that, even though we remember that the case here referred to is only that of unwillingness to forgive from the heart an offending brother who actually asks for it. Yet, if not the sin, the temptation to it is very real to us all—perhaps rather unconsciously to ourselves than consciously. For, how often is our forgiveness in the heart, as well as from the heart, narrowed by limitations and burdened with conditions; and is it not of the very essence of sectarianism to condemn without mercy him who does not come up to our demands—ay, and until he shall have come up to them to the uttermost farthing?

CHAP.
XIX

[a] For example, Shem. R. 31
[b] u. s.
[c] Bemidb. R. 19, ed. Warsh. p. 77 a
[d] Comp. Shem. R. 31

CHAPTER XX.

CHRIST'S DISCOURSES IN PERÆA—CLOSE OF THE PERÆAN MINISTRY.

(St. Luke xiii. 23–30, 31–35; xiv. 1–11, 25–35; xvii. 1–10.)

BOOK
IV

FROM the Parables we now turn to such Discourses of the Lord as belong to this period of His Ministry. Their consideration may be the more brief, that throughout we find points of correspondence with previous or later portions of His teaching.

ᵃ St. Luke
xiii. 23–30
ᵇ ver. 24;
comp. St.
Matt. vii.
13, 14; vv.
25–27;
comp. St.
Matt. viii. ,
21–23
ᶜ vv. 28, 29;
comp. St.
Matt. vii.
21–23
ᶜ vv. 28, 29;
comp. St.
Matt. viii.
11, 12
ᵈ St. Matthew and
St. Luke
ᵉ St. Luke
xiii. 23 &c.

ᶠ See also
ver. 31

Thus, the *first* of these Discourses, of which we have an outline,ᵃ recalls some passages in the 'Sermon on the Mount,'ᵇ as well as what our Lord had said on the occasion of healing the servant of the centurion.ᶜ But, to take the first of these parallelisms, the differences are only the more marked for the similarity of form. These prove incontestably, not only the independence of the two Evangelists ᵈ in their narratives, but, along with deeper underlying unity of thought in the teaching of Christ, its different application to different circumstances and persons. Let us mark this in the Discourse as outlined by St. Luke, and so gain fresh evidential confirmation of the trustworthiness of the Evangelic records.

The words of our Lord, as recorded by St. Luke,ᵉ are not spoken, as in 'The Sermon on the Mount,' in connection with His teaching to His disciples, but are in reply to a question addressed to Him by some one—we can scarcely doubt, a representative of the Pharisees:ᶠ 'Lord, are they few, the saved ones [that are being saved]?' Viewed in connection with Christ's immediately preceding teaching about the Kingdom of God in its wide and deep spread, as the great Mustard-Tree from the tiniest seed, and as the Leaven hid, which pervaded three measures of meal, we can scarcely doubt that the word 'saved' bore reference, not to the eternal state of the soul, but to admission to the benefits of the Kingdom of God—the Messianic Kingdom, with its privileges and its judgments, such as the Pharisees understood it. The question, whether 'few' were to be saved, could not have been put from the Pharisaic point of view, if understood of personal salvation;[1] while, on the other hand, if taken as applying to part in the near-expected Messianic Kingdom, it has its distinct parallel in the Rabbinic statement, that, as regarded the days of the Messiah (His Kingdom), it would be similar to what it had been at the entrance into the land of promise, when only two (Joshua and Caleb), out of all that generation, were allowed to have part in it.[a] Again, it is only when understanding both the question of this Pharisee and the reply of our Lord as applying to the Kingdom of the Messiah—though each viewing 'the Kingdom' from his own standpoint—that we can understand the answering words of Christ in their natural and obvious sense, without either straining or adding to them a dogmatic gloss, such as could not have occurred to His hearers at the time.[2]

Thus viewed, we can mark the characteristic differences between this Discourse and the parallels in 'the Sermon on the Mount,' and understand their reason. As regarded entrance into the Messianic Kingdom, this Pharisee, and those whom he represented, are told, that this Kingdom was not theirs, as a matter of course—their question as to the rest of the world being only, whether few or many would share in it—but that all must 'struggle[3] [agonise] to enter in through the narrow door.'[4] When we remember, that in 'the Sermon on the Mount' the call was only to 'enter in,' we feel that we have now reached a period, when the access to 'the narrow door' was obstructed by the enmity of so many, and when it needed 'violence' to break through, and 'take the Kingdom' 'by force.'[b] This personal breaking through the opposing multitude, in order to enter in through the narrow door, was in opposition to the many—the Pharisees and Jews generally—who were seeking to enter in, in their own way, never doubting success, but who would discover their terrible mistake. Then, 'when once the Master of the house is risen up,' to welcome His guests to the banquet, and has shut to the door, while they, standing without, vainly call upon Him to open it, and He replies: 'I know you not whence ye are,' would they begin to

CHAP.
XX

[a] Sanh.
111 a

[b] St. Matt
xi. 12

---

[1] It is difficult to understand how *Wünsche* could have referred to Sukk. 45 *b* as a parallel, since anything more thoroughly contrary to all Christ's teaching can scarcely be imagined. Otherwise also the parallel is inapt. The curious reader will find the passage in detail in *Schöttgen*, on 1 Cor. xiii. 12 (p.652).

[2] Thus, Canon *Cook* makes this distinction: 'They who are said *to* seek, seek (*i.e.* desire and wish) and no more. They

do not struggle for admission.' But would any one be refused who *sought*, in the sense of desiring, or wishing?

[3] The word implies a real combat to get at the narrow door, not 'a large crowd . . . struggling for admission.' The verb occurs besides in the following passages: St. John xviii. 36; 1 Cor. ix. 25; Col. i. 29; iv. 12; 1 Tim. vi. 12; 2 Tim. iv. 7.

[4] So according to the best reading.

remind Him of those covenant-privileges on which, as Israel after the flesh, they had relied (' we have eaten and drunk in Thy presence, and Thou hast taught in our streets '). To this He would reply by a repetition of His former words, now seen to imply a disavowal of all mere outward privileges, as constituting a claim to the Kingdom, grounding alike His disavowal and His refusal to open on their inward contrariety to the King and His Kingdom: ' Depart from Me, all ye workers of iniquity.' It was a banquet to the friends of the King: the inauguration of His Kingdom. When they found the door shut, they would, indeed, knock, in the confident expectation that their claims would at once be recognised, and they admitted. And when the Master of the house did not recognise them, as they had expected, and they reminded Him of their outward connection, He only repeated the same words as before, since it was not outward but inward relationship that qualified the guests, and theirs was not friendship, but antagonism to Him. Terrible would then be their sorrow and anguish, when they would see their own patriarchs (' we have eaten and drunk in Thy Presence') and their own prophets (' Thou hast taught in our streets') within, and yet themselves were excluded from what was peculiarly theirs—while from all parts of the heathen world the welcome guests would flock to the joyous feast. And here pre-eminently would the saying hold good, in opposition to Pharisaic claims and self-righteousness: ' There are last which shall be first, and there are first which shall be last.' [a]

[a] Comp.
also St.
Matt. xix.
30; xx. 16

As a further characteristic difference from the parallel passage in ' the Sermon on the Mount,' we note, that there the reference seems not to any special privileges in connection with the Messianic Kingdom, such as the Pharisees expected, but to admission into the Kingdom of Heaven generally.[b] In regard to the latter also the highest outward claims would be found unavailing; but the expectation of admission was grounded rather on what was *done*, than on mere citizenship and its privileges. And here it deserves special notice, that in St. Luke's Gospel, where the claim is that of fellow-citizenship (' eaten and drunk in Thy Presence, and Thou hast taught in our streets'), the reply is made, ' I know you not whence ye are;' while in ' the Sermon on the Mount,' where the claim is of what they had done in His Name, they are told: ' I never knew you.' In both cases the disavowal emphatically bears on the special plea which had been set up. With this, another slight difference may be connected, which is not brought out in the Authorised or in the Revised Version. Both in the ' Sermon on

[b] St. Matt.
vii. 21, 22

the Mount ' 'and in St. Luke's Gospel,[b] they who are bidden depart are designated as ' workers of iniquity.' But, whereas, in St. Matthew's Gospel the term (ἀνομία) really means ' lawlessness,' the word used in that of St. Luke should be rendered 'unrighteousness ' [1] (ἀδικία). Thus, the one class are excluded, despite the deeds which they plead, for their *real contrariety to God's Law*; the other, despite the plea of citizenship and privileges, for their *unrighteousness.*[c] And here we may also note, as a last difference between the two Gospels, that in the prediction of the future bliss from which they were to be excluded, the Gospel of St. Luke, which had reported the plea that He had 'taught' in their ' streets,' adds, as it were in answer, to the names of the Patriarchs,[d] mention of ' all the prophets.'

2. The next Discourse, noted by St. Luke,[e] had been spoken ' in that very day,' [2] as the last. It was occasioned by a pretended warning of ' certain of the Pharisees ' to depart from Peræa, which, with Galilee, was the territory of Herod Antipas, as else the Tetrarch would kill Him. We have previously [3] shown reason for supposing secret intrigues between the Pharisaic party and Herod, and attributing the final imprisonment of the Baptist, at least in part, to their machinations. We also remember, how the conscience of the Tetrarch connected Christ with His murdered Forerunner, and that rightly, since, at least so far as the Pharisees wrought on the fears of that intensely jealous and suspicious prince, the imprisonment of John was as much due to his announcement of the Messiah as to the enmity of Herodias. On these grounds we can easily understand that Herod should have wished to see Jesus,[f] not merely to gratify curiosity, nor in obedience to superstitious impulses, but to convince himself, whether He was really what was said of Him, and also to get Him into his power. Probably, therefore, the danger of which these Pharisees spoke might have been real enough, and they might have special reasons for knowing of it. But their suggestion, that Jesus should depart, could only have proceeded from a ruse to get Him out of Peræa, where, evidently, His works of healing [g] were largely attracting and influencing the people.

But if our Lord would not be deterred by the fears of His disciples from going into Judæa,[h] feeling that each one had his appointed working day, in the light of which he was safe, and during the brief dura-

CHAP.
XX

[a] St. Matt. vii. 23
[b] St. Luke xiii. 27

[c] Rom. 1i.

[d] St. Matt. viii. 11
[e] St. Luke xiii. 31–35

[f] St. Luke ix. 9

[g] as spoken of in St. Luke xiii. 32

[h] St. John xi. 8

---

[1] It is characteristic of 'higher' criticism when *Hilgenfeld* declares that the 'lawlessness' in St. Matthew's Gospel is intended as a covert hit at *Pauline* Christianity, and the ' unrighteousness ' in St. Luke's as a retort upon *Petrine* or Jewish Christianity!
[2] Perhaps we should rather read ' hour.'
[3] See Book III. chap. xxviii.

BOOK
IV

tion of which he was bound to 'walk,' far less would He recede before His enemies. Pointing to their secret intrigues, He bade them, if they chose, go back to 'that fox,' and give to his low cunning, and to all similar attempts to hinder or arrest His Ministry, what would be a decisive answer, since it unfolded what He clearly foresaw in the near future.

ᵃ The word
πορεύεσθαι,
ver. 31, is
also used
in ver. 32
'go,' and
ver. 33
'walk'

'Depart'?ᵃ—yes, 'depart' ye to tell 'that fox,' I have still a brief and an appointed time[1] to work, and then 'I am perfected,' in the sense in which we all readily understand the expression, as applying to His Work and Mission. 'Depart!' 'Yes, I must "depart," or go My brief appointed time: I know that at the goal of it is death, yet not at the hands of Herod, but in Jerusalem, the slaughter-house of them that "teach in her streets."'

And so, remembering that this message to Herod was spoken in the very day, perhaps the very hour that He had declared how falsely 'the workers of wickedness' claimed admission on account of the 'teaching in their streets,' and that they would be excluded from the fellowship, not only of the fathers, but of 'all the prophets' whom they called their own—we see peculiar meaning in the refer-ence to Jerusalem as the place where all the prophets perished.[2] One, Who in no way indulged in illusions, but knew that He had an appointed time, during which He would work, and at the end of which He would 'perish,' and where He would so perish, could not be deterred either by the intrigues of the Pharisees nor by the thought of what a Herod might attempt—not do, which latter was in far other hands. But the thought of Jerusalem—of what it was, what it might have been, and what would come to it—may well have forced from the lips of Him, Who wept over it, a cry of mingled

ᵇ vv. 34, 35

anguish, love, and warning.ᵇ   It may, indeed, be, that these very words, which are reported by St. Matthew in another, and manifestly most suitable, connection,ᶜ[3] are here quoted by St. Luke, because

ᶜ St. Matt.
xxiii. 37-39

they fully express the thought to which Christ here first gave distinct utterance.   But some such words, we can scarcely doubt, He did speak even now, when pointing to His near Decease in Jerusalem.

---

[1] The words 'to-day, and to-morrow, and the third day,' must not be taken as a literal, but as a well-known figurative expression. Thus we are told (Mechilta, Par. Bo, 18, towards end. ed. *Weiss*, p. 27 *b*), 'There is a "to-morrow" which is *now* [refers to the immediate present], and a "to-morrow" of a later time,' indicating a fixed period connected with the present, The latter, for example, in the passage illustrated in the Rabbinic quo-tation just made: Ex. xiii. 14, 'It shall be when thy son shall ask thee [literally] to-morrow,' in our A.V. 'in time to come.' So also Josh. xxii. 24.   'The third day' in such connection would be מהרא דמהר.

[2] Even the death of John the Baptist may, as indicated, be said to have been compassed in Jerusalem.

[3] The words will be considered in con-nection with that passage.

3. The next in order of the Discourses recorded by St. Luke ^a is that which prefaced the Parable of 'the Great Supper,' expounded in a previous chapter.^b The Rabbinic views on the Sabbath-Law have been so fully explained, that a very brief commentation will here suffice. It appears, that the Lord condescended to accept the invitation to a Sabbath-meal in the house 'of one of the Rulers of the Pharisees'—perhaps one of the Rulers of the Synagogue in which they had just worshipped, and where Christ may have taught. Without here discussing the motives for this invitation, its acceptance was certainly made use of to 'watch Him.' And the man with the dropsy had, no doubt, been introduced for a treacherous purpose, although it is not necessary to suppose that he himself had been privy to it. On the other hand, it is characteristic of the gracious Lord, that, with full knowledge of their purpose, He sat down with such companions, and that He did His Work of power and love unrestrained by their evil thoughts. But, even so, He must turn their wickedness also to good account. Yet we mark, that He first dismissed the man healed of the dropsy before He reproved the Pharisees.^c It was better so—for the sake of the guests, and for the healed man himself, whose mind quite new and blessed Sabbath-thoughts would fill, to which all controversy would be jarring.

And, after his departure, the Lord first spake to them, as was His wont, concerning their misapplication of the Sabbath-Law, to which, indeed, their own practice gave the lie. They deemed it unlawful 'to heal' on the Sabbath-day, though, when He read their thoughts and purposes as against Him, they would not answer His question on the point.^d And yet, if 'a son,'¹ or even an ox,' of any of them, had 'fallen into a pit,' they would have found some valid legal reason for pulling him out! Then, as to their Sabbath-feast, and their invitation to Him, when thereby they wished to lure Him to evil—and, indeed, their much-boasted hospitality: all was characteristic of these Pharisees—only external show, with utter absence of all real love; only self-assumption, pride, and self-righteousness, together with contempt of all who were regarded as religiously or intellectually beneath them—chiefly of 'the unlearned' and 'sinners,' those in 'the streets and lanes' of their city, whom they considered as 'the poor, and the maimed, and the halt, and the blind.'^e Even among themselves there was strife about 'the first places'—such as, perhaps, Christ had on that occasion witnessed,^f amidst mock professions of humility, when, perhaps, the master of the house had

¹ So—and not 'ass'—according to the best reading.

CHAP.
XX

^a St. Luke
xiv. 1-11
^b Chapter
xvi.

^c St. Luke
xiv. 4

^d vv. 3, 4

^e ver. 21

^f ver. 7-11

BOOK
IV

• ver. 10

afterwards, in true Pharisaic fashion, proceeded to re-arrange the guests according to their supposed dignity. And even the Rabbis had given advice to the same effect as Christ's ª—and of this His words may have reminded them.[1]

But further—addressing him who had so treacherously bidden Him to this feast, Christ showed how the principle of Pharisaism consisted in self-seeking, to the necessary exclusion of all true love.

ᵇ vv. 12-14

ᶜ Chapter xvi.

Referring, for the fuller explanation of His meaning,ᵇ to a previous chapter,ᶜ we content ourselves here with the remark, that this self-seeking and self-righteousness appeared even in what, perhaps, they most boasted of—their hospitality. For, if in an earlier Jewish record we read the beautiful words: 'Let thy house be open

ᵈ Ab. 1. 5

ᵉ Ab. de R. Nathan 7

towards the street, and let the poor be the sons of thy house,'ᵈ we have, also, this later comment on them,ᵉ that Job had thus had his house opened to the four quarters of the globe for the poor, and that, when his calamities befell him, he remonstrated with God on the ground of his merits in this respect, to which answer was made, that he had in this matter come very far short of the merits of Abraham. So entirely self-introspective and self-seeking did Rabbinism become, and so contrary was its outcome to the spirit of Christ, the inmost meaning of Whose Work, as well as Words, was entire self-forgetfulness and self-surrender in love.

ᶠ St. Luke xiv. 25-35

4. In the fourth Discourse recorded by St. Luke,ᶠ we pass from the parenthetic account of that Sabbath-meal in the house of the 'Ruler of the Pharisees,' back to where the narrative of the Phari-

ᵍ xiii. 31-35

sees' threat about Herod and the reply of Jesus had left us.ᵍ And, if proof were required of the great influence exercised by Jesus, and which, as we have suggested, led to the attempt of the Pharisees to induce Christ to leave Peræa, it would be found in the opening

ʰ ver. 25

notice,ʰ as well as in the Discourse itself which He spoke. Christ did depart—from that place, though not yet from Peræa; but with Him 'went great multitudes.' And, in view of their professed adhesion, it was needful, and now more emphatically than ever, to set before them all that discipleship really involved, alike of cost and of strength—the two latter points being illustrated by brief 'Parables' (in the wider sense of that term). Substantially, it was only what Christ had told the Twelve, when He sent them on their first

ⁱ St. Matt. x. 37, 38

Mission.[1] Only it was now cast in a far stronger mould, as befitted the altered circumstances, in the near prospect of Christ's condemnation, with all that this would involve to His followers.

[1] Almost precisely the same sayings occur in Ab. de Rabbi Nathan 25 and Vayyikra R. 1.

At the outset we mark, that we are not here told what constituted the true disciple, but what would prevent a man from becoming such. Again, it was now no longer (as in the earlier address to the Twelve), that he who loved the nearest and dearest of earthly kin more than Christ—and hence clave to such rather than to Him—was not worthy of Him; nor that he who did not take his cross and follow after Him was not worthy of the Christ. Since then the enmity had ripened, and discipleship become impossible without actual renunciation of the nearest relationship, and, more than that, of life itself.[a] Of course, the term 'hate' does not imply hatred of parents or relatives, or of life, in the ordinary sense. But it points to this, that, as *outward* separation, consequent upon men's antagonism to Christ, was before them in the near future, so, in the present, *inward* separation, a renunciation in mind and heart, preparatory to that outwardly, was absolutely necessary. And this immediate call was illustrated in twofold manner. A man who was about to begin building a tower, must count the cost of his undertaking.[b] It was not enough that he was prepared to defray the expense of the foundations; he must look to the cost of the whole. So must they, in becoming disciples, look not on what was involved in the present following of Christ, but remember the cost of the final acknowledgment of Jesus. Again, if a king went to war, common prudence would lead him to consider whether his forces were equal to the great contest before him; else it were far better to withdraw in time, even though it involved humiliation, from what, in view of his weakness, would end in miserable defeat.[c] So, and much more, must the intending disciple make complete inward surrender of all, deliberately counting the cost, and, in view of the coming trial, ask himself whether he had, indeed, sufficient inward strength—the force of love to Christ—to conquer. And thus discipleship, then, and, in measure, to all time, involves the necessity of complete inward surrender of everything for the love of Christ, so that if, and when, the time of outward trial comes, we may be prepared to conquer in the fight.[d] He fights well, who has first fought and conquered within.

Or else, and here Christ breaks once more into that pithy Jewish proverb—only, oh! how aptly, applying it to His disciples—'Salt is good;' 'salt, if it have lost its savour, wherewith shall it be salted?'[e] We have preferred quoting the proverb in its Jewish form,[f1] to show its popular origin. Salt in such condition was neither fit to improve

a St. Luke xiv. 26

b vv. 28–30

c vv. 31, 32

d ver. 33

e vv. 34, 35

f Bekhor. 8 b, lines 14, 13 from bottom

---

[1] In the Talmud: מילחא כי סרי [has an evil odour, is spoiled] במאי מלחי לה.

BOOK
IV

the land, nor, on the other hand, to be mixed with the manure. The disciple who had lost his distinctiveness would neither benefit the land, nor was he even fit, as it were, for the dunghill, and could only be cast out. And so, let him that hath ears to hear, hear the warning!

5. We have still to consider the last Discourses of Christ before the raising of Lazarus.[a] As being addressed to the disciples,[b] we have to connect them with the Discourse just commented upon. In point of fact, part of these admonitions had already been spoken on a previous occasion, and that more fully, to the disciples in Galilee.[c] Only we must again bear in mind the difference of circumstances. Here, they immediately precede the raising of Lazarus,[d] and they form the close of Christ's public Ministry in Peræa. Hence they come to us as Christ's parting admonitions to His Peræan followers.

Thus viewed, they are intended to impress on the new disciples these four things: to be careful to give no offence;[e] to be careful to take no offence;[f] to be simple and earnest in their faith, and absolutely to trust its all-prevailing power;[g] and yet, when they had made experience of it, not to be elated, but to remember their relation to their Master, that all was in His service, and that, after all, when everything had been done, they were but unprofitable servants.[h] In other words, they urged upon the disciples holiness, love, faith, and service of self-surrender and humility.

Most of these points have been already considered, when explaining the similar admonitions of Christ in Galilee.[1] The four parts of this Discourse are broken by the prayer of the Apostles, who had formerly expressed their difficulty in regard to these very requirements:[1] ' Add unto us faith.' It was upon this that the Lord spake to them, for their comfort, of the absolute power of even the smallest faith,[k] and of the service and humility of faith.[m] The latter was couched in a Parabolic form, well calculated to impress on them those feelings which would keep them lowly. They were but servants; and, even though they had done their work, the Master expected them to serve Him, before they sat down to their own meal and rest. Yet meal and rest there would be in the end. Only, let there not be self-elation, nor weariness, nor impatience; but let the Master and His service be all in all. Surely, if ever there was emphatic protest against the fundamental idea of Pharisaism, as claim-

Margin notes:
[a] St. Luke xvii. 1–10
[b] xvii. 1
[c] vv. 1–4, comp. St. Matt. xviii. 6–35; ver. 6, comp. St. Matt. xvii. 20
[d] St. John xi.
[e] St. Luke xvii. 1, 2
[f] vv. 3, 4
[g] ver. 6
[h] vv. 7–10
[i] St. Matt. xviii. 1–6, &c., 21, 22
[k] St. Luke xvii. 6
vv. 7–10

---

[1] See Book IV. chap. iii.

ing merit and reward, it was in the closing admonition of Christ's
public Ministry in Peræa: 'When ye shall have done all those things
which are commanded you, say, We are unprofitable servants; we
have done that which was our duty to do.'

And with these parting words did He most effectually and for
ever separate, in heart and spirit, the Church from the Synagogue.

CHAPTER XXI.

THE DEATH AND THE RAISING OF LAZARUS—THE QUESTION OF MIRACLES
AND OF THIS MIRACLE OF MIRACLES—VIEWS OF NEGATIVE CRITICISM
ON THIS HISTORY—JEWISH BURYING-RITES AND SEPULCHRES.

(St. John xi. 1-54.)

BOOK
IV

FROM listening to the teaching of Christ, we turn once more to follow His working. It will be remembered, that the visit to Bethany divides the period from the Feast of the Dedication to the last Paschal week into two parts. It also forms the prelude and preparation for the awful events of the End. For, it was on that occasion that the members of the Sanhedrin formally resolved on His Death. It now only remained to settle and carry out the plans for giving effect to their purpose.

This is one aspect of it. There is yet another and more solemn one. The raising of Lazarus marks the highest point (not in the Manifestation, but) in the ministry of our Lord; it is the climax in a history where all is miraculous—the Person, the Life, the Words, the Work. As regards Himself, we have here the fullest evidence alike of His Divinity and Humanity; as regards those who witnessed it, the highest manifestation of faith and of unbelief. Here, on this height, the two ways finally meet and part. And from this high point—not only from the resolution of the Sanhedrists, but from the raising of Lazarus—we have our first clear outlook on the Death and Resurrection of Christ, of which the raising of Lazarus was the typical prelude. From this height, also, have we an outlook upon the gathering of the Church at His empty Tomb, where the precious words spoken at the grave of Lazarus received their full meaning —till Death shall be no more. But chiefly do we now think of it as the Miracle of Miracles in the history of the Christ. He had, indeed, before this raised the dead; but it had been in far-off Galilee, and in circumstances essentially different. But now it would be one so well known as Lazarus, at the very gates of Jerusalem, in the sight of all men, and amidst surroundings which admitted not of mistake or doubt. If this Miracle be true, we instinctively feel all is true; and *Spinoza* was right in saying,[1] that if he could believe the raising of Lazarus, he would tear to shreds his system, and humbly accept the creed of Christians.

But is it true? We have reached a stage in this history when such a question, always most painful, might seem almost uncalled for. For, gradually and with increasing clearness, we have learned the trustworthiness of the Evangelic records; and, as we have followed Him, the conviction has deepened into joyous assurance, that He, Who spake, lived, and wrought as none other, is in very deed the Christ of God. And yet we ask ourselves here this question again, on account of its absolute and infinite importance; because this may be regarded as the highest and decisive moment in this History; because, in truth, it is to the historical faith of the Church what the great Confession of Peter was to that of the disciples. And, although such an inquiry may seem like the jarring of a discord in Heaven's own melody, we pursue it, feeling that, in so doing, we are not discussing what is doubtful, but rather setting forth the evidence of what is certain, for the confirmation of the faith of our hearts, and, as we humbly trust, for the establishment of the faith as it is in Jesus.

At the outset, we must here once more meet, however briefly, the preliminary difficulty in regard to Miracles, of which the raising of Lazarus is, we shall not say, the greatest—for comparison is not possible on such a point—but the most notable. Undoubtedly, a Miracle runs counter, not only to our experience, but to the facts on which our experience is grounded; and can only be accounted for by a direct Divine interposition, which also runs counter to our experience, although it cannot logically be said to run counter to the facts on which that experience is grounded. Beyond this it is impossible to go, since the argument on other grounds than of experience—be it phenomenal [observation and historical information] or real [knowledge of laws and principles]—would necessitate knowledge alike of all the laws of Nature and of all the secrets of Heaven.

On the other hand (as indicated in a previous part[2]), to argue this point only on the ground of experience (phenomenal or real), were not only reasoning *à priori*, but in a vicious circle. It would really amount to this: A thing has not been, because it cannot be; and it cannot be, because, so far as I know, it is not and has not been. But, to deny on such *à priori* prejudgment the possibility of Miracles,

[1] As quoted by *Godet* (ad loc.).   [2] See vol. i., p. 559.

BOOK
IV

ultimately involves a denial of a Living, Reigning God. For, the existence of a God implies at least the possibility, in certain circumstances it may be the rational necessity, of Miracles. And the same grounds of experience, which tell against the occurrence of a Miracle, would equally apply against belief in a God. We have as little ground in experience (of a physical kind) for the one as for the other. This is not said to deter inquiry, but for the sake of our argument. For, we confidently assert and challenge experiment of it, that disbelief in a God, or Materialism, involves infinitely more difficulties, and that at every step and in regard to all things, than the faith of the Christian.

But we instinctively feel that such a Miracle as the raising of Lazarus calls for more than merely logical formulas. Heart and mind crave for higher than questions of what may be logically possible or impossible. We want, so to speak, living evidence, and we have it. We have it, first of all, in the Person of the Incarnate God, Who not only came to abolish death, but in Whose Presence the continuance of disease and death was impossible. And we have it also in the narrative of the event itself. It were, indeed, an absurd demand to *prove* a Miracle, since to do so were to show that it was not a Miracle. But we may be rationally asked these three things: first, to show, that no other explanation is rationally possible than that which proceeds on the ground of its being a Miracle; secondly, to show, that such a view of it is consistent with itself and with all the details of the narrative; and, thirdly, that it is harmonious with what precedes and what follows the narrative. The second and third of these arguments will be the outcome of our later study of the history of this event; the first, that no other explanation of the narrative is rationally possible, must now be briefly attempted.

We may here dismiss, as what would not be entertained by any one familiar with historical inquiries, the idea that such a narrative could be an absolute invention, ungrounded on any faet. Again, we may put aside as repugnant to, at least English, common sense, the theory that the narrative is consistent with the idea that Lazarus was not really dead (so, the Rationalists). Nor would any one, who had the faintest sympathy with the moral standpoint of the Gospels, entertain the view of M. *Renan*,[a] that it was all a ' pious fraud ' concocted between all parties, and that, in order to convert Jerusalem by a signal miracle, Lazarus had himself dressed up as a dead body and laid in the family tomb. Scarcely more rational is M. *Renan's* latest suggestion, that it was all a misunderstanding: Martha and

[a] In the earlier editions of his Vie de Jésus

Mary having told Jesus the wish of friends, that He should do CHAP.
some notable miracle to convince the Jews, and suggesting that they XXI
would believe if one rose from the dead, when He had replied, that
they would not believe even if Lazarus rose from his grave—and
that tradition had transformed this conversation into an actual event!
Nor, finally, would English common sense readily believe (with *Baur*),
that the whole narrative was an ideal composition to illustrate what
must be regarded as the metaphysical statement: ' I am the Resurrection and the Life.' Among ourselves, at least, no serious refutation of these and similar views can be necessary.

Nor do the other theories advanced require lengthened discussion.
The mythical explanation of *Strauss* is, that as the Old Testament
had recorded instances of raising from the dead, so Christian tradition
must needs ascribe the same to the Messiah. To this (without
repeating the detailed refutation made by *Renan* and *Baur*), it is
sufficient to reply: The previous history of Christ had already offered
such instances, why needlessly multiply them? Besides, if it had
been ' a legend,' such full and minute details would not have been
introduced, and while the human element would have been suppressed,
the miraculous would have been far more accentuated. Only one
other theory on the subject requires notice: that the writer of the
Fourth Gospel, or rather early tradition, had transformed the Parable
of Dives and Lazarus into an actual event. In answer, it is sufficient to say: first, that (as previously shown) there is no connection
between the Lazarus of the Parable and him of Bethany; secondly,
that, if it had been a Parable transformed, the characters chosen
would not have been real persons, and that they were such is evident
from the mention of the family in different circumstances in the
three Synoptic Gospels,[a] of which the writer of the Fourth Gospel
was fully aware.[b] Lastly, as *Godet* remarks, whereas the *Parable*
closes by declaring that the Jews would not believe even if one rose
from the dead, the *Narrative* closes on this wise:[c] ' Many therefore
of the Jews, which came to Mary and beheld that which He did,
believed on Him.'[1]

In view of these proposed explanations, we appeal to the impartial

[a] St. Luke
x. 38 &c.;
St. Matt.
xxvi. 6 &c.
St. Mark
xiv. 3
[b] St. John
xi. 2
[c] St. John
xi. 45

[1] I do not quite understand, whether
or not Dr. *Abbott* (Encycl. Brit., Art.
'Gospels,' pp. 837, 838) holds the ' historical accuracy' of this narrative. In
a foot-note he disclaims its ' complete
discussion' as foreign to the purpose of
his essay. He refers us, however, to the
Parable of Dives and Lazarus, together
with the comments on it of *Lightfoot* in
his Horæ Hebr., and of *Wünsche* in his
Beitr. z. Erl. d. Evangelien. I have
carefully examined both, but cannot see
that either or both contribute anything
to help our understanding of the raising
of Lazarus.

reader, whether any of them rationally accounts for the origin and existence of this history in Apostolic tradition? On the other hand, everything is clear and consistent on the supposition of the historical truth of this narrative: the minuteness of details; the vividness and pictorialness of the narrative: the characteristic manner in which Thomas, Martha, and Mary speak and act, in accordance with what we read of them in the other Gospels or in other parts of this Gospel; the Human affection of the Christ; the sublime simplicity and majesty of the manner of the Miracle; and the effects of it on friend and foe. There is, indeed, this one difficulty (not objection), that the event is not mentioned in the Synoptic Gospels. But we know too little of the plan on which the Gospels, viewed as Lives of Christ, were constructed, to allow us to draw any sufficient inference from the silence of the Synoptists, whilst we do know that the Judæan and Jerusalem Ministry of Christ, except so far as it was absolutely necessary to refer to it, lay outside the plan of the Synoptic Gospels, and formed the special subject of that by St. John. Lastly, we should remember, that in the then state of thought the introduction of another narrative of raising from the dead could not have seemed to them of such importance as it appears to us in the present state of controversy—more especially, since it was soon to be followed by another Resurrection, the importance and evidential value of which far overshadowed such an event as the raising of Lazarus. Their Galilean readers had the story of the raising of the widow's son at Nain, and of Jairus' daughter at Capernaum; and the Roman world had not only all this, but the preaching of the *Resurrection*, and of pardon and life in the Name of the Risen One, together with ocular demonstration of the miraculous power of those who preached it. It remained for the beloved disciple, who alone stood under the Cross, alone to stand on that height from which he had first full and intense outlook upon His Death, and the Life which sprang from it, and flowed into all the world.

We may now, undisturbed by preliminary objections, surrender ourselves to the sublimeness and solemnity of this narrative. Perhaps the more briefly we comment on it the better.

It was while in Peræa, that this message suddenly reached the Master from the well-remembered home at Bethany, 'the village of Mary'—who, although the younger, is for obvious reasons first mentioned in this history—'and her sister Martha,' concerning their (younger) brother Lazarus: 'Lord, behold he whom Thou lovest is sick!' They are apparently the very words which 'the sisters' bade

their messeger tell. We note as an important fact to be stored in
our memory, that the Lazarus, who had not even been mentioned in
the only account preserved to us of a previous visit of Christ to
Bethany, [a] is described as 'he whom Christ loved.' What a gap of
untold events between the two visits of Christ to Bethany—and what
modesty should it teach us as regards inferences from the circumstance
that certain events are not recorded in the Gospels ! The messenger
was apparently dismissed by Christ with this reply: 'This sickness is
not unto death, but for the glory of God, in order that the Son of
God may be glorified thereby.' We must here bear in mind, that this
answer was heard by such of the Apostles as were present at the time.[1]
They would naturally infer from it that Lazarus would not die, and
that his restoration would glorify Christ, either as having foretold it,
or prayed for it, or effected it by His Will. Yet its true meaning—
even, as we now see, its literal interpretation, was, that its final upshot
was not to be the death of Lazarus, but that it was to be for the glory
of God, in order that Christ as the Son of God might be made manifest.
And we learn, how much more full are the Words of Christ than they
often appear to us; and how truly, and even literally, they may bear
quite another meaning than appears to our honest misapprehension
of them— a meaning which only the event, the future, will disclose.

And yet, probably at the very time when the messenger received
his answer, and ere he could have brought it to the sisters, Lazarus
was already dead! Nor—and this should be especially marked—did
this awaken doubt in the minds of the sisters. We seem to hear
the very words which at the time they said to each other when each
of them afterwards repeated it to the Lord: 'Lord, if Thou hadst
been here, my brother would not have died.'[2] They probably
thought the message had reached Him too late, that Lazarus would
have lived if Christ had been appealed to in time, or had been able
to come—at any rate, if He had been there. Even in their keenest
anguish, there was no failure of trust, no doubt, no close weighing of
words on their part—only the confidence of love. Yet all this while
Christ knew that Lazarus had died, and still He continued two whole
days where He was, finishing His work. And yet—and this is significantly noted before anything else, alike in regard to His delay
and to His after-conduct—He 'loved Martha, and her sister, and

---

[1] From the non-mention of Peter and
the prominence of Thomas it seems at
least doubtful, whether all the Apostles
were there.

[2] According to the best reading, the

words are the same, but the position of
the personal pronoun (μου) 'my'
brother is significantly different (see
Westcott ad loc.).

Lazarus.' Had there been no after-history, or had it not been known to us, or before it became known, it might have seemed otherwise— and in similar circumstances it often *does* seem otherwise to us. And again, what majestic calm, what Self-restraint of Human affections and sublime consciousness of Divine Power in this delay: it is once more Christ asleep, while the disciples are despairing, in the bark almost swamped in the storm! Christ is never in haste: least of all, on His errands of love. And He is never in haste, because He is always sure.

It was only after these two days that Christ broke silence as to His purposes and as to Lazarus. Though thoughts of him must have been present with the disciples, none dared ask aught, although not from misgiving, nor yet from fear. This also of faith and of confidence. At last, when His work in that part had been completed, He spoke of leaving, but even so not of going to Bethany, but into Judæa. For, in truth, His work in Bethany was not only geographically, but really, part of His work in Judæa; and He told the disciples of His purpose, just because He knew their fears and would teach them, not only for this but for every future occasion, what principle applied to them. For when, in their care and affection, they reminded the ' Rabbi '—and the expression here almost jars on us— that the Jews ' were even now seeking to stone ' Him, He replied by telling them, in figurative language, that we have each our working day from God, and that while it lasts no foe can shorten it or break up our work. The day had twelve hours, and while these lasted no mishap would befall him that walked in the way [he stumbleth not, because he seeth the light of this world]. It was otherwise when the day was past and the night had come. When our God-given day has set, and with it the light been withdrawn which hitherto prevented our stumbling—then, if a man went in his own way and at his own time, might such mishap befall him, ' because,' figuratively as to light in the night-time, and really as to guidance and direction in the way, ' the light is not in him.'

But this was only part of what Jesus said to His disciples in preparation for a journey that would issue in such tremendous consequences. He next spoke of Lazarus, their ' friend,' as ' fallen asleep '—in the frequent Jewish (as well as Christian) figurative sense of it,[1] and of His going there to wake him out of sleep. The disciples would naturally connect this mention of His going to Lazarus with His proposed visit to Judæa, and, in their eagerness to keep Him from the latter, interposed that there could be no need for

---

[1] As to the Jewish *usus* of the expression 'sleep' for death, see Book III. chap. xxvi

going to Lazarus, since sleep was, according to Jewish notions, one of the six,[a] or, according to others,[b] five symptoms or crises in recovery from dangerous illness. And when the Lord then plainly stated it, 'Lazarus died,' adding, what should have aroused their attention, that for their sakes He was glad He had not been in Bethany before the event, because now that would come which would work faith in them, and proposed to go to the dead Lazarus—even then, their whole attention was so absorbed by the certainty of danger to their loved Teacher, that Thomas had only one thought: since it was to be so, let them go and die with Jesus. So little had they understood the figurative language about the twelve hours on which God's sun shone to light us on our way; so much did they need the lesson of faith to be taught them in the raising of Lazarus!

We already know the quiet happy home of Bethany.[1] When Jesus reached it, 'He found'—probably from those who met Him by the way[c] [2]—that Lazarus had been already four days in the grave. According to custom, he would be buried the same day that he had died.[d] Supposing his death to have taken place when the message for help was first delivered, while Jesus continued after that two whole days in the place where He was, this would leave about a day for His journey from Peræa to Bethany. We do not, indeed, know the exact place of His stay; but it must have been some well-known centre of activity in Peræa, since the sisters of Bethany had no difficulty in sending their messenger. At the same time we also infer that, at least at this period, some kind of communication must have existed between Christ and His more intimate disciples and friends—such as the family of Bethany—by which they were kept informed of the general plan of His Mission-journeys, and of any central station of His temporary sojourn. If Christ at that time occupied such a central station, we can the more readily understand how some of His Galilean disciples may, for a brief space, have been absent at their Galilean homes when the tidings about Lazarus arrived. Their absence may explain the prominent position taken by Thomas; perhaps, also, in part, the omission of this narrative from the Synoptic Gospels. One other point may be of interest. Supposing the journey to Bethany to have occupied a day, we would suggest the following as the order of events. The messenger of the Sisters left Bethany on the Sunday (it could not have been on the Sabbath), and reached Jesus on the

[a] Ber. 57 b
[b] Ber. R. 20

[c] Comp. St. John xi. 20

[d] Moed K. 28 a; comp Sanh. 46 b

---

[1] See chap. v. of this Book.
[2] In that case Christ's inquiry would afford another instance of His self-exinanition in His great Humiliation of 'becoming obedient.'

BOOK
IV

Monday. Christ continued in Peræa other two days, till Wednesday, and arrived at Bethany on Thursday. On Friday the meeting of the Sanhedrists against Christ took place, while He rested in Bethany on the Friday, and, of course, on the Sabbath, and returned to Peræa and 'Ephraim' on the Sunday. This may be a convenient place for adding to the account already given,[1] in connection with the burying of the widow's son at Nain, such further particulars of the Jewish observances and rites,[2] as may illustrate the present history. Referring to the previous description, we resume, in imagination, our attendance at the point where Christ met the bier at Nain and again gave life to the dead. But we remember that, as we are now in Judæa, the hired mourners— both mourning-men (for there were such) and mourning-women— would follow, and not, as in Galilee, precede, the body.[3] From the narrative we infer that the burial of Lazarus did not take place in a common burying-ground, which was never nearer a town than 50 cubits,[a] dry and rocky places being chosen in preference. Here the graves must be at least a foot and a half apart. It was deemed a dishonour to the dead to stand on, or walk over, the turf of a grave. Roses and other flowers seem to have been planted on graves.[4] But cemeteries, or common burying-places, appear in earliest times to have been used only for the poor,[b] or for strangers.[c] In Jerusalem there were also two places where executed criminals were buried.[d] All these, it is needless to say, were outside the City. But there is abundant evidence, that every place had not its own burying-ground; and that, not unfrequently, provision had to be made for the transport of bodies. Indeed, a burying-place is not mentioned among the ten requisites for every fully-organised Jewish community.[5] The names given, both to the graves and to the burying-place itself, are of interest. As regards the former, we mention such as ' the house of silence;'[e] 'the house of stone;'[f] 'the hostelry,' or, literally, 'place where you spend the night;' 'the couch;' 'the resting-place;' 'the valley of the multitude,' or 'of the dead.' The cemetery was called 'the house of graves;'[g] or 'the court of burying;' and 'the house of eternity.' 'By a euphemism, 'to die' was designated as 'going to

[a] Baba B. 25 a

[b] 2 Kings xxiii. 6; Jer. xxvi. 23
[c] St. Matt. xxvii. 7; Acts i. 19
[d] Sanh. vi. 5

[e] Targ. on Ps. cxv. 17
[f] Moed K. 9 b

[g] Erub. iii.1; Tohar. iii. 7

---

[1] When relating the history of the raising of the widow's son at Nain, Book III. chap. xx.

[2] An interesting account (to which I would acknowledge obligations) is given in a brochure by Dr. Perles, reprinted from Frankel's Monatsschrift.

[3] Shabb. 153 a; comp. also as re-

gards Jerusalem (where the Galilean custom prevailed), Semach. iii. 6.

[4] Comp. Perles, u. s. p. 25.

[5] These were: a law court, provision for the poor, a synagogue, a public bath, a secessus, a doctor, a surgeon, a scribe, a butcher, and a schoolmaster.

rest,' 'been completed;' 'being gathered to the world' or 'to the **CHAP. XXI** home of light;' 'being withdrawn,' or 'hidden.' Burial without coffin seems to have continued the practice for a considerable time, and rules are given how a pit, the size of the body, was to be dug, and surrounded by a wall of loose stones to prevent the falling in of earth. When afterwards earth-burials had to be vindicated against the Parsee idea of cremation, Jewish divines more fully discussed the question of burial, and described the committal of the body to the ground as a sort of expiation.[a] It was a curious later practice, that children who had died a few days after birth were circumcised on their graves. Children not a month old were buried without coffin or mourning, and, as some have thought, in a special place.[b] In connection with a recent controversy it is interesting to learn that, for the sake of peace, just as the poor and sick of the Gentiles might be fed and nursed as well as those of the Jews, so their dead might be buried with those of the Jews, though not in their graves.[c] On the other hand, a wicked person should not be buried close to a sage.[d] Suicides were not accorded all the honours of those who had died a natural death, and the bodies of executed criminals were laid in a special place, whence the relatives might after a time remove their bones.[e] The burial terminated by casting earth on the grave.[f]

But, as already stated, Lazarus was, as became his station, not laid in a cemetery, but in his own private tomb in a cave—probably in a garden, the favourite place of interment. Though on terms of close friendship with Jesus, he was evidently not regarded as an apostate from the Synagogue. For, every indignity was shown at the burial of an apostate; people were even to array themselves in white festive garments to make demonstration of joy.[g] Here, on the contrary, as we gather from the sequel, every mark of sympathy, respect, and sorrow had been shown by the people in the district and by friends in the neighbouring Jerusalem. In such case it would be regarded as a privilege to obey the Rabbinic direction of accompanying the dead, so as to show honour to the departed and kindness to the survivors. As the sisters of Bethany were 'disciples,' we may well believe that some of the more extravagant demonstrations of grief were, if not dispensed with, yet modified. We can scarcely believe, that the hired 'mourners' would alternate between extravagant praises of the dead and calls upon the attendants to lament;[h] or that, as was their wont, they would strike on their breast, beat their hands, and dash about their feet,[i] or break into wails and mourning songs, alone or in chorus.[k] In all probability, however, the funeral oration would be delivered—as in the case of all distinguished persons[m]—either in

Marginal notes:
[a] Sanh. 46
[b] Keth. 20 b
[c] Gitt. 61 a
[d] Sanh. 47 a
[e] u. s. 46 a
[f] Ber. 8 a
[g] Semach. 2
[h] Semach. i. 6
[i] Moed K. 27 b
[k] u. s. 28 b, where also the text their laments
[m] Jer. Moed K. i. 5

BOOK
IV

ᵃ Baba B.
100 b
ᵇ Meg. 28
a, b
ᶜ Shabb.
153 a
ᵈ Many of
them in
Moed K. 25

the house,ᵃ or at one of the stations where the bearers changed, or at the burying-place; perhaps, if they passed it, in the Synagogue.ᵇ It has previously been noted, what extravagant value was, in later times, attached to these orations, as indicating both a man's life on earth and his place in heaven.ᶜ The dead was supposed to be present, listening to the words of the speaker and watching the expression on the face of the hearers. It would serve no good purpose to reproduce fragments from these orations.ᵈ Their character is sufficiently indicated by the above remarks.[1]

When thinking of these tombs in gardens,[2] we so naturally revert to that which for three days held the Lord of Life, that all details become deeply interesting. And it is, perhaps, better to give them here rather than afterwards to interrupt, by such inquiries, our solemn thoughts in presence of the Crucified Christ. Not only the rich, but even those moderately well-to-do, had tombs of their own, which probably were acquired and prepared long before they were needed,

ᵉ Baba B.
100 b

ᶠ Ber. 53 a
ᵍ Bets. 6 a

ʰ Meg. 26 b
ⁱ Mearta.
Babha
Mets. 85 b;
Baba B.
58 a

and treated and inherited as private and personal property.ᵉ In such caves, or rock-hewn tombs, the bodies were laid, having been anointed with many spices,ᶠ with myrtle,ᵍ aloes, and, at a later period, also with hyssop, rose-oil, and rose-water. The body was dressed and, at a later period, wrapped, if possible, in the worn cloths in which originally a Roll of the Law had been held.ʰ The 'tombs' were either 'rock-hewn' or natural 'caves'ⁱ or else large walled vaults, with niches along the sides. Such a 'cave' or 'vault' of 4 cubits' (6 feet) width, 6 cubits' (9 feet) length, and 4 cubits' (6 feet) height, contained 'niches' for eight bodies—three on each of the longitudinal sides, and two at the end opposite the entrance. Each 'niche' was 4 cubits (6 feet) long, and had a height of seven and a width of six handbreadths. As these burying 'niches' were hollowed out in the walls they were called *Kukhin*.[3] The larger caves or vaults were 6 cubits (9 feet) wide, and 8 cubits (12 feet) long, and held thirteen bodies—four along each side-wall, three opposite to, and

ᵏ Baba B.
vi. 8

one on either side of the entrance.ᵏ These figures apply, of course, only to what the Law required, when a vault had been contracted for. When a person constructed one for himself, the dimensions of the walls and the number of *Kukhin* might, of course, vary. At the entrance

---

[1] See Zunz, Zur Gesch. u. Liter. pp. 304 to 458. In Moed K. 25 b we have the miraculous portents at the death of great Rabbis: columns weeping or statues flattening or bursting, blood flowing, stars appearing, trees uprooted, arches bending, &c.

[2] *Nicolai* (De Sepulchr. Hebr., a book of no great value) gives a pictorial illustration at p. 170.

[3] Not *Kokim*. On the difference, as regards the entrance into these caves, between Jewish and Phœnician tombs, see *Conder*, 'Heth and Moab,' p. 93.

to the vault was 'a court' 6 cubits (9 feet) square, to hold the bier and
its bearers.   Sometimes two 'caves' opened on this 'court.'   But it
is difficult to decide whether the second 'cave,' spoken of, was intended
as an ossary [1] (*ossarium*).   Certain it is, that after a time the bones
were collected and put into a box or coffin, having first been anointed
with wine and oil, and being held together by wrappings of cloths.[a]
This circumstance explains the existence of the mortuary chests, or
osteophagi, so frequently found in the tombs of Palestine by late
explorers, who have been unable to explain their meaning.[2]   This
unclearness [3] is much to be regretted, when we read, for example, of
such a 'chest' as found in a cave near Bethany.[b]   One of the explorers [4] has discovered on them fragments of Hebrew inscriptions.
Up to the present, only few Hebrew memorial inscriptions have been
discovered in Palestine.   The most interesting are those in or near
Jerusalem, dating from the first century B.C. to the first A.C.[5]   There
are, also, many inscriptions found on Jewish tombs *out of Palestine* (in
Rome, and other places), written in bad Greek or Latin, containing,
perhaps, a Hebrew word, and generally ending with *shalom*, 'peace,'
and adorned with Jewish symbols, such as the Seven-branched Candlestick, the Ark, the festive emblems of the Feast of Tabernacles, and
others.[6]   In general, the advice not to read such inscriptions,[c] as it
would affect the sight, seems to imply the common practice of having
memorial inscriptions in Hebrew.   They appear to have been graven
either on the lid of the mortuary chest, or on the *Golel*, or great stone
'rolled' at the entrance to the vault, or to the 'court' leading into it,
or else on the inside walls of yet another erection, made over the vaults
of the wealthy,[d] and which was supposed to complete the burying-
place, or *Qebher*.

These small buildings surmounting the graves may have served
as shelter to those who visited the tombs.   They also served as
'monuments,' [7] of which we read in the Bible, in the Apocrypha,[e]

Margin notes:
CHAP.
XXI

[a] Jer. Moed
K. i. 5;
Semach. 12
and 13

[b] Recovery
of Jerusa-
lem, p. 494

[c] Horay.
13 *b*

[d] This is
expressly
stated in
Moed. K.
8 *b*, lines
7–9

[e] 1 Macc.
xiii. 27–29

---

[1] This partly depends whether, with
Rashi and *Perles* (p. 29), we regard
שמיא בי as an *ossarium*, or, with *Levy*, regard it as = בי טעמא, 'house of mourning,' Ber. 6 *b* (comp. *Schwab* ad loc.).
[2] Comp. letters, (*a*) by Dr. *Chaplin*,
Quart. Stat. Oct. 1873, p. 155; (*b*) by M.
Clermont-Ganneau, Ap. 1874, pp. 95,
&c.; (*c*) Dr. *Chaplin*, Quart. Stat. Jan.
1876, p. 9; (*d*) Art. by Capt. *Conder* ib.
pp. 18, &c.
[3] See, especially, Capt. *Wilson's* Report in the third Quart. Stat. (1869), pp.
66, &c.

[4] M. *Clermont-Ganneau.*
[5] The supposed ancient (pre-Christian,
Israelitish) inscriptions in the Crimea are
now generally ascribed to a much later
date. Comp. *Harkavy*, Altjüd. Denkm.
[6] See *Schürer*, Gemeinde Verf. d.
Juden in Rom. *Schürer* has collected
forty-five of the most interesting of
these inscriptions.
[7] On account of the poverty of some of
the sages, it was declared that they needed
not monuments; their deeds were their
monuments (Jer. Sheqal. ii. 7, p. 47 *a*).

BOOK
IV

a Ant. xvi.
7. 1
b Erub.v. 1;
Sheq. ii. 5

c Moed K.
i. 2
d St. Matt.
xxiii. 27
Moed K. 6 a

e Moed K.
29 a

f Baba B.
100 b

and in *Josephus*.[a][1] In Rabbinic writings they are frequently mentioned, chiefly by the name *Nephesh*,[2] 'soul,' 'person'—transferred in the sense of 'monument,'[b] or, by the more Scriptural name of *bamah*,[3] or, by the Greco-Aramaic,[4] or the Hebrew designation for a building generally. But of gravestones with inscriptions we cannot find any record in Talmudic works. At the same time, the place where there was a vault or a grave was marked by a stone, which was kept whitened,[c] to warn the passer-by against defilement.[d]

We are now able fully to realise all the circumstances and surroundings in the burial and raising of Lazarus.

Jesus had come to Bethany. But in the house of mourning they knew it not. As Bethany was only about fifteen furlongs—or about two miles—from Jerusalem, many from the City, who were on terms of friendship with what was evidently a distinguished family, had come in obedience to one of the most binding Rabbinic directions— that of comforting the mourners. In the funeral procession the sexes had been separated, and the practice probably prevailed even at that time for the women to return alone from the grave. This may explain why afterwards the women went and returned alone to the Tomb of our Lord. The mourning, which began before the burial,[5] had been shared by the friends who sat silent on the ground, or were busy preparing the mourning meal. As the company left the dead, each had taken leave of the deceased with a 'Depart in peace!'[e] Then they had formed into lines, through which the mourners passed amidst expressions of sympathy, repeated (at least seven times) as the procession halted on the return to the house of mourning.[f] Then began the mourning in the house, which really lasted thirty days, of which the first three were those. of greatest, the others, during the seven days, or the special week of sorrow, of less intense mourning. But on the Sabbath, as God's holy day, all mourning was intermitted— and so 'they rested on the Sabbath, according to the commandment.'

In that household of disciples this mourning would not have

---

[1] The first gives an exaggerated account of the great monument erected by Simon Maccabeus in honour of his father and brothers; the second refers to a monument erected by Herod over the tomb of David.
[2] On the use of the word *Nephesh* as meaning not only 'soul' and 'person,' but as applied also to the   , the reader will find some very interesting remarks in the App. Not. Miscell. to *Pocock's* Porta

Mosis, pp. 19, 20, and 75–78, and in *Pagnini*, Thes. Ling. Sanct. col. 1658, &c.
[3] Ezek. xliii. 7. Probably the second clause of Is. liii. 9 should read thus: 'And with the rich His sepulchre.'
[4] רומוס.
[5] On the subject of 'mourning' I must refer generally to the corresponding chapter in 'Sketches of Jewish Social Life.'

assumed such violent forms, as when we read that the women were in
the habit of tearing out their hair,[a] or of a Rabbi who publicly scourged
himself.[b] But we know how the dead would be spoken of.   In death
the two worlds were said to meet and kiss.[c]   And now they who
had passed away beheld God.[d]   They were at rest.   Such beautiful
passages as Ps. cxii. 6, Prov. x. 7,[e] Is. xi. 10, last clause, and Is. lvii.
2,[f] were applied to them.   Nay, the holy dead should be called 'living.'
In truth, they knew about us, and unseen still surrounded us.[g]   Nor
should they ever be mentioned without adding a blessing on their
memory.[h]

In this spirit, we cannot doubt, the Jews were now 'comforting'
the sisters.   They may have repeated words like those quoted as the
conclusion of such a consolatory speech: [i] 'May the Lord of consolations (בעל נחמות) comfort you! Blessed be He Who comforteth the
mourners!' But they could scarcely have imagined how literally a
wish like this was about to be fulfilled.   For, already, the message
had reached Martha, who was probably in one of the outer apartments of the house: Jesus is coming! She hastened to meet the
Master.   Not a word of complaint, not a murmur, nor doubt, escaped
her lips—only what during those four bitter days these two sisters
must have been so often saying to each other, when the luxury of
solitude was allowed them, that if He had been there their brother
would not have died.   And even now—when it was all too late—when
they had not received what they had asked of Him by their messenger,
it must have been, because He had not asked it, though he had said
that this sickness was not unto death; or else because he had delayed
to work it till He would come.   And still she held fast by it, that
even now God would give Him whatsoever He asked.   Or, did they
mean more: were they such words of unconscious prophecy, or sight
and sound of heavenly things, as sometimes come to us in our passion
of grief, or else winged thoughts of faith too soon beyond our vision?
They could not have been the expression of any real hope of the
miracle about to take place, or Martha would not have afterwards
sought to arrest Him, when He bade them roll away the stone.   And
yet is it not even so, that, when that comes to us which our faith had
once dared to suggest, if not to hope, we feel as if it were all too
great and impossible—that a very physical 'cannot be' separates
us from it?

It was in very truth and literality that the Lord meant it, when
He told Martha her brother would rise again, although she understood His Words of the Resurrection at the Last Day.   In answer,

CHAP.
XXI

[a] Jer. Kidd.
i. 8
[b] Ab. d. R.
Nath. 25
[c] Jer.
Yebam. 4 d
[d] Siphré,
towards
end
[e] Ber. R.49
[f] Shabb.
152 b
[g] Ber. 18 b,
19 a; comp.
Heb. xii. 1
[h] Yoma 38 b;
Taan. 28 a
[i] Kethub.
8 b

BOOK
IV

Christ pointed out to her the connection between Himself and the Resurrection; and, what He spoke, that He did when He raised Lazarus from the dead. The Resurrection and the Life are not special gifts either to the Church or to humanity, but are connected with the Christ—the outcome of Himself. The Resurrection of the Just and the General Resurrection are the consequence of the relation in which the Church and humanity in general stand to the Christ. Without the Christ there would have been no Resurrection. Most literally He *is* the Resurrection and the Life—and this, the new teaching about the Resurrection, was the object and the meaning of the raising of Lazarus. And thus is this raising of Lazarus the outlook, also, upon His own Resurrection, 'Who is ' the first-fruits from the dead.'

And though the special, then present, application, or rather manifestation of it, would be in the raising of Lazarus—yet this teaching, that accompanied it, is to 'all believers:' 'He that believeth in Me, even if [though] he die, shall live; and whosoever liveth and believeth in Me shall not die for ever' [1] (unto the Æon)—where possibly we might, for commentation, mentally insert the sign of a pause (—) between the words 'die' and 'for ever,' or 'unto the Æon.' It is only when we think of the meaning of Christ's previous words, as implying that the Resurrection and the Life are the outcome of Himself, and come to us only through Him and in Him, that we can understand the answer of Martha to His question: 'Believest thou this? Yea, Lord, I have believed that thou art the Christ, the Son of God

ᵃ St. John
xi. 4

[with special reference to the original message of Christ ᵃ], He that cometh into the world ['the Coming One into the world' [2] = the world's promised, expected, come Saviour].

What else passed between them we can only gather from the context. It seems that the Master 'called' for Mary. This message Martha now hasted to deliver, although 'secretly.' Mary was probably sitting in the chamber of mourning, with its upset chairs and couches, and other melancholy tokens of mourning, as was the custom; surrounded by many who had come to comfort them; herself, we can scarcely doubt, silent, her thoughts far away in that world to, and of which the Master was to her 'the Way, the Truth, and the Life.' As

---

[1] This is not only the literal rendering, but the parallelism of the previous member of the sentence ('even if he die, shall live')—where the 'life' is neither the spiritual nor the eternal, but life in opposition to physical death—seems to demand this, rather than the rendering of both the A.V. and the R.V.

[2] Possibly it might be: 'He that was to come,' or shouln come, like הַבָּא or הֶאָתֵי, in which case it would be another evidence of Hebraisms in the Fourth Gospel.

she heard of His coming and call, she rose 'quickly,' and the Jews followed her, under the impression that she was again going to visit, and to weep at the tomb of her brother. For, it was the practice to visit the grave, especially during the first three days.[a] When she came to Jesus, where He still stood, outside Bethany, she was forgetful of all around. It was, as if sight of Him melted what had frozen the tide of her feelings. She could only fall at His Feet, and repeat the poor words with which she and her sister had these four weary days tried to cover the nakedness of their sorrow: poor words of consolation, and poor words of faith, which she did not, like her sister, make still poorer by adding the poverty of her hope to that of her faith—the poverty of the future to that of the past and present. To Martha that had been the *maximum*, to Mary it was the *minimum* of her faith; for the rest, it was far, far better to add nothing more, but simply to worship at His Feet.

It must have been a deeply touching scene: the outpouring of her sorrow, the absoluteness of her faith, the mute appeal of her tears. And the Jews who witnessed it were moved as she, and wept with her. What follows is difficult to understand; still more difficult to explain: not only from the choice of language, which is peculiarly difficult, but because its difficulty springs from the yet greater difficulty of expressing what it is intended to describe. The expression, 'groaned in spirit,' cannot mean that Christ 'was moved with indignation in the spirit,' since this could not have been the consequence of witnessing the tears of Mary and what, we feel sure, was the genuine emotion of the Jews. Of the various interpretations,[1] that commends itself most to us, which would render the expression: 'He vehemently moved His Spirit and troubled Himself.' One, whose insight into such questions is peculiarly deep, has reminded us[2] that 'the miracles of the Lord were not wrought by the simple word of power, but that in a mysterious way the element of sympathy entered into them. He took away the sufferings and diseases of men in some sense by taking them upon Himself.' If, with this most just view of His Condescension to, and union with, humanity as its Healer, by taking upon Himself its diseases, we combine the statement formerly made about the Resurrection, as not a gift or boon but the outcome of Himself—we may, in some way, not understand, but be able to gaze into, the unfathomed depth

[a] Semach. 8; Taan. 16

---

[1] For a brief but excellent summary of the principal views on the subject, see *Westcott*, ad loc.

[2] Canon *Westcott*.

of that Theanthropic fellow-suffering which was both vicarious
and redemptive, and which, before He became the Resurrection
to Lazarus, shook His whole inner Being, when, in the words of
St. John, ' He vehemently moved His Spirit and troubled Himself.'

And now every trait is in accord. ' Where have ye laid him? '
So truly human—as if He, Who was about to raise the dead, needed
the information where he had been laid; so truly human, also, in
the underlying tenderness of the personal address, and in the absorption of the whole Theanthropic energy on the mighty burden
about to be lifted and lifted away. So, also, as they bade Him come
and see, were the tears that fell from Him ($\dot{\epsilon}\delta\acute{a}\kappa\rho\upsilon\sigma\epsilon\nu$), not like the
violent lamentation ($\ddot{\epsilon}\kappa\lambda\alpha\upsilon\sigma\epsilon\nu$) that burst from Him at sight and
prophetic view of doomed Jerusalem.[a] Yet we can scarcely think
that the Jews rightly interpreted it, when they ascribed it only to
His love for Lazarus. But surely there was not a touch either of
malevolence or of irony, only what we feel to be quite natural in the
circumstances, when some of them asked it aloud: ' Could not this
One, Which opened the eyes of the blind, have wrought so that [in
order] this one also should not die ? ' Scarcely was it even unbelief.
They had so lately witnessed in Jerusalem that Miracle, such as had
' not been heard' ' since the world began; [b] that it seemed difficult to
understand how, seeing there was the will (in His affection for Lazarus), there was not the power—not to raise him from the dead, for
that did not occur to them, but to prevent his dying. Was there,
then, a barrier in death? And it was this, and not indignation, which
once more caused that Theanthropic recurrence upon Himself, when
again ' He vehemently moved His Spirit.'

And now they were at the cave which was Lazarus' tomb. He
bade them roll aside the great stone which covered its entrance.[1]
Amidst the awful pause which preceded obedience, one voice only was
raised. It was that of Martha. Jesus had not spoken of raising
Lazarus. But what was about to be done? She could scarcely have
thought that He merely wished to gaze once more upon the face
of the dead. Something nameless had seized her. She dared not
believe; she dared not disbelieve. Did she, perhaps, not dread a
failure, but feel misgivings, when thinking of Christ as in presence of
commencing corruption before these Jews—and yet, as we so often,
still love Him even in unbelief? It was the common Jewish idea that
corruption commenced on the fourth day, that the drop of gall, which

[a] St. Luke
xix. 41

[b] St. John
ix. 32

---

[1] In St. John xi. 41 the words, ' from the place where the dead was laid,' should
be omitted, as not in the best MSS.

had fallen from the sword of the Angel and caused death, was then working its effect, and that, as the face changed, the soul took its final leave from the resting-place of the body.[a] Only one sentence Jesus spake of gentle reproof, of reminder of what He had said to her just before, and of the message He had sent when first He heard of Lazarus' illness,[b] but, oh so full of calm majesty and consciousness of Divine strength. And now the stone *was* rolled away. We all feel that the fitting thing here was prayer—yet not petition, but thanksgiving that the Father 'heard' Him, not as regarded the raising of Lazarus, which was His Own Work, but in the ordering and arranging of all the circumstances—alike the petition and the thanksgiving having for their object them that stood by, for He knew that the Father always heard Him: that so they might believe, that the Father had sent Him. Sent of the Father—not come of Himself, not sent of Satan—and sent to do His Will!

And in doing this Will, He *was* the Resurrection and the Life. One loud command spoken into that silence; one loud call to that sleeper; one flash of God's Own Light into that darkness, and the wheels of life again moved at the outgoing of The Life. And, still bound hand and foot with graveclothes ['bands,' *Takhrikhin*], and his face with the napkin, Lazarus stood forth, shuddering and silent, in the cold light of earth's day. In that multitude, now more pale and shuddering than the man bound in the graveclothes, the Only One majestically calm was He, Who before had been so deeply moved and troubled Himself, as He now bade them 'Loose him, and let him go.'

We know no more. Holy Writ in this also proves its Divine authorship and the reality of what is here recorded. The momentarily lifted veil has again fallen over the darkness of the Most Holy Place, in which is only the Ark of His Presence and the cloudy incense of our worship. What happened afterwards—how they loosed him, what they said, what thanks, or praise, or worship, the sisters spoke, and what were Lazarus' first words, we know not. And better so. Did Lazarus remember aught of the late past, or was not rather the rending of the grave a real rending from the past: the awakening so sudden, the transition so great, that nothing of the bright vision remained, but its impress—just as a marvellously beautiful Jewish legend has it, that before entering this world, the soul of a child has seen all of heaven and hell, of past, present, and future; but that, as the Angel strikes it on the mouth to waken it into this world, all of the other has passed from the mind? Again we say: We know not—and it is better so.

CHAP.
XXI

[a] Abh. Z. 20 b; Ber. R. 100; Vayyik. R. 18
[b] St. John xi 4

And here abruptly breaks off this narrative. Some of those who had seen it believed on Him; others hurried back to Jerusalem to tell it to the Pharisees. Then was hastily gathered a meeting of the Sanhedrists,[1] not to judge Him, but to deliberate what was to be done That He was really doing these miracles, there could be no question among them. Similarly, all but one or two had no doubt as to the source of these miracles. If real,[2] they were of Satanic agency—and all the more tremendous they were, the more certainly so. But whether really of Satanic power, or merely a Satanic delusion, one thing, at least, was evident, that, if He were let alone, all men would believe on Him? And then, if He headed the Messianic movement of the Jews as a nation, alike the Jewish City and Temple, and Israel as a nation, would perish in the fight with Rome. But what was to be done? They had not the courage of, though the wish for, judicial murder, till he who was the High-Priest, Caiaphas, reminded them of the well-known Jewish adage, that it 'is better one man

a Ber. R. 94; comp. also 91, and the Midr. on Eccl. ix. 18

should die, than the community perish.'[a] Yet, even so, he who spoke was the High-Priest; and for the last time, ere in speaking the sentence he spoke it for ever as against himself and the office he held, spake through him God's Voice, not as regards the counsel of murder, but this, that His Death should be 'for that nation'—nay, as St. John adds, not only for Israel, but to gather into one fold all the now scattered children of God.

This was the last prophecy in Israel; with the sentence of death on Israel's true High-Priest died prophecy in Israel, died Israel's High-Priesthood. It had spoken sentence upon itself.

This was the first Friday of dark resolve. Henceforth it only needed to concert plans for carrying it out. Some one, perhaps Nicodemus, sent word of the secret meeting and resolution of the Sanhedrists. That Friday and the next Sabbath Jesus rested in Bethany, with the same majestic calm which He had shown at the grave of Lazarus. Then He withdrew, far away to the obscure bounds of Peræa and Galilee, to a city of which the very location is now unknown.[3] And there He continued with His disciples, withdrawn from the Jews—till He would make His final entrance into Jerusalem.

---

[1] On the Sanhedrin, see further, in Book V.

[2] The doubt as to their reality would, of course, come from the Sadducees in the Sanhedrin. It will be remembered, that both Caiaphas and the Chief Priests belonged to that party.

[3] The 'city' 'called *Ephraim*' has not been localised. Most modern writers identify it with the Ephraim, or Ephron, of 2 Chron. xiii. 19, in the neighbourhood of Bethel, and near the wilderness of Bethaven. But the text seems to require a place in·Peræa and close to Galilee. Comp. p. 127.

CHAPTER XXII.

ON THE JOURNEY TO JERUSALEM—DEPARTURE FROM EPHRAIM BY WAY
OF SAMARIA AND GALILEE—HEALING OF TEN LEPERS—PROPHETIC
DISCOURSE OF THE COMING KINGDOM—ON DIVORCE: JEWISH VIEWS
OF IT—THE BLESSING TO LITTLE CHILDREN.

(St. Matt. xix. 1, 2; St. Mark x.1; St. Luke xvii. 11; St. Luke xvii. 12–19; St.
Matt. xix. 3–12; St. Mark x. 2–12; St. Matt. xix. 13–15; St. Mark x. 13–16; St.
Luke xviii. 15–17.)

THE brief time of rest and quiet converse with His disciples in the retirement of Ephraim was past, and the Saviour of men prepared for His last journey to Jerusalem. All the three Synoptic Gospels mark this, although with varying details.[a] From the mention of Galilee by St. Matthew, and by St. Luke of Samaria and Galilee—or more correctly, ' between (along the frontiers of) Samaria and Galilee,' we may conjecture that, on leaving Ephraim, Christ made a very brief detour along the northern frontier to some place at the southern border of Galilee—perhaps to meet at a certain point those who were to accompany him on his final journey to Jerusalem. This suggestion, for it is no more, is in itself not improbable, since some of Christ's immediate followers might naturally wish to pay a brief visit to their friends in Galilee before going up to Jerusalem. And it is further confirmed by the notice of St. Mark,[b] that among those who had followed Christ there were ' many women which came up with Him unto Jerusalem.' For, we can scarcely suppose that these ' many women' had gone with Him in the previous autumn from Galilee to the Feast of Tabernacles, nor that they were with Him at the Feast of the Dedication, or had during the winter followed Him through Peræa, nor yet that they had been at Bethany.[1] All these difficulties are obviated if, as suggested, we suppose that Christ had passed from Ephraim along the border of Samaria to a place in Galilee, there to meet such of His disciples as would go up with Him

CHAP.
XXII

[a] St. Matt.
xix. 1, 2;
St. Mark x.
1; St. Luke
xvii. 11

[b] St. Mark
xv. 40, 41

---

[1] Indeed, any lengthened journeying, and for an indefinite purpose, would have been quite contrary to Jewish manners. Not so, of course, the travelling in the festive band up to the Paschal Feast.

BOOK
IV

to Jerusalem. The whole company would then form one of those festive bands which travelled to the Paschal Feast, nor would there be anything strange or unusual in the appearance of such a band, in this instance under the leadership of Jesus.

Another and deeply important notice, furnished by SS. Matthew and Mark, is, that during this journey through Peræa, 'great multitudes' resorted to, and followed Him, and that 'He healed' [a] and 'taught them.' [b] This will account for the incidents and Discourses by the way, and also how, from among many deeds, the Evangelists may have selected for record what to them seemed the most important or novel, or else best accorded with the plans of their respective narratives.[1]

a St. Matthew
b St. Mark

Thus, to begin with, St. Luke alone relates the very first incident by the way,[c] and the first Discourse.[d] Nor is it difficult to understand the reason of this. To one who, like St. Matthew, had followed Christ in His Galilean Ministry, or, like St. Mark, had been the penman of St. Peter, there would be nothing so peculiar or novel in the healing of lepers as to introduce this on the overcrowded canvas of the last days. Indeed, they had both already recorded what may be designated as a *typical* healing of lepers.[e] But St. Luke had not recorded such healing before; and the restoration of *ten* at the same time would seem to the 'beloved physician' matter, not only new in his narrative, but of the deepest importance. Besides, we have already seen, that the record of the whole of this East-Jordan Ministry is peculiar to St. Luke; and we can scarcely doubt that it was the result of personal inquiries made by the Evangelist on the spot, in order to supplement what might have seemed to him a gap in the Gospels of St. Matthew and St. Mark. This would explain his fulness of detail as regards incidents, and, for example, the introduction of the history of Zacchæus, which to St. Mark, or rather to St. Peter, but especially to St. Matthew (himself once a publican), might appear so like that which they had so often witnessed and related, as scarcely to require special narration. On the same ground we account for the record by St. Luke of Christ's Discourse predictive of the Advent of the Messianic Kingdom.[f] This Discourse is evidently in its place at the beginning of Christ's last journey to Jerusalem. But the other two Evangelists merge it in the account of the fuller teaching on the same subject during the last days of Christ's sojourn on earth.[g]

c St. Luke
xvii. 12-19
d vv. 20-37

e St. Matt.
viii. 2-4;
St. Mark i.
40-45

f St. Luke
xvii. 20-37

St. Matt.
xxiv.; St.
Mark xiii.

[1] This will more fully appear when we study the history of Zacchæus and the cure of the blind man in Jericho.

It is a further confirmation of our suggestion as to the road taken by Jesus, that of the ten lepers whom, at the outset of His journey, He met when entering into a village, one was a Samaritan. It may have been that the district was infested with leprosy; or these lepers may, on tidings of Christ's approach, have hastily gathered there. It was, as fully explained in another place,[1] in strict accordance with Jewish Law, that these lepers remained both outside the village and far from Him to Whom they now cried for mercy. And, without either touch or even command of healing, Christ bade them go and show themselves as healed to the priests. For this it was, as will be remembered, not necessary to repair to Jerusalem. Any priest might declare 'unclean' or 'clean' provided the applicants presented themselves singly, and not in company,[2] for his inspection.[*] And they went at Christ's bidding, even before they had actually experienced the healing! So great was their faith, and, may we not almost infer, the general belief throughout the district, in the power of 'the Master.' And *as* they went, the new life coursed in their veins. Restored health began to be felt, just as it ever is, not before, nor yet after believing, but in the act of obedience of a faith that has not yet experienced the blessing.

But now the characteristic difference between these men appeared. Of the ten, equally recipients of the benefit, the nine Jews continued their way—presumably to the priests—while the one Samaritan in the number at once turned back, with a loud voice glorifying God. The whole event may not have occupied many minutes, and Jesus with his followers may still have stood on the same spot whence He bade the ten lepers go show themselves to the priests. He may have followed them with his eyes, as, but a few steps on their road of faith, health overtook them, and the grateful Samaritan, with voice of loud thanksgiving, hastened back to his Healer. No longer now did he remain afar off, but in humblest reverence fell on his face at the Feet of Him to Whom he gave thanks. This Samaritan[3] had received more than new bodily life and health: he had found spiritual life and healing.

But why did the nine Jews not return? Assuredly, they must have had some faith when first seeking help from Christ, and still

* Neg. iii. 1

---

[1] See Book III. chap. xv.
[2] As we note, in St. Luke xvii. 14, the direction to show themselves 'to the priests' (in the plural), this forms another point of undesigned evidence of the authenticity of the narrative.
[3] Some have seen in the reference by

St. Luke here, and in the Parable of the Good Samaritan, a peculiarly Pauline trait. But we remember St. John's reference to the Samaritans (iv.), and such sentiments in regard to the Gentiles as St. Matt. viii. 11, 12.

more when setting out for the priests before they had experienced the healing. But perhaps, regarding it from our own standpoint, we may overestimate the faith of these men. Bearing in mind the views of the Jews at the time, and what constant succession of miraculous cures —without a single failure—had been witnessed these years, it cannot seem strange that lepers should apply to Jesus. Nor yet perhaps did it, in the circumstances, involve very much greater faith to go to the priests at His bidding—implying, of course, that they were or would be healed. But it was far different to turn back and to fall down at His feet in lowly worship and thanksgiving. That made a man a disciple.

Many questions here suggest themselves: Did these nine Jews separate from the one Samaritan when they felt healed, common misfortune having made them companions and brethren, while the bond was snapped so soon as they felt themselves free of their common sorrow? The History of the Church and of individual Christians furnishes, alas! not a few analogous instances. Or did these nine Jews, in their legalism and obedience to the letter, go on to the priests, forgetful that, in obeying the letter, they violated the spirit of Christ's command? Of this also there are, alas! only too many parallel cases which will occur to the mind. Or was it Jewish pride, which felt it had a right to the blessings, and attributed them, not to the mercy of Christ, but to God; or, rather, to their own relation as Israel to God? Or, what seems to us the most probable, was it simply Jewish ingratitude and neglect of the blessed opportunity now within their reach—a state of mind too characteristic of those who know not ' the time of their visitation '—and which led up to the neglect, rejection, and final loss of the Christ? Certain it is, that the Lord emphasised the terrible contrast in this between the children of the household and ' this stranger.' [1] And here another important lesson is implied in regard to the miraculous in the Gospels. The history shows how little spiritual value or efficacy they attach to miracles, and how essentially different in this respect their tendency is from all legendary stories. The lesson conveyed in this case is, that we may expect, and even experience, miracles, without any real faith in the Christ; with belief, indeed, in His Power, but

---

[1] The equivalent for this would be נָכְרִי. This, as may be shown from very many passages, means not so much a stranger as a non-Jew. Thus, the expression Nokhri and Yisrael are constantly contrasted as non-Jews and Jews. At the same time it must be admitted that in Demai iii. 4, the Nokhri is also distinguished from the Cuthean, or Samaritan. But see the explanatory note of Maimonides referred to by Surenhusius vol. i. p. 87.

without surrender to His Rule. According to the Gospels, a man CHAP.
might either seek benefit from Christ, or else receive Christ through XXII
such benefit.   In the one case, the benefit sought was the object, in
the other, the means; in the one, it was the goal, in the other, the
road to it; in the one, it gave healing, in the other, brought salvation;
in the one, it ultimately led away from, in the other, it led to Christ
and to discipleship.   And so Christ now spake it to this Samaritan:
' Arise, go thy way; thy faith has made thee whole.'   But to all time
there are here to the Church lessons of most important distinction.

2. The Discourse concerning the Coming of the Kingdom, which
is reported by St. Luke immediately after the healing of the ten
lepers,[a] will be more conveniently considered in connection with the ᵃ St. Luke
xvii. 20–37
fuller statement of the same truths at the close of our Lord's Ministry.[b]   It was probably delivered a day or so after the healing of the ᵇ St. Matt.
xxiv.
lepers, and marks a farther stage in the Peræan journey towards
Jerusalem.   For, here we meet once more the Pharisees as questioners.[c] This circumstance, as will presently appear, is of great ᶜ St. Luke
xvii. 20
importance, as carrying us back to the last mention of an interpellation by the Pharisees.[d] ᵈ in St.
Luke xvi.
3. This brings us to what we regard as, in point of time, the next ¹⁴
Discourse of Christ on this journey, recorded both by St. Matthew,
and, in briefer form, by St. Mark.[e]   These Evangelists place it im- ᵉ St. Matt.
xix. 3–12;
mediately after their notice of the commencement of this journey.[f] St. Mark x
2–12
For reasons previously indicated, St. Luke inserts the healing of ᶠ St. Matt.
xix. 1, 2;
the lepers and the prophetic Discourse, while the other two Evan- St. Mark
x. 1
gelists omit them.   On the other hand, St. Luke omits the Discourse here reported by St. Matthew and St. Mark, because, as
we can readily see, its subject-matter would, from the standpoint of
his Gospel, not appear of such supreme importance as to demand
insertion in a narrative of selected events.

The subject-matter of that Discourse is, in answer to Pharisaic
' tempting,' an exposition of Christ's teaching in regard to the
Jewish law and practice of divorce.   The introduction of this subject
in the narratives of St. Matthew and St. Mark seems, to say the
least, abrupt.   But the difficulty is entirely removed, or, rather,
changed into undesigned evidence, when we fit it into the general
history.   Christ had advanced farther on His journey, and now once
more encountered the hostile Pharisees.   It will be remembered
that He had met them before in the same part of the country,[g] ¹ and ᵍ St. Luke
xvi. 14
answered their taunts and objections, among other things, by charg-

¹ See chap. xviii. of this Book.

BOOK
IV

* St. Luke
xvi. 17, 18

b St. Matt
xix. 3

c Gittin

ing them with breaking in spirit that Law of which they professed to be the exponents and representatives. And this He had proved by reference to their views and teaching on the subject of divorce.[a] This seems to have rankled in their minds. Probably they also imagined, it would be easy to show on this point a marked difference between the teaching of Jesus and that of Moses and the Rabbis, and to enlist popular feeling against Him. Accordingly, when these Pharisees again encountered Jesus, now on his journey to Judæa, they resumed the subject precisely where it had been broken off when they had last met Him, only now with the object of 'tempting Him.' Perhaps it may also have been in the hope that, by getting Christ to commit Himself against divorce in Peræa—the territory of Herod— they might enlist against Him, as formerly against the Baptist, the implacable hatred of Herodias.[1]

But their main object evidently was to involve Christ in controversy with some of the Rabbinic Schools. This appears from the form in which they put the question, whether it was lawful to put away a wife 'for every cause'?[b] St. Mark, who gives only a very condensed account, omits this clause; but in Jewish circles the whole controversy between different teachers turned upon this point. All held that divorce was lawful, the only question being as to its grounds. We will not here enter on the unsavoury question of 'Divorce' among the Jews,[2] to which the Talmud devotes a special tractate.[c] There can, however, be no question that the practice was discouraged by many of the better Rabbis, alike in word[3] and by their example;[4] nor yet, that the Jewish Law took the most watchful care of the interests of the woman. In fact, if any doubt were raised as to the legal validity of the letter of divorce, the Law always pronounced *against* the divorce. At the same time, in popular practice, divorce must have been very frequent; while the principles underlying Jewish legislation on the subject are most objectionable.[5] These were in turn due to a comparatively lower estimate of woman, and to an unspiritual view of the marriage-relation. Christianity has first raised woman to her proper position, not by giving her a new

---

[1] So, according to many commentators. See *Meyer*, ad loc.

[2] On the general subject I would refer to 'Sketches of Jewish Social Life,' pp. 142, 157, 158.

[3] Thus, the Talmudic tractate on 'Divorce,' while insisting on its duty in case of sin, closes with the words: 'He who divorces his first wife, the very altar sheds tears over him' (Gitt. 90 *b*, last lines;

comp. Mal. ii. 13–16).

[4] An instance of refusing to be divorced, even from a very disagreeable and quarrelsome wife, is that of R. Chiya, mentioned in Yebam. 63 *a*, towards end.

[5] Two disgusting instances of Rabbis making proclamation of their wish to be married for a day (in a strange place, and then divorced), are mentioned in Yoma 18 *b*.

one, but by restoring and fully developing that assigned to her in the Old Testament. Similarly, as regards marriage, the New Testament—which would have us to be, in one sense, ' eunuchs for the Kingdom of God,' has also fully restored and finally developed what the Old Testament had already implied. And this is part of the lesson taught in this Discourse, both to the Pharisees and to the disciples.

To begin with, divorce (in the legal sense) was regarded as a privilege accorded only to Israel, not to the Gentiles.[a] [1] On the question: what constituted lawful grounds of divorce, the Schools were divided. Taking their departure from the sole ground of divorce mentioned in Deut. xxiv. 1: ' a matter of shame [literally, nakedness],' the School of Shammai applied the expression only to moral transgressions,[b] and, indeed, exclusively to unchastity.[c] It was declared that, if a woman were as mischievous as the wife of Ahab, or [according to tradition] as the wife of Korah, it were well that her husband should not divorce her, except it be on the ground of adultery.[b] At the same time this must not be regarded as a fixed legal principle, but rather as an opinion and good counsel for conduct. The very passages, from which the above quotations are made, also afford only too painful evidence of the laxity of views and practices current. And the Jewish Law unquestionably allowed divorce on almost any grounds; the difference being, not as to what was lawful, but on what grounds a man should set the Law in motion, and make use of the absolute liberty which it accorded him. Hence, it is a serious mistake on the part of Commentators to set the teaching of Christ on this subject by the side of that of Shammai.

But the School of Hillel proceeded on different principles. It took the words, ' matter of shame ' in the widest possible sense, and declared it sufficient ground for divorce if a woman had spoiled her husband's dinner.[e] [2] Rabbi Akiba thought, that the words,[f] ' if

CHAP.
XXII

[a] Jer. Kidd.
58 c; Ber. R.
18

[b] Gitt. ix.
10
[c] Bemidb.
R. 9, ed.
Warsh. p.
29 b, about
the middle
[d] Gitt. 90 a;
Sanh. 22 a
and b

[e] Gitt. 90 a
[f] Deut.
xxiv. 1

[1] This by a very profane application to this point of the expression ' God of Israel,' in Mal. ii. 16.

[2] An extraordinary attempt has been made to explain the expression (הקדיחה תבשילו, ' burns his mess ') as meaning ' brings dishonour upon him.' But (1) in the two passages quoted as bearing out this meaning (Ber. 17 b, Sanh. 103 a, second line from bottom), the expression is not the precise equivalent for ' bringing dishonour,' while in both cases the addition of the words ' in public ' (ברבים)

marks its figurative use. The real meaning of the expression in the two passages referred to is: One who brings into disrepute (destroys) that which has been taught and learned. But (2) in Gitt. ix. 10; 90 a; Bemidb. R. 9 there is no indication of any figurative use of the expression, and the commentators explain it, as burning the dish, ' either by fire or by salt '; while (3), the expression is followed by an anti-climax giving permission of divorce if another woman more pleasing were found.

ª Yebam.
63 *b*; Gitt.
90 *a, b*
ᵇ Gitt. iv. 7
ᶜ Keth.vii. 6

she find no favour in his eyes,' implied that it was sufficient if a man had found another woman more attractive than his wife. All agreed that moral blame made divorce a duty,ª and that in such cases a woman should not be taken back.ᵇ According to the Mishnah,ᶜ women could not only be divorced, but with loss of their dowry, if they transgressed against the Law of Moses or of Israel. The former is explained as implying a breach of the laws of tithing, of setting apart the first of the dough, and of purification. The latter is explained as referring to such offences as that of going in public with uncovered head, of spinning in the public streets, or entering into talk with men, to which others add, that of brawling, or of disrespectfully speaking of her husband's parents in his presence. A

ᵈ Erub. 41 *b*
ᵉ Yebam.
63 *b*
ᶠ Gitt. iv.
7, 8

troublesome,ᵈ or quarrelsome wife might certainly be sent away;ᵉ and ill repute, or childlessness (during ten years) were also regarded as valid grounds of divorce.ᶠ

Incomparably as these principles differ from the teaching of Christ, it must again be repeated, that no real comparison is possible between Christ and even the strictest of the Rabbis, since none of them actually *prohibited* divorce, except in case of adultery, nor yet laid down those high eternal principles which Jesus enunciated. But we can understand how, from the Jewish point of view, 'tempting Him,' they would put the question, whether it was lawful to divorce a wife 'for every cause.'[1] Avoiding their cavils, the Lord appealed straight to the highest authority—God's institution of marriage. He,

ᵍ Used in
the same
sense, for
example,
Baba B. 8 *b*

Who at the beginning[2] [from the first, originally, מרישא]ᵍ had made them male and female, had in the marriage-relation 'joined them together,' to the breaking of every other, even the nearest, relationship, to be 'one flesh'—that is, to a union which was unity. Such was the fact of God's ordering. It followed, that they *were* one—and what God had willed to be one, man might not put asunder. Then followed the natural Rabbinic objection, why, in such case, Moses had commanded a bill of divorcement. Our Lord replied by pointing out that Moses had not commanded divorce, only tolerated it on account of their hardness of heart, and in such case commanded to give a bill of divorce for the protection of the wife. And this argument would appeal the more forcibly to them, that the Rabbis themselves taught that a somewhat similar concession had been

---

[1] These words are omitted by St. Mark in his condensed account. But so far from regarding, with *Meyer*, the briefer account of St. Mark as the original one, we look on that of St. Matthew as more

fully reproducing what had taken place.
[2] The clause, St. Matt. xix. 4, should, I think, be thus pointed: ' He Who made them, at the beginning made them, &c.'

made [a] by Moses in regard to female captives of war—as the Talmud has it, 'on account of the evil impulse.' [b] But such a separation, our Lord continued, had not been provided for in the original institution, which was a union to unity. Only one thing could put an end to that unity—its absolute breach. Hence, to divorce one's wife (or husband) while this unity lasted, and to marry another, was adultery, because, as the divorce was null before God, the original marriage still subsisted—and, in that case, the Rabbinic Law would also have forbidden it. The next part of the Lord's inference, that ' whoso marrieth her which is put away doth commit adultery,' is more difficult of interpretation. Generally, it is understood as implying that a woman divorced for adultery might not be married. But it has been argued,[1] that, as the literal rendering is, ' whoso marrieth her when put away,' it applies to the woman whose divorce had just before been prohibited, and not, as is sometimes thought, to ' a woman divorced [under any circumstances].' Be this as it may, the Jewish Law, which regarded marriage with a woman divorced under any circumstances as unadvisable,[e] absolutely forbade that of the adulterer with the adulteress.[d]

Whatever, therefore, may be pleaded, on account of ' the hardness of heart ' in modern society, in favour of the lawfulness of relaxing Christ's law of divorce, which confines dissolution of marriage to the one ground (of adultery), because then the unity of God's making has been broken by sin—such a retrocession was at least not in the mind of Christ, nor can it be considered lawful, either by the Church or for individual disciples. But, that the Pharisees had rightly judged, when ' tempting Him,' what the popular feeling on the subject would be, appears even from what ' His disciples ' [not necessarily the Apostles] afterwards said to Him. They waited to express their dissent till they were alone with Him ' in the house,' [e] and then urged that, if it were as Christ had taught, it would be better not to marry at all. To which the Lord replied,[f] that ' this saying ' of the disciples,[2] ' it is not good to marry,' could not be received by all men, but only by those to whom it was ' given.' For, there were three cases in which abstinence from marriage might lawfully be contemplated. In two of these it was, of course, natural; and, where it was not so, a man might, ' for the Kingdom of Heaven's sake '—that is, in the service of God and of Christ—have all his thoughts, feelings, and impulses

CHAP.
XXII

[a] Deut. xxi. 11
[b] Kidd. 21 b

[e] Pes. 112 a
[d] Sot. v. 1

[e] St. Mark x. 10

[f] St. Matt. xix. 10-12

---

[1] Canon *Cook* argues this with great ingenuity.
[2] This is the view commonly taken.

But ' the saying ' may, without much difficulty, be also applied to that of Christ.

so engaged that others were no longer existent. For, we must here beware of a twofold misunderstanding. It is not bare abstinence from marriage, together, perhaps, with what the German Reformers called *immunda continentia* (unchaste continency), which is here commended, but such inward preoccupation with the Kingdom of God as would remove all other thoughts and desires.[1] It is this which requires to be 'given' of God; and which 'he that is able to receive it'—who has the moral capacity for it—is called upon to receive. Again, it must not be imagined that this involves any command of celibacy: it only speaks of such who in the active service of the Kingdom feel, that their every thought is so engrossed in the work, that wishes and impulses to marriage are no longer existent in them.[a] [2]

ᵇ St. Matt.
xix. 13–15
St. Mark x.
13–16; St.
Luke xviii.
15–17

4. The next incident is recorded by the three Evangelists.[b] It probably occurred in the same house where the disciples had questioned Christ about His teaching on the Divinely sacred relationship of marriage. And the account of His blessing of 'infants' and 'little children' most aptly follows on the former teaching. It is a scene of unspeakable sweetness and tenderness, where all is in character—alas! even the conduct of the 'disciples' as we remember their late inability to sympathise with the teaching of the Master. And it is all so utterly unlike what Jewish legend would have invented for its Messiah. We can understand how, when One Who so spake and wrought, rested in the house, Jewish mothers should have brought their 'little children,' and some their 'infants,' to Him, that He might 'touch,' 'put His Hands on them, and pray.' What power and holiness must these mothers have believed to be in His touch and prayer; what life to be in, and to come from Him; and what gentleness and tenderness must His have been, when they dared so to bring these little ones! For, how utterly contrary it was to all Jewish notions, and how incompatible with the supposed dignity of a Rabbi, appears from the rebuke of the disciples. It was an occasion and an act when, as the fuller and more pictorial account of St. Mark informs us, Jesus 'was much displeased'—the only time

---

[1] For, it is not merely to practise outward continence, but to become in mind and heart a *eunuch*.

[2] The mistaken literalism of application on the part of *Origen* is well known. Such practice must have been not unfrequent among Jewish Christians, for, curiously enough, the Talmud refers to it, reporting a conversation between a Rabbi and such a Jewish Christian eunuch (צדוקי גיאזא), Shabb. 152 *a*. The same story is related, with slight alterations, in the Midrash on Eccles. x. 7, ed. Warsh. p. 102 *a*, last four lines. Any practice of this kind would have been quite contrary to Jewish law (Pes. 112 *b*; Shabb. 110 *b*).

this strong word is used of our Lord [1]—and said unto them: ' Suffer the little children to come to Me,[2] hinder them not, for of such is the Kingdom of God.' Then He gently reminded His own disciples of their grave error, by repeating what they had apparently forgotten,[a] that, in order to enter the Kingdom of God, it must be received as by a little child—that here there could be no question of intellectual qualification, nor of distinction due to a great Rabbi, but only of humility, receptiveness, meekness, and a simple application to, and trust in, the Christ. And so He folded these little ones in His Arms, put His Hands upon them, and blessed them,[3] and thus for ever consecrated that child-life, which a parent's love and faith brought to Him; blessed it also by the laying-on of His Hands—as it were, 'ordained it,' as we fully believe to all time, 'strength because of His enemies.'

---

[1] The other places in which the verb occurs are: St. Matt. xx. 24; xxi. 15; ?xxvi. 8; St. Mark x. 41; xiv. 4; St. Luke xiii. 14; the substantive in 2 Cor. vii. 11.

[2] The 'and' before 'hinder' should be omitted according to the best MSS.

[3] As Mr. *Brown McClellan* notes, in his learned work on the New Testament, the word is an 'intensive compound form of blessing, especially of dearest friends and relations at meeting and parting.'

CHAPTER XXIII.

THE LAST INCIDENTS IN PERÆA—THE YOUNG RULER WHO WENT AWAY SORROWFUL—TO LEAVE ALL FOR CHRIST—PROPHECY OF HIS PASSION—THE REQUEST OF SALOME, AND OF JAMES AND JOHN.

(St. Matt. xix. 16–22; St. Mark x. 17–22; St. Luke xviii. 18–23; St. Matt. xix. 23–30; St. Mark x. 23–31; St. Luke xviii. 24–30; St. Matt. xx. 17–19; St. Mark x. 32–34: St. Luke xviii. 31–34; St. Matt. xx. 20--28; St. Mark x. 35- 45.)

BOOK
IV

As we near the goal, the wondrous story seems to grow in tenderness and pathos. It is as if all the loving condescension of the Master were to be crowded into these days; all the pressing need also, and the human weaknesses of His disciples. And with equal compassion does He look upon the difficulties of them who truly seek to come to Him, and on those which, springing from without, or even from self and sin, beset them who have already come. Let us try reverently to follow His steps, and learn of His words.

As 'He was going forth into the way'[1]—we owe this trait, as one and another in the same narrative, to St. Mark—probably at early morn, as He left the house where He had for ever folded into His Arms and blessed the children brought to Him by believing parents—

ᵃ St. Luke

His progress was arrested. It was 'a young man,' 'a ruler,'ᵃ probably of the local Synagogue,[2] who came with all haste, 'running,'

ᵇ St. Mark

and with lowliest gesture [kneeling],ᵇ to ask what to him, nay to us all, is the most important question. Remembering that, while we owe to St. Mark the most graphic touches,[3] St. Matthew most fully reports the words that had been spoken, we might feel inclined to

ᶜ St. Matt.
xix. 16

adopt that reading of them in St. Matthewᶜ which is not only most strongly supported, but at first sight seems to remove some of the difficulties of exposition. This reading would omit in the address of the young ruler the word 'good' before 'Master, what good thing shall I do that I may inherit eternal life?' and would make Christ's

---

[1] This is the exact rendering.

[2] Dean *Plumptre* needlessly supposes him to have been a member of the Great Sanhedrin, and even identifies him with Lazarus of Bethany.

[3] This is well pointed out by Canon *Cook* on St. Mark x. 19.

reply read: 'Why askest thou Me concerning the good [that which
is good]? One there is Who is good.' This would meet not only
the objection, that in no recorded instance was a Jewish Rabbi
addressed as 'Good Master,' but the obvious difficulties connecteu
with the answer of Christ, according to the common reading: 'Why
callest thou Me good? none is good, save only One: God.' But
on the other side it must be urged, that the undoubted reading of
the question and answer in St. Mark's and St. Luke's Gospels agrees
with that of our Authorised Version, and hence that any difficulty of
exposition would not be removed, only shifted, while the reply of
Christ tallies far better with the words 'Good Master,' the strangeness
of such an address from Jewish lips giving only the more reason for
taking it up in the reply: 'Why callest thou Me good? none is good
save only One: God.' Lastly, the designation of God as the only One
'good' agrees with one of the titles given Him in Jewish writings:
'The Good One of the world '(עולם של טובו).[a][1]   [a] Pesiqta,
ed. Buber,
p. 161 a,
last lines

The actual question of the young Ruler is one which repeatedly
occurs in Jewish writings, as put to a Rabbi by his disciples. Amidst
the different answers given, we scarcely wonder that they also pointed
to observance of the Law. And the saying of Christ seems the more
adapted to the young Ruler when we recall this sentence from the
Talmud: 'There is nothing else that is good but the Law.'[b] But   [b] Ber. 5 a,
about
middle; Ab
Zar. 19 b
here again the similarity is only of form, not of substance. For, it
will be noticed, that, in the more full account by St. Matthew, Christ
leads the young Ruler upwards through the table of the *prohibitions*
of deeds to the first positive command of deed, and then, by a rapid
transition, to the substitution for the tenth commandment in its
negative form of this wider positive and all-embracing command:[c]   [c] Lev. xix.
18
'Thou shalt love thy neighbour as thyself.' Any Jewish 'Ruler,'
but especially one so earnest, would have at once answered a challenge on the first four commandments by 'Yes'—and that not self-
righteously, but sincerely, though of course in ignorance of their
real depth. And this was not the time for lengthened discussion and
instruction; only for rapid awakening, to lead up, if possible, from
earnestness and a heart-drawing towards the Master to real disciple-

---

[1] To really remove exegetical difficulties,
the reading should be further altered to $\grave{\epsilon}\nu$
$\grave{\epsilon}\sigma\tau\grave{\iota}$ $\tau\grave{o}$ $\grave{\alpha}\gamma\alpha\theta\grave{o}\nu$, as *Wünsche* suggests,
who regards our present reading $\epsilon\grave{\iota}\varsigma$ $\grave{\epsilon}\sigma\tau\grave{\iota}\nu$
$\acute{o}$ $\grave{\alpha}\gamma\alpha\theta\acute{o}\varsigma$, as a mistake of the translator
in rendering the neuter of the Aramaic
original by the masculine. We need
scarcely say, the suggestion, however ingenious, is not supported. And then,
what of the conversation in the other
Gospels, where we could scarcely expect
a variation of the saying from the more
easy to the more difficult? On the application to God of the term 'the Good
One,' see an interesting notice in the Jüd
Liter. Blatt, for Sept. 20, 1882, p. 152.

ship. Best here to start from what was admitted as binding—the ten commandments—and to lead from that in them which was least likely to be broken, step by step, upwards to that which was most likely to awaken consciousness of sin.

And the young Ruler did not, as that other Pharisee, reply by trying to raise a Rabbinic disputation over the ' Who is neighbour to me?' [a] but in the sincerity of an honest heart answered that he had kept—that is, so far as he knew them—' all these things from his youth.' [1] On this St. Matthew puts into his mouth the question— ' What lack I yet?' Even if, like the other two Evangelists, he had not reported it, we would have supplied this from what follows. There is something intensely earnest, genuine, generous, even enthusiastic, in the higher cravings of the soul in youth, when that youth has not been poisoned by the breath of the world, or stricken with the rottenness of vice. The soul longs for the true, the higher, the better, and, even if strength fails of attainment, we still watch with keen sympathy the form of the climber upwards. Much more must all this have been the case with a *Jewish* youth, especially in those days; one, besides, like this young Ruler, in whose case affluence of circumstances not only allowed free play, but tended to draw out and to give full scope to the finer feelings, and where wealth was joined with religiousness and the service of the Synagogue. There was not in him that pride of riches, nor the self-sufficiency which they so often engender; nor the pride of conscious moral purity and aim after righteousness before God and man; nor yet the pride of the Pharisee or of the Synagogue-Ruler. What he had seen and heard of the Christ had quickened to greatest intensity all in him that longed after God and heaven, and had brought him in this supreme moral earnestness, lowly, reverently, to the Feet of Him in Whom, as he felt, all perfectness was, and from Whom all perfectness came. He had not been first drawn to Christ, and thence to the pure, as were the publicans and sinners; but, like so many—even as Peter, when in that hour of soul-agony he said: ' To whom shall we go? Thou hast the words of eternal life,'—he had been drawn to the pure and the higher, and therefore to Christ. To some the way to Christ is up the Mount of Transfiguration, among the shining Beings of another world; to some it is across dark Kedron, down the deep Garden of Gethsemane with its agonies. What matters it, if it equally lead to Him, and equally bring the sense of need and experience

---

[1] In St. Matt. xix. 20, these words should be struck out as spurious.

of pardon to the seeker after the better, and the sense of need and experience of holiness to the seeker after pardon?

And Jesus saw it all: down, through that intense upward look; inwards, through that question, 'What lack I yet?' far deeper down than that young man had ever seen into his own heart—even into depths of weakness and need which he had never sounded, and which must be filled, if he would enter the Kingdom of Heaven. Jesus saw what he lacked; and what He saw, He showed him. For, 'look-ing at him' in his sincerity and earnestness, 'He loved him'—as He loves those that are His Own. One thing was needful for this young man: that he should not only become His disciple, but that, in so doing, he should 'come and follow' Christ. We can all perceive how, for one like this young man, such absolute and entire coming and following Christ was needful. And again, to do this, it was in the then circumstances both of this young man and of Christ neces-sary, that he should go and part with all that he had. And what was an *outward*, was also, as we perceive it, an *inward* necessity; and so, as ever, Providence and Grace would work together. For, indeed, to many of us some outward step is often not merely the means or but absolutely needful for, spiritual decision. To some it is the first open profession of Christ; to others, the first act of self-denial, or the first distinct 'No'-saying; to some, it may be, it is the first prayer, or else the first act of self-consecration. Yet it seems, as if it needed not only the word of God but a stroke of some Moses'-rod to make the water gush forth from the rock. And thus would this young Ruler have been 'perfect;' and what he had given to the poor have become, not through merit nor by way of reward, but really 'treasure in heaven.' [1]

What he lacked—was earth's poverty and heaven's riches; a heart fully set on following Christ: and this could only come to him through willing surrender of all. And so this was to him alike the means, the test, and the need. To him it was this; to us it may be something quite other. Yet each of us has a lack—something quite deep down in our hearts, which we may never yet have known, and which we must know and give up, if we would follow Christ. And without forsaking, there can be no following. This is the law of the Kingdom—and it is such, because we are sinners, because sin is not only the loss of the good, but the possession of something else in its place.

There is something deeply pathetic in the mode in which St. Mark

---

[1] The words 'take up the cross,' in the *textus receptus* of St. Mark x. 21, are spurious—the gloss of a clumsy inter-polator.

describes it: ' he was sad'—the word painting a dark gloom that overshadowed the face of the young man.[1] Did he then not lack it, this one thing? We need scarcely here recall the almost extravagant language in which Rabbinism describes the miseries of poverty;[2] we can understand his feelings without that. Such a possibility had never entered his mind: the thought of it was terribly startling. That he must come and follow Christ, then and there, and in order to do so, sell all that he had and give it away among the poor, and be poor himself, a beggar, that he might have treasure in heaven; and that this should come to him as the one thing needful from that Master in Whom he believed, from Whose lips he would learn the one thing needful, and who but a little before had been to him the All in All! It was a terrible surprise, a sentence of death to his life, and of life to his death. And that it should come from *His* lips, at Whose Feet he had run to kneel, and Who held for him the keys of eternal life! Rabbinism had never asked this; if it demanded almsgiving, it was in odious boastfulness;[3] while it was declared even unlawful to give away all one's possessions [a]— at most, only a fifth of them might be dedicated.[b]

And so, with clouded face he gazed down into what he lacked— within; but also gazed up in Christ on what he needed. And, although we hear no more of him, who that day went back to his rich home very poor, because ' very sorrowful,' we cannot but believe that he, whom Jesus loved, yet found in the poverty of earth the treasure of heaven.

Nor was this all. The deep pity of Christ for him, who had gone that day, speaks also in his warning to his disciples.[c] But surely those are not only riches in the literal sense which make it so difficult for a man to enter into the Kingdom of Heaven [4]—so difficult, as to amount almost to that impossibility which was expressed in the common Jewish proverb, that a man did not even in his dreams see an elephant pass through the eye of a needle.[d] But when in their perplexity the disciples put to each other the saddened question: Who then can be saved? He pointed them onward, then upward, as well as inward, teaching them that, what

---

[1] The word is only used in St. Matt. xvi. 3, of the lowering sky.

[2] Many sayings might here be quoted. It was worse than all the plagues of Egypt put together (Babha B. 116 a); than all other miseries (Betsah 32 b); the worst affliction that could befall a man (Shem. R. 31).

[3] See a story of boastfulness in that respect in *Wünsche*, ad loc. To make a merit of giving up riches for Christ is, surely, the Satanic caricature of the meaning of His teaching.

[4] The words in St. Mark x. 24, ' for them that trust in riches,' are most likely a spurious gloss.

was impossible of achievement by man in his own strength, God would work by His Almighty Grace.

It almost jars on our ears, and prepares us for still stranger and sadder to come, when Peter, perhaps as spokesman of the rest, seems to remind the Lord that they had forsaken all to follow Him. St. Matthew records also the special question which Simon added to it: 'What shall we have therefore?' and hence his Gospel alone makes mention of the Lord's reply, in so far as it applied only to the Apostles. For, that reply really bore on two points: on the reward which all who left everything to follow Christ would obtain;[a] and on the special acknowledgment awaiting the Apostles of Christ.[b] In regard to the former we mark, that it is twofold. They who had forsaken all 'for His sake'[c] 'and the Gospel's,'[d] 'for the Kingdom of God's sake'—and these three expressions explain and supplement each other—would receive 'in this time' 'manifold more' of new, and better, and closer relationships of a spiritual kind for those which they had surrendered, although, as St. Mark significantly adds, to prevent all possible mistakes, 'with persecutions.' But by the side of this stands out unclouded and bright the promise for 'the world to come' of 'everlasting life.' As regarded the Apostles personally, some mystery lies on the special promise to them.[1] We could quite understand, that the distinction of rule to be bestowed on them might have been worded in language taken from the expectations of the time, in order to make the promise intelligible to them. But, unfortunately, we have no explanatory information to offer. The Rabbis, indeed, speak of a renovation or regeneration of the world (מחדש את עולמו) which was to take place after the 7,000 or else 5,000 years of the Messianic reign.[e] Such a renewal of all things is not only foretold by the prophets,[f] and dwelt upon in later Jewish writings,[g] but frequently referred to in Rabbinic literature.[h] [2] But as regards the special rule or 'judgment' of the Apostles, or ambassadors of the Messiah, we have not, and, of course, cannot expect any parallel in Jewish writings. That the promise of such rule and judgment to the Apostles is not peculiar to what is called the Judaic Gospel of St. Matthew, appears from its renewal at a later period, as recorded by St. Luke.[i] Lastly, that it is in accordance with Old Testament

[a] St. Matt. xix. 29; St. Mark x. 26, 30; St. Luke xviii. 29, 30
[b] St. Matt. xix. 28
[c] St. Matthew and St. Mark
[d] St. Mark

[e] Sanh. 97 b
[f] As for example Is. xxxiv. 4; li 6; lxv. 17
[g] Book of Enoch xci. 16, 17; 4 Esd. vii. 28
[h] Targum Onkelos on Deut. xxxii. 12; Targ. Jerus. on Deut. xxxii. 1; Targ. Jon. on Habak. iii. 2; Ber, R. 12. ed. Warsh. p. 24 b. near end; Pirké de R. Eliez 51
[i] St. Luke xxii. 30

---

[1] Of course, the expression 'twelve thrones' (St. Matt. xix. 28) must not be pressed to utmost literality, or it might be asked whether St. Paul or St. Matthias occupied the place of Judas. On the other hand, neither must it be frittered away, as if the 'regeneration' referred only to the Christian dispensation, and to spiritual relations under it.

[2] This subject will be further treated in the sequel.

ᵃ Acts iii.
21; Rom.
viii. 19-21;
2 Pet. iii.
13; Rev.
xxi. 1
ᵇ 1 Cor. vi.
2, 3; Rev.
xx. 4; xxi.
14

ᶜ Comp. al-
so Acts
xxvi. 7

ᵈ St. Matt.
xx. 17-19

ᵉ St. Mat.,
xx. 16; St.
Mark x. 31

ᶠ St. Matt.
xvi. 21;
xvii. 22, 23

promise, will be seen by a reference to Dan. vii. 9, 10, 14, 27; and there are few references in the New Testament to the blessed consummation of all things in which such renewal of the world,ᵃ and even the rule and judgment of the representatives of the Church,ᵇ are not referred to.

However mysterious, therefore, in their details, these things seem clear, and may without undue curiosity or presumption be regarded as the teaching of our Lord: the renewal of earth; the share in His rule and judgment which He will in the future give to His saints; the special distinction which He will bestow on His Apostles, corresponding to the special gifts, privileges, and rule with which He had endowed them on earth, and to their nearness to, and their work and sacrifices for Him; and, lastly, we may add, the preservation of Israel as a distinct, probably tribal, nation.ᶜ As for the rest, as so much else, it is 'behind the veil,' and, even as we see it, better ‚for the Church that the veil has not been further lifted.

The reference to the blessed future with its rewards was followed by a Parable, recorded, as, with one exception, all of that series, only by St. Matthew. It will best be considered in connection with the last series of Christ's Parable's.[1] But it was accompanied by what, in the circumstances, was also a most needful warning.ᵈ Thoughts of the future Messianic reign, its glory, and their own part in it might have so engrossed the minds of the disciples as to make them forgetful of the terrible present, immediately before them. In such case they might not only have lapsed into that most fatal Jewish error of a Messiah-King, Who was not Saviour—the Crown without the Cross—but have even suffered shipwreck of their faith, when the storm broke on the Day of His Condemnation and Crucifixion. If ever, it was most needful in that hour of elation to remind and forewarn them of what was to be expected in the immediate future. How truly such preparation was required by the disciples, appears from the narrative itself.

There was something sadly mysterious in the words with which Christ had closed His Parable, that the last should be first and the first last ᵉ[2]—and it had carried dark misgivings to those who heard it. And now it seemed all so strange! Yet the disciples could not have indulged in illusions. His own sayings on at least two previous occasions,ᶠ however ill or partially understood, must have led them to expect at any rate grievous opposition and tribulations in Jerusalem, and their endeavour to deter Christ from going to

---

[1] See in Book V.
[2] The words, 'many be called, but few chosen,' seem spurious in that place.

Bethany to raise Lazarus proves, that they were well aware of the danger which threatened the Master in Judæa.[a] Yet not only 'was He now going up[1] to Jerusalem,' but there was that in His bearing which was quite unusual. As St. Mark writes, He was going ' before them'—we infer, apart and alone, as One, busy with thoughts all-engrossing, Who is setting Himself to do His great work, and goes to meet it. 'And going before them was Jesus; and they were amazed [utterly bewildered, viz. the Apostles]; and those who were following, were afraid.'[2] It was then that Jesus took the Apostles apart, and in language more precise than ever before, told them how all things that were 'written by the prophets shall be accomplished on the Son of Man'[b]—not merely, that all that had been written concerning the Son of Man should be accomplished, but a far deeper truth, all-comprehensive as regards the Old Testament: that all its true prophecy ran up into the sufferings of the Christ. As the three Evangelists report it, the Lord gave them full details of His Betrayal, Crucifixion, and Resurrection. And yet we may, without irreverence, doubt whether on that occasion He had really entered into all those particulars. In such case it would seem difficult to explain how, as St. Luke reports, 'they understood none of these things, and the saying was hid from them, neither knew they the things which were spoken;' and again, how afterwards the actual events and the Resurrection could have taken them so by surprise. Rather do we think, that the Evangelists report what Jesus had said in the light of after-events. He did tell them of His Betrayal by the leaders of Israel, and that into the hands of the Gentiles; of His Death and Resurrection on the third day—yet in language which they could, and actually did, misunderstand at the time, but which, when viewed in the light of what really happened, was perceived by them to have been actual prediction of those terrible days in Jerusalem and of the Resurrection-morning. At the time they may have thought that it pointed only to His rejection by Jews and Gentiles, to Sufferings and Death—and then to a Resurrection, either of His Mission or to such a reappearance of the Messiah, after His temporary disappearance, as Judaism expected.

But all this time, and with increasing fierceness, were terrible thoughts contending in the breast of Judas; and beneath the tramp of that fight was there only a thin covering of earth, to hide and keep from bursting forth the hellish fire of the master-passion within.

CHAP.
XXIII

[a] St. John xi. 8, 16

[b] St. Luke xviii. 31

---

[1] This is the precise rendering of the verb.

[2] This is the precise rendering of St. Mark x. 32.

BOOK
IV

One other incident, more strange and sad than any that had preceded, and the Peræan stay is for ever ended. It almost seems, as if the fierce blast of temptation, the very breath of the destroyer, were already sweeping over the little flock, as if the twilight of the night of betrayal and desertion were already falling around. And now it has fallen on the two chosen disciples, James and John—'the sons of thunder,' and one of them, 'the beloved disciple!' Peter, the third in that band most closely bound to Christ, had already had his fierce temptation,[a] and would have it more fiercely—to the uprooting of life, if the Great High-Priest had not specially interceded for him. And, as regards these two sons of Zebedee and of Salome,[b] we know what temptation had already beset them, how John had forbidden one to cast out devils, because he followed not with them,[c] and how both he and his brother, James, would have called down fire from heaven to consume the Samaritans who would not receive Christ.[d] It was essentially the same spirit that now prompted the request which their mother Salome preferred,[1] not only with their full concurrence, but, as we are expressly told,[e] with their active participation. There is the same faith in the Christ, the same allegiance to Him, but also the same unhallowed earnestness, the same misunderstanding—and, let us add, the same latent self-exaltation, as in the two former instances, in the present request that, as the most honoured of His guests, and also as the nearest to Him, they might have their places at His Right Hand and at His Left in His Kingdom.[f] Terribly incongruous as is any appearance of self-seeking at that moment and with that prospect before them, we cannot but feel that there is also an intenseness of faith and absoluteness of love almost sublime, when the mother steps forth from among those who follow Christ to His Suffering and Death, to proffer such a request with her sons, and for them.

And so the Saviour seems to have viewed it. With unspeakable patience and tenderness, He, Whose Soul is filled with the terrible contest before Him, bears with the weakness and selfishness which could cherish such thoughts and ambitions even at such a time. To correct them, He points to that near prospect, when the Highest is to be made low. 'Ye know not what ye ask!' The King is to be King through suffering—are they aware of the road which leads to that goal? Those nearest to the King of sorrows must reach the

Side notes:
[a] St. Matt. xvi. 23
[b] St. Matt. xxvii. 56; comp. St. Mark xv. 40
[c] St. Mark ix. 38
[d] St. Luke ix. 54
[e] by St. Mark (x. 35)
[f] St. Matt. xx. 20–28; St. Mark x. 35–45

[1] It is very remarkable that, in St. Matt. xx. 20, she bears the unusual title: 'the mother of Zebedee's children' (comp. also for the mention of Zebedee, St. Mark x. 35). This, evidently, to emphasise that the distinction was not asked on the ground of earthly kinship, as through Salome, who was the aunt of Jesus.

place nearest to Him by the same road as He. Are they prepared for it; prepared to drink that cup of soul-agony, which the Father will hand to Him—to submit to, to descend into that baptism of consecration, when the floods will sweep over Him?[1] In their ignorance, and listening only to the promptings of their hearts, they imagine that they are. Nay, in some measure it would be so; yet, finally to correct their mistake: to sit at His Right and at His Left Hand, these were not marks of mere favour for Him to bestow—in His own words: it ' is not Mine to give except to them for whom it is prepared of My Father.'

But as for the other ten, when they heard of it, it was only the pre-eminence which, in their view, James and John had sought, which stood out before them, to their envy, jealousy, and indignation.[a] And so, in that tremendously solemn hour would the fierce fire of controversy have broken out among them, who should have been most closely united; would jealousy and ambition have filled those who should have been most humble, and fierce passions, born of self, the world and Satan, have distracted them, whom the thought of the great love and the great sacrifice should have filled. It was the rising of that storm on the sea, the noise and tossing of those angry billows, which He hushed into silence when He spoke to them of the grand contrast between the princes of the Gentiles as they ' lord it over them,' or the ' great among them ' as they ' domineer ' [2] over men, and their own aims—how, whosoever would be great among them, must seek his greatness in service—not greatness through service, but the greatness of service; and, whosoever would be chief or rather ' first ' among them, let it be in service. And had it not been thus, was it not, would it not be so in the Son of Man—and *must* it not therefore be so in them who would be nearest to Him, even His Apostles and disciples? The Son of Man—let them look back, let them look forward—He came not to be ministered unto, but to minister. And then, breaking through the reserve that had held Him, and revealing to them the inmost thoughts which had occupied Him when He had been alone and apart, going before them on the way, He spoke for the first time fully what was the deepest meaning of His Life, Mission, and Death: ' to give His Life a ransom for

CHAP.
XXIII

[a] St. Matt,
xx. 24.
&c.; St.
Mark x. 41
&c.

---

[1] The clause in St. Matthew: ' and to be baptized with the baptism that I am baptised with,' is probably a spurious insertion, taken from St. Mark's Gospel.

[2] I have chosen these two words because the verbs in the Greek (which are the same in the two Gospels) express not ordinary ' dominion ' and ' authority,' but a forcible and tyrannical exercise of it. The first verb occurs again in Acts xix. 16, and 1 Pet. v. 3; the second only in this passage in the Gospels.

BOOK
IV
⌣⌣⌣

ᵃ St. Matt.
xx. 28;
St. Mark x.
45
ᵇ St. John
xiii.
ᶜ Rom. iii.
24: 1 Cor.
vi. 20;
1 Tim. ii. 6;
1 Pet. i. 19;
1 John iv.
10

many'ᵃ¹—to pay with His Life-Blood the price of their redemption, to lay down His Life for them: in their room and stead, and for their salvation.

These words must have sunk deep into the heart of one at least in that company.² A few days later, and the beloved disciple tells us of this Ministry of His Love at the Last Supper,ᵇ and ever afterwards, in his writings or in his life, does he seem to bear them about with him, and to re-echo them. Ever since also have they remained the foundation-truth, on which the Church has been built: the subject of her preaching, and the object of her experience.ᶜ

¹ We would here call attention to some exquisitely beautiful and forcible remarks by Dean *Plumptre* on the passage.   ² Comp. Dean *Plumptre*, u. s.

CHAPTER XXIV.

IN JERICHO AND AT BETHANY—JERICHO—A GUEST WITH ZACCHÆUS—
THE HEALING OF BLIND BARTIMÆUS—THE PLOT AT JERUSALEM—AT
BETHANY, AND IN THE HOUSE OF SIMON THE LEPER.

(St. Luke xix. 1–10; St. Matt. xx. 29–34; St. Mark x. 46–52; St. Luke xviii. 35–43;
St. John xi. 55—xii. 1; St. Matt. xxvi. 6–13; St. Mark xiv. 3–9; St. John xii.
2–11.)

ONCE more, and now for the last time, were the fords of Jordan   CHAP.
passed, and Christ was on the soil of Judæa proper.   Behind Him   XXIV
were Peræa and Galilee; behind Him the Ministry of the Gospel by
Word and Deed; before Him the final Act of His Life, towards
which all had consciously tended.   Rejected as the Messiah of
His people, not only in His Person but as regarded the Kingdom of
God, which, in fulfilment of prophecy and of the merciful Counsel
of God, He had come to establish, He was of set purpose going up
to Jerusalem, there to accomplish His Decease, 'to give His Life a
Ransom for many.'   And He was coming, not, as at the Feast of
Tabernacles, privately, but openly, at the head of His Apostles, and
followed by many disciples—a festive band going up to the Paschal
Feast, of which Himself was to be 'the Lamb' of sacrifice.

The first station reached was Jericho, the 'City of Palms,' a
distance of only about six hours from Jerusalem.   The ancient City
occupied not the site of the present wretched hamlet, but lay about
half an hour to the north-west of it, by the so-called Elisha-Spring.
A second spring rose an hour further to the north-north-west.   The
water of these springs, distributed by aqueducts, gave, under a
tropical sky, unsurpassed fertility to the rich soil along the 'plain'
of Jericho, which is about twelve or fourteen miles wide.   The Old
Testament history of the 'City of Palms' is sufficiently known.   It
was here also that King Zedekiah had, on his flight, been seized
by the Chaldeans,[a] and thither a company of 345 men returned   [a] 2 Kings
under Zerubbabel.[b]   In the war of liberation under the Maccabees   xxv. 5
[b] Ezra ii. 34

BOOK
IV

a 1 Macc. ix.
50

b Jos. Ant.
xvii. 6. 5;
Jewish War
i. 33. 6

c Cant. i. 14

d War iv.
8. 3

the Syrians had attempted to fortify Jericho.[a] These forts were afterwards destroyed by Pompey in his campaign.   Herod the Great had
first plundered, and then partially rebuilt, fortified, and adorned
Jericho.   It was here that he died.[b]   His son Archelaus also built
there a palace.   At the time of which we write, it was, of course,
under Roman dominion.   Long before, it had recovered its ancient
fame for fertility and its prosperity.   Josephus describes it as the
richest part of the country, and calls it a little Paradise.   Antony
had bestowed the revenues of its balsam-plantations as an Imperial
gift upon Cleopatra, who in turn sold them to Herod.   Here grew
palm-trees of various kinds, sycamores, the cypress-flower,[c] the myro-
balsamum, which yielded precious oil, but especially the balsam-
plant.   If to these advantages of climate, soil, and productions we
add, that it was, so to speak, the key of Judæa towards the east,
that it lay on the caravan-road from Damascus and Arabia, that it
was a great commercial and military centre, and lastly, its nearness
to Jerusalem, to which it formed the last 'station' on the road of
the festive pilgrims from Galilee and Peræa—it will not be difficult
to understand either its importance or its prosperity.

    We can picture to ourselves the scene, as our Lord on that after-
noon in early spring beheld it.   There it was, indeed, already
summer, for, as Josephus tells us,[d] even in winter the inhabitants
could only bear the lightest clothing of linen.   We are approaching
it from the Jordan.   It is protected by walls, flanked by four forts.
These walls, the theatre, and the amphitheatre, have been built by
Herod; the new palace and its splendid gardens are the work of
Archelaus.   All around wave groves of feathery palms, rising in
stately beauty; stretch gardens of roses, and especially sweet-
scented balsam-plantations—the largest behind the royal gardens,
of which the perfume is carried by the wind almost out to sea, and
which may have given to the city its name (Jericho, 'the perfumed').
It is the Eden of Palestine, the very fairyland of the old world.   And
how strangely is this gem set!   Deep down in that hollowed valley,
through which tortuous Jordan winds, to lose his waters in the slimy
mass of the Sea of Judgment.   The river and the Dead Sea are
nearly equidistant from the town—about six miles.   Far across the
river rise the mountains of Moab, on which lies the purple and
violet colouring.   Towards Jerusalem and northwards stretch those
bare limestone hills, the hiding-place of robbers along the desolate
road towards the City.   There, and in the neighbouring wilderness
of Judæa, are also the lonely dwellings of anchorites—while over all

this strangely varied scene has been flung the many-coloured mantle of a perpetual summer. And in the streets of Jericho a motley throng meets: pilgrims from Galilee and Peræa, priests who have a 'station' here, traders from all lands, who have come to purchase or to sell, or are on the great caravan-road from Arabia and Damascus—robbers and anchorites, wild fanatics, soldiers, courtiers, and busy publicans—for Jericho was the central station for the collection of tax and custom, both on native produce and on that brought from across Jordan. And yet it was a place for dreaming also, under that glorious summer-sky, in those scented groves—when these many figures from far-off lands and that crowd of priests, numbering, according to tradition, half those in Jerusalem,[a] seemed fleeting as in a vision, and (as Jewish legend had it) the sound of Temple-music came from Moriah, borne in faint echoes on the breeze, like the distant sound of many waters.[b]

It was through Jericho that Jesus, 'having entered,' was passing.[1][c] Tidings of the approach of the festive band, consisting of His disciples and Apostles, and headed by the Master Himself, must have preceded Him, these six miles from the fords of Jordan. His Name, His Works, His Teaching—perhaps Himself, must have been known to the people of Jericho, just as they must have been aware of the feelings of the leaders of the people, perhaps of the approaching great contest between them and the Prophet of Nazareth. Was He a good man; had He wrought those great miracles in the power of God or by Satanic influence—was He the Messiah or the Antichrist; would He bring salvation to the world, or entail ruin on His own nation? Conquer or be destroyed? Was it only one more in the long list of delusions and illusions, or was the long-promised morning of heaven's own day at last to break? Close by was Bethany, whence tidings had come; most incredible yet unquestioned and unquestionable, of the raising of Lazarus, so well known to all in that neighbourhood. And yet the Sanhedrin—it was well known—had resolved on His death! At any rate there was no concealment about Him; and here, in face of all, and accompanied by His followers—humble and unlettered, it must be admitted, but thoroughly convinced of His superhuman claims, and deeply attached—Jesus was going up to Jerusalem to meet His enemies!

It was the custom, when a festive band passed through a place, that the inhabitants gathered in the streets to bid their brethren

[a] Jer. Taan. iv. 2

[b] Jer. Sukk. v. 3

[c] St. Luke xix. 1-10

[1] So more accurately.

welcome. And on that afternoon, surely, scarce any one in Jericho but would go forth to see this pilgrim-band. Men—curious, angry, half-convinced; women, holding up their babes, it may be for a passing blessing, or pushing forward their children that in after years they might say they had seen the Prophet of Nazareth; traders, soldiers—a solid wall of onlookers before their gardens was this 'crowd' along the road by which Jesus 'was to pass.' Would He only pass through the place, or be the guest of some of the leading priests in Jericho; would He teach, or work any miracle, or silently go on His way to Bethany? Only one in all that crowd seemed unwelcome; alone, and out of place. It was the 'chief of the Publicans'—the head of the tax and customs department. As his name shows, he was a Jew; but yet that very name Zacchæus, 'Zakkai,' 'the just,' or 'pure,' sounded like mockery. We know in what repute Publicans were held, and what opportunities of wrong-doing and oppression they possessed. And from his after-confession it is only too evident, that Zacchæus had to the full used them for evil. And he had got that for which he had given up alike his nation and his soul: 'he was rich.' If, as Christ had taught, it was harder for any rich man to enter the Kingdom of Heaven than for a camel to pass through the eye of a needle, what of him who had gotten his riches by such means?

And yet Zacchæus was in the crowd that had come to see Jesus. What had brought him? Certainly, not curiosity only. Was it the long working of conscience; or a dim, scarcely self-avowed hope of something better; or had he heard Him before; or of Him, that He was so unlike those harsh leaders and teachers of Israel, who refused all hope on earth and in heaven to such as him, that Jesus received —nay, called to Him the publicans and sinners? Or was it only the nameless, deep, irresistible inward drawing of the Holy Ghost, which may perhaps have brought us, as it has brought many, we know not why or how, to the place and hour of eternal decision for God, and of infinite grace to our souls? Certain it is, that, as so often in such circumstances, Zacchæus encountered only hindrances which seemed to render his purpose almost impossible. The narrative is singularly detailed and pictorial. Zacchæus, trying to push his way through 'the press,' and repulsed; Zacchæus, 'little of stature,' and unable to look over the shoulders of others: it reads almost like a symbolical story of one who is seeking 'to see Jesus,' but cannot push his way because of the crowd—whether of the self-righteous, or of his own conscious sins, that seem to stand between him and the Saviour, and which will not make room for him, while he is unable to look over them because he is, so to speak, 'little of stature.'

Needless questions have been asked as to the import of Zacchæus' wish 'to see who Jesus was.' It is just this vagueness of desire, which Zacchæus himself does not understand, which is characteristic. And, since he cannot otherwise succeed, he climbs up one of those wide-spreading sycamores in a garden, perhaps close to his own house, along the only road by which Jesus can pass—'to see Him.' Now the band is approaching, through that double living wall: first, the Saviour, viewing that crowd, with, ah! how different thoughts from theirs—surrounded by His Apostles, the face of each expressive of such feelings as were uppermost; conspicuous among them, he who 'carried the bag,' with furtive, uncertain, wild glance here and there, as one who seeks to gather himself up to a terrible deed. Behind them are the disciples, men and women, who are going up with Him to the Feast. Of all persons in that crowd the least noted, the most hindered in coming—and yet the one most concerned, was the Chief Publican. It is always so—it is ever the order of the Gospel, that the last shall be first. Yet never more self-unconscious was Zacchæus than at the moment when Jesus was entering that garden-road, and passing under the overhanging branches of that sycamore, the crowd closing up behind, and following as He went along. Only one thought—without ulterior conscious object, temporal or spiritual—filled his whole being. The present absolutely held him—when those wondrous Eyes, out of which heaven itself seemed to look upon earth, were upturned, and that Face of infinite grace, never to be forgotten, beamed upon him the welcome of recognition, and He uttered the self-spoken invitation in which the invited was the real Inviter, the guest the true Host. Did Jesus know Zacchæus before—or was it only all open to His Divine gaze as 'He looked up and saw him'? This latter seems, indeed, indicated by the 'must' of His abiding in the house of Zacchæus—as if His Father had so appointed it, and Jesus come for that very purpose. And herein, also, seems this story spiritually symbolical.

As bidden by Christ, Zacchæus 'made haste and came down.' Under the gracious influence of the Holy Ghost he 'received Him rejoicing.' Nothing was as yet clear to him, and yet all was joyous within his soul. In that dim twilight of the new day, and at this new creation, the Angels sang and the Sons of God shouted together, and all was melody and harmony in his heart. But a few steps

BOOK
IV

farther, and they were at the house of the Chief Publican. Strange
hostelry this for the Lord; yet not stranger in that Life of absolute
contrasts than that first hostelry—the same, even as regards its
designation in the Gospel,[1] as when the manger had been His cradle;
not so strange, as at the Sabbath-feast of the Pharisee Rulers of the
Synagogue. But now the murmur of disappointment and anger
ran through the accompanying crowd—which perhaps had not before
heard what had passed between Jesus and the Publican, certainly,
had not understood, or else not believed its import—because He was
gone to be guest with a man that was a sinner. Oh, terribly fatal
misunderstanding of all that was characteristic of the Mission of
the Christ! oh, terribly fatal blindness and jealousy! But it was
this sudden shock of opposition which awoke Zacchæus to full consciousness. The hands so rudely and profanely thrust forward only
served to rend the veil. It often needs some such sudden shock of
opposition, some sudden sharp contest, to waken the new convert
to full consciousness, to bring before him, in clear outline, alike
the past and the present. In that moment Zacchæus saw it all:
what his past had been, what his present was, what his future
must be. Standing forth, not so much before the crowd as before
the Lord, and not ashamed, nay, scarcely conscious of the confession
it implied—so much is the sorrow of the past in true repentance
swallowed up by the joy of the present—Zacchæus vowed fourfold

[a] Ex. xxii. 1 restoration, as by a thief,[a] of what had become his through false
accusation,[2] as well as the half of all his goods to the poor. And
so the whole current of his life had been turned, in those few
moments, through his joyous reception of Christ, the Saviour of
sinners; and Zacchæus the public robber, the rich Chief of the Publicans, had become an almsgiver.

It was then, when it had been all done in silence, as mostly all
God's great works, that Jesus spake it to him, for his endless comfort,
and in the hearing of all, for their and our teaching: 'This day became
—arose—there salvation to this house,' 'forasmuch as,' truly and
spiritually, 'this one also is a son of Abraham.' And, as regards

---

[1] The word here used is καταλύω,
and the hostelry at Bethlehem (St. Luke
ii. 7) was κατάλυμα.
[2] Literally, 'if I have *sycophanted* any
man anything.' It should be remarked,
as making this restoration by Zacchæus
the more intelligible, that to a penitent
Jew this would immediately occur. In the
Talmud there is a long discussion as to
restoration by penitents in cases where
the malappropriation was open to question, when the Talmud lays down the
principle, that if any one wishes to
escape the Divine punishment, he must
restore even that which, according to
strict justice, he might not be obliged to
give up (Baba Mez. 37 a).

this man, and all men, so long as time endureth: 'For the Son of Man came to seek and to save that which was lost.'

The Evangelistic record passes with significant silence over that night in the house of Zacchæus. It forms not part of the public history of the Kingdom of God, but of that joy with which a stranger intermeddleth not. It was in the morning, when the journey in company with His disciples was resumed, that the next public incident occurred in the healing of the blind by the wayside.[a] The small divergences in the narratives of the three Evangelists are well known. It may have been that, as St. Matthew relates, there were *two* blind men sitting by the wayside, and that St. Luke and St. Mark mention only one — the latter by name as 'Bar Timæus' — because he was the spokesman. But, in regard to the other divergence, trifling as it is, that St. Luke places the incident at the arrival, the other two Evangelists at the departure of Jesus from Jericho, it is better to admit our inability to conciliate these differing notes of time, than to make clumsy attempts at harmonising them. We can readily believe that there may have been circumstances unknown to us, which might show these statements to be not really diverging. And, if it were otherwise, it would in no way affect the narrative itself. Historical information could only have been derived from local sources; and we have already seen reason to infer that St. Luke had gathered his from personal inquiry on the spot. And it may have been, either that the time was not noted, or wrongly noted, or that this miracle, as the only one in Jericho, may have been reported to him before mention was made of the reception by Christ of Zacchæus. In any case, it shows the independence of the account of St. Luke from that of the other two Evangelists.

[a] St. Matt.
xx. 29-34;
St. Mark x.
46-52; St.
Luke xviii.
35-43

Little need be said of the incident itself: it is so like the other Deeds of His Life. So to speak—it was left in Jericho as the practical commentary, and the seal on what Christ had said and done the previous evening in regard to Zacchæus. Once more the crowd was following Jesus, as in the morning He resumed the journey with His disciples. And, there by the wayside, begging, sat the blind men —there, where Jesus was passing. As they heard the tramp of many feet and the sound of many voices, they learned that Jesus of Nazareth was passing by. It is all deeply touching, and deeply symbolical. But what must their faith have been, when there, in Jericho, they not only owned Him as the true Messiah, but cried—in the deep significance of that special mode of address, as coming from Jewish

BOOK
IV

lips:[1] 'Jesus, Thou Son of David, have mercy on me!' It was quite in accordance with what one might almost have expected—certainly with the temper of Jericho, as we learned it on the previous evening, when 'many,' the 'multitude,' 'they which went before,' would have bidden that cry for help be silent as an unwarrantable intrusion and interruption, if not a needless and meaningless application. But only all the louder and more earnest rose the cry, as the blind felt that they might for ever be robbed of the opportunity that was slipping past. And He, Who listens to every cry of distress, heard this. He stood still, and commanded the blind to be called. Then it was that the sympathy of sudden hope seized the 'multitude' the wonder about to be wrought fell, so to speak, in its heavenly influences upon them, as they comforted the blind in the agony of rising despair with

[a] St. Mark x. 49

the words, 'He calleth thee.'[a] As so often, we are indebted to St. Mark for the vivid sketch of what passed. We can almost see Bartimæus as, on receiving Christ's summons, he casts aside his upper garment and hastily comes. That question: what he would that Jesus should do unto him, must have been meant for those around more than for the blind. The cry to the son of David had been only for mercy. It might have been for alms—though, as the address, so the gift bestowed in answer, would be right royal—'after the order of David.' But our general cry for mercy must ever become detailed when we come into the Presence of the Christ. And the faith of the blind rose to the full height of the Divine possibilities opened before them. Their inward eyes had received capacity for The Light, before that of earth lit up their long darkness. In the language of St. Matthew, 'Jesus had compassion on them and touched their eyes.' This is one aspect of it. The other is that given by St. Mark and St. Luke, in recording the words with which He accompanied the healing: 'Thy faith has saved thee.'[2]

And these two results came of it: 'all the people, when they saw it gave praise unto God;' and, as for Bartimæus, though Jesus had bidden him 'go thy way,' yet, 'immediately he received his sight,'

[b] St. Luke

he 'followed Jesus in the way,' glorifying God.[b] And this is Divine disobedience, or rather the obedience of the spirit as against the observance of the letter.[3]

The arrival of the Paschal band from Galilee and Peræa was not in advance of many others. In truth, most pilgrims from a distance

[1] Comp. our remarks on this point in vol. ii. p. 49.

[2] The expression is the same in St. Mark and St. Luke.

[3] The Parable of the Ten Pieces of Money will be expounded in connection with the last series of Parables.

would probably come to the Holy City some days before the Feast, for the sake of purification in the Temple, since those who for any reason needed such—and there would be few families that did not require it—generally deferred it till the festive season brought them to Jerusalem. We owe this notice, and that which follows, to St. John,[a] and in this again recognise the Jewish writer of the Fourth Gospel. It was only natural that these pilgrims should have sought for Jesus, and, when they did not find Him, discuss among themselves the probability of His coming to the Feast. His absence would, after the work which He had done these three years, the claim which He made, and the defiant denial of it by the priesthood and the Sanhedrin, have been regarded as a virtual surrender to the enemy. There was a time when He need not have appeared at the Feast—when, as we see it, it was better He should not come. But that time was past. The chief priests and the Pharisees also knew it, and they 'had given commandment that, if any one knew where He was, he would show it, that they might take Him.' It would be better to ascertain where He lodged, and to seize Him before He appeared in public, in the Temple.

But it was not as they had imagined. Without concealment Christ came to Bethany, where Lazarus lived, whom He had raised from the dead. He came there six days before the Passover—and yet His coming was such that they could not 'take Him.'[b] They might as well take Him in the Temple; nay, more easily. For, the moment His stay in Bethany became known, 'much people [1] of the Jews' came out, not only for His sake, but to see that Lazarus whom He had raised from the dead. And, of those who so came, many went away believing. And how, indeed, could it be otherwise? Thus one of their plans was frustrated, and the evil seemed only to grow worse. The Sanhedrin could perhaps not be moved to such flagrant outrage of all Jewish Law, but 'the chief priests,' who had no such scruples, consulted how they might put Lazarus also to death.[c]

Yet, not until His hour had come could man do aught against Christ or His disciples. And, in contrast to such scheming, haste, and search, we mark the majestic calm and quiet of Him Who knew what was before Him. Jesus had arrived at Bethany six days before the Passover—that is, on a Friday.[2] The day after was the Sabbath,

CHAP.
XXIV

[a] St. John xi. 55-57

[b] St. John xii. 1

[c] St. John xii. 10, 11

---

[1] Canon *Westcott* prefers the reading: 'the common people.'
[2] On the precise dates, see the Com- mentaries. It has been impossible here to discuss in detail every little difficulty. Rather has it been thought best to tell

BOOK
IV

a St. John
xii. 1

and 'they made Him a supper.'ᵃ It was the special festive meal of the Sabbath. The words of St. John seem to indicate that the meal was a public one, as if the people of Bethany had combined to do Him this honour, and so share the privilege of attending the feast. In point of fact, we know from St. Matthew and St. Mark that it took place ' in the house of Simon the Leper '—not, of course, an actual leper—but one who had been such. Perhaps his guest-chamber was the largest in Bethany; perhaps the house was nearest to the Synagogue; or there may have been other reasons for it, unknown to us—least likely is the suggestion that Simon was the

b Hengsten-
berg
c Ewald

husband of Martha,ᵇ or else her father.ᶜ But all is in character. Among the guests is Lazarus: and, prominent in service, Martha; and Mary (the unnamed woman of the other two Gospels, which do not mention that household by name), is also true to her character.[1] She had ' an alabaster '[2] of 'spikenard genuine,' which was very precious.   It held ' a litra ' (לִיטְרָא or לִיטְרָּא), which was a ' Roman pound,' and its value could not have been less than nearly

d Kerith.
6 a
e Hist. Nat.
xii. 12, 26
f xii. 12, 26

9l.   Remembering the price of Nard,ᵈ as given by *Pliny*,ᵉ and that the Syrian was only next in value to the Indian, which *Pliny* regarded as the bestᶠ ointment of ' genuine '[3] Nard—unadulterated and unmixed with any other balsam[4] (as the less expensive kinds were), such a price (300 dinars= nearly 9l.) would be by no means excessive; indeed, much lower than at Rome. But, viewed in another light, the sum spent was very large, remembering that 200 dinars (about 6l.) nearly sufficed to provide bread for 5,000 men with their families, and that the ordinary wages of a labourer amounted to only one dinar a day.

We can here offer only conjectures, But it is, at least, not unreasonable to suppose—remembering the fondness of Jewish women for such perfumes[5]—that Mary may have had that ' alabaster ' of very costly ointment from olden days, before she had learned to

the events, as we regard them as having taken place. See *Nebe*, Leidensgesch. i. pp. 23, 24.

[1] Those, if any, who identify this Mary with the Magdalene, and regard the anointing of St. Luke vii. 36, &c., as identical with that of Bethany, are referred, for full discussion and refutation, to *Nebe*, Leidensgesch. vol. i. pp. 21 &c., 30 &c.

[2] *Unguenta optime servantur in alabastris* (*Plin.* H. N. xiii. 2, 3). These ' alabasters '—for the flask itself obtained that name from the stone used—had at the top

the form of a cylinder, and are likened by *Pliny* to a closed rose-bud.

[3] The expression πιστική has given rise to much controversy. Of the various renderings, that by ' genuine ' has most in its favour. For a full discussion see *Nebe*, u. s. pp. 33, 34, and *Meyer* on St. Mark xiv. 3–9.

[4] On the various mixtures of precious ointments, their adulteration, the cost of the various ingredients, and the use made of perfumes in Palestine, see *Herzfeld*, u. s. pp. 99, 100, 191, 192.

[5] See Book III. chap. xxi.

serve Christ. Then, when she came to know Him, and must have
learned how constantly that Decease, of which He ever spoke, was
before His Mind, she may have put it aside, 'kept it,' 'against the
day of His burying.' And now the decisive hour had come. Jesus
may have told her, as He had told the disciples, what was before
Him in Jerusalem at the Feast, and she would be far more quick to
understand, even as she must have known far better than they, how
great was the danger from the Sanhedrin. And it is this believing
apprehension of the mystery of His Death on her part, and this preparation of deepest love for it—this mixture of sorrow, faith, and
devotion—which made her deed so precious, that, wherever in the
future the Gospel would be preached, this also that she had done
would be recorded for a memorial of her.[a] And the more we think
of it, the better can we understand, how at that last feast of fellowship, when all the other guests realised not—no, not even His
disciples—how near the end was, she would 'come aforehand to
anoint His Body for the burying.'[b][1] Her faith made it a twofold
anointing: that of the best Guest at the last feast, and that of preparation for that Burial which, of all others, she apprehended as so
terribly near. And deepest humility now offered, what most earnest
love had provided, and intense faith, in view of what was coming,
applied. And so she poured the precious ointment over His Head,
over His Feet [2]—then, stooping over them, wiped them with her hair,
as if, not only in evidence of service and love, but in fellowship of
His Death.[c] 'And the house was filled '—and to all time His House,
the Church, is filled—' with the odour of the ointment.'

It is ever the light which throws the shadows of objects—and
this deed of faith and love now cast the features of Judas in gigantic
dark outlines against the scene. He knew the nearness of Christ's
Betrayal, and hated the more; she knew of the nearness of His
precious Death, and loved the more. It was not that he cared for the
poor, when, taking the mask of charity, he simulated anger that such
costly ointment had not been sold, and the price given to the poor.

* St. Matt.
xxvi. 13

b St. Mark
xiv. 8

c St. John

---

[1] St. Matthew and St. Mark.
[2] St. John. There is manifestly neither
contradiction nor divergence here between the Evangelists. Mary first poured
the nard over the Head, and then over His
Feet (*Godet* sees this implied in the
κατέχεεν αὐτοῦ of St. Mark). St. John
notices the anointing of the Feet, not only
as the act of greatest humility and the
mark of deepest veneration, but from its
unusual character, while anointing of the

head was not so uncommon. We recall the
ideal picture of Aaron when anointed to
the priesthood, Ps. cxxxiii. 2, to mark
here the fulfilment of the type when the
Great High-Priest was anointed for His
Sacrifice. She who had so often sat at
His feet, now anoints them, and alike
for love, reverence, and fellowship of
His sufferings, will not wipe them but
with her hair.

For he was essentially dishonest, 'a thief,' and covetousness was the underlying master-passion of his soul. The money, claimed for the poor, would only have been used by himself. Yet such was his pretence of righteousness, such his influence as 'a man of prudence' among the disciples, and such their sad weakness, that they, or at least 'some,' [a] expressed indignation among themselves and against her who had done the deed of love, which, when viewed in the sublimeness of a faith, that accepted and prepared for the death of a Saviour Whom she so loved, and to Whom this last, the best service she could, was to be devoted, would for ever cause her to be thought of as an example of loving. There is something inexpressibly sad, yet so patient, gentle, and tender in Christ's 'Let her alone.' Surely, never could there be waste in ministry of love to Him! Nay, there is unspeakable pathos in what He says of His near Burying, as if He would still their souls in view of it. That He, Who was ever of the poor and with them, Who for our sakes became poor, that through His poverty we might be made rich, should have to plead for a last service of love to Himself, and for Mary, and as against a Judas, seems, indeed, the depth of self-abasement. Yet, even so, has this falsely-spoken plea for the poor become a real plea, since He has left us this, as it were, as His last charge, and that by His own Death, that we have the poor always with us. And so do even the words of covetous dishonesty become, when passing across Him, transformed into the command of charity, and the breath of hell is changed into the summer-warmth of the Church's constant service to Christ in the ministry to His poor.

Book V.

THE CROSS AND THE CROWN.

'Ave, Scala peccatorum,
Qua ascendit rex cœlorum,
Ut ad choros Angelorum
Homo sic ascenderet;
In te vitam reparavit
Auctor vitæ, proles David,
Et sic se humiliavit.
Ut mundum redimeret.

Ap. DANIEL, *Thes. Hymnol.* vol. v. p. 183.

'The blessing from the cloud that showers,
In wondrous twofold birth
Of heaven is and earth—
He is both yours, ye hosts, and ours:
Hosannah, David's Son,
For victory is won!

He left us with a blessing here,
And took it to the sky;
The blessing from on high
Bespeaks to us His Presence near:
Hosannah, David's Son,
For victory is won!'

(From an Ascension Hymn).—A. E.

CHAPTER I.

THE FIRST DAY IN PASSION-WEEK—PALM-SUNDAY—THE ROYAL ENTRY
INTO JERUSALEM.

(St. Matt. xxi. 1–11; St. Mark xi. 1–11; St. Luke xix. 29–44; St. John xii. 12–19.)

AT length the time of the end had come. Jesus was about to make
Entry into Jerusalem as King: King of the Jews, as Heir of David's
royal line, with all of symbolic, typic, and prophetic import attaching
to it. Yet not as Israel after the flesh expected its Messiah was
the Son of David to make triumphal entrance, but as deeply and
significantly expressive of His Mission and Work, and as of old the
rapt seer had beheld afar off the outlined picture of the Messiah-
King: not in the proud triumph of war-conquests, but in the 'meek'
rule of peace.

CHAP.
I

It is surely one of the strangest mistakes of modern criticism to
regard this Entry of Christ into Jerusalem as implying that, fired by
enthusiasm, He had for the moment expected that the people would
receive Him as the Messiah.[1] And it seems little, if at all better,
when this Entry is described as ' an apparent concession to the fevered
expectations of His disciples and the multitude . . . the grave,
sad accommodation to thoughts other than His own to which the
Teacher of new truths must often have recourse when He finds Himself misinterpreted by those who stand together on a lower level.'[2]
' Apologies ' are the weakness of ' Apologetics '—and any ' accommodation ' theory can have no place in the history of the Christ. On the
contrary, we regard His Royal Entry into the Jerusalem of Prophecy
and of the Crucifixion as an integral part of the history of Christ,
which would not be complete, nor thoroughly consistent, without it.
It behoved Him so to enter Jerusalem, because He was a King; and
as King to enter it in such manner, because He was such a King—
and both the one and the other were in accordance with the prophecy
of old.

[1] So notably *Keim*. Of course, the
theory proceeds on the *assumption* that
the Discourses reported by St. Luke are
spurious.
[2] Dean *Plumptre* on St. Matt. xxi. 5.

BOOK
V

It was a bright day in early spring of the year 29, when the festive procession set out from the home at Bethany.   There can be no reasonable doubt as to the locality of that hamlet (the modern *El–'Azarîye*, ' of Lazarus '), perched on a broken rocky plateau on the other side of Olivet.   More difficulty attaches to the identification of *Bethphage*, which is associated with it, the place not being mentioned in the Old Testament, though repeatedly in Jewish writings.   But, even so, there is a curious contradiction, since Bethphage is sometimes spoken of as distinct from Jerusalem,[a] while at others it is described as, for ecclesiastical purposes, part of the City itself.[b]   Perhaps the name Bethphage—' house of figs '—was given alike to that district generally, and to a little village close to Jerusalem where the district began.[1]   And this may explain the peculiar reference, in the Synoptic Gospels, to Bethphage (St. Matthew), and again to ' Bethphage and Bethany.'[c]   For, St. Matthew and St. Mark relate Christ's brief stay at Bethany and His anointing by Mary not in chronological order,[2] but introduce it at a later period, as it were, in contrast to the betrayal of Judas[d]   Accordingly, they pass from the Miracles at Jericho immediately to the Royal Entry into Jerusalem—from Jericho to ' Bethphage,' or, more exactly, to ' Bethphage and Bethany,' leaving for the present unnoticed what had occurred in the latter hamlet.

Although all the four Evangelists relate Christ's Entry into Jerusalem, they seem to do so from different standpoints.   The Synoptists accompany Him from Bethany, while St. John, in accordance with the general scheme of his narrative, seems to follow from Jerusalem that multitude which, on tidings of His approach, hastened to meet Him.   Even this circumstance, as also the paucity of events recorded on that day, proves that it could not have been at early morning that Jesus left Bethany.   Remembering, that it was the last morning of rest before the great contest, we may reverently think of much that may have passed in the Soul of Jesus and in the home of Bethany.   And now He has left that peaceful resting-place.   It was probably soon after His outset, that He sent the ' two disciples '—possibly Peter and John[e]—into ' the village over against ' them—presumably Bethphage.   There they would find by the side of the road an ass's colt tied, whereon never man had sat.   We mark the significant symbolism of the latter, in connection with the general

[a] Siphré,ed. Friedm. p. 55 a, last lines; Sot. 45 a; Tos. Pes. viii. 8
[b] Pes. 63 b; 91 a; Menach. 78 b; Babha Mets. 90 a
[c] St. Mark and St. Luke
[d] St. Matt. xxvi. 6-13; St. Mark xiv. 3-9
[e] Comp. St. Luke xxii. 8

---

[1] See also *Caspari*, Chron. Geogr. Einl. p. 161. The question as to the proposed identification (by some) of Bethany with the *Beth Hini*, or *Beth Hanioth*, where the Sanhedrin (apparently of Sadducees) sat after leaving the Temple and which was destroyed three years before the City, must be left here undiscussed.

[2] St. Augustine has it, *recapitulando dixerunt*.

conditions of consecration to Jehovah [a]—and note in it, as also in the
Mission of the Apostles, that this was intended by Christ to be His
Royal and Messianic Entry. This colt they were to loose and to bring
to Him.

The disciples found all as He had said. When they reached
Bethphage, they saw, by a doorway where two roads met, the colt
tied by its mother. As they loosed it, 'the owners' and 'certain of
them that stood by' [b] asked their purpose, to which, as directed by
the Master, they answered: 'The Lord [the Master, Christ] hath need
of him,' when, as predicted, no further hindrance was offered. In
explanation of this we need not resort to the theory of a miraculous
influence, nor even suppose that the owners of the colt were themselves 'disciples.' Their challenge to 'the two,' and the little more
than permission which they gave, seem to forbid this idea. Nor is
such explanation requisite. From the pilgrim-band which had accompanied Jesus from Galilee and Peræa, and preceded Him to Jerusalem, from the guests at the Sabbath-feast in Bethany, and from the
people who had gone out to see both Jesus and Lazarus, the tidings
of the proximity of Jesus and of His approaching arrival must have
spread in the City. Perhaps that very morning some had come from
Bethany, and told it in the Temple, among the festive bands—specially
among his own Galileans, and generally in Jerusalem, that on that
very day—in a few, hours—Jesus might be expected to enter the
City. Such, indeed, must have been the case, since, from St. John's
account, 'a great multitude' 'went forth to meet Him.' The latter,
we can have little doubt, must have mostly consisted, not of citizens
of Jerusalem, whose enmity to Christ was settled, but of those 'that
had come to the Feast.' [c] With these went also a number of 'Pharisees,' their hearts filled with bitterest thoughts of jealousy and hatred. [d]
And, as we shall presently see, it is of great importance to keep in
mind this composition of 'the multitude.'

If such were the circumstances, all is natural. We can understand, how eager questioners would gather about the owners of the
colt (St. Mark), there at the cross-roads at Bethphage, just outside
Jerusalem; and how, so soon as from the bearing and the peculiar
words of the disciples they understood their purpose, the owners of
the ass and colt would grant its use for the solemn Entry into the
City of the 'Teacher of Nazareth,'[1] Whom the multitude was so

CHAP.
I

[a] Num. xix.
2; Deut.
xxi. 3

[b] St. Mark;
comp. also
St. Matthew

[c] St. John
xii. 12
[d] St. Luke
xix. 39; St.
John xii. 19

---

[1] It is surely one of those instances
in which the supposed authority of MSS.
should *not* be implicitly followed, when
in St. Mark xi. 3, the R.V. adopts what
we must regard as a very jejune gloss:
'and straightway He [viz. Christ] will
send him back hither'—as if the disciples had obtained the colt by pledging

eagerly expecting; and, lastly, how, as from the gates of Jerusalem tidings spread of what had passed in Bethphage, the multitude would stream forth to meet Jesus.

Meantime Christ and those who followed Him from Bethany had slowly entered on[1] the well-known caravan-road from Jericho to Jerusalem. It is the most southern of three, which converge close to the City, perhaps at the very place where the colt had stood tied. 'The road soon loses sight of Bethany. It is now a rough, but still broad and well-defined mountain-track, winding over rock and loose stones; a steep declivity on the left; the sloping shoulder of Olivet above on the right; fig-trees below and above, here and there growing out of the rocky soil.'[2] Somewhere here the disciples who brought 'the colt' must have met Him. They were accompanied by many, and immediately followed by more. For, as already stated, Bethphage—we presume the village—formed almost part of Jerusalem, and during Easter-week must have been crowded by pilgrims, who could not find accommodation within the City walls. And the announcement, that disciples of Jesus had just fetched the beast of burden on which Jesus was about to enter Jerusalem, must have quickly spread among the crowds which thronged the Temple and the City.

As the two disciples, accompanied, or immediately followed by the multitude, brought 'the colt' to Christ, 'two streams of people met'—the one coming from the City, the other from Bethany. The impression left on our minds is, that what followed was unexpected by those who accompanied Christ, that it took them by surprise. The disciples, who understood not,[a] till the light of the Resurrection-glory had been poured on their minds, the significance of 'these things,' even after they had occurred, seem not even to have guessed, that it was of set purpose Jesus was about to make His Royal Entry into Jerusalem. Their enthusiasm seems only to have been kindled when they saw the procession from the town come to meet Jesus with palm-branches, cut down by the way, and greeting Him with Hosanna-shouts of welcome. Then they spread their garments on the colt, and set Jesus thereon—'unwrapped their loose cloaks from their shoulders and stretched them along the rough path, to form a

[a] St. John xii. 16

the Master to its immediate restoration. The gloss is the more inapt as it does not occur in the parallel passages in St. Matthew and St. Luke.

[1] They *may* have awaited in Bethany the return of the two, but the succession

followed in the text seems to me by far the most probable.

[2] The quotations are from the well-known and classical passage in Dean *Stanley's* Sinai and Palestine, pp. 189 &c.

momentary carpet as He approached.' Then also in their turn they cut down branches from the trees and gardens through which they passed, or plaited and twisted palm-branches, and strewed them as a rude matting in His way, while they joined in, and soon raised to a much higher pitch ^a the Hosanna of welcoming praise. Nor need we wonder at their ignorance at first of the meaning of that, in which themselves were chief actors. We are too apt to judge them from our standpoint, eighteen centuries later, and after full apprehension of the significance of the event. These men walked in the procession almost as in a dream, or as dazzled by a brilliant light all around—as if impelled by a necessity, and carried from event to event, which came upon them in a succession of but partially understood surprises.

They had now ranged themselves: the multitude which had come from the City preceding, that which had come with Him from Bethany following the triumphant progress of Israel's King, 'meek, and sitting upon an ass, and a colt the foal of an ass.' 'Gradually the long procession swept up and over the ridge where first begins "the descent of the Mount of Olives" towards Jerusalem. At this point the first view is caught of the south-eastern corner of the City. The Temple and the more northern portions are hid by the slope of Olivet on the right; what is seen is only Mount Zion, now for the most part a rough field.' But at that time it rose, terrace upon terrace, from the Palace of the Maccabees and that of the High-Priest, a very city of palaces, till the eye rested in the summit on that castle, city, and palace, with its frowning towers and magnificent gardens, the royal abode of Herod, supposed to occupy the very site of the Palace of David. They had been greeting Him with Hosannas! But enthusiasm, especially in such a cause, is infectious. They were mostly stranger-pilgrims that had come from the City, chiefly because they had heard of the raising of Lazarus.^b And now they must have questioned them which came from Bethany, who in turn related that of which themselves had been eyewitnesses.^c We can imagine it all—how the fire would leap from heart to heart. So He was the promised Son of David—and the Kingdom was at hand! It may have been just as the precise point of the road was reached, where 'the City of David' first suddenly emerges into view, 'at the descent of the Mount of Olives,' 'that the whole multitude of the disciples began to rejoice and praise God with a loud voice for all the mighty works that they had seen.'^d As the burning words of joy and praise, the record of what they had seen, passed from mouth

CHAP.
I

^a St. Luke xix. 37, 38

^b St. John xii. 18

^c ver. 17

^d St. Luke

BOOK
V

to mouth, and they caught their first sight of 'the City of David,' adorned as a bride to welcome her King—Davidic praise to David's Greater Son wakened the echoes of old Davidic Psalms in the morning-light of their fulfilment. 'Hosanna to the Son of David! Blessed be He that cometh in the Name of the Lord. . . . Blessed the Kingdom that cometh, the Kingdom of our father David. . . . Blessed be He that cometh in the Name of the Lord. . . . Hosanna . . . Hosanna in the highest . . .Peace in heaven, and glory in the highest.'

They were but broken utterances, partly based upon Ps. cxviii., partly taken from it—the 'Hosanna,'[1] or 'Save now,' and the 'Blessed be He that cometh in the Name of the Lord,'[a] forming part of the responses by the people with which this Psalm was chanted on certain of the most solemn festivals.[2] Most truly did they thus interpret and apply the Psalm, old and new Davidic praise mingling in their acclamations. At the same time it must be remembered that, according to Jewish tradition, Ps. cxviii. vv. 25-28, was also chanted antiphonally by the people of Jerusalem, as they went to welcome the festive pilgrims on their arrival, the latter always responding in the second clause of each verse, till the last verse of the Psalm[b] was reached, which was sung by both parties in unison, Psalm ciii. 17 being added by way of conclusion.[c] But as 'the shout rang through the long defile,' carrying evidence far and wide, that, so far from condemning and forsaking, more than the ordinary pilgrim-welcome had been given to Jesus—the Pharisees, who had mingled with the crowd, turned to one another with angry frowns: 'Behold [see intently], how ye prevail nothing! See—the world[3] is gone after Him!' It is always so, that, in the disappointment of malice, men turn in impotent rage against each other with taunts and reproaches. Then, psychologically true in this also, they made a desperate appeal to the Master Himself, Whom they so bitterly hated, to check and rebuke the honest zeal of His disciples. He had been silent hitherto—alone unmoved, or only deeply moved

[a] Ps. cxviii.
25, 26

[b] ver. 29

[c] Midr. on
Ps. cxviii.,
ed. Warsh.,
pp. 85 b,
last 3 lines,
and p. 86 a

---

[1] There can be no question that 'Ωσαννά represents אָנָּ הוֹשִׁיעָה, but probably in an abbreviated form of pronunciation אָנָּ הוֹשַׁע (comp. Siegfried in Hilgenfeld's Zeitsch. f. wissensch. Theol. for 1884, p. 385).

[2] As will be remembered, it formed the last Psalm in what was called the Hallel (Ps. cxiii.–cxviii). For the mode in which, and the occasions on which it was chanted, see 'Temple, &c.' pp. 191-193. The remarks of Godet on the subject (Comm. on St. John xii.) are not accurate.

[3] A common Jewish expression, עָלְמָא Babha Mez. 85 a, line 3 from top, or כּוּלֵי עָלְמָא Ber. 58 a, about the middle.

inwardly—amidst this enthusiastic crowd. He could be silent no longer—but, with a touch of quick and righteous indignation, pointed to the rocks and stones, telling those leaders of Israel, that, if the people held their peace, the very stones would cry out.[a][1] It would have been so in that day of Christ's Entry into Jerusalem. And it has been so ever since. Silence has fallen these many centuries upon Israel; but the very stones of Jerusalem's ruin and desolateness have cried out that He, Whom in their silence they rejected, has come as King in the Name of the Lord.

'Again the procession advanced. The road descends a slight declivity, and the glimpse of the City is again withdrawn behind the intervening ridge of Olivet. A few moments and the path mounts again, it climbs a rugged ascent, it reaches a ledge of smooth rock, and in an instance the whole City bursts into view. As now the dome of the Mosque El-Aksa rises like a Ghost from the earth before the traveller stands on the ledge, so then must have risen the Temple-tower; as now the vast enclosure of the Mussulman sanctuary, so then must have spread the Temple courts; as now the grey town on its broken hills, so then the magnificent City, with its background—long since vanished away—of gardens and suburbs on the western plateau behind. Immediately before was the Valley of the Kedron, here seen in its greatest depth as it joins the Valley of Hinnom, and thus giving full effect to the great peculiarity of Jerusalem, seen only on its eastern side—its situation as of a City rising out of a deep abyss. It is hardly possible to doubt that this rise and turn of the road—this rocky ledge—was the exact point where the multitude paused again, and "He, when He beheld the City, wept over it."' Not with still weeping ($\dot{\epsilon}\delta\acute{\alpha}\kappa\rho\upsilon\sigma\epsilon\nu$), as at the grave of Lazarus, but with loud and deep lamentation ($\overset{"}{\epsilon}\kappa\lambda\alpha\upsilon\sigma\epsilon\nu$). The contrast was, indeed, terrible between the Jerusalem that rose before Him in all its beauty, glory, and security, and the Jerusalem which He saw in vision dimly rising on the sky, with the camp of the enemy around about it on every side, hugging it closer and closer in deadly embrace, and the very 'stockade' which the Roman Legions raised around it;[b] then, another scene in the shifting panorama, and the city laid with the ground, and the gory bodies of her children among her ruins; and yet another scene: the silence and desolateness of death by the Hand of God—not one stone left upon another! We know only too well how literally this vision has become

---

[1] The expression: stones bearing witness when sin has been committed, is not uncommon in Jewish writings. See Taan. 11 *a*; Chag. 16 *a*.

BOOK
V

reality; and yet, though uttered as prophecy by Christ, and its reason so clearly stated, Israel to this day knows not the things which belong unto its peace, and the upturned scattered stones of its dispersion are crying out in testimony against it. But to this day, also do the tears of Christ plead with the Church on Israel's behalf, and His words bear within them precious seed of promise.

We turn once more to the scene just described. For, it was no common pageantry; and Christ's public Entry into Jerusalem seems so altogether different from—we had almost said, inconsistent with —His previous mode of appearance. Evidently, the time for the silence so long enjoined had passed, and that for public declaration had come. And such, indeed, this Entry was. From the moment of His sending forth the two disciples to His acceptance of the homage of the multitude, and His rebuke of the Pharisee's attempt to arrest it, all must be regarded as designed or approved by Him: not only a public assertion of His Messiahship, but a claim to its national acknowledgment. And yet, even so, it was not to be the Messiah of Israel's conception, but He of prophetic picture: ' just and having salvation; lowly, and riding upon an ass.'ᵃ It is foreign to our present purpose to discuss any general questions about this prophecy, or even to vindicate its application to the Messiah. But, when we brush aside all the trafficking and bargaining over words, that constitutes so much of modern criticism, which in its care over the lesson so often loses the spirit, there can, at least, be no question that this prophecy was intended to introduce, in contrast to earthly warfare and kingly triumph, another Kingdom, of which the just King would be the Prince of Peace, Who was meek and lowly in His Advent, Who would speak peace to the heathen, and Whose sway would yet extend to earth's utmost bounds. Thus much may be said, that if there ever was true picture of the Messiah-King and His Kingdom, it is this, and that, if ever Israel was to have a Messiah or the world a Saviour, He must be such as described in this prophecy—not merely in the letter, but in the spirit of it. And as so often indicated, it was not the letter but the spirit of prophecy—and of all prophecy—which the ancient Synagogue, and that rightly, saw fulfilled in the Messiah and His Kingdom. Accordingly, with singular unanimity the Talmud and the ancient Rabbinic authorities have applied this prophecy to the Christ.ᵇ Nor was it quoted by St. Matthew and St. John in the stiffness and deadness of the letter. On the contrary (as so often in Jewish writings, two prophets—Isa. lxii. 11, and Zech. ix. 9—are made

ᵃ Zech. ix. 9

ᵇ Ber. 56 b;
Sanh. 98 a;
Pirké de
R. El. 31;
Ber. R. 75;
98; 99;
Deb. R. 4;
Midr. on
Cant. i. 4;
Midr. on
Cant. i. 4;
Midr. on
Eccles. i. 9;
Midr.
Shemuel 14

to shed their blended light upon this Entry of Christ, as exhibiting the reality, of which the prophetic vision had been the reflex.
Nor yet are the words of the Prophets given literally—as modern
criticism would have them weighed out in the critical balances—
either from the Hebrew text, or from the LXX. rendering; but their
real meaning is given, and they are 'Targumed' by the sacred
writers, according to their wont. Yet who that sets the prophetic
picture by the side of the reality—the description by the side of
Christ's Entry into Jerusalem—can fail to recognise in the one the
real fulfilment of the other?

Another point seems to require comment. We have seen reasons
to regard the bearing of the disciples as one of surprise, and that, all
through these last scenes, they seem to have been hurried from event
to event. But the enthusiasm of the people—their royal welcome
of Christ—how is it to be explained, and how reconciled with the
speedy and terrible reaction of His Betrayal and Crucifixion? Yet
it is not so difficult to understand it; and, if we only keep clear of
unconscious exaggeration, we shall gain in truth and reasonableness
what we lose in dramatic effect. It has already been suggested, that
the multitude which went to meet Jesus must have consisted chiefly
of pilgrim-strangers. The overwhelming majority of the citizens of
Jerusalem were bitterly and determinately hostile to Christ. But
we know that, even so, the Pharisees dreaded to take the final steps
against Christ during the presence of these pilgrims at the Feast,
apprehending a movement in His favour.[a] It proved, indeed, otherwise; for these country-people were but ill-informed; they dared not
resist the combined authority of their own Sanhedrin and of the
Romans. Besides, the prejudices of the populace, and especially of
an Eastern populace, are easily raised, and they readily sway from
one extreme to the opposite. Lastly, the very suddenness and completeness of the blow, which the Jewish authorities delivered, would
have stunned even those who had deeper knowledge, more cohesion,
and greater independence than most of them who, on that Palm-
Sunday, had gone forth from the City.

[a] St. Matt.
xxvi. 3–6;
St. Mark
xiv. 2; St.
Luke xxii
2

Again, as regards their welcome of Christ, deeply significant as it
was, we must not attach to it deeper meaning than it possessed.
Modern writers have mostly seen in it the demonstrations of the Feast
of Tabernacles,[1] as if the homage of its services had been offered to

---

[1] This after *Lightfoot*. *Wünsche* (Erläut. d. Evang. p. 241) goes so far as
to put this alternative, that either the
Evangelists confounded the Passover
with the Feast of the Tabernacles, or
that they purposely transferred to the
Passover a ceremony of the Feast of
Tabernacles!

BOOK   Christt.   It would, indeed, have been symbolic of much about Israel
 V   if they had thus confounded the Second with the First Advent of
        Christ, the Sacrifice of the Passover with the joy of the Feast of
        Ingathering.   But, in reality, their conduct bears not that interpre-
        tation.   It is true that these responses from Ps. cxviii., which formed
ᵃ Ps. cxiii.-   part of what was known as the (Egyptian) Hallel,ᵃ were chanted by
cxviii.   the people on the Feast of Tabernacles also, but the Hallel was
        equally sung with responses during the offering of the Passover, at
        the Paschal Supper, and on the Feasts of Pentecost and of the Dedi-
        cation of the Temple.   The waving of the palm-branches was the
        welcome of visitors or kings,[1] and not distinctive of the Feast of
        Tabernacles.   At the latter, the worshippers carried, not simple palm-
        branches, but the *Lulabh*, which consisted of palm, myrtle, and willow
        branches interwined.   Lastly, the words of welcome from Ps. cxviii.
        were (as already stated) those with which on solemn occasions the
        people also greeted the arrival of festive pilgrims,[2] although, as being
        offered to Christ alone, and as accompanied by such demonstrations,
        they may have implied that they hailed Him as the promised King, and
        have converted His Entry into a triumph in which the people did
        homage.   And, if proof were required of the more sober, and, may
        we not add, rational view here advocated, it would be found in this,
        that not till after His Resurrection did even His own disciples under-
        stand the significance of the whole scene which they had witnessed,
        and in which they had borne such a part.

        The anger and jealousy of the Pharisees understood it better,
        and watched for the opportunity of revenge.   But, for the present,
        on that bright spring-day, the weak, excitable, fickle populace
        streamed before Him through the City-gates, through the narrow
        streets, up the Temple-mount.   Everywhere the tramp of their feet,
        and the shout of their acclamations brought men, women, and
        children into the streets and on the housetops.   The City was
        moved, and from mouth to mouth the question passed among the
        eager crowd of curious onlookers: 'Who is He?' And the multitude

---

[1] Such were, and even now are, com-
mon demonstrations in the East, to wel-
come a king, a conqueror, or a deliverer.
For a large number of heathen and
Jewish instances of the same time, comp.
Wetstein, ad loc. (i. pp. 460, 461).

[2] I am aware, that so great an authority as Professor *Delitzsch* calls this in
question (Zeitschr. für Luther. Theol. for
1855, p. 653).   But the testimony of the

Midrash is against him.   *Delitzsch* regards it as the shout of the Feast of
Tabernacles.   But how should that have
been raised before the Feast of Passover?   Again, it does not seem reasonable
to suppose, that the multitude had with
full consciousness proclaimed Jesus as
the Messiah, and intended to celebrate
there and then the fulfilment of the typical meaning of the Feast of Tabernacles.

answered—not, this is Israel's Messiah-King, but: 'This is Jesus the Prophet of Nazareth of Galilee.' And so up into the Temple!

He alone was silent and sad among this excited multitude, the marks of the tears He had wept over Jerusalem still on His cheek. It is not so, that an earthly King enters His City in triumph; not so, that the Messiah of Israel's expectation would have gone into His Temple. He spake not, but only looked round about upon all things, as if to view the field on which He was to suffer and die. And now the shadows of evening were creeping up; and, weary and sad, He once more returned with the twelve disciples to the shelter and rest of Bethany.

CHAPTER II.

THE SECOND DAY IN PASSION-WEEK—THE BARREN FIG-TREE—THE CLEANSING OF THE TEMPLE—THE HOSANNA OF THE CHILDREN.

(St. Matt. xxi. 12–22; St. Mark xi. 15–26; St. Luke xix. 45–48.)

BOOK
V

a St. Mark i. 35; St. Luke v. 16; St. Matt. xiv. 23; St. Luke vi. 12; ix. 28

b St. Mark

How the King of Israel spent the night after the triumphal Entry into His City and Temple, we may venture reverently to infer. His royal banquet would be fellowship with the disciples. We know how often His nights had been spent in lonely prayer,[a] and surely it is not too bold to associate such thoughts with the first night in Passion week. Thus, also, we can most readily account for that exhaustion and faintness of hunger, which next morning made Him seek fruit on the fig-tree on His way to the City.

It was very early[1] on the morning of the second day in Passion-week (Monday), when Jesus, with his disciples, left Bethany. In the fresh, crisp, spring air, after the exhaustion of that night, 'He hungered.' By the roadside, as so often in the East, a solitary tree[2] grew in the rocky soil. It must have stood on an eminence, where it caught the sunshine and warmth, for He saw it 'afar off,'[b] and though spring had but lately wooed nature into life, it stood out, with its wide-spreading mantle of green, against the sky. 'It was not the season of figs,' but the tree, covered with leaves, attracted His attention. It might have been, that they hid some of the fruit which hung through the winter, or else the springing fruits of the new crop. For it is a well-known fact, that in Palestine 'the fruit appears before the leaves,'[3] and that this fig-tree, whether from its exposure or soil, was precocious, is evident from the fact that it was in leaf, which is quite unusual at that season on the Mount of Olives,[4] The old fruit would, of course, have been edible, and in regard to the unripe fruit we have the distinct evidence of the

---

[1] πρωΐ, used of the last night-watch in St. Mark i. 35.

[2] ἰδὼν συκῆν μίαν, a *single* tree.

[3] *Tristram*, Nat. Hist. of the Bible, p. 352.

[4] On the fig-tree generally, see the remarks on the Parable of the Barren Fig-tree, Book IV. ch. xvi.

Mishnah,[a] confirmed by the Talmud,[b] that the unripe fruit was eaten, so soon as it began to assume a red colour—as it is expressed, 'in the field, with bread,' or, as we understand it, by those whom hunger overtook in the fields, whether working or travelling. But in the present case there was neither old nor new fruit, 'but leaves only.' It was evidently a barren fig-tree, cumbering the ground, and to be hewn down. Our mind almost instinctively reverts to the Parable of the Barren Fig-tree, which He had so lately spoken.[c] To Him, Who but yesterday had wept over the Jerusalem that knew not the day of its visitation, and over which the sharp axe of judgment was already lifted, this fig-tree, with its luxuriant mantle of leaves, must have recalled, with pictorial vividness, the scene of the previous day. Israel was that barren fig-tree; and the leaves only covered their nakedness, as erst they had that of our first parents after their Fall. And the judgment, symbolically spoken in the Parable, must be symbolically executed in this leafy fig-tree, barren when searched for fruit by the Master. It seems almost an inward necessity, not only symbolically but really also, that Christ's Word should have laid it low. We cannot conceive that any other should have eaten of it after the hungering Christ had in vain sought fruit thereon. We cannot conceive that anything should resist Christ, and not be swept away. We cannot conceive, that the reality of what He had taught should not, when occasion came, be visibly placed before the eyes of the disciples. Lastly, we seem to feel (with *Bengel*) that, as always, the manifestation of His true Humanity, in hunger, should be accompanied by that of His Divinity, in the power of His Word of judgment.[d]

With St. Matthew, who, for the sake of continuity, relates this incident after the events of that day (the Monday) and immediately before those of the next,[e] we anticipate what was only witnessed on the morrow.[f] As St. Matthew has it: on Christ's Word the fig-tree immediately withered away. But according to the more detailed account of St. Mark, it was only next morning, when they again passed by, that they noticed the fig-tree had withered from its very roots. The spectacle attracted their attention, and vividly recalled the Words of Christ, to which, on the previous day, they had, perhaps, scarcely attached sufficient importance. And it was the suddenness and completeness of the judgment that had been denounced, which now struck Peter, rather than its symbolic meaning. It was rather the Miracle than its moral and spiritual import—the storm and earthquake rather than the still small Voice—which impressed the disciples. Besides, the words of Peter are at least capable of this

CHAP.
II

[a] Shebh. iv. 7
[b] Jer. Shebh. 35 *b*, last lines

[c] St. Luke xiii. 6-9

[d] Comp. St John xi. 35-44

[e] St. Matt. xxi. 18. 22
[f] St. Mark xi. 20

BOOK
V

• *Bengel*

interpretation, that the fig-tree had withered in consequence of, rather than by the Word of Christ. But He ever leads His own from mere wonderment at the Miraculous up to that which is higher.ᵃ His answer now combined all that they needed to learn. It pointed to the typical lesson of what had taken place: the need of realising, simple faith, the absence of which was the cause of Israel's leafy barrenness, and which, if present and active, could accomplish all, however impossible it might seem by outward means.¹ And yet it was only to 'have faith in God; ' such faith as becomes those who know God; a faith in God, which seeks not and has not its foundation in anything outward, but rests on Him alone. To one who ' shall not doubt in his heart, but shall believe that what he saith cometh to pass, it shall be to him.' ² And this general principle of the Kingdom, which to the devout and reverent believer needs neither explanation nor limitation, received its further application, specially to the Apostles in their coming need: ' Therefore I say unto you, whatsoever things, praying, ye ask for, believe that ye have received them [not, in the counsel of God,³ but actually, in answer to the prayer of faith], and it shall be to you.'

These two things follow: faith gives absolute power in prayer, but it is also its moral condition. None other than this is faith; and none other than faith—absolute, simple, trustful—gives glory to God, or has the promise. This is, so to speak, the New Testament application of the first Table of the Law, summed up in the ' Thou shalt love the Lord thy God.' But there is yet another moral condition of prayer closely connected with the first—a New Testament application of the second Table of the Law, summed up in the ' Thou shalt love thy neighbour as thyself.' If the first moral condition was God-ward, the second is man-ward; if the first bound us to faith, the second binds us to charity, while hope, the expectancy of answered prayer, is the link connecting the two. Prayer, unlimited in its possibilities, stands midway between heaven and earth; with one hand it reaches up to heaven, with the other down to earth; in it, faith prepares to receive, what charity is ready to dispense. He who so prays believes in God and loves man; such prayer is not selfish, self-seeking, self-conscious; least of all, is it compatible with mindfulness of wrongs, or an unforgiving spirit. This, 'then, is the second condition of

---

¹ We remind the reader, that the expression ' rooting up mountains ' is in common Rabbinic use as a hyperbole for doing the impossible or the incredible. For the former, see Babha B. 3 *b* (טורי

עקר); for the latter (עוקר הרים) Ber. 64 *a*; Sanh. 24 *a*; Horay. 14 *a*.
² The other words are spurious.
³ So *Meyer*.

prayer, and not only of such all-prevailing prayer, but even of
personal acceptance in prayer. We can, therefore, have no doubt
that St. Mark correctly reports in this connection this as the condition which the Lord attaches to acceptance, that we previously put
away all uncharitableness.[a] We remember, that the promise had
a special application to the *Apostles* and *early disciples*; we also
remember, how difficult to them was the thought of full forgiveness
of offenders and persecutors;[b] and again, how great the temptation to
avenge wrongs and to wield miraculous power in the vindication of
their authority.[c] In these circumstances Peter and his fellow-disciples,
when assured of the unlimited power of the prayer of faith, required
all the more to be both reminded and warned of this as its second
moral condition: the need of hearty forgiveness, if they had aught
against any.

From this digression we return to the events of that second day
in Passion-week (the Monday), which began with the symbolic
judgment on the leafy, barren fig-tree. The same symbolism of
judgment was to be immediately set forth still more clearly, and that
in the Temple itself. On the previous afternoon, when Christ had
come to it, the services were probably over, and the Sanctuary comparatively empty of worshippers and of those who there carried on
their traffic. When treating of the first cleansing of the Temple, at
the beginning of Christ's Ministry, sufficient has been said to explain
the character and mode of that nefarious traffic, the profits of which
went to the leaders of the priesthood, as also how popular indignation
was roused alike against this trade and the traders. We need not
here recall the words of Christ; Jewish authorities sufficiently describe,
in even stronger terms, this transformation of ' the House of Prayer '
into ' a den of robbers.' [2] If, when beginning to do the ' business ' of
His Father, and for the first time publicly presenting Himself with
Messianic claim, it was fitting He should take such authority, and
first ' cleanse the Temple ' of the nefarious intruders who, under the
guise of being God's chief priests, made His House one of traffic,
much more was this appropriate now, at the close of His Work, when,
as King, He had entered His City, and publicly claimed authority.
At the first it had been for teaching and warning, now it was in
symbolic judgment; what and as He then began, that and so He
now finished. Accordingly, as we compare the words, and even
some of the acts, of the first ' cleansing ' with those accompanying

[a] St. Mark
xi. 25 [1]

[b] St. Matt.
xviii. 21, 22

[c] St. Luke
ix. 52–56

----

[1] Ver. 26 is in all probability a spurious
addition.

[2] See the full account in Book III.
ch. v.

BOOK
V

and explaining the second, we find the latter, we shall not'say, much more severe, but bearing a different character—that of final judicial sentence.[1]

Nor did the Temple-authorities now, as on the former occasion, seek to raise the populace against Him, or challenge His authority by demanding the warrant of 'a sign.' The contest had reached quite another stage. They heard what He said in their condemnation, and with bitter hatred in their hearts sought for some means to destroy Him. But fear of the people restrained their violence. For, marvellous indeed was the power which He wielded. With rapt

• St. Luke

attention the people hung entranced on his lips,[a] 'astonished' at those new and blessed truths which dropped from them. All was so other than it had been! By His authority the Temple was cleansed of the unholy, thievish traffic which a corrupt priesthood carried on, and so, for the time, restored to the solemn Service of God; and that purified House now became the scene of Christ's teaching, when He spake those words of blessed truth and of comfort concerning the Father—thus truly realising the prophetic promise of 'a House of

• St. Mark

Prayer for all the nations.'[b] And as those traffickers were driven from the Temple, and He spake, there flocked in from porches and Temple-Mount the poor sufferers—the blind and the lame—to get healing to body and soul. It was truly spring-time in that Temple, and the boys that gathered about their fathers and looked in turn from their faces of rapt wonderment and enthusiasm to the Godlike Face of the Christ, and then on those healed sufferers, took up the echoes of the welcome at His entrance into Jerusalem—in their simplicity understanding and applying them better—as they burst into 'Hosanna to the Son of David.'

It rang through the courts and porches of the Temple, this

[1] The grounds on which this second has to be distinguished from the first cleansing of the Temple, which is recorded only by St. John (ii. 13–23) have been explained on a previous occasion. They are stated in most commentaries, though perhaps not always satisfactorily. But intelligent readers can have no difficulty in gathering them for themselves. The difficulty lies not in the two purifications, nor yet in the silence of the Synoptists as to the first, since the early Jerusalem Ministry lay not within the scope of their narratives, but in the silence of the Fourth Gospel in regard to the *second* purification. But here we would remark that, less than any of the others, is the Fourth Gospel a *history* or successive narration; but, if we may so say, historical dogmatics—the *Logos* in the historical manifestation of His Person and Work. If so, the first included the second purification of the Temple. Again, to have introduced it, or the cursing of the fig-tree, would have been to break up the course, and mar the symmetry of the narrative (St. John xii.), which presents in successive and deepening shading the attestation of the Christ: at the Supper of Bethany, on His Entry into Jerusalem, before the Greeks in the Temple, by the Voice from Heaven before His gainsayers, and to His disciples.

Children's Hosanna.   They heard it, whom the wonders He had
spoken and done, so far from leading to repentance and faith, had
only filled with indignation.   Once more in their impotent anger
they sought, as the Pharisees had done on the day of His Entry, by
a hypocritical appeal to His reverence for God, not only to mislead,
and so to use His very love of the truth against the truth, but to
betray Him into silencing those Children's Voices.   But the un-
dimmed mirror of His soul only reflected the light.[1]   These Children's
Voices were Angels' Echoes, echoes of the far-off praises of heaven,
which children's souls had caught and children's lips welled forth.
Not from the great, the wise, nor the learned, but 'out of the mouth
of babes and sucklings' has He 'perfected praise.'[2]   And this, also,
is the Music of the Gospel.

[1] We may here note, once for all, that the manner of answering used by Christ, that of answering a question by putting another up which the answer appeared with irresistible force. was very common among the Jews (מֵשִׁיב דָּבָר מִתּוֹךְ דָּבָר).   Another mode was by an allegory—whether of word or action.

[2] So in the LXX., rightly giving the sense; in the original ' strength.'   It is perhaps one of the grandest of the grand contrasts in the Psalms: God opposing and appeasing His enemies, not by a dis-play of power, as they understand it, but by the mouth of young boys [such is the proper rendering] and sucklings.   The Eternal of Hosts has these for His armourbearers, and needs none other.   The ancient Synagogue, somewhat realis-tically, yet with a basis of higher truth, declared (in the Haggadah), that at the Red Sea little children, even the babes in the womb, had joined in Israel's song of triumph, so fulfilling this saying of the Psalmist.

CHAPTER III.

THE THIRD DAY IN PASSION-WEEK—THE EVENTS OF THAT DAY—THE
QUESTION OF CHRIST'S AUTHORITY—THE QUESTION OF TRIBUTE TO
CÆSAR—THE WIDOW'S FARTHING—THE GREEKS WHO SOUGHT TO SEE
JESUS—SUMMARY AND RETROSPECT OF THE PUBLIC MINISTRY OF
CHRIST.

(St. Matthew xxi. 23–27; St. Mark xi. 27–33; St. Luke xx. 1–8; St. Matt. xxii. 15–
22; St. Mark xii. 13–17; St. Luke xx. 20–26; St. Matt. xxii. 41–46; St. Luke
xxi. 1–4; St. John xii. 20–50.)

BOOK
V

THE record of this third day is so crowded, the actors introduced on the scene are so many, the occurrences so varied, and the transitions so rapid, that it is even more than usually difficult to arrange all in chronological order. Nor need we wonder at this, when we remember that this was, so to speak, Christ's last working-day—the last, of His public Mission to Israel, so far as its active part was concerned; the last day in the Temple; the last, of teaching and warning to Pharisees and Sadducees; the last, of his call to national repentance.

That what follows must be included in one day, appears from the circumstance that its beginning is expressly mentioned by St. Mark[a] in connection with the notice of the withering of the fig-tree, while its close is not only indicated in the last words of Christ's Discourses, as reported by the Synoptists,[b] but the beginning of another day is afterwards equally clearly marked.[c]

Considering the multiplicity of occurrences, it will be better to group them together, rather than follow the exact order of their succession. Accordingly, this chapter will be devoted to the *events* of the third day in Passion Week.

1. As usually, the day commenced[d] with teaching in the Temple.[e] We gather this from the expression: ' as He was walking,'[f] viz., in one of the Porches, where, as we know, considerable freedom of meeting, conversing, or even teaching, was allowed. It will be remembered, that on the previous day the authorities had been afraid to interfere with Him. In silence they had witnessed, with im-

[a] St. Mark
xi. 20

[b] St. Matt.
xxv. 46;
St. Mark
xiii. 37; St.
Luke xxi.
36–38

[c] St. Matt.
xxvi. 1; St.
Mark xiv.
1; St. Luke
xxii. 1

[d] St. Matthew

[e] St. Luke

[f] St. Mark

potent rage, the expulsion of their traffic-mongers; in silence they had   CHAP.
listened to His teaching, and seen His miracles.   Not till the Hosanna   III
of the little boys—perhaps those children of the Levites who acted as
choristers in the Temple [1]—wakened them from the stupor of their
fears, had they ventured on a feeble remonstrance, in the forlorn
hope that He might be induced to conciliate them.   But with the
night and morning other counsels had come.   Besides, the circumstances were somewhat different.   It was early morning, the hearers
were new, and the wondrous influence of His Words had not yet
bent them to His Will.   From the formal manner in which 'the
chief priests, the scribes, and the elders are introduced,[a] and from   [a] St. Mark
the circumstance that they so met Christ immediately on His entry
into the Temple, we can scarcely doubt that a meeting, although informal,[2] of the authorities had been held to concert measures against
the growing danger.   Yet, even so, cowardice as well as cunning
marked their procedure.   They dared not directly oppose Him, but
endeavoured, by attacking Him on the one point where he seemed
to lay Himself open to it, to arrogate to themselves the appearance
of strict legality, and so to turn popular feeling against Him.

For, there was no principle more firmly established by universal
consent than that *authoritative* teaching[3] required previous authorisation.   Indeed, this logically followed from the principle of Rabbinism.   All teaching must be authoritative, since it was traditional—
approved by authority, and handed down from teacher to disciple.
The highest honour of a scholar was, that he was like a well-plastered
cistern, from which not a drop had leaked of what had been poured
into it.   The ultimate appeal in cases of discussion was always to
some great authority, whether an individual Teacher or a Decree by
the Sanhedrin.   In this manner had the great Hillel first vindicated
his claim to be the Teacher of his time and to decide the disputes
then pending.   And, to decide differently from authority, was
either the mark of ignorant assumption or the outcome of daring
rebellion, in either case to be visited with 'the ban.'   And this was
at least one aspect of the controversy as between the chief authorities and Jesus.   No one would have thought of interfering with a

[1] For these Levite chorister-boys, comp. 'The Temple and its Services,' p. 143.
[2] There is no evidence of a formal meeting of the Sanhedrin, nor, indeed, was there any case which, according to Jewish Law, could have been laid before them.   Still less can we admit (with Dean *Plumptre*), that the Chief Priests, Scribes, and Elders represented 'the then constituent elements of the San-hedrin.'
[3] Otherwise the greatest liberty of utterance was accorded to all who were qualified to teach.

BOOK
V

b Sanh. iv. 4

b Jer. Sanh.
19 a; lines
29 &c. from
bottom

c Sanh. i. 3

d Sanh. 7 *b*

mere Haggadist—a popular expositor, preacher, or teller of legends. But authoritatively to teach, required other warrant.. In fact there was regular ordination (*Semikhah*) to the office of Rabbi, Elder, and Judge, for the three functions were combined in one. According to the Mishnah, the 'disciples' sat before the Sanhedrin in three rows, the members of the Sanhedrin being recruited successively from the front-rank of the Scholars.[a] At first the practice is said to have been for every Rabbi to accredit his own disciples. But afterwards this right was transferred to the Sanhedrin, with the proviso that this body might not ordain without the consent of its Chief, though the latter might do so without consent of the Sanhedrin.[b] But this privilege was afterwards withdrawn on account of abuses. Although we have not any description of the earliest mode of ordination, the very name—*Semikhah*—implies the imposition of hands. Again, in the oldest record, reaching up, no doubt, to the time of Christ, the presence of at least three ordained persons was required for ordination.[c] At a later period, the presence of an ordained Rabbi, with the assessorship of two others, even if unordained, was deemed sufficient.[d] In the course of time certain formalities were added. The person to be ordained had to deliver a Discourse; hymns and poems were recited; the title 'Rabbi' was formally bestowed on the candidate, and authority given him to teach and to act as Judge [to bind and loose, to declare guilty or free]. Nay, there seem to have been even different orders, according to the authority bestowed on the person ordained. The formula in bestowing *full* orders was: 'Let him teach; let him teach; let him judge; let him decide on questions of first-born;[1] let him decide; let him judge!' At one time it was held that ordination could only take place in the Holy Land. Those who went abroad took with them their 'letters of orders.'[2]

At whatever periods some of these practices may have been introduced, it is at least certain that, at the time of our Lord, no one would have ventured authoritatively to teach without proper Rabbinic authorisation. The question, therefore, with which the Jewish authorities met Christ, while teaching, was one which had a very real meaning, and appealed to the habits and feelings of the people

[1] These involved points of special difficulty in canon-law.

[2] Comp. *Hamburger*, Real-Encycl. ii. pp. 883–886. But he adds little to the learned labours of *Selden*, De Synedriis, ed. Frcf. pp. 681–713. How the notion can have arisen that in early times a key was handed at ordination (Dean *Plumptre* and many others), it is difficult to say—unless it be from a misunderstanding of St. Luke xi. 52, or from a strange mistake of *Lightfoot's* meaning ad loc.

who listened to Jesus. Otherwise, also, it was cunningly framed.
For, it did not merely challenge Him for teaching, but also asked for
His authority in what He *did*; referring not only to His Work
generally, but, perhaps, especially to what had happened on the previous day. They were not there to oppose Him; but, when a man
did as He had done in the Temple, it was their duty to verify his
credentials. Finally, the alternative question reported by St. Mark:
' or '—if Thou hast not proper Rabbinic commission—' who gave
Thee this authority to do these things?' seems clearly to point to
their contention, that the power which Jesus wielded was delegated
to Him by none other than Beelzebul.

The point in our Lord's reply seems to have been strangely over-
looked by commentators.[a] As His words are generally understood, [a] St. Matt.
xxi. 23-27;
St. Mark
xi. 27-33;
St. Luke
xx. 1-8
they would have amounted only to silencing His questioners—and
that, in a manner which would, under ordinary circumstances, be
scarcely regarded as either fair or ingenuous. It would have been
simply to turn the question against themselves, and so in turn to raise
popular prejudice. But the Lord's words meant quite other. He *did*
answer their question, though He also exposed the cunning and
cowardice which prompted it. To the challenge for His authority,
and the dark hint about Satanic agency, He replied by an appeal to
the Baptist. He had borne full witness to the Mission of Christ from
the Father, and ' all men counted John, that he was a prophet indeed.'
Were they satisfied? What was their view of the Baptism in preparation for the Coming of Christ? No? They would not, or
could not, answer! If they said the Baptist was a prophet, this
implied not only the authorisation of the Mission of Jesus, but the
call to believe on Him. On the other hand, they were afraid publicly
to disown John! And so their cunning and cowardice stood out
self-condemned, when they pleaded ignorance—a plea so grossly and
manifestly dishonest, that Christ, having given what all must have
felt to be a complete answer, could refuse further discussion with
them on this point.

2. Foiled in their endeavour to involve Him with the ecclesiastical, they next attempted the much more dangerous device of bringing Him into collision with the civil authorities. Remembering
the ever watchful jealousy of Rome, the reckless tyranny of Pilate,
and the low artifices of Herod, who was at that time in Jerusalem,[b] [b] St. Luke
xxiii. 7
we instinctively feel, how even the slightest compromise on the part
of Jesus in regard to the authority of Cæsar would have been absolutely fatal. If it could have been proved, on undeniable testimony,

BOOK
V

ᵃ Acts v. 37;
Jos. Ant.
xviii. 1. 1;
xx. 5. 2

that Jesus had declared Himself on the side of, or even encouraged, the so-called 'Nationalist' party, He would have quickly perished, like Judas of Galilee.ᵃ The Jewish leaders would thus have readily accomplished their object, and its unpopularity have recoiled only on the hated Roman power. How great the danger was which threatened Jesus, may be gathered from this, that, despite His clear answer, the charge that He preverted the nation, forbidding to give tribute to Cæsar, was actually among those brought against Him before Pilate.ᵇ

ᵇ St. Luke
xxiii. 2
ᶜ St. Matt.
xxii. 15–22;
St. Mark
xⁱⁱ. 13–17;
St. Luke
xx. 19–26
ᵈ St. Luke
ᵉ St. Matthew

The plot, for such it was,ᶜ was most cunningly concocted. The object was to 'spy' out His inmost thoughts,ᵈ and, if possible, 'entangle' Him in His talk.ᵉ For this purpose it was not the old Pharisees, whom He knew and would have distrusted, who came, but some of their disciples—apparently fresh, earnest, zealous, conscientious men. With them had combined certain of 'the Herodians'—of course, not a sect nor religious school, but a political party at the time. We know comparatively little of the deeper political movements in Judæa, only so much as it has suited Josephus to record. But we cannot be greatly mistaken in regarding the Herodians as a party which honestly accepted the House of Herod as occupants of the Jewish throne. Differing from the extreme section of the Pharisees, who hated Herod, and from the 'Nationalists,' it might have been a middle or moderate Jewish party—semi-Roman and semi-Nationalist. We know that it was the ambition of Herod Antipas again to unite under his sway the whole of Palestine; but we know not what intrigues may have been carried on for that purpose, alike with the Pharisees and the Romans. Nor is it the first time in this history, that we find the Pharisees and the Herodians combined.[1] Herod may, indeed, have been unwilling to incur the unpopularity of personally proceeding against the Great Prophet of Nazareth, especially as he must have had so keen a remembrance of what the murder of John had cost him. Perhaps he would fain, if he could, have made use of Him, and played Him off as the popular Messiah against the popular leaders. But, as matters had gone, he must have been anxious to rid himself of what might be a formidable rival, while, at the same time, his party would be glad to join with the Pharisees in what would secure their gratitude and allegiance. Such, or similar, may have been the motives which brought about this strange alliance of Pharisees and Herodians.

Feigning themselves just men, they now came to Jesus with

[1] Comp., for example, St. Mark iii. 6.

honeyed words, intended not only to disarm His suspicions, but, by an appeal to His fearlessness and singleness of moral purpose, to induce Him to commit Himself without reserve. Was it lawful for them to give tribute unto Cæsar, or not? were they to pay the capitation-tax[a] of one drachm, or to refuse it? We know how later Judaism would have answered such a question. It lays down the principle, that the right of coinage implies the authority of levying taxes, and indeed constitutes such evidence of *de facto* government as to make it duty absolutely to submit to it.[b] So much was this felt, that the Maccabees, and, in the last Jewish war, Bar Kokhabh, the false Messiah, issued a coinage dating from the liberation of Jerusalem. We cannot therefore doubt, that this principle about coinage, taxation, and government was generally accepted in Judæa. On the other hand, there was a strong party in the land; with which, not only politically but religiously, many of the noblest spirits would sympathise, which maintained, that to pay the tribute-money to Cæsar was virtually to own his royal authority, and so to disown that of Jehovah, Who alone was Israel's King. They would argue, that all the miseries of the land and people were due to this national unfaithfulness. Indeed, this was the fundamental principle of the Nationalist movement. History has recorded many similar movements, in which strong political feelings have been strangely blended with religious fanaticism, and which have numbered in their ranks, together with unscrupulous partisans, not a few who were sincere patriots or earnest religionists. It has been suggested in a former part of this book, that the Nationalist movement may have had an important preparatory bearing on some of the earlier followers of Jesus, perhaps at the beginning of their inquiries, just as, in the West, Alexandrian philosophy proved to many a preparation for Christianity.[1] At any rate, the scruple expressed by these men would, if genuine, have called forth sympathy.[2] But what was the alternative here presented to Christ? To have said *No*, would have been to command rebellion; to have said simply *Yes*, would have been to give a painful shock to deep feeling, and, in a sense, in the eyes of the people, the lie to His own claim of being Israel's Messiah-King! But the Lord escaped from this 'temptation'—because, being

CHAP.
III

[a] *Jos. Jew. War* ii. 16. 4

[b] Babha K. 113 *a*, and the instance of Abigail pleading with David that Saul's coinage was still in circulation. Jer, Sanh. 20 *b*

---

[1] For fuller particulars on this point see Book II. ch. x.

[2] Some might have even religious scruples about handling a coin of Cæsar. Such an instance is mentioned in Ab. Zar. 6 *b*, where a Rabbi is advised to throw it into the water, and pretend it had accidentally dropped from his hand. But probably that instance refers to the avoidance of all possibility of being regarded as sharing in idol-festivities.

true, it was no real temptation to Him.[1] Their knavery and hypocrisy He immediately perceived and exposed, in this also responding to their appeal of being ' true.' Once more and emphatically
must we disclaim the idea that Christ's was rather an evasion of the
question than a reply. It was a very real answer, when, pointing to
the image and inscription on the coin,[2] for which He had called, He
said, ' What *is* Cæsar's render to Cæsar, and what is God's to God.' '
It did far more than rebuke their hypocrisy and presumption; it
answered not only that question of theirs to all earnest men of that
time, as it would present itself to their minds, but it settles to all
time and for all circumstances the principle underlying it. Christ's
Kingdom is not of this world; a true Theocracy is not inconsistent
with submission to the secular power in things that are really its
own; politics and religion neither include, nor yet exclude, each
other: they are, side by side, in different domains. The State is
Divinely sanctioned, and religion is Divinely sanctioned—and both
are equally the ordinance of God. On this principle did Apostolic
authority regulate the relations between Church and State, even
when the latter was heathen. The question about the limits of
either province has been hotly discussed by sectarians on either side,
who have claimed the saying of Christ in support of one or the
opposite extreme which they have advocated. And yet, to the simple
searcher after duty, it seems not so difficult to see the distinction, if
only we succeed in purging ourselves of logical refinements and
strained inferences.

It was an answer not only most truthful, but of marvellous beauty
and depth. It elevated the controversy into quite another sphere,
where there was no conflict between what was due to God and to
man—indeed, no conflict at all, but Divine harmony and peace.
Nor did it speak harshly of the Nationalist aspirations, nor yet plead
the cause of Rome. It said not whether the rule of Rome was right
or should be permanent—but only what all must have felt to be
Divine. And so they, who had come to ' entangle ' Him, ' went
away,' not convinced nor converted, but marvelling exceedingly.[3]

[1] However pictorial, the sketch of this given by *Keim* (' Jesu von Nazara.' iii. 1, pp. 131 &c.) is—as too often—somewhat exaggerated.
[2] By a strange concurrence the coin, which on Christ's demand was handed to Him, bore ' the image ' of the Emperor. It must, therefore, have been either a foreign one (Roman), or else one of the Tetrarch Philip, who exceptionally had the image of *Tiberius* on his coins

(comp. *Schürer*, N.T. Zeitgesch. p. 231). Neither Herod nor Herod Antipas had any ' image ' on their coins, but only the usual ' devices ' of the Maccabæan period. And the coins, which the Roman emperors had struck specially for Palestine, bore till the time of Vespasian, in accommodation to Jewish prejudices, no image of any kind.
[3] ἐξεθαύμαζον according to the better reading in St. Mark.

3. Passing for the present from the cavils of the Sadducees and the gainsaying of the Scribes, we come unexpectedly on one of those sweet pictures—a historical miniature, as it is presented to us— which affords real relief to the eye amidst the glare all around.[a] From the bitter malice of His enemies and the predicted judgment upon them, we turn to the silent worship of her who gave her all, and to the words with which Jesus owned it, all unknown to her. It comes to us the more welcome, that it exhibits in deed what Christ had said to those hypocrites who had discussed it, whether the tribute given to Cæsar was not robbing God of what was His. Truly here was one, who, in the simplicity of her humble worship, gave to the Lord what was His!

Weary with the contention, the Master had left those to whom He had spoken in the Porches, and, while the crowd wrangled about His Words or His Person, had ascended the flight of steps which led from 'the Terrace' into the Temple-building. From these steps— whether those leading up to the 'Beautiful Gate,' or one of the side gates—He could gain full view into 'The Court of the Women,' into which they opened. On these steps, or within the gate (for in no other place was it lawful), He sat Him down, watching the multitude. The time of Sacrifice was past, and those who still lingered had remained for private devotion, for private sacrifices, or to pay their vows and offerings. Although the topography of the Temple, especially of this part of it, is not without its difficulties, we know that under the colonnades, which surrounded 'the Court of the Women,' but still left in the middle room for more than 15,000 worshippers, provision was made for receiving religious and charitable contributions. All along these colonnades were the thirteen trumpet-shaped boxes (*Shopharoth*); somewhere here also we must locate two chambers:[b] that of 'the silent,' for gifts to be distributed in secret to the children of the pious poor, and that where votive vessels were deposited. Perhaps there was here also a special chamber for offerings.[c] These 'trumpets' bore each inscriptions, marking the objects of contribution—whether to make up for past neglect, to pay for certain sacrifices, to provide incense, wood, or for other gifts.

As they passed to this or that treasury-box, it must have been a study of deep interest, especially on that day, to watch the givers. Some might come with appearance of self-righteousness, some even with ostentation, some as cheerfully performing a happy duty. 'Many that were rich cast in much'—yes, very much, for such was the tendency that (as already stated) a law had to be enacted,

CHAP.
III

[a] St. Mark xii. 41-44; St. Luke xxi. 1-4

[b] Sheqal. vi. 5; v. 6

[c] Midd. i 1

forbidding the gift to the Temple of more than a certain proportion of one's possessions. And the amount of such contributions may be inferred by recalling the circumstance, that, at the time of Pompey and Crassus, the Temple-Treasury, after having lavishly defrayed every possible expenditure, contained in money nearly half a million, and precious vessels to the value of nearly two millions sterling.[a]

And as Jesus so sat on these steps, looking out on the ever-shifting panorama, His gaze was riveted by a solitary figure. The simple words of St. Mark sketch a story of singular pathos. ' It was one pauper widow.' We can see her coming alone, as if ashamed to mingle with the crowd of rich givers; ashamed to have her offering seen; ashamed, perhaps, to bring it; a ' widow,' in the garb of a desolate mourner; her condition, appearance, and bearing that of a ' pauper.' He observed her closely and read her truly. She held in her hand only the smallest coins, ' two Perutahs '—and it should be known that it was not lawful to contribute a less amount.[b] Together these two Perutahs made a *guadrans*, which was the ninety-sixth part of a *denar*, itself of the value of about sevenpence. But it was ' all her living ' ($\beta \iota o s$), perhaps all that she had been able to save out of her scanty housekeeping; more probably, all that she had to live upon for that day and till she wrought for more. And of this she now made humble offering unto God. He spake not to her words of encouragement, for she walked by faith; He offered not promise of return, for her reward was in heaven. She knew not that any had seen it—for the knowledge of eyes turned on her, even His, would have flushed with shame the pure cheek of her love; and any word, conscious notice, or promise would have marred and turned aside the rising incense of her sacrifice.[1] But to all time has it remained in the Church, like the perfume of Mary's alabaster that filled the house, this deed of self-denying sacrifice. More, far more, than the great gifts of their ' superfluity,' which the rich cast in, was, and is to all time, the gift of absolute self-surrender and sacrifice, tremblingly offered by

[1] Jewish tradition, though it ever and painfully thrusts forward the *reward*, has some beautiful legends, allegories, and sayings about the gifts of the poor. One quotation must here suffice (Bemidb. R. 14). It is to the effect, that, if one who is poor, doeth charity, God says of him: This one is preventing Me. He has kept My commandments before they have come to him. I must recompense him. In Vayyikra R. 3, we read of a woman, whose offering of a handful of flour the priest despised, when God admonished him in a dream to value the gift as highly as if she had offered herself. Yet another quotation from the Mishnah. The tractate Menachoth closes with these words: ' Alike as regards burnt-offerings of beasts and those of fowls [those of the poor] and the meat-offering, we find the expression " for a sweet savour," to teach us, that to offer much or to offer little is the same, provided only that a person direct mind and heart towards God.'

the solitary mourner. And though He spake not to her, yet the sunshine of His words must have fallen into the dark desolateness of her heart; and, though perhaps she knew not why, it must have been a happy day, a day of rich feast in the heart, that when she gave up 'her whole living' unto God. And so, perhaps, is every sacrifice for God all the more blessed, when we know not of its blessedness.

Would that to all time its lesson had been cherished, not theoretically, but practically, by the Church! How much richer would have been her 'treasury': twice blessed in gift and givers. But so is not legend written. If it had been a story invented for a purpose or adorned with the tinsel of embellishment, the Saviour and the widow would not have so parted—to meet and to speak not on earth, but in heaven. She would have worshipped, and He spoken or done some great thing. Their silence was a tryst for heaven.

4. One other event of solemn joyous import remains to be recorded on that day.[a] But so closely is it connected with what the Lord afterwards spoke, that the two cannot be separated. It is narrated only by St. John, who, as before explained,[1] tells it as one of a series of progressive manifestations of the Christ: first in His Entry into the City, and then in the Temple—successively, to the Greeks, by the Voice from Heaven, and before the people.

[a] St. John xii. 20-50

Precious as each part and verse here is, when taken by itself, there is some difficulty in combining them, and in showing their connection, and its meaning. But here we ought not to forget, that we have, in the Gospel-narrative, only the briefest account—as it were, headings, summaries, outlines, rather than a report. Nor do we know the surrounding circumstances. The words which Christ spoke after the request of the Greeks to be admitted to His Presence may bear some special reference also to the state of the disciples, and their unreadiness to enter into and share His predicted sufferings. And this may again be connected with Christ's prediction and Discourse about 'the last things.'[b] For the position of the narrative in St. John's Gospel seems to imply that it was the last event of that day— nay, the conclusion of Christ's public Ministry. If this be so, words and admonitions, otherwise somewhat mysterious in their connection, would acquire a new meaning.

[b] St. Matt xxiv.

It was then, as we suppose, the evening of a long and weary day of teaching. As the sun had been hastening towards its setting in

---

[1] See ch. vi.

red, He had spoken of that other sun-setting, with the sky all aglow in judgment, and of the darkness that was to follow—but also of the better Light that would rise in it. And in those Temple-porches they had been hearing Him—seeing Him in His wonder-working yesterday, hearing Him in His wonder-speaking that day—those 'men of other tongues.' They were ' Proselytes,' Greeks by birth, who had groped their way to the porch of Judaism, just as the first streaks of the light were falling within upon its altar. They must have been stirred in their inmost being; felt, that it was just for such as they, and to them that He spoke; that this was what in the Old Testament they had guessed, anticipated, dimly hoped for, if they had not seen it—its grand faith, its grander hope, its grandest reality. Not one by one, and almost by stealth, were they thenceforth to come to the gate; but the portals were to be flung wide open, and as the golden light streamed out upon the way, He stood there, that bright Divine Personality, Who was not only the Son of David, but the Son of Man, to bid them the Father's welcome of good pleasure to the Kingdom.

And so, as the lengthening shadows gathered around the Temple-court and porches, they would fain have 'seen' Him, not afar off, but near: spoken to Him. They had became ' Proselytes of Righteous-ness,' they would become disciples of ' the Lord our Righteousness; ' as Proselytes they had come to Jerusalem ' to worship,' and they would learn to praise. Yet, in the simple self-unconscious modesty of their religious childhood, they dared not go to Jesus directly, but came with their request to Philip of Bethsaida.[1] We know not why to *him*: whether from family connections, or that his education, or previous circumstances, connected Philip with these 'Greeks,' or whether anything in his position in the Apostolic circle, or something that had just occurred, influenced their choice. And he also—such was the ignorance of the Apostles of the inmost meaning of their Master—dared not go directly to Jesus, but went to his own towns-man, who had been his early friend and fellow-disciple, and now stood so close to the Person of the Master—Andrew, the brother of Simon Peter. Together the two came to Jesus, Andrew apparently foremost. The answer of Jesus implies what, at any rate, we would have expected, that the request of these Gentile converts was granted,

---

[1] We mark here also the utter absence of all legendary embellishments as evidence of truth. So far from yielding to what, even in a book like the present, is a temptation, the narrative of the Evangelist is peculiarly meagre and void of details. We may note that only ' proselytes of righteousness,' who had submitted to circumcision, would be al-lowed fellowship in the regular worship.

though this is not expressly stated, and it is extremely difficult to determine whether, and what portion of what He spake was addressed to the Greeks, and what to the disciples. Perhaps we should regard the opening words as bearing reference to the request of the Greeks, and hence as primarily addressed to the disciples,[a] but also as serving as introduction to the words that follow, which were spoken primarily to the Greeks,[b] but secondarily also to the disciples, and which bear on that terrible, ever near, mystery of His Death, and their Baptism into it.

[a] St. John xii. 23

[b] vv. 24-26

As we see these 'Greeks' approaching, the beginning of Christ's History seems re-enacted at its close. Not now in the stable of Bethlehem, but in the Temple, are 'the wise men,' the representatives of the Gentile world, offering their homage to the Messiah. But the life which had then begun was now all behind Him—and yet, in a sense, before Him. The hour of decision was about to strike. Not merely as the Messiah of Israel, but in His world-wide bearing as 'the Son of Man,' was He about to be glorified by receiving the homage of the Gentile world, of which the symbol and the firstfruits were now before Him. But only in one way could He thus be glorified: by dying for the salvation of the world, and so opening the Kingdom of Heaven to all believers. On a thousand hills was the glorious harvest to tremble in the golden sunlight; but the corn of wheat falling into the ground, must, as it falls, die, burst its envelope, and so spring into a very manifoldedness of life. Otherwise would it have remained alone. This is the great paradox of the Kingdom of God—a paradox which has its symbol and analogon in nature, and which has also almost become the law of progress in history: that life which has not sprung of death abideth alone, and is really death, and that death is life. A paradox this, which has its ultimate reason in this, that sin has entered into the world.

And as to the Master, the Prince of Life, so to the disciples, as bearing forth the life. If, in this world of sin, He must fall as the seed-corn into the ground and die, that many may spring of Him, so must they also hate their life, that they may keep it unto life eternal. Thus serving, they must follow Him, that where He is they may also be, for the Father will honour them that honour the Son.

It is now sufficiently clear to us, that our Lord spake primarily to these Greeks, and secondarily to His disciples, of the meaning of His impending Death, of the necessity of faithfulness to Him in it, and of the blessing attaching thereto. Yet He was not unconscious of the awful realities which this involved.[c] He was true Man, and

[c] vv. 27, 28 a

BOOK
V

His Human Soul was troubled in view of it:[1] True Man, therefore He felt it; True Man, therefore He spake it, and so also sympathised with them in their coming struggle.   Truly Man, but also truly more than Man—and hence both the expressed desire, and at the same time the victory over that desire: 'What shall I say?[2] " Father, save Me from this hour?[3] But for this cause came I unto this hour!"' And the seeming discord is resolved, as both the Human and the Divine in the Son—faith and sight—join in glorious accord: 'Father, glorify Thy Name!'

Such appeal and prayer, made in such circumstances, could not have remained unacknowledged, if He was the Messiah, Son of God. As at His Baptism, so at this Baptism of self-humiliation and absolute submission to suffering, came the Voice from Heaven, audible to all, but its words intelligible only to Him: 'I both glorified *it*, and will again glorify *it*!'[a] Words these, which carried the Divine seal of confirmation to all Christ's past work, and assured it for that which was to come.   The words of confirmation could only be for Himself; 'the Voice' was for all.   What mattered it, that some spoke of it as thunder on a spring-evening, while others, with more reason, thought of Angel-Voices? To him it bore the assurance, which had all along been the ground of His claims, as it was the comfort in His Sufferings, that, as God had in the past glorified Himself in the Son, so would it be in the future in the perfecting of the work given Him to do.   And this He now spake, as, looking on those Greeks as the emblem and firstfruits of the work finished in His Passion, He saw of the travail of His Soul, and was satisfied.   Of both He spake in the prophetic present.   To His view judgment had already come to this world, as it lay in the power of the Evil One, since the Prince of it was cast out from his present rule.   And, in place of it, the Crucified Christ, 'lifted up out of the earth'—in the twofold sense— was, as the result of His Work, drawing, with sovereign, conquering power, 'all' unto Him, and up with Him.

The Jews who heard it, so far understood Him, that His words referred to His removal from earth, or His Death, since this was a common Jewish mode of expression (סלק מן העולם).[b] [4] But they failed

[a] St. John
xii. 28 *b*–33

[b] vv. 34–36 *a*

---

[1] Concurrebat horror mortis et ardor obedientiæ.—*Bengel.*

[2] Quid dicam ? non, quid eligam ?— *Bengel.*

[3] Professor *Westcott* has declared himself in favour of regarding this clause, not as a question, but as a prayer. But this seems to me incompatible alike with the preceding and the succeeding clause.

[4] This is another evidence of the Aramaic education of the writer of the Fourth Gospel.   Yet another is the peculiar Judaic use of the word שעה, *hour*, in ver. 27.   But the idea of 'Prince of this world' has no analogon in the

to understand His special reference to the manner of it. And yet,
in view of the peculiarly shameful death of the Cross, it was most
important that He should ever point to it also. But, even in what
they understood, they had a difficulty. They understood Him to
imply that He would be taken from earth; and yet they had always
been taught from the Scriptures [1] that the Messiah was, when fully
manifested, to abide for ever, or, as the Rabbis put it, that His
Reign was to be followed by the Resurrection. Or did He refer to
any other One by the expression, Son of Man'? Into the controversial part of the question the Lord did not enter; nor would it
have been fitting to have done so in that 'hour.' But to their
inquiry He fully replied, and that with such earnest, loving admonition as became His last address in the Temple. Yes; it was so!
But a little while would the Light be among them. [2] Let them
hasten to avail themselves of it, [3] lest darkness overtake them—and
he that walked in darkness knew not whither he went. Oh, that
His love could have arrested them! While they still had 'the
Light,' would that they might learn to believe in the Light, that so
they might become the children of Light!

They were His last words of appeal to them, ere He withdrew to
spend His Sabbath of soul before the Great Contest.[a] And the writer   [a] St. John
of the Fourth Gospel gathers up, by way of epilogue, the great con-   xii. 36 b
trast between Israel and Christ.[b] Although He had shown so many   [b] St. John
miracles, they believe not on Him—and this their wilful unbelief   xii. 37-43
was the fulfilment of Esaias' prophecy of old concerning the Messiah.[c]   [c] Is. liii 1
On the other hand, their wilful unbelief was also the judgment of
God in accordance with prophecy.[d] Those who have followed the   [d] Is. vi.
course of this history must have learned this above all, that the
rejection of Christ by the Jews was not an isolated act, but 'the outcome and direct result of their whole previous religious development.
In face of the clearest evidence, they did not believe, because they
could not believe. The long course of their resistance to the prophetic message, and their perversion of it, was itself a hardening of
their hearts, although at the same time a God-decreed sentence on
their resistance.[4] Because they would not believe—through this

שר העולם (or Metatron) of Rabbinism,
to whom, strangely, the designation נער
(in Zech. ii. 4 [A.V.], Babha B. 75 b, and
in Ps. xxxvii. 25, Yebam. 16 b, about
middle) is applied. And this is, on the
other hand, quite as characteristic of the
Gospel which, under Jewish forms, bears
a totally contrary spirit.

[1] It is another mark of Jewish authorship, this use of the word 'Law,' to denote the whole Scriptures.
[2] Lux ipsa manet; sed non semper in
vobis.
[3] Ambulandum, non disceptandum.
Fides non est deses, sed agilis in luce.
[4] Hence the effect which in Isa. vi. is

their mental obscuration, which came upon them in Divine judgment, although in the natural course of their self-chosen religious development—therefore, despite all evidence, they did not believe, when He came and did such miracles before them. And all this in accordance with prophecy, when Isaiah saw in far-off vision the bright glory [1] of Messiah, and spoke of Him. Thus far Israel as a nation. And though, even among their ' chief rulers,' there were many who believed on Him, yet dared they not 'make confession,' from fear that the Pharisees would put them out of the Synagogues, with all the terrible consequences which this implied. For such surrender of all were they not prepared, whose intellect might be convinced, but whose heart was not converted—who ' loved the glory of men more than the glory of God.'

Such was Israel. On the other hand, what was the summary of the Christ's activity? His testimony now rose so loud, as to be

[a] St. John xii. 44
within hearing of all ('Jesus cried').[a]   From first to last that testimony had pointed from Himself up to the Father. Its substance was the reality and the realisation of that which the Old Testament had infolded and gradually unfolded to Israel, and through Israel to the world: the Fatherhood of God. To believe on Him was really not faith in Him, but faith in Him that sent Him. A step higher: To behold Christ was to behold Him that had

[b] vv. 45-48
sent Him.[b]   To combine these two: Christ had come a light into the world, God had sent Him as the Sun of Righteousness, that by believing on Him as the God-sent, men might attain moral vision— no longer ' abide in darkness,' but in the bright spiritual Light that had risen. But as for the others, there were those who heard and did not keep [2] His words; and, again, those who rejected Him, and did not receive His words. Neither in one nor the other case was the controversy as between His sayings and men. As regarded the one class, He had come into the world with the Word of salvation, not with the sword of judgment. As regarded His open enemies, He left the issue till the evidence of His word should appear in the terrible judgment of the Last Day.

Once more, and more emphatic than ever, was the final appeal to

[c] vv. 49, 50
His Mission by the Father.[c]   From first to last it had not been His

ascribed to the prophet, is here assigned to God. We say ' decreed '—but not decreed beforehand, and irrespective of their conduct. The passage is neither quoted from the Hebrew nor from the LXX., but Targumed.

[1] The paraphrase of this passage in the

Targum Jonathan (for which see Appendix II.) is, indeed, most interesting; but the *Yeqara* or outshining splendour of Jehovah, is not that to which the Evangelist here refers.

[2] So according to the better reading

own work: what He should say, and what He should speak, the
Father 'Himself' had given Him commandment.   Nay, this commandment, and what He spoke in it, was not mere teaching, nor
Law: it was Life everlasting.   And so it is, and ever shall be—
eternal thanks to the love of Him Who sent, and the grace of Him
Who came: that the things which He spake, He spake as the Father
said unto Him.

These two things, then, are the final summary by the Apostle of
the History of the Christ in His public activity.   On the one hand,
he shows us how Israel, hardened in the self-chosen course of its
religious development, could not, and, despite the clearest evidence,
did not, believe.   And, on the other hand, he sets before us the Christ
absolutely surrendering Himself to do the Will and Work of the
Father; witnessed by the Father; revealing the Father; coming as
the Light of the world to chase away its moral darkness; speaking
to all men, bringing to them salvation, not judgment, and leaving the
vindication of His Word to its manifestation in the Last Day; and
finally, as the Christ, Whose every message is commanded of God,
and Whose every commandment is life everlasting—and therefore and
so speaking it, as the Father said unto Him.

These two things: concerning the history of Israel and their necessary unbelief, and concerning the Christ as God-sent, God-witnessed,
God-revealing, bringing light and life as the Father's gift and command—the Christ as absolutely surrendering Himself to this Mission
and embodying it—are the sum of the Gospel-narratives.   They explain their meaning, and set forth their object and lessons.

CHAPTER IV.

THE THIRD DAY IN PASSION-WEEK—THE LAST CONTROVERSIES AND DIS-
COURSES—THE SADDUCEES AND THE RESURRECTION—THE SCRIBE AND
THE GREAT COMMANDMENT—QUESTION TO THE PHARISEES ABOUT
DAVID'S SON AND LORD—FINAL WARNING TO THE PEOPLE : THE
EIGHT ' WOES '—FAREWELL.

(St. Matt. xxii. 23–33; St. Mark xii. 18–27; St. Luke xx. 27–39; St. Matt. xxii. 34–
40; St. Mark xii. 28–34; St. Matt. xxii. 41–46; St. Mark xii. 35–40; St. Luke xx.
40–47; St. Matt. xxiii.)

BOOK
V

THE last day in the Temple was not to pass without other ' temptations ' than that of the Priests when they questioned His authority, or of the Pharisees when they cunningly sought to entangle Him in His speech. Indeed, Christ had on this occasion taken a different position; He had claimed supreme authority, and thus challenged the leaders of Israel. For this reason, and because at the last we expect assaults from all His enemies, we are prepared for the controversies of that day.

We remember that, during the whole previous history, Christ had only on one occasion come into public conflict with the Sadducees, when, characteristically, they had asked of Him ' a sign from heaven.' [a] Their Rationalism would lead them to treat the whole movement as beneath serious notice, the outcome of ignorant fanaticism. Nevertheless, when Jesus assumed such a position in the Temple, and was evidently to such extent swaying the people, it behoved them, if only to guard their position, no longer to stand by. Possibly, the discomfiture and powerlessness of the Pharisees may also have had their influence. At any rate, the impression left is, that those of them who now went to Christ were delegates, and that the question which they put had been well planned.[1]

Their object was certainly not serious argument, but to use the

[a] St. Matt.
xvi. 1

---

[1] There seems some reference to this question put to Christ in what we regard as covert references to Christianity in that mysterious passage in the Talmud (Yoma 66 b) previously referred to (see pp. 193, 194). Comp. the interesting dissertation of Töttermann on R. Eliezer ben Hyrcanos (pp. 16–18).

much more dangerous weapon of ridicule. Persecution the populace might have resented; for open opposition all would have been prepared; but to come with icy politeness and philosophic calm, and by
a well-turned question to reduce the renowned Galilean Teacher to
silence, and show the absurdity of His teaching, would have been to
inflict on His cause the most damaging blow. To this day such
appeals to rough and ready common-sense are the main stock-in-
trade of that coarse infidelity, which, ignoring alike the demands of
higher thinking and the facts of history, appeals—so often, alas!
effectually—to the untrained intellect of the multitude, and—shall we
not say it?—to the coarse and lower in us all. Besides, had the Sadducees succeeded, they would at the same time have gained a signal
triumph for their tenets, and defeated, together with the Galilean
Teacher, their own Pharisaic opponents. The subject of attack was
to be the Resurrection [1]—the same which is still the favourite topic
for the appeals of the coarser forms of infidelity to 'the common
sense' of the masses. Making allowance for difference of circumstances, we might almost imagine we were listening to one of our
modern orators of materialism. And in those days the defence of
belief in the Resurrection laboured under twofold difficulty. It was
as yet a matter of hope, not of faith: something to look forward to,
not to look back upon. The isolated events recorded in the Old
Testament, and the miracles of Christ—granting that they were
admitted—were rather instances of resuscitation than of Resurrection. The grand fact of history, than which none is better attested
—the Resurrection of Christ—had not yet taken place, and was not
even clearly in view of any one. Besides, the utterances of the Old
Testament on the subject of the 'hereafter' were, as became alike
that stage of revelation and the understanding of those to whom it
was addressed, far from clear. In the light of the New Testament
it stands out in the sharpest proportions, although as an Alpine
height afar off; but then that Light had not yet risen upon it.

Besides, the Sadducees would allow no appeal to the highly
poetic language of the Prophets, to whom, at any rate, they attached
less authority, but demanded proof from that clear and precise letter
of the Law, every tittle and iota of which the Pharisees exploited
for their doctrinal inferences, and from which alone they derived
them. Here, also, it was the Nemesis of Pharisaism, that the postulates of their system laid it open to attack. In vain would the Phari-

[1] In regard to the denial of the Re-   views generally, we refer to the sketch
surrection by the Sadducees, and to their   of the three sects in Book III. ch. ii.

BOOK
V

^a Deut.
xxxi. 16

^b Cant. vii.
9
^c See Sanh.
90 b, about
the middle
^d Ber. R. 20

^e Sanh. 90 b
lines 9 &c.
from
bottom
^f Sanh. 91 b

^g Sanh, 90 b
lines 10 and
9 from
bottom
^h Sanh. 92 a

ⁱ Sanh. 90 b

sees appeal to Isaiah, Ezekiel, Daniel, or the Psalms.[1] To such an argument as from the words, 'this people will rise up,'[a] the Sadducees would rightly reply, that the context forbade the application to the Resurrection; to the quotation of Isaiah xxvi. 19, they would answer that that promise must be understood spiritually, like the vision of the dry bones in Ezekiel; while such a reference as to this, 'causing the lips of those that are asleep to speak,'[b] would scarcely require serious refutation.[c] Of similar character would be the argument from the use of a special word, such as 'return' in Gen. iii. 19,[d] or that from the twofold mention of the word 'cut off' in the original of Num. xv. 31, as implying punishment in the present and in the future dispensation.[e] Scarcely more convincing would be the appeal to such passages as Deut. xxxii. 39: 'I kill and make alive,'[f] or the statement that, whenever a promise occurs in the form which in Hebrew represents the future tense,[2] it indicates a reference to the Resurrection. Perhaps more satisfactory, although not convincing to a Sadducee, whose special contention it was to insist on proof from the Law,[g] might be an appeal to such passages as Dan. xii. 2, 13,[h] or to the restoration to life by certain of the prophets, with the superadded canon, that God had in part prefiguratively wrought by His prophets whatever He would fully restore in the future.

If Pharisaic argumentation had failed to convince the Sadducees on Biblical grounds, it would be difficult to imagine that, even in the then state of scientific knowledge, any enquiring person could have really believed that there was a small bone in the spine which was indestructible, and from which the new man would spring;[3] or that there existed even now a species of mice, or else of snails, which gradually and visibly developed out of the earth.[i] Many clever sayings of the Pharisees are, indeed, here recorded in their controversies, as on most subjects, and by which a Jewish opponent might have been silenced. But here, especially, must it have been felt that a reply was not 'always an answer, and that the silencing of an opponent was not identical with proof of one's own assertion. And the additions with which the Pharisees had encumbered the doctrine of the Resurrection would not only surround it with fresh difficulties, but deprive the simple fact of its grand majesty. Thus, it was a point in discussion, whether a person would rise in his

---

[1] *Hamburger* (Real Encykl. vol. i. p. 125) has given the Rabbinic argumentation, and *Wünsche* (ad St. Matt. xxii. 23) has reproduced it—unfortunately, with the not unnatural exaggerations of *Hamburger*.

[2] It is well known that the Hebrew has no *future* tense in the strict sense.

[3] Hence called the *os sacrum* (see again in the sequel)

clothes, which one Rabbi tried to establish by a reference to the grain of wheat, which was buried 'naked,' but rose clothed.[a] Indeed, some Rabbis held, that a man would rise in exactly the same clothes in which he had been buried, while others denied this.[b] On the other hand, it was beautifully argued that body and soul must be finally judged together, so that, in their contention to which of them the sins of man had been due, justice might be meted out to each—or rather to the two in their combination, as in their combination they had sinned.[1] Again, it was inferred from the apparition of Samuel[c] that the risen would look exactly as in life—have even the same bodily defects, such as lameness, blindness, or deafness. It is argued, that they were only afterwards to be healed, lest enemies might say that God had not healed them when they were alive, but that He did so when they were dead, and that they were perhaps not the same persons.[d] In some respects even more strange was the contention that, in order to secure that all the pious of Israel should rise on the sacred soil of Palestine,[e] there were cavities underground in which the body would roll till it reached the Holy Land, there to rise to newness of life.[f]

But all the more, that it was so keenly controverted by heathens, Sadducees, and heretics, as appears from many reports in the Talmud, and that it was so encumbered with realistic legends, should we admire the tenacity with which the Pharisees clung to this doctrine. The hope of the Resurrection-world appears in almost every religious utterance of Israel. It is the spring-bud on the tree, stript by the long winter of disappointment and persecution. This hope pours its morning carol into the prayer which every Jew is bound to say on awakening;[g] it sheds its warm breath over the oldest of the daily prayers which date from before the time of our Lord;[2] in the formula 'from age to age,' 'world without end,' it forms, so to speak, the rearguard to every prayer, defending it from Sadducean assault;[3] it is one of the few dogmas denial of which involves, according to the Mishnah, the loss of eternal life, the Talmud explaining—almost in the words of Christ—that in the retribution of God this is only 'measure according to measure;'[h] nay, it is venerable even in its exaggeration, that only our ignorance fails to perceive it in every section of the Bible, and to hear it in every commandment of the Law.

But in the view of Christ the Resurrection would necessarily

CHAP.
IV

[a] Sanh. 90 b
[b] Jer. Keth. 35 a

[c] 1 Sam. xxviii. 14

[d] Ber. R. 95, beginning

[e] Is. xlii. 5

[f] Ber. R. 96, towards the close

[g] Ber. 60 b

[h] Sanh. 90 a line 4 from bottom

---

[1] This was illustrated by a very apt Parable, see Sanh. 91 a and b.

[2] It forms the second of the eighteen Eulogies.

[3] It is expressly stated in Ber. ix. 5, that the formula was introduced for that purpose.

BOOK
V

occupy a place different from all this. It was the innermost shrine in the Sanctuary of His Mission, towards which He steadily tended; it was also, at the same time, the living corner-stone of that Church which he had builded, and its spire, which, as with uplifted finger, ever pointed all men heavenwards. But of such thoughts connected with His Resurrection Jesus could not have spoken to the Sadducees; they would have been unintelligible at that time even to His own disciples. He met the cavil of the Sadducees majestically, seriously, and solemnly, with words most lofty and spiritual, yet such as they could understand, and which, if they had received them, would have led them onwards and upwards far beyond the standpoint of the Pharisees. A lesson this to us in our controversies.

The story under which the Sadducees conveyed their sneer was also intended covertly to strike at their Pharisaic opponents. The ancient ordinance of marrying a brother's childless widow [a][1] had more and more fallen into discredit, as its original motive ceased to have influence. A large array of limitations narrowed the number of those on whom this obligation now devolved. Then the Mishnah laid it down that, in ancient times, when the ordinance of such marriage was obeyed in the spirit of the Law, its obligation took precedence of the permission of dispensation, but that afterwards this relationship became reversed.[b] Later authorities went further. Some declared every such union, if for beauty, wealth, or any other than religious motives, as incestuous,[c] while one Rabbi absolutely prohibited it, although opinions continued divided on the subject. But what here most interests us is, that what are called in the Talmud the ' Samaritans,' but, as we judge, the Sadducees, held the opinion that the command to marry a brother's widow only applied to a betrothed wife, not to one that had actually been wedded.[d] This gives point to the controversial question, as addressed to Jesus.

A case such as they told, of a woman who had successively been married to seven brothers, might, according to Jewish Law, have really happened.[2] Their sneering question now was, whose wife she

[a] Deut. xxv. 5 &c.

[b] Bekhor. 1. 7

[c] Yebam. 39 b

[d] Jer. Yebam. 1. 6. This seems also to have been the view of the School of Shammai

---

[1] The Talmud has it that the woman must have no child at all—not merely no son.

[2] Jer. Yebam. 6 b, relates what I regard as a legendary story of a man who was thus induced to wed the twelve widows of his twelve brothers, each widow promising to pay for the expenses of one month, and the directing Rabbi for those of the 13th (intercalatory) month. But to his horror, after three years the women returned, laden with thirty-six children, to claim the fulfilment of the Rabbi's promise!

On the other hand it was, however, also laid down that, if a woman had lost two husbands, she should not marry a third— according to others, if she had married three, not a fourth, as there might be some fate (מִזַל) connected with her (Yeb. 64 b). On the question of the Levirate, from the modern Jewish standpoint, see

was to be in the Resurrection. This, of course, on the assumption of the grossly materialistic views of the Pharisees. In this the Saddu- cean cavil was, in a sense, anticipating certain objections of modern materialism. It proceeded on the assumption that the relations of time would apply to eternity, and the conditions of the things seen hold true in regard to those that are unseen. But perchance it is otherwise; and the future may reveal what in the present we do not see. The reasoning as such may be faultless; but, perchance, some- thing in the future may have to be inserted in the *major* or the *minor*, which will make the conclusion quite other! All such cavils we would meet with the twofold appeal of Christ to the Word[1] and to the Power of God—how God has manifested, and how He will manifest Himself—the one flowing from the other.

In His argument against the Sadducees Christ first appealed to the *power* of God.[a] What God would work was quite other than they imagined: not a mere re-awakening, but a transformation. The world to come was not to be a reproduction of that which had passed away—else why should it have passed away—but a regenera- tion and renovation; and the body with which we were to be clothed would be like that which Angels bear. What, therefore, in our present relations is of the earth, and of our present body of sin and corruption, will cease; what is eternal in them will continue. But the power of God will transform all—the present terrestrial into the future heavenly, the body of humiliation into one of exaltation. This will be the perfecting of all things by that Almighty Power by which He shall subdue all things to Himself in the Day of His Power, when death shall be swallowed up in victory. And herein also con- sists the dignity of man, in virtue of the Redemption introduced, and, so to speak, begun at his Fall, that man is capable of such renovation and perfection—and herein, also, is 'the power of God,' that He hath quickened us together with Christ, so that here already the Church receives in Baptism into Christ the germ of the Resurrection, which is afterwards to be nourished and fed by faith, through the believer's participation in the Sacrament of fellowship with His body and Blood.[2] Nor ought questions here to rise, like dark clouds, such

CHAP.
IV

[a] St. Matt. xxii. 29, 30, and paral lels.

an interesting article by *Gutmann* in *Geiger's* Wiss. Zeitschr. f. Jüd. Theol. vol. iv. (1839), pp. 61–87.

[1] The reproach 'Ye err, not knowing the Scriptures,' occurs in almost the same form in the discussions on the Resurrection between the Pharisees and the Sadducees which are recorded in the

Talmud.

[2] Through the Resurrection of Christ resurrection has become the gift of uni- versal humanity. But, beyond this general gift to humanity, we believe that we re- ceive in Baptism, as becoming connected with Christ, the inner germ of the glori- ous Resurrection-body. Its nourishment

BOOK
V
as of the perpetuity of those relations which on earth are not only so precious to us, but so holy.　Assuredly, they will endure, as all that is of God and good; only what in them is earthly will cease, or rather be transformed with the body.　Nay, and we shall also recognise each other, not only by the fellowship of the soul; but as, even now, the mind impresses its stamp on the features, so then, when all shall be quite true, shall the soul, so to speak, body itself forth, fully impress itself on the outward appearance, and for the first time shall we then fully recognise those whom we shall now fully know—with all of earth that was in them left behind, and all of God and good fully developed and ripened into perfectness of beauty.

But it was not enough to brush aside the flimsy cavil, which had only meaning on the supposition of grossly materialistic views of the Resurrection.　Our Lord would not merely reply, He would answer the Sadducees; and more grand or noble evidence of the Resurrection has never been offered than that which He gave.　Of course as speaking to the Sadducees, He remained on the ground of the Pentateuch; and yet it was not only to the Law but to the whole Bible that He appealed, nay, to that which underlay Revelation itself: the relation between God and man.　Not this nor that isolated passage only proved the Resurrection: He Who, not only historically but in the fullest sense, calls Himself the God of Abraham, of Isaac, and of Jacob, cannot leave them dead.　Revelation implies, not merely a fact of the past—as is the notion which traditionalism attaches to it—a dead letter; it means a living relationship.　'He is not the God of the dead, but of the living, for all live unto Him.'

The Sadducees were silenced, the multitude was astonished, and even from some of the Scribes the admission was involuntarily wrung: 'Teacher, Thou hast beautifully said.'　One point, however, still claims our attention.　It is curious that, as regards both these arguments of Christ, Rabbinism offers statements closely similar.　Thus, it is recorded as one of the frequent sayings of a later Rabbi, that in the world to come there would be neither eating nor drinking, fruitfulness nor increase, business nor envy, hatred nor strife, but that the just would sit with crowns on their heads, and feast on the splendor of the Shekhinah.[a]　This reads like a Rabbinic adaptation of the saying of Christ.　As regards the other point, the Talmud reports a discussion on the Resurrection between 'Sadducees,' or perhaps Jewish heretics (Jewish-Christian heretics), in which Rabbi Gamaliel II. at

[a] Ber. 17 a, towards the end

(or otherwise) depends on our personal relationship to Christ by faith, and is carried on through the Sacrament of His Body and Blood.

last silences his opponents by an appeal to the promise [a] 'that ye CHAP. may prolong your days in the land which the Lord sware unto your IV father to give unto them '—'unto *them*,' emphasises the Rabbi, not 'unto you.'[1] Although this almost entirely misses the spiritual ª Deut. xi. 9 meaning conveyed in the reasoning of Christ, it is impossible to mistake its Christian origin. Gamaliel II. lived after Christ, but at a period when there was lively intercourse between Jews and Jewish Christians; while, lastly, we have abundant evidence that the Rabbi was acquainted with the sayings of Christ, and took part in the controversy with the Church.[2] On the other hand, Christians in his day—unless heretical sects—neither denied that Resurrection, nor would they have so argued with the Jewish Patriarch; while the Sadducees no longer existed as a party engaging in active controversy. But we can easily perceive, that intercourse would be more likely between Jews and such heretical Jewish Christians as might maintain that the Resurrection was past, and only spiritual. The point is deeply interesting. It opens such further questions as these: In the constant intercourse between Jewish Christians and Jews, what did the latter learn? and may there not be much in the Talmud which is only an appropriation and adaptation of what had been derived from the New Testament?

2. The answer of our Lord was not without its further results. As we conceive it, among those who listened to the brief but decisive passage between Jesus and the Sadducees were some 'Scribes'—*Sopherim*, or, as they are also designated, 'lawyers,' 'teachers of the Law,' experts, expounders, practitioners of the Jewish Law. One of them, perhaps he who exclaimed: Beautifully said, Teacher! hastened to the knot of Pharisees, whom it requires no stretch of the imagination to picture gathered in the Temple on that day, and watching, with restless, ever foiled malice, the Saviour's every movement. As 'the Scribe' came up to them, he would relate how Jesus had literally 'gagged' and 'muzzled'[3] the Sadducees—just as, according to the will of God, we are 'by well-doing to gag the want or knowledge of senseless men.' There can be little doubt that the report would give rise to mingled feelings, in which that prevailing would be, that, although Jesus might thus have discomfited the Sadducees, He would be unable to cope with other questions, if only

---

[1] The similar reference to Exod. vi. 4 by a later Rabbi seems but an adaptation of the argument of Gamaliel II. (See both in Sanh. 90 *b*.)

[2] We also recall that Gamaliel II. was the brother-in-law of that Eliezer b. Hyrcanos, who was rightly suspected of leanings towards Christianity (see pp. 193, 194). This might open up a most interesting field of inquiry.

[3] ἐφίμωσε (St. Matt. xxii. 34). The word occurs also in St. Matt. xxii. 12: St. Mark i. 25; iv. 39; St. Luke iv. 35; 1 Cor. ix. 9; 1 Tim. v. 18; 1 Pet. ii. 15.

ᵃ Comp. the
two ac-
counts in
St. Mat-
thew xxii.
34-40 and
in St. Mark
xii. 28-34
ᵇ Ab. ii. 1;
iv. 2
ᶜ Sanh. xi. 3
ᵈ Deb. R. 6

properly propounded by Pharisaic learning. And so we can understand how one of the number, perhaps the same Scribe, would volunteer to undertake the office;ᵃ and how his question was, as St. Matthew reports, in a sense really intended to 'tempt' Jesus.

We dismiss here the well-known Rabbinic distinctions of 'heavy'
and 'light' commandments, because Rabbinism declared the 'light'
to be as binding as 'the heavy,'ᵇ those of the Scribes more 'heavy'
(or binding) than those of Scripture,ᶜ and that one commandment
was not to be considered to carry greater reward, and to be therefore more carefully observed, than another.ᵈ That such thoughts
were not in the mind of the questioner, but rather the grand general
problem—however himself might have answered it—appears even
from the form of his inquiry: 'Which [*qualis*] is the great—'the

ᵉ St. Mark
xii. 28

first'ᵉ—commandment in the Law?' So challenged, the Lord
could have no hesitation in replying. Not to silence him, but
to speak the absolute truth, He quoted the well-remembered words
which every Jew was bound to repeat in his devotions, and which
were ever to be on his lips, living or dying, as the inmost expression
of his faith: 'Hear, O Israel, the Lord our God is one Lord.' And
then continuing, He repeated the command concerning love to God
which is the outcome of that profession. But to have stopped here
would have been to propound a theoretic abstraction without concrete reality, a mere Pharisaic worship of the letter. As God is love
—His Nature so manifesting itself—so is love to God also love[1] to
man. And so this second is 'like' 'the first and great commandment.' It was a full answer to the Scribe when He said: 'There is
none other commandment greater than these.'

But it was more than an answer, even deepest teaching, when, as
St. Matthew reports, He added: 'on these two commandments hang
all the Law and the Prophets.'ᶠ It little matters for our present

ᶠ St. Matt.
xxii. 4

purpose how the Jews at the time understood and interpreted these
two commandments.[2] They would know what it meant that
the Law and the Prophets 'hung' on them, for it was a Jewish
expression (תלוין). He taught them, not that any one commandment
was greater or smaller, heavier or lighter, than another—might be set
aside or neglected, but that all sprang from these two as their root
and principle, and stood in living connection with them. It was

---

[1] *Meyer* rightly remarks on the use of
ἀγαπήσεις here, implying moral high estimation and corresponding conduct, and
not φιλεῖν, which refers to love as an
affection. The latter could not have
been commanded, although such φιλία

of the world is forbidden (St. James iv. 4)
while the φιλεῖν of one's own ψυχή (St.
John xii. 25) and the μὴ φιλεῖν τὸν
κύριο (1 Cor. xvi. 22) are stigmatised.
[2] The Jewish view of these commands
has been previously explained.

teaching similar to that concerning the Resurrection; that, as concerning the promises, so concerning the commandments, all Revelation was one connected whole; not disjointed ordinances of which the letter was to be weighed, but a life springing from love to God and love to man. So noble was the answer, that for the moment the generous enthusiasm of the Scribe, who had previously been favourably impressed by Christ's answer to the Sadducees, was kindled. For the moment, at least, traditionalism lost its sway; and, as Christ pointed to it, he saw the exceeding moral beauty of the Law. He was not far from the Kingdom of God.[a] Whether or not he ever actually entered it, is written on the yet unread page of its history.

3. The Scribe had originally come to put his question with mixed motives, partially inclined towards Him from His answer to the Sadducees, and yet intending to subject Him to the Rabbinic test. The effect now wrought in him, and the silence which from that moment fell on all His would-be questioners, induced Christ to follow up the impression that had been made. Without addressing any one in particular, He set before them all, what perhaps was the most familiar subject in their theology, that of the descent of Messiah. Whose Son was He? And when they replied: 'The Son of David,'[1] He referred them to the opening words of Psalm cx., in which David called the Messiah 'Lord.' The argument proceeded, of course, on the twofold supposition that the Psalm was Davidic and that it was Messianic. Neither of these statements would have been questioned by the ancient Synagogue. But we could not rest satisfied with the explanation that this sufficed for the purpose of Christ's argument, if the foundation on which it rested could be seriously called in question. Such, however, is not the case. To apply Psalm cx., verse by verse and consistently, to any one of the Maccabees, were to undertake a critical task which only a series of unnatural explanations of the language could render possible. Strange, also, that such an interpretation of what at the time of Christ would have been a comparatively young composition, should have been wholly unknown alike to Sadducee and Pharisee. For our own part, we are content to rest the Messianic interpretation on the obvious and natural meaning of the words taken in connection with the general teaching of the Old Testament about the Messiah, on the undoubted interpretation of the ancient Jewish Synagogue,[2] on the authority of Christ, and on the testimony of History.

CHAP.
IV

[a] St. Mark xii. 33, 34

---

[1] This also shows that the later dogma of Messiah the Son of Joseph had not yet been invented.
[2] Comp. Appendix IX.

Compared with this, the other question as to the authorship of the
Psalm is of secondary importance.   The character of infinite, nay,
Divine, superiority to any earthly Ruler, and of course to David,
which the Psalm sets forth in regard to the Messiah, would sufficiently
support the argument of Christ.   But, besides, what does it matter,
whether the Psalm was composed by David, or only put into the
mouth of David (David's or Davidic), which, on the supposition of
Messianic application, is the only rational alternative?

But we should greatly err if we thought that, in calling the attention of His hearers to this apparent contradiction about the Christ,
the Lord only intended to show the utter incompetence of the Pharisees to teach the higher truths of the Old Testament.   Such, indeed,
was the case—and they felt it in His Presence.[a]   But far beyond
this, as in the proof which He gave for the Resurrection, and in the
view which He presented of the great commandment, the Lord would
point to the grand harmonious unity of Revelation.   Viewed separately, the two statements, that Messiah was David's Son, and that
David owned Him Lord, would seem incompatible.   But in their
combination in the Person of the Christ, how harmonious and how
full of teaching—to Israel of old, and to all men—concerning the
nature of Christ's Kingdom and of His Work!

It was but one step from this demonstration of the incompetence
of Israel's teachers for the position they claimed to a solemn warning
on this subject.   And this appropriately constitutes Christ's Farewell
to the Temple, to its authorities, and to Israel.   As might have been
expected, we have the report of it in St. Matthew's Gospel.[b]   Much
of this had been said before, but in quite other connection, and therefore with different application.   We notice this, when comparing this
Discourse with the Sermon on the Mount, and, still more, with what
Christ had said when at the meal in the house of the Pharisee in
Peræa.[c]   But here St. Matthew presents a regular series of charges
against the representatives of Judaism, formulated in logical manner,
taking up successively one point after the other, and closing with the
expression of deepest compassion and longing for that Jerusalem,
whose children He would fain have gathered under His sheltering
wings from the storm of Divine judgment.

To begin with—Christ would have them understand, that, in warning them of the incompetence of Israel's teachers for the position
which they occupied, He neither wished for Himself nor His disciples
the place of authority which they claimed, nor yet sought to incite
the people to resistance thereto.   On the contrary, so long as they
held the place of authority they were to be regarded—in the lan-

[a] St. Matt.
xxii. 46

[b] St. Matt.
xxiii.

[c] St. Luke
xi. 37–54

guage of the Mishnah [a]—as if instituted by Moses himself, as sitting in Moses' seat, and were to be obeyed, so far as merely outward observances were concerned. We regard this direction, not as of merely temporary application, but as involving an important principle. But we also recall that the ordinances to which Christ made reference were those of the Jewish canon-law, and did not involve anything which could really affect the conscience—except that of the ancient, or of our modern Pharisees. But while they thus obeyed their outward directions, they were equally to eschew the spirit which characterised their observances.[1] In this respect a twofold charge is laid against them: of want of spiritual earnestness and love,[b] and of mere externalism, vanity, and self-seeking.[c] And here Christ interrupted His Discourse to warn His disciples against the first beginnings of what had led to such fearful consequences, and to point them to the better way.[d]

This constitutes the first part of Christ's charge. Before proceeding to those which follow, we may give a few illustrative explanations. Of the opening accusation about the binding (truly in bondage: $\delta\varepsilon\sigma\mu\varepsilon\dot{\upsilon}\omega$) of heavy burdens and grievous to be borne, and laying them on men's shoulders, proof can scarcely be required. As frequently shown, Rabbinism placed the ordinances of tradition above those of the Law,[e] and this by a necessity of the system, since they were professedly the authoritative exposition and the supplement of the written Law.[f] And although it was a general rule, that no ordinance should be enjoined heavier than the congregation could bear,[g] yet (as previously stated) it was admitted, that, whereas the words of the Law contained what 'lightened' and what 'made heavy,' the words of the Scribes contained only what 'made heavy.'[h] Again, it was another principle, that, where an 'aggravation' or increase of the burden had once been introduced, it must continue to be observed.[i] Thus the burdens became intolerable. And the blame rested equally on both the great Rabbinic Schools. For, although the School of Hillel was supposed in general to make the yoke lighter, and that of Shammai heavier, yet not only did they agree on many points,[2] but the School of Hillel was not unfrequently even more strict than that of his rival.[3] In truth, their differences seem too often only prompted by a spirit of opposition, so that the serious business of religion became in their hands one of rival authority and mere wrangling.[4]

CHAP.
IV

[a] Rosh haSh. ii. 9

[b] St. Matt. xxiii. 3, 4
[c] vv. 5–7

[d] vv. 8–12

[e] See especially Jer. Ber. i. 7, p. 3 b
[f] Ab. iii. 11
[g] B. Kama 79 b

[h] Jer. Sanh. 30 a, at bottom
[i] Nidd. 66 a

---

[1] Even the literal charge of teaching and not doing is brought in Jewish writings (see, for example, Ber. R. 34).
[2] So notably on the well-known 'eight-

een points' רבר ח ה"יר Ab. Sar. 36 a.
[3] Twenty-four such are mentioned. Jer. Bets. 60 b.
[4] Many, very many of them are so

BOOK
V

ᵃ Sot. 21 b

ᵇ vol. 1. p.
101

ᵉ Jer. Ber.
4 c, lines 7
and 8 from
top
ᵈ Menach
37 b

It is not so easy to understand the second part of Christ's accusation. There were, indeed, many hypocrites among them, who might, in the language of the Talmud, alleviate for themselves and make heavy for others.[a] Yet the charge of not moving them with the finger could scarcely apply to the Pharisees as a party—not even in this sense, that Rabbinic ingenuity mostly found some means of evading what was unpleasant. But, as previously explained,[b] we would understand the word rendered ' move ' as meaning to ' set in motion,' or ' move away,' in the sense that they did not ' alleviate ' where they might have done so, or else with reference to their admitted principle, that their ordinances always made heavier, never lighter—always imposed grievous burdens, but never, not even with the finger, moved them away.

With this charge of unreality and want of love, those of externalism, vanity, and self-seeking are closely connected. Here we can only make selection from the abundant evidence in support of it. By a merely external interpretation of Exod. xiii. 9, 16, and Deut. vi. 8; xi. 18, practice of wearing Phylacteries, or, as they were called, *Tephillin*, ' prayer-fillets,' was introduced.[1] These, as will be remembered, were square capsules, covered with leather, containing on small scrolls of parchment, these four sections of the law: Exod. xiii. 1–10; 11–16: Deut. vi. 4–9; xi. 13–21. The Phylacteries were fastened by long leather straps to the forehead, and round the left arm, near the heart. Most superstitious reverence was attached to them, and in later times they were even used as amulets. Nevertheless, the Talmud itself gives confirmation that the practice of constantly wearing phylacteries—or, it might be, making them broad, and enlarging the borders of the garments, ·was intended '*for to be seen of men.*' Thus we are told of a certain man who had done so, in order to cover his dishonest practices in appropriating what had been entrusted to his keeping.[c] Nay, the Rabbis had in so many words to lay it down as a principle, that the Phylacteries were not to be worn for show.[d]

Detailed proof is scarcely required of the charge of vanity and self-seeking in claiming marked outward honours, such as the uppermost places at feasts and in the Synagogue, respectful salutations in

utterly trivial and absurd, that only the hairsplitting ingenuity of theologians can account for them: others so profane that it is difficult to understand how any religion could co-exist with them. Conceive, for example, two schools in controversy whether it was lawful to kill a louse on the Sabbath. (Schabb. 12 a; 107 b.)

[1] On the Tephillin. comp. 'Sketches of Jewish Social Life,' pp. 219–224.

the market, the ostentatious repetition of the title 'Rabbi,' or 'Abba,' 'Father,' or 'Master,'[a][1] or the distinction of being acknowledged as 'greatest.' The very earnestness with which the Talmud sometimes warns against such motives for study or for piety sufficiently establishes it. But, indeed, Rabbinic writings lay down elaborate directions, what place is to be assigned to the Rabbis, according to their rank, and to their disciples,[b] and how in the College the most learned, but at feasts the most aged, among the Rabbis, are to occupy the 'upper seats.'[c] So weighty was the duty of respectful salutation by the title Rabbi, that to neglect it would involve the heaviest punishment.[d] Two great Rabbis are described as literally complaining, that they must have lost the very appearance of learning, since in the market-place they had only been greeted with 'May your peace be great,' without the addition 'My masters.'[e]

A few further illustrations of the claims which Rabbinism preferred may throw light on the words of Christ. It reads like a wretched imitation from the New Testament, when the heathen Governor of Cæsarea is represented as rising up before Rabbis because he beheld 'the faces as it were of Angels;' or like an adaptation of the well-known story about Constantine the Great when the Governor of Antioch is described as vindicating a similar mark of respect to the Rabbis by this, that he had seen their faces and by them conquered in battle.[f] From another Rabbi rays of light are said to have visibly proceeded.[g] According to some, they were Epicuræans, who had no part in the world to come, who referred slightingly to 'these Rabbis.'[h] To supply a learned man with the means of gaining money in trade, would procure a high place in heaven.[i] It was said that, according to Prov. viii. 15, the sages were to be saluted as kings;[k] nay, in some respects, they were higher—for, as between a sage and a king, it would be duty to give the former priority in redemption from captivity, since every Israelite was fit to be a king, but the loss of a Rabbi could not easily be made up.[m] But even this is not all. The curse of a Rabbi, even if uncaused, would surely come to pass.[n] It would be too painful to repeat some of the miracles pretended to have been done by them or for them, occasionally in protection of a lie; or to record their disputes which among them was 'greatest,' or how they established their respective claims.[o] Nay, their self-assertion, extended beyond this life, and a Rabbi went so far as to order that he should be buried in white garments, to show that he was worthy of appearing before his Maker.[p] But

[1] These titles are put in the mouth of King Jehoshaphat when saluting the Rabbis.

CHAP.
IV

[a] Makk. 24a

[b] Horay. 13 b

[c] Babha B. 120 a

[d] Ber. 27 b

[e] Jer. Ber. 9 a, about the middle. Comp. Levy, Neuhebr. Wörterb. ii. 10 a

[f] Jer. Ber. 9 a, about the middle

[g] u. s.

[h] Jer. Sanh x. 1

[i] Pes. 53 b

[k] Gitt. 62 a

[m] Horay. 13 a

[n] Sanh. 90 b, line 3 from top

[o] See, for example Babha Mets. 85 b and 86 a

[p] Ber. R. 96, towards close

perhaps the climax of blasphemous self-assertion is reached in the story, that, in a discussion in heaven between God and the heavenly Academy on a Halakhic question about purity, a certain Rabbi—deemed the most learned on the subject—was summoned to decide the point! As his soul passed from the body he had exclaimed: ' Pure, pure,' which the Voice from Heaven applied to the state of the Rabbi's soul; and immediately afterwards a letter had fallen from heaven to inform the sages of the purpose for which the Rabbi had been summoned to the heavenly assembly, and afterwards another enjoining a week's universal mourning for him on pain of excommunication.[a]

ᵃ Babha
Mets. 86 a

Such daring profanities must have crushed out all spiritual religion, and reduced it to a mere intellectual display, in which the Rabbi was always chief—here and hereafter. Repulsive as such legends are, they will at least help us to understand what otherwise might seem harsh in our Lord's denunciations of Rabbinism. In view of all this, we need not discuss the Rabbinic warnings against pride and self-seeking when connected with study, nor their admonitions to humility.[1] For, the question here is, what Rabbinism regarded as pride, and what as humility, in its teachers? Nor is it maintained that all were equally guilty in this matter; and what passed around may well have led the more earnest to energetic admonitions to humility and unselfishness. But no ingenuity can explain away the facts as above stated, and, when such views prevailed, it would have been almost superhuman wholly to avoid what our Lord denounced as characteristic of Pharisaism. And in this sense, not with Pharisaic painful literalism, but as opposed to Rabbinic bearing, are we to understand the Lord's warning to His own not to claim among brethren to be ' Rabbi,' or ' Abba,' or ' guide.'[2]

ᵇ St. Mark
ix, 35; St.
Luke xiv.
11; xviii.
14

The Law of the Kingdom, as repeatedly taught,[b] was the opposite. As regarded aims, they were to seek the greatness of service; and as regarded that acknowledgment which would come from God, it would be the exaltation of humiliation.

It was not a break in the Discourse,[3] rather an intensification of it, when Christ now turned to make final denunciation of Pharisaism in its sin and hypocrisy.[c] Corresponding to the eight Beatitudes in the Sermon on the Mount with which His public Ministry began,

ᶜ St. Matt.
xxiii. 13–33

---

[1] See the quotations to that effect in *Schöttgen, Wetstein, and Wünsche* ad loc.
[2] Hac clausula (ver. 11) ostendit, se non sophistice litigasse de *vocibus*, sed *rem* potius spectasse (*Calvin*).

[3] *Keim* argues at length, but very inconclusively, that this is a different Discourse, addressed to a different audience and at a different time.

He now closed it with eight denunciations of woe.[1] These are the forthpouring of His holy wrath, the last and fullest testimony against those whose guilt would involve Jerusalem in common sin and common judgment. Step by step, with logical sequence and intensified pathos of energy, is each charge advanced, and with it the Woe of Divine wrath announced.

The first Woe against Pharisaism was on their shutting the Kingdom of God against men by their opposition to the Christ. All knew how exclusive were their pretensions in confining piety to the possession of knowledge, and that they declared it impossible for an ignorant person to be pious. Had they taught men the Scriptures, and shown them the right way, they would have been true to their office; but woe to them who, in their position as leaders, had themselves stood with their back to the door of the Kingdom, and prevented the entrance of others.

The second Woe was on their covetousness and hypocrisy. They made long prayers,[a] but how often did it only cover the vilest selfishness, even to the 'devouring' of widows' houses. We can scarcely expect the Talmud here to furnish us with illustrative instances, and yet at least one such is recorded;[b] and we recall how often broad phylacteries covered fraudulent minds.

The third Woe was on their proselytism, which issued only in making their converts twofold more the children of hell than themselves. Against this charge, rightly understood, Judaism has in vain sought to defend itself. It is, indeed, true that, in its pride and exclusiveness, Judaism seemed to denounce proselytism, laid down strict rules to test the sincerity of converts, and spoke of them in general contempt[c] as 'a plague of leprosy.'[d] Yet the bitter complaint of classical writers,[e] the statements of Josephus,[f] the frequent allusions in the New Testament and even the admissions of the Rabbis, prove their zeal for making proselytes—which, indeed, but for its moral sequences, would neither have deserved nor drawn down the denunciation of a 'woe.' Thus the Midrash, commenting on the words:[g] 'the souls that they had gotten in Haran,' refers it to the converts which Abraham had made, adding that every proselyte was to be regarded as if a soul had been created.[h][3] To this we may

a Ber. 32 b;
Yoma 29 a

b Sot. 21 b;
comp. Jer.
Sot. 19 a

c Horay,13 a
d Yeb. 47 a,
b; Nidd. 13
b
e Tacit.
Hist. v. 5;
Seneca in
August. De
Civit. Dei
vi. 11 2
f Ant. xviii.
3. 5; xx. 2,
4; Jewish
War ii. 17.
10 &c.; 20,
2; Life 23
g Gen. xii. 5
h Ber. R. 39,
ed. Warsh.
p. 72 a, and
Vayy. R. 1

---

[1] Although St. Matt. xxiii. 14 is in all probability spurious, this 'woe' occurs in St. Mark xii. 40, and in St. Luke xx. 47.

[2] For passages in proof see *Wetstein* ad loc.

[3] Anyone who would see how Jewish ingenuity can, for the purpose of misrepresenting the words of Christ, put a meaning even on Jewish documents which they can never bear, is advised to read the remarks of the learned *Jellinek* on St. Matt. xxiii. 15, in the Beth ha-Midr.

BOOK
V

[a] 2 Sam.
xxi. 1 &c.;
Yebam, 79 a
[b] Ab. Zar.
24 a

[c] Midr. on
Eccl. v. 11

[d] Shebh. iv.
13 and 35 b,
36 a

[e] Maaser, i.
1

[f] Maaser.
iv. 5

add the pride with which Judaism looked back upon the 150,000 Gibeonite converts said to have been made when David avenged the sin of Saul;[a] the satisfaction with which it looked forward to the times of Messiah as those of spontaneous conversion to the Synagogue;[b] and the not unfrequent instances in which a spirit favourable to proselytism is exhibited in Jewish writings,[1] as, also, such a saying as this, that when Israel is obedient to the will of God, He brings in as converts to Judaism all the just of the nations, such as Jethro, Rahab, Ruth, &c.[c] But after all, may the Lord not have referred, not to conversion to Judaism in general, but to proselytism to the sect of the Pharisees, which was undoubtedly sought to the compassing of sea and land?

The fourth Woe is denounced on the moral blindness of these guides rather than on their hypocrisy. From the nature of things it is not easy to understand the precise allusion of Christ. It is true that the Talmud makes the strangest distinction between an oath or adjuration, such as ' by heaven ' or ' by earth,' which is not supposed to be binding; and that by any of the letters of which the Divine Name was composed, or by any of the attributes of the Divine Being, when the oath is supposed to be binding.[d] But it seems more likely that our Lord refers to oaths or adjurations in connection with vows, where the casuistry was of the most complicated kind. In general, the Lord here condemns the arbitrariness of all such Jewish distinctions, which, by attaching excessive value to the letter of an oath or vow, really tended to diminish its sanctity. All such distinctions argued folly and moral blindness.

The fifth Woe referred to one of the best-known and strangest Jewish ordinances, which extended the Mosaic law of tithing, in most burdensome minuteness, even to the smallest products of the soil that were esculent and could be preserved,[e] such as anise. Of these, according to some, not only the seeds, but, in certain cases, even the leaves and stalks, had to be tithed.[f] And this, together with grievous omission of the weightier matters of the Law: judgment, mercy, and faith. Truly, this was ' to strain out the gnat, and swallow the camel! ' We remember that this conscientiousness in tithing constituted one of the characteristics of the Pharisees; but we could scarcely be prepared for such an instance of it, as when the Talmud gravely assures us that the ass of a certain Rabbi had been so well

vol. v. pp. xlvi. xlvii., and his rendering of the quotation from Ber. R. 28.

[1] The learned *Danzius* has collected all that can be said on that subject in *Meuschen*, Nov. Test. ex Talm. illustr., pp. 649–666. But in my opinion he exaggerates his case

trained as to refuse corn of which the tithes had not been taken![a] And experience, not only in the past but in the present, has only too plainly shown, that a religious zeal which expends itself on trifles has not room nor strength left for the weightier matters of the Law.

CHAP. IV

a Jer Dem. 21 d

From tithing to *purification* the transition was natural.[1] It constituted the second grand characteristic of Pharisaic piety. We have seen with what punctiliousness questions of outward purity of vessels were discussed. But woe to the hypocrisy which, caring for the outside, heeded not whether that which filled the cup and platter had been procured by extortion or was used for excess. And, alas for the blindness which perceived not, that internal purity was the real condition of that which was outward!

Woe similarly to another species of hypocrisy, of which, indeed, the preceding were but the outcome: that of outward appearance of righteousness, while heart and mind were full of iniquity—just as those annually-whited sepulchres of theirs seemed so fair outwardly, but within were full of dead men's bones and all uncleanness. Woe, lastly, to that hypocrisy which built and decorated sepulchres of prophets and righteous men, and by so doing sought to shelter itself from share in the guilt of those who had killed them. It was not spiritual repentance, but national pride, which actuated them in this, the same spirit of self-sufficiency, pride, and impenitence which had led their fathers to commit the murders. And were they not about to imbrue their hands in the blood of Him to Whom all the prophets had pointed? Fast were they in the Divine judgment filling up the measure of their fathers.

And thicker and heavier than ever before fell the hailstorm of His denunciations, as He foretold the certain doom which awaited their national impenitence.[b] Prophets, wise men, and scribes would be sent them of Him; and only murder, sufferings, and persecutions would await them—not reception of their message and warnings. And so would they become heirs of all the blood of martyred saints, from that of him whom Scripture records as the first one murdered, down to that last martyr of Jewish unbelief of whom tradition spoke in such terms—Zechariah,[2] stoned by the king's command in the

b vv. 34-36

---

[1] *Keim*, with keen insight, characterises the Woe which contrasts their proselytising zeal with their resistance to the progress of the Kingdom; then, the third and fourth which denounce their false teaching, the fifth and sixth their false attempts at purity, while the last sets forth their relations to those forerunners of Christ, whose graves they built.

[2] We need scarcely remind the reader that this Zechariah was the son of Jehoiada. The difference in the text of St. Matthew may either be due to family

a 2 Chron.
xxiv. 20-22
b Sanh. 96
b; Gitt, 57
b; also in
the Midr.
on Eccl. iii.
16 and x. 4.
and on
Lament. ii.
2, and iv. 14
c vv. 37-39
d Vayyik.
R. 25

Court of the Temple,[a] whose blood, as legend had it, did not dry up those two centuries and a half, but still bubbled on the pavement, when Nebuzar-adan entered the Temple, and at last avenged it.[b] And yet it would not have been Jesus, if, while denouncing certain judgment on them who, by continuance and completion of the crimes of their fathers, through the same unbelief, had served themselves heirs to all their guilt, He had not also added to it the passionate lament of a love which, even when spurned, lingered with regretful longing over the lost.[c] They all knew the common illustration of the hen gathering her young brood for shelter,[d] and they knew also what of Divine protection, blessing, and rest it implied, when they spoke of being gathered under the wings of the Shekhinah. Fain and often would Jesus have given to Israel, His people, that shelter, rest, protection. and blessing—but they would not. Looking around on those Temple-buildings—that House, it shall be left to them desolate! And He quitted its courts with these words, that they of Israel should not see Him again till, the night of their unbelief past, they would welcome His return with a better Hosanna than that which had greeted His Royal Entry three days before. And this was the 'Farewell' and the parting of Israel's Messiah from Israel and its Temple. Yet a Farewell which promised a coming again; and a parting which implied a welcome in the future from a believing people to a gracious, pardoning King!

circumstances, unknown to us, which might admit of his designation as 'the son of Barachias' (the reading is undoubtedly correct), or an error may have crept into the text—how, we know not, and it is of little moment. There can be no question that the reference is to this Zacharias. It seems scarcely necessary to refer to the strange notion that the notice in St. Matt. xxiii, 35 has been derived from the account of the murder of *Zacharias, the son of Baruch,* in the Temple during the last siege (*Jos.* War. iv. 5. 4). To this there are the following four objections: (1) *Baruch* (as in Jos.) and *Barachias* (as in St. Matt.) are quite different names, in Greek as in Hebrew—בָּרוּךְ, 'blessed,' Βαρούχ, and בֶּרֶכְיָה, 'Jehovah will bless,' Βαραχίας. Comp. for ex. LXX., Neh. iii. 20 with iii. 30. (2) Because the place of their slaughter was different, that of the one 'between the porch and the altar,' that of the other 'in the midst (ἐν μέσῳ) of the Temple'—either the court of the women, or that of the Israelites. (3) Because the murder of the Zacharias referred to by St. Matt. stood out as the crowning national crime, and as such is repeatedly referred to in Jewish legend (see references in margin), and dwelt upon with many miraculous embellishments. (4) Because the clumsiest forger would scarcely have put into the mouth of Jesus an event connected with the last siege of Jerusalem and derived from Josephus. In general, we take this opportunity strongly to assert that only unacquaintance with the whole subject could lead anyone to look to Josephus for the source of any part of the evangelic narrative. To these remarks we have to add that precisely the same error (if such it be) as in our text of St. Matthew occurs in the Targum on Lament. ii. 20, where this Zechariah is designated 'the son (= grandson) of Iddo,' comp. Ezr. v. 1, and Zech. i. 1, 7. For the correct reading ('son of Jehoiada') in the 'Gospel of the Hebrews,' comp. *Nicholson,* p. 59.

CHAPTER V.

THE THIRD DAY IN PASSION-WEEK—THE LAST SERIES OF PARABLES: TO
THE PHARISEES AND TO THE PEOPLE—ON THE WAY TO JERUSALEM:
THE PARABLE OF THE LABOURERS IN THE VINEYARD—IN THE TEMPLE:
THE PARABLE OF THE 'NO' AND 'YES' OF THE TWO SONS—THE PARA-
BLE OF THE EVIL HUSBANDMEN EVILLY DESTROYED—THE PARABLE
OF THE MARRIAGE OF THE KING'S SON AND OF THE WEDDING GARMENT.

(St. Matt. xix. 30—xx. 16; St. Matt. xxi. 28-32; St. Matt. xxi. 33-46; St. Mark xii.
1-12; St. Luke xx. 9-19; St. Matt. xxii. 1-14.)

ALTHOUGH it may not be possible to mark their exact succession, it will be convenient here to group together the last series of Parables. Most, if not all of them, were spoken on that third day in Passion-week: the first four to a more general audience; the last three (to be treated in another chapter) to the disciples, when, on the evening of that third day, on the Mount of Olives,[a] He told them of the 'Last Things.' They are the Parables of Judgment, and in one form or another treat of 'the End.'

1. *The Parable of the Labourers in the Vineyard.*[b] As treating of 'the End,' this Parable evidently belongs to the last series, although it may have been spoken previously to Passion-Week, perhaps on that Mission-journey in Peræa, in connection with which it is recorded by St. Matthew. At any rate, it stands in internal relation with what passed on that occasion, and must therefore be studied with reference to it.

We remember, that on the occasion of the rich young ruler's failure to enter the Kingdom, to which he was so near, Christ had uttered an earnest warning on the danger of 'riches.'[c] In the low spiritual stage which the Apostles had as yet attained, it was, perhaps, only natural that Peter should, as spokesman of the rest, have, in a kind of spiritual covetousness, clutched at the promised reward, and that in a tone of self-righteousness he should have reminded Christ of the sacrifices which they had made. It was most painfully incongruous, yet part of what He, the Lord. had always to bear, and bore so patiently and lovingly, from their ignorance and failure to understand

CHAP.
V

[a] St. Matt.
xxiv. 1. St.
Luke xxi.
37

[b] St. Matt.
xix. 30-xx.
16

[c] Matt. xix.
23, 24

Him and His work. And this want of true sympathy, this constant contending with the moral dulness even of those nearest to Him, must have been part of His great humiliation and sorrow, one element in the terrible solitariness of His Life, which made Him feel that, in the truest sense, 'the Son of Man had not where to lay His Head.' And yet we also mark the wondrous Divine generosity which, even in moments of such sore disappointment, would not let Him take for nought what should have been freely offered in the gladsome service of grateful love. Only there was here deep danger to the disciples: danger of lapsing into feelings kindred to those with which the Pharisees viewed the pardoned Publicans, or the elder son in the Parable his younger brother; danger of misunderstanding the right relations, and with it the very character of the Kingdom, and of work in and for it. It is to this that the Parable of the Labourers in the Vineyard refers.

The principle which Christ lays down is, that, while nothing done for Him shall lose its reward, yet, from one reason or another, no forecast can be made, no inferences of self-righteousness may be drawn. It does not by any means follow, that most work done—at least, to our seeing and judging—shall entail a greater reward. On the contrary, 'many that are first shall be last; and the last shall be first.' Not *all*, nor yet always and necessarily, but 'many.' And in such cases no wrong has been done; there exists no claim, even in view of the promises of due acknowledgment of work. Spiritual pride and self-assertion can only be the outcome either of misunderstanding God's relation to us, or else of a wrong state of mind towards others [a] —that is, it betokens mental or moral unfitness.

* St. Matt.
xx. 15

Of this the Parable of the Labourers is an *illustration*. It teaches nothing beyond this.[1] But, while illustrating how it may come that some who were first are 'last, and how utterly mistaken or wrong is the thought that they must necessarily receive more than others, who, seemingly, have done more—how, in short, work for Christ is not a ponderable quantity, so much for so much, nor yet we the judges of when and why a worker has come—it also conveys much that is new, and, in many respects, most comforting.

We mark, first, the bearing of 'the householder, who went out immediately, at earliest morn ($\H\alpha\mu\alpha$ $\pi\rho\omega\ddot{\imath}$), to hire labourers into his

---

[1] Instead of discussing the explanations of others, I prefer simply to expound that which I have to propose. The difficulties of the usual interpretations are so great that a fresh study seemed requisite. Our interpretation turns on this, that the Parable is only an *illustration* of what is said in St. Matt. xix. 30.

vineyard.' That he did not send his steward, but went himself,[a] and with the dawn of morning, shows both that there was much work to do, and the householder's anxiety to have it done. That householder is God, and the vineyard His Kingdom; the labourers, whom with earliest morning He seeks in the market-place of busy life, are His Servants. With these he agreed for a *denarius* a day, which was the ordinary wages for a day's labour,[1] and so sent them into the vineyard; in other words, He told them He would pay the reward promised to labourers. So passed the early hours of the morning. About the third hour (the Jewish working day being reckoned from sunrise to sunset), that is, probably as it was drawing towards a close, he went out again, and, as he saw 'others' standing idle in the market-place, he said to them, 'Go ye also into the vineyard.' There was more than enough to do in that vineyard; enough and more to employ them. And when he came, they had stood in the market-place ready and waiting to go to work, yet 'idle'—unemployed as yet. It might not have been precisely their blame that they had not gone before; they were 'others' than those in the market-place when the Master had first come, and they had not been there at that time. Only as he now sent them, he made no definite promise. They felt that in their special circumstances they had no claim; he told them, that whatsoever was right he would give them; and they implicitly trusted to his word, to his justice and goodness. And so happened it yet again, both at the sixth and at the ninth hour of the day. We repeat, that in none of these instances was it the guilt of the labourers—in the sense of being due to their unwillingness or refusal—that they had not before gone into the vineyard. For some reason—perhaps by their fault, perhaps not—they had not been earlier in the market-place. But as soon as they were there and called, they went, although, of course, the loss of time, however caused, implied loss of work. Neither did the Master in any case make, nor they ask for, other promise than that implied in his word and character.

These four things, then, stand out clearly in the Parable: the abundance of work to be done in the vineyard; the anxiety of the householder to secure all available labourers; the circumstance that, not from unwillingness or refusal, but because they had not been there and available, the labourers had come at later hours; and that, when they had so come, they were ready to go into the vineyard

CHAP.
V

[a] St. Matt.
xx. 1

---

[1]. In Rome, at the time of Cicero, a day-labourer received 12 *as*=about 6*d*.— that is, rather less than in Judæa (comp. *Marquardt*, Röm. Alterth. vol. v. p. 52).

without promise of definite reward, simply trusting to the truth and goodness of him whom they went to serve.   We think here of those 'last,' the Gentiles from the east, west, north, and south; ᵃ of the converted publicans and sinners; of those, a great part of whose lives has, alas! been spent somewhere else, and who have only come at a late hour into the market-place; nay, of them also whose opportunities, capacity, strength, or time have been very limited—and we thank God for the teaching of this Parable.   And if doubt should still exist, it must be removed by the concluding sentences of this part of the Parable, in which the householder is represented as going out at the last hour, when, finding others standing,[1] he asks them why they stood there all the day idle, to which they reply, that no man had hired them.   These also are, in turn, sent into the vineyard, though apparently without any expressed promise at all.[2]   It thus appears, that in proportion to the lateness of their work was the felt absence of any claim on the part of the labourers, and their simple reliance on their employer.

And now it is even.   The time for working is past, and the Lord of the vineyard bids His Steward [here the Christ] pay His labourers. But here the first surprise awaits them.   The order of payment is the inverse of that of labour: 'beginning from the last unto the first.' This is almost a necessary part of the Parable.   For, if the first labourers had been paid first, they would either have gone away without knowing what was done to the last, or, if they had remained, their objection could not have been urged, except on the ground of manifest malevolence towards their neighbours.   After having received their wages, they could not have objected that they had not received enough, but only that the others had received too much.   But it was not the scope of the Parable to charge with conscious malevolence those who sought a higher reward or deemed themselves entitled to it. Again, we notice, as indicating the disposition of the later labourers, that those of the third hour did not murmur, because they had not got more than they of the eleventh hour.   This is in accordance with their not having made any bargain at the first, but trusted entirely to the householder.   But they of the first hour had their cupidity excited.   Seeing what the others had received, they expected to have more than their due.   When they likewise received every man a *denarius*, they murmured, as if injustice had been done

---

[1] The word 'idle' in the second clause of ver. 6 is spurious, though it may, of course, be supplied from the fourth clause.

[2] The last clause in our T.R. and A.V. is spurious, though *perhaps* such a promise was understood.

them. And, as mostly in like circumstances, truth and fairness seemed on their side. For, selecting the extreme case of the cleventh hour labourers, had not the Householder made those who had wrought[1] only one hour equal to them who had 'borne the burden of the day and the heat'? Yet, however fair their reasoning might seem, they had no claim in truth or equity, for had they not agreed for one *denarius* with him? And it had not even been in the general terms of a day's wages, but they had made the express bargain of one *denarius*. They had gone to work with a stipulated sum as their hire distinctly in view. They now appealed to justice; but from first to last they had had justice. This as regards the 'so much for so much' principle of claim, law, work, and pay.

But there was yet another aspect than that of mere justice. Those other labourers, who had felt that, owing to the lateness of their appearance, they had no claim—and, alas! which of us must not feel how late we have been in coming, and hence how little we can have wrought—had made no bargain, but trusted to the Master. And as they had believed, so was it unto them. Not because they made or had any claim—·'I will, however, to give unto this last, even as unto thee'—the word 'I will' ($\theta \epsilon \lambda \omega$) being emphatically put first to mark 'the good pleasure' of His grace as the ground of action. Such a Master could not have given less to those who had come when called, trusting to His goodness, and not in their deserts. The reward was now reckoned, not of work nor of debt, but of grace.[a] In passing we also mark, as against cavillers, the profound accord between what negative critics would call the 'true Judaic Gospel' of St. Matthew, and what constitutes the very essence of 'the anti-Judaic teaching' of St. Paul—and we ask our opponents to reconcile on their theory what can only be explained on the ground that St. Paul, like St. Matthew, was the true disciple of the true Teacher, Jesus Christ.

But if all is to be placed on the new ground of *grace*, with which, indeed, the whole bearing of the later labourers accords, then (as St. Paul also shows) the labourers who murmured were guilty either of ignorance in failing to perceive the sovereignty of grace—that it is within His power to do with His own as He willeth[b]—or else of malevolence, when, instead of with grateful joy, they looked on with an evil eye—and this in proportion as 'the Householder' was good.

[a] Rom. iv. 4-6; xi. 6

[b] Rom. xi.

---

[1] I prefer not rendering with *Meyer* and the R.V. ἐποίησαν, viz., ὥραν, by 'spent,' but taking the verb as the Hebrew עשׂה = 'wrought.' And the first labourers could not have meant, that the last had 'spent,' not 'wrought,' an hour. This were a gratuitous imputation to them of malevolence and calumny.

BOOK
V

ᵃ Rom. ii.;
iii. 28–31;
ix. 18–24
ᵇ Rom. xi,
11–18
ᶜ St. Matt.
xix. 30

But such a state of mind may be equally that of the Jews,ᵃ and of the Gentiles.ᵇ And so, in this illustrative case of the Parable, 'the first shall be last, and the last first.'[1] And in other instances also, though not in all—'many shall be last that are first; and first that are last.'ᶜ But He is the God, Sovereign in grace, in Whose Vineyard there is work to do for all, however limited their time, power, or opportunity; Whose labourers we are, if His Children; Who, in His desire for the work, and condescension and patience towards the workers, goeth out into the market-place even to the eleventh hour, and, with only gentlest rebuke for not having earlier come thither and thus lost our day in idleness, still, even to the last, bids us come; Who promises what is right, and gives far more than is due to them who simply trust Him: the God not of the Jews nor of the Gentiles only, but our Father; the God Who not only pays, but freely gives of His own, and in Whose Wisdom and by Whose Grace it may be, that, even as the first shall be last, so the last shall be first.

Another point still remains to be noticed. If anywhere, we expect in these Parables, addressed to the people, forms of teaching and speaking with which they were familiar—in other words, Jewish parallels. But we equally expect that the teaching of Christ, while conveyed under illustrations with which the Jews were familiar, would be entirely different in spirit. And such we find it notably in the present instance. To begin with, according to Jewish Law, if a man engaged a labourer without any definite bargain, but on the statement that he would be paid as one or another of the labourers in the place, he was, according to some, only bound to pay the lowest wages in the place; but, according to the majority, the average between the lowest and the highest.ᵈ[2] Again, as regards the letter of the Parable itself, we have a remarkable parallel in a funeral oration on a Rabbi, who died at the early age of twenty-eight. The text chosen was: 'The sleep of a labouring man is sweet,'ᵉ and this was illustrated by a Parable of a king who had a vineyard, and engaged many labourers to work in it. One of them was distinguished above the rest by his ability. So the king took him by the hand, and walked up and down with him. At even, when the labourers were paid, this one received the same wages as the others, just as if he had wrought the whole day. Upon this the others murmured, because he who had

ᵈ Babha
Mets. 87 a,
towards
the end

ᵉ Eccl. v. 12

[1] The clause which follows in our A.V. is spurious.

[2] Some interesting illustrations of secondary importance, and therefore not here introduced, may be found at the close of Babha Mets. 83 a and the beginning of b.

wrought only two hours had received the same as they who had
laboured the whole day, when the king replied: 'Why murmur ye?
This labourer has by his skill wrought as much in two hours as you
during the whole day.'ª This in reference to the great merits of the
deceased young Rabbi.

But it will be observed that, with all its similarity of form,
the moral of the Jewish Parable is in exactly the opposite direction
from the teaching of Christ. The same spirit of work and pay
breathes in another Parable, which is intended to illustrate the idea
that God had not revealed the reward attaching to each commandment, in order that men might not neglect those which brought less
return. A king—so the Parable runs—had a garden, for which he
hired labourers without telling them what their wages would be.
In the evening he called them, and, having ascertained from each
under what tree he had been working, he paid them according to
the value of the trees on which they had been engaged. And when
they said that he ought to have told them, which trees would bring
the labourers most pay, the king replied that thereby a great part of
his garden would have been neglected. So had God in like manner
only revealed the reward of the greatest of the commandments, that
to honour father and mother,ᵇ and that of the least, about letting the
mother-bird fly away ᶜ—attaching to both precisely the same reward.ᵈ

To these, if need were, might be added other illustrations of that
painful reckoning about work, or else sufferings, and reward, which
characterises Jewish theology, as it did those labourers in theParable.ᵉ

2. The second Parable in this series—or perhaps rather illustration—was spoken within the Temple. The Saviour had been
answering the question of the Pharisees as to His authority by an
appeal to the testimony of the Baptist. This led Him to refer to
the twofold reception of that testimony—on the one hand, by the
Publicans and harlots, and, on the other, by the Pharisees.

The Parable,ᶠ which now follows, introduces a man who has two
sons. He goes to the first, and in language of affection (τέκνον)
bids him go and work in his vineyard. The son curtly and rudely
refuses; but afterwards he changes his mind¹ and goes.² Meantime

CHAP.
V

ª Midr. on
Eccl. v. 11;
Jer. Ber. ii.
8

ᵇ Ex. xx. 12
ᶜ Deut.xxii.
7
ᵈ Debar. R.
6 on Deut.
xxii. 6
ᵉ See, for
example,
Ber. 5 a
and b, but
especially
7 a

ᶠ St. Matt.
xxi. 28-32

---

¹ The word is not the same as that for
'repent' in St. Matt. iii. 2. The latter
refers to a change of heart, and means
something spiritual. The word used in
the text means only a change of mind
and purpose. It occurs besides in St.
Matt.xxvii. 3; 2 Cor. vii. 8; Heb. vii.
21.

² Looking away from the very profane
use made of the saying in the Talmud,
we may quote as a literary curiosity the
following as the origin of the proverb:
He that will not when he may, when he
will he shall have nay, כשרציתי לא רצית
עכשיו שאתה רוצה איני רוצה Ber. 7 a,
line 8 from bottom.

the father, when refused by the one, has gone to his other son on the same errand. The contrast here is marked. The tone is most polite, and the answer of the son contains not only a promise, but we almost see him going: ' I, sir!—and he did not go.' The application was easy. The first son represented the Publicans and harlots, whose curt and rude refusal of the Father's call was implied in their life of reckless sin. But afterwards they changed their mind—and went into the Father's vineyard. The other son, with his politeness of tone and ready promise, but utter neglect of obligations undertaken, represented the Pharisees with their hypocritical and empty professions. And Christ obliged them to make application of the Parable. When challenged by the Lord, which of the two had done the will of his father, they could not avoid the answer. Then it was that, in language equally stern and true, He pointed the moral. The Baptist had come preaching righteousness, and, while the self-righteous Pharisees had not believed him, those sinners had. And yet, even when the Pharisees saw the effect on these former sinners, they changed not their minds that they might believe. Therefore the Publicans and harlots would and did go into the Kingdom before them.

3. Closely connected with the two preceding Parables, and, indeed, with the whole tenor of Christ's sayings at that time, is that about the Evil Husbandmen in the Vineyard.[a] As in the Parable about the Labourers sought by the Householder at different times, the object here is to set forth the patience and goodness of the owner, even towards the evil. And as, in the Parable of the Two Sons, reference is made to the practical rejection of the testimony of the Baptist by the Jews, and their consequent self-exclusion from the Kingdom, so in this there is allusion to John as greater than the prophets,[b] to the exclusion of Israel as a people from their position in the Kingdom,[c] and to their punishment as individuals.[d] Only we mark here a terrible progression. The neglect and non-belief which had appeared in the former Parable have now ripened into rebellion, deliberate, aggravated, and carried to its utmost consequences in the murder of the King's only and loved Son. Similarly, what formerly appeared as their loss, in that sinners went into the Kingdom of God before them, is now presented alike as their guilt and their judgment, both national and individual.

The Parable opens, like that in Is. v., with a description of the complete arrangements made by the Owner of the Vineyard,[1] to show

ᵃ St. Matt.
xxi. 33 &c.
and par-
allels

ᵇ ver. 36

ᶜ ver. 43

ᵈ ver. 44

---

[1] 'An hedge' against animals or marauders, 'a winepress,' or, more specifi- cally (St. Mark), a 'winefat' ($\dot{v}\pi o\lambda\dot{\eta}$-$\nu\iota o\nu$), into which the juice of the grapes

how everything had been done to ensure a good yield of fruit, and what right the Owner had to expect at least a share in it. In the Parable, as in the prophecy, the Vineyard represents the Theocracy, although in the Old Testament, necessarily, as identified with the *nation* of Israel,[a] while in the Parable the two are distinguished, and the nation is represented by the labourers to whom the Vineyard was 'let out.' Indeed, the whole structure of the Parable shows, that the husbandmen are Israel as a nation, although they are addressed and dealt with in the persons of their representatives and leaders. And so it was spoken 'to the people,'[b] and yet 'the chief priests and Pharisees ' rightly ' perceived that He spake of them.'[c]

This vineyard the owner had let out to husbandmen, while he himself 'travelled away ' [abroad], as St. Luke adds, 'for a long time.' From the language it is evident, that the husbandmen had the full management of the vineyard. We remember, that there were three modes of dealing with land. According to one of these (*Arisuth*), 'the labourers ' employed received a certain portion of the fruits, say, a third or a fourth of the produce.[d] In such cases it seems, at least sometimes, to have been the practice, besides giving them a proportion of the produce, to provide also the seed (for a field) and to pay wages to the labourers.[e] The other two modes of letting land were, either that the tenant paid a money rent to the proprietor,[f] or else that he agreed to give the owner a definite amount of produce, whether the harvest had been good or bad.[g] Such leases were given by the year or for life: sometimes the lease was even hereditary, passing from father to son.[h] There can scarcely be a doubt that it is the latter kind of lease (*Chakhranutha*, from הכר) which is referred to in the Parable, the lessees being bound to give the owner a certain amount of fruits in their season.

Accordingly, 'when the time of the fruits drew near, he sent his servants to the husbandmen to receive his fruits '—the part of them belonging to him, or, as St. Mark and St. Luke express it, 'of the fruits of the vineyard.' We gather, that it was a succession of servants, who received increasingly ill treatment from these evil husbandmen. We might have expected that the owner would now have taken severe measures; but instead of this he sent, in his patience and goodness, ' other servants '—not ' more,' [i] which would scarcely have any meaning, but 'greater than the first,' no doubt, with the idea that

CHAP.
V

a Is. v. 7

b St. Luke
xx. 9
c St. Matt.
xxi. 45

d Jer. Bikk.
64 b

e Shem. R.
41, ed.
Warsh, p.
54 b last
line
f Tos.
Demai vi.
g Babha
Mets. 104 a
h Jer. Bikk.
64 b

i as in the
A. and R.V

flowed, and ' a tower' for the watchmen and labourers generally. We may here remark that the differences in the narration of this Parable in the three Gospels are too minute for discussion here. The principal one, in St. Matt. xxi. 40, 41, comp. with the parallels, will be briefly referred to in the text.

BOOK
V

their greater authority would command respect. And when these also received the same treatment, we must regard it as involving, not only additional, but *increased* guilt on the part of the husbandmen. Once more, and with deepening force, does the question arise, what measures the owner would now take. But once more we have only a fresh and still greater display of his patience and unwillingness to believe that these husbandmen were so evil. As St. Mark pathetically put it, indicating not only the owner's goodness, but the spirit of determined rebellion and the wickedness of the husbandmen: ' He had yet one, a beloved son—he sent him last unto them,' on the supposition that they would reverence him. The result was different. The appearance of the legal heir made them apprehensive of their tenure. Practically, the vineyard was already theirs; by killing the heir, the only claimant to it would be put out of the way, and so the vineyard become in every respect their own. For, the husbandmen proceeded on the idea, that as the owner was ' abroad ' ' for a long time,' he would not personally interfere—an impression strengthened by the circumstance that he had not avenged the former ill-usage of his servants, but only sent others in the hope of influencing them by gentleness. So the labourers. ' taking him [the son], cast him forth out of the vineyard, and killed him '—the first action indicating that by violence they thrust him out of his possession, before they wickedly slew him.

The meaning of the Parable is sufficiently plain. The owner of the vineyard, God, had let out His Vineyard—the Theocracy—to His people of old. The covenant having been instituted, He withdrew, as it were—the former direct communication between Him and Israel ceased. Then in due season He sent ' His Servants,' the prophets, to gather *His* fruits—they had had theirs in all the temporal and spiritual advantages of the covenant. But, instead of returning the fruits meet unto repentance, they only ill-treated His messengers, and that increasingly, even unto death. In His longsuffering He next sent on the same errand ' greater ' than them—John the Baptist.[a] And when he also received the same treatment, He sent last His own Son, Jesus Christ. His appearance made them feel, that it was now a decisive struggle for the Vineyard— and so, in order to gain its possession for themselves, they cast the rightful heir out of His own possession, and then killed Him!

And they must have understood the meaning of the Parable, who had served themselves heirs to their fathers in the murder of all the prophets,[b] who had just been convicted of the rejection of the

Baptist's message, and whose hearts were even then full of murderous thoughts against the rightful Heir of the Vineyard. But, even so, they must speak their own judgment. In answer to His challenge, what in their view the owner of the vineyard would do to these husband-men, the chief priests and Pharisees could only reply: '*As* evil *men* evilly will he destroy them. And the vineyard will He let out to other husbandmen, which shall render Him the fruits in their season.'[a]

CHAP. V

[a] St. Matt. xxi. 41

The application was obvious, and it was made by Christ, first, as always, by a reference to the prophetic testimony, showing not only the unity of all God's teaching, but also the continuity of the Israel of the present with that of old in their resistance and rejection of God's counsel and messengers. The quotation, than which none more applicable could be imagined, was from Ps. cxviii. 22, 23, and is made in the (Greek) Gospel of St. Mathew—not necessarily by Christ—from the LXX. Version. The only, almost verbal, difference between it and the original is, that, whereas in the latter the adoption of the stone rejected by the builders as head of the corner ('this,' *hoc*, זאת) is ascribed to Jehovah, in the LXX. its original designation (αὕτη) as head of the corner (previous to the action of the builders), is traced to the Lord. And then followed, in plain and unmistakable language, the terrible prediction, first, nationally, that the Kingdom of God would be taken from them, and 'given to a nation bringing forth the fruits thereof;' and then, individually, that whosoever stumbled at that stone and fell over it, in personal offence or hostility, should be broken in pieces,[1] but whosoever stood in the way of, or resisted its progress, and on whom therefore it fell, it would 'scatter Him as dust.'

Once more was their wrath roused, but also their fears. They knew that He spake of them, and would fain have laid hands on Him; but they feared the people, who in those days regarded Him as a prophet. And so for the present they left Him, and went their way.

4. If Rabbinic writings offer scarcely any parallel to the preceding Parable, that of the Marriage-Feast of the King's Son and the Wedding Garment[b] seems almost reproduced in Jewish tradition. In its oldest form[c] it is ascribed to Jochanan ben Zakkai, who flourished about the time of the composition of the Gospel of St. Matthew. It

[b] St. Matt. xxii. 1–14
[c] Shabb. 153 *a*, and 152 *b*

---

[1] The only Jewish parallel, even in point of form, so far as I know, is in Vayy. R. 11 (ed. Warsh., p. 18 *a*, near beginning), where we read of a king who sent his treasurer to collect tribute, when the people of the land killed and plundered him.

BOOK
V

ᵃ Midr. on
Eccles. ix.
8; Midr. on
Prov. xvi.
11
ᵇ St. Matt.
xxii. 1-9
and 10-14
ᶜ Shabb.
153 a
ᵈ Shabb.
152 b

appears with variety of, or with additional details in Jewish commentaries.ᵃ But while the Parable of our Lord only consists of *two parts*,ᵇ forming one whole and having one lesson, the Talmud divides it into two separate Parables, of which the one is intended to show the necessity of being prepared for the next world—to stand in readiness for the King's feast;ᶜ while the other[1] is meant to teach that we ought to be able to present our soul to God at the last in the same state of purity in which we had (according to Rabbinic notions) originally received it.ᵈ Even this shows the infinite difference between the Lord's and the Rabbinic use of the Parable.[2] In the Jewish Parable a King is represented as inviting to a feast,[3] without, however, fixing the exact time for it. The wise adorn themselves in time, and are seated at the door of the palace, so as to be in readiness, since, as they argue, no elaborate preparation for a feast can be needed in a palace; while the foolish go away to their work, arguing there must be time enough, since there can be no feast without preparation. (The Midrash has it, that, when inviting the guests, the King had told them to wash, anoint, and array themselves in their festive garments; and that the foolish, arguing that, from the preparation of the food and the arranging of the seats, they would learn when the feast was to begin, had gone, the mason to his cask of lime, the potter to his clay, the smith to his furnace, the fuller to his bleaching-ground.) But suddenly comes the King's summons to the feast, when the wise appear festively adorned, and the King rejoices over them, and they are made to sit down, eat and drink; while he is wroth with the foolish, who appear squalid, and are ordered to stand by and look on in anguish, hunger and thirst.

ᵉ Shabb.
152 b

The other Jewish Parableᵉ is of a king who committed to his servants the royal robes. The wise among them carefully laid them by while the foolish put them on when they did their work. After a time the king asked back the robes, when the wise could restore them clean, while the foolish had them soiled. Then the king rejoiced over the wise, and, while the robes were laid up in the treasury, they were bidden go home in peace. 'But to the foolish he commanded that the robes should be handed over to the fuller, and that they themselves should be cast into prison.' We readily see that the meaning of this Parable was, that a man might preserve His soul perfectly pure, and so enter into peace, while the careless, who had lost their original

---

[1] This Parable is only in the Talmud in this connection, not in the Midrashim.
[2] The reader will find both these Parables translated in 'Sketches of Jewish Social Life,' p. 179.
[3] In the Talmud he invites his servants; in the Midrash, others.

purity [no original sin here], would, in the next world, by suffering, both expiate their guilt and purify their souls.

CHAP.
V

When, from these Rabbinic perversions, we turn to the Parable of our Lord, its meaning is not difficult to understand. The King made a marriage[1] for his Son, when he sent his Servants to call them that were bidden to the wedding. Evidently, as in the Jewish Parable, and as before in that of the guests invited to the great Supper,[a] a preliminary general invitation had preceded the announcement that all was ready. Indeed, in the Midrash on Lament. iv. 2,[b] it is expressly mentioned among other distinctions of the inhabitants of Jerusalem, that none of them went to a feast till the invitation had been given and repeated. But in the Parable those invited would not come. It reminds us both of the Parable of the Labourers for the Vineyard, sought at different times, and of the repeated sending of messengers to those Evil Husbandmen for the fruits that were due, when we are next told that the King sent forth other servants to tell them to come, for he had made ready his 'early meal' ($\check{\alpha}\rho\iota\sigma\tau o\nu$, not 'dinner,' as in the Authorised and Revised Version), and that, no doubt with a view to the later meal, the oxen and fatlings were killed. These repeated endeavours to call, to admonish, and to invite, form a characteristic feature of these Parables, showing that it was one of the central objects of our Lord's teaching to exhibit the longsuffering and goodness of God. Instead of giving heed to these repeated and pressing calls, in the words of the Parable: 'But they [the one class] made light of it, and went away, the one to his own land, the other unto his own merchandise.'

So the one class; the other made not light of it, but acted even worse than the first. 'But the rest laid hands on his servants, entreated them shamefully, and killed them.' By this we are to understand, that, when the servants came with the second and more pressing message, the one class showed their contempt for the king, the wedding of his son, and the feast, and their preference for and preoccupation with their own possessions or acquisitions—their property or their trading, their enjoyments or their aims and desires. And, when these had gone, and probably the servants still remained to plead the message of their lord, the rest evil entreated, and then killed them—proceeding beyond mere contempt, want of interest, and preoccupation with their own affairs, to hatred and murder. The sin was the more aggravated that he was their *king*, and the messengers had invited them to a feast, and that one in which every loyal subject

ᵃ St. Luke
xiv. 16, 17

ᵇ ed.
Warsh.
p. 73 b

---

[1] This rather than 'marriage-feast.'

should have rejoiced to take part. Theirs was, therefore, not only murder, but also rebellion against their sovereign. On this the king, in his wrath, sent forth his armies, which—and here the narrative in point of time anticipates the event—destroyed the murderers, and burnt their city.[1]

But the condign punishment of these rebels forms only part of the Parable. For it still leaves the wedding unprovided with guests, to sympathise with the joy of the king, and partake of his feast. And so the narrative continues:[a] 'Then'—after the king had given commandment for his armies to go forth, he said to his servants, 'The wedding indeed is ready, but they that were bidden were not worthy. Go ye therefore into the partings of the highways [where a number of roads meet and cross], and, as many as ye shall find, bid to the marriage.' We remember that the Parable here runs parallel to that other, when, first the outcasts from the city-lanes, and then the wanderers on the world's highway, were brought in to fill the place of the invited guests.[b] At first sight it seems as if there were no connection between the declaration that those who had been bidden had proved themselves unworthy, and the direction to go into the crossroads and gather any whom they might find, since the latter might naturally be regarded as less likely to prove worthy. Yet this is one of the main points in the Parable. The first invitation had been sent to selected guests—to the Jews—who might have been expected to be 'worthy,' but had proved themselves unworthy; the next was to be given, not to the chosen city or nation, but to all that travelled in whatever direction on the world's highway, reaching them where the roads of life meet and part.

We have already in part anticipated the interpretation of this Parable. 'The Kingdom' is here, as so often in the Old and in the New Testament, likened to a feast, and more specifically to a marriage-feast. But we mark as distinctive, that the King makes it *for His Son.* Thus Christ, as Son and Heir of the Kingdom, forms the central Figure in the Parable. This is the first point set before us. The next is, that the chosen, invited guests were the ancient Convenant-people—Israel. To them God had sent first under the Old Testament. And, although they had not given heed to His call, yet a second class of messengers was sent to them under the New Testament. And the message of the latter was, that 'the early meal' was ready [Christ's

ᴸ St. Matt.
xxii 8.

ᵇ St. Luke
xiv. 21-24

---

[1] Reference is only made to that part who were murderers. Not that the others escaped suffering or loss, but, in accordance with the plan of the Parable, this is not mentioned. When we read of 'their city,' may there not here be also a reference to a commonwealth or nation?

first coming], and that all preparations had been made for the great
evening-meal [Christ's Reign].   Another prominent truth is set forth
in the repeated message of the King, which points to the goodness and
longsuffering of God.   Next, our attention is drawn to the refusal
of Israel, which appears in the contemptuous neglect and preoccupation with their own things of one party, and the hatred,
resistance, and murder by the other.   Then follow in quick succession the command of judgment on the nation, and the burning of
their city—God's army being, in this instance, the Romans—and,
finally, the direction to go into the crossways to invite all men, alike
Jews and Gentiles.

With verse 10 begins the second part of the Parable.   The
'Servants '—that is, the New Testament messengers—had fulfilled
their commission; they had brought in as many as they found, both
bad and good: that is, without respect to their previous history, or
their moral and religious state up to the time of their call; and 'the
wedding was filled with guests '—that is, the table at the marriage-
feast was filled with those who as guests 'lay around it'($\dot{\alpha}\nu\alpha\kappa\epsilon\iota\mu\acute{\epsilon}\nu\omega\nu$).
But, if ever we are to learn that we must not expect on earth—not
even at the King's marriage-table—a pure Church, it is, surely, from
what now follows.   The King entered to see His guests, and among
them he descried one who had not on a wedding-garment.   Manifestly,
the quickness of the invitation and the previous unpreparedness of
the guests did not prevent the procuring of such a garment.   As the
guests had been travellers, and as the feast was in the King's palace,
we cannot be mistaken in supposing that such garments were supplied
in the palace itself to all those who sought them.   And with this
agrees the circumstance, that the man so addressed ' was speechless '
[literally, ' gagged,' or ' muzzled '].[a]   His conduct argued utter insensibility as regarded that to which he had been called—ignorance
of what was due to the King, and what became such a feast.   For,
although no previous state of preparedness was required of the
invited guests, all being bidden, whether good or bad, yet the fact
remained that, if they were to take part in the feast, they must put
on a garment suited to the occasion.   All are invited to the
Gospel-feast; but they who will partake of it must put on the King's
wedding-garment of Evangelical holiness.   And whereas it is said in
the Parable, that only one was descried without this garment, this is
intended to teach, that the King will not only generally view His
guests, but that each will be separately examined, and that no one—
no, not a single individual—will be able to escape discovery amidst the

mass of guests, if he has not the 'wedding-garment.' In short, in that day of trial, it is not a scrutiny of Churches, but of individuals in the Church. And so the King bade the servants—διακόνοις—not the same who had previously carried the invitation (δούλοις), but others—evidently here the Angels, His 'ministers,' to bind him hand and foot, and to 'cast him out into the darkness, the outer'—that is, unable to offer resistance and as a punished captive, he was to be cast out into that darkness which is outside the brilliantly lighted guest-chamber of the King. And, still further to mark that darkness outside, it is added that this is the well-known place of suffering and anguish: 'there shall be the weeping and the gnashing of teeth.'

And here the Parable closes with the general statement, applicable alike to the first part of the Parable—to the first invited guests, Israel—and to the second, the guests from all the world: 'For' (this is the meaning of the whole Parable) 'many are called, but

e St. Matt.
xxii. 14

few chosen.' [e] For the understanding of these words we have to keep in view that, logically, the two clauses must be supplemented by the same words. Thus, the verse would read: Many are called *out of the world* by God to partake of the Gospel-feast, but few *out of the world* —*not*, out of the called—are chosen by God to partake of it. The call to the feast and the choice for the feast are not identical. The call comes to all; but it may be outwardly accepted, and a man may sit down to the feast, and yet he may not be chosen to partake of the feast, because he has not the wedding-garment of converting, sanctifying grace. And so one may be thrust even from the marriage-board into the darkness without, with its sorrow and anguish.

Thus, side by side, yet wide apart, are these two—God's call and God's choice. The connecting-link between them is the taking of the wedding-garment, freely given in the Palace. Yet, we must seek it, ask it, put it on. And so here also, we have, side by side, God's gift and man's activity. And still, to all time, and to all men, alike in its warning, teaching, and blessing, is it true: 'Many are called, but few chosen!'

CHAPTER VI.

THE EVENING OF THE THIRD DAY IN PASSION-WEEK—ON THE MOUNT OF
OLIVES : DISCOURSE TO THE DISCIPLES CONCERNING THE LAST THINGS.

(St. Matt. xxiv.; St. Mark xiii.; St. Luke xxi. 5–38; xii. 35–48.)

THE last and most solemn denunciation of Jerusalem had been
uttered, the last and most terrible prediction of judgment upon the
Temple spoken, and Jesus was suiting the action to the word. It
was as if He had cast the dust off His Shoes against 'the House'
that was to be 'left desolate.' And so He quitted for ever the
Temple and them that held office in it.

CHAP.
VI

They had left the Sanctuary and the City, had crossed black
Kidron, and were slowly climbing the Mount of Olives. A sudden
turn in the road, and the Sacred Building was once more in full
view. Just then the western sun was pouring his golden beams on
tops of marble cloisters and on the terraced courts, and glittering on
the golden spikes on the roof of the Holy Place. In the setting,
even more than in the rising sun, must the vast proportions, the
symmetry, and the sparkling sheen of this mass of snowy marble
and gold have stood out gloriously. And across the black valley,
and up the slopes of Olivet, lay the dark shadows of those gigantic
walls built of massive stones, some of them nearly twenty-four feet
long. Even the Rabbis, despite their hatred of Herod, grow enthusiastic, and dream that the very Temple-walls would have been
covered with gold, had not the variegated marble, resembling the
waves of the sea, seemed more beauteous.[a] It was probably as they
now gazed on all this grandeur and strength, that they broke the
silence imposed on them by gloomy thoughts of the near desolateness of that House, which the Lord had predicted.[b] One and
another pointed out to Him those massive stones and splendid buildings, or spake of the rich offerings with which the Temple was
adorned.[c] It was but natural that the contrast between this and
the predicted desolation should have impressed them; natural, also,

[a] Baba B.
4 a; Sukk.
51 b

[b] St. Matt.
xxiii. 37–39

[c] St. Matt.
xxiv. 1.

BOOK
V

* St. Matt.
xxiv. 3
b St. Mark
xiii. 1

' St. Mark
xiii. 3

that they should refer to it—not as matter of doubt, but rather as of question.[a] Then Jesus, probably turning to one—perhaps to the first, or else the principal—of His questioners,[b] spoke fully of that terrible contrast between the present and the near future, when, as fulfilled with almost incredible literality,[1] not one stone would be left upon another that was not upturned.

In silence they pursued their way. Upon the Mount of Olives they sat down, right over against the Temple. Whether or not the others had gone farther, or Christ had sat apart with these four, Peter and James and John and Andrew are named[c] as those who now asked Him further of what must have weighed so heavily on their hearts. It was not idle curiosity, although inquiry on such a subject, even merely for the sake of information, could scarcely have been blamed in a Jew. But it did concern them personally, for had not the Lord conjoined the desolateness of that ' House ' with His own absence? He had explained the former as meaning the ruin of the City and the utter destruction of the Temple. But to His prediction of. it had been added these words: ' Ye shall not see Me henceforth, till ye shall say, Blessed is He that cometh in the Name of the Lord.' In their view, this could only refer to His Second Coming, and to the End of the world as connected with it. This explains the twofold question which the four now addressed to Christ: ' Tell us, when shall these things be? and what shall be the sign of Thy Coming, and of the consummation of the age? '[2]

Irrespective of other sayings, in which a distinction between these two events is made, we can scarcely believe that the disciples could have conjoined the desolation of the Temple with the immediate Advent of Christ and the end of the world. For, in the very saying which gave rise to their question, Christ had placed an indefinite

---

[1] According to *Josephus* (War vii. 1. 1) the city was so upheaved and dug up, that it was difficult to believe it had ever been inhabited. At a later period Turnus Rufus had the ploughshare drawn over it. And in regard to the Temple walls, notwithstanding the massiveness of the stones, with the exception of some corner or portion of wall—left almost to show how great had been the ruin and desolation—'there is, certainly, nothing now *in situ*.' (Capt. *Wilson* in the ' Ordnance Survey ').

[2] τῆς συντελείας τοῦ αἰῶνος. *Godet* argues that the account in the Gospel of St. Matthew contains, as in other parts of that Gospel, the combined reports of addresses, delivered at different times.

That may be so, but the inference of *Godet* is certainly incorrect,—that neither the question of the disciples, nor the discourse of our Lord on that occasion primarily referred to the Second Advent (the παρουσία). When that writer remarks, that only St. Matthew, but neither St. Mark nor St. Luke refer to such a question by the disciples, he must have overlooked that it is not only implied in the ' all these things ' of St. Mark, and the ' these things ' of St. Luke—which, surely, refer to more than one thing—but that the question of the disciples about the Advent takes up a distinctive part of what Christ had said on quitting the Temple, as reported in St. Matt. xxiii. 39.

period between the two. Between the desolation of the House and their new welcome to Him, would intervene a period of indefinite length, during which they would not see Him again. The disciples could not have overlooked this; and hence neither their question, nor yet the Discourse of our Lord, have been intended to conjoin the two. It is necessary to keep this in view when studying the words of Christ; and any different impression must be due to the exceeding compression in the language of St. Matthew, and to this, that Christ would purposely leave indefinite the interval between ' the desolation of the house' and His own Return.

Another point of considerable importance remains to be noticed. When the Lord, on quitting the Temple, said: 'Ye shall not see Me henceforth,' He must have referred to Israel in their *national* capacity—to the Jewish polity in Church and State. If so, the promise in the text of visible reappearance must also apply to the Jewish Commonwealth, to Israel in their national capacity. Accordingly, it is suggested that in the present passage Christ refers to His Advent, not from the general cosmic viewpoint of universal, but from the Jewish standpoint of Jewish, history, in which the destruction of Jerusalem and the appearance of false Christs are the last events of national history, to be followed by the dreary blank and silence of the many centuries of the 'Gentile dispensation,' broken at last by the events that usher in His Coming.[a]

[a] St. Luke xxi. 24 &c.

Keeping in mind, then, that the disciples could not have conjoined the desolation of the Temple with the immediate Advent of Christ into His Kingdom and the end of the world, their question to Christ was twofold: *When* would these things be ? and, What would be the *signs* of His Royal Advent and the consummation of the 'Age' ? On the former the Lord gave no information; to the latter His Discourse on the Mount of Olives was directed. On one point the statement of the Lord had been so novel as almost to account for their question. Jewish writings speak very frequently of the so-called ' sorrows of the Messiah' (*Chebhley shel Mashiach*[b] [1]). These were partly those of the Messiah, and partly—perhaps chiefly—those coming on Israel and the world previous to, and connected with, the Coming of the Messiah. There can be no purpose in describing them in detail, since the particulars mentioned vary so much, and the descriptions are so fanciful. But they may generally be characterised as marking a period of internal corruption[c] and of outward distress, especially of

[b] Shabb. 118 a

[c] End of the Mishnic Tractate Sotah

[1] If these are computed to last nine months, it must have been from a kind of fanciful analogy with the ' sorrows' of a woman.

BOOK
V

ᵃ Comp.
Sanh. 98 a
and b

famine and war, of which the land of Palestine was to be the scene, and in which Israel were to be the chief sufferers.ᵃ As the Rabbinic notices which we possess all date from after the destruction of Jerusalem, it is, of course, impossible to make any absolute assertion on the point; but, as a matter of fact, none of them refers to desolation of the City and Temple as one of the 'signs' or 'sorrows' of the Messiah. It is true that isolated voices proclaimed that fate of the Sanctuary, but not in any connection with the triumphant Advent of Messiah;[1] and, if we are to judge from the hopes entertained by the fanatics during the last siege of Jerusalem, they rather expected a Divine, no doubt Messianic, interposition to save the City and Temple,

ᵇ Comp.
Jos. War ii.
13, 4;
and espe-
cially vi. 5.
2

even at the last moment.ᵇ When Christ, therefore, proclaimed the desolation of 'the house,' and even placed it in indirect connection with His Advent, He taught that which must have been alike new and unexpected.

This may be the most suitable place for explaining the Jewish expectation connected with the Advent of the Messiah. Here we have first to dismiss, as belonging to a later period, the Rabbinic fiction of two Messiahs: the one, the primary and reigning, the Son of David; the other, the secondary and warfaring Messiah, the Son of Ephraim or

ᶜ Sukk. 52 a
and b

of Manasseh. The earliest Talmudic reference to this second Messiahᶜ dates from the third century of our era, and contains the strange and

ᵈ Zech. xii.
12

almost blasphemous notices that the prophecy of Zechariah,ᵈ concerning the mourning for Him Whom they had pierced, referred to Messiah the Son of Joseph, Who would be killed in the war of Gog and Magog;[2] and that, when Messiah the Son of David saw it, He 'asked life' of God, Who gave it to Him, as it is written in Ps. ii.: 'Ask of Me, and I will give Thee,' upon which God informed the Messiah that His father David had already asked and obtained this for Him, according to Ps. xxi. 4. Generally the Messiah, Son of Joseph, is connected with the gathering and restoration of the ten tribes. Later Rabbinic writings connect all the sufferings of the Messiah for sin with this Son of

ᵉ See espe-
cially
Yalkut on
Is. lx. vol.
ii. par 359,
quoted at
length in
Appendix
IX.

Joseph.ᵉ The war in which 'the Son of Joseph' succumbed would finally be brought to a victorious termination by 'the Son of David,' when the supremacy of Israel would be restored, and all nations walk in His Light.

It is scarcely matter for surprise, that the various notices about the Messiah, Son of Joseph, are confused and sometimes inconsistent,

---

[1] When using the expression 'Advent' in this connection, we refer to the Advent of Messiah to reign, His Messianic manifestation—*not* His Birth.

[2] Another Rabbinic authority, however, refers it to the 'evil impulse,' which was, in the future. to be annihilated.

considering the circumstances in which this dogma originated. Its primary reason was, no doubt, controversial. When hardly pressed by Christian argument about the Old Testament prophecies of the sufferings of the Messiah, the fiction about the Son of Joseph as distinct from the Son of David would offer a welcome means of escape.[1] Besides, when in the Jewish rebellion [a] under the false Messiah ' Bar-Kokhba ' (' the Son of a Star '[b]) the latter succumbed to the Romans and was killed, the Synagogue deemed it necessary to rekindle Israel's hope, that had been quenched in blood, by the picture of two Messiahs, of whom the first should fall in warfare, while the second, the Son of David, would carry the contest to a triumphant issue.[2]

In general, we must here remember that there is a difference between three terms used in Jewish writings to designate that which is to succeed the ' present dispensation' or ' world ' (*Olam hazzeh*), although the distinction is not always consistently carried out. This happy period would begin with ' the days of the Messiah ' (ימות המשיח). These would stretch into the ' coming age ' (*Athid labho*), and end with ' the world to come ' *(Olam habba)*—although the latter is sometimes made to include the whole of that period.[3] The most divergent opinions are expressed of the duration of the Messianic period. It seems like a round number when we are told that it would last for three generations.[c] In the fullest discussion on the subject,[d] the opinions of different Rabbis are mentioned, who variously fix the period at from forty to one, two, and even seven thousand years, according to fanciful analogies.[4]

CHAP.
VI

[a] 132–135
A.D.
[b] Numb.
xxiv. 17

[c] Siphré,ed
Friedmann,
p. 134 a,
about the
middle
[d] Tanchu-
ma, as in
Note 3

---

[1] Comp. *J. M. Glæsener*, De Gemino Jud. Mess. pp. 145 &c.; *Schöttgen*, Horæ Heb. ii. pp. 360–366.

[2] So also both *Levy* (Neuhebr. Wörterb. vol. iii. p. 271 a) and *Hamburger* (Real. Encykl. f. Bib. u.Talm., Abtheil.ii.p.768). I must here express surprise that a writer so learned and independent as *Castelli* (Il Messia, pp. 224–236) should have argued that the theory of a Messiah, son of Joseph, belonged to the *oldest* Jewish traditions, and did not arise as explained in the text. The only reason which *Castelli* urges against a view, which he admits to be otherwise probable, is that certain Rabbinic statements speak also of the Son of David as suffering. Even if this were so, such inconsistencies would prove nothing, since there are so many instances of them in Rabbinic writings. But, really, the only passage which from its age here deserves serious attention is Sanh. 98 a and b. In Yalkut

the suffering Messiah is expressly designated as the Son of Ephraim.

[3] In Bemidb. R. 15 (ed. Warsh. p. 63 a, lines 9 and 8 from bottom), the ' days of the Messiah ' are specially distinguished from the ' Athid labho,' *sæculum futurum*. In Tanchuma (Eqebh, ed. Warsh. ii. p. 105 a, about the middle) it is said, ' And after the days of the Messiah comes the " Olam habba " '—so that the Messianic time is there made to include the *sæculum futurum*. Again, in Pes. 68 a and Sanh. 91 b, ' the days of the Messiah' are distinguished from the ' Olam habba,' and, lastly (not to multiply instances), in Shabb. 113 b from the *Athid labho*.

[4] 40 years = the wilderness wanderings: 1000 years = one day, Ps. xc. 4; 2000 years = ' the day of vengeance and the year of salvation ' (Is. lxiii. 4); 7000 years = the marriage-week (Is. lxii. 5), a day being = 1000 years.

Where statements rest on such fanciful considerations, we can scarcely attach serious value to them, nor expect agreement. This remark holds equally true in regard to most of the other points involved. Suffice it to say, that, according to general opinion, the Birth of the Messiah would be unknown to His contemporaries;[1] that He would appear, carry on His work, then disappear—probably for forty-five days; then reappear again, and destroy the hostile powers of the world, notably ' Edom,' ' Armilos,' the Roman Power—the fourth and last world-empire (sometimes it is said: through Ishmael). Ransomed Israel would now be miraculously gathered from the ends of the earth, and brought back to their own land, the ten tribes sharing in their restoration, but this only on condition of their having repented of their former sins.[2] According to the Midrash,[a] all circumcised Israel would then be released from Gehenna, and the dead be raised—according to some authorities, by the Messiah, to Whom God would give 'the Key of the Resurrection of the Dead.'[b] This Resurrection would take place in the land of Israel, and those of Israel who had been buried elsewhere would have to roll under ground—not without suffering pain[c]—till they reached the sacred soil. Probably the reason of this strange idea, which was supported by an appeal to the direction of Jacob and Joseph as to their last resting-place, was to induce the Jews, after the final desolation of their land, not to quit Palestine. This Resurrection, which is variously supposed to take place at the beginning or during the course of the Messianic manifestation, would be announced by the blowing of the great trumpet.[d][3] It would be difficult to say how many of these strange and confused views prevailed at the time of Christ;[d] which of them were universally entertained as real dogmas; or from what source they had been originally derived. Probably many of them were popularly entertained, and afterwards further developed—as we believe, with elements distorted from Christian teaching.

We have now reached the period of the ' coming age ' (the *Athid labho*, or sæculum futurum). All the resistance to God would be concentrated in the great war of Gog and Magog, and with it the

[a] Yalkut on Is. vol. ii. p. 42 *c*; Siphra. ed. Weiss. 112 *b*

[b] Sanh. 113 *a*

[c] Kethub. 111 *a*

[d] IV. Esd. vi. 23 &c.

[1] This confirms St. John vii. 26, and affords another evidence that it cannot have been of Ephesian authorship, but that its writer must have been a Jew, intimately conversant with Jewish belief.

[2] But here opinions are divided, some holding that they will never be restored. See both opinions in Sanh. 110 *b*.

[3] On the Resurrection-body, the bone *Luz*, the dress worn, and the reappearance of the former bodily defects, see previous remarks, pp. 398, 399.

[4] In this extremely condensed abstract, I have thought it better not to cumber the page with Rabbinic references. They would have been too numerous, and the learned reader can easily find sufficient to bear on each clause in books treating on the subject.

prevalence of all wickedness be conjoined.   And terrible would be the
straits of Israel.   Three times would the enemy seek to storm the
Holy City.   But each time would the assault be repelled—at the
last with complete destruction of the enemy.   The sacred City would
now be wholly rebuilt and inhabited.   But oh, how different from of
old! Its Sabbath-boundaries would be strewed with pearls and precious
gems.   The City itself would be lifted to a height of some nine miles
—nay, with realistic application of Is. xlix. 20, it would reach up to
the throne of God, while it would extend from Joppa as far as the
gates of Damascus!   For, Jerusalem was to be the dwelling-place
of Israel, and the resort of all nations.   But more glorious in Jerusalem would be the new Temple which the Messiah was to rear, and
to which those five things were to be restored which had been
wanting in the former Sanctuary; the Golden Candlestick, the Ark,
the Heaven-lit fire on the Altar, the Holy Ghost, and the Cherubim.
And the land of Israel would then be as wide as it had been sketched
in the promise which God had given to Abraham, and which had
never before been fulfilled—since the largest extent of Israel's rule
had only been over seven nations, whereas the Divine promise
extended it over ten, if not over the whole earth.

Strangely realistic and exaggerated by Eastern imagination as
these hopes sound, there is, connected with them, a point of deepest
interest on which, as explained in another place,[1] remarkable divergence of opinion prevailed.   It concerns the Services of the rebuilt
Temple, and the observance of the Law in Messianic days.   One party
here insisted on the restoration of all the ancient Services, and the
strict observance of the Mosaic and Rabbinic Law—nay, on its full imposition on the Gentile nations.[2]   But this view must have been at
least modified by the expectation, that the Messiah would give a new
Law.[a]   But was this new Law to apply only to the Gentiles, or also
to Israel?   Here again there is divergence of opinions.   According
to some, this Law would be binding on Israel, but not on the Gentiles,
or else the latter would have a modified or condensed series of
ordinances (at most thirty commandments).   But the most liberal
view, and, as we may suppose, that most acceptable to the enlightened, was, that in the future only these two festive seasons would
be observed: The Day of Atonement, and the Feast of Esther (or
else that of Tabernacles), and that of all the sacrifices only thank-

[a] Midr. on
Cant. ii. 13
(ex rec. R.
Martini,
Pugio
Fidei.
pp. 782,
783); Yal-
kut ii. par.
296.

[1] See Book III. ch. iii. and Appendix XIV.
[2] Such as even the wearing of the
phylacteries (comp. Ber. R. 98; Midr. on
Ps. xxi.).

offerings would be continued.[1] Nay, opinion went even further, and many held that in Messianic days the distinctions of pure and impure, lawful and unlawful, as regarded food, would be abolished.[2] There can be little doubt that these different views were entertained even in the days of our Lord and in Apostolic times, and they account for the exceeding bitterness with which the extreme Pharisaic party in the Church at Jerusalem contended, that the Gentile converts must be circumcised, and the full weight of the yoke of the Law laid on their necks. And with a view to this new Law, which God would give to his world through the Messiah, the Rabbis divided all time into three periods: the primitive, that under the Law, and that of the Messiah.[3]

It only remains briefly to describe the beatitude of Israel, both physical and moral, in those days, the state of the nations, and, lastly, the end of that 'age' and its merging into 'the world to come' (*Olam habba*). Morally, this would be a period of holiness, of forgiveness, and of peace. Without, there would be no longer enemies nor oppressors. And within the City and Land a more than Paradisiacal state would prevail, which is depicted in even more than the usual realistic Eastern language. For that vast new Jerusalem (not in heaven, but in the literal Palestine) Angels were to cut gems 45 feet long and broad (30 cubits), and place them in its gates; [a] the windows and gates were to be of precious stones, the walls of silver, gold, and gems, while all kinds of jewels would be strewed about, of which every Israelite was at liberty to take. Jerusalem would be as large as, at present, all Palestine, and Palestine as all the world.[b] Corresponding to this miraculous extension would be a miraculous elevation of Jerusalem into the air.[c] And it is one of the strangest mixtures of self-righteousness and realism with deeper and more spiritual thoughts, when the Rabbis prove by references to the prophetic Scriptures, that every event and miracle in the history of Israel would find its counterpart, or rather larger fulfilment, in Messianic days. Thus, what was recorded of Abraham [d] would, on account of his merit, find, clause by clause, its counterpart in the future: 'Let a little water be fetched,' in what is predicted in Zech. xiv. 8; 'wash your feet,' in what is predicted in Is. iv. 5; 'rest yourselves under the tree,' in what is said in Is. iv. 4; and 'I will fetch a morsel of bread,' in the promise of Ps. lxxii. 16.[e]

ᵃ Babha B 75 a

ᵇ Yalkut ii. p. 57 b, par. 363, line 3

ᶜ Babha B. 75 b

ᵈ Gen. xviii. 4, 5

ᵉ Ber. R. 48

[1] Vayyik. R. 9, 27; Midr. on Ps. lvi.; c.   [3] Yalkut on Is. xxvi.; Sanh. 97 a; Ab.
[2] Midr. on Ps. cxlvi.; Vayy. R. 13;   Z. 9 a.
Tanch., Shemini 7 and 8.

But by the side of this we find much coarse realism. The land
would spontaneously produce the best dresses and the finest cakes;[a]
the wheat would grow as high as palm-trees, nay, as the mountains,
while the wind would miraculously convert the grain into flour, and
cast it into the valleys. Every tree would become fruit-bearing;[b]
nay, they were to break forth, and to bear fruit every day;[c] daily
was every woman to bear child, so that ultimately every Israelitish
family would number as many as all Israel at the time of the Exodus.[d]
All sickness and disease, and all that could hurt, would pass away.
As regarded death, the promise of its final abolition[e] was, with
characteristic ingenuity, applied to Israel, while the statement that
the child should die an hundred years old[f] was understood as referring to the Gentiles, and as teaching that, although they would
die, yet their age would be greatly prolonged, so that a centenarian
would be regarded as only a child. Lastly, such physical and outward loss as Rabbinism regarded as the consequence of the Fall,[g]
would be again restored to man.[h][1]

It would be easy to multiply quotations even more realistic than
these, if such could serve any good purpose. The same literalism
prevails in regard to the reign of King Messiah over the nations of
the world. Not only is the figurative language of the prophets
applied in the most external manner, but illustrative details of the
same character are added. Jerusalem would, as the residence of the
Messiah, become the capital of the world, and Israel take the place
of the (fourth) world-monarchy, the Roman Empire. After the
Roman Empire none other was to rise, for it was to be immediately
followed by the reign of Messiah.[i] But that day, or rather that
of the fall of the (ten) Gentile nations, which would inaugurate the
Empire of Messiah, was among the seven things unknown to man.[k]
Nay, God had conjured Israel not to communicate to the Gentiles
the mystery of the calculation of the times.[m] But the very origin of
the wicked world-Empire had been caused by Israel's sin. It had
been (ideally) founded[2] when Solomon contracted alliance with the
daughter of Pharaoh, while Romulus and Remus rose when Jeroboam
set up the worship of the two calves. Thus, what would have
become the universal Davidic Rule had, through Israel's sin, been
changed into subjection to the Gentiles. Whether or not these

CHAP.
VI

[a] Shabb. 30
b
[b] Kethub.
111 b
[c] Shabb. 30
a, b
[d] Midr. on
Ps. xlv.
[e] Is. xxv. 8
[f] Is. lxv. 20
[g] Ber. R. 12
[h] Bemidb.
R. 13
[i] Vayyik. R.
13, end
[k] Ber. R.
65
[m] Kethub.
111 a

[1] They are the following six: His
splendour, the continuance of life, his
original more than gigantic stature, the
fruits of the ground, and of trees, and the
brightness of the heavenly lights.

[2] On that day Gabriel had descended,
cut a reed from the ocean, and planted it
in mud from the sea, and on this the city
of Rome was founded (Siphré 86 a).

BOOK
V

ᵃ Ab. Z. 24 a
ᵇ Ab. Z. 3 b;
Yeb. 24 b

Gentiles would in the Messianic future become proselytes, seems a
moot question. Sometimes it is affirmed;ᵃ at others it is stated
that no proselytes would then be received,ᵇ and for this good reason,
that in the final war and rebellion those proselytes would, from fear,
cast off the yoke of Judaism and join the enemies.

That war, which seems a continuation of that of Gog and Magog,
would close the Messianic era. The nations, who had hitherto given
tribute to Messiah, would rebel against Him, when He would destroy
them by the breath of His mouth, so that Israel alone would be left

ᶜ Tanch.,
ed. Warsh
ii. p. 115 a,
top

on the face of the earth.ᶜ The duration of that period of rebellion is
stated to be seven years. It seems, at least, a doubtful point, whether
a second or general Resurrection was expected, the more probable
view being, that there was only one Resurrection, and that of Israel

ᵈ Taan, 7 a
ᵉ Kethub.
111 b

alone,ᵈ or, at any rate, only of the studious and the pious,ᵉ and
that this was to take place at the beginning of the Messianic reign.
If the Gentiles rose at all, it would only be immediately again to

ᶠ Pirké d.
R. Eliez. 34

die.ᶠ[1]

Then the final Judgment would commence. We must here once
more make distinction between Israel and the Gentiles, with whom,
nay, as more punishable than they, certain notorious sinners, heretics,
and all apostates, were to be ranked. Whereas to Israel the Gehenna,
to which all but the perfectly righteous had been consigned at death,
had proved a kind of purgatory, from which they were all ultimately

Erub. 19 a

delivered by Abraham,ᵍ or, according to some of the later Midrashim,
by the Messiah, no such deliverance was in prospect for the heathen

ʰ As to the
latter, a
solitary
opinion,
in Moed K.
27 a

nor for sinners of Israel.ʰ The question whether the fiery torments
suffered (which are very realistically described) would at last end in
annihilation, is one which at different times received different answers,
as fully explained in another place.[2] At the time of Christ the
punishment of the wicked was certainly regarded as of eternal duration. Rabbi José, a teacher of the second century, and a representative of the more rationalistic school, says expressly, ' The fire of

ᶦPes. 54 a

Gehinnom is never quenched.' And even the passage, so often
(although only partially) quoted, to the effect, that the final torments of Gehenna would last for twelve months, after which body
and soul would be annihilated, excepts from this a number of Jewish
sinners, specially mentioned, such as hereties, Epicureans, apostates,
and persecutors, who are designated as ' children of Gehenna '

---

[1] It is, of course, not denied, that
individual voices would have assigned
part in the world to come to the pious
from among the Gentiles. But even so,
what is the *precise* import of this
admission?

[2] See Appendix XIX.

(ledorey doroth, to ' ages of ages ').[a] And with this other statements agree,[b] so that at most it would follow that, while annihilation would await the less guilty, the most guilty were to be reserved for eternal punishment.

Such, then, was the final Judgment, to be held in the valley of Jehoshaphat by God, at the head of the Heavenly Sanhedrin, composed of the elders of Israel.[c] Realistic as its description is, even this is terribly surpassed by a passage[d] in which the supposed pleas for mercy by the various nations are adduced and refuted, when, after an unseemly contention between God and the Gentiles—equally shocking to good taste and blasphemous—about the partiality that had been shown to Israel, the Gentiles would be consigned to punishment. All this in a manner revolting to all reverent feeling. And the contrast between the Jewish picture of the last Judgment and that outlined in the Gospel is so striking, as alone to vindicate (were such necessary) the eschatological parts of the New Testament, and to prove what infinite distance there is between the Teaching of Christ and the Theology of the Synagogue.

After the final judgment we must look for the renewal of heaven and earth. In the latter neither physical[e] nor moral darkness would any longer prevail, since the *Yetser haRa,* or ' Evil impulse,' would be destroyed.[f][1] And renewed earth would bring forth all without blemish and in Paradisiacal perfection, while alike physical and moral evil had ceased. Then began the ' *Olam habba,*' or ' world to come.' The question, whether any functions or enjoyments of the body would continue, is variously answered. The reply of the Lord to the question of the Sadducees about marriage in the other world seems to imply, that materialistic views on the subject were entertained at the time. Many Rabbinic passages, such as about the great feast upon Leviathan and Behemoth prepared for the righteous in the latter days,[g] confirm only too painfully the impression of grossly materialistic expectations.[2] On the other hand, passages may be

CHAP.
VI

[a] Rosh haSh. 17 a
[b] Sanh. x.3; 106 b
[c] Tanch. u. s. i. p. 71 a, b
[d] Ab. Z. 2 a to 3
[e] Ber. R. 91
[f] Yalkut 1. p. 45 c.
[g] Babha B. 74 b

[1] But it does not seem clear to me, whether this conjunction of the cessation of darkness, together with that of the *Yetser haRa,* is not intended to be taken figuratively and spiritually.

[2] At the same time, many quotations by Christian writers intended to show the materialism of Jewish views are grossly unfair. Thus, for example, Ber. 57 *b,* quoted by *Weber* (Altsynag. Theol. p. 384), certainly does *not* express the grossly carnal expectancy imputed to it. On the other hand, it is certainly grossly materialistic, when we read how the skin of slaughtered Leviathan is to be made into tents, girdles, necklets, or armlets for the blessed, according to their varying merits (Babha B. 75 *a*). Altogether the account of the nature and hunt of this Leviathan, of the feast held, the various dishes served (Babha B. 74 *b* to 75 *b*), and the wine drunk on the occasion (Targ. Pseudo-Jon. on Gen. xxvii. 25; Targ. on Cant. viii. 2; on Eccles. ix. 7), are too coarsely materialistic for quotation. But what a contrast to the

BOOK
V

ª Yalkut,
vol. i. p.
32 d. and
especially
Ber. 17 a

quoted in which the utterly unmaterial character of the 'world to come' is insisted upon in most emphatic language.ª In truth, the same fundamental divergences here exist as on other points, such as the abode of the beatified, the visible or else invisible glory which they would enjoy, and even the new Jerusalem. And in regard to the latter,[1] as indeed to all those references to the beatitudes of the world to come, it seems at least doubtful, whether the Rabbis may not have intended to describe rather the Messianic days than the final winding up of all things.

To complete this sketch of Jewish opinions, it is necessary, however briefly, to refer to the Pseudepigraphic Writings,[2] which, as will be remembered, expressed the Apocalyptic expectancies of the Jews before the time of Christ. But here we have always to keep in mind this twofold difficulty: that the language used in works of this kind is of a highly figurative character, and must therefore not be literally pressed; and that more than one of them, notably IV. Esdras, dates from post-Christian times, and was, in important respects, admittedly influenced by Christian teaching. But in the main the picture of Messianic times in these writings is the same as that presented by the Rabbis. Briefly, the Pseudepigraphic view may be thus sketched.[3] Of the so-called ' *Wars of the Messiah* ' there had been already a kind of prefigurement in the days of Antiochus Epiphanes, when armed

ᵇ 2 Macc. v. 2, 3.
ᶜ Or, Sibyll. iii. 795–806

soldiery had been seen to carry on warfare in the air.ᵇ This sign is mentioned in the Sibylline Booksᶜ as marking the coming end, together with the sight of swords in the starlit sky at night, the falling of dust from heaven, the extinction of the sunlight and the appearance of the moon by day, and the dropping of blood from the rocks. A somewhat similar, though even more realistic, picture is presented in

ᵈ IV. Esdr. v. 1–12

connection with the blast of the third trumpet in IV. (II.) Esdras.ᵈ Only that there the element of moral judgment is more clearly introduced. This appears still more fully in another passage of the

ᵉ vi. 18–28

same book,ᵉ in which, apparently in connection with the Judgment, the influence of Christian teaching, although in an externalised form, may be clearly traced. A perhaps even more detailed description of

---

description of the 'Last Things' by our Lord and His Apostles! This alone would furnish sufficient presumptive evidence in favour of the New Testament. I have tried to touch this very painful matter as delicately as I could, rather by allusions than by descriptions, which could only raise prejudices.

[1] This is the Jerusalem built of sapphire, which is to descend from heaven, and in the central sanctuary of which (unlike the worship of the Book of Revelation) Aaron is to officiate and to receive the priestly gifts (Taan. 5 a; Baba B. 75 b).

[2] See Appendix.

[3] Comp. generally *Schürer*, Neutest. Zeitgesch. pp. 579, &c.

the wickedness, distress, and physical desolation upon earth at that time, is given in the Book of Jubilees.[a]

At last, when these distresses have reached their final height, when signs are in the sky, ruin upon earth, and the unburied bodies that cover the ground are devoured by birds and wild beasts, or else swallowed up by the earth,[b] would God send 'the King,' Who would put an end to unrighteousness. Then would follow the last war against Jerusalem, in which God would fight from heaven with the nations, when they would submit to, and own Him.[c] But while in the Book of Enoch and in another work of the same class[d] the judgment is ascribed to God, and the Messiah represented as appearing only afterwards,[e][1] in the majority of these works the judgment or its execution is assigned to the Messiah.[f]

In the land thus restored to Israel, and under the rule of King Messiah, the new Jerusalem would be the capital, purified from the heathen,[g] enlarged, nay, quite transformed. This Jerusalem had been shown to Adam before his Fall,[2] but after that both it and Paradise had been withdrawn from him. It had again been shown to Abraham,[h] to Moses, and to Ezra.[i] The splendour of this new Jerusalem is described in most glowing language.[k][3] Of the glorious Kingdom thus instituted, the Messiah would be King,[m][4] although under the supremacy of God. His reign would extend over the heathen nations. The character of their submission was differently viewed, according to the more or less Judaic standpoint of the writers. Thus, in the Book of Jubilees[n] the seed of Jacob are promised possession of the whole earth; they would 'rule over all nations according to their pleasure; and after that draw the whole earth unto themselves, and inherit it for ever.' In the 'Assumption of Moses'[o] this ascendency of Israel seems to be conjoined with the idea of vengeance upon Rome,[5] although the language employed is highly figurative.[p] On the other hand, in the Sibylline Books[q] the nations are represented as, in view of the blessings enjoyed by Israel, themselves turning to acknowledge God, when perfect mental enlightenment and absolute righteousness, as well as physical well-being, would prevail under the rule and

CHAP.
VI

[a] Book of Jubilees xxiii.
[b] Orac. Sibyll. iii. 633–652
[c] u. s. 653–697; comp. the figurative acc't in the Book of Enoch xc. 16, and following
[d] Assumpt. Mos. x. 2–10
[e] Book of Enoch xc.37
[f] Or. Sibyll. iii. 652–656; Book of Enoch, u. s. : comp. ch. xlv. 3–6; xlvi.; lv. 4; lxi. 8, 9, 11, 12; lxii.; lxix. 27–29; Apoc. of Bar. xxxix. 7, 8; xl.; lxx.9;lxxii. 2, end; IV. (II.) Esdras xii. 32–34; xiii. 25–30, 34–38
[g] Psalter of Sol. xvii. 25, 33
[h] Apoc. of Baruch iv. 3–6
[i] IV. Esdr. x. 44 &c.
[k] Tob. xiii. 16–18; xiv. 5; Book of Enoch liii. 6, 7; xc. 28; Apoc. of Baruch xxxii. 4
[m] Orac. Sibyll. iii. 47–50; and especially Psalter of Solomon xvii., particularly vv. 23 &c., 32, 35, 38, 47
[n] Bk. of Jub. xxxii.
[o] Or. Sibyll. x. 8
[p] Comp.ver. 9
[q] Ass. Mos. iii. 715–726

---

[1] In the *Assumptio Mosis* there is no reference at all to the Messiah.

[2] The words do not convey to me, as apparently to Dr. *Schürer*, that the New Jerusalem actually stood in Eden, and, indeed, existed otherwise than ideally.

[3] But I do not see, with *Schürer*, a reference to its coming down from heaven, not even in the passage in Baruch to which he refers, which is as follows: 'Et postea oportet renovari in gloria, et coronabitur in perpetuum.'

[4] I cannot understand how *Schürer* can throw doubt upon this, in view of such plain statements as in Ps. of Sol. xvii., such as (in regard to the Messiah): καὶ αὐτὸς βασιλεὺς δίκαιος διδακτὸς ὑπὸ Θεοῦ ἐπ' αὐτούς.

[5] 'Et ascendes supra cervices et alas aquilæ.'

BOOK
V

^a u. s. 766. 783

judgeship (whether literal or figurative) of the Prophets.^a The most 'Grecian' view of the Kingdom, is, of course, that expressed by Philo. He anticipates, that the happy moral condition of man would ultimately affect the wild beasts, which, relinquishing their solitary habits, would first become gregarious; then, imitating the domestic animals, gradually come to respect man as their master, nay, become as affectionate and cheerful as 'Maltese dogs.' Among men, the pious and virtuous would bear rule, their dignity inspiring respect, their

^b De Præm. et Pœn. ed. Mang. ii. 422–424; ed. Fref. 923–925

terror fear, and their beneficence good will.^b Probably intermediate between this extreme Grecian and the Judaic conception of the Millennium, are such utterances as ascribe the universal acknowledgment of the Messiah to the recognition, that God had invested Him with glory and power, and that His Reign was that of

^c Book of Enoch xlviii. 4, 5; xc. 37; Ps. of Sol. xvii. 34, 35, 38–40

blessing.^c

It must have been remarked, that the differences between the Apocalyptic teaching of the Pseudepigrapha and that of the New Testament are as marked as those between the latter and that of the Rabbis. Another point of divergence is, that the Pseudepigrapha uniformly represent the Messianic reign as eternal, not broken up by

^d Book of Enoch xlv. 4, 5

any further apostasy or rebellion.[1] Then would the earth be renewed,^d[2] and this would be followed, lastly, by the Resurrection. In the

^e Ap. Bar. 1, 2, 3

Apocalypse of Baruch,^e as by the Rabbis, it is set forth that men would rise in exactly the same condition which they had borne in life, so that, by being recognised, the reality of the Resurrection would be attested, while in the re-union of body and soul each would receive its due meed for the sins committed in their state of combination while

^f Sanh. 91 a and b

upon earth.^f But after that a transformation would take place: of the just into the Angelic splendour of their glory, while, on view of

^g u. s. ll. 1–6

this, the wicked would correspondingly fade away.^g Josephus states

^h Ant. xviii. 1, 3; War ii. 8, 14

that the Pharisees taught only a Resurrection of the Just.^h As we know that such was *not* the case, we must regard this as one of the

---

[1] This is expressed in the clearest language in every one of these books. In view of this, to maintain the opposite on the ground of these isolated words in Baruch (xl. 3): 'Et erit principatus ejus stans in sæculum, donec finiatur mundus corruptionis,' seems, to say the least, a strange contention, especially when we read in lxxiii. 1.: 'Sederit in pace in æternum super throno regni sui.' We can quite understand that *Gfrörer* should propound this view in order to prove that the teaching of the New Testament is only a reflection of that of later Juda-

ism; but should an argument so untenable be repeated? IV. Esdras must not here be quoted, as admittedly containing New Testament elements.

[2] Dr. *Schürer*, following in this also *Gfrörer*, holds that one party placed the renewal of the earth after the close of the Messianic reign. He quotes in support only Bar. lxxiv. 2, 3; but the words do not convey to me that inference. For the reason stated in the preceding Note, IV. Esdras cannot here serve as authority.

many assertions made by that writer for purposes of his own—probably to present to outsiders the Pharisaic doctrine in the most attractive and rational light of which it was capable. Similarly, the modern contention, that some of the Pseudepigraphic Writings propound the same view of only a Resurrection of the Just,[1] is contrary to evidence.[2] There can be no question that, according to the Pseudepigrapha, in the general Judgment, which was to follow the universal Resurrection, the reward and punishment assigned are represented as of eternal duration, although it may be open to question, as in regard to Rabbinic teaching, which of those who had been sinners would suffer final and endless torment.

The many and persistent attempts, despite the gross inconsistencies involved, to represent the teaching of Christ concerning 'the Last Things' as only the reflection of contemporary Jewish opinion, have rendered detailed evidence necessary. When, with the information just summarised, we again turn to the questions addressed to Him by the disciples, we recall that (as previously shown) they could not have conjoined, or rather confounded, the 'when' of 'these things'—that is, of the destruction of Jerusalem and the Temple—with the 'when' of His Second Coming and the end of the 'Age.' We also recall the suggestion, that Christ referred to His Advent, as to His disappearance, from the Jewish standpoint of Jewish, rather than from the general cosmic view-point of universal, history.

As regards the answer of the Lord to the two questions of His disciples, it may be said that the first part of His Discourse [a] is intended to supply information on the two facts of the future: the destruction of the Temple, and His Second Advent and the end of the 'Age,' by setting before them the signs indicating the approach or beginning of these events. But even here the exact period of each is not defined, and the teaching given intended for purely *practical* purposes. In the second part of His Discourse [b] the Lord distinctly tells them, what they are *not* to know, and why; and how all that was communicated to them was only to prepare them for that constant watchfulness, which has been to the Church at all times the proper outcome of Christ's teaching on the subject. This, then, we

[a] St. Matt. xxiv. 4–35, and parallels

[b] St. Matt. xxiv. 36 to end, and parallels

---

[1] In support of it *Schürer* quotes Ps. of Sol. iii. 16, xiv. 2, &c. But these passages convey to me, and will, I think, to others, the very opposite. Ps. iii. 16 says nothing of the wicked, only of the righteous. But in ver. 13 *b* we have it: ἡ ἀπώλεια τοῦ ἁμαρτωλοῦ εἰς τὸν αἰῶνα, and in ver. 15, αὕτη μερὶς τῶν ἁμαρτωλῶν εἰς τὸν αἰῶνα. Ps. xiv. 2 has again only reference to the righteous, but in ver. 6 we have this plain statement, which renders any doubt impossible, διὰ τοῦτο ἡ κληρονομία αὐτων ἅδης καὶ σκότος καὶ ἀπώλεια.

[2] Comp. Book of Enoch and Apoc. of Bar.

BOOK
V
ᵃ vv. 4–35
ᵇ vv. 4–8; 9–
14; 15–28;
29–35
ᶜ St. Matt.
xxiv. 8; St.
Mark xiii.
8
ᵈ St. Matt.
xxiv. 6

may take as a guide in our study: that the words of Christ contain nothing beyond what was necessary for the warning and teaching of the disciples and of the Church.

The *first* Part of Christ's Discourse ᵃ consists of four Sections,ᵇ of which the first describes 'the beginning of the birth-woes' ᶜ [1] of the new 'Age' about to appear. The expression: 'The End is not yet' ᵈ clearly indicates, that it marks only the earliest period of the beginning—the farthest *terminus a quo* of the 'birth-woes.' [2] Another general consideration, which seems of importance, is, that the Synoptic Gospels report this part of the Lord's Discourse in almost identical language. If the inference from this seems that their accounts were derived from a common source—say, the report of St. Peter—yet this close and unvarying repetition also conveys an impression, that the Evangelists themselves may not have fully understood the meaning of what they recorded. This may account for the rapid and unconnected transitions from subject to subject. At the same time it imposes on us the duty of studying the language anew, and without regard to any scheme of interpretation. This only may be said, that the obvious difficulties of negative criticism are here equally great, whether we suppose the narratives to have been written before or after the destruction of Jerusalem.

ᵉ ver 4

1. The purely practical character of the Discourse appears from its opening words.ᵉ They contain a warning, addressed to the disciples in their individual, not in their corporate, capacity, against being 'led astray.' This, more particularly in regard to Judaic seductions leading them after false Christs. Though in the multitude of impostors, who, in the troubled times between the rule of Pilate and the destruction of Jerusalem, promised Messianic deliverance to Israel, few names and claims of this kind have been specially recorded, yet the hints in the New Testament,ᶠ and the references, however guarded, by the Jewish historian,ᵍ imply the appearance of many such seducers. And their influence, not only upon Jews, but on Jewish Christians, might be the more dangerous, that the latter would naturally regard 'the woes,' which were the occasion of their pretensions, as the judgments which would usher in the Advent of their Lord. Against such seduction they must be peculiarly on their

ᶠ Acts v. 36;
viii. 9; xxi.
38
ᵍ War ii. 13,
4, 5; Ant.
xx. 5, 1; 8,
10

---

[1] ἀρχὴ ὠδίνων, St. Matt. xxiv. 8, and so according to the better reading also in St. Mark.

[2] Generally, indeed, these are regarded as 'the birth-woes' of 'the end.' But this not only implies a logical impossibility (the birth-woes of the end), but it must be remembered that these 'travail-pains' are the judgments on Jerusalem, or else on the world, which are to usher in the new—to precede its birth.

guard.   So far for the 'things' connected with the destruction of   CHAP.
Jerusalem and the overthrow of the Jewish commonwealth.   But,   VI
taking a wider and cosmic view, they might also be misled by either
rumours of war at a distance, or by actual warfare,[1] so as to believe
that the dissolution of the Roman Empire, and with it the Advent
of Christ, was at hand.[a][2]   This also would be a misapprehension,   a St. Matt.
grievously misleading, and to be carefully guarded against.   xxiv. 6-8

Although primarily applying to them, yet alike the peculiarly
Judaic, or, it might be even Christian, and the general cosmic
sources of misapprehension as to the near Advent of Christ, must
not be limited to the times of the Apostles.   They rather indicate
these twofold grounds of misapprehension which in all ages have
misled Christians into an erroneous expectancy of the immediate
Advent of Christ: the seductions of false Messiahs, or, it may be,
teachers, and violent disturbances in the political world.   So far as
Israel was concerned, these attained their climax in the great rebellion against Rome under the false Messiah, Bar Kokhba, in the time
of Hadrian,[b] although echoes of similar false claims, or hope of them,   b A.D.
have again and again roused Israel during the night of these many   132-135
centuries into brief, startled waking.   And, as regards the more
general cosmic signs, have not Christians in the early ages watched,
not only the wars on the boundaries of the Empire, but the condition
of the state in the age of Nero, the risings, turmoils, and threaten-
ings; and so onwards, those of later generations, even down to the
commotions of our own period, as if they betokened the immediate
Advent of Christ, instead of marking in them only the beginning of
the birth-woes of the new 'Age'?

2. From the warning to Christians as *individuals*, the Lord next
turns to give admonition to the *Church* in her corporate capacity.
Here we mark, that the events now described[c] must not be regarded   c St. Matt.
as following, with strict chronological precision, those referred to in   xxiv. 9-14,
the previous verses.   Rather is it intended to indicate a general *nexus*   lels
with them, so that these events begin partly before, partly during,
and partly after, those formerly predicted.   They form, in fact, the
continuation of the 'birth-woes.'   This appears even from the
language used.   Thus, while St. Matthew writes: 'Then' ($\tau\acute{o}\tau\varepsilon$, at
that time) 'shall they deliver you up,' St. Luke places the persecu-

---

[1] Of such wars and rumours of wars
not only *Josephus*, but the Roman historians, have much to say about that
time.   See the Commentaries.

[2] We know how persistently Nero has

been identified with Anti-Christ, and
how the Church then expected the immediate return of Christ; nay, in all ages,
'the End' has been associated with
troubles in 'the Roman Empire.'

BOOK
V

ᵃ St. Luke
xxi. 12
ᵇ St. Mark
xiii. 9
ᶜ St. Matt.
xxiv. 9-14,
and
parallels
ᵈ St. Matt.
xxiv. 10-13

tions 'before all these things;'ᵃ while St. Mark, who reports this part of the Discourse most fully, omits every note of time, and only emphasises the admonition which the fact conveys.ᵇ As regards the admonition itself, expressed in this part of the Lord's Discourse,ᶜ we notice that, as formerly to individuals, so now to the Church, two sources of danger are pointed out: *internal* from heresies ('false prophets') and the decay of faith,ᵈ and *external*, from persecutions, whether Judaic and from their own kindred, or from the secular powers throughout the world. But, along with these two dangers, two consoling facts are also pointed out. As regards the persecutions in prospect, full Divine aid is promised to Christians—alike to individuals and to the Church. Thus all care and fear may be dismissed: their testimony shall neither be silenced, nor shall the Church be suppressed or extinguished; but inward joyousness, outward perseverance, and final triumph, are secured by the Presence of the Risen Saviour with, and the felt indwelling of the Holy Ghost in His Church. And, as for the other and equally consoling fact: despite the persecution of Jews and Gentiles, before the End cometh 'this the Gospel of the Kingdom shall be preached in all the inhabited

ᵉ St. Matt.
xxiv. 14

earth for a testimony to all the nations.ᵉ This, then, is really the only sign of 'the End' of the present 'Age.'

3. From these general predictions, the Lord proceeds, in the

ᶠSt. Matt.
xxiv. 15-28,
and par-
allels; note
especially
the lan-
guage of
St. Luke
ᵍ St. Matt.
xxiv. 3

ʰ vv. 4, 5

third part of this Discourse,ᶠ to advertise the Disciples of the great historic fact immediately before them, and of the dangers which might spring from it. In truth, we have here His answer to their question, 'When shall these things be?'ᵍ not, indeed, as regards the *when*, but the *what* of them. And with this He conjoins the present application of His general warning regarding false Christs, given in the first part of this Discourse.ʰ The fact of which He now, in this third part of His Discourse, advertises them, is the destruction of Jerusalem. Its twofold dangers would be—outwardly, the difficulties and perils which at that time would necessarily beset men, and especially the members of the infant-Church; and, religiously, the pretensions and claims of false Christs or prophets at a period when all Jewish thinking and expectancy would lead men to anticipate the near Advent of the Messiah. There can be no question, that from both these dangers the warning of the Lord delivered the Church. As directed by him, the members of the Christian Church fled at an early period of the siege¹ of Jerusalem to Pella, while

---

¹ So *Eusebius* (Hist. Eccl. iii. 5) relates that the Christians of Judæa fled to Pella, on the northern boundary of

Peræa, in 68 A.D. Comp. also *Jos.* War iv. 9. 1, v 10. 1.

the words in which He had told that His Coming would not be in secret, but with the brightness of that lightning which shot across the sky, prevented not only their being deceived, but perhaps even the record, if not the rise of many who otherwise would have deceived them. As for Jerusalem, the prophetic vision initially fulfilled in the days of Antiochus^a would once more, and now fully, become reality, and the abomination of desolation [1] stand in the Holy Place. This, together with tribulation to Israel, unparalleled in the terrible past of its history, and unequalled even in its bloody future. Nay, so dreadful would be the persecution, that, if Divine mercy had not interposed for the sake of the followers of Christ, the whole Jewish race that inhabited the land would have been swept away.^b But on the morrow of that day no new Maccabee would arise, no Christ come, as Israel fondly hoped; but over that carcase would the vultures gather;^c and so through all the Age of the Gentiles, till converted Israel should raise the welcoming shout: 'Blessed be He that cometh in the Name of the Lord!'

4. ^dThe Age of the Gentiles, 'the end of the Age,' and with it the new allegiance of His now penitent people Israel; 'the sign of the Son of Man in heaven,' perceived by them; the conversion of all the world, the Coming of Christ, the last Trumpet, the Resurrection of the dead—such, in most rapid sketch, is the outline which the Lord draws of His Coming and the End of the world.

It will be remembered that this had been the second question of the disciples.^e We again recall, that the disciples did not, indeed, could not have connected, as immediately subsequent events, the destruction of Jerusalem and His Second Coming, since he had expressly placed between them the period—apparently protracted—of His Absence,^f with the many events that were to happen in it—notably, the preaching of the Gospel over the whole inhabited earth.^g Hitherto the Lord had, in His Discourse, dwelt in detail only on those events which would be fulfilled before this generation should pass.^h It had been for admonition and warning that He had spoken, not for the gratification of curiosity. It had been prediction of the immediate future for practical purposes, with such dim and general indication of the more distant future of the Church as was absolutely necessary to

Marginal references:
CHAP. VI

^a 2 Macc. vi. 1-9

^b St. Matt. xxiv. 22

^c ver. 28

^d vv. 29-31

^e St. Matt. xxiv. 3

^f xxiii. 38, 39

^g xxiv. 14

^h ver. 34

---

[1] The quotation from Dan. ix. 27 is neither a literal translation of the original, nor a reproduction of the LXX. The former would be: 'And upon the wing [or corner] of the abominations the destroyer.' Our Lord takes the well-known Biblical expression in the general sense in which the Jews took it, that the heathen power (Rome, the abominable) would bring desolation—lay the city and Temple waste.

mark her position in the world as one of persecution, with promise, however, of His Presence and Help; with indication also of her work in the world, to its *terminus ad quem*—the preaching of the Gospel of the Kingdom to all nations on earth.

More than this concerning the future of the Church could not have been told without defeating the very object of the admonition and warning which Christ had exclusively in view, when answering the question of the disciples. Accordingly, what follows in ver. 29, describes the history, not of the Church—far less any visible physical signs in the literal heavens—but, in prophetic imagery, the history of the hostile powers of the world, with its lessons. A constant succession of empires and dynasties would characterise politically—and it is only the political aspect with which we are here concerned —the whole period after the extinction of the Jewish State.ᵃ Immediately after that would follow the appearance to Israel of the 'Sign' of the Son of Man in heaven, and with it the conversion of all nations (as previously predicted),ᵇ the Coming of Christ,ᶜ and, finally, the blast of the last Trumpet and the Resurrection.ᵈ

ᵃ St. Matt.
xxiv. 30

ᵇ ver 14
ᶜ ver. 30
ᵈ ver. 31

5. From this rapid outline of the future the Lord once more turned to make present application to the disciples; nay, application, also, to all times. From the fig-tree, under which, on that spring-afternoon, they may have rested on the Mount of Olives, they were to learn a 'parable.'ᵉ We can picture Christ taking one of its twigs, just as its softening tips were bursting into young leaf. Surely, this meant that summer was nigh—not that it had actually come. The distinction is important. For, it seems to prove that 'all these things,' which were to indicate to them that it[1] was near, even at the doors, and which were to be fulfilled ere this generation had passed away, could not have referred to the last signs connected with the immediate Advent of Christ,ᶠ but must apply to the previous prediction of the destruction of Jerusalem and of the Jewish Commonwealth. At the same time we again admit, that the language of the Synoptists seems to indicate, that they had not clearly understood the words of the Lord which they reported, and that in their own minds they had associated the 'last signs' and the Advent of Christ with the fall of the City. Thus may they have come to expect that Blessed Advent even in their own days.

ᵉ vv. 32, 33

ᶠ vv. 29-31

II. It is at least a question, whether the Lord, while distinctly

---

[1] Not as in the R.V. 'He.' It can scarcely be supposed that Christ would speak of Himself in the third person. The subject is evidently 'the summer' (not as *Meyer* would render θέρος= 'harvest'). In St. Luke xxi. 31 it is paraphrased 'the Kingdom of God.'

indicating these facts, had intended to remove the doubt and uncertainty of their succession from the minds of His disciples. To have done so would have necessitated that which, in the opening sentence of the Second Division of this Discourse,[a] He had expressly declared to lie beyond their ken. The ' *when* '—the day and the hour of His Coming—was to remain hidden from men and Angels.[b] Nay, even the Son Himself—as they viewed Him and as He spake to them —knew it not.[1] It formed no part of His present Messianic Mission, nor subject for His Messianic Teaching. Had it done so, all the teaching that follows concerning the need of constant watchfulness, and the pressing duty of working for Christ in faith, hope, and love— with purity, self-denial, and endurance—would have been lost. The peculiar attitude of the Church: with loins girt for work, since the time was short, and the Lord might come at any moment; with her hands busy; her mind faithful; her bearing self-denying and devoted; her heart full of loving expectancy; her face upturned towards the Sun that was so soon to rise; and her ear straining to catch the first notes of heaven's song of triumph—all this would have been lost! What has sustained the Church during the night of sorrow these many centuries; what has nerved her with courage for the battle, with steadfastness to bear, with love to work, with patience and joy in disappointments—would all have been lost! The Church would not have been that of the New Testament, had she known the mystery of that day and hour, and not ever waited as for the immediate Coming of her Lord and Bridegroom.

And what the Church of the New Testament has been, and is, that her Lord and Master made her, and by no agency more effectually than by leaving undetermined the precise time of His return. To the world this would indeed become the occasion for utter carelessness and practical disbelief of the coming Judgment.[c] As in the days of Noah the long delay of threatened judgment had led to absorption in the ordinary engagements of life, to the entire disbelief of what Noah had preached, so would it be in the future. But that day would come certainly and unexpectedly, to the sudden separation of those who were engaged in the same daily business of life, of whom one might be taken up ($\pi\alpha\rho\alpha\lambda\alpha\mu\beta\acute{\alpha}\nu\epsilon\tau\alpha\iota$, ' received '), the other left to the destruction of the coming Judgment.[d]

But this very mixture of the Church with the world in the ordinary avocations of life indicated a great danger. As in all such,

CHAP.
VI

[a] St. Matt.
xxiv. 36 to end

[b] St. Matt.
xxiv. 36

[c] vv. 37-40

[d] vv. 40, 41

---

[1] The expression does not, of course, refer to Christ in His Divinity, but to the Christ, such as they saw Him, in His Messianic capacity and office.

BOOK
V

ᵃ vv. 42–51

ᵇ St. Matt.
xxiv. 43, 44

ᶜ ver. 45,
end

ᵈ ver. 42

ᵉ ver. 44

the remedy which the Lord would set before us is not negative in the avoidance of certain things, but positive.ᵃ We shall best succeed, not by going out of the world, but by being watchful in it, and keeping fresh on our hearts, as well as on our minds, the fact that He is our Lord, and that we are, and always most lovingly, to look and long for His Return. Otherwise twofold damage might come to us. Not expecting the arrival of the Lord in the night-time (which is the most unlikely for His Coming), we might go to sleep, and the Enemy, taking advantage of it, rob us of our peculiar treasure.ᵇ Thus the Church, not expecting her Lord, might become as poor as the world. This would be loss. But there might be even worse. According to the Master's appointment, each one had, during Christ's absence, his work for Him, and the reward of grace, or else the punishment of neglect, were in assured prospect. The faithful steward, to whom the Master had entrusted the care of His household, to supply His servants with what was needful for their support and work, would, if found faithful, be rewarded by advancement to far larger and more responsible work. On the other hand, belief in the delay of the Lord's Return would lead to neglect of the Master's work, to unfaithfulness, tyranny, self-indulgence and sin.ᶜ And when the Lord suddenly came, as certainly He would come, there would be not only loss, but damage, hurt, and the punishment awarded to the hypocrites. Hence, let the Church be ever on her watch,ᵈ let her ever be in readiness! ᵉ And how terribly the moral consequences of unreadiness, and the punishment threatened, have ensued, the history of the Church during these eighteen centuries has only too often and too sadly shown.[1]

---

[1] The Parable in St. Luke xii. 35–48 is so closely parallel to this, that it seems unnecessary to enter in detail upon its consideration.

CHAPTER VII.

EVENING OF THE THIRD DAY IN PASSION-WEEK—ON THE MOUNT OF
OLIVES—LAST PARABLES: TO THE DISCIPLES CONCERNING THE LAST
THINGS—THE PARABLE OF THE TEN VIRGINS—THE PARABLE OF THE
TALENTS—SUPPLEMENTARY PARABLE OF THE MINAS AND THE
KING'S RECKONING WITH HIS SERVANTS AND HIS REBELLIOUS
CITIZENS.

(St. Matt. xxv. 1–13; St. Matt. xxv. 14–30; St. Luke xix. 11–28.)

1. As might have been expected, the Parables concerning the Last
Things are closely connected with the Discourse of the Last Things,
which Christ had just spoken to His Disciples. In fact, that of the
Ten Virgins, which seems the fullest in many-sided meaning, is, in
its main object, only an illustration of the last part of Christ's Discourse.[a] Its great practical lessons had been: the unexpectedness
of the Lord's Coming; the consequences to be apprehended from its
delay; and the need of personal and constant preparedness. Similarly, the Parable of the Ten Virgins may, in its great outlines, be
thus summarised: Be ye personally prepared; be ye prepared for
any length of time; be ye prepared to go to Him directly.

Before proceeding, we mark that this Parable also is connected
with those that had preceded. But we notice not only connection,
but progression. Indeed, it would be deeply interesting, alike
historically and for the better understanding of Christ's teaching,
but especially as showing its internal unity and development, and
the credibility of the Gospel-narratives, generally to trace this connection and progress. And this, not merely in the three series of
Parables which mark the three stages of His History—the Parables
of the Founding of the Kingdom, of its Character, and of its Consummation—but as regards the Parables themselves, that so the
first might be joined to the last as a string of heavenly pearls. But
this lies beyond our task. Not so, to mark the connection between
the Parable of the Ten Virgins and that of the Man without the
Wedding-Garment.

Like the Parable of the Ten Virgins, it had pointed to the

CHAP.
VII

[a] St. Matt.
xxiv. 36–51

future. If the exclusion and punishment of the Unprepared Guest did not primarily refer to the Last Day, or to the Return of Christ, but perhaps rather to what would happen in death, it pointed, at least secondarily, to the final consummation. On the other hand, in the Parable of the Ten Virgins this final consummation is the primary point. So far, then, there is both connection and advance. Again, from the appearance and the fate of the Unprepared Guest we learned, that not every one who, following the Gospel-call, comes to the Gospel-feast, will be allowed to partake of it; but that God will search and try each one individually. There is, indeed, a society of guests—the Church; but we must not expect either that the Church will, while on earth, be wholly pure, or that its purification will be achieved by man. Each guest may, indeed, come to the banqueting-hall, but the final judgment as to his worthiness belongs to God. Lastly, the Parable also taught the no less important opposite lesson, that each individual is personally responsible; that we cannot shelter ourselves in the community of the Church, but that to partake of the feast requireth personal and individual preparation. To express it in modern terminology: It taught Churchism as against one-sided individualism, and spiritual individualism as against dead Churchism. All these important lessons are carried forward in the Parable of the Ten Virgins. If the union of the Ten Virgins for the purpose of meeting the Bridegroom, and their à priori claims to enter in with Him—which are, so to speak, the historical data and necessary premises in the Parable—point to the Church, the main lessons of the Parable are the need of individual, personal, and spiritual preparation. Only such will endure the trial of the long delay of Christ's Coming; only such will stand that of an immediate summons to meet the Christ.

It is late at even—the world's long day seems past, and the Coming of the Bridegroom must be near. The day and the hour we know not, for the Bridegroom has been far away. Only this we know, that it is the Evening of the Marriage which the Bridegroom had fixed, and that His word of promise may be relied upon. Therefore all has been made ready within the bridal house, and is in waiting there; and therefore the Virgins prepare to go forth to meet Him on His Arrival. The Parable proceeds on the assumption that the Bridegroom is not in the town, but somewhere far away; so that it cannot be known at what precise hour He may arrive. But it *is* known that He will come that night; and the Virgins who are to meet Him have gathered—presumably in the house where the

Marriage is to take place—waiting for the summons to go forth and
welcome the Bridegroom. The common mistake, that the Virgins
are represented in verse 1 as having gone forth *on the road* to meet
the Bridegroom, is not only irrational—since it is scarcely credible
that they would all have fallen asleep by the wayside, and with lamps
in their hands—but incompatible with the circumstance,[a] that at
midnight the cry is suddenly raised to go forth and meet Him. In
these circumstances, no precise parallel can be derived from the
ordinary Jewish marriage-processions, where the bridegroom, accompanied by his groomsmen and friends, went to the bride's house,
and thence conducted the bride, with her attendant maidens and
friends, into his own or his parents' home. But in the Parable, the
Bridegroom comes from a distance and goes to the bridal house.
Accordingly, the bridal procession is to meet Him on His Arrival,
and escort Him to the bridal place. No mention is made of the
Bride, either in this Parable or in that of the Marriage of the King's
Son. This, for reasons connected with their application: since in the
one case the Wedding Guests, in the other the Virgins, occupy the
place of the Bride. And here we must remind ourselves of the
general canon, that, in the interpretation of a Parable, details must
not be too closely pressed. The Parables illustrate the Sayings of
Christ, as the Miracles His Doings; and alike the Parables and the
Miracles present only one or another, not all the aspects of the
truth.

Another archæological inquiry will, perhaps, be more helpful to our
understanding of this Parable. The ' lamps '—not ' torches '—which
the Ten Virgins carried, were of well-known construction. They
bear in Talmudic writings commonly the name *Lappid*, but the
Aramaised form of the Greek word in the New Testament also occurs
as *Lampad* and *Lampadas*.[b] The lamps consisted of a round receptacle for pitch or oil for the wick. This was placed in a hollow
cup or deep saucer—the *Beth Shiqqua*[c]—which was fastened by a
pointed end into a long wooden pole, on which it was borne aloft.
According to Jewish authorities,[d] it was the custom in the East to
carry in a bridal procession about ten such lamps. We have the less
reason to doubt that such was also the case in Palestine, since, according to rubric, ten was the number required to be present at any
office or ceremony, such as at the benedictions accompanying the
marriage-ceremonies. And, in the peculiar circumstances supposed in
the Parable, Ten Virgins are represented as going forth to meet the
Bridegroom, each bearing her lamp.

a St. Matt.
xxv. 6

b Jer. Yoma
41 a, line 24
from top

c Kel. ii. 8

d See the
Arukh, ad
voc.

The first point which we mark is, that the Ten Virgins brought, presumably to the bridal house, 'their own [1] lamps.' Emphasis must be laid on this. Thus much was there of *personal* preparation on the part of all. But while the five that were wise brought also ' oil in the vessels ' [2] [presumably the hollow receptacles in which the lamp proper stood], the five foolish Virgins neglected to do so, no doubt expecting that their lamps would be filled out of some common stock in the house. In the text the foolish Virgins are mentioned before the wise, [3] because the Parable turns on this. We cannot be at a loss to interpret the meaning of it. The Bridegroom far away is Christ, Who is come for the Marriage-Feast from ' the far country'—the Home above—certainly on that night, but we know not at what hour of it. The ten appointed bridal companions who are to go forth to meet Him are His professed disciples, and they gather in the bridal house in readiness to welcome His arrival. It is night, and a marriage-procession: therefore, they must go forth with their lamps. All of them have brought their own lamps, they all have the Christian, or, say, the Church-profession: the lamp in the hollow cup on the top of the pole. But only the wise Virgins have more than this—the oil in the vessels, without which the lamps cannot give their light. The Christian or Church-profession is but an empty vessel on the top of a pole, without the oil in the vessels. We here remember the words of Christ: 'Let your light so shine before men, that they may see your good works, and glorify your Father Which is in heaven.' [a] The foolishness of the Virgins, which consisted in this that they had omitted to bring their oil, is thus indicated in the text: 'All they which [αἵτινες] [b] *were* foolish, when they brought their own lamps, brought not with them oil: ' they brought their own lamps, but not their own oil. This (as already explained), probably, not from forgetfulness—for they could scarcely have forgotten the need of oil, but from wilful neglect, in the belief that there would be a common stock in the house, out of which they would be supplied, or that there would be sufficient time for the supply of their need after the announcement that the Bridegroom was coming. They had no conception either of any personal obligation in this matter, nor that the call would come so suddenly, nor yet that there would be so little interval between the arrival of the Bridegroom

[a] St. Matt. v. 16

[b] quæ-cunque, eæ omnes quæ

---

[1] The better reading in ver. 1. and again in ver. 7, is not αὐτῶν 'their,' but ἑαυτῶν.

[2] The word αὐτῶν in ver. 4, ' *their* vessels,' is probably spurious. In both cases, as so often, the ' improving ' copy-ists have missed the deeper meaning.

[3] In ver. 2, according to the better reading, the clauses should be inverted, and, as in ver. 3, ' the foolish ' first mentioned.

and 'the closing of the door.' And so they deemed it not necessary to undertake what must have involved both trouble and carefulness— the bringing their own oil in the hollow vessels in which the lamps were fixed.

We have proceeded on the supposition that the oil was not carried in separate vessels, but in those attached to the lamps. It seems scarcely likely that these lamps had been lighted while waiting in the bridal house, where the Virgins assembled, and which, no doubt, was festively illuminated. Many practical objections to this view will readily occur. The foolishness of the five Virgins therefore consisted, *not* (as is commonly supposed) *in their want of perseverance*— as if the oil had been consumed before the Bridegroom came, and they had only not provided themselves with a sufficient extra-supply —but in *the entire absence of personal preparation*,[1] having brought no oil of their own in their lamps. This corresponds to their conduct, who, belonging to the Church—having the ' profession '—being bridal companions provided with lamps, ready to go forth, and expecting to share in the wedding feast—neglect the preparation of grace, personal conversation and holiness, trusting that in the hour of need the oil may be supplied out of the common stock. But they know not, or else heed not, that every one must be personally prepared for meeting the Bridegroom, that the call will be sudden, that the stock of oil is not common, and that the time between His arrival and the shutting of the door will be awfully brief.

For—and here begins the second scene in the Parable—the interval between the gathering of the Virgins in readiness to meet Him, and the arrival of the Bridegroom is much longer than had been anticipated. And so it came, that both the wise and the foolish Virgins ' slumbered and slept.' Manifestly, this is but a secondary trait in the Parable, chiefly intended to accentuate the surprise of the sudden announcement of the Bridegroom. The foolish Virgins did not ultimately fail because of their sleep, nor yet were the wise reproved for it. True, it was evidence of their weakness—but then it was night; all the world was asleep; and their own drowsiness might be in proportion to their former excitement. What follows is intended to bring into prominence the startling suddenness of the Bridegroom's Coming. It is midnight—when sleep is deepest— when suddenly 'there was a cry, Behold, the Bridegroom cometh! Come ye out to the meeting of Him. Then all those Virgins awoke,

---

[1] So especially *Goebel*, to whom, in general, we would acknowledge our obligations.

BOOK
V

and prepared (trimmed) their lamps.' This, not in the sense of heightening the low flame in their lamps, but in that of hastily drawing up the wick and lighting it, when, as there was no oil in the vessels, the flame, of course, immediately died out. 'Then the foolish said unto the wise, Give us of your oil; for our lamps are going out. But the wise answered, saying: Not at all [1]—it will never [2] suffice for us and you! Go ye rather to the sellers, and buy for your own selves.'

This advice must not be regarded as given in irony. This trait is introduced to point out the proper source of supply—to emphasise that the oil must be *their own*, and also to prepare for what follows. 'But while they were going to buy, the Bridegroom came; and the ready ones [they that were ready] went in with Him to the Marriage-Feast, and the door was shut.' The sudden cry at midnight: 'The Bridegroom cometh!' had come with startling surprise both to the wise and the foolish Virgins; to the one class it had come only unexpectedly, but to the other also unpreparedly. Their hope of sharing or borrowing the oil of the wise Virgins being disappointed, the foolish were, of course, unable to meet the Bridegroom. And while they hurried to the sellers of oil, those that had been ready not only met, but entered with the Bridegroom into the bridal house, and the door was shut. It is of no importance here, whether or not the foolish Virgins finally succeeded in obtaining oil—although this seems unlikely at that time of night—since it could no longer be of any possible use, as its object was to serve in the festive procession, which was now past. Nevertheless, and when the door was shut, those foolish Virgins came, calling on the Bridegroom to open to them. But they had failed in that which could alone give them a claim to admission. Professing to be bridesmaids, they had not been in the bridal procession, and so, in truth and righteousness, He could only answer from within: 'Verily I say unto you, I know you not.' This, not only in punishment, but in the right order of things.

The personal application of this Parable to the disciples, which the Lord makes, follows almost of necessity. 'Watch therefore, for ye know not the day, nor the hour.' [3] Not enough to be in waiting with the Church; His Coming will be far on in the night; it will be sudden; it will be rapid: be prepared therefore, be ever and personally prepared! Christ will come when least expected—at mid-

---

[1] Μήποτε. See *Grimm*, ad voc. But it is impossible to give the full force of the word.
[2] The better reading is οὐ μή, which double negation I have rendered, for

want of better, by 'never.'
[3] The clause 'in which the Son of Man cometh' is spurious—an early gloss crept into the text.

night—and when the Church, having become accustomed to His long delay, has gone to sleep.   So sudden will be His Coming, that after the cry of announcement there will not be time for anything but to go forth to meet Him; and so rapid will be the end, that, ere the foolish Virgins can return, the door has been for ever closed. To present all this in the most striking manner, the Parable takes the form of a dialogue, first between the foolish and the wise Virgins, in which the latter only state the bare truth when saying, that each has only sufficient oil for what is needed when joining the marriage-procession, and no one what is superfluous.   Lastly, we are to learn from the dialogue between the foolish Virgins and the Bridegroom, that it is impossible in the day of Christ's Coming to make up for neglect of previous preparation, and that those who have failed to meet Him, even though of the bridal Virgins, shall be finally ex-cluded as being strangers to the Bridegroom.

2. *The Parable of the Talents*—their use and misuse[a]—follows closely on the admonition to watch, in view of the sudden and certain Return of Christ, and the reward or punishment which will then be meted out.   Only that, whereas in the Parable of the Ten Virgins the reference was to the *personal state*, in that of 'the Talents' it is to the *personal work* of the Disciples.   In the former instance, they are por-trayed as the bridal maidens who are to welcome His Return; in the latter, as the servants who are to give an account of their stewardship.

[a] St. Matt.
xxv. 14-30

From its close connection with what precedes, the Parable opens almost abruptly with the words: ' For [it is] like a Man going abroad, [who]called His own servants, and delivered to them His goods.' The emphasis rests on this, that they were His own *servants*, and to act for His interest.   His property was handed over to them, not for safe custody, but that they might do with it as best they could in the interest of their Master.   This appears from what immediately follows: 'and so to one He gave five talents (about 1,170*l*.), but to one two (about 468*l*.), and to one one (=6,000 denarii, about 234*l*.), to each according to his own capability'[1]—that is, He gave to each according to his capacity, in proportion as He deemed them severally qualified for larger or smaller administration.   ' And He journeyed abroad straightway.'[2] Having entrusted the management of His affairs to His servants, according to their capacity, He at once went away.

---

[1] κατὰ τὴν ἰδίαν δύναμιν.
[2] Some critics and the R.V. have drawn the word 'straightway' to the next verse, as referring to the activity of the first servant.   The reasons urged by *Goebel* against this seem to me quite convincing, besides the fact that there is no cause for thus distinguishing the first from the second faithful servant.

Thus far we can have no difficulty in understanding the meaning of the Parable. Our Lord, Who has left us for the Father's Home, is He Who has gone on the journey abroad, and to His own servants has He entrusted, not for custody, but to use for Him in the time between His departure and His return, what He claims as His own ' goods.' We must not limit this to the administration of His Word, nor to the Holy Ministry, although these may have been pre-eminently in view. It refers generally to all that a man has, wherewith to serve Christ; for, all that the Christian has—his time, money, opportunities, talents, or learning (and not only ' the Word'), is Christ's, and is entrusted to us, not for custody, but to trade withal for the absent Master—to further the progress of His Kingdom. And to each of us He gives according to our capacity for working— mental, moral, and even physical—to one five, to another two, and to another one ' talent.' This capacity for work lies not within our own power; but it *is* in our power to use for Christ whatever we may have.

And here the characteristic difference appears. ' He that received the five talents went and traded with them, and made other five talents. In like manner he *that had received* the two gained [1] other two.' As each had received according to his ability, so each worked according to his power, as good and faithful servants of their Lord. If the outward result was different, their labour, devotion, and faith-fulness were equal. It was otherwise with him who had least to do for his Master, since only one talent had been entrusted to him. He ' went away, digged up earth, and hid the money of his Lord.' The prominent fact here is, that he did not employ it for the Master, as a good servant, but shunned alike the labour and the responsi-bility, and acted as if it had been some stranger's, and not his Lord's property. In so doing he was not only unfaithful to his trust, but practically disowned that he was a servant of his Lord. Accordingly, in contradistinction to the servant who had received much, two others are introduced in the Parable, who had both received com-paratively little—one of whom was faithful, while the other in idle selfishness hid the money, not heeding that it was ' his Lord's.' Thus, while the second servant, although less had been entrusted to him, was as faithful and conscientious as he to whom much had been given, and while both had, by their gain, increased the possessions of their Master, the third had by his conduct rendered the money of his Lord a dead, useless, buried thing.

---

[1] 'κέρδησεν—in the case of the first it was ἐποίησεν, although even there ἐκέρδησεν is probably the better reading.

And now the second scene opens. ' But after a long time cometh the Lord of those servants, and maketh reckoning [1] with them.' The notice of the long absence of the Master not only connects this with the Parable of the Ten Virgins, but is intended to show, that the delay might have rendered the servants who traded more careless, while it also increased the guilt of him, who all this time had not done anything with his Master's money. And now the first of the servants, without speaking of his labour in trading, or his merit in ' making ' money, answers with simple joyousness: ' Lord, five talents deliveredst Thou unto me. See, other five talents have I gained besides.' [2] We can almost see his honest face beaming with delight, as he points to his Master's increased possession. His approval was all that the faithful servant had looked for, for which he had toiled during that long absence. And we can understand, how the Master welcomed and owned that servant, and assigned to him meet reward. The latter was twofold. Having proved his faithfulness and capacity in a comparatively limited sphere, one much greater would be assigned to him. For, to do the work, and increase the wealth of his Master, had evidently been his joy and privilege, as well as his duty. Hence also the second part of his reward—that of entering into the joy of his Lord—must not be confined to sharing in the festive meal at His return, still less to advancement from the position of a servant to that of a friend who shares his Master's lordship. It implies far more than this: even satisfied heart-sympathy with the aims and gains of his Master, and participation in them, with all that this conveys.

A similar result followed on the reckoning with the servant to whom two talents had been entrusted. We mark that, although he could only speak of two talents gained, he met his Master with the same frank joyousness as he who had made five. For he had been as faithful, and laboured as earnestly as he to whom more had been entrusted. And, what is more important, the former difference between the two servants, dependent on greater or less capacity for work, now ceased, and the second servant received precisely the same welcome and exactly the same reward, and in the same terms, as the first. And a yet deeper, and in some sense mysterious, truth comes to us in connection with the words: ' Thou hast been faithful over a few things, I will set thee over many things.' Surely, then, if not after

---

[1] συναίρει λόγον, confert, vel componit, rem seu causam.
[2] ἐπ' αὐτοῖς should, I think, be retained in the text. It must at any rate be supplied.

death, yet in that other 'dispensation,' there must be work to do for Christ, for which the preparation is in this life by faithful application for Him of what He has entrusted to us—be it much or little.   This gives quite a new and blessed meaning to the life that now is—as most truly and in all its aspects part of that into which it is to unfold. No; not the smallest share of 'talents,' if only faithfully used for Christ, can be lost, not merely as regards His acknowledgment, but also their further and wider employment.   And may we not suggest, that this may, if not explain, yet cast the halo of His purpose and Presence around what so often seems mysterious in the removal of those who had just attained to opening, or to full usefulness, or even of those who are taken from us in the early morn of youth and loveliness.   The Lord may 'have need' of them, where or how we know not—and beyond this working-day and working-world there are 'many things' over which the faithful servant in little may be 'set,' that he may still do, and with greatly enlarged opportunities and powers, the work for Christ which he had loved so well, while at the same time he also shares the joy of his Lord.

It only remains to refer to the third servant, whose sad unfaithfulness and failure of service we already, in some measure, understand. Summoned to his account, he returned the talent entrusted to him with this explanation, that, knowing his Master to be a hard man, reaping where He did not sow, and gathering (the corn) where He did not 'winnow,'[1] he had been afraid of incurring responsibility,[2] and hence hid in the earth the talent which he now restored.   It needs no comment to show that his own words, however honest and self-righteous they might sound, admitted dereliction of his work and duty as a servant, and entire misunderstanding as well as heart-alienation from his Master.   He served Him not, and he knew Him not; he loved Him not, and he sympathised not with Him.   But, besides, his answer was also an insult and a mendacious pretext.   He had been idle and unwilling to work for his Master.   If he worked it would be for himself.   He would not incur the difficulties, the self-denial, perhaps the reproach, connected with his Master's work. We recognise here those who, although His servants, yet, from self-indulgence and worldliness, will not do work for Christ with the one talent entrusted to them—that is, even though the responsibility and claim upon them be the smallest; and who deem it sufficient to hide

---

[1] διασκορπίζειν here in the same sense in which the LXX. render the Hebrew זרה in Ezek. v. 2, comp. *Trommius* Concord., and *Grimm* ad verb.

[2] *Goebel* exaggerates in supposing that the servant had done so, because any possible returns for the money would not be his own, but the Master's.

it in the ground—not to lose it—or to preserve it, as they imagine, from being used for evil, without using it to trade for Christ. The falseness of the excuse, that he was afraid to do anything with it— an excuse too often repeated in our days—lest, peradventure, he might do more harm than good, was now fully exposed by the Master. Confessedly, it proceeded from a want of knowledge of Him, as if He were a hard, exacting Master, not One Who reckons even the least service as done to Himself; from misunderstanding also of what work for Christ is, in which nothing can ever fail or be lost; and, lastly, from want of joyous sympathy with it. And so the Master put aside the flimsy pretext. Addressing him as a ' wicked and slothful servant,' He pointed out that, even on his own showing, if he had been afraid to incur responsibility, he might have ' cast ' (a word intended to mark the absence of labour) the money to ' the bankers,' when, at His return, He would have received His own, ' with interest.' Thus he might, without incurring responsibility, or much labour, have been, at least in a limited sense, faithful to his duty and trust as a servant.

The reference to the practice of lodging money, at interest, with the bankers, raises questions too numerous and lengthy for full discussion in this place. The Jewish Law distinguished between ' interest ' and ' increase ' (*neshekh* and *tarbith*), and entered into many and intricate details on the subject.[a] Such transactions were forbidden with Israelites, but allowed with Gentiles. As in Rome, the business of ' money-changers ' (*argentarii, nummularii*) and that of ' bankers ' (*collectarii, mensularii*) seem to have run into each other. The Jewish ' bankers ' bear precisely the same name (*Shulchani, mensularius, τραπεζίτης*). In Rome very high interest seems to have been charged in early times; by-and-by it was lowered, till it was fixed, first at 8½, and then at 4⅙, per cent. But these laws were not of permanent duration. Practically, usury was unlimited. It soon became the custom to charge monthly interest at the rate of 1 per cent. a month. Yet there were prosperous times, as at the close of the Republic, when the rate of interest was so low as 4 per cent.; during the early Empire it stood at 8 per cent. This, of course, in what we may call fair business transactions. Beyond them, in the almost incredible extravagance, luxury, and indebtedness of even some of the chief historical personages, most usurious transactions took place (especially in the provinces), and that by people in high position (Brutus in Cyprus, and Seneca in Britain). Money was lent at 12, 24, and even 48 per cent.; the

[a] Babha Mez. iv. especially v. 6, and the Gemara, especially Babha M. 70 b &c.

bills bore a larger sum than that actually received; and the interest was added to the capital, so that debt and interest alike grew. In Greece there were regular State banks, while in Rome such provision was only made under exceptional circumstances. Not unfrequently the twofold business of money-changing and banking was combined. Such 'bankers' undertook to make payments, to collect moneys and accounts, to place out money at interest—in short, all the ordinary business of this kind.[1] There can be no question that the Jewish bankers of Palestine and elsewhere were engaged in the same undertakings, while the dispersion of their race over the world would render it more easy to have trusted correspondents in every city. Thus, we find that Herod Agrippa borrowed from the Jewish Alabarch at Alexandria the sum of 20,000 drachms, which was paid him in Italy, the commission and interest on it amounting to no less than 8½ per cent. (2,500 drachms).[2]

We can thus understand the allusion to 'the bankers,' with whom the wicked and unfaithful servant might have lodged his lord's money, if there had been truth in his excuse. To unmask its hollowness is the chief object of this part of the Parable. Accordingly, it must not be too closely pressed; but it would be in the spirit of the Parable to apply the expression to the *indirect* employment of money in the service of Christ, as by charitable contributions, &c. But the great lesson intended is, that every good and faithful servant of Christ must, whatever his circumstances, personally and directly use such talent as he may have to make gain for Christ. Tried by this test, how few seem to have understood their relation to Christ, and how cold has the love of the Church grown in the long absence of her Lord!

But as regards the 'unprofitable' servant in the Parable, the well-known punishment of him that had come to the Marriage-Feast without the wedding-garment shall await him, while the talent, which he had failed to employ for his master, shall be entrusted to him who had shown himself most capable of working. We need not seek an elaborate interpretation for this. It points to the principle, equally true in every administration of God, that 'unto every one that hath shall be given, and he shall be placed in abundance;[3] but as to him that hath not,[4] also what he hath shall be taken away from him.' Not a cynical rule this, such as the world, in its selfishness or worship of success, caricatures it; nor yet the worship of superior

---

[1] Comp. *Marquardt*, Handb. d. Röm. Alterth. vol. v. 2, pp. 56–68.
[2] *Jos.* Antiq. xviii. 6. 3.

[3] περισσευθήσεται.
[4] So the better reading, τοῦ δὲ μὴ ἔχοντος.

force; but this, that faithful use for God of every capacity will ever open fresh opportunities, in proportion as the old ones have been used, while spiritual unprofitableness must end in utter loss even of that which, however humble, might have been used, at one time or another, for God and for good.

3. To these Parables, that of the King who on his return makes reckoning with His servants and His enemies may be regarded as supplemental. It is recorded only by St. Luke, and placed by him in somewhat loose connection with the conversion of Zacchæus.[a] The most superficial perusal will show such unmistakable similarity with the Parable of ' The Talents,' that their identity will naturally suggest itself to the reader. On the other hand, there are remarkable divergences in detail, some of which seem to imply a different standpoint from which the same truth is viewed. We have also now the additional feature of the message of hatred on the part of the citizens, and their fate in consequence of it. It may have been that Christ spoke the two Parables on the two different occasions mentioned respectively by St. Luke and St. Matthew—the one on the journey to Jerusalem, the other on the Mount of Olives. And yet it seems difficult to believe that He would, within a few days of telling the Parable recorded by St. Luke, have repeated it in almost the same words to the disciples, who must have heard it in Jericho. This objection would not be so serious, if the Parable addressed, in the first instance, to the disciples (that of the Talents) had been afterwards repeated (in the record of St. Luke) in a *wider* circle, and not, as according to the Synoptists, the opposite. If, however, we are to regard the two Parables of the Talents and of the Pieces of Money as substantially the same, we would be disposed to consider the recension by St. Matthew as the original, being the more homogeneous and compact, while that of St. Luke would seem to combine with this another Parable, that of the rebellious citizens. Perhaps it is safest to assume, that, on His way to Jerusalem, when his adherents (not merely the disciples) would naturally expect that He would inaugurate His Messianic Kingdom, Christ may have spoken the latter Parable, to teach them that the relation in which Jerusalem stood towards Him, and its fate, were quite different from what they imagined, and that His Entrance into the City and the Advent of His Kingdom would be separated by a long distance of time. Hence the prospect before them was that of working, not of reigning; after that would the reckoning come, when the faithful worker would become the trusted ruler. These points were, of course, closely connected with

[a] St. Luke xix. 11-28

the lessons of the Parable of the Talents, and, with the view of present
ing the subject as a whole, St. Luke may have borrowed details from
that Parable, and supplemented its teaching by presenting another
aspect of it.

It must be admitted, that if St. Luke had really these two
Parables in view (that of the King and of the Talents), and wished
to combine them into new teaching, he has most admirably welded
them together. For, as the Nobleman Who is about to entrust money
to His servants, is going abroad to receive a Kingdom, it was possible
to represent Him alike in relation to rebellious citizens and to His own
servants, and to connect their reward with His 'Kingdom.' And so
the two Parables are joined by deriving the illustration from political
instead of social life. It has been commonly supposed, that the
Parable contains an allusion to what had happened after the death
of Herod the Great, when his son Archelaus hastened to Rome to
obtain confirmation of his father's will, while a Jewish deputation
followed to oppose his appointment—an act of rebellion which
Archelaus afterwards avenged in the blood of his enemies. The
circumstance must have been still fresh in popular remembrance,
although more than thirty years had elapsed. But if otherwise,
applications to Rome for installation to the government, and popular
opposition thereto, were of such frequent occurrence amidst the quarrels and intrigues of the Herodians, that no difficulty could have been
felt in understanding the allusions of the Parable.

A brief analysis will suffice to point out the special lessons of this
Parable. It introduces 'a certain Nobleman,' Who has claims to
the throne, but has not yet received the formal appointment from
the suzerain power. As He is going away to receive it, He deals as
yet only with His servants. His object, apparently, is to try their
aptitude, devotion, and faithfulness: and so He hands—not to each
according to his capacity, but to all equally, a sum, not large (such
as talents), but small—to each a 'mina,' equal to 100 drachms, or
about 3l. 5s. of our money. To trade with so small a sum would, of
course, be much more difficult, and success would imply greater
ability, even as it would require more constant labour. Here we
have some traits in which this differs from the Parable of the Talents.
The same small sum is supposed to have been entrusted to all, in
order to show which of them was most able and most earnest, and
hence who should be called to largest employment, and with it to
greatest honour in the Kingdom. While 'the Nobleman' was at
the court of His suzerain, a deputation of His fellow-citizens arrived

to urge this resolution of theirs: 'We will not that this One reign over us.' It was simply an expression of hatred; it stated no reason, and only urged personal opposition, even if such were in the face of the personal wish of the sovereign who appointed him king.

In the last scene, the King, now duly appointed, has returned to His country. He first reckons with His servants, when it is found that all but one have been faithful to their trust, though with varying success (the *mina* of the one having grown into ten; that of another into five, and so on). In strict accordance with that success is now their further appointment to *rule*—work here corresponding to rule there, which, however, as we know from the Parable of the Talents, is also work for Christ: a rule that is work, and work that is rule. At the same time, the acknowledgment is the same to all the faithful servants. Similarly, the motives, the reasoning, and the fate of the unfaithful servant are the same as in the Parable of the Talents. But as regards His 'enemies,' that would not have Him reign over them—manifestly, Jerusalem and the people of Israel— who, even after He had gone to receive the Kingdom, continued the personal hostility of their 'We will not that this One shall reign over us'—the ashes of the Temple, the ruins of the City, the blood of the fathers, and the homeless wanderings of their children, with the Cain-curse branded on their brow and visible to all men, attest, that the King has many ministers to execute that judgment which obstinate rebellion must surely bring, if His Authority is to be vindicated, and His Rule to secure submission.

CHAPTER VIII.

THE FOURTH DAY IN PASSION-WEEK—JESUS IN HIS LAST SABBATIC REST
BEFORE HIS AGONY, AND THE SANHEDRISTS IN THEIR UNREST—THE
BETRAYAL—JUDAS: HIS CHARACTER, APOSTASY, AND END.

(St. Matt. xxvi. 1–5, 14–16; St. Mark xiv. 1, 2, 10, 11; St. Luke xxii. 1–6.)

BOOK
V

FROM the record of Christ's Sayings and Doings, furnished by St. Matthew, we turn once more to that of public events, as, from one or another aspect they are related by all the Evangelists. With the Discourses in the Temple the public Teaching of Christ had come to an end; with that spoken on the Mount of Olives, and its applica‧ tion in the Parables of the 'Virgins' and the 'Talents,' the instruction of the disciples had been concluded. What follows in His inter‧ course with His own is *parænetic*,[1] rather than teaching,—exhortation, advice, and consolation: rather, perhaps, all these combined.

The three busy days of Passion-Week were past. The day before that on which the Paschal Lamb was to be slain, with all that was to follow, would be one of rest, a Sabbath to His Soul before its Great Agony. He would refresh Himself, gather Himself up for the terrible conflict before Him. And He did so as the Lamb of God—meekly submitting Himself to the Will and Hand of His Father, and so fulfilling all types, from that of Isaac's sacrifice on Mount Moriah to the Paschal Lamb in the Temple; and bringing the reality of all prophecy, from that of the Woman's Seed that would crush the Serpent's head to that of the Kingdom of God in its fullness, when its golden gates would be flung open to all men, and Heaven's own light flow out to them as they sought its way of peace. Only two days more, as the Jews reckoned them[2]—that Wednesday and

---

[1] I take leave to introduce a term which has become naturalised in German theological literature. There is no other single word which so expresses the ideas.

[2] An attempt has been lately made, with great ingenuity, by the Rev. B. S. Clarke, of Boxted, to show that only the weekly Sabbath and the Day of Atonement, but not the other festive, nor yet the natural days, began with the evening. The admission in regard to Sabbaths and the Day of Atonement is, in the absence of any qualifying remark in regard to them, a *primâ facie* argument against the theory. But there is more than this. In

Thursday—and at its Even the Paschal supper! And Jesus knew it well, and He passed that day of rest and preparation in quiet retirement with His disciples—perhaps in some hollow of the Mount of Olives, near the home of Bethany—speaking to them of His Crucifixion on the near Passover. They sorely needed His words; they, rather than He, needed to be prepared for what was coming. But what Divine calm, what willing obedience, and also what outgoing of love to them, with full consciousness of what was before Him, to think and speak of this only on that day! So would not a Messiah of Jewish conception have acted; nay, He would not have been placed in such circumstances. So would not a Messiah of ambitious aims or of Jewish Nationalist aspirations have acted; He would have done what the Sanhedrin feared, and raised a 'tumult of the people,' prepared for it as the multitude was, which had so lately raised the Hosanna-cry in street and Temple. So would a disillusioned enthusiast not have acted; he would have withdrawn from the impending fate. But Jesus knew it all—far more than the agony of shame and suffering, even the unfathomable agony of soul. And the while He thought only of them in it all. Such thinking and speaking is not that of Man—it is that of the Incarnate Son of God, the Christ of the Gospels.

He had, indeed, before that, sought gradually to prepare them for what was to happen on the morrow's night. He had pointed to it in dim figure at the very opening of His Ministry, on the first occasion that he had taught in the Temple,[a] as well as to Nicodemus.[b] He had hinted it, when He spoke of the deep sorrow when the Bridegroom would be taken from them,[c] of the need of taking up His cross,[d] of the fulfilment in Him of the Jonah-type,[e] of His Flesh which He would give for the life of the world,[f] as well as in what might have seemed the Parabolic teaching about the Good Shepherd, Who laid down His life for the Sheep,[g] and the Heir Whom the evil husbandmen cast out and killed.[h] But He had also spoken of it quite directly—and this, let us specially notice, always when some high-point in His History had been reached, and the disciples might have been carried away into Messianic expectations of an exaltation without humiliation, a triumph not a sacrifice. We remember, that the first occasion on which He spoke thus clearly was immediately after that

[a] St. John ii. 19
[b] iii. 14
[c] St. Matt. ix. 15.
[d] x 38
[e] St. Matt. xii. 40
[f] St. John vi. 51
[g] St. John x. 11, 15
[h] St. Matt. xxi. 38

Chull. 83 *a* it is noted, in connection with offerings, that as in the history of the Creation the day always belonged to the previous night ('one day'), it was always to be reckoned in the same manner. Again, in Pes. 2 *a* it is stated that the day lasted till three stars became visible. Lastly, and most important in regard to the Passover, it is distinctly stated (Jer. Pes. 27 *c*, below), that it began with the darkness on the 14th Nisan.

ª St. Matt.
xvi. 21
ᵇ St. Matt.
xvii. 22
ᶜ St. Matt.
xx. 17-19

confession of Peter, which laid the foundation of the Church, against which the gates of hell should not prevail;ª the next, after descending from the Mount of Transfiguration;ᵇ the last, on preparing to make His triumphal Messianic Entry into Jerusalem.ᶜ The darker hints and Parabolic sayings might have been misunderstood. Even as regarded the clear prediction of His Death, preconceived ideas could find no room for such a fact. Deep veneration, which could not associate it with His Person, and a love which could not bear the thought of it, might, after the first shock of the words was past, and their immediate fulfilment did not follow, suggest some other possible explanation of the prediction. But on that Wednesday it was impossible to misunderstand; it could scarcely have been possible to doubt what Jesus said of His near Crucifixion.[1] If illusions had still existed, the last two days must have rudely dispelled them. The triumphal Hosannas of His Entry into the City, and the acclamations in the Temple, had given place to the cavils of Pharisees, Sadducees, and Scribes, and with a 'Woe' upon it Jesus had taken His last departure from Israel's sanctuary. And better far than those rulers, whom conscience made cowards, did the disciples know how little reliance could be placed on the adherence of the 'multitude.' And now the Master was telling it to them in plain words; was calmly contemplating it, and that not as in the dim future, but in the immediate present—at that very Passover, from which scarcely two days separated them. Much as we wonder at their brief scattering on His arrest and condemnation, those humble disciples must have loved

[1] On the evidential force of the narrative of the Crucifixion, I must refer to the singularly lucid and powerful reasoning of Dr. *Wace*, in his work on 'The Gospel and its Witnesses' (London, 1883, Lecture VI.). He first refers to the circumstance, that in the narratives of the Crucifixion, written by Apostles, or by friends of Apostles, 'the writers do not shrink from describing their own conduct, or that of their Master,' with a truthfulness which terribly reflects on their constancy, courage, and even manliness. Dr. *Wace's* second argument is so clearly put, that I must take leave to transfer his language to these pages. 'Christ crucified was, we are told by St. Paul, "unto the Jews a stumbling block, and unto the Greeks foolishness." It was a constant reproach to Christians, that they worshipped a man who had been crucified as a malefactor. The main fact, of course, could not be disguised. But that the Evangelical writers should have so diligently preserved what might otherwise have been forgotten—all the minute circumstances of their Master's humiliation, the very weakness of His flesh, and His shrinking, in the garden, from the cup He had to drink—all those marks, in fact, of His human weakness which were obliterated by His Resurrection—this is an instance of truthfulness which seems at least incompatible with any legendary origin of the narratives, at a time when our Lord was contemplated in the glory of His Ascension, and of His session at the right hand of God. But whatsoever impression of truthfulness, and of intense reality in detail, is thus created by the history of the Passion, must in justice be allowed to reflect back over the whole preceding history.' The argument is then further carried out as to the truthfulness of writers who could so speak of themselves, and concerning the fate of the Christ. But the whole subject should be studied in the connection in which Dr. *Wace* has presented it.

Him much to sit around Him in mournful silence as He thus spake, and to follow Him unto His Dying.

But to one of them, in whose heart the darkness had long been gathering, this was the decisive moment. The prediction of Christ, which Judas as well as the others must have felt to be true, extinguished the last glimmering of such light of Christ as his soul had been capable of receiving. In its place flared up the lurid flame of hell. By the open door out of which he had thrust the dying Christ 'Satan entered into Judas.'[a] Yet, even so, not permanently.[b] It may, indeed, be doubted, whether, since God is in Christ, such can ever be the case in any human soul, at least on this side eternity. Since our world's night has been lit up by the promise from Paradise, the rosy hue of its morning has lain on the edge of the horizon, deepening into gold, brightening into day, growing into midday-strength and evening-glory. Since God's Voice wakened earth by its early Christmas-Hymn, it has never been quite night there, nor can it ever be quite night in any human soul.[1]

But it is a terrible night-study, that of Judas. We seem to tread our way over loose stones of hot molten lava, as we climb to the edge of the crater, and shudderingly look down its depths. And yet there, near there, have stood not only St. Peter in the night of his denial, but mostly all of us, save they whose Angels have always looked up into the Face of our Father in heaven. And yet, in our weakness, we have even wept over them! There, near there, have we stood, not in the hours of our weakness, but in those of our sore temptation, when the blast of doubt had almost quenched the flickering light, or the storm of passion or of self-will broken the bruised reed. But He prayed for us—and through the night came over desolate moor and stony height the Light of His Presence, and above the wild storm rose the Voice of Him, Who has come to seek and to save that which was lost. Yet near to us, close to us, was the dark abyss; and we can never more forget our last, almost sliding, foothold as we quitted its edge.

A terrible night-study this of Judas, and best to make it here, at once, from its beginning to its end. We shall indeed, catch sudden glimpse of him again, as the light of the torches flashes on the traitor-face in Gethsemane; and once more hear his voice in the assemblage of the haughty, sneering councillors of Israel, when his footfall on the marble pavement of the Temple-halls; and the clink of those thirty accursed pieces of silver shall waken the echoes, wake also the dirge of despair in his soul, and he shall flee from the night of his soul into the night that for ever closes around him. But all

---

[1] This apart from the question of the exceptional sin against the Holy Ghost.

this as rapidly as we may pass from it, after this present brief study of his character and history.

We remember, that 'Judas, the man of Kerioth,' was, so far as we know, the only disciple of Jesus from the province of Judæa. This circumstance; that he carried the bag, i.e. was treasurer and adminis-trator of the small common stock of Christ and His disciples; and that he was both a hypocrite and a thief ᵃ—this is all that we know for certain of his history. From the circumstance that he was ap-pointed to such office of trust in the Apostolic community, we infer that he must have been looked up to by the others as an able and prudent man, a good administrator. And there is probably no reason to doubt, that he possessed the natural gift of administration or of 'government' (κυβέρνησις).ᵇ The question, why Jesus left him ' the bag' after He knew him to be a thief—which, as we believe, he was not at the beginning, and only became in the course of time and in the progress of disappointment—is best answered .by this other: Why He originally allowed it to be entrusted to Judas? It was not only because he was best fitted—probably, absolutely fitted—for such work, but also in mercy to him, in view of his character. To engage in that for which a man is naturally fitted is the most likely means of keeping him from brooding, dissatisfaction, alienation, and eventual apostasy. On the other hand, it must be admitted that, as mostly all our life-temptations come to us from that for which we have most aptitude, when Judas was alienated and unfaithful in heart, this very thing became also his greatest temptation, and, indeed, hurried nim to his ruin. But only *after* he had first failed inwardly. And so, as ever in like circumstances, the very things which might have been most of blessing become ·most of curse, and the judgment of hardening fulfils itself by that which in itself is good. Nor could ' the bag' have been afterwards taken from him without both ex-posing him to the others, and precipitating his moral destruction. And so he had to be left to the process of inward ripening, till all was ready for the sickle.

This very gift of 'government' in Judas may also help us to understand how he may have been first attracted to Jesus, and through what process, when alienated, he came to end in that terri-ble sin which had cast its snare about him. The 'gift of govern-ment' would, in its active aspect, imply the *desire* for it. From thence to *ambition* in its worst, or selfish, aspect, there is only a step—scarcely that: rather, only different moral premisses.[1] Judas

ᵃ St John
xii. 5, 6

ᵇ 1 Cor. xii.
28

[1] On the relation between ambition and covetousness, generally, and in the case of Judas, see p. 77.

was drawn to Jesus as the *Jewish* Messiah, and he believed in Him as such, possibly both earnestly and ardently; but he expected that His would be the success, the result, and the triumphs of the Jewish Messiah, and he also expected personally and fully to share in them. How deep-rooted were such feelings even in the best, purest, and most unselfish of Jesus' disciples, we gather from the request of the mother of John and James for her sons, and from Peter's question: 'What shall we have?' It must have been sorrow, the misery of moral loneliness, and humiliation, to Him Who was Unselfishness Incarnate, Who lived to die and was full to empty Himself, to be associated with such as even His most intimate disciples, who in this sense also could not watch with Him even one hour, and in whom, at the end of His Ministry, such heaviness was mentally and morally the outcrop, if not the outcome. And in Judas all this must have been an hundredfold more than in them who were in heart true to Christ.

He had, from such conviction as we have described, joined the movement at its very commencement. Then, multitudes in Galilee followed His Footsteps, and watched for His every appearance; they hung entranced on His lips in the Synagogue or on 'the Mount'; they flocked to Him from every town, village, and hamlet; they bore the sick and dying to His Feet, and witnessed, awestruck, how conquered devils gave their testimony to His Divine Power. It was the spring-time of the movement, and all was full of promise—land, people, and disciples. The Baptist, who had bowed before Him and testified to Him, was still lifting his voice to proclaim the near King-dom. But the people had turned after Jesus, and He swayed them. And, oh! what power was there in His Face and Word, in His look and deed. And Judas, also, had been one of them who, on their early Mission, had temporarily had power given him, so that the very devils had been subject to them. But, step by step, had come the disappointment. John was beheaded, and not avenged; on the con-trary, Jesus withdrew Himself. This constant withdrawing, whether from enemies or from success—almost amounting to flight—even when they would have made Him a King; this refusal to show Him-self openly, either at Jerusalem, as His own brethren had taunted Him, or, indeed, anywhere else; this uniform preaching of dis-couragement to them, when they came to Him elated and hopeful at some success; this gathering enmity of Israel's leaders, and His marked avoidance of, or, as some might have put it, His failure in taking up the repeated public challenge of the Pharisees to show a sign from heaven; last, and chief of all, this constant and growing reference to shame, disaster, and death—what did it all mean, if not disappointment of all those hopes and expectations which had made Judas at the first a disciple of Jesus?

He that so knew Jesus, not only in His Words and Deeds, but in His inmost Thoughts, even to His night-long communing with God on the hill-side, could not have seriously believed in the coarse Pharisaic charge of Satanic agency as the explanation of all. Yet, from the then Jewish standpoint, he could scarcely have found it impossible to suggest some other explanation of His miraculous power. But, as increasingly the moral aud spiritual aspect of Christ's Kingdom must have become apparent to even the dullest intellect, the bitter disappointment of his Messianic thoughts and hopes must have gone on, increasing in proportion as, side by side with it, the process of moral alienation, unavoidably connected with his resistance to such spiritual manifestations, continued and increased. And so the mental and the moral alienation went on together, affected by and affecting each other. As if we were pressed to name a definite moment when the process of disintegration, at least sensibly, began, we would point to that Sabbath-morning at Capernaum, when Christ had preached about His Flesh as the Food of the World, and so many of His adherents ceased to follow after Him; nay, when the leaven so worked even in His disciples, that He turned to them with the searching question—intended to show them the full import of the crisis—whether they also would leave Him? Peter conquered by grasping the moral element, because it was germane to him and to the other true disciples: ' To whom shall we go? Thou hast the words of eternal life.' But this moral element was the very cliff on which Judas made shipwreck. After this, all was wrong, and increasingly so. We see disappointment in his face when not climbing the Mount of Transfiguration, and disappointment in the failure to heal the lunatick child. In the disputes by the way, in the quarrels who was greatest among them, in all the pettiness of misunderstandings and realistic folly of their questions or answers, we seem to hear the echo of his voice, to see the result of his influence, the leaven of his presence. And in it all we mark the downward hastening of his course, even to the moment when, in contrast to the deep love of a Mary, he first stands before us unmasked, as heartless, hypocritical, full of hatred—disappointed ambition having broken down into selfishness, and selfishness slid into covetousness, even to the crime of stealing that which was destined for the poor.

For, when an ambition which rests only on selfishness gives way.

there lies close by it the coarse lust of covetousness, as the kindred passion and lower expression of that other form of selfishness. When the Messianic faith of Judas gave place to utter disappointment, the moral and spiritual character of Christ's Teaching would affect him, not sympathetically but antipathetically. Thus, that which should have opened the door of his heart, only closed and double-barred it. His attachment to the Person of Jesus would give place to actual hatred, though only of a temporary character; and the wild intenseness of his Eastern nature would set it all in flame. Thus, when Judas had lost his slender foothold, or, rather, when it had slipped from under him, he fell down, down the eternal abyss. The only hold to which he could cling was the passion of his soul. As he laid hands on it, it gave way, and fell with him into fathomless depths. We, each of us, have also some master-passion; and if, which God forbid! we should lose our foothold, we also would grasp this masterpassion, and it would give way, and carry us with it into the eternal dark and deep.

On that spring day, in the restfulness of Bethany, when the Master was taking His sad and solemn Farewell of sky and earth, of friends and disciples, and told them what was to happen only two days later at the Passover, it was all settled in the soul of Judas. 'Satan entered' it. Christ would be crucified; this was quite certain. In the general cataclysm let Judas have at least something. And so, on that sunny afternoon, he left them out there, to seek speech of them that were gathered, not in their ordinary meetingplace, but in the High-Priest's Palace. Even this indicates that it was an informal meeting, consultative rather than judicial. For, it was one of the principles of Jewish Law that, in criminal cases, sentence must be spoken in the regular meeting-place of the Sanhedrin.[a] The same inference is conveyed by the circumstance, that the captain of the Temple-guard and his immediate subordinates seem to have been taken into the council,[b] no doubt to concert the measures for the actual arrest of Jesus. There had previously been a similar gathering and consultation, when the report of the raising of Lazarus reached the authorities of Jerusalem.[c] The practical resolution adopted at that meeting had apparently been, that a strict watch should henceforth be kept on Christ's movements, and that every one of them, as well as the names of His friends, and the places of His secret retirement, should be communicated to the authorities, with the view to His arrest at the proper moment.[d]

It was probably in professed obedience to this direction, that the traitor presented himself that afternoon in the Palace of the High-

a Ab. Zar. 8 b, line before last

b St. Luke xxii. 4

c St. John xi. 47, 48

d St. John xi. 57

Priest Caiaphas.[1] Those assembled there were the 'chiefs' of the Priesthood—no doubt, the Temple-officials, heads of the courses of Priests, and connections of the High-Priestly family, who constituted what both *Josephus* and the Talmud designate as the Priestly Council.[2] All connected with the Temple, its ritual, administration, order, and laws, would be in their hands. Moreover, it was but natural, that the High-Priest and his council should be the regular official medium between the Roman authorities and the people. In matters which concerned, not ordinary misdemeanours, but political crimes (such as it was wished to represent the movement of Jesus), or which affected the *status* of the established religion, the official chiefs of the Priesthood would, of course, be the persons to appeal, in conjunction with the Sanhedrists, to the secular authorities. This, irrespective of the question—to which reference will be made in the sequel—what place the Chief Priests held in the Sanhedrin. But in that meeting in the Palace of Caiaphas, besides these Priestly Chiefs, the leading Sanhedrists ('Scribes and Elders') were also gathered. They were deliberating how Jesus might be taken by subtilty and killed. Probably they had not yet fixed on any definite plan. Only at this conclusion had they arrived—probably in consequence of the popular acclamations at His Entry into Jerusalem, and of what had since happened—that nothing must be done during the Feast, for fear of some popular tumult. They knew only too well the character of Pilate, and how in any such tumult all parties—the leaders as well as the led—might experience terrible vengeance.

It must have been intense relief when, in their perplexity, the traitor now presented himself before them with his proposals. Yet his reception was not such as he may have looked for. He probably expected to be hailed and treated as a most important ally. They were, indeed, 'glad, and covenanted to give him money,' even as he promised to dog His steps, and watch for the opportunity which they sought. In truth, the offer of the betrayer changed the whole aspect of matters. What formerly they dreaded to attempt seemed now both safe and easy. They could not allow such an opportunity to slip; it was one that might never occur again. Nay, might it not even seem, from the defection of Judas, as if dissatisfaction and disbelief had begun to spread in the innermost circle of Christ's disciples?

Yet, withal, they treated Judas not as an honoured associate, but as a common informer, and a contemptible betrayer. This was not

---

[1] About Caiaphas, see Book II. ch. xi.
[2] The evidence is collected, although not well arranged, by *Wieseler*, Beitr. pp. 205–230.

only natural but, in the circumstances, the wisest policy, alike in order to save their own dignity, and to keep most secure hold on the betrayer. And, after all, it might be said, so as to minimise his services, that Judas could really not do much for them—only show them how they might seize Him at unawares in the absence of the multitude, to avoid the possible tumult of an open arrest. So little did they understand Christ! And Judas had at last to speak it out barefacedly—so selling himself as well as the Master: 'What will ye give me?' It was in literal fulfilment of prophecy,[a] that they 'weighed out' to him [1] from the very Temple-treasury those thirty pieces of silver (about 3*l.* 15*s.*).[2] And here we mark, that there is always terrible literality about the prophecies of judgment, while those of blessing far exceed the words of prediction. And yet it was surely as much in contempt of the seller as of Him Whom he sold, that they paid the legal price of a slave. Or did they mean some kind of legal fiction, such as to buy the Person of Jesus at the legal price of a slave, so as to hand it afterwards over to the secular authorities? Such fictions, to save the conscience by a logical quibble, are not so uncommon—and the case of the Inquisitors handing over the condemned heretic to the secular authorities will recur to the mind. But, in truth, Judas could not now have escaped their toils. They might have offered him ten or five pieces of silver, and he must still have stuck to his bargain. Yet none the less do we mark the deep symbolic significance of it all, in that the Lord was, so to speak, paid for out of the Temple-money which was destined for the purchase of sacrifices, and that He, Who took on Him the form of a servant,[b] was sold and bought at the legal price of a slave.[c]

And yet Satan must once more enter the heart of Judas at that Supper, before he can finally do the deed.[d] But, even so, we believe it was only temporarily, not for always—for, he was still a human being, such as on this side eternity we all are—and he had still a conscience working in him. With this element he had not reckoned in his bargain in the High Priest's Palace. On the morrow of His condemnation would it exact a terrible account. That night in Gethsemane never more passed from his soul. In the thickening and encircling gloom all around, he must have ever seen only the torchlight glare as it fell on the pallid Face of the Divine Sufferer. In the terrible stillness before the storm, he must have ever heard only these words: 'Betrayest thou the Son of Man with a kiss?' He did not

CHAP.
VIII

[a] Zech. xi. 12

[b] Phil. ii. 7
[c] Exod. xxi 32
[d] St. John xiii. 27

---

[1] Probably such was the practice in public payments.

[2] The shekel of the Sanctuary = 4 dinars. The Jerusalem shekel is found, on an average, to be worth about 2*s.* 6*d.*

hate Jesus then—he hated nothing; he hated everything. He was utterly desolate, as the storm of despair swept over his disenchanted soul, and swept him before it. No one in heaven or on earth to appeal to; no one, Angel or man, to stand by him. Not the priests, who had paid him the price of blood, would have aught of him, not even the thirty pieces of silver, the blood-money of his Master and of his own soul—even as the modern Synagogue, which approves of what has been done, but not of the deed, will have none of him! With their 'See thou to it!' they sent him reeling back into his darkness. Not so could conscience be stilled. And, louder than the ring of the thirty silver pieces as they fell on the marble pavement of the Temple, rang it ever in his soul, 'I have betrayed innocent blood!' Even if Judas possessed that which on earth cleaves closest and longest to us—a woman's love—it could not have abode by him. It would have turned into madness and fled; or it would have withered, struck by the lightning-flash of that night of terrors.

Deeper—farther out into the night' to its farthest bounds— where rises and falls the dark flood of death. The wild howl of the storm has lashed the dark waters into fury: they toss and break in wild billows at his feet. One narrow rift in the cloud-curtain overhead, and, in the pale, deathlike light lies the Figure of the Christ, so calm and placid, untouched and unharmed, on the storm-tossed waters, as it had been that night lying on the Lake of Galilee, when Judas had seen Him come to them over the surging billows, and then bid them be peace. Peace! What peace to him now—in earth or heaven? It was the same Christ, but thorn-crowned, with nail-prints in His Hands and Feet. And this Judas had done to the Master! Only for one moment did it seem to lie there; then it was sucked up by the dark waters beneath. And again the cloud-curtain is drawn, only more closely; the darkness is thicker, and the storm wilder than before. Out into that darkness, with one wild plunge—there, where the Figure of the Dead Christ had lain on the waters! And the dark waters have closed around him in eternal silence.

.　　.　　.　　.　　.　　.　　.　　.

In the lurid morn that broke on the other shore where the flood cast him up, did he meet those searching, loving Eyes of Jesus, Whose gaze he knew so well—when he came to answer for the deeds done in the flesh?

.　　.　　.　　.　　.　　.　　.

And—can there be a store in the Eternal Compassion for the Betrayer of Christ?

CHAPTER IX.

THE FIFTH DAY IN PASSION-WEEK—'MAKE READY THE PASSOVER!'

(St. Matt. xxvi. 17-19; St. Mark xiv. 12-16; St. Luke xxii. 7-13; St. John xiii. 1.)

WHEN the traitor returned from Jerusalem on the Wednesday after-noon, the Passover, in the popular and canonical, though not in the Biblical sense, was close at hand. It began on the 14th Nisan, that is, from the appearance of the first three stars on Wednesday evening [the evening of what had been the 13th], and ended with the first three stars on Thursday evening [the evening of what had been the 14th day of Nisan]. As this is an exceedingly important point, it is well here to quote the precise language of the Jerusalem Talmud:[a] 'What means: On the *Pesach*?[1] On the 14th [Nisan].' And so Josephus describes the Feast as one of eight days,[b] evidently reckoning its beginning on the 14th, and its close at the end of the 21st Nisan. The absence of the traitor so close upon the Feast would therefore, be the less noticed by the others. Necessary preparations might have to be made, even though they were to be guests in some house—they knew not which. These would, of course, devolve on Judas. Besides, from previous conversations, they may also. have judged that 'the man of Kerioth' would fain escape what the Lord had all that day been telling them about, and which was now filling their minds and hearts.

Everyone in Israel was thinking about the Feast. For the pre-vious month it had been the subject of discussion in the Academies, and, for the last two Sabbaths at least, that of discourse in the Synagogues.[2] Everyone was going to Jerusalem, or had those near and dear to them there, or at least watched the festive processions to the Metropolis of Judaism. It was a gathering of universal Israel, that of the memorial of the birth-night of the nation, and of its Exodus, when friends from afar would meet, and new friends be

a Jer. Pes. 27 d, line before last
b Ant. ii. 15, 1

---

[1] The question is put in connection with Pes. i. 8.
[2] See the Jerusalem Gemara (Jer. Pes.

27 b, towards the end). But the detailed quotations would here be so numerous. that it seems wiser to omit them.

made; when offerings long due would be brought, and purification long needed be obtained—and all worship in that grand and glorious Temple, with its gorgeous ritual. National and religious feelings were alike stirred in what reached far back to the first, and pointed far forward to the final Deliverance. On that day a Jew might well glory in being a Jew. But we must not dwell on such thoughts, nor attempt a general description of the Feast. Rather shall we try to follow closely the footsteps of Christ and His disciples, and see or know only what on that day they saw and did.

For ecclesiastical purposes Bethphage and Bethany seem to have been included in Jerusalem. But Jesus must keep the Feast in the City itself, although, if His purpose had not been interrupted, He would have spent the night outside its walls.[1] The first preparations for the Feast would commence shortly after the return of the traitor. For, on the evening [of the 13th] commenced the 14th of Nisan, when a solemn search was made with lighted candle throughout each house for any leaven that might be hidden, or have fallen aside by accident. Such was put by in a safe place, and afterwards destroyed with the rest. In Galilee it was the usage to abstain wholly from work; in Judæa the day was divided, and actual work ceased only at noon, though nothing new was taken in hand even in the morning. This division of the day for festive purposes was a Rabbinic addition; and, by way of a hedge around it, an hour before midday was fixed after which nothing leavened might be eaten. The more strict abstained from it even an hour earlier (at ten o'clock), lest the eleventh hour might insensibly run into the forbidden midday. But there could be little real danger of this, since, by way of public notification, two desecrated thankoffering cakes were laid on a bench in the Temple, the removal of one of which indicated that the time for eating what was leavened had passed; the removal of the other, that the time for destroying all leaven had come.[2]

It was probably after the early meal, and when the eating of leaven had ceased, that Jesus began preparations for the Paschal Supper. St. John, who, in view of the details in the other Gospels, summarises, and, in some sense, almost passes over, the outward events, so that their narration may not divert attention from those

[1] Comp. St. Matt. xxvi. 30, 36; St. Mark xiv. 26, 32; St. Luke xxii. 39; St. John xviii. 1.

[2] The Jerusalem Talmud gives the most minute details of the places in which search is to be made. One Rabbi proposed that the search should be repeated at three different times! If it had been omitted on the evening of the 13th, it would be made on the forenoon of the 14th Nisan.

all-important teachings which he alone records, simply tells by way
of preface and explanation—alike of the 'Last Supper' and of what
followed—that Jesus, 'knowing that His hour was come that He
should depart out of this world unto the Father[1] . . . having loved
His own which were in the world, He loved them unto the end.'[2]
But St. Luke's account of what actually happened, being in some
points the most explicit, requires to be carefully studied, and that
without thought of any possible consequences in regard to the harmony of the Gospels. It is almost impossible to imagine anything
more evident, than that he wishes us to understand that Jesus was
about to celebrate the ordinary Jewish Paschal Supper. 'And the
Day of Unleavened Bread came, on which the Passover must be sacrificed.'[a] The designation is exactly that of the commencement of
the *Pascha*, which, as we have seen, was the 14th Nisan, and the
description that of the slaying of the Paschal Lamb. What follows
is in exact accordance with it: 'And He sent Peter and John, saying, Go and make ready for us the Pascha, that we may eat *it.*'
Then occur these three notices in the same account: 'And . . .
they made ready the Pascha;'[b] 'and when the hour was come, He
reclined [as usual at the Paschal Supper], and the Apostles with
Him;'[c] and, finally, these words of His:[d] 'With desire I have desired to eat this Pascha with you.' And with this fully agrees the
language of the other two Synoptists, St. Matt. xxvi. 17-20, and
St. Mark xiv. 12-17.[3] No ingenuity can explain away these facts.
The suggestion, that in that year the Sanhedrin had postponed the
Paschal Supper from Thursday evening (the 14th-15th Nisan) to
Friday evening (15-16th Nisan), so as to avoid the Sabbath following
on the first day of the feast—and that the Paschal Lamb was there-
fore in that year eaten on Friday, the evening of the day on which
Jesus was crucified, is an assumption void of all support in history

CHAP.
IX

a St. Luke
xxli. 7

b ver. 13

c ver. 14
d ver. 15

[1] These phrases occur frequently in
Jewish writings for dying: 'the hour has
come' 'to depart out of this world.' Thus,
in Targum on Cant. i. 7, 'when the hour
had come that Moses should depart out
of the world;' Shem. R. 33, 'what hour
the time came for our father Jacob that
he should depart out of the world.'

[2] The words may also be rendered ' to
the uttermost.' But it seems more
natural to understand the 'having loved'
as referring to all Christ's previous sayings and doings—as it were, the summing
up of the whole past, like St. Matt. xxvi.
1: 'when Jesus had finished all these
sayings'—and the other clause ('He loved

them to the end') as referring to the
final and greatest manifestation of His
love; the one being the *terminus a quo*,
the other the *terminus ad quem.*

[3] It deserves notice. that the latest Jewish writer on the subject (*Joël*, Blicke in
d. Relig. Gesch. Part II. pp. 62 &c.)—however we may otherwise differ from him—
has by an ingenious process of combination shown, that the *original* view expressed in Jewish writings was, that
Jesus was crucified on the first Paschal
day, and that this was only at a later
period modified to 'the eve of the
Pascha,' Sanh. 43 *a*, 67 *a* (the latter in
Chasr. haSh., p. 23 *b*).

BOOK
V

or Jewish tradition.[1] Equally untenable is it, that Christ had held the Paschal Supper a day in advance of that observed by the rest of the Jewish world—a supposition not only inconsistent with the plain language of the Synoptists, but impossible, since the Paschal Lamb could not have been offered in the Temple, and, therefore, no Paschal Supper held, out of the regular time. But, perhaps, the strangest attempt to reconcile the statement of the Synoptists with

^a St. John xviii. 28

what is supposed inconsistent with it in the narration of St. John[a] is, that while the rest of Jerusalem, including Christ and His Apostles, partook of the Paschal Supper, the chief priests had been interrupted in, or rather prevented from it by their proceedings against Jesus—that, in fact, they had not touched it when they feared to

^b St. John xviii. 28

enter Pilate's Judgment-Hall;[b] and that, after that, they went back to eat it, 'turning the Supper into a breakfast.'[2] Among the various objections to this extraordinary hypothesis, this one will be sufficient, that such would have been absolutely contrary to one of the plainest rubrical directions, which has it: 'The Pascha is not eaten

^c Sebbach. v. 8

but during the night, nor yet later than the middle of the night.'[c]

It was, therefore, with the view of preparing the ordinary

^d St. Luke xxii. 8

Paschal Supper that the Lord now sent Peter and John.[d] For the first time we see them here joined together by the Lord, these two, who henceforth were to be so closely connected: he of deepest feeling with him of quickest action. And their question, *where* He would have the Paschal Meal prepared, gives us a momentary glimpse of the mutual relation between the Master and His Disciples; how He was still the Master, even in their most intimate converse, and would only tell them what to do just when it needed to be done; and how they presumed not to ask beforehand (far less to propose, or to interfere), but had simple confidence and absolute submission as regarded all things. The direction which the Lord gave, while once more evidencing to them, as it does to us, the Divine foreknowledge of Christ, had also its deep human meaning. Evidently, neither the house where the Passover was to be kept, nor its owner,[3] was to be named beforehand within hearing of Judas. That last Meal with its Institution of the Holy Supper, was not to be interrupted, nor their last retreat betrayed, till all had been said and done, even to the last prayer of Agony in Gethsemane. We can scarcely err in

[1] It has of late, however, found an advocate even in the learned Bishop *Haneberg.*

[2] So Archdeacon *Watkins* (in Excursus *F,* in Bp. *Ellicott's* 'Commentary on the

N.T.,' Gospel of St. John).

[3] St. Matthew calls him 'such an one' (τὸν δεῖνα). The details are furnished by St. Mark and St. Luke, and must be gathered from those Gospels.

seeing in this combination of foreknowledge with prudence the ex-   CHAP.
pression of the Divine and the Human: the 'two Natures in One   IX
Person.' The sign which Jesus gave the two Apostles reminds us of
that by which Samuel of old had conveyed assurance and direction to
Saul.ᵃ On their entrance into Jerusalem they would meet a man—   ᵃ 1 Sam. x. 3
manifestly a servant—carrying a pitcher of water. Without accosting,
they were to follow him, and, when they reached the house, to deliver
to its owner this message:¹ 'The Master saith, My time is at hand—
with thee [i.e. in thy house: the emphasis is on this] I hold² the
Passover with My disciples.ᵇ Where is My³ hostelry [or 'hall'],   ᵇ St. Mat-
where I shall eat the Passover with My disciples?'ᶜ   thew
                                                                     ᶜ St. Mark
    Two things here deserve marked attention. The disciples were   and St.
                                                                     Luke
not bidden ask for the chief or 'Upper Chamber,' but for what we
have rendered, for want of better, by 'hostelry,' or 'hall'—κατάλυμα
—the place in the house where, as in an open Khân, the beasts of
burden were unloaded, shoes and staff, or dusty garment and burdens
put down—if an apartment, at least a common one, certainly not
the best. Except in this place,ᵈ ⁴ the word only occurs as the desig- ᵈ St. Mark
nation of the 'inn' or 'hostelry' (κατάλυμα) in Bethlehem, where   xiv. 14; St.
                                                                     Luke xxii.
the Virgin-Mother brought forth her first-born Son, and laid Him in   11
a manger.ᵉ He Who was born in a 'hostelry'—Katalyma—was   ᵉ St. Luke
content to ask for His last Meal in a Katalyma. Only, and this we   ii. 7
mark secondly, it must be His own: 'My Katalyma.' It was a
common practice, that more than one company partook of the
Paschal Supper in the same apartment.ᶠ⁵ In the multitude of those   ᶠ Pes. vii.
                                                                     13
who would sit down to the Paschal Supper this was unavoidable, for
all partook of, including women and children,ᵍ only excepting those   ᵍ Pes. viii. 1
who were Levitically unclean. And, though each company might
not consist of less than ten, it was not to be larger than that each
should be able to partake of at least a small portion of the Paschal
Lambʰ—and we know how small lambs are in the East. But, while   ʰ Pes. viii.
                                                                     2
He only asked for His last Meal in the Katalyma, some hall opening
on the open court, Christ would have it His own—to Himself, to eat
the Passover alone with His Apostles. Not even a company of
disciples—such as the owner of the house unquestionably was—nor

---

¹ We combine the words from the three   nine passages only in one, 1 Sam. ix. 22,
Synoptists.   does it stand for 'apartment.'
    ² Literally, I do.   ⁵ The Mishnah explains certain regula-
    ³ So in St. Luke and also according to tions for such cases. According to the
the better reading in St. Mark.   Targum Pseudo-Jon., each company was
    ⁴ The word occurs seven times in the not to consist of less than ten persons;
LXX. and twice in the Apocrypha (Ecclus. according to Josephus (War vi. 9. 3), of
xiv. 25; 1 Macc. iii. 45). But out of these not more than twenty.

BOOK
V

ᵃ 1 Cor. xi.
23

ᵇ Yoma 12 a;
Megill, 26 a

ᶜ St. Mark

ᵈ Babha B
vi. 4

yet, be it marked, even the Virgin-Mother, might be present; witness what passed, hear what He said, ·or be at the first Institution of His Holy Supper. To us at least this also recalls the words of St. Paul: ' I have received of the Lord that which I also delivered unto you.' ᵃ

There can be no reasonable doubt that, as already hinted, the owner of the house was a disciple, although at festive seasons unbounded hospitality was extended to strangers generally, and no man in Jerusalem considered his house as strictly his own, far less would let it out for hire.ᵇ But no mere stranger would, in answer to so mysterious a message, have given up, without further questioning, his best room. Had he known Peter and John; or recognised Him Who sent the message by the announcement that it was ' The Master; ' or by the words to which His Teaching had attached such meaning: that His time had come; or even by the peculiar emphasis of His command: ' With thee ¹ I hold the Pascha with My disciples? ' It matters little which it was—and, in fact, the impression on the mind almost is, that the owner of the house had not, indeed, expected, but held himself ready for such a call. It was the last request of the dying Master—and could he have refused it? But he would do more than immediately and unquestioningly comply. The Master would only ask for ' the hall ': as He was born in a *Katalyma*, so He would have been content to eat there His last Meal—at the same time meal, feast, sacrifice, and institution. But the unnamed disciple would assign to Him, not the Hall, but the best and chiefest, ' the upper chamber, ' or *Aliyah*, at the same time the most honourable and the most retired place, where from the outside stairs entrance and departure might be had without passing through the house. And ' the upper room ' was ' large,' ' furnished and ready.' ᶜ From Jewish authorities we know, that the average dining-apartment was computed at fifteen feet square; ᵈ the expression ' furnished,' no doubt, refers to the arrangement of couches all round the Table, except at its end, since it was a canon, that the very poorest must partake of that Supper in a *reclining* attitude, to indicate rest, safety, and liberty; ² while the term ' ready ' seems to point to the ready provision of all that was required for the Feast. In that case, all that the disciples would have to ' make ready ' would be ' the Paschal Lamb,' and perhaps that first *Chagigah*, or festive Sacrifice, which, if the Paschal Lamb itself would not suffice for Supper, was

¹ Comp. similarly, for example, St. Mark v. 41; x. 18.
² The Talmud puts it that slaves were wont to take their meals standing, and that this reclining best indicated how Israel had passed from bondage into liberty.

added to it. And here it must be remembered, that it was of religion to fast till the Paschal Supper—as the Jerusalem Talmud explains,[a] in order the better to relish the Supper.

Perhaps it is not wise to attempt lifting the veil which rests on the unnamed 'such an one,' whose was the privilege of being the last Host of the Lord and the first Host of His Church, gathered within the new bond of the fellowship of His Body and Blood. And yet we can scarcely abstain from speculating. To us at least it seems most likely, that it was the house of Mark's father (then still alive)—a large one, as we gather from Acts xii. 13. For, the most obvious explanation of the introduction by St. Mark alone of such an incident as that about the young man who was accompanying Christ as He was led away captive, and who, on fleeing from those that would have laid hold on him, left in their hands the inner garment which he had loosely cast about him, as, roused from sleep, he had rushed into Gethsemane, is, that he was none other than St. Mark himself. If so, we can understand it all: how the traitor may have first brought the Temple-guards, who had come to seize Christ, to the house of Mark's father, where the Supper had been held, and that, finding Him gone, they had followed to Gethsemane, for 'Judas knew the place, for Jesus ofttimes resorted thither with His disciples '[b]—and how Mark, startled from his sleep by the appearance of the armed men, would hastily cast about him his loose tunic and run after them; then, after the flight of the disciples, accompany Christ, but escape intended arrest by leaving his tunic in the hands of his would-be captors.

If the view formerly expressed is correct, that the owner of the house had provided all that was needed for the Supper, Peter and John would find there the Wine for the four Cups, the cakes of unleavened Bread, and probably also ' the bitter herbs.' Of the latter five kinds are mentioned,[c] which were to be dipped once in salt water, or vinegar, and another time in a mixture called *Charoseth* (a compound made of nuts, raisins, apples, almonds, &c.[1])—although this *Charoseth* was not obligatory. The wine was the ordinary one of the country, only red; it was mixed with water, generally in the proportion of one part to two of water.[2] The quantity for each of the four Cups is stated by one authority as five-sixteenths of a log, which may

---

[1] As it was symbolic of the clay on which the children of Israel worked in Egypt, the rubric has it that it must be thick (Pes. 116 *a*).

[2] The contention that it was *unfer-*mented wine is not worth serious discussion, although in *modern* practice (for reasons needless to mention) its use is allowed.

BOOK
V

be roughly computed at half a tumbler—of course mixed with water.[1] The Paschal Cup is described (according to the rubrical measure, which of course would not always be observed) as two fingers long by two fingers broad, and its height as a finger, half a finger, and one-third of a finger. All things being, as we presume, ready in the furnished upper room, it would only remain for Peter and John to see to the Paschal Lamb, and anything else required for the Supper, possibly also to what was to be offered as *Chagigah*, or festive sacrifice, and afterwards eaten at the Supper. If the latter were to be brought, the disciples would, of course, have to attend earlier in the Temple. The cost of the Lamb, which had to be provided, was very small. So low a sum as about threepence of our money is mentioned for such a sacrifice.[a] But this must refer to a hypothetical case rather than to the ordinary cost, and we prefer the more reasonable computation, from one *Sela*[b] to three *Selaim*,[c] i.e. from 2s. 6d. to 7s. 6d. of our money.

a Chag. i. 2.

b Menach.
xiii. 8

c Sheqal. ii.
4

If we mistake not, these purchases had, however, already been made on the previous afternoon by Judas. It is not likely that they would have been left to the last; nor that He Who had so lately condemned the traffic in the Courts of the Temple would have sent His two disciples thither to purchase the Paschal Lamb, which would have been necessary to secure an animal that had passed Levitical inspection, since on the Passover-day there would have been no time to subject it to such scrutiny. On the other hand, if Judas had made this purchase, we perceive not only on what pretext he may have gone to Jerusalem on the previous afternoon, but also how, on his way from the Sheep-market to the Temple, to have his lamb inspected, he may have learned that the Chief-Priests and Sanhedrists were just then in session in the Palace of the High-Priest close by.[2]

On the supposition just made, the task of Peter and John would, indeed, have been simple. They left the house of Mark with wondering but saddened hearts. Once more had they had evidence, how the Master's Divine glance searched the future in all its details. They had met the servant with the pitcher of water; they had delivered their message to the master of the house; and they had seen the large Upper Room furnished and ready. But this prescience

---

[1] The whole rubric is found in Jer. Pes. 37 c. The log = to the contents of six eggs. *Herzfeld* (Handelsgesch. p. 184) makes $\frac{1}{32}$ of a log = a dessert spoon. 12 log = 1 hin.

[2] But it may have been otherwise;

perhaps the lamb was even procured by the owner of the 'Upper Chamber,' since it might be offered for another. At the same time the account in the text seems to accord best with the Gospel-narrative.

of Christ afforded only further evidence, that what He had told of   CHAP.
His impending Crucifixion would also come true.   And now it would   IX
be time for the ordinary Evening-Service and Sacrifice.   Ordinarily
this began about   2.30 P.M.—the daily Evening-Sacrifice being
actually offered up about an hour later; but on this occasion, on
account of the Feast, the Service was an hour earlier.[1]   As at about
half-past one of our time the two Apostles ascended the Temple-
Mount, following a dense, motley crowd of joyous, chatting pilgrims,
they must have felt terribly lonely among them.   Already the
shadows of death were gathering around them.   In all that crowd how
few to sympathise with them; how many enemies!   The Temple-
Courts were thronged to the utmost by worshippers from all countries
and from all parts of the land.   The Priests' Court was filled with
white-robed Priests and Levites—for on that day all the twenty-
four Courses were on duty, and all their services would be called for,
although only the Course for that week would that afternoon engage
in the ordinary service, which preceded that of the Feast.   Almost
mechanically would they witness the various parts of the well-
remembered ceremonial.   There must have been a peculiar meaning
to them, a mournful significance, in the language of Ps. lxxxi., as the
Levites chanted it that afternoon in three sections, broken three
times by the threefold blast from the silver trumpets of the Priests.

Before the incense was burnt for the Evening Sacrifice, or yet the
lamps in the Golden Candlestick were trimmed for the night, the
Paschal-Lambs were slain.   The worshippers were admitted in three
divisions within the Court of the Priests.   When the first company
had entered, the massive Nicanor Gates—which led from the Court
of the Women to that of Israel—and the other side-gates into the
Court of the Priests, were closed.   A threefold blast from the Priests'
trumpets intimated that the Lambs were being slain.   This each
Israelite did for himself.   We can scarcely be mistaken in supposing
that Peter and John would be in the first of the three companies
into which the offerers were divided; for they must have been anxious
to be gone, and to meet the Master and their brethren in that
'Upper Room.'   Peter and John[2] had slain the Lamb.   In two rows
the officiating Priests stood, up to the great Altar of Burnt-offering.
As one caught up the blood from the dying Lamb in a golden bowl,

---

[1] If it had been the evening from
Friday to Saturday, instead of from
Thursday to Friday, it would have been
two hours earlier. See the rubric in
Pes. v. 1.

[2] Although, so far as we know, not of
practical importance here, we should
perhaps bear in mind that John was a
priest.

he handed it to his colleague, receiving in return an empty bowl; and so the blood was passed on to the Great Altar, where it was jerked in one jet at the base of the Altar.[1] While this was going on, the *Hallel* [a] was being chanted by the Levites. We remember that only the first line of every Psalm was repeated by the worshippers; while to every other line they responded by a *Halleluyah*, till Ps. cxviii. was reached, when, besides the first, these three lines were also repeated:—

> Save now, I beseech Thee, LORD;
> O LORD, I beseech Thee, send now prosperity.
> Blessed be He that cometh in the Name of the LORD.

As Peter and John repeated them on that afternoon, the words must have sounded most deeply significant. But their minds must have also reverted to that triumphal Entry into the City a few days before, when Israel had greeted with these words the Advent of their King. And now—was it not, as if it had only been an anticipation of the Hymn, when the blood of the Paschal Lamb was being shed ?

Little more remained to be done. The sacrifice was laid on staves which rested on the shoulders of Peter and John, flayed, cleansed, and the parts which were to be burnt on the Altar removed and prepared for burning. The second company of offerers could not have proceeded far in the service, when the Apostles, bearing their Lamb, were wending their way back to the home of Mark, there to make final preparations for the ' Supper.' The Lamb would be roasted on a pomegranate spit that passed right through it from mouth to vent, special care being taken that, in roasting, the Lamb did not touch the oven. Everything else, also, would be made ready: the *Chagigah* for supper (if such was used); the unleavened cakes, the bitter herbs, the dish with vinegar, and that with *Charoseth* would be placed on a table which could be carried in and moved at will; finally, the festive lamps would be prepared.

' It was probably as the sun was beginning to decline in the horizon that Jesus and the other ten disciples descended once more over the Mount of Olives into the Holy City. Before them lay Jerusalem in her festive attire. All around, pilgrims were hastening towards it. White tents dotted the sward, gay with the bright flowers of

---

[1] If we may suppose that there was a double row of priests to hand up the blood, and several to sprinkle it, or else that the blood from one row of sacrifices was handed to the priests in the opposite row, there could be no difficulty in the offering of lambs sufficient for all the ' companies,' which consisted of from ten to twenty persons.

early spring, or peered out from the gardens or the darker foliage of the olive plantations. From the gorgeous Temple buildings, dazzling in their snow-white marble and gold, on which the slanting rays of the sun were reflected, rose the smoke of the Altar of Burnt-offering. These courts were now crowded with eager worshippers, offering for the last time, in the real sense, their Paschal Lambs. The streets must have been thronged with strangers, and the flat roofs covered with eager gazers, who either feasted their eyes with a first sight of the sacred City for which they had so often longed, or else once more rejoiced in view of the well-known localities. It was the last day-view which the Lord could take, free and unhindered, of the Holy City till His Resurrection. Once more, in the approaching night of His Betrayal, would He look upon it in the pale light of the full moon. He was going forward to accomplish His Death in Jerusalem; to fulfil type and prophecy, and to offer Himself up as the true Passover Lamb—"the Lamb of God, Which taketh away the sin of the world." They who followed Him were busy with many thoughts. They knew that terrible events awaited them, and they had only shortly before been told that these glorious Temple-buildings, to which, with a national pride not unnatural, they had directed the attention of their Master, were to become desolate, not one stone being left upon the other. Among them, revolving his dark plans, and goaded on by the great Enemy, moved the betrayer. And now they were within the City. Its Temple, its royal bridge, its splendid palaces, its busy marts, its streets filled with festive pilgrims, were well known to them, as they made their way to the house where the guest-chamber had been prepared. Meanwhile, the crowd came down from the Temple-Mount, each bearing on his shoulders the sacrificial Lamb, to make ready for the Paschal Supper.'[1]

[1] 'The Temple and its Services,' pp. 194 195.

CHAPTER X.

THE PASCHAL SUPPER—THE INSTITUTION OF THE LORD'S SUPPER.

(St. Matt. xxvi. 17–19; St. Mark xiv. 12–16; St. Luke xxii. 7–13; St. John xiii. 1; St. Matt. xxvi. 20; St. Mark xiv. 17; St. Luke xxii. 14–16; St. Luke xxii. 24–30; St. Luke xxii. 17, 18; St. John xiii. 2–20; St. Matt. xxvi. 21–24; St. Mark xiv. 18–21; St. Luke xxii. 21–23; St. John xiii. 21–26; St. Matt. xxvi. 25; St. John xiii. 26–38; St. Matt. xxvi. 26–29; St. Mark xiv. 22–25; St. Luke xxii. 19, 20.)

BOOK V

* Ex. xii. 6; Lev. xxiii, 5; Numb. ix. 3, 5

THE period designated as 'between the two evenings,' [a] when the Paschal Lamb was to be slain, was past. There can be no question that, in the time of Christ, it was understood to refer to the interval between the commencement of the sun's decline and what was reckoned as the hour of his final disappearance (about 6 P.M.). The first three stars had become visible, and the threefold blast of the Silver Trumpets from the Temple-Mount rang it out to Jerusalem and far away, that the Pascha had once more commenced. In the festively-lit 'Upper Chamber' of St. Mark's house the Master and the Twelve were now gathered. Was this place of Christ's last, also that of the Church's first, entertainment; that, where the Holy Supper was instituted with the Apostles, also that, where it was afterwards first partaken of by the Church; the Chamber where He last tarried with them before His Death, that in which He first appeared to them after His Resurrection; that, also, in which the Holy Ghost was poured out, even as (if the Last Supper was in the house of Mark) it undoubtedly was that in which the Church was at first wont to gather for common prayer? [b] We know not, and can only venture to suggest, deeply soul-stirring as such thoughts and associations are.

b Acts xii. 12, 25

So far as appears, or we have reason to infer, this Passover was the only sacrifice ever offered by Jesus Himself. We remember indeed, the first sacrifice of the Virgin-Mother at her Purification. But that was *hers*. If Christ was in Jerusalem at any Passover before His Public Ministry began, He would, of course, have been a guest at some table, not the Head of a Company (which must consist of at least ten persons). Hence, He would not have been the offerer of the Paschal Lamb. And of the three Passovers since His Public Ministry had begun, at the first His Twelve Apostles had not been gathered,[a] so that He could not have appeared as the Head of a Company; while at the second He was not in Jerusalem but in the utmost parts of Galilee, in the borderland of Tyre and Sidon, where, of course, no sacrifice could be brought.[b] Thus, the first, the last, the only sacrifice which Jesus offered was that in which, symbolically, He offered Himself. Again, the only sacrifice which He brought is that connected with the Institution of His Holy Supper; even as the only purification to which He submitted was when, in His Baptism, He 'sanctified water to the mystical washing away of sin.' But what additional meaning does this give to the words which He spake to the Twelve as He sat down with them to the Supper: 'With desire have I desired to eat this Pascha with you before I suffer.'

And, in truth, as we think of it, we can understand not only why the Lord could not have offered any other Sacrifice, but that it was most fitting He should have offered this one Pascha, partaken of its commemorative Supper, and connected His own New Institution with that to which this Supper pointed. This joining of the Old with the New, the one symbolic Sacrifice which He offered with the One Real Sacrifice, the feast on the sacrifice with that other Feast upon the One Sacrifice, seems to cast light on the words with which He followed the expression of His longing to eat that one Pascha with them: 'I say unto you, I will not eat any more [1] thereof,[2] until it be fulfilled in the Kingdom of God.' And has it not been so, that this His last Pascha is connected with that other Feast in which He is ever present with His Church, not only as its Food but as its Host, as both the Pascha and He Who dispenses it? With a Sacrament did Jesus begin His Ministry: it was that of separation and consecration in Baptism. With a second Sacrament did He close His Ministry: it was that of gathering together and fellowship in the Lord's Supper. Both were into His Death: yet not as something that had power over Him, but as a Death that has been followed by the Resurrection. For, if in Baptism we are buried with Him, we also rise with Him; and if in the Holy Supper we remember His Death, it is as that of Him Who is risen again—and if we show forth that Death, it is until He come again. And so this Supper,

CHAP.

X

[a] St. John ii. 13

[b] St. Matt. xv. 21, &c.

---

[1] We prefer retaining this in the text.
[2] Such would still be the meaning, even if the accusative 'it' were regarded as the better reading.

BOOK
V

also, points forward to the Great Supper at the final consummation of His Kingdom.

Only one Sacrifice did the Lord offer. We are not thinking now of the significant Jewish legend, which connected almost every great event and deliverance in Israel with the Night of the Passover. But the Pascha was, indeed, a Sacrifice, yet one distinct from all others. It was not of the Law, for it was instituted before the Law had been given or the Covenant ratified by blood; nay, in a sense it was the cause and the foundation of all the Levitical Sacrifices and of the Covenant itself. And it could not be classed with either one, or the other of the various kinds of sacrifices, but rather combined them all, and yet differed from them all. Just as the Priesthood of Christ was real, yet not after the order of Aaron, so was the Sacrifice of Christ real, yet not after the order of Levitical sacrifices but after that of the Passover. And as in the Paschal Supper all Israel were gathered around the Paschal Lamb in commemoration of the past, in celebration of the present, in anticipation of the future, and in fellowship in the Lamb, so has the Church been ever since gathered together around its better fulfilment in the Kingdom of God.

It is difficult to decide how much, not only of the present ceremonial, but even of the Rubric for the Paschal Supper, as contained in the oldest Jewish Documents, may have been obligatory at the time of Christ. Ceremonialism rapidly develops, too often in proportion to the absence of spiritual life. Probably in the earlier days, even as the ceremonies were simpler, so more latitude may have been left in their observance, provided that the main points in the ritual were kept in view. We may take it, that, as prescribed, all would appear at the Paschal Supper in festive array. We also know, that, as the Jewish Law directed, they reclined on pillows around a low table, each resting on his left hand, so as to leave the right free. But ancient Jewish usage casts a strange light on the painful scene with which the Supper opened. Sadly humiliating as it reads, and almost incredible as it seems, the Supper began with ' a contention among them, which of them should be accounted to be greatest.' We can have no doubt that its occasion was the order in which they should occupy places at the table. We know that this was subject of contention among the Pharisees, and that they claimed to be seated according to their rank.[1] A similar feeling now appeared,

---

[1] *Wünsche* (on St. John xiii. 2) refers to Pes. 108 *a*, and states in a somewhat general way that no order of rank was preserved at the Paschal Table. But the passage he quotes does *not* imply this— only, that without distinction of rank all sat down at the same table, but not that the well-established order of sitting was

alas! in the circle of the disciples and at the Last Supper of the Lord. Even if we had not further indications of it, we should instinctively associate such a strife with the presence of Judas. St. John seems to refer to it, at least indirectly, when he opens his narrative with this notice: 'And during supper, the devil having already cast it into his heart, that Judas Iscariot, the son of Simon, shall betray Him.'[a] For, although the words form a general introduction to what follows, and refer to the entrance of Satan into the heart of Judas on the previous afternoon, when he sold his Master to the Sanhedrists, they are not without special significance as placed in connection with the Supper. But we are not left to general conjecture in regard to the influence of Judas in this strife. There is, we believe, ample evidence that he not only claimed, but actually obtained, the chief seat at the table next to the Lord. This, as previously explained, was not, as is generally believed, at the right, but at the left of Christ, not below, but above Him, on the couches or pillows on which they reclined.

From the Gospel-narratives we infer, that St. John must have reclined next to Jesus, on His Right Hand, since otherwise he could not have leaned back on His Bosom. This, as we shall presently show, would be at one end—the head of the table, or, to be more precise, at one end of the couches. For, dismissing all conventional ideas, we must think of it as a low Eastern table. In the Talmud,[b] the table of the disciples of the sages is described as two parts covered with a cloth, the other third being left bare for the dishes to stand on. There is evidence that this part of the table was outside the circle of those who were ranged around it. Occasionally a ring was fixed in it, by which the table was suspended above the ground, so as to preserve it from any possible Levitical defilement. During the Paschal Supper, it was the custom to remove the table at one part of the service; or, if this be deemed a later arrangement, the dishes at least would be taken off and put on again. This would render it necessary that the end of the table should protrude beyond the line of guests who reclined around it. For, as already repeatedly stated, it was the custom to recline at table, lying on the left side and leaning on the left hand, the feet stretching back towards the ground, and each guest occupying a separate divan or pillow. It would, therefore, have been impossible to place or remove anything from

[a] St. John xiii. 2

[b] B Bathr 57 b

infringed. The Jerusalem Talmud says nothing on the subject. The Gospel-narrative, of course, expressly states that there *was* a contention about rank among the disciples. In general, there are a number of inaccuracies in the part of *Wünsche's* Notes referring to the Last Supper.

the table from behind the guests. Hence, as a matter of necessity, the free end of the table, which was not covered with a cloth, would protrude beyond the line of those who reclined around it. We can now form a picture of the arrangement. Around a low Eastern table, oval or rather elongated, two parts covered with a cloth, and standing or else suspended, the single divans or pillows are ranged in the form of an elongated horseshoe, leaving free one end of the table,

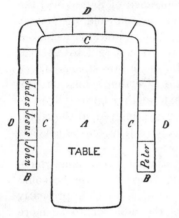

somewhat as in the accompanying woodcut. Here A represents the table, B B respectively the ends of the two rows of single divans on which each guest reclines on his left side, with his head (C) nearest the table, and his feet (D) stretching back towards the ground.

So far for the arrangement of the table. Jewish documents are equally explicit as to that of the guests. It seems to have been quite an established rule[a] that, in a company of more than two, say of three, the chief personage or Head—in this instance, of course, Christ—reclined on the middle divan. We know from the Gospel-narrative that John occupied the place on His right, at that end of the divans—as we may call it—at the head of the table. But the chief place next to the Master would be that to His left, or above Him. In the strife of the disciples, which should be accounted the greatest, this had been claimed, and we believe it to have been actually occupied, by Judas. This explains how, when Christ whispered to John by what sign to recognise the traitor,[b] none of the other disciples heard it. It also explains, how Christ would first hand to Judas the sop, which formed part of the Paschal ritual, beginning with him as the chief guest at the table, without thereby exciting special notice. Lastly, it accounts for the circumstance that, when Judas, desirous of ascertaining whether his treachery was known, dared to ask whether it was he, and received the affirmative answer,[c] no one at table knew what had passed. But this could not have been the case, unless Judas had occupied the place next to Christ; in this case, necessarily that at His left, or the post of chief honour. As regards Peter, we can quite understand how, when the Lord with such loving words rebuked their self-seeking and taught them of the greatness of Christian humility, he should, in his im-

petuosity of shame, have rushed to take the lowest place at the other
end of the table.[1]   Finally, we can now understand how Peter could
beckon to John, who sat at the opposite end of the table, over against
him, and ask him across the table, who the traitor was.[a]   The rest
of the disciples would occupy such places as were most convenient,
or suited their fellowship with one another.

a St. John
xiii. 24

The words which the Master spoke as He appeased their unseemly strife must, indeed, have touched them to the quick. First,
He showed them, not so much in the language of even gentlest reproof as in that of teaching, the difference between worldly honour
and distinction in the Church of Christ.   In the world kingship lay
in supremacy and lordship, and the title of Benefactor accompanied
the sway of power.   But in the Church the 'greater' would not
exercise lordship, but become as the less and the younger [the latter
referring to the circumstance, that age next to learning was regarded
among the Jews as a claim to distinction and the chief seats];
while, instead of him that had authority being called Benefactor,
the relationship would be reversed, and he that served would be
chief.   Self-forgetful humility instead of worldly glory, service
instead of rule: such was to be the title to greatness and to authority in the Church.[b]   Having thus shown them the character and title
to that greatness in the Kingdom, which was in prospect for them, He
pointed them in this respect also to Himself as their example.   The
reference here is, of course, not to the act of symbolic foot-washing,
which St. Luke does not relate—although, as immediately following on
the words of Christ, it would illustrate them—but to the tenor of His
whole Life and the object of His Mission, as of One Who served, not
was served.   Lastly, He woke them to the higher consciousness of
their own calling.   Assuredly, they would not lose their reward; but
not here, nor yet now.   They had shared, and would share His 'trials'[2]
—His being set at nought, despised, persecuted; but they would also
share His glory.   As the Father had 'covenanted' to Him, so He
'covenanted' and bequeathed to them a Kingdom, 'in order,' or 'so
that,' in it they might have festive fellowship of rest and of joy with
Him.   What to *them* must have been 'temptations,' and in that
respect also to Christ, they had endured: instead of Messianic glory,
such as they may at first have thought of, they had witnessed only

b St. Luke
xxii. 25, 26

---

[1] It seems almost incomprehensible,
that Commentators, who have not
thought this narrative misplaced by
St. Luke, should have attributed the
strife to Peter and John, the former being
jealous of the place of honour which 'the
beloved Disciple' had obtained.   (So
Nebe, Leidensgesch.; the former even
Calvin.)

[2] Not 'temptation'—i.e. not assaults
from within, but assaults from without.

contradiction, denial, and shame—and they had ' continued 'with Him. But the Kingdom was also coming. When His glory was manifested, their acknowledgment would also come. Here Israel had rejected the King and His Messengers, but then would that same Israel be judged by their word. A Royal dignity this, indeed, but one of service; a full Royal acknowledgment, but one of work. In that sense were Israel's Messianic hopes to be understood by them. Whether or not something beyond this may also be implied, and, in that day when He again gathers the outcasts of Israel, some special Rule and Judgment may be given to His faithful Apostles, we venture not to determine. Sufficient for us the words of Christ in their primary meaning.[1]

So speaking, the Lord commenced that Supper, which in itself was symbol and pledge of what He had just said and promised. The Paschal Supper began, as always,[a] by the Head of the Company taking the *first cup*, and speaking over it ' the thanksgiving.' The form presently in use consists really of two benedictions—the first over the wine, the second for the return of this Feastday with all that it implies, and for being preserved once more to witness it.[2] Turning to the Gospels, the words which follow the record of the benediction on the part of Christ [b] seem to imply, that Jesus had, at any rate, so far made use of the ordinary thanksgiving as to speak both these benedictions. We know, indeed, that they were in use before His time, since it was in dispute between the Schools of Hillel and Shammai, whether that over the wine or that over the day should take precedence. That over the wine was quite simple: ' Blessed art Thou, Jehovah our God, Who hast created the fruit of the Vine!' The formula was so often used in blessing the cup, and is so simple, that we need not doubt that these were the very words spoken by our Lord. It is otherwise as regards the benediction ' over the day,' which is not only more composite, but contains words expressive of Israel's national pride and self-righteousness, such as we cannot think would have been uttered by our Lord. With this exception, however, they were no doubt identical in contents with the present formula. This we infer from what the Lord added, as He passed the cup round the circle of the disciples.[3] No more, so He told them, would He speak

---

[1] The ' sitting down with Him ' at the feast is evidently a promise of joy, reward, and fellowship. The sitting on thrones and judging Israel must be taken as in contrast to the ' temptation ' of the contradiction of Christ and of their Apostolic message—as their vindication against Israel's present gainsaying.

[2] The whole formula is given in ' The Temple and its Services,' pp. 204, 205.

[3] I have often expressed my conviction that in the ancient Services there was considerable elasticity and liberty left to the individual. At present a cup is filled

the benediction over the fruit of the vine—not again utter the thanks 'over the day,' that they had been 'preserved alive, sustained, and brought to this season.' Another Wine, and at another Feast, now awaited Him—that in the future, when the Kingdom would come. It was to be the last of the old Paschas; the first, or rather the symbol and promise, of the new. And so, for the first and last time, did He speak the twofold benediction at the beginning of the Supper.

The cup, in which, according to express Rabbinic testimony,[a] the wine had been mixed with water before it was 'blessed,' had passed round. The next part of the ceremonial was for the Head of the Company to rise and 'wash hands.' It is this part of the ritual of which St. John [b] records the adaptation and transformation on the part of Christ. The washing of the disciples' feet is evidently connected with the ritual of 'handwashing.' Now this was done *twice* during the Paschal Supper: [c] the first time by the Head of the Company alone, immediately after the first cup; the second time by all present, at a much later part of the service, immediately before the actual meal (on the Lamb, &c.). If the footwashing had taken place on the latter occasion, it is natural to suppose that, when the Lord rose, all the disciples would have followed His example, and so the washing of their feet would have been impossible. Again, the footwashing, which was intended both as a lesson and as an example of humility and service,[d] was evidently connected with the dispute 'which of them should be accounted to be greatest.' If so, the symbolical act of our Lord must have followed close on the strife of the disciples, and on our Lord's teaching what in the Church constituted rule and greatness. Hence the act must have been connected with the first handwashing—that by the Head of the Company—immediately after the first cup, and not with that at a later period, when much else had intervened.

[a] Babha B. 97 *b*, lines 11 and 12 from top

[b] St. John xiii.

[c] Pes. x. 4

[d] St. John xiii. 12-16

All else fits in with this. For clearness' sake, the account given by St. John [e] may here be recapitulated. The opening words concerning the love of Christ to His own unto the end form the general introduction.[1] Then follows the account of what happened 'during Supper'—the Supper itself being left undescribed—beginning, by

[e] St. John xiii.

[f] ver. 2

for each individual, but Christ seems to have passed the one cup round among the Disciples. Whether such was sometimes done, or the alteration was designedly, and as we readily see, significantly, made by Christ, cannot now be determined.

[1] *Godet*, who regards ver. 1 as a general, and ver. 2 as a special, introduction to the foot-washing, calls attention to the circumstance that such introductions not unfrequently occur in the Fourth Gospel.

way of explanation of what is to be told about Judas, with this:
'The Devil having already cast into his (Judas') heart, that Judas
Iscariot, the son of Simon, shall betray Him.' General as this notice
is, it contains much that requires special attention. Thankfully we
feel, that the heart of man was not capable of originating the
Betrayal of Christ; humanity had fallen, but not so low. It was
the Devil who had 'cast' it into Judas' heart—with force and overwhelming power.[1] Next, we mark the full description of the name
and parentage of the traitor. It reads like the wording of a formal
indictment. And, although it seems only an introductory explanation, it also points to the contrast with the love of Christ which
persevered to the end,[a] even when hell itself opened its mouth to
swallow Him up; the contrast, also, between what Jesus and what
Judas were about to do, and between the wild storm of evil that
raged in the heart of the traitor and the calm majesty of love and
peace which reigned in that of the Saviour.

a St. John
xiii. 1

If what Satan had cast into the heart of Judas explains his conduct,
so does the knowledge which Jesus possessed account for that He was
about to do.[b][2] Many as are the thoughts suggested by the words,
'Knowing that the Father had given all things into His Hands, and
that He came forth from God, and goeth unto God'—yet, from their
evident connection, they must in the first instance be applied to the
Footwashing, of which they are, so to speak, the logical antecedent.
It was His greatest act of humiliation and service, and yet He never
lost in it for one moment aught of the majesty or consciousness of His
Divine dignity; for He did it with the full knowledge and assertion
that all things were in His Hands, and that He came forth from and
was going unto God—and He could do it, because He knew this.
Here, not side by side, but in combination, are the Humiliation and
Exaltation of the God-Man. And so, 'during Supper,' which had
begun with the first cup, 'He riseth from Supper.' The disciples
would scarcely marvel, except that He should conform to that
practice of handwashing, which, as He had often explained, was, as
a ceremonial observance, unavailing for those who were not inwardly
clean, and needless and unmeaning in them whose heart and life had
been purified. But they must have wondered as they saw Him put
off His upper garment, gird Himself with a towel, and pour water
into a basin, like a slave who was about to perform the meanest
service.

b St. John
xi

---

[2] *Bengel*: magna vis.
[1] The contrast is the more marked. as
the same verb ($\beta \acute{\alpha} \lambda \lambda \varepsilon \iota \nu$) is used both of

Satan 'casting' it into the heart of
Judas, and of Christ throwing into the
basin the water for the footwashing.

From the position which, as we have shown, Peter occupied at the end of the table, it was natural that the Lord should begin with him the act of footwashing.[1] Besides, had He first turned to others, Peter must either have remonstrated before, or else his later expostulation would have been tardy, and an act either of self-righteousness or of needless voluntary humility. As it was, the surprise with which he and the others had witnessed the preparation of the Lord burst into characteristic language when Jesus approached him to wash his feet. 'Lord—Thou—of me washest the feet!' It was the utterance of deepest reverence for the Master, and yet of utter misunderstanding of the meaning of His action, perhaps even of His Work. Jesus was now doing what before He had spoken. The act of externalism and self-righteousness represented by the washing of hands, and by which the Head of the Company was to be distinguished from all others and consecrated, He changed into a footwashing, in which the Lord and Master was to be distinguished, indeed, from the others—but by the humblest service of love, and in which He showed by His example what characterised greatness in the Kingdom, and that service was evidence of rule. And, as mostly in every symbol, there was the real also in this act of the Lord. For, by sympathetically sharing in this act of love and service on the part of the Lord, they who had been bathed—who had previously become clean in heart and spirit—now received also that cleansing of the 'feet,' of active and daily walk, which cometh from true heart-humility, in opposition to pride, and consisteth in the service which love is willing to render even to the uttermost.

But Peter had understood none of these things. He only felt the incongruousness of their relative positions. And so the Lord, partly also wishing thereby to lead his impetuosity to the absolute submission of faith, and partly to indicate the deeper truth he was to learn in the future, only told him, that though he knew it not now, he would understand hereafter what the Lord was doing. Yes, hereafter—when, after that night of terrible fall, he would learn by the Lake of Galilee what it really meant to feed the lambs and to tend the sheep of Christ; yes, hereafter—when no longer, as when he had been young, he would gird himself and walk whither he would. But, even so, Peter could not content himself with the prediction that in the future he would understand and enter into what Christ was doing in washing their feet. Never, he declared,

---

[1] *St. Chrysostom* and others unduly urge the words (ver. 6), 'He cometh to Peter.' He came to him, not after the others, but from the place where the basin and water for the purification had stood.

could he allow it. The same feelings, which had prompted him to attempt withdrawing the Lord from the path of humiliation and suffering,ᵃ now asserted themselves again. It was personal affection, indeed, but it was also unwillingness to submit to the humiliation of the Cross. And so the Lord told him, that if He washed him not, he had no part with Him. Not that the bare act of washing gave him part in Christ, but that the refusal to submit to it would have deprived him of it; and that, to share in this washing, was, as it were, the way to have part in Christ's service of love, to enter into it, and to share it.

Still, Peter did not understand. But as, on that morning by the Lake of Galilee, it appeared that, when he had lost all else, he had retained love, so did love to the Christ now give him the victory —and, once more with characteristic impetuosity, he would have tendered not only his feet to be washed, but his hands and head. Yet here, also, was there misunderstanding. There was deep symbolical meaning, not only in *that* Christ did it, but also in *what* He did. Submission to His doing it meant symbolically share and part with Him—part in His Work. *What* He did, meant His work and service of love; the constant cleansing of one's walk and life in the love of Christ, and in the service of that love. It was not a meaningless ceremony of humiliation on the part of Christ, not yet one where submission to the utmost was required; but the action was symbolic, and meant that the disciple, who was already bathed and made clean in heart and spirit, required only this—to wash his feet in spiritual consecration to the service of love which Christ had here shown forth in symbolic act. And so His Words referred not, as is so often supposed, to the forgiveness of our daily sins—the introduction of which would have been wholly abrupt and unconnected with the context—but, in contrast to all self-seeking, to the daily consecration of our life to the service of love after the example of Christ.

And still do all these words come to us in manifold and ever-varied application. In the misunderstanding of our love to Him, we too often imagine that Christ cannot will or do what seems to us incongruous on His part, or rather, incongruous with what we think about Him. We know it not now, but we shall understand it hereafter. And still we persist in our resistance, till it comes to us that so we would even lose our part in and with Him. Yet not much, not very much, does He ask, Who giveth so much. He that has washed us wholly would only have us cleanse our feet for the service of love, as He gave us the example.

They were clean, these disciples, but not all.   For He knew that
there was among them he 'that was betraying Him.'[1]   He knew it,
but not with the knowledge of an inevitable fate impending, far less
of an absolute decree, but with that knowledge which would again
and again speak out the warning, if by any means he might be saved.
What would have come, if Judas had repented, is as idle a question
as this: What would have come if Israel, as a nation, had repented
and accepted Christ?   For, from our human standpoint, we can only
view the human aspect of things—that earthwards; and here every
action is not isolated, but ever the outcome of a previous development
and history, so that a man always freely acts, yet always in consequence
of an inward necessity.

The solemn service of Christ now went on in the silence of
reverent awe.[a]   None dared ask Him nor resist.   It was ended, and   a St. John xiii. 12-17
He had resumed His upper garment, and again taken His place at the
Table.   It was His now to follow the symbolic deed by illustrative
words, and to explain the practical application of what had just been
done.   Let it not be misunderstood.   They were wont to call Him by
the two highest names of Teacher and Lord, and these designations
were rightly His.   For the first time He fully accepted and owned
the highest homage.   How much more, then, must His Service of
love, Who was their Teacher and Lord, serve as example[2] of what
was due[3] by each to his fellow-disciple and fellow-servant!   He,
Who really was Lord and Master, had rendered this lowest service to
them as an example that, as He had done, so should they do.   No
principle better known, almost proverbial in Israel, than that a servant
was not to claim greater honour than his master, nor yet he that was
sent than he who had sent him.   They knew this, and now also the
meaning of the symbolic act of footwashing; and if they acted it out,
then theirs would be the promised ' Beatitude.'[4]

This reference to what were familiar expressions among the Jews,
especially noteworthy in St. John's Gospel, leads us to supplement a
few illustrative notes from the same source.   The Greek word for 'the
towel,' with which our Lord girded Himself, occurs also in Rabbinic
writings, to denote the towel used in washing and at baths (*Luntith*
and *Aluntith*).   Such girding was the common mark of a slave, by

---

[1] So the expression in St. John xiii.
11, more accurately rendered.
[2] $ὑπόδειγμα$. The distinctive meaning
of the word is best gathered from the
other passages in the N.T. in which it
occurs, viz. Heb. iv. 11; viii. 5; ix. 23;
St. James v. 10; 2 Pet. ii. 6.   For the

literal outward imitation of this deed of
Christ in the ceremony of footwashing,
still common in the Roman Catholic
Church, see *Bingham*, Antiq. xii. 4, 10.
[3] $ὀφείλετε$.
[4] The word is that employed in the
'Beatitudes,' $μακάριοι$.

BOOK
V

ᵃ Shem. R.
20
ᵇ Ezek. xvi.
9
ᶜ Comp.
Ezek. xvi.
10; Ex. xix.
4; xiii. 21

¹ Comp. St.
John xiii.
17

ᵉ Kidd. 42 a
ᶠ Ber. R. 78

ᵍ Yalkut on
Is. lx. vol.
ii. p. 56 d,
lines 12, 13
from top

ʰ St. John
xiii. 18, 19

ⁱ Ps. xli. 9

whom the service of footwashing was ordinarily performed. And, in
a very interesting passage, the Midrash ᵃ contrasts what, in this
respect, is the way of man with what God had done for Israel. For, He
had been described by the prophet as performing for them the service of
washing,ᵇ and others usually rendered by slaves.ᶜ Again, the combination of these two designations, 'Rabbi and Lord,' or 'Rabbi, Father,
and Lord,' was among those most common on the part of disciples.¹
The idea, that if a man knows (for example, the Law) and does not
do it, it were better for him not to have been created,ᵈ is not unfrequently expressed. But the most interesting reference is in regard
to the relation between the sender and the sent, and a servant and his
master. In regard to the former, it is proverbially said, that while he
that is sent stands on the same footing as he who sent him,ᵉ yet he
must expect less honour.ᶠ And as regards Christ's statement that
'the servant is not greater than his Master,' there is a passage in
which we read this, *in connection with the sufferings of the Messiah*:
'It is enough for the servant that he be like his Master.'ᵍ

But to return. The footwashing on the part of Christ, in which
Judas had shared, together with the explanatory words that followed,
almost required, in truthfulness, this limitation: 'I speak not of you
all.' For it would be a night of terrible moral sifting to them all. A
solemn warning was needed by all the disciples. But, besides, the
treachery of one of their own number might have led them to doubt
whether Christ had really Divine knowledge. On the other hand, this
clear prediction of it would not only confirm their faith in Him, but
show that there was some deeper meaning in the presence of a Judas
among them.ʰ We come here upon these words of deepest mysterious-
ness: 'I know those I chose; but that the Scripture may be fulfilled,
He that eateth My Bread lifteth up his heel against Me!'ⁱ It were
almost impossible to believe, even if not forbidden by the context, that
this knowledge of which Christ spoke, referred to an eternal foreknowledge; still more, that it meant Judas had been chosen with such
foreknowledge in order that this terrible Scripture might be fulfilled
in him. Such foreknowledge and foreordination would be to sin, and
it would involve thoughts such as only the harshness of our human
logic in its fatal system-making could induce anyone to entertain.
Rather must we understand it as meaning that Jesus had, from the
first, known the inmost thoughts of those He had chosen to be His
Apostles; but that by this treachery of one of their number, the terrible prediction of the worst enmity, that of ingratitude, true in all

רבי ומורי or רבי אבי ואדוני ¹.

ages of the Church, would receive its complete fulfilment.[1] The word ·*that*'—'that the Scripture may be fulfilled,' does not mean 'in order that,' or 'for the purpose of;' it never means this in that connection;[2] and it would be altogether irrational to suppose that an event happened *in order* that a special prediction might be fulfilled. Rather does it indicate the higher internal connection in the succession of events, when an event had taken place in the free determination of its agents, *by which*, all unknown to them and unthought of by others, that unexpectedly came to pass which had been Divinely foretold. And herein appears the Divine character of prophecy, which is always at the same time announcement and forewarning, that is, has besides its predictive a moral element: that, while man is left to act freely, each development tends to the goal Divinely foreseen and foreordained. Thus the word 'that' marks not the connection between causation and effect, but between the Divine antecedent and the human subsequent.

There is, indeed, behind this a much deeper question, to which brief reference has already formerly been made. Did Christ know from the beginning that Judas would betray Him, and yet, so knowing, did He choose him to be one of the Twelve? Here we can only answer by indicating this as a canon in studying the Life on earth of the God-Man, that it was part of His Self-exinanition—of that emptying Himself, and taking upon Him the form of a Servant[a]—voluntarily to forego His Divine knowledge in the choice of His Human actions. So only could He, as perfect Man, have perfectly obeyed the Divine Law. For, if the Divine had determined Him in the choice of His Actions, there could have been no merit attaching to His Obedience, nor could He be said to have, as perfect Man, taken our place, and to have obeyed the Law in our stead and as our Representative, nor yet be our Ensample. But if His Divine knowledge did not guide Him in the choice of His actions, we can see, and have already indicated, reasons why the discipleship and service of Judas should have been accepted, if it had been only as that of a Judæan, a man in many

CHAP.
X

[a] Phil. ii.
5-7

---

[1] At the same time there is also a terrible literality about this prophetic reference to one who ate his bread, when we remember that Judas, like the rest, lived of what was supplied to Christ, and at that very moment sat at His Table. On Ps. xli. see the Commentaries.

[2] '*ἵνα* frequenter *ἐκβατικῶς, i.e.* de *eventu* usurpari dicitur, ut sit *eo eventu, ut; eo successu, ut, ita ut*' [Grimm, ad verb.]—Angl. 'so that.' And *Grimm*

rightly points out that *ἵνα* is *always* used in that sense, marking the internal connection in the succession of events— *ἐκβατικῶς not τελικῶς*—where the phrase occurs 'that it might be fulfilled.' This canon is most important, and of very wide application wherever the *ἵνα* is connected with the Divine Agency, in which, from our human view-point, we have to distinguish between the decree and the counsel of God.

respects well fitted for such an office, and the representative of one of the various directions which tended towards the reception of the Messiah.

We are not in circumstances to judge whether or not Christ spoke all these things continuously, after He had sat down, having washed the disciples' feet. More probably it was at different parts of the meal. This would also account for the seeming abruptness of this concluding sentence:ᵃ 'He that receiveth whomsoever I send receiveth Me.' And yet the internal connection of thought seems clear. The apostasy and loss of one of the Apostles was known to Christ. Would it finally dissolve the bond that bound together the College of Apostles, and so invalidate their Divine Mission (the Apostolate) and its authority? The words of Christ conveyed an assurance which would be most comforting in the future, that any such break would not be lasting, only transitory, and that in this respect also 'the foundation of God standeth.'

In the meantime the Paschal Supper was proceeding. We mark this important note of time in the words of St. Matthew: 'as they were eating,'ᵇ or, as St. Mark expresses it, 'as they reclined and were eating.'ᶜ According to the Rubric, after the 'washing' the dishes were immediately to be brought on the table. Then the Head of the Company would dip some of the bitter herbs into the salt-water or vinegar, speak a blessing, and partake of them, then hand them to each in the company. Next, he would break one of the unleavened cakes (according to the present ritual the middle of the three), of which half was put aside for after supper. This is called the *Aphiqomon*, or after-dish, and as we believe that 'the bread' of the Holy Eucharist was the *Aphiqomon*, some particulars may here be of interest. The dish in which the broken cake lies (not the *Aphiqomon*), is elevated, and these words are spoken: 'This is the bread of misery which our fathers ate in the land of Egypt. All that are hungry, come and eat; all that are needy, come, keep the Pascha.' In the more modern ritual the words are added: 'This year here, next year in the land of Israel; this year bondsmen, next year free!' On this the second cup is filled, and the youngest in the company is instructed to make formal inquiry as to the meaning of all the observances of that night,ᵈ when the Liturgy proceeds to give full answers as regards the festival, its occasion, and ritual. The Talmud adds that the table is to be previously removed, so as to excite the greater curiosity.ᵉ We do not suppose that even the earlier ritual represents the exact observances at the time of Christ, or that, even

ᵃ St. John xiii. 20

ᵇ St. Matt. xxvi. 21
ᶜ St. Mark xiv. 18.

ᵈ Pes. x. 4

ᵉ Pes. 115 b

if it does so, they were exactly followed at that Paschal Table of the Lord. But so much stress is laid in Jewish writings on the duty of fully rehearsing at the Paschal Supper the circumstances of the first Passover and the deliverance connected with it, that we can scarcely doubt that what the Mishnah declares as so essential formed part of the services of that night. And as we think of our Lord's comment on the Passover and Israel's deliverance, the words spoken when the unleavened cake was broken come back to us, and with deeper meaning attaching to them.

After this the cup is elevated, and then the service proceeds somewhat lengthily, the cup being raised a second time and certain prayers spoken. This part of the service concludes with the two first Psalms in the series called 'the Hallel,'[a] when the cup is raised a third time, a prayer spoken, and the cup drunk. This ends the first part of the service. And now the Paschal meal begins by all washing their hands—a part of the ritual which we scarcely think Christ observed. It was, we believe, during this lengthened exposition and service that the 'trouble in spirit' of which St. John speaks[b] passed over the soul of the God-Man. Almost presumptuous as it seems to inquire into its immediate cause, we can scarcely doubt that it concerned not so much Himself as them. His Soul could not, indeed, but have been troubled, as, with full consciousness of all that it would be to Him—infinitely more than merely human suffering —He looked down into the abyss which was about to open at His Feet. But He saw more than even this. He saw Judas about to take the last fatal step, and His Soul yearned in pity over him. The very sop which He would so soon hand to him, although a sign of recognition to John, was a last appeal to all that was human in Judas. And, besides all this, Jesus also saw, how, all unknown to them, the terrible tempest of fierce temptation would that night sweep over them; how it would lay low and almost uproot one of them, and scatter all. It was the beginning of the hour of Christ's utmost loneliness, of which the climax was reached in Gethsemane. And in the trouble of His Spirit did He solemnly 'testify' to them or the near Betrayal. We wonder not, that they all became exceeding sorrowful, and each asked, 'Lord, is it I?' This question on the part of the eleven disciples, who were conscious of innocence of any purpose of betrayal, and conscious also of deep love to the Master, affords one of the clearest glimpses into the inner history of that Night of Terror, in which, so to speak, Israel became Egypt. We can now better understand their heavy sleep in Gethsemane, their

a Ps. cxiii to cxviii.

b St. John xiii. 21

BOOK
V

forsaking Him and fleeing, even Peter's denial. Everything must have seemed to these men to give way; all to be enveloped in outer darkness, when each man could ask whether he was to be the Betrayer.

The answer of Christ left the special person undetermined, while it again repeated the awful prediction—shall we not add, the most solemn warning—that it was one of those who took part in the Supper. It is at this point that St. John resumes the thread of the narrative.[a] As he describes it, the disciples were looking one on another, doubting of whom He spake. In this agonising suspense Peter beckoned from across the table to John, whose head, instead of leaning on his hand, rested, in the absolute surrender of love and intimacy born of sorrow, on the bosom of the Master.[1] Peter would have John ask of whom Jesus spake.[2] And to the whispered question of John, 'leaning back as he was on Jesus' breast,' the Lord gave the sign, that it was he to whom He would give 'the sop' when He had dipped it. Even this perhaps was not clear to John, since each one in turn received 'the sop.'

At present, the Supper itself begins by eating, first, a piece of the unleavened cake, then of the bitter herbs dipped in *Charoseth*, and lastly two small pieces of the unleavened cake, between which a piece of bitter radish has been placed. But we have direct testimony, that, about the time of Christ,[3] 'the sop'[4] which was handed round consisted of these things wrapped together: flesh of the Paschal Lamb, a piece of unleavened bread, and bitter herbs.[b] This, we believe, was 'the sop,' which Jesus, having dipped it for him in the dish, handed first to Judas, as occupying the first and chief place at Table. But before He did so, probably while He dipped it in the dish, Judas, who could not but fear that his purpose might be known, reclining at Christ's left hand, whispered into the Master's ear, 'Is it I, Rabbi?' It must have been whispered, for no one at the Table could have heard either the question of Judas or the affirmative answer of Christ.[c] It was the last outgoing of the pitying love of Christ after the traitor. Coming after the terrible warning and woe on the Betrayer,[d] it must be regarded as the final warning and also the final attempt at rescue on the part of the

[a] St. John xiii. 22

[b] Jer.Chall. 57 b

[c] St. John xiii. 28

[d] St. Matt. xxvi. 24; St. Mark xiv. 21

---

[1] The reading adopted in the R.V. of St. John xiii. 24 represents the better accredited text, though it involves some difficulties.

[2] On the circumstance that John does not name himself in ver. 23, *Bengel* beautifully remarks: 'Optabilius est, amari ab Jesu, quam nomine proprio celebrari.'

[3] The statement is in regard to Hillel, while the Temple stood.

[4] Mark the definite article—*not* 'a sop.'

Saviour. It was with full knowledge of all, even of this that his treachery was known, though he may have attributed the information not to Divine insight but to some secret human communication, that Judas went on his way to destruction. We are too apt to attribute crimes to madness; but surely there is moral, as well as mental mania; and it must have been in a paroxysm of that, when all feeling was turned to stone, and mental self-delusion was combined with moral perversion, that Judas 'took'[1] from the Hand of Jesus 'the sop.' It was to descend alive into the grave—and with a heavy sound the gravestone fell and closed over the mouth of the pit. That moment Satan entered again into his heart. But the deed was virtually done; and Jesus, longing for the quiet fellowship of His own with all that was to follow, bade him do quickly that he did.

But even so there are questions connected with the human motives that actuated Judas, to which, however, we can only give the answer of some suggestions. Did Judas regard Christ's denunciation of ' woe ' on the Betrayer not as a prediction, but as intended to be deterrent—perhaps in language Orientally exaggerated—or if he regarded it as a prediction, did he not believe in it? Again, when after the plain intimation of Christ and His Words to do quickly what he was about to do, Judas still went to the betrayal, could he have had an idea—rather, sought to deceive himself, that Jesus felt that He could not escape His enemies, and that He rather wished it to be all over? Or had all his former feelings towards Jesus turned, although temporarily, into actual hatred which every Word and Warning of Christ only intensified? But above all and in all we have, first and foremost, to think of the peculiarly Judaic character of his first adherence to Christ; of the gradual and at last final and fatal disenchantment of his hopes; of his utter moral, consequent upon his spiritual, failure; of the change of all that had in it the possibility of good into the actuality of evil; and, on the other hand, of the direct agency of Satan in the heart of Judas, which his moral and spiritual ship-wreck rendered possible.

From the meal scarcely begun Judas rushed into the dark night. Even this has its symbolic significance. None there knew why this strange haste, unless from obedience to something that the Master had bidden him.[2] Even John could scarcely have understood the sign which Christ had given of the traitor. Some of them thought, he

---

[1] St. John xiii. 30 should be rendered, 'having taken,' not ' received.'
[2] To a Jew it might seem that with the ' sop,' containing as it did a piece of the Paschal Lamb, the chief part in the Paschal Supper was over.

had been directed by the words of Christ to purchase what was needful for the feast: others, that he was bidden go and give something to the poor. Gratuitous objection has been raised, as if this indicated that, according to the Fourth Gospel, this meal had not taken place on the Paschal night, since, after the commencement of the Feast (on the 15th Nisan), it would be unlawful to make purchases. But this certainly was not the case. Sufficient here to state, that the provision and preparation of the needful food, and indeed of all that was needful for the Feast, was allowed on the 15th Nisan.[1] And this must have been specially necessary when, as in this instance, the first festive day, or 15th Nisan, was to be followed by a Sabbath, on which no such work was permitted. On the other hand, the mention of these two suggestions by the disciples seems almost necessarily to involve, that the writer of the Fourth Gospel had placed this meal in the Paschal Night. Had it been on the evening before, no one could have imagined that Judas had gone out during the night to buy provisions, when there was the whole next day for it, nor would it have been likely that a man should on any ordinary day go at such an hour to seek out the poor. But in the Paschal Night, when the great Temple-gates were opened at midnight to begin early preparations for the offering of the *Chagigah*, or festive sacrifice, which was not voluntary but of due, and the remainder of which was afterwards eaten at a festive meal, such preparations would be quite natural. And equally so, that the poor, who gathered around the Temple, might then seek to obtain the help of the charitable.

The departure of the betrayer seemed to clear the atmosphere. He was gone to do his work; but let it not be thought that it was the necessity of that betrayal which was the cause of Christ's suffering of soul. He offered Himself willingly—and though it was brought about through the treachery of Judas, yet it was Jesus Himself Who freely brought Himself a Sacrifice, in fulfilment of the work which the Father had given Him. And all the more did He realise and express this on the departure of Judas. So long as he was there, pitying love still sought to keep him from the fatal step. But when the traitor was at last gone, the other side of His own work clearly emerged into Christ's view. And this voluntary sacrificial aspect is further clearly indicated by His selection of the terms ' Son of Man ' and ' God ' instead of ' Son ' and ' Father.' [a]   ' Now is glorified the

*St. John

---

[1] The Mishnah expressly allows the procuring even on the Sabbath of that which is required for the Passover, and the Law of the Sabbath-rest was much more strict than that of feast-days. See this in Appendix XVII., p. 783.

Son of Man, and God is glorified in Him.[1] And God shall glorify
Him in Himself, and straightway shall He glorify Him.' If the first
of these sentences expressed the meaning of what was about to take
place, as exhibiting the utmost glory of the Son of Man in the
triumph of the obedience of His Voluntary Sacrifice, the second
sentence pointed out its acknowledgment by God: the exaltation
which followed the humiliation, the reward [2] as the necessary sequel
of the work, the Crown after the Cross.

Thus far for one aspect of what was about to be enacted. As for
the other—that which concerned the disciples: only a little while would
He still be with them. Then would come the time of sad and sore
perplexity—when they would seek Him, but could not come whither
He had gone—during the terrible hours between His Crucifixion
and His manifested Resurrection. With reference to that period
especially, but in general to the whole time of His Separation
from the Church on earth, the great commandment, the bond which
alone would hold them together, was that of love one to another,
and such love as that which He had shown towards them. And this
—shame on us, as we write it!—was to be the mark to all men
of their discipleship.[a] As recorded by St. John, the words of the
Lord were succeeded by a question of Peter, indicating perplexity as
to the primary and direct meaning of Christ's going away. On this
followed Christ's reply about the impossibility of Peter's now sharing
his Lord's way of Passion, and, in answer to the disciple's impetuous
assurance of his readiness to follow the Master not only into peril,
but to lay down his Life for Him, the Lord's indication of Peter's
present unpreparedness and the prediction of His impending denial.
It may have been, that all this occurred in the Supper-Chamber and
at the time indicated by St. John. But it is also recorded by the
Synoptists as on the way to Gethsemane, and in, what we may term,
a more natural connection. Its consideration will therefore be best
reserved till we reach that stage of the history.

We now approach the most solemn part of that night: The Institution of the Lord's Supper. It would manifestly be beyond the
object, as assuredly it would necessarily stretch beyond the limits, of
the present work, to discuss the many questions and controversies
which, alas! have gathered around the Words of the Institution. On

CHAP.
X

[a] St. John
xiii. 31-35

---

[1] The first clause in ver. 32 of our
T.R. seems spurious, though it indicates
the logical *nexus* of facts.

[2] Probably the word 'reward' is
wrongly chosen, for I look on Christ's
exaltation after the victory of His Obedience as rather the necessary sequence
than the reward of His Work.

the other hand, it would not be truthful wholly to pass them by. On certain points, indeed, we need have no hesitation. The Institution of the Lord's Supper is recorded by the Synoptists, although without reference to those parts of the Paschal Supper and its Services with which one or another of its acts must be connected. In fact, while the historical *nexus* with the Paschal Supper is evident, it almost seems as if the Evangelists had intended, by their studied silence in regard to the Jewish Feast, to indicate that with this Celebration and the new Institution the Jewish Passover had for ever ceased. On the other hand, the Fourth Gospel does not record the new Institution—it may have been, because it was so fully recorded by the others; or for reasons connected with the structure of that Gospel; or it may be accounted for on other grounds.[1] But whatever way we may account for it, the silence of the Fourth Gospel must be a sore difficulty to those who regard it as an Ephesian product of symbolico-sacramentarian tendency, dating from the second century.

The absence of a record by St. John is compensated by the narrative of St. Paul in 1 Cor. xi. 23–26, to which must be added as supplementary the reference in 1 Cor. x. 16 to 'the Cup of Blessing which we bless' as 'fellowship of the Blood of Christ, and the Bread which we break' as 'fellowship of the Body of Christ.' We have thus four accounts, which may be divided into two groups: St. Matthew and St. Mark, and St. Luke and St. Paul. None of these give us the very words of Christ, since these were spoken in Aramæan. In the renderings which we have of them one series may be described as the more rugged and literal, the other as the more free and paraphrastic. The differences between them are, of course, exceedingly minute; but they exist. As regards the text which underlies the rendering in our A.V., the differences suggested are not of any practical importance,[2] with the exception of two points. First, the copula '*is*' ['This is My Body,' 'This is My Blood'] was certainly *not* spoken by the Lord in the Aramaic, just as it does not occur in the Jewish formula in the breaking of bread at the beginning of the Paschal Supper. Secondly, the words: 'Body which is given,' or, in 1 Cor. xi. 24, 'broken,' and 'Blood which is shed,' should be more correctly rendered: 'is being given,' 'broken,' 'shed.'

---

[1] Could there possibly be a *hiatus* in our present Gospel? There is not the least external evidence to that effect, and yet the impression deepens on consideration. I have ventured to throw out some hints on this subject in 'The Temple and its Services,' Appendix at close.

[2] The most important of these, perhaps, is the rendering of 'covenant' for 'testament.' In St. Matthew the word 'new' before 'covenant,' should be left out; this also in St. Mark, as well as the word 'eat' after 'take.'

If we now ask ourselves at what part of the Paschal Supper the new Institution was made, we cannot doubt that it was before the Supper was completely ended.[a] We have seen, that Judas had left the Table at the beginning of the Supper. The meal continued to its end, amidst such conversation as has already been noted. According to the Jewish ritual, *the third Cup* was filled at the close of the Supper. This was called, as by St. Paul,[b] 'the Cup of Blessing,' partly, because a special 'blessing' was pronounced over it. It is described as one of the ten essential rites in the Paschal Supper. Next, 'grace after meat' was spoken. But on this we need not dwell, nor yet on 'the washing of hands' that followed. The latter would not be observed by Jesus as a religious ceremony; while, in regard to the former, the composite character of this part of the Paschal Liturgy affords internal evidence that it could not have been in use at the time of Christ. But we can have little doubt, that the Institution of the Cup was in connection with this third 'Cup of Blessing.'[1] If we are asked, what part of the Paschal Service corresponds to the 'Breaking of Bread,' we answer, that this being really the last Pascha, and the cessation of it, our Lord anticipated the later rite, introduced when, with the destruction of the Temple, the Paschal as all other Sacrifices ceased. While the Paschal Lamb was still offered, it was the Law that, after partaking of its flesh, nothing else should be eaten. But since the Paschal Lamb has ceased, it is the custom after the meal to break and partake as *Aphikomon*, or after-dish, of that half of the unleavened cake, which, as will be remembered, had been broken and put aside at the beginning of the Supper. The Paschal Sacrifice having now really ceased, and consciously so to all the disciples of Christ, He anticipated this, and connected with the breaking of the Unleavened Cake at the close of the Meal the institution of the breaking of Bread in the Holy Eucharist.

What did the Institution really mean, and what does it mean to us? We cannot believe that it was intended as merely a sign for remembrance of His Death. Such remembrance is often equally vivid in ordinary acts of faith or prayer; and it seems difficult, if no more than this had been intended, to account for the Institution of a special Sacrament, and that with such solemnity, and as the second great rite of the Church—that for its nourishment. Again, if it were a mere token of remembrance, why the Cup as well as the Bread? Nor can

CHAP.
X

[a] St. Matt.
xxvi. 26;
St. Mark
xiv. 22

[b] 1 Cor. x. 10

---

[1] Though, of course, most widely differing from what is an attempt to trace an analogy between the Ritual of the Romish Mass and the Paschal Liturgy of the Jews, the article on it by the learned Professor *Bickell*, of Innsbruck, possesses a curious interest. See Zeitsch. für Kathol. Theol. for 1880, pp. 90–112.

we believe, that the copula ' *is* '—which, indeed, did not occur in the words spoken by Christ Himself—can be equivalent to ' *signifies*.' As little can it refer to any change of substance, be it in what is called Transubstantiation or Consubstantiation. If we may venture an explanation, it would be that ' this,' received in the Holy Eucharist, conveys to the soul as regards the Body and Blood of the Lord, the same effect as the Bread and the Wine to the body—receiving of the Bread and the Cup in the Holy Communion is, really, though spiritually, to the Soul what the outward elements are to the Body: that they are both the symbol and the vehicle of true, inward, spiritual feeding on the Very Body and Blood of Christ. So is this Cup which we bless fellowship of His Blood, and the Bread we break of His Body —fellowship with Him Who died for us, and in His dying; fellowship also in Him with one another, who are joined together in this, that for us this Body was given, and for the remission of our sins this precious Blood was shed.[1]

Most mysterious words these, yet most blessed mystery this of feeding on Christ spiritually and in faith. Most mysterious—yet ' he who takes from us our mystery takes from us our Sacrament.' [2] And ever since has this blessed Institution lain as the golden morning-light far out even in the Church's darkest night—not only the seal of His Presence and its pledge, but also the promise of the bright Day at His Coming. ' For as often as we eat this Bread and drink this Cup, we do show forth the Death of the Lord '—for the life of the world, to be assuredly yet manifested—' till He come.' ' Even so, Lord Jesus, come quickly!'

[1] I would here refer to the admirable critical notes on 1 Cor. x. and xi. by Professor *Evans* in ' The Speaker's Commentary.'

[2] The words are a hitherto unprinted utterance on this subject by the late Professor *J. Duncan*, of Edinburgh.

CHAPTER XI.

THE LAST DISCOURSES OF CHRIST—THE PRAYER OF CONSECRATION.[1]

(St. John xiv.; xv.; xvi.; xvii.)

THE new Institution of the Lord's Supper did not finally close what passed at that Paschal Table. According to the Jewish Ritual, the Cup is filled a fourth time, and the remaining part of the *Hallel* [a] repeated. Then follow, besides Ps. cxxxvi., a number of prayers and hymns, of which the comparatively late origin is not doubtful. The same remark applies even more strongly to what follows after the fourth Cup. But, so far as we can judge, the Institution of the Holy Supper was followed by the Discourse recorded in St. John xiv. Then the concluding Psalms of the *Hallel* were sung,[b] after which the Master left the 'Upper Chamber.' The Discourse of Christ recorded in St. John xvi., and His prayer,[c] were certainly uttered after they had risen from the Supper, and before they crossed the brook Kidron.[d] In all probability they were, however, spoken before the Saviour left the house. We can scarcely imagine such a Discourse, and still less such a Prayer, to have been uttered while traversing the narrow streets of Jerusalem on the way to Kidron.

1. In any case there cannot be doubt, that the first Discourse [e] was spoken while still at the Supper-Table. It connects itself closely with that statement which had caused them so much sorrow and perplexity, that, whither He was going, they could not come.[f] If so, the Discourse itself may be arranged under these four particulars: *explanatory and corrective*;[g] *explanatory and teaching*;[h] *hortatory and promissory*;[i] *promissory and consolatory.*[k] Thus there is constant and connected progress, the two great elements in the Discourse being: teaching and comfort.

At the outset we ought, perhaps, to remember the very common Jewish idea, that those in glory occupied different abodes, correspond-

CHAP.
XI

a Ps. cxv.-cxviii.

b St. Matt.
xxvi. 30; St. Mark
xiv. 26
c St. John
xvii.
d St. John
xviii. 1

e Recorded
in St. John
xiv.

f St. John
xiii. 33

g vv. 1-4
h vv. 5-14
i vv. 15-24
k vv. 24-31

---

[1] As this chapter is really in the nature of a commentation on St. John xiv., xv., xvi., xvii., the reader is requested to peruse it with the Bible-text beside him. Without this it could scarcely be intelligently followed.

ᵃ Babha
Mets. 83 b,
line 13 from
top, and
other pas-
sages

ing to their ranks. ᵃ If the words of Christ, about the place whither they could not follow Him, had awakened any such thoughts, the explanation which He now gave must effectually have dispelled them. Let not their hearts, then, be troubled at the prospect. As they believed in God, so let them also have trust in Him.[1] It was His Father's House of which they were thinking, and although there were 'many mansions, ' or rather 'stations,' in it—and the choice of this word may teach us something—yet they were all in that one House. Could they not trust Him in this? Surely, if it had been otherwise, He would have told them, and not left them to be bitterly disappointed in the end. Indeed, the object of His going was the opposite of what they feared: it was to prepare by His Death and Resurrection a place for them. Nor let them think that His going away would imply permanent separation, because He had said they could not follow Him thither. Rather did His going, not away, but to prepare a place for them, imply His Coming again, primarily as regarded individuals at death, and secondarily as regarded the Church —that He might receive them unto Himself, there to be with Him. Not final separation, then, but ultimate gathering to Himself, did His present going away mean. 'And whither I go, ye know the way.'ᵇ

Jesus had referred to His going to the Father's House, and implied that they knew the way which would bring them thither also. But His Words had only the more perplexed, at least some of them. If, when speaking of their not being able to go whither He went, He had not referred to a separation between them in that land far away, whither was He going? And, in their ignorance of this, how could they find their way thither? If any Jewish ideas of the disappearance and the final manifestation of the Messiah lurked beneath the question of Thomas, the answer of the Lord placed the matter in the clearest light. He had spoken of the Father's House of many 'stations, ' but only one road led thither. They must all know it: it was that of personal apprehension of Christ in the life, the mind, and the heart. The way to the Father was Christ; the full manifestation of all spiritual truth, and the spring of the true inner life were equally in Him. Except through Him, no man could consciously come to the Father. Thomas had put his twofold question thus: What was the goal? and, what was the way to it? ᶜ In His answer Christ significantly reversed this order, and told them first what was the way—Himself; and then what was the goal. If they

---

[1] I prefer retaining the rendering of the A.V., as more congruous to the whole context.

had spiritually known Him as the way, they would also have known   CHAP.
the goal, the Father, and now, by having the way clearly pointed   XI
out, they must also know the goal, God; nay, He was, so to speak,
visibly before them—and, gazing on Him, they saw the shining track
up to heaven, the Jacob's ladder at the top of which was the Father.[a]   [a] St. John xiv. 7

But once more appeared in the words of Philip that carnal
literalising, which would take the words of Christ in only an external
sense.[b] Sayings like these help us to perceive the absolute need of   [b] ver. 8
another Teacher, the Holy Spirit. Philip understood the words of
Christ as if He held out the possibility of an actual sight of the
Father; and this, as they imagined, would for ever have put an end
to all their doubts and fears. We also, too often, would fain have
such solution of our doubts, if not by actual vision, yet by direct
communication from on high. In His reply Jesus once more and
emphatically returned to this truth, that the vision, which was that
of faith alone, was spiritual, and in no way external; and that this
manifestation had been, and was fully, though spiritually and to
faith, in Him. Or did Philip not believe that the Father was really
manifested in Christ, because he did not actually behold Him?
Those words which had drawn them and made them feel that heaven
was so near, they were not His own. but the message which He had
brought them from the Father; those works which He had done, they
were the manifestation of the Father's 'dwelling' in Him. Let them
then believe this vital union between the Father and Him—and, if
their faith could not absolutely rise to that height, let it at least
rest on the lower level of the evidence of His works. And so would
He still lead us upwards, from the experience of what He does to the
knowledge of what He is. Yea, and if they were ever tempted to
doubt His works, faith might have evidence of them in personal
experience. Primarily, no doubt, the words[c] about the greater   [c] ver 12
works which they who believed in Him would do, because He went
to the Father, refer to the Apostolic preaching and working in its
greater results after the outpouring of the Holy Spirit. To this also
must primarily refer the promise of unlimited answer to prayer in
His Name.[d] But in a secondary, yet most true and blessed, sense,   [d] vv. 13. 14
both these promises have, ever since the Ascension of Christ, also
applied both to the Church and to all individual Christians.

A twofold promise, so wide as this, required, it must be felt, not
indeed limitation, but qualification—let us say, definition—so far as
concerns the indication of its necessary conditions. Unlimited power
of working by faith and of praying in faith is qualified by obedience

BOOK
V

to His Commandments, such as is the outcome of personal love to Him.[a] And for such faith, which compasseth all things in the obedience of love to Christ, and can obtain all by the prayer of faith in His Name, there will be a need of Divine Presence ever with them.[b] While He had been with them, they had had one *Paraclete*,[1] or ' Advocate,' Who had pleaded with them the cause of God, explained and advocated the truth, and guarded and guided them. Now that His outward Presence was to be withdrawn from earth, and He was to be their Paraclete or Advocate in Heaven with the Father,[c] He would, as His first act of advocacy, pray the Father, Who would send them another Paraclete, or Advocate, who would continue with them for ever. To the guidance and pleadings of that Advocate they could implicitly trust themselves, for He was ' the Spirit of Truth.' The world, indeed, would not listen to His pleadings, nor accept Him as their Guide, for the only evidence by which they judged was that of outward sight and material results. But theirs would be other Empirics: an experience not outward, but inward and spiritual. They would know the reality of His Existence and the truth of His pleadings by the continual Presence with them as a body of this Paraclete, and by His dwelling in them individually.

Here (as *Bengel* justly remarks) begins the essential difference between believers and the world. The Son was sent into the *world*; not so the Holy Spirit. Again, the world receives not the Holy Spirit, because it knows Him not; the disciples know Him, because they possess Him. Hence ' to have known ' and ' to have ' are so conjoined, that not to have known is the cause of not having, and to have is the cause of knowing.[d] In view of this promised Advent of the other Advocate, Christ could tell the disciples that He would not leave them ' orphans ' in this world. Nay, in this Advocate Christ Himself came to them. True, the world, which only saw and knew what fell within the range of its sensuous and outward vision (ver. 17), would not behold Him, but *they* would behold Him, because He lived, and they also would live—and hence there was fellowship of spiritual life between them.[2] On that day of the Advent of His Holy Spirit would they have full knowledge, because experience, of the Christ's Return to the Father, and of their own being in Christ, and of His

ᵃ St. John
xiv. 15
ᵇ ver. 16

ᶜ 1 John ii
1

ᵈ ver. 17

---

[1] Without entering on the discussion of what has engaged so much attention, I must content myself here with indicating the result at which I have arrived. This is simply to abide by the real and natural meaning of the word, alike in the Greek and in Rabbinic usage. This is: not Comforter but Advocate, or, it may be, according to circumstances, Defender, Representative, Counsellor, and Pleader.

[2] Ver. 19 should, I think, be rendered: ' But you behold Me, because [for] I live, and ye shall live.'

being in them. And, as regarded this threefold relationship, this must be ever kept in view: to be in Christ meant to love Him, and this was: to have and to keep His commandments; Christ's being in the Father implied, that they who were in Christ or loved Him would be loved also of His Father; and, lastly, Christ's being in them implied, that He would love them and manifest Himself to them.[a]

One outstanding novel fact here arrested the attention of the disciples. It was contrary to all their Jewish ideas about the future manifestation of the Messiah, and it led to the question of one of their number, Judas—not Iscariot· 'Lord, what has happened, that to us Thou wilt manifest Thyself, and not to the world?' Again they thought of an outward, while He spoke of a spiritual and inward manifestation. It was of this coming of the Son and the Father for the purpose of making 'station' with them [1] that He spoke, of which the condition was love to Christ, manifested in the keeping of His Word, and which secured the love of the Father also. On the other hand, not to keep His Word was not to love Him, with all that it involved, not only as regarded the Son, but also the Father, since the Word which they heard was the Father's.[b]

Thus far then for this inward manifestation, springing from life-fellowship with Christ, rich in the unbounded spiritual power of faith, and fragrant with the obedience of love. All this He could say to them now in the Father's Name—as the first Representative, Pleader, and 'Advocate,' or Paraclete. But what, when He was no longer present with them? For that He had provided 'another Paraclete,' Advocate, or Pleader. This 'Paraclete, the Holy Spirit, Whom the Father will send in My Name, that same will teach you all things, and bring to your remembrance all things that I said to you.' It is quite evident, that the interpretation of the term Paraclete as 'the Comforter' will not meet the description here given of His twofold function as teaching all, and recalling all, that Christ Himself had said. Nor will the other interpretation of 'Advocate' meet the requirements, if we regard the Advocate as one who pleads for *us*. But if we regard the Paraclete or Advocate as the Representative of Christ, and pleading, as it were, for *Him*, the cause of Christ, all seems harmonious. Christ came in the Name of the Father, as the first Paraclete, as His Representative; the Holy Spirit comes in the Name of Christ, as the second Paraclete, the Representative of Christ, Who is in the Father. As such the second Paraclete is sent by the

CHAP.
XI

[a] St. John xiv. 20, 21

[b] vv. 22-24

[1] καὶ μονὴν παρ' αὐτῷ ποιησόμεθα. Of course only 'a station,' as the reference is only to the state of believers while on earth.

BOOK
V

Father in Name of the first Paraclete, and He would both complete in them, and recall to them, His Cause.

And so at the end of this Discourse the Lord returned again, and now with fuller meaning, to its beginning. Then He had said: 'Let not your heart be troubled; ye believe in God, believe also in Me.' Now, after the fuller communication of His purpose, and of their relation to Him, He could convey to them the assurance of peace, even His Own peace, as His gift in the present, and His legacy for the future.ᵃ In their hearing, the fact of His going away, which had filled them with such sorrow and fear, had now been conjoined with that of His Coming¹ to them. Yes, as He had explained it, His departure to the Father was the necessary antecedent and condition of His Coming to them in the permanent Presence of the other Paraclete, the Holy Ghost. That Paraclete, however, would, in the economy of grace, be sent by the Father alone. In the dispensation of grace, the final source from whence all cometh, Who sendeth both the Son and the Holy Ghost, is God the Father. The Son is sent by the Father, and the Holy Ghost also, though proceeding from the Father and the Son, is sent by the Father in Christ's Name. In the economy of grace, then, the Father is greater than the Son. And the return of the Son to the Father marks alike the completion of Christ's work, and its perfection, in the Mission of the Holy Ghost, with all that His Advent implies. Therefore, if, discarding thoughts of themselves, they had only given room to feelings of true love to Him, instead of mourning they would have rejoiced because He went to the Father, with all that this implied, not only of rest and triumph to Him, but of the perfecting of His Work—since this was the condition of that Mission of the Holy Ghost by the Father, Who sent both the Son and the Holy Spirit. And in this sense also should they have rejoiced, because, through the presence of the Holy Ghost in them, as sent by the Father in His ' greater ' work, they would, instead of the present selfish enjoyment of Christ's Personal Presence, have the more power of showing their love to Him in apprehending His Truth, obeying His Commandments, doing His Works, and participating in His Life.² Not that Christ expected them to understand the full

ᵃ St. John
xiv. 27

---

¹ The word ' again ' before ' come unto you ' is spurious, as also are the words ' I said ' before ' I go to the Father.'

² The great difficulty in understanding the last part of ver. 28 lies not in any one of the clauses, nor in the combination of two, but in that of three of them. We could understand that, if they loved Him, they would rejoice that He went to the Father, as marking the completion of His work ; and again, that they should rejoice in His going to the Father, Who was greater, and would send the Holy Ghost, as implying benefit to themselves. But the difficulty of combining all these, so that love to Christ should induce a

meaning of all these words. But afterwards, when it had all come to pass, they would believe.[a]

With the meaning and the issue of the great contest on which He was about to enter thus clearly before Him, did He now go forth to meet the last assault of the ' Prince of this World.'[b] But why that fierce struggle, since in Christ ' he hath nothing ' ? To exhibit to ' the world ' the perfect love which He had to the Father; how even to the utmost of self-exinanition, obedience, submission, and suffering He was doing as the Father had given Him commandment, when He sent Him for the redemption of the world. In the execution of this Mission He would endure the last sifting assault and contest on the part of the Enemy, and, enduring, conquer for us. And so might the world be won from its Prince by the full manifestation of Christ, in His infinite obedience and righteousness, doing the Will of the Father and the Work which He had given Him, and in His infinite love doing the work of our salvation.[c]

2. The work of our salvation! To this aspect of the subject Christ now addressed Himself, as He rose from the Supper-Table. If in the Discourse recorded in the fourteenth chapter of St. John's Gospel the Godward aspect of Christ's impending departure was explained, in that of the fifteenth chapter the new relation is set forth which was to subsist between Him and His Church. And this— although epigrammatic sayings are so often fallacious—may be summarised in these three words: Union, Communion, Disunion. The Union between Christ and His Church is corporate, vital, and effective, alike as regards results and blessings.[d] This Union issues in Communion—of Christ with His disciples, of His disciples with Him, and of His disciples among themselves. The principle of all these is love: the love of Christ to the disciples, the love of the disciples to Christ, and the love in Christ of the disciples to one another.[e] Lastly, this Union and Communion has for its necessary counterpart Disunion, separation from the world. The world repudiates them for their union with Christ and their communion. But, for all that, there is something that must keep them from going out of the world. They have a Mission in it, initiated by, and carried on in the power of, the Holy Ghost—that of uplifting the testimony of Christ.[f]

As regards the relation of the Church to the Christ Who is about

[a] ver. 29

[b] St. John
xiv. 30.

[e] ver. 31

[d] xv. 1-8

[e] vv. 9-17

[f] vv. 18-27

wish that He should go to the Father, because He was greater, seems one, of which I can only see the natural solution in the interpretation which I have ventured to suggest.

BOOK
V

to depart to the Father, and to come to them in the Holy Ghost as His Representative, it is to be one of *Union—corporate, vital,* and *effective.* In the nature of it, such a truth could only be set forth by *illustration.* When Christ said: 'I am the Vine, the true one, and My Father is the Husbandman;' or again, 'Ye are the branches' —bearing in mind that, as He spake it in Aramaic, the copulas 'am,' 'is,' and 'are,' would be omitted—He did not mean that He *signified* the Vine or was its *sign,* nor the Father that of the Husbandman, nor yet the disciples that of the branches. What He meant was, that He, the Father, and the disciples, stood in exactly the same relationship as the Vine, the Husbandman, and the branches. That relationship was of corporate union of the branches with the Vine for the production of fruit to the Husbandman, Who for that purpose pruned the branches. Nor can we forget in this connection, that,

a There the two could with difficulty be separated. Hence the vine the symbol of Israel, the sages being the ripe grapes, Chull. 92 a

in the old Testament, and partially in Jewish thought,[a] the Vine was the symbol of Israel, not in their national but in their Church-capacity. Christ, with His disciples as the branches, *is* 'the Vine, the true One'—the reality of all types, the fulfilment of all promises. They are many branches, yet a grand unity in that Vine; there is one Church of which He is the Head, the Root, the Sustenance, the Life. And in that Vine will the object of its planting of old be realised: to bring forth fruit unto God.

Yet, though it be one Vine, the Church must bear fruit not only in her corporate capacity, but individually in each of the branches. It seems remarkable that we read of branches in Him that bear not fruit. This must apparently refer to those who have by Baptism been inserted into the Vine, but remain fruitless—since a merely outward profession of Christ could scarcely be described as 'a branch in' Him. On the other hand, every fruit-bearing branch the Husbandman 'cleanseth'[1]—not necessarily nor exclusively by pruning, but in whatever manner may be requisite—so that it may produce the largest possible amount of fruit. As for them, the process of cleansing had 'already' been accomplished through, or because of [the meaning is much the same], the Word which He had spoken unto them. If that condition of fruit-bearing now existed in them in consequence of the impression of His Word, it followed as a cognate condition that they must abide in Him, and He would abide in them. Nay, this was a vital condition of fruit-bearing, arising from the fundamental fact that He was the Vine and they the branches. The proper, normal condition of every branch in that Vine was to bear

[1] $\alpha \ddot{\iota} \rho \epsilon \iota - \kappa \alpha \theta \alpha \dot{\iota} \rho \epsilon \iota$: Suavis rhythmus (*Bengel*).

much fruit, of course, in proportion to its size and vigour.   But, both figuratively and really, the condition of this was to abide in Him, since ' apart ' from Him they could do nothing.   It was not like a force once set in motion that would afterwards continue of itself.   It was a life, and the condition of its permanence was continued union with Christ, from Whom alone it could spring.

And now as regarded the two alternatives: he that abode not in Him was the branch ' cast outside ' and withering, which, when ready for it, men would cast into the fire—with all of symbolic meaning as regards the gatherers and the burning that the illustration implies. On the other hand, if the corporate and vital union was effective, if they abode in Him, and in consequence, His Words abode in them, then: ' Whatsoever ye will ye shall ask, and it shall be done to you.' It is very noteworthy that the unlimitedness of prayer is limited, or, rather, conditioned, by our abiding in Christ and His Words in us,[1] just as in St. John xiv. 12–14 it is conditioned by fellowship with Him, and in St. John xv. 16 by permanent fruitfulness.[2]   For, it were the most dangerous fanaticism, and entirely opposed to the teaching of Christ, to imagine that the promise of Christ implies such absolute power—as if prayer were magic—that a person might ask for anything, no matter what it was, in the assurance of obtaining his request.[3]   In all moral relations, duties and privileges are correlative ideas, and in our relation to Christ conscious immanence in Him and of His Word in us, union and communion with Him, and the obedience of love, are the indispensable conditions of our privileges.   The believer may, indeed, ask for anything, because he may always and absolutely go to God; but the certainty of special answers to prayer is proportionate to the degree of union and communion with Christ.   And such unlimited liberty of prayer is connected with our bearing much fruit, because thereby the Father is glorified and our discipleship evidenced.[a][4]

a St. John
xv. 7, 8.

This union, being inward and moral, necessarily unfolds into *communion*, of which the principle is *love*.   'Like as the Father loved Me, even so loved I you.   Abide in My love.   If ye keep My commandments, ye shall abide in the love *that is* Mine ($\dot{\epsilon}\nu\ \tau\tilde{\eta}\ \dot{a}\gamma\dot{a}\pi\eta$

---

[1] Canon *Westcott* beautifully observes: ' Their prayer is only some fragment of His teaching transformed into a supplication, and so it will necessarily be heard.'

[2] Every unprejudiced reader will feel that St. Matt. xviii. 19, 20. *so far as it does not belong to an entirely different sphere*, is subject to similar conditions.

[3] Some, to me at least, horrible instances of this supposed absolute licence of prayer have appeared in a certain class of American religious literature which of late has found too wide circulation among us.

[4] Preces ipsæ sunt fructus, et fructum augent (*Bengel*).

BOOK
V

<del>∼∽∼∽</del>

τῇ ἐμῇ).' We mark the *continuity* in the scale of love: the Father towards the Son, and the Son towards us; and its *kindredness* of forthgoing. And now all that the disciples had to do was to *abide* in it. This is connected, not with sentiment nor even with faith, but with obedience.[1] Fresh supplies are drawn by faith, but continuance in the love of Christ is the manifestation and the result of obedience. It was so even with the Master Himself in His relation to the Father. And the Lord immediately explained [a] what His object was in saying this. In this, also, were they to have *communion* with Him: communion in that joy which was His in consequence of His perfect obedience. ' These things have I spoken to you, in order that the joy *that is* Mine (ἡ χαρὰ ἡ ἐμή) may be [2] in you, and your joy may be fulfilled [completed].'

a St. John
xv. 11

But what of those commandments to which such importance attached? Clean as they now were through the Words which He had spoken, one great commandment stood forth as specially His Own, consecrated by His Example and to be measured by His observance of it. From whatever point we view it, whether as specially demanded by the pressing necessities of the Church; or as, from its contrast to what Heathenism exhibited, affording such striking evidence of the power of Christianity;[3] or, on the other hand, as so congruous to all the fundamental thoughts of the Kingdom: the love of the Father in sending His Son for man, the work of the Son in seeking and saving the lost at the price of His Own Life, and the new bond which in Christ bound them all in the fellowship of a common calling, common mission, and common interests and hopes—love of the brethren was the one outstanding Farewell-Command of Christ.[b] And to keep His commandments was to be His friend. And they were His friends. ' No longer ' did He call them servants, for the servant knew not what his lord did. He had now given them a new name, and with good reason: ' You have I called friends, because all things which I heard of My Father I made known to you.' And yet deeper did He descend, in pointing them to the example and measure of His love as the standard of theirs towards one another. And with this teaching He combined what He had said before, of bearing fruit and of the privilege of fellowship with Himself. They were His friends; He had proved it by treating them as such in now opening up before them the whole

b vv. 12-14

---

[1] We would fain here correct another modern religious extravagance.

[2] So according to the better reading.

[3] 'The heathen are wont to exclaim with wonder, See how these Christians love one another!' (*Tertullian,* apud *Westcott.*)

counsel of God. And that friendship: 'Not you did choose Me, but I did choose you'—the object of His 'choosing' [that to which they were 'appointed'] being, that, as they went forth into the world, they should bear fruit, that their fruit should be permanent, and that they should possess the full privilege of that unlimited power to pray of which He had previously spoken.[a] All these things were bound up with obedience to His commands, of which the outstanding one was to 'love one another.'[b]

But this very choice on His part, and their union of love in Him and to one another, also implied not only *separation* from, but repudiation by, the world.[c] For this they must be prepared. It had come to Him, and it would be evidence of their choice to discipleship. The hatred of the world showed the essential difference and antagonism between the life-principle of the world and theirs. For evil or for good, they must expect the same treatment as their Master. Nay, was it not their privilege to realise, that all this came upon them for His sake? and should they not also remember, that the ultimate ground of the world's hatred was ignorance of Him Who had sent Christ?[d] And yet, though this should banish all thoughts of personal resentment, their guilt who rejected Him was truly terrible. Speaking to, and in, Israel, there was no excuse for their sin—the most awful that could be conceived; since, most truly: 'He that hateth Me, hateth My Father also.' For, Christ was the Sent of God, and God manifest. It was a terrible charge this to bring against God's ancient people Israel. And yet there was, besides the evidence of His Words, that of His Works.[e] If they could not apprehend the former, yet, in regard to the latter, they could see by comparison with the works of other men that they were unique.[2] They saw it, but only hated Him and His Father, ascribing it all to the power and agency of Beelzebul. And so the ancient prophecy had now been fulfilled: 'They hated Me gratuitously.'[f] But all was not yet at an end: neither His Work through the other Advocate, nor yet theirs in the world. 'When the Advocate is come, Whom I will send to you from the Father—the Spirit of the Truth—Who pro-

CHAP.
XI

[a] St. John xv. 16

[b] ver. 17

[c] ver. 18

[d] vv. 19-21

[e] vv. 22-24

[f] Ps. xxxv. 19; lxix. 4

---

[1] This, although the primary meaning of ver. 17 is: 'in order that ye love one another'—such is the object and scope of what He commanded them. It ought perhaps to be noted, that, as the company of Priests that had ministered in the Temple for the week gave place to their successors, this farewell prayer was spoken: He that dwelleth in this house put among you brotherhood, love, peace, and friendship (Jer. Ber. 3 c).

[2] Canon *Westcott* writes: 'The works are characterised (*which none other did*); the words are undefined (*come and spoken*). The works of Christ might be compared with other works: His words had an absolute power.'

ceedeth from the Father [goeth forth on His Mission as sent by the Father[1]], this Same will bear witness about Me.   And ye also bear witness,[2] because ye are with Me from the beginning.'

3. The last of the parting Discourses of Christ, in the sixteenth chapter of St. John, was, indeed, interrupted by questions from the disciples.   But these, being germane to the subject, carry it only forward.   In general, the subjects treated in it are: the new relations arising from the departure of Christ and the coming of the other Advocate.   Thus the last point needed would be supplied—chap. xiv. giving the comfort and teaching in view of His departure; chap. xv. describing the personal relations of the disciples towards Christ, one another, and the world; and chap. xvi. fixing the new relations to be established.

The chapter appropriately opens by reflecting on the predicted enmity of the world.[a]   Christ had so clearly foretold it, lest this should prove a stumbling-block to them.   Best, to know distinctly that they would not only be put out of the Synagogue, but that everyone who killed them would deem it 'to offer a religious service to God.'   So, no doubt, Saul of Tarsus once felt, and so did many others who, alas! never became Christians.   Indeed, according to Jewish Law, 'a zealot' might have slain without formal trial those caught in flagrant rebellion against God—or in what might be regarded as such, and the Synagogue would have deemed the deed as meritorious as that of Phinehas.[b]   It was a sorrow, and yet also a comfort, to know that this spirit of enmity arose from ignorance of the Father and of Christ.   Although they had in a general way been prepared for it before, yet He had not told it all so definitely and connectedly from the beginning, because He was still there.[c]   But now that He was going away, it was absolutely necessary to do so. For even the mention of it had thrown them into such confusion of personal sorrow, that the main point, *whither* Christ was going, had not even emerged into their view.[d][3]   Personal feelings had quite engrossed them, to the forgetfulness of their own higher interests. He was going to the Father, and this was the condition, as well as the antecedent of His sending the Paraclete.

a St. John xvi.

b Sanh. 81 b; Bemid. R. 21

c St. John xvi. 1-4

d ver. 5

[1] On this meaning of the words see the Note of Canon *Westcott*.

[2] For the fulfilment of this predicted twofold testimony, see Acts v. 32.

[3] The question of Thomas (St. John xiv. 5) bore as to the way, rather than the goal; that of Peter (xiii. 36) seemed founded either on the Jewish idea that the Messiah was to disappear, or else referred to Christ's going among enemies and into danger, whither Peter thought he would follow Him. But none of the questions contemplated the Messianic Return of the Son to the Father with a view to the Mission of the Holy Ghost.

But the Advent of the 'Advocate' would mark a new era, as regarded the Church^a and the world. It was their Mission to go forth into the world and to preach Christ. That other Advocate, as the Representative of Christ, would go into the world and convict on the three cardinal points on which their preaching turned. These three points on which all Missioning proceeds, are —Sin, Righteousness, and Judgment. And on these would the New Advocate convict the world. Bearing in mind that the term 'convict' is uniformly used in the Gospels[1] for clearly establishing or carrying home guilt,[2] we have here three separate facts presented to us. As the Representative of Christ, the Holy Ghost will carry home to the world, establish the fact of its guilt in regard to *sin*— on the ground that the world believes not in Christ. Again, as the Representative of Christ, He will carry home to the world the fact of its guilt in regard to *righteousness*—on the ground that Christ has ascended to the Father, and hence is removed from the sight of man. Lastly, as the Representative of Christ, He will establish the fact of the world's guilt, because of this: that its Prince, Satan, has already been judged by Christ—a judgment established in His sitting at the Right Hand of God, and which will be vindicated at His Second Coming. Taking, then, the three great facts in the History of the Christ: His First Coming to salvation, His Resurrection and Ascension, and His Sitting at the Right Hand of God, of which His Second Coming to Judgment is the final issue, this Advocate of Christ will in each case convict the world of guilt; in regard to the first—concerning sin, because it believes not on Him Whom God has sent; in regard to the second—concerning righteousness, because Christ *is* at the Father's Right Hand; and, in regard to the third—concerning judgment, because that Prince whom the world still owns has already been judged by Christ's Session at the Right Hand of God, and by His Reign, which is to be completed in His Second Coming to Earth.

Such was the cause of Christ which the Holy Spirit as the Advocate would plead to the world, working conviction as in a hostile guilty party. Quite other was that cause of Christ which, as His Advocate, He would plead with the disciples, and quite other in their case the effect of His advocacy. We have, even on the present occasion, marked how often the Lord was hindered, as well as

CHAP.
XI

^a St. John
xvi. 7

---

[1] It occurs besides this place in St. Matt. xviii. 15; St. Luke iii. 19; St. John iii. 20; viii. (9) 46.
[2] Closely similar to the above is the use of the verb ἐλέγχω in St. James ii. 9, and in Rev. iii. 19. This may be called the Hebraic *usus* of the word. In the Epistles of St. Paul it is more general; in that to the Hebrews (xii. 5) it seems to stand for punishing.

BOOK
V

grieved, by the misunderstanding and unbelief of man. Now it was the self-imposed law of His Mission, the outcome of His Victory in the Temptation in the Wilderness, that He would not achieve His Mission in the exercise of Divine Power, but by treading the ordinary path of humanity. This was the limitation which He set to Himself—one aspect of His Self-exinanition. But from this His constant sorrow must also have flowed, in view of the unbelief of even those nearest to Him. It was, therefore, not only expedient, but even necessary for them, since at present they could not bear more, that Christ's Presence should be withdrawn, and His Representative take His place, and open up His Cause to them. And this was to be His special work to the Church. As Advocate, not speaking from [1] Himself, but speaking whatsoever He shall hear—as it were, according to His heavenly 'brief'—He would guide them into all truth. And here His first 'declaration' would be of 'the things that are coming.' A whole new order of things was before the Apostles—the abolition of the Jewish, the establishment of the Christian Dispensation, and the relation of the New to the Old, together with many kindred questions. As Christ's Representative, and speaking not from Himself, the Holy Spirit would be with them, not suffer them to go astray into error or wrong, but be their 'way-leader' into all truth. Further, as the Son glorified the Father, so would the Spirit glorify the Son, and in analogous manner—because He shall take of His and 'declare' it unto them. This would be the second line, as it were, in the 'declarations' of the Advocate, Representative of Christ. And this work of the Holy Spirit, sent by the Father, in His declaration about Christ, was explained by the circumstance of the union and communication between the Father and Christ.[a] And so—to sum up, in one brief Farewell, all that He had said to them—there would be 'a little while' in which they would not 'behold' Him (οὐκέτι θεωρεῖτέ με), and again a little while and they would 'see' Him (ὄψεσθέ με), though in quite different manner, as even the wording shows.[b] [2]

If we had enter ined any doubt of the truth of the Lord's previous words, that in their absorbedness in the present the disciples had not thought of the 'whither' to which Christ was going, and that it was needful for them that He should depart and the other Advocate come,[c] this conviction would be forced upon us by their

ᵃ St. John xvi. 8-15

ᵇ ver. 16

ᶜ vv. 5-7

---

[1] This meaning of the word is not only most important but well marked. Canon *Westcott* calls attention to its use also in the following passages: v. 19; vii. 18; xi. 51; xv. 4.

[2] The words, 'because I go to the Father,' are spurious in ver. 16.

perplexed questioning among themselves as to the meaning of the
twofold ' little while,' and of all that He had said about, and connected with, His going to the Father. They would fain have asked,
yet dared not. But He knew their thoughts, and answered them.
That first ' little while ' comprised those terrible days of His Death
and Entombment, when they would weep and lament, but the world
rejoice. Yet their brief sorrow would be turned into joy. It was
like the short sorrow of childbearing—afterwards no more remembered
in the joy that a human being had been born into the world. Thus
would it be when their present sorrow would be changed into the
Resurrection-joy—a joy which no man could ever afterwards take
from them. On that day of joy would He have them dwell in
thought during their present night of sorrow. That would be,
indeed, a day of brightness, in which there would be no need of
their making further inquiry of Him (ἐμὲ οὐκ ἐρωτήσετε).ᵃ All
would then be clear in the new light of the Resurrection. A day
this, when the promise would become true, and whatsoever they asked
the Father (αἰτήσητε), He would give it them in Christ's Name.¹
Hitherto they had not yet asked in His Name; let them ask: they
would receive, and so their joy be completed. Ah! that day of
brightness. Hitherto He had only been able to speak to them, as it
were, in parables and allegory, but then would He ' declare ' to them
in all plainness about the Father. And, as He would be able to speak
to them directly and plainly about the Father, so would they then
be able to speak directly to the Father—as the Epistle to the
Hebrews expresses it, come with ' plainness ' ² or ' directness ' to the
throne of grace. They would ask directly in the Name of Christ;
and no longer would it be needful, as at present, first to come
to Him that He may ' inquire ' of the Father ' about ' them (ἐρωτήσω
περὶ ὑμῶν). For, God loved them as lovers of Christ, and as recognising that He had come forth from God. And so it was—He had
come forth from out the Father ³ when He came into the world,
and, now that He was leaving it, He was going to the Father.

The disciples imagined that they understood this at least.
Christ had read their thoughts, and there was no need for anyone

ᵃ St. John
xvi. 23
comp. ver
19

---

¹ According to the better reading of
ver. 23: ' He will give it you in My
Name.'
² The same word (παῤῥησία) is used
of Christ's ' plainly' declaring the Father
(ver. 25), and of our liberty in prayer in
Heb. iv. 16; comp. also x. 19. For the
Johannine use of the word, comp. St.

John vii. 4, 13, 26; x. 24; xi. 14, 54;
xvi. 25, 29; xviii. 20; 1 John ii. 28; iii.
21; iv. 17; v. 14.
³ According to the better reading: ἐκ
τοῦ πατρός. Surely, if words have any
meaning, these teach the unity of Essence of the Son and the Father.

BOOK
V

ª St. John
xvi. 30

ᵇ St. John
xvi. 32
xiv. 1

ᵈ xvi. 33

ᵉ St. John
xvii.

ᶠ vv. 1–5; 6–
19; 20–26

ᵍ vv. 1–5

to put express questions.ª He knew all things, and by this they believed—it afforded them evidence—that He came forth from [1] God. But how little did they know their own hearts! The hour had even come when they would be scattered, every man to his own home, and leave Him alone—yet, truly, He would not be alone, because the Father would be with Him.ᵇ Yet, even so, His latest as His first thoughtᶜ was of them; and through the night of scattering and of sorrow did He bid them look to the morning of joy. For, the battle was not theirs, nor yet the victory doubtful: 'I [emphatically] have overcome [it is accomplished] the world.'ᵈ

We now enter most reverently what may be called the innermost Sanctuary.ᵉ For the first time we are allowed to listen to what was really 'the Lord's Prayer,' [2] and, as we hear, we humbly worship. That Prayer was the great preparation for His Agony, Cross, and Passion; and, also, the outlook on the Crown beyond. In its three partsᶠ it seems almost to look back on the teaching of the three previous chapters,[3] and convert them into prayer.[4] We see the great High-Priest first solemnly offering up Himself, and then consecrating and interceding for His Church and for her work.

The first part of that Prayerᵍ is the consecration of Himself by the Great High-Priest. The final hour had come. In praying that the Father would glorify the Son, He was really not asking anything for Himself, but that 'the Son' might [5] 'glorify' the Father. For, the glorifying of the Son—His support, and then His Resurrection, was really the completion of the work which the Father had given Him to do, as well as its evidence. It was really in accordance ('even as') with the power or authority which the Father gave Him over 'all flesh,'[6] when He put all things under His Feet as the Messiah—the object of this Messianic Rule being, 'that the totality' (the all, πᾶν) 'that Thou hast given Him, He should give to them eternal life.' The climax in His Messianic appointment, the object of His Rule over all flesh, was the Father's gift to Christ of the Church as a totality and a unity; and in that Church Christ gives to

---

[1] Very significantly, however, they use neither παρά, nor ἐκ, but ἀπό.

[2] That in St. Matt. xi. 25–27 is a brief thanksgiving.

[3] Comp. each chapter with the corresponding section of verses in ch. xvii.

[4] I cannot agree with Canon *Westcott* that these last Discourses and this Prayer were spoken in the Temple. It is, indeed, true, that on that night the Temple was thrown open at midnight, and speedily thronged. But if our Lord had come before that time, He would have found its gates closed; if after that time, He could not have found a place of retirement and quiet, where it is conceivable that could have been said and prayed which is recorded in St. John xiv., xv., xvi., xvii.

[5] The word 'also' should be struck out.

[6] We mark this Hebraism in the Fourth Gospel.

each individually eternal life. What follows [a] seems an intercalated sentence, as shown even by the use of the particle 'and,' with which the all-important definition of what is 'eternal life' is introduced, and by the last words in the verse. But although embodying, so to speak, as regards the form, the record which St. John had made of Christ's Words, we must remember that, as regards the substance, we have here Christ's own Prayer for that eternal life to each of His own people. And what constitutes 'the eternal life'? Not what we so often think, who confound with the thing its effects or else its results. It refers not to the future, but to the present. It is the realisation of what Christ had told them in these words: 'Ye believe in God, believe also in Me.' It is the pure sunlight on the soul, resulting in, or reflecting the knowledge of Jehovah; the Personal, Living, True God, and of Him Whom He did send, Jesus Christ. These two branches of knowledge must not so much be considered as co-ordinate, but rather as inseparable. Returning from this explanation of 'the eternal life' which they who are bathed in the Light possess even now and here, the Great High-Priest first offered up to the Father that part of His work which was on earth and which He had completed. And then, both as the consummation and the sequel of it, He claimed what was at the end of His Mission: His return to that fellowship of essential glory, which He possessed together with the Father before the world was.[b]

The gift of His consecration could not have been laid on more glorious Altar. Such Cross must have been followed by such Crown.[c] And now again His first thought was of them for whose sake He had consecrated Himself. *These He now solemnly presented to the Father.*[d] He introduced them as those (the individuals) whom the Father had specially given to him out of the world. As such they were really the Father's, and given over to Christ—and He now presented them as having kept the Word of the Father. Now they knew that all things whatsoever the Father had given the Son were of the Father. This was the outcome, then, of all His teaching, and the sum of all their learning—perfect confidence in the Person of Christ, as in His Life, Teaching, and Work sent not only of God, but of the Father. Neither less nor yet more did their 'knowledge' represent. All else that sprang out of it they had yet to learn. But it was enough, for it implied everything; chiefly these three things—that they *received* the words which He gave them as from the Father; that they *knew truly* that Christ had come out from the Father; and that they *believed* that the Father had sent Him. And,

CHAP.
XI

[a] in St. John xvii. 3

[b] vv. 4, 5

[c] Phil. ii. 8 11

[d] St. John xvii. 6-10

indeed, reception of Christ's Word, knowledge of His Essential Nature, and faith in His Mission: such seem the three essential characteristics of those who are Christ's.

ᵃ St. John
xvii. 9-12

And now He brought them in *prayer* before the Father.ᵃ He was interceding, not for the 'world' that was His by right of His Messiahship, but for them whom the Father had specially given Him. They were the Father's in the special sense of covenant-mercy, and all that in that sense was the Father's was the Son's, and all that was the Son's was the Father's. Therefore, although all the world was the Son's, He prayed not now for it; and although all in earth and heaven were in the Father's Hand, He sought not now His blessing on them, but on those whom, while He was in the world, He had shielded and guided. They were to be left behind in a world of sin, evil, temptation, and sorrow, and He was going to the Father. And this was His prayer: 'Holy Father, keep them in Thy Name which Thou hast given Me, that so (in order that) they may be one (a unity, ἕν), as We *are*.' The peculiar address, 'Holy Father,' shows that the Saviour once more referred to the keeping in holiness, and what is of equal importance, that 'the unity' of the Church sought for was to be primarily one of spiritual character, and not a merely outward combination. Unity in holiness and of nature, as was that of the Father and Son, such was the great object sought, although such union would, if properly carried out, also issue in outward unity. But while moral union rather than outward unity was in His view, our present 'unhappy divisions,' arising so often from wilfulness and unreadiness to bear slight differences among ourselves—each other's burdens—are so entirely contrary not only to the Christian, but even to the Jewish, spirit, that we can only trace them to the heathen element in the Church.

While He was 'with them,' He 'kept' them in the Father's Name. Them whom the Father had given Him, by the effective drawing of His grace within them, He guarded (ἐφύλαξα), and none from among them was lost, except the son of perdition—and this, according to prophecy. But ere He went to the Father, He prayed thus for them, that in this realised unity of holiness the joy that was

ᵇ ver. 13

His [1] (τὴν χαρὰν τὴν ἐμήν), might be 'completed' in them.ᵇ And there was the more need of this, since they were left behind with nought but His Word in a world that hated them, because, as Christ, so they also were not of it ['from' it, ἐκ]. Nor yet did Christ ask with a view to their being taken out of the world, but with this

---

[1] Comp. here St. John xv. 11.

'that' [in order that] the Father should 'keep them [preserve, CHAP.
τηρήσῃς] from the Evil One.'[1] And this the more emphatically, XI
because, even as He was not, so were they not 'out of the world,'
which lay in the Evil One. And the preservative which He sought
for them was not outward but inward, the same in kind as while He
had been with them,[a] only coming now directly from the Father. It a St. John
xvii. 12
was sanctification 'in the truth,'[2] with this significant addition:
'The word that is Thine (ὁ λόγος ὁ σός) is truth.'[b] b vv. 12-17

In its last part this intercessory Prayer of the Great High-Priest
bore on the work of the disciples and its fruits. As the Father had
sent the Son, so did the Son send the disciples into the world—in
the same manner, and on the same Mission. And for their sakes He
now solemnly offered Himself, 'consecrated' or 'sanctified' Himself,
that they might 'in truth'[3]—truly—be consecrated. And in view
of this their work, to which they were consecrated, did Christ pray not
for them alone, but also for those who, through their word, would
believe in Him, 'in order,' or 'that so,' 'all may be one'—form a
unity. Christ, as sent by the Father, gathered out the original
'unity;' they, as sent by Him, and consecrated by His consecration,
were to gather others, but all were to form one great unity, through
the common spiritual communication. 'As Thou in Me, and I also
in Thee, so that [in order that] they also may be in Us, so that [in
order that] the world may believe that Thou didst send Me.' 'And
the glory that Thou hast given Me'—referring to His Mission in the
world, and His setting apart and authorisation for it—'I have given
to them, so that [in order that] [in this respect also] they may be
one, even as We are One [a unity].[4] I in them, and Thou in Me, so
that they may be perfected into One'—the ideal unity and real character of the Church, this—'so that the world may know that Thou
didst send Me, and lovedst them as Thou lovedst Me.'

After this unspeakably sublime consecration of His Church, and
communication to her of His glory as well as of His Work, we cannot
marvel at what follows and concludes 'the Lord's Prayer.'[c] We c vv. 24-26
remember the unity of the Church—a unity in Him, and as that
between the Father and the Son—as we listen to this: 'That which
Thou hast given Me, I will that, where I am, they also may be with

---

[1] This meaning is ruled by a reference
to 1 John v. 18, 19, and, if so, it seems
in turn to rule the meaning of the petition: 'Deliver us from the Evil One.'
[2] Not, 'by Thy truth.'
[3] Not, as in the A.V. (ver. 19),

'through the truth' (ἐν ἀληθείᾳ).
[4] It need scarcely be said that by the
term 'unity' we refer not to unity of
Person, but of Nature, Character, and
Work.

Me—so that they may gaze [behold] on the glory that is Mine, which Thou hast given Me [be sharers in the Messianic glory]: because Thou lovedst Me before the foundation of the world.'

And we all would fain place ourselves in the shadow of this final consecration of Himself and of His Church by the Great High-Priest, which is alike final appeal, claim, and prayer: 'O Righteous Father, the world knew Thee not, but I know Thee, and these know that Thou sentest Me. And I made known unto them Thy Name, and will make it known, so that [in order that] the love wherewith Thou lovedst Me may be in them, and I in them.' This is the charter of the Church: her possession and her joy; her faith, her hope also, and love; and in this she standeth, prayeth, and worketh.

CHAPTER XII.

GETHSEMANE.

(St. Matt. xxvi. 30–56; St. Mark xiv. 26–52; St. Luke xxii. 31–53; St. John xviii. 1–11.)

WE turn once more to follow the steps of Christ, now among the last He trod upon earth. The 'hymn,' with which the Paschal Supper ended, had been sung. Probably we are to understand this of the second portion of the *Hallel*,[a] sung some time after the third Cup, or else of Psalm cxxxvi., which, in the present Ritual, stands near the end of the service. The last Discourses had been spoken, the last Prayer, that of Consecration, had been offered, and Jesus prepared to go forth out of the City, to the Mount of Olives. The streets could scarcely be said to be deserted, for, from many a house shone the festive lamp, and many a company may still have been gathered; and everywhere was the bustle of preparation for going up to the Temple, the gates of which were thrown open at midnight.

Passing out by the gate north of the Temple, we descend into a lonely part of the valley of black Kidron, at that season swelled into a winter torrent. Crossing it, we turn somewhat to the left, where the road leads towards Olivet. Not many steps farther (beyond, and on the other side of the present Church of the Sepulchre of the Virgin) we turn aside from the road to the right, and reach what tradition has since earliest times—and probably correctly—pointed out as 'Gethsemane,' the 'Oil-press.' It was a small property enclosed ($\chi\omega\rho\acute{\iota}o\nu$), 'a garden' in the Eastern sense, where probably, amidst a variety of fruit trees and flowering shrubs, was a lowly, quiet summer-retreat, connected with, or near by, the 'Olive-press.' The present Gethsemane is only some seventy steps square, and though its old gnarled olives cannot be those (if such there were) of the time of Jesus, since all trees in that valley—those also which stretched their shadows over Jesus—were hewn down in the Roman siege, they may have sprung from the old roots, or from the odd kernels. But we love to think of this 'Garden' as the place where

Jesus ' often '—not merely on this occasion, but perhaps on previous visits to Jerusalem—gathered with His disciples. It was a quiet resting-place, for retirement, prayer, perhaps sleep, and a trysting-place also where not only the Twelve, but others also, may have been wont to meet the Master. And as such it was known to Judas, and thither he led the armed band, when they found the Upper Chamber no longer occupied by Jesus and His disciples. Whether it had been intended that He should spend part of the night there, before returning to the Temple, and whose that enclosed garden was—the other Eden, in which the Second Adam, the Lord from heaven, bore the penalty of the first, and in obeying gained life—we know not, and perhaps ought not to inquire. It may have belonged to Mark's father. But if otherwise, Jesus had loving disciples even in Jerusalem, and, we rejoice to think, not only a home at Bethany, and an Upper Chamber furnished in the City, but a quiet retreat and trysting-place for His own under the bosom of Olivet, in the shadow of the garden of ' the Oil-press.'

The sickly light of the moon was falling full on them as they were crossing Kidron. It was here, we imagine, after they had left the City behind them, that the Lord addressed Himself first to the disciples generally. We can scarcely call it either prediction or warning. Rather, as we think of that last Supper, of Christ passing through the streets of the City for the last time into that Garden, and especially of what was now immediately before Him, does what He spake seem natural, even necessary. To them—yes, to them all —He would that night be even a stumbling-block. And so had it been

foretold of old,ᵃ that the Shepherd would be smitten, and the sheep scattered. Did this prophecy of His suffering, in its grand outlines, fill the mind of the Saviour as He went forth on His Passion? Such Old Testament thoughts were at any rate present with Him, when, not unconsciously nor of necessity, but as the Lamb of God, He went to the slaughter. A peculiar significance also attaches to His prediction that, after He was risen, He would go before them into Galilee.ᵇ For, with their scattering upon His Death, it seems to us, the Apostolic circle or College, as such, was for a time broken up. They continued, indeed, to meet together as individual disciples, but the Apostolic bond was temporarily dissolved. This explains many things: the absence of Thomas on the first, and his peculiar position on the second Sunday; the uncertainty of the disciples, as evidenced by the words of those on the way to Emmaus; as well as the seemingly strange movements of the Apostles—all which are quite

ᵃ Zech. xiii. 7

ᵇ St. Matt. xxvi.32; St. Mark. xiv. 28

changed when the Apostolic bond is restored. Similarly, we mark, that only seven of them seem to have been together by the Lake of Galilee,[a] and that only afterwards the Eleven met Him on the mountain to which He had directed them.[b] It was here that the Apostolic circle or College was once more re-formed, and the Apostolic commission renewed,[c] and thence they returned to Jerusalem, once more sent forth from Galilee, to await the final events of His Ascension, and the Coming of the Holy Ghost.

a St. John
xxi. 2
b St. Matt.
xxviii. 16
c u. s. vv.
18-20

But in that night they understood none of these things. While all were staggering under the blow of their predicted scattering, the Lord seems to have turned to Peter individually. What He said, and how He put it, equally demand our attention: 'Simon, Simon '[d] —using his old name when referring to the old man in him—'Satan has obtained [out-asked, $\dot{\varepsilon}\xi\eta\tau\dot{\eta}\sigma\alpha\tau o$] you, *for the purpose* of sifting like as wheat. But I have made supplication for thee, that thy faith fail not.' The words admit us into two mysteries of heaven. This night seems to have been 'the power of darkness,' when, left of God, Christ had to meet by Himself the whole assault of hell, and to conquer in His own strength as Man's Substitute and Representative. It is a great mystery: but quite consistent with itself. We do not, as others, here see any analogy to the permission given to Satan in the opening chapters of the Book of Job, always supposing that this embodies a real, not an allegorical story. But in that night the fierce wind of hell was allowed to sweep unbroken over the Saviour, and even to expend its fury upon those that stood behind in His Shelter. Satan had 'out-asked,' obtained it—yet not to destroy, nor to cast down, but 'to sift,' like as wheat[1] is shaken in a sieve to cast out of it what is not grain. Hitherto, and no farther, had Satan obtained it. In that night of Christ's Agony and loneliness, of the utmost conflict between Christ and Satan, this seems almost a necessary element.

d St. Luke
xxii. 31

This, then, was the first mystery that had passed. And this sifting would affect Peter more than the others. Judas, who loved not Jesus at all, had already fallen; Peter, who loved Him—perhaps not most intensely, but, if the expression be allowed, most extensively—stood next to Judas in danger. In truth, though most widely apart in their directions, the springs of their inner life rose in close proximity. There was the same readiness to kindle into enthusiasm, the same desire to have public opinion with him, the same shrinking from the Cross, the same moral inability or unwillingness to

---

[1] It is very probable that the basis of the figure is Amos ix. 9.

stand alone, in the one as in the other.   Peter had abundant courage
to sally out, but not to stand out.   Viewed in its primal elements
(not in its development), Peter's character was, among the disciples,
the likest to that of Judas.   If this shows what Judas might have
become, it also explains how Peter was most in danger that night;
and, indeed, the husks of him were cast out of the sieve in his
denial of the Christ.   But what distinguished Peter from Judas
was his ' faith ' of spirit, soul, and heart—of spirit, when he apprehended the spiritual element in Christ; [a] of soul, when he confessed
Him as the Christ; [b] and of heart, when he could ask Him to sound
the depths of his inner being, to find there real, personal love to Jesus. [c]

[a] St. John
vi. 68
[b] St. Matt.
xvi. 16
[c] St. John
xxi. 15-17

The second mystery of that night was Christ's supplication for
Peter.   We dare not say, as the High-Priest—and we know not when
and where it was offered.   But the expression is very strong, as of
one who has need of a thing.[1]   And that for which He made such supplication was, that Peter's faith should not fail.   This, and not that
something new might be given him, or the trial removed from Peter.
We mark, how Divine grace presupposes, not supersedes, human
liberty.   And this also explains why Jesus had so prayed for Peter,
not for Judas.   In the former case there was *faith*, which only
required to be strengthened against failure—an eventuality which,
without the intercession of Christ, was possible.   To these words of
His, Christ added this significant commission: ' And thou, when thou
hast turned again, confirm thy brethren.'[2]   And how fully he did this,
both in the Apostolic circle and in the Church, history has chronicled.
Thus, although such may come in the regular moral order of things,
Satan has not even power to 'sift' without leave of God; and thus
does the Father watch in such terrible sifting over them for whom
Christ has prayed.   This is the first fulfilment of Christ's Prayer,
that the Father would 'keep them from the Evil One.'[d]   Not by any
process from without, but by the preservation of their faith.   And
thus also may we learn, to our great and unspeakable comfort, that
not every sin—not even conscious and wilful sin—implies the failure
of our faith, very closely though it lead to it; still less, our final
rejection.   On the contrary, as the fall of Simon was the outcome of
the natural elements in him, so would it lead to their being brought

[d] St. John
xvii. 15

---

[1] This even philologically, and in all
the passages in which the word is
used. Except in St. Matt. ix. 38, it
occurs only in the writings of St. Luke
and St. Paul.

[2] Curiously enough, Roman Catholic
writers see in the prediction of his fall
by implication an assertion of Peter's
supremacy. This, because they regard
Peter as the representative and head of
the others.

to light and removed, thus fitting him the better for confirming his brethren. And so would light come out of darkness. From our human standpoint we might call such teaching needful: in the Divine arrangement it is only the Divine sequent upon the human antecedent.

We can understand the vehement earnestness and sincerity with which Peter protested against the possibility of any failure on his part. We mostly deem those sins farthest which are nearest to us; else, much of the power of their temptation would be gone, and temptation changed into conflict. The things which we least anticipate are our falls. In all honesty—and not necessarily with self-elevation over the others—he said, that even if all should be offended in Christ, he never could be, but was ready to go with Him into prison and death. And when, to enforce the warning, Christ predicted that before the repeated crowing of the cock [1] ushered in the morning,[2] Peter would thrice deny that he knew Him, Peter not only persisted in his asseverations, but was joined in them by the rest. Yet—and this seems the meaning and object of the words of Christ which follow—they were not aware how terribly changed the former relations had become, and what they would have to suffer in consequence.[a] When formerly He had sent them forth, both without provision and defence, had they lacked anything? No! But now no helping hand would be extended to them; nay, what seemingly they would need even more than anything else would be 'a sword'—defence against attacks, for at the close of His history He was reckoned with transgressors.[3] The Master a crucified Malefactor—what could His followers expect? But once more they only understood Him in a grossly realistic manner. These Galileans, after the custom of their countrymen,[b] had provided themselves with short swords,

[a] St. Luke xxii. 35–38

[b] Jos. War iii. 3, 2

---

[1] This crowing of the cock has given rise to a curious controversy, since, according to Rabbinic law, it was forbidden to keep fowls in Jerusalem, on account of possible Levitical defilements through them (Baba K. vii. 7). *Reland* has written a special dissertation on the subject, of which *Schöttgen* has given a brief abstract. We need not reproduce the arguments, but *Reland* urges that, even if that ordinance was really in force at the time of Christ (of which there is grave doubt), Peter might have heard the cock crow from Fort Antonia, occupied by the Romans, or else that it might have reached thus far in the still night air from outside the walls of Jerusalem. But there is more than doubt as to the existence of this ordinance at the time. There is repeated mention of the 'cock-crow' in connection with the Temple-watches, and if the expression be regarded as not literal, but simply a designation of time, we have in Jer. Erub. x. 1 (p. 26 *a*, about middle) a story in which a cock caused the death of a child at Jerusalem, proving that fowls must have been kept there.

[2] St. Matthew speaks of 'this night,' St. Mark and St. Luke of 'this day,' proving, if such were needed, that the day was reckoned from evening to evening.

[3] Omit the article.

which they concealed under their upper garment.   It was natural for men of their disposition, so imperfectly understanding their Master's teaching, to have taken what might seem to them only a needful precaution in coming to Jerusalem.   At least two of them—among them Peter—now produced swords.[1]   But this was not the time to reason with them, and our Lord simply put it aside.   Events would only too soon teach them.

They had now reached the entrance to Gethsemane.   It may have been that it led through the building with the ' oil-press, ' and that the eight Apostles, who were not to come nearer to the ' Bush burning, but not consumed, ' were left there.   Or they may have been taken within the entrance of the Garden, and left there, while, pointing forward with a gesture of the Hand, He went ' yonder ' and prayed.[a] According to St. Luke, He added the parting warning to pray that they might not enter into temptation.

a St. Matt
xxvi. 36

Eight did He leave there.   The other three—Peter, James, and John—companions before of His glory, both when He raised the daughter of Jairus [b] and on the Mount of Transfiguration [c]—He took with Him farther.   If in that last contest His Human Soul craved for the presence of those who stood nearest Him and loved Him best, or if He would have them baptized with His Baptism, and drink of His Cup, these were the three of all others to be chosen.   And now of a sudden the cold flood broke over Him.   Within these few moments He had passed from the calm of assured victory into the anguish of the contest.   Increasingly, with every step forward, He became ' sorrowful,' full of sorrow, ' sore amazed,' and ' desolate.' [2] He told them of the deep sorrow of His Soul ($\psi v \chi \acute{\eta}$) even unto death, and bade them tarry there to watch with Him.   Himself went forward to enter the contest with prayer.   Only the first attitude of the wrestling Saviour saw they, only the first words in that Hour of Agony did they hear.   For, as in our present state not uncommonly in the deepest emotions of the soul, and as had been the case on the Mount of Transfiguration, irresistible sleep crept over their frame.   But what, we may reverently ask, was the cause of this sorrow unto death of the Lord Jesus Christ? Not fear, either of bodily or mental suffering: but Death.   Man's nature, created of God immortal, shrinks (by the law of its nature)

b St. Mark
v. 37
c St. Matt.
xvii. 1

---

[1] The objection has been raised, that, according to the Mishnah (Shabb. vi. 4), it was not lawful to carry swords on the Sabbath.   But even this Mishnah seems to indicate that there was divergence of opinion on the subject, even as regarded the Sabbath, much more a feast-day.

[2] We mark a climax.   The last word ($\dot{\alpha}\delta\eta\mu o\nu\epsilon\hat{\imath}\nu$ (used both by St. Matthew and St. Mark seems to indicate utter loneliness, desertion, and desolateness.

from the dissolution of the bond that binds body to soul. Yet to fallen man Death is not by any means fully Death, for he is born with the taste of it in his soul. Not so Christ. It was the Unfallen Man dying; it was He, Who had no experience of it, tasting Death, and that not for Himself but for every man, emptying the cup to its bitter dregs. It was the Christ undergoing Death by man and for man; the Incarnate God, the God-Man, submitting Himself vicariously to the deepest humiliation, and paying the utmost penalty: Death—all Death. No one as He could know what Death was (not dying, which men dread, but Christ dreaded not); no one could taste its bitterness as He. His going into Death was His final conflict with Satan for man, and on his behalf. By submitting to it He took away the power of Death; He disarmed Death by burying his shaft in His own Heart. And beyond this lies the deep, unutterable mystery of Christ bearing the penalty due to our sin, bearing our death, bearing the penalty of the broken Law, the accumulated guilt of humanity, and the holy wrath of the Righteous Judge upon them. And in view of this mystery the heaviness of sleep seems to steal over our apprehension.

Alone, as in His first conflict with the Evil One in the Temptation in the wilderness, must the Saviour enter on the last contest. With what agony of soul He took upon Him now and there the sins of the world, and in taking expiated them, we may learn from this account of what passed, when, with strong crying and tears unto Him that was able to save Him from death,' He 'offered up prayers and supplications.'[a] And—we anticipate it already—with these results: that He was heard; that He learned obedience by the things which He suffered; that He was made perfect; and that He became: to us the Author of Eternal Salvation, and before God, a High-Priest after the order of Melchizedek. Alone—and yet even this being 'parted from them' ($\dot{\alpha}\pi\varepsilon\sigma\pi\dot{\alpha}\sigma\theta\eta$),[b] implied sorrow.[c][1] And now, 'on His knees,' prostrate on the ground, prostrate on His Face, began His Agony. His very address bears witness to it. It is the only time, so far as recorded in the Gospels, when He addressed God with the personal pronoun: 'My Father.'[d][2] The object of the prayer was, that, 'if it were possible, the hour might pass away from Him.'[e] The subject of the prayer (as recorded by the three Gospels) was, that the Cup itself might pass away, yet always with the limitation, that not His Will but the Father's might be done. The petition of Christ, there-

a Heb. v. 7

b St. Luke xxii. 41
c Comp. Acts. xxi.

d St. Matt. xxvi. 39. 42
e St. Mark xiv. 36

---

[1] The Vulgate renders: 'avulsus est.' *Bengel* notes: 'serio affectu.'

[2] *St. Jerome* notes: 'dicitque blandiens: Mi Pater.'

BOOK
V

fore, was subject not only to the Will of the Father, but to His own Will that the Father's Will might be done.[1] We are here in full view of the deepest mystery of our faith: the two Natures in One Person. Both Natures spake here, and the 'if it be possible' of St. Matthew and St. Mark is in St. Luke 'if Thou be willing.' In any case, the 'possibility' is not physical—for with God all things are possible— but moral: that of inward fitness. Was there, then, any thought or view of 'a possibility,' that Christ's work could be accomplished without that hour and Cup? Or did it only mark the utmost limit of His endurance and submission? We dare not answer; we only reverently follow what is recorded.

It was in this extreme Agony of Soul almost unto death, that the Angel appeared (as in the Temptation in the wilderness) to 'strengthen' and support His Body and Soul. And so the conflict went on, with increasing earnestness of prayer, all that terrible hour.[a] For, the appearance of the Angel must have intimated to Him, that the Cup could not pass away.[2] And at the close of that hour—as we infer from the fact that the disciples must still have seen on His Brow the marks of the Bloody Sweat[3]—His Sweat, mingled with Blood,[4] fell in great drops on the ground. And when the Saviour with this mark of His Agony on His Brow[5] returned to the three, He found that deep sleep held them. While He lay in prayer, they lay in sleep; and yet where soul-agony leads not to the one, it often induces the other. His words, primarily addressed to 'Simon,' roused them, yet not sufficiently to fully carry to their hearts either the loving reproach, the admonition to 'Watch and pray' in view of the coming temptation, or the most seasonable warning about the weakness of the flesh, even where the spirit was willing, ready and ardent (πρόθυμον).

The conflict had been virtually, though not finally, decided, when the Saviour went back to the three sleeping disciples. He now returned to complete it, though both the attitude in which He prayed (no longer prostrate) and the wording of His Prayer—only slightly altered as it was—indicate how near it was to perfect victory. And

a St. Matt.
xxvi. 40

---

[1] This explains the ἀπὸ τῆς εὐλαβείας of Hebr. v. 7.

[2] Bengel: 'Signum bibendi calicis.'

[3] The pathological phenomenon of blood being forced out of the vessels in bloody sweat, as the consequence of agony, has been medically sufficiently attested. See the Commentaries.

[4] No one who has seen it, can forget the impression of Carlo Dolce's picture, in which the drops as they fall kindle into heavenly light.

[5] They probably knew of the Bloody Sweat by seeing its marks on His Brow, though those who did not follow Him on His capture may have afterwards gone, and in the moonlight seen the drops on the place where He had knelt.

once more, on His return to them, He found that sleep had weighted their eyes, and they scarce knew what answer to make to Him. Yet a third time He left them to pray as before. And now He returned victorious. After three assaults had the Tempter left Him in the wilderness; after the threefold conflict in the Garden he was vanquished. Christ came forth triumphant. No longer did He bid His disciples watch. They might, nay they should, sleep and take rest, ere the near terrible events of His Betrayal—for, the hour had come when the Son of Man was to be betrayed into the hands of sinners.

A very brief period of rest this,[1] soon broken by the call of Jesus to rise and go to where the other eight had been left, at the entrance of the Garden—to go forward and meet the band which was coming under the guidance of the Betrayer. And while He was speaking, the heavy tramp of many men and the light of lanterns and torches indicated the approach of Judas and his band. During the hours that had passed all had been prepared. When, according to arrangement, he appeared at the High-Priestly Palace, or more probably at that of Annas, who seems to have had the direction of affairs, the Jewish leaders first communicated with the Roman garrison. By their own admission they possessed no longer (for forty years before the destruction of Jerusalem) the power of pronouncing capital sentence.[a] It is difficult to understand how, in view of this fact (so fully confirmed in the New Testament), it could have been imagined (as so generally) that the Sanhedrin had, in regular session, sought formally to pronounce on Jesus what, admittedly, they had not the power to execute. Nor, indeed, did they, when appealing to Pilate, plead that they had pronounced sentence of death, but only that they had a law by which Jesus should die.[b] It was otherwise as regarded civil causes, or even minor offences. The Sanhedrin, not possessing the power of the sword, had, of course, neither soldiery, nor regularly armed band at command. The 'Temple-guard' under their officers served merely for purposes of police, and, indeed, were neither regularly armed nor trained.[c] Nor would the Romans have tolerated a regular armed Jewish force in Jerusalem.

We can now understand the progress of events. In the fortress of Antonia, close to the Temple and connected with it by two stairs,[d] lay the Roman garrison. But during the Feast the Temple itself was guarded by an armed Cohort, consisting of from 400 to 600 men,[2] so

[a] Sanh. 41

[b] St. John xviii. 31; St. John xix. 7

[c] Jos. War iv. 4. 6

[d] Jos. War v. 5, 8

---

[1] It will be noticed that we place an interval of time, however brief, between St. Matt. xxvi. 45 (and similarly St. Mark xiv. 41) and the following verse. So

already St. *Augustine*
[2] The number varied. See *Marquardt*, Röm. Alterthumsk. vol. v. 2, pp. 359, 386, 441. Canon *Westcott* suggests that it

as to prevent or quell any tumult among the numerous pilgrims.[a] It would be to the captain of this 'Cohort' that the Chief Priests and leaders of the Pharisees would, in the first place, apply for an

armed guard to effect the arrest of Jesus, on the ground that it might lead to some popular tumult. This, without necessarily having to state the charge that was to be brought against Him, which might have led to other complications. Although St. John speaks of 'the band' by a word ($\sigma\pi\varepsilon\tilde{\iota}\rho\alpha$) which always designates a 'Cohort' —in this case 'the Cohort,' the definite article marking it as that of the Temple—yet there is no reason for believing that the whole Cohort was sent. Still, its commander would scarcely have sent a strong detachment out of the Temple, and on what might lead to a riot, without having first referred to the Procurator, Pontius Pilate. And if further evidence were required, it would be in the fact that

the band was led not by a Centurion, but by a Chiliarch,[b] which, as there were no intermediate grades in the Roman army, must represent one of the six tribunes attached to each legion. This also explains not only the apparent preparedness of Pilate to sit in judgment early next morning, but also how Pilate's wife may have been disposed for those dreams about Jesus which so affrighted her.

This Roman detachment, armed with swords and 'staves'—with the latter of which Pilate on other occasions also directed his soldiers

to attack them who raised a tumult[c]—was accompanied by servants from the High-Priest's Palace, and other Jewish officers, to direct the arrest of Jesus. They bore torches and lamps placed on the top of

poles, so as to prevent any possible concealment.[d]

Whether or not this was the 'great multitude' mentioned by St. Matthew and St. Mark, or the band was swelled by volunteers or curious onlookers, is a matter of no importance. Having received this band, Judas proceeded on his errand. As we believe, their first move was to the house where the Supper had been celebrated. Learning that Jesus had left it with His disciples, perhaps two or three hours before, Judas next directed the band to the spot he knew so well: to Gethsemane. A signal by which to recognise Jesus seemed almost necessary with so large a band, and where escape or resistance might be apprehended. It was—terrible to say—none other than a kiss. As soon as he had so marked Him, the guard were to seize, and lead Him safely away.

might have been, not a cohort, but a 'manipulus' (of about 200 men); but, as himself points out, the expression as used in the N.T. seems always to indicate a cohort.

Combining the notices in the four Gospels, we thus picture to ourselves the succession of events. As the band reached the Garden, Judas went somewhat in advance of them,[a] and reached Jesus just as He had roused the three and was preparing to go and meet His captors. He saluted Him, 'Hail, Rabbi,' so as to be heard by the rest, and not only kissed but covered Him with kisses, kissed Him repeatedly, loudly, effusively ($\kappa\alpha\tau\epsilon\phi\iota\lambda\eta\sigma\epsilon\nu$). The Saviour submitted to the indignity, not stopping, but only saying as He passed on: 'Friend, that for which thou art here;'[b][1] and then, perhaps in answer to his questioning gesture: 'Judas, with a kiss deliverest thou up the Son of Man?'[c] If Judas had wished, by thus going in advance of the band and saluting the Master with a kiss, even now to act the hypocrite and deceive Jesus and the disciples, as if he had not come with the armed men, perhaps only to warn Him of their approach, what the Lord said must have reached his inmost being. Indeed, it was the first mortal shaft in the soul of Judas. The only time we again see him, till he goes on what ends in his self-destruction, is as he stands, as it were sheltering himself, with the armed men.[d]

It is at this point, as we suppose, that the notices from St. John's Gospel[e] come in. Leaving the traitor, and ignoring the signal which he had given them, Jesus advanced to the band, and asked them: 'Whom seek ye?' To the brief spoken, perhaps somewhat contemptuous, 'Jesus the Nazarene,' He replied with infinite calmness and majesty: 'I am He.' The immediate effect of these words was, we shall not say magical, but Divine. They had no doubt been prepared for quite other: either compromise, fear, or resistance. But the appearance and majesty of that calm Christ—heaven in His look and peace on His lips—was too overpowering in its effects on that untutored heathen soldiery, who perhaps cherished in their hearts secret misgivings of the work they had in hand. The foremost of them went backward, and they fell to the ground. But Christ's hour had come. And once more He now asked them the same question as before, and, on repeating their former answer, He said: 'I told you that I am *He*; if therefore ye seek Me, let these go their way,'—the Evangelist seeing in this watchful care over His own the inital fulfilment of the words which the Lord had previously spoken concerning their safe preservation,[f] not only in the sense of their outward

CHAP.
XII

[a] St. Luke

[b] St. Matt xxvi. 49; comp. St. Mark xiv. 45

[c] St. Luke xxii. 48

[d] St. John xviii. 5

[e] xviii. 4–9

[f] St. John xvii. 12

---

[1] We cannot, as many interpreters, take the words in an interrogative sense. I presume that Christ spoke both what St. Matthew and what St. Luke record. Both bear internal marks of genuineness.

BOOK
V

* St. Matt.
xxvi. 50 b
b St. Mark
xiv. 46
c St. John
xviii. 11. 26

d St. Mat-
thew
e St. John

f St. Luke

g St. John

preservation, but in that of their being guarded from such tempta
tions as, in their then state, they could not have endured.

The words of Christ about those that were with Him seem to
have recalled the leaders of the guard to full consciousness—perhaps
awakened in them fears of a possible rising at the incitement of His
adherents. Accordingly, it is here that we insert the notice of St.
Matthew,ᵃ and of St. Mark,ᵇ that they laid hands on Jesus and took
Him. Then it was that Peter,ᶜ seeing what was coming, drew the
sword which he carried, and putting the question to Jesus, but
without awaiting His answer, struck at Malchus,¹ the servant² of the
High-Priest—perhaps the Jewish leader of the band—cutting off his
ear. But Jesus immediately restrained all such violence, and rebuked all self-vindication by outward violence (the taking of the
sword that had not been received)—nay, with it all merely outward
zeal, pointing to the fact how easily He might, as against this
'cohort,' have commanded Angelic legions.ᵈ³ He had in wrestling
Agony received from His Father that Cup to drink,ᵉ⁴ and the Scriptures must in that wise be fulfilled. And so saying, He touched the
ear of Malchus, and healed him.ᶠ

But this faint appearance of resistance was enough for the guard.
Their leaders now bound Jesus.ᵍ It was to this last, most unde-
served and uncalled-for indignity that Jesus replied by asking them,
why they had come against Him as against a robber—one of those
wild, murderous Sicarii. Had He not been all that week daily in
the Temple, teaching? Why not then seize Him? But this 'hour'
of theirs that had come, and 'the power of darkness'—this also had
been foretold in Scripture!

And as the ranks of the armed men now closed around the bound
Christ, none dared to stay with Him, lest they also should be bound
as resisting authority. So they all forsook Him and fled. But
there was one there who joined not in the flight, but remained,

---

¹ The name *Malchus*, which occurs also
in *Josephus* (Ant. i. 15. 1.; xiv. 5. 2; 11.
4; War i. 8. 3), must not be derived, as
is generally done, from מֶלֶךְ a king. Its
Hebrew equivalent, apparently, is *Mal-
luch*, 'Counsellor,' a name which occurs
both in the Old Testament and in the
LXX. (1 Chron. vi. 44; Neh. x. 4, &c.),
and as a later Jewish name in the
Talmud. But both *Frankel* (Einl. in d.
Jer. Talm. p. 114) and *Freudenthal* (Hell.
Stud. p. 131) maintain that it was not
a Jewish name, while it was common
among Syrians, Phœnicians, Arabians,

and Samaritans. The suggestion therefore lies near, that Malchus was either a
Syrian or a Phœnician by birth.
² The definite article here marks that
he was, in a special sense, *the* servant of
the High-Priest—his body-servant.
³ A legion had ten cohorts.
⁴ This reference to the 'cup which
the Father had given Him to drink' by
St. John, implies the whole history of the
Agony in Gethsemane, which is not recorded in the Fourth Gospel. And this
is, on many grounds, very instructive·

a deeply interested onlooker. When the soldiers had come to seek Jesus in the Upper Chamber of his home, Mark, roused from sleep, had hastily cast about him the loose linen garment or wrapper[1] that lay by his bedside, and followed the armed band to see what would come of it. He now lingered in the rear, and followed as they led away Jesus, never imagining that they would attempt to lay hold on him, since he had not been with the disciples nor yet in the Garden. But they,[2] perhaps the Jewish servants of the High-Priest, had noticed him. They attempted to lay hold on him, when, disengaging himself from their grasp, he left his upper garment in their hands, and fled.

So ended the first scene in the terrible drama of that night.

---

[1] σινδών. This, no doubt, corresponds to the *Sadin* or *Sedina* which, in Rabbinic writings, means a linen cloth, or a loose linen wrapper, though, possibly, it may also mean a night-dress (see *Levy*, ad voc.).

[2] The designation 'young men' (St. Mark xiv. 51) is spurious.

CHAPTER XIII.

THURSDAY NIGHT—BEFORE ANNAS AND CAIAPHAS—PETER AND JESUS.

(St. John xviii. 12–14; St. Matt. xxvi. 57, 58; St. Mark xiv. 53, 54; St. Luke xxii.
54, 55; St. John xviii. 24, 15–18; St. John xviii. 19–23; St. Matt. xxvi. 69, 70;
St. Mark xiv. 66–68; St. Luke xxii. 56, 57; St. John xviii. 17, 18; St. Matt. xxvi.
71, 72; St. Mark xiv. 69, 70; St. Luke xxii. 58; St. John xviii. 25; St. Matt. xxvi.
59–68; St. Mark xiv. 55–65; St. Luke xxii. 67–71, 63–65; St. Matt. xxvi. 73–75;
St. Mark xiv. 70–72; St. Luke xxii. 59–62; St. John xviii. 26, 27.)

BOOK
V

IT was not a long way that they led the bound Christ. Probably through the same gate by which He had gone forth with His disciples after the Paschal Supper, up to where, on the slope between the Upper City and the Tyropœon, stood the well-known Palace of Annas. There were no idle saunterers in the streets of Jerusalem at that late hour, and the tramp of the Roman guard must have been too often heard to startle sleepers, or to lead to the inquiry why that glare of lamps and torches. and Who was the Prisoner, guarded on that holy night by both Roman soldiers and servants of the High-Priest.

If every incident in that night were not of such supreme interest, we might dismiss the question as almost idle, why they brought Jesus to the house of Annas, since he was not at that time the actual High-Priest. That office now devolved on Caiaphas, his son-in-law, who, as the Evangelist significantly reminds us,[a] had been the first to enunciate in plain words what seemed to him the political necessity for the judicial murder of Christ.[b] There had been no pretence on his part of religious motives or zeal for God; he had cynically put it in a way to override the scruples of those old Sanhedrists by raising their fears. What was the use of discussing about forms of Law or about that Man? it must in any case be done; even the friends of Jesus in the Council, as well as the punctilious observers of Law, must regard His Death as the less of two evils. He spoke as the bold, unscrupulous, determined man that he was; Sadducee in heart rather than by conviction; a worthy son-in-law of Annas.

a St. John
xviii. 14

b xi. 50

No figure is better known in contemporary Jewish history than that of Annas; no person deemed more fortunate or successful, but none also more generally execrated than the late High-Priest. He had held the Pontificate for only six or seven years; but it was filled by not fewer than five of his sons, by his son-in-law Caiaphas, and by a grandson. And in those days it was, at least for one of Annas' disposition, much better to have been than to be High-Priest. He enjoyed all the dignity of the office, and all its influence also, since he was able to promote to it those most closely connected with him. And, while they acted publicly, he really directed affairs, without either the responsibility or the restraints which the office imposed. His influence with the Romans he owed to the religious views which he professed. to his open partisanship of the foreigner, and to his enormous wealth. The Sadducean Annas was an eminently safe Churchman, not troubled with any special convictions nor with Jewish fanaticism, a pleasant and a useful man also, who was able to furnish his friends in the Prætorium with large sums of money. We have seen what immense revenues the family of Annas must have derived from the Temple-booths, and how nefarious and unpopular was the traffic. The names of those bold, licentious, unscrupulous, degenerate sons of Aaron were spoken with whispered curses.ᵃ ᵃ Pes. 57 a Without referring to Christ's interference with that Temple-traffic, which, if His authority had prevailed, would, of course, have been fatal to it, we can understand how antithetic in every respect a Messiah, and such a Messiah as Jesus, must have been to Annas. He was as resolutely bent on His Death as his son-in-law, though with his characteristic cunning and coolness, not in the hasty, bluff manner of Caiaphas. It was probably from a desire that Annas might have the conduct of the business, or from the active, leading part which Annas took in the matter; perhaps for even more prosaic and practical reasons, such as that the Palace of Annas was nearer to the place of Jesus' capture, and that it was desirable to dismiss the Roman soldiery as quickly as possible—that Christ was first brought to Annas, and not to the actual High-Priest.

In any case, the arrangement was most congruous, whether as regards the character of Annas, or the official position of Caiaphas. The Roman soldiers had evidently orders to bring Jesus to the late High-Priest. This appears from their proceeding directly to him, and from this, that apparently they returned to quarters immediately on delivering up their prisoner.[1] And we cannot ascribe this to any

[1] No further reference whatever is made to the Roman guard.

BOOK
V

official position of Annas in the Sanhedrin, first, because the text implies that it had not been due to this cause,[1] and, secondly, because, as will presently appear, the proceedings against Christ were *not* those of the ordinary and regular meetings of the Sanhedrin.

No account is given of what passed before Annas. Even the fact of Christ's being first brought to him is only mentioned in the Fourth Gospel. As the disciples had all forsaken Him and fled, we can understand that they were in ignorance of what actually passed, till they had again rallied, at least so far, that Peter and 'another disciple,' evidently John, 'followed Him into the Palace of the High-priest'—that is, into the Palace of Caiaphas, not of Annas. For as, according to the three Synoptic Gospels, the Palace of the High-Priest Caiaphas was the scene of Peter's denial, the account of it in the Fourth Gospel[a][2] must refer to the same locality, and not to the Palace of Annas, while the suggestion that Annas and Caiaphas occupied the same dwelling is not only very unlikely in itself, but seems incompatible with the obvious meaning of the notice,[b] ' Now Annas sent Him bound unto Caiaphas the High-Priest.' But if Peter's denial, as recorded by St. John, is the same as that described by the Synoptists, and took place in the house of Caiaphas, then the account of the examination by the High-Priest,[c] which follows the notice about Peter, must also refer to that by Caiaphas, not Annas.[3] We thus know absolutely nothing of what passed in the house of Annas—if, indeed, anything passed—except that Annas sent Jesus bound to Caiaphas.[4]

a St. John
xviii. 15-18

b ver. 24

c St. John
xviii. 19-23

[1] We read (St. John xviii. 13): 'For he was father-in-law to Caiaphas.'

[2] And hence also that of the two disciples following Christ.

[3] In this argument we lay little stress on the designation, 'High-Priest,' which St. John (ver. 19) gives to the examiner of Christ, although it is noteworthy that he carefully distinguishes between Annas and Caiaphas, marking the latter as ' the High-Priest' (vv. 13, 24).

[4] According to our argument, St. John xviii. 24 is an intercalated notice, referring to what had previously been recorded in vv. 15-23. To this two critical objections have been raised. It is argued, that as ἀπέστειλεν is in the aorist, not pluperfect, the rendering must be, 'Annas sent,' not 'had sent Him.' But then it is admitted, that the aorist is occasionally used for the pluperfect. Secondly, it is insisted that, according to the better reading, οὖν should be inserted after ἀπέστειλεν which Canon *Westcott* renders: ' Annas therefore sent Him.' But notwithstanding Canon *Westcott's* high authority, we must repeat the critical remark of *Meyer*, that there are 'important witnesses' against as well as for the insertion of οὖν, while the insertion of other particles in other Codd. seems to imply that the insertion here of any particle was a later addition.

On the other hand, what seem to me two irrefragable arguments are in favour of the retrospective application of ver. 24. First, the preceding reference to Peter's denial must be located in the house of Caiaphas. Secondly, if vv. 19-23 refer to an examination by Annas, then St. John has left us absolutely no account of anything that had passed before Caiaphas—which, in view of the narrative of the Synoptists, would seem incredible.

Of what occurred in the Palace of Caiaphas we have two accounts.
That of St. John[a] seems to refer to a more private interview between
the High-Priest and Christ, at which, apparently, only some personal
attendants of Caiaphas were present, from one of whom the Apostle   [a] St. John
may have derived his information.[1] The second account is that of   xviii. 19-23
the Synoptists, and refers to the examination of Jesus at dawn of
day[b] by the leading Sanhedrists, who had been hastily summoned   [b] St. Luke
for the purpose.   xxii. 66

It sounds almost like presumption to say, that in His first interview with Caiaphas Jesus bore Himself with the majesty of the Son
of God, Who knew all that was before Him, and passed through it as
on the way to the accomplishment of His Mission. The questions of
Caiaphas bore on two points: the disciples of Jesus, and His teaching
—the former to incriminate Christ's followers, the latter to incriminate the Master. To the first inquiry it was only natural that
He should not have condescended to return an answer. The reply to
the second was characterised by that ' openness ' which He claimed for
all that He had said.[c][2] If there was to be not unprejudiced, but   [c] St. John
even fair inquiry, let Caiaphas not try to extort confessions to which   xviii. 20
he had no legal right, nor to ensnare Him when the purpose was
evidently murderous. If he really wanted information, there could
be no difficulty in procuring witnesses to speak to His doctrine: all
Jewry knew it. His was no secret doctrine ('in secret I spake
nothing'). He always spoke 'in Synagogue and in the Temple,
whither all the Jews gather together.'[3] If the inquiry were a fair
one, let the judge act judicially, and ask not Him, but those who had
heard Him.

It must be admitted, that the answer sounds not like that of one
accused, who seeks either to make apology, or even greatly cares to
defend himself. And there was in it that tone of superiority which

---

[1] Canon *Westcott* supposes that the Apostle himself was present in the audience chamber. But, although we readily. admit that John went into the house, and was as near as possible to Christ, many reasons suggest themselves why we can scarcely imagine John to have been present, when Caiaphas inquired about the disciples and teaching of Jesus.

[2] I cannot think that the expression τῷ κόσμῳ 'to the world,' in ver. 20 can have any implied reference to the great world in opposition to the Jews (as so many interpreters hold). The expression 'the world' in the sense of 'everybody' is common in every language. And its Rabbinic use has been shown on p. 368, Note 3. Christ proves that He had had no 'secret' doctrine, about which He might be questioned, by three facts: 1. He had spoken παρρησίᾳ 'without reserve'; 2. He had spoken τῷ κόσμῳ to everybody, without confining Himself to a select audience; 3. He had taught in the most public places—in Synagogue and in the Temple, whither all Jews resorted.

[3] So according to the better reading, and literally.

even injured human innocence would have a right to assume before a nefarious judge, who sought to ensnare a victim, not to elicit the truth. It was this which emboldened one of those servile attendants, with the brutality of an Eastern in such circumstances, to inflict on the Lord that terrible blow. Let us hope that it was a heathen, not a Jew, who so lifted his hand. We are almost thankful that the text leaves it in doubt, whether it was with the palm of the hand, or the lesser indignity—with a rod. Humanity itself seems to reel and stagger under this blow. In pursuance of His Human submission, the Divine Sufferer, without murmuring or complaining, or without asserting His Divine Power, only answered in such tone of patient expostulation as must have convicted the man of his wrong, or at least have left him speechless. May it have been that these words and the look of Christ had gone to his heart, and that the now strangely-silenced malefactor became the confessing narrator of this scene to the Apostle John?

2. That Apostle was, at any rate, no stranger in the Palace of Caiaphas. We have already seen that, after the first panic of Christ's sudden capture and their own flight, two of them at least, Peter and John, seem speedily to have rallied. Combining the notices of the Synoptists [a] with the fuller details, in this respect, of the Fourth Gospel,[b] we derive the impression that Peter, so far true to his word, had been the first to stop in his flight and to follow ' afar off.' If he reached the Palace of Annas in time, he certainly did not enter it, but probably waited outside during the brief space which preceded the transference of Jesus to Caiaphas. He had now been joined by John, and the two followed the melancholy procession which escorted Jesus to the High-Priest. John seems to have entered ' the court' along with the guard,[c] while Peter remained outside till his fellow-Apostle, who apparently was well known in the High-Priest's house, had spoken to the maid who kept the door—the male servants being probably all gathered in the court [1]—and so procured his admission.

Remembering that the High-Priest's Palace was built on the slope of the hill, and that there was an outer court, from which a door led into the inner court, we can, in some measure, realise the scene. As previously stated, Peter had followed as far as that inner door, while John had entered with the guard. When he missed his fellow-disciple, who was left outside this inner door, John ' went out,'

[a] St. Matt. xxvi. 58; St. Mark xiv. 54; St. Luke xxii, 54, 55
[b] St. John xviii. 15–18

[c] St John xviii. 15

---

[1] The circumstance that *Josephus* (Ant. vii. 2. 1) on the ground of 2 Sam. iv 6 (LXX.) speaks of a female 'porter,' and that Rhoda opened the door in the house of the widowed mother of John Mark (Acts xii. 13), does not convince me, that in the Palace of the High-Priest a female servant regularly discharged that office.

and, having probably told the waiting-maid that this was a friend of his, procured his admission. While John now hurried up to be in the Palace, and as near Christ as he might, Peter advanced into the middle of the court, where, in the chill spring night, a coal fire had been lighted. The glow of the charcoal, around which occasionally a blue flame played, threw a peculiar sheen on the bearded faces of the men as they crowded around it, and talked of the events of that night, describing, with Eastern volubility, to those who had not been there what had passed in the Garden, and exchanging, as is the manner of such serving-men and officials, opinions and exaggerated denunciations concerning Him Who had been captured with such unexpected ease, and was now their master's safe Prisoner. As the red light glowed and flickered, it threw the long shadows of these men across the inner court, up the walls towards the gallery that ran round, up there, where the lamps and lights within, or as they moved along apartments and corridors, revealed other faces: there, where, in an inner audience-chamber, the Prisoner was confronted by His enemy, accuser, and judge.

What a contrast it all seemed between the Purification of the Temple only a few days before, when the same Jesus had overturned the trafficking tables of the High-Priest, and as He now stood, a bound Prisoner before him, at the mercy of every menial who might curry favour by wantonly insulting Him? It was a chill night when Peter, down ' beneath,' [a] looked up to the lighted windows. There, among the serving-men in the court, he was in every sense ' without.' [b] He approached the group around the fire. He would hear what they had to say; besides, it was not safe to stand apart; he might be recognised as one of those who had only escaped capture in the Garden by hasty flight. And then it was chill—and not only to the body, the chill had struck to his soul. Was he right in having come there at all? Commentators have discussed it as involving neglect of Christ's warning. As if the love of any one who was, and felt, as Peter, could have credited the possibility of what he had been warned of; and, if he had credited it, would, in the first moments of returning flood after the panic of his flight, have remembered that warning, or with cool calculation acted up to the full measure of it! To have fled to his home and shut the door behind him, by way of rendering it impossible to deny that he knew Christ, would not have been Peter nor any true disciple. Nay, it would itself have been a worse and more cowardly denial than that of which he was actually guilty. Peter followed afar off, thinking of nothing else but his imprisoned Master,

CHAP.
XIII

[a] St. Mark xiv. 66
[b] St. Matt. xxvi. 69

BOOK
V

and that he would see the end, whatever it might be. But now it was chill, very chill, to body and soul, and Peter remembered it all; not, indeed, the warning, but that of which he had been warned. What good could his confession do? perhaps much possible harm; and why was he there?

° The Syn
optists
ᵇ St. John

Peter was very restless, and yet he must seem very quiet. He 'sat down' among the servants,ª then he stood up among them.ᵇ It was this restlessness of attempted indifference which attracted the attention of the maid who had at the first admitted him. As in the uncertain light she scanned the features of the mysterious stranger,

° St. John

she boldly charged him,ᶜ though still in a questioning tone, with being one of the disciples of the Man Who stood incriminated up there before the High-Priest. And in the chattering of his soul's fever, into which the chill had struck, Peter vehemently denied all knowledge of Him to Whom the woman referred, nay, of the very meaning of what she said. He had said too much not to bring soon another charge upon himself. We need not inquire which of the slightly varying reports in the Gospels represents the actual words of the woman or the actual answer of Peter. Perhaps neither; perhaps all—certainly, she said all this, and, certainly, he answered all that, though neither of them would confine their words to the short sentences reported by each of the Evangelists.

What had he to do there? And why should he incriminate himself, or perhaps Christ, by a needless confession to those who had neither the moral nor the legal right to exact it? That was all he now remembered and thought; nothing about any denial of Christ. And so, as they were still chatting together, perhaps bandying words, Peter withdrew. We cannot judge how long time had passed, but this we gather, that the words of the woman had either not made any impression on those around the fire, or that the bold denial of Peter had satisfied them. Presently, we find Peter walking away

ᵈ St.Matthew
ᵉ St. Mark

down 'the porch,'ᵈ which ran round and opened into 'the outer court.'ᵉ He was not thinking of anything else now than how chilly it felt, and how right he had been in not being entrapped by that woman. And so he heeded it not, while his footfall sounded along the marble-paved porch, that just at this moment 'a cock crew.' But there was no sleep that night in the High-Priest's Palace. As he walked down the porch towards the outer court, first one maid met him; and then, as he returned from the outer court, he once more encountered his old accuser, the door-portress; and as he crossed the inner court to mingle again with the group around the fire, where he had formerly found safety, he was first accosted by one man, and then they all

around the fire turned upon him—and each and all had the same thing
to say, the same charge, that he was also one of the disciples of Jesus
of Nazareth. But Peter's resolve was taken; he was quite sure it was
right; and to each separately, and to all together, he gave the same
denial, more brief now, for he was collected and determined, but more
emphatic—even with an oath.ª And once more he silenced suspicion
for a time. Or, perhaps, attention was now otherwise directed.

3. For, already, hasty footsteps were heard along the porches
and corridors, and the maid who that night opened the gate at the
High-Priest's Palace was busy at her post. They were the leading
Priests, Elders, and Sanhedrists,[1] who had been hastily summoned to
the High-Priest's Palace, and who were hurrying up just as the first
faint streaks of gray light were lying on the sky. The private examination by Caiaphas we place (as in the Gospel of St. John) between
the first and second denial of Peter; the first arrival of Sanhedrists
immediately after his second denial. The private inquiry of Caiaphas
had elicited nothing; and, indeed, it was only preliminary. The
leading Sanhedrists must have been warned that the capture of
Jesus would be attempted that night, and to hold themselves in
readiness when summoned to the High-Priest. This is not only
quite in accordance with all the previous and after circumstances in
the narrative, but nothing short of a procedure of such supreme importance would have warranted the presence for such a purpose of
these religious leaders on that holy Passover-night.

But whatever view be taken, thus much at least is certain, that
it was no formal, regular meeting of the Sanhedrin. We put aside,
as à priori reasoning, such considerations as that protesting voices
would have been raised, not only from among the friends of Jesus,
but from others whom (with all their Jewish hatred of Christ) we
cannot but regard as incapable of such gross violation of justice and
law. But all Jewish order and law would have been grossly infringed
in almost every particular, if this had been a formal meeting of the
Sanhedrin.[2] We know what their forms were, although many of
them (as so much in Rabbinic accounts) may represent rather the
ideal than the real—what the Rabbis imagined should be, rather than

---

[1] The expression 'all the council'
must evidently be taken in a general,
not literal sense. No one would believe,
for example, that either Nicodemus or
Gamaliel was present. I would not,
however, attach any great importance to
this. The reference to the 'Elders' (in
St. Matt.) is spurious.

[2] This is also the conclusion of the
calmest and most impartial Jewish his-

torian, my lamented friend, the late Dr.
Jost (Gesch. d. Judenth. i. pp. 402–409).
He designates it 'a private murder
(Privat-Mord), committed by burning
enemies, not the sentence of a regularly
constituted Sanhedrin. The most prominent men who represented the Law, such
as Gamaliel, Jochanan b. Zakkai, and
others, were not present.' The defence of
the proceedings as a right and legal pro-

BOOK
V

what was; or else what may date from later times. According to Rabbinic testimony, there were three tribunals. In towns numbering less than 120 (or, according to one authority, 230 [1]) male inhabitants, there was only the lowest tribunal, that consisting of three Judges.[2] Their jurisdiction was limited, and notably did not extend to capital causes.[3] The authority of the tribunal of next instance—that of twenty-three [4]—was also limited, although capital causes lay within its competence. The highest tribunal was that of seventy-one, or the Great Sanhedrin, which met first in one of the Temple-Chambers, the so-called *Lishkath haGazith*—or Chamber of Hewn Stones—and at the time of which we write in ' the booths of the sons of Annas.'[5] The Judges of all these Courts were equally set apart by ordination *(Semikhah)*, originally that of the laying on of hands. Ordination was conferred by *three*, of whom one at least must have been himself ordained, and able to trace up his ordination through Joshua to

[a] Sanh. 2 a;
Maim.
Sanh. iv.
1-3

Moses.[a] This, of course, on the theory that there had been a regular succession of ordained Teachers, not only up to Ezra, but beyond him to Joshua and Moses. The members of the tribunals of twenty-three

[b] Sanh. 2 a;
15 b

were appointed by the Great Sanhedrin.[b] The members of the tribunals of three were likewise appointed by the Great Sanhedrin, which entrusted to men, specially accredited and worthy, the duty of travelling through the towns of Palestine and appointing and ordain-

[c] Sanh. 88
b; *Maim.* u.
s. ch. ii. 7, 8

ing in them the men best fitted for the office.[c] The qualifications mentioned for the office remind us of those which St. Paul indicates

[d] 1 Tim.
iii.; Tit. 1.

as requisite for the Christian eldership.[d]

Some inferences seem here of importance, as throwing light on early Apostolic arrangements—believing, as we do, that the outward

---

cedure by the Sanhedrin, as made by *Salvador* (Gesch. d. Mos. Instit. [German Transl.] vol. ii. pp. 67–79) is, from the critical point of view, so unsatisfactory, that I can only wonder the learned *Saalschütz* should, even under the influence of Jewish prejudice, have extended to it his protection (Mos. Recht, pp. 623–626). At the same time, the refutation of *Salvador* by *M. Dupin* (reproduced as App. to vol. iii. of the German translation of *Salvador*) is as superficial as the original attack. *Cohen's* ' Les Déicides' is a mere party-book which deserves not serious consideration. *Grätz* (Gesch. d. Juden, iii. p. 244) evades the question.

[1] In Sanh. i. 6, the reasons for the various numbers are given; but we can scarcely regard them as historical.

[2] Various modern writers have of late denied the existence of tribunals of three.

But the whole weight of evidence is against them. A number of passages might here be quoted, but the reader may be generally referred to the treatment of the subject in *Selden*, de Synedriis, ii. c. 5, and especially to *Maimonides*, Hilkh. Sanh.

[3] In the case of a *Mumcheh* or admitted authority, even one Judge could in certain civil cases pronounce sentence (Sanh. 2 b; 3 a).

[4] In Jerusalem there were said to have been two such tribunals; one whose *locale* was at the entrance to the Temple-Court, the other at that to the inner or Priest-Court.

[5] It is a mistake to identify these with the four shops on the Mount of Olives. They were the Temple-shops previously described.

form of the Church was in great measure derived from the Synagogue.
First, we notice that there was regular ordination, and, at first at
least, by the laying on of hands.   Further, this ordination was *not*
requisite either for delivering addresses or conducting the liturgy in
the Synagogue, but for *authoritative* teaching, and especially for
judicial functions, to which would correspond in the Christian Church
the power of the Keys—the administration of discipline and of the
Sacraments as admitting into, and continuing in the fellowship of the
Church.   Next, ordination could only be conferred by those who had
themselves been rightly ordained, and who could, therefore, through
those previously ordained, trace their ordination upwards.   Again,
each of these ' Colleges of Presbyters ' had its Chief or President.
Lastly, men entrusted with supreme (Apostolic) authority were sent
to the various towns 'to appoint elders in every city.' [a]   [a] Tit. 1. 5

The appointment to the highest tribunal, or Great Sanhedrin,
was made by that tribunal itself, either by promoting a member of
the inferior tribunals or one from the foremost of the three rows, in
which ' the disciples ' or students sat facing the Judges.   The latter
sat in a semicircle, under the presidency of the *Nasi* (' prince ') and
the vice-presidency of the *Ab-beth-din* (' father of the Court of Law ').[1]
At least twenty-three members were required to form a *quorum*.[b]   [b] Bemidb.
We have such minute details of the whole arrangements and pro-   R. 1
ceedings of this Court as greatly confirms our impression of the
chiefly ideal character of some of the Rabbinic notices.   Facing the
semicircle of Judges, we are told, there were two shorthand writers,
to note down, respectively, the speeches in favour and against the
accused.   Each of the students knew, and sat in his own place.   In
capital causes the arguments in defence of and afterwards those
incriminating the accused, were stated.   If one had spoken in favour,
he might not again speak against the panel.   Students might speak
for, not against him.   He might be pronounced ' not guilty ' on the
same day on which the case was tried; but a sentence of ' guilty '
might only be pronounced on the day following that of the trial.   It
seems, however, at least doubtful, whether in case of profanation of
the Divine Name (*Chillul haShem*), judgment was not immediately
executed.[c]   Lastly, the voting began with the youngest, so that   [c] Kidd, 40 a

---

[1] *Kuenen*, and after him *Schürer*
(Neutest. Zeitgesch.) have denied the
existence of this arrangement, but, as
I think, on quite insufficient grounds.
They have been answered by *D. Hoffmann* (see the very able ed. of the *Pirqé
Abhoth*, by that learned and accurate
scholar, Prof. *Strack* of Berlin, p. 9,
notes).   Comp. also *Levy*, Neuhebr.
Worterb., s. v. *Schürer* has to account
for other passages besides those which he
quotes (p. 413)—notably for the very
clear statement in Chag. ii. 2.

BOOK
V

juniors might not be influenced by the seniors; and a bare majority was not sufficient for condemnation.

These are only some of the regulations laid down in Rabbinic writings. It is of greater importance to enquire, how far they were carried out under the iron rule of Herod and that of the Roman Procurators. Here we are in great measure left to conjecture. We can well believe that neither Herod nor the Procurators would wish to *abolish* the Sanhedrin, but would leave to them the administration of justice, especially in all that might in any way be connected with purely religious questions. Equally we can understand, that both would deprive them of the power of the sword and of decision on all matters of political or supreme importance. Herod would reserve to himself the final disposal in all cases, if he saw fit to interfere, and so would the Procurators, who especially would not have tolerated any attempt at jurisdiction over a Roman citizen. In short, the Sanhedrin would be accorded full jurisdiction in inferior and in religious matters, with the greatest show, but with the least amount, of real rule or of supreme authority. Lastly, as both Herod and the Procurators treated the High-Priest, who was their own creature, as the real head and representative of the Jews; and as it would be their policy to curtail the power of the independent and fanatical Rabbis, we can understand how, in great criminal causes or in important investigations, the High-Priest would always preside—the presidency of the *Nasi* being reserved for legal and ritual questions and discussions. And with this the notices alike in the New Testament and in Josephus accord.

Even this brief summary about the Sanhedrin would be needless, if it were a question of applying its rules of procedure to the arraignment of Jesus. For, alike Jewish and Christian evidence establish the fact, that Jesus was not formally tried and condemned by the Sanhedrin. It is admitted on all hands, that forty years before the destruction of the Temple the Sanhedrin ceased to pronounce capital sentences. This alone would be sufficient. But, besides, the trial and sentence of Jesus in the Palace of Caiaphas would (as already stated) have outraged every principle of Jewish criminal law and procedure. Such causes could only be tried, and capital sentence pronounced, in the regular meeting-place of the Sanhedrin,[a][1] not, as here, in the High-Priest's Palace; no process, least of all such an one,

[a] Ab Zar.
B b

---

[1] There is truly not a tittle of evidence for the assumption of commentators, that Christ was led from the Pala e of Caiaphas into the Council-Cha b r. The whole proceedings took place in the former, and from it Christ was brought to Pilate (St. John xviii. 28).

might be begun in the night, not even in the afternoon,[a1] although if the discussion had gone on all day, sentence might be pronounced at night.[b] Again, no process could take place on Sabbaths or Feastdays,[c] or even on the eves of them,[d2] although this would not have nullified proceedings, and it might be argued on the other side, that a process against one who had seduced the people should preferably be carried on, and sentence executed, at the great public Feasts,[e] for the warning of all. Lastly, in capital causes there was a very elaborate system of warning and cautioning witnesses,[3] while it may safely be affirmed, that at a regular trial Jewish Judges, however prejudiced, would *not* have acted as the Sanhedrists and Caiaphas did on this occasion.

But as we examine it more closely, we perceive that the Gospel-narratives do not speak of a formal trial and sentence by the Sanhedrin. Such references as to 'the Sanhedrin' ('council'), or to 'all the Sanhedrin,' must be taken in the wider sense, which will presently be explained. On the other hand, the four Gospels equally indicate that the whole proceedings of that night were carried on in the Palace of Caiaphas, and that during that night no formal sentence of death was pronounced. St. John, indeed, does not report the proceedings at all; St. Matthew[f] only records the question of Caiaphas and the answer of the Sanhedrists; and even the language of St. Mark does *not* convey the idea of a formal sentence.[g] And when in the morning, in consequence of a fresh consultation, also in the Palace of Caiaphas, they led Jesus to the Prætorium, it was not as a prisoner condemned to death of whom they asked the execution,[h] but as one against whom they laid certain accusations worthy of death, while, when Pilate bade them judge Jesus according to Jewish Law, they replied, not: that they had done so already, but, that they had no competence to try capital causes.[k]

4. But although Christ was not tried and sentenced in a formal meeting of the Sanhedrin, there can, alas! be no question that His Condemnation and Death were the work, if not of the Sanhedrin, yet of the Sanhedrists—of the whole body of them ('all the council'), in the sense of expressing what was the judgment and purpose of

CHAP. XIII

[a] Shabb. 9 b
[b] Sanh. 32 a
[c] Bets. 36
[d] Baba K. 113 a
[e] Sanh. xi. 4; Tos. Sanh. xi. 6

[f] St. Matt. xxvi. 66

[g] St. Mark xiv. 64: 'condemned Him to be worthy of death'

[h] St. John xviii. 29, 30

[i] St. Luke xxiii. 2; St. Matt. xxvii. 12

[k] St. John xviii. 31.

---

[1] The ordinary Court-hours were from after morning-service till the time of the meal (Shabb. 10 a).

[2] In civil cases at least no process was carried on in the months of Nisan and Tishri (comp. *Bloch*, Civil Process-Ordnung).

[3] The details on these points are given in most commentaries. (Comp. the Tractate Sanhedrin and the Gemara on it.)

In a capital cause not only would the formal and very solemn warning charge against false testimony have been addressed to the witnesses, but the latter would be tested by the threefold process known as *Chaqiroth, Derishoth*, and *Bediqoth*; the former two referring to questions on the main points, the third or secondary points in the evidence.

all the Supreme Council and Leaders of Israel, with only very few exceptions. We bear in mind, that the resolution to sacrifice Christ had for some time been taken. Terrible as the proceedings of that night were, they even seem a sort of concession—as if the Sanhedrists would fain have found some legal and moral justification for what they had determined to do. They first sought 'witness,' or as St. Matthew rightly designates it, 'false witness' against Christ.[1] Since this was throughout a private investigation, this witness could only have been sought from their own creatures. Hatred, fanaticism, and unscrupulous Eastern exaggeration would readily misrepresent and distort certain sayings of Christ, or falsely impute others to Him. But it was altogether too hasty and excited an assemblage, and the witnesses contradicted themselves so grossly, or their testimony so notoriously broke down, that for very shame such trumped-up charges had to be abandoned. And to this result the majestic calm of Christ's silence must have greatly contributed. On directly false and contradictory testimony it must be best not to cross-examine at all, not to interpose, but to leave the false witness to destroy itself.

Abandoning this line of testimony, the Priests next brought forward probably some of their own order, who on the first Purgation of the Temple had been present when Jesus, in answer to the challenge for 'a sign' in evidence of His authority, had given them that mysterious 'sign' of the destruction and upraising of the Temple of His Body.[a][2] They had quite misunderstood it at the time, and its reproduction now as the ground of a criminal charge against Jesus must have been directly due to Caiaphas and Annas. We remember, that this had been the first time that Jesus had come into collision, not only with the Temple authorities, but with the avarice of 'the family of Annas.' We can imagine how the incensed High-Priest would have challenged the conduct of the Temple-officials, and how, in reply, he would have been told what they had attempted, and how Jesus had met them. Perhaps it was the only real inquiry which a man like Caiaphas would care to institute about what Jesus said. And here,

---

[1] The Pharisaic Law of witnesses was very peculiar. Witnesses who contradicted each other were *not* considered in Rabbinic Law as false witnesses, in the sense of being punishable. Nor would they be so, even if an *alibi* of the accused were proved—only if the *alibi* of the witnesses themselves were proved (comp. *Bähr*, Gesetz ü. Falsche Zeug., pp. 29, &c.). Thus the 'Story of Susanna' is bad in Jewish Law, unless, as *Geiger* supposes, it embodies an earlier mode of pro-

cedure in Jewish criminal jurisprudence.
[2] Critically also this is of interest. The first Purgation of the Temple is not related by the Synoptists, but they here confirm St. John's account of it. On the other hand, St. John's account of the Temple-purgation confirms that of the Synoptists, which St. John does not relate. And the evidence is the stronger, that the two sets of accounts are manifestly independent of each other, and that of the Fourth Gospel younger than that of the Synoptists.

in its grossly distorted form, and with more than Eastern exaggeration of partisanship it was actually brought forward as a criminal
charge!

Dexterously manipulated, the testimony of these witnesses might
lead up to two charges. It would show that Christ was a dangerous
seducer of the people, Whose claims might have led those who believed
them to lay violent hands on the Temple, while the supposed assertion,
that He would [a] or was able [b] to build the Temple again within three
days, might be made to imply Divine or magical pretensions.[1] A
certain class of writers have ridiculed this part of the Sanhedrist plot
against Jesus. It is, indeed, true, that, viewed as a Jewish charge, it
might have been difficult, if not impossible, to construe a capital
crime out of such charges, although, to say the least, a strong popular
prejudice might thus have been raised against Jesus—and this, no
doubt, was one of the objects which Caiaphas had in view. But it
has been strangely forgotten that the purpose of the High-Priest was
not to formulate a capital charge in *Jewish* Law, since the assembled
Sanhedrists had no intention so to try Jesus, but to formulate a
charge which would tell before the Roman Procurator. And here
none other could be so effective as that of being a fanatical seducer of
the ignorant populace, who might lead them on to wild tumultuous
acts. Two similar instances, in which the Romans quenched Jewish
fanaticism in the blood of the pretenders and their deluded followers,
will readily recur to the mind.[2] In any case, Caiaphas would
naturally seek to ground his accusation of Jesus before Pilate on
anything rather than His claims to Messiahship and the inheritance
of David. It would be a cruel irony if a Jewish High-Priest had to
expose the loftiest and holiest hope of Israel to the mockery of
a Pilate; and it might prove a dangerous proceeding, whether

CHAP.
XIII

[a] St. Mark
[b] St. Matt.

---

[1] At the same time neither this, nor
even the later charge of 'blasphemy,'
would have made Jesus what was technically called either a *Massith*, or a
Maddiach. The former is described as
an *individual* who *privately* seduces
private individuals into idolatry (Sanh.
vii. 10; Jer. Yeb. 15 *d*), it being added
that he speaks with a loud voice (in praise
of some false god) and uses the Holy
(Hebr.) language (Jer. Sanh. 25 *d*). On
the other hand, the *Maddiach* is one who
publicly seduces the people to idolatry,
using, as it is added, the language spoken
commonly by the people. The two Talmudic stories, that witnesses had lain in
wait to hear and report the utterances
of Christ (Sanh. 67 *a*), and that forty

days before His execution heralds had
summoned any exculpatory evidence in
His favour (Sanh. 43 *a*), may be dismissed
without comment.

[2] Besides other movements, we refer
here specially to that under Theudas,
who led out some 400 persons under
promise of dividing Jordan, when both
he and his adherents were cut down by
the Romans (*Jos.* Ant. xx. 5. 1). At a
later time an Egyptian Jew gathered
3,000 or 4,000 on the Mount of Olives,
promising to cast down the walls of
Jerusalem by the breath of his mouth
(u. s. xx. 8, 6). Another impostor of that
kind was Simon of Cyprus (u. s. xx. 7. 2),
and, of course, Bar Kokhabh.

as regarded the Roman Governor or the feelings of the Jewish people.

But this charge of being a seducer of the people also broke down, through the disagreement of the two witnesses whom the Mosaic Law required,[a] and who, according to Rabbinic ordinance, had to be separately questioned.[b] But the divergence of their testimony does not exactly appear in the differences in the accounts of St. Matthew and of St. Mark. If it be deemed necessary to harmonise these two narratives, it would be better to regard both as relating the testimony of these two witnesses. What St. Mark reported may have been followed by what St. Matthew records, or *vice versâ*, the one being, so to speak, the basis of the other. But all this time Jesus preserved the same majestic silence as before, nor could the impatience of Caiaphas, who sprang from his seat to confront, and, if possible, browbeat his Prisoner, extract from Him any reply.

Only one thing now remained. Jesus knew it well, and so did Caiaphas. It was to put the question, which Jesus could not refuse to answer, and which, once answered, must lead either to His acknowledgment or to His condemnation. In the brief historical summary which St. Luke furnishes, there is an inversion of the sequence of events, by which it might seem as if what he records had taken place at the meeting of the Sanhedrists [1] on the next morning. But a careful consideration of what passed there obliges us to regard the report of St. Luke as referring to the night-meeting described by St. Matthew and St. Mark. The motive for St. Luke's inversion of the sequence of events may have been,[2] that he wished to group in a continuous narrative Peter's threefold denial, the third of which occurred *after* the night-sitting of the Sanhedrin, at which the final adjuration of Caiaphas elicited the reply which St. Luke records, as well as the other two Evangelists. Be this as it may, we owe to St. Luke another trait in the drama of that night. As we suppose, the simple question was first addressed to Jesus, whether He was the Messiah? to which He replied by referring to the needlessness of such an enquiry, since they had predetermined not to credit His claims, nay, had only a few days before in the Temple refused[c] to discuss them.[d] It was upon this that the High-Priest, in the most solemn manner, adjured the True One by the Living God, Whose Son He was, to say it, whether He were the Messiah and Divine—the two being so joined together, not

a Deut.
xvii. 6
b Rosh
haSh. ii. 6

c St. Matt.
xxii. 41-46
d St. Luke
xxii. 67, 68;
the clause
'nor let Me
go' is
spurious

[1] It seems, to say the least, strange to explain the expression 'led Him into their συνέδριον' as referring to the regular Council-*chamber* (St. Luke xxii. 66).

[2] At the same time I confess myself in no way anxious about an accord of *details* and *circumstances*. when, admittedly, the *facts* entirely agree—nay, in such case, the accord of facts would be only the more striking.

in Jewish belief, but to express the claims of Jesus. No doubt or hesitation could here exist. Solemn, emphatic, calm, majestic, as before had been His silence, was now His speech. And His assertion of what He was, was conjoined with that of what God would show Him to be, in His Resurrection and Sitting at the Right Hand of the Father, and of what they also would see, when He would come in those clouds of heaven that would break over their city and polity in the final storm of judgment.

They all heard it—and, as the Law directed when blasphemy was spoken, the High Priest rent both his outer and inner garment, with a rent that might never be repaired.[a] But the object was attained. Christ would neither explain, modify, nor retract His claims. They had all heard it; what use was there of witnesses, He had spoken *Giddupha*,[1] 'blaspheming.' Then, turning to those assembled, he put to them the usual question which preceded [2] the formal sentence of death. As given in the Rabbinical original, it is: [3] 'What think ye, gentlemen? And they answered, if for life, "For life!" and if for death, "For death." '[b] But the formal sentence of death, which, if it had been a regular meeting of the Sanhedrin, must now have been spoken by the President,[c] was not pronounced.[4]

[a] Sanh. vii.
5
Moed K.
26 a

[b] Tanchuma Piqqudey, ed.
Warsh. i. p.
132 b

[c] Sanch. iii.
7

There is a curious Jewish conceit, that on the Day of Atonement the golden band on the High Priest's mitre, with the graven words, 'Holiness unto Jehovah,' atoned for those who had blasphemed.[d] It stands out in terrible contrast to the figure of Caiaphas on that awful night. Or did the unseen mitre on the True and Eternal High-Priest's Brow, marking the consecration of His Humiliation to Jehovah, plead for them who in that night were gathered there, the blind leaders of the blind? Yet amidst so many most solemn thoughts, some press prominently forward. On that night of terror, when all the enmity of man and the power of hell were unchained, even the falsehood of malevolence could not lay any crime to His charge, nor yet any accusation be brought against Him other than the misrepresentation of His symbolic Words. What testimony to Him this solitary false and ill-according witness! Again: 'They all condemned Him to be worthy of death.' Judaism itself would not now re-echo this sentence of the Sanhedrists. And yet is it not

[d] Jer. Yoma
44 c

---

[1] Other designations for it are *Chillul haShem*, and, euphemistically, *Berkhath haShem*.

[2] But this does not seem to me to have been the actual sentence. In regard to the latter, see the formalities detailed in

Sanh. iii. 7.

[3] סברי מרנן והם אומרים אם לחיים
לחיים ואם למיתה למתה.

[4] The President of the Judges said: 'Such an one, thou . . . art guilty' (Sanh. iii. 7).

after all true—that He was either the Christ, the Son of God, or a blasphemer? This Man, alone so calm and majestic among those impassioned false judges and false witnesses; majestic in His silence, majestic in His speech; unmoved by threats to speak, undaunted by threats when He spoke; Who saw it all—the end from the beginning; the Judge among His judges, the Witness before His witnesses: which was He—the Christ or a blaspheming impostor? Let history decide; let the heart and conscience of mankind give answer. If He had been what Israel said, He deserved the death of the Cross; if He is what the Christmas-bells of the Church, and the chimes of the Resurrection-morning ring out, then do we rightly worship Him as the Son of the Living God, the Christ, the Saviour of men.

5. It was after this meeting of the Sanhedrists had broken up, that, as we learn from the Gospel of St. Luke, the revolting insults and injuries were perpetrated on Him by the guards and servants of Caiaphas. All now rose in combined rebellion against the Perfect Man: the abject servility of the East, which delighted in insults on One Whom it could never have vanquished, and had not even dared to attack; that innate vulgarity, which loves to trample on fallen greatness, and to deck out in its own manner a triumph where no victory has been won; the brutality of the worse than animal in man (since in him it is not under the guidance of Divine instinct), and which, when unchained, seems to intensify in coarseness and ferocity; [1] and the profanity and devilry which are wont to apply the wretched witticisms of what is misnomered common sense and the blows of tyrannical usurpation of power to all that is higher and better, to what these men cannot grasp and dare not look up to, and before the shadows of which, when cast by superstition, they cower and tremble in abject fear! And yet these insults, taunts, and blows which fell upon that lonely Sufferer, not defenceless, but undefending, not vanquished, but uncontending, not helpless, but majestic in voluntary self-submission for the highest purpose of love—have not only exhibited the curse of humanity, but also removed it by letting it descend on Him, the Perfect Man, the Christ, the Son of God. And ever since has every noblehearted sufferer been able on the strangely clouded day to look up, and follow what, as it touches earth, is the black misty shadow, to where, illumined by light from behind, it passes into the golden light—a

---

[1] Have we advanced much beyond this, when the Parisian democracy can inscribe on its banners such words as ' Ecrasez l'Infâme '—and, horrible to relate it, teach its little children to bring to this its floral offerings?

mantle of darkness as it enwraps us, merging in light up there where its folds seem held together by the Hand from heaven.

This is *our* Sufferer—the Christ or a blasphemer; and in that alternative which of us would not choose the part of the Accused rather than of His judges? So far as recorded, not a word escaped His Lips; not a complaint, nor murmur; nor utterance of indignant rebuke, nor sharp cry of deeply sensitive, pained nature. He was drinking, slowly, with the consciousness of willing self-surrender, the Cup which His Father had given Him. And still His Father—and this also specially in His Messianic relationship to man.

We have seen that, when Caiaphas and the Sanhedrists quitted the audience-chamber, Jesus was left to the unrestrained licence of the attendants. Even the Jewish Law had it, that no 'prolonged death' (*Mithah Arikhta*) might be inflicted, and that he who was condemned to death was not to be previously scourged.[a] At last they were weary of insult and smiting, and the Sufferer was left alone, perhaps in the covered gallery, or at one of the windows that overlooked the court below. About one hour had passed[b] since Peter's second denial had, so to speak, been interrupted by the arrival of the Sanhedrists. Since then the excitement of the mock-trial, with witnesses coming and going, and, no doubt, in Eastern fashion repeating what had passed to those gathered in the court around the fire; then the departure of the Sanhedrists, and again the insults and blows inflicted on the Sufferer, had diverted attention from Peter. Now it turned once more upon him; and, in the circumstances, naturally more intensely than before. The chattering of Peter, whom conscience and consciousness made nervously garrulous, betrayed him. This one also was with Jesus the Nazarene; truly, he was of them—for he was also a Galilean! So spake the bystanders; while, according to St. John, a fellow-servant and kinsman of that Malchus, whose ear Peter, in his zeal, had cut off in Gethsemane, asserted that he actually recognised him. To one and all these declarations Peter returned only a more vehement denial, accompanying it this time with oaths to God and imprecations on himself.

The echo of his words had scarcely died out—their diastole had scarcely returned them with gurgling noise upon his conscience—when loud and shrill the second cock-crowing was heard. There was that in its harsh persistence of sound that also wakened his memory. He now remembered the words of warning prediction which the Lord had spoken. He looked up; and as he looked, he saw, how up there, just at that moment; the Lord turned round [1] and looked upon him—yes, in all that assembly, upon Peter! His eyes spake His Words; nay, much more; they searched down to the innermost depths of Peter's heart, and broke them open. They had pierced through all self-delusion, false shame, and fear: they had reached the man, the disciple, the lover of Jesus. Forth they burst, the waters of conviction, of true shame, of heart-sorrow, of the agonies of self-condemnation; and, bitterly weeping, he rushed from under those suns that had melted the ice of death and burnt into his heart—out from that cursed place of betrayal by Israel, by its High Priest—and even by the representative Disciple.

Out he rushed into the night. Yet a night lit up by the stars of promise—chiefest among them this, that the Christ up there—the conquering Sufferer—had prayed for him. God grant us in the night of our conscious self-condemnation the same star-light of His Promises, the same assurance of the intercession of the Christ, that so, as *Luther* puts it, the particularness of the account of Peter's denial, as compared with the briefness of that of Christ's Passion, may carry to our hearts this lesson: 'The fruit and use of the sufferings of Christ is this, that in them we have the forgiveness of our sins.'

---

[1] There is not any indication in the text that, as Commentators suppose, Christ was at that moment led bound across the Court; nor, indeed, that till the morning He was at all removed from near the place where He had been examined.

CHAPTER XIV.

THE MORNING OF GOOD FRIDAY.

(St. Matt. xxvii. 1, 2, 11–14; St. Mark xv. i–5; St. Luke xxiii. 1–5; St. John xviii. 28–38; St. Luke xxiii. 6–12; St. Matt. xxvii. 3–10; St. Matt. xxvii. 15–18; St. Mark xv. 6–10; St. Luke xxiii. 13–17; St. John xviii. 39, 40; St. Matt. xxvii. 19; St. Matt. xxvii. 20–31; St. Mark xv. 11–20; St. Luke xxiii. 18–25; St. John xix. 1–16.)

THE pale grey light had passed into that of early morning, when the CHAP.
Sanhedrists once more assembled in the Palace of Caiaphas.[1] A XIV
comparison with the terms in which they who had formed the gathering
of the previous night are described will convey the impression, that
the number of those present was now increased, and that they who
now came belonged to the wisest and most influential of the Council.
It is not unreasonable to suppose, that some who would not take
part in deliberations which were virtually a judicial murder might,
once the resolution was taken, feel in Jewish casuistry absolved from
guilt in advising how the informal sentence might best be carried
into effect.   It was this, and not the question of Christ's guilt, which
formed the subject of deliberation on that early morning.   The
result of it was to 'bind' Jesus and hand Him over as a malefactor
to Pilate, with the resolve, if possible, not to frame any definite
charge;[a] but, if this became necessary, to lay all the emphasis on   [a] St. John
the purely political, not the religious aspect of the claims of Jesus.[b2]   xviii. 29, 30
                                                                            [b] St. Luke
To us it may seem strange, that they who, in the lowest view of   xxiii. 2
it, had committed so grossly unrighteous, and were now coming on
so cruel and bloody a deed, should have been prevented by religious
scruples from entering the 'Prætorium.'   And yet the student of
Jewish casuistry will understand it; nay, alas, history and even
common observation furnish only too many parallel instances of
unscrupulous scrupulosity and unrighteous conscientiousness.   Alike
conscience and religiousness are only moral tendencies natural to
man; whither they tend, must be decided by considerations outside

---

[1] This is so expressly stated in St. John xviii. 28, that it is difficult to understand whence the notion has been derived that the Council assembled in their ordinary council-chamber.

[2] Comp. St. Matt. xxvii. 1 with xxvi. 59, where the words 'and elders' must be struck out; and St. Mark xv. 1 with xiv. 55.

BOOK
V

of them: by enlightenment and truth.[1] The ' Prætorium,' to which
the Jewish leaders, or at least those of them who represented the
leaders—for neither Annas nor Caiaphas seems to have been personally present—brought the bound Christ, was (as always in the
provinces) the quarters occupied by the Roman Governor. In
Cæsarea this was the Palace of Herod, and there St. Paul was afterwards a prisoner. But in Jerusalem there were two such quarters:
the fortress Antonia, and the magnificent Palace of Herod at the
north-western angle of the Upper City. Although it is impossible
to speak with certainty, the balance of probability is entirely in
favour of the view that, when Pilate was in Jerusalem with his wife,
he occupied the truly royal abode of Herod, and not the fortified
barracks of Antonia.[2] From the slope at the eastern angle, opposite
the Temple-Mount, where the Palace of Caiaphas stood, up the narrow
streets of the Upper City, the melancholy procession wound to the
portals of the grand Palace of Herod. It is recorded, that they
who brought Him would not themselves enter the portals of the
Palace, ' that they might not be defiled, but might eat the Passover.'

Few expressions have given rise to more earnest controversy than
this. On two things at least we can speak with certainty. Entrance
into a heathen house *did* Levitically render impure for that day—
that is, till the evening.[3] The fact of such defilement is clearly

[1] These are the *Urim* and *Thummim*
of the ' anima naturaliter Christiana.'

[2] This is, of course, not the traditional
site, nor yet that which was formerly in
favour. But as the Palace of Herod
undoubtedly became (as all royal resi-
dences) the property of the State, and as
we have distinct evidence that Roman
Procurators resided there, and took their
seat in front of that Palace on a raised
pavement to pronounce judgment (*Jos.*
War ii. 14. 8; comp. *Philo*, ad Caj. § 38),
the inference is obvious, that Pilate,
especially as he was accompanied by his
wife, resided there also.

[3] The various reasons for this need not
here be discussed. As these pages are
passing through the press (for a second
edition)my attention has been called to Dr.
Schürer's brochure (' Ueber φαγεῖν τὸ
πάσχα,' Giessen, 1883), intended to controvert the interpretation of St. John xviii.
28, given in the text. This is not the
place to enter on the subject at length.
But I venture to think that, with all his
learning, Dr. *Schürer* has not quite met the
case, nor fully answered the argument as

put by *Kirchner* and *Wieseler*. Putting
aside any argument from the supposed
later date of the ' Priest-Codex,' as compared with Deuter., and indeed the
purely Biblical argument, since the
question is as to the views entertained
in the time of Christ, *Schürer* argues: 1.
That the *Chagigah* was not designated
by the term *Pesach*. 2. That the defilement from entering a heathen house
would not have ceased in the evening (so
as to allow them to eat the Passover),
but have lasted for seven days, as being
connected with the suspicion that an
abortus—i.e. a dead body—might be
buried in the house. On the first point
we refer to Note 1 on the next page,
only adding that, with all his ingenuity,
Schürer has not met all the passages
adduced on the other side, and that the
view advocated in the text is that
adopted by many Jewish scholars.

The argument on the second point is
even more unsatisfactory. The defilement
from entering the *Prætorium*, which the
Sanhedrists dreaded, might be—or rather,
in this case must have been—due to other

attested both in the New Testament [a] and in the Mishnah, though its reasons might be various.[b] A person who had so become Levitically unclean was technically called *Tebhul Yom* ('bathed of the day'). The other point is, that, to have so become 'impure' for the day, would *not* have disqualified for eating the Paschal Lamb, since the meal was partaken of *after* the evening, and when a new day had begun. In fact, it is distinctly laid down[c] that the 'bathed of the day,' that is, he who had been impure for the day and had bathed in the evening, *did* partake of the Paschal Supper, and an instance is related,[d] when some soldiers who had guarded the gates of Jerusalem 'immersed,' and ate the Paschal Lamb. It follows that those Sanhedrists could not have abstained from entering the Palace of Pilate because by so doing they would have been disqualified for the Paschal Supper.

The point is of importance, because many writers have interpreted the expression 'the Passover' as referring to the Paschal Supper, and have argued that, according to the Fourth Gospel, our Lord did not on the previous evening partake of the Paschal Lamb, or else that in this respect the account of the Fourth Gospel does not accord with that of the Synoptists. But as, for the reason just stated, it is impossible to refer the expression 'Passover' to the Paschal Supper, we have only to inquire whether the term is not also applied to other offerings. And here both the Old Testament[e] and Jewish writings[1]

CHAP.
XIV

[a] Acts x 28
[b] Ohol. xviii. 7; To-har. vii. 3

[c] Pes. 92 a

[d] Jer. Pes. 36 b, lines 14 and 15 from bottom

[e] Deut. xvi. 1-3; 2 Chron. xxxv. 1, 2, 6, 18

causes than that the house might contain an *abortus* or a dead body. And of such many may be conceived, connected either with the suspected presence of an idol in the house or with contact with an idolator. It is, indeed, true that *Ohol.* xviii. 7 refers to the suspicion of a buried *abortus* as the cause of regarding the houses of Gentiles as defiled; but even so, it would be too much to suppose that a bare suspicion of this kind would make a man unclean for seven days. For this it would have been necessary that the dead body was actually within the house entered, or that what contained it had been touched. But there is another and weightier consideration. *Ohol.* xviii. 7 is not so indefinite as Dr. *Schürer* implies. It contains a most important limitation. In order to make a house thus defiled (from suspicion of an *abortus* buried in it), it states that *the house must have been inhabited by the heathen for forty days*, and even so the custody of a Jewish servant or maid would have rendered needless a *bediqah*, or investigation (to clear the house of

suspicion). Evidently, the *Prætorium* would not have fallen under the category contemplated in *Ohol.* xviii. 7, even if (which we are not prepared to admit) such a case would have involved a defilement of seven days. Thus *Schürer's* argument falls to the ground. Lastly, although the *Chagigah* could only be brought by the offerer in person, the Paschal Lamb might be brought for another person, and then the *tebhul yom* partake of it. Thus, if the Sanhedrists had been defiled in the morning they might have eaten the Pascha at night. Dr. *Schürer* in his *brochure* repeatedly appeals to *Delitzsch* (Zeitschr. f. Luther. Theol. 1874, pp. 1-4); but there is nothing in the article of that eminent scholar to bear out the special contention of *Schürer*, except that he traces the defilement of heathen houses to the cause in *Ohal.* xviii. 7. *Delitzsch* concludes his paper by pointing to this very case in evidence that the N.T. documents date from the *first*, and not the second century of our era.

[1] The subject has been so fully discussed in *Wieseler*, Beitr., and in

BOOK
V

show, that the term *Pesach*, or ' Passover,' was applied not only to the
Paschal Lamb, but to all the Passover sacrifices, especially to what
was called the *Chagigah*, or festive offering (from *Chag*, or *Chagag*, to
bring the festive sacrifice usual at each of the three Great Feasts).'
According to the express rule (Chag. i. 3) the *Chagigah* was brought
on the first festive Paschal Day.[1] It was offered immediately after
the morning-service, and eaten on that day—probably some time
before the evening, when, as we shall by-and-by see, another ceremony
claimed public attention. We can therefore quite understand that,
not on the eve of the Passover, but on the first Paschal day, the Sanhedrists would avoid incurring a defilement which, lasting till the
evening, would not only have involved them in the inconvenience of
Levitical defilement on the first festive day, but have actually prevented their offering on that day the Passover, festive sacrifice, or
Chagigah. For, we have these two express rules: that a person could
not in Levitical defilement offer the *Chagigah*; and that the *Chagigah*
could not be offered for a person by some one else who took his place
(Jer. Chag. 76 *a*, lines 16 to 14 from bottom). These considerations
and canons seem decisive as regards the views above expressed. There
would have been no reason to fear ' defilement ' on the morning of
the Paschal Sacrifice; but entrance into the *Prœtorium* on the morning of the first Passover-day would have rendered it impossible for
them to offer the *Chagigah*, which is also designated by the term *Pesach*.

It may have been about seven in the morning, probably even
earlier,[2] when Pilate went out to those who summoned him to dispense justice. The question which he addressed to them seems to
have startled and disconcerted them. Their procedure had been
private; it was of the very essence of proceedings at Roman Law
that they were in public. Again, the procedure before the Sanhedrists had been in the form of a criminal investigation, while it
was of the essence of Roman procedure to enter only on definite
accusations.[3] Accordingly, the first question of Pilate was, what

Kirchner, Jüd. Passahfeier, not to speak
of many others, that it seems needless to
enter further on the question. No competent Jewish archæologist would care
to deny that 'Pesach' *may* refer to the
'*Chagigah*,' while the motive assigned
to the Sanhedrists by St. John implies,
that in this instance it *must* refer to this,
and not to the Paschal Lamb.

[1] יום טוב הראשון של פסח. But concession was made to those who had
neglected it on the first day to bring it

during the festive week, which in the
Feast of Tabernacles was extended to
the *Octave*, and in that of Weeks (which
lasted only one day) over a whole week
(see Chag. 9 *a*; Jer. Chag. 76 *c*). The
Chagigah could not, but the *Paschal
Lamb* might. be offered by a person on
behalf of another.

[2] Most commentators suppose it to
have been much earlier. I have followed
the view of *Keim*.

[3] Nocens, nisi accusatus fuerit, con-

accusation they brought against Jesus. The question would come upon them the more unexpectedly, that Pilate must, on the previous evening, have given his consent to the employment of the Roman guard which effected the arrest of Jesus. Their answer displays humiliation, ill-humour, and an attempt at evasion. If He had not been 'a malefactor, they would not have 'delivered'[1] Him up! On this vague charge Pilate, in whom we mark throughout a strange reluctance to proceed—perhaps from unwillingness to please the Jews, perhaps from a desire to wound their feelings on the tenderest point, perhaps because restrained by a Higher Hand—refused to proceed. He proposed that the Sanhedrists should try Jesus according to Jewish Law. This is another important trait, as apparently implying that Pilate had been previously aware both of the peculiar claims of Jesus, and that the action of the Jewish authorities had been determined by 'envy.'[a] But, under ordinary circumstances, Pilate would *not* have wished to hand over a person accused of so grave a charge as that of setting up Messianic claims to the Jewish authorities, to try the case as a merely religious question.[b] Taking this in connection with the other fact, apparently inconsistent with it, that on the previous evening the Governor had given a Roman guard for the arrest of the prisoner, and with this other fact of the dream and warning of Pilate's wife, a peculiar impression is conveyed to us. We can understand it all, if, on the previous evening, after the Roman guard had been granted, Pilate had spoken of it to his wife, whether because he knew her to be, or because she might be interested in the matter. Tradition has given her the name *Procula*;[c] an Apocryphal Gospel describes her as a convert to Judaism;[d] while the Greek Church has actually placed her in the Catalogue of Saints. What if the truth lay between these statements, and Procula had not only been a proselyte, like the wife of a previous Roman Governor,[2] but known about Jesus and spoken of Him to Pilate on that evening? This would best explain his reluctance to condemn Jesus, as well as her dream of Him.

As the Jewish authorities had to decline the Governor's offer to proceed against Jesus before their own tribunal, on the avowed ground that they had not power to pronounce capital sentence,[3] it

[a] St. Matt.
xxvii. 18

[b] Acts. xxii.
30; xxiii.
28, 29; xxiv.
9, 18–20

[c] *Nicephorus,*
H.E. 1. 30
[d] Gospel
according
to Nicod.
ch. ii.

---

demnari non potest. In regard to the publicity of Roman procedure, comp. Acts xvi. 19; xvii. 6; xviii. 12; xxv. 6; *Jos.* War ii. 9. 3; 14. 8; 'maxima frequentia amplissimorum ac sapientissimorum civium adstante' (Cicero).

[1] Significantly the word is the same as that in reference to the *betrayal* of Judas.
[2] Saturninus (*Jos.* Ant. xviii. 3, 5).
[3] The apparently strange statement, St. John xviii. 32, affords another un-

THE CROSS AND THE CROWN.

now behoved them to formulate a capital charge. This is recorded by St. Luke alone.ᵃ It was, that Jesus had said, He Himself was Christ a King. It will be noted, that in so saying they falsely imputed to Jesus their own political expectations concerning the Messiah. But even this is not all. They prefaced it by this, that He perverted the nation and forbade to give tribute to Cæsar. The latter charge was so grossly unfounded, that we can only regard it as in their mind a necessary inference from the premiss that He claimed to be King. And, as telling most against Him, they put this first and foremost, treating the inference as if it were a fact—a practice this only too common in controversies, political, religious, or private.

This charge of the Sanhedrists explains what, according to all the Evangelists, passed within the Prætorium. We presume that Christ was within, probably in charge of some guards. The words of the Sanhedrists brought peculiar thoughts to Pilate. He now called Jesus and asked Him: 'Thou art the King of the Jews?' There is that mixture of contempt, cynicism, and awe in this question which we mark throughout in the bearing and words of Pilate. It was, as if two powers were contending for the mastery in his heart. By the side of uniform contempt for all that was Jewish, and of that general cynicism which could not believe in the existence of anything higher, we mark a feeling of awe in regard to Christ, even though the feeling may partly have been of superstition. Out of all that the Sanhedrists had said, Pilate took only this, that Jesus claimed to be a King. Christ, Who had not heard the charge of His accusers, now ignored it, in His desire to stretch out salvation even to a Pilate. Not heeding the implied irony, He first put it to Pilate, whether the question—be it criminal charge or inquiry—was his own, or merely the repetition of what His Jewish accusers had told Pilate of Him. The Governor quickly disowned any personal inquiry. How could he raise any such question? he was not a Jew, and the subject had no general interest. Jesus' own nation and its leaders had handed Him over as a criminal: what had He done?

The answer of Pilate left nothing else for Him Who, even in that supreme hour, thought only of others, not of Himself, but to bring before the Roman directly that truth for which his words had

designed confirmation of the Jewish authorship of the Fourth Gospel. It seems to imply, that the Sanhedrin might have found a mode of putting Jesus to death in the same informal manner in which Stephen was killed and they sought to destroy Paul. The Jewish law recognised a form of procedure, or rather a want of procedure, when a person caught *in flagrante delicto* of blasphemy might be done to death without further inquiry.

given the opening.   It was not, as Pilate had implied, a *Jewish*   CHAP.
question: it was one of absolute truth; it concerned all men.   The   XIV
Kingdom of Christ was not of this world at all, either Jewish or
Gentile.   Had it been otherwise, He would have led His followers
to a contest for His claims and aims, and not have become a prisoner
of the Jews.   One word only in all this struck Pilate.   'So then a
King art Thou!'   He was incapable of apprehending the higher
thought and truth.   We mark in his words the same mixture of
scoffing and misgiving.   Pilate was now in no doubt as to the nature
of the *Kingdom*; his exclamation and question applied to the *Kingship*.   That fact Christ would now emphasise in the glory of His
Humiliation.   He accepted what Pilate said; He adopted his words.
But He added to them an appeal, or rather an explanation of His
claims, such as a heathen, and a Pilate, could understand.   His
Kingdom was not of this world, but of that other world which He
had come to reveal, and to open to all believers.   Here was *the*
truth!   His Birth or Incarnation, as the Sent of the Father, and
His own voluntary Coming into this world—for both are referred to
in His words [a]—had it for their object to testify of the truth con-   [a] St. John
cerning that other world, of which was His Kingdom.   This was no   xviii. 37
Jewish-Messianic Kingdom, but one that appealed to all men.   And
all who had moral affinity to 'the truth' would listen to His testimony, and so come to own Him as 'King.'

But these words struck only a hollow void, as they fell on
Pilate.   It was not merely cynicism, but utter despair of all that is
higher—a moral suicide—which appears in his question: 'What is
truth?'   He had understood Christ, but it was not in him to respond
to His appeal.   He, whose heart and life had so little kinship to 'the
truth,' could not sympathise with, though he dimly perceived, the
grand aim of Jesus' Life and Work.   But even the question of Pilate
seems an admission, an implied homage to Christ.   Assuredly, he
would not have so opened his inner being to one of the priestly
accusers of Jesus.

That man was no rebel, no criminal!   They who brought Him
were moved by the lowest passions.   And so he told them, as he
went out, that he found no fault in Him.   Then came from the
assembled Sanhedrists a perfect hailstorm of accusations.   As we
picture it to ourselves, all this while the Christ stood near, perhaps
behind Pilate, just within the portals of the Prætorium.   And to
all this clamour of charges He made no reply.   It was as if the
surging of the wild waves broke far beneath against the base of the

BOOK
V

rock, which, untouched, reared its head far aloft to the heavens.   But as He stood in the calm silence of Majesty, Pilate greatly wondered. Did this Man not even fear death; was He so conscious of innocence, so infinitely superior to those around and against Him, or had He so far conquered Death, that He would not condescend to their words? And why then had He spoken to him of His Kingdom and of that truth?

Fain would he have withdrawn from it all; not that he was moved for absolute truth or by the personal innocence of the Sufferer, but that there was that in the Christ which, perhaps for the first time in his life, had made him reluctant to be unrighteous and unjust.   And so, when, amidst these confused cries, he caught the name Galilee as the scene of Jesus' labours, he gladly seized on what offered the prospect of devolving the responsibility on another.   Jesus was a Galilean, and therefore belonged to the jurisdiction of King Herod.   To Herod, therefore, who had come for the Feast to Jerusalem, and there occupied the old Maccabean Palace, close to that of the High-Priest, Jesus was now sent.[a][1]

a St. Luke
xxiii. 6-12

To St. Luke alone we owe the account of what passed there, as, indeed, of so many traits in this last scene of the terrible drama.[2] The opportunity now offered was welcome to Herod.   It was a mark of reconciliation (or might be viewed as such) between himself and the Roman, and in a manner flattering to himself, since the first step had been taken by the Governor, and that, by an almost ostentatious acknowledgment of the rights of the Tetrarch, on which possibly their former feud may have turned.   Besides, Herod had long wished to see Jesus, of Whom he had heard so many things.[b]   In that hour coarse curiosity, a hope of seeing some magic performances, was the only feeling that moved the Tetrarch.   But in vain did he ply Christ with questions.   He was as silent to him as formerly against the virulent charges of the Sanhedrists.   But a Christ Who would or could do no signs, nor even kindle into the same denunciations as the Baptist, was, to the coarse realism of Antipas, only a helpless figure that might be insulted and scoffed at, as did the Tetrarch and his men of war.[3]   And so Jesus was once more sent back to the Prætorium.

b St. Luke
ix. 7-9

[1] ἀνέπεμψεν. Meyer marks this as the technical term in handing over a criminal to the proper judicial authority.
[2] It is worse than idle—it is trifling to ask, whence the Evangelists derived their accounts.   As if those things had been done in a corner, or none of those who now were guilty had afterwards become disciples!
[3] It is impossible to say, whether 'the gorgeous apparel' in which Herod arrayed Christ was purple, or white. Certainly it was not, as Bishop Haneberg suggests (Relig. Alterth. p. 554), an old high-priestly garment of the Maccabees.

It is in the interval during which Jesus was before Herod, or
probably soon afterwards, that we place the last weird scene in the life
of Judas, recorded by St. Matthew.[a] We infer this from the circumstance, that, on the return of Jesus from Herod, the Sanhedrists do
not seem to have been present, since Pilate had to call them together,[b]
presumably from the Temple. And here we recall that the Temple
was close to the Maccabean Palace. Lastly, the impression left on
our minds is, that henceforth the principal part before Pilate was
sustained by 'the people,' the Priests and Scribes rather instigating
them than conducting the case against Jesus. It may therefore
well have been, that, when the Sanhedrists went from the Maccabean
Palace into the Temple, as might be expected on that day, only a
part of them returned to the Prætorium on the summons of Pilate.

But, however that may have been, sufficient had already passed
to convince Judas what the end would be. Indeed, it is difficult to
believe that he could have deceived himself on this point from the first,
however he had failed to realise the fact in its terrible import till after
his deed. The words which Jesus had spoken to him in the Garden
must have burnt into his soul. He was among the soldiery that fell
back at His look. Since then Jesus had been led bound to Annas, to
Caiaphas, to the Prætorium, to Herod. Even if Judas had not been
present at any of these occasions, and we do not suppose that his conscience had allowed this, all Jerusalem must by that time have been
full of the report, probably in even exaggerated form. One thing he
saw: that Jesus was condemned. Judas did not 'repent' in the Scriptural sense; but 'a change of mind and feeling' came over him.[1] Even
had Jesus been an ordinary man, and the relation to Him of Judas
been the ordinary one, we could understand his feelings, especially
considering his ardent temperament. The instant before and after sin
represents the difference of feeling as portrayed in the history of the
Fall of our first parents. With the commission of sin, all the bewitching, intoxicating influence, which incited to it, has passed away, and
only the naked fact remains. All the glamour has been dispelled; all
the reality abideth. If we knew it, probably scarcely one out of many
criminals but would give all he has, nay, life itself, if he could recall
the deed done, or awake from it to find it only an evil dream. But it
cannot be; and the increasingly terrible is, that it *is* done, and done
for ever. Yet this is not 'repentance,' or, at least, God alone knows
whether it is such; it may be, and in the case of Judas it only was,

CHAP.
XIV

[a] St. Matt.
xxvii. 3–10
[b] St Luke
xxiii. 13;
comp. St.
Matt.
xxvii. 17

---

[1] The verb designating Scriptural repentance is μετανοέω; that here used is
μεταμέλομαι, as in St. Matt. xxi. 29,
32; 2 Cor. vii. 8; Heb. vii. 21.

'change of mind and feeling' towards Jesus. Whether this might have passed into repentance, whether, if he had cast himself at the Feet of Jesus, as undoubtedly he might have done, this would have been so, we need not here ask. The mind and feelings of Judas, as regarded the deed he had done, and as regarded Jesus, were now quite other; they became increasingly so with ever-growing intensity. The road, the streets, the people's faces—all seemed now to bear witness against him and for Jesus. He read it everywhere; he felt it always; he imagined it, till his whole being was on flame. What had been; what was; what would be! Heaven and earth receded from him; there were voices in the air, and pangs in the soul—and no escape, help, counsel, or hope anywhere.

It was despair, and his a desperate resolve. He must get rid of these thirty pieces of silver, which, like thirty serpents, coiled round his soul with terrible hissing of death. Then at least his deed would have nothing of the selfish in it: only a terrible error, a mistake, to which he had been incited by these Sanhedrists. Back to them with the money, and let them have it again! And so forward he pressed amidst the wondering crowd, which would give way before that haggard face with the wild eyes, that crime had made old in those few hours, till he came upon that knot of priests and Sanhedrists, perhaps at that very moment speaking of it all. A most unwelcome sight and intrusion on them, this necessary but odious figure in the drama—belonging to its past, and who should rest in its obscurity. But he would be heard; nay, his words would cast the burden on them to share it with him, as with hoarse cry he broke into this: ' I have sinned—in that I have betrayed—innocent blood!' They turned from him with impatience, in contempt, as so often the seducer turns from the seduced—and, God help such, with the same fiendish guilt of hell: 'What is that to us? See thou to it!' And presently they were again deep in conversation or consultation. For a moment he stared wildly before him, the very thirty pieces of silver that had been weighed to him, and which he had now brought back, and would fain have given them, still clutched in his hand. For a moment only, and then he wildly rushed forward, towards the Sanctuary itself,[1] probably to where the Court of Israel bounded on that of the Priests, where generally the penitents stood in waiting, while in the Priests' Court the sacrifice was offered for them. He bent forward, and with all his might hurled from him [2] those thirty

---

[1] The expression ναός is always used in the N.T. of the Sanctuary itself, and not of the outer courts; but it would include the Court of the Priests, where the sacri-

fices were offered.

[2] I so understand the ῥίψας of St. Matt. xxvii. 5.

pieces of silver, so that each resounded as it fell on the marble pavement.

Out he rushed from the Temple, out of Jerusalem, 'into solitude.'[1] Whither shall it be? Down into the horrible solitude of the Valley of Hinnom, the 'Tophet' of old, with its ghastly memories, the Gehenna of the future, with its ghostly associations. But it was not solitude, for it seemed now peopled with figures, faces, sounds. Across the Valley, and up the steep sides of the mountain! We are now on 'the potter's field' of Jeremiah—somewhat to the west above where the Kidron and Hinnom valleys merge. It is cold, soft clayey soil, where the footsteps slip, or are held in clammy bonds. Here jagged rocks rise perpendicularly: perhaps there was some gnarled, bent, stunted tree.[2] Up there he climbed to the top of that rock. Now slowly and deliberately he unwound the long girdle that held his garment. It was the girdle in which he had carried those thirty pieces of silver. He was now quite calm and collected. With that girdle he will hang himself[3] on that tree close by, and when he has fastened it, he will throw himself off from that jagged rock.

It is done; but as, unconscious, not yet dead perhaps, he swung heavily on that branch, under the unwonted burden the girdle gave way, or perhaps the knot, which his trembling hands had made, unloosed, and he fell heavily forward among the jagged rocks beneath, and perished in the manner of which St. Peter reminded his fellow-disciples in the days before Pentecost.[a][4] But in the Temple the priests knew not what to do with these thirty pieces of money. Their unscrupulous scrupulosity came again upon them. It was not lawful to take into the Temple-treasury, for the purchase of sacred things, money that had been unlawfully gained. In such cases the Jewish Law provided that the money was to be restored to the donor, and, if he insisted on giving it, that he should be induced to spend it for something for the public weal. This explains the apparent discrepancy between the accounts in the Book of Acts and by St. Matthew. By a fiction of law the money was still considered to be Judas', and to have been applied by him[b] in the purchase of the well-known 'potter's field,' for the charitable purpose of burying in

a Acts i. 18, 19

b Acts. i. 18

---

[1] ἀνεχώρησε.
[2] The topographical notice is based on *Bädeker-Socin's* Palästina, pp. 114–116.
[3] This, not with any idea that his death would expiate for his sin. No such idea attached to suicide among the Jews.

[4] As presented in the text, there is no real divergence between the accounts of St. Matthew and the Book of Acts. *Keim* has formulated the supposed differences under five particulars, which are discussed *seriatim* by *Nebe*, Leidensgesch. vol. ii. pp. 12 &c.

it strangers.ᵃ But from henceforth the old name of ' potter's field,' became popularly changed into that of ' field of blood ' (*Haqal Dema*). And yet it was the act of Israel through its leaders: ' they took the thirty pieces of silver—the price of him that was valued, whom they of the children of Israel did value, and gave them for the potter's field!' It was all theirs, though they would have fain made it all Judas': the valuing, the selling, and the purchasing. And ' the potter's field'—the very spot on which Jeremiah had been Divinely directed to prophesy against Jerusalem and against Israel: ᵇ how was it now all fulfilled in the light of the completed sin and apostasy of the people, as prophetically described by Zechariah! This Tophet of Jeremiah, now that they had valued and sold at thirty shekel Israel's Messiah-Shepherd—truly a Tophet, and become a field of blood! Surely, not an accidental coincidence this, that it should be the place of Jeremy's announcement of judgment: not accidental, but veritably a fulfilment of his prophecy! And so St. Matthew, targuming this prophecy in form [1] as in its spirit, and in true Jewish manner stringing to it the prophetic description furnished by Zechariah, sets the event before us as the fulfilment of Jeremy's prophecy.[2]

We are once more outside the Prætorium, to which Pilate had summoned from the Temple Sanhedrists and people. The crowd was momentarily increasing from the town.[3] It was not only to see what was about to happen, but to witness another spectacle, that of the release of a prisoner. For it seems to have been the custom, that at the Passover[4] the Roman Governor released to the Jewish populace some notorious prisoner who lay condemned to death. A very significant custom of release this, for which they now began to clamour. It may have been, that to this also they were incited by the Sanhedrist who mingled among them. For if the stream of popular sympathy might be diverted to Bar-Abbas, the doom of Jesus would be the more securely fixed. On the present occasion it might be the more easy to influence the people, since Bar-Abbas belonged to that

[1] The alterations in the words quoted are, as previously explained, a ' targuming' of them.
[2] Most Commentators, however, regard the word ' Jeremy' as a lapse of memory, or an oversight by the Evangelist, or else as a very early error of transcription. Other explanations (more or less unsatisfactory) may be seen in the commentaries. *Böhl* (Alttest. Cit. p. 78), following *Valckenar*, thinks the mistake arose from confounding $Z_{\rho\iota o \upsilon}$ (written abbreviated) with $I_{\rho\iota o \upsilon}$ But the whole question is of no real importance.
[3] According to the better reading of St. Mark xv. 8 ' the multitude was going up.'
[4] How can they who regard the Johannine account as implying that Christ was crucified on the morning *before* the Passover, explain the words of St. John, ' Ye have a custom, that I should release unto you one *at the Passover* ' ?

class, not uncommon at the time, which, under the colourable pretence of political aspirations, committed robbery and other crimes. But these movements had deeply struck root in popular sympathy. A strange name and figure, Bar-Abbas. That could scarcely have been his real name. It means 'Son of the Father.'[1] Was he a political Anti-Christ? And why, if there had not been some conjunction between them, should Pilate have proposed the alternative of Jesus or Bar-Abbas, and not rather that of one of the two malefactors who were actually crucified with Jesus?

But when the Governor, hoping to enlist some popular sympathy, put this alternative to them—nay, urged it, on the ground that neither he nor yet Herod had found any crime in Him, and would even have appeased their thirst for vengeance by offering to submit Jesus to the cruel punishment of scourging, it was in vain. It was now that Pilate sat down on 'the judgment seat.' But ere he could proceed, came that message from his wife about her dream, and the warning entreaty to have nothing to do 'with that righteous man.' An omen such as a dream, and an appeal connected with it, especially in the circumstances of that trial, would powerfully impress a Roman. And for a few moments it seemed as if the appeal to popular feeling on behalf of Jesus might have been successful.[a] But once more the Sanhedrists prevailed. Apparently, all who had been followers of Jesus had been scattered. None of them seem to have been there; and if one or another feeble voice might have been raised for Him, it was hushed in fear of the Sanhedrists. It was Bar-Abbas for whom, incited by the priesthood, the populace now clamoured with increasing vehemence. To the question—half bitter, half mocking —what they wished him to do with Him Whom their own leaders had in their accusation called 'King of the Jews,' surged back, louder and louder, the terrible cry: 'Crucify him!' That such a cry should have been raised, and raised by Jews, and before the Roman, and against Jesus, are in themselves almost inconceivable facts, to which the history of these eighteen centuries has made terrible echo. In vain Pilate expostulated, reasoned, appealed. Popular frenzy only grew as it was opposed.

All reasoning having failed, Pilate had recourse to one more expedient, which, under ordinary circumstances, would have been effective.[b] When a Judge, after having declared the innocence of the accused, actually rises from the judgment-seat, and by a symbolic act pronounces the execution of the accused a judicial murder,

a St. Mark
xv. 11

b St. Matt.
xxvii. 24, 25

---

[1] The ancient reading 'Jesus Bar-Abbas' is not sufficiently attested to be adopted.

BOOK
V

from all participation in which he wishes solemnly to clear himself, surely no jury would persist in demanding sentence of death. But in the present instance there was even more. Although we find allusions to some such custom among the heathen,[1] that which here took place was an essentially Jewish rite, which must have appealed the more forcibly to the Jews that it was done by Pilate. And, not only the rite, but the very words were Jewish.[2] They recall not merely the rite prescribed in Deut. xxi. 6, &c., to mark the freedom from guilt of the elders of a city where untracked murder had been committed, but the very words of such Old Testament expressions as in 2 Sam. iii. 28, and Ps. xxvi. 6, lxxiii. 13,[a] and, in later times, in Sus. ver. 46. The Mishnah bears witness that this rite was continued.[b] As administering justice in Israel, Pilate must have been aware of this rite.[3] It does not affect the question, whether or not a judge could, especially in the circumstances recorded, free himself from guilt. Certainly, he could not; but such conduct on the part of a Pilate appears so utterly unusual, as, indeed, his whole bearing towards Christ, that we can only account for it by the deep impression which Jesus had made upon him. All the more terrible would be the guilt of Jewish resistance. There is something overawing in Pilate's, 'See ye to it'—a reply to the Sanhedrists' 'See thou to it,' to Judas, and in the same words. It almost seems, as if the scene of mutual imputation of guilt in the Garden of Eden were being re-enacted. The Mishnah tells us, that, after the solemn washing of hands of the elders and their disclaimer of guilt, priests responded with this prayer: 'Forgive it to Thy people Israel, whom Thou hast redeemed, O Lord, and lay not innocent blood upon Thy people Israel!' But here, in answer to Pilate's words, came back that deep, hoarse cry: 'His Blood be upon us,' and—God help us!—'on our children!' Some thirty years later, and on that very spot, was judgment pronounced against some of the best in Jerusalem; and among the 3,600 victims of the Governor's fury, of whom not a few were scourged and crucified right over against the Prætorium, were many of the noblest of the citizens of Jerusalem.[c] A few years more, and hundreds of crosses bore Jewish mangled bodies within sight of Jerusalem. And still have these wanderers seemed to bear, from century to century, and from land to land, that burden of blood; and still does it seem to weigh 'on us and our children.'

[a] In the LXX. version

[b] Sot. ix. 6

[c] Jos. War 14, 8, 9

---

[1] See the quotations in Wetstein, ad loc., and Nebe, u. s. p. 104.
[2] ἀθῷος ἀπὸ τοῦ αἵματος is a Hebraism=מִדַּם נָקִי.

[3] The Evangelist put what he said into the well-remembered Old Testament words.

The Evangelists have passed as rapidly as possible over the last
scenes of indignity and horror, and we are too thankful to follow
their example. Bar-Abbas was at once released. Jesus was handed
over to the soldiery to be scourged and crucified, although final and
formal judgment had not yet been pronounced.[a] Indeed, Pilate
seems to have hoped that the horrors of the scourging might still
move the people to desist from the ferocious cry for the Cross.[b] For
the same reason we may also hope, that the scourging was not
inflicted with the same ferocity as in the case of Christian martyrs,
when, with the object of eliciting the incrimination of others, or
else recantation, the scourge of leather thongs was loaded with lead,
or armed with spikes and bones, which lacerated back, and chest, and
face, till the victim sometimes fell down before the judge a bleeding
mass of torn flesh. But, however modified, and without repeating
the harrowing realism of a Cicero, scourging was the terrible introduction to crucifixion—'the intermediate death.' Stripped of His
clothes, His hands tied and back bent, the Victim would be bound
to a column or stake, in front of the Prætorium. The scourging
ended, the soldiery would hastily cast upon Him His upper
garments, and lead Him back into the Prætorium. Here they
called the whole cohort together, and the silent, faint Sufferer
became the object of their ribald jesting. From His bleeding Body
they tore the clothes, and in mockery arrayed Him in scarlet or
purple.[1] For crown they wound together thorns, and for sceptre
they placed in His Hand a reed. Then alternately, in mock proclamation they hailed Him King, or worshipped Him as God, and
smote Him or heaped on Him other indignities.[2]

Such a spectacle might well have disarmed enmity, and for ever
allayed worldly fears. And so Pilate had hoped, when, at his bidding,
Jesus came forth from the Prætorium, arrayed as a mock-king, and

CHAP.
XIV

[a] St. John
xix. 1,
following

[b] St. John
xix. 4,
following

---

[1] The *Sagum*, or short woollen military
cloak, scarlet or purple (the two colours
are often confounded, comp. *Wetstein*
ad loc.), fastened by a clasp on the right
shoulder. It was also worn by Roman
generals, and sometimes (in more costly
form and material) presented to foreign
kings.

[2] *Origen* already marks in this a
notable breach of military discipline.
Keim (Jesu von Naz. iii. 2, pp. 393, &c.)
gives a terribly graphic and realistic
account of the whole scene. The soldiers
were, as mostly in the provinces, chiefly
provincials—in this case, probably
Syrians. They were all the more bitterly

hostile to the Jews (*Jos.* Ant. xix. 9. 1;
War ii. 12, 1. 2; v. 11, 1—there also
derision at execution). A strange illustration of the scene is afforded by what
happened only a few years afterwards at
Alexandria, when the people in derision
of King Agrippa I., arrayed a well-known
maniac (Karabas) in a common door-
mat, put a papyrus crown on his head,
and a reed in his hand, and saluted him
' Maris,' lord (*Philo*, In Flacc. ed. *Mang.*
ii. 522; *Wetstein*, N.T, i. p. 535). On all
the classical illustrations and corrobora-
tions of the whole proceedings in every
detail, the reader should consult *Wetstein*,
ad loc.

the Governor presented Him to the populace in words which the Church has ever since treasured: ' Behold the Man!' But, so far from appeasing, the sight only incited to fury the ' chief priests' and their subordinates. This Man before them was the occasion, that on this Paschal Day a heathen dared in Jerusalem itself insult their deepest feelings, mock their most cherished Messianic hopes! ' Crucify!' ' Crucify!' resounded from all sides. Once more Pilate appealed to them, when, unwittingly and unwillingly, it elicited this from the people, that Jesus had claimed to be the Son of God.

If nothing else, what light it casts on the mode in which Jesus had borne Himself amidst those tortures and insults, that this state-ment of the Jews filled Pilate with fear, and led him to seek again converse with Jesus within the Prætorium. The impression which had been made at the first, and been deepened all along, had now passed into the terror of superstition. His first question to Jesus was, whence He was? And when, as was most fitting—since he could not have understood it—Jesus returned no answer, the feelings of the Romans became only the more intense. Would He not speak; did He not know that he had absolute power ' to release or to crucify' Him?[1] Nay, not absolute power—all power came from above; but the guilt in the abuse of power was far greater on the part of apostate Israel and its leaders, who knew whence power came, and to Whom they were responsible for its exercise.

So spake not an impostor; so spake not an ordinary man—after such sufferings and in such circumstances—to one who, whencesoever derived, *had* the power of life or death over Him. And Pilate felt it—the more keenly, for his cynicism and disbelief of all that was higher. And the more earnestly did he now seek to release Him. But, proportionately, the louder and fiercer was the cry of the Jews for His Blood, till they threatened to implicate in the charge of rebellion against Cæsar the Governor himself, if he persisted in unwonted mercy.

Such danger a Pilate would never encounter. He sat down once more in the judgment-seat, outside the Prætorium, in the place called ' Pavement,' and, from its outlook over the City, ' Gabbatha,'[2] ' the rounded height.' So solemn is the transaction that the Evan-gelist pauses to note once more the day—nay, the very hour, when

---

[1] This is the proper order of the words. To 'release' is put first to in-duce Christ to speak.
[2] The derivation of *Wünsche* (גב הבית) ' back of the Temple,' is on every ground to be rejected. *Gabbath* (גַּבַּת) or *Gab-betha* means ' a rounded height.' It occurs also as the name of a town (Jer. Taan. 69 *b*).

the process had commenced. It had been the Friday in Passover- week,[1] and between six and seven of the morning.[2] And at the close Pilate once more in mockery presented to them Jesus: ' Behold your King!'[3] Once more they called for His Crucifixion—and, when again challenged, the chief priests burst into the cry, which pre- ceded Pilate's final sentence, to be presently executed: ' We have no king but Cæsar!'

With this cry Judaism was, in the person of its representatives, guilty of denial of God, of blasphemy, of apostasy. It committed suicide; and, ever since, has its dead body been carried in show from land to land, and from century to century: to be dead, and to remain dead, till He come a second time, Who is the Resurrection and the Life!

---

[1] I have simply rendered the $\pi\alpha\rho\alpha$-$\sigma\kappa\epsilon\nu\dot{\eta}$ $\tau o\tilde{v}$ $\pi\acute{\alpha}\sigma\chi\alpha$ by Friday in Pass- over-week. The evidence for regarding $\pi\alpha\rho\alpha\sigma\kappa\epsilon\nu\dot{\eta}$, in the Gospels, as the *terminus technicus* for Friday, has been often set forth. See *Kirchner*, D. jud. Passahf. pp. 47, &c.

[2] The hour ('about the sixth') could only refer to when the process was taken in hand.

[3] I ought to mention that the verb $\grave{\epsilon}\kappa\acute{\alpha}\theta\iota\sigma\epsilon\nu$ in St. John xix. 13, has been taken by some critics in the transitive sense: ' Pilate . . . brought Jesus forth and seated Him in the judgment-seat,' implying an act of mock-homage on the part of Pilate when, in presenting to the Jews their King, he placed Him on the judgment-seat. Ingenious as the sug- gestion is, and in some measure sup- ported, it does not accord with the whole tenour of the narrative.

CHAPTER XV.

'CRUCIFIED, DEAD, AND BURIED.'

(St. Matt. xxvii. 31–43: St. Mark xv. 20–32 ª; St. Luke xxiii. 26–38; St. John xix. 16–24; St. Matt, xxviii. 44; St. Mark xv. 32 ᵇ; St. Luke xxiii. 39–43; St. John xix. 25–27; St. Matt. xxvii. 45–56; St. Mark xv. 33–41; St. Luke xxiii. 44–49; St. John xix. 28–30; St. John xix. 31–37; St. Matt. xxvii. 57–61; St. Mark xv. 42–47; St. Luke xxiii. 50–56; St. John xix. 38–42; St. Matt. xxvii. 62–66.)

BOOK
V

ª St. John
xix. 16

ᵇ ver. 6

IT matters little as regards their guilt, whether, pressing the language of St. John,ª we are to understand that Pilate delivered Jesus to the Jews to be crucified, or, as we rather infer, to his own soldiers. This was the common practice, and it accords both with the Governor's former taunt to the Jews,ᵇ and with the after-notice of the Synoptists. They, to whom He was ' delivered,' 'led Him away to be crucified: ' and they who so led Him forth ' compelled ' the Cyrenian Simon to bear the Cross. We can scarcely imagine, that the Jews, still less the Sanhedrists, would have done this. But whether formally or not, the terrible crime of slaying, with wicked hands, their Messiah-King rests, alas, on Israel.

Once more was He unrobed and robed. The purple robe was torn from His Wounded Body, the crown of thorns from His Bleeding Brow. Arrayed again in His own, now blood-stained, garments, He was led forth to execution. Only about two hours and a half had passed ᶜ since the time that He had first stood before Pilate (about half-past six),ᵈ when the melancholy procession reached Golgotha (at nine o'clock A.M.). In Rome an interval, ordinarily of two days, intervened between a sentence and its execution; but the rule does not seem to have applied to the provinces,[1] if, indeed, in this case the formal rules of Roman procedure were at all observed.

ᶜ St. Mark
xv. 25

ᵈ St. John
xix. 25

The terrible preparations were soon made: the hammer, the nails, the Cross, the very food for the soldiers who were to watch under each Cross.[2] Four soldiers would be detailed for each Cross,

[1] The evidence is collected by *Nebe*, u. s. vol. ii. p. 166, 167.

[2] *Keim* seems to imagine that, not in-deed the whole ' cohort,' but a *manipulus* of about 120, or a *centuria* of about 60 men, accompanied the procession. But

the whole being under the command of a centurion. As always, the
Cross was borne to the execution by Him Who was to suffer on it— perhaps His Arms bound to it with cords. But there is happily no evidence—rather, every indication to the contrary—that, according to ancient custom, the neck of the Sufferer was fastened within the *patibulum*, two horizontal pieces of wood, fastened at the end, to which the hands were bound. Ordinarily, the procession was headed by the centurion,[1] or rather, preceded by one who proclaimed the nature of the crime,[2] and carried a white, wooden board, on which it was written. Commonly, also, it took the longest road to the place of execution, and through the most crowded streets, so as to attract most public attention. But we would suggest, that alike this long circuit and the proclamation of the herald were, in the present instance, dispensed with. They are not hinted at in the text, and seem incongruous to the festive season, and the other circumstances of the history.

Discarding all later legendary embellishments,[3] as only disturbing, we shall try to realise the scene as described in the Gospels. Under the leadership of the centurion, whether or not attended by one who bore the board with the inscription, or only surrounded by the four soldiers, of whom one might carry this tablet, Jesus came forth bearing His Cross. He was followed by two malefactors—'robbers' —probably of the class then so numerous, that covered its crimes by pretensions of political motives. These two, also, would bear each his cross, and probably be attended each by four soldiers. Crucifixion was not a Jewish mode of punishment, although the Maccabee King Jannæus had so far forgotten the claims of both humanity and religion as on one occasion to crucify not less than 800 persons in Jerusalem itself.[a] But even Herod, with all his cruelty, did not resort to this mode of execution. Nor was it employed by the Romans till after the time of Cæsar, when, with the fast increasing cruelty of punishments, it became fearfully common in the provinces. Especially does it seem to characterise the domination of Rome in Judæa under every Governor. During the last siege of Jerusalem

[a] *Jos.* Ant. xiii. 14, 2; War i. 4, 6

---

of this there is not evidence, and all in-dications lead to a contrary inference.

[1] Tradition calls him Longinus.

[2] This was the Jewish practice also (Sanh. vi. 2). At the same time it must be remembered, that this was chiefly to elicit testimony in favour of the criminal, when the execution would be immediately arrested; and also that, as the Sanhedrin had, for centuries before

the redaction of the Mishnah, been de-prived of the power of life and death, such descriptions read very like *ideal* arrangements. But the practice seems also to have been Roman ('per præconem pronunciati').

[3] Such as concerning Veronica and the bearing of the Virgin-Mother (Acta Pilati, vii. x.; Mors Pilati [Tischendorf] 433).

BOOK
V

hundreds of crosses daily arose, till there seemed not sufficient room nor wood for them, and the soldiery diversified their horrible amusement by new modes of crucifixion. So did the Jewish appeal to Rome for the Crucifixion of Israel's King come back in hundredfold echoes. But, better than such retribution, the Cross of the God-Man hath put an end to the punishment of the cross, and instead, made the Cross the symbol of humanity, civilisation, progress, peace. and love.

As mostly all abominations of the ancient world, whether in religion or life, crucifixion was of Phœnician origin, although Rome adopted, and improved on it. The modes of execution among the Jews were: strangulation, beheading, burning, and stoning. In all ordinary circumstances the Rabbis were most reluctant to pronounce sentence of death. This appears even from the injunction that the Judges were to fast on the day of such a sentence.[a] Indeed, two of the leading Rabbis record it, that no such sentence would ever have been pronounced in a Sanhedrin of which they had been members. The indignity of hanging—and this only after the criminal had been otherwise executed—was reserved for the crimes of idolatry and blasphemy.[b] The place where criminals were stoned (*Beth haSeqilah*) was on an elevation about eleven feet high, from whence the criminal was thrown down by the first witness. If he had not died by the fall, the second witness would throw a large stone on his heart as he lay. If not yet lifeless, the whole people would stone him.[1] At a distance of six feet from the place of execution the criminal was undressed, only the covering absolutely necessary for decency being left.[c][2] In the case of Jesus we have reason to think that, while the mode of punishment to which He was subjected was un-Jewish, every concession would be made to Jewish custom, and hence we thankfully believe that on the Cross He was spared the indignity of exposure. Such would have been truly un-Jewish.[3]

Three kinds of Cross were in use: the so-called St. Andrew's Cross (×, the *Crux decussata*), the Cross in the form of a T (*Crux Commissa*), and the ordinary Latin Cross (+, *Crux immissa*). We believe that Jesus bore the last of these. This would also most readily

[a] With application of Lev. xix. 26, Sanh. 63 *a*.

[b] Sanh. vi. 4

[c] Sanh. vi. 3, 4

---

[1] This explains how 'the witnesses' at the stoning of St. Stephen laid down their garments at the feet of Paul.

[2] This opinion, however, was not shared by the majority of Rabbis. But, as already stated, all those notices are rather ideal than real.

[3] According to the Rabbis, when we read in Scripture generally of the punishment of death, this refers to the lightest, or strangulation (Sanh. 52 *b*). Another mode of execution reads like something between immuring alive and starvation (Sanh. 81 *b*)—something like the manner in which in the Middle Ages people were starved to death.

admit of affixing the board with the threefold inscription, which we know His Cross bore. Besides, the universal testimony of those who lived nearest the time (*Justin Martyr, Irenæus*, and others), and who, alas! had only too much occasion to learn what crucifixion meant, is in favour of this view. This Cross, as St. John expressly states, Jesus Himself bore at the outset. And so the procession moved on towards Golgotha. Not only the location, but even the name of that which appeals so strongly to every Christian heart, is matter of controversy. The name cannot have been derived from the skulls which lay about, since such exposure would have been unlawful, and hence must have been due to the skull-like shape and appearance of the place. Accordingly, the name is commonly explained as the Greek form of the Aramæan *Gulgalta*, or the Hebrew *Gulgoleth*, which means a skull.

Such a description would fully correspond, not only to the requirements of the narrative, but to the appearance of the place which, so far as we can judge, represents Golgotha. We cannot here explain the various reasons for which the traditional site must be abandoned. Certain it is, that Golgotha was ' outside the gate,' [a] and ' near the City.' [b] In all likelihood it was the usual place of execution. Lastly, we know that it was situated near gardens, where there were tombs, and close to the highway. The three last conditions point to the north of Jerusalem. It must be remembered that the third wall, which afterwards surrounded Jerusalem, was not built till several years after the Crucifixion. The new suburb of Bezetha extended at that time outside the second wall. Here the great highway passed northwards; close by, were villas and gardens; and here also rockhewn sepulchres have been discovered, which date from that period. But this is not all. The present Damascus Gate in the north of the city seems, in most ancient tradition, to have borne the name of St. Stephen's Gate, because the Proto-Martyr was believed to have passed through it to his stoning. Close by, then, must have been the place of execution. And at least one Jewish tradition fixes upon this very spot, close by what is known as the Grotto of Jeremiah, as the ancient ' place of stoning (*Beth haSeqilah*). And the description of the locality answers all requirements. It is a weird, dreary place, two or three minutes aside from the high road, with a high, rounded, skull-like rocky plateau, and a sudden depression or hollow beneath, as if the jaws of the skull had opened. Whether or not the ' tomb of the Herodian period in the rocky knoll to the west of Jeremiah's Grotto ' was the most sacred spot upon earth—the ' Sepulchre in the

[a] Heb. xiii 12

[b] St. John xix. 20

BOOK
V

Garden,' we dare not positively assert, though every probability attaches to it.[1]

Thither, then, did that melancholy procession wind, between eight and nine o'clock on that Friday in Passover week. From the ancient Palace of Herod it descended, and probably passed through the gate in the first wall, and so into the busy quarter of Acra. As it proceeded, the numbers who followed from the Temple, from the dense business-quarter through which it moved, increased. Shops, bazaars, and markets were, indeed, closed on the holy feast-day. But quite a crowd of people would come out to line the streets and to follow; and, especially, women, leaving their festive preparations, raised loud laments, not in spiritual recognition of Christ's claims, but [a St. Luke] in pity and sympathy.[a][2] And who could have looked unmoved on such a spectacle, unless fanatical hatred had burnt out of his bosom all that was human? Since the Paschal Supper Jesus had not tasted either food or drink. After the deep emotion of that Feast, with all of holiest institution which it included; after the anticipated betrayal of Judas, and after the farewell to His disciples, He had passed into Gethsemane. There for hours, alone—since His nearest disciples could not watch with Him even one hour—the deep waters had rolled up to His soul. He had drunk of them, immersed, almost perished in them. There had He agonised in mortal conflict, till the great drops of blood forced themselves on His Brow. There had He been delivered up, while they all had fled. To Annas, to Caiaphas, to Pilate, to Herod, and again to Pilate; from indignity to indignity, from torture to torture, had He been hurried all that livelong night, all that morning. All throughout He had borne Himself with a Divine Majesty, which had awakened alike the deeper feelings of Pilate and the infuriated hatred of the Jews. But if His Divinity gave its true meaning to His Humanity, that Humanity gave its true meaning to His voluntary Sacrifice. So far, then, from seeking to hide its manifestations, the Evangelists, not indeed needlessly but unhesitatingly, put them forward.[3] Unrefreshed by food or

---

[1] This view was first propounded by *Thenius*, and afterwards advocated by *Furrer* (Wander. d. Paläst, pp. 70, &c.), but afterwards given up by him. As to the locality, comp. 'Quart. Statement of Pal. Explor. Fund,' Oct. 1881, pp. 317–319; *Conder's* 'Handbook to the Bible,' pp. 355, 356, and for the description of Jeremiah's Grotto, *Baedeker-Socin*, u. s. p. 126. Of course, proof is in the nature of things impossible; yet to me this seems the most sacred and precious locality in Jerusalem.

[2] I cannot conceive any sufficient ground, why *Keim* should deny the historical character of this trait. Surely, on *Keim's* own principles, the circumstance, that only St. Luke records it, would not warrant this inference. On the other hand, it may be characterised as perhaps one of the most natural incidents in the narrative.

[3] I can only account for it by the prejudices of party feeling, that one of such

sleep, after the terrible events of that night and morning, while His
pallid Face bore the blood-marks from the crown of thorns, His
mangled Body was unable to bear the weight of the Cross.   No
wonder the pity of the women of Jerusalem was stirred.   But ours
is not pity, it is worship at the sight.   For, underlying His Human
Weakness was the Divine Strength which led Him to this voluntary
self-surrender and self-exinanition.   It was the Divine strength of
His pity and love which issued in His Human weakness.

Up to that last Gate which led from the 'Suburb' towards the
place of execution did Jesus bear His Cross.   Then, as we infer, His
strength gave way under it.   A man was coming from the opposite
direction, one from that large colony of Jews which, as we know, had
settled in Cyrene.[1]   He would be specially noticed; for, few would at
that hour, on the festive day, come 'out of the country,'[2] although
such was not contrary to the Law.   So much has been made of this,
that it ought to be distinctly known that travelling, which was forbidden on Sabbaths, was *not* prohibited on feast-days.[3]   Besides, the place
whence he came—perhaps his home—might have been within the
ecclesiastical boundary of Jerusalem.   At any rate, he seems to have
been well known, at least afterwards, in the Church—and his sons
Alexander and Rufus even better than he.[a]   Thus much only can   [a] St. Mark
xv. 21
we say with certainty; to identify them with persons of the same
name mentioned in other parts of the New Testament can only be
matter of speculation.[4]   But we can scarcely repress the thought
that Simon the Cyrenian had not before that day been a disciple;
had only learned to follow Christ, when, on that day, as he came in
by the Gate, the soldiery laid hold on him, and against his will
forced him to bear the Cross after Christ.   Yet another indication
of the need of such help comes to us from St. Mark,[b] who uses an   [b] xv. 22
expression[5] which conveys, though not necessarily that the Saviour
had to be borne, yet that He had to be supported to Golgotha from
the place where they met Simon.

Here, where, if the Saviour did not actually sink under His

---

fine and sympathetic tact as *Keim* should
so strangely have missed this, and imputed, especially to St. John, a desire of
obscuring the element of weakness and
forsakenness (u. s. p. 401).
[1] See vol. i. pp. 62, 63, 119.
[2] Certainly *not* 'from the field.' The
original, it is now generally admitted,
does not mean this, and, as *Wieseler*
aptly remarks (Beitr. p. 267). a person

would scarcely return from labour in the
field at nine o'clock in the morning (St.
Mark xv. 25).
[3] This is shown in Tosaph. to Chag.
17 *b*, and admitted by all Rabbinic
writers. (See *Hoffmann*, Abh. ü.d. Pentat.
Ges. p. 66.)
[4] Acts xiii. 1; Rom. xvi. 13.
[5] φέρουσιν.

BOOK
V

* St. Luke
xxiii. 27–31

b as St.
Luke also
records

c Hos. ix. 14

d War vi.
3, 4

e Hos. x. 8

f Rev. vi. 10

burden, it yet required to be transferred to the Cyrenian, while Himself henceforth needed bodily support, we place the next incident in
this history.[a] While the Cross was laid on the unwilling Simon,
the women who had followed with the populace closed around the
Sufferer, raising their lamentations.[1] At His Entrance into Jerusalem,[b]
Jesus had wept over the daughters of Jerusalem; as He left it for
the last time, they wept over Him. But far different were the
reasons for His tears from theirs of mere pity. And, if proof were
required of His Divine strength, even in the utmost depth of His
Human weakness—how, conquered, He was Conqueror—it would
surely be found in the words in which He bade them turn their
thoughts of pity where pity would be called for, even to themselves
and their children in the near judgment upon Jerusalem. The time
would come, when the Old Testament curse of barrenness[c] would be
coveted as a blessing. To show the fulfilment of this prophetic lament
of Jesus, it is not necessary to recall the harrowing details recorded
by *Josephus*,[d] when a frenzied mother roasted her own child, and in
the mockery of desperateness reserved the half of the horrible meal
for those murderers who daily broke in upon her to rob her of what
scanty food had been left her; nor yet other of those incidents,
too revolting for needless repetition, which the historian of the last
siege of Jerusalem chronicles. But how often, these many centuries,
must Israel's women have felt that terrible longing for childlessness,
and how often must the prayer of despair for the quick death of falling mountains and burying hills rather than prolonged torture[e] have
risen to the lips of Israel's sufferers! And yet, even so, these words
were also prophetic of a still more terrible future![f] For, if Israel
had put such flame to its 'green tree' how terribly would the Divine
judgment burn among the dry wood of an apostate and rebellious
people, that had so delivered up its Divine King, and pronounced
sentence upon itself by pronouncing it upon Him!

And yet natural, and, in some respects, genuine, as were the tears
of 'the daughters of Jerusalem,' mere sympathy with Christ almost
involves guilt, since it implies a view of Him which is essentially the
opposite of that which His claims demand. These tears were the
emblem of that modern sentiment about the Christ which, in its
effusiveness, offers insult rather than homage, and implies rejection
rather than acknowledgment of Him. We shrink with horror from

---

[1] ἐκόπτοντο καὶ ἐθρήνουν αὐτόν.   ad gestus), ita θρηνεῖν est oris et ocu-
Gerhard remarks: ' ut κόπτεσθαι sive   lorum (*Bengel*: ad, fletum et vocem
plangere est manuum (*Bengel* : pertinet   flebilem).

the assumption of a higher standpoint, implied in so much of the modern so-called criticism about the Christ. But even beyond this, all mere sentimentalism is here the outcome of unconsciousness of our real condition. When a sense of sin has been awakened in us, we shall mourn, not for what Christ has suffered, but for what He suffered for us. The effusiveness of mere sentiment is impertinence or folly: impertinence, if He was the Son of God; folly, if He was merely Man And, even from quite another point of view, there is here a lesson to learn. It is the peculiarity of Romanism ever to present the Christ in His Human weakness. It is that of an extreme section on the opposite side, to view Him only in His Divinity. Be it ours ever to keep before us, and to worship as we remember it, that the Christ is the Saviour God-Man.

It was nine of the clock when the melancholy procession reached Golgotha, and the yet more melancholy preparations for the Crucifixion commenced. Avowedly, the punishment was invented to make death as painful and as lingering as the power of human endurance. First, the upright wood was planted in the ground. It was not high, and probably the Feet of the Sufferer were not above one or two feet from the ground. Thus could the communication described in the Gospels take place between Him and others; thus, also, might His Sacred Lips be moistened with the sponge attached to a short stalk of hyssop. Next, the transverse wood (*antenna*) was placed on the ground, and the Sufferer laid on it, when His Arms were extended, drawn up, and bound to it. Then (this not in Egypt, but in Carthage and in Rome) a strong, sharp nail was driven, first into the Right, then into the Left Hand (the *clavi trabales*). Next, the Sufferer was drawn up by means of ropes, perhaps ladders;[1] the transverse either bound or nailed to the upright, and a rest or support for the Body (the *cornu* or *sedile*) fastened on it. Lastly, the Feet were extended, and either one nail hammered into each, or a larger piece of iron through the two. We have already expressed our belief that the indignity of exposure was not offered at such a Jewish execution. And so might the crucified hang for hours, even days, in the unutterable anguish of suffering, till consciousness at last failed.

It was a merciful Jewish practice to give to those led to execution a draught of strong wine mixed with myrrh so as to deaden con-

---

[1] But *Nebe* denies the use of ladders, and, in general, tries to prove by numerous quotations that the whole Cross was first erected, and then the Sufferer lifted up to it, and, only after that, the nails fastened into His Arms and Feet. Strange though it may seem, the question cannot be absolutely decided.

BOOK
V

sciousness.[a] This charitable office was performed at the cost of, if
not by, an association of women in Jerusalem.[b] That draught was
offered to Jesus when He reached Golgotha.[1] But having tasted it,
and ascertained its character and object, He would not drink it. It
was like His former refusal of the pity of the 'daughters of Jerusalem.' No man could take His Life from Him; He had power to lay
it down, and to take it up again. Nor would He here yield to the
ordinary weakness of our human nature; nor suffer and die as if it
had been a necessity, not a voluntary self-surrender. He would meet
Death, even in his sternest and fiercest mood, and conquer by submitting to the full. A lesson this also, though one difficult, to the
Christian sufferer.

And so was He nailed to His Cross, which was placed between,
probably somewhat higher than, those of the two malefactors crucified with Him.[2] One thing only still remained: to affix to His Cross
the so-called 'title' (*titulus*), on which was inscribed the charge on
which He had been condemned. As already stated, it was customary
to carry this board before the prisoner, and there is no reason for
supposing any exception in this respect. Indeed, it seems implied in
the circumstance, that the 'title' had evidently been drawn up under
the direction of Pilate. It was—as might have been expected,
and yet most significantly[3]—trilingual: in Latin, Greek, and Aramæan. We imagine, that it was written in that order,[4] and that the
words were those recorded by the Evangelists (excepting St. Luke,[5]
who seems to give a modification of the original, or Aramæan, text).
The inscription given by St. Matthew exactly corresponds with that

which *Eusebius*[c] records as the Latin *titulus* on the cross of one of
the early martyrs. We therefore conclude, that it represents the
Latin words. Again, it seems only natural, that the fullest, and to
the Jews most offensive, description should have been in Aramæan,

---

[1] The two alleged discrepancies, be-
between St. Matthew and St. Mark,
though, even if they did exist, scarcely
worth mention, may be thus explained:
1. If St. Matthew wrote 'vinegar' (although the best MSS. read 'wine'), he,
no doubt, so translated literally the word
Chomets (חֹמֶץ) which, though literally,

'vinegar,' refers to an inferior kind of wine
which was often mixed (comp. Pes. 42 b).
2. If our Greek text of St. Matthew speaks
of 'wormwood' (as in the LXX.)—not
'gall'—and St. Mark of myrrh, we must
remember, that both may have been
regarded as stupefying, perhaps both
used, and that possibly the mistake may
have arisen from the similarity of the

words and their writing—*Lebhonah*,
'myrrh,' *Laanah*, 'wormwood'—when
לבונה may have passed into לענה—the
ב into ע.
[2] *Sepp*, vol. vi. p. 336, recalls the execution of Savonarola between Fra
Silvestro and Fra Domenico, and the
taunt of his enemies: 'Now, brother!'
[3] Professor *Westcott* beautifully re-
marks:These three languages gathered up
the result of the religious, the social, the
intellectual preparation for Christ, and in
each witness was given to His office.
[4] See next page, note 1.
[5] The better reading there is, ὁ
βασιλεὺς τῶν Ἰουδαίων οὗτος.

which all could read. Very significantly this is given by St. John. It follows, that the inscription given by St. Mark must represent that in Greek. Although much less comprehensive, it had the same number of words, and precisely the same number of letters, as that in Aramæan, given by St. John.[1]

It seems probable, that the Sanhedrists had heard from some one, who had watched the procession on its way to Golgotha, of the inscription which Pilate had written on the 'titulus '—partly to avenge himself on, and partly to deride, the Jews. It is not likely that they would have asked Pilate to take it down after it had been affixed to the Cross; and it seems scarcely credible, that they would have waited outside the Prætorium till the melancholy procession commenced its march. We suppose that, after the condemnation of Jesus, the Sanhedrists had gone from the Prætorium into the Temple, to take part in its services. When informed of the offensive tablet, they hastened once more to the Prætorium, to induce Pilate not to allow it to be put up. This explains the inversion in the order of the account in the Gospel of St. John,[a] or rather, its location in that narrative in immediate connection with the notice, that the Sanhedrists were afraid the Jews who passed by might be influenced by the inscription. We imagine, that the Sanhedrists had originally no intention of doing anything so un-Jewish as not only to gaze at the sufferings of the Crucified, but to even deride Him in His Agony-—that, in fact, they had not intended going to Golgotha at all. But when they found that Pilate would not yield to their remonstrances, some of them hastened to the place of Crucifixion, and, mingling with the crowd, sought to incite their jeers, so as to prevent any deeper impression[2] which the significant words of the inscription might have produced.[3]

Before nailing Him to the Cross, the soldiers parted among them the poor worldly inheritance of His raiment.[4] On this point there are

CHAP.
XV

[a] St. John xix. 21. 22

---

[1] Probably it would read *Jeshu han-Notsri malka dihudaey* (יֵשׁוּ הַנֹּצְרִי מַלְכָּא דִיהוּדָאֵי—יֵשׁוּע הַנֹּצְרִי). Both have four words and, in all, twenty letters. The Latin inscription (St. Matthew) would be, *Hic est Jesus Rex Judæorum*—five words and twenty-two letters. It will be seen how each would fill a line of about the same length. The notice of the three languages in St. Luke is spurious We retain the *textus receptus* of St. John xix. 19, as in any case it seems most unlikely that Pilate

would have placed the Latin in the middle and not at the top. The Aramæan would stand last.

[2] Comp. here the account of St. Matt. (xxvii. 39–43) and of the other Synoptists.

[3] Thus, the notice in St. John xix. 21, 22, would be parenthetic, chronologically belonging to an earlier part, and inserted here for the sake of historical connection.

[4] It is generally stated, that this was the common Roman custom. But of this there is no evidence, and in later times

slight seeming differences[1] between the notices of the Synoptists and the more detailed account of the Fourth Gospel. Such differences, if real, would afford only fresh evidence of the general trustworthiness of the narrative. For, we bear in mind that, of all the disciples, only St. John witnessed the last scenes, and that therefore the other accounts of it circulating in the early Church must have been derived, so to speak, from second sources. This explains, why perhaps the largest number of seeming discrepancies in the Gospels occurs in the narrative of the closing hours in the Life of Christ, and how, contrary to what otherwise we might have expected, the most detailed as well as precise account of them comes to us from St. John. In the present instance these slight seeming differences may be explained in the following manner. There was, as St. John states, first a division into four parts—one to each of the soldiers—of such garments of the Lord as were of nearly the same value. The head-gear, the outer cloak-like garment, the girdle, and the sandals, would differ little in cost. But the question, which of them was to belong to each of the soldiers, would naturally be decided, as the Synoptists inform us, by lot.

But, besides these four articles of dress, there was the seamless woven inner garment,[2] by far the most valuable of all, and for which, as it could not be partitioned without being destroyed, they would specially cast lots[3] (as St. John reports). Nothing in this world can be accidental, since God is not far from any of us. But in the History of the Christ the Divine purpose, which forms the subject of all prophecy, must have been constantly realised; nay, this must have forced itself on the mind of the observer, and the more irresistibly when, as in the present instance, the outward circumstances were in such sharp contrast to the higher reality. To St. John, the loving and loved disciple, greater contrast could scarcely exist than between this rough partition by lot among the soldiery, and the character and claims of Him Whose garments they were thus apportioning, as if He had been a helpless Victim in their hands. Only one explanation

it was expressly forbidden (*Ulpianus*, Digest. xlviii. 20, 6). I cannot see how *Keim*, and, after him, *Nebe*, should infer from this as certain, that the law had formerly been the opposite.

[1] Strangely, I confess, to my thinking, they seem to have been a source of anxiety and distress to St. *Augustine*, that he might find their true conciliation.

[2] It is deeply significant that the dress of the priests was not sewed but woven (Zehbach. 88 *a*), and especially so that of the High-Priest (Yoma 72 *b*). According to tradition, during the seven days of consecration, Moses ministered in a seamless white dress, woven throughout. (Taan. 11 *b*.)

[3] It is impossible to determine in what manner this was done. The various modes of casting the lot are described by *Adam*, Roman Antiq. pp. 397–399. Possibly, however, it was much more simple and rough than any of these.

could here suggest itself: that there was a special Divine meaning in the permission of such an event—that it was in fulfilment of ancient prophecy. As he gazed on the terrible scene, the words of the Psalm[a][1] which portrayed the desertion, the sufferings, and the contempt even unto death of the Servant of the Lord, stood out in the red light of the Sun setting in Blood. They flashed upon his mind—for the first time he understood them;[2] and the flames which played around the Sufferer were seen to be the sacrificial fire that consumed the Sacrifice which He offered. That this quotation is made in the Fourth Gospel alone, proves that its writer was an eyewitness; that it was made in the Fourth Gospel at all, that he was a Jew, deeply imbued with Jewish modes of religious thinking. And the evidence of both is the stronger, as we recall the comparative rareness, and the peculiarly Judaic character of the Old Testament quotations in the Fourth Gospel.[3]

It was when they thus nailed Him to the Cross, and parted His raiment, that He spake the first of the so-called 'Seven Words': 'Father, forgive them, for they know not what they do.'[4] Even the reference in this prayer to 'what they do' (not in the past, nor future) points to the soldiers as the primary, though certainly not the sole object of the Saviour's prayer.[b][5] But higher thoughts also come to us. In the moment of the deepest abasement of Christ's Human Nature, the Divine bursts forth most brightly. It is, as if the Saviour would discard all that is merely human in His Sufferings, just as before He had discarded the Cup of stupefying wine. These soldiers were but the unconscious instruments: the form was nothing; the contest was between the Kingdom of God and that of darkness, between the Christ and Satan, and these sufferings were but the necessary path of obedience, and to victory and glory. When He is most human (in the moment of His being nailed to the Cross), then is He most Divine, in the utter discarding of the human elements of human instrumentality and of human suffering. Then also in the

CHAP. XV

[a] Ps. xxii. 18

[b] Comp. Acts iii. 17 1 Cor. ii. 8

---

[1] *Strauss* calls Ps. xxii. 'the programme of the Passion of Christ.' We may accept the description, though not in his sense.

[2] The Scripture quotation in the t. r. of St. Matthew, and, in all probability, that also in St. Mark, is spurious.

[3] Altogether there are fifteen such quotations in the Fourth Gospel. Of these at most only two (St. John vi. 31 and vii. 38) could be described as Alexandrian in character, the rest are truly Judaic.

[4] The genuineness of these words has been called in question. But alike external and internal evidence demands their retention.

[5] It would be presumptuous to seek to determine *how far* that prayer extended. Generally—I agree with *Nebe*—to all (Gentiles and Jews) who, in their participation in the sufferings inflicted on Jesus, acted in ignorance.

BOOK
V

utter self-forgetfulness of the God-Man—which is one of the aspects of the Incarnation—does He only remember Divine mercy, and pray for them who crucify Him; and thus also does the Conquered truly conquer His conquerors by asking for them what their deed had forfeited.   And lastly, in this, that alike the first and the last of His Utterances begin with ' Father,' does He show by the unbrokenness of His faith and fellowship the real spiritual victory which He has won.   And He has won it, not only for the martyrs, who have learned from Him to pray as He did, but for everyone who, in the midst of all that seems most opposed to it, can rise, beyond mere forgetfulness of what is around, to realising faith and fellowship with God as ' the Father,'—who through the dark curtain of cloud can discern the bright sky, and can feel the unshaken confidence, if not the unbroken joy, of absolute trust.

This was His first Utterance on the Cross—as regarded them; as regarded Himself; and as regarded God.   So, surely, suffered not Man.   Has this prayer of Christ been answered?   We dare not doubt it; nay, we perceive it in some measure in those drops of blessing which have fallen upon heathen men, and have left to Israel also, even in its ignorance, a remnant according to the election of grace.[1]

And now began the real agonies of the Cross—physical, mental, and spiritual.   It was the weary, unrelieved waiting, as thickening darkness gradually gathered around.   Before sitting down to their melancholy watch over the Crucified,[a] the soldiers would refresh themselves, after their exertion in nailing Jesus to the Cross, lifting it up, and fixing it, by draughts of the cheap wine of the country. As they quaffed it, they drank to Him in their coarse brutality, and mockingly came to Him, asking Him to pledge them in response. Their jests were, indeed, chiefly directed not against Jesus personally, but in His Representative capacity, and so against the hated, despised Jews, whose King they now derisively challenged to save Himself.[b]   Yet even so, it seems to us of deepest significance, that He was so treated and derided in His Representative Capacity and as the King of the Jews.   It is the undesigned testimony of history, alike as regarded the character of Jesus and the future of Israel.   But what from almost any point of view we find so difficult to understand is, the—

a St. Matthew

b St. Luke

---

[1] In reference to this *St. Augustine* writes: 'Sanguinem Christi, quem sævientes fuderunt, credentes biberunt.' The question why Christ did not Himself forgive, but appeal for it to the Father, is best answered by the consideration, that it was really a *crimen læsæ majestatis* against the *Father*, and that the vindication of the Son lay with God the Father.

unutterable abasement of the Leaders of Israel—their moral suicide
as regarded Israel's hope and spiritual existence. There, on that
Cross, hung He, Who at least embodied that grand hope of the
nation; Who, even on their own showing, suffered to the extreme
for that idea, and yet renounced it not, but clung fast to it in unshaken confidence; One, to Whose Life or even Teaching no objection could be offered, save that of this grand idea. And yet, when
it came to them in the ribald mockery of this heathen soldiery, it
evoked no other or higher thoughts in them; and they had the
indescribable baseness of joining in the jeer at Israel's great hope,
and of leading the popular chorus in it!

For, we cannot doubt, that—perhaps also by way of turning aside
the point of the jeer from Israel—they took it up, and tried to direct
it against Jesus; and that they led the ignorant mob in the piteous
attempts at derision. And did none of those who so reviled Him in
all the chief aspects of His Work feel, that, as Judas had sold the
Master for nought and committed suicide, so they were doing in
regard to their Messianic hope? For, their jeers cast contempt on
the four great facts in the Life and Work of Jesus, which were also
the underlying ideas of the Messianic Kingdom: the new relationship
to Israel's religion and the Temple (' Thou that destroyest the Temple,
and buildest it in three days'); the new relationship to the Father
through the Messiah, the Son of God ('if Thou be the Son of God ');
the new all-sufficient help brought to body and soul in salvation ('He
saved others'); and, finally, the new relationship to Israel in the fulfilment and perfecting of its Mission through its King ('if He be the
King of Israel'). On all these, the taunting challenge of the Sanhedrists, to come down from the Cross, and save Himself, if He would
claim the allegiance of their faith, cast what St. Matthew and St. Mark
characterise as the ' blaspheming ' [1] of doubt. We compare with theirs
the account of St. Luke and of St. John. That of St. Luke reads like
the report of what had passed, given by one who throughout had been
quite close by, perhaps taken part in the Crucifixion [2]—one might
almost venture to suggest, that it had been furnished by the Centurion. [3] The narrative of St. John reads markedly like that of an

[1] The two Evangelists designate by
this very word the bearing of the passers-
by, rendered in the A.V. 'reviled' and
'railed.'
[2] The peculiarities in it are (besides
the *titulus*): what passed on the procession to Golgotha (St. Luke xxiii. 27–
31); the prayer, when affixed to the Cross

(ver. 34 *a*); the bearing of the soldiers
(vv. 36, 37); the conversion of the penitent thief; and the last words on the
Cross (ver. 46).
[3] There is no *evidence*, that the Centurion was still present when the soldier
'came' to pierce the Saviour's side (St.
John xix. 31–37).

eyewitness, and he a Judæan.[1] And as we compare both the general
Judæan cast and Old Testament quotations in this with the other parts
of the Fourth Gospel, we feel as if (as so often), under the influence
of the strongest emotions, the later development and peculiar thinking
of so many years afterwards had for the time been effaced from the
mind of St. John, or rather given place to the Jewish modes of conception and speech, familiar to him in earlier days. Lastly, the
account of St. Matthew seems as if written from the priestly point of
view, as if it had been furnished by one of the Priests or Sanhedrist-
party, present at the time.

Yet other inferences come to us. First, there is a remarkable
relationship between what St. Luke quotes as spoken by the soldiers:
'If Thou art the King of the Jews, save Thyself,' and the report of
the words in St. Matthew:[a] 'He saved others—Himself He cannot
save. He[2] is the King of Israel! Let Him now come down from
the Cross, and we will believe on Him!' These are the words of the
Sanhedrists, and they seem to respond to those of the soldiers, as
reported by St. Luke, and to carry them further. The 'if' of the
soldiers: 'If Thou art the King of the Jews,' now becomes a direct
blasphemous challenge. As we think of it, they seem to re-echo, and
now with the laughter of hellish triumph, the former Jewish challenge
for an outward, infallible sign to demonstrate His Messiahship. But
they also take up, and re-echo, what Satan had set before Jesus in
the Temptation of the wilderness. At the beginning of His Work,
the Tempter had suggested that the Christ should achieve absolute
victory by an act of presumptuous self-assertion, utterly opposed to
the spirit of the Christ, but which Satan represented as an act of trust
in God, such as He would assuredly own. And now, at the close of
His Messianic Work, the Tempter suggested, in the challenge of the
Sanhedrists, that Jesus had suffered absolute defeat, and that God
had publicly disowned the trust which the Christ had put in Him.
'He trusteth in God: let Him deliver Him now, if He will have Him.'[3]
Here, as in the Temptation of the Wilderness, the words misapplied
were those of Holy Scripture—in the present instance those of
Ps. xxii. 8. And the quotation, as made by the Sanhedrists, is the
more remarkable, that, contrary to what is generally asserted by
writers, this Psalm[b] *was* Messianically applied by the ancient

ª St. Matt.
xxvii. 42

ᵇ Ps. xxii.

---

[1] So from the peculiar details and O.T.
quotations.
[2] The word 'if' [if He] in our A.V.
is spurious.

[3] This is the literal rendering. The
'will have Him'= has pleasure in Him,
like the German: 'Wenn Er Ihn will.'

Synagogue.[1] More especially was this verse,[a] which precedes the mocking quotation of the Sanhedrists, expressly applied to the sufferings and the derision which Messiah was to undergo from His enemies: 'All they that see Me laugh Me to scorn: they shoot out the lip, they shake the head.'[b] [2]

CHAP.
XV

[a] Ps. xxii. 7

[b] Yalkut on
Is. lx., vol.
ii. p. 56 d,
lines 12 &c.
from bot-
tom

The derision of the Sanhedrists under the Cross was, as previously stated, not entirely spontaneous, but had a special motive. The place of Crucifixion was close to the great road which led from the North to Jerusalem. On that Feast-day, when, as there was no law to limit, as on the weekly day of rest, locomotion to a 'Sabbath day's journey,' many would pass in and out of the City, and the crowd would naturally be arrested by the spectacle of the three Crosses. Equally naturally would they have been impressed by the *titulus* over the Cross of Christ. The words, describing the Sufferer as 'the King of the Jews,' might, when taken in connection with what was known of Jesus, have raised most dangerous questions. And this the presence of the Sanhedrists was intended to prevent, by turning the popular mind in a totally different direction. It was just such a taunt and argumentation as would appeal to that coarse realism of the common people, which is too often misnamed 'common sense.' St. Luke significantly ascribes the derision of Jesus only to the Rulers,[3] and we repeat, that that of the passers by, recorded by St. Matthew and St. Mark, was excited by them. Thus here also the main guilt rested on the leaders of the people.[4]

One other trait comes to us from St. Luke, confirming our impression that his account was derived from one who had stood quite close to the Cross, probably taken official part in the Crucifixion. St. Matthew and St. Mark merely remark in general, that the derision of the Sanhedrists and people was joined in by the thieves on the Cross.[5] A trait this, which we feel to be not only psychologically

[1] See Appendix IX.

[2] *Meyer* actually commits himself to the statement, that Ps. xxii. was not Messianically applied by the Jews. Other writers follow his lead. The objection, that the Sanhedrists could not have quoted this verse, as it would have branded them as the wicked persons described in the Psalm, has no force when we remember the loose way in which the Jews were in the habit of quoting the Old Testament.

[3] The words, 'with them,' in St. Luke xxiii. 35, are spurious.

[4] St. Mark introduces the mocking speeches (xv. 29) by the particle οὐά

('Ah') which occurs only here in the N.T. It is evidently the Latin '*Vah*,' an exclamation of ironical admiration. (See *Bengel* and *Nebe*, ad loc.) The words literally were: 'Ha! the downbreaker of the sanctuary and upbuilding it in three days, save Thyself.' Except the introductory particle and the order of the words, the words are the same in St. Matthew. The ὁ καταλύων is used in the sense of a substantive (comp. *Winer*, Gram. p. 122, and especially p. 316).

[5] The language of St. Matthew and St. Mark is quite general, and refers to 'the thieves;' that of St. Luke is precise and detailed. But I cannot agree with

true, but the more likely of occurrence, that any sympathy or possible alleviation of their sufferings might best be secured by joining in the scorn of the leaders, and concentrating popular indignation upon Jesus. But St. Luke also records a vital difference between the two 'robbers' on the Cross.[1] The impenitent thief takes up the jeer of the Sanhedrists: 'Art Thou not the Christ?[2] Save Thyself and us!' The words are the more significant, alike in their bearing on the majestic calm and pitying love of the Saviour on the Cross, and on the utterance of the 'penitent thief,' that—strange as it may sound—it seems to have been a terrible phenomenon, noted by historians,[3] that those on the cross were wont to utter insults and imprecations on the onlookers, goaded nature perhaps seeking relief in such outbursts. Not so when the heart was touched in true repentance.

If a more close study of the words of the 'penitent thief' may seem to diminish the fulness of meaning which the traditional view attaches to them, they gain all the more as we perceive their historic reality. His first words were of reproof to his comrade. In that terrible hour, amidst the tortures of a slow death, did not the fear of God creep over him—at least so far as to prevent his joining in the vile jeers of those who insulted the dying agonies of the Sufferer?[4] And this all the more, in the peculiar circumstances. They were all three sufferers; but they two justly, while He Whom he insulted had done nothing amiss. From this basis of fact, the penitent rapidly rose to the height of faith. This is not uncommon, when a mind is learning the lessons of truth in the school of grace. Only, it stands out here the more sharply, because of the dark background against which it is traced in such broad and brightly shining

those who, for the sake of 'harmony,' represent the penitent thief as joining in his comrade's blasphemy before turning to Christ. I do not deny, that such a sudden change might have taken place; but there is no evidence for it in the text, and the supposition of the penitent thief first blaspheming gives rise to many incongruities, and does not seem to fit into the text.

[1] Tradition names the impenitent thief *Gestas*, which *Keim* identifies with στεγανός, silenced, hardened—although the derivation seems to me forced. The penitent thief is called *Dysmas*, which I would propose to derive from δυσμή in the sense of 'the setting,' viz., of the sun: he who turns to the setting sun.

Sepp very fancifully regards the penitent thief as a Greek (Japhetisch), the impenitent as a negro.

[2] So according to the right reading.

[3] See the quotations in *Nebe*, ii. 258.

[4] 'Dost not thou even fear God, seeing thou art in the same condemnation?' Condemnation here means that to which one is condemned: the sufferings of the cross; and the expostulation is: Suffering as thou art like Him and me, canst thou join in the jeers of the crowd? Dost thou not even fear God—should not fear of Him now creep over thy soul, or at least prevent thee from insulting the dying Sufferer? And this all the more, since the circumstances are as immediately afterwards described.

outlines. The hour of the deepest abasement of the Christ was, as
all the moments of His greatest Humiliation, to be marked by a manifestation of His Glory and Divine Character—as it were, by God's
testimony to Him in history, if not by the Voice of God from heaven.
And, as regarded the 'penitent' himself, we notice the progression in
his soul. No one could have been ignorant—least of all those who
were led forth with Him to crucifixion, that Jeśus did not suffer for
any crime, nor for any political movement, but because He professed
to embody the great hope of Israel, and was rejected by its leaders.
And, if any had been ignorant, the 'title' over the Cross and the
bitter enmity of the Sanhedrists, which followed Him with jeers
and jibes, where even ordinary humanity, and still more Jewish feeling, would have enjoined silence, if not pity, must have shown what
had been the motives of 'the condemnation' of Jesus. But, once the
mind was opened to perceive all these facts, the progress would be
rapid. In hours of extremity a man may deceive himself and fatally
mistake fear for the fear of God, and the remembrance of certain
external knowledge for spiritual experience. But, *if* a man really
learns in such seasons, the teaching of years may be compressed into
moments, and the dying thief on the Cross might outdistance the
knowledge gained by Apostles in their years of following Christ.

One thing stood out before the mind of the 'penitent thief,' who
in that hour *did* fear God. Jesus had done nothing amiss. And
this surrounded with a halo of moral glory the inscription on the
Cross, long before its words acquired a new meaning. But how did
this Innocent One bear Himself in suffering? Right royally—not
in an earthly sense, but in that in which alone He claimed the
Kingdom. He had so spoken to the women who had lamented Him,
as His faint form could no longer bear the burden of the Cross; and
He had so refused the draught that would have deadened consciousness and sensibility. Then, as they three were stretched on the
transverse beam, and, in the first and sharpest agony of pain, the
nails were driven with cruel stroke of hammer through the quivering
flesh, and, in the nameless agony that followed the first moments of
the Crucifixion, only a prayer for those who in ignorance, were the
instruments of His torture, had passed His lips. And yet He was
innocent, Who so cruelly suffered. All that followed must have only
deepened the impression. With what calm of endurance and majesty
of silence He had borne the insult and jeers of those who, even to
the spiritually unenlightened eye, must have seemed so infinitely far
beneath Him! This man did feel the 'fear' of God, who now learned

the new lesson in which the fear of God was truly the beginning of wisdom. And, once he gave place to the moral element, when under the fear of God he reproved his comrade, this new moral decision became to him, as so often, the beginning of spiritual life. Rapidly he now passed into the light, and onwards and upwards: 'Lord, remember me, when Thou comest in Thy Kingdom!'

The familiar words of our Authorised Version—'When Thou comest into Thy Kingdom'—convey the idea of what we might call a more spiritual meaning of the petition. But we can scarcely believe, that at that moment it implied either that Christ was then going into His Kingdom, or that the 'penitent thief' looked to Christ for admission into the Heavenly Kingdom. The words are true to the Jewish point of vision of the man. He recognised and owned Jesus as the Messiah, and he did so, by a wonderful forthgoing of faith, even in the utmost Humiliation of Christ. And this immediately passed beyond the Jewish standpoint, for he expected Jesus soon to come back in His Kingly might and power, when he asked to be remembered by Him in mercy. And here we have again to bear in mind that, during the Life of Christ upon earth, and, indeed, before the outpouring of the Holy Ghost, men always first learned to believe in the Person of the Christ, and then to know His teaching and His Mission in the forgiveness of sins. It was so in this case also. If the 'penitent thief' had learned to know the Christ, and to ask for gracious recognition in His coming Kingdom, the answering assurance of the Lord conveyed not only the comfort that his prayer was answered, but the teaching of spiritual things which he knew not yet, and so much needed to know. The 'penitent' had spoken of the future, Christ spoke of 'to-day'; the penitent had prayed about that Messianic Kingdom which was to come, Christ assured him in regard to the state of the disembodied spirits, and conveyed to him the promise that he would be there in the abode of the blessed— 'Paradise'—and that through means of Himself as the Messiah: 'Amen, I say unto thee—To-day with Me shalt thou be in the Paradise.' Thus did Christ give him that *spiritual* knowledge which he did not yet possess—the teaching concerning the 'to-day,' the need of gracious admission into Paradise, and that with and through Himself—in other words, concerning the forgiveness of sins and the opening of the Kingdom of Heaven to all believers. This, as the first and foundation-creed of the soul, was the first and foundation-fact concerning the Messiah.

This was the Second Utterance from the Cross. The first had been of utter self-forgetfulness; the second of deepest, wisest, most gracious spiritual teaching. And, had He spoken none other than these, He would have been proved to be the Son of God.[1]

Nothing more would require to be said to the 'penitent' on the Cross. The events which followed, and the words which Jesus would still speak, would teach him more fully than could otherwise have been done. Some hours—probably two—had passed since Jesus had been nailed to the Cross. We wonder how it came that St. John, who tells us some of the incidents with such exceeding particularity, and relates all with the vivid realisation of a most deeply interested eyewitness, should have been silent as to others—especially as to those hours of derision, as well as to the conversion of the penitent thief. His silence seems to us to have been due to absence from the scene. We part company with him after his detailed account of the last scene before Pilate.[a] The final sentence pronounced, we suppose him to have hurried into the City, and to have acquainted such of the disciples as he might find—but especially those faithful women and the Virgin-Mother—with the terrible scenes that had passed since the previous evening. Thence he returned to Golgotha, just in time to witness the Crucifixion, which he again describes with peculiar fulness of details.[b] When the Saviour was nailed to the Cross, St. John seems once more to have returned to the City—this time, to bring back with him those women, in company of whom we now find him standing close to the Cross. A more delicate, tender, loving service could not have been rendered than this. Alone, of all the disciples, he is there—not afraid to be near Christ, in the Palace of the High-Priest, before Pilate, and now under the Cross. And alone he renders to Christ this tender service

[a] St. John
xix. 2-16

[b] vv. 17-24

---

[1] Fully to understand it, we ought to realise what would be the Jewish ideas of the 'penitent thief,' and what his understanding of the words of Christ. Broadly, one would say, that as a Jew he would expect that his 'death would be the expiation of his sins.' Thoughts of need of forgiveness through the Messiah would not therefore come to him. But the words of Christ must have supplied all this. Again, when Christ spoke of 'Paradise,' His hearer would naturally understand that part of Hades in which the spirits of the righteous dwelt till the Resurrection. On both these points there are so many passages in Rabbinic writings that it is needless to quote (see for ex. *Wetstein*, ad loc., and our remarks on the Parable of Lazarus and Dives). Indeed, the prayer: let my death be the expiation of my sins, is still in the Jewish office for the dying, and the underlying dogma is firmly rooted in Rabbinic belief. The words of our Lord, so far from encouraging this belief, would teach him that admission to Paradise was to be granted by Christ. It is scarcely necessary to add, that Christ's words in no way encouraged the realistic conceptions which Judaism attached to Paradise (פרדס). In Biblical Hebrew the word is used for a choice garden : in Eccl. ii. 5 ; Cant. iv. 13; Nehem. ii. 8. But in the LXX. and the Apocr. the word is already used in our sense of Paradise. Lastly, nothing which our Lord had said to the 'penitent thief' about being 'to-day' with Him in Paradise, is in any way inconsistent with, rather confirms, the doctrine of the Descent into Hades.

of bringing the women and Mary to the Cross, and to them the protection of his guidance and company. He loved Jesus best; and it was fitting that to his manliness and affection should be entrusted the unspeakable privilege of Christ's dangerous inheritance.[1]

^a St. John
xix. 25–27

The narrative[a] leaves the impression that with the beloved disciple these four women were standing close to the Cross: the Mother of Jesus, the Sister of His Mother, Mary the wife of Clopas, and

b St. Matt.
xxvii. 55
c St. Mark
xv. 40, 41

Mary of Magdala.[2] A comparison with what is related by St. Matthew[b] and St. Mark[c] supplies further important particulars. We read there of only three women, the name of the Mother of our Lord being omitted. But then it must be remembered that this refers to a later period in the history of the Crucifixion. It seems as if John had fulfilled to the letter the Lord's command: 'Behold thy mother,' and literally 'from that very hour' taken her to his own home. If we are right in this supposition, then, in the absence of St. John— who led away the Virgin-Mother from that scene of horror—the other three women would withdraw to a distance, where we find them at the end, not 'by the Cross,' as in St. John xix. 25, but 'beholding from afar,' and now joined by others also, who had loved and followed Christ.

We further notice that, the name of the Virgin-Mother being omitted, the other three are the same as mentioned by St. John; only, Mary of Clopas is now described as 'the mother of James and

d St. Mark
e St. Matthew

Joses,'[3] and Christ's 'Mother's Sister' as 'Salome'[d] and 'the mother of Zebedee's children.'[e] Thus Salome, the wife of Zebedee and St. John's mother, was the sister of the Virgin, and the beloved disciple the cousin (on the mother's side) of Jesus, and the nephew of the Virgin. This also helps to explain why the care of the Mother had been entrusted to him. Nor was Mary the wife of Clopas unconnected with Jesus. What we have every reason to regard as a trust-

f Hegesip-
pus in
Euseb. H.E.
iii. 11 and
iv. 22

worthy account[f] describes Clopas as the brother of Joseph, the husband of the Virgin. Thus, not only Salome as the sister of the Virgin, but Mary also as the wife of Clopas, would, in a certain sense,

[1] The first impression left is, of course, that the 'brothers' of Jesus were not yet, at least in the full sense, believers. But this does not by any means necessarily follow, since both the presence of John under the Cross, and even his outward circumstances, might point him out as the most fit custodian of the Virgin-Mother. At the same time it seems the more likely supposition, that the brothers of Jesus were converted by the appearance to

James of the Risen One (1 Cor. xv. 7).

[2] This view is now generally adopted.

[3] There is, of course, the difficulty that Judas (Lebbæus) and Simon Zelotes are not here mentioned as her sons. But they may have been her stepsons, or there may have been other reasons for the omission. 'Judas of James' could scarcely have been the son of James, and Simon is expressly mentioned by Hegesippus as the son of Clopas.

have been His aunt, and her sons His cousins. And so we notice among the twelve Apostles five cousins of the Lord: the two sons of Salome and Zebedee, and the three sons of Alphæus or Clopas[1] and Mary: James, Judas surnamed Lebbæus and Thaddæus, and Simon surnamed Zelotes or Cananæan.[2]

We can now in some measure realise events. When St. John had seen the Saviour nailed to the Cross, he had gone to the City and brought with him for a last mournful farewell the Virgin, accompanied by those who, as most nearly connected with her, would naturally be with her: her own sister Salome, the sister-in-law of Joseph and wife (or more probably widow) of Clopas, and her who of all others had experienced most of His blessed power to save—Mary of Magdala. Once more we reverently mark His Divine calm of utter self-forgetfulness and His human thoughtfulness for others. As they stood under the Cross, He committed His Mother to the disciple whom He loved, and established a new human relationship between him and her who was nearest to Himself.[3] And calmly, earnestly, and immediately did that disciple undertake the sacred charge, and bring her—whose soul the sword had pierced—away from the scene of unutterable woe to the shelter of his home.[4] And this temporary absence of John from the Cross may account for the want of all detail in his narrative till quite the closing scene.[a]

Now at last all that concerned the earthward aspect of His Mission—so far as it had to be done on the Cross—was ended. He had prayed for those who had nailed Him to it, in ignorance of what they did; He had given the comfort of assurance to the penitent, who had owned His Glory in His Humiliation; and He had made the last provision of love in regard to those nearest to Him. So to speak, the relations of His Humanity—that which touched His Human Nature in any direction—had been fully met. He had done with the Human

[a] St. John xix. 28

---

[1] Alphæus and Clopas are the same name. The first occurs in the Babylon Talmud as *Ilphai*, or *Ilpha* (אילפא), as in R. haSh. 17 *b*, and often; the other in the Jerusalem Talmud as *Chilphai* (חילפיי), as for ex. in Jer. B. Kama 7 *a*.

[2] I regard the Simon Zelotes of the list of Apostles as the Simon son of Clopas, or Alphæus, of *Hegesippus—first*, because of his position in the lists of the Apostles along with the two other sons of Alphæus; *secondly*, because, as there were only two prominent Simons in the N.T. (the brother of the Lord, and Zelotes), and

Hegesippus mentions him as the son of Clopas, it follows that the Simon son of Clopas was Simon Zelotes. Levi Matthew was, indeed, also a son of Alphæus, but we regard this as another Clopas than the husband of Mary.

[3] Incongruous though the interruption be, we cannot help noticing that the introduction of such a scene seems inconsistent with the whole theory of an Ephesian authorship of the Fourth Gospel. On the other hand, it displays evidence of the true human interest of an actor in the scene.

[4] Nothing is really known of the later history of the Blessed Virgin.

BOOK
V

* St. Matt.
xxvii. 51

aspect of His Work and with earth. And, appropriately, Nature seemed now to take sad farewell of Him, and mourned its departing Lord, Who, by His Personal connection with it, had once more lifted it from the abasement of the Fall into the region of the Divine, making it the dwelling-place, the vehicle for the manifestation, and the obedient messenger of the Divine.

For three hours had the Saviour hung on the Cross. It was midday. And now the Sun was craped in darkness from the sixth to the ninth hour. No purpose can be served by attempting to trace the source of this darkness. It could not have been an eclipse, since it was the time of full moon; nor can we place reliance on the later reports on this subject of ecclesiastical writers.[1] It seems only in accordance with the Evangelic narrative to regard the occurrence of the event as supernatural, while the event itself might have been brought about by natural causes; and among these we must call special attention to the earthquake in which this darkness terminated.* For, it is a well-known phenomenon that such darkness not unfrequently precedes earthquakes. On the other hand, it must be freely admitted, that the language of the Evangelists seems to imply that this darkness extended, not only over the land of Israel, but over the inhabited earth. The expression must, of course, not be pressed to its full literality, but explained as meaning that it extended far beyond Judæa and to other lands. No reasonable objection can be raised from the circumstance, that neither the earthquake nor the preceding darkness are mentioned by any profane writer whose works have been preserved, since it would surely not be maintained that an historical record must have been preserved of every earthquake that occurred, and of every darkness that may have preceded it.[2] But the most

[1] I do not think the testimony of *Phlegon*, as quoted by *Eusebius*, is available (see the discussion in *Wieseler's* Synopse, p. 387, note 1). Still, if the astronomical calculations of *Ideler* and *Wurm* are correct, 'the eclipse' recorded by *Phlegon* [whether 'eclipse' in the *scientific* sense, or 'darkness,'] would have taken place in the very year of our Lord's death, A.D. 29, but, as they reckon, on November 24. I do not possess the special knowledge requisite to verify these calculations; but that it is described by *Phlegon* as an 'eclipse'— which this could not have been—does not necessarily invalidate the argument, since he might have used the term inaccurately. It is in this sense that St. Luke (xxiii. 45) uses the verb—that is, if we adopt the amended reading. What

Nebe writes on this subject (vol. ii. p. 301), and the illustrations of the popular use of the word from *Pliny* and *Plutarch*, deserve the most serious consideration. But, I repeat, I cannot attach weight in this argument to such testimonies, nor yet to the sayings of *Origen*, *Tertullian*, &c., nor to the Acta Pilati (the ecclesiastical testimonies are discussed by *Nebe*, u. s. p. 299).

[2] There are frequent notices in classical writers of eclipses preceding disastrous events or the death of great men, such as of Cæsar (*Nebe*, u. s. p. 300). But these were, if correctly related, eclipses in the true sense, and, as such, natural events, having in no way a supernatural bearing, and hence in no sense analogous to this 'darkness' at the Crucifixion.

unfair argument is that, which tries to establish the unhistorical character of this narrative by an appeal to what are described as Jewish sayings expressive of similar expectancy.[1] It is quite true that in old Testament prophecy—whether figuratively or really—the darkening, though not only of the sun, *but also of the moon and stars*, is sometimes connected, not with the Coming of Messiah, still less with His Death, but with the final Judgment.[2] But Jewish tradition never speaks of such an event in connection with Messiah, or even with the Messianic judgments, and the quotations from Rabbinic writings made by negative critics must be characterised as not only inapplicable but even unfair.[3]

But to return from this painful digression. The three hours' darkness was such not only to Nature; Jesus, also, entered into darkness: Body, Soul, and Spirit. It was now, not as before, a contest—but suffering. Into this, to us, fathomless depth of the mystery of His Sufferings, we dare not, as indeed we cannot, enter. It was of the Body; yet not of the Body only, but of physical life. And it

[1] So *Strauss* (after *Wetstein*) and even *Keim*. Painful as controversy is in connection with the last hours of Jesus, I would not have shrunk from contesting the positions of *Keim*, if I had not felt that every unprejudiced person must see, that most of them are mere assertions, without an attempt at anything like historical evidence.

[2] *Strauss* (ii. p. 556), and more fully *Keim* (iii. p. 438, Note 3), quote Joel ii. 10, 31; Amos viii. 9; Is. xiii. 10; 1. 3; Job ix. 7; Jer. xv. 9. Of these passages some have no bearing, however remote, on the subject, while the others refer not to the Messiah but to the final judgment.

[3] To be quite fair, I will refer to *all* the passages quoted in connection with the darkening of the sun as a token of mourning. The first (quoted by *Wetstein*) is from the Midrash on Lament. iii. 28 (ed. Warsh. p. 72 *a*). But the passage, evidently a highly figurative one, refers to the destruction of Jerusalem and the dispersion of Israel, and, besides the darkening of the sun, moon, and stars (not the sun only), refers to a realistic fulfilment of Nah. i. 3 and Lament. iii. 28 in God's walking in dust and keeping silence. The second quotation of *Wetstein*, that when a great Rabbi dies it is as portentous as if the sun went down at midday—has manifestly no bearing whatever on the matter in hand (though *Strauss* adduces it). The last and only

quotation really worth mention is from Sukk. 29 *a*. In a somewhat lengthened statement there, the meaning of an obscuration of the sun or moon is discussed. I have here to remark (1) that these phenomena are regarded as 'signs' in the sense of betokening coming judgments, such as war, famine, &c., and that these are supposed to affect various nations according as the eclipse is towards the rising or setting of the sun. The passage therefore *can* have no possible connection with such a phenomenon as the death of Messiah. (2) This is further confirmed by the enumeration of certain sins for which heavenly luminaries are eclipsed. Some are not fit for mention, while others are such as false witness-bearing, the needless cutting down of fruit-trees, &c. (3) But the unfairness, as well as the inaptitude, of the quotation appears from this, that only the beginning of the passage is quoted (*Strauss* and *Keim*): 'At a time when the sun is obscured, it is an evil sign to all the world,' while what follows is omitted: 'When the sun is obscured, it is an evil sign to the nations of the world; when the moon is obscured, it is an evil sign to Israel, because Israel reckons according to the moon, the nations of the world according to the sun.' And yet *Wünsche* (Erläuter. pp. 355, 356) quotes both that which precedes and that which follows this passage, but leaves out this passage itself. (Comp. Mechilta, p. 3 *b*.)

BOOK   was of the Soul and Spirit; yet not of them alone, but in their con-
V   scious relation to man and to God. And it was not of the Human
       only in Christ, but in its indissoluble connection with the Divine:
of the Human, where it reached the utmost verge of humiliation to
body, soul, and spirit—and in it of the Divine, to utmost self-exinanition. The increasing, nameless agonies of the Crucifixion[1] were
deepening into the bitterness of death. All nature shrinks from
death, and there is a physical horror of the separation between body
and soul which, as a purely natural phenomenon, is in every instance
only *overcome*, and that only by a higher principle. And we conceive that the purer the being the greater the violence of the
tearing asunder of the bond with which God Almighty originally
bound together body and soul. In the Perfect Man this must have
reached the highest degree. So, also, had in those dark hours the
sense of man-forsakenness and of His own isolation from man; so,
also, had the intense silence of God, the withdrawal of God, the sense
of His God-forsakenness and absolute loneliness. We dare not here
speak of punitive suffering, but of forsakenness and loneliness. And
yet as we ask ourselves how this forsakeness can be thought of as
so complete in view of His Divine consciousness, which at least could
not have been wholly extinguished by His Self-exinanition, we feel
that yet another element must be taken into account. Christ on the
Cross suffered *for* man; He offered Himself a sacrifice; He died for
our sins, that, as death was the wages of sin, so He died as the
Representative of man—for man and in room of man; He obtained

* αἰωνίαν
λύτρωσιν,
Hebr. ix. 12

for man 'eternal redemption,'[a] having given His Life 'a ransom,'[b]
for many. For, men were 'redeemed' with the 'precious Blood of

b λύτρον, St.
Matt. xx. 28

Christ, as of a Lamb without blemish and without spot;'[c] and Christ

c 1 Pet. i. 19

'gave Himself for us, that He might "redeem" us from all iniquity;'[d]

d Tit. ii. 14

He 'gave Himself "a ransom" for all;'[e] Christ died for all;'[f]

e ἀντίλυτρον
ὑπὲρ πάντων
1 Tim. ii. 6

Him, Who knew no sin, God 'made sin for us;' 'Christ redeemed
us from the curse of the Law, having become a curse for us'—and

f ὑπὲρ πάν-
των, 2 Cor.
v. 15

this, with express reference to the Crucifixion.[g] This sacrificial,

g Gal. iii. 13

vicarious, expiatory, and redemptive character of His Death, if it
does not explain to us, yet helps us to understand, Christ's sense of
God-forsakenness in the supreme moment of the Cross; if one might
so word it—the passive character of His activeness through the
active character of His passiveness.

It was this combination of the Old Testament idea of sacrifice,

---

These are described with terrible realism by *Keim*.

and of the Old Testament ideal of willing suffering as the Servant of Jehovah, now fulfilled in Christ, which found its fullest expression in the language of the twenty-second Psalm. It was fitting—rather, it was true—that the willing suffering of the true Sacrifice should now find vent in its opening words: 'My God, My God, why hast Thou forsaken Me?'—*Eli, Eli, lema sabachthanei?*[1] These words, cried with a loud voice[2] at the close of the period of extreme agony,[3] marked the climax and the end of this suffering of Christ, of which the utmost compass was the withdrawal of God and the felt loneliness of the Sufferer. But they that stood by the Cross, misinterpreting the meaning, and mistaking the opening words for the name *Elias*, imagined that the Sufferer had called for Elias. We can scarcely doubt, that these were the soldiers who stood by the Cross. They were not necessarily Romans; on the contrary, as we have seen, these Legions were generally recruited from Provincials. On the other hand, no Jew would have mistaken *Eli* for the name of Elijah, not yet misinterpreted a quotation of Psalm xxii. 1 as a call for that prophet. And it must be remembered, that the words were not whispered, but cried with a loud voice. But all entirely accords with the misunderstanding of non-Jewish soldiers, who, as the whole history shows, had learned from His accusers and the infuriated mob snatches of a distorted story of the Christ.

And presently the Sufferer emerged on the other side. It can scarcely have been a minute or two from the time that the cry from the twenty-second Psalm marked the high-point of His Agony, when the words 'I thirst'[a] seem to indicate, by the prevalence of the merely human aspect of the suffering, that the other and more terrible aspect of sin-bearing and God-forsakenness was past. To us, therefore, this seems the beginning, if not of Victory, yet of Rest, of the End. St. John alone records this Utterance, prefacing it with this distinctive statement, that Jesus so surrendered Himself to the human feeling, seeking the bodily relief by expressing His thirst: 'knowing that all things were now finished, that the Scripture might

CHAP. XV

St. John xix. 28

---

[1] So in St. Matthew, according to the best reading. In St. Mark, *Eloi, Eloi* [apparently the Syriac form], *lema sabachthanei?* Might it be that St. Matthew represents the current Judæan or Galilean dialect, and St. Mark the Syrian, and that this casts light alike on the dialects in Palestine at the time of Christ, and even, to some extent, on the composition of the Gospels, and the land in which they were written? The Targum renders Ps. xxii. 2: *Eli, Eli, metul mah shebhaqtani?* ('On account of what hast Thou forsaken me?')

[2] This in the extreme agony of soul, not to mark His Divinity.

[3] 'About the ninth hour.' I cannot bring myself here to discuss the supposed analogous quotations of Ps. xxii. 1 in Rabbinic writings. The comparison is equally inapt and irreverent.

BOOK
V

be fulfilled.'[1] In other words, the climax of Theanthropic Suffering in His feeling of God-forsakenness, which had led to the utterance of Psalm xxii. 1, was now, to His consciousness, the end of all which in accordance with Scripture-prediction He had to bear. He now could and did yield Himself to the mere physical wants of His Body.

It seems as if St. John, having perhaps just returned to the scene, and standing with the women 'afar off,' beholding these things,[a] had hastened forward on the cry from Psalm xxii.,[2] and heard Him express the feeling of thirst, which immediately followed. And so St. John alone supplies the link between that cry and the movement on the part of the soldiers, which St. Matthew and St. Mark, as well as St. John, report. For, it would be impossible to understand why, on what the soldiers regarded as a call for Elijah, one of them should have hastened to relieve His thirst, but for the Utterance recorded in the Fourth Gospel. But we can quite understand it, if the Utterance, ' I thirst,' followed immediately on the previous cry.

One of the soldiers—may we not be allowed to believe, one who either had already learned from that Cross, or was about to learn, to own Him Lord—moved by sympathy, now ran to offer some slight refreshment to the Sufferer by filling a sponge with the rough wine of the soldiers and putting it to His lips, having first fastened it to the stem ('reed') of the caper ('hyssop'), which is said to grow to the height of even two or three feet.[3] But, even so, this act of humanity was not allowed to pass unchallenged by the coarse jibes of the others who would bid him leave the relief of the Sufferer to the agency of Elijah, which in their opinion He had invoked. Nor should we perhaps wonder at the weakness of that soldier himself, who, though he would not be hindered in his good deed, yet averted the opposition of the others by apparently joining in their mockery.[b]

By accepting the physical refreshment offered Him, the Lord

[1] The words last quoted can, of course, and have by most writers been connected with the thirst of Christ, as the fulfilment of Ps. lxix. 21. But the structure of the sentence leads rather to the punctuation adopted in the text, while I have the greatest difficulty in applying Ps. lxix. 21 in the manner proposed, and still more grave objection to the idea that Christ uttered the words in order to fulfil the Psalm, although the word 'that' must, as previously shown (p. 503), not be taken in the sense of 'in order that.'

There is, of course, a *tertium quid*, and the Evangelist may be supposed to have expressed only his own sense that the Scripture was fulfilled, when he saw the thirst of the Saviour quenched in the 'vinegar' of the soldiers. But in that case we should expect the words ' that the Scripture might be fulfilled,' placed *after* the 'I thirst.'

[2] Whether or not he heard the words of the cry.

[3] Comp. *Tristram* Nat. Hist. of the Bible, p. 457.

once more indicated the completion of the work of His Passion. For, as He would not enter on it with His senses and physical consciousness lulled by narcotised wine, so He would not pass out of it with senses and physical consciousness dulled by the absolute failure of life-power. Hence He took what for the moment restored the physical balance, needful for thought and word. And so He immediately passed on to 'taste death for every man.' For, the two last 'sayings' of the Saviour now followed in rapid succession: first, that with a loud voice, which expressed it, that the work given Him to do, as far as concerned His Passion, was 'finished;'[a] and then, that in the words of Psalm xxxi. 5, in which He commended His Spirit into the Hands of the Father.[b] Attempts at comment could only weaken the solemn thoughts which the words awaken. Yet some points should be noted for our teaching. His last cry 'with a loud voice' was not like that of one dying. St. Mark notes, that this made such deep impression on the Centurion.[c] In the language of the early Christian hymn, it was not Death which approached Christ, but Christ Death: He died without death.[1] Christ encountered Death, not as conquered, but as the Conqueror. And this also was part of His work, and for us: now the beginning of His Triumph. And with this agrees the peculiar language of St. John, that He 'bowed the Head, and gave up the Spirit'($\tau\grave{o}$ $\pi\nu\epsilon\tilde{v}\mu\alpha$).

[a] St. John
[b] St. Luke
[c] St. Mark xv. 39

Nor should we fail to mark the peculiarities of His last Utterance. The 'My God' of the fourth Utterance had again passed into the 'Father' of conscious fellowship. And yet neither in the Hebrew original of this Psalm, nor in its Greek rendering by the LXX., does the word 'Father' occur. Again, in the LXX. translation of the Hebrew text this word expressive of entrustment—the commending— is in the future tense; on the lips of our Lord it is in the present tense.[2] And the word, in its New Testament sense, means not merely commending: it is to deposit, to commit for safe keeping.[3] That in dying—or rather meeting and overcoming Death—He chose and adapted these words, is matter for deepest thankfulness to the Church. He spoke them *for* His people in a twofold sense: on their behalf, that they might be able to speak them; and 'for them,' that henceforth they might speak them after Him. How many thousands have pillowed their heads on them when going to rest! They were

---

[1]   En pessima, non tu
Pervenis ad Christum, sed Christus pervenit ad te,
Cui licuit sine morte mori.
        Sedulius.

[2] So according to the better reading.
[3] Comp. the use of the verb $\pi\alpha\rho\alpha\tau\acute{\iota}\theta\eta\mu\iota$ in such passages as St. Luke xii. 48; Acts xiv. 23; xx. 32; 1 Tim. i. 18; 2 Tim. ii. 2.

the last words of a Polycarp, a Bernard, Huss, Luther, and Melanchthon. And to us also they may be the fittest and the softest lullaby. And in ' the Spirit ' which He had committed to God did He now descend into Hades, ' and preached unto the spirits in prison.' [a] But behind this great mystery have closed the two-leaved gates of brass, which only the Hand of the Conqueror could burst open.

[a] 1 Pet. iii. 18, 19

And now a shudder ran through Nature, as its Sun had set. We dare not do more than follow the rapid outlines of the Evangelic narrative. As the first token, it records the rending of the Temple-Veil in two from the top downward to the bottom; as the second, the quaking of the earth, the rending of the rocks and the opening of the graves. Although most writers have regarded this as indicating the strictly chronological succession, there is nothing in the text to bind us to such a conclusion. Thus, while the rending of the Veil is recorded first, as being the most significant token to Israel, it may have been connected with the earthquake, although this alone might scarcely account for the tearing of so heavy a Veil from the top to the bottom. Even the latter circumstance has its significance. That some great catastrophe, betokening the impending destruction of the Temple, had occurred in the Sanctuary about this very time, is confirmed by not less than four mutually independent testimonies: those of Tacitus,[1] of Josephus,[2] of the Talmud,[3] and of earliest Christian tradition.[4] The most important of these are, of course, the Talmud and Josephus. The latter speaks of the mysterious extinction of the middle and chief light in the Golden Candlestick, forty years before the destruction of the Temple; and both he and the Talmud refer to a supernatural opening by themselves of the great Temple-gates that had been previously closed, which was regarded as a portent of the coming destruction of the Temple. We can scarcely doubt, that some historical fact must underlie so peculiar and widespread a tradition, and we cannot help feeling that it may be a distorted version of the occurrence of the rending of the Temple-Veil (or of its report) at the Crucifixion of Christ.[5]

---

[1] Hist. v. 13.
[2] Jew. War vi. 5, 3.
[3] Jer. Yoma 43 c; Yoma 39 b.
[4] So in the Gospel according to the Hebrews, from which St. Jerome quotes (in Matt. xxvii. 51, and in a letter to Hedibia) to the effect, that the huge lintel of the Temple was broken and splintered, and fell. St. Jerome connects the rending of the Veil with this, and it would seem an obvious inference to connect again this breaking of the lintel with an earthquake.

[5] A story is told in Jewish tradition (Gitt, 56 b, about the middle; Ber. R. 10; Vayyik. R. 22, and in other places) to the effect that, among other vilenesses, ' Titus the wicked' had penetrated into the Sanctuary, and cut through the Veil of the Most Holy Place with his sword, when

But even if the rending of the Temple-Veil had commenced with the earthquake, and, according to the Gospel to the Hebrews, with the breaking of the great lintel over the entrance, it could not be wholly accounted for in this manner. According to Jewish tradition, there were, indeed, two Veils before the entrance to the Most Holy Place.[a] The Talmud explains this on the ground that it was not known, whether in the former Temple the Veil had hung inside or outside the entrance and whether the partition-wall had stood in the Holy or Most Holy Place.[b] Hence (according to *Maimonides*)[c] there was not any wall between the Holy and Most Holy Place, but the space of one cubit, assigned to it in the former Temple, was left unoccupied, and one Veil hung on the side of the Holy, the other on that of the Most Holy Place. According to an account dating from Temple-times, there were altogether thirteen Veils used in various parts of the Temple—two new ones being made every year.[d] The Veils before the Most Holy Place were 40 cubits (60 feet) long, and 20 (30 feet) wide, of the thickness of the palm of the hand, and wrought in 72 squares, which were joined together; and these Veils were so heavy, that, in the exaggerated language of the time, it needed 300 priests to manipulate each. If the Veil was at all such as is described in the Talmud, it could not have been rent in twain by a mere earthquake or the fall of the lintel, although its composition in squares fastened together might explain, how the rent might be as described in the Gospel.

Indeed, everything seems to indicate that, although the earthquake might furnish the physical basis, the rent of the Temple-Veil was—with reverence be it said—really made by the Hand of God. As we compute, it may just have been the time when, at the Evening-Sacrifice, the officiating Priesthood entered the Holy Place, either to burn the incense or to do other sacred service there. To see before them, not as the aged Zacharias at the beginning of this history the Angel Gabriel, but the Veil of the Holy Place rent from top to bottom—that beyond it they could scarcely have seen—and hanging in

CHAP.
XV

[a] Yoma v. 1

[b] Yoma 51 *b*
[c] Hilkh.
Beth ha-
Bech, iv. 2.
ed. Amst.
vol. iii. p.
149 *b*

[d] Yoma 54 *a*
Kethub.
106 *a*;
Sheqal.
viii. 5.

blood dropped down. I mention the legend to express my emphatic protest against the manner in which Dr. *Joel* (Blicke in d. Religionsgesch. i. pp. 7, 8, treating of the passage in the Midr. on Lam. ii. 17) has made use of it. He represents it, as if the Veil had been *rent* (Zerreissen des Vorhanges bei d. Tempelzerstörung) — not cut through by Titus, and on the basis of this misrepresentation has the boldness to set a legend about Titus side by side with the Evangelic account of the rending of the Temple-Veil! I write thus strongly because I am sorry to say that this is by no means the only instance in which Jewish writers adapt their quotations to controversial purposes. *Joel* refers to Dr. *Sachs*, Beitr. i. p. 29, but that learned writer draws no such inference from the passage in question.

BOOK
V

two parts from its fastenings above and at the side, was, indeed, a terrible portent, which would soon become generally known, and must, in some form or other, have been preserved in tradition. And they all must have understood, that it meant that God's Own Hand had rent the Veil, and for ever deserted and thrown open that Most Holy Place where He had so long dwelt in the mysterious gloom, only lit up once a year by the glow of the censer of him, who made atonement for the sins of the people.[1]

Other tokens were not wanting. In the earthquake the rocks were rent, and their tombs opened. This, as Christ descended into Hades. And when He ascended on the third day, it was with victorious saints who had left those open graves. To many in the Holy City on that ever-memorable first day, and in the week that followed, appeared the bodies of many of those saints who had fallen on sleep in the sweet hope of that which had now become reality.[2]

But on those who stood under the Cross, and near it, did all that was witnessed make the deepest and most lasting impression. Among them we specially mark the Centurion under whose command the soldiers had been. Many a scene of horror must he have witnessed in those sad times of the Crucifixion, but none like this. Only one conclusion could force itself on his mind. It was that which, we cannot doubt, had made its impression on his heart and conscience. Jesus was not what the Jews, His infuriated enemies, had described Him. He was what He professed to be, what His bearing on the Cross and His Death attested Him to be: 'righteous,' and hence, 'the Son of God.' From this there was only a step to personal allegiance to Him, and, as previously suggested, we may possibly owe to him some of those details which St. Luke alone has preserved.

The brief spring-day was verging towards the 'evening of the Sabbath.' In general, the Law ordered that the body of a criminal should not be left hanging unburied over night.[a] Perhaps in ordinary circumstances the Jews might not have appealed so confidently to Pilate as actually to ask[3] him to shorten the sufferings

ᵃ Deut. xxi.
23 ; comp.
Jos. War
iv. 5, 2

[1] May this phenomenon account for the early conversion of so many priests recorded in Acts vi. 7 ?

[2] I dare express myself dogmatically on the precise import of St. Matt. xxvii. 52, 53. Does it mean that they were actually clothed with the Resurrection-body, or with the body which they had formerly borne, or that many saints from out Hades appeared to those who loved them, and with them had waited for the Kingdom, in the forms which they had known ? We know too little of the connection between the other world and this, and the mode in which the departed may communicate with those here, to venture on any decided statement, especially as we take into account the unique circumstances of the occasion.

[3] ἠρώτησαν, they 'asked,' St. John xix. 31.

of those on the Cross, since the punishment of crucifixion often CHAP.
lasted not only for hours but days, ere death ensued.   But here XV
was a special occasion.   The Sabbath about to open was a 'high-day'
—it was both a Sabbath and the second Paschal Day, which was
regarded as in every respect equally sacred with the first—nay,
more so, since the so-called Wavesheaf was then offered to the Lord.
And what the Jews now proposed to Pilate was, indeed, a shortening, but not in any sense a mitigation, of the punishment.   Sometimes there was added to the punishment of crucifixion that of
breaking the bones(*crurifragium*, σκελοκοπία)by means of a club or
hammer.   This would not itself bring death, but the breaking of the
bones was always followed by a *coup de grâce*, by sword, lance, or
stroke (the *perforatio* or *percussio sub alas*), which immediately put an
end to what remained of life.[1]   Thus the ' breaking of the bones ' was
a sort of increase of punishment, by way of compensation for its
shortening by the final stroke that followed.

It were unjust to suppose, that in their anxiety to fulfil the letter
of the Law as to burial on the eve of that high Sabbath, the Jews
had sought to intensify the sufferings of Jesus.   The text gives no
indication of this; and they could not have asked for the final stroke
to be inflicted without the 'breaking of the bones,' which always
preceded it.   The irony of this punctilious care for the letter of the
Law about burial and the high Sabbath by those who had betrayed
and crucified their Messiah on the first Passover-day is sufficiently
great, and, let us add, terrible, without importing ficticious elements.
St. John, who, perhaps, immediately on the death of Christ, left the
Cross, alone reports the circumstance.   Perhaps it was when he con-
certed with Joseph of Arimathæa, with Nicodemus, or the two
Marys, measures for the burying of Christ, that he learned of the
Jewish deputation to Pilate, followed it to Prætorium, and then
watched how it was all carried out on Golgotha.   He records, how
Pilate acceded to the Jewish demand, and gave directions for the
crurifragium, and permission for the after-removal of the dead
bodies, which otherwise might have been left to hang, till putrescence
or birds of prey had destroyed them.   But St. John also tells us
what he evidently regards as so great a prodigy that he specially
vouches for it, pledging his own veracity, as an eyewitness, and
grounding on it an appeal to the faith of those to whom his Gospel
is addressed.   It is, that certain 'things came to pass [*not* as in

[1] Comp. *Friedlieb*, Archæol. d. Leidensgesch. pp. 163-168; but especially *Nebe*,
u. s. ii. pp. 394, 395.

BOOK
V

our A.V., 'were done'] that the Scripture should be fulfilled,' or, to put it otherwise, by which the Scripture was fulfilled. These things were two, to which a third phenomenon, not less remarkable, must be added. For, first, when, in the *crurifragium*, the soldiers had broken the bones of two malefactors, and then came to the Cross of Jesus, they found that He was dead already, and so 'a bone of Him' was 'not broken.' Had it been otherwise, the Scripture concerning the Paschal Lamb,[a] as well that concerning the Righteous Suffering Servant of Jehovah,[b] would have been broken. In Christ alone these two ideas of the Paschal Lamb and the Righteous Suffering Servant of Jehovah are combined into a unity and fulfilled in their highest meaning. And when, by a strange concurrence of circumstances, it 'came to pass' that, contrary to what might have been expected, 'a bone of Him' was 'not broken,' this outward fact served as the finger to point to the predictions which were fulfilled in Him.

[a] Ex. xii. 46; Numb. ix. 12

[b] Ps. xxxiv. 20

Not less remarkable is the second fact. If, on the Cross of Christ, these two fundamental ideas in the prophetic description of the work of the Messiah had been set forth: the fulfilment of the Paschal Sacrifice, which, as that of the Covenant, underlay all sacrifices, and the fulfilment of the ideal of the Righteous Servant of God, suffering in a world that hated God, and yet proclaiming and realising His Kingdom, a third truth remained to be exhibited. It was not in regard to the character, but the effects, of the Work of Christ—its reception, alike in the present and in the future. This had been indicated in the prophecies of Zechariah,[c] which foretold how, in the day of Israel's final deliverance and national conversion, God would pour out the spirit of grace and of supplication, and as 'they shall look on Him Whom they pierced,' the spirit of true repentance would be granted them, alike nationally and individually. The application of this to Christ is the more striking, that even the Talmud refers the prophecy to the Messiah.[d] And as these two things really applied to Christ, alike in His rejection and in His future return,[e] so did the strange historical occurrence at His Crucifixion once more point to it as the fulfilment of Scripture prophecy. For, although the soldiers, on finding Jesus dead, broke not one of His Bones, yet, as it was necessary to make sure of His Death, one of them, with a lance, 'pierced His Side, with a wound so deep, that Thomas might afterwards have thrust his hand into His Side.'

[c] Zech. xii. 10

[d] Sukk. 52 a

[e] Rev. i. 7

[f] St. John xx. 27

And with these two, as fulfilling Holy Scripture, yet a third phenomenon was associated, symbolic of both. As the soldier pierced the side of the Dead Christ, 'forthwith came thereout Blood and

Water.' It has been thought by some,[1] that there was physical cause for this—that Christ had literally died of a broken heart, and that, when the lance pierced first the lung filled with blood and then the pericardium filled with serous fluid,[2] there flowed from the wound this double stream.[3] In such cases, the lesson would be that reproach had literally broken His Heart.[a] But we can scarcely believe that St. John could have wished to convey this without clearly setting it forth—thus assuming on the part of his readers knowledge of an obscure, and, it must be added, a scientifically doubtful phenomenon. Accordingly, we rather believe that to St. John, as to most of us, the significance of the fact lay in this, that out of the Body of One dead had flowed Blood and Water—that corruption had not fastened on Him. Then, there would be the symbolic meaning conveyed by the Water (from the pericardium) and the Blood (from the heart)—a symbolism most true, if corruption had no power nor hold on Him—if in Death He was not dead, if He vanquished Death and Corruption, and in this respect also fulfilled the prophetic ideal of not seeing corruption.[b] To this symbolic bearing of the flowing of Water and Blood from His pierced side, on which the Evangelist dwells in his Epistle,[c] and to its eternal expression in the symbolism of the two Sacraments, we can only point the thoughtful Christian. For, the two Sacraments mean that Christ had come; that over Him, Who was crucified for us and loved us unto death with His broken heart, Death and Corruption had no power; and that He liveth for us with the pardoning and cleansing power of His offered Sacrifice.

Yet one other scene remains to be recorded. Whether before, or, more probably, after the Jewish deputation to the Roman Governor, another and a strange application came to Pilate. It was from one apparently well known, a man not only of wealth and standing,[d] but whose noble bearing[4] corresponded to his social condition, and who was known as a just and a good man.[e] Joseph of Arimathæa was a Sanhedrist,[5] but he had not consented either to the counsel or

Marginal notes:

CHAP. XV

[a] Ps. lxix. 20

[b] Ps. xvi. 10

[c] 1 John v. 6

[d] St. Matthew

[e] St. Luke

---

[1] So, with various modifications, which need not here be detailed, first, Dr. Gruner (Comment. Antiq. Med. de Jesu Christi Morte, Hal. 1805), who, however, regarded Jesus as not quite dead when the lance pierced the heart, and, of late, Dr. Stroud (The Physical Cause of the Death of Christ, 1871), and many interpreters (see Nebe, u. s. pp. 400, 401).

[2] But certainly not through a separation of the serum and the cruor, which is the mark of beginning putrefaction.

[3] The fullest and most satisfactory physical explanation is that given by the Rev. S. Haughton, M.D., and reprinted in the Speaker's Commentary on 1 John, pp. 349, 350. It demonstrates, that this phenomenon would take place, but only if a person who was also being crucified died of rupture of the heart.

[4] This seems implied in the expression εὐσχήμων (A.V. 'honourable'), St. Mark xv. 43.

[5] Taken in connection with St. Luke xxiii. 51, this is probably the meaning of βουλευτής. Otherwise we would have

the deed of his colleagues.   It must have been generally known,
that he was one of those 'which waited for the Kingdom of God.'
But he had advanced beyond what that expression implies.   Although
secretly, for fear of the Jews:ᵃ he was a disciple of Jesus.   It is in
strange contrast to this 'fear,' that St. Mark tells us, that, 'having
dared,'¹ 'he went in unto Pilate and asked for the Body of Jesus.'
Thus, under circumstances the most unlikely and unfavourable,
were his fears converted into boldness, and he, whom fear of the
Jews had restrained from making open avowal of discipleship during the life-time of Jesus, not only professed such of the Crucified
Christ,² but took the most bold and decided step before Jews and
Gentiles in connection with it.   So does trial elicit faith, and the
wind, which quenches the feeble flame that plays around the outside,
fan into brightness the fire that burns deep within, though for a
time unseen.   Joseph of Arimathæa, now no longer a secret disciple,
but bold in the avowal of his reverent love, would show to the
Dead Body of his Master all veneration.   And the Divinely ordered
concurrence of circumstances not only helped his pious purpose, but
invested all with deepest symbolic significance.   It was Friday
afternoon, and the Sabbath was drawing near.³   No time therefore
was to be lost, if due honour were to be paid to the Sacred Body.
Pilate gave it to Joseph of Arimathæa.   Such was within his power,
and a favour not unfrequently accorded in like circumstances.⁴   But
two things must have powerfully impressed the Roman Governor,
and deepened his former thoughts about Jesus: first, that the death
on the Cross had taken place so rapidly, a circumstance on which he
personally questioned the Centurion,ᵇ and then the bold appearance
and request of such a man as Joseph of Arimathæa.⁵   Or did the
Centurion express to the Governor also some such feeling as that
which had found utterance under the Cross in the words: 'Truly
this Man was the Son of God'?

regarded him rather as a member of ' the
Council of Priests' (*Beth Din shel
Kohanim*, Kethub. i. 5) which met in
what anciently was called the *Lishkath
Bulvatin* (Chamber of Councillors) in
the Temple (Jer. Yoma 38 *c*; Yoma 8 *b*).
The Greek work itself has passed into
Rabbinic language as *Bulyutos*, and in
other modifications of the word.
    ¹ τολμήσας.
    ² At the same time I feel, that this
might have been represented by the Jews
as not quite importing what it really
was—as rather an act of *pietas* towards

the Rabbi of Nazareth than of homage to
the Messiahship of Jesus.
    ³ The ἡμέρα παρασκευῆς in connec-
tion with 'the Sabbath' (St. Luke xxiii. 54)
shows, that the former expression refers
to 'the preparation' for the *Sabbath*, or
the Friday.
    ⁴ See the proof in *Wetstein*, ad loc.
    ⁵ The Arimathæa of Joseph is probably
the modern Er-Ram, two hours north of
Jerusalem, on a conical hill, somewhat
east of the road that leads from Jerusalem to Nablus (*Jos. Ant.* viii. 12. 3)—
the Armathaim of the LXX.   The ob-

The proximity of the holy Sabbath, and the consequent need of haste, may have suggested or determined the proposal of Joseph to lay the Body of Jesus in his own rock-hewn new tomb,[1] wherein no one had yet been laid.[a] The symbolic significance of this is the more marked, that the symbolism was undesigned. These rock-hewn sepulchres, and the mode of laying the dead in them, have been very fully described in connection with the burying of Lazarus.[2] We may therefore wholly surrender ourselves to the sacred thoughts that gather around us. The Cross was lowered and laid on the ground; the cruel nails drawn out, and the ropes unloosed. Joseph, with those who attended him, 'wrapped' the Sacred Body 'in a clean linen cloth,' and rapidly carried It to the rock-hewn tomb in the garden close by. Such a rock-hewn tomb or cave (*Meartha*) had niches (*Kukhin*), where the dead were laid. It will be remembered, that at the entrance to 'the tomb'—and within 'the rock'—there was 'a court,' nine feet square, where ordinarily the bier was deposited, and its bearers gathered to do the last offices for the Dead. Thither we suppose Joseph to have carried the Sacred Body, and then the last scene to have taken place. For now another, kindred to Joseph in spirit, history, and position, had come. The same spiritual Law, which had brought Joseph to open confession, also constrained the profession of that other Sanhedrist, Nicodemus. We remember, how at the first he had, from fear of detection, come to Jesus by night, and with what bated breath he had pleaded with his colleagues not so much the cause of Christ, as on His behalf that of law and justice.[b] He now came, bringing 'a roll' of myrrh and aloes, in the fragrant mixture well known to the Jews for purposes of anointing or burying.

It was in 'the court' of the tomb that the hasty embalmment—if such it may be called—took place. None of Christ's former disciples seem to have taken part in the burying. John may have withdrawn to bring tidings to, and to comfort the Virgin-Mother; the others

[a] St. Luke

[b] St. John vii. 50

---

jections of *Keim* (which it would take too long to discuss in a note) are of no force (comp. his Jesu von Naz. iii. p. 516). It is one of the undesigned evidences of the accuracy of St. Luke, that he described it as belonging to Judæa. For, whereas Ramah in Mount Ephraim originally belonged to Samaria, it was afterwards separated from the latter and joined to the province of Judæa (comp. 1 Macc. x. 38; xi. 28, 34).

[1] *Meyer* regards the statement of St. Matthew to that effect (xxvii. 60) as inconsistent with the notice in St. John xix. 42. I really cannot see any inconsistency, nor does his omission of the fact that the tomb was Joseph's seem to me fatal. The narrative of St. John is concentrated on the burying rather than its accessories. Professor *Westcott* thinks that St. John xix. 41, implies 'that the sepulchre in which the Lord was laid was not chosen as His final resting-place.' But of this also I do not perceive evidence.

[2] See Book IV. ch. xxi.

BOOK
V
~~~~~~
a St. Luke

b St. Luke

c Sanh. 47 b
d Ohal. ii 4

also, that had ' stood afar off, beholding,' appear to have left. Only a few faithful ones,[a] notably among them Mary Magdalene and the other Mary, the mother of Joses, stood over against the tomb, watching at some distance where and how the Body of Jesus was laid. It would scarcely have been in accordance with Jewish manners, if these women had mingled more closely with the two Sanhedrists and their attendants. From where they stood they could only have had a dim view of what passed within the court, and this may explain how, on their return, they ' prepared spices and ointments '[b] for the more full honours which they hoped to pay the Dead after the Sabbath was past.[1] For, it is of the greatest import-ance to remember, that haste characterised all that was done. It seems as if the ' clean linen cloth ' in which the Body had been wrapped, was now torn into ' cloths ' or swathes, into which the Body, limb by limb, was now ' bound,'[2] no doubt, between layers of myrrh and aloes, the Head being wrapped in a napkin. And so they laid Him to rest in the niche of the rock-hewn new tomb. And as they went out, they rolled, as was the custom, a ' great stone '—the *Golel* —to close the entrance to the tomb,[c] probably leaning against it for support, as was the practice, a smaller stone—the so-called *Dopheq*.[d] It would be where the one stone was laid against the other, that on the next day, Sabbath though it was, the Jewish authorities would have affixed the seal, so that the slightest disturbance might become apparent.[3]

.   .   .   .

' It was probably about the same time, that a noisy throng prepared

---

[1] St. John computes it at about 100 *litras*. As in all likelihood this would refer to Roman pounds, of about twelve ounces each, the amount is large, but not such as to warrant any reasonable ob-jection. A servant could easily carry it, and it is not said that it was all used in the burying. If it were possible to find any similar use of the expression (λίτρας), one might be tempted to regard the *litras* as indicating not the weight, but a *coin*. In that sense the word *litra* is used, sometimes as = 100 denars, in which case 100 litras would be = about 250 *l.*, but more frequently as=4 drachms, in which case 100 litras would be=about 12*l.* (comp. *Herzfeld*, Handelsgesch. p. 181). But the linguistic difficulty seems very great, while any possible objection to the weight of the spices is really in-considerable. For the kind of spices used in the burying, see Book IV. ch. xxi.

(at the burying of Lazarus). In later times there was a regular rubric and prayers with Kabbalistic symbolism (see *Perles*, Leichenfeierlichk. p. 11, Note 12). No doubt, the wounds in the Sacred Body of our Lord had been washed from their gore.

[2] The Synoptists record, that the Body of Jesus was ' wrapped ' in a ' linen cloth '; St. John tells us that it was ' bound ' with the aloes and myrrh of Nicodemus into ' swathes ' or ' cloths,' even as they were found afterwards in the empty tomb, and by their side ' the napkin,' or *soudarion*, for the head. I have tried to combine the account of the Synoptists and that of St. John into a continuous narrative.

[3] But it must be admitted, that there are difficulties on this particular. See the remarks on this point at pp. 623 and 631, but especially pp, 636, 637.

to follow delegates from the Sanhedrin to the ceremony of cutting CHAP.
the Passover-sheaf. The Law had it, "he shall bring a sheaf [lite- XV
rally, the Omer] with the first-fruits of your harvest, unto the
priest; and he shall wave the Omer before Jehovah, to be accepted
for you." This Passover-sheaf was reaped in public the evening
before it was offered, and it was to witness this ceremony that the
crowd had gathered around the elders. Already on the 14th Nisan
the spot whence the first sheaf was to be reaped had been marked
out, by tying together in bundles, while still standing, the barley
that was to be cut down, according to custom, in the sheltered Ashes-
Valley across Kidron. When the time for cutting the sheaf had
arrived—that is, on the evening of the 15th Nisan, even though it
were a Sabbath, just as the sun went down, three men, each with a
sickle and basket, set to work. Clearly to bring out what was distinctive in the ceremony, they first asked of the bystanders three
times each of these questions: " Has the sun gone down? " " With this
sickle? " " Into this basket? " " On this Sabbath? (or first Passover-
day)"—and, lastly, "Shall I reap?" Having each time been answered
in the affirmative, they cut down barley to the amount of one ephah,
or about three pecks and three pints of our English measure. This
is not the place to follow the ceremony farther—how the corn was
threshed out, parched, ground, and one omer of the flour, mixed
with oil and frankincense, waved before the Lord in the Temple on
the second Paschal day (or 16th of Nisan). But, as this festive
procession started, amidst loud demonstrations, a small band of
mourners turned from having laid their dead Master in His resting-
place. The contrast is as sad as it is suggestive. And yet, not in
the Temple, nor by the priest, but in the silence of that garden-
tomb, was the first Omer of the new Paschal flour to be waved before
the Lord.'[1]

.   .   .   .

' Now on the morrow, which is after the preparation [the Friday],
the chief priests and the Pharisees were gathered together unto
Pilate, saying, Sir, we remember that that deceiver said, while He
was yet alive, After three days I rise again. Command, therefore,
that the sepulchre be made sure until the third day, lest haply His
disciples come and steal Him away, and say unto the people, He is
risen from the dead: so the last error shall be worse than the first.
Pilate said unto them, Take a guard, go your way, make it as sure as

[1] See 'The Temple and its Services,' pp. 221-224.

ye can. So they went, and made the sepulchre sure, sealing the
stone, the guard being with them.'

.   .   .   .

But was there really need for it?   Did they, who had spent what
remained of daylight to prepare spices wherewith to anoint the Dead
Christ, expect His Body to be removed, or did they expect—perhaps
in their sorrow even think of His word: 'I rise again'?   But on that
holy Sabbath, when the Sanhedrists were thinking of how to make
sure of the Dead Christ, what were the thoughts of Joseph of
Arimathæa and Nicodemus, of Peter and John, of the other disciples,
and especially of the loving women who only waited for the first
streak of Easter-light to do their last service of love?   What were
their thoughts of God—what of Christ—what of the Words He had
spoken, the Deeds He had wrought, the salvation He had come to
bring, and the Kingdom of Heaven which He was to open to all
believers?

Behind Him had closed the gates of Hades; but upon them rather
than upon Him had fallen the shadows of death.   Yet they still loved
Him—and stronger than death was love.

CHAPTER XVI.

ON THE RESURRECTION OF CHRIST FROM THE DEAD.

THE history of the Life of Christ upon earth closes with a Miracle as great as that of its inception. It may be said that the one casts light upon the other. If He was what the Gospels represent Him, He must have been born of a pure Virgin, without sin, and He must have risen from the Dead. If the story of His Birth be true, we can believe that of His Resurrection; if that of His Resurrection be true, we can believe that of His Birth. In the nature of things, the latter was incapable of strict historical proof; and, in the nature of things, His Resurrection demanded and was capable of the fullest historical evidence. If such exists, the keystone is given to the arch; the miraculous Birth becomes almost a necessary postulate, and Jesus is the Christ in the full sense of the Gospels. And yet we mark, as another parallel point between the account of the miraculous Birth and that of the Resurrection, the utter absence of details as regards these events themselves. If this circumstance may be taken as indirect evidence that they were not legendary, it also imposes on us the duty of observing the reverent silence so well-befitting the case, and not intruding beyond the path which the Evangelic narrative has opened to us.

CHAP.
XVI

That path is sufficiently narrow, and in some respects difficult; not, indeed, as to the great event itself, nor as to its leading features, but as to the more minute details. And here, again, our difficulties arise, not so much from any actual disagreement, as from the absence of actual identity. Much of this is owing to the great compression in the various narratives, due partly to the character of the event narrated, partly to the incomplete information possessed by the narrators—of whom only one was strictly an eyewitness, but chiefly to this, that to the different narrators the central point of interest lay in one or the other aspect of the circumstances connected with the Resurrection. Not only St. Matthew,[1] but also St. Luke, so

[1] So Canon *Westcott*.

BOOK
V

* Acts. i. 3

b Acts xii.
12

c 1 Cor. xv.
4-8

compresses the narrative that 'the distinction of points of time' is almost effaced. St. Luke seems to crowd into the Easter Evening what himself tells us occupied forty days.ᵃ His is, so to speak, the pre-eminently Jerusalem account of the evidence of the Resurrection; that of St. Matthew the pre-eminently Galilean account of it. Yet each implies and corroborates the facts of the other.[1] In general we ought to remember, that the Evangelists, and afterwards St. Paul, are not so much concerned to narrate the whole *history* of the Resurrection as to furnish the evidence for it. And here what is distinctive in each is also characteristic of his special view-point. St. Matthew describes the impression of the full evidence of that Easter morning on friend and foe, and then hurries us from the Jerusalem stained with Christ's Blood back to the sweet Lake and the blessed Mount where first He spake. It is, as if he longed to realise the Risen Christ in the scenes where he had learned to know Him. St. Mark, who is much more brief, gives not only a mere summary,[2] but, if one might use the expression, tells it as from the bosom of the Jerusalem family, from the house of his mother Mary.ᵇ St. Luke seems to have made most full inquiry as to all the facts of the Resurrection, and his narrative might almost be inscribed: 'Easter Day in Jerusalem.' St. John paints such scenes—during the whole forty days, whether in Jerusalem or Galilee—as were most significant and teachful of this threefold lesson of his Gospels: that Jesus was the Christ, that He was the Son of God, and that, believing, we have life in His Name. Lastly, St. Paul—as one born out of due time—produces the testimony of the principal witnesses to the fact, in a kind of ascending climax.ᶜ And this the more effectively, that he is evidently aware of the difficulties and the import of the question, and has taken pains to make himself acquainted with all the facts of the case.

---

[1] The reader who is desirous of further studying this point is referred to the admirable analysis by Canon *Westcott* in his notes prefatory to St. John xx. At the same time I must respectfully express dissent from his arrangement of some of the events connected with the Resurrection (u. s., p. 288 a).

[2] I may here state that I accept the genuineness of the concluding portion of St. Mark (xvi. 9-20). If, on internal grounds, it must be admitted that it reads like a postscript; on the other hand, without it the section would read like a mutilated document. This is not the place to discuss the grounds on which I have finally accepted the genuine-

ness of these verses. The reader may here be referred to Canon *Cook's* 'Revised Version of the first three Gospels,' pp. 120-125, but especially to the masterly and exhaustive work by Dean *Burgon* on 'The last twelve verses of the Gospel according to St. Mark.' At the same time I would venture to say, that Dean *Burgon* has not attached sufficient importance to the adverse impression made by the verses in question on the ground of internal evidence (see his chapter on the subject, pp. 136-190). And it must be confessed, that, whichever view we may ultimately adopt, the subject is beset with considerable difficulties.

The question is of such importance, alike in itself and as regards this whole history, that a discussion, however brief and even imperfect,[1] preliminary to the consideration of the Evangelic narrations, seems necessary.

What thoughts concerning the Dead Christ filled the minds of Joseph of Arimathæa, of Nicodemus, and of the other disciples of Jesus, as well as of the Apostles and of the pious women? They believed Him to be dead, and they did not expect Him to rise again from the dead—at least, in our accepted sense of it. Of this there is abundant evidence from the moment of His Death, in the burial-spices brought by Nicodemus, in those prepared by the women (both of which were intended as against corruption), in the sorrow of the women at the empty tomb, in their supposition that the Body had been removed, in the perplexity and bearing of the Apostles, in the doubts of so many, and indeed in the express statement: 'For as yet they knew not the Scripture, that He must rise again from the dead.'[a] And the notice in St. Matthew's Gospel,[b] that the Sanhedrists had taken precautions against His Body being stolen, so as to give the appearance of fulfilment to His prediction that He would rise again after three days[2]—that, therefore, they knew of such a prediction, and took it in the literal sense—would give only more emphasis to the opposite bearing of the disciples and their manifest non-expectancy of a literal Resurrection. What the disciples expected, perhaps wished, was not Christ's return in glorified corporeity, but His Second Coming in glory into His Kingdom.

But if they regarded Him as really dead and not to rise again in the literal sense, this had evidently no practical effect, not only on their former feelings towards Him, but even on their faith in Him as the promised Messiah.[3] This appears from the conduct of Joseph and Nicodemus, from the language of the women, and from the whole bearing of the Apostles and disciples. All this must have been very different, if they had regarded the Death of Christ, even on the Cross, as having given the lie to His Messianic Claims.[4] On

[a] St. John xx. 9

[b] St. Matt. xxvii. 62-66

---

[1] I have purposely omitted detailed references to, and refutation of, the arguments of opponents.

[2] But it must be truthfully admitted that there is force in some, though not in all, the objections urged against this incident by *Meyer* and others. It need scarcely be said that this would in no way invalidate the truth of the narrative. Further than this, which we unhesitatingly state, we cannot at present enter on the question. See pp. 636, 637.

[3] The statement of the two on the way

to Emmaus (St. Luke xxiv. 21): 'But we trusted that it was He Which should redeem Israel,' refers only to the disappointment of their Jewish hopes of a present Messianic Kingdom.

[4] It can scarcely be supposed, that their whole ideas of His Messiahship had in those few hours undergone a complete change, and that in a philosophico-rationalistic direction, such as would have been absolutely and wholly foreign to minds and training like theirs.

the contrary, the impression left on our minds is, that, although they deeply grieved over the loss of their Master, and the seeming triumph of His foes,ª yet His Death came to them not unexpectedly, but rather as of internal necessity and as the fulfilment of His often repeated prediction. Nor can we wonder at this, since He had, ever since the Transfiguration, laboured, against all their resistance and reluctance, to impress on them the fact of His Betrayal and Death. He had, indeed—although by no means so frequently or clearly—also referred to His Resurrection. But of this they might, according to their Jewish ideas, form a very different conception from that of a literal Resurrection of that Crucified Body in a glorified state, and yet capable of such terrestrial intercourse as the Risen Christ held with them. And if it be objected that, in such case, Christ must have clearly taught them all this, it is sufficient to answer, that there was no need for such clear teaching on the point at that time; that the event itself would soon and best teach them; that it would have been impossible really to teach it, except by the event; and that any attempt at it would have involved a far fuller communication on this mysterious subject than, to judge from what is told us in Scripture, it was the purpose of Christ to impart in our present state of faith and expectancy. Accordingly, from their point of view, the prediction of Christ might have referred to the continuance of His Work, to His Vindication, or to some apparition of Him, whether from heaven or on earth—such as that of the saints in Jerusalem after the Resurrection, or that of Elijah in Jewish belief—but especially to His return in glory; certainly, not to the Resurrection as it actually took place. The fact itself would be quite foreign to Jewish ideas, which embraced the continuance of the soul after death and the final resurrection of the body, but not a state of spiritual corporeity, far less, under conditions such as those described in the Gospels.[1] Elijah, who is so constantly introduced in Jewish tradition, is never represented as sharing in meals or offering his body for touch; nay, the Angels who visited Abraham are represented as only making show of, not really, eating.[2] Clearly, the Apostles had not learned

[1] But even if a belief in His Resurrection had been a requirement in their faith, as *Keim* rightly remarks, such realistic demonstration of it would not have been looked for. Herod Antipas did not search the tomb of the Baptist when he believed him risen from the dead—how much more should the disciples of Christ have been satisfied with evidence far less realistic and frequent than that described in the Gospels. This

consideration shows that there was no motive for inventing the details connected with the history of the Resurrection.
[2] So *Josephus* (Ant. xi. 1. 2), and, to show that this was not a rationalistic view, Baba Mets. 65 *b*, Ber. R. 48. Later tradition (Tos. to B. Mets.; Bemidb. R. 10), indeed, seems to admit the literal eating, but as representing travellers, and in acknowledgment of Abraham's hos-

the Resurrection of Christ either from the Scriptures—and this
proves that the narrative of it was not intended as a fulfilment of
previous expectancy—nor yet from the predictions of Christ to that
effect; although without the one, and especially without the other,
the empty grave would scarcely have wrought in them the assured
conviction of the Resurrection of Christ.[1]

This brings us to the real question in hand. Since the Apostles
and others evidently believed Him to be dead, and expected not His
Resurrection, and since the fact of His Death was not to them a
formidable, if any, objection to His Messianic Character—such as
might have induced them to invent or imagine a Resurrection—how
are we to account for the history of the Resurrection with all its
details in all the four Gospels and by St. Paul? The details, or
'signs' are clearly intended as *evidences* to all of the reality of the
Resurrection, without which it would not have been believed; and
their multiplication and variety must, therefore, be considered as
indicating what otherwise would have been not only numerous but
insuperable difficulties. Similarly, the language of St. Paul[a] implies
a careful and searching inquiry on his part;[2] the more rational,
that, besides intrinsic difficulties and Jewish preconceptions against
it, the objections to the fact must have been so often and coarsely
obtruded on him, whether in disputation or by the jibes of the Greek
scholars and students who derided his preaching.[b]

[a] Gal. i. 18

[b] Acts xvii.
32

Hence, the question to be faced is this: Considering their
previous state of mind and the absence of any motive, how are we to
account for the change of mind on the part of the disciples in regard
to the Resurrection? There can at least be no question, that they
came to believe, and with the most absolute certitude, in the Resurrection as an historical fact; nor yet, that it formed the basis and
substance of all their preaching of the Kingdom; nor yet, that St.
Paul, up to his conversion a bitter enemy of Christ, was fully persuaded of it; nor—to go a step back—that Jesus Himself expected
it. Indeed, the world would not have been converted to a dead Jewish
Christ, however His intimate disciples might have continued to love
His memory. But they preached everywhere, first and foremost,
the Resurrection from the dead! In the language of St. Paul: 'If
Christ hath not been raised, then is our preaching vain, your faith
also is vain. Yea, and we are found false witnesses of God . . . ye

pitality. *Onkelos* simply renders literally, but the Targum Pseudo-Jon. seems
purposely to leave the point undetermined.

[1] This is well argued by *Weiss*, Leben
Jesu, vol. ii. p. 608.
[2] This is conveyed by the verb
ἱστορέω.

BOOK
V

*1 Cor. xv.
14, 15, 17

are yet in your sins.'ᵃ We must here dismiss what probably underlies the chief objection to the Resurrection: its miraculous character. The objection to Miracles, as such, proceeds on that false Supranaturalism, which traces a Miracle to the immediate *fiat* of the Almighty without any intervening links; [1] and, as already shown, it involves a vicious *petitio principii*. But, after all, the Miraculous is only the to us unprecedented and uncognisable—a very narrow basis on which to refuse historical investigation. And the historian *has* to account for the undoubted fact, that the Resurrection was the fundamental personal conviction of the Apostles and disciples, the basis of their preaching, and the final support of their martyrdom. What explanation then can be offered of it?

1. We may here put aside two hypotheses, now universally discarded even in Germany, and which probably have never been seriously entertained in this country. They are that of gross fraud on the part of the disciples, who had stolen the Body of Jesus—as to which even *Strauss* remarks, that such a falsehood is wholly incompatible with their after-life, heroism, and martyrdom;—and again this, that Christ had not been really dead when taken from the Cross, and that He gradually revived again. Not to speak of the many absurdities which this theory involves,[2] it really shifts—if we acquit the disciples of complicity—the fraud upon Christ Himself.

2. The only other explanation, worthy of attention, is the so-called 'Vision-hypothesis:' that the Apostles really believed in the Resurrection, but that mere visions of Christ had wrought in them this belief. The hypothesis has been variously modified. According to some, these visions were the outcome of an excited imagination, of a morbid state of the nervous system. To this there is, of course, the preliminary objection, that such visions presuppose a previous expectancy of the event, which, as we know, is the opposite of the fact. Again, such a 'Vision-hypothesis' in no way agrees with the many details and circumstances narrated in connection with the Risen One, Who is described as having appeared not only to one or another in the retirement of the chamber, but to many, and in a manner and circumstances which render the idea of a mere vision impossible. Besides, the visions of an excited imagination would not have endured and led to such results; most probably they would soon have given place to corresponding depression.

---

[1] The whole subject of miracles requires fuller and clearer treatment than it has yet received.

[2] Such as this, how with pierced Feet He could have gone to Emmaus.

The 'Vision-hypothesis' is not much improved, if we regard the supposed vision as the result of reflection—that the disciples, convinced that the Messiah could not remain dead (and this again is contrary to fact) had wrought themselves first into a persuasion that He must rise, and then into visions of the Risen [1] One. Nor yet would it commend itself more to our mind, if we were to assume that these visions had been directly sent from God Himself,[2] to attest the fact that Christ lived. For, we have here to deal with a series of facts that cannot be so explained, such as the showing them His Sacred Wounds; the offer to touch them; the command to handle Him, so as to convince themselves of His real corporeity; the eating with the disciples; the appearance by the Lake of Galilee, and others. Besides, the 'Vision-hypothesis' has to account for the events of the Easter-morning, and

---

[1] This argument might, of course, be variously elaborated, and the account in the Gospels represented as the form which it afterwards took in the belief of the Church. But (a) the whole 'Vision-hypothesis' is shadowy and unreal, and the sacred writers themselves show that they knew the distinction between visions and real appearances; (b) it is impossible to reconcile it with such occurrences as that in St. Luke xxiv. 38–43 and St. John xxi. 13, and, if possible, even more so, to set aside all these details as the outcome of later tradition, for which there was no other basis than the desire of vindicating a vision; (c) it is incompatible with the careful inquiry of St. Paul, who, as on so many other occasions, is here a most important witness. (d) The theory involves the most arbitrary handling of the Gospel-narratives, such as that the Apostles had *at once* returned to Galilee, where the sight of the familiar scenes had kindled in them this enthusiasm; that all the notices about the 'third day' are to be rejected, &c. (e). What was so fundamental a belief as that of the Resurrection could not have had its origin in a delusive vision. This, as Keim has shown, would be incompatible with the calm clearness of conviction and strong purpose of action which were its outcome. Besides, are we to believe that the enthusiasm had first seized the women, then the Apostles, and so on? But how, in that case, about the 500 of whom St. Paul speaks? They could scarcely all have been seized with the same mania. (f) A mere vision is unthinkable under such circumstances as the walk to Emmaus, the conversation with Thomas,

with Peter, &c. Besides, it is incompatible with the giving of such definite promises by the Risen Christ as that of the Holy Spirit, and of such detailed directions as that of Evangelising the world. (g) Lastly, as Keim points out, it is incompatible with the fact that these manifestations ceased with the Ascension. We have eight or at most nine such manifestations in the course of six weeks, and then they suddenly and permanently cease! This would not accord with the theory of visions on the part of excited enthusiasts. But were the Apostles such? Does not the perusal of the Gospel-narratives leave on the impartial reader exactly the opposite impression?

[2] These two modes of accounting for the narrative of the Resurrection: by fraud, and that Christ's was not real death, were already attempted by *Celsus*, 1700 years ago, and the first, by the Jews long before that. *Keim* has subjected them, as modified by different advocates, to a searching criticism, and, with keen irony, exhibited their utter absurdity. In regard to the supposition of fraud he says: it shows that not even the faintest idea of the holy conviction of the Apostles and first Christians has penetrated these spirits. The objection that the Risen One had only manifested Himself to *friends*, not before enemies, is also as old as *Celsus*. It ignores that, throughout, the revelation of Christ does not supersede, but imply faith; that there is no such thing in Christianity as forcing conviction, instead of eliciting faith; and that the purpose of the manifestations of the Risen Christ was to confirm, to comfort, and to teach His disciples. As for His

BOOK
V

ᵃ St. Luke
xxiv. 38-43

especially for the empty tomb from which the great stone had been
rolled, and in which the very cerements [1] of death were seen by those
who entered it.   In fact, such a narrative as that recorded by St. Luke ᵃ
seems almost designed to render the 'Vision-hypothesis' impossible.
We are expressly told, that the appearance of the Risen Christ, so far
from meeting their anticipations, had affrighted them, and that they
had thought it spectral, on which Christ had reassured them, and bidden
them handle Him, for 'a spirit hath not flesh and bones, as ye behold Me
having.'   Lastly, who removed the Body of Christ from the tomb?   Six
weeks afterwards, Peter preached the Resurrection of Christ in Jerusalem.   If Christ's enemies had removed the Body, they could easily
have silenced Peter; if His friends, they would have been guilty of
such fraud, as not even *Strauss* deems possible in the circumstances.
The theories of deception, delusion,[2] and vision being thus impossible, and the *à priori* objection to the fact, as involving a Miracle,
being a *petitio principii*, the historical student is shut up to the
simple acceptance of the narrative.   To this conclusion the unpreparedness of the disciples, their previous opinions, their new testimony unto martyrdom, the foundation of the Christian Church, the
testimony of so many, singly and in company, and the series of recorded manifestations during forty days, and in such different circumstances, where mistake was impossible, had already pointed with
unerring certainty.[3]   And even if slight discrepancies, nay, some
not strictly historical details, which might have been the outcome of
earliest tradition in the Apostolic Church, could be shown in those
accounts which were not of eyewitnesses, it would assuredly not

enemies, the Lord had expressly declared
that they would not see Him again till
the judgment.

[1] Exaggeration would, of course, be
here out of the question.

[2] The most deeply painful, but also
interesting study is that of the conclusion
at which *Keim* ultimately arrives (Gesch.
Jesu v. Naz. iii. pp. 600-605). It has
already been stated with what merciless
irony he exposes the fraud and the non-
death theory, as well as the arguments of
Strauss.   The 'Vision-hypothesis' he
seems at first to advocate with considerable ingenuity and rhetorical power. And
he succeeds in this the more easily, that,
alas, he surrenders—although most ar-
bitrarily—almost every historical detail
in the narrative of the Resurrection! And
yet what is the result at which he ultimately arrives ? He shows, perhaps more
conclusively than any one else, that the
'vision-hypothesis' is also impossible!

Having done so, he virtually admits that
he cannot offer any explanation as to 'the
mysterious exit' of the life of Jesus.
Probably the visions of the Risen Christ
were granted directly by God Himself
and by the glorified Christ (p. 602).
'Nay, even the bodily appearance itself
may be conceded to those who without
it fear to lose all' (p. 603). But from
this there is but a very small step to the
teaching of the Church. At any rate,
the greatest of negative critics has, by
the admission of his inability to explain
the Resurrection in a natural manner,
given the fullest confirmation to the fundamental article of our Christian faith.

[3] *Reuss* (Hist. Evang. p. 698) well remarks, that if this fundamental dogma
of the Church had been the outcome of
invention, care would have been taken
that the accounts of it should be in the
strictest and most literal agreement.

invalidate the great fact itself, which *may unhesitatingly be pro-*
nounced that best established in history. At the same time we
would carefully guard ourselves against the admission that those
hypothetical flaws really exist in the narratives. On the contrary,
we believe them capable of the most satisfactory arrangement, unless
under the strain of hypercriticism.

The importance of all this cannot be adequately expressed in
words. A dead Christ might have been a Teacher and Wonder-
worker, and remembered and loved as such. But only a Risen and
Living Christ could be the Saviour, the Life, and the Life-Giver—
and as such preached to all men. And of this most blessed truth
we have the fullest and most unquestionable evidence. We can,
therefore, implicitly yield ourselves to the impression of these narratives, and, still more, to the realisation of that most sacred and
blessed fact. This is the foundation of the Church, the inscription
on the banner of her armies, the strength and comfort of every
Christian heart. and the grand hope of humanity:

'The Lord is risen indeed.' [1]

---

[1] *Godet* aptly concludes his able discussion of the subject by observing that,
if *Strauss* admits that the Church would
have never arisen if the Apostles had not
had unshaken faith in the reality of
Christ's Resurrection, we may add, that
this faith of the Apostles would have
never arisen unless the Resurrection had
been a true historical fact.

CHAPTER XVII.

'ON THE THIRD DAY HE ROSE AGAIN FROM THE DEAD; HE ASCENDED INTO
HEAVEN.'

(St. Matt. xxviii. 1–10; St. Mark xvi. 1–11; St. Luke xxiv. 1–12; St. John xx. 1–18;
St. Matt. xxviii. 11–15; St. Mark xvi. 12, 13; St. Luke xxiv. 13–35; 1 Cor. xv. 5;
St. Mark xvi. 14; St. Luke xxiv. 36–43; St. John xx. 19–25; St. John xx. 26–29;
St. Matt. xxviii. 16; St. John xxi. 1–24; St. Matt. xxviii. 17–20; St. Mark xvi.
15–18; 1 Cor. xv. 6; St. Luke xxiv. 44–53; St. Mark xvi. 19, 20; Acts i. 3–12.)

BOOK
V

GREY dawn was streaking the sky, when they who had so lovingly
watched Him to His Burying were making their lonely way to the
rock-hewn Tomb in the Garden.[1] Considerable as are the difficulties of exactly harmonising the details in the various narratives—
if, indeed, importance attaches to such attempts—we are thankful
to know that any hesitation only attaches to the arrangement of
minute particulars,[2] and not to the great facts of the case. And
even these minute details would, as we shall have occasion to show,
be harmonious, if only we knew all the circumstances.

The difference, if such it may be called, in the names of the
women, who at early morn went to the Tomb, scarce requires
elaborate discussion. It may have been, that there were two parties,
starting from different places to meet at the Tomb, and that this also
accounts for the slight difference in the details of what they saw and
heard at the Grave. At any rate, the mention of the two Marys and
Joanna is supplemented in St. Luke [a] by that of the 'other women
with them,' while, if St. John speaks only of Mary Magdalene,[b] her
report to Peter and John: 'We know not where they have laid Him,'
implies, that she had not gone alone to the Tomb. It was the first
day of the week [3]— according to Jewish reckoning the third day from

[a] St. Luke
xxiv. 10
[b] St. John
xx. 1

---

[1] I must remain uncertain, however
important, whether the ὀψὲ σαββάτων
refers to Saturday evening or early
Sunday morning.

[2] The reader who is desirous of comparing the different views about these
seeming or real small discrepancies is
referred to the various Commentaries.
On the strictly orthodox side the most

elaborate and learned attempt at conciliation is that by Mr. McClellan (New Test.,
Harmony of the Four Gospels, pp. 508–
538), although his ultimate scheme of
arrangement seems to me too composite.

[3] μία σαββάτων, an expression which
exactly answers to the Rabbinic אחד
בשבת.

His Death.[1] The narrative leaves the impression that the Sabbath's rest had delayed their visit to the Tomb; but it is at least a curious coincidence that the relatives and friends of the deceased were in the habit of going to the grave up to the third day (when presumably corruption was supposed to begin), so as to make sure that those laid there were really dead.[a] Commenting on this, that Abraham descried Mount Moriah on the third day,[b] the Rabbis insist on the importance of 'the third day' in various events connected with Israel, and specially speak of it in connection with the resurrection of the dead, referring in proof to Hos. vi. 2.[c] In another place, appealing to the same prophetic saying, they infer from Gen. xlii. 17, that God never leaves the just more than three days in anguish.[d] In mourning also the third day formed a sort of period, because it was thought that the soul hovered round the body till the third day, when it finally parted from its earthly tabernacle.[e]

Although these things are here mentioned, we need scarcely say that no such thoughts were present with the holy mourners who, in the grey of that Sunday-morning,[2] went to the Tomb. Whether or not there were two groups of women who started from different places to meet at the Tomb, the most prominent figure among them was Mary Magdalene[3]—as prominent among the pious women as Peter was among the Apostles. She seems to have first reached the Grave,[2] and, seeing the great stone that had covered its entrance rolled away, hastily judged that the Body of the Lord had been removed. Without waiting for further inquiry, she ran back to inform Peter and John of the fact. The Evangelist here explains, that there had been a great earthquake, and that the Angel of the Lord, to human sight as lightning and in brilliant white garment, had rolled back the stone, and sat upon it, when the guard, affrighted by what they heard and saw, and especially by the look and attitude of heavenly power in the Angel, had been seized with mortal faintness. Remembering the events connected with the Crucifixion, which had no doubt been talked about among the soldiery, and bearing in mind the impression of such a sight on such minds, we could readily understand the effect on the two sentries who that long night had kept guard over the solitary

CHAP.
XVII

[a] Mass. Semach. viii. p. 29 d
[b] Gen. xxii. 4

[c] Ber. R. 56, ed. Warsh. p. 102 b, top of page
[d] Ber. R. 91

[e] Moed K. 28 b; Ber. R. 100

---

[1] Friday, Saturday, Sunday.
[2] I cannot believe that St. Matthew xxviii. 1 refers to a visit of the two Marys on the Saturday evening, nor St. Mark xvi. 1 to a purchasing at that time of spices.
[3] The accounts imply, that the women knew nothing of the sealing of the stone and of the guard set over the Tomb.

This may be held as evidence, that St. Matthew could not have meant that the two Marys had visited the grave on the previous evening (xxviii. 1). In such case they must have seen the guard. Nor could the women in that case have wondered who would roll away the stone for them.

Tomb. The event itself (we mean: as regards the rolling away of the stone), we suppose to have taken place after the Resurrection of Christ, in the early dawn, while the holy women were on their way to the Tomb. The earthquake cannot have been one in the ordinary sense, but a shaking of the place, when the Lord of Life burst the gates of Hades to re-tenant His Glorified Body, and the lightning-like Angel descended from heaven to roll away the stone. To have left it there, when the Tomb was empty, would have implied what was no longer true. But there is a sublime irony in the contrast between man's elaborate precautions and the ease with which the Divine Hand can sweep them aside, and which, as throughout the history of the Christ and of His Church, recalls the prophetic declaration: 'He that sitteth in the heavens shall laugh at them.'

While the Magdalene hastened, probably by another road, to the abode of Peter and John, the other women also had reached the Tomb, either in one party, or, it may be, in two companies. They had wondered and feared how they could accomplish their pious purpose—for, who would roll away the stone for them? But, as so often, the difficulty apprehended no longer existed. Perhaps they thought that the now absent Mary Magdalene had obtained help for this. At any rate, they now entered the vestibule of the Sepulchre. Here the appearance of the Angel filled them with fear. But the heavenly Messenger bade them dismiss apprehension; he told them that Christ was not there, nor yet any longer dead, but risen, as, indeed, He had foretold in Galilee to His disciples; finally, he bade them hasten with the announcement to the disciples, and with this message, that, as Christ had directed them before, they were to meet Him in Galilee. It was not only that this connected, so to speak, the wondrous present with the familiar past, and helped them to realise that it was their very Master; nor yet that in the retirement, quiet, and security of Galilee, there would be best opportunity for fullest manifestation, as to the five hundred, and for final conversation and instruction. But the main reason, and that which explains the otherwise strange, almost exclusive, prominence given at such a moment to the direction to meet Him in Galilee, has already been indicated in a previous chapter.[1] With the scattering of the Eleven in Gethsemane on the night of Christ's betrayal, the Apostolic College was temporarily broken up. They continued, indeed, still to meet together as individual disciples, but the bond of the Apostolate was, for the moment, dissolved. And the Apostolic circle was to be

---

[1] See this Book, ch. xii.

re-formed, and the Apostolic Commission renewed and enlarged, in Galilee; not, indeed, by its Lake, where only seven of the Eleven seem to have been present,[a] but on the mountain where He had directed them to meet Him.[b] Thus was the end to be like the beginning. Where He had first called, and directed them for their work, there would He again call them, give fullest directions, and bestow new and amplest powers. His appearances in Jerusalem were intended to prepare them for all this, to assure them completely and joyously of the fact of His Resurrection—the full teaching of which would be given in Galilee. And when the women, perplexed and scarcely conscious, obeyed the command to go in and examine for themselves the now empty niche in the Tomb, they saw two Angels[1]—probably as the Magdalene afterwards saw them—one at the head, the other at the feet, where the Body of Jesus had lain. They waited no longer, but hastened, without speaking to any one, to carry to the disciples the tidings of which they could not even yet grasp the full import.[2]

2. But whatever unclearness of detail may rest on the narratives of the Synoptists, owing to their great compression, all is distinct when we follow the steps of the Magdalene, as these are traced in the Fourth Gospel. Hastening from the Tomb, she ran to the lodging of Peter and to that of John—the repetition of the preposition 'to' probably marking, that the two occupied different, although perhaps closely adjoining, quarters.[c] Her startling tidings induced them to go at once—'and they went towards the sepulchre.' 'But they began to run, the two together'—probably so soon as they were outside the town and near 'the Garden.' John, as the younger, outran Peter.[3] Reaching the Sepulchre first, and stooping down, 'he

[a] St. John xxi. 2
[b] St. Matt. xxviii. 16

[c] So already Bengel

---

[1] It may, however, have been that the appearance of the one Angel was to one company of women, that of two Angels to another.

[2] While I would speak very diffidently on the subject, it seems to me as if the Evangelists had compressed the whole of that morning's events into one narrative: 'The Women at the Sepulchre.' It is this compression which gives the appearance of more events than really took place, owing to the appearance of being divided into scenes, and the circumstance that the different writers give prominence to different persons or else to different details in what is really one scene. Nay, I am disposed—though again with great diffidence—to regard the appearance of Jesus 'to the women' (St. Matt. xxviii. 9) as the same with that to Mary Mag-

dalene, recorded in St. John xx. 11–17, and referred to in St. Mark xvi. 9—the more so as the words in St. Matt. xxviii. 9 'as they went to tell His disciples' are spurious, being probably intended for harmonistic purposes. But, while suggesting this view, I would by no means maintain it as one certain to my own mind, although it would simplify details otherwise very intricate.

[3] It may be regarded as a specimen of what one might designate as the imputation of sinister motives to the Evangelists, when the most 'advanced' negative criticism describes this 'legend' as implying the contest between Jewish and Gentile Christianity (Peter and John) in which the younger gains the race! Similarly, we are informed that the penitent thief on the Cross is intended

seeth' (βλέπει) the linen clothes, but, from his position, not the napkin which lay apart by itself. If reverence and awe prevented John from entering the Sepulchre, his impulsive companion, who arrived immediately after him, thought of nothing else than the immediate and full clearing up of the mystery. As he entered the sepulchre, he 'steadfastly (intently) beholds' (θεωρεῖ) in one place the linen swathes that had bound the Sacred Limbs, and in another the napkin that had been about His Head. There was no sign of haste, but all was orderly, leaving the impression of One Who had leisurely divested Himself of what no longer befitted Him. Soon 'the other disciple' followed Peter. The effect of what he saw was, that he now believed in his heart that the Master was risen—for till then they had not yet derived from Holy Scripture the knowledge that He must rise again. And this also is most instructive. It was not the belief previously derived from Scripture, that the Christ was to rise from the Dead, which led to expectancy of it, but the evidence that He had risen which led them to the knowledge of what Scripture taught on the subject.

3. Yet whatever light had risen in the inmost sanctuary of John's heart, he spake not his thoughts to the Magdalene, whether she had reached the Sepulchre ere the two left it, or met them by the way. The two Apostles returned to their home, either feeling that nothing more could be learned at the Tomb, or to wait for further teaching and guidance. Or it might even have been partly due to a desire not to draw needless attention to the empty Tomb. But the love of the Magdalene could not rest satisfied, while doubt hung over the fate of His Sacred Body. It must be remembered that she knew only of the empty Tomb. For a time she gave way to the agony of her sorrow; then, as she wiped away her tears, she stooped to take one more look into the Tomb, which she thought empty, when, as she 'intently gazed' (θεωρεῖ), the Tomb seemed no longer empty. At the head and feet, where the Sacred Body had lain, were seated two Angels in white. Their question, so deeply true from their knowledge that Christ had risen: 'Woman, why weepest thou?' seems to have come upon the Magdalene with such overpowering suddenness, that, without being able to realise—perhaps in the semi-gloom—who it was that had asked it, she spake, bent only on obtaining the information she sought: 'Because they have taken away

to indicate the Gentiles, the impenitent the Jews! But no language can be too strong to repudiate the imputation, that so many parts of the Gospels were intended as covert attacks by certain tendencies in the early Church against others—the Petrine and Jacobine against the Johannine and Pauline directions.

my Lord, and I know not[1] where they have laid Him.' So is it often with us, that, weeping, we ask the question of doubt or fear, which, if we only knew, would never have risen to our lips; nay, that heaven's own 'Why?' fails to impress us, even when the Voice of its Messengers would gently recall us from the error of our impatience.

But already another answer was to be given to the Magdalene. As she spake, she became conscious of another Presence close to her. Quickly turning round, 'she gazed' ($\theta\varepsilon\omega\rho\varepsilon\hat{\iota}$) on One Whom she recognised not, but regarded as the gardener, from His presence there and from His question: 'Woman, why weepest thou? Whom seekest thou?' The hope, that she might now learn what she sought, gave wings to her words—intensity and pathos. If the supposed gardener had borne to another place the Sacred Body, she would take It away, if she only knew where It was laid. This depth and agony of love, which made the Magdalene forget even the restraints of a Jewish woman's intercourse with a stranger, was the key that opened the Lips of Jesus. A moment's pause, and He spake her name in those well-remembered accents, that had first unbound her from sevenfold demoniac power and called her into a new life. It was as another unbinding, another call into a new life. She had not known His appearance, just as the others did not know Him at first, so unlike, and yet so like, was the glorified Body to that which they had known. But she could not mistake the Voice, especially when It spake to her, and spake her name. So do we also often fail to recognise the Lord when He comes to us 'in another form'[a] than we had known. But we cannot fail to recognise Him when He speaks to us and speaks our name.

Perhaps we may here be allowed to pause, and, from the non-recognition of the Risen Lord till He spoke, ask this question: With what body shall *we* rise? Like or unlike the past? Assuredly, most like. Our bodies will then be *true*; for the soul will body itself forth according to its past history—not only *im*press itself, as now on the features, but *ex*press itself—so that a man may be known by what he is, and as what he is. Thus, in this respect also, has the Resurrection a moral aspect, and is the completion of the history of

[a] St. Mark xvi. 12

---

[1] When *Meyer* contends that the plural in St. John xx. 2, 'We know not where they have laid Him,' does not refer to the presence of other women with the Magdalene, but is a general expression for: We, all His followers, have no knowledge of it—he must have overlooked that, when alone, she repeats the same words in ver. 13, but markedly uses the *singular* number: 'I know not.'

mankind and of each man. And the Christ also must have borne in His glorified Body all that He was, all that even His most intimate disciples had not known nor understood while He was with them, which they now failed to recognise, but knew at once when He spake to them.

It was precisely this which now prompted the action of the Magdalene—prompted also, and explains, the answer of the Lord. As in her name she recognised His Name, the rush of old feeling came over her, and with the familiar ' Rabboni!' [1]—my Master—she would fain have grasped Him. Was it the unconscious impulse to take hold on the precious treasure which she had thought for ever lost; the unconscious attempt to make sure that it was not merely an apparition of Jesus from heaven, but the real Christ in His corporeity on earth; or a gesture of veneration, the beginning of such acts of worship as her heart prompted? Probably all these; and yet probably she was not at the moment distinctly conscious of either or of any of these feelings. But to them all there was one answer, and in it a higher direction, given by the words of the Lord: ' Touch Me not, for I am not yet ascended to the Father.' Not the Jesus appearing from heaven—for He had not yet ascended to the Father; not the former intercourse, not the former homage and worship. There was yet a future of completion before Him in the Ascension, of which Mary knew not. Between that future of completion and the past of work, the present was a gap—belonging partly to the past and partly to the future. The past could not be recalled, the future could not be anticipated. The present was of reassurance, of consolation, of preparation, of teaching. Let the Magdalene go and tell His ' brethren ' of the Ascension. So would she best and most truly tell them that she had seen Him; so also would they best learn how the Resurrection linked the past of His Work of love for them to the future: ' I ascend unto My Father, and your Father, and to my God, and your God.' Thus, the fullest teaching of the past, the clearest manifestation of the present, and the brightest teaching of the future—all as gathered up in the Resurrection—came to the Apostles through the mouth of love of her out of whom He had cast seven devils.

4. Yet another scene on that Easter morning does St. Matthew relate, in explanation of how the well-known Jewish calumny had arisen that the disciples had stolen away the Body of Jesus. He

[1] This may represent the *Galilean* form of the expression, and, if so, would be all the more evidential.

tells, how the guard had reported to the chief priests what had hap- CHAP.
XVII
pened, and how they in turn had bribed the guard to spread this
rumor, at the same time promising that if the fictitious account
of their having slept while the disciples robbed the Sepulchre should
reach Pilate, they would intercede on their behalf. Whatever else
may be said, we know that from the time of *Justin Martyr*[a][1] this a Dial. c.
Tryph.
xvii.; cviii.
has been the Jewish explanation.[2] Of late, however, it has, among
thoughtful Jewish writers, given place to the so-called 'Vision-hypothesis,' to which full reference has already been made.

5. It was the early afternoon of that spring-day perhaps soon after
the early meal, when two men from that circle of disciples left the
City. Their narrative affords deeply interesting glimpses into the
circle of the Church in those first days. The impression conveyed
to us is of utter bewilderment, in which only some things stood out
unshaken and firm: love to the Person of Jesus; love among the
brethren; mutual confidence and fellowship; together with a dim
hope of something yet to come—if not Christ in His Kingdom, yet
some manifestation of, or approach to it. The Apostolic College
seems broken up into units; even the two chief Apostles, Peter and
John, are only 'certain of them that were with us.' And no wonder;
for they are no longer 'Apostles'—sent out. Who is to send them
forth? Not a dead Christ! And what would be their commission,
and to whom and whither? And above all rested a cloud of utter
uncertainty and perplexity. Jesus *was* a Prophet mighty in word
and deed before God and all the people. But their rulers had crucified Him. What was to be their new relation to Jesus; what to
their rulers? And what of the great hope of the Kingdom, which
they had connected with Him?

Thus they were unclear on that very Easter Day even as to His
Mission and Work: unclear as to the past, the present, and the
future. What need for the Resurrection, and for the teaching which
the Risen One alone could bring! These two men had on that very
day been in communication with Peter and John. And it leaves
on us the impression, that, amidst the general confusion, all had
brought such tidings as they had, or had come to hear them, and
had tried but failed, to put it all into order or to see light around it.
'The women' had come to tell of the empty Tomb and of their vision
of Angels, who said that He was alive. But as yet the Apostles had

---

[1] In its coarsest form it is told in the
so-called *Toldoth Jeshu*, which may be
seen at the end of *Wagenseil's* Tela
Ignea Satanæ.

[2] So *Grätz*, and most of the modern
writers.

BOOK
V

• St. Mark
xvi. 11

no explanation to offer.   Peter and John had gone to see for themselves.   They had brought back confirmation of the report that the
Tomb was empty, but they had seen neither Angels nor Him Whom
they were said to have declared alive.   And, although the two had
evidently left the circle of the disciples, if not Jerusalem, before the
Magdalene came, yet we know that even her account did not carry
conviction to the minds of those that heard it,ᵃ

Of the two, who on that early spring afternoon left the City in
company, we know that one bore the name of Cleopas.¹   The other,
unnamed, has for that very reason, and because the narrative of that
work bears in its vividness the character of personal recollection, been
identified with St. Luke himself.   If so, then, as has been finely remarked,² each of the Gospels would, like a picture, bear in some dim
corner the indication of its author: the first, that of the 'publican;'
that by St. Mark, that of the young man, who, in the night of the
Betrayal, had fled from his captors; that of St. Luke in the companion of Cleopas; and that of St. John, in the disciple whom Jesus
loved.   Uncertainty, almost equal to that about the second traveller
to Emmaus, rests on the identification of that place.³   But such

---

¹ This may be either a form of Alphæus,
or of Cleopatros.

² By *Godet*.

³ Not less than four localities have been
identified with Emmaus.   But some
preliminary difficulties must be cleared.
The name Emmaus is spelt in different
ways in the Tulmud (comp. *Neubauer*,
Geogr. d. Talm. p. 100, Note 3). *Josephus*
(War iv. 1. 3; Ant. xviii. 2. 3) explains
the meaning of the name as 'warm baths,'
or thermal springs.   We will not com-
plicate the question by discussing the
derivation of Emmaus.   In another place
(War vii. 6. 6) *Josephus* speaks of
Vespasian having settled in an Emmaus,
sixty furlongs from Jerusalem, a colony
of his soldiers.   There can be little
doubt that the Emmaus of St. Luke and
that of *Josephus* are identical.   Lastly,
we read in the Mishnah (Sukk. iv. 5) of a
Motsa whence they fetched the willow
branches with which the altar was
decorated at the Feast of Tabernacles,
and the Talmud explains this Moza as Kolonieh, which again is identified by Christian writers with Vespasian's colony of
Roman soldiers (*Caspari,*Chronol Geogr.
Einl. p. 207; Quart. Rep. of the Pal.
Explor. Fund, July, 1881, p. 237 [not
without some slight inaccuracies]).   But

an examination of the passage in the
Mishnah must lead us to dismiss this
part of the theory.   No one could imagine
that the worshippers would walk sixty
stadia (seven or eight miles) for willow
branches to decorate the altar, while the
Mishnah, besides, describes this Moza as
below, or south of Jerusalem, whereas the
modern *Kolonieh* (which is identified
with the Colonia of *Josephus*) is north-
west of Jerusalem.   No doubt, the
Talmud, knowing that there was an
Emmaus which was a ' Colonia,' blunder-
ingly identified with it the Moza of the
willow branches. This, however, it seems
lawful to infer from it, that the Emmaus
of *Josephus* bore popularly the name of
Kolonieh.   We can now examine the
four proposed identifications of Emmaus.
The oldest and the youngest of these may
be briefly dismissed.   The most common,
perhaps the earliest identification, was
with the ancient *Nicopolis*, the modern
Amwâs, which in Rabbinic writings also
bears the name of Emmaus (*Neubauer*,
u. s.).   But this is impossible, as Nicopolis is twenty miles from Jerusalem.
The latest proposed identification is that
with *Urtas*, to the south of Bethlehem
(Mrs. *Finn*, Quart. Rep. of Pal. Exlor.
Fund, Jan. 1883, p. 53).   It is impossible

great probability attaches, if not to the exact spot, yet to the locality,
or rather the valley, that we may in imagination follow the two
companions on their road.

We leave the City by the Western Gate. A rapid progress for
about twenty-five minutes, and we have reached the edge of the
plateau. The blood-stained City, and the cloud-and-gloom-capped
trysting-place of the followers of Jesus, are behind us; and with
every step forward and upward the air seems fresher and freer, as if
we felt in it the scent of mountain, or even the far-off breezes of the
sea. Other twenty-five or thirty minutes—perhaps a little more,
passing here and there country-houses—and we pause to look back,
now on the wide prospect far as Bethlehem. Again we pursue our
way. We are now getting beyond the dreary, rocky region, and are
entering on a valley. To our right is the pleasant spot that marks
the ancient *Nephtoah*,[a] on the border of Judah, now occupied by the   [a] Josh. xv.
village of *Lifta*. A short quarter of an hour more, and we have
left the well-paved Roman road and are heading up a lovely valley.
The path gently climbs in a north-westerly direction, with the height
on which Emmaus stands prominently before us. About equidistant
are, on the right Lifta, on the left Kolonieh. The roads from these
two, describing almost a semicircle (the one to the north-west, the
other to the north-east), meet about a quarter of a mile to the south
of Emmaus (Hammoza, Beit Mizza). What an oasis this in a region
of hills! Along the course of the stream, which babbles down, and
low in the valley is crossed by a bridge, are scented orange- and
lemon-gardens, olive-groves, luscious fruit trees, pleasant enclosures,
shady nooks, bright dwellings, and on the height lovely Emmaus.

here to enter into the various reasons urged by the talented and accomplished proposer of this identification. Suffice it, in refutation, to note, that, *admittedly*, there were 'no natural hot-baths,' or thermal springs, here, only 'artificial Roman baths,' such as, no doubt, in many other places, and that 'this Emmaus was Emmaus *only* at the particular period when they (St. Luke and *Josephus*) were writing' (u. s. p. 62). There now only remain two localities, the modern *Kolonieh* and *Kubeibeh*—for the strange proposed identification by Lieut. *Conder* in the Quarterly Rep. of the Pal. Explor. Fund, Oct. 1876 (pp. 172–175) seems now abandoned even by its author. *Kolonieh* would, of course, represent the *Colonia* of *Josephus*, according to the Talmud = Emmaus. But this is only 45 furlongs from Jerusalem. But at the head of the same valley, in the Wady Buwai, and at a distance of about three miles north, is Kubeibeh, the Emmaus of the Crusaders, just sixty furlongs from Jerusalem. Between these places is *Beit Mizza*, or *Hammoza*, which I regard as the real Emmaus. It would be nearly 55 or 'about 60 furlongs' (St. Luke)—sufficiently near to *Kolonieh* (Colonia) to account for the name, since the 'colony' would extend up the valley, and sufficiently near to *Kubeibeh* to account for the tradition. The Palestine Exploration Fund has now apparently fixed on *Kubeibeh* as the site (see Q. Report, July, 1881, p. 237, and their N.T. map.

A sweet spot to which to wander on that spring afternoon;[1] a most suitable place where to meet such companionship, and to find such teaching, as on that Easter Day.

It may have been where the two roads from Lifta and Kolonieh meet, that the mysterious Stranger, Whom they knew not, their eyes being 'holden,' joined the two friends. Yet all these six or seven miles[2] their converse had been of Him, and even now their flushed faces bore the marks of sadness[3] on account of those events of which they had been speaking—disappointed hopes, all the more bitter for the perplexing tidings about the empty Tomb and the absent Body of the Christ. So is Christ often near to us when our eyes are holden, and we know Him not; and so do ignorance and unbelief often fill our hearts with sadness, even when truest joy would most become us. To the question of the Stranger about the topics of a conversation which had so visibly affected them,[4] they replied in language which shows that they were so absorbed by it themselves, as scarcely to understand how even a festive pilgrim and stranger in Jerusalem could have failed to know it, or perceive its supreme importance. Yet, strangely unsympathetic as from His question He might seem, there was that in His Appearance which unlocked their inmost hearts. They told Him their thoughts about this Jesus; how He had showed Himself a Prophet mighty in deed and word before God and all the people;[5] then, how their rulers had crucified Him; and, lastly, how fresh perplexity had come to them from the tidings which the women had brought, and which Peter and John had so far confirmed, but were unable to explain. Their words were almost childlike in their simplicity, deeply truthful, and with a pathos and earnest craving for guidance and comfort that goes straight to the heart. To such souls it was, that the Risen Saviour would give His first teaching. The very rebuke with which He opened it must have brought its comfort. We also, in our weakness, are sometimes sore distrest when we hear what, at the moment, seem to us insuperable

---

[1] Even to this day this seems a favourite resort of the inhabitants of Jerusalem for an afternoon (comp. *Conder's* Tent-Work in Palestine, i. pp. 25-27).

[2] 60 furlongs about = 7½ miles.

[3] I cannot persuade myself that the right reading of the close of ver. 17 (St. Luke xxiv.) can be 'And they stood still, looking sad.' Every reader will mark this as an incongruous, jejune 'break-up in the vivid narrative, quite

unlike the rest. We can understand the question as in our A.V., but scarcely the standing-still and looking sad on the question as in the R.V.

[4] Without this last clause we could hardly understand how a stranger would accost them, and ask the subject of their conversation.

[5] *Meyer's* rendering of ὃς ἐγένετο in ver. 19 as implying: se præstitit, se præbuit, is more correct than the 'which was' of both the A.V. and R.V.

difficulties raised to any of the great truths of our holy faith; and, in perhaps equal weakness, feel comforted and strengthened, when some 'great one' turns them aside, or avows himself in face of them a believing disciple of Christ. As if man's puny height could reach up to heaven's mysteries, or any big infant's strength were needed to steady the building which God has reared on that great Corner-stone! But Christ's rebuke was not of such kind. Their sorrow arose from their folly in looking only at the things seen, and this, from their slowness to believe what the prophets had spoken. Had they attended to this, instead of allowing themselves to be swallowed up by the outward, they would have understood it all. Did not the Scriptures with one voice teach this twofold truth about the Mes-siah, that He was to suffer and to enter into His glory? Then why wonder—why not rather expect, that He had suffered, and that Angels had proclaimed Him alive again?

He spake it, and fresh hope sprang up in their hearts, new thoughts rose in their minds. Their eager gaze was fastened on Him as He now opened up, one by one, the Scriptures, from Moses and all the prophets, and in each well-remembered passage interpreted to them the things concerning Himself. Oh, that we had been there to hear —though in the silence of our hearts also, if only we crave for it, and if we walk with Him, He sometimes so opens from the Scriptures —nay, from all the Scriptures, that which comes not to us by critical study: 'the things concerning Himself.' All too quickly fled the moments. The brief space was traversed, and the Stranger seemed about to pass on from Emmaus—not feigning it, but really: for, the Christ will only abide with us if our longing and loving con-strain Him. But they could not part with Him. 'They constrained Him.' Love made them ingenious. It was toward evening; the day was far spent; He must even abide with them. What a rush of thought and feeling comes to us, as we think of it all, and try to realise times, scenes, circumstances in our experience, that are blessedly akin to it.

The Master allowed Himself to be constrained. He went in to be their guest, as they thought, for the night. The simple evening-meal was spread. He sat down with them to the frugal board. And now He was no longer the Stranger; He was the Master. No one asked, or questioned, as He took the bread and spake the words of blessing, then, breaking, gave it to them. But that moment it was, as if an unfelt Hand had been taken from their eyelids, as if suddenly the film had been cleared from their sight. And as they knew Him, He vanished from their view—for, that which He had come to do had been done. They were unspeakably rich and happy now. But, amidst it all, one thing forced itself ever anew upon them, that, even while their eyes had yet been holden, their hearts had burned within them, while He spake to them and opened to them the Scriptures. So, then, they had learned to the full the Resurrection-lesson—not only that He was risen indeed, but that it needed not His seen Bodily Presence, if only He opened up to the heart and mind all the Scriptures concerning Himself. And this, concerning those other words about 'holding' and 'touching' Him—about having converse and fellowship with Him as the Risen One, had been also the lesson taught the Magdalene, when He would not suffer her loving, worshipful touch, pointing her to the Ascension before Him. This is the great lesson concerning the Risen One, which the Church fully learned in the Day of Pentecost.

6. That same afternoon, in circumstances and manner to us unknown, the Lord had appeared to Peter.[a] We may perhaps suggest, that it was *after* His manifestation at Emmaus. This would complete the cycle of mercy: first, to the loving sorrow of the woman; next, to the loving perplexity of the disciples; then, to the anxious heart of the stricken Peter—last, in the circle of the Apostles, which was again drawing together around the assured fact of His Resurrection.

7. These two in Emmaus could not have kept the good tidings to themselves. Even if they had not remembered the sorrow and perplexity in which they had left their fellow-disciples in Jerusalem that forenoon, they could not have kept it to themselves, could not have remained in Emmaus, but must have gone to their brethren in the City. So they left the uneaten meal, and hastened back the road they had travelled with the now well-known Stranger—but, ah, with what lighter hearts and steps!

They knew well the trysting-place where to find 'the Twelve'— nay, not the Twelve now, but 'the Eleven'—and even thus their circle was not complete, for, as already stated, it was broken up, and at least Thomas was not with the others on that Easter-Evening of the first 'Lord's Day.' But, as St. Luke is careful to inform us,[b] with them were the others who then associated with them. This is of extreme importance, as marking that the words which the Risen Christ spake on that occasion were addressed not to the Apostles as such—a thought forbidden also by the absence of Thomas—but to the Church, although it may be as personified and represented by such of the 'Twelve,' or rather 'Eleven,' as were present on the occasion.

When the two from Emmaus arrived, they found the little band
as sheep sheltering within the fold from the storm. Whether they
apprehended persecution simply as disciples, or because the tidings
of the empty Tomb, which had reached the authorities, would stir
the fears of the Sanhedrists, special precautions had been taken.
The outer and inner doors were shut, alike to conceal their gathering and to prevent surprise. But those assembled were now sure
of at least one thing. Christ *was* risen. And when they from
Emmaus told their wondrous story, the others could antiphonally
reply by relating how He had appeared, not only to the Magdalene,
but also to Peter. And still they seem not yet to have understood His Resurrection; to have regarded it as rather an Ascension
to Heaven, from which He had made manifestation, than as the
reappearance of His real, though glorified Corporeity.

They were sitting at meat [a]—if we may infer from the notice of ^a St. Mark
St. Mark, and from what happened immediately afterwards, discussing, xvi. 14
not without considerable doubt and misgiving, the real import of these
appearances of Christ. That to the Magdalene seems to have been
put aside—at least, it is not mentioned, and, even in regard to the
others, they seem to have been considered, at any rate by some,
rather as what we might call spectral appearances. But all at once
He stood in the midst of them. The common salutation—on His
Lips not common, but a reality—fell on their hearts at first with
terror rather than joy. They had spoken of spectral appearances,
and now they believed they were ' gazing ' ($\theta\epsilon\omega\rho\epsilon\tilde{\iota}\nu$) on ' a spirit.'
This the Saviour first, and once for all, corrected, by the exhibition
of the glorified marks of His Sacred Wounds, and by bidding them
handle Him to convince themselves, that His was a real Body, and
what they saw not a disembodied spirit.[1] The unbelief of doubt now
gave place to the not daring to believe all that it meant, for very
gladness, and for wondering whether there could now be any longer
fellowship or bond between this Risen Christ and them in their
bodies. It was to remove this also, which, though from another
aspect, was equally unbelief, that the Saviour now partook before
them of their supper of broiled fish,[2] thus holding with them true
human fellowship as of old.[3]

---

[1] I cannot understand why Canon
Cook (' Speaker's Commentary' ad loc.)
regards St. Luke xxiv. 39 as belonging
' to the appearance on the octave of the
Resurrection.' It appears to me, on the
contrary, to be strictly parallel to St.
John xx. 20.

[2] The words ' and a honeycomb ' seem
spurious.
[3] Such seems to me the meaning of His
eating; any attempt at explaining, we
willingly forego in our ignorance of the
conditions of a glorified body, just as we
refuse to discuss the manner in which

BOOK
V

It was this lesson of His continuity—in the strictest sense—with the past, which was required in order that the Church might be, so to speak, reconstituted now in the Name, Power, and Spirit of the Risen One Who had lived and died. Once more He spake the 'Peace be unto you!' and now it was to them not occasion of doubt or fear, but the well-known salutation of their old Lord and Master. It was followed by the re-gathering and constituting of the Church as that of Jesus Christ, the Risen One. The Church of the Risen One was to be the Ambassador of Christ, as He had been the Delegate of the Father. 'The Apostles were [say rather, 'the Church was'] commissioned to carry on Christ's work, and not to begin a new one.'[1] 'As the Father has sent Me [in the past, for His Mission was completed], even so send [2] I you [in the constant present, till His Coming again].' This marks the threefold relation of the Church to the Son, to the Father, and to the world, and her position in it. In the same manner, for the same purpose, nay, so far as possible, with the same qualification and the same authority as the Father had sent Christ, does He commission His Church. And so it was that He made it a very real commission when He breathed on them, not individually but as an assembly, and said: 'Take ye the [3] Holy Ghost;' and this, manifestly not in the absolute sense, since the Holy Ghost was not yet given,[4] but as the connecting link with, and the qualification for, the authority bestowed on the Church. Or, to set forth another aspect of it by somewhat inverting the order of the words: Alike the Mission of the Church and her authority to forgive or retain sins are connected with a personal qualification: 'Take ye the Holy Ghost;'—in which the word 'take' should also be marked. This is the authority which the Church possesses, not *ex opere operato*, but as connected with the taking and the indwelling of the Holy Ghost in the Church.

He suddenly appeared in the room while the doors were shut. But I at least cannot believe, that His body was then in a 'transition state,' not perfected nor quite glorified till His Ascension.

[1] *Westcott.*

[2] The words in the two clauses are different in regard to the sending of Christ (ἀπέσταλκέν με) and in regard to the Church (πέμπω ὑμᾶς). No doubt, there must be deeper meaning in this distinction, yet both are used alike of Christ and of the disciples. It may be as *Cremer* seems to hint (Bibl. Theol. Lex. of the N.T. p. 529) that ἀποστέλλω, from which 'apostle' and 'apostolate' are derived, refers to a mission with a definite commission, or rather for a defi-

nite purpose, while πέμπω is sending in a general sense. See the learned and ingenious Note of Canon *Westcott* (Comm. on St. John, p. 298).

[3] In the original the definite article is omitted. But this, though significant, can surely not be supposed to prove that the expression is equivalent to 'a gift of the Holy Ghost.' For, as *Meyer* has pointed out, the word is used in other passages without the article, where the Holy Ghost is referred to (comp. St. John i. 33; vii. 39; Acts i. 2, 5).

[4] This alone would suffice to show what misinterpretation is sometimes made, by friend and foe, of the use of these words in the English Ordinal.

It still remains to explain, so far as we can, these two points: in what this power of forgiving and retaining sins consists, and in what manner it resides in the Church. In regard to the former we must first inquire what idea it would convey to those to whom Christ spake the words. It has already been explained,[a] that the power of 'loosing' and 'binding' referred to the legislative authority claimed by, and conceded to, the Rabbinic College. Similarly, as previously stated, that here referred to applied to their juridical or judicial power, according to which they pronounced a person either 'Zakkai,' innocent or 'free'; 'absolved,' 'Patur'; or else 'liable,' 'guilty,' 'Chayyabh' (whether liable to punishment or sacrifice). In the true sense, therefore, this is rather administrative, disciplinary power, 'the power of the keys'—such as St. Paul would have had the Corinthian Church put in force—the power of admission and exclusion, of the authoritative declaration of the forgiveness of sins, in the exercise of which power (as it seems to the present writer) the authority for the administration of the Holy Sacraments is also involved. And yet it is not, as is sometimes represented, 'absolution from sin,' which belongs only to God and to Christ as Head of the Church, but absolution of the sinner, which He has delegated to His Church: 'Whosoever sins ye forgive, they are forgiven.' These words also teach us, that what the Rabbis claimed in virtue of their office, that the Lord bestowed on His Church in virtue of her receiving, and of the indwelling of, the Holy Ghost.

In answering the second question proposed, we must bear in mind one important point. The power of 'binding' and 'loosing' had been primarily committed to the Apostles,[b] and exercised by them in connection with the Church.[c] On the other hand, that of forgiving and retaining sins, in the sense explained, was primarily bestowed on the Church, and exercised by her through her representatives, the Apostles, and those to whom they committed rule.[d] Although, therefore, the Lord on that night committed this power to His Church, it was in the person of her representatives and rulers. The Apostles alone could exercise legislative functions,[1] but the Church has to the end of time 'the power of the keys.'

8. There had been absent from the circle of disciples on that Easter-Evening one of the Apostles, Thomas. Even when told of the marvellous events at that gathering, he refused to believe, unless he had personal and sensuous evidence of the truth of the report.

CHAP.
XVII

[a] Book III. ch. xxxvii.

[b] St. Matt. xvi. 19; xviii. 18

[c] Acts xv. 22, 23

[d] 1 Cor. v. 4, 5, 12, 13; 2 Cor. ii. 6, 10

---

[1] The decrees of the first Councils should be regarded not as legislative, but either as disciplinary, or else as explanatory of Apostolic teaching and legislation.

It can scarcely have been, that Thomas did not believe in the fact that Christ's Body had quitted the Tomb, or that He had really appeared. But he held fast by what we may term the Vision-hypothesis, or, in this case, rather the spectral theory. But until this Apostle also had come to conviction of the Resurrection in the only real sense—of the identical though glorified Corporeity of the Lord, and hence of the continuity of the past with the present and future, it was impossible to re-form the Apostolic Circle, or to renew the Apostolic commission, since its primal message was testimony concerning the Risen One. This, if we may so suggest, seems the reason why the Apostles still remained in Jerusalem, instead of hastening, as directed, to meet the Master in Galilee.

A quiet week had passed, during which—and this also may be for our twofold learning—the Apostles excluded not Thomas,[1] nor yet Thomas withdrew from the Apostles. Once more the day of days had come—the Octave of the Feast. From that Easter-Day onwards the Church must, even without special institution, have celebrated the weekly-recurring memorial of His Resurrection, as that when He breathed on the Church the breath of a new life, and consecrated it to be His Representative. Thus, it was not only the memorial of His Resurrection, but the birthday of the Church, even as Pentecost was her baptismal day. On that Octave, then, the disciples were again gathered, under circumstances precisely similar to those of Easter, but now Thomas was also with them. Once more— and it is again specially marked : ' the doors being shut '[2]—the Risen Saviour appeared in the midst of the disciples with the well-known salutation. He now offered to Thomas the demanded evidence ; but it was no longer either needed or sought. With a full rush of feeling he yielded himself to the blessed conviction, which, once formed, must immediately have passed into act of adoration : ' My Lord and my God ! ' The fullest confession this hitherto made, and which truly embraced the whole outcome of the new conviction concerning the reality of Christ's Resurrection. We remember how, under similar circumstances, Nathanael had been the first to utter fullest confession.[a] We also remember the analogous reply of the Saviour. As then, so now, He pointed to the higher : to a faith which was not the outcome of sight, and therefore limited and bounded

a St. John
i. 45-51

---

[1] It must, however, be remembered that Thomas did not deny that Christ was risen—except as in the peculiar sense of the Resurrection. Had he denied the other, he would scarcely have continued in the company of the Apostles.

[2] Significantly, the expression ' for fear of the Jews ' no longer occurs. That apprehension had for the present passed away.

by sight, whether of the senses or of perception by the intellect. As one has finely remarked: 'This last and greatest of the Beatitudes is the peculiar heritage of the later Church'[1]—and thus most aptly comes as the consecration gift of that Church.

CHAP.
XVII

9. The next scene presented to us is once again by the Lake of Galilee. The manifestation to Thomas, and, with it, the restoration of unity in the Apostolic Circle, had originally concluded the Gospel of St. John.[a] But the report which had spread in the early Church, that the Disciple whom Jesus loved was not to die, led him to add to his Gospel, by way of Appendix, an account of the events with which this expectancy had connected itself. It is most instructive to the critic, when challenged at every step to explain why one or another fact is not mentioned or mentioned only in one Gospel, to find that, but for the correction of a possible misapprehension in regard to the aged Apostle, the Fourth Gospel would have contained no reference to the manifestation of Christ in Galilee, nay, to the presence of the disciples there before the Ascension. Yet, for all that, St. John had it in his mind. And should we not learn from this, that what appear to us strange omissions, which, when held by the side of the other Gospel-narratives, seem to involve discrepancies, may be capable of the most satisfactory explanation, if we only knew all the circumstances?

[a] St. John xx. 30, 31

The history itself sparkles like a gem in its own peculiar setting. It is of green Galilee, and of the blue Lake, and recalls the early days and scenes of this history. As St. Matthew has it,[b] 'the eleven disciples went away into Galilee'—probably immediately after that Octave of the Easter.[2] It can scarcely be doubted, that they made known not only the fact of the Resurrection, but the trysting which the Risen One had given them—perhaps at that Mountain where He had spoken His first 'Sermon.' And so it was, that 'some doubted,'[c] and that He afterwards appeared to the five hundred at once.[d] But on that morning there were by the Lake of Tiberias only seven of the disciples. Five of them only are named. They are those who most closely kept in company with Him—perhaps also they who lived nearest the Lake.

[b] St. Matt. xxviii. 16

[c] St. Matt xxviii. 17
[d] 1 Cor. xv 6

The scene is introduced by Peter's proposal to go a-fishing. It seems as if the old habits had come back to them with the old associations. Peter's companions naturally proposed to join him.[3]

[1] Canon *Westcott*.
[2] The account of St. Luke (xxiv. 44–48) is a condensed narrative—without distinction of time or place—of what occurred during all the forty days.
[3] The word 'immediately' in St. John xxi. 3 is spurious.

All that still, clear night they were on the Lake, but caught nothing. Did not this recall to them the former event, when James and John, and Peter and Andrew were called to be Apostles, and did it not specially recall to Peter the searching and sounding of his heart on the morning that followed? ª   But so utterly self-unconscious were they, and, let us add, so far is this history from any trace of legendary design,[1] that not the slightest indication of this appears. Early morning was breaking, and under the rosy glow above the cool shadows were still lying on the pebbly ' beach.'   There stood the Figure of One Whom they recognised not—nay, not even when He spake.   Yet His Words were intended to bring them this knowledge.   The direction to cast the net to the right side of the ship brought them, as He had said, the haul for which they had toiled all night in vain.   And more than this: such a multitude of fishes, that they were not able to draw up the net into the ship.   This was enough for ' the disciple whom Jesus loved,' and whose heart may previously have misgiven him.   He whispered it to Peter: ' It is the Lord,' and Simon, only reverently gathering about him his fisher's upper garment,[2] cast himself into the sea.   Yet even so, except to be sooner by the side of Christ, Peter seems to have gained nothing by his haste.   The others, leaving the ship, and transferring themselves to a small boat, which must have been attached to it, followed, rowing the short distance of about one hundred yards,[3] and dragging after them the net, weighted with the fishes.

They stepped on the beach, hallowed by His Presence, in silence, as if they had entered Church or Temple.   They dared not even dispose of the netful of fishes which they had dragged on shore, until He directed them what to do.   This only they noticed, that some unseen hand had prepared the morning meal, which, when asked by the Master, they had admitted they had not of their own. And now Jesus directed them to bring the fish they had caught. When Peter dragged up the weighted net, it was found full of great fishes, not less than a hundred and fifty-three in number.   There is no need to attach any symbolic import to that number, as the Fathers and later writers have done.   We can quite understand—nay, it seems almost natural, that, in the peculiar circumstances, they should have counted the large fishes in that miraculous draught that still

---

[1] Yet St. John must have been acquainted with this narrative, recorded as it is by all the three Synoptists.
[2] This notice also seems specially in-

dicative that the narrator is himself from the Lake of Galilee.
[3] About 200 cubits.

left the net unbroken.[1] It may have been, that they were told to
count the fishes—partly, also, to show the reality of what had taken
place. But on the fire of coals there seems to have been only one
fish, and beside it only one bread.[2] To this meal He now bade them,
for they seem still to have hung back in reverent awe, nor durst they
ask Him, Who He was, well knowing it was the Lord. This, as
St. John notes, was the third appearance of Christ to the disciples as
a body.[3]

10. And still this morning of blessing was not ended. The
frugal meal was past, with all its significant teaching of just sufficient
provision for His Servants, and abundant supply in the unbroken net
beside them. But some special teaching was needed, more even
than that to Thomas, for him whose work was to be so prominent
among the Apostles, whose love was so ardent, and yet in its very
ardour so full of danger to himself. For, our dangers spring not
only from deficiency, but it may be from excess of feeling, when that
feeling is not commensurate with inward strength. Had Peter not
confessed, quite honestly, yet, as the event proved, mistakingly, that
his love to Christ would endure even an ordeal that would disperse
all the others?[a] And had he not, almost immediately afterwards,
and though prophetically warned of it, thrice denied his Lord?
Jesus had, indeed, since then appeared specially to Peter as the
Risen One. But this threefold denial still stood, as it were, uncan-
celled before the other disciples, nay, before Peter himself. It was to
this that the threefold question of the Risen Lord now referred.
Turning to Peter, with pointed though most gentle allusion to the
danger of self-confidence—a confidence springing from only a sense
of personal affection, even though genuine—He asked: 'Simon, son
of Jona'—as it were with fullest reference to what he was naturally
—'lovest thou Me more than these?' Peter understood it all. No
longer with confidence in self, avoiding the former reference to the
others, and even with marked choice of a different word to express
his affection[4] from that which the Saviour had used, he replied, appealing rather to his Lord's, than to his own consciousness: 'Yea,
Lord, Thou knowest that I love Thee.' And even here the answer of

[a] St. Matt.
xxvi. 33;
St. John
xiii. 37

---

[1] Canon *Westcott* gives, from St.
Augustine, the points of difference be-
tween this and the miraculous draught
of fishes on the former occasion (St.
Luke v.). These are very interesting.
Not so the fanciful speculations of the
Fathers about the symbolic meaning of
the number 153.

[2] This seems implied in the absence of
the article in St. John xxi. 9.
[3] St. John could not have meant His
third appearance in general, since himself had recorded three previous manifestations.
[4] Christ asks: $\dot{\alpha}\gamma\alpha\pi\tilde{\alpha}\varsigma$ $\mu\varepsilon$, and Peter
answers: $\sigma\grave{v}$ $o\tilde{i}\delta\alpha\varsigma$ $\ddot{o}\tau\iota$ $\phi\lambda\tilde{\omega}$ $\sigma\varepsilon$.

Christ is characteristic. It was to set him first the humblest work,
that which needed most tender care and patience: ' Feed [provide with
food] My Lambs.'

Yet a second time came the same question, although now without
the reference to the others, and, with the same answer by Peter, the
now varied and enlarged commission: ' Feed [shepherd, ποίμαινε] My
Sheep.' Yet a third time did Jesus repeat the same question, now
adopting in it the very word which Peter had used to express his
affection. Peter was grieved at this threefold repetition. It recalled
only too bitterly his threefold denial. And yet the Lord was not
doubtful of Peter's love, for each time He followed up His question
with a fresh Apostolic commission; but now that He put it for the
third time, Peter would have the Lord send down the sounding-line
quite into the lowest deep of his heart: ' Lord, Thou knowest all
things—Thou perceivest [1] that I love Thee!' And now the Saviour
spake it: ' Feed [provide food for] My Sheep.' His Lambs, His
Sheep, to be provided for, to be tended as such! And only love can
do such service.

Yes, and Peter did love the Lord Jesus. He had loved Him when
he said it, only too confident in the strength of his feelings, that he
would follow the Master even unto death. And Jesus saw it all—
yea, and how this love of the ardent temperament which had once
made him rove at wild liberty, would give place to patient work of
love, and be crowned with that martyrdom which, when the beloved
disciple wrote, was already matter of the past. And the very
manner of death by which he was to glorify God was indicated in
the words of Jesus.

As He spake them, He joined the symbolic action to His ' Follow
Me.' This command, and the encouragement of being in death
literally made like Him—following Him—were Peter's best strength.
He obeyed; but as he turned to do so, he saw another following.
As St. John himself puts it, it seems almost to convey that he had
longed to share Peter's call, with all that it implied. For, St. John
speaks of himself as the disciple whom Jesus loved, and he reminds us
that in that night of betrayal he had been specially a sharer with
Peter, nay, had spoken what the other had silently asked of him. Was
it impatience, was it a touch of the old Peter, or was it a simple
inquiry of brotherly interest which prompted the question, as he
pointed to John: ' Lord—and this man, what?' Whatever had
been the motive, to him, as to us all, when, perplexed about those

[1] γινώσκεις.

who seem to follow Christ, we ask it—sometimes in bigoted narrowness, sometimes in ignorance, folly, or jealousy—is this the answer: 'What is that to thee? follow thou Me.' For John also had his lifework for Christ. It was to 'tarry' while He was coming [1]—to tarry those many years in patient labour, while Christ was coming.

But what did it mean? The saying went abroad among the brethren that John was not to die, but to tarry till Jesus came again to reign, when death would be swallowed up in victory. But Jesus had not so said, only: 'If I will that he tarry while I am coming.' What that 'Coming' was, Jesus had not said, and John knew not. So, then, there are things, and connected with His Coming, on which Jesus has left the veil, only to be lifted by His own Hand—which He means us not to know at present, and which we should be content to leave as He has left them.

11. Beyond this narrative we have only briefest notices: by St. Paul, of Christ manifesting Himself to James, which probably finally decided him for Christ, and of His manifestation to the five hundred at once; by St. Matthew, of the Eleven meeting Him at the mountain, where He had appointed them; by St. Luke, of the teaching in the Scriptures during the forty days of communication between the Risen Christ and the disciples.

But this twofold testimony comes to us from St. Matthew and St. Mark, that then the worshipping disciples were once more formed into the Apostolic Circle—Apostles, now, of the Risen Christ. And this was the warrant of their new commission: 'All power (authority) has been given to Me in heaven and on earth.' And this was their new commission: 'Go ye, therefore, and make disciples of all the nations, baptizing them into the Name of the Father, and of the Son, and of the Holy Ghost.' And this was their work: 'Teaching them to observe all things whatsoever I commanded you.' And this is His final and sure promise: 'And lo, I am with you alway, even unto the end of the world.'

12. We are once more in Jerusalem, whither He had bidden them go to tarry for the fulfilment of the great promise. The Pentecost was drawing nigh. And on that last day—the day of His Ascension—He led them forth to the well-remembered Bethany. From where He had made His last triumphal Entry into Jerusalem before His Crucifixion, would He make His triumphant Entry visibly into

---

[1] So Canon *Westcott* renders the meaning. The 'coming' might refer to the second Coming, to the destruction of Jerusalem, or even to the firm establishment of the Church. The tradition that St. John only slept in his grave at Ephesus is mentioned even by St. *Augustine*.

Heaven. Once more would they have asked Him about that which seemed to them the final consummation—the restoration of the Kingdom to Israel. But such questions became them not. Theirs was to be work, not rest; suffering, not triumph. The great promise before them was of spiritual, not outward, power: of the Holy Ghost —and their call not yet to reign with Him, but to bear witness for Him. And, as He so spake, He lifted His Hands in blessing upon them, and, as He was visibly taken up, a cloud received Him. And still they gazed, with upturned faces, on that luminous cloud which had received Him, and two Angels spake to them this last message from Him, that He should so come in like manner—as they had beheld Him going into heaven.

And so their last question to Him, ere He had parted from them, was also answered, and with blessed assurance. Reverently they worshipped Him; then, with great joy, returned to Jerusalem. So it was all true, all real—and Christ 'sat down at the Right Hand of God!' Henceforth, neither doubting, ashamed, nor yet afraid, they 'were continually in the Temple, blessing God.' 'And they went forth and preached everywhere, the Lord working with them, and confirming the word by the signs that followed. Amen.'

Amen! It is so. Ring out the bells of heaven; sing forth the Angelic welcome of worship; carry it to the utmost bounds of earth! Shine forth from Bethany, Thou Sun of Righteousness, and chase away earth's mist and darkness, for Heaven's golden day has broken!

.   .   .   .

Easter Morning, 1883.—Our task is ended—and we also worship and look up. And we go back from this sight into a hostile world, to love, and to live, and to work for the Risen Christ. But as earth's day is growing dim, and, with earth's gathering darkness, breaks over it heaven's storm, we ring out—as of old they were wont, from church-tower, to the mariners that hugged a rock-bound coast—our Easter-bells to guide them who are belated, over the storm-tossed sea, beyond the breakers, into the desired haven. Ring out, earth, all thy Easter-chimes; bring your offerings, all ye people; worship in faith, for—

'This Jesus, Which was received up from you into heaven, shall so come, in like manner as ye beheld Him going into heaven.' 'Even so, Lord Jesus, come quickly!'

APPENDICES.

APPENDIX I.

PSEUDEPIGRAPHIC WRITINGS.

(See vol. i. pp. 37, 38, and other places.)

ONLY the briefest account of these can be given in this place; barely more than an enumeration.

I. *The Book of Enoch.*—As the contents and the literature of this remarkable book, which is quoted by St. Jude (vv. 14, 15), have been fully described in Dr. *Smith's* and *Wace's* Dictionary of Christian Biography (vol. ii. pp. 124–128), we may here refer to it the more shortly.

It comes to us from Palestine, but has only been preserved in an Ethiopic translation (published by Archbishop *Laurence* [Oxford, 1838; in English transl. 3rd ed. 1821–1838; German transl. by *A. G. Hoffmann*], then from five different MSS. by Professor *Dillmann* [Leipzig, 1851; in German transl. Leipzig, 1853]). But even the Ethiopic translation is not from the original Hebrew or Aramaic, but from a Greek version, of which a small fragment has been discovered (ch. lxxxix. 42–49; published by Cardinal *Mai.* Comp. also *Gildemeister*, Zeitschr. d. D. Morg. Ges. for 1855, pp. 621–624, and *Gebhardt*, Merx' Arch. ii. 1872, p. 243).

As regards the contents of the work: An Introduction of five brief chapters, and the book (which, however, contains not a few spurious passages) consists of five parts, followed by a suitable Epilogue. The most interesting portions are those which tell of the Fall of the Angels and its consequences, of Enoch's rapt journeys through heaven and earth, and of what he saw and heard (ch. vi.–xxxvi.); the Apocalyptic portions about the Kingdom of Heaven and the Advent of the Messiah (lxxxiii.–xci.); and, lastly, the hortatory discourses (xci.–cv.). When we add, that it is pervaded by a tone of intense faith and earnestness about the Messiah, 'the last things,' and other doctrines specially brought out in the New Testament, its importance will be understood. Altogether the Book of Enoch contains 108 chapters.

From a literary point of view, it has been arranged (by *Schürer* and others) into *three parts*:—1. *The Original Work* (*Grundschrift*), ch. i.–xxxvi.; lxxii.–cv. This portion is supposed to date from about 175 B.C. 2. *The Parables*, ch. xxxvii.–liv. 6; lv. 3–lix.; lxi.–lxiv.; lxix. 26–lxxi. This part also dates previous to the Birth of Christ—perhaps from the time of Herod the Great. 3. *The so-called Noachian Sections*, ch. liv. 7–lv. 2; lx.; lxv.–lxix. 25. To these must be added ch. cvi., cvii., and the later conclusion in ch. cviii. On the dates of all these portions it is impossible to speak definitely.

II. Even greater, though a different interest, attaches to the *Sibylline Oracles*, written in Greek hexameters.[1] In their present form they consist of twelve books,

---

[1] We have in the main accepted the learned criticism of Professor *Friedlieb* (Oracula Sibyllina, 1852.

together with several fragments. Passing over two large fragments, which seem to have originally formed the chief part of the introduction to Book III., we have (1) the two first Books. These contain part of an older and Hellenist Jewish Sibyl, as well as of a poem by the Jewish Pseudo-Phocylides, in which heathen myths concerning the first ages of man are curiously welded with Old Testament views. The rest of these two books was composed, and the whole put together, not earlier than the close of the second century, perhaps by a Jewish Christian. (2) The third Book is by far the most interesting. Besides the fragments already referred to, vv. 97–807 are the work of a Hellenist Jew, deeply imbued with the Messianic hope. This part dates from about 160 before our era, while vv. 49–96 seem to belong to the year 31 B.C. The rest (vv. 1–45, 818–828) dates from a later period. We must here confine our attention to the most ancient portion of the work. For our present purpose, we may arrange it into three parts. In the first, the ancient heathen theogony is recast in a Jewish mould—Uranus becomes Noah; Shem, Ham, and Japheth are Saturn, Titan, and Japetus, while the building of the Tower of Babylon is the rebellion of the Titans. Then the history of the world is told, the Kingdom of Israel and of David forming the centre of all. What we have called the second is the most curious part of the work. It embodies ancient heathen oracles, so to speak, in a Jewish recension, and interwoven with Jewish elements. The third part may be generally described as anti-heathen, polemical, and Apocalyptic. The Sibyl is thoroughly Hellenistic in spirit. She is loud and earnest in her appeals, bold and defiant in the tone of her Jewish pride, self-conscious and triumphant in her anticipations. But the most remarkable circumstance is, that this Judaising and Jewish Sibyl seems to have passed—though possibly only in parts—as the oracles of the ancient Erythræan Sibyl, which had predicted to the Greeks the fall of Troy, and those of the Sibyl of Cumæ, which, in the infancy of Rome, Tarquinius Superbus had deposited in the Capitol, and that as such it is quoted from by Virgil (in his 4th Eclogue) in his description of the Golden Age.

Of the other Sibylline Books little need be said. The 4th, 5th, 9th, and 12th Books were written by Egyptian Jews at dates varying from the year 80 to the third century of our era. Book VI. is of Christian origin, the work of a Judaising Christian, about the second half of the second century. Book VIII., which embodies Jewish portions, is also of Christian authorship, and so are Books X. and XI.

III. The collection of eighteen hymns, which in their Greek version bear the name of *the Psalter of Solomon*, must originally have been written in Hebrew, and dates from more than half a century before our era. They are the outcome of a soul intensely earnest, although we not unfrequently meet expressions of Pharisaic self-righteousness.[1] It is a time of national sorrow in which the poet sings, and it almost seems as if these 'Psalms' had been intended to take up one or another of the leading thoughts in the corresponding Davidic Psalms, and to make, as it were, application of them to the existing circumstances.[2] Though somewhat Hellenistic in its cast, the collection breathes ardent Messianic expectancy, and firm faith in the resurrection, and eternal reward and punishment (iii. 16; xiii. 9, 10; xiv. 2, 6, 7; xv. 11 to the end).

IV. Another work of that class—'*Little Genesis*,' or '*The Book of Jubilees*'—

---

[1] Comp. for example, ix. 7, 9.
[2] This view which, so far as I know, has not been suggested by critics, will be confirmed by an attentive perusal of almost every 'Psalm' in the collection (comp. the first three with the three opening Psalms in the Davidic Psalter). Is our 'Psalter of Solomon,' as it were, an historical commentary by the typical 'sage?' And is our collection only a fragment?

has been preserved to us in its Ethiopic translation (though a Latin version of part of it has lately been discovered) and is a Haggadic Commentary on Genesis. Professing to be a revelation to Moses during the forty days on Mount Sinai, it seeks to fill *lacunæ* in the sacred history, specially in reference to its chronology. Its character is hortatory and warning, and it breathes a strong anti-Roman spirit. It was written by a Palestinian in Hebrew, or rather Aramæan, probably about the time of Christ. The name, ' Book of Jubilees,' is derived from the circumstance that the Scripture-chronology is arranged according to Jubilee periods of forty-nine years, fifty of these (or 2,450 years) being counted from the Creation to the entrance into Canaan.

V. Among the Pseudepigraphic Writings we also include the *4th Book of Esdras,* which appears among our Apocrypha as 2 Esdras ch. iii.–xiv. (the two first and the two last chapters being spurious additions). The work, originally written in Greek, has only been preserved in translation into five different languages (Latin, Arabic, Syriac, Ethiopic, and Armenian). It was composed probably about the end of the first century after Christ. From this circumstance, and the influence of Christianity on the mind of the writer, who, however, is an earnest Jew, its interest and importance can be scarcely exaggerated. The name of Ezra was probably assumed, because the writer wished to treat mainly of the mystery of Israel's fall and restoration.

The other Pseudepigraphic Writings are:—

VI. *The Ascension* (ch. i.–v.) *and Vision* (ch. vi.–xi.) *of Isaiah,* which describes the martyrdom of the prophet (with a Christian interpolation [ch. iii. 14–iv. 22] ascribing his death to prophecy of Christ, and containing Apocalyptic portions), and then what he saw in heaven. The book is probably based on an older Jewish account, but is chiefly of Christian heretical authorship. It exists only in translations, of which that in Ethiopic (with Latin and English versions) has been edited by Archbishop *Laurence.*

VII. *The Assumption of Moses* (probably quoted in St. Jude ver. 9) also exists only in translation, and is really a fragment. It consists of twelve chapters. After an Introduction (ch. i.), containing an address of Moses to Joshua, the former, professedly, opens to Joshua the future of Israel to the time of Varus. This is followed by an Apocalyptic portion, beginning at ch. vii. and ending with ch. x. The two concluding chapters are dialogues between Joshua and Moses. The book dates probably from about the year 2 B.C., or shortly afterwards. Besides the Apocalyptic portions the interest lies chiefly in the fact that the writer seems to belong to the Nationalist party, and that we gain some glimpses of the Apocalyptic views and hopes—the highest spiritual tendency—of that deeply interesting movement. Most markedly, this Book at least is strongly anti-Pharisaic, especially in its opposition to their purifications (ch. vii.). We would here specially note a remarkable resemblance between 2 Tim. iii. 1–5 and this in Assump. Mos. vii. 3–10: (3) ' Et regnabunt de his homines pestilentiosi et impii, dicentes se esse iustos, (4) et hi suscitabunt iram animorum suorum, qui erunt homines dolosi, sibi placentes, ficti in omnibus suis et omni hora diei amantes convivia, devoratores gulæ (5) . . . (6) [paupe] rum bonorum comestores, dicentes se haec facere propter misericordiam eorum, (7) sed et exterminatores, queruli et fallaces, celantes se ne possint cognosci, impii in scelere, pleni et iniquitate ab oriente usque ad occidentem, (8) dicentes: habebimus discubitiones et luxuriam edentes et bibentes, et potabimus nos, tamquam principes erimus. (9) Et manus eorum et dentes inmunda tractabunt, et os eorum loquetur ingentia, et superdicent: (10) noli [tu me] tangere, ne inquines me . . .' But it is very significant, that instead of the denunciation of the Pharisees in vv. 9, 10 of the *Assumptio*, we have in 2 Tim. iii. 5. the words 'having the form of godliness, but denying the power thereof.'

VIII. *The Apocalypse of Baruch.*—This also exists only in Syriac translation, and is apparently fragmentary, since the vision promised in ch. lxxvi. 3 is not reported, while the Epistle of Baruch to the two and a half tribes in Babylon, referred to in lxxvii. 19, is also missing. The book has been divided into seven sections (i.–xii.; xiii.–xx.; xxi.–xxxiv.; xxxv.–xlvi.; xlvii.–lii.; liii.–lxxvi.; lxxvii.– lxxxvii.). The whole is in a form of revelation to Baruch, and of his replies, and questions, or of notices about his bearing, fast, prayers, &c. The most interesting parts are in sections v. and vi. In the former we mark (ch. xlviii. 31–41) the reference to the consequence of the sin of our first parents (ver. 42; comp. also xvii. 3; xxiii. 4; liv. 15, 19), and in ch. xlix. the discussion and information: with what body and in what form the dead shall rise, which is answered, not as by St. Paul in 1 Cor. xv.—though the question raised (1 Cor. xv. 35) is precisely the same—but in the strictly Rabbinic manner, described by us in vol. ii. pp. 398, 399. In section vi. we specially mark (ch. lxix.–lxxiv.) the Apocalyptic descriptions of the Last Days, and of the Reign and Judgment of Messiah. In general, the figurative language in that Book is instructive in regard to the phraseology used in the Apocalyptic portions of the New Testament. Lastly, we mark that the views on the consequences of the Fall are much more limited than those expressed in 4 Esdras. Indeed, they do not go beyond physical death as the consequence of the sin of our first parents (see especially liv. 19: Non est ergo Adam causa, nisi animæ suæ tantum; nos vero unusquisque fuit animæ suæ Adam). At the same time, it seems to us, as if perhaps the reasoning rather than the language of the writer indicated hesitation on his part (liv. 14–19; comp. also first clause of xlviii. 43). It almost seems as if liv. 14–19 were intended as against the reasoning of St. Paul, Rom. v. 12 to the end. In this respect the passage in Baruch is most interesting, not only in itself (see for ex. ver. 16: Certo enim qui credit recipiet mercedem), but in reference to the teaching of 4 Esdras, which, as regards original sin, takes another direction than Baruch. But I have little doubt that both allude to the—to them— novel teaching of St. Paul on that doctrine. Lastly, as regards the question when this remarkable work was written, we would place its composition *after* the destruction of Jerusalem. Most writers date it before the publication of 4 Esdras, Even the appearance of a Pseudo-Baruch and Pseudo-Esdras are significant of the political circumstances and the religious hopes of the nation.

For criticism and fragments of other Old Testament Pseudepigrapha, comp. *Fabricius*, Codex Pseudepigraphus Vet. Test., 2 vols. (ed. 2, 1722). The Psalter of Sol., IV. Esdr. (or, as he puts it, IV. and V. Esd.), the Apocal of Baruch, and the Assumption of Mos., have been edited by *Fritzsche* (Lips. 1871); other Jewish (Hebrew) O. T. Pseudepigraphs—though of a later date—in *Jellinek's* Beth haMidrash (6 vols.), *passim*. A critical review of the literature of the subject would here be out of place.

APPENDIX II.

PHILO OF ALEXANDRIA AND RABBINIC THEOLOGY.

(See vol. i. pp. 42, 45, 47, 53).

(AD. vol. i. p. 42, note 4.) In comparing the allegorical Canons of Philo with those of Jewish traditionalism, we think first of all of the seven exegetical canons which are ascribed to *Hillel*. These bear chiefly the character of logical deductions, and as such were largely applied in the Halakhah. These seven canons were next expanded by *R. Ishmael* (in the first century) into thirteen, by the analysis of one of them (the 5th) into six, and the addition of this sound exegetical rule, that where two verses seem to be contradictory, their conciliation must be sought in a third passage. The real rules for the Haggadah—if such there were—were the thirty-two canons of *R. José* the Galilean (in the second century). It is here that we meet so much that is kindred in form to the allegorical canons of *Philo.*[1] Only they are not rationalising, and far more brilliant in their application. Most taking results—at least to a certain class of minds—might be reached by finding in each consonant of a word the initial letter of another (*Notariqon*). Thus, the word *MiSBeaCH* (altar) was resolved into these four words, beginning respectively with M, S, B, CH: Forgiveness, Merit, Blessing, Life. Then there was *Gematria*, by which every letter in a word was resolved into its arithmetical equivalent. Thus, the two words, Gog and Magog = 70, which was the supposed number of all the heathen nations. Again, in *Athbash* the letters of the Hebrew alphabet were transposed (the first for the last of the alphabet, and so on), so that SHeSHaKH (Jer. xxv. 26; li. 41) became *BaBeL*, while in *Albam*, the twenty-two Hebrew letters were divided into two rows, which might be exchanged (L for A, M for B, &c.).

In other respects also the Palestinian had the advantage of the Alexandrian mode of interpretation. There was at least ingenuity, if not always truth, in explaining a word by resolving it into two others,[2] or in discussing the import of exclusive particles (such as 'only,' 'but,' 'from,'), and inclusives (such as 'also,' 'with,' 'all'), or in discovering shades of meaning from the derivation of a word, as in the eight synonyms for 'poor'—of which one (*Ani*), indicated simply 'the poor'; another (*Ebhyon*, from *abhah*), one who felt both need and desire; a third (*misken*), one humiliated; a fourth (*rash* from *rush*), one who had been emptied of his property; a fifth (*dal*), one whose property had become exhausted; a sixth (*dakh*), one who felt broken down; a seventh (*makh*), one who had come down; and the eighth (*chelekh*), one who was wretched—or in discussing such dif-

---

[1] The reader who will take our outline of Philo's views to pieces, and compare it with the 'XXV. Theses de modis et formulis quibus pr. Hebr. doctores SS. interpretari etc. soliti fuerunt' (in *Surenhusius'* Βίβλος Καταλ-λαγῆς, pp. 57 to 88), will convince himself of the truth of this.

[2] As, for example, *Malqosh*, the latter rain = Mal-Qash, fill the stubble.

ferences as between *amar*, to speak gently, and *dabhar*, to speak strongly—and many others.[1] Here intimate knowledge of the language and tradition might be of real use. At other times striking thoughts were suggested, as when it was pointed out that all mankind was made to spring from one man, in order to show the power of God, since all coins struck from the same machine were precisely the same, while in man, whatever the resemblance, there was still a difference in each.

2. (Ad vol. i. p. 45, and note 3.) The distinction between the unapproachable God and God as manifest and manifesting Himself, which lies at the foundation of so much in the theology of Philo in regard to the ' intermediary beings '—' Potencies ' —and the Logos, occurs equally in Rabbinic theology,[2] though there it is probably derived from a different source. Indeed, we regard this as explaining the marked and striking avoidance of all anthropomorphisms in the Targumim. It also accounts for the designation of God by two classes of terms, of which in our view, the first expresses the idea of God as revealed, the other that of God as revealing Himself; or, to put it otherwise, which indicate, the one a state, the other an act on the part of God. The first of these classes of designations embraces two terms: *Yeqara*, the excellent glory, and *Shekhinah*, or *Shekhintha*, tne abiding Presence.[3] On the other hand, God, as in the act of revealing himself, is described by the term *Memra*, the ' Logos,' ' the Word.' A distinction of ideas also obtains between the terms *Yeqara* and *Shekhinah*. The former indicates, as we think, the inward and upward, the latter the outward and downward, aspect of the revealed God. This distinction will appear by comparing the use of the two words in the Targumim, and even by the consideration of passages in which the two are placed side by side (as for ex., in the Targum Onkelos on Ex. xvii. 16; Numb. xiv. 14; in Pseudo-Jonathan, Gen. xvi. 13, 14; in the Jerusalem Targum, Ex. xix. 18; and in the Targum Jonathan, Is. vi. 1, 3; Hagg. i. 8). Thus, also, the allusion in 2 Pet. i. 17, to ' the voice from the excellent glory ' ($\tau\tilde{\eta}s$ $\mu\epsilon\gamma\alpha\lambda o\pi\rho\epsilon\pi o\tilde{\upsilon}s$ $\delta\delta\xi\eta s$) must have been to the *Yeqara*.[4] The varied use of the terms *Shekhinah* and *Yeqara*, and then *Memra*, in the Targum of Is. vi., is very remarkable. In ver. 1 it is the *Yeqara* and its train—the heavenward glory—which fills the Heavenly Temple. In ver. 3

---

[1] Comp. generally, *Hamburger*, vol. ii. pp. 181-212, and the ' History of the Jewish Nation,' pp. 567-580, where the Rabbinic Exegesis is fully explained.

[2] Besides the designations of God to which reference is made in the text, Philo also applies to Him that of τόπος, ' place,' in precisely the same manner as the later Rabbis (and especially the Kabbalah) use the word מָקוֹם. To Philo it implies that God is extramundane. He sees this taught in Gen. xxii. 3, 4, where Abraham came ' unto the place of which God had told him; but, when he ' lifted up his eyes,' 'saw the place afar off ' Similarly, the Rabbis when commenting on Gen. xxviii. 11, assign this as the reason why God is designated מָקוֹם, that He is extramundane; the discussion being whether God is the place of His World or the reverse, and the decision in favour of the former—Gen. xxviii. 11 being explained by Ex. xxxiii. 21, and Deut xxxiii. 27 by Ps. xc. 1 (Ber. R. 68, ed. Warsh. p 125 b).

[3] I think it is *Köster* (Trinitätslehre vor Christo) who distinguishes the two as God's Presence within and without the congregation. In general his *brochure* is of little real value. Dr. S. *Maybaum* (Anthropomorphien

u. Anthropopathien ber Onkelos) affords a curious instance of modern Jewish criticism. With much learning and not a little ingenuity he tries to prove by a detailed analysis, that the three terms *Memra*, *Shekhinah*, and *Yeqara* have not the meaning above explained! The force of ' tendency-argumentation ' could scarcely go farther than his essay.

[4] Not as *Grimm* (Clavis N.T. p. 107 a) would have it, the *Shekhinah*, though he rightly regards the N T. δόξα, in this signification of the word, as the equivalent of the Old Testament יְקָר כָּבוֹד. Clear notions on the subject are so important that we give a list of the chief passages in which the two terms are used in the Targum Onkelos, viz. *Yeqara*: Gen. xvii. 22; xviii. 33; xxviii. 13; xxxv. 13; Ex. iii. 1, 6; xvi. 7, 10; xvii. 16; xviii. 5: xx. 17, 18; xxiv. 10, 11, 17; xxix. 43; xxxiii. 18, 22, 23,: xl. 34, 38; Lev. ix. 4, 6, 23; Numb. x. 36: xii. 8; xiv. 14, 22. *Shekhinah*: Gen. ix. 27; Ex. xvii. 7, 16; xx. 21: xxv. 8; xxix. 45, 46; xxxiii. 3, 5. 14-16, 20; xxxiv. 6, 9; Numb. v. 3; vi. 25: xi. 20; xiv. 14, 42; xxiii. 21; xxxv. 34; Deut. i. 42; iii. 24; iv. 39; vi. 15; vii. 21; xii. 5, 11, 21; xiv. 23, 24; xvi. 2, 6, 11, xxiii. 15; xxvi. 2; xxxii. 10; xxxiii. 26.

we hear the *Trishagion* in connection with the dwelling of His *Shekhintha*, while the splendour (*Ziv*) of His *Yeqara* fills the earth—as it were, flows down to it. In ver. 5 the prophet dreads, because he had seen the *Yeqara* of the Shekhinah, while in ver. 6 the coal is taken from before the Shekhintha (which is) upon the throne of the Yeqara (a remarkable expression, which occurs often; so especially in Ex. xvii. 16). Finally, in ver. 8, the prophet hears the voice of the *Memra* of Jehovah speaking the words of vv. 9, 10. It is intensely interesting to notice that in St. John xii. 40, these words are prophetically applied in connection with Christ. Thus St. John applies to the Logos what the Targum understands of the *Memra* of Jehovah.

But, theologically, by far the most interesting and important point, with reference not only to the Logos of Philo, but to the term *Logos* as employed in the Fourth Gospel, is to ascertain the precise import of the equivalent expression *Memra* in the Targumim. As stated in the text of this book (vol. i. p. 47), the term *Memra* as applied to God, occurs 176 times in the Targum Onkelos, 99 times in the Jerusalem Targum, and 321 times in the Targum Pseudo-Jonathan. We subjoin the list of these passages, arranged in three classes. Those in *Class I.* mark where the term does not apply to this, or where it is at least *doubtful*; those in *Class II.* where the *fair* interpretation of a passage shows; and *Class III.* where it is *undoubted* and unquestionable, that the expression *Memra* refers to God as revealing Himself, that is, the Logos.

Classified List of all the Passages in which the term 'Memra' occurs in the Targum Onkelos.

(The term occurs 176 times. Class III., which consists of those passages in which the term Memra bears *undoubted* application to the Divine Personality as revealing Himself, comprises 79 passages.) [1]

CLASS I. *Inapplicable or Doubtful*: Gen. xxvi. 5; Ex. ii. 25; v. 2; vi. 8; xv. 8, 10, 26; xvi. 8; xvii. 1; xxiii. 21, 22; xxv. 22; xxxii. 13; Lev. xviii. 30; xxii. 9; xxvi. 14, 18, 21, 27; Num. iii. 39, 51; iv. 37, 41, 45, 49; ix. 18 (bis), 19, 20 (bis), 23 quat.; x. 13; xiii. 3; xiv. 11, 22, 30, 35; xx. 12, 24; xxiii. 19; xxiv. 4, 16; xxvii. 14; xxxiii. 2, 38· xxxvi. 5; Deut. i. 26; iv. 30; viii. 3, 20; xiii. 5, 19 (in our Version 4, 18); xv. 5; xxvi. 15, 18; xxvii. 10; xxviii. 1, 2, 15, 45, 62; xxx. 2, 8, 10, 20.

An examination of these passages would show that, for caution's sake, we have sometimes put down as 'inapplicable' or 'doubtful' what, viewed in connection with other passages in which the word is used, appears scarcely doubtful. It would take too much space to explain why some passages are put in the *next* class, although the term Memra *seems* to be used in a manner parallel to that in Class I. Lastly, the reason why some passages appear in Class III., when others, somewhat similar, are

---

[1] As these sheets are passing through the press for a second edition, the classic edition of the Targum Onkelos by Dr. *Berliner* (in 2 vols. Berlin, 1884) has reached me. Vol. i. gives the text after the *editio Sabioneta* (of the year 1557). Vol. ii. adds critical notes to the text (pp. 1–70), which are followed by very interesting *Prolegomena*, entering fully on all questions connected with this Targum, historical, exegetical, and critical, and treating them with equal learning and breadth and sobriety of judgment. On comparing our ordinary text with that published by Dr. *Berliner* I find that in the three passages italicised (Gen. vii. 16, vi. 6, *once*, and xxviii. 21) the *ed. Sabion.* has not the word *Memra*. This is specially noteworthy as regards the very important passage, Gen. xxviii. 21.

placed in Class II., must be sought in the context and connection of a verse. We must ask the reader to believe that each passage has been carefully studied by itself, and that our conclusions have been determined by careful consideration, and by the fair meaning to be put on the language of Onkelos.

CLASS II. *Fair*: Gen. vii. 16; xx. 3; xxxi. 3, 24; Ex. xix. 5; Lev. viii. 35; xxvi. 23; Numb. xi. 20, 23; xiv. 41; xxii. 9, 18, 20; xxiii. 3, 4, 16; xxvii. 21; xxxvi. 2; Deut. i. 32; iv. 24, 33, 36; v. 24, 25, 26; ix. 23 (bis); xxxi. 23; xxxiv. 5.

CLASS III. *Undoubted*: Gen. iii. 8, 10; vi. 6 (bis), 7; viii. 21; ix. 12, 13, 15, 16, 17; xv. 1, 6; xvii. 2, 7, 10, 11; xxi. 20, 22, 23; xxii. 16; xxiv. 3; xxvi. 3, 24, 28; xxviii. 15, 20, 21; xxxi. 49, 50; xxxv. 3; xxxix. 2, 3, 21, 23; xlviii. 21; xlix. 24, 25; Ex. iii. 12; iv. 12, 15; x. 10; xiv. 31; xv. 2; xviii. 19; xix. 17; xxix. 42, 43; xxx. 6; xxxi. 13, 17; xxxiii. 22; Lev. xx. 23; xxiv. 12; xxvi. 9, 11, 30, 46; Numb. xiv. 9 (bis), 43; xvii. 19 (in our Version v. 4); xxi. 5; xxiii. 21; Deut. i. 30; ii. 7; iii. 22; iv. 37; v. 5; ix. 3; xviii. 16, 19; xx. 1; xxiii. 15; xxxi. 6, 8; xxxii. 51; xxxiii. 3, 27.

Of most special interest is the rendering of *Onkelos* of Deut. xxxiii. 27, where instead of 'underneath are the everlasting arms,' *Onkelos* has it: 'And by His Memra was the world made,' exactly as in St. John i. 10. This divergence of *Onkelos* from the Hebrew text is utterly unaccountable, nor has any explanation of it, as far as I know, been attempted. *Winer*, whose inaugural dissertation 'De Onkeloso ejusque Paraphrasi Chaldaica' (Lips. 1820), most modern writers have simply followed (with some amplifications, chiefly from *Luzatto's* 'Philoxenus,' אהב הגר makes no reference to this passage, nor do his successors, so far as I know. It is curious that, as our present Hebrew text has *three* words, so has the rendering of *Onkelos*, and that both end with the same word.

In classifying the passages in which the word *Memra* occurs in the Jerusalem Targum and the Targum Pseudo-Jonathan, we have reversed the previous order, and Class I. represents the passages in which the term *undoubtedly* applies to the Personal manifestation of God; Class II., in which this is the *fair* interpretation; Class III., in which such application is, to say the most, *doubtful*.

Classified List of Passages (*according to the above scheme*) *in which the term 'Memra' occurs in the Targum Jerushalmi on the Pentateuch.*

CLASS I. Of *undoubted* application to a Personal Manifestation of God: Gen. i. 27; iii. 9, 22; v. 24; vi. 3; vii. 16; xv. 1; xvi. 3; xix. 24; xxi. 33; xxii 8, 14; xxviii. 10; xxx. 22 (bis; xxxi. 9; xxxv. 9 (quat.); xxxviii. 25; xl. 23; Exod. iii. 14; vi. 3; xii. 42 (quat.); xiii. 18; xiv. 15, 24, 25; xv. 12, 25 (bis); xix. 5, 7, 8, 9 (bis); xx. 1, 24; Lev. i. 1; Numb. ix. 8; x. 35, 36; xiv. 20; xxi. 6; xxiii. 8 (bis); xxiv. 6, 23; xxv. 4; xxvii. 16; Deut. i. 1; iii. 2; iv. 34; xxvi. 3, 14, 17, 18; xxviii. 27, 68; xxxii. 15, 39, 51; xxxiii. 2, 7; xxxiv. 9, 10, 11.

CLASS II. Where such application is *fair*: Gen. v. 24; xxi. 33; Ex. vi. 3; xv. 1; Lev. i. 1; Numb. xxiii. 15, 21; xxiv. 4, 16; Deut. xxxii. 1, 40.

CLASS III. Where such application is *doubtful*: Gen. vi. 6; xviii. 1, 17; xxii. 14 (bis); xxx. 22; xl. 23; xlix. 18; Ex. xiii. 19; xv. 2, 26; xvii. 16; xix. 3; Deut. i. 1; xxxii. 18; xxxiv. 4, 5.

Classified List of Passages in which the term 'Memra' occurs in the Targum Pseudo-Jonathan on the Pentateuch.

CLASS I. *Undoubted*: Gen. ii. 8; iii. 8, 10, 24; iv. 26; v. 2; vii. 16; ix. 12, 13, 15, 16, 17; xi. 8; xii. 17; xv. 1; xvii. 2, 7, 10, 11; xviii. 5; xix. 24 (bis); xx. 6, 18; xxi. 20, 22, 23, 33; xxii. 1; xxiv. 1, 3; xxvi. 3, 24, 28; xxvii. 28, 31; xxviii. 10, 15, 20; xxix. 12; xxxi. 3, 50; xxxv. 3, 9; xxxix. 2, 3, 21, 23; xli. 1; xlvi. 4; xlviii. 9, 21; xlix. 25; l. 20; Exod. i. 21; ii. 5; iii. 12; vii. 25; x. 10; xii. 23, 29; xiii. 8, 15, 17; xiv. 25, 31; xv. 25; xvii. 13, 15, 16 (bis); xviii. 19; xx. 7; xxvi. 28; xxix. 42, 43; xxx. 6, 36; xxxi. 13, 17; xxxii. 35; xxxiii. 9, 19; xxxiv. 5; xxxvi. 33; Lev. i. 1 (bis); vi. 2; viii. 35; ix. 23; xx. 23; xxiv. 12 (bis); xxvi. 11, 12, 30, 44, 46; Numb. iii. 16, 39, 51; iv. 37, 41, 45, 49; ix. 18 (bis), 19, 20 (bis), 23 (ter); x. 13, 35, 36; xiv. 9, 41, 43; xvi. 11, 26; xvii. 4; xxi. 5, 6, 8, 9, 34; xxii. 18, 19, 28; xxiii. 3, 4, 8 (bis), 16, 20, 21; xxiv. 13; xxvii. 16; xxxi. 8; xxxiii. 4; Deut. i. 10, 30, 43; ii. 7, 21; iii. 22; iv. 3, 7 (bis), 20, 24, 33, 36; v. 5 (bis), 11, 22, 23, 24 (bis), 25, 26; vi. 13, 21, 22; ix. 3; xi. 23; xii. 5, 11; xviii. 19; xx. 1; xxi 20; xxiv. 18, 19; xxvi. 5, 14, 18; xxviii. 7, 9, 11, 13, 20, 21, 22, 25, 27, 28, 35, 48, 49, 59, 61, 63, 68; xxix. 2, 4; xxx. 3, 4, 5, 7; xxxi. 5, 8, 23; xxxii. 6, 9, 12, 36; xxxiii. 29; xxxiv. 1, 5, 10, 11.

CLASS II. *Fair*: Gen. v. 24; xv. 6; xvi. 1, 13; xviii. 17; xxii. 16; xxix. 31; xxx. 22; xlvi. 4; Ex. ii. 23; iii. 8, 17, 19; iv. 12; vi. 8; xii. 27; xiii. 5, 17; xxxii. 13; xxxiii. 12, 22; Lev. xxvi. 44; Numb. xiv. 30; xx. 12, 21; xxii. 9, 20; xxiv. 4, 16, 23; Deut. viii. 3; xi. 12; xxix. 23; xxxi. 2, 7; xxxii. 18, 23, 26, 38, 39, 43, 48, 50, 51; xxxiii. 3, 27; xxxiv. 6.

CLASS III. *Doubtful*: Gen. vi. 3, 6 (bis), 7 (bis); viii. 1, 21; xxii. 18; xxvi. 5 (bis); Ex. iv. 15; v. 2; ix. 20, 21; x. 29; xiv. 7; xv. 2, 8; xvi. 3, 8; xix. 5; xxv. 22; Lev. xviii. 30; xxii. 9; xxvi. 40; Numb. vi. 27; ix. 8; xii. 6; xiv. 11, 22, 35; xv. 34; xx. 24; xxiii. 19; xxvii. 14; xxxiii. 2. 38; xxxvi. 5; Deut. i. 26, 32; iv. 30; v. 5; viii. 20; ix. 23; xi. 1; xiii. 18; xv. 5; xix. 15; xxv. 18; xxvi. 17; xxvii. 10; xxviii. 1, 15, 45, 62; xxx. 2, 8, 9, 10; xxxi. 12; xxxiii. 9.

(Ad vol. i. p. 53, note 4.) Only one illustration of *Philo's* peculiar method of interpreting the Old Testament can here be given. It will at the same time show how he found confirmation for his philosophical speculations in the Old Testament, and further illustrate his system of moral theology in its most interesting, but also most difficult, point. The question is, how the soul was to pass from its state of sensuousness and sin to one of devotion to reason, which was religion and righteousness. It will be remarked that the change from the one state to the other is said to be accomplished in one of three ways: by *study*, by *practice*, or through a *good natural disposition* (μάθησις, ἄσκησις, εὐφυΐα) exactly as Aristotle put it. But Philo found a symbol for each, and for a preparatory stage in each, in Scripture. The three Patriarchs represented this threefold mode of reaching the supersensuous: Abraham, study; Jacob, practice; Isaac, a good disposition; while Enos, Enoch, and Noah, represented the respective preparatory stages. *Enos* (hope), the first real ancestor of our race, represented the mind awakening to the existence of a better life. *Abraham* (study) received command to leave 'the land' (sensuousness). But all study was threefold. It was, first, *physical*—Abram in the land of Ur, contemplating the starry sky, but not knowing God. Next to the physical was that 'intermediate' (μέση) study, which embraced the ordinary 'cycle of knowledge' (ἐγκύκλιος παιδεία). This was Abram after he left Haran, and that know-

APP.
II

ledge was symbolised by his union with Hagar, who tarried (intermediately) between Kadesh and Bered. But this stage also was insufficient, and the soul must reach the third and highest stage, that of Divine philosophy (truly, the love of wisdom, $\phi\iota\lambda o\sigma o\phi\iota\alpha$) where eternal truth was the subject of contemplation. Accordingly, Abram left Lot, he became Abraham, and he was truly united to Sarah, no longer Sarai. Onwards and ever upwards would the soul now rise to the knowledge of virtue, of heavenly realities, nay, of the nature of God Himself.

But there was yet another method than 'study,' by which the soul might rise —that of *askesis*, discipline, practice, of which Scripture speaks in Enoch and Jacob. *Enoch*—whom 'God took, and he was not' (Gen. v. 24)—meant the soul turning from the lower to the higher, so that it was no longer found in its former place of evil. From Enoch, as the preparatory stage, we advance to *Jacob*, first merely fleeing from sensuous entanglements (from Laban), then contending with the affections, ridding himself of five of the seventy-five souls with which he had entered Egypt (Deut. x. 22, comp. with Gen. xlvi. 27), often nearly misled by the Sophists (Dinah and Hamor), often nearly failing and faint in the conflict (Jacob's wrestling), but holpen by God, and finally victorious, when Jacob became Israel.

But the highest of all was that spiritual life which came neither from study nor discipline, but through a good natural disposition. Here we have, first of all, *Noah*, who symbolises only the commencement of virtue, since we read not of any special virtue in him. Rather is he *rest*—as the name implies—good, relatively to those around. It was otherwise with *Isaac*, who was perfect before his birth (and hence chosen), even as *Rebekah* meant constancy in virtue. In that state the soul enjoyed true rest (the Sabbath, Jerusalem) and joy, which Isaac's name implied. But true virtue, which was also true wisdom. was Paradise, whence issued the one stream (goodness), which again divided into four branches (the four Stoic virtues):—*Pison*, 'prudence' ($\phi\rho\acute{o}\nu\eta\sigma\iota\varsigma$); *Gihon*, 'fortitude' ($\grave{\alpha}\nu\delta\rho\acute{\iota}\alpha$); *Tigris*, 'desire' ($\grave{\epsilon}\pi\iota\theta\upsilon\mu\acute{\iota}\alpha$), and *Euphrates*, 'justice' ($\delta\iota\kappa\alpha\iota o\sigma\acute{\upsilon}\nu\eta$). And yet, though these be the Stoic virtues, they all spring from Paradise, the Garden of God—and all that is good, and all help to it, comes to us ultimately from God Himself, and is in God.

APPENDIX III.

RABBINIC VIEWS AS TO THE LAWFULNESS OF IMAGES, PICTORIAL REPRESENTATIONS ON COINS, ETC.

(See vol. i. p. 89, note 3.)

ON this point, especially as regarded images, statues, and coins, the views of the Rabbis underwent (as stated in the text) changes and modifications according to the outward circumstances of the people. The earlier and strictest opinions, which absolutely forbade any representation, were relaxed in the Mishnah, and still further in the Talmud.

In tracing this development, we mark as a first stage that a distinction was made between *having* such pictorial representations and *making use of them*, in the sense of selling or bartering them; and again between *making* and *finding* them. The Mishnah forbids only such representations of human beings as carry in their hand some symbol of power, such as a staff, bird, globe, or, as the Talmud adds, a sword, or even a signet-ring (Ab. Z. iii. 1). The Commentaries explain that this must refer to the making use of them, since their possession was, at any rate, prohibited. The Talmud adds (Ab. Z. 40 *b*, 41 *a*) that these were generally representations of kings, that they were used for purposes of worship, and that their prohibition applied only to villages, not to towns, where they were used for ornament. Similarly the Mishnah directs that everything bearing a representation of sun or moon, or of a dragon, was to be thrown into the Dead Sea (Ab. Z. iii. 3). On the other hand, the Talmud quotes (Ab. Z. 42 *b*) a proposition (*Boraita*), to the effect that all representations of the planets were allowed, except those of the sun and moon,[1] likewise all statues except those of man, and all pictures except those of a dragon, the discussion leading to the conclusion that in two, if not in all the cases mentioned, the Talmudic directions refer to finding, not making such. So stringent, indeed, was the law as regarded signet-rings, that it was forbidden to have raised work on them, and only such figures were allowed as were *sunk* beneath the surface, although even then they were not to be used for sealing (Ab. Z. 43 *b*). But this already marks a concession, accorded apparently to a celebrated Rabbi, who had such a ring. Still further in the same direction is the excuse, framed at a later period, for the Rabbis who worshipped in a Synagogue that had a statue of a king, to the effect that they could not be suspected of idolatry, since the place, and hence their conduct, was under the inspection of all men. This more liberal tendency had, indeed, appeared at a much earlier period, in the case of the Nasi Gamaliel II., who made use of a public bath at Acco in which there was a statue of Aphrodite.

---

[1] The Nasi R. Gamaliel made use of representations of the moon in questioning ignorant witnesses with a view to fixing (by the new moon) the beginning of the month. But this must be regarded as a necessary exception to the Mishnic rule.

The Mishnah (Ab. Z. iii. 4) puts this twofold plea into his mouth, that he had not gone into the domain of the idol, but the idol came into his, and that the statue was there for ornament, not for worship. The Talmud endorses, indeed, these arguments, but in a manner showing that the conduct of the great Gamaliel was not really approved of (Ab. Z. 44 *b*). But a statue used for idolatrous purposes was not only to be pulverized, but the dust cast to the winds or into the sea, lest it might possibly serve as manure to the soil! (Ab. Z. iii. 3.) This may explain how Josephus ventured even to blame King Solomon for the figures on the brazen sea and on his throne (Ant. viii. 7. 5), and how he could excite a fanatical rabble at Tiberias, to destroy the palace of Herod Antipas because it contained ' figures of living creatures ' (Life 12).[1]

---

[1] Following the insufficient reasoning of *Ewald* (Gesch. d. Volkes Isr. vol. v. p. 83), *Schürer* represents the non-issue of coins with the image of Herod as a concession to Jewish prejudices, and argues that the coins of the Emperors struck in Palestine bore no effigy. The assertion is, however, unsupported, and St. Matt. xxii. 20 proves that coins with an image of Cæsar were in general circulation. *Wieseler* (Beitr. pp. 83-87 had shown that the absence of Herod's effigy on coins proves his inferior position relatively to Rome, and as this has an important bearing on the question of a Roman census during his reign, it was scarcely fair to simply ignore it. The Tulmud (Baba K. 97 *b*) speaks of coins bearing on one side David and Solomon (? their effigies or their names), and on the other ' Jerusalem, the holy City.' But if it be doubtful whether these coins had respectively the effigies of David or of Solomon, there can be no doubt about the coins ascribed in Ber. R. (Par. 39, ed. Warshau, p. 71 *b*) to Abra-ham, Joshua, David, and Mordecai—that of Abraham being described as bearing on one side the figures of an old man and an old woman (Abraham and Sarah), and on the other those of a young man and a young woman (Isaac and Rebekah). The coins of Joshua are stated to have borne cn one side a bullock, on the other a ram, according to Deut. xxxiii. 17. There could, therefore, have been no such abhorrence of such coins, and if there had been, Herod was scarcely the man to be deterred by it. On these supposed coins of David, &c., see the very curious remarks of *Wagenseil*, Sota, pp. 574, and following. The fullest and most accurate information on all connected with the coins of the Jews is contained in the large and learned work of Mr. *Madden*, ' Coins of the Jews ' (vol. ii. of ' The International Numismata Orientalia,' 1881). Comp. also the Review of this book in the Journal of the Royal Archæological Inst. for 1882, vol. xxxix. pp. 203-206.

APPENDIX IV.

AN ABSTRACT OF JEWISH HISTORY FROM THE REIGN OF ALEXANDER THE GREAT TO THE ACCESSION OF HEROD.

(See Book I. ch. viii.)

THE political connection of Israel with the Grecian world, and, with it, the conflict with Hellenism, may be said to have commenced with the victorious progress of Alexander the Great through the then known world (333 B.C.).[1] It was not only that his destruction of the Persian empire put an end to the easy and peaceful allegiance which Judæa had owned to it for about two centuries, but that the establishment of such a vast Hellenic empire, as was the aim of Alexander, introduced a new element into the old world of Asia. Everywhere the old civilisation gave way before the new. So early as the commencement of the second century before Christ, Palestine was already surrounded, north, east, and west, with a girdle of Hellenic cities, while in the interior of the land itself Grecianism had its foothold in Galilee and was dominant in Samaria. But this is not all. After continuing the frequent object of contention between the rulers of Egypt and Syria, Palestine ultimately passed from Egyptian to Syrian domination during the reign of Seleucus IV. (187–175 B.C.). His successor was that Antiochus IV., Epiphanes (175–164), whose reckless determination to exterminate Judaism, and in its place to substitute Hellenism, led to the Maccabean rising. Mad as this attempt seems, it could scarcely have been made had there not been in Palestine itself a party to favour his plans. In truth, Grecianism, in its worst form, had long before made its way, slowly but surely, into the highest quarters. For the proper understanding of this history its progress must be briefly indicated.

After the death of Alexander, Palestine passed first under Egyptian domination. Although the Ptolemies were generally favourable to the Jews (at least of their own country), those of Palestine at times felt the heavy hand of the conqueror (*Jos.* Ant. xii. 1. 1). Then followed the contests between Syria and Egypt for its possession, in which the country must have severely suffered. As *Josephus* aptly remarks (Ant. xii. 3. 3), whichever party gained, Palestine was 'like a ship in a storm which is tossed by the waves on both sides.' Otherwise it was a happy time, because one of comparative independence. The secular and spiritual power was vested in the hereditary High-Priests, who paid for their appointment (probably annually) the sum of twenty (presumably Syrian) talents, amounting to five ordinary talents, or rather less than 1,200*l.*[2] Besides this personal, the country

APP.
IV

---

[1] We do not here discuss the question, whether or not Alexander really entered Jerusalem. Jewish legend has much to tell of him, and reports many supposed inquiries on his part or discussions between him and the Rabbis, that prove at least the deep impression which his appearance had made, and the permanent results which followed from it.

[2] Comp. *Herzfeld,* Gesch. d. Volkes Isr. vol. ii. *passim,* but specially pp. 181 and 211.

paid a general tribute, its revenues being let to the highest bidder. The sum levied on Judæa itself has been computed at 81,900*l*. (350 ordinary talents). Although this tribute appears by no means excessive, bearing in mind that in later times the dues from the balsam-district around Jericho were reckoned at upwards of 46,800*l*. (200 talents), the hardship lay in the mode of levying it by strangers, often unjustly, and always harshly, and in the charges connected with its collection. This cause of complaint was, indeed, removed in the course of time, but only by that which led to far more serious evils.

The succession of the High-Priests, as given in Nehem. xii. 10, 11, 22, furnishes the following names: Jeshua, Joiakim, Eliashib, Joiada, Johanan,[1] Jonathan, and Jaddua, who was the contemporary of Alexander the Great. After the death of Jaddua, we have the following list:[2] *Onias I.* (*Jos.* Ant. xi. 8. 7), *Simon I. the Just*[3] (Ant. xii. 2. 5), *Eleazar, Manasseh* (Ant. xii. 4. 1), *Onias II., Simon II.* (Ant. xii. 4. 10), *Onias III., Jason* (Ant. xii. 5. 1), *Menelaus,* and *Alcimus* (Ant. xii. 9. 7), with whom the series of the Pontiffs is brought down to the time of the Maccabees. Internal peace and happiness ceased after the death of Simon the Just (in the beginning of the third century B.C.), one of the last links in that somewhat mysterious chain of personages, to which tradition has given the name of ' the Great Assemblage,' or ' Great Synagogue.'[4]

Jewish legend has much that is miraculous to tell of Simon the Just, and connects him alike with events both long anterior and long posterior to his Pontificate. Many of these traditions read like the outcome of loving, longing remembrance of a happy past which was never to return. Such a venerable form would never again be seen in the Sanctuary (Ecclus. l. 1–4), nor would such miraculous attestation be given to any other ministrations[5] (Yoma 39 *a* and *b*; Jer. Yoma v. 2; vi. 3). All this seems to point to the close of a period when the High-Priesthood was purely Jewish in spirit, just as the hints about dissensions among his sons (Jer. Yoma 43 *d*, at top) sound like faint reminiscences of the family—and public troubles which followed. In point of fact he was succeeded not by his son Onias,[6] who was under age, but by his brother Eleazar, and he, after a Pontificate of twenty years, by his brother Manasseh. It was only twenty-seven years later, after the death of Manasseh, that Onias II. became High-Priest. If Eleazar, and especially Manasseh, owed their position, or at least strengthened it, by courting the favour of the ruler of Egypt, it was almost natural that Onias should have taken the opposite or Syrian part. His refusal to pay the High-Priestly tribute to Egypt could scarcely have been wholly due to avarice, as *Josephus* suggests. The anger and threats of

---

[1] I have placed Johanan (Neh. xii. 22) *before* Jonathan, in accordance with the ingenious reasoning of *Herzfeld*, ii. p. 372. The chronology of their Pontificates is almost inextricably involved. In other respects also there are not a few difficulties. See *Zunz*, Gottesd. Vortr. p. 27, and the elaborate discussions of *Herzfeld*, whose work, however, is very faulty in arrangement.

[2] Happily no divergence exists as to their succession.

[3] Some Christian and all Jewish writers assign the designation of ' The Just ' to Simon II. This is directly contrary to the express statement of *Josephus*. *Herzfeld* (i. 377) appeals to Abhoth i. 2, 3, Men. 109 *b*, and Jer. Yoma vi. 3, but immediately relinquishes the two latter references as otherwise historically untenable. But surely no historical *inference*—for such it is—from Ab.

i. 2, 3 is worth setting against the express statement of *Josephus*. Besides, *Zunz* has rightly shown that the expression *Qibbel* must not be too closely pressed, as indeed its use throughout the Perek seems to indicate (Gottesd. Vortr. p. 37, Note).

[4] Of this more in the sequel. He is called: מיריי, בנסת הגדולה, which however does not seem necessarily to imply that he was actually a member of it.

[5] It deserves notice that in these same Talmudic passages reference is also made to the later entire cessation of the same miracles, as indicating the coming destruction of the Temple.

[6] Or as he is designated in the Talmud; Chonyi, Nechunyah, and even Nechunyon. Onias is a Grecianised form—itself a significant fact.

the king were appeased by the High-Priest's nephew Joseph, who claimed descent from the line of David. He knew how to ingratiate himself at the court of Alexandria, and obtained the lease of the taxes of Cœle-Syria (which included Judæa), by offering for it double the sum previously paid. The removal of the foreign tax-gatherer was very grateful to the Jews, but the authority obtained by Joseph became a new source of danger, especially in the hands of his ambitious son, Hyrcanus. Thus we already mark the existence of three parties: the Egyptian, the Syrian, and that of the 'sons of Tobias' (Ant. xii. 5. 1), as the adherents of Joseph were called, after his father. If the Egyptian party ceased when Palestine passed under Syrian rule in the reign of Antiochus III. the Great (223–187 B.C.), and ultimately became wholly subject to it under Seleucus IV. (187–173), the Syrian, and especially the Tobias-party, had already become Grecianised. In truth, the contest now became one for power and wealth in which each sought to outbid the other by bribery and subserviency to the foreigner. As the submission of the people could only be secured by the virtual extinction of Judaism, this aim was steadily kept in view by the degenerate priesthood.

The storm did not, indeed, break under the Pontificate of Simon II., the son and successor of Onias II., but the times were becoming more and more troublous. Although the Syrian rulers occasionally showed favour to the Jews, Palestine was now covered with a network of Syrian officials, into whose hands the temporal power mainly passed. The taxation also sensibly increased, and, besides crown-money, consisted of a poll-tax, the third of the field-crops, the half of the produce of trees, a royal monopoly of salt and of the forests, and even a tax on the Levitical tithes and on all revenues of the Temple.[1] Matters became much worse under the Pontificate of Onias III., the son and successor of Simon II. A dispute between him and one Simon, a priest, and captain of the temple-guard,[2] apparently provoked by the unprincipled covetousness of the latter, induced Simon to appeal to the cupidity of the Syrians by referring to the untold treasures which he described as deposited in the Temple. His motive may have been partly a desire for revenge, partly the hope of attaining the office of Onias. It was ascribed to a supernatural apparition, but probably it was only superstition which arrested the Syrian general at that time. But a dangerous lesson had been learned alike by Jew and Gentile.

Seleucus IV. was succeeded by his brother Antiochus IV., Epiphanes (175–164). Whatever psychological explanation may be offered of his bearing—whether his conduct was that of a madman, or of a despot intoxicated to absolute forgetfulness of every consideration beyond his own caprice by the fancied possession of power uncontrolled and unlimited—cruelty and recklessness of tyranny were as prominently his characteristics as revengefulness and unbounded devotion to superstition. Under such a reign the precedent which Simon, the Captain of the Temple, had set, was successfully followed up by no less a person than the brother of the High-Priest himself. The promise of a yearly increase of 360 talents in the taxes of the country, besides a payment of 80 talents from another revenue (2 Macc. iv. 8, 9), purchased the deposition of Onias III.—the first event of that kind recorded in Jewish history—and the substitution of his brother Joshua, Jesus, or Jason (as

---

[1] In 1 Macc. x. 29–33; Jos. Ant. xii. 3. 3; xiii. 2. 3. In view of these express testimonies the statement of Ewald (Gesch. d. V. Isr. vol. iv. p. 373), to the effect that Palestine, or at least Jerusalem, enjoyed immunity from tax-

ation, seems strange indeed. Schürer (u. s. p. 71) passes rather lightly over the troubles in Judæa before Antiochus Epiphanes.

[1] Herzfeld rightly corrects 'Benjamin' in 2 Macc. iii. 4. Comp. u. s. p. 218.

APP.
IV

he loved to Grecianise his name), in the Pontificate.[1] But this was not all. The necessities, if not the inclinations, of the new High-Priest, and his relations to the Syrian king, prescribed a Grecian policy at home. It seems almost incredible, and yet it is quite in accordance with the circumstances, that Jason should have actually paid to Antiochus a sum of 150 talents for permission to erect a Gymnasium in Jerusalem, that he entered citizens of Antioch on the registers of Jerusalem, and that on one occasion he went so far as to send a deputation to attend the games at Tyre, with money for purchasing offerings to Heracles! And in Jerusalem, and throughout the land, there was a strong and increasing party to support Jason in his plans, and to follow his lead (2 Macc. iv. 9, 19). Thus far had Grecianism already swept over the country, as not only to threaten the introduction of views, manners, and institutions wholly incompatible with the religion of the Old Testament, but even the abolition of the bodily mark which distinguished its professors (1 Macc. i. 15; *Jos.* Ant. xii. 5. 1).

But the favour which Antiochus showed Jason was not of long duration. One even more unscrupulous than he, Menelaus (or, according to his Jewish name, Onias), the brother of that Simon who had first excited the Syrian cupidity about the Temple treasure, outbade Jason with Antiochus by a promise of 300 talents in addition to the tribute which Jason had paid. Accordingly, Menelaus was appointed High-Priest. In the expressive language of the time: 'he came, bringing nothing worthy of the High-Priesthood, but having the fury of a cruel tyrant and the rage of a savage beast' (2 Macc. iv. 25). In the conflict for the Pontificate, which now ensued, Menelaus conquered by the help of the Syrians. A terrible period of internal misrule and external troubles followed. Menelaus and his associates cast off every restraint, and even plundered the Temple of some of its precious vessels. Antiochus, who had regarded the resistance to his nominee as rebellion against himself, took fearful vengeance by slaughter of the inhabitants of Jerusalem and pillage of the Temple. But this was not all. When checked in his advance against Egypt, by the peremptory mandate of Rome, Antiochus made up for his disappointment by an expedition against Judæa, of which the avowed object was to crush the people and to sweep away Judaism. The horrors which now ensued are equally recorded in the Books of the Maccabees, by *Josephus*, and in Jewish tradition.[2] All sacrifices, the service of the Temple, and the observance of the Sabbath and of feast-days were prohibited; the Temple at Jerusalem was dedicated to Jupiter Olympius; the Holy Scriptures were searched for and destroyed; the Jews forced to take part in heathen rites; a small heathen altar was reared on the great altar of burnt-offering—in short, every insult was heaped on the religion of the Jews, and its every trace was to be swept away. The date of the final profanation of the Temple was the 25th *Chislev* (corresponding to our December)—the same on which, after its purification by Judas Maccabee,[3] its services were restored, the same on which the Christian Church celebrates the dedication of a better Temple. that of the Holy Ghost in the Incarnation of Jesus Christ.

[1] The notice in *Jos.* Ant. xii. 5. 1 must be corrected by the account in 2 Macc. Comp. *Herzfeld*, u. s.

[2] Besides Talmudic and Midrashic notices, we here refer to that most interesting and ancient *Megillath Taanith*, or 'Rolls of Fasts,' of which a translation is given in Appendix V. The passages bearing on this period are collected in *Derenbourg*, Hist. de la Palestine, pp. 59–63, although his reference to that

on the 28th of Adar is at least open to controversy.

[3] The designation 'Maccabee' was originally given to *Judas* (1 Macc. ii. 4, 66; iii. 1; v. 24, 34). The name was, like that of Charles *Martel*, probably derived from מקב, or in Chaldee מקבא, a hammer. Comp. *Josippon ben Gorion*, iii. 9. 7 (ed. *Breithaupt*, p. 200)—only that he writes the name with a כ and not a ק.

But the relentless persecution, which searched for its victims in every part of the land, also called forth a deliverer in the person of *Mattathias*. The story of the glorious rising and final deliverance of the country under the *Maccabees* or *Asmonæans*, as they are *always* called in Jewish writings,[1] is sufficiently known. Only the briefest outline of it can here be attempted. Mattathias died before it came to any actual engagement with the Syrians, but victory after victory attended the arms of his son, *Judas the Maccabee*, till at last the Temple could be purified and its services restored, exactly three years after its desecration (25 Chislev, 165 B.C.). The rule of the Jewish hero lasted other five years, which can scarcely be described as equally successful with the beginning of his administration. The first two years were occupied in fortifying strong positions and chastising those hostile heathen border-tribes which harassed Judæa. Towards the close of the year 164 Antiochus Epiphanes died. But his successor, or rather Lysias, who administered the kingdom during his minority, was not content to surrender Palestine without a further contest. No deeds of heroism, however great, could compensate for the inferiority of the forces under Judas' command.[2] The prospect was becoming hopeless, when troubles at home recalled the Syrian army, and led to a treaty of peace in which the Jews acknowledged Syrian supremacy, but were secured liberty of conscience and worship.

But the truce was of short duration. As we have seen, there were already in Palestine two parties—that which, from its character and aims, may generally be designated as the *Grecian*, and the *Chasidim* (Assideans). There can be little doubt that the latter name originated in the designation *Chasidim*, applied to the pious in Israel in such passages as Ps. xxx. 5 (4 in our A.V.); xxxi. 23 (A.V. 24; xxxvii. 28). Jewish tradition distinguishes between the 'earlier' and the 'later' Chasidim (Ber. v. 1 and 32 *b*; Men. 40 *b*). The descriptions of the former are of so late a date, that the characteristics of the party are given in accordance with views and practices which belong to a much further development of Rabbinical piety. Their fundamental views may, however, be gathered from the four opening sentences of the Mishnic Tractate 'Abhoth,'[3] of which the last are ascribed to José the son of Joezer, and José the son of Jochanan, who, as we know, still belonged to the 'earlier Chasidim.' These flourished about 140 B.C., and later. This date throws considerable light upon the relation between the 'earlier' and 'later' Chasidim, and the origin of the sects of the Pharisees and Sadducees. Comparing the sentences of the earlier Chasidim (Ab. i. 2–4) with those which follow, we notice a marked simplicity about them, while the others either indicate a rapid development of Rabbinism, or are echoes of the political relations subsisting, or else seem to allude to present difficulties or controversies. We infer that the 'earlier' Chasidim represented the 'pious' in Israel—of course, according to the then standpoint—who, in opposition to the Grecian party, rallied around Judas Maccabee and his successor, Jonathan. The assumption of the High-Priestly dignity by Jonathan the Maccabee, on the nomination of the Syrian king (about 152), was a step which the ultra-orthodox party never forgave the Asmonæans. From that period, therefore, we date the alienation of the Chasidim—or rather the cessation of the 'earlier' Chasidim.

---

[1] חשמנאים. *Josephus* (Ant. xii. 6. 1) derives the word from *Asmonæus*, the great-grandfather of Mattathias. Others derive it from the word חשמנים ('princes' in A.V. Ps. lxviii. 31).

[2] The Syrian force is said to have amounted to 100,000 footmen, 20,000 horsemen, and 32 war-elephants (1 Macc. vi. 30).

[3] We regard the opening sentence of Abhoth as marking out the general principles and aims of the so-called 'Great Assembly.'

Henceforth the party, as such, degenerated, or, to speak more correctly, ran into extreme religious views, which made them the most advanced section of the Pharisees.[1] The latter and the Sadducees henceforth represented the people in its twofold religious direction. With this view agrees the statement of *Josephus* (Ant. xiii. 5. 9), who first mentions the existence of Pharisees and Sadducees in the time of Jonathan, and even the confused notice in Aboth de Rabbi Nathan 5, which ascribes the origin of the Sadducees to the first or second generation of Zadok's disciples, himself a disciple of Antigonus of Socho, which would bring the date to nearly the same time as *Josephus*.

From this digression, necessary for the proper understanding of the internal relations in Judæa, we return to the political history. There was another change on the throne of Syria. Demetrius, the new king, readily listened to the complaints of a Jewish deputation, and appointed their leader, Alcimus (Jakim or Eljakim) High-Priest. At first the Chasidim were disposed to support him, as having formerly filled a high post in the priesthood, and as the nephew of José the son of Jazer, one of their leaders. But they suffered terribly for their rashness. Aided by the Syrians, Alcimus seized the Pontificate. But Judas once more raised the national standard against the intruder and his allies. At first victory seemed to incline to the national side, and the day of the final defeat and slaughter of the Syrian army and of Nicanor their general was enrolled in the Jewish Calendar as one on which fasting and mourning were prohibited (the 13th Adar, or March). Still, the prospect was far from reassuring, the more so as division had already appeared in the ranks of the Jews. In these circumstances Judas directed his eyes towards that new Western power which was beginning to overshadow the East. It was a fatal step—the beginning of all future troubles—and, even politically, a grave mistake, to enter into a defensive and offensive alliance with Rome. But before even temporary advantage could be derived from this measure, Judas the Maccabee had already succumbed to superior numbers, and heroically fallen in battle against the Syrians.

The war of liberation had lasted seven years, and yet when the small remnant of the Asmonæan party chose Jonathan, the youngest brother of Judas, as his successor, their cause seemed more hopeless than almost at any previous period. The Grecian party were dominant in Judæa, the Syrian host occupied the land, and Jonathan and his adherents were obliged to retire to the other side Jordan. The only hope, if such it may be called, lay in the circumstance that after the death of Alcimus the Pontificate was not filled by another Syrian nominee, but remained vacant for two years. During this time the nationalists must have gained strength, since the Grecian party now once more sought and obtained Syrian help against them. But the almost passive resistance which Jonathan successfully offered wearied out the Syrian general and led to a treaty of peace (1 Macc. ix. 58–73). In the period which followed, the Asmonæan party steadily increased, so that when a rival king claimed the Syrian crown, both pretenders bade for the support of Jonathan. He took the side of the new monarch, Alexander Balas, who sent him a crown of gold and a purple mantle, and appointed him High-Priest, a dignity which Jonathan at once accepted.[2] The Jewish Pontiff was faithful to his patron

---

[1] A somewhat analogous change, at least of theological opinions, distinguishes the later from the earlier 'Puritans.' Theological schools which are partly political in their early history often degenerate either into political partisans or else into extreme sectaries, as either one or the other of their *rationes vivendi* ceases.

[2] The Pharisees never forgave this. It is quite true that this plea for their opposition to

even against a new claimant to the crown of Syria.' And such was his influence, that the latter, on gaining possession of the throne, not only forgave the resistance of Jonathan, but confirmed him in the Pontificate, and even remitted the taxation of Palestine on a tribute (probably annual) of 300 talents. But the faithlessness and ingratitude of the Syrian king led Jonathan soon afterwards to take the side of another Syrian pretender, an infant, whose claims were ostensibly defended by his general Trypho. In the end, however, Jonathan's resistance to Trypho's schemes for obtaining the crown for himself led to the murder of the Jewish High-Priest by treachery.

The government of Judæa could not, in these difficult times, have devolved upon one more fitted for it than Simon, an elder brother of Judas Maccabee. His father had, when making his dying disposition, already designated him 'as the man of counsel' among his sons (1 Macc. ii. 65). Simon's policy lay chiefly in turning to good account the disputes in Syria, and in consolidating such rule as he had acquired (143–135 B.C.). After the murder of his brother by Trypho, he took the part of the Syrian claimant (Demetrius) to whom Trypho was opposed. Demetrius was glad to purchase his support by a remission of all taxation for all time to come. This was the first great success, and the Jews perpetuated its memory by enrolling its anniversary (the 27th Iyar, or May) in their Calendar. An even more important date, alike in the 'Calendar' (Meg. Taan. Per. 2) and in Jewish history (1 Macc. xiii. 51), was the 23rd Iyar, when the work of clearing the country of the foreigner was completed by the Jewish occupation of the Acra, or fortress of Jerusalem, hitherto occupied by the Syrian party. The next measures of Simon were directed to the suppression of the Grecian party in Judæa, and the establishment of peace and security to his own adherents. To the popular mind this 'Golden Age,' described in glowing language in 1 Macc. xiv. 8–14, seemed to culminate in an event by which the national vanity was gratified and the future safety of their country apparently ensured. This was the arrival of a Roman embassy in Judæa to renew the league which had already been made both by Judas Maccabee and by Jonathan. Simon replied by sending a Jewish embassy to Rome, which brought a valuable shield of gold in token of gratitude. In their intoxication the Jews passed a decree, and engraved it on tables of brass, making Simon 'their High-Priest and Governor for ever, until there should arise a faithful prophet;' in other words, appointing him to the twofold office of spiritual and secular chief, and declaring it hereditary (1 Macc. xiv. 41–45). The fact that he should have been appointed to dignities which both he and his predecessor had already held, and that offices which in themselves were hereditary should now be declared such in the family of Simon, as well as the significant limitation: 'until there should arise a faithful prophet,' sufficiently indicate that there were dissensions among the people and opposition to the Asmonæans. In truth, as the Chasidim had been alienated, so there was a growing party among the Pharisees, their successors, whose hostility to the Asmonæans increased till it developed into positive hatred. This antagonism was, however, not grounded on their possession of the secular power, but on their occupancy of the Pontificate, perhaps on their combination of the two offices. How far their enmity went,

the Asmonæans is for the first time reported during a later reign—that of John Hyrcanus I.—and that it was then ostensibly based on the ground of Hyrcanus' mother having been a captive of war. But see our remarks on this point further on.
1 The story, however, differently told by

Josephus (Ant. xiii. 4. 3). I have followed the account in 1 Macc., which is generally regarded as the more trustworthy, though I am not without misgivings, since *Josephus* evidently had the Book of Maccabees before him.

APP.
IV

will appear in the sequel. For a time it was repressed by the critical state of affairs. For, the contest with the Syrians had to be once more renewed, and although Simon, or rather his sons, obtained the victory, the aged High-Priest and two of his sons, Mattathias and Judas, fell by the treachery of Ptolomæus, Simon's son-in-law.

The Pontificate and the government now devolved upon the only one of Simon's sons still left, known as John Hyrcanus I. (Jochanan Horkenos,[1] Jannai [2]), 135–105 B.C. His first desire naturally was to set free his mother, who was still in the power of Ptolomæus, and to chastise him for his crimes. But in this he failed. Ptolemy purchased immunity by threatening to kill his captive, and afterwards treacherously slew her. Soon after this a Syrian army besieged Jerusalem. The City was reduced to great straits. But when at the Feast of Tabernacles the Syrian king not only granted a truce to the besieged, but actually provided them with what was needed for the services of the Temple, Hyrcanus sought and obtained peace, although the Syrian councillors urged their king to use the opportunity for exterminating Judaism. The conditions, though hard, were not unreasonable in the circumstances. But fresh troubles in Syria gave a more favourable turn to affairs in Judæa. First, Hyrcanus subjected Samaria, and then conquered Idumæa, whose inhabitants he made proselytes by giving them the alternative of circumcision or exile. Next, the treaty with the Romans was renewed, and finally Hyrcanus availed himself of the rapid decay of the Syrian monarchy to throw off his allegiance to the foreigner. Jewish exclusiveness was further gratified by the utter destruction of Samaria, of which the memorial-day (the 25th Marcheshvan, November) was inserted in the festive 'Calendar' (Meg. Taan. Per. 8).[3] Nor was this the only date which his successors added to the calendar of national feasts.[4]

But his reign is of the deepest importance in our history as marking the first public contest between the two great parties, the Pharisees and the Sadducees, and also as the turning-point in the history of the Maccabees. Even the coins of that period are instructive. They bear the inscription: ' Jochanan, the High-Priest, and the *Chebher* of the Jews;' or else, ' Jochanan the High-Priest, Chief, and the *Chebher* of the Jews.'[5] The term *Chebher*, which on the coins occurs only in connection with ' High-Priest,' unquestionably refers, not to the Jewish people generally, but to them in their ecclesiastical *organisation*, and points therefore to the acknowledgment of an ' Eldership,' or representative ecclesiastical body, which presided over affairs along with and under the ' High-Priest' as ' Chief.'[6] In this respect the presence or absence of the word ' *Chebher*,' or even of mention of the Jews, might afford hints as to the relationship of a Maccabee chief to the ecclesiastical leaders

---

[1] The derivation of the name Hyrcanus, or in Rabbinical writings *Horqenos*, proposed by *Grätz* (Gesch. d. Juden. vol. iii. p. 55), and supported by *Hamburger* (Real. Encycl. für Bibel u. Talmud, sect. ii. p. 421, note 15) is untenable, in view of the fact, that not a few Rabbinical authorities bore the same name (comp. Ab. ii. 8; Sanh. 58 *a*). It could not, therefore, have been an appellation derived from the victory of Hyrcanus ' over *Cendebæus*, the Hyrcanian.'

[2] The name *Jannai* is supposed to have been an abbreviation of Jochanan. Many Rabbinical teachers of that name are mentioned. *Derenbourg* (Hist. de la Palest. p. 95) regards it as an abbreviation of Jonathan, but his reasoning is not convincing.

[3] According to Jer. Sotah ix. 13, and Sot.

33 *a*, a ' *Bath Qol*,' or Heavenly Voice, issuing from the Most Holy Place, had announced to Hyrcanus, while officiating in the Temple, the victory of his sons at Samaria. *Josephus* (Ant. xiii. 10. 7), assigns on this ground to Hyrcanus the prophetic, as well as the priestly and royal, title.

[4] These are the 15th and 16th Sivan, the 16th Adar, and the 7th Iyar. Comp. the Meg. Taan.

[5] *Schürer* (Neutest. Zeitg. p. 113) does not give this inscription correctly. Comp. *Levy*, Gesch. d. Jud. Münzen, pp. 52, 53. See especially *Madden*. ' Coins of the Jews,' pp. 74–81, where all the varieties of inscription are given.

[6] We dismiss the fanciful readings and explanations of the word חבר by *De Saulcy*

of the people. It has already been explained that the Chasidim, viewed as the National party, had ceased, and that the leaders were now divided into Pharisees and Sadducees. By tradition and necessity Hyrcanus belonged to the former, by tendency and, probably, inclination to the latter. His interference in religious affairs was by no means to the liking of the Pharisees, still less to that of their extreme sectaries, the Chasidim. Tradition ascribes to Hyrcanus no less than *nine* innovations, of which only *five* were afterwards continued as legal ordinances. *First*, the payment of tithes (both of the Levitical and the so-called 'poor's tithe') was declared no longer obligatory on a *seller*, if he were one of the *Am ha-Arets*, or country people, but on the buyer.[1] Complaints had long been made that this heavy impost was not paid by the majority of the common people, and it was deemed better to devolve the responsibility on the buyer, unless the seller were what was called '*neeman*,' trusted; i.e., one who had solemnly bound himself to pay tithes. In connection with this, *secondly*, the declaration ordered in Deut. xxvi. 3–10 was abrogated as no longer applicable. *Thirdly*, all work that caused noise was forbidden during the days intermediate between the first and the last great festive days of the Passover and of the Feast of Tabernacles. *Fourthly*, the formula: 'Awake, why sleepest Thou, O Lord' (Ps. xliv. 23), with which, since the Syrian persecution, the morning service in the Temple had commenced, was abolished. *Fifthly*, the cruel custom of wounding the sacrificial animals on the head was prohibited and rings fastened in the pavement to which the animals were attached (Jer. Maas. Sh. v. 9; Jer. Sot. ix. 11; Tos. Sot. 13; Sotah 48 *a*). The *four* ordinances of Hyrcanus which were abolished referred to the introduction in official documents, after the title of the High-Priest, of the expression 'El Elyon'—the Most High God; to the attempt to declare the Syrian and Samaritan towns liable to tithes (implying their virtual incorporation) while, according to an old principle, this obligation only applied when a place could be reached from Judæa without passing over heathen soil; to the abrogation by Hyrcanus of a former enactment by José ben Joezer, which discouraged emigration by declaring all heathen soil defiled, and which rendered social intercourse with Gentiles impossible by declaring vessels of glass capable of contracting Levitical defilement (Jer. Shabb. 1. 4; Shabb. 14 *b*)— and which was re-enacted; and, lastly, to the easy terms on which the King had admitted the Idumæans into the Jewish community.

From all this it is not difficult to form an idea of the relations between Hyrcanus and the Pharisees. If Hyrcanus had not otherwise known of the growing aversion of the Pharisees, a Sadducean friend and councillor kept him informed, and turned it to account for his party. The story of the public breach between Hyrcanus and the Pharisees is told by *Josephus* (Ant. xiii. 10. 5, 6), and in the Talmud (Kidd. 66 *a*), with only variations of names and details. Whether from a challenge thrown out to the Pharisees (according to the Talmud), or in answer to a somewhat strange request by Hyrcanus, to point out any part of his conduct which was not in accordance with the law (so *Josephus*), one of the extreme section of the Pharisees,[2] at a feast given to the party, called upon Hyrcanus to be content with secular power, and to resign the Pontificate, on the ground that he was disqualified for it, because

---

and *Ewald*. But I cannot agree with *Schürer* in applying it to the people as a whole. Even the passage which he quotes (Ber. iv. 7, with which the corresponding *Gemara* should be compared), proves that the word is not used loosely for the people, but with reference to their ecclesiastical *nexus*. Comp. also Meg. 27 *b*.

[1] Comp. 'Sketches of Jewish Social Life in the Time of Christ,' pp. 233, 234.

[2] *Josephus* calls him Eleazar, but the Talmud (Kidd. 66 *a*) Jehudah ben Gedidim, for which *Hamburger* would read *Nedidim*, the sect of 'the solitaries,' which he regards as another designation for the extreme Chasidim.

his mother had been a captive of war. Even the Talmud admits that this report was calumnious, while it offered a gratuitous insult to the memory of a really noble, heroic woman, all the more unwarrantable that the Pontificate had, by public decree, been made hereditary in the family of Simon, the father of Hyrcanus, which could not have been the case if the charge now brought had been other than a pretext to cover the hostility of the Chasidim. The rash avowal was avenged on the whole party. In the opinion of Hyrcanus they all proved themselves accomplices, when, on being questioned, they declared the offender only guilty of 'stripes and bonds.' Hyrcanus now joined the Sadducees, and, although the statement of the Talmud about the slaughter of the leading Pharisees is incorrect, there can be no doubt that they were removed from power and exposed to persecution. The Talmud adds this, which, although chronologically incorrect, is significant, 'Jochanan the High-Priest served in the Pontificate eighty years, and at the end of them he became a Sadducee.' But this was only the beginning of troubles to the Pharisaic party, which revenged itself by most bitter hatred — the beginning, also, of the decline of the Maccabees.

Hyrcanus left five sons. To the oldest of them, Aristobulus (in Hebrew Jehudah), he bequeathed the Pontificate, but appointed his own widow to succeed him in the secular government. But Aristobulus cast his mother into prison, where she soon afterwards perished—as the story went, by hunger. The only one of his brothers whom he had left at large, and who, indeed, was his favourite, soon fell also a victim to his jealous suspicions. Happily his reign lasted only one year (105–104 B.C.). He is described as openly favouring the Grecian party, although, on conquering Ituræa, a district east of the Lake of Galilee,[1] he obliged its inhabitants to submit to circumcision.

On the death of Aristobulus I., his widow, Alexandra Salome, released his brothers from prison, and apparently married the eldest of them, Alexander Jannæus (or in Hebrew Jonathan), who succeeded both to the Pontificate and the secular government. The three periods of his reign (104–78 B.C.) seem indicated in the varying inscriptions on his coins.[2] The first period, which lasted eight or ten years, was that in which Jannai was engaged in those wars of conquest, which added the cities on the maritime coast to his possessions.[3] During that time Salome seems to have managed internal affairs. As she was devoted to the Pharisaic party—indeed one of their leaders, Simeon ben Shetach, is said to have been her brother (Ber. 48 a) —this was the time of their ascendency. Accordingly, the coins of that period bear the inscription, 'Jonathan the High-Priest and the *Chebher* of the Jews.' But on his return to Jerusalem he found the arrogance of the Pharisaic party ill accordant with his own views and tastes. The king now joined the Sadducees, and Simeon ben Shetach had to seek safety in flight (Jer. Ber. vii. 2 p. 11 b). But others of his party met a worse fate. A terrible tragedy was enacted in the Temple itself. At the Feast of Tabernacles Jannai, officiating as High-Priest, set the Pharisaic custom at open defiance by pouring the water out of the sacred vessel on the ground instead of upon the altar. Such a high-handed breach of

---

[1] By a curious mistake, *Schürer* locates Ituræa north instead of east of the Lake of Galilee, and speaks of 'Jewish tradition' as drawing such a dark picture of Aristobulus. Dr. S. must refer to *Josephus*, since Jewish tradition never named Aristobulus (Neutest. Zeitg. p. 118).

[2] For the coins of that reign comp. *Madden*,

u. s. pp. 83–90. I have, however, arranged them somewhat differently.
[5] Accordingly, on the second series of coins, which date from his return to Jerusalem, and breach with the Pharisees, we have on the reverse the device of an anchor with two cross-bars.

what was regarded as most sacred, excited the feelings of the worshippers to the highest pitch of frenzy. They pelted him with the festive *Ethrogs* (citrons), which they carried in their hands, and loudly reproached him with his descent from 'a captive.' The king called in his foreign mercenaries, and no fewer than 6,000 of the people fell under their swords. This was an injury which could neither be forgiven nor atoned for by conquests. One insurrection followed after the other, and 5,000 of the people are said to have fallen in these contests. Weary of the strife, Jannai asked the Pharisaic party to name their conditions of peace, to which they caustically replied, 'Thy death' (*Jos.* Ant. xiii. 13. 5). Indeed, such was the embitterment that they actually called in, and joined the Syrians against him. But the success of the foreigner produced a popular revulsion in his favour, of which Jannai profited to take terrible vengeance on his opponents. No fewer than 800 of them were nailed to the cross, their sufferings being intensified by seeing their wives and children butchered before their eyes, while the degenerate Pontiff lay feasting with abandoned women. A general flight of the Pharisees ensued. This closes the second period of his reign, marked on the coin by the significant absence of the words '*Chebher* of the Jews,' the words being on one side in Hebrew, 'Jonathan the king,' and on the other in Greek, 'Alexander the king.'

The third period is marked by coins which bear the inscription 'Jehonathan the High-Priest and the Jews.' It was a period of outward military success, and of reconciliation with the Pharisees, or at least of their recall—notably of Simeon ben Shetach, and then of his friends—probably at the instigation of the queen (Ber. 48 *a*; Jer. Ber. vii. 2). Jannai died in his fiftieth year, after a reign of twenty-seven years, bequeathing the government to his wife Salome. On his death-bed he is said to have advised her to promote the Pharisees, or rather such of them as made not their religiousness a mere pretext for intrigue: 'Be not afraid of the Pharisees, nor of those who are not Pharisees, but beware of the painted ones, whose deeds are like those of Zimri, and who seek the reward of Phinehas' (Sot. 22 *b*). But of chief interest to us is, that this period of the recall of the Pharisees marks a great internal change, indicated even in the coins. For the first time we now meet the designation '*Sanhedrin*.' The *Chebher*, or eldership, had ceased as a ruling power, and become transformed into a *Sanhedrin*, or ecclesiastical authority, although the latter endeavoured, with more or less success, to arrogate to itself civil jurisdiction, at least in ecclesiastical matters.[1]

The nine years of Queen Alexandra's (in Hebrew Salome) reign were the Golden Age of the Pharisees, when heaven itself smiled on a land that was wholly subject to their religious sway. In the extravagant language of the Talmud (Taan. 23 *a*, second line from top): 'In the days of Simeon ben Shetach, the rains came down in the nights of fourth days,[2] and on those of the Sabbaths, so that the grains of corn became like kidneys, those of barley like the stones of olives, and lentils like gold dinars, and they preserved a specimen (*dogma*) of them for future generations to show them what disastrous results may follow upon sin.' That period of

---

[1] Jewish tradition, of course, vindicates a much earlier origin for the Sanhedrin, and assumes its existence not only in the time of Moses, David, and Solomon, but even in that of Mordecai! (Comp. *Buxtorf*, Lex. Chald. Talmud col. 1514.)

[2] In quoting this passage, *Derenbourg* (u. s. p 111) and *Schürer* leave out these words. [They are omitted in the corresponding account of this story in Vayy. R. 35, ed.

Warsh. p. 54 *a*; in Siphre, ed. *Friedmann*, p. 80 *a*; also in Siphra, ed. *Weiss*, p. 110 *d*, where the whole connection is very much as in Vayy. R.] Yet the words are, in one sense, most significant, since these fertilising rains, descending on these two nights when it was specially forbidden to go out, since on them innumerable demons haunted the air (Pes. 112 *b*, line 10 from the bottom), indicated an exceptional blessing. The reason why these

miraculous blessing was compared to the equally miraculous dispensation of heaven during the time that the Temple of Herod was building, when rain only fell at night, while the morning wind and heat dried all, so that the builders could continue their work without delay.[1] Queen Salome had appointed her eldest son, Hyrcanus II., a weak prince, to the Pontificate. But, as *Josephus* puts it (Ant. xiii. 16. 2), although Salome had the title, the Pharisees held the real rule of the country, and they administered it with the harshness, insolence, and recklessness of a fanatical religious party which suddenly obtains unlimited power. The lead was, of course, taken by Simeon ben Shetach, whom even the Talmud characterises as having ' hot hands' (Jer. Sanh. vi. 5,[2] p. 23 *b*). First, all who were suspected of Sadducean leanings were removed by intrigue or violence from the Sanhedrin. Next, previous ordinances differing from Pharisaical views were abrogated, and others breathing their spirit substituted. So sweeping and thorough was the change wrought, that the Sadducees never recovered the blow, and whatever they might teach, yet those in office were obliged in all time coming to conform to Pharisaic practice (*Jos*. Ant. xviii. 1. 4; Tos. Yoma i. 8).

But the Pharisaic party were not content with dogmatical victories, even though they celebrated each of them by the insertion in the Calendar of a commemorative feast-day. Partly ' to discourage the Sadducees,' partly from the supposed ' neces-sities of the time, and to teach others' (to make an example; Siphré on Deut.), they carried their principles even beyond their utmost inferences, and were guilty of such injustice and cruelty, that, according to tradition, Simeon even con-demned his own innocent son to death, for the sake of logical consistency.[3] On the other hand, the Pharisaic party knew how to flatter the queen, by intro-ducing a series of ordinances which protected the rights of married women and rendered divorce more difficult.[4] The only ordinance of Simeon ben Shetach, which deserves permanent record, is that which enjoined regular school attendance by all children, although it may have been primarily intended to place the education of the country in the hands of the Pharisees. The general discontent caused by the tyranny of the Pharisees must have rallied most of the higher classes to the party of the Sadducees. It led at last to remonstrance with the queen, and was probably the first occasion of that revolt of Aristobulus, the younger son of Salome, which darkened the last days of her reign.

Salome died (in the beginning of 69 B.C.) before the measures proposed against Aristobulus could be carried out. Although Hyrcanus II. now united the royal office with the Pontificate, his claims were disputed by his brother Aristobulus II., who conquered, and obliged his brother to abdicate in his favour his twofold dignity. To cement their reconciliation, Alexander the son of Aristobulus married Alexan-dra the daughter of Hyrcanus. They little thought how ill-fated that union would prove. For already another power was intriguing to interpose in Jewish affairs,

---

two nights are singled out as dangerous is, that Chanina b. Dosa, of whom Rabbinic tradition has so many miracles to relate, conceded them to the hurtful sway of *Agrath bath Machlath* and her 18 myriads of Angels. See App. xiii. In view of this, M. *Derenbourg's* explanatory note would seem to require to be modified. But, in general, rain even on the night before the Sabbath was regarded as a curse (Vayy. R. 35), and it has been ingeniously suggested that the רְכִיעוֹת in the Midrash must be taken in the sense in which that word is explained in

Taan. 6 *a*, viz. as the ordinary time of rain. Why the night before Wednesday and Friday night are represented as left in the power of hurtful demons might open an interesting field for speculation.
[1] This notice is followed by the somewhat blasphemous story of the achievements of *Choni* (*Onias*) *hammeaggel*, to which reference will be made in the sequel.
[2] *Chammumoth.*
[3] Comp. also Sanh. 46 *a*.
[4] Comp. *Derenbourg*, pp. 108, 109.

with which it was henceforth to be identified. Alexander Jannai had appointed one Antipas, or Antipater—of whose origin the most divergent accounts are given [1] —to the governorship of Idumæa. He was succeeded by a son of the same name. The dissension between the two Asmonæans seemed to offer the opportunity for realising his ambitious schemes. Of course, he took the part of the weak Hyrcanus as against the warlike Aristobulus, and persuaded the former that he was in danger of his life. Ultimately he prevailed on him to fly to Aretas, King of Arabia, who, in consideration of liberal promises, undertook to reinstate Hyrcanus in the government. The Arab army proved successful, and was joined by a large proportion of the troops of Aristobulus, who was not shut up within the fortified Temple-buildings. To add to the horrors of war, a long famine desolated the land. It was during its prevalence that Onias, reputed for his omnipotence in prayer, achieved what procured for him the designation 'hammeaggel'—the 'circle drawer.' [2] When his prayer for rain remained unanswered, he drew a circle around him, declaring his determination not to leave it till the Almighty had granted rain, and that not in drops, nor yet in desolating floods (which successively happened), but in copious, refreshing showers. It could serve no good purpose to reproduce the realistic manner in which this supposed power of the Rabbi with God is described (Taan. 23 a). But it were difficult to say whether this is more repugnant to feelings of reverence, or the reported reproof of Simeon ben Shetach, who forbore to pronounce the ban upon him because he was like a spoilt child who might ask anything of his father, and would obtain it. But this supposed power ultimately proved fatal to Onias during the siege of Jerusalem by Hyrcanus and Aretas. [3] Refusing to intercede either for one or the other of the rival brothers, he was stoned to death (Ant. xiv. 2. 1).

But already another power had appeared on the scene. Pompey was on his victorious march through Asia when both parties appealed to him for help. Scaurus, whom Pompey detached to Syria, was, indeed, bought by Aristobulus, and Aretas was ordered to raise the siege of Jerusalem. But Pompey quickly discovered that Hyrcanus might, under the tutelage of the cunning Idumæan, Antipater, prove an instrument more likely to serve his ulterior purposes than Aristobulus. Three deputations appeared before Pompey at Damascus—those of the two brothers, and one independent of both, which craved the abolition of the Asmonæan rule and the restoration of the former mode of government, as we understand it, by the 'Chebher' or Eldership under the presidency of the High-Priest. It need scarcely be said that such a demand would find no response. The consideration of the rival claims of the Asmonæans Pompey postponed. The conduct of Aristobulus not only confirmed the unfavourable impression which the insolent bearing of his deputies had made on Pompey, but sealed his own fate and that of the Jewish people. Pompey laid siege to Jerusalem. The adherents of Hyrcanus surrendered the City, but those of Aristobulus retired into the Temple. At last the sacred precincts were taken by storm amidst fearful carnage. The priests, who were engaged in their

---

[1] According to some (Ant. xiv. 1. 3), he was of noble Jewish, according to others, of heathen and slave descent. The truth lies probably between these extremes.

[2] It almost seems as if this repugnant story were a sort of Jewish imitation of the circle which Popilius Lænas drew around Antiochus Epiphanes, bidding him decide, ere he left

it, whether or not he would comply with the demand of the Romans.

[3] Both *Josephus* and the Talmud (Sotah 49 b) give an account, though in different version, of the manner in which the besieged sought a supply of sacrifices from the besiegers.

APP.
IV

sacred functions,[1] and who continued them during this terrible scene, were cut down at the altar. No fewer than 12,000 Jews are said to have perished.

With the taking of Jerusalem by Pompey (63 B.C.) the history of the Maccabees as a reigning family, and, indeed, that of the real independence of Palestine, came to an end. So truly did Jewish tradition realise this, that it has left us not a single notice either of this capture of Jerusalem or of all the subsequent sad events to the time of Herod. It is as if their silence meant that for them Judæa, in its then state, had no further history. Still, the Roman conquerer had as yet dealt gently with his prostrate victim. Pompey had, indeed, penetrated into the Most Holy Place in contemptuous outrage of the most sacred feelings of Israel; but he left the treasures of the Temple untouched, and even made provision for the continuance of its services. Those who had caused the resistance of Jerusalem were executed, and the country made tributary to Rome. But Judæa not only became subject to the Roman Governor of Syria, its boundaries were also narrowed. All the Grecian cities had their independence restored; Samaria was freed from Jewish supremacy; and the districts comprised within the so-called Decapolis (or 'ten cities') again obtained self-government. It was a sadly curtailed land over which Hyrcanus II., as High-Priest, was left Governor, without being allowed to wear the diadem (Ant. xx. 10). Aristobulus II. had to adorn as captive the triumphal entry of the conquerer into Rome. [2]

The civil rule of Hyrcanus as Ethnarch must from the first have been very limited. It was still more contracted when, during the Proconsulate of Gabinius (57–55 B.C.),[3] Alexander, a son of Aristobulus, who had escaped from captivity, tried to possess himself of the government of Judæa (Ant. xiv. 5. 2–4). The office of Hyrcanus was now limited to the Temple, and the Jewish territory, divided into five districts, was apportioned among five principal cities, ruled by a council of local notables ($\check{\alpha}\rho\iota\sigma\tau\sigma\iota$). Thus, for a short time, monarchical gave place to aristocratic government in Palestine. The renewed attempts of Aristobulus or of his family to recover power only led to fresh troubles, which were sadly diversified by the rapacity and severity of the Romans. The Triumvir Crassus, who succeeded Gabinius (55–53 B.C.), plundered the Temple not only of its treasures but of its precious vessels. A new but not much happier era began with Julius Cæsar. If Aristobulus and his son Alexander had not fallen victims to the party of Pompey, the prospects of Hyrcanus and Antipater might now have been very unpromising. But their death and that of Pompey (whom they had supported) changed the aspect of matters. Antipater not only espoused the cause of the victor of Pharsalus, but made himself eminently useful to Cæsar. In reward, Hyrcanus was confirmed as Pontiff and Ethnarch of Judæa, while Antipater was made a Roman citizen and nominated *Epitrophos*, or (Roman) administrator of the country. Of course, the real power was in the hands of the Idumæan, who continued to hold it, despite the attempts of Antigonus, the only surviving son of Aristobulus. And from henceforth Cæsar made it part of his policy to favour the Jews (comp. the decrees in their favour, Ant. xiv. 10).

Meantime Antipater had, in pursuance of his ambitious plans, appointed his son Phasael Governor of Jerusalem, and Herod Governor of Galilee. The latter,

---

[1] According to *Josephus*, it was on the Day of Atonement; according to *Dio Cassius*, apparently on a Sabbath. Comp. the remarks of *Derenbourg* on these conflicting statements (u. s. p. 117, note).
[2] The captives then brought to Rome and

sold as slaves became the nucleus of the Jewish community in the imperial city.
[5] Comp. the masterly survey of the state of matters in Syria and Judæa in *Marquardt*, Handb. d. Röm. Alterth., vol. iv. pp. 247–260.

although only twenty-five years of age, soon displayed the vigour and sternness which characterised his after-career. He quelled what probably was a 'nationalist' rising in Galilee, in the blood of Ezekias, its leader, and of his chief associates. This indeed secured him the favour of Sextus Cæsar, the Governor of Syria, a relative of the great *Imperator*. But in Jerusalem, and among the extreme Pharisaic party, it excited the utmost indignation. They foresaw the advent of a foe most dangerous to their interests and liberty, and vainly sought to rid themselves of him. It was argued that the government of the country was in the hands of the High-Priest, and that Herod, as Governor of Galilee, appointed by a foreign administrator, had no right to pronounce capital punishment without a sentence of the Sanhedrin. Hyrcanus yielded to the clamour; but Herod appeared before the Sanhedrin, not as a criminal, but arrayed in purple, surrounded by a body-guard, and supported by the express command of Sextus Cæsar to acquit him. The story which is related, though in different version, and with different names), in the Talmud (Sanh. 19 *a*), and by *Josephus* (Ant. xiv. 9. 3-5), presents a vivid picture of what passed in the Sanhedrin. The appearance of Herod had so terrified that learned body that none ventured to speak, till their president, Shemajah (Sameas), by his bold speech, rallied their courage. Most truly did he foretell the fate which overtook them ten years later, when Herod ruled in the Holy City. But Hyrcanus adjourned the meeting of the Sanhedrin, and persuaded Herod to withdraw from Jerusalem. His was, however, only a temporary humiliation. Sextus Cæsar named Herod Governor of Cœle-Syria, and he soon appeared with an army before Jerusalem, to take vengeance on Hyrcanus and the Sanhedrin. The entreaties of his father and brother induced him, indeed, to desist for the time, but ten years later alike Hyrcanus and the members of the Sanhedrin fell victims to his revenge.

Another turn of affairs seemed imminent when Cæsar fell under the daggers of the conspirators (15 March, 44), and Cassius occupied Syria. But Antipater and Herod proved as willing and able to serve him as formerly Cæsar. Antipater, indeed, perished through a court- or perhaps a 'Nationalist' plot, but his murderers soon experienced the same fate at the hands of those whom Herod had hired for the purpose. And still the star of Herod seemed in the ascendant. Not only did he repel attempted inroads by Antigonus, but when Antonius and Octavianus (in 42 B.C.) took the place of Brutus and Cassius, he succeeded once more in ingratiating himself with the former, on whom the government of Asia devolved. The accusations made by Jewish deputations had no influence on Antony. Indeed, he went beyond his predecessors in appointing Phasael and Herod tetrarchs of Judæa. Thus the civil power was now nominally as well as really in their hands. But the restless Antigonus was determined not to forego his claim. When the power of Antony was fast waning, in consequence of his reckless indulgences, Antigonus seized the opportunity of the incursion of the Parthians into Asia Minor to attend the great object of his ambition. In Jerusalem the adherents of the two parties were engaged in daily conflicts, when a Parthian division appeared. By treachery Phasael and Hyrcanus were lured into the Parthian camp, and finally handed over to Antigonus. Herod, warned in time, had escaped from Jerusalem with his family and armed adherents. Of his other opponents Antigonus made sure. To unfit Hyrcanus for the Pontificate his ears were cut off, while Phasael destroyed himself in his prison. Antigonus was now undisputed High-Priest and king. His brief reign of three years (40-37 B.C.) is marked by coins which bear in Hebrew the device: Matthatjah the High-Priest, and in Greek: King Antigonus.

The only hope of Herod lay in Roman help. He found Antony in Rome. What difficulties there were, were removed by gold, and when Octavian gave his consent, a decree of the Senate declared Antigonus the enemy of Rome, and at the same time appointed Herod King of Judæa (40 B.C.). Early in the year 39 B.C. Herod was in Palestine to conquer his new kingdom by help of the Romans. But their aid was at first tardy and reluctant, and it was 38, or more probably 37, before Herod could gain possession of Jerusalem itself. Before that he had wedded the beautiful and unhappy Mariamme, the daughter of Alexander and grand-daughter of Hyrcanus, to whom he had been betrothed five years before. His conquered capital was desolate indeed, and its people impoverished by exactions. But Herod had reached the goal of his ambition. All opposition was put down, all rivalry rendered impossible. Antigonus was beheaded, as Herod had wished; the feeble and aged Hyrcanus was permanently disqualified for the Pontificate; and any youthful descendants of the Maccabees left were absolutely in the conqueror's power. The long struggle for power had ended, and the Asmonæan family was virtually destroyed. Their sway had lasted about 130 years.

Looking back on the rapid rise and decline of the Maccabees, on their speedy degeneration, on the deeds of cruelty with which their history soon became stained, on the selfishness and reckless ambition which characterised them, and especially on the profoundly anti-nationalist and anti-Pharisaic, we had almost said anti-Jewish, tendency which marked their sway, we can understand the bitter hatred with which Jewish tradition had followed their memory. The mention of them is of the scantiest. No universal acclamation glorifies even the deeds of Judas the Maccabee; no Talmudic tractate is devoted to that 'feast of the dedication' which celebrated the purging of the Temple and the restoration of Jewish worship. In fact such was the feeling, that the priestly course of Joiarib—to which the Asmonæans belonged—is said to have been on service when the first and the second Temple were destroyed, because 'guilt was to be punished on the guilty.' More than that, ' R. Levi saith: *Yehoyaribh* [" Jehovah will contend "], the man [the name of the man or family]; *Meron* ["rebellion," evidently a play upon Modin, the birthplace of the Maccabees], the town; *Mesarbey* ["the rebels," evidently a play upon Makkabey]—(*masar beitha*) He hath given up the Temple to the enemies.' Rabbi Berachjah saith: ' *Yah heribh* [Jehoiarib], God contended with His children, because they revolted and rebelled against Him ' (Jer. Taan. iv. 8, p. 68 *d*, line 35 from bottom).[1] Indeed, the opprobrious designation of rebellion, and *Sarbaney El*, rebels against God, became in course of time so identified with the Maccabees. that it was used when its meaning was no longer understood. Thus *Origen* (Euseb. Hist. Eccl. vi. 25) speaks of the (Apocryphal) books of the Maccabees as ' inscribed Sarbeth Sarbane El' (= סרבת סרבני אל), the disobedience, or rebellion (resistance) of the disobedient, or rebels, against God.[2] So thoroughly had these terms become identified in popular *parlance*, that even the tyranny and cruelty of a Herod could not procure a milder judgment on the sway of the Asmonæans.

---

[1] Comp. *Geiger*, Urschrift, p. 204; *Deren-bourg*, p. 119, note.
[2] Comp. *Geiger*, u. s. p 205, Note, *Hamburger*, u. s. p. 367. Various strange and most unsatisfactory explanations have been proposed of these mysterious words, which yet, on consideration, seem so easy of understanding. Comp. the curious explanations of *Grimm*, *Ewald*, and others, in *Grimm's* Exeget. Handb. zu d. Apokryphen, 3te Lief. p. xvii. *Deren'ourg* (Hist. de la Palest. pp. 450–452) regards σαρβηδ as a corruption for σαβαβηδ, and would render the whole by ' Book of the family of the Chief (שׂר) of the people of God.'

APPENDIX V.

RABBINIC THEOLOGY AND LITERATURE.

(Vol. i. Book I. ch. viii.)

1. *The Traditional Law.*—The brief account given in vol. i. p. 100, of the character and authority claimed for the traditional law may here be supplemented by a chronological arrangement of the *Halakhoth* in the order of their supposed introduction or promulgation.

In the *first* class, or 'Halakhoth of Moses from Sinai,' tradition enumerates *fifty-five*,[1] which may be thus designated: *religio-agrarian*, four;[2] *ritual*, including questions about 'clean and unclean,' twenty-three;[3] concerning *women* and intercourse between the sexes, three;[4] concerning *formalities* to be observed in the copying, fastening, &c., of the Law and the phylacteries, eighteen;[5] *exegetical*, four;[6] *purely superstitious*, one;[7] *not otherwise included*, two.[8] *Eighteen* ordinances are ascribed to Joshua, of which only one is ritual, the other seventeen being agrarian and police regulations.[9] The other traditions can only be briefly noted. Boaz, or else 'the tribunal of Samuel,' fixed, that Deut. xxiii. 3 did not apply to alliances with Ammonite and Moabite *women*. Two ordinances are ascribed to David, two to Solomon, one to Jehoshaphat, and one to Jehoiada. The period of Isaiah and of Hezekiah is described as of immense Rabbinic activity. To the prophets at Jerusalem three ritual ordinances are ascribed. Daniel is represented as having prohibited the bread, wine, and oil of the heathen (Dan. i. 5). Two ritual determinations are ascribed to the prophets of the Exile.

---

[1] The numbers given by *Maimonides*, in his Preface to the Mishnah, and their arrangement, are somewhat different, but I prefer the more critical (sometimes even hypercritical) enumeration of *Herzfeld*. They are also enumerated in *Peiser's Nachlath Shimoni*, Part I. pp. 47–49 *b*.

[2] Peah ii. 6; Yad. iv. 3; Tos. Peah iii. 2; Orlah iii. 9.

[3] Erub. 4 *a*; Nidd. 72 *b*; Ker. 6 *b*; Ab. d. R.N. 19, 25; Tos. Chall. 1. 6; Shabb 70 *a*; Bekh. 16 *a*; Naz. 28 *b*; Chull. 27 *a*, 28 *a*; 42 *a*, 43 *a*; Moed Q. 3 *b*. Of these, the most interesting to the Christian reader are about the 11 ingredients of the sacred incense (Ker. 6 *b*); about the 26 kinds of work prohibited on the Sabbath (Shabb. 70 *a*); that the father, but not the mother, might dedicate a child under age to the Nazirate (Naz. 28 *b*); the 7 rules as to slaughtering animals; to cut the neck; to cut through the trachea, and, in the case of four-footed animals, also through the gullet; not to pause while slaughtering; to use a knife perfectly free of all notches, and quite sharp; not to strike with the knife; not to cut too near the head; and not to stick the knife into the throat; certain determinations about the Feast of Tabernacles, such

as about the pouring out of the water, &c.

[4] Ab. Z. 36 *b*; Niddah 45 *a*. 72 *b*.

[5] Jer. Meg. i. 9; Shabb. 28 *b*; Men. 32 *a*; 35 *a*.

[6] Ned. 37 *b*. These four Halakhoth are: as to the authoritative pronunciation of certain words in the Bible; as to the *Ittur Sopherim*, or syntactic and stylistic emendation in the following five passages: Gen. xviii. 5, xxiv. 55; Numb. xxxi. 2; Ps. lxviii. 22 (A.V. 21); xxxvi. 7 (A.V. 6); about the *Qeri velo Kethibh*, words *read* but *not written* in the text; and the *Kethibh velo Qeri*, words *written* but *not read* in the text.

[7] Pes. 110 *b*. Not to eat two pieces (even numbers) of an egg, a nut, or cucumber, &c.

[8] Eduy. viii. 7; Tanch. 60 *a*. The first of these *Halakhoth* speaks of the activity of Elijah in preparation for the coming of the Messiah (Mal. iii. 23, 24, A.V. iv. 5, 6), as directed to restore those of pure Israelitish descent who had been improperly extruded, and to extrude those who had been improperly admitted.

[9] Baba K. 81 *a*; Tos. Baba M. 11; Jer. Baba K. iii. 2. Among the police regulations is this curious one, that all were allowed to fish in the Lake of Galilee, but not to lay down nets, so as not to impede the navigation.

After the return from Babylon traditionalism rapidly expanded, and its peculiar character more and more clearly developed. No fewer than twelve traditions are traced back to the three prophets who flourished at that period, while four other important legal determinations are attributed to the prophet Haggai individually. It will readily be understood that Ezra occupied a high place in tradition. Fifteen ordinances are ascribed to him, of which some are ritual. Three of his supposed ordinances have a general interest. They enjoin the general education of children, and the exclusion of Samaritans from admission into the Synagogue and from social intercourse. If only one legal determination is assigned to Nehemiah, 'the men of the Great Synagogue' are credited with fifteen, of which six bear on important critical and exegetical points connected with the text of the Scriptures, the others chiefly on questions connected with ritual and worship. Among the 'pairs' (*Zug-oth*) which succeeded the 'Great Synagogue,' three 'alleviating' ordinances (of a very punctilious character) are ascribed to José, the son of Joezer,[1] and two, intended to render all contact with heathens impossible, to him and his colleague. Under the Maccabees the feast of the dedication of the Temple was introduced. To Joshua the son of Perachya, one punctilious legal determination is ascribed. Of the decrees of the Maccabean High-Priest Jochanan we have already spoken in another place; similarly, of those of Simon the son of Shetach and of his learned colleague. Four legal determinations of their successors Shemayah and Abhtalion are mentioned. Next in order comes the prohibition of Greek during the war between the Maccabean brothers Hyrcanus and Aristobulus. This brings us to the time of Hillel and Shammai, that is, to the period of Jesus, to which further reference will have to be made in another place.

2. *The Canon of Scripture.*—Reference has been made in the text (vol. i. p. 107) to the position taken by Traditionalism in reference to the written as compared with what was regarded as the oral Revelation. Still, nominally, the Scriptures were appealed to by the Palestinians as of supreme authority. The views which *Josephus* expresses in this respect, although in a popular and Grecianised form, were substantially those entertained by the Rabbis and by his countrymen generally (comp. Ag. Apion, i. 7, 8).[2] A sharp distinction was made between canonical and non-canonical books. The test of the former was inspiration, which had ceased in the time of Artaxerxes, that is, with the prophet Malachi. Accordingly, the work of the elder Jesus the son of Sirach (Jeshua ben Sira, ben Eliezer) was excluded from the Canon, although it is not unfrequently referred to by Rabbinic authorities in terms with which ordinarily only Biblical quotations are introduced.[3] According to the view propounded by Josephus, not only were the very words inspired in which a prediction was uttered, but the prophets were unconscious and passive vehicles of the Divine message (Ant. iv. 6. 5; comp. generally, Ant ii. 8. 1; vi. 8, 2; viii. 13, 3; ix. 3, 2; 8, 6; x. 2, 2; 4, 3). Although pre-eminence in this respect was assigned to Moses (Ant. iv. 8, 49), yet Divine authority equally attached to the

---

[1] According to tradition (Sot. 47 *a* and *b*) the *Eshko'oth*, or 'bunches of grapes,' ceased with Josè. The expression refers to the Rabbis, and *Herzfeld* ingeniously suggests this explanation of the designation, that after Jos' they were no longer undivided like bunches of grapes, but divided in their opinions. For other explanations comp. *Deren'ourg*, u s pp. 88, 456-458

[2] For a detailed account of the views of *Josephus* on the *Canon* and on *Inspiration*, I take leave to refer to my article in ' *Smith's* Dictionary of Christian Biography,' vol. iii. pp 453, 454.

[3] Comp. *Zunz*, Gottesd Vortr. pp. 101, 102, and *C. Seligmann*, d Buch d Weish. d. Jesus Sirach. The Talmudic quotations from the work of the elder Jesus have been repeatedly collated I may here take leave to refer to my collection and translation of them in Append. II. to the 'History of the Jewish Nation.'

sayings of the prophets, and even, though perhaps in a still inferior degree, to the 'Hymns,' as the Hagiographa generally were called from the circumstance that the Psalter stood at the head of them (comp. *Philo*, De Vita contempl., ed. *Mangey*, vol. ii. p. 475; St. Luke xxiv. 44). Thus the division of the Bible into three sections —the Law, the Prophets, and the other 'Writings'—which already occurs in the prologue to the work of Jesus the son of Sirach,[1] seems to have been current at the time. And here it is of great interest, in connection with modern controversies, that Josephus seems to attach special importance to the prophecies of Daniel as still awaiting fulfilment (Ant. x. 10. 4; 11. 7).

That the Rabbis entertained the same views of inspiration, appears not only from the distinctive name of 'Holy Writings' given to the Scriptures, but also from the directions that their touch defiled the hands,[2] and that it was duty on the Sabbath to save them from conflagration, and to gather them up if accidentally scattered, and that it was not lawful for heirs to make division of a sacred roll (comp. Shabb. xvi. 1; Erub. x. 3; Kel. xv. 6; Yad. iii. 2-5; iv. 5 [where special reference is made to Daniel] 6). From what we know of the state of feeling, we might have inferred, even if direct evidence had not existed, that a distinctive and superior place would be ascribed to the Books of Moses. In point of fact, the other books of Scripture, alike the Prophets and the Hagiographa,[3] are only designated as *Qabbalah* ('received,' handed down, tradition), which is also the name given to oral tradition.[4] It was said that the *Torah* was given to Moses (Jer. Sheq. vi. 1) 'in (letters of) white fire graven upon black fire,' although it was matter of dispute whether he received it volume by volume or complete as a whole (Gitt. 60 *a*). But on the question of its inspiration not the smallest doubt could be tolerated. Thus, to admit generally, that 'the Torah as a whole was from heaven, except this (one) verse, which the Holy One, blessed be He, did not speak, but Moses of himself' was to become an infidel and a blasphemer (Sanh. 99 *a*).[5] Even the concluding verses in Deuteronomy had been dictated by God to Moses, and he wrote them down—not repeating them, however, as before, but weeping as he wrote. It will readily be understood in what extravagant terms Moses himself was spoken of. It is not only that the expression 'man of God' was supposed to imply, that while as regarded the lower part of his nature Moses was man, as regarded the higher he was Divine, but that his glorification and exaltation amount

---

[1] Comp. also *1* Macc. ii. 13, 14.

[2] The general statement that this decree was intended to prevent a common or profane use of the Scripture does not explain its origin. The latter seems to have been as follows: At first the priests in the Temple were wont to deposit the *Terumah* near the copy of the Law there kept (Shabb 14 *a*). But as mice were thereby attracted, and damage to the Sacred Roll was apprehended, it was enacted that the Sacred Roll in the Temple rendered all meat that touched it unclean. This decree gave rise to another, by way of further precaution, that even the hands which touched the Sacred Roll. or any other part of the Bible, became unclean (so that, having touched the latter, they could not touch the *Terumah*). Then followed (in the course of development) a third decree, that such touch defiled also outside the Temple. Finally, the first decree was modified to the effect that the Sacred Roll in the Temple did *not* defile the hands, while all other Scriptures (anywhere else) defiled them

(Chel xv. 6) The explanation offered to the Sadducees by R. Jochanan b. Zakkai is evidently intended to mislead (Yad iv. 6), Comp *Levy*. Neuhebr. Wörterb. vol. ii. pp. 163, 164.

[3] The difference in the degree of inspiration between the Prophetic and the Hagiographic books is not accurately defined. Later Jewish theologians rather evade it by describing the former as given by 'the spirit of prophecy,' the latter 'by the Holy Spirit.' It must, however, be admitted that in Jewish writings 'the Holy Spirit' is not only *not* a Personality, but an influence very inferior to what we associate with the designation.

[4] The proof-passages are quoted in *Zunz*, u. s. p. 44 note, also in J. *Delitzsch*, De Inspir. Script. S. pp. 7, 8.

[5] At the same time, in Meg. 31 *b* the formulation of the curses by Moses in Lev. xxvi. is said to have been מִפִּי הַגְּבוּרָה (from God directly), while that in Deut. xxviii, was מִפִּי עַצְמוֹ (from Moses himself).

to blasphemy.[1] So far as inspiration or ' revelation ' is concerned, it was said that Moses ' saw in a clear glass, the prophets in a dark one '—or, to put it otherwise: ' he saw through one glass, they through seven.' Indeed, although the opening words of Ps. lxxv. showed, that the Psalms were as much revelation as the Law, yet, ' if Israel had not sinned, they would have only received the Pentateuch, and the Book of Joshua,' and, in the time to come, of all Scripture the Pentateuch alone would retain its place. It was somewhat contemptuously remarked, that the Prophets uttered nothing as regarded practice that had not already been told in the Pentateuch (Taan. 9 a). It was but natural for Rabbinism to declare that the Law alone fully explained its meaning (at least according to their interpretation of it), while the Prophets left much in obscurity.[2] To mark the distinction, it was forbidden to put the Law in the same wrapper with the Prophets, so as not to place perhaps the latter on the top of the former (Tos. Meg. iv. 20). Among the Prophets themselves there was a considerable difference, not only in style and training but even in substance (Sanh. 89 a), although all of them had certain common qualifications (comp. Ab. de R. Nathan, 37). Of all the prophets Isaiah was greatest, and stood next to Moses. Ezekiel saw all that Isaiah saw—but the former was like a villager, the latter like a townsman who saw the king (Chag. 13 b). Jeremiah and Amos were, so to speak, scolding, owing to the violence of their temperament, while Isaiah's was the book of consolation, especially in response to Jeremiah.

The Hagiographa or ' Kethubhim ' also bear in the Talmud the general designation of ' Chokhmah,' wisdom. It has been asserted that, as the Prophetic Books, so the Hagiographa, were distinguished into ' anterior ' (Psalms, Proverbs, Job) and ' posterior,' or else into ' great ' and ' small.' But the statement rests on quite insufficient evidence.[3] Certain, however, it is, that the Hagiographa, as we possess them, formed part of the Canon in the time of Jesus the son of Sirach—that is, even on the *latest* computation of his authorship,[4] about the year 130 B.C.[5] Even so, it would not be easy to vindicate, on historical grounds, the so-called Maccabean authorship of the Book of Daniel, which would fix its date about 105 B.C. For, if other considerations did not interfere, few students of Jewish history would be disposed to assert that a book, which dated from 105 B.C., could have found a place in the Jewish Canon.[6] But, as explained in vol. i. p. 26, we would assign a much earlier date to the Book of Sirach. The whole question in its bearing on the New Testament is so important, that one or two further remarks may be allowed. Leaving aside most serious critical objections, and the unquestionable fact, that

---

[1] A more terribly repulsive instance of this can scarcely be conceived than in Debar. R. 11, of which the worst parts are reproduced in Yalkut 304 a, b, c.

[2] Comp. generally *Hamburger's* Real. Encycl. vols. i. and ii. See also *Delitzsch's* work already quoted, and *Fürst,* Kanon d. Alten Test. nach Talmud u. Midrasch.

[3] *Fürst,* u. s. pp. 57–59,-quotes Ber. 57 b and Sot. 7 b, Ab. de R. Nathan 40. But no one who reads either Ber. 57 b, or Ab. de R. Nathan 40, would feel inclined to draw from passages so strange and repulsive any serious inference, while Sot. 7 b is far too vague to serve as a basis. In general, this is one of the many instances in which *Fürst,* as, indeed, many modern Jewish writers, propounds as matters of undoubted fact, what, on critical examination, is seen to rest on no certain his-

torical basis—sometimes on no basis at all.

[4] Which in another place we have shown to be erroneous.

[5] *Fürst.* p. 56. See also *Reuss,* Gesch. d. Heil. Schr. A.T. (p. 550), who gives its date as 132.

[6] *Fürst,* who holds the Maccabean origin of the Book of Daniel, is so frequently inconsistent with himself in the course of his remarks on the subject, that it is sometimes difficult to understand him. Occasionally, when argument is wanting, he asserts that a thing is self-evident (es versteht sich von selbst). Such a ' self-evident ' assertion, for which, however, no historical evidence is offered—which, indeed, runs in the opposite direction—is summarised on page 100. But the word ' self-evident ' has no place in historical discussions, where only that is evident which rests on *historical* grounds.

no amount of ingenuity can conciliate the Maccabean application of Dan. ix. 24-27 with the chronology of that period,[1] while the Messianic interpretation fits in with it,[2] other, and seemingly insuperable difficulties are in the way of the theory impugned. It implies, that the Book of Daniel was not only an Apocryphal, but a Pseudepigraphic work; that of all such works it alone has come down to us in its Hebrew or Chaldee original; that a Pseudepigraphic work, nearly contemporary with the oldest portion of the Book of Enoch, should not only be so different from it, but that it should find admission into the Canon, while Enoch was excluded; that a Pseudepigraphon younger than Jesus the Son of Sirach should have been one of the Khethubhim; and, finally, that it should have passed the repeated revision of different Rabbinic 'Colleges'—and that at times of considerable theological activity—without the suspicion being even raised that its authorship dated from so late a period as a century and a half before Christ. And we have evidence that since the Babylonish exile, at least *four* revisions of the Canon took place within periods sufficiently distant from each other.

The question hitherto treated has been exclusively of the *date* of the composition of the Book of Daniel, without reference to who may have been its author, whether its present is exactly the same as its original form, and, finally, whether it ever belonged to those books whose right to canonicity, though not their age, was in controversy, that is, whether it belonged, so to speak, to the Old Testament ἀντιλεγόμενα. As this is not the place for a detailed discussion of the canonicity of the Book of Daniel—or, indeed, of any other in the Old Testament canon—we shall only add, to prevent misunderstanding, that no opinion is here expressed as to possible, greater or less, interpolations in the Book of Daniel, or in any other part of the Old Testament. We must here bear in mind that the moral view taken of such interpolations, as we would call them, was entirely different in those times from ours; and it may perhaps be an historically and critically not unwarranted proposition, that such interpolations were, to speak moderately, not at all unusual in ancient documents. In each case the question must be separately critically examined in the light of internal and (if possible) external evidence. But it would be a very different thing to suggest that there may be an interpolation, or, it may be, a re-arrangement in a document (although at present we make no assertions on the subject, one way or the other), and to pronounce a whole document a fabrication dating from a much later period. The one would, at any rate, be quite in the spirit of those times; the other implies, besides insuperable critical difficulties, a deliberate religious fraud, to which no unprejudiced student could seriously regard the so-called Pseudepigrapha as forming any real *analogon*.

But as regards the Book of Daniel, it is an important fact that the right of the Book of Daniel to canonicity was never called in question in the ancient Synagogue. The fact that it was distinguished as 'visions' (*Chezyonoth*) from the other 'prophecies' has, of course, no bearing on the question, any more than the circumstance that later Rabbinism, which, naturally enough, could not find its way through the Messianic prophecies of the book, declared that even Daniel was mistaken in, and could not make anything of the predictions concerning the 'latter days'

---

[1] This is admitted even by Mr. *Drummond* ('Jewish Messiah,' pp. 246, 254-257, 260). Mr. *Drummond's* book is quoted as representing the advocacy by a distinguished English scholar of the Maccabean theory of the authorship of Daniel.
[2] *Drummond*, u. s. p. 261.

APP.
V

(Ber. R. 98).[1] On the other hand, Daniel was elevated to almost the same pinnacle as Moses, while it was said that, as compared with heathen sages, if they were all placed in one scale, and Daniel in the other, he would outweigh them all. We can readily understand that, in times of national sorrow or excitement, these prophecies would be eagerly resorted to, as pointing to a glorious future.

But although the Book of Daniel was not among the *Antilegomena*, doubts were raised, not indeed about the age, but about the right to canonicity of certain other portions of the Bible. Thus, certain expressions in the prophecies of Ezekiel were questioned as apparently incompatible with statements in the Pentateuch[2] (Men. 45 a), and although a celebrated Rabbi, Chananyah, the son of Chizkiyah, the son of Garon (about the time of Christ), with immense labour, sought to conciliate them, and thus preserved the Book of Ezekiel (or, at least, part of it) from being relegated among the Apocrypha, it was deemed safest to leave the final exposition of the meaning of Ezekiel 'till Elijah come,' as the restorer of all things.

The other objections to canonicity apply exclusively to the third division of the Old Testament, the *Kethubhim* or Hagiographa. Here even the Book of Proverbs seems at one time to have been called in question (Ab. de R. Nathan 1), partly on the ground of its secular contents, and partly as containing ' supposed contradictory statements '[3] (Shabb. 30 b). Very strong doubts were raised on the Book of Ecclesiastes (Yad. iii. 5; Eduy. v. 3), first, on the ground of its contradiction of some of the Psalms[4] (Shabb. 30 a); secondly, on that of its inconsistencies[5] (Shabb. 30 b); and, thirdly, because it seemed to countenance the denial of another life, and, as in Eccl. xi. 1, 3, 9, other heretical views (Vayyikra R. 28, at the beginning).[6] But these objections were finally answered by great ingenuity, while an appeal to Eccl. xii. 12, 13, was regarded as removing the difficulty about another life and future rewards and punishments. And as the contradictions in Ecclesiastes had been conciliated, it was hopefully argued that deeper study would equally remove those in the Book of Proverbs (Shabb. 30 b).[7] Still, the controversy about the canonicity of Ecclesiastes continued so late as the second century of our era (comp. Yad. iii. 5). That grave doubts also existed about the Song of Solomon, appears even from the terms in which its canonicity is insisted upon (Yad. u. s.), not to speak of express statements in opposition to it (Ab. de R. Nathan 1). Even when by an allegorical interpretation it was shown to be the ' wisdom of all wisdom,' the most precious gem, the holy of holies, tradition still ascribed its composition to the *early* years of Solomon (Shir haSh. R. 1). It had been his first work, and was followed by Proverbs, and finally by Ecclesiastes.[8] But perhaps the greatest objec-

---

[1] And yet there are frequent indications that Rabbinism sought guidance on these very subjects in the prophecies of Daniel. Thus, in the Pirqe de R. Eliezer there are repeated references to the four monarchies—the Persian, Median, Macedonian,and Roman—when, in the time of the fifth monarchy, that of the children of Ishmael—after a terrible war against Rome, the Messiah would come (comp. Pirqé de R. El. 19, and especially 28, 30, and 48).

[2] Among them the following may be mentioned (Chull. 37 b); Ezek. iv. 14 &c., and (Men. 45 a), Ezek. xliv. 31 were regarded as suggesting that these prohibitions applied only to *priests;* (Moed. K. 5 a) Ezek. xliv. 19, seemed to imply that an ordinary Israelite

might perform sacrificial service, while Ezek. xlv. 18 appeared to enjoin a sacrifice nowhere mentioned in the Pentateuch.

[3] For ex. Prov. xxvi. 4, 5.,

[4] As for ex. Ps. cxv. 17 compared with Eccl. iv. 2 and ix. 4.

[5] For ex. Eccl. ii. 2 comp. with vii. 3; and again, viii 15, or iv. 2 comp. with ix. 4.

[6] The school of Shammai was *against.* that of Hillel in *favour* of the Canonicity of Ecclesiastes (Eduy. v. 3). In Tos. Yad. ii. Ecclesiastes is said to be uninspired, and to contain only the wisdom of Solomon.

[7] But it must be admitted that some of these conciliations are sufficiently curious.

[8] But on this subject opinions differ very widely (see Shir haSh. R. 1, ed. Warshau. pp.

tions were those taken to the Book of Esther (Meg. 7 *a*). It excited the enmity of other nations against Israel, and it was outside the canon. Grave doubts prevailed whether it was canonical or inspired by the Holy Spirit (Meg. u. s.; Yoma 29 *a*). The books of Ezra and Nehemiah were anciently regarded as one—the name of the latter author being kept back on account of his tendency to self-exaltation (Sanh. 93 *b*). Lastly, the genealogical parts of the Book of Chronicles were made the subject of very elaborate secret commentation (Pes. 62 *b*).

Two points still require brief mention. Even from a comparison of the LXX. Version with our Hebrew text, it is evident that there were not only many variations, but that spurious additions (as in Daniel) were eliminated. This critical activity, which commenced with Ezra, whose copy of the Pentateuch was, according to tradition, placed in the Temple, that the people might correct their copies by it, must have continued for many centuries.[1] There is abundant evidence of frequent divergences—though perhaps minute—and although later Rabbinism laid down the most painfully minute directions about the mode of writing and copying the rolls of the Law, there is such discrepancy, even where least it might be expected,[2] as to show that the purification of the text was by no means settled. Considering the want of exegetical knowledge and historical conscientiousness, and keeping in view how often the Rabbis, for Haggadic purposes, alter letters, and thus change the meaning of words, we may well doubt the satisfactory character of their critical labours. Lastly, as certain omissions were made, and as the Canon underwent (as will be shown) repeated revision, it *may* have been that certain portions were added as well as left out, and words changed as well as restored.

For, ancient tradition ascribes a peculiar activity to certain 'Colleges'—as they are termed—in regard to the Canon. In general, the well-known *Baraita* (Baba B. 14 *b*, 15 *a*) bears, that Moses wrote the Pentateuch, the book (Prophecies ?) of Balaam, and Job; Joshua the work that bears his name, and the last eight verses of Deuteronomy;[3] Samuel the corresponding books, Judges and Ruth; David with the 'ten Elders,' Adam, Melchisedek, Abraham, Moses, Heman, Jeduthun, Asaph, and the three sons of Korah, the Psalter; Jeremiah wrote his prophecies, Lamentations, and Kings; King Hezekiah and his Sanhedrin compiled, or edited, the Prophecies of Isaiah, Proverbs, the Song, and Ecclesiastes; and the men of the 'Great Synagogue' the Prophecies of Ezekiel, of the twelve Minor Prophets, and the books of Daniel and Esther; Ezra wrote his own book and Chronicles, the work being completed by Nehemiah, the son of Chakaliah. The last verse of Joshua were written by Eleazar and Phinehas; the last chapters of Samuel by Gad and Nathan.[4]

Loose and uncritical as these statements may appear, they so far help our in-

---

[3] *b* and [4] *a*) the only point on which all are agreed being that he wrote Ecclesiastes last —Rabbi Jonathan irreverently remarking that when a man is old he utters *dibhrê habhalim*—vain words!

[1] In Jer. Taan. 68 *a* we read of three codices of the Pentateuch, respectively named after one word in each codex, the reading of which was either rejected or adopted on comparison with the others.

[2] Thus, we have different notices about the number of verses in the Bible, the arrangement of the Psalter, the medial letter and medial word in the Pentateuch, and the number of its sections and chapters (Kidd. 30 *a*; Yalkut i. § 855). But the sum total of verses in the Bible (23,199) differs by 99 from that in our present text. Similarly, one of the most learned Rabbinic critics of the third century declares himself at a loss about the exact medial letter, word, and verse of the Pentateuch, while in Palestine the Pentateuch seems to have been arranged into 1,085, in Babalonia into 378 chapters (comp. *Fürst*, Kultur-u. Liter. Gesch. p. 62).

[3] But comp. an opinion, previously quoted, about the last verses in Deut.

[4] 'History of the Jewish Nation,' p. 418.

APP.
V

vestigations as to show that, according to tradition, certain portions of Scripture were compiled or edited by one or another Rabbinic 'College,' and that there were several 'Colleges' which successively busied themselves with the codification and revision of the Canon. By these 'Colleges,' we are not to understand gatherings of certain members, who discussed and decided a question at one or more of their meetings. They rather indicate the learned activity of the authorities during a certain *period*, which are respectively designated by the generic names of 'the Sanhedrin of Hezekiah,' 'The Men of the Synagogue,' the 'Legal Court of the Maccabees,' and finally, 'Chananyah and his College.' We have thus somewhat firmer historical ground. If in Prov. xxv. 1, we read of the activity about the Canon of 'the Men of Hezekiah,' and bear in mind the Scriptural account of the religious revival of that reign (for ex. 2 Chron. xxix. 25–30; 2 Chron. xxx. 1), we scarcely require the frequent and elaborate glorification of tradition to lead us to infer that, if the collection of the Book of Proverbs was due to their activity, they must have equally collated the other portions of Scripture then existing, and fixed the Canon as at their time. Again, if we are to credit the statement that they equally collected and edited the Prophecies of Isaiah, we are obliged to infer that the continuance of that College was not limited to the life of Hezekiah, since the latter died before Isaiah (Tos. Baba Bathra; Yeb. 49 *b*).

What has just been indicated is fully confirmed by what we know of the activity of Ezra (Ezra vii. 6, 10), and of his successors in the Great Synagogue. If we are to attach credit to the notice in 2 Macc. ii. 13,[1] it points to such literary activity as tradition indicates. That the revision and determination of the Canon must have been among the main occupations of Ezra and his successors of 'the Great Synagogue'—whatever precise meaning may be attached to that institution—seems scarcely to require proof. The same remark applies to another period of religious reformation, that of the so-called Asmonæan College. Even if we had not the evidence of their exclusion of such works as those of Ben Sirach and others, there could be no rational doubt that in their time the Canon, as presently existing, was firmly fixed, and that no work of comparatively late date could have found admission into it. The period of their activity is sufficiently known, and too near what may be called the historical times of Rabbinism, for any attempt in that direction, without leaving traces of it. Lastly, we come to the indications of a critical revision of the text by 'Chananyah and his College.'[2] shortly before the time of our Lord. Thus we have, in all, a record of *four* critical revisions of the Canon up to the time of Christ.

3. Any attempt to set forth in this place a detailed exposition of the *Exegetical Canons of the Rabbis*, or of their application, would manifestly be impossible. It would require almost a treatise of its own; and a cursory survey would neither be satisfactory to the writer nor instructive to the general reader. Besides, on all subjects connected with Rabbinic exegesis, a sufficient number of learned treatises exists, which are easily accessible to students, while the general reader can only be interested in such general results as have been frequently indicated throughout these volumes. Lastly, the treatment of certain branches of the subject, such as a criticism of the *Targumim*, really belongs to what is known as the science of 'Introduction,' either to the Old or the New Testament, in manuals of which, as well

---

[1] The expression 'the epistles of the kings concerning the holy gifts' must refer to the official Persian documents concerning gifts to the Temple, &c.

[2] Shabb. 13 *b*; Chag. 13 *a*; Men. 45 *a*.

as in special treatises, all such subjects are fully discussed. Besides these the student may be referred, for a general summary, to the labours of Dr. *Hamburger* (Real-Encycl.). Special works on various branches of the subject cannot here be named, since this would involve an analysis and critical disquisition. But for a knowledge of the Rabbinic statements in regard to the *Codices* and the text of the Old Testament, reference may here be made to the short but masterly analysis of Professor *Strack* (Prolegomena Critica), in which, first, the various codices of the Old Testament, and then the text as existing in Talmudical times, are discussed, and the literature of the subject fully and critically given. The various passages are also mentioned in which the Biblical quotations in the Mishnah and Gemara differ from our present text.[1] Most of them are, however, of no exegetical importance. On the exegesis of the Rabbis generally, I would take leave to refer to the sketch of it given in the ' History of the Jewish Nation,' ch. xi., and especially in App. V., on ' Rabbinical Exegesis,' where all its canons are enumerated. Some brief notices connected with Rabbinic Commentaries quoted in this work will be found at the beginning of vol. i.

4. Somewhat similar observations must be made in regard to the mystical Theology of the Synagogue, or the so-called Kabbalah. Its commencement must certainly be traced to, and before, the times described in these volumes. For a discussion of its origin and doctrines I must once more take leave to refer to the account given in the ' History of the Jewish Nation ' (pp. 435, &c.). The whole modern literature of the subject, besides much illustrative matter, is given in the Italian text annexed to *David Castelli's* edition of *Sabbatai Donnolo's* Hebrew Commentary on the Book *Yetsirah*, or the Book of Creation. For, the Kabbalah busies itself with these two subjects: the History of the Creation (*Yetsirah*, perhaps rather 'formation' than Creation), and the ' *Merkabhah*,' or the Divine apparition as described by Ezekiel. Both refer to the great question, underlying all theosophic speculation: that of God's connection with His creatures. They treat of the mystery of Nature and of Providence, with especial bearing on Revelation; and the question, how the Infinite God can have any connection or intercourse with finite creatures, is attempted to be answered. Of the two points raised, that of Creation is of course the first in the order of thinking as well as of time—and the book *Yetsirah* is the oldest Kabbalistic document.

' The *Sepher Yetsirah* is properly a monologue on the part of Abraham, in which, by the contemplation of all that is around him, he ultimately arrives at the conviction of the Unity of God.

' We distinguish the substance and the form of creation; that which is, and the mode in which it is. We have already indicated that the original of all that exists

---

[1] There are in the Mishnah sixteen variations: Lev. xi. 33; xxv. 36; Numb. xxviii. 5; xxxii. 22; Deut. xxiv. 19; Josh. viii. 33; 2 Sam. xv. 6; Is. x. 13; Ezek. xlvi. 21; Amos ix. 14: Mal. iii. 16, 23 (A.V. iv. 5); Ps. lxviii. 27; Job i. 1; Prov. xxii. 28; 2 Chron. xxviii. 15. In the Talmud 105 such variations occur, viz., Gen. vii. 8, 23; xx. 2; xxv. 6, xxxv. 18; Ex. xii. 3, 6; xiii. 16; xxiv. 5; xxv. 13 xxxi. 1; Lev. iv. 25, 30, 34; x. 12; xv. 10; xviii. 18; Numb. v. 19; xviii. 16; Deut. vi. 7, 9, 20; xxiii. 1; xxv. 7; xxxiii. 27; xxxiv. 6; Josh. iii. 17; x. 11; xiv. 7, 10; xvi. 6; xxiii. 15; Judg. xv. 20; xvi. 31; 1 Sam. ii 24; 2 Sam. iii. 25; xxiv. 15; 2 Kings xvii. 31; xxiii. 17; Is. ii. 3; xxxviii. 16; xlii. 5; lviii. 7; Jer. ii. 22; xxix. 11; Ezek. xl. 48; xliv. 9; xlvii. 1; Hos. iv. 11; Amos. iv. 6; viii. 11; ix. 14; Hag. ii. 8; Mich. iv. 2; Zech. xii. 10; Mal. ii. 12; Ps. v. 5; xvi. 10 (where the difference is important); xxvi. 5, 6; xxxvii. 32; lvi. 11; lxii. 12; lxviii. 21; xcv. 5: xcvii. 7; cxxvii. 5; cxxxix. 5; Prov. viii. 13; xi. 17, 25; xv. 1; Job ii. 5, 6, 8; xiii. 4 xiv. 16; xxxvi. 5, 11; Ruth. iii. 15; iv. 11; Eccl. ix. 14, 15; x. 5; Dan. ii. 29; iv. 14; vi. 18; x. 13; Ezr. iv. 3; Neh. iv. 16; viii. 8 (bis), 15, 17; 1 Chron. iii. 17; iv. 10; v. 24; xvi. 5; xvii. 9; xxvi. 8, 23; xxvii. 34; 2 Chron. xxvi. 2; xxxi. 5, 13.

is Divine. 1st, We have God; 2nd, God manifest, or the Divine *entering* into form; 3rd, That Divine in its form, from which in turn all original realities are afterwards derived. In the *Sepher Yetsirah*, these Divine realities (the substance) are represented by the ten numerals, and their form by the twenty-two letters which constitute the Hebrew alphabet—language being viewed as the medium of connection between the spiritual and the material; as the form in which the spiritual appears. At the same time, number and language indicate also the arrangement and the mode of creation, and, in general, its boundaries. "By thirty-two wonderful paths," so begins the *Sepher Yetsirah*, "the Eternal, the Lord of Hosts, the God of Israel, the Living God, the King of the World, the merciful and gracious God, the glorious One, He that inhabiteth eternity, Whose Name is high and holy, has created the world." But these ten numerals are in reality the ten *Sephiroth*, or Divine emanations, arranged in triads, each triad consisting of two opposites (flowing or emanating from a superior triad until the Divine Unity is reached), and being reconciled in a middle point of connection. These ten *Sephiroth*, in the above arrangement, recur everywhere, and the sacred number ten is that of perfection. Each of these *Sephiroth* flows from its predecessor, and in this manner the Divine gradually evolves. This emanation of the ten *Sephiroth* then constitutes the substance of the world; we may add, it constitutes everything else. In God, in the world, in man, everywhere we meet these ten *Sephiroth*, at the head of which is God manifest, or the *Memra* (*Logos*, the Word). If the ten *Sephiroth* give the substance, the twenty-two letters are the form of creation and of revelation. "By giving them form and shape, and by interchanging them, God has made the soul of everything that has been made, or shall be made." "Upon those letters, also, has the Holy One, Whose Name be praised, founded His holy and glorious Name." These letters are next subdivided, and their application in all the departments of nature is shown. In the unit creation, the triad; world, time and man are found. Above all these is the Lord. Such is a very brief outline of the rational exposition of the Creation, attempted by the *Sepher Yetsirah*.' [1]

We subjoin a translation of the book *Yetsirah*, only adding that much, not only as regards the meaning of the expressions but even their translation, is in controversy. Hence, not unfrequently, our rendering must be regarded rather as our interpretation of the mysterious original.

THE BOOK YETSIRAH.

PEREQ. I.

Mishnah 1. *In thirty-two wonderful paths of wisdom, Jah, Jehovah Tsebhaoth, the God of Israel, the Living God, and King of the World, God merciful and gracious, High and Exalted, Who dwelleth to Eternity, high and holy is His Name, hath ordered* [established, created?] (the world) *by three Sepharim* [books]: *by Sepher* [the written Word], *Sephar* [number, numeral] *and Sippur* [spoken word]. Others, pointing the words differently, render these mysterious terms: Number, Word, Writing; others, Number, Numberer, Numbered; while still others see in it a reference to the threefold division of the letters of the Hebrew alphabet, of which more afterwards.

1 'History of the Jewish Nation,' pp. 435, 436.

Mishnah 2. *Ten Sephiroth* [emanations] *belimah* [1] [without anything, i.e. before these, the sole elements out of which all else evolved], *twenty-two letters of foundation* (these constitute the Hebrew Alphabet, and the meaning seems that the *Sephiroth* manifest themselves in that which is uttered): *three mothers* (*Aleph*, the first letter of *Avveyr*, air; *Mem*, the first letter of *Mayim*, water; and *Shin*, the last letter of *Esh*, fire—although this may represent only one mystical aspect of the meaning of the term ' mothers,' as applied to these letters), *seven duplex* [2] (pronounced ' soft' or ' hard,' viz. Beth, Gimel, Daleth, Kaph, Pe, Resh, Tau, which are, or were, in Hebrew capable of modification by a Dagesh—but this also must be mystically understood) *and twelve simple ones* [3] (the simple letters of the Hebrew Alphabet).

Mishnah 3. *Ten Sephiroth belimah* (the analogy is now further traced in God and in man), *the number of the ten fingers, five against five, and the covenant of the One Only* (God) *placed between them* (the covenant relationship between God and man in the midst, even as it is symbolised in the person of man which is between the twice five fingers) *by the word of the tongue* (this, the relation Godward) *and by the word of sexualness* [*nuditas*] (the relation earthwards—the one has become dual.)

Mishnah 4. *Ten Sephiroth belimah—ten and not nine, ten and not eleven—be informed in wisdom, and be wise in information; examine in them, search out from them, and put the thing in its reality* (certitude, proper state?), *and place again the Creator in His place.*

Mishnah 5. *Ten Sephiroth belimah—their measurement ten, which have no end* (limitation): *depth of beginning* (past) *and depth of ending* (future), *depth of good and depth of evil, depth of height and depth of profundity* (or, above and beneath), *depth of east and depth of west, depth of north and depth of south—One only Lord, God, the true* (approved) *King, Who reigneth over all from His holy dwelling and unto all eternity.*

Mishnah 6. *Ten Sephiroth belimah—their appearance like the sheen of lightning* (reference here to Ezek. i. 14), *and their outgoings* (goal) *that they have no end, His word is in them* (the Logos manifest in the Sephiroth), *in running and in returning, and at His word like storm-wind they pursue* (follow), *and before His throne they bend* (in worship).

Mishnah 7. *Ten Sephiroth belimah—their end is joined to their beginning, like the flame that is bound up with the coal, for the Lord is One only, and there is no second to Him, and before One what countest thou?*

Mishnah 8. *Ten Sephiroth belimah—shut thy mouth, that it speak not, and thy heart, that it think not, and if thy heart run away, bring it back to its place, for on this account is it said* (Ezek. i. 14) ' *they run and return,' and on this condition has the Covenant been made.*

Mishnah 9 and 10. *Ten Sephiroth belimah—One: the Spirit of the living God, blessed and again blessed be the Name of Him Who liveth for ever—Voice and Spirit and Word, and this is the Holy Ghost.*

Two: Wind (air, spirit?) *from* (out of) *Spirit—thereby ordered and hewed He the twenty-two letters of foundation, three mothers, and* 7 *duplicate, and* 12 *simple ones, and one Spirit from* (among) *them. Three: Water from breath* (wind), *He designed and hewed in them tohu vavohu, slime and dung—designed them like a bed*

---

[1] The expression occurs already in Job xxvi. 7.
[2] Probably ' twofold ' might best express the meaning.

[3] Mark also the symbolical significance of the numbers 3, 7, 12 as the manifestation of God—the Archetype of all else.

(a garden bed), *hewed them like a wall, covered them like pavement. Four: Fire from water, He designed it and hewed in it the throne of glory, the Ophanim and Seraphim, the sacred living creatures, and the angels of service, and of these three He founded His dwelling place, as it is said, He maketh His angels breaths* (winds), *and His ministers a flaming fire.*

Mishnah 11. *Five: Three letters from out the simple ones: He sealed spirit on the three, and fastened them in His Great Name* יי (Jehovah, of which these three letters are the abbreviation; what follows shows how the permutation of these three letters marks the varied relationship of God to creation in time and space, and at the same time, so to speak, the immanence of His manifestation in it). *And He sealed with them six outgoings* (ends, terminations): *He turned upwards, and He sealed it with* יהו. *Six: He sealed below, turned downwards, and sealed it with* יוה. *Seven: He sealed eastward, He turned in front of Him, and sealed it with* הוי. *Eight: He sealed westward, and turned behind, and sealed it with* הוי. *Nine: He sealed southward, and turned to His right, and sealed it with* ויה. *Ten: He sealed northward, and turned to His left, and sealed it with* והי.

Mishnah 12. *These are the Sephiroth belimah—one: Spirit of the living God, and wind* (air, spirit? the word *ruach* means all these), *water, and fire; and height above and below, east and west, north and south.*

PEREQ II.

Mishnah 1. *Twenty-and-two letters of foundation: three mothers, seven duplex, and twelve simple ones—three mothers* אמש, *their foundation the scale of merit and the scale of guilt, and the tongue of statute trembling* (deciding) *between them.* (This, to be mystically carried out, in its development, and application to all things: the elements, man, &c.)

Mishnah 2. *Twenty-two letters of foundation: He drew them, hewed them, weighed them, and interchanged them, melted them together* (showing how in the permutation of letters all words—viewed mystically as the designation of things—arose), *He formed by them the nephesh of all that is formed* (created), *and the nephesh of everything that is to be formed* (created).

Mishnah 3. *Two-and-twenty letters of foundation: drawn in the voice, hewn in the wind* (air, spirit?) *fastened on the mouth in five places:* אחהע (the gutturals among the Hebrew letters), בומף (the labials), גיכק (the palatals), דטלנת (the linguals), זסשרץ (the dentals).

Mishnah 4. *Twenty-two letters of foundation, fastened in a circle in 231 gates* (marking how these letters are capable of forming, by the permutation of two of them, in all 231 permutations); *and the circle turns forwards and backwards, and this is the indication of the matter: as regards what is good, there is nothing higher than* ענג (oneg), *'delight,' and nothing lower than* נגע (negah), *'plague'* (stroke). *In such manner He weighed them and combined them,* א *with them all, and them all with* א ב *with them all, and them all with* ב, *and thus the rest, so that it is found that all that is formed and all that is spoken proceeds from one Name* (the name of God being, as it were, the fundamental origin of everything).

Mishnah 5. *He formed from Tohu that which has substance, and made that which is not into being, and hewed great pillars from the air, which cannot be handled; and this is the indication: beholding and speaking He made all that is formed and all words by one Name—and the indication of the matter: twenty-two numbers and one body.*

Pereq III.

Mishnah 1. *Three mothers*—אמש: *their foundation, the scale of guilt and the scale of merit, and the tongue of the statute trembling* (deciding) *between them.*

Mishnah 2. *Three mothers*—אמש—*a great mystery, marvellous and hidden, and sealed with six signets, and from them go forth fire and water, and divide themselves into male and female. Three mothers,* אמש *their foundation, and from them were born the fathers* (rerum naturæ semina), *from which everything is created* (fire is regarded as the male principle, water as the female principle, and air as combining the two: א is the first letter of the Hebrew word for air, מ for that of water, ש the last for that of fire).

Mishnah 3. *Three letters,* אמש—*in the world: air, water, fire; the heavens were created in the beginning from fire, and the earth was created from water, and the air trembles* (the same word as that in regard to the tongue between the scales of the balance, indicating the intermediate, inclining to the one or the other) *between the fire and the water.*

Mishnah 4. *Three mothers,* אמש—*in the year: fire, and water, and wind. Heat is created from fire, cold from water, and the moderate from the wind* (air) *that is intermediate between them. Three mothers,* אמש—*in the nephesh: fire, water, and wind. The head was created from fire, and the belly from water, and the body from wind that is intermediate between them.*

Mishnah 5. *Three mothers,* אמש—*He drew them, and hewed them, and melted them together, and sealed with them the three mothers in the world, the three mothers in the year, and the three mothers in the nephesh—male and female.*

(Now follows a further mystical development and application.) *The letter* א *He made King in the Spirit, and bound upon him the crown* (this refers to farther mystical signs indicated in the Kabbalistic figure drawn on p. 438 of the 'History of the Jewish Nation'), *and melted them one with the other, and sealed with them: in the world the air, in the soul life, and in the nephesh* (living thing) *body—the male with* אמש, *the female with* אשמ. מ *He made King in the waters, and bound on it the crown, and melted them one with the other, and sealed: in the world earth, and in the year cold, and in the nephesh the belly—male and female, male in* מאש, *and female in* משא. ש *He made King in the fire, and bound on it the crown, and melted them one with the other, and sealed with it: in the upper world the heavens, in the year heat, in the nephesh the head—male and female.*

Pereq IV.

Mishnah 1. *Seven duplex letters,* בגר כפרת (it will here be noticed that we now proceed from the numeral 3 to the further mystic numeral 7), *accustomed* (habituated, adapted, fitted) *for two languages* (correlate ideas); *life, and peace, and wisdom, and riches, grace, and seed, and government* (the mystic number 7 will here be noted), *and accustomed* (fitted) *for two tongues* (modes of pronunciation) בב', גג' דר' ככ' פפ' רר' תת',—*the formation of soft and hard, the formation of strong and weak* (the dual principle will here be observed); *duplicate, because they are opposites: the opposites—life and death; the opposites—peace and evil; the opposites —wisdom and folly; the opposites—riches and poverty; the opposites—grace and ugliness; the opposites—fertility and desolation; the opposites—rule and servitude.*

Mishnah 2. *Seven duplex letters,* בגר כפרת; *corresponding to the seven out goings; from them seven outgoings: above and below, east and west, north and south, and the holy Temple in the middle, and it upbears the whole.*

Mishnah 3. *Seven duplex,* בגר כפרת*; He drew them, and hewed them, and melted them, and formed from them, in the world the stars* (the planets), *in the year the days, in the nephesh the issues, and with them He drew seven firmaments, and seven earths, and seven Sabbaths, therefore He loves the seventh under all heavens.*

Mishnah 4. *Two letters build two houses* (here the number of possible permutations are indicated). *Three letters build six houses, four build twenty-four houses, five build* 120 *houses, six build* 720 *houses, and from thence go onward and think what the mouth is not able to speak, and the ear not able to hear. And these are the stars in the world—seven: the Sun, Venus, Mercury, the Moon, Saturn, Jupiter, Mars. And these are the days in the year; the seven days of creation; and the seven gates of issue in the nephesh: two eyes, two ears, and a mouth, and the two nostrils. And with them were drawn the seven firmaments, and the seven earths, and the seven times; therefore loved He the seventh above all that is of delight under the heavens.*

Pereq V.

Mishnah 1. *The properties of the twelve simple letters* (or their attributes)— הוז חטי לן סע צק*—their foundation: sight, hearing, smell, speech, eating, concubitus, working, walking, anger, laughter, thinking, sleep. Their measurements twelve boundaries in the hypothenuse* (points in transverse lines); *the boundary N.E., the boundary S.E., the boundary E. upwards, the boundary E. downwards; the boundary N. upwards, the boundary N. downwards, the boundary S.W., the boundary N.W., the boundary W. upwards, the boundary W. downwards, the boundary S. upwards, the boundary S. downwards, and they extend and go on into the eternal* (boundless space), *and they are the arms of the world.*

(Mishnah 2. *Twelve simple letters,* הוז חטי לן סע צק. *He drew them, and melted them, and formed of them the twelve constellations in the world* (signs of the Zodiac): *Aries, Taurus, Gemini, Cancer, Leo, Virgo, Libra, Scorpio, Sagittarius, Capricornus, Aquarius, Pisces* (these are expressed in the original in an abbreviated, contracted form). *These are the twelve months of the year: Nisan, Iyar, Sivan, Tammuz, Abh, Elul, Tishri, Marcheshvan, Kislev, Tebheth, Shebhat, Adar* (thus the number twelve is marked, first in the functions of man, then in the points of the compass, then in the starry skies, and then in the year). *And these are the twelve leaders in nephesh* (living beings): *two hands, and two feet, and two kidneys, the spleen, the liver, the gall, the intestine, the upper stomach, the lower stomach* (perhaps gullet, stomach, and intestine—at any rate, three organs connected with deglutition and digestion). *He made them like a land* (province), *and set them in order like war, and also—this as against that, ordered God. Three mothers, which are three fathers, because from them issue fire, wind, and water. Three mothers, and seven duplicate, and twelve simple ones.*

Mishnah 3. *These are the twenty-two letters with which the Holy One has founded* (all), *blessed be He, Jah, Jehovah Tsebhaoth, the Living God, the God of Israel, high and lifted up, dwelling eternally, and holy is His Name, exalted and holy is He.*

Pereq VI.

Mishnah 1. *Three fathers and their generations, seven subduers and their hosts* (planets?), *seven boundaries of hypothenuse—and the proof of the matter: faithful witnesses are the world, the year, and the nephesh. The law* (statute, settled order) *of the twelve, and of the seven, and of the three, and they are appointed over the heavenly dragon, and the cycle, and the heart. Three: fire, and water, and wind* air); *the fire above, the water below, and the wind* (air) *the statute intermediate between them. And the demonstration of the matter: the fire bears the water, מ is silent, ש hisses, and א is the statute intermediate between them* (all these have further mystic meaning and application in connection with words and ideas).

Mishnah 2. *The dragon is in the world like a king on his throne; the cycle is in the year like a king in his land; the heart is in the nephesh like a king in war. Also in all that is pursued God has made the one against the other* (opposite poles and their reconciliation): *the good against the evil; good from good, and evil from evil; the good trying the evil, and the evil trying the good; the good is kept for the good, and the evil is kept for the evil.*

Mishnah 3. *Three are one, that standeth alone; seven are divided, three as against three, and the statute intermediate between them. Twelve are in war: three loving, three hating, three giving life, three giving death. The three loving ones: the heart, the ears, and the mouth; the three hating ones: the liver, the gall, and the tongue—and God a faithful king reigning over all: one (is) over three, three over seven, seven over twelve, and they are all joined together, the one with the other.*

Mishnah 4. *And when Abraham our father had beheld, and considered, and seen, and drawn, and hewn, and obtained it, then the Lord of all revealed Himself to him, and called him His friend, and made a covenant with him and with his seed: and he believed in Jehovah, and it was imputed to him for righteousness. He made with him a covenant between the ten toes, and that is circumcision; between the ten fingers of his hand, and that is the tongue; and He bound two-and-twenty letters on his tongue, and showed him their foundation. He drew them with water, He kindled them with fire, He breathed them with wind* (air); *He burnt them in seven; He poured them forth in the twelve constellations.*

The views expressed in the Book *Yetsirah* are repeatedly referred to in the Mishnah and in other of the most ancient Jewish writings. They represent, as stated at the outset, a direction long anterior to the Mishnah, and of which the first beginnings and ultimate principles are of deepest interest to the Christian student. The reader who wishes to see the application to Christian metaphysics and theology of the Kabbalah, of which *Yetsirah* is but the first word, is referred to a deeply interesting and profound work, strangely unknown to English scholars: *Molitor*, Philosophie d. Gesch. oder über d. Tradition, 4 vols. English readers will find much to interest them in the now somewhat rare work of the Rev. *John Oxley*: The Christian Doctrine of the Trinity and Incarnation (London, 1815, 2 vols.).

The principles laid down in the Book *Yetsirah* are further carried out and receive their fullest (often most remarkable) development and application in the book Zohar ('Splendour'—the edition used by us is the 8vo. edition, Amsterdam, 1805, in 3 vols., with the Amsterdam edition of the Tikkuné Zohar; other Kabbalistic books used by us need not here be mentioned). The main portion of the Zohar is in the form of a Commentary on the Pentateuch, but other tractates are interspersed throughout the volumes.

5. *Dogmatic Theology.*—This is fully treated of in the text of these volumes.

6. *Historic Theology.*—To describe and criticise the various works which come under this designation would require the expansion of this Appendix into a Tractate. Some of these compositions have been referred to in the text of these volumes. For a general account and criticism of them I must again refer to the 'History of the Jewish Nation' (see especially the chapters on 'The Progress of

Arts and Sciences among the Jews,' and 'Theological Science and Religious Belief in Palestine '). For the historical and critical account of Rabbinic historical works the student is referred to *Zunz*, Gottesd. Vortr. d. Juden, ch. viii. The only thing which we shall here attempt is a translation of the so-called *Megillath Taanith*, or 'Roll of Fasts '; rather, a Calendar of the days on which fasting and mourning was *prohibited*. The oldest part of the document (referred to in the Mishnah, Taan. ii. 8) dates from the beginning of the second century of our era, and contains elements of even much greater antiquity. That which has come down of it is here given in translation:[1]—

MEGILLATH TAANITH, OR ROLL OF FASTS.

These are the days on which it is not lawful to fast, and during some of them mourning must also be intermitted.

I. NISAN.

1. From the 1st day of the month Nisan, and to the 8th of it, it was settled about the daily sacrifice (that it should be paid out of the Temple-treasury)—mourning is prohibited.

2. And from the 8th to the end of the Feast (the 27th) the Feast of Weeks was re-established—mourning is interdicted.

II. IYAR.

1. On the 7th Iyar the dedication of the wall of Jerusalem—mourning is prohibited.

2. On the 14th is the day of the sacrifice of the little (the second) Passover—mourning is prohibited.

3. On the 23rd the sons of Acra[2] issued from Jerusalem.

4. On the 27th the imposts were removed from Judæa and Jerusalem.

III. SIVAN.

1. On the 17th Sivan the tower of Zur was taken.

2. On the 15th and 16th the men of Bethshean and of the plain were exiled.

3. On the 25th the tax-gatherers were withdrawn from Judah and Jerusalem.

IV. TAMMUZ.

1. On the 14th Tammuz the Book of Decisions (' aggravating ordinances ') was abrogated—mourning is prohibited.

V. ABH.

1. On the 15th Abh the season of wood-offerings (for the Temple use) of priests (comp. *Jos.* War ii. 17. 6)—mourning is prohibited.

2. On the 24th we returned to our Law.

---

[1] All the glosses on and in the text have been omitted. The edition of the Tractate in its *present* form used by us is that of Warshau, 1874, and consists (with comments) of 20 octavo (double) pages. For the criticism of the work see specially *Grätz*, Gesch. d. Juden, vol. iii. pp. 415–428, and *Derenbourg*, Hist. de la Palest. pp. 439–446. A special tractate on the subject is *Schmilg's* inaugural dissertation, Leipzig. 1874. It need scarcely be said that these writers entertain different views as to the historical dates specially commem-orated in the Megillath Taanith, and the events to which they refer. Comp. also *Wolfius*, Biblioth. Rabb. vol. i. p. 385, vol. ii. p. 1325, vol. iii. p. 1196. My edition of *Wolfius* has the great advantage of the marginal notes and corrections by the great Jewish historian, the late Dr. *Jost*, who, many years ago, gave me his copy.

[2] We abstain from giving historical notes. For the different explanations of the commemorative dates the reader is referred to the books already mentioned.

VI. Elul.

1. On the 7th of Elul the day of the Dedication of Jerusalem—mourning prohibited.

2. On the 17th the Romans withdrew from Judæa and Jerusalem.

3. On the 22nd we returned to kill the apostates.

VII. Tishri.

1. On the 3rd Tishri the mention of the Divine Name was removed from public deeds.

VIII. Marcheshvan.

1 On the 23rd Marcheshvan the *Sorigah* (a partition-wall in the Temple, supposed to have been erected by the heathen, comp. 1 Macc. iv. 43–46) was removed from the Temple-court.

2. On the 25th the wall of Samaria was taken.

3. On the 27th the meat offering was again brought on the altar.

IX. Kislev.

1. On the 3rd the Simavatha (another heathen structure) was removed from the court or the Temple,

2. On the 7th is a feast day.

3. On the 21st is the day of Mount Garizim—mourning is prohibited.

4. On the 25th the eight days of the Feast of Lights (Chanukah) begin—mourning is prohibited.

X. Tebheth.

1. On the 28th the congregation was re-established according to the Law. (This seems to refer to the restoration of the Sanhedrin after the Sadducean members were removed, under the rule of Queen Salome. See the historical notices in Appendix IV.)

XI. Shebhat.

1. On the 2nd a feast day [1]—mourning is prohibited.

2. On the 22nd the work, of which the enemy said that it was to be in the Temple, was destroyed—mourning is interdicted. (This seems to refer to the time of Caligula, when, on the resistance of the Jews, the statue of the Emperor was at last not allowed to be in the Temple.)

3. On the 28th King Antiochus was removed from Jerusalem (supposed to refer to the day of the death of Antiochus, son of Antiochus Epiphanes, in his expedition against the Parthians).

XII. Adar.

1. On the 8th and the 9th, days of joy on account of rain-fall.

2. On the 12th is the day of Trajan.

3. On the 13th is the day of Nicanor (his defeat).

---

[1] This feast seems to refer to the death of King Herod; that on the 7th Kislev to the death of King Jannæus.

4. On the 14th and on the 15th are the days of Purim (Feast of Esther)—mourning is prohibited.

5. On the 16th was begun the building of the wall of Jerusalem—mourning is prohibited.

6. On the 17th rose the heathens against the remnant of the Scribes in the country of Chalcis and of the Zabedæans, and Israel was delivered.

7. On the 20th the people fasted for rain, and it was granted to them.

8. On the 28th the Jews received good tidings that they would no longer be hindered from the sayings of the Law—mourning is prohibited.

On these days every one who has before made a vow of fasting is to give himself to prayer.

(In extenuation of the apparent harshness and literality of our renderings, it should be stated, that both the *Sepher Yetsirah* and the *Megillath Taanith* are here for the first time translated into English.)

APPENDIX VI.

LIST OF THE MACCABEES, OF THE FAMILY OF HEROD, OF THE HIGH PRIESTS, THE ROMAN PROCURATORS OF JUDÆA, AND ROMAN GOVERNORS OF SYRIA.

(See vol. i. Bk. II. ch. ii.)

I. THE MACCABEAN FAMILY.

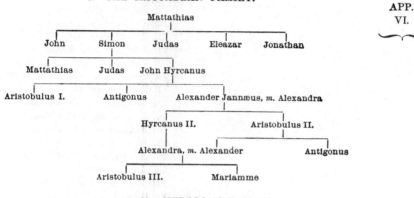

```
                        Mattathias
    ┌──────────┬──────────┬──────────┬──────────┐
   John      Simon      Judas     Eleazar   Jonathan
    │
 ┌──────────┬──────────┐
Mattathias  Judas   John Hyrcanus
    ┌──────────────┬──────────────────┐
Aristobulus I.  Antigonus   Alexander Jannæus, m. Alexandra
                        ┌──────────────┬──────────────┐
                    Hyrcanus II.          Aristobulus II.
                        │              ┌──────────────┐
                 Alexandra, m. Alexander          Antigonus
                    ┌──────────────┐
            Aristobulus III.    Mariamme
```

II. HERODIAN FAMILY.

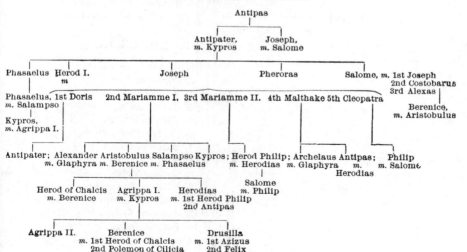

```
                        Antipas
              ┌────────────────┬────────────────┐
           Antipater,        Joseph,
           m. Kypros         m. Salome
 ┌────────┬──────────────┬────────────────┬────────────────┬────────────────┐
Phasaelus Herod I.     Joseph          Pheroras      Salome, m. 1st Joseph
           m                                                   2nd Costobarus
                                                               3rd Alexas
Phasaelus, 1st Doris   2nd Mariamme I,  3rd Mariamme II.  4th Malthake 5th Cleopatra
m. Salampso                                                    Berenice,
   │                                                          m. Aristobulus
Kypros,
m. Agrippa I.

Antipater; Alexander Aristobulus Salampso Kypros; Herod Philip; Archelaus Antipas;   Philip
          m. Glaphyra m. Berenice m. Phasaelus    m. Herodias  m. Glaphyra    m.   m. Salome
                                                                           Herodias

        Herod of Chalcis  Agrippa I.   Herodias        Salome
          m. Berenice    m. Kypros   m. 1st Herod Philip  m. Philip
                                        2nd Antipas

     Agrippa II.      Berenice              Drusilla
                  m. 1st Herod of Chalcis   m. 1st Azizus
                     2nd Polemon of Cilicia    2nd Felix
```

APP.　III.　LIST OF HIGH-PRIESTS FROM THE ACCESSION OF HEROD THE
VI　　　　GREAT TO THE DESTRUCTION OF JERUSALEM.

Appointed by	
Herod the Great . . .	1. Ananel. 2. Aristobulus. 3. Jesus, son of Phabes. 4. Simon, son of Boethos. 5. Matthias, son of Theophilos. 6. Joazar, son of Boethos.
Archelaus	7. Eleazar, son of Boethos. 8. Jesus, son of Sié.
Quirinius	9. Ananos (Annas).
Valerius Gratus . . .	10. Ishmael, son of Phabi. 11. Eleazar, son of Ananos. 12. Simon, son of Camithos. 13. Joseph (Caiaphas).
Vitellius	14. Jonathan, son of Ananos. 15. Theophilos, son of Ananos.
Agrippa I.	16. Simon Cantheras, son of Boethos. 17. Matthias, son of Ananos. 18. Elionaios, son of Cantheras.
Herod of Chalcis . .	19. Joseph, son of Camithos. 20. Ananias, son of Nedebaios.
Agrippa II. . . .	21. Ishmael, son of Phabi. 22. Joseph Cabi, son of Simon. 23. Ananos, son of Ananos. 24. Jesus, son of Damnaios. 25. Jesus, son of Gamaliel. 26. Matthias, son of Theophilos.
The People during the last war	27. Phannias, son of Samuel.

IV.　LIST OF PROCURATORS OF JUDÆA.

3 B.C. to 66 A.D.	1. Ethnarch Archelaus. 2. Coponius. 3. M. Ambivius. 4. Annius Rufus. 5. Valerius Gratus. 6. Pontius Pilate. 7. Marcellus. 8. King Agrippa. 9. Cuspius Fadus. 10. Tiberius Alexander. 11. Ventidius Cumanus. 12. Antonius Felix. 13. Porcius Festus. 14. Albinus. 15. Gessius Florus.

V. LIST OF ROMAN GOVERNORS OF SYRIA.

6 B.C. to 69 A.D.

1. P. Quinctilius Varus.
2. M. Lollius.
3. C. Marcius Censorinus (?)
4. L. Volusius Saturninus.
5. P. Sulpic. Quirinius.
6. Qu. Cæcilius Creticus Silanus.
7. Cn. Calpurn. Piso.
8. Cn. Sent. Saturninus (?)
9. Aelius Lamia.
10. L. Pompon. Flaccus.
11. L. Vitellius.
12. P. Petronius.
13. C. Vibius Marsus.
14. C. Cass. Longinus.
15. C. U. Quadratus.
16. { Domitius Corbulo.
17. { C. Itius (conjoined).
18. Cestius Gallus.
19. C. Lic. Mucianus.

APPENDIX VII.

ON THE DATE OF THE NATIVITY OF OUR LORD.

(Vol. i. Book II. ch. iii. and other passages.)

So much, that is generally accessible, has of late been written on this subject, and such accord exists on the *general* question, that only the briefest statement seems requisite in this place, the space at our command being necessarily reserved for subjects which have either not been treated of by previous writers, or in a manner or form that seemed to make a fresh investigation desirable.

At the outset it must be admitted, that absolute certainty is impossible as to the exact date of Christ's Nativity—the precise year even, and still more the month and the day. But in regard to the year, we possess such *data* as to invest it with such probability, as almost to amount to certainty.

1. The first and most certain date is that of the death of Herod the Great. Our Lord was born *before* the death of Herod, and, as we judge from the Gospel-history, very shortly before that event. Now the year of Herod's death has been ascertained with, we may say, absolute certainty, as shortly before the Passover of the year 750 A.U.C., which corresponds to about the 12th of April of the year 4 before Christ, according to our common reckoning, More particularly, shortly before the death of Herod there was a lunar eclipse (*Jos. Ant. xvii. 6. 4*), which, it is astronomically ascertained, occurred on the night from the 12th to the 13th of March of the year 4 before Christ. Thus the death of Herod must have taken place between the 12th of March and the 12th of April—or, say, about the end of March (comp. Ant. xvii. 8. 1). Again, the Gospel-history necessitates an interval of, at the least, seven or eight weeks before that date for the birth of Christ (we have to insert the purification of the Virgin—at the earliest, six weeks after the Birth—The Visit of the Magi, and the murder of the children at Bethlehem, and, at any rate, some days more before the death of Herod). Thus the birth of Christ could not have possibly occurred after the beginning of Febuary 4 B.C., and most likely several weeks earlier. This brings us close to the ecclesiastical date, the 25th of December, in confirmation of which we refer to what has been stated in vol. i. p. 187, see especially note 3. At any rate, the often repeated, but very superficial objection, as to the impossibility of shepherds tending flocks in the open at that season, must now be dismissed as utterly untenable, not only for the reasons stated in vol. i. p. 187, but even for this, that if the question is to be decided on the ground of rain-fall, the probabilities are in favour of December as compared with February—later than which it is impossible to place the birth of Christ.

2. No certain inference can, of course, be drawn from the appearance of 'the star' that guided the Magi. That, and on what grounds, our investigations have

pointed to a confirmation of the date of the Nativity, as given above, has been fully explained in vol. i. ch. viii. (see specially p. 213).

3. On the taxing of Quirinius, see vol. i. pp. 181, 182.

4. The next historical *datum* furnished by the Gospels is that of the beginning of St. John the Baptist's ministry, which, according to St. Luke, was in the fifteenth year of Tiberius, and when Jesus was 'about thirty years old' (St. Luke iii. 23). The accord of this with our reckoning of the date of the Nativity has been shown in vol. i. p. 264.

5. A similar conclusion would be reached by following the somewhat vague and general indication furnished in St. John ii. 20.

6. Lastly, we reach the same goal if we follow the historically somewhat uncertain guidance of the date of the Birth of the Baptist, as furnished in this notice (St. Luke i. 5) of his annunciation to his father, that Zacharias officiated in the Temple as one of 'the course of Abia' (see here vol. i. p. 135). In Taan. 29 *a* we have the notice, with which that of Josephus agrees (War vi. 4, 1, 5), that at the time of the destruction of the Temple 'the course of Jehoiarib,' which was the first of the priestly courses, was on duty. That was on the 9–10 *Ab* of the year 823 A.U.C., or the 5th August of the year 70 of our era. If this calculation be correct (of which, however, we cannot feel quite sure), then counting 'the courses' of priests backwards, the course of Abia would, in the year 748 A.U.C. (the year before the birth of Christ) have been on duty from the 2nd to the 9th of October. This also would place the birth of Christ in the end of December of the following year (749), taking the expression 'sixth month' in St. Luke i. 26, 36, in the sense of the running month (from the 5th to the 6th month, comp. St. Luke i. 24). But we repeat that absolute reliance cannot be placed on such calculations, at least so far as regards month and day. (Comp. here generally *Wieseler*, Synopse, and his Beiträge.)

APPENDIX VIII.

RABBINIC TRADITIONS ABOUT ELIJAH, THE FORERUNNER OF THE MESSIAH.

(Vol. i. Book II. ch. iii. p. 143.)

APP.
VIII

To complete the evidence, presented in the text, as to the essential difference between the teaching of the ancient Synagogue about 'the Forerunner of the Messiah' and the history and mission of John the Baptist, as described in the New Testament, we subjoin a full, though condensed, account of the earlier Rabbinic traditions about Elijah.

Opinions differ as to the descent and birthplace of Elijah. According to some, he was from the land of Gilead (Bemid. R. 14), and of the tribe of Gad (Tanch. on Gen. xlix. 19). Others describe him as a Benjamite, from Jerusalem, one of those 'who sat in the Hall of Hewn Stones' (Tanch. on Ex. xxxi. 2), or else as paternally descended from Gad and maternally from Benjamin.[1] Yet a third opinion, and to which apparently most weight attaches, represents him as a Levite, and a Priest—nay, as the great High-Priest of Messianic days. This is expressly stated in the Targum Pseudo-Jon. on Ex. xl. 10, where it also seems implied that he was to anoint the Messiah with the sacred oil, the composition of which was among the things unknown in the second Temple, but to be restored by Elijah (Tanch. on Ex. xxiii. 20, ed. Warsh. p. 91 a, lines 4 and 5 from the top). Another curious tradition identifies Elijah with Phinehas (Targum Pseudo-Jon. on Ex. vi. 18). The same expression as in the Targum ('Phinehas—that is Elijah') occurs in that great storehouse of Rabbinic tradition, Yalkut (vol. i. p. 245 b, last two lines, and col. c). From the pointed manner in which reference is made to the parallelism between the zeal of Phinehas and that of Elijah, and between their work in reconciling God and Israel, and bringing the latter to repentance, we may gather alike the origin of this tradition and its deeper meaning.[2]

For (as fully explained in Book II. ch. v.) it is one of the principles frequently expressed by the ancient Synagogue, in its deeper perception of the unity and import of the Old Testament, that the miraculous events and Divine interpositions of Israel's earlier history would be re-enacted, only with wider application, in Messianic days. If this idea underlay the parallelism between Phinehas and Elijah, it is still more fully carried out in that between Elijah and Moses. On comparing the Scriptural account of these two messengers of God we are struck with the close correspondence between the details of their history. The Synagogue is careful to trace this analogy step by step (Yalkut, vol. ii. p. 32 d) to the final deliverance of

---

[1] This question is fully discussed in Ber. R. 71 towards the close. Comp. also Shem. R. 40. For fuller details we refer to our remarks on Gen. xlix. 19 in Appendix IX.
[2] I cannot agree with either of the explana-

tions of this passage offered by *Castelli* (Il Messia, p. 199), whose citation is scarcely as accurate as usually. The passage quoted is in the Par. Pinchas, opening lines.

Israel, marking that, as that by Moses had for ever freed his people from the domination of Egypt, so would the final deliverance by Elijah for ever break the yoke of all foreign rule.   The allusion here is to the part which Elijah was expected to take in the future ‘ wars of Gog and Magog ’ (Seder Olam R. c. xvii.). Indeed, this parallelism is carried so far, that tradition has it, that, when Moses was commissioned by God to go to Pharaoh, he pleaded that God should rather send by him whom He designed to send for the far greater deliverance in the latter days.   On this it was told him that Elijah’s mission would be to Israel, while he (Moses) was sent to Pharaoh (Pirqé de R. Eliez. 40).[1]   Similarly, it is asserted that the cave from which Moses beheld the Divine Presence passing before him (Ex. xxxiii. 22) was the same as that in which Elijah stood under similar circumstances—that cave having been created. not with the rest of the world, but specially on the eve of the world’s first Sabbath (Siphré on Deut., ed. *Friedmann*, p. 147 *a*, last line).   Considering this parallelism between them, the occurrence of the somewhat difficult expression will scarcely surprise us, that in the days of the Messiah Moses and Elijah would come together—‘ as one ’ (Debar. R. 3, at the end).[2]

It has been noted in the text that the activity of Elijah, from the time of his appearance in the days of Ahab to that of his return as the forerunner of the Messiah, is represented in Jewish tradition as *continuous*, and that he is almost constantly introduced on the scene, either as in converse with some Rabbi, or else as busy about Israel’s welfare, and connected with it.   Thus Elijah chronicles in heaven the deeds of man (Seder Olam R. xvii.), or else he writes down the observance of the commandments by men, and then the Messiah and God seal it (Midrash on Ruth ii. 14, last line, ed. Warsh. p. 43 *b*).   In general, he is ever interested in all that concerns Israel’s present state or their future deliverance (Sanh. 98 *a*).   Indeed, he is connected with the initiatory rite of the covenant, in acknowledgment of his zeal[3] in the restoration of circumcision, when, according to tradition, it had been abrogated by the ten tribes after their separation from Judah. God accordingly had declared: ‘ Israel shall not make the covenant of circumcision, but thou shalt see it,’ and the sages decreed that (at circumcision) a seat of honour shall be placed for the Angel of the Covenant (Mal. iii. 2; Pirqé de R. Eliez. 29, end).   Tradition goes even further.   Not only was he the only ambassador to whom God had delegated His three special ‘ keys ’: of birth, of the rainfall, and of waking the dead (Yalkut, vol. ii. 32 *c*), but his working was almost Divine (Tanch. Bereshith 7; ed. Warsh. p. 6 *b*, last line, and 7 *a*).

We purposely pass over the activity of Elijah in connection with Israel, and especially its Rabbis and saints, during the interval between the Prophet’s death and his return as the Forerunner of the Messiah, such as Jewish legend describes it.

---

[1] *Castelli* writes: *Lo Prega a mandare in tuogo suo Elic, già esistente almeno in ispirito; e Dio risponde, che è predestinato non a quella, ma alla finale redenzione.*   But there are three inaccuracies here, for (1) Moses does not *name* Elijah;   (2) there is not a hint that Elijah was pre-existing in spirit;   while (3) God’s reply to Moses is as in our text.

[2] The question has been raised whether Jeremiah (or even Isaiah) was also to appear in Messianic days.   In favour of this view 2 Macc. ii. 1–8 and xv. 14–16 afford, to say the least, presumptive evidence.   We do not refer to 4 Esdras ii. 18, because the two first and the two last chapters of that book in our Apocrypha (2 Esdras) are spurious, being of much later, probably Christian, authorship. *Gfrörer* thinks that 4 Esdras v. (2 Esdras vii. 28) refers to Jeremiah and Isaiah (Urchrist vol. ii. p. 230).   But I cannot draw the same inference from it.   On the other hand, there is a remarkable passage in Mechilta on Ex. xvi. 33 (ed. *Weiss*, p. 59 *b*), which not only seems to conjoin Jeremiah with the Messiah (though the inaccurate rendering of *Wetstein,* Nov. Test. vol. i. p. 430 conveys an exaggerated and wrong impression of this), but reminds us of 2 Macc. ii. 1–8.

[3] In this passage also reference is made to the zeal of Phinehas as corresponding to that of Elijah.

APP.
VIII

No good purpose could be served by repeating what so frequently sounds not only utterly foolish and superstitious, but profane. In Jewish legend Elijah is always introduced as the guardian of the interests of Israel, whether theologically or personally—as it were the constant living *medium* between God and his people, the link that binds the Israel of the present—with its pursuits, wants, difficulties and interests—to the bright Messianic future of which he is the harbinger. This probably is the idea underlying the many, often grotesque, legends about his sayings and doings. Sometimes he is represented as, in his well-meant zeal, going so far as to bear false witness in order to free Rabbis from danger and difficulty (Berach. 58 *a*). In general, he is always ready to instruct, to comfort, or to heal, condescending even to so slight a malady as the toothache (Ber. R. 96, end). But most frequently is he the adviser and friend of the Rabbis, in whose meetings and studies he delighteth. Thus he was a frequent attendant in Rabh's Academy—and his indiscretion in divulging to his friends the secrets of heaven had once procured for him in heaven the punishment of fiery stripes (Babha Mets. 85 *b*). But it is useless to do more than indicate all this. Our object is to describe the activity of Elijah in connection with the coming of the Messiah.

When, at length, the time of Israel's redemption arrived—then would Elijah return. Of two things only are we sure in connection with it. Elijah will not 'come yesterday'—that is, he will be revealed the same day that he comes—and he will not come on the eve of either a Sabbath or feast-day, in order not to interrupt the festive rest, nor to break the festive laws (Erub. 43 *b*, Shabb. 33 *a*). Whether he came one day (Er. 43 *b*) or three days before the Messiah (Yalkut, vol. ii. p. 53 *c*, about the middle) his advent would be *close* to that of the Messiah (Yalkut, vol. i. p. 310 *a*. line 21 from bottom).[1] The account given of the three days between the advent of Elijah and of the Messiah is peculiar (Yalkut, vol. ii. p. 53 *c*). Commenting on Is. lii. 7, it is explained, that on the first of those three days Elijah would stand on the mountains of Israel, lamenting the desolateness of the land, his voice being heard from one end of the world to the other, after which he would proclaim: 'Peace' cometh to the world; 'peace' cometh to the world! Similarly on the second day he would proclaim, 'Good' cometh to the world; 'good' cometh to the world! Lastly, on the third day, he would, in the same manner as the two previous days, make proclamation: '*Jeshuah*[2] (salvation) cometh to the world; *Jeshuah* (salvation) cometh to the world,' which, in order to mark the difference between Israel and the Gentiles, would be further explained by this addition: 'Saying unto Zion—Thy King cometh!'

The period of Elijah's advent would, according to one opinion (Pirqé de R. Eliez. 43), be a time of genuine repentance by Israel, although it is not stated that this change would be brought about by his ministry. On the other hand, his peculiar activity would consist in settling ceremonial and ritual questions, doubts, and difficulties, in making peace, in restoring those who by violence had been wrongfully excluded from the congregation and excluding those who by violence had been wrongfully introduced (Bab. Mets. i. 8; ii. 8; iii. 4, 5; Eduy. vii. 7). He would also restore to Israel these three things which had been lost: the golden

---

[1] *Schöttgen* (Horæ Hebr. tomus ii. p. 534) has not correctly apprehended the meaning of this passage. It is not '*statim* cum ipso Messiæ adventu,' but *prope* or *proxime* (סמוך לביאה). *Schöttgen* writes inaccurately, והביאה.

[2] Of course this is the Hebrew word used in Is. lii. 7 ('that publisheth *salvation*'). None the less significant, however, in this connection, is the fact that the word is pronounced like the Name of Jesus.

pot of Manna (Ex. xvi. 33), the vessel containing the anointing oil, and that with the waters of purification—according to some, also Aaron's rod that budded and bore fruit.[1] Again, his activity is likened to that of the Angel whom God had sent before Israel to drive out and to vanquish the hostile nations (Tanch. on Ex. xxiii. 20, § 18 at the close; ed. Warsh. p. 106 b). For. Elijah was to appear, then to disappear, and to appear again in the wars of Gog and Magog [2] (Seder Olam R. xvii.). But after that time general peace and happiness would prevail, when Elijah would discharge his peculiar functions. Finally, to the ministry of Elijah some also ascribed the office of raising the dead (Sotah ix. 15, closing words).[3]

Such is a summary of ancient Jewish tradition concerning Elijah as the forerunner of the Messiah. Comparing it with the New Testament description of John the Baptist, it will at least be admitted that, from whatever source the sketch of the activity and mission of the Baptist be derived, it cannot have been from the ideal of the ancient Synagogue, nor yet from popularly current Jewish views. And, indeed—could there be a greater contrast than between the Jewish forerunner of the Messiah and him of the New Testament?

---

[1] The reader will find, in our remarks on Ps. cx. 2 in Append. IX. the curious traditions about this rod of Aaron, as given in Bemid. R. 18 and Yalkut on Ps. cx. 2. The story of the wonder-working rod is told somewhat differently in the Targum Pseudo-Jon. on Ex. ii. 20, 21 and iv. 20; and again, with other variations, in Pirkê de R. Eliez. 40. In the latter passage we are told, that this rod had passed from the possession of Joseph (after his death) into the palace of Pharaoh. Thence Jethro, who was one of the magicians of Egypt, had removed it to his own home. The ability of Moses to read the writing on the rod—according to other traditions, to uproot it out of the garden—indicated him to Jethro as the future deliverer of Israel, and determined him to give to Moses Zipporah for his wife (in preference to all other suitors). According to other traditions, Moses had been for many years imprisoned, and ministered to by Zipporah, who loved him. It may be added, that, according to very ancient tradition, the rod of Aaron was one of the things created

on the eve of the world's first Sabbath (Siphre, ed. Friedmann, p. 147 a, last line).
[2] We have purposely omitted all reference to the connection between Elijah and the 'second' Messiah, the son of Ephraim, because that line of tradition belongs to a later period than that of Christ.
[3] The view of the Apocrypha on the Mission of Elijah may be gathered from Ecclus. xlviii. 1–12. Some additional Talmudic notices about Elijah will be found at the close of Append. IX. The Sepher Eliyahu (Apocalypse of Elijah), published in Jellinek's Beth ha-Midr. part ii. pp. 65–68, adds nothing to our knowledge. It professes to be a revelation by the Angel Michael to Elijah of the end and the last days, at the close of the fourth monarchy. As it is simply an Apocalyptic account of the events of those days, it cannot here find a place, however interesting the Tractate. I have purposely not referred to the abominable story about Elijah told in Yoma 19 b, last lines.

APPENDIX IX.

LIST OF OLD TESTAMENT PASSAGES MESSIANICALLY APPLIED IN ANCIENT RABBINIC WRITINGS.

(Vol. i. Book II. ch. v.)

APP. IX

THE following list contains the passages in the Old Testament applied to the Messiah or to Messianic times in the most ancient Jewish writings. They amount in all to 456, thus distributed : 75 from the Pentateuch, 243 from the Prophets, and 138 from the Hagiographa, and supported by more than 558 separate quotations from Rabbinic writings. Despite all labour and care, it can scarcely be hoped that the list is quite complete, although, it is hoped, no important passage has been omitted. The Rabbinic references might have been considerably increased, but it seemed useless to quote the same application of a passage in many different books. Similarly, for the sake of space, only the most important Rabbinic quotations have been translated *in extenso*. The Rabbinic works from which quotations have been made are : the *Targumim*, the two *Talmuds*, and the *most ancient Midrashim*, but neither the *Zohar* (as the date of its composition is in dispute), nor any other Kabbalistic work, nor yet the younger Midrashim, nor, of course, the writings of later Rabbis. I have, however, frequently quoted from the well-known work *Yalkut*, because, although of comparatively late date, it is really, as its name implies, a collection and selection from more than fifty older and accredited writings, and adduces passages now not otherwise accessible to us. And I have the more readily availed myself of it, as I have been reluctantly forced to the conclusion that even the *Midrashim* preserved to us have occasionally been tampered with for controversial purposes. I have quoted from the best edition of *Yalkut* (Frankfort a. M., 1687), but in the case of the other Midrashim I have been obliged to content myself with such more recent reprints as I possessed, instead of the older and more expensive editions. In quoting from the Midrashim, not only the Parashah, but mostly also the folio, the page, and frequently even the lines are referred to. Lastly, it only remains to acknowledge in general that, so far as possible, I have availed myself of the labours of my predecessors—specially of those of *Schöttgen*. Yet, even so, I may, in a sense, claim these references also as the result of my own labours, since I have not availed myself of quotations without comparing them with the works from which they were adduced—a process in which not a few passages quoted had to be rejected. And if any student should arrive at a different conclusion from mine in regard to any of the passages hereafter quoted, I can at least assure him that mine is the result of the most careful and candid study I could give to the consideration of each passage. With these prefatory remarks I proceed to give the list of Old Testament passages Messianically applied in ancient Rabbinic writings.

In *Gen.* i. 2, the expression, 'Spirit of God,' is explained of 'the Spirit of the King Messiah,' with reference to *Is.* xi. 2, and the 'moving on the face of the deep' of 'repentance,' according to *Lam. ii.* 19. So in Ber. R. 2, and in regard to the first point also in Ber. R. 8, in Vayyik. R. 14, and in other places.

Gen. ii. 4 : 'These are the generations—תוֹלְדוֹת—of the heavens and of the earth,' taken in connection with *Gen. iii.* 15 and *Ruth iv.* 18. Here we note one of the most curious Messianic interpretations in Ber. R. 12 (ed. Warsh. p. 24 *b*). It is noted that the word 'generations' (תוֹלְדוֹת) is always written in the Bible without the וֹ which is the equivalent for the numeral 6, except in Gen. ii. 4 and Ruth iv. 18. This to indicate that subsequent to Gen. ii. 4 the Fall took place, in which Adam lost וֹ—six—things : his glorious sheen (Job xiv. 20) ; life (Gen. iii. 19) ; his stature (Gen. iii. 8—either by 100, by 200, by 300, or even by 900 cubits) ; the fruit of the ground ; the fruits of the trees (Gen. iii. 17) ; and the heavenly lights. We have now seen why in Gen. ii. 4—that is, previous to the Fall—the וֹ is still in תוֹלְדוֹת, since at that time these six things were not yet lost. But the וֹ reappears in the word תוֹלְדוֹת in Ruth iv. 18, because these six things are to be restored to man by ' the son of Pharez '—or the Messiah (comp. for each of these six things : Judg. v. 31 *b* ; Is. lxviii. 22 ; Lev. xxvi. 13 ; Zech. viii. 12 ; Is. xxx. 26). It is added that although—according to the literal rendering of Ps. xlix. 12 (in Heb. ver. 13)—man did not remain unfallen one single night, yet, for the sake of the Sabbath, the heavenly lights were not extinguished till after the close of the Sabbath. When Adam saw the darkness, it is added, he was greatly afraid, saying : Perhaps he, of whom it is written, ' he shall bruise thy head, and thou shalt bruise his heel,' cometh to molest and attack me, and he said, ' Surely the darkness shall cover me.' This curious extract at least shows in what context the Synagogue applied Gen. iii. 15. The same occurs substantially in Shem. R. 30.

Gen. iii. 15. This well-known passage is paraphrased, with express reference to the Messiah, in the Targum Pseudo-Jonathan and the so-called Jerusalem Targum. *Schöttgen* conjectures that the Talmudic designation of ' heels of the Messiah ' (Sot. 49 *b*, line 2 from top) in reference to the near Advent of the Messiah in the description of the troubles of those days (comp. St. Matt. x. 35, 36) may have been chosen partly with a view to this passage.

Gen. iv. 25. The language of Eve at the birth· of Seth : ' another seed,' is explained as meaning ' seed which comes from another place,' and referred to the Messiah in Ber. R. 23 (ed. Warsh. p. 45 *b*, lines 8, 7 from the bottom). The same explanation occurs twice in the Midrash on Ruth iv. 19 (in the genealogy of David, ed. Warsh. p. 46 *b*), the second time in connection with Ps. xl. 8 (' in the volume of the book it is written of me '—*bim'gillath sepher*—Ruth belonging to the class מְגִלֹּת).

In connection with *Gen. v.* 1 it is noted in Ber. R. 24, that King Messiah will not come till all souls predestined for it have appeared in human bodies on earth.

In *Gen. viii.* 11 the Targum Pseudo-Jonathan notes that the olive-leaf, brought by the dove, was taken from the Mount of the Messiah.

Gen. ix. 27. The promise, that Japhet shall dwell in the tents of Shem, is paraphrased in the Targum Pseudo-Jon. as meaning, that his descendants should become proselytes, and dwell in the schools of Shem—which seems to refer to Messianic times.

In connection with *Gen. xiv.* 1, we are reminded in Ber. R. 42, that when we see the nations warring together, we may expect the coming of the Messiah.

The promise in *Gen. xv.* 18 is expected to be finally fulfilled in the time of Messiah, in Ber. R. 44.

In connection with *Gen. xviii.* 4, 5 it is noted (Ber. R. 48, ed. Warsh. p. 87 *b*) that the words of Abraham to his Angelic guests were to be returned in blessing to Abraham's descendants, in the wilderness, in the land of Canaan, and in the latter (Messianic) days. Referring only to this last point, the words 'let a little water be fetched,' is paralleled with the ' living waters ' in Zech. xiv. 8; ' wash your feet,' with Is. iv. 4 (the washing away of the filth of the daughters of Zion) ; ' rest under the tree,' with Is. iv. 6 : ' there shall be a tabernacle for a shadow in the daytime from the heat ; ' ' I will fetch a morsel of bread,' with the provision, Ps. lxxii. 16 : ' there shall be a handful of corn in the earth,' &c. So also the words: ' Abraham ran unto the herd,' are paralleled with Is. vii. 21 (which is most significantly here applied to Messianic times); and lastly, the words, ' he stood by them,' with Mic. ii. 13: ' the breaker is come up before them.' [1] The same interpretation occurs in Bemid. R. 14 (ed. Warsh. p. 55 a), the references to Messianic days there being to Is. xiv. 2 ; xxx. 25 ; xli. 18 ; iv. 4 ; and iv. 6.

The last clause of *Gen. xix.* 32 is interpreted (Ber. R. 51, ed. Warsh. p. 95 a), as referring, like the words of Eve about Seth, to the Messiah—the sin of the daughters of Lot being explained on the ground of their believing that all mankind had been destroyed in the judgment that overthrew Sodom.

The promise in *Gen. xxii.* 18 is also explained Messianically in Bemid. R. 2 (ed. W. p. 5 b), in connection with Num. ii. 32, where it is somewhat curiously shown in what sense Israel is to be like the sand of the sea.

Gen. xxxiii. 1. The Midrash conjoins this with Is. lxvi. 7, and notes that, before the first oppressor was born, the last Redeemer was already born.

In *Gen. xxxv.* 21 the Targum Pseudo-Jon. paraphrases ' the tower of Eder' (at Bethlehem) as the place whence the Messiah would be revealed.

On *Gen. xxxviii.* 1, 2 there are very remarkable Messianic comments in Ber. R.85.

Gen. xlix. 1. The Targum Pseudo-Jon. notes, that the end for which the Messiah would come was not revealed to Jacob. A similar statement is found in the Midrash on the passage (Ber. R. 98, ed. Warsh. p. 173 a), where it is said of Jacob and Daniel that they saw the end, and yet it was afterwards hid from them. The passage quoted in the case of Daniel is Dan. xii. 4.

Gen. xlix. 9. The expression ' lion's whelp,' is explained of the Messiah in Yalkut 160 (vol. i. p. 49 c), no less than five times ; while the term ' he couched,' is referred to the Messiah in Ber. R. 98.

Gen xlix. 10. This well-known prediction (on which see the full and interesting discussion in *Raym. Martini,* Pugio Fidei) is in Yalkut, u. s., applied to the Messiah, with a quotation of Ps. ii. 9. The expression ' Shiloh' is also applied to the Messiah, with the curious addition, that in the latter days all nations would bring gifts to Him. Alike the Targum Onkelos, Pseudo-Jonathan, and the Jerusalem Targum, as well as Sanh. 98 b, the Midrash on the passage, and that on Prov. xix. 21, and on Lam. i. 16, where it is rendered *shelo,* ' whose it is,' refer the expression ' Shiloh,' and, indeed, the whole passage, to the Messiah; the Midrash Ber. R. (99, ed. Warsh. p. 178 b) with special reference to Is. xi. 10, while the promise with reference to the ass's colt is brought into connection with Zech. ix. 9, the fulfilment of this prophecy being expected along with that in Ezek. xxxvi. 25 (' I will sprinkle clean water'). Another remarkable statement occurs in the Midrash on the passage (Ber. R. 98, ed. Warsh. p. 174 b), which applies the verse to the coming of Him of Whom it is written, Zech. ix. 9. Then He would

---

[1] Indeed, this Parashah in Ber. R. contains other similar parallelisms between Gen. xvii. and Messianic times.

wash his garment in wine (Gen. xlix. 11), which is explained as meaning the teaching of the Law to Israel, and His clothes in the blood of grapes, which is explained as meaning that He would bring them back from their errors. One of the Rabbis, however, remarks that Israel would not require to be taught by the King Messiah in the latter days, since it was written (Is. xi. 10), 'to it shall the Gentiles seek.' If so, then why should the Messiah come, and what will He do to the congregation of Israel ? He will redeem Israel, and give them thirty commandments, according to Zech. xi. 12. The Targum Pseudo-Jon. and the Jer. Targum also apply *verse* 11 to the Messiah. Indeed, so general was this interpretation, that, according to popular opinion, to see a palm-tree in one's dreams was to see the days of the Messiah (Berach. 57 *a*).

Gen. xlix. 12 is also applied to the Messiah in the Targum Pseudo-Jon. and the Jerusalem Targum. So also is *verse* 18, although not in express words.

In *Gen. xlix.* 17, last clause, in its connection with ver. 18, the Midrash (Ber. R. 98) sees a reference to the disappointment of Jacob in mistaking Samson for the Messiah.

In the prophecy of Gad in *Gen. xlix.* 19 there is an allusion to Messianic days, as Elijah was to be of the tribe of Gad (Ber. R. 99, ed. Warsh. p. 179 *a*). There is, however, in Ber. R. 71, towards the close, a dispute whether he was of the tribe of Gad, or of the tribe of Benjamin, at the close of which Elijah appears, and settles the dispute in a rather summary manner.

On *Gen. l.* 10 the Midrash, at the close of Ber. R., remarks that as they had mourned, so in Messianic days God would turn their mourning into joy, quoting Jer. xxxi. 13 and Is. li. 3.

Ex. iv. 22 is referred to the Messiah in the Midr. on Ps. ii. 7.

On *Exod. xii.* 2, 'let this be the beginning of months,' it is remarked in Shem. R. 15 (ed. Warsh. p. 24 *b*) that God would make new ten things in the latter days, these being marked by the following passages : Is. lx. 19 ; Ezek. xlvii. 9 ; xlvii. 12 ; Ezek. xvi. 55 ; Is. liv. 11 ; Is. xi. 7 ; Hos. ii. 20 ; Is. lxv. 19 ; Is. xxv. 8 ; Is. xxxv. 10. Similarly on Num. xii. 1 we have, in Shem. R. 51, a parallelism between Old Testament times and their institutions and those of the latter days, to which Is. xlix. 12 and lx. 8 are supposed to apply.

On *Exod. xii.* 42 the Jerus. Targum notes that there were 4 remarkable nights: those of creation, of the covenant with Abraham, of the first Passover, and of the redemption of the world ; and that as Moses came out of the desert, so would the Messiah come out of Rome.

Exod. xv. 1. It is noted in Mekhilta (ed. *Weiss*, p. 41 *a*) that this song would be taken up in Messianic days, only with far wider reach, as explained in Is. lx. 5 ; lviii. 8 ; xxxv. 5, 6 ; Jer. xxxi. 13 ; and Ps. cxxvi. 2.

Ex. xvi. 25 is applied to the Messiah, it being said that, if Israel only kept one Sabbath according to the commandment, the Messiah would immediately come (Jer. Taan. 64 *a*).

Ex. xvi. 33. This manna, it is noted in Mechil. ed. *Weiss*, p. 59 *b*, was to be preserved for the days of the Messiah. Is. xxx. 15 is similarly explained in Jer. Taan. i. 1.

Ex. xvii. 16 the Targum Pseudo-Jonathan refers to Messianic times.

Exod. xxi. 1. Shem. R. 30, ed Warsh. p. 44 *b*, 45 *a*, notes on the word 'judgments' a number of things connected with judgment, showing how Balaam could not have wished the advent of the future deliverance (Numb. xxiv. 17), since he was to perish in it ; but that Israel should cleave to the great hope

APP.
IX

pressed in Gen. xlix. 18 ; Is. lvi. 1 ; lix. 16 ; and especially Zech. ix. 9, of which a different rendering is proposed.

On *Exod. xl.* 9, 11 there is in the Targum Pseudo-Jon. distinct reference to the King Messiah, on whose account the anointing oil was to be used.

The promise (*Lev. xxvi.* 12) is also referred to the latter, or Messianic, days in Yalkut 62 (vol. i. p. 17 *b*).

Lev. xxvi. 13 is applied to Messianic times. See our remarks on Gen. ii. 4.

The promise of peace in the Aaronic benediction *Num. vi.* 26 is referred to the peace of the Kingdom of David, in accordance with Is. ix. 7 (Siphré on Num. par. 42, ed. *Friedmann*, p. 12 *b*).

Num. vii. 12. In connection with this it is marked that the six blessings which were lost by the Fall are to be restored by the son of Nahshon, i.e. the Messiah (Bem. R. 13, ed. W. p. 51 *a*).

In the Jerusalem Targum on *Num. xi.* 26 the prophecy of Eldad and Medad is supposed to have been with regard to the wars of the latter days against Jerusalem, and to the defeat of Gog and Magog by the Messiah.

In *Num. xxiii.* 21 the term 'King' is expressly referred to the Messiah in Targum Pseudo-Jon. So also *Num. xxiv.* 7 in the Jer. Targum.

In *Num. xxiv.* 17 Balaam's prediction of the Star and Sceptre is referred to the Messiah in the Targum Onkelos and the Targum Pseudo-Jonathan, as well as in Jer. Taan. iv. 8 ; Deb. R. 1 ; Midr. on Lament. ii. 2. Similarly, *verses* 20 *and* 24 of that prophecy are ascribed in the Targum Pseudo-Jon. to the Messiah.

Num. xxvii. 16. In connection with this verse it is noticed that His one Spirit is worth as much as all other spirits, according to Is. xi. 1 (Yalkut, vol. i. p. 247 *a*).

Deut. i. 8 is applied to the days of the Messiah in Siphré, 67 *a*.

In the comments of Tanchuma on *Deut. viii.* 1. (ed. Warsh. p. 104 *b*, 105 *a*) there are several allusions to Messianic days.

Deut. xi. 21 is applied in Siphré, Par. 47 (ed. *Friedmann*, p. 83 *a*) to the days of the Messiah.

In *Deut. xvi.* 3 the record of the deliverance from Egypt is supposed to be carried on to the days of the Messiah, in Siphré, Par. 130 (ed. *Friedmann*, p. 101 *a*). See, also, Ber. i. 5.

On *Deut. xix.* 8, 9 it is noted, in Siphré on Deut., Par. 185 (ed. *Friedm.* p. 108 *b*), that as three of these cities were in territory never possessed by Israel, this was to be fulfilled in Messianic times. See also Jer. Macc. ii. 7.

In Tanchuma on *Deut. xx.* 10 (Par. 19, ed. Warsh. p. 114 *b*) the offer of peace to a hostile city is applied to the future action of Messiah to the Gentiles, in accordance with Zech. ix. 10 ; Is. ii. 4 ; and Ps. lxviii. 32 ; while, on the other hand, the resistance of a city to the offer of peace is likened to rebellion against the Messiah, and consequent judgment, according to Is. xi. 4.

Deut. xxiii. 11 is typically applied to the evening of time, when God would wash away the filth of the daughters of Zion (Is. iv. 4) ; and the words : ' when the sun is down ' to when King Messiah would come (Tanchuma on Par. Ki Thetse 3, ed. Warsh. p. 115 *b*).

Deut. xxv. 19 and *Deut. xxx.* 4 are referred by the Targum Pseudo-Jon. to Messianic times. In the latter passage the gathering of dispersed Israel by Elijah, and their being brought back by Messiah, are spoken of. Comp. also Bem. R., last three lines.

On *Deut. xxxii.* 7 Siphré (Par. 210, ed. *Friedm.* p. 134 *a*) makes the beautiful observation, that in all Israel's afflictions they were to remember the good and comfortable things which God had promised them for the future world, and in connection with this there is special reference to the time of the Messiah.

On *Deut. xxxii.* 30 Siphré (p. 138 *a*) marks its fulfilment in the days of the Messiah.

On *Deut. xxxiii.* 5 the Jer. Targum speaks of a king whom the tribes of Israel shall obey, this being evidently the King Messiah.

Deut. xxxiii. 17. Tanchuma on Gen. i. Par. 1 (ed. Warsh. p. 4 *a*) applies this to the Messiah. So also in Bemidb. R. 14.

Deut. xxxiii. 12. The expression, 'he shall cover him,' is referred to this world; 'all the day long,' to the days of the Messiah; and 'he shall dwell between his shoulders,' to the world to come (Sebach. 118 *b*).

Judg. v. 31: 'let them that love Him be as the sun when he goeth forth in his might,' is applied to Messianic times in Ber. R. 12. See our remarks on Gen. ii. 4.

On *Ruth ii.* 14: 'come hither at the time of meat,' the Midr. R. Ruth 5 (ed. Warsh. p. 43 *a* and *b*), has a very remarkable interpretation. Besides the application of the word 'eat,' as beyond this present time, to the days of the Messiah, and again to the world to come, which is to follow these days, the Midrash applies the whole of it mystically to the Messiah, viz. 'Come hither,' that is, draw near to the Kingdom, 'and eat of the bread,' that is, the bread of royalty, 'and dip thy morsel in vinegar'—these are the sufferings, as it is written in Is. liii. 5, 'He was wounded for our transgressions.' 'And she sat beside the reapers'—because His Kingdom would in the future be put aside from Him for a short time, according to Zech. xiv. 2; 'and he reached her parched corn'—because He will restore it to Him, according to Is. xi. 4. R. Berachiah, in the name of R. Levi, adds, that the second Redeemer should be like the first. As the first Redeemer (Moses) appeared, and disappeared, and reappeared after three months, so the second Redeemer would also appear, and disappear, and again become manifest, Dan. xii. 11, 12 being brought into connection with it. Comp. Midr. on Cant. ii. 9; Pesik. 49 *a*, *b*. Again, the words, 'she ate, and was sufficed, and left,' are thus interpreted in Shabb. 113 *b* : she ate—in this world ; and was sufficed—in the days of the Messiah ; and left—for the world to come.

Again, the Targum on *Ruth i.* 1 speaks of the Messiah; and again on *Ruth iii.* 15 paraphrases the six measures of barley as referring to six righteous ones, of which the last was the Messiah, and who were each to have six special blessings.

Ruth iv. 18. The Messiah is called 'the son of Pharez,' who restores what had been lost to humanity through the fall of Adam. See our remarks on Gen. ii. 4.

The Messianic interpretation of *Ruth iv.* 20 has already been given under Gen. iv. 25.

1 *Sam. ii.* 10. The latter clause of this promise is understood by the Targum (and also in some of the Midrashim) as applying to the Kingdom of the Messiah.

2 *Sam. xxii.* 28. In a Talmudic passage (Sanh. 98 *a*, line 19, &c., from the bottom), which contains many references to the coming of the Messiah, His advent is predicted in connection with this passage.

2 *Sam. xxiii.* 1 is applied by the Targum to the prophecy of David concerning the latter Messianic days.

2 *Sam. xxiii.* 3. The 'ruling in the fear of God' is referred in the Targum to the future raising up of the Messiah.

In 2 *Sam. xxiii.* 4 the morning light at sunrise is explained in the Midrash on the passage (par. 29, ed. Lemberg, p. 56 *b*, lines 7-9 from the top), as applying to the appearance of the Messiah.

The expression, 1 *Kings iv.* 33, that Solomon spoke of trees, is referred in the Targum to his prophecy concerning kings that were to reign in this age, and in that of the Messiah.

On the name ' Anani,' in 1 *Chr. iii.* 24, the Targum remarks that this is the Messiah, the interpretation being that the word Anani is connected with the word similarly written (not punctuated) in Dan. vii. 13, and there translated 'clouds,' of which the explanation is given in Tanchuma (Par. Toledoth 14, p. 37 *b*).

Ps. ii., as might be expected, is treated as full of Messianic references. To begin with, *Ps. ii.* 1 is applied to the wars of Gog and Magog in the Talmud (Berach. 7 *b* and Abhod. Zarah 3 *b*), and also in the Midrash on Ps. ii. Similarly, *verse* 2 is applied to the Messiah in Abhod. Zarah, u. s., in the Midrash on Ps. xcii. 11 (ed. Warsh. p. 70 *b*, line 8 from the top); in Pirqué de R. Eliez. c. 28 (ed. Lemberg, p. 33 *b*, line 9 from top). In Yalkut (vol. ii. par. 620, p. 90 *a*, line 12 from the bottom), we have the following remarkable simile on the words, ' against God, and His Messiah,' likening them to a robber who stands defiantly behind the palace of the king, and says, If I shall find the son of the king, I shall lay hold on him, and crucify him, and kill him with a cruel death. But the Holy Spirit mocks at him, 'He that sitteth in the heavens shall laugh.' On the same verse the Midrash on Ps. ii. has a curious conceit, intended to show that each who rose against God and His people thought he was wiser than he who had preceded him. If Cain had killed his brother while his father was alive, forgetful that there would be other sons, Esau proposed to wait till after his father's death. Pharaoh, again, blamed Esau for his folly in forgetting that in the meantime Jacob would have children, and hence proposed to kill all the male children, while Haman, ridiculing Pharaoh's folly in forgetting that there were daughters, set himself to destroy the whole people; and, in turn, Gog and Magog, ridiculing the shortsightedness of all, who had preceded them, in taking counsel against Israel so long as they had a Patron in heaven, resolved first to attack their heavenly Patron, and after that Israel. To which apply the words, 'against the Lord, and against His Anointed.'

But to return. *Ps. ii.* 4 is Messianically applied in the Talmud (Abhod. Z. u. s.). *Ps. ii.* 6 is applied to the Messiah in the Midrash on 1 Samuel xvi. 1 (Par. 19, ed. Lemberg, p. 45 *a* and *b*), where it is said that of the three measures of sufferings [1] one goes to the King Messiah, of whom it is written (Is. liii.) ' He was wounded for our transgressions.' They say to the King Messiah: Where dost Thou seek to dwell ? He answers : Is this question also necessary ? In Sion My holy hill (Ps. ii. 6). (Comp. also Yalkut ii. p. 53 *c*.)

Ps. ii. 7 is quoted as Messianic in the Talmud, among a number of other Messianic quotations (Sukk. 52 *a*). There is a very remarkable passage in the Midrash on Ps. ii. 7 (ed. Warsh. p. 5 *a*), in which the unity of Israel and the Messiah in prophetic vision seems clearly indicated. Tracing the 'decree' through the Law, the Prophets, and the Hagiographa, the first passage quoted is Exod. iv 22 : ' Israel is My first-born son ; ' the second, from the Prophets, Is. lii. 13 : ' Behold My servant shall deal prudently,' and Is. xlii. 1 : ' Behold My servant, whom I uphold; ' the third, from the Hagiographa, Ps. cx. 1 : ' The Lord said unto my Lord,' and again, Ps. ii. 7 : ' The Lord said unto Me, Thou art My Son,' and yet this other saying (Dan. vii. 13): ' Behold, one like the Son of Man came with the clouds of heaven.' Five lines further down, the same Midrash, in reference to the words ' Thou art My Son,' observes that, when that hour comes, God speaks to

---

[1] As to these three measures of sufferings, and the share falling to the age of the Messiah, see also the Midrash on Ps. ii. 7.

Him to make a new covenant, and thus He speaks : ' This day have I begotten Thee '—this is the hour in which He becomes His Son.

Ps. ii. 8 is applied in Ber. R. 44 (ed. Warsh. p. 80 *a*) and in the Midrash on the passage, to the Messiah, with the curious remark that there were three of whom it was said ' Ask of Me '—Solomon, Ahaz,[1] and the Messiah. In the Talmud (Sukk. 52 *a*) the same passage is very curiously applied, it being suggested that, when the Messiah, the Son of David, saw that the Messiah, the Son of Joseph,[2] would be killed, He said to the Almighty, I seek nothing of Thee except life. To which the reply was : Life before Thou hadst spoken, as David Thy father prophesied of Thee, Ps. xxi. 4.

Ps. ii. 9 will be referred to in our remarks on Ps. cxx.

Ps. xvi. 5 is discussed in Ber. R. 88, in connection with the cup which Pharaoh's butler saw in his dream. From this the Midrash proceeds to speak of the four cups appointed for the Passover night, and to explain their meaning in various manners, among others, contrasting the four cups of fury, which God would make the nations drink, with the four cups of salvation which He would give Israel in the latter days, viz. Ps. xvi. 5 ; Ps. cxvi. 13 ; Ps. xxiii. 5. The expression, Ps. cxvi. 13, rendered in our A.V. ' the cup of salvation,' is in the original, ' the cup of salvations '—and is explained as implying one for the days of the Messiah, and the other for the days of Gog.

On *verse* 9, the Midrash on the passage says : ' My glory shall rejoice in the King Messiah, Who in the future shall come forth from me, as it is written in Is. iv. 5 : "upon all the glory a covering." ' And the Midrash continues ' my flesh also shall dwell in safety '—i.e. after death, to teach us that corruption and the worm shall not rule over it.

Ps. xviii. 31 (in the Heb. verse 32). The Targum explains this in reference to the works and miracles of the Messiah.

Ps. xviii. 50 is referred in the Jer. Talmud (Ber. ii. 4, p. 5 *a*, line 11 from the top), and in the Midr. on Lam. i. 16, to the Messiah, with this curious remark, implying the doubt whether He was alive or dead : ' The King Messiah, whether He belong to the living or the dead, His Name is to be David, according to *Ps. xviii.* 50.'

Ps. xxi. 1 (2 in the Hebrew)—the King there spoken of is explained by the Targum to be the King Messiah. The Midrash on the passage identifies him with Is. xi. 10, on which Rabbi Chanina adds that the object of the Messiah is to give certain commandments to the Gentiles (not to Israel, who are to learn from God Himself), according to the passage in Isaiah above quoted, adding that the words ' his rest shall be glorious' mean that God gives to King Messiah from the glory above, as it is said : 'In Thy strength shall the king rejoice,' which strength is a little afterwards explained as the Kingdom (ed. Warsh. p. 30 *a* and *b*).

Verse 3 is Messianically applied in the Midrash on the passage.

Ps. xxi. 3 (4 in the Hebrew). Only a few lines farther down in the same Midrash, among remarkable Messianic applications, is that of this verse to the Messiah, where also the expressions ' Jehovah is a man of war,' and ' Jehovah Zidkenu,' are applied to the Messiah.[3] Comp. also Shemoth R. 8, where it is noted that God will crown Him with His own crown.

---

[1] The Midrash gives two very curious explanations of his name.

[2] On the twofold Messiah, or rather the device of the Jews on this subject, see in the text of the chapter. I cannot but suspect that the words ' Son of Joseph ' in the Talmud are a later and clumsy emendation, since what follows evidently applies to the Son of David.

[3] The idea of an organic connection between Israel and the Messiah seems also to underlie this passage.

Verse 4 is Messianically applied in Sukk. 52 *a*.

Ps. xxi. 5 (6 in the Hebrew). The first clause of this verse Yalkut on Num. xxvii. 20 (vol. i. p. 248 *a*, line 10 from the bottom) applies to the glory of the King Messiah, immediately quoting the second clause in proof of its Messianic application. This is also done in the Midrash on the passage. But perhaps one of the most remarkable applications of it is in Bemidbar R. 15, p. 63 *b*, where this passage is applied to the Messiah.

Finally in *Ps. xxi.* 7 (8 in the Hebrew), the expression 'king' is applied in the Targum to the Messiah.

On the whole, then, it may be remarked that Ps. xxi. was throughout regarded as Messianic.

On *Ps. xxii.* 7 (8 in the Hebrew) a remarkable comment appears in Yalkut on Is. lx., applying this passage to the Messiah (the second, or son of Ephraim), and using almost the same words in which the Evangelists describe the mocking behaviour of the Jews at the Cross.

Ps. xxii. 15 (16 in the Hebrew). There is a similarly remarkable application to the Messiah of this verse in Yalkut.

The promise in *Ps. xxiii.* 5 is referred in Bemid. R. 21 to the spreading of the great feast before Israel in the latter days.

Ps. xxxi. 19 (20 in the Hebrew) is in the Midrash applied to the reward that in the latter days Israel would receive for their faithfulness. Also in Pesiqta, p. 149 *b*, to the joy of Israel in the presence of the Messiah.

The expression in *Ps. xxxvi.* 9, 'In Thy light shall we see light,' is applied to the Messiah in Yalkut on Isaiah lx. (vol. ii. p. 56 *c*, line 22 from the bottom).

The application of *Ps. xl.* 7 to the Messiah has already been noted in our remarks on Gen. iv. 25.

Ps. xlv. is throughout regarded as Messianic. To begin with; the Targum renders *verse* 2 (3 in the Hebrew) : 'Thy beauty, O King Messiah, is greater than that of the sons of men.'

Verse 3 (4 in the Hebrew) is applied in the Talmud (Shabb 63 *a*) to the Messiah, although other interpretations of that verse immediately follow.

The application of *verse* 6 (7 in the Hebrew), to the Messiah in a MS. copy of the Targum has already been referred to in another part of this book, while the words, 'Thy throne is for ever and ever' are brought into connection with the promise that the sceptre would not depart from Judah in Ber. R. 99, ed. Warsh. p. 178 *b*, line 9 from the bottom.

On *verse* 7 the Targum, though not in the Venice edition (1568), has : 'Thou, O King Messiah, because Thou lovest righteousness,' &c. Comp. *Levy*, Targum. Wörterb. vol. ii. p. 41 *a*.

The Midrash on the Psalm deals exclusively with the inscription (of which it has several and significant interpretations) with the opening words of the Psalm, and with the words (ver. 16), 'Instead of thy fathers shall be thy children,' but at the same time it clearly indicates that the Psalm applies to the latter, or Messianic, days.

On *Ps. l.* 2 Siphré (p. 143 *a*) notes that four times God would appear, the last being in the days of King Messiah.

Ps. lx. 7. Bemidbar R. on Num. vii. 48, Parash. 14 (ed. Warsh p. 54 *a*) contains some very curious Haggadic discussions on this verse. But it also broaches the opinion of its reference to the Messiah.

Ps. lxi. 6 (7 in the Hebrew). 'Thou shalt add days to the days of the king,' is rendered by the Targum : 'Thou shalt add days to the days of King Messiah.'

There is a curious gloss on this in Pirqé d. R. Eliez. c. 19 (ed. Lemberg, p. 24 *b*), in which Adam is supposed to have taken 70 of his years, and added them to those of King David. According to another tradition, this accounts for Adam living 930 years, that is, 70 less than 1,000, which constitute before God one day, and so the threatening had been literally fulfilled : In the day thou eatest thereof, thou shalt die.

Ps. lxi. 8 (9 in the Hebrew). The expression, ' that I may daily perform my vows,' is applied in the Targum to the day in which the Messiah is anointed King.

Ps. lxviii. 31 (32 in the Hebrew). On the words ' Princes shall come out of Egypt,' there is a very remarkable comment in the Talmud (Pes. 118 *b*) and in Shemoth R. on Ex. xxvi. 15, &c. (ed. Warsh. p. 50 *b*), in which we are told that in the latter days all nations would bring gifts to the King Messiah, beginning with Egypt. ' And lest it be thought that He (Messiah) would not accept it from them, the Holy One says to the Messiah : Accept from them hospitable entertainment,' or it might be rendered, 'Accept it from them; they have given hospitable entertainment to My son.'

Ps. lxxii. This Psalm also was viewed by the ancient Synagogue as throughout Messianic, as indicated by the fact that the Targum renders the very first verse : ' Give the sentence of Thy judgment to the King Messiah, and Thy justice to the Son of David the King,' which is re-echoed by the Midrash on the passage (ed. Warsh. p. 55 *b*) which applies it explicitly to the Messiah, with reference to Is. xi. 1. Similarly, the Talmud applies *ver.* 16 to Messianic times (in a very hyperbolical passage, Shabb. 30 *b*, line 4 from the bottom). The last clause of verse 16 is applied, in Keth. 111 *b*, line 21 from top, and again in the Midr. on Eccl. i. 9, to the Messiah sending down manna like Moses.[1]

Verse 17. In Sanh. 98 *b* ; Pes. 54 *a* ; Ned. 39 *b*, the various names of the Messiah are discussed, and also in Ber. R. 1 ; in Midr. on Lam. i. 16, and in Pirqé de R. Eliez. c. 3. One of these is stated to be Jinnon, according to Ps. lxxii. 17.

Verse 8 is applied in Pirqé de R. El. c. 11, to the Messiah. Yalkut (vol. ii.) on Is. lv. 8 (p. 54 *c*), speaks of the ' other Redeemer ' as the Messiah, applying to him Ps. lxxii. 8.

In commenting on the meeting of Jacob and Esau, the Midr. Ber. R. (78, ed. Warsh. p. 141 *b*) remarks that all the gifts which Jacob gave to Esau, the nations of the world would return to the King Messiah—proving it by a reference to *Ps. lxxii.* 10 ; while in Midrash Bemidbar R. 13 it is remarked that as the nations brought gifts to Solomon, so they would bring them to the King Messiah.

In the same place, a little higher up, Solomon and the Messiah are likened as reigning over the whole world, the proof passages being, besides others, *Ps. lxxii.* 8, *Daniel vii.* 13, and *ii.* 35.

On the application to the Messiah of *verse* 16 we have already spoken, as also on that of *verse* 17.

Ps. lxxx. 17 (in the Hebrew 18). The Targum paraphrases ' the Son of Man ' by ' King Messiah.'

Ps. lxxxix. 22–25 (23–26 in the Hebrew). In Yalkut on Is. lx. 1 (vol. ii. p. 56 *c*) this promise is referred to the future deliverance of Israel by the Messiah.

Again, *verse* 27 (28 in the Hebrew) is applied in Shemoth R. 19, towards the end, to the Messiah, special reference being made to Ex. iv. 22, ' Israel is My first-born son.'

Verse 51 (52 in the Hebrew). There is a remarkable comment on this in the Midrash on the inscription of Ps. xviii. (ed. Warsh. p. 24 *a*, line 2 from the bottom),

---

[1] See the passage in Sanh. 96 *b* &c. given at the close of this Appendix.

in which it is set forth that as Israel and David did not sing till the hour of persecution and reproach, so when the Messiah shall come—'speedily, in our days'—
the song will not be raised until the Messiah is put to reproach, according to Ps.
lxxxix. 52 (51), and till ,here shall fall before Him the wicked idolaters referred
to in Dan. ii. 42, and the four kingdoms referred to in Zech. xiv. 2. In that hour
shall the song be raised, as it is written Ps. xcviii. 1.

In the Midr. on Cant. ii. 13 it is said : If you see one generation after another
blaspheming, expect the feet of the King Messiah, as it is written, *Ps. lxxix.* 53.

Ps. xc. 15. The Midr. (ed. Warsh. p. 67 *b*) remarks : The days wherein Thou
hast afflicted us—that is, the days of the Messiah. Upon which follows a discussion upon the length of days of the Messiah, R. Eliezer holding that they are 1,000
years, quoting the words 'as yesterday,' one day being 1,000 years. R. Joshua
holds that they were 2,000 years, the words 'the days' implying that there were
two days. R. Berachiah holds that they were 600 years, appealing to Is. lxv. 22,
because the root of the tree perishes in the earth in 600 years. R. José thinks that
they are 60 years, according to Ps. lxxii. 5, the words 'throughout all generations'
(dor dorim) being interpreted : Dor = 20 years ; Dorim = 40 years : 20 + 40 = 60.
R. Akiba says: 40 years, according to the years in the wilderness. The Rabbis say:
354 years, according to the days in the lunar year. R. Abahu thinks 7,000 years,
reckoning the 7 according to the days of the bridegroom.

On *Ps. xc.* the Midrash concludes by drawing a contrast between the Temple
which men built, and which was destroyed, and the Temple of the latter or Messianic days, which God would build, and which would not be destroyed.

Ps. xcii., verses 8, 11, *and* 13 (7, 10, and 12 in our A. V.), are Messianically interpreted in Pirqé de R. El. c. 19. In the Midrash on *verse* 13 (12 in our A. V.),
among other beautiful applications of the figure of the Psalm, is that to the Messiah
the Son of David. The note of the Midrash on the expression 'like a cedar of
Lebanon,' as applied to Israel, is very beautiful, likening it to the cedar, which,
although driven and bent by all the winds of heaven, cannot be rooted up from its
place.

Ps. xcv. 7, *last clause.* In Shem. R. 25 and in the Midrash on Cant. v. 2 (ed.
Warsh. p. 26 *a*), it is noted that, if Israel did penitence only one day [or else properly observed even one Sabbath], the Messiah the Son of David would immediately come. [The whole passage from which this reference is taken is exceedingly
interesting. It introduces God as saying to Israel : My son, open to Me a door
of penitence only as small as a needle's eye, and I will open to you doors through
which carriages and waggons shall come in. It almost seems a counterpart of the
Saviour's words (Rev. iii. 20) : 'Behold, I stand at the door and knock ; if any
man hear My voice and open the door, I will come in to him.'] Substantially the
same view is taken in Sanh. 98 *a*, where the tokens of the coming of the Messiah
are described—and also in Jer. Taan. 64 *a.*

Ps. cii. 16 (17 in the Hebrew) is applied in Bereshith R. 56 (ed. Warsh. p. 104 *b*)
to Messianic times.

Ps. cvi. 44. On this there is in the Midrash a long Messianic discussion, setting
forth the five grounds on which Israel is redeemed : through the sorrows of Israel,
through prayer, through the merits of the patriarchs, through repentance towards
God, and in the time of 'the end.'

Ps. cx. is throughout applied to the Messiah. To begin with, it evidently underlies the Targumic rendering of *ver.* 4. Similarly, it is propounded in the Midr. on

Ps. ii. (although there the chief application of it is to Abraham). But in the Midrash on Ps. xviii. 36 (35 in our A. V.), *Ps. cx. verse* 1, ' Sit thou at My right hand ' is specifically applied to the Messiah, while Abraham is said to be seated at the left.

Verse 2, ' The rod of Thy strength.' In a very curious mystic interpretation of the pledges which Tamar had, by the Holy Ghost, asked of Judah, the seal is interpreted as signifying the kingdom, the bracelet as the Sanhedrin, and the staff as the King Messiah, with special reference to Is. xi. and *Ps. cx.* 2 (Beresh. R. 85, ed. Warsh. p. 153 *a*) Similarly in Bemid. R. 18, last line, the staff of Aaron, which is said to have been in the hands of every king till the Temple was destroyed, and since then to have been hid, is to be restored to King Messiah, according to this verse ; and in Yalkut on this Psalm (vol. ii. Par. 869, p. 124 *c*) this staff is supposed to be the same as that of Jacob with which he crossed Jordan, and of Judah, and of Moses, and of Aaron, and the same which David had in his hand when he slew Goliath, it being also the same which will be restored to the Messiah.

Verse 7 is also applied in Yalkut (u. s. col. *d*) to Messianic times, when streams of the blood of the wicked should flow out, and birds come to drink of that flood.

Ps. cxvi. 9 is in Ber. R. 96 supposed to indicate that the dead of Palestine would live first in the days of the Messiah.

Ps. cxvi. 13 has been already commented upon.

On *Ps. cxix.* 33 the Midrash remarks that there were three who asked wisdom of God : David, Solomon, and the King Messiah, the latter according to Ps. lxxii. 1.

Ps. cxx. 7 is applied to the Messiah in the Midrash (p. 91 *a*, ed. Warsh.), the first clause being brought into connection with Is. lvii. 19, with reference to the Messiah's dealings with the Gentiles, the resistance being described in the second clause, and the result in Ps. ii. 9.

Ps. cxxi. 1 is applied in Tanchuma (Par. Toledoth 14, ed. Warsh. p. 37 *b*. See also Yalkut, vol. ii. 878, p. 127 *c*) to the Messiah, with special reference to Zech. iv. 7 and Is. lii. 7.

Ps. cxxvi. 2. In Tanchuma on Ex. xv. i. (ed. Warsh. p. 87 *a*) this verse is applied to Messianic times in a rapt description, in which successively Is. lx. 5, Is. lviii. 8, Is. xxxv. 5, 6, Jer. xxxi. 13, and *Ps. cxxvi.* 2, are grouped together as all applying to these latter days.

The promise in *Ps. cxxxii.* 18 is applied in Pirké de R. El. c. 28 to Messianic times, and *verse* 14 in Ber. R. 56.

So is *Ps. cxxxiii.* 3 in Ber. R. 65 (p. 122 *a*), closing lines.

The words in *Ps. cxlii.* 5 are applied in Ber. R. 74 to the resurrection of Israel in Palestine in the days of Messiah.

The words, ' When thou awakest,' in *Prov. vi.* 22 are Messianically applied in Siphré on Deut. (ed. *Friedmann*, p. 74 *b*).

In Midr. on *Eccl. i.* 9 it is shown at great length that the Messiah would re-enact all the miracles of the past.

The last clause of Eccl. i. 11 is applied to the days of the Messiah in the Targum.

Eccl. vii. 24 is thus paraphrased in the Targum : ' Behold, it is remote from the sons of men that they should know what was done from the beginning of the world, but a mystery is the day of death—and the day when shall come King Messiah, who can find it out by his wisdom ?'

In the Midr. on *Eccl. xi.* 8 it is noted that, however many years a man might study, his learning would be empty before the teaching of Messiah. In the Midr. on *Eccl. xii.* 1 it is noted that the evil days are those of the woes of Messiah.

Canticles. Here we have first the Talmudic passage (Sheb. 35 *b*) in which the principle is laid down, that whenever throughout that book Solomon is named, except in chap. viii. 12, it applies, not to Solomon, but to Him Who was His peace (there is here a play on these words, and on the name Solomon).

To *Cant. i.* 8 the Targum makes this addition : 'They shall be nourished in the captivity, until the time that I shall send to them the King Messiah, Who will feed them in quietness.'

So also on *verse* 17 the Targum contrasts the Temple built by Solomon with the far superior Temple to be built in the days of the Messiah, of which the beams were to be made of the cedars of Paradise.

Cant. ii. 8, although applied by most authorities to Moses, is by others referred to the Messiah (Shir haShirim R., ed. Warsh., p. 15 *a*, about the middle ; Pesiqta, ed. *Buber*, p. 47 *b*). *Cant. ii.* 9 is Messianically applied in Pesiqta, ed. *Buber*, p. 49, *a* and *b*.

The same may be said of *verse* 10 ; while in connection with *verse* 12, in similar application, Is. lii. 7 is quoted.

In connection with *verse* 13, in the same Midrash (p. 17 *a*), Rabbi Chija bar Abba speaks of a great matter as happening close to the days of the Messiah, viz., that the wicked should be destroyed, quoting in regard to it Is. iv. 3.

Cant. iii. 11, ' the day of his espousals.' In Yalkut on the passage (vol. ii. p. 178 *d*) this is explained : ' the day of the Messiah, because the Holy One, blessed be His Name, is likened to a bridegroom ; " as the bridegroom rejoiceth over the bride " '—and 'the day of the gladness of his heart,' as the day when the Sanctuary is rebuilt, and Jerusalem is redeemed.

On *Cant. iv.* 5 the Targum again introduces the twofold Messiah, the one the son of David, and the other the son of Ephraim.

Cant. iv. 16. According to one opinion in the Midrash (p. 25 *b*, line 13 from the bottom) this applies to the Messiah, Who comes from the north, and builds the Temple, which is in the south. See also Bemidbar R. 13, p. 48 *b*.

On *Cant. v.* 10 Yalkut remarks that He is white to Israel, and red to the Gentiles, according to Isaiah lxiii. 2.

On *Cant. vi.* 10 Yalkut (vol. ii. p. 184 *b*) has some beautiful observations, first, likening Israel in the wilderness, and God's mighty deeds there, to the morning ; and then adding that, according to another view, this morning-light is the redemption of the Messiah : For as, when the morning rises, the darkness flees before it, so shall darkness fall upon the kingdoms of this world when the Messiah comes. And yet again, as the sun and moon appear, so will the Kingdom of the Messiah also appear—the commentation going on to trace farther illustrations.

Cant. vii. 6. The Midrash thus comments on it (among other explanations): How fair in the world to come, how pleasant in the days of the Messiah !

On *Cant. vii.* 13, the Targum has it : ' When it shall please God to deliver His people from captivity, then shall it be said to the Messiah : The time of captivity is past, and the merit of the just shall be sweet before Me like the odour of balsam.'

Similarly on *Cant. viii.*1, the Targum has it : ' And at that time shall the King Messiah be revealed to the congregation of Israel, and the children of Israel shall say to Him, Come and be as a brother to us, and let us go up to Jerusalem, and there suck with thee the meaning of the Law, as an infant its mother's breast.'

On *Cant. viii.* 2 the Targum has it : ' I will take Thee, O King Messiah, and make thee go up into my Temple, there Thou shalt teach me to tremble before the Lord, and to walk in His ways. There we shall hold the feast of leviathan, and drink the old wine, which has been kept in its grapes from the day the world was created, and of the pomegranates and of the fruits which are prepared for the just in the Garden of Eden.'

On *verse* 4 the Targum says : ' The King Messiah shall say : I adjure you, My people, house of Israel, why should you rise against the Gentiles, to go out of captivity, and why should you rebel against the might of Gog and Magog ? Wait a little, till those nations are consumed which go up to fight against Jerusalem, and then shall the Lord of the world remember you, and it shall be His good will to set you free.'

Chap. viii. 11 is applied Messianically in the Talmud (Shebhu. 35 *b*), and so is *verse* 12 in the Targum.

(It should, however, be remarked that there are many other Messianic references in the comments on the Song of Solomon.)

Is. i. 25, 26, is thus explained in the Talmud (Sanh. 98 *a*) : ' The Son of David shall not come till all the judges and rulers in Israel shall have ceased.'

Similarly *Is. ii.* 4 is Messianically interpreted in Shabb. 63 *a*.

Is. iv. 2 the Targum distinctly applies to the times of the Messiah.

Is. iv. 4 has been already commented upon in our remarks on Gen. xviii. 4, **5,** and again on Deut. xxiii. 11.

Verses 5 and 6 are brought into connection with Israel's former service in contributing to, and making the Tabernacle in the wilderness, and it is remarked that in the latter days God would return it to them by covering them with a cloud of glory. This, in Yalkut (vol. i. p. 99 *c*), and in the Midrash on Ps. xiii., as also in that on Ps. xyi. 9.

Is. vi. 13 is referred in the Talmud (Keth. 112 *b*) to Messianic times.

The reference of *Is. vii.* 21 to Messianic times has already been discussed in our notes on Gen. xviii. 7.

Is. viii. 14 is also Messianically applied in the Talmud (Sanh. 38 *a*).

Is. ix. 6 is expressly applied to the Messiah in the Targum, and there is a very curious comment in Debarim R. 1 (ed. Warsh., p. 4 *a*) in connection with a Haggadic discussion of Gen. xliii. 14, which, however fanciful, makes a Messianic application of this passage—also in Bemidbar R. 11.

Verse 7, ' Of the increase of his government and peace there shall be no end,' has already been referred to in our comments on Num. vi. 26.

Is. x. 27 is in the Targum applied to the destruction of the Gentiles before the Messiah. *Is. x.* 34, is quoted in the Midrash on Lam. i. 16, in evidence that somehow the birth of the Messiah was to be connected with the destruction of the Temple.

Is. xi., as will readily be believed, is Messianically interpreted in Jewish writings. Thus, to begin with, in the Targum on *verses* 1 and 6 ; in the Talmud (Jer. Berach. 5 *a* and Sanh. 93 *b*) ; and in a number of passages in the Midrashim. Thus, *verse* 1 in Bereshith R. 85 on Gen. xxxviii. 18, where also Ps. cx. 2 is quoted, and in Ber. R. 99, ed. Warsh., p. 178 *b*. In Yalkut (vol. i. p. 247 *d*, near the top),

APP.
IX

where it is described how God had shown Moses all the spirits of the rulers and prophets in Israel, from that time forward to the Resurrection, it is said that all these had one knowledge and one spirit, but that the Messiah had one spirit which was equal to all the others put together, according to *Is. xi.* 1.

On the *2nd verse* see our remarks on Gen. i. 2, while in Yalkut on Prov. iii. 19, 20 (vol. ii. p. 133 *a*) the verse is quoted in connection with Messianic times, when by wisdom, understanding, and knowledge the Temple will be built again. On that verse see also Pirq. d. R. El. 3.

On *Is. xi.* 3 the Talmud (Sanh. 93 *b*, lines 21 &c. from the top) has a curious explanation. After quoting ch. xi. 2 as Messianic, it makes a play on the words, 'of quick understanding,' or 'scent,' as it might be rendered, and suggests that this word וַהֲרִיחוֹ is intended to teach us that God has laden Him with commandments and sufferings like *millstones* (כְּרֵיחַיִם). Immediately afterwards, from the expression 'He shall not judge after the sight of His eyes, but reprove with equity for the meek of the earth,' it is inferred that the Messiah knew the thoughts of the heart, and it is added that, as Bar Kokhabh was unable to do this, he was killed.

Verse 4, 'he shall smite the earth with the rod of his mouth,' is Messianically applied in the Midrash on Ps. ii. 2, and in that on Ruth ii. 14—also in Yalkut on Is. lx.

Verse 7 has been already noticed in connection with Ex. xii. 2.

On *verse* 10 see our remarks on Gen. xlix. 10 and Ps. xxi. 1.

Verse 11 is Messianically applied in Yalkut (vol. i. p. 31 *b* and vol. ii. 38 *a*), as also in the Midrash on Ps. cvii. 2.

Verse 12 is Messianically applied in that curious passage in the Midrash on Lamentations i. 2, where it is indicated that, as the children of Israel sinned from א to ת, so God would in the latter days comfort them from א to ת (i.e. through the whole alphabet), Scripture passages being in each case quoted.

The Messianic application of *Is. xii.* 3 is sufficiently established by the ancient symbolic practice of pouring out the water on the Feast of Tabernacles.

In connection with *Is. xii.* 5 the Midrash on *Ps. cxviii.* 23 first speaks of the wonderment of the Egyptians when they saw the change in Israel from servitude to glory on their Exodus, and then adds, that the words were intended by the Holy Ghost to apply to the wonders of the latter days (ed. Warsh. p. 85 *b*).

On *Is. xiv.* 2, see our comments on Gen. xviii. 4, 5.

Is. xiv. 29, *xv.* 2, *xvi.* 1, and *xvi.* 5 are Messianically applied in the Targum.

Is. xviii. 5 is similarly applied in the Talmud (Sanh. 98 *a*); and *Is. xxiii.* 15 in Sanh. 99 *a*.

Is. xxi. 11, 12 is in Jer. Taan. 64 *a*, and in Shem. R. 18, applied to the manifestation of the Messiah.

In *Is. xxiii.* 8 the Midr. on Eccl. i. 7 sees a curious reference to the return of this world's wealth to Israel in Messianic days.

Is. xxiii. 15 is Messianically applied in the Talmud (Sanh. 99 *a*) where the expression 'a king' is explained as referring to the Messiah.

Is. xxiv. 23 is Messianically applied in the curious passage in Bemidbar R. quoted under Gen. xxii. 18; also in Bemidbar R. 13 (ed. Warsh. p. 51 *a*).

The remarkable promise in *Is. xxv.* 8 is applied to the times of the Messiah in the Talmud (Moed Q. 28 *b*), and in that most ancient commentary Siphra. (Yalkut i. p. 190 *d* applies the passage to the world to come). But the most remarkable interpretation is that which occurs in connection with Is. lx. 1 (Yalkut ii. 56 *c*, line 16 from the bottom), where the passage (*Is. xxv.* 8) is, after an expostulation on the part of Satan with regard to the Messiah, applied to the casting into Gehenna of Satan and of the Gentiles. See also our remarks on Ex. xii. 2. In Debar. R. 2, *Isaiah xxv.* 8 is applied to the destruction of the *Jetser ha-Ra* and the abolishing of death in Messianic days; in Shem. R. 30 to the time of the Messiah.

Verse 9. Tanchuma on Deuteronomy opens with a record of how God would work all the miracles, which He had shown in the wilderness, in a fuller manner for Zion in the latter days, the last passage quoted in that section being *Is. xxv.* 9. (Tanchuma on Deut. ed. Warsh. p. 99 *a*, line 5 from the bottom).

Of *Is. xxvi.* 19 there is Messianic application in the Midrash on Ecclesiastes i. 7.

On *Is. xxvii.* 10 Shem. R. 1, and Tanchuma on Exod. ii. 5 (ed. Warsh. p. 64 *b*) remark that, like Moses, the Messiah, Who would deliver His own from the worshippers of false gods, should be brought up with the latter in the land.

Verse 13 is quoted in the Talmud (Rosh. haSh. 11 *b*) in connection with the future deliverance. So also in Yalkut. i. p. 217 *d*, and Pirqé de R. El. c. 31.

Is. xxviii. 5 is thus paraphrased in the Targum : ' At that time shall the Messiah of the Lord of hosts be a crown of joy.'

Is. xxviii. 16 the Targum apparently applies to the Messiah. At least, so Rashi (on the passage) understands it.

Is. xxx. 18 is Messianically applied in Sanh. 97 *b*; *verse 15* in Jer. Taan. i. 1.

The expression in *Is. xxx.* 19, ' he shall be very gracious unto thee,' is applied to the merits of the Messiah in Yalkut on Zeph. iii. 8 (p. 84 *c*).

On *verse 25* see our remarks on Gen. xviii. 4.

Verse 26 is applied to Messianic times in the Talmud (Pes. 68 *a*, and Sanh. 91 *b*), and similarly in Pirqé de R. El. 51, and Shemoth R. 50. So also in Ber. R. 12. See our remarks on Gen. ii. 4.

Is. xxxii. 14, 15. On this passage the Midrash on Lam. iii. 49 significantly remarks that it is one of the three passages in which mention of the Holy Ghost follows upon mention of redemption, the other two passages being Is. lx. 22, followed by lxi. 1, and Lam. iii. 49.

Is. xxxii. 20. The first clause is explained by Tanchuma (Par. 1, ed. Warsh. p. 4 *a*, first three lines) to apply to the study of the Law, and the second to the two Messiahs, the son of Joseph being likened to the ox, and the son of David to the ass, according to Zech. ix. 9; and similarly the verse is Messianically referred to in Deb. R. 6 (ed. Warsh. vol. iii. p. 15 *b*), in a very curious play on the words in Deut. xxii. 6, 7, where the observance of that commandment is supposed to hasten the coming of King Messiah.

Is. xxxv. 1. This is one of the passages quoted in Tanchuma on Deut. i. 1 (ed. Warsh. p. 99 *a*) as among the miracles which God would do to redeemed Zion in the latter days. So also is *verse 2* in this chapter.

Is. xxxv. 5, 6 is repeatedly applied to Messianic times. Thus, in Yalkut i. 78 *c*, and 157 *a*; in Ber. R. 95; and in the Midrash on Ps. cxlvi. 8.

Verse 10 is equally applied to Messianic times in the Midrash on Ps. cvii. 1, while at the same time it is noted that this deliverance will be accomplished by God Himself, and not either by Elijah, nor by the King Messiah.[1] A similar refer-

---

[1] Signor *Castelli* remarks in his learned treatise (Il Messia, p. 164) that redemption is always ascribed to God, and not to the Messiah. But the distinction is of no importance, seeing that this is indeed the work of God, but carried out by the Messiah, while, on the other hand, Rabbinic writings frequently refer Israel's deliverance to the agency of the Messiah.

ence occurs in Yalkut (vol. ii. p. 162 *d*), at the close of the Commentary on the Book of Chronicles, where it is remarked that in this world the deliverance of Israel was accomplished by man, and was followed by fresh captivities, but in the latter or Messianic days their deliverance would be accomplished by God, and would no more be followed by captivity. See also Shemoth R. 15 and 23.

Is. xl. 1 is one of the passages referred to in our note on Is. xi. 12, and also on Is. xxxv. 1.

The same remark applies to *verses* 2 *and* 3.

Verse 5 is also Messianically applied in Vayyikra R. 1; Yalk. ii. 77 *b* about the middle.

On *verse* 10 Yalkut, in discussing Ex. xxxii. 6 (vol. i. p. 108 *c*) broaches the opinion, that in the days of the Messiah Israel would have a double reward, on account of the calamities which they had suffered, quoting *Is. xl.* 10.

Is. xli. 18 has been already noted in our remarks on Gen. xviii. 4, 5.

Verse 25 is Messianically applied in Bem. R. 13, p. 48 *b*.

The expression 'The first,' in *ch. xli.* 27, is generally applied to the Messiah; in the Targum, according to Rashi; in Bereshith R. 63; in Vayyikra R. 30; and in the Talmud (Pes. 5 *a*); so also in Pesiqta (ed. *Buber*) p. 185 *b*.

Is. xlii. 1 is applied in the Targum to the Messiah, as also in the Midrash on Ps. ii.; and in Yalkut ii. p. 104 *d*. See also our comments on Ps. ii. 7.

On *Is. xliii.* 10, the Targum renders 'My servant' by 'My servant the Messiah.'

The promise in *Is. xlv.* 22 is also among the future things mentioned in the Midrash on Lamentations, to which we have referred in our remarks on Is. xi. 12.

Is. xlix. 8. There is a remarkable comment on this in Yalkut on the passage, to the effect that the Messiah suffers in every age for the sins of that generation, but that God would in the day of redemption repair it all (Yalk. ii. p. 52 *b*).

Is. xlix. 9 is quoted as the words of the Messiah in Yalkut (vol. ii. p. 52 *b*).

Verse 10 is one of the passages referred to in the Midrash on Lamentations, quoted in connection with Is. xi. 12.

Verse 12 has already been noticed in our remarks on Ex. xii. 2.

From the expression 'comfort' in *verse* 13, the Messianic title 'Menachem' is derived. Comp. the Midrash on Prov. xix. 21.

Verse 14 is Messianically applied in Yalkut ii. p. 52 *c*.

Verse 21 is also one of the passages referred to in the Midrash on Lamentations, quoted under Ps. xi. 12.

On *verse* 23 it is remarked in Vayyikra R. 27 (ed. Warsh. p. 42 *a*), that Messianic blessings were generally prefigured by similar events, as, for example, the passage here quoted in the case of Nebuchadnezzar and Daniel.

A Messianic application of the same passage also occurs in Par. 33 and 36, as a contrast to the contempt that Israel experiences in this world.

The second clause of *verse* 23 is applied to the Messiah in the Midrash on Ps. ii. 2, as to be fulfilled when the Gentiles shall see the terrible judgments.

Verse 26 is similarly applied to the destruction of the Gentiles in Vayyikra R. 33 (end).

Is. li. 12 is one of the passages referred to in the Midrash on Lamentations, quoted in our comments on Is. xi. 12.

Is. li. 12 *and* 17 are among the passages referred to in our remarks on Is. xxv. 9

Is. lii. 3 is Messianically applied in the Talmud (Sanh. 97 *b*), while the last clause of *verse* 2 is one of the passages quoted in the Midrash on Lamentations (see Is. xi. 12).

The well-known Evangelic declaration in *Is. lii.* 7 is thus commented upon in Yalkut (vol. ii. p. 53 *c*) : In the hour when the Holy One, blessed be His Name, redeems Israel, three days before Messiah comes Elijah, and stands upon the mountains of Israel, and weeps and mourns for them, and says to them : Behold the land of Israel, how long shall you stand in a dry and desolate land ? And his voice is heard from the world's end to the world's end, and after that it is said to them : Peace has come to the world, peace has come to the world, as it is said : How beautiful upon the mountains, &c. And when the wicked hear it, they rejoice, and they say one to the other: Peace has come to us. On the second day he shall stand upon the mountains of Israel, and shall say : Good has come to the world, good has come to the world, as it is written : That bringeth good tidings of good. On the third day he shall come and stand upon the mountains of Israel, and say : Salvation has come to the world, salvation has come to the world, as it is written : That publisheth salvation.

Similarly, this passage is quoted in Yalkut on Ps. cxxi. 1. See also our remarks on Cant. ii. 13.

Verse 8 is one of the passages referred to in the Midrash on Lamentations quoted above, and frequently in other places as Messianic.

Verse 12 is Messianically applied in Shemoth R. 15 and 19.

Verse 13 is applied in the Targum expressly to the Messiah. On the words ' He shall be exalted and extolled ' we read in Yalkut ii. (Par. 338, p. 53 *c*, lines 7 &c. from the bottom): He shall be higher than Abraham, to whom applies Gen. xiv. 22 ; higher than Moses, of whom Num. xi. 12 is predicated ; higher than the ministering angels, of whom Ezek. i. 18 is said. But to Him there applies this in Zech. iv. 7 : ' Who art thou, O great mountain ? ' ' And He was wounded for our transgressions, and bruised for our iniquities, and the chastisement of our peace was upon Him, and with His stripes we are healed.' R. Huna says, in the name of R Acha : All sufferings are divided into three parts ; one part goes to David and the Patriarchs, another to the generation of the rebellion (rebellious Israel), and the third to the King Messiah, as it is written (Ps. ii. 7), ' Yet have I set My King upon My holy hill of Zion.' Then follows a curious quotation from the Midrash on Samuel, in which the Messiah indicates that His dwelling is on Mount Zion, and that guilt is connected with the destruction of its walls.

In regard to *Is. liii.* we remember, that the Messianic name of ' Leprous ' (Sanh. 98 *b*) is expressly based upon it. *Is. liii.* 10 is applied in the Targum on the passage to the Kingdom of the Messiah.

Verse 5 is Messianically interpreted in the Midrash on Samuel (ed. Lemberg, p. 45 *a*, last line), where it is said that all sufferings are divided into three parts, one of which the Messiah bore—a remark which is brought into connection with Ruth ii. 14. (See our comments on that passage.)

Is. liv. 2 is expected to be fulfilled in Messianic times (Vayyikra R. 10).

Is. liv. 5. In Shemoth R. 15 this is expressly applied to Messianic days.

Is. liv. 11 is repeatedly applied to the Messianic glory, as, for example, in Shemoth R. 15. (See our comments on Ex. xii. 2.)

So is *verse* 13, as in Yalkut (vol. i. p. 78 *c*) ; in the Midrash on Ps. xxi. 1 ; and in other passages.

Is. lv. 12 is referred to Messianic times, as in the Midrash on Ps. xiii.

Is. lvi. 1. See our comments on Exod. xxi. 1.

Verse 7 is one of the passages in the Midrash on Lamentations which we have quoted under Is. xi. 12.

On *Is. lvii.* 14 Bemidbar R. 15 (ed. Warsh. p. 64 *a*) expresses a curious idea about the stumbling-block, as mystically the evil inclination, and adds that the promise applies to God's removal of it in the world to come, or else it may be in Messianic days.

Verse 16 receives in the Talmud (Yeb. 62 *a* and 63 *b*) and in the Midr. on Eccl. i. 6 the following curious comment: ' The Son of David shall not come till all the souls are completed which are in the Guph '—(i.e. the pre-existence of souls is taught, and that they are kept in heaven till one after another appears in human form, and that the Messiah is kept back till all these shall have appeared), proof of this being derived from *Is. lvii.* 16.

Similarly *chap. lix.* 15 is applied to Messianic times in Sanh. 97 *a*, and Midr. on Cant. ii. 13 ; and *verse* 19 in Sanh. 98 *a*.

Verse 17 is applied to Messianic times in Pesiqta, ed. *Buber*, p. 149 *a*.

Verse 20 is one of the passages mentioned in the Midrash on Lamentations quoted above. (See Is. xi. 12.)

Is. lix. 19, 20, is applied to Messianic times in Sanh. 98 *a*. In Pesiqta 166 *b* it is similarly applied, the peculiar form (*plene*) in which the word *Goel* (Redeemer) is written being taken to indicate the Messiah as the Redeemer in the full sense.

Is. lx. 1. This is applied in the Targum to Messianic times. Similarly, it is explained in Ber. R. i. with reference to Dan. ii. 2 ; in Ber. R. 2 ; and also in Bemidbar R. 15 and 21. In Yalkut we have some very interesting remarks on the subject. Thus (vol. i. Par. 363, p. 99 *c*), commenting on Exod. xxv. 3 &c., in a very curious description of how God would in the world to come return to Israel the various things which they had offered for the Tabernacle, the oil is brought into connection with the Messiah, with reference to Ps. cxxxii. 17 and *Is. lx.* 1. Again, on p. 215 *c* (at the commencement of the Parashah Behaalothekha) we have, first, a very curious comparison between the work of the Tabernacle and that of the six days of Creation, after which the question is put: Why Moses made seven lights, and Solomon seventy ? To this the reply is given, that Moses rooted up seven nations before Israel, while Solomon reigned over all the seventy nations which, according to Jewish ideas, constitute the world. Upon this it is added, that God had promised, that as Israel had lighted for His glory the lights in the Sanctuary, so would He in the latter days fill Jerusalem with His glory, according to the promise in *Is. lx.* 1, and also set up in the midst of it lights, according to Zeph. i. 12. Still more clearly is the Messianic interpretation of *Is. lx.* brought out in the comments in Yalkut on that chapter. One part of it is so curious that it may here find a place. After explaining that this light for which Israel is looking is the light of the Messiah, and that Gen. i. 4 really referred to it, it is added that this is intended to teach us that God looked forward to the age of the Messiah and His works before the Creation of the world, and that He hid that light for the Messiah and His generation under His throne of glory. On Satan's questioning Him for whom that light was destined, the answer is: For Him Who in the latter days will conquer thee, and cover thy face with shame. On which Satan requests to see Him, and when he is shown Him, falls on his face and says: I confess that this is the Messiah Who will in the latter days be able to cast me, and all the Gentiles, into Gehenna, according to Is. xxv. 8. In that hour all the nations will tremble, and say before God: Who is this into Whose hand we fall, what is His Name, and what is His purpose? On which God replies: This is Ephraim, the Messiah [the second Messiah, the son of Joseph]; My Righteousness is His Name.' And so the commentation goes on to touch on Ps. lxxxix. 23, 24, and 26, in a manner most deeply interesting, but which it would be impossible here fully to give (Yalkut, vol. ii. Par. 359, p. 56 c). In col. *d* there are farther remarkable discussions about the Messiah, in connection with the wars in the days when Messiah should be revealed, and about Israel's final safety. But the most remarkable passage of all, reminding us almost of the history of the Temptation, is that which reads as follows (line 22 &c. from the top): It is a tradition from our Rabbis that, in the hour when King Messiah comes, He stands on the roof of the Temple, and proclaims to them, that the hour of their deliverance has come, and that if they believed they would rejoice in the light that had risen upon them, as it is written (*Is. lx.* 1), 'Arise, shine, for thy light is come.' This light would be for them alone, as it is written (*ver.* 2), 'For darkness shall cover the earth.' In that hour also would God take the light of the Messiah and of Israel, and all should walk in the light of Messiah and of Israel, as it is written (*ver.* 3), 'The Gentiles shall come to thy light, and kings to the brightness of thy rising.' And the kings of the nations should lick the dust from under the feet of the Messiah, and should all fall on their faces before Him and before Israel, and say: Let us be servants to Thee and to Israel. And so the passage goes on to describe the glory of the latter days. Indeed, the whole of this chapter may be said to be full of Messianic interpretations.

After this it will scarcely be necessary to say that *verses* 2, 3, and 4 are similarly applied in the Midrashim. But it is interesting to notice that *verse 2* is specifically applied to Messianic times in the Talmud (Sanh. 99 *a*), in answer to the question when the Messiah should come.

On *verse 4* the Midrash on Cant. i. 4, on the words 'we will be glad and rejoice in thee,' has the following beautiful illustration. A Queen is introduced whose husband and sons and sons-in-law go to a distant country. Tidings are brought to her: Thy sons are come back. On which she says: Cause for gladness have I, my daughters-in-law will rejoice. Next, tidings are brought her that her sons-in-law are coming, and she is glad that her daughters will rejoice. Lastly, tidings are brought: The king, thy husband, comes. On which she replies: This is indeed perfect joy, joy upon joy. So in the latter days would the prophets come, and say to Jerusalem: 'Thy sons shall come from far' (*verse 4*), and she will say: What gladness is this to me!—'and thy daughters shall be nursed at thy side,' and again she will say: What gladness is this to me! But when they shall say to her (Zech. ix. 9): ' Behold, thy king cometh unto thee; he is just, and having salvation,' then shall Zion say: This indeed is perfect joy, as it is written (Zech. ix. 9), 'Rejoice greatly, O daughter of Zion,' and again (Zech. ii. 10), 'Sing and rejoice, O daughter of Zion.' In that hour she will say (Is. lxi. 10): ' I will greatly rejoice in the Lord, my soul shall be joyful in my God.'

Verse 7 is Messianically applied in the Talmud (Abod. Sar. 24 *a*).

Verse 8 is Messianically applied in the Midrash on Ps. xlviii. 13.

In connection with *verse 19* we read in Yalkut (vol. i. p. 103 *b*) that God said to Israel: In this world you are engaged (or busied) with the light for the Sanctuary, but in the world to come, for the merit of this light, I send you the King Messiah, Who is likened to a light, according to Ps. cxxxii. 17 and *Is. lx.* 19, 'the Lord shall be unto thee an everlasting light.'

Verse 21 is thus alluded to in the Talmud (Sanh. 98 *a*): 'Rabbi Jochanan said, The Son of David shall not come, until all be either just or all be unjust:' the former according to Is. *lx.* 21, the latter according to Is. lix. 16.

Verse 22 is also Messianically applied in the Talmudic passage above cited.

Is. lxi. 1 has already been mentioned in our remarks on Is. xxxii. 14, 15.

On *verse* 5 there is a curious story related (Yalkut, vol. i. Par. 212, p. 64 *a*, lines 23–17 from the bottom) in which, in answer to a question, what was to become of the nations in the days of the Messiah, the reply is given that every nation and kingdom that had persecuted and mocked Israel would see, and be confounded, and have no share in life; but that every nation and kingdom which had not so dealt with Israel would come and be husbandmen and vinedressers to Israel in the days of the Messiah. A similar statement to this is found in the Midrash on Eccl. ii. 7.

Verse 9 is also applied to Messianic times.

Verse 10 is one of the passages referred to in Tanchuma on Deut. i. 1 quoted under Is. xxv. 9. In Pesiqta, ed. *Buber,* p. 149 *a*, the verse is explained as applying to the glory of Messiah's appearance.

Is. lxii. 10 has already been referred to in our remarks on Is. lvii. 14.

Is. lxiii. is applied to the Messiah, Who comes to the land after having seen the destruction of the Gentiles, in Pirqé de R. Eliez. c. 30.

Verse 2 has been referred to in our comments on Cant. v. 10. It is also quoted in reference to Messianic days in Pesiqta, ed. *Buber,* p. 149 *a*.

Verse 4 is explained as pointing to the days of the Messiah, which are supposed to be 365 years, according to the number of the solar days (Sanh. 99 *a*); while in other passages of the Midrashim, the destruction of Rome and the coming of the Messiah are conjoined with the day of vengeance. See also the Midr. on Eccl. xii. 10.

Is. lxiv. 4 (3 in the Hebrew). In Yalkut on Is. lx. (vol. ii. p. 56 *d*, line 6, &c., from the bottom) Messianic application is made of this passage in a legendary account of the seven tabernacles which God would make for the Messiah, out of each of which proceed four streams of wine, milk, honey, and pure balsam. Then God is represented as speaking of the sufferings which Messiah was to undergo, after which the verse in question is quoted.

Is. lxv. 17 is quoted in the Midrash on Lamentations, referred to in our remarks on Is. xi. 12.

Verse 19 is one of the passages referred to in Tanchuma on Deut. i. 1. See Isaiah xxv. 9.

To *verse* 25 we have the following curious illustrative reference in Ber. R. 20 (ed. Warsh. p. 38 *b*, line 6 from the bottom) in connection with the Fall: In the latter days everything shall be healed again (restored again) except the serpent (Is. lxv. 25) and the Gibeonites (Ezek. xlviii. 19). But a still more strange application of the verse occurs in the same Midrash (Par. 95, ed. Warsh. p. 170 *a*), where the opening clauses of it are quoted with this remark: Come and see all that the Holy One, blessed be His Name, has smitten in this world, He will heal in the latter days. Upon which a curious disquisition follows, to prove that every man would appear after death exactly as he had been in life, whether blind, dumb, or halting, nay, even in the same dress, as in the case of Samuel when Saul saw him—but that afterwards God would heal the diseased.

Is. lxvi. 7 is applied to Messianic times in Vayyikra R. 14 (last line), and so are some of the following verses in the Midrashim, notably on Gen. xxxiii. 1.

Is. lxviii. 22 is applied to Messianic times in Ber. R. 12. See our remarks on Gen. ii. 4.

Jer. iii. 17 is applied to Messianic days in Yalkut on Joshua iii. 9 &c. (vol. ii. p. 3 *c*, line 17 from the top), and so is *verse* 18 in the commentation on the words in Cant. i. 16 ' our bed is green,' the expression being understood of the ten tribes, who had been led captive beyond the river Sabbatyon ; but when Judah's deliverance came, Judah and Benjamin would go to them and bring them back, that they might be worthy of the days of the Messiah (vol. ii. p. 176 *d*, line 9 &c. from the bottom).

Jer. v. 19 is mentioned in the Introd. to Echa R. as one of three passages by which to infer from the apostasy of Israel the near advent of Messiah.

The expression ' speckled bird ' in *Jer. xii.* 9 is applied to the Messiah in Pirqé de R. Eliez. c. 28.

The last word in *Jer. xvi.* 13 is made the basis of the name *Chaninah*, given to the Messiah in the Talmud (Sanh. 98 *b*), and in the Midr. on Lam. i. 16.

On *verse* 14 Mechilta has it, that in the latter days the Exodus would no more be mentioned on account of the greater wonders then experienced.

On *Jer. xxiii.* 5, 6, the Targum has it : ' And I will raise up for David the Messiah the Just.' This is one of the passages from which, according to Rabbinic views, one of the Names of the Messiah is derived, viz. : Jehovah cur Righteousness. So in the Talmud (Babha Bathra 75 *b*), in the Midrash on Ps. xxi. 1, Prov. xix. 21, and in that on Lamentations i. 16.

On *verse* 7 see our remarks on Jer. xvi. 14. In the Talmud (Ber. 12 *b*) this verse is distinctly applied to Messianic days.

Jer. xxx. 9 is Messianically applied in the Targum on the passage.

Jer. xxx. 21 is applied to the Messiah in the Targum, and also in the Midrash on Ps. xxi. 7.

On *Jer. xxxi.* 8, *3rd clause,* Yalkut has a Messianic interpretation, although extremely far-fetched. In general, the following verses are Messianically interpreted in the Midrashim.

Verse 20 is Messianically applied in Yalkut (ii. p. 66 *c*, end), where it is supposed to refer to the Messiah when imprisoned, when all the nations mock and shake their heads at Him. A more remarkable interpretation still occurs in the passage on Is. lx. 1, to which we have already referred. Some farther extracts from it may be interesting. Thus, when the enemies of the Messiah flee before Him, God is supposed to make an agreement with the Messiah to this effect : The sins of those who are hidden with Thee will cause Thee to be put under an iron yoke, and they will do with Thee as with this calf, whose eyes are covered, and they will choke Thy spirit under the yoke, and on account of their sins Thy tongue shall cleave to Thy mouth. On which the Messiah inquires whether these troubles are to last for many years, and the Holy One replies that He has decreed a week, but that if His soul were in sorrow, He would immediately dispel these sorrows. On this the Messiah says : Lord of the world, with gladness and joy of heart I take it upon Me, on condition that not one of Israel should perish, and that not only those alone should be saved who are in My days, but also those who are hid in the dust ; and that not only the dead should be saved who are in My days, but also those who have died from the days of the first Adam till now ; and not only those, but also those who have been prematurely born. And not only these, but also those who have come into Thy knowledge to create them, but have not yet been created. Thus I agree, and thus I take all upon Me. In the hebdomad when the Son of

David comes, they shall bring beams of iron, and shall make them a yoke to His neck, until His stature is bent down. But He cries and weeps, and lifts up His voice on high, and says before Him: Lord of the world, what is My strength, My spirit, and My soul, and My members? Am I not flesh and blood? In that hour David (the Son of David) weeps, and says: 'My strength is dried up like a potsherd.' In that hour the Holy One, blessed be His Name, says: Ephraim the Messiah, My righteous one, Thou hast already taken this upon Thee before the six days of the world, now Thy anguish shall be like My anguish; for from the time that Nebuchadnezzar, the wicked one, has come up and destroyed My house, and burned My Sanctuary, and I have sent into captivity My children among the children of the Gentiles, by My life, and by the life of Thy head, I have not sat down on My throne. And if Thou wilt not believe Me, see the dew which is on My head, as it is said (Cant. v. 2) 'My head is filled with dew.' In that hour the Messiah answers Him: Lord of the world, now I am quieted, for it is enough for the servant that he is as his Master (this reminding us of our Lord's saying, St. Matt. x. 25). R. Isaac then remarks that in the year when the King Messiah shall be revealed, all nations shall rise up against each other (we have already quoted this passage in another place, as also that about the Messiah standing upon the roof of the Temple). Then follows this as a tradition of the Rabbis: In the latter days the Fathers shall stand up in the month of Nisan, and say to Him: Ephraim, the Messiah, our Righteousness, though we are Thy Fathers, yet Thou art better than we, because Thou hast borne all the sins of our sons, and hard and evil measure has passed upon Thee, such as has not been passed either upon those before or upon those after. And Thou hast been for laughter and derision to the nations for the sake of Israel, and Thou hast dwelt in darkness and in mist, and Thine eyes have not seen light, and Thy light clung to Thee alone, and Thy body was dried up like wood, and Thine eyes were darkened through fasting, and Thy strength was dried up like a potsherd. And all this on account of the sins of our children. Is it Thy pleasure that our sons should enjoy the good thing which God had displayed to Israel? Or perhaps on account of the anguish which Thou hast suffered for them, because they have bound Thee in the prison-house, wilt Thou not give unto them thereof? He says to them: Fathers of the world, whatever I have done I have only done for your sakes, and for the sake of your children, that they may enjoy that goodness which the Holy One, blessed be He, has displayed to Israel. Then say to Him the Fathers of the world: Ephraim, Messiah, our Righteousness, be Thou reconciled to us, because Thou hast reconciled Thy Maker and us. R. Simeon, the son of Pasi, said: In that hour the Holy One, blessed be His Name, exalts the Messiah to the heaven of heavens, and spreads over Him the splendour of His glory, because of the nations of the world, and because of the wicked Persians. Then the Fathers of the world say to Him: Ephraim, Messiah, our Righteousness, be Thou their judge, and do to them what Thy soul desireth. For unless mercies had been multiplied on Thee. they would long ago have exterminated Thee suddenly from the world. as it is written (*Jer. xxxi.* 20) 'Is Ephraim My dear son?' And why is the expression: 'I will surely have mercy' [in the Hebrew reduplicated: 'having mercy I will have mercy'], but that the first expression 'mercy' refers to the hour when He was bound in prison, when day by day they gnashed with their teeth, and winked with their eyes, and nodded with their heads, and wide-opened their mouths, as it is written in Ps. xxii. 7 [8 in Hebrew]; while the second expression 'I will have mercy' refers to the hour when He came out of the prison-house, when not only one kingdom, nor two, came against Him, but 140 kingdoms came round about Him, and the Holy One, blessed be His Name, says to Him: Ephraim, Messiah, My righteous one, be not afraid, for all these shall perish by the breath of Thy mouth, as it is written (Is. xi. 4). Long as this quotation may be, its interest seems sufficient to warrant its insertion.

Jer. xxxi. 31, 33, and 34 are applied to Messianic times in Yalkut (vol. i. p. 196 c ; 78 c ; and in vol. ii. p. 54 b, and p. 66 d).

Jer. xxxiii. 13. The close of the verse is thus paraphrased in the Targum : ' The people shall yet learn by the hands of the Messiah,' while in Yalkut (vol. i. p. 105 d) mention is made of a tenfold gathering together of Israel, the last—in connection with this verse—in the latter days.

On *Lam. i.* 16 there is in the Midrash R. (ed. Warsh. p. 64 b) the curious story about the birth of the Messiah in the royal palace of Bethlehem, which also occurs in the Jer. Talmud.

Lam. ii. 22, *first clause.* The Targum here remarks : Thou wilt proclaim liberty to Thy people, the house of Israel, by the hand of the Messiah.

Lam. iv. 22, *first clause.* The Targum here remarks : And after these things thy iniquity shall cease, and thou shalt be set free by the hands of the Messiah and by the hands of Elijah the Priest

Ezek. xi. 19 is applied to the great spiritual change that was to take place in Messianic days, when the evil desire would be taken out of the heart (Deb. R. 6, at the end ; and also in other Midrashic passages).

Ezek. xvi. 55 is referred to among the ten things which God would renew in Messianic days—the rebuilding of ruined cities, inclusive of Sodom and Gomorrah, being the fourth (Shem. R. 15, ed. Warsh. p. 24 b).

Ezek. xvii. 22 and 23 is distinctly and very beautifully referred to the Messiah in the Targum.

Ezek. xxv. 14 is applied to the destruction of all the nations by Israel in the days of the Messiah in Bemidbar R. on Num. ii. 32 (Par. 2, ed. Warsh. p. 5 b).

Ezek. xxix. 21 is among the passages applied to the time when the Messiah should come, in Sanh. 98 a.

So is *Ezek. xxxii.* 14.

Ezek. xxxvi. 25 is applied to Messianic times alike in the Targum and in Yalkut (vol. i. p. 235 a), as also in the Talmud (Kidd. 72 b).

On *verse* 27 see our remarks on chap. xi. 19.

Ezek. xxxix. 2 is Messianically applied in Bemidbar R. 13, ed. Warsh. p. 48 b.

Ezek. xlvii. 9 and 12 are quoted as the second and the third things which God would renew in the latter days (Shem. R. 15)—the second being, that living waters should go forth out of Jerusalem, and the third, that trees should bear fruit every month, and the sick be healed by them.

On *Ezek. xlviii.* 19 the Talmud (Baba B. 122 a) has the following curious comment, that the land of Israel would be divided into thirteen tribes, the thirteenth belonging to the Prince, and this verse is quoted as proof.

Dan. ii. 22 is Messianically applied in Ber. R. 1, and in the Midr. on Lament. i. 16, where it gives rise to another name of the Messiah : the Lightgiver.

Verse 35 is similarly applied in the Pirqé de R. Eliez. c. 11, and *verse* 44 in c. 30.

Dan. vii. 9. This passage was interpreted by R. Akiba as implying that one throne was set for God, and the other for the Messiah (Chag. 14 a).

Dan. vii. 13 is curiously explained in the Talmud (Sanh. 98 a), where it is said that, if Israel behaved worthily, the Messiah would come in the clouds of heaven; if otherwise, humble, and riding upon an ass.

Dan. vii. 27 is applied to Messianic times in Bem. R. 11.

Dan. viii. 13, 14.   By a very curious combination these verses are brought into connection with Gen. iii. 22 (' man has become like one of us '), and it is argued, that in Messianic days man's primeval innocence and glory would be restored to him, and he become like one of the heavenly beings, Ber. R. 21 (ed. Warsh. p. 41 *a*).

Dan. ix. 24.   In Naz. 32 *b* it is noted that this referred to the time when the second Temple was to be destroyed.   So also in Yalkut, vol. ii. p. 79 *d*, lines 16 &c. from the bottom.

Dan. xii. 3 is applied to Messianic times in a beautiful passage in Shem. R. 15 (at the end).

Dan. xii. 11, 12.   These two verses receive a peculiar Messianic interpretation, and that by the authority of the Rabbis.   For it is argued that, as Moses, the first Redeemer, appeared, and was withdrawn for a time, and then reappeared, so would the second Redeemer; and the interval between His disappearance and reappearance is calculated at 45 days, arrived at by deducting the 1,290 days of the cessation of the sacrifice (Dan. xii. 11) from the 1,335 days of Dan. xii. 12 (Midr. on Ruth ii. 14, ed. Warsh. p. 43 *b*).

Hos. ii. 2 is explained in the Midr. on Ps. xlv. 1 as implying that Israel's redemption would be when they were at the lowest.

Hos. ii. 13 is one of the three passages referred to on Jer. v. 19.

Hos. ii. 18 is quoted in Shem. R. 15 (on Ex. xii. 2) as the seventh of the ten things which God would make new in Messianic days.

Hos. iii. 5 is applied to the Messiah in the Targum, and from it the Jer. Talm. (Ber. 5 *a*) derives the name David as one of those given to the Messiah.

Hos. vi. 2 is Messianically applied in the Targum.

Hos. xiii. 14 is applied to the deliverance by the Messiah of those of Israel who are in Gehinnom, whom He sets free;—the term Zion being understood of Paradise. See Yalk. on Is. Par. 269, comp. Maas. de R. Joshua in Jellinek's Beth ha-Midr. ii. p. 50.

Hos. xiv. 7 is Messianically applied in the Targum.

Joel ii. 28 is explained in the Midrashim as referring to the latter days, when all Israel will be prophets (Bemidbar R. 15; Yalkut i. p. 220 *c*, and other places).

Joel iii. 18 is similarly applied in the Midrashim, as in that on Ps. xiii. and in others.   The last clause of this verse is explained in the Midr. on Eccl. i. 9 to imply that the Messiah would cause a fountain miraculously to spring up, as Moses did in the wilderness.

Amos iv 7 is in Midr. on Cant. ii. 13 applied to the first of the seven years before Messiah come.

Amos v. 18 is one of the passages adduced in the Talmud (Sanh. 98 *b*) to explain why certain Rabbis did not wish to see the day of the Messiah.

Amos viii. 11 is applied to Messianic times in Ber. R. 25.

Amos ix. 11 is a notable Messianic passage.   Thus, in the Talmud (Sanh. 96 *b*) where the Messiah is called the ' Son of the Fallen,' the name is explained by a reference to this passage.   Again, in Ber. R. 88, last three lines (ed. Warsh. p. 157 *a*), after enumerating the unexpected deliverances which Israel had formerly experienced, it is added: Who could have expected that the fallen tabernacle of David should be raised up by God, as it is written (*Amos ix.* 11) and who should have expected that the whole world should become one bundle (be gathered into one Church)? Yet it is written Zeph. iii. 9. Comp. also the long discussion in Yalkut on this passage (vol. ii. p. 80 a and b).

Obadiah verses 18 and 21 are applied to the Kingdom and time of the Messiah in Deb. R. 1.

Micah ii. 13. See our remarks on Gen. xviii. 4, 5. The passage is also Messianically quoted in the Midrash on Prov. vi. (ed. Lemberg, p. 5 a, first two lines).

The promise in *Micah iv.* 3 is applied to the times of the Messiah in the Talmud (Shabb. 63 a).

So is the prediction in *verse* 5 in Shemoth R. 15; while *verse* 8 is thus commented upon in the Targum: ' And thou Messiah of Israel, Who shalt be hidden on account of the sins of Zion, to thee shall the Kingdom come.'

The well-known passage, *Micah v.* 2, is admittedly Messianic. So in the Targum, in the Pirqé de R. Eliez. c. 3, and by later Rabbis.

Verse 3 is applied in the Talmud to the fact that the Messiah was not to come till the hostile kingdom had spread for nine months over the whole world (Yoma 10 a), or else, over the whole land of Israel (Sanh. 98 b).

Similarly *Micah vii.* 6 is applied to Messianic times in Sanh. 97 a, and in Sotah 49 b; also in the Midr. on Cant. ii. 13. And so is *verse* 15 in Yalkut (vol. ii. p. 112 b.

In *Micah vii.* 8, the expression, Jehovah shall be light to me, is referred to the days of the Messiah in Deb. R. 11, ed. Warsh. vol. v. p. 22 a.

Nahum ii. 1. See our remarks on Is. lii. 7.

Habakkuk ii. 3. This is applied to Messianic times in a remarkable passage in Sanh. 97 b, which will be quoted in full at the close of this Appendix ; also in Yalkut, vol. ii. p. 83 b.

Habakkuk iii. 18 is applied to Messianic times in the Targum.

Zephaniah iii. 8. The words rendered in our A.V. 'the day that I rise up to the prey' are translated ' for testimony' and applied to God's bearing testimony for the Messiah (Yalkut, vol. ii. p. 84 c, line 6 from the top).

Verse 9 is applied to the voluntary conversion of the Gentiles in the days of the Messiah in the Talmud (Abhod. Zarah, 24 a) ; and in Ber. R. 88; and *verse* 11 in Sanh. 98 a.

Haggai ii. 6 is expressly applied to the coming redemption in Deb. R. 1 (ed. Warsh. p. 4 b, line 15 from the top).

Zech. i. 20. The four carpenters there spoken of are variously interpreted in the Talmud (Sukk. 52 b), and in the Midrash (Bemidbar R. 14). But both agree that one of them refers to the Messiah.

Zech. ii. 10 is one of the Messianic passages to which we have referred in our remarks on Is. lx. 4. It has also a Messianic cast in the Targum.

Zech. iii. 8. The designation ' Branch' is expressly applied to King Messiah in the Targum. Indeed, this is one of the Messiah's peculiar names.

Verse 10 is quoted in the Midrash on Ps. lxxii. (ed. Warsh. p. 56 a, at the top) in a description of the future time of universal peace.

Zech. iv. 7 is generally applied to the Messiah, expressly in the Targum, and also in several of the Midrashim. Thus, as regards both clauses of it, in Tanchuma (Par. Toledoth 14, ed. Warsh. p. 37 b and 38 a).

Verse 10 is Messianically explained in Tanchuma (u. s.).

Zech. vi. 12 is universally admitted to be Messianic. So in the Targum, the Jerusalem Talmud (Ber. 5 a), in the Pirqé de R. Eliez. c. 48, and in the Midrashim.

Zech. vii. 13 is one of the three passages supposed to mark the near advent of Messiah. See our remarks on Jer. v. 19.

Zech. viii. 12 is applied to Messianic times in *Ber. R.* 12. See our remarks on Gen. ii. 4.

Zech. viii. 23 is one of the predictions expected to be fulfilled in Messianic days, it being however noted that it refers to instruction in the Law in that remarkable passage on Is. lx. 1 in Yalkut ii. p. 56 *d,* to which we have already referred.

In *Zech. ix.* 1 the name ' Chadrakh ' is mystically separated into ' Chad,' sharp, and ' rakh,' gentle, the Messiah being the one to the Gentiles and the other to the Jews (Siphré on Deut. p. 65 *a,* Yalkut i. p. 258 *b*).

Verse 9. The Messianic application of this verse in all its parts has already repeatedly been indicated. We may here add that there are many traditions about this ass on which the Messiah is to ride ; and so firm was the belief in it, that, according to the Talmud, ' if anyone saw an ass in his dreams, he will see salvation ' (Ber. 56 *b*). The verse is also Messianically quoted in Sanh. 98 *a,* in Pirqé de R. Eliez. c. 31, and in several of the Midrashim.

On *verse* 10 see our remarks on Deut. xx. 10.

Zech. x. 4 is Messianically applied in the Targum.

Zech. xi. 12 is Messianically explained in Ber. R. 98, but with this remark, that the 30 pieces of silver apply to 30 precepts, which the Messiah is to give to Israel.

Zech. xii. 10 is applied to the Messiah the Son of Joseph in the Talmud (Sukk. 52 *a*), and so is *verse* 12, there being, however, a difference of opinion whether the mourning is caused by the death of the Messiah the Son of Joseph, or else on account of the evil concupiscence (Yetser haRa).

Zech. xiv. 2 will be readily understood to have been applied to the wars of Messianic times, and this in many passages of the Midrashim, as, indeed, are *verses* 3, 4, 5, *and* 6.

Verse 7. The following interesting remark occurs in Yalkut on Ps. cxxxix. 16, 17 (vol. ii. p. 129 *d*) on the words ' none of them.' This world is to last 6,000 years ; 2,000 years it was waste and desolate, 2,000 years mark the period under the Law, 2,000 years that under the Messiah. And because our sins are increased, they are prolonged. As they are prolonged, and as we make one year in seven a Sabbatic year, so will God in the latter days make one day a Sabbatic year, which day is 1,000 years—to which applies the verse in Zechariah just quoted. See also Pirqé de R. Eliez. c. 28.

Verse 8 is Messianically applied in Ber. R. 48. See our remarks on Gen. xviii 4, 5.

Verse 9 is, of course, applied to Messianic times, as in Yalkut i. p. 76 *c,* 266 *a,* and vol. ii. p. 33 *c,* Midr. on Cant. ii. 13, and in other passages.

Malachi iii. 1 is applied to Elijah as forerunner of the Messiah in Pirqé de R. Eliez. c. 29.

Verse 4. In Bemidbar R. 17, a little before the close (ed. Warsh. p. 69 *a*), this verse seems to be applied to acceptable sacrifices in Messianic days.

On *verse* 16 Vayyikra R. 34 (ed. Warsh. p. 51 *b,* line 4 from the bottom) has the following curious remark : If any one in former times did the Commandment, the prophets wrote it down. But now when a man observes the Commandment, who writes it down ? Elijah and the King Messiah and the Holy One, blessed be His Name, seal it at their hands, and a memorial book is written, as it is written *Mal. iii.* 16.

The promise in *verse* 17 is extended to Messianic days in Shemoth R. 18.

On *Mal. iv.* 1 (in Hebrew iii. 19) the following curious comment occurs in Bereshith R. 6 (p. 14 *b*, lines 15 &c. from the bottom): ' The globe of the sun is encased, as it is said, He maketh a tabernacle for the sun (Ps. xix.). And a pool of water is before it. When the sun comes out, God cools its heat in the water lest it should burn up the world. But in the latter days the Holy One takes it out of its sheath, and with it burns up the wicked, as it is written Mal. iv. 1.'

Verse 2 (iii. 20 in Hebrew) is in Shemoth R. 31 quoted in connection with Ex. xxii. 26, and explained ' till the Messiah comes.'

Verse 5 is, of course, applied to the forerunner of the Messiah. So in many places, as in the Pirqé de R. Eliez. c. 40; Debarım R. 3; in the Midrash on Cant. i, 1 ; in the Talmud, and in Yalkut repeatedly.[1]

To the above passages we add some from the Apocryphal Books, partly as indicating the views concerning the Messiah which the Jews had derived from the Old Testament, and partly because of their agreement with Jewish traditionalism as already expounded by us. These passages must therefore be judged in connection with the Rabbinical ideas of the Messiah and of Messianic days. It is in this sense that we read, for example, the address to Jerusalem, *Tobit xiii.* 9 *to the end.* Comp. here, for example, our quotations on Amos ix. 11.

Similarly *Tobit xiv.* 5–7 may be compared with our quotations on Ps. xc., Is. lx. 3, and especially on Zech. viii. 23, also on Gen. xlix. 11.

Wisdom of Solomon iii. 7, 8 may be compared with our remarks on Is. lxi. 1.

Ecclus. xliv. 21 *&c. and xlvii.* 11 may be compared with our quotations on Ps. lxxxix. 22–25 ; Ps. cxxxii. 18; Ezek. xxix. 21.

Ecclus. xlviii. 10, 11. See the comments on Is. lii. 7, also our references on Mal. iii. 1 ; Mal. iv. 5 ; Deut. xxv. 19 and xxx. 4 ; Lam. ii. 22. In Sotah ix. 15 Elijah is represented as raising the dead.

Baruch ii. 34, 35 ; *iv.* 29 *&c.* ; *and ch. v.* are so thoroughly in accordance with Rabbinic, and, indeed, with Scriptural views, that it is almost impossible to enumerate special references.

The same may be said of 1 *Macc. ii.* 57 ; while such passages as *iv.* 46 and *xiv.* 41 point forward to the ministry of Elijah as resolving doubts, as this is frequently described in the Talmud (Shekalim ii. 5 ; Men. 45 *a*, Pes. 13 *a* ; and in other places).

Lastly, 2 *Macc. ii.* 18 is fully enlarged on in the Rabbinic descriptions of the gathering of Israel.

Perhaps it may be as well here to add the Messianic discussion in the Talmud, to which such frequent reference has been made (Sanhedrin, beginning at the two last lines of p. 96 *b*, and ending at p 99 *a*). The first question is that asked by one Rabbi of the other, whether he knew when the Son of the Fallen would come? Upon which follows an explanation of that designation, based on Amos ix. 11, after which it is added that it would be a generation in which the disciples of the sages would be diminished, and the rest of men consume their eyes for sorrow, and terrible sorrows so follow each other, that one had not ceased before the other began. Then a description is given of what was to happen during the hebdomad when the Son of David would come. In the first year it would be according to Amos iv. 7 ; in the second year there would be darts of famine ; in the third year great

---

[1] From the above review of Old Testament passages, all reference to sacrifices have been omitted, because, although the Synagogue held the doctrine of the vicariousness and atoning character of these sacrifices, no mention occurs of the Messiah in connection with them.

famine and terrible mortality, in consequence of which the Law would be forgotten by those who studied it. In the fourth year there would be abundance, and yet no abundance; in the fifth year great abundance and great joy, and return to the study of the Law; in the sixth year voices (announcements); in the seventh wars, and at the end of the seventh the Son of David would come. Then follows some discussion about the order of the sixth and seventh year, when Ps. lxxxix. 51 is referred to. Next we have a description of the general state during those days. Sacred places (Academies) would be used for the vilest purposes, Galilee be desolated, Gablan laid waste, and the men of Gebul wander from city to city, and not find mercy. And the wisdom of the scribes would be corrupted, and they who fear sin be abhorred, and the face of that generation would be like that of a dog, and truth should fail, according to Is. lix. 15. (Here a side issue is raised.) The Talmud then continues in much the same terms to describe the Messianic age as one, in which children would rebel against their parents, and as one of general lawlessness, when Sadduceeism should universally prevail, apostasy increase, study of the Law decrease; and, generally, universal poverty and despair of redemption prevail—the growing disregard of the Law being pointed out as specially characterising the last days. R. Kattina said: The world is to last 6,000 years, and during one millennium it is to lie desolate, according to Is. ii. 17. R. Abayi held that this state would last 2,000 years, according to Hosea vi. 2. The opinion of R. Kattina was, however, regarded as supported by this, that in each period of seven there is a Sabbatic year—the day here = 1,000 years of desolateness and rest—the appeal being to Is. ii. 17; Ps. xcii. 1, and xc 4. According to another tradition the world was to last 6,000 years: 2,000 in a state of chaos, 2,000 under the Law, and 2,000 being the Messianic age. But on account of Israel's sins those years were to be deducted which had already passed. On the authority of Elijah it was stated that the world would not last less than eighty-five jubilees, and that in the last jubilee the Son of David would come. When Elijah was asked whether at the beginning or at the end of it, he replied that he did not know. Being further asked whether the whole of that period would first elapse or not, he similarly replied, his meaning being supposed to be that until that term people were not to hope for the Advent of Messiah, but after that term they were to look for it. A story is related of a man being met who had in his hands a writing in square Hebrew characters, and in Hebrew, which he professed to have got from the Persian archives, and in which it was written that after 4,290 years from the Creation the world would come to an end. And then would be the wars of the great sea-monsters, and those of Gog and Magog, and the rest of the time would be the times of the Messiah, and that the Holy One, blessed be His Name, would only renew His world after the 7,000 years; to which, however, one Rabbi objects, making it 5,000 years. Rabbi Nathan speaks of Habakkuk ii. 3 as a passage so deep as to go down to the abyss, reproving the opinion of the Rabbis who sought out the meaning of Daniel vii. 25, and of Rabbi Samlai, who similarly busied himself with Ps. lxxx. 5, and of Rabbi Akiba, who dwelt upon Haggai ii. 6. But the first kingdom (Babylonian?) was to last seventy years; the second (Asmonæan?) fifty-two years; and the rule of the son of Kozebhah (Bar Kokhabh, the false Messiah) two and a half years. According to Rabbi Samuel, speaking in the name of Rabbi Jonathan: Let the bones of those be broken who calculate the end, because they say, The end has come, and the Messiah has not come, therefore He will not come at all. But still expect Him, as it is said (Hab. ii. 3), 'Though it tarry, wait for it.' Perhaps thou wilt say: We wait for Him, but He does not wait for it. On this point read Is. xxx. 18. But if so, what hinders it? The quality of judgment. But in that case, why should we wait? In order to receive the reward, according to the last clause of Is. xxx. 18. On which follows a further discussion. Again, Rabh maintains that all the limits of time as regards the Messiah are past, and that it now only depends on repentance and good works when He shall come. To this Rabbi Samuel objected, but Rabh's view was supported by Rabbi Eliezer, who said that if Israel repented they would be redeemed, but if not they would not be redeemed. To which Rabbi Joshua added, that in the latter case God would raise over them a King whose decrees would be hard like those of Haman, when Israel would repent. The opinion of Rabbi Eliezer was further supported by Jer. iii. 22, to which Rabbi Joshua objected by quoting Is. lii. 3, which seemed to imply that Israel's redemption was not dependent on their repentance and good works. On this Rabbi Eliezer retorted by quoting Mal. iii. 7, to which again Rabbi Joshua replied by quoting Jer. iii. 14, and Rabbi Eliezer by quoting Is. xxx. 15. To this Rabbi Joshua replied from Is. xlix. 7. Rabbi Eliezer then urged Jer. iv. 1, upon which Rabbi Joshua retorted from Dan. xii. 7, and so effectually silenced Rabbi Eliezer. On this Rabbi Abba propounded that there was not a clearer mark of the Messianic term than that in Is. xxxvi. 8. To which Rabbi Eliezer added Zech. viii. 10. On this the question is raised as to the meaning of the words ' neither was there any peace to him that went out or came in.' To this Rabh gave answer that it applied to the disciples of the sages, according to Ps. cxix. 165. On which Rabbi Samuel replied that at that time all the entrances would be equal (i.e. that all should be on the same footing of danger). Rabbi Chanina remarked that the Son of David would not come till after fish had been sought for for the sick and not found, according to Ezek. xxxii. 14 in connection with Ezek. xxix. 21. Rabbi Chamma, the son of Rabbi Chanina, said that the Son of David would not come until the vile dominion over Israel had ceased, appealing to Is. xviii. 5, 7. R. Seira said that Rabbi Chanina said : The Son of David would not come till the proud had ceased in Israel, according to Zeph. iii. 11, 12. Rabbi Samlai, in the name of Rabbi Eliezer the son of Rabbi Simeon, said that the Son of David would not come till all judges and rulers had ceased in Israel, according to Is. i. 26. Ula said: Jerusalem is not to be redeemed, except by righteousness, according to Is. i. 27. We pass over the remarks of Rabbi Papa, as not adding to the subject. Rabbi Jochanan said: If thou seest a generation that increasingly diminishes, expect Him, according to 2 Sam. xxii. 28. He also added: If thou seest a generation upon which many sorrows come like a stream, expect Him, according to Is. lix. 19, 20. He also added: The Son of David does not come except in a generation where all are either righteous, or all guilty—the former idea being based on Is. lx. 21, the latter on Is. lix. 16 and xlviii. 11. Rabbi Alexander said, that Rabbi Joshua the son of Levi referred to the contradiction in Is. lx. 22 between the words ' in his time ' and again ' I will hasten it,' and explained it thus : If they are worthy, I will hasten it, and if not, in His time. Another similar contradiction between Dan. vii. 13 and Zech. ix. 9 is thus reconciled : If Israel deserve it, He will come in the clouds of heaven ; if they are not deserving, He will come poor, and riding upon an ass. Upon this it is remarked that Sabor the King sneered at Samuel, saying: You say that the Messiah is to come upon an ass : I will send Him my splendid horse. To which the Rabbi replied : Is it of a hundred colours, like His ass? Rabbi Joshua, the son of Levi, saw Elijah, who stood at the door of Paradise. He said to him: When shall the Messiah come? He replied: When that Lord shall come (meaning God). Rabbi Joshua, the son of Levi, said: I saw two [himself and Elijah], and I heard the voice of three [besides the former two the Voice of God]. Again he met Elijah standing at the door of the cave of Rabbi Simon the son of Jochai, and said to him: Shall I attain the world to come? Elijah replied: If it pleaseth to this Lord. Upon which follows the same remark: I have seen two, and I have heard the voice of three. Then the Rabbi asks Elijah: When shall the Messiah come? To which the answer is: Go and ask Him thyself. And where does He abide? At the gate of the city (Rome). And what is His sign? He abides among the poor, the sick, the stricken. And all unbind, and bind up again the wounds at the same time, but He undoes (viz. the bandage) and rebinds each separately, so that if they call for Him they may not find Him engaged.[1] He went to meet Him and said: Peace be to Thee, my Rabbi and my Lord. He replied to him: Peace be to thee, thou son of Levi. He said to Him: When wilt Thou come, my Lord? He replied to him: To-day. Then he turned to Elijah, who said to him: What has He said to thee? He said to me: Son of Levi, peace be to thee. Elijah said to him: He has assured thee and thy father of the world to come. He said to him: But He has deceived me in that He said: I come to-day, and He has not come. He said to him that by the words 'to-day' He meant: To-day if ye will hear My voice (Ps. xcv. 7). Rabbi José was asked by his disciples: When will the Son of David come? To this he replied: I am afraid you will ask me also for a sign. Upon which they assured him they would not. On this he replied: When this gate (viz. of Rome) shall fall, and be built, and again fall, and they shall not have time to rebuild it till the Son of David comes. They said to him: Rabbi, give us a sign. He said to them: Have ye not promised me that ye would not seek a sign? They said to him: Notwithstanding do it. He said to them: If so, the waters from the cave of Pamias (one of the sources of the Jordan) shall be changed into blood. In that moment they were changed into blood. Then the Rabbi goes on to predict that the land would be overrun by enemies, every stable being filled with their horses. Rabh said that the Son of David would not come till the kingdom (i.e. foreign domination) should extend over Israel for nine months, according to Micah v. 3. Ula said: Let Him come, but may I not see Him, and so said Raba. Rabbi Joseph said: Let Him come, and may I be found worthy to stand the shadow of the dung of His ass (according to some: the tail of his ass). Abayi said to Raba: Why has this been the bearing of your words? If on account of the sorrows of the Messiah, we have the tradition that Rabbi Eliezer was asked by his disciples, what a man should do to be freed from the sorrows of the Messiah; on which they were told: By busying yourselves with the Torah, and with good works. And you are a master of the Torah, and you have good works. He answered: Perhaps sin might lead to occasion of danger. To this comforting replies are given from Scripture, such as Gen. xxviii. 15, and other passages, some of them being subjected to detailed commentation.

Rabbi Jochanan expressed a similar dislike of seeing the days of the Messiah, on which Resh Lakish suggested that it might be on the ground of Amos v. 19, or rather on that of Jer. xxx. 6. Upon this, such fear before God is accounted for by the consideration that what is called service above is not like what is called service below (the family above is not like the family below), so that one kind may outweigh the other. Rabbi Giddel said, that Rabh said, that Israel would rejoice in the years of the Messiah. Rabbi Joseph said: Surely, who else would rejoice in them? Chillak and Billak? (two imaginary names, meaning no one). This, to

---

[1] The Vienna edition of the Talmud has several lacunæ on this page (98 a).

exclude the words of Rabbi Hillel, who said: There is no more Messiah for Israel, seeing they have had Him in the time of Hezekiah. Rabh said: The world was only created for David; Samuel, for Moses; and Rabbi Jochanan, for the Messiah. What is His Name? The school of Rabbi Shila said: Shiloh is His Name, according to Gen. xlix. 10. The school of Rabbi Jannai said: Jinnon, according to Ps. lxxii. 17. The school of Rabbi Chanina said: Chaninah, according to Jer. xvi. 13. And some say: Menachem, the son of Hezekiah, according to Lam. i. 16. And our Rabbis say: The Leprous One of the house of Rabbi is His Name, as it is written Is. liii. 4. Rabbi Nachman said: If He is among the living, He is like me, according to Jer. xxx. 21. Rabh said: If He is among the living, He is like Rabbi Jehudah the Holy, and if among the dead He is like Daniel, the man greatly beloved. Rabbi Jehudah said, Rabh said: God will raise up to them another David, according to Jer. xxx. 9, a passage which evidently points to the future. Rabbi Papa said to Abaji: But we have this other Scripture Ezek. xxxvii. 25, and the two terms (Messiah and David) stand related like Augustus and Cæsar. Rabbi Samlai illustrated Amos v. 18, by a parable of the cock- and the bat which were looking for the light. The cock said to the bat: I look for the light, but of what use is the light to thee? So it happened to a Sadducee who said to Rabbi Abahu: When will the Messiah come? He answered him: When darkness covers this people. He said to him: Dost thou intend to curse me? He replied: It is said in Scripture Is. lx. 2. Rabbi Eliezer taught: The days of the Messiah are forty years, according to Ps. xcv. 10. Rabbi Eleazar, the son of Asariah, said: Seventy years, according to Is. xxiii. 15, 'according to the days of a King,' the King there spoken of being the unique king, the Messiah. Rabbi said: Three generations, according to Ps. lxxii. 5. Rabbi Hillel said: Israel shall have no more Messiah, for they have had Him in the days of Hezekiah. Rabbi Joseph said: May God forgive Rabbi Hillel: when did Hezekiah live? During the first Temple. And Zechariah prophesied during the second Temple, and said Zech. ix. 9. We have the tradition that Rabbi Eliezer said: The days of the Messiah are forty years. It is written Deut. viii. 3, 4, and again in Ps. xc. 15 (showing that the days of rejoicing must be like those of affliction in the wilderness). Rabbi Dosa said: Four hundred years, quoting Gen. xv. 13 in connection with the same Psalm. Rabbi thought it was 365 years, according to the solar year, quoting Is. lxiii. 4. He asked the meaning of the words: 'The day of vengeance is in My heart,' Rabbi Jochanan explained them: I have manifested it to My heart, but not to My members, and Rabbi Simon ben Lakish: To My heart, and not to the ministering angels. Abimi taught that the days of the Messiah were to last for Israel 7,000 years (a Divine marriage-week), according to Is. lxii. 5. Rabbi Jehudah said, that Rabbi Samuel said, that the days of the Messiah were to be as from the day that the world was created until now, according to Deut. xi. 21. Rabbi Nachman said: As from the days of Noah till now, according to Is. liv. 9. Rabbi Chija said, that Rabbi Jochanan said: All the prophets have only prophesied in regard to the days of the Messiah; but in regard to the world to come, eye has not seen, O God, beside Thee, what He hath prepared for him that waiteth for Him (Is. lxiv. 4). And this is opposed to what Rabbi Samuel said, that there was no difference between this world and the days of the Messiah, except that foreign domination would cease. Upon which the Talmud goes off to discourse upon repentance, and its relation to perfect righteousness.

Lengthy as this extract may be, it will at least show the infinite difference between the Rabbinic expectation of the Messiah, and the picture of Him presented in the New Testament. Surely the Messianic idea, as realised in Christ, could not have been derived from the views current in those times!

APPENDIX X.

ON THE SUPPOSED TEMPLE-SYNAGOGUE.

(Vol. i. Book II. ch. x. p. 246.)

APP.

X

PUTTING aside, as quite untenable, the idea of a regular *Beth ha-Midrash* in the Temple (though advocated even by *Wünsche*), we have here to inquire whether any historical evidence can be adduced for the existence of a Synagogue within the bounds of the Temple-buildings. The notice (Sot. vii. 8) that on every Sabbatic year lection of certain portions was made to the people in the 'Court,' and that a service was conducted there during public fasts on account of dry weather (Taan. ii. 5), can, of course, not be adduced as proving the existence of a regular Temple-Synagogue. On the other hand, it is expressly said in Sanh. 88 *b*, lines 19, 20 from top, that on the Sabbaths and feast-days the members of the Sanhedrin went out upon the *Chel* or Terrace of the Temple, when questions were asked of them and answered. It is quite true that in Tos. Sanh. vii. (p. 158, col. *d*) we have an inaccurate statement about the second of the Temple-Sanhedrin as sitting on the *Chel* (instead of at the entrance to the Priests' Court, as in Sanh. 88 *b*), and that there the Sabbath and festive discourses are loosely designated as a 'Beth ha-Midrash' which was on 'the Temple-Mount.'[1] But since exactly the same description—indeed, in the same words—of what took place is given in the Tosephta as in the Talmud itself, the former must be corrected by the latter, or rather the term 'Beth ha-Midrash' must be taken in the wider and more general sense as the 'place of Rabbinic exposition,' and not as indicating any permanent Academy. But even if the words in the Tosephta were to be taken in preference to those in the Talmud itself, *they contain no mention of any Temple-Synagogue.*

Equally inappropriate are the other arguments in favour of this supposed Temple-Synagogue. The first of them is derived from a notice in Tos. Sukkah. iv. 4, in which R. Joshua explains how, during the first night of the Feast of Tabernacles, the pious never 'saw sleep,' since they went, first 'to the Morning Sacrifice, thence to the Synagogue, thence to the Beth ha-Midrash, thence to the festive sacrifices, thence to eat and to drink, thence again to the Beth ha-Midrash, thence to the Evening Sacrifice, and thence to the "joy of the house of water-drawing"' (the night-feast and services in the Temple-Courts). The only other argument is that from Yoma vii. 1, 2, where we read that while the bullock and the goat were burned the High-Priest read to the people certain portions of the Law, the roll of which was handed by the *Chazzan* of the Synagogue (it is not said which Synagogue) to the head of the Synagogue, by him to the Sagan, and by the Sagan to the High-Priest.[2] How utterly inconclusive inferences from these notices

---

[1] So also by *Maimonides*, Yad ha-Chas. vol. iv. p. 241 *a* (Hilc. Sanh. ch. iii.).

[2] A similar arrangement is described in Sot. vii. 8 as connected with the reading of

the Law by the kings of Israel to the people, according to Deut. xxxi. 10. Will it be argued from this that there was a Synagogue in the Temple in the early days of the kings?

are, need not be pointed out. More than this—the existence of a Temple-Synagogue seems entirely incompatible with the remark in Yoma vii. 2, that it was impossible for anyone present at the reading of the High-Priest to witness the burning of the bullock and goat—and that, *not* because the former took place in a regular Temple-Synagogue, but ' because the way was far and the two services were exactly at the same time.' Such, so far as I know, are all the Talmudical passages from which the existence of a regular Temple-Synagogue has been inferred, and with what reason, the reader may judge for himself.

It is indeed easy to understand that Rabbinism and later Judaism should have wished to locate a Synagogue and a Beth ha-Midrash within the sacred precincts of the Temple itself. But it is difficult to account for the circumstance that such Christian scholars as *Reland, Carpzov,* and *Lightfoot* should have been content to repeat the statement without subjecting its grounds to personal examination. *Vitringa* (Synag. p. 30) almost grows indignant at the possibility of any doubt— and that, although he himself quotes passages from *Maimonides* to the effect *that the reading of the Law by the High-Priest on the Day of Atonement took place in the Court of the Women,* and hence not in any supposed Synagogue. Yet commentators generally, and writers on the Life of Christ have located the sitting of our Lord among the Doctors in the Temple in this supposed Temple-Synagogue ! [1]

---

[1] In a former book ('Sketches of Jewish Life in the Time of our Lord') I had expressed hesitation and misgivings on the subject. These (as explained in the text), a fuller study has converted into absolute certitude against the popularly accepted hypothesis. And what, indeed, could have been the meaning of a Synagogue—which, after all, stood as substitute for the Temple and its Services— within the precincts of the Temple; or how could the respective services be so arranged as not to clash ; or, lastly, have not the prayers of the Synagogue, admittedly, taken the place of the Services and Sacrifices of the Temple ?

APPENDIX XI.

ON THE PROPHECY, IS. XL. 3.

(See vol. i. Book II. ch. xi. p. 260, Note 2.)

ACCORDING to the Synoptic Gospels, the public appearance and preaching of John was the fulfilment of the prediction with which the second part of the prophecies of Isaiah opens, called by the Rabbis, 'the book of consolations.' After a brief general preface (Is. xl. 1, 2), the words occur which are quoted by St. Matthew and St. Mark (Is. xl. 3), and more fully by St. Luke (Is. xl. 3–5). A more appropriate beginning of 'the book of consolations' could scarcely be conceived.

The quotation of Is. xl. 3 is made according to the LXX., the only difference being the change of 'the paths of our God' into 'His paths.' The divergences between the LXX. and our Hebrew text of Is. xl. 4, 5 are somewhat more numerous, but equally unimportant—the main difference from the Hebrew original lying in this, that, instead of rendering 'all flesh shall see it together,' we have in the LXX. and the New Testament, 'all flesh shall see the salvation of God.' As it can scarcely be supposed that the LXX. read ישׁעי for יחדו, we must regard their rendering as *Targumic*. Lastly, although according to the accents in the Hebrew Bible we should read, 'The Voice of one crying: In the wilderness prepare,' &c., yet, as alike the LXX., the Targum, and the Synoptists render, 'The Voice of one crying in the wilderness: Prepare,' their testimony must be regarded as outweighing the authority of the accents, which are of so much later date.

But the main question is, whether Is. xl. 3, &c., refers to Messianic times or not. Most modern interpreters regard it as applying to the return of the exiles from Babylon. This is not the place to enter on a critical discussion of the passage; but it may be remarked that the insertion of the word 'salvation' in v. 5 by the LXX. seems to imply that they had viewed it as Messianic. It is, at any rate, certain that the Synoptists so understood the rendering of the LXX. But this is not all. The quotation from Is. xl. was regarded by the Evangelists as fulfilled, when John the Baptist announced the coming Kingdom of God. We have proof positive that, on the supposition of the correctness of the announcement made by John, they only took the view of their contemporaries in applying Is. lx. 3, &c., to the preaching of the Baptist. The evidence here seems to be indisputable, for *the Targum renders the close of v. 9* ('say unto the cities of Judah, Behold your God!') *by the words: 'Say to the cities of the House of Judah, the Kingdom of your God shall be manifested.'*

In fact, according to the Targum, 'the good tidings' are *not* brought *by* Zion nor *by* Jerusalem, but *to* Zion and *to* Jerusalem.

APPENDIX XII.

ON THE BAPTISM OF PROSELYTES.

(See vol. i. Book II. ch. xi. p. 273.)

ONLY those who have made study of it can have any idea how large, and sometimes bewildering, is the literature on the subject of Jewish Froselytes and their
Baptism. Our present remarks will be confined to the Baptism of Proselytes.

1. Generally, as regards proselytes (*Gerim*) we have to distinguish between the
Ger ha-Shaar (proselyte of the gate) and *Ger Toshabh* (' sojourner,' settled among
Israel), and again the *Ger hatstsedeq* (proselyte of righteousness) and *Ger habberith*
(proselyte of the covenant). The former are referred to by *Josephus* (Ant. xiv. 7. 2),
and frequently in the New Testament, in the Authorised Version under the designation of those who 'fear God,' Acts xiii. 16, 26; are 'religious,' Acts xiii. 43;
'devout,' Acts xiii. 50; xvii. 4, 17; 'worship God,' Acts xvi. 14; xviii. 7.
Whether the expression 'devout' and 'feared God' in Acts x. 2, 7 refers to proselytes of the gate is doubtful. As the 'proselytes of the gate' only professed their
faith in the God of Israel, and merely bound themselves to the observance of the
so-called seven Noachic commandments (on which in another place), the question
of 'baptism' need not be discussed in connection with them, since they did not
even undergo circumcision.

2. It was otherwise with 'the proselytes of righteousness,' who became 'children of the covenant,' 'perfect Israelites,' Israelites in every respect, both as regarded duties and privileges. All writers are agreed that three things were
required for the admission of such proselytes: *Circumcision* (*Milah*), *Baptism*
(*Tebhilah*), and a *Sacrifice* (*Qorban*, in the case of women: baptism and sacrifice)—
the latter consisting of a burnt-offering of a heifer, or of a pair of turtle doves or of
young doves (*Maimonides*, Hilkh. Iss. Biah xiii. 5). After the destruction of the
Temple promise had to be made of such a sacrifice when the services of the
Sanctuary were restored. On this and the ordinances about circumcision it is not
necessary to enter further. That *baptism* was absolutely necessary to make a
proselyte is so frequently stated as not to be disputed (See *Maimonides*, u. s.; the
tractate *Massekheth Gerim* in *Kirchheim's* Septem Libri Talm. Parvi, pp. 38–44
[which, however, adds little to our knowledge]; Targum on Ex. xii. 44; Ber. 47 *b*;
Kerith. 9 *a*; Jer. Yebam. p. 8 *d*; Yebam. 45 *b*, 46 *a* and *b*, 48 *b*, 76 *a*; Ab. Sar. 57 *a*,
59 *a*, and other passages). There was, indeed, a difference between Rabbis Joshua
and Eliezer, the former maintaining that baptism alone without circumcision, the
latter that circumcision alone without baptism, sufficed to make a proselyte, but
the sages decided in favour of the necessity of both rites (Yebam. 46 *a* and *b*).
The baptism was to be performed in the presence of three witnesses, ordinarily
Sanhedrists (Yebam. 47 *b*), but in case of necessity others might act. The person
to be baptized, having cut his hair and nails, undressed completely, made fresh pro-

fession of his faith before what were designated 'the fathers of the baptism' (our Godfathers, Kethub. 11 a; Erub. 15 a), and then immersed completely, so that every part of the body was touched by the water. The rite would, of course, be accompanied by exhortations and benedictions (*Maimonides*, Hilkh. Milah iii. 4; Hilkh. Iss. Biah xiv. 6). Baptism was not to be administered at night, nor on a Sabbath or feast-day (Yebam. 46 b). Women were attended by those of their own sex, the Rabbis standing at the door outside. Yet unborn children of proselytes did not require to be baptized, because they were born 'in holiness' (Yebam. 78 a). In regard to the little children of proselytes opinions differed. A person under age was indeed received, but not regarded as properly an Israelite till he had attained majority. Secret baptism, or where only the mother brought a child, was not acknowledged. In general, the statements of a proselyte about his baptism required attestation by witnesses. But the children of a Jewess or of a proselyte were regarded as Jews, even if the baptism of the father was doubtful.

It was indeed a great thing when, in the words of *Maimonides*, a stranger sought shelter under the wings of the Shekhinah, and the change of condition which he underwent was regarded as complete. The waters of baptism were to him in very truth, though in a far different from the Christian sense, the 'bath of regeneration' (Titus iii. 5). As he stepped out of these waters he was considered as 'born anew'—in the language of the Rabbis, as if he were 'a little child just born' (Yeb. 22 a; 48 b; 97 b), as 'a child of one day' (Mass. Ger. c. ii.). But this new birth was not 'a birth from above' in the sense of moral or spiritual renovation, but only as implying a new relationship to God, to Israel, and to his own past, present, and future. It was expressly enjoined that all the difficulties of his new citizenship should first be set before him, and if, after that, he took upon himself the yoke of the law, he should be told how all those sorrows and persecutions were intended to convey a greater blessing, and all those commandments to redound to greater merit. More especially was he to regard himself as a new man in reference to his past. Country, home, habits, friends, and relations were all changed. The past, with all that had belonged to it, was past, and he was a new man—the old, with its defilements, was buried in the waters of baptism. This was carried out with such pitiless logic as not only to determine such questions as those of inheritance, but that it was declared that, except for the sake of not bringing proselytism into contempt, a proselyte might have wedded his own mother or sister (comp. Yeb. 22 a; Sanh. 58 b). It is a curious circumstance that marriage with a female proselyte was apparently very popular (Horay. 13 a, line 5 from bottom; see also Shem. R. 27), and the Talmud names at least three celebrated doctors who were the offspring of such unions (comp. *Derenbourg*, Hist. de la Palest., p. 223, note 2). The praises of proselytes and proselytism are also sung in Vayy. R. 1.

If anything could have further enhanced the value of such proselytism, it would have been its supposed antiquity. Tradition traced it up to Abraham and Sarah, and the expression (Gen. xii. 5) ' the souls that they had gotten ' was explained as referring to their proselytes, since 'every one that makes a proselyte is as if he made (created) him ' (Ber. R. 39, comp also the Targums Pseudo-Jon. and Jerus. and Midr. on Cant. i. 3). The Talmud, differing in this from the Targumim, finds in Exod. ii. 5 a reference to the baptism of Pharaoh's daughter (Sotah 12 b, line 3; Megill. 13 a, line 11). In Shem. R. 27 Jethro is proved to have been a convert, from the circumstance that his original name had been Jether (Exod.

IV. 18), an additional letter (Jethro). as in the case of Abraham, having been added to his name when he became a proselyte (comp. also Zebhach. 116 *a* and Targum Ps.-Jon. on Exod. xviii. 6, 27, Numb. xxiv. 21. To pass over other instances, we are pointed to Ruth (Targum on Ruth i. 10, 15), and to Nebuzaradan —who is also described as a proselyte (Sanh. 96 *b*, line 19 from the bottom). But it is said that in the days of David and Solomon proselytes were not admitted by the Sanhedrin because their motives were suspected (Yeb. 76 *a*), or that at least they were closely watched.

But although the baptism of proselytes seems thus far beyond doubt, Christian theologians have discussed the question, whether the rite was practised at the time of Christ, or only introduced after the destruction of the Temple and its Services, to take the place of the Sacrifice previously offered. The controversy, which owed its origin chiefly to dogmatic prejudices on the part of Lutherans, Calvinists, and Baptists, has since been continued on historical or quasi-historical grounds. The silence of Josephus and Philo can scarcely be quoted in favour of the later origin of the rite. On the other hand, it may be urged that, as Baptism did not take the place of sacrifices in any other instance, it would be difficult   account for the origin of such a rite in connection with the admission of proselytes.

Again, if a Jew who had become Levitically defiled, required immersion, it is difficult to suppose that a heathen would have been admitted to all the services of the Sanctuary without a similar purification. But we have also positive testimony (which the objections of *Winer*, *Keil*, and *Leyrer*, in my opinion do not invalidate), that the baptism of proselytes existed in the time of Hillel and Shammai. For, whereas the school of Shammai is said to have allowed a proselyte who was circumcised on the eve of the Passover, to partake after baptism of the Passover,[1] the school of Hillel forbade it. This controversy must be regarded as proving that at that time (previous to Christ) the baptism of proselytes was customary [2] (Pes. viii. 8, Eduy. v. 2).

[1] The case supposed by the school of Shammai would, however, have been impossible, since, according to Rabbinic directions, a certain time must have elapsed between circumcision and baptism.

[2] The following notice from *Josephus* (Ant. xviii. 5. 2) is not only interesting in itself, but for the view which it presents of baptism. It shows what views rationalising Jews took of the work of the Baptist, and how little such were able to enter into the real meaning of his baptism. 'But to some of the Jews it appeared, that the destruction of Herod's army came from God, and, indeed, as a righteous punishment on account of what had been done to John, who was surnamed the Baptist. For Herod ordered him to be killed, a good man, and who commanded the Jews to exercise virtue, both as to righteousness towards one another, and piety towards God. and so to come to baptism. For that the baptizing would be acceptable to Him, if they made use of it, not for the putting away (remission) of some sins, but for the purification of the body, after that the soul had been previously cleansed by righteousness. And when others had come in crowds, for they were exceedingly moved by hearing these words, Herod, fearing lest such influence of his over the people might lead to some rebellion, for they seemed ready to do anything by his council, deemed it best, before anything new should happen through him, to put him to death, rather than that, when a change should arise in affairs, he might have to repent,' &c. On the credibility of this testimony see the Article on *Josephus*, in *Smith's* 'Dictionary of Christian Biography,' vol. iii. pp. 441–460 (see especially pp. 458, 459).

APPENDIX XIII.

APP.
XIII

WITHOUT here entering on a discussion of the doctrine of Angels and devils as presented in Holy Scripture, the Apocrypha, and the Pseudepigrapha, it will be admitted that considerable progression may be marked as we advance from even the latest Canonical to Apocryphal, and again from these to the Pseudepigraphic Writings. The same remark applies even more strongly to a comparison of the latter with Rabbinic literature. There we have comparatively little of the Biblical in its purity. But, added to it, we now find much that is the outcome of Eastern or of prurient imagination, of national conceit, of ignorant superstition, and of foreign, especially Persian, elements. In this latter respect it is true—not, indeed, as regards the doctrine of good and evil Angels, but much of its Rabbinic elaboration—that 'the names of the Angels (and of the months) were brought from Babylon' (Jer. Rosh. haSh. 56 d; Ber. R. 48), and with the 'names,' not a few of the notions regarding them. At the same time, it would be unjust to deny that much of the symbolism which it is evidently intended to convey is singularly beautiful.

I. ANGELOLOGY.

1. *Creation, Number, Duration, and Location of the Angels.* We are now considering. not the *Angel-Princes* but that vast unnumbered 'Host' generally designated as 'the ministering Angels' (מלאכי השרת). Opinions differ (Ber. R. 3) whether they were created on the *second* day as being 'spirits,' 'winds' (Ps. civ. 4), or on the *fifth* day (Is. vi. 2) in accordance with the works of Creation on those days. Viewed in reference to God's Service and Praise, they are 'a flaming fire': in regard to their office, winged messengers (Pirqé de R. El. 4). But not only so: every day ministering Angels are created, whose apparent destiny is only to raise the praises of God, after which they pass away into the fiery stream (*Nahar de-Nur*) whence they originally issued [1] (Chag. 14 a; Ber. R. 78). More than this—a new Angel is created to execute every behest of God, and then passeth away (Chag. u. s.). This continual new creation of Angels, which is partly a beautiful allegory, partly savours of the doctrine of 'emanation,' is Biblically supported by an appeal to Lament. iii. 23. Thus it may be said that daily a *Kath*, or company, of Angels is created for the daily service of God, and that every word which proceedeth from His mouth becomes an 'Angel' [Messenger—mark here the ideal unity of Word and Deed], (Chag. 14 a).

The vast number of that Angelic Host, and the consequent safety of Israel as

---

[1] This stream issues from under the throne of God, and is really the sweat of the 'living creatures' in their awe at the glory of God (Ber. R. 78).

against its enemies, was described in the most hyperbolic language. There were 12 *Mazzaloth* (signs of the Zodiac), each having 30 chiefs of armies, each chief with 30 legions, each legion with 30 leaders, each leader with 30 captains, each captain with 30 under him, and each of these with 365,000 stars—and all were created for the sake of Israel! (Ber. 32. *b*). Similarly, when Nebuchadnezzar proposed to ascend into heaven, and to exalt his throne above the stars, and be like the Most High, the Bath Qol replied to this grandson of Nimrod that man's age was 70, or at most 80 years, while the way from earth to the firmament occupied 500 years,[a] the thickness of the firmament was 500 years, from one firmament to the other occupied other 500 years, the feet of the living creatures were equal to all that had preceded, and the joints of their feet to as many as had preceded them, and so on increasingly through all their members up to their horns, after which came the Throne of Glory, the feet of which again equalled all that had preceded, and so on (Chag. 13 *a*b).[1] In connection with this we read in Chag. 12 *b* that there are seven heavens: the *Vilon*, in which there is the sun; *Reqia*, in which the sun shines, and the moon, stars, and planets are fixed; *Shechaqim*, in which are the millstones to make the manna for the pious; *Zebhul*, in which the Upper Jerusalem, and the Temple and the Altar are, and in which Michael, the chief Angel-Prince, offers sacrifices; *Maon*, in which the Angels of the Ministry are, who sing by night and are silent by day for the sake of the honour of Israel (who now have their services); *Machon*, in which are the treasuries of snow, hail, the chambers of noxious dews, and of the receptacles of water, the chamber of the wind, and the cave of mist, and their doors are of fire; lastly, *Araboth*, wherein Justice, Judgment, and Righteousness are, the treasures of Life, of Peace, and of Blessing, the souls of the righteous, and the spirits and souls of those who are to be born in the future, and the dew by which the dead are to be raised. There also are the Ophanim, and the Seraphim, and the living creatures, and the ministering Angels, and the Throne of Glory, and over them is enthroned the Great King. [For a description of this Throne and of the Appearance of its King, see Pirqé de R. Eliez. 4.] On the other hand, sometimes every power and phenomenon in Nature is hypostatised into an Angel—such as hail, rain, wind, sea, &c.; similarly, every occurrence, such as life, death, nourishment, poverty, nay, as it is expressed: 'there is not a stalk of grass upon earth but it has its Angel in heaven' (Ber. R. 10). This seems to approximate the views of Alexandrian Mysticism. So also, perhaps, the idea that certain Biblical heroes became after death Angels. But as this may be regarded as implying their service as messengers of God, we leave it for the present.

2. *The Angel-Princes, their location, names, and offices.* Any limitation, as to duration or otherwise, of the Ministering Angels does not apply either to the Ophanim (or wheel-angels), the Seraphim, the Chayoth (or living creatures), nor to the Angel-Princes (Ber. R. 78).[2] In Chag. 13 *a*, *b* the name *Chashmal* is given to the 'living creatures.' The word is explained as composed of two others which mean silence and speech—it being beautifully explained, that they keep silence when the Word proceeds out of the mouth of God, and speak when He has ceased. It would be difficult exactly to state the number of the Angel-Princes. The 70 nations, of which the world is composed, had each their Angel-Prince (Targ. Jer. on Gen. xi.7, 8; comp. Ber. R. 56; Shem. R. 21; Vayyi. R. 29; Ruth R. ed. Warsh. p. 36 *b*), who plead their cause with God. Hence these Angels are really hostile to Israel, and

APP.
XIII

[a] In Jer. Ber 2 *c* it is 50 years

[b] See also Pes. 94 *b*

---

[1] Some add the Cherubim as another and separate class.

[2] According to Jer. Ber. ix. 1, the abode of the living creatures was to an extent of 515

years' journey, which is proved from the numerical value of the word ישרה 'straight' (Ezek. i. 7).

APP.
ΧΙΙΙ

may be regarded as not quite good Angels, and are cast down when the nationality which they represent is destroyed. It may have been as a reflection on Christian teaching that Israel was described as not requiring any representative with God, like the Gentiles. For, as will soon appear, this was not the general view entertained. Besides these Gentile Angel-Princes there were other chiefs, whose office will be explained in the sequel. Of these 5 are specially mentioned, of whom four surround the Throne of God: Michael, Gabriel, Rephael, and Uriel. But the greatest of all is Metatron, who is under the Throne, and before it. These Angels are privileged to be within the *Pargod*, or cloudy veil, while the others only hear the Divine commands or counsels outside this curtain (Chag. 16 a, Pirqé d. R. El. iv.). It is a slight variation when the Targum Pseudo-Jonathan on Deut. xxxiv. 6 enumerates the following as the 6 principal Angels: Michael, Gabriel, Metatron, Yophiel, Uriel, and Yophyophyah. The Book of Enoch (ch. xx.) speaks also of 6 principal Angels, while Pirqé d. R. Eliez. iv. mentions seven. In that very curious passage (Berakhoth 51 a) we read of three directions given by Suriel, Prince of the Face, to preserve the Rabbis from the Techaspith (company of Evil Angels), or, according to others, from Istalganith (another company of Evil Angels). In Chag. 13 b we read of an Angel called Sandalpon, who stands upon the earth, while his head reaches 500 years' way beyond the living creatures. He is supposed to stand behind the Merkabah (the throne-chariot), and make crowns for the Creator, which rise of their own accord. We also read of Sagsagel, who taught Moses the sacred Name of God, and was present at his death. But, confining ourselves to the five principal Angel-chiefs, we have,

a. *Metatron,*[1] who appears most closely to correspond to the Angel of the Face, or the Logos. He is the representative of God. In the Talmud (Sanh. 38 b) a Christian is introduced as clumsily starting a controversy on this point, that, according to the Jewish contention, Exod. xxiv. 1 should have read, ' Come up to Me.' On this R. Idith explained that the expression referred to the Metatron (Exod. xxxiii. 21), but denied the inference that Metatron was either to be adored, or had power to forgive sins, or that he was to be regarded as a Mediator. In continuation of this controversy we are told (Chag. 15 a, b) that, when an apostate Rabbi had seen Metatron sitting in heaven, and would have inferred from it that there were two supreme powers, Metatron received from another Angel 60 fiery stripes so as to prove his inferiority ! In Targ. Ps.-Jon. on Gen. v. 24 he is called the Great Scribe, and also the Prince of this world. He is also designated as ' the Youth,' and in the Kabbalah as ' the Little God,' who had 7 names like the Almighty, and shared His Majesty. He is also called the ' Prince of the Face,' and described as the Angel who sits in the innermost chamber (Chag. 5 b), while the other Angels hear their commands outside the Veil (Chag. 16 a). He is represented as showing the unseen to Moses (Siphré, p. 141 a), and as instructing infants who have died without receiving knowledge (Abhod. Zar. 3 b). In the Introduction to the Midrash on Lamentations there is a revolting story in which Metatron is represented as proposing to shed tears in order that God might not have to weep over the destruction of Jerusalem, to which, however, the Almighty is made to refuse His assent. We hesitate to quote further from the passage. In Siphré on Deut. (ed. *Friedm.* p. 141 a) Metatron is said to have shown Moses the whole of Palestine. He is also said to have gone before Israel in the wilderness

---

[1] On the controversy on the meaning of the name Metatron, whether it means under the throne, or behind the throne, or is the same as Metator, divider, arranger, representative, we will not enter.

b. Michael ('who is like God?'), or the Great Prince (Chag. 12 *b*). He stands at the right hand of the throne of God. According to Targ. Ps.-Jon. on Exod. xxiv. 1, he is the Prince of Wisdom. According to the Targum on Ps. cxxxvii. 7, 8, the Prince of Jerusalem, the representative of Israel. According to Sebach. 62 *a* he offers upon the heavenly Altar; according to some, the souls of the pious; according to others, lambs of fire. But, although Michael is the Prince of Israel, he is not to be invoked by them (Jer. Ber. ix. 13 *a*). In Yoma 77 *a* we have an instance of his ineffectual advocacy for Israel before the destruction of Jerusalem. The origin of his name as connected with the Song of Moses at the Red Sea is explained in Bemidb. R. 2. Many instances of his activity are related. Thus, he delivered Abraham from the fiery oven of Nimrod, and afterwards, also, the Three Children out of the fiery furnace. He was the principal or middle Angel of the three who came to announce to Abraham the birth of Isaac, Gabriel being at his right, and Rephael at his left. Michael also saved Lot. Michael and Gabriel wrote down that the primogeniture belonged to Jacob, and God confirmed it. Michael and Gabriel acted as 'friends of the bridegroom' in the nuptials of Adam. Yet they could not bear to look upon the glory of Moses. Michael is also supposed to have been the Angel in the bush (according to others, Gabriel). At the death of Moses, Michael prepared his bier, Gabriel spread a cloth over the head of Moses, and Sagsagel over his feet. In the world to come Michael would pronounce the blessing over the fruits of Eden, then hand them to Gabriel, who would give them to the patriarchs, and so on to David. The superiority of Michael over Gabriel is asserted in Ber. 4 *b*, where, by an ingenious combination with Dan. x. 13, it is shown that Is. vi. 6 applies to him (both having the word אחד, one). It is added that Michael flies in one flight, Gabriel in two, Elijah in four, and the Angel of Death in eight flights (no doubt to give time for repentance).

c. Gabriel ('the Hero of God') represents rather judgment, while Michael represents mercy. Thus he destroyed Sodom (Bab. Mez. 86 *b*, and other places). He restored to Tamar the pledges of Judah, which Sammael had taken away (Sot. 10 *b*). He struck the servants of the Egyptian princess, who would have kept their mistress from taking Moses out of the water (Sot. 12 *b*); also Moses, that he might cry and so awaken pity. According to some, it was he who delivered the Three Children; but all are agreed that he killed the men that were standing outside the furnace. He also smote the army of Sennacherib. The passage in Ezek. x. 2, 7 was applied to Gabriel, who had received from the Cherub two coals, which, however, he retained for six years, in the hope that Israel might repent.[a] He is supposed to be referred to in Ezek. ix. 4 as affixing the mark on the forehead which is a ת, drawn, in the case of the wicked, in blood (Shabb. 55 *a*). We are also told that he had instructed Moses about making the Candlestick, on which occasion he had put on an apron, like a goldsmith; and that he had disputed with Michael about the meaning of a word. To his activity the bringing of fruits to maturity is ascribed—perhaps because he was regarded as made of fire, while Michael was made of snow (Deb. R. 5). These Angels are supposed to stand beside each other, without the fire of the one injuring the snow of the other. The curious legend is connected with him (Shabb. 56 *b*, Sanh. 21 *b*), that, when Solomon married the daughter of Pharaoh, Gabriel descended into the sea, and fixed a reed in it, around which a mudbank gathered, on which a forest sprang up. On this site imperial Rome was built. The meaning of the legend—or perhaps rather allegory—seems (as explained in other parts of this book) that, when Israel began to decline from God, the punishment through its enemies was prepared, which

[a] Gabriel was also designated *Itmon*, because he stops up the sins of Israel (Sanh. 45 *b*)

culminated in the dominion of Rome. In the future age Gabriel would hunt and slay Leviathan. This also may be a parabolic representation of the destruction of Israel's enemies.

d. Of *Uriel* ('God is my light') and *Rephael* ('God heals') it need only be said, that the one stands at the left side of the Throne of glory, the other behind it.[1]

3. *The Ministering Angels and their Ministry.* The ministry of the Angels may be divided into two parts, that of praising God, and that of executing His behests. In regard to the former, there are 694,000 myriads who daily praise the Name of God. From sunrise to sundown they say: Holy, holy, holy, and from sundown to sunrise: Blessed be the Glory of God from its place. In connection with this we may mention the beautiful allegory (Shem. R. 21) that the Angel of prayer weaves crowns for God out of the prayers of Israel. As to the execution of the Divine commands by the Angels, it is suggested (Aboth d. R. Nathan 8) that their general designation as ministering Angels might have led to jealousy among them. Accordingly, their names were always a composition of that of God with the special commission entrusted to them (Shem. R. 29), so that the name of each Angel depended on his message, and might vary with it (Ber. R. 78). This is beautifully explained in Yalkut (vol. ii. Par. 797), where we are told that each Angel has a tablet on his heart, in which the Name of God and that of the Angel is combined. This change of names explained the answer of the Angel to Manoah (Bemidb. R. 10). It is impossible to enumerate all the instances of Angelic activity recorded in Talmudic writings. Angels had performed the music at the first sacrifice of Adam; they had announced the consequences of his punishment; they had cut off the hands and feet of the serpent; they had appeared to Abraham in the form of a baker, a sailor, and an Arab. 120,000 of them had danced before Jacob when he left Laban; 4,000 myriads of them were ready to fight for him against Esau; 22,000 of them descended on Sinai and stood beside Israel when, in their terror at the Voice of God, they fled for twelve miles. Angels were directed to close the gates of heaven when the prayer of Moses with the All-powerful, Ineffable Name in it, which he had learnt from Sagsagel, would have prevented his death. Finally, as they were pledged to help Israel, so would they also punish every apostate Israelite. Especially would they execute that most terrible punishment of throwing souls to each other from one world to another. By the side of these debasing superstitions we come upon beautiful allegories, such as that a good and an evil Angel always accompanied man, but especially on the eve of the Sabbath when he returned from the Synagogue, and that for every precept he observed God sent him a protecting Angel. This idea is realistically developed in Pirké d. R. El. 15, where the various modes and times in which the good Angels keep man from destruction are set forth.

It is quite in accordance with what we know of the system of Rabbinism, that the heavenly host should be represented as forming a sort of consultative Sanhedrin. Since God never did anything without first taking counsel with the family above (Sanh. 38 *b*),[2] it had been so when He resolved to create man. Afterwards the Angels had interceded for Adam, and, when God pointed to his disobedience, they had urged that thus death would also come upon Moses and Aaron, who were sinless, since one fate must come to the just and the unjust. Similarly,

---

[1] The names of the four Angel-Princes— Michael, Gabriel, Uriel, and Raphael—are explained in Bemid. R. 2.

[2] According to Jer. Ber. ix. 7 (p. 14 *b*), God only takes counsel with His Sanhedrin

when He takes away, not when He giveth (Job i. 21)—and it is argued that, wherever the expression 'and Jehovah' occurs, as in the last clause of 1 Kings xxii. 23, it means God and His Sanhedrin.

they had interceded for Isaac, when Abraham was about to offer him, and finally dropped three tears on the sacrificial knife, by which its edge became blunted. And so through the rest of Israel's history, where on all critical occasions Jewish legend introduces the Angels on the scene.

4. *Limitation of the power of the Angels.* According to Jewish ideas, the faculties, the powers, and even the knowledge of Angels were limited. They are, indeed, pure spiritual beings (Vayyikra R. 24), without sensuous requirements (Yoma 75 *b*), without hatred, envy, or jealousy (Chag. 14), and without sin (Pirqé d. R. El. 46). They know much, notably the future (Ab. d. R. Nath. 37), and have part in the Divine Light. They live on the beams of the Divine Glory (Bem. R. 21), are not subject to our limitations as to movement, see but are not seen (Ab. d. R. Nath. u. s.), can turn their face to any side (Ab. d. R. Nath. 37), and only appear to share in our ways, such as in eating (Ber. R. 48). Still, in many respects they are inferior to Israel, and had been employed in ministry (Ber. R. 75). They were unable to give names to the animals, which Adam did (Pirqé d. R. El. 13). Jacob had wrestled with the Angel and prevailed over him when the Angel wept (Chull. 92 *a*). Thus it was rather their nature than their powers or dignity which distinguished them from man. No Angel could do two messages at the same time (Ber. R. 50). In general they are merely instruments blindly to do a certain work, not even beholding the Throne of Glory (Bemidb. R. 14), but needed mutual assistance (Vayyikra R. 31). They are also liable to punishments (Chag. 16 *a*). Thus, they were banished from their station for 138 years, because they had told Lot that God would destroy Sodom, while the Angel-Princes of the Gentiles were kept in chains till the days of Jeremiah. As regards their limited knowledge, with the exception of Gabriel, they do not understand Chaldee or Syriac (Sot. 33 *a*). The realistic application of their supposed ignorance on this score need not here be repeated (see Shabb. 12 *b*). As the Angels are inferior to the righteous, it follows that they are so to Israel. God had informed the Angels that the creation of man was superior to theirs, and it had excited their envy. Adam attained a place much nearer to God than they, and God loved Israel more than the Angels. And God had left all the ministering Angels in order to come to Moses, and when He communicated with him it was directly, and the Angels standing between them did not hear what passed. In connection with this ministry of the Angels on behalf of Biblical heroes a curious legend may here find its place. From a combination of Ex. xviii. 4 with Ex. ii. 15 the strange inference was made that Moses had actually been seized by Pharaoh. Two different accounts of how he escaped from his power are given. According to the one, the sword with which he was to be executed rebounded from the neck of Moses, and was broken, to which Cant. vii. 5 was supposed to refer, it being added that the rebound killed the would-be executioner. According to another account, an Angel took the place of Moses, and thus enabled him to fly, his flight being facilitated by the circumstance that all the attendants of the king were miraculously rendered either dumb, deaf, or blind, so that they could not execute the behests of their master. Of this miraculous interposition Moses is supposed to have been reminded in Ex. iv. 11, for his encouragement in undertaking his mission to Pharaoh. In the exaggeration of Jewish boastfulness in the Law, it was said that the Angels had wished to receive the Law, but that they had not been granted this privilege (Job xxviii. 21). And sixty myriads of Angels had crowned with two crowns every Israelite who at Mount Sinai had taken upon himself the Law (Shabb. 88 *a*). In view of all

APP.
XIII

this we need scarcely mention the Rabbinic prohibition to address to the Angels prayers, even although they bore them to heaven (Jer. Ber. ix. 1), or to make pictorial representations of them (Targ. Ps.-Jon. on Ex. xx. 23 ; Mechilta on the passage, ed. *Weiss*, p. 80 *a*).

5. *The Angels are not absolutely good.* Strange as it may seem, this is really the view expressed by the Rabbis. Thus it is said that, when God consulted the Angels, they opposed the creation of man, and that, for this reason, God had concealed from them that man would sin. But more than this—the Angels had actually conspired for the fall of man (the whole of this is also related in Pirqé d. R. El. 13). Nor had their jealousy and envy been confined to that occasion. They had accused Abraham, that, when he gave a great feast at the weaning of Isaac, he did not even offer to God a bullock or a goat. Similarly, they had laid charges against Ishmael, in the hope that he might be left to perish of thirst. They had expostulated with Jacob, because he went to sleep at Bethel. But especially had they, from envy, opposed Moses' ascension into heaven; they had objected to his being allowed to write down the Law, falsely urging that Moses would claim the glory of it for himself, and they are represented, in a strangely blasphemous manner, as having been with difficulty appeased by God. In Shabb. 88 *b* we have an account of how Moses pacified the Angels, by showing that the Law was not suitable for them, since they were not subject to sinful desires, upon which they became the friends of Moses, and each taught him some secret, among others the Angel of death how to arrest the pestilence. Again, it is said, that the Angels were wont to bring charges against Israel, and that, when Manasseh wished to repent, the Angels shut the entrance to heaven, so that his prayer might not penetrate into the presence of God.

Equally profane, though in another direction, is the notion that Angels might be employed for magical purposes. This had happened at the siege of Jerusalem under Nebuchadnezzar, when, after the death of that mighty hero Abika, the son of Gaphteri, Chananeel, the uncle of Jeremiah, had conjured up ministering Angels, who affrighted the Chaldees into flight. On this God had changed their names, when Chananeel, unable any longer to command their services, had summoned up the Prince of the World by using the Ineffable Name, and lifted Jerusalem into the air, but God had trodden it down again, to all which Lam. ii. 1 referred (Yalk. vol. ii. p. 166 *c* and *d*, Par. 1001). The same story is repeated in another place (p. 167, last line of col. *c*, and col. *d*), with the addition that the leading inhabitants of Jerusalem had proposed to defend the city by conjuring up the Angels of Water and Fire, and surrounding their city with walls of water, of fire, or of iron ; but their hopes were disappointed when God assigned to the Angels names different from those which they had previously possessed, so that when called upon they were unable to do what was expected of them.

6. *The Names of the Angels.* Besides those already enumerated, we may here mention,[1] the *Sar ha-Olam*, or 'Prince of the World' (Yeb. 16 *b*) ; the *Prince of the Sea*, whose name is supposed to have been *Rahab*, and whom God destroyed because he had refused to receive the waters which had covered the world, and the smell of whose dead body would kill every one if it were not covered by water. *Dumah* is the Angel of the realm of the dead (Ber. 18 *b*). When the soul of the righteous leaves the body, the ministering Angels announce it before God, Who deputes them to meet it. Three hosts of Angels then proceed on this errand,

---

[1] *Akhtariel*—perhaps ' the crown of God'—seems to be a name given to the Deity (Ber. 7 *a*).

each quoting successively one clause of Is. lvii. 2. On the other hand, when the wicked leave the body, they are met by three hosts of destroying Angels, one of which repeats Is. xlviii. 22, another Is. l. 11, and the third Ezek. xxxii. 19 (Keth. 104 *a*). Then the souls of all the dead, good or bad, are handed over to Dumah. *Yorqemi* is the Prince of hail. He had proposed to cool the fiery furnace into which the Three Children were cast, but Gabriel had objected that this might seem a deliverance by natural means, and being himself the Prince of the fire, had proposed, instead of this, to make the furnace cold within and hot without, in order both to deliver the Three Children and to destroy those who watched outside (Pes. 118 *a* and *b*).[1] *Ridya*, or *Radya* is the Angel of rain. One of the Rabbis professed to describe him from actual vision as like a calf whose lips were open, standing between the Upper and the Lower Deep, and saying to the Upper Deep, Let your waters run down, and to the Lower, Let your waters spring up. The representation of this Angel as a calf may be due to the connection between rain and ploughing, and in connection with this it may be noticed that Ridya means both a plough and ploughing (Taan. 25 *b*). Of other Angels we will only name the *Ruach Pisqonith*, or Spirit of decision, who is supposed to have made most daring objection to what God had said, Ezek. xvi. 3, in which he is defended by the Rabbis, since his activity had been on behalf of Israel (Sanh. 44 *b*); *Naqid*, the Angel of Food; *Nabhel*, the Angel of Poverty; the two *Angels of Healing*; the *Angel of Dreams*, *Lailah*; and even the *Angel of Lust*.[a]

It is, of course, not asserted that all these grossly materialistic superstitions and profane views were entertained in Palestine, or at the time of our Lord, still less that they are shared by educated Jews in the West. But they certainly date from Talmudic times; they embody the only teaching of Rabbinic writings about the Angels which we possess, and hence, whencesoever introduced, or however developed, their roots must be traced back to far earlier times than those when they were propounded in Rabbinic Academies. All the more that modern Judaism would indignantly repudiate them, do they bear testimony against Rabbinic teaching. And one thing at least must be evident, for the sake of which we have undertaken the task of recording at such length views and statements repugnant to all reverent feeling. The contention of certain modern writers that the teaching about Angels in the New Testament is derived from, and represents Jewish notions, must be perceived to be absolutely groundless and contrary to fact. In truth, the teaching of the New Testament on the subject of Angels represents, as compared with that of the Rabbis, not only a return to the purity of Old Testament teaching, but, we might almost say, a new revelation.

II. SATANOLOGY AND FALL OF THE ANGELS.

The difference between the Satanology of the Rabbis and of the New Testament is, if possible, even more marked than that in their Angelology. In general we note that, with the exception of the word *Satan*, none of the names given to the great enemy in the New Testament occurs in Rabbinic writings. More important still, the latter *contain no mention of a Kingdom of Satan*. In other words, the power of evil is not contrasted with that of good, nor Satan with God. The

APP.
XIII

[a] See also the names of the five angels of destruction of whom Moses was afraid on his descent from the Mount. Against three of the three Patriarchs were to fight, God Himself being asked, or else proposing, to combat along with Moses against the other two (Shem. R. 41; 44)

---

[1] It is said that Gabriel had proposed in this manner to deliver Abraham when in similar danger at the hands of Nimrod. And, although God had by His own Hand delivered the patriarch, yet Gabriel had obtained this as the reward of his proposal, that he was allowed to deliver the Three Children from the fiery furnace.

devil is presented rather as the enemy of man, than of God and of good. This marks a fundamental difference. The New Testament sets before us two opposing kingdoms, or principles, which exercise absolute sway over man. Christ is 'the Stronger one' who overcometh 'the strong man armed,' and taketh from him not only his spoils, but his armour (St. Luke xi. 21, 22). It is a *moral contest* in which Satan is vanquished, and the liberation of his subjects is the consequence of his own subdual. This implies the deliverance of man from the power of the enemy, not only externally but internally, and the substitution of a new principle of spiritual life for the old one. It introduces a moral element, both as the ground and as the result of the contest. From this point of view the difference between the New Testament and Rabbinism cannot be too much emphasised, and it is no exaggeration to say that this alone—the question here being one of principle not of details—would mark the doctrine of Christ as fundamentally divergent from, and incomparably superior to, that of Rabbinism. 'Whence hath this Man this wisdom?' Assuredly, it may be answered, not from His contemporaries.

Since Rabbinism viewed the 'great enemy' only as the envious and malicious opponent of man, the spiritual element was entirely eliminated.[1] Instead of the personified principle of Evil, to which there is response in us, and of which all have some experience, we have only a clumsy and—to speak plainly—often a stupid hater. This holds equally true in regard to the threefold aspect under which Rabbinism presents the devil: as *Satan* (also called *Sammael*); as the *Yetser haRa*, or evil impulse personified; and as the *Angel of Death*—in other words, as the Accuser, Tempter, and Punisher. Before explaining the Rabbinic views on each of these points, it is necessary to indicate them in regard to—

1. *The Fall of Satan and of his Angels.* This took place, not antecedently, but *subsequently to the creation of man.* As related in Pirqé de R. Eliezer, ch. 13, the primary cause of it was jealousy and envy on the part of the Angels.[2] Their opposition to man's creation is also described in Ber. R. 8, although there the fall of man is not traced to Satanic agency. But we have (as before stated) a somewhat blasphemous account of the discussions in the heavenly Sanhedrin, whether or not man should be created. While the dispute was still proceeding God actually created man, and then addressed the ministering Angels: 'Why dispute any longer? Man is already created.' In the Pirqé de R. Eliezer, we are only told that the Angels had in vain attempted to oppose the creation of man. The circumstance that his superiority was evidenced by his ability to give names to all creatures, induced them to 'lay a plot against Adam,' so that by his fall they might obtain supremacy. Now of all Angel-Princes in heaven Sammael was the first—distinguished above

[1] An analogous remark would apply to Jewish teaching about the good angels, who are rather Jewish elves than the high spiritual beings of the Bible.

[2] As a curious illustration how extremes meet, we subjoin the following from *Jonathan Edwards.* After describing how 'Satan, before his fall, was the chief of all the angels . . . nay, . . . the Messiah or Christ (!), as he was the Anointed, so that in this respect, Jesus Christ is exalted unto his place in heaven'; and that 'Lucifer or Satan, while a holy angel . . . was a type of Christ,' the great American divine explains his fall as follows: 'But when it was revealed to him, high and glorious as he was, that he must be a ministering spirit to the race of mankind which he had seen newly created, which appeared so feeble, mean, and despicable, so vastly inferior not only to him, the prince of the angels, and head of the created universe, but also to the inferior angels, and that he must be subject to one of that race which should hereafter be born, he could not bear it. This occasioned his fall' (Tractate on 'The Fall of the Angels,' Works, vol. ii. pp. 608, 609, 610). Could *Jonathan Edwards* have heard of the Rabbinic legends, or is this only a strange coincidence? The curious reader will find much quaint information, though, I fear, little help, in Prof. *W. Scott's* vol. 'The Existence of Evil Spirits,' London, 1843.

Taking the company of Angels subject to him, he came down upon earth, and selected as the only fit instrument for his designs the serpent, which at that time had not only speech, but hands and feet, and was in stature and appearance like the camel. In the language of the Pirqé de R. Eliezer, Sammael took complete possession of the serpent, even as demoniacs act under the absolute control of evil spirits. Then Sammael, in the serpent, first deceived the woman, and next imposed on her by *touching* the tree of life (although the tree cried out), saying, that he had actually ·touched' the tree, of which he pretended the touch had been forbidden on pain of death (Gen. iii. 3)[1]—and yet he had not died! Upon this Eve followed his example, and touched the tree when she immediately saw the Angel of Death coming against her. Afraid that she would die and God give another wife to Adam, she led her husband into the sin of disobedience. The story of the Fall is somewhat differently related in Ber. R. 18, 19. No mention is there made either of Sammael or of his agency, and the serpent is represented as beguiling Eve from a wish to marry her, and for that purpose to compass the death of Adam.

Critical ingenuity may attempt to find a symbolic meaning in many of the details of the Jewish legend of the Fall, although, to use moderate language, they seem equally profane and repulsive. But this will surely be admitted by all, that the Rabbinic account of the fall of the Angels, as connected with the fall of man, equally contrasts with the reverent reticence of the Old Testament narrative and the sublime teaching of the New Testament about sin and evil.

2. *Satan, or Sammael, as the accuser of man.* And clumsy, indeed, are his accusations. Thus the statement (Gen. xxii. 1) that 'God tempted Abraham' is, in Jewish legend, transformed (Sanh. 89 *b*) into a scene, where, in the great upper Sanhedrin (Ber. R. 56), Satan brings accusation against the Patriarch.[2] All his previous piety had been merely interested; and now when, at the age of one hundred, God had given him a son, he had made a great feast and not offered aught to the Almighty. On this God is represented as answering, that Abraham was ready to sacrifice not only an animal but his own son; and this had been the occasion of the temptation of Abraham. That this legend is very ancient, indeed, *pre-Christian* (a circumstance of considerable importance to the student of this history) appears from its occurrence, though in more general form, in the Book of Jubilees, ch. xvii. In Ber. R. 55 and in Tanchuma (ed. Warsh. p. 29 *a* and *b*), the legend is connected with a dispute between Isaac and Ishmael as to their respective merits, when the former declares himself ready to offer up even his life unto God. In Tanchuma (u. s.) we are told that this was one of the great merits of man, to which the Almighty had pointed when the Angels made objection to his creation.

3. *Satan, or Sammael, as the seducer of man.* The statement in Baba B. 16 *a* which identifies *Satan* with the *Yetser haRa*, or evil impulse in man, must be regarded as a rationalistic attempt to gloss over the older teaching about Sammael, by representing him as a personification of the evil inclination within us. For, the Talmud not only distinguishes between a personal Satan without, and evil inclination within man, but expressly ascribes to God the creation of the *Yetser haRa* in man as he was *before the Fall*, the occurrence of two ' ' in the word וייצר ('and He formed,' Gen. ii. 7) being supposed to indicate the existence of two impulses in

---

[1] The Rabbis point out, how Eve had *added* to the words of God. He had only commanded them not to *eat* of the tree, while Eve added to it, that they were not to *touch* it. Thus adding to the words of God had led to

the first sin, with all the terrible consequences connected with it.

[2] In Ber. R. 56 the accusation is stated to have been brought by the ministering angels

us—the *Yetser Tobh* and the *Yetser haRa* (Ber. 61 *a*). And it is stated that this existence of evil in man's original nature was of infinite comfort in the fear which would otherwise beset us in trouble (Ber. R. 14). More than this (as will presently be shown), the existence of this evil principle within us was declared to be absolutely necessary for the continuance of the world (Yoma 69 *b*, Sanh. 64 *a*).

Satan, or Sammael, is introduced as the seducer of man in all the great events of Israel's history. With varying legendary additions the story of Satan's attempts to prevent the obedience of Abraham and the sacrifice of Isaac is told in Sanh. 89 *b*, Ber. R. 56, and Tanchuma, p. 30 *a* and *b*. Yet there is nothing even astute, only a coarse realism, about the description of the clumsy attempts of Satan to turn Abraham from, or to hinder him in, his purpose; to influence Isaac; or to frighten Sarah. Nor are the other personages in the legend more successfully sketched. There is a want of all higher conception in the references to the Almighty, a painful amount of downright untruthfulness about Abraham, lamentable boastfulness and petty spite about Isaac, while the Sarah of the Jewish legend is rather a weak old Eastern woman than the mother in Israel. To hold such perversions of the Old Testament by the side of the New Testament conception of the motives and lives of the heroes of old, or the doctrinal inferences and teaching of the Rabbis by those of Christ and His Apostles, were to compare darkness with light.

The same remarks apply to the other legends in which Satan is introduced as seducer. Anything more childish could scarcely be invented than this, that, when Sammael could not otherwise persuade Israel that Moses would not return from Mount Sinai, he at last made his bier appear before them in the clouds (Shab. 89 *a*), unless it be this story, that when Satan would seduce David he assumed the form of a bird, and that, when David shot at it, Bath-Sheba suddenly looked up, thus gaining the king by her beauty (Sanh. 107 *a*). In both these instances the obvious purpose is to palliate the guilt whether of Israel or of David, which, indeed, is in other places entirely explained away as not due to disobedience or to lust (comp. Ab. Zar. 4 *b*, 5 *a*).

4. *As the Enemy of man, Satan seeks to hurt and destroy him; and he is the Angel of Death.* Thus, when Satan had failed in shaking the constancy of Abraham and Isaac, he attacked Sarah (Yalkut, i. Par. 98, last lines p. 28 *b*). To his suggestions, or rather false reports, her death had been due, either from fright at being told that Isaac had been offered (Pirqé de R. El. 32, and Targum Ps.-Jon.), or else from the shock, when after all she learned that Isaac was not dead (Ber. R. 58). Similarly, Satan had sought to take from Tamar the pledges which Judah had given her. He appeared as an old man to show Nimrod how to have Abraham cast into the fiery oven, at the same time persuading Abraham not to resist it, &c. Equally puerile are the representations of Satan as the Angel of Death. According to Abod. Zar. 20 *b*, the dying sees his enemy with a drawn sword, on the point of which a drop of gall trembles. In his fright he opens his mouth and swallows this drop, which accounts for the pallor of the face and the corruption that follows. According to another Rabbi, the Angel of Death really uses his sword, although, on account of the dignity of humanity, the wound which he inflicts is not allowed to be visible. It is difficult to imagine a narrative more repulsive than that of the death of Moses according to Deb. R. 11. Beginning with the triumph of Sammael over Michael at the expected event, it tells how Moses had entreated rather to be changed into a beast or a bird than to die; how Gabriel

and Michael had successively refused to bring the soul of Moses; how Moses, knowing that Sammael was coming for the purpose, had armed himself with the Ineffable Name; how Moses had in boastfulness recounted to Sammael all his achievements, real and legendary; and how at last Moses had pursued the Enemy with the Ineffable Name, and in his anger taken off one of his horns of glory and blinded Satan in one eye. We must be excused from further following this story through its revolting details.

But, whether as the Angel of Death or as the seducer of man, Sammael has not absolute power. When Israel took the Law upon themselves at Mount Sinai, they became entirely free from his sway, and would have remained so, but for the sin of the Golden Calf. Similarly, in the time of Ezra, the object of Israel's prayer (Neh. viii. 6) was to have Satan delivered to them. After a three days' fast it was granted, and the Yetser haRa of idolatry, in the shape of a young lion, was delivered up to them. It would serve no good purpose to repeat the story of what was done with the bound enemy, or now his cries were rendered inaudible in heaven. Suffice it that, in view of the requirements of the present world, Israel liberated him from the ephah covered with lead (Zech. v. 8), under which, by advice of the prophet Zechariah, they had confined him, although for precaution they first put out his eyes (Yoma, 69 *b*). And yet, in view, or probably, rather, in ignorance, of such teaching, modern criticism would derive the Satanology of the New Testament and the history of the Temptation from Jewish sources!

Over these six persons—Abraham, Isaac, Jacob, Moses, Aaron, and Miriam, with whom some apparently rank Benjamin—the Angel of Death had no power (Baba B. 17 *a*). Benjamin, Amram, Jesse, and Chileb (the son of David) are said to have died (only) through 'the sin of the serpent.' In other cases, also, Sammael may not be able to exercise his sway till, for example, he has by some ruse diverted a theologian from his sacred study. Thus he interrupted the pious meditations of David by going up into a tree and shaking it, when, as David went to examine it, a rung of the ladder, on which he stood, broke, and so interrupted David's holy thoughts. Similarly, Rabbi Chasda, by occupation with sacred study, warded off the Angel of Death till the crackling of a beam diverted his attention. Instances of the awkwardness of the Enemy are related (Kethub. 77 *b*), and one Rabbi—Joshua—actually took away his sword, only returning it by direct command of God. Where such views of Satan could even find temporary expression, superstitious fears may have been excited; but the thought of moral evil and of a moral combat with it could never have found lodgment.

III. Evil Spirits (*Shedim, Ruchin, Ruchoth, Lilin*).

Here also, as throughout, we mark the presence of Parsee elements of superstition. In general, these spirits resemble the *gnomes, hobgoblins, elves,* and *sprites* of our fairy tales. They are cunning and malicious, and contact with them is dangerous; but they can scarcely be described as absolutely evil. Indeed, they often prove kind and useful; and may at all times be rendered innocuous, and even made serviceable.

1. *Their origin, nature, and numbers.* Opinions differ as to their origin, in fact, they variously originated. According to Ab. 12 *b*, Ber. R. 7, they were created on the eve of the first Sabbath. But since that time their numbers have greatly increased. For, according to Erub. 18 *b*. Ber. R. 20 (ed. Warsh. p. 40 *b*), multitudes of them were the offspring of Eve and of male spirits, and of Adam with female spirits,

or with Lilith (the queen of the female spirits), during the 130 years that Adam had been under the ban, and before Seth was born (Gen. v. 3):[1] comp. Erub. 18 b. Again, their number can scarcely be limited, since they propagate themselves (Chag. 16 a), resembling men in this as well as in their taking of nourishment and dying. On the other hand, like the Angels they have wings, pass unhindered through space, and know the future. Still further, they are produced by a process of transformation from vipers, which, in the course of four times seven years, successively pass through the forms of vampires, thistles and thorns, into Shedim (Bab. K. 16 a)—perhaps a parabolic form of indicating the origination of Shedim through the fall of man. Another parabolic idea may be implied in the saying that Shedim spring from the backbone of those who have not bent in worship (u. s.).

Although Shedim bear, when they appear, the form of human beings, they may assume any other form. Those of their number who are identified with dirty places are represented as themselves black (Kidd. 72 a). But the reflection of their likeness is not the same as that of man. When conjured up, their position (whether with the head or the feet uppermost) depends on the mode of conjuring. Some of the Shedim have defects. Thus, those of them who lodge in the caper bushes are blind, and an instance is related when one of their number, in pursuit of a Rabbi, fell over the root of a tree and perished (Pes. 111 b). Trees, gardens, vineyards, and also ruined and desolate houses, but especially dirty places, were their favourite habitation, and the night-time, or before cock-crowing, their special time of appearance.[2] Hence the danger of going alone into such places (Ber. 3 a, b; 62 a). A company of two escaped the danger, while before three the Shed did not even appear (Ber. 43 b). For the same reason it was dangerous to sleep alone in a house (Shabb. 151 b), while the man who went out before cock-crow, without at least carrying for protection a burning torch (though moonlight was far safer) had his blood on his own head. If you greeted anyone in the dark you might unawares bid Godspeed to a Shed (Sanh. 44 a). Nor was the danger of this inconsiderable, since one of the worst of these Shedim, especially hurtful to Rabbis, was like a dragon with seven heads, each of which dropped off with every successive lowly bending during Rabbi Acha's devotions (Kidd. 29 b). Specially dangerous times were the eves of Wednesday and of the Sabbath. But it was a comfort to know that the Shedim could not create or produce anything; nor had they power over that which had been counted, measured, tied up and sealed (Chull. 105 b); they could be conquered by the ' Ineffable Name;' and they might be banished by the use of certain formulas, which, when written and worn, served as amulets.

The number of these spirits was like the earth that is thrown up around a bed that is sown. Indeed, no one would survive it, if he saw their number. A thousand at your right hand and ten thousand at your left, such crowding in the Academy or by the side of a bride; such weariness and faintness through their malignant touch, which rent the very dress of the wearers! (Ber. 6 a.) The queen of the female spirits had no less a following than 180,000 (Pes. 112 b). Little as we imagine it, these spirits lurk everywhere around us: in the crumbs on

---

[1] From the expression 'a son in his own likeness,' &c., it is inferred that his previous offspring during the 138 years was not in his likeness.

[2] The following Haggadah will illustrate both the power of the evil spirits at night and how amenable they are to reasoning. A Rabbi was distributing his gifts to the poor at night when he was confronted by the Prince of the Ruchin with the quotation Deut. xix. 34 ('Thou shalt not remove thy neighbour's landmark'), which seemed to give the 'spirit' a warrant for attacking him. But when the Rabbi replied by quoting Prov. xxi. 14 ('a gift in secret appeaseth wrath'), the 'spirit' fled in confusion (Jer. Peah viii. 9, p. 21 b).

the floor, in the oil in the vessels, in the water which we would drink, in the diseases which attack us, in the even-numbered cups of our drinking, in the air, in the room, by day and by night.

2. *Their arrangement.* Generally, they may be arranged into *male* and *female* spirits, the former under their king *Ashmedai,* the latter under their queen *Lilith,* probably the same as *Agrath bath Machlath*—only that the latter may more fully present the hurtful aspect of the demoness. The hurtful spirits are specially designated as *Ruchin, Mazziqin* (harmers), *Malakhey Chabbalah* (angels of damage), &c. From another aspect they are arranged into *four* classes (Targ. Pseudo-Jon. Numb. vi. 24): the *Tsaphriré,* or morning spirits (Targ. on Ps. cxxi. 6; Targ. Cant. iv. 6); the *Tiharé,* or midday spirits (Targ. Pseudo-Jon. Deut. xxxii 24; Targ. Cant. iv. 6); the *Telané,* or evening spirits (Targ. Cant. iii. 8; iv. 6; Targ. Eccles. ii. 5); and the *Lilin,* or night spirits (Targ. Pseudo-Jon. on Deut. xxxii. 34; Targ. Is. xxxiv. 14). [According to 2 Targ. Esther ii. 1, 3, Solomon had such power over them, that at his bidding they executed dances before him.]

a. Ashmedai (perhaps a Parsee name), *Ashmodi, Ashmedon,* or *Shamdon,* the king of the demons (Gitt. 68 *a, b*; Pes. 110 *a*). It deserves notice, that this name does *not* occur in the Jerusalem Talmud nor in older Palestinian sources.[1] He is represented as of immense size and strength, as cunning, malignant, and dissolute. At times, however, he is known also to do works of kindness—such as to lead the blind, or to show the road to a drunken man. Of course, he foreknows the future, can do magic, but may be rendered serviceable by the use of the 'Ineffable Name,' and especially by the signet of King Solomon, on which it was graven. The story of Solomon's power over him is well known, and can here only be referred to in briefest outline. It is said, that as no iron was to be used in the construction of the Temple, Solomon was anxious to secure the services of the worm *Shamir,* which possessed the power of cutting stones (see abou him Ab. Z. 12 *a*; Sot. 48 *b*; Gitt. 68 *a, b*). By advice of the Sanhedrin, Solomon conjured up for this purpose a male and a female Shed, who directed him to Ashmedai. The latter lived at the bottom of a deep cistern on a high mountain. Every morning on leaving it to go into heaven and hear the decrees of the Upper Sanhedrin, he covered the cistern with a stone, and sealed it. On this Benayah, armed with a chain, and Solomon's signet with the Ineffable Name, went and filled the cistern with wine, which Ashmedai, as all other spirits, hated. But as he could not otherwise quench his thirst, Ashmedai became drunk, when it was easy, by means of the magical signet, to secure the chain around him. Without entering on the story of his exploits, or how he indicated the custody of Shamir, and how ultimately the worm (which was in the custody of the moor-cock[2]) was secured, it appears that, by his cunning, Ashmedai finally got released, when he immediately hurled Solomon to a great distance, assumed his form, and reigned in his stead; till at last, after a series of adventures, Solomon recovered his signet, which Ashmedai had flung away, and a fish swallowed. Solomon was recognised by the Sanhedrin and Ashmedai fled at sight of his signet. [Possibly the whole of this is only a parabolic form for the story of Solomon's spiritual declension, and final repentance.]

b. Lilith, the queen of female spirits—to be distinguished from the *Lilin* or

---

[1] *Hamburger* ascribes this to the anxiety of the Palestinians to guard Judaism from Gnostic elements. We are, however, willing to recognise in it an indirect influence of Christianity.

[2] The *Tarnegol Bera* — a mythical animal reaching from earth to heaven (Targ. on Ps. l. 11)—also called *Naggar Tura* (Gitt. 68 *b*) from his activity in cleaving mountains.

night-spirits, and from *Lela* or *Lailah*, an Angel who accompanied Abraham on his expedition against Chedorlaomer (Sanh. 96 *a*). Here we recognise still more distinctly the Parsee elements. Lilith is 'the queen of Zemargad' (Targ. on Job i. 15)—'Zemargad' representing all green crystals, malachite, and emerald—and the land of Zemargad being 'Sheba.' Lilith is described as the mother of Hormiz or Hormuz[1] (Baba B. 73 *a*). Sometimes she is represented as a very fair woman, but mostly with long, wild-flowing hair, and winged (Nidd. 24 *b*; Erub. 100 *b*). In Pes. 111 *a* we have a formula for exorcising Lilith. In Pes. 112 *b* (towards the end) we are told how Agrath bath Machlath (probably the Zend word Agra—'smiting, very wicked'—bath Machlath 'the dancer') threatened Rabbi Chanina with serious mischief, had it not been that his greatness had been 'proclaimed in heaven, on which the Rabbi would have shown his power by banning her from all inhabited places, but finally gave her liberty on the eve of the fourth day and of the Sabbath, which nights accordingly are the most dangerous seasons.

3. *Character and habits of the Shedim.* As many of the Angels, so many of the Shedim, are only personifications. Thus, as diseases were often ascribed to their agency, there were Shedim of certain diseases, as of asthma, croup, canine rabies, madness, stomachic diseases, &c. Again, there were local *Shedim*, as of Samaria, Tiberias, &c. On the other hand, Shedim might be employed in the magic cure of diseases (Shabb. 67 *a*). In fact, to conjure up and make use of demons was considered lawful, although dangerous (Sanh. 101 *a*), while a little knowledge of the subject would enable a person to avoid any danger from them. Thus, although Chamath, the demon of oil, brings eruptions on the face, yet the danger is avoided if the oil is used out of the hollow of the hand, and not out of a vessel. Similarly, there are formulas by which the power of the demons can be counteracted. In these formulas, where they are not Biblical verses, the names of the demons are inserted. This subject will be further treated in another Appendix.

In general, we may expect to find demons on water, oil, or anything else that has stood uncovered all night; on the hands before they have been washed for religious purposes, and on the water in which they have been washed; and on the breadcrumbs on the floor. Demons may imitate or perform all that the prophets or great men of old had wrought. The magicians of Egypt had imitated the miracles of Moses by demoniacal power (Shem. R. 9). So general at the time of our Lord was the belief in demons and in the power of employing them, that even *Josephus* (Ant. viii. 2, 5) contended that the power of conjuring up, and driving out demons, and of magical cures had been derived from King Hezekiah, to whom God had given it. *Josephus* declares himself to have been an eye-witness of such a wonderful cure by the repetition of a magical formula. This illustrates the contention of the Scribes that the miraculous cures of our Lord were due to demoniac agency.

Legions of demons lay in waiting for any error or failing on the part of man. Their power extended over all even numbers.[2] Hence, care must be had not to drink an even number of cups (Ber. 51 *b*), except on the Passover night, when the demons have no power over Israel (Pes. 109 *b*). On the other hand, there are demons who might almost be designated as familiar spirits, who taught the Rabbis,

---

[1] *Hamburger* renders it *Ahriman*, but it seems rather like *Hormuzd*. Perhaps the Rabbis wished to combine both. *Ahriman* is written *Ahurmin*, Sanh. 39 *a*, in that very curious notice of a controversy with a Mage.

[2] The superstition 'There's luck in odd numbers' has passed to all nations.

Shed Joseph (Pes. 110 *a*) and the Shed Jonathan (Yeb. 122 *a*). Rabbi Papa had a young Shed to wait upon him (Chull. 105 *b*). There can, however, be no difficulty in making sure of their real existence. As Shedim have cock's feet, nothing more is required than to strew ashes by the side of one's bed, when in the morning their marks will be perceived (Ber. 6 *a*; Gitt. 68 *b*). It was by the shape of his feet that the Sanhedrin hoped to recognise, whether Ashmedai was really Solomon, or not, but it was found that he never appeared with his feet uncovered. The Talmud (Ber. 6 *a*) describes the following as an infallible means for actually seeing these spirits: Take the afterbirth of a black cat which is the daughter of a black cat—both mother and daughter being firstborn—burn it in the fire, and put some of the ashes in your eyes. Before using them, the ashes must be put into an iron tube, and sealed with an iron signet. It is added, that Rabbi Bibi successfully tried this experiment, but was hurt by the demons, on which he was restored to health by the prayers of the Rabbis.[1]

Other and kindred questions, such as those of amulets, &c., will be treated under demoniac possessions. But may we not here once more and confidently appeal to impartial students whether, in view of this sketch of Jewish Angelology and Satanology, the contention can be sustained that the teaching of Christ on this subject has been derived from Jewish sources?

---

[1] Dr. *Kohut's* comparison of Rabbinic Angelology and Demonology with Parseeism (Ueber d. jüd. Angelol u. Dämonol. in ihrer Abhäng. vom Parsismus) is extremely interesting, although not complete and its conclusions sometimes strained. The negative arguments derived from Jewish Angelology and Satanology by the author of 'Supernatural Religion' are based on inaccurate and uncritical information, and do not require detailed discussion.

APPENDIX XIV.

THE LAW IN MESSIANIC TIMES.

(See vol. i. Book III. ch. iii. p. 341.)

APP.
XIV

THE question as to the Rabbinic views in regard to the binding character of the Law, and its imposition on the Gentiles, in Messianic times, although, strictly speaking, not forming part of this history, is of such vital importance in connection with recent controversies as to demand special consideration. In the text to which this Appendix refers it has been indicated, that a new legislation was expected in Messianic days. The ultimate basis of this expectancy must be sought in the Old Testament itself—not merely in such allusions as to the intrinsic worthlessness of sacrifices, but in such passages as Deut. xviii. 15, 18, and its prophetic commentary in Jer. xxxi. 31, &c. It was with a view to this that the Jewish deputation inquired whether John the Baptist was 'that Prophet.' For, as has been shown, Rabbinism associated certain reformatory and legislative functions with the appearance of the Forerunner of the Messiah (Eduy. viii. 7).

There were, indeed, in this, as in most respects, diverging opinions according to the different standpoints of the Rabbis, and, as we infer, not without controversial bearing on the teaching of Christianity. The strictest tendency may be characterised as that which denied the possibility of any change in the ceremonial Law, as well as the abrogation of festivals in the future. Even the destruction of the Temple, and with it the necessary cessation of sacrifices—if, indeed, which is a moot question, all sacrifices did at once and absolutely cease—only caused a gap; just as exile from the land could only free from such laws as attached to the soil of Israel.[1] The reading of the sacrificial sections in the Law (Meg. 31 b; Ber. R. 44)—at any rate, in conjunction with prayers (Ber. 2 b), but especially study of the Law (Men. 110 a), took in the meantime the place of the sacrifices. And as regarded the most sacred of all sacrifices, that of the Day of Atonement, it was explained that the day rather than the sacrifices brought reconciliation (Sifra c. 8). This party held the principle that not only those Divine, but even those Rabbinic, ordinances, which apparently had been intended only for a certain time or for a certain purpose, were of eternal duration (Bezah 5 b). 'The law is never to cease; there are the commandments—since there is no prophet who may change a word in them.'[2]

---

[1] In the Book *Cusari* (iii. 49, ed. *Cassel*, p. 274) an inference somewhat inconvenient to Rabbinism is drawn from this. If, as it asserts, Levitical uncleanness and holiness are correlative terms, the one implying the other, would it not follow that with the cessation of the Jewish economy the whole ceremonial Law would also cease? See *Cassel's* note.

[2] For further particulars I refer to *Stein*, Schrift des Lebens, i. pp. 319-336 (ch. on 'The Messiah'), to the article on the Messiah in *Hamburger's* Real-Encycl. ii. pp. 747, 748, and especially to that most interesting *brochure* of Rabbi *Holdheim*, Das Ceremonialges. im Messias-Reich. I have not read a more clear demonstration of the impossibility of Rabbinism, nor—strange as it may sound—a fuller vindication of the fundamental positions of Christianity.

So far were these views carried, that it was asserted: 'Israel needs not the teaching of the King Messiah,' but that 'He only comes to gather the dispersed, and to give to the Gentiles thirty commandments, as it is written (Zechar. xi. 12), "they weighed me my price, thirty pieces of silver"' (Ber. R. 98). But even these extreme statements seem to imply that keen controversy had raged on the subject. Besides, the most zealous defenders of the Law admitted that the Gentiles were to receive laws in Messianic times. The smallest and most extreme section held that, the laws, as Israel observed them, would be imposed on the Gentiles (*Chull.* 92 *a*); others that only thirty commandments, the original Noachic ordinances, supposed to be enumerated in Lev. xix., would become obligatory,[1] while some held, that only *three* ordinances would be binding on the new converts: two connected with the Feast of Tabernacles, the third, that of the phylacteries (Midr. on Ps. xxxi. 1, ed. Warsh., p. 30 *b*). On the other hand, we have the most clear testimony that the prevailing tendency of teaching was in a different direction. In a very curious passage (Yalkut ii. 296, p. 46 *a*), in which the final restitution of 'the sinners of Israel and of the righteous of the Gentiles' who are all in Gehinnom, is taught in very figurative language, we are told of a '*new* Law which God will give by the Messiah' in the age to come—thanksgiving for which calls forth that universal *Amen*, not only on earth but in Gehinnom, which leads to the deliverance of those who are in the latter. But as this may refer to the time of the final consummation, we turn to other passages. The Midrash on Song ii. 13, applying the passage in conjunction with Jer. xxxi. 31, expressly states that the Messiah would give Israel a new law, and the Targum, on Is. xii., 3, although perhaps not quite so clearly, also speaks of a 'new instruction.' It is needless to multiply proofs (such as Vayyikra R. 13). But the Talmud goes even further, and lays down the two principles, that in the 'age to come' the whole ceremonial Law and all the feasts were to cease.[2] And although this may be regarded as merely a general statement, it is definitely applied to the effect, that all sacrifices except the thank-offering, and all fasts and feasts except the Day of Atonement, or else the Feast of Esther, were to come to an end—nay (in the Midr. on the words 'the Lord looseth the bound,' Ps. cxlvi. 7), that what had formerly been 'bound' or forbidden would be 'loosed' or allowed, notably that the distinctions between clean and unclean animals would be removed.

There is the less need of apology for any digression here, that, besides the intrinsic interest of the question, it casts light on two most important subjects. For, first, it illustrates the attempt of the narrowest Judaic party in the Church to force on Gentile believers the yoke of the whole Law; the bearing of St. Paul in this respect; his relation to St. Peter; the conduct of the latter; and the proceedings of the Apostolic Synod in Jerusalem (Acts xv.). St. Paul, in his opposition to that party, stood even on Orthodox Jewish ground. But when he asserted, not only a new 'law of liberty,' but the typical and preparatory character of the whole Law, and its fulfilment in Christ, he went far beyond the Jewish standpoint. Further, the favourite modern theory as to fundamental opposition in principle between Pauline and Petrine theology in this respect, has, like many kindred theories, no support in the Jewish views on that subject, unless we suppose that Peter had belonged to the narrowest Jewish school, which his whole history seems to forbid. We can also understand, how the Divinely granted vision of the abrogation of the distinction between clean and unclean animals (Acts x. 9–16)

---

[1] *Stein,* u. s. pp. 327, 328.   [2] Comp. on this *Holdheim,* Das Ceremonialges, p. 46.

APP.
XIV

may, though coming as a surprise, have had a natural basis in Jewish expectancy,[1] and it explains how the Apostolic Synod, when settling the question,[2] ultimately fell back on the so-called Noachic commandments, though with very wider-reaching principles underlying their decision (Acts xv. 13–21). Lastly, it seems to cast even some light on the authorship of the Fourth Gospel; for, the question about 'that prophet' evidently referring to the possible alteration of the Law in Messianic times, which is reported only in the Fourth Gospel, shows such close acquaintance with the details of Jewish ideas on this subject, as seems to us utterly incompatible with its supposed origination as 'The Ephesian Gospel' towards the end of the second century, the outcome of Ephesian Church-teaching—an 'esoteric and eclectic' book, designed to modify 'the impressions produced by the tradition previously recorded by the Synoptists.'

[1] The learned reader will find a very curious illustration of this in that strange Haggadah about the envy of the serpent being excited on seeing Adam fed with meat from heaven—where another equally curious Haggadah is related to show that 'nothing is unclean which cometh down from heaven.'

[2] Yalkut i. 15, p. 4, d, towards the middle A considerable part of vol. iii. of 'Supernatural Religion' is devoted to argumentation on this subject. But here also the information of the writer on the subject is neither accurate nor critical, and hence his reasoning and conclusions are vitiated.

APPENDIX XV.

THE LOCATION OF SYCHAR, AND THE DATE OF OUR LORD'S VISIT TO SAMARIA.

(See vol. i. Book III. ch. viii.)

I. THE LOCATION OF SYCHAR.

ALTHOUGH modern writers are now mostly agreed on this subject, it may be well briefly to put before our readers the facts of the case.

Till comparatively lately, the Sychar of St. John iv. was generally regarded as representing the ancient Shechem. The first difficulty here was the *name*, since Shechem, or even Sichem, could scarcely be identified with Sychar, which is undoubtedly the correct reading. Accordingly, the latter term was represented as one of opprobrium, and derived from '*Shekhar*' (in Aramæan *Shikhra*), as it were, 'drunken town,' or else from '*Sheqer*' (in Aramæan *Shiqra*), 'lying town.' But, not to mention other objections, there is no trace of such an alteration of the name Sychar in Jewish writings, while its employment would seem wholly incongruous in such a narrative as St. John iv. Moreover, all the earliest writers distinguished Sychar from Shechem. Lastly, in the Talmud the name *Sokher*, also written *Sik.íra*, frequently occurs, and that not only as distinct from Shechem, but in a connection which renders the hypothesis of an opprobrious by-name impossible. Professor *Delitzch* (Zeitschrift für Luther. Theol. for 1856, ii. pp. 242, 243) has collected seven passages from the Babylon Talmud to that effect, in five of which Sichra is mentioned as the birthplace of celebrated Rabbis—the town having at a later period apparently been left by the Samaritans, and occupied by Jews (Baba Mez. 42 *a*, 83 *a*, Pes. 31 *b*, Nidd. 36 *a*, Chull. 18 *b*, and, without mention of Rabbis, Baba K. 82 *b*, Menach. 64 *b*. See also Men. x. 2, and Jer. Sheq. p. 48 *d*). If further proof were required, it would be sufficient to say that a woman would scarcely have gone a mile and a half from Shechem to Jacob's well to fetch water, when there are so many springs about the former city. In these circumstances, later writers have generally fixed upon the village of 'Askar, half a mile from Jacob's Well, and within sight of it, as the Sychar of the New Testament, one of the earliest to advocate this view having been the late learned Canon Williams. Little more than a third of a mile from 'Askar is the reputed tomb of Joseph. The transformation of the name Sychar into 'Askar is explained, either by a contraction of '*Ain 'Askar*, 'the well of Sychar,' or else by the fact that in the Samaritan Chronicle the place is called Iskar, which seems to have been the vulgar pronunciation of Sychar. A full description of the place is given by Captain Conder (Tent-Work in Palestine, vol. i. pp. 71 &c., especially pp. 75 and 76), and by M. Guérin, 'La Samarie,' vol. i. p. 371, although the latter writer, who almost always absolutely follows tradition, denies the identity of Sychar and 'Askar (pp. 401, 402).

II. Time of our Lord's Visit to Sychar.

This question, which is of such importance not only for the chronology of this period, but in regard to the unnamed Feast at Jerusalem to which Jesus went up (St. John v. 1), has been discussed most fully and satisfactorily by Canon Westcott (Speaker's Commentary, vol. ii. of the New Testament, p. 93). The following data will assist our inquiries.

1. Jesus spent some time after the Feast of Passover (St. John ii. 23) in the province of Judæa. But it can scarcely be supposed that this was a long period, for—

2ndly, in St. John iv. 45 the Galileans have evidently a fresh remembrance of what had taken place at the Passover in Jerusalem, which would scarcely have been the case if a long period and other festivals had intervened. Similarly, the 'King's Officer' (St. John iv. 47) seems also to act upon a recent report.

3rdly, the unnamed Feast of St. John v. 1 forms an important element in our computations. Some months of Galilean ministry must have intervened between it and the return of Jesus to Galilee. Hence it could not have been Pentecost. Nor could it have been the Feast of Tabernacles, which was in autumn, nor yet the Feast of the Dedication, which took place in winter, since both are expressly mentioned by their names (St. John vii. 2, x. 22). The only other Feasts were: the Feast of Wood-Offering (comp. 'The Temple,' &c., p. 295), the Feast of Trumpets, or New Year's Day, the Day of Atonement, and the Feast of Esther, or Purim.

To begin with the latter, since of late it has found most favour. The reasons against Christ's attendance in Jerusalem at Purim seem to me irresistible. Canon Westcott urges that the discourse of Christ at the unnamed Feast has not, as is generally the case, any connection with the thoughts of that festival. To this I would add, that I can scarcely conceive our Lord going up to a feast observed with such boisterous merriment as Purim was, while the season of the year in which it falls would scarcely tally with the statement of St. John v. 3, that a great multitude of sick people were laid down in the porches of Bethesda.[1]

But if the unnamed Feast was not Purim, it must have been one of these three, the Feast of the Ingathering of Wood, the Feast of Trumpets, or the Day of Atonement. In other words, it must have taken place late in summer, or in the very beginning of autumn. But if so, then the Galilean ministry intervening between the visit to Samaria and this Feast leads to the necessary inference that the visit to Sychar had taken place in early summer, probably about the middle or end of May. This would allow ample time for Christ's stay at Jerusalem during the Passover and for His Judæan ministry.

As we are discussing the date of the unnamed Feast, it may be as well to bring the subject here to a close. We have seen that the only three Feasts to which reference could have been made are the Feast of Wood Offering, the Feast of Trumpets, and the Day of Atonement. But the last of these could not be meant, since it is designated, not only by Philo, but in acts xxvii. 9, as 'the fast,' not the feast $\nu\eta\sigma\tau\epsilon\iota\alpha$, not $\dot{\epsilon}o\rho\tau\dot{\eta}$ (comp. LXX., Lev. xiv. 29 &c., xxiii. 27 &c.). As between the Feast of the Wood Offering and that of Trumpets I feel at considerable loss. Canon Westcott has urged on behalf of the latter reasons which I confess are very

---

[1] I must here correct the view expressed in my book on 'The Temple,' p. 291, due to a misunderstanding of St. John iv. 35. Of course, if the latter had implied that Jesus was at Sychar in December, the unnamed feast must have been *Purim*.

weighty. On the other hand, the Feast of Trumpets was not one of those on which people generally resorted to Jerusalem, and as it took place on the 1st of Tishri (about the middle of September), it is difficult to believe that anyone going up to it would not rather have chosen, or at least remained over, the Day of Atonement and the Feast of Tabernacles, which followed respectively, on the 10th and 15th days of that month. Lastly, the Feast of Wood Offering, which took place on the 15th Ab (in August), was a popular and joyous festival, when the wood needed for the altar was brought up from all parts of the country (comp. on that feast 'The Temple and its Services,' &c., pp. 295, 296). As between these two feasts, we must leave the question undecided, only noting that barely six weeks intervened between the one and the other feast.

APPENDIX XVI.

ON THE JEWISH VIEWS ABOUT ' DEMONS' AND ' THE DEMONISED,' TOGETHER WITH SOME NOTES ON THE INTERCOURSE BETWEEN JEWS AND JEWISH CHRISTIANS IN THE FIRST CENTURIES.

(See vol. i. Book III. ch. xiv.)

APP,
XVI

IT is not, of course, our purpose here to attempt an exhaustive account of the Jewish views on ' demons' and 'the demonised.' A few preliminary strictures are, however, necessary on a work upon which writers on this subject have too implicitly relied. I refer to *Gfrörer's* Jahrhundert des Heils (especially vol. i. pp. 378— 424). Gfrörer sets out by quoting a passage in the Book of Enoch on which he lays great stress, but which the critical inquiries of *Dillmann* and other scholars have shown to be of no value in the argument. This disposes of many pages of negative criticism on the New Testament which Gfrörer founds on this quotation. Similarly, 4 Esdras would not in our days be adduced in evidence of pre-Christian teaching. As regards Rabbinic passages, Gfrörer uncritically quotes from Kabbalistic works which he mixes up with quotations from the Talmud and from writings of a later date. Again, as regards the two quotations of Gfrörer from the Mishnah (Erub. iv. 1; Gitt. vii. 1), it has already been stated (vol. i. p. 481, note 4) that neither of these passages bears any reference to demoniac possessions. Further, Gfrörer appeals to two passages in Sifrè which may here be given *in extenso*. The first of these (ed. *Friedmann*, p. 107 *b*) is on Deut. xviii. 12, and reads thus: ' He who joins himself (cleaves) to uncleanness, on him rests the spirit of uncleanness; but he who cleaves to the Shechinah, it is meet that the Holy Spirit should rest on him.' The second occurs in explanation of Deut. xxxii. 16, and reads as follows (u. s. p. 136 *b*): 'What is the way of a "demon" (*Shed*)! He enters into a man and subjects him.' It will be observed that in both these quotations reference is made to certain moral, not to physical effects, such as in the case of the demonised. Lastly, although one passage from the Talmud which Gfrörer adduces (though not quite exactly) applies, indeed, to demoniacal possessions, but is given in an exaggerated and embellished form.

If from these incorrect references we turn to what Jewish authorities really state on the subject, we have:—

1. To deal with the *Writings of Josephus.* In Antiq. vi. 8. 2, *Josephus* ascribes Saul's disorder to demoniac influence, which 'brought upon him such suffocations as were ready to choke him.' In Antiq. vi. 8. 2, the demon-spirit is said to enter into Saul, and to disorder him. In Antiq. viii. 2. 5, *Josephus* describes the wisdom, learning, and achievements of Solomon, referring specially to his skill in expelling demons who caused various diseases. According to Josephus, Solomon had exercised this power by incantations, his formulæ and words of exorcism being still

known in Josephus's days. In such manner a certain Eleazar had healed a 'demoniac' in the presence of Vespasian, his officers, and troops, by putting to his nostrils a ring 'that held a root of one of those mentioned by Solomon,' by which the demon was drawn out amidst convulsions of the demoniac, when the demon was further adjured not to return by frequent mention of the name of Solomon, and by 'incantations which he [Solomon] had composed.' To show the reality of this, a vessel with water had been placed at a little distance, and the demon had, in coming out, overturned it. It is probably to this 'root' that Josephus refers in War. vii. 6. 3, where he names it *Baaras*, which I conjecture to be the equivalent of the form בּוֹעֲרָא, *boara*, 'the burning,' since he describes it as of colour like a flame, and as emitting at even a ray like lightning, and which it would cost a man's life to take up otherwise than by certain magical means which Josephus specifies. From all this we infer that Josephus occupied the later Talmudical standpoint, alike as regards exorcism, magical cures, and magical preventions. This is of great importance as showing that these views prevailed in New Testament times. But when Josephus adds, that the demons expelled by *Baaras* were 'the spirits of the wicked,' he represents a superstition which is *not* shared by the earlier Rabbis, and may possibly be due to a rationalising attempt to account for the phenomenon. It is, indeed, true that the same view occurs in comparatively late Jewish writings, and that in Yalkut on Is. 46 *b* there appears to be a reference to it, at least in connection with the spirits of those who had perished in the flood; but this seems to belong to a different cycle of legends.

2. *Rabbinic views*.[1] Probably the nearest approach to the idea of Josephus that 'demons' were the souls of the wicked, is the (perhaps allegorical) statement that the backbone of a person who did not bow down to worship God became a *Shed*, or demon (Baba K. 16 *a*; Jer. Shabb. 3 *b*). The ordinary names for demons are 'evil spirits,' or 'unclean spirits' (*ruach raah*,[2] *ruach tumeah*), *Seirim* (lit. goats). *Shedim* (*Sheyda*, a demon, male or female, either because their chief habitation is in desolate places, or from the word 'to fly about,' or else from 'to rebel'), and *Mazzikin* (the hurtful ones). A demoniac is called *Gebher Shediyin* (Ber. R. 65). Even this, that demons are supposed to eat and drink, to propagate themselves, and to die, distinguishes them from the 'demons' of the New Testament. The food of demons consists of certain elements in fire and water, and of certain odours. Hence the mode of incantation by incense made of certain ingredients. Of their origin, number, habitation, and general influence, sufficient has been said in the Appendix on Demonology. It is more important here to notice these two Jewish ideas: that demons entered into, or took possession of, men; and that many diseases were due to their agency. The former is frequently expressed. The 'evil spirit' constrains a man to do certain things, such as to pass beyond the Sabbath-boundary (Erub. 41 *b*), to eat the Passover-bread, &c. (Rosh ha-Sh. 28 *a*). But it reads more like a caustic than a serious remark when we are informed that these three things deprive a man of his free will and make him transgress: the Cuthæans, an evil spirit, and poverty (Erub. u.s.). Diseases—such as *rabies*, *angina*, *asthma*, or accidents—such as an encounter with a wild bull, are due to their agency, which, happily, is not unlimited. As stated in App. XIII. the most dangerous demons are those of dirty (secret) places (Shabb. 67 *a*). Even numbers (2, 4, 6, &c.) are always dangerous, so is anything that comes from unwashen hands. For such, or similar oversights, a whole legion

---

[1] I would here generally acknowledge my obligations to Dr. *Brecher's* tractate on the subject.

[2] Erub. 41 *b*; Pes. 112 *a*. The more common designation is *r. tumeah*; but there are others.

of demons is on the watch (Ber. 51 *a*). On the evening of the Passover the demons are bound, and, in general, their power has now been restricted, chiefly to the eves of Wednesday and of the Sabbath (Pes. 109 *b* to 112 *b*, *passim*). Yet there are, as we shall see, circumstances in which it would be foolhardiness to risk their encounter. Without here entering on the views expressed in the Talmud about prophecy, visions. and dreams, we turn to the questions germane to our subject.

A. *Magic and Magicians.* We must here bear in mind that the practice of magic was strictly prohibited to Israelites, and that—as a matter of principle at least—witchcraft, or magic, was supposed to have no power over Israel, if they owned and served their God (Chull. 7 *b*; Nedar. 32 *a*). But in this matter also —as will presently appear—theory and practice did not accord. Thus, under certain circumstances, the repetition of magical formulas was declared lawful even on the Sabbath (Sanh. 101 *a*). Egypt was regarded as the home of magic (Kidd. 49 *b*; Shabb. 75 *a*). In connection with this, it deserves notice that the Talmud ascribes the miracles of Jesus to magic, which He had learned during His stay in Egypt, having taken care, when He left, to insert under His skin its rules and formulas, since every traveller, on quitting the country, was searched, lest he should take to other lands the mysteries of magic (Shabb. 104 *b*).

Here it may be interesting to refer to some of the strange ideas which Rabbinism attached to the early Christians, as showing both the intercourse between the two parties, and that the Jews did not deny the gift of miracles in the Church, only ascribing its exercise to magic. Of the existence of such intercourse with Jewish Christians there is abundant evidence. Thus, R. Joshua, the son of Levi (at the end of the second century), was so hard pressed by their quotations from the Bible that, unable to answer, he pronounced a curse on them, which, however, did not come. We gather, that in the first century Christianity had widely spread among the Jews, and R. Ishmael, the son of Elisha, the grandson of that High-Priest who was executed by the Romans (Josephus, War i. 2, 2), seems in vain to have contended against the advance of Christianity. At last he agreed with R. Tarphon that nothing else remained but to burn their writings. It was this R. Ishmael who prevented his nephew Ben Dama from being cured of the bite of a serpent by a Christian, preferring that he should die rather than be healed by such means (Abod. Zar. 27 *b*, about the middle). Similarly, the great R. Eliezer ben Hyrcanus, also in the first century, was so suspected of the prevailing heresy that he was actually taken up as a Christian in the persecution of the latter. Though he cleared himself of the suspicion, yet his contemporaries regarded him for a time doubtfully, and all agreed that the troubles which befell him were in punishment for having listened with pleasure to the teaching of the heretics (Ab. Z. 16 *b*, 17 *a*.[1] The following may be mentioned as instances of the magic practiced by these heretics. In Jer. Sanh. 25 *d*, we are told about two great Rabbis who were banned by a heretic to the beam of a bath. In return the Rabbis, by similar means, fastened the heretic to the door of the bath. Having mutually agreed to set each other free, the same parties next met on board a ship. Here the heretic by magical means clave the sea, by way of imitating Moses. On this the Rabbis called upon him to walk through the sea, like Moses, when he was immediately overwhelmed through the ban of R. Joshua ! Other stories of a similar and even more absurd character might be quoted. But if such opinions were entertained of Jewish Christians, we can scarcely wonder that all their books were

[1] See more on this subject in vol. ii. pp. 193, 194.

ordered to be burnt (Bemid. R. 9), that even a roll of the Law written by a heretic was to be destroyed (Gitt. 45 b), and that Jewish Christians were consigned to eternal punishment in Gehinnom (Rosh. haSh. 17 a), from which even the token of circumcision should not deliver them since an Angel would convert it into uncircumcision (Shem R. 19[1]).

But to return. Talmudic writings distinguish several classes of magicians. The *Baal Obh*, or conjuror of the dead, evoked a voice from under the armpit, or from other members of the dead body, the arms or other members being struck together, for the purpose of eliciting the sound. Necromancy might be practised in two different ways. The dead might be called up (by a method which scarcely bears description), in which case they would appear with the feet upwards. But this must not be practised on the Sabbath. Or again, a skull might, by magical means, be made to answer. This might be done on the Sabbath also (Sanh. 65 a and b) Or a demon might be conjured up by a certain kind of incense, and then employed in magic. A second class of magicians (called *Yideoni*) uttered oracles by putting a certain bone into their mouth. Thirdly, there was the *Chabar*, or serpent charmer, a distinction being made between a great and a small Chabar, according as larger or smaller serpents were charmed. Fourthly, we have the *Meonen*, who could indicate what days or hours were lucky and unlucky. Fifthly, there was the '*searcher after the dead*,' who remained fasting on graves in order to communicate with an unclean spirit; and, lastly, the *Menachesh*, who knew what omens were lucky and what unlucky (Sanh. 66 a). And if they were treated only as signs and not as omens, the practice was declared lawful (Chull. 95 b).

In general the black art might be practised either through demons, or else by the employment of magical means. Among the latter we reckon, not only incantations, but magic by means of the thumb, by a knife with a black handle, or by a glass cup (Sanh. 67 b), or by a cup of incantation (Baba Mets. 29 b). But there was danger here, since, if all proper rules and cautions were not observed the magician might be hurt by the demon. Such an instance is related, although the Rabbi in question was mercifully preserved by being swallowed by a cedar, which afterwards burst and set him free (Sanh. 101 a). Women were specially suspected of witchcraft (Jer. Sanh. vii. 25 d), and great caution was accordingly enjoined. Thus, it might even be dangerous to lift up loaves of bread (though not broken pieces) lest they should be bewitched (Erub. 64 b). A number of instances are related in which persons were in imminent danger from magic, in some of which they suffered not only damage but death, while in others the Rabbis knew how to turn the impending danger against their would-be assailants. (Comp. for example Pes. 110 b; Sot. 22 a; Gitt. 45 a; Sanh. 67 b). A very peculiar idea is that about the Teraphim of Scripture. It occurs already in the Targum Ps.-Jon. on Gen. xxxi. 19, and is found also in the Pirqé de R. Eliez. c. 36. It is stated that the Teraphim were made in the following manner: a first-born was killed, his head cut off, and prepared with salt and spices, after which a gold plate, upon which magical formulas had been graven, was placed under his tongue, when the head was supposed to give answer to whatever questions might be addressed to it.

B. After this we can scarcely wonder, that so many diseases should have been

---

[1] We have here only been able to *indicate* this most interesting subject. Much more remains to be said concerning Eliezer b. Hyrcanus, and others. There seem even to have been regular meeting-places for discussion between Jews and Christians. Nay, the practice of some early Christians to make themselves eunuchs is alluded to in the Talmud (Shabb. 152 a).

imputed to magical or else to demoniac influences, and cured either by magical means or by exorcism. For our present purpose we leave aside not only the question, whether and what diseases were regarded as the punishment of certain sins, but also all questions as to their magical causes and means of cure. We confine our remarks to the supposed power of evil spirits in the production of diseases. Four things are mentioned as dangerous on account of demons, of which we shall only mention three: To walk between two palm-trees,[1] if the space is wider than four cubits; to borrow drinking-water; and to walk over water that has been poured out, unless it have been covered with earth, or spat upon, or you have taken off your shoes (Pes. 111 a). Similarly, the shadow of the moon, of certain trees, and of other objects, is dangerous, because demons love to hide there. Much caution must also be observed in regard to the water with which the hands are washed in the morning, as well as in regard to oil for anointing, which must never be taken from a strange vessel which might have been bewitched.

Many diseases are caused by direct demoniac agency. Thus, leprosy (Horay. 10 a), rabies (Yoma 83 b), heart-disease (Gitt. 67 b), madness, asthma (Bechor. 44 b), croup (Yoma 77 b; Taan. 20 b), and other diseases, are ascribed to special demons. And although I cannot find any notices of demoniac possession in the sense of permanent indwelling, yet an evil spirit may seize and influence a person. The nearest approach to demoniac possession is in a legend of two Rabbis who went to Rome to procure the repeal of a persecuting edict, when they were met on board ship by a demon, *Ben Temalion*, whose offer of company they accepted, in hope of being able to do some miracle through him. Arrived in Rome, the demon took possession of the daughter of Cæsar. On this he was exorcised by the Rabbis ('Ben Temalion, come out! Ben Temalion, come out!'), when they were rewarded by the offer of anything they might choose from the Imperial Treasury, on which they removed from it the hostile decree (Meilah 17 b, about the middle).

As against this one instance, many are related of cures by magical means. By the latter we mean the superstitious and irrational application of means which could in no way affect any disease, although they might sometimes be combined with what might be called domestic remedies. Thus, for a bad cold in the head this remedy is proposed: Pour slowly a quart of the milk of a white goat over three cabbage stalks, keep the pot boiling and stir with a piece of 'Marmehon-wood' (Gitt. 69 a, b). The other remedy proposed is the excrement of a white dog mixed with balsam. It need scarcely be said, that the more intractable the disease, the more irrational are the remedies proposed. Thus against blindness by day it is proposed to take of the spleen of seven calves and put it on the basin used by surgeons for bleeding. Next, some one outside the door is to ask the blind man to give him something to eat, when he is to reply: How can I open the door—come in and eat—on which the latter obeys, taking care, however, to break the basin, as else the blindness might strike him. We have here an indication of one of the favourite modes of healing disease—that by its transference to another. But if the loss of the power of vision is greater at night than by day, a cord is to be made of the hair of some animal, one end of which is to be tied to the foot of the patient, the other to that of a dog. The children are to strike together pieces of crockery behind the dog, while the patient repeats these words: 'The dog is old and the cock is foolish.' Next seven pieces of meat are to be taken from seven

---

[1] In general palm-trees and their fruit are dangerous, and you should always wash your hands after eating dates.

different houses, and hung up on the doorposts, and the dog must afterwards eat the meat on a dunghill in an open place. Lastly, the cord is to be untied when one is to repeat: 'Let the blindness of M. the son of N. leave M. the son of N. and pierce the eyeballs of the dog!' (Gitt, 69 a).

We have next to refer to strictly magical cures. These were performed by amulets—either preventive, or curative of disease—or else by exorcism. An amulet was regarded as *probate*, if three cures had been performed by it. In such case it might be put on even on the Sabbath. It consisted either of a piece of parchment (the *Pithqa*, Sanh. 78 b), on which certain magical words were written, or of small bundles of certain plants or herbs (also designated as *Qemia*, an amulet, Shabb. 61 a; Kidd. 73 b). However, even probate amulets might fail, owing to the adverse constellation under which a person was. In any case the names and numbers of the demons, whose power it was wished to counteract, required to be expressly stated. Sometimes the amulet contained also a verse from the Bible. It need scarcely be said, that the other words written on the amulet had—at least, in their connection—little if any sensible meaning. But those learned in these arts and the Rabbis had the secret of discovering them, so that there was at least no mystery about them, and the formulas used were well known. If the mischief to be counteracted was due to demoniac agency, it might be prevented or removed by a kind of incantation, or by incantation along with other means, or in difficult cases by exorcism. As instances of the first we may quote the following. To ward off any danger from drinking water on a Wednesday or Sabbath-Evening, when evil spirits may rest on it, it is advised either to repeat a passage of Scripture in which the word *Qol* ('Voice') occurs seven times (Ps. xxix. 3-9), or else to say this: 'Lul, Shaphan, Anigron, Anirdaphin—between the stars I sit, betwixt the lean and the fat I walk!' (Pes. 112 a). Against flatulence, certain remedies are recommended (such as drinking warm water), but they are to be accompanied by the following formula: '*Qapa, Qapa*, I think of thee, and of thy seven daughters, and eight daughters-in-law!' (Pes. 116 a). Many similar prescriptions might be quoted. As the remedy against blindness has been adduced to point the contrast to the Saviour's mode of treatment, it may be mentioned that quite a number of remedies are suggested for the cure of a bloody flux—of which perhaps wine in which Persian onions, or anise and saffron, or other plants have been boiled, seem the most rational—the medicament being, however, in each case accompanied by this formula: 'Be cured of thy flux!'

Lastly, as regards incantation and exorcism, the formulas to be used for the purpose are enumerated. These mostly consist of words which have little if any meaning (so far as we know), but which form a rhyme or alliteration when a syllable is either omitted or added in successive words. The following, for example, is the formula of incantation against boils: 'Baz, Baziyah, Mas, Masiya, Kas, Kasiyah, Sharlai and Amarlai—ye Angels that come from the land of Sodom to heal painful boils! Let the colour not become more red, let it not farther spread, let its seed be absorbed in the belly. As a mule does not propagate itself, so let not this evil propagate itself in the body of M. the son of M.' (Shabb, 67 a). In other formulas the demons are not invoked for the cure, but threatened. We have the following as against another cutaneous disease: 'A sword drawn, and a sling outstretched! His name is not Yokhabh, and the disease stand still!' Against danger from the demon of foul places we have the following: 'On the head of the

cast him into a bed of cresses, and beat him with the jawbone of an ass' (Shabb 67 a). On the other hand, it is recommended as a precaution against the evil eye to put one's right thumb into the left hand and one's left thumb into the right hand, and to say: 'I, M. N. belong to the house of Joseph over whom the evil eye has no power' (Ber. 55 b). A certain Rabbi gave this as information derived from one of the chief of the witches, by which witchcraft might be rendered harmless. The person in danger should thus address the witches: 'Hot filth into your mouths from baskets with holes, ye witching women! Let your head become bald, and the wind scatter your breadcrumbs. Let it carry away your spices, let the fresh saffron which you carry in your hands be scattered. Ye witches, so long as I had grace and was careful, I did not come among you, and now I have come, and you are not favourable to me' (Pes. 110 a, b). To avoid the danger of two or more persons being separated by a dog, a palm-tree, a woman, or a pig, we are advised to repeat a verse from the Bible which begins and ends with the word El (Almighty). Or in passing between women suspected of witchcraft it may be well to repeat this formula: 'Agrath, Azelath, Asiya, Belusiya are already killed by arrows.' Lastly, the following may be quoted as a form of exorcism of demons: 'Burst, curst, dashed, banned be Bar-Tit, Bar-Tema, Bar-Tena, Chashmagoz, Merigoz, and Isteaham!'

It has been a weary and unpleasant task to record such abject superstitions, mostly the outcome of contact with Parsee or other heathen elements. Brief though our sketch has been, we have felt as if it should have been even more curtailed. But it seemed necessary to furnish these unwelcome details in order to remove the possibility of comparing what is reported in the New Testament about the 'demonised' and 'demons' with Jewish notions on such subjects. Greater contrast could scarcely be conceived than between what we read in the New Testament and the views and practices mentioned in Rabbinic writings—and if this, as it is hoped, has been firmly established, even the ungrateful labour bestowed on collecting these unsavoury notices will have been sufficiently repaid.

APPENDIX XVII.

THE ORDINANCES AND LAW OF THE SABBATH AS LAID DOWN IN THE MISHNAH AND THE JERUSALEM TALMUD.

(See Book III. ch. xxxv. in vol. ii. p. 52.)

THE terribly exaggerated views of the Rabbis, and their endless, burdensome rules about the Sabbath may best be learned from a brief analysis of the *Mishnah*, as further explained and enlarged in the Jerusalem Talmud.[1] For this purpose a brief analysis of what is, confessedly, one of the most difficult tractates may here be given.

APP.
XVII

The Mishnic tractate *Sabbath* stands at the head of twelve tractates which together form the second of the six sections into which the Mishnah is divided, and which treats of Festive Seasons (*Seder Moed*). Properly to understand the Sabbath regulations, it is, however, necessary also to take into account the second tractate in that section, which treats of what are called 'commixtures' or 'connections' (*Erubin*). Its object is to make the Sabbath Laws more bearable. For this purpose, it is explained how places, beyond which it would otherwise have been unlawful to carry things, may be connected together, so as, by a legal fiction, to convert them into a sort of private dwelling. Thus, supposing a number of small private houses to open into a common court, it would have been unlawful on the Sabbath to carry anything from one of these houses into the other. This difficulty is removed if all the families deposit before the Sabbath some food in the common court, when 'a connection' is established between the various houses, which makes them one dwelling. This was called the 'Erubh of Courts.' Similarly, an extension of what was allowed as a 'Sabbath journey' might be secured by another 'commixture,' the 'Erubh' or 'connection of boundaries.' An ordinary Sabbath day's journey extended 2,000 cubits beyond one's dwelling.[2] But if at the boundary of that 'journey' a man deposited on the Friday food for two meals, he thereby constituted it his dwelling, and hence might go on for other 2,000 cubits. Lastly, there was another 'Erubh,' when narrow streets or blind alleys were connected into 'a private dwelling' by laying a beam over the entrance, or extending a wire or rope along such streets and alleys. This, by a legal fiction, made them 'a private dwelling,' so that everything was lawful there which a man might do on the Sabbath in his own house.

Without discussing the possible and impossible questions about these *Erubin* raised by the most ingenious casuistry, let us see how Rabbinism taught Israel to

---

[1] The Jerusalem Talmud is not only the older and the shorter of the two *Gemaras*, but would represent most fully the Palestinian ideas.

[2] On the Sabbath-journey, and the reason for fixing it at a distance of 2,000 cubits, see *Kitto's* Cyclop. (last ed.) 'Sabbath-way,' and 'The Temple and its Services,' p. 148.

APP.
XVII

observe its Sabbath. In not less than twenty-four chapters,[1] matters are seriously discussed as of vital religious importance, which one would scarcely imagine a sane intellect would seriously entertain. Through 64½ folio columns in the Jerusalem, and 156 double pages of folio in the Babylon Talmud does the enumeration and discussion of possible cases, drag on, almost unrelieved even by Haggadah.[2] The Talmud itself bears witness to this, when it speaks (no doubt exaggeratedly) of a certain Rabbi who had spent no less than two and a half years in the study of only one of those twenty-four chapters! And it further bears testimony to the unprofitableness of these endless discussions and determinations. The occasion of this is so curious and characteristic, that it might here find mention. The discussion was concerning a beast of burden. An ass might not be led out on the road with its covering on, unless such had been put on the animal previous to the Sabbath, but it was lawful to lead the animal about in this fashion in one's courtyard.[3] The same rule applied to a packsaddle, provided it were not fastened on by girth and back-strap. Upon this one of the Rabbis is reported as bursting into the declaration that this formed part of those Sabbath Laws (comp. Chag. i. 8) which were like mountains suspended by a hair! (Jer. Shabb. p. 7, col. *b*, last lines). And yet in all these wearisome details there is not a single trace of anything spiritual— not a word even to suggest higher thoughts of God's holy day and its observance,

The tractate on the Sabbath begins with regulations extending its provisions to the close of the Friday afternoon, so as to prevent the possibility of infringing the Sabbath itself, which commenced on the Friday evening. As the most common kind of labour would be that of carrying, this is the first point discussed. The Biblical Law forbade such labour in simple terms (Ex. xxxvi. 6; comp. Jer. xvii. 22). But Rabbinism developed the prohibition into eight special ordinances,[1] by first dividing 'the bearing of a burden' into two separate acts—lifting it up and putting it down—and than arguing, that it might be lifted up or put down from two different places, from a public into a private, or from a private into a public place. Here, of course, there are discussions as to what constituted a 'private place' (רשות היחיד); 'a public place' (רשות הרבים); 'a wide space,' which belongs neither to a special individual nor to a community, such as the sea, a deep wide valley; or else the corner of a property leading out on the road or fields—and, lastly, a 'legally free place.'[4] Again, a 'burden' meant, as the lowest standard of it, the weight of 'a dried fig.' But if 'half a fig' were carried at two different times—lifted or deposited from a private into a public place, or *vice versâ*—were these two actions to be combined into one so as to constitute the sin of Sabbath desecration? And if so, under what conditions as to state of mind, locality, &c.? And, lastly, how many different sins might one such act involve? To give an instance of the kind of questions that were generally discussed. The standard measure for forbidden food was the size of an olive, just as that for carrying burdens was the weight of a fig. If a man had swallowed forbidden food of the size of half an olive, rejected it, and

---

[1] In the Jerusalem Talmud a Gemara is attached only to the first twenty chapters of the Mishnic tractate *Shabbath*; in the Babylon Talmud to all the twenty-four chapters.
[2] I have counted about thirty-three Haggadic pieces in the tractate.
[3] In the former case it might be a burden or lead to work, while in the latter case the covering was presumably for warmth.
[4] Such a free place (מָקוֹם פָּטוּר) must cover less than four square cubits—for ex., a pillar would be such. To this no legal deter-

mination would apply. The 'wide space' is called *Karmelith* (כַּרְמְלִית). The Mishnah, however, expressly mentions only the 'private' and the 'public' place (or 'enclosed' and 'open'), although the *Karmelith* is implied in x. 2; xi. 4, 5. The *Karmelith* was in certain circumstances treated as 'public,' in others as 'private' property. The explanation of the terms and legal definitions is in Jer. Shabb. 12 *d*; 13 *a*; Shabb. 6, *a*, *b*; Toseft. Shabb. 1.

again eaten of the size of half an olive, he would be guilty, because the palate had altogether tasted food to the size of a whole olive; but if one had deposited in another locality a burden of the weight of half a fig, and removed it again, it involved no guilt, because the burden was altogether only of half a fig, nor even if the first half fig's burden had been burnt and then a second half fig introduced. Similarly, if an object that was intended to be worn or carried in front had slipped behind it involved no guilt, but if it had been intended to be worn or carried behind, and it slipped forward, this involved guilt, as involving labour.

Similar difficulties were discussed as to the guilt in case an object were thrown from a private into a public place, or the reverse. Whether, if an object was thrown into the air with the left, and caught again in the right hand, this involved sin, was a nice question, though there could be no doubt a man incurred guilt if he caught it with the same hand with which it had been thrown, but he was not guilty if he caught it in his mouth, since, after being eaten, the object no longer existed, and hence catching with the mouth was as if it had been done by a second person. Again, if it rained, and the water which fell from the sky were carried, there was no sin in it; but if the rain had run down from a wall it would involve sin. If a person were in one place, and his hand filled with fruit stretched into another, and the Sabbath overtook him in this attitude, he would have to drop the fruit, since if he withdrew his full hand from one locality into another, he would be carrying a burden on the Sabbath.

It is needless to continue the analysis of this casuistry. All the discussions to which we have referred turn only on the *first* of the legal canons in the tractate 'Sabbath.' They will show what a complicated machinery of merely external ordinances traditionalism set in motion; how utterly unspiritual the whole system was, and how it required no small amount of learning and ingenuity to avoid committing grievous sin. In what follows we shall only attempt to indicate the leading points in the Sabbath-legislation of the Rabbis.

Shortly before the commencement of the Sabbath (late on Friday afternoon) nothing new was to be begun;[1] the tailor might no longer go out with his needle, nor the scribe with his pen; nor were clothes to be examined by lamp-light. A teacher might not allow his pupils to read, if he himself looked on the book. All these are precautionary measures. The tailor or scribe carrying his ordinary means of employment, might forget the advent of the holy day; the person examining a dress might kill insects,[2] which is strictly forbidden on the Sabbath, and the teacher might move the lamp to see better, while the pupils were not supposed to be so zealous as to do this.

These latter rules, we are reminded, were passed at a certain celebrated discussion between the schools of Hillel and Shammai, when the latter were in the majority. On that occasion also opposition to the Gentiles was carried to its farthest length, and their food, their language, their testimony, their presence, their intercourse, in short, all connection with them denounced. The school of Shammai also forbade to make any mixture, the ingredients of which would not be wholly dissolved and assimilated, before the Sabbath. Nay, the Sabbath law was declared to apply even to lifeless objects. Thus, wool might not be dyed if the process was

---

[1] Here such questions are raised as what constitutes the beginning, for ex., of shaving or of a bath.

[2] To kill such vermin is, of course, strictly forbidden (to kill a flea is like killing a camel).

Rules are given how to dispose of such insects. On the same occasion some curious ideas are broached as to the transformation of animals, one into another.

not completed before the Sabbath. Nor was it even lawful to sell anything to a heathen unless the object would reach its destination before the Sabbath, nor to give to a heathen workman anything to do which might involve him in Sabbath work. Thus, Rabbi Gamaliel was careful to send his linen to be washed three days before the Sabbath. But it was lawful to leave olives or grapes in the olive or wine-press. Both schools were agreed that, in roasting or baking, a crust must have been formed before the Sabbath, except in case of the Passover lamb. The Jerusalem Talmud, however, modifies certain of these rules. Thus the prohibition of work to a heathen only implies, if they work in the house of the Jew, or at least in the same town with him. The school of Shammai, however, went so far as to forbid sending a letter by a heathen, not only on a Friday or on a Thursday, but even on a Wednesday, or to embark on the sea on these days.

It being assumed that the lighting of the Sabbath lamp was a law given to Moses on Mount Sinai, the Mishnah proceeds, in the second chapter of the tractate on the Sabbath, to discuss the substances of which respectively the wick and the oil may be composed, provided always that the oil which feeds the wick is not put in a separate vessel, since the removal of that vessel would cause the extinction of the lamp, which would involve a breach of the Sabbath law. But if the light were extinguished from fear of the Gentiles, of robbers, or of an evil spirit, or in order that one dangerously ill might go to sleep, it involved no guilt. Here, many points in casuistry are discussed, such as whether twofold guilt is incurred if in blowing out a candle its flame lights another. The Mishnah here diverges to discuss the other commandments, which, like that of lighting the Sabbath lamp, specially devolve on women, on which occasion the Talmud broaches some curious statements about the heavenly Sanhedrin and Satan, such as that it is in moments of danger that the Great Enemy brings accusations against us, in order to ensure our ruin; or this, that on three occasions he specially lies in ambush: when one travels alone, when one sleeps alone in a dark house, and when one crosses the sea. In regard to the latter we may note as illustrative of St. Paul's warning not to travel after the fast (Day of Atonement), that the Jewish proverb had it: 'When you bind your *Lulabh* [1] (at the Feast of Tabernacles) bind also your feet'—as regards a sea-voyage (Jer. Shabb. 5 *b*, Ber. R. 6).

The next two chapters in the tractate on the Sabbath discuss the manner in which food may be kept warm for the Sabbath, since no fire might be lighted. If the food had been partially cooked, or was such as would improve by increased heat, there would be temptation to attend to the fire, and this must be avoided. Hence the oven was immediately before the Sabbath only to be heated with straw or chaff ; if otherwise, the coals were to be removed or covered with ashes. Clothes ought not to be dried by the hot air of a stove. At any rate, care must be taken that the neighbours do not see it. An egg may not be boiled by putting it near a hot kettle, nor in a cloth, nor in sand heated by the sun. Cold water might be poured on warm, but not the reverse (at least such was the opinion of the school of Shammai), nor was it lawful to prepare either cold or warm compresses. 'Nay, a Rabbi went so far as to forbid throwing hot water over one's self, for fear of spreading the vapour, or of cleaning the floor thereby! A vessel might be put under a lamp to catch the falling sparks, but no water might be put into it, because it was

---

[1] The *Lulabh* (לוּלָב) consisted of a palm with myrtle and willow branch tied on either side of it, which every worshipper carried on the Feast of Tabernacles ('Temple and its Services,' p. 238).

not lawful to extinguish a light. Nor would it have been allowed on the Sabbath to put a vessel to receive the drops of oil that might fall from the lamp. Among many other questions raised was this: whether a parent might take his child in his arms. Happily Rabbinic literality went so far as not only to allow this, but even in the supposed case that the child might happen to have a stone in its hands, although this would involve the labour of carrying that stone ! Similarly, it was declared lawful to lift seats, provided they had not, as it were, four steps, when they must be considered as ladders. But it was not allowed to draw along chairs, as this might produce a rut or cavity, although a little carriage might be moved, since the wheels would only compress the soil but not produce a cavity (comp. in the Bab. Talmud, Shabb. 22 *a*; 46; and Bets. 23 *b*).

Again, the question is discussed, whether it is lawful to keep the food warm by wrapping around a vessel certain substances. Here the general canon is, that all must be avoided which would increase the heat: since this would be to produce some outward effect, which would be equivalent to work.

In the fifth chapter of the tractate we are supposed to begin the Sabbath morning. Ordinarily, the first business of the morning would, of course, have been to take out the cattle. Accordingly, the laws are now laid down for ensuring Sabbath rest to the animals. The principle underlying these is, that only what serves as ornament, or is absolutely necessary for leading out or bringing back animals, or for safety, may be worn by them; all else is regarded as a burden. Even such things as might be put on to prevent the rubbing of a wound, or other possible harm, or to distinguish an animal, must be left aside on the day of rest.

Next, certain regulations are laid down to guide the Jew when dressing on the Sabbath morning, so as to prevent his breaking its rest. Hence he must be careful not to put on any dress which might become burdensome, nor to wear any ornament which he might put off and carry in his hand, for this would be a 'burden.' A woman must not wear such headgear as would require unloosing before taking a bath, nor go out with such ornaments as could be taken off in the street, such as a frontlet, unless it is attached to the cap, nor with a gold crown, nor with a necklace or nose-ring, nor with rings, nor have a pin [1] in her dress. The reason for this prohibition of ornaments was, that in their vanity women might take them off to show them to their companions, and then, forgetful of the day, carry them, which would be a 'burden.' Women are also forbidden to look in the glass on the Sabbath, because they might discover a white hair and attempt to pull it out, which would be a grievous sin; but men ought not to use looking-glasses even on weekdays, because this was undignified. A woman may walk about her own court, but not in the street, with false hair. Similarly, a man was forbidden to wear on the Sabbath wooden shoes studded with nails, or only one shoe, as this would involve labour; nor was he to wear phylacteries nor amulets, unless, indeed, they had been made by competent persons (since they might lift them off in order to show the novelty). Similarly, it was forbidden to wear any part of a suit of armour. It was not lawful to scrape shoes, except perhaps with the back of a knife, but they might be touched with oil or water. Nor should sandals be softened with oil, because that would improve them. It was a very

[1] Literally, a needle which has not an eyelet Of course, it would not be lawful for a modern Jew—if he observe the Rabbinic Law—to carry a stick or a pencil on the Sabbath, to drive, or even to smoke.

serious question, which led to much discussion, what should be done if the tie of a sandal had broken on the Sabbath. A plaster might be worn, provided its object was to prevent the wound from getting worse, not to heal it, for that would have been a work. Ornaments which could not easily be taken off might be worn in one's courtyard. Similarly, a person might go about with wadding in his ear, but not with false teeth nor with a gold plug in the tooth. If the wadding fell out of the ear, it could not be replaced. Some, indeed, thought that its healing virtues lay in the oil in which it had been soaked, and which had dried up, but others ascribed them to the warmth of the wadding itself. In either case there was danger of healing—of doing anything for the purpose of a cure—and hence wadding might not be put into the ear on the Sabbath, although if worn before it might be continued. Again, as regarded false teeth: they might fall out, and the wearer might then lift and carry them, which would be sinful on the Sabbath. But anything which formed part of the ordinary dress of a person might be worn also on the Sabbath, and children whose ears were being bored might have a plug put into the hole. It was also allowed to go about on crutches, or with a wooden leg, and children might have bells on their dresses; but it was prohibited to walk on stilts, or to carry any heathen amulet.

The seventh chapter of the tractate contains the most important part of the whole. It opens by laying down the principle that, if a person has either not known, or forgotten, the whole Sabbath law, all the breaches of it which he has committed during ever so many weeks are to be considered as only one error or one sin. If he has broken the Sabbath law by mistaking the day, every Sabbath thus profaned must be atoned for; but if he has broken the law because he thought that what he did was permissible, then every separate infringement constitutes a separate sin, although labours which stand related as *species* to the *genus* are regarded as only one work. It follows, that guilt attaches to the state of mind rather than to the outward deed. Next, forty less one chief or ' fathers ' of work (*Aboth*) are enumerated, all of which are supposed to be forbidden in the Bible. They are: sowing, ploughing, reaping, binding sheaves, threshing, winnowing, sifting (selecting), grinding, sifting in a sieve, kneading, baking; shearing the wool, washing it, beating it, dyeing it, spinning, putting it on the weaver's beam, making two thrum threads, weaving two threads, separating two threads, making a knot, undoing a knot, sewing two stitches, tearing in order to sew two stitches; catching deer, killing, skinning, salting it, preparing its skin, scraping off its hair, cutting it up, writing two letters, scraping in order to write two letters; building, pulling down, extinguishing fire, lighting fire, beating with the hammer, and carrying from one possession into the other.

The number thirty-nine is said to represent the number of times that the word ' labour ' occurs in the Biblical text, and all these *Aboth* or ' fathers ' of work are supposed to be connected with some work that had been done about the Tabernacle, or to be kindred to such work. Again, each of these principal works involved the prohibition of a number of others which were derived from them, and hence called their ' descendants ' (*toledoth*). The thirty-nine principal works have been arranged in four groups: the first (1–11) referring to the preparation of bread; the second (12–24) to all connected with dress; the third (25–33) to all connected with writing; and the last (34–39) to all the work necessary for a private house. Another Rabbi derives the number thirty-nine (of these Aboth) from the numerical value of the initial word in Exod. xxxv. 1, although in so doing he has to change

the last letter (לאה, the ה must be changed into a ח to make thirty-nine).[1]
Further explanations must here be added. If you scatter two seeds, you have
been sowing. In general, the principle is laid down, that anything by which
the ground may be benefited is to be considered a 'work' or 'labour,' even if
it were to sweep away or to break up a clod of earth. Nay, to pluck a blade of
grass was a sin. Similarly, it was sinful labour to do anything that would promote the ripening of fruits, such as to water, or even to remove a withered leaf.
To pick fruit, or even to lift it from the ground, would be like reaping. If, for
example, a mushroom were cut, there would be a twofold sin, since by the act of
cutting, a new one would spring in its place. According to the Rabbis of Cæsarea,
fishing, and all that put an end to life, must be ranked with harvesting. In
connection with the conduct of the disciples in rubbing the ears of corn on the
Sabbath, it is interesting to know that all work connected with food would be
classed as one of the *toledoth*, of binding into sheaves. If a woman were to roll
wheat to take away the husks, she would be guilty of sifting with a sieve. If she
were rubbing the ends of the stalks, she would be guilty of threshing. If she were
cleaning what adheres to the side of a stalk, she would be guilty of sifting. If she
were bruising the stalk, she would be guilty of grinding. If she were throwing it
up in her hands, she would be guilty of winnowing. Distinctions like the following
are made: A radish may be dipped into salt, but not left in it too long, since
this would be to make pickle. A new dress might be put on, irrespective of the
danger that in so doing it might be torn. Mud on the dress might be crushed in
the hand and shaken off, but the dress must not be rubbed (for fear of affecting the
material). If a person took a bath, opinions are divided, whether the whole body
should be dried at once, or limb after limb. If water had fallen on the dress,
some allowed the dress to be shaken but not wrung; others, to be wrung but not
shaken. One Rabbi allowed to spit into the handkerchief, and that although
it may necessitate the compressing of what had been wetted; but there is a grave
discussion whether it was lawful to spit on the ground, and then to rub it with the
foot, because thereby the earth may be scratched. It may, however, be done on
stones. In the labour of grinding would be included such an act as crushing salt.
To sweep, or to water the ground, would involve the same sin as beating out the
corn. To lay on a plaster would be a grievous sin; to scratch out a big letter,
leaving room for two small ones, would be a sin, but to write one big letter occupying the room of two small letters was no sin. To change one letter into another
might imply a double sin. And so on through endless details!

The Mishnah continues to explain that, in order to involve guilt, the thing
carried from one locality to another must be sufficient to be entrusted for safe
keeping. The quantity is regulated: as regards the food of animals, to the
capacity of their mouth; as regards man, a dried fig is the standard. As regards
fluids, the measure is as much wine as is used for one cup, that is—the measure
of the cup being a quarter of a log, and wine being mixed with water in the proportion of three parts water to one of wine—one-sixteenth of a log.[2] As regards milk,
a mouthful; of honey, sufficient to lay on a wound; of oil, sufficient to anoint the
smallest member; of water, sufficient to wet eyesalve; and of all other fluids, a
quarter of a log.

<hr>

[1] The Rabbis contend for the lawfullness
of changing the ה into a ח for the sake of
an interpretation. So expressly here (Jer.
Shabb. 9 *b*) and in Jer. Peah 20 *b* (הלולים

into חלולים in Lev. xix. 24).
[2] It has been calculated by *Herzfeld* that a
log = 0·36 of a litre; 'six hen's eggs.'

As regarded other substances, the standard as to what constituted a burden was whether the thing could be turned to any practical use, however trifling. Thus, two horse's hairs might be made into a birdtrap; a scrap of clean paper into a custom-house notice; a small piece of paper written upon might be converted into a wrapper for a small flagon. In all these cases, therefore, transport would involve sin. Similarly, ink sufficient to write two letters, wax enough to fill up a small hole, even a pebble with which you might aim at a little bird, or a small piece of broken earthenware with which you might stir the coals, would be 'burdens!'

Passing to another aspect of the subject, the Mishnah lays it down that, in order to constitute sin, a thing must have been carried from one locality into another entirely and immediately, and that it must have been done in the way in which things are ordinarily carried. If an object which one person could carry is carried by two, they are not guilty. Finally, like all labour on the Sabbath, that of cutting one's nails or hair involves mortal sin, but only if it is done in the ordinary way, otherwise only the lesser sin of the breach of the Sabbath rest. A very interesting notice in connection with St. John v., is that in which it is explained how it would not involve sin to carry a living person on a pallet, the pallet being regarded only as an accessory to the man; while to carry a dead body in such manner, or even the smallest part of a dead body, would involve guilt.

From this the Mishnah proceeds to discuss what is analogous to carrying, such as drawing or throwing. Other 'labours' are similarly made the subject of inquiry, and it is shown how any approach to them involves guilt. The rule here is, that anything that might prove of lasting character must not be done on the Sabbath. The same rule applies to what might prove the beginning of work, such as letting the hammer fall on the anvil; or to anything that might contribute to improve a place, to gathering as much wood as would boil an egg, to uprooting weeds, to writing two letters of a word—in short, to anything that might be helpful in, or contribute towards, some future work.

The Mishnah next passes to such work in which not quantity, but quality, is in question—such as catching deer. Here it is explained that anything by which an animal might be caught is included in the prohibition. So far is this carried that, if a deer had run into a house, and the door were shut upon it, it would involve guilt, and this, even if, without closing the door, persons seated themselves at the entry to prevent the exit of the animal.

Passing over the other chapters, which similarly illustrate what are supposed to be Biblical prohibitions of labour as defined in the thirty-nine *Aboth* and their *toledoth*, we come, in the sixteenth chapter of the tractate, to one of the most interesting parts, containing such Sabbath laws as, by their own admission, were imposed only by the Rabbis. These embrace: 1. Things forbidden, because they might lead to a transgression of the Biblical command; 2. Such as are like the kinds of labour supposed to be forbidden in the Bible; 3. Such as are regarded as incompatible with the honour due to the Sabbath. In the first class are included a number of regulations in case of a fire. All portions of Holy Scripture, whether in the original or translated, and the case in which they are laid; the phylacteries and their case, might be rescued from the flames. Of food or drink only what was needful for the Sabbath might be rescued; but if the food were in a cupboard or basket the whole might be carried out. Similarly, all utensils needed for the Sabbath meal, but of dress only what was absolutely necessary, might be saved, it being, however, provided, that a person might put on a dress, save it, go back and put on another, and so on. Again, anything in the house might be covered with a skin so as to save it from the flames, or the spread of the flames might be arrested by piling up vessels. It was not lawful to ask a Gentile to extinguish the flame, but not duty to hinder him, if he did so. It was lawful to put a vessel over a lamp, to prevent the ceiling from catching fire; similarly, to throw a vessel over a scorpion, although on that point there is doubt. On the other hand, it is allowed, if a Gentile has lighted a lamp on the Sabbath, to make use of it, the fiction being, however, kept up that he did it for himself, and not for the Jew. By the same fiction the cattle may be watered, or, in fact, any other use made of his services.

Before passing from this, we should point out that it was directed that the Hagiographa should not be read except in the evening, since the daytime was to be devoted to more doctrinal studies. In the same connection it is added, that the study of the Mishnah is more important than that of the Bible, that of the Talmud being considered the most meritorious of all, as enabling one to understand all questions of right and wrong. Liturgical pieces, though containing the Name of God, might not be rescued from the flames. The Gospels and the writings of Christians, or of heretics, might not be rescued. If it be asked what should be done with them on weekdays, the answer is, that the Names of God which they contain ought to be cut out, and then the books themselves burned. One of the Rabbis, however, would have had them burnt at once, indeed, he would rather have fled into an idolatrous temple than into a Christian church: 'for the idolators deny God because they have not known Him, but the apostates are worse.' To them applied Ps. cxxxix. 21, and, if it was lawful to wash out in the waters of jealousy the Divine Name in order to restore peace, much more would it be lawful to burn such books, even though they contained the Divine Name, because they led to enmity between Israel and their Heavenly Father.

Another chapter of the tractate deals with the question of the various pieces of furniture—how far they may be moved and used. Thus, curtains, or a lid, may be regarded as furniture, and hence used. More interesting is the next chapter (xviii.), which deals with things forbidden by the Rabbis because they resemble those kinds of labour supposed to be interdicted in the Bible. Here it is declared lawful. for example, to remove quantities of straw or corn in order to make room for guests, or for an assembly of students, but the whole barn must not be emptied, because in so doing the floor might be injured. Again, as regards animals, some assistance might be given, if an animal was about to have its young, though not to the same amount as to a woman in childbirth, for whose sake the Sabbath might be desecrated. Lastly, all might be done on the holy day needful for circumcision. At the same time, every preparation possible for the service should be made the day before. The Mishnah proceeds to enter here on details not necessarily connected with the Sabbath law.

In the following chapter (xx.) the tractate goes on to indicate such things as are only allowed on the Sabbath on condition that they are done differently from ordinary days. Thus, for example, certain solutions ordinarily made in water should be made in vinegar. The food for horses or cattle must not be taken out of the manger, unless it is immediately given to some other animal. The bedding straw must not be turned with the hand, but with other parts of the body. A press in which linen is smoothed may be opened to take out napkins, but must not be screwed down again, &c.

The next chapter proceeds upon the principle that, although everything is to be avoided which resembles the labours referred to in the Bible, the same prohibition does not apply to such labours as resemble those interdicted by the Rabbis. The application of this principle is not, however, of interest to general readers.

In the twenty-second chapter the Mishnah proceeds to show that all the precautions of the Rabbis had only this object: to prevent an ultimate breach of a Biblical prohibition. Hence, where such was not to be feared, an act might be done. For example, a person might bathe in mineral waters, but not carry home the linen with which he had dried himself. He might anoint and rub the body, but not to the degree of making himself tired; but he might not use any artificial remedial measures, such as taking a shower-bath. Bones might not be set, nor emetics given, nor any medical or surgical operation performed.

In the last two chapters the Mishnah points out those things which are unlawful as derogatory to the dignity of the Sabbath. Certain things are here of interest as bearing on the question of purchasing things for the feast-day. Thus, it is expressly allowed to borrow wine, or oil, or bread on the Sabbath, and to leave one's upper garment in pledge, though one should not express it in such manner as to imply it was a loan. Moreover, it is expressly added that if the day before the Passover falls on a Sabbath, one may in this manner purchase a Paschal lamb, and, presumably, all else that is needful for the feast. This shows how Judas might have been sent on the eve of the Passover to purchase what was needful, for the law applying to a feast-day was much less strict than that of the Sabbath. Again, to avoid the possibility of effacing anything written, it was forbidden to read from a tablet the names of one's guests, or the *menu*. It was lawful for children to cast lots for their portions at table, but not with strangers, for this might lead to a breach of the Sabbath, and to games of chance. Similarly, it was improper on the Sabbath to engage workmen for the following week, nor should one be on the watch for the close of that day to begin one's ordinary work. It was otherwise if religious obligations awaited one at the close of the Sabbath, such as attending to a bride, or making preparations for a funeral.[1] On the Sabbath itself it was lawful to do all that was absolutely necessary connected with the dead, such as to anoint or wash the body, although without moving the limbs, nor might the eyes of the dying be closed—a practice which, indeed, was generally denounced.

In the last chapter of the tractate the Mishnah returns to the discussion of punctilious details. Supposing a traveller to arrive in a place just as the Sabbath commenced, he must only take from his beast of burden such objects as are allowed to be handled on the Sabbath. As for the rest, he may loosen the ropes and let them fall down of themselves. Further, it is declared lawful to unloose bundles of straw, or to rub up what can only be eaten in that condition; but care must be taken that nothing is done which is not absolutely necessary. On the other hand, cooking would not be allowed—in short, nothing must be done but what was absolutely necessary to satisfy the cravings of hunger or thirst. Finally, it was declared lawful on the Sabbath to absolve from vows, and to attend to similar religious calls.

Detailed as this analysis of the Sabbath law is, we have not by any means exhausted the subject. Thus, one of the most curious provisions of the Sabbath law

---

[1] It is curious as bearing upon a recent controversy, to note that on this occasion it is said that an Israelite may be buried in the coffin and grave originally destined for a Gentile, but not *vice versâ*.

was, that on the Sabbath only such things were to be touched or eaten as had been expressly prepared on a weekday with a view to the Sabbath (Bez. 2 *b*).[1] Anything not so destined was forbidden, as the expression is 'on account of *Muqtsah*' (מוקצה), i.e. as not having been the 'intention.' Jewish dogmatists enumerate nearly fifty cases in which that theological term finds its application. Thus, if a hen had laid on the Sabbath, the egg was forbidden, because, evidently, it could not have been destined on a weekday for eating, since it was not yet laid, and did not exist; while if the hen had been kept, not for laying but for fattening, the egg might be eaten as forming a part of the hen that had fallen off! But when the principle of *Muqtsah* is applied to the touching of things which are not used because they have become ugly (and hence are not in one's mind). so that. for example, an old lamp may not be touched, or raisins during the process of drying them (because they are not eatable then), it will be seen how complicated such a law must have been.

Chiefly from other tractates of the Talmud the following may here be added. It would break the Sabbath rest to climb a tree, to ride, to swim, to clap one's hands, to strike one's side, or to dance. All judicial acts, vows, and tilling were also prohibited on that day (Bez. v. 2). It has already been noted that aid might be given or promised for a woman in her bed. But the Law went further. While it prohibited the application or use on the Sabbath of any remedies that would bring improvement or cure to the sick, 'all actual danger to life,' (כל ספק נפש'ת הוחה את חשבת, Yoma viii. 6) superseded the Sabbath law, but nothing short of that. Thus, to state an extreme case, if on the Sabbath a wall had fallen on a person, and it were doubtful whether he was under the ruins or not, whether he was alive or dead, a Jew or Gentile, it would be duty to clear away the rubbish sufficiently to find the body. If life were not extinct the labour would have to be continued; but if the person were dead nothing further should be done to extricate the body. Similarly, a Rabbi allowed the use of remedies on the Sabbath in throat diseases, on the express ground that he regarded them as endangering life. On a similar principle a woman with child or a sick person was allowed to break even the fast of the Day of Atonement, while one who had a maniacal attack of morbid craving for food (בולמוס)=βούλιμος might on that sacred day have even unlawful food (Yoma viii. 5, 6).

Such are the leading provisions by which Rabbinism enlarged the simple Sabbath-law as expressed in the Bible,[2] and, in its anxiety to ensure its most exact observance, changed the spiritual import of its rest into a complicated code of external and burdensome ordinances. Shall we then wonder at Christ's opposition to the Sabbath-ordinances of the Synagogue, or, on the other hand, at the enmity of its leaders? and can greater contrast be imagined than between the teaching of Christ on this subject, and that of his most learned and most advanced contemporaries? And whence this difference unless Christ was the 'Teacher come from God,' Who spake as never before man had spoken?

---

[1] This destination or preparation is called *Hachanah*.
[2] Ex. xx. 8-11; xxiii. 12; xxxi. 12-17; xxxiv. 21; xxxv. 1-3; Deut. v. 12-15.

APPENDIX XVIII.

HAGGADAH ABOUT SIMEON KEPHA (LEGEND OF SIMON PETER.)

(אגרתא דשמעין כיפא)

(Vol. ii. Book III. ch. xxxviii.)

APP.
XVIII

THIS Haggadah exists in four different Recensions (comp. *Jellinek*, Beth ha-Midrash, Pt. V. and Pt. VI., pp. ix., x). The first of these, reproduced by Jellinek (u. s. Pt. V. p. xxvi. &c., and pp. 60–62) was first published by *Wagenseil* in his collection of Antichristian writings, the *Tela Ignea Satanæ*, at the close of that blasphemous production, the *Sepher Toledoth Jeshu* (pp. 19–24). The second Recension is that by Huldrich (Leyden, 1705); the third has been printed, as is inferred, at Breslau in 1824; while the fourth exists only in MS. Dr. Jellinek has substantially reproduced (without the closing sentences) the text of Wagenseil's (u. s. Pt. V.), and also Recensions III. and IV. (u. s. Pt. VI.). He regards Recension IV. as the oldest; but we infer from its plea against the abduction of Jewish children by Christians and against forced baptisms, as well as from the use of certain expressions, that Recension IV. is younger than the text of Wagenseil, which seems to present the legend in its most primitive form. Even this, however, appears a mixture of several legends; or perhaps the original may afterwards have been interpolated. It were impossible to fix even approximately the age of this oldest Recension, but in its present form it must date after the establishment of Christianity in Rome, and that of the Papacy, though it seems to contain older elements. It may be regarded as embodying certain ancient legends among the Jews about St. Peter, but adapted to later times, and cast in an apologetic form. A brief criticism of the document will best follow an abstract of the text, according to the first or earlier Recension.

The text begins by a notice that the strife between the Nazarenes and the Jews had grown to such proportions that they separated, since any Nazarene who saw a Jew would kill him. Such became the misery for thirty years, that the Nazarenes increased to thousands and myriads, and prevented the Jews from going up to the feasts of Jerusalem. And the distress was as great as at the time of the Golden Calf. And still the opposing faith increased, and twelve wicked men went out, who traversed the twelve kingdoms. And they prophesied false prophecies in the camp, and they misled Israel, and they were men of reputation, and strengthened the faith of Jesus, for they said that they were the Apostles of the Crucified. And they drew to themselves a large number from among the children of Israel. On this the text describes, how the sages in Israel were afflicted and humbled themselves, each confessing to his neighbour the sins which had brought this evil, and earnestly asking of God to give them direction how to arrest the advance of Nazarene doctrine and persecution. As they finished their prayer, up rose an elder from their midst, whose name was Simeon Kepha, who had formerly put into requisition the *Bath Kol* and said: 'Hearken to me, my brethren and my people! If my words are good in your sight, I will separate those sinners from the congregation of the children of Israel, and they shall have neither part nor inheritance in the midst of Israel, if only you take upon you the sin. And they all answered and said: We will take upon us the sin, if only thou wilt do what thou hast said.' Upon this, the narrative proceeds, Peter went into the Sanctuary, wrote the Ineffable Name, and inserted it in his flesh. Having learnt the Ineffable Name, he went to the metropolis ('*metropolin*') of the Nazarenes, and proclaimed that every believer in Christ should come to him, since he was an Apostle. The multitudes required that he should prove his claim by a sign ('*oth*') such as Jesus had done while He was alive, when Peter, through the power of the Ineffable Name, restored a leper, by laying on of hands, and raised the dead. When the Nazarenes saw this, they fell on their faces, and acknowledged his Apostolate. Then Peter delivered this as his message, first bidding them swear to do as he would command: 'Know (said he) that the Crucified hated Israel and their law, as Isaiah prophesied: "Your new moons and your feasts my soul hateth;" know also, that he delighteth not in Israel, as Hosea prophesied: "You are not my people." And although it is in His power to extirpate them from the world in a moment, from out of every place, yet He does not purpose to destroy them, but intends to leave them, in order that they be in memory of His Crucifixion and lapidation to all generations. Besides, know that He bore all those great sufferings and afflictions to redeem you from Gehenna. And now He admonishes and commands you, that you should do no evil to the Jews: and if a Jew says to a Nazarene, "Go with me one *parasang*" (Persian mile about three English miles), let him go with him two *parasangs*. And if a Jew smites him on the left cheek, let him present to him also the right cheek, in order that they may have their reward in this world, while in the next they will be punished in Gehenna. And if you do thus, you will deserve to sit with Him in His portion. And behold, what He commands you is, that ye shall not observe the Feast of the Passover, but observe the day of His death. And instead of the Feast of Pentecost observe forty days from the time that He was slain to when He went up into heaven. And instead of the Feast of Tabernacles observe the day of His birth, and on the eighth day after His birth observe that on which He was circumcised.'

To these commands all agreed, on condition that Peter should remain with them. This he consented to do, on the understanding that he would not eat anything except bread of misery and water of affliction—presumably not only to avoid forbidden food, but in expiatory suffering for his sin—and that they should build him a tower in the midst of the city, in which he would remain unto the day of his death, all which provisions were duly carried out. It is added, that in this tower he served the God of his fathers, Abraham, Isaac, and Jacob. What is still stranger, it is added, that he wrote many *Piutim*—a certain class of liturgical poems which form part of the Synagogue service—and that he sent these throughout all Israel to be in perpetual memory of him, and especially that he despatched them to the Rabbis. The remark is the more noteworthy, as other Jewish writers also describe the Apostle Peter as the author of several liturgical poems, of which one is still repeated in the Synagogue on Sabbaths and Feast-days (comp. Jellinek, *Beth ha-Midr.*, part v., p. 61, note). But to return. Peter is said to have remained in that tower for six years, when he died, and by his direction was buried within the tower. But the Nazarenes raised there a great fabric, 'and this tower may be seen in Rome, and they call it Peter, which is the word for a stone, because he sat on a stone till the day of his death. But after his death another person named Elijah came, in the wickedness and cunning of his heart to mislead them. And he said to them that Simon had deceived them, for that Jesus had commanded him to tell them: it had not come into His heart to despise the Law of Moses; that if any one wished to circumcise, he should circumcise; but if any one did not wish to be circumcised, let him be immersed in foul waters. And even if he were not immersed, he would not thereby be in danger in the world. And he commanded that they should not observe the seventh day, but only the first day, because on it were created the heavens and the earth. And he made to them many statutes which were not good. But the people asked him: Give us a true sign that Jesus hath sent thee. And he said to them: What is the sign that you seek? And the word had not been out of his mouth when a great stone of immense weight fell and crushed his head. So perish all Thine enemies, O God, but let them that love Thee be as the sun when he goeth forth in his strength!'

Thus far what we regard as the oldest Recension. The chief variations between this and the others are, that in the third Recension the opponent of Peter is called Abba Shaul (St. John also is mentioned; Jellinek, u.s. part vi., p. 156), while in the fourth Recension (in MS.), which consists of nineteen chapters, this opponent is called Elijah. In the latter Recension there is mention of Antioch and Tiberias, and other places connected with the lives of St. Peter and St. Paul, and the early history of the Church. But the occurrence of certain Romanic words, such as Papa, Vescova, &c., shows its later date. Again, we mark that, according to Recensions III. and IV., Peter sent his liturgical pieces to *Babylon*, which may either indicate that at the time of the document 'Babylon' was the centre of the Jewish population, or else be a legendary reminiscence of St. Peter's labours in 'the Church that is in Babylon' (1 Pet. v. 13). In view of modern controversies it is of special interest that, according to the Jewish legend, Peter, secretly a Jew, advised the Christians to throw off completely the law of Moses, while Paul, in opposition to him, stands up for Israel and the Law, and insists that either circumcision or baptism may be practised. It will be further noted, that the object of the document seems to be: 1st, to serve as an 'apology' for Judaism, by explaining how it came that so many Jews, under the leadership of Apostles, embraced the new faith. This seems to be traced to the continued observance of Jewish legal practices by the Christians. Simon Peter is supposed to have arrested the progress of Christianity by separating the Church from the Synagogue, which he did by proclaiming that Israel were rejected, and the Law of Moses abolished. On the other hand, St. Paul is represented as the friend of the Jews, and as proclaiming that the question of circumcision or baptism, of legal observances or Christian practices, was a matter of indifference. This attempt to heal the breach between the Church and the Synagogue had been the cause of Divine judgment on him. 2ndly, The legend is intended as an apology for the Jews, with a view to ward off persecution. 3rdly, It is intended to show that the leaders of the Christians remained in heart Jews. It will perhaps not be difficult—at least, hypothetically —to separate the various legends mixed up, or perhaps interpolated in the tractate. From the mention of the *Piutim* and the ignorance as to their origin, we might be disposed to assign the composition of the legend in its present form to about the eighth century of our era.

APPENDIX XIX.

ON ETERNAL PUNISHMENT, ACCORDING TO THE RABBIS AND THE NEW TESTAMENT.

(See vol. ii. Book V. ch. vi.)

THE Parables of the 'Ten Virgins' and of the 'Unfaithful Servant' close with a Discourse on 'the Last Things,' the final Judgment, and the fate of those at Christ's Right Hand and at His Left (St. Matt. xxv. 31–46). This final Judgment by our Lord forms a fundamental article in the Creed of the Church. It is the Christ Who comes, accompanied by the Angelic Host, and sits down on the throne of His Glory, when all nations are gathered before Him. Then the final separation is made, and joy or sorrow awarded in accordance with the past of each man's history. And that past, as in relationship to the Christ—whether it have been 'with' Him or 'not with' Him, which latter is now shown to be equivalent to an 'against' Him. And while, in the deep sense of a love to Christ which is utterly self-forgetful in its service and utterly humble in its realisation of Him to Whom no real service can be done by man, to their blessed surprise, those on 'the Right' find work and acknowledgment where they had never thought of its possibility, every ministry of their life, however small, is now owned of Him as rendered to Himself—partly, because the new direction, from which all such ministry sprang, was of 'Christ in' them, and partly, because of the identification of Christ with His people. On the other hand, as the lowest service of him who has the new inner direction is Christward, so does ignorance, or else ignoration, of Christ ('When saw we Thee. . . . ?') issue in neglect of service and labour of love, and neglect of service proceed from neglect and rejection of Christ. And so is life either 'to' Christ or 'not to' Christ, and necessarily ends in 'the Kingdom prepared from the foundation of the world' or in 'the eternal fire which is prepared for the Devil and his angels.'

Thus far the meaning of the Lord's Words, which could only be impaired by any attempt at commentation. But they also raise questions of the deepest importance, in which not only the head, but perhaps much more the heart, is interested, as regards the precise meaning of the term 'everlasting' and 'eternal' in this and other connections, so far as those on the Left Hand of Christ are concerned. The subject has of late attracted renewed attention. The doctrine of the Eternity of Punishments, with the proper explanations and limitations given to it in the teaching of the Church, has been set forth by Dr. *Pusey* in his Treatise: 'What is of Faith as to Everlasting Punishment?' Before adverting, however, briefly, to the New Testament teaching, it seems desirable with some fulness to set forth the *Jewish* views on this subject. For the views held at the time of

APP.
XIX

Christ, whatever they were, must have been those which the hearers of Christ entertained; and whatever these views, Christ did not, at least directly, contradict or, so far as we can infer, intend to correct them.[1] And here we have happily sufficient materials for a history of Jewish opinions at different periods on the Eternity of Punishments; and it seems the more desirable carefully to set it forth, as statements both inaccurate and incomplete have been put forward on the subject.

Leaving aside the teaching of the Apocrypha and Pseudepigraphic Writings (to which Dr. Pusey has sufficiently referred), the first Rabbinic utterances come to us from the time immediately before that of Christ, from the Schools of Shammai and Hillel (Rosh haSh. 16 *b* last four lines, and 17 *a*).[2] The former arranged all mankind into three classes: the perfectly righteous, who are 'immediately written and sealed to eternal life;' the perfectly wicked, who are 'immediately written and sealed to Gehenna;' and an intermediate class, 'who go down to Gehinnom, and moan, and come up again,' according to Zech. xiii. 9, and which seemed also indicated in certain words in the Song of Hannah (1 Sam. ii. 6)   The careful reader will notice that this statement implies belief in Eternal Punishment on the part of the School of Shammai. For (1) The perfectly wicked are spoken of as 'written and sealed unto Gehenna'; (2) The School of Shammai expressly quotes, in support of what it teaches about these wicked, Dan. xii. 2, a passage which undoubtedly refers to the final judgment after the Resurrection; (3) The perfectly wicked, so punished, are expressly distinguished from the third, or intermediate class, who merely 'go down to Gehinnom,' but are not 'written and sealed,' and 'come up again.

Substantially the same, as regards Eternity of Punishment, is the view of the School of Hillel (u. s. 17 *a*). In regard to sinners of Israel and of the Gentiles it teaches, indeed, that they are tormented in Gehenna for twelve months, after which their bodies and souls are burnt up and scattered as dust under the feet of the righteous; but it significantly excepts from this number certain classes of transgressors 'who go down to Gehinnom and are punished there to ages of ages.' That the Niphal form of the verb used, נִדּוֹנִין; must mean 'punished' and not 'judged,' appears, not only from the context, but from the use of the same word and form in the same tractate (Rosh haSh. 12 *a*, lines 7 &c. from top), when it is said of the generation of the Flood that 'they were punished' surely not 'judged'—by 'hot water.' However, therefore, the School of Hillel might accentuate the mercy of God, or limit the number of those who would suffer Eternal Punishment, it did teach Eternal Punishment in the case of some. And this is the point in question.

But, since the Schools of Shammai and Hillel represented the theological teaching in the time of Christ and His Apostles, it follows, that the doctrine of Eternal Punishment was that held in the days of our Lord, however it may afterwards have been modified. Here, so far as this book is concerned, we might rest the case. But for completeness' sake it will be better to follow the historical development of Jewish theological teaching, at least a certain distance.

The doctrine of the Eternity of Punishments seems to have been held by the Synagogue throughout the whole first century of our era. This will appear from the sayings of the Teachers who flourished during its course. The Jewish Parable

---

[1] Of course, we mean their general direction, not the details.
[2] In view of the strange renderings and in-

terpretations given of Rosh haSh. 16 *b*, 17 *a*, I must call special attention to this *locus classicus*.

of the fate of those who had not kept their festive garments in readiness or apeared in such as were not clean (Shabb. 152 *b*, 153 *a*) has been already quoted in our exposition of the Parables of the Man without the Wedding-garment and of the Ten Virgins. But we have more than this. We are told (Ber. 28 *b*) that, when that great Rabbinic authority of the first century, Rabbi Jochanan ben Zakkai—'the light of Israel, the right hand pillar, the mighty hammer'—lay a dying and wept, he accounted for his tears by fear as to his fate in judgment, illustrating the danger by the contrast of punishment by an earthly king 'whose bonds are not eternal bonds nor his death eternal death,' while as regarded God and His judgment: 'if He is angry with me, His Wrath is an Eternal Wrath, if He binds me in fetters, His fetters are Eternal fetters, and if He kills me, His death is an Eternal Death.' In the same direction is this saying of another great Rabbi of the first century, Elieser (Shabb. 152 *b*, about the middle), to the effect that 'the souls of the righteous are hidden under the throne of glory,' while those of the wicked were to be bound and in unrest (זוממות והוֹכנות), one Angel hurling them to another from one end of the world to the other—of which latter strange idea he saw confirmation in 1 Sam. xxv. 29. To the fate of the righteous applied, among other beautiful passages, Is. lvii. 2, to that of the wicked Is. lvii. 21. Evidently, the views of the Rabbis of the first century were in strict accordance with those of Shammai and Hillel.

In the second century of our era, we mark a decided difference in Rabbinic opinion. Although it was said that, after the death of Rabbi Meir, the ascent of smoke from the grave of his apostate teacher had indicated that the Rabbi's prayers for the deliverance of his master from Gehenna had been answered (Chag. 15 *b*), most of the eminent teachers of that period propounded the idea, that in the last day the sheath would be removed which now covered the sun, when its fiery heat would burn up the wicked (Ber. R. 6). Nay, one Rabbi maintained that there was no hell at all, but that that day would consume the wicked, and yet another, that even this was not so, but that the wicked would be consumed by a sort of internal conflagration.

In the third century of our era we have once more a reaction, and a return to the former views. Thus (Kethub. 104 *a*, about the middle) Rabbi Eleasar speaks of the three bands of Angels, which successively go forth to meet the righteous, each with a welcome of their own, and of the three bands of Angels of sorrow, which similarly receive the wicked in their death—and this, in terms which leave no doubt as to the expected fate of the wicked. And here Rabbi José informs us (Tos. Ber. vi. 15), that 'the fire of Gehenna which was created on the second day is not extinguished for ever.' With this view accord the seven designations which, according to Rabbi Joshua ben Levi, attach to Gehenna (Erub. 19 *a*, line 11, &c., from bottom—but the whole page bears on the subject). This doctrine was only modified, when Ben Lakish maintained, that the fire of Gehenna did not hurt sinners from among the Jews (Kethub. u. s.). Nor does even this other saying of his (Nedar. 8 *b*, last four lines) necessarily imply that he denied the eternity of punishment: 'There is no Gehinnom in the world to come '—since it is qualified by the expectation that the wicked would be punished (נידוֹנין), not annihilated, by the heat of the sun, which would be felt as healing by the righteous. Lastly, if not universal beatification, yet a kind of universal moral restoration seems implied in the teaching of Rabbi Jehudah to the effect that in the *sæculum futurum* God would destroy the *Yetser haRa*.

Tempting as the subject is, we must here break off this historical review, for want of space, not of material. Dr. Pusey has shown that the Targumim also teach the doctrine of Eternal Punishment—though their date is matter of discussion—and to the passages quoted by him in evidence others might be added. And if on the other side the saying of Rabbi Akiba should be quoted (Eduy. ii. 10) to the effect that the judgment of the wicked in Gehenna was one of the five things that lasted for twelve months, it must be remembered that, even if this be taken seriously (for it is really only a *jeu d' esprit*), it does not necessarily imply more than the teaching of Hillel concerning that intermediate class of sinners who were in Gehenna for a year—while there was another class the duration of whose punishment would be for ages of ages. Even more palpably inapt is the quotation from Baba Mez. 58 *b* (lines 5, &c., from the bottom). For, if that passage declares that all are destined to come up again from Gehenna, *it expressly excepts* from this these three classes of persons: adulterers, those who put their fellow-men publicly to shame, and those who apply an evil name to their neighbors.

But there can at least be no question, that the passage which has been quoted at the outset of these remarks (Rosh haSh. 16 *b*, 17 *a*), proves beyond the possibility of gainsaying that both the Great Schools, into which Rabbinic teaching at the time of Christ was divided, held the doctrine of Eternal Punishments. This, of course, entirely apart from the question who—how many, or rather, how few— were to suffer this terrible fate. And here the cautions and limitations, with which Dr. Pusey has shown that the Church has surrounded her teaching, cannot be too often or earnestly repeated. It does, indeed, seem painfully strange that, if the meaning of it be at all realised, some should seem so anxious to contend for the extension to so many of a misery from which our thoughts shrink in awe. Yet this we are well assured, that the Judge of all the Earth will judge, not only righteously, but mercifully. He alone knows all the secrets of heart and life, and He alone can apportion to each the due meed. And in this assured conviction may the mind trustfully rest as regards those who have been dear to us.

But if on such grounds we shrink from narrow and harsh dogmatism, there are certain questions which we cannot quite evade, even although we may answer them generally rather than specifically. We put aside, as an unhealthy and threatening sign of certain religious movements, the theory, lately broached, of a so-called 'Conditional Immortality.' So far as the reading of the present writer extends, it is based on bad philosophy and even worse exegesis. But the question itself, to which this 'rough-and-ready' kind of answer has been attempted, is one of the most serious. In our view, an impartial study of the Words of the Lord, recorded in the Gospels—as repeatedly indicated in the text of these volumes—leads to the impression that His teaching in regard to reward and punishment should be taken in the ordinary and obvious sense, and not in that suggested by some. And this is confirmed by what is now quite clear to us, that the Jews, to whom He spoke, believed in Eternal Punishment, however few they might consign to it. And yet we feel that this line of argument is not quite convincing. For might not our Lord, as in regard to the period of His Second Coming, in this also have intended to leave His hearers in incertitude? And, indeed, is it really necessary to be quite sure of this aspect of eternity?

And here the question arises about the precise meaning of the words which Christ used. It is, indeed, maintained that the terms $\alpha i \acute{\omega} \nu \iota o \varsigma$ and kindred expres-

sions always refer to eternity in the strict sense. But of this I cannot express myself convinced (see ad voc. *Schleusner*, Lex., who, however, goes a little too far;
Wahl, Clavis N.T.; and *Grimm*, Clavis N.T.), although the balance of evidence is
in favour of such meaning. But it is at least conceivable that the expressions
might refer to the end of all time, and the merging of the 'mediatorial regency'
(1 Cor. xv. 24) in the absolute kingship of God.

In further thinking on this most solemn subject, it seems to the present writer
that exaggerations have been made in the argument. It has been said that, the
hypothesis of annihilation being set aside, we are practically shut up to what is
called *Universalism*. And again, that Universalism implies, not only the final restoration of *all* the wicked, but even of Satan and his angels. And further, it has
been argued that the metaphysical difficulties of the question ultimately resolve
themselves into this: why the God of all foreknowledge had created beings—be
they men or fallen angels—who, as He foreknew, would ultimately sin? Now
this argument has evidently no force as against absolute Universalism. But even
otherwise, it is rather specious than convincing. For we only possess *data* for
reasoning in regard to the sphere which falls within our cognition, which the absolutely Divine—the pre-human and the pre-created—does not, except so far as it
has been the subject of Revelation. This limitation excludes from the sphere of
our possible comprehension all questions connected with the Divine foreknowledge,
and its compatibility with that which we know to be the fundamental law of
created intelligences, and the very condition of their moral being: personal freedom
and choice. To quarrel with this limitation of our sphere of reasoning, were to
rebel against the conditions of human existence. But if so, then the question of
Divine foreknowledge must not be raised at all, and the question of the fall of
angels and of the sin of man must be left on the (to us) alone intelligible basis:
that of personal choice and absolute moral freedom.

Again—it seems at least an exaggeration to put the alternatives thus: absolute
eternity of punishment—and, with it, of the state of rebellion which it implies, since
it is unthinkable that rebellion should absolutely cease, and yet punishment continue; annihilation; or else universal restoration. Something else is at least think-
able, that may not lie within these hard and fast lines of demarcation. It is at
least conceivable that there may be a *quartum quid*—that there may be a purification or transformation (*sit venia verbis*) of all who are capable of such—or, if it is
preferred, an unfolding of the germ of grace, present before death, invisible though
it may have been to other men, and that in the end of what we call time or 'dispensation,' only that which is morally incapable of transformation—be it men or
devils—shall be cast into the lake of fire and brimstone (Rev. xx. 10, 14, 15; xxi.
8). And here, if, perhaps just, exception is taken to the terms 'purification' or
'transformation' (perhaps spiritual development), I would refer in explanation to
what Dr. Pusey has so beautifully written—although my reference is only to this
point, not to others on which he touches (Pusey, What is of Faith, &c., pp. 116–
122). And, in connection with this, we note that there is quite a series of
Scripture-statements, which teach alike the final reign of God ('that God may be
all in all'), and the final putting of all things under Christ—and all this in connection with the blessed fact that Christ has 'tasted death for every man,' 'that
the world through Him might be saved,' and, in consequence, to 'draw all' unto
Himself, comp. Col. i. 19, 20 (comp. St. John iii. 17; xii. 32; Rom. v. 18–24;
1 Cor. xv. 20–28; Eph. i. 10; Col. i. 19, 20; 1 Tim. ii. 4, 6; iv. 10; Heb. ii. 9;

APP.
XIX

1 John ii. 2; iv. 14—all which passages must, however, be studied in their connection).

Thus far it has been the sole aim of the present writer to set before the reader, so far as he can, all the elements to be taken into consideration. He has pronounced no definite conclusion, and he neither wishes nor purposes to do so. This only he will repeat, that to his mind the Words of our Lord, as recorded in the Gospels, convey this impression, that there *is* an eternity of punishment; and further, that this was the accepted belief of the Jewish schools in the time of Christ. But of these things does he feel fully assured: that we may absolutely trust in the loving-kindness of our God; that the work of Christ is for all and of infinite value, and that its outcome must correspond to its character; and. lastly, for practical purposes, that in regard to those who have departed (whether or not we know of grace in them) our views and our hopes should be the widest (consistent with Scripture teaching), and that as regards ourselves, personally and individually, our views as to the need of absolute and immediate faith in Christ as the Saviour, of holiness of life, and of service of the Lord Jesus, should be the closest and most rigidly fixed.

INDEX I.

OF SUBJECTS.

INDEX II.

OF PASSAGES FROM THE FOUR GOSPELS REFERRED TO IN THESE VOLUMES.

3 G

EXPLANATORY NOTES AND CORRECTIONS

FOR THE SECOND VOLUME.

Page 15[a]: The Targum is quoted from the Venice edition.

" 16[g]: However, the word has also been translated in the wider sense of 'garment.' But see Rosh haSh., and compare also what is said about the *Tephillin*, which cannot be otherwise interpreted than in the text.

" 21[a]: But the passage is a somewhat difficult one, and it has received different interpretations. See *Levy* as in note 1, and *Lightfoot* ad loc. Line 10, read: 'by a vow from anything by which he might be profited (or rather have enjoyment) from his son.' And so as regards note 2, various interpretations and comments are given. But the principle that a vow would exclude parents from being 'profited' is clearly established in Ned. ix. 1.

" 116[a]: Simon b. Shetach compares him to a son who sins against his father, and yet he does what the child pleases, so Chony, although he was sinning against God, yet He answered that very prayer.

" 162[cde]: Of course, these were only the extreme inferences from their principles, and not intended *literatim*.

" 156, note 1: On the Octave of the Feast probably Ps. xii. was chanted (see Sopher. xix. beg.).

" 182[d]: One of the prohibitions there would be exactly parallel to the making of clay.

" 290, note 2, end : I refer here especially to Bemid. R. 2. It would be difficult to find anything more realistically extravagant in its exaltation of Israel over all the nations (*delete* 28). The note sets forth the general impression left on the mind, and is, of course, not intended as a citation.

" 297[d]: The reference is to one who hesitates to forgive injury to his name when asked to do so by the offender. At the same time I gladly admit how beautifully Rabbinism speaks about mercy and forgiveness. In this respect also are the Gospels historically true, since the teaching of Christ here sprang from, and was kindred to the highest teaching of the Rabbis. But, to my mind, it is just where Rabbinism comes nearest to Christ that the essential difference most appears. And from even the highest Rabbinic sayings to the forgiveness of Christ in its freeness, absoluteness, internalness, and universality (to Jew and Gentile) there is an immeasurable distance.

" 388, note 1: In Vayy. R. 3, there is another beautiful story of a poor man who offered every day half his living, and whose sacrifice was presented before that of King Agrippa.

Page 409[d]:   As regards the view given of Jer. Ber. 9 *a*, I refer to *Levy*, **Neuhebr**
Wörterb. II., p. 10 *a*.'

"   411[h]:   Comp. also Vayy. R. 1.

"   431[a]:   It was described as more beautiful than the waves of the sea.

"   437[a]:   The quotation of the Midrash on Cant. is again from the unmutilate**d**
citation in R. *Martini*, Pugio Fidei (ed. Carpz), pp. 782, 783.

"   note 1:   The citations refer to the Jerusalem from heaven.   For the rest se**e**
Weber, Altsynag. Theol., p. 386.   But probably the last clause ha**d**
best be omitted.

"   479, line 9:   'What is the *Pascha*,' &c.; rather: 'What is " on the *Pesach ?*
On the 14 Nisan'—in the original: *BaPesach*, i.e. the beginning o**f**
the Passover.

"   556, line 7:   for 'on public Feast-days' read 'at the great public Feasts.'

"   609:   The reference [d] applies to the end of the sentence.   On the thirtee**n**
Veils comp. *Maimonides* (Kel. haMiqd. vii. 17).